OXFORD PAPERBACK

A Concise Encyclopedia

A Concise Encyclopedia

OXFORD
UNIVERSITY PRESS

OXFORD
UNIVERSITY PRESS
Great Clarendon Street, Oxford OX2 6DP

Oxford University Press is a department of the University of Oxford.
It furthers the University's objective of excellence in research,
scholarship, and education by publishing worldwide in

Oxford New York

Auckland Bangkok Buenos Aires Cape Town Chennai
Dar es Salaam Delhi Hong Kong Istanbul Karachi Kolkata
Kuala Lumpur Madrid Melbourne Mexico City Mumbai Nairobi
São Paolo Shanghai Singapore Taipei Tokyo Toronto

First published 1987 as *The New Macmillan Encyclopedia*
This revised and updated edition published as an
Oxford University Press paperback 2004

British Library Cataloguing in Publication Data
Data available

Library of Congress Cataloging in Publication Data
Data available

ISBN 0-19-280595-9

1

Typeset in Swift by Market House Books Ltd.

Printed in Great Britain by Clays Ltd, St Ives plc

Contents

Editors

Alan Isaacs
Jonathan Law

Contributors

John Daintith
Jessica Foote
Amanda Isaacs
Sven Lidman
Elizabeth Martin
Anne Stibbs
Margaret Tuthill

Preface

This *Concise Encyclopedia* sets out to cover the whole range of human knowledge—arts, sciences, ideas, history, biography, and geography—in a single handy volume. Apart from breadth and balance of coverage, the editors have recognized three main priorities: accurate and up-to-date information; concise, accessible language; and a clear, user-friendly presentation. The result is a compact but comprehensive reference book that will meet the needs of a wide range of readers, whether at school, in the workplace, or at home. The book has been compiled with the National Curriculum in mind and should prove invaluable for coursework and other school projects.

The format of the *Concise Encyclopedia* makes it extremely easy to use; entries are arranged in strict alphabetical order and there is an extensive network of cross-references, making the text more-or-less self-indexing. Cross-references are indicated in two ways. Where a cross-reference occurs in the middle of a sentence, an asterisk is used to indicate that further information about the entry being read will be found at the article on the word or phrase so marked. In all other cases, cross-references to other articles are printed in SMALL CAPITALS.

An additional resource is provided by the quick-reference section at the end of the book, which gathers a number of useful tables together for ease of use.

Two further matters may require a word of explanation:

1. Chinese transliterations. This Concise Encyclopedia follows official Chinese practice in using the pinyin system of transliterating Chinese names. The Wade-Giles equivalent (formerly the system most commonly used in the English-speaking world) and, when it exists, the conventional Western name is given in brackets following the pinyin name. However, a small number of names—including Chiang Kai-shek, Mao Tse-tung, and Yangtze River—are so well known in their Wade-Giles or conventional Western forms that we have decided to retain these very familiar spellings.

2. Population figures for towns and cities. Wherever possible, these refer to the town or city proper rather than to the urban area of which it forms part.

This book is dedicated to Alan Isaacs, editor for over twenty years (1981–2002) of the *Macmillan Encyclopedia*, from the text and databases of which the current volume was compiled. Alan was working on the preparation of the *Concise Encyclopedia* at the time of his death earlier this year. We trust that we have completed the job to the standards that he would have expected.

JL

2004

Key to Abbreviations Used in Maps

ABBREVIATION ON MAP	STANDS FOR
A.	Albania
Afg.	Afghanistan
Ar.	Armenia
Au.	Austria
Az.	Azerbaidzhan
B.	Belgium
Ban.	Bangladesh
Be.	Benin
BH.	Bosnia-Hercegovina
Bots.	Botswana
Bu.	Burkina Faso
Bul.	Bulgaria
C.	Croatia
CAR.	Central African Republic
Congo (Dem. Rep.)	Democratic Republic of Congo
Congo (B.)	Congo-Brazzaville
CZ.	Czech Republic
Den.	Denmark
El Salv.	El Salvador
Eq. Guinea	Equatorial Guinea
E.T.	East Timor
Fin.	Finland
G.	Germany
G.-B.	Guinea-Bissau
Gab.	Gabon
Gam.	The Gambia
Gh.	Ghana
H.	Hungary
Is.	Israel
Kazak.	Kazakhstan
Kir.	Kirgizstan
L.	Lebanon
Li.	Lithuania
Lu.	Luxembourg
M.	Macedonia
Mol.	Moldova
N.	Netherlands
Nor.	Norway
Nth. Korea	North Korea
Pol.	Poland
Q.	Qatar
R.	Romania
Rep. of Ireland	Republic of Ireland
Rep. of Sth. Africa	Republic of South Africa
S.	Slovakia
Sen.	Senegal
Sl.	Slovenia
Sth. Korea	South Korea
Sw.	Swaziland
Sw.	Switzerland
Swe.	Sweden
Taj.	Tadzhikistan
Tu.	Turkmenistan
U.A.E.	United Arab Emirates
U.K.	United Kingdom
Ug.	Uganda
Ukr.	Ukraine
Uzb.	Uzbekistan
U.S.M.	Union of Serbia and Montenegro
Zam.	Zambia
Zimb.	Zimbabwe

A

Aachen (French name: Aix-la-Chapelle) 50 46N 06 06E A spa city in W Germany, in North Rhine-Westphalia near the Belgian and Dutch borders. It is an important industrial centre with iron and steel, textiles, and light engineering. *History*: it was the N capital of Charlemagne's empire and many Holy Roman Emperors were crowned in the cathedral (founded c. 796 AD). It was annexed by France in 1801 and passed to Prussia (1815). Extensively damaged during World War II, it was captured by the Allies in 1944. Population (1999 est): 243 600.

Aalborg *See* ÅLBORG.

Aalto, Alvar (1898–1976) Finnish architect. His reputation is based on the Paimio tuberculosis sanatorium (1933). Other buildings include a hall of residence at the Massachusetts Institute of Technology (1948) and the Helsinki Hall of Culture (1958).

aardvark (Afrikaans: earth pig) A nocturnal African mammal, *Orycteropus afer*, also called ant bear. It is about 1.5 m long, lives in grassland, and has a long snout, large ears, and a thick tail. Its strong claws are used to tear open the mounds of termites, which are picked up with its long sticky tongue. The aardvark is the only member of its order (*Tubulidentata*).

Aaron In the Old Testament, the elder brother of *Moses. Although he allowed the golden calf to be built, he and his descendants became the priests of the Jews.

Aarhus *See* ÅRHUS.

abacus A calculating device consisting of balls strung on wires or rods set in a frame, probably of Babylonian origin. Its use declined in Europe with the introduction of *Arabic numerals in about the 10th century AD.

Abadan 30 20N 48 15E A city in SW Iran, on an island in the Shatt (river) al-Arab. Much of Iran's oil is brought here by pipeline for refining or exporting. Population (1996): 206 073.

abalone A marine *gastropod mollusc belonging to the widely distributed family *Haliotidae*, of rocky coasts, also called ear shell or ormer. Up to 30 cm long, their dishlike shells have a row of holes along the outer edge through which deoxygenated water and waste products are expelled from the body. The large foot is considered a delicacy and the shells are used as mother-of-pearl for ornaments.

Abbado, Claudio (1933–) Italian conductor, associated with La Scala, Milan (1968–86), the Vienna State Opera (1986–91), and the Berlin Philharmonic (1989–2001).

'Abbasids A dynasty of caliphs, which ruled the Muslim empire from 750 to 1258. Descended from Mohammed's uncle al-Abbas (566–652), they seized power from the *Umayyads in Damascus and moved their capital to Baghdad. Their rule saw a flowering of culture and scholarship.

Abbevillian A culture of the Lower *Palaeolithic in Europe, characterized by crude stone hand axes made by hammering flakes off a flint with another stone. Named after Abbeville in France, the Abbevillian also appears in Britain but in Africa similar early hand axes are designated *Acheulian.

Abbey Theatre A Dublin theatre opened in 1904. Annie Horniman (1860–1937), a friend of W. B. *Yeats, initiated the building for the Irish National Dramatic Society, a company founded by the actors Frank Fay (1870–1931) and his brother W. G. Fay (1872–1947). The Abbey Theatre gained an international reputation performing mainly plays by Irish playwrights on Irish subjects. The original playhouse burnt down in 1951 and was replaced in 1966.

abdomen In mammals (including humans), the region of the body extending from the lower surface of the diaphragm to the pelvis.

a

The abdomen contains the intestines, liver, pancreas, kidneys, gall bladder, and—in females—the ovaries and womb. In arthropods, the abdomen is the posterior section of the body, which is usually segmented.

Abdullah I (1882–1951) Emir of Transjordan (1921–46) and first King of Jordan (1946–51). He fought with T. E. *Lawrence in the Arab revolt against Turkish rule during World War I. He was assassinated.

Abdullah II (1962–) King of Jordan (1999–). The eldest son of King *Hussein by his second wife, he is married to the Palestinian-born Queen Rania (1970–).

Abel *See* CAIN.

Abel, Niels Henrik (1802–29) Norwegian mathematician. One of the great mathematical problems of Abel's day was to find a general solution for a class of equations called quintics. Abel proved that such a solution was impossible, but died before his achievement was recognized.

Abelard, Peter (1079–1142) French philosopher. His ill-fated marriage with Heloïse, niece of a canon of Notre Dame, Paris, ended when Abelard was castrated by thugs hired by the canon (1118). He retired to a monastery and she became a nun. Despite his great fame as a teacher, Abelard was perpetually in trouble with the church authorities. His *Sic et Non* (*For and Against*), had a major influence on the development of *scholasticism by listing points on which acknowledged authorities differed.

Abercrombie, Sir (Leslie) Patrick (1879–1957) British town planner and architect, best known for his detailed schemes for London, *The County of London Plan* (1943) and *The Greater London Plan* (1944). Later plans include those for Edinburgh, Hull, and the West Midlands.

Aberdeen 1. 57 10N 2 04W A city and port in NE Scotland, in City of Aberdeen council area, on the North Sea coast between the mouths of the Rivers Don and Dee. Aberdeen is an old cathedral city with a university dating from 1494 (King's College). Fishing has always been important, as has the working of local granite; the "Granite City" provided stone for London's cobbled streets in the 18th century. Other industries include engineering, paper making, textiles, and chemicals. Aberdeen's proximity to North Sea oil has transformed it into an important service centre for the oil industry. Population (1996 est): 217 260. **2. City of Aberdeen.** A council area in NE Scotland, established in 1996. Area: 186 sq km (72 sq mi). Population (2001): 212 125.

Aberdeen Angus A breed of polled (naturally hornless) beef cattle, originating from NE Scotland. Short, stocky, and usually black (some have red coats), they are hardy and adapt well to different climates. Angus bulls are commonly mated with dairy breeds to produce a polled beef cross.

Aberdeenshire A council area of NE Scotland, on the North Sea. In 1975 the historic county of Aberdeenshire became part of Grampian Region; it was restored as an independent unitary authority (with adjusted borders) in 1996. The City of Aberdeen forms a separate council area. Agriculture is important (especially stock raising). Industries include fish processing, tourism, whisky distilling, and those associated with North Sea oil. Area: 6318 sq km (2439 sq mi). Population (2001): 226 871. Administrative centre: Aberdeen.

aberration 1. A defect in a lens or mirror that causes blurring or distortion of the image. **Spherical aberration** is caused by rays from the outside of the lens or mirror being brought to a focus at a different point from those nearer to the centre. In **chromatic aberration**, different colours are focused at different points, since the refractive index of glass varies with the wavelength. *See also* ASTIGMATISM. **2.** An apparent displacement in the position of a star or other heavenly body due to the motion of the observer with the earth in its orbit round the sun.

Aberystwyth 52 25N 4 05W A town and resort in Wales, in Ceredigion on Cardigan Bay. A college of the University of Wales was established in 1872 and the National Library of Wales, in 1911. Population (1991 est): 11 154.

Abidjan 5 19N 4 00W The former capital of Côte d'Ivoire, off the Gulf of Guinea. A small village until developed by the French in the 1920s, it became the capital in 1934. It is now an important port, linked to the sea by the Vridi Canal. Population (1995): 2 797 000.

Abkhazia (*or* **Abkhaz Republic**) An administrative division of Georgia. Most of the population is Abkhazian or Georgian and lives along the narrow subtropical coastal lowland. The region is predominantly agricultural; the chief mineral is coal. *History*: invaded by the Romans, it later gained independence before coming under the Ottoman Turks in the 16th century. It became a Russian protectorate in 1810 and an autonomous republic of the Soviet Union in

1921. In 1992 it declared independence, leading to a conflict (1993–94) in which Georgian troops unsuccessfully attempted to regain control. The political situation remains unresolved. Area: 8600 sq km (3320 sq mi). Population (1993 est): 516 600. Capital: Sukhumi.

Abolition Movement The campaign to abolish slavery in the USA. Opponents of slavery formed an antislavery society in 1833. They helped runaway slaves escape to Canada via their secret Underground Railroad route; such publications as *Uncle Tom's Cabin* (1851–52) by Harriet Beecher Stowe unveiled the slavery issue, which was settled by the Civil War.

Abominable Snowman A creature, also called Yeti (Tibetan: Snowman), that is believed to live at high altitudes in the Himalayas. There have been no authenticated sightings, but footprints in the snow have been photographed (which may have other causes).

Aborigines The dark-skinned hunters and gatherers who inhabited Australia before European settlement. Material culture was rudimentary, while kinship organization and terminology were complex. Aboriginal mythology was elaborate and included accounts of creation during the primordial dawn, which they call "Dream Time." There are roughly 136 000 people of Aboriginal descent in Australia. The small proportion who maintain a nomadic way of life are threatened by encroachments upon their lands. In 1993 Aborigines were granted the right to reclaim land formerly held under native title but this was curtailed by further legislation in 1998.

abortion The expulsion or removal of a fetus from the womb before it is capable of independent survival. In the UK a fetus is not legally viable until 24 weeks old. Expulsion of a dead fetus at any later time is called a stillbirth. Abortion may be spontaneous (a miscarriage) or induced for therapeutic or social reasons. In the UK (excluding Northern Ireland) induced abortion is legal if it is carried out under the terms of the Abortion Act (1967) and the Abortion Regulations (1991): two doctors must agree that termination of the pregnancy is necessary (e.g. to prevent the birth of a severely deformed or abnormal child or to preserve the health of the mother) and the operation must be performed in approved premises. Unless there are exceptional circumstances, the abortion must be carried out in or before the 24th week. Methods used include *dilatation and curettage, suction of the womb using an aspirator, and the administration of certain drugs (e.g. mifepristone).

Aboukir, Battle of (25 July 1799) The battle in which Napoleon defeated the Ottoman Turks during his occupation of Egypt. The 7000-strong French army defeated the unruly Turkish force of 18 000.

Abraham In the Old Testament, patriarch and founder of the Hebrew nation (Genesis 11–25). Born in Ur in about 2000 BC, he travelled to Canaan with his wife Sarah, where God established a covenant with him in which Abraham agreed to circumcise himself and to have all his male descendants circumcised. After the birth of their son, **Isaac**, God commanded Abraham to sacrifice him; when Abraham was about to obey, a ram was substituted and God reaffirmed his promises. Isaac's son *Jacob had 12 sons, the ancestors of the 12 tribes of Israel. Abraham is also "the father of Faith" to Christians and Muslims.

Abraham, Plains of A plateau in E Canada, on the W edge of Quebec citadel. Here Gen James *Wolfe defeated the French under Gen Montcalm (13 September 1759), leading to British control over Canada.

Abruzzi (*or* **Abruzzo**) A region in E central Italy. It consists of the Apennines in the W and a coastal region in the E. Agriculture is limited, producing mainly cereals. Manufacturing industry is primarily for local needs but there is also a large fishing fleet. Area: 10 794 sq km (4167 sq mi). Population (2000 est): 1 279 016. Capital: L'Aquila.

abscess A pus-filled cavity surrounded by inflamed tissue, usually caused by bacterial infection. Abscesses may form anywhere in the body. They usually require draining and sometimes also treatment with antibiotics.

absinthe A highly alcoholic drink made from spirits infused with herbs, including aniseed and wormwood. Absinthe has been banned in many countries because of the harmful effects of wormwood, and substitutes (e.g. anis) are drunk instead.

absolute zero The lowest temperature that can theoretically be attained. It is equal to −273.15°C or 0 K. In practice, absolute zero can never be reached, although temperatures of a few thousandths of a degree above absolute zero have been achieved. *See* CRYOGENICS.

absolutism A political system, characteristic of European monarchies between the 16th and 18th centuries, in which the sovereign attempted to centralize power in his own person.

a

Louis XIV of France is often regarded as the typical absolute monarch. Justified by the theory of the divine right of kings, absolutism was associated in the 18th century with enlightened despotism but was challenged by the ideals of the American and French Revolutions.

absorption *See* ADSORPTION.

abstract art A nonrepresentational form of art. Tendencies to abstraction can be found in almost any age or school of art, particularly oriental and decorative art. However, the widespread use of *photography in the 20th century to create a permanent visual record of people, places, events, etc., made the strictly representational function of painting much less important, enabling artists to explore various forms of abstraction. In about 1910 Wassily Kandinsky (1866–1944) produced a watercolour that is usually considered the first modern abstract. Two main tendencies of abstract art have since developed; whereas *cubism led to the geometric abstract style of such painters as Piet *Mondrian and Kasimir Malevich (1878–1935), the abstract expressionists (*see* ABSTRACT EXPRESSIONISM), such as Jackson *Pollock, emphasized spontaneous free expression. A characteristic of abstract sculpture is the use of new materials, such as plastic, glass, and steel. *See also* ACTION PAINTING; CONSTRUCTIVISM; MINIMAL ART.

abstract expressionism An art movement that developed in New York in the years after World War II, characterized by an emphasis on spontaneous subjective expression. It is associated with experimental improvisational techniques, notably the *action painting of Jackson *Pollock. Other artists associated with the movement include *de Kooning and *Rothko.

Abu Dhabi *See* UNITED ARAB EMIRATES.

Abuja 9 10N 7 06E The federal capital of Nigeria; the seat of government moved to this new city in December 1991. Population (1996 est): 350 100.

Abu Simbel A monumental rock-cut temple complex constructed about 1250 BC by Pharaoh Ramses II in *Nubia. Four colossal statues of Ramses, each 20 m (66 ft) high, at the entrance were raised to escape inundation by Lake Nasser (1968).

Abydos An ancient city in Upper Egypt, founded before 3000 BC and continuously occupied until Roman times. It was a principal centre of *Osiris worship. The most impressive remaining structure is Seti I's Great Temple (c. 1300 BC), with shrines for six deities and the god pharaoh. The Table of Abydos, a king list carved on its walls, provides information about earlier pharaohs.

abyssal zone The ocean depths lying below 1000 m. It is the zone of greatest ocean depth, lying seawards of the continental slope (*see* CONTINENTAL SHELF). Since no light penetrates to these depths, they contain relatively little marine life and the temperature never rises above 4°C. The ocean depths below 6000 m, the deep-sea trenches, may be classified separately as the **hadal zone**.

Abyssinian cat A breed of short-haired cat, many individuals of which are descendants of one exported to the UK from Abyssinia in the 19th century. They have slender bodies and wedge-shaped heads with large ears. The reddish-brown coat has black or brown markings. The Red Abyssinian is a rich copper-red.

Acacia A genus of tropical and subtropical trees and shrubs (over 700 species), particularly abundant in Australia (*see* WATTLE). Acacias have clusters of yellow or white flowers, produce long flattened pods, and usually have compound leaves consisting of many small leaflets. In some species the leaflets do not develop and the leafstalks assume their function, being broad and flattened. Acacias yield a number of useful products: gums (including gum arabic), tannins, dyes, and woods suitable for furniture. Many are grown as ornamental plants. Family: *Leguminosae*.

Académie Française The French literary academy founded by Cardinal de Richelieu in 1634 (incorporated 1635) to preserve the French literary heritage. Its membership is limited at any one time to 40 "immortals," who have included Corneille, Racine, and Voltaire. It is continuously engaged in the revision of the official French dictionary.

Academy, Greek The college founded (c. 385 BC) near Athens by Plato, which continued in various guises until its dissolution by Justinian in 529 AD. It is famed mainly for contributions to philosophy and science.

Academy of Motion Picture Arts and Sciences An organization founded in Hollywood in 1927 to raise the artistic and technical standards of the film industry. It is responsible for the annual presentation of the **Academy Awards**, popularly known as Oscars, for excellence in acting, writing, directing, and other aspects of film production.

Acanthus A genus of perennial herbaceous

plants (about 50 species), mostly native to the Mediterranean region: *A. mollis* and *A. spinosus* are the species most commonly planted in temperate gardens. Growing to a height of 1–1.5 m, they have tough, often spiny, leaves and spikes of purple and white flowers. The fruit—a capsule—explodes to disperse the seeds. Family: *Acanthaceae*.

Acapulco 16 51N 99 56W A seaside resort in S Mexico, on the Pacific Ocean. Known as the Riviera of Mexico, it has fine sandy beaches and many hotels. Population (2000 est): 619 253.

acceleration The rate of change of a body's velocity. Linear acceleration is the rate of change of linear velocity. It is measured in metres per second per second. Angular acceleration is the rate of change of angular velocity and is measured in radians per second per second.

acceleration of free fall (*g*) Formerly called acceleration due to gravity; the acceleration of a falling body when air resistance is neglected. Caused by gravitational attraction between the body and the earth, it varies slightly at different points on the earth's surface. Its standard value is 9.806 metres per second per second.

accelerators Large machines used for accelerating beams of charged particles (electrons, protons, etc.) to very high speeds primarily for research in *particle physics. The particles are accelerated by electric fields either in a straight line, as in the *linear accelerator, or in a circle, as in the *cyclotron, *synchrotron, and *synchrocyclotron. The beam is confined to its path by magnetic fields. Particle accelerators are used by directing a beam of particles at a stationary target or, for greater energy, by colliding two beams of particles together. Accelerators are also used to create artificial isotopes and in *radiotherapy. The first accelerator was a linear accelerator, produced in 1932 by *Cockcroft and *Walton. *See also* CERN.

accessory In law, a person who incites another to commit a crime but is not present when the crime is committed is an accessory before the fact. (An abettor is distinguished from an accessory before the fact by being present at the commission of a crime.) A person who assists another whom he knows has committed a crime is an accessory after the fact.

accomplice In law, a person concerned with one or more other persons in committing a crime, either as its actual perpetrator or as an abettor or *accessory.

accordion A portable musical instrument invented in Berlin in 1822. A member of the reed-organ family, the accordion is a boxlike instrument in which bellows force air through reeds mounted in end panels. In the modern **piano accordion** a small piano-like keyboard supplies the melody, while buttons operated by the other hand produce chords.

Accra 5 32N 0 12W The capital of Ghana, a port on the Gulf of Guinea. It is built on the site of three 17th-century trading fortresses founded by the English, Dutch, and Danish. It became the capital of the Gold Coast in 1877. Following the opening of a railway to the agricultural hinterland (1923) it developed rapidly into the commercial centre of Ghana. The University of Ghana was founded in 1948 at Legon, just outside Accra. Population (1998 est): 1 446 000 (metropolitan area).

accumulator A cell or battery that can be recharged by passing a current through it in the direction opposite to that of the discharge current. The most common example is the lead-acid accumulator used in motor vehicles. This consists, when charged, of a positive lead dioxide electrode and a negative spongy lead electrode, both immersed in sulphuric acid with a relative density of 1.20–1.28. During discharge lead sulphate forms on the electrodes and the acid density falls.

Nickel-iron (NiFe) accumulators with an electrolyte of 20% potassium hydroxide are also used. Interest in *electric cars has stimulated accumulator development.

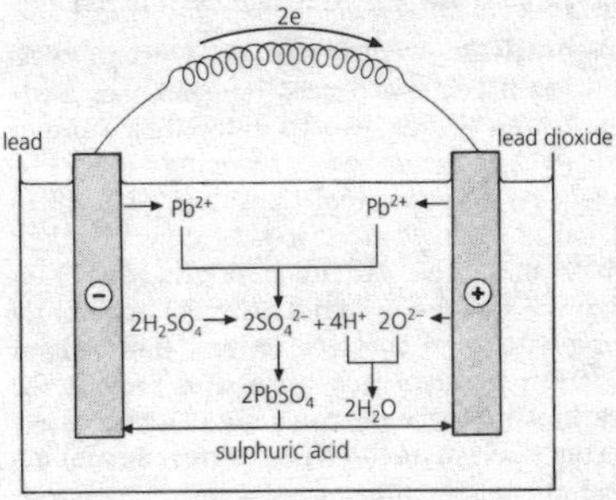

accumulator. A single cell of a lead (Pb) sulphuric acid (H_2SO_4) accumulator. The reactions shown are those taking place during discharge. During charging the lead sulphate ($PbSO_4$) is converted to lead dioxide (PbO_2) and sulphuric acid, the density of which rises.

ACE inhibitors (angiotensin-converting enzyme inhibitors) A class of drugs used in the treatment of high blood pressure and heart failure, often in combination with a *diuretic. They prevent artery constriction by interfering with the enzyme that converts angiotensin into an artery constrictor. Examples include captopril and enalapril.

acetylcholine A chemical that transmits impulses between the ends of two adjacent nerves and is confined largely to the parasympathetic nervous system. Acetylcholine is released on stimulation of the nerve and diffuses across the gap of the *synapse to stimulate the adjacent nerve. It is rapidly converted to an inactive form by the enzyme cholinesterase, permitting the passage of a further impulse.

acetylene *See* ALKYNES.

Achebe, Chinua (1930–) Nigerian novelist of the Ibo people. His first novel, *Things Fall Apart* (1958), deals with the arrival of missionaries and colonial government in the Ibo homeland. His other works include the novels *A Man of the People* (1966) and *Anthills of the Savannah* (1987), as well as short stories, poems, and essays.

achene A small dry *fruit having a single seed that is attached to the fruit wall at one point only. The fruit does not open at maturity (i.e. the fruit is indehiscent) and the seed is thus retained until germination. Lettuce fruits are examples of achenes.

Acheron A river in N Greece, in Greek mythology the chief river of the underworld. In Dante, it is the river across which the souls of the dead are ferried to hell by *Charon.

Acheulian A culture of the Lower *Palaeolithic. It is characterized by hand axes made by hammering flakes off a flint with a hammer of wood, antler, or bone, producing a more regular and effective tool than the *Abbevillian hand axe. Named after St Acheul near Amiens (N France), the Acheulian occurs widely in Eurasia and also in Africa, where it apparently originated and survived longest (until about 58 000 years ago). Acheulian sites provide the earliest evidence of man's use of fire and are often associated with *Homo erectus* remains (*see* HOMO).

Achilles In Greek mythology, the greatest Greek warrior in the Trojan War. The son of Peleus, King of Thessaly, and Thetis, a sea nymph, he was dipped by his mother in the River Styx as a child, which made his whole body invulnerable except for the heel by which she had held him. After a quarrel with *Agamemnon he ceased fighting until the death of his friend Patroclus at the hand of *Hector. Achilles then slew Hector and was himself later killed by Paris, who shot a poisoned arrow into his heel.

acid rain Rain that contains sulphuric and nitric acids as a result of the absorption of sulphur dioxide and nitrogen oxides, mostly from industrial and vehicle emissions, in the atmosphere. It is contended that the effects can include destruction of fish, crops, and trees, as well as damage to buildings. In 1985 19 countries agreed to make substantial reductions in the emission of sulphur dioxide by 1993.

acids and bases Acids are chemical compounds containing hydrogen that can be replaced by a metal atom to produce a *salt. They have a sour taste and turn litmus red. When dissolved in water they dissociate into ions. Hydrochloric acid (HCl), for instance, gives chloride ions and hydrogen ions: $HCl + H_2O \rightarrow Cl^- + H^+ + H_2O$. The hydrogen ion is associated with a water molecule, a combination referred to as a hydroxonium ion (H_3O^+).

Bases are compounds that react with acids to form salts and water. Bases that dissolve in water, known as **alkalis**, produce hydroxide ions (OH^-). Many are metal hydroxides, such as sodium hydroxide (NaOH). The neutralization of an acid by a base in solution is a reaction in which hydrogen and hydroxide ions combine to give water. The concept of an acid has been extended to include any compound that can donate a proton and a base as a proton acceptor. This (the Brönsted-Lowry theory) can be applied to reactions in nonaqueous solvents. A further extension of the terms (Lewis theory) defines an acid as an acceptor of an unshared electron pair and a base as a pair donor. *See also* PH.

acne A skin condition, common in adolescence, affecting the face, chest, and back. Acne is caused by overactivity and inflammation of the sebaceous glands: oily sebum accumulates in the hair follicles, producing pustules and blackheads. Severe cases can be treated with antibiotics, retinoids (e.g. isotretinoin), or other drugs.

Aconcagua, Mount (Spanish name: Cerro Aconcagua) 32 40S 70 02W A mountain in W Argentina, in the Andes, regarded as being the highest point in the W hemisphere. It is of volcanic origin. Height: 6960 m (22 835 ft).

aconite A European herbaceous plant, *Aconitum napellus*, also known as monkshood. Growing to a height of 1 m, its flowers are usually purplish-blue and hood-shaped; the bulbous roots yield poisonous alkaloids, including aconitine, which have been used in medicine as narcotics and analgesics. Winter aconite is a related plant, *Eranthis hyemalis*, with yellow flowers. Family: *Ranunculaceae* (buttercup family).

acornworm A wormlike marine invertebrate animal, 5–180 cm long, that burrows in soft sand or mud. A filter feeder, it has an acorn-shaped head with the mouth at the base. Chief genera: *Balanoglossus*, *Saccoglossus*; phylum: *Hemichordata*.

acoustics The branch of physics concerned with the production, propagation, reception, properties, and uses of sound. **Architectural acoustics** is concerned with the design of public auditoriums so that sounds can be heard in all parts of them with the maximum clarity and the minimum distortion. *Ultrasonics is the study of very high frequency sound (above about 20 000 hertz). The structure and function of sound sources, such as loudspeakers, and sound receptors, such as microphones, also form part of acoustics. Other fields include speech communication and the design of machines that can understand spoken instructions.

acquittal In law, the clearing of an accused person of the charge against him, usually by court verdict. In England there must be a verdict of "not guilty"; in Scotland the verdict may be either "not guilty" or "not proven." Acquittal prevents a person from being prosecuted for the same offence again. Anyone charged as an *accessory to a crime is automatically acquitted if the principal is acquitted.

acromegaly A rare disease in which a noncancerous tumour of the pituitary gland secretes abnormally large amounts of growth hormone. This causes enlargement of the face, hands, feet, and heart. The tumour can be destroyed by X-rays, surgically removed, or treated with drugs (e.g. bromocriptine).

acropolis (Greek: high town) In ancient Greek towns, the isolated rocky plateau on which stood the religious and administrative nucleus of the town and which served as a citadel in time of war. The most famous is the Acropolis of Athens, which is still adorned by remains of buildings (including the Propylaea, *Parthenon, and Erectheum) erected by *Cimon, *Themistocles, and *Pericles.

acrylics Synthetic materials produced by *polymerization of acrylonitrile (vinyl cyanide; CH_2:CHCN). Acrylic resins are used in paints and plastics, the most common being *Perspex. Acrylic fibre is widely used in textiles, mainly for knitwear, furnishing fabrics, and carpets. **Acrylic paints** are easily applied and enable artists to produce a bright smooth finish.

Actaeon A mythological Greek hunter, son of the god Aristaeus and Autonoe, daughter of Cadmus, King of Thebes. Ovid, in his *Metamorphoses*, relates how Actaeon accidentally caught sight of the goddess Artemis bathing naked and was turned by her into a stag and killed by his own hounds.

ACTH (adrenocorticotrophic hormone) A peptide hormone, secreted by the anterior lobe of the pituitary gland, that stimulates the cortex of the adrenal glands to produce three types of *corticosteroid hormones. Secretion of ACTH is stimulated by physical stress and is regulated by secretions of the *hypothalamus of the brain.

actinides A group of related chemical elements in the periodic table ranging from actinium (atomic number 89) to lawrencium (atomic number 103). They are radioactive and include a number of *transuranic elements. Chemically, they resemble the *lanthanides.

actinium (Ac) A highly radioactive metal that occurs naturally in uranium minerals. It is the first of the actinide series of elements and is chemically similar to the lanthanide elements. It was discovered in 1899 by A. L. Debierne (1874–1949). The **actinium series** of radioactive decay is headed by uranium-235, which undergoes a series of alpha and beta decays ending with the stable isotope lead-207. At no 89; at wt (227); mp 1051°C; bp 3200 ± 300°C; half-life of ^{227}Ac 21.6 yrs.

action painting A modern art technique, mainly associated with *abstract expressionism, in which paint is sprayed, splashed, or dribbled over a large canvas to form an unpremeditated and usually abstract design. Jackson *Pollock invented it in 1947 to give free expression to his emotions.

Actium, Battle of (31 BC) The decisive land and sea battle that ended the civil war in ancient Rome. Octavian, later *Augustus (the first Roman emperor), defeated the forces of *Mark Antony and Cleopatra.

Actors' Studio An actors' workshop founded in New York in 1947 by Elia *Kazan and others. Under its director Lee Strasberg (1901–82), who joined it in 1950, it became famous for its emphasis on "method" acting, which was developed from the theories of *Stanislavsky. Film actors influenced by it in-

a

clude Marlon *Brando, Rod Steiger (1925–2002), and James *Dean.

Acts of the Apostles The fifth book of the New Testament, written by Luke about 63 AD as a sequel to his Gospel. Starting with the ascension of Christ, it deals with the spread of the Christian Church from a single congregation in Jerusalem to Paul's first missionary journey and his eventual imprisonment in Rome.

actuary A mathematician employed by an *insurance company to calculate the premiums payable on policies. The calculations are based on statistically determined risks and eventualities (e.g. sickness, life expectancy). In the UK qualifications are awarded by the Institute of Actuaries through examination.

acupuncture A traditional Chinese system of healing in which thin metal needles are inserted into selected points in the body. The needles are stimulated either by manual rotation or electrically. Acupuncture is used in the Far East to relieve pain and in China as an anaesthetic for surgical operations. The traditional explanation of its effectiveness relates to balancing the opposing life forces *yin and yang. Recent research in the West suggests that the needles may activate deep sensory nerves, which cause the pituitary and midbrain to release endorphins (natural pain killers; *see* ENCEPHALINS).

Adam, Adolphe-Charles (1803–56) French composer. He composed over 60 operas but is primarily remembered for his romantic ballet *Giselle* (1841), the earliest full-length traditional ballet.

Adam and Eve In the Old Testament, the first human beings. According to Genesis (2.7–3.24), Jehovah created Adam from dust in his own image and put him in the Garden of Eden. His wife Eve was created from one of his ribs. Tempted by the serpent (the devil) to eat the forbidden fruit of the Tree of Knowledge, Eve induced Adam to eat the fruit also; as a result they were expelled from Eden. Their sons included Cain and Abel.

Adam, Robert (1728–92) British architect and interior designer. The son of the Palladian architect **William Adam** (1689–1748), he evolved a unique style that blended the *rococo and *neoclassicism, although he occasionally used gothic forms. After visiting Italy (1755–58), Robert, often in collaboration with his brother **James Adam** (1732–94), built many country houses, notably Kenwood House (1768), the interior of Syon House (1769), and Osterley Park (1780). His building of town houses in London, such as Apsley House (1775), led him into severe financial difficulties. In his last years in Edinburgh he produced much of his finest work, for instance Charlotte Square (1791).

Adams, Gerry (Gerard A.; 1948–) Northern Irish politician, president of Sinn Féin (1983–). He was a leading participant in the talks that produced the Good Friday Agreement of 1998 and subsequent attempts to resolve the issue of the decommissioning of IRA weapons. Since 1983 he has been several times elected to the British parliament but declines to take his seat.

Adams, John (1735–1826) US statesman; first vice president (1789–97) and second president of the USA (1797–1801). During the American Revolution he successfully mobilized European support for the North American cause. His term as president was troubled by disputes with his vice president, Thomas *Jefferson, over US policy towards Revolutionary France. Adams was defeated by Jefferson in the election of 1800. His son **John Quincy Adams** (1767–1848) was sixth president of the USA (1825–29). As secretary of state (1817–25) he was largely responsible for the *Monroe Doctrine (1823). His presidency was made difficult by the opposition of Andrew Jackson, who defeated Adams in the presidential election in 1828. From 1831 Adams served in the House of Representatives, where he campaigned against slavery.

adaptation In biology, a change in a physical characteristic of an animal or plant that makes it better suited to survive in a particular environment. For example, cacti have adapted to desert environments by evolving swollen water-storing stems. *See also* ADAPTIVE RADIATION.

adaptive radiation The process by which a uniform population of animals or plants evolves into a number of different forms. The original population increases in size and spreads to occupy different habitats. It forms several subpopulations, each adapted to the particular conditions of its habitat. In time—and if the subpopulations differ sufficiently—a number of new species will be formed from the original stock. The Australian marsupials evolved in this way into burrowers, fliers, carnivores, herbivores, and many other different forms.

adder A widely distributed European *viper, *Vipera berus*, about 80 cm long, common in heathland areas. It is usually greyish with a broad black zigzag line along its back and black spots on its sides. Although venomous, its bite is rarely fatal. It is one of the three species of snakes found in Britain. The name adder is also given to a highly venomous Australian snake (death adder) of the cobra family and to some harmless North American snakes. *See also* PUFF ADDER.

Addington, Henry, 1st Viscount Sidmouth (1757–1844) British statesman; prime minister (1801–04), replacing Pitt the Younger. Addington was attacked for his management of the Napoleonic Wars and resigned. As home secretary (1812–21) he has been held responsible for the *Peterloo Massacre.

Addis Ababa 9 02N 38 43E The capital of Ethiopia, on a central plateau 2440 m (8000 ft) above sea level. It became the capital in 1889 and was capital of Italian East Africa (1936–41). It is the country's administrative centre and chief market place and its major industries produce cement, tobacco, textiles, and shoes. A railway line links the city with the port of Djibouti on the Gulf of Aden. It is also an important pan-African centre with the headquarters of the African Union and the UN Economic Commission for Africa. Population (1994 est): 2 316 400.

Addison, Joseph (1672–1719) British essayist and poet. He became an undersecretary in the Whig administration in 1706 and was elected to parliament in 1708. He began to contribute to Richard *Steele's journal, the *Tatler*, and in 1711 Addison and Steele founded the *Spectator*. He is also remembered for the tragedy *Cato* (1713).

Addison's disease A rare disease of the adrenal glands, first described by the British physician Thomas Addison (1793–1860), characterized by a reduced secretion of corticosteroid hormones. This leads to weakness, intestinal upsets, darkening of the skin, low blood pressure, and collapse. Formerly fatal, Addison's disease can now be readily treated with synthetic steroids.

Adelaide 34 56S 138 36E The capital of South Australia, on the Torrens River. Founded in 1837, the city was laid out in wide straight streets. Extensive parklands separate the city from its suburbs. It is an important commercial centre with a harbour at Port Adelaide. Industries include the manufacture of cars and textiles, oil refining, and electronics. Population (1995 est): 1 081 000.

Aden 12 50N 45 03E The main port and commercial centre of Yemen, on the **Gulf of Aden**, an arm of the Indian Ocean connecting with the Red Sea. Taken by the British in 1839, Aden was an important coaling station on the Suez route to India. It became part of the Federation of Saudi Arabia in 1963 and was the scene of fighting between rival nationalist groups until 1968, when it became the capital of the independent republic of South Yemen, now part of Yemen. Economic activity centres on the port and an oil refinery. Population (1995 est): 562 000.

Adenauer, Konrad (1876–1967) German statesman. He was a successful Rhineland politician until the Nazi government forced him out of public life (1934) and imprisoned him (1934, 1944). In 1946 Adenauer re-emerged as chairman of the Christian Democratic Union (CDU) and became the first chancellor (1949–63) of the Federal Republic of Germany. He presided over Germany's economic miracle and did much to restore its international prestige.

adenoids Two masses of tissue situated at the back of the nose. They consist of lymphatic tissue, which destroys disease-causing microbes in the throat. In children they are normally large, and when associated with recurrent throat infections or persistent breathing through the mouth are usually removed surgically. This operation is often combined with tonsillectomy (removal of the tonsils) as the tonsils also tend to be infected.

adiabatic process Any process in which heat neither enters nor leaves a system. Usually, such a process changes the temperature of the system. An example is the sudden compression of a gas, causing its temperature to rise. The compression is assumed to take place so quickly that the gas loses none of its acquired heat.

Ádi Granth The canonical scriptures of Sikhism, compiled in 1604 by Arjun Mal (1581–1606). It consists of about 6000 hymns. Although Sikhs do not worship images, the Ádi Granth is itself an object of worship.

Adirondack Mountains A mountain range in the USA, in N New York state. It consists of a glaciated plateau rising to 1629 m (5344 ft) at Mount Marcy. Its scenery and lakes make it a popular tourist area.

adjutant stork A large carrion-eating *stork, *Leptotilos dubius*, occurring in Asia and similar to the related *marabou. It has a white plumage with dark-grey back, wings, and tail, a short neck, and a heavy pointed bill. Its head and neck are naked and a bald pouch hangs from the throat. Order: *Ciconiiformes.*

Adler, Alfred (1870–1937) Austrian psychiatrist who introduced the concept of the *inferiority complex. Initially an associate of Sigmund *Freud, Adler came to disagree with Freud and by 1911 he had founded his own school. Adler viewed each individual as a unique entity striving to compensate for feelings of inferiority resulting from physical or social disabilities (*The Neurotic Constitution*, 1912) and regarded sex as an opportunity to express dominance.

Admiral's Cup A biennial sailing competition held by the Royal Ocean Racing Club since 1957. Three yachts represent each nation and the competition comprises three races in the Solent and two offshore races: from Cherbourg to the Isle of Wight and from Plymouth to the Fastnet Rock off SW Ireland and back (the Fastnet Cup).

Admiralty Islands A group of about 40 islands in the SW Pacific Ocean, in Papua New Guinea in the Bismarck Archipelago. Copra and pearls are exported. The main island is Manus with the chief town, Lorengau. Area: about 2000 sq km (800 sq mi). Population (1995): 35 200.

Adonis In Greek mythology, a youth from Cyprus, loved by *Aphrodite for his great beauty. *Zeus decreed that his time should be divided between Aphrodite on earth, Persephone, queen of the underworld, and himself. He was celebrated in many festivals, his death and resurrection representing seasonal change.

adoption The process enabling a natural parent's legal rights and duties towards an unmarried minor to be transferred to another adult. The Adoption Act (1976), as amended by the Children's Act (1989), controls the work of adoption societies, the rights of the natural parents, and the adopted child's right to know his original name. Birth control, abortion, and the acceptance of one-parent families has decreased the number of children available for adoption in recent years. However, greater publicity has been given to finding adoptive homes for children with special needs, e.g. older children, children of mixed race, and the physically or mentally handicapped.

adrenal glands Two small pyramid-shaped endocrine glands in man and other mammals, one at the upper end of each of the kidneys. Each gland has an outer cortex, controlled by hormones secreted by the pituitary gland, and an inner medulla producing *adrenaline and *noradrenaline, controlled directly by the nervous system. The cortex secretes three classes of steroid hormones that regulate the balance of salts and water, the use of carbohydrates, and the activity of the sex glands (*see* CORTICOSTEROIDS). *See also* ADDISON'S DISEASE; CUSHING'S DISEASE.

adrenaline (*or* **epinephrine**) A hormone secreted by the medulla of the *adrenal glands. A *catecholamine derived from the amino acid tyrosine, adrenaline increases heart rate, raises blood pressure, and increases the level of blood glucose. Its release is triggered by stress in preparation by the body for "fight or flight." Adrenaline is also secreted by nerve endings of the sympathetic nervous system. *See also* NORADRENALINE.

Adrian IV (Nicholas Breakspear; c. 1100–59) Pope (1154–59). The only English pope, also known as Hadrian IV, he was unanimously elected after leading the mission to the Scandinavian churches (1152). His claim that the Holy Roman Empire was held by papal grant occasioned a major quarrel with Emperor Frederick Barbarossa.

Adriatic Sea A northern arm of the Mediterranean Sea, extending between Italy and Croatia for about 750 km (466 mi). Its principal ports are Brindisi, Bari, Venice, Trieste, and Rijeka. The Italian and Croatian coasts are strikingly different: the one flat and sandy, the other rocky and irregular with many offshore islands.

adsorption The production of a layer of atoms or molecules of a substance on a solid or liquid surface. The adsorbed atoms or molecules may be strongly held by chemical bonds (**chemisorption**), in which case the adsorbed layer is usually only one molecule thick. Adsorption may also occur through weaker physical forces (**physisorption**), often giving rise to several molecular layers. In contrast, **absorption** involves material penetrating into the bulk of a solid or liquid.

adultery Voluntary sexual intercourse between a married person and a person of the opposite sex to whom he or she is not married. In many countries, including some US states, adultery is a crime; under some systems, such as Islamic law, it may carry the death penalty. More generally it is a ground for *divorce or judicial separation; in English law it has traditionally been considered proof of the "irretrievable breakdown" of a marriage.

Advent (from Latin: *adventus*, coming) The first season of the church year, leading to *Christmas. It begins on the Sunday nearest St Andrew's Day (30 Nov). From the 6th century it has been observed as a solemn preparation for celebrating Christ's birth and for his Second Coming.

adventists Several Protestant Christian denominations that stress a belief in the imminent Second Coming of Christ. In the USA adventism began in 1831 with the millenarian preaching of William Miller (1782–1849), who predicted the Second Coming for 1843–44, but postponed the date when his prediction proved false. In the UK a similar movement was founded in 1832 as the Catholic Apostolic Church. There have been many adventist movements, the Seventh-Day Adventists now being the best known.

advocate In Scotland and in some countries, such as France, having a legal system based on Roman law, a person whose profession is to plead the cases of others in a court of justice. The English equivalent is a barrister. In Scotland, the **Lord Advocate** is the chief law officer of the Crown, generally equivalent to the *attorney general in England.

Aegean civilizations The prehistoric settlements on the islands of the Aegean Sea (between mainland Greece and Asia Minor). At the beginning of the Bronze Age (c.3000 BC) an influx of immigrants to the Cyclades islands (S Aegean) brought sophistication and prosperity, which can be seen from the excavations on Thera (*or* Santorini). The subsequent Minoan civilization was at its greatest between the 17th and 15th centuries BC. At the end of the 15th century BC the related Mycenaean civilization asserted its supremacy.

Aegean Sea A section of the NE Mediterranean Sea, lying between Greece and Turkey and containing many islands, including the Cyclades, Dodecanese, and N Sporades.

Aeneas A legendary Trojan leader, son of Anchises and *Aphrodite, and hero of Virgil's *Aeneid*. After the Greek victory in the Trojan War, he sailed away from burning Troy with his family and other survivors and was shipwrecked near Carthage. He fell in love with *Dido but abandoned her to continue his divinely ordained voyage to Italy, where he founded what was to become Rome.

Aeolus The Greek god of the winds and ruler of Aeolia. In Homer's *Odyssey* he gave Odysseus a bag containing contrary winds; Odysseus' companions untied it, causing his ship to be blown back to Aeolia. An **aeolian harp**, a wooden resonating box strung with gut string produces chordal sounds that vary according to the wind pressure, when hung in the open air.

aerial (*or* **antenna**) An electrical conductor that transmits and receives radio or other electromagnetic waves. An oscillating *electromagnetic field, caused by waves from a distant source, induces an oscillating current in the receiving aerial. A transmitting aerial works by the same process in reverse. A modern aerial for UHF (ultra-high frequency) and VHF (very high frequency) consists of a dipole formed from two metal rods, each approximately one-quarter of the operating wavelength. In the **Yagi aerial** named after H. Yagi (1886–1976), a reflector rod is set behind the dipole and several director rods are placed in front of it to provide a more directional array. It is widely used as a receiving and transmitting aerial for television.

aerodynamics The study of the behaviour and flow of air around objects. As air is a viscous fluid any object moving through it experiences a drag. Aerodynamics is important in the design of vehicles travelling at more than 50 km per hour (31 mph), buildings and bridges, engines, furnaces, as well as aircraft (*see* AERONAUTICS) and missiles.

aeronautics The science and history (*see also* AIRCRAFT) of flight. An object flying through air is subject to four basic forces: its own weight (vertically downwards as a result of gravity), lift (to counterbalance its weight and keep it in the air), thrust (to force it through the air), and drag (resulting from friction between the body and the air). Birds and insects use their wings to provide both lift and thrust; man, in his heavier-than-air fixed-wing craft, uses an **aerofoil** to provide the lift and an *internal-combustion engine (propeller or jet) to provide the thrust (*see also* AIRCRAFT; GLIDERS). Helicopters use rotating aerofoils to provide lift, while *rockets use no lift surfaces, the jet of expanding gas providing both lift and thrust. The use of aerofoils as lift surfaces depends on Bernoulli's theorem, according to which the total energy of a flowing fluid remains constant; thus, if the velocity of the fluid increases, its pressure decreases in proportion. An aerofoil is a wing so shaped that (at subsonic speeds) air is accelerated over its rounded leading edge and curved upper surface, causing a reduced pressure above it. A smaller reduction in air velocity on its underside causes a slightly increased pressure below it. The combination of these pressure differences provides the lift. At supersonic speeds these forces are somewhat altered (*see* SOUND BARRIER) and the aerofoil has to be more sweptback and more streamlined. *See also* AIRSHIPS; BALLOONS.

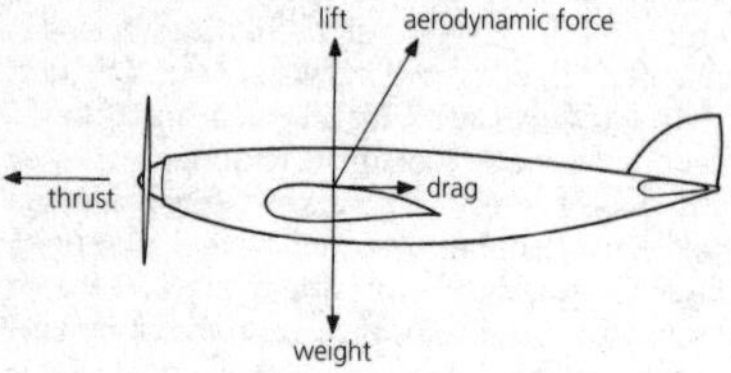

forces acting on aircraft

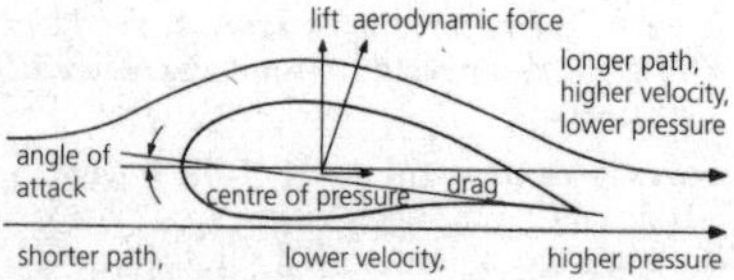

cross-section of aerofoil

aeronautics. The forces acting on an aircraft. The aerofoil cross-section shows how the lift, which keeps it in the air, results from the passage of the aerofoil through the air, causing a lower pressure above it and a higher pressure below it.

aerosol A colloidal suspension of particles of liquid or solid in a gaseous medium. Fog, mist, and smoke are common natural examples. By means of pressurized packages, aerosols can be produced from a huge range of substances, including insecticides, paints, hairsprays, etc. In these, the substance is mixed with an easily liquefied gas (often a chlorofluorocarbon, CFC), which acts as a propellant when the pressure is released. Because there is evidence that CFCs cause damage to the ozone layer, safer propellants are being sought.

Aeschylus (c. 525–456 BC) Greek tragic dramatist, the first of the great trio of Athenian tragedians that included *Sophocles and *Euripides. He wrote over 80 plays, of which only 7 survive: *The Persians* (472), *Seven against Thebes* (467), the *Oresteia* trilogy (*Agamemnon*, *Libation Bearers*, and *Eumenides*; 458), *Suppliant Women*, and *Prometheus Bound*. His introduction of a second actor, allowing dialogue and action independent of the chorus, and his innovations in scenery, transformed drama.

Aesop The supposed author of a collection of Greek fables, said by Herodotus to be a slave from Samos who lived in the 6th century BC. Originating in folklore, the fables are anecdotal stories whose animal characters illustrate a moral point. The Roman poet Phaedrus popularized them in the 1st century AD, and the French poet La Fontaine wrote more sophisticated versions in the 17th century.

Aesthetic movement A British literary and artistic movement of the late 19th century, summarized in the slogan "art for art's sake." Reacting against the ugliness of industrialism and against contemporary utilitarian social philosophies, its followers sought to create beauty for its own sake, self-consciously divorcing art from life. They included Oscar Wilde, Aubrey Beardsley, and other contributors to the periodical *The Yellow Book* (1894–97). *See also* DECADENTS.

aesthetics The philosophical study of art. It includes questions concerning the nature of beauty and how we arrive at standards of judgment. Objective views hold that beauty is in the object and that aesthetic judgments are true or false. Subjective views see value as something an observer brings to the work—it may be purely a matter of personal preference or, as *Kant held, something that can be universally agreed upon.

Aetius, Flavius (d. 454 AD) Roman general. He became virtual ruler of the western Empire, dominating the emperor, Valentian III (reigned 425–55). Aetius defeated the Huns under Attila at the Catalaunian Plains (451) but was powerless to halt their invasion of Italy. He was subsequently murdered by Valentian.

Afghan hound A breed of large dog having long legs, large drooping ears, and a very long silky coat, which may be of any colour. The Afghan probably originated in ancient Egypt and was later used in Afghanistan to hunt leopards and gazelles. Height: 68–73 cm (dogs); 61–66 cm (bitches).

Afghanistan, Republic of A state in central Asia. The country is mountainous, the Hindu Kush range rising over 6000 m (20 000 ft). The only lower-lying areas are along the River Amu Darya (ancient name: Oxus) in the N and the delta of the River Helmand in the SW. The population consists of mixed ethnic groups, the largest being the Pathans and the Tadzhiks. *Economy*: virtually all forms of economic activity have been devastated by 25 years of civil war. The cultivation of opium poppies and the production and sale of narcotics, although officially discouraged, are now the country's main source of revenue. Agriculture is now mainly at subsistence level. Attempts made during the 1970s to develop industry, exploit mineral and natural gas resources, and to improve communications have all been halted. *History*: before the opening up of international sea routes in the 15th century Afghanistan was an important centre on the overland routes across central Asia. For centuries under the rule of different powers, including the Mongol Genghis Khan in the 13th century, it became an independent kingdom in 1747. During the 19th century Afghanistan became involved in the struggle between Britain and Russia for influence in central Asia. After two wars with Britain (1839–42 and 1878–80) it became a buffer state between British India and Russia, with Britain controlling its foreign policy. Independence was achieved in 1921 under Amanollah Khan (1892–1960) after the third Afghan War. In 1926 Amanollah declared himself king. He was deposed in 1929 by a brigand chief, Habibullah, who was in turn defeated by Nader Khan. When the latter was assassinated in 1933 he was succeeded by his son, King Zahir. Since World War II there has been friction with Pakistan over the question of an independent Pathan state in Pakistan. In 1973 the monarchy was overthrown by Mohammed Daud and in 1977 a republic was set up with Daud as president. In 1978 he was killed in a military coup and a new government was set up by the Marxist People's Democratic Party. In 1979 Babrak Karmal came to power with Soviet aid; he was succeeded in 1986 by Mohammad Najibullah (1947–96). Soviet military occupation of Afghanistan provoked worldwide condemnation. After nine years of fighting against Mujahidin guerrillas, Soviet forces withdrew in 1989; Najibullah's government was finally overthrown in 1992. Fierce fighting continued between rival factions and in 1996 the Taleban militia ousted the Kabul government and imposed strict Islamic law. By late 1998 they had defeated anti-Taleban forces in the N (the Northern Alliance) to take control of virtually the whole country. In October–November 2001 Afghan cities suffered massive US airstrikes after the Taleban refused to hand over Osama *Bin Laden, whose Afghan-based *al-Qaida organization was widely held responsible for the events of *September 11 (*see also* WAR ON TERRORISM). As the Taleban regime collapsed, the Northern Alliance reoccupied Kabul and other major cities. An interim administration was established under Hamid Karzai, who became president in 2002. Fighting between US-led forces and Taleban/al-Qaida fighters has continued intermittently. The conflict has greatly exacerbated Afghanistan's already severe refugee and food supply problems. A new constitution was promulgated in 2004 and democratic elections are planned for later in the year. Official languages: Pushtu and Dari Persian. Currency: afghani of 100 puls. Area: 657 500 sq km (250 000 sq mi). Population (2003 est): 28 717 000. Capital: Kabul.

Africa The second largest continent in the world. A notable feature of the NE is the Great Rift Valley, which contains an extensive system of freshwater lakes as well as the continent's highest point, Mount *Kilimanjaro. The principal rivers are the Nile, Niger, Congo, and Zambezi. Africa's climate and vegetation vary considerably from the arid desert of the Sahara to the tropical rainforest of the Congo basin. The inhabitants of Africa are principally of Negroid origin, although the originators of the Berber language group remain dominant in N Africa and the Sahara and there are a few Cushite-speaking peoples in the NE. *History*: Africa's long history has been substantiated by Louis Leakey's finds of hominoid man at Olduvai Gorge. The earliest African civilization was established in Egypt in about 3400 BC. From the 7th century AD Arab influence was strong and Islam spread with the trans-Saharan and East African coastal trade. Several African kingdoms and empires emerged during this period, notably the Sudanese empires of Ghana, Mali, and Songhai. From the 15th century European exploration and exploitation began, initiated by the Portuguese. Slaves, ivory, and gold were exported from Africa from the 17th to the late 19th centuries. From 1880 to 1912 most of Africa was partitioned by the European powers, which imposed political boundaries upon the continent that bore no relationship to former political and social organizations; this resulted in long-standing problems (*see also* SOUTH AFRICA, REPUBLIC OF). In the 1950s there was movement towards independence and Africa now consists of independent nations. Nevertheless, large areas of the continent have remained politically unstable and economically undeveloped, as well as being prey to natural disasters, such as the droughts that affected E and S Africa in the 1980s and 1990s. The 1990s saw a trend away from dictatorship and one-party rule towards multiparty democracy, as well as the final disappearance of White-dominated regimes (in Namibia and South Africa). Area: about 30 300 000 sq km (11 700 000 sq mi). Population (1998 est): 755 919 000. See illustration on p. 14.

a

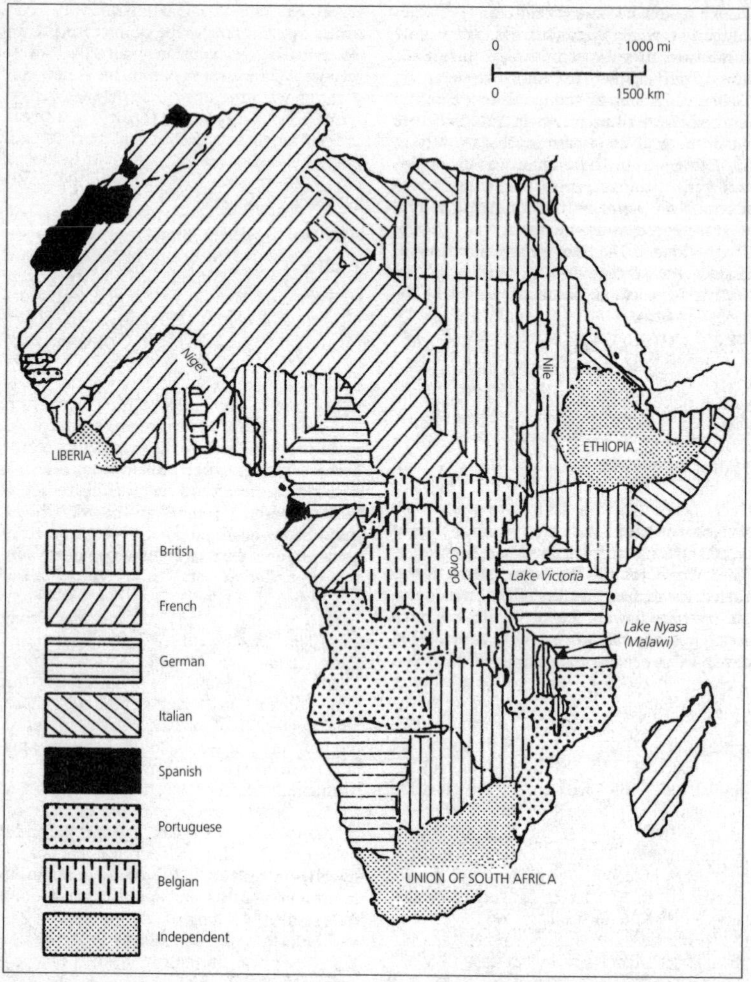

Africa. In the so-called "scramble for Africa" (1880–1912) the European powers annexed most of the continent. The map shows the position in 1914.

African languages A geographical classification of the languages spoken in the African continent. The Hamito-Semitic group extends across N Africa from Mauretania to Somalia. The Nilo-Saharan group is spoken in many dialects in central Africa, and the *Niger-Congo languages, many of them *Bantu languages, cover most of the area S of the Sahara. In S Africa the *Khoisan languages survive. There are up to a thousand indigenous languages of the continent. Malagasy, of Austronesian origin, is spoken in Madagascar. *Swahili is a lingua franca in East Africa. Certain African languages are unique in using click sounds in their phonology; predominance of certain consonantal groups (kp, gb, mb, nd) is also common in Africa.

African National Congress (**ANC**) A

Black nationalist movement in S Africa. Founded in 1912, it fought apartheid from 1948, turning to guerrilla activity after being outlawed by the South African government in 1960. ANC leaders, including Nelson *Mandela, were released from prison in 1989 and 1990, when the ANC was legalized. The ANC played an active role in devising South Africa's interim constitution, signed in 1993, and won multiracial elections in 1994. In 1998 Mandela was succeeded as president of the ANC by Thabo *Mbeki. The ANC greatly increased its majority in elections held in 1999 and Mbeki became president of South Africa; it was re-elected in 2004.

African Union (**AU**) An organization of African States created in 2002 as the successor to the **Organization of African Unity (OAU)** (founded in 1963). It aims to extend the OAU's policy of seeking cooperative solutions to the continent's political and economic problems, with the longer-term goal of establishing an economic union and a Pan-African parliament.

African violet A flowering plant, *Saintpaulia ionantha*, native to tropical East Africa. The plants have rosettes of hairy, often deeply ridged, leaves, bear clusters of pink, blue, purple, or white flowers, and grow to a height of 10–15 cm. Many varieties and hybrids have been developed as ornamentals. Family: *Gesneriaceae*.

Afrikaner A South African of Dutch or *Huguenot descent. The Afrikaners comprise about 60% of the Republic's White population. Formerly called "Boers" (farmers), they have undergone considerable urbanization since the 1930s. In the 18th and 19th centuries they led a seminomadic life, resisting governmental control from Cape Town. Their two independent states, the South African Republic and the Orange Free State, came under British rule after the second Boer War. Their language, **Afrikaans**, derives, but is distinct, from Dutch and together with English has been an official language of South Africa since 1925. *See also* GREAT TREK.

Afro-Asiatic languages *See* HAMITO-SEMITIC LANGUAGES.

Agadir 30 30N 9 40W A port in SW Morocco, on the Atlantic coast. An earthquake in 1960 destroyed much of the town and killed about 12 000 people. Population (1994 est): 155 244.

agama A common African broad-headed lizard belonging to the family *Agamidae* (50 species). 30–45 cm long, agamas feed on insects. The common agama (*Agama agama*) is variously coloured: dominant males have a brick-red head, blue body and legs, and banded tail; other males are duller coloured, like the females.

Agamemnon King of Mycenae and commander of the Greek army in the Trojan War. His quarrel with Achilles is the main theme of Homer's *Iliad*. After his return from Troy with Cassandra, the captured daughter of King Priam, Agamemnon was murdered by his wife Clytemnestra and her lover Aegisthus.

agaric A fungus belonging to a large worldwide family (*Agaricaceae*). The group includes many edible mushrooms, such as the field mushroom (*A. campestris*), as well as the poisonous death cap. The visible part of the fungus consists of a stalk bearing a cap with gills on the undersurface. Phylum: *Basidiomycota*. *See also* FLY AGARIC; MUSHROOM.

agate A banded or concentrically patterned form of *chalcedony. The colours, ranging from white, milky blue, yellow, and brown to red, are due to traces of mineral or organic matter. Being hard, it is used for mortars for grinding, and also for ornamental purposes.

Agave A genus of plants (about 300 species) of the S USA and tropical America, many of which are grown for ornament. Agaves have a basal tuft of thick fleshy leaves and a cluster of flowers that—in some species—grows on a tall stalk (up to 12 m high). It may be 60 or more years before flowers are produced; after flowering the plant dies. Several species are commercially important as a source of fibre, especially *sisal; the fermented juice of others is used as an alcoholic drink (pulque) or distilled to produce spirits (*see* TEQUILA). Family: *Agavaceae* (or *Amaryllidaceae*).

agglomerate A rock composed of a mixture of coarse angular fragments and finer material formed by volcanic explosions; it is usually found in or near the volcanic vent.

Agincourt, Battle of (25 October 1415) The battle that took place during the *Hundred Years' War at Agincourt (now in the Pas-de-Calais), in which the French were defeated by an English army led by Henry V. The decisive English victory, which owed much to their outstanding archers, was achieved with not more than 1600 dead; the French may have lost as many as 6000 men.

Agni The Hindu god of fire, who protects humans from evil, guards the home, and, by cleansing humans from sin, bestows immortality.

a

agnosticism The philosophical view that doubts the existence of God and other spiritual phenomena, claiming that if they exist it is impossible to know anything about them. The word was coined by T. H. Huxley in 1869. Agnosticism was subsequently embraced by rationalists, who hesitated on philosophical or social grounds to adopt outright atheism.

agora A central feature of ancient Greek town planning. As with the Roman *forum, the primary function of the agora was as the town market. In addition, however, it also became the main social and political meeting place. Together with the *acropolis, it normally contained the most important buildings of the town.

agoraphobia *See* PHOBIA.

agouti A rabbit-sized rodent belonging to a genus (*Dasyprocta*; 13 species) of Central and South American forests. Agoutis have long legs, small ears, and a very short hairless tail. Family: *Dasyproctidae* (agoutis and pacas); suborder: *Hystricomorpha*.

Agra 27 09N 78 00E A city in India, in Uttar Pradesh on the River Jumna. Former capital of the Mogul Empire (1566–69 and 1601–58), it fell to the British in 1803 and from 1835 until 1862 was capital of the North-West Provinces. Notable buildings include the *Taj Mahal. Population (1991): 899 195.

Agricola, Gnaeus Julius (40–93 AD) Roman governor of Britain and father-in-law of his biographer Tacitus. Sent to govern Britain in 78, after holding previous legionary posts there, he followed a policy of romanization, exploration, and expansion before his recall in 84.

agricultural revolution The changes in agriculture in Britain that took place mainly in the 18th century. The open-field system of strip farming was replaced by larger enclosed fields, hedged and ditched, in which improved agricultural methods and new implements could be used (*see* TULL, JETHRO); the quality of cattle and sheep was improved by scientific stock breeding. This resulted in a greater production of food for the growing industrial population (*see* INDUSTRIAL REVOLUTION), although it meant hardship for those farmers who were displaced by enclosure.

agriculture The practice or study of farming. Settled farming probably dates back to the 10th millennium BC, when in many regions of the world it began to replace man's activities as a hunter and gatherer of food. The domestication of cattle, goats, sheep, and pigs together with the cropping of wheat, barley, rice, etc., enabled settled communities to evolve and primitive civilizations to flourish in such regions as the fertile river basins of the Tigris, Euphrates, and Nile.

Until the end of the 19th century farming was based entirely on energy derived from man and his draught animals. However, during the 20th century, especially in developed countries, the tractor has become the primary energy source. In this century, too, there has been great success in improving breeds of plants and animals, improving soil fertility (*see* FERTILIZERS), increasing mechanization, and control of plant and animal pests, measures that have enormously increased the quantity and quality of food produced. These measures are now being applied in the developing world, where they are bringing about the Green Revolution that is needed to feed the world's growing population. However, reconciling maximum food production and conservation of the environment is one of the principal tasks of the UN *Food and Agriculture Organization. *See also* ARABLE FARMING; LIVESTOCK FARMING.

Agrigento 37 19N 13 35E A seaport in Italy, in S Sicily. Founded about 580 BC, it has famous ancient temples and is the birthplace of the philosopher Empedocles. Sulphur mining is the main occupation. Population (latest est): 56 372.

Agrippa, Marcus Vipsanius (?63–12 BC) Roman general and associate of the Emperor Augustus, whose daughter Julia was his third wife. After military successes in Gaul (38 BC) Agrippa became consul (37 BC). He played an important part in the defeat of Mark Antony at Actium (31 BC) and contributed to the military successes of Augustus.

Agrippina the Younger (15–59 AD), was notorious for her political intrigues. She probably murdered her uncle, the Emperor Claudius, who was also her third husband, to make way for the succession of her son, Nero. She exerted considerable influence early in Nero's reign, but after they quarrelled he had her murdered.

agronomy The management of land, especially for the production of arable crops. Agronomy involves the determination of the nature of a soil and how its fertility may be improved by such processes as drainage, irrigation, the application of natural and artificial fertilizers, and husbandry techniques (e.g. crop rotation). Equally important is the breeding of crop plants that are suited to a particular soil.

Aguascalientes 21 51N 102 18W A city in central Mexico. A commercial centre, its industries include ceramics production, tanning, and railway engineering. There are medicinal hot springs nearby. Population (2000 est): 594 056.

Ahern, Bertie (1951–) Irish statesman. Leader of Fianna Fáil (1994–), he became prime minister of Ireland in 1997 and was an architect of the Good Friday Agreement for Northern *Ireland of 1998. He presided over an economic boom and was re-elected in 2002.

Ahmadabad (*or* **Ahmedabad**) 23 03N 72 40E An industrial city in central India, in Gujarat. Founded in 1411, it is a major rail and textile centre (established 1859–61). Its university was established in 1949. Population (1991 est): 2 872 865.

ai *See* SLOTH.

Aidan, St (c. 600–51 AD) Irish monk and bishop. A monk at *Iona until his consecration as bishop of Northumbria in 635, he founded the monastery at Lindisfarne (*see* HOLY ISLAND), the centre of his extensive missionary activity in N England. His life is described by *Bede in his *Ecclesiastical History*. Feast day: 31 Aug.

AIDS (*a*cquired *i*mmune *d*eficiency *s*yndrome) A viral disease characterized by a decrease of certain T-lymphocytes, resulting in a breakdown of the immune system and increased susceptibility to other diseases. The causative agent, the human immunodeficiency virus (HIV), is transmitted in blood, semen, vaginal fluid, and breast milk; a high proportion of HIV-positive people (virus carriers) may develop symptoms of the disease, although this may take up to ten years after infection. In the western world AIDS is found most frequently in homosexual males and intravenous drug users, but the virus can also be transmitted by heterosexual intercourse and transfusions of infected blood (all of which is now tested). Such drugs as zidovudine (*or* AZT) and the protease inhibitors only slow the progress of the disease and do not yet offer a cure; clinical trials of vaccines are being planned. By the end of 2003, AIDS had resulted in an estimated 27 million deaths worldwide (including over 10 000 in Britain), while those suffering from AIDS or HIV were estimated at over 40 million. Some 80% of deaths from AIDS (and nearly 80% of new cases of HIV infection) now occur in central and southern Africa.

aikido A Japanese martial art, primarily for self-defence by means of dodging an attacker and leading him in the direction in which his momentum takes him before subduing him without injury.

AIM (Alternative Investment Market) *See* STOCK EXCHANGE.

Ainu A Mongoloid people living on certain islands of Japan and Russia (Hokkaido, Sakhalin, Kurile Islands). They were once noted for their profusion of body hair, but intermarriage has made them resemble the Japanese. Although their traditional culture has largely disappeared and they are now few in number, they speak a language not related to any other.

air *See* ATMOSPHERE.

aircraft Any machine capable of flying. Aircraft fall into two categories: lighter-than-air machines (*see* AIRSHIPS; BALLOONS) and heavier-than-air machines. The latter include *helicopters and fixed-wing aircraft, first *gliders and then powered aeroplanes. 19th-century experience of gliding, especially by Otto Lilienthal (1849–96) in Germany, provided the Wright Brothers with the information they needed to build their first powered aircraft in 1907 using the Otto-Daimler *internal-combustion engine. In 1909 the Frenchman Louis *Blériot flew across the English Channel. By the beginning of World War I, aircraft were sufficiently advanced to be used for reconnaissance and their usefulness as bombers soon became evident. Fast manoeuvrable fighters to shoot down the slower heavily laden bombers were an obvious subsequent development. By the end of the war aerial combat was established as an integral part of modern warfare. After the war air circuses and flying clubs using World War I aircraft sprang up all over the world, heralding the age of civil aviation. In 1924 Imperial Airways was formed in the UK, using Handley Page airliners, and during the 1930s a worldwide network of commercial routes developed. The Atlantic was first flown solo nonstop (from New York to Paris) in 1927 by Charles *Lindbergh and by 1939 there was a transatlantic flying-boat service, using Class C Short flying boats with in-flight refuelling.

By the outbreak of World War II aircraft of all kinds were poised for aerial combat. During the war many British bombers (including Wellingtons, Blenheims, Halifaxes, and Lancasters) were in service against the German Heinkel 111, Dornier 17, and Junkers 88. Domi-

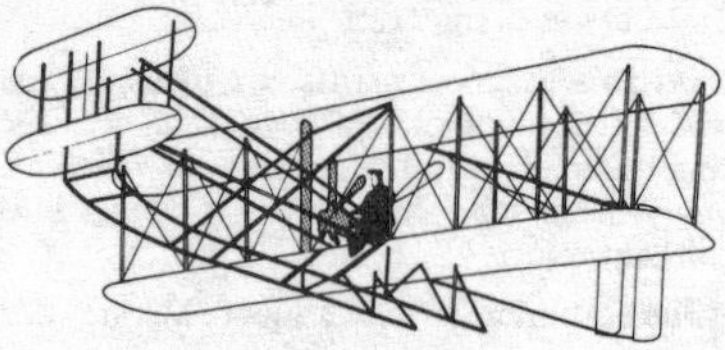

Wright Brothers' Flyer The first powered flight at Kitty Hawk, North Carolina, USA, on 17 December 1903 lasted 12 seconds.

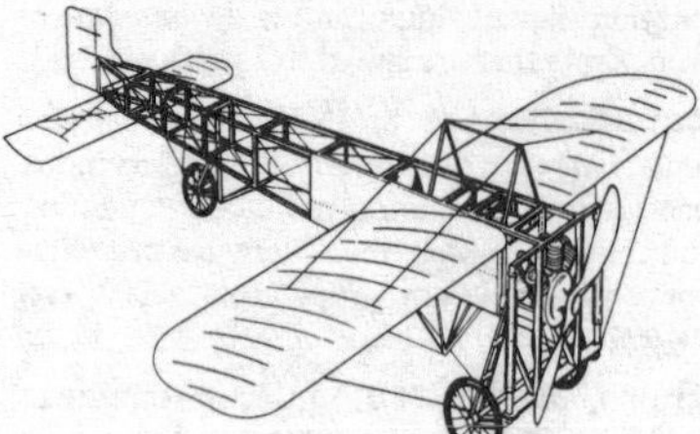

Blériot XI Louis Blériot's 30-minute flight from Calais to Dover on 25 July 1909 was the first cross-channel flight.

Handley Page 42E Hannibal In 1928 the British airline, Imperial Airways, brought eight HP42 aircraft. The 24-seater Hannibal had a top speed of 100 mph (160 km/hr).

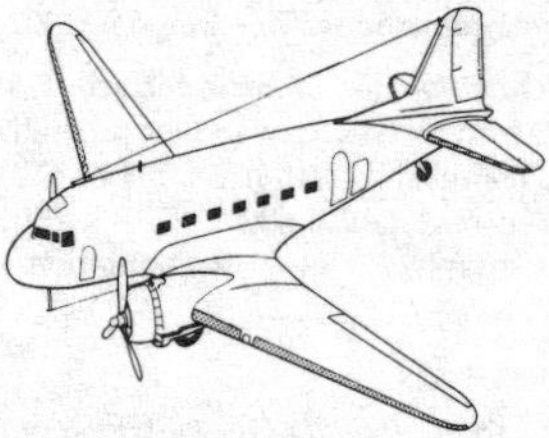

Douglas DC3 Introduced in 1936, it was widely used in World War II as the Dakota transport. Its Pratt and Whitney 1200 hp engines gave it a maximum speed of 200 mph (320 km/hr).

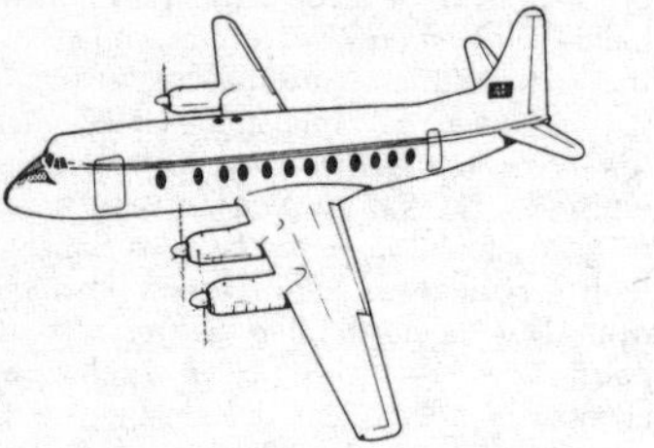

Vickers Viscount Introduced into service in 1950, it was the first successful turboprop airliner. Powered by four Rolls-Royce Dart engines, it carried 60 passengers.

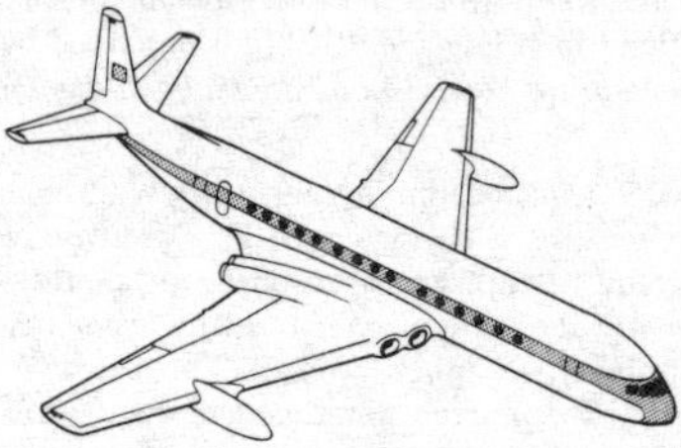

De Havilland Comet I The first jet airliner, it went into service in 1952. Crashes due to metal fatigue caused its withdrawal and in 1958 it was replaced by the Comet IV.

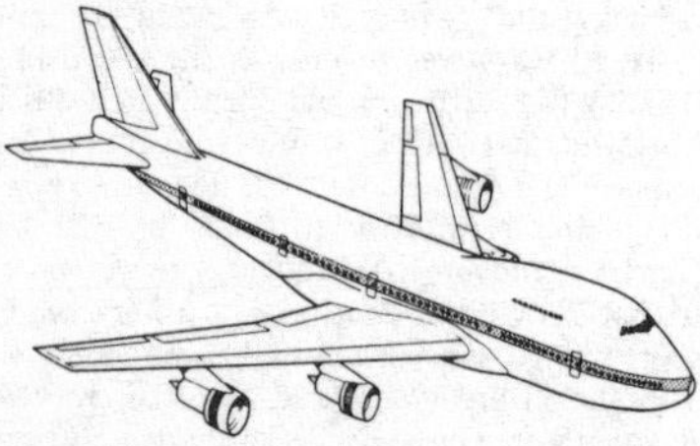

Boeing 747 Nicknamed the "jumbo jet" this wide-bodied jetliner, which can carry up to 500 passengers, has been in service with many airlines since 1970.

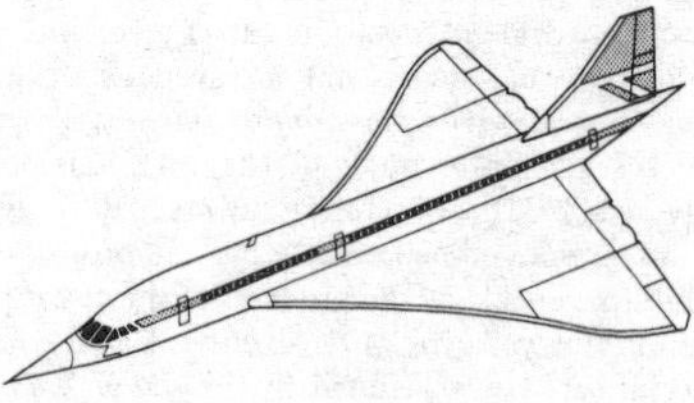

Concorde The first supersonic airliner, it was built by the French and British in cooperation. Powered by four Rolls-Royce Olympus engines, it came into service in 1976.

civil aircraft

Sopwith Camel A highly manoeuvrable fighter, first delivered in 1917. Its 130 hp Clerget engine gave it a top speed of 113 mph (181 km/hr).

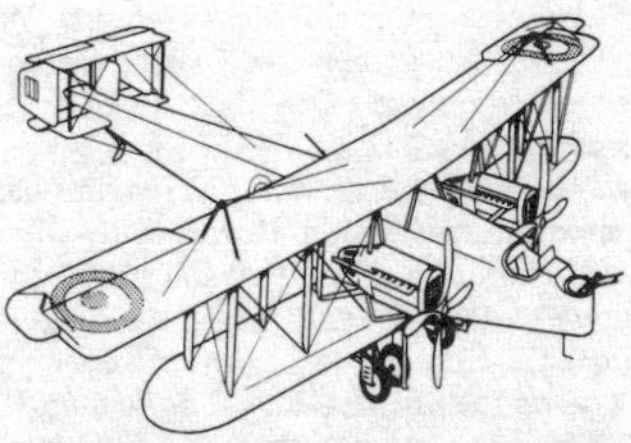

Handley Page 0/400 The largest World War I bomber. Its twin 360 hp engines enabled it to carry 2000 lbs (907 kg) of bombs.

Supermarine Spitfire British fighter. Originally powered by a Rolls-Royce Merlin engine, it later had the Griffon engine, giving it a top speed of 450 mph (724 km/hr).

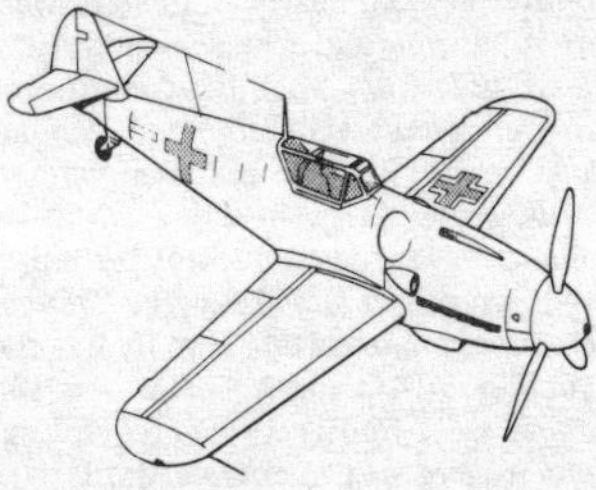

Messerschmitt 109 German fighter, designed in 1935. The latest version (109G) had an 1800 hp engine enabling it to fly at 430 mph (692 km/hr).

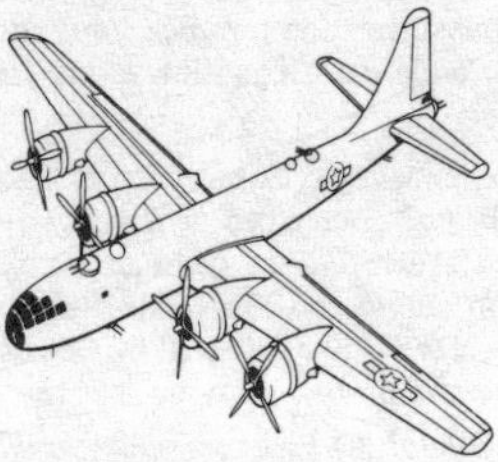

Boeing B-29 Superfortress This enormous US bomber entered the war in 1943 and was used to drop the atom bombs on Japan.

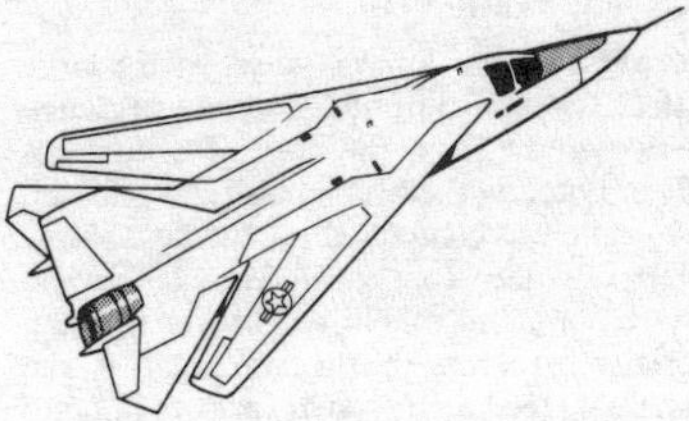

General Dynamics F-111 US fighter and fighter-bomber, the first warplane to have swing wings (1967). It was powered by a Pratt and Whitney TF30 turbo fan.

Hawker Siddeley Harrier British VTOL aircraft developed in 1969. Two movable nozzles direct the thrust of its engine downwards for vertical take-off.

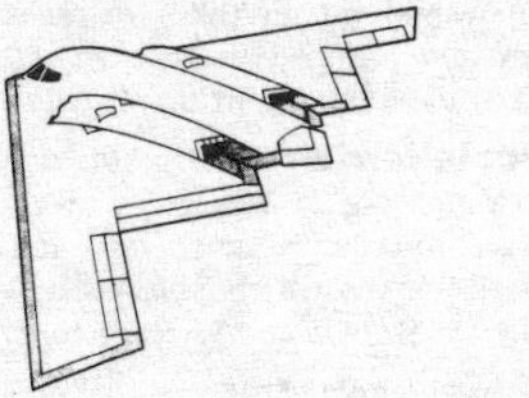

Northrop B2 stealth bomber US bomber, publicly revealed in 1989. The most expensive warplane ever developed, costing £350 million each, its revolutionary 'flying wing' design is alleged to make it invisible to enemy radar.

military aircraft

nant British fighters were the Supermarine Spitfire and the Hawker Hurricane, against the main German fighter, the Messerschmitt Me Bf109. The British jet-powered Gloster Meteor entered service in 1944, as did the German Messerschmitt Me 262 jet.

Since the end of war, the *jet engine has dominated aircraft design. However, the first postwar generation of civil aircraft used the jet engine to drive propellers (e.g. the Vickers Viscount), the first true jet to enter passenger service being the British Comet. The Boeing 707 (with its four engines in pods suspended below the wings) followed in 1954.

The first aircraft to break the *sound barrier were military and nearly all modern warplanes are supersonic and armed with missiles. Examples include the British Hawker Hunter and Avro Vulcan; the US McDonnell Douglas Phantom, Convair Hustler, and General Dynamics Swingwing F111; the French Mirage; and the Soviet MiGs. The US B2 Stealth bomber was introduced in the late 1980s. The first supersonic passenger aircraft (SST) to fly was the Soviet Tupolev Tu-144 in 1968. This was followed a year later by the Anglo-French Concorde, which remained in service until 2003. Long- and medium-range passenger services are dominated by the wide-bodied (jumbo) jets, such as the Boeing 747 and the European Airbus. *See also* AERONAUTICS.

aircraft carrier A naval vessel with a large flat deck for launching and landing warplanes. The first flight from the deck of a ship was made in 1910, and the first true aircraft carrier, HMS *Argus*, was completed for the Royal Navy in 1918, too late for World War I. Carriers played a dominant role in World War II, being especially effective in the war against the Japanese. After World War II carriers came to be regarded chiefly as tactical units, although they saw considerable action in the Korean and Vietnam Wars. The USS *Enterprise*, the first nuclear-powered carrier (1961), displaced 76 000 tonnes and steamed more than 432 000 km (270 000 mi) before requiring refuelling.

Airedale terrier The largest breed of *terrier, originating in Yorkshire. It has a long squarish muzzle, a short tail, and a tan-coloured wiry coat with a black saddle region. Height: 58–61 cm (dogs); 56–58 cm (bitches).

airships Dirigible *balloons that obtain their thrust from a propeller. The first airship to fly was a French steam-powered machine, designed in 1852 by H. Giffard; however, the first practical airship was the electrically powered *La France* (1884), built by Renard and Krebs. By 1900 the initiative in airships had passed to Germany, with the machines of Count Ferdinand von Zeppelin (1838–1917) leading the field. Between 1910 and 1914 Zeppelins were in extensive passenger service, carrying some 35 000 passengers, without mishap. In World War I these machines were used by the Germans to bomb England. Thereafter, a series of disasters destroyed the credibility of hydrogen-filled airships. The British *R101* caught fire at Beauvais in 1930, the US *Shenandoah* and the *Akron* were lost in 1933, and the German *Hindenberg* was destroyed in 1937.

Aix-en-Provence (Latin name: Aquae Sextiae) 43 31N 5 27E A city in S France, in the Bouches-du-Rhône department. The capital of Provence in the middle ages, it has a gothic cathedral and a university (1409). Cézanne was born here. An agricultural centre, it trades in olive oil and fruit. Population (1999): 134 222.

Aix-la-Chapelle *See* AACHEN.

Ajaccio 41 51N 8 43E The capital of Corsica, a port on the Gulf of Ajaccio. Napoleon I was born here. Tourism is important. Population (latest est): 55 279.

Ajanta 20 30N 75 48E A village in W India, in Maharashtra. Its Buddhist caves, dating from the 1st century BC to the 7th century AD, consist of monasteries and temples, some containing remarkable paintings illustrating the life of the times.

Ajax A legendary Greek hero, son of Telamon, King of Salamis. Described in Homer's *Iliad* as great in stature and in courage, he fought *Hector in single combat. He became insane with rage after being defeated by Odysseus in the contest for the armour of the dead *Achilles. Sophocles' play *Ajax* depicts the hero recovering his sanity, only to be driven by shame to suicide.

Akbar (I) the Great (1542–1605) The third Mogul emperor (1556–1605). Akbar embarked on a series of military campaigns and conquered all of N India. Late in his reign he conquered the Deccan to the south. He was noted for his able administration, his encouragement of trade, and his tolerance towards non-Muslims. Mogul architecture also reached a peak during his reign.

Akhenaton (*or* **Ikhnaton**) King of Egypt (1379–1362 BC) of the 18th dynasty, one of whose wives was Nefertiti. He replaced the traditional Amon cult with the monotheistic worship of the sun god, Aton, and built a new capital, Akhetaton, at Tell el-Amarna. Internal disorder during his reign enabled the Hittite king, Suppiluliumas, to remove N Syria from Egyptian control.

Akhmatova, Anna (Anna Andreevna Gorenko; 1889–1966) Russian poet. Her first books, *Evening* (1912) and *Beads* (1914), were an immediate success. She was married to Nikolai Gumiliov (1886–1921), founder of acmeism, from 1910 until 1918. After the Revolution she wrote about public life as well as personal themes. Her works were banned (1922–40) but in the 1960s were restored to favour.

Akihito (1933–) Emperor of Japan (1989–). The son of *Hirohito, he was the first Crown Prince to marry a commoner, Michido Shoda (1934–).

Akkad The capital city and dynastic name of a S Mesopotamian kingdom established about 2300 BC, N of Sumer. Akkad, the site of which is still unidentified, was founded by Sargon. The Semitic language of Akkad, Old Akkadian, spread to much of the Middle East, developing later into the languages of both Babylonia and Assyria. About 2150 BC, barbarian invasions brought about Akkad's decline and the short-lived reascendancy of Ur.

Aksum (*or* **Axum**) 14 05N 38 40E An ancient town in N Ethiopia. It was capital of the Christian Aksumite Empire (1st–6th centuries AD). According to tradition, the Ark of the Covenant was brought here from Jerusalem.

Alabama A state in the SE USA, on the Gulf of Mexico. Except for the forested uplands in the NE it consists of an undulating plain, drained by the Alabama and Tombigbee Rivers. The iron and steel industry around the state's largest city, Birmingham, is the most important. Mobile is an important seaport. Cotton production in the central Black Belt is a principal crop along with peanuts, soya beans, wheat, and maize; the raising of cattle and poultry is also important. *History*: first explored by the Spanish in the 16th century, it passed to the British (1763) following disputes with the Spanish and French. In 1783 it came under US control and with an area to the S added in the Louisiana Purchase (1803) became a state in 1819. New settlers established large cotton plantations based on slave labour and following secession from the Union (1861), the state sent most of its White male population to fight against the N. Area: 135 776 sq km (52 423 sq mi). Population (2000): 4 447 100. Capital: Montgomery.

alabaster A pure fine-grained white form of *gypsum. Often translucent and attractively veined, it has long been worked ornamentally, for carvings, etc. The alabaster of Volterra, Tuscany, is well known.

Alain-Fournier (Henri-Alban Fournier; 1886–1914) French novelist. The son of a country schoolmaster, he became a literary journalist in Paris and was killed in World War I. His one completed novel, *Le Grand Meaulnes* (1913), is nostalgic and almost mystical; set in the French countryside of his childhood, it describes a young man's search for a girl he has glimpsed only briefly.

Alamo, the A mission in the USA, in San Antonio, Texas. During the Texas revolution it was defended from 24 Feb until 6 March 1836, by less than 200 Texan volunteers (including the legendary Davy Crockett), who were all massacred during the onslaught of 4000 Mexican troops led by Santa Anna. Six weeks later a victory at San Jacinto secured Texan independence.

Åland Islands (Finnish name: Ahvenanmaa Islands) A group of over 6000 islands and islets, under Finnish administration but semi-autonomous, at the entrance to the Gulf of Bothnia. Population (1992): 24 847. Language: Swedish. Capital: Mariehamn.

Alaska The largest state in the USA, occupying the NW corner of the North American continent. It is a mountainous volcanic area, rising over 6000 m (20 000 ft) to Mount McKinley, the highest peak in North America. The numerous rivers include the Yukon flowing W into the Bering Sea. Oil production (discovered 1950) is the major industry and there are rich supplies of natural gas. Coal, gold, and copper are mined. Fishing, especially salmon, and forestry are also major industries. Agricultural development is hindered by the short growing season and severe climate. *History*: first settled by Russians following voyages by the Dane, Vitus Bering (1728, 1741), it was under the trade control of the Russian American company until 1867 when it was purchased by the USA. A number of gold rushes in the late 19th century helped to swell the sparse population. It became the 49th state in 1959. A 2437 km (1523 mi)-road from Dawson Creek, Canada to Fairbanks, Alaska, called the **Alaska Highway** was built for defence against Japan (1942). Area: 1 700 138 sq km (656 424 sq mi). Population (2000): 626 932. Capital: Juneau.

Alba, Fernando Alvarez de Toledo, Duke of (*or* **Alva**; 1507–83) Spanish general, who commanded Habsburg forces against

Protestants in Germany and the French in Italy. Philip II of Spain placed him in command of the Netherlands (1567–73), where his ruthless attempts to subdue the Dutch Protestants made him very unpopular and led to his recall. He led the expedition against Portugal (1580–81). *See also* REVOLT OF THE NETHERLANDS.

albacore A fast-swimming *tuna fish, *Thunnus alalunga*, found in warm seas. Up to 1 m long, it has very long pectoral fins. It is the chief source of tuna for canning.

Alban, St (3rd century AD) The first English martyr. A pagan soldier, he protected a Christian priest and was converted by him. On admitting this to the Roman authorities, he was scourged and beheaded on a site subsequently dedicated to him as the Abbey of St Albans. Feast day: 22 or 17 June. Emblem: a stag.

Albania, Republic of (Albanian name: Shqiperia) A country in SE Europe, occupying part of the Balkan Peninsula on the Adriatic Sea. It consists of a mountainous interior, rising to over 2700 m (9000 ft), with extensive forests and fertile coastal lowlands. The people belong to two main groups, the Ghegs (N of the River Shkumbi) and the Tosks (S). *Economy*: mainly agricultural, although industrial development is increasing. There have been attempts to develop the rich mineral resources as well as the rich natural-gas deposits. Main exports include crude oil, bitumen, chrome ore, copper wire, tobacco, fruit, and vegetables. Under communism the economy was subject to rigid central control and Albania became one of the poorest countries in Europe. Despite subsequent liberalization the economy remains very weak, owing in part to widespread corruption. *History*: became independent in 1912 after more than four centuries of Turkish rule. Following a civil war, in which Italy intervened, Albania became a republic in 1925 and a monarchy in 1928, when its president, Ahmed Beg Zogu (1895–1961), was proclaimed as King Zog. After occupation by Italy and Germany during World War II, another republic was set up in 1946, with a communist-controlled assembly. It aligned itself with the Soviet Union but after the death of Stalin relations between the two countries weakened and diplomatic relations were broken off from 1961 to 1990. Albania maintained close relations with China but otherwise remained isolated until the 1980s. Enver Hoxha (1908–85), as first party secretary, was executive leader from 1946 to 1985. Pressure for change led to free elections in 1991 but in 1997 the collapse of fraudulent saving schemes led to street violence and the resignation of the government. Elections in 1997 resulted in victory for the Socialists. In 1998 violent protests in Tirana forced the government to flee the capital and Fatos Nano resigned as prime minister; a new Western-style constitution was subsequently approved in a referendum. In 1999 the crisis in neighbouring *Kosovo led to a massive influx of refugees and tensions with both Serbia and Macedonia. Nano returned as prime minister in 2002. Official language: Albanian. Currency: lek of 100 qindars. Area: 28 748 sq km (11 101 sq mi). Population (2003 est): 3 166 000. Capital: Tirana.

Albany 42 40N 73 49W A city in the USA, the capital of New York state on the Hudson River. Founded in 1614 by the Dutch, it is one of North America's oldest cities. Economic growth accelerated with the building of the Erie Canal (1825) and today its main manufactures are electrical goods, textiles, dental goods, chemicals, and building materials. Population (2000): 95 658.

albatross A large seabird belonging to a family (*Diomedeidae*; 14 species) that occurs mainly in southern oceans. It has a hooked bill; usually a white or brown plumage often with darker markings, and very long narrow wings (the wandering albatross, *Diomedea exulans*, has the largest wingspan of any bird, reaching up to 3.5 m). Albatrosses can glide for hours over the open sea, feeding on squids and cuttlefish; they come ashore only to breed. Order: *Procellariiformes* (*see* PETREL).

albedo A measure of the reflecting power of a nonluminous object, such as a planet or natural satellite. It is the ratio of the amount of light reflected in all directions from the object to the amount of incident light. Clouds, snow, and ice have high albedos while volcanic rocks have very low albedos.

Albee, Edward (1928–) US dramatist. His early one-act plays, notably *Zoo Story* (1958) and *The Death of Bessie Smith* (1960), analyse contemporary social tensions using techniques of the *Theatre of the Absurd. His first three-act play, *Who's Afraid of Virginia Woolf?* (1962), which dramatizes the love-hate relationship of an academic couple, was very successful. Later plays include *A Delicate Balance* (1967, Pulitzer Prize), *Marriage Play* (1986), *Three Tall Women* (1991, Pulitzer Prize), and *Goat* (2004).

Albéniz, Isaac Manuel Francisco (1860–1909) Spanish composer and pianist. A child prodigy, he frequently ran away from home, giving recitals in North and South

America and Europe. He began serious composition after studying with d'Indy and Dukas in Paris. His works include operas, songs, and *Iberia* (1906–09), a collection of 12 piano pieces.

Albert I (1875–1934) King of the Belgians (1909–34). As commander in chief of the Belgian army, Albert led his country's heroic but unsuccessful resistance to the German invasion (1914) and contributed to the Allied victory in World War I.

Albert, Prince (1819–61) Prince Consort of the United Kingdom and younger son of Ernest I, Duke of Saxe-Coburg-Gotha. In 1840 he married his cousin Queen Victoria and became her chief adviser. Although he was initially unpopular, his devotion to duty and patronage of the arts, science, and industry won him respect. He is remembered for his organization of the *Great Exhibition (1851). He died of typhoid.

Alberta A province of W Canada, mostly on the Great Plains. It consists mainly of a plateau, rising to the foothills of the *Rocky Mountains in the SW. The undulating S prairie and parkland further N support profitable ranches and grain farms. Alberta is Canada's largest oil and gas producer, possesses vast coalfields, and includes the Athabasca tar sands, one of the world's largest oil reserves (at present untapped). *History*: first explored in the 18th century, Alberta became Canadian territory in 1869. The arrival of the railway from E Canada (1883) facilitated agricultural settlement, and Alberta became a province in 1905. Area: 644 389 sq km (248 799 sq mi). Population (2001): 3 664 249. Capital: Edmonton.

Alberti, Leon Battista (1404–72) Italian Renaissance architect, also a painter, writer, musician, and scientist. As his façade of Sta Maria Novella in Florence demonstrates, he adapted classical rules to 15th-century requirements. His most significant buildings were the churches of S Sebastiano and S Andrea in Mantua and the incomplete Tempio Malatestiano in Rimini. His treatise *De re aedificatoria* (*On Architecture*; 1452) was translated into several European languages in the 16th century.

Albigenses Followers of the Christian heresy of Catharism (*see* CATHARI), who flourished in southern France in the 12th and 13th centuries. Named after the town of Albi in Languedoc, they were the object of the Albigensian Crusade, launched in 1208 and led by the father of Simon de Montfort. They were finally suppressed by the Inquisition in about 1233.

albinism An inherited disorder in which tyrosinase, one of the enzymes required for the formation of the pigment *melanin, is absent. Albinos have abnormally pale skin, fair hair, and pink or light-blue irises. The condition can be eased by the use of spectacles to treat the lens abnormalities common in albinos and by protection of the skin and eyes from direct sunlight. Albinism, which can affect all human races, is also seen in animals.

Albinoni, Tomaso (1671–1750) Italian composer and court musician to the Duke of Mantua. His works, which influenced J.S. Bach, include 50 operas, a violin concerto, and two oboe concertos. The *Adagio* for organ and strings often attributed to Albinoni was in fact composed by his Italian biographer Remo Giazotto (1910–) and incorporates a fragment of a bass part by Albinoni.

Ålborg (*or* **Aalborg**) 57 03N 09 56E A city and seaport in Denmark, in N Jutland. Founded in 1342 AD, it has a gothic cathedral and a 16th-century castle. A university was established in 1974. Its industries include shipbuilding, cement manufacture, and textiles. Population (2000): 161 161.

albumins A class of proteins that are soluble in both water and dilute aqueous salt solutions. Serum albumins are constituents of blood; α-lactalbumin is found in milk; and ovalbumin is part of egg white. Preparations of albumins are used in therapeutic transfusions.

Albuquerque 35 05N 106 38W A city in the USA, in New Mexico on the Rio Grande. The state's largest city, it is situated in a rich agricultural area and food canning and the manufacture of livestock products are its principal industries. It is the home of the University of New Mexico (1892). Population (2000): 448 607.

Alcatraz An island in the USA, in W California in San Francisco Bay. It was the site of a notorious maximum security prison from 1934 until 1962.

alchemy A pseudoscience combining practical *chemistry with mystical views of the universe. Originating independently in China and Egypt, probably before the 3rd century BC, alchemy remained a legitimate branch of science and philosophy in Asia, Europe, and the Islamic lands for over 1500 years. It had three principal goals: the elixir of life (to ensure immortality), the panacea (or universal medicine), and the means of transmuting base metals into gold (*see* PHILOSOPHER'S STONE). In China, *Taoism, which highly esteemed long life, fos-

a

tered alchemical experimentation in search of the elixir. In Europe, concentration upon gold-making brought alchemy into disrepute.

Alcibiades (c. 450–404 BC) Athenian general and politician. Brought up by *Pericles, he was the pupil and lover of *Socrates. Alcibiades encouraged Athenian imperialism during the *Peloponnesian War (431–404) until, accused of desecrating monuments in Athens, he defected to Sparta (415). He regained Athenian favour (410) and was a successful commander until defeat, the fault of a subordinate, forced him into exile (406). He was murdered in Phrygia.

Alcmaeon In Greek mythology, the son of Amphiarus, one of the Seven Against Thebes, and Eriphyle. He killed his mother to avenge the death of Amphiarus, and was pursued by the Furies. His first wife was Arsinoë, daughter of King Pegeus of Psophis, but on his wanderings he married the daughter of the river god Achelous, and was pursued and killed by Pegeus and his sons. His own sons later avenged his death by killing Pegeus.

Alcock, Sir John (William) (1892–1919) British aviator. He served with the Royal Naval Air Service in World War I and in 1919, accompanied by **(Sir) Arthur Brown** (1886–1948), was the first to fly the Atlantic Ocean. They flew a Vickers-Vimy from St John's, Newfoundland, to Clifden, Co Galway, in 16 hours 27 minutes. A few months later Alcock was killed in a flying accident.

Alcoholics Anonymous A voluntary organization started in the USA in 1934 to help alcoholics. Members, who must genuinely want to stop drinking, help one another on the basis of group therapy by sharing their experiences of alcoholism. There are local autonomous groups in over 170 countries, including the UK, which has more than 1000 groups. An associated organization, **ALANON**, provides support for the close relatives of alcoholics.

alcoholism An illness caused by physical and psychological dependence on alcohol. Alcoholism causes mood changes, deterioration in personal standards, and periods of memory loss. Continued heavy consumption will eventually lead to cirrhosis of the liver, heart disease, and damage to the nerves. Sudden withdrawal may produce tremor, delusions, and hallucinations. Treatment, which is lengthy and difficult, includes initial alcohol withdrawal (with appropriate sedation) accompanied and followed by adequate psychological support. Drugs such as disulfiram (Antabuse), which cause vomiting after drinking alcohol, may assist the treatment. *See* ALCOHOLICS ANONYMOUS.

alcohols The class of organic compounds that includes *ethanol (ethyl alcohol; C_2H_5OH) and *methanol (methyl alcohol; CH_3OH). Ethanol is the alcohol found in intoxicating drinks. Alcohols contain at least one hydroxyl group and have the general formula ROH, where R is a *hydrocarbon group. They react with acids to give *esters and water. Primary alcohols oxidize to form *aldehydes and secondary alcohols to form *ketones.

alcohol strength The measurement of the percentage volume of *ethanol (ethyl alcohol) in alcoholic drinks in order to calculate government duty on them. In the USA, 100° proof is 50% alcohol by volume. Until January 1980, the UK used a similar system for spirits, but with 57.06%, measured at 15°C, as the standard (100° proof), pure alcohol being 175° proof. France and Italy formerly used the Gay-Lussac scale, which simply states the percentage volume of alcohol, measured at 15°C. The **OMIL** (International Organization of Legal Metrology) system, now used throughout the EU, is based on percentage volume of alcohol at 20°C. Thus a bottle of spirits labelled in the EU "35% vol" is approximately equivalent to 61° proof in the former UK system or 70° proof in the US system.

Alcott, Louisa May (1832–88) US novelist. Her first book, *Flower Fables* (1854), was written when she was 16 to raise money for her family. *Hospital Sketches* (1863) recounted her experiences as a nurse in the Civil War. *Little Women* (1868–69), her most famous book, was largely autobiographical. Other works include *An Old-Fashioned Girl* (1870), *Little Men* (1871), and *Jo's Boys* (1886).

Aldeburgh 52 9N 1 35E A small resort in SE England in Suffolk. Once an important port, it is now famous for its annual music festival established in 1948 by Benjamin *Britten and the singer Peter Pears (1910–86), who lived here. It is the birthplace of the poet George *Crabbe, and Dr Elizabeth Garrett Anderson (1836–1917) was elected the first woman mayor in England here in 1908. Population (1991): 2654.

aldehydes A class of organic chemicals that contain the –CHO group. They are prepared by the oxidation of alcohols and are themselves oxidized to form carboxylic acids. Common aldehydes are formaldehyde and acetaldehyde.

alder A tree or shrub of the genus *Alnus*. The leaves are roundish and toothed; the flowers grow as separate male and female catkins on the same tree. The fruit is a woody cone containing small winged nuts. The black alder (*A. glutinosa*), about 20 m high, is found in wet places throughout Europe and Asia and in N Africa. Its timber is used in general turnery. Family: *Betulaceae* (birch family).

alderfly An insect, also known as a fish fly, having two pairs of delicate finely veined wings and long antennae. Up to 50 mm long (including the wings), alderflies live near fresh water, feeding on smaller insects and laying their eggs on reeds. The larvae, which are also carnivorous, live in the water and crawl out to pupate in burrows in the soil. Family: *Sialidae*; order: *Neuroptera* (lacewings, etc.).

alderman (from Anglo-Saxon *ealdorman*, a local official) In the UK, senior members of the major local authorities, normally elected by the directly elected members, until the Local Government Act (1972) abolished the office as an active rank except in the City of London. In the USA, many cities call their local-government officers aldermen but their powers vary from city to city.

Aldermaston 51 23N 1 09W A village in S England, in West Berkshire unitary authority, Berkshire. It is associated with protest marches (1958–63) organized by the Campaign for Nuclear Disarmament and is the site of the Atomic Weapons Research Establishment. Population (latest est): 2157.

Alderney (French name: Aurigny) 49 43N 2 12W The third largest of the Channel Islands, separated from France by the dangerous Race of Alderney channel. Its economy is based on dairy farming and tourism. Area: 8 sq km (3 sq mi). Population (2001): 2294. Chief town: St Anne.

Aldershot 51 15N 0 47W A town in S England, in Hampshire. It is the chief garrison town and army training centre in the UK. Population (1991): 51 536.

Aldrin, Jr, Edwin Eugene (1930–) US astronaut, the second man to walk on the moon. Known as "Buzz," he was an air force pilot during the Korean War before becoming an astronaut in 1963. He was lunar module pilot (under Neil *Armstrong) in Apollo 11 when it made the first moon landing in 1969.

aldosterone A steroid hormone that acts on the kidneys to regulate the levels of salts and water in the body.

aleatoric music Music that incorporates elements of chance. The term (from Latin *alea*, a game of dice), was first used in the 1950s to describe John *Cage's experiments in determining pitch, rhythm, structure, and dynamics by the use of the I Ching, a classic Chinese work on divination. Boulez, Stockhausen, and others have experimented with this type of music. Computers have also been used to generate aleatoric music.

Aleppo (Arabic name: Halab) 36 14N 37 10E A town in NW Syria. The Crusaders tried in vain to capture it, and from 1516 to 1919 Aleppo was part of the Ottoman Empire. After World War II, it was incorporated into independent Syria. It is now an industrial centre and the terminus of a pipeline from Iraq; its university was founded in 1960. Population (1994 est): 1 591 400.

Aletsch Glacier The largest glacier in Europe, in Switzerland in the Bernese Oberland lying SE of the Aletschhorn mountain. Length: 26 km (16 mi).

Aleutian Islands A chain of volcanic Alaskan islands lying between the Bering Sea and the Pacific Ocean, divided politically between Russia and the USA. The chief settlements are on Unalaska. Russian exploitation of supplies after 1741 greatly reduced the population, but fishing and seal, otter, and fox hunting are now regulated. There are strategic US military stations on the islands and underground nuclear tests have been made here (since 1971).

Alexander I (c. 1077–1124) King of the Scots (1107–24), who ruled the highlands while his brother and successor David ruled the lowlands. He was noted for his reform of the Scottish church and his foundation of the monastery of Scone (1114). He aided Henry I of England's campaign against Wales (1114).

Alexander II (1198–1249) King of the Scots (1214–49). Hoping to regain the northern counties of England, he supported the unsuccessful Barons' War (1215–17) against King John. In 1221 he married Joan, the sister of Henry III of England, and gave up his claims to English territory in 1237, when the present border between England and Scotland was fixed.

Alexander (III) the Great (356–323 BC) King of Macedon (336–323), who between 334 and his death conquered most of the world known to antiquity. Alexander, who was a pupil of Aristotle, inherited a plan to invade Persia from his father Philip II; having secured his position in Macedon and Greece, he put this plan into action. In 333 he defeated the Persian king Darius III at Issus; in 332 he reduced Tyre in his greatest victory. Alexander then proceeded to conquer Egypt and Babylon (331). Moving on to Media and then east into central Asia, he finally embarked on the Indian expedition (327–325). He crossed the River Indus and conquered the Punjab. Forced to turn back by his reluctant army, he died at Babylon shortly after the marathon return journey.

Alexander III (1241–86) King of the Scots (1249–86). He married (1251) Margaret, daughter of Henry III of England. Under his leadership, the Scots defeated the Norwegians at the battle of Largs (1263) and by the Treaty of Perth (1266) gained the Isle of Man and the Hebrides from Norway.

Alexander VI (Rodrigo Borgia; c. 1431–1503) Pope (1492–1503), notorious for his immorality, nepotism, and extravagance. Father of four illegitimate children, he used papal wealth to further the career of his son, Cesare Borgia, who pursued Alexander's territorial ambitions in Italy. He was a generous patron of the arts.

Alexander of Tunis, Harold, 1st Earl (1891–1969) British field marshal. In World War II he commanded the evacuation from Dunkirk and was the last man to leave France. He became commander in chief in the Middle East (1942) and then, as Eisenhower's deputy, directed the offensive that defeated the Germans in N Africa (1943). He ended the war as Allied supreme commander in the Mediterranean and was subsequently governor general of Canada (1946–52) and Conservative minister of defence (1952–54).

Alexandra (1844–1925) A Danish princess who married (1863) Edward VII of the United Kingdom, when he was the Prince of Wales. In 1902 she founded Queen Alexandra's Imperial (now Royal) Army Nursing Corps and in 1912 she instituted the Alexandra Rose Day in aid of hospitals.

Alexandra (1872–1918) The wife from 1894 of *Nicholas II of Russia. A German princess and granddaughter of Queen Victoria, Alexandra fell under the evil influence of *Rasputin. His disastrous domination of her government while Nicholas was supreme commander of the Russian forces in World War I precipitated the Russian Revolution and the execution of Alexandra and her family by the Bolsheviks.

Alexandria (Arabic name: al-Iskandariyah) 31 13N 22 55E The chief seaport and second largest city in Egypt, between Lake Mareotis and the Mediterranean Sea. It handles most of Egypt's trade and the chief export is cotton; industries include oil refining and cotton ginning. *History*: founded in 332 BC by Alexander the Great it remained the Egyptian capital for over a thousand years. It was a Greek and Jewish cultural centre with a famous library founded by Ptolemy I Soter in the 3rd century BC, which was largely destroyed by fire in 97 BC. In 30 BC Alexandria fell to the Romans, becoming their most important regional capital. It declined following the discovery of the Cape of Good Hope passage and the removal of the capital to Cairo. It was bombarded by the British in 1882, Pompey's Pillar being one of the few ancient monuments to escape destruction. Two obelisks (*see* CLEOPATRA'S NEEDLES), were removed and one is now in London, the other in New York. Population (1996): 3 328 196.

alexandrine A verse metre consisting of a line of 12 syllables usually with major stresses on the sixth and final syllables. The name is derived from 12th-century French poems about Alexander the Great. It was the dominant verse form in 17th-century French poetry, when it was used by *Racine and *Corneille.

alfalfa A perennial flowering plant, *Medicago sativa*, also called lucerne. Growing to a height of 1 m, it resembles clover, having clusters of small purple flowers. Native to Europe, it is widely grown as forage for cattle and because of its ability to fix nitrogen. Family: *Leguminosae*.

Alfred the Great (849–99) King of Wessex (871–99). He prevented the Danish conquest of England, defeating them at Edington (878) after a campaign of guerrilla warfare. The legend of the king, travelling incognito, being reprimanded for burning the peasant housewife's cakes, possibly refers to this unsettled period of his life. After his victory he allowed the Danes to keep their conquests in Mercia and East Anglia provided that Guthrum, their king, converted to Christianity. Alfred built a navy to defend the south coast against further Danish invasions (885–86; 892–96) and protected Wessex with a chain of fortifications. He took London (886), thus gaining control of all England save the Danish areas.

algae A vast group of simple organisms (about 25 000 species) traditionally regarded as plants but now usually placed in the kingdom *Protoctista*. Algae contain the green pigment chlorophyll (and can therefore carry out photosynthesis) but have no true stems, roots, or leaves (*see* THALLOPHYTA). They range from single-celled organisms to the giant seaweeds. Most algae are aquatic, although some live in damp places on land—on rocks, trees, or in soils. A few are parasitic or associate with other organisms (*see* LICHENS). Reproduction is extremely variable and may involve asexual means, such as cell division, fragmentation, or spore production, and/or sexual means by gamete production. The more advanced algae often alternate between sexual and asexual phases. Algae provide a valuable food source for aquatic herbivorous animals and many are used as fertilizers and in industry. They include the green, yellow-green, brown, and *red algae; blue-green algae are now classified as bacteria.

Algarve A region in S Portugal, bordering on Spain and the Atlantic Ocean, mostly corresponding to the modern administrative district of Faro. It became a Moorish kingdom in 1140 and was the last stronghold of the Moors in Portugal, being reconquered in 1249. Sparsely populated inland, its fertile coastal belt is densely populated and produces maize, figs, almonds, and olives; tourism and fishing are important.

algebra The branch of mathematics that uses symbols to represent unknown quantities. The first treatise on the subject was written by Diophantus of Alexandria in the 3rd century AD and the name derives from the Arabic *al-jabr*, a term used by the mathematician *al-Khwarizmi to denote the addition of equal quantities to both sides of an equation and later adopted as the name for the whole subject. Algebra was used in ancient Babylon, Egypt, and India and brought to Europe by the Arabs. In classical algebra symbols, such as x and y, represent ordinary numbers, the magnitude of which are determined by the solution of equations. Modern, or abstract, algebra is concerned with any system of quantities that obey a particular set of general rules and relationships.

Algeciras 36 08N 5 27W A port in S Spain, in Andalusia on the Bay of Gibraltar. Founded in 713 AD, it was destroyed by Alfonso XI of Castile (1311–50; reigned 1312–50) in 1344. The present town was rebuilt in 1760. In 1906 it was the site of the Algeciras Conference, a meeting of European powers to solve their dispute over Morocco. Its exports include oranges and cork. Population (1998 est): 101 972.

Algeria, Democratic and Popular Republic of A country in N Africa, on the Mediterranean Sea. It consists chiefly of the N Sahara Desert, with the Atlas Mountains in the N and small fertile areas near the coast. The inhabitants, who live almost entirely in the N, are mainly Arabs and Berbers. *Economy*: mainly agricultural although industrialization has proceeded rapidly since independence, financed by the discovery of oil (the main export) in the desert areas, and natural gas, which since 1996 has been piped directly to Spain. *History*: a former province of the Roman Empire, Algeria was subjugated in the 7th century by the Arabs, who introduced Islam. Overrun by Turks in the 16th century, it became a pirate state in the 18th century under the domination of *deys*, independent rulers who preyed on Mediterranean shipping. Algeria was annexed by the French in the 19th century and in 1881 the N section became part of Metropolitan France. A war of independence, waged by the *Front de Libération nationale (FLN), lasted from 1954 to 1962 when independence was granted by de Gaulle, following referendums held in both Algeria and France. A republic was set up under Ahmed Ben Bella but was overthrown in 1965 by a Council of Revolution. Col Houari Boumédienne (1925–78) became president; following Boumédienne's death, Col Benjedid Chadli became the new president. A multiparty system was introduced in 1989, but when Islamic fundamentalists were poised to win a general election in 1992 the elections were cancelled and a transitional government was installed. Some 100 000 people died in the ensuing guerilla war, including the head of state, Mohammed Boudiaf, who was assassinated in 1992. In 1996 a new constitution, designed to exclude religious parties from politics, was endorsed in a referendum. Elections in 1997 resulted in victory for the government. The country's first free presidential elections, held in 1999, were marred by the withdrawal of all the opposition candidates. A peace plan unveiled by the new president, Abdelaziz Bouteflika, was backed in a referendum and by January 2000 the main insurgent group had agreed to disband. However, violence by more extreme Islamic groups has since increased, as has agitation by Berber separatists. Official languages: Arabic and Berber languages. Currency: dinar of 100 centimes. Area: 2 381 745 sq km (919 595 sq mi). Population (2003 est): 31 800 000. Capital: Algiers.

Algiers (Arabic name: al-Jaza'ir; French name: Alger) 36 45N 3 05E The capital of Algeria, a port on the Mediterranean Sea. Exports include wine, citrus fruits, and iron ore. The University of Algiers was founded in 1879 and the University of Science and Technology in 1974. *History*: founded by the Phoenicians, it was re-established by the Arabs in the 10th century.

a

Overrun by Turks in the 16th century, it became a base for Barbary pirates until taken by the French in 1830. During World War II it was the headquarters of the Allied forces in N Africa and, for a time, the seat of the French government in exile. Population (1998): 1 519 570.

Algonquian A group of North American Indian languages, including *Cree, *Cheyenne, Blackfoot, and others, spoken by tribes living to the S and E of Hudson Bay and in the eastern woodland zone. The Algonquian tribes lived by hunting and fishing and roamed widely in small family groups and bands.

Alhambra A castle on a hilly terrace outside *Granada (Spain), built between 1238 and 1358. It was the last stronghold of the Muslim kings of Granada. Combining citadel and palace, it is an outstanding example of Moorish architecture, with magnificent courts and gardens. The name derives from Arabic *al-hamra*, the red, an allusion to the red stucco used on the walls.

Ali (c. 600–61) A cousin of *Mohammed, who became his son-in-law by marriage to *Fatimah. Born at Mecca, he was the second, or perhaps the first, person to embrace Islam. He became the fourth caliph in 656, but faced much opposition and was murdered in 661 at Kufa, Iraq. His tomb is venerated at Najaf. According to *Shiite Muslims, Ali was the only legitimate successor of Mohammed and only his descendants can be imams.

Ali, Muhammad (Cassius Marcellus Clay; 1942–) US boxer. A gold medallist in the 1960 Olympic Games, he became professional world heavyweight champion (1964). On becoming a Black Muslim he changed his name and was soon afterwards stripped of his title for three years because of his refusal to join the US army. Defeated (1971) by Joe Frazier, he again became champion in 1974 by defeating George Foreman. In 1978 he lost the title briefly to Leon Spinks; his defeat of Spinks later that year made him the only boxer to become world champion three times. He now suffers from Parkinson's disease, possibly as a result of blows to the head.

Alicante 38 21N 0 29W A port in SE Spain, in Valencia on the Mediterranean Sea. Exports include wine, olive oil, and fruits. Industries include oil refining, textiles, chemicals, soap, tobacco, and tourism. Population (1998 est): 272 432.

Aligarh 27 42N 78 25E A city in N India, in Uttar Pradesh. An agricultural trading centre, it is the site of the notable Aligarh Muslim University (founded as a college in 1875). Population (1991): 479 978.

alimentary canal *See* DIGESTION.

aliphatic compounds Organic chemical compounds that are not aromatic. They include the *alkanes, *alkenes, and *alkynes as well as some cyclic compounds (cycloalkanes).

alkali *See* ACIDS AND BASES.

alkali metals The elements forming group I of the *periodic table: lithium, sodium, potassium, rubidium, caesium, and francium. All are highly reactive soft, silvery-white *metals with low densities, melting points, and boiling points. In chemical reactions they tend to form positive ions and have a valence of 1. The oxides and hydroxides are alkalis.

alkaline-earth metals The elements forming group II of the *periodic table: beryllium, magnesium, calcium, strontium, barium, and radium. They are similar to the *alkali metals in appearance and chemistry, but are harder, have higher melting and boiling points, and are somewhat less reactive. They have a valence of 2. The **alkaline earths** are the oxides of these metals.

alkaloids A group of nitrogen-containing basic compounds produced by plants and having diverse effects on the body. Many alkaloids are used as medicinal drugs, including quinine, reserpine, morphine, scopolamine, and atropine. Others, such as strychnine and coniine (from hemlock) are poisons. Caffeine, nicotine, and LSD are also alkaloids.

alkanes (*or* **paraffins**) A series of hydrocarbons containing only single bonds between the carbon atoms. They have the general formula C_nH_{2n+2}. The first four members of the series methane (CH_4), ethane (C_2H_6), propane (C_3H_8), and butane (C_4H_{10}) are gases; higher members are liquids or waxes. They are obtained from natural gas or oil and they and their substitution products have many uses.

alkanet A herbaceous plant of the genus *Anchusa*, native to Eurasia but widely grown for ornament (*A. azurea* is a common garden plant). It may reach a height of 50–120 cm, with clusters of small blue or white flowers and narrow or oval leaves. Family: *Boraginaceae*. A similar and related plant, *Pentaglottis sempervirens*, is also called alkanet.

alkenes (*or* **olefins**) Hydrocarbons that contain at least one carbon–carbon double bond in their molecules. The simplest types, with one double bond, have the general formula C_nH_{2n}; *ethene is the first member of this series. The alkenes are more reactive than the *alkanes, undergoing addition and polymerization reactions. They are obtained by cracking petroleum and their main use is as starting materials in industrial chemistry.

al-Khwarizmi, Muhammed ibn Musa (c. 780–c. 850 AD) Arabic mathematician, who introduced the Hindu decimal system and the use of zero into Arabic mathematics. He also extended the work of Diophantus on algebraic equations in a book the title of which included the word *al-jabr* ("transposition"), from which the modern word "algebra" is derived.

alkynes (*or* **acetylenes**) Hydrocarbons that contain at least one carbon–carbon triple bond in their molecules. The simplest types, with one triple bond, have the general formula C_nH_{2n-2}; ethyne (*or* acetylene, C_2H_2) is the first member of this series. The alkynes, like the *alkenes, undergo addition and polymerization reactions. They are extremely reactive, tending to explode under pressure, and are difficult to use in large quantities.

Allah (Arabic, probably from *al-ilah*: the god) The Islamic name of God. Allah was worshipped in pre-Islamic Arabia as early as the 3rd century BC. In Mecca he was given special rank as "the god," but lesser tribal gods continued to be worshipped alongside him until *Mohammed proclaimed Allah as the one omnipotent and omniscient God, the same God as worshipped by Jews and Christians. He is eternal, the creator of the universe, the judge of men, merciful and compassionate. His word is embodied in the *Koran.

Allahabad 25 57N 81 50E A city in N India, in Uttar Pradesh at the confluence of the Rivers Ganges and Jumna. It is principally an administrative and educational centre; its university was established in 1887. There is an annual religious festival and a much larger one every 12 years. Population (1991): 806 447.

Allegheny Mountains A mountain range in the USA, extending from North Carolina to Pennsylvania. Part of the Appalachian Mountains, it consists of well-rounded uplands rising to 1480 m (4860 ft) at Spruce Knob.

allegory A verse or prose narrative in which characters and events in the plot hold a deeper, usually moral, meaning. It is similar to but usually longer than the fable and the parable. Examples of allegory include the French *Roman de la rose* (13th century), Bunyan's *The Pilgrim's Progress* (1678), and Orwell's *Animal Farm* (1945).

Allegri, Gregorio (1582–1652) Italian composer of church music. He wrote two volumes of concertinas, two volumes of motets, and a *Miserere* for nine voices.

allele Any one of the various alternative forms of a *gene that can occur at the same site on a *chromosome. In *Drosophila* fruit flies, for example, several alternative eye colours are possible depending on which of the various alleles of the gene for eye colour is present in the individual.

Allen, Ethan (1739–89) American soldier, who pursued the independence from New York and New Hampshire of the Green Mountain region (now Vermont). Between 1770 and 1775 he commanded the Green Mountain Boys, who helped to capture Fort Ticonderoga (1775), the first American victory in the American Revolution. He was imprisoned by the British (1775–78) and died shortly before Vermont achieved statehood in 1789.

Allen, Woody (Allen Stewart Konigsberg; 1935–) US film actor and director. His films include *Play It Again, Sam* (1972), *Annie Hall* (1977), *Manhattan* (1979), *Hannah and Her Sisters* (1986), *Crimes and Misdemeanours* (1990), *Deconstructing Harry* (1997), and *Hollywood Ending* (2002).

Allenby, Edmund Henry Hynman, 1st Viscount (1861–1936) British field marshal. After experience in the Boer War, he commanded the Third Army in France in World War I. In 1917, appointed commander in chief of the Egyptian Expeditionary Force against the Turks in Palestine, he captured (9 Dec) Jerusalem and then went on to devastate the Turks at Megiddo (1918). He ended his career as high commissioner in Egypt (1919–25).

Allende (Gossens), Salvador (1908–73) Chilean statesman; president of Chile (1970–73), the first Marxist to come to power through free elections. A founder of the Chilean Socialist Party, Allende governed a coalition of left-wing parties. His nationalization policies created much opposition and he was overthrown and killed in a US-backed military coup.

allergy An abnormal reaction by the body that is provoked by certain substances, including pollen, house-dust mites, certain foods and drugs, moulds, etc. Normally all foreign substances (antigens) entering the body are destroyed by *antibodies. Allergic people,

a

however, become hypersensitive to certain antigens (called allergens), so that when they are encountered they stimulate not only the normal antibody reaction but also the specific symptoms of the allergy. Allergic conditions include *hay fever, some forms of *asthma and dermatitis, and *urticaria. Treatment includes the use of *antihistamines, corticosteroids, and desensitization.

Allied Powers The nations united in opposition to the Central Powers in World War I and to the Axis Powers in World War II. In World War I the Allies were initially the UK, France, and Russia, bound by the Treaty of London (1914), and later included Italy, Japan, and Portugal; the USA was an associated power from 1917. In World War II the chief Allies were the UK, France (1939–40, 1944–45), the Soviet Union (from June 1941), the USA (from December 1941), and China.

alligator A large broad-snouted reptile belonging to the genus *Alligator* (2 species). Each side of the jaw contains 17–22 teeth, which are all covered when the mouth is closed. The American alligator (*A. mississippiensis*) is mainly black and lives in rivers of the SE USA, reaching a length of 5–6 m; the rare Chinese alligator (*A. sinensis*) of the Yangtze River is smaller. They dig burrows in which they hibernate during cold weather. Order: *Crocodilia* (*see* CROCODILE).

Allium A genus of herbaceous plants (about 450 species), including the *onion, *shallot, *garlic, *leek, *chive, etc. They have bulbs, those of several species being widely used in temperate regions for food and flavouring, and in many the flowers are replaced by small bulbs (bulbils), by means of which the plants can be propagated. Family: *Liliaceae* (or *Alliaceae* according to some authorities).

Allosaurus A large bipedal dinosaur of the Jurassic and Cretaceous periods (200–65 million years ago). Up to 11 m long, it had large hind limbs, a well-developed tail, small forelegs, and thick protective knobs of bone over the eyes. Although fairly slow, it hunted prey, possibly in groups, and was equipped with sharp claws and pointed teeth. Order: *Saurischia*.

alloy A blend of a metal with other metals or nonmetals. The first alloy was probably *bronze, which was first used in Europe in about 2000 BC. *Steel and *brass are the most widely used alloys. Alloys of aluminium are also common, especially in the aircraft industry. Alloys may be intermetallic compounds, solid solutions, heterogenous mixtures, or any combination of these forms. In general, intermetallic compounds tend to be hard and brittle: iron carbide, which strengthens iron to form steel is an example. Solid solutions, on the other hand, are usually soft and ductile: cartridge-case brass is a typical example. Most alloys melt over a range of temperatures unlike a pure metal, which has a specific melting point. **Eutectic alloys** consist of solid solutions having the lowest melting point of all the possible mixtures of the components. They are used in fuses and other safety mechanisms.

All Saints' Day A Christian feast commemorating all saints, whether known or unknown. In the Eastern Churches it has always been observed on the first Sunday after Pentecost. In the West its date varied until fixed as 1 Nov by Gregory III. *See also* HALLOWE'EN.

All Souls' Day A Christian feast in the Western Church commemorating all Christians who have died (the "faithful departed"). It is observed on 2 Nov. Requiem masses, containing the *Dies Irae*, are celebrated.

allspice (*or* **pimento**) A widely used aromatic spice, so named because it combines the flavours of several different spices. It is derived from the powdered dried unripe berries of an evergreen tree, *Pimenta dioca*, which is native to Central America and the West Indies. Family: *Myrtaceae*.

Alma Ata 43 19N 76 55E (name until 1921: Verny) The former capital of Kazakhstan. Situated in the foothills of the Trans-Alay Alatau (mountains), it has food and tobacco processing industries and there is a thriving film industry. The capital transferred to Akmola (later renamed Astana) in 1997. Population (1995 est): 1 150 500.

almanac A calendar of the months and days of the year containing astronomical and other miscellaneous data. It usually includes information about eclipses, phases of the moon, positions of the planets, times of sunset and sunrise and of high and low tides, as well as religious and secular holidays. Modern almanacs include official government publications listing national statistics.

Alma-Tadema, Sir Lawrence (1836–1912) British painter of Dutch birth, who lived in England from 1870. Many of his paintings were inspired by Egyptian and classical antiquity.

Almodóvar, Pedro (1949–) Spanish film director, noted for his provocative black comedies, often on sexual themes. His films include *Women on the Verge of a Nervous Breakdown*

(1988), *Tie Me Up! Tie Me Down!* (1989), *The Flower of My Secret* (1995), *All About My Mother* (1999), and *Talk to Her* (2002).

almond A tree, *Prunus amygdalus*, native to SW Asia but widely grown in warm regions. The edible nuts are produced by a variety called sweet almond; the nuts of the bitter almond yield aromatic almond oil, used as a flavouring. Almond trees grow to a height of 7 m; they have pink flowers and are sometimes grown for ornament. Family: *Rosaceae*. *See also* PRUNUS.

Aloe A genus of succulent herbaceous plants (about 200 species), all native to Africa. A stem is usually absent, the toothed fleshy leaves forming a basal rosette, up to 40 cm in diameter. The flowers are red or yellow; the juice of some species, especially *A. vera*, is used as an emollient. Family: *Liliaceae*.

alpaca A shaggy-coated hoofed mammal, *Lama pacos*, traditionally bred in the South American Andes. Its dark fleece reaches nearly to the ground and is shorn every two years, each animal yielding about 3 kg of wool. Alpacas thrive at high altitudes, keeping to damp grassy plateaus. Family: *Camelidae* (camels).

alphabets Writing systems in which each symbol represents a speech sound (*see* PHONETICS). Many pictographic writing systems developed as far as ideography and even *syllabaries, but the breakthrough to true alphabetic phonetic writing took place, it seems, only on the E shores of the Mediterranean around 2000 BC. From this Semitic alphabet all the major alphabets in use today—Roman, Greek, Cyrillic, Hebrew, Arabic, and Devanagari—are ultimately derived. *See also* INTERNATIONAL PHONETIC ALPHABET.

alpha particle The nucleus of a helium-4 atom, consisting of two protons and two neutrons. It is extremely stable and is emitted by some radioactive nuclei in the process known as **alpha decay**, which reduces the mass number of the nucleus by four and its atomic number by two. An example is the decay of uranium-238 into thorium-234.

Alphege, St (954–1012) English martyr. He became Bishop of Winchester in 984 and was appointed Archbishop of Canterbury in 1006. He was captured by the Danes in 1011 and murdered because he refused to save himself at the expense of his tenants. Feast day: 19 April.

alphorn A musical instrument used in Switzerland for calling cattle. Made of wood, it is commonly 2 m long or more. Being valveless, it plays only harmonics.

Phoenician
Early Hebrew
Early Aramaic
Early Greek
Classical Greek
Etruscan
Early Latin
Classical Latin
Russian-Cyrillic
Modern Roman
A B C D E F G H I J K L M N O P Q R S T U V W X Y Z

alphabets. The letters of the modern Roman alphabet have developed from the ancient Phoenician syllabary. This script in its Aramaic form was also the ultimate source of the Arabic alphabet and probably of the Brahmi alphabet, from which the many scripts of modern India are derived. The Cyrillic alphabet was derived directly from the Greek, whereas the Roman came through Etruscan and Latin.

Alps The highest mountain range in Europe. It extends some 800 km (497 mi) in an arc roughly E–W through France, Switzerland, Italy, and Austria, and rises to 4807 m (15 771 ft) at Mont Blanc near the W end. Several major rivers rise here, including the Rhône, Rhine, Drava, and Po. The snowline varies between

a

2400 m and 3000 m (7874 ft and 9843 ft) and many of the lower slopes are used as pasture in summer, while in winter the Alps are Europe's major skiing area. There are several road and rail routes across the chain, including a number of tunnels. *See also* MARITIME ALPS.

al-Qaida (Arabic: the base) The international terrorist organization created by Osama *Bin Laden that carried out the attacks on America on *September 11 2001. The seeds of al-Qaida were sown during Bin Laden's guerrilla campaign against the Soviets in Afghanistan (1979–89), but the organization took definitive shape when he moved to Sudan (1991), where he trained terrorists for a holy war against the USA. Bomb attacks on US servicemen in Yemen (1992), Somalia (1993), and Saudi Arabia (1995) followed and in 1998 al-Qaida blew up the US embassies in Kenya and Tanzania, killing around 200. From 1996 al-Qaida had its command centre in S Afghanistan, where it forged links with the *Taleban. Following September 11, al-Qaida's headquarters and training camps became the prime targets in the US-led *war on terrorism. Although it suffered some losses, al-Qaida cells are still active in many countries. It is thought to have been involved in the Bali bombing of Oct 2002 and the Madrid railway bombing of March 2004, in each of which some 200 people were killed.

Alsace (German name: Elsass) A planning region and former province in NE France, separated from Germany by the River Rhine. It is a fertile agricultural area and has important potassium deposits. *History*: it was often a scene of conflict between France and Germany. Under Roman occupation from the 1st century AD, it became a Frankish duchy in the 5th century and was part of the Holy Roman Empire from the 10th to the 17th centuries. The French gained control of Alsace in 1648, after the Thirty Years' War, but it was lost to Germany in 1871, after the Franco-Prussian War, and linked with *Lorraine to form the German imperial territory of **Alsace-Lorraine**. This existed until it reverted to France in 1919. It came under German control again in World War II and was restored to France in 1945. Area: 8310 sq km (3208 sq mi). Population (1999): 1 734 145.

Alsatian dog *See* GERMAN SHEPHERD DOG.

Altai Mountains A mountain system in Asia, extending from Siberia, Russia, into China and Mongolia. It rises to 4506 m (14 783 ft) at Belukha in Russia.

Altamira Upper *Palaeolithic cave site in N Spain, recognized in 1879, noted for the 150 magnificent paintings of animals on the cave's ceiling. Bison, painted in red ochre with black manganese manes, tails, and hooves, are the chief species depicted. *See also* MAGDALENIAN.

Altdorfer, Albrecht (c. 1480–1538) German artist. His masterpieces, few of which survive, show his love of forested mountains and include *The Battle of Issus* and *St George* (both Alte Pinakothek, Munich). He became the city architect of Regensburg.

alternating current (ac) Electrical current that periodically reverses its direction. It is the form of current produced when a coil of wire rotates in a magnetic field and, as this is the way in which current is produced in *power stations by *electric generators, it is the form of current most widely used, especially because its voltage can be easily increased or decreased by a transformer. The electromotive force (emf), E, produced by a generator is equal to $E'\sin \omega t$, where E' is the maximum emf, ω is the angular velocity of rotation, and t is the time. Thus the current has the form of a sine wave, with a frequency $\omega/2\pi$. In the UK the frequency used is 50 hertz (60 hertz in the USA). The voltage at which it is transmitted is several hundred kilovolts, which is transformed down to 240 volts for domestic use. *See also* ELECTRICITY SUPPLY.

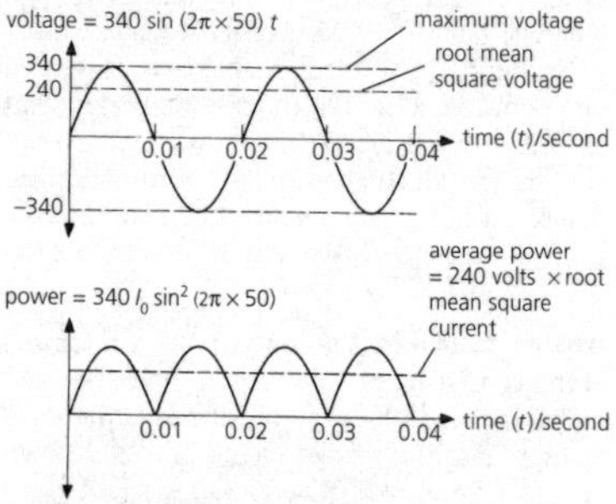

alternating current. The voltage and power waveforms in a 240-volt, 50-hertz domestic mains supply. The current ($I = I_0 \sin(2\pi \times 50)t$) has a similar waveform to the voltage.

alternation of generations A phenomenon occurring in the *life cycles of many plants and some animals (particularly cnidarians) in which there is an alternation between two distinct forms (generations), which differ from each other in structure, reproduction, and also often in habit. In plants the generation reproducing sexually is the gametophyte and the asexual generation is the sporophyte. Either phase may be predominant in a particular species; for example, the gametophyte is dominant in mosses and the sporophyte in flowering plants. In cnidarians sedentary asexual polyps alternate with free-living sexual forms called medusae.

alternative energy The use of renewable energy sources from the environment. Most countries now rely heavily on *fossil fuels (oil, coal, and natural gas) and nuclear power for their energy needs. To combat the *greenhouse effect resulting from the use of fossil fuels and the environmental hazards of nuclear-waste disposal, the UK government in 2002, in accordance with the *Kyoto agreement, imposed a **renewables obligation** on all energy suppliers, who must take 3% of their energy from renewable sources. This rises to 10% in 2010. In the late 1990s in the UK some 2.3 million tonnes of oil equivalent was provided by renewable sources (80% *biomass energy, 17% *hydroelectric power, 2.5% wind power, and 0.5% solar power). To meet the Kyoto obligations, the largest investment is going into wind power, with the development of wind farms. Wave power, tidal power, and geothermal energy are also being developed.

alternative medicine (*or* **complementary medicine**) Treatment of physical and mental illness by alternative methods to those of orthodox medicine. It includes such specialties as *osteopathy, *homeopathy, *acupuncture, and *hypnosis, which are recognized and practised by some qualified doctors. Other branches include *chiropractic, *aromatherapy, naturopathy, herbalism, dietary treatments, the laying on of hands, and self-healing (e.g. by yoga, biofeedback, etc.). *See also* HOLISTIC MEDICINE.

Althing The parliament of Iceland, the oldest in the world, founded in about 930 AD. Since independence in 1944 it has been the country's sovereign legislature. It has 60 members in two houses of equal power.

Althorp House A country house in Northamptonshire, the childhood home and burial place of *Diana, Princess of Wales. It has been the seat of the Spencer family since 1508. A museum dedicated to the life of Diana opened in 1998.

altimeter A device for measuring altitude in one of two ways. A **pressure altimeter** consists of an aneroid *barometer calibrated in metres (or feet) above sea level. A **radio altimeter** consists of a device that measures the time taken for a radio or radar signal to reach the ground and return.

altitude The angular distance of an astronomical body above or below an observer's horizon. It reaches a maximum of 90° when the body is directly overhead. It is used with the angular distance **azimuth**, measured eastwards along the horizon from the direction of N, to specify the position of an astronomical body on the *celestial sphere.

Altman, Robert (1922–) US film director, screenwriter, and producer. His films, mainly black comedies and satires, include *M*A*S*H* (1970), *Nashville* (1975), *Short Cuts* (1994), and *Gosford Park* (2002).

alto A high adult male singing voice produced by falsetto. Range: that of the *countertenor and *contralto.

altocumulus cloud (Ac) A medium type of *cloud appearing as globular masses in bands across the sky.

altostratus cloud (As) A medium type of *cloud appearing as a greyish sheet, sometimes thin enough for the sun to be seen through it. It usually heralds rain.

aluminium (Al) A light silvery-white metal first isolated by Friedrich Wöhler in 1827. It is the most abundant metal in the earth's crust and the main source is *bauxite, an impure hydrated oxide. The metal is extracted by electrolysis of the oxide dissolved in a flux of low melting point with the mineral cryolite. Its most important uses depend on its lightness (relative density 2.70), ductility, and good electrical conductivity. It is used in electrical power cables, kitchen utensils, and many industrial applications. Pure aluminium is soft, but its alloys with copper, magnesium, and other elements have considerable strength. This combined with their low densities makes such alloys important in aircraft construction. The hydroxide ($Al(OH)_3$) is used in glass manufacture and as an antacid in medicine. At no 13; at wt 26.9815; mp 660.4°C; bp 2520°C.

Alyssum A genus of low-growing herbaceous plants (about 150 species), mostly native to S Europe but widely grown in gardens. Alyssums have small flowers grouped in terminal clusters. Varieties of sweet alyssum (*A. maritimum*) have white or pink flowers and are grown as annuals. Perennial alyssums include *A. saxatile*, which has yellow flowers. Family: *Cruciferae*.

a

Alzheimer's disease A degenerative disease that affects nerve cells of the brain. It causes speech disturbances, progressive loss of memory and other mental faculties, and changes in behaviour and personality; though it may occur in middle age it is more common in elderly people. Its cause is uncertain, but some forms of Alzheimer's disease are inherited. Named after the German neurologist Alois Alzheimer (1864–1915).

amalgam An alloy of mercury with various other metals, including silver, gold, and palladium. Amalgams of mercury with silver and tin are used in dentistry to fill tooth cavities.

Amaranthus A genus of herbaceous plants (50–60 species) native to tropical and subtropical regions but now widely distributed (as pigweed). The small petalless flowers grow in long drooping spikes. Several species are grown for ornament, including *A. caudatus* (love-lies-bleeding), 60–100 cm tall with dark-red flowers, *A. tricolor* (Joseph's coat), with purple flowers and red, yellow, and green leaves. Family: *Amaranthaceae.*

amaryllis A perennial herbaceous plant, *Amaryllis belladonna*, also called belladonna lily, native to South Africa but widely cultivated for ornament. Growing from bulbs, it has strap-shaped leaves and a 45 cm long stem bearing 5–12 funnel-shaped sweet-scented flowers, usually rose-pink. Family: *Amaryllidaceae.*

Amati A family of violin makers in Cremona, Italy. **Andrea Amati** (c. 1520–c. 1578) developed the design that became the standard modern violin. His sons **Antonio Amati** (?1550–1638) and **Girolamo Amati** (1551–1635) worked as a team. Girolamo's son **Nicolò Amati** (1596–1684) was the family's greatest craftsman and taught Andrea *Guarneri (d. 1698) and *Stradivari.

Amazon, River (Portuguese name: Rio Amazônas) The largest river system and the second longest river in the world. Rising as the Río Marañón in the Andes, in Peru, it flows generally W–E to enter the Atlantic Ocean in NE Brazil. Its drainage basin extends over much of Brazil, and parts of Venezuela, Colombia, Ecuador, Peru, and Bolivia. It is covered by a mantle of tropical rain forest (selva) and is navigable to oceangoing vessels as far as Iquitos, 3700 km (2300 mi) upstream. Destruction of the rain forest in recent years has caused concern on ecological grounds. Length: 6440 km (4000 mi). Drainage basin area: about 5 827 500 sq km (2 250 000 sq mi).

Amazons (Greek: breastless ones) A mythical nation of female warriors who were believed by the ancient Greeks to live in Pontus, near the Black Sea. Trained for war and hunting, the Amazons got their name from their habit of removing the right breast to facilitate the drawing of bows. They intervened in the *Trojan War against the Greeks, but Achilles killed their queen, Penthesilea. They also invaded Attica but were defeated by *Theseus, who took their queen Hippolyte captive.

amber A translucent or opaque yellow fossil resin exuded by coniferous trees; insects and leaves are often preserved in the mineral, having been trapped on the sticky surface prior to hardening. It is found predominantly in Tertiary deposits around the S Baltic coast. It is used for beads, ornaments, and amber varnish.

ambergris A waxy substance found in the intestines of sperm whales. Mainly cholesterol, with fatty oils and steroids, it has a musky scent and is used in making perfumes.

Ambrose, St (c. 339–97 AD) Italian bishop of Milan and Doctor of the Church. Born at Trier, he was appointed a provincial governor in 370 with his headquarters at Milan. He was made Bishop of Milan in 374. He championed orthodoxy and the rights of the church against the civil power.

ambrosia The food of the gods in Greek mythology. Bestowing eternal life on those who ate it, ambrosia was (according to Homer and others) taken with the drink **nectar**; it was also described as a perfume.

Amenhotep III King of Egypt (c. 1417–1379 BC) of the 18th dynasty. He controlled Palestine and Syria through vassal kings and maintained good relations with Babylon. Many of the monumental buildings at Karnak and Luxor were erected by him. He was the father of Akhenaton.

American eagle *See* BALD EAGLE.

American football *See* FOOTBALL.

American Indians A diverse group of peoples of North, Central, and South America and the Caribbean Islands. In many respects they resemble the Mongoloid peoples of Asia, which has led to their classification as a subtype of the *Mongoloid race. However, their physical diversity, and the possession of certain features not common among Mongoloids, suggests other origins. Their ancestors probably migrated to the Americas from Asia via Alaska between 10 000 and 20 000 years ago. They have coarse dark straight hair, yellowish-brown skins, and sparse body hair. They speak a variety of languages and culturally range from primitive hunters and gatherers to the creators of the *Aztec, *Maya, and *Inca civilizations. *See also* NORTH AMERICAN INDIANS.

American Revolution (*or* **American War of Independence**; 1775–83) The conflict in which the 13 colonies of North America gained independence from Britain. American resentment at Britain's authoritative rule focused in the mid-18th century on taxation. Protests against such legislation as the *Stamp Act (1765) and Townshend Acts (1767) culminated in the *Boston Tea Party (1773), to which Britain responded with the punitive Intolerable Acts (1774). The first Continental Congress was summoned at Philadelphia and, after attempts by both sides at negotiation had failed, the first shots of the war were fired at Lexington and Concord (April 1775). In the autumn the Americans invaded Canada, taking Montreal and besieging Quebec until forced to withdraw to Ticonderoga in Spring, 1776. On 4 July the second Continental Congress issued the *Declaration of Independence. Gen William Howe landed on Long Island in August and defeated the newly appointed American commander in chief, George *Washington, near White Plains. At the beginning of January 1777, however, Washington dealt a counterblow at Princeton before settling in winter quarters. Britain's strategy in 1777 was based on a plan for Gen John Burgoyne to march S from Canada and join Howe at the Hudson River. Burgoyne arrived at the Hudson (Aug) but Howe had left New York by sea, landed at Chesapeake Bay, and defeated Washington at the Brandywine, taking Philadelphia (Sept). Burgoyne, meanwhile, was forced to surrender his army at *Saratoga, a defeat that proved a turning point by bringing France into the war on the American side. In 1778 the British began an offensive in the S. Howe's successor, Clinton, took Charleston, South Carolina, and Cornwallis defeated Gates at Camden (1780). In early 1781 the British lost badly at Cowpens (17 Jan) but won, with heavy casualties, the battle of Guilford Court House (15 March). Cornwallis now moved into Virginia, establishing a base at Yorktown. There besieged by a Franco-American force under the Comte de Rochambeau (1725–1807) and Washington, on 19 October Cornwallis surrendered. American victory was now assured although conflict continued, chiefly at sea. The British navy had been threatened throughout by American privateers and the activities of such commanders as John Paul Jones, but the main threat at sea came from America's European allies—the French, Spanish (from 1779), and Dutch (from 1780), who gained control of the English Channel and threatened invasion. Rodney's success (1782) in the West Indies enabled Britain to regain control of the Atlantic. In 1783 Britain acknowledged American independence in the Treaty of *Paris.

America's Cup A sailing race held periodically off Newport, Rhode Island (USA) and elsewhere, in which US yachts are challenged for a cup won by the US *America* off the Isle of Wight in 1851. The USA retained the cup until 1983, when it was won by the Australian *Australia II*. The USA won again in 1987 and 1992. New Zealand won it in 1995.

americium (Am) The fourth transuranic element, synthesized (1944) by G. T. Seaborg and others by addition of neutrons to plutonium followed by β-decay. It forms the oxide (AmO_2) and such trihalides as $AmCl_3$; it is strongly radioactive. At no 95; at wt (243); mp 1176°C.

amethyst A gemstone comprising a purple variety of *quartz. Its colour is due to impurities, particularly iron oxide. The best crystals are found in Brazil and the Urals. It is used for jewellery. Birthstone for February.

Amiens 49 54N 2 18E A city in NE France, the capital of the Somme department situated on the River Somme. Known as Samarobriva in pre-Roman times, it was the ancient capital of Picardy. The **Peace of Amiens** (1802) marked a respite in the Revolutionary and Napoleonic Wars. Its gothic cathedral survived the damage of both World Wars. An important railway junction, Amiens' industries include textiles, tyres, and chemicals. Population (1999): 135 501.

Amin (Dada), Idi (c. 1925–2003) Ugandan politician; president (1971–79). He rose rapidly in the army, becoming commander in 1966. He overthrew Milton *Obote to become president and in 1972 ordered the expulsion of 80 000 non-Ugandan Asians. He and his government were notorious for their brutality; Amin was overthrown in a Tanzanian-backed coup after which he went into exile.

amines A class of basic organic compounds derived from ammonia (NH_3), in which one (primary amines), two (secondary amines), or three (tertiary amines) of the hydrogen atoms are replaced by organic groups. *See also* AMINO ACIDS.

amino acids A group of organic acids characterized by having at least one carboxyl group (–COOH) and at least one amino group (–NH_2). About 20 different amino acids comprise the basic constituents of *proteins. Certain essen-

a

tial amino acids cannot be manufactured by the body and must be supplied in the diet. In man these are: arginine, histidine, isoleucine, leucine, lysine, methionine, phenylalanine, threonine, tryptophan, and valine.

Amis, Sir Kingsley (1922–95) British novelist and poet, one of the *Angry Young Men. His first novel, *Lucky Jim* (1954), was a popular success. Later novels include *I Want It Now* (1968), *Jake's Thing* (1978), *The Old Devils* (1986), which won the Booker Prize, and *The Folks that Live on the Hill* (1990). He published several volumes of poetry and his memoirs appeared in 1991. His son **Martin Amis** (1949–), also a novelist, wrote *The Rachel Papers* (1974), *Money* (1984), *London Fields* (1989), *The Information* (1995), and *Yellow Dog* (2003). His autobiography, *Experience*, was published in 2000.

Amish A US and Canadian Protestant sect and a conservative faction of the Mennonites. Jakob Ammann, a Mennonite bishop in Switzerland, founded the sect in the 1690s, and by 1727 his followers had begun to settle in Pennsylvania. The Amish dress uniformly and depend on farming for their livelihood.

Amman 31 57N 35 56E The capital of Jordan. Amman was the capital of the biblical Ammonites, and there are some Greek and Roman remains. Under the British mandate in Palestine, the town grew from a small village, and in 1946 it became the capital of independent Jordan. The city has had large influxes of refugees following fighting in the Arab-Israeli Wars (1948, 1967, and 1973); in 1970 tension resulting from the refugee presence led to fighting on the streets of Amman between Jordanian forces and Palestinians. The university was founded in 1962. Amman is now an important communications centre, with some manufacturing industry. Population (1994 est): 963 490.

ammeter An instrument for measuring electric current. The two most common types are the moving-coil and the moving-iron ammeters. The moving-coil ammeter is more sensitive but will only measure direct current. The moving-iron ammeter will measure both alternating and direct current but is less sensitive and its scale is nonlinear. Some modern instruments are electronic and have a digital display.

ammonia (NH_3) A colourless toxic basic gas used for the manufacture of fertilizers, nitric acid, explosives, and synthetic fibres. It is made by the *Haber-Bosch process.

ammonite A *cephalopod mollusc belonging to the subclass *Ammonoidea* (over 600 genera), abundant during the late Palaeozoic and Mesozoic eras, becoming extinct 100 million years ago. Their fossilized remains have either straight or coiled shells, some up to 200 cm in diameter, containing many chambers, which provided buoyancy for the free-swimming animal.

Ammonites An ancient Semitic tribe who were descended from Ben-ammi, the son of Lot, and lived E of Jordan. They worshipped the god Moloch and often fought the Israelites.

amnesia Loss of memory resulting from such causes as head injuries, drugs, hysteria, senility, or psychological illness. The memory loss may be for events before the injury or disease (**retrograde amnesia**) or for events after it (**anterograde amnesia**). In some cases specific areas of the brain show pathological changes. Treatment is related to the cause.

Amnesty International An organization, founded by Peter Benenson in the UK in 1961, aiming to defend freedom of speech, opinion, and religion in all parts of the world. It campaigns for the release of "prisoners of conscience," against torture, and for human rights and is concerned for the welfare of refugees. It has some 1.5 million members in over 150 countries and is funded by voluntary contributions. It won the Nobel Peace Prize in 1977.

amniocentesis A form of prenatal diagnosis in which a small quantity of the fluid (amniotic fluid) that surrounds an unborn baby in the mother's womb is removed for examination. The specimen may be taken by needle through the abdominal wall or, later in pregnancy, the opening of the womb. Tests on the amniotic fluid may reveal the presence of certain diseases or congenital disorders in the baby (e.g. Down's syndrome or spina bifida). If serious abnormality is detected, the possibility of abortion can be considered. Amniocentesis is offered to women when there is a family history of congenital disease and to pregnant women over 35 years of age.

Amoeba A genus of free-living microscopic animals (*see* PROTOZOA). They occur widely in soil and water and their flexible cells assume various shapes. The common amoeba (*A. proteus*) may be up to 0.5 mm long. Amoebas move by extending their cytoplasm into lobes (pseudopodia), which also engulf food particles and liquids. They reproduce by binary *fission and under adverse conditions form protective cysts. Some related forms are parasitic, including *Entamoeba histolytica*, which causes amoebic dysentery in man. Phylum: *Rhizopoda*.

Amon The supreme Egyptian deity. Originally a Theban god, he acquired major status in the ascendancy of the 18th (Theban) dynasty in about 1570 BC. He became associated with the rival god Ra and as Amon-Ra became the national god. Great temples were built to him at Luxor and Karnak (c. 1400 BC). Amon-Ra remained supreme god until 663 BC.

Amorites Semitic nomads of Palestine and Syria, who invaded the centres of civilization of Mesopotamia during the late 3rd millennium and 2nd millennium BC. They occupied *Babylonia, assimilated its culture and established numerous small kingdoms. Many Babylonian kings, including Hammurabi, were of Amorite stock.

Amos (early 8th century BC) An Old Testament prophet of Judah. The **Book of Amos** contains his prophecies delivered in Israel. He denounced the luxury and injustice of the privileged nation and predicted God's judgment by means of an Assyrian invasion and natural calamities.

amount of substance A quantity proportional to the number of particles, such as atoms or ions, in a sample. The constant of proportionality is the *Avogadro number. In *SI units amount of substance is measured in *moles.

ampere (A) The SI unit of electric current equal to the current that when passed through two parallel infinitely long conductors placed 1 metre apart in a vacuum produces a force between them of 2×10^{-7} newton per metre of length. This 1948 definition replaced all former definitions including that of the international ampere based on the rate of deposition of silver from a solution of silver nitrate. Named after A. M. *Ampère.

Ampère, André Marie (1775–1836) French physicist. He introduced the important distinctions between electrostatics and electric currents and between current and voltage, demonstrated that current-carrying wires exert a force on each other, and gave an explanation of magnetism in terms of electric currents. **Ampère's law** states that the strength of the magnetic field at any point produced by a current (I) flowing through a conductor of length l is proportional to Il/d^2, where d is the distance between the point and the conductor. The unit of electric current is named after him.

amphetamine A stimulant drug that produces a feeling of alertness and wellbeing, increases muscular activity, and reduces fatigue and appetite. Because of the risk of addiction, particularly when combined with barbiturates ("purple hearts"), amphetamine is now rarely prescribed. It is occasionally used (in the form of dexamphetamine) to treat attention deficit disorder in children.

amphibian An animal belonging to the class *Amphibia*, which contains over 2500 species of frogs, toads, newts, salamanders, and caecilians. Adult amphibians breathe through lungs and have adapted to a wide range of habitats; however they require damp surroundings in order to minimize loss of body fluids through their thin, moist and usually scaleless skin. Generally amphibians lay their eggs in ponds or rivers. The eggs hatch into aquatic tadpole larvae that breathe using gills and develop into adults by a complete bodily transformation known as *metamorphosis.

amphiboles A group of rock-forming minerals, mostly complex hydrous ferromagnesian silicates. Horneblende and tremolite are examples. Amphiboles are common in igneous and metamorphic rocks and often occur in fibrous or acicular forms, including some forms of *asbestos.

amphitheatre An elliptical or circular building with tiers of seats surrounding an arena, designed by the Romans as a setting for gladiatorial and wild-beast shows, etc. The earliest stone amphitheatre is that at Pompeii (c. 70 BC). The largest is the *Colosseum in Rome but there are also remains of amphitheatres in Arles, Nîmes, Capua, Verona, Sicily, and N Africa.

Amphitryon In Greek mythology, a grandson of Perseus who was betrothed to Alcmene, daughter of the King of Mycenae. While he was at war, Zeus assumed his appearance and seduced Alcmene, who conceived Heracles.

Amphitrite The Greek goddess of the sea. Poseidon chose her to be his wife when he saw her dancing with her sister Nereids. She rejected him and fled to the island of Naxos, but he sent a dolphin to reclaim her. She bore him three sons, Triton, Rhodos, and Benthesicyma.

amphora An ancient Greek two-handled vase used as a container for liquids and fruit, and sometimes as an urn for holding ashes of the dead. The most important are the Black Figure vases (600–480 BC) of black-painted red earthenware depicting mythological scenes.

Other undecorated types, sometimes tapering to a pointed base, were used for transporting oil and wine.

amplifier An electronic device for intensifying an electrical signal in an alternating-current circuit, with an external steady voltage supply. Amplifiers are designed to multiply the input (current, voltage, or power) by a specific factor, known as the gain. Often an amplifier consists of several stages, the output from one stage becoming the input to the next stage. This method is used in the amplifiers in sound-reproduction systems.

Amritsar 31 35N 74 56E A city in NW India, in Punjab. Founded in 1577 by the fourth guru of the Sikhs, Ram Das, it has become the centre of the Sikh faith. In 1919 hundreds of Indian nationalists were killed here when fired upon by troops under British control. In 1984 about 1000 people died when the Sikh shrine, the Golden Temple, was fortified by Sikh extremists and stormed by the Indian army. The subsequent assassination of Indira *Gandhi was a reprisal for this event. A commercial, cultural, and communications centre, it manufactures textiles and silk. Population (1991): 709 456.

Amsterdam 52 21N 4 54E The official capital of the Netherlands, in North Holland province on the Rivers Amstel and IJ. The government seat is at The Hague. Linked to the North Sea by canal (1876), it is a major seaport. It is also an important financial and industrial centre, with a diamond cutting and polishing trade. Industries include shipbuilding, dairy produce, tobacco, and brewing. The city is mostly built on piles and linked with a radial system of canals and approximately 1000 bridges. *History*: chartered in 1300, it joined the Hanseatic League in 1369. It became the capital in 1808. Population (1999 est): 727 053.

Amu Darya, River A river in central Asia. Rising in the Pamirs, it flows mainly NW through the Hindu Kush, Turkmenistan, and Uzbekistan to join the Aral Sea through a large delta. It forms part of the N border of Afghanistan and is important for irrigation. It is navigable for over 1450 km (800 mi). Length: 2400 km (1500 mi).

Amundsen, Roald (1872–1928) Norwegian explorer, the first person to reach the South Pole. After sailing the *Northwest Passage in the *Gjöa* (1903–06) he abandoned his plan to reach the North Pole on hearing of Peary's success (1909). He himself beat *Scott to the South Pole in 1911. In 1926 he flew a dirigible over the North Pole with Umberto Nobile (1885–1928). Amundsen died while searching for Nobile following the latter's dirigible crash in the Arctic Ocean. A small section of the S Pacific Ocean, bordering on Ellsworth Land in Antarctica, is called **Amundsen Sea** after him.

Amur, River (Chinese name: Heilong Jiang *or* Hei-Lung Chiang) A river in NE Asia. Rising in N Mongolia, it flows generally SE and NE through Mongolia, Russia, and China, to the Sea of Okhotsk. It forms the border between Russia and Manchuria. Length: 4350 km (2700 mi).

Anabaptists (from Greek: rebaptizers) Any of various radical religious groups originating in several continental countries during the *Reformation. They were called Anabaptists because they rejected infant baptism in favour of baptizing adults when they professed their faith. Persecuted by Roman Catholics and Protestants, they were accused of fanaticism, heresy, and immorality. They believed in pacifism, common ownership of goods, and millenarianism, and held radical political views. Their modern descendants, such as the Mennonites, number more than 500 000.

anabolic steroids *See* ANDROGENS.

anabolism *See* METABOLISM.

anaconda A nonvenomous South American *constrictor snake, *Eunectes murinus*. Up to 10 m long, it is typically dark green with oval black spots and lives in swamps and rivers, feeding on fish and small caymans and also hunting deer, peccaries, and birds along the water's edge.

Anacreon (6th century BC) Greek lyric poet. He fled from his native island of Teos before the Persian invasion, and lived at Samos and then Athens, under the patronage of Hipparchus. His work, only fragments of which survive, consisted chiefly of love lyrics and drinking songs.

anaemia A reduction in the number of red cells or the quantity of red pigment (*see* HAEMOGLOBIN) in the blood. It may be due to loss of blood, for example after an accident or operation or from chronic bleeding of a peptic ulcer, or lack of the iron necessary for the production of haemoglobin. **Haemolytic anaemias** are caused by increased destruction of the red blood cells, as may occur in certain blood diseases (e.g. *sickle-cell disease and thalassaemia) and malaria or because of the presence of toxic chemicals. Anaemia can also result from the defective production of red cells, as occurs in **pernicious anaemia** (when it is due to deficiency of *vitamin B_{12}).

anaesthesia A state of insensitivity to pain. Anaesthesia occurs in certain diseases of the nervous system, but is induced artificially for surgical operations. Alcohol and opium derivatives have been used as anaesthetics for centuries, but it was not until the 1840s that the first anaesthetic gases—ether, nitrous oxide, and chloroform—were used to induce **general anaesthesia** (total unconsciousness). This procedure now involves premedication (including administration of sedatives) to prepare the patient for surgery, followed by induction of anaesthesia by injecting a short-acting barbiturate (usually sodium thiopentone). Anaesthesia is maintained by inhalation of an anaesthetic gas (e.g. halothane). **Local anaesthesia** involves injection of a local anaesthetic (e.g. lignocaine) and is used for dental surgery and other minor operations. **Spinal anaesthesia** (epidural or subarachnoid) produces loss of sensation in a particular part of the body by injecting a local anaesthetic into the space round the spinal cord. It may be used, for example, during childbirth.

Anaheim 33 50N 117 56W A city in the USA, in S California near Los Angeles. It is a major tourist centre, containing the famous Disneyland opened in 1955. Population (2000): 328 014.

analgesics A class of drugs that relieve pain. **Narcotic analgesics**, such as *morphine, are powerful pain killers that act directly on the brain. Some anaesthetics also have analgesic properties. Aspirin and paracetemol are examples of **antipyretic analgesics**, which also reduce fever. These drugs are not addictive but are less potent than the narcotics.

analytic geometry The study of geometrical relations by algebraic methods. Geometrical figures are placed in a coordinate system, each point in the figure being represented by its coordinates, which satisfy an algebraic equation. It is also known as coordinate geometry or Cartesian geometry, after its inventor René *Descartes.

anaphylaxis A severe and immediate allergic response (*see* ALLERGY) that follows the interaction of the foreign substance (allergen) with antibody that is bound to the surface of certain cells (mast cells). This leads to the release of bradykinin, *histamine, and other chemicals, which cause the symptoms. Symptoms are either local (such as rash or swelling) or general (shock and collapse). The latter is a medical emergency; it is treated with injections of adrenaline, corticosteroids, and antihistamines.

anarchism A political theory advocating abolition of the state and all governmental authority. Most anarchists believe that voluntary cooperation between individuals and groups is not only a fairer and more moral way of organizing society but is also more effective and orderly. Anarchism aims at maximizing personal freedom and holds that societies in which freedom is limited by coercion and authority are inherently unstable. As an influential political force, anarchism was defeated in Russia by communism but persisted in Europe, especially in Spain until the end of the Civil War (1939).

Anastasia (1901–?1918) The youngest daughter of *Nicholas II of Russia. Although she was believed to have been executed after the Russian Revolution, a Mrs Anna Anderson (d. 1984) claimed from 1920 that she was Anastasia. Her claim was officially rejected in 1961 and finally proved false by DNA testing in 1993.

Anatolia *See* ASIA MINOR.

anatomy The study of the structure of living organisms. Early studies of human anatomy were made by the Greek physician Galen, in the 2nd century AD, but it was not until the 16th century that the prejudice against dissecting human cadavers was overcome and anatomists—notably Vesalius—made valuable contributions to the science. In the 17th century William *Harvey discovered the circulation of blood, while the development of the microscope enabled advances in the detailed structure of the body to be made by such microscopists as Malpighi, *Leeuwenhoek, and Swammerdam. In the 20th century anatomy received a valuable tool with the development of the electron microscope, which greatly extended the investigation of microscopic structure. Specialized branches of anatomy include embryology (the study of development), *histology (tissues), and *cytology (cells).

Anaxagoras (c. 500–428 BC) Greek philosopher, born at Clazomenae (Asia Minor). In about 480 he moved to Athens, but because of his influence on *Pericles, he was banished (450) on a trumped-up charge of impiety. He believed that the physical universe was made up of an infinite number of substances and that matter was infinitely divisible. He was the first to explain solar eclipses.

Anaximander (c. 610–c. 546 BC) Greek philosopher, born in Miletus (Asia Minor). He held that the physical universe came from something unlimited, rather than one particular kind of matter, and maintained that the earth lay unsupported at the centre of the universe. He was also an early evolutionist, believing that the origin of life arose in the sea, and that man evolved from some more primitive species.

ANC *See* AFRICAN NATIONAL CONGRESS.

ancestor worship The belief held by many members of prescientific societies that the spirits of their ancestors may be invoked to exert powers in their favour, especially in hunting, warfare, or other such enterprises. Ancestor cults can be socially important in reinforcing the powers of the community's living elders, who are believed to act as mouthpieces of the spirits. Festivals to propitiate the dead were features of both Greek and Roman religions, and ancestor cults formed part of Chinese and Japanese traditional religions.

anchor Any device for mooring a vessel to the bottom of a body of water. In ancient times a heavy stone was used, attached to the vessel by a rope. Modern anchors are designed for different kinds of bottom—sandy, rocky, muddy, etc.—and usually dig into the bottom with their bladelike flukes. They are attached to the vessel by heavy chain in large boats and ships or by rope (usually of nylon) in small boats.

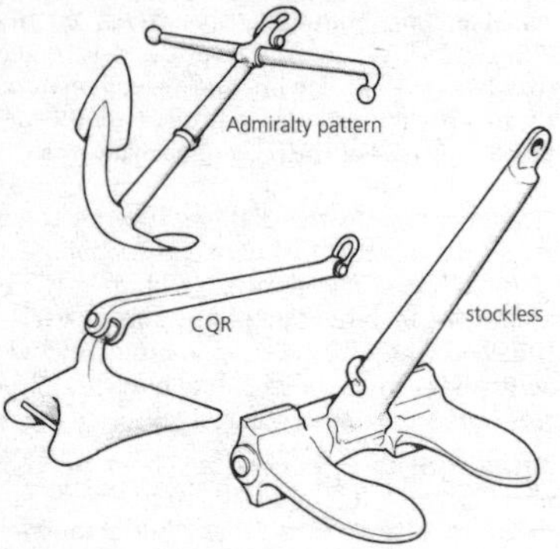

anchor. Three common forms of anchor.

Anchorage 61 10N 150 00E A city and port in the USA, in S Alaska at the head of Cook Inlet. Founded in 1914 as the terminus of the Alaska Railroad, its main industries are defence projects. Population (2000): 260 283.

anchovy A small herring-like fish belonging to the tropical and warm-temperate family *Engraulidae* (100 species). 10–25 cm long, anchovies have a large mouth extending behind the eye, a small lower jaw, and a pointed snout. They live in shoals, chiefly in coastal waters, and are fished for food, bait, and animal feeds.

Ancona 43 37N 13 31E A seaport in central Italy, the capital of Marche on the Adriatic Sea. It dates from 1500 BC, when it was founded by the Dorians. Its industries are connected with shipbuilding, engineering, and sugar refining. Population (1994 est): 100 597.

Andalusia (Spanish name: Andalucía) The southernmost region of Spain, bordering on the Atlantic Ocean and Mediterranean Sea. It chiefly occupies chiefly the river basin of the Guadalquivir and is one of Spain's most fertile regions producing citrus fruit, olives, and wine. Under Roman control after the 2nd century BC, the region was named Andalusia (after its 5th-century Vandal settlers) by the Muslims, who invaded the region in the early 8th century; much evidence of the Muslim occupation remains. In the 15th century Castile finally recovered Andulusia from the Muslims. After the Moriscos (Christians of Moorish descent) were expelled in 1609 the region's prosperity diminished. Its coastal resorts are popular with tourists, as are the Moorish buildings of Granada, Seville, and Córdoba. It became an autonomous region in 1981. Population (2001): 7 357 558.

Andaman and Nicobar Islands A Union Territory of India, comprising two island groups in the E Bay of Bengal. The Andaman forests support plywood and match industries. Coconuts, rubber, and coffee are also important. The Nicobar Islands 120 km (75 mi) S of the Andaman Islands, produce coconuts, areca nuts, and fish. Area: 8293 sq km (3215 sq mi). Population (2001): 356 265. Capital: Port Blair.

Andersen, Hans Christian (1805–75) Danish author, famous for his fairy tales. The son of a shoemaker, he attended Copenhagen University before travelling widely in Europe, writing novels, plays, and travel books. His international reputation, however, was earned by the 168 fairy tales that he wrote between 1835 and 1872. These include such classics as "The Snow Queen" and "The Ugly Duckling."

Anderson, Elizabeth Garrett (1836–1917) British physician, who pioneered the admission of women into the medical profession. Refused admission to medical schools, she studied privately and in 1865 was granted a licence to practise. She helped to establish the London hospital for women named after her.

Andes (Spanish name: Cordillera de los Andes) A mountain system in W South America. It extends N for about 7250 km (4500 mi) from Cape Horn to the Isthmus of Panama, reaching 6960 m (22 835 ft) at Mount Aconcagua and separating a narrow coastal belt from the rest of the continent. Comprising a series of parallel mountain ranges, it is chiefly of volcanic origin and contains several active volcanoes, including *Cotopaxi; earthquakes are common phenomena. It is rich in mineral wealth; the chief metals extracted include gold, silver, platinum, mercury, copper, and lead.

Andhra Pradesh A state in E central India, on the Bay of Bengal. The coastal plain rises westwards over the Eastern *Ghats into the Deccan plateau. Rice, sugar cane, cotton, tobacco, and pulses are farmed. Large forests provide teak, bamboo, and fruit trees. Manganese, iron ore, mica, and coal are mined. Industries include textiles, machinery, oil refining, and shipbuilding, which has been developed with cheap hydroelectricity. The region was struck by a severe earthquake in 1993. Area: 275 068 sq km (106 204 sq mi). Population (2001): 75 727 541. Capital: Hyderabad. Chief seaport: Vishakhapatnam.

Andorra, Principality of (Catalan name: Valls d'Andorra; French name: Les Vallées d'Andorre) A small principality in the E Pyrenees, between France and Spain. It is mountainous with peaks reaching heights of almost 3000 m (about 9500 ft). *Economy*: tourism and agriculture (wheat, potatoes, livestock raising, and tobacco) are the principal industries. Financial services are also important. *History*: in 1278 it was placed under the joint overlordship of the Bishop of Urgel in Spain and the Comte de Foix in France. The latter's rights passed in the 16th century to the French Crown and are now held by the president. Andorra pays dues in alternate years of 960 francs to France and 460 pesetas to the bishopric respectively. In 1993 a new constitution was approved, giving Andorra greater autonomy, and in 1994 Andorra's first sovereign government took office. Andorra is a tax haven and immigration has been substantial in recent years. Official language: Catalan. Currency: euro of 100 cents. Area: 465 sq km (179 sq mi). Population (2003 est): 66 900. Capital: Andorra la Vella.

Andrea del Sarto (Andrea d'Agnolo; 1486–1530) Florentine painter, whose work, through its influence on his pupils Jacopo da Pontormo (1494–1557), Giovanni Battista Rosso (1494–1540), and Giorgio Vasari (1511–74), became a starting point for Tuscan *mannerism. Andrea spent most of his life in Florence, producing frescoes in the Scalzi and SS Annunziata. Among his most important paintings are several representing the Holy Family and the *Madonna of the Harpies* (1517; Uffizi).

Andrew, St In the New Testament, one of the 12 Apostles. Originally a fisherman with his brother Simon Peter, he was a disciple of John the Baptist before following Jesus. Apparently crucified, he is the patron saint of Scotland and Russia. Feast day: 30 Nov.

Androcles The hero of a story by Aulus Gellius (?125–?165 AD). Androcles was an escaped slave who removed a thorn from the paw of a lion. The lion later recognized the recaptured slave in the arena and spared him; both were freed. The story was satirized by G. B. Shaw in his play *Androcles and the Lion* (1913).

androgens A group of steroid hormones that influence the development and function of the male reproductive system and determine male secondary sexual characteristics, such as the growth of body hair and deepening of the voice at puberty. The major androgens are *testosterone and androsterone, produced by the testes in higher animals and man and also in small amounts by the adrenal glands and ovaries in mammals. Natural and synthetic androgens are used in medicine to treat conditions caused by androgen deficiency. Some synthetic androgens (**anabolic steroids**) promote the growth of muscle and bone and are administered to debilitated patients. Their use by athletes is banned by most athletic authorities.

Andromache In Greek mythology, the wife of Hector. She appears in Homer's *Iliad*. After the fall of Troy she became the slave of Neoptolemus, son of Achilles, and bore him three sons.

Andromeda (astronomy) A constellation in the N sky near Cassiopeia. The brightest star is the 2nd-magnitude Alpheratz. The constellation contains the spiral **Andromeda galaxy**, the largest of the nearby galaxies in the Local Group.

Andromeda (Greek mythology) The daughter of the Ethiopian king, Cepheus, and Cassiopeia. Her mother's boasts of Andromeda's beauty enraged Poseidon, who sent a sea monster to whom Andromeda was to be sacrificed. Chained to a rock to await her fate, she was rescued by *Perseus, who married her.

Aneirin (6th century AD) Welsh poet. His poem "Y Gododdin," preserved in the manuscript *Book of Aneirin* (c. 1250), celebrates the he-

a

roes of an expedition sent from Edinburgh to recapture Catterick from the Saxons. Out of 300 warriors only one survived.

anemometer An instrument for measuring the velocity of a fluid, often the wind. In one type, the fluid drives a small windmill or set of cups, the rate of rotation of which is a measure of the fluid velocity. Other types of anemometer are the *Pitot tube and the *Venturi tube.

Anemone A genus of herbaceous perennial plants (about 150 species) mostly native to N temperate regions. The leaves are segmented and the flowers lack true petals. The Eurasian wood anemone (*A. nemorosa*), 10–15 cm high, has white flowers. Many species are cultivated as ornamentals for their colourful flowers, including the poppy and Japanese anemones (*A. coronaria* and *A. japonica*). Family: *Ranunculaceae.*

aneurysm A swelling in the wall of an artery, due to a weakness in the wall. The most common cause in the western world is now *atherosclerosis. Aneurysms may rupture, causing fatal haemorrhage. Treatment consists of surgical removal of the aneurysm and its replacement with a graft.

angelfish **1.** A fish of the tropical marine family *Chaetodontidae*, having a narrow oval laterally compressed body, a small mouth, and often an elongated snout. Up to 70 cm long, angelfish are solitary, living around coral reefs. They are usually patterned in a variety of brilliant colours. **2.** A South American *cichlid fish of the genus *Pterophyllum*, especially *P. scalare*, which is valued as an aquarium fish.

Angelica A genus of tall perennial herbs (about 70 species) distributed in the N hemisphere and New Zealand. They grow up to 2 m tall and have umbrella-like clusters of white or greenish flowers. The Eurasian species *A. archangelica* yields an oil used in liqueur and perfume making, and its stems are candied to make the confectionary angelica. *A. sylvestris* (wild angelica) is native to Europe and Asia and introduced in Canada. Family: *Umbelliferae.*

Angelico, Fra (Guido di Pietro; c. 1400–55) Italian painter of the early Renaissance, born in Vicchio (Tuscany). In the early 1420s he became a Dominican monk in Fiesole. His order transferred in 1436 to St Mark's Convent, Florence, where he painted several frescoes, including a famous *Annunciation*. From 1445 to about 1450 he painted fresco cycles in the Vatican but only the *Scenes from the Lives of SS Stephen and Lawrence* has survived. He was an exclusively religious painter, whose spiritual serenity is reflected in his popular name.

angels (Greek: messengers) In Christianity, Judaism, and Islam, supernatural beings created before the material universe. Their primary role was to praise and serve God. Many, however, followed Lucifer in his rebellion, becoming devils in hell. In the Bible angels appear mainly as messengers from God to man. Dionysius the Areopagite systematized angelology into nine orders. Later medieval theologians debated such questions as the nature of angels' bodies, which are often depicted as winged humans. In Christian belief **archangels** are ranked above angels in the celestial hierarchy.

angina pectoris Chest pain caused by a reduction in the supply of blood to the heart due to narrowing of the coronary blood vessels. *See* CORONARY HEART DISEASE.

angioplasty *See* CORONARY HEART DISEASE.

angiosperm Any flowering plant. Angiosperms comprise a vast group of leafy green plants (about 240 000 species) in which the seeds are formed within an ovary, which becomes the *fruit. They may have evolved from early *gymnosperms in the Jurassic period (about 180 million years ago), rapidly radiating and becoming the dominant plants in the mid-Cretaceous (about 100 million years ago). They include many trees and shrubs but most are herbaceous. The 300 families are grouped into two classes: the *monocotyledons and *dicotyledons.

Angkor A ruined city in Cambodia, founded about 880 AD as capital of the Khmer empire. It was rediscovered, covered by jungle, in 1860. Its temples, decorated with relief sculptures, were intended to emulate mountains; chief of these are the Angkor Wat (early 12th century) and Bayon (c. 1200).

anglerfish A marine fish, also called goosefish, belonging to the order *Lophiiformes*. Anglerfish are generally small and have flat bodies, large heads, and wide mouths. The first ray of the spiny dorsal fin is modified to form a "fishing line" ending with a fleshy flap of skin—the "bait," which is often luminous in deep-sea species. Fish, invertebrates, and even seabirds are lured and snapped up by the huge mouth.

Angles A Germanic tribe originating from the Angeln district of Schleswig, which with the *Saxons and *Jutes invaded and conquered most of England during the 5th century AD. England is named after them.

Anglesey (Welsh name: Ynys Môn; Latin name: Mona) A low-lying island off the NW coast of Wales, linked to the mainland by road and rail bridges over the Menai Strait. Part of Gwynedd from 1974 until 1996, it has now been reinstated as a separate county. The chief agricultural activity is sheep rearing. Area: 705 sq km (272 sq mi). Population (2001): 66 828. Administrative centre: Llangefni.

Anglican Communion The fellowship of episcopal Churches in communion with the see of Canterbury. Until 1786, when the consecration of bishops for foreign sees was legalized, it consisted of the Churches of England, Ireland, and Wales and the Episcopal Church of Scotland. In 1787 the Protestant Episcopal Church of the USA was founded and thereafter Anglican dioceses were formed in all parts of the British Empire and elsewhere. The member churches are fully autonomous, comprising about 350 dioceses; they meet for consultation at the *Lambeth Conferences. Total membership is estimated at 70 million. *See also* CHURCH OF ENGLAND.

angling Fishing with a baited hook line and usually a rod. There are four main categories. Game fishing for salmon and trout takes place in fast streams and rivers. Coarse fishing for members of the carp family, such as roach and bream is a sport in which the fish are returned to the water. Sea fishing for mackerel, flatfish, etc, is popular in shallow waters round the UK. Big-game fishing for shark, tuna, and swordfish require specially equipped motorboats. Competitions were common in Britain by the 18th century. The National Angling Championship was instituted in 1906 and in 1957 the first world championship was staged.

Anglo-Catholicism A movement within the *Anglican Communion that stresses the continuity of the Church of England with Catholic Christianity. The main impetus of modern Anglo-Catholicism was provided by the 19th-century *Oxford Movement. Anglo-Catholics emphasize the historic episcopate, the sacramental life of the Church, and traditional Catholic practices with regard to the celebration of the Eucharist, vestments, etc. Some Anglo-Catholics left the Church of England following the decision (1992) to ordain women as priests.

Anglo-Saxons The Germanic conquerors of Britain during the 5th century AD (*see* ANGLES; SAXONS; JUTES). They first established a number of separate kingdoms, principally *Northumbria, *Mercia, and *Wessex, but eventually England was unified under an Anglo-Saxon dynasty. Kings ruled with the assistance of a *witan or council of wise men. Popular government and justice at the local level took the form of hundred courts. They were converted to Christianity as a result of the mission of St *Augustine of Canterbury. The Anglo-Saxons developed a rich art and literature. Their language is also known as Old English. *See also* ENGLISH.

Angola, Republic of A country in SW Africa, on the Atlantic Ocean. The Cabinda district lies to the N of the River Congo and is separated from the rest of the country by a section of the Democratic Republic of Congo. The country consists of a narrow coastal plain and a broad dissected plateau that reaches heights of over 2000 m (6500 ft). The inhabitants are almost all Black Africans (mainly of Bantu origin) with small numbers of mixed race. *Economy*: agriculture is run on a cooperative basis and the main crops are sugar cane and coffee. Angola is rich in mineral resources and diamonds have long been an important source of revenue. There is considerable oil production, especially offshore from Cabinda, and hydroelectricity is being harnessed. Main exports include oil, coffee, diamonds, and iron ore. The economy has been severely disrupted by 27 years of civil war and there are serious food shortages. *History*: discovered and settled by the Portuguese in the late 15th century, the area remained a Portuguese colony (apart from a brief period of Dutch occupation from 1641 to 1648) until 1951 when it became an overseas province of Portugal. During the 1950s and 1960s there was a rise in nationalism and in 1974 Portugal agreed to independence; however, lack of internal unity led to civil war. The various groups took over different parts of the country and in November 1975, Portugal granted independence to the "Angolan people" rather than to any one group. The People's Republic of Angola was declared by the MPLA (Popular Movement for the Liberation of Angola), with its capital in Luanda, supported by the Soviet Union and Cuba. The MPLA gained control of the country in 1976 but opposition from the National Front for the Liberation of Angola (FNLA) and the National Union for the Total Independence of Angola (UNITA), backed by South Africa, continued. South African and Cuban troops began to leave in 1988. A ceasefire was agreed in 1991, but broke down following the MPLA's victory in multiparty elections (1992). In 1994 the MPLA and UNITA agreed to

a

form a unity government but negotiations broke down in 1998 and UNITA launched a new offensive. In April 2002 a ceasefire ended 27 years of civil war which had claimed one million lives. Official language: Portuguese. Currency: kwanza of 100 lwei. Area: 1 246 700 sq km (481 351 sq mi). Population (2003 est): 10 776 000. Capital: Luanda.

Angora goat A breed of goat, originating in Turkey, whose long silky hair is regularly sheared and used commercially to make mohair, a wool-like fabric or yarn used in clothing etc. Mohair is now also obtained from several other goat breeds derived from the Angora.

Angora rabbit A breed of domesticated rabbit, originating in France in the 17th century, of which there are now both English and French varieties. The long wool, which is usually white but can be black or blue, is used in clothing manufacture (**Angora wool**).

Angry Young Men A group of British novelists and dramatists in the 1950s, mainly of working-class or lower middle-class origin, whose attitudes included dissatisfaction with postwar British society. The phrase "angry young man" was first applied to the dramatist John *Osborne. Associated with this group were the novelists Kingsley *Amis, John Wain (1925–94), and John Braine (1922–86), the dramatist Arnold *Wesker, and the critic Colin Wilson (1931–).

Ångström, Anders Jonas (1814–74) Swedish physicist and astronomer. He was a founder of spectroscopy, his work on solar spectra leading to the discovery (1862) of hydrogen in the sun. The **angstrom**, a unit of wavelength equal to 10^{-10} m (one tenth of a nanometre), is named after him.

Anguilla 18 14N 63 05W A West Indian island in the E Caribbean Sea, in the Leeward Islands. Formerly part of the UK Associated State of St Kitts-Nevis-Anguilla, it became a separate British dependency in 1980. Its economy is based on stock raising, salt production, boatbuilding, and fishing. Area: 90 sq km (35 sq mi). Population (1998 est): 12 394. *See also* ST KITTS-NEVIS, FEDERATION OF.

Angus A council area of E Scotland, on the North Sea. In 1975 the historic county of Angus was incorporated into Tayside Region. In 1996 it was restored as an independent unitary authority with adjusted borders; the city of Dundee now forms a separate authority. Agriculture is important; other sources of income include fishing, textiles, and engineering. Area: 2181 sq km (842 sq mi). Population (2001): 108 400. Administrative centre: Forfar.

aniline (*or* **phenylamine**; $C_6H_5NH_2$) A colourless oily liquid *amine used to make dyes, plastics, and drugs. It is made by the reduction of nitrobenzene obtained from coal tar.

animal A living organism belonging to the kingdom *Animalia*. Animals are typically mobile and feed on *plants, other animals, or their remains. Their body *cells lack the rigid cellulose wall of plant cells and they require specialized tissues, such as bone, for protection and support. Because of their activity, animals have specialized organs for sensing the nature of their environment; information from the sense organs is transmitted and coordinated by means of a nervous system. There are over one million species of animals, grouped into over 30 phyla. *See also* LIFE; TAXONOMY.

animal rights movement A campaign conducted by several organizations to protest against cruelty to and exploitation of animals. Targets of the movement, which developed in the 1970s, include zoos, research using experimental animals, foxhunting, and retailers of animal products. Some groups, such as the League Against Cruel Sports, favour parliamentary action, while others, such as the Animal Liberation Front, condone criminal acts, including damage to property.

animism **1.** The belief that the physical world is permeated by a spirit sometimes called the **anima mundi**. Georg Ernst Stahl (1660–1734) was its chief proponent. **2.** In anthropology, all forms of belief in spiritual agencies. Sir Edward Tylor (1832–1917), who coined this usage, distinguished between the souls of the dead (*see* ANCESTOR WORSHIP) and other personalized supernatural entities.

anise An annual Mediterranean herb, *Pimpinella anisum*, growing to a height of up to 75 cm and having umbrella-like clusters of small yellow-white flowers. It is cultivated for its liquorice-flavoured seeds (aniseed), which are used in cookery and yield an oil used to flavour drinks, etc. Family: *Umbelliferae*.

Ankara 39 55N 32 50E The capital of Turkey, in the W central region of the country. Conquered by Alexander the Great in the 4th century BC, it later came within the Roman and Byzantine Empires. It was attacked by Persians and Arabs, and in the 11th century it was defeated by the Turks. It became the capital of modern Turkey in 1923; it has three universities. Population (1997): 2 984 099.

phylum (approx. no. species)	*important classes*	*representative members*
Porifera (5000)		sponges
Cnidaria (9000)	Hydrozoa	Hydra, Portuguese man-of-war
	Scyphozoa	jellyfish
	Anthozoa	sea anemones, corals
Platyhelminthes (18 500)	Turbellaria	planarians
	Trematoda	flukes
	Cestoda	tapeworms
Nematoda (12 000)		roundworms
Mollusca (50 000)	Gastropoda	snails, slugs
	Bivalvia	mussels, oysters, cockles
	Cephalopoda	squids, octopus
Annelida (12 000)	Oligochaeta	earthworms
	Polychaeta	lugworms
	Hirudinea	leeches
Arthropoda (>1 000 000)	Arachnida	spiders, scorpions
	Crustacea	lobsters, crabs, woodlice
	Insecta	beetles, wasps, ants, flies, bugs
	Chilopoda	centipedes
	Diplopoda	millipedes
Echinodermata (6500)	Asteroidea	starfish
	Ophiuroidia	brittle stars
	Echinoidea	sea urchins
	Holothuroidea	sea cucumbers
Chordata (55 000)	Chondrichthyes	sharks, rays
	Osteichthyes	bony fish (salmon, carp, eels, perch, etc.)
	Amphibia	frogs, toads, newts, salamanders
	Reptilia	lizards, snakes, crocodiles,turtles
	Aves	birds
	Mammalia	mammals, including humans

A simplified classification of the animal kingdom (major phyla only)

ankylosaur A heavily armoured dinosaur of the late Cretaceous period, which ended 65 million years ago. Ankylosaurs were low and flat and their backs were covered with hard protective bony plates. *Euoplocephalus* (or *Ankylosaurus*) reached a length of 5 m, weighed 3 tonnes, and its plated tail ended in a large bony knob. Order: *Ornithischia*.

Annaba (former name: Bône) 36 57N 7 39E A large port in E Algeria, on the Mediterranean Sea. An early centre of Christianity, it held the bishopric of St Augustine (396–430 AD). In 1832 it was captured by the French. Mineral exports are important, particularly phosphates and iron ore. Industries include flour milling and iron and steel processing. Population (1998): 348 554.

Annam A region in central Vietnam, long ruled from Hue. The Chinese, who had occupied it in 111 BC, were driven out in AD 939; it was a powerful independent state until becoming a French protectorate in 1884. In 1949 it became part of independent Vietnam.

Annan, Kofi (1938–) Ghanaian international civil servant; secretary general of the United Nations (1996–). He formerly worked for the UN in Geneva and New York. Annan and the UN were jointly awarded the 2001 Nobel Peace Prize.

Annapurna, Mount 28 34N 83 50E A massif in NW central Nepal, in the Himalayas. Its highest peak **Annapurna I**, at 8078 m (26 504 ft), was first climbed in 1950 by a French team.

Anne (1665–1714) Queen of England and Scotland (Great Britain from 1707) and Ireland (1702–14). Anne, the last Stuart monarch, was the daughter of the Roman Catholic James II but was herself brought up as a Protestant. Following the overthrow (1688) of James, she supported the accession of her Protestant brother-in-law, William III, whose heiress she became. She married (1683) Prince George of Denmark (1653–1708) and was pregnant 18 times by him; none of her five children born alive survived childhood. Anne therefore agreed to the Act of *Settlement (1701), which

a

provided for the Hanoverian succession after her death.

Anne (Elizabeth Alice Louise) (1950–) Princess of the United Kingdom, who became Princess Royal in 1987. The only daughter of Elizabeth II, she is eighth in line of succession to the throne. In 1973 she married Mark Phillips (1948–); following their divorce in 1992 she married Cmdr Timothy Laurence. An accomplished horsewoman, she is president of the Save the Children Fund.

annelid worm An invertebrate animal belonging to a phylum (*Annelida*) of about 12 000 species, widely distributed in salt water, fresh water, and on land. The body is characteristically a muscular cylinder divided into many fluid-filled segments. Annelids are divided into three classes: the Polychaeta, or bristleworms (*see* RAGWORM; LUGWORM; FANWORM); the Oligochaeta (*see* EARTHWORM; TUBIFEX), and the Hirudinea (*see* LEECH).

Anne of Bohemia (1366–94) The first wife (from 1382) of Richard II of England and daughter of Emperor Charles IV. Her household extravagance was a cause of dissension between Richard and parliament.

Anne of Cleves (1515–57) The fourth wife of Henry VIII of England. The marriage (January 1540) was arranged to effect an alliance with German Protestant rulers but Henry found Anne unattractive and quickly divorced her (July 1540).

Anne of Denmark (1574–1619) The wife (from 1589) of James I of England and VI of Scotland. She spent heavily on building and court entertainments (appearing herself in Ben Jonson's masques) and was suspected of Roman Catholic sympathies.

annihilation The conversion of a particle and its antiparticle into electromagnetic radiation (annihilation radiation) as a result of a collision. The energy of the radiation is equivalent to the combined mass of the two particles. *See also* ANTIMATTER.

annual rings (*or* **growth rings**) A pattern of rings visible in a cross section of a tree trunk, produced by different rates of wood growth: the wood appearing in spring consists of large cells corresponding to vigorous growth; autumn wood has small cells as growth slows down, and in winter growth ceases. The number of rings provides an estimate of the age of the tree. *See also* DENDROCHRONOLOGY.

annuals Plants that complete their life cycle—from germination, flowering, and seed production to death—within one year. Many annuals are used as bedding plants and flower extensively in the summer months. *Compare* PERENNIALS.

annuity A form of pension in which an *insurance company makes a series of periodic payments to a person (annuitant) or his or her dependents over a number of years (term), in return for either a lump sum or regular instalments. An immediate annuity begins at once and a deferred annuity after a fixed period. An annuity certain is for a specific number of years. A life annuity is paid from a certain age until death. A perpetuity continues indefinitely.

annulment The process establishing that a marriage is not legally valid, as opposed to *divorce, which ends a valid marriage. An invalid marriage is considered void, never to have existed. A marriage is void if, for example, the husband or wife is insane, too young, or already married. When the husband or wife is unable or unwilling to consummate the marriage, it may be declared void if either partner wishes it.

Annunciation In the Bible, the announcement by the archangel Gabriel to the Virgin Mary of her conception of Christ (Luke 1.26–38). The feast, in full called the Annunciation of the Blessed Virgin Mary, or Lady Day, is celebrated on 25 March.

anode The positive electrode of an electrolytic cell, valve, etc. It is the electrode by which the electrons leave the system. *Compare* CATHODE.

anodizing A process in which a light metal or alloy, usually aluminium, is covered with a protective layer by oxidation in an electrolytic cell. Usually the cell contains chromic acid; the metal treated is the anode of the cell. A porous layer of oxide is formed, which can be dyed to give a coloured finish.

anointing of the sick *See* SACRAMENT.

Anopheles A widespread genus of mosquitoes (about 350 species), the females of which are important as vectors of the malarial parasite *Plasmodium*. The best-known malaria carrier is *A. maculipennis*. Some species transmit filariasis and encephalitis. Unlike other mosquitoes the larvae lack a siphon and lie flat on the surface of the water.

anorexia nervosa A psychological illness in which the patient, usually an adolescent girl, refuses food over a long period. It often starts with dieting to lose weight, which becomes obsessional: the patient becomes emaciated and may—without treatment—starve to death. The psychological causes are complex, often involving disturbances in family relationships. Hospitalization may be required for the treatment, which involves intensive nursing, sedation, and *psychotherapy and may involve forced feeding.

Anouilh, Jean (1910–87) French dramatist, who achieved his first success in 1937 with *Traveller without Luggage*. His plays include reworkings of Greek myths (*Antigone*, 1944), social comedies (*Ring Round the Moon*, 1950), and historical dramas (*L'Alouette*, 1953; *Becket*, 1959).

Anschluss (German: union; 1938) The union of Austria with Germany. Following the forced resignation of the Austrian chancellor Kurt von Schuschnigg (1897–1977), Nazi forces entered Austria on 14 March and Schuschnigg was imprisoned. *Anschluss* was declared and ratified by a plebiscite.

Anselm of Canterbury, St (c. 1033–1109) Italian theologian and philosopher, Archbishop of Canterbury, and Doctor of the Church. Appointed to the see of Canterbury in 1093, Anselm defended church rights against William II Rufus until he went into exile to Rome in 1097. Recalled by *Henry I in 1100, he eventually reached an uneasy compromise with him. He is the leading early scholastic philosopher and is perhaps best known for his formulation of the ontological argument for the existence of God, which states that if God is "that than which nothing greater can be conceived," then the existence of God is necessary, for it is possible to conceive of a greater entity than a nonexistent God. Feast day: 21 April.

ant An insect belonging to the family *Formicidae* (over 10 000 species). Ants occur in almost all terrestrial habitats, are 0.05–25 cm long, and show a high degree of social organization. A colony consists of wingless sterile female workers and a smaller number of fertile males and females, usually the progeny of a single queen. The young males and females fly from the nest to mate, after which the males die and the young queens found new colonies. Ant societies range from simple groups of a few individuals to large complex nests comprising millions of ants and sometimes involving a second species taken as slaves to work in the colony. Some ants have stings; others secrete burning acids (such as formic acid) as a defence. Order: *Hymenoptera*.

Antananarivo (former name: Tananarive) 18 52S 47 30E The capital of Madagascar. It was occupied by the French in 1895. A cultural centre, it has a university (1961) and two cathedrals. Industries include tobacco and leather goods. Population (1993): 1 052 835.

Antarctica The most southerly continent, surrounding the South Pole. An almost circular ice-covered plateau, it is indented by the Weddell and Ross Seas and contains about 90% of the world's ice. The continent's climate is the severest in the world and although it lacks vegetation it has abundant wildlife including whales, seals, and penguins. Scientific stations were established during the International Geophysical Year (1957–58). Some nations (*see* AUSTRALIAN ANTARCTIC TERRITORY; BRITISH ANTARCTIC TERRITORY; NORWEGIAN ANTARCTIC TERRITORY) have political claims to territory in Antarctica; Argentina and Chile have also laid claims to portions of British Antarctic Territory. Under the **Antarctic Treaty** (1959; extended 1998) 43 nations have agreed to freeze all political claims, to refrain from military activities and mineral extraction, and to cooperate on scientific ventures in the continent. *History*: in his voyage of 1772–75 Capt James Cook circumnavigated the continent. Many explorations took place during the 19th century culminating in the race for the South Pole. This was reached first by Roald *Amundsen of the Norwegian Antarctic Expedition on 14 December 1911, and a month later by *Scott of the British Expedition, which perished on the return journey. Area: about 14 200 000 sq km (5 500 000 sq mi).

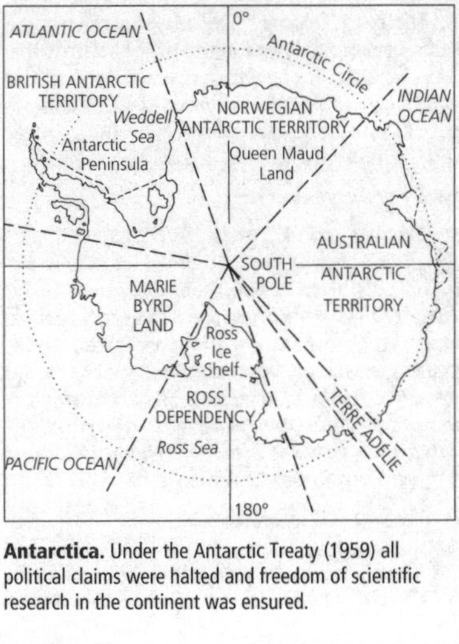

Antarctica. Under the Antarctic Treaty (1959) all political claims were halted and freedom of scientific research in the continent was ensured.

a

Antarctic Ocean The sections of the S Atlantic, Pacific, and Indian Oceans around Antarctica. Except in the height of summer (late Feb to early March), it is covered by drifting pack ice.

anteater A long-tailed animal belonging to a family (*Myrmecophagidae*; 3 species) occurring in tropical South America. It is toothless and has a narrow snout with a long sticky tongue used to pick up ants and termites after tearing open their nests with its powerful claws. The giant anteater (*Myrmecophaga tridactyla*) reaches 1.8 m in length and has grey and black fur and a bushy tail. The lesser anteater or tamandua (*Tamandua tetradactyla*) is a smaller arboreal animal with a prehensile tail. Order: *Edentata*. Several other unrelated animals that feed on ants or termites are called anteaters; these include the *pangolins (scaly anteaters), *echidnas (spiny anteaters), and *aardvark.

Antelami, Benedetto (active 1177–1233) Italian sculptor. He developed a style that marked the transition between the romanesque and the gothic. His best-known works are the reliefs on the doors of the baptistry at Parma, of which he was probably also the architect.

antelope A fast-running hoofed mammal belonging to the family *Bovidae* and occurring chiefly in Africa but occasionally in Asia. The shoulder height varies from 25 cm in the *royal antelope to 180 cm in the *eland. All male antelopes and some females have horns. *See also* GAZELLE; GNU; KUDU.

antenna 1. (zoology) The sensory feeler of insects, crustaceans, and many other arthropods, one or two pairs of which are attached to the head. They are usually jointed threadlike structures containing receptors of sound, smell, touch, and temperature. **2.** (radio) *See* AERIAL.

anther *See* STAMEN.

Anthony of Egypt, St (c. 251–356 AD) Egyptian hermit and founder of Christian monasticism. An ascetic from the age of 20, he withdrew into isolation for 34 years, when he emerged to organize a monastic community. When he was about a hundred years old, he preached against Arianism. His combat with temptation in the desert is described in Athanasius's *Life of Saint Anthony*; it became a frequent subject in Christian art.

Anthony of Padua, St (1195–1231) Portuguese friar and Doctor of the Church, known for preaching and converting heretics in N Italy and the Albigenses in S France. He became professor of theology to the Franciscan Order in 1223. He is often invoked as a finder of lost property.

anthracene ($C_{14}H_{10}$) An aromatic compound consisting of three fused benzene rings. It is obtained from coal tar and used to make dyes.

anthracite *See* COAL.

anthrax A contagious disease of many animals, including farm livestock, that can be transmitted to man. Caused by the bacterium *Bacillus anthracis*, it is usually contracted by eating contaminated food. Onset is often sudden with a rise in temperature, staggering, respiratory distress, convulsions, and death. In horses and pigs a subacute form may occur, with progressive swelling of the throat and neck resulting in laboured breathing and choking. In many countries the authorities must be notified of any outbreaks. Treatment is with antibiotics and prevention is by vaccination of herds. Humans may develop localized swellings after handling infected carcasses or acquire a pneumonia from inhaling the bacterial spores (woolsorters' disease).

Although several governments and terrorist groups are believed to have developed anthrax as a biological weapon, it has never been used in conflict.

anthropoid ape A tailless *primate belonging to the family *Pongidae*, which includes the gibbons, chimpanzees, orang-utans, and gorillas. *See* APE.

anthropology The scientific study of man in his physical and social aspects. It includes *archaeology, *linguistics, cultural or social anthropology, and physical anthropology. Physical anthropology is concerned with the origins and evolution of man through the examination of his fossil remains, and the study and classification of the races (*see also* ANTHROPOMETRY). Cultural anthropology is concerned with the evolution of human society and culture, including language, and with the systematic comparison of social, linguistic, technical, and behavioural diversity.

anthropometry The science concerned with the measurement of the human body, particularly with respect to the variation that exists between different populations and races. Anthropometry ranges from the measurement of structural characteristics, such as height and cranial capacity, to the analysis of chemical constituents of the body, such as blood groups. By comparing fossil and present-day measurements anthropometry has also helped to reveal the sequence of events that has occurred during the evolution of man (*see* ANTHROPOLOGY).

anthropomorphism The human tendency to ascribe the motives, feelings, etc., of human beings to nonhuman entities. The anthropomorphism of ancient Greek religion was ridiculed by Xenophanes of Colophon (6th century BC) but God in Christianity has not escaped from an implicit anthropomorphism. Religious art can scarcely avoid being anthropomorphic.

antiballistic missiles High-speed nuclear weapons used to attack hostile *ballistic missiles. Operated by ground-based radar and computers, they rely for their final attack on their own guidance systems, destroying the target by radiation from their warheads. Short-range versions with low-yield warheads (e.g. US *Sprint*) are designed to seek and destroy targets within the earth's atmosphere; long-range missiles with high-yield warheads operate in space (e.g. US *Spartan*).

antibiotics Drugs derived from microorganisms or synthetically to treat infections caused by bacteria or fungi. Bacteriocidal antibiotics, such as *penicillin, kill bacteria, whereas bacteriostatic antibiotics, such as *tetracycline and *chloramphenicol, simply halt their growth. Examples of antifungal antibiotics are nystatin and griseofulvin. Possible adverse effects of antibiotic treatment include allergic reactions. The appearance of resistant strains of bacteria, due to the indiscriminate use of antibiotics, has resulted in the development of certain life-threatening infections that do not respond to most existing drugs.

antibody A protein produced by certain white blood cells (lymphocytes) that reacts specifically with and neutralizes a foreign protein (e.g. a bacterium), which is known as the **antigen**. Antibody production is stimulated by contact with the antigen: subsequent exposure to the antigen produces a greater antibody response, which provides the basis of *immunity. Antibodies contribute to the body's resistance to infection and are responsible for the rejection of foreign tissue or organ transplants. *See also* MONOCLONAL ANTIBODY.

Antichrist In the New Testament, a person or institution opposed to Christ, who will appear before Christ's second coming (John 2.18–22). Some early Christians believed Nero to be the Antichrist; many reformers, such as Luther, saw the pope in this role.

anticline An arch-shaped *fold or upfold in folded rock strata, the oldest rocks occurring at the core. In areas of complex folding an upfold may have its youngest rocks at the core, the resulting structure being termed an antiform. *Compare* SYNCLINE.

anticoagulants Drugs, such as heparin and warfarin, that interfere with blood clotting. They are used when there has been, or there is a risk of, clots forming in the blood vessels, as after *thrombosis of the leg veins.

anticyclone (*or* **high**) An area of atmospheric pressure higher than the surrounding air with one or more isobars of approximately circular form around its centre. Winds, generally light, circulate around the high pressure centre in a clockwise direction in the N hemisphere and anticlockwise in the S hemisphere. Calm settled weather is usually synonymous with anticyclones in temperate latitudes.

antidepressants A class of drugs used to relieve depression. The most widely used are the tricyclic antidepressants, which include amitriptyline and imipramine, and the SSRIs (selective serotonin reuptake inhibitors), such as fluoxetine (Prozac). The MAO inhibitors prevent the action of the enzyme monoamine oxidase in breaking down adrenaline and related compounds that affect mood. These antidepressants may have serious side effects and are therefore restricted to the treatment of severe psychological disorders.

Antietam, Battle of (17 September 1862) A decisive engagement in the US Civil War, which prevented the Confederate capture of Washington, DC. In the last of a series of battles, the advance of the Confederate general Robert E. *Lee, was checked at Antietam by the Federal general George B. McClellan (1826–85). The South lost about 10 000 men but McClellan allowed Lee to withdraw into Virginia.

Antigone In Greek mythology, the daughter of *Oedipus and Jocasta, whose story forms the basis of Sophocles' tragedy *Antigone*. When her father was banished from Thebes she accompanied him into exile in Colonus. Her brothers Eteocles and Polyneices had agreed to reign alternately in Thebes, but Eteocles' refusal to yield the crown led to their killing each other. Despite the Theban senate's decree prohibiting the burial of Polyneices, Antigone performed the funeral rites for her brother. She was consequently ordered to be buried alive by Creon, ruler of Thebes, and hanged herself.

Antigua and Barbuda A West Indian

a

country in the E Caribbean Sea, comprising the islands of Antigua, Barbuda, and Redonda. Tourism is the chief source of revenue; sugar and cotton production are also important and financial services are being developed. *History*: Antigua was discovered by Columbus (1493) and colonized by British settlers in 1632. It formed an associated state within the British Commonwealth from 1967 until gaining independence in 1981. It is a member of CARICOM. Elections in 2004 resulted in defeat for the ruling Labour Party, which had held power since 1976. Currency: dollar of 100 cents. Area: 440 sq km (170 sq mi). Population (2003): 76 800. Capital: St John's.

antihistamine A drug that interferes with the action of *histamine. Some antihistamines (e.g. chlorpheniramine) prevent histamine from causing allergic reactions and are used to treat hay fever and other allergies; some of these drugs are also used to prevent travel sickness and as sedatives. Other antihistamines (e.g. ranitidine) prevent histamine stimulating the secretion of gastric juice and are used to treat peptic ulcers.

Antilles The islands of the West Indies, excluding the Bahamas. The group is divided into the *Greater Antilles and the *Lesser Antilles.

antimatter Hypothetical matter in which the constituent atoms consist of **antiparticles**. For every elementary particle (*see* PARTICLE PHYSICS) there exists an antiparticle that is identical except for certain of its properties, such as electric charge and isospin number, which are of equal magnitude but opposite in sign. An atom of antimatter would contain a nucleus of antiprotons and antineutrons surrounded by positrons (antielectrons). *See also* ANNIHILATION.

antimony (Sb) A metallic element that occurs in nature as the element and more commonly in the sulphide stibnite (Sb_2S_3). The element exists in two forms: the normal metallic form, which is brittle bluish-white and flaky, and an amorphous grey form. It forms the oxide (Sb_2O_3) by burning in air and the volatile hydride, stibine (SbH_3), which like many antimony compounds is toxic. Pure antimony is used in making *semiconductors; other uses include addition to lead to increase its hardness in battery plates and as oxides or sulphides in paints, glasses, and ceramics. At no 51; at wt 121.75; mp 630.7°C; bp 1587°C.

Antioch (modern Turkish name: Antakya) 36 12N 36 10E A town in central S Turkey, near the coast and the Syrian border. Founded in 301 BC, it had a large early Christian community, and there are notable Roman mosaics in the Archaeological Museum. Population (1994 est): 137 200.

antioxidant A substance that inhibits oxidation of such products as food, paints, plastics, fuels, etc. Natural antioxidants, such as ascorbic acid (vitamin C), vitamin E, and beta-carotene, reduce damage to cells caused by free *radicals.

antipope A person raised to the papacy in opposition to a lawfully elected pope. Hippolitus, the first of some 40 antipopes, was created in the early 3rd century. During the later Roman Empire and the middle ages most antipopes represented rival factions supporting different political or doctrinal claims. In the 11th and 12th centuries some 14 antipopes were chosen by the Holy Roman Emperors, who resented the Church's growing independence from lay control. From 1378, following the *Great Schism, the popes remaining in Avignon under French control were styled antipopes. The Council of Pisa (1409) elected a new pope to end the Schism, but he too was regarded as an antipope until unity was restored at the Council of *Constance (1515). There have been no antipopes since the mid-15th century.

antipsychotics A group of drugs used to quieten disturbed patients with schizophrenia, brain damage, mania, delirium, or agitated depression. They include the phenothiazines (e.g. chlorpromazine) and the butyrophenones as well as the more recent so-called atypical antipsychotics (e.g. clozapine, risperidone), which have less severe side-effects.

Antirrhinum A genus of chiefly Mediterranean and W North American herbaceous plants (about 40 species). The most widely cultivated species is the ornamental snapdragon (*A. majus*), 30–80 cm high with brightly coloured two-lipped tubular flowers adapted to pollination by bees. Family: *Scrophulariaceae*.

antisemitism Hostility towards Jews, which has characterized their existence since the diaspora (6th century BC). Represented as God's chosen people in the Old Testament and the betrayers of Christ in the New Testament, the Jews appeared as a threateningly coherent minority in Christian Europe, especially as many served as moneylenders to Christians, who were forbidden by canon law to lend money for interest (usury). As a result of expulsion, persecution, the Inquisition (1478), and papal bull (1555) medieval Europe lost large numbers of its Jews, many of whom enriched the Muslim countries of N Africa and Turkey. It was not until the 18th-century Enlightenment had introduced religious freedom that they returned in any numbers. However, in the 19th century the earlier church-led antisemitism was replaced by a spurious jingoism, especially in Germany. In France, it became public in the *Dreyfus affair. In Russia, government-tolerated pogroms were common in the late 19th century. Antisemitism reached its peak in Hitler's final solution (*see* WANNSEE CONFERENCE), which cost the Jews six million lives (*see* HOLOCAUST). Since the establishment of the state of Israel, antisemitism has to some extent been replaced by Arab anti-Zionism. It does, however, persist, especially in E Europe.

antiseptic A substance that kills bacteria and other dangerous microorganisms and can be applied to the skin (to cleanse wounds, before surgery, etc.) or taken internally. Antiseptics are generally distinguished from disinfectants, which are too toxic to be used on or within the body.

antitoxin An *antibody produced against a toxin. Antitoxins can be isolated from inoculated healthy animals and used to treat or prevent specific infections; for example, an antitoxin against tetanus is obtained from the plasma of animals inoculated against tetanus.

antitrust acts US legislation to control *monopolies and preserve a competitive market. The Sherman Antitrust Act (1890), the first of several measures, prohibited contracts "in restraint of trade." Interpreted narrowly at first, these laws were strengthened by successive legislation (including the Clayton Act 1914 and the Antimerger Act 1950) prohibiting or restricting interlocking directorships, price fixing, and takeovers. In the UK, the less stringent Fair Trading Act (1973) performs similar functions.

antlers The paired bony structures growing from the heads of deer, generally confined to males. In temperate regions the antlers begin to grow in early summer: they are at first covered with velvety skin, which is later shed. Used for fighting and display, the antlers are shed each year at the end of the mating season. Deer grow their first set of antlers, which are usually straight spikes, at the age of 1–2 years. The number of points is increased in successive years.

antlion An insect belonging to a family (*Myrmeleontidae*) in which the adults resemble dragonflies and live only long enough to mate and lay eggs. The predatory larva lives 1–3 years, generally at the bottom of a conical pit in loose sand: any insect that falls into the pit is snapped up with its large jaws, which protrude from the sand. Order: *Neuroptera*.

Antofagasta 21 51S 102 18W A city in NW Chile, a port on the Pacific Ocean. It is a commercial and Industrial centre. The chief industries are metal refining and founding; export include nitrates and copper. The University of the North was established here in 1956. Population (1999 est): 243 048.

Antonello da Messina (c. 1430-c. 1479) Italian painter, born in Messina (Sicily). He trained in Naples, where he probably learned the Flemish technique of oil painting; this he introduced to Venice during a visit in 1475. The realism of Flemish art also deeply influenced his style, particularly in *St Jerome in His study* and *Portrait of a Man* (both National Gallery, London).

Antonescu, Ion (1882–1946) Romanian general and politician. A pro-Nazi, he became prime minister (1940), replacing Carol II's government with a totalitarian regime. In 1941 he commanded the army in Bessarabia. He was executed for war crimes.

Antonine Wall A Roman frontier defence work 58.5 km (36.5 mi) long, linking the Firths of Forth and Clyde in S Scotland and still surviving in places. It was built about 142 AD by Lollius Urbicus, governor of Britain, for the emperor *Antoninus Pius, and abandoned in 196 AD. A military road linked 29 small forts along a turf wall 3 m (10 ft) high and 4.3 m (14 ft) wide, behind a substantial ditch. *See also* HADRIAN'S WALL.

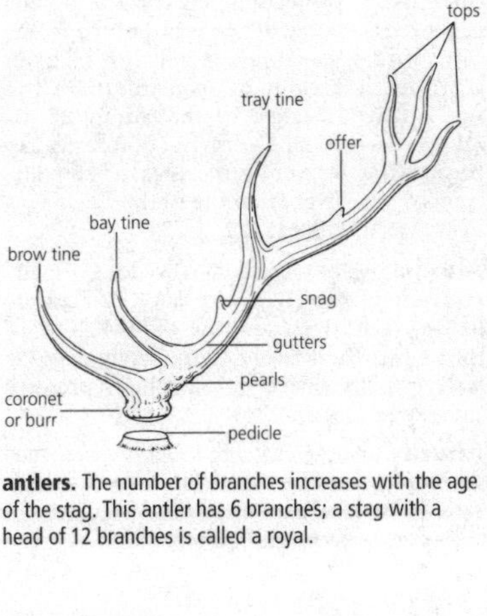

antlers. The number of branches increases with the age of the stag. This antler has 6 branches; a stag with a head of 12 branches is called a royal.

a

Antoninus Pius (86–161 AD) Roman emperor (138–61). Antoninus was admitted by Emperor Hadrian to his advisory council and adopted as his successor in 138. His reign was generally prosperous; minor campaigns were fought abroad and noted legal reforms were introduced; the *Antonine Wall was built during his reign. He was deified after his death.

Antonioni, Michelangelo (1912–) Italian film maker. In 1939 he moved to Rome to work for the magazine *Cinema*. His first films were *Gente del Po* (1943–47) and *Cronaca di un amore* (1950). Later films include *L'avventura* (1959), *La notte* (1961), *Blow-Up* (1966), *Zabriskie Point* (1970), *The Passenger* (1975), and *Beyond the Clouds* (1995).

Antrim **1.** A historic county of NE Northern Ireland, on the Atlantic Ocean and the Irish Sea. Its administrative powers were devolved to the new district councils in 1973. On the N coast is the famous *Giant's Causeway. Outside Belfast the county is agricultural. Industry includes the manufacture of man-made fibres, which has largely replaced linen production. Area: 3100 sq km (1200 sq mi). **2.** A district in Northern Ireland, in Co Antrim. Area: 415 sq km (160 sq mi). Population (2001): 48 366.

Antwerp (Flemish name: Antwerpen; French name: Anvers) 51 13N 4 25E A city in Belgium, on the River Scheldt. Antwerp is one of the largest seaports in the world and has important shipbuilding and ship-repairing industries. Other industries include oil refining, diamond cutting, textiles, and electronics. It possesses many fine buildings, including the 14th-century gothic cathedral and the 16th-century Butchers' Hall. There is a large Flemish-speaking population. *History*: the leading commercial centre of western Europe in the 16th century, its decline began with religious strife and its sacking by Spaniards (1576); this was further hastened by the closure of the River Scheldt (1648). The revival of its economy began when Belgium purchased the shipping rights of the river from the Netherlands. Population (2000 est): 446 525.

Anubis Egyptian god of the dead, usually represented as a crouching jackal or a jackal-headed man. He supervised the weighing of the souls of the dead and the embalming of the body (originally devised, it is said, to preserve the body of Osiris).

Anura An order of amphibians (over 2000 species) comprising the *frogs and *toads. Anurans are specialized for jumping, having a short backbone, no tail, and large hind legs. The eggs hatch into tadpoles, which undergo *metamorphosis. This order is also called the *Salientia*.

Anyang 36 04N 114 20E A city in E China, in Henan province. The last capital (1384–1111 BC) of the Shang dynasty, it has many archaeological remains. Industries include cotton and steel. Population (1999 est): 527 982.

ANZAC The Australian and New Zealand Army Corps, which served in World War I in Europe and the Middle East. On **ANZAC Day**, 25 April (the day of the ANZAC landing in Gallipoli in 1915), the dead of both World Wars are remembered.

aoudad A tawny-coloured sheep, *Ammotragus lervia*, also called Barbary sheep. The only wild sheep in Africa, aoudads live in dry rocky northern regions and obtain water mainly from vegetation and dew. They stand 102 cm at the shoulder and have outward-curving horns and long hair hanging from the neck and chest.

Apache A North American Indian people with six major divisions: the Jicarillos, Mescaleros, Chiricahuas, and Western Apache of the S Plains and SW region of the USA; and the Lipan and Kiowa-Apache living further to the east. Their language is of Athabascan type. They were feared raiders, who frequently attacked the villages of Pueblo Indians and Spanish settlements. In addition to hunting, some groups practised farming. Normally tribal unity was slight but in the late 19th century, under such chiefs as Geronimo and Victorio, they would form groups to attack the Americans. There are today about 10 000 Apaches on reservations.

apartheid (Afrikaans: apartness) The policy of separate development of the White and non-White populations in South Africa. Apartheid, which was introduced by the Afrikaner National Party in 1948, aimed to divide South Africa into separate regions for Whites and Blacks. The White minority that governed South Africa attracted worldwide hostility for this policy and in 1961 South Africa was forced to withdraw from the British Commonwealth. In 1985 non-Whites won limited constitutional rights and interracial marriage was allowed. Increased internal unrest, combined with sporting and financial pressure from outside, led *de Klerk to start dismantling apartheid. In 1992 Whites voted in a referendum to admit Blacks to the political process and in 1993 a new constitution enfranchised all South African adults; in 1994 Nelson *Mandela was elected the first Black President of South Africa.

apatite The commonest phosphorous mineral, of composition $Ca_5(PO_4)_3(OH,F,Cl)$. It is found as an accessory mineral in many igneous rocks and is used in the production of fertilizers. The enamel of teeth is composed almost entirely of apatite (*see also* FLUORIDATION) and the chief inorganic constituent of bone is hydroxyapatite, $Ca_{10}(PO_4)_6(OH)_2$.

Apatosaurus A huge herbivorous dinosaur, which has also been called *Brontosaurus*, of the late Jurassic period, which ended about 135 million years ago. Up to 21 m long and weighing up to 30 tonnes, it had massive pillar-like legs, a long neck and tail, and spent most of its time in swamps, coming ashore to lay eggs. With its nostrils placed high on its head, it was able to stand almost fully submerged. Order: *Saurischia*.

ape A highly intelligent tailless *primate belonging to the family *Pongidae* (11 species), found in central Africa and S Asia. There are two subfamilies: the arboreal *Hylobatinae* (*see* GIBBON; SIAMANG) and the ground-dwelling *Ponginae* (*see* CHIMPANZEE; ORANG-UTAN; GORILLA), also called great apes. Forest apes are often solitary but ground-dwelling apes live in complex societies and all have highly developed means of communication. Some tailless primates of other families are also called apes.

Apennines (Italian name: Appennini) A mountain range in Italy. It extends about 1050 km (652 mi) down the Italian peninsula from the Maritime Alps in the NW to the Strait of Messina in the S. The range is not generally very high, the highest peak being Monte Corno at 2914 m (9560 ft). The Apennines are volcanic in the S (*see* VESUVIUS).

aphelion The point in the orbit of a body around the sun at which the body is furthest from the sun. The earth is at aphelion on 3 July. *Compare* PERIHELION.

aphid An insect, also called a plant louse, belonging to a family (*Aphidae*) of plant pests. Small, soft, and often wingless, aphids have long thin antennae and weak legs and are usually green (greenfly), red, or brown. There are two thin tubes projecting from the abdomen from which honeydew is secreted. Aphids feed on plant sap, piercing plant tissues with sharp beaklike mouthparts, causing leaf curl, retardation of growth, and often forming galls. Order: *Hemiptera*.

Aphrodite In Greek mythology, the goddess of love, called *Venus by the Romans. According to Homer she was the daughter of Dione and Zeus; Hesiod says that she was born from the foam after *Uranus had been castrated and his genitals thrown into the sea. She was the wife of Hephaestus but had an affair with Ares. Paris' choice of her as the most beautiful of the three goddesses at the wedding feast of Peleus and Thetis (the others were Hera and Athena) caused the *Trojan War. Revered throughout Greece as the personification of spiritual love, she also embodied sensual lust.

Apis The Egyptian bull god. Originally a minor fertility god, he became associated with Ptah and later Osiris (when he became known as Serapis). A bull sacred to him was kept until another with appropriate markings was found; it was then ritually drowned in the Nile and its body mummified in the Serapeum vault at Saqqarah.

apocalypse (Greek: revelation) In the New Testament, the Book of *Revelation. The term is also used of various noncanonical writings, such as the Book of Enoch, and of parts of the Old Testament books of Isaiah, Ezekiel, and Daniel. Full of symbolism and imagery, they describe visions of a great new era that will supersede the present age of suffering.

Apocrypha (Greek: hidden things) Twelve books taken by the early Christian Church from the Greek version of the Old Testament but not forming part of the Hebrew Bible. They originated in the Hellenistic Judaism of Alexandria but were not accepted as canonical by orthodox Jews. In the *Vulgate, most of them are printed with the Old Testament but they are omitted or printed as a separate section in Protestant versions of the Bible. They are: I Esdras, Tobit, Judith, the Rest of Esther, the Wisdom of Solomon, Ecclesiasticus, Baruch with the Epistle of Jeremy, the Song of the Three Holy Children, the History of Susanna, Bel and the Dragon, the Prayer of Manasses, and I and II Maccabees.

apogee The point in the orbit of the moon or of an artificial satellite around the earth at which the body is furthest from the earth. *Compare* PERIGEE.

Apollinaire, Guillaume (Wilhelm de Kostrowitzky; 1880–1918) French poet. Born in Italy, he settled in Paris in 1900. His poetry, first collected in *Alcools* (1913), blends lyricism with experiment. Having been wounded in World War I, he wrote a surrealist play, *Les Mamelles de Tirésias* (1917), and a modernist manifesto, *L'Esprit nouveau et les poètes*, during his recuperation. The poems in *Calligrammes* (1918) included typographical experiments.

a

Apollo A Greek god, symbol of light, of reason, and of male beauty. He is also associated with medicine, prophecy, music and poetry, the care of animals and crops, morality, and the maintenance of society. He and his sister *Artemis were the children of *Zeus by *Leto. He established his oracle at Delphi after killing Python, its dragon guardian.

Apollo moon programme The US programme to land men on the moon by 1970, announced by President Kennedy in 1961. The programme was directed by *NASA. A Saturn V rocket launched the Apollo spacecraft towards the moon and, once the craft was in lunar orbit, the lunar module descended to the moon's surface carrying two astronauts. The third astronaut remained in the orbiting craft. At the end of the surface mission the lunar module's descent stage was left on the moon while its ascent stage was shot into lunar orbit and docked with the orbiting craft. Following the transfer of the two astronauts, the ascent stage was jettisoned and the spacecraft returned to earth. The astronauts travelled to and from the moon in the command module, the rocket engines for in-flight manoeuvres, fuel cells, etc., being carried in the separate service module, which was jettisoned prior to re-entering the earth's atmosphere.

The first six Apollo missions were unmanned test flights, the next four being manned. Apollo 11 made the first manned lunar landing in July 1969. Of the six ensuing missions, all, except Apollo 13, were highly successful.

Apostles In the New Testament, the 12 men chosen by Jesus as his disciples who, after his death, were to spread his teaching throughout the Roman world. Originally they were: Andrew, Bartholomew (*or* Nathaniel), James son of Alphaeus, James son of Zebedee, John, Jude (*or* Thaddeus), Judas Iscariot, Matthew (*or* Levi), Philip, Simon Peter, Simon the Zealot, and Thomas. After his suicide Judas Iscariot was replaced by Matthias. St Paul is also included among the Apostles because of his claim to have seen Jesus after the resurrection.

Apostles' Creed A Christian profession of faith in three sections concerning God the Father, Jesus Christ, and the Holy Spirit. Widely used in the Western Churches, it is of uncertain date but its present title first occurs in a letter of St Ambrose of about 390 AD.

apostolic succession A Christian doctrine held by the Roman Catholic and Orthodox Churches and by some Anglicans. Its upholders claim that the Apostles appointed the first bishops and that there is thus a continuous line of succession from the Apostles to the present ministries of these Churches, along which the power and authority given by Christ to the former have passed to the latter.

Appalachian Mountains A mountain range in North America. It extends NE–SW from the Gaspé Peninsula, in Canada, to Alabama and separates the Mississippi-Missouri lowlands from the Atlantic coastal plain. It consists of a series of mountain ranges and plateaus, including the Allegheny Mountains, the Catskill Mountains, and the White Mountains of New Hampshire. Its highest point is

craft	*astronauts*	*launch date*	*comments*
Apollo 7	W. Schirra W. Cunningham D. Eisele	11 October 1968	first manned flight of Apollo spacecraft
Apollo 8	F. Borman J. Lovell W. Anders	21 December 1968	first manned flight around moon
Apollo 9	J. McDivitt D. Scott R. Schweickart	3 March 1969	complete Apollo craft tested in earth orbit
Apollo 10	T. Stafford J. Young E. Cernan	18 May 1969	rehearsal of moon landing
Apollo 11	N. Armstrong E. Aldrin M. Collins	16 July 1969	first manned moon landing, 20 July
Apollo 12	C. Conrad A. Bean R. Gordon	14 November 1969	second moon landing
Apollo 13	J. Lovell F. Haise J. Swigert	11 April 1970	mission aborted after in-flight explosion in service module
Apollo 14	A. Shepard E. Mitchell S. Roosa	31 January 1971	third moon landing
Apollo 15	D. Scott J. Irwin A. Worden	26 July 1971	fourth moon landing
Apollo 16	J. Young C. Duke T. Mattingly	16 April 1972	fifth moon landing
Apollo 17	E. Cernan H. Schmitt R. Evans	7 December 1972	last moon landing

Apollo moon programme

Mount Mitchell, at 2038 m (6684 ft). Coalmining is important and iron ore is also extracted. It also contains the **Appalachian Trail**, the longest continuous footpath in the world.

Appaloosa An American breed of spotted riding horse. Height: 1.47–1.60 m (14½–15¾ hands).

appeal In law, the review of a court decision by a higher court, usually at the request of one of the parties to the case. The decisions of some administrative or professional bodies may also be appealed against in the courts. Appeals in *common law systems are usually based on alleged errors of law in the original trial, but may sometimes also be based on errors of fact. *See also* COURTS OF LAW.

appeasement In the 1930s, the policy of the British prime minister, Neville *Chamberlain, and his French counterpart, Édouard Daladier, of accepting the demands of Hitler and Mussolini in the hope of maintaining peace. It culminated in the Munich Agreement (1938), which was totally discredited in 1939, when Hitler seized Czechoslovakia and precipitated World War II by marching into Poland. Strongly opposed by Winston Churchill, appeasement has since been excused by some as an attempt by Britain and France to buy time to rearm.

appendix (*or* **vermiform appendix**) A thin blind-ended tube, 7–10 cm long, that opens from the end of the large intestine. It has no known function in man and is prone to infection, causing inflammation known as **appendicitis**. Surgical removal of an inflamed appendix is often necessary to prevent rupture and subsequent *peritonitis. In herbivorous animals (e.g. rabbits and cows) the appendix is large and functions in the digestion of vegetable matter.

Appian Way The road, built about 312 BC by the statesman Appius Claudius, between Rome and Capua. It was the first in the strategic network of Roman roads. A short stretch is still visible near Rome.

apple A deciduous tree or shrub of the genus *Malus* (about 35 species), native to N temperate regions and widely cultivated for their rounded fleshy fruits (pomes). Several species have been cultivated, especially *M. pumila* of W Asia, with the development of numerous varieties of dessert, cooking, and cider apples. Apples are also used for soft drinks and as a source of pectin. Family: *Rosaceae*. *See also* CRAB APPLE.

Appleton layer *See* IONOSPHERE.

Appomattox 37 21N 78 51W A town in the USA in Virginia. The US Civil War ended here when Robert E. Lee surrendered to Ulysses Grant on 9 April 1865.

apricot A tree, *Prunus armenica*, native to China and widely grown in warm temperate countries, especially Spain, for its fruits. It is 6–9 m tall and has white five-petalled flowers and toothed heart-shaped leaves. The orange-yellow fruits have sweet flesh. Family: *Rosaceae*.

apse A semicircular or polygonal eastern end of a church used in the basilica and in romanesque and Norman architecture. The clergy were seated in the apse behind the central altar.

Apulia (*or* **Puglia**) A region in SE Italy, on the Adriatic Sea. It consists of lowlands in the N and S and a hilly central area. Wheat, tobacco, vegetables, olives, figs, vines, and almonds are the main products. Manufacturing is being developed, particularly at Taranto. Area: 19 347 sq km (7470 sq mi). Population (2000 est): 4 085 239. Capital: Bari.

Aqaba 29 32N 35 00E A port in Jordan, on the **Gulf of Aqaba**, a narrow inlet at the NE end of the Red Sea. Aqaba was the Roman stronghold of Aelana. Being Jordan's only port, it has been considerably expanded to export phosphates. Population (1990 est): 46 090.

aquamarine A pale blue or green variety of *beryl. Many fine specimens of this gemstone come from Brazil, Madagascar, and California.

aquarium A receptacle containing fresh or salt water for maintaining fish, aquatic plants, etc. or a building in which such receptacles are displayed. A water heater (for tropical species), aerator, and filter may be necessary. The first public aquarium was opened at the London Zoo in 1853.

aquatint An etching technique that produces a result similar to a wash drawing. The method was invented in the 1760s by a Frenchman, Jean Baptiste Le Prince (1733–81). Sharply defined areas of tone are employed, usually in conjunction with etched lines. A printing plate is sprinkled with powdered asphaltum or resin, which is fixed to the plate by heating. Stopping-out varnish is used to mask different areas as the plate is immersed for varying lengths of time in an acid bath. Goya and Picasso used the technique with outstanding effect.

aquavit A spirit distilled from grains and

a

flavoured with caraway seeds. Drunk predominantly in Scandinavia, it is served ice cold.

aqueduct A narrow bridge, channel, or conduit designed to enable water to flow at a steady rate over irregular natural terrain, such as a valley. Aqueducts were built by the Greeks, but the technique was developed by the Romans. Impressive Roman examples still survive at Nîmes, Segovia, and Rome.

Aquilegia A genus of perennial herbaceous plants (100 species) of temperate regions, commonly known as columbines. Their flowers have petals with long honey-secreting spurs. Many modern hybrids are derived from the European columbine (*A. vulgaris*). Family: *Ranunculaceae*.

Aquinas, St Thomas (c. 1225–74) Italian Dominican theologian, scholastic philosopher, and Doctor of the Church, known as *Doctor Angelicus*. The son of Count Landulf of Aquino, he was educated at Monte Cassino and at the University of Naples. Joining the Dominican Order in 1244 in spite of parental opposition, he became a pupil of Albertus Magnus in Paris (1245) and followed him to Cologne in 1248. He was a theological adviser (1259–69) to the papal Curia before teaching in Paris until 1272, when he was appointed a professor at Naples. He was canonized in 1323. His most influential works are the *Summa contra gentiles* (1259–64), written for missionaries, and the uncompleted *Summa theologica* (1266–73), the first systematic work of Latin theology. Feast day: 7 March.

Aquino, Cory (Corazón Aquino; 1933–) Philippine stateswoman; president (1986–92). She succeeded her assassinated husband **Benigno S. Aquino** (1933–83) as leader of the opposition and became head of state when the corrupt *Marcos regime came to an end.

Aquitaine (Latin name: Aquitania) A planning region in SW France, bordering on the Bay of Biscay. Formerly an administrative region in Roman Gaul, it extended from the Pyrenees N to the River Loire. It became an independent duchy under the Merovingians (7th century). The marriages of Eleanor of Aquitaine to Louis VII of France and then to Henry II of England resulted in rival French-English claims to the territory (*see* HUNDRED YEARS' WAR). Area: 41 408 sq km (15 984 sq mi). Population (1999): 2 908 359.

Arab horse An ancient breed of horse originally bred by the Bedouins in Arabia. It is usually grey, chestnut, or bay with a long silky mane and tail, a wedge-shaped head, and an arched neck. The Arab is prized as a riding horse for its speed, hardiness, and docile temperament. Height: 1.42–1.52 m (14–15 hands).

Arabia A peninsula in the Middle East, forming the SW tip of Asia and bordered by the Red Sea, the Gulf of Aden, the Gulf of Oman, and the Persian Gulf. It consists of Saudi Arabia, Yemen, Oman, the United Arab Emirates, Qatar, Bahrain, and Kuwait. *History*: as remains of irrigation systems show, S Arabia was the site of technologically advanced ancient civilizations. It was conquered briefly by the Persians in 575 AD and later unified from Mecca by Islam in the 7th century, when the previously warring Arab tribes turned their attention to the conquest of N Africa, SW Asia, and S Europe. From the 16th century until World War I the Ottoman Turks held nominal control over much of the peninsula, challenged chiefly by the Wahhabiyah. From the mid-19th century until the late 1960s the UK was the chief foreign presence.

Arabian Desert **1.** A desert chiefly in Saudi Arabia. Area: about 2 300 000 sq km (887 844 sq mi). **2.** A desert in E Egypt between the River Nile and the Red Sea.

Arabian Sea A section of the NW Indian Ocean between Arabia and India. Connected to the Mediterranean Sea by the Red Sea and the Suez Canal, it forms a major shipping route.

Arabic A member of the Semitic group of languages. It is written from right to left. Arabic is the mother-tongue of some 110 million people inhabiting SW Asia (the Middle East) and the countries of N Africa. Arabic can be roughly classified into three parts: (a) Classical Arabic, the language of the *Koran and the great Arab writers and poets; (b) Modern Literary, or Standard, Arabic, the language of the press and broadcasting; and (c) the colloquial dialects (vernaculars), which differ in a greater or lesser degree from country to country.

Arabic numerals The number symbols 0, 1, 2, 3, 4, 5, 6, 7, 8, 9. They are believed to have originated in India and were introduced into Europe by the Arabs in about the 10th century AD. *Compare* ROMAN NUMERALS.

Arab League An organization formed to promote Arab unity and cooperation. Formed in Cairo in 1945, it consisted of those Arab countries that were then independent; others joined on attaining independence. Palestine, represented by the PLO, is a member. The League has had some success in the scientific and cultural field but in politics has been split between its conservative and progressive members. In 1979, following the Egyptian-Israeli peace treaty, Egypt was expelled from the League, which was relocated in Tunis: it returned to Cairo following Egypt's readmission in 1989.

arable farming The cultivation of plants for food, fibres, vegetable oils, etc. Arable farming is often carried out in conjunction with livestock farming, enabling the farmer to grow his own animal feeds and to make use of animal manures as *fertilizers. Grass is the chief feed for *ruminant livestock and a major arable crop. Apart from grazing, grass is cut and conserved for winter food.

Cereal crops are a principal source of food and animal feedstuffs. The major cereals are wheat, barley, rice, and maize with oats, millet, sorghum, and rye cultivated to a lesser extent. Wheat may be sown either in autumn or spring, according to the variety, and is harvested in late summer when the grain is hard.

Beans are grown as a major source of vegetable protein, the most important being soyabean, produced chiefly in China and the USA. They are harvested mechanically using a specially adapted combine harvester. Harvesting root crops, such as potatoes and sugar beet, requires specialized machines that excavate the crop and remove soil. Crops grown for their oil content include sunflower, groundnut, linseed, cottonseed, and rape. Modern pesticides and fertilizers, together with innovations in mechanization, irrigation, and plant breeding have resulted in dramatic increases in crop yields, bringing about a Green Revolution, especially in developing countries.

Arabs A Semitic people originally inhabiting the Arabian peninsula. They are roughly divided into two cultural groups: the nomadic *Bedouin tribes and the settled communities of the towns and oases. Wealth from oil has recently led to industrialization and westernization in the towns, but Islam remains a strong conservative force in social customs, particularly in women's role in society. The Arabs appeared as a power in world history early in the 7th century AD, with the rise of Islam, and they carried their language (*see* ARABIC), religion, and culture as far as Spain in the W and Indonesia in the E.

Arachne In Greek mythology, a girl from Lydia who defeated Athena in a tapestry-weaving contest. The jealous goddess destroyed all Arachne's work; she attempted to hang herself, but Athena changed her into a spider.

arachnid An invertebrate animal belonging to a class (*Arachnida*; 65 000 species) of chiefly terrestrial *arthropods, including the *spiders, *scorpions, harvestmen, *ticks, and *mites. An arachnid's body is divided into two parts: a combined head and thorax (cephalothorax) and an abdomen. The cephalothorax bears four pairs of legs and two pairs of head appendages, one of which consists of strong pincer-like claws. Arachnids are mostly carnivorous; many secrete poison from specialized glands to kill prey or enemies. Others are parasites, some of which are carriers of disease. Arachnids usually lay eggs, which hatch into immature adults.

Arafat, Yassir (1929–) Palestinian leader. In the 1950s he was a founder of al-*Fatah and in 1968 he became president of the *Palestine Liberation Organization (PLO). Since 1983 his leadership has been rejected by some factions of the PLO. In 1993 he signed a peace agreement with Israel, which led to the award of the 1994 Nobel Peace Prize (jointly with *Rabin and *Peres). Following Israel's partial withdrawal from the *West Bank he was elected first president of the new Palestinian National Authority in 1996. He signed a further land-for-peace deal with Israel in 1998 but subsequent talks (2000) ended in impasse, leading to renewed violence. Since 2001 Arafat's inability to restrain Palestinian suicide bombers and Israel's reoccupation of much of the West Bank have greatly weakened his authority.

Aragon An autonomous region and medieval kingdom in NE Spain, of which Ramoir I (d. 1063) was the first king (1035–63). Union with Catalonia was secured by marriage in 1140. Later expansion gave the Aragonese Sicily (1282) and Sardinia (1320) and culminated in the conquest by Alfonso the Magnanimous (1385–1458) of the kingdom of Naples (1442). In 1469 Ferdinand the Catholic (1452–1516), heir to the Aragonese throne, married Isabella the Catholic (1451–1504) of Castile and on his accession in 1479 the two kingdoms were united. Area: 47 609 sq km (18 382 sq mi). Population (2000 est): 1 189 909.

Aragon, Louis (1897–1982) French poet, novelist, and journalist. In 1919 he and André Breton founded the surrealist journal *Littérature*; his first books of poetry, *Feu de joie* (1920) and *Le Mouvement perpétuel* (1925), and his prose work *Le Paysan de Paris* (1926) are surrealist in style. He became a communist after a visit to the Soviet Union in 1930 and then turned to social realism, especially in the novel series *Le Monde réel* (1933–51).

a

Aral Sea A salt-water lake in W Asia in Kazakhstan and Uzbekistan, now considered one of the world's worst ecological disasters. Once the fourth largest lake in the world, overuse of its source rivers (the Amu Darya and Syr Darya) for irrigation has reduced its water volume by more than half. It is heavily polluted by agricultural chemicals. Area (including salt flats): about 66 000 sq km (25 477 sq mi).

Aramaic A western branch of the Semitic group of languages. Its 22-character alphabet is the ancestor of both Hebrew and Arabic alphabets. Originally the speech of Aram (the biblical name for Syria), Aramaic became the official language of the Persian Empire under Darius I. It replaced Hebrew as the language of the Jews from about the time of the Exile in 605 BC until after the rise of Islam and was the language spoken by Jesus and his disciples.

Ararat, Mount (Turkish name: Ağrı Dağı) 39 44N 44 15E A mountain in E Turkey, near the Armenian and Iranian borders. It is volcanic in origin and isolated but for a secondary peak 12 km (7 mi) away. Traditionally, Noah's ark came to rest here after the flood (Genesis 8.4). Height: 5165 m (16 946 ft).

Araucaria A genus of coniferous trees (about 15 species), native to Australasia and South America (it is named after a district of Chile). They have whorled horizontal branches covered with scale leaves, and male and female flowers usually grow on separate trees. The genus includes the ornamental *monkey puzzle and several trees yielding useful timber, including the Norfolk Island pine (*A. heterophylla*); the hoop pine (*A. cunninghamii*) and the bunya bunya (*A. bidwillii*), both from E Australia; and the parana pine (*A. angustifolia*), of Brazil. Family: *Araucariaceae*.

Arawak Indians of the Greater Antilles and northern and western areas of the Amazon basin. Their languages are the most widespread of the South American Indian languages and include Goajiro in Colombia, Campa and Machiguenga in Peru, and Mojo and Bauré in Bolivia. They are farmers growing manioc and maize. Prior to the Spanish conquests they were divided into numerous hereditary chiefdoms. They were never a warlike people and in the Caribbean area *Carib tribes frequently raided Arawak groups and enslaved Arawak women. The tribal gods were the spirits of chiefs represented by a hierarchy of idols called zemis, which were housed in temples.

arbor vitae A coniferous tree of the genus *Thuja* (6 species), native to North America and E Asia. They have scalelike leaves, which densely cover the flattened stems, and small scaly cones, 1–1.8 cm long. The Chinese arbor vitae or cedar (*T. orientalis*), which grows to a height of 30 m, is a popular ornamental tree; the giant arbor vitae, or western red cedar (*T. plicata*), of W North America, grows to a height of 40 m and yields a valuable timber. Family: *Cupressaceae*.

Arbutus A genus of evergreen trees and shrubs (about 20 species) distributed in Central and North America and W Europe. The small white or pinkish flowers are borne in terminal clusters and the berries are reddish. The leaves are dark green, toothed, and shiny above. The strawberry tree (*A. unedo*) of SW Europe is widely grown as an ornamental, reaching a height of 9 m. Family: *Ericaceae*.

Arcadia A mountainous region of ancient Greece, in the central Peloponnesus, that was identified in the literature of Greece, Rome, and the Renaissance (e.g. in Sidney's *Arcadia*) as an earthly paradise. It is a modern department.

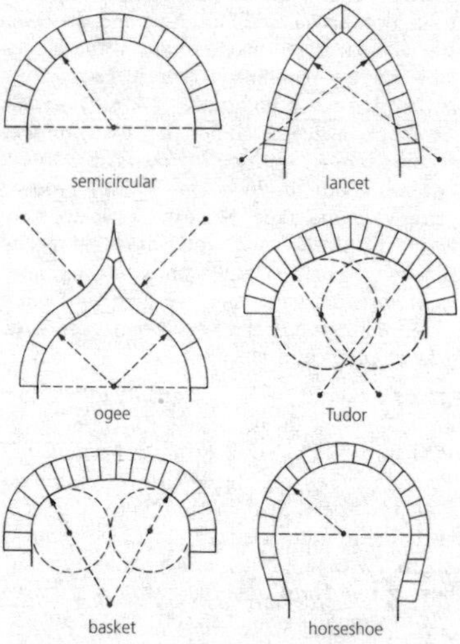

arch. The semicircular arch characterized Roman, Romanesque, and Norman architecture; the lancet, ogee, Tudor, and basket arches were gothic and later medieval developments; the horseshoe arch is typical of Islamic architecture.

Arc de Triomphe A ceremonial arch standing at the centre of the Étoile at the top of the Champs Elysées in Paris. It was commissioned to celebrate the victories of *Napoleon I and

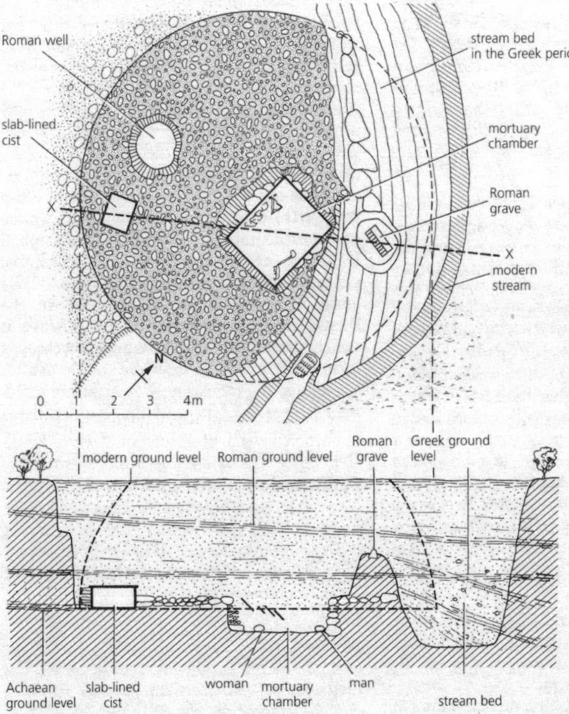

(a) A plan of an ancient Greek burial mound showing the relative positions of the original mortuary chamber and other burials in the mound.

(b) A strategic section (through XX) of the same mound showing the comparative levels of the ground at various periods.

archaeology

built between 1806 and 1836 to the designs of Jean Chalgrin (1739–1811).

arch In architecture, a structure (invented by the Romans) for spanning a horizontal space. By using interlocking and mutually supporting pieces of stone, greater distances can be spanned than with single megaliths; also arches can be employed to provide a more even distribution of pressure throughout a building. The basic forms of arch are the pointed, or gothic, arch, and the rounded, or classical, arch.

archaeology The scientific study of the material remains of human history. Archaeology may be supplemented by written records, where they exist, but its techniques are principally concerned with nonliterary evidence for man's social and cultural development. Modern archaeology has numerous specialized branches—classical, industrial, underwater, etc. Before the 19th century, digging was carried out to plunder precious objects from ruins. Scientific excavation followed the realization that often more could be learnt from the surroundings in which objects are discovered than from the objects themselves. Essential techniques include stratigraphy, based on the principle that in any sequence of deposits the uppermost is latest and the lowest earliest, and typology, the study of changes in forms (e.g. of pottery). Methods of dating include radiometric dating, *palaeomagnetism, thermoluminescence, *varve dating, and *dendrochronology.

Archaeopteryx A genus of extinct primitive birds, fossils of which date from the Jurassic period (160–120 million years ago). It had many reptilian features, such as numerous teeth, a long bony tail, and claws on the hand, but was fully feathered and is believed to be the ancestor of modern birds. *Archaeopteryx* lived in dense forests, climbing trees using its claws and gliding down in search of food.

a

Archangel (Russian name: Arkhangelsk) 64 32N 40 40E A port in NW Russia, on the River Dvina, 50 km (30 mi) from the White Sea. Founded in 1584, it was Russia's leading port until the early 18th century. The country's largest timber-exporting port, it has timber-processing and shipbuilding industries and also supports a fishing fleet. Population (1999 est): 366 200.

archery A sport in which a specified number of arrows are shot at a target over a prescribed distance. The modern bow developed from the medieval longbow, but the skill of shooting arrows from a bow dates back 30 millennia. **Target archery** consists of shooting at a target of standard size marked with five or ten circular scoring zones. Different competitions require different permutations of distances and numbers of arrows. **Field archery** consists of shooting at large animal figures with superimposed scoring rings. In **clout shooting** arrows are shot into the air to fall on a target marked on the ground, while in **flight shooting** the purpose is to achieve the maximum distance. Archery is an amateur sport, governed internationally by the Fédération internationale de Tir à l'Arc (founded 1931).

Archimedes (c. 287–c. 212 BC) Greek mathematician and inventor, regarded as the greatest scientist of classical times. Archimedes was born in Syracuse and studied in Alexandria, afterwards returning to Sicily, where he remained for the rest of his life. He is best known for his discovery of Archimedes' principle, supposedly in response to the King of Syracuse asking him to determine whether a gold crown had been adulterated with silver. Legend has it that he made his discovery while taking a bath and ran through the streets of Syracuse shouting "Eureka!" **Archimedes' principle** states that when a body is partly or wholly immersed in a fluid its apparent loss of weight is equal to the weight of the liquid displaced. He is also credited with the invention of **Archimedes' screw**, a device for raising water consisting of an inclined helical screw rotated about a central axis in a trough of water, although the device was probably already known to the Egyptians. He was killed during the Roman invasion of Syracuse.

architecture The art of designing and constructing buildings that are both functionally and aesthetically satisfying. Factors principally influencing an architect are: the use to which the building will be put; the materials obtainable; the resources available in money and labour; and contemporary artistic taste. The earliest civilizations built on a monumental scale for their gods or the deified dead (*see* PYRAMIDS; ZIGGURAT). Secular architecture reflected the needs of local rulers for security, comfort, and—very important—display. The Greeks were the first to develop the concepts of proportion and harmony that still influence western architectural theory. Roman engineers greatly extended flexibility of design by their use of arches and domes. Medieval European architecture reached its zenith in the gothic cathedral but the Renaissance brought a resurgence of interest in the principles of classical architecture. This was followed by a gothic revival at the beginning of the 19th century. In the 20th century technical advances in the use of prestressed concrete opened the way to modern architecture; while the necessities of engineering increasingly determine a building's appearance, the best modern architects demonstrate that architecture can still survive as an art form.

Arcimboldo, Giuseppe (1527–93) Mannerist painter, born in Milan. He moved to Prague in 1562, becoming painter and designer of court pageants to the Habsburg emperors. His grotesque portraits include the head of a cook composed of pots and pans, fish, and meat.

Arctic Circle The area around the North Pole enclosed by the parallel of latitude 66°32′N. It includes parts of Greenland, Russia, the USA, Canada, and Scandinavia and extensive areas of ice-covered ocean, notably the Arctic Ocean. The population consists mainly of Eskimos, who live by hunting. *History*: during the 16th century exploration of the Arctic by the Dutch and English began in the search for a Northeast or Northwest Passage to the Far East. In 1725–42 the Russian Imperial Navy carried out exploration. In 1879 a US expedition under G. W. De Long (1844–81) became trapped in the ice while attempting to reach the North Pole and its ship was crushed. Wreckage found off the coast of Greenland having drifted across the Arctic Ocean suggested that a sea route through the ice was possible. The Norwegian Fridtjof *Nansen in the *Fram* drifted for nearly two years (1893–95) through the ice and proved that the North Pole was within an ice-covered sea. Robert E. Peary was the first to reach the North Pole (1909). Since then extensive mapping and geological and meteorological studies have been carried out; the Soviet Union was particularly active and, like the USA, established several drifting scientific stations.

Arctic fox A small fox, *Alopex lagopus*, found throughout tundra regions. It feeds on birds and small mammals, especially lemmings and Arctic hares, and grows a dense woolly coat of fur in winter. There are two colour varieties: the white fox, which has a white winter coat and a brown summer coat; and the blue fox, which is dark grey in summer and pale grey in winter. Arctic foxes have been farmed commercially for their fur.

Arctic Ocean The world's smallest ocean, almost completely enclosed by North America, Eurasia, and Greenland. Explored since the 17th century, it is covered by ice.

The orders of classical architecture

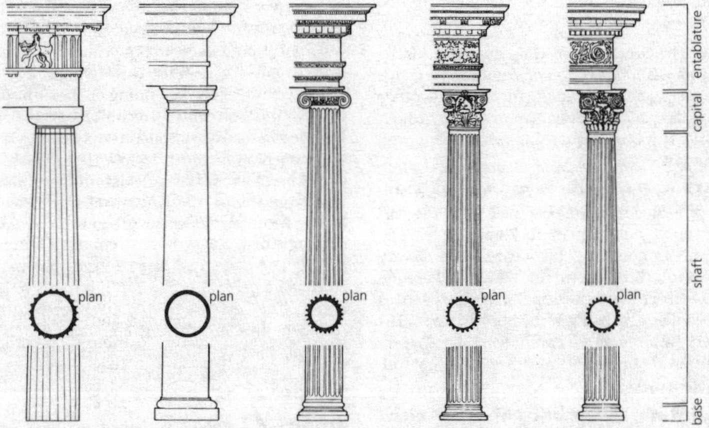

Some terms in classical architecture

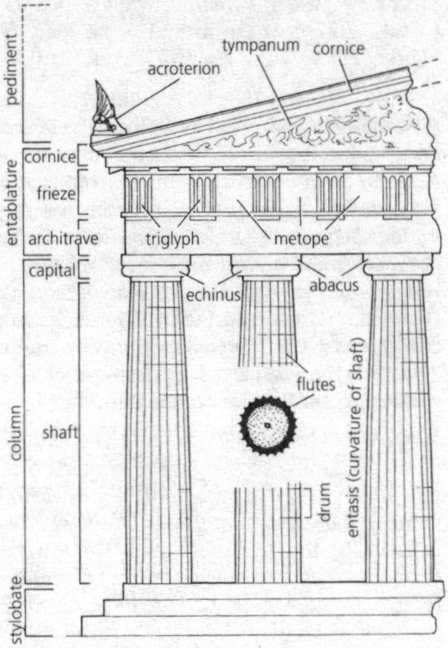

Some terms in gothic architecture

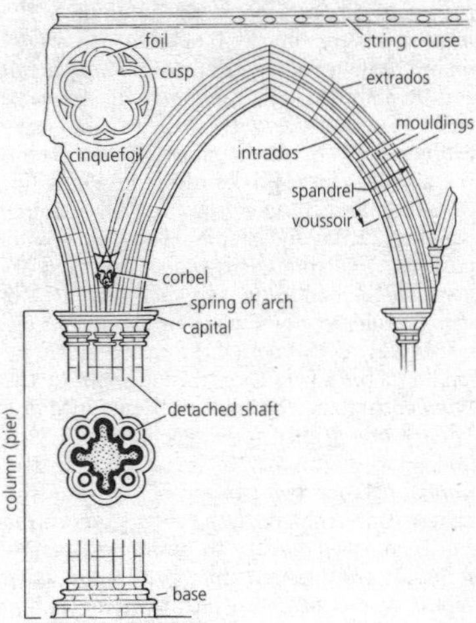

architecture

a

Ardennes A chain of hills in W Europe. It extends through N Luxembourg, S Belgium, and NE France at an average height of about 500 m (1640 ft), forming the watershed between the Rivers Meuse and Moselle.

Ards A district in Northern Ireland, in Co Down. Area: 368 sq km (142 sq mi). Population (2001): 73 244.

are (a) A unit of area in the *metric system equal to 100 square metres. The *hectare (100 ares) is more frequently used.

Ares The Greek god of war, identified by the Romans with *Mars. Son of Zeus and Hera, his popularity never rivalled that of the other Olympian gods. He loved *Aphrodite, by whom he had three offspring, Deimos, Phobos, and Harmonia.

Aretino, Pietro (1492–1556) Italian satirist. Son of a shoemaker, he claimed to be the bastard son of a nobleman. In Rome (1517–27) he became famous for his satires and bawdy lyrics. He then settled in Venice, where he made a fortune by writing scurrilous satires on people or by being bribed not to do so. His letters, published in six volumes (1537–57), provide a vivid portrait of his times. He also wrote five comedies.

Argentina, Republic of The second largest country in South America. It consists chiefly of subtropical plains and forests (the Gran Chaco) in the N, the fertile temperate pampas in the centre, the Andes in the W, and the semidesert Patagonian plateau in the S. The inhabitants are almost all of European origin, mainly Italian and Spanish, with a very small and dwindling Indian population. *Economy*: chiefly agricultural with stock rearing, especially cattle. The main industries have traditionally been meat processing and packing but there has been recent growth in oil refining, plastics, textiles, and chemicals. Natural-gas deposits have been intensively developed and Argentina is practically self-sufficient in oil. *History*: colonized by the Spanish from 1515 onwards. During this period the native Indian inhabitants put up a fierce resistance but by the 19th century they had almost been wiped out. The country gained its independence in 1816, under José de San Martín, and a new constitution in 1853 marked the end of civil war and unrest. Since the late 19th century Argentina has been ruled mostly by military dictatorships. Most prominent among the rulers since World War II has been Lt Gen Juán *Perón, who came to power in 1946. Following the death (1952) of his popular wife, Eva, he was overthrown in a military revolution (1955). In 1973 he returned to power but died the following year. He was succeeded by his second wife, Isabel, but as the economic situation deteriorated and unrest increased, allegations of corruption were made against her government. In 1976 Lt Gen Jorge Rafael Videla came to power at the head of a three-man junta and severe measures were used to suppress opposition. Gen Leopoldo Galtieri led a further coup and became president in December 1981. On 2 April 1982, Argentina launched an invasion of the Falkland Islands (which it calls the Islas Malvinas) to which it laid claim. Following armed conflict with a task force sent by the UK, Argentinian troops were forced to surrender on 14 June 1982; a defeat that forced Galtieri's resignation. Raúl Alfonsín was elected president in 1983, ending seven years of military rule. The Péronist Carlos Saúl Menem was president from 1989 until 1999, when he was succeeded by Fernando de la Rua, whose attempts in December 2001 to arrest a financial crisis provoked riots and a general strike, leading to his resignation. The Perónist Nestor Kirchner became president in 2003. Official language: Spanish. Currency: peso of 100 centavos. Area: 2 777 815 sq km (1 072 515 sq mi). Population (2003 est): 36 846 000. Capital: Buenos Aires.

argon (Ar) A noble gas that occurs in the atmosphere (0.94%). It was first isolated in 1894 by Rayleigh and Ramsay, by the distillation of liquid air. Because it is chemically inert, it is used to fill fluorescent lamps and as an inert gas blanket for welding reactive metals. At no 18; at wt 39.948; mp −189.2°C; bp −185.7°C.

Argonauts In Greek mythology, the 50-man crew of Jason's ship *Argo*, on the quest of the *Golden Fleece. Accounts of its composition vary, but all agree that it included the shipbuilder Argo, the tireless helmsman Tiphys, the keen-sighted Lynceus, *Heracles and his follower Hylas, and even *Orpheus and the Dioscuri, *Castor and Pollux. The Argonauts encountered such perils as the *Sirens, the *Harpies, the Symplegades (moving rocks that crushed ships) and the bronze giant Talos.

Argos 37 38N 22 43E A town in the NE Peloponnese (S Greece). Belonging in Homeric times to a follower of *Agamemnon, Argos gave its name to the surrounding district (the Argolid). Eclipsed by nearby Sparta after the 6th century BC, Argos remained neutral or the ineffective ally of Athens during the 5th century. Considerable remains of the city survive.

Argus In Greek mythology, a giant with 100

eyes who was beheaded by Hermes. He was (at the command of Hera) the guardian of Io, who was desired by Zeus; when he was killed Hera set his eyes in the tail of the peacock.

Argyll and Bute A council area of W Scotland, on the Atlantic Ocean and the North Channel. In 1975 the historic county of Argyll and the county and island of Bute became a single district within Strathclyde Region. This district became an independent unitary authority in 1996 (with slightly adjusted borders). It includes the islands of Mull, Islay, and Jura among many others. Fishing (including salmon farming) and livestock are important, as are tourism, whisky distilling, and textiles. Area: 6930 sq km (2676 sq mi). Population (2001): 91 306. Administrative centre: Lochgilphead.

Århus (*or* **Aarhus**) 56 10N 10 13E A seaport in Denmark, in E Jutland. One of the oldest cities in Denmark, it has a gothic cathedral and a university (1928). Its industries include electronic goods, machinery, and textiles. Population (2000 est): 540 600.

aria (Italian: air) A solo song with instrumental accompaniment, usually in an opera or oratorio. The name was also used of instrumental pieces but its meaning became restricted with the development of the three part *aria da capo* by Monteverdi, Scarlatti, and Handel. Attacked by reformers, such as Gluck and Wagner, the aria form is little used in modern opera.

Ariadne In Greek legend, the daughter of *Minos, King of Crete, and Pasiphaë. She helped *Theseus to kill the Minotaur and escape from its labyrinth. He abandoned her on the island of Naxos, where she was found by *Dionysus, who married her.

Arianism A Christian heresy started by Arius, which held that the Son of God, Jesus Christ, was not truly divine. In 325 AD the Council of Nicaea banished the Arians, including several bishops, and affirmed that the Father and the Son were coequal, coeternal, and "of one substance." Although the Arians were soon restored and a version of the heresy was accepted for a time, Arianism was finally defeated at the Council of Constantinople in 381 AD.

Arias Sánchez, Oscar (1941–) Costa Rican statesman; president (1986–90). His Central American peace plan was intended to end regional conflicts by 1988 but had only limited success. He won the Nobel Peace Prize in 1987.

Ariosto, Ludovico (1474–1533) Italian poet. He spent most of his life in the service of the Este, the ducal family of Ferrara. He wrote plays and much lyric verse but is best known for his epic poem, *Orlando furioso* (1516). It was published in its revised form in 1532. Its precursor was the *Orlando innamorato* (1483) of Boiardo.

Aristarchus of Samos (c. 310–230 BC) Greek astronomer, who maintained that the earth rotates upon its axis and orbits the sun. He made the first attempts to estimate trigonometrically the size and distance from the earth of the sun and the moon.

Aristophanes (c. 450–c. 385 BC) Greek comic dramatist. He wrote about 40 plays, of which 11 survive: *The Acharnians* (425), *The Knights* (424), *The Clouds* (423), *The Wasps* (422), *The Peace* (421), *The Birds* (414), *Lysistrata* (411), *Thesmophoriazusae* (410), *The Frogs* (405), *Women in Parliament* (393), and *Plutus* (388). His plots were satirical fantasies on contemporary topics.

Aristotelianism Tendencies in philosophical thought that originated with Aristotle. Interpretations of his work were preserved by Arab scholars, culminating in the 12th-century commentaries of Averroes. Aquinas in the 13th century made Aristotle the metaphysical basis of Christian theology but the Latin Averroists produced their own theories, holding (for instance) that a proposition can be philosophically true although theologically false.

Aristotle (384–322 BC) Greek philosopher and scientist. His father was court physician in Macedonia. Aristotle joined Plato's Academy at Athens (367–347) but, failing to become head of the Academy at Plato's death, he accepted the protection of Hermeias, ruler of Atarneus in Asia Minor, and married his patron's niece. About 343 *Philip of Macedon appointed Aristotle tutor to his son Alexander, then aged 13. After Alexander's accession in 336, Aristotle founded the *Lyceum at Athens (a research community with library and museum). When Alexander died in 323 BC, anti-Macedonian reaction forced Aristotle to withdraw to Chalcis, where he died. Aristotle wrote over 400 books; those that survive (about one-quarter), edited by Andronicus of Rhodes about 40 BC, are apparently memoranda for his students' use, not intended for general publication.

arithmetic The branch of mathematics that deals with elementary theories of numbers, measurement, and computation. The fundamental operations of arithmetic are addition, subtraction, multiplication, and division. Addition and multiplication are assumed to obey the *associative law, the commutative law, and the distributive law. Other operations in arithmetic include extracting roots, raising a number to a power, and taking *logarithms. Arithmetic is also concerned with fractions and the various number systems, such as the *decimal system and the *binary system.

arithmetic progression (*or* **arithmetic sequence**) A sequence of numbers in which successive terms have a constant difference, for example, 1, 4, 7, 10, 13....

Arizona A state in the SW USA. It falls into two natural regions: in the NE lies part of the Colorado Plateau, an area of dry plains and escarpments, and in the S and W is an area of desert basins and gentle valleys, drained by the Gila and Salt Rivers. The Colorado River flows through the Grand Canyon in the NW of the state. In such an arid region inadequate water supplies have long been a problem and a number of major irrigation projects have been built. Most of the population lives in urban settlements in the S and W. Manufacturing (electrical, communications, aeronautical, and aluminium products) is the major industry. The state produces over half of the USA's copper as well as gold, silver, oil, and timber. Tourism is an important source of revenue. The main crops are cotton, vegetables, and citrus fruits; livestock is also important. It has the largest Indian population in the USA; the main tribes are the Navajo, Hopi, and Apache. *History*: inhabited by Indians as early as 25 000 BC, the area was explored by the Spanish in the 16th century. Following the Mexican War, Arizona, then part of New Mexico, was ceded to the USA (1848). It was swept by Apache wars until 1877 and became a state in 1912. Area: 295 023 sq km (113 909 sq mi). Population (2000): 5 130 632. Capital: Phoenix.

Arkansas A state in the S central USA, lying W of the Mississippi River. It consists chiefly of the largely forested uplands of the N and W, descending to the Mississippi alluvial plain in the E and the West Gulf coastal plain in the S. The **Arkansas River** (2335 km; 1450 mi) bisects the state from W to E. The state is no longer primarily agricultural although the Mississippi Plain provides fertile land; soya beans and rice have replaced cotton as the major crop. There are major lumbering, petroleum, and gas developments around Smackover and El Dorado and coal deposits in the Arkansas River Valley. The state produces 90% of US bauxite. Manufactures include electronic equipment and wood products. *History*: explored by the Spanish and French in the 16th and 17th centuries, it formed part of the *Louisiana Purchase by the USA in 1803. It became a state in 1836, seceded from the Union in 1861, and was readmitted in 1868. Area: 137 539 sq km (53 104 sq mi). Population (2000): 2 673 400. Capital: Little Rock.

Ark of the Covenant In the Old Testament, the sacred chest of the Israelites that contained the tablets of the law (the Ten Commandments) and was symbolic both of God's presence and his *covenant with Israel. Made of acacia wood, and covered with gold, it was eventually placed in the Temple of Jerusalem. It probably disappeared during the Babylonian exile.

Arkwright, Sir Richard (1732–92) British inventor and industrialist, who invented a spinning frame powered by water, the so-called water frame (patented in 1769). Arkwright subsequently mechanized other spinning processes and his mills were vandalized by spinners put out of work by the incipient factory system.

Arlington National Cemetery The largest cemetery in the USA, comprising 170 hectares (420 acres) just outside Washington DC. Since 1864 it has been the burial ground of Americans killed in action and of eminent public servants.

Armada, Spanish The fleet of 130 ships sent by Philip II of Spain in 1588 to invade England. After indecisive encounters with the English fleet led by Howard of Effingham, under whom Sir John Hawkins held command, the Armada anchored off Calais only to be dispersed by English fireships during the night of 28 July. A major engagement off Gravelines followed, in which the Armada was defeated. It suffered further losses in storms as it escaped round Scotland and Ireland, arriving in Spain with 86 ships. The defeat was a major blow to Spain, which had claimed divine authority for its crusade against Protestant England. *See also* DRAKE, SIR FRANCIS.

armadillo A mammal belonging to the family *Dasypodidae* (12 species), widespread in open country in the southern USA and South America. Armadillos have a covering of jointed bands or horny plates that enables them to roll themselves into a ball for protection. They have long-clawed toes for burrowing, simple peglike teeth, and feed on insects and other invertebrates. Armadillos range in size from the giant armadillo (*Priodontes giganteus*), about 120 cm long, to the rare pink fairy armadillo (*Chlamyphorus truncatus*), 12 cm long. Order: *Edentata*.

a

Armageddon *See* MEGIDDO.

Armagh 1. A historic county in S Northern Ireland. Its administrative powers were devolved to the new district councils in 1973. Armagh is predominantly agricultural; produce includes potatoes, flax, and apples. Area: 1326 sq km (512 sq mi). **2.** A district in Northern Ireland, in Co Armagh. Area: 667 sq km (258 sq mi). Population (2001): 54 263.

Armani, Giorgio (1934–) Italian fashion designer. His fashion house, established in 1975, produces elegant ready-to-wear designs for men and women.

Armenia, Republic of A densely populated and mountainous republic in W Asia. *Economy*: industries include food processing, metallurgy, and chemicals. The rich mineral deposits include copper, lead, and zinc. The raising of livestock is the chief agricultural activity. In the 1990s the economy suffered from embargoes imposed by Turkey and Azerbaidzhan because of the *Nagorno-Karabakh dispute and there was large-scale emigration. More recent years have seen an economic recovery. *History*: the region formed the E part of the historic area inhabited by the *Armenians. It was acquired by Russia in 1828. The Russian province declared its independence in 1918 but it subsequently formed part of the Transcaucasian Soviet Federated Republic. It became a separate Soviet republic in 1936 and an independent state in 1991. Demands for the return of the disputed Nagorno-Karabakh region from Azerbaidzhan led to civil conflict in the late 1980s and a state of virtual war between the two countries from 1991; a ceasefire was agreed in 1994. Armenia declared independence in 1991 and a new constitution was promulgated following a referendum in 1995. Presidential elections in 1998 resulted in victory for the hardline nationalist Robert Kocharyan. In October 1999 the prime minister was shot dead in parliament by maverick extremists. Presidential elections in 2003 saw Kocharyan reelected amidst accusations of vote-rigging. Official language: Armenian. Currency: dram of 100 luma. Area: 29 800 sq km (11 490 sq mi). Population (2003): 3 061 000. Capital: Yerevan.

Armenians A people of NE Turkey and Armenia speaking an Indo-European language. Approximately 1.5 million live in Turkey, Europe, and America and 3 million in Armenia, with smaller numbers in Georgia and Azerbaidzhan. Their culture is ancient, with a literature written in an alphabet derived from Greek and Syriac script. Their language is the only representative of a distinct branch of the Indo-European family. They call themselves Hay and their land Hayastan. They mainly belong to the Armenian Church, founded by St Gregory the Illuminator (*c.* 240–332) about 300 AD. During the 19th and 20th centuries they suffered massacres at the hands of the Ottoman Turks.

armour Defensive equipment used as a protection in warfare. Body armour (helmet, breastplate, greaves) was used in Bronze Age Greece. The Romans evolved heavier armour for both men and horses. In the early Middle Ages chainmail was widely used but after about 1300 plate armour, often sumptuously decorated and encasing the whole body, was worn by knights on horseback. Gunpowder gradually rendered most body armour obsolete. However, steel helmets were revived in World War I as a protection against shrapnel and body armour is now again in use by military personnel.

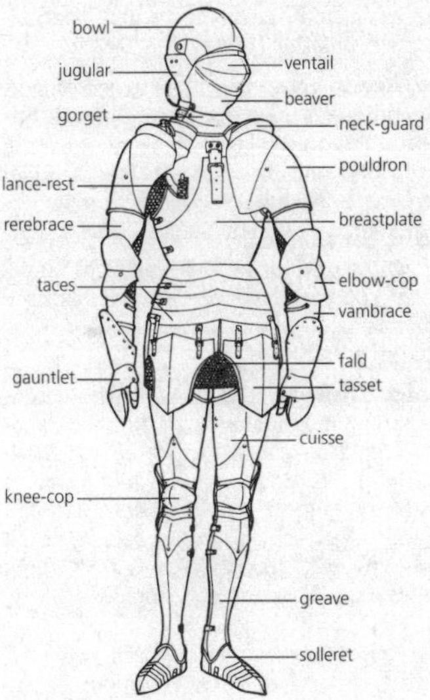

armour. The skill of the European armourer reached its height in the late 15th and early 16th centuries, when suits of plate armour were made to cover the entire body.

Armstrong, Louis (1900–71) US Black jazz trumpeter and singer, known as "Satchmo." Born in New Orleans, he learned to play the cornet in the orphanage in which he was brought up. His career took him to Chicago, where he made many recordings (some of them with Earl Hines), which earned him a worldwide reputation. He later played with several large orchestras and toured widely. His gravelly singing voice and superb trumpet playing were featured in many films.

Armstrong, Neil (Alden) (1930–) US astronaut, the first man to walk on the moon. A navy pilot during the Korean War, he worked for NASA, (1955–71) and became an astronaut in 1962. He was commander of Apollo 11 (1969). As he stepped onto the moon he said "That's one small step for a man, one giant leap for mankind."

Arnhem 52 00N 5 53E A city in the E Netherlands, the capital of Gelderland province. In World War II a large airborne landing of British troops attempted to secure a bridgehead over the River Rhine here to facilitate an Allied invasion of Germany. The attempt failed with heavy casualties in the ensuing battle (17–27 September 1944). A railway junction, its industries include engineering and pharmaceuticals. Population (1999 est): 137 222.

Arno, River A river in central Italy. Rising in the Apennines, it flows mainly W through Florence and Pisa to the Ligurian Sea. It burst its banks in 1966 causing disastrous floods in Florence. Length: 240 km (150 mi).

Arnold, Sir Malcolm (1921–) British composer, who began his musical career as an orchestral trumpet player. He has written nine symphonies and several concertos as well as much film music.

Arnold, Thomas (1795–1842) British educator. Appointed headmaster of Rugby School (1828), Arnold reformed the school and instituted the prefectorial system, which came to characterize English public schools. Arnold's piety was infectious, and Rugby became noted for "muscular Christianity." *Tom Brown's Schooldays* provides a record of Arnold's achievement.

His son **Matthew Arnold** (1822–88) was a poet and critic. He worked as a government inspector of schools from 1851 to 1886. His critical works include *Essays in Criticism* (1865; 1888) and *Culture and Anarchy* (1869), in which he advocated literary and cultural values as an antidote to the progressive materialism of Victorian society. His poetry included "Dover Beach" (1867) and the narrative poems "The Scholar Gypsy" (1853) and "Sohrab and Rustum" (1853).

aromatherapy A form of *alternative medicine using plant essential oils to enhance physiological functions. They may be inhaled or applied, with massage, to the skin. An art practised in classical Greece, it became popular in the West in the 1990s.

aromatic compound A type of cyclic organic chemical compound that includes *benzene and its derivatives. On conventional theories of valence these compounds appear to be unsaturated (i.e. contain double bonds). However, benzene and similar compounds are much less reactive than the *alkenes, tending to undergo substitution reactions rather than addition reactions. The explanation for the stability of the benzene ring lies in a model in which the carbon atoms are joined by single bonds and the extra six valence electrons are free to move around the ring in a delocalized orbital. Aromatic compounds were originally distinguished from *aliphatic compounds because of the distinctive properties of benzene compounds, many of which have a fragrant odour.

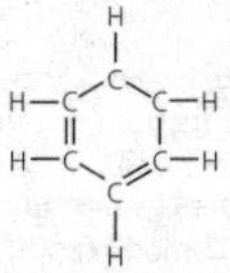

The conventional formula of benzene devised by F. A. Kekulé von Stradonitz (1829–96). With alternating double bonds it would be unsaturated and have properties similar to the alkenes.

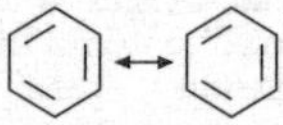

In the benzene molecule the bonds are actually intermediate between single and double bonds. This is often represented as a resonance hybrid between the two conventional structures.

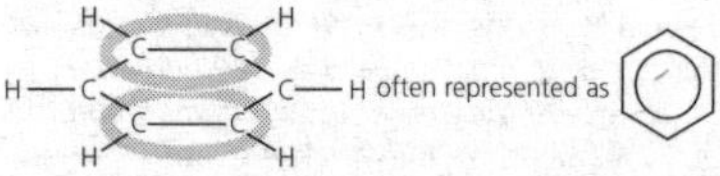

The modern explanation of the bonding involves a delocalized orbital above and below the ring. The six valence electrons (one from each carbon atom) are free to move in this orbital. This explains the properties of benzene and the fact that all C-C bonds are equal.

aromatic compound

Arp, Jean (Hans) (1887–1966) French sculptor and poet. He was one of the founders of the *dada movement (1916) and later associated with the surrealist movement in Paris. Arp experimented with collages and produced numerous painted wood reliefs. In about 1930 he began his abstract sculptures suggesting organic rather than geometric forms. His wife and occasional collaborator was the artist Sophie Tauber (1889–1943).

Arrhenius, Svante August (1859–1927) Swedish physicist and chemist, who became a professor of the University of Stockholm in 1895. He won the 1903 Nobel Prize for Chemistry for his theory of electrolytic dissociation. He later worked on the application of physical chemistry to living processes.

arrowroot A herbaceous perennial plant, *Maranta arundinacea*, native to Guyana but widely cultivated in the West Indies for the fine starch that is extracted from its underground fleshy tubers and used in cooking. The plant is about 1.5 m high and has short-stalked white flowers and broad-bladed leaves with long narrow sheaths. Family: *Marantaceae*.

Arrow War *See* OPIUM WARS.

ars antiqua (Latin: old art) A style of European music of the 13th century. It was particularly associated with composers of the Parisian school, such as Pérotin (c. 1155–c. 1202) and Léonin (late 12th century), and characterized by the use of complex forms of organum. It was succeeded by **ars nova*.

arsenic (As) A brittle semimetal that occurs in nature in a variety of forms: native, as the sulphides realgar (As_2S_2) and orpiment (As_2S_3), as sulpharsenides, such as arsenopyrite (FeSAs), and as arsenates. The element occurs in several forms and was known to the ancients. Pure arsenic has important uses as a dopant in the semiconductor industry. Arsenic and its common compounds are extremely poisonous. Compounds include the white oxide (As_2O_3), the gaseous hydride arsine (AsH_3), and arsenates, some of which are used as insecticides. At no 33; at wt 74.9216; mp 817°C (28 atm); sublimes 613°C.

ars nova (Latin: new art) A style of European music of the 14th century, which succeeded **ars antiqua*. The name was taken from the title of a treatise by Philippe de Vitry (1291–1361), which set out new principles for the composition of *motets and for the notation of complex rhythms.

arson At common law, maliciously setting fire to something, including buildings, vehicles, etc. As a distinct offence, arson was abolished in English law by the Criminal Damage Act (1971), which is the statute covering all types of criminal damage (the destruction or damage of property belonging to another). Criminal damage committed by fire is still, however, charged as arson.

Art Deco The style of design predominant in the decorative arts of the 1920s and 1930s. The name derives from the 1925 Exposition Internationale des Arts Décoratifs in Paris. In deliberate contrast to *Art Nouveau, Art Deco was characterized by emphatic geometrical lines and shapes, vibrant colour schemes, and the use of man-made substances, such as plastic. Influenced by the *Bauhaus, Art Deco included among its practitioners René Lalique (1860–1945) and Erté (Romaine de Tirtoff; 1892–1990). It was debased by shoddy mass production, but interest in it rekindled in the late 20th century.

Artemis In Greek mythology, the daughter of Zeus and Leto and twin sister of Apollo. Settled in *Arcadia, she and her band of Oceanids and nymphs spent their time hunting. Artemis demanded chastity from her followers and rigorously punished all transgressors. *Actaeon was killed for watching her bathe and *Orion for raping her. Despite this severity she was protectress of both animal and human young. Ephesus was the most famous centre of her worship. She was associated with the moon and identified by the Romans with *Diana. *Compare* HECATE.

Artemis, Temple of One of the Seven Wonders of the World, built at *Ephesus in 356 BC. The deity worshipped here was the many-breasted fertility goddess called Diana of the Ephesians in Acts 19.28, rather than the classical *Artemis.

arteriosclerosis The loss of elasticity in the walls of arteries. It covers various conditions of the arteries and arterioles (small arteries) associated with the ageing process. It is also used as a synonym for *atherosclerosis.

artery A thick-walled blood vessel that carries oxygen-rich blood away from the *heart to supply all the tissues and organs of the body. The largest is the aorta, which leads directly from the heart and descends into the abdomen, giving rise to all the other arteries of the body. In middle age the lining of the arteries commonly becomes thickened by *atherosclerosis, which may lead to various diseases caused by obstruction of blood flow (e.g. strokes, heart attacks). *See also* BLOOD PRESSURE.

artesian well A well sunk into an aquifer (a water-saturated rock stratum) that is confined between two layers of impermeable rock and through which water flows upwards under pressure. The aquifer reaches the surface and receives rainfall where the water table is higher than the site of the well, resulting in a head of pressure.

arthritis Inflammation of one or more joints, causing pain, swelling, and restriction of movement. Many different diseases can cause arthritis, the most important of which are *osteoarthritis, rheumatoid arthritis, and *gout. **Rheumatoid arthritis**, which is more common in women, usually affects the hands and feet and often also the hips, knees, and shoulders. The synovial membrane lining the joint becomes inflamed, resulting in damage to the cartilage over the joint with consequent pain and deformity. An autoimmune disease (*see* AUTOIMMUNITY), it is diagnosed by a blood test (the blood contains the rheumatoid factor) and X-rays. Treatment is usually based on analgesic and anti-inflammatory drugs; some patients benefit from gold salts and steroids, while severe cases may require surgical replacement of the affected joint(s).

arthropod An invertebrate animal belonging to the largest and most diverse phylum (*Arthropoda*) of the animal kingdom, containing about a million species (i.e. 75% of all known species). Arthropods include *arachnids, *crustaceans, *insects, *centipedes, and *millipedes. An arthropod has a segmented body with a hard outer skeleton (cuticle) made of chitin, which is shed periodically to allow the body to grow. Jointed appendages are modified for swimming, walking, feeding, respiration, reproduction, etc. Young arthropods often go through *metamorphosis to reach the adult form. Many are harmful—as pests, parasites, or vectors of disease—but others are beneficial to man, as pollinators, food sources, predators of pests, and decomposers of organic wastes.

Arthurian legend The medieval romances concerning the legendary British king Arthur and his knights. Arthur emerged as a figure of romance in the *Historia Regum Britanniae* of *Geoffrey of Monmouth. In the legend, he is the son of Uther Pendragon, was born at Tintagel in Cornwall, became king of Britain at 15, and won a number of famous victories. He married Guinevere and held court at Caerleon in Wales (or, in some versions, at Camelot, which may have been near South Cadbury, Somerset). Involved in a war at Rome, he left his kingdom in the charge of his nephew Modred, who betrayed him and abducted Guinevere. Arthur returned to Britain and defeated Modred but was himself wounded. He was taken to the Isle of Avalon (the Celtic paradise, associated with Glastonbury) to be healed. The Anglo-Norman poet Wace (c. 1100–c. 1175) introduced the knightly fellowship of the Round Table, Layamon (early 13th century) added magical elements, and *Chrétien de Troyes focused on the quest of the *Holy Grail. Other legendary characters were the magician Merlin and the sorceress Morgan le Fay (Arthur's sister). Sir Thomas Malory's *Morte d'Arthur* (c. 1470) concluded the medieval accounts, while Tennyson's *Idylls of the King* (from 1842) and T. H. White's *The Once and Future King* (1958) gave later versions.

artichoke A perennial thistle-like herbaceous plant, *Cynara scolemus*, also known as globe artichoke, native to central and W Mediterranean regions and widely grown in warm temperate areas for its nutty-tasting immature flower heads. The hairy indented straplike leaves, 1 m long, arise each year from the base of the short annual stems, which carry branched flower stalks bearing purplish flowers. Family: *Compositae*. *See also* JERUSALEM ARTICHOKE.

Articles of Confederation The first constitution of the USA (written 1776–77, adopted 1781), which was replaced by the Constitution of 1789. The leaders of the American Revolution feared the abuses of a centralized government and adopted a federal system that guaranteed each state its "sovereignty, freedom, and independence." The Continental Congress could not levy taxes but could wage war and borrow and issue money.

artificial insemination The artificial introduction of semen into the vagina of a female at or shortly after ovulation. Although practised in the 14th century by Arab horse breeders, the techniques were developed largely for livestock in the Soviet Union during the early 20th century. Semen collected from a single male can be stored at low temperatures for months before being used to fertilize many females. This has resulted in dramatic breed improvements and the control of venereal disease. Artificial insemination is also used in human medicine; for an infertile husband, semen is obtained from a donor (DI–donor insemination). Although donors are currently anonymous, children conceived after April 2005 will have the right to find out who their natural father is when they reach the age of 18. Semen may be provided by the husband in cases of impotence (artificial insemination husband—AIH). When the wife is infertile the husband's semen may be used to artificially inseminate a surrogate mother. This woman gives birth to the child, usually for money, and must then be prepared to relinquish all claims on it to the natural father and his wife. Commercial surrogacy is growing in the USA, but in the UK the Surrogacy Arrangements Act (1985) prohibits commercial agencies from engaging women as surrogate mothers. *See also* TEST-TUBE BABY.

artificial intelligence (**AI**) The design of computer programs to perform tasks that involve intelligence when carried out by human beings. Tasks performed by AI include playing games, learning, understanding natural language and speech, formulating plans, proving theorems, and visual perception. Perceptual tasks involve unconscious computation in humans, which is hard to simulate. AI programs sometimes simulate human behaviour by building computer models of cognitive processes, but in most cases they adopt any technique that will do the task set or do it better than it has been done before.

artificial respiration The restoration of the flow of air into and out of the lungs when the patient's own breathing movements have ceased, for example after drowning, poisoning, etc. Mouth-to-mouth respiration—the "kiss of life"—involves a person breathing out into the patient's mouth: carbon dioxide in this exhaled air acts as a stimulus for the natural breathing reflexes. In hospitals artificial respiration by a *respirator is sometimes provided during surgery, severe pneumonias, and after head injuries.

artillery Firearms with a calibre in excess of 20 mm, used to bombard enemy positions, provide cover, etc. Early guns were classed by projectile weight, e.g. 12-pounder. Modern weapons are identified by calibre: light (below 120 mm), medium (121–160 mm), heavy (161–210 mm), and super or very heavy (above 211 mm). Gun projectiles have flat trajectories, while *mortars and *howitzers have high trajectories, with correspondingly short ranges. Artillery rockets deliver more explosive further, without needing heavy launchers. Modern electronic equipment enables artillery fire to score a direct hit with near certainty on any visible target; as this also applies to the guns themselves artillery is now usually remote controlled.

Artiodactyla An order of hoofed mammals (150 species), distributed worldwide except for Australasia and Antarctica. Artiodactyls are terrestrial herbivores having two or four toes on each foot and often bearing horns. The group is divided into three suborders: *Suiformes* (pigs, peccaries, and hippopotamuses); *Tylopoda* (camels and llamas); and *Ruminantia* (*see* RUMINANT), which comprises deer, cattle, antelopes, giraffes, pronghorns, and chevrotains. *Compare* PERISSODACTYLA.

Art Nouveau A decorative style pervading all visual art forms in Britain, France, Germany (Jugendstil), Austria (Sezessionstil), Belgium, Spain, and the USA in the 1890s and early 1900s. It is characterized by designs of naturalistic foliage and shapes linked by undulating lines. In Britain it is associated with the *Arts and Crafts movement of William *Morris, the designs of Charles Rennie Mackintosh (1868–1928), and the graphic work of Aubrey *Beardsley. On the Continent leading examples are the Parisian metro designs of Hector Guimard (1867–1942), the extravagant Barcelona flats and hotels of Antonio Gaudí (1852–1926), and the Belgian stores and houses of Victor Horta (1861–1947).

Arts and Crafts movement An English 19th-century aesthetic movement derived from William *Morris and his Pre-Raphaelite associates, whose firm was founded (1861) to produce handmade furnishings. The movement revived the principles of medieval craftsmanship and respect for materials. It culminated in the establishment of the Century Guild for Craftsmen (1882) and the Arts and Crafts Exhibition Society (1888). It helped to create the emerging *Art Nouveau style.

Arts Councils Four bodies, the Arts Councils of England, Scotland, Wales, and Northern Ireland, that channel government support for the arts. Founded originally in 1946 as the Arts Council of Great Britain, the Councils have since 1995 been responsible for distributing the proceeds of the National Lottery allocated to the arts.

Aruba 12 30N 70 00W A West Indian island, formerly (until 1986) part of the Netherlands Antilles, now a separate Dutch territory. Oil refining is important. Area: 193 sq km (75 sq mi). Population (2001 est): 97 200. Chief town: Oranjestad.

arum (*or* **arum lily**) A plant of the tropical African genus *Zantedeschia* (8 species), especially *Z. aethiopica*, widely grown as an ornamental. It has arrow-shaped leaves and a flower head of tiny yellow flowers surrounded by a white funnel-shaped bract (spathe). *Araceae*. The European genus *Arum*, of the same family, contains the *cuckoopint. The related bog arum, or wild calla (*Calla palustris*), grows in swamps of N temperate and subarctic regions. It has heart-shaped leaves and small flowers enveloped in a white spathe.

Arunachal Pradesh (name until 1972: North-East Frontier Agency) A state in NE India, stretching N from the Brahmaputra Valley to the Himalayas. There it shares a disputed border with Tibet, from which Chinese troops have twice invaded since 1945. It became the 24th state of India in 1987. Mostly rainforest, it is inhabited by hill tribes. Area: 83 743 sq km (32 648 sq mi). Population (2001): 1 091 117. Capital: Itanagar.

Arundel 50 51N 0 34W A market town in SE England, in West Sussex on the River Arun. Its 11th-century castle (mainly rebuilt in the 19th century) is the seat of the Dukes of Norfolk. Other notable buildings include the 19th-century cathedral. Population (1991): 3033.

Aryans Peoples speaking Indo-European, Indo-Iranian, or Indo-Aryan languages. It has been claimed that all the Indo-European peoples originated from an Aryan people who dispersed from a common homeland into Europe and N India. Indo-Aryan-speaking peoples invaded and settled in N India in the second millennium BC. They were tribal herdsmen who became farmers. The earliest literature of India, the Vedas, written in *Sanskrit, contains details of Aryan ritual practices.

ASA rating The American Standards Association measure of the sensitivity or speed of photographic *film. A film rated at 200 is twice as fast (i.e. needs half the exposure time) as 100 ASA film. General-purpose films have speeds between 50 and 160 ASA. High-speed films for poor light are rated between 200 and 1000 ASA.

asbestos A fibrous form of certain silicate minerals, particularly the *amphiboles anthophyllite, tremolite, riebeckite, and actinolite, or a fibrous form of *serpentine, called chrysotile. Blue asbestos is crocidolite, a fibrous riebeckite. Asbestos is heat-resistant, chemically inert, and has a high electrical resistance; it is much used in industry. The fibres are spun and woven or made into blocks. The main producer is Canada. *See also* ASBESTOSIS.

asbestosis A lung disease caused by the inhalation of asbestos fibres. It is an occupational disease to which those exposed to large amounts of the mineral are particularly prone: tighter factory health controls have greatly reduced its incidence. It affects the air sacs of the lungs, which become thickened and scarred, causing breathlessness: patients are liable to develop lung cancer.

Ascension 7 57S 14 22W A rocky island in the S Atlantic Ocean, a dependency of St Helena. It has little vegetation and was uninhabited until 1815. A British telecommunications centre, it is also a US air base and space research station. Area: 88 sq km (35 sq mi). Population (2001): 980. Chief settlement: Georgetown.

Ascension In the Christian calendar, the day on which it is believed Christ ascended into Heaven. Since the 4th century it has been celebrated 40 days after Easter.

asceticism Systematic spiritual self-discipline, usually involving fasting, vigils, sexual abstinence, and renunciation of worldly pleasures. *Stoicism advocated ascetic practices in order to subdue passions. Christian asceticism is based on the theory of identifying with Christ's sufferings and is viewed not as an end in itself but as a means to contemplation of and spiritual union with the divine. It became an important element in certain monastic orders and in Christian mysticism. In Islam, asceticism is particularly associated with *sufism; there is also a strong tradition of asceticism in Buddhism and Hinduism.

Asclepius (*or* **Aesculapius**) In Greek mythology, a son of *Apollo and the god of medicine. He was instructed by the centaur *Chiron in hunting and medicine. When he restored Hippolytus to life as a favour to Artemis, Zeus became angry and struck him dead with a thunderbolt. The sick, believing in Asclepius's power to cure them through dreams, came to sleep in his temples, the chief of which were at Epidaurus and on the island of Cos.

Ascomycota A large phylum of fungi (over 30 000 species), known as sac fungi because their spores are formed in a saclike structure (called an ascus). The nonreproductive part of these fungi is often a microscopical meshwork of cells. The group includes the *truffles, *yeasts, *Penicillium*, and *Aspergillus*.

Ascot 51 25N 0 41W A village in S England, in Bracknell Forest unitary authority, Berkshire. The construction of its famous racecourse was ordered by Queen Anne in 1711. Traditionally the sovereign opens the Royal Ascot meeting in June, driving in an open carriage round the course from nearby Windsor Castle. Population (latest est): 13 500, with Sunningdale.

ASEAN *See* ASSOCIATION OF SOUTH-EAST ASIAN NATIONS.

Asgard In Norse mythology, the home of the gods and of heroes killed in battle, comprising over 12 kingdoms and palaces, as well as Valhalla. From earth it was reached by the bridge Bifrost (the rainbow).

ash A tree of the genus *Fraxinus* (about 50 species), native to the N hemisphere. Many species yield a pale-yellow wood of commercial importance. Reaching a height of 30 m, ashes have compound leaves made up of pairs of oval or lance-shaped leaflets, small inconspicuous flowers, and winged fruits ("ash keys"). Most species are deciduous, including the European ash (*F. excelsior*). Family: *Oleaceae* (olive family). *See also* MOUNTAIN ASH.

Ashanti A people of the S part of Ghana, who speak Twi. They are an agricultural people producing crops for local markets and cocoa for export. Their social organization is based upon matrilineal kin groups living in villages governed by headmen. The Ashanti established an empire in S Ghana during the 18th and 19th centuries. They worship a pantheon of gods and practise an ancestor cult.

Ashcroft, Dame Peggy (1907–91) British actress. She made her debut in 1926. Her most notable performances included Juliet in 1935, Hedda Gabler in 1954, and roles in plays by Pinter and Beckett. She won an Oscar for her performance in the film *A Passage to India* (1984).

Ashdown, Paddy, Baron (Jeremy John Durham A.; 1941–) British politician, leader of the Social and Liberal Democrats (1988–99). He entered parliament in 1983 after service in the Commandos and the Special Boat Section. He was appointed to the powerful position of UN high representative in Bosnia in 2002.

Ashes A mock trophy awarded to the winning team in cricket Test matches between England and Australia. It originated with the first Australian victory (1882), when an obituary for English cricket in the *Sporting Times* ended with the words: "The body will be cremated and the ashes taken to Australia." In 1883 the victorious English captain was presented with an urn (now kept in the pavilion at *Lord's cricket ground) containing the ashes of the stumps used in the match.

Ashkenazim Jews of German or Eastern European origin, as opposed to *Sephardim. Forming some 85% of world Jewry, they have a distinct way of pronouncing Hebrew, and other customs, and until this century they mostly spoke *Yiddish. The first Ashkenazy synagogue in London was founded in 1690.

Ashkenazy, Vladimir (1937–) Russian pianist and conductor. He won the 1955 Warsaw Chopin Competition and was joint winner of the 1962 Tchaikovsky Competition. In 1973 he settled in Iceland.

Ashkhabad 37 58N 58 24E The capital of Turkmenistan, rebuilt after an earthquake (1948). Products include foods, carpets, glass, and machinery. Population: (1999 est): 605 000.

Ashley, Laura (born Laura Mountrey; 1925–85) British fashion designer, who married Bernard Ashley in 1949, and opened her first London boutique in 1967. This became the model for an international chain. Her husband and sons took over the business after her death.

Ashmolean Museum A museum in Oxford, housing paintings and archaeological collections. The collection was donated to Oxford University in 1675 by Elias Ashmole (1617–92) and put on public display in 1683. Now in the neoclassical building (1845) of Charles Robert Cockerell (1788–1863), it includes Italian Renaissance paintings and English 19th-century works.

Ashton, Sir Frederick (William Mallandaine) (1904–88) British ballet dancer and choreographer, born in Ecuador. He joined the Sadler's Wells Ballet in 1935, became an associate director in 1952, and was director of the Royal Ballet from 1963 to 1970. His works include *Cinderella* (1948), *Ondine* (1958), *La Fille mal gardée* (1960), and many ballets choreographed for Margot Fonteyn.

Ashur The oldest Assyrian capital (modern Qalat Sharqat) on the River Tigris in Iraq. Named after its guardian sun-god, Ashur became capital of the rising Assyrian empire (14th century BC) to which it gave its name. With its later cocapitals *Nimrud and *Nineveh it was destroyed in 612 BC. First excavated in 1903, Ashur's ruins include major temples and a *ziggurat.

Ashurbanipal King of Assyria (668–?627 BC), son of Esarhaddon. He suppressed two revolts during his reign and conquered the city of Tyre. He founded a remarkable library at Nineveh, some of the items in which are now in the British Museum.

Ash Wednesday In the Christian calendar, the first day of *Lent, so named from the custom, probably dating from the 8th century, of marking the foreheads of the congregation with ashes as a sign of penitence.

a

Asia The largest continent in the world, it occupies about one-third of the dry land. Extending W to the Ural Mountains, it is separated from Africa by the Red Sea and bounded on the N by the Arctic Ocean. It includes the islands of Indonesia, Japan, the Philippines, and Taiwan. It contains the world's highest point (Mount *Everest) and also its lowest (the *Dead Sea). Its central mass of mountains and plateaus has historically formed a major barrier between N and S Asia. Vast alluvial plains border the major rivers, including the Rivers Ganges, Mekong, and Ob and the Yangtze and Yellow Rivers. Containing about half of the world's total population, it is the most populous continent. There are three main population groups: Negroid (in the Philippines), Mongoloid (including the Chinese, Japanese, and Koreans), and Caucasoid (including the Arabs, Afghans, and Pakistanis). Other groups, including the Malays, are a mixture of these main races. Christianity, Judaism, Hinduism (with the largest following), Buddhism, Islam, Confucianism (in China), and Shintoism (in Japan) all originated in Asia. Agriculture employs about two-thirds of the total population. Asia has important mineral resources, notably the oil and natural-gas deposits of the Arab states. Area: 44 391 162 sq km (17 139 445 sq mi). Population (1998 est): 3 589 233 000.

Asia Minor (*or* **Anatolia**) The westernmost part of Asia between the Black Sea and the Mediterranean Sea approximating to present-day Turkey. For much of the second millennium BC, Asia Minor was the centre of the *Hittite empire. After the Hittites' collapse (12th century BC) central and W Asia Minor were dominated by *Phrygia, which reached its zenith in the 8th century, when the Assyrian Empire conquered SE Asia Minor. Phrygia fell to *Lydia in the 6th century but in 546 Cyrus the Great established Achaemenian control over Asia Minor. In 333 it was conquered by Alexander the Great and after his death, during the *Hellenistic age, the S was contested by the *Seleucids and the Macedonian rulers of Egypt. Asia Minor came under Roman control in the 2nd and 1st centuries BC, forming part of the *Roman Empire and then the Eastern Roman (subsequently Byzantine) Empire. Conquered by the Seljuq Turks in the 11th century AD and overrun by the Mongols in the 13th, Asia Minor was incorporated in the Ottoman Empire during the 14th and 15th centuries.

Asimov, Isaac (1920–92) US science fiction writer and biochemist, born in Russia. His many books include the *Foundation Trilogy* (1951–53; sequel 1982) and collections of short stories, notably *I, Robot* (1950), *Nightfall* (1969), and *The Edge of Tomorrow* (1986). He also wrote books popularizing scientific topics.

Asmara (*or* **Asmera**) 15 20N 38 49E The capital of Eritrea, in the central highlands. The population still includes many Italians, Eritrea having been an Italian colony from 1890 until Allied occupation (1941). Industries include meat processing, distilling, and clothes manufacture. Population (1995 est): 431 000.

Asoka (died c. 232 BC) Indian king of the Maurya dynasty, who ruled over almost all of India (c. 270–c. 272 BC). A devoted Buddhist, he advocated tolerance and non-violence (**ahimsa**).

asp An aggressive European *viper, *Vipera aspis*, that lives in dry habitats. About 60 cm long, it is grey-brown to coppery brown with dark bars or zigzags, grey, yellowish, or blackish underparts, and a yellow patch under the tail tip. The snout is upturned into a small spike. The asp that killed Cleopatra was probably the Egyptian cobra (*Naja haje*).

Asparagus A genus of herbaceous plants (about 300 species), with creeping underground stems (rhizomes), found throughout the Old World. *A. officinalis* is cultivated in temperate and subtropical regions for its young edible shoots, which are considered a delicacy. Several African species are ornamental: *A. plumosus*, known as **asparagus fern**, produces attractive feathery sprays of branchlets. Family: *Liliaceae*.

aspen One of several *poplar trees having slender flattened leafstalks, so that the leaves tremble in the faintest breeze. The European aspen (*Populus tremula*), which grows to a height of 25 m has rounded toothed leaves. Its soft white wood is used for matches and paper pulp.

Asperger's syndrome A mild form of *autism characterized by a lack of empathy with others, stilted and pedantic speech, and an obsessive preoccupation with detail and specialized subjects. Sufferers are often highly intelligent. Named after Austrian paediatrician Hans Asperger (1906–80).

Aspergillus A genus of fungi, including many common moulds, such as *A. flavus*, which infects peanuts and produces the poison aflatoxin.

asphalt A black highly viscous or solid hydrocarbon compound, used in road construction and the manufacture of roofing materials. It is obtained from the distillation of certain crude oils and from surface deposits (asphalt lakes), which occur naturally after the lighter fractions of a crude oil reservoir have evaporated.

asphodel A white- or yellow-flowered lily-like plant of the mostly Mediterranean genera *Asphodelus* and *Asphodeline*. In Greek mythology, the asphodel said to grow in the Elysian fields was *Asphodeline lutea*. The asphodel of the early English and French poets was probably the daffodil. The bog asphodel (*Narthecium ossifragum*), of NW Europe, grows to a height of 30 cm in swampy regions. Family: *Liliaceae*.

Aspidistra A genus of herbaceous plants (8 species) native to E Asia. *A. elatior* is commonly grown as a hardy pot plant for its long ornamental leaves. It may produce purple bell-shaped flowers. Family: *Liliaceae*.

aspirin Acetylsalicylic acid: a drug widely used to treat mild pain, such as headache and toothache. It also relieves inflammation and is therefore helpful in the treatment of rheumatoid arthritis, and it reduces fever and helps to prevent coronary thrombosis and strokes. In some people aspirin may cause bleeding from the stomach and it is no longer used for children under 12. *See also* ANALGESICS.

Asquith, Herbert Henry, 1st Earl of Oxford and (1852–1928) British statesman and Liberal prime minister (1908–16). Asquith's government introduced important social reforms, including noncontributory old-age pensions (1908 budget) and the National Insurance Act (1911); it ended the veto power of the House of Lords with the 1911 Parliament Act. After the outbreak of World War I Asquith headed a Liberal-Conservative coalition government (1915–16). He remained leader of the Liberal Party until 1926.

ass A small fast-running mammal belonging to the genus *Equus* (horses), native to Africa and Asia. Asses are about 200 cm long, weighing up to 250 kg, and have characteristically long ears. The Asiatic wild ass (*E. hemionus*) has a grey or tan hide and a dark stripe along the back. The African wild ass (*E. asinus*) is the ancestor of the domestic donkey. *See also* MULE.

Assad, Hafiz al- (1928–2000) Syrian statesman; president (1971–2000). In 1966, following the coup in Syria by the radical Ba'athists, he became minister of defence. In 1970 he led a coup by the military wing of the Ba'ath party and was elected president the following year. In foreign affairs he remained hostile to Israel and the West until the early 1990s, from which point he began to mend relations. He was succeeded by his son, **Bashar al-Assad** (1965–).

Assam A state in NE India, mostly in the Brahmaputra Valley beyond Bangladesh. High rainfall supports tea, Assam's economic mainstay. Rice, jute, sugar cane, and cotton are also grown. Assam produces half of India's oil, as well as coal. *History*: a flourishing region by 1000 BC, Assam received later migrants from China and Burma. Burmese invasions led Britain to assume control (1826). In World War II Assam played a strategic role in the Allied advance into Burma. In recent years the region has been troubled by ethnic unrest. Area: 78 523 sq km (30 310 sq mi). Population (2001 est): 26 638 407. Capital: Dispur.

Assassins (Arabic: hashish eaters) A sect of the Ismaili. In Persia and Syria in the 12th and 13th centuries they were notorious for their practice of stabbing opponents, especially Muslims. It was commonly believed that the stabbings were carried out while they were under the influence of hashish, hence their name.

Assisi 43 04N 12 37E A town in central Italy, in Umbria. It is the birthplace of St *Francis of Assisi, who founded the Franciscan Order in 1209, and is the site of a Franciscan convent, which has two gothic churches containing frescoes by Giotto. Population (1990): 24 790.

Association football *See* FOOTBALL.

Association of South-East Asian Nations (ASEAN) An international organization, founded in 1967, to assist the development of its member states (now Brunei, Indonesia, Laos, Malaysia, Myanmar (Burma), the Philippines, Singapore, Thailand, and Vietnam). It aims to eliminate trade barriers, promote cultural exchanges, facilitate communications, and improve technology, commerce, and industry.

associative law The mathematical rule, obeyed by addition and multiplication in ordinary *arithmetic, that the order in which successive identical operations are performed does not affect the result: for addition $a + (b + c) = (a + b) + c$; for multiplication $a(bc) = (ab)c$.

assurance A form of insurance against an event that is certain to occur, e.g. death. The main types are **term assurance**, which only pays out if death occurs within a stipulated period, such as during a particular business trip; **whole-life assurance**, which pays out on the death of the assured, whenever it occurs; **endowment assurance**, which pays out either on the death of the assured, whenever it occurs, or after a fixed period (e.g. on the assured's 65th birthday). *See also* ANNUITY.

Assyrian Empire An ancient kingdom on the Upper Tigris (now N Iraq), where the Assyrians (named after their god Ashur) settled in about 2500 BC, forming a dependency of Babylon. Ashur-uballit I (c. 1365–c. 1330) laid the foundations of the Empire, which was extended by Tiglath-pileser I (1120–1074), who conquered the city of Babylon. A new era of aggressive expansion was initiated by Ashurnasirpal II (883–859). The Assyrian domain was extended to Syria and Palestine under Shalmaneser III (858–824) and Assyrian ascendancy reached its zenith under Tiglath-pileser III (745–727). *Nineveh, the capital, fell to Media and Babylon in 612.

Astaire, Fred (Frederick Austerlitz; 1899–1987) US dancer and film star. He began his career as a music-hall dancer. His best-known films are the 1930s musicals in which he partnered Ginger Rogers. These include *Top Hat* (1935), *Follow the Fleet* (1936), and *Shall We Dance* (1937). His later costars included Judy Garland, Leslie Caron, and Audrey Hepburn.

Astana (name until 1961 and 1994–98: Akmola; name 1961–94: Tselinograd) 51 10N 71 25E A city in N Kazakhstan; it replaced Alma Ata as the capital of Kazakhstan in 1997. Population (1999 est): 313 000.

Astarte The Phoenician goddess of love and fertility, equivalent to the Babylonian Ishtar and sometimes regarded as the counterpart of Aphrodite. She was associated with the moon and often represented by a crescent.

astatine (At) A short-lived radioactive *halogen. Its longest-lived isotope, At–210, has a half-life of 8.1 hours. Small amounts exist in nature as a result of uranium and thorium decay. At no 85; at wt (210); mp 302°C; bp 337°C.

Aster A genus of perennial herbaceous plants (about 500 species), many of which are native to N temperate regions and are grown as the garden plants known as Michaelmas daisies. 60–100 cm tall, they have flowers with blue, red, or white rays and a central yellow disc. *A. amellus* and *A. aeris* are common ornamental species. Family: *Compositae*.

asteroid *See* MINOR PLANET.

asthma A disorder in which breathlessness and wheezing are aggravated by certain stimuli, which cause the bronchi to become constricted. Bronchial asthma may be an allergic reaction (*see* ALLERGY), it may occur secondarily to respiratory infection, or it may be brought on by exertion, certain drugs, or strong emotion. The most common treatment is by means of bronchodilator drugs, usually in the form of aerosol inhalers; severe attacks require corticosteroid inhalers. Cardiac asthma is associated with some forms of heart disease and requires a different treatment.

astigmatism A form of *aberration that can occur in mirrors and lenses (including the eye). It results when the curvature is different in two mutually perpendicular planes; rays in one plane may then be in focus while rays in the other are out of focus. It is corrected in the eye by the use of cylindrical lenses.

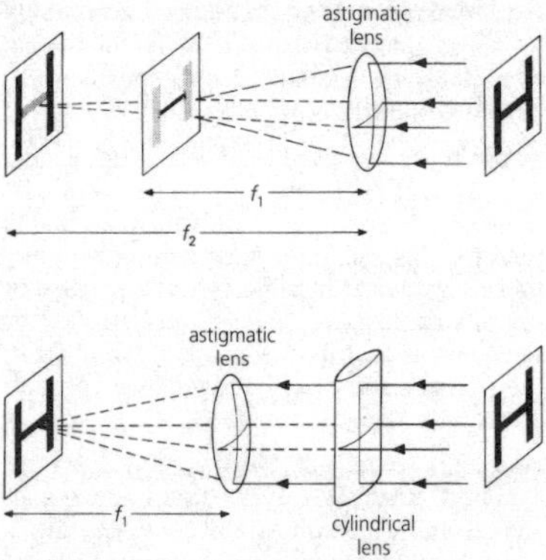

astigmatism. An astigmatic lens cannot focus vertical and horizontal lines at the same time. Here the vertical focal length f_1 is shorter than the horizontal focal length f_2. In the human eye this would be corrected by spectacles with cylindrical lenses, reducing the overall focal length in the horizontal plane only, so that both vertical and horizontal lines are in sharp focus at distance f_1.

Astor, Nancy Witcher, Viscountess (1879–1964) US-born British politician, the first woman MP to sit in the House of Commons (1919–45). She championed the causes of women's rights and education, representing the constituency that was formerly that of her husband **Waldorf, 2nd Viscount Astor** (1879–1952). An MP from 1910 to 1919, Astor was proprietor (1919–45) of the *Observer* newspaper.

Astrakhan 46 22N 48 04E A port in SE Russia, on the River Volga. The city was an important trading centre, declining after the Revolution. Astrakhan fur, from the Karakul lamb of central Asia, was first brought to Russia by Astrakhan traders. More than half the population is employed in fishing or allied occupations. Population (1999 est): 488 000.

astrolabe An instrument used in navigation and astronomy, invented in about 200 BC. It was replaced in the 18th century by the *sextant. It consists of a disc calibrated round its circumference in degrees. It was fitted with a sighting pointer (alidade), the angle of which, when aligned with the sun or a prominent star, enabled time and latitude and longitude to be calculated.

astrology The study of the positions of the heavenly bodies in relation to their presumed influence upon human affairs. Astrology originated in *Babylonia and then passed to Greece, India, China, and the Islamic lands. In medieval Europe astrologers had a respected role in public and personal life. Astrology is based upon an elaborate system of hypothetical relationships: each "house" (*see* ZODIAC), for instance, imparts a particular character to those born under its influence and the sun, moon, and principal planets in various positions predispose people to good or ill. The two branches of astrology are "natural" (concerned mainly with observations and theory) and "judicial" (foretelling events by means of a horoscope). The subject has no scientific basis. *See also* BIRTHSTONE.

astronomer royal An eminent British astronomer appointed by the sovereign on the advice of the prime minister. Until 1971 the astronomer royal was also head of the Royal Observatory (formerly at Greenwich, then at Herstmonceux, and at Cambridge from 1990). The first holder was John Flamsteed, appointed in 1675 when the Observatory was founded. The present holder is Sir Martin Rees.

astronomical unit (AU) A unit of length equal to the mean distance between the earth and the sun (1.495×10^{11} metres, 92.9×10^{6} miles).

astronomy The study of celestial bodies. One of the most ancient of the sciences, naked-eye astronomy flourished in China, Babylonia, Egypt, and classical Greece (*see* ARISTARCHUS OF SAMOS; HIPPARCHUS; PTOLEMAIC SYSTEM). After the decline of ancient Greek culture, interest in astronomy was the preserve of the Arabs for many centuries. European interest in the heavens, transmitted from the Arabs through Spain, reawakened in the 16th century with the work of *Copernicus and Tycho *Brahe, who were able to separate the science of astronomy from astrological pseudoscience. But it was not until 1609 that Galileo's refracting *telescope enabled the sky to be investigated in any detail; in 1671 Newton devised the more effective reflecting telescope. These devices provided the means for the development of astrometry and *celestial mechanics. In the 19th century, the use of spectroscopy (*see* SPECTRUM) provided the basis for the new sciences of *astrophysics and astrochemistry.

Until the 1930s all observations of the heavens were made by observing the light that passed through the atmosphere. Jansky's discovery (1932) that radio waves are emitted by celestial bodies marked the beginnings of *radio astronomy.

The advent of high-altitude balloons and rockets and then artificial satellites orbiting above the atmosphere has enabled the radiation from space that is absorbed by the atmosphere—gamma rays, X-rays, ultraviolet, and most wavelengths of infrared radiation—to provide information, for example, on the birth of stars and the more violent cosmic phenomena. In addition planetary probes and spacecraft have greatly increased our knowledge of many members of the solar system.

astrophysics The study of the physical and chemical processes and characteristics associated with celestial objects. It is based on theories developed in astronomy, physics, and chemistry and on observations of the radiation emitted by the objects. Originally only studies at optical and then at radio and infrared wavelengths were made, but with the recent advent of rockets and artificial satellites, sources of X-rays, gamma rays, and ultraviolet radiation can also be observed. *See also* COSMOLOGY.

Asunción 25 15S 57 40W The capital of Paraguay, an important port in the S on the River Paraguay. Founded in 1536, it was for a time the centre of the Spanish settlements in the area. The National University was founded in 1890 and the Catholic University in 1960. Industries include flour milling, food processing, and textiles. Population (1992): 502 426.

Aswan (*or* **Assuan**; Greek name: Syene) 24 05N 32 56E A city in S Egypt, on the River Nile. Some ruins of the ancient city of Syene remain. Nearby quarries supplied granite for many Egyptian monuments. The **Aswan High Dam** and earlier **Aswan Dam** are also nearby and have stimulated growth within the city. The High Dam was begun in 1960 and financed by the Soviet Union; it was completed in 1970. It is about 5 km (3 mi) long and 100 m (328 ft) high; its reservoir, **Lake Nasser**, extends for about 560 km (350 mi) behind the dam. Since its construction the famous annual Nile floods have been controlled and water is available for irrigation and for hydroelectric power. Ancient Nubian monuments (notably the *Abu Simbel and Philae temples) that were threatened with permanent flooding were moved to new sites. About 7 km (4 mi) downstream is the earlier Aswan Dam (completed 1902); 2 km (1.2 mi) long and 54 m (177 ft) high, this provides irrigation water. Population (1996): 219 017.

asymptote A straight line that a two-dimensional curve approaches but never meets as the curve is extended infinitely.

Asyut (*or* **Assiut**; ancient name: Lycopolis) 27 14N 31 07S The largest city in Upper Egypt, on the River Nile. It is an important commercial centre and is renowned for its handicrafts and its textile industries. Below the city the Asyut barrage provides water for irrigation. It has a university (1957). Population (1996): 343 498.

Atacama Desert (Spanish name: Desierto de Atacama) A cool arid area in N central Chile, extending for about 1100 km (700 mi) S from the Peruvian border. It consists chiefly of a series of salt basins and is one of the driest areas in the world. There are valuable deposits of copper and it is a major source of nitrates. Area: about 80 290 sq km (31 000 sq mi).

Atalanta A swift-footed huntress of Greek mythology. Hippomenes (or Meilanion), on her promise to marry any man who could outrun her, raced with her. Furnished with three of the Hesperides' golden apples by *Aphrodite, which he dropped to distract her, he won the race and married her.

Atatürk, Kemal (Mustafa Kemal; 1881–1938) Turkish statesman, the founder of modern Turkey; president (1923–38). Born in Salonika, he entered the army and distinguished himself in World War I. After the war he opposed the humiliating Treaty of *Versailles and as president of the provisional government organized the defeat of the Greek invasion of Asia Minor (1920). In 1922 the Ottoman sultan was deposed and Kemal became the first president of Turkey. From then until his death he worked to make Turkey a modern secular state. He took the surname Atatürk (Father of the Turks) in 1934.

ataxia Loss of muscular coordination, often caused by disease of the part of the brain (the cerebellum) that controls movement. Ataxia may accompany severe vitamin B_{12} and folic acid deficiencies or follow a brain haemorrhage.

Athanasian Creed A Christian profession of faith traditionally attributed to St Athanasius (296–373 AD) but probably dating from the 5th century. Its central statements concern the doctrines of the *Trinity and of the *Incarnation. Once popular in the Western Churches, it is now little used.

atheism The denial of the existence of God (or gods). Historically atheism has taken many different forms. In theocratic societies charges of atheism were frequently made against individuals or groups suspected of antisocial behaviour or of dissent from the prevailing orthodoxy. Philosophical materialists, such as Hobbes, were also attacked as atheists but the spread of rationalism in the 18th century created a climate sympathetic to atheism. In the 19th century, scientific advances challenged the old arguments for the existence of God, making atheism respectable. Atheists now hold either that the concept of God, being untestable, is meaningless (*see* LOGICAL POSITIVISM) or that all we know by scientific means about the universe suggests that God is a false notion (*see* HUMANISM). *Compare* AGNOSTICISM.

Athelstan (d. 939) King of England (925–39), succeeding his father Edward the Elder; he was crowned King of Mercia in 924. He defeated a Scottish invasion force in 937 and is also known for six extant legal codes.

Athena (*or* **Pallas Athena**) The virgin Greek goddess of war and of wisdom, the protectress of Athens which is named after her. Born from the head of Zeus, fully armed with a javelin, she was his favourite child. In the Trojan War she constantly aided the Greeks. She also helped Heracles in his labours and guided Perseus on his expedition against the Gorgons. She is identified with the Roman *Minerva.

Athens (Modern Greek name: Athínai) 37 59N 23 42E The capital of Greece, situated on a plain in the SE of the country. It is the administrative, cultural, and economic centre of the country and adjoins its port and industrial sector, *Piraeus. Athens combines the ancient and the modern, with only one or two small Byzantine and neo-Byzantine churches surviving to testify to the period between Roman times and the early 19th century. The remains of ancient Athens found on the Acropolis include the *Parthenon, the Ionic Erechtheum, the Propylaea (a gateway), and the tiny temple of Athena Nike. To the NW, the recently restored Agora (market), contains the Theseum (5th century BC), probably the best-preserved ancient temple. To the N and E lies modern Athens. *History*: there is evidence of settlements dating back to the 3rd millennium BC. Athens probably enjoyed its first rise to fame under Pisistratus and his sons in the 6th century BC. Around 506 Cleisthenes established a democracy for the free men of Athens. During the following century it became the leading Greek city state and defeated the Persians with the aid of its powerful navy (*see* GREEK-PERSIAN WARS). The Long Walls, connecting the city to Piraeus, and the Parthenon date from this period. Under *Pericles, it reached a peak of intellectual brilliance with the philosophy of Socrates and the drama of Aeschylus, Sophocles, and Euripides. Defeated by Sparta in the *Peloponnesian War (431–404 BC), it recovered slowly, regaining its intellectual supremacy with such figures as Plato, Aristotle, and Aristophanes. Defeated by Philip of Macedon in 338 BC, it came under the rule of Rome in the 2nd century BC. Owing to the influence of Hellenic culture on the Romans it continued to prosper and, despite being overrun by Germanic tribes in the 4th century AD, maintained its academic standing until the closure of the schools of philosophy by Justinian in 529. The city fell to the Crusaders in 1204 and was under Turkish occupation from 1456 until 1833, when it became the capital of the newly independent kingdom of Greece. Population (1991): 748 110.

atherosclerosis (*or* **atheroma**) Patchy thickening of the lining of arteries caused by the deposition of fatty material and fibrous tissue. This tends to obstruct the blood flow and predisposes to *thrombosis, which may lead to a heart attack or a stroke. In the Western world atherosclerosis is common in adults: its cause is believed to be associated with a diet high in animal fats (*see* CHOLESTEROL), cigarette smoking, and obesity. *See also* CORONARY HEART DISEASE.

athletics Sports that involve running, walking, throwing, and jumping competitions. They are divided into track and field events. At international level the track events include races over 100 m, 200 m, 400 m, 800 m, 1500 m, 5000 m, and 10 000 m; the 110 m and 400 m hurdles (*see* HURDLING); the 4 × 100 and 4 × 400 m relay races; the 3000 m steeplechase; the *marathon; and the 20 km walk (*see* WALKING). The standard field events are *high jump, *long jump, *triple jump, *pole vault, *shot put, *discus throw, *hammer throw, and *javelin throw. In addition there are the *decathlon (for men), the *pentathlon or *heptathlon (for women), and the modern pentathlon. The governing body is the International Amateur Athletic Federation.

Athos, Mount 1. 40 10N 24 19E A mountain in NE Greece, at the end of Aktí, the easternmost promontory of Chalcidice. Height: 2033 m (6670 ft). **2.** An autonomous Greek Orthodox monastic republic occupying the mountain. Area: 80 sq km (31 sq mi). Population (1991): 1557.

Atlanta 33 45N 84 23W A city in the USA, the capital of Georgia, situated at the foot of the Appalachian Mountains. Founded in 1837 and partly destroyed by Gen Sherman in 1864, it is now the industrial, administrative, transportation, and cultural centre of the SE USA. Population (2000): 416 474.

Atlantic, Battle of the *See* WORLD WAR II.

Atlantic Charter (1941) A declaration made by Franklin D. Roosevelt and Winston Churchill stating common national policies. These included freedom of choice of government, improved economic and social conditions, freedom of the seas, and the total abolition of Nazism.

Atlantic Ocean The world's second largest ocean, extending between Antarctica, America, Europe, and Africa. Its major currents include the *Gulf Stream crossing it W–E. Its floor is rich in minerals, oil and gas now being exploited. The Mid-Atlantic Ridge rises above sea level as islands, such as the Azores. The youngest ocean, the Atlantic was formed when the continents now surrounding it split apart 200 million years ago.

Atlantis In Greek legend, a large island civilization in the Atlantic beyond the Pillars of Hercules (Straits of Gibraltar), which, according to Plato's dialogues the *Timaeus* and *Critias*, was destroyed by earthquake. The story, transmitted to the Greeks by the Egyptians, may refer to a cataclysmic volcanic eruption (c. 1450 BC) on the island of Thera in the Cyclades N of Crete.

Atlas In Greek mythology, the brother of Prometheus and son of the Titan Iapetus and the nymph Clymene. As a punishment for his part in the revolt of the Titans against the Olympians he was forced to hold up the pillars separating heaven from earth. From the 16th century this was depicted in the frontispieces of books of maps, which thus came to be called atlases.

Atlas Mountains A mountain system in NW Africa, extending generally NE from the Atlantic coast of Morocco to Tunisia. It consists of several mountain chains and plateaus and rises to 4165 m (13 664 ft) at Mount Toubkal in the Moroccan Great Atlas range.

atman (Sanskrit: breath, soul) A fundamental concept of Hinduism, signifying the individual soul or the eternal essential self. When the body dies the *atman* is continuously reincarnated until final spiritual release is achieved. In the later *Upanishads, and in the Hindu philosophical schools of Samkhya and orthodox Vedanta, the function of *atman* and its relation to *Brahman is the central issue.

atmosphere (meteorology) The gaseous envelope surrounding the earth or any other celestial body. The earth's atmosphere is composed of nitrogen (78.08%), oxygen (20.95%), argon (0.93%), and carbon dioxide (0.03%), together with small proportions of other gases and variable amounts of water vapour. In the lowest layer of the earth's atmosphere, the **troposphere**, air temperature decreases as height increases. The thickness of this layer varies from about 7 km (4.5 mi) to about 16 km (9.9 mi) at the equator. It is here that most meteorological phenomena occur. In the **stratosphere**, which goes up to about 50 km (31 mi), temperature is fairly constant because the sun's radiation counteracts the effect of decreasing density. Above this is the *ionosphere. The outermost layer, from about 400 km (248 mi), is called the **exosphere**. From 100 km (62 mi) upwards the oxygen dissociates into atoms. There is little nitrogen above 150 km (93 mi). The atmosphere protects the earth from excessive radiation and cosmic particles and is important in maintaining the heat balance of the earth. *See also* OZONE.

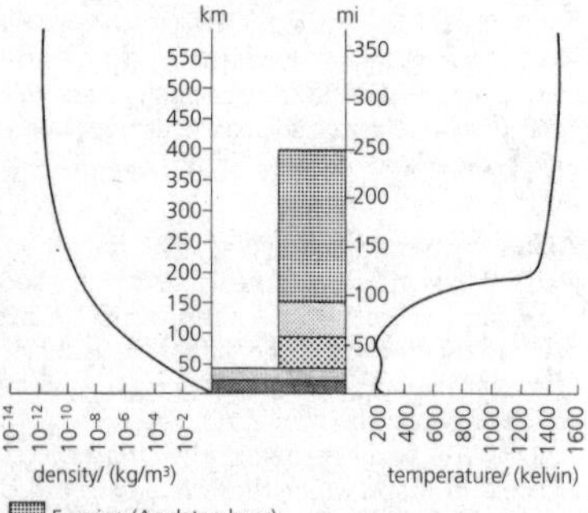

atmosphere. The density of the atmosphere falls off sharply with height above the earth's surface. The more complicated temperature variation is shown in the graph, which also illustrates the regions of the ionosphere.

atmosphere (unit) A unit of pressure equal to 101 325 pascals or 760 mm of mercury.

atmospheric pollution The release into the atmosphere of gases, droplets of liquid, or solid particles that have an undesirable effect on people, vegetation, buildings, etc. The main sources of pollution are vehicle and aircraft emissions, power stations, and other industrial plants. The gaseous pollutants include the oxides of carbon (*see* GREENHOUSE EFFECT), sulphur, and nitrogen (*see* ACID RAIN). The liquid pollutants include droplets of diesel oil and contaminated water spray, while carbon particles, soot, and coal dust are the most common solid pollutants. Natural causes of pollutions include volcanoes, forest fires, and dust storms.

atmospheric pressure The pressure exerted by the atmosphere. It decreases with altitude and, at ground level, varies around 760 millimetres of mercury, 101 325 pascals, or 1013.25 millibars.

atom *See* ATOMIC THEORY.

atomic bomb *See* NUCLEAR WEAPONS.

atomic clock A highly accurate clock based on the frequency at which certain atoms or molecules vibrate between two states. For example, the nitrogen atom in the ammonia molecule vibrates through the plane of the three hydrogen atoms and back again with a frequency of 23 870 hertz. In the ammonia clock, a quartz-crystal oscillator feeds energy into ammonia gas at this frequency. The ammonia only absorbs energy at this frequency, enabling a feedback circuit to control the frequency of the oscillator. The caesium clock depends on the energy difference between states of the caesium nucleus in a magnetic field.

atomic energy *See* NUCLEAR ENERGY.

Atomic Energy Authority A UK body established in 1954 to research into and develop nuclear energy. Its principal research establishments are situated at Harwell and Culham, both in Oxfordshire.

atomic force microscope (**AFM**) A high-resolution microscope useful in magnifying nonconducting samples, such as biochemical molecules. It consists of a small diamond probe attached to an arm that slowly scans the specimen. The tracking force between the diamond tip and the specimen's surface is monitored and the height of the probe is adjusted to keep the force constant. A computer-generated contour map of the surface can thus be generated, which identifies the individual atoms of the specimen.

atomic mass unit (amu) A unit of mass equal to one-twelfth of the mass of an atom of carbon-12 ($1.660\,33 \times 10^{-27}$ kg). Relative atomic masses (atomic weights) are based on this unit. The unit is also called the dalton (after John Dalton).

atomic number (Z) The number of protons in a nucleus of an atom. It determines the position of the element in the *periodic table and, in a neutral atom, is equal to the number of electrons surrounding the nucleus. It is also known as proton number.

atomic theory The theory that an atom is the smallest particle of an element that can take part in a chemical reaction. *Democritus is credited with first conceiving the idea, which was, however, vigorously attacked by *Aristotle. The concept fell from favour until the early 19th century, when John *Dalton used it to explain how elements combine in simple proportions. The structure of the atom was first investigated by Lord *Rutherford, who discovered that it consisted of a heavy positively charged core (the *nucleus) surrounded by *electrons. Niels Bohr elaborated on this model (the Bohr atom) but the modern concept of the atom was not finally elucidated until the advent of Schrödinger's *wave mechanics.

Almost all of the atom's mass is concentrated in the nucleus, which consists of positively charged *protons and neutral *neutrons of almost equal mass (the mass of the electron is only 1/1836 that of the proton). The number of electrons in a neutral atom is equal to the number of protons in the nucleus, as the charge on the proton is equal but opposite to that of the electron. The electrons can be thought of as existing in a series of shells around the nucleus, each shell corresponding to a particular energy level. The chemical behaviour of an atom is largely determined by the number of electrons in its outermost shell, as atoms are most stable when they have no partly filled shells, a state often achieved by chemical combination. See illustration on p. 80. *See also* PARTICLE PHYSICS; CHEMICAL BOND.

atonality The use in music of all 12 notes of the scale in such a way as to avoid *tonality. Atonality arose from the increasing chromaticism of the music of the late 19th century. *See also* SERIALISM.

ATP (adenosine triphosphate) An energy-rich compound (a nucleotide) with an important role in the metabolism of living organisms. On its formation from ADP (adenosine diphosphate) in the mitochondria of cells, ATP incorporates a large amount of energy that, on release, is used by cells to manufacture proteins, carbohydrates, etc., and to provide energy for muscle contraction and other dynamic processes.

Atreus In Greek mythology, King of Mycenae, the son of Pelops and father of Agamemnon and Menelaus. His house was cursed as a result of a feud between him and his brother Thyestes over the throne of Mycenae. After Thyestes had seduced his wife, Atreus killed Thyestes' sons and served them at a feast. Another son of Thyestes, Aegisthus, later killed Atreus.

atrium 1. Originally part of a Roman house, a central, partly covered court, frequently colonnaded, which often contained the shrine to the household god. Around it were the entrances to the main rooms. Later it became the main reception room of the house. **2.** An open area or courtyard in front of early Christian churches. **3.** A central hall in a large building, such as a hotel, that extends to several storeys and is often covered by a glass roof.

atropine An alkaloid, extracted from deadly nightshade, that acts on certain nerves of the autonomic nervous system. It is used during anaesthesia to decrease lung secretions, which lowers the risk of postoperative chest infections, and to treat asthma, diarrhoea, colic, peptic ulcers, and parkinsonism. It also dilates the pupil and speeds up the heart rate.

Attenborough, Richard, Baron (1923–) British film actor, director, and producer. A versatile character actor, he has appeared in such films as *Brighton Rock* (1947), *10 Rillington Place* (1971), and *Jurassic Park* (1993). As director, his films include *A Bridge Too Far* (1977), *Gandhi* (1982), *Cry Freedom* (1987), *Shadowlands* (1994), and *In Love and War* (1996). His brother **Sir David Attenborough** (1926–) is a naturalist and broadcaster, whose television series include *Life on Earth* (1978), *The Living Planet* (1983), *Trials of Life* (1990), *The Life of Birds* (1998), and *The Life of Mammals* (2003).

attention deficit disorder (*or* **hyperactivity disorder**) A psychiatric disorder of young children, associated with learning difficulties, hyperactivity, and disruptive behaviour. It occurs most frequently in epileptic, brain-damaged, or intellectually impaired children. The condition is managed by family

There is no simple way to illustrate an atom:

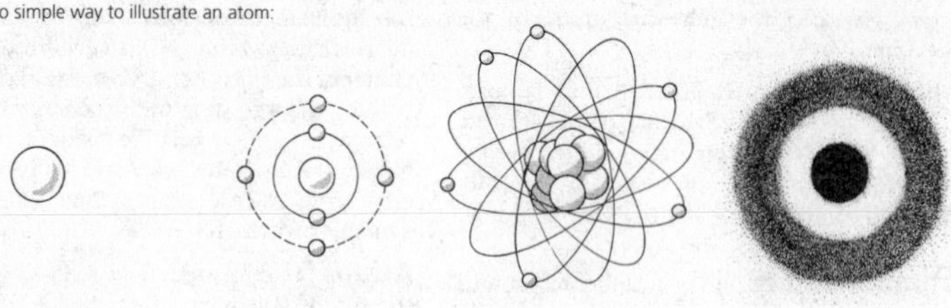

by the 19th century it was regarded as a minute solid billiard ball;

with the work of Rutherford between 1906 and 1914 and Bohr in 1913 it was depicted as a miniature solar system with a central nucleus and orbiting electron;

Sommerfeld's refinements of quantum theory in 1916 led to a model with precessing elliptical orbits and spinning electrons;

by 1926 Schrödinger's wave mechanics had been published, based on de Broglie's dual wave–particle concept of electrons. The atom is now regarded as a nucleus surrounded by a "haze" of probabilities that electrons will occur in certain positions.

The main characteristic of an atom, as the smallest particle of matter, is not what our models of it look like but the way it absorbs and emits energy.

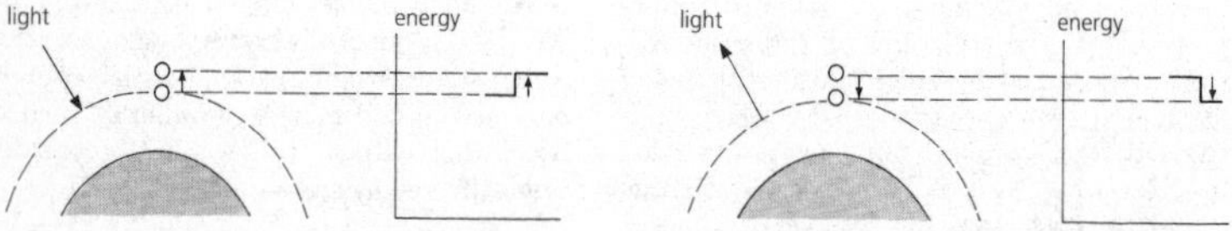

When an atom absorbs energy (e.g. when light of the right wavelength falls on it) its electrons jump to a higher energy level.

When these electrons fall back to their original (ground) state they emit energy (as light, ultraviolet, etc.).

All matter and therefore all atoms, according to modern physics, consists of two kinds of particles: leptons and quarks. Electrons are leptons; the particles of the nucleus (protons and neutrons) are each made up of different arrangements of three quarks.

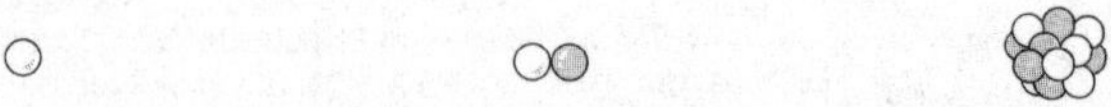

The simplest atomic nucleus is the hydrogen nucleus consisting of one proton.

An isotope of hydrogen, deuterium, has a nucleus consisting of one proton and one neutron.

All other nuclei consist of arrangements of protons and neutrons. The carbon nucleus consists of six protons and six neutrons.

atomic theory

therapy and such drugs as Dexedrine (dexamphetamine) and Ritalin (methylphenidate).

Attica A region of ancient E central Greece. According to Greek legend the 12 towns of Attica were united by Theseus into a single state, which was dominated by Athens by the 5th century BC.

Attila (c. 406–53) King of the Huns (434–53), known as the Scourge of God. After murdering his brother and coruler, Bleda, he extended his possessions in central Europe and attacked (441–43) the eastern frontier of the Roman Empire. In 451 he invaded Gaul and suffered his only defeat, at the battle of the Catalaunian Plains. His campaigns in Italy (452) caused much destruction. The pope paid him to spare Rome and Attila died shortly afterwards.

Attlee, Clement (Richard), 1st Earl (1883–1967) British statesman; Labour prime minister (1945–51). A barrister by profession, he was elected MP for Limehouse in 1922, was leader of the Labour Party (1935–55), and deputy prime minister of the wartime coalition government (1942–45). As the first postwar prime minister he introduced the welfare state, nationalized major industries, and gave independence to India.

attorney general The chief law officer of the Crown in England and Wales and its representative in the courts. He is legal adviser to the government and the House of Commons, of which he is always a member and to which he is answerable, and is head of the English bar. He advises on the drafting of Acts of Parliament. With his subordinate, the director of public prosecutions, he prosecutes crimes in the sovereign's name. *See* CROWN PROSECUTION SERVICE.

Atwood, Margaret (1939–) Canadian novelist, poet, and short-story writer. Her novels include *The Handmaid's Tale* (1986), *The Robber Bride* (1993), *The Blind Assassin* (2000), and *Oryx and Crake* (2003).

aubergine A spiny herbaceous plant, *Solanum melongena*, native to S Asia and also known as eggplant. It is commonly grown in warmer regions for its fruit, a large white, yellow, or purple berry that is eaten as a vegetable. The plant grows to a height of 60–100 cm. Family: *Solanaceae*.

Aubrey, John (1626–97) English antiquary and biographer. He is best known for his *Lives of Eminent Men* (1813) and *Brief Lives* (1898), which were first published in bowdlerized editions long after his death. He was also an active archaeologist.

Aubrietia (*or* **Aubrieta**) A genus of trailing herbaceous perennial flowering plants (about 15 species), native to mountainous areas of E Europe and W Asia. *A. deltoidea* is commonly grown in rock gardens, bearing small purple, red, or pink flowers. Family: *Cruciferae*.

Auckland 36 55S 174 47E The largest city and port in New Zealand, on North Island. Founded in 1840, it was the capital of New Zealand until 1865. The University of Auckland was established in 1882 and there are two cathedrals (Roman Catholic and Anglican). The city is connected with the mainly residential North Shore by the Auckland Harbour Bridge (1959). Auckland is a major industrial centre with engineering, food processing, shipbuilding, and chemical industries. Population (1996 est): 353 670.

Auden, W(ystan) H(ugh) (1907–73) British poet. His early volumes, beginning with *Poems* (1930) and *Look, Stranger!* (1936), established him as a leading left-wing poet of the 1930s. He also wrote verse dramas in collaboration with Christopher *Isherwood, with whom he went to the USA in 1939. He became a US citizen in 1946, returning to England while he was professor of poetry at Oxford (1956–61). He wrote several opera libretti, notably for Stravinsky's *The Rake's Progress* (1951).

audio frequency A frequency in the range 20 to 20 000 hertz, i.e. the range of frequencies to which the human ear is sensitive.

Aughrim, Battle of (12 July 1691) The final defeat of the main army of the former King James II of England by the army of William III in Ireland. It was the most disastrous battle in Irish history, with 7000 Jacobite dead. It is still celebrated, together with the battle of the *Boyne, by Ulster Unionists on its anniversary (*see also* ORANGE ORDER).

Augsburg 48 21N 10 54E A city in S Germany, in Bavaria at the confluence of the Rivers Wertach and Lech. It is a major industrial centre; its manufactures include textiles, chemicals, cars, aircraft, and printing machinery. Many of its historic buildings, including the 10th-century cathedral, survived the bombardment of World War II. *History*: founded by the Romans in 15 BC, it became an important banking and commercial centre in the 15th and 16th centuries. An imperial free city from 1276, it was the seat of the notable diets of 1530 (*see* AUGSBURG CONFESSION) and 1555, which issued the religious compromise establishing the coexistence of Catholicism and Lutheranism, known as the **Peace of Augsburg**. Population (1999 est): 254 400.

Augsburg Confession The main and distinctive confession of faith of the Lutheran Churches. Drawn up in its original form by Melancthon and approved by Luther, it was presented to the imperial diet that Emperor Charles V had summoned at Augsburg in 1530 to judge Luther's controversial preaching.

Augustine of Canterbury, St (died c. 604) Italian churchman, the first Archbishop of Canterbury. Chosen by Pope *Gregory I to evangelize England in 596, he converted Ethelbert I of Kent and successfully established Canterbury as the primatial see. Feast day: 26 or 27 May.

Augustine of Hippo, St (354–430 AD) North African theologian; Father and Doctor of

a

the Church, born at Tagaste. After studying at Carthage, he became a Manichaean, but under the influence of St Ambrose, Bishop of Milan, he converted to Christianity in 386. On his return to Africa, he lived as a monk until he was ordained at Hippo in 391. He became Bishop of Hippo in 396 and died there during a Vandal siege. His *The City of God*, a defence of Christianity in 22 books, and his spiritual autobiography, *The Confessions*, are the most important books written by an early Father of the Church. **Augustinians** are members of religious orders that follow the Rule of St Augustine, especially the orders of the Augustinian (*or* Austin) Canons, founded in the 11th century, and the Augustinian Hermits (*or* Austin Friars), founded in the 13th century. Feast day: 28 Aug.

Augustus (*or* **Octavian**; 63 BC–14 AD) The first Roman emperor, who restored the greatness of the Roman world following the disintegration of the Republic. Born Gaius Octavius, he was the great-nephew and adopted son of Julius Caesar. After Caesar's assassination in 44, Augustus (now Gaius Julius Caesar Octavianus; *or* Octavian) came to an agreement with *Mark Antony and in 43 they formed the second Triumvirate with Lepidus. Lepidus was forced to retire in 36 and Augustus' relations with Mark Antony failed to withstand Antony's abandonment of his wife Octavia (Augustus' sister) for Cleopatra. Antony's defeat at Actium in 31 allowed Augustus to establish his personal supremacy at the head of an autocratic government known as the principate. In 27 he was proclaimed Augustus (sacred). With the military assistance of Agrippa, and later of his own stepson *Tiberius, he secured and then expanded the Empire. In 4 AD he named Tiberius his heir. Augustus was deified after his death.

auk A stout-bodied seabird belonging to a family (*Alcidae*; 22 species) occurring in the N hemisphere and having a black and white plumage and short pointed wings. The family includes *puffins, *razorbills, *guillemots, and the extinct flightless great auk (*Pinguinus impennis*). Order: *Charadriiformes* (gulls, plovers, etc.).

Aung San (c.1914–47) Burmese statesman; leader of the independence movement. Committed to radical politics from his student days at Rangoon University, Aung San founded the Anti-Fascist People's Freedom League in 1944. He played a crucial role in the negotiations that led to Burmese independence from Britain but was assassinated before it was fully attained.

His daughter, **Aung San Suu Kyi** (1945–), cofounded the National League for Democracy and led protests against martial law. Placed under house arrest in 1989, she became a symbol of opposition to military rule. Her supporters won free elections in 1990 but the military held on to power by force. She was awarded the Nobel Peace Prize in 1991. Although she was released in 1995, the government placed her under renewed house arrest in 2000–02 and again from 2003.

aurora A display of diffuse changing coloured light seen high in the earth's atmosphere, often taking the form of red or green streamers. Aurorae occur predominantly in polar regions when energetic charged particles from the sun become trapped in the earth's magnetic field. The rapidly moving particles interact with atoms and molecules in the upper atmosphere and cause them to emit light. In the N hemisphere they are called the Northern Lights.

Auschwitz *See* OŚWIĘCIM.

Austen, Jane (1775–1817) British novelist. She was the daughter of a clergyman and lived an outwardly uneventful life with her family in the south of England, settling in Chawton in Hampshire in 1809. Her six major novels are *Sense and Sensibility* (1811), *Pride and Prejudice* (1813), *Mansfield Park* (1814), *Emma* (1815–16), *Northanger Abbey* (1818), and *Persuasion* (1818).

austenite A form of *steel that exists when the metal is heated to about 1000°C, in which the carbon exists as a solid solution in the iron. Austenitic steels retain this structure at room temperature because of the presence of an alloying element, such as manganese. Austenite is nonmagnetic and has a high ductility. Named after Sir William C. Roberts-Austen (1843–1902).

Austerlitz, Battle of (2 December 1805) The battle in which Napoleon's 68 000-strong army outmanoeuvred and defeated almost 90 000 Russians and Austrians led by Mikhail Kutuzov (1745–1813). It took place near Austerlitz (now Slavkov u Brna, in the Czech Republic). Napoleon's great victory forced the Austrians to make peace with France by the Treaty of Pressburg and the Russian army to return to Russia.

Australia, Commonwealth of A country in the S Pacific, comprising the whole of the smallest continent and the island of Tasmania to the SE. External territories include *Norfolk Island, *Christmas Island, the Cocos (Keeling) Islands, and the *Australian Antarctic Territory. Much of the country has a hot dry climate and a large part of the vast central plains are desert or semidesert. The most fertile areas are in the E, along the coastal plains, and in the extreme SW. The Great Barrier Reef lies off the tropical NE coast and the highest mountains, rising over 2000 m (7000 ft), are in the Great Dividing Range, which runs parallel to the E coast. The Murray River and its tributaries in the SE form the main river system. The inhabitants are very largely of European, especially British, origin but there are about 100 000 Aborigines and people of mixed race living in the interior. Since World War II the population has increased dramatically, largely as a result of immigration. *Economy*: agriculture continues to make a substantial contribution to the economy, the main crops being cereals, sugar cane, and fruit. Livestock, particularly sheep and cattle, is also important. Since the 1960s, however, there has been marked growth in iron and steel products. Mining is now of vital importance, especially the extraction of coal, iron, bauxite, uranium, copper, lead, and zinc; about 70% of oil for home consumption is now produced in Australia. The main exports are coal and gas, iron and iron ore, nonferrous ores, and cereals. *History*: the country was inhabited by the Aborigines, immigrants from SE Asia, for approximately 20 000 years before the arrival of the Europeans, beginning with the Portuguese in the 16th century and the Dutch in the early 17th century. In 1770 Captain Cook claimed the fertile E coast for Britain, which was first used as a penal colony. After the introduction of the merino sheep, however, civilian settlements were established further to the N and W towards the interior, eventually reaching the far side of the Blue Mountains in 1813. Colonies were developed in Tasmania, Western Australia, Victoria, South Australia, and Queensland. By 1829 the whole continent was a British dependency. The discovery of gold in Victoria in 1851 attracted large numbers of immigrants and from this period the colonies struggled for greater independence. In 1901 the six colonies were federated to form the Commonwealth, becoming an independent dominion of the British Empire. In 1911 the Australian Capital Territory (the site for the federal capital) and the Northern Territory were added to the Commonwealth. Since World War II closer economic ties have been developed with Japan. In 1978 the Northern Territory achieved self-government although the federal government retained control over uranium. Australia is a member of the Commonwealth. Constitutional links with the UK were ended in 1986. The 1980s and 1990s saw growing support for Australia becoming a republic: however, despite the fact that a people's Constitutional Convention (elected in 1997) voted to sever links with the crown, a referendum motion to replace the Queen with an appointed president was defeated in 1999. A conservative coalition led by John Howard has held power since 1996. Official language: English. Currency: dollar of 100 cents. Area: 7 686 884 sq km (2 967 283 sq mi). Population (2003 est): 19 880 000. Capital: Canberra.

Australian Alps A mountain range in SE Australia. Part of the *Great Dividing Range, it extends from E Victoria into SE New South Wales and contains the *Snowy Mountains and Mount *Kosciusko, Australia's highest mountain. It is a popular winter-sports area.

Australian Antarctic Territory The area of Antarctica claimed by Australia. It includes all the land lying S of latitude 60°S and between longitudes 45°E and 160°E, excluding Terre Adélie. Several research stations are sited here.

Australian Capital Territory An administrative division of SE Australia. It was created in 1911 from the Limestone Plains region of New South Wales as a site for *Canberra, the capital of Australia. Jervis Bay was transferred to the territory in 1915 for development as a seaport. It is the site of the Australian Academy of Science, the Royal Military College, and the Royal Australian Naval College (at Jervis Bay). Area: 2432 sq km (939 sq mi). Population (2000 est): 308 400.

Australian Rules *See* FOOTBALL.

Australopithecus A genus of fossil manlike higher primates of the late Pliocene and Pleistocene eras of S and E Africa. Although small in brain size, their cranial and skeletal structures were more like those of modern man than of apes. They walked erect and ate fruit, seeds, and meat. The earliest australopithecines, dated between 4 and 3 million years ago, included *A. anamensis* and *A. afarensis*. They probably evolved into various other species, some of which were the ancestors of modern man while others, such as *A. robustus*, probably coexisted with early forms of man before becoming extinct. Significant fossil finds of *Australopithecus* were made by Louis and Richard Leakey at Olduvai and Lake Turkana. *See* HOMO.

Austria, Republic of (German name: Österreich) A country in central Europe, on the

N side of the Alps. A large part of the country is mountainous but the E area consists of lower hills and plains, with the River Danube flowing through the NE. Most of the inhabitants are German but there are minorities of Croats, Slovenes, and others. *Economy*: although agriculture and forestry are important, there is considerable heavy industry, based particularly on iron and steel. Hydroelectric power is a valuable source of energy. Main exports include iron and steel, machinery, textiles, paper and paper products, and wood. *History*: Austria has a long history going back to the Celtic settlements of the early Iron Age. The area was part of the Roman Empire from 15 BC until the 5th century AD when it was overrun by Germanic tribes. In succeeding centuries it was occupied in turn by Slavs and Magyars from whom it was taken in 955 by the Holy Roman Emperor *Otto (I) the Great. He conferred it upon Leopold of Babenberg, who founded the first Austrian dynasty. In 1282 the *Habsburgs acquired Austria, which was to become the core of their vast empire. In 1526 Bohemia and Hungary were united under the Austrian Crown. The Austrian Empire continued to hold a predominant position in Europe until the middle of the 19th century when its power was lessened by successive defeats, especially in the *Austro-Prussian War. In 1867 the Habsburgs formed the Dual Monarchy of *Austria-Hungary, under the Emperor *Francis Joseph. During his reign there was considerable unrest, especially among the Slavs; the assassination of the Archduke Francis Ferdinand by Serbian nationalists in 1914 was the immediate cause of World War I. In 1918 Austria became a republic. In spite of efforts on the part of the chancellor *Schuschnigg to maintain independence, it was annexed by Nazi Germany in 1938 (*see* ANSCHLUSS). After World War II it was occupied jointly by the Allies, regaining its independence as a republic in 1955. Bruno Kreisky led a socialist government from 1970 until 1983. Austria became a member of the EU in 1995 and adopted the single European currency in 1999–2002. A series of socialist-led coalitions governed until 1999, when the left was defeated in elections. The subsequent formation (2000) of a coalition containing members of the extreme right-wing Freedom Party led EU and other countries to impose diplomatic sanctions. Elections in 2002 resulted in victory for the conservatives under Wolfgang Schüssel. Official language: German. Currency: euro of 100 cents. Area: 85 853 sq km (32 375 sq mi). Population (2003 est): 8 054 000. Capital: Vienna.

Austria-Hungary, Dual Monarchy of The Habsburg monarchy from 1867 to 1918, established in response to the militant demands of Hungarian nationalism. The empire of Austria and the kingdom of Hungary each had its own laws, parliament, and ministries but were united by the monarch (Emperors *Francis Joseph and then Charles), minister for foreign affairs and minister for war, and by the biannual meetings of delegations of representatives of each parliament. The Dual Monarchy disappeared in 1918 with the proclamation of an Austrian republic.

Austrian Succession, War of the (1740–48) The war between Austria and Prussia, in which Britain supported Austria and France and Spain were allied to Prussia. It was brought about by the disputed succession of *Maria Theresa to the Austrian lands. Hostilities were begun by Frederick the Great of Prussia, who annexed the Austrian province of Silesia in 1740. The war was ended by the Treaty of Aix-la-Chapelle, at which Prussia obtained the greater share of Silesia.

Austro-Prussian War (*or* **Seven Weeks' War**; 1866) A war between German states led respectively by Austria and Prussia. The Prussian victory was an important landmark in Bismarck's strategy for uniting Germany under Prussian leadership.

Authorized Version *See* KING JAMES VERSION.

autism A rare and severe mental illness that starts in early childhood. Autistic children do not form normal personal relationships but they can become emotionally attached to things. They do not communicate normally, often cannot form abstract concepts, and they are very upset by tiny changes in their familiar surroundings. Most, but not all, have learning disabilities. Autism can be caused by brain damage and can also be inherited. Lengthy specialized education is usually necessary for autistic children. *See also* ASPERGER'S SYNDROME.

auto-da-fé (Portuguese: act of faith) The public ceremony at which persons convicted of crimes by the *Inquisition in Portugal, Spain, and their colonies were sentenced. Punishment of victims, including the burning of heretics, was the responsibility of the secular authorities. The first *auto-da-fé* was held in Seville in 1481 and the last, in Mexico in 1815.

autogiro An aircraft with large horizontal freely rotating blades to obtain lift. It differs from the *helicopter in that a propeller provides forward motion, which in turn causes the rotation of the unmotorized horizontal blades.

autoimmunity A condition in which the body produces antibodies (called autoantibodies) that damage or destroy its own tissues. This produces symptoms of various **autoimmune diseases**, the majority of which are poorly understood. Rheumatoid *arthritis is caused by the production of autoantibodies against joint tissue; the disease can be diagnosed by the detection of these antibodies in the serum. A more general production of autoantibodies causes systemic *lupus erythematosis, which can affect most tissues in the body.

autopsy (**necropsy** *or* **postmortem**) The dissection and examination of a dead body. An autopsy is performed when the cause of death is uncertain: it may provide further information on a poorly understood disease or evidence of criminal involvement. Except for sudden death or death due to obscure causes, permission for autopsy must be granted by the relatives.

autumn crocus A herbaceous perennial European plant, *Colchicum autumnale*, also called meadow saffron. It has narrow strap-shaped leaves, up to 30 cm long, and a single purple-blue crocus-like flower, which appears in autumn after the leaves have died. The drug colchicine, extracted from the corms, is used in the treatment of gout and in genetic research. Some plants of the genus are cultivated for ornament. Family: *Liliaceae*. *Compare* CROCUS.

Auvergne A planning region and former province in S central France. Its name derives from the Averni, who strongly resisted Roman control of the area. Crossed by the volcanic Auvergne Mountains that rise to over 1800 m (6000 ft), it has many mineral springs and some level fertile districts. It is predominantly agricultural and is noted for the growing of wheat and grapes and the rearing of cattle; cheese and wine are also produced. Area: 25 988 sq km (10 032 sq mi). Population (1999): 1 308 878.

auxin An organic substance, produced within a plant, that stimulates, inhibits, or modifies growth of the plant. Auxins are sometimes known as plant hormones. The main auxin is indoleacetic acid (IAA). Auxins are responsible for a variety of effects, for example shoot curvature, leaf fall, and fruit growth. Synthetic auxins, such as 2,4-dichlorophenoxyacetic acid (2,4-D), are used as weedkillers for broad-leaved weeds.

Avalon *See* ARTHURIAN LEGEND.

Avebury 51 27N 1 51W A village in S England, in Wiltshire, on the site of a large complex of Neolithic and early Bronze Age stone circles, banks, and ditches. The principal circle, with its ditch and outer bank, encloses over 12 hectares (30 acres); within it are two smaller ones. Nearby is *Silbury Hill.

avens A perennial herbaceous plant of the genus *Geum* (about 40 species), native to temperate and Arctic regions. Most species rarely exceed 60 cm in height. Their flowers, 2–3 cm long, are white, yellow, orange, or red, either solitary or in clusters. *G. coccineum* is a common ornamental. Family: *Rosaceae*.

Averroes (Ibn Rushd; 1126–98) Muslim philosopher and a judge in Córdoba and Seville. Averroes' main works were his commentaries on Aristotle, which greatly influenced the philosophy of medieval Christianity. He defended philosophy as the highest form of enquiry, holding that faith and reason are separate ways of arriving at the truth.

aversion therapy A form of *conditioning used to treat some kinds of undesirable behaviour, such as sexual deviation, alcoholism, and drug addiction. An unpleasant stimulus (e.g. an electric shock) is associated with a stimulus related to the problem behaviour (e.g. the taste of alcohol). *See also* BEHAVIOURISM.

Avesta The sacred scriptures of Zoroastrianism (*see* ZOROASTER). Written in Old Iranian, the five books of the *Avesta* contain prayers (probably by Zoroaster himself) hymns, ritual and liturgical instruction, and the main body of Zoroastrian law. Its surviving form dates from about the 6th century AD.

Avicenna (980–1037) Persian philosopher and physician. Avicenna received extensive education in science and philosophy and served various rulers during his life, as government official and physician. His encyclopedia of philosophy, *Ash-Shifa* (*The Recovery*), encompasses logic, psychology, metaphysics, and natural sciences and parts were subsequently translated into Latin. Avicenna's *Canon of Medicine*, based on Roman and Arabic medicine and his own medical knowledge, became a popular text throughout the Middle East and Europe.

Avignon 43 56N 4 48E A town in SE France, the capital of the Vaucluse department on the River Rhône. The papacy, under French control, was removed to Avignon (1309–77; *see* AVIGNON PAPACY) and there were subsequently rival popes at Rome and Avignon until 1417 (*see* GREAT SCHISM). Famous sights include the

a

14th-century papal palace and the 12th-century bridge, of which only four arches remain. A tourist centre, Avignon trades in wine and has chemical, soap, and cement industries. Population (latest est): 89 440.

Avignon papacy (1309–77) The period during which the popes resided in Avignon (France) rather than Rome. The papal court was established in Avignon by Clement V, who, like his six successors in Avignon, was French. English and German criticism of French dominance over the papacy eventually forced its return to Rome under Gregory XI. Shortly afterwards the division in the Church known as the *Great Schism occurred, largely in response to the increased power acquired by the cardinals during the Avignon papacy (*see also* ANTIPOPE).

avocado A tree, *Persea americana*, up to 18 m tall, native to Mexico and Central America but now extensively cultivated in Florida, California, and South Africa for its fruit. These fruits—**avocado pears**—may reach a weight of 2 kg: they have a green to dark-purple skin, a fatty flesh rich in fat, protein, and vitamins A and B, and a single hard seed.

avocet A wading bird of the genus *Recurvirostra*, having long slender legs and a long thin upcurved bill used to skim the surface of mud or water in search of small invertebrates. The Eurasian avocet (*R. avosetta*), 50 cm long, has a black-and-white plumage and is protected in Britain. Family: *Recurvirostridae*; order: *Charadriiformes* (gulls, plovers, etc.).

Avogadro, Amedeo, Conte di Quaregna e Ceretto (1776–1856) Italian physicist, who became professor of physics at the University of Turin. He developed Gay-Lussac's hypothesis that equal volumes of gases contain equal numbers of particles, establishing the difference between atoms and molecules. Because he made this vital distinction the theory is now known as **Avogadro's hypothesis**. His name is also commemorated in the **Avogadro number** (*or* the Avogadro constant), the number of molecules in one mole of substance (it has the value $6.022\,52 \times 10^{23}\ \mathrm{mol}^{-1}$). Avogadro's work was not acknowledged until Cannizzaro brought it to public notice in 1854.

Avon, (Robert) Anthony Eden, 1st Earl of (1897–1977) British statesman; Conservative prime minister (1955–57). Foreign secretary from 1935 to 1938, he resigned in opposition to Neville Chamberlain's policy of *appeasement. At the beginning of World War II he was secretary for war and then (1940–45; 1951–55) foreign secretary. He succeeded Churchill as prime minister and following Nasser's nationalization (1956) of the *Suez Canal and an Israeli attack on Egypt, joined France in an offensive against Egypt. Egypt retained control of Suez and Eden was much criticized: he resigned shortly afterwards. He became Earl of Avon in 1961.

Avon, River The name of several rivers in the UK, including: **1.** A river in central England, flowing SW from Northamptonshire to the River Severn at Tewkesbury. Length: 154 km (96 mi). **2.** A river in SW England, flowing S and W from Gloucestershire to the Severn estuary at Avonmouth. Length: 120 km (75 mi). **3.** A river in S England, flowing S from Wiltshire to the English Channel. Length: 96 km (60 mi).

AWACS (*A*irborne *W*arning *a*nd *C*ontrol *S*ystem) A US radar system mounted on an aircraft to give early warning of the movements of enemy aircraft and, if appropriate, to direct intervention measures against them.

Axis Powers The coalition of Germany, Italy, and Japan that opposed the Allied Powers in *World War II. It originated in agreements going back to 1936 and it culminated in the Tripartite Pact (1940).

axolotl A salamander, *Ambystoma mexicanum*, occurring in Mexican lakes. It reaches a length of 25 cm, has a long tail and weak limbs, and is typically dark brown. Axolotls retain their larval characteristics permanently, reproducing in this state, although under certain conditions they may develop into adults. Family: *Ambystomatidae*.

Ayckbourn, Sir Alan (1939–) British dramatist. After working in provincial repertory theatre, he gained his first London success with *Relatively Speaking* (1967). His comedies include *Absurd Person Singular* (1973), the trilogy *The Norman Conquests* (1974), *A Chorus of Disapproval* (1985), *Body Language* (1990), and *House and Garden* (2000), all characterized by detailed observation of middle-class life. He directs a repertory theatre in Scarborough. He was knighted in 1997.

aye-aye A rare arboreal prosimian primate, *Daubentonia madagascariensis*, occurring only in the coastal forests of N Madagascar. It is 86–104 cm long including the tail (50–60 cm) and has dark shaggy fur and large ears used to detect wood-boring insects, extracting them with its incisor teeth and narrow elongated third finger. Family: *Daubentoniidae*.

Ayer, Sir Alfred (Jules) (1910–89) British

philosopher; Wykeham Professor of Logic at Oxford (1959–78). Ayer's major contribution to British philosophy was his bringing to England the teachings of the *Vienna Circle, in particular the doctrine of *logical positivism, which he expounded in *Language, Truth and Logic* (1936). His later books include *The Foundations of Empirical Knowledge* (1940), *The Problem of Knowledge* (1956), and two volumes of autobiography (1977, 1984).

Ayers Rock (Aboriginal name, Uluru) The largest monolith in the world, in Australia, in SW Northern Territory. It consists of a vast red rock, 335 m (1099 ft) high and 10 km (6.25 mi) in circumference. Its colour varies according to atmospheric changes and the position of the sun.

Aylesbury 51 50N 0 50W A market town in S central England, the administrative centre for Buckinghamshire. Lying in an agricultural area, it has food-processing, insurance, and various light industries. Population (1991): 58 058.

Aylward, Gladys (1903–70) British missionary. From 1930 she worked as an independent missionary in China. Her life story was the subject of a popular film, *The Inn of the Sixth Happiness* (1958), in which she was played by Ingrid Bergman.

Ayrshire A historic county of SW Scotland, bordered by the Firth of Clyde and including the island of Arran. In 1975 it became part of Strathclyde Region. Further reorganization in 1996 led to the creation of three new council areas, East Ayrshire, North Ayrshire, and South Ayrshire.

Ayrshire cattle A breed of red or brown and white cattle originating in Ayrshire, SW Scotland. A hardy breed, Ayrshires are primarily producers of good quality milk, used especially in cheese making. Many herds have been replaced by the higher yielding Friesians.

Ayub Khan, Mohammad (1907–74) Pakistani statesman; president (1958–69). After a distinguished military career he became defence minister in 1954. Following President Iskander Mirza's coup in 1958, Ayub Khan became chief martial law administrator and then ousted Mirza to become president. With Shri Lal Ba'hadur Shastri he negotiated (1966) the ceasefire agreement following the India-Pakistan war of 1965. He was forced to resign following civil unrest in East Pakistan.

azalea A deciduous shrub of the genus *Rhododendron*. (Most horticulturalists prefer to restrict the term rhododendron to the large evergreen species.) Growing to a height of up to 2 m, azaleas are native to North America and S Asia but are widely cultivated as ornamentals. The attractive flowers are funnel-shaped (about 6 cm in diameter) and of various colours. Family: *Ericaceae*.

Azerbaidzhan, Republic of A republic in W Asia, on the Caspian Sea. Most of the population are Shiite Muslims. *Economy*: agricultural products include cotton, tobacco, and fruit. Oil and gas are the most important industries. *History*: the region was acquired by Russia from Persia in the early 19th century, proclaimed its independence in 1918, but subsequently formed part of the Transcaucasian Soviet Federated Socialist Republic; it became a separate Soviet republic in 1936 and an independent state in 1991. In 1988–90 riots over Armenian claims to the disputed *Nagorno-Karabakh area escalated into a state of virtual civil war. Azerbaidzhani troops fought Armenian forces in the region from 1991 until 1994, when a ceasefire was declared. In 1993 the former communist leader Heidar Aliyev became head of state after a military coup; he was re-elected in 1998, amidst widespread allegations of fraud, and succeeded by his son, Ilham Aliyev, in 2003. Official language: Azeri. Currency: manat of 100 gopik. Area: 86 600 sq km (33 430 sq mi). Population (2003 est): 8 235 000. Capital: Baku.

azimuth *See* ALTITUDE.

Azores (Portuguese name: Açôres) 38 30N 28 00W Three groups of volcanic islands in the N Atlantic Ocean, in Portugal. The chief islands include São Miguel, Terceira, Faial, and Flores. Settled by the Portuguese in the 15th century, they were previously uninhabited. Naval fighting between the English and Spanish took place here in the 16th and 17th centuries. The site of US air bases, they produce fruit, tobacco, and wine. Area: 2300 sq km (888 sq mi). Population (2001): 242 073. Capital: Ponta Delgada, on São Miguel.

Aztecs A Nahuatl-speaking people who ruled an empire in central and S Mexico before their defeat by Hernán Cortés in the 16th century. They had an advanced, elaborate, and rich civilization centred on their capital Tenochtitlán and other cities. They constructed large palaces and temples in which they worshipped many gods, especially Huitzilopochtli to whom they sacrificed human victims, captives of warfare, by ripping out their hearts while they still lived. Authority and influence were vested in a class of chiefs and priests and in the kings, the last of whom was Montezuma.

B

Ba'ath Party An Arab political party committed to the creation of a united socialist Arab nation. The Ba'athists rose to power in Syria in 1963 and in Iraq (where Saddam *Hussein became their leader) in 1968. The Syrian and Iraqi wings of the party have been deeply divided since the 1970s. The Iraqi Ba'athists lost power as a result of the *Iraq War of 2003.

Babbage, Charles (1792–1871) British mathematician and inventor. In an attempt to produce more accurate mathematical tables, Babbage conceived the idea of a mechanical computer that could store information. Although he never completed the machine, it was the forerunner of the modern computer.

Babel, Isaac Emmanuilovich (1894–1941) Russian short-story writer. Of Jewish descent, he served in the imperial army, but fought for the Bolsheviks in 1917. His *Odessa Tales* were published in 1916. *Red Cavalry* (1926) was a series of sketches based on his experience in the war against Poland. He died in a Siberian prison camp, a victim of Stalin, but was posthumously rehabilitated in the 1950s.

Babel, Tower of In the old Testament (Genesis 11.1–9) a tower intended to reach to heaven. Jehovah, angered by this presumptuous behaviour, caused the builders to speak different languages so that, incomprehensible to each other, they had to abandon the work. The legend is an attempt to account for diversity of language.

Babi faith A religion founded in 1844 by Mirza 'Ali Mohammed (1819–50), who became known as the Bab (the Gate). It was the immediate precursor of the *Baha'i faith.

baboon A large *Old World monkey belonging to the genus *Papio* (5 species), of African and Asian grassland. Baboons are 95–185 cm long including the tail (45–70 cm) and have a shaggy mane and a long doglike face with large teeth. They feed on insects, small vertebrates, and vegetable matter. Baboons live in well-organized troops containing 40–150 individuals arranged in a social hierarchy according to age and sex.

Babylon The capital of ancient Babylonia, strategically positioned on the River *Euphrates S of modern Baghdad. Its first period of prominence was about 2150 to 1740 BC, under a dynasty of which Hammurabi was the most illustrious member. Subsequently, rising Assyrian power threatened Babylonian independence, though some Babylonians, such as Nebuchadnezzar I (reigned c. 1146–1123), temporarily reversed the trend. Sacked in 689 BC by the king of Assyria, Sennacherib (d. 681 BC), Babylon was rebuilt from 625 BC onwards, especially during the reign (c. 605–562) of *Nebuchadnezzar II. It was the remains of this city that were excavated (1899–1917) by the German archaeologist Robert Koldewey (1855–1925). In 539 BC Babylon surrendered to Cyrus the Great of Persia (d. 529 BC); by 275 BC it was virtually depopulated. *See also* HANGING GARDENS OF BABYLON; ZIGGURAT.

Babylonia The area of *Mesopotamia on the alluvial plain on the lower reaches of the River Euphrates, which was controlled by ancient *Babylon. Before about 2000 BC approximately the same area was known as *Sumer, of which *Ur was the capital.

Bacchanalia The Roman form of the Hellenistic mystery rites in honour of Bacchus (*see* DIONYSUS). The cult reached Rome from S Italy in the 2nd century BC. Originally involving only women, Bacchic worship included ecstatic rituals and secret orgies. In 186 BC a decree of the Senate prohibited Bacchanalia in Rome.

Bacchus *See* DIONYSUS.

Bach, Johann Sebastian (1685–1750) German composer and keyboard player, the greatest member of a large musical family. He became a chorister in Lüneburg and in 1703 a violinist at the Weimar court, later becoming organist there. In 1707 he married his cousin Maria Barbara Bach (1684–1720); after her death he married Anna Magdalena Wilcken (1701–60). He became kapellmeister at the court of Prince Leopold of Anhalt at Köthen in 1717 and finally cantor of St Thomas' Church, Leipzig, in 1723. Among his greatest works are the *St John Passion* (1723), the *St Matthew Passion* (1729), and the *Mass in B minor* (1733–38), as well as over 200 cantatas. His compositions for orchestra include violin and harpsichord concertos and the *Brandenburg Concertos* (1721). For the harpsichord and clavichord he composed a collection of 48 preludes and fugues entitled *The Well-Tempered Clavier* (Part I, 1722; Part II, 1744) and the *Goldberg Variations* (1742). Bach's music did not become widely known until Mendelssohn revived it.

Of Bach's 20 children, 3 sons became famous musicians. His eldest son **Wilhelm Friedemann Bach** (1710–84) studied in Leipzig and became church organist in Dresden (1733–46) and subsequently in Halle (1746–64). He ended his life in poverty, leaving cantatas, concertos, and symphonies.

His third son **Carl Philipp Emanuel Bach** (1714–88) became musician to Frederick the Great in Berlin and subsequently director of the principal church in Hamburg in succession to Telemann. He developed a new monophonic style of composition in his symphonies, concertos, and keyboard music that became the basis of the classical style.

J. S. Bach's 11th son **Johann Christian Bach** (1735–82), known as the English (or London) Bach, studied in Berlin and after holding posts in Italy became music master to the British royal family. He composed 13 operas, as well as concertos, church music, and piano pieces.

bacillus Any rod-shaped bacterium, specifically a bacterium of the genus *Bacillus*: spore-forming species including parasites of plants and animals. *B. anthracis* was first shown to cause anthrax in livestock by Robert Koch (1843–1910).

backgammon A board game for two players that was known in ancient Mesopotamia, Greece, and Rome and in medieval England (as "the tables"). Each player has 15 pieces, which are moved round the 24 chevrons (points) marked on the board, according to the throws of two dice. From their starting positions the players move in opposite directions. Each tries to bring all his pieces into the last quarter after which he can remove them from the board. Simultaneously he must block his opponent's moves.

background radiation Low-intensity radiation naturally present on the earth. It results either from the bombardment of the earth by *cosmic rays or from naturally occurring radioactive substances in the earth's crust.

backswimmer A *water bug, belonging to the worldwide family *Notonectidae* (nearly 200 species), that swims on its back, using a pair of oarlike legs for propulsion. Backswimmers can fly but are normally found in fresh water, preying voraciously on insects, tadpoles, and small fish. They must return to the surface periodically to replenish their air store.

Bacon, Francis (1909–92) British painter, born in Dublin of English parentage. Self-taught, he was assured a place in British art with his *Three Studies* (of figures for the base of a *Crucifixion*; 1945). Another of his well-known paintings is *Study after Velázquez* (1951), a version of Velázquez's portrait of pope Innocent X.

Bacon, Francis, 1st Baron Verulam, Viscount St Albans (1561–1626) English lawyer and philosopher. He was called to the Bar in 1582 and became an MP in 1584. Under James I, Bacon became attorney general (1613) and Lord Chancellor (1618). In 1621, however, he was found guilty of bribery and corruption, fined £40,000, and banished from office.

In 1597 he published his first group of *Essays*; further such discourses appeared in 1625. *The Advancement of Learning* (1605) presented a new classification of sciences and was expanded in the *De augmentis scientiarum* of 1623. In *Novum organum scientiarum* (1620) he advocated the scientific method of *induction. His other works include the *New Atlantis* (1626), which describes his ideal state.

Bacon, Roger (c. 1214–c. 1292) English monk, scholar, and scientist, called Doctor Mirabilis for his diverse skills and learning. In three books written for Pope Clement IV he attempted to systematize the current state of knowledge; other works prophesied aeroplanes, microscopes, steam engines, and telescopes; he also detected errors in the Julian *calendar and has been credited with the invention of *gunpowder and of the magnifying glass.

bacteria Microscopic single-celled organisms found wherever life is possible. Bacteria form a kingdom of organisms distinguished from all others by the structure of their cells, which lack a nucleus. They are divided into two groups, the archaebacteria and the eubacteria. Archaebacteria lack a rigid cell wall and are found in hot springs, volcanic vents, and other inhospitable environments. The eubacteria (so-called "true bacteria") are generally 0.0001–0.005 mm long; they may be spherical (coccus), rodlike (*see* BACILLUS), or spiral-shaped (spirillum) and often occur in chains or clusters of cells. True bacteria have a rigid cell wall, which may be surrounded by a slimy capsule, and they often have long whiplike flagella for locomotion and short hairlike pili used in a form of sexual reproduction. A few bacteria can grow on simple inorganic substrates using carbon dioxide from the atmosphere to manufacture their own nutrients, but the majority require a source of organic carbon and other nutrients for growth. Some bacteria can reproduce every 15 minutes, leading to rapid population growth.

The most important role of bacteria is in decomposing dead plant and animal tissues and releasing their constituents to the soil (*see* CARBON CYCLE).

bacteriophage (*or* **phage**) A *virus that infects a bacterium. 25–800 nanometres in size, phages may be spherical, filamentous, or tadpole-shaped with a head and tail. They consist of a protein coat surrounding a core of nucleic acid (either DNA or RNA) that is inserted into the bacterium. The viral genes then use the protein-synthesis apparatus of the bacterium to produce new phages, which are released from the cell, usually causing its destruction. Phages are used in genetic engineering to transfer foreign DNA into bacterial hosts.

Baden-Powell, Robert Stephenson Smyth, 1st Baron (1857–1941) British general and founder of the Boy Scouts (*see* SCOUT ASSOCIATION). He achieved fame through his defence of Mafeking in the Boer War (1899–1900). Utilizing the experience of character training he had gained overseas, he founded the Boy Scouts in 1908 and, with his sister Agnes, the Girl Guides in 1910 (*see* GUIDES ASSOCIATION).

Baden-Württemberg A *Land* in SW Germany, bordering on France and Switzerland, formed by an amalgamation of three former *Länder* (1952). Area: 35 751 sq km (13 800 sq mi). Population (1995 est): 10 272 000. Capital: Stuttgart.

Bader, Sir Douglas (1910–82) British fighter pilot. After losing his legs in a flying accident (1931), Bader argued himself back into the RAF at the start of World War II. Becoming a national hero, he was finally shot down and imprisoned by the Germans, who only prevented his escape by depriving him of his artificial legs. In 1976 he was knighted for his work for the disabled.

badger A nocturnal burrowing mammal of the *weasel family (*Mustelidae*). The largest of the eight species is the gregarious Eurasian badger (*Meles meles*), about 90 cm long, with short strong legs, long coarse greyish hair on the body, and a black and white striped head. It lives in a complex of burrows (a set) and feeds on insects, rodents, worms, berries, etc.

Bad Godesberg *See* GODESBERG.

badminton An indoor court game for two or four players, played with rackets and a shuttlecock of nylon or cork and feathers. It originated in about 1870, probably from battledore and shuttlecock and may have first been played

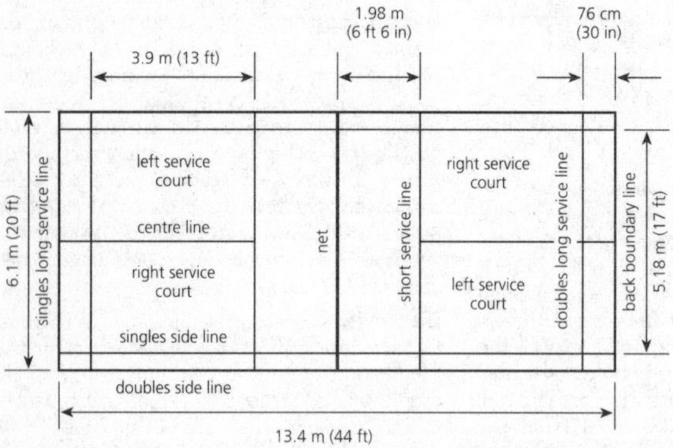

badminton. The dimensions of the court. The top of the net at the centre is 1.5 m (5 ft) above the floor.

in the park of Badminton House, in the village of Badminton (Avon). It is a volleying game (the shuttles do not bounce) and points are scored only by the serving side. If the serving side fails to make a good return the service changes (in doubles games both partners serve before their opponents). A game is usually played to 15 points (women's singles go to 11 points).

Baekeland, Leo Hendrik (1863–1944) US industrial chemist, born in Belgium. He invented Bakelite (*see* PLASTICS), the first synthetic thermosetting plastic. The discovery was made while Baekeland was searching for a synthetic substitute for *shellac.

Baffin Island The largest island of the Canadian Arctic, lying N of Hudson Strait, named after William Baffin (c. 1584–1622). It is separated from Greenland by a Strait forming **Baffin Bay** (in the N) and Davis Strait. Mountainous with many glaciers and snowfields, its sparse population is concentrated in Frobisher Bay. Since April 1999 it has formed part of the new Inuit territory of *Nunavut. Area: 476 068 sq km (183 810 sq mi).

Baghdad 33 20N 44 26E The capital of Iraq, on the River Tigris near the centre of the country. Built by the caliph Mansur in the 8th century, it was a centre of commerce, learning, and religion until sacked by the Mongols in 1258. It became the capital of independent Iraq (1927) and has three universities (1947, 1957, and 1963). It was severely damaged by US bombing in the *Iraq War (2003). Population (1995 est): 4 478 000.

bagpipes A reed-pipe instrument of ancient origin, found in many countries. Air is forced into a windbag either by the mouth (Scottish bagpipes) or by a bellows (Northumbrian pipes). By pressing the bag under his arm the player pushes air into the sounding pipes, which consist of one to three drones (each sounding a single note) and a chanter pipe. Bagpipes are regarded as the national instrument of Scotland, having been introduced to the British Isles in the 13th century.

Baha'i faith A religion founded in Persia in 1863 by Mirza Husain 'Ali (1817–92), who was known as Baha' Allah (Glory of God). He proclaimed himself to be the Promised One whose coming was foretold by the Bab (*see* BABI FAITH). His eldest son and then his great-grandson led the Baha'is after his death until 1957. Since 1963 the faith has been governed by the Universal House of Justice, a council at Haifa, Israel, elected by national spiritual assemblies. The basic tenet of the faith is that God reveals himself to man through prophets who appear at various stages in history and the most recent of these is Baha' Allah.

Bahamas, Commonwealth of the A state consisting of about 700 islands and innumerable cays in the West Indies, off the SE coast of Florida. The principal islands, which are mainly low lying, include New Providence, Grand Bahama, Abaco, Eleuthera, Andros, and Watling Island (San Salvador). The majority of the population is of African descent. *Economy*: tourism accounts for over 50% of revenue and employment. It is also an offshore financial centre, 90% of companies being foreign-owned. Efforts are now being made to develop agriculture, fisheries, and industry. *History*: in 1492 Columbus made his first landing in the W hemisphere on the island of San Salvador. The first European occupation comprised an English religious settlement in the mid-17th century, and the islands became a British crown colony in 1717. In 1973 the Bahamas attained full independence within the Commonwealth. Official language: English. Currency: Bahamian dollar of 100 cents. Area: 13 864 sq km (5353 sq mi). Population (2003 est): 314 000. Capital: Nassau.

Bahrain, Kingdom of An independent sheikdom in the Arabian Gulf, occupying a low-lying archipelago between Saudi Arabia and the Qatar Peninsula. The two main islands, Bahrain and Al-Muharraq, are connected by a causeway and there are also plans for a causeway to Saudi Arabia. The inhabitants are mainly Arabs. *Economy*: almost totally dependent upon oil. A large refinery processes local oil and much larger amounts coming from Saudi Arabia by pipeline. Efforts are being made to develop other industry with some success. *History*: the islands were under Portuguese rule from 1521 until 1602, and during parts of the 17th century Iran had control, eventually being expelled by the Khalifa family, who have ruled the area for most of the time since. It was a British protected state from 1861 until 1971 when full independence was declared by the emir, Sheik Isa ibn Sulman al-Khalifa (1933–99). Bahrain became a member of OPEC in 1970. The National Assembly was dissolved in 1975 following political unrest, but growing opposition to the regime in the mid-1990s led the emir to set up an appointed consultative council. In 2000 Emir Hamad took the title of king and a new constitution was enacted; parliamentary elections were held but boycotted by some opposition groups. Official language: Arabic. Currency: dinar of 1000 fils. Area: 660 sq km

(255 sq mi). Population (2003 est): 674 000. Capital: Manama.

b

bail The release by a court of an imprisoned person, usually while awaiting trial, into the keeping of people who agree to ensure his reappearance at a particular date and time. If these people, called "sureties," then fail to produce him, they forfeit whatever sum of money the court has set for bail. The person bailed must also stand as surety for himself; if thought trustworthy, he may be bailed without other sureties, "in his own recognizance."

Bainbridge, Dame Beryl (1934–) British novelist and playwright. Born in Liverpool, she has written such novels as *The Dressmaker* (1973), *An Awfully Big Adventure* (1989), *Master Georgie* (1998), and *According to Queenie* (2001). She was appointed DBE in 2000.

Baird, John Logie (1888–1946) British electrical engineer, who invented an early television system. In 1924 he first succeeded in transmitting the outline of shapes, although his 240-line system was not adopted by the BBC. Baird also worked on radar and fibre optics.

Bakhtaran (name until 1987: Kermanshar) 34 19N 47 04E A town in W Iran, with a largely Kurdish population. Population (1996): 692 986.

Bakhtyari An Islamic tribe of W Iran of some 400 000 members speaking the Luri dialect of Persian. About one-third are still nomadic herdsman living in tents. They migrate 150 miles from their winter pastures on the plains to the summer pastures in the mountains.

baking powder A mixture, usually of sodium bicarbonate and tartaric acid or cream of tartar, used in baking. It generates carbon dioxide on heating or wetting, thus making the dough rise.

Baku 40 22N 49 53E The capital of Azerbaidzhan, a port on the Caspian Sea. Its ancient buildings include mosques and a 17th-century palace. It has been a centre of oil production since the 19th century. Population (1997 est): 1 727 200.

Bala, Lake (Welsh name: Llyn Tegid) The largest natural lake in Wales, in Gwynedd. The town of Bala lies at its N end. Length: 6 km (4 mi).

Balaclava, Battle of (25 October 1854) An indecisive battle between Russian and British-Turkish forces in the *Crimean War. It is notorious for the heavy British casualties caused by misunderstanding between Lord *Raglan, the British commander in chief, and Lord Lucan (1800–88), the cavalry commander. The courageous Light Brigade charged Russian artillery in a narrow valley and 113 of its 673 men were killed. The charge was made famous by Tennyson's poem "Charge of the Light Brigade".

balalaika A Russian instrument of the guitar family, having a long fretted fingerboard, a triangular body, and three wire strings that are plucked with a plectrum. Small versions are held like a guitar and the larger ones balanced on the floor like a double bass.

balance A sensitive device for comparing two masses, consisting of a beam pivoted at its centre (usually on an agate knife edge) with pans hanging from each of its ends. The material of unknown mass is placed in one pan and standard weights are placed in the other. A pointer indicates when the beam is horizontal and the whole device is enclosed in a glass case to avoid draughts and temperature changes. A standard balance will weigh to the nearest 0.0001 g, while extremely sensitive **microbalances** can be used to weigh objects with a mass of only 1 microgram.

balance of payments The difference between a country's income and its expenditure abroad. The current account records the country's balance-of-trade earnings or deficit on visible goods and invisible earnings on such items as insurance, transport, tourism, and some kinds of government spending. The capital account records all long- and short-term capital flows. If the sum of the current and capital accounts shows a deficit there will be a net loss of foreign exchange.

balance of power The principle that no nation or group of nations should be permitted to become too dominant. It was adopted in Europe in the alliance system of 15th-century Italy and by the Congress of *Vienna at the start of the 19th century. In the 20th century the concept was largely replaced by the nuclear deterrent.

balance of trade The difference in money between the value of a country's imports and its exports. Together with the invisibles account and capital transfers it makes up the *balance of payments. The balance of trade can be in deficit without necessarily meaning that the balance of payments will also be in deficit.

Balanchine, George (Georgy Melitonovich Balanchivadze; 1904–83) US ballet dancer and choreographer, born in Russia. He worked for

Diaghilev's Ballets Russes in Europe from 1924 and went to the USA in 1933, becoming artistic director of the New York City Ballet. His ballets include *Firebird* (1950) and *Don Quixote* (1965).

bald eagle A large sea *eagle, *Haliaetus leucocephalus*, also called the American eagle; it is the national emblem of the USA and an endangered species. It is dark brown with a white head and tail and has a prominent curved beak and unfeathered legs. It feeds on carrion and fish.

Baldwin, James Arthur (1924–87) US Black novelist, essayist, and dramatist. His first novel, *Go Tell It on the Mountain* (1953), is based on his experience in Harlem, New York City, where he was born. He lived in Paris from 1948 to 1957, when he returned to the USA as an active civil-rights campaigner. His works include novels, plays, and collections of essays.

Baldwin of Bewdley, Stanley, 1st Earl (1867–1947) British statesman, who was Conservative prime minister (1923–24, 1924–29, 1935–37), when he dealt with the *General Strike (1926) and Edward VIII's abdication (1936). Baldwin was criticized for condoning Italy's conquest of Ethiopia and his reluctance to rearm in the face of Germany's military build-up.

Balearic Islands An archipelago in the W Mediterranean Sea comprising an autonomous region of Spain. It includes the chief islands of *Majorca, *Minorca, *Ibiza, and Formentera, together with several islets. The islands were conquered by Aragon from the Moors in the 14th century. Area: 5014 sq km (1936 sq mi). Population (2000 est): 845 630. Capital: Palma, on Majorca.

Balenciaga, Cristóbal (1895–1972) Spanish fashion designer, known for his simple but elegant suits and evening dresses in the 1950s.

Balfour Declaration (1917) The decision of the British Government, made known in a letter of 2 Nov from the British foreign secretary, Arthur Balfour (1848–1930), to Lionel, Baron Rothschild (1868–1937), the chairman of the British Zionist Federation, to support the establishment of a national Jewish home in Palestine. Although the Declaration was abandoned in 1939, it helped to justify the partition of Palestine and the creation of the State of Israel in 1948.

Bali An Indonesian island off E Java. Mountainous and volcanic, it has southern fertile plains that produce chiefly rice. *History*: Hindu since the 7th century AD, Bali resisted the 16th–17th century spread of Islam through Indonesia. Dutch rule began in 1908 and Bali became part of Indonesia in 1945. In the 1965–67 purge of communists 40 000 people were killed. In 2002 a bomb planted in a night club in Kuta Beach by Islamic terrorists killed over 200 people. Area: 5558 sq km (2146 sq mi). Population (1995 est): 2 902 200. Chief town: Denpasar.

Balkan Mountains (Bulgarian name: Stara Planina) A mountain range extending 500 km (311 mi) E–W for the entire width of central Bulgaria. It rises to 2376 m (7795 ft) at Botev Peak.

Balkans An area in SE Europe consisting of present-day Greece, Albania, Croatia, Bosnia-Hercegovina, the Former Yugoslav Republic of Macedonia, Serbia and Montenegro, Bulgaria, part of Romania, and the European part of Turkey. Part of the Roman empire from the 2nd century BC and of the Eastern Roman (Byzantine) Empire from the 5th century AD, the Balkans were ruled by the Ottoman Turks from the 15th to the early 20th century, when independence was granted (*see also* BALKAN WARS). All the Balkan states, except Greece, became communist after *World War II. In the 1990s the region was once again plunged into turmoil with the disintegration of Yugoslavia, the savage civil war in Bosnia-Hercegovina, and the *Kosovo war.

Balkan Wars (1912–13) In the first Balkan War (1912–13) the Balkan League (Bulgaria, Serbia, Greece, and Montenegro) defeated Turkey. In the concluding Treaty of London, Turkey lost all its European possessions except E Thrace. In the second Balkan War (1913) the victors fought over their acquisitions in Macedonia, from most of which Bulgaria was excluded by the Treaty of Bucharest; Turkey regained Thrace.

ballet A dramatic art in which dancing and mime, accompanied by music, combine to tell a story or evoke a mood. Ballet originated in the formal dances of French court entertainments, notably under Louis XIV. In the 18th century ballet established itself in the public theatre but still as an adjunct to *opera or other forms of drama. Dancing on the tips of the toes (*sur les pointes*) was introduced early in the 19th century, which saw the heyday of romantic ballet. Modern ballet arose in the early 20th century when *Fokine and *Diaghilev (*see also* BALLETS RUSSES) combined the polished technique of the imperial Russian dancers with the natural-

b

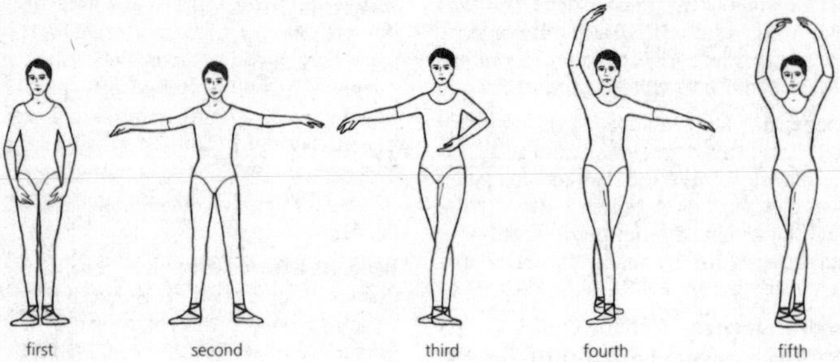

The five ballet positions

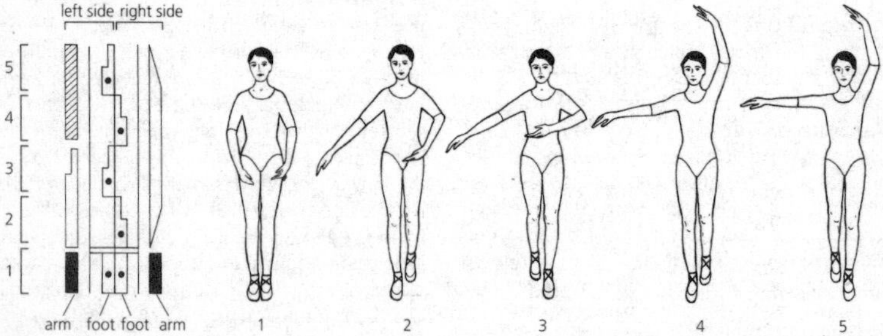

Labanotation

ballet. Rudolph Laban (1879–1958) published his system for recording dance movements (Labanotation) in 1928, since when it has gained widespread acceptance. In this simple example, the initial positions of the legs and arms are indicated at (1). Subsequent positions (2–5) are seen by reading upwards from the bottom. The dancer, starting with feet together and arms at her sides, takes four even steps forward, beginning with the right foot, and moves her arms upwards and outwards (the different shadings representing low, middle, and high positions).

ism advocated by the American Isadora *Duncan.

Ballets Russes A Russian ballet company (1909–29) founded in Paris by *Diaghilev. It gave the West its first opportunity to see Russian imperial dancers and greatly influenced the subsequent development of ballet. Its choreographers included *Fokine, *Massine, *Balanchine, and *Nijinsky, who was also one of its principal dancers. *Ravel and *Stravinsky composed music for several of its ballets.

ballistic missiles Rocket-powered nuclear missiles that are propelled to desired altitudes and then follow an unpowered trajectory. Intercontinental ballistic missiles (ICBMs) are capable of reaching any point on the surface of the earth. Both the USA and the former Soviet republics possess large numbers of these, some of which (MIRVs—multiple independently targeted re-entry vehicles) have up to ten separate warheads. *See also* ANTIBALLISTIC MISSILES.

ball lightning A luminous moving sphere, several centimetres in diameter, occurring just above the ground on rare occasions during thunderstorms. It hisses, has a distinct odour, and may be either red, orange, or yellow. It lasts for only a few seconds and then either dies away or explodes. The phenomenon is not fully understood.

balloons Lighter-than-air craft, consisting of a bag of gas that displaces a volume of air of greater mass than the total mass of the balloon and its contents. The first successful balloon flight was made in 1783 by the *Montgolfier brothers' hot-air balloon; it flew 9 km across Paris. Two years later a hydrogen balloon designed by J. A. C. Charles (1746–1823), flew across the Channel. The use of balloons in war began with Napoleon's observation balloons in 1794, after which they were little used until their extensive use in both World Wars in the form of barrage balloons. The sport of **ballooning**

enjoyed a revival in the latter half of the 20th century, using a hot-air balloon carrying its own propane air heater. The height record for a manned balloon is 30 480 m (D. Simons, US Air Force, 1957). The first crossing of the Atlantic Ocean by helium balloon was achieved in 1978. In 1999 Brian Jones of the UK and Bertrand Piccard of Switzerland made the first circumnavigation of the globe in a hot-air balloon.

Ballymena A district in central Northern Ireland, in Co Antrim. Area: 634 sq km (247 sq mi). Population (2001): 58 610.

Ballymoney A district in Northern Ireland, in Co Antrim. Area 417 sq km (161 sq mi). Population (2001): 26 894.

Balmoral Castle The principal country residence of the British monarch in Scotland, situated in SW Aberdeenshire by the River Dee. It was bought by the royal family in 1848 and rebuilt in the 1850s.

balsa An evergreen tree, *Ochroma pyramidale*, native to Central and South America, also called corkwood. About 12 m tall, it is the source of an extremely light pale-coloured wood, which is widely used for corks, canoes, floats, etc. Family: *Bombacaceae*.

balsam An aromatic resinous substance derived from the Central American leguminous tree *Myroxylon peneirae*, grown in El Salvador. It is used in medicine and perfumes.

Baltic Sea A section of the Atlantic Ocean in N Europe, bounded by Denmark, Sweden, Finland, Latvia, Lithuania, Estonia, Russia, Poland, and Germany. To the W, it leads into the Little Belt, the Great Belt, and the Sound, and to the E, the Gulfs of Bothnia, Finland, and Riga. Receiving rivers draining almost one-fifth of Europe, it has low salinity, and can freeze.

Baltic states The republics of Latvia, Lithuania, and Estonia. They were independent states between World Wars I and II and constituent republics of the Soviet Union from 1940 to 1991. They joined the EU in 2004.

Baltimore 39 25N 76 40W A city in the USA, in Maryland at the mouth of the Patapsco River. Established in 1729, it was named after the first Baron Baltimore who founded Maryland. It was the starting point of the USA's first railway (1827). Baltimore contains a number of universities, including the prestigious Johns Hopkins University (founded 1876); in the 1980s considerable rebuilding in the port area revitalized the city. Industries include steel, sugar and food processing, oil refining, and chemicals. Population (2000): 651 154.

Baluchistan A province in W Pakistan, on the Arabian Sea and the Iranian and Afghani borders. Mostly rough arid highlands, it is inhabited by pastoral Pathans, Baluchs, and other peoples. The NW deserts are practically uninhabited but the coastal plain and E lowlands support cereals and herbs. *History*: on trade routes from India to the Middle East, Baluchistan has flourished since ancient times. It usually enjoyed autonomy until Britain won control (19th century). In 1947 it became part of Pakistan. Area: 347 190 sq km (134 050 sq mi). Population (1998): 6 511 000. Capital: Quetta.

Balzac, Honoré de (1799–1850) French novelist. A lawyer's clerk, he wrote popular novels under pseudonyms. In 1828, bankruptcy forced him to turn to writing; *Les Chouans* (1829) was his first successful novel, and in the next 20 years he added over 40 novels to the cycle *La Comédie humaine*. In these novels, which included *Eugénie Grandet* (1833), *Le Père Goriot* (1834), and *La Cousine Bette* (1846), he developed new techniques of realism.

Bamako 12 40N 7 59W The capital of Mali, a port in the S on the River Niger. A centre of Muslim learning under the medieval Mali Empire, it had dwindled to a small village by the end of the 19th century. It became the capital of the French Sudan in 1905. Population (1996 est): 809 552.

bamboo A treelike plant of the tribe *Bambuseae*, native to tropical and subtropical regions, particularly in SE Asia. From an underground stem (rhizome) arise hollow woody jointed stems, which may reach a height of 40 m in some species. These are used for building, etc., while the young shoots are eaten. Family: *Gramineae* (grasses).

Banaba *See* OCEAN ISLAND.

banana A palmlike plant of the Old World tropical genus *Musa*, especially *M. paradisiaca sapientum*. The "trunk," up to 9 m high, is composed of the overlapping bases of the leaves, which are often 3 m or more long. The tip of the flowering stem bears male flowers; clusters of female flowers, further up the stem, develop into seedless fruits, up to 30 cm long, without being fertilized. (All cultivated bananas are sterile hybrids: the plants are propagated from suckers arising from the underground rhizome.) Varieties called plantains are cooked and eaten when still green in Africa and the Caribbean. Family: *Musaceae*.

Banbridge A district in S Northern Ireland,

in Co Down. Area: 442 sq km (170 sq mi). Population (2001): 41 392.

b

Bandaranaike, S(olomon) W(est) R(idgeway) D(ias) (1899–1959) Sri Lankan statesman; prime minister (1956–59) and founder (1951) of the Sri Lanka Freedom Party (SLFP). After his assassination his wife, **Sirimavo Bandaranaike** (1916–2000) succeeded him as head of the SLFP and became the world's first female prime minister (1960–65, 1970–77, 1994–2000). In 1980 she was expelled from parliament on the grounds of misuse of power. In 1994 their daughter **Chandrika Bandaranaike Kumaratunga** (1945–) became prime minister, but after 3 months was elected president. Her mother then became prime minister for the third time.

Bandar Seri Begawan (former name: Brunei Town) 4 56N 114 58E The capital of Brunei, a port in the NE near the mouth of the Brunei River. Population (1994): 49 902.

bandicoot A ratlike *marsupial mammal of a family (*Peramelidae*; 20 species) occurring in Australia (including Tasmania) and New Guinea. About the size of rabbits, bandicoots are mainly carnivorous, eating insects, worms, and grubs.

Bandung 6 57S 107 34E A city in Indonesia, in W Java. Its chief industries are chemicals, quinine, plastics, metal processing, and textiles. It has two universities and a nuclear research centre (1964). Population (1995 est): 2 368 200.

Bangalore 12 58N 77 35E A city in S India, the capital of Karnataka. Founded in the 16th century, it fell to the British in 1791. Its modern industries include machine tools, aircraft assembly, and electronics. Population (1991): 2 650 659.

Bangkok (Thai name: Krung Threp) 13 44N 100 30E The capital and main port of Thailand, in the SW near the mouth of the River Chao Phraya. It became a royal city and the capital in 1782. Distinctive features of the city are its canal system and the many Buddhist temples. It is the centre of most of the country's industry and commerce and it has eight universities. Population (1999 est): 5 647 799.

Bangladesh, People's Republic of A country in the Indian subcontinent in the delta of the Rivers Ganges and Brahmaputra. *Economy*: Its population, mostly Bengali, is largely occupied in agriculture, rice being by far the most important crop. Bangladesh produces 70% of the world's raw jute, its main export. Fishing, is also important. The economy has grown rapidly in the 2000s but Bangladesh remains one of the world's poorest countries. *History*: the area formed part of the kingdom of Bengal, and its conquest by the Afghans in the 12th century led to the growth of the Islamic religion. It was part of British India from 1857 until 1947 when it became a province of Pakistan (East Pakistan). Discontent led to civil war in 1971, Indian forces coming to the aid of the Bengalis. In 1972 East Pakistan achieved independence within the Commonwealth as Bangladesh, and Sheikh Mujibur Rahman (1920–75) became prime minister. In 1974 floods and famine led to political unrest and terrorism; Mujib assumed absolute power in 1975 but was assassinated soon after. Gen Ziaur Rahman assumed power in 1976, was elected president in 1978, but was assassinated in 1981. The military, led by Lt Gen Hussain Mohammed Ershad, took power in 1982, and in 1983 Ershad became president; political unrest led to his resignation in 1990. In 1991 Gen Ziaur's widow, Begum Khaleda Zia, was elected prime minister and Abdur Rahman Biswas became president under a new constitution. In 1996 continuing political crisis led Begum Zia to step down and she was succeeded by Mujibur's daughter, Sheikha Hasina Wajded. In 1998 floods left about two-thirds of the land area under water and some 25 million people homeless. Begum Zia's Bangladesh Nationalist Party was returned to power in 2001. Official language: Bengali. Currency: taka of 100 paise. Area: 142 797 sq km (55 126 sq mi). Population (2003 est): 133 107 000. Capital: Dhaka.

Bangui 4 23N 19 20E The capital of the Central African Republic, a port in the SW on the Ubangi River. Founded in 1889, the port handles goods for both the Central African Republic and Chad; its main exports are cotton and coffee. Population (1995 est): 553 000.

banjo An originally American guitar-type instrument with 4–9 strings. It consists of a round metal hoop covered with parchment and a fretted fingerboard. It was common in jazz bands, folk music, and minstrel shows.

Banjul (name until 1973: Bathurst) 13 20N 16 38W The capital of The Gambia, a port in the W at the mouth of the River Gambia, founded by the British in 1816. Population (1993): 42 407.

Bank of England The British central bank, which was nationalized in 1946. It was originally incorporated in 1694, being set up by a group of London merchants to lend money to William III. Since the mid-19th century it has been the only bank authorized to issue bank-notes. The Bank is responsible for financing the national debt and holding the country's gold reserves. Since 1997 it has had responsibility for setting the **bank rate**, the rate of interest at which the Bank of England lends to the discount houses.

bankruptcy The legal process by which the property of a person who cannot pay his debts is distributed among his creditors. In England bankruptcy was originally a branch of the criminal law aimed at preventing fraudulent traders evading their creditors, but since the reign of Queen Anne the law has also sought to protect the bankrupt by ending his obligation to repay most of his past debts. The Bankruptcy Act (1914) and the Insolvency Acts (1976, 1986) stipulate the circumstances in which a person may be made bankrupt, what portion of his property is to be distributed, and the creditors who are to be paid in priority to others. Liquidation is the equivalent process applicable to a company.

Bannister, Sir Roger (Gilbert) (1929–) British doctor and middle-distance runner, who on 6 May 1954, was the first man to run a mile in under 4 minutes (3 minutes 59.4 seconds).

Bannockburn 56 06N 3 55W A village in Scotland, near Stirling on the Bannock Burn (a tributary of the River Forth). 1.5 km (1 mi) NW is Scotland's most famous battlefield, where in 1314 Robert the Bruce, King of the Scots, routed the English under Edward II, who had come to relieve the besieged Stirling Castle. Population (1991): 2675.

Banting, Sir Frederick Grant (1891–1941) Canadian physiologist, who, with C. H. *Best, discovered a technique for the successful isolation of the hormone *insulin from pancreatic tissue in 1921, enabling *diabetes to be treated. Banting was awarded a Nobel Prize (1923).

Bantu A large subgroup of African languages of the Niger-Congo group spoken over the whole of the S half of Africa by about 60 million people. It includes Zulu, Xhosa, and Kongo; perhaps the most widely known representative is *Swahili, the language of Tanzania and lingua franca of E Africa.

Bantu Homelands (*or* **Bantustans**) The areas of South Africa designated for the Black populations from 1950 until 1994, comprising just over 13% of the land area. Acts of parliament in 1913 and 1936 controlled the extent of African lands and prohibited Blacks from holding land in White areas. Limited self-government was granted to these areas from 1963 and some were granted full independence (not internationally recognized) from 1976. Bantustan policy was opposed by most African leaders and many of the territories resisted self-government, regarding it as a poor substitute for majority rule in South Africa. Following multiracial elections in 1994 the Homelands were reintegrated into South Africa.

banyan A tropical Asian tree, *Ficus benghalensis*, related to the fig and reaching a height of 30 m. Supporting aerial roots, which grow down to penetrate the soil, subsequently give rise to thorny branches of their own. Family: *Moraceae*.

baobab A tropical African tree, *Adansonia digitata*, with a tapering conical trunk (the base of which may exceed 10 m in diameter) reaching a height of 18 m and bearing branches at its apex. The fruits contain an edible pulp surrounded by a tough woody capsule and the bark yields a fibre of local importance. Family: *Bombacaceae*.

baptism A ceremony of initiation, occurring in many religions, involving the use of water as a symbol of purification from sin. In the Christian Church, it is a *sacrament. Both the *Baptists and the modern descendants of the *Anabaptists practise adult baptism, but most other Churches prefer infant baptism.

Baptists Protestant Christians who baptize, by immersion, only those old enough consciously to accept the Christian faith. "General Baptist" Churches, owed their origin in 1612 to John Smyth (c. 1554–1612) and Thomas Helwys (c. 1550–c. 1616), while "Particular Baptist" Churches, founded in 1633 by Calvinists, believed that salvation was only for a particular few. Both movements merged into the Baptist Union in 1891. The first Baptist Church in America was established at Providence, Rhode Island, by Roger Williams in 1639.

Baqqarah A cattle-herding Arab people of Chad and the Sudan. As a result of intermarriage with local peoples they have dark skins and speak a distinct dialect of Arabic. They migrate between northern wet-season grazing lands and southern dry-season river areas.

bar A unit of pressure equal to 10^5 pascals (0.987 atmosphere). The commonly used unit is the millibar (one-thousandth of a bar).

Barbados, State of An island state in the West Indies, E of the Windward Islands. Most of the population is of African descent. *Economy*: tourism is now the chief economic activity, although sugar cane, the main crop, remains important. The discovery of oil and natural gas has assisted the growth of small industries. *History*: a British colony from 1627 until 1966, it became independent within the Commonwealth. In 1998 a constitutional commission recommended that Barbados should become a republic but remain inside the Commonwealth. Official language: English. Currency: Barbados dollar of 100 cents. Area: 430 sq km (166 sq mi). Population (2003 est): 272 000. Capital: Bridgetown.

Barbary A region in N Africa stretching from Egypt to the Atlantic Ocean that is named after the *Berbers. Between the 16th and 18th centuries, Barbary was notorious for its pirates, who caused havoc in the Mediterranean. The **Barbary ape** is a large monkey, *Macaca sylvana*, also called magot. They are tailless and roam in bands over the forest floor, feeding on seeds, leaves, insects, etc.

barbel A long slender freshwater fish, belonging to the genus *Barbus*, that is related to *carp and occurs in clear fresh waters of Asia, Africa, and Europe. It has four fleshy thread-like appendages (barbels) near its mouth, which detect prey while exploring the river bed. *B. barbus* of Europe is usually 30–50 cm long.

Barber, Samuel (1910–81) US composer. Two of his works, the opera *Vanessa* (1958) and the piano concerto (1963), won Pulitzer Prizes. His output includes chamber music, choral works, symphonies, and concertos. His best-known work is the *Adagio for Strings*, an arrangement of the slow movement of his string quartet (1936).

barber's shop Unaccompanied close-harmony singing that originated in barbers' shops in the USA in the late 19th century. It had several revivals in the 20th century.

barbiturates A class of drugs that act by depressing the activity of the brain. The short-acting barbiturate thiopentone is used to induce *anaesthesia, while the long-acting phenobarbitone is used to control some forms of epilepsy. Barbiturates were formerly used as sleeping tablets but because they are habit-forming and have toxic side-effects, their use is now severely limited.

Barcelona 41 25N 2 10E A city in NE Spain, in Catalonia on the Mediterranean Sea. Manufactures include locomotives, textiles, and electrical equipment. The focus of Catalan art and literature, it has many educational establishments including the university (1430), and a 14th-century cathedral. It is also famous for its Art Nouveau buildings designed by Antonio Gaudi. *History*: founded by the Carthaginians, it was taken by the Moors in 713 AD and by Charlemagne in 801 AD. In 1137 Catalonia and Aragón united and Barcelona became the capital. It was the seat of the Catalan autonomous government and later of the Republican government, during the Spanish Civil War (1936–39). The 1992 Olympics were held here. Population (1995 est): 1 614 571.

Bardeen, John (1908–91) US physicist, who shared the 1956 Nobel Prize for his part in the invention of the transistor (with W. B. *Shockley and W. H. *Brattain) while working at the Bell Telephone Laboratories in 1948. He also shared the 1972 Nobel Prize for his work on the theory of superconductivity (with L. N. Cooper and J. R. Schrieffer).

Bardot, Brigitte (1934–) French film actress. Her films include *And God Created Woman* (1956) and *Viva Maria* (1965). She became probably the best-known sex symbol of the 1960s but subsequently turned her back on the cinema and devoted herself to animal welfare.

Barebones Parliament The assembly, also known as the parliament of saints, called by Oliver *Cromwell in July 1653. It consisted mainly of merchants and lesser gentry, "godly men" nominated by the congregations, and was named after one of them, Praisegod Barebone (c. 1596–1679).

Barenboim, Daniel (1942–) Israeli pianist and conductor. In 1967 he married the cellist **Jacqueline du Pré** (1945–87), with whom he gave recitals. Barenboim conducted the Orchestre de Paris from 1975 to 1989, and became music director of the Chicago Symphony Orchestra in 1991. Since 1992 he has been the director of the Staatsoper in Berlin. In recent years he has organized musical projects to promote reconciliation between Arabs and Israelis.

Barents Sea A section of the Arctic Ocean between Eurasia and Svalbard. It covers part of the Eurasian continental shelf and is rich in fish. It is named after the Dutch navigator Willem Barents (1550–97).

baritone A deep adult male singing voice, lower than tenor and higher than bass. Range: G at the bottom of the bass stave to G two octaves above.

barium (Ba) A silvery reactive metal that resembles calcium in its behaviour. It was discovered in 1808 by Sir Humphry Davy and occurs naturally as barytes ($BaSO_4$) and witherite ($BaCO_3$). The sulphate is used as a white pigment in paint and, because of its opacity to X-rays, is used in X-ray diagnosis. All soluble barium compounds are toxic, the carbonate being used as rat poison. At no 56; at wt 137.327; mp 729°C; bp 1805°C.

bark The dead outer layer of the stems and roots of woody plants, which protects the inner tissues. Antiseptic deposits, such as tannins, give the colour. Bark may include layers of insulating *cork, which is responsible for the characteristic ridges and patterns on some tree trunks. Bark is a source of cinnamon, quinine, and various other products.

bark beetle A hard cylindrical beetle, also called an engraver beetle, belonging to a family (*Scolytidae*; 7000 species) of wood borers. It is usually less than 6 mm long, coloured red-brown or black, and causes considerable damage to trees. It burrows underneath the bark to lay eggs that develop into burrowing larvae. Certain species also transmit diseases (*see* ELM BARK BEETLE) and can be serious economic pests.

Bar Kokhba (Simeon bar Kosiba; d. 135 AD) Jewish freedom fighter. In 132 he launched a revolt against Roman rule and attempted to set up an independent Jewish state. He was hailed as Messiah by some but was killed when his last stronghold, Betar, fell.

barley A *cereal grass of the genus *Hordeum*, especially *H. vulgare*, which produces its grain in four rows; *H. distichon* (two-rowed barley); and *H. hexadistichon* (six-rowed barley). It is used in brewing, as an animal feed, and to produce pearl barley.

Bar Mitzvah (Hebrew: son of the commandment) The ceremony marking the rite of passage of a Jewish boy into the adult community at the age of 13. It is customary for him to read a passage from the Torah in a synagogue on the first Saturday after his birthday. In some communities a similar ceremony, called a **Bat Mitzvah**, exists for girls.

Barnabas, St In the New Testament (Acts), a Christian Apostle of the 1st century. After going with St Paul to evangelize Cyprus (his birthplace), he clashed with him and they parted company. He is regarded as the founder of the Cypriot Church. Feast day: 11 June.

barnacle A marine *crustacean belonging to the class *Cirripedia* (1000 species). Some members of the group are parasites, but the typical (nonparasitic) barnacles live attached to rocks, ships, etc., and filter food particles from the water with long feathery appendages, which protrude from the calcareous shell. Goose barnacles (e.g. *Lepas anatifera*) are attached by means of a stalk; others, including the acorn barnacle (*Balanus*), are unstalked. Barnacles are hermaphrodite; their larvae are free-swimming, but later settle and become fixed to a surface by means of a cement-like substance secreted by their antennae.

Barnard, Christiaan Neethling (1922–2001) South African surgeon, who (in 1967 at the Groote Schuur Hospital in Cape Town) performed the world's first successful heart transplant operation. After his retirement in 1983 he entered politics.

Barnardo, Thomas John (1845–1905) British doctor and philanthropist. In 1867 Barnardo founded the first of his many homes at Stepney, London, to care for destitute children.

barn owl An *owl belonging to a family (*Tytonidae*; 9 species) with a worldwide distribution. Barn owls have heart-shaped faces, long feathered legs, and usually a reddish plumage with pale underparts. The common barn owl (*Tyto alba*), 30–45 cm long, nests in old barns and hunts for small rodents.

Barnsley 1. 53 34N 1 28W A town in N England, in Barnsley unitary authority, South Yorkshire on the River Dearne. Formerly a coalmining centre, it now has various industries including electronics, new technology, glass manufacture, and textiles. Population (1991): 75 120. **2.** A unitary authority in N England, in South Yorkshire. Area: 329 sq km (127 sq mi). Population (2001): 218 062.

Baroda *See* VADODARA.

barometer An instrument for measuring atmospheric pressure. In the mercury barometer, atmospheric pressure forces mercury from a reservoir into a vertical evacuated glass tube marked with a scale. The height of the mercury column is directly proportional to the atmospheric pressure. In the smaller, but less sensitive aneroid barometer, variations in the atmospheric pressure on the lid of an evacuated metal box cause a pointer to move round a dial. See illustration on p. 100.

Barons' Wars 1. (1215–17) The civil war between King John of England and his barons. John's failure to honour the *Magna Carta led the barons to offer the English Crown to the future Louis VIII of France, who invaded Eng-

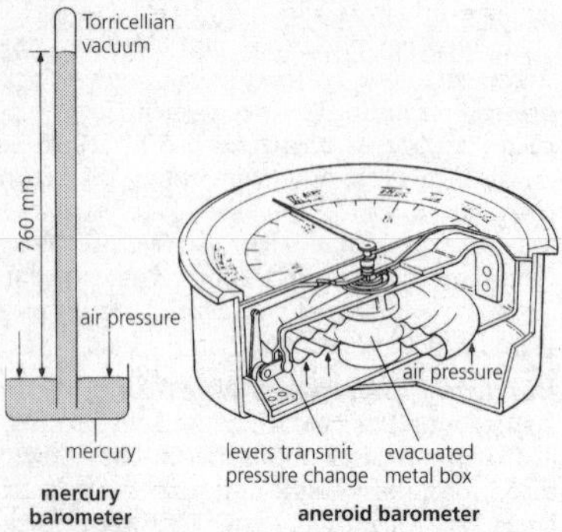

barometer. In the mercury barometer the height of the mercury column is directly proportional to the air pressure and is independent of the diameter of the tube. In the aneroid barometer movements of the lid of the evacuated metal box are transmitted to the pointer by the levers.

land. John's death and the reissue of Magna Carta (1216) removed many baronial grievances but war continued until the barons' defeat at Lincoln and Sandwich (1217). **2.** (1264–67) The civil war between Henry III of England and his barons led by Simon de *Montfort, following Henry's repudiation of the Provisions of *Oxford. He was captured at the battle of *Lewes (1264) and England was controlled by de Montfort until his death at Evesham (1265). Hostilities continued until the royalist capture of the Isle of Ely in 1267.

baroque In architecture, a style dominant in European Roman Catholic countries in the 17th and early 18th centuries. Beginning in Italy as a reaction against *classicism, it was characterized by curved and broken lines, ornate decoration (which led to the rococo), and elaborate spatial effects. English architects, such as *Wren and *Vanbrugh, were influenced by it. In art and sculpture, the baroque was a complementary style that developed from Italian *mannerism. Leading baroque painters include *Caravaggio and *Rubens, while *Bernini is the principal exponent in sculpture. In music, the compositions of the 17th and early 18th centuries, from Monteverdi to Bach, are frequently called baroque music.

Barquisimeto 10 03N 69 18W A city in NW Venezuela. It is the commercial centre of a coffee-growing area and has a university (1963). Population (2000 est): 875 790.

barracuda A shoaling fish of the family *Sphyraenidae* (about 20 species), found in all tropical seas and caught for food and sport. Its body is up to 1.8 m long and bears two dorsal fins. Barracudas feed voraciously on other fish and the larger species are considered dangerous to man. Order: *Perciformes*.

Barranquilla 11 00N 74 50W An important port in NW Colombia, on the Río Magdalena near its mouth on the Caribbean Sea. Its manufactures include textiles, vegetable oils, and chemicals. It has two universities (1941, 1967). Population (1999 est): 1 223 260.

Barrie, Sir James (Matthew) (1860–1937) British dramatist and novelist. The son of a Scots weaver, he came to London as a freelance writer in 1885. After two successful novels about Scottish rural life he wrote mostly for the theatre. His best-known plays are *The Admirable Crichton* (1902), *Peter Pan* (1904), which has also remained a popular children's book, and *Dear Brutus* (1917).

barrister In England and Wales or Northern Ireland, a member of the legal profession who has been "called to the Bar," i.e. awarded the title barrister-at-law by one of the *Inns of Court. Barristers argue cases in courts and advise clients through their *solicitors. Until 1990 they had the exclusive right to argue cases in the higher courts. Barristers are known as advocates in Scotland and elsewhere as advocates or attorneys.

barrow A prehistoric burial mound, also called a tumulus or cairn. From about 2000 BC earth barrows, concealing stone or timber passages and burial chambers, were built all over Europe for the interment of warrior chiefs. Long (i.e. rectangular or trapezoidal) barrows, such as at West Kennet (S England), were used for Neolithic multiple burials. Round barrows were more usual in Bronze Age cultures. Barrows continued in use in Iron Age Europe, and as late as the 7th century AD.

Barry, Sir Charles (1795–1860) British architect, who worked in both classical and gothic styles. In 1836 he won the competition to rebuild the Houses of Parliament (*see* PALACE OF WESTMINSTER), which, assisted by Augustus Pugin (1812–52), he designed in the gothic manner. He also designed the Reform Club (1837) in London.

Barrymore, Lionel (1878–1954) US actor remembered for his performances in the first series of *Dr Kildare* films. His sister **Ethel Barrymore** (1879–1959) acted with Sir Henry Irving in London, and later became a leading stage actress in the USA. Their brother **John**

Barrymore (1882–1942) was also an actor. His greatest stage success was his performance of Hamlet in 1922. As a film star during his later career he was famous for such films as *Grand Hotel* (1932) and for his tempestuous private life. His granddaughter **Drew Barrymore** (1975–) became a child star in *E.T.* (1982) and later found success in such films as *The Wedding Singer* (1998).

Barthes, Roland (1915–80) French literary critic and writer. His early works, such as *Mythologies* (1957), in which he pioneered the study of popular culture, and *On Racine* (1963), made him a leading figure in the structuralist movement (*see* STRUCTURALISM). Later works include *The Pleasure of the Text* (1975).

Bartholdi, Frédéric August (1834–1904) French sculptor, remembered chiefly for his *Statue of Liberty.

Bartók, Béla (1881–1945) Hungarian composer. Bartók studied and taught at the Budapest Academy of Music, where he and Zoltan Kodály (1882–1967) undertook research into Hungarian folksong. In 1940 he went to live in the USA, where he died in poverty. A virtuoso pianist, he composed three piano concertos, *Mikrokosmos* (1926–37), and other piano works. His stage works include the opera *Duke Bluebeard's Castle* (1911) and the ballet *The Miraculous Mandarin* (1919). In his six string quartets and *Music for Strings, Percussion, and Celesta* (1936) he explored unusual sonorities. His most popular work is the *Concerto for Orchestra* (1943).

Bartolommeo, Fra (Baccio della Porta; c. 1472–1517) Florentine Renaissance painter. After training under Cosimo Rosselli (1439–1507), he became a supporter of *Savonarola, whose death moved him to join the Dominican monastery of S Marco (1500) and abandon painting until 1504. His works include *St Mark* and the *Pietà* (both Palazzo Pitti, Florence).

baryon A collective term for *nucleons and other elementary particles that have a proton or neutron in their decay products. All baryons have a *quantum number called the baryon number, which is equal to +1 and is always conserved in an interaction. *See* PARTICLE PHYSICS.

basalt A volcanic rock of basic composition, typically dark, heavy, and fine textured. Three broad groups of basalt are recognized: alkali basalt, high-alumina basalt, and tholeiite. Basalt constitutes over 90% of volcanic rocks.

baseball A nine-a-side bat-and-ball game that evolved from *rounders, played mainly in the USA, Japan, and Latin America. The object for each team while batting is to score as many runs as possible and while fielding to prevent the other team from doing so. A team bats until three players are out; one turn at bat for both teams constitutes an inning, of which there are usually nine in a game. The pitcher, standing at the pitcher's mound, throws the ball to the batter, standing at home plate, who tries to hit it into fair territory and run. He scores a home run by making a complete circuit of the bases (first, second, third, and home). A player may be struck out (if he misses the ball or hits it into foul territory in each of three attempts), caught out, tagged out (if he or the base he is running towards is touched by a player with the ball), or put out by being hit by a batted ball while running.

Basidiomycota (*or* **Basidiomycetes**) A large phylum of fungi (22 000–25 000 species) that includes many *mushrooms, the bracket fungi, *puffballs, etc., as well as microscopic forms, such as the parasitic *rusts and *smuts of crops. They reproduce by basidia, which are typically club-shaped and produce spores at the tips of stalklike projections.

Basie, Count (William B.; 1904–84) US Black jazz pianist and band leader. He became famous for his distinctive "big band" style and recorded many albums, including *Atomic Mr Basie* and *Straight Ahead.*

basil An annual herbaceous plant of the Indian genus *Ocimum*, cultivated as a pot herb. Sweet basil (*O. basilicum*), up to 30 cm high, has toothed leaves and small white or bluish flowers. Family: *Labiatae.*

Basildon 51 34N 0 25E A town in SE England, in Essex. Created as a new town in 1949 from several townships, its industries include engineering, printing, and tobacco. Population (1991): 100 924.

basilica **1.** A Roman public meeting hall. In imperial times, many had a layout similar to the Basilica of Maxentius in Rome: rectangular ground plan, colonnaded aisles, entrance porch (narthex), and windows in the upper storey (clerestory). **2.** A Christian church based on a similar plan (e.g. S Giovanni in Laterano in Rome).

basilisk **1.** An arboreal lizard belonging to the tropical American genus *Basiliscus.* Up to 60 cm long, it has a narrow body, a long whiplike tail, and a flat lobe protruding from the back of its head. It has long hind legs with lobed toes fringed with scales, enabling it to run over the surface of water. **2.** A legendary snakelike serpent of ancient Greece and Rome whose glance was believed to be fatal to all living things except the weasel.

Basingstoke 51 16N 1 05W A town in S England, in Hampshire. Its manufactures include agricultural machinery, scientific instruments, and leather goods. It is also a warehousing and distribution centre for southern England. Population (1991): 77 837.

basketball A five-a-side court game invented in the USA (1891) by James Naismith (1861–1939). The object is to toss or put an inflated ball into the opponents' basket, a net mounted 3.05 m (10 ft) above the floor on a backboard. Players use only their hands, passing the ball or dribbling it by bouncing, and they may not run with it. The premier professional basketball league is the National Basketball Association in the USA (founded in 1949).

basking shark A large *shark belonging to the family *Cetorhinidae*. Up to 15 m long, they are grey-brown or blackish and inhabit cold and temperate regions of the Atlantic, Pacific, and Indian Oceans. Basking sharks usually occur in shoals near the surface and float or swim slowly, feeding on plankton.

Basle (French name: Bâle; German name: Basel) 47 33N 7 36E The second largest city in Switzerland, on the River Rhine where the French, German, and Swiss borders meet. Industries include chemicals, pharmaceuticals, and engineering. The Bank for International Settlements was established here in 1929. Population (1996 est): 174 007.

Basle, Council of A general council of the Roman Catholic Church summoned by Pope Martin V in 1431 to consider the heretical *Hussites and the nature of papal power. Martin's successor, moved it to Ferrara. However, a minority of councillors remained at Basle, electing the antipope, Felix V, in 1439. He resigned in 1449 and the council was brought to an end.

Basque A non-Indo-European language spoken by some 500 000 Basque people of the W Pyrenean areas of Spain and France. The Basques are strongly Roman Catholic and traditionally enjoyed a degree of regional autonomy, forming an independent government (1936–37) during the Spanish Civil War. The Basque Provinces became an autonomous region of Spain in 1978. Nationalism remains a significant force and the Basque Separatist movement is still active. Since 1968 guerrilla tactics have been adopted by the ETA (*Euskadi ta Azkatasuna*) and the French-based *Enbata* groups. ETA declared a ceasefire in 1998, leading to direct contacts with the Spanish government, but returned to violence in 2000.

Basra 30 30N 47 50E A town in SE Iraq, on the Shatt (river) al-Arab. It is linked by rail and river steamer to Baghdad; the modern port (Al Ma'qil) was constructed by the British during World War I. It was occupied by the British once more during the *Iraq War (2003). Population (latest est): 406 296.

bass (fish) One of several perchlike *bony fish of the order *Perciformes*. The majority belong to the family *Serranidae* (*see* SEA BASS), which includes the common European bass (*Dicentrarchus labrax*). This can grow up to 1 m long and has a grey or blue back with a white or yellowish belly. North American freshwater bass belong to the family *Centrarchidae*.

bass (music) **1.** The deepest adult male singing voice. Range: E below the bass stave to E two octaves above. **2.** The lowest voice or instrumental part of a piece of music.

Bassano, Jacopo (Jacopo *or* Giacomo da Ponte; c. 1517–92) Italian painter of the Venetian school, born in Bassano, the son of a painter. He was one of the earliest painters of rustic life, in both secular, e.g. *Pastoral* (Lugano), and religious scenes, e.g. *Adoration of the Kings* (National Gallery, Edinburgh).

basset hound A breed of dog originating in France. It has a long body with very short legs and a narrow face with drooping ears. They were formerly popular hunting dogs. Height: 33–38 cm.

bassoon A woodwind instrument. Its conically bored tube is about 2.5 m (8 ft) long and is bent back on itself. It has a metal crook into which a double reed is inserted. Its extensive compass (about three and a half octaves above B flat below the bass stave) allows it a melodic as well as a bass role.

Bass Strait A channel separating the mainland of Australia from Tasmania. It has valuable oil and natural gas deposits. Length: 290 km (180 mi). Maximum width: 240 km (150 mi).

Bastille A fortress in Paris, It was built in about 1370 to protect the wall around Paris against English attack and became a state prison under Cardinal de *Richelieu. The storming of the Bastille on 14 July 1789, is regarded as the beginning of the *French Revolution.

bat A flying mammal belonging to the order *Chiroptera* (981 species), distributed in most temperate and tropical regions. There are two suborders: the *fruit bats (*Megachiroptera*; 150 species) and the insect-eating bats (*Microchiroptera*; 831 species). The wings are extensions of skin that are supported between the forelimb, with its very long fingers, the hind limbs, and the tail. Insectivorous bats use *echolocation for navigation and catching prey whereas fruit bats have eyes adapted for night vision.

bateleur An African snake *eagle, *Terathopius ecaudatus*, having very long wings and a short tail. It flies vast distances, preying on reptiles, mammals, and carrion, which it seizes with its short rough powerful toes.

Bateson, William (1861–1926) British biologist, whose experiments on inheritance helped found the science of genetics. His results (1905–08) corroborated the findings of Gregor *Mendel published in 1865 although he refused to accept the chromosome theory proposed by T. H. Morgan.

Bath 51 23N 2 22W A city in SW England, in Bath and NE Somerset unitary authority, Somerset, on the River Avon. It was an early Roman centre known as Aquae Sulis because of its hot natural springs. The Roman baths have survived and are considered the best Roman remains in the UK. Bath became fashionable as a spa town in the 18th century when many of the finest buildings were built, including the Royal Crescent and the Assembly Rooms. The Bath Spa Project, which includes a new high-tech spa as well as restored 18th-century facilities, is due to open in 2004. Bath Abbey, mainly 16th-century, lies in the centre. Population (1991): 85 202.

Bath, Order of the A British order of knighthood, formed by George I in 1725 as a successor to the Knights of the Bath, traditionally founded by Henry IV in 1399. It comprises the sovereign, knights and dames grand cross (GCB), knights and dames commanders (KCB), and companions (CB). Its name is derived from the bathing ceremony that formed the principal rite of admission to the original order.

Bath and North East Somerset A unitary authority in SW England, in Somerset; it was formerly (1974–96) part of the county of Avon. Area: 351 sq km (136 sq mi). Population (2001): 169 045.

Bathsheba In the Old Testament, the wife of Uriah, the Hittite. She had an adulterous relationship with King David, who, having sent Uriah to his death in battle, married her. After repenting, in the face of God's displeasure at his duplicity, David fathered a son, who became King Solomon.

Baton Rouge 30 30N 91 10W A city in the USA, the capital of Louisiana situated on the Mississippi River. It is a major deepwater port with oil and sugar refineries. Population (1996 est): 215 882.

battered baby syndrome Injuries inflicted on babies or young children by their parents. Battering commonly takes the form of facial bruises, cigarette burns, head injuries (often with brain damage), and fractured bones. The parents are often emotionally disturbed or have themselves suffered from physical abuse in infancy. A care order is often necessary to safeguard a child from further abuse.

Battle 50 55N 0 29E A town in S England, in East Sussex. It was the scene of the Battle of Hastings (1066) in which Harold II was defeated by William the Conqueror, who built Battle Abbey to commemorate his victory. Population (1991): 5234.

Baudelaire, Charles (1821–67) French poet. He inherited his father's fortune in 1842 and lived extravagantly until what was left of the capital was placed in trust by his family (1844). In 1852 he discovered Edgar Allan *Poe, publishing several translations of his works (1856–65). His only volume of poetry, *Les Fleurs du mal* (1857, revised 1861), contained several erotic poems, which led to his being convicted for obscenity.

Baudouin I (1930–93) King of the Belgians (1951–93), succeeding his father Leopold III. He was interned by the Nazis in World War II. He married Fabiola de Mora y Aragón in 1960. In 1990 he abdicated for two days to avoid signing an act legalizing abortion.

Bauhaus A German school of design founded in 1919 at Weimar and closed by the Nazis in 1933. From 1925 to 1932 it was housed at Dessau in a building designed by *Gropius (its director until 1928), itself a work of great influence. The Bauhaus sought to produce a practical synthesis of all the arts and to develop a style appropriate for the industrial 20th century. *See also* KANDINSKY, WASSILY; KLEE, PAUL.

bauxite The chief ore of aluminium. It is a residual deposit formed by the weathering of aluminium-rich rocks (mainly syenites) under tropical conditions and consists mainly of hydrated aluminium oxide.

b

Bavaria (German name: Bayern) The largest *Land* of Germany, bordering on Austria and the Czech Republic. Mainly agricultural, it produces rye, wheat, and barley. *History*: a duchy and later a kingdom ruled by the Wittelsbachs from 1180 to 1918, it then became a republic. Area: 70 547 sq km (29 232 sq mi). Population (2000 est): 12 155 000. Capital: Munich.

Bax, Sir Arnold Edward Trevor (1883–1953) British composer. His tone poems, such as *Tintagel* (1917) and *The Garden of Fand* (1916), and his seven symphonies remain his most popular works. He was Master of the King's Music from 1941 until his death.

bay A Mediterranean evergreen tree, *Laurus nobilis*. It can reach a height of 20 m, has aromatic dark-green lance-shaped leaves used to season food. Family: *Lauraceae* (*see* LAUREL).

Bayeux 49 16N 0 42W A town in NW France, in the Calvados department on the River Aure. There is a fine 13th-century cathedral. Industries include dairy foods and plastics. The **Bayeux Tapestry** is an 11th-century embroidered linen strip, 69 m (231 ft) long, which depicts the Norman conquest of England (1066). The tapestry was reputedly commissioned for Bayeux cathedral by its bishop, Odo, the half-brother of William the Conqueror, whose wife Matilda is traditionally credited with its making. Some experts have concluded, however, that it was made in England. It is now exhibited in a former seminary close to the cathedral. Population (latest est): 14 704.

Bay of Pigs (Spanish name: Bahia de los Cochinos) A bay on the SW coast of Cuba where on 17 April 1961, about 1200 Cuban exiles attempted to invade the country. Hoping to overthrow Fidel Castro, and supported by the US *Central Intelligence Agency, the invasion was unsuccessful largely because it lacked sufficient US military backing.

Bayreuth 49 27N 11 35E A town in S Germany, in Bavaria. It was the home of Richard *Wagner, who designed its Festival Theatre (1872–76), where his operas are performed annually. Population (1991): 72 780.

bazooka Originally a 2.36 inch (60 mm) antitank rocket launcher fired from the shoulder and used by the US army in World War II, but later any similar weapons. The name came from a tubular wind instrument.

BBC *See* BRITISH BROADCASTING CORPORATION.

BCG (bacille Calmette Guérin) A vaccine consisting of a weakened form of the tuberculosis bacterium, which is injected to give partial protection against tuberculosis. A successful vaccination produces a lump at the injection site.

beagle A long-established breed of dog originating in the UK. It has a deep chest, strong shoulders, and drooping ears. Beagles have long been used as hunting hounds; more recently, they have become popular household pets. Height: 33–40 cm.

bean The seed or fruit of certain herbs, shrubs, or trees of the family *Leguminosae*. *See* BROAD BEAN; FRENCH BEAN; LIMA BEAN; MUNG BEAN; RUNNER BEAN; SOYA BEAN.

bear A large heavy mammal belonging to a family (*Ursidae*; 8 species) found in Europe, Asia, and America. Bears have a shaggy coat and a short tail and walk flat on the soles of their broad feet. They can stand erect and most of them are vegetarian. Newborn bears are very small (about the size of rats), blind, and toothless. Order: *Carnivora*. *See* BLACK BEAR; BROWN BEAR; POLAR BEAR; SPECTACLED BEAR; SUN BEAR.

bearbaiting A *blood sport formerly popular in Britain and Europe. A bear, sometimes blinded, was chained to a stake in a bear pit or bear garden and dogs were let loose to attack it. **Bullbaiting** used bulls in a similar way. Both bearbaiting and bullbaiting were made illegal in the UK in 1835.

bearded vulture *See* LAMMERGEIER.

Beardsley, Aubrey Vincent (1872–98) British illustrator of the periodicals *The Yellow Book* and *The Savoy* and of several books, including Wilde's *Salome* and Pope's *Rape of the Lock*, he achieved notoriety with his grotesque and erotic imagery. His curved lines, characteristic of *Art Nouveau, contrast with dense areas of black ink.

Beas, River A river in NW India, flowing mainly W from the Himalayas to the River Sutlej. It forms part of the Punjab irrigation scheme. Length: 470 km (290 mi).

beating the bounds A traditional ceremony that takes place in several English towns and villages on Ascension Day. Primarily a religious event, it evolved during the reign of Elizabeth I, and is derived from the earlier ceremonies of Rogationtide. A priest leads those present round the parish boundaries offering prayers for the harvest while young boys beat the boundary stones with sticks. An equivalent Scottish ceremony is called riding the marches.

Beatitudes In the New Testament, the eight blessings with which Jesus opened the Sermon on the Mount (Matthew 5.3–12). They describe such Christian virtues as meekness, mercy, and purity of heart (e.g. "Blessed are the meek: for they shall inherit the earth."). The word derives from the Latin of the *Vulgate, *beati sunt* (blessed are).

Beatles A British rock group, which achieved worldwide popularity during the 1960s. The Beatles appeared at the Cavern Club in Liverpool in 1962 and subsequently recorded "Love Me Do" and "She Loves You," which became a British number one in 1963. By this time the group consisted of George Harrison (1943–2001), John *Lennon, Paul *McCartney, and Ringo Starr (1940–); they toured the USA successfully, made two films, and were awarded MBEs in 1965. Their later albums include *Sergeant Pepper's Lonely Hearts Club Band* (1967). In 1970 they disbanded to pursue separate careers.

Beat movement US literary and social movement of the 1950s that sought personal liberation through art, drugs, sex, and any other "consciousness-expanding" means. The movement centred on the artistic communities of Greenwich Village in New York and of San Francisco and Los Angeles. Among its prominent writers were Allen Ginsberg (1926–97) and Jack Kerouac (1922–69).

Beaton, Sir Cecil (Walter Hardy) (1904–80) British photographer. From the 1920s onwards he became famous for his society portraits, many taken for *Vanity Fair* and *Vogue* magazines. After World War II he turned also to scenery and costume designs, notably for *My Fair Lady*.

Beatrix (1938–) Queen of the Netherlands since the abdication (1980) of her mother Queen Juliana. Her marriage (1966) to the German Claus von Amsberg (1926–2002) caused some controversy.

beats Variations in the intensity of sound when two tones of nearly equal frequency are heard. The effect is similar to that of *interference. At certain times, the amplitudes of the waves reinforce each other and, at intermediate times, they tend to cancel each other out. The frequency of the beats is equal to the difference in the frequencies of the two notes.

Beatty, David, 1st Earl (1871–1936) British admiral. In World War I, Beatty took part in the destruction of three German cruisers in Heligoland Bight (1914) and the sinking of the *Blücher* near Dogger Bank (1915). He also fought in the Battle of Jutland (1916). As commander of the Grand Fleet, he received the German naval surrender in 1918.

Beaufort scale A scale of wind speed devised in 1805 by Admiral Sir Francis Beaufort (1774–1857).

Beaumarchais, Pierre-Augustin Caron de (1732–99) French dramatist. Son of a watchmaker, he became rich and famous with *The Barber of Seville* (1775) and *The Marriage of Figaro* (1778), which inspired operas by *Rossini and *Mozart. Constantly involved in lawsuits, he wrote *Mémoires* (1773–75) in self-defence.

Beaune 47 02N 4 50E A town in E central France, in the Côte-d'Or department. The centre for the wine trade of Burgundy, it has a wine museum. Population (latest est): 21 127.

Beaufort number	*description of wind*	*wind speed knots*	*wind speed metres per second*
0	calm	< 1	0.0– 0.2
1	light air	1– 3	0.3– 1.5
2	light breeze	4– 6	1.6– 3.3
3	gentle breeze	7–10	3.4– 5.4
4	moderate breeze	11–16	5.5– 7.9
5	fresh breeze	17–21	8.0–10.7
6	strong breeze	22–27	10.8–13.8
7	near gale	28–33	13.9–17.1
8	gale	34–40	17.2–20.7
9	strong gale	41–47	20.8–24.4
10	storm	48–55	24.5–28.4
11	violent storm	56–63	28.5–32.6
12	hurricane	≥64	≥32.7

Beaufort scale

b

Beauvais 49 26N 2 05E A market town in N France, in the Oise department. Its fine cathedral (begun 1227) was damaged during World War II and the factory in which the famous Gobelin tapestries had been made since 1664 was completely destroyed and subsequently moved to Paris. Population (latest est): 56 280.

Beauvoir, Simone de (1908–86) French novelist and essayist. The constant companion of Jean-Paul *Sartre, whom she met at the Sorbonne in 1929, her novels include *The Blood of Others* (1948), *The Mandarins* (1956), and *All Said and Done* (1975). *The Second Sex* (1953) argued for the liberation of women from their traditional roles.

Beaux-Arts A French classical-revival architectural style that flourished at the École des Beaux Arts, Paris, in the late 19th century. The Paris Opera (1861) and Monte Carlo Casino (1878) were built by J. L. C. Garnier (1825–98) in this style.

beaver A large aquatic *rodent, *Castor fiber*, of Europe, Asia, and North America. Over 1 m long and weighing up to 40 kg, beavers have a dark sleek waterproof coat and a broad flat tail used for balance and swimming. They build a "lodge" of sticks and mud using their large incisor teeth to cut wood. During the summer they feed on vegetation. Family: *Castoridae*.

Beaverbrook, Max(well) Aitken, 1st Baron (1879–1964) British newspaper proprietor and politician, born in Canada. In 1919 he bought a majority interest in the *Daily Express*, in 1921 he founded the *Sunday Express*, and in 1929 bought the *Evening Standard* (London). He served in Lloyd George's World War I cabinet as minister of information (1918) and in Churchill's World War II cabinet as minister of aircraft production (1940–41).

Bechet, Sidney (1897–1959) US Black jazz clarinetist and soprano saxophone player. He achieved wide recognition after a tour of Europe in 1919, subsequently worked with Duke Ellington, and after World War II lived in Paris.

Becket, St Thomas (c. 1118–70) English churchman. The son of a London merchant, Becket became chancellor to Henry II in 1154 and archbishop of Canterbury in 1162. After quarrelling with Henry he refused to swear allegiance to the Constitutions of Clarendon and was exiled to France (1164–70). Subsequent attempts to resolve the dispute failed and on 29 December 1170 he was murdered in Canterbury Cathedral by four courtiers who took literally Henry's frustrated remark "Will no-one rid me of this turbulent priest?' He was canonized in 1173.

Beckett, Samuel (1906–89) Irish novelist, dramatist, and poet. After studying at Trinity College, Dublin he settled in Paris in 1937. He wrote in both French and English. His plays, which include *Waiting for Godot* (1954), and his prose works, such as the trilogy *Molloy* (1951), *Malone Dies* (1951) and *The Unnamable* (1953), treat human existence with a nihilism tempered by desperate humour. His later works, such as *Breath* (1972) and *Not I* (1973), are notably brief and concentrated. He won the Nobel Prize in 1969.

Beckham, David (1975–) British Association footballer. A midfielder, he has played for England since 1996 and became captain in 2000. He and his wife, Victoria, a former member of the Spice Girls pop group ("Posh Spice"), moved to Spain in 2003, when he joined Real Madrid.

Becquerel, (Antoine) Henri (1852–1908) French physicist, who was professor at the Conservatoire des Arts et Métiers in Paris. He discovered radioactivity (1896) by chance, on finding that invisible rays from uranium salts could affect a photographic plate even through a light-proof wrapper. For his research on these radiations, Becquerel shared the Nobel Prize (1903) with his associates Pierre and Marie *Curie. The SI unit of activity (radioactivity), the **becquerel** (Bq), is named after him. It is equal to the number of atoms of a radioactive substance that disintegrate in one second.

bedbug A flat wingless insect, about 5 mm long, belonging to a family (*Cimicidae*; 30 species) of blood-sucking parasites. In temperate regions *Cimex lectularius* is the species that most commonly attacks man, hiding by day in bedding, furniture, etc., and becoming active at night. Order: *Hemiptera* (bugs).

Bedchamber Crisis (1839) A constitutional crisis that arose over Queen Victoria's ladies of the bedchamber. After the resignation of Lord Melbourne, a Whig, Peel attempted to form a Tory ministry and requested that Victoria dismiss her Whig ladies. She refused and Melbourne remained in office until his government fell in 1841, when Victoria consented to the dismissal of three ladies.

Bede, St (c. 673–735 AD) English historian, known as the Venerable Bede. After 682 he lived at the monastery of Jarrow in Northumberland. His *Ecclesiastical History of the English People* (c. 731), written in Latin and later translated into English is an important source for Anglo-Saxon history (5th–8th centuries). He was the author of many grammatical, scientific, and historical works. Feast day: 27 May.

Bedford 52 08N 0 29W A town in S England, the administrative centre of Bedfordshire on the River Ouse. John *Bunyan was born nearby and spent 12 years in Bedford gaol. Business includes manufacturing, distribution, and call centres. Population (1991): 73 917.

Bedfordshire A county in the South Midlands of England. It is chiefly low lying, rising to the Chiltern Hills in the SW, and is drained by the Great Ouse River. Agricultural products include wheat and vegetables. The chief industries are centred on Luton, Dunstable, and Bedford. Area: 1192 sq km (460 sq mi). Population (2001, excluding Luton): 381 571. Administrative centre: Bedford.

Bedlington terrier A breed of dog originating in Bedlington, N England, in the early 19th century. It has long legs and a narrow face and is a sporting dog. The thick coat may be blue or sandy. Height: about 40 cm.

Bedouin The nomadic *Arab tribes of the Syrian and Arabian deserts. Their economy is based on camels, sheep, and goats. Courageous fighters, the Bedouin played an active role in the early Arab conquests, but are under pressure to take up a settled existence.

bee A four-winged insect (10–30 mm long) belonging to the worldwide superfamily *Apoidea* (about 12 000 species). Bees feed on pollen and nectar and are important pollinators. The ovipositor is used to sting attackers and in some species is barbed, remaining in the wound. Most solitary bees nest in soil, hollow trees, or wall cavities. Some, however, tunnel into wood (the carpenter bee) or construct nests using earth (*see* MASON BEE) or leaves (*see* LEAFCUTTER BEE). The female lays one or more eggs in a nest that is then sealed. The social bees (families *Apidae* and *Halictidae*) live in communities organized into castes—workers (infertile females), drones (males, developed from unfertilized eggs), and a queen (a fertile female). Colonies are established in trees, walls, or cliffs (*see also* HONEYBEE). Order: *Hymenoptera*.

beech A tree of the genus *Fagus* (10 species), native to N temperate regions, occasionally reaching a height of 40 m. Beeches have smooth grey bark. The leaves are oval, the flowers are unisexual and inconspicuous, and the fruits are seeds enclosed in husks (beechnuts or mast). The common beech of Europe and Asia is *Fagus sylvatica*, the timber of which is used for furniture and flooring. Family: *Fagaceae*.

Beecham, Sir Thomas (1879–1961) British conductor. He used his inherited fortune for the advancement of English music. He promoted the work of Richard Strauss, Sibelius, and—particularly—Delius. He founded the London Philharmonic Orchestra (1932) and the Royal Philharmonic Orchestra (1947).

bee-eater A brightly coloured bird belonging to a family (*Meropidae*; 24 species) occurring mainly in tropical Old World regions. Bee-eaters have pointed wings, long central tail feathers, a slender curved bill, and, commonly, a black eye stripe. They nest in burrows and feed in flight, chiefly on bees and wasps. Order: *Coraciiformes* (hornbills, kingfishers, etc.).

beer An alcoholic drink made from fermented malt flavoured with hops. Beer is brewed by malting barley, or other grain, by allowing it to germinate; the resulting malt is dried (kilned), ground, and heated with water (mashed). Starch in the grain is converted into soluble carbohydrates by enzymes in the malt. The resulting liquid wort is boiled with hops to concentrate the wort and utilize the bitter flavour of the hops. Yeast is added and the carbohydrates in the wort are converted into alchohol by fermentation. Beer was drunk in ancient Egypt and is now enjoyed worldwide. **Ale** was originally a stronger drink than beer, brewed without hops. The terms are now interchangeable, although ale is sometimes reserved for stronger brews fermented at higher temperatures. **Mild** beer is made with fewer hops than **bitter** and a darker malt is used to impart colour. **Lager** is traditionally a light beer matured over a long period at low temperature. **Stout** is made from a blend of roasted barley and malts.

Beerbohm, Sir Max (1872–1956) British caricaturist and writer. His only novel, *Zuleika Dobson* (1911), is an Oxford romance. From 1911 he lived in Rapallo, Italy, returning to England only during World War II.

Beersheba 31 15N 34 47E A town in S Israel, the largest in the Negev. In World War I it was the scene of a British victory over the Turks. Population (1999 est): 163 700.

beeswax A substance produced by bees to build honeycombs. It is collected by heating the honeycomb in water so that the floating wax can be separated. Beeswax (melting point

61–69°C) is used in high-quality polishes, candles, etc.

beet A herbaceous plant, *Beta vulgaris*, native to Europe and the Mediterranean region. Several varieties are cultivated in temperate areas, in particular the *sugar beet. The taproot of the red or garden beet yields beetroot, while the mangel-wurzel (*B. vulgaris vulgaris*) is an important fodder. Family: *Chenopodiaceae*.

Beethoven, Ludwig van (1770–1827) German composer, born in Bonn. His father, a court musician, attempted to exploit him as a child prodigy. He settled in Vienna in 1792 after studying there with Haydn. At the age of 30 he began to go deaf. About 600 of Beethoven's works survive, among them 9 symphonies, 5 piano concertos, 1 violin concerto, 16 string quartets, 10 violin and piano sonatas, 32 piano sonatas, 2 ballets, 2 masses, the opera *Fidelio* (1805–14), and about 200 song settings. His last works include the *Missa Solemnis* (1818–23), the ninth symphony (1817–23), and the innovative late string quartets.

beetle An insect belonging to the largest order (*Coleoptera*; about 278 000 species) of the animal kingdom. The forewings are specialized as hard structures (called elytra), which cover the functional hindwings when these are not in use. The elytra and the thick cuticle provide protection against predation and desiccation and enable aquatic species to trap a store of air. Many beetles are pests of crops, timber, etc.; others are useful by preying on insect pests. *See also* WEEVIL.

Beeton, Isabella Mary (1836–65) British author of one of the most famous English cookery books, *The Book of Household Management* (1861), first published in a women's magazine founded by her husband. She died of puerpural fever at the age of 29 after the birth of her third child.

Begin, Menachem (1913–92) Israeli statesman; prime minister (1977–83). Born in Russia, he commanded Jewish forces in Palestine from 1942. In 1948 he founded the Freedom (Herut) Movement and in 1973 became joint chairman of the Unity Party. In 1979 he negotiated the Camp David peace agreement with *Sadat, for which they shared the Nobel Peace Prize.

Begonia A genus of generally succulent herbaceous plants (about 1000 species) native to the tropics. They are grown as ornamental plants for their colourful flowers. Family: *Begoniaceae*.

Behan, Brendan (1923–64) Irish playwright. His first play, *The Quare Fellow* (1954), and his autobiography, *Borstal Boy* (1958), were based on his imprisonment for IRA activities. His best-known play was *The Hostage* (1957).

behaviourism A school of psychology, founded in the USA by J. B. Watson (1878–1958) in the early 20th century, that aims to predict observable behaviour. The approach was successful in describing how animals learnt tasks in the laboratory but cannot fully account for such complex processes as emotion, language, and relationships. **Behaviour therapy** is a method of treating psychological problems by assuming that they are the result of faulty learning. It was developed mainly by Hans Eysenck (1916–97) from behaviourism. Conditioning may be used to teach new behaviour, such as better ways of relating to people, or to eliminate undesirable behaviour, such as excessive drinking (*see* AVERSION THERAPY). It includes treatment for *phobias, in which repeated exposure to the feared object or situation reduces the subject's fear of it.

Beiderbecke, Bix (Leon Bismarck B.; 1903–31) US jazz cornetist and pianist. He played with Louis Armstrong and in the band of Paul Whiteman (1891–1967), becoming a jazz legend because of his great originality and his early death from alcoholism.

Beijing (**Peking** *or* **Pei-ching**) 39 55N 116 25E The capital of the People's Republic of China, an autonomous city situated in the NE of the country in Hobei province. The city has expanded considerably since 1949 and there has been rapid development of industries. *History*: the site has a long history of human habitation. As Ta-tu, it first became the capital (of N China) under the Yuan dynasty in 1272. The capital was later moved to Nanjing, returning to Beijing (1420) under the third Ming emperor. In 1928 the Nationalist (Guomindang) government moved the capital to Nanjing. Beijing became the capital of the People's Republic of China in 1949. In 1989 thousands of students demonstrating for reform were massacred in Tiananmen Square. Population (1999 est): 6 633 929.

Beirut 33 52N 35 30E The capital of the Lebanon, on the E Mediterranean. After centuries of Turkish domination, it was held by the French from World War I until 1941, when it became the capital of the newly independent Lebanon. It was badly damaged in the civil war (1975–76) and in 1982 when Israeli forces besieged the city and forced the Palestine Liberation Organization to leave. It was then the scene of fighting between religious factions until the private militias withdrew in 1990. Population (1998 est): 1 500 000.

Belarus (**Belorussia**, **Byelorussia** *or* **White Russia**) A republic in E Europe. The majority of its inhabitants are Belarussians, a Slav people. *Economy*: dairy and meat farming are important. Owing to the lack of mineral resources, industry declined after the collapse of the Soviet Union; in 1994 Belarus entered an economic union with Russia to try to solve this problem. *History*: Belarus was part of Lithuania, Poland, and then Russia before becoming a constituent republic of the Soviet Union in 1919. It became an independent republic in 1991. Although a multiparty constitution was adopted, the former communists have continued to dominate politics. In the late 1990s President Aleksandr Lukashenko signed controversial treaties with Russia establishing joint economic and foreign policies and assumed near-dictatorial powers. He was reelected by a landslide in 2001 but foreign observers condemned the poll as unfair. The regime's suppression of opposition has provoked much criticism. Official languages: Belarussian and Russian. Currency: rouble of 100 kopeks. Area: 207 600 sq km (80 134 sq mi). Population (2003 est): 9 881 000. Capital: Minsk.

Belau, Republic of (name until 1981: Palau *or* Pelew) A country in the W Pacific Ocean comprising a group of islands, eight of which are inhabited. *Economy*: fishing is the main source of income; tourism is being developed. *History*: formerly part of the Spanish Empire, the islands were administered successively by Germany, Japan, and the USA before becoming a UN Trust Territory in 1947. Self-government was achieved in 1981 (with the USA retaining control of foreign and defence policy) and full independence in 1994. Official languages: Palauan and English. Currency: US dollar of 100 cents. Area: 488 sq km (188 sq mi). Population (2003 est): 20 200. Capital: Koror.

Belém 1 27S 48 29W A port in N Brazil, the capital of Pará state on the Rio do Pará. It exports products from the Amazon basin including nuts, jute, and rubber. Population (1996): 851 705.

Belfast **1.** 54 40N 5 50W The capital of Northern Ireland, a seaport situated where the River Lagan enters Belfast Lough in Belfast district, Co Antrim and Co Down. The principal buildings include the City Hall (1906) and Parliament Buildings (1932) at Stormont. *History*: Belfast grew with the expansion of the linen-making and shipbuilding industries in the 19th century; it became a city in 1888. The parliament of Northern Ireland sat in the city from 1921 to 1972. Its recent history has been marked by conflict between Protestant and Roman Catholic communities. The British army has maintained a presence since 1969 (much reduced since the terrorist ceasefires of the mid-1990s). Population (1991): 279 237. **2.** A district of W Northern Ireland in Co Antrim and Co Down. Area: 115 sq km (44 sq mi). Population (2001): 277 391.

Belgae The Germanic tribes occupying NE *Gaul in Roman times. Julius Caesar, who named them, defeated them in 57 BC but they continued their opposition to the Romans from SE Britain.

Belgium, Kingdom of (French name: Belgique; Flemish name: België) A country in NW Europe, on the North Sea. It is low lying except for the Ardennes in the SE. The population is divided between the French and the Flemish, with other small minorities. *Economy*: highly industrialized, with engineering, food processing, brewing, textiles, and chemicals. The service sector is of growing importance. Agriculture is intensive but produces only for the home market. In 1921 a customs union was formed with Luxembourg and in 1948 both joined with the Netherlands to form the *Benelux Economic Union. Belgium is a member of the EU and almost two-thirds of its trade is with other members. *History*: the area was part of the Roman Empire until about the end of the 2nd century AD, when it was invaded by Germanic tribes. In medieval times the cities of Ghent, Bruges, and Ypres rose to virtual independence and prosperity through the wool industry. Its strategic position gave Belgium considerable importance in the balance of power in Europe and after being occupied by France during the Napoleonic Wars, it was joined to the Netherlands in 1815. Following an uprising, it became independent in 1830, and the National Congress elected Prince Leopold of Saxe-Coburg as King of the Belgians in 1831. It was attacked and occupied by Germany in both World Wars. When the Germans invaded in 1940, King *Leopold III surrendered immediately but the government struggled on in exile in London. In 1950 the king abdicated in favour of his son, *Baudouin, who was succeeded in 1993 by his brother, Albert II. Since World War II there has been tension between the French-speaking Walloons in the S and the Flemish-speaking community in the N. In 1977 Belgium was divided into the semiautonomous regions of Flanders, Wallonia, and Brussels, the regions acquiring greater autonomy under a new federal constitution in 1993. Dr Wilifried Martens (1936–) was prime minister from 1979 to 1992. Belgium adopted the European single currency in 1999–2002. Official languages: French, Flemish, Dutch, and German. Currency: euro of 100 cents. Area: 30 513 sq km (11 781 sq mi). Population (2003 est): 10 341 000. Capital: Brussels.

Belgrade (Serbo-Croat name: Beograd) 44 50N 20 30E The capital of the Union of Serbia and Montenegro and of Serbia, situated at the confluence of the Rivers Danube and Sava. It became the Serbian capital in the early 15th century. It later suffered Turkish and Austrian occupations but again became capital of Serbia in the late 19th century and of Yugoslavia after World War I. It was occupied by the Germans in World War II and has expanded considerably since. Population (2000 est): 1 194 878.

Belize (name until 1973: British Honduras) A country in Central America between Mexico and Guatemala. It is generally low lying, rising to the Maya Mountains in the SW. The population is of African, Spanish-American, and Mayan Indian descent, with other small minorities. *Economy*: mainly agricultural; with sugar, citrus, cocoa, and timber exports. Agriculture was devastated by hurricanes in 1998 and 2001. Tourism grew rapidly in the early 2000s. *History*: once a Mayan settlement, Belize was discovered by Columbus in 1502 but the first European occupation was a settlement of British woodcutters, which held out against the Spanish throughout the 17th century; in 1862 it became a British colony under Jamaica, becoming an independent colony in 1884; it attained self-government in 1964. Claims, based on early Spanish treaties, were made to it by Guatemala but it was granted full independence within the Commonwealth in 1981. The 1999 elections were won by the People's United Democratic Party led by Said Musa. Official language: English. Currency: Belize dollar of 100 cents. Area: 22 963 sq km (8867 sq mi). Population (2003 est): 269 000. Capital: Belmopan.

Belize City 17 29N 88 10W The chief port of Belize, on the Caribbean coast. It was formerly capital of Belize but following a severe hurricane (1961), Belmopan, which became capital in 1970, was constructed inland. Population (1994): 48 655.

Bell, Alexander Graham (1847–1922) Scottish-born US scientist and inventor. He went to Canada in 1870 and to the USA in 1873, becoming professor of vocal physiology at Boston University. Bell's work in telegraphy and telephony led to the invention of the telephone, which he patented in 1876.

belladonna *See* DEADLY NIGHTSHADE.

Bellerophon In Greek mythology, the grandson of Sisyphus and son of Glaucus, King of Corinth. Sent by Iobates, King of Lycia, to kill the *Chimera, he was able to carry out his task by flying above the dragon on Pegasus, a winged horse.

Bellini, Jacopo (c. 1400–c. 1470) Venetian painter, who was a pupil of *Gentile da Fabriano. Although few of his paintings survive, his two sketchbooks (British Museum and Louvre) reveal a remarkable understanding of perspective. They influenced his son-in-law Andrea *Mantegna and his two sons, who trained under him. The elder, **Gentile Bellini** (c. 1429–1507), is best known for his portraits and procession scenes. The younger, **Giovanni Bellini** (c. 1430–1516), was an important influence on Venetian art, especially through his pupils *Titian and *Giorgione. His paintings included several altarpieces.

Bellini, Vincenzo (1801–35) Italian composer. Of his 11 operas, *La somnambula* and *Norma* (both 1831) and *I Puritani* (1835) remain popular.

Belloc, (Joseph-Pierre) Hilaire (1870–1953) British poet and essayist. Born in France, he served (1906–10) as a Liberal MP. His works include light verse, essays, biographies, and satirical novels, often illustrated by his friend G. K. *Chesterton. A Roman Catholic apologist, he opposed the socialism of G. B. *Shaw and H. G. *Wells.

Bellow, Saul (1915–) Canadian-born US novelist, the son of Russian Jewish immigrants. His first novel, *Dangling Man* (1944), was influenced by *existentialism. Later novels, such as *Herzog* (1964), *Humboldt's Gift* (1975), *The Dean's December* (1982), and *Ravelstein* (2000) are ironic studies of harassed Jewish intellectuals. He won the Nobel Prize in 1976.

Belmopan 17 12N 88 00W The capital of Belize, on the River Belize about 80 km (50 mi) inland from Belize City, which it succeeded as the capital in 1970 after the latter was damaged by a hurricane in 1961. Population (2000 est): 8130.

Belo Horizonte 19 54S 43 54W A city in SE Brazil, in Minas Gerais state. Founded in 1897, it was Brazil's first planned city. Distinctive architecture includes Oscar Niemayer's Chapel of São Francisco. The chief industries include cotton textiles, meat processing, and iron and steel. Population (2000): 2 229 697.

Belorussia *See* BELARUS.

beluga 1. A giant *sturgeon, *Huso huso*, up to 8.4 m long, that occurs in the Caspian and Black Seas and the River Volga of E Europe. It is a highly prolific egg producer and the source of the best caviar. **2.** *See* WHITE WHALE.

bends *See* DECOMPRESSION SICKNESS.

Benedictines The monks and nuns belonging to the Roman Catholic Order of St Benedict (OSB), a union of independent abbeys, which follow the Rule of **St Benedict of Nursia** (c. 480–c. 550). Benedict, the father of Western monasticism, drew up his Rule at Monte Cassino, Italy, in 525; it requires residence in one place, common ownership of property, and a life of work, prayer, and study. The Benedictines were largely responsible for preserving the learning of antiquity after the fall of the Roman Empire. The liqueur Bénédictine is made by the order at Fécamp, France.

benefit of clergy The development in England of the 12th-century canon law that criminal clerics should not be tried by both ecclesiastical and secular courts. Henry II established that all clerics had the right to be tried solely in ecclesiastical courts, which could not inflict capital punishment. This privilege was much abused in the middle ages and although limited during the Reformation was not abolished until the early 19th century.

Benelux The customs union formed by *Bel*gium, the *Ne*therlands, and *Lux*embourg in 1948. It was the first free-trade market in Europe. All three countries are now members of the European Union, which has similar aims.

Beneš, Edvard (1884–1948) Czechoslovak statesman. In 1918 Beneš helped Tomáš *Masaryk to found Czechoslovakia and became foreign minister. He became president in 1935 but spent World War II as head of a provisional government in London, returning to Czechoslovakia in 1945. He resigned in 1948, when Czechoslovakia became a communist state.

Bengal A region of the NE Indian subcontinent on the limb of the Indian Ocean known as the **Bay of Bengal**, around the Ganges and Brahmaputra deltas; it is divided between India and Bangladesh. *History*: the centre of Buddhist (8th–12th centuries), Hindu (11th–13th centuries), and Islamic dynasties, Bengal became the base for British expansion through India. It was partitioned between India and Pakistan at independence (1947).

Bengali An Indo-Aryan language spoken by 80 million people in Bangladesh and West Bengal (India). The literary form of the language uses many *Sanskrit words. There is a distinct colloquial form.

Benghazi (*or* **Banghazi**; Italian name: Bengasi) 32 07N 20 05E The second largest city in Libya, on the Gulf of Sidra. Severely damaged during World War II, it has grown with the development of local oilfields: other industries include light engineering. Population (1995 est): 650 000.

Ben-Gurion, David (David Gruen; 1886–1973) Israeli statesman; Israel's first prime minister (1948–53, 1955–63). In 1917 he joined the British Army's Jewish Legion to free Palestine from Ottoman control (achieved in 1918) and to establish a Jewish home in Palestine, as promised in the *Balfour Declaration. In 1920 he founded the General Federation of Labour (the Histadrut) and in 1930 the Israeli Workers' Party (Mapai). He led the Zionist effort to establish a Jewish state, finally achieved in 1948. After resigning in 1963, he was leader of the opposition party, the Rafi, until 1970.

Benin, Republic of (name until 1975: Dahomey) A country in West Africa, on the Gulf of Guinea. Flat forests and swamps in the S rise to plateaus in the centre and to mountains in the N. The population is mainly Fon and Yoruba in the N and Somba and Bariba in the S. *Economy*: chiefly agricultural; cotton has been introduced in the N and coffee in the S, and these provide the main exports. Offshore oil has been found but production, which began in the 1980s, has so far proved disappointing. There is a huge external debt. *History*: the powerful Aja kingdom of Dahomey was a centre of the slave trade in the 17th century but was conquered by the French in 1893 and became part of French West Africa. Dahomey attained self-government in 1958 and became an independent republic within the French Community in 1960. A series of military coups ensued, in the last of which (1972) Brig Gen Mathieu Kérékou seized power. In 1974 he established a Marxist-Leninist state. Unrest led to the adoption of a pluralistic constitution (1990) but in 1996 Kérékou was re-elected as president. Official language: French. Currency: CFA franc of 100 centimes. Area: 112 600 sq km (43 464 sq mi). Population (2003 est): 7 041 000. Capital: Porto Novo.

Benin City 6 19N 5 41E A city in Nigeria. It is an important centre for the rubber industry

b

and also exports palm oil. Population (1996 est): 229 400.

Bennett, Alan British actor and writer. He appeared in and cowrote the Cambridge Footlights revue *Beyond the Fringe* (1959). His plays include *Forty Years On* (1968), *The Madness of George III* (1991), and *The History Boys* (2004). His *Talking Heads* (1988, 1998) were monologues for TV. *Writing Home* (1994) is a collection of diaries and essays.

Bennett, (Enoch) Arnold (1837–1931) British novelist. He published his first novel, *A Man from the North*, in 1898 and lived in Paris from 1902 to 1912. His best-known novels are about life in the Potteries area of Staffordshire, where he grew up. They include *Anna of the Five Towns* (1902), *The Old Wives' Tale* (1908), and *Clayhanger* (1910).

Bennett, Richard Rodney (1936–) British composer and pianist, known primarily for his scores for such films as *Far from the Madding Crowd* (1967), *Murder on the Orient Express* (1974), and *Four Weddings and a Funeral* (1994), and for his five major operas, including *The Mines of Sulphur* (1963) and *Victory* (1969).

Ben Nevis 56 48N 5 00W The highest mountain in the British Isles, in Highland, Scotland, in the Grampians. Height: 1343 m (4406 ft).

Bentham, Jeremy (1748–1832) British philosopher, pioneer of *utilitarianism. From a wealthy middle-class background, he studied law, but preferred theory to practice and in 1776 published *A Fragment on Government*. In 1789 *Principles of Morals and Legislation* presented utilitarianism. He retired to the country in 1814 and wrote copiously on politics and ethics until his death.

Benue, River A river in West Africa. Rising in N Cameroon, it flows W across Nigeria to join the River Niger at Lokoja. Length: 1400 km (870 mi).

Benxi (*or* **Pen-ki**) 41 21N 123 45E A city in NE China, in Liaoning province. It is a centre of iron and steel production. Population (1999 est): 827 203.

Benz, Karl (Friedrich) (1844–1929) German engineer and car manufacturer. In 1885 he built the first car to be driven by an internal-combustion engine. The Benz Company merged with Daimler in 1926 to form Daimler-Benz, the makers of Mercedes-Benz cars.

benzene (*or* **benzol**; C_6H_6) A colourless highly flammable liquid. It is the simplest aromatic compound, its molecules consisting of a ring of six carbon atoms each with a hydrogen atom attached. Benzene is obtained from *oil and from *coal tar. It is widely used in the chemical industry.

benzodiazepines A class of tranquillizing drugs that act by depressing specific areas of the brain. Benzodiazepines, such as diazepam (Valium) and chlordiazepoxide (Librium), are used as *sedatives. Nitrazepam (Mogadon) is used as a sleeping pill (a hypnotic). Both nitrazepam and diazepam are habit forming. Recent years have seen mounting concern about the effects of long-term usage and abuse of benzodiazepines, particularly of temazepam (Normison), which is now a controlled drug.

Beowulf An Anglo-Saxon epic poem preserved in a late 10th-century manuscript. Probably composed in the 8th century by a Christian poet sympathetic to pagan ideals, it alludes to historical events of early 6th-century Scandinavia. In the first part the hero, Beowulf, kills the marauding monster, Grendel; in the second part, Beowulf, now king of the Swedish tribe of Geats, slays a dragon but is mortally wounded.

Berberis A widely distributed genus of deciduous or evergreen spiny shrubs (over 400 species). The small yellow or orange flowers usually grow in clusters and the fruits are red or blue berries. Berberis is implicated in a rust disease of wheat and is therefore outlawed in some areas. Family: *Berberidaceae*.

Berbers A Muslim people occupying parts of N Africa (Morocco, Algeria, Tunisia, and adjacent regions) and speaking a non-Semitic language. Prior to the introduction of Arabic speech in the 7th century AD, Berber languages were spoken over the whole of the area and are still spoken by an estimated ten million people; Morocco is still predominantly Berber in population. The Berbers played an important role in the Islamic conquest of the Iberian peninsula in the 8th century.

Berg, Alban (1885–1935) Austrian composer. A friend and pupil of *Schoenberg, he adopted *atonality and used *serialism. His greatest works are the operas *Wozzeck* (1915–21) and *Lulu* (1928–35), the intensely personal *Lyric Suite* (for string quartet; 1925–26), and a violin concerto (1935).

bergamot A tree, *Citrus bergamia*, closely related to the orange. An essence (oil of bergamot) extracted from the rind of its fruit is used in perfumery. The name is also given to two plants of the mint family (*Labiatae*): *Men-*

tha citrata, which yields an extract similar to oil of bergamot, and *Monarda citriodora* (lemon bergamot) sometimes used in a tealike beverage.

Bergen 60 23N 5 20E The second largest city in Norway, a sea port situated in the SW. Founded about 1070 AD, it became the chief commercial city and the country's capital (12th–13th centuries). It had connections with Hanseatic merchants (14th–18th centuries). It was rebuilt after damage by fire in 1702, 1855, and 1916 and by bombing during World War II. It exports fish products and base metals. Population (1997 est): 224 130.

Bergenia A genus of herbaceous perennial plants (6 species), native to central and E Asia but often cultivated for their attractive foliage and early-blooming pink or white flowers. Family: *Saxifragaceae*.

Bergius, Friedrich (1884–1949) German chemist, who shared the 1931 Nobel Prize with C. Bosch for inventing a process for making motor fuels from coal or petroleum residues by treating them with hydrogen under high pressure and temperature (1913). This process was used extensively by Germany in World War II.

Bergman, Ingmar (1918–) Swedish film and stage director. His films, many of which explore tense psychological relationships and issues of religious belief, include *The Seventh Seal* (1956), *Wild Strawberries* (1957), *Persona* (1966), *Cries and Whispers* (1972), and *Fanny and Alexander* (1982).

Bergman, Ingrid (1915–82) Swedish actress. She went to Hollywood in 1939 and became an international film star, appearing in such films as *Casablanca* (1942), *Gaslight* (1944), and *Anastasia* (1956).

Bergson, Henri (1859–1941) French philosopher and psychologist. To reconcile free will and *determinism, Bergson distinguishes between consciousness, an indivisible flow of cumulative states in which (free) will operates, and the external physical world where causality reigns. His works include *Matière et mémoire* (1896) and *L'Évolution créatrice* (1907). He won the Nobel Prize for Literature in 1927.

beriberi A disease caused by deficiency of *vitamin B_1 (thiamine), common in areas where the staple diet is polished rice (thiamine occurs mainly in the rice husks). Dry beriberi affects the peripheral nerves, causing muscular weakness and pain. Wet beriberi is probably the result of combined protein malnutrition and thiamine deficiency: it causes accumulation of fluid and swelling of the limbs, leading eventually to heart failure. Treatment consists of providing a diet with adequate thiamine and vitamin supplements.

Bering Sea A section of the N Pacific Ocean between Russia, Alaska, and the Aleutian Islands. Navigation is difficult, with storms and a partial ice covering in winter. The NE continental shelf contains oil and gas, as yet unexploited. The **Bering Strait** is a narrow shallow channel between Asia and North America, connecting the Bering Sea with the Arctic Ocean. During the Ice Age it bridged the continents when the sea level fell.

Berkeley, George (1685–1753) Irish bishop and idealist philosopher. In *A New Theory of Vision* (1709), *Principles of Human Knowledge* (1710), and *Three Dialogues between Hylas and Philonous* (1713), he argued that the material world exists only in being perceived by the mind.

Berkeley, Sir Lennox (1903–89) British composer. He studied under Nadia Boulanger and taught at the Royal Academy of Music from 1946 to 1968. Berkeley's compositions include the *Serenade for Strings* (1939), *Four Poems of St Teresa* for contralto and strings (1947), and the fourth symphony (1978).

berkelium (Bk) A synthetic transuranic element synthesized by Seaborg at the University of California at Berkeley in 1949. The longest-lived isotope, ^{249}Bk, has a half-life of 314 days. At no 97; at wt (247).

Berkshire A historic county of S England. In 1974 it lost a substantial part of the NW to Oxfordshire, while gaining part of SW Buckinghamshire. In 1998 Berkshire county council was abolished, with administrative powers being devolved to six unitary authorities: Bracknell Forest, Reading, Slough, West Berkshire, Windsor and Maidenhead, and Wokingham. The county consists mainly of lowlands rising to the Berkshire Downs in the N. It is predominantly agricultural; industries include paints, plastics, and pharmaceutical goods at Slough and light engineering and horticulture at Reading. Area: 1256 sq km (485 sq mi).

Berlin 52 31N 13 20E The capital city and a *Land* of Germany, in the NE of the country on the River Spree. *History*: founded in the 13th century, it was an important member of the Hanseatic League. Its independence was reduced by the Hohenzollern Electors of Brandenburg from the 15th century, but it became their capital and grew in importance with their increasing power, becoming the capital of Prussia in the 18th century and of the German Empire in 1871. Badly damaged in World War II, it was occupied by the four major powers after the defeat of Germany. In 1948 Berlin became two separate administrative units: Soviet-controlled East Berlin and West Berlin, formed from the US, UK, and French zones. The Soviet Union blockaded the city for almost a year in 1948–49 (*see* BERLIN AIRLIFT). From 1949–90 East Berlin was the capital of East Germany; West Berlin remained an enclave within East Germany, administratively linked with West Germany. In 1961 the Berlin wall was built by the East Germans to curb the flow of refugees from E to W. Demolition of the wall began in 1989; full reunification was achieved in 1990, when Berlin became capital of the reunited Germany. The federal government was moved here in 1999. It is a major industrial and cultural centre. Population (1999 est): 3 392 900.

Berlin, Congress of (1878) A meeting of European powers, which revised the Treaty of San Stefano that had ended the 1877–78 Russo-Turkish War. The Congress limited Russian naval expansion, permitted Austria-Hungary to occupy Bosnia-Hercegovina, and gained Turkish recognition of the independence of Serbia, Romania, and Montenegro.

Berlin, Sir Isaiah (1909–97) British philosopher and historian, who was also a diplomat in Washington and Moscow. His works, which defend liberal humanism, include *The Inevitability of History* (1954), *Two Concepts of Liberty* (1959), and *Four Essays on Liberty* (1969).

Berlin airlift (1948–49) An operation by the Allies to supply isolated West Berlin with the necessities of life after the Soviet Union cut off all rail, road, and water links with the city in an attempt to force the Allies to abandon their rights there. The airlift continued until the blockade was lifted as a result of an embargo on exports from the E European states.

Berlioz, (Louis) Hector (1803–69) French Romantic composer and conductor. His first successful work, the *Symphonie Fantastique* (1830–31), was influenced by his love for his future wife, the Irish actress, Harriet Smithson (1800–54). His dramatic symphony *Harold in Italy* (1834) and choral symphony *Romeo and Juliet* (1839) were popular successes. The oratorio *The Childhood of Christ* (1850–54) was his last major success, for his two-part opera *The Trojans* (1856–59) was not performed complete in his lifetime. He was the author of a famous treatise on orchestration and a volume of memoirs.

Berlusconi, Silvio (1936–) Italian politician and media tycoon; prime minister (1994, 2001–). A controversial figure, he founded the populist Forza Italia movement in 1993 and led a centre-right coalition to victory in the elections of 2001.

Bermejo, Río A river of S central South America. Rising in S Bolivia, it flows SE into Argentina to join the River Paraguay. Length: 1046 km (650 mi).

Bermuda A United Kingdom overseas territory comprising some 300 coral islands (of which 20 are inhabited), in the W Atlantic Ocean. The largest island is Bermuda (*or* Great Bermuda), while smaller ones include Somerset, Ireland, and St George. Approximately three-quarters of the population is Black. *Economy*: tourism and agriculture are the main activities. *History*: visited by the Spanish navigator Juan de Bermudez in 1515, the islands were first settled in 1609 by British colonists shipwrecked there on the way to Virginia. They became the responsibility of the British Crown in 1684 and self-governing in 1968. Demands for independence led to serious unrest in the 1970s, but in 1995 the people voted against independence in a referendum. In 1998 the Labour Party formed a government under Jennifer Smith. Official language: English. Currency: Bermuda dollar of 100 cents. Area: 53 sq km (20 sq mi). Population (2002 est): 63 600. Capital: Hamilton.

Bermuda Triangle The most notorious of several geographic regions, all lying roughly between 30° and 40° of latitude, in which numerous ships and aircraft have vanished without trace. The Triangle covers about 3 900 000 sq km (1 500 000 sq mi) between Bermuda, Florida, and Puerto Rico. No generally satisfactory explanation of these disappearances has been advanced, but the powerful currents may explain the lack of wreckage.

Bern (French name: Berne) 46 57N 95 58W The capital of Switzerland, on the River Aare. Founded as a military post in the 12th century, it joined the Swiss Confederation in 1353 and became the capital in 1848. It has considerable industry and contains the headquarters of several international organizations. Population (1999 est): 123 254.

Bernadette of Lourdes, St *See* LOURDES.

Bernadotte, Jean Baptiste Jules (c. 1763–1844) French marshal, who was King of Sweden (1818–44) as Charles XIV John, founding the present Swedish royal house. Rising from the ranks he became a marshal under Napoleon, with whose support he was adopted as heir by the dying Charles XIII of Sweden. Turning against Napoleon, Bernadotte contributed to his defeat at Leipzig (1813). In 1814 he forced Denmark to cede Norway to the Swedish monarchy.

Berne Convention An international *copyright agreement of 1866. Its main provision guarantees copyright in all signatory countries of any work copyrighted in any one of them. The USA is still not a signatory.

Bernhardt, Sarah (Sarah Henriette Rosine Bernard; 1844–1923) French actress. Plays in which she gave worldwide performances include *Phèdre* (1879), *La Dame aux camélias*, and *L'Aiglon* by Edmond Rostand. She was also manager of several theatres in Paris.

Bernini, Gian Lorenzo (1598–1680) Italian *baroque sculptor and architect, born in Naples, the son of a sculptor. His first major sculptures were for Cardinal Scipione Borghese and included *Apollo and Daphne* (1622–24; Borghese Gallery, Rome). Encouraged by Urban VIII, he extended his talents into architecture, major works being the baldachin over the tomb of St Peter (1624–33) and the piazza and colonnade (1656–67) of St Peter's, Rome. Later sculptures included fountains for Roman piazzas.

Bernoulli's principle The principle of conservation of energy applied to fluid flow. If the effects of friction are neglected the total energy of the flow at any point in a pipe is equal to the sum of the kinetic energy due to the flow velocity, the gravitational potential energy due to height, and the energy of pressure in the fluid itself. Bernoulli's theorem states that the sum of these three components is constant throughout a flow system. Named after the Swiss scientist Daniel Bernoulli (1700–82).

Bernstein, Leonard (1918–90) US conductor, composer, and pianist. From 1958 to 1969 he was musical director and conductor of the New York Philharmonic Orchestra. His compositions, including symphonies, choral works, and songs, often contain jazz and folk elements. His musicals, such as *On the Town* (1944) and *West Side Story* (1957), have been widely popular.

Berruguete, Pedro (c. 1450–c. 1504) Castillian Renaissance painter. In the 1470s he worked in Italy at the court of Urbino, where he painted *Federigo da Montefeltro and his Son* (Urbino). On returning to Spain (1482) he painted frescoes for Toledo cathedral and altarpieces for the Dominican order in Avila. His son **Alonso Berruguete** (c. 1489–1561) was a mannerist painter and sculptor, who worked in Italy (c. 1504–c. 1517) and became court painter to Emperor Charles V (1518).

berserkers (Old Norse: bear-shirts) In Scandinavian mythology, savage warriors whose frenzy in battle transformed them from men into wolves or bears gave them immunity from harm by the sword or fire—hence the phrase "to go berserk." They were devotees of *Odin and, in early Scandinavian history, warriors called berserkers were often employed as bodyguards to nobles.

Berthelot, Marcelin (1827–1907) French chemist and politician. A pioneer of organic chemistry he demolished the theory that organic compounds contained a "vital force." In chemical thermodynamics he distinguished between endo- and exo-thermic reactions. He became a senator in 1881 and foreign secretary in 1895.

Berthollet, Claude Louis, Comte (1748–1822) French chemist and physician. He introduced bleaching by chlorine; he also showed that ammonia consists of hydrogen and nitrogen. Berthollet, working with *Lavoisier, developed a new chemical nomenclature. He travelled to Egypt as scientific adviser to Napoleon, who made him a senator and a count.

Bertolucci, Bernardo (1940–) Italian film director. His earlier films were influenced by Marxism, notably *Before the Revolution* (1965) and the epic *1900* (1977). He achieved commercial success with the controversial *Last Tango in Paris* (1972); other films include *The Last Emperor* (1988), *Stealing Beauty* (1996), and *Beseiged* (1999).

beryl A mineral consisting of beryllium aluminosilicate, found principally in granites and granite pegmatites. It occurs as crystals up to one metre in length and is white, pale blue, or green. Aquamarine and *emerald are gem varieties.

beryllium (Be) A light (relative density 1.85) alkaline-earth metal that was discovered in 1828 by F. Wöhler and A. Bussy (1794–1882) independently. It occurs in nature in such minerals as *beryl and phenacite (Be_2SiO_4). It is transparent to X-rays and is used as windows on X-ray tubes. Alloys with copper are extensively used and the oxide (BeO), having a high melting point (2530°C), is used as a ceramic. Its salts are poisonous. At no 4; at wt 9.0122; mp 1289°C; bp 2472°C.

Berzelius, Jöns Jakob, Baron (1779–1848) Swedish chemist, who found the atomic compositions of many chemical compounds. He also discovered the elements selenium (1817), silicon (1824), and thorium (1828) and determined the atomic and molecular weights of more than 2000 elements and compounds. He introduced the current notation for chemical formulae and the use of oxygen as a standard for atomic weights.

Bes The Egyptian god of recreation, also associated with children and childbirth. Images of the god, represented as a grotesque dwarf with a tail, were kept in homes as protection against evil.

Bessarabia A region in E Europe, largely in Moldova and Ukraine, with a predominantly Moldovan population. The main activity is agricultural processing. *History*: the region was colonized by the Greeks and later fell successively to the Romans, Huns, Magyars, Mongols, and Turks, passing to Russia in 1812. In 1918 Bessarabia declared its independence, later voting for union with Romania, which ceded it (1940) to the Soviet Union; it remained under Soviet control until 1991. Area: about 44 300 sq km (17 100 sq mi).

Bessemer process A steelmaking process invented by the British engineer Sir Henry Bessemer (1813–98) in 1855. A long cylindrical vessel (Bessemer converter) is charged with molten pig iron; air is blown through the iron to oxidize the carbon, silicon, and manganese impurities. Phosphorus is removed by reaction with the converter's basic refractory lining. Carbon, in the form of spiegel, is added to give steel of the required carbon content. It has been largely replaced by the basic-oxygen process.

Best, Charles Herbert (1899–1978) US physiologist, who, as an undergraduate research assistant to *Banting, helped to isolate the hormone insulin.

beta blocker A drug, such as propranolol, that prevents certain nerve endings (beta receptors) of the sympathetic nervous system from being stimulated, thus reducing heart activity. Developed by Sir James *Black, they are used to treat angina, arrhythmia, and hypertension.

beta decay A radioactive process in which a neutron within a nucleus decays by the *weak interaction into a proton, an electron (beta particle), and an antineutrino; alternatively, a proton may decay into a neutron, a positron, and a neutrino. Since the nuclear charge changes by one in both cases, the nucleus is converted into the nucleus of another element.

betatron A type of particle *accelerator used for producing very high energy electrons. The electrons are accelerated round a circular path in an evacuated torus-shaped chamber, by means of a large pulsed magnetic field. Electron energies up to 300 MeV are possible.

betel A mixture of the boiled dried seeds (**betel nuts**) of the areca, or betel palm (*Areca catechu*), and the leaves of the betel pepper (*Piper betle*), which produces copious salivation when chewed with lime—common in India.

Betelgeuse An immense conspicuous red *supergiant, over 500 light years distant, the second brightest star in *Orion. It is a variable star with its magnitude ranging from 0.3 to 0.9 over a period of about 5.8 years.

Bethlehem 31 42N 35 12E A town on the *West Bank of the River Jordan, near Jerusalem. The Church of the Nativity was built in 326 over the grotto that is the presumed birthplace of Jesus Christ. Population (latest est): 91 010.

Betjeman, Sir John (1906–84) British poet. He published his first book of poetry in 1933. His verse autobiography, *Summoned by Bells* (1960), shows the nostalgia and gentle social satire characteristic of his other poems. He took a keen interest in Victorian and Edwardian architecture. He was poet laureate from 1972.

betony A widespread perennial herb, *Stachys officinalis* (or *Betonica officinalis*), up to 30 cm high. It has round-toothed leaves and a dense head of reddish-purple tubular flowers. The leaves may be used for tea and for herbal tobacco. Family: *Labiatae*.

Bevan, Aneurin (1897–1960) British Labour politician, a brilliant orator on the party's left. As minister of health (1945–51), he was the architect of the *National Health Service. He was also minister of labour in 1951. His wife **Jenny, Baroness Lee** (1904–88), a Labour MP (1929–31, 1945–70), was minister for the arts (1967–70).

Beveridge, William Henry Beveridge, 1st Baron (1879–1963) British economist, writer, and academic. Beveridge became an authority on unemployment. His best-known work was the *Report on Social Insurance and Allied Services* (1942), the so-called **Beveridge Report**, on which the welfare state was based.

Bevin, Ernest (1881–1951) British politician and trade-union leader. In 1937 Bevin became chairman of the TUC and in 1940 he was appointed minister of labour, serving in Churchill's war cabinet. He was foreign secretary (1945–51) in the postwar Labour Government, when he helped to form NATO.

bezique A card game, usually for two players, that became popular in France about 1860. Two packs of 32 cards are used (standard packs with the cards from two to six removed). Each player is dealt eight cards; the next card indicates the trump suit and the rest form the stockpile. The object is to score points by collecting melds (certain combinations of cards) and to take tricks containing brisques (aces and tens). Play continues until one player's score reaches 1000 or 1500.

Bhagavadgita (Sanskrit: Song of the Lord) Hindu poem probably composed about 300 BC, forming part of the epic *Mahabharata*. It blends a number of Hindu philosophies. Arjuna, one of the five Pandava brothers, is compelled to battle with his kinsmen, the Kauravas; he is persuaded by *Krishna, acting as his charioteer, of the virtue of selflessly performing the duties of caste.

Bhaskhara II (1114–c. 1185) Indian mathematician, who was the first to use the decimal system in a written work, invented the + and – convention, and used letters to represent unknown quantities as in modern algebra.

Bhavachakra (Sanskrit: wheel of becoming) In Buddhism, an image of the cyclical nature of earthly existence, in the form of a wheel held by the demon of impermanence. At the centre, turning the wheel, are greed, hatred, and delusion, depicted as a cockerel, snake, and pig, biting each other's tails. Around the rim, the 12 stages in the cycle of life are symbolically expressed.

Bhopal 23 17N 77 28E A city in India, the capital of Madhya Pradesh. Notable buildings include the unfinished Taj-ul-Masjid, the largest mosque in India. Bhopal's varied manufactures include vehicle parts and cotton textiles. In 1984 over 2000 people died after poisonous isocyanate gas escaped from the US-owned Union Carbide factory. Population (1991): 1 063 662.

Bhutan, Kingdom of (Bhutanese name: Druk-yul) A small country in the E Himalayas, between India and Tibet. It is entirely mountainous, rising over 7300 m (21 900 ft) in the N. Over half the population are of Tibetan origin, known as Bhutias, with minorities of Nepalese in the S and Indians in the E. *Economy*: mainly agricultural; forests cover almost 60% of the land; hydroelectricity is being developed. *History*: in 1865 part of S Bhutan was annexed by the British and a treaty was concluded in which Britain agreed to pay an annual subsidy. In 1910 Britain agreed not to interfere in Bhutan's internal affairs and Sir Ugyen Wangchuk was elected the first hereditary maharaja (now referred to as king). In 1969 the absolute monarchy was replaced by a "democratic monarchy" and power is now between the king, the Council of Ministers, and the National Assembly. A process of devolving key powers from the king to the Assembly began in 1998. The 1990s saw ethnic tensions between Bhutias and Nepalese, many of whom fled to Nepal. Official language: Dzongkha Bhutanese. Currency: ngultrum of 100 chetrums. Area: 46 600 sq km (18 000 sq mi). Population (2003 est): 685 000. Capital: Thimphu.

Bhutto, Benazir (1953–) Pakistani politician; prime minister (1988–90, 1993–96). She was the first female leader of a Muslim country. Twice dismissed from office for alleged corruption, she was convicted (in absentia) of corruption in 1999 and sentenced to five years' imprisonment; in 2001 Pakistan's Supreme Court ordered a retrial and in 2002 she was given a three-year sentence for failing to appear before the court.

Her father, **Zulfikar Ali Bhutto** (1928–79), formed the Pakistan People's Party in 1967; after the secession of East Pakistan (Bangladesh) he became president (1971–73) and prime minister (1973–77). He was ousted by a military coup, defeated in the subsequent election, and executed for conspiracy to murder an opponent.

Biafra The secessionist eastern region of Nigeria (1967–70). In an attempt to protect their interests the *Ibo people declared unilateral independence under Lieut Col Odumegwu Ojukwu (1933–). The federal government under Gen Yakuba Gowon (1934–) refused to recognize the new state and attacked it. The Ibo were decimated.

Białystok 53 09N 23 10E A city in NE Poland. It grew mainly under the Branicki family in the 18th century. In World War II the Germans killed half the population and destroyed the industry but cloth manufacture has been revived. Population (1999 est): 283 937.

biathlon 1. An athletic event first included in the Winter Olympic Games in 1960; competitors ski 20 km (12.5 mi) with rifles and ammunition and at each of four points along the course take five shots at 150 m (164 yd). **2.** An athletic event consisting of running 4000 m (2.5 mi) and swimming 300 m (328 yd), introduced in 1968 by the Modern Pentathlon Association of Great Britain.

Bible (Greek *biblia*, books) The collected books of the *Old Testament, the *New Testament, and the *Apocrypha. The canon of the Hebrew Old Testament was definitively established by the rabbinical council of Jamnia (90–100 AD), although most of the books had acquired authority much earlier. The New Testament canon was also established gradually but had essentially its present form by the 3rd century AD. To Christians it represented the complete fulfilment of the prophecies of the Old Testament. Both Jews and Christians have traditionally regarded their scriptures as divinely inspired, hence correct in every particular. Almost all Christians agreed, until relatively recently, on the literal truth of the contents, a belief slowly eroded by the development of science from the 17th century. Despite attempts to condemn scientific findings when these appeared to conflict with scripture, as in the case of Galileo, scientific method was soon applied to the study of the Bible itself. As a result, many traditional assumptions about the Bible's content and authorship are no longer tenable. Most modern biblical criticism accepts that the scriptures must be interpreted within their historical context. The oldest extant complete manuscript of the Old Testament dates from the 11th century AD, but there are much earlier versions of such parts of the text as the Pentateuch (*see also* DEAD SEA SCROLLS). The earliest fragments of the New Testament date from the 2nd century AD; thereafter there are an extremely large number of manuscripts of quite early date. *Translations*: the first translation of the Bible is the Latin *Vulgate of St Jerome. Major English versions are: the version prefaced by *Wycliffe (1382–88), the last manuscript Bible written before the introduction of printing; the New Testament (1525) by Tyndale; the Bible of Miles Coverdale; the Great Bible (1539), supervised by Coverdale under the patronage of Thomas Cromwell; the *Geneva Bible; the Bishops' Bible (1568); the *Douai Bible; the *King James Version; the *Revised Version* (1881–95); the *Revised Standard Version* (1946–57); and *The New English Bible* (1961–70).

Bibliothèque Nationale The national library of France in Paris, containing around seven million volumes. It is based on the royal libraries of Charles the Wise (1364–80) and his successors. From 1537 it received a copy of every book published in France.

bicycles Light vehicles, the two wheels of which are moved by cranks attached to pedals operated by the rider. Bicycles developed in the 19th century from a two-wheeled hobby-horse or dandy-horse. Around 1840 a Scotsman, Kirkpatrick Macmillan, applied the dandy-horse principle to models with pedals. The first true bicycles, with rotary cranks on their front wheels, went into production in Paris in 1865. To increase efficiency the front wheel was gradually made larger, resulting in the 20-year vogue of the ordinary (*or* pennyfarthing) bicycle. This was superseded by the so-called safety bicycle (1876), which had a chain and sprocket drive to the rear wheel and was essentially the same as the modern bicycle. Pneumatic rubber tyres (1889), a freewheeling mechanism (1894), and variable gears (1899) were later refinements. The current trend is for wide-tyred machines called mountain bikes or all-terrain bikes (ATBs), with up to 24 gears. The first race was held in France in 1868.

Biddle, John (1615–62) English founder of Unitarianism (*see* UNITARIANS). While a schoolmaster he wrote his *Twelve Arguments* against the deity of the Holy Ghost, for which he was imprisoned in 1645. Although his adherents began to meet openly from 1652, he was arrested and banished under Cromwell and finally died in prison in London.

Biedermeier style A style of furniture and painting that flourished in Austria, Germany, and Scandinavia from about 1816 to about 1848. It was satirically named after the fictional Gottlieb Biedermeier, created by the poet Ludwig Eichrocht (1827–92) to characterize bourgeois bad taste. Biedermeier furniture utilized French *Empire style design for modern functional purposes. Biedermeier paintings aimed at extreme naturalism in outdoor scenes and intimacy in interiors and portraits.

bigamy The criminal offence of marrying a person while being married to another. Defences include an honest belief in the death of the original marriage partner, or that the first marriage was invalid. Although a person would not be guilty of bigamy in such cases, the second marriage will still be invalid.

big-bang theory A cosmological theory (*see* COSMOLOGY), first proposed in the 1920s, that all the matter and radiation in the universe originated in an immense explosion about 10 to 20 thousand million years ago. As the universe so created expanded, the initially high temperature decreased, enabling hydrogen and helium to form. This matter eventually interacted to form galaxies. The theory also predicts that the radiation formed shortly after the explosion should by now have cooled to about three kelvin. This is indeed the temperature of the isotropic microwave background radiation, detected in 1965 and now considered strong evidence for the big-bang theory.

Big Ben The 14-ton bell in the clock tower of the *Palace of Westminster (London), named after Sir Benjamin Hall (1802–67), commissioner of works when the clock was installed (1859). Both the clock and the tower itself are also known by this name.

bighorn A mountain sheep, *Ovis canadensis*, of North America. There is considerable variation within the species, ranging from the small Nelson's bighorn to the largest Rocky Mountain bighorns, which stand 100 cm at the shoulder.

Bihar A state in N India, bordering on Nepal. The densely populated rural Ganges plain produces rice, sugar cane, pulses, and vegetables. There is little industry and Bihar remains India's poorest state. *History*: the centre of N Indian civilization from 1500 BC, it was the scene of the early development of Buddhism and Jainism. More recently Bihar has seen conflict between Maoist insurgents and right-wing militias. In 2000 a large area of S Bihar became the new state of *Jharkand. Area: 99 225 sq km (38 301 sq mi). Population (2001 est): 82 878 000. Capital: Patna.

Bikini Atoll 11 35N 165 20E An atoll in the central Pacific Ocean in the *Marshall Islands. It was the site of US atomic and hydrogen bomb tests (some underwater) from 1946 to 1958.

Biko, Steven (1946–77) Black South African medical student, who cofounded the Black Consciousness movement in 1972. His arrest and death in police custody caused international concern and made him a hero of the struggle against *apartheid.

Bilbao 43 15N 2 56W A port in N Spain, the largest city in the Basque Provinces on the River Nervión. One of Spain's chief ports, its exports include iron ore, lead, and wine. Frank Gehry's Guggenheim Art Museum was opened here in 1997. Population (1998 est): 358 467.

bilberry A deciduous shrub, *Vaccinium myrtillus*, 30–60 cm high, also known as blaeberry, huckleberry, and whortleberry. It is found on acid moors and mountains in N Europe and N Asia. The angular stems bear small pointed leaves that turn red in autumn. The globular pink flowers develop into blue berries, which may be eaten raw or cooked or used to make preserves or wine. Family: *Ericaceae* (heath family).

bile A greenish alkaline fluid secreted by the liver and stored in the *gall bladder. Contraction of the gall bladder, which is triggered by a hormone released from the duodenum in the presence of food, causes the bile to be expelled through the common bile duct into the intestine. Bile is composed of a mixture of bile salts (which emulsifies fatty foods for digestion) and bilirubin (a breakdown product of the blood pigment haemoglobin).

bilharziasis *See* SCHISTOSOMIASIS.

billiards A game for two players using cues and balls on a table. In **English billiards** the table measures 12 × 6 ft (3.6 × 1.8 m) and has six pockets (holes round the edges of the table); points are scored using two white cue balls and one red ball, all 2 in (5.2 cm) in diameter. A cannon, in which the cue ball strikes both the other balls, scores two points; a winning hazard, in which the cue ball pockets another ball, scores two points (white) or three (red); a losing hazard, in which the cue ball is pocketed after striking another ball, scores two points (off white) or three (off red). A turn (*or* break) lasts until the player fails to score. **Carom billiards** is played on a smaller table with no pockets and scoring is by cannons (*or* caroms). **Bar billiards** is played on a small table with a timing device and holes in the surface, into which balls are potted off each other until the time runs out. *See also* SNOOKER.

Billingsgate A fish market in London, situated from the 16th century on the N bank of the River Thames by London Bridge. In 1982 it was moved to its present location on the Isle of Dogs.

Bill of Rights 1. (1689) An act of parliament incorporating the Declaration of Rights, the conditions on which the English throne was offered to William and Mary (*see* GLORIOUS REVOLUTION). It curtailed the royal prerogative. MPs were to be freely elected and guaranteed freedom of speech. Roman Catholics were barred from the throne. **2.** (1791) The first ten amendments to the US Constitution, described by Jefferson as "what the people are entitled to against every government on earth." They include freedom of press, speech, and religion and the right to a fair and public trial.

binary star Two stars moving around each

other under mutual gravitational attraction. Possibly 50% of stars are members of binary or other multiple systems. The components of a **visual binary** can be distinguished by telescope whereas a **spectroscopic binary** can only be detected by spectroscope measurements, the components usually being very close. In an **eclipsing binary** the orbital plane is so orientated that one component passes alternately in front of and then behind the other, causing the combined brightness to fluctuate. In a **close binary** the two components are close enough to exchange gaseous matter and can even share gas.

binary system A number system that uses only two digits 0 and 1. Numbers are expressed in powers of 2 instead of powers of 10, as in the decimal system. In binary notation, 2 is written as 10, 3 as 11, 4 as 100, 5 as 101, and so on. Computers calculate in binary notation, the two digits corresponding to two switching positions (e.g. on or off) in the logic circuits.

binding energy The energy released when protons and neutrons bind together to form an atomic nucleus. The mass of a nucleus is always less than the sum of the masses of the constituent protons and neutrons. The missing mass is converted into the binding energy according to Einstein's law $E = mc^2$.

bindweed A widely distributed climbing plant of the temperate and subtropical genera *Convolvulus* and *Calystegia*. Bindweeds twine their stems around other plants for support and can be persistent weeds. The leaves are large and arrow-shaped and the conspicuous white, pink, or yellow flowers are funnel-shaped. Family: *Convolvulaceae*.

bingo (former names: tombola; housy-housy) A gambling game developed in the 1880s from the children's game of lotto. Each player buys a card containing lines of random numbers (from 1 to 75 in the USA and usually from 1 to 90 in the UK). As numbers are called out, the players cover corresponding squares on their cards with counters; the first person to complete a line or the card wins. It became popular in the UK following a relaxation of the gaming laws during the 1960s, many local cinemas being converted into bingo halls.

Bin Laden, Osama (1957–) Saudi-born leader of the *al-Qaida terrorist movement. The heir to a vast fortune from his father's construction business, Bin Laden dedicated himself to militant Islamic activities in the late 1970s. His role in organizing guerrilla resistance to the Soviet invaders in Afghanistan (1979–89) made him a hero to many Muslims. However, his opposition to the stationing of US troops on Saudi soil (in 1990) then led him to organize a series of attacks on US military and diplomatic targets from Sudan (from 1992). In 1996 Bin Laden transferred these operations to Afghanistan, where he forged links with the *Taleban. In 2001 he achieved worldwide notoriety as the presumed instigator of the attacks on New York and Washington on *September 11. Although the USA's subsequent *war on terrorism destroyed al-Qaida's Afghan bases, Bin Laden is thought to have survived; his whereabouts are unknown.

binoculars A portable optical instrument used for magnifying distant objects. It consists of two telescopes fixed side by side, one for each eye, inside which there are a number of lenses for magnifying and focusing the image and usually prisms for altering the direction of the light and thus increasing the effective length of the telescope.

binomial nomenclature A system devised by *Linnaeus in the 18th century for the scientific naming of plants and animals, each species being identified by two Latin names—the name of the genus (written with an initial capital letter) followed by the name of the species. The specific name may be followed by the author's name, usually abbreviated. Thus the wolf is *Canis lupus* L (for Linnaeus).

binomial theorem The theorem, discovered by *Newton in 1676, that the quantity $(a+n)^n$, where n is an integer, can be expanded in a series: $(a+b)^n = a^n + na^{n-1}b + [n(n-1)\,a^{n-2}b^2]\,/\,2! + [n(n-1)(n-2)\,a^{n-3}b^3]\,/\,3! + \ldots + b^n$ where, for example, 3! (called factorial three) is $3 \times 2 \times 1$.

binturong A mammal, *Arctictis binturong*, of SE Asia, closely related to the *palm civets. It has a dark-grey shaggy coat, tufted ears, short legs, and a bushy prehensile tail (60 cm long). Binturongs live in trees and feed mainly on fruit and other vegetation.

biochemistry The scientific study of the chemical composition and reactions of living organisms. Central to biochemistry is *metabolism and the determination of the complex sequence of reactions involved in the digestion of food, the utilization of energy, the manufacture of new tissues, etc. Biochemists are also concerned with the role of *genes, *hormones, and *enzymes in initiating and controlling metabolic reactions.

biodegradable substances Materials that can be broken down by such processes as decomposition by fungi and bacteria—and can therefore be reused by living organisms. Substances that are **nonbiodegradable**, such as plastics, persist in the environment, causing pollution.

biological control The control of pests by the use of living organisms. The controlling agent is usually a predator, parasite, or disease of the pest. For example, the virus disease myxomatosis was introduced into Australia and Britain to control the rabbit population. Recent methods of controlling insect pests include the release of sterile males to mate among the population. Biological control avoids the environmental pollution of chemical pesticides.

biological warfare The use of disease-causing microorganisms as weapons. In World War I, the Germans infected Allied cavalry horses with bacteria causing *glanders. Although biological warfare is now officially banned by the major powers, research continues in developing new strains of such organisms as the plague bacterium (*Pasteurella pestis*) and the smallpox virus. The organisms are required to be highly virulent and could be delivered in the warhead of a missile. Alternatively, they could be added to water or food supplies. A more recent concern is so-called **bioterrorism**, such as the anthrax attacks on US and Pakistani targets in late 2001.

bioluminescence The production of light by living organisms, including certain bacteria, fungi, and animals (e.g. fireflies and glow-worms). In some the *luminescence is due to symbiotic light-producing bacteria. The light is emitted by the compound luciferin when it is oxidized: the reaction is catalysed by an enzyme, luciferase.

biomass The total weight (mass) of all living organisms (or of all members of a particular species) found in a given area. Biomass is expressed as mass per unit area.

biomass energy Energy obtained from the methane (biogas) generated by sewage or farm, industrial, and household organic waste, from specially cultivated organisms, or from crops, such as trees and sugar cane. Known collectively as **biofuels**, these alternative energy sources already supply some 4% of US fuel requirements.

biophysics The scientific discipline concerned with the explanation of biological phenomena in terms of the laws of physics. Biophysics emerged in the 1940s with the work of such scientists as Max *Perutz and John *Kendrew, who applied the phenomenon of X-ray diffraction to determine the structure of biological molecules. More recent topics include the nature of the nervous impulse and the operation of sense organs.

biopsy The removal of a sample of living tissue from the body for microscopic examination. Biopsies are used to assist in the diagnosis of diseases, including cancer, jaundice and anaemia.

biotin *See* VITAMIN B COMPLEX.

bipolar disorder *See* MANIC-DEPRESSIVE PSYCHOSIS.

birch A deciduous tree or shrub of the genus *Betula* (40 species), of the N hemisphere. Birches grow up to 25 m and have smooth grey bark, that peels off in strips. The glossy leaves are usually triangular, with toothed edges. The flowers are male and female catkins producing tiny winged nuts. Birch wood, especially that of the Eurasian silver birch (*B. pendula*), is used for turned articles. Family: *Betulaceae*.

bird A warm-blooded animal belonging to the class *Aves* (about 8600 species), adapted for flight by having fore limbs modified as wings and a body covering of feathers. Other adaptations include a light skeleton with hollow bones and a large breastbone providing attachment for the powerful flight muscles. The jaws are elongated into a horny bill (teeth are absent or reduced). Birds have good eyesight and colour vision and most are active by day. Many communicate by song (*see* SONGBIRD) and some undergo seasonal migrations.

Birds are of great economic importance to man. The eggs and flesh of many provide food (game or poultry). Wildfowl and game birds are hunted for sport, and the feathers of some birds provide ornamental plumes, etc. Other species are pests, for example by damaging crops. Modern birds include both flying and flightless species (ratites); they are grouped into 28 orders, the largest of which is the *Passeriformes* (*see* PASSERINE BIRD). *See also* ORNITHOLOGY.

bird of paradise A bird, 30–65 cm long, belonging to a family (*Paradisaeidae*; 40 species) occurring in New Guinea and neighbouring islands. The male is usually brightly coloured, with long tail feathers and ornamental plumes, and performs an acrobatic display to attract the dull-coloured female.

bird of prey A bird that hunts other animals for food, also called raptor. Birds of prey are divided into the nocturnal hunters, comprising the owls (order *Strigiformes*), and those that hunt by day, comprising the eagles, falcons, hawks, secretary bird, and the vultures (order *Falconiformes*). Live prey is normally taken but the vultures specialize in feeding on carrion. Birds of prey are characterized by their strong hooked bills for tearing flesh, clawed talons, and powerful flight with a high-speed dive onto prey.

bireme *See* SHIPS.

Birkenhead 53 24N 3 02W A port in NW England, in Wirral unitary authority, Merseyside, linked with Liverpool by road and rail tunnels. Population (1991): 93 087.

Birkenhead, F(rederick) E(dwin) Smith, 1st Earl of (1872–1930) British Conservative politician. A barrister, Birkenhead entered parliament in 1906. As attorney general (1915–19) he was famous for his prosecution of Sir Roger Casement (1864–1916) and while lord chancellor (1919–22) he introduced major land-law reforms. He was secretary for India (1924–28).

Birmingham 1. 52 30N 1 50W A city in central England, in Birmingham unitary authority, West Midlands. Britain's second largest city, it is a centre of engineering and metalworking. A cultural centre, it possesses three universities, an art gallery (1874–81), a symphony orchestra, a ballet company, a repertory theatre, and Symphony Hall (1991). Among postwar developments are a modern shopping complex centred on the Bull Ring (rebuilt 2002–03) and the National Exhibition Centre (1976). *History*: an Anglo-Saxon settlement, its development dates largely from the industrial revolution although its metalworking tradition is much older. It was severely bombed during World War II. Population (1994 est): 965 928. **2.** A unitary authority in Central England, in West Midlands. Area: 283 sq km (109 sq mi). Population (2001): 977 091. **3.** 33 30N 86 55W A city in the USA, in Alabama. Settled in 1813, it is the state's largest city and the main industrial centre of the South. It has an important iron and steel industry. Population (2000): 242 820.

Biró, Laszlo (1900–85) Hungarian inventor, who in 1938 patented the ballpoint pen containing quick-drying ink. Such pens are now commonly known as biros.

birthstone In *astrology, a gemstone associated with a birth month. The ancient belief that certain gems had supernatural powers led to them being worn for luck. The modern list of birthstones is usually: January—garnet; February—amethyst; March—bloodstone; April—diamond; May—emerald; June—pearl; July—ruby; August—sardonyx; September—sapphire; October—opal; November—topaz; December—turquoise.

Birtwistle, Sir Harrison (1934–) British composer. His compositions include the operas *Punch and Judy* (1966–67), *Gawain* (1991), and *The Last Supper* (2001), *Endless Parade* (for trumpet and orchestra; 1987), and the large-scale orchestral work *Exody* (1998). He was knighted in 1988 and appointed CH in 2000.

Biscay, Bay of (French name: Golfe de Gascogne; Spanish name: Golfo de Vizcaya) An inlet of the Atlantic Ocean, off the coast of W France and N Spain. It is comparatively deep and subject to rough seas. Width: about 320 km (199 mi).

Bishkek (*or* **Pishpek**; name 1925–91: Frunze) 42 53N 74 46E The capital of Kirgizstan, on the River Chu. Manufactures include machinery and textiles. Population (1999 est): 619 000.

Bismarck, Otto Eduard Leopold, Prince von (1815–98) Prussian statesman; first chancellor of the German Empire (1871–90). A conservative, known as the Iron Chancellor, Bismarck came to prominence after the collapse of the Revolution of 1848. After victory in the *Franco-Prussian War (1870–71) William I of Prussia accepted the imperial crown and Bismarck became chancellor of the new German Empire. He came into conflict (the Kulturkampf) with the Roman Catholic Church and, abroad, presided over the Congress of *Berlin (1878) and formed the *Triple Alliance with Austria and Italy. Losing the support of William II, Bismarck resigned in 1890 over the abolition of antisocialist laws.

Bismarck Archipelago A group of volcanic islands in the SW Pacific Ocean, in Papua New Guinea. It includes New Britain, New Ireland, and the Admiralty Islands. Area: 49 658 sq km (19 173 sq mi). Population (1995 est): 424 000.

bismuth (Bi) A dense white brittle metal, similar in properties to tin and lead. It is obtained as a by-product of lead, copper, tin, silver, and gold refining and also occurs naturally as the pure metal, the sulphide (Bi_2S_3), and the oxide (Bi_2O_3). It has unusual properties for a metal, having low thermal and electrical conductivity, and decreasing in volume on melting. With tin and cadmium it is used to make low-melting alloys in fire prevention systems.

At no 83; at wt 208.98037; mp 271.4°C; bp 1564±5°C.

bison A massive hoofed mammal belonging to the genus *Bison* (2 species). The North American bison (*B. bison*) was once abundant on the plains but is now found only on reserves. Over 150 cm at the shoulder and weighing up to 1000 kg, it has a shaggy mane and low-slung head with incurved horns. The smaller European bison (*B. bonasus*), also called wisent, is now found only in zoos. Family: *Bovidae*.

Bissau 11 50N 15 37N The capital and chief port of Guinea-Bissau, on the Geba estuary. Founded by the Portuguese in 1687, it became capital of Portuguese Guinea in 1941. Population (1999 est): 274 000.

bit A *b*inary dig*it*. The basic unit of information in information theory and computer memory stores. It is the amount of information needed to specify one of two alternatives, i.e. to distinguish between 1 and 0 in the binary notation.

bittern A bird belonging to the subfamily *Botaurinae*, occurring throughout the world in swamps and reedbeds. The European bittern (*Botaurus stellaris*) is a solitary bird, 70 cm long, with a yellow-brown dark-streaked plumage that provides camouflage. The little bittern (*Ixobrychus minutus*) is 34 cm long with buffish-white wing patches. Family: *Ardeidae* (herons, etc.).

bitumen The tarry residue left after *distillation of oil, lignite, or coal, consisting almost entirely of a mixture of carbon with large *hydrocarbon molecules. Its principal uses are in roadmaking and binding cement.

bivalve A *mollusc belonging to the class *Bivalvia* (also called *Pelecypoda* or *Lamellibranchia*; about 10 000 species). Bivalves are characterized by having two hinged shell plates (valves) and include *clams, *mussels, *oysters, and *scallops. Bivalves inhabit both salt and fresh water. Most bivalves are of separate sexes but some are hermaphrodite. Some hermaphrodite bivalves, including *Ostrea* oysters, incubate the fertilized eggs.

Bizet, Georges (Alexandre César Léopold B.; 1838–75) French composer. In 1855 he produced his first major work, the symphony in C major. Among his best-known works are the music to Alphonse Daudet's play *L'Arlésienne* (1872) and the opera *Carmen* (1873–74).

Black, Sir James (Whyte) (1924–) British biochemist. His discovery of beta blockers and his work on drugs for peptic ulcers won him a Nobel Prize (1988). He was appointed to the OM in 2000.

b

Black and Tans The irregular forces recruited by the British Government to fight the IRA in Ireland in 1920–21. Their name derives from their uniform, khaki with black caps and belts. They acted with great severity and were hated by the Irish.

black bear The native bear of North American forests, *Ursus* (or *Euarctos*) *americanus*. American black bears grow to a weight of 150 kg; they climb well and eat berries, pine cones, and grass as well as small animals. The Himalayan black, or moon, bear, *Selenarctos thibetanus*, inhabits forests of central and E Asia and has a white V-shaped mark on its chest.

black beetle *See* COCKROACH.

blackberry (*or* **bramble**) A prickly shrub, *Rubus fruticosus* (an aggregate species), occurring throughout Europe. The stems, up to 5 m long, root wherever they touch the ground. The dark-green leaves usually consist of five oval toothed leaflets and the pinkish-white flowers are borne in terminal clusters. The edible fruits consist of an aggregate of several small berries. Family: *Rosaceae*.

blackbird A songbird, *Turdus merula*, that is one of the commonest European birds, particularly in urban areas. The male, about 25 cm long, is black with a bright-yellow bill and eye ring; the larger female is dark brown with a dark bill. Blackbirds feed chiefly on worms and other invertebrates but will also eat scraps. Family: *Turdidae* (thrushes).

black body A theoretical body that absorbs all the electromagnetic radiation falling upon it. When heated it emits radiation (black-body radiation) having a continuous distribution of wavelengths with a maximum at a particular wavelength, which depends only on the temperature of the body.

Blackburn 53 45N 2 29W A town in NW England, in Blackburn with Darwen unitary authority, Lancashire, on the Leeds–Liverpool Canal. Traditionally a cotton-weaving town, it now has engineering and electronics industries. Population (1991): 105 994.

Blackburn with Darwen A unitary authority in NW England, in Lancashire. Area: 137 sq km (53 sq mi). Population (2001): 137 471.

blackcap A European *warbler, *Sylvia atricapillus*. About 14 cm long, it has an olive-brown plumage with paler underparts and a darker cap (black in the male and reddish-brown in the female). Blackcaps feed chiefly on insects but—before migrating—they eat fruit to build up energy reserves.

b

Black Country, the An industrial area of central England. Situated NW of Birmingham, it grew up around the coalfield in what was then S Staffordshire. It gained its name from the grime produced by intense industrialization in the 19th century.

blackcurrant A shrub, *Ribes nigrum*, native to most of Europe and N Asia and widely cultivated. The stems and three-lobed leaves emit a characteristic smell. The drooping clusters of greenish bell-shaped flowers develop into edible black berries. Family: *Grossulariaceae* (gooseberry family).

Black Death The worst outbreak of *plague, principally bubonic but also pneumonic and septicaemic, of the medieval period. Originating in the Far East, it spread through Europe and England in May 1348. Estimates of mortality rates vary from 20% to more than 50%. The outbreak had a profound effect not only on demographic trends but also upon rural society and the economy as a whole. Further outbreaks followed in the 1350s and 1370s.

black earth *See* CHERNOZEM.

blackfly Any black *aphid, especially the bean aphid (*Aphis fabae*). Bean aphids occur in masses on beans (especially broad beans), spinach, dock, etc., in summer months. They overwinter as fertilized eggs in *Euonymus*, *Viburnum*, and *Philadelphus* trees.

black grouse A Eurasian *grouse, *Lyrurus tetrix*, of moorlands. The male (also called blackcock), 50 cm long, has a glossy black plumage and a lyre-shaped tail; the female is reddish brown. Both have conspicuous red wattles above the eyes.

black hole A celestial "object" that has undergone such total *gravitational collapse that no light can escape from it. Once a collapsing object's radius has shrunk below a critical value (the Schwarzschild radius) it becomes a black hole; for a star, this radius is about 10 km or less. The surface having this radius is called the event horizon of the black hole. The object will continue to contract until compressed to an infinite density at a single central point—a singularity. Black holes of 10^6 to 10^9 solar masses are now thought to exist at the centres of certain galaxies, possibly including our own, and to be the powerful sources of energy in *quasars.

Black Hole of Calcutta A small cell (5.5 m × 4.5 m) in which over one hundred British soldiers were allegedly confined overnight in 1756, less than 25 men surviving. The outrage was perpetrated by the Nawab of Bengal, who, objecting to the fortification of Calcutta by the East India Company, defeated the British garrison.

blackjack *See* PONTOON.

black mass A blasphemous parody of the Roman Catholic mass, celebrated by satanists in honour of the devil. A naked woman is usually present at or on the altar and participants take hallucinatory drugs.

Black Mountains A mountain range in SE Wales and W central England, in Powys, Monmouthshire, and Herefordshire, mainly in the Brecon Beacons National Park. It rises to 811 m (2660 ft) at Wann Fach.

Black Muslims Members of the Nation of Islam movement founded in Detroit (USA) in 1930 by W. D. Fard, believed by Black Muslims to be the Saviour. After the disappearance of Fard in 1933, the movement was led by Elijah Muhammad (1897–1975); *Malcolm X was a leading member until 1964. It aims to establish a new Black Islamic state and follows many Muslim practices.

Blackpool 1. 53 50N 3 03W A coastal resort in NW England, in Blackpool unitary authority, Lancashire, famous for its 160 m (520 ft) high Tower (modelled on the Eiffel Tower), Pleasure Beach, and illuminations. Population (1991): 146 262. **2.** A unitary authority in NW England, in Lancashire. Area: 35 sq km (13 sq mi). Population (2001): 142 284.

Black Prince, Edward the *See* EDWARD, THE BLACK PRINCE.

Black Rod An official of the House of Lords, first appointed in 1522, having been called usher of the Order of the *Garter since 1350. He maintains order in the House and when the monarch delivers a speech, summons members of the Commons by knocking on their door with his staff of office (black rod).

Black Sea An inland sea bounded by Bulgaria, Romania, Moldova, Ukraine, Russia, Georgia, and Turkey; it is connected to the Mediterranean Sea via the Bosporus in the SW and to the sea of Azov in the N. Its salinity is kept low principally by the influx of fresh water from the Rivers Danube and Dnepr.

blackthorn (*or* **sloe**) A thorny shrub, *Prunus spinos*, forming dense thickets, up to 4 m high, in many parts of Europe and Asia. The clusters of white flowers usually appear before the leaves, which are oval and toothed. The bitter-tasting blue-black stone fruits are used to flavour sloe gin. Family: *Rosaceae.*

black widow A venomous *spider, also called button or redback spider, that belongs to a genus (*Latrodectus*; about 6 species) found in tropical and subtropical regions. The female of *L. mactans*, the most common North American species, has a shiny black body, 25 mm long, with red markings on the abdomen. (The male is about 6 mm long and usually killed and eaten by the female after mating.) The bite is serious but rarely fatal. Family: *Theridiidae.*

bladder In anatomy, any hollow organ containing fluid, especially the urinary bladder, into which urine drains from the *kidneys.

bladderwort A plant of the widely distributed genus *Utricularia* (about 200 species, many tropical). Most bladderworts are submerged aquatic plants with finely divided leaves bearing small bladders, which trap tiny aquatic animals by a trapdoor mechanism triggered by sensitive hairs. The two-lipped tubular flowers protrude above the water. Family: *Lentibulariaceae.*

Blaenau Gwent A county borough in SE Wales, created in 1996 from part of N Gwent. Area: 109 sq km (42 sq mi). Population (2001): 70 058. Administrative centre: Ebbw Vale.

Blair, Tony (Anthony Charles Lynton B.; 1953–) British Labour politician: prime minister (1997–). He entered parliament in 1983 and served as shadow home secretary (1992–94) before becoming party leader (1994). Having reformed the party's constitution and modernized its image, he led it to a landslide victory in the general election of 1997. His government enacted devolution in Scotland and Wales, negotiated a new settlement in Northern Ireland, and promised reform of public services; it was re-elected with a large majority in 2001. Blair committed British forces to military action in *Kosovo (1999) and Afghanistan (2001; *see* WAR ON TERRORISM). In 2003 he sent British troops to support US forces in the *Iraq War, on the grounds that Iraq possessed weapons of mass destruction; when no such weapons were found his leadership faced severe criticism.

Blake, Robert (1599–1657) English admiral. A Parliamentarian in the Civil War, Blake became one of Cromwell's most successful commanders and in 1650 destroyed Prince Rupert's Royalist fleet. In the first *Dutch War, Blake was largely responsible for the English victory and sank 16 Spanish ships at Santa Cruz off Tenerife (1657). He died while returning to Plymouth.

Blake, William (1757–1827) British poet, painter, and engraver. His poems, the texts of which he engraved and illustrated, include *Songs of Innocence* (1789), *Songs of Experience* (1794), various "Prophetic Books," *Milton* (1808), and *Jerusalem* (1820). His watercolours for *The Book of Job* (1826) and Dante's *Divine Comedy* (1827) were inspired by his visions and engravings after Michelangelo. Although unrecognized by his generation, except by a few friends, he was a precursor of Romanticism.

Blantyre (*or* **Blantyre-Limbe**) 15 46S 35 00E The largest city in Malawi, in the Shire Highlands. In 1956 it was linked with Limbe, a major railway centre. Blantyre is Malawi's chief industrial centre and its executive and judicial capital. Population (1994 est): 446 800.

blast furnace A furnace used in the *smelting of ore. In steel making, iron ore, coke, and limestone are poured in at the top of a vertical furnace and a blast of hot air is blown in at the bottom to burn the coke. Molten iron is drawn off at the bottom. A glassy waste, called slag, is also produced.

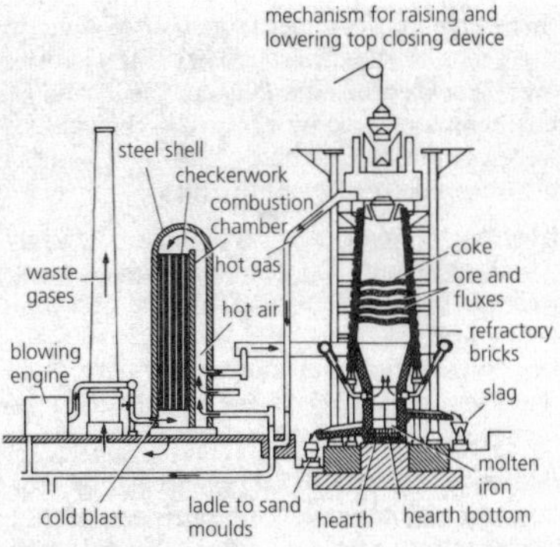

blast furnace

Blaue Reiter, Der (German: The Blue Rider) A group of artists formed in Munich in 1911 by *Kandinsky and Franz Marc (1880–1916). Their symbolic and expressionist style (*see* EXPRESSIONISM) shows the influence of primitive art and children's pictures. The group, which also included Paul *Klee and August Macke (1887–1914), disbanded during World War I.

bleaching The whitening, lightening, or removing of colour by chemical treatment or exposure to sunlight. Most bleaching agents are oxidizing agents, which convert a pigment into an oxidized colourless form. Examples are hydrogen peroxide, *bleaching powder, and hypochlorites. In some processes reducing agents, such as sulphur dioxide, are used.

bleaching powder (*or* **chloride of lime**) A whitish powder containing calcium hypochlorite ($Ca(OCl)_2$), calcium chloride ($CaCl_2$), calcium hydroxide ($Ca(OH)_2$), and water. It reacts with dilute acids to produce chlorine, which acts as a bleaching agent.

bleeding heart An ornamental plant of the genus *Dicentra*, especially *D. spectabilis* from Siberia and Japan and *D. eximia* from North America. They are perennials with arching stems, up to 90 cm long, bearing strings of large rose-red heart-shaped flowers with whitish tips. Family: *Fumariaceae*.

Blenheim, Battle of (13 August 1704) The battle won by the Duke of *Marlborough and Prince Eugène of Savoy (1663–1736) against the French in the War of the *Spanish Succession. It was fought at Blenheim (now Blindheim) on the Danube River.

Blenheim Palace The baroque palace built between 1705 and 1725 at Woodstock, Oxfordshire (England), as a gift from Queen Anne to the Duke of *Marlborough for his victories over the French, especially at the Battle of Blenheim. Designed by Vanbrugh, the gardens were laid out by Capability *Brown. It was the birthplace of Winston Churchill.

blenny A small fish belonging to a family (*Bleniidae*; about 300 species) found among rocks in shallow waters of tropical and temperate seas. Blennies have an elongated scaleless body with a blunt nose. Many have small tentacles on their heads. The name is also used for several other fish of the order *Perciformes*.

Blériot, Louis (1872–1936) French aviator. Beginning his career as a motorcar engineer he was the first to fly the English Channel (1909), from Calais to Dover, in a monoplane. He later became a manufacturer of aircraft.

Bletchley Park A house in Buckinghamshire that became the headquarters of Allied codebreakers in World War II. Here the German Enigma machine's coded messages were deciphered using one of the first electronic computers. This enabled German plans for the Battle of the Atlantic to be given to the Royal Navy in advance.

Bligh, William (1754–1817) British admiral. He accompanied *Cook on his second voyage round the world and in 1787 sailed to Tahiti on the *Bounty*. While setting sail for home, his crew mutinied under Fletcher Christian, leaving Bligh and 18 officers aboard a small boat without maps. He eventually reached safety. In 1805 he was made governor of New South Wales.

blight A severe disease of plants caused by pests, fungi, or other agents. Symptoms commonly include spotting followed by wilting and death. The notorious potato blight that devastated Ireland in the mid-19th century was caused by the fungus *Phytophthora infestans*.

Bliss, Sir Arthur (Edward Drummond) (1891–1975) British composer. Director of music at the BBC (1942–44), Bliss was knighted in 1950 and was Master of the Queen's Music (1953–75). His works include *A Colour Symphony* (1922), music for the film *The Shape of Things to Come* (1935), a piano concerto (1938), the opera *The Olympians* (1948–49), and a cello concerto (1970).

blister beetle A brightly coloured beetle, about 10–15 mm long, belonging to a widely distributed family (*Meloidae*; about 2000 species), which also includes the *oil beetles. The larvae are parasitic upon other insects, while the adults generally feed on plants. Their secretion of cantharidin, a powerful blistering agent, has led to the medicinal use of various species, especially *Spanish fly.

Blitzkrieg (German: lightning war) A military tactic aiming to disorganize enemy forces by suprise attacks using tanks and aerial bombardment. It was extensively used by the Germans in *World War II. The **Blitz** refers to the intensive German air raids on London during the battle of Britain in *World War II.

Bloch, Ernest (1880–1959) Swiss-born composer of Jewish descent who moved to the USA in 1916. His opera *Macbeth* (1903–09), a rhapsody for cello and orchestra entitled *Schelomo* (1916), *Concerto Grosso* (1925), and *Sacred Service* (1930–33) incorporate Jewish musical elements.

Bloch, Felix (1905–83) US physicist, born in Zurich, who moved to the USA when Hitler came to power. He developed the nuclear magnetic resonance technique for which he shared the Nobel Prize (1952) with E. M. Purcell. During World War II he worked on the development of the atomic bomb. In 1954 he became the first director of CERN.

Bloemfontein 29 07S 26 14E The judicial capital of South Africa and the capital of Free State. Founded in 1846, it is an important agricultural centre and new gold mines have been opened nearby. Population (1991): 126 867.

blood The red body fluid consisting of a watery *plasma in which are suspended various blood cells—the red cells (*see* ERYTHROCYTE) and several kinds of white cells (*see* LEUCOCYTE). The *platelets are small particles involved in blood clotting. Blood pumped round the vascular system by the heart acts as a medium for transporting oxygen, carbon dioxide, digested food, hormones, waste materials, salts, and many other substances to and from the tissues. An average adult has about 70 millilitres of blood per kilogram of body weight (i.e. about 5 litres in an average man). Blood is present in all animals with a circulatory system: its functions are similar to that of human blood although its composition varies. *See also* BLOOD CLOTTING; BLOOD GROUPS; CIRCULATION OF THE BLOOD.

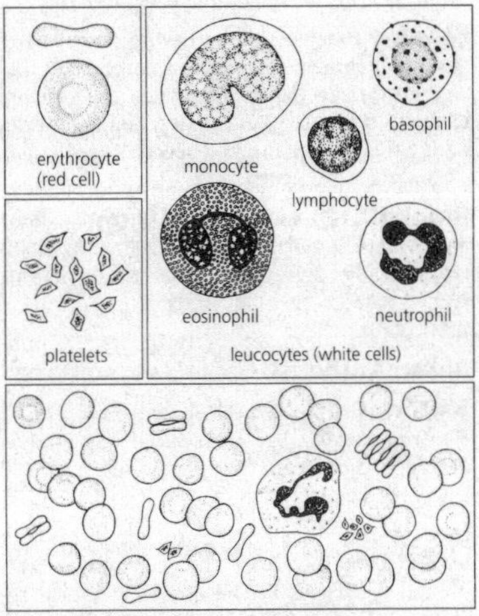

blood. Blood cells and platelets, showing surface and side views of a red cell and five types of white cell (above). Human blood, magnified about 1500 times (below), containing a single white cell, a mass of red cells, and two clusters of platelets.

blood clotting The mechanism by which blood is converted from a liquid to a solid state to prevent loss of blood after injury. The process involves chemical reactions between soluble proteins (clotting factors) in the blood in the presence of *platelets, resulting in the formation of a fibrous protein (fibrin), which forms the basis of the blood clot. *See also* THROMBOSIS.

blood fluke A parasitic flatworm of the genus *Schistosoma* (3 species), which causes the disease *schistosomiasis in many parts of the world. The flukes are carried by freshwater snails and enter their human hosts to inhabit blood vessels, feeding on blood and causing severe debilitation. *See also* FLUKE.

blood groups The different types of blood, classified on the basis of the presence of certain proteins (*see* ANTIBODY) on the surface of the red cells, which is genetically determined. The major grouping is the ABO system, discovered in 1900 by Karl Landsteiner (1868–1943). It consists of four groups: A, B, AB, and O. Group A cells carry the A antigen and the plasma contains *antibodies against B antigen (anti-B antibodies); the converse applies to group B blood. Transfusion of blood between these groups causes destruction of the donor blood cells (*see* BLOOD TRANSFUSION). Group O blood contains neither antigen and can therefore be used in transfusions to people of groups A and B. Group AB blood contains neither anti-A nor anti-B antibody: people of this blood group can accept both A and B blood during transfusion. *See also* RHESUS FACTOR.

bloodhound An ancient breed of dog with a keen sense of smell, originating around the Mediterranean and used for tracking. It has a sturdy frame and a large head with long drooping ears and wrinkled skin around the eyes. Height: 63–69 cm (dogs); 58–64 cm (bitches).

blood pressure The pressure that blood exerts on the walls of the arteries, due to the pumping action of the heart. Blood pressure is at its lowest between heartbeats (i.e. at diastole) and at its highest when the ventricles of the heart are contracting (i.e. systole). It is recorded, using a *sphygmomanometer, as the height in millimetres of a column of mercury (mmHg). A healthy adult might have a systolic pressure of about 120 mmHg and a diastolic pressure of 80 mmHg, expressed as 120/80. *See also* HYPERTENSION.

bloodstone A mineral of a green colour speckled with red. It is a variety of *chalcedony. Birthstone for March.

blood transfusion Usually the transfer of blood from a **blood bank** to a person who has suffered extensive loss of blood; for example, during surgery or following an accident. Some people (e.g. Jehovah's Witnesses) object to transfusion on religious grounds. The blood is stored at 4°C and used within 3–4 weeks. The *blood group of the recipient must match that of the donor.

b

Bloody Assizes *See* JEFFREYS OF WEM, GEORGE, 1ST BARON.

Bloody Sunday **1.** The massacre of unarmed protestors by Russian police in St Petersburg on 22 January 1905. 100 people were killed, precipitating the *Revolution of 1905. **2.** The violent events of 21 November 1920 when the IRA assassinated 11 men believed to be British spies. The *Black and Tans responded by killing 12 innocent spectators at a Dublin football match. **3.** The events in Londonderry on 30 January 1972 when British paratroops fired into a crowd during a minor disturbance in a civil-rights demonstration, killing 13 innocent people.

Bloomsbury group A group of English writers and artists active in the 1910s and 1920s who met initially in private houses in Bloomsbury, London. The group included the writers Virginia *Woolf and Lytton Strachey, the art critics Clive Bell (1881–1964) and Roger *Fry, and the economist J. M. *Keynes. Their belief in the importance of personal relations and aesthetic experience was influenced by G. E. Moore's *Principia Ethica* (1903).

blowfly A large buzzing fly belonging to the family *Calliphoridae*. Some blowflies lay their eggs in human food, but more commonly the larvae develop in decaying organic material. The larvae of certain species (e.g. of the American genus *Cochliomyia*) are serious pests of sheep and cattle. Chief genera: *Calliphora* (bluebottles), *Lucilia* (greenbottles).

bluebell One of several plants having bell-shaped blue flowers. In England the bluebell is *Endymion non-scriptus*, up to 50 cm high, which overwinters as a bulb. Family: *Liliaceae*. In Scotland the name is applied to the *harebell.

bluebottle *See* BLOWFLY.

blue-green bacteria Bacteria belonging to the phylum *Cyanobacteria*; they were formerly classified as algae (blue-green algae; division *Cyanophyta*). They contain a blue pigment (phycocyanin), in addition to the green chlorophyll. Reproduction is asexual. They occur on moist surfaces and in the soil, where they contribute to *nitrogen fixation. Aquatic blue-green bacteria are a constituent of plankton.

blue gum *See* EUCALYPTUS.

Blue Mountains A mountain range in Australia, in New South Wales. Part of the *Great Dividing Range, it reaches 1180 m (3871 ft) at Bird Rock.

blues A type of US folk music that evolved from the Negro spirituals and work songs of the 1860s. It is characterized by mournful or bitter-sweet lyrics and the use of "blue notes" (flattened thirds and sevenths). The first published blues were "Memphis Blues" (1912) by W. C. Handy (1873–1958) and Jelly Roll Morton's "Jelly Roll Blues" (1915). The blues influenced the development of jazz and rock music and stimulated composers, such as George Gershwin, who wrote the orchestral *Rhapsody in Blue* (1924).

bluetit A European tit, *Parus caeruleus*, with a blue crown and wings, a yellow breast, and white face. Bluetits feed chiefly on insect larvae.

bluets A tufted herb of the genus *Houstonia* (about 25 species), native to North America and widely grown in rock gardens. The small funnel-shaped flowers are borne singly or in clusters. Some species provide ground cover in shade. Family: *Rubiaceae* (madder family).

blue whale The largest living *whale, *Balaenoptera musculus*, growing to over 30 m and weighing over 150 tonnes. They are nearing extinction due to overhunting and have been designated an endangered species. Family: *Balaenopteridae* (*see* RORQUAL).

Blunkett, David (1947–) British Labour politician; home secretary (2001–). Blind from childhood, he entered parliament in 1987 and was secretary of state for education (1997–2001).

Blunt, Anthony *See* MACLEAN, DONALD.

Blyton, Enid (1897–1968) British writer of children's books. She introduced her famous character Noddy in 1949 and wrote over 600 books for children.

boa A snake belonging to the subfamily *Boinae* (40–60 species) of the *constrictor family and occurring in Old and New World regions. 20–760 cm long, boas are usually green or yellowish with a camouflaging pattern. They kill their prey by biting and then constricting. The boa constrictor (*Boa constrictor*), occurring from Mexico to Argentina, is about 3.5 m long.

Boadicea (Latin name: Boudicca; d. 61 AD) Queen of the *Iceni. Her husband Prasutagus ruled in what is now Norfolk (England). At his death in 61, Roman officials raped Boadicea and her daughters. She led the Iceni into rebellion, sacking Colchester, London, and St Albans. The Roman governor Suetonius Paulinus defeated the rebels at or near Fenny Stratford. Boadicea committed suicide.

boar, wild A Eurasian wild *pig, *Sus scrofa*, once common in European forests. Up to 1.5 m long and 1 m high at the shoulder, they have a rough greyish bristly coat. The ancestors of domestic pigs, males have four tusks.

Boat Race An annual rowing race on the River Thames between Oxford and Cambridge Universities, first held in 1829 at Henley. The present course of 6.8 km (4.25 mi) from Putney to Mortlake was established in 1845. By 2004 Cambridge had won 78 races and Oxford 71, with one dead heat (1877).

bobcat A short-tailed cat *Felis rufa*, resembling a lynx, found in North America. About 90 cm long, it is brown with greyish markings and has large ears.

bobsledding The sport of racing bobsleds (also called bobsleighs or bobs), which was developed by British sportsmen at St Moritz (Switzerland) in the late 19th century. A bobsled is a steel-bodied toboggan with two pairs of runners, the front pair steerable, and a rear brake, holding two or four people. The bobsleds slide down a narrow chute some 1500 m (1640 yd) long with high walls, reaching speeds of over 130 km per hour (81 mph).

Boccaccio, Giovanni (1313–75) Italian writer and poet. Son of a merchant of Florence, he wrote *Filocolo*, a prose romance, *Filostrato*, which supplied the plot of Chaucer's *Troilus and Criseyde*, and *Teseida*, the source of Chaucer's *Knight's Tale*. Between 1348 and 1353 he composed the *Decameron*, a collection of a hundred stories told by a party escaping from plague-stricken Florence in 1348.

Bodhisattva In Mahayana Buddhism, the title of a person who is to become a Buddha; also the Buddha (Gautama) before his enlightenment. The Bodhisattva ideal is that of the individual who seeks enlightenment not for himself alone but for all beings.

Bodleian Library The major library of Oxford University, first established in 1409 and restored and enlarged by Sir Thomas Bodley from 1598 to 1602. Since 1610 it has been entitled to receive a free copy of every book published in Britain; it contains well over 2.5 million volumes.

Boeotia A region of central Greece, N and W of *Attica. Its rich central plains are surrounded by hills and mountains. The dozen or so city states that shared the territory formed a federal state dominated by *Thebes in 446 BC.

Boer Wars (*or* **South African Wars**) The wars fought against the British by the Boers or *Afrikaners of South Africa. In the first (1880–81) the Boers of the Transvaal under *Kruger rebelled against British rule. After inflicting a massive defeat on the British garrison at Majuba Hill, the Transvaal regained its independence under the *Pretoria Convention. In the second Boer War (1899–1902) the Boer forces were initially successful, besieging Ladysmith, Mafeking, and Kimberley. They suffered reverses during 1900 but were able to hold off the British under Kitchener and F. S. Roberts (1832–1914). The British devastated the countryside, rounded up Boer women and children, of whom some 20 000 died in concentration camps, and finally defeated the Boers, who lost their independence in the Peace of Vereeniging (1902).

Boethius, Anicius Manlius Severinus (c. 480–524 AD) Roman statesman and philosopher. A patrician, he became chief minister under Theodoric but later earned the emperor's displeasure and was imprisoned, tortured, and executed. His most famous work is *The Consolation of Philosophy*, written while he was in prison.

Bogarde, Sir Dirk (Derek van den Bogaerde; 1921–99) British film actor of Dutch descent. His major films include *The Damned* (1969), *Death in Venice* (1970), and *Providence* (1978). He was also the author of several autobiographical volumes and novels.

Bogart, Humphrey (1899–1957) US film actor, usually cast in tough-guy roles. His films include *Casablanca* (1942), *To Have and Have Not* (1944), in which Lauren Bacall (1924–   ), whom he subsequently married, made her screen debut, *The Big Sleep* (1946), *The African Queen* (1951), and *The Caine Mutiny* (1954).

Bogotá, Santa Fé de 4 38N 74 15W The capital of Colombia, on a fertile central plateau of the E Andes at an altitude of 2640 m (8600 ft). Founded by the Spanish in the early 16th century on the site of the conquered Indian settlement of Bacatá, it became the capital of the viceroyalty of New Grenada. Population (1999 est): 6 260 862.

Bohemia (Czech name: Čechy; German name: Böhmen) An area of the W Czech Republic. It consists chiefly of a plateau enclosed by mountains. It is the most industrialized part of the Czech Republic; agriculture and mining are also important. *History*: Bohemia derives its name from the Boii (the first known inhabitants), who were displaced by the Czechs (1st-5th centuries AD). Bohemia became part of the greater Moravian empire in the 9th century. It achieved the height of its power following the acquisitions of the Přemyslid Otakar II (1230–78; reigned 1253–78). The Přemyslid dynasty came to an end with the assassination of Wencelas III (1289–1306; reigned 1305–06) and John of Luxembourg was subsequently elected king (1310). The golden age of Bohemia was established by his son Charles I (Emperor Charles IV).

Bohr, Niels Henrik David (1885–1962) Danish physicist, who worked with J. J. *Thomson at Cambridge and *Rutherford at Manchester. He made an immense contribution to atomic theory by combining Rutherford's nuclear model with Planck's quantum theory. The Bohr model of the atom, in which a central nucleus is surrounded by electrons confined to circular orbits corresponding to fixed energy levels, was modified by Sommerfeld but is the basis for modern atomic theory. Bohr also invented the concept of complementarity to combine the particle and wave aspects of subatomic particles. Bohr later worked at Los Alamos on the atom bomb, after escaping from German-occupied Denmark. He shared the 1975 Nobel Prize for Physics with his son Aage Bohr (1922–).

boiling point The temperature at which the vapour pressure of a liquid is equal to the atmospheric pressure (101 325 pascals).

Boise 43 38N 116 12W A city in the USA, the capital and largest city of Idaho. The centre of a gold rush in 1862, it has timber, food-processing, and agricultural industries. Population (2000): 185 787.

Boletus A genus of mushrooms (about 50 species). The undersurface of the cap bears a series of vertical tubes (instead of gills), in which the spores are formed. Most grow near trees and they are generally edible (*see* CEP), except Satan's boletus (*B. satanas*), which is poisonous. It has a short stalk and a grey cap 10–20 cm in diameter. Family: *Boletaceae*; phylum: *Basidiomycota*.

Boleyn, Anne (c. 1507–36) The second wife (from 1533) of Henry VIII and the mother of Elizabeth I. When she failed to produce a male heir for Henry she was accused of committing adultery and executed.

Bolingbroke, Henry St John, 1st Viscount (1678–1751) English statesman and philosopher. A Tory MP, he became secretary of war (1704–08) and secretary of state (1710–14). As a supporter of the *Jacobites, he fled to France after the accession of George I and helped to organize the Fifteen Rebellion. He also wrote several philosophical works. Returning to England in 1725, he became a leading opponent of Robert *Walpole. His political writings include *The Idea of a Patriot King* (1749).

Bolívar, Simón (1783–1830) South American soldier, known as the Liberator. The son of a wealthy Venezuelan creole family, his travels in Europe instilled a lasting admiration for the ideas of the Enlightenment. He returned to Latin America in 1807 and devoted the rest of his life to its liberation from Spain. In 1813 he seized Caracas but after defeat in 1814 went into exile until 1817. His victory at the battle of Boyacá (1819) achieved the liberation of New Granada (renamed Colombia). Bolívar became its president and, after liberating Venezuela and Quito (Ecuador) in 1821, organized a federation of the three newly independent states. Latin America was finally freed of the Spanish by campaigns in Peru, Upper Peru taking the name Bolivia in his honour.

Bolivia, Republic of An inland country in South America consisting of low plains in the N and E, crossed by extensive river systems; in the W, the Andes rise to over 6400 m (21 000 ft) and the Altiplano, a plateau averaging about 3900 m (13 000 ft), contains Lakes Titicaca and Poopó. Bolivia has some of the world's highest inhabited regions, with most of the population, of mixed Indian and Spanish descent, living at altitudes of over 3000 m (10 000 ft). *Economy*: Mineral resources include tin, silver, zinc, lead, antimony, and copper. Mining, gas, and petroleum are the main industries. The main crops are sugar cane, soya beans, potatoes, and bananas. The illegal trade in coca also thrives. *History*: ruins near Tiahuanaco indicate a pre-Inca civilization (the Aymaras) going back to the 10th century. The area later became part of the Inca Empire and was conquered by the Spanish in the 16th century, when it became known as Upper Peru. The discovery of tin and silver led to great prosperity. In 1776 it became part of the viceroyalty of Buenos Aires. After a long war it gained its independence with the help of Simón Bolívar in 1825 and became a republic with Antonio José de *Sucre (1795–1830) as first president. During the remainder of the century struggles with neighbouring countries cost Bolivia much territory. Political unrest and violent changes of government continued for most of the 20th century and in 1971 a military coup brought Gen Hugo Banzer Suárez to power; he was overthrown in a coup in 1978. By 1985 Bolivia had the highest rate of inflation in the world and massive foreign debts. The former dictator Banzer was elected president in 1997. Elections in 2002 resulted in victory for Gonzalo Sánchez de Lozada (previously president in 1993–97). Disputes with Peru and Chile continue over access to the Pacific coast. Official languages: Spanish, Quechua, and Aymara. Currency: boliviano of 100 centavos. Area: 1 098 580 sq km (424 051 sq mi). Population (2003 est): 8 586 000. Capital: La Paz.

boll weevil A brownish *weevil, *Anthonomus grandis*. Originally a native of the New World tropics, it is now a major insect pest of cotton crops in the W hemisphere. The female lays a single egg within each cotton boll, which thus fails to develop.

Bologna 44 30N 11 20E A city in N Italy, the capital of Emilia-Romagna. The site dates from Etruscan times, but it did not become a free city until the middle ages; the Emperor Charles V was crowned here in 1530. Regarded as Italy's gastronomic centre, its industries include engineering and food processing. Population (2000 est): 381 161.

Bolsheviks One of the two factions into which the Russian Social Democratic Workers' Party split in 1903 in London (the other was the Mensheviks). The Bolsheviks, which means those in the majority, were led by *Lenin, who believed that the revolution must be guided by a single centralized party of professional revolutionaries. The Bolsheviks came to power in the *Russian Revolution (1917).

Bolshoi Ballet The principal Russian ballet company, based at the Bolshoi Theatre in Moscow. It originated from a dancing class established by the Moscow orphanage in the late 18th century and moved into its present premises in 1856 after fire had destroyed the first Bolshoi Theatre. It first appeared in the West in London in 1956. From 1964 to 1998 it was directed by the choreographer Yuri Grigorovich (1927–).

Bolt, Robert Oxton (1924–95) British dramatist. His plays include *A Man for All Seasons* (1960), a study of Sir Thomas *More. He wrote screenplays for *Lawrence of Arabia* (1962) and other films directed by David *Lean.

Bolton 1. 53 35W 2 26W A town in NW England, in Bolton unitary authority, Greater Manchester. Traditionally a cotton-spinning town, Bolton also manufactures machinery and chemicals. Population (1991): 139 020. **2.** A unitary authority in NW England, in Greater Manchester. Area: 140 sq km (54 sq mi). Population (2001): 261 035.

Boltzmann, Ludwig Eduard (1844–1906) Austrian physicist, who developed statistical mechanics with James Clerk *Maxwell and J. W. *Gibbs. In thermodynamics, he elucidated the relationship between entropy and molecular disorder.

Bombay (official name from 1995: Mumbai) 18 56N 72 51E A city in India, the capital of Maharashtra and the country's main seaport on the W coast. The city occupies a group of islands united by a system of causeways. Its natural harbour, 11 km (7 mi) wide, is the focus of most of India's international trade. The Tata hydroelectric system powers much of Bombay's industry, which includes cotton textiles, food processing, and oil refining. The population is mainly Hindu but there are large Muslim, Christian, and Jewish minorities. *History*: ceded to the Portuguese in 1534, it passed to Charles II of England in 1661 and to the British East India Company in 1668. The railways, the opening of the Suez Canal, and land reclamation led to expansion in the 19th century. Population (1991): 9 909 547.

Bombay duck A fish, *Harpodon nehereus*, found in the estuaries of N India, where it is widely used for food. It has a grey or brown body, about 40 cm long, with small dark speckles and large fins. Order: *Myctophiformes*.

bone A rigid tissue that forms most of the skeleton of higher animals and man. Most bones have a central cavity filled with *marrow. Bone is composed of a matrix of fibres of the protein collagen, responsible for their strength, and bone salts, chiefly calcium salts (*see* APATITE). This tissue is formed by activity of bone cells (osteoblasts), which become enclosed in the matrix when they have ceased to function. Bone formation starts during embryonic life. Most bones develop from cartilage and the process is complete at birth. Membrane bones (e.g. the skull bones) are formed directly in connective tissue, the process being completed after birth (hence the gap (called a fontanelle) in a newborn baby's skull).

bongo An antelope, *Boocerus euryceros*, of African forests. About 120 cm high at the shoulder, bongos are red-brown with white body stripes and markings on the head. The male has spiralled horns up to 100 cm long. Bulls are solitary; cows and calves live in small herds.

Bonhoeffer, Dietrich (1906–45) German

b

pastor and theologian. He opposed the pro-Nazi part of the Lutheran Church; during the war he became involved with anti-Hitler conspirators. He was arrested in 1943, sent to Buchenwald concentration camp, and finally hanged. His *Letters and Papers from Prison* (1953) and theological writings are still widely read.

Bonington, Sir Chris (Christian John Storey B.; 1934–) British mountaineer, author, and photographer. He made the first British ascent of the N face of the Eiger (1962) and climbed Everest in 1985.

Bonn 50 43N 7 07E A city in NW Germany, in North Rhine-Westphalia on the River Rhine. The old part of the town contains the cathedral (12th–13th centuries) and Beethoven's birthplace (now a museum). *History*: settled by the Romans, it was destroyed by the Normans (9th century), and was the seat of the Electors of Cologne (13th to 16th centuries). It passed from France to Prussia in 1815 and was the capital of West Germany from 1949 to 1990. Although Berlin became the capital of the reunited Germany, the seat of government remained in Bonn until 2000. Population (1999 est): 304 100.

Bonnard, Pierre (1867–1947) French painter. Originally a lawyer, he attracted attention with his lithographs, *Aspects of the Life of Paris* (1895), and illustrations for Verlaine's book *Parallèlement* (1900). After 1900 his paintings of interiors, landscapes, and bathing women were treated increasingly with dazzling colour and light.

Bonnie Prince Charlie *See* CHARLES EDWARD STUART, THE YOUNG PRETENDER.

bonsai An ordinary shrub or tree, such as a conifer or flowering cherry, that is developed as a miniature (up to about 60 cm high). The technique was first practised in China over 700 years ago. It was later perfected by the Japanese and has now spread to the W hemisphere. Both branches and roots of potted cuttings are trained and pruned. The trees may take ten years to acquire an aged appearance, and some live 300–400 years.

bony fish Any fish belonging to the class *Osteichthyes* (or *Pisces*), which includes the majority of food and game fishes (*see* TELEOST). They have bony skeletons and their gills are covered by a structure called an operculum. Many species use a swim bladder for buoyancy control and even for breathing air (*see* LUNGFISH). Subclasses: *Actinopterygii*; *Sarcopterygii*.

booby A large tropical seabird belonging to the family *Sulidae* (gannets, etc.; 9 species) characterized by a large head, a long tapering bill, and a wedge-shaped tail. Boobies are 65–85 cm long and typically have a white plumage with brown markings. Boobies dive into the sea to catch fish.

boogie-woogie A popular *blues piano style in which the left hand plays a repetitive pattern with eight beats to the bar, often in ascending broken octaves, and the right hand provides a syncopated melodic line. The style was developed in the USA in the 1920s by such pianists as Pinetop Smith (1904–29).

Booker Prize An annual prize of £50,000 for a work of British, Irish, or Commonwealth fiction in the English language. It has been awarded since 1969 by the British food trading company Booker, in conjunction with the Publishers' Association. Since 2002 it has been known as the **Man Booker Prize** under a new sponsorship agreement with the Man Group.

Book of the Dead 1. A collection of ancient Egyptian texts dating from the 16th century BC. They consist of charms and spells written on papyrus and placed inside mummy cases for use by the dead in the afterlife. **2.** (Buddhist name: Bar-do Thödol) The **Tibetan Book of the Dead**, an ancient Buddhist text that purports to describe the experiences of the soul after death. It is thought to show the influence of shamanic practices on Tibetan Buddhism.

Boole, George (1815–64) British mathematician, who applied the methods of algebra to logic. By replacing logical operations by symbols, Boole showed that the operations could be manipulated to give logically consistent results. His method, known as Boolean algebra or symbolic logic, led to mathematics being given a logically consistent foundation. The subject was further developed by *Frege, Bertrand *Russell and A. N. *Whitehead.

boomerang A curved hand-thrown wooden missile used by Australian Aborigines to kill game or as a weapon of war. The angled shape and the spin given to the missile when thrown enables them to return to the thrower if they miss their target. Up to 75 cm (30 in) long, they can be effective to a distance of 45 m (50 yd).

boomslang A venomous green snake, *Dispholidus typus*, occurring in Africa and reaching 1.8 m in length. It feeds on birds and chameleons, often holding its body erect and motionless before striking. Its venom can cause fatal haemorrhaging in humans. Family: *Colubridae*.

Booth, William (1829–1912) British preacher

year	*winner*	*title*
1969	P H Newby	*Something to Answer For*
1970	Bernice Rubens	*The Elected Member*
1971	V S Naipaul	*In a Free State*
1972	John Berger	*G*
1973	J G Farrell	*The Siege of Krishnapur*
1974	Nadine Gordimer	*The Conservationist*
	Stanley Middleton	*Holiday*
1975	Ruth Prawer Jhabvala	*Heat and Dust*
1976	David Storey	*Saville*
1977	Paul Scott	*Staying On*
1978	Iris Murdoch	*The Sea, The Sea*
1979	Penelope Fitzgerald	*Offshore*
1980	William Golding	*Rites of Passage*
1981	Salman Rushdie	*Midnight's Children*
1982	Thomas Keneally	*Schindler's Ark*
1983	J M Coetzee	*Life and Times of Michael K*
1984	Anita Brookner	*Hotel du Lac*
1985	Keri Hulme	*The Bone People*
1986	Kingsley Amis	*The Old Devils*
1987	Penelope Lively	*Moon Tiger*
1988	Peter Carey	*Oscar and Lucinda*
1989	Kazuo Ishiguro	*The Remains of the Day*
1990	A S Byatt	*Possession*
1991	Ben Okri	*The Famished Road*
1992	Michael Ondaatje	*The English Patient*
	Barry Unsworth	*Sacred Hunger*
1993	Roddy Doyle	*Paddy Clarke Ha Ha Ha*
1994	James Kelman	*How Late It Was, How Late*
1995	Pat Barker	*The Ghost Road*
1996	Graham Swift	*Last Orders*
1997	Arundhati Roy	*The God of Small Things*
1998	Ian McEwan	*Amsterdam*
1999	J M Coetzee	*Disgrace*
2000	Margaret Atwood	*The Blind Assassin*
2001	Peter Carey	*The True History of the Kelly Gang*
2002	Yann Martel	*Life of Pi*
2003	D B C Pierre	*Vernon God Little*

(Man) Booker Prize

and founder of the *Salvation Army. He was born in Nottingham and became an itinerant Methodist preacher. He established a mission in Whitechapel in 1865. The reluctance of established churches to accept his slum converts led to the foundation of the Salvation Army (1877).

Bootle 53 28N 3 00W A town in NW England in Sefton unitary authority, Merseyside. It has extensive modern docks. Population (1991): 65 454.

bop (*or* **bebop**) A type of jazz that originated in the USA in the 1940s as a reaction against swing. Bop emphasized the art of melodic improvisation but was also characterized by harmonic and rhythmic experimentation. In New York City, Dizzy Gillespie and Charlie "Bird" Parker established small bop bands that required the audience to listen rather than dance.

borage A widely grown annual Mediterranean herb, *Borago officinalis*. Up to 60 cm high, with terminal clusters of small blue flowers with backward-pointing petals, borage is used in herbal remedies, beverages, etc. Family: *Boraginaceae*.

Bordeaux (Latin name: Burdigala) 44 50N 0 34W A city in SW France, the capital of the Gironde department on the River Garonne. It is a major seaport and wine centre. Industries include shipbuilding, engineering, and oil and sugar refining. *History*: an important centre under the Romans, it became the capital of Aquitania (*see* AQUITAINE). It was the seat of the French government for a brief period in 1914 and again in 1940. Population (1999): 215 118.

b

border terrier A breed of working dog originating in the border region of England and Scotland. It has a deep narrow body, triangular forward-falling ears, and a short strong muzzle. Weight: 6–7 kg (dogs); 5–6 kg (bitches).

bore A tidal flood wave occurring in certain estuaries and travelling upstream several kilometres at great speed. It occurs when the spring flood tide brings sea water into an estuary more quickly than it can travel up the river.

Borghese An Italian family that originated in Siena and rose to fame in Rome in 1605 after **Camillo Borghese** (1552–1621) became Pope Paul V. His adopted nephew **Scipione Caffarelli** (1576–1633), sponsored *Bernini in the building of the Villa Borghese (now an art gallery) in Rome.

Borgia, Cesare (c. 1475–1507) Duke of the Romagna and captain general of the armies of the Church. The illegitimate son of Pope Alexander VI, Borgia became Archbishop of Valencia and a cardinal. He surrendered his cardinalship to marry the sister of the king of Navarre and to become captain general of the Church. He won the Romagna in three campaigns (1499–1502) but was forced to relinquish it after Alexander's death (1502). He escaped from imprisonment and died in the employ of the Navarrese king. His sister **Lucrezia Borgia** (1480–1519), unfairly notorious for her immorality, was married three times by her father Alexander VI to further his political aims. Her third husband Alfonso (1486–1534) became Duke of Este and she presided over a distinguished court at Ferrara.

Boris III (1894–1943) King of Bulgaria (1918–1943). Boris ruled as a dictator from 1938 and supported the Axis Powers in World War II. He apparently died of a heart attack but may have been assassinated.

Bormann, Martin (1900–45) German Nazi leader, who became Hitler's personal secretary in 1942. He was sentenced to death in absentia at Nuremberg. In 1973 it was established that he had committed suicide in 1945.

Born, Max (1882–1970) British physicist, born in Germany. He shared the 1954 Nobel Prize with W. Bothe for his work in statistical mechanics. With *Heisenberg he developed matrix mechanics. Born was professor of natural philosophy at Edinburgh University from 1936 to 1953.

Borneo A mountainous island SE of Peninsular Malaysia, in the Greater Sunda Islands. During the 19th century Borneo was settled and partitioned by the Dutch and British. It now consists of the Indonesian territory of *Kalimantan, the Malaysian states of *Sabah and *Sarawak, and the sultanate of *Brunei. The chief population groups are the coastal Malays and indigenous Dyaks. It possesses valuable resources of oil, coal, and gold. Area: 750 000 sq km (290 000 sq mi).

Bornholm 55 02N 15 00E A Danish island in the Baltic Sea, SE of Sweden. Dairy farming and pottery are the main activities. Area: 588 sq km (227 sq mi). Population (2001): 44 126. Chief town: Rønne.

Borobudur A huge Buddhist stupa (shrine) in central Java, built about 800 AD and abandoned, unfinished, about 1000. It has five square terraces of diminishing size, one on top of the other, on the vertical surfaces of which is carved a relief depicting the Buddha's life. On top, three circular terraces support 72 stupas. Restored (1973–83) at a cost of £20 million, it was badly damaged in a terrorist attack in 1985.

Borodin, Aleksandr Porfirevich (1833–87) Russian composer, one of the *Five, and a professor of chemistry. He produced two symphonies (1867 and 1876), the tone poem *In the Steppes of Central Asia* (1880), three string quartets, and the opera *Prince Igor* (completed by *Rimsky-Korsakov and Glazunov in 1890).

boron (B) A nonmetallic element isolated (1808) by Sir Humphry Davy. It has two forms: an impure brownish amorphous powder and pure brown crystals. The main source, kernite ($Na_2B_4O_7.4H_2O$), is mined in California. Boron is used in semiconductors and in hardened steel. The isotope boron-10 absorbs neutrons: boron carbide (B_4C) and boron alloys are used in the control rods and shielding of nuclear reactors. The compound borax ($Na_2B_4O_7.10H_2O$) is used in glass manufacture. At no 5; at wt 10.81; mp 2092°C; bp 4002°C.

borough In England and Wales, an urban area enjoying various privileges (often including a degree of self-government) by special charter. Boroughs originated in Anglo-Saxon England. In the UK, county boroughs were set up by the Local Government Act (1888) but were wound up by the Local Government Act (1972). Boroughs remain the units of local government in *London (outside the City). During the 1990s county boroughs were reintroduced in Wales and many of the former English county boroughs were reinstated in the form of unitary authorities. The Scottish equivalent of the borough is the burgh.

Borstal system An English penal system established by the Prevention of Crime Act (1908) for the rehabilitation of offenders aged between 15 and 21. The name derives from the prison at Borstal near Rochester, Kent, where the system was introduced. It was abolished by the Criminal Justice Act (1982), since when offenders under 21 have been detained in a young offender institution.

borzoi A breed of large dog originating in Russia, also called Russian wolfhound, and used originally for hunting wolves. It has a long silky coat. Height: about 70 cm.

Bosch, Carl (1874–1940) German chemist, who developed the Haber process for converting atmospheric nitrogen into ammonia, so that it could be used industrially. This Haber-Bosch process has been widely used to manufacture nitrates for explosives and fertilizers.

Bosch, Hieronymus (Jerome van Aeken; c. 1450–c. 1516) Dutch painter. He was born in 's Hertogenbosch (hence his name), where from 1486 he belonged to the Roman Catholic Brotherhood of Our Lady. The often inexplicable symbolism of his half-animal half-human creatures and devils was inspired by contemporary proverbs. Among his major works are *The Haywain* (El Escorial) and *Garden of Earthly Delights* (Prado).

Bosnia-Hercegovina A republic in SE Europe. It is mainly agricultural but there is some heavy industry. However, Bosnia has suffered almost total economic disruption from the civil war of the early 1990s. *History*: part of ancient Illyria, the region was inhabited by Slavs from the 7th century AD onwards. Bosnia became a separate political entity in the 10th century but later came under the control of Hungary. It became an independent kingdom in the late 14th century and annexed Hercegovina but fell to the Turks in 1463. In 1908 it was annexed to Austria-Hungary; Serbian opposition to this led to the assassination of Archduke Francis Ferdinand, precipitating World War I. In 1918, Bosnia was incorporated into Yugoslavia, which became a communist state after World War II. In 1992 the Bosnian people, most of whom are Muslims and Croats, voted for independence, but this was opposed by the Bosnian Serbs, leading to civil war. Serbian forces took control of the N of the country and besieged Sarajevo. The conflict involved brutal "ethnic cleansing," mostly of Muslims by Serbs. In 1995 Croatia invaded W Bosnia, repulsing Serb forces, and NATO bombed Serb positions. In Dec 1995 a US-brokered peace deal stated that Bosnia should remain a single state but should consist of a Muslim-Croat Federation in the W and a Bosnian Serb Republic in the N and E. Following elections (1996), the president, Alija Izetbegović, became chairman of a new joint presidency, comprising representatives from the three communities. Ultimate authority lies with the UN High Representative (since 2002, Lord *Ashdown). Official language: Serbo-Croat. Currency: euro of 100 cents. Area: 51 129 sq km (19 737 sq mi). Population (2003 est): 3 720 000. Capital: Sarajevo.

boson A class of elementary particles with integral spin. Bosons include all the *mesons and the *photon. *See* PARTICLE PHYSICS.

Bosporus (Turkish name: Karadeniz Boğazi) A strait separating Europe and Asia and connecting the Black Sea with the Sea of Marmara. It is spanned by one of the world's longest suspension bridges. Length: about 30 km (19 mi). Width: about 0.6–4 km (0.4–2.5 mi).

Boston 42 20N 71 05W A city in the USA, the capital of Massachusetts. It is an important port and financial centre. Boston is a major cultural and educational centre. It is the site of Boston University (1869), Northeastern University (1898), and Boston Latin School (established in 1635 and one of the country's first free secondary schools). Harvard Medical School is also situated here. *History*: founded in 1630 by Puritan Englishmen, it became a centre of opposition to the British prior to the American Revolution (*see* BOSTON TEA PARTY). It was a leading force in the antislavery movement during the 1830s. Population (2000): 589 141.

Boston Tea Party (1773) An expression of colonial hostility towards Britain before the *American Revolution. A group of American radicals objecting to the import of cheap tea, enforced by the Tea Act to rid the East India Company of its surplus stocks, threw a cargo of tea into Boston harbour. Britain retaliated with the Intolerable Acts. *See also* STAMP ACT.

Boswell, James (1740–95) Scottish writer, the biographer of Samuel *Johnson. Son of an Edinburgh advocate, he first met Johnson in 1763. The biography, published in 1791, was widely acclaimed.

Bosworth Field, Battle of (22 August 1485) The battle fought near Market Bosworth, Leicestershire, in which Henry Tudor defeated Richard III, ending the Wars of the *Roses.

Richard was killed in the battle and Henry became the first *Tudor monarch, as Henry VII.

botany The scientific study of plants. Scientific botany dates from the 4th century BC, with the studies of the ancient Greeks—notably Theophrastus and Dioscorides. The basic principles of modern plant classification were laid down by John Ray at the end of the 17th century, and by the middle of the 18th century *Linnaeus had published his works, which established the principles of *taxonomy still in use. The invention of the microscope in the 16th century enabled detailed studies of plant structure, culminating in Schleiden's theory of the cellular nature of plants in the 1830s. The 18th century saw the discovery of *photosynthesis. During the 19th century the origin of plant species was elucidated in Charles Darwin's theory of evolution and Gregor *Mendel established the mechanisms of inheritance. Botany in the 20th century was revolutionized by advances in physiology, biochemistry, cell biology, breeding techniques, and genetic engineering.

Botany Bay An inlet of the Tasman Sea, in SE Australia. It was the site of Capt Cook's first landing in Australia (1770), is now surrounded by the suburbs of Sydney. Area: about 42 sq km (16 sq mi).

bot fly A hairy beelike fly belonging to the families *Gasterophilidae* (horse bot flies), *Calliphoridae* (e.g. the deer bot fly), or *Oestridae* (e.g. the sheep bot fly). The larvae are parasitic in mammals, often living within nasal cavities or the digestive tract to cause irritation and vertigo. When mature the larvae pass out with the faeces. *Compare* WARBLE FLY.

Botha, Pieter Willem (1916–) South African statesman; prime minister (1978–84) and president (1984–89). Although a vehement supporter of *apartheid, he presided over the new constitution of 1984, which allowed some non-Whites limited political power.

Botham, Ian Terence (1955–) British cricketer. A brilliant all-rounder, he played for Somerset (1973–86), Worcestershire (1987–91), Durham (1991–93), and England (1977–93), captaining the side (1980–81). He held a record number of test wickets (1986–88) and scored over 3000 runs in Test matches.

Bothnia, Gulf of A shallow section of the Baltic Sea, between Sweden and Finland. It remains frozen for about five months of the year. Area: about 117 000 sq km (45 200 sq mi).

Bothwell, James Hepburn, 4th Earl of (c. 1535–78) The third husband of Mary, Queen of Scots. He was almost certainly responsible for the murder of her second husband *Darnley in 1567. Following their defeat at Carberry Hill, Bothwell escaped to Denmark, where he died, insane, in captivity.

bo tree An Indian tree, *Ficus religiosa*, up to 30 m high, also called the peepul or pipal. It has heart-shaped leaves and globular purple fruits. Related to the fig, the bo tree is sacred to Buddhists, because Buddha sat beneath one when he attained enlightenment. Family: *Moraceae* (mulberry family).

Botswana, Republic of (former name until 1966: Bechuanaland) A country in the centre of S Africa, lying between the Rivers Zambezi and Molopo. It is largely an arid plateau, with the Kalahari Desert in the S and W. The River Okavango in the N is important for irrigation. The majority of the population, consisting mainly of the Bantu-speaking Tswana group, lives along the E border. The original inhabitants, the Bushmen, are now a small minority. *Economy*: chiefly agricultural. Large quantities of minerals, including coal and diamonds, were discovered in the 1960s and by the late 1990s diamonds were providing over three-quarters of export revenue. Botswana now has one of the fastest growing economies in Africa. *History*: the area became the British Protectorate of Bechuanaland in 1885 and was annexed to the Cape Colony in 1895. It later became a British High Commission Territory, gaining internal self-government in 1965 and full independence in 1966 as the Republic of Botswana within the Commonwealth. Until 1980 it was under the democratic rule of Sir Seretse Khama (1921–80). Dr Quette Masire was head of state from 1980 until 1998, when he retired in favour of Festus Mogae. Official language: English. Currency: pula of 100 thebe. Area: 575 000 sq km (222 000 sq mi). Population (2003 est): 1 663 000. Capital: Gaborone.

Botticelli, Sandro (Alessandro di Mariano Filipepi; c. 1445–1510) Florentine *Renaissance painter, called by his brother's nickname, meaning "little barrel." His chief patrons were the Medici, for whom he produced illustrations for Dante's *Divine Comedy* and allegorical paintings, such as *Primavera*, *Birth of Venus* (both Uffizi), and *Mars and Venus* (National Gallery, London). In 1481–82 he worked on frescoes for the Sistine Chapel in the Vatican.

bottlebrush An evergreen Australian shrub or tree of the genus *Callistemon* (25 species). Growing to a height of about 6 m, it has stiff narrow leaves, 5 cm long. The flower heads consist mainly of bunches of fluffy red or yellow stamens, resembling bottle brushes. The fruits are woody. Family: *Myrtaceae.*

bottlenose A *dolphin, *Tursiops truncatus*, grey-blue and growing to 4 m. They are a shallow-water species, popular in dolphinariums and for research into the social behaviour of whales.

botulism A rare and serious form of food poisoning from foods containing the toxin produced by the bacterium *Clostridium botulinum*. The toxin can affect the cardiac and respiratory centres of the brain and may result in death. The bacterium thrives in improperly preserved foods but is invariably destroyed in cooking.

Bouaké 7 42N 5 00W A city in central Côte d'Ivoire. It is an important trade centre, linked to Abidjan. Population (1995 est): 330 000.

Boucher, François (1703–70) French *rococo painter. Born in Paris, the son of a lacemaker, he was influenced by *Watteau. He worked for Louis XV, and Madame de Pompadour, whom he painted (National Gallery of Scotland). He became director of the Gobelins tapestry factory (1755) and the French Academy (1765).

Boudicca *See* BOADICEA.

Boudin, Eugène (1824–98) French painter and forerunner of *impressionism, born in Honfleur. He painted his coastal scenes in the open air.

Bougainville A volcanic forested island in the SW Pacific Ocean, the largest in the *Solomon Islands; a province of Papua New Guinea. Copra, cocoa, timber, and tortoise shell are exported. It has one of the world's largest open-cast copper mines. Rebels declared independence in 1990 but the island was reoccupied by government troops in 1992. A peace treaty was signed in 1998; Bougainville was subsequently (2001) granted autonomy with the option of total independence by 2016. Area: about 10 360 sq km (4000 sq mi). Population (2000): 175 160. Chief town: Kieta.

Bougainvillea A genus of tropical South American shrubs (18 species) climbing by means of hooked thorns. The shrubs bear numerous showy "flowers" for most of the year. The coloured parts are actually large bracts, which surround the small inconspicuous flowers. Family: *Nyctaginaceae.*

Boulanger, Nadia (Juliette) (1887–1979) French composer, teacher, and conductor. Lennox *Berkeley and Aaron *Copland were among her pupils. Her works include the cantata *La Sirène* (1908; awarded the Prix de Rome), and the opera *La Ville morte* (1911).

Boulez, Pierre (1925–) French composer and conductor, a pupil of Messiaen, he was influenced by Schoenberg, Webern, and Cage. He has used *serialism in such works as *Structures I and II* (for two pianos; 1951–52 and 1956–61) and has set poems by René Char and Mallarmé. His more recent works include *Dérive 2* (1993).

Boulle, André Charles (*or* **Buhl**; 1642–1732) French cabinetmaker in the service of Louis XIV. Boullework (*or* buhlwork) is a style of marquetry using brass, tortoiseshell, etc., inlaid on ebony.

Boulogne-sur-Mer 50 43N 1 37E A port and resort in N France, in the Pas-de-Calais. It was severely damaged in World War II. It is the country's main fishing port and has a ferry service to England. Population (latest est): 44 244.

Boult, Sir Adrian (Cedric) (1889–1983) British conductor of the BBC Symphony Orchestra (1930–49) and the London Philharmonic Orchestra (1949–57). He was associated particularly with the works of Elgar, Holst, and Vaughan Williams.

Bourbons A European dynasty that originated in Bourbonnais (now Allier, central France). It acquired ducal status in 1272, when Agnès Bourbon married the sixth son of Louis IX. The first Bourbon king of France was *Henry IV (reigned 1589–1610) and Bourbons continued to rule until the *French Revolution (1792). The present pretender to the French throne is Henry, Count of Clermont (1933–).

The Bourbon Louis XIV's grandson became (1700) *Philip V of Spain, where the Bourbons ruled almost continuously until the abdication of Alfonso XIII in 1931. His grandson *Juan Carlos was restored to the Spanish throne in 1975. In Naples and Sicily Bourbons ruled between 1734 and 1860.

Bourges (Latin name: Avaricum) 47 05N 2 23E A city in central France, the capital of the Cher department. An important town of Aquitaine, it became the capital of Berry in the 12th century and the centre of power following the Battle of Agincourt (1415). Population (latest est): 75 609.

Bourguiba, Habib (1903–2000) Tunisian statesman; president (1957–87). A leading figure in the struggle for Tunisian independence, he

b

spent ten years between 1934 and 1955 in French prisons. After independence in 1956 he became president, and in 1975 became life president; he was deposed in a bloodless coup.

Bournemouth 1. 50 43N 1 54W A resort in S England, in Bournemouth unitary authority, Dorset, on Poole Bay. It has a famous symphony orchestra. Population (1991 est): 155 488. **2.** A unitary authority in S England, in E Dorset. Area: 46 sq km (17 sq mi). Population (2001): 163 441.

Bovidae A family of hoofed *ruminant mammals (about 128 species), comprising antelopes, cattle, sheep, and goats. Several species have been domesticated for meat, milk, hides, and wool. Order: *Artiodactyla.*

Bow, Clara (1905–65) US film actress. She personified the 1920s "flapper" in such films as *Mantrap* (1926) and *It* (1927), becoming known as the "It" girl.

bowerbird A songbird belonging to a family (*Ptilonorhynchidae*; 18 species) found in Australasian forests. 22–35 cm long, it is related to the bird of paradise. Males court females by building dome-shaped bowers with twigs, moss, etc., often decorating them with feathers and shells.

Bowie, David (David Jones; 1947–) British pop singer and songwriter, noted for his changes of style and image. His albums include *Ziggy Stardust* (1972), *Heroes* (1977), *Let's Dance* (1983), and *Heathen* (2002). He has also acted in films.

bowling (*or* **tenpin bowling**) A game in which players compete by attempting to knock down standing pins with rolling balls. The ten pins, 38.1 cm (15 in) high and each weighing about 1.5 kg (3.5 lb), are placed in a triangle (frame) 18.29 m (20 yd) distant at the end of a wooden lane. The balls, which have a thumb hole and two finger holes, have a maximum circumference of 68.5 cm (27 in) and a maximum weight of 7.26 kg (16 lb). Ten frames comprise a game.

bowls A game in which biased bowls ("woods") are rolled towards a smaller one (the "jack"). **Flat green bowls** is played on a level grass surface 40–44 yd (36.6–40.2 m) square. Matches are usually played between two sides of four, each player using two bowls; a contest consists of three to six simultaneous matches. The jack is rolled onto the green by the first player and is followed by the other bowls in turn, the object being to position them as near the jack as possible. **Crown green bowls** is played, mainly in N England, on a green 30–60 yd (27.4–54.9 m) square and sloping up to a central area raised 6–12 in (15–30 cm). Matches are usually singles lasting until one player reaches a score of 21.

box A small evergreen tree, *Buxus sempervirens*, up to 9 m high. The leaves are small and glossy and being slow growing, box is widely grown as hedges for topiary. Family: *Buxaceae.*

boxer A breed of working dog originating in Germany. It has a powerful frame with long straight legs and a broad muzzle. Height: 56–61 cm (dogs); 53–58 cm (bitches).

Boxer Rising (1900) A rebellion in China so called because the rebels belonged to a secret society named the Fists of Righteous Harmony. They opposed the Western presence in China and, wearing yellow sashes, marched on Peking, killing and pillaging as they went. The rebellion was suppressed by an international force.

boxing Fist-fighting between men wearing gloves in a roped-off ring. Organized boxing in modern times began in 18th-century England. The **Queensberry Rules**, drawn up under the patronage of the Marquess of Queensberry (1844–1900) and published in 1867, lay down the rules. In professional boxing the ring is 14 × 20 ft (4 × 6 m) square. The weight limits for professional boxers are: flyweight, 112 lb (50.8 kg); bantamweight, 118 lb (53.5 kg); featherweight, 126 lb (57.2 kg); lightweight, 135 lb (61.2 kg); light welterweight, 140 lb (63.5 kg); welterweight, 147 lb (66.7 kg); light middleweight, 154 lb (69.8 kg); middleweight, 160 lb (72.6 kg); light heavyweight, 175 lb (79.4 kg); heavyweight, unlimited. A bout consists of up to 15 3-minute rounds, separated by 1-minute intervals. A fight may be decided on points (marks awarded by the judges after each round), by disqualification, or by knockout (defined as being unable to rise within ten seconds). World titles are offered by the World Boxing Council, the World Boxing Association, the International Boxing Federation, and the World Boxing Organization. Concern has been expressed regarding the danger to health (especially brain damage) of this sport.

box turtle A terrestrial turtle belonging to the North American genus *Terrapene* (6 species). Up to 18 cm long, they have a high-domed carapace and a hinged plastron, which allows the shell to form a protective box. Family: *Emydidae.*

Boyle, Robert (1627–91) Irish scientist. His

The Skeptical Chymist (1661), distinguished between elements, compounds, and mixtures and dismissed the Aristotelian concept of the four elements. His work on gases led to **Boyle's law** (1663), stating that the pressure of unit mass of an ideal gas at constant temperature is inversely proportional to its volume. This law is only approximately true for real gases.

Boyne, Battle of the (1 July 1690) The victory of William III of England over the former King James II in Ireland. The battle was fought at the River Boyne, N of Dublin, where James hoped to halt the Williamites' advance southwards. The battles of the Boyne and of *Aughrim are still celebrated by Ulster Unionists on the latter's anniversary, 12 July.

Boyoma Falls (former name: Stanley Falls) A series of seven cataracts in NE central Democratic Republic of Congo, on a 100-km (62-mi) stretch of the River Lualuba, where it becomes the Congo River.

Boy Scouts *See* SCOUT ASSOCIATION.

Brachiopoda A phylum of primitive marine invertebrate animals (about 250 species) called lamp shells because of their resemblance to Roman oil lamps. The body is protected by two shell valves, usually attached to the sea bed by a fleshy stalk (peduncle). Eggs and sperm are discharged into the sea and produce free-swimming larvae.

bracken (*or* **brake**) A widely distributed *fern, *Pteridium aquilinum*. Its black underground rhizome creeps extensively, producing aerial fronds, up to 5 m high, with stalks bearing triangular blades made up of branches of paired leaflets. Spore capsules occur in brownish clusters (sori) under the leaflets. Family: *Dennstaedtiaceae*.

Bracknell 51 26N 0 46W A town in SE England, in Bracknell Forest unitary authority, Berkshire, developed as a new town since 1949. It is a centre for high-tech electronic industries and services. The Meteorological Office is here. Population (1991 est): 60 895.

Bracknell Forest A unitary authority in SE England, in SE Berkshire. Area: 109 sq km (42 sq mi). Population (2001): 109 606.

bract A modified leaf found at the base of a flower or inflorescence (flower cluster). Occasionally bracts are large and brightly coloured, resembling petals, as in the poinsettias. Smaller bracts (bracteoles) may be found on the flower stalk.

Bradbury, Sir Malcolm Stanley (1932–2000) British novelist and critic, who established his reputation with *The History Man* (1975). His other works include the comic novels *Eating People is Wrong* (1959), *Rates of Exchange* (1983), and *To the Hermitage* (2000). He also wrote for television. He was knighted in 2000.

Bradbury, Ray (1920–   ) US science-fiction writer. His novels include *The Illustrated Man* (1951), *Fahrenheit 451* (1953), *Death is a Lonely Business* (1986), and *A Graveyard for Lunatics* (1990).

Bradford 1. 53 48N 1 45W A city in N England, in Bradford unitary authority, West Yorkshire. It is the foremost wool textile town in the UK. Financial services are of growing importance, as is tourism. Population (1991): 289 376. **2.** A unitary authority in N England, in West Yorkshire. Area: 370 sq km (143 sq mi). Population (2001): 467 668.

Bradman, Sir Donald George (1908–2001) Australian cricketer, who was the most successful batsman of his era (1928–48). He scored 117 centuries in 338 first-class innings and in Test matches averaged 99.94 runs. His best score was 452 not out (1929–30). As Australian captain (1936–48) he never lost a series.

Braemar 57 01N 2 34W A village in NE Scotland, in Aberdeenshire on Clunie Water (a tributary of the River Dee). It hosts the annual Highland games.

Bragança (*or* **Braganza**) The ruling dynasty of Portugal from 1640 to 1910 and of Brazil from 1822 to 1889. The family was descended from Alfonso, illegitimate son of John I (1357–1433; reigned 1385–1433) and 1st Duke of Bragança. The first Bragança king was John IV (1604–56; reigned 1640–56) and the last was Manuel II (1889–1932; reigned 1908–10), after whose deposition Portugal became a republic. When Brazil became independent (1822), it was ruled by two members of the family, Pedro I (1798–1834; reigned 1822–31) and Pedro II (1825–91; reigned 1831–89), before becoming a republic (1889).

Bragg, Sir William Henry (1862–1942) British physicist, who worked in Australia from 1886 to 1908. His early research is described in *Studies in Radioactivity* (1912). With his son **Sir (William) Lawrence Bragg** (1890–1971) he discovered **Bragg's law** of X-ray diffraction, stating that if two parallel X-rays of wavelength λ are reflected by adjacent planes, distance d apart, in a crystal lattice and the rays then constructively interfere, then $2d\sin\theta = n\lambda$, where n is an integer and θ the angle between the X-rays and the planes. Together they wrote *X-rays and Crystal Structure* (1915) and were jointly awarded the Nobel Prize in 1915.

Brahe, Tycho (1546–1601) Danish astronomer, who made accurate astronomical instruments enabling him to revise existing astronomical tables. As a result of observing a nova in 1572, King Frederick II had two observatories built for him, where he worked from 1580 to 1597. He believed in a compromise between Copernicus' heliocentric system and the Ptolemaic view that the earth is immobile. He thought that the sun and moon revolve round a static earth, but that all other bodies revolve round the sun. After Frederick's death, he moved to Prague, where *Kepler became his student. After Tycho's death, Kepler used his teacher's observations to test his laws of planetary motion.

Brahma The creator god of later Vedic religion. Arising from the cosmic Golden Egg, he brings into existence the cyclical process of the creation and destruction of the world. His four heads and arms represent the four *Vedas, castes, and yugas (ages of the world). Brahma represents the creative aspect of supreme deity in the trimurti triad but since the 7th century his worship has been superseded by that of Siva and *Vishnu.

Brahman In the *Upanishads, the changeless source of the phenomenal universe, seen as an all-pervading infinite Being, who is both the basis of existence and the state of one who has achieved release (*see* ATMAN). Brahman originally meant "the sacred Word," and was the exclusive domain of the literate priestly caste. In its extended significance it came to be the proper spiritual object of that class alone. *See* BRAHMANISM. *See also* ZEBU.

Brahmanas Commentaries on the *Vedas, written in Sanskrit between about 1000 and 600 BC. They are major sources of Indian philosophy, theology, and myth. *See also* UPANISHADS.

Brahmanism An early speculative rather than devotional form of *Hinduism, derived from the *Vedas and characterized by the veneration of an elite priestly caste, who, as the privileged keepers of religious knowledge embodied the sacred word. *See also* BRAHMAN.

Brahmaputra River A river in S Asia. Rising in SW Tibet as the Tsangpo, it flows generally E across the Himalayas before turning S into the Assam Valley of NE India as the Dihang. From here, as the Brahmaputra, it flows WSW across NE India to join the River *Ganges N of Gaolundo Ghat. Length: 2900 km (1800 mi).

brahmin (*or* **brahman**) The first of the four major Hindu castes, that of the priests, they alone are able to perform the most important religious tasks, to study and recite the scriptures. Since in India spiritual and secular knowledge are virtually inseparable, brahmins frequently wield considerable intellectual and political power.

Brahms, Johannes (1833–97) German composer, born in Hamburg. Brahms moved to Vienna in 1863 and later became musical director of the Gesellschaft der Musikfreunde (Society of Friends of Music; 1872–75). His main orchestral works comprise four symphonies, two piano concertos, a violin concerto, and a concerto for violin and cello. His choral works include *A German Requiem* (1868) and the *Alto Rhapsody* (1869). He wrote a large quantity of chamber music and composed much piano music and many songs.

Braille, Louis (1809–52) French teacher, who, blinded by an accident at the age of three, published a system of writing that allows the blind to read by touch. Modern **Braille** consists of 63 characters, each of which is made up of one to six embossed dots.

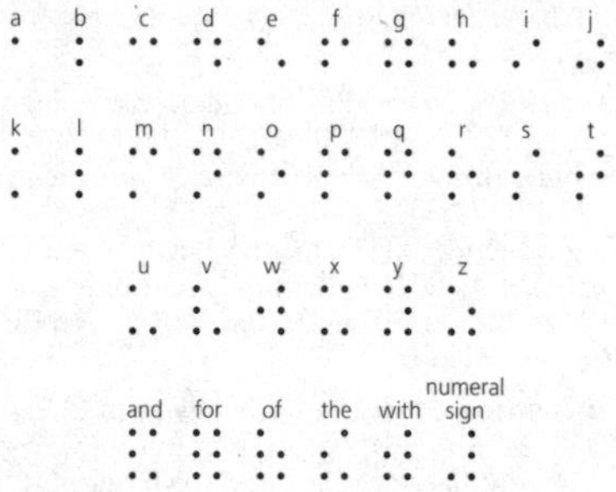

Braille. The alphabet.

brain The nervous tissue that lies within the skull and is ensheathed by three membranes (meninges). It is the organ of the mind and it controls many bodily activities. The hindmost part of the brain, joining the *spinal cord, is the medulla oblongata: this ascends to the pons, which joins the midbrain. These parts, together called the brainstem, control breathing and heartbeat and regulate the level of consciousness. They also convey information to and from the cerebrum. The cerebellum, connected to

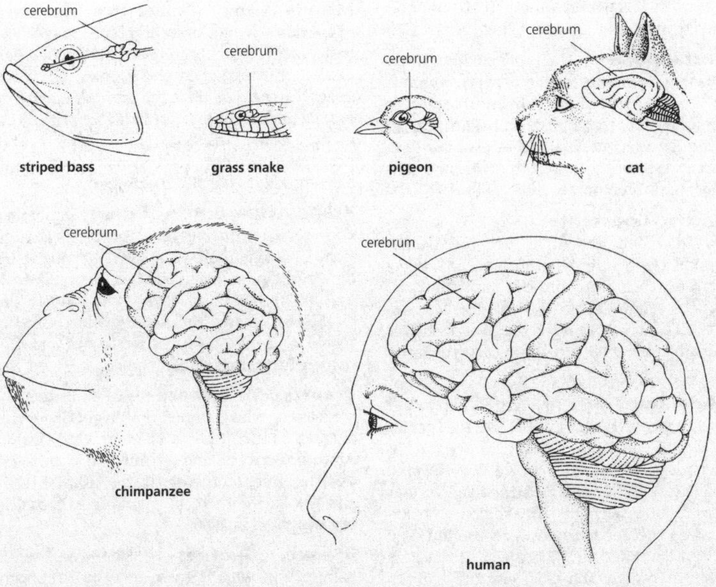

brain. The brains of these representative vertebrates (drawn to the same scale) show a progressive increase in the size and complexity of the cerebrum. In humans this development is such that the cerebrum covers or encloses all the other parts of the brain.

the brainstem, ensures the coordination of movements. The upper end of the brainstem is connected to the most highly developed part of the brain—the cerebrum. This consists of two cerebral hemispheres joined by a tract of nerve fibres. Its surface is intricately folded and is made up of an outer layer of nerve cell bodies (grey matter) and an inner mass of nerve fibres (white matter). The cerebrum is largely responsible for understanding language, thought, and the voluntary control of movements. The hemispheres differ in function: one hemisphere controls the dominant side of the body (normally the left hemisphere in right-handed people) and that hemisphere controls speech. The nondominant hemisphere specializes in analysing how things are arranged in space. Deep within the cerebrum and brainstem lie cavities (ventricles) filled with *cerebrospinal fluid. The brain of vertebrate animals is similar but less highly developed than the human brain; in lower animals a collection of ganglia (nerve cell bodies) functions as the brain.

Bramante, Donato (1444–1514) Italian painter and architect of the Renaissance. From about 1498 he lived in Rome, where he built the Tempietto di S Pietro in Montorio (1502) and the (now destroyed) Palazzo Caprini (1514). He is considered the founder of Roman High Renaissance architecture; his plans for St Peter's formed a basis for the later designs of *Michelangelo.

brambling A finch, *Fringilla montifringilla*, 14.5 cm long, that breeds in Asia and N Europe and migrates south in winter. It has a brown-speckled plumage with white wing bars and orange underparts but in winter the male has a black head and back.

Bran A legendary Celtic god-king of Britain, whose story is told in the *Mabinogion. A giant, he once waded across the Irish sea. His severed head lived on for some 80 years, giving good advice before being finally buried in London to protect Britain from invasion.

Branagh, Kenneth (1961–) British actor and director. He founded the Renaissance Theatre Company in 1986 and appeared in both Shakespearean and contemporary plays. His films include *Henry V* (1989), *Mary Shelley's*

Frankenstein (1994), and *Hamlet* (1997). He was formerly married to Emma *Thompson.

Branchiopoda A class of small, mostly fresh-water *crustaceans (over 800 species). They include the fairy shrimps, *tadpole shrimps, *water fleas, and clam shrimps, all bearing flat fringed appendages used for locomotion, respiration, and filter feeding. Parthenogenesis is common.

Brancusi, Constantin (1876–1957) Romanian sculptor, who moved to Paris in 1904. His stone and metal sculptures, such as the *Sleeping Muse* series beginning in 1906 and the *Birds* variations (1912–40), possess an abstract simplicity. In contrast, his wood sculptures, such as the *Prodigal Son* (1915), utilize angular forms inspired by African art.

Brandenburg 1. 52 24N 12 31E A city in E Germany, on the River Havel. It was the former capital of the province of Brandenburg and has been largely rebuilt since World War II. Population (latest est): 93 660. **2.** A *Land* and former electorate of E Germany. The region was conquered by the Germans between the 10th and 12th centuries and in 1157 Albert (I) the Bear became margrave, and then elector, of Brandenburg. Under Frederick William, the Great Elector (1640–88), Brandenburg gained suzerainty of Prussia and became a leading German power. In 1701 the Elector of Brandenburg became Frederick I of Prussia. After World War II some Eastern parts of Brandenburg became Polish. It was reinstated as a *Land* in 1990. Population (2000 est): 2 601 200.

Brandenburg Gate A ceremonial gateway in Berlin, built (1789) in the neoclassical style by the architect C.G. Langhans (1732–1808). Situated at the W end of Unter den Linden, it became the symbol of the modernized city.

Brando, Marlon (1924–2004) US film actor, influenced by the "method" of the New York *Actors' Studio in the 1950s. His films include *A Streetcar Named Desire* (1951), *On the Waterfront* (1954), *The Godfather* (1972), *Apocalypse Now* (1979), and *Don Juan de Marco* (1995).

Brandt, Willy (1913–92) German statesman; chairman of the Social Democratic Party (1964–87) and chancellor of West Germany (1969–74). In Norway from 1933, he was a leader of the resistance movement against the Nazis throughout World War II. As chancellor he negotiated treaties with Russia, Poland, and East Germany and in 1971 was awarded the Nobel Peace Prize. He resigned when it was revealed that one of his aides was an East German spy.

brandy A spirit distilled from fermented grape juice (wine) or other fruit juices. The best types of wine brandy are matured in oak casks and named after the Cognac and Armagnac districts of France. Marc (French) or grappa (Italian) brandy is made from the refermented grape pips, skins, and stems left after pressing for wine. VSOP—very superior old pale—brandy is usually 20–25 years old.

Brandywine, Battle of the (11 September 1777) A battle during the *American Revolution. Sir William Howe (1729–1814), advancing on Philadelphia, encircled Gen George Washington's troops in an attempt to cut off the city. Howe crossed the Brandywine Creek, defeated Washington's surprised troops, and subsequently occupied Philadelphia.

Branson, Sir Richard (1950–) British entrepreneur who founded the Virgin Group, including Virgin Records (sold in 1992), Virgin Atlantic Airways, and Virgin Rail Group. He was the first to cross both the Atlantic (1987) and the Pacific (1991) in a hot-air balloon. He was knighted in 2000.

Braque, Georges (1882–1963) French painter, who with *Picasso developed *cubism. Notable among Braque's innovations were the use of lettering in compositions, e.g. *The Portuguese* (1911; Basle), mixing paint with sand to produce interesting textures, and papiers collés (paper pasted on canvases).

Brasília 16 0S 48 10W The capital and a federal district of Brazil, situated on the central plateau. It was inaugurated in 1960, the chief designer being Lúcio Costa and the principal architect, Oscar *Niemeyer. Its modern buildings include the National Congress Building and the cathedral. Population (2000): 1 954 442.

brass An *alloy of copper and zinc. Brasses containing less than 36% zinc are ductile when cold, those with more are harder. It does not rust but exposure to sea water causes leaching out of the zinc. This is partially prevented by the addition of tin (1%) in Naval Brass, sometimes with about 0.05% of arsenic.

Brassica A genus of mainly annual or biennial herbs (about 40 species), with erect clusters of four-petalled yellow flowers. The genus includes many important vegetables, including broccoli, Brussels sprout, cabbage, cauliflower, kale, rape, swede, and turnip.

brass instruments Wind instruments made of brass. The *French horn, *trumpet, *trombone, and *tuba are used in orchestras; brass bands also include *bugles and *cornets.

Brass instruments have either a cup-shaped or cone-shaped mouthpiece, the shape of which influences the tone quality, as does the type of bore, which may be conical (horn) or cylindrical (trumpet). A brass instrument plays the harmonic series natural to its length; additional series are made available by the use of crooks, slides, or valves.

Bratislava (German name: Pressburg; Hungarian name: Pozsony) 48 10N 17 10E The capital of Slovakia, on the River Danube. It was the capital of Hungary (1526–1784). Notable buildings include the gothic cathedral (13th century), where many of the kings of Hungary were crowned. It is an industrial centre and river port. Population (2000 est): 448 292.

Brattain, Walter Houser (1902–87) US physicist, who shared the 1956 Nobel Prize for his part in the invention of the transistor (with W. B. *Shockley and John Bardeen).

Braun, Eva (1910–45) The mistress and finally the wife of Adolf Hitler. Their relationship probably began in 1933 and they were married shortly before their suicides on 30 April 1945.

Brazil, Federative Republic of (Portuguese name: Brasil) A country comprising almost half the area of South America. The N of the country is dominated by the Amazon basin with its tropical rain forests. The land rises to the Guiana Highlands in the N and the Brazilian Highlands in the S, with large tracts of grassland in between. The population is largely of European descent, with a small and dwindling Indian minority. In recent years destruction of the Amazon rain forests has caused worldwide concern. *Economy*: agriculture remains important, the chief crops being sugar cane, manioc, maize, rice, and beans. Brazil is the world's largest producer of coffee. Cocoa, bananas, and oranges are also important. Livestock breeding has increased and Brazil is now ahead of Argentina as a cattle producer. The fishing industry is nationalized. Brazil is exceptionally rich in mineral resources; the iron-ore reserves are estimated to be the largest in the world. Large deposits of phosphates have been discovered, as well as uranium, manganese, gold, and copper. 90% of power comes from hydroelectric sources. Oil production only provides a fraction of Brazil's domestic needs although offshore fields have been found near Campos. *History*: claimed by the Portuguese in 1494, it became a Portuguese settlement. During the Napoleonic Wars the Portuguese court was transferred to Brazil and in 1815 it was made a kingdom. In 1822 independence was declared by Pedro I (1798–1834), son of John VI of Portugal, with a constitution that proclaimed him emperor. In 1889 his son Pedro II (1825–91) was deposed and Brazil became a republic. From 1930 to 1945 it was ruled by the benevolent dictator Getúlio Vargas (1883–1954). Less stable governments followed. Elections were held in 1985, ending 20 years of military rule. Subsequent governments have struggled with a series of economic and financial crises. The social democrat F. H. Cardoso was president from 1995 to 2002, when he was succeeded by a socialist, Luiz Inacio Lula da Silva. Official language: Portuguese. Currency: real of 100 centavos. Area: 8 511 865 sq km (3 286 000 sq mi). Population (2003 est): 178 470 000. Capital: Brasilia.

Brazil nut The seed of a tall forest tree, *Bertholletia excelsa*, up to 45 m high, native to tropical South America. The tree produces fluffy flowers that develop into woody fruits, each containing 12–24 seeds (the nuts). Family: *Lecythidaceae*.

brazilwood An evergreen tree, *Caesalpinia brasiliensis*, of tropical South America. The leaves are bipinnate and the orange flowers develop into seed pods. The tree yields a very hard wood used for cabinetwork. Family: *Leguminosae*.

Brazzaville 4 07W 15 15E The capital of Congo-Brazzaville, situated on the Congo River opposite Kinshasa (in the Democratic Republic of Congo). Founded in the 1880s, Brazzaville became capital of French Equatorial Africa in 1910. During World War II it was the centre of the Free French forces in Africa. It became capital of the newly independent Republic of Congo (now Congo-Brazzaville) in 1960. Population (1995 est): 937 579.

breadfruit The starchy fruit of a tropical tree *Artocarpus communis*. When roasted it forms a staple part of the diet in the Pacific islands. The tree grows to a height of 30 m and has shiny divided leaves. The large round fruits have a thick rind and develop from long female catkins. Family: *Moraceae*.

bream One of several *teleost fishes, especially *Abramis brama*, a food and game fish related to *carp that occurs in European lakes and slow-moving rivers. Its deep body, 30–70 cm long, is bluish grey or brown above and silvery below. *See also* SEA BREAM.

Bream, Julian Alexander (1933–) British guitarist and lutenist, whose repertoire includes arrangements of baroque and Renaissance pieces as well as works written for him by Britten and Henze.

b

breathalyzer A roadside test used by the police to estimate the amount of alcohol in the breath. In the UK a suspected driver blows through a tube into a device, which records the level of alcohol in the breath. If the level is above the legal limit (35 µg of alcohol per ml of breath or 80 mg per 100 ml of blood), the suspect is arrested and taken to a police station, where a further specimen of breath (or blood or urine) is taken for analysis. It is this specimen that provides evidence for prosecution for drunken driving offences.

Brecht, Bertolt (1898–1956) German dramatist and poet. He studied medicine and was converted to Marxism in 1928. *The Threepenny Opera* was an adaptation of John Gay's *The Beggar's Opera*, with music by Kurt Weill. In 1933 he moved to Scandinavia and the USA (1941–47). During these years he wrote *Galileo* (1938), *Mother Courage* (1939) and *The Caucasian Chalk Circle* (1949). In 1949 he returned to East Berlin and founded his Berliner Ensemble Company.

Breda 51 35N 4 46E An industrial town in the SW Netherlands, in North Brabant province. Its capture by the Spanish in 1625 is depicted in Velázquez' famous painting, *The Surrender of Breda*. Population (1999 est): 159 042.

Brehon Laws A collection of ancient Irish laws, dating back to the 8th century, which constitute one of the most important sources for the history of contemporary Irish society. The Brehon was an official who pronounced upon the law. The Laws describe conditions of tenure and transfer of land and fixes penalties and fines for criminal acts.

Bremen 1. 53 05N 8 48E The second largest port in Germany, capital of the *Land* of Bremen. Its industries include shipbuilding, oil refining, and food processing. Population (1999 est): 542 300. **2.** The smallest *Land* of Germany, comprising the cities of *Bremen and *Bremerhaven enclosed by the *Land* of Lower Saxony. Area: 404 sq km (156 sq mi). Population (2000): 673 100.

Bremerhaven 53 33N 8 35E A city in NW Germany, in Bremen on the Weser estuary. It is a major fishing, freight, and passenger port, its industries include fish processing and shipbuilding. Population (1999 est): 123 800.

bremmstrahlung Electromagnetic radiation emitted by a charged particle when it is decelerated on passing close to a nucleus. The effect is most often observed with electrons since they are light and therefore easily decelerated. Cosmic rays dissipate their energy as bremmstrahlung on entering the earth's atmosphere.

Bren gun A gas-operated light machine gun with interchangeable barrels first built at *Br*no, Czechoslovakia (1933), and later manufactured at *En*field, UK (1935). Widely used in World War II, it was accurate and reliable and used 0.303 calibre ammunition.

Brenner Pass 47 02N 11 32E The lowest of the chief passes in the Alps, on the Austrian-Italian border. Important since Roman times, it links Innsbruck (Austria) with Verona (Italy).

Brescia 45 33N 10 13E A city in Italy, in Lombardy. It has Roman remains, 9th-century and 17th-century cathedrals, and a 12th-century palace. Population (2000 est): 191 317.

Breslau *See* WROCŁAW.

Bresson, Robert (1907–99) French film director and screenwriter. His films, which are mainly austere treatments of moral and spiritual dilemmas, include *Le Journal d'un curé de campagne* (1950), *Mouchette* (1967), and *L'Argent* (1983).

Brest 1. (name until 1921: Brest-Litovsk; Polish name: Brześć nad Bu-giem) 52 08N 23 40E A port in Belarus, near the Polish border. It is a major industrial centre. Population (1998 est): 297 000. **2.** 48 23N 4 30W A port and naval base in NW France, in the Finistère department on the Atlantic Ocean. A German U-boat base in World War II, it was almost entirely destroyed by Allied bombing. Industries include fishing, chemicals, and clothing. Population (1999): 149 634.

Brethren Members of the Protestant Brethren Churches. The largest, called the Church of the Brethren, was founded in Germany in the early 18th century. Persecution forced its members to emigrate to America, where they became known as "Tunkers," "Dunkers," or "German Baptists." They believe in temperance and pacifism and practise adult baptism by triple immersion.

Brétigny, Treaty of (1360) The treaty that concluded the first phase of the *Hundred Years' War. Never fully effective, it promised a ransom of £500,000 for *John (II) the Good of France (1319–64; reigned 1350–64; captured at Poitiers in 1356) and granted territories, including Aquitaine, to Edward III of England. In return, Edward was to renounce his claim to the French throne.

Breton A Celtic language with four distinct

dialects spoken in Brittany by about one million people. Originally introduced by immigrants from SW England, it is related to Cornish and Welsh but has been strongly influenced by French. It has a literature that dates from the 15th century.

Bretton Woods Conference (1944) A conference held at Bretton Woods, New Hampshire (USA), at which the USA, UK, and Canada established the financial rules that led to the setting up of the *International Monetary Fund (IMF) and the *International Bank for Reconstruction and Development (World Bank). Each country agreed to maintain its currency within 1% of a value fixed for gold and to back the IMF in bridging any temporary payments imbalances. The system collapsed in 1971, following the US Government's suspension of convertibility from dollars to gold.

Brezhnev, Leonid Ilich (1906–82) Soviet statesman; secretary of the Soviet Communist Party (1964–82) and president of the Soviet Union (1977–82). Brezhnev, a metallurgist, was a political leader in the Red Army during World War II. He and *Kosygin forced Khrushchev to resign in 1964. His rule was marked by detente with the West, intervention in the affairs of other E European countries, and social and economic stagnation at home.

briar A shrubby rambling *rose with arching prickly stems, found in hedgerows and scrub in many parts of Europe. The principal species are *Rosa rubiginosa*, *R. micrantha*, *R. agrestis*, and *R. elliptica*. *See also* SWEET BRIAR.

Briar is also the name of a shrubby white *heath (*Erica arborea*), the roots of which are used for making briar pipes.

bribery and corruption The giving of a gift to a person in a position of trust, to induce him to act contrary to his duty. If such a gift is secretly given it is presumed to be corrupt. Bribery of public servants is illegal according to the Public Bodies Corrupt Practices Act (1889). Obtaining a title or similar honour by bribery is a crime according to the Honours (Prevention of Abuses) Act (1925). Bribery in connection with parliamentary and other elections is a corrupt practice forbidden by the Parliamentary Elections Act (1868) and the Representation of the People Act (1949).

bricks A traditional building material in the form of a rectangular block usually measuring 225 × 112 × 75 mm. They are normally made from clay and baked or fired in a kiln at about 900°C. Water is driven off, organic matter becomes oxidized, and some of the clay minerals fuse and fill the gaps between the clay particles. Iron oxide gives the brick its reddish colour. London stock bricks are yellowish on account of the sand and alumina they contain. Bricks are laid in various patterns, known as bonds.

bridge A card game deriving from whist. **Straight bridge** was first played in Britain about 1880; having overtaken whist in popularity, about 1911 it was displaced by its descendant, **auction bridge**, in which the opposing pairs of partners competed to decide the trump suit. By 1929 **contract bridge**, which had developed in the USA, was popularized by Ely Culbertson (1891–1955). Two pairs of partners bid to name the trump suit (or to play without a trump suit) and "contract" to win a specified number of tricks above the six tricks of the "book." A game consists of 100 points, with each spade or heart trick counting 30, each diamond or club 20, and for a bid in no trumps 40 for the first trick and 30 for subsequent tricks. Only the tricks contracted for in the bidding are counted towards game; extra points are awarded separately for "honours" (ace to ten of trumps), overtricks, and for slams (when the partners have bid for and won all the tricks or all but one trick in a hand). Penalty points are awarded to the opponents for undertricks. The side winning two games consecutively or two games out of three wins the rubber, which counts as either 500 or 700 extra points.

bridges Structures that provide a means of crossing a river, valley, road, or railway. There are three basic designs. **Beam** (*or* **girder**) **bridges** are supported at their ends by the ground, with the weight thrusting downwards. The cantilever is a more complex form of girder. **Arch bridges** thrust outwards as well as downwards at their ends and are in compression. **Suspension bridges** use cables under tension to pull inwards against anchorages in the ground. The roadway, or a truss supporting it, hangs from the main cables by a network of vertical cables. See illustration on p. 146.

Bridge, Frank (1879–1941) British composer. His orchestral suite *The Sea* (1910–11) earned him early popularity but his later works, such as *Oration* (for cello and orchestra; 1930), are in a highly individual modern idiom. He was the teacher of Benjamin *Britten.

Bridgend A county borough of S Wales, created in 1996 from part of Mid Glamorgan. Area: 264 sq km (102 sq mi). Population: (2001): 128 650.

Bridge of Sighs (Italian name: Ponte dei Sospiri) A covered bridge in Venice (Italy) link-

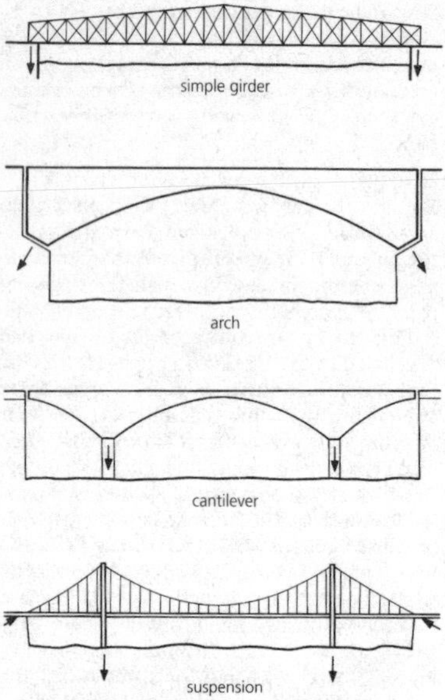

bridges. The arrows show how forces are exerted onto or away from the foundations in each of the basic structural types.

ing the Doge's Palace with the prison; named from the sighs of the prisoners crossing it.

Bridget, St (**St Bride** *or* **St Brigit**; died c. 523 AD) Irish abbess and second patron saint of Ireland. She is believed to have founded the first Irish convent, at Kildare. Feast day: 1 Feb.

Bridgetown 14 05N 59 35W The capital of Barbados, a port in the SW on Carlisle Bay, founded in 1628. Population (latest est): 6070.

Bridgewater Canal A waterway constructed in 1759–61 by James *Brindley for the Duke of Bridgewater; it ran from Worsley to Manchester (later extended to Liverpool) and was used for transporting coal. The first British canal, it is constructed on an aqueduct across the Irwell Valley.

Brie An area in N France, between the Rivers Seine and Marne. Predominantly agricultural, it produces wheat and sugar beet and is noted for its cheese. Area: 6500 sq km (2510 sq mi).

Bright, Richard (1789–1858) British physician, who described many disorders, particularly the group of symptoms, including oedema (retention of body fluid), that he showed to be due to kidney disease. This is sometimes called **Bright's disease** (*see* NEPHRITIS).

Brighton 50 50N 0 10W A resort in S England, in Brighton and Hove unitary authority, East Sussex. Originally a fishing village, its growth began with the development of sea bathing in the 1750s and the patronage of the Prince Regent (later George IV), who had the Royal Pavilion redesigned by John *Nash in oriental style. Other notable features include the Lanes (famous for their antique shops) and the boating marina (completed in 1979). Population (1991 est): 133 400.

Brighton and Hove A city and unitary authority in S England, in East Sussex. Area: 72 sq km (28 sq mi). Population (2001): 247 820.

Brigit A Celtic goddess of fire, fertility, and culture. Elements of her cult were passed into the traditions surrounding St *Bridget, notably the burning of a sacred fire by her shrine.

brill An edible *flatfish, *Scophthalmus rhombus*, related to *turbot, that occurs in European coastal waters. Its smooth body is sandy with light and dark spots above.

brimstone A lemon-yellow butterfly, *Gonopteryx rhamni*, found in Europe, N Africa, and parts of Asia. Adults hibernate, flying early in spring. The next generation emerges in June or later, the caterpillars feeding on buckthorn. Family: *Pieridae*.

Brindley, James (1716–72) British canal builder. He designed and built some 588 km of canals, including the *Bridgewater Canal, without ever using diagrams or calculations.

Brisbane 27 30S 153 00E The third largest city in Australia, the capital and chief port of Queensland. Exports include wool, meat, mineral sands, and wheat. Notable buildings include Parliament House (1869), the Observatory (1829) built by convicts, and the Queen Elizabeth II Stadium built for the 1982 Commonwealth Games. *History*: originally a penal colony, the settlement was opened to colonists in 1842. Population (1998 est): 848 741.

bristlecone pine A *pine tree, *Pinus aristata*, native to mountainous regions of Colorado, Arizona, and New Mexico. Up to 15 m tall. Bristlecone pines are among the longest-lived trees: some trees have reached an age of 5000 years and have been used to date archaeological sites (*see* DENDROCHRONOLOGY).

bristletail A slender wingless insect, 5–20 mm long, that has two or three long tail bristles and belongs to the orders *Thysanura* (three-pronged bristletails) or *Diplura* (two-pronged bristletails). Most bristletails live in damp sheltered places and feed on plant detritus (*see also* SILVERFISH).

Bristol 1. 51 27N 2 35W A port and industrial city in SW England, mainly in Bristol unitary authority. A major port in the 17th and 18th centuries, trading mostly with the Americas (and prospering greatly from the slave trade), its docks at Avonmouth and Portishead (including the modern Portbury dock) are still active. Nearby is the Avon Gorge, spanned by Brunel's Clifton Suspension Bridge (1832–64). Population (1991): 407 992. **2.** A unitary authority in SW England, created in 1996 from part of Avon. Area: 100 sq km (42 sq mi). Population (2001): 380 615.

Bristol Channel An inlet of the Atlantic Ocean in the UK, between South Wales and SW England. It forms an extension of the Severn Estuary and has the greatest tidal range in England. Length: about 137 km (85 mi).

Britain, Battle of *See* WORLD WAR II.

British Academy A learned society formed in 1901 to provide British representation of the humanities at the International Association of Academies. Incorporated in 1902, it promotes the study of languages and literatures, history, archaeology, philosophy, religion, law, economics, and the visual arts.

British Antarctic Territory A British colony established in 1962 that consists of the South Orkney and South Shetland islands and a part of the Antarctic. It is used as a base for the British Antarctic Survey stations.

British Broadcasting Corporation (**BBC**) A broadcasting authority in the UK. The BBC was first set up as a private company in 1922 and was incorporated as a public body under royal charter in 1927; it is responsible to parliament and is politically neutral and independent. It has national television and radio stations and a number of local radio stations. It relies on revenue from television licences as it is not permitted to carry advertising. The BBC provides external services in 43 languages.

British citizenship A form of citizenship introduced on 1 January 1983 by the British Nationality Act (1981). With British Dependent Territories citizenship and British Overseas citizenship, it replaced the composite citizenship of the UK and Colonies created by the British Nationality Act (1948). From 1983 until 2002 full British citizenship could be acquired by birth in the UK to a parent who was either a British citizen or a settled resident there, by descent, by registration, or by naturalization. In 2002 the government restored full British citizenship to UK Overseas (formerly Dependent) Territories and Overseas citizens. British citizens have automatic citizenship of the EU.

British Columbia The westernmost province of Canada, on the Pacific Ocean. It is bounded by the *Rocky Mountains in the E and the Coast Range in the W. The main rivers (the Fraser, Kootenay, Thompson, and Columbia) and their tributaries are swift flowing and there are many lakes and waterfalls. Forests cover over 55% of the surface. There are rich mineral resources; gold, silver, lead, zinc, copper, coal, and oil are all produced. Only a small area is farmed, and half the population lives in the Lower Mainland. *History*: the area was visited by Captain Cook (1778) and a British colony established on Vancouver Island (1849) spread to the mainland when gold was discovered (1858). Entry into Canada (1871) and the transcontinental railway (1885) encouraged development. Area: 930 528 sq km (359 277 sq mi). Population (2001 est): 4 095 900. Capital: Victoria.

British Council An institution set up in 1934 and incorporated by royal charter in 1940. The Council's chief aims are to promote a knowledge of the UK abroad, to promote the teaching of English, and to foster cooperation between the developing countries and the UK.

British Council of Churches A body, set up in 1947, of representatives of the major Churches in Britain and Ireland except the Roman Catholic Church (although this sends observers to meetings). The recommendations it makes to member Churches are designed to effect unity. It founded Christian Aid and is an Associate Council of the *World Council of Churches.

British Dependent Territories *See* UNITED KINGDOM OVERSEAS TERRITORIES.

British Empire *See* EMPIRE, BRITISH.

British Indian Ocean Territory A United Kingdom Overseas Territory established in 1965 consisting of the Chagos Archipelago, the largest island of which is Diego Garcia (claimed by Mauritius). Aldabra, Farquhar, and Desroches were returned to the Seychelles in 1976. Under an agreement of 1966 the islands were made available to the US military. Construction of a major US naval and airbase on Diego Garcia was accompanied by the expulsion of all

2000 inhabitants from the islands. In 2000 the British High Court ruled that this action had been illegal and that the islanders had the right to return.

British Legion *See* ROYAL BRITISH LEGION.

British Library The national library, formed in 1973 from the British Museum Library, founded in 1753, and other collections; it consists of some 18 million books. The first reading room of a purpose-built library in St Pancras (London) opened in 1997.

British Museum The national museum founded in 1753 to house the private collection of the naturalist Sir Hans Sloane (1660–1753); it now occupies Sir Robert Smirke's neoclassical building (1847) in Bloomsbury, London. Its collections are unique and include Egyptian mummies, the Elgin Marbles, and the Rosetta Stone. The natural history exhibits were transferred to a building in South Kensington, known as the Natural History Museum. *See also* BRITISH LIBRARY.

British Standards Institution (BSI) An institution founded in 1901 (renamed in 1931) to establish minimum standards of quality for various products and to avoid duplication of design, sizes, and patterns. Products that conform to BSI standards bear the Kite mark. The BSI is a member of the *International Organization for Standardization.

British thermal unit (btu) An obsolete unit of energy equal to the amount of heat required to raise the temperature of 1 lb of water through 1°F. It is equal to 1055.06 joules (251.997 calories).

Britons The indigenous inhabitants of Britain before the Anglo-Saxon settlements. They spoke languages of the Brythonic branch of the Celtic language family. At the Roman conquest (1st century AD) Britain was divided into tribal kingdoms with a common Celtic culture (*see* LA TÈNE).

Brittany (Breton name: Breiz; French name: Bretagne) A planning region and former province in NW France. It consists of a peninsula between the Bay of Biscay and English Channel. It was part of ancient Armorica and in 56 BC was conquered by Julius Caesar. During the 5th–6th centuries AD Celts from Britain migrated here to escape the Anglo-Saxon invasion. Finally incorporated into France in 1532, it has retained its own distinctive culture. Area: 27 184 sq km (10 494 sq mi). Population (1999): 2 906 197.

Britten, (Edward) Benjamin, Baron (1913–76) British composer. A pupil of Frank *Bridge, he spent the years 1939–42 in the USA and subsequently founded the English Opera Group (1947) and the Aldeburgh Festival (1948) in the Suffolk town in which he lived with his partner, the tenor **Sir Peter Pears** (1910–86). Among Britten's compositions are the operas *Peter Grimes* (1945), *Billy Budd* (1951), and *Death in Venice* (1973); the orchestral works *Variations on a Theme by Frank Bridge* (1937) and the *Cello Symphony* (1964); choral works, such as *A War Requiem* (1962); and many chamber works.

brittle star A marine invertebrate animal, also called sand star or serpent star, belonging to a subclass (*Ophiuroidea*) of *echinoderms. It has a small disclike body bearing five long fragile arms, used for locomotion. Class: *Stelleroidea* (starfish and brittlestars).

Brno (German name: Brünn) 49 12N 16 40E The second largest city in the Czech Republic, formerly (1918–49) the capital of the province of Moravia. A fortified town in the middle ages, it contains the Spilberk fortress, an Austrian political prison (1621–1857). The botanist Gregor Mendel devised the principles of heredity here (1865). Brno is now an important industrial centre. Population (2000 est): 383 569.

broad bean An annual plant, *Vicia faba*, 60–150 cm tall, with a ribbed stem and compound grey-green leaves. The large pod has a woolly lining surrounding large flat edible beans, for which the plant is cultivated. *See also* BEAN.

broadbill A brightly coloured passerine bird belonging to a family (*Eurylaimidae*; 14 species) of tropical African and Asian forests. It is about 12 cm long with a large head, partly joined toes, and a very broad short bill. Most species are insectivorous.

Broads, the A low-lying area in E England, mainly in Norfolk but extending into Suffolk. It consists of shallow lakes, believed to have originated as medieval peat diggings, linked to the Rivers Bure and Yare and their tributaries. These now provide holiday boating and fishing facilities. The Broads was given a status equivalent to a National Park in 1989.

broccoli A cultivated variety of wild *cabbage (*Brassica oleracea*) with a stout upright stem and a loose cluster of flower heads at the top. Sprouting broccoli has purple or white flowers. Calabrese or green sprouting broccoli is an Italian variety, often with fused parallel stems. Both are eaten as vegetables.

broch A circular dry-stone defensive structure built in N Scotland and adjacent islands, probably in the period 100 BC to 100 AD. The six-storey-high broch at Mousa (Shetland) is a famous example.

bromine (Br) A dense reddish-brown liquid element, discovered by A. J. Balard (1802–76) in 1826. It is extracted from sea water and other natural brines by electrolysis or by displacement with chlorine. The liquid element is volatile and its vapour has a pungent smell reminiscent of chlorine with severe irritating effects. Compounds include silver bromide (AgBr), used in photography. At no 35; at wt 79.904; mp −7.2°C; bp 58.78°C.

bronchitis Inflammation of the bronchi (*see* LUNGS). Acute bronchitis is often due to a virus infection. Chronic bronchitis is common in middle-aged men in the UK, being aggravated by cigarette smoking. Irritation of the mucus-secreting glands in the bronchi results in a persistent cough, with the production of large amounts of sputum. The patient is breathless and liable to chest infections. Treatment consists of the prompt management of any chest infection.

Brontë sisters Three British novelists, daughters of the rector of Haworth, an isolated village in Yorkshire. After attending a local boarding school, **Charlotte Brontë** (1816–55) and **Emily Brontë** (1818–48) rejoined their sister **Anne Brontë** (1820–49) at home. Their early writings chronicled the imaginary kingdoms of Angria and Gondal. All the sisters worked for brief periods as governesses and teachers to help pay off the debts of their alcoholic artist brother, **Patrick Branwell Brontë** (1817–48). In 1846 the sisters published *Poems by Currer, Ellis, and Acton Bell* and in 1847, under the same pseudonyms, the novels *Jane Eyre* (by Charlotte), *Wuthering Heights* (by Emily), and *Agnes Grey* (by Anne). In 1848 Emily died of tuberculosis, as did Anne in 1849. Charlotte published *Shirley* (1849) and *Villette* (1853). She married her father's curate in 1854 and died in pregnancy a year later.

Brontosaurus *See* APATOSAURUS.

Brontotherium A genus of extinct North American hoofed mammals—titanotheres—that lived during the Oligocene epoch (between 38 and 26 million years ago). Standing 2.5 m at the shoulder, *Brontotherium* had a large skull with a pair of bony horns.

bronze An *alloy of copper and (4–11%) tin. Because it melts between 900°C and 1000°C, it was one of the first metals to be used for making weapons and utensils, being known around 2000 BC in Britain. It is harder than pure copper. *See also* GUN METAL.

Bronze Age The cultural phase during which metallurgical technology, based first on copper (in the Chalcolithic period) and then on bronze, replaced the stone technology of the *Neolithic period. In Eurasia the development of international trade, literacy, the plough, and the wheel took place during this phase, which began at varying dates according to locality (the earliest being about 6500 BC in Anatolia); it gave way to the *Iron Age in about 1000 BC. In Africa, iron, discovered about 800 BC, replaced stone without an intervening Bronze Age. In the Americas, copper, discovered about 100 AD, was followed rapidly by iron.

Bronzino, Il (Agnolo di Cosimo; 1503–72) Florentine mannerist painter (*see* MANNERISM). His religious and allegorical works, such as *Venus, Cupid, and Folly* (National Gallery, London), were influenced by Michelangelo. As court painter to Cosimo I de' Medici he painted many portraits, including *Eleanor of Toledo and Her Son Giovanni* (Uffizi), a characteristic work.

Brooke, Rupert (Chawner) (1887–1915) British poet. His charm and good looks gained him many friends in literary circles. He received a naval commission in 1914 but died of blood poisoning on a hospital ship in the Aegean, without having seen action. The idealistic patriotism of *1914 and Other Poems* (1915) made him a national hero.

Brookner, Anita (1928–) British writer and art historian. Her novels include the Booker prizewinner *Hotel du Lac* (1984), *Fraud* (1992), and *The Next Big Thing* (2002).

broom A deciduous shrub, *Sarothamnus scoparius* (or *Cytisus scoparius*), 60–200 cm high, with shiny green five-angled stems and small pointed compound leaves. The bright-yellow flowers are clustered at the ends of the twigs. Broom is found in heaths and woodland glades in Europe. It is poisonous to livestock but is often grown as an ornamental. Family: *Leguminosae*.

Brouwer, Adriaen (c. 1605–38) Flemish painter, who worked in Holland, initially as a pupil of *Hals, and later in Antwerp. He excelled in small paintings of brawling and drunken peasants.

Brown, Sir Arthur *See* ALCOCK, SIR JOHN (WILLIAM).

Brown, Capability (Lancelot B.; 1716–83) British landscape gardener, who carried on the work of William *Kent. Abandoning the formal continental style, Brown's gardens sought to create a stylized imitation of nature, in the landscaped English park (as at Blenheim Palace, 1765). He was also an architect, designing houses and garden buildings. His nickname arose because he frequently told his patrons that their grounds had "capabilities" for landscaping.

Brown, Ford Madox (1821–93) British painter, born in Calais. Influenced by the Pre-Raphaelites, he painted chiefly historical themes, although his most famous paintings, *Work* (Manchester) and *The Last of England* (Birmingham), are of contemporary subjects.

Brown, (James) Gordon (1951–) British Labour politician; chancellor of the exchequer (1997–). He entered parliament in 1983 and was shadow chancellor (1992–97). As chancellor he presided over a period of stability and growth.

Brown, John (1800–59) US abolitionist, who raided the Federal Arsenal at Harpers Ferry, Virginia, in an attempt to establish a slave refuge and a base for promoting slave uprisings. He was captured and executed for treason; he is the hero of the song "John Brown's Body."

Brown, Robert (1773–1858) Scottish botanist, who in 1831 first recognized the *nucleus as a fundamental constituent of cells. Four years earlier, while observing a solution of pollen grains in water under a microscope, he discovered the continuous random movement of the grains, now known as the **Brownian movement**. Although Brown was unable to exlain it, it is now known to be due to collisions between the atoms and molecules of the fluid with the particles.

brown algae Algae of the phylum *Phaeophyta* (1500 species), which contain a brown pigment (fucoxanthin) in addition to and sometimes masking the green chlorophyll. Brown algae include all the larger *seaweeds, such as wracks and kelps. Many show an *alternation of generations.

brown bear A large shaggy mostly brown bear, *Ursus arctos*, of the N hemisphere. There are many local races and subspecies—the reputedly ferocious grizzly bear (*U. arctos horribilis*), of N Canada and Alaska, reaches a length of 2.5 m and a weight of 550 kg; the Alaskan Kodiac bear—a giant grizzly—is the largest living land carnivore, reaching a length of 2.8 m and a weight of 760 kg.

Browning, Robert (1812–89) British poet. The son of a bank clerk, he wrote several verse dramas and numerous dramatic monologues, including the famous "My Last Duchess" (1842). The poem cycle *The Ring and the Book* (1868–69) was his last major work. His wife **Elizabeth Barrett Browning** (1806–61) was also a poet. A spinal injury when she was 15 made her a lifelong semi-invalid. In 1846 she defied her domineering father and eloped with Browning to Italy. Here she wrote her most famous work, *Sonnets from the Portuguese* (1850).

Browning Automatic Rifle (**BAR**) A gas-operated automatic *rifle designed in 1917 by John Moses Browning (1855–1926). The standard automatic weapon in the US army until the Korean War, it weighed over 8.6 kg (19 lbs).

Brownshirts The colloquial name for the Nazi Sturmabteilung (SA; stormtroopers). They were founded in 1921 and reorganized by Ernst Röhm (1887–1934) in 1930. Squads of thugs, who eliminated the Nazis' opponents, they numbered two million by 1933. In 1934 Hitler eliminated Röhm himself and reduced their power. *See also* SS.

Bruce, Robert *See* ROBERT (I) THE BRUCE.

brucellosis (*or* **undulant fever**) An infectious disease of farm animals caused by the bacterium *Brucella abortus*. Symptoms include fever weakness, cough, joint pain, and sometimes swelling of the lymph nodes. Tetracycline usually cures the disease, which can be contracted by humans from contaminated milk.

Bruch, Max (1838–1920) German composer, best known for his first violin concerto (1868) and *Kol Nidrei* (1880) for cello and orchestra, based on a Jewish hymn.

Brücke, Die (German: The Bridge) A German organization founded in 1905 to promote modern art. Its members, notably Ernst Kirchner (1880–1938), were influenced, like their French contemporaries, the fauves (*see* FAUVISM), by *Van Gogh, *Gauguin, *Munch, and primitive art. Although the group broke up in 1913, their crudely painted, vibrantly coloured works had a lasting influence on the graphic arts. *See also* EXPRESSIONISM.

Bruckner, Anton (1824–96) Austrian composer. A professor at the Vienna conservatoire (1871–91), he was granted a pension and apartments in the Belvedere palace in Vienna in 1891, where he worked on his ninth (unfinished) symphony (1887–96). His 11 symphonies had a mixed reception during his lifetime and were frequently performed in shortened versions. Bruckner also composed choral and chamber music and a *Te Deum* (1881–84).

Brueghel the Elder, Pieter (*or* **Bruegel**; 1525–69) Flemish painter, popularly called Peasant Brueghel, whose patrons included Cardinal de Granvelle (1517–86). Influenced by *Bosch in such works as the macabre *Triumph of Death* (Prado), in 1563 he settled in Brussels, where he executed his best-known works, e.g. *Peasant Wedding* (Kunsthistorisches Museum, Vienna), and a landscape series entitled the *Labours of the Months*. Many of his paintings were copied by his eldest son **Pieter Brueghel the Younger** (?1564–?1638). His younger son **Jan Brueghel the Elder** (1568–1625) is noted for his flower and landscape paintings.

Bruges (Flemish name: Brugge) 51 13N 3 14E A town in NW Belgium. It was the capital of Flanders in the 12th century and during the 13th and 14th centuries it became the centre of the Hanseatic League. It has many fine gothic buildings, including the 14th-century cathedral, the Church of Notre Dame and the Market Hall (13th–15th centuries) with its famous belfry. It is linked by canal to many European ports. Population (2000 est): 116 246.

Brummel, George Bryan (1778–1840) British dandy, known as Beau Brummel. He was a prominent member of fashionable society and a close friend of the Prince Regent, later George IV. After becoming bankrupt he fled to France and died in an asylum.

Brunei, State of A small sultanate in NW Borneo, consisting of two separate areas, bounded by the Malaysian state of Sarawak. The people are mainly Malays, while about a quarter of the population are Chinese or other minorities. *Economy*: dominated by oil since the discovery of the Seria oilfield in 1929 and the later offshore oilfields. A deepwater port and a natural-gas liquefaction plant have been built. Agriculture is being encouraged. The economy suffered from the Asian financial crisis of 1997 and the fall in oil prices. *History*: a powerful state in the 16th century controlling the whole of Borneo, it became a British protected state in 1888. In 1962 there was a revolt against the proposal to join the Federation of Malaysia, and since then the sultan has ruled by decree. In 1967 Hassanal Bolkia Mu'izuddin Waddaulah (1946–) succeeded his father as sultan. Self-government was achieved in 1971 and full independence in 1984. Unemployment and social unrest rose during the 1990s. Offical language: Malay. Currency: Brunei dollar of 100 cents. Area: 5800 sq km (2226 sq mi). Population (2003 est): 344 000. Capital: Bandar Seri Begawan.

Brunel, Isambard Kingdom (1806–59) British engineer, whose most famous works were the Clifton suspension bridge (1864) and his ships the *Great Western* (1837), the *Great Britain* (1843), and the *Great Eastern* (1858). Much of his work was done for the Great Western Railway, for which he built over 1600 km of track. His father **Sir Marc Isambard Brunel** (1769–1849) was also an engineer. Born in France, he worked in New York after fleeing the French Revolution. He moved to England in 1799, where he became famous for his tunnelling shield, which allowed tunnels to be dug below water. His tunnel under the River Thames from Rotherhithe to Wapping took from 1825 to 1842 to complete.

Brunelleschi, Filippo (1377–1446) Italian Renaissance architect, who began his career as a goldsmith. His taste for classical architecture is demonstrated by his most famous construction, the dome of Florence cathedral (1430s). The Ospedale degli Innocenti (1419–26) is often regarded as the first architectural expression of the Renaissance.

Brunhild (*or* **Brynhild**) A heroine of Norse and Germanic legend. In the *Volsungasaga* she is the daughter of Odin, doomed to sleep on a fire-encircled rock until wakened by a mortal (*see* SIEGFRIED). In the *Nibelungenlied* she is the queen of Issland.

Brunswick (German name: Braunschweig) 52 15N 10 30E A city in N Germany, in Lower Saxony on the River Oker. It was the capital of the former duchy of Brunswick. Notable buildings include the castle and the romanesque cathedral (both 12th-century), the old town hall (14th-15th centuries), and the ducal palace (1768–69). Population (1999 est): 246 800.

Brussels (French name: Bruxelles) 50 51N 4 22E The capital of Belgium, situated on the River Senne. The headquarters of the EU and NATO, it has many fine buildings including the 15th-century gothic town hall, the 13th-century Maison du Roi, the 18th-century Palais de la Nation (parliament building), and the Royal Palace. *History*: settled by the French in the 7th century AD, it developed into a centre of the wool industry in the 13th century. It became the capital of the Spanish Netherlands in the 15th century and later of the Austrian S Netherlands. In 1830 it was chosen as capital of the new kingdom of Belgium. Population (1995 est, urban area): 1 121 000.

b

Brussels sprout A variety of wild cabbage, *Brassica oleracea* var. *gemmifera*, cultivated for its large edible buds. The stout shoots, up to 80 cm high, have curly leaves arranged spirally up the stem; the large buds grow in the angle between the leaf bases and the stem. *See also* BRASSICA.

Brutus, Marcus Junius (?85–42 BC) Roman soldier, who supported Pompey against Caesar in the civil war, was pardoned by Caesar and made governor of Cisalpine Gaul (46). He subsequently joined the conspiracy to murder Caesar (44) and committed suicide after his defeat by Antony at Philippi (42).

bryony Either of two unrelated Eurasian plants. **Black bryony** (*Tamus communis*) is a herbaceous climber with heart-shaped leaves. The bell-shaped yellow flowers are borne in separate male and female spikes. The fruits are scarlet berries, and the plant overwinters as a tuber. Family: *Dioscoreaceae* (yam family). **White bryony** (*Bryonia dioica*) is a perennial climbing herb. The hairy stem arises from a large rootstock and the leaves are palmately lobed. Greenish male and female flowers occur on separate plants and produce poisonous scarlet berries. Family: *Cucurbitaceae* (gourd family).

bryophytes A group of flowerless green plants comprising the hornworts, *liverworts, and mosses. The plant body is either differentiated into stems and leaves or is a flat branching structure (thallus). Bryophytes lack true vascular (conducting) tissues and roots (the rootlike rhizoids serve mainly for anchorage). They show *alternation of generations: the plant itself is the sexual (gametophyte) phase, which bears male and female sex organs (antheridia and archegonia, respectively). Fertilization of an egg cell results in the development of a spore capsule—the asexual (sporophyte) phase—which remains attached to the gametophyte. The spores germinate to form new plants.

Bryozoa (*or* **Ectoprocta**) A phylum of aquatic colonial invertebrate animals (about 6000 species), called moss animals, found chiefly in seas as matlike encrustations on rocks. A colony consists of individuals, each up to 3 mm long and with a chitinous or gelatinous case and a ring of ciliated tentacles around the mouth. These waft food particles into the U-shaped digestive tract.

Brythonic languages *See* CELTIC LANGUAGES.

BSE (bovine spongiform encephalopathy) A fatal disease of cattle causing degeneration of brain tissue and popularly known as "mad cow disease". It is caused by an abnormal protein (prion), which accumulates in the brain and can be passed on from infected cows to their calves. It can also be transmitted to other species by ingestion of beef products from infected animals. The first cases were recorded in the UK in 1986 and concern that BSE might spread to humans led the government to ban (1989) the use of beef offal in human foods. However, it was not strictly enforced and in 1996 several people died from a new strain of *Creutzfeldt-Jakob disease, which was probably caused by eating BSE-infected beef products. The EU then imposed a worldwide ban on British beef until an agreed programme of cattle slaughter had been completed (the ban was lifted in 1999). From 1997 until 1999 the British also government banned the sale of beef on the bone. In 2000 an official enquiry into the origin and spread of BSE blamed intensive farming practices, the animal feed industry, and lack of openness by the British government.

bubonic plague *See* PLAGUE.

Buchan, John, 1st Baron Tweedsmuir (1875–1940) British novelist. *Prester John* (1910) was the first of a series of vigorous adventure novels that included *The Thirty-Nine Steps* (1915). Director of Information during World War 1, he was made governor general of Canada in 1935.

Bucharest (Romanian name: București) 44 25N 26 07E The capital of Romania, in the SE on a tributary of the Danube. *History*: a fortress was built in the 15th century and it became capital of Walachia in 1659. Bucharest became capital of Romania in 1862. It was badly damaged by German bombing in World War II. Population (1997 est): 2 027 512.

Buckingham, George Villiers, 1st Duke of (1592–1628) A favourite of James I of England from 1615, he became Earl of Buckingham (1617), Lord High Admiral (1619), and Duke of Buckingham (1623). His attempt to negotiate the marriage of Prince Charles to the daughter of the Spanish king failed (1623); he was assassinated after his unsuccessful expedition to relieve the Huguenots at La Rochelle (1627). His son **George Villiers, 2nd Duke of Buckingham** (1628–87) was a member of the *Cabal group of ministers under Charles II. After his father's death he was brought up in the royal family, with whom he went into exile after the royalist defeat in the Civil War (1651). He became a privy councillor at the Restoration. He wrote the satirical play *The Rehearsal* (1671).

Buckingham Palace The London residence of the British monarch. It was built about 1705 for the Duke of Buckingham, becoming a royal residence in 1761. It was completely redesigned by Nash for George IV, although its main façade was not added until 1913. It was opened to the public in 1993.

Buckinghamshire A county in the south Midlands of England. Under local government reorganization in 1974 it lost part of the S, including Slough, to Berkshire. Milton Keynes became an independent unitary authority in 1997. The land rises gently N from the River Thames to the Chiltern Hills before descending to the fertile Vale of Aylesbury. It is mainly agricultural; industry includes the manufacture of furniture at High Wycombe. Area (excluding Milton Keynes): 1568 sq km (605 sq mi). Population (2001, excluding Milton Keynes): 479 028. Administrative centre: Aylesbury.

buckminsterfullerene A form of carbon molecule that contains 60 carbon atoms arranged in a ball-like structure; resembling the geodesic dome designed by R. Buckminster Fuller, after whom it is named.

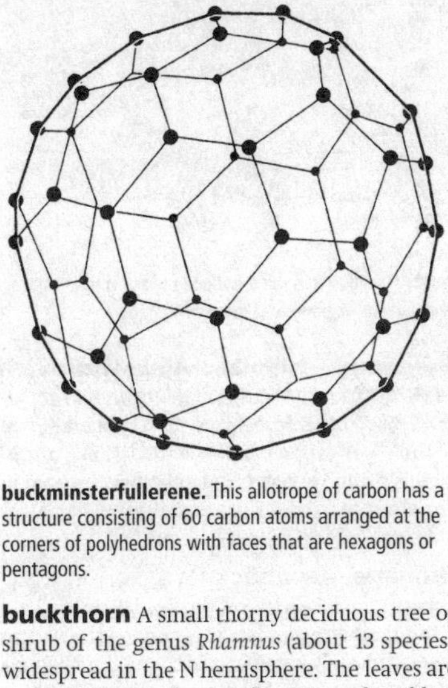

buckminsterfullerene. This allotrope of carbon has a structure consisting of 60 carbon atoms arranged at the corners of polyhedrons with faces that are hexagons or pentagons.

buckthorn A small thorny deciduous tree or shrub of the genus *Rhamnus* (about 13 species), widespread in the N hemisphere. The leaves are oval and the small green flowers produce blue-black berries. The alder buckthorn (*Frangula alnus*) is a similar and related shrub that lacks thorns. Family: *Rhamnaceae*.

buckwheat A herbaceous plant of the genus *Fagopyrum*, especially *F. esculentum*. Up to 60 cm tall, they have arrow-shaped leaves and clusters of densely packed small pink or white flowers. Buckwheats are native to Asia but widely cultivated for their seed, used as a cereal substitute. Family: *Polygonaceae* (dock family).

Budapest 47 33N 19 03E The capital of Hungary, situated in the N of the country on the River Danube. Most of Hungary's industry, including machinery, iron, and steel, is sited here. *History*: from the 14th century the fortress of Buda, on the W bank of the Danube, was the seat of the Magyar kings. After occupation by the Turks, it came under Habsburg rule in the 17th century. In 1872 it united with Pest, on the E bank, to form the city that became the capital of Hungary in 1918. In 1956 it was the scene of a popular rising, suppressed by Soviet troops. Population (2000 est): 1 811 552.

Buddhism The nontheistic religion founded in the late 6th century BC by Gautama Siddhartha (the **Buddha**), following his attainment of enlightenment under a sacred bo tree in Buddh Gaya in Bihar, India. His followers seek to emulate his example of perfect morality, wisdom, and compassion, culminating in a transformation of consciousness known as enlightenment. The apparent substantiality of all objects, including the self, is illusion. The central beliefs of Buddhism are based on the Buddha's *Four Noble Truths, the last of which is the *Eightfold Path by which enlightenment may be attained and the individual self annihilated in *nirvana. Buddhism is not dogmatic, but has developed into many schools (*see* MAHAYANA; ZEN BUDDHISM). It has over 500 million followers in Sri Lanka, Nepal, Japan, and elsewhere.

Buddleia A widespread genus of trees and shrubs (about 100 species). The small four-petalled flowers are usually clustered in dense heads; the fruit is a capsule or berry. Many species are grown as ornamentals, especially *B. davidii* (butterfly bush), 4–5 m high, the long purple flower heads of which attract butterflies; and *B. globosa*, which has round orange flower heads. Family: *Buddleiaceae*.

budgerigar A small *parakeet, *Melopsitticus undulatus*, occurring in large flocks in Australia. It is 19 cm long and has a green and yellow plumage. Since its introduction to Britain in 1840 it has become a popular cagebird. Selective breeding has produced birds of many colours.

b

Buenaventura 3 54N 77 02W A port in W Colombia, on the Pacific Ocean. Exports include coffee and sugar from the Cauca Valley and gold and platinum from the Chocó district. Population (1999 est): 224 336.

Buenos Aires 34 50S 58 37W The capital of Argentina situated on the Río de la Plata estuary. The financial, commercial, and industrial centre of the country, its chief exports are beef and wool. It possesses a national library and a famous opera house (the Teatro Colón). *History*: founded in 1580, after Indian attacks on earlier settlements, it became capital of the newly created viceroyalty of the Río de la Plata in 1776 and of the new Republic of Argentina in 1880. In the late 19th and early 20th centuries its population was greatly swelled by European immigrants. Population (1999 est, urban area): 2 904 192.

buffalo A large African hoofed mammal, *Syncerus caffer*, also called Cape buffalo. Weighing over 700 kg and measuring 110–150 cm at the shoulder, buffaloes have massive curved horns and a smooth black coat. They live in large herds in grassy areas where both tree cover and water are available. Family: *Bovidae*. *Compare* BISON; WATER BUFFALO.

Buffalo 42 52N 78 55W A city in the USA, in New York state on Lake Erie and the Niagara River. It is linked to New York City by the New York State Barge Canal (formerly Erie Canal). Population (2000): 292 648.

bug A common name for any insect-like animal. Specifically, the term refers to insects of the order *Hemiptera* (the true bugs), especially the *bedbug and insects of the suborder *Heteroptera* (plant bugs, water bugs, etc.).

Bug, River 1. (*or* **Western Bug**) A river in E central Europe, rising in SW Ukraine and flowing NW as part of the border between Ukraine and Poland to the River Vistula. Length: 724 km (450 mi). **2.** (*or* **Southern Bug**) A river in Ukraine, rising in the W and flowing SE to the Dnieper estuary on the Black Sea. Length: 853 km (530 mi).

Buganda A former kingdom in East Africa, now comprising an administrative region of Uganda bordering on Lake Victoria.

bugle A high-pitched brass instrument with a wide conical tube, a cup-shaped mouthpiece, and a small bell. It lacks valves and so can only play a single harmonic series (usually having the fundamental of C). Formerly much used for military signalling, it is now used on ceremonial occasions.

Bukovina (*or* **Bucovina**) An area in E Europe, in the NE Carpathian Mountains. As part of the principality of Moldavia, it fell to the Turks in 1512 and was ceded to Austria in 1775. Occupied by the Romanians in 1918, the N part was ceded to the Soviet Union (1940) and is now part of independent Ukraine. S Bukovina remained a Romanian province until it was abolished in 1952.

Bulawayo 20 10S 28 43E The second largest city in Zimbabwe. It was founded in 1894 by the British, near to Lobengula, the centre of the Ndebele tribe. The city is the country's chief industrial centre. Population (1998 est): 790 000.

bulb A modified underground stem of certain perennial herbaceous plants, for example onions and tulips, that serves as an overwintering organ. Food is stored in overlapping fleshy leaves or leaf bases, borne on a very short stem, and is used to produce one or more plants the following season.

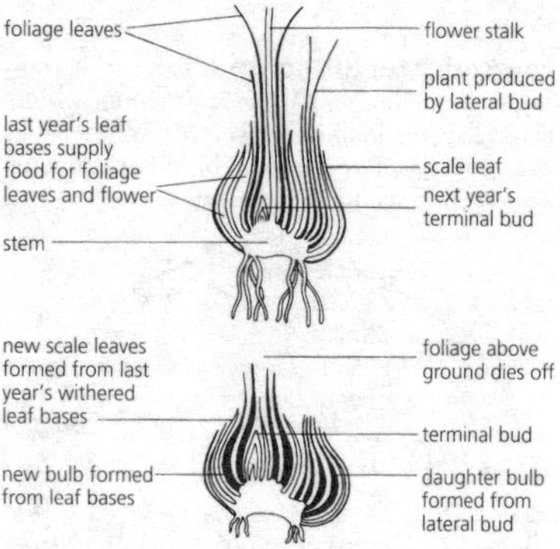

bulb. A section through a daffodil bulb in spring (above) and summer (below) to show growth cycle.

Bulganin, Nikolai Aleksandrovich (1895–1975) Soviet statesman; prime minister (1955–58). Bulganin became (1944) a member of Stalin's war cabinet and in 1947, defence minister. As prime minister, Bulganin participated in the attempt to oust Khrushchev in 1957 and was subsequently dismissed.

Bulgaria, Republic of A country in SE Europe, in the E Balkans on the Black Sea. The low-lying Danube basin in the N rises to the Balkan Mountains in the centre; further S the Rhodope Mountains reach heights of almost 3000 m (10 000 ft). The inhabitants are mainly Bulgars, with minorities of Macedonians, Turks, and Gipsies. *Economy*: industrialization proceeded rapidly after World War II. Coal, iron, and other minerals are mined and hydroelectricity and nuclear energy contribute to power supplies. Oil and natural gas have been found offshore in the Black Sea. Agriculture has been mechanized; the main crops include wheat, maize, and beet. In 1991 legislation permitted the return of collectivized land to individual owners and the privatization of state companies. *History*: following the invasion of the Bulgars in the 7th century AD and their gradual adoption of the culture of the conquered Slavs, Bulgaria became a significant power in SE Europe. Under Turkish rule from 1396, the Bulgars retained their national identity over the centuries until they became independent in 1908. Bulgaria aligned itself with Germany in both World Wars. In 1944 it was occupied by the Soviet Union; power was seized by the left-wing Fatherland Front, which formed a pro-Soviet government that declared war on Germany. In 1946 a People's Republic was proclaimed. Under a new constitution (1971) Todor Zhivkov became head of state. Democratic multiparty elections were held in 1990. The former Communists, now styled Socialists, returned to power in 1994 but a nonsocialist president was elected in 1996. In 1997 economic crisis led to mass protest against the government and parliamentary elections were won by a centre-right coalition. A new centrist party led by the former King Simeon II was victorious in the elections of 2001. Bulgaria joined NATO in 2004. Official language: Bulgarian. Currency: levi of 100 stotinki. Area: 110 912 sq km (42 823 sq mi). Population (2003 est): 7 786 000. Capital: Sofia.

Bulgarian A language belonging to the South Slavonic group spoken by eight million people in Bulgaria, Greece, Romania, Moldova, and Ukraine. It differs from other Slavonic languages in lacking declensions for nouns and shares grammatical features with other non-Slavonic Balkan languages. The literature written in Bulgarian dates from the 9th century.

bulk modulus *See* ELASTIC MODULUS.

bull (from Latin: *bulla*, seal) Originally, the seal attached to papal edicts it later referred to the documents themselves, now only to important missives. Issued to assert doctrine, they are named by their opening phrase, for example *Pastor Aeternus* (Eternal Father; 1870).

bulldog A breed of dog originating in England, where it was used in bull- and bearbaiting. It has a compact rounded body with short sturdy legs and a short tail. The relatively large head has an undershot jaw and loose folds of skin. Weight: 25 kg (dogs); 23 kg (bitches).

bullfighting The national spectator sport of Spain, it is also popular in parts of France and Latin America; mounted bullfighting, in which the bulls are not killed, is practised in Portugal. At a Spanish *corrida de toros* (bullfight) three matadors kill two bulls each. Following the initial ceremonial procession the first bull enters the ring. Preliminary passes are made by the *banderilleros* (assistants) with their capes to attract the bull's attention. The matador then makes his first series of passes with his cape, controlling the bull's charge. During the next stage, the matadors make the bull charge at a mounted picador, who uses a lance to stab the bull's neck, so that it lowers its head. This procedure is repeated up to three times. During the following stage the neck muscle is further weakened by pairs of barbed sticks (*banderillas*) thrust into it by the *banderilleros*. In the final stage the matador performs a series of passes with his *muleta* (a small red cape folded over a stick) to weaken the bull until he can sever its aorta with his sword.

bullfinch A woodland *finch, *Pyrrhula pyrrhula*, of N Eurasia. It is about 14 cm long and has a grey back, a pinkish breast, and black head. Bullfinches strip trees and shrubs and are often regarded as pests.

bullfrog A large frog, *Rana catesbiana*, of North America. Dull green with a slightly warty skin, bullfrogs grow to about 20 cm. Females are larger than males. Other large frogs—*Pyxicephalus adspersus* in Africa and *Rana tigrina* in India—are also called bullfrogs.

bull mastiff A breed of dog resulting from crosses between bulldogs and mastiffs. It is sturdily built with a short broad muzzle and folds of skin surrounding the face. The short coat is red-brown. Height: 63–68 cm (dogs); 61–66 cm (bitches).

Bull Run, Battles of (*or* **Battles of Manassas**) Two battles in the US *Civil War fought in NE Virginia. Both were Confederate victories. In the first (21 July 1861), Federal forces failed to prevent the unification of Confederate forces under Gen P.G.T. Beauregard (1818–93) and Gen Joseph E. Johnstone (1807–91) at Manassas Junction near a stream named Bull Run. The second (29–30 August 1862) followed an unsuccessful Federal attempt to capture Gordonsville, the Confederate capital. The 70 000 Federal troops, awaiting reinforcements were attacked by Stonewall *Jackson and forced to retreat to Washington.

b

bull terrier A breed of dog originating in the UK from crosses between bulldogs and terriers. It is strongly built with a courageous temperament. Height: 48–56 cm. (Miniature bull terriers must not exceed 36 cm in height.) **Pit bull terriers** resemble Staffordshire bull terriers but are larger; since 1991 they must be registered with the police and muzzled in public.

bulrush A widely distributed perennial herbaceous plant, *Scirpus lacustris*, growing in ponds, rivers, etc. 1–3 m high, it has cylindrical leafless stems bearing branched clusters of small reddish-brown flowers. Family: *Cyperaceae* (sedges, etc.). The name is also applied to the *reedmace; the biblical bulrush is the *papyrus.

bumblebee A social *bee belonging to a genus (*Bombus*) found mainly in temperate regions. Bumblebees, 15–25 mm long, are usually black with yellow or orange bands. They live in colonies containing 100–400 workers in the summer. Their life cycle is like that of the *honeybee, although only young fertilized queens survive the winter. Solitary parasitic bumblebees belong to the genus *Psithyrus*. Family: *Apidae*.

Bunker Hill, Battle of (17 June 1775) A battle of the *American Revolution actually fought on Breed's Hill (next to Bunker Hill) in Charlestown, near Boston. The Americans defended the strategic hill from two British attacks but Sir William Howe (1729–1814) displaced them at the third attempt.

Bunsen, Robert Wilhelm (1811–99) German chemist. Working with *Kirchhoff, Bunsen developed the technique of spectroscopy, using a **Bunsen burner** to heat the substance. This gas burner, consisting of a vertical tube with a variable air inlet at its base, was not invented by Bunsen but he popularized it as a convenient laboratory tool. In 1860 Bunsen and Kirchhoff used spectroscopy to discover the elements *rubidium and *caesium.

bunting A sparrow-like bird belonging to a subfamily (*Emberizinae*) of the finches. Buntings are 12–20 cm long and usually have a brownish or greyish plumage. The subfamily includes the *yellowhammer and the *snow bunting.

Buñuel, Luis (1900–83) Spanish film director whose surrealistic films, made mainly in France and Mexico, include *Un Chien andalou* (1928), *The Discreet Charm of the Bourgeoisie* (1972), and *That Obscure Object of Desire* (1977).

Bunyan, John (1628–88) British writer. Son of a tinker, he fought in the parliamentary army during the Civil War. After being converted to religion, he became the leader of a group of Baptists in Bedford and he was imprisoned for preaching without a licence (1660). During his 12 years in prison he wrote his spiritual autobiography, *Grace Abounding* (1666), and began his imaginative allegory *The Pilgrim's Progress* (1678).

burbot A food fish, *Lota lota*, related to the ling. Up to 1.1 m long, it lives on the bottom in cold fresh waters, feeding on other fish.

Burgas 42 30N 29 29E A city in E Bulgaria, on the Black Sea. Its industries include fishing, mining, and oil refining. Population (1999 est): 195 240.

Burgenland A federal state in E Austria, bordering on Hungary. It was ceded to Austria by Hungary following World War I. It is predominantly agricultural. Area: 3965 sq km (1531 sq mi). Population (2001): 278 600. Capital: Eisenstadt.

Burgess, Anthony (John Anthony Burgess Wilson; 1917–93) British novelist and writer. His novels include *A Clockwork Orange* (1962), *Nothing like the Sun* (1964), *Earthly Powers* (1980), *Any Old Iron* (1989), and *A Dead Man in Deptford* (1993).

Burgess, Guy *See* MACLEAN, DONALD.

Burghley, William Cecil, Lord (1520–98) English statesman; close adviser to Elizabeth I. He served both Somerset and Northumberland under Edward VI and outwardly espoused Roman Catholicism under Mary I. His pragmatism is evident in Elizabeth's religious settlement (*see* REFORMATION). He influenced Elizabeth's pro-Protestant foreign policy and helped to prepare for the Spanish invasion (*see* ARMADA, SPANISH). He secured the execution of Mary, Queen of Scots. He was succeeded as royal adviser by his son **Robert Cecil, 1st Earl of Salisbury** (c. 1563–1612), who negotiated the accession of James VI of Scotland to the English throne as James I (1603). As lord treasurer (1608–12), he was James's chief adviser.

Burgos 42 21N 3 41W A city in N Spain, in Old Castile. Its cathedral (13th–16th centuries) contains the remains of the legendary hero El Cid. Population (1999 est): 161 984.

Burgundy A planning region and former province of France, E of the Rivers Rhône and

Saône. It is a major wine-producing area. A Scandinavian people occupied the region in the 4th century AD, establishing a kingdom that was conquered by the Franks in 534. The NW part of the region became a duchy in the 9th century, passing to the French Crown in the mid-14th century. Area: 31 582 sq km (12 191 sq mi). Population (1999 est): 1 610 067.

Buridan, Jean (c. 1297–c. 1358) French philosopher. He is associated with "Buridan's ass," an animal that has free will but starves through being unable to choose between equally attractive piles of hay.

Burke, Edmund (1729–97) British political philosopher. An MP from 1765, he attacked George III's exalted view of the monarch's political role in the pamphlet *Thoughts on the Cause of the Present Discontents* (1770) and blamed the unrest in the American colonies on British misgovernment. An opponent of democracy on the grounds that it brought demagogues to the fore, he advocated responsible aristocratic government and emphasized the dangers of large schemes of speculative reform. Both these ideas were expounded in his condemnation of the French Revolution (*Reflections on the Revolution in France*, 1790). He also wrote *A Philosophical Enquiry into the Origin of Our Ideas of the Sublime and Beautiful* (1757).

Burkina Faso (name until 1984: Upper Volta) A landlocked country in West Africa. It consists mainly of a low-lying plateau, crossed by the headwaters of the River Volta. The population is almost entirely African, the largest groups being the Mossi and Fulani. *Economy*: chiefly based on subsistence farming. Production of crops is being increased by improved water supplies. Some minerals, including manganese, have been found. Cotton is now the main export. *History*: the area was occupied by powerful Mossi states from the 14th century. It became part of the French protectorate of Soudan in 1898 and in 1919 the separate protectorate of Upper Volta was formed. In 1932 it was divided between Niger, Ivory Coast, and Soudan but was reconstituted in 1947. In 1958 Upper Volta became an autonomous republic, gaining full independence in 1960. A military coup in 1966 brought Lt Col (later Gen) Sangoulé Lamizana to power; he was overthrown in a coup in 1980. In 1983, after another coup, Capt Thomas Sankara assumed power; he died in 1987 in a coup led by Capt Blaise Compaoré, who reintroduced democracy. He was elected president in 1991 (re-elected 1998) and his party won the 1992, 1997, and 2002 elections. Official language: French. Currency: CFA franc of 100 centimes. Area: 274 002 sq km (105 764 sq mi). Population (2003 est): 13 228 000. Capital: Ouagadougou.

Burma *See* MYANMAR, UNION OF.

Burmese A language of the Tibeto-Burman branch of Sino-Tibetan, spoken by 20 million people in Myanmar (Burma), where it is the official language. Written in an alphabet derived from the Pali script of India, Burmese literature dates from the 11th century AD.

Burne-Jones, Sir Edward Coley (1833–98) British Pre-Raphaelite painter and designer. After meeting *Rossetti (1856) he abandoned his studies at Oxford, for an art career. Typical of his romantic paintings is *King Cophetua and the Beggar Maid* (Tate Gallery). More influential were his designs for stained glass and tapestries, often for the firm of William *Morris.

burnet A slender perennial herb of the genera *Sanguisorba* (about 3 species) and *Poterium* (about 25 species), of N temperate regions. 500–1000 cm high, they have pinnate toothed leaves and oval heads of crimson or greenish petal-less flowers. Family: *Rosaceae*.

Burnet, Sir Frank Macfarlane (1899–1985) Australian physician, who discovered the phenomenon of acquired immunological tolerance to foreign tissue transplants, for which he shared a Nobel Prize (1960) with Sir Peter *Medawar. He received the OM in 1957.

Burns, Robert (1759–96) Scottish poet. Son of a poor farmer in Ayrshire, Burns became the Scottish national poet. *Poems, Chiefly in the Scottish Dialect* (1786) won him immediate fame. His return to farming was a failure and from 1789 he worked for the excise service. His poems range from love lyrics to broad humour, as in "Tam o'Shanter" (1788), and scathing satire, as in "The Twa Dogs" (1786). He also collected and wrote numerous songs. **Burns Night** (25th Jan) commemorates his birth and is celebrated by Scots all over the world.

Bursa 40 12N 29 04E A town in NW Turkey. It was the capital of the Ottoman Turks for most of the 14th century. Population (1997): 1 066 559.

Burton, Richard (Richard Jenkins; 1925–84) British actor, born in Wales. He first achieved success in Shakespearean roles, but from the 1950s acted mainly in films. These included *Look Back in Anger* (1959), *Becket* (1964), and *Who's Afraid of Virginia Woolf?* (1966). He was twice married to Elizabeth Taylor.

Burton-upon-Trent 52 49N 1 36W A town

in central England, in E Staffordshire on the River Trent. Its brewing tradition dates back to brewing by the Benedictine monks of Burton Abbey (founded 1002). Population (1991): 60 525.

Burundi, Republic of A small inland country in central Africa, bordering on Lake Tanganyika. It consists chiefly of high plateau along the Nile-Congo dividing range, descending to the Great Rift Valley in the W. Most of the population belongs to the Hutu, a Bantu tribe, but the rulers are Tutsi and there are other tribal minorities. *Economy*: mainly subsistence agriculture; coffee accounts for 80% of exports and tea and cotton are also important. Minerals have been found although industry provides only minimal revenue. The economy has been devastated by 10 years of civil war and the imposition (from 1996) of a trading blockade by many African countries. *History*: the area became part of German East Africa in 1890 and from 1919 was administered by Belgium, first under League of Nations mandate and then as a UN trust territory. It became independent in 1962. In 1966 the hereditary ruler Mwami Mwambutsa IV was deposed by his son, who was enthroned as Mwami Ntare V. In the same year, following a military coup, Capt (later Lt Gen) Michel Micombero set up a republic with himself as president, assuming absolute powers in 1972. In 1976 Jean-Baptiste Bagaza became president in a coup; he was overthrown in 1987 by Maj Pierre Buyoya. A Hutu, Melchior Ndadaye, was elected president in 1993 in Burundi's first democratic elections. He was killed after only months in office, as was his Hutu successor the following year. Ethnic fighting intensified with wholesale massacres on both sides and some 500 000 refugees fled the country. A power-sharing government was set up but ethnic violence continued, culminating in a Tutsi-led coup (July 1996) and the reinstatement of Buyoya as president. Despite the formation of another multiethnic administration and the signing of a peace agreement in 2001 fierce fighting has continued. Official languages: French and Kirundi. Currency: Burundi franc of 100 centimes. Area: 27 834 sq km (10 759 sq mi). Population (2003 est): 6 096 000. Capital: Bujumbura.

Bury A unitary authority in NW England, in Greater Manchester. Area: 99 sq km (38 sq mi). Population (2001): 180 612.

burying beetle A strong beetle, also called a sexton beetle, belonging to a genus (*Necrophorus*) occurring in N temperate regions. 1.5–35 mm long, many have black and orange markings. They feed and lay their eggs on the dead bodies of small animals, which they first bury. Family: *Silphidae* (carrion beetles).

Bury St Edmunds 52 15N 0 43E A market town in E England, in Suffolk. Its ruined abbey was built as a shrine to St Edmund, last King of East Anglia (martyred in 870 AD). Population (1991): 31 237.

Bush, George (Herbert Walker) (1924–) US statesman; Republican president (1989–93). Ambassador to the UN (1971–72), he was director of the CIA (1976–77) and vice president (1981–88) under Ronald Reagan. In 1991 he authorized US military action against Iraq in the *Gulf War; he was defeated in the 1992 elections and awarded an honorary knighthood (1993). His son **George W(alker) Bush** (1946–) also became Republican president (2001–), having previously been governor of Texas (1995–2001). Following a legal battle that ended in the Supreme Court, he emerged victorious over his Democrat opponent, Al Gore, in a bitterly disputed election (2000). In office Bush was accused of isolationism after pulling the USA out of several international treaties. Following *September 11, 2001, he launched a massive US attack on targets in Afghanistan (*see* WAR ON TERRORISM) and with the support of Britain, but not the UN, invaded Iraq (2003), toppling Saddam *Hussein (*see* IRAQ WAR).

bushbaby A small nocturnal *prosimian primate of the genus *Galago* (4 species), of African forests. They are 27–80 cm long including the tail (15–40 cm). Common bushbabies (*G. senegalensis*) have soft dense greyish fur and a long bushy tail. They live in small groups. Family: *Lorisidae*.

bushel A unit of capacity (dry or liquid) equal to 8 gallons or 2219.36 cubic inches in the UK and 2150.42 cubic inches in the USA.

Bushido The code of the Japanese *samurai class. It originated in about the 13th century, although the term was not used until the 17th. Obedience to one's lord and fearlessness were its main virtues; in the 13th–14th centuries it was influenced by Zen Buddhism and in the 17th–19th centuries, by Confucianism. In the mid-19th century it became the basis of Japanese emperor worship and nationalism. *See also* MARTIAL ARTS.

bushmaster A pit viper, *Lachesis muta*, occurring in scrub and forests of Central and South America. The longest venomous snake (its venom can be fatal) of the New World, it reaches a length of 1.8 m and is brownish pink with dark diamond-shaped blotches.

bushrangers Australian outlaws in the late-18th and 19th centuries. They robbed farmsteads and stagecoaches, murdered, and plundered; some shared their gains with the poor. The most famous was Ned *Kelly.

bustard A large omnivorous bird of the family (*Otididae*; 22 species) occurring in grasslands of the Old World and having long legs adapted for running. Bustards have a long stout neck, broad wings, and a grey or brown mottled plumage. The great bustard (*Otis tarda*), 120 cm long and weighing 14 kg, is the largest European land bird. Order: *Gruiformes* (cranes, rails, etc.).

butadiene ($H_2C{:}CHHC{:}CH_2$) A colourless flammable gas made from *butanes and butenes. It is used in making synthetic rubbers.

butane (C_4H_{10}) A colourless flammable gaseous *alkane. It is used in the manufacture of synthetic rubber and, in its pressurized liquefied form, as a fuel.

Bute A Scottish island in the Firth of Clyde, in Argyll and Bute council area, separated from the mainland by the Kyles of Bute. The island serves Glasgow as a holiday resort. Area: 121 sq km (47 sq mi). Population (latest est): 8000. Chief town: Rothesay.

Butler, Samuel (1835–1902) British novelist. Son of a clergyman, he rejected his family and religion in 1859 to emigrate to New Zealand. In 1864 he returned wealthy and turned to literature. *Erewhon* (1872), which made him famous, satirizes Victorian ideals. The autobiographical *The Way of All Flesh* (1903) recounts his liberation from his family background.

buttercup An annual or perennial plant of the genus *Ranunculus*. Most species, including the common buttercup (*Ranunculus acris*), have yellow flowers. Family: *Ranunculaceae*.

butterflies and moths Insects belonging to the order *Lepidoptera* (about 100 000 species), distributed worldwide. The adults have two pairs of scale-covered wings, which are often highly coloured and patterned; the wingspan ranges from 4 mm to up to 300 mm. They all undergo a complete metamorphosis comprising a four-stage life cycle: egg, larva (*see* CATERPILLAR), *pupa (chrysalis), and adult (imago). The caterpillars feed mainly on plants, in some cases becoming serious crop pests; the adults feed mainly on nectar and other plant juices using a long tubular proboscis and may aid plant pollination in the process. Butterflies generally are active by day and rest with their wings vertical; moths, which are mainly nocturnal, generally rest with their wings horizontal. Antennae, which are smooth and club-shaped in butterflies and plumed or feathery in moths.

butterwort A *carnivorous plant of the genus *Pinguicula* (about 30 species), found in the N hemisphere and South America. 12–15 cm high, they have a rosette of yellow-green leaves covered with sticky glands, on which insects are trapped, and a single funnel-shaped violet or pink flower. Family: *Lentibulariaceae*.

button quail A small ground-dwelling bird belonging to a family (*Turnicidae*; 15 species) found in warm Old World grassland regions. Button quails are 13–19 cm long with a brown streaked plumage, short wings, and a slender bill. The female courts the male, who incubates the eggs and tends the young. Order: *Gruiformes* (cranes, rails, etc.).

Buxtehude, Dietrich (1637–1707) Danish composer. He settled in Germany in 1668 as organist at the Marienkirche, Lübeck. J. S. Bach walked 200 miles to Lübeck to hear Buxtehude's music. One of the most influential of the North German organists, he composed much sacred organ music.

Buxton 53 17N 1 55W A spa and resort in N central England, in the Peak District of Derbyshire on the River Wye. Its mineral waters were first used by the Romans. During the 1970s Buxton Opera House, built in 1903 and formerly used only as a theatre and cinema, was restored to its original condition. Population (1991): 19 854.

buzzard A *hawk belonging to a widespread genus (*Buteo*) characterized by broad wings, a rounded tail, and brown plumage. Buzzards hunt for small mammals, reptiles, etc., and soar gracefully. The common Eurasian buzzard (*B. buteo*), 55 cm long, occurs in a number of races; the migratory rough-legged buzzard (*B. lagopus*) is distinguished by its feathered legs.

buzz bomb *See* V-1.

Byatt, Dame A(ntonia) S(usan) British novelist and writer. Her novels include *The Virgin in the Garden* (1978), the Booker-prizewinning *Possession* (1990), and *A Whistling Woman* (2002). Her sister is Margaret *Drabble.

Byblos 34 08N 35 38E A Phoenician city state on the E Mediterranean coast, now Jubeil (Lebanon). Egyptian records from the 14th to the 10th centuries BC attest a thriving trade with Byblos. Under Greek and Roman rule Byblos dwindled in importance but remained a centre of orgiastic worship of Astarte (*see* APHRODITE). *See also* TYRE.

b

Byng, John (1704–57) British admiral who, in 1756, failed to relieve Minorca, then under attack by the French, and retreated to Gibraltar. He was made a scapegoat and shot for failing to do his duty—or, in Voltaire's satirical view, as a warning to his colleagues ("pour encourager les autres").

Byrd, William (?1543–1623) English composer, who, in spite of being a Roman Catholic, became organist of Lincoln Cathedral and subsequently of the Chapel Royal (1572). His compositions include Catholic masses and motets, Anglican services, anthems, and keyboard music.

Byron, George Gordon, 6th Baron (1788–1824) British poet. Born with a clubfoot, he was lionized by London society after the publication of *Childe Harolde's Pilgrimage* (1812). His many lovers included his half-sister Augusta Leigh, Lady Caroline Lamb, and Claire Clairmont (by whom he had a daughter, Allegra). His marriage (1815) to Annabella Milbanke lasted one year; their daughter, Augusta, became the Countess of Lovelace and a noted mathematician. Byron then left England to stay near Geneva with *Shelley. In Italy in 1818 he began writing the satire *Don Juan*. He died in Greece while training troops at Missolonghi for the Greek war of independence.

Byzantine Empire *See* EASTERN ROMAN EMPIRE.

Byzantium *See* ISTANBUL.

C

Cabal Five ministers of Charles II of England who dominated politics from 1667 to about 1674. They were Sir Thomas Clifford (1630–73), Lord Ashley (later 1st Earl of Shaftesbury), the 2nd Duke of Buckingham, the Earl of Arlington (1618–85), and the Earl of Lauderdale (1616–82).

cabbage A flowering plant, *Brassica oleracea* var. *capitata*, widely cultivated as a vegetable. The short stem bears a round heart, up to 25 cm in diameter, of tightly compressed leaves. All cabbages and many other brassicas are derived from the wild cabbage (*B. oleracea*), a perennial herb native to coastal regions of W Europe. Family: *Cruciferae*.

cabbage white butterfly A white butterfly belonging to the genus *Pieris*, whose caterpillars eat cabbages and related vegetables. The species are the large white (*P. brassicae*), the green-veined white (*P. napi*), and the small white (*P. rapae*). Family: *Pieridae*.

cabinet A committee of the executive heads of government. In the UK the cabinet originated in the 16th-century cabinet council, a committee of the *Privy Council. Cabinet power was enhanced by William III's recognition that his ministers should be selected from the political group prominent in parliament and by the emergence in the 18th century of the *prime minister. By the end of the 19th century the principle of collective cabinet responsibility to parliament had been established. Cabinets now consist of some 20 leading ministers, from either house of parliament, whom the prime minister has appointed to head executive departments.

cachalot *See* SPERM WHALE.

cactus A flowering plant belonging to the family *Cactaceae* (over 2000 species). These perennial herbs and shrubs grow chiefly in the drier regions of tropical America and the West Indies. Plant size and shape varies widely; the larger species may grow to a height of 10 m or more. Cacti show pronounced modifications to prevent water loss—their leaves or shoots are reduced to spines, they have thick waxy outer layers, and many possess succulent stems that store water. The flowers, borne singly, are large and brightly coloured.

caddis fly A mothlike insect, also called sedge fly, belonging to the worldwide order *Trichoptera* (about 5000 species). Caddis flies—1.5–40 mm long, with long antennae—are found in cool damp places and feed on nectar. The omnivorous larvae (called caddis worms) live in flowing fresh water, often in portable cases constructed from sand, stones, pieces of leaf, etc.

Cade, Jack (d. 1450) English peasant who led a Kentish rebellion in 1450 against Henry VI. The rebels demanded an end to high taxation and court corruption and the recall of Richard Plantagenet, Duke of York, from Ireland. In spite of initial successes, the rebellion was soon put down and Cade was killed.

Cader Idris A mountain ridge in NW Wales, in Gwynedd, in Snowdonia National Park. It rises to 892 m (2927 ft) at Pen-y-Gader.

Cádiz 36 32N 6 18W A city and seaport in SW Spain, in Andalusia on the Gulf of Cádiz. It was founded by Phoenician merchants (c. 1100 BC). Following the discovery of America it prospered as a base for the Spanish treasure fleet; the harbour was burned by Sir Francis Drake in 1587. Population (1998 est): 143 121.

cadmium (Cd) A soft dense metal, discovered in 1817 by Friedrich Strohmeyer (1776–1835). Cadmium occurs naturally as the mineral greenockite (CdS) and in zinc, copper, and lead sulphide ores. It is chemically similar to lead and is a component of low-melting-point alloys. It is used in the control rods of nuclear reactors, in light meters, television-tube phosphors, batteries, solders, and in special low-friction alloys for bearings. At no 48; at wt 112.411; mp 321.1°C; bp 767°C.

Caen 49 11N 0 22W A city and port in NW France, the capital of the Calvados department on the River Orne. Caen has iron, silk, and leather industries. The 19th-century ship canal made it an important port; it was badly damaged in World War II. Population (1999): 113 987.

Caernarfon (English name: Caernarvon) 53 08N 4 16W A town in North Wales, on the Menai Strait, the administrative centre of Gwynedd. Caernarfon is a tourist centre, market town, and small port. Its castle (built by Edward I in 1284) is the likely birthplace of Edward II, the first Prince of Wales, and was the scene of the investiture of Prince Charles as Prince of Wales in 1969. Population (1991): 9695.

Caerphilly **1.** 51 35N 3 14W A market town in South Wales, in Caerphilly county borough. In a former coalmining area, it is known for Caerphilly cheese (originally made here) and its castle, the largest in Wales. Population (1991): 28 481. **2.** A county borough in SE Wales, created in 1996 from parts of Mid Glamorgan and Gwent. Area: 275 sq km (106 sq mi). Population (2001): 169 521.

Caesar, (Gaius) Julius (100–44 BC) Roman general and statesman, whose career marked the end of the Roman Republic. Caesar, born of a patrician family, allied himself with the popular party by his marriage in 84 to Cinna's daughter Cornelia. After her death in 68, he married Pompeia, whom he divorced in 62, and in 59 he married Calpurnia.

During the 60s Caesar ascended the political ladder, joining *Pompey and *Crassus in the first Triumvirate (60) and becoming consul (59) and then governor of Gaul. Caesar's subjugation of Gaul (58–50), and his brief campaigns in Britain (55, 54), confirmed his military reputation and made him a popular hero. When the Triumvirate ended (50) the Senate, with Pompey's support, asked Caesar to resign his armies. He refused and, crossing the River Rubicon into Italy (49), initiated the civil war. Caesar defeated Pompey at *Pharsalus (48) and spent the following winter in Alexandria with Cleopatra, who became his lover. He later defeated the remnants of Pompey's party at Thapsus (46) and Munda (45), after which he returned to Rome as dictator. On the Ides of March (15 March 44), Caesar was assassinated in the Senate House by republicans, including *Brutus and Cassius, who feared his monarchical aspirations.

Caesar wrote outstanding accounts of his campaigns in Gaul (*De bello gallico*) and the civil war (*De bello civili*).

Caesarean section A surgical operation in which a baby is delivered through an incision made in the abdominal wall and the womb, so called because Julius Caesar was believed to have been born in this way. Perhaps a more plausible etymology is that it derives from *caesus* (past participle of Latin *caedere*, to cut). Caesarean section is employed when a baby cannot be delivered through the vagina; for instance, because it is abnormally positioned in the womb or is too large to pass through the birth canal.

caesium (Cs) The most reactive and electropositive alkali metal. It was discovered by Bunsen and Kirchhoff in 1860 and occurs naturally in the mica lepidolite and as pollucite, $(Cs,K)AlSi_2O_6.nH_2O$. It is used in photoelectric cells. At no 55; at wt 132.905; mp 28.39°C; bp 671°C.

caffeine (*or* **theine**; $C_8H_{10}O_2N_4$) The substance in coffee and tea that acts as a stimulant. In its pure form it is white and crystalline.

Cage, John (1912–92) Avantgarde US composer. His works include *4 minutes 33 seconds* (1954), silence in three movements for any instrument(s), *Apartment Building 1776* (1976), *Thirty Pieces for Five Orchestras* (1981), and *Europeras 3 and 4* (1990).

Cagney, James (1899–1986) US actor. He began making films in the 1930s, after working in vaudeville, and became famous for his portrayals of tough gangsters. His films include *Public Enemy* (1931) and *The Roaring Twenties* (1939).

Cain In the Old Testament, the elder son of Adam and Eve. He became jealous of his younger brother **Abel**, whose burnt offerings were accepted by God in preference to his own. He killed Abel and was banished, marked as the world's first murderer.

Caine, Sir Michael (Maurice Micklewhite; 1933–) British film actor. His numerous films include *The Ipcress File* (1965), *Get Carter* (1971), *Educating Rita* (1983), *Little Voice* (1999), and *The Quiet American* (2002). He was knighted in 2000.

Cainozoic era *See* CENOZOIC ERA.

Cairngorm Mountains A mountain range in NE Scotland, in Aberdeenshire and Highland, forming a N extension of the Grampians. Its highests peaks include Ben Macdhui at 1309 m (4296 ft) and Braeriach at 1296 m (4252 ft). The area is popular for winter sports, centred on Aviemore. It was designated a national park (the UK's largest) in 2003.

cairn terrier A breed of small dog originating in the Scottish Highlands, where it was used to flush game from cover (such as stone cairns). It has a long outer coat and a short soft undercoat; the colour varies from red, sandy, or grey to almost black. Height: about 25 cm.

Cairo (Arabic name: El Qahira) 30 01N 31 14E The capital of Egypt, situated in the N of the country on the E bank of the River Nile. It is the largest city in Africa. Its many mosques include the Mosque of Omar (643 AD), Cairo's earliest remaining Arabic building. Population (1996 est): 9 900 000. *See also* GIZA, EL.

caisson disease *See* DECOMPRESSION SICKNESS.

calabash A tree, *Crescentia cujete*, 7.5–15 m tall, native to tropical America (particularly Brazil). Funnel-shaped flowers are borne on the old stems and produce gourdlike fruits, up to 50 cm long. These fruits have woody outer layers and, after removal of the inner pulp, are used as pots, cooking utensils, etc. Family: *Bignoniaceae*.

Calabria A mountainous region occupying the southern "toe" of Italy. Crotone is the main industrial centre. Area: 15 080 sq km (5822 sq mi). Population (2000 est): 2 050 478. Capital: Catanzaro.

Calais 50 57N 1 52E A port in N France, in the Pas-de-Calais department. It lies on the shortest sea route to England. Calais produces lace, tulle, and other textiles. *History*: besieged and captured by the English under Edward III in 1346, Calais remained in English hands until 1558. Population (1995 est): 75 309.

calamine An ore of zinc. In English usage it refers to zinc carbonate (smithsonite) and in the USA it refers to zinc silicate (hemimorphite). A skin lotion of the same name contains zinc oxide.

Calceolaria A genus of perennial herbs and shrubs (300–400 species) native to temperate South America. The plants grow to a height of 30–70 cm and bear brightly coloured slipper-shaped flowers. Some species and hybrids are grown as ornamentals. Family: *Scrophulariaceae*.

calcite A common rock-forming mineral consisting of crystalline calcium carbonate. It is usually colourless or white. It occurs in igneous, metamorphic, and sedimentary rocks. *See also* LIMESTONE.

calcium (Ca) A reactive metal, first isolated by Sir Humphry Davy in 1808. It occurs in nature as calcite ($CaCO_3$), *fluorite (CaF_2), and *gypsum ($CaSO_4.2H_2O$) and is an essential constituent of shells, bones, and teeth. The element is extracted by electrolysis of the molten chloride ($CaCl_2$). At no 20; at wt 40.08; mp 842 ± 2°C; bp 1494°C.

calculus The mathematical techniques, developed by *Newton and *Leibniz, that are based on the concept of infinitely small changes in continuously varying quantities. For example, calculus is used to define the velocity of a moving body as the rate of change of its position at any instant. Velocity (v) is said to be the derivative of position (x) with respect to time (t); in calculus it is written $v = dx/dt$. In this notation dt is a vanishingly small time interval and dx is the distance the body travels in this time. If x is a known function of t, values

1. The derivative dx/dt at P gives the slope of the curve at P. When the function has a stationary (e.g. a maximum as at A or a minimum as at B) value, $dx/dt = 0$.

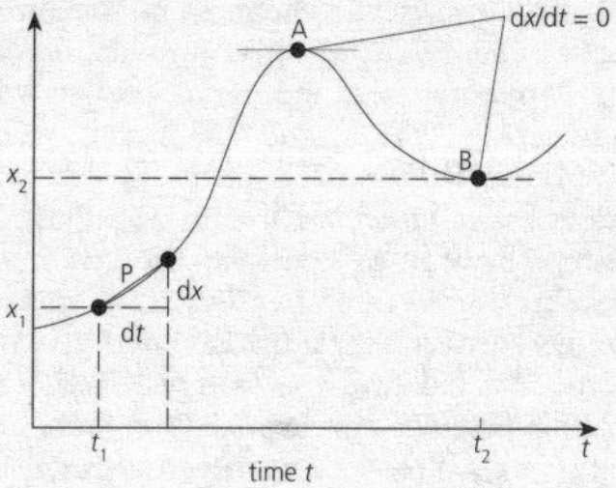

2. The integral $\int_{t_1}^{t_2} v.dt$ (= $x_2 - x_1$) is the shaded area, i.e. it is the sum of all the areas $v.dt$ of the infinitely thin slices. The area between A and B is subtracted since v is negative.

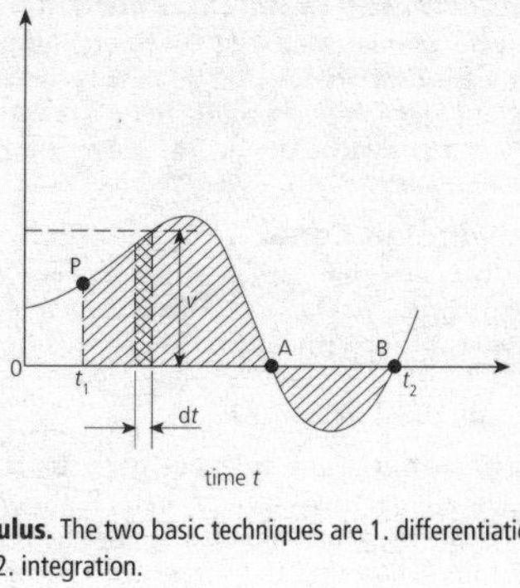

calculus. The two basic techniques are 1. differentiation and 2. integration.

for v at any time can be obtained by calculating the derivative of (differentiating) this function with respect to time. Similarly, the derivative of the velocity (or the second derivative of position) at any instant gives its acceleration (a), i.e. $d^2x/dt^2 = dv/dt = a$. The **differential calculus** is the technique for making such calculations. On a graph, the derivative of a function is the gradient of the curve at any point.

The **integral calculus** is concerned with the reverse process. If velocity is a continuously varying function of time, the change in position over a measurable time interval is calculated by summing the products of v and dt for each of the infinitessimally small intervals of time (dt) that make up the measurable interval. As with differential calculus, the extraction of integrals follows general rules. On a graph, the area between the curve of a function and the horizontal axis is the integral of the function over the specified interval.

Calcutta (official name from 1999: Kolkata) 22 35N 88 21E A city in India, the capital of West Bengal on the River Hooghly. It is a major industrial centre and the most important seaport on the E coast of India. Jute manufacturing dominates the industrial sector, while engineering, cotton, and chemicals are also important. The conurbation has a vast population, many of whom live in appalling conditions. By way of contrast, the city centre contains many imposing buildings, situated around Fort William (a British building dating from 1758). Calcutta was founded in 1692 as a trading post for the British East India Company (*see also* BLACK HOLE OF CALCUTTA). Population (1991 est, urban area): 10 916 272.

Calderdale A unitary authority in N England, in West Yorkshire. Area: 364 sq km (140 sq mi). Population (2001): 192 396.

Calderón (de la Barca), Pedro (1600–81) Spanish dramatist at the court of Philip IV. After the death of Lope de Vega he became the leading Spanish playwright. His plays include *Life is a Dream* (1635) and *The Mayor of Zalamanca* (1640).

Caledonian Canal A system of lochs and canals in Scotland, linking the North Sea with the Irish Sea, via the Great Glen. Engineered by Thomas Telford, it was opened to navigation in 1822. It is now used mainly by small craft. Length: about 100 km (60 mi).

calendar Any of a variety of systems for the reckoning of time over an extended period. Calendars are usually based on the earth's orbital period around the sun (a year), although in some systems the moon's orbital period around the earth (a month) is used. Since the seasons recur after each tropical *year (which contains 365.2422 days), the length of the calendar year, averaged over many years, should correspond as closely as possible to that of the tropical year. This is achieved by using leap years, which contain one more day than the usual calendar year.

In 46 BC, Julius Caesar established the so-called **Julian calendar** in which a period of three years, each of 365 days, was followed by a leap year of 366 days. The average length of the year was therefore 365.25 days. Since this was over 11 minutes longer than the tropical year, an extra day appeared about every 128 years. This discrepancy was amended by the **Gregorian calendar**, which was introduced in Roman Catholic countries in 1582 by Pope Gregory XIII, was made law in Britain and its colonies in 1752, and is now in almost worldwide use. Leap years are restricted to century years divisible by 400 (e.g. 1600 and 2000) and any other year divisible by four. This reduces the average length of the calendar year to a much more acceptable 365.2425 days.

Calgary 51 05N 114 05W A city in W Canada, in Alberta. It is the centre of Canada's petroleum industry and the distribution and farming centre of S Alberta. The Calgary Stampede, a famous rodeo, is celebrated annually. Population (1996): 768 082.

Cali 3 24N 76 30W The third largest city in Columbia. It is a commercial and industrial centre, with a university founded in 1945. Population (1999 est): 2 077 386.

calico A simple woven cotton fabric that originated as a printed fabric from Calicut, India (now named *Kozhikode). Strong and serviceable with a wide range of textures, it is used mainly for dresses and domestic purposes.

California The third largest state in the USA, on the W coast. It consists of a narrow coastal plain rising to the Coast Range, with the fertile central valleys of the Sacramento and San Joaquin Rivers, deserts in the S, and the Sierra Nevada Mountains in the E. It is the most populous and prosperous state in the USA; the predominantly urban population is concentrated along the coast. Oil is exploited along with natural gas, cement, sand and gravel, and borate. Aircraft and ship construction are important industries, as well as general construction and food processing; wine production is especially important. Since the 1980s the area S of San Francisco has become known as Silicon Valley

Gregorian calendar	*Hebrew calendar*	*Islamic calendar*	*Chinese calendar*	
solar year of 365.2425 days	lunar year; the year 5750 started on 1 January 1990	lunar year; the year 1410 started on 18 September 1990	lunar and solar cycles; 24 fortnightly periods	
January (31 d)	Shevat (30 d) (Jan/Feb)	Muharram (30 d)	Xiao Han Da Han	Jan Jan/Feb
February (28 d; 29 days in leap year)	Adar (29 d) (Feb/Mar)	Safar (29 d)	Li Chun Yu Shui	Feb Feb/Mar
March (31 d)	Nisan (30 d) (Mar/Apr)	Rabī' I (30 d)	Jing Zhe Chun Fen	Mar Mar/Apr
April (30 d)	Iyar (29 d) (Apr/May)	Rabī' II (29 d)	Qing Ming Gu Yu	Apr Apr/May
May (31 d)	Sivan (30 d) (May/June)	Jumādā I (30 d)	Li Xia Xiao Man	May May/June
June (30 d)	Tammuz (29 d) (June/July)	Jumādā II (29 d)	Mang Zhong Xia Zhi	June June/July
July (31 d)	Av (30 d) (July/Aug)	Rajab (30 d)	Xiao Shu Da Shu	July July/Aug
August (31 d)	Elul (29 d) (Aug/Sept)	Sha'ban (29 d)	Li Qiu Chu Shu	Aug Aug/Sept
September (30 d)	Tishri (30 d) (Sept/Oct)	Ramadān (30 d)	Bai Lu Qui Fen	Sept Sept/Oct
October (31 d)	Heshvan (29 or 30 d) (Oct/Nov)	Shawwāl (29 d)	Han Lu Shuang Jiang	Oct Oct/Nov
November (30 d)	Kislev (29 or 30 d) (Nov/Dec)	Dhūal-Qa'dah (30 d)	Li Dong Xiao Xue	Nov Nov/Dec
December (31 d)	Tevet (29 d) (Dec/Jan)	Dhūal-Hijjah (20 or 30 d)	Da Xue Dong Zhi	Dec Dec/Jan

Calendars still in use

owing to the concentration of high-tech industry. The state also produces grapes, tomatoes, cotton, sugar beet, strawberries, citrus fruits, hay, beef cattle, and turkeys. *History*: first discovered by the Spanish (1542) it remained under their control until it was ceded to the USA (1848). In the same year gold was discovered, leading to a rapid increase in the number of immigrants. California became a state in 1850. Area: 411 013 sq km (158 693 sq mi). Population (2000): 33 871 648. Capital: Sacramento.

californium (Cf) A synthetic transuranic element first isolated in 1950. Californium-252 is an intense neutron emitter. It is used as a neutron source in instruments for determining moisture contents and discovering precious metals. At no 98; at wt (251).

Caligula (Gaius Caesar; 12–41 AD) Roman emperor (37–41), son of Germanicus Caesar and Agrippina the Elder. Succeeding Tiberius, he initially enjoyed great popularity but his subsequent tyrannical and extravagant behaviour brought allegations of madness, from both contemporaries and historians, and he was assassinated.

calisaya *See* CINCHONA.

Callaghan, (Leonard) James, Baron (1912–) British statesman; Labour prime minister (1976–79). He entered parliament in 1945 and was chancellor of the exchequer (1964–67), home secretary (1967–70), and foreign secretary (1974–76). He became prime minister when Harold Wilson resigned and was defeated in the 1979 election.

Callas, Maria (Maria Kalogeropoulos; 1923–77) US-born soprano of Greek parentage. She possessed a brilliant coloratura voice and fine acting ability. From 1950 she was prima donna of La Scala, Milan.

C

Calliope In Greek legend, goddess of epic poetry and the chief of the nine *Muses. She was loved by Apollo; her children included Hymen, Ialemus, and *Orpheus.

calorie A former unit of heat replaced by the joule. Formerly defined as the amount of heat required to raise the temperature of 1 gram of water through 1°C, the calorie is now defined as 4.1868 joules. The kilocalorie or Calorie (1000 calories) is still used to express the energy value of foods.

Calvary A hill beyond the walls of Jerusalem on which Christ was crucified. The Hebrew name is Golgotha (a skull). Its precise location is unknown but traditionally it has been taken as the spot, now within the Church of the Holy Sepulchre, where St Helena discovered a supposed relic of the Cross in 327 AD.

Calvin, John (1509–64) French Protestant reformer. He studied law and theology and in the early 1530s openly sided with Protestantism. Settling in Basle in 1536, he published the first edition of his influential *Institutes* setting out his beliefs. During a visit to Geneva in 1536 he met the Protestant reformer, Guillaume Farel (1489–1565), who persuaded him to stay. Their efforts to organize the Reformation in the city resulted in their exile (1538). Calvin then preached in Strasbourg, but was invited back to Geneva in 1541, remaining there as its virtual dictator until his death. His theological teachings, known as **Calvinism**, form the basis of the doctrines of most of the reformed Churches that are not Lutheran, including the state Churches of the Netherlands and Scotland (*see* PRESBYTERIANISM), various Nonconformist Churches, and some Churches in North America and Germany. Calvin's systematic writings stress the transcendant power of God and man's total depravity outside God's redeeming grace. Like Luther, Calvin believed that faith must be based on Scripture alone, that justification (that is, righteousness in God's eyes) could only be achieved through faith. Unlike Luther, he believed that some people, the elect, were predestined for salvation and the rest for damnation. He also believed that the church should control the state.

Calvino, Italo (1923–85) Italian novelist and writer. His witty and erudite fantasies include the trilogy *Our Forefathers* (1952–60) and *Invisible Cities* (1972).

Calypso A Greek nymph, the daughter of *Atlas, who kept *Odysseus with her on the island of Ogygia for several years before allowing him to return home.

calypso orchid A rare and highly prized perennial orchid, *Calypso bulbosa*, also known as the fairy slipper orchid, native to cold N temperate regions. 8–10 cm high, it has a solitary pink flower with brown, purple, and yellow markings and a single crinkled dark-green leaf.

Camargue, la The Rhône delta area in S France, between the river channels of the Grand Rhône and the Petit Rhône. Once chiefly marshy, much land reclamation has occurred and cattle, especially bulls for the bullring, and horses are reared. Rice is also grown here. Area: about 560 sq km (215 sq mi).

Camberwell beauty A *nymphalid butterfly, *Nymphalis antiopa*, occurring in temperate Eurasia and in North America, where it is called mourning cloak because of its sombre coloration: purple wings with cream edges. The adults hibernate and the caterpillars feed on various trees.

cambium A layer of cells in woody plants that is responsible for producing additional *xylem and *phloem tissue, bringing about an increase in girth. The cambium also produces bark and protective callus tissue after injury. *See also* MERISTEM.

Cambodia A country in SE Asia, in the Indochina Peninsula on the Gulf of Thailand. It consists mainly of an alluvial plain drained by the River Mekong and enclosed by mountains. Most of the inhabitants are Khmers, with small minorities of Vietnamese and Chinese. *Economy*: mainly agricultural, the staple crop being rice. Production was severely reduced during the Khmer Rouge regime, but is now recovering. Industry was suspended entirely during the Khmer Rouge period but now includes garment making. Cambodia is rich in forests, and phosphates, gemstones, and gold are produced; there are also known quantities of unexploited iron ore and manganese. There is an abundance of freshwater fish. Tourism is developing. *History*: the kingdom of Funan (1st–6th centuries AD) was conquered by the Buddhist *Khmers. Following the collapse of their empire in the 15th century, Cambodia was prey to attack from the Thais and Vietnamese until 1863, when it became a French protectorate. In 1887 it became part of the Union of *Indochina. In 1949 it achieved self-government as a member of the French Union, gaining full independence in 1953. Under Prince *Sihanouk Cambodia was used as a base by North Vietnamese (communist) forces (*see* VIETNAM WAR); following the failure of his attempts to negotiate their withdrawal, he was deposed (1970) by Gen

Lon Nol (1913–85), who was supported by the USA. Shortly afterwards US and South Vietnamese troops invaded the renamed Khmer Republic to support Lon Nol against the communist Khmer Rouge guerrillas. In the ensuing civil war the Khmer Rouge was finally victorious in 1974, and in 1975 the country was renamed Kampuchea. The Khmer Rouge Government, led by Pol Pot (1925–98), attempted to reshape the country's economy on cooperative lines by forcing Cambodians out of the towns, depriving them of their property, and killing many thousands of the aged, sick, or dissenting. Altogether some two million people died as a result of these policies. The Vietnamese invaded the country in December 1978; Pol Pot was overthrown and a government set up under Heng Samrin. In 1982 the Khmer Rouge, with two other exiled factions, formed the Coalition Government of Democratic Kampuchea (CGDK), with a seat at the UN. Guerrilla attacks by CGDK forces on the forces of prime minister Hun Sen continued after the Vietnamese withdrew in 1989. In 1991 UN peace talks led to the creation of a new governing coalition. Sihanouk returned as head of state and a democratic monarchist constitution was adopted in 1993. However, the Khmer Rouge boycotted multiparty elections and continued fighting: the later 1990s saw splits in the movement, leading to its effective demise by 1999. Elections in 1998 and 2003 resulted in victory for Hun Sen's party. Official language: Khmer; French is widely spoken. Currency: riel of 100 sen. Area: 181 000 sq km (71 000 sq mi). Population (2003): 13 125 000. Capital: Phnom Penh.

Cambrian Mountains A mountain system in Wales, extending N–S from Gwynedd, through Powys to Carmarthenshire. The name is sometimes used for all the Welsh mountains and sometimes reserved for the central range, i.e. excluding Snowdonia in the NW and the Brecon Beacons and Black Mountains in the SE.

Cambrian period The earliest geological period of the *Palaeozoic era. It began about 590 million years ago and lasted at least 70 million years, lying between the Precambrian and Ordovician periods. Rocks of this period are the first to contain an abundance of fossils, including primitive representatives of most invertebrates living today. Trilobites were very abundant, as well as brachiopods and gastropods. The Cambrian period is divided into Lower, Middle, and Upper.

Cambridge **1.** 52 12N 0 07E A city in E England, the administrative centre of Cambridgeshire on the River Cam (*or* Granta), a tributary of the Great Ouse. The city is dominated by the federation of colleges that form **Cambridge University**. The oldest college, Peterhouse, dates from 1284. Kings College was founded in 1441 and its chapel (built 1446–1515 in the perpendicular gothic style) is a distinctive landmark. The largest college, Trinity, was founded by Henry VIII in 1546. The first college for women, Girton, opened in 1869. Industries in the town include electronics, high-tech research and development, biotechnology, and the manufacture of scientific instruments. It is also an important market centre for East Anglia. Population (1994 est): 113 800. **2.** 42 22N 71 06W A city in the USA, in Massachusetts on the Charles River opposite Boston. A famous educational centre, it is the site of Harvard University (1636) and the Massachusetts Institute of Technology (MIT). Industries include printing and publishing. Population (2000): 101 355.

Cambridgeshire A county of E England. In 1965 it was combined with the Isle of Ely and in 1974 it absorbed Huntingdon and Peterborough as well as parts of W Suffolk. Peterborough became an independent unitary authority in 1998. It consists chiefly of low-lying fenland, crossed by the Rivers Ouse and Nene. It is predominantly agricultural, the main products being cereals, fruit, and vegetables. Area (excluding Peterborough): 3068 sq km (1184 sq mi). Population (2001, excluding Peterborough): 552 655. Administrative centre: Cambridge.

camel A hoofed mammal belonging to the genus *Camelus* (2 species). Camels are used for riding, as pack animals, and as a source of milk, meat, wool, and hides. The one-humped Arabian camel (*C. dromedarius*) is about 2 m high at the shoulder and generally brown in colour. The dromedary is a long-legged breed of Arabian camel, developed for racing and riding. The heavier two-humped Bactrian camel (*C. bactrianus*) is native to central Asian steppes, where wild herds still exist.

Adapted to living in sandy deserts, camels can close their nostrils and have heavy protective eyelashes. Although unable to store water, camels can store fat in the hump. Family: *Camelidae*; order: *Artiodactyla*.

Camellia A genus of evergreen shrubs and trees (80–100 species) native to India, China, and Japan. Several species are widely grown as ornamentals. The best known, *C. japonica*, grows to a height of 9 m and has attractive glossy oval leaves. The genus also includes the *tea plant. Family: *Theaceae*.

Camelot The legendary capital of King Arthur's kingdom (*see* ARTHURIAN LEGEND). Cadbury Camp, near Yeovil, and Winchester are among the places identified with it.

C

Camembert 48 52N 0 10E A village in NW France, in the Orne department. Camembert is famous for the creamy cheese named after it.

camera, photographic A device for producing a photographic image. Basically, a camera consists of a light-tight box containing a lens and light-sensitive *film or plate. The light image coming through the lens is brought into focus on the film by adjusting the distance between the film and the lens. A picture is taken by opening the shutter over the lens for a certain period to expose the film. The exposure time is determined by the shutter speed. The diameter of the opening (aperture) in front of the lens is measured by its *f-number. Shutter speed and lens aperture determine the light available to record the image on the film.

In a **digital camera**, the light-sensitive film is replaced by a medium that records the image in digital form, so that it can be seen on a small screen forming part of the camera. The digital information can be fed into a computer, viewed on the screen as a single image, improved or manipulated in a variety of ways using computer software, and printed using a colour printer.

camera, television A camera for the instantaneous transmission of moving pictures. The scene to be televised is focused onto a screen in the electronic camera tube. This optical image is scanned in horizontal lines, fast enough to appear as a continuous moving picture to the human eye; in most cameras, the image is scanned 25 to 30 times per second. The intensity of light at each point of the image is converted to an electrical signal, which is amplified before being transmitted together with the sound and synchronization signals.

Cameroon, Republic of (French name: République du Cameroun) A country in W Africa, on the Gulf of Guinea. Hot swampy coastal plains rise to forested plateaus in the centre and to the Adamwa Highlands in the N. The main river is the Sanaga. The population consists of over a hundred different ethnic groups, the most numerous being the Bamileke. *Economy*: chiefly subsistence agriculture with varied crops; the main cash crops are cocoa and coffee. Aluminium smelting is the chief industry. Oil was discovered in 1973 and provides half the country's revenue. *History*: in 1884 the German protectorate of Kamerun was established and after World War I it was divided into the French and British Cameroons, which were governed from 1922 under League of Nations mandate and from 1946 as UN trust territories. The French Cameroons attained self-government in 1957 and became independent as the Federal Republic of the Cameroon in 1960. After a plebiscite in the British Cameroons in 1961, the S joined Cameroon (which became a united republic in 1972) and the N joined Nigeria. The early 1990s saw mounting opposition to one-party rule. In 1992 Paul Biya (1933–) was re-elected president amid allegations of fraud, leading to riots and a state of emergency. Legislative elections in 1992, 1997, and 2002 likewise returned the ruling party but were marred by allegations of unfairness. Cameroon joined the Commonwealth in 1995. Official languages: French and English. Currency: CFA franc of 100 centimes. Area: 475 442 sq km (183 530 sq mi). Population (2003 est): 15 746 000. Capital: Yaoundé.

Camões, Luis de (c. 1524–80) Portuguese poet and soldier. After 17 years wandering in the Portuguese colonies in the East, he returned destitute to Lisbon. In 1572 he published *The Lusiad*, an epic celebrating the 1497 voyage of da *Gama. His lyrical poetry is also much admired.

camomile (*or* **chamomile**) A perennial scented European herb, *Anthemis nobilis* (or *Chamaemelum nobile*). The spreading much-branched stems (10–30 cm in length) carry long-stalked daisy-like flowers. and partially webbed feet (they are expert swimmers). The capybara is the only member of its family (*Hydrochoeridae*).

Campaign for Nuclear Disarmament (**CND**) An organization formed in 1958 to campaign for Britain's nuclear disarmament. In the late 1950s and early 1960s, led by Canon John Collins (1905–82) and Bertrand *Russell, it organized large demonstrations, including the Aldermaston marches. It revived in the early 1980s amid new fears of nuclear war but membership has since declined with lessening of East–West tensions.

Campanula A genus of annual and perennial herbaceous plants (about 300 species), often known as bellflowers, native to N temperate zones and tropical mountains. 15–120 cm high, they bear spikes of blue, pink, or white bell-shaped flowers. The fruit is a capsule. Some species (including *Canterbury bell) are grown as ornamentals. Family: *Campanulaceae*.

Campbell, Sir Malcolm (1885–1949) British motor engineer, who broke the land-speed record nine times between 1924 and 1935 and the water-speed record three times between 1937 and 1939. He was the first man to exceed 483 km per hour (300 mph; 1935). His son **Donald Malcolm Campbell** (1921–67) also set land- and water-speed records, including 648.7 km per hour (403.1 mph) for a wheel-driven car at Lake Eyre (1964). He was killed in an attempt to break his own water-speed record on Coniston Water. The speed at which he crashed, 527.9 km per hour (328 mph), was the unofficial record for several years. His daughter **Gina Campbell** (1948–) broke the women's water-speed record in 1984.

Campbell-Bannerman, Sir Henry (1836–1908) British statesman; Liberal prime minister (1905–08). Campbell-Bannerman's government granted the Transvaal and Orange River Colony responsible government and passed the Trades Disputes Act (1906), which gave trades unionists greater freedom to strike. Resigning shortly before his death, he left his successor *Asquith a strong and united Liberal Party.

Camus, Albert (1913–60) French novelist, an exponent of *existentialism. Born in poverty in Algiers, he won a school scholarship and studied philosophy at university. During World War II he edited *Combat*, a journal of the French Resistance. Camus published several collections of essays and plays, and three novels, notably *The Outsider* (1942), *The Plague* (1947), and *The Rebel* (1953). In 1957 he won the Nobel Prize.

Canaan An area roughly corresponding to modern Israel, W Jordan, and S Syria, known from the Bible as the land promised by God to the Israelites before the Exodus.

Canada A country occupying the entire northern half of the North American continent (except for Alaska). More than half of Canada consists of the Canadian Shield, at the centre of which lies the Hudson Bay lowlands. The Western Cordillera, which is partly made up of the Coast Mountains and the Rocky Mountains, runs parallel to the Pacific coast. Between the Rocky Mountains and the Canadian Shield lie the Interior Lowlands (consisting of prairies, plains, and the Mackenzie Lowlands). The SE region of Canada is dominated by the St Lawrence River and the *Great Lakes and is the most densely populated area in the country. The population is mainly of British and French descent but there are several substantial minorities, including Germans, Italians, Ukrainians, and Dutch as well as the original inhabitants, the Indians and Inuit. *Economy*: both agriculture and industry are highly developed and the numerous manufacturing industries (concentrated mainly in Ontario and Quebec) include paper, iron and steel, motor vehicles, telecommunications equipment, and food processing. Canada is the world's largest producer of zinc, potash, and uranium: other mineral resources include asbestos, nickel, cadmium, sulphur, molybdenum, silver, and gold. Oil production has increased since the discovery of large oilfields in Alberta and natural gas is also produced. Agriculture is important, with cereals in the Prairie Provinces and considerable fruit growing in British Columbia and Ontario. There is a valuable fishing industry; forestry has long been important to Canada's economy and the other traditional industry, the fur trade, continues. Exports include motor vehicles and parts, wood, wood pulp, and paper, oil, gas, and petroleum products. *History*: there is evidence of Viking settlement in the NE of Canada around 1000 AD. In 1497 John Cabot reached Newfoundland and Nova Scotia, the first being claimed for England in 1583. In 1534 Jacques Cartier explored the Gulf of St Lawrence and in 1608 Champlain established the first permanent settlement at Quebec. Known as New France, this became a royal province in 1663. Later in the 17th century, when the *Iroquois defeated the *Huron Indians, the French colony was almost completely destroyed. The fur trade was of great importance to all settlers and in 1670 the English set up the Hudson's Bay Company. By 1696 the French and English were in conflict: in 1713 the Treaty of Utrecht gave Acadia (former French colony centred on present-day Nova Scotia), Newfoundland, and Hudson Bay to Britain and after the Seven Years' War, during which Gen Wolfe defeated the French under Gen Montcalm (1759), Canada was ceded to Britain by the Treaty of Paris (1763). In the late 18th century the United Empire Loyalists, fleeing from the American Revolution, settled in Canada. The ensuing racial tension led to the division of Quebec into French-speaking Lower Canada and English-speaking Upper Canada (1791), which were reunited in 1841. By the British North America Act (1867) a confederation of Lower Canada (Quebec), Upper Canada (Ontario), Nova Scotia, and New Brunswick was established. In 1869 Rupert's Land was bought from the Hudson's Bay Company; the province of Manitoba was created from it a year later. In 1871 British Columbia and in 1873 Prince Edward Island joined the confederation. Alberta and Saskatchewan were created from the NW Territories in 1905. Canada's constitutional independence was defined by the Statute of Westminster in 1931. The main political problem in recent decades has been the French-Canadian separatist agitation, led by the Quebec Liberation Front. Since 1982, when a new constitution for Canada was signed by Elizabeth II, Quebec has acted outside the constitution, despite attempts (1985) to achieve reconciliation. Proposals to give Quebec greater autonomy were rejected in a national referendum (1992), while Quebec voters narrowly rejected (1995) the proposal that the province should become a sovereign state. The Liberal Party, which had held office for most of the previous 43 years, lost power to the Progressive Conservatives in 1979 but regained it in 1993 and was re-elected in 1997 and 2000. In 1999 a vast area of the Arctic NE was designated as an autonomous Inuit territory named *Nunavut. Official languages: English and French. Currency: Canadian dollar of 100 cents. Area: 9 976 169 sq km (3 851 809 sq mi). Population (2003 est): 31 590 000. Capital: Ottawa.

Canada balsam A transparent resin obtained from fir trees. It is used as an adhesive in optical instruments because its refractive index is similar to that of glass.

Canada goose A large *goose, *Branta canadensis*, that breeds in Canada and Alaska, migrating in flocks to the southern USA for the winter. It is 60–100 cm long and has a black head and neck, white throat, dark-brown back, and pale underparts.

Canaletto (Antonio Canal; 1697–1768) Venetian painter, famous for his views of Venice. He trained under his father, a theatrical-scenery painter, before visiting Rome (1719–20), where he designed opera sets. His popularity with English collectors led to a stay in England (1746–55), where he painted views of London.

canals Man-made open water channels. They are divided into two categories: conveyance canals and navigation canals. The former carry water for irrigation, power, or drainage; the latter, to facilitate transportation, often connect two natural waterways. Canals have been dug from ancient times. The Grand Canal in China, started in 109 BC, was 1000 km (620 mi) long by the 8th century and carried 1.8 million tonnes of freight per annum. Some modern ship canals achieve spectacular reductions in voyage distances, especially the *Suez Canal (completed in 1869) and the *Panama Canal (1914). Others of considerable local importance include the Corinth Canal (1893) and the St Lawrence Seaway (1959) connecting the Great Lakes.

canary A small songbird, *Serinus canarius*, native to the Canary Islands, Madeira, and the Azores. Wild canaries have an olive-green plumage with yellow to grey underparts streaked with black. Popular as cagebirds since the 15th century, they have been selectively bred both for their musical song and attractive yellow plumage. Subfamily: *Carduelinae*; family: *Fringillidae* (finches).

Canary Islands (Spanish name: Islas Canarias) A group of Spanish islands of volcanic origin in the Atlantic Ocean, close to NW Africa; an autonomous region of Spain. Since 1927 they have constituted two provinces named after their capitals of Las Palmas (including the islands of Fuerteventura, Gran Canaria, and Lanzarote) and Santa Cruz de Tenerife (including the islands of Ferro, Gomera, La Palma, and Tenerife). The islands became Spanish possessions in the 15th century. Fruit is grown for export. Tourism is also important. Total area: 7270 sq km (2807 sq mi). Population (2000 est): 1 716 216.

Canaveral, Cape (name from 1963 until 1973: Cape Kennedy) A barrier island in the USA, in E central Florida separated from the mainland by lagoons. It is the site of operations by NASA at the Kennedy Space Center.

Canberra 35 15S 149 10E The capital of Australia, in the Australian Capital Territory on the Molonglo River. Formally inaugurated in 1927, the establishment of the National University in 1946 and the growth of government departments have led to sizeable increases in population. Population (1998 est): 306 000.

cancer A group of diseases caused by the abnormal and uncontrolled division of cells to form tumours that invade and destroy the tissues in which they arise. Such tumours are described as malignant: their cells spread (metastasize) through the bloodstream or lymphatic system or across body cavities to set up secondary tumours at other sites in the body. The cause of cancer remains uncertain, although it is known that exposure to certain substances (*see* CARCINOGEN) will produce it; a genetic element, diet, and certain viruses are also implicated. Cancer can arise in almost any tissue: in the western world the breasts, colon, lungs, bronchi, prostate gland, and stomach are common sites. Carcinomas are cancers arising in epithelium; less common but more malignant are sarcomas—cancers of connective tissue (bone, cartilage, muscle, etc.). Leukaemia, affecting the bone marrow and other blood-forming tissues, and lymphoma, cancer of the lymph nodes, are forms of sarcoma. Treatment of cancer includes *chemotherapy, *radiotherapy, and surgery.

Cancer (Latin: Crab) An inconspicuous constellation in the N sky, lying on the *zodiac between Leo and Gemini. It contains the star cluster Praesepe.

candela (cd) The SI unit of luminous intensity equal to the intensity of 1/600 000 square metre of the surface of a black body maintained at the freezing point of platinum.

Candia *See* IRÁKLION.

candidiasis An infection caused by a species of yeast (*Candida albicans*). Popularly known as thrush, it affects the mouth and vagina most frequently; it may develop after treatment with certain antibiotics and with diseases (e.g. leukaemia, AIDS) and drugs (e.g. steroids) that reduce the natural immunity of the body. The infection is cleared readily by such antifungals as nystatin.

Candlemas The Christian feast of the Purification of the Virgin Mary and the Presentation of Christ in the Temple (Luke 2.22–38), which is observed on 2 Feb. It is so called because of the distribution of candles, symbolizing Christ's appearance as the "light of the world."

cane The stem of certain large grasses and of some palms. In some species it is hollow and jointed, e.g. *reeds (*Phragmites* species), *bamboo (*Bambusa* species), and *sugar cane; in others it is solid, e.g. *rattan and Malacca (*Calamus* species) used for making furniture, walking sticks, etc.

Canea (Greek name: Khaniá) 35 31N 24 01E The capital of Crete, on the Gulf of Khaniá. The island's main port, it exports leather, olives, olive oil, and fruit. Population (1991 est): 133 060.

Canidae The dog family: a family of mammals belonging to the order *Carnivora*. It includes the dogs, wolves, jackals, coyote, and foxes.

cannabis The resin (hashish) or crushed leaves and flowers (marihuana, "grass," or "pot") obtained from certain species of *hemp. The drug is eaten or inhaled and produces euphoria, distortion of time sense, as well as sight, sound, and memory. Anxiety may also be experienced and cannabis can cause dependence as well as progression to "hard" drugs. For these reasons a legal ban on its sale and use has been maintained in most countries. In the UK possession of small amounts of cannabis for one's personal use is no longer (from 2004) an arrestable offence although dealing in the substance is. *See also* HALLUCINOGENS.

Cannae, Battle of (216 BC) The battle, fought at the village of Cannae in Apulia (SE Italy), in which *Hannibal and the Carthaginians killed almost 50 000 Romans.

Cannes 43 33N 7 00E A resort in S France, in the Alpes-Maritimes department on the French Riviera. Its development as a fashionable resort dates from 1834, when the British statesman Lord Brougham (1778–1868) built a villa here. An annual film festival is held here. Population (latest est): 69 363.

cannibalism The practice of eating human flesh, either as food or for ritual or magical purposes. In ritual cannibalism certain parts of a defeated enemy may be eaten in order to absorb his strength and courage or to prevent his spirit taking revenge. In other cases (endocannibalism) it forms part of rituals performed at the death of a kinsman. The word is derived from the *Arawak term for the *Carib Indians among whom it was common. Ritual cannibalism was practised also by the New Zealand Maoris, the Fijian islanders, in Polynesia, in parts of Africa, in New Guinea, and among some North American Indian peoples.

Canning, George (1770–1827) British statesman; foreign secretary (1807–09, 1822–27) and Tory prime minister (1827). An MP from 1793, he held office under Pitt and contributed (1797–98) to the weekly *Anti-Jacobin*, which opposed the French Revolution. He became foreign secretary but resigned in 1809 in opposition to the management of the Napoleonic Wars by Castlereagh. He again became foreign secretary after Castlereagh's suicide before briefly becoming prime minister. His son **Charles John, Earl Canning** (1812–62) was governor general of India (1856–62).

cannon An early form of *artillery firearm used primarily until 1670 as a siege gun. A 14th-century invention (by the German monk, Berthold Schwarz), early cannon were made of wrought-iron rods welded together, covered in lead, and wrapped with iron bands. Cast guns were made in England after 1500. Modern cannons include guns, *mortars, and *howitzers.

canonization In the Christian Church, the conferring of the status of *saint on a dead

C

Archbishop of Canterbury	term of office
Randall Thomas Davidson (1848–1930)	1903–28
Cosmo Gordon Lang (1864–1945)	1928–42
William Temple (1881–1944)	1942–44
Geoffrey Francis Fisher (1887–1972)	1945–61
Arthur Michael Ramsey (1904–88)	1961–74
Frederick Donald Coggan (1909–2000)	1974–80
Robert Alexander Kennedy Runcie (1921–2000)	1980–91
George Leonard Carey (1935–)	1991–2002
Rowan Douglas Williams (1950–)	2002–

Archbishops of Canterbury since 1903

person. In the Roman Catholic Church this is done by a formal declaration of the pope after a long investigation. Beatification, by which the Church permits the veneration of a person, with the title "Blessed," within a particular diocese, order, or other limited area, precedes canonization and depends on evidence of the person's exceptional virtue and miracles regarded as authentic. The Church then puts the case for the canonization and appoints the *Promotor Fidei* (Latin: promoter of the faith, popularly known as the devil's advocate), to oppose it, and completes the process after satisfactory evidence of further miracles.

canon law The laws of Christian Churches, particularly the Roman Catholic, Anglican, and Orthodox Churches. They include regulations governing the clergy, the ecclesiastical courts, matters of worship and doctrine, and so on. In the 12th century Gratian (died c. 1179) produced his *Decretum*, a collection of rules that the Roman Catholic Church recognized as authoritative. The *Decretum* in turn formed part of a later collection, the Corpus Juris Canonici, which in 1917 was revised to form the Codex Juris Canonici, the present Roman Catholic code of law. The ecclesiastical law of the Church of England was mainly contained in the early-17th-century *Book of Canons*, but new laws were introduced in the 1960s.

Canova, Antonio (1757–1822) Italian neoclassical sculptor, who worked in Venice, Rome, and Paris, where he worked for Napoleon. His classical works included *Cupid and Psyche* (1792) and the *Three Graces* (1813–16).

Cantabrian Mountains (Spanish name: Cordillera Cantábrica) A mountain range in N Spain extending E–W along the Atlantic coast and rising to 2648 m (8868 ft).

Canterbury 51 17N 1 05E A city in SE England, in Kent on the River Stour. The cathedral (11th–15th centuries), where Thomas *Becket was martyred in 1170, is the seat of the Archbishop and Primate of the Anglican Church. The first Archbishop of Canterbury was St *Augustine. The present Archbishop is Rowan *Williams. The University of Kent (1960) overlooks the city. Population (1991): 36 464.

Canterbury bell An annual or biennial flowering plant, *Campanula medium*, native to S Europe and frequently grown as a garden ornamental. The plant grows to a height of 75 cm and bears spikes of pink, rose, lavender, blue, or white bell-shaped flowers, each 5 cm or more long. Family: *Campanulaceae*.

Canton (Chinese names: Guangzhou *or* Kuang-chou) 23 08N 113 20E A port in S China, the capital of Guangdong province on the Zhu Jiang (Pearl River) delta. Densely populated, it is the commercial and industrial centre of S China; industries include steel, shipbuilding, paper, textiles, and the manufacture of machinery and chemicals. Population (1999 est): 3 306 277.

Cantonese *See* CHINESE.

Cantor, Georg (1845–1918) Russian mathematician, born in St Petersburg. Cantor's family moved in 1856 to Germany, where he spent the rest of his life. He set the concept of infinity on a rigorous mathematical foundation. His ideas created great controversy and were viciously attacked, by Leopold Kronecker (1823–91) in particular. He broke down in 1884 under the strain and died in a mental asylum.

Canute II (*or* **Cnut**; c. 994–1035) Danish King of England after defeating Edmund Ironside (1016). He became King of Denmark (1019) and of Norway (1028). He defended England from Viking attacks (1017, 1026, 1028) and subjected Malcolm II of Scotland (1028). According to legend, he proved to flatterers the limits of his powers by demonstrating his inability to induce the waves to recede.

Capablanca y Graupera, José Raúl (1888–1942) Cuban chess player, who was world champion from 1921 to 1927.

capacitance The ability of an electrical component (a **capacitor** or formerly a condenser) to store charge. It is measured in *farads and defined as the ratio of the stored charge in coulombs to the voltage drop across the component. Capacitance is one of the factors that control the frequency response of circuits and components to alternating currents.

Cape Breton Island An island in SE Canada, in Nova Scotia, separated from the mainland by the Strait of Canso. It was ceded to Britain by the French (1763). Area: 10 280 sq km (3975 sq mi). Population (1991): 120 098.

Cape Cod A sandy peninsula in the USA, in Massachusetts between Cape Cod Bay and the Atlantic Ocean. A popular summer resort area, it also produces cranberries and asparagus. Length: 105 km (65 mi).

Cape Horn (Spanish name: Cabo de Hornes) The most southerly point in South America, at the S end of Horn Island, Chile. It is notorious for its stormy weather.

Cape of Good Hope A headland in South Africa, in the SW extremity of Cape Province. It was discovered (1488) by Dias, who named it the Cape of Storms.

Cape Province (official name: Cape of Good Hope Province; Afrikaans name: Kaapprovinsie) A former province in South Africa, in the extreme S. In 1994 it was replaced by the new regions **Northern Cape**, **Western Cape**, **Eastern Cape**, and part of **North West**. The area consists chiefly of plateaus separated by mountain ranges. Western Cape produces most of South Africa's fruit and vegetables for export and has many vineyards; sheep and cattle rearing is extensive and wheat and alfalfa are grown. Diamonds and copper are the chief minerals, others being asbestos, manganese, and iron ore. *History*: first settled by the Dutch (1652), it was ceded to Britain in 1814, becoming known as the Cape Colony. The discovery of diamonds in Griqualand West led to its annexation to the Cape Colony (1871). In 1910 the colony became a province in the Union of South Africa.

caper A bramble-like spiny shrub, *Capparis spinosa*, native to drier regions of S Europe. The pickled flower buds are the capers used in flavouring. The fruit is a berry. Family: *Capparidaceae*.

capercaillie The largest European *grouse, *Tetrao urogallus*, of Eurasian coniferous forests, where it feeds on pine buds and needles. The male, almost 100 cm long, is black with a blue-green gloss and red wattles above the eyes. The smaller female is brown with black and white markings.

Cape Town (Afrikaans name: Kaapstad) 33 56S 18 28E The legislative capital of South Africa on the S shore of Table Bay. Founded by Jan van Riebeeck in 1652 as a supply post for the Dutch East India Company, it is the oldest White settlement in South Africa. Cape Town is a major port and is an important commercial and industrial city besides being a popular holiday centre. Its industries include oil refining, chemicals, motor vehicles, and textiles. Population (1996, urban area): 2 415 408.

Cape Verde, Republic of (Portuguese name: Cabo Verde) A country occupying an archipelago in the N Atlantic Ocean, off the coast of West Africa. It consists of ten islands and five islets, most of which are mountainous. The majority of the population is of mixed African and European descent. *Economy*: mainly subsistence agriculture. Fish and fish products are the main exports. Refuelling services for ships and planes are an important source of revenue. *History*: the Cape Verde Islands were settled by the Portuguese in the mid-15th century, becoming a Portuguese colony in the 19th century and gaining full independence in 1975. Multiparty elections (1991) ended 15 years of one-party rule, when the ruling PAICV (African Party for the Independence of Cape Verde) was defeated by the opposition Movement for Democracy (MPD). The PAICV returned to power in 2001. Official language: Portuguese. Currency: escudo of 100 centavos. Area: 4033 sq km (1557 sq mi). Population (2003 est): 438 000. Capital: Praia.

capital *See* ORDERS OF ARCHITECTURE.

capital-gains tax (**CGT**) A UK tax, introduced in 1965, on the profit arising from the disposal of an asset by sale or gift (and until 1971 by death). It applies to stocks and shares (except some government stocks), to dwellings that are not the owner's only residence, and to all other saleable assets with some exceptions (e.g. cars). The rate of tax is the taxpayer's marginal rate of income tax on the gain; however the first £7,700 (from 2002) of a person's gains in any year are exempt and certain reductions apply to shares in a company held by employees.

capitalism An economic and political system that developed following the *industrial revolution. Essential features of the system are uncontrolled free markets, based on the profit motive, and unrestricted ownership of the means of production (capital). If the system is allowed to develop without restriction it has certain undesirable attributes (*see* LAISSEZ-FAIRE). This has led Western countries to restrict capitalism by a greater or lesser degree of government regulation.

capital punishment The punishment of a convicted criminal by execution. In 18th-century Britain over 200 offences carried the death penalty, including such crimes as petty theft and forgery. In 1868 public executions were abolished and by the Homicide Act (1957) only certain kinds of murder remained punishable by death (murder committed in the course or furtherance of theft, in resisting arrest, etc.). In 1965 the death penalty was suspended for all crimes except treason, violent piracy, and (until 1971) arson in royal dockyards. In 1999 the death penalty was formally abolished for all peacetime offences. Several US states revived it in 1976.

Capodimonte porcelain A valuable soft-paste *porcelain made (1743–59) near Naples at a factory started by Charles IV of Naples. Typical pieces were peasant figures and vessels and services modelled like local sea shells and seaweeds.

Capone, Al (1899–1947) US gangster, probably born in Italy, who dominated the Chicago underworld of organized crime in the late 1920s. He was imprisoned in 1931 for income-tax evasion.

Capra, Frank (1897–1992) US film director, born in Italy. His best-known films include several popular sentimental comedies, notably *It Happened One Night* (1934), *Arsenic and Old Lace* (1942), and *It's a Wonderful Life* (1946).

Capri, Island of (Latin name: Capreae) An Italian island at the SW entrance to the Bay of Naples. Its mild climate, fine scenery, and beaches have made it a popular resort since Roman times. The Blue Grotto, a cavern accessible only by sea, is a notable feature. Area: about 13 sq km (5 sq mi). Population (latest est): 8000.

Capsicum A genus of annual and perennial flowering plants (about 50 species), native to Central and South America. The fruits (berries) of some species, particularly the various cultivated varieties of *C. annuum* and *C. frutescens*, are the chillies and peppers used in cookery. Large fruits (up to about 10 cm long) are the sweet peppers, which have a mild taste and are used in salads, etc. They are usually green but may be red (the red varieties—paprika—can be ground to produce a spice). Smaller berries (about 2 cm long) are the hot-tasting red peppers (or chillies); when dried and ground these form cayenne pepper. Dwarf varieties are grown for ornament. Family: *Solanaceae*.

capsule In botany, a type of dry *fruit that releases its seeds at maturity through pores, teeth, or slits: an example is the poppy capsule. The term also refers to the spore-producing structures of mosses and liverworts and the slimy envelope surrounding some bacterial cells. In zoology, it is the layer of connective tissue surrounding some organs, for example the kidney.

capuchin monkey A long-tailed *monkey belonging to the genus *Cebus* (4 species), of South America. Capuchins are 70–90 cm long including the tail (40–50 cm) and live in large troops in the treetops, feeding chiefly on fruit but also eating insects, birds, and eggs. Family: *Cebidae*.

Capuchins A Roman Catholic order of friars founded in 1525. They are reformed Franciscans, named after the pointed cowl (capuche) they wear in emulation of St *Francis. Opposed by the established Franciscans, they were almost suppressed in 1542, but survived to become important during the Counter-Reformation, being recognized in 1619 as one of the three independent branches of the Franciscan order.

capybara The largest living rodent, *Hydrochoerus hydrochaeris*. Resembling giant guinea-pigs, up to 1.25 m long and 50 cm high, capybaras graze on river banks in Central and South America, living in groups of up to 20 individuals. They have short coarse yellowish-brown hair and partially webbed feet (they are expert swimmers). The capybara is the only member of its family (*Hydrochoeridae*).

car A self-propelled road vehicle. The search for a means of replacing the horse as a means of transport began seriously at the beginning of the 18th century, when *Newcomen and *Watt had shown that steam could be harnessed to produce power. Joseph Cugnot (1725–1804) in 1770 used a steam engine to drive a gun tractor and in 1808 Richard Trevithick built a working steam carriage. But these vehicles were no more than cumbersome novelties. An effective horseless carriage needed a more compact power source. This was eventually provided by two German engineers, Nikolaus

Benz 8hp 1600 of these "horseless carriages" were sold between 1898 and 1900. Described as the first reliable car offered to the public, its twin-cylinder 1570 cc engine gave it a top speed of 18 mph (29 km/hr).

Rolls-Royce Silver Ghost First built in 1907 (and continuing in production until 1927) it quickly established itself as "the best car in the world." Its 7-litre 6-cylinder engine gave it a top speed of 65 mph (105 km/hr).

Ford Model T 15 million of this first mass-produced car (nicknamed the "Tin Lizzie") were made between 1908 and 1927. Its 4-cylinder, 2898 cc engine gave it a top speed of 40 mph (64 km/hr).

Bugatti Royale Made to compete with the Rolls-Royce, this 13-litre 8-cylinder car cost over £5000 in 1927 – too much for even its intended royal customers. Six were sold. In 1987 one survivor was sold for £5.5 M.

Volkswagen Nicknamed "the Beetle," this 1937 German design by Ferdinand Porsche was still selling in the 1970s, making it the best selling car ever made. Its air-cooled slow-revving rear engine increased from 1131 to 1600 cc over the years.

MG TC This post-war British sports car (1946-55) was little changed from the TA model first built in 1937. The TC had a 1250 cc engine.

Buick This 1949 US car represented a release from wartime restrictions and set the trend for a generation of large American cars.

Mini The best selling British car ever made. Designed by Alec Issigonis, the mini was introduced in 1959. Its frontwheel drive, transverse engine, and 10-inch wheels made it an extremely roomy car for its size.

Chrysler Voyager A US people carrier with up to seven seats introduced in the 1990s. Engine options include a 3.3 litre V-6 petrol engine and a 2.5 litre 4-cylinder turbocharged diesel.

C

*Otto and Gottlieb *Daimler, who in 1876 patented the Otto-cycle *internal-combustion engine. In 1885, another German, Karl *Benz, used a 3 hp version of this engine to power a tricycle capable of 15 mph (20 km per hour). By 1890 both Daimler and Benz were selling motorized dog carts and in France, during the closing decade of the 19th century, Panhard, Comte Albert de Dion, Georges Bouton, and Peugeot were all selling cars. In the USA, Henry Ford built his first car in 1896. In the UK, however, the development of the motor car was hampered by legislation introduced in 1865, which insisted that they must be preceded on the roads by a man carrying a red flag. This law was not repealed until 1896. Some ten years later Henry *Royce, dissatisfied with the quality of imported cars, decided to build his own. In partnership with C. S. Rolls, he sold his first Rolls-Royce Silver Ghost in 1907.

By the start of World War I, some 130 000 cars were registered in the UK. In the early 1920s a family Ford, Austin, Citroën, Morris, or Renault cost about £500. During the 1920s and 1930s the price of cars steadily declined until at the beginning of World War II a British-made Ford 8 or Austin 7 cost about £100. But the real mass market did not develop until after World War II, since when a model has to sell a million vehicles to be a commercial success. Cars now are more reliable and made safer by the use of seat belts and inflatable air bags. However, as a mass producer of carbon dioxide (*see* GREENHOUSE EFFECT), toxic gases, and lead (*see* TETRAETHYL LEAD), the modern car is the enemy of conservationists and town planners. *See also* ELECTRIC CAR.

Caracas 10 35N 66 56W The capital of Venezuela, situated near the N coast and linked by road to its port, La Guaira. It was founded by the Spanish as Santiago de León de Caracas in the 16th century. It is the birthplace of Simón Bolívar. Population (2000 est): 1 975 787.

carat 1. A unit of weight for precious stones, formerly defined as 4 grains (Troy), but now equal to 0.200 grams. **2.** A measure of the fineness of gold equal to the number of parts of gold by weight in 24 parts of the alloy. Thus 18-carat gold contains 18/24ths pure gold.

Caratacus (*or* **Caractacus**; 1st century AD) King of the Catuvellauni. The son of Cunobelinus (Cymbeline), Caratacus organized resistance to the Roman invasion of 43 AD. Defeated, he fled first to Wales then to the north British queen, Cartimandua, who betrayed him. He was pardoned by Emperor Claudius but died in exile.

Caravaggio (Michelangelo Merisi; 1573–1610) Italian *baroque painter, whose nickname derives from his birthplace. In Rome he painted scenes of the life of St Matthew in S Luigi dei Francesi. He also executed numerous altarpieces, some of which, e.g. *Death of the Virgin* (Louvre), were condemned for depicting sacred personages as coarse peasants. Caravaggio is noted for his dramatic contrasts of light and shade in such paintings as *Supper at Emmaus* (National Gallery, London).

caraway A perennial flowering plant, *Carum carvi*, native to N temperate regions from Europe to the Himalayas. The much-branched stem grows to a height of 25–60 cm and terminates in clusters of small white flowers. The fruit is an oblong capsule containing the familiar caraway seeds, used in cookery. Family: *Umbelliferae*.

carbohydrate One of a large group of chemical compounds containing the elements carbon, hydrogen, and oxygen and having the general formula $C_x(H_2O)_x$. Green plants manufacture carbohydrates—such as *sugars and starch—during *photosynthesis and their cell walls consist largely of carbohydrates—predominantly *cellulose. Hence plant carbohydrates are the primary source of food energy for animals. Glycogen is a carbohydrate energy reserve found in animals, while chitin is a structural carbohydrate occurring in arthropods (and also in fungi).

carbolic acid *See* PHENOLS.

carbon (C) A chemical element that is unique in terms of the huge number and variety of its compounds. The element occurs naturally in two main forms: *graphite, which is a soft greyish-black mineral, and *diamond, the hardest substance known. A third form, buckminsterfullerene, contains ball-shaped carbon structures. Charcoal and *coke are also composed of carbon. The extensive chemistry of carbon results from its ability to form single, double, and triple bonds with itself and other elements and to form chains and rings. At no 6; at wt 12.011; sublimes at 3367 ± 25°C.

carbon cycle The process by which carbon (in the form of carbon dioxide) in the atmosphere is taken up by plants during photosynthesis and transferred from one organism to the next in a *food chain, i.e. the plants are eaten by herbivorous animals that are themselves eaten by carnivores. At various stages carbon is returned to the environment with the release of carbon dioxide at *respiration and through decay.

carbon dioxide (CO_2) A colourless odourless noncombustible gas. It is present (about 0.03% by volume) in air, being produced by combustion of carbon compounds and by respiration. Industrially, CO_2 is made from chalk or limestone and is used as a coolant in nuclear reactors, as a refrigerant, in fire extinguishers, and in "fizzy" drinks.

carbon fibres Black silky threads of pure carbon made by heat treating organic textile fibres, so that all molecular side chains are removed. Eight times stronger than steel, they are used to reinforce resinous or metallic substances to make jet engine and rocket components, providing great strength at high temperatures.

Carboniferous period A geological period of the *Palaeozoic era occurring about 370–280 million years ago between the Devonian and Permian periods. During the period land plants increased prolifically and led to the formation of the world's major coal deposits. Amphibians became more common and by the end of the period some reptiles had evolved. The Carboniferous is divided into Lower and Upper (Mississippian and Pennsylvanian). Limestone deposits were widespread in the Lower Carboniferous; millstone grits and the Coal Measures (alternating beds of coal, sandstone, shale, and clay), in the Upper.

carbon monoxide (CO) A colourless odourless flammable gas. It is produced by the incomplete combustion of carbon compounds (e.g. coke or natural gas). CO is highly toxic, combining with red blood cells and preventing them from carrying oxygen. It is present in the exhaust fumes of internal-combustion engines.

carborundum A dark crystalline compound (silicon carbide) manufactured by heating silica (sand) with carbon (coke). It is used as an abrasive and as a refractory material.

carboxylic acids *See* FATTY ACID.

carburettor The device formerly used in a petrol engine to vaporize the fuel and mix it with air in the correct proportions. In most modern petrol engines the carburettor is replaced by a fuel-injection system.

carcinogen An agent that causes cancer. Carcinogens can be chemicals, radiation, and some viruses. Chemical carcinogens include tar (such as that produced by cigarette smoking), aniline, and azo dyes. Large doses of radiation and several viruses are also known to cause cancer.

cardamom (**cardamum** *or* **cardamon**) A perennial herb, *Elettaria cardamomum*, native to India. 1.5–3 m tall, it has large leaves, green and purple veined flowers, and small capsules filled with hard angular seeds. The spice cardamon consists of whole or ground dried fruit or seeds. It is cultivated in India, Sri Lanka, and Guatemala. Family: *Zingiberaceae* (ginger family).

Cardiff (Welsh name: Caerdydd) **1.** 51 30N 3 13W The capital of Wales (since 1955), a city situated in the SE of the principality at the mouth of the River Taff. Its port still handles general cargo but employment is now largely dependent on service occupations (especially banking and insurance). At the centre of the city lies the Norman castle, rebuilt in the 1870s. University College, Cardiff (founded 1883), the University of Wales Institute of Science and Technology (UWIST), the Welsh National School of Medicine, and the National Museum of Wales are all located in the city. Since May 1999 Cardiff has been home to the Welsh Assembly. In addition to Cardiff Arms Park, the traditional home of Welsh rugby, a Millennium stadium was constructed for the 1999 rugby World Cup. *History*: originally a small Roman fort, the site was reoccupied by the Normans. It received its first royal charter in 1581. Cardiff's modern prosperity was based on coal from the valleys to the N of the city; by 1913 it was the largest coal-exporting port in the world. The Cardiff Bay area, including the port and quayside, was redeveloped as a commercial, residential, and leisure area in the 1990s. Population (1992): 295 600. **2.** A county borough in SE Wales, created in 1996 from part of South Glamorgan. Area: 139 sq km (54 sq mi). Population (2001): 305 340.

Cardigan, James Thomas Brudenell, 7th Earl of (1797– 1868) British cavalry officer. In 1854, during the Crimean War, he led the fatal charge of the Light Brigade at *Balaclava, made famous by Tennyson. The woollen garment known as a cardigan was named after him.

cardinals, college of (*or* **Sacred College**) The body of the highest dignitaries next to the pope in the *Roman Catholic Church. Originating in the advisory roles played by the parish priests and deacons of the city of Rome, the present membership of 125 cardinals was established under John XXIII and Paul VI. They assist the pope as a privy council, conducting the temporal affairs of the Church, advising on questions of doctrine, etc.; they elect the pope from among their own number.

C

Carey, Peter (1943–) Australian novelist and writer, who won the Booker Prize with both *Oscar and Lucinda* (1988) and *The True History of the Kelly Gang* (2001). Other novels include *Illywhacker* (1985) and *My Life as a Fake* (2003).

cargo cults Religious cults found chiefly in Melanesia since the late 19th century. Their adherents believe that a new paradise will be heralded mainly by the arrival of a supernatural cargo of goods brought by spirits, who are variously viewed as gods, ancestors, or White foreigners.

Carib An American Indian people of the Lesser Antilles and northern South America, after whom the Caribbean was named. The maritime island Caribs were warriors and cannibals, who before the advent of the Spaniards expelled the *Arawak Indians from the Lesser Antilles, enslaving the women and killing and eating the men. As a consequence, in these islands men spoke Carib and women, Arawak. The mainland Caribs were less aggressive and their culture was adapted to the tropical forest region.

Caribbean Sea A section of the Atlantic Ocean, between the West Indies, E Central America, and N South America. Area: 2 718 200 sq km (1 049 500 sq mi). Maximum depth: 7686 m (25 216 ft).

caribou *See* REINDEER.

caries Cavities in the teeth caused by bacterial erosion of the enamel and dentine. The bacteria feed on sugar from the diet: the sugar and bacteria become attached to the teeth to form a layer called plaque, and acid formed by bacterial breakdown of the sugar causes the damage of caries. *See also* FLUORIDATION.

Carlisle 54 54N 2 55W A city in NW England, the administrative centre of Cumbria on the River Eden. Once a Roman military centre (Luguvallum) and important fortress in the border wars with the Scots, it has a 12th-century cathedral and a castle (11th–13th centuries). Industries include metal goods, food processing, and textiles but most employment is now in the service sector. Population (1991): 72 439.

Carlow (Irish name: Ceatharlach) A county in the E Republic of Ireland, in Leinster. Chiefly low lying, it rises to mountains in the E. Agriculture is intensive producing barley, wheat, and sugar beet. Area: 896 sq km (346 sq mi). Population (2002 est): 45 845. County town: Carlow.

Carlyle, Thomas (1795–1881) Scottish historian and essayist. *Sartor Resartus*, a blend of fiction, philosophy, and autobiography, was published in 1836 and was followed by his major work, *The French Revolution*, in 1837. This and later works express his view of history as shaped by the "Hero," or inspired individual.

Carmarthenshire (Welsh name: Sir Caerfyrddin) A county in SW Wales, on Carmarthen Bay. In 1974 it became part of Dyfed but was reinstated as a county in 1996. The county is predominantly agricultural, with dairy farming the main activity. New industries have been introduced to the former coalmining and steel-working area in the SE. Area: 2380 sq km (919 sq mi). Population (2001): 173 635. Administrative centre: Carmarthen.

Carmelites A Roman Catholic religious order founded around the mid-12th century by St Berthold (died c. 1195), who established a monastery at **Mount Carmel** (height 546 m; 1791 ft) in what is now N Israel. With the collapse of the Crusader kingdoms, the order moved to Europe. In 1452 an order of Carmelite nuns was instituted. In the 16th century the order was reformed by St *Teresa of Àvila and emphasized the cultivation of the contemplative life.

Carmina Burana A miscellany of 13th-century Latin and German poems and six religious dramas found in a Benedictine monastery in Bavaria. It was transformed by the German composer Carl Orff (1895–1982) into an oratorio (1935–36), which has become a popular concert work.

Carnap, Rudolf (1891–1970) German-born logical positivist philosopher. A founder of the *Vienna Circle, he was professor of philosophy successively at universities in Vienna, Prague, Chicago, and Los Angeles. He worked on formal logic and its applications to science and *epistemology, believing that the analysis and clarification of knowledge should be the purpose of philosophy. By developing logical syntax and *semantics, he tried to construct a formal language for the empirical sciences to eliminate confusion, ambiguity, and similar obstacles to knowledge.

carnation A large-flowered cultivated form of the clove pink (*Dianthus caryophyllus*). These perennials grow to heights of 40–60 cm, have tufts of dense grasslike foliage, and double flowers in white, yellow, orange, pink, red, or lavender. Flowers of carnations (and pinks) are noted for their clovelike fragrance. Family: *Caryophyllaceae*. *See also* DIANTHUS.

Carnivora An order of mammals adapted for hunting and eating flesh. Carnivores have strong jaws, with sharp incisor teeth and pointed canine teeth. They are the major predators and most species are terrestrial, stalking or pouncing on their prey. The 252 species are divided into seven families: *Canidae* (dogs); *Ursidae* (*see* BEAR); *Procyonidae* (*see* RACCOON; PANDA); *Mustelidae* (weasels, skunks, etc.); *Viverridae* (genets, mongooses, etc.); and *Felidae* (cats).

carnivorous plant A plant that obtains at least some of its nutrients by the digestion of insects and other small animals. Carnivorous, or insectivorous, plants show remarkable structural adaptations for their mode of life. Butterworts and *sundews trap and digest insects by means of the sticky secretions produced by glands in the leaves. The *Venus flytrap traps its prey between bilobed hinged leaves with marginal teeth. Another common method of capture and digestion is by means of liquid-filled "pitchers" into which the insects fall (*see* PITCHER PLANT).

Carnot, (Nicolas Léonard) Sadi (1796–1832) French engineer and soldier, whose investigations on the efficiency of steam engines laid the basis for the science of thermodynamics. The **Carnot theorem** states that no engine can be more efficient than a reversible engine working between the same temperatures. The **Carnot cycle** is a thermodynamic cycle of the pressure and temperature changes in the gas in an ideal heat engine.

Caroline Islands An archipelago in the W Pacific Ocean, consisting of *Belau and the Federated States of *Micronesia. Spain claimed the islands in 1899 but sold them to Germany. They were controlled by Japan (1914–44) and the USA (1944–47) before becoming part of the UN Trust Territory of the Pacific Islands. Tourism is important and copra is the main export. Area: 1183 sq km (457 sq mi). Population (latest est): 115 208.

Caroline of Ansbach (1683–1737) The wife of George II of Great Britain and a strong supporter of Sir Robert *Walpole. She was appointed regent during George's absences abroad.

Caroline of Brunswick (1768–1821) The wife of George IV of the United Kingdom. After their separation (1796), he forbade her to see their child Charlotte. When George became king (1820), his attempt to divorce Caroline failed owing to popular support for her but she was excluded from the coronation (1821).

carotenoids A group of yellow, orange, or red pigments manufactured by bacteria, fungi, and plants and essential in the diet of animals. There are two groups—carotenes (including beta-carotene, a precursor of *vitamin A) and xanthophylls. Carotenoid pigments are important for display and camouflage colouring in both plants and animals and also as eye pigments.

carp An omnivorous freshwater fish, *Cyprinus carpio*, native to Asia but widely introduced elsewhere and raised for food. It has an elongated body, usually about 35 cm long, with large scales, greenish or brownish above and paler below, four barbels on the upper lip, and a long dorsal fin. Family: *Cyprinidae* (about 2000 species); order: *Cypriniformes*.

Carpaccio, Vittore (c. 1460–c. 1525) Venetian painter, noted for his paintings of his native city and his narrative cycles. His works, influenced by Gentile and Giovanni *Bellini, include a cycle of *Scenes from the Life of St Ursula* and *The Miracle of the Cross* (Accademia, Venice).

Carpathian Mountains A mountain range in Slovakia, Poland, Hungary, Ukraine, Moldova, and Romania. They form a rough semicircle about 1450 km (900 mi) long (including the Transylvanian Alps, which are also known as the **Southern Carpathians**) between Bratislava and the Iron Gate, both on the River Danube. The highest peak is Mount Gerlachovka, at 2663 m (8737 ft), in N Slovakia.

carpel The female organ of a flower, consisting of the *stigma, style, and ovary. *See also* PISTIL.

Carrantuohill 52 00N 9 45W The highest mountain in Ireland, in Co Kerry, in Macgillicuddy's Reeks. Height: 1041 m (3414 ft).

Carrickfergus A district in E Northern Ireland, in Co Antrim. Area: 85 sq km (33 sq mi). Population (2001): 37 659.

carrion crow An omnivorous Eurasian crow, *Corvus corone corone*, about 46 cm long with a pure-black plumage and a harsh croaking call. It is a notorious egg thief.

Carroll, Lewis (Charles Lutwidge Dodgson; 1832–98) British writer and mathematician. He lectured in mathematics at Oxford University from 1855 to 1881. The children's classic *Alice's Adventures in Wonderland* (1865) was written for the young Alice Liddell, the daughter of the head of his Oxford College. It and the sequel, *Through the Looking-Glass* (1872), combine elements of fantasy, logic, and nonsense and have had a lasting appeal to adults as well as children. He also wrote nonsense verse, notably *The Hunting of the Snark* (1876).

carrot A biennial flowering plant, *Daucus carota*, found in grassy places in temperate regions from Europe to India. The stem grows to a height of 30–100 cm and bears a head of small white flowers. *Daucus carota sativus* is the cultivated carrot grown as an annual for its orange edible root. Family: *Umbelliferae*.

Carter, Angela (1940–92) British novelist and writer. Her novels, which blend fantasy, satire, and macabre humour, include *The Magic Toyshop* (1967), *Nights at the Circus* (1984), and *Wise Children* (1991).

Carter, Jimmy (James Earl C.; 1924–) US statesman; Democratic president (1977–81). A peanut farmer, he left business for politics becoming governor of Georgia (1970–74). He is best known for bringing about the peace treaty between Egypt and Israel (1979). Subsequently he won respect as an international peacebroker in Ethiopia, Korea, Haiti, and elsewhere. He was awarded the Nobel Peace Prize in 2002.

Cartesian coordinates *See* COORDINATE SYSTEMS.

Carthage (Punic name: *Kart-Hadasht*, New City) An ancient city of N Africa, near modern Tunis. Traditionally founded 814 BC by *Dido and exiles from *Tyre, Carthage rapidly became leader of the Phoenician trading cities of N Africa, waging intermittent war with the Greeks of Marseilles and Sicily. From 264 BC Carthage fought the three *Punic Wars with *Rome, her former ally, and was totally destroyed (146 BC). Refounded by Julius *Caesar (45 BC), Carthage became administrative capital of Roman Africa, the capital of the *Vandal kingdom (439–533 AD), and a Byzantine outpost, until destroyed by the Muslims in 697 AD.

Carthusians A contemplative Roman Catholic religious order founded in 1084 by St Bruno and named after the first community, La Grande Chartreuse, near Grenoble. Although originally without a written rule, the Carthusians observed a rigorous life of fasting and solitude and were vowed to silence. The French monks are noted for the liqueur Chartreuse, which they make.

Cartier-Bresson, Henri (1908–2004) French photographer and pioneer of photojournalism. His photographs, collected in such books as *The Decisive Moment* (1952), concentrate on ordinary people in everyday settings. As a film maker, he collaborated with Jean *Renoir in the late 1930s.

cartilage A flexible supportive tissue consisting chiefly of a polysaccharide—chondroitin sulphate—in which elastic or collagen fibres may be embedded. Cartilage lines the bone ends at joints and also provides the skeleton of the nose, external ear, and parts of the throat (larynx) and airways of the respiratory tract. A tough cartilage forms the intervertebral discs between the bones of the spine. During development a large amount of *bone is formed from pre-existing cartilage.

cartilaginous fish Any *fish belonging to the class *Chondrichthyes*, comprising the *sharks, rays, and *chimaeras. They have a cartilaginous skeleton and the males have pelvic fins modified to form copulatory organs (claspers). Fertilization occurs inside the female's body. Some species deposit their eggs on the sea bed while in others the eggs are retained and develop internally resulting in the birth of live young.

Cartwright, Edmund (1743–1823) British inventor and industrialist, In 1785 he invented a power loom and then set up a factory in Doncaster for weaving and spinning yarn. Four years later he invented a machine for combing wool. In 1793 his business failed but parliament recognized his achievements in 1809 with an award of £10,000.

Caruso, Enrico (1873–1921) Italian tenor, born in Naples. The greatest lyric tenor of his time, he was acclaimed worldwide.

caryatid A carved column in the shape of a draped female figure that first appeared in Greek architecture around 500 BC. The most notable caryatids to have survived are on the Erechtheum on the Acropolis of Athens. Caryatids were infrequent in Roman architecture but enjoyed a limited revival in 19th-century classicism.

Casablanca (Arabic name: Dar-el-Beida) 33 39N 7 35W The largest city and port in Morocco, on the Atlantic coast. First established by the Portuguese (1515), it was taken by the French in 1907. During World War II it was the scene of the **Casablanca Conference** (1943), a summit meeting between Franklin D. Roosevelt and Sir Winston Churchill. Major industries include textiles, electronics, chemicals, cement, and food processing. Fishing and tourism are also important. Population (1994 est): 523 279.

Casals, Pablo (Pau C.; 1876–1973) Spanish cellist, conductor, and composer. Casals revolutionized the style and technique of cello playing.

Casanova, Giovanni Giacomo, Chevalier de Seingalt (1725–98) Italian adventurer. He lived in many European cities, working at different times as a violinist, a spy, and a librarian. His adventures, which included a dramatic escape from prison in Venice in 1756 and many romantic liaisons, are recorded in his memoirs.

Cascade Range A volcanic mountain range in North America. It extends N–S, nearly parallel to the Pacific coast, between the Fraser River in British Columbia (Canada) and N California (USA), where it becomes continuous with the *Sierra Nevada. It reaches 4392 m (14 408 ft) at Mount Rainier.

casein The major protein present in milk. Casein is easily digested and contains a good balance of essential *amino acids, making it a high-quality dietary protein. Casein is also used industrially to make thermoplastics (e.g. knife handles).

Casement, Sir Roger (1864–1916) British consular official and Irish nationalist, executed by the British for treason. In World War I he tried unsuccessfully to obtain German help for Irish nationalists. After returning to Ireland in a German submarine he was arrested, tried, and executed. His diaries, disclosing his homosexuality, were released by the British government to quell international pressure for a reprieve. They were claimed to have been forged but are now regarded as genuine.

cashew A tree, *Anacardium occidentale*, native to tropical America and cultivated widely in the tropics. It grows to a height of about 12 m and has sweet-scented red flowers. The fruit is a kidney-shaped nut that develops at the end of a hanging pear-shaped receptacle. The edible kernel—the cashew nut—is extracted after the fruit is roasted. Family: *Anacardiaceae*.

cashmere A warm soft wool-like fabric made from the undercoat of the *Kashmir goat, produced mainly in China, Mongolia, and Iran. Originally used in shawls from Kashmir, it is expensive as each goat produces only small quantities of fine soft hair and processing is costly.

Caspian Sea The largest inland sea in the world, bounded by Iran, Russia, Azerbaidzhan, Kazakhstan, and Turkmenistan and fed chiefly by the River Volga. Its surface is 28.5 m (93.5 ft) below sea level and is generally becoming lower due to irrigation and increased evaporation from the Volga. The chief ports are Astrakhan in Russia and Baku in Azerbaidzhan. Area: about 370 000 sq km (142 827 sq mi).

Cassandra A legendary Trojan prophetess, daughter of King Priam of Troy. After she had refused to submit to Apollo's advances, he condemned her prophecies to eternal disbelief. When Troy fell she was taken by Agamemnon, with whom she was later murdered.

cassava A shrubby flowering plant, *Manihot esculentus* (or *M. utilissimus*), also known as manioc, native to tropical America. Many varieties of this species—divided into two groups, sweet and bitter cassavas—are cultivated in the tropics for their edible starchy tuberous roots. These can be processed into tapioca, ground to produce manioc or cassava meal (Brazilian arrowroot), used as animal fodder, or eaten as a vegetable. Family: *Euphorbiaceae* (spurge family).

Cassia A genus of trees, shrubs, and herbs (500–600 species) of tropical and warm regions of Asia, Africa, and America. The laxative drug senna is extracted from the dried leaves and pods (fruits) of many cultivated species. The fruit of *C. fistula* (cassia pods or purging cassia) is also used as a laxative. Some species are grown as ornamentals. Family: *Leguminosae*.

cassiterite The only commercial ore of tin, consisting of stannic oxide. It is found in association with acid igneous rocks and as alluvial deposits.

Cassius Longinus, Gaius (d. 42 BC) Roman general. Cassius supported *Pompey until Pompey's defeat by Julius Caesar at *Pharsalus. He was then pardoned by Caesar but joined the conspiracy to assassinate him in 44. Outlawed, Cassius committed suicide after defeat in the battle of *Philippi.

Casson, Sir Hugh (Maxwell) (1910–99) British architect. A planning adviser to many war-damaged areas in England after World War II, he became director of architecture for the Festival of Britain in 1948.

cassowary A large flightless bird belonging to a family (*Casuariidae*; 3 species) occurring in rain forests of Australia and New Guinea. The largest cassowary (*Casuarius casuarius*) is 150 cm tall and has a black plumage, two red throat wattles, and a blue head with a protective bony helmet. Cassowaries have long powerful legs, each having a long sharp claw, and feed on seeds and berries. Order: *Casuariiformes*.

Castagno, Andrea del (Andrea di Bartolo

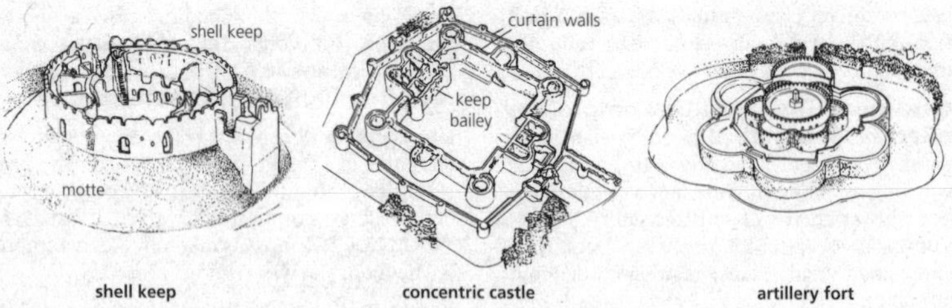

castle. The early medieval shell keep gave way to the massive fortifications of the 14th and 15th centuries, which were in turn superseded by the artillery fort with its low walls and sweeping lines of fire.

de Simone; c. 1421–57) Italian *Renaissance painter, who was born near Castagno but settled in Florence. His major frescoes depict the *Last Supper* and the *Passion* (Sta Apollonia, Florence). Later works, showing the influence of *Donatello, include the equestrian portrait of *Niccolò da Tolentino* (Duomo, Florence).

caste A system of social stratification in which social boundaries are very definite. A pure caste system consists of a hierarchy of hereditary endogamous occupational groups, in which positions are fixed and mobility from one caste to another is prevented. The Hindu caste system provides the cardinal example. Traditionally there are four main castes: brahmins (priests), ksatriyas (warriors), vaisyas (merchants), and sundras (serfs). Outside these groups are the "outcastes" or "untouchables." Despite legislation (1947) abolishing "untouchability" and prohibiting discrimination on the basis of caste, prejudice remains.

Castile A former kingdom in central Spain. Originally a district at the foot of the Cantabrian Mountains, Castile expanded in the 9th and 10th centuries, becoming a united country. In 1035 it became a kingdom and in 1230 was united with the kingdom of León, a union dominated by Castile. In 1479 Spain was virtually united following the marriage of Isabella of Castile to Ferdinand the Catholic and Castile became the political, administrative, cultural, and linguistic centre of Spain.

cast iron A form of impure iron containing between 2.5% and 4.5% of carbon by weight. The high carbon content makes it relatively hard and brittle and it tends to crack under tension. Cast iron is made by casting *pig iron and adjusting its composition to improve the strength. It is used for casting into complicated shapes.

castle A fortified defensive building. Its name deriving from Latin *castellum*, a small fortified place, the castle underwent many changes in its history to counteract the development of increasingly powerful weapons. In the early middle ages a castle consisted of a simple building on a mound of earth surrounded by a wooden fence (the motte and bailey castle), a design later copied in stone. Later designs became more complicated, involving extensive outworks of battlemented towers and walls.

Castlereagh A district of E Northern Ireland, in Co Down. Area: 84 sq km (32 sq mi). Population (2001): 66 488.

Castlereagh, Robert Stewart, Viscount (1769–1822) British statesman, foreign secretary (1812–22). An MP in the Irish parliament (1780), he became Viscount Castlereagh in 1796. He was appointed chief secretary for Ireland in 1798 but resigned in 1801, when George III rejected Catholic Emancipation. His policies as secretary for war (1807–09) were attacked by *Canning, with whom Castlereagh fought a duel. As foreign secretary he played an important role at the Congress of *Vienna (1814–15).

Castor and Pollux Twin heroes of classical mythology, also known as the Dioscuri. Pollux was immortal, the son of *Zeus and *Leda; Castor was mortal, the son of Tyndareus and Leda. When Castor died, Pollux asked Zeus to allow them to remain unseparated. Transformed into the Gemini constellation, they were the patrons of mariners.

castor oil A pale yellow viscous oil extracted from the seeds of the *castor-oil plant. It is used as a laxative and is also a raw material for the manufacture of resins, plastics, and lubricants.

castor-oil plant A flowering plant, *Ricinus communis*, up to 12 m high, native to tropical Africa and Asia. It is cultivated widely, in the tropics for its seeds, from which castor oil is extracted, and in temperate regions as an ornamental shrub. Family: *Euphorbiaceae* (spurge family).

castration Removal of the testes (orchidectomy) or ovaries (oophorectomy). In medicine, castration may be performed in cases of cancer of the testes: it always produces sterility but—unless done before puberty—need not cause impotence. Castration is widely used in livestock management to increase meat production or docility. Castration was also performed before puberty on church choristers in the 17th and 18th centuries to ensure that soprano voice quality remained in adulthood. Such eunuch singers were called **castrati**. The practice was ended by Leo XIII in 1878.

Castro (Ruz), Fidel (1926–) Cuban statesman; president of Cuba (1976–). The son of a wealthy sugar planter, Castro became an opponent of the dictator Fulgencio Batista (1901–73). On 26 July 1953, he led an unsuccessful attack on the Moncada barracks and was imprisoned until 1955. In 1956 he invaded Cuba from Mexico with a small armed band and after a long guerrilla war he defeated government troops. He entered Havana on 1 January 1959. Castro established a socialist government, which the USA attempted to subvert (*see* BAY OF PIGS). As a result, Cuba became heavily dependent on the Soviet Union. A defiant and influential leader during the 1970s, Castro has become an increasingly isolated figure since the collapse of the Soviet Union (1991).

cat A carnivorous mammal belonging to the family *Felidae* (36 species). Most cats have sheathed claws and sharp canine teeth to kill their prey. Their acute vision (especially in poor light), sense of smell, and hearing are adaptations for hunting stealthily, often at night. With no natural enemies, the kittens (or cubs) are born blind and toothless and learn hunting techniques through play.

The wide range of different breeds of domestic cat (*Felis catus*), including Persian, Siamese, and Abyssinian, are thought to have been developed from the African wildcat, or cafer cat (*F. lybica*) and possibly the European *wildcat. Wild species range in size from the *tiger to the tiny South African black-footed cat (*F. nigripes*).

catabolism *See* METABOLISM.

catacombs Subterranean cemeteries, especially those containing early Christian graves. The earliest and biggest catacombs are in Rome, particularly those of St Calixtus and St Sebastian along the *Appian Way. With the acceptance of Christianity they fell into disuse, although some remained as centres of pilgrimage.

Catalan A Romance language spoken by about five million people in Catalonia and the Balearic Islands in Spain, Andorra, and the Roussillon region of France. It is closely related to Spanish and to the Occitan language of France.

catalepsy A condition associated with certain abnormal mental states, including schizophrenia and hysteria, in which the patient, usually female, remains motionless, often with the limbs in fixed positions, for a variable length of time.

Catalonia (Spanish name: Cataluña; Catalan name: Catalunya) A mainly mountainous region of NE Spain, on the Mediterranean Sea. Agriculture is important, the main crops being cereals, olives, and grapes. It is the most highly industrialized region in Spain. *History*: united with Aragon in 1137 and Castile in 1497, Catalonia has nevertheless maintained a strong separatist tradition. In 1932 an autonomous government was established and this lasted throughout the Civil War (1936–39), in which Catalonia was on the Republican side. The Catalan government was restored provisionally in 1978. Area: 31 932 sq km (12 329 sq mi). Population (2000 est): 6 261 999. Capital: Barcelona.

catalysis The acceleration of a *chemical reaction by a substance (catalyst) that is not itself consumed in the reaction. The catalyst allows the reaction to proceed via a different lower-energy pathway. Since the reverse reaction is also accelerated, catalysis does not shift the chemical equilibrium, it merely speeds its attainment. Catalysis is used in industrial chemical processes. In living organisms enzymes are catalysts for biochemical reactions. The **catalytic converter** is a device, first developed in the 1950s, for removing carbon monoxide, oxides of nitrogen, and hydrocarbons from the exhaust gases of motor vehicles by passing them over catalysts in the exhaust system. In **catalytic cracking** in oil refining, the large molecules of crude oil are decomposed by heat and pressure in the presence of a catalyst.

catamaran A modern sailing vessel with two identical hulls, rigidly fastened parallel to one another, and, usually, a single mast with a triangular mainsail and jib. Because of their buoyancy, the hulls of a catamaran offer very little resistance to the water, making it extremely fast. The same principle has been adopted for some modern high-speed car ferries. The original catamaran was a native canoe-like vessel of the SW Pacific.

cataract Opacities in the lens of the eye resulting in blurred vision and caused by the deposition of small crystals or changes in the composition of the lens substance. The former condition increases with age; such cataracts are a common cause of blindness in the elderly. Certain diseases, such as poorly controlled diabetes mellitus, can also lead to cataracts. Cataracts are usually treated by surgical replacement of the opaque lens by a plastic lens.

catecholamines Amine derivatives of catechol (pyrocatechol or 1,2 dihydroxy-benzene; $CH_6H_4(OH)_2$). They include *adrenaline, *noradrenaline, and dopamine, which act as neurotransmitters and/or hormones.

categorical imperative The fundamental moral law in *Kant's ethical theory: an act is moral only if the principle on which it is justified is universally applicable.

catenary The curve obtained by suspending a string between two points. If the middle of the string, the lowest point, is at height *a* above a reference level, then the height, *y*, at distance *x* along the string from the middle is given by: $y = \frac{1}{2}a\,(e^{x/a} + e^{-x/a})$.

caterpillar The larva of *butterflies and moths. Soft-bodied and wingless, all caterpillars have a head and 13 body segments with 3 pairs of true thoracic legs and 5 pairs of abdominal prolegs, which aid in locomotion. The mouthparts are adapted for chewing leaves or feeding on sap. Some species are serious crop pests. Caterpillars exhibit a wide variety of camouflaging colours and shapes. Some produce irritating or poisonous secretions.

Catesby, Robert *See* FAWKES, GUY.

catfish **1.** A *bony fish of the order *Siluriformes* (about 2500 species), with a stout scaleless body, 4–450 cm long, a broad flat head, and long whisker-like barbels. Freshwater catfish (family *Ictaluridae*), sometimes called bullheads, occur worldwide; marine catfish (family *Ariidae*) inhabit tropical and coastal waters and are generally bottom-dwelling scavengers used as food, game, and aquarium fish. **2.** A marine fish of the family *Anarhichadidae* (order *Perciformes*).

Cathari (*or* **Cathars**) A heretical sect that spread from Bulgaria to W Europe in the 11th century. They flourished in France (*see* ALBIGENSES) and in Italy until they were wiped out in the 14th century by the Inquisition. Their doctrine taught that the material world was irredeemably evil but that man's soul was good. They were divided into two classes, the believers and the perfect; the latter lived in celibacy, sex being regarded as evil.

Catherine (II) the Great (1729–96) Empress of Russia (1762–96), who gained the throne in a coup in which her unpopular husband, Emperor Peter III (1728–62; reigned 1762), was murdered. Catherine's reign marked the expansion of Russian territory as a result of her successful wars against the Turks (1768–74, 1787–92) and the partition of Poland (1772, 1793, 1795). Influenced by the ideas of the Enlightenment, she had to abandon her scheme to emancipate the serfs in the face of opposition from their masters. Of her many lovers, only Grigori Potemkin (1739–91) exerted a durable influence on government.

Catherine de' Medici (1519–89) Regent of France (1560–63) during the minority of her second son, Charles IX, and virtual ruler until his death (1574). The daughter of Lorenzo de' Medici, Duke of Urbino, she married Henry II of France in 1533. Intent on upholding royal authority during the *Wars of Religion, she advocated tolerance for the *Huguenots but later supported the Catholics. She was largely responsible for the *St Bartholomew's Day Massacre.

Catherine of Aragon (1485–1536) The first wife (1509–33) of Henry VIII of England and the mother of Mary I. Failing to bear him a son, she was divorced by Henry, who argued that their marriage was invalid because Catherine was the widow of his brother Arthur. The pope's refusal to accept their divorce provoked the English *Reformation.

Catherine of Braganza (1638–1705) The wife (from 1662) of Charles II of England. A Portuguese princess and a devout Roman Catholic, her unpopularity was intensified by her failure to produce an heir to the throne.

cathode The negative electrode of an electrolytic cell, valve, etc. It is the electrode by which the electrons enter the system. *Compare* ANODE.

cathode-ray tube (CRT) A vacuum tube that converts electrical signals into visible form by projecting a beam of electrons onto a fluorescent screen. The electron beam is produced by an electron gun, and deflected horizontally and vertically by an arrangement of plates and magnets, which move it back and forth across the screen and focus it by creating an *electromagnetic field, the strength of which varies according to input signals. In a television tube the beam intensity varies to form the light and dark regions of the picture. In the **cathode-ray oscilloscope** (CRO) it is used to show the variation of a signal strength with time or with some other electrical quantity.

Catholic emancipation A campaign in Britain and Ireland to secure full civil and political rights for Roman Catholics. In the late 18th century several relief acts were passed but parliamentary representation was still denied. The opposition of the Tory establishment and the monarchy continued until O'Connell's efforts achieved the Catholic Emancipation Act of 1829.

Cato the Elder (Marcus Porcius C.; 234–149 BC) Roman statesman, who wrote the first history of Rome. A moral and political conservative, Cato as censor (184) legislated against luxury and sponsored improvements in public works. His great-grandson, **Cato the Younger**, (Marcus Porcius C.; 95–46 BC) was an opponent of Julius Caesar. Caesar, with Pompey and Crassus, created the first Triumvirate (60) in part to neutralize Cato's opposition to their political ambitions. Forced to support Pompey in the civil war in an attempt to save the Republic, Cato escaped after Pompey's death to Utica, in Africa. There, on hearing of Caesar's victory at Thapsus, he committed suicide.

Catullus, Valerius (c. 84–c. 54 BC) Roman poet. Born in Verona, he became the leading member of a group of young innovatory poets in Rome. 116 poems survive, of which the most famous are the 25 lyrics addressed to a married woman named Lesbia.

Caucasian languages *See* NORTHEAST CAUCASIAN LANGUAGES; NORTHWEST CAUCASIAN LANGUAGES; SOUTH CAUCASIAN LANGUAGES.

Caucasoid A race or group of races and peoples originally inhabiting Europe, North Africa, and the Near East. They are characterized by skin pigmentation ranging from very pale to dark brown, straight to curly hair, narrow high-bridged noses, plentiful body hair, and a high frequency of Rh-negative blood type.

Caucasus Mountains (Russian name: Kavkaz) Two mountain ranges in SE Europe and W Asia extending NW–SE between the Black Sea and the Caspian Sea and separated by the River Kura: the **Great Caucasus**, some 1000 km (621 mi) long, to the N and the **Little Caucasus**, about half that length, along the Turkish borders of Georgia, Armenia, and Azerbaidzhan. Their highest point is Mount Elbrus.

cauliflower A variety of wild *cabbage, *Brassica oleracea* var. *botrytis*, cultivated as a vegetable. The short stem bears a round white heart, up to 25 cm in diameter, of tightly compressed flower buds surrounded by green leaves. *See also* BRASSICA.

Cavafy, Constantine (C. Kavafis; 1863–1933) Greek poet, who lived in Alexandria. His poems were often on subjects from the ancient Hellenistic world or erotic homosexual works.

Cavalier poets A group of English poets connected with the court of Charles I (1625–49), including Richard *Lovelace and Robert *Herrick. Their love lyrics and poems about war and honour were characterized by a sophisticated elegance.

Cavaliers The royalist party during the English *Civil War. After the *Restoration of the monarchy (1660) the name was kept by the court party and was given to the parliament that sat from 1661 to 1679. The cavaliers were distinguished by their elaborate dress, with lace ruffles, feathers, and velvet, in contrast to the sober attire of the *Roundheads.

Cavan (Irish name: Cabhán) A county in the NE Republic of Ireland, in Ulster. It is generally hilly, drained chiefly by the River Erne, with lakes and *drumlins. Agriculture is the mainstay of the economy, producing oats, potatoes, and dairy products. Some small industries exist in the towns. Area: 1890 sq km (730 sq mi). Population (2002): 56 416. County town: Cavan.

Cavell, Edith (1865–1915) British nurse. From 1907 she worked at a training institute for nurses in Brussels. She was executed by the Germans in 1915 for helping Allied soldiers to escape from German-occupied Belgium. Before she died she is reputed to have said "I realize that patriotism is not enough. I must have no hatred or bitterness towards anyone."

Cavendish, Henry (1731–1810) British physicist; grandson of the Duke of Devonshire, from whom he inherited a fortune. He discovered hydrogen and investigated its properties. He also identified the gases in the atmosphere and showed that water is a compound. The first to measure accurately the universal gravitational constant, he used it to calculate the mass of the earth.

caves Underground hollows, usually opening directly onto the ground surface or connected with it by a passage. In limestone regions, where most caves occur, many constitute part of a system of natural underground drainage and are connected by subterranean streams. These caves are excavated by the slow solution of limestone by slightly acidic rain water percolating through its joints. The other main type of cave is that eroded from the base of a cliff by the sea. Such caves are located at some point of weakness in an otherwise resistant rock, such as a fault plane or bed of softer material.

caviare A Russian delicacy, eaten as an hors d'oeuvre, which consists of sturgeon's roe, salted and freed from all fat. The roe of the beluga is considered the best, although caviare is also obtained from other types of sturgeon.

Cavour, Camillo Benso di, Count (1810–61) Italian statesman; the architect of Italian unification. In 1852 he formed his first government under *Victor Emmanuel II of Sardinia-Piedmont. Cavour accepted an alliance with France and Britain during the Crimean War and negotiated a further alliance with France at Plombières in 1859 to oust Austria from Italy. He resigned when France came to terms with Austria but became prime minister again in 1860, negotiating the union of Sardinia-Piedmont with Parma, Modena, Tuscany, and the Romagna. By 1861 he had achieved the establishment of a united Italy.

cavy A small South American *rodent belonging to the genus *Cavia* (6 species); the ancestor of the domestic guinea pig. Cavies are mainly nocturnal and live in groups in scrub and grassland, digging burrows and feeding on vegetation and seeds. Family: *Caviidae*.

Caxton, William (c. 1422–91) The first English printer. A cloth merchant, Caxton lived in Bruges from 1446 until 1470, when he moved to Cologne. There he learned the technique of printing and in 1474 set up a press that produced the first printed book in English, *Recuyell of the Historyes of Troye* (1475). On returning to England (1476), he set up a press at Westminster, where he printed a long and varied list, including Chaucer's *Canterbury Tales* (1478).

Cayenne 4 55N 52 18W The capital and main Atlantic port of French Guiana, in the NW of the Île de Cayenne. Founded by the French in 1643, it served as a French penal settlement (1854–1938). Cayenne pepper derives its name from a plant grown in the area. Population (1999): 50 594.

cayman (*or* **caiman**) An amphibious reptile occurring in rivers of Central and South America. 1.2–4.5 m long, it feeds on fish, birds, and insects. Genera: *Caiman* (2 species), *Melanosuchus* (1 species), *Paleosuchus* (2 species); subfamily: *Alligatorinae* (alligators and caimans); order: *Crocodilia* (*see* CROCODILE).

Cayman Islands A United Kingdom overseas territory in the Caribbean Sea, consisting of three low-lying coral islands (Grand Cayman, Little Cayman, and Cayman Brac) lying about 320 km (200 mi) NW of Jamaica. The population is mainly of mixed African and European descent. The Cayman Islands are a tax haven and tourist centre. The main exports are turtle shell, dried turtle meat, and tropical fish. *History*: discovered in 1503 by Columbus, who named them Las Tortugas because of the abundance of turtles. Formerly attached to Jamaica, they gained a certain measure of self-government in 1959 and became a separate British colony in 1962. Official language: English. Currency: Cayman Islands dollar of 100 cents. Area: 260 sq km (100 sq mi). Population (2000 est): 40 900. Capital: Georgetown.

cedar A conifer of the genus *Cedrus* (4 species), native to the Mediterranean region and the Himalayas and widely planted for ornament and timber. Cedars usually grow to a height of 40 m. Their stiff needle-like leaves grow in tufts of 10–40 on short spurs and their cones are erect and barrel-shaped, 5–14 cm long. The best-known species are the *deodar; the Atlas cedar (*C. atlantica*), from the Atlas mountains; and the cedar of Lebanon (*C. libani*), of the E Mediterranean. Family: *Pinaceae*.

Celebes *See* SULAWESI.

celeriac A variety of cultivated *celery, *Apium graveolens* var. *rapaceum*, also known as turnip-rooted or knob celery, grown for its globular edible root.

celery The cultivated form of wild celery, or smallage (*Apium graveolens*), a biennial herb native to grassy coastal areas from Europe to India and Africa. Many varieties of cultivated celery have been developed for their edible leafstalks (up to 30 cm in length), which may be pink, yellow, or green. Family: *Umbelliferae*.

celesta A small keyboard instrument the quiet bell-like tone of which is produced by hammers striking steel plates hung over wooden resonators. Invented about 1880, the celesta was used by Tchaikovsky in his ballet *Casse-Noisette*.

celestial mechanics The study of the motions of celestial bodies subject to mutual gravitational interaction through the application of the laws of *gravitation and of *mechanics.

celestial sphere The imaginary sphere at the centre of which lies the earth and on the inner surface of which can be projected the stars and other celestial bodies. The directions of these bodies, as seen from earth, are measured in terms of their angular distances from certain points and circles on the celestial sphere. These circles include the *ecliptic, the observer's horizon, and the **celestial equator**, where the earth's equatorial plane meets the celestial sphere. The reference points include the equinoxes, the *zenith, and the **celestial poles**, where the earth's axis meets the celestial sphere. The earth's daily rotation causes an apparent and opposite rotation of the celestial sphere.

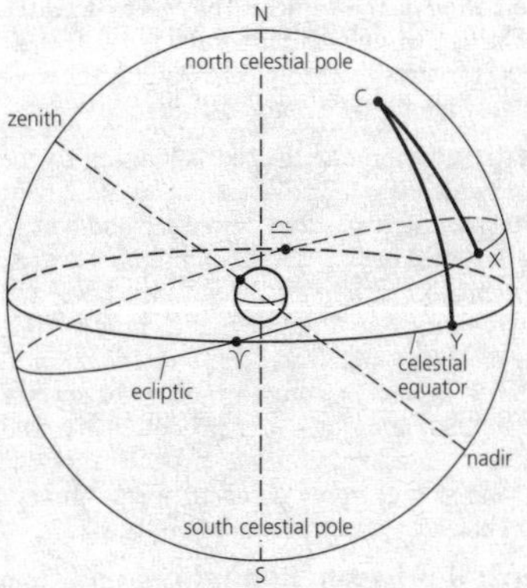

♈ first point of Aries; vernal equinox
♎ first point of Libra; autumnal equinox
C celestial object
♈Y right ascension of C (in hours anticlockwise from ♈)
♈X celestial longitude of C (in degrees anticlockwise from ♈)
YC declination of C
XC celestial latitude of C

celestial sphere

cell The basic unit of living matter, which performs the vital processes of producing energy, synthesizing new molecules from raw materials, division, and self-replication. All plants and animals are composed of cells, the average size of which ranges from 0.01 to 0.1 mm; the simplest organisms (bacteria, protozoa, etc.) consist only of a single cell. The fundamental importance of cells was first recognized by Schleiden and Schwann in 1838–39. All cells except those of bacteria and mammalian red blood cells possess a *nucleus, containing the genetic material, and cytoplasm, within which are structures (organelles) specialized for different metabolic functions. The cells of the body that are not involved in reproduction (somatic cells) divide by *mitosis to produce daughter cells identical to themselves. The reproductive cells divide by *meiosis to produce gametes, each containing half the number of chromosomes of the somatic cells. The difference between plant and animal cells is the presence in the former of a rigid cellulose cell wall and chlorophyll (*see* CHLOROPLAST).

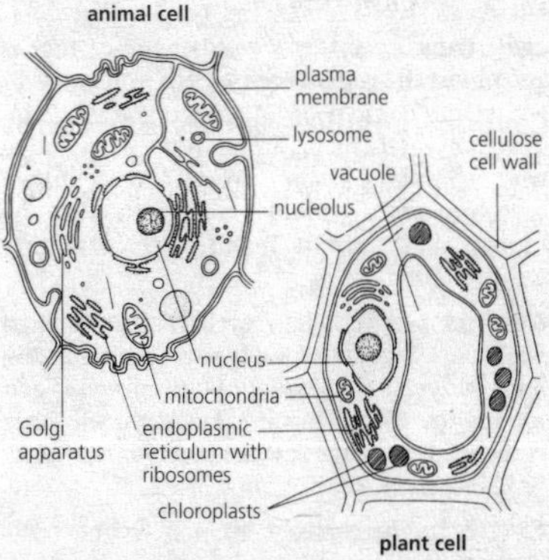

cell. Plant and animal cells are basically similar but plant cells are supported by cellulose cell walls and contain the green pigment chlorophyll within chloroplasts. Plant cells often also have large fluid-filled vacuoles, which help to control turgidity of the cell.

Cellini, Benvenuto (1500–71) Florentine goldsmith and sculptor, famous for his autobiography (1558–62). Cellini worked chiefly as a medallist and craftsman for the papacy in Rome, the Medici in Florence, and Francis I in France. His *Perseus* (Loggia dei Lanzi, Florence) attests to his skills as a sculptor.

cello (full name: violoncello) A musical instrument of the *violin family, held between the knees and supported at its lower end by an adjustable pin. It has an extensive range above its lowest note (C two octaves below middle C). Its four strings are tuned C, G, D, A. It emerged as a solo instrument in the 18th and 19th centuries.

cellular network Any of the networks enabling mobile telephones to connect to the main telephone system. Established originally in the UK jointly by British Telecom and Securicor (as Cellnet), it consists of adjacent cells, each about 5 km across, except in cities, where the cells are smaller and more numerous. Each cell has a transmit/receive station connected to the main telephone network. All transmitters work at the same frequency. The mobile telephone has a battery-powered radio transmitter, which sends speech signals to the receiver in its cell. As subscribers move from one cell to another (e.g. by car), a computerized control system automatically receive signals from the new area.

celluloid A highly flammable thermoplastic material made from cellulose nitrate and camphor. It became the first commercially made plastic (patented 1870).

cellulose $(C_6H_{10}O_5)_n$ A *carbohydrate that is an important constituent of the cell walls of plants and consists of linked glucose units. Industrially, it is made from wood pulp and is used to manufacture rayon and cellulose-acetate plastics. Cellulose is important in the human diet since it forms part of dietary *fibre.

Celsius scale A temperature scale devised by Anders Celsius (1701–44), who originally designated zero as the boiling point of water and 100° as the freezing point. The scale was later reversed. Until 1948 it was known as the centigrade scale.

Celtic languages A branch of the Indo-European language family formerly widespread in W Europe. It is divided into two subgroups: Gaulish and Insular Celtic. The Gaulish languages are now extinct, being superseded in early medieval times by Romance, Germanic, and other languages. Insular Celtic can be further divided into Goidelic (including Manx and *Gaelic) and Brythonic (including *Welsh, *Cornish, and Breton).

Celtic Sea The part of the Atlantic Ocean between Ireland, Wales, SW England, and Brittany.

Celts A people who occupied a large part of Iron Age Europe. They were known to the Greeks as Keltoi and to the Romans as Gauls. There were numerous Celtic tribes and chiefdoms sharing a culture that can be traced back to the Bronze Age of central Europe (c. 1200 BC). *See also* DRUIDS.

cement A powdered mixture of calcium silicates and aluminates. On mixing with water it undergoes complex hydration processes and sets into a hard solid mass. **Portland cement** and similar materials are made by heating limestone with clay and grinding the product. Portland cement was invented by a British stonemason, Joseph Aspdin (1799–1855), and named after the stone quarried at Portland, Dorset, which it resembles. It is used extensively in *mortars and in *concrete.

Cenozoic era (*or* **Cainozoic era**) The part of the *geological time scale beginning about 65 million years ago and following the *Mesozoic era. It is usually taken to include both the Tertiary and Quaternary periods. During this era the mammals flourished, after the extinction of most of the reptiles dominant in the Mesozoic; the Cenozoic is sometimes known as the age of mammals. Birds and flowering plants also flourished.

centaur In Greek legend, one of a race of wild creatures, half-human and half-horse, living in the mountains of Thessaly and descended from Ixion, King of the Lapiths. They were defeated by the Lapiths in a battle resulting from their characteristically unruly behaviour at the wedding of Ixion's son. *See also* CHIRON.

centipede An *arthropod belonging to the worldwide class (or subclass) *Chilopoda* (about 2800 species). It has long antennae and a slender flattened body of 15–181 segments. The first segment bears a pair of poison claws and nearly all the remaining segments bear a single pair of legs (*compare* MILLIPEDE). The tropical order *Scolopendrida* contain the largest species, up to 280 mm long. Centipedes are found under stones, logs, and leaf litter during the day and at night prey on earthworms, insects, etc. They lay eggs or produce live young.

Central African Republic (name from 1976 until 1979: Central African Empire) A country in central Africa, consisting mainly of a plateau lying at about 900 m (3000 ft). The dense forests in the S are drained by the River Ubangi, an important channel of communication. Most of the population belongs to the Banda and Baya tribes. *Economy*: chiefly subsistence agriculture. Diamonds are the chief export; others are cotton, coffee, and timber. There is also a state uranium mine. An IMF-backed programme of economic reforms was instituted in 1994. *History*: as Ubangi-Shari it was one of the four territories of French Equatorial Africa and from 1958 had internal self-government as a member of the French Community. It became independent in 1960 as the Central African Republic. After seizing power in a military coup (1965), Jean Bédel Bokossa had himself declared emperor (1976) but was ousted (1979) and exiled, following allegations of massacres. Free presidential elections (1993) were won by Ange Félix Patasse and a coalition government was formed that same year. A military rebellion was suppressed (1996) with the help of French troops and there was a failed coup attempt in 2001. Official language: French; Sango is the national language. Currency: CFA franc of 100 centimes. Area: 625 000 sq km (241 250 sq mi). Population (2003 est): 3 684 000. Capital: Bangui.

Central America An isthmus of S North America, extending from the Isthmus of Tehuantepec to the NW border of Colombia and comprising an area of 596 000 sq km (230 000 sq mi). It consists of Belize, Costa Rica, El Salvador, Guatemala, Honduras, Nicaragua, and Panama, together with four Mexican states.

Central Intelligence Agency (**CIA**) A US government department established in 1947 to coordinate US intelligence operations. It is not permitted to operate within the USA.

centre of gravity A fixed point through which the resultant gravitational force on a body always passes no matter what its orientation.

centrifugal force *See* CENTRIPETAL FORCE.

centripetal force A force that acts on a moving body causing it to move in a curved path. An object is constrained to move in a circle by a centripetal force directed towards the centre. It has an acceleration towards the centre of v^2/r, where v is the objects' velocity and r the radius of the circle. The centripetal force is necessary to overcome the object's tendency to move in a straight line and appears to be balanced by an equal **centrifugal force** directed radially outwards.

ceorl The free peasant (as distinct from the slave) of Anglo-Saxon England. The economic pressures of the Danish invasions and the Norman conquest contributed to the ceorl's declining status and eventual absorption amongst the unfree *villeins. Thus "churl" has come to mean an uncouth person.

cep (*or* **cèpe**) An edible mushroom, *Boletus edulis*. Common in temperate woodlands from August to November, it has a stout whitish or brown stalk and a hemispherical cap, brown to white in colour and 6–20 cm in diameter.

cephalopod A *mollusc belonging to the class *Cephalopoda* (about 600 species), which includes octopuses, *squids, and cuttlefishes. The most advanced of the molluscs, cephalopods are carnivorous and mostly free swimming, with a ring of tentacles around the mouth, well-developed eyes, and shells that are reduced and often absent. They are found in both shallow and deepwater marine habitats. In cephalopods the sexes are usually separate and fertilization is internal, often preceded by courtship behaviour.

Cepheid variable A highly luminous supergiant star the brightness of which varies very regularly in a period (1–70 days) that depends on the *luminosity of the star. By measuring the period and the average apparent *magnitude of a Cepheid, its distance can be determined. *See also* VARIABLE STARS. Cepheids occur in ours and other galaxies and are a major means of measuring distances of galaxies up to about 20 million light years away.

Cerberus In Greek legend, the monstrous dog who guarded the entrance to the underworld, usually portrayed as having three heads and a dragon's neck and tail. The final task of *Heracles was to overpower this monster.

cereals Cultivated grasses selected for their high yields of grain, which constitutes a major item in the diet of man and livestock. Wheat, *rice, and *maize are the most important cereals, but *barley, *oats, *rye, and *millet are also widely cultivated. *See also* ARABLE FARMING.

cerebral palsy Damage to the developing brain resulting in uncoordinated movements and muscular weakness and paralysis. The brain damage may be caused by injury during birth, insufficient oxygen before, during, or immediately after birth, or a viral infection of the brain. Posture and speech are often affected. Treatment includes physiotherapy to improve movement and speech therapy; special education may also be needed.

cerebrospinal fluid The fluid that surrounds the *brain and *spinal cord. It is produced by special blood vessels inside the cerebrum and is reabsorbed by special bunches of veins. It acts as a shock absorber and support for the central nervous system. A normal adult has 130 ml of clear fluid; samples of it are taken for diagnostic tests for diseases of the nervous system.

Ceredigion A county of W Wales, on Cardigan Bay. In 1974 the historical county of Cardiganshire became part of Dyfed; in 1996 it was reinstated as a unitary authority under its Welsh name, Ceredigion. It consists of a narrow coastal plain rising to rolling uplands in the E and N. Agriculture and tourism are the chief economic activities. The county is a stronghold of the Welsh language. Area: 1793 sq km (692 sq mi). Population (2001): 75 384. Administrative centre: Aberaeron.

C

Ceres (astronomy) The largest *minor planet, 1003 km in diameter, and the first to be discovered (in 1801 by Piazzi). It orbits at between 2.55 and 2.98 astronomical units from the sun, with a period of 4.6 years.

Ceres (mythology) *See* DEMETER.

cerium (Ce) The most abundant lanthanide element, discovered in 1803 by Berzelius and others. It occurs naturally in several minerals including monazite, $(Ce,La,Th)PO_4$, and allanite, a complex aluminosilicate. It is used as a catalyst in self-cleaning ovens and as a polishing agent. At no 58; at wt 140.115; mp 798°C; bp 3443°C.

CERN (European Laboratory for Particle Physics; formerly Organisation (previously Conseil) européenne pour la Recherche nucléaire) A W European organization founded in 1954 to carry out nuclear research. Its headquarters are in Geneva. It runs a 28GeV proton synchrotron *accelerator, with an intersecting storage ring system, which is 300 m (328 yd) in diameter, and the Large Electron-Positron Collider (LEP), the world's largest accelerator. In 1994 CERN decided to build a £2 billion accelerator called the large hadron collider (LHC), which is due to open in 2006, when it will be used to attempt to detect the *Higgs boson. *See also* PARTICLE PHYSICS..

Cervantes, Miguel de (1547–1616) Spanish novelist. In 1569 he went to Italy and fought at the battle of Lepanto in 1571. Returning to Spain in 1575, he was captured by pirates and held for five years. After 1580 he held minor jobs in the civil service while writing a pastoral novel, *La Galatea* (1585), and several plays. *Don Quixote* (Part I, 1605; Part II, 1615), his revolutionary picaresque novel, won him fame throughout Europe.

cervical cancer Cancer of the neck (cervix) of the womb. An increased risk of the disease occurring is associated with certain strains of human papillomavirus. Regular **cervical screening** has cut the mortality of the condition. This is based on the **cervical smear test** (or Pap test, after its inventor G. N. Papanicolaou, 1883–1962) in which a few cells are scraped from the lining of the cervix for microscopic examination.

Ceylon *See* SRI LANKA, DEMOCRATIC SOCIALIST REPUBLIC OF.

Cézanne, Paul (1839–1906) French postimpressionist painter, born in Aix-en-Provence, the son of a banker. After studying law, he was encouraged by his childhood friend Emile *Zola to settle in Paris (1861). His crude and often erotic early paintings failed to find favour. In 1872, while working with *Pissarro in Pontoise, he turned to *impressionism but soon rejected it in favour of more stability and solidity. His approach influenced the development of *cubism. Living mainly in Provence, he painted portraits, e.g. *The Card Players* (Louvre), still lifes, landscapes, especially of Mont St Victoire and L'Éstaque, and a series of *Bathers*.

c.g.s. system A metric system of units based on the centimetre, gram, and second. It includes dynes, ergs, and both electrostatic and electromagnetic units. It has been replaced for scientific purposes by *SI units.

Chablis 47 49N 3 48E A village in central France, in the Yonne department. Chablis is famous for the white wine named after it.

Chabrol, Claude (1930–) French film director. He was a leading member of the New Wave group of French directors in the late 1950s. His films, many of which are influenced by Alfred Hitchcock and use tense murder plots to illuminate bourgeois social relationships, include *Le Beau Serge* (1958), *Le Boucher* (1969), and *Au coeur du mensonge* (1999).

Chad, Republic of (French name: Tchad) A country covering an extensive area in N central Africa, consisting mainly of poor semidesert. The land rises from Lake Chad in the SW to the Tibesti Mountains in the N, reaching heights of about 3400 m (11 000 ft). The majority of the rather sparse population (concentrated in the S) is Sara, a Bantu people; most of the nomadic peoples of the N are Muslims. *Economy*: mainly subsistence agriculture with livestock and fishing. The main exports are cotton and meat. Chad is one of Africa's poorest countries. *History*: one of the four territories of French Equatorial Africa, it had internal self-government as a member of the French Community from 1958, gaining independence in 1960. Since 1963 there has been considerable unrest in the N. Rebel forces led by Hissene Habré seized power in 1982, leading to eight years of virtual civil war. In 1990 Habré's government was overthrown and the new president, Idriss Deby, established multiparty democracy. A new constitution took steps approved by referendum (1996) and Deby was re-elected in free elections in 1996 and 2001. A peace agreement with the northern rebels was signed in 2002. Official language: French. Currency: CFA franc of 100 centimes. Area: 1 284 000 sq km (495 624 sq mi). Population (2003 est): 9 253 000. Capital: N'djamena.

Chadwick, Sir James (1891–1974) British physicist, who worked at Cambridge with *Rutherford and went on to discover the *neutron in 1932 by analysing the radiation emitted by beryllium when bombarded with alpha particles. He was awarded the 1935 Nobel Prize.

chafer A herbivorous beetle belonging to the family *Scarabaeidae* (*see* SCARAB BEETLE). Chafers cause much damage to trees and crops by eating the foliage and flowers; the larvae, which live in the soil, attack the roots. Chief genera: *Melolontha* (*see* COCKCHAFER), *Cetonia* (rose chafers), and *Phyllopertha* (garden chafers).

chaffinch A *finch, *Fringilla coelebs*, about 15 cm long, that is common in woods and parks in Europe, W Asia, and N Africa. The male chaffinch has a chestnut back, pinkish breast, greyish-blue crown and nape, and two conspicuous white wing bars. The female has a duller plumage with an olive-green back. Chaffinches are often migratory.

Chagall, Marc (1887–1985) Russian-born painter and printmaker of Jewish parentage. After studying in St Petersburg (1907–10), he visited Paris (1910). There he painted some of his best-known works, recalling Russian village life, such as *Me and the Village* (1911; New York). His childlike figures, distorted in scale and often upside down, influenced the surrealists. During World War II he lived in the USA, where he designed ballet sets and costumes; he later worked on mosaics and tapestries for the Israeli Knesset building (1966).

Chagos Islands *See* BRITISH INDIAN OCEAN TERRITORY.

chain 1. A measure of length equal to 66 feet. **2.** A measuring device used in surveying. A Gunter's chain is 66 feet long (consisting of 100 links), whereas an Engineer's chain is 100 feet long (also 100 links).

Chain, Sir Ernst Boris (1906–79) British biochemist, born in Germany. Coming to England in 1933, Chain worked first at Cambridge and then at Oxford with Lord Florey on the isolation and purification of penicillin. For their work, Chain, Florey, and Sir Alexander *Fleming (the discoverer of penicillin) were awarded a Nobel Prize (1945).

chain reaction A series of reactions in which the product of each reaction sets off further reactions. In a nuclear chain reaction each nuclear fission is induced by a neutron ejected by a previous fission. For example, the fission of a uranium-235 nucleus produces either two or three neutrons each of which can induce the fission of another uranium-235 nucleus. Chain reactions are used as a source of energy in *nuclear reactors and *nuclear weapons. *See also* CRITICAL MASS.

chalcedony A cryptocrystalline (submicroscopically grained) sometimes fibrous *silica mineral. The numerous varieties include carnelian (red); agate, onyx, and sardonyx (banded); jasper (red or brown); and chert and flint (opaque grey or black).

Chalcidice (Modern Greek name: Khalkidhikí) A peninsula in NE Greece. It ends in three promontories, the northernmost of which contains Mount *Athos. There are fertile low-lying areas but it is mostly wooded and mountainous. It is named after Chalcis, the capital of the Greek island of Euboea, which originally established a colony here. Area: 2945 sq km (1149 sq mi).

chalcopyrite The principal ore of copper, sometimes called copper pyrites, of composition $CuFeS_2$. It is brassy yellow with a greenish black streak and occurs mainly in veins associated with the upper part of an acid igneous intrusion.

Chaldea (*or* **Chaldaea**) The region of S Babylonia in which the new Babylonian empire was established by Nabopolassar (d. 605 BC) in 625 in the last years of the Assyrian empire. At its height under *Nebuchadnezzar II (reigned 604–562), the Chaldean empire, centred on the rebuilt city of Babylon, dominated the Middle East for about 70 years until overthrown by the Achaemenians in 539.

chalk A sedimentary rock that is a pure-white fine-grained variety of *limestone (calcium carbonate). Coccoliths (the calcareous remains of extinct unicellular organisms) are the main constituents of chalk although other invertebrate remains are included. Chalk is very characteristic of the Upper Cretaceous period in W Europe and the Chalk is sometimes used synonymously with the Upper Cretaceous.

chamberlain An officer appointed by a monarch, nobleman, or corporation to perform ceremonial duties. The chamberlains of medieval England were financial officers and were figures of great political importance in the 12th century. The chamberlain was succeeded by the Lord Chamberlain, who is responsible for the administration of the royal household. Until 1968 he also licensed plays for public performance.

Chamberlain, Joseph (1836–1914) British politician. He was mayor of Birmingham (1873–76), and became a Liberal MP in 1876. In 1886 he split the Liberal Party with his opposition to Irish Home Rule. In 1895 he became colonial secretary in the Conservative government, but his commitment to imperial preference in tariff rates caused a rift in the Conservative ranks, which contributed to electoral defeat in 1906. His eldest son **Sir (Joseph) Austen Chamberlain** (1863–1937) became a Liberal-Unionist MP in 1892. He was chancellor of the exchequer (1919–21) and then foreign secretary (1924–29), when he negotiated the *Locarno Pact and won a Nobel Peace Prize (1925). Joseph's son by his second marriage, **(Arthur) Neville Chamberlain** (1869–1940), was a Conservative MP and prime minister of the National Government (1937–40), when he advocated a policy of *appeasement towards the fascist powers. He recognized Italy's conquest of Ethiopia and kept out of the Spanish Civil War. To avoid a European war he visited Hitler three times in 1938, coming to the *Munich Agreement and claiming to have brought "peace for our time". Hitler's invasion of Czechoslovakia, however, forced him to abandon appeasement. He declared war on Germany after Hitler's attack on Poland but his ineffective direction of the war led to his resignation in May 1940.

chamber music Music written to be played in the intimacy of a room rather than in a large hall. In the baroque period chamber sonatas were distinguished from church sonatas and in the late 18th century Haydn, Mozart, and Beethoven established the piano trio (violin, cello, and piano), the duo sonata (one instrument and piano), and the string quartet (two violins, viola, and cello) as the main chamber music forms. Chamber music has been written for other combinations of players, including the clarinet quintet (clarinet and string quartet) and the piano quintet (piano and string quartet).

chameleon An arboreal lizard belonging to the Old World family *Chamaeleontidae* (84 species) and characterized by its ability to change its skin colour by concentration or dispersion of pigment in skin cells. 17–25 cm long, chameleons have a narrow body, an extensile tongue for capturing insects, and bulging eyes that can move independently. They may be green, yellow, cream, or dark brown, often with spots. Genera: *Brookesia, Chamaeleo.*

chamois An agile hoofed *mammal, *Rupicapra rupicapra*, of mountainous regions in Europe and SW Asia. Chamois grow to about 75 cm high at the shoulder and have distinctive narrow upright horns with backward-pointing hooked tips. Their tawny coat becomes darker and longer in winter. Their hide was formerly used for chamois (or shammy) leather. Family: *Bovidae.*

champagne A sparkling wine produced around Reims and Épernay, NE France. Champagne is usually made from black (*pinot noir*) and white (*pinot chardonnay*) grapes. After fermentation sugar and yeast are added to the still wine, which, when bottled, undergoes a secondary fermentation, which produces the sparkle. A dosage of sugar syrup determines whether it will be sweet (*sec*) or dry (*brut*).

Champagne A former province in NE France, now incorporated in the planning region of **Champagne-Ardenne**. Ruled by counts during the middle ages, it became important for its trade fairs and at the end of the 17th century began to produce the *champagne for which it is famous.

Chancery, Court of In English law, the court in which the system of *equity developed. It originated in the 15th century as the personal court of the king's chief law officer, the Lord Chancellor, in which he dealt with cases for which the *common law was inadequate. These included partnerships, the administration of estates, and the execution of trusts. In 1875 it was merged with the Supreme Court of Judicature; it survives as the Chancery Division of the High Court.

Chandigarh 30 43N 76 47E A Union Territory and modern (1953) city in NW India, on the Haryana–Punjab border. The joint capital of both states, it was planned by *Le Corbusier in 30 rectangular sectors for housing, government, and industry. Punjab University was established here in 1947. Area: 114 sq km (44 sq mi). Population (1991): 640 725.

Chandler, Raymond (1888–1959) US novelist. Educated at Dulwich College, England, he returned to the USA and worked in business before starting to write detective stories in the 1930s. The detective Philip Marlowe features in all his nine novels, which include *The Big Sleep* (1939), and *The Long Goodbye* (1954).

change ringing The sounding of a peal of church bells (which contains from 5 to 12 bells) in a fixed order. Each bell is rung by a single individual. The changes are prescribed by numerical order, e.g. 12345, 21345, 23145.

Channel Islands (French name: Îles Anglo-Normandes *or* Îles de la Manche) A group of islands in the English Channel, off the coast of NW France. The chief islands comprise *Jersey (the largest), *Guernsey, *Alderney, and *Sark. Since the Norman conquest (1066) they have been a dependency of the British Crown. During World War II they were the only British territory to come under German occupation. Tourism is important but the islands are also noted for their early flowers, fruit, potatoes, and tomatoes. Area: 194 sq km (75 sq mi). Population (2001 est): 153 700.

Channel tunnel (*or* **Chunnel**) A tunnel linking Britain with France. First suggested to Napoleon in 1802, digging was actually started by private companies in each country in 1882. A press outcry in Britain forced the government to abandon the scheme on security grounds in 1883. In 1964 the two governments revived the project; the tunnel was agreed upon and in the early 1970s work again started, to be abandoned on economic grounds in 1974. In 1987 Britain and France began to build a high-speed rail tunnel between Folkstone and Coquelles, which was officially opened in 1994. It is 49.4 km (30.7 mi) long.

chanterelle An edible *mushroom, *Cantharellus cibarius*, occurring in temperate woodlands. It is funnel-shaped and yellow with the gills clearly visible and measures 3–10 cm across the cap. Family: *Cantharellaceae*; phylum: *Basidiomycota*.

Chaos In earliest Greek mythology, the goddess representing the primeval emptiness from which evolved Night, Erebus (darkness), Tartarus (the underworld), and Eros (desire).

Chaplin, Charlie (Sir Charles C.; 1889–1977) British film actor. He was recruited by the Keystone Studio while touring the USA with Fred Karno's pantomine company in 1913. He gained immediate popular and financial success with his portrayals of a sensitive but pathetic tramp dressed in baggy trousers and a bowler hat. From 1918 he wrote and directed his own films. These included *The Gold Rush* (1924), *City Lights* (1931), *Modern Times* (1936), and *The Great Dictator* (1940). Accused of having communist sympathies, he left the USA in 1952 to live in Switzerland.

char (*or* **charr**) A food and game fish belonging to the genus *Salvelinus*, related to *trout, especially *S. alpinus*, found in Arctic coastal waters and fresh waters of Europe and North America. Its torpedo-shaped body, about 30 cm long, is olive-green with yellow spots above and silvery or bright red below.

Chardin, Jean-Baptiste-Siméon (1699–1779) French painter of still lifes and domestic interiors after the Dutch tradition of *Vermeer, noted for the simplicity of his paintings, e.g. *The Housewife* (Louvre) and *The Young Schoolmistress* (National Gallery, London).

Charente, River A river in W central France. Rising in the Haute-Vienne department, it flows mainly W to the Bay of Biscay. Length: 362 km (225 mi).

Chari, River (*or* **R. Shari**) A river in N central Africa. Rising in the N Central African Republic, it flows N to Lake Chad. Length: 2250 km (1400 mi).

Charing Cross A district in the Greater London borough of the city of Westminster. The

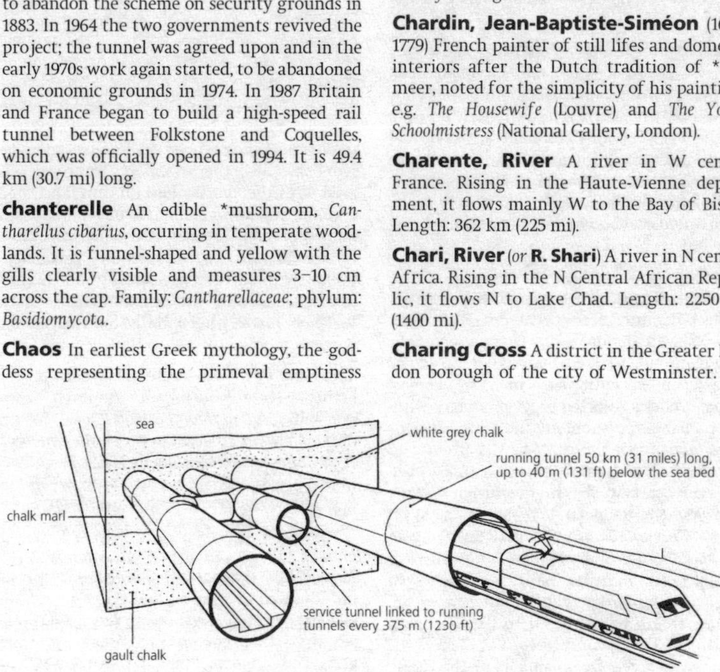

Channel tunnel. A 100-mph (160 km/hr) rail shuttle ("Le Shuttle") ferrying motor vehicles between the terminals at Folkestone, England, and Coquelles, France, began to operate in 1994. The following year Eurostar began to provide a passenger service between London and Paris or Brussels. The tunnel consists of two running tunnels linked by a service tunnel.

last of 12 crosses, marking the resting places of Queen Eleanor's coffin on its journey from Nottinghamshire, where she died, to Westminster Abbey, was erected here (1290) by Edward I.

charismatic movement A Christian movement that emphasizes the charismatic (divinely bestowed) gifts of speaking in tongues, laying on of hands, and baptism by the Holy Spirit. The practice began with the *Pentecostal Churches, but since the 1960s many charismatics have preferred to remain in their own Roman Catholic, Protestant, or Orthodox churches.

Charlemagne (c. 742–814) King of the Franks (771–814) and the first postclassical western emperor (800–14). The son of Pepin the Short, he conquered the Saxon tribes (772–81) and became King of Lombardy (773). In 778 he campaigned in NE Spain, where at Roncesvalles his paladin Roland was killed. In 800, having conquered most of western Christendom, he was crowned emperor of the West by Pope Leo III.

Charles (Philip Arthur George) (1948–) Prince of Wales and heir-apparent to the throne of the United Kingdom as the eldest son of Elizabeth II. He was married (1981–96) to *Diana, Princess of Wales, with whom he had two sons, Prince William (1982–) and Prince Harry (1984–), before their separation (1992) and divorce (1996). His views on modern architecture and ecological issues have aroused controversy.

Charles I (1600–49) King of England, Scotland, and Ireland (1625–49), succeeding his father James I. His first three parliaments (1625; 1626; 1628–29) were dominated by Puritan members, who attempted to make financial grants to the king dependent on his agreement to their demands. Charles resorted to levying taxes without parliamentary consent and ruled without parliament from 1629 to 1640. His attempt to impose *Laud's Anglican prayer book on Presbyterian Scotland led to the Bishops' Wars (1639–40). The financial demands of the Wars forced Charles to summon parliament again but the so-called Short Parliament (April–May 1640) proved so critical that he soon dissolved it. The *Long Parliament, summoned in November following Charles' defeat by the Scots, demanded far-reaching reforms. Charles attempted to arrest five members of the House of Commons and in April 1642 war broke out (*see* CIVIL WAR, ENGLISH). After his defeat at Naseby (1645), he surrendered to the Scots at Newark in 1646. Charles was tried at Westminster Hall, found guilty of treason, and beheaded.

Charles (II) the Bald (823–77) Holy Roman Emperor (875–77) and, as Charles I, King of France (843–77). After the death of his father Louis I, civil war broke out between Charles and his three older brothers. By 843 Charles had procured by the Treaty of Verdun the nucleus of what was to become France.

Charles II (1630–85) King of England, Scotland, and Ireland (1660–85). He fought with his father, Charles I, in the Civil War and, after his father's execution (1649), was crowned by the Scots. Defeated by Cromwell (1651), he was forced into exile. After the fall of the Protectorate (1659), Charles became king after promising a general pardon and liberty of conscience in the Declaration of Breda. Charles was forced to dismiss his adviser, the Earl of *Clarendon, after the failure of the *Dutch War of 1665–67 and replaced him with a group of ministers known as the *Cabal. His Roman Catholic sympathies became clear with his Declaration of Indulgence (1672), which annulled the penal laws against Dissenters and Roman Catholics. Parliament responded with the Test Act (1673) excluding Dissenters and Roman Catholics from office, which together with the unpopular Dutch War of 1672–74 served to destroy the Cabal. Fear of Catholicism came to a head with the *Popish Plot (1678), a fabricated Catholic plot to murder Charles and place his Roman Catholic brother, later James II, on the throne. Charles resisted subsequent parliamentary attempts to exclude James from the succession and ruled without parliament from 1681. On his deathbed he acknowledged his Roman Catholicism.

Charles (V) the Wise (1337–80) King of France (1364–80) during the Hundred Years' War with England. As regent (1356–60) for his father John II, Charles suppressed the peasants' revolt known as the Jacquerie (1358). From 1369 to 1375 he regained most of the territory lost to England by the Treaty of Brétigny (1360).

Charles V (1500–58) Holy Roman Emperor (1519–56). Charles inherited Burgundy and the Netherlands (1506) from his father Philip of Burgundy (1478–1506); he became King of Spain and Naples (1516) on the death of his maternal grandfather Ferdinand II of Aragon and Holy Roman Emperor on the death of his paternal grandfather Maximilian I. Charles' vast possessions provoked intermittent warfare with Francis I of France (1494–1547; reigned 1515–47): in 1525, having defeated Francis at Pavia,

Charles briefly took the French king prisoner and in 1527, in response to an alliance between France, the papacy, Venice, and Milan, Charles' troops sacked Rome. Their contest for European hegemony ended inconclusively with the Treaty of Crépy (1544).

Charles' reign saw the emergence of the *Reformation and in 1521 he presided over the Diet of Worms, which condemned *Luther. His subsequent attempts to conciliate the Protestants failed and in 1546 Charles took up arms against the Protestant Schmalkaldic League, defeating it at Mühlberg (1547). In 1551, however, two German Protestant rulers allied with Henry II of France and Charles was forced to accept Protestant demands. Exhausted by the problems of his Empire, Charles retired to a Spanish monastery, dividing his possessions between his son, who became *Philip II of Spain, and his brother, Emperor Ferdinand I (1503–64).

Charles (VI) the Well-Beloved (1368–1422) King of France (1380–1422). Charles suffered attacks of insanity from 1392 and the ensuing conflict for the regency led to civil war between the Armagnacs and the Burgundians. In 1415 Henry V of England invaded France and defeated the French at *Agincourt. After further campaigns Henry married (1420) Charles' daughter Catherine of Valois (1401–37) and was named as regent of France and Charles' heir.

Charles VI (1685–1740) Holy Roman Emperor (1711–40). His claim (1700) to the Spanish throne gave rise to the War of the *Spanish Succession (1701–14), in which he was unsuccessful. In 1716–18 and 1736–39 he fought the Turks and in 1733–38 he fought and lost the War of the Polish Succession. In 1713 he issued the Pragmatic Sanction, settling the succession of his Austrian possessions on his daughter, *Maria Theresa; this led to the war of the *Austrian Succession on his death.

Charles VII (1403–61) King of France (1422–61). He suffered losses to the invading English and their Burgundian allies until 1429 when, with *Joan of Arc, he liberated Orleans. By 1453, he had driven the English from all of France, except Calais. *See also* HUNDRED YEARS' WAR.

Charles VII (1697–1745) Holy Roman Emperor (1742–45) during the War of the *Austrian Succession. The Elector of Bavaria (1726–45), Charles joined the alliance against Maria Theresa when she claimed the Austrian inheritance. He was elected emperor in opposition to Maria Theresa's husband Francis (subsequently Emperor Francis I).

Charles IX (1550–74) King of France (1560–74) during the *Wars of Religion. His mother *Catherine de' Medici dominated his reign and was largely responsible for the Saint Bartholomew's Day Massacre of Huguenots that Charles ordered in 1572.

Charles X (1757–1836) King of France (1824–30). Charles lived abroad after the French revolution, returning at the Bourbon restoration (1815), when he became leader of the ultraroyalist party. His reactionary rule led to his overthrow (1830) and he fled to England.

Charles Edward Stuart, the Young Pretender (1720–88) The son of the Old Pretender, *James Edward Stuart. Romantically known as Bonnie Prince Charlie, in 1745 he landed in Scotland, rallied his *Jacobite supporters and marched S to claim the English throne. Lack of support forced his withdrawal again to Scotland. Defeated in battle at Culloden (1746), he escaped to exile in Europe.

Charles's law For a gas at constant pressure, its volume is directly proportional to its absolute temperature. The law is not strictly obeyed but is closely approximated in gases above their *critical state. An alternative statement of the law is that gases expand by 1/273 of their volume at 0°C for every 1°C rise in temperature. Named after Jacques Charles (1746–1823).

Charleston 32 48N 79 58W A city in the USA, in South Carolina near the Atlantic coast. Founded in 1670, it was here that the US Civil War started with the bombardment of Fort Sumter by Confederate troops in 1861. The ballroom dance called the **Charleston** originated here, having been a popular Black dance in the early 1900s. It became a craze in the 1920s with its syncopated rhythms and twisting toe-in steps. A major port, its manufactures include fertilizer, paper, and steel. Population (1992 est): 81 301.

Charleston, Battles of Two battles of the *American Revolution fought at Charleston, South Carolina. In the first (1776) the Americans repulsed the British, whose invasion of the South was thus delayed. In the second battle the Americans surrendered (12 May 1780) Charleston after a 45-day siege.

charm A property of matter, expressed as a *quantum number, postulated to account for the unusually long lifetime of the psi particle (discovered in 1974). According to this hypothesis a quark (*see* PARTICLE PHYSICS) exists having the property called charm. Charm is believed to be conserved in *strong interactions and in electromagnetic interactions.

Charon In Greek legend, the ferryman who carried the souls of the dead over the Rivers Styx and Acheron to the underworld. Only the correctly buried dead were taken. A coin placed in the mouth of the corpse was his payment.

Chartism A British working-class movement for political reform, centring on the London Working Men's Association (LWMA). Founded in June 1836 by William Lovett (1800–77), the LWMA drew up a People's Charter (1838) of six points: universal male suffrage, the secret ballot, equal electoral districts, abolition of the property qualifications for MPs, payment of MPs, and annual general elections. The Chartists quickly gained support throughout the country and presented their Charter with 1.2 million signatures to parliament (1839). It was rejected, as were their two later petitions (1842, 1848). Chartism lost support in the 1840s because of lack of organization, rivalry between its leaders, and reviving trade and prosperity.

Chartres 48 27N 1 30E A town in N central France, the capital of the Eure-et-Loire department on the River Eure. The gothic cathedral (begun c. 1194) is famous, especially for its 13th-century stained glass. Chartres is the principal market town of the Beauce region. Population (latest est): 41 850.

Charybdis *See* SCYLLA AND CHARYBDIS.

chat A songbird belonging to the *thrush family. True chats include *stonechats, *whinchats, wheatears, and *redstarts although the name is also given to certain Australian wrens (family *Muscicapidae*) and to American wood warblers (family *Parulidae*).

Chatham 51 23N 0 32E A town in SE England, in Medway unitary authority, Kent, on the Medway estuary. Its naval base, dating from Tudor times, closed in 1984. Population (1991): 71 691.

Chaucer, Geoffrey (c. 1342–1400) English poet. Chaucer made various journeys to Europe as a soldier and diplomat and held positions in the customs service. His poems *The Book of the Duchess* and *The Parliament of Fowls* derive from the French tradition of the allegorical dream poem. Chaucer also parodied Dante's *Divine Comedy* in *The House of Fame* and used Boccaccio's poem *Il filostrato* as the basis for *Troilus and Criseyde*. His best-known work is *The Canterbury Tales*, a collection of stories told by a group of pilgrims travelling from London to Canterbury.

Chechenia (**Chechenya** *or* **Chechnya**) A constituent republic of Russia in the N Caucasus. Chechenia has an oilfield and deposits of natural gas and minerals. Its main industries are engineering, chemicals, and food canning. *History*: the Chechens and Ingushes, neighbouring Muslim peoples, were conquered by Russia in the late 1850s. Each nationality became (1922 and 1924 respectively) a separate autonomous region before uniting (1936) to become the Checheno-Ingush Autonomous Republic. After the break-up (1991) of the Soviet Union, the republic declared independence from Russia and then Chechenia and Ingushetia declared independence from each other (1992). In 1994 the Russian army suppressed the Chechen secessionists, virtually destroying Grozny. Violence continued until the Russian troops withdrew (1996), leaving the rebels in control. In 1999 Russia launched a renewed assault, causing widespread civilian casualties. Chechen forces abandoned the city to Russian troops in early 2000 and the republic was placed under direct presidential control. However, terrorist activities by Chechen militants have continued; the republic's pro-Moscow president, Akhmad Kalyrov, was assassinated in May 2004. Area (including Ingushetia): 19 300 sq km (7350 sq mi). Population (2000 est): 574 000. Capital: Grozny.

Cheddar 51 17N 2 46W A village in SW England, in Somerset, famous for its cheese and for the caves and rare limestone flora of the **Cheddar Gorge**, a pass through the Mendip Hills. Population (1991): 4484.

cheese A dairy product made from separated milk solids (curd). Curd is made by coagulating milk with rennet or some other enzyme and removing the liquid (whey). It is then salted, pressed into blocks, and left to mature. Cheese is a rich source of protein and calcium. It contains fat but little carbohydrate since most of it is left in the whey.

cheetah A large *cat, *Acinonyx jubatus*, of Africa and SW Asia, also called hunting leopard. It has a reddish-yellow coat with black spots and grows to about 2 m in length. Cheetahs have nonretractable claws and rough pads and they hunt by running down prey. They are the fastest mammals, sprinting at up to 110 km per hour (70 mph).

Chekhov, Anton Pavlovich (1860–1904) Russian dramatist and short-story writer. He studied medicine at Moscow University and developed as a writer after graduating. Suffering from tuberculosis, he bought a farm at Melikhovo in 1892 and, after a haemorrhage in 1897, lived at Yalta in the Crimea. His first play, *The Seagull* (1896), failed at first but succeeded triumphantly when revived in 1898 by Stanislavsky's Moscow Art Theatre. His other major plays were *Uncle Vanya* (1897), *The Three Sisters* (1901), and *The Cherry Orchard* (1904).

Chelonia An order of reptiles (600 species) comprising the aquatic *turtles and *terrapins and the terrestrial *tortoises, widely distributed in warm and temperate regions. They have a protective shell consisting of an upper carapace and a lower plastron joined together at the sides with openings for the head, tail, and limbs. The neck is long and mobile and can be withdrawn into the shell.

Chelsea porcelain A pioneer soft-paste *porcelain made at Chelsea (London) between 1743 and 1785. From early sparsely decorated figures and small dishes the factory improved to become one of the most important in contemporary Europe. *See also* DERBY WARE.

Cheltenham 51 54N 2 04W A town in SW England, in Gloucestershire. A fashionable spa town in the 18th century, it is famous for its schools (Cheltenham College, a boys' public school, and Cheltenham Ladies' College) and racecourse. Population (1997 est): 106 500.

chemical bond The force that holds the atoms together in a molecule or the ions together in a crystalline solid. In general, atoms combine to form molecules and ions combine to form crystals in order to increase their stability by sharing or transferring outer electrons in such a way that the stable noble-gas configuration results (*see* ATOMIC THEORY). In **covalent bonds**, atoms are held together by sharing pairs of electrons in their outer shells. In the **electrovalent** (*or* **ionic**) **bond** an outer electron is transferred from one atom to another so that ions are formed. The electrostatic force between the ions holds the molecule or crystal together. **Coordinate** (*or* **dative**) **bonds** are covalent bonds in which both electrons are donated by the same atom.

chemical engineering The design, maintenance, and operation of equipment used in industrial chemical processes. Chemical engineers study both chemistry and engineering subjects. In the UK the profession is controlled by the Institution of Chemical Engineers.

chemical reaction A process in which one or more chemical substances change to other substances, either spontaneously or as a result of heat, irradiation, etc. Chemical reaction involves rearrangement of electrons between reacting species to form different molecules. A chemical reaction can be expressed quantitatively in a **chemical equation**.

chemiluminescence The emission of light, without heat, in a *chemical reaction. It occurs when the molecules resulting from its reaction are produced in an excited energy state. Light is emitted as the excited molecules revert to their ground state.

chemistry The scientific study of matter, especially the changes and interactions it can undergo. Chemistry can be said to have originated with Aristotle's four-element (earth, air, fire, water) analysis of matter. This view persisted unchallenged through some 2000 years of *alchemy, until it was finally demolished by Robert *Boyle in his *Skeptical Chymist* (1661). The modern concept of an element was provided by Boyle, who also correctly distinguished between elements, compounds, and mixtures. The elucidation of the structure of compounds in terms of the elements they contain was developed by such 18th-century chemists as *Cavendish, *Priestley, and *Lavoisier. Berzelius' law of constant proportions and Dalton's atomic theory, produced at the beginning of the 19th century, established chemistry on a quantitative basis. However, it was not until the beginning of the 20th century that the work of J. J. Thomson and Rutherford (*see* ATOMIC THEORY) had established the structure of the atom, enabling the electronic theory of *valence to emerge. This theory made sense of the work of Newlands and *Mendeleyev in ordering the elements into the structure of the *periodic table. **Inorganic chemistry** is concerned with the study of all these elements (except carbon) and their compounds and interactions. **Organic chemistry** is the study of the enormous number of compounds of carbon. **Physical chemistry** is concerned with the application of physics to a quantitative assessment of the structures and properties of compounds and the laws that control chemical reactions.

Chemnitz (name from 1953 until 1990: Karl-Marx-Stadt) 50 49N 12 50E A city in SE Germany, on the River Chemnitz. A textile centre since the 14th century, it became famous for machine construction in the 19th century. Population (1999 est): 266 000.

chemoreception The reception by an organism of chemical stimuli. In man and other air-breathing vertebrates, chemicals ingested in food, etc., are sensed by taste buds on the tongue and walls of the mouth, while airborne chemicals are detected by smell (olfactory) receptors in the lining of the nasal passages (*see also* PHEROMONE). Both smell and taste organs are present in fish; worms and other lower animals have only a general sensitivity to chemicals over the body surface. Chemoreception is used by animals for locating and identifying other organisms and food sources.

chemotherapy The treatment of disease by means of drugs. The term was originally coined by Paul *Ehrlich (1854–1915), for the synthetic chemicals used to treat infectious diseases (e.g. salvarsan for syphilis), but it was later expanded to include antibiotics. Chemotherapy now commonly refers to the chemical treatment of cancer—by means of cytotoxic and other drugs—as distinct from treatment with X-rays (*see* RADIOTHERAPY).

Cheney, Richard B(ruce) (1941–) US politician, Republican vice-president under George W. Bush (2001–).

Chequers A country house in S England, in Buckinghamshire near Princes Risborough. Dating from 1565, it was given to the nation by Arthur Hamilton, 1st Viscount Lee of Fareham (1868–1947), and has been the official country residence of British prime ministers since 1921.

Cherbourg 49 38N 1 37W A seaport in NW France, in the Manche department on the Cotentin Peninsula. Cherbourg has civil and military docks and large shipbuilding yards. In the heyday of ocean liners Cherbourg was an important transatlantic port; the cross-channel service to Southampton remains important. Population (latest est): 30 112.

Cherenkov, Pavel Alekseievich (1904–90) Russian physicist, who discovered **Cherenkov radiation** in 1934. This radiation consists of blue-white light emitted by the atoms of a medium through which a high-energy charged particle is passing at a speed in excess of the speed of light in that medium. Three years later the effect was explained by James Franck (1882–1964) and Igor Tamm (1895–1971). The three physicists shared the 1958 Nobel Prize for their work.

Chernobyl 51 17N 30 15E A town in N Ukraine. In 1986 the nuclear reactor here exploded, causing the deaths of 31 people at the time (a further 219 died later) and the release of a radioactive cloud. Mass evacuation of people living near the reactor followed; the reactor itself was subsequently entombed in concrete. The accident led to widespread reviews of the safety of nuclear power.

chernozem (*or* **black earth**) A type of soil that is characteristic of the grasslands of the continental interiors. There is a dark surface layer rich in alkaline humus, underlain by calcium carbonate concretions. Chernozems are agriculturally among the richest soils in the world.

Cherokee A North American Indian people of the hill country of E Tennessee and North Carolina, speaking an Iroquoian language. They lived in farming towns of 30 to 60 log cabins.

cherry A tree or shrub of the genus *Prunus*, of N temperate regions, having small rounded juicy fruits surrounding a hard stone containing a seed. Cherry trees produce clusters of white or pinkish flowers in spring, and some varieties are grown only for ornament. Cherries cultivated for their fruits are of two main types—sour and sweet. Sour cherries have been developed from *P. cerasus*. Morello—the best variety—has dark-red fruits used in jams and liqueurs. Sweet dessert cherries arose from the gean (*P. avium*), native to Eurasia and N Africa. Found in woods and hedges, it grows to 25 m. Fruits of cultivated forms vary from pale yellow to dark red.

cherubim and seraphim Supernatural beings who are the two highest orders of *angels in the celestial hierarchy. The seraphim are described by Isaiah (Isaiah 6.2–7) as six-winged attendants upon God's throne. The cherubim, who are traditionally depicted as winged heads, appear in the Bible as guardians of the divine presence (e.g. Genesis 3.24).

chervil An annual herb, *Anthriscus cerefolium*, 30–50 cm high, grown for its leaves, used for salads and seasonings. Its white flowers grow in umbrella-like clusters. A native of central, E, and S Europe, it now grows on hedgebanks and waste ground throughout Europe, the Americas, N Africa, and New Zealand. Family: *Umbelliferae*.

Cheshire A county in NW England, bordering on Wales. It consists chiefly of the low-lying Cheshire Plain rising to the Pennines in the E. It is predominantly agricultural. In 1974 the industrial part of the Wirral Peninsula became part of Merseyside and the NE passed to Greater Manchester. Warrington and Halton (Widnes and Runcorn) became independent unitary authorities in 1998. Industries include chemicals, based on the Cheshire salt fields, and textiles. Area (excluding unitary authorities):

2077 sq km (802 sq mi). Population (2001, excluding unitary authorities): 673 777. Administrative centre: Chester.

Cheshire, (Geoffrey) Leonard, Baron (1917–92) British philanthropist. In the RAF during World War II, he won the Victoria Cross. Appalled by the atomic bombing of Nagasaki, he devoted himself to the relief of suffering by founding the Cheshire Foundation Homes for the incurably sick (of which there are now 330) and launching the World War Memorial Fund for Disaster Relief (in 1989). He was made a life peer in 1991. He married (1959) **Sue, Baroness Ryder** (1923–2000), who founded the Sue Ryder Foundation for the Sick and Disabled of All Age Groups.

chess A board game for two players, each of whom controls 16 pieces. The pieces are moved according to strict rules, the object of the game being to force the opponent's king into a position from which it cannot escape. A player attempts to weaken his opponent's position by capturing his pieces (other than the king). The game is immensely complicated and there is a vast literature devoted to chess strategy. Well known to 5th-century Hindus, it seems to have reached Europe, via Persia and Arabia, in the 10th century. The rules of the game have hardly changed since the 16th century, although the identities of some of the pieces have. Since 1922 the rules have been controlled by the Fédération internationale des Échecs (FIDE), which also organizes world championships. In 1993 a rival organization, the Professional Chess Association, held its own world championships. See illustration on p. 200.

Chester 53 12N 2 54W A city in NW England, the administrative centre of Cheshire on the River Dee. It was a Roman fortress (Deva) and a medieval walled city and port (the walls remain intact and there are many half-timbered buildings). The Rows are two-tiered arcades of shops with covered balustrades. Its cathedral dates from the 11th century. Chester is a commercial and railway centre, with clothing and metallurgical industries. Population (1995): 120 100.

Chesterfield 53 15N 1 25W A town in N central England, in Derbyshire. Its 14th-century parish church has a famous crooked spire. Chesterfield's industries include engineering, glass, plastics, and packaging. Population (1997 est): 100 300.

Chesterton, G(ilbert) K(eith) (1874–1936) British writer. His detective stories, beginning with *The Innocence of Father Brown* (1911), featured a Roman Catholic priest. With Hilaire Belloc, he opposed the socialism of G. B. Shaw and H. G. Wells. Chesterton converted to Roman Catholicism in 1922, and thereafter wrote mainly on religious subjects, for example *St Francis of Assisi* (1923). He published over 100 volumes, including *Dickens* (1906) as well as the novels *The Napoleon of Notting Hill* (1904), and *The Man Who Was Thursday* (1908).

chestnut A tree, *Castanea sativa*, also called sweet or Spanish chestnut, bearing large brown edible nuts inside prickly burs. Native to Europe and N Africa and widely introduced, it grows to a height of 30 m. The North American chestnut (*C. dentata*)—once one of the largest common trees of eastern areas—has been largely destroyed by the chestnut blight fungus. Family: *Fagaceae* (beech family). *Compare* HORSE CHESTNUT.

Chevalier, Maurice (1888–1972) French singer and actor. Starting as an entertainer in Parisian revues, he went to Hollywood in the 1930s and starred in many successful musical films. These included *Love Me Tonight* (1932), *Love in the Afternoon* (1957), and *Gigi* (1958).

Cheviot Hills A range of hills in the UK. They extend along the border between Scotland and England, mainly in Northumberland, reaching 816 m (2677 ft) at The Cheviot. The woollen fabric called **cheviot** is spun from the fleece of the sheep found in the Cheviot Hills.

chevrotain A small hoofed mammal of the family *Tragulidae*. Asiatic chevrotains (genus *Tragulus*; 3–6 species), also called mouse deer, of SE Asia, measure 20–33 cm at the shoulder and resemble small deer, but lack antlers and have a three-chambered stomach. The African water chevrotain (*Hyemoschus aquaticus*) is very similar.

Cheyenne An Algonkian-speaking North American Indian people of the Plains region. They orginally lived in what is now Minnesota but intertribal wars forced the abandonment of their agriculturalist life in favour of the nomadic buffalo-hunting culture of the Plains.

Cheyenne 41 08N 104 50W A city in the USA, the capital and largest city of Wyoming. It is an agricultural trading centre. Population (latest est): 50 008.

Chhattisgarh A state of E central India, created in 2000 from the SE part of Madhya Pradesh. It consists of an undulating plain surrounded by hillier country; there are extensive forests. Rice and grain are produced in large quantities; industry includes food processing with some mining and quarrying. *History*: the area was ruled by the Haihaya dynasty from the 8th century. Under British rule it consisted of 14 princely kingdoms under a British agent based in Raipur. Area: 135 194 sq km (52 199 sq mi). Population (2001): 20 79 956. Capital: Raipur.

Chiang Kai-shek (*or* **Jiang Jie Shi**; 1887–1975) Nationalist Chinese soldier and statesman. He took part in the overthrow of the *Qing dy-

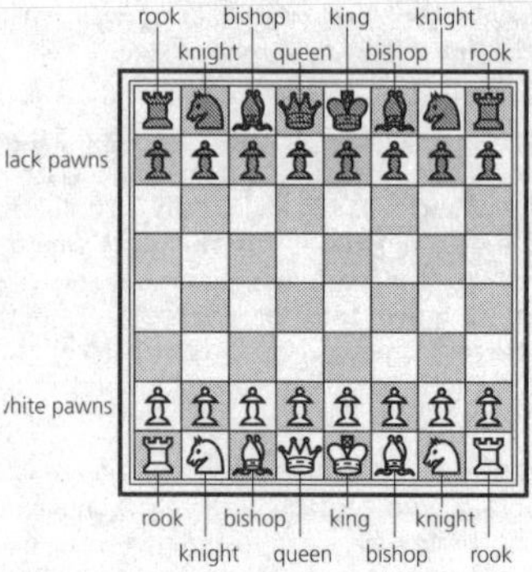

The chessboard ready for play. A white square is always on the player's right. The queen always starts on a square of her own colour.

BLACK

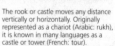

	a	b	c	d	e	f	g	h	
8	QR1 QR8	QN1 QN8	QB1 QB8	Q1 Q8	K1 K8	KB1 KB8	KN1 KN8	KR1 KR8	1
7	QR2 QR7	QN2 QN7	QB2 QB7	Q2 Q7	K2 K7	KB2 KB7	KN2 KN7	KR2 KR7	2
6	QR3 QR6	QN3 QN6	QB3 QB6	Q3 Q6	K3 K6	KB3 KB6	KN3 KN6	KR3 KR6	3
5	QR4 QR5	QN4 QN5	QB4 QB5	Q4 Q5	K4 K5	KB4 KB5	KN4 KN5	KR4 KR5	4
4	QR5 QR4	QN5 QN4	QB5 QB4	Q5 Q4	K5 K4	KB5 KB4	KN5 KN4	KR5 KR4	5
3	QR6 QR3	QN6 QN3	QB6 QB3	Q6 Q3	K6 K3	KB6 KB3	KN6 KN3	KR6 KR3	6
2	QR7 QR2	QN7 QN2	QB7 QB2	Q7 Q2	K7 K2	KB7 KB2	KN7 KN2	KR7 KR2	7
1	QR8 QR1	QN8 QN1	QB8 QB1	Q8 Q1	K8 K1	KB8 KB1	KN8 KN1	KR8 KR1	8
	a	b	c	d	e	f	g	h	

WHITE

Chess notations. In the algebraic notation each square is referred to by a file letter a–h and a rank number 1–8. In the descriptive notation the files bear the names of the piece on the first rank. The ranks are counted 1–8 away from the player.

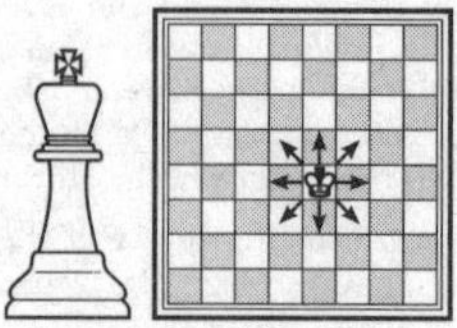

The king, weak and vulnerable, moves only one square at a time (in any direction). The name of the game is a corruption of the Persian word for king–shah.

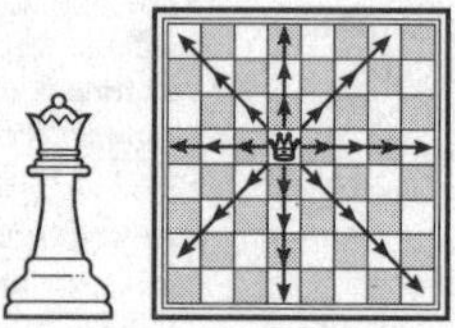

The queen, the most powerful piece, moves any distance in any direction. Originally known as the counsellor, its present name and moves were adopted in the 15th century.

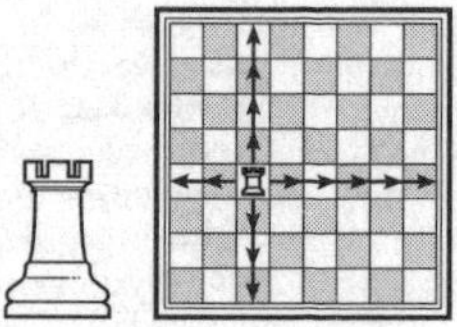

The rook or castle moves any distance vertically or horizontally. Originally represented as a chariot (Arabic: rukh), it is known in many languages as a castle or tower (French: tour).

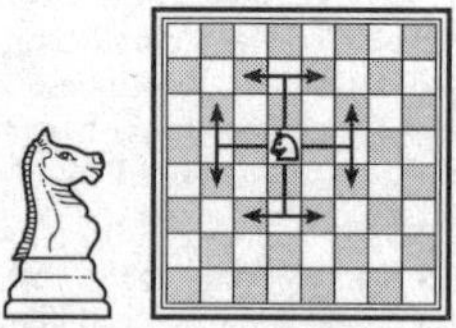

The knight, the only piece to jump over other pieces, moves one square horizontally and two vertically or two horizontally and one vertically. Usually represented by a horse's head, it is sometimes known as the horse (as it was in the Arabic version).

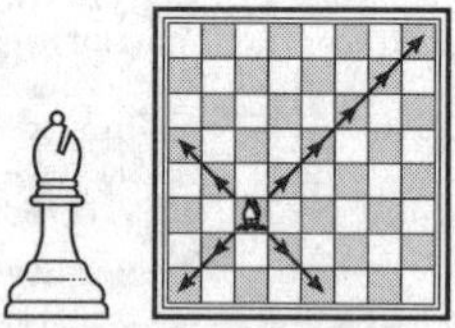

The bishop moves in any direction diagonally. In the Hindu and Arabic games the piece was called an elephant. In the European games the piece has acquired a variety of identities: a bishop in English, a jester (fou) in French, a runner (Laufer) in German, but still an elephant (slon) in Russian.

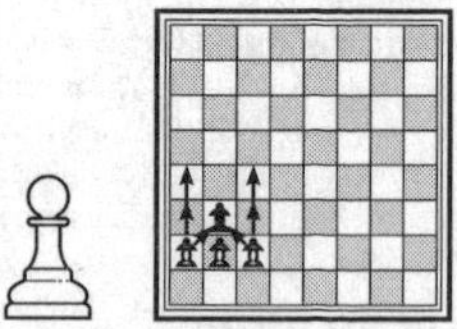

The pawn moves forward one square (or two on its first move). In Arabic it was called a foot-soldier, the English word deriving from the Latin pes, pedis. In some European languages the piece is called a peasant (e.g. German: Bauer).

chess

nasty in 1911 and in 1925 became leader of the Guomindang (Nationalist People's Party). The Nationalists began fighting their former allies, the Communists, in 1927; following Japan's defeat in World War II civil war again broke out. Chiang was forced to flee to *Taiwan in 1949, where he established the Republic of China. His son **Jiang Jing Guo** (*or* Chiang Ching-kuo; 1910–88) was prime minister (1971–78) and president (1978–88) of Taiwan.

chiaroscuro (Italian: light-dark) The pattern of light and shade in a picture. Controlled chiaroscuro was an important element of *Renaissance composition, while strong contrasts of light and shade were a main feature of *baroque painting. Chiaroscuro is displayed to supreme effect in etchings by Rembrandt and *Whistler.

Chicago 41 50N 87 45N A city and major port in the USA, in Illinois on Lake Michigan. The third largest city in the country, it was formerly known for its stockyards but now manufactures iron and steel, textiles, and chemicals. The first of its towering skyscrapers was built in 1887 and the Sears Tower (1974) was for many years the world's tallest office building, 443 m (1454 ft) high. *History*: founded in 1803 near the site of Fort Dearborn, it became a city in 1837 and expanded rapidly with the construction of the railways. In 1871 it was almost completely destroyed by a disastrous fire, in which several hundred people were killed. Chicago was subsequently rebuilt in stone and steel. Population (1996 est): 2 721 547.

Chichén Itzá A Maya city in N Yucatán (Mexico) that was the political and religious centre of a wide area under Toltec influence from the late 10th to the 13th centuries. Remains include El Castillo (a pyramidal temple mound), an astronomical observatory, and a cenote (natural well), from which gold, jade, and other sacrificial objects have been recovered.

Chichester 50 50N 0 48W A market town in SW England, the administrative centre of West Sussex. Chichester has Roman remains, including its street plan. Its cathedral dates from the 11th century. Other notable buildings include the Festival Theatre (1962). Population (1991): 26 572.

chickenpox A common very infectious virus disease. It is usually contracted in childhood and one attack normally gives an immunity that lasts for life. At the end of the incubation period (about a fortnight) the patient develops a fever and an irritating rash. Small raised spots appear on the chest and spread—in the next few days—over the body, face, and limbs. The patient is infectious until the last blister has flaked off. *See also* SHINGLES.

chick pea An annual plant, *Cicer arietinum*, up to 40 cm high, with whitish flowers and edible pealike seeds. It is the chief pulse crop of India, where the cooked seeds are called dhal. Probably native to W Asia, it has long been cultivated in S Europe. Family: *Leguminosae*.

chicory A perennial herb, *Cichorium intybus*, 30–120 cm high, with bright-blue flowers. The dried ground roots yield chicory, a coffee additive, while the blanched leaves are used in salads. A native of Eurasia and N Africa, it is widely cultivated elsewhere. Family: *Compositae*. *See also* ENDIVE.

chiffchaff A woodland *warbler, *Phylloscopus collybita*, about 10 cm long, with a grey-green plumage and whitish underparts. It occurs in Europe and W Asia during the summer and winters in S Europe and Africa. It resembles the willow warbler but can usually be distinguished by its "chiff-chaff" call.

Chihuahua A breed of dog originating from an ancient Mexican breed and developed in the USA. Its coat is variable in colour and either smooth and glossy or long and soft. Height: about 13 cm.

child abuse The physical or sexual abuse of children, usually by a relative (sometimes a parent). Child protection registers kept by local authority social services departments hold the names of children considered to be at risk. Several charities have been set up to attempt to alleviate these problems. *See also* BATTERED BABY SYNDROME.

Children's Crusade (1212) A bizarre episode of the *Crusades, in which some 50 000 children set out from France and Germany to capture Jerusalem. None reached their destination, most being sold as slaves.

Child Support Agency (**CSA**) In the UK, a government agency established in 1993 to administer the Child Support Act (1991) by assessing and collecting child maintenance payments from absent parents. The agency has caused a good deal of controversy and reforms of its methods of assessment were announced in 2003.

Chile, Republic of A country in South America, extending in a narrow strip along the W coast of the S half of the continent. There are many islands off the coast, some of which (including *Easter Island) are well out into the

Pacific Ocean. Chile also includes half of the island of Tierra del Fuego. The country is dominated by the Andes, which are separated from a lower coastal range by a central valley. The majority of the population is of mixed Spanish and Indian descent. *Economy*: based chiefly on the export of minerals, found principally in the N. Chile is one of the world's largest producers and exporters of copper, while the production of iron ore now exceeds that of nitrates. Coal is also mined in quantity. Oil and natural gas are produced but quantities are now declining. The main crops are wheat, sugar beet, potatoes, and maize. Fruit and forest production is growing and there is now an important wine industry. *History*: when Magellan, the first European to set eyes on Chile, sailed through (1520) the strait named after him, S Chile was occupied by Mapuche Indians. A Spanish colony was founded at Santiago in 1541 and Chile was attached to the viceroyalty of Peru. The revolt against Spain began in 1810, when a provisional republic was declared, but victory over the Spaniards was achieved only in 1817 with the military help of the Argentine liberator José de *San Martin. In 1818 the Republic of Chile was established under Bernardo *O'Higgins. The early 20th century saw economic decline and growing instability. The socialist president Salvador *Allende was overthrown by Gen *Pinochet in 1973. After a period of brutal dictatorship Pinochet stepped down in 1990 and democracy was restored. In 1998 Chile's bitter political divisions were reopened by the arrest of Pinochet for alleged human-rights violations. Presidential elections in 2000 were won by the socialist Ricardo Lagos. Chile is a member of the OAS and the LAIA. Official language: Spanish. Currency: Chilean peso of 100 centavos. Area: 741 767 sq km (286 397 sq mi). Population (2003 est): 15 326 000. Capital: Santiago.

chilli *See* CAPSICUM.

Chiltern Hills A chalk escarpment in S central England. It extends NE from the Goring Gap in the Thames Valley, reaching 255 m (852 ft) at Coombe Hill.

chimaera (*or* **chimera**) An organism composed of cells of two genetically different types. Plants with variegated leaves are chimaeras resulting from a mutation in a cell in the growing region (apical meristem). Plant chimaeras can also be produced by *grafting, being known as graft hybrids.

Chimborazo, Mount 1 29S 78 52W An extinct volcano in the Andes, the highest point in Ecuador. Height: 6267 m (20 681 ft).

Chimera A legendary Greek fire-breathing monster with a lion's head, a goat's body, and a serpent's tail. After ravaging Lycia she was killed by Bellerophon.

chimpanzee An ape, *Pan troglodytes*, of West African forests. Chimpanzees are 100–170 cm tall when standing erect and live in small groups, mostly on the ground, feeding chiefly on fruit and leaves but occasionally eating meat. They communicate by facial expressions and calls and possess considerable intelligence.

China, People's Republic of A country in E Asia, covering vast areas of land ranging from the low-lying and densely populated plains of the NE to the high peaks of the Tibetan Plateau in the W. China proper falls into three natural regions, formed around the three main rivers: the Yellow River in the N, the Yangtze in the centre, and the Xi Jiang in the S. Over 90% of the inhabitants are Han Chinese. *Economy*: mainly dependent upon agriculture, which was formerly socialized through a system of communes but has now been fragmented into small private holdings. The emphasis is on foodcrops, rice in the S, wheat and millet in the N, as well as livestock, especially pigs. Cotton is grown in the N and tea in the S. Coal is extensively mined and is the major source of power. China has been self-sufficient in oil since 1973 and small amounts of natural gas are produced. Iron ore is the most important mineral deposit and China is the main world producer of tungsten ore. Other minerals include antimony, lead, bauxite, and manganese. Recent decades have seen large-scale development of modern industries, especially textiles, steel, electronics, and chemicals; state control of the economy has been loosened and there has been a huge increase in foreign trade. Exports include farm produce, textiles, metals and manufactured goods. *History*: China is one of the world's oldest civilizations, with a history of organized society going back over nearly four millenniums. The first important recorded dynasty was the Shang in the valley of the Yellow River (18th-12th centuries BC). From the 12th to the 3rd centuries BC the *Zhou spread S and E. Under the *Qin, in the 3rd century BC, a unified empire came into being and the first Great Wall was built. The rule of the *Han dynasty, from the 3rd century BC to the early 3rd century AD, saw spectacular advances in technology and manufacturing but its decline was followed by centuries of struggle between different parts of the empire. With the *Tang dynasty (7th–10th centuries) China was once more reunited and reached the high point of its civilization. It was followed by the Song (10th–13th centuries), the *Mongol (13th–14th centuries), the *Ming (14th–17th centuries), and the *Qing, which lasted until 1912. From the 16th century Europeans came to China and set up trading posts despite opposition from the Qing. British efforts to open up the country to free trade led to the Opium War in 1839 and to the opening of treaty ports (and also to the cession of Hong Kong). Later other trade concessions were made to several European countries; Chinese opposition to these moves included the Taiping Rebellion (1851–64) and the antiforeign Boxer Rebellion (1899–1900). In 1911 a revolution under the leadership of Sun Yat-sen ousted the Qing and a republic was set up. The 1920s saw the rise of the Guomindang (Nationalist People's Party) under Gen *Chiang Kai-shek and the foundation of the Chinese Communist Party. In 1926 relations between them broke down and a struggle began that continued until after World War II. In the 1930s threats from Japan culminated in open attack and the occupation of parts of the country, which lasted until the end of World War II. This put a temporary halt to internal struggles, but in 1949 the Guomindang was defeated by the communists and a People's Republic was set up by *Mao Tse-tung. Chiang Kai-shek retreated to Taiwan, where he set up the Republic of China. During the early years of communism relations with the Soviet Union were close but they later deteriorated. In 1966 Mao launched the Cultural Revolution, designed to eradicate "revisionism" and to prevent the rise of a ruling class. Mao died in 1976 and was succeeded by the moderate Hua Guo Feng (1920–). Attempts by a "radical" faction (known as the Gang of Four and including Mao's widow Jiang Qing) to gain power were thwarted by the arrest of its members. *Deng Xiao Ping then became the dominant force in government. His rule was marked by economic liberalization but rejection of political reform. In 1984 the government authorized the massacre of thousands of protesting students in Tiananmen Square, Beijing. Following Deng's death in 1997, *Jiang Zemin emerged as the country's paramount leader. *Hu Jintao succeeded him as president in 2003. The former British crown colony of Hong Kong was returned to China in 1997, as was the Portuguese overseas territory of Macao in 1999. Since 1971 China has had a seat at the UN. Official language: Mandarin Chinese. Currency: yuan of 10 chiao or 10 fen. Area: 9 597 000 sq km (3 704 440 sq mi). Population (2003 est): 1 288 892 000. Capital: Beijing.

china clay A mineral deposit consisting mainly of kaolin, a hydrous aluminium silicate. Kaolin is produced by weathering or by hydrothermal processes acting on the feldspars in granite. It is used for making high-grade ceramic products and in many industrial processes.

chinchilla A *rodent belonging to the genus *Chinchilla* (2 species), widely bred for its valuable long soft blue-grey fur. Measuring 30–50 cm long, wild chinchillas are found high in the Andes, living among rocks and feeding at night on vegetation. South American captive chinchillas are mostly short-tailed (*C. brevicaudata*) while in North America the long-tailed species (*C. laniger*) is bred. Family: *Chinchillidae.*

Chinchilla cat A breed of long-haired cat. Chinchillas have a compact body with short legs and a broad head with a snub nose and small tufted ears. The white fur is tipped with black on the back, flanks, head, ears, and tail, giving it a silvery lustre. The eyes are emerald or blue-green.

Chindits The 77th Indian Brigade, organized by Orde *Wingate in 1943 in Burma (now Myanmar) as a "long-range penetration" infantry division. A guerrilla force, the Chindits were so called after the mythological Burmese temple guardian, the *chinthe*, and because they operated beyond the River Chindwin. Initially successful in severing Japanese lines of communication they were later in danger of being encircled and were forced to return to India in groups.

Chindwin, River A river in N Myanmar (Burma), flowing S to join the Irrawaddy River near Myingyan. Length: 1046 km (650 mi).

Chinese A language or group of languages of the Sino-Tibetan family spoken in E Asia. The many distinct forms or dialects of Chinese, which include Mandarin, Min, Kan, Hakka, Hsiang, Wu, and Cantonese (or Yüeh), are mutually unintelligible. In China there have been attempts recently to standardize the language, using Mandarin as a basis. Chinese is a tonal language, many words, otherwise identical, having quite distinct meanings according to intonation. Words are usually monosyllabic and do not change their form to indicate part of speech. The language is written in logographic characters or symbols of pictorial origin (*see* IDEOGRAPHIC WRITING SYSTEMS), which enables them to be understood by speakers of any Chinese dialect. There are as many as 40 000 of these of which 10 000 are in common use. Literacy requires knowledge of about 2000 of them. For transliteration purposes, Pinyin (phonetic spelling) has replaced the older Wade-Giles system (and is generally used in this book).

Chinese lantern plant A hardy ornamental, *Physalis alkekengi*, also called bladder cherry or winter cherry. A native of S and central Europe, it grows to a height of 20–60 cm. The edible fruit is enclosed in a reddish inflated calyx resembling a lantern. Family: *Solanaceae*.

chinoiserie Decorative art and architecture that incorporated Chinese motifs into European fantasy designs and was popular in the late 17th and 18th centuries. The fashion was inspired by importation into Europe of Chinese porcelain, lacquer, etc., in the 17th century. Instances of chinoiserie in England include the *willow pattern, combining Chinese elements into a new design; the interior of the Brighton Royal Pavilion is an architectural example.

Chinook A North American Indian people of the NW Pacific coast of the USA. The Chinook language forms part of a division of the Penutian language family. The Chinook were salmon fishers and traders, their location along the lower Columbia River being ideally suited for exchanging goods with peoples to the N and S and in the interior. Chinook Jargon, a combination of Chinook, Nootka, and other Indian languages mixed with English and French words, became the trading language of the entire W coast of America.

chipmunk A ground squirrel belonging to the genus *Tamias* (18 species), of North America and Asian forests. Chipmunks are 15–30 cm long and have a black and white striped back and strong feet and claws for digging. They live in burrows and, in the winter, do not hibernate but feed on a store of nuts and dried fruit carried under ground in their large cheek pouches.

Chippendale, Thomas (1718–79) British cabinetmaker, famous for his furniture designs, especially his chairs. His illustrated collection of rococo furniture designs was widely influential in England and America, although his later neoclassical styles are considered the finest. His son, also **Thomas Chippendale** (died c. 1822), continued the business.

Chirac, Jacques (1932–) French statesman; president (1995–), prime minister (1974–76; 1986–88). Having reorganized the Gaullists in the late 1970s, he became (1986) prime minister under *Mitterrand. He was also mayor of Paris (1977–95). As president he implemented unpopular austerity measures to prepare France for the introduction (January 1999) of the single European currency. In 2002 he won a landslide victory in the presidential elections.

Chiron In Greek legend, a *centaur, son of Cronos and the sea nymph Philyra. Unlike his fellow centaurs, he was revered for his wisdom and knowledge of medicine. After being accidentally wounded by Heracles he bequeathed his immortality to Prometheus and was transformed into the constellation Sagittarius.

chiropractic An alternative medical specialty based on the assumption that most diseases originate from disorders of the nervous system, particularly as a result of compression of the nerve roots as they emerge from the spine. A chiropractor attempts to relieve symptoms by manipulating the spine with his hands.

Chittagong 22 20N 91 48E A city and major port in Bangladesh, on the Indian Ocean. The focal point of road, rail, and air routes, it is the second most important industrial centre in the country. Population (1991): 1 599 000.

chivalry The code of conduct of medieval European knights. The code encompassed the military virtues of bravery and loyalty as well as honour and courtesy. The latter was related to the ideal of *courtly love. The chivalric ideal enshrined a commitment to uphold Christianity and was a major factor in the *Crusades.

chive A small hardy perennial plant, *Allium schoenoprasum*, native to Europe. It has small white bulbs and produces clumps of thin tubular leaves and spherical heads of bluish flowers. The onion-flavoured leaves are used for seasoning foods. Family: *Liliaceae*.

chloramphenicol An *antibiotic usually reserved for severe bacterial infections. It is particularly useful in the treatment of typhoid fever and some forms of pneumonia and meningitis.

chlorine (Cl) A greenish poisonous *halogen gas, discovered in 1774 by C. W. Scheele. It is found in nature only in compounds, especially common salt (NaCl), sylvite (KCl), and carnallite ($KMgCl_3.6H_2O$). Chlorine is liberated by the electrolysis of brine. It irritates the respiratory system and was used as a poisonous gas in World War I. Chlorine gas is reactive and combines directly with most elements. Its oxidizing properties make it useful for disinfecting water. It is used in the manufacture of many compounds. At no 17; at wt 35.453; mp −100.98°C; bp −34.6°C.

chloroform (*or* **trichloromethane**; $CHCl_3$) A colourless volatile liquid made by reacting *bleaching powder with acetone, acetaldehyde, or ethanol. Its main use is now in the manufacture of *fluorocarbons but it is also used as a solvent and as an anaesthetic.

chlorophyll A green pigment present in organisms capable of *photosynthesis. Higher plants possess chlorophylls *a* and *b*, located in *chloroplasts; chlorophyll *c* is found in some primitive marine plants, and bacteriochlorophyll occurs in photosynthetic bacteria. The chlorophylls absorb red and blue light, trapping light energy for photosynthesis.

chloroplast A structure within a plant cell in which the process of *photosynthesis takes place. It is bounded by a membrane and contains the green pigment *chlorophyll. Chloroplasts vary greatly in shape and number within a cell. The greatest concentration occurs in the palisade mesophyll tissue of the leaves—the main photosynthesizing region.

chloroquine A drug used to prevent and treat malaria. It acts by preventing the digestion of haemoglobin (the red pigment of blood) by the malaria parasite. Chloroquine is also used in the treatment of rheumatoid arthritis and related diseases.

chocolate *See* COCOA AND CHOCOLATE.

cholera An acute infection of the intestine caused by the bacterium *Vibrio cholerae*, which is transmitted in drinking water contaminated by faeces of a patient. Epidemics of cholera occur in regions where sanitation is poor. After an incubation period of 1–5 days, cholera causes severe vomiting and diarrhoea, which—untreated—leads to dehydration that can be fatal. Treatment consists of replacement of fluid and salts by intravenous injections. Vaccinations against cholera provide only temporary immunity.

cholesterol A compound derived from steroids and found in many animal tissues. Cholesterol is manufactured mainly by the liver and is carried to other tissues in the form of low-density lipoproteins (LDLs); its derivatives form constituents of cell membranes, bile, blood, and gallstones. High levels of LDL-cholesterol in the blood have been associated with an increased risk of heart disease, as a result of fatty deposits in the walls of arteries. *See also* ATHEROSCLEROSIS.

Chomsky, Noam (1928–) US linguist, under whose influence the aims and methods of general linguistic theory and especially of grammar were radically revised. *Syntactic Structures* (1957) and *Aspects of the Theory of Syntax* (1965) develop the idea of transformations by which a sentence may be generated from an underlying "deep structure." He is also an outspoken critic of US foreign policy.

Chopin, Frédéric (François) (1810–49) Polish composer and pianist of French descent. He studied in Warsaw but later settled in Paris, where he lived with the novelist George *Sand from 1838 to 1847. A fervent nationalist, he wrote mazurkas and polonaises influenced by Polish folk music. He developed a highly characteristic style of writing for the piano, for which he composed 2 concertos, 3 sonatas, 4 ballads, 4 scherzos, 24 preludes, and many waltzes, nocturnes, and studies. He also wrote a cello sonata, a piano trio, and songs.

chordate Any animal distinguished by a hollow dorsal nerve cord; a rodlike *notochord that forms the basis of the internal skeleton; and paired gill slits in the wall of the pharynx behind the head, although in higher chordates these are apparent only in early embryonic stages. Chordates comprise the tunicates, lancelets, and vertebrates. Some authorities place these three groups in a single phylum, *Chordata*, while others divide them into separate phyla: *Urochordata*, *Cephalochordata*, and *Craniata* (*see* VERTEBRATA), respectively.

chorea Involuntary jerky movements caused by disease of the brain. It is a feature of **Huntington's disease** (or **chorea**), a hereditary disease that is also associated with mental deterioration. **Sydenham's chorea**, formerly known as St Vitus's dance, is often associated with rheumatic fever in children. It can be treated with antibiotics.

choreography The art of composing *ballet and other theatrical dances. Choreography originally referred only to a dance notation, the lack of which has made precise reconstruction of many ballets difficult. The most comprehensive system for recording dance steps is that devised by the Hungarian dancer Rudolph Laban (1879–1958), known as Labanotation (*see* BALLET). The modern choreographer is usually a professional dancer, who selects, arranges into sequences, and teaches the dancers each step of the ballet.

Chou En-lai (*or* **Zhou En Lai**; 1898–1976) Chinese communist statesman; prime minister (1949–76) and foreign minister (1949–58). Chou studied in Japan, France, and Germany. He led workers in the 1927 general strike in Shanghai, after which he escaped *Guomindang (Nationalist) assassins and fled to Nanchang, where he helped to organize an uprising. After the establishment in 1949 of the People's Republic of China, he gained prominence as a diplomat and was largely responsible for establishing communist China's bureaucracy.

chough A large black songbird, *Pyrrhocorax pyrrhocorax*, about 37 cm long, with red legs and a long red down-curved bill. It occurs in the Alps, Spain, and a few sea cliffs around Britain. The yellow-billed Alpine chough (*P. graculus*) occurs at high altitudes in European mountains. Family: *Corvidae* (crows).

chow chow A breed of dog originating in China more than 200 years ago. The chow has a compact body and a blue-black tongue. The thick coat forms a mane around the neck and shoulders. Height: 46–51 cm.

Chrétien de Troyes (12th century AD) French poet, author of the earliest romances dealing with the *Arthurian legend. He was a native of Champagne and a member of the court of Marie, countess of Champagne, to whom his romance *Lancelot* was dedicated. His romances include *Erec*, *Cligés*, *Yvain*, and *Perceval* (or *Conte del Graal*), in which the *Holy Grail appears in a literary work for the first time.

Christchurch 43 33S 172 40E A city in New Zealand, on E South Island. Founded in 1850, it has a gothic-style cathedral (completed in 1901) and many fine parks. Industries are primarily associated with the rich agriculture of the Canterbury Plains; these include meat processing, tanning, chemicals, and flour milling. Population (1999 est): 324 300.

Christian Aid A British organization founded in 1949 by the *British Council of Churches to direct the use of donations made to the developing world. It supports development programmes in agriculture, health, and education and gives relief aid in emergencies.

Christian Democrats Political parties having programmes based on Christian principles and generally of a conservative nature. The German **Christlich-Demokratische Union** (Christian Democratic Union; CDU), founded in 1945, held power in alliance with the Christlich-Soziale Union (Christian Social Union; CSU), from 1948 to 1969 under Konrad *Adenauer. Since 1982 it has been the main party in the coalition led by Helmut Kohl. In Italy the **Democrazia Cristiana** (Christian Democratic Party; DC), founded in 1943 as the successor to the Partito Popolare Italiano (Italian Popular Party), dominated government from 1945 until 1993. Other Christian Democratic parties are found in Austria, Belgium, France, Norway, and Spain.

Christianity The religious faith based on the person and teachings of *Jesus Christ, which had its origin in *Judaism. Its believers hold that Jesus is the Messiah prophesied in the Old Testament. Chiefly through the missionary activities of St Paul, Christianity spread rapidly through the Roman Empire, despite persecutions under Nero and later emperors. Christian belief was at first taught by the Apostles by word of mouth; however, the need for a written record of Jesus' life and teaching was soon fulfilled by the *Gospels. The definition of Christian belief and the authority of bishops and scriptures was well developed when Constantine became emperor (312). A series of general councils, the first held in 325 at *Nicaea, defined orthodox Christian belief. Constantine's establishment of his new capital, Constantinople, led to a growing polarization between the Eastern *Orthodox Church and the Western *Roman Catholic Church. Despite the collapse of the Western Empire, Western Christianity, under the Bishop of Rome who claimed authority as St Peter's successor, spread vigorously. The Orthodox Church, not so rigorously centralized, became increasingly isolated, and with the development of doctrinal differences the two Churches drifted apart. The date of the formal separation is generally regarded as 1054. By the end of the first millennium the Roman church was rapidly gaining power, the papacy reaching the zenith of its influence in the 13th century under Pope Innocent III. In the later middle ages the assertion of power by temporal rulers weakened the united structure of the papacy and *Holy Roman Empire.

By the 16th century the Church no longer had the power to override national interests; in this weakened state it was unable to resist the inevitable fragmentation caused by the *Reformation. Some reformers, such as the followers of Martin *Luther and the English Church, were comparatively conservative, while the Calvinists, centred in Geneva, were more radical. Coinciding with the exploration of the globe, the Reformation and the Roman Catholic response to it, the *Counter-Reformation, stimulated the spread of Christianity throughout the world, giving rise to many different Christian denominations and communions The total number of Christians has been estimated at over 1999 million (2000), or approximately 33% of the world population.

Christian Science A religious movement founded by Mary Baker *Eddy. Having been influenced by P. P. Quimby (d. 1866), a spiritual leader, she formulated a set of principles of faith healing based on Christ's healing powers, which she claimed to have discovered and which she expounded in *Science and Health* (1875). The First Church of Christ, Scientist, opened in Boston, Massachusetts, in 1879. The movement spread throughout the world; by 2000 there were some 350 000 adherents and 2000 churches. The movement emphasizes healing, primarily of sin and secondarily of disease.

Christie, Dame Agatha (1890–1976) British author of detective fiction and playwright. She introduced her most famous character, the Belgian detective Hercule Poirot, in *The Mysterious Affair at Styles* (1920). Later novels include *The Murder of Roger Ackroyd* (1926) and *Death on the Nile* (1937). In all, she wrote over 50 popular novels, creating other well-known fictional detectives, including Miss Jane Marple. Several stories have been filmed, and her play *The Mousetrap* has had an unparalleled long run in London since its opening in 1952.

Christmas The Feast of the Nativity of Christ. In the West it has been celebrated on 25 Dec since 336 AD, partly in order to replace the pagan sun worship on the same date. In the East, both the Nativity and Epiphany were originally celebrated on 6 Jan, but by the end of the 4th century 25 Dec was almost universally accepted, although the Armenian Church still celebrates Christmas on 6 Jan.

Christmas Island **1.** An island in the Indian Ocean, SW of Java. It became a territory of the Commonwealth of Australia in 1958. The only commercial activity is phosphate mining. Area: 135 sq km (52 sq mi). Population (1994 est): 2000. **2.** (*or* **Kiritimati**) A large coral atoll in the W central Pacific Ocean, in Kiribati in the Line Islands. British and US nuclear tests were held here between 1957 and 1962. It has coconut plantations. Area: 359 sq km (139 sq mi). Population (1995): 3225.

Christmas rose A perennial herbaceous plant, *Helleborus niger*, about 35 cm tall, native to central and S Europe and Asia Minor. Grown in gardens for its attractive white or pink winter-flowering blossoms, it prefers rich moist shady sites. The poisonous rhizomes are irritant to the skin when fresh. Dried, they have been used medicinally. Family: *Ranunculaceae*.

Christopher, St (3rd century AD) Christian martyr of Syria. According to legend, he carried a child across a river where he was working as a ferryman. The child grew heavier and he learned that it was in fact Christ and he was thus carrying the weight of the world. He is the patron saint of travellers. Feast day: 25 July.

chromium (Cr) A hard grey transition metal, discovered in 1798 by Louis Nicolas Vauquelin (1763–1829). It occurs in nature principally as chromite ($FeCr_2O_4$). The metal is extracted by reducing the oxide (Cr_2O_3) with aluminium. The chief uses of chromium are in electroplating steel and in making alloys with iron. All chromium compounds are coloured. At no 24; at wt 51.996; mp 1863 ± 20°C; bp 2472°C.

chromosome One of the threadlike structures that carry the genetic information (*see* GENE) of living organisms and are found in the nuclei of their cells. Chromosomes consist of a central axis of *DNA with associated *RNA and proteins. Before cell division, the long filamentous threads contract and thicken and each chromosome can be seen as two identical threads (**chromatids**) joined at the centromere. The chromatids later separate to become the daughter chromosomes (*see* MITOSIS). Chromosome number is characteristic of a species. For example, a normal human body cell has 46 chromosomes comprising 22 matched pairs (called autosomes) and two *sex chromosomes. A human sperm or egg cell has half this number of chromosomes (*see* MEIOSIS). Abnormal numbers or parts of chromosomes often lead to abnormalities in the individual concerned.

chromosphere The layer of a star's atmosphere that lies between the *photosphere and the *corona. It is very much less dense than the photosphere. The sun's chromosphere is a few thousand kilometres thick; the temperature increases rapidly from about 4000°C near the photosphere to about 500 000°C at the base of the corona. The solar chromosphere cannot be seen without special equipment, except at a total solar *eclipse.

chronic fatigue syndrome A condition that sometimes follows a serious viral disease, especially glandular fever. Extreme fatigue, which may be associated with a sore throat, muscular pain, and headache, lasts for many months. With no cause established, treatment is confined to relieving symptoms and providing psychological support. The condition has also been called **myalgic encephalopathy** (ME).

Chronicles, Books of Two Old Testament books covering the history of Judah from the Creation to the end of the Babylonian exile (538 BC). They were probably written in the 4th century BC and originally formed a continuous history with the books of Ezra and Nehemiah. After opening with genealogies from Adam, they describe the reigns of David and Solomon and the succeeding Kings of Judah. Special emphasis is given to the building of the Temple at Jerusalem.

chrysalis The *pupa of most insects of the order Lepidoptera. *See also* BUTTERFLIES AND MOTHS.

Chrysanthemum A genus of herbaceous plants and shrubs (about 200 species) native to Eurasia, Africa, and North America. The showy forms are widely and easily cultivated, having colourful single or double long-lasting flower heads. The different varieties may bloom at any time from early spring to autumn. Family: *Compositae. See also* PYRETHRUM.

chub One of several freshwater fish related to *carp, found in Europe and North America. The European chub (*Leucixus cephalus*) has a plump elongated body, usually 30–40 cm long, and is dark blue or green above and silvery below. Certain unrelated freshwater fish of the genus *Leucichthys* (order: *Salmoniformes*) are also called chub.

Churchill, Lord Randolph Henry Spencer (1849–95) British Conservative politician; third son of the 7th Duke of Marlborough and the father of Sir Winston *Churchill. A 'Tory Democrat', he entered parliament in 1874, serving as secretary for India (1885–86), and chancellor of the exchequer (1886). He married (1874) Jeanette (Jennie) Jerome (1854–1921), an American.

Churchill, Sir Winston (Leonard Spencer) (1874–1965) British statesman and author. The son of Lord Randolph *Churchill, he served in the army and as a war correspondent in the second Boer War before becoming a Conservative MP in 1900. In 1904 he joined the Liberals and subsequently served as president of the Board of Trade (1908–10), home secretary (1910–11), and first lord of the admiralty (1911–15). In 1915, during World War I, he rejoined the army and served in France. In 1917 he became minister of munitions, supporting the development of the *tank. Churchill lost his parliamentary seat in 1922 but was re-elected as a constitutionalist in 1924, becoming chancellor of the exchequer in Baldwin's government. From 1929 he was out of office until the outbreak of World War II, when he became first lord of the admiralty and then, in 1940, prime minister of a coalition government. During World War II, his remarkable oratory and outstanding qualities as a leader made him a symbol of British resistance to tyranny. He was largely responsible for Britain's victorious alliance with the Soviet Union and the USA (1941) but came to view Soviet communism as a future threat. Churchill's coalition government was defeated in 1945 but he returned as Conservative prime minister in 1951, serving until his resignation in 1955. His writings include *The Second World War* (1948–54) and *A History of the English-Speaking Peoples* (1956–58); he won the 1953 Nobel Prize for Literature.

Churchill River A river in W Canada, flowing from NW Saskatchewan E and NE through Manitoba to Hudson Bay. Length: 1610 km (1000 mi).

Church in Wales The Welsh Anglican Church, which was the Established Church of Wales from the 16th century until 1920, when it was disestablished. Since then the Church in Wales has been an autonomous province of the *Anglican Communion. One of its six diocesan bishops is elected Archbishop of Wales. The church has 1142 parishes and 700 stipendiary clergy.

Church of England The Established Church in England, which embodies Protestant elements but also claims continuity with the English Church as established by St Augustine, the first Archbishop of Canterbury. Prior to the mission of Augustine (597), the native Church was dominated by Celtic missionaries from Ireland and Scotland. Conflicts between the indigenous Celtic Church and Rome were resolved in favour of Roman usage at the Synod of *Whitby (664), and thereafter the English Church remained under papal authority until the *Reformation. Under *Henry VIII, papal supremacy was rejected and the king was acknowledged Supreme Head of the Church, but there were no doctrinal changes. The two bases of Anglican doctrine and worship were formulated in the succeeding reigns: the Book of *Common Prayer, introduced in the reign of *Edward VI, and the *Thirty-Nine Articles, published under Elizabeth I, whose excommunication (1570) by the pope completed the break with Rome. By the 19th century three parties had developed within the Church and these continue to the present: the Low

Church or Evangelical group, which emphasizes the Protestant tradition; the High Church group (*see* ANGLO-CATHOLICISM); and a Liberal group stressing adaptation to modern ideas. The two provinces of the Church are the archbishoprics of Canterbury and York, each of which is further divided into bishoprics. Ecclesiastical affairs are supervised by the General Synod (established 1970 to replace the Church Assembly), composed of bishops, clergy, and laity. In 1992 the Synod voted to admit women to the priesthood. Church property and endowments are administered by the Church Commissioners for England (established 1948). *See also* ANGLICAN COMMUNION; CHARISMATIC MOVEMENT; HOLY ORDERS; LAMBETH CONFERENCES; LATITUDINARIANISM.

Church of Scotland The Established Church in Scotland. The Scottish Church's secession from Rome was effected in 1560, largely under the influence of John *Knox. The argument over Church government between Episcopalians and Presbyterians' continued until the reign of William of Orange, who established the Presbyterian Church in 1690. During the 18th century, disputes arose between traditional Evangelicals and Moderates; this, together with the question of patronage, led to secessions. During the 19th and 20th centuries many of these divisions were healed.

CIA *See* CENTRAL INTELLIGENCE AGENCY.

cicada An insect belonging to the mainly tropical family *Cicadidae* (over 2000 species). Cicadas are 20–50 mm long and have large membranous wings. Males produce loud noises by vibrating two membranes at the base of the abdomen (stridulation). Cicadas usually inhabit trees and the females lay eggs in the wood. The *nymphs drop to the ground and burrow to feed on plant juices from roots. After 1–17 years they emerge as adults. Order: *Hemiptera*.

Cicero, Marcus Tullius (106–43 BC) Roman orator and statesman. Elected consul in 63 BC, his execution of the Catiline conspirators without trial lost him support and he was exiled in 58 BC for 18 months. During the civil war he supported Pompey against Caesar. After the assassination of Caesar in 44 BC he made a series of attacks on Antony, the *Philippics*, for which he was later arrested and killed. He also wrote treatises on rhetoric and philosophical works influenced by Greek political theory.

cichlid A freshwater fish of the family *Cichlidae* (over 6000 species), found in tropical regions, especially Africa. Cichlids have a brightly coloured body, up to 30 cm long, and a single long dorsal fin; they feed on plants or animals. Many are popular aquarium fish. Order: *Perciformes*.

cider An alcoholic drink made from fermented apple juice. In England cider is made predominantly in the West Country, from apples grown specifically for cider making. Sweet cider has a large amount of unfermented sugar, dry cider little sugar, and rough cider is dry cider with some acetic acid.

Ciliophora A phylum of microscopic single-celled organisms (*see* PROTOZOA), the ciliates, having two nuclei and tracts of hairlike cilia over the cell surface, used for feeding and swimming. Most are free-swimming (e.g. *Paramecium*) but some are attached to the substrate by a stalk (*see* STENTOR; VORTICELLA). Most ciliates feed on organic detritus, etc., but some are parasitic, especially on fish.

Cimon (died c. 450 BC) Athenian general and politician. He opposed Themistocles' policy of enmity towards the Spartans, believing Persia was the common Greek enemy, and in about 466 he scored a great victory against the Persians. His opponents, including *Pericles, caused him to be ostracized (461) but after his return to Athens, Cimon negotiated a truce with Sparta (c. 450) and died fighting the Persians in Cyprus.

Cinchona A genus of trees (40 species) of the South American Andes, now cultivated elsewhere in the tropics, especially India. One of the most important species is calisaya (*C. calisaya*). The bark yields powerful medicinal drugs, including *quinine and quinidine. Cultivation is now less important, owing to the development of synthetic drugs lacking side-effects. Family: *Rubiaceae*.

Cincinnati 39 10N 84 30W A city in the USA, in SW Ohio on the Ohio River. Founded in 1788, it developed as a meat-packing centre in the 19th century. Today it is an important inland port and major manufacturing centre. Population (2000): 331 285.

cinema The first motion picture exhibited to a public audience was made in 1895 by the French brothers Louis and Auguste Lumière and the first commercial success was the American film *The Great Train Robbery* (1903). Influential pioneers of the silent cinema in the USA were D.W. *Griffith, Mack Sennett, and Charlie *Chaplin. In Europe, technological developments were creatively exploited by such directors as F.W. Murnau (1889–1931) in Germany and *Eisenstein in Russia. The end of the era of silent films was signalled by the success of Al Jolson's *The Jazz Singer* (1927), which had a synchronized musical score; colour film, introduced in the 1930s, added further popular appeal. Between 1930 and 1945 the cinema industry in the USA became essentially an entertainment factory, controlled by the giant Hollywood studios such as MGM and Paramount. The decline in cinema audiences from the early 1950s because of the rival attraction of television caused the break-up of the Hollywood system: subsequently many of the most significant developments in the cinema have been achieved by directors elsewhere. Prominent British directors included Carol Reed, David Lean, and Alfred Hitchcock; directors elsewhere included *Fellini, *Antonioni, *Bergman, *Buñuel, and Godard in Europe, Kurosawa in Japan, and Satyajit Ray in India. By the late 1970s cinema had become a truly global medium. Since the 1980s Hollywood has regained some of its dominance with big-budget action spectaculars featuring the latest special effects, as in the work of *Spielberg. Recently, this trend has been boosted by the increasingly sophisticated techniques now available for the computer manipulation of images.

cineraria A herbaceous perennial pot plant developed from *Senecio cruentus* of the Canary Islands. There are numerous horticultural varieties, noted for their handsome daisy-like flowers. Family: *Compositae*.

Cinna, Lucius Cornelius (d. 84 BC) Roman politician. Expelled from Rome by his opponent Sulla (87), Cinna returned with Marius and captured Rome. He tried to restrain Marius' brutal revenge on their opponents and as consul (86–84) restored order. He was killed in a mutiny shortly before Sulla's return to Italy.

cinnabar (moth) A moth, *Callimorpha jacobaeae*, of Europe and Asia. Both the adults—scarlet and black—and the caterpillars—striped black and yellow—have warning coloration to discourage predators. Superfamily: *Caradrinoidea* (noctuids, tiger moths, etc.).

cinnabar (ore) A mineral consisting of mercury sulphide, the chief ore of mercury. It is bright red and occurs in veins and impregnations associated with volcanic rocks.

cinnamon An evergreen tree, *Cinnamomum zeylanicum*, 7–10 m high, native to Sri Lanka and cultivated widely in the tropics. It is coppiced, the bark of the twigs being peeled off and rolled up to form the spice. Family: *Lauraceae*.

Cinque Ports An association of five English ports (Sandwich, Dover, Hythe, New Romney, Hastings) in Kent and Sussex formed during the 11th century to defend the Channel coast. After the Norman conquest they were granted considerable privileges in return for providing the nucleus of the navy. Winchelsea and Rye were later added to their number. The Lord Warden of the Cinque Ports survives as an honorary office.

Circe Legendary Greek sorceress, who had the power to transform men into beasts. Odysseus, who visited her island of Aeaea on his voyage from Troy, was protected by the herb moly, and forced her to restore his men to human form.

circulation of the blood The passage of blood through the heart and the network of arteries and veins associated with it. By supplying the tissues with blood, the circulatory system effects the transport of oxygen, nutrients, etc., and the removal of waste products. Oxygen-rich blood is pumped out of the *heart into the aorta and then, via the arteries, to all the tissues of the body. Here oxygen is removed, and deoxygenated blood returns, through the veins, to the heart. This blood is then pumped to the lungs, where it is reoxygenated, and returned to the heart to repeat the circuit. The circulation of the blood was first discovered by William *Harvey in 1628.

circumcision The removal of all or part of the foreskin of the penis. In many traditional societies circumcision forms part of a rite of passage. Among some Islamic peoples it is performed just before marriage; Jewish babies are circumcised when they are eight days old. Its origin is unknown but it has hygienic advantages, especially in hot climates, and cancer of the penis very rarely occurs among circumcised men. The incidence of AIDS in African tribes that practise male circumcision is much lower than in tribes that do not. Recent research has shown that the outermost keratin layer of skin cannot be penetrated by HIV but because the inner side of the foreskin (like the mucosa lining the vagina and the anus) has no keratin layer it enables HIV to enter the body. Circumcision is also carried out if the opening of the foreskin is too narrow (phimosis). So-called **female circumcision** ranges from removal of the skin around the clitoris to infibulation, in which all the external genitalia are removed. These mutilations, illegal in the UK since 1985, are still common in Africa and the Middle East.

Cirencester 51 44N 1 59W A market town in SW England, in Gloucestershire. In Roman times it was the second largest town in Britain (Corinium) and it was an important wool centre in the middle ages. The Royal Agricultural College is situated in Cirencester. Population (1991): 15 221.

cirrhosis Destruction of the cells of the liver followed by their replacement with fibrous tissue, which eventually produces symptoms of liver failure (e.g. jaundice, swelling of the legs and abdomen, and vomiting of blood). Cirrhosis may be caused by *alcoholism, *hepatitis, obstruction of the bile duct, and heart failure, but often the cause is not known. Treatment is determined by the underlying condition.

cirrocumulus cloud (Cc) A high *cloud with a mottled appearance composed of ice crystals; it is sometimes known as "mackerel sky."

cirrostratus cloud (Cs) A high thin veil of *cloud composed of ice crystals, visible as a halo around the sun or moon.

cirrus cloud (Ci) A high detached *cloud occurring in the troposphere above 6000 m (20 000 ft), composed of ice crystals and appearing wispy and fibrous. It is usually associated with fair weather.

Cistercians An order of Roman Catholic monks founded by St Robert of Molesme (c. 1027–1111) as a stricter offshoot of the *Benedictine order. The mother house at Cîteaux, France, was founded in 1098. *See also* TRAPPISTS.

citric acid An organic compound that occurs in plant and animal tissues and is involved in the series of metabolic reactions called the *Krebs cycle. A commercial preparation of citric acid is used as a flavouring agent in foods.

citron A citrus tree, *Citrus medica*, 2–3 m high. Originally from the Far East, it was introduced into the Mediterranean region in about 300 BC; this remains the main centre of commercial cultivation. The rough yellowish sour fruits are used to make candied peel, produced by soaking in brine and preserving in sugar.

citronella A *grass, *Cymbopogon nardus*, cultivated in tropical regions of Africa and Asia and introduced into tropical America. It forms dense tufts and contains geraniol or citronella oil, used in cosmetics and insect repellents.

Citrus The largest and most important genus of tropical and subtropical fruits (10 species), originating in SE Asia. All the species are small evergreen trees or shrubs with simple glossy leaves and five-petalled, usually white, flowers. The juicy fruits are rich in vitamin C, citric acid, and pectin (used in jam making). The most important are the *orange, *lemon, *lime, *grapefruit, *citron, bergamot, and *tangerine. Family: *Rutaceae*.

City Hall The headquarters of the mayor of London. An asymmetrical egg-shaped building designed by Norman *Foster, it opened in 2002 and stands opposite the Tower of London on the River Thames. It contains a circular debating chamber for the Greater London Assembly.

city states Independent municipalities, each comprising a town and its surrounding countryside, characteristic of ancient Greece. There were several hundreds of city states, of which Athens was the largest.

Ciudad Juárez 31 42N 106 29W A city in N Mexico, on the Rio Grande. Its importance is due to its location on the US border and as a marketing centre for cotton. Population (2000 est, urban area): 1 190 000.

civet A solitary nocturnal mammal belonging to the family *Viverridae*. The African civet (*Viverra civetta*) is cat-like, about 1.2 m long with coarse greyish spotted fur. Mainly carnivorous, civets also eat fruit and roots. The secretion of their anal glands is used in perfumes as a fixative, making other scents last longer. *See also* PALM CIVET.

civil engineering The branch of *engineering that deals with the design and construction of buildings and public structures, such as roads, railways, dams, canals, etc. The term was first used in 1750 by John Smeaton (1724–92) to distinguish his work from that of military engineers.

civil law The body of law governing the rights of private individuals and their relationships with each other rather than with the state. It is also called private law, as distinguished from public law and *criminal law. The term is also used of the European legal systems derived from *Roman law, which are different from *common law systems in important respects. For example, in civil law court decisions have no legal force in the decision of similar cases. English-speaking countries generally use common law, although the law of Scotland is more closely related to civil law.

civil list In the UK, the sum given annually from the Consolidated Fund to the monarch and her consort to meet their expenses. Until

1993 the Queen's children (except the Prince of Wales, who receives the revenues of the Duchy of Cornwall) were also on the list. The list was introduced in 1689, became law in 1697, and in 1830 all government expenses were removed from it. Originally parliament voted at the monarch's accession the sum to be paid annually but it is now, because of inflation, reviewed every ten years. **Civil list pensions**, charged to the Consolidated Fund but not forming part of the civil list, are awarded by the monarch on the advice of the prime minister to distinguished persons.

civil rights The individual's rights to liberty, equality of treatment, education, etc., under the law and safeguarded by the state. In countries with a written constitution, such as the USA, they form part of the constitution. In England there have been a number of unsuccessful attempts to codify these rights, which are still only protected by the general law. *See also* BILL OF RIGHTS.

Civil War, English (1642–51) The war between Charles I and parliament, which led to the execution of the king (1649) and the establishment of Oliver Cromwell's *Protectorate (1653). The Civil War was the outcome of a struggle for power between king and parliament, culminating in the events of the *Long Parliament. War was precipitated by Charles' rejection of parliament's Nineteen Propositions in June 1642, and on 22 Aug he raised his standard at Nottingham. The first battle, at Edgehill, ended indecisively but during 1643 the royalists (*or* *Cavaliers) gained ground in the N and W. The parliamentarian (*see* ROUNDHEADS) negotiation of the Solemn League and Covenant with the Scots led to their victory at *Marston Moor (1644); the formation of the *New Model Army brought about the decisive defeat of Charles at *Naseby (1645). In 1646 Charles surrendered to the Scots at Newark and the first Civil War was brought to an end. He was handed over to parliament in January 1647, but was seized by the army in June. He escaped to the Isle of Wight and in December reopened negotiations with the Scots. The second Civil War ensued (1648), with royalist uprisings in Wales and Kent, ending with Cromwell's defeat of the Scots at Preston in August. In the following year, Charles was tried and executed and the *Commonwealth was established by the Rump Parliament. The Civil War was concluded by Cromwell's subjection of Ireland (1649–50), his defeat of Charles' heir (later Charles II) at Dunbar (1650), and his victory against the Scots at Worcester in 1651.

Civil War, US (1861–65) The conflict between the Federal government of the USA and the 11 *Confederate States in the South, arising from the conflict of interest between the agricultural slave-owning South and the industrialized North. The election of a president, Abraham Lincoln, opposed to slavery precipitated the secession of the southern states under Jefferson Davis, and war broke out when the Confederates opened fire on Fort Sumter, South Carolina. The opening campaigns in Virginia culminated in the Confederate victory at the first battle of *Bull Run (July). Early in 1862 the Confederate Stonewall Jackson conducted a brilliant campaign in the Shenandoah Valley but on 4 May the Federal Army captured Yorktown and defeated Robert E. Lee's force in the Seven Days' battles (25 June–1 July). The Confederates won a victory at the second battle of Bull Run in August and Lee pushed N into Maryland. Defeated at *Antietam (Sept), the Confederates were then victorious at Fredericksburg (Dec). In Tennessee, meanwhile, the Confederate success at Shiloh (6–7 April) was followed by a reverse at Stones River (31 Dec–2 Jan). In 1863, following his victory at Chancellorsville, Virginia (1–5 May), Lee began his second invasion of the N, only to be defeated at *Gettysburg (July). In the W, Federal troops under Ulysses S. Grant besieged Vicksburg, Mississippi, which fell on 4 July, and, after defeat at Chickamauga (19–20 Sept), won the victory of Chatanooga (23–25 Nov). In 1864 Grant, now the Federal general in chief, advanced against Lee, whom he encountered inconclusively at *Cold Harbor (June). Sherman, who held the Federal command in the W, took Atlanta (Sept) before making his historic March to the Sea. After capturing Savannah in September, Sherman moved N through the Carolinas and on 9 April 1865, Lee surrendered at Appomatox Court House. By 2 June the Federal victory was complete.

Clackmannanshire A council area of central Scotland, lying N of the Firth of Forth. In 1975 the small county of Clackmannanshire was absorbed into Central Region; it became an independent unitary authority in 1996. It is chiefly agricultural, with distilling and some light industry. Area: 157 sq km (60 sq mi). Population (2001): 48 077. Administrative centre: Alloa.

clairvoyance *See* EXTRASENSORY PERCEPTION.

clam A *bivalve mollusc with two equal shells and a muscular burrowing foot. Burrowing clams live buried in sand and mud, mainly in shallow coastal waters; they feed by taking in water through a tube (siphon) extended into the water. The largest burrowing clam is the geoduck (*Panopea generosa*), weighing up to 5 kg, while the giant clam (*Tridacna gigas*) can exceed 250 kg.

clan A group tracing descent from a common ancestor. Clans are frequently important divisions in traditional societies, as in the pre-18th-century Scottish Highlands. The Scottish clans, until their suppression following the *Jacobite rebellions of 1715 and 1745, controlled distinctive territories and were frequently rivals. The members of a clan wore characteristic clothing (*see* HIGHLAND DRESS) and often bore the name of its founder preceded by Mac (son of).

Clare (Irish name: Chláir) A county in the W Republic of Ireland, in Munster situated between Galway Bay and the Shannon estuary. It consists of a low-lying central plain rising E to mountains and W to the limestone area of the Burren. Agriculture is the chief occupation. Area: 3188 sq km (1231 sq mi). Population (2002): 94 000. County town: Ennis.

Clare, John (1793–1864) British poet, the self-educated son of a farm labourer in Northamptonshire. His first book, *Poems Descriptive of Rural Life and Scenery* (1820), brought him fame and patronage in London. Subsequent volumes, including *The Shepherd's Calendar* (1827), were less successful, and he lived in great poverty. In 1837 he became insane and in 1841 was confined to a lunatic asylum in Northampton, where he wrote some of his best poems.

Clarendon, Edward Hyde, 1st Earl of (1609–74) English statesman and historian. He served as the king's chancellor of the exchequer during the English Civil war and went into exile in 1646, settling eventually with the future Charles II in France. At the Restoration (1660) he became Lord Chancellor. His daughter Anne married the future James II. Criticized for the sale of Dunkirk to France (1662) and for his handling of the second Dutch War (1664–67), he fell from power and went again into exile, where he completed his monumental *History of the Rebellion and Civil Wars in England* (1702–04).

Clare of Assisi, St (1194–1253) Italian nun, founder of the "Poor Clares." Influenced by the teaching of St *Francis of Assisi, she gave up all her possessions and followed him. St Francis established a community of women with Clare as abbess in 1215. She was canonized in 1255. Because of an incident in which she saw mass celebrated at a distance, she was proclaimed patron saint of television in 1958. Feast day: 12 Aug.

clarinet A woodwind instrument with a single reed and a cylindrical bore. It is a transposing instrument existing in several sizes and generally has a fundamental of A or B flat; it has a range of three and a half octaves. The clarinet did not become a regular member of the orchestra until the late 18th century. The **bass clarinet** is pitched an octave lower than the B flat clarinet.

Clarke, Kenneth Harry (1940–) British Conservative politician; chancellor of the exchequer (1993–97). His previous posts included home secretary (1992–93).

classicism The aesthetic qualities embodied in the visual arts and literature of ancient Greece and Rome that served as ideals for later European artistic movements. Qualities associated with the concept include harmony and balance of form, clarity of expression, and emotional restraint. The Italian Renaissance of the 15th and 16th centuries was the first attempt to revive these qualities in the arts. Its achievements in art and architecture inspired artists throughout Europe during the next two centuries. In literature, Renaissance interpretations of Aristotle's *Poetics* influenced writers all over Europe in the 17th and 18th centuries. Towards the end of the 18th century there was a general reaction against rigid neoclassicist doctrines.

Classics The five annual English flat races (Derby; Oaks, One Thousand Guineas; St Leger; Two Thousand Guineas) for three-year-old horses only.

Claude Lorraine (Claude Gellée; 1600–82) French landscape painter, born in Lorraine. His paintings of the Roman countryside include biblical or classical figures and his seascapes are remarkable for their sunlight.

Claudius I (10 BC–54 AD) Roman emperor (41–54), who owed his accession to the chaos that followed the murder of his nephew Emperor *Caligula. His rule was efficient: he extended the Empire, taking part in the invasion of Britain (43), but his susceptibility to the influence of his third wife Valeria Messalina alienated the Senate. Agrippina the Younger, his niece and fourth wife, was suspected of his murder. Taught by Livy, Claudius also wrote histories.

Clausewitz, Karl von (1780–1831) Prussian general and military theorist. In 1812 Clausewitz negotiated the Treaty of Tauroggen, which set in motion the joint Prussian, Russian, and British war effort against Napoleon. Of his many military works the posthumously published *Vom Kriege* is the most famous.

C

Clausius, Rudolf Julius Emanuel (1822–88) German physicist, who in 1854 formulated the concept of *entropy and used it in a statement of the second law of thermodynamics. He also contributed to the development of the *kinetic theory of gases and suggested that electrolysis involved the dissociation of molecules into charged particles.

claustrophobia *See* PHOBIA.

clavichord A keyboard instrument, popular from the 15th to the 18th centuries. Its delicate tone is produced by small brass plates fixed to the end of each key, which strike the strings. It is strung lengthways and has a range of about four octaves.

clavicle The collar bone. There are two clavicles, each running from the upper end of the breastbone to form a joint with the shoulder blade. They brace the shoulders and help to support the arms.

cleavage The repeated division of a fertilized egg cell (zygote) to produce a ball of cells that forms the blastula. In holoblastic cleavage, which occurs in egg cells with little yolk, the entire cell divides. Meroblastic cleavage occurs in yolky egg cells, such as those of birds, when only the yolk-free region divides.

Cleese, John (1939–) British comic actor and writer, best known for his TV series *Monty Python's Flying Circus* (1969–74) and *Fawlty Towers* (1974, 1978). Films include *A Fish Called Wanda* (1988).

clef (French: key) The symbol placed at the beginning of a musical stave to indicate the pitch of the notes. The treble clef, a decorative G, indicates that the second line up of the stave is the G above middle C; the bass clef, an archaic F, indicates that the fourth line up is the F below middle C. The C clef can be set on any of the lines of the stave to establish it as middle C; the alto clef (used for viola music) has the C on the middle line; the tenor clef (used for cello music) has the C on the fourth line up.

cleft palate An abnormality caused by failure of the left and right halves of the palate to fuse during embryonic development. It leaves the nasal and oral cavities in continuity and it may be associated with a harelip. The cleft can be repaired surgically at 16 to 18 months of age.

Clematis A genus of herbaceous or woody plants (about 250 species), mainly climbing perennials, widely distributed in temperate regions. There are many horticultural varieties, with purple, pink, or white flowers. Family: *Ranunculaceae*.

Clemenceau, Georges (1841–1929) French statesman; prime minister (1906–09, 1917–20). A member of the chamber of deputies from 1876 to 1893, he subsequently devoted much of his energy to journalism. During the prewar years he urged military preparation against Germany and then attacked the World War I government for defeatism. As prime minister for the second time, he led France to victory.

Cleopatra VII (69–30 BC) Queen of Egypt (51–48, 47–30), the mistress of Julius Caesar and then of Mark Antony. Cleopatra was coruler with her brother Ptolemy XIII (61–48), who ousted her in 48. Restored by Caesar, she accompanied him to Rome and gave birth to (allegedly) his son Caesarion. After Caesar's murder, Cleopatra returned to Egypt and in 41 she met Antony. In 37 he abandoned his wife Octavia and lived with Cleopatra, who bore him three sons. Antony's brother-in-law Octavian defeated Antony and Cleopatra at *Actium in 31 and in 30 they both committed suicide.

Cleopatra's Needles A pair of ancient Egyptian obelisks carved in the reign of Thutmose III (c. 1475 BC) at Heliopolis. They were moved by *Augustus Caesar to Alexandria in 12 BC. They were moved again in 1878, one being set up on the Victoria Embankment, London, the other in Central Park, New York.

Cleveland 41 30N 81 41W A city in the USA, in Ohio on Lake Erie. It is a major Great Lakes port and the largest city in Ohio. One of the country's leading iron and steel centres, its other industries include oil refining, food processing, and the manufacture of motor vehicles. Population (2000): 478 403.

Cleveland, Stephen Grover (1837–1908) US statesman; Democratic president (1885–89, 1893–97). In his first term as president he tried to stamp out graft and excessive tariff protection. His second term was troubled by a financial crisis and labour strife.

Cleveland Bay A breed of horse developed in the Cleveland region of N Yorkshire, England, and always reddish brown (bay) with black mane, tail, and legs. Formerly a pack and coach horse, Clevelands are now used mainly for crossing with Thoroughbreds to produce showjumpers. Height: 1.57–1.68 m (15½–16½ hands).

click beetle A long narrow flat beetle, also called skipjack beetle, belonging to a large and worldwide family (*Elateridae*; 8000 species). If upturned it rights itself by springing into the air with a clicking sound. The larvae, known as wireworms, are serious pests of root crops.

Clinton, Bill (William Jefferson C.; 1946–) US statesman; Democratic president (1993–2001). His first term saw US-brokered peace deals in Bosnia-Hercegovina and the Middle East and an economic boom. He was re-elected in 1996. In 1998 he confessed to a sexual affair with a White House trainee, despite his previous denial on oath. The House of Representatives voted for his impeachment for perjury and obstruction of justice but he was found not guilty (1999) by the Senate. His wife, **Hillary Rodham Clinton** (1947–), was elected to the Senate in 2000.

clipper ship A fast sailing vessel developed in the 19th century for international commerce, so called because it clipped the time required for a given passage.

Clive, Robert, Baron Clive of Plassey (1725–74) British soldier and colonial administrator, who established British supremacy in India. He joined the East India Company in 1743 and made his name by capturing Arcot (1751). In 1757 he recaptured Calcutta from the Nawab of Bengal, whom he then defeated at Plassey. This assured the East India Company control of Bengal, of which Clive was virtual ruler until 1760, when he returned to England. He was appointed governor and commander in chief of Bengal (1764–67). He was subsequently named in an inquiry into the East India Company's affairs, was vindicated (1773), but committed suicide shortly afterwards.

cloaca The posterior chamber of the body in all vertebrate animals except the placental mammals, into which the digestive, urinary, and genital tracts open. Faeces, urine, and eggs or sperm are discharged through its vent.

clock A device for measuring the passage of time. Clockwork has two essential components: an energy store (a raised weight or a coiled spring) and an escapement that regulates the release of energy from the store. The earliest recorded escapement was in a giant Chinese astronomical clock (c. 1090 AD). Early European clocks (called turret clocks from their usual position in church towers) were crude ironwork with verge escapements, driven by falling weights and recording time by striking on the hour. The 14th-century Italian family of Dondi introduced dials and the innovation of mainsprings about 1500 enabled portable clocks (*see also* WATCH) to be made. Refinements in the 17th century were the anchor escapement (1671) and the use of pendulums (*see* HUYGENS, CHRISTIAAN). An important advance in the 18th century was the development of an accurate marine chronometer, used by navigators to determine position. Scientific advances in the 20th century have led to the development of clocks regulated by the natural vibrations of atoms (*see* ATOMIC CLOCK).

clone A population of organisms produced from a single parent cell by asexual division—for example by vegetative reproduction in

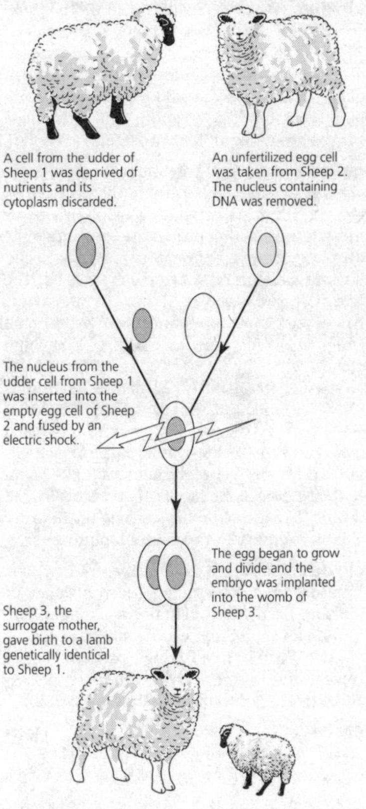

A cell from the udder of Sheep 1 was deprived of nutrients and its cytoplasm discarded.
An unfertilized egg cell was taken from Sheep 2. The nucleus containing DNA was removed.
The nucleus from the udder cell from Sheep 1 was inserted into the empty egg cell of Sheep 2 and fused by an electric shock.
The egg began to grow and divide and the embryo was implanted into the womb of Sheep 3.
Sheep 3, the surrogate mother, gave birth to a lamb genetically identical to Sheep 1.

clone. The stages involved in producing the first clone of a higher animal.

plants or parthenogenesis in animals. The individuals of a clone are genetically identical. The first successful **cloning** of a higher animal took place in Scotland in 1996, when the nucleus of a body cell taken from an adult sheep was fused with an egg cell that had had its own nucleus removed and was stimulated to divide by an electric shock. The resulting embryo was inserted into the womb of a surrogate sheep, leading to the birth of a lamb genetically identical to the first sheep. In the UK all experiments on human embryos are subject to strict controls by the Human Fertilization and Embryology Authority. In 1998 the Authority ruled that research into cloned human tissue for surgical transplant could proceed but that reproductive human cloning could not.

clothes moth A small *tineid moth whose larvae feed on clothes, carpets, blankets, etc. There are a number of species of widespread distribution. Adults generally have a wingspan of 12–25 mm and are pale grey-brown in colour. Pesticides, dry cleaning, and man-made fibres have reduced their damaging effects.

cloud A mass of minute water droplets or ice crystals, or a combination of both, produced by the condensation of water vapour in the atmosphere. When conditions are favourable the droplets grow and precipitation may occur. Various classifications of clouds exist but the one most extensively used by meteorologists is based on cloud appearance and height and comprises ten principal forms. The high clouds, normally above 5000 m (16 000 ft) are cirrus (Ci), cirrostratus (Cs), and cirrocumulus (Cc). The medium clouds at 2000–5000 m (6500–16 000 ft) comprise altocumulus (Ac) and altostratus (As). Below this level the low clouds are stratus (St), stratocumulus (Sc), and *nimbostratus (Ns). Some clouds grow vertically and cannot be classified solely by height; these are chiefly cumulus (Cu) and cumulonimbus.

cloud chamber A device, invented by C. T. R. *Wilson, used for studing the properties of ionizing particles. It contains a chamber containing a vapour that can be made supersaturated. When an ionizing particle passes through the chamber drops of liquid condense along its trail, thus making the trail visible.

clove An evergreen Indonesian tree, *Eugenia caryophyllata*, growing to a height of 12 m. The dried flower buds are used as spice. The whole tree is aromatic, clove oil being distilled from the buds, stalks, and leaves for use in medicine and as artificial vanilla. Family: *Myrtaceae*.

clover An annual or perennial plant of the genus *Trifolium* (about 290 species), which also includes the trefoils. Clovers, which occur mainly in N temperate regions, have leaves divided into three leaflets and dense heads of flowers. They are valuable as fodder plants and for their nitrogen-fixing ability. Family: *Leguminosae*.

clubmoss A perennial mosslike plant, also called ground pine, belonging to a genus (*Lycopodium*; about 200 species) of flowerless vascular plants, found mainly in tropical and subtropical forests and mountainous regions. It has a creeping stem with wiry branches, densely covered with green, yellowish, or greyish needle-like leaves. The spore capsules occur at the base of special leaves (sporophylls), which are often arranged in conelike clusters (strobili). Order: *Lycopodiales*; phylum: *Lycophyta*.

Cluny 46 25N 4 39E A town in E France, in the Saône-et-Loire department. Its famous Benedictine abbey (founded 910 AD) became the centre of the Cluniac order, a reformed Benedictine order that was widely influential in Europe (c. 950–c. 1130). Population (latest est): 4724.

cluster of galaxies A group of *galaxies that are physically associated by mutual gravitational effects. Most galaxies are members of a cluster: our own Galaxy belongs to the Local Group. The densest clusters contain a thousand or more galaxies. Adjacent clusters are loosely grouped into **superclusters**.

clutch A device enabling two rotating shafts to be coupled and uncoupled. Positive clutches have square or spiral jaws allowing no slipping and normally both shafts have to be at rest for engagement. Friction clutches provide for slipping while the shafts are being engaged, but do not have to be stopped for engagement. In a plate clutch flat discs attached to each shaft press against each other; in a hydraulic clutch radial vanes attached to the shafts are immersed in a fluid.

Clutha River A river in New Zealand, the longest river in South Island. It flows generally S from Lake Wanaka, in the Southern Alps, to enter the Pacific Ocean near Kaitangata. Length: 340 km (210 mi).

Clyde, River A river in W Scotland. Rising in the hills of South Lanarkshire, it flows NW through Glasgow and S of *Clydebank to enter the Atlantic Ocean at the Firth of Clyde. Length: 170 km (106 mi).

Clydebank 55 54N 4 24W A town in W central Scotland, in West Dunbartonshire Region on the River Clyde. Shipbuilding has been replaced by more varied economic activities. Population (1991): 29 171.

Clydesdale A breed of draught horse developed in the Clydesdale region of Scotland in the 18th century. It has a compact body with strong legs and feet and may be bay, brown, black, or chestnut. Height: about 1.75 m (17 hands).

Clytemnestra In Greek legend, the daughter of Tyndareus, King of Sparta, and Leda, and wife of *Agamemnon. She and her lover Aegisthus killed Agamemnon after the Trojan War and she herself was killed by her son *Orestes.

cnidarian An aquatic invertebrate animal of the phylum *Cnidaria* (about 9000 species), including *Hydra*, jellyfish, sea anemones, corals, etc. There are two different generations of the life cycle (*see* POLYP; MEDUSA) and either or both may occur. The body cavity has a single opening (mouth) and stinging cells (nematocysts) are used for defence or catching prey.

coal A carbonaceous mineral deposit used as a fuel and raw material for the chemical industry. Coal results from the compaction and heating of partially decomposed fossil vegetable matter. During the coalification process the plant remains are changed progressively from a peatlike material into lignite (brown coal), sub-bituminous and bituminous coal, semi-anthracite, and anthracite. During this process the percentage of carbon present increases and the moisture and volatile content decreases; anthracite is about 90% carbon. These coals are known as the humic coals. The sapropelic coals (cannel coal and boghead coal) are derived from finely divided vegetable matter (algae, spores, and fungal material). Most coal was formed in the Carboniferous period, although some of the younger coals, for example lignite, date from Mesozoic and Tertiary times.

Coal has been mined in Britain since Roman times but on a small scale until the industrial revolution. In about 1800 coal was first carbonized on a commercial scale to produce *coal gas for gas lighting and coke for smelting iron ore. By the middle of the 19th century, interest in the by-products (coal tar, ammonia, and pitch) was awakening. The chemistry of coal tar developed into the study of organic chemistry, and the aromatic compounds from coal tar led to the development of the dyestuffs and explosives industries. In the 20th century these products also became the foundation of the plastics industry. During the 1920s and 1930s processes were also developed (mainly in Germany) for converting coal into oil. Subsequently, *natural gas has largely replaced coal gas and petrochemicals (*see* OIL) have to a considerable extent replaced coal tar as sources of raw materials. In 1947 the UK coal mines were nationalized under the National Coal Board but in 1994 the Coal Industry Act authorized the issuing of licences to private companies. The government decided to close many of the UK's mines in the 1990s and by 2003 there were only 9 deep mines still in operation.

coal gas A gas consisting mainly of hydrogen (50%) and methane (30%), with some carbon monoxide (8%) and other gases. It is made by destructive distillation of coal, a process that involves heating it to 1000°C. Coal gas was formerly supplied to homes for heating and cooking, but it has now been largely replaced, in the UK, by *natural gas from the North Sea.

Coal Measures *See* CARBONIFEROUS PERIOD.

coastguard A paranaval force formed by some countries during the 19th century to hinder smuggling. In Britain it now deals principally with lifesaving and maritime safety through a network of coast-watching stations and provides a meteorological service.

Coast Mountains A mountain range of W Canada, extending from the US border 1600 km (1000 mi) N into Alaska. Very rugged, it rises steeply from the Pacific coast. It includes Canada's largest mountain mass and a long glacier belt. Mount Waddington at 3978 m (13 260 ft) is the highest point.

cobalt (Co) A transition metal similar to iron and noted for its deep-blue colour when reacted in ceramics. It was discovered by G. Brandt (1694–1768) in 1735 and occurs naturally as cobaltite (CoAsS) and in copper, nickel, iron, silver, and lead ores. It is used as an alloy in the manufacture of cutting steels and magnets. The isotope ^{60}Co is a strong gamma-emitter produced in nuclear reactors and used in radiotherapy (the **cobalt bomb**) and in industry. At no 27; at wt 58.9332; mp 1495°C; bp 2928°C.

Cobbett, William (1763–1835) British journalist, who championed the cause of the rural poor in his weekly *The Political Register* (from 1802). After army service in Canada he accused his officers of corruption and was forced to flee Britain (1792), returning in 1800. He was imprisoned (1810–12) for attacking the flogging of militiamen and in 1817 was again forced to flee to the USA. Returning to Britain in 1819, he began in 1821 the country tours described in *Rural Rides* (1830).

C

cobra A highly venomous snake occurring in warm regions of Africa and Asia and able to expand its neck ribs to form a hood. The king cobra (*Ophiophagus hannah*) of S Asia is over 3.6 m long, making it the largest venomous snake; it preys chiefly on other snakes. The common Indian cobra (*Naja naja*), used by snake charmers, is 1.7 m long and frequently enters houses at night in search of rats. Family: *Elapidae* (cobras, mambas, coral snakes).

coca A Peruvian tree, *Erythroxylon coca*, cultivated in Java, South America, and Sri Lanka for its leaves, which—when dried—yield cocaine. Coca leaves have been chewed for centuries in South America for their effect in relieving fatigue and hunger; prolonged use can cause addiction and mental and physical damage. Family: *Erythroxylaceae*.

cocaine An alkaloid ($C_{17}H_{21}O_4N$) derived from *coca leaves and also made synthetically. The first drug to be used as a local anaesthetic, it has largely been replaced by safer drugs for this purpose (e.g. procaine) although it is still used in pain-killing mixtures for treating people with terminal illnesses (e.g. cancer). Cocaine, an addictive stimulant, is taken for the euphoria it produces. **Crack** is a highly addictive derivative of cocaine; it can induce violence in habitual users.

cochineal A natural red dye obtained from the dried bodies of certain female scale insects, especially *Dactylopius coccus* of Mexico. It has now been largely replaced by synthetic dyes, but continues to be used for colouring foodstuffs and cosmetics.

cochlea *See* EAR.

cockatiel A small Australian *cockatoo, *Nymphicus hollandicus*, of interior grasslands. It is 32 cm long and has a grey plumage with white wing patches, a yellow head and crest, and reddish ear patches.

cockatoo A *parrot belonging to a genus (*Cacatua*; 17 species) ranging throughout Australia, Malaysia, and the Philippines. Cockatoos are usually white, often with a pink or yellow blush, although some species are black; all have a long erectile crest and a large hooked bill used to crack nuts and extract grubs from wood.

cockchafer A European beetle, *Melolontha melolontha*, also called maybug, that is very destructive to plants (*see* CHAFER). Up to 35 mm long, it is black with reddish-brown legs and wing cases and has a loud buzzing flight. The larvae—which cause the most damage, particularly to cereals and grasses—are also called white grubs or rookworms.

Cockcroft, Sir John Douglas (1897–1967) British physicist, who shared the 1951 Nobel Prize with Ernest *Walton for their development of the first particle *accelerator in 1932, which was used for accelerating protons to split an atomic nucleus (of lithium) for the first time. In World War II he worked on the atom bomb and in 1946 became director of the Atomic Energy Research Establishment at Harwell.

Cockerell, Sir Christopher Sydney (1910–99) British engineer and inventor of the *hovercraft. After working on radar in World War II, he concentrated upon hydrodynamics. He filed his first patent for an air-cushion vehicle in 1955. The first practical hovercraft, the SR.NI, was launched in 1959.

cocker spaniel A breed of gundog, thought to be of Spanish origin. It is compact with short legs, a short tail, and long droopy ears. The long flat silky coat is usually black, red, or cream, either plain or in mottled combinations. Height: 39–41 cm (dogs); 38 cm (bitches).

cockle A *bivalve mollusc of the family *Cardiidae* (about 250 species). The ribbed shell valves, 1–23 cm in diameter, are rounded, producing a relatively globular bivalve. Cockles burrow in sand or mud, straining food particles from water drawn in through their protruding siphons. The European cockle (*Cardium* (or *Cerastoderma*) *edule*) is edible.

cockroach A nocturnal insect belonging to the mainly tropical family *Blattidae* (3500 species). It has a black or brown flat body, 12–50 mm long, with long antennae and leathery forewings. Cockroaches seldom fly; they feed on plant and animal materials and can be household pests. A widely distributed species is the common cockroach, or black beetle (*Blatta orientalis*). Order: *Dictyoptera*.

cocoa and chocolate Foods derived from the seeds of the cacao tree (*Theobroma cacao*), native to tropical America and cultivated mainly in West Africa. The tree is pruned and woody pods, 23–30 cm long, grow directly from its trunk. The pods contain seeds (cocoa, or cacao, beans) embedded in a whitish pulp, which are scraped out, fermented, and dried before export. Manufacturing is carried out mainly in the importing countries, where the beans are shelled, roasted, and ground. From them cocoa powder and chocolate are made. Cocoa butter, a fat retained in chocolate but removed from cocoa powder, is a rich source of food energy. Family: *Sterculiaceae.*

coconut The fruit of the coconut *palm, *Cocos nucifera*; one of the most important tropical crops. The tree has a slender trunk, up to 25 m high, which bears a crown of giant featherlike leaves. The coconuts take a year to ripen and have a thick fibrous husk surrounding a single-seeded nut. The hollow core contains coconut milk; the white kernel is eaten raw or dried to yield copra, from which coconut oil is extracted for use in soaps, synthetic rubbers, and edible oils. The residual coconut cake is used as a livestock feed and the coarse husk fibre (coir) is used for matting, etc.

Cocos Islands (*or* **Keeling Islands**) Two Australian coral atolls in the E Indian Ocean. They were visited by Charles Darwin (1836). First settled in 1826, they were under Australian administration from 1955 and became part of Northern Territory in 1984. Copra is produced and there is an important meteorological station. Area: 13 sq km (5 sq mi). Population (1993): 593.

Cocteau, Jean (1889–1963) Versatile French poet, artist, and filmmaker. He made his name with the novel *Les Enfants terribles* (1929) and sketches written for Diaghilev's ballet company, such as *Parade* (1917). In World War I he served as an ambulance driver and became acquainted with *Picasso, *Modigliani, and other leading painters and writers. His creative work includes poetry (*L'Ange Heurtebise*, 1925), plays (*Orphée*, 1926), films (*Le Sang d'un poète*, 1929; and *Orphée*, 1949), and graphic work.

cod A carnivorous fish, *Gadus morhua*, that lives near the bottom in temperate N Atlantic waters and is commercially fished for food and liver oil. Its elongated body, up to 1.8 m long, is generally dark grey with spots and has three dorsal fins, two anal fins, and a whisker-like barbel on its lower jaw. *G. macrocephalus* is a similar N Pacific species. Family: *Gadidae*; order: *Gadiformes.*

codeine An *analgesic drug used to relieve mild pain. It is a derivative of morphine but less toxic and less addictive. Codeine depresses the cough centre of the brain and is therefore often added to cough mixtures. It is also used in the treatment of diarrhoea.

Code Napoléon The systematic collection of the *civil law of France. Drafted by a commission set up by *Napoleon I when he was first consul, the code—properly called the *Code Civil*—was brought into force in 1804. It and the other codes subsequently produced under Napoleon's administration remain the basis of present French law and served as a model for civil law codes elsewhere.

coelacanth A *bony fish of the suborder *Coelacanthini.* Once thought to have been extinct for 60 million years, several living representatives have been found since the discovery, in 1938, of *Latimeria chalumnae* off the coast of SE Africa. It has a heavy body, up to 1.5 m long, with a short head and limblike fins, and crawls on the bottom, feeding on other fish. Order: *Crossopterygii.*

coeliac disease A disease in which the small intestine is abnormally sensitive to gliadin (a component of the protein *gluten, found in wheat). It results in abnormalities in the cells of the intestine, which cannot digest or absorb food. The symptoms include diarrhoea, stunted growth, and general malaise, the condition is treated by a gluten-free diet.

coelom The body cavity of many animals. In mammals (including humans) the embryonic coelom is divided into three cavities, which become occupied by the lung, heart, and intestines. In the fully developed mammal the coelom is reduced to the virtually nonexistent spaces between the membranes lining the heart (the pericardium), the lungs (the pleura), and the intestines (the peritoneum).

coenzyme A nonprotein substance that forms a complex with certain enzymes and is essential for the proper functioning of these enzymes. Coenzymes include nucleotide derivatives (e.g. *ATP and NAD), coenzyme A (important in the *Krebs cycle), and *vitamins of the B complex.

Coetzee, J(ohn) M(axwell) (1940–) South African novelist and writer. *The Life and Times of Michael K* (1983) and *Disgrace* (1999) both won the Booker Prize. Other novels include *In the Heart of the Country* (1977) and *The Master of Petersburg* (1994). He received the 2003 Nobel Prize for literature.

coffee The seeds (called beans) of certain tropical evergreen trees of the genus *Coffea*, which yield a stimulating drink. *C. arabica* is the most widely grown coffee tree, producing the best quality beans. *C. canephora* is more disease resistant, longer living, and can be grown at lower altitudes. *C. liberica*, of still lower quality, is grown in Malaysia and Guyana. The coffee beans are usually fermented, then sun dried before export. Family: *Rubiaceae*.

Cognac 45 42N 0 19W A town in W France, in the Charente department. Under French law, the name Cognac may only be applied to brandy produced in a certain area around the town. Population (latest est): 20 995.

coke A fuel consisting mainly of carbon. It is made by heating coal in the absence of air and is produced as a by-product of *coal gas. Coke is used in *blast furnaces and other industrial processes as well as for domestic heating.

cola *See* KOLA.

Colchester 51 54N 0 54E A market town in SE England, in Essex on the River Colne. Founded by Cymbeline (Cunobelinus) in about 10 AD, Colchester was an important Roman town (Camulodunum); the Roman walls remain in part and there is a Norman castle. Essex University (1961) is nearby. Colchester's industries include engineering and printing. Population (1993 est): 149 100.

Cold Harbor, Battles of Two battles in the US *Civil War fought near Richmond, Virginia, the Confederate capital. In the first (27 June 1862) the Confederate general, Robert E. *Lee defeated the Federal forces under George B. McClellan (1826–85), both sides suffering heavy losses. In the second (3–12 June 1864), the Federal advance on Richmond under Ulysses S. *Grant was temporarily halted when he encountered Lee's entrenched forces.

Colditz 51 08N 12 49E A town in E Germany, on the River Mulde. Its castle, built by *Augustus II on a cliff above the town, was used as a top-security prisoner-of-war camp during World War II. Many escapes were attempted, some of which were successful.

Cold War The hostility between the USA and the Soviet Union, and their respective allies, following World War II. The term was first used in 1947 by the US politician Bernard Baruch (1870–1965). Fear of nuclear war prevented military confrontation; the Cold War was fought on economic, political, and ideological fronts. Most virulent in the 1950s, it had given way by the 1970s to the movement towards detente; despite renewed tensions in the 1980s, it was formally ended in 1990 following the collapse of communism in the East.

Coleraine A district in N Northern Ireland, in Co Londonderry. Area: 477 sq km (184 sq mi). Population (2001): 56 315.

Coleridge, Samuel Taylor (1772–1834) British poet and critic. In 1795 he met William *Wordsworth and their joint publication of *Lyrical Ballads* (first edition 1798) marked a decisive break with 18th-century poetry. His finest poems, such as *Kubla Khan* (1797) and *The Rime of the Ancient Mariner* (1797–98), were written at this time, but his personal life was troubled by his marriage, his poverty, and his increasing opium addiction. His subsequent creative energies were committed to journalism, lectures, and the writing of the critical and metaphysical *Biographia Literaria* (1817).

Coleridge-Taylor, Samuel (1875–1912) British composer, the son of a doctor from Sierra Leone and a British mother. Educated at the Royal College of Music, he is best known for the trilogy *Song of Hiawatha* (for solo voices, chorus, and orchestra; 1898–1900).

Colet, John (c. 1466–1519) English theologian and humanist. After his ordination, he lectured at Oxford, collaborating with Thomas More and Erasmus, prior to his appointment as dean of St Paul's Cathedral. He founded St Paul's School in 1509. He was a fierce opponent of Church corruption and published numerous theological works.

Coleus A genus of herbaceous or shrubby plants (150 species) originating in the Old World tropics. Many cultivated varieties of the species *C. blumei* are grown for their variegated leaves of a diversity of colours. Family: *Labiatae*.

colitis Inflammation of the large intestine (the colon), causing abdominal pain and diarrhoea (sometimes with the passage of blood). Colitis can be caused by bacterial infection (e.g. dysentery) or by *Crohn's disease. Ulcerative colitis, in which the colon becomes ulcerated, is treated with corticosteroids or sulphasalazine (a sulphonamide drug). Surgery may be required for severe cases.

collagen A structural protein that is the main component of the white fibres of connective tissue. Inelastic but with great tensile strength, it is found in tendons and ligaments and also in skin, bone, and cartilage.

College of Arms (*or* **Heralds' College**) An English heraldic society, comprising three kings of arms, six heralds, and four pursuivants of arms. Its origins lie in the royal officers of arms, who received a charter from Richard III in 1484. The College was reincorporated in 1555. Its functions include the settling of rights to bear arms, which the kings may grant by letters patent.

collie A breed of dog originating in Scotland and widely used as a sheepdog. The rough-coated collie has a long dense coat and bushy tail; the smooth-coated variety has a shorter smooth coat and the bearded collie has a long coat with a shaggy beard. Collies are grey, fawn, or sandy, with or without white markings. Height: 56–61 cm (dogs); 51–56 cm (bitches).

Collins, Michael (1890–1922) Irish nationalist. A leading member of Sinn Fèin, he masterminded the IRA's campaign against British forces in 1919–21. Subsequently he played a major role in the negotiations that established (1921) the Irish Free State and led the Free State army in the ensuing civil war. He was killed in an ambush.

colloid A system in which a disperse phase is present in a dispersion medium in the form of particles 10^{-9} to 10^{-6} m in length. If the disperse phase is solid and the dispersion medium is liquid the colloid is known as a **sol** (examples include milk). If both are liquid the colloid is known as an **emulsion** (e.g. mayonnaise). A colloidal suspension in which the particles of the disperse phase link together, with the dispersion medium circulating through the meshwork, is called a **gel** (e.g. a photographic emulsion). *See also* AEROSOL.

Cologne (German name: Köln) 50 56N 06 57E A city in W Germany on the River Rhine. A port and major commercial centre, it is the site of a university (1388) and the largest gothic cathedral in N Europe (founded 1248 and reconstructed after World War II). *History*: founded by the Romans, it became the capital of the northern empire in 258 AD and later the seat of Frankish kings. In 1798 it was annexed by France, passing to Prussia in 1815. Population (1999 est): 963 200.

Colombia, Republic of A country in NW South America, on the Pacific Ocean and the Caribbean Sea. The majority of the population is of mixed Spanish and Indian descent. *Economy*: the chief product is coffee, which accounts for over half the total exports. There is also widespread illegal trafficking in and processing of cocaine. The country is rich in mineral resources; gold, silver, copper, lead, and mercury are mined and Colombia is one of the world's richest sources of platinum and emeralds. There are also large reserves of oil, coal, and natural gas. *History*: inhabited by Indians before the Spanish colonization of the 16th century. In 1819 Simón Bolívar secured the independence of Greater Colombia, which included what are now Panama, Venezuela, and Ecuador as well as Colombia. This lasted until 1830 when Venezuela and Ecuador broke away; Panama became independent in 1903. Since 1975 there has been almost continuous unrest, including strikes, kidnappings, and left-wing guerrilla activity. Despite government campaigns the drug cartels remain extremely powerful and a major source of corruption, violence, and instability. In January 1999 substantive talks began with the main left-wing guerrilla organization (FARC) but the peace process suffered frequent setbacks and collapsed in early 2002; government forces immediately moved against FARC-held territory in the S. Elections in 2002 resulted in victory for Alvaro Uribe, who announced a new clampdown on the insurgents and drug producers. Official language: Spanish. Currency: Colombian peso of 100 centavos. Area: 1 138 914 sq km (456 535 sq mi). Population (2003 est): 41 662 000. Capital: Bogotá.

Colombo 6 55N 79 52E The capital and main port of Sri Lanka, on the W coast at the mouth of the River Kelani. Population (1997 est): 800 982.

Colombo Plan An agreement, signed in Colombo (Ceylon) in 1951, designed to foster economic development in the countries of S and SE Asia. It now has 26 members—20 countries within the region and Australia, Canada, Japan, New Zealand, the UK, and the USA.

colon *See* INTESTINE.

Colorado One of the Mountain States in the W central USA. Most of the population lives and works in a transition zone, the Colorado Piedmont, between the Rocky Mountains in the W and the Great Plains of the E. Manufacturing is the most important sector of the economy, especially the production of machinery, chemicals, military equipment, and food products. Colorado also produces molybdenum, coal, and oil. Tourism, especially winter sports, is of growing importance. *History*: explored by the Spanish, part of Colorado was acquired by the USA in the Louisiana Purchase (1803) and part from Mexico in 1848. Following the discovery of gold (1859), it became a territory in 1861 and a state in 1876. Area: 269 998 sq km (104 247 sq mi). Population (2000): 4 301 261. Capital: Denver.

Colorado potato beetle A brown and yellow striped *leaf beetle, *Leptinotarsa decemlineata*, about 10 mm long. Both the adults and the larvae eat potato leaves: the larvae also attack the tubers. The beetle is native to W North America but has spread eastwards, throughout Europe, to become a serious pest.

Colorado River A river in the W USA, rising in the Rocky Mountains and flowing SW through Colorado, Utah, and Arizona (where it passes through the *Grand Canyon) to the Gulf of California in Mexico. It is extensively used for irrigation and as a source of hydroelectric power. Length: 2320 km (1440 mi).

Colosseum An *amphitheatre in Rome. One of the most impressive of all Roman remains, the Colosseum was begun (c. 70 AD) by the emperor *Vespasian. It is an elliptical building, four storeys high, 188 m (617 ft) long, and 156 m (512 ft) wide. It could seat 47 000 people and was used mainly for gladiatorial and wild-beast fights.

Colossians, Epistle of Paul to the A New Testament book written by the Apostle Paul about 60 AD to the church in Colossae in W Asia Minor. Its theme is that the Christian faith is sufficient and that speculative philosophy diverts attention from this truth.

Colossus of Rhodes A gigantic statue of the sun god *Helios by the harbour of Rhodes. Cast in bronze by Chares of Lindos about 280 BC and standing about 31 m (100 ft) tall, it was counted among the *Seven Wonders of the World. An earthquake destroyed it 50 years after its completion.

colour The sensation produced when light of different wavelengths falls on the human eye. Although it is actually continuous, the visible spectrum is usually split into seven major colours: red, orange, yellow, green, blue, indigo, and violet, in order of decreasing wavelength (from about 6.5×10^{-7} m for red light to 4.2×10^{-7} m for violet). A mixture of all these colours in equal proportions gives white light; other colours are produced by varying the proportions or omitting components. Coloured pigments, dyes, and filters selectively absorb certain wavelengths, transmitting or reflecting the rest. Thus a red book illuminated by white light absorbs all the components of white light except red, which is reflected. This is a subtractive process, since the final colour is that remaining after absorption of the others. Combining coloured lights, on the other hand, is an additive process. A mixture of the whole spectrum gives white light, as will a mixture of lights of three *primary colours.

colour blindness The inability to distinguish certain colours. There are various forms, the most common of which is red-green colour blindness (the inability to distinguish red and green). Colour blindness is usually an inherited and incurable condition. Because it is a recessive trait carried on the X chromosome it is far more common in men than women (about 8% of males of Caucasian origin are colour blind). Very occasionally colour blindness may be due to disease of the retina (the light-sensitive layer of the eye).

Colt revolver A *revolver with a five-shot cylinder rotated and locked in line with the single barrel by cocking the weapon. Invented by the US engineer Samuel Colt (1814–62) in 1835, it became the standard .45 US army and navy revolver, remaining in service until 1945.

colugo An arboreal mammal belonging to the genus *Cyanocephalus* and order *Dermoptera* (2 species), also called flying lemur, found in Asia, Borneo, and the Philippines. About 60 cm long, colugos have a membrane of skin, extending from the chin via the fore and hind limbs to the tail, with which they can glide up to 70 m. Colugos feed on leaves and fruit.

Columba, St (c. 521–597 AD) Irish missionary and abbot. Ordained in 551, he founded churches and monasteries in Ireland before setting up a monastery on Iona. From here, Scotland was evangelized. Feast day: 9 June.

Columbia 34 00N 81 00W A city in the USA, the capital of South Carolina. It is an important commercial centre; its industries include textiles, plastics, and machinery. Fort Jackson (a major US Army post) is adjacent to the city. Population (2000): 116 728.

Columbia River A river in North America, flowing SW from British Columbia, through Washington State, to the Pacific Ocean at Oregon. It is an important source of hydroelectric power and forms the only deepwater harbour N of San Francisco. Length: 1930 km (1200 mi).

Columbus 39 59N 83 03W A city in the USA, the capital of Ohio on the Scioto River. It is a major industrial and commercial centre of a rich agricultural area; its manufactures include aircraft, machinery, and footwear. Population (2000): 711 470.

Columbus, Christopher (1451–1506) Italian navigator, who pioneered European contact with America. He was born in Genoa, became a pirate, and in 1476 was shipwrecked off the coast of Portugal, where he settled. He conceived the idea of reaching the East by sailing westwards but his plan was rejected by the

Portuguese king (John the Perfect); he eventually won the patronage of the Spanish monarchs Ferdinand and Isabella and on 3 August 1492, set sail in the *Santa Maria*, accompanied by the *Pinta* and the *Niña*. On 12 Oct he landed in the Bahamas and in November visited Hispaniola. On his second voyage (1493–96) he visited Guadeloupe, Puerto Rico, and Jamaica. On his third voyage (1498–1500) he reached Trinidad and the mainland of South America but the expedition ended in disaster: in 1499, following a revolt against his command, a Spanish governor was dispatched to relieve Columbus, who was sent back in chains to Spain. On his arrival, however, he was released and compensated and shortly afterwards set off on his last voyage (1502–04). From this he returned ill, dying shortly afterwards in Valladolid.

Comanche A North American Indian people of the southern Plains. They speak a language of the Uto-Aztecan group, closely related to Shoshone. They migrated to this area from Wyoming in the 18th century. Horse breeders and fierce warriors, they often attacked white settlers in Texas until they agreed to settle in Oklahoma in 1867.

combustion A chemical reaction in which a substance combines with oxygen, producing heat and light. The oxidation reactions in combustion are generally chain reactions involving free radicals, the principal overall reactions being the oxidation of carbon to carbon dioxide and the oxidation of hydrogen to water ($C + 2H_2 + 2O_2 \rightarrow CO_2 + 2H_2O$).

Comédie-Française The French national theatre, founded in 1680 and reconstituted in 1803 by Napoleon. It is organized as a cooperative society, owned by its members. Despite its strong emphasis on tradition, it has produced many of France's most original actors.

comet A small body that moves, usually in a very elongated orbit, around the sun. A typical comet consists of a small nucleus of ice and dust surrounded by an immense tenuous luminous cloud of gas and dust, the coma. Tails of gas and of dust only appear when a comet is near the sun; they point away from the sun and may be millions of kilometres long. A comet eventually decays to produce a stream of meteoroids around its orbit.

comfrey A perennial herbaceous plant, *Symphytum officinale*, also called boneset. Up to 100 cm high, it has drooping creamy or purplish flowers. Native to Europe and temperate Asia and formerly used medicinally, it is now grown as a garden flower. Family: *Boraginaceae*.

Comintern *See* INTERNATIONAL.

commedia dell'arte An Italian form of popular theatre that flourished throughout Europe from the 16th to the 18th centuries. It was performed by professional actors whose comic and often vulgar improvisations were based on a set of stock situations and stereotyped characters. These included the clown *Harlequin, the cuckold Pantaloon, and the lover Inamorato.

commensalism A relationship between two individuals of different species in which one (the commensal) lives in, on, or with the other (the host), from which it derives food, shelter, support, or transport. An example is provided by certain barnacles, which live attached to whales. *See also* SYMBIOSIS.

commercial banks Institutions that offer a deposit, transfer, and loan service to companies and private individuals. In the UK, the commercial banks (or high-street banks) are public limited companies (joint-stock banks), which emerged from World War I as the big five: Barclays Bank, Lloyds Bank (now Lloyds TSB), Midland Bank (now HSBC), National Provincial Bank, and Westminster Bank (in 1968 the last two merged to form the National Westminster Bank, now called NatWest and owned by the Royal Bank of Scotland). Others now include the Abbey (formerly Abbey National), the Halifax, and the Woolwich, which were formerly building societies.

Common Agricultural Policy (**CAP**) The agricultural policy adopted by members of the EC. The aims of the policy are to ensure reasonable living standards for farmers and to secure regular supplies and reasonable prices for consumers. CAP involves the distribution of grants and a price-support system. The system's production of embarrassing surpluses (e.g. the butter "mountain" and wine "lake" of the 1970s) led to the imposition of production quotas in the 1980s.

common law The part of the law of England and of most English-speaking countries that was originally unwritten and based on the common customs of the country. Its growth was the result of judicial precedent, by which an earlier judgment or decision was binding in deciding a similar case. Such decisions can only be overruled by statute or by a higher court. It is distinguished from the statute law established by Acts of Parliament, from *equity, administered by the Court of *Chancery, and from the *civil law of most European countries.

Common Prayer, Book of The official liturgy of the Church of England. After the Reformation, Thomas *Cranmer and others began to formulate an order of worship in English. The first Prayer Book was published under Edward VI in 1549; criticism led to a more Protestant revision in 1552. The Roman Catholic Queen Mary abolished the Prayer Book, and from the accession of Elizabeth I to the end of the Civil War, it was reinstated, further revised, and again abolished, this time by the Puritans. The version of 1662, established by the Act of Uniformity, is still in use; a revised version was authorized in 1928. The 1980 *Alternative Service Book*, in modern English, was the preferred version of the Church of England until 2000–2001, when it was superseded by *Common Worship*, a book that includes both modern-language and traditional services.

Commonwealth (1649–53) The period in English history between the execution of Charles I and the *Protectorate; the term is sometimes used synonymously with Interregnum to refer to the entire period between the execution of Charles I and the *Restoration in 1660.

Commonwealth A loose association of 54 independent nations, most of which were once subject to the imperial government of the UK (*see* EMPIRE, BRITISH). The British Commonwealth of Nations was established by the Statute of Westminster (1931), which was based on the autonomy, equality, and common allegiance to the Crown of member states. Its name was modified to the Commonwealth after World War II. Its member states are currently Antigua and Barbuda, Australia, the Bahamas, Bangladesh, Barbados, Belize, Botswana, Brunei, Cameroon, Canada, Cyprus, Dominica, Fiji, The Gambia, Ghana, Grenada, Guyana, India, Jamaica, Kenya, Kiribati, Lesotho, Malawi, Malaysia, Maldives, Malta, Mauritius, Mozambique, Namibia, New Zealand, Nigeria, Pakistan, Papua New Guinea, St Kitts-Nevis, St Lucia, St Vincent and the Grenadines, Samoa, Seychelles, Sierra Leone, Singapore, Solomon Islands, South Africa, Sri Lanka, Swaziland, Tanzania, Tonga, Trinidad and Tobago, Uganda, the UK, Vanuatu, Zambia, and Zimbabwe (suspended from 2002). Nauru and Tuvalu are special members and are not represented at the meetings of Commonwealth heads; there are in addition a number of associated states and dependent territories. Commonwealth heads of government meet every two years.

Commonwealth of Independent States (**CIS**) A community of nations founded by Russia, Ukraine, and Belarus to maintain unity in such areas as economic policy after the collapse of the Soviet Union. Nine other former Soviet republics subsequently joined.

communications satellite An unmanned artificial satellite by which long-distance television broadcasting, telephone communications, and computer data links are achieved. High-frequency radio signals are sent from one transmitting station to the satellite, where they are amplified and retransmitted to one or more receiving stations. The first active satellite was the US Telstar 1, launched in 1962. Telstar and other early satellites were in relatively low elliptical orbits and were only visible for a short portion of their orbit. A communications satellite is now usually placed in a geostationary orbit. This is a circular orbit lying about 36 000 km above the earth's equator. The satellite completes such an orbit in the same time (24 hours) as the earth rotates on its axis and thus to a ground-based radio station appears to remain nearly stationary in the sky. Three or more satellites, suitably placed around the equatorial orbit, can provide worldwide communications links. Various organizations, serving commercial, private, or government interests, have been set up to provide worldwide communications; notably **Intelsat** (International Telecommunications Satellite Organization), founded in 1964, which now has over 100 member countries.

communism A movement based on the principle of communal ownership of all property. It is associated with *The Communist Manifesto* (1848) of Marx and Engels according to which the capitalist profit-based system of private ownership is replaced by a society in which the means of production are communally owned. This process, initiated by the overthrow of the bourgeoisie (*see* MARXISM), passes through a phase marked by the dictatorship of the proletariat and the preparatory stage of *socialism.

In the second half of the 19th century Marxist theories motivated several social democratic parties in Europe, although their policies later aimed at reforming capitalism (hence the epithet "reformist") rather than overthrowing it. The exception was the Russian Social Democratic Labour Party, which finally demolished the Tsar's regime in the Revolution of November 1917. In 1918 this party changed its name to the Communist Party of the Soviet Union, thus establishing the distinction between communism and socialism (*see* LENIN, VLADIMIR ILICH).

After the success of the Russian Revolution many socialist parties in other countries became communist parties, owing allegiance of varying degrees to the Soviet Communist Party (*see* INTERNATIONAL). In 1944–46 communist regimes were set up with the aid of the Soviet army in several E European countries. In 1949 the communists in China, again with Soviet support, overthrew the Nationalists and inaugurated the People's Republic of China. In the early 1970s the term **Eurocommunism** was introduced to refer to the policies of communist parties in W Europe. Communist parties have been electorally significant in France and Italy. In 1989 communist rule collapsed in Poland, Hungary, Czechoslovakia, Bulgaria, Romania, and East Germany; the Soviet Communist Party was suspended following the failed coup attempted by hardliners in 1991. However, communist governments have since been reelected in several of these countries.

Communism Peak (Russian name: Pik Kommunizma) 38 59N 72 01E The highest mountain in Tadzhikistan, in the Pamirs; the highest mountain in the former Soviet Union. Height: 7495 m (24 589 ft).

community In ecology, an interdependent group of living organisms that occupies a particular habitat. The plants and animals of a community are closely associated with each other in various ecological relationships: for example, they depend on one another for food (*see* FOOD CHAIN). The size and composition of the community depend on the habitat and climate; it may show seasonal changes. During ecological *succession, the structure of a community constantly changes until the stable climax community is established. *See also* ECOLOGY.

community service A form of sentence introduced in the UK by the Criminal Justice Act (1972). It requires an offender to work for a prescribed number of hours on behalf of the community instead of being imprisoned or fined. In the UK the offender must be aged 16 or over, have given consent, and have committed no violence.

Como 45 48N 09 05E A city in N Italy, in Lombardy on Lake Como. Known as Comum in Roman times, it is the birthplace of the elder and younger Pliny. It has a 15th-century marble cathedral and a gothic town hall. Como is an important tourist centre and its industries include the famous silk factories. Population (1995 est): 96 900.

Comoros, Union of the A country consisting of a group of islands in the Indian Ocean, between Madagascar and the African mainland. The main islands are Grand Comoro, Anjouan, and Mohéli; another island, Mayotte, has remained French. The population is of mixed African and Arab descent. *Economy*: almost entirely agricultural. Sugar cane was formerly the main crop but others, such as vanilla and perfume plants, are now increasing in importance. *History*: became a French colony in the 19th century. At first joined to Madagascar, the Comoros became a separate French overseas territory in 1947. In a referendum in 1974 the islands (except Mayotte) voted in favour of independence, recognized by France in 1976. From 1979 to 1989 effective control lay with the mercenary leader Bob Denard; he was ousted by the French after the assassination of President Ahmed Abdallah in 1989. In 1997 Anjouan and Mohéli declared independence from Comoros, seeking a resumption of French rule. In December 2001 voters backed a new federal constitution under which each of the three main islands will have financial and legislative autonomy. Official languages: French and Arabic; Swahili is also used commercially. Currency: CFA franc of 100 centimes. Area: 1862 sq km (719 sq mi). Population (2003 est): 584 000. Capital: Moroni.

compact disc (**CD**) A 120 mm plastic disc used for storing digitized information, especially in the high-fidelity recording of music. They are also used as high-capacity read-only memories (**CD-ROM**) for computers. Re-recordable CDs (**CD-RW**) are increasingly popular for data storage. Digital versatile disks (**DVD**) are similar to CDs but have a higher capacity; they are increasingly replacing videos as a means of recording films for home entertainment. *See* INTERACTIVE COMPACT DISC.

Companions of Honour, Order of the (**CH**) British order of chivalry, instituted in 1917. It comprises the sovereign and not more than 65 men and women who have made conspicuous contributions to the nation.

compass A device for determining the direction of magnetic north. The magnetic compass, which has been in use as an aid to navigation probably since the 2nd century BC, consists of a magnetic needle balanced on a point, allowing it to pivot freely. The S end of the magnet indicates magnetic N. Magnetic compasses are subject to interference from nearby ferrous metal objects and fittings, and compasses must be adjusted to compensate for distortion. Compensation must also be made, in the reading of a compass, for magnetic N not being in the same direction as geographic N in most longitudes. A more sophisticated kind of compass,

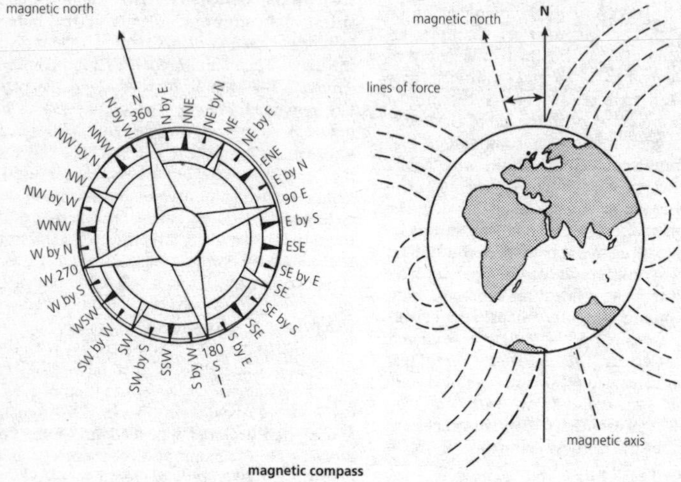

magnetic compass

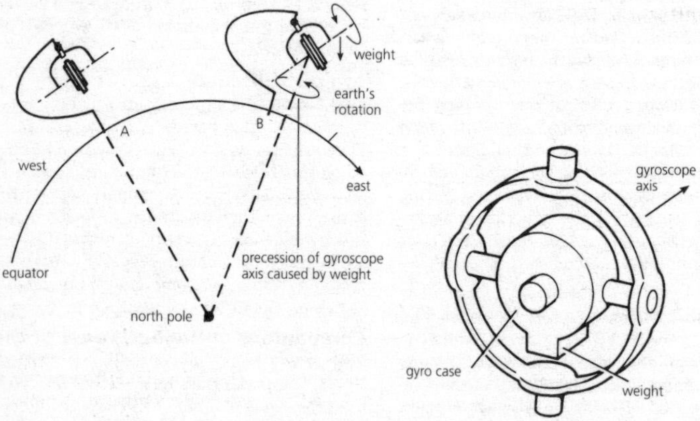

gyrocompass

compass. In the magnetic compass, the magnetized needle lines up with the earth's magnetic field. In the gyrocompass a spinning gyroscope is suspended on three mutually perpendicular frames. The axis of spin of a free gyroscope shifts round as the earth rotates: as the axis of the gyrocompass moves from the horizontal at position A to position B, a weight pulls it downwards. As a result of the gyroscopic effect, the axis shifts round at right angles to the gravitational force (precesses) and describes a circle around the N–S direction. When the precession is damped, the gyroscope axis settles down pointing N.

used on larger vessels and in aircraft, is the **gyrocompass**, which employs the effect of the earth's rotation on the orientation of a spinning object's axis of rotation.

compass plant A perennial herbaceous plant, *Silphium laciniatum*, of the North American prairie. Its oval leaves are orientated N–S to avoid the intense midday radiation. 1–2 m high, it is sometimes cultivated and is also known as turpentine plant, from the substances that ooze from the stem. Family: *Compositae*.

Compiègne 49 25N 2 50E A town and resort in N France, in the Oise department on the River Oise. Joan of Arc was captured here by the English in 1430. A railway coach in the forest of Compiègne was the scene of the signing of the Armistice (1918) ending World War I and of the agreement made between the Pétain government and Hitler in 1940. Population (latest est): 44 703.

complementary medicine *See* ALTERNATIVE MEDICINE.

complex numbers Quantities that consist of a real number and an imaginary number. They may be written in the form $a + ib$, where a and b are real numbers and $i = \sqrt{-1}$. Two complex numbers can be added and subtracted: for example $(a + ib) + (c + id) = (a + c) + i(b + d)$. They may also be multiplied and divided into each other. A complex number $a + ib$ may be thought of as a pair of ordered numbers (a,b) similar to a pair of Cartesian coordinates (x,y) (*see* COORDINATE SYSTEMS). Then (a,b) can be regarded as a point on a plane called the complex plane or Argand diagram in which the real axis is taken as horizontal and the imaginary axis as vertical.

Compositae (*or* **Asteraceae**) The largest family of flowering plants (about 900 genera and 14 000 species). They vary from small herbs to trees and are found worldwide. The tiny flowers are grouped into heads that resemble a single large flower. The individual florets may be similar, as in thistles, or of two types (disc and ray flowers), as in daisies. Many composites are cultivated as ornamentals (e.g. chrysanthemums and dahlias); others are agricultural weeds (daisies, dandelions, etc.) and some are edible (e.g. lettuce).

Composite order *See* ORDERS OF ARCHITECTURE.

comprehensive schools Secondary schools attended by children of all abilities. In the UK the widespread introduction of comprehensive schools was started in 1965 by the Labour Government and by the late 1990s some 92% of the secondary-school population attended comprehensives. This resulted in many former grammar schools becoming comprehensives. Since 1979 Local Education Authorities (LEAs) have no longer been required to abolish selective schools; however, since 1998 they will be obliged to do so if a ballot of local parents supports such a move.

Compton, Arthur Holly (1892–1962) US physicist, who in 1923 discovered the **Compton effect** (increase in wavelength of electromagnetic radiation when scattered by free electrons). He could only explain the effect by assuming that the radiation consisted of photons, then still a novel idea. He shared the 1927 Nobel Prize with C. T. R. *Wilson.

Compton-Burnett, Dame Ivy (1892–1969) British novelist. *Pastors and Masters* (1925) was the first of a series of 17 novels set in a stylized Victorian-Edwardian upper-class world. The series includes *Manservant and Maidservant* (1947) and *Mother and Son* (1955).

computer A device for processing information at high speeds, by electronic methods. The principles behind the modern computer were conceived by Charles Babbage in the 19th century. The first practical machines were built in Britain and the USA during World War II. Postwar developments in information theory and the invention of the transistor made possible the computer revolution of the next 20 years. Since the 1970s, advances in integrated circuits using silicon chips have led to the successive development of minicomputers, microcomputers (or personal computers), lap top computers, and personal digital assistants.

A **digital computer** processes information in the form of groups of binary numbers (*see* BIT), which are represented by the on and off positions of electronic switches. The sequence of operations it performs on this information is controlled by a program, and the suite of programs that enables a computer to perform useful functions is called its software. The physical equipment, or hardware, of a computer generally has three main components: the central processing unit (CPU), main memory, and peripheral devices that enable information to be fed into the machine, display it in a readable form, or act as auxiliary memory. Input, formerly by punched tape or cards, is now by keyboard at a visual display unit (VDU) or by methods of automatic data capture, such as optical character recognition (OCR). Output is by printout on paper, VDU, or magnetic disc or tape. New developments, such as the development of CPUs that work much faster by using optical rather than electrical impulses, promise further increases in the power of computers. The transputer, which harnesses several microprocessors in parallel, now offers microcomputer users the computing speed of a large mainframe.

An **analog computer** is a device that deals with continuously varying physical quantities, such as current or voltage. They are used mainly for simulation or monitoring and controlling continuous processes in industry or scientific research.

computer virus An unauthorized computer program that exploits weaknesses in a computer's operating system to insert itself into the system; it then propagates itself to other machines via networks or disks. It interferes with the machine's operation, and in some cases destroys data held on the machine.

Comte, Auguste (1798–1857) French philosopher. Often said to be the founder of sociology, he coined the term, although work of a sociological nature had been done long before. He is best remembered for his positivism (the view that society could be studied scientifically by natural-science methods and was subject to general laws). His principal work is *Cours de philosophie positive* (6 vols, 1830–42).

Conakry (*or* **Konakry**) 9 25N 13 56W The capital of Guinea, a port in the SW on Tombo Island, which is linked to the mainland by a causeway. It was founded by the French in 1884 and became capital in 1893. Population (1999 est): 1 764 000.

concentration camp A prison camp in which large numbers of people are held without legal process, usually because of their politics or ethnicity; they may be subjected to coercion (forced labour) or even extermination. The first such camps were established by the British during the Boer War in order to isolate the Boer guerrillas from the civilian population. Some 20 000 people, mostly women and children, died. From 1933 the name was used by the German Nazis for their labour and death camps. It is estimated that 20 million people died in the camps before and during World War II, from deliberate murder, starvation, exposure, etc. (*see* HOLOCAUST). Forced labour camps were used in the Soviet Union (the Gulags) and other totalitarian states.

concerto A musical composition for one or more solo instruments and orchestra, usually in three movements (a *sonata form movement, a slow movement, and a rondo finale). In the late 18th century Mozart perfected the form in his piano concertos; subsequent concertos have been written in a number of different styles.

conch A heavy-shelled marine *snail of the family *Strombidae* (about 80 species). Conch shells have a triangular outer whorl with a broad lip and can be 2–35 cm long. Indo-Pacific spider conchs (genus *Lambis*) have long horns around the aperture of their shell.

Concord 42 28N 71 17W A city in the USA, in Massachusetts on the Concord River. The first battle of the American Revolution occurred here on 19 April 1775. Population (latest est): 17 080.

Concorde An Anglo-French four-engined supersonic passenger aircraft. Test-flown in 1969, it went into regular transatlantic service in 1976. In July 2000 a Concorde crashed on take-off from Paris, killing 115 people, and all Concordes were immediately grounded for modifications. Although they returned to service in 2001 they were finally withdrawn on the grounds of high cost in 2003.

concrete A building material that was used by the Romans but in its modern form came into use after the invention of Portland *cement in 1824. Concrete consists of a mixture of a cement, usually Portland cement, and an aggregate of sand, gravel, and broken stones. Water is added to this mixture and complex hydration reactions cause the cement to harden around the aggregate. The material can be reinforced with steel bars (usually up to 50 mm in diameter) to increase its tensile strength. **Reinforced concrete** was invented in France in about 1850. In **prestressed concrete** the concrete is maintained in a state of compression by stretching the steel reinforcing wires (usually 6 mm in diameter) and keeping them in a state of tension after the concrete has set around them. Prestressed concrete is now widely used as a structural material as it has a reduced tendency to bend under load.

condensation 1. A change of physical state from a gas or vapour to a liquid. Thus as a gas is cooled below a certain temperature it may (depending on the pressure) condense to the liquid. Condensation occurs in buildings when warm moist air comes in contact with cold surfaces, such as windows and uninsulated walls. **2.** A type of organic chemical reaction in which two molecules combine to form a larger molecule with elimination of a smaller molecule, such as water or methanol.

conditioned reflex A *reflex response evoked by a stimulus other than that which normally produces it. A classic example is provided by Pavlov's experiments with dogs. The normal stimulus causing salivation (i.e. food) was paired with a different stimulus (a ringing bell) so often that eventually the bell by itself caused the dogs to salivate. A conditioned reflex gradually disappears if the stimulus is presented repeatedly; this process is called extinction. *See also* CONDITIONING.

conditioning The process of modifying behaviour by changing the stimuli (and therefore responses) associated with it. Classical conditioning occurs when a response is associated with a stimulus by pairing the stimulus with an event that causes the response by reflex (*see* CONDITIONED REFLEX). Operant conditioning is brought about by either rewarding or punishing an action by the subject, which thus either encourages or discourages the behaviour (*see also* AVERSION THERAPY). Behaviourism uses both forms of conditioning to explain how people learn.

condom *See* CONTRACEPTION; SEXUALLY TRANSMITTED DISEASE.

condor A huge South American *vulture, *Vultur gryphus*, found high in the Andes. It is black with a white ruff, bare pink head and neck, and has a wingspan of 3 m. It feeds chiefly on carrion but also takes lambs and young deer. The very rare Californian condor (*Gymnogyps californianus*) is smaller with a bare yellow head and red neck.

conduction 1. (thermal) The transfer of heat from a region of high temperature to one of lower temperature, without the transfer of matter. It occurs as a result of the transfer of kinetic *energy by collisions between atoms and molecules in gases, liquids, and nonmetallic solids. In metals, which are the best thermal and electrical conductors, the energy is transferred by collisions between the free electrons that move through the crystal lattice and the ions of the lattice. **2.** (electrical) The passage of an electric current through a substance. In metals, the best conductors, it results from the passage of free electrons moving in one direction under the influence of an electric field. In an electrolyte it is due to the passage of positive ions in one direction and negative ions in the other. In gases it is due to positive ions flowing in one direction and electrons in the other. In *semiconductors it results from the passage of electrons in one direction and positive holes in the other.

cone The structure, also called a strobilus, that bears the reproductive organs (sporophylls) in some pteridophytes (club mosses, horsetails, etc.) and the gymnosperms (conifers and related plants). In conifers both male and female cones are produced: the familiar woody cones of pines, larches, etc., are female strobili, made up of overlapping woody structures called bract scales, which bear the sporophylls in their axils.

Confederate States The 11 southern states of the USA that seceded from the Union (1860–61), precipitating the US *Civil War: South Carolina, Georgia, Texas, Virginia, Arkansas, Tennessee, North Carolina, Mississippi, Florida, Alabama, and Louisiana.

Confederation of British Industry (**CBI**) The employers' federation in the UK. The CBI formulates industry's views on economic matters and is consulted by the government.

confession The admission of sins by a penitent seeking forgiveness. As a religious practice it originated in Judaism and was taken over by the early Christian Church. The fourth Lateran Council (1215) made private confession to a priest empowered to grant absolution (auricular confession) incumbent on all Christians once a year. In the Roman Catholic and Orthodox Churches auricular confession is part of the *sacrament of penance. In most Protestant churches general confession by the whole congregation is practised.

confirmation A Christian rite generally held to complete the initiation of a member into the Church. In the Eastern Orthodox Church, it is administered by a priest immediately after baptism and followed by Holy Communion; in the West, it is conferred by a bishop—in the Roman Catholic Church not before the seventh birthday and in the Anglican Churches after the candidate has undergone instruction in the faith (traditionally at the age of 11 or 12 but now often as an adult).

Confucius (Kong Zi *or* K'ung-fu-tzu; c.551–479 BC) Chinese philosopher, the founder of **Confucianism**. As a minor official, he gathered numerous disciples, mainly young gentlemen who wished to enter government service. Promoted to ministerial rank, he became famous for his just and effective policies, but on the ruler's refusing to heed his advice, he resigned (c.496). The teaching of Confucianism is contained in five books. While retaining the concept of a divine will (*ming*), Confucianism emphasizes man's duty to his fellows. It was the official religion of China until the 1960s.

Congo, Democratic Republic of (name from 1971 until 1997: Zaïre) A large country in central equatorial Africa, with a short coastline on the Atlantic Ocean. It is drained by the Congo River and fringed along its E border by a chain of lakes, including Lake Tanganyika, comprising part of the Great Rift Valley. Most of the population is African, the largest groups being Luka, Mongo, and Kongo. *Economy*: agricultural production has fallen owing to drought and recurrent civil wars. The chief cash crops are palm oil, coffee, and cotton. The chief export is copper and the country is the world's chief producer of industrial diamonds and cobalt. Other minerals include manganese, zinc, gold, and uranium; offshore oil has been exploited since 1975. *History*: when the Portuguese penetrated the region in the late 15th century it was dominated by the kingdom of the Kongo. In the late 19th century it was explored by Livingstone and, under Belgian auspices, Stanley. Leopold II of the Belgians established personal rule over the Congo Free State, which was internationally recognized at the Conference of Berlin (1884–85). In 1908, annexed by Belgium, it became the colony of the Belgian Congo. It became independent as the Democratic Republic of the Congo (1960). Civil war followed and in 1965 Mobutu Sese Seko seized power. The country was renamed Zaïre in 1971. In 1977–78 invasion forces twice tried to topple Mobutu. Zaïre was a one-party state from 1978 until 1991, when moves were made towards a multi-party system and a transitional government was elected (1992). However, Mobutu's attempts to block this process led to economic collapse. In 1996, civil war broke out when Tutsi rebels attacked Hutu militiamen who had taken refuge from Rwanda. By June 1997 the rebels held most of the country and Mobutu fled. The rebel leader, Laurent Kabila, became head of state and the country reverted to the name Democratic Republic of Congo. Civil war erupted again (August 1998) when many of Kabila's former supporters rebelled against him. The rebels were backed by Rwanda and Uganda, while Angolan, Zimbabwean, and Sudanese forces came to the aid of Kabila. Although the national governments signed a ceasefire agreement (1999), fighting has continued. Laurent Kabila was killed during a coup attempt in January 2001 and succeeded by his son Maj-Gen Joseph Kabila. In 2002 Rwanda withdrew its forces and Kabila agreed to establish a transitional power-sharing administration pending elections in 2004. Official language: French. Currency: Congolese franc. Area: 2 345 409 sq km (895 348 sq mi). Population (2003 est): 52 771 000. Capital: Kinshasa.

Congo-Brazzaville, Republic of (name until 1960: Middle Congo; name from 1960 to 1999: Republic of Congo) A country in W central Africa, bordering on the Congo River. The uplands give way to plains in the NE. The population is composed chiefly of Bantu tribes. *Economy*: largely agricultural, the main cash crops being sugar cane, palm oil, cocoa, and tobacco. Minerals include lead, zinc, and gold; oil was discovered in 1969 and is now an important source of revenue. *History*: in the 15th century the Portuguese established trading relations with the Congo kingdom. In the 19th century the exploration of the Frenchman Pierre de Brazza (1852–1905) led to the establishment of the colony of Middle Congo, which in 1910 became one of the four territories of French Equatorial Africa. In 1958 it attained internal self-government as a member of the French Community and in 1960 became independent. Maj Marien Ngouabi came to power in a military coup (1968) but was assassinated (1977) and the government taken over by a military committee. Plans for a multiparty system were endorsed by a referendum (1992) and elections were held in 1993. However, the result was disputed, leading to fighting between rival militias. In 1997 the former military leader Denis Sassou Nguesso was reinstated in a coup; he was elected president in 2002. Sporadic fighting has continued. Official language: French. Currency: CFA franc of 100 centimes. Area: 342 000 sq km (132 018 sq mi). Population (2003 est): 3 724 000. Capital: Brazzaville.

Congo River (name from 1971 until 1997: Zaïre River) The second longest river in Africa. Its true source is disputed, one headstream being the River Lualaba and the other the River Chambezi. Below their confluence it flows N, as the Congo River after Boyoma Falls. It flows W then SW to enter the Atlantic Ocean at Boma. The river is an important source of hydroelectric power since the construction of dams in the 1970s. Length: 4820 km (3000 mi).

Congregationalism In Christianity, a form of church government in which centralized authority is rejected and each congregation is autonomous. Congregationalist groups were active at the time of the Reformation, and in England the Independents, as they were known, were prominent during the Civil War and Commonwealth. Congregationalism spread to America, where it flourished. In England, the United Reformed Church was founded in 1972 by the union of the Congregationalists with the Presbyterians.

Congress The legislature of the USA instituted by the constitution (1789) and comprising the Senate, the upper house, and the House of Representatives, the lower house. The Senate serves as a check on the larger House of Representatives, with which it has equal legislative responsibility as well as further powers to ratify treaties and confirm appointments. Each state in the Union is equally represented by two senators. There are 435 seats in the House of Representatives, which are allocated among the states according to population.

Congreve, William (1670–1729) British dramatist. Educated in Ireland, he returned to England in 1688 to study law but under the patronage of *Dryden entered the literary world instead. The comedies *Love for Love* (1695) and *The Way of the World* (1700) are his best-known plays.

conic sections Geometrical figures produced by the intersection of a plane and a cone. If the plane cuts the cone at right angles to its axis the figure is a circle. If the plane is tilted slightly an *ellipse is formed. If the plane is tilted further, until it lies parallel to the side of the cone, the figure is a *parabola. Tilted more, the figure becomes a *hyperbola in which the plane also intersects another cone the vertex of which touches the vertex of the first cone, so that a hyperbola has two branches.

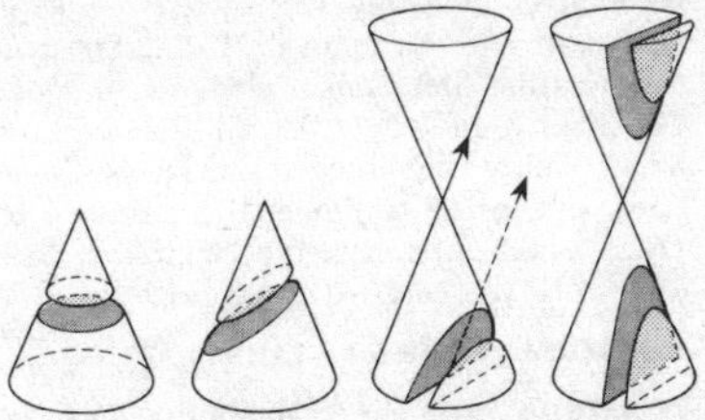

conic section. The circle, ellipse, parabola, and hyperbola are produced by slicing through the cone as shown.

conifer A *gymnosperm tree of the widely distributed phylum *Coniferophyta* (550 species), most abundant in the colder temperate zones, especially in the north; elsewhere they are usually found at high altitudes. Nearly all conifers are evergreen (larches are exceptions), with simple needle-like or scalelike leaves. The reproductive organs are typically borne in separate male and female *cones, usually on the same tree, and produce winged seeds that are dispersed by wind. The principal families are the *Pinaceae* (pines, cedars, spruces, firs, larches, hemlocks, etc.); *Cupressaceae* (cypresses, junipers, arbor vitae, etc.); *Taxodiaceae* (sequoias, swamp cypress, etc.); *Taxaceae* (yews); and *Araucariaceae* (monkey puzzle, etc.).

conjugation The process by which exchange of genetic material occurs in certain lower organisms by means of a connection between the cytoplasm of the two "mating" individuals. In ciliate protozoa and certain algae it is a type of sexual reproduction, the gametes (or gametic nuclei) passing through a cytoplasmic bridge (protozoa) or a conjugation tube (algae). In bacteria the connection between cells is by means of special hairs (pili) or cell-to-cell bridges.

conjunctivitis Inflammation of the conjunctiva—the membrane that covers the surface of the eye and lines the eyelids. Popularly known as pinkeye, it is marked by itching, redness, and watering of the eye. It may be caused by allergy to drugs or pollen; bacterial infection; or mechanical irritation.

Connacht (*or* **Connaught**) A province and ancient kingdom of the NW Republic of Ireland. It consists of the counties of Galway, Leitrim, Mayo, Roscommon, and Sligo. Area: 17 122 sq km (6611 sq mi). Population (2002): 464 050.

Connecticut A state in the NE USA, in New England. It is one of the most densely populated states in the USA. Manufacturing is important. Yale University is at New Haven. *History*: one of the original 13 colonies in the USA, it was first explored by the Dutch in the early 17th century. The first settlement was by English colonists from the Massachusetts Bay Colony (1633–35). Area: 12 973 sq km (5009 sq mi). Population (2000): 3 405 565. Capital: Hartford.

connective tissue The tissue that supports, binds, or separates the specialized tissues and organs of the body. Connective tissue consists of a semifluid ground substance of polysaccharide and protein in which are embedded white collagen fibres, yellow elastic fibres, and various cells (including fibroblasts, which produce the ground substance and the fibres). The amount of collagen determines the toughness of the tissue. Specialized connective tissue includes fatty tissue, blood, bone, and cartilage.

Connemara An area in the W Republic of Ireland, in Co Galway bordering on the Atlantic Ocean. It contains many lakes, peat bogs, and the Twelve Bens, a group of quartzite mountains.

Connery, Sir Sean (Thomas C.; 1929–) Scottish film actor who became famous as James Bond, a role he first played in *Doctor No* (1962). Other films include *The Name of the Rose* (1986) and *Entrapment* (1999).

conquistador (Spanish: conqueror) One of the men who conquered the Indians of Central and South America for Spain in the first half of the 16th century. Few in number, the conquistadores were driven by a fanatical desire to find fame and gold and to serve the Roman Catholic Church. The most famous were Hernán *Cortés and Francisco *Pizarro.

Conrad, Joseph (Teodor Josef Konrad Watęcz Korzeniowski; 1857–1924) Polish-born British novelist, who knew no English before he was 20. Orphaned at the age of 11, he went to Marseilles in 1874, where he became a sailor. Conrad published his first novel, *Almayer's Folly*, in 1895. His seagoing experiences influenced both the themes of his fiction and his own moral outlook. His major novels include *Lord Jim* (1900), *Nostromo* (1904), *The Secret Agent* (1907), and *Under Western Eyes* (1911).

Conservative Party A UK political party that grew out of the *Tory party in the 1830s under the leadership of Sir Robert *Peel. His repeal of the *Corn Laws (1846) caused a split in the party, with the Peelites later joining the Liberal Party. Under the leadership of *Disraeli the Conservatives acquired a distinct philosophy that combined identification with the monarchy, the British Empire, and the Church of England with social reform. Under *Salisbury and then Balfour the party was almost continuously in power from 1886 to 1905 and again, under Bonar *Law, *Baldwin, Neville *Chamberlain, and *Churchill, from 1922 to 1945, being the dominant party in the coalitions of 1931–35 and 1940–45. It was again in office from 1951 to 1964, led successively by Churchill, Eden (*see* AVON, (ROBERT) ANTHONY EDEN, 1ST EARL OF), *Macmillan, and Home, from 1970 to 1974 under *Heath, and from 1979 to 1997 under *Thatcher and then John *Major. The party's disunity over European integration contributed to its heavy defeat in 1997, after which William Hague became leader. The Conservatives suffered a second crushing defeat in 2001 and Hague resigned. Iain Duncan Smith took over the leadership, but was replaced by Michael *Howard in 2003.

Constable, John (1776–1837) British landscape painter. After working for his father, he trained in London at the Royal Academy schools. He painted the Suffolk countryside, Hampstead Heath, and Salisbury Cathedral with a particular concern for changing weather conditions, exemplified in *The Leaping Horse* (1825; Royal Academy) and *Dedham Vale* (1828; National Gallery, Edinburgh).

Constance, Council of (1414–18) The 16th ecumenical council of the Roman Catholic Church, held in the German town of Constance, which ended the *Great Schism by electing Pope Martin V (1417). It decreed that the authority of a general council was superior to that of the pope.

Constance, Lake (German name: Bodensee) A lake on the River Rhine in W Germany, Switzerland, and Austria. Area: 531 sq km (205 sq mi).

constantan An alloy of 55% copper and 45% nickel. It is used in electrical equipment, such as resistors and *thermocouples, because it has a high electrical resistance that does not change with temperature.

Constantine the Great (?285–337 AD) Roman emperor in the West (312–24) and sole emperor (324–37). The son of Constantius (c. 250–306), Roman emperor in the West (305–06), Constantine was acclaimed as his father's successor by his troops at York but did not secure his position until he defeated his rival Maxentius (d. 312). He became sole emperor after defeating the Eastern emperor Licinius (c. 270–325; reigned 311–24). Constantine was the first Roman emperor to adopt Christianity. In 313 he issued the Edict of Milan, which established toleration of Christians, and in 325 summoned the Council of *Nicaea, the first general council of the Church. He was baptized on his deathbed.

Constantinople *See* ISTANBUL.

constellations The 88 areas into which the N and S hemispheres of the sky are now divided, using established boundaries. Each star, galaxy, or other celestial body lies within, or sometimes overlaps, the boundaries of one of the constellations and is often named in terms of this constellation. They originally had no fixed limits but were groups of stars forming a distinctive pattern outlining a mythological hero, animal, etc.

constitution The principles according to which a country is governed. The UK has an unwritten constitution comprising some statutes, much *common law, and a good deal of custom. In many countries, the constitution is written. The **US constitution** was drawn up in 1787, ratified in 1788, and came into effect in 1789. It contains 7 articles and 27 amendments of which 10 constitute the *Bill of Rights (1791). It defines the separation of powers, designed as a system of checks and balances, between the legislature, the executive, and the judiciary. Amendments subsequent to the Bill of Rights include the abolition of slavery (13), universal suffrage (15), and prohibition of liquor (18).

constrictor A snake belonging to the family *Boidae* (70 species) occurring chiefly in tropical regions. Constrictors are nonvenomous and kill their prey by coiling their thick muscular body around it and squeezing until it suffocates. They often have claws, which are vestigial limbs. The family comprises two subfamilies, *Boinae* (*see* BOA) and *Pythoninae* (*see* PYTHON).

constructivism A movement in abstract sculpture, architecture, and design, which was launched in Russia by the *Realist Manifesto* (1920) of the brothers Naum Gabo (1890–1977) and Antoine Pevsner (1886–1962) with the aim of freeing contemporary art from political and social overtones. The chief principles of constructivism were functionalism, the articulation of space, and the use of modern materials, such as plastic and steel.

consuls The two magistrates who held supreme civil and military authority under the *Roman Republic. They were elected annually by the Comitia Centuriata and presided over the Senate. Under the Empire they were nominated by the emperor and held office for only two to four months, the posts becoming honorary.

contact lenses A removable form of lens worn directly against the eye to replace spectacles for long or short sight or to protect the eye in some disorders of the outer transparent layer (cornea). Modern plastic contact lenses are hard (corneal), gas-permeable (allowing oxygen to permeate the cornea), or soft (hydrophilic).

contempt of court An act or omission that tends to undermine the authority of a court or that is likely to prejudice a fair trial. Examples are insulting a presiding judge or failing to comply with a court order; magistrates are not empowered to commit for contempt. The publication of matters on which the court is to decide is also a contempt. A person found in contempt is liable to a fine or imprisonment.

continental drift The theory, first set out in 1912 by Alfred Wegener, that the continents are not fixed in position but drift slowly (*see also* PLATE TECTONICS). Wegener's work was based on similarities in geological structures, flora and fauna, and coastal outlines; in recent years geophysical data, particularly from geomagnetic studies, have provided firmer evidence. It is believed that about 200 million years ago a supercontinent (termed Pangaea) began to break up (*see* GONDWANALAND; LAURASIA) and the fragments drifted apart until the continents reached their present positions. It is probable that continents have been joining together and breaking up throughout the earth's history.

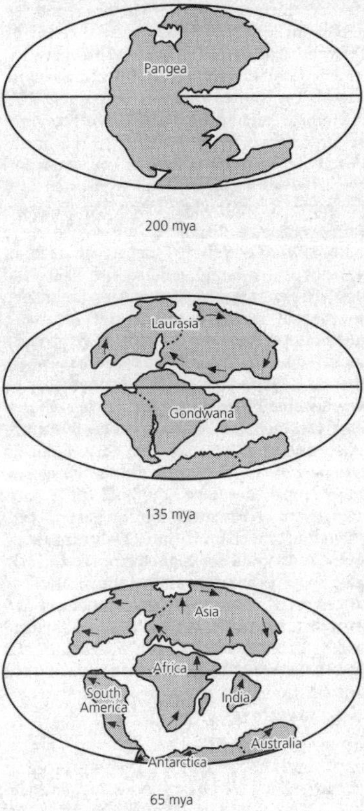

continental drift. The position of the continents (from top to bottom) 200 million years ago, 135 million years ago, and 65 million years ago.

C

continental shelf The area of sea floor adjacent to the continents, dipping gently from the shoreline to a depth of about 200 m. At this depth, the shelf edge, the continental slope begins, dipping more steeply to the ocean bottom. Shelves tend to be wider off low-lying regions than mountainous regions; the average width is about 70 km.

contraception The prevention of unwanted pregnancy, also known as birth control and family planning. The rhythm method and coitus interruptus are the most simple but least reliable. In the former intercourse is avoided around the middle of the menstrual cycle, when ovulation is most likely to occur; in the latter the penis is withdrawn before ejaculation. Barrier methods include the condom (or sheath), which is worn over the penis, and the diaphragm, which is fitted over the cervix of the womb and should be used with a spermicidal jelly. Condoms also offer protection against sexually transmitted diseases, including AIDS. The female condom (e.g. Femidom) offers similar protection. More reliable is the intrauterine device (IUD)—a loop or coil, often impregnated with copper, that is inserted into the womb. Its method of action is not known. Some women are unable to use an IUD as it causes side effects (heavy menstrual bleeding or recurrent infection). Since the 1960s, the most efficient means of preventing pregnancy has been by taking hormonal pills (*see* ORAL CONTRACEPTIVE), but this, too, may produce side effects and is unsuitable for some women. Alternatively, hormonal contraceptives may be administered by means of skin patches. A long-term contraceptive method is the intramuscular injection, at two- or three-monthly intervals, of a synthetic hormone (progestogen). Recently developed methods for women include the hormonal "morning-after" pill, which must be taken within 72 hours of intercourse and should not be used more frequently than once per month; the administration of progestogen by means of a subcutaneous implant or a vaginal ring, which release the hormone; and hormonal IUDs (e.g. Mirena). *See also* STERILIZATION; STOPES, MARIE (CHARLOTTE CARMICHAEL).

contract In law, an enforceable promise or bargain, usually written but sometimes oral. A simple promise for which nothing is given in exchange is not a contract and is only enforceable at law as a *deed. Something of value, called "consideration," must be exchanged in return for the promise; the value must be real but need not be equivalent. Breach of contract, meaning failure to fulfil its conditions, may result in the offender being sued for damages by the other party.

contralto The deepest female singing voice. Range: F below middle C to D an octave and a sixth above.

convection The transfer of heat within a fluid by means of motion of the fluid. Convection may be natural or forced. In natural convection, the fluid flows by virtue of the warmer part being less dense than the cooler part. Thus the warmer fluid rises and the colder fluid sinks under the influence of gravity. In forced convection, some external cause, such as a fan, drives colder fluid into a warmer one, or vice versa.

convergence (*or* **convergent evolution**) The development in unrelated animals of similarities resulting from adaption to the same way of life. Thus whales (mammals) and fish, both aquatic, have evolved similar features independently.

conversos (Spanish: converts) Spanish Jews who were forced to become Roman Catholics during the late 14th and 15th centuries. The Spanish *Inquisition was created largely to prevent the apostasy of conversos and **Moriscos** (Muslims forced to convert to Catholicism). Jews who adopted Spanish names and professed Christianity to avoid death at the hands of the Inquisition were called **Marranos** (Spanish: pigs).

Convocations of Canterbury and York The assemblies of the clergy of the two provinces of the Church of England. Dating from at least the 8th century, they were originally assemblies of bishops only. They later divided into two houses, an upper house composed of diocesan bishops and a lower house composed of certain lower clergy. The extent of their powers fluctuated, but they maintained the right to tax the clergy until after the Restoration. From 1717 to 1852 they were prevented by the Crown from dealing with questions of business and held only formal meetings. In 1969 many of their powers were assumed by the General Synod of the Church of England.

Convolvulus A widely distributed genus of annual or perennial twining plants (about 250 species). The flowers are funnel or bell-shaped and attractive. The Eurasian *bindweed (*C. arvensis*) is a noxious weed with deep persistent roots and rapidly growing stems. Some species, such as *C. althaeoides*, are cultivated in gardens.

Some have medicinal (purgative) properties. Family: *Convolvulaceae*.

Conwy 1. 53 18N 3 52W A market town and resort in North Wales, in Conwy county borough on the estuary of the River Conwy. It has a 13th-century castle. A tunnel under the estuary opened in 1991. Population (1991): 13 627. **2.** A county borough in N Wales created in 1996 from parts of Gwynedd and Clwyd. Area: 1130 sq km (436 sq mi). Population (2001): 109 597.

Cook, Captain James (1728–79) British navigator and cartographer. He joined the Royal Navy (1755) and served in the Seven Years' War (1756–63), during which he surveyed the St Lawrence River. His observations on the eclipse of the sun in 1766 were presented to the Royal Society, which gave him command of an expedition to Tahiti to observe the transit of the planet Venus across the sun and to discover Terra Australis, a presumed southern continent. The expedition set sail in the *Endeavour* in 1768 and, Venus observed, Cook went on to discover and chart New Zealand and the E coast of Australia, returning to England in 1771. His second voyage (1772–75) in the *Resolution*, accompanied by the *Adventure*, achieved the circumnavigation of the Antarctic. He charted Easter Island and discovered New Caledonia, the South Sandwich Islands, and South Georgia. On his return he received the Royal Society's Copley Medal for his dietary work (on avoiding scurvy). On his third voyage (1776–79) he was killed by Hawaiians.

Cook, Mount (Maori name: Aorangi) 43 37S 170 08E The highest mountain in New Zealand, in South Island in the Southern Alps. Height: 3764 m (12 349 ft).

Cook Islands A group of scattered islands in the SE Pacific Ocean, a New Zealand dependency. The chief islands are Rarotonga, Atiu, and Aitutaki. Fruit, copra, and mother-of-pearl are exported. Area: 241 sq km (93 sq mi). Population (1994): 18 500. Capital: Avarua.

Cookstown A district in central Northern Ireland in Co Tyrone. Area: 512 sq km (198 sq mi). Population (2001): 32 581.

coolabar A tree, *Eucalyptus microtheca*, growing to 25 m, common inland in W Australia. The wood is grey near the outside, deep red within. Also called jinbul, moolar, blackbox, and dwarf box, it is used for building. Family: *Myrtaceae*. *See also* EUCALYPTUS.

Coolidge, John Calvin (1872–1933) US statesman; Republican president (1923–29). His presidency followed the scandals of the administration (1921–23) of Warren Harding (1865–1923) but Coolidge's own honesty was never questioned. He supported US business at home and abroad, but did little to curb the speculation on the stock market that ended in the 1929 financial crash.

Cooper, Gary (Frank James C.; 1901–61) US film actor. He is best known for his portrayals of tough but sensitive heroes in Hollywood westerns. These include *The Virginian* (1929), *The Westerner* (1940), and *High Noon* (1952).

cooperative societies Societies set up to manufacture, buy, or sell produce, either without profit or with profits distributed to members or shareholders as dividends. The cooperative movement was inspired by the British philanthropist Robert *Owen in the early 19th century and was seen as an alternative to the hardship that seemed to be caused by competition. Cooperative societies in agriculture, in which machinery is shared and produce is marketed jointly, are common in both the advanced and developing countries. In the UK the largest cooperative is the Cooperative Wholesale Society (CWS).

coordinate systems Geometrical systems that locate points in space by a set of numbers. In **Cartesian coordinates**, devised by René *Descartes, a point is located by its distance from intersecting axes. In a plane (two dimensions) there are two axes and in space (three dimensions) there are three. Usually the axes are at right angles to each other and are known as rectangular axes, but oblique axes can also be used. **Polar coordinates** denote position by distance and direction. A fixed point, called the origin, and a fixed line, called the polar axis, are taken as the references. For any point, the polar coordinates are the length, r, of the radius of the circle centred at the origin and passing through the point, and the angle, θ, between this radius and the polar axis. In three dimensions, **spherical polar coordinates** are used. The radius of a sphere centred at the origin and the two angles it makes with the polar axis define the point. See illustration on p. 236.

coot An aquatic *rail of the genus *Fulica* (9 species). Coots have broadly lobed toes, diving deeply to feed on invertebrates and aquatic plants. The European coot (*F. atra*) occurs throughout the Old World and is 37 cm long with black plumage and a white bill and frontal shield.

Copenhagen (Danish name: København) 55 40N 12 35E The capital and chief port of Denmark, on the E coast of Sjælland. Notable buildings include the 17th-century Charlottenborg Palace (now the Royal Academy of Arts) and Christiansborg Palace (now the parliamentary and government buildings). *History*: already a human settlement in the year 900 AD, it became capital of Denmark in 1443. It was attacked by the Hanseatic League in the middle ages and by Sweden in the 17th century. In 1801 the Danish fleet was destroyed by Nel son at the battle of Copenhagen. In 1728, and again in 1795, it was badly destroyed by fire. Occupied by the Germans in World War II, it became the centre of a strong resistance movement. Population (2000 est): 485 699.

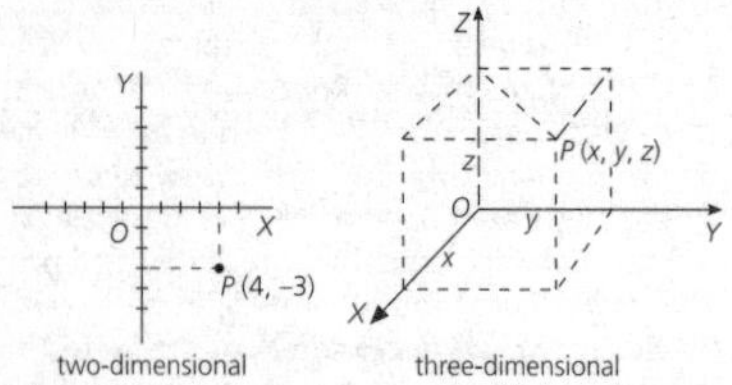

Cartesian coordinates

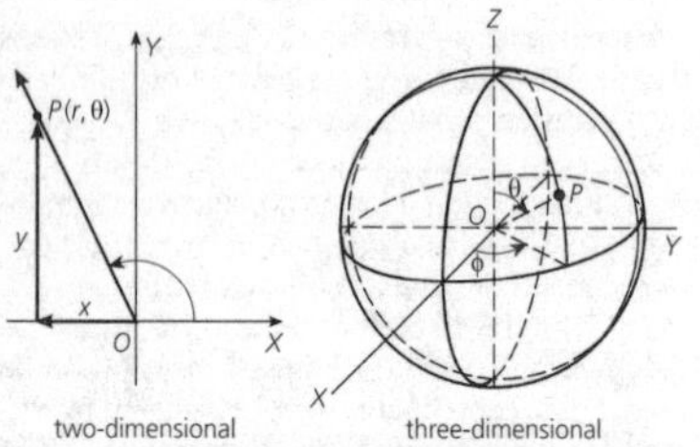

polar coordinates

coordinate systems. In two-dimensional Cartesian coordinates a point *P* is located by giving its *x*- and *y*-coordinates, in this case 4 and –3 (always given in this order, as shown). In three-dimensional Cartesian coordinates *P* is located in terms of three axes. In polar coordinates *P* is located by a radius *r* and an angle θ. In three dimensions a second angle, ϕ, is required. In the diagrams Cartesian coordinates are superimposed on the polar coordinates.

Copepoda A class of *crustaceans (7500 species), mostly 0.5–2 mm long, that have long antennae, a single median eye, and no carapace. There are 11 pairs of appendages on the head and thorax and forked tail filaments (furca). Copepods occur in abundance in fresh and salt water, forming a constituent of plankton. Most feed on microscopic plants or animals but some are parasitic on fish, other crustaceans, etc. *See also* CYCLOPS.

Copernicus, Nicolaus (1473–1543) Polish astronomer, formulator of the modern heliocentric theory of the solar system. After studying mathematics and music at Cracow and Bologna, Copernicus became interested in the problem of calculating planetary positions, since existing tables were out of date. He noticed that by using a system in which the earth revolved round the sun, instead of Ptolemy's geocentric system, these calculations would be much easier to make. Realizing that these ideas were at variance with the Church's view that the earth was at the centre of the universe, Copernicus only circulated them to a few friends. The full text of his book *De revolutionibus orbium coelestium* was published in 1543.

Copland, Aaron (1900–90) US composer, also active as a teacher, pianist, and champion of contemporary music. He is best known for his compositions in a popular style, such as the ballets *Billy the Kid* (1938) and *Rodeo* (1942). His other works employ a variety of styles and include a piano concerto (1927) in a jazz idiom, a *Piano Fantasy* (1950), and the tone poem *Inscape* (1967).

copper (Cu) A reddish-brown metal, known from prehistoric times and named after the island of Cyprus, which was the principal source in Roman times. It occurs naturally as the native element, the sulphide chalcopyrite ($CuFeS_2$), the carbonate malachite ($CuCO_3.Cu(OH)_2$), and other minerals. Copper is extracted by smelting and electrolysis. It is malleable, ductile, and is important because of its good electrical (second only to silver) and thermal conductivity. Copper is widely used in the electrical industry and in the form of copper pipes in plumbing. It is contained in the alloys *brass and *bronze. At no 29; at wt 63.546; mp 1084.7°C; bp 2563°C.

copra *See* COCONUT.

Coptic Church The largest Christian Church in Egypt. The Copts trace the history of their Church to St *Mark. As a result of its Monophysite beliefs, which were condemned at the Council of Chalcedon (451), the Coptic Church became somewhat isolated from other Christian bodies. The Muslim conquest of Egypt in 642, together with language and cultural differences, widened the division. The Church suffered some persecution under Arab dominion. In 1741 a number of Copts entered the Roman Catholic communion, becoming the Uniat Coptic Church. Alexandria held an eminent position in the early Church and remains the seat of the Coptic patriarch, who presides over the Church with 12 diocesan bishops. The Copts are in communion with the Armenian and Syrian (Orthodox) Churches.

copyright A type of intellectual property consisting of the rights of authors, composers, artists, photographers, publishers and others who create or publish original works to reproduce their works. In the UK protection is given by the Copyright Act (1956), the Copyright, Designs, and Patents Act (1988), and the European Single Market Act (1992). The Copyright (Computer Software) Amendment Act (1985) extends copyright to computer programs. In EU countries copyright protection now lasts for 70 years after the death of the copyright holder (or the date of publication, if later). In the USA (since 1998) it lasts for 70 years after the death of the copyright holder or 95 years after publication when the holder is a corporation. In contrast to a patent, copyright cannot exist in an idea, method, or scheme, but only in its expression. Infringement of copyright is known as piracy. Under the Universal Copyright Convention (1952, revised 1971), works must be marked with the symbol ©, the name of the copyright holder, and the date of first publication.

coracle An ancient boat, usually round, made of wickerwork or laths over which a waterproofed animal skin has been stretched. Coracles were used in Ireland and in Wales and other parts of W Britain.

coral A sedentary marine animal belonging to a class (*Anthozoa*) of cnidarians. They are found in all oceans, feeding mainly on small animals. Reproduction can be asexual (by budding) or sexual, the eggs being fertilized in the water.

The stony (*or* true) corals (order *Madreporaria*; about 1000 species) secrete a rigid external skeleton made of almost pure calcium carbonate. **Coral reefs** are slowly produced by succeeding generations of stony corals, occurring in dense colonies, chiefly at depths of less than 50 m and at temperatures above 20°C. Within this zone symbiotic algae (zooxanthellae) stimulate the growth of coral skeletons.

Coral Sea A section of the SW Pacific Ocean off NE Australia. It contains the *Great Barrier Reef.

coral snake A New World burrowing venomous snake that preys on other snakes. The main genus, *Micrurus* (40 species), ranges from the S USA to Argentina; most species are ringed with red, black, and yellow or white. Old World coral snakes are similar and found in SE Asia (genus *Calliophis*) and Africa (genus *Elaps*). Family: *Elapidae* (cobras, mambas, coral snakes). The rear-fanged false coral snakes have similar patterning but belong to the family *Colubridae* (grass snakes, etc.).

cor anglais A double-reeded musical instrument, the alto member of the oboe family. It is a transposing instrument, the notes sounding a fifth lower than written. It has a range of two and a half octaves from the E below middle C.

Cordaitales An order of extinct *gymnosperm trees that—with *Calamites*—formed vast forests during the Carboniferous and Permian periods (370–240 million years ago). The trees probably grew up to 30 m high, with strap-shaped leaves, up to 1 m long.

Córdoba 37 53N 4 46W A city in S Spain, in Andalusia on the River Guadalquivir. It became the capital of Moorish Spain in 756 AD and by the 10th century was Europe's largest cultural centre. Its immense Moorish cathedral (8th–10th centuries) was originally a mosque. Population (1998 est): 309 961.

Cordon Bleu Originally, the blue ribbon of the knight's grand cross of the Order of the Holy Spirit, the first order of the Bourbon kings. The term is now used to describe food, or a chef, that achieves a very high standard.

Corelli, Arcangelo (1653–1713) Italian violinist and composer. He established the concerto grosso, in which a small group of soloists (typically two violins and cello) is contrasted with the full orchestra. His most famous work is the *Christmas Concerto* for strings and continuo.

Corfu (Latin name: Corcyra; Modern Greek name: Kérkira *or* Kérkyra) A Greek island in the NE Ionian Sea. It has belonged to many powers, including Venice (1386–1797) and Britain (1815–64). The local produce includes olives, figs, and citrus fruit, and tourism is important. Area: 641 sq km (250 sq mi). Population (1991): 107 592. Chief town: Corfu.

corgi One of two breeds of working dog originating in SW Wales. The Cardigan Welsh corgi has a long tail, rounded ears, and a shortish coat, which may be reddish brown, streaked brown, or black and tan; the Pembroke Welsh corgi has a short tail, pointed ears, and a finer coat of red, sable, fawn, or black and tan. Height: 30 cm (Cardigan); 25–30 cm (Pembroke).

coriander An annual plant, *Coriander sativum*, 20–70 cm high, with small pink or white flowers. Probably native to the Mediterranean, it is cultivated for its spicy seeds. Family: *Umbelliferae*.

Corinth (Greek name: Kórinthos) 37 56N 22 55E A port in S Greece. *History*: a settlement before 3000 BC, it became the second largest and richest of the Greek city states after Athens, rivalry between the two culminating in the *Peloponnesian War. Destroyed by the Romans in 146 BC, Corinth was later revived as a Roman colony (44 BC). Population (1995 est): 26 600.

Corinthian order *See* ORDERS OF ARCHITECTURE.

Corinthians, Epistles of Paul to the Two New Testament books written by the apostle Paul to the Christian Church at Corinth in about 57 AD. In the first he answers questions on practical and doctrinal issues, for example marriage and celibacy, the resurrection of the dead, and the Eucharist. In the second he defends himself against his opponents at Corinth.

Coriolis force A force required to account for the motion of a body as seen by an observer in a rotating frame of reference. It is often referred to as a fictitious force as it disappears on changing to a nonrotating frame. For example, a shell shot from a gun at the centre of a rotating table appears to an outside observer to travel in a straight line. To an observer on the table it appears to have a curved path. The Coriolis force is required to account for this apparent tangential acceleration. The Coriolis force is responsible for the formation and direction of rotation of anticyclones and whirlpools. Named after the French physicist Gaspard de Coriolis (1792–1843).

cork Tissue that forms the outer layer of *bark in woody plants. The cork oak (*Quercus suber*) is cultivated in Portugal and SW Spain as the source of commercial cork. The cork is stripped from the tree every 8–10 years.

Cork (Irish name: Corcaigh) **1.** 51 54N 8 28W The second largest city in the Republic of Ireland and county town of Co Cork. The settlement grew up around a monastery (founded in about the 6th century AD) and has many notable buildings, especially its cathedrals and St Ann's Shaldon Church. It is an industrial and trading centre with a harbour. Population (2002): 123 338. **2.** The largest county in the Republic of Ireland, in Munster. Mountains in the W extend eastwards intersected by valleys, notably that of the River Blackwater. Its many coastal inlets include Bantry Bay and Cork Harbour. Agriculture and fishing are important. Its many castles include Blarney Castle, famous for the Blarney Stone. Area: 7459 sq km (2880 sq mi). Population (2002 est): 448 181. County town: Cork.

corm A fleshy underground stem base of certain perennial herbaceous plants that acts as an overwintering structure. Growth the following season occurs by one or more buds: if two or more plants are produced the corm is acting as an organ of vegetative reproduction.

cormorant A slender long-necked waterbird belonging to a family (*Phalacrocoracidae*; 30 species) and found on most coasts and some inland waters. 50–100 cm in length, cormorants are typically glossy black and have webbed feet and a long hook-tipped bill. Order: *Pelecaniformes* (gannets, pelicans, etc.).

corncrake A migratory bird, *Crex crex*, also called landrail, that breeds in Eurasian grasslands, wintering in S Africa and Asia. It is 26 cm long with a streaked brown plumage and a rasping call. Family: *Rallidae* (rails).

cornea The transparent outer layer of the eyeball. Corneal grafts have been used successfully; since the cornea has no blood supply the graft cannot be rejected by blood-borne antibodies.

Corneille, Pierre (1606–84) French dramatist. His *Le Cid* (1636), the seminal play of French classical tragedy, excited much controversy. Here and in *Horace* (1640), *Cinna* (1641), and *Polyeucte* (1643) he pioneered a dramatic genre subsequently perfected by *Racine.

cornet A trumpet-like valved brass instrument, with cup-shaped mouthpiece and conical bore. Pitched in B flat, it has a range of two and a half octaves from the E below middle C.

cornflower An annual, sometimes overwintering, herbaceous plant, *Centaurea cyanus*, growing to about 75 cm high; a cereal crop weed. Flower heads are bright blue with a purplish centre. Family: *Compositae*.

Cornish A Celtic language of the Brythonic group, formerly spoken in Cornwall. It became extinct in about 1800 but has subsequently been revived.

Corn Laws The British laws that regulated (1360–1846) the import and export of corn to guarantee farmers' incomes. These laws were bitterly resented by the working classes, because they kept the price of bread high, and by the manufacturers, who argued that little money was left for the purchase of manufactured goods. The Anti-Corn Law League was led by Richard Cobden (1804–65) and John Bright

(1811–89). In 1846 Sir Robert Peel's government repealed them.

corn poppy An annual, or sometimes biennial, poppy, *Papaver rhoeas*, with scarlet flowers. Also called field poppy, it is widespread as a weed and grows to a height of 50 cm.

cornucopia A decorative motif from Greek antiquity denoting abundance and wealth. It consists of a goat's horn filled with fruit and flowers.

Cornwall (Celtic name: Kernow) The most southwesterly county of England, bordering on the Atlantic Ocean and the English Channel. It is mainly hilly, rising to Bodmin Moor in the E. Tourism is a chief source of income. Agriculture is important; the long-established tin mines were abandoned in the 1990s. In 1998 Cornwall was officially recognized as the poorest region in the UK owing to the crises in farming and fishing. Area: 3546 sq km (1369 sq mi). Population (2001): 499 114. Administrative centre: Truro.

Cornwall, Duchy of A private estate of some 130 000 acres, mostly in Cornwall, Devon, and Somerset, belonging to the eldest son of the sovereign, who becomes Duke of Cornwall at birth or from the moment his parent is crowned.

corona The outer layer of a star's atmosphere. The sun's corona has two main components. The **inner corona** lies above the chromosphere and consists of rapidly moving electrons. Its temperature reaches about 2 000 000°C some 75 000 km above the visible solar surface (the photosphere). The **outer corona** extends for millions of kilometres and consists of comparatively slow-moving dust particles. *See also* SOLAR WIND.

coronary heart disease The most common form of heart disease in the Western world. It is caused by *atherosclerosis of the coronary arteries, which reduces the blood flow to the heart. This may precipitate the formation of a blood clot in these arteries—**coronary thrombosis**. The patient experiences sudden pain in the chest (*see* ANGINA PECTORIS) and the result may be a heart attack, when the blood flow to the heart is suddenly stopped (*see* MYOCARDIAL INFARCTION). **Coronary bypass surgery** is a procedure in which a piece of vein from the leg or mammary artery is used as a graft to bypass a section of coronary artery blocked by atherosclerosis. In **coronary angioplasty** a catheter is inserted into a narrowed coronary artery and a balloon at the tip of the catheter is inflated to dilate the blood vessel.

coroner In England and Wales, an officer of the Crown appointed for life by a county council from among suitably qualified barristers, solicitors, or qualified medical practitioners. The main duty of a coroner is to inquire into a death resulting from an act of violence or suspicious circumstances, or occurring in prison. He is often assisted by a jury of 7 to 11 people. A jury verdict of manslaughter or murder is equivalent to an indictment, and the coroner can commit the accused for trial. A coroner also inquires into cases of *treasure trove. In Scotland, the coroner's duties are carried out by the procurator fiscal.

Corot, Jean Baptiste Camille (1796–1875) French landscape painter. Although he exhibited at the Paris Salon from 1827, he did not achieve critical acclaim until the 1850s, with his poetical misty landscapes populated by nymphs. More popular today are his open-air sketches, small landscapes, and figure studies.

corporation tax A tax levied on the profits of a company on an annual basis. In the UK, the rate of tax is announced by the chancellor of the exchequer in his budget.

Corpus Christi, Feast of (Latin: body of Christ) A Christian feast honouring the institution of the Eucharist, observed in the West on the second Thursday after *Whit Sunday. The chief rite of the feast is the procession of the Blessed Sacrament. It is not generally observed by Protestant Churches.

Correggio (Antonio Allegri; c. 1494–1534) Italian Renaissance painter, born at Correggio, near Modena. He worked chiefly in Parma, where he decorated the Camera di S Paolo, the domed vaulting of S Giovanni Evangelista, and the cathedral with frescoes that anticipate the *baroque.

Corsica (French name: Corse) An island in the Mediterranean Sea, a region of France. It is mountainous and largely covered with *maquis*, a dense scrub type of vegetation. Agriculture produces citrus fruits, olives, vegetables, and tobacco; sheep and goats are reared and tourism is important. *History*: under Genoese control from the 14th century, it was sold to France in 1768. During World War II it came under Italian occupation but was liberated by the French in 1943. Area: 8680 sq km (3367 sq mi). Population (1999): 260 196. Capital: Ajaccio.

Cortés, Hernán (1485–1547) Spanish conquistador. In Hispaniola and Cuba from 1504, he led a small expedition to Mexico in 1519 and reached Tenochtitlán, the capital of the Aztec Empire. In the absence of Cortés, the Aztecs launched an attack on Tenochtitlán, forcing the Spaniards' retreat—the *noche triste* (night of sorrows). Cortés rebuilt his forces and destroyed Tenochtitlán (1521) and the Aztec Empire, founding New Spain. After further expeditions he died in poverty in Spain.

cortex The outer tissues of an animal or plant organ. In plants the cortex is situated between the *epidermis and vascular (conducting) tissues of stems and roots. Its cell walls may contain corky and woody materials or silica, providing strength, and also stored food, usually starch. In animals the outer tissue of the adrenal gland, the cerebrum, and the *kidney is called the cortex.

corticosteroids Steroid hormones secreted by the cortex of the adrenal glands (also a group of synthetic drugs with similar properties). The glucocorticoids (e.g. cortisone, prednisolone, and dexamethasone) affect carbohydrate metabolism. As anti-inflammatory drugs, they are used to treat allergic conditions, inflammatory disorders, and autoimmune diseases. The mineralocorticoids (e.g. aldosterone, fludrocortisone) control salt and water balance in the body.

corundum A mineral consisting mainly of aluminium oxide, the accessory minerals giving rise to a variety of colours. Sapphire is a blue variety containing iron and titanium; ruby contains chromium. The nongem varieties are used as abrasives (corundum is the second hardest mineral to diamond).

Cos (Modern Greek name: Kos) A Greek island in the Dodecanese. It was a member of the Delian League and the home of Hippocrates. It produces fruit, silk, and tobacco. Cos lettuce originally came from here. Area: 282 sq km (109 sq mi). Population (latest est): 21 000.

cosmic rays A continuous stream of very high-energy particles that bombard the earth from space. The primary radiation consists of *protons and light nuclei with smaller numbers of neutral particles, such as *photons and *neutrinos. These particles collide with atomic nuclei in the earth's atmosphere producing large numbers of elementary particles, known as secondary radiation. One primary particle may produce a large number of secondary particles on colliding with a nucleus. This effect is called a shower. Some cosmic rays are believed to come from the sun, others from outside the solar system.

cosmology The study of the origin, evolution, and structure of the universe. A variety of cosmological models have been suggested through the ages. Two simple but incorrect common-sense models are the flat earth draped by a canopy of stars and the earth-centred (geocentric) universe, the *Ptolemaic system. More accurate theories emerged as instruments were developed to study the heavens (*see* ASTRONOMY). *See also* BIG-BANG THEORY; STEADY-STATE THEORY.

Cossacks A people of S and SW Russia descended from independent Tatar groups and escaped serfs from Poland, Lithuania, and Muscovy. They established a number of independent self-governing communities, which were given special privileges by Russian or Polish rulers in return for military service. Known for their horsemanship, the Cossacks slowly lost their autonomy as Russia expanded in the 17th and 18th centuries. Many fled Russia after the Revolution (1918–21) and collectivization subsumed remaining Cossack communities.

Costa Rica, Republic of A country in the Central American isthmus between Nicaragua and Panama. It includes the island of Cocos, 483 km (186 mi) to the SW. The Caribbean lowlands rise to a central plateau area, with volcanic peaks reaching 3819 m (12 529 ft). The inhabitants are mainly of Spanish and mixed descent, with a dwindling Indian population. *Economy*: chiefly agricultural, the main crops being coffee, bananas, and sugar. Almost 75% of the land is forested with valuable woods, such as mahogany, rosewood, and cedar. Mineral resources include gold, haematite ore, and sulphur. Manufacturing is important and now includes computer parts, processed foods, and textiles. Tourism is now the chief source of income. The country's infrastructure and farming were devastated by Hurricane Mitch (1998). *History*: discovered by Columbus in 1502, it became a Spanish colony in the 15th century and the native Indian population was practically wiped out. It was part of the captaincy general of Guatemala until it gained independence in 1821. From 1824 until 1838 it formed part of the Central American Federation. The country has remained relatively stable since 1948, although economic difficulties in the 1990s caused some unrest. Miguel Angel Rodriguez was elected president in 2002. Official language: Spanish. Currency: colon of 100 céntimos. Area: 50 900 sq km (19 653 sq mi). Population (2003 est): 4 171 000. Capital: San José.

cot death (*or* **sudden infant death syndrome**; **SIDS**) The death of a baby, usually occurring overnight in its cot, from an unidentifiable cause. In 1991–93 a campaign encouraging mothers to lie babies on their backs and not to overwrap or smoke over them resulted in a 55% decrease in cot deaths in the UK.

Côte d'Ivoire, Republic of (name until 1986: Ivory Coast) A country in West Africa, on the Gulf of Guinea. Swamps and tropical forests give way to savanna to the N. The diverse African population includes Baule, Bete, Senufo, and Malinke. *Economy*: chiefly agricultural, livestock being important as well as crops, including maize, yams, and other tropical plants. The main cash crop is cocoa, of which Côte d'Ivoire is the world's leading producer. Exports of cocoa and coffee account for about 40% of GDP. Mineral resources are sparse. Industry, including tourism, is being developed. *History*: explored by the Portuguese in the late 15th century, the area was disputed by several European trading nations, becoming a French colony in 1893. It became part of French West Africa in 1904 and an overseas territory in 1946. It had internal self-government as a member of the French Community from 1958 and became fully independent in 1960. Falls in world cocoa prices led to economic crisis in the 1980s. An IMF reform programme partially stabilized the economy in the 1990s. Félix Houphouët-Boigny, president from 1960 to 1993, introduced multiparty democracy in 1990. In 1999 Gen Robert Guei seized power in a military coup. He lost power in elections in 2000 and was killed while attempting to mount a further coup in 2001. In 2002–03 violence intensified, despite the arrival of French peacekeeping troops. Official language: French. Currency: CFA franc of 100 centimes. Area: 322 463 sq km (124 470 sq mi). Population (2003 est): 16 631 000. Capital: Yamoussoukro.

Cotoneaster A genus of shrubs and small trees (about 50 species) of N temperate regions of the Old World. Some species are evergreen. *C. horizontalis* is a popular ground and wall cover; *C. hybrida pendula* is a weeping standard. Family: *Rosaceae*.

Cotonou 6 24N 2 31E The chief city in Benin, on the Gulf of Guinea. A deepwater port, it is the nation's main commercial centre. Population (1994 est): 750 000.

Cotopaxi 0 40S 78 28W The world's highest active volcano, in N central Ecuador, in the Andes. Height: 5896 m (19 457 ft).

Cotswold Hills A range of limestone hills in SW central England, mainly in Gloucestershire. It is noted for its picturesque towns and villages.

cotton A herbaceous plant of the genus *Gossypium* (20 or 67 species, according to the classification system), native to tropical and subtropical regions. Several species are cultivated for the whitish outer fibres of their seeds. Usually 1–2 m high, cotton plants bear whitish flowers and produce seed pods (bolls), which burst when filled with the soft masses of fibres. The bolls are harvested mechanically and the fibres separated from the seeds (ginning) and cleaned and aligned (carding), ready for spinning into yarn. Cotton forms a light durable cloth used in a wide range of garments, furnishings, etc. The seeds are crushed to yield cottonseed oil, used in margarines, cooking oils, soaps, etc., and the residual meal is fed to livestock. Family: *Malvaceae*.

cotyledon The seed leaf of seed-bearing plants (gymnosperms and angiosperms): a food store within seeds providing the embryo plant with sufficient energy to germinate. Flowering plants with one cotyledon are classified as *monocotyledons; those with two as *dicotyledons. *See* GERMINATION.

couch grass A *grass, *Agropyron repens*, also known as quack grass or twitch, native to Europe and naturalized in other N temperate regions. 30–120 cm high, it is a serious weed of arable crops.

cougar A red-brown *cat, *Felis concolor*, of North and South America, also called puma, mountain lion, and catamount. It is 1.5–3 m long including its tail (50–80 cm), with long hind legs enabling a powerful leap. It feeds on a variety of animals.

coulomb (C) The SI unit of electric charge equal to the quantity of electricity transferred by a current of one ampere in one second. Named after Charles de Coulomb (1736–1806), French physicist.

Coulomb's law *See* ELECTRIC CHARGE.

Council of Europe An association of European states, founded in 1949, that is pledged to uphold parliamentary democracy and to promote the economic and social progress of its members. Its seat is in Strasbourg.

council tax In the UK, a tax to finance local government that replaced the community charge (*see* POLL TAX) in 1993. Adult residents of private households are liable for the tax, which is calculated by the local council according to the market value of the dwelling. There

C

counterpoint. An example of counterpoint from J. S. Bach's *Fantasia in C minor.*

are discounts for sole occupants and those on low incomes.

counterpoint The art of combining two or more melodic lines simultaneously in music. The word derives from the Latin *punctus contra punctum*, point against point (i.e. note against note). The use of counterpoint continued beyond the end of the polyphonic period (*see* POLYPHONY). In the 20th century contrapuntal techniques were used by Stravinsky, Hindemith, Tippett, and others.

Counter-Reformation A movement within the *Roman Catholic Church to combat the effects of the Protestant *Reformation. Extending from the middle of the 16th to the middle of the 17th century, it witnessed the emergence of the *Jesuits, the Council of *Trent, the extension of the *Inquisition, and a revival of Catholic spirituality.

countertenor A natural high male singing voice, higher than tenor, common in England in the 17th and 18th centuries. It is distinguished from the male *alto voice, which is produced by falsetto, and has the same range as contralto.

country and western A type of US popular music that evolved from the hillbilly ballads of the Appalachian Mountains and the cowboy songs of the West. The singer is accompanied by the guitar and other stringed instruments. Influenced by other styles of popular music, country and western has its own offshoots, such as bluegrass.

county A geographical subdivision of a country, often with powers of local government. In the UK counties are long established: the name was applied by the Normans to the Anglo-Saxon shire. In England and Wales the Local Government Act (1972; effective 1974) amalgamated some old counties and established new ones and placed a variety of public services in the hands of elected county councils. The Local Government (Scotland) Act (1973) created nine new regions and three island areas. Northern Ireland has six historic counties but administration is now carried out by 26 district councils. In the 1990s Local Government Acts for Scotland and Wales (1994; effective 1996) replaced the Scottish system with 32 council areas and reorganized Wales into 10 counties and 12 county boroughs (all unitary authorities). In England several counties were abolished and their powers devolved to the district councils (now unitary authorities).

Couperin, François (1668–1733) French composer, called le Grand, the most famous member of a family that produced five generations of musicians. He was organist to Louis XIV and at St Gervais and is best known for his harpsichord music.

courgette A variety of *marrow, also called zucchini, eaten when small and immature (up to 15 cm long). Mature courgettes resemble ordinary marrows.

Courtauld Institute of Art A college and gallery for the study of art history in London. The industrialist Samuel Courtauld (1876–1947) left his house in Portman Square with his collection of impressionist paintings to London University in 1931. In 1990 the Institute moved to more spacious premises in the west wing of Somerset House in the Strand.

courtly love A literary convention describing passionate love, arising in 12th-century Provence in the poems of the *troubadours. It is not certain to what extent courtly love actually existed as a social phenomenon. In the literary convention the aristocratic lover is abjectly devoted to his chosen lady, whose virtues are idealized with quasi-religious fervour and who remains unobtainable because she is married to someone else. The lover is bound by rules of *chivalry and is ennobled by his attachment to the beloved. On the other hand, he suffers enormously from the capricious behaviour of his lady, etc. The convention spread from Provence to Italy, N France, Germany, and England, where it was treated in detail by Chaucer. It continued as an important element in the Elizabethan sonnet through the influence of *Petrarch.

court-martial A court, consisting of commissioned officers in the army, navy, or air force, convened to try a member of any of these services for an offence against military discipline or against ordinary law. An appeal court was established in 1951 and is now governed by the Courts-Martial (Appeals) Act (1968). An offender is not immune from trial by ordinary courts, but they must take into account any punishment to which he was sentenced by the court-martial.

courts of law Assemblies in which the law is administered. In England and Wales *civil law (*see also* COMMON LAW; EQUITY) is administered by the County Courts and the High Court of Justice and *criminal law is administered by the Magistrates' Courts and the Crown Court. Appeals from the civil law courts lie to the civil division of the Court of Appeal and those from the criminal law courts lie from Magistrate's Courts to the Crown Court and from the Crown Court to the criminal division of the Court of Appeal. Two or more judges of the High Court, when sitting together, may constitute a Divisional Court, which hears appeals on points of law from Magistrates' Courts, Crown Courts, and certain tribunals. The Divisional Court can either (1) order the lower court to continue its hearing of the case in point while directing how the law should be applied or (2) allow or dismiss the appeal itself, if all the facts of the case have already been heard and decided by the lower court. The House of Lords is currently the Supreme Court of Appeal in both criminal and civil cases, although the government has announced plans to create a new Supreme Court. The High Court of Justice and the Court of Appeal together with the Crown Court form the Supreme Court of Judicature.

The County Courts have jurisdiction over most civil law actions. All divorce petitions start in the County Courts but are transferred to the High Court if defended. The High Court of Justice comprises the *Chancery, Queen's Bench (including the Admiralty Court (*see* MARITIME LAW) and the Commercial Court), and Family Divisions.

A criminal case comes first before a Magistrates' Court (*see* MAGISTRATE), which has jurisdiction in less serious cases (e.g. traffic offences) but commits more serious cases for trial at the Crown Court. The Crown Court, which was created in 1971 to replace the Courts of Assize and Courts of Quarter Session, is organized in six circuits (Midland and Oxford, North Eastern, Northern, South Eastern, Wales and Chester, and Western). A Crown Court sits in London as the Central Criminal Court (Old Bailey). *See also* JUDGE.

In Scotland the supreme court for civil cases is the Court of Session, established in 1532, and the supreme court for criminal cases is the High Court of Judiciary. Appeals from the former lie to the House of Lords and from the latter to a tribunal of three judges of the High Court of Justiciary. *See also* CROWN PROSECUTION SERVICE.

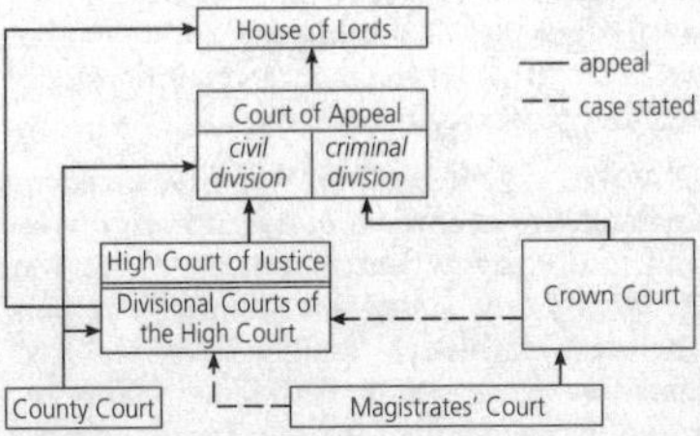

courts of law

Cousteau, Jacques Yves (1910–97) French naval officer and underwater explorer. He shared in the invention of the aqualung (1943) and invented a way of using television under water. In 1945 he founded the Undersea Research Group of the French navy at Marseilles and in 1950 became commander of the oceanographic research vessel *Calypso*. He was famous for such films as *The Silent World* (1953) and *The Living Sea* (1963) and for his environmental campaigns.

covenant 1. (law) A binding agreement between two parties whereby each promises to do something for the other (*see also* DEED). **2.** In the Old Testament, the agreement between God and Israel, which forms the basis of the Jewish religion. In return for obedience to the Law (the Ten Commandments) as delivered to Moses, the Israelites were privileged as God's chosen people.

Covenanters Scottish Presbyterians who in the 16th and 17th centuries covenanted to defend their church. The National Covenant of 1638 was signed by thousands of Scottish Presbyterians after Charles I's attempt to introduce the English Prayer Book, this opposition culminating in the Bishops' Wars. In the English *Civil War the Covenanters joined the parliamentarians in 1643 in return for the promise of church reform. After the Restoration (1660) they were persecuted until the re-establishment of Presbyterianism in Scotland after the Glorious Revolution (1688).

Covent Garden The principal English opera house, officially named the Royal Opera House. The first theatre on the site was opened in 1732, and the present building dates from the 1850s; it is currently the home of both the Royal Opera and the Royal Ballet Company. It takes its name from a square (originally a convent garden) onto which it backs, which was laid out in 1631 by Inigo *Jones. For many years London's fruit and vegetable market occupied the square but in 1973 it moved to Nine Elms (Wandsworth) and the square was redeveloped as a shopping precinct.

Coventry 1. 52 25N 1 30W A city in central England, in Coventry unitary authority, West Midlands. Heavily bombed during World War II, the city centre was almost entirely rebuilt. The new cathedral, designed by Sir Basil Spence, was opened in 1962 and retains the ruins of the old cathedral, which was bombed in 1940. Population (1991): 299 316. **2.** A unitary authority in central England, in West Midlands. Area: 97 sq km (37 sq mi). Population (2001): 300 844.

Coward, Sir Noel (1899–1973) British dramatist, composer, and actor. He first established his reputation with *The Vortex* (1924), a domestic drama, but his best-known plays are elegant comedies of manners, such as *Hay Fever* (1925) and *Blithe Spirit* (1941). He also contributed to revues, musicals, and films, notably *In Which We Serve* (1942) and *Brief Encounter* (1946).

Cowes 50 45N 1 18W A town in S England, situated on the Isle of Wight. It is a resort and yachting centre. Population (1991): 16 335.

cowpea An annual African plant, *Vigna unguiculata*, widely grown for food in tropical areas. There are two forms: a short erect one grown in Africa and America, whose seeds are used dried, and a tall climbing one grown in SE Asia, whose long pods are eaten when young. Family: *Leguminosae*.

Cowper, William (1731–1800) British poet. His publications include *Olney Hymns* (1779; with John Newton), "John Gilpin's Ride" (1783), a comic ballad, and *The Task* (1785), a long poem on rural themes. He was mentally unstable throughout his life, and frequently attempted suicide.

cowpox A contagious virus disease of cattle that can be contracted by humans. Edward *Jenner used fluid from cowpox blisters to produce the first effective smallpox vaccine.

cowrie A *gastropod mollusc of the family *Cypraeidae* (about 160 species), mostly found in warm seas. 1–15 cm long, cowries have glossy shells with inrolled lips and feed at night on small animals.

cowslip A perennial spring-flowering Eurasian herb, *Primula veris*, growing to a height of 20 cm. It has bright-yellow flowers and is found from lowland meadows to alpine pastures. Family: *Primulaceae* (primrose family).

coyote A wild *dog, *Canis latrans*, of Central and North American grassland, also called prairie wolf. Coyotes are about 120 cm long, including the bushy tail (30 cm), and have yellowish fur. They hunt alone or in packs.

coypu A South American aquatic *rodent, *Myocaster coypus*. About 60 cm long (excluding a long hairless tail), it has thick brown fur and webbed hind feet. The underfur of the belly is known as nutria, and coypus are farmed for fur. Family: *Capromyidae*.

crab A *crustacean belonging to the tribes *Brachyura* (true crabs; about 4500 species) or *Anomura* (about 1300 species). True crabs have a wide flat body covered by a hard carapace. There is a large pair of pincers and four pairs of legs used for walking (typically sideways) or swimming. They are carnivores or scavengers and most species are marine. Order: *Decapoda*.

crab apple A tree, *Malus sylvestris*, 2–10 m high: one of the species from which cultivated *apples have been developed. A native of Europe and Asia, it is sometimes grown as an ornamental. Family: *Rosaceae*.

Crabbe, George (1754–1832) British poet, doctor, and cleric, born in Aldeburgh, Suffolk, scene of many of his poems. *The Village* (1783) was a brutally realistic portrayal of rural life, as were the verse tales of *The Borough* (1810) and *Tales of the Hall* (1819).

Crab nebula A turbulent expanding mass of gas, lying about 6000 light years distant in the constellation Taurus. It is the remnant of a *supernova observed in 1054. Within the nebula lies the **Crab pulsar**. This optical *pulsar rotates with a period of only 0.033 seconds.

Cracow *See* KRAKÓW.

Craigavon A district in central Northern Ireland, in Co Armargh. Area: 279 sq km (108 sq mi). Population (2001): 80 671.

crake A small shy bird belonging to the *rail family, commonly found in marshes and swamps. The Eurasian spotted crake (*Porzana porzana*) is 23 cm long and has a red ring at the base of the bill.

Cranach the Elder, Lucas (Lucas Müller;

1472–1553) German artist. Because of his portraits of Reformation leaders including his friend Luther, he is sometimes called the Reformation painter. He is also noted for his stylized but sensuous nudes, e.g. *Adam and Eve* (Courtauld Institute, London).

cranberry A low evergreen shrub of the genus *Vaccinium*, bearing red edible berries and growing in acidic boggy areas. *V. oxycoccus* occurs in Europe, N Asia, and North America. *V. macrocarpon* of North America has larger fruits (about 1.5 cm across). Family: *Ericaceae* (heath family).

crane A long-legged bird belonging to a family (*Gruidae*; 14 species) occurring in Old World regions and North America. Up to 140 cm tall with a wingspan of over 200 cm, cranes vary from grey to white with black wingtips; some species are crested. They feed on grain, shoots, and small animals; northern species are migratory. Order: *Gruiformes* (rails, etc.). *See also* DEMOISELLE; WHOOPING CRANE.

cranefly A harmless fly, also called daddy longlegs, belonging to the family *Tipulidae*. Craneflies are 6–75 mm long with long delicate legs and wings. The larvae generally occur in water or rotting vegetation. However some—the leatherjackets—are plant pests.

cranesbill A herbaceous plant of the genus *Geranium* (about 400 species), widely distributed, and usually having pink or purple flowers. They take their name from the long slender beaklike carpels. The meadow cranesbill (*G. pratense*), a perennial up to 60 cm high, has violet-blue flowers. Family: *Geraniaceae*.

Cranmer, Thomas (1489–1556) Anglican reformer and martyr. He was consecrated Archbishop of Canterbury in 1532, following his support of *Henry VIII in the king's divorce dispute with the pope. He is especially remembered for his contributions to the Prayer Books of 1549 and 1552. Under Queen Mary he was tried as a heretic and burned at the stake.

Crassus, Marcus Licinius (c. 115–53 BC) Roman politician, nicknamed *Dives* (wealthy). Crassus suppressed Spartacus' revolt (71) and joined Pompey and Caesar in the first Triumvirate (60). He was killed during an invasion of Parthia.

crayfish A freshwater *crustacean, also called crawfish and crawdad, belonging to the superfamily *Nephropidea*. It has a small lobster-like body, 25–75 mm long, and feeds on plant and animal material. Some species are edible. Order: *Decapoda*.

Crécy, Battle of (26 August 1346) The first land battle of the *Hundred Years' War, fought in N France, in which the English, led by *Edward III, defeated the French under Philip VI.

Cree An Algonkian-speaking North American Indian people. They lived by hunting and trapping in small wandering bands. One group, known as Plains Cree, moved into the Plains and adopted the buffalo-hunting culture of this region often raiding for horses.

Creek A Muskogean-speaking North American Indian people divided into the Muskogee of Georgia and the Hitchiti of Alabama. They were cultivators and hunters and tattooed their bodies heavily. A confederacy of Creek towns fought the encroaching whites in the 18th and early 19th centuries. On their defeat in the 1830s they were removed to Oklahoma.

Cremona 45 08N 10 01E A town in N Italy, in Lombardy. It has a 12th-century cathedral and a 13th-century palace. From the 16th to the 18th centuries it was famous for the manufacture of violins. Population (latest est): 75 160.

creosote A substance produced by distilling tar. The creosote used for preserving wood is obtained from *coal tar and is a brownish mixture of aromatic hydrocarbons and *phenols. Creosote made from wood tar is a mixture of phenols and is used in pharmacy.

cresol (*or* **methylphenol**; $CH_3C_6H_4OH$) A liquid *aromatic compound obtained from *coal tar. It has three *isomers, a mixture of which is used as a disinfectant.

cress A plant of the mustard family (*Cruciferae*) the leaves of which are used in salads, especially garden cress, or peppergrass (*Lepidium sativum*). The seedlings are eaten, often with those of white mustard (*Sinapis alba*). The European winter, or land, cress (*Barbarea verna*) grows to a height of 100 cm.

Cretaceous period A geological period of the Mesozoic era, between about 135 and 65 million years ago, divided into the Lower and Upper Cretaceous. The dinosaurs and other giant reptiles, as well as the ammonites and many other invertebrates, became extinct at the end of the Cretaceous.

Crete (Modern Greek name: Kríti) The largest of the Greek islands, in the E Mediterranean Sea. It is generally mountainous, rising over 2400 m (7874 ft). The economy is based primarily on agriculture and tourism. *History*: colonized probably in the 6th millennium BC from

Asia Minor, Crete achieved extensive maritime power during the Middle Minoan period (c. 2000–c. 1700 BC). Relics include the palace at *Knossos and clay tablets bearing two different scripts known as *Linear A and *Linear B. Politically insignificant in the history of classical Greece, it fell to Rome (67 BC), Byzantium (395 AD), and the Muslims (826). In 1204 it was sold to the Venetians, who gave both the island and Iráklion the name Candia. It fell to Turkey in 1669 and was officially incorporated into Greece in 1913. Area: 8332 sq km (3217 sq mi). Population (2001): 601 159. Capital: Khaniá.

Creutzfeldt-Jakob disease (CJD) A fatal neurological disease characterized by rapidly progressive dementia and involuntary jerking movements, first described by German psychiatrists H. G. Creutzfeldt (1885–1964) and A. M. Jakob (1884–1931). It is believed to be caused by deposits of an abnormal form of a brain protein (prion), which destroys surrounding brain cells. Sporadic and inherited forms of CJD are rare and typically affect elderly people, but the disease can be transmitted accidentally (e.g. through injections of prion-infected growth hormone), appearing many years after the initial infection. In the mid-1990s a variant form of CJD arose in the UK, which was thought to be linked to the consumption of beef products from cattle infected with *BSE.

Crewe 53 05N 2 27W A town in NW England, in Cheshire. Crewe developed as a railway junction with railway engineering and workshops; it now has varied industries, including high technology. Population (1991): 63 351.

Crick, Francis Harry Compton (1916–2004) British biophysicist, who (with James D. *Watson) proposed a model for the molecular structure of *DNA (1953). Following this breakthrough, Crick helped to determine the mechanism of protein synthesis. He shared a Nobel Prize (1962) with Watson and Maurice *Wilkins and was appointed to the OM in 1991.

cricket (sport) An 11-a-side bat-and-ball team game, in which the object is to score the most runs. It originated in England among shepherds using their crooks as bats; its rules were laid down in 1744 and the game is played almost exclusively in the UK and its former empire. It is presided over by two umpires (from 1993 a third umpire may make certain decisions in test matches with the aid of video replays). It is played on a grass pitch 22 yd (20.12 m) long having at each end a wicket of three stumps surmounted by two bails. The cork and twine ball, encased in leather, is 8.8–9 in (22.4–22.9 cm) in circumference and weighs 5.5–5.75 oz (155.9–163 g). The members of one team take turns to bat in pairs, one defending each wicket; the batsmen's objective is to score runs by hitting the ball and exchanging ends. Each player bats until he is bowled, caught, stumped, run out, or judged lbw (leg before wicket). The members of the other team field, some taking turns to bowl the ball. International cricket is played mainly in Test matches between England, Australia, the West Indies, New Zealand, India, Pakistan, Sri Lanka, and South Africa. In England first-class cricket chiefly involves the 18 professional first-class county teams.

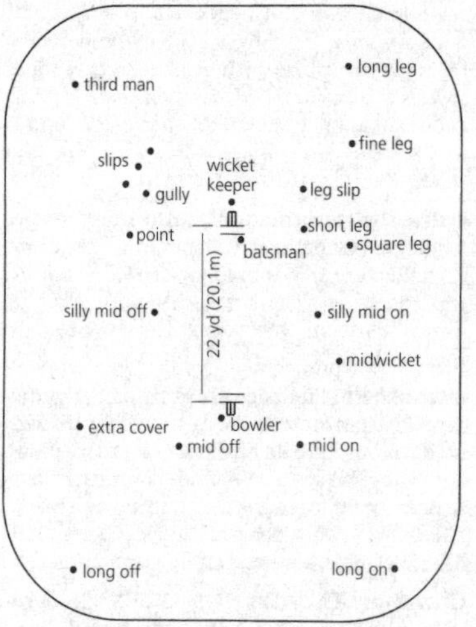

cricket. The pitch, showing the usual fielding positions (for a right-handed batsman).

cricket (zoology) An insect, resembling a grasshopper but with longer antennae, belonging to one of several families of the order *Orthoptera*. The males stridulate (i.e. make a chirping noise) by rubbing the front wings together. True crickets (family *Gryllidae*; 2400 species) have black or brown flattened bodies, 3–50 mm long, with long tail appendages (cerci) and short forewings (they do not fly). The females have long needle-like ovipositors for depositing eggs in soil or crevices. True crickets are omnivorous.

Crimea (Russian name: Krym) A peninsula and autonomous region (*oblast*) in the S Ukraine. It is mainly flat but rises to 1545 m

(5069 ft) in the S. Iron ore is mined here and wheat, tobacco, and wine are produced. *History*: colonized by Greeks in the 6th century BC, the Crimea was invaded by Goths, Huns, and others and in 1239 was made a khanate by Tatars. This was overthrown by Turks in 1475, and the area was annexed by Russia in 1783. Following the break-up of the Soviet Union in 1991, many Crimeans now favour union with Russia or total independence. Area: about 27 000 sq km (10 423 sq mi). Population (2001): 2 031 000. Capital: Simferopol. *See also* CRIMEAN WAR.

Crimean War (1853–56) The war between Russia, on one side, and Britain, France, the Ottoman (Turkish) Empire, and (from 1855) Sardinia-Piedmont, on the other. Caused by Russia's expansionist ambitions in the Balkans, the war culminated in the year-long siege of Sevastopol and the battles of *Balaclava and *Inkerman. The Russians eventually evacuated the port in September 1855 and peace was formally concluded at Paris (1856). Over 250 000 men were lost by each side, many from disease in the appalling hospitals of the Crimea. *See also* NIGHTINGALE, FLORENCE.

criminal law The body of law determining the acts and circumstances that amount to a crime (a wrong against society prohibited by law) and the punishment for crimes. Criminal law derives in England chiefly from *common law, although statute law has contributed significantly to its development. Most crimes entail both an act (*actus reus*) and a mental element (*mens rea*). However, there is a growing number of crimes in which no mental element is necessary (called crimes of strict liability), such as most motoring offences. Insanity, infancy (children under the age of ten), or duress (an act committed under threat of death or serious personal injury) may excuse a crime, but ignorance of the law does not if, in cases involving a mental element, the offender intends the result of his acts. In England all criminal cases appear first before a Magistrates' Court and may then be committed to the Crown Court (*see* COURTS OF LAW).

crinoid A marine invertebrate animal belonging to a class (*Crinoidea*; about 700 species) of *echinoderms. It has a small cup-shaped body covered with calcareous plates and with five radiating pairs of feathery flexible arms surrounding the mouth at the top. Sea lilies are fixed to the sea bottom, coral reefs, etc., by a stalk. Feather stars, e.g. *Antedon*, are free-swimming. Crinoids occur mainly in deep waters and feed on microscopic plankton and detritus. The larvae are sedentary.

critical mass The mass of fissile substance that is just capable of sustaining a *chain reaction within it. Below the critical mass, too many of the particles that might have induced a reaction escape.

critical state The state of a gas at its critical temperature, pressure, and volume. The critical temperature is the temperature above which a gas cannot be liquefied by increased pressure alone. The vapour pressure of the gas at this temperature is the critical pressure and its volume, the critical volume. In the critical state the density of the vapour is equal to the density of the liquid.

Croatia (Serbo-Croat name: Hrvatska) A republic in SE Europe, on the Adriatic Sea. It is chiefly mountainous, with plains in the NE. *Economy*: mainly agricultural, producing cereals, potatoes, tobacco, fruit, and livestock. Industries include food processing, metallurgy, and textiles. Tourism is reviving. *History*: settled by the Croats in the 7th century AD, the region was successively controlled by Hungary, Turkey, and Austria until the formation of the kingdom of the Serbs, Croats, and Slovenes (later Yugoslavia) in 1918. Following occupation by the Axis Powers in World War II, Croatia became an independent state (1941), rejoining Yugoslavia in 1945. In 1991 there was fighting between Croatian nationalists and the Serb-led Yugoslav army. Croatia's independence was recognized in 1992. The mainly Serb Krajina region declared itself independent from Croatia but was recaptured by government troops in 1995. Croatia was involved in the Bosnian civil war between 1991 and 1995. In the late 1990s there was growing opposition to the authoritarian rule of Franjo Tudjman and following his death (1999) his nationalists were heavily defeated by the centre-left in parliamentary elections (2000). Official language: Croatian. Currency: kuna. Area: 56 538 sq km (22 050 sq mi). Population (2003 est): 4 428 000. Capital: Zagreb.

Croce, Benedetto (1866–1952) Italian philosopher. His system is expounded in *Philosophy of Mind* (1900–10). The only reality is mental and this reality is divided into theoretical and practical. Theoretical reality comprises intuition (art and aesthetics) and conception (philosophy or history), while practical reality comprises individual will (political and economic activity) and universal will (morality).

crocodile A reptile belonging to either of two genera, *Crocodylus* or *Osteolaemus*, and distinguished from alligators and caymans by having a more pointed snout and fewer teeth, the fourth tooth of the lower jaw remaining visible when the mouth is closed. Crocodiles occur chiefly in tropical fresh waters although the estuarine crocodile (*C. porosus*), which reaches a length of 6 m, occurs in coastal waters of SE Asia and Australia. Crocodiles belong to the order *Crocodilia* (about 20 species). Crocodilians are amphibious mainly nocturnal carnivores and rivers, where they prey chiefly on fish but also on water birds and land animals. They have long powerful jaws and a covering of protective bony plates; the ears and nostrils can be closed by valves when under water. The female builds a nest of mud or vegetation in which over a hundred shelled eggs may be laid.

crocodile bird An African riverbank courser, *Pluvianus aegyptius*, that feeds on parasites picked from crocodiles. It is 23 cm long and is black with white markings.

Crocus A genus of low-growing plants (75 species), native to Mediterranean regions and widely planted in gardens. Spring-flowering species include *C. vernus*, with white, blue, or purple flowers, and *C. aureus*, with deep-yellow flowers. *C. speciosus* is a purple autumn-flowering species. An Asian species (*C. sativus*) is the source of *saffron. Family: *Iridaceae*. *Compare* AUTUMN CROCUS.

Croesus (died c.546 BC) The last king of *Lydia (c. 560–c. 546 BC), famous for his wealth. He conquered the Greek cities on the coast of Asia Minor but was defeated by the Persian king Cyrus (II) the Great (d. 529) in 546. According to legend, Croesus was saved by Apollo from execution by Cyrus.

Crohn's disease An inflammatory disorder of the intestinal tract named after the US physician B. B. Crohn (1884–1983). Symptoms include abdominal pain and diarrhoea. Its cause is not known. Patients are treated with drugs; some cases require surgery.

Cro-Magnon A prehistoric race of men. Skeletal remains were found (1868) at Cro-Magnon SW France and similar bones of tall broad-faced individuals have been found at other European sites. They first appeared about 35 000 years ago. The Cro-Magnon hunted reindeer, bison, and wild horse and produced the earliest known examples of cave art (*see* LASCAUX). *See also* HOMO.

Crompton, Samuel (1753–1827) British inventor of the spinning mule (1779). It was able to produce yarn of a higher quality and at a greater speed than had previously been possible. Crompton sold his idea for very little money but in 1812 he was awarded a parliamentary grant of £5,000.

Cromwell, Oliver (1599–1658) English soldier and statesman; Lord Protector of England (1653–58). Cromwell was MP for Huntingdon in the parliament of 1628–29 and a critic of Charles I in the *Long Parliament, summoned in 1640. After the outbreak of the *Civil War he raised a troop of cavalry, the nucleus of his Ironsides (formed 1643), and fought at Edgehill (1642). He held command at *Marston Moor (1644) and was instrumental in the formation of the *New Model Army under Fairfax, which with Cromwell as second in command decisively defeated Charles at *Naseby (1645). Cromwell acted as mediator between the king, parliament, and the New Model Army but his conciliatory attitude hardened after Charles' flight to the Isle of Wight; when the second Civil War ended in Charles' defeat (1648), Cromwell signed the king's death warrant. After the establishment of the Commonwealth he ruthlessly subjected Ireland (1649–50) and defeated Charles' heir at Dunbar (1650) and Worcester (1651). In 1653 he expelled the Rump of the Long Parliament and following the failure of the *Barebones Parliament (formed in 1653 and named after one of its members, Praisegod Barebones), he accepted the Instrument of Government, which established the *Protectorate. As Lord Protector, Cromwell established Puritanism but permitted religious toleration. He ended the first Dutch War, allied with France against Spain (gaining Dunkirk), and conquered Jamaica (1655). He refused parliament's offer of the crown in 1657. He was succeeded as Lord Protector by his son **Richard Cromwell** (1626–1712), who was forced to abdicate in 1659.

Cromwell, Thomas, Earl of Essex (c.1485–1540) English statesman, who drafted the legislation that made the English Church independent of Rome (*see* REFORMATION). He entered *Wolsey's service in 1514, became an MP in 1529 and chancellor of the exchequer in 1533. He ended the marriage of Henry VIII to Catherine of Aragon by a series of Acts that made the king head of the English Church. Between 1536 and 1540 he organized the dissolution of the monasteries, after which his negotiation of Henry's disastrous marriage to Anne of Cleves led to his execution for treason.

Cronus A Greek deity, the youngest of the Titans. He ruled the universe after castrating his father Uranus. He swallowed all the children he fathered by his sister Rhea except Zeus, for whom a stone was substituted. Zeus was reared secretly in Crete and eventually overthrew Cronus.

Crookes, Sir William (1832–1919) British physicist, who showed that cathode rays consisted of charged particles rather than electromagnetic radiation, since they were deflected by a magnetic field. He invented the Crookes radiometer and Crookes glass, containing cerium, to protect the eyes of the industrial workers. He also discovered the element thallium.

croquet A ball-and-mallet game that probably developed from *paille-maille*, a French game played certainly by the 13th century. It is played on a grass lawn, ideally 35 × 28 yd (32 × 25.6 m), with an arrangement of six hoops and one peg. Two to four players attempt to follow a prescribed course through the hoops, each using a distinctively coloured ball, the winner being the first to hit the peg with his ball.

Crosby, Bing (Harry Lillis C.; 1904–77) US popular singer. He achieved worldwide fame during the 1930s and 1940s with such hits as "White Christmas" (1942). He starred in many films, often with Bob *Hope, and also in his own radio and television shows.

crossbill A finch of the genus *Loxia* (3 species), 14.5-17 cm long, whose unique cross-tipped bill is specialized for extracting seeds from unopened cones. The common crossbill (*L. curvirostra*) of Eurasia and North America feeds on spruce seeds. The male is red and the female grey-green. The parrot crossbill (*L. pytyopsittacus*) feeds on pine seeds

crossbow A short bow mounted on a stock, used in Europe throughout the middle ages. Crossbows were composite, made of wood, horn, tendons, and by the early 15th century of steel (called an arbalest). They were drawn by hand, a belt hook, or a winch. The bolt or *quarrel* was short, iron-tipped, fletched with wood, leather, or brass, and capable of penetrating armour.

Crossopterygii An order of bony fish, most of which are now extinct. The suborder *Rhipidistia* were predatory freshwater fishes of the Devonian and Carboniferous periods (about 400–280 million years ago), some of which evolved into the amphibians. The suborder *Coelacanthini* contains the coelacanth, the only surviving member of the order. Subclass: *Sarcopterygii.*

Croton A genus of tropical trees and shrubs (750 species) many of which are of economic importance. *C. tiglium* of SE Asia produces croton oil, a powerful laxative now considered unsafe. The bark of *C. cascarilla* and *C. eluteria*, trees of the Bahamas, produces cascarilla, used in tonics. *C. laccifer* from India and Sri Lanka provides a lac used in varnishes. Several Brazilian species produce dragon's-blood resin. Family: *Euphorbiaceae* (spurge family).

croup An acute infection of the respiratory tract, usually caused by viruses, resulting in inflammation and obstruction of the larynx (voice box). Croup occurs most commonly in children under five years of age; symptoms include difficulty in breathing. Treatment consists of steam inhalations and sedatives; severe cases may require surgery.

crow A large songbird of the widely distributed family *Corvidae* (102 species). 30–65 cm long, crows typically have a black or brightly coloured plumage and a stout bill. Their food includes carrion and they have a distinctive call. The typical crows are the carrion, hooded, and American crows but the family also includes the *rooks, *ravens, *choughs, jays, and *jackdaws.

crown dependencies *See* UNITED KINGDOM OVERSEAS TERRITORIES.

crown jewels Royal insignia and regalia and the personal jewellery inherited or acquired by a sovereign. The British Crown Jewels, kept in the Tower of London, were mainly amassed after the Restoration, the earlier set having been destroyed under Cromwell. Those used for coronations include a replica of St Edward's crown, the Sword of State, the Orb, and the Sceptre. Those used for other state occasions include the Imperial State Crown and another Sword of State.

crown of thorns **1.** A Madagascan shrub, *Euphorbia splendens*, often cultivated for ornament. Up to 100 cm high, it has spiny stems and clusters of small flowers. *See* EUPHORBIA. **2.** A spiny vigorous shrub, *Zizyphus spina-christi.* It is widespread in the Mediterranean region and is said to be the source of Christ's crown of thorns. Family: *Rhamnaceae* (buckthorn family).

crown-of-thorns starfish A reddish starfish, *Acanthaster planci*, that has a spiny body, up to 45 cm across, with 12–19 arms. With the decimation of its chief predator—the Pacific triton (*Charonia tritonis*)—by shell collectors, it has spread throughout the South Pacific.

Crown Prosecution Service An independent prosecuting body established in England

and Wales in 1986 to decide whether a case should be pursued in the courts. It deals with cases brought by the police (excluding traffic offences) and is headed by the Director of Public Prosecutions. In 2004 the government announced plans to rename it the Public Prosecution Service.

Cruciferae (*or* **Brassicaceae**) A family of plants (about 1900 species), mainly annual or perennial herbs, abundant in N temperate regions. The flowers are four-petalled and cross-shaped. Many crucifers are of economic importance as food plants, cattle food, ornamentals, and weeds. Some, such as cabbage and other brassicas, have been grown since ancient times.

Cruikshank, George (1792–1872) British painter and illustrator. He illustrated such books as Dickens' *Oliver Twist* and Ainsworth's *Tower of London*. His etchings of *The Bottle* and painting of *The Worship of Bacchus* (Tate Gallery) are moralizing sermons on alcoholism.

Cruise, Tom (Thomas Cruise Mapother IV; 1962–) US film actor. His films include *The Outsiders* (1983), *Born on the Fourth of July* (1989), *Eyes Wide Shut* (1999), and *Magnolia* (2000). He was married to Nicole *Kidman.

cruiser A fast heavily armed warship, smaller than a battleship but larger than a *destroyer. Cruisers with increased firepower, nuclear power, and greater versatility have replaced most of the world's battleships.

Crusades The military expeditions organized in western Christendom primarily to recover the Holy Places of Palestine from Muslim occupation. The first Crusade (1095–99) was launched under the aegis of the papacy. Jerusalem was captured and the Crusader states of the Kingdom of Jerusalem, the County of Edessa, Antioch, and Tripoli were created. The fall (1144) of Edessa inspired the unsuccessful second Crusade (1147–48) and the capture of Jerusalem by *Saladin in 1187 led to the inconclusive third Crusade (1189–92), led by *Philip II Augustus of France, Emperor Frederick I Barbarossa, and *Richard (I) the Lionheart of England. The fourth Crusade (1202–04) was diverted from its initial objective, Egypt, and sacked Constantinople (1204). The four Crusades of the 13th century failed to recover lost ground and Acre, the last foothold of the West in Palestine, was lost in 1291. *See also* CHILDREN'S CRUSADE.

crustacean An *arthropod of the subphylum or superclass *Crustacea* (over 35 000 species), which includes the *barnacles, *woodlouse, *shrimps, *lobsters, *crabs, etc. The head bears two pairs of antennae and three pairs of jaws; the head and thorax together are usually covered by a chitinous carapace. There are numerous pairs of forked appendages, which are modified for different functions. Crustaceans are predominantly aquatic, breathing by means of gills. The larvae pass through several stages (*see* METAMORPHOSIS) to reach the adult form.

cryogenics The production, effects, and uses of very low temperatures, usually meaning from −150°C down to *absolute zero. The most common method of producing cryogenic temperatures is to use adiabatic processes. Cryogenic effects include changes in electrical properties, such as *superconductivity, and changes in mechanical properties, such as superfluidity (*see* SUPERFLUID). Cryogenics has been applied to food preservation, life-support systems in space, and liquid propellants.

Crystal Palace A building designed by Joseph *Paxton (1801–65) to house the *Great Exhibition of 1851. The Crystal Palace, which had an area of 69 892 sq m (772 289 sq ft), was built in Hyde Park, London, of prefabricated glass and iron. It was later reassembled at Sydenham in SE London but burnt down in 1936.

crystals Solids that have a regular geometrical shape because the constituent atoms, ions, or molecules are arranged in an ordered repeating pattern, known as a crystal lattice. There are seven crystal systems, into which all

system	*edges*	*angles*
cubic	$a = b = c$	$\alpha = \beta = \gamma = 90°$
tetragonal	$a = b \neq c$	$\alpha = \beta = \gamma = 90°$
orthorhombic	$a \neq b \neq c$	$\alpha = \beta = \gamma = 90°$
hexagonal	$a = b \neq c$	$\alpha = \beta = 90°; \gamma = 120°$
trigonal	$a = b \neq c$	$\alpha = \beta = \gamma = 90°$
monoclinic	$a \neq b \neq c$	$\alpha = \gamma \neq \beta = 90°$
triclinic	$a \neq b \neq c$	$\alpha \neq \beta \neq \gamma$

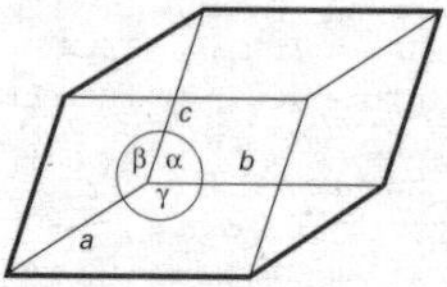

unit cell

crystals. The classification of crystals.

crystals are classified. Crystal structures are studied by a variety of techniques, including X-ray diffraction and electron microscopy. **Crystallography** is concerned with the structure and properties of crystals. Noncrystalline solids, such as glass, are said to be amorphous.

ctenophore A marine invertebrate animal, also called comb jelly, sea gooseberry, and sea walnut, belonging to the phylum *Ctenophora* (about 80 species). Its transparent gelatinous body is usually rounded and bears eight rows of ciliated comblike plates, used for locomotion. Ctenophores often occur in swarms in coastal waters, feeding on planktonic animals.

Cuba, Republic of A country in the Caribbean Sea, off the S coast of Florida. It consists of two main islands, Cuba and the Isla de la Juventud, together with over 1500 small islands and keys. On the island of Cuba fertile plains rise to mountains in the centre and SE and hills in the NW. The population is mainly of European origin, with large African and mixed minorities. *Economy*: mainly state controlled, it is dependent upon its sugar crop. Tobacco is another important export crop and meat production is important in the domestic economy. Mineral resources include nickel. The country has lost almost all its foreign trade following the collapse of the Soviet Union. Tourism is now the main source of revenue. *History*: discovered by Columbus in 1492, it was a Spanish colony (except in 1762–63, when it was occupied by the British) until 1898, when Spain withdrew following war with the USA. After three years of US occupation Cuba became a republic (1901) but the USA continued to intervene in Cuba's affairs until 1934. In 1940 Fulgencio Batista (1901–73) took Cuba into World War II on the Allied side. His corrupt dictatorship was overthrown (1959) in a socialist revolt led by Fidel *Castro, after which relations with the USA became increasingly strained and Cuba moved closer in its international relations to the Soviet Union. In 1961 an invasion of Cuban exiles with US support was defeated at the *Bay of Pigs and in 1962 the Soviet installation of missile bases in Cuba resulted in a US naval blockade. The crisis was resolved when the Soviet Union agreed to remove the bases. In the 1980s Cuban troops were involved in revolutionary conflicts in both Africa and the Caribbean. Since the collapse of the Soviet Union (1991) Cuba has suffered economic and political isolation. Official language: Spanish. Currency: Cuban peso of 100 centavos. Area 148 124 sq km (46 736 sq mi). Population (2003 est): 11 295 000. Capital: Havana.

cubism A style of painting and sculpture, originating in the works of *Picasso and *Braque in about 1907. It started as an intellectual investigation of how a solid form can be represented in two dimensions without resorting to illusionism. Volume was suggested by the fusion of multiple viewpoints of an object, which was presented as a complex of geometrical shapes. After 1911 the development of cubism led to the introduction of collage. Cubism was the principal catalytic influence on the evolution of *abstract art.

cuckoo A bird belonging to a family (*Cuculidae*; 128 species) occurring worldwide and ranging from 16–70 cm in length. The European cuckoo (*Cuculus canorus*), grey with white barring, belongs to a subfamily of parasitic cuckoos (*Cuculinae*; 47 species); these lay their eggs in the nests of other birds, which rear their young. Order: *Cuculiformes* (cuckoos and turacos).

cuckoopint A perennial herbaceous European plant, *Arum maculatum*, also called lords-and-ladies. 30–50 cm tall, it has a cylindrical cluster of tiny flowers, which protrudes from a funnel-shaped bract (spathe). The flowers give rise to poisonous red berries. Family: *Araceae*.

cucumber An annual vine, *Cucumis sativus*, widely cultivated since ancient times. The long green juicy fruits, up to 60 cm long, are eaten raw, cooked, or pickled (*see* GHERKIN). Family: *Cucurbitaceae* (gourd family).

cuisine minceur A style of gourmet cookery in which the traditional generous use of butter, cream, and other rich ingredients is minimized. Cuisine minceur was elaborated by the French chef Michel Guérard (1933–) in the 1970s at his restaurant at Eugénie-les-Bains in SW France.

Cullinan diamond An exceptional diamond weighing 3106 metric carats (c. 621 g) when found in the Premier Mine, South Africa, in 1905. It was cut into 9 major and 96 small stones. The two largest (Star of Africa and Cullinan II) are set in the British royal regalia.

Culloden Moor A moor in N Scotland, in the Highland Region near Inverness. In 1746 it was the scene of the last land battle to be fought in Britain, in which the Young Pretender, Charles Edward Stuart, was defeated by the Duke of Cumberland, thus ending the *Jacobite cause in Britain.

Culpeper, Nicholas (1616–54) English herbalist, physician, and astrologer. In 1649 he published an unauthorized translation of the official London Pharmacopoeia. This was followed by his famous and equally popular *Complete Herbal* (1653).

Cultural Revolution, Great Proletarian (1966–69) A political movement launched in China by *Mao Tse-tung with the professed aim of eliminating bureaucracy and reinvigorating revolutionary attitudes. Many leading officials were dismissed, the formal educational system was abolished, and reforms to foster correct political views were introduced. Young people, mobilized as *Red Guards, attacked Party officials and destroyed cultural objects. The result was a reign of anarchy and terror.

Cumbria A county in NW England, bordering on the Irish Sea. It was created in 1974 from Westmorland, Cumberland, and parts of NW Lancashire and NW Yorkshire. It consists of the *Lake District, enclosed by coastal lowlands and the Pennine uplands. Agricultural activity includes sheep, dairy, and arable farming. New industries, including chemicals, have largely replaced the traditional ones of coal, iron, and steel. Atomic energy establishments exist at Sellafield and Calder Hall. Area: 6809 sq km (2628 sq mi). Population (2001): 487 607. Administrative centre: Carlisle.

cumin An annual herb, *Cuminum cyminum*, up to 30 cm high with small whitish flowers and bristly fruits. Native to the Mediterranean, it has long been cultivated in Europe, India, and China for its bitter fruits, which are used in curry powders, to flavour liqueurs, etc. Family: *Umbelliferae*.

cumulus cloud (Cu) A low type of *cloud of convective origin having a heaped appearance and developing vertically from a flat base. **Cumulonimbus cloud** is heavy and dense, extending vertically to about 6000 m (20 000 ft), and is associated with thunderstorms. Its upper part often spreads out to form an anvil shape.

cuneiform The oldest writing system of which records survive, used to represent a number of ancient Near Eastern languages. The name derives from the wedge-shaped marks (Latin *cuneus*, a wedge) made by the imprint of a stylus in soft clay. Originally pictographic, by the 3rd millennium BC cuneiform pictures had become stylized in the form of groups of wedge-shaped imprints, many representing the sounds of syllables. Probably devised by the Sumerians not later than 3100 BC, cuneiform spread to other language groups in the area. By 100 BC, however, it had largely been superseded by the North Semitic script that was used to represent the Aramaic language.

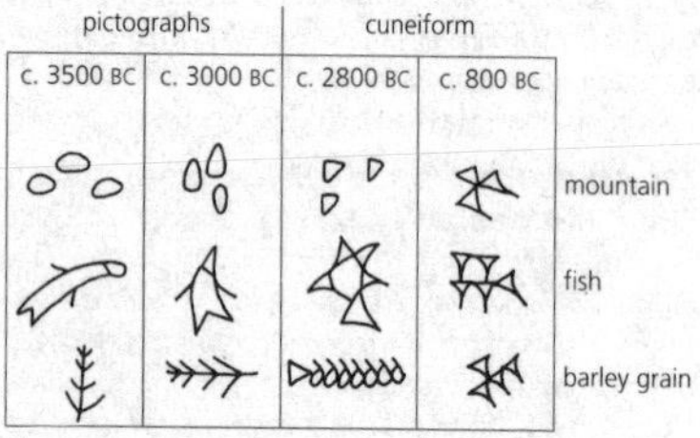

cuneiform. The wedge-shaped strokes of cuneiform writing developed gradually from pictographs.

Cupid The Roman god of love, identified with the Greek Eros, and lover of Psyche. He is usually portrayed as a winged boy shooting arrows of love.

cupronickel A corrosion-resistant alloy of 75% copper and 25% nickel (by weight). In the UK the Coinage Act (1946) substituted cupronickel coinage for silver alloy; the four cupronickel coins now in circulation are the 5p, 10p, 20p, and 50p pieces.

Curaçao A West Indian island, the largest in the Netherlands Antilles. Discovered in 1499, it was settled by the Spanish before being colonized by the Dutch in 1634. The refining of oil from Venezuela is of major importance; other industries include the production of Curaçao liqueur and calcium-phosphate mining. Area: 444 sq km (173 sq mi). Population (2000 est): 143 387. Chief town: Willemstad.

curare A resinous substance obtained from South American trees of the genera *Strychnos* and *Chondodendron*, used as an arrow poison by South American Indians. Curare blocks the action of *acetylcholine and causes muscular contraction; curare-like compounds (e.g. tubocurarine) are injected during general anaesthesia to relax muscles.

Curia Regis The King's Court of early medieval Europe. It fulfilled all the functions of royal government—and from its specialist departments developed the public government offices, such as, in England, the Chancery and the Exchequer, as well as the courts of law and parliament.

curie (Ci) A unit of radioactivity equal to the amount of an isotope that decays at the rate of 3.7×10^{10} disintegrations per second. Named after Pierre *Curie.

Curie, Marie (1867–1934) Polish chemist, renowned for her research into *radioactivity. Born Marya Skłodowska, she emigrated to France and married (1895) **Pierre Curie** (1859–1906), a French physicist. Marie Curie noticed in 1898 that one particular uranium ore emitted an anomalously large amount of radiation. Realizing that the radiation was caused by a new element, she and her husband spent four years isolating one gram of radium salt from eight tons of the ore. The Curies, together with Henri Becquerel, were awarded the 1903 Nobel Prize for Physics and, for her discovery of radium and polonium, she won the 1911 Nobel Prize for Chemistry. Pierre Curie discovered the *piezoelectric effect (1880) and showed that ferromagnetism reverts to paramagnetism (*see* MAGNETISM) above a certain temperature, now known as the Curie point (1895). He was killed in a road accident; she died as a result of the radiation to which she had been exposed. Their daughter **Irène Joliot-Curie** (1896–1956) married the French physicist **Frédéric Joliot** (1900–59) in 1926. They were the first to produce radioactivity artificially. For this work they were awarded the Nobel Prize for Chemistry in 1935.

curium (Cm) An artificial transuranic element discovered by Seaborg and others in 1944 and named after Marie and Pierre Curie. All 13 isotopes are radioactive and some intensely so. Curium is a silvery reactive metal. Its compounds include the oxides (CmO_2, Cm_2O_3) and halides (CmF_3, $CmCl_3$). At no 96; at wt (247); mp 1340 ± 40°C.

curlew A streaked brown or grey bird belonging to the genus *Numenius* (8 species). Curlews have a long neck and long curved bill. They breed in inland subarctic regions and migrate south in winter to marshes and mudflats, feeding on worms and crabs. The common Eurasian curlew (*N. arquata*) is almost 60 cm long and ranges from Britain to central Asia. Family: *Scolopacidae* (snipe, sandpipers, etc.).

curling A target game played on ice with stones fitted with handles, played since at least the early 16th century in Scotland. Two teams of four players take it in turns to slide two curling stones, each up to 36 m (39 yd), along the ice towards the "house," a series of concentric circles at the end of the rink. A team scores one point for each stone finishing nearer the centre of the house than any of its opponents'.

currant **1.** One of several species of shrubs belonging to the genus *Ribes*. Some are cultivated for their fruit, for example *blackcurrant and *redcurrant, and others, such as the *flowering currant, are grown as ornamentals. Family: *Grossulariaceae*. **2.** The dried berry of a small seedless *grape, grown in the Mediterranean region and used in cooking.

currawong An Australasian songbird of the genus *Strepera* (6 species). About 50 cm long, currawongs are usually black, sometimes with white markings, and have a long hook-tipped bill. They feed on insects, small mammals, and birds and frequently destroy fruit crops. Family: *Cracticidae* (Australian magpies).

cuscus A cat-sized *marsupial mammal belonging to the genus *Phalanger*, found in forests of NE Australia, New Guinea, and nearby islands. Cuscuses have a prehensile tail and climb slowly around trees at night, eating mainly leaves and fruit but sometimes catching lizards or birds. Family: *Phalangeridae* (*see* PHALANGER).

Cushing's disease A disorder resulting from excess *corticosteroid hormones in the body, named after H.W. Cushing (1869–1939). The symptoms include obesity, loss of minerals from the bones, and reddening of the face and neck; it may be associated with the symptoms of *diabetes mellitus and high blood pressure. It may be caused by a tumour of the pituitary gland or the adrenal gland or by prolonged therapy with high doses of corticosteroids: the treatment is determined by the cause.

custard apple A small tree of the genus *Annona* so called because of the custard-like flavour of its fruits. The common custard apple (*A. reticulata*), 5–8 m high and widely grown in the West Indies, produces reddish many-seeded fruits, 8–12 cm in diameter. Family: *Annonaceae*.

Custer, George A(rmstrong) (1839–76) US cavalry general. After earning distinction in the Civil War, he commanded the Seventh Cavalry during the western campaigns against the Indians. Sent to round up Sioux and Cheyenne forces under Chief *Sitting Bull in S Dakota's Black Hills in 1876, he and his force of about 260 were massacred at the *Little Bighorn (Custer's Last Stand).

cuttlefish A *cephalopod mollusc belonging to the family *Sepiidae* (about 100 species), of temperate coastal waters. 2.5–90 cm long, the body is supported by an internal calcareous shell—the cuttlebone—which gives buoyancy. When alarmed, the animal emits an inky fluid.

Cuzco 13 32S 71 57W A city in S Peru, in the Andes 3416 m (11 207 ft) above sea level. It was the capital of the Inca Empire prior to the Spanish conquest in 1533; Inca ruins include the Temple of the Sun. Population (1998 est): 278 590.

Cybele An Asiatic earth goddess identified by the Greeks with *Rhea. The centre of her worship was Phrygia, whence her cult spread to Athens and later to Rome. She represented the powers of nature and was a protectress of wild animals. Her priests were eunuchs known as Corybantes.

cybernetics The study of communication and control between men, machines, and organizations. The name was derived from the Greek word meaning "steersman" by Norbert *Wiener, who pioneered the subject. The human ability to adapt to changing circumstances and to make decisions is simulated in the design of computer-controlled systems.

cycad A *gymnosperm plant belonging to the phylum *Cycadophyta* (about 100 species), native to warm and tropical regions. They resemble small palms, having short stout stems with a crown of frondlike leaves. Reproductive organs are in the form of separate male and female cones borne on different trees. The stems of some species yield a type of *sago.

Cyclades (Modern Greek name: Kikládhes) A group of some 220 Greek islands in the S Aegean Sea, including Ándros, Delos, Íos, Míkonos, Melos, Náxos (the largest), Páros, and Syros. Total area: 2578 sq km (995 sq mi). Population (1991): 94 005. Capital: Hermopolis (on Syros).

Cyclamen A genus of perennial plants (15 species) native from the European Mediterranean to Iran and widely cultivated. The pot varieties are grown from *C. persicum*. The garden cyclamens include dwarf varieties, 5–8 cm high. All cyclamens produce corms but most can be grown from seed. They have drooping flowers with red, pink, or white reflexed petals. Family: *Primulaceae*.

cyclone An area of relatively low atmospheric pressure with a series of closed isobars around its centre. In the N hemisphere wind circulates in an anticlockwise direction around its centre, in the S hemisphere it is clockwise. Except in the tropics, cyclones are now usually referred to as *depressions or lows. Tropical cyclones include *hurricanes and *typhoons.

Cyclops A genus (44 species) of very small freshwater crustaceans of the class *Copepoda*, so named because of their single median eye. In Africa and Asia they transmit the parasitic Guinea worm larvae to humans if accidentally swallowed.

cyclostome An eel-like jawless aquatic vertebrate of the class *Cyclostomata*, which includes the *lamprey and *hagfish. Cyclostomes have a long cylindrical body with fins arranged singly (*compare* FISH), a cartilaginous skeleton, and a sucking mouth with numerous horny teeth. They occur mainly in temperate fresh waters and salt waters and many are parasitic on fish. Subphylum: *Agnatha*.

cyclotron A type of particle *accelerator in which charged particles are accelerated in an outward spiral path inside two hollow D-shaped conductors (called dees) placed back to back. The maximum energy of the particles is about 25 MeV. *See also* SYNCHROCYCLOTRON.

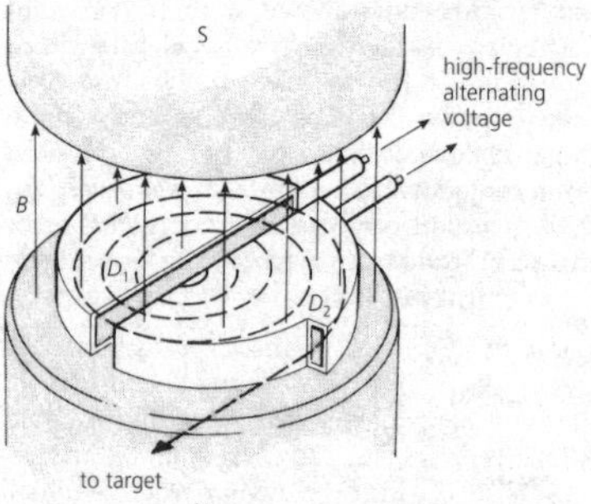

cyclotron. The charged particles are accelerated in the two D-shaped conductors (D_1 and D_2), which are supported in the magnetic field B.

Cymbidium A genus of tropical and subtropical *orchids (40–70 species), native to Asia and Australia. Most species have pseudobulbs and sprays of 6–20 flowers on each flower stalk. Cymbidiums are among the most popular orchids in cultivation today.

Cynics The followers of the Greek moral philosopher *Diogenes of Sinope, who were active from the early 3rd century BC. They were outspoken critics of accepted social values and often lived unconventional lives. Positive freedom could be attained by self-realization, but often it was the negative side of the Cynics' beliefs that was emphasized. Their distinction between natural and artificial values strongly influenced other ancient philosophies.

cypress A conifer of the genus *Cupressus* (true cypresses; 20 species), native to S Europe, E Asia, and North America and widely planted for ornament and timber. Cypresses have tiny scale-like leaves and rounded cones, 1–4 cm in diameter. The Italian or funeral cypress (*C. sempervirens*), of the Mediterranean region, is 25–45 m high. Family: *Cupressaceae*.

Related trees of the genus *Chamaecyparis* (6 species), of North America and SE Asia, are known as false cypresses. An example is Lawson's cypress C. lawsoniana. *See also* SWAMP CYPRESS.

Cyprus, Republic of (Greek name: Kypros; Turkish name: Kibris) An island state in the E Mediterranean Sea. A central plain rises to the Kyrenia Range in the N, and in the SW the Troödos Massif rises over 1800 m (6000 ft). Most of the population is Greek or Turkish, the former being in the majority. *Economy*: mainly agricultural. Mineral resources include iron pyrites, asbestos, chromite, and copper ores. Tourism is now the main source of revenue. The Turkish sector remains relatively poor, despite attempts to create a self-sufficient economy. Exports include wine, citrus fruits, potatoes, and metals. *History*: there was already a Greek colony on Cyprus almost 4000 years ago. It was conquered by Egypt in the 6th century BC and later formed part of the Persian, Macedonian, Roman, Byzantine, and Arab empires. In 1193 it became a Frankish kingdom and in 1489 a Venetian dependency. In 1571 it was conquered by the Turks and this occupation lasted until 1878 when it came under British administration. In the 1930s Greek Cypriots began advocating Enosis (Union with Greece), and in 1955 a Greek Cypriot organization (EOKA), led by Archbishop Makarios and Gen Grivas, began guerrilla warfare against the British. Cyprus became a republic in 1960 and a member of the Commonwealth in 1961. There were fierce clashes between the Greek and Turkish communities in the 1960s and in 1964 a UN peacekeeping force was sent to the island. Following a Greek-supported military coup in 1974, in which Makarios was temporarily overthrown, Turkey invaded the island leading to its virtual partition. In 1975 the Turks set up their own government in the N; this declared itself an independent state in 1983 but has not been recognized internationally. A UN plan to end the division of Cyprus (1992) failed to find acceptance and tensions between the communities have persisted. The EU's decision to admit Cyprus in May 2004 (excluding the Turkish N if there was no reunification) led to a new UN unity plan; in referendums held in April 2004 this was backed by Turkish Cypriots but rejected by Greek Cypriots. Official languages: Greek and Turkish. Currency: Cyprus pound of 1000 mils. Area: 9251 sq km (3572 sq mi). Population (2003 est): 714 000. Capital: Nicosia.

Cyrano de Bergerac, Savinien (1619–55) French writer and dramatist. He wrote a comedy, *Le Pédant joué* (1654), tragedies, and two satirical romances (published posthumously). He was noted for his comically long nose as well as his chivalrous nature and is the subject of Rostand's play *Cyrano de Bergerac*.

Cyrillic alphabet The alphabet used for Russian, Belarussian, Ukrainian, Bulgarian, Serbian, and various other languages of the former Soviet Union. It was developed from a Greek alphabet of the 9th century AD and is traditionally attributed to the Greek brothers, St Cyril (c. 827–69 AD) and St Methodius (c. 825–49 AD). It originally consisted of 43 letters, but modern versions have reduced this number to about 30.

cystic fibrosis A hereditary disease affecting the mucus-secreting and sweat glands. Symptoms, which appear in early childhood, are due to the production of thick mucus, which obstructs the pancreatic duct, intestinal glands, and bronchi. Patients suffer from malnutrition and recurrent chest infections. Current treatment, aimed at relieving symptoms, includes antibiotics, physiotherapy, a low-fat high-protein diet, and the administration of pancreatic enzymes.

cytology The study of the structure and function of cells. It began with the development of techniques for the study of materials under the light microscope, which enabled the *nucleus and other organelles to be observed. This led to the identification of chromosomes. More recent developments have included the use of phase-contrast and electron microscopy, and the use of such techniques as cell separation and analysis, autoradiography, and tissue culture. Cytological tests provide the basis for diagnosis of many diseases, including cancer.

cytoplasm *See* CELL.

cytotoxic drugs Drugs used to kill cancer cells. These drugs have led to improvements in the treatment of some cancers (e.g. leukaemia) but often cause severe side effects, including damage to bone marrow.

Czech A West Slavonic language spoken by over ten million people, mostly in the Czech Republic, where it is the official language. It is written in the Latin alphabet in a standardized form based on the dialect of Prague.

Czechoslovakia (Official name: Czech and Slovak Federative Republic) A former country in central Europe. The population was about two-thirds Czech and almost a third Slovak. Czechoslovakia was created, under Tomáš *Masaryk and Edvard Beneš, in 1918 following the collapse of the Austrian Empire. The new state was unable to withstand the expansionist ambitions of Hitler's Germany, which had taken control of all Czechoslovakia by 1939. Following the war Ruthenia was ceded to the Soviet Union, and some three million Germans were expelled from Czechoslovakia. By 1948 the Communist Party was in power and Czechoslovakia was closely allied with the Soviet Union. In 1968 a liberalization programme initiated by Dubček provoked a Soviet invasion. In 1989 pressure for liberal reform led to the fall of the Communist regime; a new government was formed with Václav Havel as president. Pressure for Slovakian independence led to Slovakia and the Czech Republic becoming separate states on 1 January 1993.

Czech Republic A landlocked country in central Europe. It is mainly wooded and mountainous. *Economy*: industry was entirely nationalized during the communist era (1948–89) and agriculture organized in collectives and state farms. A major privatization programme began in 1992. Principal crops include beet, wheat, potatoes, and barley. Industrial products include motor vehicles, glass, beer, and ceramics. Forestry is important. *History*: the Czech Republic, which comprises the historic provinces of Bohemia and Moravia, was a federal republic of Czechoslovakia until 1 January 1993. Václav *Havel, the former president of Czechoslovakia, was elected president of the new state. The Czech Republic joined NATO in 1999 and the EU in May 2004. Elections in 2002 led to the formation of a centre-left coalition led by Vladimir Spidla. In 2003 Havel was succeeded as president by Vaclav Kraus. Official language: Czech. Currency: koruna of 100 hellers. Area: 78 838 sq km (30 431 sq mi). Population (2003 est): 10 202 000. Capital: Prague.

D

dab One of several *flatfish of the family *Pleuronectidae*, especially the genus *Limanda* found in N Atlantic and N Pacific waters. The European *L. limanda* is an important food fish.

dabchick A small *grebe, *Tachybaptus ruficollis*, common in quiet inland waters of Europe, S Asia, and Africa. It has a dark-brown back, pale underparts, and a bright chestnut breast, neck, and cheeks. It feeds on small fish and aquatic invertebrates.

dace A slender lively fish belonging to the family *Cyprinidae*, which includes chub, roach, minnow, etc. The European dace (*Leuciscus leuciscus*) is up to 30 cm long, silvery coloured, and lives in schools in fast-flowing streams and rivers, eating both plant and animal material.

Dachau 48 15N 11 26E A town in S Germany, in Bavaria. It was the site of a Nazi concentration camp (1933–45). Population (latest est): 33 200.

dachshund A breed of dog originating in Germany, where they were developed to pursue badgers to earth. There are two size varieties—standard and miniature—and three coat types—long-haired, smooth-haired, and wire-haired. They are usually brownish or black and tan.

dada A European art and literary movement, beginning in Zürich in 1916 and aimed at deflating the status of the art-object. Its ideology was transmitted in such periodicals as *L'Intransigeant* in France. Manufactured objects were favoured both in graphic art and sculpture, as in the collages of *Arp, *Ernst, and Kurt Schwitters and the ready-mades of *Duchamp, who exported dada to the USA. Although dada petered out in the early 1920s, *surrealism absorbed many of its characteristics.

Daedalus A legendary Greek craftsman and sculptor, said to have built the labyrinth for King *Minos of Crete. Minos imprisoned him but he created wings for himself and his son **Icarus** and flew away; Icarus was killed when the sun melted his wings but Daedalus reached Sicily.

daffodil A perennial European plant, *Narcissus pseudonarcissus*, that is widely grown as a garden bulb. It has narrow leaves and yellow flowers, each with a trumpet shaped central crown surrounded by six segments. Family: *Amaryllidaceae*.

Dagestan Republic A constituent republic of Russia, on the Caspian Sea. The Caucasus Mountains lie to the S. Over 30 different nationalities, many of whom are Muslim, inhabit the republic. *Economy*: there are large engineering, oil, chemical, and food industries and power stations are under construction. Crops include wheat and fruit. *History*: conquered by Arabs, Turks, Mongols, and Persians, Dagestan was annexed by Russia in 1813. It was an autonomous Soviet Republic from 1921 until 1991. The 1990s saw growing agitation by Muslim separatists, leading to armed conflict with Russian troops (1999). Area: 50 278 sq km (19 416 sq mi). Population (2000 est): 2 149 000. Capital: Makhachkala.

Daguerre, Louis-Jacques-Mandé (1789–1851) French inventor of the first practicable photographic process (the daguerreotype). Working initially with Joseph Niepce (1765–1833), who had produced the first permanent photographic image (the heliograph), Daguerre succeeded during the 1830s in producing a photograph by focusing light onto a copper plate that had been coated with a silver salt. Daguerreotypes were widely made in the mid-19th century.

Dahlia A genus of herbaceous perennial tropical American plants (12 species), originally cultivated as a food crop for their tubers but now grown mainly for ornament. The brightly coloured flowers may be single or double. The varieties known as flat heads and pompoms are derived from *D. pinnata*; cactus-type flowers with pointed petals are varieties of *D. juarezii*. Family: *Compositae*.

Dáil Éireann The representative assembly of the Republic of Ireland. It is the more important house in the National Parliament, the other house being the Seanad Éireann (the Senate). There are 166 members elected by proportional representation, at least once every 5 years. The president (the nominal head of state) summons and dissolves the Dáil on the advice of the prime minister.

Daimler, Gottlieb (Wilhelm) (1834–1900) German inventor, who contributed to the development of the internal-combustion engine. Daimler started to build his own engines in 1883, which were soon sufficiently light and efficient to power motorcycles; in 1890 he founded a company to manufacture motor *cars.

daisy A herbaceous plant of the genus *Bellis* (15 species), with flower heads consisting of small central yellow disc florets surrounded by white or purple petal-like ray florets. The entire head is surrounded by bracts. Many species are garden ornamentals, some with double-flowered varieties. The common wild Eurasian daisy is *B. perennis*, a perennial up to 6 cm high, common in grasslands and lawns. Family: *Compositae*.

Dakar 14 45N 17 08W The capital and main port of Senegal, on Cape Verde peninsula, and the main industrial centre of the country. Population (1998 est): 1 999 000.

Dalai Lama The title of the spiritual and political ruler of Tibet and head of the Gelukpa Buddhist school. The title, originating in the 14th century, signifies the incarnation of the *Bodhisattva of compassion. Chosen by oracles after the death of the previous incumbent, the Dalai Lama is regarded as infallible. The 14th Dalai Lama went into exile in India in 1959 after a failed uprising against the occupying Chinese. He won the Nobel Peace Prize in 1989.

Dali, Salvador (1904–89) Spanish surrealist painter. He joined the Paris surrealists (1929) and, inspired by Freudian theories of the unconscious, painted startling dream images with photographic realism during self-induced hallucinatory states. While living in New York (1940–55), he turned to religious subjects and became a Roman Catholic.

Dalian *See* LÜDA.

Dallas 32 47N 96 48W A city in the USA, in NE Texas on the Trinity River. The discovery of oil in E Texas during the 1930s accelerated the city's growth, which was further enhanced by the introduction of the aircraft and electronics industries during World War II. Today Dallas is the state's second largest city and the financial and commercial centre of the SW. President John F. Kennedy was assassinated here in 1963. Population (2000): 1 188 580.

Dalmatian dog A breed named after Dalmatia, a coastal belt in Croatia on the Adriatic Sea, whence they were exported to the UK. Dalmatians are strongly built and were formerly used as carriage dogs. The short sleek coat has a pure white background with black or liver (brown) spots.

dalton *See* ATOMIC MASS UNIT.

Dalton, John (1766–1844) British chemist and originator of the modern *atomic theory of matter. His earliest researches led to **Dalton's law of partial pressures**, stating that the total pressure exerted by a certain volume of a gaseous mixture is equal to the sum of the pressures exerted by each gas, if it alone occupied the same volume. He believed that gases consist of particles, extending his theory in 1803 to suggest that all matter is particulate.

dam A barrier across a river. Dams are used for diverting the flow of water; raising the water level for navigation purposes; storing water for irrigation, industrial use, or water control; and providing a high-pressure source of water for *hydroelectric power. Gravity dams, usually made of concrete, have a flat vertical face upstream. They are no longer used for the largest dams. Arch dams consist of curved concrete structures presenting their convex faces upstream.

Daman and Diu A Union Territory in W India, formerly (until 1987) part of Goa, Daman, and Diu. Diu is an island off the coast of Gujarat. Area: 112 sq km (43 sq mi). Population (2001): 158 059. Chief town: Daman.

Damascus (Arabic name: Esh Sham) 33 30N 36 19E The capital of Syria, in the SE of the country close to the Lebanese border. It is thought to be the oldest continually inhabited city in the world. Under Ottoman rule from 1516 until 1918, Damascus was taken by the French (1920) and became capital of Syria in 1941. Population (1994): 1 394 322.

Damocles Legendary courtier of Dionysius I of Syracuse in the 9th century BC. Dionysius seated him at a banquet beneath a sword suspended by a single hair, thus illustrating the insecurity of human life, irrespective of wealth or power.

damson The edible plumlike stone fruit of *Prunus damascena*, a slender twisted tree found across the N hemisphere. It has small white flowers that develop into purple fruits. Family: *Rosaceae*. *See also* PLUM.

Danae In Greek legend, the daughter of Acrisius, King of Argos. He imprisoned her because an oracle said he would be killed by her child; Zeus visited her, however, and she gave birth to *Perseus. Acrisius cast mother and son out to sea but Polydectes, King of Seriphos, rescued them.

Da Nang (former name: Tourane) 16 04N 108 14E A port in S central Vietnam, on the South China Sea. It was the site of a major US airbase during the Vietnam War. Population (1992 est): 382 674.

dandelion A weedy perennial herbaceous plant of the worldwide genus *Taraxacum*, with a basal rosette of jagged toothed leaves and a solitary flower head of bright-yellow florets. The seeds have parachutes of fine white hairs and are dispersed by wind. The common dandelion (*T. officinale*) is found throughout the N hemisphere. Family: *Compositae*.

Danelaw The area of Anglo-Saxon England E of Watling Street from the River Tees to the River Thames within which Danish laws and customs prevailed from the late 9th to the late 11th centuries.

Daniel (6th century BC) An Old Testament prophet and Jewish exile in Babylon. **The Book of Daniel** is usually credited to him, the first six chapters telling of various mainly supernatural episodes involving Daniel and his companions under Kings Nebuchadnezzar and Belshazzar.

Daniell cell An electric cell whose positive pole consists of copper immersed in a solution of copper sulphate and whose negative pole consists of zinc in a solution of sulphuric acid or zinc sulphate. It has an almost constant emf of 1.08 volts. Named after J. F. Daniell (1790–1845), British chemist.

Danish The official language of Denmark, spoken by about five million people. It belongs to the East Scandinavian branch of the North Germanic languages. Closely related to other Scandinavian languages, it is the most altered form of the common ancestral tongue.

Dante Alighieri (1265–1321) Italian poet. Born into a noble Guelf family of Florence (*see* GUELFS AND GHIBELLINES), he became involved in the political struggle between the Black Guelfs and the White Guelfs, leading to his exile (c. 1301) from Florence. Dante's major works include the autobiographical love poem *La vita nuova* (c. 1292), the epic poem *The Divine Comedy* (c. 1307), and two influential treatises on the value of vernacular Italian as a literary language.

Danube, River The second longest river in Europe after the River Volga. Rising in the Black Forest in Germany, it flows mainly ESE across central and SE Europe to enter the Black Sea in Romania. Immensely important commercially, it is linked by the River Altmühl with canals to the Rivers Main and Rhine. Major cities along its course include Vienna, Budapest, and Belgrade. Length: 2850 km (1770 mi).

Daphne (botany) A genus of evergreen and deciduous shrubs (70 species) of the Old World, including many important ornamentals. The leaves are arranged spirally up the stem. The small bell-shaped flowers occur in clusters. The genus includes the deciduous mezereon (*D. mezereum*), with reddish-purple flowers and red berries, and the evergreen spurge laurel (*D. laureola*), with greenish flowers and black berries. Family: *Thymeleaceae*.

Daphne (Greek mythology) A mountain nymph who rejected Apollo and, to escape him, was transformed by Gaea into a laurel tree. Apollo made the laurel a symbol of honour and victory.

Daphnia *See* WATER FLEA.

Daphnis In Greek legend, a Sicilian shepherd who was punished with blindness for infidelity in love. He consoled himself with songs and was thus revered as the inventor of pastoral poetry and song.

Da Ponte, Lorenzo (1749–1838) Italian author, originally a priest. Banished from Italy in 1779, he settled in Vienna and there wrote the libretti for Mozart's operas *The Marriage of Figaro* (1786), *Don Giovanni* (1787), and *Cosi fan tutte* (1790). In 1805 he went to the USA.

Dardanelles (Ancient name: Hellespont) A strait separating European and Asian Turkey and connecting the Sea of Marmara with the Aegean Sea. It was the scene of an unsuccessful campaign in *World War I. Length: 60 km (37 mi); width: 1.5–6.5 km (1–4 mi).

Dar es Salaam 6 48S 39 12E The capital and main port of Tanzania, on the Indian Ocean. Founded in 1862, it was capital of German East

Africa (1891–1916) and of Tanganyika (1916–64). It is an important commercial and industrial centre. Population (latest est): 1 360 850.

darkling beetle A black or dark brown flightless beetle belonging to a widely distributed family (*Tenebrionidae*; 15 000 species), particularly common in warm regions. Nearly all are scavengers, feeding on decaying vegetation, dung, fungi, or stored grains and cereals. Mealworms (larvae of *Tenebrio molitor*) are common pests of flour mills, etc., and are also reared commercially as food for birds and fish.

d

Darling, Grace (1815–42) British heroine, the daughter of a lighthouse keeper on the Northumberland coast. In 1838 she helped her father rescue five people from a ship (*Forfarshire*) that had struck the rocks during a storm.

Darling River A river in E Australia, rising in the Great Dividing Range and flowing generally SW across New South Wales before joining the Murray River at Wentworth. Length: 2740 km (1702 mi).

Darlington 1. 54 31N 1 34W A town in NE England, in Darlington unitary authority, Co Durham. The Stockton–Darlington railway (1825) was the world's first passenger railway. Darlington has engineering, construction, and communications industries. Population (1991): 86 767. **2.** A unitary authority in NE England, in Durham. Area: 198 sq km (77 sq mi). Population (2001): 97 822.

Darmstadt 49 52N 08 39E A city in central Germany, in Hesse. It has a 16th-century palace. Manufactures include machinery and chemicals. Population (1999 est): 137 600.

Darnley, Henry Stuart, Lord (1545–67) The second husband of Mary, Queen of Scots, and father of James I of England. He married Mary, his cousin, in 1565. He was involved in the murder of her secretary David Riccio (1566) and was himself murdered, probably by *Bothwell.

darter A slender elongated bird belonging to a family (*Anhingidae*; 4 species) occurring in tropical and subtropical inland waters. Darters are about 88 cm long and black or brown with white markings; males have plumes on the head and neck. They have thin pointed bills for catching fish underwater. Order: *Pelecaniformes* (gannets, pelicans, etc.).

Dartford 51 27N 0 14E A town in SE England, in Kent linked with Thurrock (Essex) by the Dartford Tunnel (opened in 1963) under the River Thames. A bridge was opened in 1991. Population (1991): 59 411.

Dartmoor A moorland area of England, in SW Devon. A national park since 1951, it consists of a rolling granite upland rising to tors, the highest of which is High Willhays at 621 m (2039 ft). Its many historic remains include stone circles and Bronze Age and Iron Age settlements. A major tourist attraction, it is also used extensively as a military training area. Dartmoor prison was opened in 1806. Area: 945 sq km (365 sq mi).

Dartmouth 50 21N 3 35W A port and resort in SW England, in Devon on the Dart estuary. The Royal Naval College (1905) is situated here. Population (1991): 5676.

Darwin 12 23S 130 44E A city in Australia, the capital and chief port of the Northern Territory. It had to be largely rebuilt after a cyclone in 1974. Population (1994): 78 100.

Darwin, Charles Robert (1809–1882) British naturalist, who originated the concept that living things evolve by means of natural selection. Following attempts to study medicine and theology, Darwin's interest in natural history led him to sail with HMS *Beagle* on an expedition to South America and the Pacific (1831–36). As ship's naturalist, Darwin made exhaustive observations of the geology and natural history of the region.

Following the voyage, Darwin analysed his observations and formed them into a coherent view of nature. In 1859 he published his findings in *Origin of Species by Means of Natural Selection* (*see* DARWINISM). His views aroused controversy because they conflicted with the account of the Creation in the Bible. This culminated in the debate at Oxford in 1860 between Darwin's supporters, led by T.H. *Huxley, and Bishop Samuel Wilberforce. Huxley's arguments won the day. In *The Descent of Man* (1871), Darwin applied his theories to humans; they are now accepted as a fundamental principle of biology. His grandfather **Erasmus Darwin** (1731–1802) was a successful physician noted for his radical views, especially on biology. Among his ideas were speculations about the nature of evolution that anticipated later theories, particularly those of *Lamarck.

Darwinism The theory of *evolution based on the work of Charles *Darwin. Darwin drew his conclusions from the following observations: (1) in any population the organisms show individual variations; (2) the size of the population remains constant although more offspring are produced than are necessary to maintain it. He concluded that the forces acting on the population—competition, disease, climate, etc.—resulted in the survival of those best fitted to the environment, a process he called **natural selection**. The survivors would breed, thus passing on their inheritable advantageous variations to their offspring. In a gradually changing environment this process would result in a change in the whole population and ultimately the evolution of new *species.

Darwin's theory has been modified by subsequent discoveries in genetics, which have revealed the source of the variation on which it is based (mostly genetic mutations). The modern version of his theory is known as **neo-Darwinism**.

dasyure A small carnivorous *marsupial mammal belonging to a family (*Dasyuridae*; 45 species) occurring in Australia and New Guinea. Dasyures are nocturnal and good climbers. See also TASMANIAN DEVIL.

data processing The organization, transmission, and storage of information by computers. In batch processing, data is grouped and coded before processing. In on-line processing each user feeds data into the system continuously. Many systems incorporate both of these forms of processing for different types of work. The Data Protection Act (1998; in force from 2000), which supplements and strengthens earlier legislation (1984), provides protection for individuals by controlling the processing of information about them stored on computers.

date A *palm tree, *Phoenix dactylifera*, native to N Africa and SW Asia and cultivated from Morocco to India for its sugar-rich fruits. Male and female flowers grow on separate trees, the female flowers developing into large clusters of single-seeded berries.

dating techniques *See* DENDROCHRONOLOGY; HELIUM DATING; POTASSIUM-ARGON DATING; RADIOCARBON DATING; RUBIDIUM-STRONTIUM DATING; URANIUM-LEAD DATING.

dauphin From 1350 until 1830 the title of the heirs to the French Crown. It was the personal name, and later became the title, of the rulers of a former province of SE France, the Dauphiné, which was purchased by the future Charles V in 1350. After becoming king (1364), he granted the Dauphiné and its accompanying title to his son, thus establishing a precedent.

David (d. 962 BC) King of Israel (c. 1000–962). David was anointed by Samuel as the successor of Saul, the first King of Israel. He became a close friend of Saul's son, Jonathan, but his successes against the Philistines, in cluding the slaying of Goliath, aroused Saul's jealousy and he became an outlaw. After the death of Saul and Jonathan, David was proclaimed King of Hebron and then of all Israel. He conquered Jerusalem, making it the nation's political and religious centre, finally defeated the Philistines, and united the tribes of Israel. His reign was troubled by the revolt of his son Absalom. David was succeeded by Solomon, his son by Bathsheba. According to the Jewish prophets, the Messiah must be a descendant of David.

David I (1084–1153) King of the Scots (1124–53). He recognized Matilda as successor to Henry I of England, and invaded N England (1138) after Stephen had seized the throne. Stephen defeated him in the battle of the Standard (1138), near Northallerton. David founded or refounded over a dozen monasteries.

David, Jacques Louis (1748–1825) French neoclassical painter. His mature works depicted heroic scenes from Republican Rome and ancient Greece, e.g. *Oath of the Horatii* (Louvre). During the Revolution he painted some of its martyrs, e.g. *Death of Marat*, and as court painter to Napoleon I (from 1804) his paintings illustrate imperial successes, e.g. *Napoleon Crowning Josephine* (Louvre).

David, St (*or* **St Dewi**; c. 520–600 AD) The patron saint of Wales and first abbot of Menevia (now St David's). He was also a missionary and the founder of many churches in Wales. Feast day: 1 March.

David ap Gruffudd (d. 1283) The brother of *Llywelyn ap Gruffudd, after whose death (1282) David claimed the title Prince of Wales. He was executed by Edward I for leading the Welsh in rebellion against him.

Davies, Sir Peter Maxwell (1934–) British composer and conductor. He was director (1970–87) of the chamber ensemble The Fires of London. Some of his works blend medieval musical techniques with modern compositional devices. His output includes film music, operas, seven symphonies, and the ten Strathclyde Concertos. He was appointed Master of the Queen's Music in 2004.

Davis, Bette (Ruth Elizabeth D.; 1908–89) US film actress. From the 1930s to the 1950s she gave intense performances in such films as *Jezebel* (1938), *Dark Victory* (1939), and *All About Eve* (1950). In later years she played elderly eccentric or neurotic women.

d

Davis, Sir Colin (1927–) British conductor. He has conducted the BBC Scottish Symphony Orchestra, the English Chamber Orchestra, and the orchestras of the Metropolitan Opera, New York, and the Royal Opera, Covent Garden, becoming conductor of the London Symphony Orchestra in 1995. He was appointed CH in 2001.

Davis, John (*or* **J. Davys**; c.1550–1605) English navigator. He went on three voyages in search of the *Northwest Passage (1585, 1586, 1587), passing through the strait named after him to Baffin Bay. In 1592, seeking the Magellan Strait, he discovered the Falkland Islands.

Davis, Miles (1926–91) US jazz trumpeter and composer, one of the originators of cool jazz. His albums include *Birth of the Cool* (1948), the innovatory *Kind of Blue* (1960), and *Bitches Brew* (1969), in which he pioneered the fusion of jazz with rock.

Davis, Steve (1957–) British snooker player. He won the world professional championship in 1981, 1983, 1984, and 1987–89.

Davis Cup An international tennis trophy for competing teams of men, donated in 1900 by Dwight Filley Davis (1879–1945). Recent winners have been USA (1990, 1992, 1995), France (1991, 1996, 2001), Germany (1993), Sweden (1994, 1997, 1998), Australia (1999, 2003), Spain (2000), and Russia (2002).

Davy, Sir Humphry (1778–1829) British chemist and inventor of the miner's safety lamp (1815), known as the Davy lamp. For discovering the value of nitrous oxide as an anaesthetic Davy was invited to join the Royal Institution in London; here his most important work was the discovery of many new metallic elements—potassium in 1807 and sodium, calcium, barium, magnesium and strontium in 1808. He employed the young Michael *Faraday as his assistant at the Royal Institution.

DBE *See* ORDER OF THE BRITISH EMPIRE, THE MOST EXCELLENT.

DDT (dichlorophenyltrichloroethane) An organochlorine compound that was formerly widely used as a contact *insecticide. It is active against many insects, including mosquitoes, flies, fleas, and bedbugs. However, many have become resistant to DDT, which is a very stable compound and accumulates not only in their tissues but also in the tissues of the animals that prey on them, causing toxic effects. Its use is banned in the UK.

deadly nightshade (*or* **belladonna**) A branching perennial herb, *Atropa belladonna*, native to Eurasia. It has solitary purple or greenish bell-shaped flowers. The shiny black berries taste sweet but contain a deadly poison. The plant is a source of a variety of alkaloids, especially hyoscyamine and atropine. Family: *Solanaceae*. *See also* NIGHTSHADE.

Dead Sea A lake in E Israel and W Jordan. It is fed by the River Jordan and, having no outlet, is highly saline and supports no life. Area: 1050 sq km (401 sq mi).

Dead Sea Scrolls A group of Hebrew and Aramaic manuscript scrolls found in caves in the area of Khirbat Qumran, NW of the Dead Sea. The first were discovered in 1947. The 500 different documents, dating from 250 BC to 70 AD, seem to have formed the library of a Jewish, perhaps *Essene, community that existed from about 125 BC to 66–70 AD. They include texts of many Old Testament books, commentaries, prayers, psalms, and material peculiar to the community. They are particularly valuable as evidence of the accuracy of previously known Old Testament texts.

Dean, James (James Byron; 1931–55) US film actor who trained at the *Actors' Studio, and became a cult hero for his generation. His films were *East of Eden* (1954), *Rebel without a Cause* (1955), and *Giant* (1955), released following his death in a car crash.

death The permanent cessation of all bodily functions in an organism. A person is medically pronounced dead when his heartbeat and breathing movements have ceased permanently, but since the advent of mechanical ventilators the heartbeat may be maintained long after "natural" breathing has stopped as a result of irreversible brain damage. Brain death is defined on the basis of brain function: when the parts of the brain that control respiration and other vital reflexes have ceased to function the patient is said to be brain dead, i.e. truly dead, although his heart may continue to beat for some time with the aid of mechanical life-support systems.

death cap A highly poisonous mushroom, *Amanita phalloides*, fairly common in and near deciduous woodlands. Its cap is usually pale greenish yellow. The stalk is white or greenish white, with a baglike sheath (volva) at its base.

death's-head moth A *hawk moth, *Acherontia atropos*, with a wingspan of 125 mm, found in Europe, Africa, and Asia. Its thoracic markings resemble a skull and crossbones.

deathwatch beetle A widely distributed wood-boring beetle, *Xestobium rufovillosum*, about 7 mm long, that can cause immense damage to old buildings and furniture. It lays its eggs in small crevices in the wood and the larvae tunnel in, eventually reducing it to powder. The pupae often make knocking sounds by repeatedly striking their heads against the walls of their burrows. Family: *Anobiidae.*

debenture stock A document setting out the terms of a fixed-interest loan to a company. A **secured debenture** is secured against a specified asset belonging to the company (fixed charge) or against all the company's assets (floating charge). An **unsecured debenture** has no such security, but if it cannot be paid back on the repayment date, debenture holders can force the company into liquidation and they then take priority over other shareholders in having their capital repaid. An **irredeemable debenture** is never repaid, being bought only for the interest it earns.

de Broglie, Louis Victor, 7th Duc (1892–1987) French physicist, who won the 1929 Nobel Prize for his theory that elementary particles have associated waves, known as **de Broglie waves**. The theory was confirmed by the subsequent observation of *electron diffraction and forms the basis of the branch of quantum mechanics known as *wave mechanics.

Debussy, Claude (Achille) (1862–1918) French composer. He spent most of his life in Paris and is regarded as the originator of musical impressionism. His most famous works include *Prélude à l'après-midi d'un faune* (for orchestra; 1892–94), the opera *Pelléas et Mélisande* (1892–1902), *La Mer* (three symphonic sketches; 1903–05), a string quartet, and a sonata for flute, viola, and harp.

Decadents A group of late-19th-century French symbolist poets and their contemporaries in England. They aimed to create a literature liberated from all moral and social responsibilities. Poets linked with the movement included *Rimbaud, *Verlaine, and *Mallarmé in France, and Arthur Symons and Oscar *Wilde in England. *See also* AESTHETIC MOVEMENT.

Decapoda A worldwide order of *crustaceans (over 8500 species), with five pairs of thoracic appendages—anterior pincers and four pairs of walking legs. They include the *shrimps and *prawns (suborder: *Natantia*, "swimming forms") and *lobsters, *crayfish, and *crabs (suborder: *Reptantia*, "walking forms").

decathlon An athletic competition for men, consisting of ten events over two days. On the first are 100 m sprint, long jump, shot put, high jump, and 400 m sprint; on the second are 110 m hurdles, discus throw, pole vault, javelin throw, and 1500 m run.

decibel (dB) A unit used to compare two power levels on a logarithmic scale. Two power levels P and P_0 differ by n decibels when $n = 10 \log_{10} P/P_0$. The unit is often used to express a sound intensity in which case P_0 is usually taken as the intensity of the lowest audible note of the same frequency as P.

decimal system The number system in common use, having a base 10 and thus using ten separate numerals. It also involves the use of a decimal point to express numbers less than one, as in 0.25. The decimal system was invented by the Hindus and adopted by the Arabs in the 9th century (*see also* MATHEMATICS). The use of decimal fractions originated in Italy in the 12th century but use of the decimal point did not occur until the early 18th century. Decimalization of currency systems was introduced by France after the Revolution and followed by most other European and American countries, except for Britain, which did not decimalize until 1971. *See also* METRIC SYSTEM.

Declaration of Independence (4 July 1776) The declaration, adopted by the 13 colonies of North America, that announced their independence from Great Britain. Written by Thomas *Jefferson between 11 June and 2 July and revised before adoption, the Declaration is both specific (in its enumeration of grievances) and general (in its statement of principles of governance) and is one of the most influential proclamations in the Western political tradition.

declination *See* MAGNETIC DECLINATION; RIGHT ASCENSION.

decompression sickness (*or* **caisson disease**) An occupational hazard of pilots and underwater divers caused by too rapid a return to normal atmospheric pressure. At high pressures large amounts of gas can be carried in the blood. A rapid return to normal pressure causes nitrogen (the main component of inhaled air) to form bubbles in the blood; this interrupts the blood supply to the tissues, producing joint pain (the bends), general discomfort, and respiratory problems (the chokes). Decompression sickness is prevented by a slow return to atmospheric pressure; it is treated by placing the patient in a hyperbaric chamber.

Decorated The style of gothic architecture predominant in England between 1300 and 1370. In contrast to the geometric restraint of its predecessor, *Early English, Decorated is characterized by complex flowing patterns, especially in window tracery. Roof vaults were intricately ribbed and the ogee or double curved arch with elaborate ornamentation became common.

d

Dee, River The name of three rivers in the UK. **1.** A river in NE Scotland, flowing E to the North Sea at Aberdeen. Length: 140 km (87 mi). **2.** A river in North Wales and NW England, rising in Gwynedd and flowing E and N through Chester to the Irish Sea. Length: 112 km (70 mi). **3.** A river in S Scotland, flowing S to the Solway Firth. Length: 80 km (50 mi).

deed In law, a document in writing, signed, sealed, and delivered, transferring a right over property (title-deed) or creating an obligation on its maker. To be binding it need not fulfil conditions applicable to a *contract. A deed may be between two parties, to establish mutual obligations, or it may involve one party only (deed poll).

deer A *ruminant mammal of the family *Cervidae* (41 species), occurring mainly in the N hemisphere, although a few are found in South America and N Africa and they have been introduced to SE Asia and Australasia. Nearly all deer have bony antlers that are shed and replaced every year. Deer range in size from the *elk to the small South American pudu.

defamation In law, a false and derogatory statement about another person that tends to lower him in the estimation of members of the community generally. It is libel if made in a permanent form (e.g. in newspapers, broadcasts) and slander if made in a transient form, by spoken words or gestures. The remedy for both types of defamation is by civil proceedings, although libel may also be a crime if its publication is calculated to provoke a breach of the peace. Not only the originator of a libel but everyone who has subsequently repeated or published it may be sued by the person libelled. Action for libel cannot be brought against "privileged" proceedings or statements such as judicial and parliamentary proceedings. A statement judged to be a fair comment on a matter of public interest is also not actionable as defamation.

deficit financing The fiscal policy of stimulating the economy by government spending in excess of revenue by borrowing to finance the resultant deficit. Deficit financing was advocated by the British economist J. M. *Keynes and became normal practice from 1945 until the 1980s, when monetarist ideas became influential (*see* NATIONAL DEBT).

deflation A government action to slow down the economy, with the aim of easing *inflation or cutting down on imports and thus helping the *balance of payments. Both monetary policy (credit "squeeze") and fiscal policy (increasing taxes, cutting government spending) can be used to deflate the economy.

Defoe, Daniel (1660–1731) British novelist, economist, and journalist. His early career as a merchant ended in bankruptcy in 1692. He worked as a journalist and informer for both Whigs and Tories and suffered imprisonment (1702) for one of his pamphlets. From 1704 to 1713 he wrote most of the thrice-weekly *Review* himself. His famous novels were written late in his career, *Robinson Crusoe* in 1719 and *Moll Flanders* and *Colonel Jack* in 1722.

defoliant A chemical applied to foliage in order to cause premature shedding of leaves. Defoliants are used to aid mechanical harvesting of cotton and for other peaceful uses. They are also employed in chemical warfare.

Degas, (Hilaire Germain) Edgar (1834–1917) French painter and sculptor. His early works were portraits and history paintings. From the mid-1860s he turned to painting contemporary scenes, particularly of ballet and racecourses, characterized by informal poses and unusual angles. His pastels of women at their toilet shocked his contemporaries but are among his finest works. He exhibited frequently with the impressionists but was little influenced by their style.

de Gaulle, Charles André Joseph Marie (1890–1970) French general and statesman who was an outstanding international figure in the mid-20th century; president (1958–69). An advocate of mechanized warfare during the 1930s, he was promoted early in World War II to general (1940). He opposed the Franco-German armistice, becoming leader of the Free French in London and a symbol of French patriotism. De Gaulle resented his dependence on Britain and the USA and the antagonism between them was to continue after the war. In 1958 he was summoned from retirement to deal with the crisis in *Algeria. He became president of the new Fifth Republic in 1959 and moved towards the achievement of Algerian independence (1962). He subsequently pursued his vision of a Europe of nationally self-conscious states, free of US influence. He thus opposed the postwar multinational organizations, refusing to sign the *Nuclear Test-Ban Treaty (1963) and withdrawing France from the military structure of NATO (1966). He was also passionately opposed to UK membership of the EEC. At home his position was greatly weakened by the student and industrial unrest of May 1968, and in 1969 he resigned. His policies, however, have endured in the right-wing Gaullist movement in French politics.

De Havilland, Sir Geoffrey (1882–1965) British aircraft designer and manufacturer, who produced some of the first jet-propelled aircraft. During both World Wars he designed several military aircraft, including the Mosquito of World War II.

dehydration A potentially serious condition resulting from excessive loss of water from the body. The water that is continuously lost from the body in urine, sweat, expired air, and faeces must be replaced by drinking. Dehydration may result from insufficient intake of water or from excessive loss in fever, vomiting, diarrhoea, or from the skin in hot climates. It may lead, if not treated, to shock and death.

deism A system of belief in God that, in contrast to *theism, discounts revealed religion and takes God as the philosophical first cause. More specifically, deism was a rationalistic anti-Christian movement in England in the late 17th and early 18th centuries with its roots in John *Locke's empiricism; its adherents regarded dogmatic religions as corruptions of man's natural relation with God.

Dekabrists (*or* **Decembrists**) Members of an unsuccessful anti-Tsarist revolt in December 1825, following the death of Alexander I. They were members of various clandestine organizations formed after the Napoleonic Wars by discontented former military officers.

de Klerk, F(rederik) W(illem) (1937–) South African statesman; president (1989–94). He dismantled apartheid and in 1993 signed South Africa's new multiracial (transitional) constitution. After the ANC won multiracial elections (1994), de Klerk became second deputy president. In 1996 he withdrew his party from the ruling coalition and resigned (1997) as party leader. He was awarded the 1993 Nobel Peace Prize jointly with Nelson Mandela.

de Kooning, Willem (1904–97) US painter of Dutch birth. He painted both figurative and abstract compositions but by the late 1940s was regarded as a leader of *abstract expressionism. In his later years he produced many paintings while suffering from Alzheimer's disease.

Delacroix, Eugène (1798–1863) French Romantic painter, influenced by Théodore Géricault (1791–1824), *Rubens, and *Constable. His richly coloured paintings were often inspired by incidents in Dante, Shakespeare, and Byron, and by contemporary events, e.g. *Massacre at Chios* (1824), based on a Turkish atrocity in Greece.

de la Mare, Walter (1873–1956) British poet, novelist, and anthologist, whose work is imbued with an atmosphere of mystery and magic. His works include the poem "The Listeners" (1912), the novel *Memoirs of a Midget* (1921), and the anthology *Love* (1943).

Delaunay, Robert (1885–1941) The earliest French painter of completely abstract compositions. In his series of *Discs* (1912–13) he pioneered orphism (which he called *simultaneisme*), a style in which colour alone was the subject matter.

Delaware The second smallest state in the USA. It occupies part of the low-lying Atlantic coastal plain with higher ground in the NW, where most of the state's population and industry is concentrated. It is one of the most industrialized states; Wilmington contains the administrative centres of several large chemical companies. Motor vehicles, synthetic rubber, textiles, and food products are also produced. *History*: the Dutch established a settlement (1631) but it was the Swedes who founded the first permanent settlement Fort Christiana (now Wilmington) in 1638. Delaware was subsequently captured by the Dutch (1655) and the English (1664). It became part of Pennsylvania in 1682 and shared a governor with that colony until 1776. It was the first of the original 13 states of the USA. Area: 5328 sq km (2057 sq mi). Population (2000): 783 600. Capital: Dover.

Delft 52 01N 4 21E A town in the W Netherlands, in South Holland province. Since the late 16th century it has been famous for its pottery and porcelain known as delftware. Population (1991 est): 89 000.

Delhi 28 40N 77 14E The capital of India, situated midway between the Ganges and Indus Valleys on the W bank of the River Jumna. It consists of the old city (Old Delhi), which was built in 1639 on the site of former cities of Delhi that date from the 15th century BC, and New Delhi, which replaced Calcutta as the capital of British India in 1912. Both the old and new cities together with the surrounding area comprise the Union Territory of Delhi, an administrative unit of some 1418 sq km (553 sq mi). The massive Red Fort of Old Delhi contains the Imperial Palace (1638–48) of Shah Jahan, and the Jami Masjid (Principal Mosque). New Delhi, with its spacious tree-lined streets and imposing government buildings, was designed chiefly by Sir Edwin Lutyens. Population (1991): 7 206 704.

Delian League A confederacy of Greek city states formed in 478 BC during the *Greek-Persian Wars under the leadership of Athens. Members met on the sacred island of Delos. After the peace between Greece and Persia (c. 450) Athens regarded its allies as subjects. The League was disbanded after Athens' defeat (404) in the Peloponnesian War but was revived in defence against Sparta in 378, lasting until the defeat (338) of Athens and Thebes at Chaeronea.

Delibes, Leo (1836–91) French composer. He wrote operas and operettas but his best-known works are the ballets *Coppélia* (1870) and *Sylvia* (1876).

deliquescence The process in which some crystalline substances, such as calcium chloride ($CaCl_2$), absorb water from the atmosphere to such an extent that they dissolve; this is extreme hygroscopic (water-attracting) behaviour. Deliquescent substances are used in several industries to provide dry atmospheres.

Delius, Frederick (1862–1934) British composer of German descent. Largely self-taught, he was influenced by Debussy and Grieg. His works include *Paris, the Song of a Great City* (1899), *On Hearing the First Cuckoo in Spring* (1912), and *North Country Sketches* (1913–14). Delius became blind in 1925 but continued to compose with the help of his amanuensis, Eric Fenby (1906–97).

Della Robbia, Luca (1400–82) Florentine Renaissance sculptor. Working first in marble, Luca produced the relief *Cantoria* (1431–38) for the Duomo, Florence. Later he specialized in enamelled terracotta sculptures.

Delos (Modern Greek name: Dhílos) 37 23N 25 15E A Greek island in the S Aegean Sea, one of the Cyclades. It was of great importance in antiquity (*see* DELIAN LEAGUE), and many ancient temples and other buildings have been excavated. Area: 3 sq km (1 sq mi).

Delphi A village in central Greece. In antiquity, it was the principal sanctuary and oracle of *Apollo. The oracle's advice, interpreted from the trance utterances of a priestess, was widely sought by individuals and the Greek states. As traditional beliefs declined after the 4th century BC the oracle lost influence. It was closed by the Christian emperor, Theodosius (390 AD).

Delphinium A genus of annual or perennial herbs (250 species), also called larkspur, with tall spikes of deep-blue flowers. Delphiniums, native to the N hemisphere, are popular garden plants. Cultivated varieties have single or double flowers in shades of blue, pink, purple, or white. Family: *Ranunculaceae*.

delta A large fan-shaped accumulation of sediment deposited at the mouth of a river, where it discharges into a sea or lake. It forms when the river's flow is slowed down on meeting the comparatively static sea or lake, resulting in a reduction of the river's load-bearing capacity. Clay particles also coagulate on meeting salt water and are deposited. The river is increasingly divided by the deposition into channels. Being fertile, deltas (such as the Nile Delta) are often extensively cultivated but are also prone to flooding.

Demeter A Greek corn goddess and mother goddess, sister of *Zeus. She was worshipped at Eleusis, whose people helped her in her search for her daughter *Persephone, abducted to the underworld. In gratitude she instructed them in agriculture and religion. She was identified with the Roman goddess Ceres.

democracy A form of government in which people either rule themselves, as in ancient Athens, or elect representatives to rule in their interests, as in most modern democracies. Elections, to be democratic, must be held regularly, be secret, and provide a choice of candidates; the elected assembly must also be free to legislate and to criticize government policy. Modern democratic ideas stem from 18th-century *utilitarianism.

Democratic Party One of the two major political parties in the USA (*compare* REPUBLICAN PARTY). Originating in Jefferson's Republican Democrats in 1792, it became the Democratic Party during the presidency (1829–37) of Andrew Jackson. In 1860, just before the Civil War, the Democrats split over the issue of *slavery into northern and southern factions and the party, dominated by southern Democrats, was eclipsed until regaining northern support in the 1880s. With F. D. Roosevelt's *New Deal programme in the 1930s, the Democrats again became identified as a progressive party. Democratic presidents include

Woodrow Wilson, F.D.Roosevelt, J.F.Kennedy, and Bill Clinton.

Democritus (c.460–370 BC), Greek philosopher and scientist. His atomism, developed from Leucippus, considered that all matter consists of minute particles—atoms—the multifarious arrangement of which accounts for different properties of matter apparent to our senses. Democritus wrote also on cosmology, biology, perception, music, and ethics.

demography A branch of the social sciences concerned with the statistical study of the sizes, distribution, and composition of human populations. It includes analysis of birth, death, and marriage rates for whole populations or groups within them.

demoiselle A *crane, *Anthropoides virgo*, of dry grassy regions of central Europe and Asia. It is grey with a black head and neck, long black breast feathers, and long white plumes behind each eye.

Demosthenes (384–322 BC) Athenian orator and statesman. He attacked Philip of Macedon's imperial ambitions in Greece in a series of orations called the *Philippics* (351, 344, 341) and promoted an Athenian alliance with Thebes against Philip. This was defeated by Philip at Chaeronea (338), whereby Macedonian supremacy in Greece was assured. After the death of Philip's son, Alexander the Great (323), Demosthenes again encouraged a Greek revolt. Condemned to death by Alexander's successors, Demosthenes fled Athens and committed suicide.

demotic script A form of Egyptian hieroglyphic writing. Pictorial hieroglyphics became less realistic and increasingly cursive from about 2500 BC until in the 7th century BC they developed into the cursive script called demotic. This continued in common use until the 5th century AD. *See also* ROSETTA STONE.

Denbighshire A county in North Wales on the Irish Sea. In 1974 it was absorbed into Clwyd and Gwynedd but reinstated (with different boundaries) in 1996. It is mainly hilly. Agriculture is the chief economic activity and tourism is important. Area: 844 sq km (327 sq mi). Population (2001): 93 092. Administrative centre: Ruthin.

Dench, Dame Judi (Olivia) (1934–) British actress, noted for her Shakespearean roles. Film roles include Queen Victoria in *Mrs Brown* (1997), Elizabeth I in *Shakespeare in Love* (1999), and Iris Murdoch in *Iris* (2001).

dendrochronology (*or* **tree-ring dating**) An archaeological dating technique based on the *annual rings of trees. Variations in ring widths have been shown to correspond to rainfall and temperature variations and thus very old tree trunks can give a record of past climates. Any construction incorporating timber can be dated by comparing the timber-ring patterns with a specimen of known age.

Deng Xiao Ping (1904–07) Chinese statesman. He was dismissed during the Cultural Revolution but subsequently became vice premier (1973–76; 1977–80). Subsequently he held various posts and titles but was effectively China's supreme leader until his death. His rule saw liberalization of the economy but continuing political repression.

denim A coarse twill-woven cloth, named after the French fabric *serge de Nîmes*. It is made of cotton, often with an admixture of nylon, and usually dyed blue. Originally popular for work garments, denim became fashionable for jeans and other casual clothes in the 1970s.

De Niro, Robert (1943–) US film actor of the Method school; he won Oscars for *The Godfather Part II* (1974) and *Raging Bull* (1979). Other films include *Taxi Driver* (1976), *Goodfellas* (1990), and *Analyze This* (1999).

Denis, St (3rd century) The patron saint of France. Of Italian birth, he was sent to Gaul as a missionary and there became the first Bishop of Paris. He was martyred under the Emperor Valerian. His shrine is in the Benedictine abbey at St Denis near Paris. Feast Day: 9 Oct.

Denmark, Kingdom of (Danish name: Danmark) A country in N Europe, between the Baltic and the North Seas. It consists of the N section of the Jutland peninsula and about a hundred inhabited islands. *Greenland and the *Faeroe Islands are also part of the Danish kingdom. The country is almost entirely flat. *Economy*: agriculture is important. Since World War II, however, industry has predominated, with manufacturing, engineering, chemicals, brewing, and food processing. Financial and service industries are major employers. Exports include meat and meat products, dairy produce, cereals, fish, porcelain, glassware, and metal goods. *History*: Viking kingdoms occupied the area from the 8th to the 10th century, when Denmark became a united Christian monarchy under Harald Bluetooth. His grandson, Canute, ruled over Denmark, Norway, and England, forming the Danish Empire, which was dissolved soon after his death. In 1363 Norway again came under the Danish Crown by

d

royal marriage. In 1397 Denmark and Norway joined with Sweden to form the Kalmar Union, which lasted until 1523. The Peace of Copenhagen (1660) concluded a long period of conflict between Denmark and Sweden. It then became an absolute monarchy until 1849, when a more liberal government was formed. Having supported Napoleon in the Napoleonic Wars, Denmark was compelled to cede Norway to Sweden by the Treaty of Kiel (1814). During World War II Denmark was occupied by Germany but a resistance movement aided the Allied victory. Iceland, which had previously been united with Denmark, became independent in 1944. A new constitution was enacted in 1953, with a single-chamber parliament. In 1973 Denmark joined the EC (now the EU). The Maastricht Treaty (*See* EUROPEAN COMMUNITY) was rejected in two referendums (1992, 1993) but later accepted. Membership of the single European currency was rejected in a referendum (2000). Denmark's first right-wing government in more than 75 years was elected in 2001, when Anders Fogh Rasmussen became prime minister. A bridge and causeway linking Denmark and Sweden was completed in 2000. Official language: Danish. Currency: krone of 100 øre. Area: 43 074 sq km (16 631 sq mi). Population (2003 est): 5 387 000. Capital: Copenhagen.

density The mass of unit volume of a substance. In *SI units it is measured in kilograms per cubic metre; water has a density of 1000 kg m^{-3} at 4°C. **Relative density** (formerly called "specific gravity") is the density of a substance divided by the density of water at 4°C. The density of a gas (vapour density) is often expressed as the mass of unit volume of the gas divided by the mass of the same volume of hydrogen at standard temperature and pressure.

dentistry The branch of medical science concerned with the care of the teeth, gums, and mouth. Restorative dentistry is concerned with the repair of teeth damaged by *caries and the replacement of teeth lost through injury or extraction. Orthodontics deals with the correction of badly positioned teeth, usually by means of braces or other appliances but sometimes by surgery on the jaw. Periodontics includes the care of the gums and other structures supporting the teeth and the treatment of periodontal disease.

Denver 39 45N 105 00W A city in the USA, the capital of Colorado on the South Platte River. Founded in 1858 during the Colorado gold rush, Denver is the financial, administrative, and industrial centre for a large agricultural area. Population (2000): 554 636.

deodar A tall *cedar, *Cedrus deodara*, native to the Himalayas, where it forms vast forests, and widely planted for ornament in temperate regions and for timber in S Europe. It has young branches that droop down and large barrel-shaped cones.

depression (economics) A period during the *trade cycle in which demand is low compared to industry's capacity to satisfy it. Profits, and therefore confidence and investment, are also correspondingly low. A depression is also characterized by high unemployment, as occurred in the 1930s (*see* DEPRESSION). Governments after World War II adopted *deficit financing policies to counter depressions, but the combination of depression and *inflation in the 1970s led to widespread adoption of *monetarism. A depression is also called a slump.

depression (psychiatry) Severe and persistent misery. It can be a normal reaction to distressing events (reactive depression). Sometimes, however, it is out of all proportion to the situation or may have no apparent external cause (endogenous depression): it can then be a sign of mental illness. In *manic-depressive psychosis the depression is severe and leads the sufferer to despairing and guilty beliefs; sleep, appetite, and concentration can all be disturbed. In depressive neurosis the symptoms are less extreme but may still lead to suicide. Treatment with *antidepressant drugs is often effective and psychotherapy is helpful. Severe cases may need *electroconvulsive therapy.

Depression The period, also called the Slump, during the early 1930s, when worldwide economic collapse precipitated commercial failure and mass unemployment. Starting in the USA in 1929, when share prices fell so disastrously that thousands were made bankrupt, the Depression caused international repercussions. Overseas trade almost ceased, industrial production dropped, millions in industrialized countries were unemployed, and agricultural countries were impoverished. Roosevelt's *New Deal (1934) brought Americans hope of recovery, but Britain, despite abandoning free trade to protect its industries, never regained its commercial pre-eminence. In Germany the Depression contributed to the rise of Hitler's Nazi movement.

Derain, André (1880–1954) French postimpressionist painter. In his bold designs and vibrant colours, he was initially a leading exponent of *fauvism, but after 1907 he came under the influence of *Cézanne and painted in a cubist manner. He later reverted to a more traditional style. He produced some notable scenery and costume designs for Diaghilev's *Ballets Russes.

Derby A flat race for three-year-old horses, run over 2.4 km (1.5 mi) at Epsom in early June. The most prestigious of the English Classics, it was instituted (1780) by the 12th Earl of Derby.

Derby 1. 52 55N 1 30W A city in central England, in Derby unitary authority, Derbyshire, on the River Derwent. Its growth as a manufacturing centre began in the late 17th century (*see* DERBY WARE). Today Derby is an important engineering centre (with Rolls-Royce aero engines) and has large railway workshops. Population (1991): 222 500. **2.** A unitary authority in central England, in Derbyshire. Area: 78 sq km (30 sq mi). Population (1996 est): 233 700.

Derbyshire A county in N central England. In 1974 it lost part of the NE to South Yorkshire, while gaining part of NE Cheshire; Derby city became an independent unitary authority in 1997. It consists of lowlands in the SE rising to the uplands of the *Peak District in the NW. The main rivers are the Derwent, Trent, Dove, and Rother. Sheep and dairy farming are important. Heavy industry and mining are in decline and service industries are increasingly important. Area (excluding Derby city): 2551 sq km (985 sq mi). Population (2001, excluding Derby city): 734 581. Administrative centre: Matlock.

Derby ware Porcelain first produced by William Duesbury (1725–86) at Derby in the 1750s. Early manufactures resemble *Chelsea porcelain and Duesbury later bought the Chelsea works (1770). Utility products were decorated in bold blue, red, and gilt "Japan" patterns, but important portrait and fictional figures were also made in quantity. Products of the factory between 1786 and 1811 are called Crown Derby.

dermatology *See* SKIN.

Derry 1. A district in NE Northern Ireland, in Co Londonderry. Area: 373 sq km (144 sq mi). Population (2001): 106 066. **2.** *See* LONDONDERRY.

Derwent, River Any of several rivers in England, including: **1.** A river in N central England, flowing SE from N Derbyshire to the River Trent. Length: 96 km (60 mi). **2.** A river in N England, flowing S from the North York Moors to join the River Ouse between Selby and Goole. Length: 92 km (57 mi). **3.** A river in NW England, flowing N and W from the Borrowdale Fells, Cumbria, to the Irish Sea. Length: 54 km (34 mi).

desalination The removal of salt from brine to produce fresh water. Desalination is used to irrigate arid regions in which sea water is available, especially if solar power can be used as an energy source. Methods commonly employed are evaporation of the sea water, the condensed vapour forming relatively pure water, and freezing of the sea water, which produces pure ice. Freezing requires less energy than evaporation but the process is slower and technically more difficult.

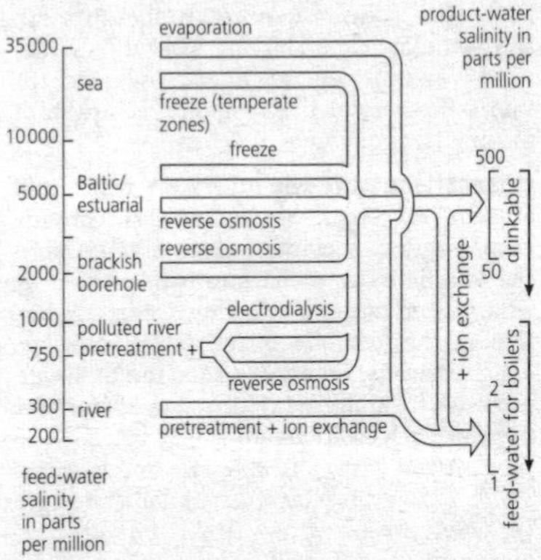

desalination. The initial and final salinities for various desalination techniques and feed-water sources.

Descartes, René (1596–1650) French philosopher and mathematician. After a Jesuit education he spent nine years in travel and military service before turning to study, primarily in Holland. Descartes' *Discourse on Method* (1637) introduced his technique of methodical doubt, which he developed in his greatest work the *Meditations* (1641). Asking "How and what do I know?" he arrived by a process of reduction at his famous statement "Cogito ergo sum" ("I think, therefore I am"). From this he proved to his own satisfaction God's existence (he was a sincere and lifelong Roman Catholic) and hence the existence of everything else. The importance of this approach lies in making *epistemology the gateway to knowledge. Equally influential was his dualism: he considered that the world was composed of mind, the essence of human beings, and matter—but never satisfactorily answered the problem of how mind and matter can interact. Descartes also contributed to the foundations of geometry (*see* COORDINATE SYSTEMS) and optics.

desert A virtually barren area of land where precipitation is minimal and sporadic, limiting vegetation growth. The mean annual rainfall is usually taken as being below 250 mm (10 in) for desert conditions. Deserts may occur in areas of high atmospheric pressure, such as the *Sahara, or near the W coast of continents cooled by cold ocean currents (e.g. the Atacama and *Kalahari Deserts). They are also found in continental interiors where mountain barriers restrict precipitation, such as the *Gobi Desert. Many deserts are characterized by stony scrublands with occasional resistant rock uplands and some areas of shifting sand dunes. The wind is an important agent of erosion and the rain, falling as violent downpours, is capable of moving large amounts of debris.

desertification The process by which arid or semiarid areas become deserts through human action or climatic change. Removal of the topsoil, by artificial means or erosion by wind, water, or desiccation, results in a reduction in the ground's water-storage capacity, which can cause crops to fail and famine. Overintensive farming and the cutting of trees for firewood helped to create the *Dust Bowl in the USA and have caused deserts in Africa and SW Asia to advance by several kilometres each year. Solutions are now based on effective management of surface cover and climate.

desert rat *See* JERBOA.

De Sica, Vittorio (1901–74) Italian film director. His postwar films, in which he treated contemporary social themes with compassion and political awareness, included *Shoeshine* (1946), *Bicycle Thieves* (1948), and *Umberto D* (1952).

Des Moines 41 35N 93 35W A city in the USA, the capital of Iowa. Founded in 1843, it is an important industrial and commercial centre. Population (2000): 198 682.

destroyer A fast heavily armed naval vessel that is smaller than a *cruiser, has a displacement of about 3000 tonnes, and is 110–150 m (330–450 ft) long. Destroyers are not armoured. Because of their speed, armament, and versatility, they are employed in antisubmarine warfare, in convoy work, and in attack groups consisting of one carrier and five or six destroyers.

detached retina A condition in which the retina—a layer of specialized light-sensitive cells at the back of the eye—becomes separated from the layer beneath it. It happens slowly and painlessly and the patient loses part of his vision. It is caused by injury to the eye or inflammation in the eye and is most common in very short-sighted people. Detached retina is treated surgically using a laser beam to weld the retina in place.

detergents Chemicals used for cleansing. Although the term includes *soaps it is usually applied to synthetic *surfactants. Such detergents have large molecules, typically composed of a hydrocarbon oil-soluble part and a water-soluble part. These compounds are thus able to promote the solution of oil, grease, etc., in water. Household detergents may also contain water softeners, bleaches, and fabric brighteners.

determinism The philosophical theory that every event has a cause and that all events are determined by causal physical laws. Applied to human actions, determinism appears to conflict with the concept of *free will. If even desires, intentions, and motives are determined and if actions are, in principle, predictable, this contradicts the idea that actions are freely chosen, and hence the concept of moral responsibility. However, some philosophers believe that determinism and free will are compatible and that a person acts freely if his desires are the cause of his actions. *See also* PREDESTINATION.

Detroit 42 23N 83 05W A city and port in the USA, in Michigan on the Detroit River. Founded in 1701, it is the fifth largest city in the USA. It is dominated by the motor-vehicle industry. Population (2000): 951 270.

deuterium (*or* **heavy hydrogen**; D *or* ^{2}H) An *isotope of *hydrogen having a nucleus consisting of one proton and one neutron. It occurs naturally in hydrogen (0.0156%) and is used as a radioactive tracer. Heavy water (deuterium oxide; D_2O) is used in *nuclear reactors as a moderator (*see also* THERMONUCLEAR REACTOR). At no 1; at wt 2.014.

De Valera, Eamon (1882–1975) Irish statesman; prime minister (1932–48, 1951–54, 1957–59) and president (1959–73). A commandant in the 1916 *Easter Rising, he nevertheless escaped execution and in 1917 was elected to the British parliament and became the president of *Sinn Féin. From 1919 he was president of the self-declared Irish Republic but rejected the terms of the Anglo-Irish treaty of 1921 (*see* HOME RULE) and backed the republicans in the ensuing civil war. In 1926 he founded *Fianna Fáil.

de Valois, Dame Ninette (Edris Stannus;

1898–2001) British ballet dancer and choreographer, born in Ireland. During the 1920s she worked with Diaghilev's Ballets Russes. In 1931 she founded the Sadler's Wells Ballet, which became the *Royal Ballet in 1956; she directed it until 1963. She was appointed to the OM in 1992.

devaluation A downward change in the value of one country's currency in terms of other currencies. A country that devalues makes its exports cheaper and its imports more expensive; thus devaluation should help correct a balance-of-payments deficit by increasing the volume of exports and decreasing the volume of imports. Under the Bretton Woods fixed-rate system (*see* BRETTON WOODS CONFERENCE) devaluations only occurred occasionally but were large and destabilizing. In the floating-rate system that replaced it, the value of a currency was determined by supply and demand with a minimum of government interference, so producing gradual devaluations. The *European Monetary System was intended to stabilize EC currencies, making devaluation unnecessary, but had clearly failed in this aim by September 1992, when market pressures forced the UK to leave the system. In 1999–2002 12 EU states adopted the single European currency.

developing countries Countries that do not have sophisticated industries and consequently have a low per capita income. They include almost all the countries in Africa, Asia, and South America. Their economies are characterized by abundant cheap unskilled labour and a scarcity of capital for investment. Nearly 80% of the world's population lives in developing countries in largely agricultural economies from which poverty, hunger, disease, and illiteracy have not been eliminated. Many of these economies rely shakily on one main crop, which in years of crop failure, poor world demand, or low market prices can cause severe hardship.

Devil In Christian tradition, the personification of evil, who seeks to tempt mankind away from the path of salvation and rules in *hell. Judaeo-Christian doctrine holds that God created the Devil good and he became evil of his own free will by committing sin (commonly thought to have been the sin of pride). The Devil is identified with such Old Testament figures as the archangel **Lucifer** (who sought to make himself God's equal and was expelled from heaven), the serpent that tempted Eve (Genesis 3.1–6), and **Satan** the tormentor of Job. Similar figures exist in Islam and Zoroastrianism.

devolution The delegation of political powers from a central government to regional governments. In the UK the establishment of the *Stormont parliament in Northern Ireland was the first important act of devolution. Growing nationalist sentiment in Scotland and Wales led to the introduction of two devolution bills in 1976 and the holding of referendums in March 1979. In Wales there was a majority against the devolution plans; in Scotland an insufficiently large majority favoured them. In 1997 new plans to establish a Welsh assembly and a Scottish parliament were endorsed in referendums and the first elections to these bodies took place in May 1999. Following the Good Friday Agreement (1998), an assembly with a power-sharing executive was established in Northern Ireland and power was devolved in late 1999; however, failure to achieve progress on the decommissioning of terrorist weapons and the ending of paramilitary activity led the British government to suspend the new institutions from February to May 2000 and again from October 2002.

Devon A county of SW England, bordering the Atlantic Ocean in the N and the English Channel in the S. It consists mainly of the mid-Devon plain, rising to *Dartmoor in the S and *Exmoor in the NE. The chief rivers are the Dart, Exe, and Tamar. Tourism and agriculture are important while industry is concentrated around Exeter and Plymouth, a major naval base. Plymouth and Torbay became unitary authorities in 1998. Area (excluding unitary authorities): 6569 sq km (2536 sq mi). Population (2001, excluding unitary authorities): 704 499. Administrative centre: Exeter.

Devonian period A geological period of the Upper Palaeozoic era between the Silurian and Carboniferous periods, about 415 to 370 million years ago. It is divided into seven stages, based on invertebrate fossil remains, such as corals, brachiopods, ammonoids, and crinoids. The rocks containing these fossils were marine deposits but the Devonian period also shows extensive continental deposits (Old Red Sandstone). Fossils from these rocks include fish, land plants, and freshwater molluscs.

dew The condensation of moisture, which forms on the ground or on objects near the ground, especially at night. It occurs when the air near the ground cools to the **dew point**, at which it becomes saturated and the water vapour present condenses into water droplets.

Dewar flask (**Thermos flask** *or* **vacuum**

d

flask) A flask, used to store a substance at constant temperature. It has double glass walls, the space between the walls being evacuated to prevent heat loss by conduction. The inside wall is silvered to prevent heat loss by radiation and the flask is tightly stoppered to prevent heat loss by convection or evaporation. It was invented by the Scottish scientist Sir James Dewar (1842–1923).

Dewey Decimal Classification An international system for classifying the books in a library, originated in 1873 by the US librarian Melvil Dewey (1851–1931). Books are divided according to subject matter into ten groups, each group having a hundred numbers; principle subdivisions within each group are divided by ten, and with the use of decimal numbers further subdivisions can be generated without limit.

Dhaka (name until 1984: Dacca) 23 42N 90 22E The capital of Bangladesh, situated in the SE of the country, on the Burhi Ganga River. It is a riverport and commercial and industrial centre. The capital of the Bengal province of the Mogul Empire in the 17th century, it came under British rule in the 18th century and upon independence in 1947 was made capital of East Pakistan. Population (1991): 3 839 000.

diabetes One of several diseases with a common symptom—the production of large quantities of urine. The term usually refers to **diabetes mellitus** (*or* sugar diabetes), in which the body is unable to utilize sugars to produce energy due to a deficiency of the pancreatic hormone *insulin. Symptoms include thirst, weight loss, and a high level of glucose in the urine and in the blood (hyperglycaemia). Treatment involves a controlled diet, often with insulin injections or pills to reduce the amount of sugar in the blood. **Diabetes insipidus** is a rare disease due to a deficiency of the pituitary hormone vasopressin, which regulates water balance in the body. The patient produces large quantities of watery urine and is always thirsty. It is treated with doses of the hormone.

Diaghilev, Sergei (Pavlovich) (1872–1929) Russian ballet impresario. The outstanding success of his season of Russian ballet (1909) resulted in the organization of a permanent company (1911), known as the *Ballets Russes, which Diaghilev directed until his death.

dialect A variant of a language spoken in a particular district or by a particular group of people. The distinction between language and dialect is not clear cut. As a general rule any two dialects of a language may be expected to be mutually comprehensible. Dialects develop as a result of geographical separation, usually within a generation or so of the time of separation.

dialectical materialism The official philosophy of *Marxism, derived by Marx and Engels from a combination of contemporary (1850) science and *Hegel's idealism. **Historical materialism**, expounded in the *Communist Manifesto*, is a coherent account of history on an economic basis: for every system of production there is an appropriate organization of class and property. While economic forces continually develop production systems, the class and property structure remains unchanged, causing tension between economic forces and social relations, which continues until the ultimate rational socialist society evolves.

dialysis A process, discovered by Thomas Graham (1804–69), for separating mixtures of fluids by diffusion through a semipermeable membrane. Different substances in a solution diffuse at different rates. The passage of large particles is almost completely blocked by a semipermeable membrane, whereas salt solutions pass through easily. The technique of dialysis is used in artificial kidney machines, or dialysers, which take over the function of diseased kidneys by filtering waste material from the blood but leaving behind proteins, blood cells, and other large particles.

diamond The hardest known mineral, comprising a cubic variety of crystalline *carbon, formed under intense heat and pressure. Diamonds are used industrially, mainly for cutting and grinding tools, the others being used as gems. The largest diamond yet discovered is the *Cullinan diamond. Many industrial diamonds are produced synthetically from graphite subjected to very high temperatures and pressures.

Diana The Roman goddess identified with the Greek Artemis, associated with women and childbirth and with the moon. She is usually represented as a virgin huntress armed with bow and arrows.

Diana, Princess of Wales (1961–97) Former wife of Prince Charles and mother of Prince William (1982–) and Prince Harry (1984–), famous as a fashion icon as well as for her committed work with many charities. She was killed in a car crash in Paris with her companion Dodi Fayed; her premature death caused an unprecedented display of public grief.

Dianthus A genus of annual and perennial herbs (300 species), mainly from Europe and Asia, having flower stems (often branched) with swollen joints and showy white, pink, or red flowers. Common species include *D. barbatus* (*see* SWEET WILLIAM), *D. caryophyllus* (*see* CARNATION), and *D. plumarius* (*see* PINK). Family: *Caryophyllaceae*.

diaspora (Greek: dispersion) The collective term for Jewish communities outside the land of Israel. Beginning with the Babylonian exile (6th century BC), Jews spread to most parts of the world, while continuing to regard Israel as their homeland. In the late 19th century there was a massive exodus of Jews from Russia and Poland, and the Nazi *holocaust destroyed many old European communities. The main centre is now the USA, with some six million Jews.

diatoms Microscopic *algae belonging to a phylum (*Diatoms* or *Bacillariophyta*; about 16 000 species) occurring abundantly as single cells or colonies in fresh water and oceans (forming an important constituent of *plankton) and also in soil. They have silicon-rich cell walls, often beautifully sculptured, forming a shell (called a test) composed of two halves that fit together. Fossilized tests form a porous rock called diatomaceous earth (*or* kieselguhr), used in filters, insulators, abrasives, etc.

Dicentra A genus of annual and perennial herbaceous plants (about 300 species) from North America and E Asia. They have divided compound leaves and sprays of hanging flowers that are flattened sideways. Many species are ornamentals (*see* BLEEDING HEART). Family: *Fumariaceae*.

Dickens, Charles (1812–70) British novelist. He began his career by contributing to popular magazines, achieving sudden fame with *The Pickwick Papers* (1837), which he followed with *Oliver Twist* (1838), *Nicholas Nickleby* (1839), and the very successful *Old Curiosity Shop* (1840–41); like all his novels, these first appeared in monthly instalments. *David Copperfield* (1849–50) was a strongly autobiographical work. His later novels, from *Bleak House* (1853) to the incomplete *Edwin Drood* (1870), were increasingly pessimistic in tone; *Great Expectations* (1860–61) and *Our Mutual Friend* (1864–65) depict the destructive powers of money and ambition.

Dickinson, Emily (1830–86) US poet. From the age of 30 she lived a largely secluded life in Amherst, Massachusetts. Of her 1700 poems, which are mainly brief intense lyrics on themes of love and death, only seven appeared in her lifetime.

dicotyledons The larger of the two main groups of flowering plants, which includes hardwood trees, shrubs, and many herbaceous plants (*compare* MONOCOTYLEDONS). Dicots are characterized by having two seed leaves (cotyledons) in the embryo. Typically the flower parts are arranged in fours or fives (or multiples of these) and the leaves have a netlike pattern of veins. *See also* ANGIOSPERM.

Diderot, Denis (1713–84) French philosopher and writer. With *Voltaire, Diderot helped create the *Enlightenment, mainly through the *Encyclopédie*, which he edited after 1750 (*see* ENCYCLOPEDISTS).

Dido In Greek legend, the daughter of a king of Tyre, who fled to Africa when her husband was murdered; there she founded *Carthage. According to legend she burnt herself to death on a funeral pyre to avoid marriage to Iarvas of Numidia; in Virgil's *Aeneid* she killed herself after being abandoned by her lover *Aeneas.

dielectric A substance that acts as an electrical insulator and can sustain an electric field. When a voltage is applied across a perfect dielectric there is no energy loss and the electric field strength changes simultaneously with voltage. In real dielectrics, such as air or wax, there is always a small energy loss.

Dien Bien Phu, Battle of (March–May 1954) The decisive battle of the Indochina war, in NE Vietnam, in which Vietnamese forces defeated the French. It coincided with the Geneva Conference, which ended French control of Indochina.

Dieppe 49 55N 1 05E A port and resort in N France, in the Seine-Maritime department on the English Channel. Population (1990): 36 600.

Diesel engine *See* INTERNAL-COMBUSTION ENGINE.

dietetics The study of the principles of nutrition and their application to the selection of appropriate diets both to maintain health and as part of the treatment of certain diseases. A balanced diet should contain foods with adequate amounts of all the nutrients—carbohydrates, fats, proteins, minerals, and vitamins—as well as foods with a high content of dietary *fibre.

Dietrich, Marlene (Maria Magdalene von Losch; 1904–92) German film actress and singer. Her image of sultry beauty was developed by the Austrian-born director Josef von Sternberg

(1894–1969) in such films as *The Blue Angel* (1930), *Blonde Venus* (1932), and *Shanghai Express* (1932).

diffraction The spreading or bending of light waves as they pass the edge of an object or pass through an aperture. The diffracted waves subsequently interfere with each other producing regions of alternately high and low intensity. This phenomenon can be observed in the irregular boundary of a shadow of an object cast on a screen by a small light source. A similar effect occurs with sound waves. *See also* INTERFERENCE.

diffusion 1. The mixing of different fluids, or the distribution of a substance from a region of high concentration to one of lower concentration, by means of the random thermal motion of its constituents. The rates at which gases diffuse are inversely proportional to their densities (Graham's law). **2.** The scattering of a beam of radiation on reflection from a rough surface or on transmission through certain media. When diffusion occurs the laws of reflection and refraction are not obeyed.

digestion The process by which food is converted into substances that can be absorbed by the *intestine. The process begins in the mouth, where the food is chewed and mixed with saliva, and continues with the action of digestive enzymes secreted by the *stomach, duodenum, and *pancreas. Rhythmic contractions of the muscular layer of the intestinal wall (called peristalsis) ensures a constant mixing of enzymes and food and the propulsion of food along the intestine. The products of digestion include amino acids, various sugars (such as lactose, maltose, and glucose), and fat molecules; these are absorbed by the intestine and conveyed to the bloodstream.

digitalis A drug prepared from the dried leaves of foxglove plants. Digitalis is purified to digoxin, digitoxin, and lanatoside C. These drugs are used to improve the action of a failing or inefficient heart and to reduce a dangerously fast heart rate.

digital mapping The production of a map using a system in which the points and lines that make it up are converted, or digitized, into computer data. Subsequent reproduction may be of the whole map or of a selected part; it may be at a different scale and/or on a transformed projection. A print of the map can be produced or it may be displayed on a visual display unit. Changes can be made without the whole map having to be redrawn. In the UK the *Ordnance Survey began to digitize its data in 1973 and completed this programme in 1995.

digital photography *See* CAMERA, PHOTOGRAPHIC.

Dijon 47 20N 5 02E A city in France, the capital of the Côte-d'Or department on the Burgundy Canal. The former capital of Burgundy, it is the site of the palace of the Dukes of Burgundy and has a cathedral (13th–14th centuries). It is famous for its mustard. Population (1999): 149 867.

dilatation and curettage (D and C) An operation in which the neck (cervix) of the womb is dilatated (widened) and the lining of the womb is scraped out. D and C may be performed for the removal of any residual membranes after a miscarriage or abortion, removal of cysts or tumours, and removal of a specimen of tissue in the diagnosis of gynaecological disorders.

dill A widely cultivated annual or biennial European herb, *Anethum graveolens*, 60 cm high. The smooth stem bears feathery leaves and umbrella-like clusters of small yellow flowers, which produce small hard flat fruits. The young leaves and fruits are used to flavour soups, cakes, salads, fish, and pickled cucumbers. Family: *Umbelliferae*.

D'Indy, Vincent (1851–1931) French composer. The pupil and biographer of Franck, he was greatly influenced by Wagner and wrote a number of large-scale orchestral compositions, as well as operas and chamber music. His most famous work is the *Symphony on a French Mountaineer's Song* (for piano and orchestra; 1886).

dingo An Australian wild *dog, *Canis familiaris* (formerly *C. dingo*), introduced from Asia. It has a tan-coloured coat. It is nocturnal and generally solitary.

Dinka A Nilotic people of the Nile basin region of the Sudan. Warlike and independent, the Dinka move with their cattle from dry-season pastures by the rivers to wet-season settlements, where they grow millet. There are many independent tribes.

dinosaur An extinct reptile that was the dominant terrestrial animal during the Jurassic and Cretaceous periods (200–65 million years ago). Dinosaurs first appeared about 225 million years ago, ranging in size from about 60 cm to such mighty creatures as *Diplodocus*, which reached 27 m in length. There were two orders: the *Saurischia*, which were mostly carnivores and included the bipedal *Allosaurus* and *Tyrannosaurus*; and the *Ornithischia*, which were all herbivores and included the bipedal *Iguanodon*, the horned *Triceratops*, and *Stegosaurus*.

Why both orders died out at the end of the Cretaceous period along with other reptiles, such as *ichthyosaurs, *pterosaurs, and *plesiosaurs, is still not certain. Dinosaurs had large bodies with heavy bones and protective armour and were probably unable to adapt to climatic changes and the effects of a rise in the sea level, which flooded their coastal habitats.

Diocletian(us), Gaius Aurelius Valerius (245–313 AD) Roman emperor (284–305). He rose to prominence in the army, to which he owed his accession. In 293 he established the tetrarchy to govern the Empire more effectively in a time of civil strife: the Empire was divided into East and West, with each ruled by an emperor and his associate. Diocletian ruled in the East with Galerius, abdicating in 305.

diode *See* SEMICONDUCTOR DIODE; THERMIONIC VALVE.

Diogenes of Sinope (412–322 BC) The founder of the philosophical sect of the *Cynics. Diogenes claimed, in contrast to almost all Greek thinkers, total freedom and self-sufficiency for the individual. Unlike modern anarchists, he saw no need for violent rebellion to assert his independence, which he thought he already had. His disregard for social conventions made him the subject of many stories.

Dionysus (*or* **Bacchus**) The Greek god of wine, originally a vegetation god. He was the son of Semele (daughter of Cadmus) by Zeus. A common theme of many Dionysian legends is a people's refusal to accept his divinity and his subsequent retribution.

dioptre A unit used to measure the power of a lens equal to the reciprocal of its focal length in metres. The power of a converging lens is taken to be positive and that of a diverging lens as negative.

Dioscuri *See* CASTOR AND POLLUX.

diphtheria An acute bacterial infection primarily affecting the nose, throat, or larynx. Virtually eliminated from most Western nations by extensive immunization, it formerly caused the death of many children. It is still found in Africa and India. Diphtheria produces a membrane across the throat that chokes the child. The disease can be cured using penicillin and antitoxin.

Diplodocus An amphibious dinosaur of the Jurassic period (200–136 million years ago) and the largest terrestrial vertebrate ever to exist, reaching a length of 27 m. It had a narrow body with massive legs, a long neck with a tiny head, and a long tail. It fed on vegetation in swamps and shallow lakes. Order: *Saurischia*.

dipper An aquatic songbird of the family *Cinclidae* (4 species) of Eurasia and America. Dippers are found near fast-flowing mountain streams, diving into the water to search for insects and small fish. The Eurasian white-breasted dipper (*Cinclus cinclus*) is about 17 cm long and has a dense dark-brown plumage with a white breast.

Diptera An order of insects comprising the two-winged, or true, flies. *See* FLY.

Dirac, Paul Adrien Maurice (1902–84) British physicist. In 1928 he introduced a general formulation of quantum theory. Two years later he incorporated *relativity into quantum theory and produced an equation that predicted the existence of antiparticles. He shared the 1933 Nobel Prize with Erwin *Schrödinger.

direction finder Equipment for locating the source of a radio signal, such as a ship at sea. It consists of one or more directive *aerials (usually in the form of a loop), designed to detect signals from a specific direction, and a receiver. Frequencies normally used are between 0.1 and 2 megahertz. Radar is a form of direction finding based on picking up reflections of a transmitted signal.

discus throw A field event in athletics. The circular discus is made of wood and metal, the men's weighing 2 kg (4.4 lb) and the women's 1 kg (2.2 lb). It is thrown as far as possible with one hand from within a circle 2.5 m (8.2 ft) in diameter.

disinfectant A substance or process that kills germs or prevents them multiplying. Carbolic acid (phenol) was introduced for this purpose in medicine in the 1870s by Joseph *Lister. It is still used in cleaning materials and, in weaker solutions, in skin disinfectants. Chlorine and such compounds as sodium hypochlorite kill bacteria and also some viruses. Other chemical disinfectants include chlorinated phenols, hydrogen peroxide (H_2O_2), iodine (I_2), and formaldehyde (HCHO). Dry heating to 140°C for about 3 hours will kill all disease-causing germs. Boiling water and ultraviolet light are also effective disinfectants.

Disney, Walt (1901–66) US film producer and animator. His most famous cartoon character, Mickey Mouse, was designed in 1928. His films include full-length cartoon features, such as *Snow White and the Seven Dwarfs* (1938), *Pinocchio* (1939), and *Bambi* (1943), nature documentaries, and live-action films, such as *Mary Poppins* (1964). His *Fantasia* (1940) used cartoons to accompany several pieces of classical music. He opened Disneyland, an amusement park, in California in 1955 and Walt Disney World in Florida was opened in 1971. Similar parks were opened in Tokyo (1983) and near Paris (1992).

d

Disraeli, Benjamin, 1st Earl of Beaconsfield (1804–81) British statesman; Conservative prime minister (1868, 1874–80). Becoming an MP in 1837, Disraeli was critical of Peel's Conservative Government (1841–46) and opposed the repeal of the *Corn Laws. Three times chancellor of the exchequer in Derby's governments (1852, 1858–59, 1866–68), he was largely responsible for the 1867 Reform Act. He succeeded Derby in 1868, but soon lost office to the Liberals under Gladstone. During Disraeli's second premiership the Conservative Party came to be clearly identified with policies that upheld the monarchy, Empire, and Church of England, while sponsoring social reform. In 1875 he bought Britain a major stake in the Suez Canal and in 1876 secured passage of a bill that conferred the title Empress of India on Queen Victoria. A flamboyant and witty parliamentarian, Disraeli was also a writer, whose novels include *Coningsby, or the New Generation* (1844) and *Sybil, or the Two Nations* (1845).

distillation A method of purifying or separating the components of a liquid by boiling or evaporating the liquid and condensing the vapour. It is used for separating either liquids from solids or a mixture of liquids whose components have different boiling points (known as fractional distillation). Distillation is employed in petroleum refineries to separate the various *hydrocarbons, in the production of alcoholic spirits, and in extracting pure water from sea water.

District of Columbia A federal district of the E USA, coextensive with the federal capital, *Washington. Area: 178 sq km (69 sq mi).

dittany A perennial European herbaceous plant, *Dictamnus albus*, also known as the gas plant. A strong-scented gland-covered plant, it gives off an aromatic oil. Dittany produces a drooping spike of white or pink flowers. Family: *Rutaceae*.

Diu *See* DAMAN AND DIU.

diuretics A large class of drugs that increase the excretion of urine by the kidneys. Diuretics are used in the treatment of diseases in which fluid accumulates in the tissues, such as heart failure, kidney failure, and some liver diseases (such as cirrhosis).

diver A large aquatic bird belonging to a family (*Gaviidae*; 3 species) occurring in the N hemisphere, also called loon. Divers breed on lakes and ponds and spend the winter in temperate coastal waters. They have small pointed wings and black and white plumage and they dive deeply, feeding on fish, frogs, and aquatic insects. Order: *Gaviiformes*.

dividend A share in the profits of a company paid to shareholders. The rate of dividend is declared at the company's annual general meeting to reflect the preceding year's profit. It is usually expressed as a percentage of the par value of the share (e.g. a 5% dividend on a 20p share would pay 1p per share). The dividend **yield** of the share is the income it produces expressed as a percentage of its current value (e.g. a 5% dividend on a 20p share that has a current value of 35p is $20/35 \times 5 = 2.86\%$). Dividends are usually paid twice yearly, an interim dividend and a final dividend.

divine right of kings A political doctrine claiming that monarchs are responsible only to God and that their subjects owe them unquestioning obedience. The theory originated in the middle ages and was most fully developed in the 16th and 17th centuries, especially in England under the Stuart kings and in France under Louis XIV.

diving beetle An aquatic beetle of the family *Dytiscidae*, with a flattened body and oar-like hind legs. They are efficient predators, and breathe by raising the end of the abdomen above the water to fill a cavity under their wings with air.

divorce The legal process by which a marriage is ended. Until the Matrimonial Causes Act (1857), which established a Divorce Court, divorce in England was possible only by special Act of Parliament. Jurisdiction is now vested in the High Court and county courts (*see* COURTS OF LAW). Since 1971, the only ground for divorce has been that the marriage has irretrievably broken down; the current law is contained in the Matrimonial Causes Act (1973). The party who is applying for the divorce (the petitioner) must substantiate such breakdown by presenting evidence of adultery, desertion, or unreasonable behaviour by the other party (the respondent) or that the parties have lived apart for at least two years (if the respondent agrees to the divorce) or at least five years (if he or she does not). If the respondent contests these allegations, the suit must be heard in open court;

if not, an immediate decree nisi can be granted, followed six weeks later by the decree absolute, leaving the parties free to remarry. During the proceedings the parties must have reached agreements about money and the care of any children. The Family Law Act, passed in 1996, contained provisions that aimed to reform divorce proceedings by replacing the emphasis on apportioning blame with a more consensual approach. However, pilot schemes for the new measures in 1997–99 were considered unsuccessful and those sections of the Act dealing with divorce were never implemented.

Diwali (Festival of Light, from Sanskrit *dīpawalī*, row of lights) An important Hindu religious festival held during October or November. It honours *Lakshmi, the goddess of wealth (or in Bengal, Kali). There is feasting, gambling, and lighting of lamps in honour of *Rama. Jains commemorate at this time the death of their saint Mahavira.

Dixieland A type of jazz played by White musicians in imitation of the traditional *New Orleans style. It emerged in the early 20th century but declined during the swing and bebop eras.

Djibouti, Republic of (name until 1977: the French Territory of the Afars and the Issas) A small country in NE Africa, on the Gulf of Aden at its entrance to the Red Sea. It consists chiefly of an arid rocky coastal plain rising to a plateau inland. The main population groups are Somalis (chiefly Issas) and Afars, with Arabic and European minorities. *Economy*: the port of Djibouti (a free port since 1949) is the country's economic focus handling an important transshipment trade. The port is linked by rail to Ethiopia and handles about half of that country's trade. *History*: French involvement, centred on the port, began in the mid-19th century. It was made a French colony known as French Somaliland in 1896 and proclaimed an overseas territory in 1967. It became independent in 1977 as Djibouti with Hassan Gouled Aptidon as its first president. The country suffered from the disruption of trade caused by civil wars and famine in Ethiopia and Somalia and the arrival from those countries of large numbers of refugees. Following a guerrilla war (1991) against Gouled's one-party rule, multiparty democracy was established (1992) and peace agreements were signed (1993 and 2000) with the rebels. Gouled was succeeded by his ally Ismael Omar Guelleh in 2001. Official languages: Hamitic languages of Somali. Currency: Djibouti franc of 100 centimes. Area: 21 783 sq km (8409 sq mi). Population (2003 est): 457 000. Capital: Djibouti.

DNA (deoxyribonucleic acid) A nucleic acid that is the chief constituent of the *chromosomes, carrying genetic information, in the form of *genes, necessary for the organization and functioning of living cells.

The molecular structure of DNA, proposed by J. D. *Watson and F. H. *Crick in 1953, consists of a double helix of two strands coiled around each other. Each strand is made up of alternating pentose sugar (deoxyribose) and phosphate groups, with an organic base attached to each pentose group. There are four possible bases: adenine (A), guanine (G), cytosine (C), and thymine (T). The bases on each strand are joined by hydrogen bonds and are always paired in the same way: A always binds with T and G with C. During replication, the strands of the helix separate and each provides a template for the synthesis of a new complementary strand, thus producing two identical copies of the original helix. This special property for accurate self-replication enables DNA to duplicate the genes of an organism during the cell divisions of growth (*see* MITOSIS) and the production of germ cells for the next generation (*see* MEIOSIS).

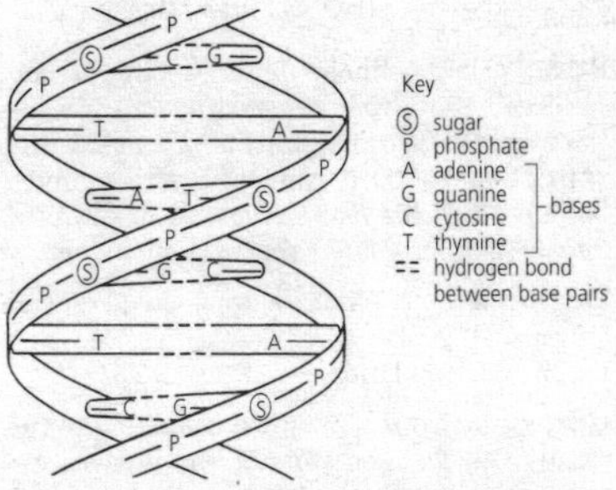

DNA. The structure of a DNA molecule takes the form of a double helix. The sequence of base pairs constitutes the genetic code, which controls the inheritance of characteristics.

Dnepr, River (*or* **R. Dnieper**) A river in NE Europe. Rising in the Valdai Hills, NE of Smolensk, it flows mainly SE through Russia, Belarus, and E Ukraine to enter the Black Sea. Length: 2286 km (1420 mi).

Dnepropetrovsk (name from 1787 until 1796 and from 1802 until 1826: Ekaterinoslav) 48 29N 35 00E A city in E Ukraine on the River Dnepr. It is one of the country's largest industrial cities, producing especially iron and steel. Population (1998 est): 275 000.

Dnestr, River (*or* **R. Dniester**) A river in NE Europe. It flows mainly SE from the Carpathian Mountains, through Ukraine and Moldova to the Black Sea near Odessa. Length: 1411 km (877 mi).

d

Dobermann pinscher A breed of dog developed by Louis Dobermann in Germany in the late 19th century. It has a powerful streamlined body and a long muzzle. The short smooth coat is black, brown, or blue-grey with tan markings. Dobermanns are widely used as police, guard, and guide dogs.

dock A plant (usually perennial) of the genus *Rumex*, of temperate regions. It has a deep stout root and large lance-shaped leaves. The small greenish flowers borne in small clusters produce small nutlets, often surrounded by the reddish papery remains of the petals. Dock leaves are the traditional antidote to nettle stings. Family: *Polygonaceae*. *See also* SORREL.

Dodecanese A group of some 20 Greek islands and islets in the SE Aegean Sea, including Cos, *Rhodes (the largest), and Pátmos. They were taken from Turkey by Italy in 1912 and passed to Greece in 1947. Total area: 2719 sq km (1050 sq mi). Population (1991): 162 439. Capital: Rhodes.

dodo A large clumsy flightless bird, *Raphus cucullatus*, that lived on Mauritius but was extinct by 1681. It had a grey-blue plumage, tiny wings, a tuft of curly white tail feathers, and a large head with a massive hooked bill. Family: *Raphidae*; order: *Columbiformes* (pigeons, etc.

Dodoma 6 10S 35 40E A town in E central Tanzania. It replaced Dar es Salaam as the capital in 1983. Population (latest est): 203 833.

dog A carnivorous mammal belonging to the family *Canidae*. Ancestors of the modern domestic dog (*Canis familiaris*), probably derived from wolves or jackals, were first domesticated over 10 000 years ago. Wild dogs generally live and hunt in packs, relying on speed and cooperation to secure their prey. They are specialized hunters with long legs, sharp teeth, strong jaws, and acute hearing and smell.

The intelligence and social nature of dogs have led to their selective breeding by man for a variety of purposes, principally as sporting dogs, working dogs, and household pets. There are up to 400 modern breeds.

doge The title of the chief magistrate of Venice from about 697 AD to the fall of the Venetian Empire in 1797. The doge was elected for life and wielded considerable power until 1172 when his authority was restricted by the creation of a supreme Great Council of 480 members. Further constitutional checks made the doge little more than a figurehead. The present richly decorated **Doge's Palace** originated in the early 14th century.

dogfish A small *shark belonging to one of a number of families. *Scyliorhinus stellaris* and *S. canicula* are brown-spotted dogfish commonly found in Mediterranean and British coastal waters. They are edible and purchased as "rock salmon."

Dogger Bank A vast sandbank in the central North Sea, 17–36 m (55–120 ft) below water. It is a major fishing ground.

dog rose A shrubby *rose, *Rosa canina*, with arching stems that grows in woods, hedges, and roadsides of Europe, North Africa, and SW Asia.

dogwood A shrub or small tree of the genus *Cornus* (about 45 species), mostly of the N hemisphere. It has oval pointed leaves with prominent curved veins and dense clusters of four-petalled flowers. The fruit is a berry. The common European dogwood (*C. sanguinea*) has white flowers, blood-red shoots and autumn leaves, and black berries. Family: *Cornaceae*.

Doha 25 15N 51 36E The capital of Qatar, on the E coast. Population (1997): 264 009.

Dohnányi, Ernö (Ernst von D.; 1877–1960) Hungarian composer and pianist, who spent his last years in the USA. Unlike his contemporaries, Bartók and Kodály, Dohnányi remained uninfluenced by Hungarian folksong. His best-known composition is the *Variations on a Nursery Theme* (for piano and orchestra; 1913).

Dolby system Tradename of an electronic device for reducing the hiss in sound reproduction, particularly in *tape recorders. It was invented by Ray Dolby (1933–). The system selectively boosts the higher frequencies in the sound signal before recording it, to drown out the constant hiss produced by the tape, and attenuates them when playing back. It operates only when the music is quiet enough for the hiss to be heard.

doldrums The equatorial belt within which the trade-wind zones converge. Winds are light and variable but the strong upward movement of air caused by the convergence produces frequent thunderstorms, heavy rains, and squalls.

Dollfuss, Engelbert (1892–1934) Austrian statesman; chancellor (1932–34). His chancellorship was increasingly strained by his inability

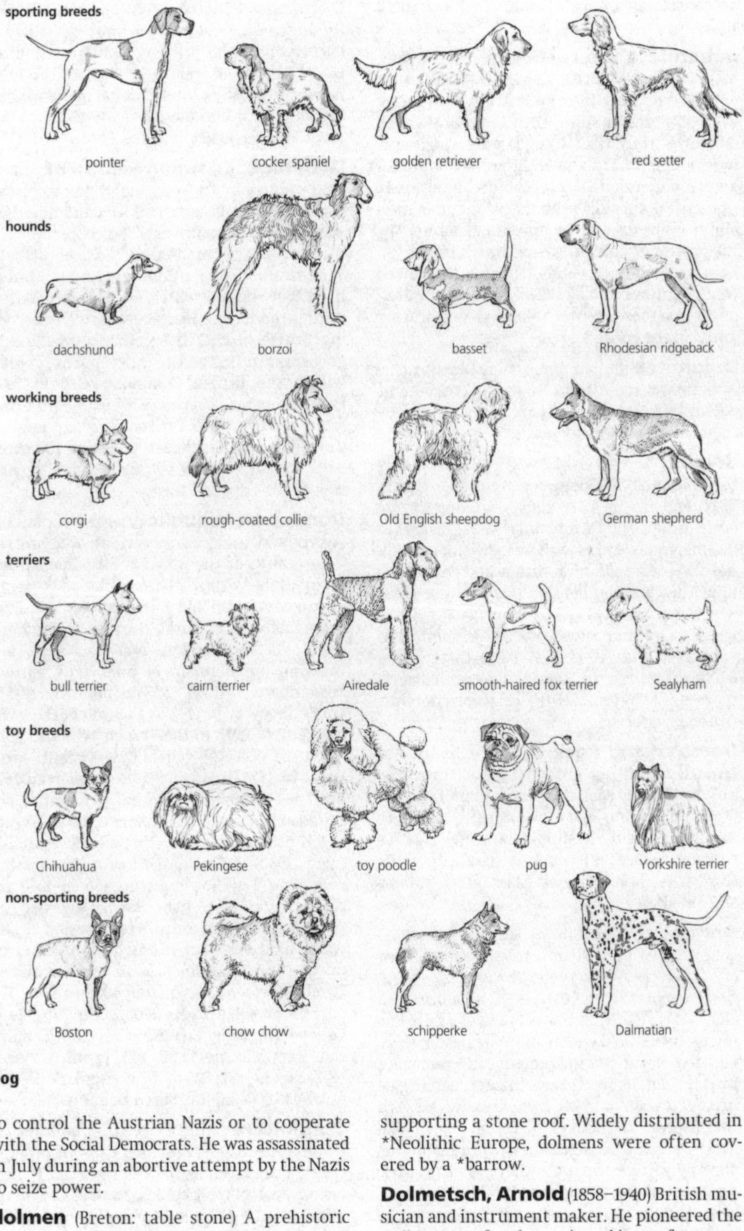

dog

to control the Austrian Nazis or to cooperate with the Social Democrats. He was assassinated in July during an abortive attempt by the Nazis to seize power.

dolmen (Breton: table stone) A prehistoric tomb made of huge stone slabs set upright and supporting a stone roof. Widely distributed in *Neolithic Europe, dolmens were often covered by a *barrow.

Dolmetsch, Arnold (1858–1940) British musician and instrument maker. He pioneered the rediscovery of early music and its performance on contemporary instruments in its original style.

dolomite A mineral consisting of calcium magnesium carbonate, $CaMg(CO_3)_2$, colourless or white or grey in colour. Rocks containing over 15% magnesium carbonate are called dolomites, those containing less are magnesian limestones, and those containing both dolomite and calcite are dolomitic limestones. Dolomite occurs as a primary sediment, in metalliferous veins and in limestones altered by the process of dolomitization, by which the calcium carbonate is wholly or partly converted to dolomite by magnesium-rich sea water, or by magnesium-rich solutions permeating joints in the rock.

Dolomites (Italian name: Alpi Dolomitiche) A section of the Alps in NE Italy. Composed of dolomitic limestone, they are characterized by their steep-sided rocky peaks.

dolphin **1.** A toothed *whale of the family *Delphinidae* (about 50 species). Agile and streamlined and up to 4.5 m long, dolphins live in large groups and feed mainly on fish. They are intelligent creatures with well-developed abilities for social communication and *echolocation. The common dolphin (*Delphinus delphus*), which grows to 2.1 m, is blue-black with a white belly and striped body. *See also* BOTTLENOSE; PORPOISE. **2.** A large fast-moving marine fish of the family *Coryphaenidae* (2 species) that resembles the cetaceous dolphin. Order: *Perciformes*.

Dome of the Rock The great mosque in Jerusalem, built in 691 AD by the *Umayyad caliph, 'Abd al-Malik, to commemorate the Muslim tradition that Mohammed ascended to Paradise from the Temple Mount (*see* TEMPLE OF JERUSALEM) on which it stands. It is the third most holy place of Islam, after *Mecca and *Medina.

Domesday Book (1086) The survey of England ordered by William I to assess the extent of his own possessions and the value for taxation purposes of the estates of his tenants in chief. Parts of N and NW England and some towns, including London and Winchester, were omitted. Royal commissioners collected, shire by shire, details about each *manor, naming its present owner and its owner under Edward the Confessor, changes in its size since Edward's reign, the numbers of its inhabitants and the services or rents they owed, and the numbers of its ploughteams, mills, and fisheries. The survey, in two volumes, is now in the Public Record Office.

Domingo, Placido (1941–) Spanish tenor. He sings a wide range of roles but specializes in Puccini and Verdi, starring in film versions of *La Traviata* (1983) and *Otello* (1986). In the 1990s he reached a huge international audience performing with Luciano Pavarotti (1935–) and José Carreras (1946–) as the Three Tenors.

Dominica, Commonwealth of An island country in the West Indies, the largest of the Windward Islands. It is of volcanic origin and very mountainous. The population is mainly of African descent. *Economy*: chiefly agricultural. *History*: discovered by Columbus in 1493, it was alternately French then British during the 18th century before finally becoming British in 1783. It became internally self-governing in 1967 and an independent republic within the British Commonwealth in 1978. Dame Eugenia Charles was prime minister from 1980 until 1995. Official language: English. Currency: East Caribbean dollar of 100 cents. Area: 728 sq km (289 sq mi). Population (2003 est): 69 700. Capital: Roseau.

Dominican Republic A largely mountainous country in the Caribbean Sea, occuping the E two-thirds of the island of Hispaniola (Haiti occupies the W third). The population is mainly of mixed African and European descent. *Economy*: chiefly agricultural. The principal mineral export is ferro-nickel. Manufacturing and tourism are increasingly important. *History*: becoming a Spanish colony following the island's discovery in 1492 by Columbus, the E was ceded, 1795–1809, to the French, who had colonized the W. The E gained independence from Spain in 1821. It was held by Haiti from 1822 until 1844, when the Dominican Republic was founded. Political and economic instability led to US occupation (1916–22) and the establishment (1930) of Trujillo's 30-year dictatorship. Following Trujillo's assassination in 1962 the elected president, Juan Bosch, was deposed (1963) in a military coup. After a period of civil war, a new democratic constitution was introduced (1966). Joaquín Balaguer was president from 1966 to 1978 and from 1986 to 1996. The current president (since 2000) is Hipólito Mejía. Official language: Spanish. Currency: Dominican Republic peso of 100 centavos. Area: 48 442 sq km (18 700 sq mi). Population (2003 est): 8 716 000. Capital: Santo Domingo.

Dominicans (Latin *Ordo Praedicatorum*: Order of Preachers) A Roman Catholic order of friars, also known as Black Friars, Friar Preachers, or (in France) Jacobins, founded by St Dominic (c. 1170–1221) and formally organized at Bologna in 1220–21. As preachers and teachers the friars lived mendicant lives. Among their scholars was St Thomas *Aquinas. They were prominent defenders of orthodoxy in the *Inquisition. There are also two orders of Dominican nuns.

Don, River A river in SW Russia, flowing mainly S to the Sea of Azov. A canal links it to the River Volga. Length: 1981 km (1224 mi).

Donatello (Donato de Nicolo di Betti Bardi; c. 1386–1466) Florentine sculptor. A pioneer of the Renaissance style, Donatello's marble sculptures are lifelike rather than idealized figures. Simultaneously he developed a new form of relief sculpture in which he created perspective. Working also in bronze from the early 1420s, he produced *David* (c. 1430–35; Florence), the influential equestrian monument in Padua known as the *Gattamelata* (1447–53), and the high altar for S Antonio, Padua (1446–50).

Doncaster 1. 53 32N 1 07W An industrial town in N England, in Doncaster unitary authority, South Yorkshire, with railway workshops; coalmining is in decline. Population (1991): 71 595. **2.** A unitary authority in N England, in South Yorkshire. Area: 582 sq km (225 sq mi). Population (2001): 286 865.

Donegal (Irish name: Dún Na Ngall) A county in the N Republic of Ireland, in Ulster bordering on the Atlantic Ocean. Chiefly mountainous, it has a rugged indented coastline. Area: 4830 sq km (1865 sq mi). Population (2002): 137 383. County town: Lifford.

Dönitz, Karl (1891–1980) German admiral. A U-boat commander in World War I, in World War II he developed the "pack" system of submarine attack. In 1943 he became grand admiral and then commander in chief of the German navy. He was appointed chancellor after Hitler's death and was imprisoned (1946–56) for war crimes.

Donizetti, Gaetano (1797–1848) Italian composer of operas. His 75 stage works rely on coloratura display, the popular characteristic of his age. They include *Lucia di Lammermoor* (1835) and *Daughter of the Regiment* (1840).

Don Juan The great aristocratic libertine of European literature. In Tirso de Molina's play *El burlador de Sevilla* (1630) he kills the father of his latest victim; he mockingly invites the old man's statue to dinner, and it drags him off to hell. This plot is retained in subsequent versions, most notably Molière's *Don Juan* (1665) and Mozart's *Don Giovanni* (1787). In satirical treatments by *Byron (*Don Juan*, 1819–24) and G. B. *Shaw (*Man and Superman*, 1903) Juan is more hunted than hunter.

donkey A domesticated *ass more commonly used for pack and draught work than for riding. *See also* MULE.

Donne, John (1572–1631) English metaphysical poet. Failing to gain secular advancement, despite having several influential patrons, he became an Anglican priest in 1615 and was appointed Dean of St Paul's in 1621. His poetry combines passionate feeling for God, woman, and humanity with brilliant intellectual wit. Almost all of it, even religious works, such as *La Corona* (1607), was written before 1615.

Doppler effect The apparent change in the frequency of a wave caused by relative motion between the source and the observer. When the source and the observer are approaching each other, the apparent frequency of the wave increases; when one is travelling away from the other, the apparent frequency decreases. An example is the change in pitch of a train whistle as the train passes through a station. The effect can also be observed as a shifting of the wavelength of light from a receding star towards the red end of the spectrum; this is known as the *redshift. Named after Christian Doppler (1803–53), Austrian physicist.

Dorchester 50 43N 2 26W A market town in S England, the administrative centre for Dorset on the River Frome. Population (1991): 15 037.

Dordogne, River A river in SW France. Rising in the Auvergne Mountains, it flows SW and W to enter the Gironde estuary NNE of Bordeaux. It is important for hydroelectric power and has famous vineyards along its lower course. Length: 472 km (293 mi).

Doré, (Paul) Gustave (Louis Christophe) (1832–83) French illustrator, painter, and sculptor, born in Strasbourg. He established his popularity in the 1850s with his illustrations of works by Rabelais and Balzac. These were followed by illustrations to Dante, Cervantes, Tennyson, etc., showing his taste for the grotesque and dramatic. His realistic scenes of poverty in *London* influenced Van Gogh.

Dorians Iron Age Greek conquerors of the S Aegean region (c. 1100–1000 BC). Moving southward from Epirus and SW Macedonia, they displaced the Achaeans and brought about the final collapse of the Bronze Age *Mycenaean civilization. They settled chiefly in the Peloponnese.

Doric order *See* ORDERS OF ARCHITECTURE.

dormancy A period of reduced metabolic activity during which a plant or animal or a reproductive body (e.g. seeds or spores) can survive unfavourable environmental conditions. The onset may be triggered by, for example, changes in temperature, daylength (photoperiodism), and availability of water, oxygen, and carbon dioxide. The dormant phase of a life cycle is represented as spores in bacteria and fungi, cysts in protozoans and some invertebrates, and seeds, buds, and bulbs or similar organs in plants. *See also* HIBERNATION.

d

dormouse A climbing *rodent belonging to the family *Gliridae* (about 10 species) of Eurasia and Africa. The common dormouse (*Muscardinus avellanarius*) is reddish, about 6 cm long with a 5-cm bushy tail. It feeds at night on nuts, berries, and seeds, hibernating during winter.

Dorset A county of SW England, bordering on the English Channel. In 1974 it gained part of SW Hampshire. Bournemouth and Poole became independent unitary authorities in 1997. It consists of lowlands in the SE with several ranges of hills. The chief rivers are the Frome and the Stour. Agriculture is predominant, especially livestock farming. Tourism is important, notably in Bournemouth and Weymouth. Many towns are associated with the writings of Thomas *Hardy. Area (excluding unitary authorities): 2544 sq km (982 sq mi). Population (2001, excluding unitary authorities): 390 986. Administrative centre: Dorchester.

Dortmund 51 32N 07 27E A city in NW Germany, in North Rhine-Westphalia in the *Ruhr. A port on the Dortmund–Ems Canal and a major industrial and brewing centre. Population (1999 est): 590 300.

Dortmund–Ems Canal A major canal in Germany. Opened in 1899, it links the Ruhr industrial area with the North Sea near Emden. Length: about 270 km (168 mi).

Dostoievski, Fedor Mikhailovich (1821–81) Russian novelist. He lived in W Europe from 1867 to 1871, plagued by his epilepsy and compulsive gambling. He returned to Russia in 1871 and became relatively prosperous, stable, and conservative. His major novels, in which he explored moral and political themes with psychological realism, are *Crime and Punishment* (1866), *The Idiot* (1868–69), *The Possessed* (1869–72), and *The Brothers Karamazov* (1879–80).

dotterel A small Eurasian *plover, *Eudromias morinellus*, that nests in tundra regions and migrates to the Mediterranean and SW Asia for the winter. It has a broad white eye stripe and a grey breast separated by a narrow white band from its russet belly.

Douai Bible The Roman Catholic version of the Bible in English, translated from the *Vulgate by Roman Catholic scholars from Oxford, who had fled to Europe during the reign of Elizabeth I and who were members of the English College at Douai. The New Testament was published at Reims in 1582 and the Old Testament at Douai in 1609–10. Its language influenced the translators of the *King James Version.

Douala 4 04N 9 43E The largest city in Cameroon, on the River Wouri estuary. A deepwater port and the chief export point of the country, it is also a major West African industrial centre. Population (1992 est): 1 200 000.

double bass The lowest-pitched musical instrument of the violin family. Its four strings are tuned in fourths (E, A, D, G), giving it a range of over three octaves, from the E an octave below the bass stave. The double bass is a member of the symphony orchestra; it is also played in jazz and dance bands, usually by plucking the strings.

Douglas 54 09N 4 29W The capital of the Isle of Man, on the E coast. It is a port and resort, its buildings including the House of Keys (parliament house) and the Manx Museum. Population (1998): 23 487.

Douglas fir A conifer, *Pseudotsuga taxifolia*, native to W North America and cultivated widely both for ornament and for its timber. 60–90 m high, it has flexible blunt needles and cylindrical cones. Family: *Pinaceae*.

Douglas-Home, Sir Alec *See* HOME OF THE HIRSEL, ALEC DOUGLAS-HOME, BARON.

Doulton English pottery works, established at Lambeth (London) in 1815, specializing in salt-glazed stoneware. Brown stoneware vessels with relief moulded portrait and landscape ornament were typical of the period to 1850. From 1856 unique studio pottery in coloured glazes was produced, using wood-fired kilns.

Douro, River (Spanish name: Duero) A river in SW Europe. Flowing W from N central Spain, it forms part of the border between Spain and Portugal before entering the Atlantic Ocean at Oporto. Length: 895 km (556 mi).

dove *See* PIGEON.

Dover 51 08N 1 19E A port in SE England, in Kent on the Strait of Dover. A Cinque Port, it is the UK's chief ferry and Hovercraft port for the Continent. Population (1993 est): 106 100.

Dowding, Hugh Caswall Tremenheere, 1st Baron (1882–1970) British air chief marshal, who was head of the RAF Fighter Command in 1940. His strategic and tactical genius in coordinating early warning radar, pilots, and equipment played a major role in winning the Battle of Britain.

Dow Jones index A weighted average of the prices on the New York Stock Exchange of 30 industrial shares, computed each working day by Dow Jones and Co. First devised in 1897 using only 11 shares, it is the principal indicator of movements in share prices in the USA.

Down 1. A historic county in SE Northern Ireland, bordering on the Irish Sea. Its administrative powers were devolved to the new district councils in 1973. It consists of lowlands in E rising to the Mourne Mountains in the SW. Agriculture is the chief occupation. Area: 2466 sq km (952 sq mi). **2.** A district in SE Northern Ireland, in Co Down. Area: 638 sq km (246 sq mi). Population (2001): 63 828.

Downing Street A London street adjoining Whitehall. No 10 is the official residence of the prime minister; the chancellor of the exchequer resides at No 11. It was named after the English statesman Sir George Downing (1623–84).

Downs, North and South Two roughly parallel ranges of chalk hills in SE England, separated by the Weald. The **North Downs** extend W–E between Guildford, in Surrey, and Dover, in Kent. The **South Downs** extend generally SE from Winchester, in Hampshire, to Beachy Head. In 1999 plans were announced to designate the South Downs as a national park. The Downs have traditionally been sheep-farming areas.

Down's syndrome A condition that results from the presence of one extra copy of chromosome 21 and is present at birth; it is named after J. L. H. Down (1828–96), English physician. Affected children often have learning difficulties and their faces resemble those of people from the Far East; heart defects may be present. They are usually cheerful and with special education can live relatively normal lives. Down's syndrome is more common in babies of mothers over 40; it can be detected during pregnancy (*see* AMNIOCENTESIS).

Doyle, Sir Arthur Conan (1859–1930) Scottish author, creator of the detective Sherlock Holmes. Conan Doyle graduated in medicine but soon turned to writing. Holmes first appeared in the novel *A Study in Scarlet* (1887), narrated, as are nearly all the short stories and novels about him, by Dr John H. Watson. Conan Doyle also created the brilliant Professor Challenger in *The Lost World* (1912) but he valued most highly his historical novels, such as *The White Company* (1890).

Doyle, Roddy (1958–) Irish novelist and playwright. His works include *The Commitments* (1988), *Paddy Clarke Ha Ha Ha* (1993), which won the 1993 Booker Prize, and *A Star Called Henry* (1999).

D'Oyly Carte, Richard (1844–1901) British theatre impresario and manager. He produced most of the comic operas of Gilbert and Sullivan at the Savoy Theatre, London, which he opened in 1881.

Drabble, Margaret (1939–) British novelist. Most of her novels concern the moral and emotional problems of women in contemporary society. They include *The Millstone* (1965), *The Needle's Eye* (1972), *The Radiant Way* (1987), and *The Seven Sisters* (2002). She also edited the 1985 *Oxford Companion to English Literature*. Her sister is A. S. *Byatt.

Draco (7th century BC) Athenian lawgiver. His legal system was so harsh that "draconian" has since been used to describe any rigorous or cruel law. Draco's code prescribed the death penalty for most offences, taking retribution out of the hands of private citizens.

dragonfly A strong agile brightly coloured insect belonging to the widely distributed suborder *Anisoptera* (about 4500 species). It has a long body, large eyes, and transparent veined wings (spanning up to 180 mm). Both the adults and freshwater nymphs (naiads) are active carnivores and control many insect pests, such as mosquitoes, flies, and gnats. Order: *Odonata*.

drag racing 1. A form of *motor racing that originated in the USA. It is held in heats of two cars on a straight strip a quarter of a mile (402 m) long. Using a standing start, races depend heavily on acceleration. Speeds have exceeded 400 km per hour (250 mph) in specially constructed light powerful vehicles. **2.** A form of motorcycle racing organized in the same way.

Drake, Sir Francis (1540–96) English navigator and admiral. Drake's first important voyages were trading expeditions to Guinea and the West Indies and in 1567 he accompanied Sir John *Hawkins to the Gulf of Mexico. In 1572 he embarked on a plundering expedition, destroying towns on the Isthmus of Panama and capturing much booty. In 1578 he became the first Englishman to navigate the Straits of Magellan, intending to raid the Pacific coast. Alone out of five ships, his *Golden Hind* sailed N but unable to find a way back to the Atlantic Ocean crossed the Pacific Ocean, returning home in 1580 via the Cape of Good Hope. Drake crowned his career by helping to defeat the Spanish *Armada at Gravelines (1588).

d

Drakensberg Mountains (*or* **Quathlamba**) The chief mountain range in S Africa, extending from SE South Africa along the E border of Lesotho to Swaziland, reaching 3482 m (11 425 ft) at Thaba Ntlenyana.

draughts (US name: checkers) A board game for two players, developed in 12th-century Europe from an ancient Egyptian game. Each player has 12 disc-shaped pieces which are placed at the opposite ends of a chessboard. The pieces move only on theblack squares and black always starts. One piece per turn is moved diagonally forwards onto an adjacent square. If the next square is occupied by one of the opponent's pieces but the square beyond that is vacant, the playing piece must jump onto the vacant square, removing the opponent's piece from the board. If a piece reaches the opposing back line it becomes a "king" and it may then move forwards or backwards. The winner is the player who takes or immobilizes all his opponent's pieces.

Dravidian languages A large language family of up to 20 languages spoken mainly in S India. The major languages of the family are *Tamil, Kanarese (*or* Kannada), Telugu, Malayalam, and Tulu. These are all spoken in a continuous area in India, and Tamil is also spoken in Sri Lanka.

Dresden 51 5N 13 41E A city in SE Germany, on the River *Elbe, the capital of Saxony. One of the world's most beautiful cities prior to its devastation by bombs in 1945, it has since been rebuilt. Dresden is a centre of culture, light industry, and market gardening. Population (1999 est): 477 700.

Dresden porcelain *See* MEISSEN PORCELAIN.

dressage The training of a riding (*or* carriage) horse to make it calm, supple, and responsive to its rider (*or* driver). Originally a training for military charges, the present, more humane, methods developed in the 18th century. The most advanced stage is *haute école* equitation in which a horse is taught to perform intricate leaps and movements. Dressage competitions consist of a sequence of complex prescribed movements.

Dreyfus, Alfred (1859–1935) French Jewish army officer. Unjustly accused of revealing state secrets to the German military attaché in Paris, in 1894 Dreyfus, the victim of antisemitism, was deported for life to the penal colony on Devil's Island (off the coast of French Guiana). His case was reopened in 1898, becoming the focus of conflict between royalist, nationalist, and militarist elements on the one hand and socialist, republican, and anticlerical factions on the other. Following a retrial in 1899, Dreyfus was pardoned but not completely cleared until 1906.

dromedary *See* CAMEL.

Drosophila A genus of small *fruit flies (about 1000 species). Most species feed on fermenting materials, such as rotting or damaged fruit. Some species, especially *D. melanogaster*, have been used extensively in laboratory studies of heredity and evolution because of the large chromosomes in their salivary glands and their short life cycle. Family: *Drosophilidae*.

drugs Compounds that alter the physiological state of living organisms (including humans). **Medicinal drugs** are widely used for the treatment, prevention, and diagnosis of disease. The wide range of drugs available for this purpose includes the anaesthetics (*see* ANAESTHESIA), *analgesics, *antibiotics, *cytotoxic drugs, *diuretics, hormonal drugs, and *tranquillizers.

Some drugs are taken solely for their pleasurable effects. Many such drugs are addictive. In the UK these dangerous drugs are known as **controlled drugs**. They are classified as: Class A (heroin, cocaine, ecstasy, etc.) attracting the severest penalties; Class B (amphetamines, barbiturates, etc.) less severe penalties; Class C (including steroids and from 2004 cannabis) still illegal but treated more leniently.

Druids Ancient Celtic priests who were also revered as teachers and judges. They worshipped nature gods, believed in the immortality of the soul and *reincarnation, and also taught astronomy. Their central religious rite involved the sacred oak tree. They sacrificed humans, usually criminals, on behalf of those near to death. In Gaul and Britain they were wiped out by the Romans, their last stand being in Anglesey (61 AD), but in Ireland they survived until the arrival of Christian missionaries.

drumlin A small streamlined hill, formed through glaciation and composed of glacial till or drift, sometimes with a rock core. Drumlins usually occur in groups or swarms (sometimes called basket-of-eggs topography), their long axes parallel to the direction of ice flow.

drupe A stone fruit, such as a cherry, plum, or peach. The fruit wall (pericarp) develops into three layers: an outer skin (epicarp), succulent flesh (mesocarp), and a stone (endocarp) containing the seed.

Drury Lane Theatre The oldest theatre in London, first opened in 1663. The present building dates from 1813. It has housed every form of dramatic production. Its early managers included David *Garrick and R. B. *Sheridan, and it has strong associations with the actors Edmund *Kean and Sir Henry *Irving.

Druses (*or* **Druzes**) Adherents of a religious sect living mainly in Syria, the Lebanon, and Israel. Druses are not generally accepted as Muslims. Their scriptures are based on the Bible, the Koran, and on Sufi writings.

Dryden, John (1631–1700) British poet and critic. He welcomed the Restoration of the monarchy and wrote several successful plays for the recently reopened theatres, such as *All for Love* (1677). He also wrote brilliant verse satires, notably *Absalom and Achitophel* (1681) and *MacFlecknoe* (1682), and many translations.

dry rot The decay of timber caused by cellulose-digesting fungi, especially *Serpula lacrymans*. Spores are liable to germinate in timber having a moisture content of over 20% and the fungus appears as a whitish mass on the surface. The timber becomes cracked and crumbly and the infection may spread to adjoining dry timbers. Treatment is by removal of infected timbers and application of fungicide to the remaining parts. *Compare* WET ROT.

Dubai *See* UNITED ARAB EMIRATES.

Du Barry, Marie Jeanne Bécu, Comtesse (?1743–93) The last mistress of *Louis XV of France from 1768 until his death (1774), when she was banished from court. She was guillotined during the French Revolution.

Dublin (Irish name: Baile Átha Cliath) **1.** 53 20N 6 15W The capital of the Republic of Ireland, on Dublin Bay. An important commercial and cultural centre, it is also the largest manufacturing centre and the largest port in the Republic. Its industries include whiskey distilling, brewing, clothing, glass, and food processing. It is noted for its wide streets and 18th-century Georgian squares. The Easter Rising of 1916 took place here. Population (2002): 495 101. **2.** A county in the E Republic of Ireland, in Leinster bordering on the Irish Sea. Chiefly low lying, it rises in the S to the Wicklow Mountains and is drained by the River Liffey. Area: 922 sq km (356 sq mi). Population (2002): 1 122 600. County town: Dublin.

Dubrovnik (Italian name: Ragusa) 42 40N 18 07E A port and tourist resort in W Croatia on the Adriatic coast. In 1991 it was damaged during the civil war that followed Croatia's secession from Yugoslavia. Population (1991): 49 730.

Duchamp, Marcel (1887–1968) French artist. His first success was *Nude Descending a Staircase* (1912; Philadelphia), influenced by *cubism and futurism. This was followed by his controversial ready-made objects, for example a urinal, first exhibited in New York. He lived in New York after 1915 and became leader of its *dada art movement. His best-known work is the glass and wire picture of *The Bride Stripped Bare by Her Bachelors, Even* (1915–23; Philadelphia).

duck A small short-necked waterbird belonging to the family *Anatidae* (ducks, geese, and swans), occurring in salt and fresh waters throughout the world except Antarctica. Ducks are adapted for swimming and diving, having a dense waterproofed outer plumage with a thick underlayer of down. The blunt spatulate bill is covered with a sensitive membrane and has internal horny plates for sifting food from water. The 200 species of duck are mostly gregarious; many are migratory. Dabbling ducks feed at the surface of the water, while diving ducks dive to forage in deeper water. Order: *Anseriformes* (ducks and geese).

duck-billed platypus An aquatic *monotreme mammal, *Ornithorhynchus anatinus*, of Australia and Tasmania. Platypuses have webbed feet and a broad flat toothless beak for sieving invertebrates from stream bottoms. The female lays two eggs and after incubation suckles the tiny young. Family: *Ornithorhynchidae*.

Dudley A unitary authority in W central England, in West Midlands. Area: 98 sq km (38 sq mi). Population (2001): 305 164.

Dufay, Guillaume (c. 1400–74) Burgundian composer and priest. One of the outstanding composers of the middle ages, he wrote masses, motets, magnificats, and French and Italian chansons.

Dufy, Raoul (1877–1953) French painter. His

early influences were *impressionism and then *fauvism. He later developed an individual style in lively racecourse and regatta scenes.

dugong A marine herbivorous mammal, *Dugong dugon*, of the Indo-Pacific region. Dugongs, also known as sea cows, have blue-grey rough skin and a bristly snout; the males have short tusks. Their forelimbs are flippers and they lack hind limbs, having a flukelike tail for swimming. Family: *Dugongidae*; order: *Sirenia*.

d

dulcimer A musical instrument consisting of a shallow resonating box with strings stretched over two moveable bridges. It is played with two small hammers and is much used in European and Asian folk music.

Dumas, Alexandre (1802–70) French novelist and dramatist, often called Dumas *père*. He is noted for his historical romances, including *The Count of Monte Cristo* (1844–45), *The Three Musketeers* (1844), and *The Black Tulip* (1850). His son **Alexandre Dumas** (1824–95), a dramatist, was often called Dumas *fils*. His best-known work is the novel *La Dame aux camélias* (1848), the basis of a play and Verdi's opera *La Traviata*.

Du Maurier, George (Louis Palmella Busson) (1834–96) British caricaturist and novelist, born in Paris, who contributed caricatures to *Punch* and other magazines. His novel *Trilby* (1894), remembered for its sinister hypnotist Svengali, is based on his life as an art student in Paris. The best-known works of his granddaughter **Dame Daphne Du Maurier** (1907–89) are romances, usually set in Cornwall. They include *Rebecca* (1938) and *My Cousin Rachel* (1951).

Dumfries and Galloway A council area in SW Scotland, bordering on the Solway Firth. Formed in 1975 from the counties of Dumfries, Kirkudbright, and Wigtown, it became a unitary authority in 1996. It consists of uplands in the N descending to coastal lowlands in the S and has an indented coastline. The region is predominantly agricultural. Area: 6369 sq km (2460 sq mi). Population (2001): 147 765. Administrative centre: Dumfries.

Dunbarton (*or* **Dunbartonshire**) A historic county of W Scotland. In 1975 its boundaries were adjusted to form Dunbarton District, in Strathclyde Region. Further reorganization in 1996 involved the creation of two council areas, *East Dunbartonshire and *West Dunbartonshire.

Duncan I (d. 1040) King of the Scots (1034–40). His claim to the throne was challenged by Macbeth, by whom he was murdered.

Duncan, Isadora (1878–1927) US dancer. She lived mostly in Europe, where she gained a reputation for both her innovative modern interpretive dancing and her flamboyant lifestyle.

Dundee 1. 56 28N 3 00W A city and port in E Scotland, in Dundee City council area, on the Firth of Tay. It provides supplies and services for the North Sea oil industry and is also a fast-growing centre for biotechnology and genetic research. Population (1993 est): 153 710. **2. Dundee City**. A council area in E Scotland. Area: 65 sq km (25 sq mi). Population (2001): 145 663.

Dunedin 45 52S 170 30E A port in New Zealand, in SE South Island at the head of Otago Harbour. Founded by Scottish Presbyterians in 1848, it has two cathedrals (Anglican and Roman Catholic) and the University of Otago (the oldest in the country, founded in 1869). Population (1999 est): 119 600.

Dunfermline 56 04N 3 29W A town in E Scotland, in Fife Region on the Firth of Forth. Several Scottish kings, including Robert the Bruce, are buried in the 11th-century abbey. Population (1991): 55 083.

Dungannon A district in S Northern Ireland, in Co Tyrone. Area: 763 sq km (294 sq mi). Population (2001): 47 735.

dung beetle A *scarab beetle, usually small and dark, that has the habit of rolling dung into balls, which serve as a food source for both the adults and larvae.

Dungeness 50 55N 0 58E A shingle headland in SE England, in Kent extending into the English Channel. Two nuclear power stations and an automatic lighthouse are located here.

Dunkirk (French name: Dunkerque) 51 02N 2 23E A port in N France, in the Nord department on the Strait of Dover. During *World War II some 338 200 Allied troops were successfully evacuated from its beaches (1940) following the fall of France. Dunkirk is a rapidly growing industrial centre and has an oil refinery and naval shipbuilding yards. Population (1990): 71 071.

Dun Laoghaire 53 17N 6 08W A port in the E Republic of Ireland, in Co Dublin. It is the terminus of a ferry service from Holyhead, Wales. Population (2002): 191 389.

dunlin A common *sandpiper, *Calidris alpina*, that breeds in far northern regions, ranging south to N Britain. It has a bill with a curved tip and a black and russet plumage that changes to grey in winter.

Dunlop, John Boyd (1840–1921) Scottish inventor, who is credited with inventing the pneumatic tyre (1887). Dunlop began to produce his tyres commercially in 1890, contributing to the development of motor cars.

dunnock A shy songbird, *Prunella modularis*, also called hedge sparrow. About 14 cm long, the dunnock has a brown plumage with a greyish throat and breast. It has a sharp bill and feeds on insects. Family: *Prunellidae* (accentors).

Duns Scotus, John (c. 1260–1308) Scottish-born Franciscan philosopher, who, with Roger *Bacon and William of Ockham, carried on controversy against *Aquinas. Duns Scotus held that what makes one thing distinct from another is its form or essence—that is, its essential properties rather than its accidental properties, as the latter may be removed or changed without altering its identity. Although nicknamed the Subtle Doctor by contemporaries, Duns Scotus suffered Renaissance ridicule, his name giving rise to the derisive label "dunce."

Dunstan, St (924–88 AD) English churchman and monastic reformer. Appointed Abbot of Glastonbury in 943, he rebuilt its monastery and revived English monasticism. The chief minister under Kings Eadred and Edgar, he became Bishop of Worcester (957), Bishop of London (959), and Archbishop of Canterbury (960). Feast day: 19 May.

duodenum *See* INTESTINE.

Durban 29 53S 31 00E The main seaport in South Africa, on the Indian Ocean. Population (1996, urban area): 2 117 650.

Dürer, Albrecht (1471–1528) German *Renaissance painter, engraver, draughtsman, and woodcut designer. He was influenced by Italian artists but his woodcuts of the *Apocalypse* (1498) are still gothic in style. In about 1500, he became preoccupied with the study of human proportions. Paintings of this period include the *Self-Portrait* as Christ (1500) and *Adoration of the Magi* (1504). He executed his most famous engravings, including *Knight, Death, and the Devil*, in the period 1512–19.

Durham 1. 54 47N 1 34W A city in NE England, the administrative centre of Co Durham on the River Wear. It has a Norman cathedral and an 11th-century castle. Population (1991): 36 937. **2.** A county in NE England, on the North Sea. It consists of lowlands, rising W to the uplands of the Pennines and is drained by the Rivers Wear and Tees. Agriculture includes sheep and dairy farming. Coalmining was formerly important, but the last deep pits closed in the 1990s. Light engineering, services, and clothing manufacture are now the chief industries. In 1974 it lost the NE and SE to Tyne and Wear and Cleveland respectively. In 1996 Cleveland was abolished and the former SE boundary restored for ceremonial purposes: these areas are now administered by the unitary authorities of Hartlepool and Stockton-on-Tees. Darlington became an independent unitary authority in 1997. Area (excluding unitary authorities): 2434 sq km (960 sq mi). Population (2001, excluding unitary authorities): 493 470. Administrative centre: Durham.

durra A variety of *sorghum, *S. vulgare*, also called millet. It is cultivated in arid lands in S Europe, Asia, and Africa and is used as a cereal, as animal feed, and for the manufacture of sugar and syrup.

Durrell, Lawrence George (1912–90) British novelist and poet. His best-known work is *The Alexandria Quartet*, comprising *Justine* (1957), *Balthazar* (1958), *Mountolive* (1958), and *Clea* (1960). His later work includes *The Avignon Quintet* (1974–85). His brother **Gerald Durrell** (1925–95) was a naturalist and popular writer, known for such books as *My Family and Other Animals* (1956).

durum *See* WHEAT.

Dushanbe (name until 1929: Dyushambe; name 1929–61: Stalinabad) 38 38N 68 51E The capital of Tadzhikistan, on the River Dushanbinka. It has food and textile industries. Since 1992 it has been the scene of fighting between rival political factions. Population (1998 est): 513 000.

Düsseldorf 51 13N 6 47E A city in NW Germany, capital of North Rhine-Westphalia on the River Rhine. A port and major commercial and industrial centre of the *Ruhr, its main industry is iron and steel. Population (1999 est): 568 500.

Dust Bowl, the An area in the USA, extending across W Kansas, Oklahoma, and Texas, and into Colorado and New Mexico. During the 1930s droughts and overfarming caused topsoil erosion.

Dutch The national language of the Netherlands, belonging to the West Germanic language group. In Belgium it is one of the two official languages and is known as Flemish (*or* Vlaams). It is derived from Low Franconian, the speech of the Salic Franks, who settled in this area, and has numerous local variants.

Dutch elm disease A serious disease, first described in the Netherlands in 1919, that reached epidemic proportions in Britain in the 1970s, killing millions of elm trees. The fungus responsible, *Ceratocystus ulmi*, blocks the vessels that carry water to the leaves, which wilt and eventually die. The disease is carried by the elm bark beetle. Protective measures can be taken but are too expensive for widespread use.

d

Duvalier, François (1907–71) Haitian politician, known as Papa Doc; president (1957–71). He used his secret police, the Tonton Macoutes, to suppress opposition and exploited Black nationalism and voodoo rites to maintain popular support. In 1964 he became president for life, a post in which his son **Jean-Claude Duvalier** (1951–), known as Baby Doc, succeeded him, but had to flee to France after an uprising in 1986.

DVD *See* COMPACT DISC.

Dvořák, Antonín (1841–1904) Czech composer. He wrote his famous ninth symphony, entitled "From the New World," while director of the National Conservatory in New York, 1892–95. Besides the symphonies he wrote concertos for piano, violin, and cello, orchestral tone poems, chamber music, piano music, and songs. His Czech nationalism is particularly evident in his famous *Slavonic Dances* for piano duet (1878–86).

Dylan, Bob (Robert Allen Zimmerman; 1941–) US singer and songwriter. An outstanding lyricist, he spoke for the protest movement of the 1960s with such folk albums as *The Times They Are a-Changin'* (1964); later albums include *Blonde on Blonde* (1966), *Blood on the Tracks* (1975) and, following his conversion to Christianity, *Slow Train Coming* (1979). More recent records include *Time Out of Mind* (1997) and *Love & Theft* (2001).

dynamite An explosive plastic solid consisting of 75% nitroglycerine and 25% kieselguhr, a porous form of silicon dioxide (SiO_2). It was invented in 1866 by *Nobel. Nitroglycerine alone is very sensitive to shock. The kieselguhr makes it safe to handle. Dynamite is used for blasting, particularly under water.

dynamo *See* ELECTRIC GENERATOR.

dyne The unit of force in the *c.g.s. system equal to the force that will impart to a mass of one gram an acceleration of one centimetre per second per second.

dysentery An infection of the large bowel causing painful diarrhoea that often contains blood and mucus. It may be caused either by bacteria of the genus *Shigella* or by amoebae. It can occur wherever there is poor sanitation, but amoebic dysentery is much more common in tropical countries. Treatment for bacillary dysentery is usually by administration of fluids to prevent dehydration, but for amoebic dysentery drugs to kill the amoebae are also given.

dyslexia Difficulty in learning to write, spell, and read. It is commonly discovered at school. Dyslexic children are usually of normal intelligence and with special teaching can improve greatly. In some cases the cause is genetic.

dysprosium (Dy) A lanthanide element discovered in 1886. It forms the oxide (Dy_2O_3) and halides (for example DyF_3) and can be separated from the other lanthanides by ion-exchange techniques. At no 66; at wt 162.50; mp 1412°C; bp 2567°C.

E

Eadred (d. 955) King of England (946–55), who reconquered Northumbria by expelling Eric Bloodaxe (954), its Norwegian king.

Eadwig (*or* **Edwy**; d. 959) King of England from 955 to 957, when he lost Mercia and Northumbria, and thereafter of Kent and Wessex.

eagle A large broad-winged bird of prey occurring throughout the world, mostly in remote mountainous regions. Eagles have a large hooked bill and strong feet with large curved talons and are typically dull brown. With a wingspan of 1.3–2.4 m, they can soar for long periods searching for food. Family: *Accipitridae* (hawks and eagles). *See also* BALD EAGLE; GOLDEN EAGLE.

Eagle owl Europe's largest owl, *Bubo bubo*; it has a body length of 65–70 cm, and is yellowish brown with darker stripes and ear tufts. The eagle owl is endangered, and active measures have been taken to breed it.

ealdorman The chief royal official of the Anglo-Saxon shire. Almost always of noble rank, he presided over the shire court, executed royal orders, and raised the shire military levy. Ealdormen later became the hereditary earls, and the sheriffs succeeded to their duties.

ear The organ of hearing and balance in vertebrates (including man). The human ear is divided into external, middle, and inner parts. Sound waves are transmitted through the auditory meatus and cause the eardrum (tympanic membrane) to vibrate. These vibrations are transmitted through the three small bones (ossicles) of the middle ear to the fenestra ovalis, which leads to the inner ear. A duct (the Eustachian tube) connects the middle ear to the back of the throat (pharynx), enabling the release of pressure that builds up in the middle ear. The cochlea—a spiral organ of the inner ear—contains special cells that convert the sound vibrations into nerve impulses, which are transmitted to the hearing centres of the brain via the cochlear nerve. The inner ear also contains the organs of balance: three semicircular canals, each of which registers movement in a different plane.

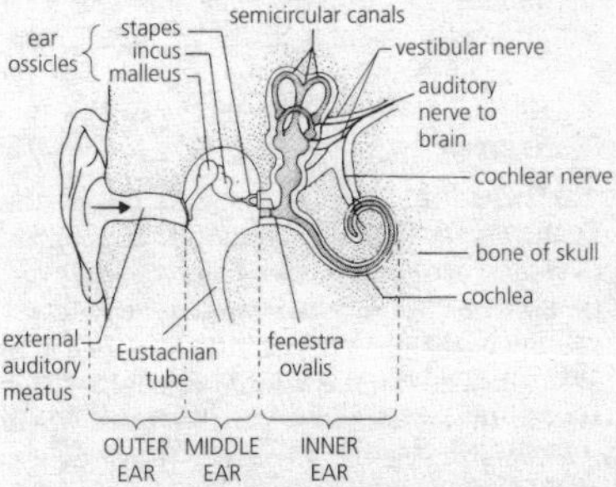

ear. A vertical section through the human ear shows its internal structure; the middle and inner ears are embedded in the bone of the skull. The arrow indicates the direction of sound waves entering the ear.

Earhart, Amelia (1898–1937) US aviator, who was the first woman to fly solo across the Atlantic (1932) and Pacific (1935) Oceans. She died on an attempted flight around the world.

Earl Marshal A hereditary post held by the Duke of Norfolk since 1672. As the senior member of the College of Arms, the Earl Marshal oversees state ceremonies, his staff of office being a golden rod with a black ring at each end.

Early English The style of gothic architecture predominant in England in the 13th century. It is characterized by narrow pointed windows and arches, in contrast to the rounded features of the preceding period.

earth The third planet from the sun, at an average distance of 149.6 million km (93 million mi) from it. Its diameter at the equator is 12 756 km (7926 mi), slightly less at the Poles; its shape is therefore a flattened sphere. It completes an orbit of the sun in 365.26 days, and makes one rotation on its axis every 23.93 hours. The earth is believed to be about 4600 million years old. Geologists divide this time into eras, periods, and epochs (*see* GEOLOGICAL TIME SCALE). The earth consists of an inner core of solid iron, surrounded by an outer core of molten iron. Surrounding this is the solid mantle, inner and outer, which is separated from the crust by the Mohorovičić Discontinuity. The crust consists of basaltic oceanic crust surmounted by less dense granitic continental crust, which forms the continents. The crust varies in thickness from 5 km under the oceans to 60 km under mountain ranges. The composition of the crust is approximately 47% oxygen, 28% silicon, 8% aluminium, 4.5% iron, 3.5% calcium, 2.5% each sodium and potassium, and 2.2% magnesium. All other elements present occur to an extent of less than 1% each. 70.8% of the earth's surface is ocean.

earthquake A series of shocks felt at the earth's surface, ranging from mild tremblings to violent oscillations, resulting from the fracturing of brittle rocks within the earth's crust and upper mantle. The magnitude of an earthquake depends on the amount of energy liberated in the seismic waves at the focus, where the overstrained rocks fracture. The *Richter scale is used for comparing earthquake magnitudes. The majority of earthquakes occur in certain well-defined seismic zones, corresponding with the junction of lithospheric plates (*see* PLATE TECTONICS).

earthworm A terrestrial *annelid worm belonging to a class (*Oligochaeta*) found all over the world. Earthworms feed on rotting vegetation, pulling the dead leaves down into their burrows and improving the fertility of the soil. The body consists of about 100 segments.

earwig A nocturnal usually herbivorous insect belonging to an order (*Dermaptera*; about 1100 species) found in Europe and warm regions. It has a dark slender body, a pair of pincers (cerci) at the end of the abdomen, and two pairs of wings.

East Ayrshire A council area of SE Scotland, consisting of the E part of the historic county of Ayrshire. Absorbed into Strathclyde Region in 1975, it became an independent unitary authority in 1996. It consists mainly of a rich agricultural plain. Dairying and cattle breeding are the main agricultural activities. Area: 1252 sq km (483 sq mi). Population (2001): 120 235. Administrative centre: Kilmarnock.

Eastbourne 51 00N 0 44W A resort in S England, on the East Sussex coast near Beachy Head, where the South Downs reach the sea. Population (1991): 94 793.

East Dunbartonshire A council area of central Scotland, comprising part of the historic county of Dunbarton. Absorbed into Strathclyde Region in 1975, it became an independent unitary authority in 1996. It is mainly low-lying and agricultural. Area: 172 sq km (66 sq mi). Population (2001): 108 243. Administrative centre: Kirkintilloch.

Easter The feast of the resurrection of Christ. Associated by the early Church with the Jewish Passover, the date of celebrating Easter was a matter of controversy. At the Council of Nicaea in 325 AD, it was agreed that it would be linked to the full moon on or following the vernal equinox and might thus fall on any Sunday between 22 March and 25 April. *See also* GOOD FRIDAY; LENT.

Easter Island (*or* **Rapanui**) 27 05S 109 20W A Chilean island of volcanic origin in the S Pacific Ocean. It is famed for its tall stone sculptures. The population is of Polynesian stock. Area: 166 sq km (64 sq mi). Population (latest est): 2000. Chief settlement: Hanga-Roa.

Eastern Roman Empire (*or* **Byzantine Empire**) The Roman territories E of the Balkans separated from the western Roman Empire by Diocletian in 293 AD. An eastern emperor and magistrates coexisted with their western counterparts at Rome. Under Constantine the Great the Empire became Christian. Constantinople (previously Byzantium; now Istanbul) was inaugurated as the "New Rome" in 330 AD. The Eastern Empire survived until the fall of Constantinople to the Ottoman Turks in 1453.

Easter Rising (1916) An armed insurrection mainly in Dublin against the British Government. Patrick Pearse, a leader of the Irish Republican Brotherhood, and James Connolly with his Citizen Army, a total of 2000 men, occupied strategic positions in the city and proclaimed the establishment of the Irish Republic. Serious fighting ensued with the government employing artillery. The insurgents surrendered unconditionally and 15 of the leaders were executed.

East India Company 1. (British) A commercial company that was incorporated in 1600 to trade in East Indian spices and came to wield considerable political power in British India. Its dominance was established at the expense of the French East India Company (founded 1664) by Robert Clive's victories in the Seven Years' War (1756–63). For the next decade the Company controlled government, its powers then being restricted by a series of Government of India Acts. The Company ceased to exist in 1873. **2.** (Dutch) A commercial company founded in 1602 to foster Dutch trade in the East Indies. By the late 17th century, it concentrated almost exclusively on the administration of Java.

East Lothian A council area of SE Scotland, on the Firth of Forth and the North Sea. In 1975 the boundaries of the historic county of East Lothian were adjusted to form a district of the same name, in Lothian Region. In 1996 this became an independent unitary authority. Coastal plains in the N rise to hills in the SW. Agriculture, fishing, and tourism are the main economic activities. Area: 678 sq km (262 sq mi). Population (2001): 90 088. Administrative centre: Haddington.

Eastman, George (1854–1932) US inventor of the Kodak camera (1888) and founder of the Eastman Kodak Company (1892). In 1884 he patented a photographic film consisting of a paper base on which the necessary chemicals were fixed rather than being applied to photographic plates when required; the paper base was replaced by celluloid in 1889. In 1928 he developed a process for colour photography.

East Renfrewshire A council area of W central Scotland, consisting of part of the historic county of Renfrewshire. Absorbed into Strathclyde Region in 1975, it became a unitary authority in 1996. It is mainly an upland farming area apart from the N, which is a residential area for Glasgow. Area: 173 sq km (67 sq mi). Population (2001): 89 311. Administrative centre: Giffnock.

East Riding A county in NE England, a historical division of Yorkshire, on the North Sea and Humber estuary. In 1974 it was incorporated into the new county of Humberside. In 1996 Humberside was abolished and separate unitary authorities were created for the East Riding and Kingston upon Hull: the latter is considered part of the East Riding for ceremonial purposes. The area is mainly flat rising to the Yorkshire Wolds in the N. The main economic activities are farming, fishing, and tourism. Area (excluding Kingston upon Hull): 1748 sq km (675 sq mi). Population (2001, excluding Kingston upon Hull): 314 076. Administrative centre: Beverley.

East River A river in the E USA, a tidal strait and navigable waterway flowing through New York City and connecting New York Harbour with Long Island Sound. Length: 26 km (16 mi).

East Sussex A county of SE England, formerly part of Sussex, on the English Channel. Brighton and Hove became an independent unitary authority in 1997. It consists mainly of undulating land with the South Downs in the S. It is predominantly agricultural. Coastal resorts include Brighton and Eastbourne. Area (excluding Brighton and Hove): 1795 sq km (693 sq mi). Population (2001, excluding Brighton and Hove): 492 324. Administrative centre: Lewes.

East Timor (Portuguese name: Timor-Leste) A country in SE Asia, occupying the E part of the island of Timor with a small enclave in W Timor (Indonesia). It is mountainous, with a monsoon climate. The great majority of the population are Roman Catholics. *Economy*: lack of natural resources, underdevelopment, and 25 years of repression and conflict have left East Timor the poorest nation in Asia. 90% of the population live off the land; the main crops are coffee (the chief export), coconuts, and sandalwood. Offshore oil and gas began to be exploited in 2004. *History*: in 1859 Timor was divided between Holland, which took the W part, and Portugal, which took the E. In 1975 East Timor declared its independence but this provoked a military invasion by Indonesia (which had incorporated W Timor in 1949). Wholesale massacres of the Timorese population followed. Formal annexation by Indonesia in 1976 was not recognized by the UN. In a referendum in 1999, 78.5% of the population voted for independence. A campaign of terror followed initiated by anti-independence militias. In October of that year Indonesian troops were withdrawn, leaving a UN administration to oversee the transition to independence, finally achieved in May 2002, with the former guerrilla leader, Xanana Gusmão, having been elected president. Official languages: Portuguese and Tetum (a lingua franca). Currency: US dollar of 100 cents. Area: 14 874 sq km (5743 sq mi). Population (2003 est): 778 000. Capital: Dili.

Eastwood, Clint (1930–) US film actor and director. He became popular playing taciturn tough guys in such films as *A Fistful of Dollars* (1964) and *Dirty Harry* (1971); his films as a director include *Unforgiven* (1992) and *Mystic River* (2003).

ebony The valuable heartwood of several tropical evergreen trees of the genus *Diospyros*. Ebony is very hard, dark, and heavy. It is used for cabinetwork, inlaying, etc. The most important species of trees are *D. ebenum* from India and Sri Lanka and *D. reticulata* from Mauritius. Family: *Ebenaceae*.

e

Eccles, Sir John Carew (1903–97) Australian physiologist who showed how the different nerve endings could either allow the transmission of nervous impulses to other nerves (excitatory) or prevent their passage (inhibitory). He was awarded the 1963 Nobel Prize with A. F. *Huxley and A. L. Hodgkin.

Ecclesiastes (Greek: the preacher) An Old Testament book consisting of a series of largely pessimistic reflections on human life. Although traditionally ascribed to *Solomon, it is in fact one of the later books to be accepted as part of the Hebrew Bible.

echidna A monotreme mammal belonging to the family *Tachyglossidae* (2 species), of Australia and New Guinea. The Australian echidna (*Tachyglossus aculeatus*), or spiny anteater, is about 45 cm long, with very long spines among its fur, and digs for ants, picking them up with its long sticky tongue. The single egg is incubated in a pouch on the female's belly. The young echidna is suckled at a teat in the pouch.

Echidna In Greek legend, a monster, half woman and half serpent. By the monster Typhon she gave birth to many other legendary monsters, including Chimera, Cerberus, Orthus, Scylla, the Sphinx, and the dragons of the Hesperides and of Colchis.

echinoderm A marine invertebrate animal of the phylum *Echinodermata* (over 6500 species), including *starfish, *sea urchins, *crinoids, *sea cucumbers, etc. Echinoderms usually have a skin-covered skeleton of calcareous plates, often bearing spines. They use hydrostatic pressure to extend numerous small saclike organs (tube feet) used in locomotion, respiration, feeding, etc. Echinoderms generally occur on the sea floor.

Echo In Greek legend, a nymph deprived of speech by Hera and able to repeat only the final words of others. Her hopeless love for *Narcissus caused her to fade away until only her voice remained.

echolocation A method by which certain animals can sense and locate surrounding objects by emitting sounds and detecting the echo. Insectivorous bats detect the echo by means of large ears or folds of the nostril, and are able to locate their prey when hunting on the wing. Toothed whales and porpoises emit brief intense clicks, enabling them to discriminate very small objects.

echo sounding The use of sound waves to measure the depth of the sea below a vessel or to detect other vessels or obstacles. The device used consists of a source of ultrasonic pulses and an electronic circuit to measure the time taken for the pulse to reach the target and its echo to return to the transducer. The device was developed originally by the Allied Submarine Detection Investigation Committee (ASDIC) in 1920 and was formerly known by this acronym. The name was changed to sonar (*so*und *na*vigation and *r*anging) in 1963.

eclipse The passage of all or part of an astronomical body into the shadow of another. A **lunar eclipse** occurs when the moon can enter the earth's shadow at full moon. The gradual obscuration of the moon's surface is seen wherever the moon is above the horizon. A **solar eclipse**, which is strictly an *occultation, occurs at new moon, but only when the moon passes directly in front of the sun. The moon's shadow falls on and moves rapidly across the earth. Observers in the outer shadow region (the penumbra) will see a **partial eclipse**, with only part of the sun hidden. Observers in the dark inner (umbral) region of the shadow will see a **total eclipse**, in which the sun's disc is completely but briefly obscured; the *corona can, however, be seen. If the moon is too far away totally to cover the sun, an **annular eclipse** is observed, in which a rim of light is visible around the eclipsed sun.

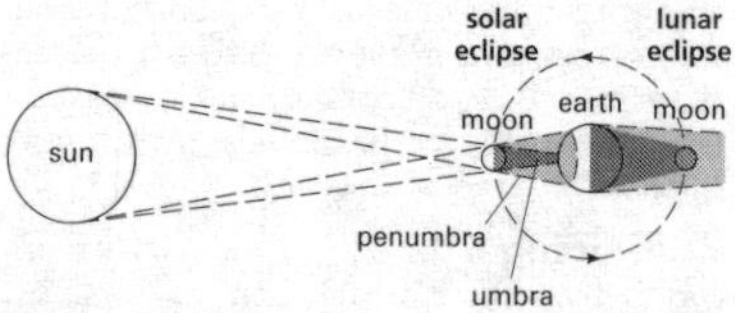

eclipse

ecliptic The great circle in which the plane of the earth's orbit around the sun meets the *celestial sphere. It marks the apparent path of the sun across the celestial sphere, relative to the background stars, over the course of a year.

ecology The scientific study of organisms in their natural environment. Modern ecology is concerned with the relationships of different species with each other and with the environment (habitat). A *community of organisms and their habitat is called an **ecosystem**. Ecologists can calculate the productivity of various ecosystems in terms of energy, with important applications in agriculture. In addition, the effects of man's intervention on natural ecosystems can be predicted, enabling the effective conservation of wildlife and management of game and fish.

e-commerce The use of the *Internet to buy and sell goods and services. Payment is usually by credit card, but other methods, such as digitized e-cash, are available.

economics A social science concerned with the production of goods and services, their distribution, exchange, and consumption. **Microeconomics** is concerned with the problems facing individuals and firms, while **macroeconomics** is concerned with the economy of a country and regulation of the economy by governments. *See also* MONETARISM.

ecstasy A street name for the illegal hallucinogen 3,4-methylene dioxymethamphetamine (MDMA), which first became a popular recreational drug in the 1980s. Side-effects include overheating and dehydration, which may cause users to drink dangerous amounts of water. Persistent use may also cause memory loss.

ectopic pregnancy Pregnancy occurring elsewhere than in the womb, most commonly in a Fallopian tube. It may lead to abortion or, more seriously, to rupture of the tube, with pain, bleeding, and shock. The usual treatment is surgical removal of the fetus and tube.

Ecuador, Republic of A country in NW South America, lying on the Equator, from which it takes its name. It includes the *Galápagos Islands. It consists chiefly of a coastal plain in the W, separated from the tropical jungles and rivers of the Amazon basin by the Andes (containing several active volcanoes). There are frequent earthquakes. The population is largely of Indian and mixed race, with minorities of European and African descent. *Economy*: mainly agricultural, with cash crops (bananas, coffee, and cocoa) grown in the lower coastal areas. Much of the country is forested and valuable hardwoods are produced. Fishing and the oil industry are important. *History*: the Andean kingdom of Quito had already been conquered by the Incas when the Spanish established a colony in 1532. It gained independence in 1821 and in 1822 joined Gran Colombia under *Bolívar. In 1830 it became the independent republic of Ecuador. Between 1934 and 1972 the would-be dictator Velasco Ibarra (1893–1979) was five times elected president but each time deposed by the military. A new democratic constitution was introduced in 1979 and free elections were held: since then governments have faced problems of economic crisis, unrest, and threatened military intervention. Financial and economic crisis in 2000 led to the resignation of the cabinet, the adoption of the US dollar, rising disorder, and a coup led by the military. In 2002 the left-wing populist Lucio Gutiérerrez was elected president. Official language: Spanish. Currency: US dollar of 100 cents. Area: 270 670 sq km (104 505 sq mi). Population (2003): 13 003 000. Capital: Quito.

eczema Inflammation of the skin, often without obvious cause. Eczema resulting from contact with irritant or allergy-provoking substances, infections, drugs, or radiation is usually called dermatitis.

Eddy, Mary Baker (1821–1910) US religious leader, founder of *Christian Science. Often ill as a young woman, Mrs Eddy was influenced by the spiritual leader Phineas Parkhurst Quimby (1802–66). She published her beliefs in *Science and Health* (1875) and in 1879 founded the Church of Christ, Scientist, in Boston.

edelweiss A common perennial alpine plant, *Leontopodium alpinum*, from Europe and South America, often grown in rock gardens. About 15 cm high, it has woolly leaves and tiny yellow flowers surrounded by whitish felted bracts. Family: *Compositae* (daisy family).

Eden, Anthony *See* AVON, (ROBERT) ANTHONY EDEN, 1ST EARL OF.

Edgar (c. 943–75) The first king of a united England (959–75). He allowed his Danish subjects to retain Danish laws. Edgar promoted a monastic revival, encouraged trade by reforming the currency, and improved naval defence.

Edgar the Aetheling (c. 1050–c. 1130) The grandson of Edmund II Ironside; his title Aetheling means royal prince. His claim to the English throne was rejected in 1066 owing to his minority and ill health. In 1068 and 1069 he led revolts against William I but came to terms with him in 1074.

Edinburgh **1.** 55 57N 3 13W The capital of Scotland, a city in the E centre of the country, in City of Edinburgh council area, on the Firth of Forth. In the old town, atop steep basalt cliffs that rise above the city, stands the castle. The Royal Mile extends E from the castle rock to the Palace of Holyrood House (begun c. 1500). The other famous thoroughfare is Princes Street. The new town contains fine Georgian architecture situated around a network of broad streets, squares, and circuses. *History*: strategically important in medieval times in the wars between England and Scotland, Edinburgh emerged as the national capital in the 15th century. After James VI of Scotland (James I of England) moved his court to London in 1605 Edinburgh suffered a decline, but by the mid-18th century it was a centre of learning. The annual Edinburgh International Festival was founded in 1947. The city has been the seat of the Scottish Parliament since 1999. Population (1991): 401 910. **2. City of Edinburgh.** A council area in E central Scotland, created from part of Lothian Region in 1996. Area: 262 sq km (101 sq mi). Population (2001): 448 624.

Edison, Thomas Alva (1847–1931) US inventor, owning a large research laboratory in Menlo Park, New Jersey. His most famous invention, the electric light bulb, was constructed in 1879. By 1881 Edison had built a generating station and was supplying electricity to over 80 customers. Among his other 1300 inventions were the gramophone and improvements to Bell's telephone. He also discovered thermionic emission, enabling J. A. *Fleming to produce the first thermionic valve.

Edmonton 53 34N 113 25W A city in W Canada, the capital of Alberta on the North Saskatchewan River. Population (1996): 616 306.

Edmund I (921–46) King of England (939–46), who expelled the Norse king Olaf from Northumbria (944).

Edmund II Ironside (c. 981–1016) The son of Ethelred II of England. His struggle with Canute for the vacant throne ended in Edmund's defeat at Ashingdon (1016). Canute agreed on the partition of England with Edmund, but after Edmund's sudden death Canute acquired the whole kingdom.

Edward I (1239–1307) King of England (1272–1307), succeeding his father Henry III. He married (1254) *Eleanor of Castile. He encouraged parliamentary institutions at the expense of feudalism and subdued Wales, on which he imposed the English system of administration. He later tried to assert his authority over Scotland and died while on his way to fight Robert Bruce (*see* ROBERT (I) THE BRUCE).

Edward II (1284–1327) King of England (1307–27), succeeding his father Edward I. He became the first English Prince of Wales (1301). He married (1308) Isabella of France (1292–1358). His reign was troubled by his extravagance, his military disasters in Scotland, notably at Bannockburn (1314), and the unpopularity of his favourites, Piers Gaveston (d. 1312) and Hugh le Despenser (1262–1326), which led to his murder.

Edward III (1312–77) King of England (1327–77), succeeding his father Edward II. He assumed effective power in 1330 after imprisoning his mother Isabella of France (1292–1358) and executing her lover Roger de Mortimer. Thereafter his reign was dominated by military adventures, his victories in Scotland encouraging him to plan (1363) the union of England and Scotland. Through his mother he claimed the French throne, thus starting (1337) the *Hundred Years' War. His son *John of Gaunt dominated the government during his last years.

Edward IV (1442–83) King of England (1461–70, 1471–83) during the Wars of the *Roses. The Yorkist leader, he was crowned after defeating the Lancastrians at Mortimer's Cross and Towton (1461). He was forced from the throne (1470) by the Earl of *Warwick but regained it after defeating the Lancastrians at Tewkesbury (1471).

Edward V (1470–?1483) King of England (1483), succeeding his father Edward IV. His uncle, the Duke of Gloucester, imprisoned Edward and his brother Richard in the Tower of London, deposed Edward after a reign of only three months, and had himself crowned as Richard III. The two boys, known as the Princes in the Tower, were probably murdered in 1483.

Edward VI (1537–53) King of England (1547–53) and the son of Henry VIII, whom he succeeded, and Jane *Seymour. Effective power was held by the protector, the Duke of *Somerset, until 1550, when the Duke of *Northumberland seized power. Edward became a fervent Protestant and during his reign the *Reformation in England made substantial progress.

Edward VII (1841–1910) King of the United Kingdom (1901–10), succeeding his mother Queen Victoria. He married (1863) *Alexandra of Denmark. As Prince of Wales his indiscretions caused Victoria to exclude him from all affairs of state, but he became a popular king.

Edward VIII (1894–1972) King of the United Kingdom (1936), succeeding his father George V. He abdicated on 11 December 1936, because of constitutional objections to his liaison with the twice-divorced Mrs Wallis Simpson

(1896–1986), whom he married in France in 1937. He became Duke of Windsor and was governor of the Bahamas during World War II. He subsequently lived in France until his death.

Edward, the Black Prince (1330–76) Prince of Wales and the eldest son of Edward III. His nickname may refer to the black armour he was said to have worn at Crécy (1346). He won victories against France in the *Hundred Years' War and ruled Aquitaine from 1360 until ousted (1371).

Edward the Confessor (c. 1003–66) King of England (1042–66), nicknamed for his piety and his foundation of a new Westminster Abbey (consecrated 1065). His early reign was dominated by rivalry between his Norman favourites and his father-in-law Earl Godwin (d. 1053). After 1053 the Godwins were in the ascendant. Edward's childlessness resulted in rival claims to the throne by two named heirs (*see* HAROLD II; WILLIAM (I) THE CONQUEROR) and led ultimately to the Norman conquest. He was canonized in 1161.

Edward the Elder (d. 924) King of England (899–924), succeeding his father Alfred the Great. He defeated the Danes (918), taking East Anglia, and also conquered Mercia (918) and Northumbria (920).

Edward the Martyr (c. 963–78) King of England (975–78), succeeding his father Edgar. He was murdered at Corfe Castle in Dorset and canonized in 1001. Feast day: 18 March.

Edwin (c. 585–633) King of Northumbria (616–33), who became overlord of all English kingdoms S of the Humber, except for Kent. His marriage to Ethelburh, a Christian, led to his conversion and that of his people to Christianity (627). He was killed in battle against Penda of Mercia.

eel A snakelike *bony fish of the worldwide order *Anguilliformes* (or *Apodes*; over 500 species) having, usually, a scaleless body, no pelvic fins, and long dorsal and anal fins. Most species are marine, occurring mainly in shallow waters and feeding on other fish. The freshwater eels (family *Anguillidae*) migrate to the sea to breed—the *Sargasso Sea in the case of European and American species—and the young eels (elvers) return to rivers and streams. *See also* ELECTRIC EEL.

eelgrass A perennial herbaceous marine plant of the genus *Zostera*, especially *Z. marina*, which grows in muddy intertidal flats and estuaries on the coasts of Europe and North America. It has creeping underground stems (rhizomes), which help to stabilize mudbanks, and broad dark-green grasslike leaves. Family: *Zosteraceae*.

EFTA *See* EUROPEAN FREE TRADE ASSOCIATION.

egg (*or* **ovum**) The female reproductive cell (*see* GAMETE), which—when fertilized by a male gamete (sperm)—develops into a new individual. Animal eggs are surrounded by nutritive material (yolk) and—usually—one or more protective membranes, for example a jelly coat in amphibian eggs, the shell and other layers in birds' eggs. In mammals the egg is nourished from the maternal circulation and thus has less yolk than the eggs of other egg-laying animals in which the embryo is nourished by the yolk. *See also* OVARY.

eglantine *See* SWEET BRIAR.

ego In *psychoanalysis, the part of the mind that is closely in touch with the demands of external reality and operates rationally. It includes some motives (such as hunger and ambition), the individual's learned responses, and his (or her) conscious thought. It has to reconcile the conflicting demands of the *id, the *superego, and the outside world.

egret A white bird belonging to the *heron subfamily. The great white egret (*Egretta alba*) has long silky ornamental plumes in the breeding season. The smaller cattle egret (*Aroleola ibis*) is 50 cm long and follows large grazing animals.

Egypt, Arab Republic of A country in NE Africa, extending into SW Asia. It consists mostly of desert—the *Sinai Peninsula, the Eastern Desert (a vast upland area), and the Western Desert (an extensive low plateau); most of the population is concentrated along the fertile Nile Valley. *Economy*: the introduction of modern irrigation schemes, such as the *Aswan High Dam, has led to an increase in the quantity and diversity of agricultural products, especially cotton. There has been considerable expansion of the industrial sector since the 1950s. Oil was discovered in 1909 and production has greatly increased; petroleum refining is an important industry. Natural gas is also being exploited. Egypt's many historical and archaeological remains make tourism important, although this is threatened by Islamic terrorism. *History*: ancient Egyptian history is traditionally divided into 30 dynasties, beginning in about 3100 BC with the union of Upper and Lower Egypt by Menes and ending in 343 BC with the death of the last Egyptian *pharaoh, Nectanebo II. The dynasties are grouped into the Old Kingdom (3rd–6th dynasties; c. 2686–c. 2160), the First Intermediate Period (7th–11th dynasties; c. 2160–c. 2040), the Middle Kingdom (12th dynasty; c. 2040–c. 1786), the Second Intermediate Period (13th–17th dynasties; c. 1786–c. 1567), and the New Kingdom (18th–20th dynasties; c. 1570–1085). During the New Kingdom there was territorial expansion and, later, trouble with the Sea Peoples; the 20th dynasty also saw the priests' power rise at the kings' expense. The outcome of Egypt's decline under the 21st–25th dynasties (1085–664) was the Assyrian invasion under Esarhaddon (671) and the 26th dynasty (664–525) was brought to an end by the Persian Achaemenians. Achaemenian rule was interrupted by the native 28th, 29th, and 30th dynasties (404–343) and was finally ended by Alexander the Great of Macedon, who obtained Egypt in 332.

On Alexander's death Egypt was acquired by the Macedonian Ptolemy I Soter. The Ptolemies ruled until the suicide of *Cleopatra VII in 30 BC, when Egypt passed under Roman rule. In 395 AD, Egypt became part of the Byzantine (Eastern Roman) Empire. The Arabs conquered Egypt in 642 and it was then governed by representatives of the caliphate of Baghdad, under whom Islam was introduced. After 868 it gained virtual autonomy under a series of ruling dynasties. The last of these, the Fatimids, were overthrown by *Saladin, who restored Egypt to the caliphate in 1171. It was ruled by the Mamelukes from 1250 until 1517, when it was conquered by the Ottoman Turks. By the early 18th century power was largely in the hands of the Mameluke elite.

In 1798 Napoleon established a French protectorate over Egypt, which in 1801 was overthrown by the British and Ottomans. Mehemet 'Ali was brought to power as viceroy in 1805, and in 1840 he was recognized by the Ottomans as hereditary ruler. In 1869 the opening of the Suez Canal enhanced Egypt's international significance and from 1882 the British dominated Egyptian government in spite of nominal Ottoman suzerainty. Egypt was a British protectorate from 1914 until independence under King Fu'ad I was granted in 1922. In 1936 his son Farouk signed a treaty of alliance with Britain, which retained rights in the Suez Canal zone, and in World War II Egypt joined the Allies. The immediate postwar period saw the first Arab-Israeli War (1948–49) and a military coup (1952) that overthrew the monarchy and brought *Nasser to power (1954). Nasser's nationalization of the Suez Canal in 1956 precipitated an invasion by Israeli and Anglo-French forces, which were compelled by the UN to withdraw. In 1958 Egypt, Syria, and subsequently North Yemen formed the United Arab Republic. Conflict with Israel erupted again in 1967, when in the Six Day War Egypt lost the Sinai peninsula, which was partly regained in the fourth war (1973). In 1970 Nasser was succeeded by Sadat, who in 1972 brought Egypt's close relationship with the Soviet Union to an end. In 1979, under US influence, Egypt and Israel signed a peace treaty and Egypt was expelled from the Arab League. Opposition to Sadat's policies culminated in his assassination by Islamic extremists in 1981. He was succeeded by Hosni Mubarak (1929–). Egypt was readmitted to the Arab League in 1989 but suffered a resurgence of terrorist attacks by Islamic extremists during the 1990s. Official language: Arabic. Currency: Egyptian pound of 100 piastres. Area: 1 000 000 sq km (386 198 sq mi). Population (2003 est): 68 185 000. Capital: Cairo.

Ehrlich, Paul (1854–1915) German bacteriologist, who studied acquired immunity to disease and, with Emil Behring (1854–1917), prepared a serum against diphtheria. In 1910 he produced an arsenical compound (Salvarsan) for treating syphilis. Ehrlich shared a Nobel Prize (1908) with I. I. Metchnikov (1845–1916).

Eichmann, Adolf (1906–62) German Nazi politician, appointed at the *Wannsee Conference to implement the planned extermination of European Jews. After World War II he went into hiding in Argentina; traced and captured by the Israelis in 1960, he was tried and hanged for war crimes.

eider A large sea *duck, *Somateria mollissima*, of far northern sea coasts. About 55 cm long, males are mostly white with a black crown, belly, and tail; females are mottled dark brown. The soft breast feathers of the female are the source of eiderdown.

Eiffel Tower A metal tower in Paris, 300 m (984 ft) high, built for the 1889 Centennial Exposition by the French engineer Alexandre-Gustave Eiffel (1832–1923).

Eiger 46 34N 8 01E A mountain in central S Switzerland, in the Bernese Oberland. Its difficult N face was first climbed successfully in 1938. Height: 3970 m (13 025 ft).

Eightfold Path (*or* **The Noble Eightfold Path**) In Buddhism the fourth of the *Four Noble Truths, which summarizes the eight ways that lead the Buddhist to enlightenment. They are: right understanding, right resolve, right speech, right action, right livelihood, right effort, right mindfulness, and right meditation.

Eilat (**Elat** *or* **Elath**) 29 33N 34 57E A resort and port in extreme S Israel, on the Gulf of Aqaba. The modern city was founded in 1949. Population (latest est): 26 000.

Einstein, Albert (1879–1955) German physicist. While working at the Patent Office in Berne, Switzerland, he continued his researches into theoretical physics and in 1905 published four highly original papers. One gave a mathematical explanation of the Brownian movement (*see* BROWN, ROBERT), the second explained the photoelectric effect in terms of *photons, the third announced his special theory of *relativity, and the fourth related mass to energy. In 1916 he extended the theory of relativity to the general case. He received the 1921 Nobel Prize for Physics. Einstein was lecturing in California when Hitler came to power in 1933. Being Jewish, he remained in the USA, spending the rest of his life at the Institute for Advanced Study in Princeton, unsuccessfully seeking a *unified field theory. He became a US citizen in 1940. Einstein was persuaded in 1939 to write to President Roosevelt warning him that an atom bomb could now be made and that Germany might make one. He took no part in its manufacture and became a postwar advocate of nuclear disarmament.

einsteinium (Es) An artificial transuranic element discovered by Ghiorso and others in 1952 and named after Albert Einstein. It behaves chemically as a trivalent actinide. Its 11 isotopes are all radioactive; the longest-lived has a half-life of 275 days. At no 99; at wt (252).

Eisenhower, Dwight D(avid) (1890–1969) US general and statesman; Republican president (1953–61). In World War II he was commander of US troops in Europe (1942), of Allied forces in N Africa and Italy (1942–43), and then supreme commander of Allied forces in Europe (1943). He commanded the forces in the D-Day invasion of Normandy. In 1951 he became supreme commander of NATO. A popular president, "Ike" initiated social welfare programmes. His administration spanned the Cold War years and was marred by the anticommunist agitation of Joseph *McCarthy. The **Eisenhower Doctrine** (1957) offered economic and military help to Middle Eastern nations to impede communist advances.

Eisenstein, Sergei (1898–1948) Russian film director. His films, which include *Battleship Potemkin* (1925), *Alexander Nevsky* (1938), and *Ivan the Terrible* (1942–46), used advanced editing and montage techniques.

eisteddfod A Welsh festival of literature, music, and drama. A medieval tradition, it later declined but was revived as the chief national cultural event during the 19th century.

Ekaterinburg (name from 1924 until 1991: Sverdlovsk) 56 52N 60 35E A city in NW Russia. Nicholas II and his family were all executed here in 1918. Population: (1999 est): 1 272 900.

eland A large horned antelope belonging to the genus *Taurotragus* (2 species), of African plains. The common eland (*T. oryx*) is light brown with thin vertical white stripes towards the shoulders. The Derby eland (*T. derbianus*) has a black neck with a white band at the base. Both species have a black-tufted tail and dewlap.

elastic modulus The ratio of the stress on a body obeying Hooke's law to the strain produced. The strain may be a change in length (Young's Modulus) or a change in volume (bulk modulus).

Elba An Italian island in the Tyrrhenian Sea. Napoleon I was exiled here (1814–15) following his abdication. Area: 223 sq km (86 sq mi). Population (1991 est): 27 722.

Elbe, River (Czech name: Labe) A river in central Europe, flowing mainly NW from the N Czech Republic, through Germany to the North Sea at Hamburg. It is connected by various canal systems to the Rivers Weser and Rhine as well as to the River Oder. Length: 1165 km (724 mi).

El Cid (Rodrigo Diáz de Vivar; c. 1040–99) Spanish warrior, immortalized in the epic poem *Cantar del mio Cid*. A vassal of Alfonso VI of Castile, he was exiled by the king in 1079 and became a soldier of fortune, fighting for both Spaniard and Moor. Always loyal to his king, he was returned to favour and became protector and then ruler of Valencia.

elder A shrub or tree of the genus *Sambucus* (40 species), found in temperate and subtropical areas. The cream-coloured flowers, grouped into flat-topped clusters, can be used in tea or wine. The red or black berries are used in wine, jams, and jellies. The common European elder is *S. nigra*. Family: *Caprifoliaceae*.

Eldorado (Spanish: the golden one) An Indian ruler in Colombia who, according to legend, ritually coated himself in gold dust before bathing in a lake. The name was later applied to a region of fabulous wealth suggested by this legend. The conquest of South America in the 16th century was hastened by expeditions seeking Eldorado, notably those of Francisco *Pizarro (1539) and Jiménez de Quesada (1569–72).

Eleanor of Aquitaine (c. 1122–1204) The wife (1137–52) of Louis VII of France and, after the annulment of their marriage, the wife (1154–89) of Henry II of England. Henry imprisoned her (1174–89) for complicity in their sons' rebellion against him. After Henry's death she helped to secure their peaceful accession as Richard I (1189) and John (1199).

Eleanor of Castile (1246–90) The wife (from 1254) of Edward I of England. Edward erected the **Eleanor Crosses** (e.g. Charing Cross) wherever her body rested on its way from Nottinghamshire, where she died, to her funeral in London.

electoral college An indirect electoral system used in the US for electing the president and vice president. Each state chooses by popular vote a number of electors to send to an electoral college. This number is equal to its number of representatives in the House of Representatives plus its two senators. All the electors chosen by a state pledge themselves to vote for the presidential candidate with the highest popular vote in the state. Thus the majority of the elected president is enhanced in the college, giving an increased influence to the more populous states.

Electra In Greek legend, the daughter of Agamemnon and Clytemnestra. She helped her brother Orestes escape after the murder of Agamemnon and later helped him to kill Clytemnestra and her lover Aegisthus.

electric car A car driven by one or more electric motors, which are powered by batteries. Diminishing oil reserves and the pollution problems associated with the *internal-combustion engine have intensified the search for an effective electric car (*see* GREENHOUSE EFFECT). Although milk floats have been in use since the 1930s, no electric car can yet compete with a petrol-driven car, as even a light car using 280 kg of expensive nickel-cadmium batteries with regenerative braking only has a 50–60 mile range. Two lines of research are therefore being pursued: improving accumulators and making workable *fuel cells. The hybrid electric car carries its own petrol-engine-driven generator for use outside towns.

electric charge A property of certain elementary particles (*see* PARTICLE PHYSICS) that causes them to undergo *electromagnetic interactions. The magnitude of the charge is always the same and is equal to 1.6021×10^{-19} coulomb (although quarks have a fractional charge). Charge is of two kinds, arbitrarily called positive and negative. Like charges repel each other and unlike charges attract each other. The force (F) between charges q_1 and q_2 is given by Coulomb's law, $F = q_1q_2/4\pi\varepsilon_0 d^2$, where ε_0 is the electric constant and d is the distance between charges.

electric constant (ε_0) A constant that appears in Coulomb's law (*see* ELECTRIC CHARGE). Its value is 8.854×10^{-12} farad per metre. It is also known as the absolute *permittivity of free space. *Compare* MAGNETIC CONSTANT.

electric eel An eel-like freshwater fish, *Electrophorus electricus*, that occurs in NE South America. Up to 3 m long, it has electric organs—modified muscle tissue—in the tail, which produce shocks capable of killing prey and of stunning a human being. Family: *Electrophoridae*; order: *Gymnotiformes*.

electric field The pattern of the lines of force that surround an electric charge. The field strength at any point is inversely proportional to the square of the distance of that point from the charge (Coulomb's law). Any other charge placed in this field experiences a force proportional to the field strength and to the magnitude of the introduced charge. The force is attractive if the charges are opposite and repulsive if they are alike.

electric generator A device for converting mechanical energy into electricity, usually by *electromagnetic induction. A simple electromagnetic generator, or dynamo, consists of a conducting coil rotated in a magnetic field. Current induced in this coil is fed to an external circuit by slip rings in an alternating-current generator (called an alternator) or by a commutator, which rectifies the current, in a direct-current generator.

Most of the electricity from *power stations is produced by alternators as three-phase alternating current, i.e. there are three windings on each generator, producing three separate output voltages. For transmission there are three conductor wires with a common neutral wire. Generally, all three phases are supplied to large factories but the supply is split to single phase for homes, shops, and offices.

electricity The phenomena that arise as a result of *electric charge. Electricity has two forms: *static electricity, which depends on

Modern life depends on electricity in so many ways, yet it is not known exactly what it is.

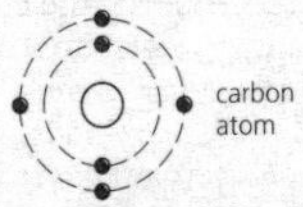

Atoms consist of electrons, protons, and neutrons. The electrons cluster round the central nucleus of protons and neutrons.

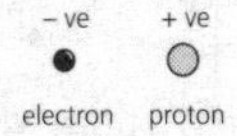

Electrons have a negative electric charge — protons are positively charged. The charges are equal but opposite.

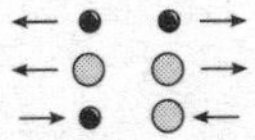

Similar charges repel each other, opposite charges attract each other. These are the forces harnessed to make electricity.

An electrical current consists of a flow of electrons in one direction. But in many atoms, such as helium, they are tightly bound to the nucleus. To flow as a current electrons have to be free.

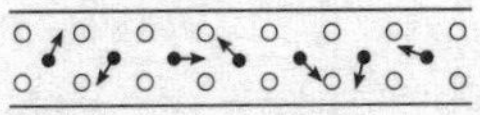

In a metal wire some of the electrons are free to move about between the metal ions (atoms that have lost an electron). Normally they move about at random and no current flows.

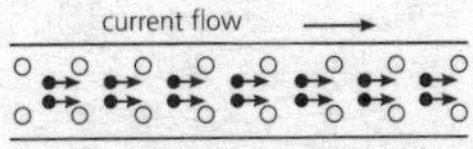

When the majority of electrons flow in one direction this is an electric current. 1 ampere is equivalent to a flow of 6×10^{18} electrons per second.

There are two main methods of making electrons flow to generate a current.

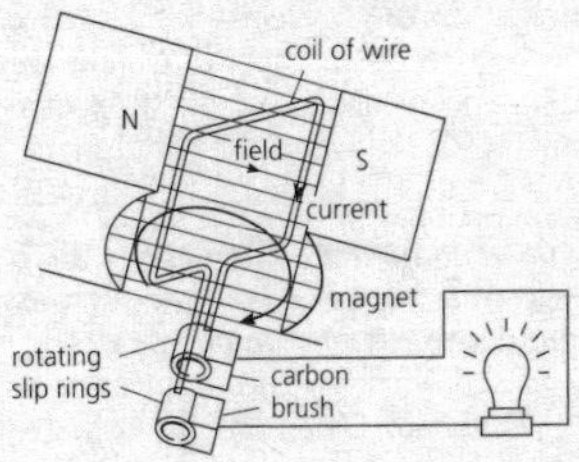

One method is to subject them to a changing magnetic field — this is the principle of the dynamo. If a coil of wire is rotated between the poles of a magnet, the electrons are forced round the coil. This is the power-station method; coal or oil is burned to raise steam to drive a turbine, which rotates the coils.

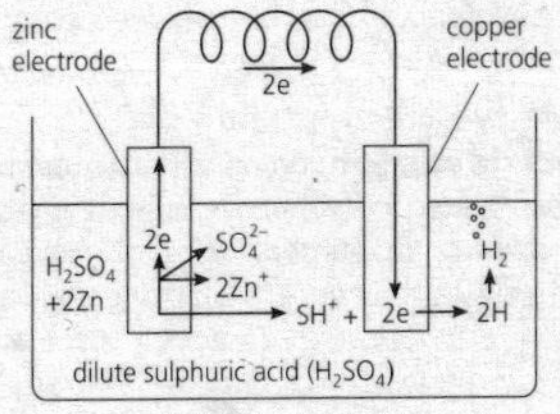

The other way is to make use of a chemical reaction in an electric cell to dissociate the electrons from their atoms and molecules. The separated charges then flow in opposite directions as a result of the forces between them. This is how a battery works. The sulphuric acid dissolves the zinc electrode producing 2 electrons, a sulphate ion (SO_4^{2-}), 2 zinc ions (Zn^+), and 2 hydrogen ions (H^+).

electricity

stationary charges, and current electricity, which consists of a flow of charges, specifically *electrons. Current electricity was first demonstrated by Volta in 1800 and investigated by *Ampère during the next 25 years. Oersted's discovery (1820) that a magnetic needle was deflected by an electric current inspired *Faraday to a deep investigation of the relationship between electricity and magnetism, which led him to the discovery of *electromagnetic induction, the *electric generator, and the *electric motor. The theory of electromagnetism was elucidated by Clerk *Maxwell in the mid-1850s.

electricity supply The system that generates (*see* POWER STATION), transmits, and distributes the electric power in an industrialized society. Power stations are interconnected by transmission lines to form a grid. Grid-control centres continuously monitor the load from factories, offices, homes, etc., and match it with the best combination of available generating

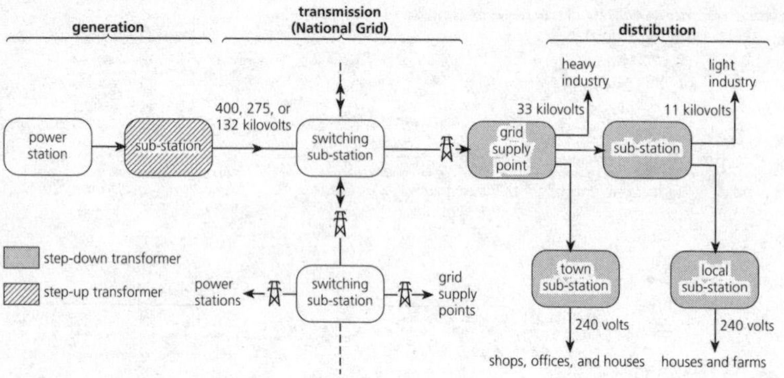

electricity supply. A schematic diagram of the UK system.

capacity, maintaining the supply at a constant voltage and frequency. Base-load stations run continuously. These are usually the larger or cheaper-to-run nuclear and gas- or coal-fired stations. Less economic or smaller stations that are easier to start up and shut down are brought in to supply the peak demand. The grid voltage is reduced at substations for area distribution and further reduced at local substations to the UK domestic supply voltage of 240 volts.

electric motor A device that converts electrical energy into mechanical energy, usually for driving machinery. They depend on the principle that a current-carrying conductor in a magnetic field experiences a force and that when two electromagnets are placed close together the two magnetic fields force them apart. The simplest type of motor uses this principle to turn a single coil of wire (the armature or rotor) between the poles of a permanent magnet. Practical motors use a stationary winding (stator) in place of a permanent magnet. Most motors work on an alternating-current (ac) supply. In the induction motor, current is fed to the stator, which induces a current in the rotor; interaction between the magnetic field of the stator and the induced rotor current causes the rotor to rotate. In the synchronous ac motor, current is also fed to the rotor (through slip rings) and the rate of rotation is proportional to the supply frequency. In a dc motor current is fed to the rotor through a commutator. *See also* LINEAR MOTOR.

electric ray A fish, also called torpedo ray, belonging to a family (*Torpedinidae*) found mainly in shallow waters of warm and temperate regions. Electric organs—modified muscle tissue—on each side of the disclike head produce electric shocks used in defence and food capture. Order: *Batoidea* (*see* RAY).

electrocardiography Examination of the electrical activity of the heart. Impulses generated by the contraction of the heart muscle are transmitted through electrodes attached to the skin to a recording apparatus (electrocardiograph). The recording itself, an electrocardiogram (ECG), indicates the rhythm of the heart and aids in the diagnosis of heart disease.

electroconvulsive therapy (**ECT**) A treatment for mental disorders, such as endogenous depression, in which an electric current is passed through the brain in order to cause a convulsion. The convulsion is greatly reduced by giving an anaesthetic and drugs to relax the muscles.

electroencephalography The measurement of the electrical activity of the brain and the recording of the brain waves in the form of a tracing—an electroencephalogram (EEG). Brain waves were first recorded from electrodes on the scalp in 1926. Electroencephalography is now used widely to diagnose diseases of the brain and to study brain function. *See also* MAGNETIC RESONANCE IMAGING.

electrolysis The chemical decomposition of a substance by passing an electric current through it. If a voltage is applied across two electrodes placed in a liquid (electrolyte) containing ions, the positive ions will drift towards the negative electrode (cathode) and the negative ions towards the positive electrode (anode). At the electrodes, the ions may give up their charge and form molecules. Alternatively, the atoms of the electrode may ionize and pass into solution. Electrolysis is used to electroplate metals and in the manufacture of a number of chemicals, such as sodium and chlorine.

electromagnet *See* MAGNET.

electromagnetic field A concept describing electric and magnetic forces that, like gravitational forces, act without physical contact (action at a distance). The interaction of electricity and magnetism was first investigated in the 19th century. Faraday explained the electromagnetic interaction in terms of magnetic lines of force, forming a field of force, which is distorted by the presence of a current-carrying conductor or by another magnet. James Clerk *Maxwell developed the theory that electricity and magnetism are different manifestations of the same phenomenon (the electromagnetic field), magnetism being the result of relative motion of *electric fields.

electromagnetic induction The production of voltage in an electrical conductor when it is in a changing magnetic field or if it moves in relation to a steady magnetic field. The direction of the induced *electromotive force opposes the change or motion causing it. Since a current-carrying conductor itself induces a magnetic field, if the current changes, **self-inductance** occurs, opposing the current change. **Mutual inductance** occurs between two adjacent conductors that carry changing currents.

electromagnetic interaction An interaction that occurs between elementary particles that possess an electric charge. The interaction can be visualized as the exchange of virtual photons (*see* VIRTUAL PARTICLE) between the interacting particles. The electromagnetic interaction is 200 times weaker than the *strong interaction but 10^{10} times stronger than the *weak interaction. *See also* PARTICLE PHYSICS.

electromagnetic radiation Transverse waves consisting of electric and magnetic fields vibrating perpendicularly to each other and to the direction of propagation. In free space the waves are propagated at a velocity of 2.9979×10^8 metres per second, known as the velocity of light (symbol: c). Their *wavelength, λ, and *frequency, f, are related by the equation $\lambda f = c$. Those with the highest frequencies are known as *gamma radiation; then in descending order of frequency the **electromagnetic spectrum** includes X-rays, *ultraviolet radiation, visible *light, *infrared radiation, *microwaves, and *radio waves. Electromagnetic radiation exhibits typical wave properties, such as *refraction, *diffraction, *interference, and polarization. However, it has a dual nature in that it can also be regarded as a stream of massless elementary particles called *photons.

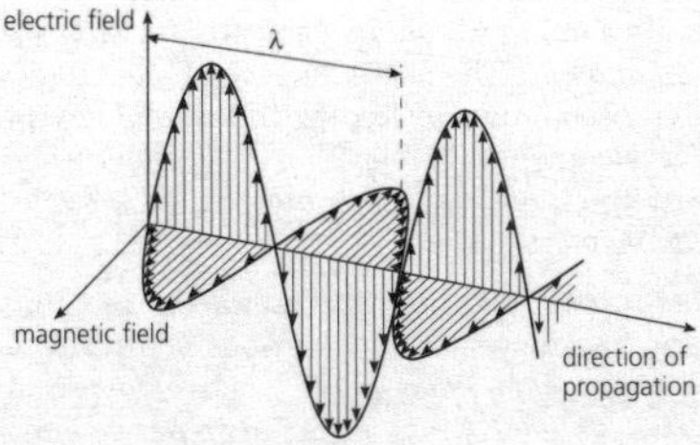

electromagnetic radiation

electromotive force (emf) The electrical potential difference or voltage between two points in an electric circuit. It causes the movement of charge that constitutes an electric current.

electron A stable negatively charged elementary particle with mass $9.109\,56 \times 10^{-31}$ kilogram and spin ½. Electrons are responsible for almost all commonly observed electrical and magnetic effects and, since they orbit the nucleus in atoms, are also responsible for most chemical processes. A **free electron** is one that has become detached from an atom. An electric current passing through a metal or low-pressure gas consists of a flow of free electrons; a current of 1 ampere is equivalent to a flow of 6×10^{18} electrons per second.

electronic fund transfer (**EFT**) A means of charging a sale to a customer's bank account or credit card by a computer at the retail outlet connected to the telephone network. For example, supermarket sales can be paid for by using a debit card, which instantly debits the customer's bank or building society account.

electronic mail (*or* **e-mail**) A means of transmitting and receiving text using a system of computers connected to the telephone network. Subscribers send messages by keyboarding them into a microprocessor and transmitting them by telephone line to a central computer. To receive a communication, a subscriber calls up the central computer and receives any communications addressed to it on its microprocessor and printer.

electronics The study of devices that control

and utilize the movement of *electrons and other charged particles. Originating with the invention of thermionic valves, it expanded rapidly during World War II to include radar, missile guidance systems, and *computers. The replacement of bulky *thermionic valves by *semiconductor components, such as *transistors, and later by *integrated circuits has resulted in much more compact and reliable equipment. The social impact of electronics has been immense, leading for example to the development of television, communications satellites, and the computerization of office and factory systems.

electronic tagging A method of monitoring the movements of persons convicted of certain offences as an alternative to prison. The offender wears a microchip device emitting a signal to a transmitter attached to a telephone. If the offender moves out of a 75-metre (250-ft) range, the telephone sends a message to a controlling computer.

electron microscope A type of microscope in which a beam of electrons is focused by means of magnetic and electrostatic lenses onto a specimen and scattered by it to produce an image. Typically an electron microscope can resolve two points 10^{-9} metre apart and produce magnifications of up to a million.

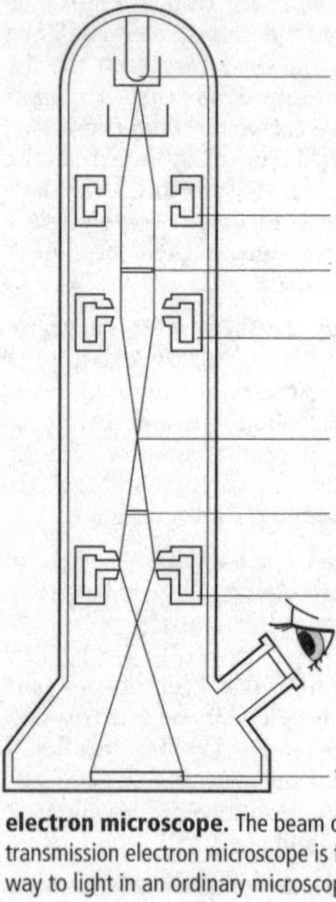

electron microscope. The beam of electrons in the transmission electron microscope is focused in a similar way to light in an ordinary microscope.

electronvolt (eV) A unit of energy equal to the increase in the energy of an electron when it passes through a rise in potential of one volt. $1\ \text{eV} = 1.6 \times 10^{-19}$ joule.

electroplating The process of depositing a layer of one metal on another by making the object to be plated the cathode in an electrolytic bath (*see* ELECTROLYSIS). Metals used for electroplating include silver (*see* SILVERPLATE), gold, chromium, cadmium, copper, zinc, and nickel; they usually form the anode in the bath.

elements Substances that cannot be broken down into simpler fragments by chemical means. A sample of an element contains atoms that are chemically identical, since they have the same *atomic number and thus the same number of electrons around the nucleus. Samples of a given element may consist of a mixture of *isotopes. Over 100 elements are known, of which about 90 occur naturally, the rest having been synthesized in nuclear reactions. *See also* PERIODIC TABLE.

elephant A mammal of the order *Proboscidea*: the African elephant (*Loxodonta africana*) or the Indian elephant (*Elephas maximus*). (The extinct *mammoths also belonged to this order.) Elephants have a tough brownish-grey skin and a prehensile trunk—an extension of the nose and upper lip used to convey food (vegetation) and water to the mouth. The upper incisor teeth are continually growing ivory tusks. Elephants live in herds. The African elephant is the largest land mammal, standing 3–4 m high at the shoulder. The smaller Indian elephant—intelligent and readily trained—is used for transport and heavy work.

elephantiasis A chronic infection caused by nematode worms, called filariae. The worms block the lymphatic channels causing swelling of the legs and scrotum (or vulva). Elephantiasis occurs only in the tropics.

elephant seal A large seal belonging to the genus *Mirounga* (2 species). The male Antarctic elephant seal (*M. leonina*) grows to over 6 m; females are about half that size. The slightly smaller northern elephant seal (*M. angustirostris*) lives off the W coast of North America.

Elgar, Sir Edward (1857–1934) British composer. A professional violinist, Elgar wrote choral works, two symphonies, concertos for violin and cello, and chamber music. His most famous works are the *Dream of Gerontius* (1900), the *Enigma Variations* (1899), and the *Pomp and Circumstance* marches (1901–30).

Elgin Marbles Ancient Greek marble sculptures, mostly a frieze from the *Parthenon, sold to the British Museum in 1816 by Lord Elgin for £35,000. He acquired them from the Turks occupying Athens, who were using the Parthenon for target practice. The British government has not yielded to Greek agitation for their return.

El Greco (Domenikos Theotokopoulos; 1541–1614) Painter of Greek parentage, born in Crete, who worked mainly in Spain. He trained in Venice under Titian in the 1560s and in 1577 moved to Spain, settling in Toledo. His early Spanish works were Venetian in inspiration, but his later paintings of saints and his masterpiece, *The Burial of Count Orgaz* (1586–88), are characterized by strident colours and dramatically elongated figures.

Eliot, George (Mary Ann Evans; 1819–80) British novelist, noted for her depiction of provincial English society. She wrote the novels *Adam Bede* (1859), *The Mill on the Floss* (1860), *Silas Marner* (1861), the pioneering and influential *Middlemarch* (1871–72), and *Daniel Deronda* (1876).

Eliot, T(homas) S(tearns) (1888–1965) Anglo-American poet, critic, and dramatist, born in Missouri. His first volume of poetry was the innovatory *Prufrock and Other Observations* (1917). *The Waste Land* (1922) and *Four Quartets* (1935–41) are other major poetic achievements. In 1927 he became an Anglo-Catholic and a British subject. From 1922 to 1939 he edited *The Criterion*, a critical review. His verse dramas include *Murder in the Cathedral* (1935) and *The Cocktail Party* (1949). He was awarded the Nobel Prize in 1948.

Elizabeth I (1533–1603) Queen of England and Ireland (1558–1603), daughter of Henry VIII and Anne *Boleyn. Her mother's execution and Elizabeth's imprisonment by Mary I made her cautious and suspicious but her devotion to England made her one of its greatest monarchs. Her religious compromise (1559–63) established moderate Protestantism in England (*see* REFORMATION). England won a great naval victory in 1588 by destroying the Spanish *Armada. Elizabeth never married and was called the Virgin Queen.

Elizabeth II (1926–) Queen of the United Kingdom (1952–), noted for her scrupulous fulfilment of the roles of constitutional monarch and head of the Commonwealth. She married Prince *Philip in 1947; their four children are Prince *Charles, Princess *Anne, Prince Andrew, Duke of York (1960–), and Prince Edward, Earl of Wessex (1964–).

Elizabeth the Queen Mother (1900–2002) The consort of *George VI and mother of *Elizabeth II and Princess Margaret. Formerly Lady Elizabeth Bowes-Lyon, she married in 1923 and was widowed in 1952.

elk The largest deer, *Alces alces*, found in forests of N Eurasia and also in N North America, where it is called a moose. Up to 2 m high at the shoulder, elks have a broad curved muzzle and a short neck with a heavy dewlap. The coat is grey-brown and males grow large palmate antlers. They feed on leaves and water plants and form herds in winter.

Ellesmere Island The most northerly of the Canadian Arctic islands, in Baffin Bay W of

African elephant

Indian elephant

elephant. The African elephant can be distinguished from the smaller Indian species by its larger ears, flatter forehead, smooth skin, and concave back.

Greenland. It is mountainous with deep fjords, and is covered by glaciers. It has few permanent inhabitants. Area: 212 688 sq km (82 119 sq mi).

Ellice Islands *See* TUVALU, STATE OF.

Ellington, Duke (Edward Kennedy E.; 1899–1974) US Black jazz composer, band leader, and pianist. In New York he established a group of musicians that remained the core of his band for 30 years. In later years Ellington concentrated on large-scale works for jazz orchestra.

ellipse A closed curve having the shape of an elongated circle. The sum of the distances from any point on the circumference to each of two fixed points, known as the foci, is a constant. The ellipse is one of a family of curves known as *conic sections.

elm A tree of the genus *Ulmus* (about 30 species), of N temperate regions. Up to 40 m high, elms have toothed leaves, clusters of small reddish flowers, and winged nuts. Elms are widely planted for shade and ornament and for their durable timber, but the number in Europe and North America has been greatly reduced by *Dutch elm disease. Species include the English elm (*U. procera*), the Eurasian wych elm (*U. glabra*), and the American elm (*U. americana*). Family: *Ulmaceae*.

elm bark beetle A wood-boring beetle that tunnels under the bark of elm trees and carries the fungus *Ceratostomella ulni*, which causes *Dutch elm disease. Family: *Scolytidae* (*see* BARK BEETLE).

El Niño (Spanish: the Christ child) Widespread weather disruption resulting from reversal of the trade winds and sea currents in the equatorial Pacific region, so called as it tends to begin at around Christmas. Normally, trade winds blow from east to west, pushing warm water westwards and bringing heavy rainfall to Indonesia and cool waters with dry weather to Peru. As a result of El Niño a huge mass of warm water moves eastward, causing torrential rain and floods in Peru and the southern USA, while drought and forest fires occur in Indonesia and Australia. El Niño events can extend as far west as Africa, resulting in storms and flooding in the E and drought in the S. El Niño usually lasts about 18 months. Since the late 1970s it has recurred on average every 4 years.

El Salvador, Republic of A country in Central America, on the Pacific Ocean. Narrow coastal lowlands rise to a fertile plateau, which is enclosed by volcanic mountains. Most of the population is of mixed European and Indian descent. *Economy*: mainly agricultural, dominated by coffee since the late 19th century. Most of the cultivated land is controlled by a few families. *History*: the Aztec population was conquered by the Spaniards in 1526 and after the overthrow of Spanish rule the region formed part of the Central American Federation (1823–38). In 1841 it became an independent republic. Tensions arising from the emigration of Salvadoreans to Honduras culminated in war in 1965 and again in 1969. In 1978–79 the repressive regime of Gen Carlos Humberto Romero provoked rising unrest. Romero was deposed in 1979 and a junta took control but violence continued. Civilian rule returned in 1982. After 12 years of virtual civil war with the Farabundo Martí National Liberation Front (FMLN), a peace agreement was reached in 1992. Elections were held in 1994 in which the FMLN took part. The country has since been governed by a right-wing coalition led by the ARENA party, with Francisco Flores as president since 1999. El Salvador is a member of the OAS. Official language: Spanish. Currency: US dollar of 100 cents. Area 21 393 sq km (8236 sq mi). Population (2003 est): 6 515 000. Capital: San Salvador.

Elsinore *See* HELSINGØR.

Ely 52 24N 0 16E A city in E England, in Cambridgeshire on the River Ouse. The Isle of Ely is an area of higher ground surrounded by fenland. Ely's 12th-century cathedral dominates the fen landscape. Population (1991): 10 329.

Elysium (*or* **Elysian Fields**) In Greek mythology, the fields on the banks of the River Oceanus where those favoured by the gods live in eternal happiness. In Roman mythology Elysium is part of the underworld.

e-mail *See* ELECTRONIC MAIL.

Emancipation Proclamation (1863) The edict issued by President Abraham *Lincoln that freed slaves in the rebellious southern states of the USA. Its provisions were extended and confirmed by the 13th Amendment, which abolished *slavery throughout the nation (1865).

embolism The sudden blocking of an artery by a clot or other material that has come from another part of the body via the bloodstream. A clot most commonly forms in the leg and pieces break away and lodge in the arteries of the lung—a **pulmonary embolism**. A clot may sometimes come from the heart and lodge in

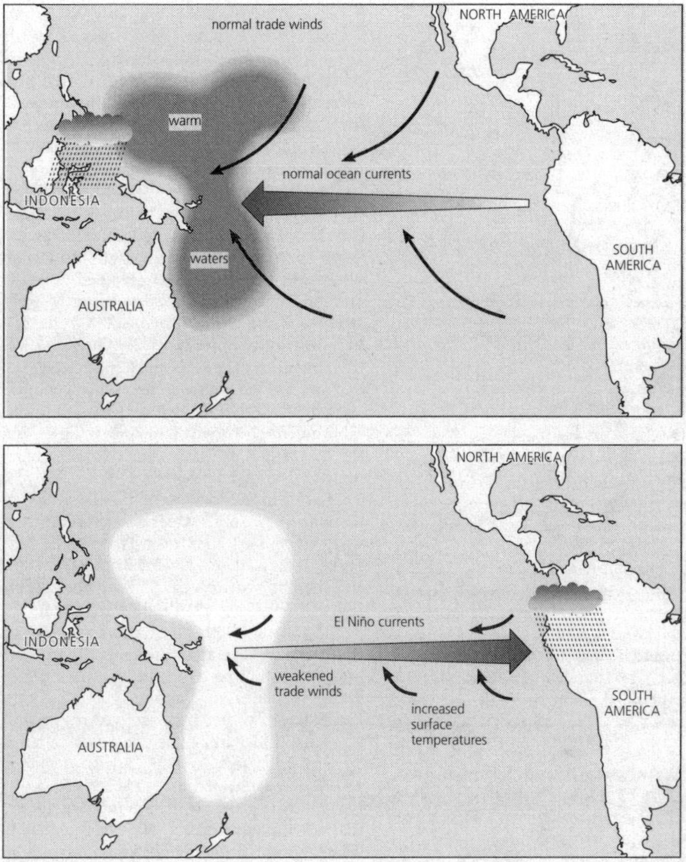

El Niño. Showing the ocean currents that bring flooding to parts of South America, leaving Indonesia and parts of Australia in drought.

the brain, causing a *stroke. *See also* THROMBOSIS.

embryo An animal or plant in the earliest stages of its development. In vertebrate animals the embryonic stage lasts from the first division of the fertilized egg until the young animal either hatches from the egg or is expelled from the womb at birth. A human embryo is called a *fetus from the eighth week of pregnancy. In invertebrate animals the embryo is generally called a *larva. In plants, the embryo lies within the *seed. **Embryology** is the study of the development of embryos. See illustration on p. 306.

emerald A green variety of *beryl, highly valued as a gemstone. It occurs mainly in metamorphic rocks, the finest specimens coming from Muzo, Colombia.

Emerson, Ralph Waldo (1803–82) US essayist and poet, a leading transcendentalist. He published *Nature*, his transcendentalist creed, in 1836 and expressed his optimistic humanism in *Representative Men* (1850) and *The Conduct of Life* (1860).

emery A granular greyish-black rock consisting of *corundum with magnetite, hematite, or spinel. It occurs mainly in metamorphic rocks or sediments and is used as an abrasive.

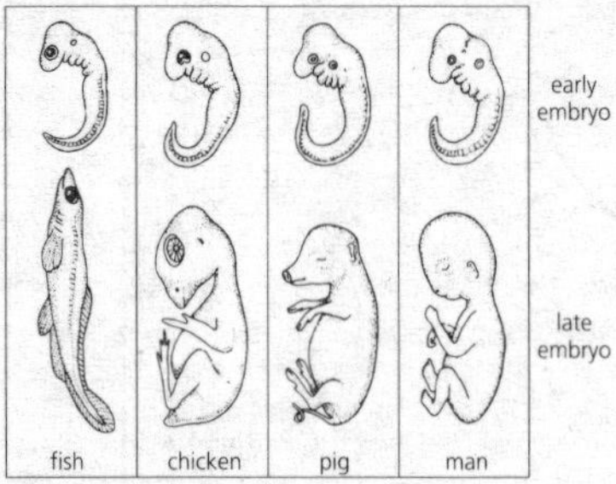

The different species are hard to distinguish in the early stages of development; later they develop individual characteristics.

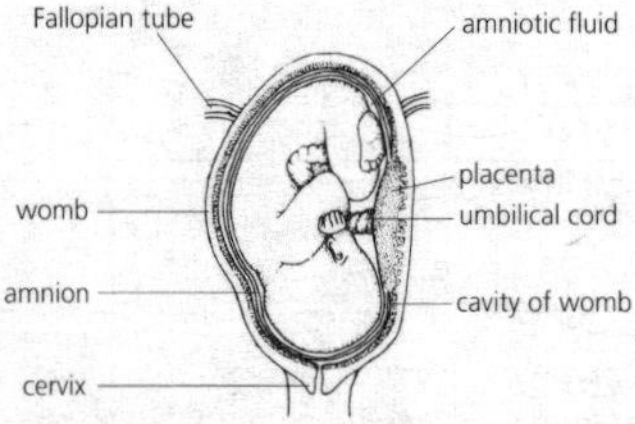

embryo. Various vertebrate embryos (above); a human embryo (below).

Empedocles (c. 490–430 BC) Sicilian Greek philosopher. He founded the doctrine that earth, air, fire, and water make up the world, and that love and strife (attraction and antipathy) govern their distribution.

emperor penguin A large *penguin, *Aptenodytes forsteri*. 1.2 m tall, it is the largest seabird and has a blue-grey plumage with a black head and throat, a white belly, and orange patches on the neck.

emphysema A progressive disease of the lungs characterized by destruction of lung tissue and distension of the air spaces. It is most commonly caused by smoking and is often accompanied by chronic *bronchitis. Patients become very breathless on exertion.

Empire, British Britain's overseas possessions from the 16th to mid 20th centuries. Although the empire originated in the discovery of Cape Breton Island (1497), permanent settlements in North America were not established until the early 17th century, when colonists, some escaping religious persecution, were granted charters by the Crown to settle Virginia, Maryland, and New England. The American colonies were lost in 1783 (*see* AMERICAN REVOLUTION). In Canada the English came into conflict with the French and only established control in the *Seven Years' War (1756–63), from which they also emerged victorious in India. Robert Clive's victory at Plassey (1757) assured British, rather than French, dominance in India and the East India Company continued to govern until 1857, when its authority was replaced by the Crown's.

The Napoleonic Wars in the early 19th century brought possessions in the West Indies (Trinidad, Tobago, St Lucia) as well as Mauritius, Ceylon, and, in Africa, the Cape. Substantial possessions in Africa were not obtained until the late 18th century with the acquisition of what are now Sierra Leone, Ghana, and Nigeria. The 19th-century colonial expansion in Africa was fired by missionary zeal, which motivated such explorers as *Livingstone, as well as commercial activities. The late 19th century saw the establishment of British dominance in Egypt and the Sudan but in South Africa it was undermined by *Afrikaner hostility.

Colonies in Australia were initially penal settlements: New South Wales was settled in 1778, Tasmania in 1803, and Queensland in 1824. New Zealand was controlled by the British from 1840 and the 19th century also achieved the acquisition of Hong Kong (1841) and Burma (1886).

The colonies were supervised from 1801 by the Colonial Office, and were generally self-governing. In the mid-19th century, the self-governing colonies in Canada, Australia, New Zealand, and South Africa received responsible government, whereby governors were advised by local ministers. In 1907 Canada, Australia, and New Zealand (and in 1910 South Africa), by now federated, were termed dominions. In 1931 the *Commonwealth of Nations was established, giving the dominions autonomy, and in the following decades Britain's other colonies gradually achieved full independence.

Empire style The neoclassical style in the decorative arts that developed during the Napoleonic empire (1804–14). It was inspired by classical Greek, Roman, and Egyptian models and reflected contemporary interest in archaeology (e.g. Pompeii). Dark woods, such as rosewood, were favoured, sparsely ornamented with *ormolu. Shapes tended to be plain but caryatids were used as supports. The grandiose **Second Empire style** was the official architectural style of the French Government under Emperor Napoleon III (1852–70).

emu A large flightless long-legged Australian bird, *Dromaius novaehollandiae*, found in open plains and forests. It has a dark-brown hairlike plumage with a naked blue spot on each side of the neck, and can run at high speeds.

emulsion *See* COLLOID.

encephalins (*or* **enkephalins**) Short peptide molecules, found in parts of the brain and spinal cord, that are thought to relieve pain. These and similar compounds are called **endorphins**. In the spinal cord encephalins are believed to inhibit painful sensations by reacting with specific receptor sites on the sensory nerve endings. In the brain their function is less certain but may be associated with mood. The pain-relieving effects of acupuncture may be due to the release of the body's encephalins.

encephalitis Inflammation of the brain. It usually occurs as a result of a virus infection, but can be caused by malaria, fungi, or parasites (rarely by bacteria). The patient is often drowsy and fevered and has a bad headache. There is no specific treatment for viral encephalitis but the patient usually recovers.

Encke's comet A comet that has a period of only 3.3 years (decreasing by 2.5 hours/revolution) and has been very closely studied during its numerous apparitions. Its period was first established by the German astronomer J. F. Encke (1791–1865).

Encyclopedists (French name: Encyclopédistes) The French intellectuals who contributed to *Diderot's monumental *Encyclopédie*, published in 28 volumes between 1751 and 1772. Five more volumes were published in 1776–77. Over 200 experts, including such leading figures of the *Enlightenment as Voltaire and Rousseau, contributed articles. By their appeal to reason rather than faith the Encyclopedists threatened the authority of Church and state.

endangered species A plant or animal species that is in danger of extinction. Some 34 000 vascular-plant species and 5000 animal species are currently endangered, mostly through destruction of natural habitats, pollution, and hunting and trapping. During the 20th century the number of endangered species grew dramatically, and in 1948 the International Union for the Conservation of Nature and Natural Resources (IUCN) was founded to devise measures to protect them. The IUCN publishes the Red Data Book, which lists all known endangered species. Trade in endangered species is regulated by CITES—the Convention on International Trade in Endangered Species. This has been signed by 96 countries, including the UK. *See also* WORLD WIDE FUND FOR NATURE.

endive An annual or biennial plant, *Cichorium endivia*, probably native to S Asia and N China and cultivated widely. It has a rosette of shiny leaves, either curled and narrow (var. *crispa*), used for salads, or broad (*latifolia*), used for cooking. Family: *Compositae*. *See also* CHICORY.

endocrine glands Ductless glands that secrete *hormones into the bloodstream. Most are regulated by hormones from the *pituitary gland, which is itself controlled by neurohormones secreted by the *hypothalamus. Other endocrine glands include the thyroid, adrenal, and *parathyroid glands, parts of the *pancreas (the islets of Langerhans), and the ovaries and testes. The study of the endocrine glands is called **endocrinology**.

endorphins *See* ENCEPHALINS.

Endymion In Greek legend, a beautiful youth who was put into an everlasting sleep by Selene, goddess of the moon, so that she could enjoy his beauty forever.

energy A property of a system that enables it to do work, i.e. to move the point of application of a force. The several forms of energy can be converted into each other under appropriate conditions. Kinetic energy is energy of motion, whereas *potential energy is stored energy, for example the energy stored in a body by virtue of its position in a gravitational or electric field. Other forms of energy include heat (the kinetic energy of the atoms and molecules in a body), chemical energy (the potential energy stored in the chemical bonds between atoms), nuclear energy (the potential energy stored in the atomic nucleus), and radiant energy (the energy associated with electromagnetic waves). As a consequence of the special theory of relativity, mass has also to be regarded as a form of energy. Energy is measured in joules (SI units), calories or ergs (c.g.s. units), kilowatt-hours or British thermal units (Imperial units).

Energy sources: the combustion of wood and fossil fuels (asphalt, coal, oil, natural gas) is a process, long known to man, in which chemical energy is converted into heat energy. The *industrial revolution and the later advent of motorized transport brought explosive increases in the demand for energy and consequently for fossil fuels. The total world energy consumption is of the order of 4×10^{20} joules per year, nearly 88% of which is provided by fossil fuels. Concern both about fossil fuel reserves and the 2.5×10^{10} tonnes of CO_2 they produce each year (*see* GREENHOUSE EFFECT) is directing attention to *alternative energy sources as well as nuclear energy.

energy band A concept used to explain the electrical properties of solids, particularly *semiconductors. It is a band of allowed energies for electrons in a solid. The distribution of the bands in a solid determines the conducting properties of the solid.

Engels, Friedrich (1820–95) German socialist and chief collaborator of Karl *Marx. He was able to introduce Marx to English economic conditions and the British working-class movement. Among other works he wrote the *Condition of the Working Class in England in 1844* (1845). After Marx's death, he edited the last volume of *Das Kapital* (1885).

engineering The systematic application of scientific knowledge to the design, creation, and use of structures and machines. Civil engineering arose from the study and design of such static structures as bridges, dams, buildings, etc., whereas mechanical engineering is concerned with dynamical systems, such as machinery and engines. Other important branches of engineering are electrical engineering, aeronautical engineering, and *chemical engineering.

England The largest political division in the *United Kingdom. With Wales to the W and Scotland to the N, it is separated from the mainland of Europe by the North Sea and the English Channel and from Ireland by the Irish Sea. It consists of two main zones: the lowlands, which extend across the Midlands, the SE, East Anglia, and the Fens, and the highlands of the Pennines and the Lake District in the N and the uplands of Dartmoor and Exmoor in the SW. The chief rivers are the Thames and the Severn. The centre of government and administration of the UK, England is also the wealthiest and most populous of the UK countries. *Economy*: the development of industry has been a major contributor to England's wealth. The exploitation of North Sea oil and gas continues to make an important contribution to the economy. Coalmining was formerly of major importance but there are now only 8 deep mines in operation (compared to some 800 in the 1950s). Despite the expansion of industries based on advanced technology, the decline of heavy industry (including shipbuilding), has led to high unemployment in the North and on Merseyside. Agriculture has increased in productivity but employs a declining number of people. Dairy farming is dominant in the W, while livestock rearing (especially sheep and cattle) is important in the hilly areas of the N and SW. The major crops, mainly from the E and SE, are cereals, potatoes, and sugar beet. Over 75% of the workforce are now employed in service industries. Tourism is an important source of revenue. *History*: there is much archaeological evidence of prehistoric settlement in England but historical records begin with the Roman occupation, from 43 AD until the early 5th century. Christianity was introduced in the 4th century, and conquests between the 3rd and 7th centuries by *Angles, *Saxons, and *Jutes led to the establishment of independent kingdoms (*see* MERCIA; NORTHUMBRIA; WESSEX), which were united in the 9th century under the leadership of Wessex. By the late 800s the Danes had established themselves in the area that came to be known as the *Danelaw and from 1016 to 1042 the English were ruled successively by the Danish kings Canute and *Hardecanute. The *Norman conquest (1066) ended the *Anglo-Saxon period and established a new dynasty of Norman kings. In 1455 the rival claims of the Houses of *Lancaster and *York precipitated the Wars of the *Roses, which lasted until Richard III's defeat at Bosworth (1485) by Henry *Tudor. The 16th century saw the establishment of Protestantism in England (*see* REFORMATION), the formal union of England and Wales (*see* UNION, ACTS OF), and, under Elizabeth I, a significant development in overseas exploration and trade. The Tudors were succeeded by the *Stuarts in 1603, when James VI of Scotland ascended the English throne as *James I. The unpopularity of James and his son Charles I, especially with parliament, brought about the *Civil War, which ended with Charles' execution (1649) and the establishment of republican government. The Stuart *Restoration (1660) followed the fall of Oliver Cromwell's *Protectorate but the authoritarian and pro-Catholic policies of James II brought about his deposition in 1688 and the succession of William of Orange and his Stuart wife Mary. The crisis of the Glorious Revolution saw the emergence of the rival political groups known as *Whigs (later Liberals) and *Tories (later Conservatives). The Tories' association with the *Jacobites, who in 1714 threatened the Hanoverian succession (*see* SETTLEMENT, ACT OF), led to their political isolation. The 18th century saw union with Scotland (1707) and the loss of the American colonies (1783; *see* AMERICAN REVOLUTION). Following union with Ireland in 1801, England, Wales, Scotland, and Ireland became the United Kingdom of Great Britain and Ireland. Area: 130 360 sq km (50 332 sq mi). Population (2001): 49 138 831. Capital: London. *See also* UNITED KINGDOM.

English A West Germanic language spoken originally in Britain but now also in the USA, Canada, New Zealand, Australia, and many other parts of the world. It is the world's most widely known and used language, with a unique role as the international language of science, commerce, computing and the Internet, and mass entertainment. Its history may be divided into three periods. In the Old English period (c. 407–1100 AD), four dialects were spoken: Northumbrian, Mercian, Kentish, and West Saxon. The last became the standard form. Middle English refers to the period from 1100 to 1500, when five dialects were spoken: Northern (developed from Northumbrian), West and East Midlands (diverging from Mercian), South Western (from West Saxon) and South Eastern (from Kentish). Each developed in characteristic ways but in general the influence of French after the Norman conquest brought new vocabulary and sound patterns. Modern English covers the period from 1500 and was much influenced by the speech of London. Its vocabulary is about half Germanic and half Romance with many other borrowings.

English Channel (French name: La Manche) An arm of the Atlantic Ocean in NW Europe, between England and France. It is one of the busiest shipping lanes in the world. *See also* CHANNEL TUNNEL.

engraving A method of producing a reproductive plate by chiselling, carving, or biting the design onto a metal or wood plate. Intaglio engraving denotes such methods as *etching, mezzotint, and soft- or hard-ground engraving, in which the printed impression pulls ink from inside the carved grooves. By contrast, relief engraving denotes methods, such as *woodcut, in which the carved-away areas are not inked. Intaglio engraving allows for delicacy and detail; relief engraving is often exploited when force and clarity are needed.

Enlightenment (*or* **Age of Reason**) An 18th-century philosophical movement that sought to replace authoritarian beliefs with rational scientific inquiry. During the 17th century, as scientific knowledge increased, such scholars as Newton, Pascal, and Descartes questioned many accepted beliefs. In France the Philosophes (e.g. Voltaire) attacked religion; the Enlightenment beliefs in individual liberty and equality were embodied in the work of Voltaire, Rousseau, and other *Encyclopedists. The movement helped to inspire the French Revolution but came to an end in the era of war and political reaction that followed.

entomology The study of insects. Modern entomology dates from the 17th century, when the introduction of microscopy enabled fine details of insect anatomy to be described. Attention is now focused on insect pests, since knowledge of them is important in their control.

entropy A measure of the disorder of a system, used in *thermodynamics. Thus a solid has less entropy than a liquid since the constituent particles in a solid are in a more ordered state. The change in entropy of a reversible system is equal to the energy absorbed by the system divided by the thermodynamic temperature at which the change takes place. The entropy of a closed system never decreases during a thermodynamic process.

E number *See* FOOD ADDITIVES.

environment The surroundings in which an organism lives, which are affected by physical and chemical factors as well as by other organisms. The damage to the earth caused by human activities has been a major concern during the last 50 years. In the UK, the Department for Environment, Food, and Rural Affairs is responsible for a wide range of activities, including conservation areas, land use, and energy resources. *See* ACID RAIN; ENDANGERED SPECIES; GREENHOUSE EFFECT; OZONE; POLLUTION.

enzymes A group of proteins that act as biological catalysts, i.e. they speed up (or slow down) the rate of chemical reactions in living organisms. Enzymes are manufactured by cells according to the *genetic code carried by the chromosomes; because each enzyme catalyses a specific reaction, it is the enzymes that determine the function of the cell. Control of *metabolism is largely by regulation of enzyme production and activity.

Eocene epoch *See* TERTIARY PERIOD.

eohippus An extinct (Eocene) ancestor of the *horse. About 28 cm tall, it was a browsing forest dweller and had four toes on the forefoot and three on the hindfoot.

Ephesians, Epistle of Paul to the A New Testament book written as a circular letter from the Apostle Paul to churches in Asia Minor in about 60 AD; it stresses the equality of Jewish and Gentile Christians.

Ephesus An ancient Greek city and trading centre on the Ionian coast of *Asia Minor. It maintained its prosperity under the Persians and Alexander the Great and in Roman times was rivalled only by *Alexandria as a commercial centre. It was sacked by the *Goths in 262 AD. *See also* ARTEMIS, TEMPLE OF.

Epicureanism A school of thought founded by the Greek philosopher **Epicurus** (341–270 BC) around 300 BC in Athens. He taught that the highest good was pleasure and the avoidance of pain, based on tranquillity of mind and conscience.

Epidaurus A city state of ancient Greece, situated across the Saronic Gulf from *Athens. Its sanctuary of *Asclepius was famous in antiquity for its medical cures. The 4th-century BC theatre (part of the temple complex) is sufficiently preserved to be still used for plays.

epidemiology The science that investigates the incidence and causative factors of diseases that are associat ed with a particular environment or way of life. Epidemiologists have enlarged their studies from the classical epidemics of communicable diseases, such as typhus and cholera, to include noncommunicable diseases, such as cancer.

epidermis The outermost layer of cells in animals and plants. In higher animals (including mammals) it forms the outer layer of the skin.

epididymis *See* TESTIS.

epidural *See* ANAESTHESIA.

epiglottis A leaf-shaped flap of cartilage at the root of the tongue that prevents food and fluid from entering the windpipe during swallowing.

epilepsy A disease characterized by seizures (periods of sudden loss of consciousness): sufferers included Dostoievski, Van Gogh, and Julius Caesar. In tonic-clonic seizures (formerly called grand mal epilepsy) the patient suddenly becomes stiff, loses consciousness, and has convulsions for a few minutes. Absence seizures (formerly called petit mal) most commonly affect children, who suddenly lose consciousness for a few seconds but usually do not fall down. These and other forms of epilepsy are treated with anticonvulsant (antiepileptic) drugs.

epinephrine *See* ADRENALINE.

Epiphany (*or* **Twelfth Day**) A Christian feast celebrated on 6 Jan. In Eastern Orthodox Churches it commemorates the baptism of Jesus. Introduced to the West in the 4th century, it developed as a celebration of the coming of the *Magi to Bethlehem, representing the manifestation (Greek: *epiphaneia*) of Christ to the Gentiles. **Twelfth Night** is the night preceding Epiphany and traditionally devoted to festivities.

epiphyte A plant that grows on another plant for support. Epiphytes are not parasites: some obtain nourishment from decaying plant remains and many solve the problem of obtaining water by developing such structures as aerial roots.

epistemology The philosophical discipline that considers the nature, basis, and limits of knowledge. It is one of the three main branches of modern philosophy and is considered fundamental to all philosophical and scientific enquiry.

Epistles The 21 books of the *New Testament that were written as letters, mostly by Paul (13). The remainder are attributed to James, Peter (2), John (3), Jude, and an unknown author. In the liturgy of many Christian Churches, the Epistle is the name of the first of two passages of Scripture (usually taken from the New Testament Epistles) recited at the celebration of the Eucharist, the second being the Gospel.

epoxy resin A type of synthetic *resin containing the –O– atom (epoxy group). They are viscous liquids but set to hard clear solids on the addition of curing agents. They are extensively used as adhesives, the resin and the curing agent being mixed immediately before use.

Epstein, Sir Jacob (1880–1959) British sculptor of US birth, working in London after 1905. From 1912 he experimented with avantgarde sculpture, provoking criticism with such works as *Genesis* (1931). His bronze portrait busts of Einstein (1933), T. S. Eliot, and Vaughan Williams (1950) were more favourably received. His last works included *St Michael and the Devil* (1958) for Coventry Cathedral.

equator The great circle around the earth at latitude 0°, lying midway between the poles in a plane at right angles to the earth's axis. It is 40 076 km (24 902 mi) long and divides the N from the S hemisphere.

Equatorial Guinea, Republic of A small country in W central Africa, on the Gulf of Guinea. It consists of two main parts: mainland Río Muni and the island of Bioko (formerly Macías Nguema), as well as the island of Pagalu (formerly Annobón) and several smaller islands. The inhabitants are mainly *Fang, Fernandinos, and the indigenous Bubi (descendants of slaves from West Africa), who inhabit Bioko. *Economy*: chiefly agricultural. Although the discovery of offshore oil made Equatorial Guinea the world's fastest growing economy in the early 2000s, it remains one of the world's poorest countries. *History*: formerly a Spanish colony, the area became two Spanish provinces in 1959 and gained independence in 1968. In 1979 the life president Francisco Macías Nguema (1924–79) was overthrown and executed in a coup led by Lt Col Teodoro Obiang Nguema Mbasogo, who became president. Multiparty elections held in 1993 resulted in victory for the ruling party but were condemned as unfair by international observers. Opposition parties were declared illegal in 1997–98 and human rights violations continue to concern the UN. Official languages: Spanish and French. Currency: CFA franc of 100 centimes. Area: 28 051 sq km (10 831 sq mi). Population (2003 est): 494 000. Capital: Malabo.

equinox Either of the two points at which the *ecliptic intersects the celestial equator (*see* CELESTIAL SPHERE). The ecliptic represents the apparent annual path of the sun around the celestial sphere. The sun crosses the celestial equator from S to N at the **vernal** (*or* **spring**) **equinox**, usually on 21 March. It crosses from N to S at the **autumnal equinox**, usually on 23 Sept. At the equinoxes night and day are of almost equal duration.

equity (law) The body of rules developed by the Court of *Chancery to achieve a fair result in cases in which the application of *common law would fail to do so. The rules of equity developed separately from but by the same method (judicial precedent) as the common law. The two systems were amalgamated in 1875 with the establishment of the High Court of Justice. Now all courts administer both law and equity, the rules of equity prevailing if in conflict with the common law. *See also* COURTS OF LAW.

Erasmus, Desiderius (1466–1536) Christian humanist and writer, born at Rotterdam. A highly influential Renaissance thinker, he studied and taught all over Europe. He produced many original works and compilations, including *Encomium Moriae* (*Praise of Folly*; 1509), written for Thomas *More. He also produced the first translation of the Greek New Testament.

erbium (Er) A lanthanide element that forms an oxide (Eb_2O_3) and halides (e.g. $EbCl_3$). It is added to phosphors, glasses, and alloys. At no 68; at wt 167.26; mp 1529°C; bp 2868°C.

Erfurt 50 59N 11 00E A city in S Germany, on the River Gera. One of the oldest German cities, it became a member of the Hanseatic League in the 15th century and was of great commercial importance in the 16th century. Population (1999 est): 202 102.

erg The unit of energy in the *c.g.s. system equal to the work done when a force of one dyne acts through a distance of one centimetre. 1 erg = 10^{-7} joule.

ergonomics The study of the psychological and physical factors that can be used to improve the design of both machines and systems for human use.

ergot A disease caused by the fungus *Claviceps purpurea*, which affects cereals and grasses, especially rye. In affected plants a hard black fungal body develops in place of the grain. Consumption of bread made with diseased grain produces the symptoms of **ergotism**: gangrene of the fingers and toes or convulsions.

Erie, Lake The fourth largest of the Great Lakes in North America, between Canada and the USA. Linked with Lake Ontario via the Welland Ship Canal, it forms part of the St Lawrence Seaway system. It is closed to navigation during winter due to freezing. Area: 25 718 sq km (9930 sq mi).

Erinyes (*or* **furies**) In Greek legend, spirits of vengeance who lived in the underworld and ruthlessly pursued all evildoers. They were three in number and were named (in later writers) Allecto, Tisiphone, and Megaera. After *Orestes was acquitted of his mother's murder, the pursuing Erinyes became known as the **Eumenides** or 'kindly ones'. In Roman legend they were known as the Furies (Latin *Furiae* or *Dirae*).

Eris A Greek goddess personifying strife. She threw a golden apple inscribed "To the Fairest" among the gods. Aphrodite, Hera, and Athena each claimed the apple. *Paris, who had to decide, chose Aphrodite because she offered him in return the most beautiful woman as his wife. This myth, the Judgment of Paris, explains the origin of the *Trojan War.

Eritrea A country in NE Africa, bordering on the Red Sea. It consists of a narrow coastal plain rising inland to the Ethiopian plateau. *Economy*: agriculture and industry, producing sorghum, livestock, hides, and textiles, were devastated in the war of independence but are now being restored. *History*: a former Italian colony, it came under British administration in 1941. Its integration with Ethiopia in 1962 gave rise to political discontent, which developed during the 1970s and 1980s into civil war between separatists and Ethiopian government forces. The war ended in 1991, when Eritrea achieved *de facto* independence; full independence was internationally recognized in 1993. In 1998–99 and 2000 there were fierce border skirmishes between Eritrea and Ethiopia. Official languages: English and Arabic. Currency: nakfa. Area: 93 679 sq km (36 170 sq mi). Population (2003 est): 4 141 000. Capital: Asmara.

Ernst, Max (1891–1976) German artist. He was a founder in 1919 of the Cologne *dada movement. He excelled in collage, particularly of cut-out illustrations, and became a leading practitioner of *surrealism in Paris. In 1941 he moved to the USA.

Eros The Greek god of love, the son of Aphrodite by Zeus, Hermes, or Ares. He was usually portrayed as a winged youth armed with bow and arrows. He was identified with the Roman Cupid.

erythrocyte (*or* **red blood cell**) A disc-shaped blood cell, about 0.007 mm in diameter, that lacks a nucleus and contains *haemoglobin, which combines reversibly with oxygen and is the means by which blood transports oxygen from the lungs to the tissues. A deficiency of red blood cells (below about 4.5 million per mm^3 of blood) or haemoglobin is called *anaemia.

escape velocity The initial velocity required by a projectile to enable it, without any further source of power, to escape from the gravitational field of a celestial body. It depends on the mass and diameter of the celestial body. For the earth the escape velocity is 11 200 metres per second.

Escoffier, Auguste (1846–1935) French chef. He gained an international reputation while supervising the kitchens at the Savoy and the Carlton hotels in London.

Eskimo *See* INUIT.

Eskimo-Aleut languages *See* INUIT-ALEUT LANGUAGES.

ESP *See* EXTRASENSORY PERCEPTION.

Esperanto An artificial language invented by a Polish philologist, L. L. Zamenhof (1859–1917), in 1887. Intended as a universal medium of communication, it is spoken by over 100 000 people. Grammatically it is entirely regular, its pronunciation is consistent with its spelling, and as well as grammatical rules it has the potential for the formation of new words.

Essen 51 27N 6 57E A city in W Germany, in North Rhine-Westphalia near the River Ruhr. It has a 9th-century cathedral. It is the administrative centre of the *Ruhr. Population (1999 est): 600 700.

Essenes An ancient Jewish sect active between the 2nd century BC and the 2nd century AD in Palestine. The *Dead Sea Scrolls may be relics of an Essene community.

essential oils Substances with a characteristic scent produced by the glands of aromatic plants. They are used in perfumes, food flavourings, and medicines. Examples include lavender oil and clove oil.

Essex A county of E England, bordering on the North Sea and Greater London, which incorporated the SW of the county in 1965. Southend-on-Sea and Thurrock became independent unitary authorities in 1998. It is mainly low lying, rising gently towards the chalk uplands of the NW. Agriculture is important. Industry is located mainly in the SW. Harwich is a major ferry port. Area (excluding unitary authorities): 3446 sq km (1330 sq mi). Population (2001, excluding unitary authorities): 1 310 922. Administrative centre: Chelmsford.

Essex, Robert Devereux, 2nd Earl of (?1566–1601) English soldier and courtier to Elizabeth I. He was appointed Master of the Horse (1587) after distinguishing himself against Spain. He commanded an expedition (1591–92) sent to aid Henry IV of France and in 1596 he took part in the sack of Cádiz. He was dismissed (1600) after failing to suppress an Irish rebellion and in 1601 raised a riot in London, for which he was executed.

esters Organic compounds produced by the reaction of an alcohol with an acid, with the elimination of water. Common organic esters are formed from carboxylic acids and have the general formula R.CO.OR′. The lighter ones often have a pleasant smell and taste and are widely used in perfumes and flavourings.

Esther In the Old Testament, the queen of the Persian King Ahasuerus. The **Book of Esther** tells how she used her influence to prevent a massacre of Persian Jews, commemorated in the Jewish feast of *Purim.

Estonia, Republic of A republic in NE Europe. It has many lakes and includes numerous islands in the Baltic Sea. Some 30% of the population are Russians. *Economy*: fishing is important. Industries include machine building, textiles, and food processing. *History*: Estonia was ceded to Russia in 1721. Rebellions in the 19th century culminated in a declaration of independence (1918), which was recognized by Soviet Russia in 1920. Estonia was assigned to the Soviet Union by the Nazi-Soviet Pact (1939), becoming a Soviet republic in 1940. It was occupied by Germany in World War II. Separatist feeling grew in the 1980s, culminating in independence in 1991. In 1993 a new law denying citizenship to non-Estonian-speaking residents increased tension between Estonians and Russians. Since 1995 the country has been governed by a series of centrist coalitions. Estonia joined both the EU and NATO in 2004. Official language: Estonian. Currency: kroon of 100 sents. Area: 45 100 sq km (17 410 sq mi). Population (2003 est): 1 353 000. Capital: Tallinn.

Estonian A language of the Baltic-Finnic branch of the Finno-Ugric division of the Uralic language family. The official language of Estonia, it is related to Finnish.

etching A method of making prints from a metal plate covered with an acid-resistant ground, on which a design is drawn with a needle. The plate is then placed in acid, the exposed lines being eaten away. These recessed lines retain ink and the design is transferred to paper.

ethane (C_2H_6) A colourless gas, the second member of the *alkane series. It occurs in *natural gas.

ethanol (*or* **ethyl alcohol**; C_2H_5OH) A colourless flammable liquid that is the active constituent of alcoholic drinks. It is prepared by fermentation or by the catalytic hydration of *ethylene. It is used as a solvent, a raw material for producing other chemicals, and a fuel.

Ethelbert (c. 552–616 AD) King of Kent, who became overlord of all England south of the Humber. Encouraging the conversion of his people to Christianity, he received Augustine's mission from Rome. He wrote the first extant English code of laws.

Ethelred I (d. 871 AD) King of England (866–71), in whose reign the Vikings launched a full-scale invasion of England. Ethelred died after his victory at Ashdown, leaving his brother *Alfred the Great to fight on.

Ethelred the Unready (968–1016) King of England (978–1016). In the face of Danish raids, he was forced to pay huge tributes (Danegeld) to the enemy. He was driven into exile by King Sweyn of Denmark in 1013 but returned after Sweyn's death (1014).

ethene (*or* **ethylene**; C_2H_4) A colourless flammable gaseous *alkene. It is made by cracking petroleum and is used to make *polythene (polyethylene).

ether Any member of the group of organic compounds with the general formula R–O–R′, which are formed by the condensation of two alcohols. Diethyl ether, $C_2H_5OC_2H_5$, often known simply as ether, is a volatile liquid and is used as an anaesthetic and solvent.

ethics The science of morality, also called moral philosophy. It is one of the three main branches of modern philosophy and seeks to discover a consistent principle by which human actions can be judged. Until about a century ago, ethics aimed to be a guide to human conduct. Now it is more descriptive, attempting to discover how moral decisions are actually made. In utilitarianism the good of society is the criterion and this is now the basis of commercial, legal, and social ethics; however, conscience remains the guide of most individuals. *See also* HEDONISM; RATIONALISM.

Ethiopia, Federal Democratic Republic of (former name: Abyssinia) A country in NE Africa, on the Red Sea. It consists of deserts in the SE and NE and a central plateau, crossed by river valleys (including that of the Blue Nile) and by mountain ranges. The population consists of many ethnic groups, including the Galla and Amhara. *Economy*: Ethiopia remains one of the poorest countries in the world and agriculture is chiefly at subsistence level. The situation has been worsened in recent years by serious crop failures, causing famines. All land was nationalized in 1975 and farmed cooperatively until 1992, when private ownership was reintroduced. *History*: Ethiopia has a long history, legend claiming the descent of its rulers from Solomon and the Queen of Sheba. From the 2nd to the 9th century AD there was considerable prosperity and expansion; in the 4th century Ethiopia became the first Christian country in Africa. This period was followed by centuries of struggles (especially with the Muslims) and of internal divisions. Only in the 19th century was the country reunited. In 1896 Italian attempts to conquer Ethiopia were defeated but in 1935 Italy (under Mussolini) invaded. In 1936 Addis Ababa fell and the emperor, Haile Selassie, fled to England. Ethiopia then formed part of Italian East Africa (with Eritrea and Italian Somaliland). In 1941 the Allies liberated Ethiopia and Haile Selassie returned to the throne. Eritrea was fully integrated into Ethiopia in 1962; it became independent in 1993. Haile Selassie was deposed in 1974 and a provisional military government came to power. After the execution of members of the ruling military council in 1977, the government became known as the Derg (Provisional Military Administrative Council) with Mengistu Haile Mariam (1937–) as president. During this unsettled period liberation movements in Eritrea and the Somali-speaking Ogaden area increased their armed struggle; in 1977 Ethiopian troops beat off a Somali invasion of the Ogaden. Successive droughts (1982, 1984, 1987, 1989, 1999–2000, 2002) led to famine and resettlement from the N to the fertile west; one million people died in the famine of 1984. Massive foreign aid was hampered by internal strife and disorganization. Armed rebellion in the province of Tigré led to civil war and the fall of Mengistu in 1991, when a provisional government was installed. A new constitution was ratified in 1994. In 1998–99 and 2000 there was fierce border fighting with Eritrea. Official language: Amharic. Currency: birr of 100 cents. Area: 1 128 221 sq km (435 608 sq mi). Population (2003 est): 66 558 000. Capital: Addis Ababa.

ethology The study of animal behaviour, founded in Europe in the 1930s by the work of Konrad *Lorenz and Niko Tinbergen (1907–88), who studied animals in their natural states. Ethologists are concerned with how animals respond to signals or stimuli, how they sense these signals, and what their response means to other animals and to themselves. They demonstrate the interactions between the inherited (instinctive) aspects of behaviour and those determined by experience (learning).

Etna, Mount 37 45N 15 00E A volcano in E Sicily. The first recorded eruption was in 476 BC and in the last hundred years significant eruptions have occurred in 1928, 1949, 1971, 1991, 2000, and 2002. Height: 3263 m (10 705 ft).

Eton 51 31N 0 37 W A town in SE England, in Maidenhead and Windsor unitary authority, Berkshire, opposite Windsor on the River Thames. Eton College, the famous public school, was founded by Henry VI in 1440. Population (1991, excluding Eton College): 1974.

Etruscans The ancient inhabitants of Etruria (now Tuscany) in central Italy N of Rome. From the 8th to the 5th centuries BC their cities, forming a loose political confederacy, dominated their neighbours but after 396 they were rapidly absorbed by the Romans. The Etruscans had extensive trading links. Their origins are mysterious. Their language was non-Indo-European but is still untranslated.

etymology The study of the history of words, in which words are traced back to their earliest recorded forms, or even beyond these to hypothetical reconstructed forms. Most English words are derived either from Proto-Germanic (*see* GERMANIC LANGUAGES) or from Latin and French. Many learned English words were taken from Greek or made up from Greek elements, while in the past 200 years English has borrowed words from languages in every part of the world.

EU *See* EUROPEAN UNION.

Eucalyptus A genus of tropical and subtropical evergreen trees (about 600 species) native to Australia but cultivated elsewhere. Eucalypts—also known as gum trees—are among the tallest trees in the world, 90–100 m high. The blue-grey bark is smooth and often peeling and the mature leaves are long and narrow. Fast-growing and drought-resistant, eucalypts are important sources of timber. The best known species are the blue gum and the red gum. All parts of the trees contain essential oils. Family: *Myrtaceae* (myrtle family).

Eucharist (Greek *eucharistia*: thanksgiving) The chief *sacrament and central act of worship of the Christian Churches. Also known as Holy Communion, the Lord's Supper, and the Mass, its institution is described in the three Synoptic Gospels. At the last meal of Christ and the apostles, bread and wine were blessed by Christ and shared, representing his death on the cross and the subsequent redemption of mankind.

Euclid (c. 300 BC) Greek mathematician, famous for his book entitled *Elements* in which he derived all that was known of geometry from a few simple axioms. The geometry that obeys Euclid's axioms is known as Euclidean geometry, all other kinds being called non-Euclidean.

Euglena A genus of single-celled microorganisms found chiefly in fresh water. They are spindle-shaped, with a flexible cell wall and a gullet from which protrudes a long whiplike flagellum, used for locomotion. They are regarded by some authorities as algae and by others as protozoans.

Eulenspiegel, Till A German peasant folk hero, a crafty and often savage joker whose exploits inspired numerous folktales and many literary and musical works, notably the epic poem (1928) by Gerhart Hauptmann (1862–1946) and the tone poem by Richard *Strauss.

Eumenides *See* ERINYES.

euphonium Brass instrument with a wide conical bore, a cup-shaped mouthpiece, four valves, and a range of just over three octaves rising from the third B flat below middle C.

Euphorbia A worldwide genus of herbs and small trees (1600 species), having clusters of small flowers each surrounded by conspicuous petal-like bracts. The genus includes some ornamental shrubs such as poinsettia. The herbaceous euphorbias are known as *spurges. Family: *Euphorbiaceae*.

Euphrates, River A river in SW Asia, rising in E Turkey and flowing SE through Syria into Iraq. 190 km (118 mi) from the Persian Gulf, it joins the River Tigris to form the Shatt al-Arab. It flows past the historic sites of Babylon, Ur, Nippur, and Sippara. Length: 2700 km (1678 mi).

EURATOM *See* EUROPEAN ATOMIC ENERGY COMMUNITY.

eurhythmics A system of teaching music by developing the student's physical response to rhythm. Devised by Émile Jaques-Dalcroze (1865–1950) in about 1905, it has been used in physical education and *ballet and modern dance training.

Euripides (c. 480–406 BC) Greek dramatist, the third (after *Aeschylus and *Sophocles) of the three major writers of Attic tragedy. Of approximately 90 plays, 19 survive, including the tragedies *Medea* (431), *Hippolytus* (428), *Electra* (415), *The Trojan Women* (415), *The Bacchae* (405), and *Iphigenia at Aulis* (405). His technical innovations included naturalistic dialogue and a diminution of the role of the chorus. He also explored feminine psychology.

euro The currency unit of certain member states of the European Union that was launched in January 1999 and replaced the national currencies for all forms of monetary transaction in January–March 2002. It is subdivided into 100 cents. *See* EUROPEAN MONETARY SYSTEM.

Europa In Greek mythology, the daughter of King Agenor of Tyre. Carried to Crete by Zeus in the form of a bull, she bore him three sons: Minos, Rhadamanthus, and Sarpedon.

Europe A continent bordering on the Arctic Ocean (N), the Atlantic Ocean (W), and the Mediterranean Sea (S); the Ural Mountains, the River Ural, and the Caspian Sea form its E boundary. Europe is the second smallest continent but has exerted a disproportionate influence on the rest of the world. A central plain, extending from the Ural Mountains to the Atlantic Ocean and divided by uplands and the English Channel, comprises two-thirds of the continent. It rises in the S to a series of mountain systems (e.g. the Pyrenees, Alps, Apennines, Carpathian Mountains), and in the N to the mountainous region of Scandinavia and Scotland. The chief rivers flow from the Valdai Hills (e.g. Volga, Don, Dnieper) or the Alps (e.g. Danube, Rhine, Rhône, Po). Its four **climatic zones** are characterized by mild winters, cool summers, and rain all the year round (NW); mild winters, hot summers, and chiefly spring and autumn rain (Mediterranean); cold winters, warm summers, and chiefly summer rain (Central Europe); and very cold winters (E Europe). **Vegetation zones** comprise, from N to S: tundra; a coniferous forest belt; a deciduous forest belt; and the mainly evergreen and scrub vegetation of the Mediterranean. Steppe and semidesert characterize the SE. Forest once covered some 80% of Europe but intense agriculture since the middle ages and industrialization since the 19th century have reduced it to 30% of the land mass. Europe possesses important mineral resources. Coalfields, especially in Germany, Poland, Russia, and Ukraine, continue to be an important source of power, and oil and natural-gas reserves are found in Russia, Romania, Albania, and beneath the North Sea. Iron-ore deposits are found on a large scale only in countries of the former Soviet Union, which also have reserves of nickel, tin, and manganese, but nonmetallic minerals occur widely. Europe's high-density population is concentrated in industrial regions. Most of the large number of national groups in Europe speak an Indo-European language. Europeans may be subdivided into racial types (e.g. Nordic, Germanic, Alpine, and Mediterranean) but extensive intermixing has occurred. Christianity, in various forms, is the dominant religion. Europe's medieval and modern history is that of its diverse nations, conflicts between which culminated in the 20th century in the two World Wars. The postwar period saw a split between the communist countries of E Europe, dominated by the Soviet Union until its collapse, and the countries of W Europe, which have sought to resolve their rivalries in the EUROPEAN UNION. Area: about 10 400 000 sq km (4 000 000 sq mi). Population (1996 est): 729 370 000.

European Atomic Energy Community (EURATOM) An international organization founded in 1958 to promote peaceful uses of atomic energy in Europe. In 1967 the executive and legislative bodies of EURATOM and the European Coal and Steel Community merged with those of the European Economic Community.

European Community (**EC** *or* **European Communities**) An economic and political organization of W European states created in 1967 when the executive and legislative bodies of the European Economic Community merged with those of the European Coal and Steel Community and the European Atomic Energy Community. The original members, Belgium, France, Italy, Luxembourg, the Netherlands, and West Germany, were joined by Denmark, Ireland, and the UK in 1973; Greece joined in 1981, and Spain and Portugal joined in 1986. In 1985 Greenland left the EC, having attained home rule.

Agreements were reached on the removal of customs tariffs between members, the setting of a Common External Tariff for imports from nonmember states, and the abolition of barriers to free movement of labour, services, and capital between members. The EC controlled the Common Agricultural Policy (CAP) and initiated a Common Fisheries Policy (1983). British passports in a common European format were introduced in the UK in 1988. Under the terms of the **Maastricht Treaty** (signed Feb 1992) members agreed to closer political, economic, and monetary union (*see* EUROPEAN MONETARY SYSTEM), which led to the establishment of the *European Union in 1993.

European Economic Community (**EEC** *or* **Common Market**) An organization of W European states created by the Treaty of Rome (1957) to foster economic cooperation, with the eventual aim of economic, and some political, unity. The EEC implemented a Common Agricultural Policy (CAP) in 1962 (modified 1968) and promoted the removal of customs tariffs. In 1967 its legislative and executive bodies merged with those of EURATOM and the European Coal and Steel Community to form the *European Community.

European Free Trade Association (**EFTA**) An association, now consisting of four states (Iceland, Norway, Switzerland, and Liechtenstein), founded in 1960 to foster free trade between members. In 1984 free trade was established between the EC and EFTA. In 1994 the EU and EFTA (excluding Switzerland) formed the **European Economic Area** (EEA), the world's richest open market.

European Monetary System (**EMS**) A system created by the European Community (now the EU) in 1979 to stabilize exchange rates between members and as a possible step towards European Monetary Union (EMU). Participating states limited fluctuations in their exchange rates through the **Exchange Rate Mechanism** (ERM) and linked their currencies to the European Currency Unit (ECU), the value of which was based on a basket of currencies. In 1992 the ERM failed when market pressures forced the British and Italian governments to withdraw and the Spanish peseta also fell below its floor value. Despite the failure of the ERM, plans to introduce a single European currency (the euro) and a **European Central Bank** (ECB) advanced rapidly in the late 1990s. By 2001 12 EU countries (excluding Denmark, Sweden, and the UK) had committed themselves to EMU. Their currencies were locked together and the euro was launched for all noncash transactions in January 1999; the first notes and coins were issued in January 2002 and the national currencies were withdrawn by March. A referendum (2000) in Denmark rejected the euro and the UK and Sweden are committed to referendums before joining. EU countries outside EMU will be able to join ERM II based on the euro and supervised by the ECB.

European Space Agency (**ESA**) An organization responsible for Europe's space programme, formed in 1975 from the merger of the European Space Research Organization (founded 1962) and the European Launcher Development Organization. There are at present 15 full-member nations, including the UK. Since 1979 all ESA *satellites have been launched by the ESA launcher **Ariane**. In 1996 the launcher Ariane-5 was destroyed on its maiden flight.

European Union (**EU**) An organization established in 1993 by the terms of the Maastricht Treaty (*see* EUROPEAN COMMUNITY). It comprises the EC, with the addition of a common foreign and security policy and cooperation between members in justice and policing. In 1995 Austria, Sweden, and Finland joined. (Greek) Cyprus, the Czech Republic, Estonia, Hungary, Latvia, Lithuania, Malta, Poland, Slovenia, and Slovakia all joined in May 2004.

The **European Commission** (until 1993 the Commission of the European Communities) is in Brussels and consists of one member or two appointed by each member country; its president is elected for a four-year term. The Commission acts as an advisory body to, and is responsible for implementing policy decided upon by, the Council of Ministers of the European Union. The current Commission is headed by José Manuel Durão Barroso. Also in Brussels, the Council comprises ministers from the governments of the member countries. The heads of government meet triannually as the European Council. The **European Parliament** at

Strasbourg or Luxembourg comments on the Commission's legislative proposals; it must be consulted on the annual budgets and may dismiss the Commission. Members are (since 1979) elected by direct vote in the member countries and sit as political groups in the Parliament. The long-planned single European currency (*see* EUROPEAN MONETARY SYSTEM) was introduced in 1999–2002. Controversial proposals for an EU constitution, which would create an EU president and foreign minister and further limit the right of national veto, were agreed in 2004.

europium (Eu) A *lanthanide element, used in television-tube phosphors. At no 63; at wt 151.96; mp 822°C; bp 1527°C.

Eurydice In Greek legend, a dryad, the wife of *Orpheus. She died of a snake bite. Orpheus descended to the underworld to recover her but lost her forever when he violated the condition of her release and turned to look at her before emerging.

euthanasia (Greek: easy death) The taking of life to relieve suffering from painful and incurable diseases. Voluntary euthanasia includes both active steps for taking life (e.g. administration of drugs) and the withholding of life-supporting treatment (passive euthanasia). With compulsory euthanasia the patient—for example, a severely deformed baby—is unable to express his own wishes and the responsibility for deciding to terminate life rests on society or a person acting on authority. Many societies (e.g. The Voluntary Euthanasia Society, or Exit) promote voluntary euthanasia. Voluntary euthanasia was effectively decriminalized in the Netherlands in 1993 and made fully legal under certain conditions in 2001. Euthanasia has been legalized in strictly defined circumstances in Oregon, USA (1998) and Belgium (2002).

Evans, Sir Arthur John (1851–1941) British archaeologist. His life's work was the excavation in Crete of *Knossos (1899–1935). In *The Palace of Minos* (1921–36) he firmly established the chronology and main features of *Minoan civilization.

Evelyn, John (1620–1706) English author, best known for his *Diary*, a detailed personal record of the years 1641–1706.

evening primrose A herbaceous plant of the genus *Oenothera* (100 species), 90–100 cm tall, native to the Americas but widespread in Europe. The fragrant yellow flowers open in the evening.

Everest, Mount 27 59N 86 56E The highest mountain in the world, on the Nepal–Tibet border in the Himalayas. Climbing attempts started in 1920 and the 12th expedition, led by Col John Hunt (later Baron Hunt; 1910–98), was the first to succeed: (Sir) Edmund *Hillary (1919–) and Sherpa *Tenzing Norgay (c. 1914–86) reached the summit on 29 May 1953. Height: 8846 m (29 023 ft).

evergreen plants Plants the foliage of which is retained throughout the year. The leaves, which are tough and waxy, are produced and shed at different times all the year round, individual leaves often remaining on the tree for several years. Most conifers and many tropical broad-leaved trees are evergreen. **Deciduous plants** produce softer leaves, which are all shed before winter, leaving only the woody parts and protected buds exposed.

evolution In biology, the gradual and continuous process by which the first and most primitive of living organisms have developed into the diversity of plant and animal life known today. Until the 18th century it was generally believed that each group of organisms was separately and divinely created. Work by Linnaeus and Buffon indicated that this was incorrect.

The first theory of evolution was published by Lamarck, in 1809 (*see* LAMARCKISM). His idea of the inheritance of acquired characteristics lacked definite proof, although it has had its supporters. A more satisfactory theory was put forward by Charles *Darwin and A. R. *Wallace in 1858: they proposed that new species arose by a process of natural selection acting on individual inheritable variations in a population (*see* DARWINISM). Later work has proved that these heritable changes result from spontaneous genetic mutations, and Darwin's theory—with some modifications—is now generally accepted.

Excalibur King Arthur's magic sword. In one legend Arthur succeeds in drawing it from a stone, thereby proving his claim to the English throne. In another he receives it from the Lady of the Lake, to whom it is thrown back at his death. *See also* ARTHURIAN LEGEND.

excitation In physics, the raising of a system from its lowest energy level (the ground state) to a higher energy level (the excited state). It is most frequently caused by the absorption of a *photon by an atom or ion.

excommunication The exclusion of a Christian from the community of the Church for misconduct. In the early Church, exclusion from the sacraments was frequently used as a means of censure, and in the middle ages the papacy used it to apply political pressure against sovereigns. It is still used by the Roman Catholic Church.

Exeter 50 43N 3 31W A city in SW England, the administrative centre of Devon on the River Exe. It has a 13th-century cathedral and an ancient Guildhall. Population (1993 est): 105 100.

existentialism A philosophical movement that rejects metaphysics and concentrates on the individual's existence in the world. The forerunner of existentialism was *Kierkegaard, whose pragmatic philosophy of existence was adapted by French intellectuals, especially *Sartre, after World War II. Sartre's existentialism allows individuals freedom in a nihilistic universe. A man is responsible for his effect on others, but only *his* existence is real to him and he is ultimately his own judge.

Exmoor A high moorland and national park of SW England, extending from NE Devon into W Somerset, reaching 520 m (1707 ft) at Dunkery Beacon. It supports heather, bracken, and grass and is grazed by the small hardy Exmoor ponies, wild red deer, and sheep. Parts are now being ploughed. Area: 686 sq km (265 sq mi).

Exodus (Greek: going out) The second book of the Bible, traditionally ascribed to Moses, and probably compiled between the 9th and 4th centuries BC, relating events that may have occured in the 15th century BC. It recounts the events culminating in the departure of the Israelites from Egypt, where they had lived as slaves since the time of Joseph, and their arrival at Mount Sinai, where the Ten Commandments are given to Moses.

expanding universe The theory that the universe is expanding was first confirmed by Edwin Hubble (1889–1953) in 1929 following observations that the light from distant galaxies is subject to a *redshift, which arises from the recession of the galaxies from us (and from each other). The expansion can be explained by the *big-bang theory. *See also* HUBBLE CONSTANT.

explosives Substances that can be made to produce a large volume of gas very suddenly. The energy of the expanding gases may be used for a number of industrial or military purposes. Most explosives used are **chemical explosives**. These include *TNT, *nitroglycerin, *dynamite, and *gelignite. Modern high explosives are often in the form of water gels, which are plastic, water resistant, and easy to handle safely. In **nuclear explosives**, there is an almost instantaneous release of nuclear energy, which is used for bombs and occasionally for mining.

exposure meter A device for measuring the intensity of light falling on a photographic *camera, used to determine the film exposure time and lens *f-number needed to suit the lighting conditions. The aperture and shutter speed can then be set manually or sometimes automatically.

expressionism A movement in the arts of the early 20th century in which the force of human emotion was allowed to distort the presentation of the external world. In the visual arts the chief exponents were Die *Brücke and Der *Blaue Reiter groups in Germany. Expressionism was also significant in the cinema and the theatre.

extrasensory perception (**ESP**) Acquisition of information not accessible through normal perceptual processes. Three phenomena are usually classified under this heading: clairvoyance (knowledge of distant events and concealed objects), telepathy (thought transference between people), and precognition (knowledge of future events). Evidence for all three tends to be anecdotal.

eye The organ of sight. The human eyes lie within two bony sockets in the skull and are attached by six muscles, which produce eye movements. At the front of the eye the white fibrous outer layer (sclera) is replaced by the transparent cornea. A delicate membrane (the conjunctiva) covers the white of the eye and lines the eyelids. Light entering the eye is refracted by the cornea and passes through the

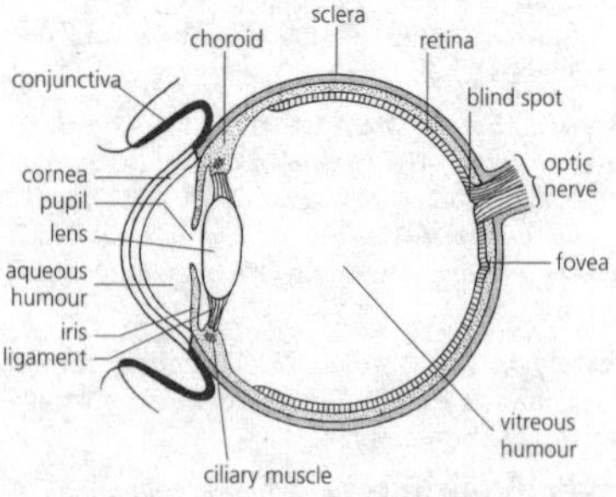

eye. The structure of the human eye is revealed in this section. The blind spot, where the optic nerve leaves the eye, contains no visual cells and is therefore insensitive to light. The fovea is the area of acutest vision.

watery aqueous humour and pupil to the lens. The pigmented *iris controls the amount of light entering the eye. The shape of the lens can be adjusted by means of the ciliary muscles so that an image is focused through the jelly-like vitreous humour onto the *retina. Contraction of the ciliary muscles causes the lens to become flattened for focusing distant objects; relaxation of the muscles increases the curvature of the lens for focusing near objects. Light-sensitive cells in the retina send impulses to the brain via the optic nerve. *See also* LONGSIGHTEDNESS; OPHTHALMOLOGY; SHORT-SIGHTEDNESS.

Eyre, Lake A shallow salt lake of NE South Australia. It is normally dry except during the rainy season when heavy rains are fed into the lake. Area: about 9100 sq km (3500 sq mi).

F

Fabergé, Peter Carl (1846–1920) Russian goldsmith and jeweller. He designed elegant *objets d'art* and was patronized by European royalty. He was especially famous for jewelled Easter eggs containing gifts.

Fabian Society A society, named after *Fabius Maximus, formed in London in 1884 for the purpose of peacefully promoting socialist ideas and establishing a socialist state in Britain. Members included George Bernard *Shaw and Sidney and Beatrice *Webb. The Fabians were active in the establishment of the Labour Party.

Fabius Maximus, Quintus (d. 203 BC) Roman general of the second Punic War. Appointed dictator after Hannibal's defeat of the Romans at Trasimene in 217, Fabius adopted a policy of attrition, harassing Hannibal but avoiding pitched battles. Hannibal's victory at *Cannae in 216 proved the wisdom of Fabius' tactics.

Factory Acts A series of UK parliamentary Acts that regulate conditions of work in factories. A response to the appalling conditions resulting from the *industrial revolution, the early Factory Acts (1802, 1819, 1833) were primarily concerned with the employment of children. Anthony Ashley Cooper (later Lord Shaftesbury), leader of the ten-hour movement, was largely responsible for the Acts of 1844 and 1847, the achievements of which were consolidated in subsequent 19th-century legislation. The safety, health, and welfare of factory workers is now regulated by the Factories Act (1961), which is increasingly being replaced by the Health and Safety at Work Act (1974).

factory farming The intensive farming of livestock in which animals are kept in confined artificial environments, with controlled lighting, heating, etc., to maximize production. Battery cages for laying hens, crates for veal calves, factory systems for bacon pigs and beef cattle are examples. Critics argue that animals suffer distress and that the edible products contain high levels of hormones and antibiotics. In 1999 EU countries agreed to end battery-egg production by 2013.

Faeroe Islands (*or* **Faroe Islands**) A Danish group of 22 self-governing islands in the N Atlantic Ocean, between the Shetland Islands and Iceland, the chief ones being Strømø, Østerø, and Vaagø. Fishing and fish processing is important. Official currency: krone of 100 øre. Area: 1400 sq km (540 sq mi). Population (2001 est): 46 600. Capital: Thorshavn, on Strømø.

Fahd bin Abdul Aziz (1922–) King of Saudi Arabia (1982–). He succeeded his half-brother Khalid Ibn Abdul Aziz.

Fahrenheit scale A temperature scale in which the temperature of melting ice is taken as 32 degrees and the temperature of boiling water, as 212 degrees. Named after the German physicist Gabriel Daniel Fahrenheit (1686–1736).

faience Several kinds of tin-glazed earthenware made in France. The name derives from *porcellana di Faenza*, a species of *maiolica made in Faenza, Italy. The technique of coating fragile porous earthenware with impervious hard white opaque tin glaze was brought to France by Italian potters in the 16th century. Centres of production during the 17th and 18th centuries were Lyons, Marseilles, Moustiers, Nevers, and Rouen.

Fairbanks, Douglas (Julius Ullman; 1883–1939) US film actor. With D. W. Griffith, Charlie Chaplin, and his wife Mary Pickford he founded United Artists in 1919. His films, in which he played handsome athletic heroes, include *The Mark of Zorro* (1920) and *The Black Pirate* (1926). His son **Douglas Fairbanks Jr** (1909–2000) was also a film actor, playing similar roles, as in *The Prisoner of Zenda* (1937).

Fair Isle 59 32N 1 38W A sparsely inhabited island in the North Sea, off the N coast of Scotland between the Orkney and Shetland Islands.

It is famous for its knitted goods with intricate patterns. Area: 16.5 sq km (6 sq mi).

Faisal I (1885–1933) King of Iraq (1921–33). He played an important part in the Arab revolt during World War I. After the war he was briefly King of Syria before the French occupation (1920). In 1921 the British installed him as king in mandatory Iraq.

Faisal Ibn Abdul Aziz (1905–75) King of Saudi Arabia (1964–75). He became the real ruler of Saudi Arabia in 1958, although his brother Saud was still nominally king until his abdication in 1964. His reign saw the increased international importance of Saudi Arabia as an oil-producing country. He was assassinated by his nephew.

Falange Española The Spanish Fascist party, created in 1933 by José António Primo de Rivera (1870–1936). The Falange wanted to regenerate Spain by means of revolution but rejected socialism. In 1937 Franco merged the Falange with the various Nationalist parties to create the National Movement, which became Spain's only legal party after the Civil War.

Falashas An Ethiopian tribe, who practise an early form of Judaism. In early 1985 the Israelis organized a secret airlift of over 7000 Falashas to Israel from famine-stricken Ethiopia.

falcon A ground-nesting bird of prey belonging to a widely distributed family (*Falconidae*; 58 species). Falcons are characterized by long pointed wings and a notched hooked bill. True falcons belong to the genus *Falco;* they kill small birds in flight with their claws or seize small mammals from the ground. Order: *Falconiformes* (falcons, hawks, etc.). *See also* GYRFALCON; KESTREL; MERLIN; PEREGRINE FALCON. The sport of hunting small animals or birds with falcons, other hawks, or sometimes eagles is known as **falconry**. It was practised in Asia from the 8th century BC and in Europe from late medieval times to the 17th century. The birds are taken as fledglings (eyasses) or caught as one-year-old birds (passagers) or fully mature birds (haggards), but because many hunting birds are now protected species, they are often bred in captivity. They are trained to sit hooded on the gloved fist and, by the use of a lure (an imitation bird with meat attached), to hunt and kill (but not retrieve).

Falkirk A council area in central Scotland, on the Firth of Forth. Formerly part of Stirling, it was absorbed into Central Region in 1974 and became a unitary authority in 1996. It is mainly agricultural, with petrochemicals in Grangemouth. Area: 299 sq km (4700 sq mi). Population (2001): 145 191. Administrative centre: Falkirk.

Falkland Islands (Argentine name: Islas Malvinas) An island group and United Kingdom overseas territory in the S Atlantic Ocean. The main islands are East and West Falkland; *South Georgia and the South Sandwich group to the SE now form a separate overseas territory. The population is almost entirely of British origin. Fishing is a major source of revenue and sheep farming produces wool for export. *History*: the first landing was by Capt John Strong in 1690. In the early 19th century the islands became a British colony. Argentina has long made claims to the group and on 2 April 1982, invaded the islands, triggering the **Falklands War**. Attempts at a diplomatic settlement failed and a task force sent by the UK recaptured first South Georgia and then the Falkland Islands on 14 June, after considerable loss of life on both sides. Argentina refused to declare a cessation of hostilities until 1989. The declaration of a fishing zone (1987) led to tripling of the islands' income. The economy has benefited from a new trade in squid, and is expected to be revolutionized by the exploitation of newly discovered oil resources. Currency: Falkland pound of 100 pence. Area: 12 173 sq km (4700 sq mi). Population (2001): 2564. Capital: Stanley.

Falla, Manuel de (1876–1946) Spanish nationalist composer. His music was heavily influenced by Spanish folksong and he is best known for his ballet scores *Love the Magician* (1915) and *The Three-Cornered Hat* (1919), *Nights in the Gardens of Spain* (for piano and orchestra; 1909–15), and a concerto for harpsichord and chamber ensemble.

Fallopian tubes *See* OVARY.

fallout Radioactive particles deposited from the atmosphere after a nuclear explosion. Local fallout consists of large particles deposited within a radius of a few hundred kilometres during the first few hours after the explosion. Tropospheric fallout may occur anywhere along the same line of latitude as the explosion during the first week after the explosion. Particles drawn high into the atmosphere can cause stratospheric fallout for several years.

fallow deer A *deer, *Dama dama*, native to Mediterranean forests but widely kept in parks and woodlands. About 90 cm high at the shoulder, fallow deer are fawn with white spots in summer, becoming greyish in winter.

Famagusta 35 07N 33 57E A port in Cyprus,

on the E coast. Founded in the 3rd century BC, it did not develop until the 13th century AD, when Christians fled here from Palestine. Many residents left in 1974 on the Turkish invasion of N Cyprus. Population (1994): 67 167.

Fang A Bantu people of West Africa comprising tribes in N Gabon, Equatorial Guinea, and S Cameroon.

fanworm A marine annelid worm belonging to the family *Sabellidae*, also called peacock or feather-duster worm. Fanworms build a parchment-like tube, up to 45 cm long, from which protrudes a feathery crown of tentacles that trap food particles and absorb oxygen. Class: *Polychaeta*.

FAO *See* FOOD AND AGRICULTURE ORGANIZATION.

farad (F) The SI unit of electrical capacitance equal to the capacitance of a parallel-plate capacitor with a potential difference of one volt across its plates when the capacitor is charged with one coulomb, i.e. $1\,F = 1\,CV^{-1}$. Named after Michael *Faraday.

Faraday, Michael (1791–1867) British chemist and physicist. In 1813 he became assistant to Sir Humphry *Davy at the Royal Institution, eventually succeeding Davy there as professor of chemistry (1833). His major work was on electricity and electrochemistry. Continuing Davy's work on electrolysis (1832) he went on to quantify the process in **Faraday's laws of electrolysis** (1833). These are: (1) the mass of a substance produced by an electrolytic reaction varies directly with the amount of electricity passed through the cell; (2) the masses of substances produced by a given amount of electricity are proportional to the equivalent masses of the substances. The **Faraday constant** is the quantity of electricity equivalent to 1 mole of electrons, i.e. the product of Avogadro's number and the electronic charge. It has the value 96 487 coulombs per mole. In electricity, he discovered the connection between electricity and magnetism and, independently of Joseph Henry (1797–1878), first showed that electromagnetic induction was possible. He used induction to produce the first electrical generator (1831) and also the first transformer.

Fargo, William *See* WELLS, HENRY.

Farnborough 51 17N 0 46W A town in S England, in Hampshire. The Royal Aircraft Establishment, the UK's chief aeronautical research centre, was situated here until 1991; there are plans to develop the site as a heritage centre. Population (1991): 52 535.

Farne Islands (*or* **The Staples**) 55 38N 1 36W A group of about 30 islets and rocks in NE England, off the Northumberland coast. St Cuthbert lived on Inner Farne. In 1838 a heroic rescue by Grace *Darling took place from Longstone Island lighthouse.

Farouk I (1920–65) The last king of Egypt (1936–52). His inability to prevent British intervention in Egyptian affairs, and defeat in the first Arab-Israeli War (1948–49), led to his overthrow.

Fasciola *See* LIVER FLUKE.

fascism A political movement that first became organized in Italy in 1919 under *Mussolini. Economic backwardness, fear of communist revolution, and frustrated national ambitions enabled Mussolini's Blackshirts to come to power in 1922. Fascism emphasized an imagined national or racial superiority, and concentrated authority on a dictatorial cult figure. In Germany Hitler added antisemitism to fascist militarism, secret police, and anticommunism. World War II destroyed Mussolini's and Hitler's dictatorships and fascism won little support in other countries, except in Spain, where Franco's regime survived almost 40 years.

fast reactor A nuclear reactor (*see* NUCLEAR ENERGY) in which natural uranium enriched with uranium-235 or plutonium-239 is used without a moderator, the chain reaction being sustained by fast neutrons. In these reactors the core is surrounded by a blanket of natural uranium into which neutrons escape. These neutrons collide with U-238 nuclei to form U-239 nuclei, which decay to the fissionable isotope Pu-239. By suitable design, more Pu-239 can be produced in the blanket than is required to enrich the fuel in the core. These reactors are therefore called **breeder reactors**. They are 50 times more economical in uranium usage than *thermal reactors. The temperature is so high that a liquid metal (usually sodium) has to be used as coolant and safety considerations have precluded their use.

Fatah, al- (Arabic: the victory) A Palestinian organization, also known as the Palestine National Liberation Movement, established in the late 1950s. Led by Yassir *Arafat, al-Fatah began guerrilla warfare against Israel in the mid-1960s. The organization subsequently split into factions pro and anti Arafat and his role in the Arab-Israeli peace process of the 1990s.

Fates In Greek mythology, three goddesses who determine human destinies. The daughters of Zeus and Themis, they are: Lachesis, who assigns a person's position at birth; Clotho, who spins out the thread of his existence; and Atropos, who cuts the thread at death.

fathom A unit used to express depths of water, equal to six feet.

Fatimah (d. 632) The daughter of *Mohammed. She married *Ali and was the mother of his sons, Hasan and Husayn, from whom most of the Shiite imams were descended. The Fatimid caliphs claimed descent from her.

fats and oils Lipid substances formed by the combination of glycerol with *fatty acids. Fats occur widely in animals and plants as an energy store and as insulating material. Vegetable fats and oils are used in making soaps, margarines, cooking oils, paints, and lubricants. Animal fats are used in foods, soaps, and candles. Oils are distinguished from fats by being liquid at 20°C, whereas fats are solid. Mineral oils are hydrocarbons rather than lipids (*see* OIL).

fatty acid (*or* **carboxylic acid**) An organic acid that comprises one or more carboxyl groups (–COOH) attached to an alkyl group. Fatty acids combine with glycerol to form glycerides, the main constituents of *fats and oils. Animal fats tend to be hard because they contain a high proportion of saturated fatty acids; soft fats, such as vegetable and fish oils, contain greater proportions of unsaturated and polyunsaturated fatty acids (containing one or more double bonds). The risk of heart disease associated with dietary fat is thought to be reduced if the fat consumed is rich in polyunsaturated fatty acids.

fatwa An edict issued by a Muslim religious leader. The most notorious such edict was the *fatwa* issued by Ayatollah *Khomeini in 1989, which demanded the assassination of Salman *Rushdie.

Faulkner, William (1897–1962) US novelist. *Sartoris* (1929) was the first of his stories set in the fictitious Yoknapatawpha County, based on his native northern Mississippi. His major novels include *The Sound and the Fury* (1929) and *Absalom, Absalom!* (1936). He was awarded the Nobel Prize in 1949.

fault A fracture plane in the rocks of the earth's crust, the rocks on each side being displaced relative to one another, either vertically, horizontally, or obliquely. Faulting occurs as a result of accumulated strain in the rocks, usually at plate margins (*see* PLATE TECTONICS). A rift valley is a downward vertical displacement between parallel faults.

Fauré, Gabriel (Urbain) (1845–1924) French composer and organist. His works include the well-known *Requiem* (1886–87), incidental music for Maeterlinck's play *Pelléas and Mélisande* (1898), the opera *Pénélope* (1913), the orchestral *Pavane* (1887), songs, such as those in the cycle *La Bonne Chanson* (1891–92), and much piano music and chamber music.

Faust A legendary medieval German scholar and magician who sold his soul to the Devil in exchange for knowledge and power. He has has inspired numerous literary works, notably by *Marlowe (1592), *Goethe (1808, 1832), and Thomas *Mann (1947), as well as musical works, including operas by *Gounod.

fauvism A movement in French painting at the turn of the 19th century, characterized by the aggressive use of strong colours. Under the leadership of *Matisse, the fauves included *Dufy, *Braque, *Rouault, and Vlaminck.

Fawkes, Guy (1570–1606) English convert to Roman Catholicism, who became involved in the Gunpowder Plot, led by Robert Catesby (1573–1605), to blow up James I and parliament. The conspirators were informed upon and Fawkes was discovered (5 November 1605) with the gunpowder in a cellar of the Palace of Westminister. Catesby was killed resisting arrest and Fawkes was executed. Nov 5 continues to be celebrated with fireworks and the burning on a bonfire of effigies of Fawkes (so-called "guys").

fax (*or* **facsimile transmission**) A method of sending images (text or pictures) through the normal telephone network. The document is scanned optically to break it into a pattern of dots, which are transmitted as electrical pulses. The receiving device reconstructs the image from this information and prints it out.

FBI *See* FEDERAL BUREAU OF INVESTIGATION.

Federal Bureau of Investigation (FBI) The organization within the US Department of Justice that carries out investigations into possible breaches of federal law, especially those related to security. Founded as the Bureau of Investigation in 1908, it became the FBI in 1935; under J. Edgar *Hoover (director 1924–72) it developed considerable autonomy. It campaigned against organized crime in the 1930s and participated in the anticommunist activities of Joseph *McCarthy in the 1950s.

Fédération internationale de Foot-

ball association (**FIFA**) The world governing body of association football, formed in Paris in 1904. Based in Zürich, it has over 140 members. It runs the World Cup competition.

feedback In electronics and communications theory, the process of returning to the input of a device a fraction of the output signal. **Negative feedback**, in which the feedback opposes and therefore reduces the input, is often used in *amplifier circuits. It compensates for noise and distortion in the output signal, although it also reduces the overall amplification. **Positive feedback** reinforces the input signal. If it becomes too high, the circuit oscillates and the output becomes independent of the input.

The principle of negative feedback also operates in biological systems, especially in controlling some biochemical reactions: the product of the reaction inhibits further activity of the enzyme catalysing it.

feldspars The most important group of rock-forming minerals and the major constituents of igneous rocks. There are four components of feldspars: anorthite (calcium plagioclase, $CaAl_2Si_2O_8$); albite (sodium plagioclase, $NaAlSi_3O_8$); orthoclase (potassium feldspar, $KAlSi_3O_8$); and celsian (barium feldspar, $BaAl_2Si_2O_8$).

Fellini, Federico (1920–93) Italian film director. His films, many of which are characterized by autobiographical elements, include *La strada* (1954), *La Dolce Vita* (1960), *8½* (1963), *Amarcord* (1974), *Intervista* (1987), and *The Voice of the Moon* (1990).

fencing The art of combat with a sword, of which there are three main forms in sport: foil, épée, and sabre. Bouts are fought on a *piste*, or marked-out area. The winner is the first to score five hits (for men) or four (for women) in a time limit of six minutes (for men) or five (for women), the form of the hit varying between the three weapons.

feng shui An ancient Chinese art that claims to determine the best location for buildings and their furnishings. Adherence to its principles is claimed to enhance the flow of *ch'i* (positive energy) in an environment.

Fenians Members of a secret Irish-American revolutionary society, the Irish Republican Brotherhood (IRB), formed in 1858 by James Stephens (1825–1901). The IRB's influence continued into the 20th century, when it was superseded by the IRA.

fennel A strong-smelling perennial herb, *Foeniculum vulgare*, native to S Europe and cultivated throughout temperate Eurasia. The feathery dark-green leaves and the greenish seeds (which taste of aniseed) are used to flavour food. Florence, or sweet, fennel (*F. dulce*) is cultivated for its bulblike leafstalks, which may be eaten cooked as a vegetable or raw in salads. Family: *Umbelliferae.*

Fens, the A low-lying highly fertile area in E England, W and S of the Wash extending across parts of Cambridgeshire, Lincolnshire, Norfolk, and Suffolk. Once waterlogged, the first drainage attempt was made by the Romans. This was resumed during the 17th century by the Duke of Bedford. The Fens are now virtually all drained.

fenugreek An annual herb, *Trigonella foenum-graecum*, native to the Mediterranean but widely cultivated. The brownish seeds are used to flavour curry and chutney. Family: *Leguminosae.*

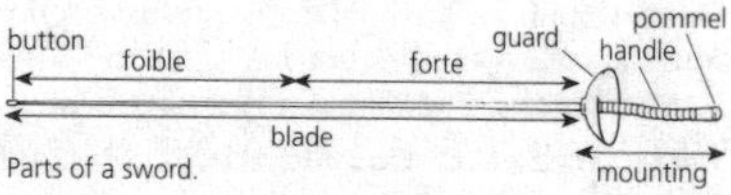

Parts of a sword.

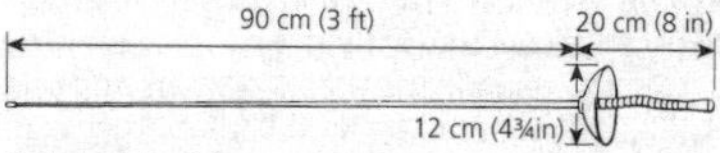

foil. The foil weighs a maximum of 500 g. Its blade is quadrangular and very flexible.

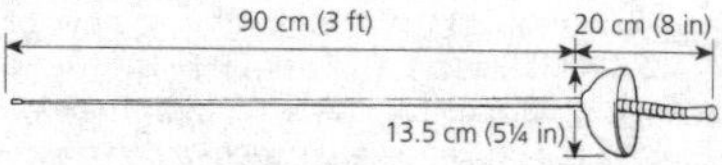

épée. The épée weights a maximum of 770 g. Its blade is triangular and stiffer than that of the foil.

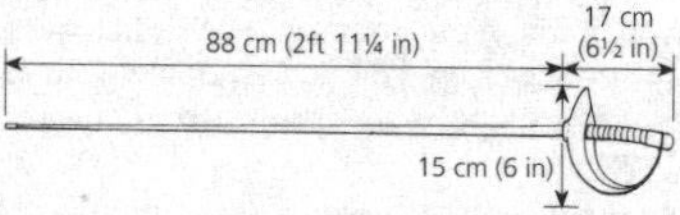

sabre. The sabre weighs a maximum of 500 g. Its blade is a flattened V-shape.

fencing

Ferdinand (V and II) the Catholic (1452–1516) King of Castile as Ferdinand V (1474–1504) and of Aragon as Ferdinand II (1479–1516). He ruled Castile jointly with his wife *Isabella (I) the Catholic of Castile and after her death was regent for their daughter, Joanna the Mad. Ferdinand's accession to the

Aragonese throne effected the union of Castile and Aragon, to which Granada, taken from the Moors in 1492, was added. The introduction of the Inquisition (1480) and the expulsion of the Jews (1492) aimed to strengthen both church and monarchy.

Fermanagh A county and district of SW Northern Ireland (the new administrative district created in 1973 has the same boundaries as the historic county). It contains Upper and Lower Lough Erne. Fermanagh is mainly agricultural; traditional manufactures include cotton and tweeds. Area (including loughs): 1851 sq km (715 sq mi). Population (2001): 57 527.

Fermat, Pierre de (1601–65) French mathematician who founded *number theory and, with Blaise *Pascal, *probability theory.

fermentation The process by which microorganisms and tissues respire in the absence of oxygen (i.e. anaerobically). It can cause the decomposition of organic materials. The fermentation of carbohydrates by yeasts to form alcohol is the basis of making wines and beers and the production of industrial alcohol. Other types of fermentation produce lactic acid, as in the souring of milk by bacteria.

Fermi, Enrico (1901–54) US physicist, born in Italy. His early work in Italy was concerned with the mathematical statistics of nuclear particles. For his work on the bombardment of uranium by thermal neutrons he was awarded the 1938 Nobel Prize. He moved in 1938 to the USA. He achieved the first controlled nuclear chain reaction and later played a central role in the development of the atom bomb at Los Alamos. He bitterly opposed *Teller in the development of the hydrogen bomb.

fermium (Fm) An artificial transuranic element, named after Fermi and found in debris from the 1952 hydrogen-bomb explosion. The most stable isotope, ^{257}Fm, the most stable isotope, has a half-life of 100.5 days. At no 100; at wt (257).

fern A perennial spore-producing vascular plant of the phylum *Filicinophyta* (or *Pterophyta* according to some classification schemes; about 9000–15 000 species), most abundant in tropical regions but widely distributed elsewhere. The life cycle shows *alternation of generations. The fern plant itself is the asexual (sporophyte) generation, which has a creeping underground stem (rhizome) bearing roots and aerial fronds, which reach a height of 25 m in the *tree ferns. The fronds are feather-like and usually divided into leaflets. Asexual spores are produced in capsules, which usually occur in clusters on the underside of the leaflets. The spores develop into the inconspicuous sexual (gametophyte) generation—a tiny heart-shaped plant (called a prothallus) producing egg and sperm cells. The fertilized egg cell develops into a new sporophyte plant, which grows up from the prothallus.

ferret A domesticated form of *polecat, *Mustela putorius*, that is slightly smaller than the European polecat and lighter in colour (sometimes albino). They are used to drive rats and rabbits from their burrows.

ferrimagnetism A form of magnetism occurring in certain antiferromagnetic materials. The behaviour is weakly ferromagnetic below the Néel temperature and paramagnetic above it.

ferrite 1. A compound of iron with the general chemical formula MFe_2O_4, where M is a metal. Most ferrites are ferromagnetic or ferrimagnetic ceramic materials and they are used in transformers and computer memories. **2.** Iron in its body-centred cubic crystal structure, either pure or as a constituent of *steel.

ferromagnetism The property of a material that enables it to become a permanent magnet, i.e. ferromagnetic materials when placed in a *magnetic field develop a very strong internal field and retain some of it when the external field is removed. The most common ferromagnetic substances are iron, cobalt, nickel, and alloys of these metals. Ferromagnetism, like *paramagnetism, is caused by the unbalanced spin of atomic electrons, which produces the effect of a tiny magnet. In ferromagnetic substances, the application of an external field causes groups of these tiny magnets, called domains, to become aligned. Above a certain temperature, the Curie point, thermal agitation destroys the domain structure and the substance becomes paramagnetic.

Fertile Crescent A strip of land in the Middle East roughly comprising the lower Nile Valley, the E Mediterranean coast, Syria, and *Mesopotamia. Formerly enjoying a wetter climate, it was the cradle of civilization, with sites showing evidence of settled communities from at least 9000 BC.

fertility drugs Drugs given to infertile women to stimulate the release of an egg cell from the ovary. The best known are the gonadotrophins—hormones normally released by the pituitary gland to control activity of the ovary.

f

fertilization The union of a male and a female *gamete, involving the fusion of hereditary material. The resulting cell, which is called a zygote, undergoes division (*see* CLEAVAGE), growth, and development to form a new individual, in which half the chromosomes are of paternal origin and half of maternal origin. In **self-fertilization** both gametes are produced by the same individual; in **cross-fertilization** they derive from different individuals. In most aquatic animals the gametes are expelled into the water and fertilization is external; in most terrestrial animals the sperms are introduced into the body of the female, where fertilization takes place.

fertilizers Substances added to soils to maintain or improve soil fertility. Natural farmyard manures have long been used as a source of plant nutrients and humus, which maintains the physical structure of the soil. Other traditional fertilizers have included bone meal, dried blood, and other animal products. Modern artificial fertilizers have provided the means for dramatic increases in crop yields. The major plant nutrients required are nitrogen (chiefly provided as ammonium nitrate derived from fixation of atmospheric nitrogen), phosphate (derived from naturally occurring rock phosphate), and potassium (from mined potash deposits). Artificial fertilizers have been of immense benefit in helping to feed a rapidly expanding human population, although excessive application can lead to pollution of rivers.

Fès (*or* **Fez**; Arabic name: Fas) 34 05N 5 00W A city in N Morocco. In the 14th century the Islamic city reached its peak as a major centre for commerce and learning. It has two mosques; the Qarawiyin Mosque is the oldest in Africa and contains a university (859 AD). Population (1994 est): 263 828.

fescue A *grass of the genus *Festuca* (about 100 species), native to temperate and cold regions of the N hemisphere. It grows in tufts. Meadow fescue (*F. pratensis*) is sown as a pasture grass and used for livestock fodder; sheep's fescue (*F. ovina*) grows on mountains and in dry and exposed soil. Red or creeping fescue (*F. rubra*) is common in grass mixtures for lawns.

fetishism 1. In anthropology, the practice of using charms magically, found among W African tribes and, hence, in the West Indies. Sir Edward Tylor (1832–1917) reserved the term for the idea of spirits embodied in or associated with material objects. **2.** In psychiatry, the abnormal condition in which sexual satisfaction is obtained by handling or otherwise using nongenital objects (fetishes). The fetish may be an article of clothing, rubber objects, leather, etc.

fetus (*or* **foetus**) The developing baby in the womb from the beginning of the ninth week of pregnancy until birth. The fetus is protected by a series of membranes enclosing a fluid (amniotic fluid), which can be extracted and used for diagnostic purposes. The fetus is connected through the *umbilical cord and *placenta to the mother's bloodstream.

feudalism The type of land tenure, characteristic of medieval Europe, in which property was held by a vassal of a lord in return for military service and a pledge of homage. Feudalism originated in the 8th and 9th centuries. It led to a fragmentation of authority, which was reflected in the rapid growth of feudal armies, the development of the castle as an administrative and military centre, and the growth of justice administered by local lords rather than by a central authority. From the 12th century these implications of feudal tenure were challenged by the growing power of Western rulers, especially in England, where it was abolished in 1661. Their governments increasingly depended on a royal bureaucracy and an army of mercenaries rather than the feudal bands. The growth of towns, outside the feudal framework, also contributed to the decline of feudalism.

Feynman, Richard Phillips (1918–88) US physicist, who shared the 1965 Nobel Prize with Julian Schwinger (1918–94) and Shinitiro Tomonaga (1906–79) for their development of quantum electrodynamics.

Fianna Fáil (Irish: Soldiers of Destiny) Irish political party, founded in 1926 by Eamon *De Valera from moderate *Sinn Féin members. The ruling party in the years 1932–48, 1951–54, 1957–73, 1977–81, 1982, 1987–94, and from 1997, its leaders have been De Valera (until 1959), Sean Lemass (until 1966), Jack Lynch (until 1979), Charles *Haughey (until 1992), Albert Reynolds (until 1994), and Bertie Ahern.

fibre (*or* **dietary fibre**) The constituent of the human diet that is not digested. It consists of the cell walls of plants, i.e. cellulose, lignin, hemicellulose, and pectic substances. Significant amounts are present in wholewheat cereals and flour, root vegetables, nuts, and fruit: refined foods, such as sugar, have a low fibre content. Dietary fibre is considered helpful in preventing constipation, diverticular disease, obesity, diabetes mellitus, and colonic cancer.

fibreglass (**glass fibre** *or* **spun glass**) Material made from glass drawn into fine threads. Glass fibre has excellent heat- and fire-resistant properties and is a good electrical insulator. It is spun and woven into curtain material; made into glass wool for heat, electrical, and sound insulation; woven into coarse mats for filters; and used in reinforcing moulded plastics for boats, car bodies, etc.

fibre optics The use of thin flexible glass fibres for transmitting light. Each fibre, which may be used singly or in bunches, has a high refractive index. The light inside the fibre is totally internally reflected and travels through the fibre with little loss of intensity. The fibres are highly polished and coated with a substance of lower refractive index to reduce dispersion further. Glass fibres are used in communications and for examining otherwise inaccessible places, for example in medical diagnosis and in specialized industrial processes.

fiddler crab A small burrowing *crab, 25–30 mm long, belonging to the genus *Uca* (about 65 species). The brightly coloured male has an enlarged claw. Fiddler crabs are found on salt marshes and sandy beaches of tropical and temperate regions.

field In physics, a region of space in which a body possessing certain properties can exert a force on similar bodies, when they are not in contact. For example, a body having mass exerts an attractive force on all other massive bodies as a result of its gravitational field. Similarly, an electrically charged body exerts a force (attractive or repulsive, depending on polarity) on other charged bodies and a magnetized body will have a magnetic field around it. A field is often represented by lines of force to indicate the direction in which the force acts at that point.

Fielding, Henry (1707–54) British novelist and dramatist. He wrote about 25 plays, mostly satirical and topical comedies, between 1728 and 1737. His major novels include *Joseph Andrews* (1742), the ironical *Jonathan Wild* (1743), and *Tom Jones* (1749).

fieldmouse A small nocturnal long-tailed *mouse, *Apodemus sylvaticus*, of Europe, Asia, and N Africa. About 9 cm long, with an 8-cm tail, it has a rich brown coat with white underparts. Fieldmice feed on seeds and grain and can become a pest.

Field of the Cloth of Gold (1520) The meeting near Calais of Henry VIII of England and Francis I of France. Francis hoped for English support against Emperor Charles V, with whom, however, Henry subsequently formed an alliance.

Fields, Gracie (Dame Grace Stansfield; 1898–1979) British popular entertainer. She began her career as a music-hall singer and comedian and made several films during the 1930s. During World War II she gave many concerts for the troops; she later lived in Capri.

FIFA *See* FÉDÉRATION INTERNATIONALE DE FOOTBALL ASSOCIATION.

fife A small transverse *flute, pitched in B flat and used in military fife-and-drum bands.

Fife A council area in E Scotland, bordering on the North Sea, coextensive with the historic county of Fife. It consists of a lowland peninsula located between the Firths of Forth and Tay. Agriculture is most important in the N with industry concentrated in the S. Area: 1323 sq km (511 sq mi). Population (2001): 349 429. Administrative centre: Glenrothes.

fig A spreading tree or shrub, *Ficus carica*, probably native to W Asia but widely cultivated in warm temperate and subtropical regions. The large dark-green leaves are usually deeply lobed. The tiny flowers are borne inside a fleshy pear-shaped structure, which develops into the edible fig after fertilization. Figs are eaten fresh, dried, or preserved. Family: *Moraceae* (mulberry family).

fighting fish One of several labyrinth fishes, especially of the genus *Betta*, found in SE Asia and the Malay Archipelago and named for the aggression shown by the males towards each other and to immature females. The Siamese fighting fish (*B. splendens*) is about 6.5 cm long and greenish or brown in colour.

Fiji, Republic of A country in the S Pacific Ocean. It consists of over 800 islands, only 106 of which are inhabited; the largest are Viti Levu and Vanua Levu. Most of the population are Indians and Fijians with some Europeans, Chinese, and other Pacific islanders. *Economy*: chiefly agricultural, sugar cane being the main cash crop. *History*: discovered by Abel Tasman in 1643, the islands were visited by Capt Cook in 1774 and ceded to Britain in 1874. Fiji became independent within the British Commonwealth in 1970. It left the Commonwealth in 1987, when it declared itself a republic after two military coups led by Maj Gen Sitveni Rabuka; a new constitution was passed guaranteeing native Fijians political dominance over ethnic Indians. Fiji was readmitted to the Commonwealth in 1997, the racial elements in the constitution were revoked, and in 1999 Fiji elected its first ethnic Indian prime minister, Mahenda Chaudry. However, in May 2000 he and his cabinet were taken hostage by native Fijians opposed to multiracial government. The military took control, suspended the 1997 constitution, and installed a new government. This government, led by Laisenia Qarase, was returned to power in elections (August 2001). Official language: English. Currency: Fiji dollar of 100 cents. Area: 18 272 sq km (7055 sq mi). Population (2003 est): 827 000. Capital: Suva.

f

filaria A parasitic *nematode worm, mainly of central Africa, Asia, and the SW Pacific. The species *Wuchereria bancrofti* and *Brugia malayi* cause the disease **filariasis**. The tiny larval worm enters the body in the saliva of a biting mosquito or mite. It then grows up to 8 cm long in lymph and blood vessels, causing swelling and pain (*see* ELEPHANTIASIS).

film A thin flexible strip of cellulose acetate, or similar transparent plastic, coated with a light-sensitive emulsion. A black-and-white photographic emulsion usually consists of gelatin containing tiny suspended crystals of silver halide. After exposure to light in a *camera, these crystals are reduced to metallic silver when treated with the chemicals in the developer, to produce a reversed (or negative) image. In colour photography, the film has three layers of light-sensitive emulsion, one for each of the primary colours. The final image is generally produced using a process of subtractive colour reversal. The sensitivity (speed) of film is quoted as an *ASA rating. *See also* PHOTOGRAPHY.

filter A device that allows one substance to pass through it but not others. For example, a filter is used to remove solid particles from a liquid or gas by passing the mixture through a porous substance, such as paper or *fibreglass, the holes in which are fine enough to prevent the passage of the particles. Such filters are used in some air-conditioning units, for water purification, etc. In optics, coloured glass filters are used to select light with a certain range of wavelengths. In electronics, filters are circuits used to allow alternating currents of a certain frequency range to pass, while currents with frequencies outside the range are stopped.

finch A songbird belonging to a family (*Fringillidae*; 176 species) occurring in most regions of the world except Australia. Finches have hard conical bills used to crack open seeds, although they also feed on buds and fruit. There are two subfamilies: the *Fringillinae*, including the finer-billed *chaffinch and *brambling of the Old World, and the *Carduelinae*, comprising the heavier-billed species found in both the Old World and North America. *Compare* WEAVERFINCH.

Fine Gael (Irish: Tribe of Gaels) Irish political party, formed in 1933. It was the senior member of ruling coalitions in Ireland (1948–51, 1954–57, 1973–77, 1981–Jan 1982, Dec 1982–87, and 1994–97), led successively by John Costello, Liam Cosgrave, Dr Garret *Fitzgerald, and John Bruton. The current leader (from 2001) is Enda Kenny.

fingerprint The impression made by the pattern of ridges on the palmar side of the end joint of the fingers and thumbs. The taking of a person's fingerprints, which are virtually unique, for the purpose of identifying habitual criminals was introduced into the UK in 1901, largely as a result of the work of Sir William Herschel (1833–1917) and Sir Edward Henry (1859–1931). Fingerprints left at the scene of a crime may be taken by photography. Classification relies on a numerical value given to a print, which identifies the finger and the pattern of ridges. *See also* GENETIC FINGERPRINTING.

Finisterre, Cape 42 52N 9 16W The most westerly point in Spain, on the Atlantic coast.

Finland, Republic of (Finnish name: Suomi) A country in N Europe, with S and W coastlines on the Baltic Sea. It includes the Åland Islands, situated at the mouth of the Gulf of Bothnia. The land is generally low lying.

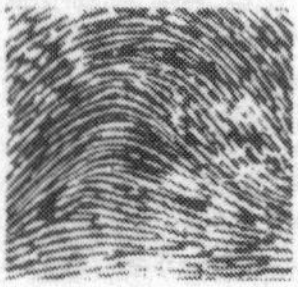
arch

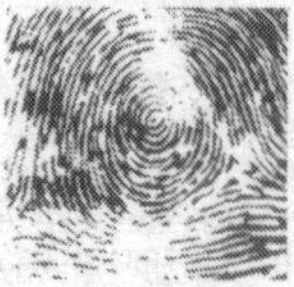
whorl

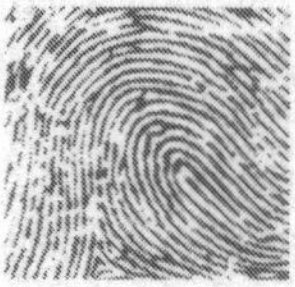
loop

fingerprint. Loops are the commonest form of pattern (c. 65%), followed by whorls (c. 30%), and then arches (c. 5%).

Over 10% of the area consists of lakes, which, together with rivers and canals, provide an extensive network of inland waterways. The majority of the population are Finns, with minorities of Swedes, Lapps, and Russians. *Economy*: agriculture is highly mechanized and, together with cereals, dairy produce is of particular importance. Over 70% of the land is under forest, providing ample resources for the timber and pulp and paper industries. Hydroelectricity provides the main source of power. *History*: prehistorically the Finnic peoples migrated into Finland, gradually driving the Lapps northwards. Conquered by Sweden in the 12th century AD, Finland had a considerable degree of independence, becoming a grand duchy in the 16th century. In the 18th century the SE was occupied by Russia and in 1809 the rest of the country was ceded to Russia, becoming an autonomous grand duchy. It became independent in 1917, following the Russian Revolution, and a republic two years later. In 1939 it was invaded by Soviet forces and in 1940, and again in 1944, was forced to cede certain territories to the Soviet Union. A treaty of friendship between the two countries, first signed in 1948, continued in force until 1991. It was replaced in 1992 by a similar treaty with Russia. Finland became a member of the EU in 1995 and adopted the European single currency in 1999–2002. Paavo Lipponen has led a centre-left government since 1995. Official languages: Finnish and Swedish. Currency: euro of 100 cents. Area: 305 745 sq km (117 913 sq mi). Population (2003 est): 5 212 000. Capital: Helsinki.

Finney, Albert (1936–) British actor. Following his early successful performances in plays by modern dramatists he made several films, notably *Saturday Night and Sunday Morning* (1960), *The Dresser* (1983), and *Erin Brockovich* (2000).

Finno-Ugric languages A large group of languages of the Uralic family, spoken by more than 20 million people in dispersed communities in Scandinavia, E Europe, and W Asia. Thought to have diverged about five millennia ago, the Finnic and Ugric languages can be further divided into Ugric (*Hungarian and Ob-Ugric) and Finnic (Finnish, Estonian, Lapp, Mari, Permic, and a number of other languages).

fins Organs of locomotion and balance in fish and some other aquatic animals. The fins of fish are supported by bony or cartilaginous fin rays and are either median or paired. The median fins include the tail (or caudal) fin, typically used for propulsion (in conjunction with the muscular body) and the dorsal and anal fins, used for balancing. The paired pectoral fins, just behind the gills, and pelvic fins, further back, are used for steering (although in rays the large pectorals provide motive force).

fir A coniferous tree of the genus *Abies* (about 50 species). Mostly native to N temperate regions, these trees are also called silver firs, as many species have leaves with a silvery undersurface. Firs have blunt-tipped needles and erect stout woody cones; they are important softwood trees. The European silver fir (*A. alba*), which forms pure forests in the mountains of central Europe, is widely grown for its timber: it reaches a height of 50 m. Another widely planted timber tree is the grand, or giant, fir (*A. grandis*), which grows up to 90 m in its native W North America. Family: *Pinaceae*.

firefly A nocturnal beetle belonging to a family (*Lampyridae*; 2000 species) common in tropical and temperate regions. Fireflies emit a greenish light—often as short rhythmic flashes—from organs on the abdomen (*see* BIOLUMINESCENCE). Many have conspicuous orange or yellow markings. The wingless females and larvae are called **glowworms**.

Fire of London (2–5 September 1666) The fire that started in a baker's shop in Pudding Lane and destroyed four-fifths of the City. More than 13 000 buildings, including the medieval St Paul's Cathedral, were razed to the ground. Sir Christopher *Wren played a major part in the subsequent rebuilding. The **Monument**, which he designed in 1671, stands close to Pudding Lane to commemorate the Fire.

fireworks Combustible devices, used for signals, flares, and displays. Gunpowder rockets and fire crackers were first used in ancient China for military purposes and celebrations and in Europe from the middle ages. The basic explosive, usually gunpowder, is coloured by the addition of metallic salts: sodium salts for yellow, barium for green, strontium for red, and copper for blue. Metal filings are added for sparks and aniline dyes provide coloured smokes.

firn (*or* **névé**) A stage in the transformation of fresh snow to glacier ice. Compaction and recrystallization of the snow increases its density and it becomes firn at a relative density of 0.5. Under further compaction firn may be transformed to glacier ice, this occurring at a relative density of 0.89–0.90.

Fischer-Tropsch reaction The formation

of light liquid *hydrocarbons by passing a mixture of hydrogen and carbon monoxide over catalysts at around 200°C. The reaction enables synthetic liquid fuels to be produced from coal. It was invented by F. Fischer (1852–1932) and H. Tropsch (1839–1935) in 1925 and was extensively used in Germany during World War II.

fish A cold-blooded aquatic vertebrate belonging to either of the two classes *Chondrichthyes*

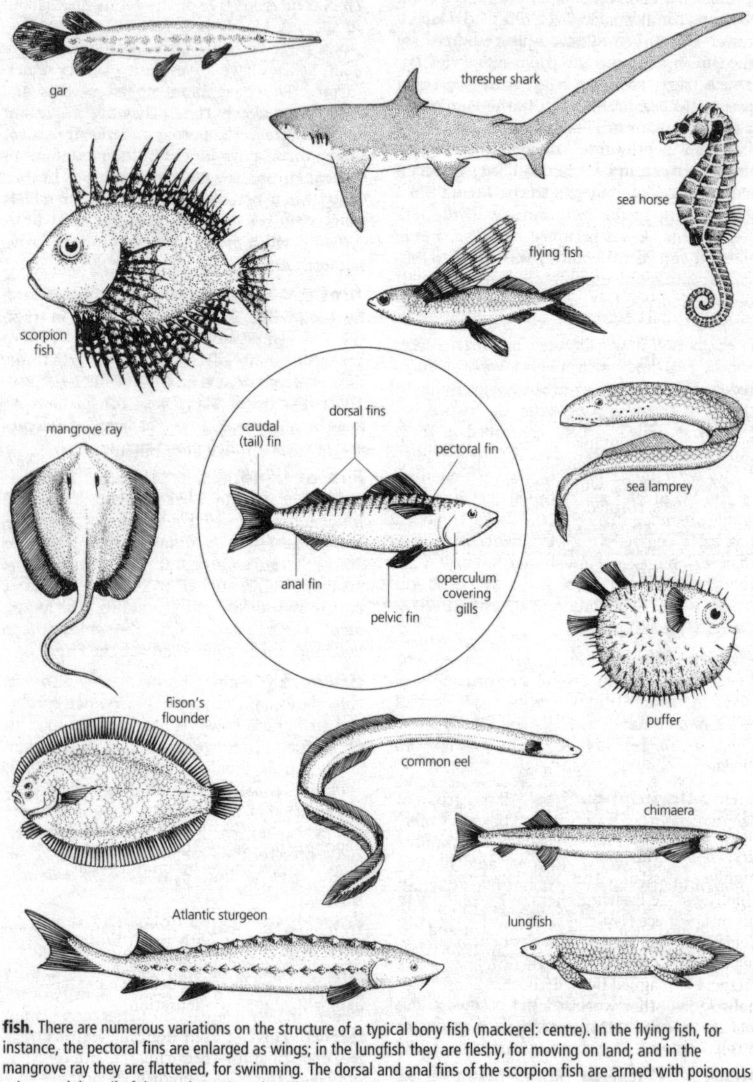

fish. There are numerous variations on the structure of a typical bony fish (mackerel: centre). In the flying fish, for instance, the pectoral fins are enlarged as wings; in the lungfish they are fleshy, for moving on land; and in the mangrove ray they are flattened, for swimming. The dorsal and anal fins of the scorpion fish are armed with poisonous spines and the tail of the sea horse is prehensile.

(*see* CARTILAGINOUS FISH) or *Osteichthyes* (*see* BONY FISH; FLATFISH), which together comprise over 30 000 species occurring worldwide in seas and fresh waters. They have streamlined bodies with a covering of bony scales, a fin-bearing tail, an anal fin, one or more dorsal fins, and paired lateral, pectoral (anterior), and pelvic (ventral) fins, which are used in swimming. Oxygen is obtained from water by means of *gills situated in the wall of the mouth cavity, although a few species can also breathe air (*see* LUNGFISH). The majority of fish are carnivorous, feeding mainly on other fish and invertebrates, although some eat plants. Large numbers of small eggs are laid and are usually fertilized externally.

fish hawk *See* OSPREY.

fission (biology) A form of asexual reproduction in which an individual splits into two (binary fission) or more (multiple fission) equal parts, each part becoming a new individual. It occurs in a variety of plants, bacteria, protozoa, and some multicellular animals (e.g. corals).

fission (physics) *See* NUCLEAR ENERGY.

fission-track dating A method of dating based on the spontaneous nuclear fission of uranium-238 in the sample. The fissions are recorded as tracks, which are then compared to the tracks formed by inducing fission in the uranium-235 present. A comparison of the numbers of tracks is used as a measure of the age of the sample.

Fitzgerald, Edward (1809–83) British poet. His famous *Rubaiyat of Omar Khayyam* (1859) was a free adaptation of the 12th-century Persian original.

Fitzgerald, Ella (1918–96) US Black jazz singer. She performed with such musicians as Duke Ellington and Oscar Peterson, and made many albums, including *Hello Love*, *Duke Ellington's Song Book*, and the *Gershwin Song Books*.

Fitzgerald, F(rancis) Scott (Key) (1896–1940) US novelist. His autobiographical first novel, *This Side of Paradise* (1920), was highly successful. After 1924 Fitzgerald lived chiefly on the French Riviera, where he wrote his masterpiece *The Great Gatsby* (1925). His wife Zelda suffered increasingly from schizophrenia and after 1930 was confined to an asylum. Fitzgerald, plagued by guilt, declined into alcoholism. His other works include *The Beautiful and the Damned* (1922) and *Tender is the Night* (1934).

Fitzgerald, Garret (1926–) Irish statesman; prime minister of Ireland (1981–82; 1982–87). He was leader of the Fine Gael party 1977–87 and negotiated the Anglo-Irish Agreement of 1985.

Fiume *See* RIJEKA.

Five, the A group of 19th-century Russian composers dedicated to the formation of a nationalist musical tradition based on folk music. Led by Mili Balakirev, the other members were *Borodin, César Cui, *Mussorgski, and *Rimsky-Korsakov.

fives A British court game that originated in handball and developed in different forms at three public schools, Eton, Rugby, and Winchester. It is played with gloved hands by two or four players on a three- or four-walled court, each side returning the ball in turn to certain areas of wall.

fjord (*or* **fiord**) A long narrow sea inlet lying between steep mountain slopes, especially in Norway. Usually U-shaped, fjords are glaciated valleys that have been flooded by the sea. Many are extremely deep, but near their mouths they usually have a considerably shallower bar or threshold.

flag A Eurasian iris, *Iris pseudacorus* (yellow flag), growing in marshes and ditches. Up to 1.2 m high, it has yellow flowers and long bladelike leaves. The sweet flag (*Acorus calamus*) is a perennial herbaceous plant native to Asia and North America and naturalized in Britain, growing at the margins of ponds, rivers, etc. About 1 m high, it has wavy-edged leaves, which smell of tangerines when crushed, and the small yellow flowers are tightly packed on a tapering spikelike spadix. Family: *Araceae*.

flagella Long threadlike structures that project from the surface of a cell and produce lashing or undulating movements, used for locomotion or the production of water currents. Flagella occur in certain protozoa, motile gametes (usually sperms), lower plants, and sponges, in which they have a complex internal structure. Bacteria have flagella of a simpler structure. Because of this difference, many biologists prefer the term "undulipodia" for nonbacterial flagella.

flageolet A musical instrument similar to the *recorder but with two thumb holes on the underside and a more complex head fitted with a slender ivory mouthpiece containing a sponge to absorb condensation.

Flamboyant In French gothic architecture, the predominant style during the 15th century. Similar to the earlier English Decorated style, Flamboyant takes its name from its characteristic slender and elaborate curves that wind into flamelike patterns, especially in window tracery. St Maclou, Rouen (begun 1432), is a fine Flamboyant church.

flamboyant tree A tree, *Delonix regia*, also called royal poinciana, flame tree, and peacock flower. It has showy flame-coloured flowers with long protruding stamens. Native to Madagascar, it is widely planted in the tropics for shade and ornament. Family: *Leguminosae*.

f

flamenco A type of Spanish music originating in Andalusia, typically consisting of a song accompanied by dancing, in which the men perform intricate toe and heel tapping steps (*zapateados*) and the women rely on graceful hand and body movements. It was developed by gipsies and shows signs of Moorish influence. Flamenco guitar playing employs a different technique from that of the "classical" guitar, including a percussive effect obtained by tapping the body of the guitar with the fingers.

flame tree One of several unrelated trees with flame-coloured showy flowers. The name is most commonly applied to *Brachychiton acerifolium* (or *Sterculia acerifolia*), a deciduous Australian tree that bears masses of small scarlet bell-like flowers on leafless branches. It may also refer to the *flamboyant tree.

flamingo A wading bird belonging to a family (*Phoenicopteridae*; 4 species) occurring in large flocks on saltwater lakes in warm regions of the world. Flamingos have a long neck, a broad wingspan, and white plumage, tinged with pink. They separate algae, diatoms, small molluscs, etc., from mud using their bills, which are lined with sievelike filters. Order: *Ciconiiformes* (herons, storks, etc.).

Flaminius, Gaius (d. 217 BC) Roman popular leader. An advocate of the plebeians' rights, he often challenged or disregarded senatorial authority. In 220, as consul, he built the Flaminian Way, Rome's road to N Italy. Elected in 217 as leader against *Hannibal, he was defeated and killed at Trasimene.

Flamsteed, John (1646–1719) English astronomer, who established, with the permission of Charles II, a national observatory at Greenwich and was appointed the first astronomer royal in 1675. His star catalogue gave the positions of more than 3000 stars.

Flanders A historic region in Europe, in the SW of the Low Countries. It now comprises the provinces of East Flanders and West Flanders in Belgium and parts of N France and the Netherlands. In the middle ages Flanders formed an autonomous region ruled by the Counts of Flanders and after the 12th century it became a major industrial and commercial centre, its cloth being especially important. The scene of many battles during its history, it saw heavy fighting in both World Wars. *See also* FLEMINGS.

flatfish Any carnivorous *bony fish of the order *Pleuronectiformes* (about 600 species), including many important food fishes, such as *halibut, *plaice, *sole, and *turbot. They have a laterally flattened body fringed with dorsal and anal fins. Both eyes occur on the same side of the head and they lie on their "blind" side, usually on sandy or muddy bottoms of coastal waters; the upper surface is coloured to blend with their surroundings. In the larval stage one eye migrates over the head to lie near the other.

flat racing A form of horse racing in which the horses are not required to jump obstacles. Flat races are usually run over distances between 0.8 km (0.5 mi) and 2.4 km (1.5 mi). Thoroughbred horses are used, mainly as two- and three-year-olds. Weight handicaps are allotted in most races. The most prestigious races are the English *Classics, the US Triple Crown, and the French Prix de l'Arc de Triomphe.

flatworm A flat-bodied wormlike animal of the invertebrate phylum *Platyhelminthes* (9000 species). Some flatworms are free-living (planarians) but the majority are parasitic (*see* FLUKE; TAPEWORM). They range in size from 1 mm to 15 m. Many are hermaphrodite.

Flaubert, Gustave (1821–80) French novelist. His first novel, *Madame Bovary* (1856), was controversially explicit. Other major works include *Salammbô* (1862), *L'Éducation sentimentale* (1870), *La Tentation de Saint Antoine* (1874), and the brilliant short stories in *Trois contes* (1877).

flax A herbaceous plant of the genus *Linum* (230 species), mostly of the N hemisphere. Cultivated flax (*L. usitatissimum*) is an annual with narrow leaves and blue flowers. Its stem fibres are used to make linen, fine writing paper, and cigarette paper. The seeds contain *linseed oil. Flax is cultivated throughout Europe. Family: *Linaceae*.

flea A small wingless insect belonging to the widely distributed order *Siphonaptera* (about 1600 species). Fleas are bloodsucking parasites of birds and mammals. Their legs are modified for jumping. Fleas have irritating bites and act as carriers of some serious diseases. Two important and widely distributed species are the human flea (*Pulex irritans*) and the oriental rat flea (*Xenopsylla cheopis*), which transmits bubonic plague and typhus to man.

Flémalle, Master of (c. 1378–1444) One of the founders (with the *van Eyck brothers) of the Flemish school of painting. He is usually identified as Robert Campin. His works display the careful realistic rendering of details from everyday life that characterizes the Flemish school as a whole.

Fleming, Sir Alexander (1881–1955) British microbiologist, who discovered the antibiotic *penicillin. In 1928 Fleming noticed that a mould contaminating a bacterial culture had destroyed the bacteria in its vicinity. He identified the mould but could not isolate or identify the antibiotic. This was later achieved by Lord *Florey and Sir Ernst *Chain, with whom Fleming shared the 1945 Nobel Prize.

Fleming, Ian (Lancaster) (1908–64) British author and journalist, famous for his creation of the archetypal secret agent, James Bond, in 12 novels and 7 short stories, most of them filmed.

Fleming, Sir John Ambrose (1849–1945) British electrical engineer, who constructed the first rectifying diode (*see* THERMIONIC VALVE) in 1904. His invention greatly stimulated the development of radio and led to the invention of the triode two years later by Lee De Forest (1873–1961).

Flemings Inhabitants of N and W Belgium (*Flanders) who speak Flemish, a dialect of *Dutch known by them as Vlaams. They number approximately 5 500 000. Like the Dutch they are descended from the Salic Franks, a Germanic people, who settled the area during the 3rd and 4th centuries AD. They retain a cultural identity distinct from that of French-speaking Belgians (*see* WALLOONS).

flight recorder A strong box containing a multitrack tape record of an aircraft's flight parameters (instrument readings, position of control surfaces, etc.) and the voices of the pilot and crew. Recordings are made every second. If found after a crash it can provide information as to its cause.

flint A variety of *chalcedony. It is grey to black, is dense and tough, and breaks with a conchoidal (curved) fracture, leaving sharp edges (hence its use by Stone Age man for tools and weapons). It occurs in nodules in chalk along the bedding planes and as pebbles in river gravels and beach material.

flint glass A durable, brilliant, and highly refractive glass. Also known as lead glass and crystal glass, it is used in high-quality glassware and also in lenses and prisms since it absorbs very little light.

Flintshire A county in NE Wales, on the Dee estuary and the Irish Sea. In 1974 it became part of Clwyd; it was reinstated as a county (with different borders) in 1996. The Deeside region is heavily industrialized, while the S and W are agricultural. Area: 437 sq km (169 sq mi). Population (2001): 148 565. Administrative centre: Mold.

f

Flodden, Battle of (9 September 1513) The battle in which the English under Thomas Howard, Earl of Surrey (1443–1524), defeated the Scots under *James IV at Flodden Edge, Northumberland. The Scots had invaded England after allying with France against Henry VIII.

Florence (Italian name: Firenze) 43 47N 11 15E A city in Italy, the capital of Tuscany on the River Arno. The principal industry is tourism. Its many famous buildings include the 13th-century cathedral of Sta Maria del Fiore, the campanile of Giotto, the baptistery, and many churches (including Sta Maria Novella and Sta Croce). The Ponte Vecchio (1345) across the River Arno connects the *Uffizi gallery to the Palazzo Pitti (now an art gallery). Art treasures in Florence include works by Michelangelo, Donatello, Masaccio, Giotto, Fra Angelico, Botticelli, Raphael, Titian, and Rubens. *History*: an early Roman colony, it had developed into an important centre of trade and industry by the 12th century. It was torn by the struggles between the *Guelfs and Ghibellines (13th and 14th centuries) but flourished financially and culturally (14th–16th centuries). The rule of the *Medici family began in 1434 and continued almost uninterrupted for three centuries. Following a period of Austrian rule, Florence became part of the new kingdom of Italy in 1861 and was the provisional capital (1865–71). Population (2000 est): 376 682.

Florey, Howard Walter, Baron (1898–1968) Australian pathologist, who, working with Sir Ernst *Chain, isolated and purified the antibiotic *penicillin, first discovered by Sir Alexander *Fleming in 1928. Florey and Chain developed techniques for producing the pure drug in large quantities. In 1941 they conducted the first clinical trials, in which penicillin proved very effective in combating bacterial infections. Florey shared the 1945 Nobel Prize with Chain and Fleming.

Florida A state in the far SE of the USA, between the Atlantic Ocean and the Gulf of Mexico. It is a low-lying peninsula with many lakes and rivers. Tourism, based on its subtropical climate, is the most important industry, with many popular resorts, such as Miami Beach and Palm Beach. The John F. Kennedy Space Center is at Cape Canaveral. Florida produces some 75% of the USA's citrus fruits, as well as large quantities of vegetables. *History*: following its exploration by the Spanish, it was ceded to the British in 1763 but returned to Spain after the American Revolution. It passed to the USA in 1819, becoming a state in 1845. It was a supporter of the Confederate cause during the US Civil War. The **Florida Keys** are a chain of small islands, separated from the S coast of Florida by Florida Bay. They include the islands of Key West and Key Largo and extend for over 160 km (100 mi). The islands are linked by the Overseas Highway, a complex of roads and 42 bridges. Mainland area: 151 670 sq km (58 560 sq mi). Population (2000): 15 982 378. Capital: Tallahassee.

flotsam, jetsam, and lagan Goods cast into the sea that respectively remain afloat, sink, or would sink but have attached to them a buoy, which keeps them afloat. Unless claimed by the owner, they belong to the Crown.

flounder A common name for any *flatfish or for certain species. An example is *Platichthys flesus*, which lives in European coastal and fresh waters. It has a greenish or brownish mottled upper surface and is an important food and game fish.

flour The powdered grain of wheat or other cereals, used in baking, chiefly bread. When the two proteins in wheat, glutenin and gliadin, are mixed with water they form gluten, which permits the dough to expand and retain the carbon dioxide resulting from fermentation of the yeast in bread dough. The principal commercial flours are whole wheat (100%), wholemeal and stoneground (92%), wheatmeal (80–90%), and white flours (70–72%). Whole wheat and wholemeal flour retain more of the bran (the outer skin of the wheat grain) and have more iron and calcium than white flour, and so are favoured by nutritionists. They are also a good source of dietary *fibre. Flour with a high gluten content (strong flour) is best when yeast is called for, as in dough for bread. A softer flour with a lower gluten content (fine flour) is used for cakes, shortbread, etc. Plain flour is an all-purpose flour, with a moderate gluten content. Self-raising flour is plain flour with the addition of raising agents.

flower The reproductive organ of flowering plants (angiosperms), which is essential for the production of seeds and fruits. It is made up of the perianth (petals and sepals) and the sexual organs—the *stamens producing pollen (male gametes) and the *carpels containing the female gametes. The petals and sepals serve to protect the sexual organs and—in flowers pollinated by animals—are brightly coloured, scented, and secrete *nectar to attract insects and birds. Wind-pollinated flowers are typically small and inconspicuous and may lack a perianth.

flowering currant An ornamental garden shrub, *Ribes sanguineum*, native to North America. Its drooping spikes of pink tubular flowers appear before the maple-shaped leaves. The fruit is a blue-black berry. The shrub has an odour of blackcurrants. Family: *Grossulariaceae* (*see* CURRANT).

flowering rush A perennial freshwater plant, *Butomus umbellatus*, native to Eurasia but common throughout N temperate regions: it is a popular garden plant. It has long tapering leaves and an umbrella-shaped cluster of pinkish flowers at the tip of a long stalk. Family: *Butomaceae*.

fluidics The use of jets of fluid in a circuit to carry out electronic functions. Fluidic circuits can resist much higher temperatures than electronic circuits and are also unaffected by ionizing radiation and magnetic fields. They therefore have uses in nuclear reactors and spacecraft. They are also used as delay lines since they respond much more slowly than electronic circuits.

fluidization The process of supporting very fine solid particles in a stream of gas so that the combination of solid and fluid behaves like a liquid. The process is used, for example, in transporting coal dust.

fluid mechanics The study of the mechanical properties of fluids. Hydrostatics is concerned with the study of fluids at rest and hydrodynamics (*or* fluid dynamics) with fluids that are flowing. Hydraulics deals with the practical applications of these sciences. Two important aspects of hydrodynamics are the conservation of energy in fluid flow and the distinction between streamline and turbulent flow. *See also* AERODYNAMICS.

fluke A parasitic *flatworm of the class *Trematoda* (over 6000 species). Typically leaf-shaped, some are elongated to fit the body cavities they inhabit. Monogenetic flukes have a single host and are generally external parasites of fishes; the digenetic flukes have life cycles involving up to four different hosts and are mainly internal parasites of vertebrates, passing early larval stages in various invertebrates.

fluorescence *See* LUMINESCENCE.

fluorescent lamp A lamp that uses fluorescence (*see* LUMINESCENCE) as its source of light. It consists of a glass tube containing a low pressure gas, such as mercury vapour. As a current passes through the gas, collisions between the electrons and atoms of the gas excite the atoms, which emit *ultraviolet radiation when they return to the ground state. The radiation strikes a phosphor coating on the inner surface of the tube, causing the phosphor to fluoresce emitting visible light.

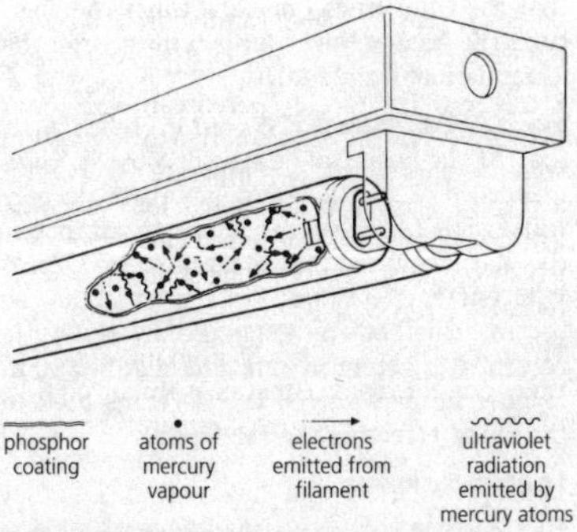

fluorescent lamp. Electrons from the filament collide with atoms of mercury vapour in the tube producing ultraviolet radiation. This is converted to visible light by the fluorescent coating on the tube.

fluoridation The addition of fluoride (usually sodium fluoride) to drinking water to reduce dental *caries (tooth decay), especially in children. The fluoride combines with apatite—the chief constituent of tooth enamel—to form fluoroapatite, which has a greater resistance to bacterial decay. The recommended level is one part of fluoride per million. In the UK the decision to implement this recommendation rests with local authorities.

fluorine (F) A highly reactive pale-yellow halogen gas, the most electronegative element known. It was first isolated by H. Moissan in 1886 and occurs naturally in volcanic gases and as *fluorite (CaF_2) and cryolite (Na_3AlF_6). It is prepared by electrolysis of potassium hydrogen fluoride (KHF_2) solution in dry hydrofluoric acid (HF). The gas uranium hexafluoride (UF_6) allows separation of the fissile ^{235}U isotope from ^{238}U by gaseous diffusion. Hydrofluoric acid is used to etch glass. Fluorocarbons are chemically unreactive and have many important uses. *See also* FLUORIDATION. At no 9; at wt 18.9984; mp −219.62°C; bp −188.14°C.

fluorite (*or* **fluorspar**) A mineral consisting of calcium fluoride. It occurs in hydrothermal veins, often in ore deposits, and in some igneous rocks. Most fluorite is used as a flux in iron and steel making; it is also used as a source of fluorine. Blue John is a deep blue or purple variety used for ornamental purposes.

fluorocarbons Synthetic compounds of carbon and fluorine (sometimes also containing atoms of other halogens). They are extremely resistant to chemical attack, even at very high temperatures, and are nontoxic and nonflammable. They are used as refrigerants, anaesthetics, heat-transfer agents, and high-temperature lubricants. The fluoroanalogue of polythene, polytetrafluoroethylene (Teflon), is a useful plastic in corrosive environments and has a very low coefficient of friction. Its stability at high temperatures enables it to be used for nonstick coatings in cooking utensils. **Chlorofluorocarbons** (CFCs), containing both fluorine and chlorine, were formerly much used as propellants for aerosols, although their use is now limited on environmental grounds as photochemical reactions in the upper atmosphere may lead to depletion of the *ozone layer.

flute A woodwind instrument of ancient origin, existing in many different cultures. The modern side-blown flute (in which a column of air is made to vibrate by blowing across an elliptical mouth hole) and the *recorder are members of the same family. Originally made of wood, most flutes are now metal. The modern orchestral flute is about 0.6 m (2 ft) long and has a range of three octaves above middle C.

flux 1. The net amount of a directional quantity passing through a surface area at right angles to the surface. The concept of flux is used to describe phenomena that involve forces or the flow of energy, such as electric flux, magnetic flux, and luminous flux. **2.** A substance used in brazing and soldering to aid the formation of the joint. It lowers the melting point of the solder and also removes oxides from the metal surfaces allowing the solder to unite with a clean metal surface.

fly An insect belonging to the order *Diptera*

(over 85 000 species)—the so-called true, or two-winged, flies—of great economic importance in transmitting disease. The adults have only two wings (the front pair), the hind pair being reduced to balancing organs. The mouthparts are adapted for piercing or sucking, and most species feed on plant juices or suck the blood of mammals. The larvae—often called maggots—are typically scavengers on plant and animal refuse. Bloodsucking species, such as mosquitoes and tsetse flies, may transmit such diseases as malaria, sleeping sickness, and yellow fever. The order also includes the *houseflies, *blowflies, *craneflies, and *horse flies.

Various flying insects of other orders are also called flies, e.g. the alderfly, firefly, and mayfly.

fly agaric A poisonous mushroom, *Amanita muscaria*, found in woodlands, especially of birch and conifers. Its cap is scarlet or orange-red with white scales and the white stalk has a membranous collar beneath the cap. Fly agaric is seldom fatal.

flycatcher A small active songbird belonging to an Old World family (*Muscicapidae*; 378 species) and feeding on insects, typically caught in flight. They have delicate legs used only for perching. The typical flycatchers are dull coloured and include the grey-and-brown European spotted flycatcher (*Muscicapa striata*) and the black-and-white pied flycatcher (*Ficedula hypoleuca*). The tropical blue flycatchers and paradise flycatchers are beautifully coloured and ornamented. *Compare* TYRANT FLYCATCHER.

flying fish A fish of the family *Exocoetidae* (about 40 species). Flying fish swim just below the surface in warm oceanic waters. If disturbed they launch themselves from the water by rapidly beating the tail and glide through the air using large winglike pectoral fins.

flying fox A fruit *bat belonging to the genus *Pteropus* (51 species), ranging from Africa to Australia. Flying foxes have foxlike heads and a wingspan of up to 1.5 m.

flying lemur *See* COLUGO.

flying lizard A lizard belonging to the genus *Draco* (15 species) of SE Asia, having large folds of skin between the legs supported by ribs that are spread out when the lizard jumps from a tree. They have greenish bodies and brightly coloured "wings." Family: *Agamidae* (agamas).

flying snake A slender diurnal arboreal snake belonging to the genus *Chrysopelea* (3 species), occurring in S Asia and the East Indies. They can glide short distances by launching themselves in the air and flattening their belly scales. Family: *Colubridae*.

flying squirrel A nocturnal *squirrel of the subfamily *Petauristinae* (37 species), occurring in SE Asia, North America, and Eurasia. Flying squirrels have a flap of loose skin from elbow to knee that is stretched tight by extending the legs, enabling them to glide from branch to branch.

Flynn, Errol (1909–59) Australian actor. He played the handsome adventurous hero in such Hollywood films as *Captain Blood* (1935), *Gentleman Jim* (1942), and (as John Barrymore) *Too Much Too Soon* (1958). His private life was candidly recounted in two autobiographies.

f-number The ratio of the focal length of a camera lens to the diameter of the shutter opening (aperture). For example, f-8 means that the focal length is eight times the aperture. The smaller the f-number, the greater the illumination of the film.

Foch, Ferdinand (1851–1929) French marshal. At the outbreak of World War I he commanded the Ninth Army and was largely responsible for halting the German advance at the Marne and for the Allied victory at Ypres (1915). After the Somme offensive (1916), he became chief of the general staff (1917). He returned to action in 1918 and as Allied commander in chief forced the Germans back to the Rhine, effecting their defeat.

foetus *See* FETUS.

fog A cloud near the ground surface, within which visibility is reduced to less than 1 km (0.6 mi). Fog is the result of the condensation of water vapour on tiny particles in the lower layers of air, usually through the cooling of air to below its *dew point; it is most likely to occur with light wind conditions and a clear sky at night. There is a greater incidence in industrial areas.

föhn A warm dry wind that descends down the leeward side of mountains. It is a frequent occurrence in the Alps (where the name originated), the Rocky Mountains (where it is known as the **chinook**), and the Andes. In winter it can cause extremely rapid thaws of lying snow, resulting in avalanches.

Fokine, Michel (Mikhail F.; 1880–1942) Russian ballet dancer and choreographer. From 1909 he worked with Diaghilev's Ballets Russes in Paris, for which he choreographed such revolutionary ballets as *The Firebird* (1910) and

Petrushka (1911). He became a naturalized US citizen in 1932.

fold A buckling of sedimentary rock strata produced by compressional forces acting on it. Large-scale folding produces mountain ranges; this occurs where two continental plates collide (*see* PLATE TECTONICS) and the sediment along their margins is compressed and folded. A simple upfold is called an *anticline and a downfold, a *syncline; however, most folds are much more complex.

folic acid *See* VITAMIN B COMPLEX.

Folies-Bergère A Parisian variety theatre opened in 1869 and celebrated chiefly for its elaborate revues featuring dancing girls and striptease acts.

folk dance A form of dance developed by country people, usually for their own amusement. Folk dances derive from ancient ritual dances used in religious worship and to invoke the fertility of the land (the original purpose of the maypole dance). They have greatly influenced other forms of dances, notably court dancing, 18th- and 19th-century ballroom dances (such as the waltz and polka), and *ballet. In England the most popular types are country dancing and the Morris dance.

Folkestone 51 5N 1 11E A resort and port in SE England, in Kent. The English terminal of the *Channel tunnel is here. Population (1991): 45 587.

folk music Song or dance music developed from a communal aural tradition, e.g. Irish ballads and cowboy songs. The melody and words of folksongs are often changed by a succession of performances. Folk music is characterized by modal melody and simple forms, such as dances, lullabies, work songs, and love ballads.

Fonda, Henry (1905–82) US film actor and director, associated particularly with the portrayal of men of solid integrity, notably in *The Grapes of Wrath* (1940). Other films include *War and Peace* (1956), *Twelve Angry Men* (1957), which he directed, and *On Golden Pond* (1981), which earned him his first Oscar and also starred his daughter **Jane Fonda** (1937–). Her other films include *Klute* (1971), *Julia* (1977), and *Old Gringo* (1989). His son **Peter Fonda** (1939–) and granddaughter **Bridget Fonda** (1964–) are also film actors.

Fontainebleau 48 24N 2 42E A town in N central France, in the Seine-et-Marne department. The surrounding forest inspired the Barbizon school of painters. The 16th century Royal Palace was largely built by Francis I. Fontainebleau was the headquarters of NATO from 1954 to 1966. Population (latest est): 18 753.

Fonteyn, Dame Margot (Margaret Hookham; 1919–91) British ballet dancer. She was a member of the Sadler's Wells company and the Royal Ballet from 1934 to 1959 and often performed in partnership with Rudolf *Nureyev.

food additives Substances added to food to alter its taste, texture, appearance, keeping qualities, or other properties. Although additives play a vital role in food preservation, consumer resistance to them has grown following recent reports of their toxic, carcinogenic, or allergic effects. In the UK prepacked and processed foods must list their ingredients, including any additives. About 280 of these currently have an **E number**, meaning that they have been approved for use in the EU. Additives without an E number must be listed by name.

Food and Agriculture Organization (**FAO**) A specialized agency of the *United Nations constituted in 1945 to coordinate international efforts to raise levels of nutrition and food production and to improve the management of forests. The headquarters are in Rome.

food chain A series of living organisms associated in a feeding relationship: each animal feeds on the one below it in the series. Most commonly, green plants are at the base of a food chain. They are eaten by herbivores, which in turn may be consumed by carnivores. Parasites are also part of the chain, and different food chains are often interconnected to form a **food web**. Other food chains are based on decomposers—organisms that feed on dead organic remains. See illustration on p. 338.

fool's gold *See* PYRITE.

foot-and-mouth disease An infectious virus disease affecting cattle, sheep, goats, pigs, and many wild animals. Typically it causes fever and blisters in the mouth and feet, with consequent reluctance to feed, listlessness, and lameness. The virus can be transmitted to other animals by direct contact or indirectly by infected dung, etc.; it can also be carried by contaminated vehicles, people, and wild animals. The disease is currently endemic in N South America, central Africa, the Middle East, and S Asia. It also occurs sporadically in China and NW Africa. In Europe it was eradicated by a programme of compulsory mass vaccination of cattle during the 1950s and 1960s, combined with 'stamping out' of any subsequent disease by slaughter of infected animals. However, the UK suffered a major outbreak in 2001, when over 5.6 million animals were destroyed.

football A field game played throughout the world, the object of which is to score goals with an inflated ball. The modern games evolved during the 19th century.

American football is played with an oval ball on a field marked out as a gridiron. There are 22 players on the field at any one time, but groups of differently specialized players are used in different phases of the game. After kick off, the game progresses in downs, or periods when the offensive team is advancing the ball towards the goal by passing or running with it. The team has four downs in which to advance the ball 10 yd (9 m). If it fails, the other team is given possession, having the chance to substitute offensive for defensive players. If the 10 yd is covered, the team maintains possession of the ball. A touchdown, in which the ball is taken across the opponents' goal line, scores six points; a conversion after a touchdown, in which the ball is taken over the goal line again from scrimmage or is kicked between the goalposts scores respectively two points or one point; a field goal (kicked from anywhere on the field) scores three points. Players must wear protective clothing.

Association football (*or* soccer) dates back to the founding in England of the Football Association (1863). It is an 11-a-side game played with a spherical ball weighing 14–16 oz (396–453 g) and having a circumference of 27–28 in (69–71 cm). The traditional positions of the players are: goalkeeper; right and left back; right, centre, and left half-back; outside right, inside right, centre forward, inside left, and outside left. These positions have now become very flexible. The teams toss for the first kick (the kick-off), following which the teams try to kick or head the ball into the opponents' goal. Only the goalkeeper may use his hands, and then only in his penalty area. Played all over the world, the game is governed internationally by the *Fédération internationale de Football association.

Australian Rules is a fast 18-a-side game played with an oval ball measuring 22.75 by 29.5 in (57.2 by 73.6 cm), with which players may run as long as they bounce it every 9 m (10 yd). The ball must be punched instead of thrown. There are four goalposts without crossbars at each end. A goal, kicked between the two inner posts, scores six points; a behind, kicked between an inner and an outer post, scores one point.

Canadian football is similar to American football but is played with 12-a-side teams on a larger field and has slightly different scoring and rules.

Rugby football uses an oval ball that is kicked or passed by hand. The game was first played at Rugby School, England, according to tradition in 1823. In 1871 the Rugby Football Union was formed, but its ban on professionalism led in 1893 to the secession of the Rugby League (then called the Northern Union); there are therefore two types of rugby. Rugby Union

food chain. The feeding relationships between some plants and animals of a meadow habitat are simplified in this food web; in practice many more links and various other organisms are involved.

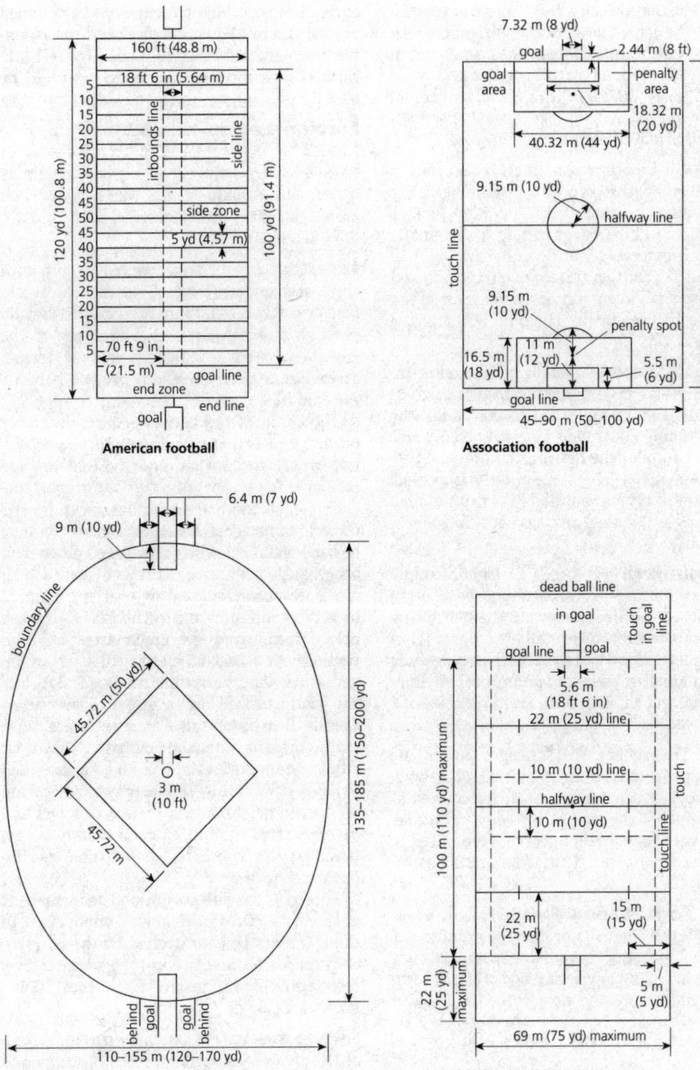

football. Dimensions of pitches.

football (*or* rugger) is a 15-a-side game played throughout the world. The ball is 11–11.25 in (27.9–28.6 cm) long. A try, in which the ball is touched down behind the opponents' goal line, is worth five points; a goal (a try "converted" by kicking the ball over the crossbar of the goalposts), seven points total; a penalty goal, resulting from a kick awarded as a penalty, or a drop goal, from the field, score three points. A scrum, in which the forwards of both teams battle for the ball in a tight mass, is used to restart the game after minor infringements. The ban on professionalism was abandoned in 1995. Rugby League football is a 13-a-side game with slightly different rules and scoring in which professionalism has always been allowed; it is played mainly in N England.

Football League An English association football competition for professional teams. It was created in the N in 1888 to help finance professional clubs by providing a systematic series of matches, The Second Division was added in 1892 with a system of promotion and relegation between the divisions soon after; the Third Division was added in 1920 and the Fourth in 1958.

football pools A system of gambling involving postal betting on the results of football matches. First appearing in the UK in 1923, they are now controlled by a few companies registered under the Betting, Gaming and Lotteries Act (1963). The stake money is pooled, some 30% of which is available as prize money (30% goes in running costs and 40% in government duty).

Foraminifera An order of small single-celled organisms (protozoa) found on the sea bed or as part of the *plankton. They form tiny calcareous often multichambered shells from which they extend fine branching pseudopodia to trap small protozoans and algae. Phylum: *Granuloreticulosa*; kingdom: *Protoctista*. *See also* GLOBIGERINA.

force The agency that changes either the speed or the direction of motion of a body (symbol: *F*). It is a *vector quantity defined as the product of the mass of the body and the acceleration produced on it. Force is measured in newtons. *See also* CENTRIPETAL FORCE; CORIOLIS FORCE.

Ford, Ford Madox (Ford Hermann Hueffer; 1873–1939) British novelist, the grandson of the Pre-Raphaelite artist Ford Madox Brown. Among his many novels and books of criticism and memoirs are the novels *The Good Soldier* (1915) and *Parade's End* (1924–28), a tetralogy. He founded and edited the *English Review* (1908).

Ford, Gerald R(udolph) (1913–) US statesman; Republican president (1974–77) following Nixon's resignation.

Ford, Harrison (1942–) US film actor. His films, mostly adventure fantasies, include *Star Wars* (1977) and its sequels, *Raiders of the Lost Ark* (1981), and *What Lies Beneath* (2000).

Ford, Henry (1863–1947) US car manufacturer. The Ford Motor Company was founded in 1903 and in 1912 Ford introduced the assembly line to manufacture the famous Model T, 15 million of which had been mass-produced by 1928.

Foreign Legion A French military force formed in 1831 to serve in France's African colonies. Its recruits are international but its officers are usually French. The headquarters are at Aubagne, near Marseille, with units in Corsica and Djibouti.

forest An area of land covered largely with trees and undergrowth. Over 20% of world land area is forest, both natural and artificially planted, making forests a vital part of the global ecosystem as major suppliers of oxygen as well as timber. They also provide habitats for wildlife.

The species of trees growing depends mainly on climate. Northern coniferous forests consist largely of pine, spruce, and firs and provide softwood for paper pulp, furniture, construction, etc. In more temperate regions forests consist primarily of mixed deciduous trees, especially oak, ash, elm, beech, sycamore, and other hardwoods, used mainly in furniture. In Mediterranean climates, the trees are adapted to hot dry summers and include the evergreen oaks. Broad-leaved evergreen trees are also found in New Zealand and South America, together with southern conifers. Tropical forests are characterized by a great diversity of species, usually of tall evergreen trees, with many climbing vines and epiphytes. The major tropical rain forests are in the Amazon and Orinoco river basins, with others in Africa and SE Asia. In neighbouring regions of lower and more seasonal rainfall, an open savanna forest predominates, consisting of scattered deciduous trees.

Forestry, the cultivation and management of forests, is of major economic importance. In the UK, forestry is controlled by the Forestry Commission (established in 1919), which is now responsible for the production of most home-grown softwoods.

forget-me-not An annual or perennial herb of the genus *Myosotis* (50 species), of temperate regions. It has long spikes of small flowers, usually blue with white centres. Several species are grown as garden flowers. Family: *Boraginaceae*.

Forman, Miloš (1932–) Czech film director. His earlier films, such as *The Fireman's Ball* (1967), blend humour and social criticism. In 1968 he went to the USA, where he made *One Flew over the Cuckoo's Nest* (1975). More recent films include *Amadeus* (1983), and *The People vs Larry Flint* (1996).

formic acid (*or* **methanoic acid**; HCOOH) A colourless corrosive liquid *fatty acid with a pungent smell. It is used in textile finishing and chemical manufacture. Formic acid occurs naturally in nettles and insects. Its name comes from the Latin *formica*, ant, whose sting is due to the secretion of formic acid.

Forster, E(dward) M(organ) (1879–1970) British novelist. His fiction and social criticism stress the importance of human affection and the need to cultivate both the intellect and the imagination. His novels include *Where Angels Fear to Tread* (1905), *A Room with a View* (1908), *Howards End* (1910), and *A Passage to India* (1924).

Forsythia A genus of shrubs (about 7 species), native to E Europe and Asia and widely grown as garden ornamentals. The masses of four-petalled yellow flowers appear before the leaves. The slender stems make the plants suitable for wall shrubs and hedges. The most common garden forsythia is the hybrid *F.× intermedia*. Family: *Oleaceae* (olive family).

Forth, River A river in SE Scotland, rising on the NE slopes of Ben Lomond and flowing 104 km (65 mi) E through Stirling to Alloa. The river then expands into the **Firth of Forth** (an inlet of the North Sea) extending 82 km (51 mi) in length and 31 km (19 mi) wide at its mouth. It is spanned by the cantilever iron Forth Rail Bridge (designed in the 1880s by Benjamin Baker) and a road bridge (1964).

Fort Knox 37 54N 85 59W A military base in the USA, in N Kentucky. Established in 1917, it is the site of the US Depository, which contains US gold reserves. Population (latest est): 38 277.

Fortuna The Roman goddess of fortune and good luck. She was usually portrayed standing on a ball or wheel, indicating her mutability, and holding a cornucopia from which she distributes her favours. She is identical with Tyche.

Fort Worth 32 45N 97 20W A city in the USA, in NE Texas near Dallas, centre of the N Texas industrial area. Population (2000): 534 694.

forum A Roman marketplace; the forum was the town's civic centre, containing all the main temples and public buildings. *See also* AGORA.

Fosse Way A Roman road from Exeter through Cirencester to Lincoln. It marked the frontier in the first phase of the Roman conquest of Britain (c. 47 AD). Its characteristically straight course is now followed partly by the modern A429.

fossil The remains or traces of a plant or animal that lived in the past, usually preserved in sedimentary rock. It may be the whole or part of the organism itself that is preserved, usually chemically altered; alternatively it may have dissolved away leaving an impression (mould), which preserves its exact shape, or a cast, when it has been replaced exactly by mineral matter. Examples of fossils are whole mammoths preserved in ice, insects preserved in amber, and coal (the carbonized remains of extinct swamp plants). Trace fossils include excrement, burrows, or fossil tracks. The study of fossils is called *palaeontology. See table on p. 342.

fossil fuels The mineral fuels *coal, *oil, and *natural gas that occur in rock formations. They were formed by the deposition millions of years ago of the remains of vegetation (coal) and living organisms (oil and gas), which were buried under subsequent deposition and later subjected to heat and pressure. Fossil fuels supply a large proportion of our current *energy needs, but the reserves are finite (*see also* GREENHOUSE EFFECT).

Foster, Norman, Baron (1935–) British architect. His high-tech designs include Stansted Airport (1991), the Berlin Reichstag (1999), and *City Hall, London (2002).

Fourier, Jean Baptiste Joseph, Baron (1768–1830) French mathematician and physicist, noted for his method of expanding a periodic function in terms of sine and cosine waves, now known as **Fourier analysis**.

Four Noble Truths The fundamental doctrine of Buddhism, set forth by Gautama in the first discourse at Benares. The Truths are: existence is characterized by suffering; the cause of suffering is craving; to end craving is to end suffering; the way to achieve this is the *Eightfold Path.

four o'clock plant A bushy perennial herb, *Mirabilis jalapa*, native to tropical America but widely grown as an ornamental. It bears clusters of red, pink, white, yellow, or streaked flowers, which are tubular with a wide flared mouth and open in the late afternoon. Family: *Nyctaginaceae*.

fowl, domestic A domesticated form of the red *jungle fowl, *Gallus gallus*, native to Asian forests. It was first domesticated about 4000 years ago as a religious and sacrificial animal and was used by the Romans for food. Since the 19th century, a large number of breeds and va-

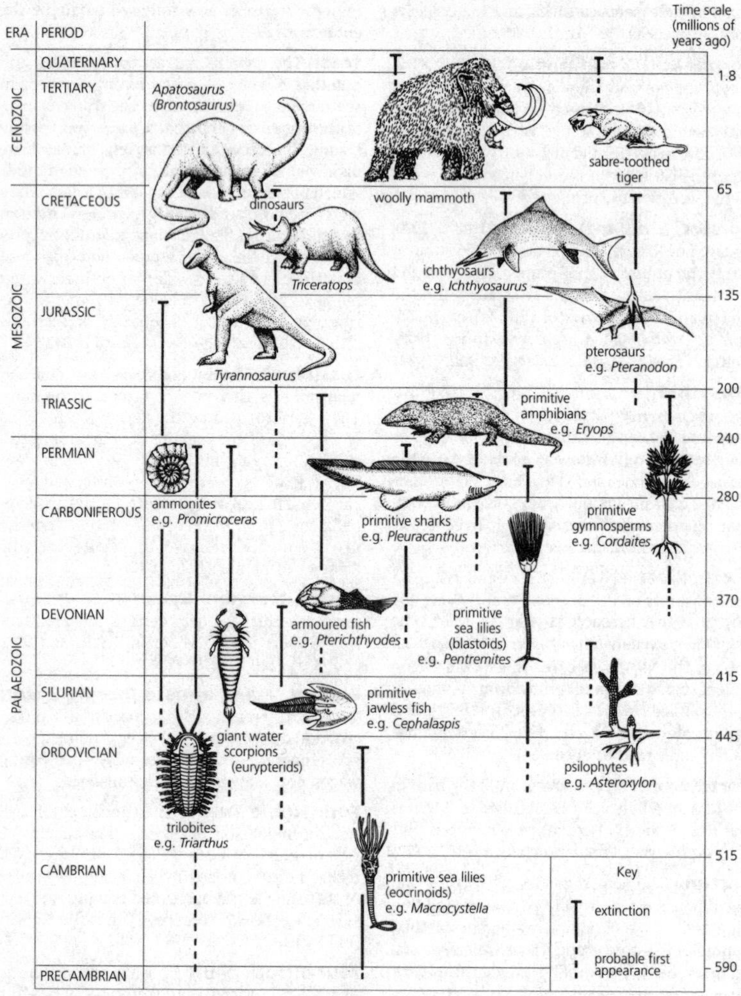

fossil. Some extinct animals and plants from past geological ages.

rieties have been selected for size, resistance to disease, egg production, shell colour, fertility, and food conversion efficiency. *See also* LIVESTOCK FARMING.

Fowles, John (1926–) British novelist, whose works treat philosophical, psychological, and social themes in a rich and often fantastic manner. His novels include *The Collector* (1963), *The Magus* (1966), *The French Lieutenant's Woman* (1969), and *The Maggot* (1985); he has also written the short stories *The Ebony Tower* (1974).

fox A carnivorous mammal belonging to the *dog family (*Canidae*). Foxes have pointed ears, short legs, and large bushy tails. Generally nocturnal, they are solitary stealthy hunters. The most familiar is the red fox (*Vulpes vulpes*), found in forest and woodland and now venturing into suburban gardens (*see* FOXHUNTING).

Some species are specialized for life in difficult habitats, such as the *Arctic fox and the fennec (desert fox). Chief genera: *Vulpes* (9 species), *Dusicyon* (South American foxes; 8 species).

Fox, Charles James (1749–1806) British Whig politician; the first British foreign secretary (1782). He entered parliament (1768) as a supporter of Lord *North but opposed North's American policy. Fox resigned over George III's appointment of the Earl of Shelburne (1737–1805) as prime minister in 1782 and joined North in a coalition that briefly took office under the Duke of Portland (1738–1809) in 1783. He supported the French Revolution, over which many Whigs joined the Tories, and in 1798 he was dismissed from the privy council for opposing war with Revolutionary France.

Fox, George (1624–91) English religious leader, founder of the *Quakers. A Puritan by upbringing, Fox became dissatisfied with established Christianity and the state's control of the church. In 1646 he had a personal revelation and thereafter preached a gospel of love, stressing the immediate guidance of the Holy Spirit. He was frequently imprisoned for his beliefs.

foxglove A herbaceous plant of the genus *Digitalis*, especially *D. purpurea*, a biennial herb native to W Europe but naturalized elsewhere. Foxgloves have large grey-green leaves and tall spikes of drooping bell-shaped flowers, purple, yellow, or white in colour. The dried leaves contain *digitalis. Family: *Scrophulariaceae*.

foxhunting A sport in which huntsmen on horseback pursue a fox with a pack of 20 to 30 specially bred dogs, called **foxhounds**, which hunt by scent. It has been organized in the UK since the 18th century. The hunt officials, who are traditionally dressed in scarlet coats, are the master of foxhounds, who directs the hounds, and one or more whippers-in, who help to control them. Mounted followers (the field) accompany the hunt. Hunting, supported by many country people, also has its detractors (notably the League against Cruel Sports). In 2001 and 2002 the House of Commons voted for an outright ban on hunting with hounds, but the House of Lords has so far blocked the measure. Hunting with hounds is now illegal in Scotland following a vote by the Scottish Parliament (2002).

fox terrier A breed of dog, either smooth-haired or wire-haired, developed in England for hunting foxes and badgers. It is sturdy with a broad tapering muzzle and small drooping ears. The coat is mainly white with black and tan markings. Height: 37–39 cm.

fracture The breaking of a bone. This usually occurs as a result of injury but it may happen very easily in bones diseased with cancer or osteoporosis (pathological fracture). In a simple fracture the ends of the broken bone are not displaced; in a compound fracture the broken bone pierces the skin. Fractures are treated by aligning the ends of the broken bone and immobilizing them. Sometimes, it is necessary to pin fractures surgically.

Fragonard, Jean Honoré (1732–1806) French *rococo painter whose light-hearted and delicately erotic subjects include *The Swing* and *The Progress of Love*. Dutch influence can be seen in a number of his landscapes and portraits.

France, Anatole (Jacques Anatole François Thibault; 1844–1924) French novelist. His intervention in the *Dreyfus case (1897) marked the beginning of his commitment to socialism and, during his final years, communism. In such novels as *L'Île des pingouins* (1909) and *Les Dieux ont soif* (1913) his view of mankind is deeply pessimistic. He was awarded the Nobel Prize in 1921.

France, Republic of A country in W Europe, bordering on the English Channel in the N, the Atlantic Ocean in the W, and the Mediterranean Sea in the S. It includes the island of Corsica and several overseas regions (Martinique, Guadeloupe, and French Guiana). Overseas territories include French Polynesia and New Caledonia. Fertile lowlands cover most of the N and W of France, rising to the Pyrenees in the S, the Massif Central in the SE, and the Vosges, Jura, and Alps in the E. The principal rivers are the Seine, the Loire, and the Rhône. *Economy*: agriculture is important, especially animal products; the wine industry is a major source of revenue. There were large-scale developments in the industrial sector after World War II but economic growth has slowed down in recent decades. *History*: France today approximates to the ancient region of *Gaul, which was conquered by Julius Caesar in the 1st century BC. It became part of the Roman Empire and in the 1st century AD Christianity was introduced to the provinces into which Gaul was divided. From the 3rd to the 5th centuries, it was overrun by German tribes, including the Goths, Vandals, and *Franks (from whom the name France is derived). The Frankish kingdom reached its peak under Charlemagne (reigned 768–814) and his Carolingian dynasty continued to rule in France until 987, when Hugh Capet became the first Capetian king. During the 10th century Norsemen (Vikings) established themselves in what became Normandy and in 1066 invaded England. The claims of English kings to French territory were realized on a large scale by the Angevins and consequent conflict between France and England culminated in the *Hundred Years' War (1337–1453), as a result of which the English were expelled from all of France, except Calais. The Capetians were succeeded by the *Valois dynasty (1328–1589), a period that saw the beginning of France's long rivalry with Spain for hegemony in Europe. During the *Wars of Religion the first *Bourbon, Henry IV, came to the throne (1589). The first half of the 17th century was dominated by Cardinal de *Richelieu and his protégé and successor as chief minister, Cardinal Mazarin (1602–61). They were responsible for France replacing Spain, after the Thirty Years' War, as the supreme European power (1659). During the reign (1643–1715) of *Louis XIV France reached

regions	*area (sq km)*	*population (1999)*	*chief town*
Alsace	8280	1734145	Strasbourg
Aquitaine	41308	2908359	Bordeaux
Auvergne	26013	1173878	Clermont-Ferrand
Basse-Normandie	17589	1422193	Caen
Bourgogne (Burgundy)	31582	1276846	Dijon
Bretagne (Brittany)	27208	2906197	Rennes
Centre	39151	2440329	Orléans
Champagne-Ardenne	25606	1342363	Châlons-sur-Marne
Corse (Corsica)	8680	260196	Ajaccio
Franche-Comté	16202	1117059	Besançon
Haute-Normandie	12317	1780192	Rouen
Île-de-France	12012	9962011	Paris
Languedoc-Roussillon	27376	2295648	Montpellier
Limousin	16942	710939	Limoges
Lorraine	23547	2310376	Metz
Midi-Pyrénées	45348	2558687	Toulouse
Nord-Pas-de-Calais	12414	3996588	Lille
Pays de la Loire	32082	3222061	Nantes
Picardie	19399	1857834	Amiens
Poitou-Charentes	25810	1301407	Poitiers
Provence-Alpes-Côte d'Azur	31400	4476151	Marseille
Rhône-Alpes	43698	5645407	Lyon
Overseas departments	*Chief town*		
Guadeloupe	Basse-Terre		
Guiana	Cayenne		
Martinique	Fort-de-France		
Réunion	Saint-Denis		
Territorial collectivities	*Chief town*		
Mayotte	Dzaoudzi		
St Pierre and Miquelon	St Pierre		
Overseas territories	*Chief town*		
Southern and Antarctic Territories	–		
New Caledonia	Nouméa		
French Polynesia	–		
Wallis and Futuna	Mata-Utu		

Republic of France

the zenith of its power and brilliance. Decline, however, began before his death and gathered speed in the following decades. The disastrous *Seven Years' War forced France to recognize British supremacy in North America and India and the political reaction and economic incompetence of the later Bourbon kings precipitated the *French Revolution in 1789. The First Republic was proclaimed (1792) and Louis XVI was guillotined (1793) in spite of the military opposition of the major European powers (*see* REVOLUTIONARY AND NAPOLEONIC WARS). In 1799 Napoleon Bonaparte overthrew the Directory, becoming first consul and, in 1804, emperor. By 1808 he had brought most of continental Europe under his sway but in 1815 he was finally defeated at Waterloo and exiled. The Bourbons were restored until 1830, when the July Revolution raised Louis Philippe to the throne. Overthrown in the Revolution of 1848, the monarchy was replaced by the Second Republic of which Louis Napoleon became president; in 1852 he proclaimed himself emperor as *Napoleon III. During the Second Empire France underwent the beginnings of industrialization but its prosperity was not sufficient to achieve victory in the *Franco-Prussian War, in which Napoleon's ignominious leadership led to his overthrow (1870). The subsequent Third Republic lasted until 1940, in spite of *World War I and political dissension. After the outbreak of World War II France fell to Germany and a pro-German government was established at Vichy, while *de Gaulle led the Free French resistance in London. In 1944 France was liberated by the Allies and de Gaulle established a provisional government that gave way (1946) to the Fourth Republic. The immediate postwar period was overshadowed by war in Indochina and by the crisis in Algeria that precipitated the fall of the Fourth Republic (1958). De Gaulle was recalled from retirement and, as president of the Fifth Republic, instituted firm government. In May 1968, however, the Republic was shaken by serious revolts among students and a wave of strikes and in 1969 he resigned. Gaullist principles nevertheless continued to influence government under his successors Pompidou and Giscard d'Estaing. Mitterrand's election (1981) made him the first socialist to hold the office of president in 35 years. The 1995 presidential elections showed a swing to the right, with the election of Jacques Chirac. He was re-elected in 2002, with Jean-Marie Le Pen, the candidate of the extreme right, as runner-up. France adopted the single European currency in 1999–2002. Official language: French. Currency: euro of 100 cents. Area: 543 814 sq km (209 912 sq mi). Population (2003 est): 59 773 000. Capital: Paris.

Francis Ferdinand (1863–1914) Archduke of Austria and heir apparent to his uncle, Emperor *Francis Joseph. His assassination (28 June 1914) by a Serbian nationalist at Sarajevo precipitated *World War I.

Francis Joseph (1830–1916) Emperor of Austria (1848–1916) and King of Hungary (1867–1916). His long reign saw the rise of national tensions in the Empire, which led to the establishment of the Dual Monarchy of *Austria-Hungary, under which Austria and Hungary coexisted as equal partners under the Austrian Crown. He was defeated in the Austro-Prussian War of 1866 but in 1879 he allied with the recently formed German Empire and in 1882 with Italy, forming the *Triple Alliance. His ultimatum to Serbia, following the assassination by a Serbian nationalist of his nephew, Archduke *Francis Ferdinand (1914), led to *World War I.

Francis of Assisi, St (Giovanni di Bernardone; c. 1182–1226) Italian friar, born in Assisi. He renounced his worldly life in 1205 to live in poverty and devote himself to charitable works. Gaining followers, he founded his order, the **Franciscans**, in 1209. He travelled throughout Spain, the Holy Land, and Egypt. He received the stigmata in 1224 and was canonized in 1228. Feast day: 4 Oct. The Franciscan order has remained an important missionary and charitable branch of the Roman Catholic Church.

Francis Xavier, St (1506–52) Spanish *Jesuit missionary. While studying in Paris (1523–34) he met St Ignatius of Loyola and helped him found the Jesuit order. From 1541 he established missions in the Indies, India, and Japan. Feast day: 3 Dec.

francium (Fr) The heaviest alkali metal, a very unstable radioactive element discovered in 1939 by Perey. The longest-lived isotope ^{223}Fr has a half-life of 22 minutes; traces of the element exist in nature. At no 87; at wt (223); mp 27°C; bp 677°C.

Franck, César Auguste (1822–90) Belgian composer, organist, and teacher, who settled in Paris in 1834. Franck was influenced by Bach and evolved a highly chromatic form of harmony. He also developed "cyclic form," the use of the same theme in more than one movement of a work. His compositions include *Symphonic Variations* (for piano and orchestra; 1885), a symphony (1886–88), and a string quartet (1889).

Franco, Francisco (1892–1975) Spanish general and statesman; dictator from 1939 until his death. He became chief of the General Staff in 1935 and on 18 July 1936, staged a military uprising against the Republican Government of Manuel Azaña (1880–1940) that precipitated the *Spanish Civil War. In October 1936, he became head of state in the Nationalist Zone and commander in chief of the rebel forces. By 1939, with help from Hitler and Mussolini, he had defeated the Republican forces and become the absolute leader of Spain. Franco's government, in which the National Movement (*see* FALANGE ESPAÑOLA) was the only political party, remained sympathetic to Hitler but stayed neutral throughout World War II. Spain was excluded from the newly formed UN in 1945 but was admitted during the Cold War, when Franco's anticommunism made him a more attractive ally. Although his government achieved considerable economic advance for Spain, he operated a dictatorship that tolerated no opposition.

Franco-Prussian War (1870–71) A war between France and Prussia. Fearing Bismarck's proposals to make a relative of William I of Prussia the king of Spain, France declared war. Napoleon III and his army were soon defeated at the battle of *Sedan but French resistance continued. Napoleon was deposed and the Third Republic was established. The Treaty of Frankfurt imposed a huge indemnity on France, which ceded Alsace and Lorraine to the newly established German Empire; France was left economically weakened and politically divided.

frangipani A tropical American tree, *Plumeria rubra*, cultivated throughout the tropics. It has tapering long-stalked leaves and round clusters of fragrant pink, reddish-purple, white, or yellow flowers, used to make perfume. Family: *Apocynaceae*.

Frank, Anne (1929–45) German Jewish girl, who died in a German concentration camp. Her diary became a symbol of Jewish resistance and courage following its publication in 1947. She wrote it while hiding from the Nazis in Amsterdam in 1942–43. After being betrayed she was sent to Belsen, where she died.

Frankfurt am Main 50 06N 8 41E A city in W Germany, in Hessen on the River Main. A major banking and commercial centre, it is famed for its trade fairs, especially the annual book fair. It was the seat of the imperial elections (9th to 18th centuries) and coronations (1562–1792) of the Holy Roman emperors and the original home of the Rothschilds. Population (1999 est): 644 700.

frankincense (*or* **olibanum**) An aromatic gum resin obtained chiefly from trees of the genus *Boswellia*, especially *B. carteri*, which grows in the Middle East. It smells of balsam when heated, and burns brightly giving off a fragrant odour. Frankincense has been known since ancient Egyptian times and is still used as an *incense, in fumigants, and in perfumes.

Franklin, Benjamin (1706–90) US diplomat, scientist, and author. His experiments with static electricity established the electrical nature of thunderstorms and led him to invent the lightning conductor. In the disputes that led to the American Revolution he represented Pennsylvania's case to Britain (1757–62, 1766–75) and as a member of the Continental Congress helped frame the Declaration of Independence (1775). As a diplomat in Paris (1776–85), he enlisted French help for the colonies and later negotiated peace with Britain (1783).

Franks A Germanic people, who invaded Roman *Gaul from the Rhineland between the 3rd and 5th centuries AD. One of the Frankish tribes, the Salian Franks, gained control of most of Gaul under their ruler Clovis (d. 511) and were converted to Christianity. The Frankish state was ruled by the *Merovingian dynasty (named after Clovis' grandfather, Merovech) until its replacement by the Carolingians (named after *Charlemagne) in 751. The Carolingian empire lasted until its division in 843. The western Frankish kingdom was the nucleus of France.

Franz Josef Land (Russian name: Zemlya Frantsa Iosifa) A Russian archipelago of about 85 icebound islands in the N Barents Sea. They were discovered in 1873 by Austrians and annexed by the Soviet Union in 1926. Total area: about 20 700 sq km (79 905 sq mi).

Fraser River A river in W Canada, the chief river of British Columbia. Rising near Mount Robson, it flows rapidly through mountain gorges and eventually empties into the Strait of Georgia near Vancouver. Length: 1370 km (850 mi).

fraud In law, making a false representation, by words or conduct or by withholding facts where there is a duty to disclose them, in order to obtain a material advantage. To prove fraud it is necessary to show that a false representation was made (1) knowingly, (2) without belief in its truth, or (3) recklessly, without concern whether it was true or not.

Frazer, Sir James George (1854–1941) British anthropologist and writer. Frazer's major work was *The Golden Bough* (first edition 1890). The results of his work were far-reaching, influencing people outside the anthropological field.

Frederick (I) Barbarossa (c. 1123–90) Holy Roman Emperor (1152–90; crowned 1155). He was engaged in a long struggle with the papacy and was excommunicated in 1160. His warring against the Lombard cities was ultimately unsuccessful; they regained their independence in 1183. He failed to subdue his powerful cousin, Henry the Lion (?1129–95), but established his authority in Poland, Hungary, Bohemia, and Burgundy.

Frederick II (1194–1250) Holy Roman Emperor (1220–50) and, as Frederick I, King of Sicily (1198–1250). As leader of the sixth Crusade (1228–29) he captured Jerusalem but remained an opponent of papal policy and was excommunicated three times (1227, 1239, 1245). He was a man of wide learning but neglected the government of his possessions.

Frederick (II) the Great (1712–86) King of Prussia (1740–86), who made Prussia a major European power. He liberalized the Prussian legal code and introduced economic and social reforms that reinvigorated Prussian society and institutions. His conquest of Silesia (1740) gave rise to the War of the *Austrian Succession (1740–48), after which his possession of the region was confirmed. His victory in the *Seven Years' War (1756–63) established the military supremacy of Prussia.

freemasonry A secret society for men, which declares itself to be based on brotherly love, faith, and charity. It probably developed from the medieval stonemasons' guilds. In its modern form freemasonry dates from the establishment (1717) in England of the Grand Lodge, to which some 9250 private lodges are now affiliated. During the 18th century masonry spread to America and the colonies as well as to continental Europe. Its ceremonies, which are allegorical and illustrated by symbols, demand a vow of secrecy as well as a belief in God and are based on Old Testament anecdotes and moralities.

Opposition to masonry orginated with a papal bull (1738) excommunicating masons, since when Roman Catholics have never accepted its principles or its secrecy.

Freesia A genus of ornamental South African plants (20 species), cultivated commercially, especially as a source of cut flowers. Growing from corms, they have sword-shaped leaves and clusters of funnel-shaped lemon-scented flowers of various colours. Most cultivated varieties are hybrids derived from *F. refracta* (with yellowish flowers) and *F. armstrongii* (rose-purple flowers). Family: *Iridaceae*.

Freetown 8 20N 13 05W The capital and main port of Sierra Leone, on the Atlantic coast. It was founded in the late 18th century as a refuge for freed slaves and was capital of British West Africa (1808–74), becoming the capital of Sierra Leone in 1961. Population (1999 est): 822 000.

free will In philosophy and theology, the ability of man to choose his own destiny, as opposed to the idea that everything that happens to him is inevitable. Philosophers are concerned to discover what the presuppositions and implications of free will are, compared to those of *determinism. They are also concerned to discover to what extent free will and determinism can be compatible. In a theistic context, determinism is replaced by *predestination, the view that all events, including human choice, are fixed by the will of God.

freezing The preservation of food by keeping it frozen, thereby arresting the development of the microorganisms responsible for the decay of the food. Home freezers keep food at a temperature of about −18°C (−0.4°F). Most foods are well preserved by freezing, with little loss in nutritional value but some with a high water content within the cells of the food, such as strawberries and cucumbers, become soggy after freezing as a result of damage to the cell structure by ice formation. Most vegetables are blanched (boiled for 2–4 minutes) before freezing to arrest the action of enzymes. It is the residual enzymic action that determines the recommended storage time. In **freeze drying** food is rapidly frozen under very low pressure. Any water present freezes and then sublimes under the low pressure.

Frege, Gottlob (1848–1925) German mathematician and logician, who extended *Boole's work on symbolic logic by using logical symbols not already used in mathematics (symbols for *or*, *if-then*, etc.). This is now standard practice in logic.

Fremantle 32 07S 115 44E A major seaport in Western Australia, SW of Perth at the mouth of the Swan River. Kwinana, an important industrial complex with oil and nickel refineries and bulk-grain facilities, is nearby. Population (latest est): 23 981.

French A Romance language spoken by 45 million people in France, and extensively in Canada, Belgium, Switzerland, and elsewhere. It is the official language of 21 countries. Standard French, based upon the Parisian dialect known as Francien, has been France's official administrative language since 1539. It has replaced most northern dialects, known collectively as *langue d'oïl*, and has superseded the Occitan dialects of S France, known as *langue d'oc* (*see* PROVENÇAL). During the 17th century the *Académie Française and the publication of a standard dictionary (1680) quickly stabilized the language.

French bean An annual herb, *Phaseolus vulgaris*, also called kidney bean, probably native to South America but widely cultivated. It has large heart-shaped leaves and white pealike flowers. Both dwarf and twining varieties are grown for their *beans, usually eaten in the pod. The **haricot bean** is a variety of French bean grown in warm climates; the seeds are used for making baked beans.

French Community An association of states, comprising France and its former colonies, established by the new Fifth Republic after a constitutional referendum (1958). In addition to France it includes Guadeloupe, French Guiana, Martinique, Mayotte, La Réunion, St Pierre and Miquelon, Southern and Antarctic Territories, French Polynesia, New Caledonia, and Wallis and Futuna.

French Guiana A French overseas region on the NE coast of South America. A narrow fertile coastal belt rises to a mountainous interior, which is covered in dense forest rich in valuable timber. *History*: Europeans in search of *Eldorado explored the region from the early 16th century, but it was not settled until the 17th century, when the French, Dutch, Portuguese, and English competed for possession. In 1817 it was finally obtained by the French, who established penal colonies, including the notorious one on Devil's Island, in the territory. The French Guianese have had full French citizenship since 1848. Area: about 91 000 sq km (34 740 sq mi). Population (2001 est): 168 000. Capital: Cayenne.

French horn An orchestral brass instrument, which evolved from the hunting horn. It consists of a long narrow coiled tube with a wide bell and a cup-shaped mouthpiece. In the 18th century crooks of tubing of different length were inserted to enable it to play in various keys. In the 19th century valves were fitted giving the horn in F a complete range of about three octaves. It is a transposing instrument: its music is written a fifth higher than it sounds.

French Polynesia (former name: French Settlements in Oceania) A French overseas territory in the S Pacific Ocean consisting of several island groups. The most important of these are the Gambier Islands, the Society Archipelago, the Tuamotu Archipelago, the Tubuai Islands, and the Marquesas Islands. Area: about 4000 sq km (1500 sq mi). Population (2001 est): 238 000. Capital: Papeete.

French Republican calendar The calendar adopted (1793) in France during the French Revolution and retained until 1806, when the Gregorian *calendar was reintroduced. The year began on 22 Sept (the date in 1792 when the Republic came into being) and had 365 days divided into 12 months of 30 days each.

French Revolution The overthrow of the French monarchy as a reaction to the corrupt, feudal, and incompetent government of the Bourbon kings. In 1789 Louis XVI was forced to summon the *States General but its Third Estate, opposing aristocratic attempts to dominate proceedings, formed its own National Assembly. Riots followed, the Bastille was stormed, the king was mobbed at Versailles, and the Assembly (from July the Constituent Assembly) promulgated the Declaration of the Rights of Man. Feudalism was abolished and in September 1791, a new constitution was accepted by the king following his thwarted attempt to flee France (the flight to Varennes). However, his uncooperativeness fostered the growing republicanism of what became the Legislative Assembly (October 1791) and then the National Convention (September 1792). The Convention proclaimed a republic and in January 1793, Louis was executed. The moderate Girondins, discredited by France's war reverses (*see* REVOLUTIONARY AND NAPOLEONIC WARS), were now ousted by the Jacobins and power passed to the Committee of Public Safety. Under *Robespierre the Committee conducted a *Reign of Terror in which thousands of suspected antirevolutionaries were executed. His extremism, however, brought his downfall (1794) and led to the establishment of the Directory (1795), which struggled with economic crises until Napoleon's coup d'état (1799) brought the Revolution to an end.

French Southern and Antarctic Territories A French overseas territory (since 1955) comprising Terre Adélie in Antarctica with the islands of Amsterdam and St Paul and the Kerguelen and Crozet archipelagos in the Indian Ocean.

frequency The number of cycles completed by a vibrating system in unit time, usually one second (symbol: ν or f). The unit of frequency is the hertz (*see* HERTZ, HEINRICH RUDOLF). The angular frequency, ω, is related to the frequency by the equation $\omega = 2\pi f$ and is measured in radians per second.

frequency modulation *See* MODULATION.

fresco A classical and Renaissance method of wall decoration in which pure pigments dissolved in water were applied to the wet lime-plastered surface of a wall, producing a chemical reaction that made the colours a permanent part of the wall. Up to about 1500 the design was sketched freehand onto the rough plaster surface. Separate areas of the sketch were then filled in with fine smooth plaster and detailed colour was applied in layers of different pigments. Subsequently the cartoon, as used by Michelangelo, Raphael, Holbein, and others, allowed for more complicated premeditated design. The composition was drawn on sheets of paper, later applied to the wall, and the design pricked through with a stylus or with charcoal dust forced through the stylus piercings. Fresco painting was revived in the 20th century by the Mexican muralists Orozco and *Rivera.

Freud, Sigmund (1856–1939) Austrian pioneer of psychoanalysis. Freud studied medicine and, in 1882, joined the staff of a psychiatric clinic in Vienna. An interest in hypnosis developed through his collaboration with Josef Breuer (1842–1925) and Jean-Martin Charcot (1825–93). Following the publication with Breuer of *Studies in Hysteria* (1895), Freud evolved his theory that neuroses were rooted in suppressed sexual desires and sexual experiences of childhood. In *The Interpretation of Dreams* (1899), he analysed the content of dreams in terms of unconscious desires. His emphasis on the sexual origin of mental disorders aroused great controversy. In 1902 Freud established a circle in Vienna, which later (1910) became the International Psycho-Analytical Society. However, many of its members, including Carl *Jung and Alfred *Adler, resigned over disagreements. Freud left Vienna in 1938, following the Nazi invasion, joining his son in London. His other books include *The Psychopathology of Everyday Life* (1904), *Totem and Taboo* (1913), and *Beyond the Pleasure Principle* (1920). His grandson **Lucian Freud** (1922–) is a painter, who became a British citizen in 1939. His bleakly realistic portraits and nudes are extremely highly regarded and command enormous prices.

Freyja (*or* **Freya**) The Norse goddess of love and fertility, the sister of Frey, the god of sunshine, rain, and fertility. She is the Norse counterpart of Venus and is the leader of the *Valkyries. In some sources she is identified with *Frigga.

friction A force exerted at the boundary between two solids or fluids that retards motion between them. In solid friction a distinction is drawn between sliding friction and rolling friction. Sliding friction is further divided into dynamic friction, defined as the minimum force needed to keep a body sliding, and static friction, defined as the minimum force needed to move a stationary body. The latter is slightly greater than the former. In rolling friction the force of resistance is less than in sliding friction as the rolling body moves up the side of a depression made in the stationary body. The coefficient of friction is defined as the ratio of the frictional force to the perpendicular reaction between the surfaces. Friction is caused primarily by the two surfaces interlocking at the microscopic level. It is reduced by the use of lubricants, such as grease or graphite.

Friedman, Milton (1912–) US economist, known for his theories on monetary supply, which contradict those of *Keynes. His published work, which argues for the free market economy, includes *A Theory of the Consumption Function* (1957), *Capitalism and Freedom* (1962), and *Money Mischief* (1992). He won the 1976 Nobel Prize.

Friends of the Earth A British environmental pressure group. Established in 1971, it campaigns on environmental issues through demonstrations, public meetings, and parliamentary legislation. Targets have included motorway projects, commercial whaling, and industrial pollution (including nuclear power plants). The organization also has branches in 70 countries, directed from the Netherlands.

Friesian cattle A breed of black-and-white cattle originating from the province of Friesland in the Netherlands. They were exported to North America by early settlers and there developed as Holstein-Friesians. They are high-yielding milk producers and crosses, especially with a Charolais or Hereford bull, give good beef.

frigate bird A seabird belonging to the genus *Fregata* and family *Fregatidae* (5 species), occurring in tropical and subtropical oceanic regions, also called man-of-war bird because it often steals food from other birds in midair. 80–115 cm long, frigate birds have narrow wings spanning up to 2.3 m, a long hooked bill, and a forked tail. Males are glossy black and develop an inflatable red throat sac in the breeding season; females are brownish black with white underparts. Order: *Pelecaniformes* (gannets, pelicans, etc.).

Frigga (*or* **Frigg**) The Norse goddess of married love and the hearth, the wife of *Odin. In some legends she is identified with *Freyja; her name is preserved in *Friday*.

Frisian Islands A chain of islands in the North Sea extending along the coast of, and politically divided between, the Netherlands, Germany, and SW Denmark. The chain comprises three main groups: the West, North, and East Frisian Islands. The **Frisian language** was formerly spoken along the North Sea coastal region of Holland as far as Schleswig in Germany. It is now principally confined to Friesland province in Holland and certain offshore islands including Helgoland in the North Frisian islands.

fritillary (botany) A bulbous perennial plant of the genus *Fritillaria* (80 species), mostly native to N temperate regions. The leaves are narrow and the bell-shaped flowers droop from slender stalks. The European snake's head (*F. meleagris*) has reddish-purple chequered flowers. The crown imperial (*F. imperialis*), native to N India, has a cluster of pendant red flowers at the top of a tall (120 cm) stem, topped by a tuft of leaves. Both species are popular garden plants. Family: *Liliaceae*.

fritillary (zoology) A *nymphalid butterfly, usually brown or orange marked with black. Chief genera: *Boloria, Melitaea*.

Friuli-Venezia Giulia A semiautonomous region in the extreme NE of Italy. It was formed in 1947 and incorporated Trieste in 1954. It consists of mountains along the N border with Austria and a coastal plain in the S. There is arable or livestock farming throughout the region. Area: 7850 sq km (3031 sq mi). Population (2000 est): 1 185 172. Capital: Trieste.

Froebel, Friedrich Wilhelm August (1782–1852) German pioneer of nursery education. He applied the concept of harmonious growth to the development of children in *The Education of Man* (1826). His view that children should spend time together in creative play led him to found the first kindergarten (1837) at Blankenburg.

frog A tail-less amphibian of the family *Ranidae*, which includes bullfrogs, hairy frogs, and leopard frogs. Many other so-called frogs, such as *tree frogs, are actually toads. The European frog (*Rana temporaria*) grows to 10 cm. Greenish-brown with black markings, it spends most of its life on land, feeding on insects, and only returns to water to breed. Order: *Anura*.

froghopper A small jumping insect belonging to the family *Cercopidae* (about 2000 species). Froghoppers feed on plant juices, sometimes becoming pests. Eggs are laid on stems or roots and the *nymphs remain stationary until adult. They often protect themselves against predators and desiccation with a cover of white froth ("cuckoo spit"), produced by blowing air mixed with fluid from the anus through a valve in the abdomen. For this reason they are often known as cuckoo-spit insects and spittlebugs. Order: *Hemiptera*.

front In meteorology, the interface between two air masses of different thermal characteristics and origins. Where the air masses converge the warm air, being lighter, rises and slopes over the cold air. Distinctive weather phenomena are associated with fronts, particularly the development of depressions, and they are important in weather forecasting.

Front de Libération nationale (**FLN**) An Algerian nationalist group that organized the war of independence against France (1954–62). Formed in 1954, the FLN began a campaign of terrorism and sabotage. In 1956 it organized itself like a government, sending diplomatic missions abroad, and in 1958 set up a provisional government in Tunis. In 1962 the French agreed to Algerian independence and when Ahmed Ben Bella (1916–) became president in 1963 the FLN became Algeria's sole political party.

frost A weather condition that occurs when the temperature falls below 0°C (32°F). It is recognized by the icy deposit that forms but if the air is very dry this will not occur. In weather forecasting grades of severity of frost are distinguished as slight (−0.1 to −3.5°C), moderate (−3.6 to −6.4°C), severe (−6.5 to −11.5°C), and very severe (below −11.5°C). A distinction is made between ground frost, measured at grass level, and air frost, measured at a height of 1.4 m (4 ft).

Frost, Robert (Lee) (1874–1963) US poet. He became famous with the publication of *A Boy's Will* (1913) and *North of Boston* (1914). His work, which is often pastoral, has a dark undercurrent of anxiety and suffering.

frostbite Damage to part of the body, usually a hand or foot, resulting from exposure to extreme cold. The blood vessels to the affected limb constrict so that little blood (and therefore essential oxygen) reaches the skin, nerves, and muscles. This may lead to loss of sensation, ulcers, and eventually gangrene, necessitating amputation. Initial treatment is gently to warm the affected part.

fructose A simple sugar $C_6H_{12}O_6$ that is sweeter than sucrose and present in green leaves, fruits, and honey.

fruit The fertilized ovary of a flower, which contains the seed (or seeds) and may incorporate other parts of the flower (e.g. the receptacle in strawberries, the bracts in pineapples). The variation in the structure of fruits reflects the different means they have evolved to ensure dispersal of the seeds, which is essential to prevent overcrowding and enable the plant to spread and colonize new habitats. Fleshy fruits, for example, are usually eaten by animals, the seeds passing out with their faeces. Animals can also carry hooked or sticky fruits on their bodies. Seeds dispersed by wind are usually very light: they are either forcibly ejected from their fruits, for example from the *capsule of poppy and the pods of leguminous plants, or they remain attached to the fruit, which can itself remain airborne for considerable distances. Some fruits are distributed by

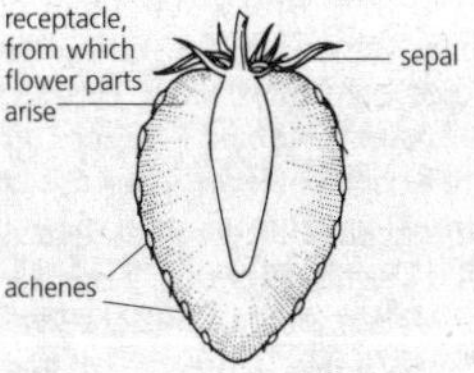

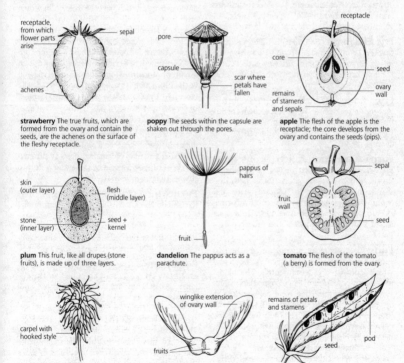

strawberry The true fruits, which are formed from the ovary and contain the seeds, are the achenes on the surface of the fleshy receptacle.

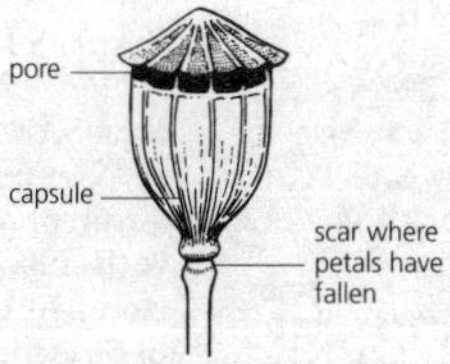

poppy The seeds within the capsule are shaken out through the pores.

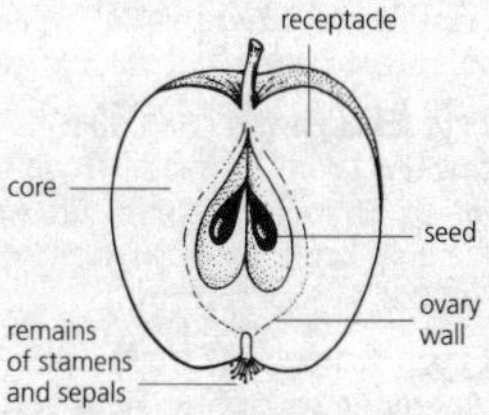

apple The flesh of the apple is the receptacle; the core develops from the ovary and contains the seeds (pips).

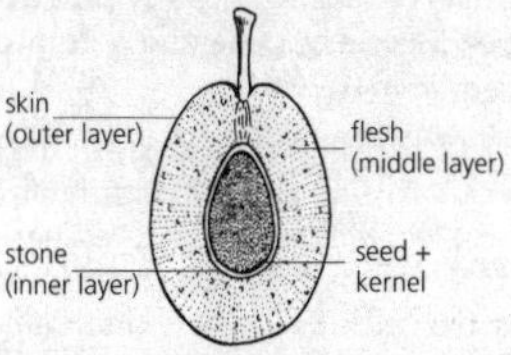

plum This fruit, like all drupes (stone fruits), is made up of three layers.

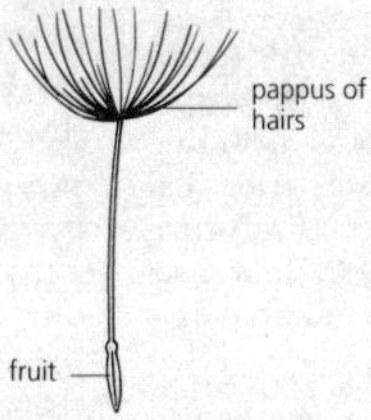

dandelion The pappus acts as a parachute.

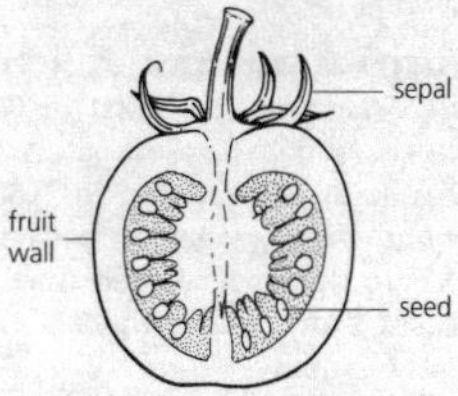

tomato The flesh of the tomato (a berry) is formed from the ovary.

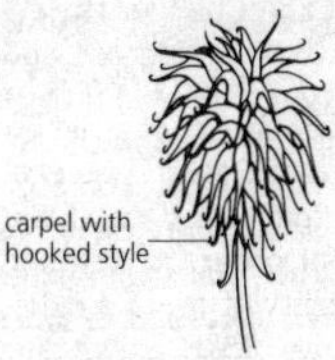

herb bennet The hooks cling to the fur of animals, which thus disperse the seeds.

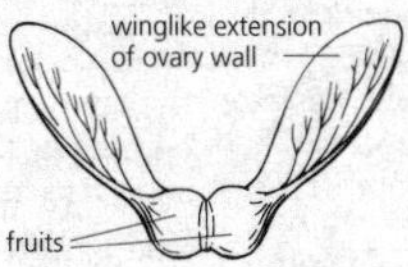

sycamore The two winged fruits separate and are carried away by the wind.

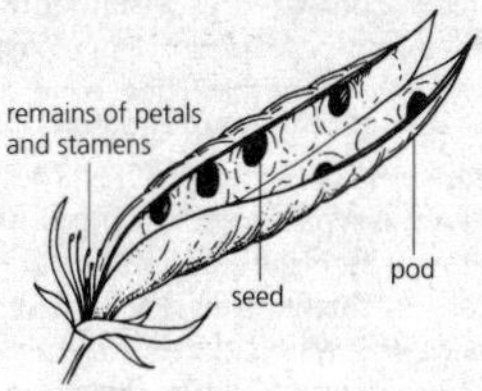

lupin When ripe, the pod splits open and curls back, ejecting the seeds.

fruit

water: coconut fruits can be transported several hundred miles by sea. The word fruit is popularly restricted to the fleshy edible fruits.

fruit bat A vegetarian *bat belonging to the family *Pteropidae* and suborder *Megachiroptera* (150 species). Fruit bats occur in tropical and subtropical regions of the Old World. They are typically larger than insect-eating bats and have better vision; only one genus (*Rousettus*, 13 species) uses *echolocation. Most eat fruit although some feed on flowers or nectar. *See also* FLYING FOX.

f

fruit fly A fly belonging to the family *Trypetidae* (1200 species)—the true fruit flies. (Insects of the family *Drosophilidae* are known as small fruit flies: *see* DROSOPHILA.) True fruit flies have spotted or banded wings and the larvae of many species feed on fruit, often causing serious damage. For example, the Mediterranean fruit fly (*Ceratitis capitata*) is a pest of almost all succulent fruits.

Fry, Elizabeth (1780–1845) British prison reformer. From 1813 she strove to improve the lot of women prisoners in Newgate Prison, London. Later, she visited prisons throughout Europe, urging reform.

Fry, Roger (Eliot) (1866–1934) British painter and art critic. He is best known for his influential writings on art, e.g. *Vision and Design* (1920), and artists, e.g. *Bellini* (1899) and *Cézanne* (1927).

Fuchs, Klaus Emil Julian (1911–88) British physicist and spy, born in Germany. During World War II he worked on atomic bomb research in Britain and in 1950 was tried and found guilty of having passed secret information to the Soviet Union since 1943. He was released from prison in 1959 and emigrated to East Germany.

Fuchsia A genus of shrubs and herbs (100 species) mostly native to tropical America and widely cultivated as ornamentals. The plants range from creeping forms, bushes, and small trees to epiphytes. They have deep-pink, red, or purple drooping flowers all along the branches; each flower has four long flaring coloured sepals surrounding the shorter petals, below which the stamens and stigma protrude. Most cultivated forms are varieties of *F. magellanica*, *F. coccinea*, and *F. arborescens* or hybrids between them. Family: *Onagraceae* (willowherb family).

fuel cell A device that converts the energy of a chemical reaction directly into an electric current. In the simplest type oxygen and hydrogen are fed through two separate porous nickel plates into an electrolytic solution. The gases combine to form water and thus set up a potential difference between the two plates. Fuel cells are distinguished from *accumulators in that the latter need to be recharged and do not consume their chemicals (which in fuel cells need to be replenished). Fuel cells provide a clean source of power.

fuel injection The pumping of fuel in the form of a spray directly into the cylinders of an *internal-combustion engine. In petrol engines it is increasingly used to replace the carburettor as it gives a more even fuel distribution in the combustion chamber. Fuel injection is also used in Diesel engines and continuous-combustion engines.

fugue A piece of polyphonic music, generally having three or four parts (*or* voices), in which each part enters in turn with a statement of the main theme (*or* subject). After stating the subject each voice continues with the secondary theme (*or* counter-subject). Fugues are not composed to strict patterns; episodes in different tonalities are often interspersed with subsequent groups of entries of the voices. At the climax the voices are overlapped in close succession (*stretto*).

Fujiyama (English name: Mount Fuji) 35 23N 138 42E The highest mountain in Japan, it is a dormant volcano in S central Honshu. Long regarded as a symbol of Japan, it has a symmetrical snow-capped (Oct–May) cone and a Shinto shrine. Height: 3776 m (12 388 ft).

Fukuoka 33 39N 130 21E A port in Japan in N Kyushu on Hakata Bay. An ancient commercial centre, *Kublai Khan was twice defeated here (1274, 1281). Kyushu University was established in 1910. Industries include textiles and shipbuilding. Population (latest est): 1 284 741.

Fulani A Muslim people scattered over a large area of W Africa from Lake Chad to the Atlantic coast. They are a mixed Negroid and, probably, Berber racial type. Their language, known as Fulfulde (*or* Fula), belongs to the Atlantic division of the Niger-Congo family. Their social and cultural patterns are varied. In N Nigeria many adopted the *Hausa language and culture and, as a result of religious wars (1804–10), established a Muslim empire in which they were the ruling elite.

fullerene *See* CARBON.

fulmar A maritime North Atlantic bird, *Fulmarus glacialis*. It is about 46 cm long and dark grey above with white underparts. Family: *Procellariidae* (petrels).

Funchal 32 40N 15 55W The capital of the Madeira Islands, on the S coast of Madeira, and a popular tourist resort. Population (latest est): 44 111.

functionalism A doctrine principally associated with the *international style. Its main tenet is that the more fitted to its purpose a building is, the more beautiful it will be. Developed under Louis Sullivan in the 1890s, the doctrine's most vocal advocate was *Le Corbusier. Functionalism led to a very severe style, lacking in all ornamentation and idiosyncracy. Its dominance faded after 1930.

fundamental interactions The basic forces that occur in nature. *See* ELECTROMAGNETIC INTERACTION; GRAVITATIONAL INTERACTION; STRONG INTERACTION; WEAK INTERACTION.

fundamentalism A form of religion in which traditional beliefs are held uncompromisingly. Jewish and Christian fundamentalists reject any scientific theories, such as those of cosmology and evolution, that conflict with a literal interpretation of the Bible. Christian fundamentalism has strong support among Protestants in parts of the USA. Islamic fundamentalists adhere strictly to the teachings of the Koran and expect the state to adopt Islamic law. A strong upsurge of Islamic fundamentalism began in the late 1970s when Ayatollah Khomeini became leader of Iran. Islamic fundamentalism has also inspired terrorist groups in the Middle East and the international *al-Qaida network.

fungi Unicellular or multicellular organisms belonging to the kingdom *Fungi* (about 50 000 known species) and including mushrooms, mildews, moulds, yeasts, etc. Fungi were formally classified as plants; however all fungi lack chlorophyll and therefore (unlike plants) cannot manufacture their own food by photosynthesis. Some are saprophytes, feeding on dead organic matter by means of digestive enzymes; others are parasites of plants or animals. The body of most fungi consists of a network of branching threadlike structures (hyphae), forming a mycelium. Sexual reproduction results in the formation of spores, which may be produced in a specialized structure called a fruiting body: this is the visible part of mushrooms, puffballs, etc. Other fungi consist of single cells, which can reproduce asexually by simple division into two daughter cells. Fungi are distributed worldwide in terrestrial, freshwater, and marine habitats. Some live in the soil and play a vital role in bringing about decomposition of dead organic matter. Other fungi (e.g. *Penicillium* and *Streptomyces*) are of great importance as a source of *antibiotics. Many parasitic fungi cause disease in animals and humans (*see* INFECTION) or in plants (e.g. the smuts and rusts), while some saprotrophs are destructive to timber (*see* DRY ROT). Some fungi form associations with other organisms, most notably with algae to form *lichens. *See also* ASCOMYCOTA; BASIDIOMYCOTA.

furlong A unit of length equal to 220 yards (⅛ mile), used in horseracing.

Furness A peninsula in NW England, in Cumbria between the Irish Sea and Morecambe Bay. Chief town: Barrow-in-Furness.

Fushun 41 51N 123 53E A city in NE China, in Liaoning province. Its oil, steel, and chemical industries are based on its oil-shale and vast coal deposits. Aluminium production is also important. Population (1999 est): 1 271 113.

fusion *See* NUCLEAR ENERGY.

Futuna Islands *See* WALLIS AND FUTUNA.

Fuzhou (**Fu-chou** *or* **Foochow**) 26 10N 119 20E A port in SE China, the capital of Fujian province on the Min delta. An ancient capital, it was the centre of foreign trade from the 10th to the 19th centuries. Population (1999 est): 1 057 372.

Fyn (German name: Fünen) The second largest Danish island, situated between the Little Belt and the Great Belt. Fishing is important and its fertile soil supports cereal growing, dairy farming, and cattle rearing. It was joined to Sjaelland by a suspension bridge in 1998. Area: 3481 sq km (1344 sq mi). Population (2001): 472 064.

G

Gable, Clark (1901–60) US film actor. He established his popularity during the 1930s, when he played many tough masculine roles. His films include *It Happened One Night* (1934), *Gone with the Wind* (1939), and *The Misfits* (1961).

Gabon (official name: Gabonese Republic) An equatorial country in West Africa. The population is mainly Fang. *Economy*: almost three-quarters of the land is forested and timber was formerly the most important resource. Now, however, its vast mineral wealth forms the basis of the economy. Agriculture consists chiefly of subsistence farming. *History*: trading posts were set up by the Portuguese in the late 15th century and the area later became a centre of the slave trade. Settled by the French in the mid-19th century, it became part of French Equatorial Africa in 1910. It gained internal self-government in 1958 and became independent in 1960. A one-party political system was instituted under Omar Bongo in 1967; in the 1980s the opposition was led by an underground group known as the *morena*. Continuing unrest led to multiparty legislative elections being held in 1990; in 1993 and 1998 Bongo was victorious in multiparty presidential elections, amidst widespread accusations of fraud. Official language: French. Currency: CFA franc of 100 centimes. Area: 267 000 sq km (103 089 sq mi). Population (2003 est): 1 329 000. Capital: Libreville.

gaboon viper A highly venomous *puff adder, *Bitis gabonica*, occurring in African rain forests. Up to 2 m long, it has hornlike projections on its snout and is patterned with buff, brown, and purple rectangles and triangles. It feeds on small vertebrates.

Gaborone (former name: Gaberones) 24 45S 25 55E The capital of Botswana. The seat of government was transferred here from Mafeking in 1965. Population (1997 est): 183 487.

Gaddafi, Moammar al- (*or* **Qaddafi**; 1942–) Libyan colonel and statesman. In 1969 he led a revolt that overthrew the Libyan monarchy and in 1970 became chairman of the Revolutionary Command Council. His Arab nationalist and Islamic socialist policies led to a reorganization of Libyan society and brought him into conflict with the West, which accused him of backing international terrorism. A new era of cooperation with the West began in 2004, when Gaddafi announced that he had abandoned plans to build nuclear weapons.

Gaddi, Taddeo (c. 1300–?1366) Florentine painter, who was the pupil and assistant of *Giotto. His works include the *Life of the Virgin* (Baroncelli Chapel, Sta Croce, Florence). His son **Agnolo Gaddi** (c. 1350–96), painted the *Story of the True Cross* in Sta Croce and the *Life of the Virgin* (Duomo, Prato).

gadolinium (Gd) A *lanthanide element named after the Finnish chemist J. Gadolin (1760–1852). It is used in television-tube phosphors. At no 64; at wt 157.25; mp 1313°C; bp 3273°C.

Gadsden Purchase (1853) About 77 700 sq km (30 000 sq mi) of land in what are now New Mexico and Arizona, bought by the USA from Mexico for $10 million. The purchase was named after its negotiator, James Gadsden (1788–1858).

Gaelic A language of the Goidelic group of *Celtic languages. Irish Gaelic is spoken in Ireland as a first language by around 100 000 people and as a second language by around 700 000. Scottish Gaelic (*or* Erse), which is spoken in NW Scotland, is an offshoot of Irish Gaelic.

Gagarin, Yuri Alekseevich (1934–68) Soviet cosmonaut, who on 12 April 1961, became the first person to orbit the earth reaching a height of about 301 km (187 mi). He died when a plane he was testing crashed.

Gaia (*or* **Gaea**) A Greek goddess personifying the earth. The wife and mother of Uranus (Heaven), by whom she bore the *Titans, the

*Cyclops, and the *Gigantes, she incited the revolt of the Titans against him.

Gainsborough, Thomas (1727–88) British portrait and landscape painter. The elegant style of Van Dyck is reflected in Gainsborough's *Countess Howe* (Kenwood House, London) and the *Blue Boy* (San Marino, California) while his landscapes were influenced by *Ruisdael, Meindert Hobbema (1638–1709), and later by *Rubens, particularly the *Harvest Wagon* (Barber Institute, Birmingham). After 1774 he successfully rivalled *Reynolds; in his later years he painted idyllic rustic scenes, the so-called "fancy" pictures.

galago *See* BUSHBABY.

Galahad In *Arthurian legend, the son of *Lancelot and Elaine. As the most perfect exemplar of knighthood, he was (in many romances) the only knight to succeed in the quest of the *Holy Grail.

Galápagos Islands (Spanish name: Archipiélago de Colón) An archipelago in the Pacific Ocean, W of Ecuador. It consists of 12 main islands and several smaller ones, all of volcanic origin. Visited by Charles *Darwin in 1835, the islands contain many endemic species, including the Galápagos giant tortoise (*Testude elephantopus*), up to 1.5 m long and weighing up to 150 kg. Many islands now form nature reserves. Area: 7428 sq km (2868 sq mi). Population (2000 est): 17 000.

Galatea 1. In Greek legend, a nymph who loved the shepherd Acis and was loved by Polyphemus. When Acis was killed by his rival she turned him into a river. **2.** The name of a statue that came to life in answer to the prayers of *Pygmalion.

galaxies Huge assemblies of stars, gas, and dust, bound together by gravitational interactions. **Spiral galaxies** are large flattened systems with spiral arms containing much interstellar gas and dust from which stars can form. Spirals have a mass of 10^{10} to 10^{11} solar masses. **Elliptical galaxies** are actually spheroidal with no clear internal structure. They vary in size and mass, the largest giant ellipticals exceeding 10^{12} solar masses. **Irregular galaxies** have no definite shape and are relatively small, with a high content of interstellar matter.

Galaxy (*or* **Milky Way system**) The spiral *galaxy to which the sun belongs. It contains about a hundred thousand million (10^{11}) stars. Most lie in its two spiral arms, the sun lying about 33 000 light years from the centre. Light cannot penetrate the dust in the innermost regions of the Galaxy but radio, infrared, and X-ray observations have shown complex phenomena to be occurring, possibly arising from the presence of a *black hole at the galactic centre.

Galbraith, John Kenneth (1908–) US economist and diplomat. His works in the Keynesian tradition include *The Affluent Society* (1958), *Economics and the Public Purpose* (1973), and *The Culture of Contentment* (1992).

Galen (129–c. 199 AD) Greek physician and scholar, whose ideas dominated medicine until the Renaissance. Galen showed the importance of the spinal cord in muscle activity, the role of the ureter in kidney and bladder function, and that arteries carry blood rather than air despite holding mistaken views on blood circulation. Galen also wrote on philosophy, law, and mathematics.

galena The principal ore of lead. It is a grey soft metallic mineral, found as cubic crystals of lead sulphide in hydrothermal veins and as replacement deposits in limestones. Galena ore bodies usually contain silver.

Galicia 1. A medieval kingdom in NW Spain, now an autonomous region. Colonized by the *Visigoths, it became a subkingdom of Castile in the late 11th century. **2.** A historical region of E Europe, now in Poland and Ukraine.

Galilean satellites The four largest *satellites of Jupiter—Io, Europa, Ganymede, and Callisto—discovered by Galileo (1610) and studied in detail by the US *Voyager probes (1979). Io is the most active volcanic body known in the solar system.

Galilee A district of N Israel, bordering the River Jordan, associated with the early ministry of Jesus Christ, Crusader battles, and Jewish settlement after the fall of Jerusalem (70 AD). Zionist settlements, begun in 1892, became part of Israel in 1949. **The Sea of Galilee** (Sea of Tiberias; Lake of Gennesaret; Lake Kinneret) is a lake in NE Israel. It is fed mainly by and drained by the River Jordan; its surface is 209 m (686 ft) below sea level. It was the scene of many episodes in the life of Christ. Area: 166 sq km (64 sq mi).

Galileo Galilei (1564–1642) Italian mathematician, physicist, and astronomer. Born in Pisa, legend has it that he demonstrated that the rate of fall of a body is independent of its mass by dropping weights from the Leaning Tower of Pisa. He is also reputed to have worked out that the period of a pendulum is independent of its amplitude by watching a swinging chandelier in Pisa Cathedral. In 1609 Galileo designed a telescope and used it to discover sunspots and Jupiter's satellites. His book *Dialogue on Two World Systems* (1632) denounced the Ptolemaic system of astronomy in favour of Copernicus' system. As the Roman Catholic Church had condemned Copernicus' work in 1616, Galileo was forced by the Inquisition to recant his views and placed under house arrest for the rest of his life. He was cleared of heresy by a Vatican commission in 1992.

g

Galla A people of Ethiopia numbering about 10 million and making up about 40% of the Ethiopian population. They were originally nomads who spread from the SE region during the 16th century. Their language belongs to the Hamito-Semitic family.

gall bladder A saclike organ (7–10 cm long) that receives and stores *bile (formerly called gall) formed by the liver. The gall bladder is connected to the liver by the hepatic ducts and to the intestine by the common bile duct. Crystallization of bile components forms **gallstones**, which may block the bile duct or cause gall bladder infections (cholecystitis) and may necessitate surgical removal of the gall bladder (cholecystectomy).

Gallic Wars (58–51 BC) The campaigns in which Julius Caesar annexed Transalpine *Gaul (France). Caesar's intervention in Gallic intertribal warfare was prompted by concern for Italian security. NE Gaul was pacified by 57 BC and the tribes along the Atlantic coast by 56 BC. In 52 Caesar defeated the tribes of central Gaul, led by Vercingetorix. Caesar's own account of the Gallic Wars has survived.

gallinule A bird belonging to the family *Rallidae* (rails). Gallinules are widely distributed, occurring on semistagnant water edged by dense vegetation, and commonly have blue, green, or purple plumage for camouflage. They are 30–45 cm long and have long slender toes enabling them to run over floating vegetation. *See also* MOORHEN.

Gallipoli (Turkish name: Gelibolu) 40 25N 26 41E A seaport in Turkey, on the NE coast of the Dardanelles. Strategically important for the defence of Istanbul, the town had to be rebuilt after the Gallipoli campaign (*see* WORLD WAR I). Population (latest est): 14 721.

gallium (Ga) A metallic element with a low melting point and high boiling point, discovered in 1875 by Lecoq de Boisbaudran. **Gallium arsenide** (GaAs) is a *semiconductor that is widely used in electronic devices, particularly the field-effect *transistor and the Gunn diode. At no 31; at wt 69.72; mp 29.77°C; bp 2205°C.

gallon An Imperial unit of volume equal to the volume occupied by ten pounds of distilled water under precisely defined conditions. The US gallon is equal to 0.832 68 British gallons.

Galsworthy, John (1867–1933) British novelist and dramatist. *The Man of Property* (1906) began the famous novel series *The Forsyte Saga*, chronicling the decline of a rich English family. His plays include *Strife* (1909).

Galvani, Luigi (1737–85) Italian physician, who pioneered research into the electrical properties of living things. Observing the twitching of frog muscles when touched with metal, he wrongly attributed the phenomenon to an innate animal electricity. This inspired Alessandro Volta (1745–1827) to discover the electric cell. The *galvanometer is named after Galvani.

galvanized steel Steel coated with zinc to prevent corrosion. The zinc may be deposited by electroplating the steel in molten zinc, spraying with molten zinc, or by coating it with zinc powder and heating it.

galvanometer An instrument for measuring small electric currents, named after Luigi *Galvani. The moving-coil galvanometer consists of a coil of wire suspended in a magnetic field. A current passing through the coil causes it to rotate until balanced by the opposing torsion in the suspending thread. The angle of rotation is used to measure the current. In the moving-magnet instrument the magnet is suspended in the earth's magnetic field and deflection is caused by a current passing through the surrounding coil.

Galway (Irish name: Contae Na Gaillimhe) A county in the W Republic of Ireland, in Connacht. Low lying E of Lough Carrib, it rises to Connemara (an area of moors and bogs) in the W. Offshore islands include the Aran Islands. Cattle and sheep rearing are important. Area: 5939 sq km (2293 sq mi). Population (2002): 208 826. County town: Galway.

Gama, Vasco da (c. 1469–1524) Portuguese navigator. In 1497, he departed with three ships to continue the search by Bartolomeu Dias (c. 1450–c. 1500) for the route to India. He rounded the Cape of Good Hope and crossed to Calicut (1498). Received with hostility by the Indians, he withdrew. In 1502 da Gama was sent out on a punitive expedition to establish Portugal's influence in the Indian Ocean, returning to Portugal with much booty. Some 20 years later he went back to India as Portuguese viceroy.

Gambia, Republic of The A country in West Africa, surrounded by Senegalese territory. Swamps along the River Gambia give way to savanna. The majority of the inhabitants are Mandingo. *Economy*: overwhelmingly agricultural, producing groundnuts and rice. In 1988 it agreed a free-trade zone with Senegal. Tourism is being encouraged. *History*: in the 15th century the mouth of the River Gambia was explored by the Portuguese, and in 1661 the English established a trading settlement on James Island. The area was administered by the British from 1807 until it achieved independence in 1965, with Sir Dawda Jawara as first president; it became a republic within the British Commonwealth in 1970. Close ties with Senegal were reinforced with the formation of the Senegambia Confederation (1982–89). In 1994 Lt Yayah Jammeh replaced Jawara as president in a military coup; a civilian constitution was adopted in 1996. Jammeh was re-elected in 2001. Official language: English. Currency: dalasi of 100 butut. Area: 10 689 sq km (4125 sq mi). Population (2003 est): 1 426 000. Capital: Banjul.

Gambia, River A river in West Africa. Rising in Guinea, it flows NW through Senegal and The Gambia to the Atlantic Ocean. Length: 1126 km (700 mi).

Gambier Islands 23 10S 135 00W A group of coral islands in the S Pacific Ocean, in French Polynesia. They have been used for French nuclear tests. Area: 30 sq km (11 sq mi). Population (latest est): 582. Chief settlement: Rikitea.

gamboge (*or* **camboge**) A hard brittle gum resin obtained from various SE Asian trees of the genus *Garcinia*. It is orange to brown in colour and turns bright yellow when powdered. Artists use gamboge as a pigment and to colour varnishes. In medicine it is used as a strong purgative.

gamete A reproductive cell—either male or female—produced in the sex organs of plants or animals and containing half the number of *chromosomes present in a body (somatic) cell. On *fertilization the new individual therefore has a complete set of chromosomes, half from each parent. The female gamete (*see* EGG) is large and immotile and contains abundant cytoplasm, while the male gamete (*see* SPERM) is motile, with little cytoplasm.

game theory The branch of mathematics that seeks to analyse and solve problems arising in economic, business, or military situations on the assumption that each participant adopts strategies that will maximize gain (payoff) and minimize loss, as in playing a game. Worked out originally by John von *Neumann and Oskar Morganstern (1907–77), it was successfully used in World War II in an analysis of submarine warfare.

gametophyte *See* ALTERNATION OF GENERATIONS.

gamma globulin *See* GLOBULIN.

gamma radiation Highly energetic electromagnetic radiation emitted by certain radioactive substances as a result of transitions of nucleons from a higher to a lower energy level and when an elementary particle and its antiparticle annihilate each other. The wavelength of gamma radiation is between 10^{-10} and 10^{-14} metre.

Ganda A Bantu people of the region W and N of Lake Victoria. They are agriculturalists, whose staple crop is bananas. The largest tribe in Uganda, they were formerly ruled by a king (Kabaka) in their own kingdom of *Buganda.

Gandhi, Indira (1917–84) Indian stateswoman; prime minister (1966–77; 1980–84). Daughter of Jawaharlal *Nehru, she succeeded Lal Bahadur Shastri as prime minister and leader of the *Indian National Congress. In 1975 she was accused of electoral malpractices and threatened with the loss of her seat. She was defeated in the elections of 1977 but returned to power in 1980. In the wake of sectarian violence, she was assassinated in 1984 by Sikh members of her bodyguard. Her elder son **Rajiv Gandhi** (1942–91) succeeded her as prime minister (1984–89); he was also assassinated. Rajiv's widow, the Italian-born **Sonia Gandhi** (1946–), became leader of the Congress Party in 1998; although she led the party to victory in the election of 2004 she declined the post of prime minister.

Gandhi, Mohandas Karamchand (1869–1948) Indian nationalist leader. Mahatma ("Great Soul") Gandhi was born in W India and went to England in 1888 to study law. In 1893 he moved to South Africa to practise law and became a champion of the rights of the Indian community, introducing a policy of noncooperation (satyagraha) with the civil authorities. After returning to India, he became leader of the *Indian National Congress. Following imprisonment (1922–24) for civil disobedience, Gandhi campaigned against the degradation of untouchables. In 1930 he walked from Ahmedabad to the sea, where he distilled salt from sea water in protest against the government's salt monopoly, and was again imprisoned. In 1932 he undertook his first "fast unto death," against the government's attitude to untouchables. During World War II Gandhi had to reconcile Indian support for Britain with his beliefs in nonviolence and an independent India. His demand that the British should withdraw immediately from India led the British to gaol Gandhi and other Congress leaders until 1944.

Subsequently, Gandhi played a crucial part in independence talks and finally accepted the establishment of Pakistan. When violence broke out in Bengal, Gandhi undertook a fast in an attempt to halt the conflict. His advocacy of friendship between Hindus and Muslims caused resentment among Hindu fanatics, one of whom (Nathuram Godse) assassinated him. Ghandi was for many years regarded as both a saint and the supreme Indian leader.

Gandzha (name from 1813 until 1920: Yelisavetpol; name from 1935 until 1990: Kirovabad) 40 39N 46 20E A city in NW Azerbaidzhan. A medieval commercial centre, it is now important for industry. Population (1997 est): 291 900.

Ganesha (*or* **Ganesa**) One of the principal Hindu deities, who is portrayed as having an elephant's head on a human body. His father *Shiva beheaded him, but then replaced his human head with that of the first creature he found. He is the patron of prosperity and learning.

Ganges, River (*or* **Ganga**) The great river of N India. Formed by headstreams in the Himalayas, it flows E across the Ganges plain to the Brahmaputra River, thereafter continuing as the River Padma, which empties into the Bay of Bengal by way of the largest delta in the world. It is the Hindus' most sacred river. Length: 2507 km (1557 mi).

gangrene Death of tissues, most commonly those of a limb. This usually results from narrowing of the blood vessels of the legs by *atherosclerosis or because of diabetes. If the tissues become infected the condition is called wet gangrene. Treatment is aimed at improving the blood flow to the limbs by surgery or by rest; in advanced cases amputation may be necessary.

gannet A seabird of the family *Sulidae*, distributed worldwide. (Tropical members are called boobies.) The North Atlantic gannet (*Sula bassana*), also called solan goose, 90 cm long, is white with black wingtips. Gannets feed on fish and nest in colonies on rocky islands and cliffs. Order: *Pelecaniformes* (cormorants, pelicans, etc.).

Ganymede (Greek mythology) A Trojan prince of great beauty carried off by Zeus to be his cupbearer in exchange for some immortal horses or a golden vine.

Gaoxiong (*or* **Kao-hsiung**; Japanese name: Takao) 22 36N 120 17E A city in SW Taiwan, the second largest on the island and its leading port. Under Japanese occupation (1895–1945) it became an important naval base. Population (2000 est): 1 475 505.

Garbo, Greta (Greta Gustafson; 1905–90) Swedish actress. Her aloof beauty contributed much to her portrayal of tragic heroines in such films as *Grand Hotel* (1932), *Anna Karenina* (1935), and *Camille* (1936). As a comedienne she excelled in *Ninotchka* (1939).

García Lorca, Federico (1898–1936) Spanish poet and dramatist. He won international fame with *Gipsy Ballads* (1928). His masterpiece is the trilogy of folk tragedies *Blood Wedding* (1933), *Yerma* (1934), and *The House of Bernarda Alba* (1936). He was shot by Nationalist partisans in the Spanish Civil War.

García Márquez, Gabriel (1928–) Colombian novelist; his novels include *One Hundred Years of Solitude* (1967) and *Chronicle of a Death Foretold* (1981). He won a Nobel Prize in 1982.

Garda, Lake (Latin name: Lacus Benacus) A lake in central N Italy. Sheltered on the N by the Alps, it has a temperate climate that attracts holidaymakers. Area: 370 sq km (143 sq mi).

Gardenia A genus of ornamental shrubs and trees (60–100 species) native to tropical and subtropical Africa and Asia. Many are richly scented and used in perfumes and tea. *G. jasminoides* is a popular pot plant. Family: *Rubiaceae* (madder family).

garfish *See* NEEDLEFISH.

Garibaldi, Giuseppe (1807–82) Italian soldier, a hero of the movement for Italian unification (*see* RISORGIMENTO). Influenced by Mazzini, he joined an attempted republican revolution in Sardinia-Piedmont (1834) and was forced to flee to South America. He returned to Italy to join the Revolution of 1848, fighting the Austrians and play a leading part in the unsuccessful defence of Rome against the French.

Following another period of exile, he joined the unification movement led by *Cavour and Victor Emmanuel II. In 1860 he set out from Genoa on the Expedition of a Thousand, achieving the conquest of Sicily and Naples and their incorporation in the new kingdom of Italy. He also fought for the French in the Franco-Prussian War (1870–71).

Garland, Judy (Frances Gumm; 1922–69) US singer and film actress. She began her career at the age of five in vaudeville. Her films included *The Wizard of Oz* (1939), *Meet Me in St Louis* (1944), and *A Star is Born* (1954). Although an unhappy private life interfered with her career, she maintained her reputation as a superstar. Her daughter **Liza Minnelli** (1946–) is also a singer and actress, best known for her starring role in *Cabaret* (1972); other films include *Arthur* (1981) and *Stepping Out* (1991).

garlic A widely cultivated perennial herb, *Allium sativum*, native to Asia and naturalized in S Europe and North America. Its leafless flower stem grows to a height of 60 cm. The bulb, with its pungent taste, is used in cooking.

garnet A group of minerals, with varying compositions, that occur chiefly in metamorphic rocks. They are used as abrasives and semiprecious stones. Birthstone for January.

Garonne, River A river in SW France. Rising in the central Pyrenees, it enters the Atlantic Ocean by the Gironde estuary. Length: 580 km (360 mi).

Garrick, David (1717–79) English actor. He went to London with Samuel *Johnson in 1737 and began his long theatrical career with a highly acclaimed performance as Richard III in 1741. As manager of the Drury Lane Theatre from 1747 to 1776, he introduced innovations in production, lighting, and scenery.

Garter, Order of the A British order of knighthood, traditionally founded by Edward III in 1348 and comprising chiefly the sovereign and 25 knights companions. Its motto, *Honi soit qui mal y pense* (The shame be his who thinks badly of it), supposedly the words of Edward III on tying to his leg a garter dropped by a lady, is inscribed on a blue garter worn below the left knee. The order's chapel is St George's Chapel, Windsor.

Gascony A former duchy of SW France. After Roman rule Gascony was conquered by the Visigoths and then by the Franks. It fell to Aquitaine in 1052 and came under English control in the 12th century. It was regained by the French at the end of the Hundred Years' War (1453).

gases Substances that distribute themselves evenly throughout a closed container. The behaviour of a gas under variations of temperature, pressure, and volume is fairly accurately described by the *gas laws and the *kinetic theory of gases.

Gaskell, Elizabeth Cleghorn (1810–65) British novelist. In 1832 she married a Unitarian minister and settled in Manchester, the industrial setting of her first novel, *Mary Barton* (1848). Her other novels include *Cranford* (1853) and *North and South* (1855). She also wrote the first biography of her friend Charlotte Brontë (1857).

gas laws Relationships between the thermodynamic temperature (T), pressure (p), and volume (V) of a gas. Boyle's law (*see* BOYLE, ROBERT) ($p \propto 1/V$) and *Charles's law ($V \propto T$) are combined in the ideal gas equation: $pV = nRT$, where R is the gas constant, which has the value 8.314 $\mathrm{J\,K^{-1}\,mol^{-1}}$, and n is the number of moles present. Only ideal gases obey these laws exactly. Later modifications of these equations attempt to cover real gases.

gastropod A single-shelled *mollusc belonging to the class *Gastropoda* (about 40 000 species), including *snails and *slugs, *limpets, and sea hares. 0.1–20 cm long, gastropods occupy terrestrial, freshwater, and marine habitats. They move by undulating the muscular foot and have two pairs of retractable sensory head tentacles, one pair bearing simple eyes. They feed by scraping plant or animal matter with a rasping tongue (radula). Most gastropods have internal fertilization: the mating individuals may be of separate sexes or hermaphrodite.

gas turbine A form of *internal-combustion engine consisting of a *turbine in which the power to drive the blades is provided by hot gas. It consists of a compressor, a combustion chamber, and the turbine. Atmospheric air is fed under pressure from the compressor to the combustion chambers, where a fuel, such as natural gas, paraffin, or oil is burnt; the hot gases then drive the turbine, which in turn drives the compressor. Power is supplied either in the form of thrust from a jet or rotation of the turbine shaft.

Gates, Bill (William Henry G; 1955–) US business man, whose Microsoft company (founded 1975) has dominated the computer software industry worldwide since the early

1980s. The company's success was consolidated by its Windows system, first introduced in 1985. One of the world's richest men, he was awarded an honorary British knighthood in 2004.

Gateshead 1. 54 58N 1 35W A town in NE England, in Gateshead unitary authority, Tyne and Wear, on the River Tyne. Industries include engineering and clothing. Landmarks include the new Baltic art gallery and Millennium Bridge and the Angel of the North, the UK's largest outdoor sculpture. Population (1991): 83 159. **2.** A unitary authority in NE England, in Tyne and Wear. Area: 142 sq km (55 sq mi). Population (2001): 191 151.

g

Gatwick 51 08N 0 11W A village in SE England, 43 km (27 mi) S of London, in W Sussex. It is the site of one of London's two subsidiary airports (*see also* STANSTED).

Gauguin, Paul (1848–1903) French postimpressionist painter. After five years at sea he became a stockbroker (1871), painting as a hobby. He became a full-time painter in 1883 and developed a style called synthetism in such paintings as *Vision after the Sermon* (National Gallery, Edinburgh). He visited Martinique in 1887 and stayed with Van Gogh in Arles in 1888. Seeking the inspiration of a primitive civilization, he moved to Tahiti (1891), where the symbolism in such paintings as *Nevermore* (Courtauld Institute, London) was influenced by native superstitions.

Gaul An ancient region of Europe. It was divided by the Romans into Transalpine Gaul (the area bound by the Rhine, Alps, and Pyrenees) and Cisalpine Gaul (N Italy). Transalpine Gaul was settled from about 1500 BC by Celtic tribes, who inhabited Cisalpine Gaul after around 500 BC. Subsequent Gallic expansion southwards brought conflict with Rome, which the Gauls sacked in 390. In 121 the Romans annexed S Transalpine Gaul, which they called Gallia Narbonensis, and between 58 and 50 Caesar subdued the rest of Gaul, finally crushing the Gallic tribal leader Vercingetorix at Alesia. Gaul was extensively romanized and prospered until the barbarian invasions in the 5th century.

Gauss, Karl Friedrich (1777–1855) German mathematician, regarded as one of the greatest mathematicians of all time. He influenced all aspects of mathematics and much of physics. His greatest contributions were in the fields of probability theory, number theory, complex numbers, algebra, and electricity and magnetism.

gavial (*or* **gharial**) A long-snouted reptile, *Gavialis gangeticus*, occurring in N Indian rivers and sacred to Hindus. 4–5 m long, it has long slender sharp-toothed jaws, which it uses to catch fish. It is the only member of its family (*Gavialidae*). Order: *Crocodilia* (*see* CROCODILE).

Gawain In Arthurian legend, a knight of the Round Table, the nephew of King Arthur and the son of King Lot of Norway and the Orkneys. He was known for his purity and courage.

Gaya 24 48N 85 00E A city in NE India, in Bihar. A centre of Hindu pilgrimage, it is situated 10 km (6 mi) S of Buddh Gaya, which is sacred to Buddhists. Population (1991): 291 220.

Gay-Lussac, Joseph Louis (1778–1850) French chemist and physicist. He discovered boron (1808) and the law that gases combine in a simple ratio by volume (**Gay-Lussac's law**). He also discovered *Charles's law independently of Charles and published his results first.

Gaza Strip A strip of coastal territory, 50 km (30 mi) long, on the SE corner of the Mediterranean Sea. Agriculture is the chief pursuit, especially the growing of citrus fruit. Following the Arab-Israeli War of 1948–49, it was the only part of Palestine held by Egypt. Held by the Israelis for a short time in 1956–57, it was taken by them again in 1967. Under the Camp David agreement (1979), eventual self-government for the area was planned. The Gaza Strip suffers from extreme overpopulation, with many Palestinian refugees being housed in squalid camps. In 1994 Palestinian self-government commenced (*see* PALESTINE LIBERATION ORGANIZATION). Violent protests intensified in 2001–2002, provoking Israeli air and rocket attacks and repeated military incursions. In March 2004 Israel announced a controversial plan to withdraw from Gaza unilaterally but to hold on to settlements in the *West Bank. Population (1993): 748 000.

gazelle A slender antelope of the genus *Gazella* (about 12 species), of Africa and Asia. 50–90 cm high at the shoulder, gazelles are distinguished from other antelopes by horizontal stripes on the face. In most species both sexes have lyre-shaped horns.

Gdańsk (German name: Danzig) 54 22N 18 41E A port in N Poland. It is an industrial centre with metallurgy, chemicals, and food processing. The city's famous shipyards closed in 1997. *History*: it was under Prussian control (1793–1807 and 1814–1919), becoming a free city under the League of Nations in 1919. In 1939 it was annexed by Germany; the city was returned to Poland in 1945. Population (1999 est): 458 988.

Gdynia 54 31N 18 30E A port in N Poland. Originally a fishing village, it has become Poland's main shipbuilding centre and naval base. Population (1999 est): 253 521.

gecko A slender long-tailed nocturnal lizard belonging to the widely distributed family *Gekkonidae* (650 species), found in a wide range of habitats. 3–35 cm long, many geckos have fleshy toe pads covered with microscopic hooks enabling them to cling to smooth surfaces. They feed on insects and have well-developed vocal cords. The **tokay** (*Gekko gecko*) of E Asia is a large arboreal gecko.

Geelong 38 10S 144 26E A city and major port in Australia, in S Victoria. Wool, wheat, and oil are the principal exports. Population (1998 est): 186 307.

Geiger counter A device that detects and quantifies ionizing radiation and particles. Essentially it consists of a metal cylinder containing low-pressure gas and a wire anode. Ionizing particles passing into the tube through a window at one end induce discharges, which can be counted by a suitable circuit. Named after the German physicist Hans Geiger (1882–1945).

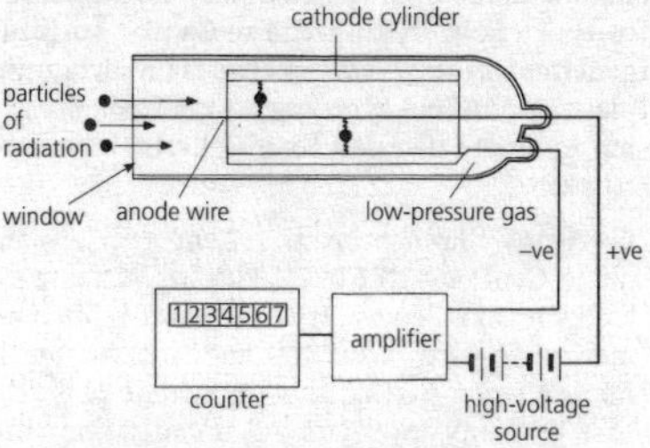

Geiger counter. The radiation entering the tube causes an electrical discharge through the gas between the anode and cathode, sending an electrical pulse to the counter.

geisha A Japanese woman whose profession is to entertain men in a restaurant. Geishas, who are not prostitutes, sing and dance or engage their clients in conversation.

gel *See* COLLOID.

gelada A large *Old World monkey, *Theropithecus gelada*, of Ethiopian mountains. 120–150 cm long including the tufted tail (70–80 cm), it has a cape of dark-brown hair with two bare patches on the chest and lives in large groups, feeding on roots, leaves, and fruit.

gelatin A protein derived from bones and skins. In solution it forms a reversible gel that becomes fluid as the temperature rises and solidifies on cooling. It is widely used in the food industry, in drug preparations, and in photographic emulsions.

Geldof, Bob (1952–) Irish rock musician. Born in Dublin, Geldof made successful recordings with the Boomtown Rats before becoming involved in fund raising for the starving in Africa in 1984. His efforts, culminating in a massive concert held simultaneously in the UK and the USA in 1985, generated widespread support and unprecedented donations to charity. He received an honorary knighthood in 1986.

gelignite A high explosive consisting of nitroglycerin, cellulose nitrate, potassium nitrate, and woodpulp.

Gell-Mann, Murray (1929–) US physicist, who won the 1969 Nobel Prize for his work on elementary particles. In 1953 he introduced the concept of *strangeness to account for the absence of certain expected interactions. He also formulated the theory of unitary symmetry and the concept of quarks (*see also* PARTICLE PHYSICS).

Gemini (Latin: Twins) A conspicuous constellation in the N sky near Orion, on the *zodiac between Cancer and Taurus. The brightest stars are Pollux and Castor.

gene A unit of the hereditary material of an organism that provides the genetic information necessary to fulfil a single function. The term was first coined by W. L. Johannsen (1857–1927) in 1909. Genes were initially conceived as a string of beads comprising the *chromosome. However, with the discovery of the structure of *DNA and the molecular basis of heredity, a gene is now regarded as being a functional unit (cistron) corresponding to a specific sequence of the *genetic code. *See also* GENE THERAPY; GENOME.

General Agreement on Tariffs and Trade (GATT) An organization set up in 1948 by a UN initiative to regulate and reduce barriers to world trade. GATT was succeeded by the *World Trade Organization in 1996.

General Strike (1926) A national stoppage of work by members of Britain's major industries, lasting from 3 to 12 May. It began when the Trades Union Council (TUC) called out its members in support of the miners, who had refused to accept a reduction in wages. The government under Stanley *Baldwin kept essential services going and nine days later the TUC called off the Strike.

Genesis The first book of the Bible, traditionally ascribed to Moses. It recounts the creation of the universe and of man, the fall of Adam, the Flood, and the scattering of the nations at Babel. The remainder of the book focuses on the lives of *Abraham, Isaac, Jacob, and Joseph, introducing the covenant between God and the Israelites.

genet A carnivorous mammal of the genus *Genetta* (9 species) of Africa and Europe. Genets range from the 50-cm Abyssinian genet (*G. abyssinica*) to the 100-cm African giant genet (*G. victoriae*). They have retractile claws, long tails (up to 50 cm), foxlike heads, and pale fur with dark spots or stripes. Genets are nocturnal, preying on birds and small mammals. Family: *Viverridae*.

gene therapy The treatment of diseases using genetic engineering. It is targeted at somatic (rather than germ) cells and aims to treat both genetic diseases and some cancers. Genetic diseases, such as haemophilia, muscular dystrophy, and cystic fibrosis, are caused by a faulty gene failing to produce a vital protein; the treatment is designed to introduce into the patients body the correct version of the gene, which can restore the missing protein. In treating cancers, gene transfer can enable genes acting specifically against tumour cells to be inserted into these cells.

genetic code The way in which information encoded in DNA and RNA molecules is used for the organization and function of living cells. The nature of the code was elucidated in the 1960s by the work of *Crick, M. W. Nirenberg (1927–), Har Gobind Khorana (1922–), and others. The basic symbol of the code is a sequence of three consecutive bases of messenger RNA (which is transcribed from DNA).

genetic counselling Advice given to those with a family history of inherited diseases, such as cystic fibrosis and muscular dystrophy. Parents are told of the likelihood of their children being affected, and the means of prevention and treatment available.

genetic engineering (genetic modification *or* **recombinant DNA technology)** Alteration of the genetic constitution of organisms, usually bacteria, in order to obtain gene products beneficial to man. Typically, a sequence of desirable genes is inserted into the DNA of a host bacterium. This altered DNA (*or* recombinant DNA) then directs the bacterial cell to synthesize the desired gene product (for example, insulin). Genetic engineering has been used to improve crop plants, for example by conferring resistance to pests or herbicides or prolonging storage time. The resultant **genetically modified organisms** (GMOs) include tomatoes, maize, and soya. Because the long-term effects of GM crops are not known, in the UK their commercial exploitation is controversial. In 2004 the government permitted GM maize to be grown for animal consumption.

genetic fingerprinting (*or* **DNA fingerprinting**) An identification technique based on DNA examination. DNA is extracted from sample cells (e.g. from blood or semen) and broken into fragments using enzymes. These fragments, containing the genetic code unique to each individual, are compared with fragments obtained from a blood sample of the test subject. In 1987 the technique was first used in the UK as forensic evidence, since when its use has become widespread.

genetics The study of heredity and variation in living organisms. The science of genetics is founded on the work of Gregor *Mendel. In the early 20th century *chromosomes and their *genes were established as the carriers of information determining inheritable characteristics, and with the discovery of the structure of *DNA in 1953, the molecular basis of genetics was revealed. Genetics is important in plant and animal breeding and in understanding inherited diseases. *See also* GENETIC ENGINEERING.

Geneva (French name: Genève; German name: Genf) 46 13N 6 09E A city in SW Switzerland, on Lake Geneva. It is a cultural and commercial centre, banking and international finance being particularly important. It is the base of many international organizations including the International Red Cross and the World Health Organization. *History*: originally a prehistoric lake dwelling, it was later a Roman city. It became the centre of the Calvinist Reformation and a refuge for persecuted Protestants. Population (1999 est): 172 809.

Geneva Bible An English translation of the Bible published in 1560 by Puritan exiles in Geneva. It is also called the Breeches Bible because of the use of the word in the translation of Genesis 3.7.

Geneva Conventions International agreements covering the care and protection of noncombatants and wounded troops in wartime. Inspired by the establishment of the Interna-

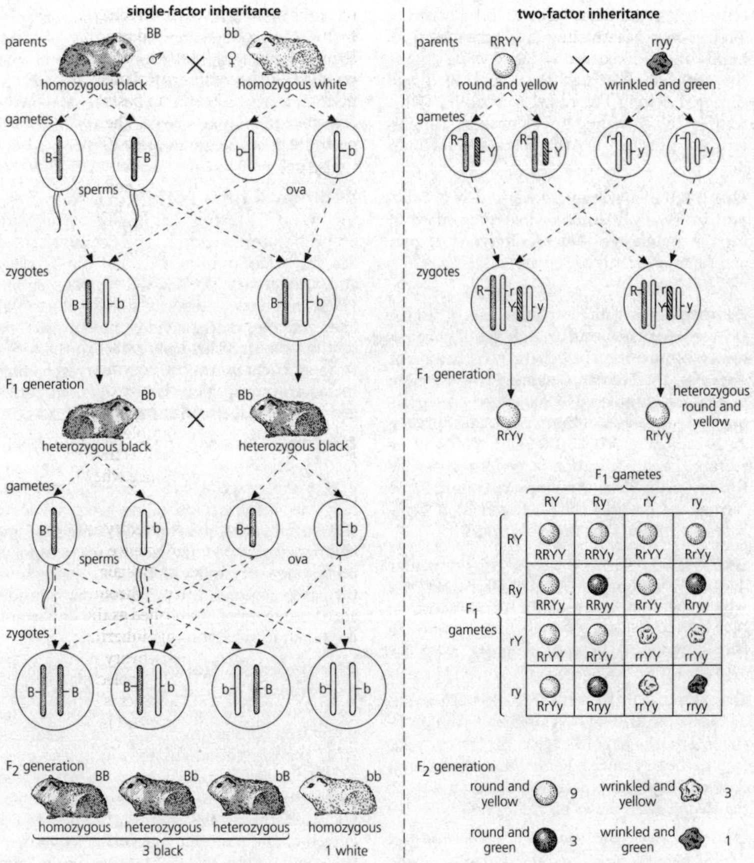

genetics. When a purebred (homozygous) black guinea pig (BB) mates with a purebred white one (bb) all the offspring (F1 generation) will be black (Bb), since the gene for black is dominant. Mating of this heterozygous F1 generation will produce both black and white guinea pigs (F2 generation) in the ratio 3:1, since each of the parents carries a white recessive gene. The same principle applies to the inheritance of two factors — seed colour and texture — in pea plants. When a plant with round yellow seeds (RRYY — dominant) is crossed with one producing wrinkled green seeds (rryy — recessive) the offspring will all have round yellow seeds (RrYy — heterozygous). Crossing of this generation results in the segregation and reassortment of the genes so that their offspring will show all four possibilities of seed colour and texture in the proportions 9:3:3:1. These examples of single- and two-factor inheritance obey Mendel's laws.

tional *Red Cross, a code of practice for the treatment of wounded soldiers was agreed in 1864. Subsequent agreements (1906, 1929, 1949) cover assistance for forces at sea, the treatment of prisoners of war, and the protection of civilians.

Geneva, Lake (French name: Lac Léman) A lake on the River Rhône between Switzerland and France. The city of Geneva and the towns of Montreux, Lausanne, and Evian stand on its shores. It is dominated by the Alps to the N. Area: 577 sq km (223 sq mi).

Genghis Khan (c. 1162–1227) The founder of the Mongol empire. Originally called Tamujin, he adopted the title Genghis Khan (Emperor of All) in 1206 after uniting the nomadic Mongol tribes of the Siberian steppes and destroying Tatar power. Organizing his horsemen into highly mobile squadrons called *ordus* (hence "hordes"), he breached the Great Wall and captured Peking but failed to conquer China completely. Advancing westwards, Genghis crushed resistance in Afghanistan, Persia, and S Russia.

Genoa (Italian name: Genova) 44 24N 08 56E A port in NW Italy. A major maritime city during the middle ages, Genoa is Italy's chief port and a major industrial centre. Population (2000 est): 636 104.

g

genome The full complement of genes (i.e. DNA sequences) within a single set of chromosomes, comprising the genetic constitution of a species. The **Human Genome Project**, begun in 1988 and completed in 2003, succeeded in sequencing the bases of human DNA, comprising an estimated 30 000–35 000 genes. This will facilitate the identification of genes responsible for many diseases, enabling accurate genetic testing and possibly the development of gene-based treatments for these disorders.

gentian A herbaceous plant of the widely distributed genus *Gentiana* (about 400 species), which includes many alpine perennials. The blue flowers usually form a bell or funnel with spreading lobes. The fruit of most species is a capsule. Family: *Gentianaceae*.

Gentile da Fabriano (Niccolo di Giovanni di Massio; c. 1370–1427) Florentine painter of the international gothic style. His fresco cycles for the Doge's Palace, Venice, and the Lateran Basilica, Rome, have perished. The *Adoration of the Magi* (Uffizi) shows his rich style.

geochronology The study of dating geological events, rocks, sediments, and organic remains. Absolute dating involves radioactive dating techniques giving an actual date BP (before present). Relative dating establishes the order of geological events in relation to each other, using fossil correlation, pollen analysis, etc.

Geoffrey of Monmouth (c. 1100–54) English chronicler. His major work, the fanciful *Historia Regum Britanniae*, was the main source for the whole body of medieval European literature concerned with the Arthurian legend.

geography The study of the features of the earth's surface, especially in terms of the human environment. Modern geography was founded in the early 19th entury by the German scholars Alexander von Humboldt and Carl Ritter and is now divided between the physical and social sciences. Physical geography includes geomorphology (the study of landforms), biogeography (the study of soils and the distribution of animals and plants), and climatology (the study of climate). The main branches of human geography are historical geography, economic geography, urban geography, and political geography.

geological time scale A time scale covering the earth's history. The largest divisions are eras (Palaeozoic, Mesozoic, and Cenozoic); these are subdivided into periods and the Tertiary and Quaternary periods are further subdivided into epochs; epochs consist of several ages, and ages can be divided into chrons. The stratomeric standard scale refers to the rocks formed in these intervals; the corresponding terms are group (era), system (period), series (epoch), stage (age), and chronozone (chron).

geology The study of the earth: its origin, history, structure, composition, and the natural processes acting on it. The branches of geology are historical (including geochronology, stratigraphy, and palaeontology); physical (including geomorphology, geophysics, petrology, mineralogy, crystallography, and geochemistry); and economic, involving the distribution and occurrence of the economically important rocks and minerals.

geomagnetic field The earth's magnetic field, causing a compass needle to align north–south. It is believed to be caused by the liquid-iron core acting as a dynamo resulting from the convection currents in it. The magnetic poles do not coincide with the geographic poles, and their positions vary with time. Reversals of the earth's magnetic field have occurred in the past. The **magnetic elements** of the earth's field are the *magnetic dip, the *magnetic declination, and the horizontal field strength.

geometrid moth A moth of the family *Geometridae*, occurring in Europe, Asia, and North America. The name is derived from the looping method of locomotion of the caterpillars, which are known as inch worms, loopers, or measuring worms. The adults, known as pugs, umbers, carpet moths, etc., have slender bodies, a weak flight, and camouflaging coloration.

geometry A branch of mathematics concerned with the properties of space and shapes. In Euclidean geometry the space corresponds to common ideas of physical space and the shapes are idealizations of the common shapes that occur in real life. Other branches of geometry include non-Euclidean geometry, Riemannian geometry, and *analytic geometry. *See also* TOPOLOGY.

era	period	epoch	millions of years ago
Cenozoic	Quaternary	Holocene	
		Pleistocene	1.8
	Tertiary	Pliocene	
		Miocene	
		Oligocene	
		Eocene	
		Palaeocene	65
Mesozoic	Cretaceous		135
	Jurassic		200
	Triassic		240
Palaeozoic	Permian		280
	Carboniferous		370
	Devonian		415
	Silurian		445
	Ordovician		515
	Cambrian		590
Precambrian	Precambrian		4500

geological time scale

geophysics The study of the physical forces acting on and within the earth. Important branches of geophysics are seismology, geomagnetism, vulcanology, natural radioactivity, and the gravitational field.

George I (1660–1727) The first Hanoverian King of Great Britain and Ireland (1714–27) and Elector of Hanover (1698–1727). He divorced his wife for infidelity (1694) and imprisoned her for 32 years. A successful soldier and a shrewd diplomat, he was unpopular in Britain because he seemed to subordinate British to Hanoverian interests. He never learnt English and left government to his Whig ministers.

George II (1683–1760) King of Great Britain and Ireland and Elector of Hanover (1727–69). His reliance on such ministers as Sir Robert *Walpole influenced the development of constitutional monarchy. In the War of Austrian Succession he fought at Dettingen (1743), the last British king to appear in battle. He was a patron of musicians, notably Handel.

George III (1738–1820) King of Great Britain and Ireland (1760–1820) and Elector (1760–1815) and King (1815–20) of Hanover. He shared with Lord *North the blame for the loss of the American colonies but was more astute in backing William Pitt the Younger as prime minister (1783–1801). He suffered periods of insanity from the 1780s (attributed to *porphyria) and was permanently insane by 1811, after which the Prince of Wales (later George IV) acted as regent (*see also* REGENCY STYLE).

George IV (1762–1830) King of the United Kingdom and of Hanover (1820–30). He secretly married a Roman Catholic, Maria Fitzherbert, in 1785 but the marriage was invalid and in 1795 he married *Caroline of Brunswick. George's dissipation and his treatment of his wife undermined the prestige of the monarchy.

George V (1865–1936) King of the United Kingdom (1910–36), second son of Edward VII, whose heir he became on the death (1892) of his elder brother Albert Victor. In 1893 George married Mary of Teck.

George VI (1895–1952) King of the United Kingdom (1936–52). Second son of George V, he succeeded to the throne when Edward VIII abdicated. He married Lady Elizabeth Bowes-Lyon (*see* ELIZABETH THE QUEEN MOTHER) in 1923.

George, St The patron saint of England and of soldiers. His cult was brought to England by Crusaders returning from Palestine, where he was believed to have been martyred during Emperor Diocletian's rule. In art he is usually portrayed slaying a dragon, a legend that probably derives from the *Pegasus myth. Feast day: 23 April.

George Cross The highest British decoration for civilian bravery, awarded since 1940. A silver cross superscribed *For Gallantry*, it has twice been awarded collectively: to the island of Malta (1942) and the Royal Ulster Constabulary (1999). The **George Medal**, the second highest decoration for civilian bravery, was also instituted in 1940.

Georgetown (*or* **Penang**) 5 26N 100 16E A city in NW Peninsular Malaysia, the capital of Penang state. It is now Malaysia's chief port. Population (1991): 219 376.

Georgetown 6 46N 58 10W The capital and main port of Guyana. Founded by the British in 1781, it was later occupied by the French and the Dutch. Population (1999 est): 275 000.

Georgia (USA) A state on the SE coast of the USA. It can be divided into two physical regions: the Appalachian Mountains in the N and a coastal plain with forests and swamps in the S. Agriculture is important; poultry has replaced cotton as the major item and Georgia is a leading producer of peanuts. *History*: named after George II, it was founded in 1732. Settlement of the state expanded after the American Revolution; a supporter of the Confederate cause in the US Civil War, it suffered considerable damage during Gen Sherman's March to the Sea (1864). During the last hundred years it has suffered from a decline in the cotton industry and troubled race relations. Area: 152 488 sq km (58 876 sq mi). Population (2000): 8 186 453. Capital: Atlanta.

Georgia (Asia) A republic in W Asia. It is a mountainous region with many holiday resorts on the Black Sea coast. The population is mostly Georgian. *Economy*: Georgia is rich in minerals, especially manganese and coal. It also has hydroelectric resources. The main crop is tea; citrus fruits, grapes, and tobacco are also important. *History*: Christianity was introduced in the 4th century AD. An independent kingdom for most of the middle ages, Georgia was divided between Persia and Turkey in 1555, passing to Russia in the 19th century. It became independent in 1918 but subsequently formed part of the Transcaucasian Soviet Federated Republic. It became a separate republic in the USSR in 1936. Independence was declared in 1990; in 1992 the dictatorial president Zviad Gamsakhurdia was overthrown, government passed to a state council under Eduard Shevardnadze, Georgia's independence was recognized, and free elections were held. The early 1990s saw fighting between state troops and separatists in Abkhazia and South Ossetia (supported by Russia). Greater stability was achieved after Georgia and Russia signed an economic cooperation agreement (1994). A new constitution (1995) granted considerable autonomy to Abkhazia and South Ossetia (renamed Tskhinvali) but pressure for complete independence has continued. In 2003 disputed election results provoked massive demonstrations and Shevardnadze was forced to resign; he was succeeded by the opposition leader Mikhail Saakashvili. Official language: Georgian. Currency: lari of 100 tetri. Area: 69 493 sq km (26 831 sq mi). Population (2003 est): 4 934 000. Capital: Tbilisi.

Georgian The language spoken by the Georgian peoples of Georgia, Azerbaidzhan, Turkey, and Iran. It belongs to the Kartvelian or South Caucasian group and is written in a script derived from Aramaic with Greek influences and has a literature dating from the 5th century AD. It is the official language of Georgia.

Georgian style A style of British architecture prevalent during the reigns of George I to George IV (1714–1830). The period was subject to several different influences but was dominated by Palladianism and *neoclassicism. Georgian architecture was characterized by the symmetrical use of twelve-paned sash windows and the restrained use of classical features.

geostationary orbit *See* COMMUNICATIONS SATELLITE.

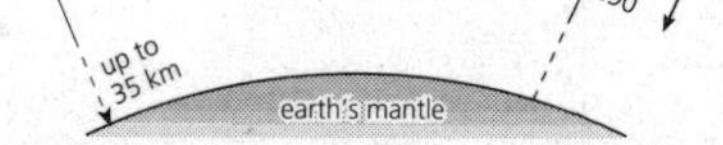

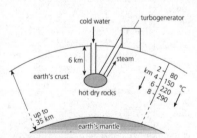

geothermal power. In the UK the absence of volcanoes and geysers means that hot-dry-rock (HDR) technology has to be used. In this, cold water is pumped some 6 km down in the earth's crust, where it percolates through fissures in the hot dry rocks; the resulting superheated steam is brought to the surface, where it drives a turbogenerator. HDR technology is still experimental.

geothermal power Heat produced in the earth's interior. Volcanoes, geysers, and hot springs are all sources of geothermal power, although only the latter two provide convenient energy sources. It supplies about 0.1% of the world's energy requirements.

geranium A herbaceous plant of the genus *Pelargonium* (250 species), most species of which are native to South Africa. They have showy flowers, usually red or pink. Most horticultural geraniums are hybrids. Family: *Geraniaceae*. Horticultural geraniums should be distinguished from related plants of the genus *Geranium* (*see* CRANESBILL).

gerbil A small *rodent belonging to the subfamily *Gerbillinae* (over 100 species) of Africa and Asia, also called jird and sand rat. Ranging in size from 5–20 cm, gerbils have long hind legs. They spend the day in underground burrows, feeding at night on seeds and roots. Chief genera: *Gerbillus*, *Tatera*; family: *Cricetidae*.

Géricault, (Jean Louis André) Théodore (1791–1824) French painter. His famous *Raft of the Medusa* (1819) was based on a contemporary shipwreck. He is also noted for his paintings of horses and a late series of portraits of insane people. He died in a riding accident.

German A language of the West Germanic language group. It is the official language of Germany and Austria and one of the four official languages of Switzerland. High German, the official and written form, developed from dialects of the highland areas of Germany and Austria. Old High German was spoken before 1100 AD when Middle High German, based on Upper German dialects, became the standard form. Modern High German developed from the 16th-century dialect of Luther. Low German exists only in a spoken form in N Germany and is derived from Old Saxon and Middle Low German speech.

Germanic languages A subgroup of the Indo-European language group. There are three recognized subgroups: East Germanic, North Germanic, and West Germanic. The first of these is now extinct. North Germanic covers the *Scandinavian languages, West Germanic includes modern English and German among its descendants as well as *Dutch (Netherlandic) and Frisian. All three branches can be traced back to an unrecorded Proto-Germanic language, which has been reconstructed by philologists by comparing and tracing back similar modern languages.

germanium (Ge) A brittle grey-white metalloid, discovered by C. A. Winkler (1838–1904) in 1886. Like *gallium it is present in coal and is concentrated in chimney soot as well as in the flue dusts of zinc smelters, from which it is obtained commercially. The element is a *semiconductor and is used in the electronics industry. At no 32; at wt 72.61; mp 938.35°C; bp 2834°C.

German measles A common contagious disease of children and young adults caused by a virus. Known medically as rubella, it is a mild infection producing a pink rash and a sore throat. If a woman is infected in pregnancy she may give birth to a malformed child.

German shepherd dog (*or* **Alsatian**) A breed of large dog originating in Germany. It has a coarse coat that can range in colour from white to black but is often black and tan. German shepherds are used as working dogs, as guard dogs, and as guide dogs for the blind. Height: 61–66 cm (dogs); 56–61 cm (bitches).

Germany, Federal Republic of A country in central Europe; since 1990 it has comprised the former East Germany (the German Democratic Republic) and the former West Germany (the Federal Republic of Germany). For administrative purposes, Germany is divided into 16 *Länder* (German, states). Extensive plains in the N, which border on the North Sea, the Baltic Sea, and Denmark, rise to a central hilly area, including the Harz Mountains and Thuringian Forest, with the Erzgebirge in the SE and the peaks of the Alps in the extreme S. The chief rivers are the Rhine, Danube, Oder, Ems, Weser, and Elbe. *Economy*: in what was then West Germany, rapid reconstruction of the industrial sector followed World War II. East Germany's centrally controlled economy was also highly industrialized, but remained undynamic by Western standards. The cost of restructuring it has proved far higher than anticipated, and as a result Germany spent most of the 1990s in recession. Considerable mineral resources include coal, lignite, iron ore, lead and zinc, and potash. The agricultural sector has declined in importance, but there is a considerable amount of forestry and an important wine industry. Manufacturing industry remains the mainstay of the economy. Tourism is an important source of revenue. *History*: The region was occupied by German tribes from about 500 BC and came repeatedly into conflict with the Romans from the 2nd century BC. Overrun by the Huns in the 4th and 5th centuries, the area was dominated by the *Franks from the 6th century and was Christianized in the late-7th to 8th centuries. After the failure of the Frankish dynasty the German kings became nominally elective but medieval Germany was in practice ruled by a series of

g

hereditary dynasties claiming the title of Holy Roman Emperor. In the 13th century the first *Habsburg emperor was elected and from the 15th century the imperial title remained almost continuously in the family. In the later middle ages the power of the princes was challenged by the *Hanseatic League. The 16th and 17th centuries were dominated by religious strife, following Luther's inception of the *Reformation at Wittenberg in 1520. The religious conflict was not resolved until the conclusion (1648) of the *Thirty Years' War. In the 17th century the Hohenzollern Electors of Brandenburg acquired Prussia, which became the dominant German state and, under *Frederick (II) the Great, a major European power. In 1806 the Holy Roman Empire was brought to an end by Napoleon, who formed the Confederation of the Rhine in its place. The post-Napoleonic German confederation was dominated by Austria and Prussia and in 1834 the latter was the moving influence behind the formation of the *Zollverein (customs union). Prussian power increased further with victory in the *Austro-Prussian War (1866), and in the *Franco-Prussian War (1870–71). In 1871 Bismarck achieved his cherished ambition of creating a German Empire. The late 19th and early 20th centuries saw rapid industrialization, an aggressive armaments programme, and the rise of Germany as a colonial power, especially in Africa; its international aspirations were a major cause of *World War I. Defeated in 1918, the Empire came to an end (1919) and was replaced by the *Weimar Republic, which was plagued by the economic difficulties that facilitated Hitler's rise to power in the early 1930s. His aggressive foreign policy and absurd racial theories led to attempts to establish a new German empire by an unprecedented ruthlessness which precipitated World War II. Following Germany's defeat the country was divided into British, French, Soviet, and US zones before the subsequent formation of two separate states, the German Democratic Republic and the Federal Republic of Germany.

East Germany or the **German Democratic Republic** (GDR; German name: Deutsche Demokratische Republik) was formed from the Soviet-occupied zone of Germany following World War II. It was given a provisional constitution in 1949, becoming independent in 1954, with membership of COMECON and the Warsaw Pact and (from 1973) a seat in the UN. The capital was East Berlin. The early years of economic austerity and curbs on civil liberties led to much discontent; the flow of refugees to West Germany continued until 1961, when the *Berlin Wall was erected. Low living standards and the government's refusal to consider liberal reform led to mass protests in 1989 and the departure of thousands of refugees to the West. President Erich Honecker resigned and a multiparty democracy was instituted. A conservative alliance won free elections in March 1990 and union with West Germany was achieved in Oct 1990.

West Germany or the **Federal Republic of Germany** (FRG; German name: Bundesrepublik Deutschland) was formed from the British-, French-, and US-occupied zones following World War II, and became fully independent in 1955. The capital was transferred to Bonn although West Berlin remained a part of the Federal Republic. In the postwar years it enjoyed a spectacular economic recovery making it the most prosperous country in W Europe.

Elections for the reunited Germany were held in Dec 1990, with victory for Helmut Kohl and the Christian Democrats. Kohl was replaced as chancellor by Gerhard Schröder in 1999, when the Christian Democrats were defeated by the Social Democrats. Germany is a member of NATO. German forces saw military action for the first time since 1945 in the NATO air war against Yugoslavia (1999). Germany adopted the single European currency in 1999–2002. Official language: German. Currency: euro of 100 cents. Area: 356 798 sq km (137 746 sq mi). Population (2003 est): 82 604 000. Capital: Berlin.

germination The process by which an embryo plant within a seed is transformed into a recognizable plant with roots, stem, and leaves. Water, warmth, and oxygen stimulate germination, which begins with the emergence of the root (radicle) and is followed by the shoot (plumule). Energy for the process is provided by the *cotyledons (seed leaves), which either remain below ground (hypogeal germination, as in the broad bean) or form the first leaves of the seedling (epigeal germination, as in the marrow).

Gershwin, George (Jacob Gershvin; 1898–1937) US composer and songwriter. He wrote many songs for musical shows and films, his jazz-inspired orchestral works include *Rhapsody in Blue* (1924) and *An American in Paris* (1928). The opera *Porgy and Bess* (1935) is still widely performed. His brother **Ira Gershwin** (1896–1983) wrote the lyrics to many of his songs.

Gestalt psychology A school of *psychology that originated in Germany in the early 20th century: Wolfgang Köhler (1887–1967) and

Kurt Koffka (1886–1941) were its founders. It regards mental processes as wholes (gestalts) that cannot be analysed into smaller components.

Gestapo (German: *Ge*heime *Sta*ats*po*lizei, secret state police) The Nazi secret police, formed in 1933 under Göring and administered from 1936 by the *SS. The two organizations were responsible for carrying out the atrocities perpetrated by the Germans in Europe.

Getty, J(ean) Paul (1892–1976) US businessman, who lived in the UK. He made his fortune in oil, becoming a millionaire at the age of 22. He founded the J. Paul Getty Museum at Malibu, California. His son, **Paul Getty Jr.** (1932–2003), was a noted philanthropist.

Gettysburg, Battle of (1–3 July 1863) The most significant battle of the US *Civil War, fought in S central Pennsylvania as part of the Confederacy's second invasion of the North. After three days of fighting the Confederates withdrew; the North lost 23 000 men and the South 25 000. The **Gettysburg Address**, one of the shortest and most famous of modern speeches, was delivered (19 November 1863) by President Abraham Lincoln at Gettysburg battlefield.

geysers Jets of hot water and steam issuing intermittently from holes in the earth's crust, some reaching heights of up to 70 m. Geysers are found in volcanically active or recently active regions. They occur when water from deep within the crust becomes superheated and suddenly boils.

Ghana, Republic of A country in West Africa, on the Gulf of Guinea. Coastal plains rise to undulating country around Accra, and, in the centre, the basin of the River Volta rises to plateaus, especially in the N and W. *Economy*: chiefly agricultural. The main cash crop is cocoa, of which Ghana is among the world's chief producers. Gold and diamonds are mined, as well as manganese, bauxite, and limestone. Hydroelectricity is an important source of power and oil was found offshore in 1978. The 1990s saw steady economic improvement. *History*: from the middle ages several small kingdoms flourished in what is now Ghana. In 1472 the Portuguese and subsequently other Europeans set up trading posts in the region, which they called the Gold Coast. The area became the British colony of the Gold Coast in 1874. In 1957, together with the British part of Togo, it became independent, its new name, Ghana, being that of a medieval N African empire. In 1960 it became a republic within the British Commonwealth under Kwame Nkrumah, who was deposed in 1969. There followed a series of military coups, in the last of which (1981) Fl Lt Jerry Rawlings came to power. Multiparty elections in 1992 led to victory for Rawlings, although the result was contested by opposition parties. Rawlings was re-elected in 1996 but defeated by the opposition leader John Kufuor in 2000. Official language: English. Currency: cedi of 100 pesewas. Area: 238 305 sq km (92 010 sq mi). Population (2003 est): 20 468 000. Capital: Accra.

gharial *See* GAVIAL.

Ghats Two mountain ranges lying along the W and E coasts of India. The **Western Ghats**, which extend about 1500 km (932 mi) from N of Bombay to Cape Comorin, rise to 2693 m (8840 ft). They have dense natural vegetation and are used for tea planting. The **Eastern Ghats** extend about 1400 km (880 mi) from near Cuttack to the Nilgiri Hills.

Ghent (Flemish name: Gent; French name: Gand) 51 02N 3 42E A city in Belgium, at the confluence of the canalized Rivers Scheldt and Lys. One of Belgium's oldest cities, it is a major port and the country's textile centre. Population (2000 est): 224 180.

gherkin A trailing West Indian vine, *Cucumis anguria*. It is cultivated for its prickly edible fruit, 2.5–7.5 cm long, used when immature for pickling. Family: *Cucurbitaceae* (gourd family).

Ghibellines *See* GUELFS AND GHIBELLINES.

Ghiberti, Lorenzo (c. 1378–1455) Florentine Renaissance sculptor, who made his name in 1402, by winning the competition for the bronze relief sculptures for the north doors of the Baptistry of the Florentine Duomo. Finished in 1424, these New Testament scenes, mainly in the international gothic style, were followed by Old Testament scenes (1425–52). Simultaneously he wrote *I commentarii*, which included histories of ancient and early Renaissance art and an autobiography.

Ghirlandaio, Domenico (Domenico di Tommaso Bigordi; 1449–94) Florentine painter of the early *Renaissance. From 1481 to 1482 he worked on a fresco in the Sistine Chapel but his major undertaking was the fresco cycle (1486–90) in Sta Maria Novella, Florence. The tenderly painted *Old Man and Boy* (Louvre) is a fine example of his portraiture.

Giacometti, Alberto (1901–66) Swiss sculptor and painter. He was influenced initially by *cubism and primitive art and later by *surrealism, particularly in his abstract construction of sticks, glass, wire, etc., entitled *The Palace at 4 am* (New York). After breaking with surrealism in 1935, he developed a unique figure style.

Giambologna (Giovanni da Bologna *or* Jean de Boulogne; 1529–1608) Italian mannerist sculptor of Flemish birth. Working from 1557 in Florence, where he was patronized by the Medici, he produced fountains, religious sculptures, and small bronze statues.

Giant's Causeway 55 14N 6 32W A promontory in N Northern Ireland, in Antrim. It consists of several thousand closely packed basaltic columns, mainly hexagonal in shape, formed by an outpouring of lava into the sea. According to legend it was built as a bridge to enable the giants to cross from Ireland to Scotland.

giant star A large very luminous star that has a very tenuous atmosphere but a dense core. It is in a late stage of evolution, having exhausted the normal source of energy in its core (hydrogen), and must obtain energy from other nuclear fusion reactions. *See also* RED GIANT.

gibberellins A group of organic compounds that stimulate plant growth. First isolated from the fungus *Gibberella fujikuroi*, over 30 gibberellins are now known. They stimulate the growth of leaves, stems, flowers, and fruit and break the dormancy of seeds and tubers.

gibbon A small *ape belonging to the genus *Hylobates* (7 species), of S Asia. 45–65 cm long, they have long arms and hooked fingers used to swing through trees. They live in family groups, feeding chiefly on fruit and leaves, and have a whooping call. Family: *Hylobatidae*. *See also* SIAMANG.

Gibbon, Edward (1737–94) British historian. His ironic treatment of Christianity in his monumental *The History of the Decline and Fall of the Roman Empire* (1776–88) aroused controversy, but its scope and style ensured its survival.

Gibbons, Grinling (1648–1721) English wood carver and sculptor, born in Rotterdam. Patronized by Charles II and subsequent British monarchs, he produced decorative carvings of flowers, fruit, etc. His best-known works are the choir stalls and organ screen in St Paul's Cathedral.

Gibbons, Orlando (1583–1625) English composer, organist, and virginalist. He wrote madrigals, church music, and string fantasias and contributed pieces to *Parthenia* (1611), the first anthology of keyboard music to be printed in England.

Gibbs, Josiah Willard (1839–1903) US physicist. Gibbs founded chemical thermodynamics, which is largely based on the function known as the Gibbs free energy. He is also known for his phase rule, relating the number of parameters that can be varied in a system of more than one phase.

Gibraltar A UK overseas territory occupying a peninsula at the southern tip of Spain. The isthmus that links it to the Spanish mainland rises sharply to the 427 m (1400 ft) limestone Rock of Gibraltar. The population is mainly of Spanish, Genoese, and Portugese descent. *Economy*: Britain's defence presence on Gibraltar was the mainstay of the economy until the mid-1980s, when the naval dockyards closed. Offshore financial services and tourism are now the main economic activities. Fees for services to shipping are also an important source of revenue. *History*: settled by the Moors in 711 AD, the Rock of Gibraltar was taken by Castile in 1462, becoming part of united Spain. It was captured in 1704 by the British to whom it was formally ceded by the Treaty of Utrecht (1713). The colony became an important British naval base. Claims to Gibraltar have long been made by Spain but a UN proposal to end British occupation was defeated in a referendum in 1967. In 1969 Spain closed its frontier with Gibraltar leading to the subsequent import of Moroccan labour. The border was reopened in 1985. In 1998–99 a new dispute led to Spain imposing a semi-blockade. Anglo-Spanish talks aimed at agreeing a new international status for Gibraltar began in 2001. However, Gibraltarians voting in a 2002 referendum rejected any form of shared sovereignty by almost 99%. Official languages: English and Spanish. Currency: Gibraltar pound of 100 pence. Area: 6.5 sq km (2.5 sq mi). Population (2000 est): 27 033.

Gibraltar, Strait of A strait between Gibraltar and Africa, joining the Atlantic Ocean and the Mediterranean Sea. It narrows to 13 km (8 mi) and is of great strategic importance.

Gibson Desert A desert in central Western Australia. It consists of a vast arid area of active sand dunes and desert grass. Area: 220 000 sq km (85 000 sq mi).

Gide, André (1869–1951) French novelist and critic. Much of his work reflects his homosexuality and consequent conflict with conventional morality. In 1895 he married his cousin Madeleine Rondeaux, the inspiration of two short works, *The Immoralist* (1902) and *Strait Is the Gate* (1909). His longer novels are *The Vatican Cellars* (1914) and *The Counterfeiters* (1926). His *Journal*, which he kept from 1885 until his death, is a major work of literary autobiography. He won the Nobel Prize in 1947.

Gielgud, Sir (Arthur) John (1904–2000) British actor. He was noted for his distinguished voice and his many fine performances in Shakespearean productions. He was appointed to the OM in 1997.

Gigantes In Greek mythology, the giant sons of *Uranus (Heaven) and *Gaia (Earth), whose rebellion against the Olympian gods was defeated with the help of Heracles. They were subsequently associated with earthquakes and volcanoes.

Gijón 43 32N 5 40W A port in NW Spain, on the Bay of Biscay. Its many ancient buildings include Roman baths and medieval palaces. Population (1998 est): 265 491.

Gilbert, William (1544–1603) English physicist and physician to Elizabeth I. His *De magnete* (1600) listed many experimental observations concerning magnets, including the discovery of magnetic dip. He was the first English scientist to accept the ideas of *Copernicus and coined such terms as *electricity* and *magnetic pole*.

Gilbert, Sir W(illiam) S(chwenk) (1836–1911) British comic dramatist. He wrote comic verses, published as *Bab Ballads* (1869), while studying law. In 1870 he met Arthur *Sullivan, the composer for whom he wrote the libretti for 14 popular operas.

Gilbert Islands *See* KIRIBATI, REPUBLIC OF.

Gillespie, Dizzy (John Birks G.; 1917–93) US Black jazz trumpeter, band leader, and composer, who was one of the originators of *bop.

gills The respiratory organs of aquatic animals: specialized thin-walled regions of the body surface through which dissolved oxygen is taken into the blood and carbon dioxide released into the water. The gills of fish lie in gill slits on each side of the gullet. The gills of molluscs and fanworms are ciliated and trap food particles in the respiratory currents. The external gills of amphibian larvae (tadpoles) are feathery structures projecting from the body wall.

gilt-edged security A UK government fixed-interest stock. Most are redeemable at par on a specified date. Short-term gilts ("shorts") are redeemable within 5 years, "mediums" in 5–15 years, and "longs" in over 15 years. The price of gilts depends upon prevailing interest rates. Most gilts are issued in units of £100 (the par value). Consols are irredeemable.

gin A spirit distilled usually from grain flavoured with juniper berries (the name is derived from the Dutch *jenever*, juniper). Gin is almost pure alcohol, with little flavour. It is generally drunk with tonic water, vermouth, fruit juice, etc.

ginger A perennial herbaceous plant, *Zingiber officinale*, native to SE Asia and widely grown in the tropics for its pungent underground stems (rhizomes), used as a spice, food, and flavouring and in medicine. The plants are sterile, and propagation is by cuttings from the rootstocks. Family: *Zingiberaceae*.

ginkgo A deciduous *gymnosperm tree, *Ginkgo biloba*, also called maidenhair tree, that is the sole living representative of a group of trees that flourished in the Carboniferous period (370–280 million years ago). Growing to a height of 30 m, it has fleshy yellow fruits containing edible kernels. The ginkgo is native to China and widely planted for ornament. Family: *Ginkgoaceae*; phylum: *Ginkgophyta*.

ginseng An extract of the forked roots of either of two herbs, *Panax quinquefolium* or *P. schinseng*, used as a stimulant drug in the Far East and to make aromatic bitters. Family: *Araliaceae* (ivy family).

Giorgione (c. 1477–1510) Italian painter of the Venetian school. He trained under Giovanni *Bellini and worked with *Titian. Most of his paintings are small secular pictures, including the *Tempest* (Accademia, Venice), notable for their dreamlike mood. His portraits, e.g. *Laura* (Vienna), influenced many Venetian painters.

Giotto (Giotto di Bondone; c. 1266–1337) Italian painter and architect, who laid the foundation for *Renaissance painting. He painted the innovative frescoes of scenes from the lives of Joachim and Anne and the Virgin and Christ in the Arena Chapel, Padua, and frescoes in Sta Croce, Florence. In 1334 he became architect of the city and surveyor of Florence Cathedral, for which he designed the campanile.

Gipsies A wandering people found on most continents. The name "Gipsy" is derived from "Egyptian," but they probably originated in India. One group is thought to have migrated through Egypt and North Africa and another through Europe reaching NW Europe during the 15th and 16th centuries. They live largely by seasonal work, itinerant trade, and fortune telling. They have been persecuted frequently, half a million being killed by the Nazis during World War II. Their native language is *Romany.

giraffe A hoofed *mammal, *Giraffa camelopardalis*, of tropical African grasslands. Measuring 3 m at the shoulder, with a neck 2.5 m long, giraffes are marked with reddish-brown blotches on a buff-coloured background. They feed on leaves; both sexes have permanent skin-covered horns. Family: *Giraffidae.*

g

giro A low-cost system for transferring money. It originated in Austria in 1883 and the British National Giro was set up by the Post Office in 1968, becoming independent in 1988 as Girobank PLC. All accounts are held at the Giro Centre (in Bootle, Merseyside), which transfers money from one account to another on receipt of a completed form. Bank giro operates similarly, but accounts are held at bank branches.

Gironde, River An estuary in SW France, on the Bay of Biscay. Formed by the confluence of the Rivers Garonne and Dordogne near Bordeaux, it is used by oceangoing vessels. Length: 72 km (45 mi).

Giscard d'Estaing, Valéry (1926–) French statesman; president (1974–81). A successful minister of finance, he succeeded Pompidou as president but was subsequently defeated by Mitterand.

Gish, Lillian (1893–1993) US actress, who began her career as a child actress on stage with her sister **Dorothy Gish** (1898–1968). Both acted for D.W. *Griffith in early silent films, including *The Birth of a Nation* (1916). Lillian's later films include *Duel in the Sun* (1946) and *The Night of the Hunter* (1955).

Giulio Romano (Giulio Pippi; c.1499–1546) Italian mannerist painter and architect (*see* MANNERISM). He was the pupil of *Raphael, whom he assisted in the decoration of the Vatican apartments and the Villa Farnesina. In 1524 he settled in Mantua, where he designed and decorated the Palazzo del Tè.

Giza, El (*or* **al-Jizah**) 30 01N 31 12E A city in N Egypt, forming a suburb of Cairo. Nearby are the great pyramids of Khafre, *Khufu, and Menkaure and the Sphinx. Population (1990 est): 2 516 000.

glacier A mass of ice and *firn of limited width lying chiefly, or completely, on land and moving downslope from its source. **Cirque glaciers** are contained in depressions on mountain slopes or valley heads. **Valley glaciers** are contained within pre-existing valleys, originating either from cirque glaciers or from an icesheet. The longest of these is the Lambert Glacier, 400 km (250 mi) long. Where a glacier emerges from a valley onto a lowland area, a lobe-shaped **piedmont glacier** results; an example is the Malaspina Glacier in Alaska. **Glaciation** is the action of glacier ice on the land surface. The main landforms resulting from glaciation are either erosional or depositional. Erosional features include U-shaped valleys and rounded rock basins known as cirques. Those of depositional origin include glacial drift and till.

gladiators The slaves, prisoners of war, condemned criminals, or volunteers who fought to the death in amphitheatres for the entertainment of the ancient Roman people. Gladiatorial combats began as a feature of funeral games but their popularity was soon so great that statesmen sponsored shows to enhance their political prestige.

Gladiolus A genus of ornamental perennial herbaceous plants (300 species), native to Europe, Africa, and the Mediterranean regions and widely cultivated. Growing from a corm, the flowering stem reaches a height of 1.2 m, with funnel-shaped flowers. Principal garden forms are *G. cardinalis, G. primulinus, G. psittacinus, G. purpurea-auratus,* and *G. saundersii.* Family: *Iridaceae.*

Gladstone, W(illiam) E(wart) (1809–98) British statesman; Liberal prime minister (1868–74, 1880–85, 1886, 1892–94). Elected to parliament in 1832, he was initially a Tory but supported Peel in the repeal of the *Corn Laws, after which the Peelites joined the Whigs (shortly to be termed Liberals). As chancellor of the exchequer (1852–55, 1859–66) Gladstone reduced tariffs and expenditure. His first ministry disestablished the Irish Church (1869) and introduced the Education Act (1870), the first Irish Land Act (1870), and the Ballot Act (introducing secret ballots). Defeated in the 1874 election, he resigned the Liberal leadership but reemerged as a critic of British policy towards the Balkans. His second ministry achieved further parliamentary reform (1884) but its failure to save *Gordon from Khartoum led to Gladstone's resignation. His last ministries followed his conversion to Irish *Home Rule but both his Home Rule bills were rejected (1886, 1893). An impressive speaker, Gladstone with his Conservative opponent Disraeli dominated British politics in the late 19th century.

Glamorgan A historic county of South Wales. In 1974 it was divided to form the counties of Mid Glamorgan, South Glamorgan, and West Glamorgan. In 1996 administrative powers passed to the new county of Swansea and the county boroughs of Bridgend, Caerphilly, Cardiff, Merthyr Tydfil, Neath and Port Talbot, Rhondda Cynon Taff, and Vale of Glamorgan.

gland An organ specialized for synthesizing a specific chemical substance (secretion) from constituents of the blood and releasing its secretion for use by the body. Man and higher animals have two kinds of glands. The *endocrine glands lack ducts and release their secretions (hormones) directly into the bloodstream. The exocrine glands have ducts through which their products are secreted. Exocrine glands include the salivary glands, the sweat and sebaceous glands in the skin, and the pancreatic cells that secrete digestive enzymes. Plants also have glands, which secrete latex, resin, nectar, tannin, etc.

glanders A highly contagious disease of horses, donkeys, and related animals caused by the bacterium *Pfeifferella mallei*, which can also infect other animals and man. Slaughter of infected animals is compulsory in most countries.

glandular fever (*or* **infectious mononucleosis**) An infection characterized by fatigue, sore throat, headache, muscular pain, and enlarged lymph nodes. Most common in children and young adults, it is caused by the Epstein–Barr virus, which can be transmitted in saliva (for example during kissing). Treatment is with bed rest and painkillers.

Glasgow 1. 55 53N 4 15W A city in central Scotland, mainly in Glasgow City council area, on the River Clyde. Formerly an important port, Glasgow has engineering, textile, chemical, brewing, and whisky-blending industries. *History*: after the union with England (1707), Glasgow's wealth grew rapidly through trade, especially in tobacco and sugar from the New World, and through industry in the industrial revolution. Population (1991): 662 954. **2. Glasgow City.** A council area in W central Scotland. Area: 175 sq km (68 sq mi). Population (2001): 577 869.

glasnost A policy of increased freedom in social and cultural matters introduced in the Soviet Union by Mikhail *Gorbachov in 1986. A Russian word meaning openness, *glasnost* was adopted in conjunction with *perestroika* (meaning progress), which heralded a new flexibility in the economy of the USSR, and an improvement of relations with the West.

glass A translucent and usually transparent noncrystalline substance that behaves as a solid although it has many of the properties of a liquid. Glass itself was known in the 3rd millennium BC but glassblowing was not invented until about 100 BC (in Syria) and windows were not in use until about 100 AD. Ordinary soda glass, used for windows, etc., consists of silica (sand), sodium carbonate, and calcium carbonate (limestone). Flint glass, used for crystal glassware, contains silica, potassium carbonate, potassium nitrate, and lead oxide. Heat-resistant glass also contains borates and alumina; optical glass contains additional elements to control the refractive index and other optical properties. Blown glass is melted and blown inside a mould until it fills the mould. Flint glass is usually blown by hand. Pressed glass is made by pressing the molten glass into a mould. Plate glass, for windows, etc., is now made by floating a rolled sheet of glass on molten tin. *See also* FIBREGLASS.

glass snake A legless lizard belonging to the genus *Ophisaurus*, occurring in Europe, S and E Asia, N Africa, and North America. Glass snakes feed on insects, lizards, mice, and birds' eggs. Unlike true snakes, they have ears, eyelids, and rigid jaws. When attacked, they shed their tail. Family: *Anguidae*.

Glastonbury 51 09N 2 43W A market town in SW England, in Somerset. Here by tradition Joseph of Arimathea founded England's first church and King Arthur is said to be buried. The Glastonbury Festival, the world's largest open-air music event, is held nearby. Population (1991): 7747.

glaucoma An eye disease caused by raised pressure inside the eye. Acute glaucoma is often caused by a sudden block to the drainage of the watery fluid (aqueous humour) inside the eye. It leads to pain and disturbed vision, which will result in blindness without urgent treatment. Chronic glaucoma—one of the commonest causes of blindness—comes on slowly and painlessly.

Glazunov, Aleksandr Konstantinovich (1865–1936) Russian composer and a pupil of Rimsky-Korsakov. Glazunov's works, which were influenced by Wagner and Liszt rather than by Russian musical nationalism, included eight symphonies, concertos, ballets, and string quartets.

Glencoe A glen in W Scotland, in the Highland Region. It was the scene of the massacre of the Macdonalds by the Campbells and English (1692).

Glendower, Owen (Welsh name: Owain Glyndwr; c. 1359–c. 1416) Welsh rebel. Allying with Henry IV's opponents, Glendower controlled most of Wales by 1404 but was subsequently defeated and turned to guerrilla warfare. He disappeared in 1416.

Glenn, John (1921–) US astronaut and politician, who on 20 February 1962, became the first American to orbit the earth. He became a US senator in 1975. In 1998 he returned to space as part of the research into the effects of space travel on the ageing human body.

g

gliders Light fixed-wing engineless aircraft, sometimes called sailplanes. They are launched into the air by a winch or catapult or by being towed by a car or powered aircraft. Once airborne a glider is lifted by warm air currents. The height record is 14.1 km (P. F. Bikle; 1961) and the distance record 1460.8 km (H. W. Grosse; 1972). Pioneered by Otto Lilienthal (1848–96), gliders were used by the *Wright brothers in designing their powered aircraft. Since the 1920s gliding has been a popular sport, controlled in the UK by the British Gliding Association (1924). *See also* HANG-GLIDING.

Glinka, Mikhail Ivanovich (1804–57) Russian composer. He composed the first truly Russian opera *Ivan Susanin* (*A Life for the Tsar*; 1836), piano music, songs, and a second opera *Russlan and Ludmilla* (1842).

Global Positioning System (GPS) A US satellite-based system enabling people, ships, aircraft, etc. equipped with a GPS receiver to determine their position on the earth to within 100 metres. It was developed for the US Department of Defense but now has a range of civilian uses, including the rescue and emergency services.

global warming *See* GREENHOUSE EFFECT.

globefish *See* PUFFER.

Globe Theatre An Elizabethan theatre, in Southwark, in which most of Shakespeare's plays were first produced. A cylindrical wooden building open to the sky, it was built in 1599, burnt down in 1613, rebuilt in 1614, and finally demolished in 1644. Its remains were rediscovered in 1989. A replica of the Globe was erected near the original site and opened for performances in 1996.

Globigerina A genus of protozoan animals that are common components of marine plankton. Ranging in size from 0.3 to 2 mm, their chalky skeletons are a major constituent of the grey mud on some sea beds, forming globigerina ooze. Order: *Foraminifera*.

globulin A type of protein that is generally insoluble in water. Gamma globulins, one of a class of globulins occurring in the blood (serum globulins), include the immunoglobulins (antibodies), which are manufactured by animals and humans to combat infections (*see* IMMUNITY). Injections of gamma globulin are used for immunization against hepatitis A. Other globulins occur in eggs, nuts, and seeds.

glockenspiel (German: bell play) A tuned percussion instrument having a keyboard-like arrangement of steel bars played with two small hammers. The notes of its two-and-a-half-octave compass above bottom G of the bass stave sound two octaves higher.

Glomma, River (Norwegian name: Glåma) A river in SE Norway and the longest river in Scandinavia. Length: 588 km (365 mi).

Glorious Revolution (1688) The overthrow of James II of England and the establishment of his daughter Mary and her husband William of Orange on the throne. The opposition to James' pro-Catholic and absolutist policies requested William's armed intervention; James fled to France. As William III and Mary II, the joint monarchs accepted the *Bill of Rights.

Gloucester 51 53N 2 14W A market town in W England, the administrative centre of Gloucestershire on the River Severn. First developed under the Romans (Glevum) it is noted for its cathedral. Population (1997 est): 107 400.

Gloucestershire A county of W England, bordering Wales. In 1996 the SW part of the historic county (part of Avon since 1974) became a unitary authority called South Gloucestershire; it is administered separately but is part of Gloucestershire for ceremonial purposes. Gloucestershire consists of three regions: the Cotswold Hills, the Severn Valley, and the Forest of Dean. It is predominantly agricultural. Area (excluding South Gloucestershire): 2638 sq km (1019 sq mi). Population (2001, excluding South Gloucestershire): 564 559. Administrative centre: Gloucester.

glowworm *See* FIREFLY.

gloxinia An ornamental herb, *Sinningia speciosa*, native to Brazil. Gloxinias have large bell-shaped velvety flowers, usually violet, purple, or pink. New plants can regenerate from the base of the leafstalks. Family: *Gesneriaceae*.

Gluck, Christoph Willibald (1714–87) German composer. He reformed *opera seria and composed the operas *Orfeo ed Euridice* (1762) and *Alceste* (1767). He also composed over 40 dramatic works.

glucose (*or* **dextrose**) A simple sugar ($C_6H_{12}O_6$) and an essential substance in the carbohydrate metabolism of living organisms. Carbohydrates (such as starch and glycogen) in food or tissue reserves are broken down to glucose, which is easily transported to cells where it undergoes *glycolysis. Organisms can also manufacture glucose from fats and proteins. Glucose levels in blood are regulated by the hormones *insulin and glucagon.

gluten A protein mixture derived from wheat. In bread making, dough rises because the gluten in wheat flour expands, trapping the carbon dioxide bubbles in an elastic network. *See also* COELIAC DISEASE.

glycerol (*or* **glycerine**; $CH_2OHCHOHCH_2OH$) A colourless syrupy liquid with a sweet taste. It is made from fats and oils or by fermentation and is used in explosives, cosmetics, and antifreeze solutions.

glycogen A starchlike carbohydrate found in animal tissues as a reserve energy source. It consists of branched chains of *glucose molecules: when required to provide energy, glycogen is broken down to glucose under the influence of hormones.

glycolysis The sequence of chemical reactions occurring in most living cells by which glucose is partially broken down to provide usable energy in the form of *ATP. Glycolysis can take place in the presence or absence of oxygen but only a small amount of the available energy is released, most being released via the *Krebs cycle.

Glyndebourne An estate near Lewes, in East Sussex, home of an annual international festival of opera. The opera house was built by John Christie (1882–1962), who founded the Glyndebourne Festival in 1934 for his wife, the opera singer Audrey Mildmay (1900–53). The opera house was completely rebuilt (1992–94).

GM crops *See* GENETIC ENGINEERING.

gnat Any of the smaller delicate species of two-winged flies (*Diptera*). They include the less virulent mosquitoes and phantom gnats (family *Culicidae*), winter gnats (family *Trichoceridae*), fungus gnats (family *Mycetophilidae*), craneflies (family *Tipulidae*), and several others.

gneiss A coarse-grained metamorphic rock consisting predominantly of bands of quartz and feldspar alternating with bands of micas and amphiboles. Gneisses are formed during regional metamorphism; those derived from igneous rocks are termed **orthogneiss**, those from sedimentary rocks **paragneiss**.

Gnosticism A religious movement that flourished in the early Christian era. It contained elements of pagan thought but is most fully recorded as a group of heretical Christian sects. The Gnostics' defining characteristic was their belief in *gnosis* (Greek: knowledge)—a special revelation from God to initiates, which would ensure their salvation. They interpreted Christ (whose humanity they denied) as being sent to rescue particles of spirit (souls) entrapped in matter.

GNP *See* GROSS NATIONAL PRODUCT.

gnu A large ungainly antelope belonging to the genus *Connochaetes* (2 species), also called wildebeest, of African plains. The brindled gnu (*C. taurinus*) grows to 140 cm high at the shoulder and is blue-grey with a long black mane, black facial tufts, and a black-tufted tail. The smaller white-tailed gnu (*C. gnou*) has a long white tail and is very rare.

Goa The 25th state of India, formerly part of Goa, Daman, and Diu Union Territory. A Portuguese overseas territory from 1510 until annexed by India in 1961, it has many fine examples of Portuguese colonial architecture, including the church in which the remains of St Francis Xavier are preserved. Area: 3702 sq km (1429 sq mi). Population (2001): 1 343 498.

goat A hoofed *ruminant mammal belonging to the genus *Capra* (5 species). Related to sheep, goats are 60–85 cm tall at the shoulder and have hollow horns; males have a scent gland beneath the tail and a beard. Wild goats, found in mountainous regions of Eurasia, live in herds. Goats were first domesticated over 10 000 years ago and are still used to provide milk, meat, and hides in many semiarid regions. Family: *Bovidae*. *See also* IBEX; MARKHOR.

goat moth A large moth, *Cossus cossus*, of Europe, Asia, and N Africa. Mottled grey and brown, it has a wingspan of 70 mm. The reddish caterpillar bores under the bark of trees and emits a characteristic strong odour.

Gobelins, Manufacture nationale des A French state-controlled tapestry factory, founded in Paris as a dyeworks in the 15th century by Jean and Philibert Gobelin. Manufacturing tapestries from 1529, it was incorpo-

g

rated by Henry IV in 1607. Since 1826 carpets have also been made here.

Gobi Desert A vast desert of SE Mongolia and N China. On a plateau 900–1500 m (2950–4920 ft) high, it is rocky with salt marshes and streams that disappear into the sand. It is rich in prehistoric remains. Area: about 1 295 000 sq km (500 000 sq mi).

goby A fish of the suborder *Gobioidei* (over 800 species), especially the family *Gobiidae* (true gobies). True gobies have smooth elongated bodies, two dorsal fins, and a suction disc formed from fused pelvic fins. Most are 5–10 cm long, although *Pandaka pygmaea* of the Philippines is the smallest known vertebrate at under 13 mm long. They are found chiefly in tropical coastal regions. Order: *Perciformes.*

g

Godard, Jean-Luc (1930–) French film director, a member of the New Wave. His films, characterized by experimental narrative and editing techniques, include *A Bout de souffle* (*Breathless*; 1959), *Week-End* (1967), *Tout va bien* (1972), *Je Vous salue, Marie* (1985), and *Eloge de l'amour* (2001).

Godavari, River A river in central India. Rising in the Western Ghats, it flows ESE to the Bay of Bengal. It is sacred to the Hindus. Length: 1500 km (900 mi).

Godesberg (*or* **Bad Godesberg**) 50 41N 7 10E A spa in W West Germany, in North Rhine-Westphalia on the River Rhine; since 1968 a district of Bonn.

Godiva, Lady (d. ?1080) The English woman who, according to the chronicler Roger of Wendover (d. 1236), rode naked through the market place of Coventry in order to persuade her husband Leofric, Earl of Mercia, to reduce his taxes on the town. The story was later embellished with a Peeping Tom who, ignoring Godiva's request that the townspeople remain indoors, was struck blind.

Godunov, Boris (Fedorovich) (c. 1551–1605) Russian statesman and tsar (1598–1605). Godunov rose to power under Ivan the Terrible and became regent for Fyodor I, whose younger brother and heir, Dimitrii, Godunov may have murdered in 1591. After Fyodor's death (1598), Godunov was elected tsar. His authority was challenged by the first False Dimitrii, a pretender who succeeded Godunov.

Godwin Austen, Mount *See* K2.

godwit A long-legged long-billed migratory bird belonging to a genus (*Limosa*; 4 species) that breeds in N Eurasia and North America. The black-tailed godwit (*L. limosa*) is 40 cm long and has a distinctive black-banded white tail. Family: *Scolopacidae* (plovers, sandpipers, etc.).

Goebbels, (Paul) Joseph (1897–1945) German Nazi politician. Appointed minister of propaganda by Hitler in 1933, he established a vast machine for the control of public information, the arts, cinema, and theatre, all of which he manipulated with a cynical disregard for truth. He committed suicide with his wife after taking the lives of his six children during the collapse of the Third Reich.

Goethe, Johann Wolfgang von (1749–1832) German poet and statesman. His discovery of Shakespeare inspired him to write an epic drama, *Götz von Berlichingen* (1773) while the autobiographical novel *The Sorrows of Young Werther* (1774) won him international fame. In 1775 he settled at the court of the Duke of Saxe-Weimar, whom he served as prime minister until 1785. At Weimar he fell in love with Charlotte von Stein, who inspired some of his greatest lyric poetry. A visit to Italy (1786–88) made him an advocate of classicism, influencing such plays as *Iphigenia on Tauris* (1787) and *Torquato Tasso* (1790). After the novel *Wilhelm Meister's Apprentice Years* (1795–96) he published the first part of his greatest work *Faust* (1808), a poetic drama of the aspirations of man. He published *Wilhelm Meister's Journeyman Years* in 1829 and completed the second part of *Faust* shortly before his death.

Gog and Magog In Revelation and other books of the Bible, attendant powers of Satan. In British folklore they appear as the survivors of a race of giants destroyed by Brutus, the legendary founder of Britain.

Gogol, Nikolai Vasilievich (1809–52) Russian novelist and dramatist. Early ambitions to become a poet and an actor and to emigrate all failed, but two volumes of stories based on his Ukrainian childhood won him acclaim from *Pushkin and other writers. To escape the controversy aroused by his satirical play *The Government Inspector* (1836) he went to Rome, where he wrote his best-known work, *Dead Souls* (1842), a grotesque lampoon of Russian feudalism. In his last years he became a depressive and a religious maniac.

Goiânia 16 43S 49 18W A city in central Brazil, the capital of Goiás state. Founded in 1933 to replace the old capital, it serves a cattle-raising and coffee-growing area. Population (2000): 1 083 396.

Goidelic languages *See* CELTIC LANGUAGES.

goitre Swelling in the neck caused by enlargement of the thyroid gland. A goitre is called simple if the thyroid is functioning normally; this occurs in areas where iodine is deficient in the water supply and it may occur sporadically in adolescent girls. A goitre may also be seen when the thyroid is overactive or underactive.

Golan Heights A range of hills in SW Syria, under Israeli administration. They are of great strategic importance; Israeli forces stormed the heights in June 1967, when most of the local populace fled. Jewish settlements have since been established.

gold (Au) A soft dense yellow metal valued since ancient times. It occurs in nature as the element and in compounds with tellurium, in rock veins and alluvial deposits. The metal is the most malleable and ductile known. It alloys with other metals, is a good conductor of heat and electricity, and is chemically unreactive. The major uses for the element are for jewellery, electrical contacts, and as a currency standard (*see* GOLD STANDARD). Purity is measured in *carats. At no 79; at wt 196.967; mp 1064.43°C; bp 2857°C.

goldcrest A tiny agile songbird, *Regulus regulus*, occurring chiefly in coniferous woodland of N Europe and Asia and feeding on insects and spiders. It is about 9 cm long and has a yellow-green plumage and an orange crest. Family: *Muscicapidae* (Old World flycatchers).

golden eagle A large dark-brown *eagle, *Aquila chrysaetos*, occurring in mountainous regions of North America and Eurasia. It is 70–85 cm long and has a wingspan of up to 230 cm; they catch small mammals and gamebirds.

goldeneye A diving duck, *Bucephala clangula*, that breeds in N Eurasia and winters in more southerly regions. It is 41–45 cm long and males are black and white with a greenish head and a circular white patch on the cheek; females are grey with white markings and a brown head.

Golden Fleece The fleece of a sacred winged ram, the recovery of which was the goal of *Jason and the *Argonauts. Athamas, King of Thebes, had two children, Phrixus and Helle, by his first wife Nephele. His second wife, Ino, hated her stepchildren and plotted their death. They fled across the sea on the golden ram but Helle fell in and drowned. Phrixus reached Colchis, sacrificed the ram to Zeus and hung the fleece in a grove sacred to Ares, where it was guarded by a dragon. The **Order of the Golden Fleece** was founded in 1430 by Philip the Good, taking as its badge Jason's fleece. After Burgundy was united with the Habsburg empire (1477), the order became confined to Austria and Spain.

golden retriever A large strongly built breed of dog whose ancestors possibly included labradors, setters, and spaniels. The dense water-resistant wavy coat is gold or cream; they are used as gun dogs, guide dogs, etc. Height: 56–61 cm (dogs); 51–56 cm (bitches).

goldenrod A perennial herb of the genus *Solidago* (about 120 species), up to 2.5 m tall and mostly native to North America. The stem bears small yellow flowers. Canadian goldenrod (*S. canadensis*) is often grown as a garden ornamental. Family: *Compositae*.

goldfinch A Eurasian *finch, *Carduelis carduelis*. About 12 cm long, it has a brown back, black wings with a broad yellow stripe, black-and-white tail and head, and a red face. It uses its pointed bill to extract seeds from thistles and dandelions and flocks of goldfinches (called charms) are commonly seen on farmland.

goldfish A freshwater fish, *Carassius auratus*, also called golden carp, of E Asian origin but introduced elsewhere as an ornamental fish. In its natural state it is greenish brown or grey and up to 30 cm long. However, the breeding of abnormal specimens has produced over 125 varieties often with a red-gold coloration. It requires cold well-oxygenated water and is omnivorous.

Golding, Sir William (1911–93) British novelist. His best-known novel, *Lord of the Flies* (1954), concerns the savagery of a group of schoolboys isolated on a desert island. His other novels include *Pincher Martin* (1956), *The Spire* (1964), *Rites of Passage* (1980), which won the Booker prize, and *Fire Down Below* (1989). He was awarded the Nobel Prize in 1983.

Goldsmith, Oliver (1730–74) Anglo-Irish writer. He arrived penniless in London in 1756 and became a friend of Johnson and Boswell. His best-known works are the poem *The Deserted Village* (1770), the novel *The Vicar of Wakefield* (1776), and the play *She Stoops to Conquer* (1773).

gold standard A monetary system in which paper money was convertible on demand into gold. Rates of exchange between currencies were fixed by their values in gold. In classical economics imbalances in international trade were rectified automatically by the gold standard. A country in deficit would have depleted gold reserves and would therefore reduce its money supply. The resulting fall in demand would reduce imports and the lowering of prices would boost exports, thus rectifying the deficit. It was finally abandoned in 1931. *See also* INTERNATIONAL MONETARY FUND.

Goldwyn, Samuel (S. Goldfish; 1882–1974) US film producer, born in Poland. In 1916 he cofounded Goldwyn Pictures, a production company that was absorbed into Metro-Goldwyn-Mayer (MGM) in 1924. His many successful films as an independent producer include *Wuthering Heights* (1939) and *Guys and Dolls* (1955).

golem In medieval Jewish folklore, an automaton or artificial human being that can be brought to life by a charm. The best-known legend is that of a golem created by a rabbi of Prague, which he used as a servant. The word originally referred to anything incomplete or embryonic.

golf A game for two or four players played on a golf course. It almost certainly originated in Scotland. A standard course is usually between 4572 m (5000 yd) and 6400 m (7000 yd) and is divided into 18 holes (9 on a small course), each of which is between 90 m (100 yd) and 540 m (600 yd) long. A "hole" comprises the flat starting point, called the "tee," a strip of mown grass about 27–90 m (30–100 yd) wide, called the "fairway," and a smooth putting green. On the green is the actual hole, which has a diameter of 10.8 cm (4.25 in). There are also obstacles around the course, such as trees, ditches, and sand bunkers. The object of the game is to hit a rubber-cored ball from each tee into each hole with as few strokes as possible ("par" for a hole is the standard number of strokes needed by a first-class player; one stroke less than par is called a "birdie," and an "eagle" is two strokes less). To achieve this a player has a set of clubs of which there are three basic types: woods, irons, and putters.

Golgi apparatus (*or* **Golgi complex**) A structure present in the cytoplasm of nearly all cells, composed of stacks of flattened sacs bounded by membranes and associated with vesicles. Discovered by Camillo Golgi (1843–1926), it is thought to function in the synthesis and concentration of certain materials, especially secretory products, which are then packaged into the vesicles and transported within the cell.

Golgotha *See* CALVARY.

goliath beetle A large beetle belonging to the group of flower *chafers. The African goliath beetle (*Goliathus giganteus*) has the largest body of all the insects, about 96 mm in length. It is white with black stripes and brown wing cases. The larvae are found in rotten logs.

gomuti A *palm tree, *Arenga pinnata* (or *A. saccharifera*), also called sugar palm, occurring in SE Asia. The sap yields palm sugar and the fermented juice (palm wine) is distilled to produce arrack. A form of sago is obtained from the pith and the leaf fibres are used to make cord, ropes, etc.

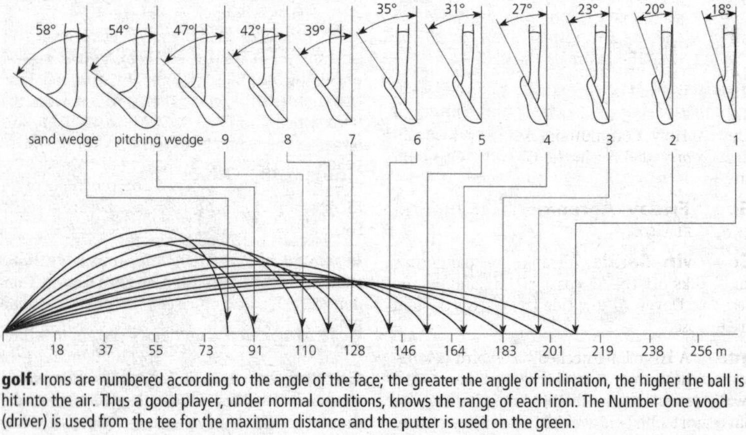

golf. Irons are numbered according to the angle of the face; the greater the angle of inclination, the higher the ball is hit into the air. Thus a good player, under normal conditions, knows the range of each iron. The Number One wood (driver) is used from the tee for the maximum distance and the putter is used on the green.

gonadotrophin One of several hormones that control the activity of the testes and ovaries (the gonads) in mammals. The pituitary gland produces three gonadotrophins: luteinizing hormone (LH), which stimulates ovulation and *oestrogen production by the ovaries and the production of *androgens by the testes; follicle-stimulating hormone (FSH), which promotes ovulation and sperm production; and *prolactin, which triggers lactation. LH and FSH are glycoproteins and are usually released together. Human chorionic gonadotrophin (HCG) is produced by the placenta, reaching a peak level in the urine in early pregnancy. Gonadotrophins are also used in *fertility drugs.

Goncourt, Edmond de (1822–96) French writer, who with his brother **Jules de Goncourt** (1830–70) wrote art criticism, social histories, and novels, notably *Germinie Lacerteux* (1864) and *Madame Gervaisais* (1869). They are best known for their *Journal*, a record of French literary life, and for Edmond's legacy, the Académie Goncourt, which awards France's prestigious annual literary prize, the **Prix Goncourt**.

Gondwanaland The supercontinent in the S hemisphere believed to have existed prior to 200 million years ago, when the drift of the continents to their present positions began. It probably consisted of South America, Africa, Australia, Antarctica, Arabia, and India. *See also* LAURASIA.

gonorrhoea A sexually transmitted disease caused by a bacterium (the gonococcus). Symptoms in men are discharge from the penis and a burning pain on passing urine. Women may have vaginal discharge and pain on urinating. Gonorrhoea can be treated with penicillin.

Good Friday The Friday before *Easter, when Christ's crucifixion is commemorated. It is a fast day, and in the Roman Catholic Church the Mass is not celebrated. In the Anglican Church Holy Communion is rarely held, although provided for in the Book of *Common Prayer.

Good Friday Agreement *See* (NORTHERN) IRELAND.

Goodwin Sands A range of dangerous sandbanks off the SE coast of England, in the Strait of Dover. At low tide large areas of sand are exposed.

goose A large long-necked waterbird belonging to the family *Anatidae* (ducks, geese, and swans), occurring in the N hemisphere. Geese have short bills and webbed feet. They chiefly feed on grass, grain, etc., and are migratory, flying in V-formations and honking in flight. Genera: *Anser* (grey geese), *Branta* (black geese); order: *Anseriformes*. *See also* CANADA GOOSE; GREYLAG GOOSE.

gooseberry A fruit bush of the genus *Ribes*, especially *R. uva-crispa* (or *R. grossularia*), which is widely cultivated in the Old World for its hairy edible berries. Family: *Grossulariaceae*.

gopher *See* SOUSLIK.

Gorbachov, Mikhail Sergeevich (1931–) Soviet statesman; general secretary of the Soviet Communist Party (1985–91) and president (1988–91). As general secretary he began a radical programme of political and economic reform (*see* GLASNOST). He signed major arms limitation treaties with the USA (1987) and NATO (1990) and in 1990 under his leadership the Communist Party voted to give up its monopoly of power. In August 1991 he survived a coup attempted by Communist hardliners. He resigned following his failure to prevent the break-up of the Soviet Union. He was awarded the Nobel Peace Prize in 1990.

Gordian knot A knot binding the yoke and beam of the chariot of Gordius, a legendary king of Phrygia. According to legend, whoever could unloose the knot would become the ruler of Asia. In 333 BC Alexander the Great is said to have cut the knot with his sword.

Gordimer, Nadine (1923–) South African novelist. Her earlier novels, which include *The Lying Days* (1953), *The Conservationist* (1974), and *My Son's Story* (1990), condemn *apartheid; later works, such as *The House Gun* (1997), explore the subsequent changes in South Africa. She was awarded the Nobel Prize in 1991.

Gordon, Charles George (1833–85) British general. Gordon served in the Crimean War and then in China and Egypt. From 1877 to 1880 he was British governor of the Sudan; in 1884 he returned to the Sudan to evacuate Europeans and Egyptians, following al *Mahdi's revolt. Gordon was besieged for ten months in Khartoum, which fell two days before a relief force arrived. Gordon was murdered.

Gordon Riots (1780) Anti-Roman Catholic riots in London fomented by Lord George Gordon (1751–93), who opposed the Roman Catholic Relief Act (1778). The riots were crushed; Gordon was arrested but acquitted of treason.

Gorgon In Greek legend, an underworld monster. Hesiod refers to three Gorgons, the sisters Stheno, Euryale, and *Medusa. They were usually portrayed as winged females with snakes for hair and boars' tusks for teeth.

gorilla The largest living *ape, *Gorilla gorilla*, of tropical African forests. Male gorillas can grow to 1.8 m with a weight of 300 kg. They walk on their feet and knuckles, feeding on plant stems and fruit. Troops are led by a dominant adult male and are generally not aggressive.

Göring, Hermann Wilhelm (1893–1946) German Nazi politician. He served in the air force in World War I and became a Nazi in 1922, taking command of Hitler's Brownshirts. When Hitler came to power in 1933, Göring was appointed air minister of Germany and prime minister of Prussia. He established the *Gestapo and probably engineered the Reichstag fire (1933). He directed the development of the Luftwaffe. Hitler declared him his successor in 1939 but expelled him from the party shortly before the Nazi collapse. Condemned to hang at Nuremburg, he committed suicide.

Gorki, Maksim (Aleksei Maksimovich Peshkov; 1868–1936) Russian novelist. His early life is recounted in his trilogy *Childhood* (1913–14), *In the World* (1915–16), and *My Universities* (1923). He established his literary reputation with romantic short stories and followed these with several novels and plays, including *Mother* (1906) and *The Lower Depths* (1906). He lived in exile from 1906 to 1913 and again from 1921 to 1928. He then returned to Russia, becoming an exponent of Stalinism.

Gorlovka (*or* **Horlivka**) 48 17N 38 05E A city in SE Ukraine, in the Donets Basin. It is one of the largest coalmining and industrial centres of the area. Population (1998 est): 309 300.

gorse (*or* **furze**) A spiny shrub, *Ulex europaeus*, up to 4 m high, with bright-yellow sweet-scented flowers. The fruit is a black hairy pod that splits open explosively to release the seeds. Gorse is native to grassy areas and heaths throughout Europe and has been introduced elsewhere. Family: *Leguminosae*.

goshawk A large powerful *hawk, *Accipiter gentilis*, ranging throughout forests of the N hemisphere and formerly used in falconry. It is 60 cm long with a wingspan of 130 cm and grey plumage.

Gospels (Old English: good news) The four New Testament accounts of Christ's life, ascribed to *Matthew, *Mark, Luke, and *John. The first three are known as the Synoptic Gospels, since they report approximately the same synopsis of the events. Material that is not found in Mark but is common to Matthew and Luke is believed to derive from a single lost source, known as Q. The fourth Gospel, John, may presuppose a knowledge of the Synoptic Gospels.

Gossaert, Jan (c. 1478–c. 1532) Flemish painter, whose popular surname, Mabuse, derives from his birthplace Maubeuge. One of the first Flemish artists to work in the Italian Renaissance style, he painted sculptural nudes against Italian architectural backgrounds, e.g. *Neptune and Amphitrite* (Berlin).

Göteborg (English name: Gothenburg) 57 45N 12 00E An important ice-free port in SW Sweden, at the mouth of the River Göta. Sweden's second largest city, it expanded with the opening of the Göta Canal (1832). Population (2000 est): 462 470.

gothic art and architecture The styles flourishing in Europe from the mid-12th to the end of the 15th centuries. "Gothic" originated as a derisory term used by Renaissance artists, who blamed the destruction of classical art on the Goths who invaded the Roman Empire. The

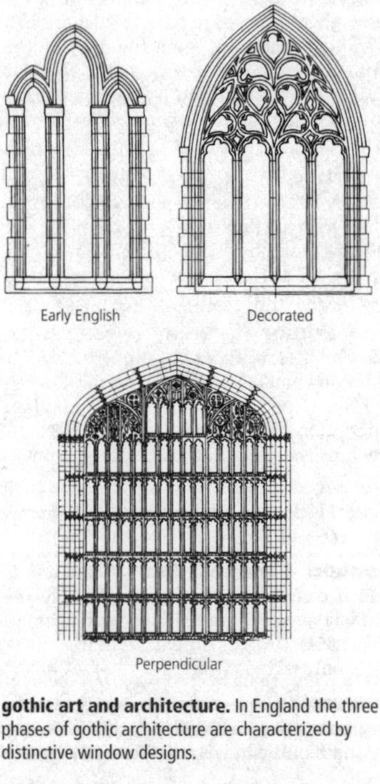

gothic art and architecture. In England the three phases of gothic architecture are characterized by distinctive window designs.

hallmarks of gothic design in church architecture are the rib and shaft ceiling, the pointed arch, and the flying buttress. It was initiated in France in such edifices as the cathedrals of Notre-Dame (begun 1163) and Chartres (begun c. 1194). In England it has been subdivided into three phases: *Early English (c. 1200–c. 1300; e.g. Lincoln Cathedral), *Decorated (c. 1300–70; e.g. Exeter Cathedral), and *Perpendicular (c. 1370–1540; e.g. Winchester Cathedral). Stained glass was developed in the period, while gothic sculpture sought a stylized elegance. Early gothic painting was restricted to manuscript illumination. Its full flowering in panel and manuscript painting came with the international gothic style of the early 15th century. The **gothic revival** of the 19th century is seen in such buildings as the Houses of Parliament and the Law Courts in London.

gothic novel An English genre, popular in the late 18th and early 19th centuries, characterized by a prevailing atmosphere of mystery and terror and pseudomedieval settings. Examples include Horace Walpole's *Castle of Otranto* (1765) and Ann Radcliffe's *The Mysteries of Udolpho* (1794).

Goths Germanic peoples who originated in Scandinavia (Gotland) and had moved into the Ukraine by the end of the 2nd century AD. Shortly afterwards they invaded the Roman Empire N of the Danube and expanded into the Balkans. Converted to Arian Christianity in the mid-4th century, their empire was soon destroyed by the *Huns and their two groups, the *Ostrogoths and *Visigoths, separated.

Gotland (**Gothland** *or* **Gottland**) The largest of the Swedish islands, in the Baltic Sea. Long disputed between Denmark and Sweden, it was finally ceded to Sweden in 1645. Area: 3140 sq km (1225 sq mi). Population (2001 est): 57 313, including associated islands. Capital: Visby.

Göttingen 51 32N 9 57E A city in E West Germany. With its famous university and the Max Planck Association for the furtherance of science, it is a noted educational centre. Population (1999 est): 127 366.

Gounod, Charles François (1818–93) French composer. His most successful works were the operas *Faust* (1852–59) and *Romeo and Juliet* (1864). Towards the end of his life he composed only sacred music.

gourami One of several freshwater tropical labyrinth fishes, especially *Osphronemus goramy*. It has a brown or grey oval body, up to 60 cm long, and a filamentous ray extending from each pelvic fin.

gourd The fruit of certain plants of the family *Cucurbitaceae*, especially the white-flowered bottle gourd (*Lagenaria siceraria*). Other gourds are grown as ornamentals. The dishcloth gourd is used as a bath sponge and the *snake gourd is grown for food.

gout Sudden attacks of arthritis caused by the presence of uric acid crystals in the joints. The big toe is most commonly affected, becoming hot, red, and very painful.

Gower Peninsula A peninsula in South Wales, in the county of Swansea, noted for its coastal scenery.

Goya (y Lucientes), Francesco (Jose) de (1746–1828) Spanish painter. After studying in Italy, he settled in Madrid (1775), where he painted scenes of Spanish life for the royal tapestry factory. As court painter from 1789 he produced realistic portraits of the royal family. He became deaf in 1792, and his works grew pessimistic, as in his etchings *Los Caprichos* and *The Disasters of War*. His best-known paintings are *Maja Clothed*, *The Shootings of 3 May 1808*, and the so-called black paintings, such as *Satan Devouring His Children* (all Prado).

Gozzoli, Benozzo (Benozzo di Lese; 1420–97) Florentine painter. His major works are the frescoes of the *Journey of the Magi* (Palazzo Medici-Riccardi, Florence), which are noted for their detailed landscapes, and portraits of his contemporaries.

Grace, W(illiam) G(ilbert) (1848–1915) British cricketer, who captained England in 13 Test matches. In his long career (1865–1908) he scored 54 896 runs, including 126 centuries, took 2876 wickets, and held 877 catches.

Graces In Greek mythology, the three daughters of Zeus and Hera, representing beauty, grace, and charm. They were named Aglaia, Euphrosyne, and Thalia.

Graf, Steffi (1969–) German tennis player. Her victories include the Wimbledon singles championship in 1988, 1989, 1991, 1992, 1993; 1995, and 1996; in 1988 she won a grand slam of the four major singles championships. She married the tennis player André Agassi in 2001.

grafting 1. (horticulture) The transfer of part of one plant, usually a shoot or a bud, onto another plant. It is used as a means of vegetative propagation, particularly for fruit trees and roses. The *cambium (a region of actively dividing cells) of the transplanted piece (the scion) is aligned with that of the recipient plant (the stock): the wound tissue thus formed binds the graft together. **2.** (surgery) *See* TRANSPLANTATION.

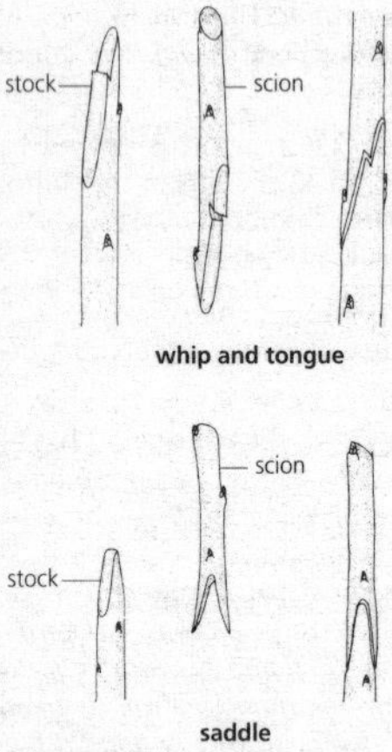

grafting. Two commonly used grafting methods. After stock and scion are fitted together they are held securely by tape, string, etc., and protected from desiccation by covering the point of union with wax or moist material.

Graham, Billy (1918–) US evangelist. His carefully staged meetings, in which the audience are invited to "take a decision for Christ," have attracted very large crowds throughout the world.

Graham, Martha (1893–1991) US ballet dancer and choreographer. Her ballets include *Primitive Mysteries* (1931), *Circe* (1963), and *Acts of Light* (1981).

Grahame, Kenneth (1859–1932) British writer. His best-known book is the children's classic, *The Wind in the Willows* (1908), adapted as a play, *Toad of Toad Hall* (1929), by A. A. *Milne.

Grahamstown (Afrikaans name: Grahamstad) 33 19S 26 32E A town in South Africa, in SE Cape Province. It was the focus of British settlement in 1820. Population (latest est): 75 000.

Graiae In Greek legend, three goddesses personifying old age, the sisters and protectors of the *Gorgons. They shared one eye and one tooth. *Perseus stole the eye in order to take the Gorgons by surprise.

Grainger, Percy (Aldridge) (1882–1961) Australian-born composer and pianist. He was a friend of Grieg and Delius and studied and recorded English folksong. His compositions include *Shepherds' Hey* (1913), and *Harvest Hymn* (1933), as well as the "clog dance" *Handel in the Strand* (1913).

gram (g) A unit of mass equal to 1/1000 of a *kilogram.

grammar schools Secondary schools in the UK providing a largely academic education for children aged 12 to 18. The original grammar schools, established in the middle ages, were preparatory institutions for university or for jobs in which a knowledge of Latin was essential. After World War II, with the growing demand for academic excellence, grammar schools were compelled to restrict entry to those passing the eleven-plus examination. Most grammar schools were replaced in the 1970s by *comprehensive schools.

Grampians 1. A range of mountains in central Scotland, mainly in Perth and Kinross and Aberdeenshire. Its chief summits include Ben Nevis at 1343 m (4406 ft) and Ben Macdhui at 1309 m (4296 ft). **2.** A mountain range in Australia. It extends SW from Victoria, reaching 1166 m (3827 ft) at Mount William.

grampus A small toothed *whale, *Grampus griseus*, of warm and temperate waters, also called Risso's dolphin. About 3.7 m long, dark-grey with a pale belly, grampuses migrate towards the Poles in summer and the equator in winter.

Granada 37 10N 3 35W A city in S Spain, in Andalusia. Formerly the capital of the kingdom of Granada, it includes many Moorish buildings (notably the Alhambra). Population (1998 est): 241 471.

Granados, Enrique (1867–1916) Spanish composer and pianist. He and his wife were drowned during World War I when HMS *Sussex* was torpedoed. Granados is best remembered for the piano pieces entitled *Goyescas* (1911), inspired by Goya.

Gran Chaco A vast plain in South America. A long-standing dispute over the territory led to the Chaco War between Paraguay and Bolivia (1932–35), following which most of the area was incorporated into Paraguay. Area: 780 000 sq km (300 000 sq mi).

Grand Canal (Chinese name: Da Yunhe) A canal in E China, the longest in the world, extending about 1600 km (1000 mi) N–S from Beijing to *Wuhan.

Grand Canyon A vast gorge in the USA, in

Arizona on the Colorado River. It became the **Grand Canyon National Park** in 1919. Length: 451 km (280 mi). Width: 6–29 km (4–18 mi). Greatest depth: 1.5 km (1 mi).

Grand Coulee Dam A large gravity *dam on the Columbia River in Washington (USA). It is 1272 m long at its crest, 108 m high, and has a reservoir capacity of 11 600 million cubic metres.

Grande Dixence Dam A gravity *dam on the River Dixence (Switzerland). Until 1970 it was the tallest dam in the world (284 m high).

Grand Guignol A type of sensational drama that flourished in Paris in the late 19th century. The term derives from the name of a theatre at which these plays were performed, and from Guignol, a stock character in French puppet shows.

grand mal *See* EPILEPSY.

Grand National Steeplechase The world's most famous *steeplechase, run in March at Aintree near Liverpool (England) over 30 assorted obstacles. It was first run in 1839.

granite A coarse-grained plutonic rock of acid composition resulting from the high silica content. Granites contain quartz, feldspar (usually alkali), and mafic (dark-coloured) minerals, usually muscovite and biotite (micas). Most granites crystallize from magma in igneous intrusions known as batholiths, but some are produced by the action of granitic fluids rising from great depths.

Gran Paradiso 45 33N 7 17E The highest mountain in Italy, in the Alps. Height: 4061 m (13 323 ft).

Grant, Cary (Archibald Leach; 1904–86) US film actor, born in England. He established his reputation in such films as *Bringing Up Baby* (1938) and *The Philadelphia Story* (1940). His films for Alfred Hitchcock include *To Catch a Thief* (1955) and *North By Northwest* (1959).

Grant, Ulysses S(impson) (1822–85) US general and statesman; Republican president (1869–77). As supreme commander of the Federal armies (1864–65) he defeated the Confederates by battering them into submission. The great losses to his own side earned him the nickname Grant the Butcher. As president, he acquiesced in Reconstruction attempts to enfranchise Blacks, fought inflation, and unsuccessfully planned to annex the Dominican Republic.

grape The fruit of vines of the genus *Vitis* (about 60 species), especially *V. vinifera*, native to N Asia but cultivated throughout Mediterranean regions. The fruit is green, red, or blue-black and used to make *wine, brandy, and liqueurs or eaten fresh or dried (as raisins, sultanas, and currants).

grapefruit A tree, *Citrus paradisi*, 6–12 m high, cultivated in the tropics and subtropics. Its fleshy yellow-skinned fruits, 10–15 cm in diameter, are eaten fresh, tinned, or crushed to make beverages. *See* CITRUS.

grape hyacinth A perennial herbaceous plant of the genus *Muscari* (50 species), mostly native to the Mediterranean region and widely grown as spring-blooming garden bulbs. The blue, pink, or white flowers are borne at the tip of a stalk, up to 15 cm high. Family: *Liliaceae*.

graphite An iron-grey to black form of pure carbon, found in many metamorphic rocks. It occurs in a laminar or massive form. It is soft, flaky, and greasy to the touch. Graphite is used for making metallurgical crucibles, as a lubricant, in paint, rubber, and pencil leads, in batteries and for other electrical purposes, and as a moderator in nuclear reactors. It has often been called plumbago or black lead, since it was formerly mistaken for lead.

Grappelli, Stephane (1908–97) French jazz violinist. A member of the Hot Club de France (1934–39), he made recordings with Earl Hines and Yehudi *Menuhin among others.

graptolite A small colonial marine animal belonging to the extinct class *Graptolithina*. Their fossils occur in rocks of the Upper Cambrian to Carboniferous periods, about 420–250 million years ago.

grass A monocotyledonous annual or perennial herbaceous plant belonging to the family *Poaceae* (or *Gramineae*; 6000–10 000 species), distributed worldwide. The leaves consist of a basal sheath and a long narrow blade. The flowering stems (culms) bear inconspicuous flowers. The single-seeded fruit (the grain) is known as a caryopsis, with the ovary wall (pericarp) and seed coat fused. Many species are important in agriculture (*see* CEREALS; SUGAR CANE). See illustration on p. 384.

Grass, Günter (1927–) German novelist. His first novel, *The Tin Drum* (1959) established him as a moral spokesman for his generation. His other novels include *The Flounder* (1977), *The Rat* (1986), *Toad Croaks* (1992), and *Crabwalk* (2002). He received the Nobel Prize for Literature in 1999.

grassfinch A songbird belonging to a subfamily of weaverfinches, occurring chiefly in

Australasia. About 10 cm long, grassfinches have long tails and stout bills.

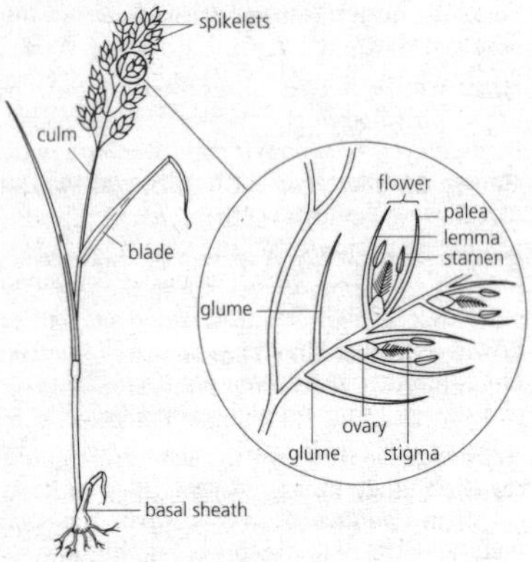

grass. The typical structure of a grass is seen in the meadow fescue (*Festuca pratensis*). The flowers are grouped into spikelets and each consists only of male and female parts surrounded by bracts; petals and sepals are absent.

grasshopper A jumping insect belonging to the family *Acrididae* (about 5000 species). 24–110 mm long, both sexes produce sound by rubbing the hind legs against the front wings. Some species can fly, (*see* LOCUST). Grasshoppers feed on low vegetation and the females lay eggs in the soil. Order: *Orthoptera*.

grass monkey A small African *guenon monkey, *Cercopithecus aethiops*, inhabiting wooded regions. The West African green monkey, the East African grivet monkey, and the South African vervet or blue monkey are all local races of grass monkey.

grass snake A nonvenomous snake, *Natrix natrix*, also called water snake, occurring throughout Europe. 75–95 cm long, it has a green back with two rows of black spots, vertical black bars along its sides, and a yellow neck patch. Its prey includes fish and small mammals. Family: *Colubridae*.

grass tree A woody plant of the genus *Xanthorrhoea* (about 5 species), native to E Australia. They often have palmlike stems, 5 m tall, that end in a tuft of rigid grasslike leaves, from which extend flower spikes. A red or yellow resin, used for varnishes, exudes from the bases of old leaves. Family: *Xanthorrhoeaceae*.

Gravenhage, 's *See* HAGUE, THE.

Graves, Robert (Ranke) (1895–1985) British poet, critic, and novelist. *Goodbye to All That* (1929) recounts his experiences in World War I. His other writings include poems, *I Claudius* (1934), and *The White Goddess* (1948).

Gravettian A culture of the Upper *Palaeolithic, succeeding the Aurignacian in W Europe. Named after the cave at La Gravette in the Dordogne (SW France), the Gravettian is characterized by small pointed stone blades (Gravette points) and dates from between 26 000 and 20 000 BC. The well-known small female figurines called Venuses are of Gravettian origin. The term Eastern Gravettian is applied to similar material from sites in Russia and E Europe. *Compare* PERIGORDIAN.

gravitation An attractive force that occurs between all bodies that possess mass. It was first described by Sir Isaac *Newton in a law stating that the force between two bodies is directly proportional to the product of their masses and inversely proportional to the square of the distance between them. The constant of proportionality, the universal **gravitational constant**, G, has the value 6.673×10^{-11} newton metre squared per kilogram squared. Gravitation is more accurately described by the general theory of *relativity.

gravitational collapse The sudden collapse of the core of a *star when thermonuclear fusion ceases. The star's internal gas pressure can no longer support the star's weight and the initial result may be a *supernova explosion. The gravitational pull of the remains of the star causes it to contract, producing a *white dwarf, *neutron star, or *black hole.

gravitational interaction One of the four kinds of interaction that occur between elementary particles (*see* PARTICLE PHYSICS) and by far the weakest (about 10^{40} times weaker than the *electromagnetic interaction). The interaction occurs between all particles with mass and can be explained as the exchange of *virtual particles called gravitons.

gray (Gy) The SI unit of absorbed dose of ionizing radiation equal to the energy in joules absorbed by one kilogram of irradiated material.

Gray, Thomas (1716–71) British poet. His most famous poem is *Elegy Written in a Country Churchyard* (1751), a classical meditation on the graves of the villagers of Stoke Poges, Buckinghamshire.

grayling A troutlike fish of the genus *Thymallus*, sometimes placed in a distinct family (*Thymallidae*). Graylings have a silvery-purple body, up to 50 cm long, with a sail-like dorsal fin, and live in fresh waters of Eurasia and N North America, feeding on aquatic insects. They are important food and game fish. Family: *Salmonidae*.

Graz 47 05N 15 22E The second largest city in Austria, the capital of Styria. Its historical buildings include a cathedral (1438–62) and a clock tower (1561). Population (2001): 226 424.

Great Artesian Basin An artesian basin of E Australia. The largest area of artesian water in the world, it extends S from Queensland into South Australia and New South Wales. Area: 1 750 000 sq km (676 250 sq mi).

Great Barrier Reef The largest coral reef in the world, off NE Australia. 2012 km (1250 mi) long, its exotic plant and animal life makes it popular with tourists.

Great Basin A large semiarid area in the USA. It extends over most of Nevada, Utah, and parts of California and Oregon.

Great Bear *See* URSA MAJOR.

Great Bear Lake A lake in N Canada, on the Arctic Circle. Frozen eight months of the year, it is the fourth largest lake in North America. Area: 31 792 sq km (12 275 sq mi).

Great Britain *England, *Scotland, and *Wales, including those adjacent islands governed from the mainland (i.e. excluding the Isle of Man and the Channel Islands). The name was introduced as early as 1603. Area: 229 523 sq km (88 619 sq mi). Population (2001): 57 103 927.

great circle A circle that is the intersection on the surface of a sphere of a plane passing through the centre of that sphere. On the earth, each meridian of longitude is half of a great circle; the equator is the only parallel of latitude that is a great circle.

Great Dane A breed of large dog originating in Germany, where they were developed for hunting boar. The short sleek coat can be golden, black, streaked brown, blue-grey, or white. Height: 76 cm minimum (dogs); 71 cm minimum (bitches).

Great Dividing Range (Great Divide *or* Eastern Highlands) The E highlands of Australia. It extends for about 3700 km (2300 mi) from Cape York Peninsula to the Grampians of Victoria, reaching 2230 m (7316 ft) at Mount *Kosciusko.

Greater Antilles The four largest West Indian islands, in the N Caribbean Sea, comprising Cuba, Hispaniola, Jamaica, and Puerto Rico.

Greater Manchester A metropolitan county of NW England, created in 1974 from SE Lancashire and parts of NE Cheshire and SW Yorkshire. In 1986 administrative powers were devolved to the unitary authorities of Wigan, Bolton, Bury, Rochdale, Salford, Oldham, Manchester, Trafford, Stockport, and Tameside. Area: 1285 sq km (496 sq mi).

Great Exhibition (1851) A display of the products of industrial Britain and Europe, planned by Prince Albert and held in the *Crystal Palace in Hyde Park, London. It contained about 13 000 exhibits.

Great Glen (*or* **Glen More**) A rift valley extending across N Scotland from Fort William to Inverness. The *Caledonian Canal was constructed along its length.

Great Lakes Five large lakes along the US-Canadian border: Lakes *Superior, *Michigan, *Huron, *Erie, and *Ontario. They comprise the world's largest freshwater surface and together with the *St Lawrence River form the St Lawrence Seaway.

Great Ouse River (*or* **R. Ouse**) A river in E England, rising in Northamptonshire and flowing NE to the Wash. Length: 257 km (160 mi).

Great Plains An extensive area in North America. It consists of plains extending from the Mackenzie River Delta in Canada to the Rio Grande in the S. Length: about 4828 km (3000 mi). Average width: about 644 km (400 mi).

Great Rift Valley (*or* **East African Rift System**) An extensive rift valley in the Middle East and East Africa. It extends from the Jordan Valley in Syria along the Red Sea into Ethiopia and through Kenya, Tanzania, and Malawi into Mozambique. Length: about 6400 km (4000 mi).

Great Salt Lake A salt lake in the USA, in NW Utah in the Great Basin. Its area has fluctuated from less than 2500 sq km (1000 sq mi) to over 5000 sq km (2000 sq mi).

Great Sandy Desert A desert of N Western Australia. It stretches SE from the Indian Ocean to the Gibson Desert. Area: 415 000 sq km (160 000 sq mi).

Great Schism (1378–1417) The split in the Roman Catholic Church following the election of two rival popes to succeed Gregory XI. When Urban VI determined to reform the College of Cardinals, they responded by electing an *antipope at Avignon, Clement VII. The Schism was ended by the Council of *Constance (1414–18) and the election of Martin V in 1417.

Great Trek The movement from the mid-1830s to mid-1840s of Dutch settlers (Afrikaners) in South Africa northwards from the Cape. The so-called Voortrekkers, under such leaders as Andries Pretorius (1799–1853), moved away from British rule at the Cape in search of more farmland that they could administer themselves. They established the republics of the Transvaal and the Orange Free State.

Great Victoria Desert A desert of Western and South Australia. It consists of a vast region of sand hills and salt marshes. Area: 323 750 sq km (125 000 sq mi).

g

Great Wall of China A medieval defensive fortification in N China. Stretching from the Yellow Sea N of Beijing nearly 2400 km (1500 mi) inland, it is the world's largest building achievement. Originally begun in 214 BC as a defence against nomads, it was rebuilt of stone in the 15th and 16th centuries. It is about 9 m (30 ft) high, with numerous watch towers along its length.

Great Zimbabwe The largest of the ruined Bantu royal centres in Zimbabwe. The word *zimbabwe* is derived from the Bantu for "revered houses." Great Zimbabwe reached its zenith in the late 14th century and traces of widespread trade, based on local gold, have been discovered, including Chinese pottery. Parts of the so-called Elliptical Building (a compound enclosing now vanished huts) stand 10.5 m (35 ft) high.

grebe A bird belonging to a primitive family (*Podicipitidae*; 21 species) occurring in rivers and lakes worldwide. Grebes have short wings, a very small tail, and partially webbed feet. They feed chiefly on fish and aquatic invertebrates. Grebes are grey, black, or brown, usually with white underparts, and in the breeding season many have brightly coloured erectile crests and ear tufts. Order: *Podicipediformes*. *See also* DABCHICK.

Greece, Republic of (official name: Hellenic Republic; Greek name: Ellás) A country in SE Europe, occupying the S section of the Balkan Peninsula. Numerous islands, lie to the S, E, and W; the largest is *Crete. *Economy*: industry has now replaced agriculture as the mainstay of the economy. Mineral resources, including lignite, bauxite, and iron ore, have been intensively exploited. The principal crops include wheat, barley, maize, tobacco, sugar beet, tomatoes, and dried and fresh fruits. Tourism is also important. In the 1990s austerity measures were imposed as a prelude to joining the single European currency. *History*: the centuries following the collapse of the *Mycenaean civilization (c. 1200 BC) saw the rise of the Greek city states and establishment of Greek colonies overseas. The 5th century was dominated by the abortive attempt of the Persians to annex Greece and the Peloponnesian War between rival Athens and Sparta. Sparta's subsequent supremacy in Greece lasted until its defeat by Thebes in 371. Greece fell to Philip of Macedon in 338 and was incorporated in the empire of his son Alexander the Great. Following Alexander's death (323), the Greek city states repeatedly attempted to assert their independence until the last Macedonian War (171–168) allowed Rome to dominate Greece. Roman rule lasted until 395 AD, when Greece became part of the Byzantine (Eastern Roman) Empire, centred on Constantinople. In the middle ages Greece was subject to invasions by the Franks, Normans, and the Latin Crusaders. In the early 14th century Byzantium reasserted its control over the area but by 1460 control had passed to the Ottoman Turks. Apart from a Venetian occupation (1686–1715), Greece remained under Ottoman rule until it achieved independence in 1829. In 1832 the Greek Crown was offered to a Bavarian prince, who became Otto I; after his deposition in 1862 a Danish prince became king as George I. Greek demands for Crete led to a disastrous war with Turkey in 1897, but in the Balkan Wars (1912–13) Greece gained the island together with territory in Thrace and Macedonia. In 1917 Greece entered World War I on the Allied side and the immediate postwar period saw renewed conflict with Turkey, in which Greece lost Smyrna. In 1924 Greece became a republic, which lasted until George II was restored in 1935. In World War II an unsuccessful Italian invasion (1940) was followed by the German occupation (1941–44), after which civil war lasted until 1949. The 1950s were dominated by the question of union with Cyprus. A military coup (1967) deposed Constantine II and led to a succession of military governments. A new constitution (1975) saw the reintroduction of democratic government. Greece became a member of the EC (now the EU) in 1981. Andreas Papandreou (1919–96) led Socialist governments from 1981 to 1989 and 1993 to 1996; he was succeeded by Costas Simitis. Greece adopted the single European currency in 2001–02. Following elections in 2004 a centre-right government took office under Costas Karamanlis. Official language: Greek. Currency: euro of 100 cents. Area: 131 986 sq km (50 960 sq mi). Population (2003 est): 11 001 000. Capital: Athens.

Greek language An Indo-European language spoken chiefly in Greece and the E Mediterranean islands. Well documented since the 14th century BC (*see* LINEAR B), ancient Greek was a highly complex inflected language. It had many dialect forms, the main groupings being Ionic (E Greece and Asia Minor), Aeolic (Boeotia and Thessaly), and Doric (the Peloponnese). From Ionic developed the Attic dialect, centred on Athens, which became the chief literary language of classical Greece. When the Greek city states lost their independence (4th century BC), their dialects gave way to a new common dialect (*koine*), which became the language of Hellenistic Greece and the New Testament. Modern Greek has two widely differing forms: the classically based Katharevusa (purified tongue) used in official publications, and Demotic, the living language of speech, poetry, and fiction.

Greek Orthodox Church Strictly, the Orthodox Church in Greece, although the term is often applied to the Orthodox Churches as a whole, to distinguish them from the Latin Church of the West. The Church in Greece dates from the 1st century and St Paul's activities, especially at Corinth. Under the patriarchate of Constantinople Greece was, from the acceptance of Christianity by Constantine, one of the main Christian centres. It is now a self-governing Church, the see of Athens holding a primacy of honour after the separation from the patriarchate of Constantinople in 1833.

Greek-Persian Wars An intermittent conflict between the Greeks and Persians. Persian encroachment on Greek territory began in 499 BC, when the Greek cities of Ionia revolted against their Persian overlords and were crushed by Darius I. In 490 the Persians were defeated by a small force of Athenians at Marathon. Darius died in 486 and in 480 Xerxes I crossed the Hellespont with a large force. The Greeks and Persians fought at Thermopylae, where the Spartans (under Leonidas I) heroically held the pass. Xerxes now attacked Attica and Athens was evacuated. At the battle of Salamis the Persians were defeated by the Greek fleet commanded by Themistocles and were again defeated at Plataea (479). Intermittent warfare continued until 449, when the Persians abandoned hope of annexing Greece.

green algae Algae of the phylum *Chlorophyta* (about 6000 species), which are bright green, owing to the predominance of the green pigment chlorophyll. Green algae range from simple unicellular plants, for example *Chlamydomonas*, to complex seaweeds. They are aquatic (mainly freshwater) or terrestrial in moist areas. Reproduction can be sexual or asexual.

green belt A zone of open, mostly agricultural, land surrounding a town to prevent it from spreading. Sir Ebenezer Howard's garden cities of the early 1900s provided the first practical examples; in 1935 the London County Council initiated the steps towards a London green belt that were realized in the Green Belt Act (1938) and the Town and Country Planning Act (1947). Since the 1950s restrictions against building in green belts have been relaxed and the 1990s and 2000s saw growing pressure for major residential developments in the countryside.

Greene, (Henry) Graham (1904–91) British novelist. He converted to Roman Catholicism in 1927, and an intense concern with questions of morality is central to many of his novels, including *Brighton Rock* (1938), *The Power and the Glory* (1940), *The Human Factor* (1978), and *The Captain and the Enemy* (1988). He also wrote literary thrillers, including *The Ministry of Fear* (1943), *The Third Man* (1950), and *Our Man in Havana* (1958).

greenfinch A Eurasian *finch, *Carduelis chloris*, about 14 cm long with an olive-green body and a pale bill. The male has a bright yellow-green breast and both sexes show bright-yellow wing flashes in flight.

greenfly *See* APHID.

greengage A bush or small tree, *Prunus italica*, related to the *plum, probably native to Asia Minor and widely cultivated. It bears round green fruits, which are used in preserves and for canning.

greenhouse effect An atmospheric effect in which some of the energy of ultraviolet radiation and visible light from the sun is retained by the earth as heat. The radiation is transmitted through the atmosphere to the earth's surface, where it is reradiated as longer wavelength infrared radiation. As the atmosphere only partially transmits the infrared back into space, some of it is absorbed by atmospheric gases, especially carbon dioxide, causing a rise in temperature. The phenomenon takes its name from a greenhouse, in which a similar effect occurs. In recent years CO_2 in the atmosphere has increased as a result of the burning of forests and increased use of fossil fuels, causing global warming. In the past century the world's average temperature has risen by over 0.6%, 1998, 2001, 2002, and 2003

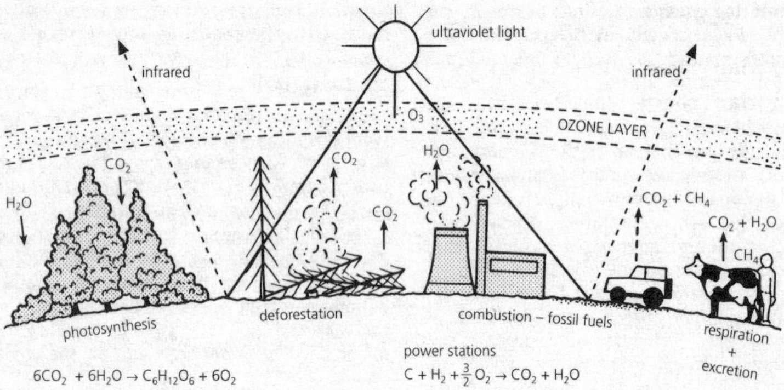

greenhouse effect. The sun's ultraviolet light is reradiated as infrared radiation, some of which is absorbed by the greenhouse gases (CO_2, CH_4, etc.).

being the four warmest years since records began in 1860. *See* KYOTO AGREEMENT.

Greenland (Danish name: Grønland; Greenlandic name: Kalaallit Nunaat) A large island off NE North America. Lying chiefly within the Arctic Circle, it is largely covered by a vast ice cap. Many glaciers emerge from this, including the Humboldt Glacier, breaking off to form icebergs along the coast. About 80% of the population are Inuit, the remainder being chiefly Danish. *Economy*: fishing is the chief occupation. Whaling and seal hunting have declined. Sheep are reared in the SW. Lead and zinc have been exploited since the early 1970s; uranium is also present. *History*: in about 986 AD the Norwegian Eric the Red discovered the island, which he named Greenland to attract settlers. Norse colonies on the island disappeared during the 15th century. A Danish colony from 1721, Greenland became an integral part of Denmark in 1953. In 1979 it gained self-government under Danish sovereignty. In 1985 Greenland left the EC. Official language: Inupik (Greenland Inuit). Currency: Danish krone of 100 øre. Area: 2 175 600 sq km (840 000 sq mi). Population (2002 est): 56 600. Capital: Nuuk.

Greenland Sea An extension of the Arctic Ocean, between Greenland, Svalbard, and Iceland. Covered by drifting ice, it links with the Atlantic Ocean.

green monkey disease An acute, often fatal, viral infection first described in Marburg, Germany, and therefore sometimes called Marburg disease. It occurs in vervet monkeys and may be transmitted to humans.

Green Party A British political party, founded in 1973 as the Ecology Party. Dedicated to protecting the environment, the party attracted growing support in the 1980s before being eclipsed by the increasingly "green" attitudes of the major political parties. Similar parties have achieved greater power elsewhere in Europe, notably in Germany.

Greenpeace An international environmental pressure group founded in 1971. It campaigns primarily against nuclear power, dumping nuclear waste, and commercial whaling. Its use of direct action has sometimes led to confrontation.

green turtle A large brown-green marine turtle, *Chelonia mydas*, formerly used to make turtle soup. Up to 1 m long and weighing up to 140 kg, they occur in warm Atlantic coastal waters feeding on marine algae and migrate to lay their eggs on Central American beaches. It is now an endangered species.

Greenwich A borough of E Greater London, on the S bank of the River Thames. The first Renaissance building in England, the Queen's House designed by Inigo *Jones (1616), was completed in 1637. The Greenwich Royal Hospital, designed by *Wren, became the Royal Naval College in 1873. Wren also designed the original *Royal Greenwich Observatory. The tea clipper *Cutty Sark* and Sir Francis Chichester's *Gipsy Moth IV* are at Greenwich Pier. *See also* MILLENNIUM DOME.

Greenwich Mean Time (**GMT**) The local time at Greenwich, London, located on the 0° meridian (*see* LATITUDE AND LONGITUDE), from which the standard times of different areas of the globe are calculated, 15° longitude representing one hour in time. In 1986 it was succeeded by Coordinated Universal Time.

Gregorian calendar *See* CALENDAR.

Gregorian chant The official liturgical plainchant of the Roman Catholic Church as codified during the papacy of *Gregory I. It consists of single unaccompanied melodic lines sung to flexible rhythms.

Gregory I, St (c. 540–604 AD) Pope (590–604), known as Gregory the Great. As pope he made peace with the Lombards and limited imperial authority over the Church. He reformed the papal states and sponsored Augustine (of Canterbury) in his mission to convert England. He also introduced the use of *Gregorian chant into the liturgy. Feast day: 3 September.

Gregory VII, St (Hildebrand; c. 1021–85) Pope (1073–85). He asserted the independence of the Church from lay control but created considerable opposition, especially in France and Germany, where Emperor *Henry IV declared his deposition (1076). He in turn excommunicated Henry and released his subjects from allegiance. Henry submitted to Gregory at Canossa (1077) but then appointed Wibert, Archbishop of Ravenna, antipope (1080), invaded Italy, and captured Rome (1084). Gregory was rescued by Norman troops but was nevertheless forced to flee. Feast day: 25 May.

Grenada An island country in the West Indies, in the Windward Islands. It also includes some of the Grenadine Islands. The majority of the population is of mixed European and Indian descent. *Economy*: largely agricultural, the chief products are cocoa, bananas, citrus fruits, sugar, and nutmeg (the main export). *History*: discovered by Columbus in 1493, it was colonized by the French and ceded to the British in 1763. In 1974 it became an independent state within the British Commonwealth. In March 1979, the government of Sir Eric Gairy was overthrown in a nearly bloodless coup led by Maurice Bishop. Following an uprising in 1983, during which Bishop was killed, the USA invaded the country and democratic government was restored. The current prime minister, Dr Keith Mitchell, took office following elections in 1995. Official language: English. Currency: East Caribbean dollar of 100 cents. Area: 344 sq km (133 sq mi). Population (2003 est): 102 000. Capital: St George's.

Grenadine Islands A chain of West Indian islets, extending for about 100 km (60 mi) between St Vincent and Grenada and administratively divided between the two.

Grenoble 45 11N 5 43E A city in SE France. The capital of the Dauphiné until 1341, it is the principal tourist centre of the French Alps. Population (1999): 153 317.

Grey, Lady Jane (1537–54) Queen of England for nine days (1553). The Protestant great-granddaughter of *Henry VII, Lady Jane was proclaimed queen by the Duke of *Northumberland when Edward VI died. However, Mary, the rightful heiress, had popular support and Jane abdicated. She was executed for treason with her husband Lord Guildford Dudley, Northumberland's son.

greyhound An ancient breed of dog used for hare coursing and racing. It has a slender deep-chested streamlined body with long legs and a long muscular neck. The short smooth coat can be of various colours. Greyhounds can reach speeds of up to 70 km per hour. Height: 71–76 cm (dogs); 68–71 cm (bitches).

greylag goose A grazing *goose, *Anser anser*, occurring in N and E Europe and central Asia. 75–87 cm long, it has a heavy orange bill and is dark grey above with pale wings, a finely barred neck, and pink legs.

Grieg, Edvard Hagerup (1843–1907) Norwegian composer. The influence of Norwegian folk music is apparent in many of his works, which include the *Lyric Pieces* (1867–1901), a very popular piano concerto (1868), incidental music to Ibsen's play *Peer Gynt* (1876), chamber music, and many songs.

griffin A mythological creature with the head and wings of an eagle, the body of a lion, and often a serpent's tail. It is common in many ancient eastern mythologies.

Griffith, Arthur (1872–1922) Irish journalist and politician, who founded *Sinn Féin in 1905. In 1919–20 he was acting head of the self-declared republican government in Ireland and in 1921 he helped to negotiate the treaty establishing the Irish Free State. He became head of the provisional government but died soon afterward.

Griffith, D(avid) W(ark) (1875–1948) US film director: the most influential pioneer of the cinema in the USA. His major films are *The Birth of a Nation* (1915), *Intolerance* (1916), and *Broken Blossoms* (1919).

griffon A breed of toy dog originating in Belgium and of terrier ancestry. It has a square compact body, a docked tail, and a large head covered with long coarse hair. The coat may be red, black, or black and tan. Weight: 2–5 kg.

g

griffon vulture One of the largest Old World *vultures, *Gyps fulvus*. It is 100 cm long and occurs in mountainous regions of S Europe, South Africa, and Asia. It is grey-brown with darker wingtips and a white head and ruff.

Grimm Two brothers, German philologists and folklorists. After early work on medieval German texts, **Jakob Grimm** (1785–1863) and **Wilhelm Grimm** (1786–1859) set about collecting German folktales, published in 1812–14 as *Kinder- und Hausmärchen*. The *Deutsche Grammatik* (1819, 1822) contains observations on the regularity of sound changes in Indo-European languages, known as **Grimm's law**. Their *Deutsches Wörterbuch* is a historical and descriptive German dictionary.

Grimsby 53 35N 0 05W A seaport in NE England, in North East Lincolnshire unitary authority, Lincolnshire, near the mouth of the Humber estuary. It is the largest fishing port in England, but the size of the fleet has been much reduced due to overfishing. Population (1991): 90 703.

grizzly bear *See* BROWN BEAR.

Grodno 53 40N 23 50E A port in W central Belarus. Possessed by Lithuania and then by Poland, it includes a medieval castle and a 16th-century palace. Population (1996 est): 301 000.

Gromyko, Andrei (1909–89) Soviet diplomat; foreign minister (1957–85) and president of the Soviet Union (1985–88). He was a major influence on Soviet foreign policy for over forty years.

Groningen A province in the Netherlands, bordering on the North Sea. Low lying and fertile, it is intensively cultivated. Area: 2350 sq km (900 sq mi). Population (2000): 562 600. Capital: Groningen.

Gropius, Walter (1883–1969) German architect, one of the pioneers of the international modern style of architecture. His first major building, a factory at Alfeld (1911) is a very early example of the new style. As director of the *Bauhaus (1919–28) he was able to influence all aspects of contemporary design. The rise of Nazi power forced him to move to America where he continued to design buildings.

Grossglockner 47 05N 12 44E The highest mountain in Austria, in the Alps. The Grossglockner Road (built 1930–35) crosses it, rising to 2576 m (7852 ft). Height: 3797 m (12 457 ft).

gross national product (**GNP**) A measure of the total annual output of a country, including net income from abroad. GNP can be calculated in three ways: based on income, output, or expenditure. All incomes accruing to residents of the country as a result of economic activity (excluding, for instance, pensions) can be summed. On the basis of output, the value added to a product at each stage of production can be summed. Alternatively the expenditure on consumption products can be calculated. **Gross domestic product** (GDP) is GNP excluding net income from abroad and gives some indication of the strength of domestic industry. **Net national product** makes a provision for depreciation, i.e. the using up of the country's capital stock.

ground beetle A heavily armoured long-legged beetle belonging to a family (*Carabidae*; 25 000 species) that is particularly common in temperate regions. Ground beetles are dark in colour or have a metallic sheen and are from 2 to 85 mm long. Most are nocturnal; the adults and most larvae are active carnivores, preying on insects, slugs, and snails.

groundhog *See* MARMOT.

groundnut The fruit of *Arachis hypogea*, also called peanut or earthnut, native to tropical South America but widely cultivated in the tropics. The plant is an annual, 30–45 cm high, with yellow flowers. After fertilization the pod ripens underground. The pod contains one to three seeds (the nuts), which are highly nutritious. Family: *Leguminosae*.

grouper One of several food and game fish of the family *Serranidae* (*see* SEA BASS), especially the genera *Epinephelus* and *Mycteroperca*, widely distributed in warm seas. Groupers have a dull-green or brown heavy body, up to or exceeding 2 m long, and a large mouth. Some are poisonous.

group therapy A form of *psychotherapy in which several patients meet to understand their problems, usually with the help of a therapist. Sometimes the aim is to increase patients' insight, sometimes to act out distressing events, and sometimes to provide support in overcoming a common problem (such as alcoholism).

grouse A game bird, 30–88 cm long, belonging to a family (*Tetraonidae*; about 18 species) of the N hemisphere. Grouse are mostly ground-living, with short round wings, a short strong bill, and feathered legs. They are noted for their spectacular courtship displays (called *leks*). The family includes the *black grouse, *red grouse, and *capercaillie of N Europe; the *ptarmigans; and the North American ruffed grouse (*Bonasa umbellus*) and *sage grouse. In Britain the grouse-shooting season is from 12 Aug to 10 Dec. Order: *Galliformes*.

growth hormone (*or* **somatotrophin**) A protein hormone that promotes the metabolic processes involved in growth of bone and muscle. It is secreted by the pituitary gland and stimulates protein synthesis, mobilizes fat reserves, increases glucose levels in the blood, and affects mineral metabolism. Lack of growth hormone in children causes dwarfism.

Grozny 43 21N 45 42E A city in S Russia, the capital of Chechenia, in one of the country's richest oil-producing areas. The city was devastated by Russian bombs during the Russian-Chechen conflict (1994–95) and again in 1999–2000, when Russian troops reoccupied the city. Population (1999 est): 186 000.

Grünewald, Matthias (Mathis Gothardt; d. 1528) German painter. His favourite subject was the crucifixion, as in the *Isenheim Altarpiece* (Colmar, France), noted for its dazzling colour. His style influenced 20th-century German expressionists (*see* EXPRESSIONISM).

grunt A small food fish, belonging to the family *Pomadasyidae* (about 75 species), that can produce piglike grunts. It has a colourful elongated body and a large mouth; it occurs in the warm and tropical coastal waters. Order: *Perciformes*.

Guadalajara 1. 20 30N 103 20W The second largest city in Mexico, at an altitude of 1650 m (5413 ft). Founded by the Spanish (1530), it is a communications centre across the Sierra Madre Occidental. Population (2000 est): 1 647 000. **2.** 40 37N 3 10W A town in NE Spain. Its palace was virtually destroyed during the Spanish Civil War but has since been restored. Population (1991): 67 200.

Guadalcanal 9 30S 160 00E The largest of the Solomon Islands, in the S Pacific Ocean. During World War II the first major US offensive against the Japanese took place here (1942–43). Area: 6475 sq km (2500 sq mi). Population (1997 est): 61 243. Chief settlement: Honiara.

Guadalquivir, River The main river of S Spain. It flows WSW to the Gulf of Cádiz and is navigable to Seville by oceangoing vessels. Length: 560 km (348 mi).

Guadalupe Hidalgo (name from 1931 until 1971: Gustavo A. Madero) 19 29N 99 07W A city in central Mexico, a NE suburb of Mexico City. The Basilica of the Virgin of Guadalupe, which was built after an Indian convert reported seeing a vision of the Virgin Mary here in 1531, is a famous place of pilgrimage. The Treaty of Guadalupe Hidalgo, which ended the Mexican War, was signed here. Population (2000 est): 668 500.

Guadeloupe A French overseas region in the West Indies, in the E Caribbean Sea. It comprises two main islands, Grande Terre and Basse Terre, together with the island dependencies of Marie Galante, La Désirade, Îles des Saintes, St Barthélemy, and the N part of *St Martin. The economy is based on agriculture; sugar cane is the chief crop. Area: 1702 sq km (657 sq mi). Population (2001 est): 432 000. Capital: Basse-Terre.

guaiacum A small evergreen tree of the genus *Guaiacum*, especially *G. officinale* of tropical America, also called lignum vitae. It has blue flowers, yellow fruits, and hard wood, used to make bowling balls. The resin is distilled for medicinal use. Family: *Zygophyllaceae*.

Guam 13 30N 144 40E An island and US unincorporated territory in the West Pacific Ocean, the largest of the Mariana Islands. Spanish from 1565 to 1898, it was occupied by the Japanese (1941–44). It is a major naval and air base, especially important during the Vietnam War. Area: 450 sq km (210 sq mi). Population (2001 est): 158 000. Capital: Agaña.

Guangzhou *See* CANTON.

guano The accumulated excrement of certain animals, especially seabirds, seals, and bats. It contains 10–18% nitrogen, 8–12% phosphoric acid, and 2–3% potash, according to the age and origin of the deposit. It has been widely used as a fertilizer.

Guantánamo 20 09N 75 14W A city in SE Cuba, N of Guantánamo Bay. It is the centre of an agricultural area producing sugar cane and coffee. Population (1994 est): 207 796.

Guarani A group of South American Indian peoples of Paraguay and neighbouring areas of Brazil and Argentina who speak languages of the Tupian group. Few now retain their original culture, based on hunting and maize cultivation, warfare, and cannibalism.

Guardi, Francesco (1712–93) Venetian painter, who sometimes collaborated with his elder brother, **Giovanni Antonio Guardi** (1699–1760). His views of Venice were sometimes copied from *Canaletto but they are distinguished by their romantic style.

Guarini, Guarino (1624–83) Italian baroque architect, philosopher, and mathematician. Although influenced by Francesco Borromini (1599–1667), his work shows great originality and technical skill. Probably his most successful building is the church of S Lorenzo, Turin (1668–87).

Guarneri An Italian family of violin makers, famous in the 17th and 18th centuries. **Andrea Guarneri** (d. 1698) was a pupil (with Stradivari) of Amati in Cremona. Andrea's grandson **Giuseppe Guarneri** (1698–1744), known as "del Gesù," was the most famous member of the family; influenced by the makers of the Brescian school, he signed his violins "Guarnerius."

Guatemala, Republic of A country in Central America, on the Pacific Ocean, with a small outlet on the Caribbean Sea. Tropical forests rise to a central mountainous region, containing a fertile plateau. About half the population are *Maya Quiché Indians and most of the rest are of mixed Spanish and Indian descent. *Economy*: mainly agricultural. The main crops are coffee, sugar, bananas, and cotton, which are the principal exports. Minerals include zinc and lead concentrates. Oil was discovered in 1974. *History*: there is extensive archaeological evidence of pre-Spanish civilizations, especially that of the Maya, and, from the 12th century, the Aztecs. From 1524 to 1821 the area was part of the Spanish captaincy general of Guatemala, which included most of Central America. It formed the nucleus of the Central American Federation until 1839, when it became independent. During the next 150 years periods of democratic government alternated with military dictatorships and there was almost continuous political unrest; Guatemala has often been criticized for its human rights record. In 1996 Alvaro Arzú became president and signed a peace agreement with the URNG (left-wing, mostly Maya Quiché Indian, guerrillas) guaranteeing the rights of indigenous peoples. The presidency of Alfonso Portillo (1999–2003) was marked by corruption scandals and rising social unrest; he was succeeded by Oscar Berger in 2004. Official language: Spanish. Currencies: quetzal of 100 centavos and US dollar. Area: 108 889 sq km (42 042 sq mi). Population (2003 est): 12 347 000. Capital: Guatemala City.

Guatemala City 14 38N 90 22W The capital of Guatemala. Founded in 1776, it was the capital of the captaincy general of Guatemala and later of the Central American Federation. Population (2000 est, urban area): 2 578 526.

guava A tropical American tree, *Psidium guajava*, about 10 m tall. Its white flowers develop into yellow pear-shaped fruits containing many small seeds. Guava fruits are used to make jam and jelly, stewed for desserts, or canned. Family: *Myrtaceae* (myrtle family).

Guayaquil (*or* **Santiago de Guayaquil**) 2 13S 79 54W The largest city and chief port of Ecuador, on the River Guayas. Population (1997 est): 1 973 880.

gudgeon A freshwater shoaling fish, *Gobio gobio*, related to *carp, found in Europe and N Asia. Used as bait, it has a slender greyish body, up to 20 cm long, with a row of blackish spots along each side and a pair of barbels at the corners of the mouth.

guelder rose A small tree or shrub, *Viburnum opulus*, 4–5 m high, found throughout Eurasia. It has clusters of flowers, 5–10 cm across, in which the outer flowers are large and sterile and the inner ones are small and fertile. The fruits are red translucent berries. Family: *Caprifoliaceae* (honeysuckle family).

Guelfs and Ghibellines The propapal and proimperial factions respectively in medieval Germany and Italy. Arising from a German struggle between rival claimants to the Holy Roman Empire, the Guelfs (named after Welf, the family name) and Ghibellines (named after Waiblingen, a Hohenstaufen castle), their conflict acquired an Italian context because of papal opposition to the Hohenstaufen. The Italian city states were led by Florence (Guelf) and Pisa (Ghibelline).

guenon An *Old World monkey belonging to the genus *Cercopithecus* (10 species), of African forests. They are 83–160 cm long including the tail (50–88 cm) and move in troops, feeding on leaves, fruits, and insects. The mona monkey (*C. mona*) is a strikingly marked guenon. *See also* GRASS MONKEY.

Guercino (Giovanni Francesco Barbieri; 1591–1666) Italian painter. His masterpiece, the ceiling frescos in the Casino Ludovisi, Rome, commissioned by Pope Gregory XV in 1621, were influenced by the Carracci. While in Rome (1621–23) he also painted the *Burial of St Petronilla* (Capitoline Museum, Rome).

Guericke, Otto von (1602–86) German physicist, renowned for his investigation of vacuums. In 1650 he invented the air pump, which he used to perform a series of experiments culminating in a demonstration in which two teams of horses failed to separate a pair of large hemispheres (called the Magdeburg hemispheres after his home town) placed together and evacuated. When air was admitted to the hemispheres they fell apart.

Guernica 43 19N 2 40W A historic Basque town in N Spain, on the Bay of Biscay. During the Spanish Civil War it was virtually destroyed by German planes supporting the Nationalists on 27 April 1937. This is depicted in a painting by Picasso. Population (latest est): 16 378.

Guernsey 49 27N 2 35W The second largest of the Channel Islands, in the English Channel. It is low lying in the N and hilly in the S with rugged coastal cliffs. The finance industry is important, together with horticulture and dairy farming (the Guernsey breed of cattle originated here). Guernsey is a popular tourist resort. Area: 63 sq km (24.5 sq mi). Population (2001 est): 64 300. Capital: St Peter Port.

Guevara, Che (Ernesto G.; 1928–67) Argentine revolutionary, who became the hero of left-wing youth in the 1960s. A doctor, he joined Castro's invasion of Cuba (1956). After Castro's victory, Guevara influenced Cuba's foreign relations and directed its land-reform policies. In 1967 he was killed while attempting to instigate a revolt in Bolivia.

guide dogs Dogs specially trained to guide the blind. The first training schools were established in Germany (1911–18) and the British Guide Dog Association was founded in 1931. The most suitable breeds for the four-month training course are German Shepherd dogs (Alsatians), Labradors, and golden retrievers.

Guides Association An association founded (as the Girl Guides Association) by Robert and (his sister) Agnes Baden Powell in 1910 to encourage the physical, mental, and spiritual development of girls. The three classes of members are Brownie Guides (aged 7–10), Guides (10–15), and Ranger Guides (14–20). Its counterpart for boys is the Scout Association. The Association dropped the word "Girl" from its title in 1992.

Guildford 51 14N 0 35W A city in SE England, in Surrey on the River Wey. It is a market and residential town; its buildings include Guildford Cathedral (1936). Population (1991): 65 998.

guilds (*or* **gilds**) Associations formed in medieval Europe to further their members' common purposes. Originally religious or social, the first guilds are recorded in the 9th century. Merchant guilds were created in many towns in the 11th century to organize trade and became a powerful force in local government. Craft guilds, restricted to specific crafts or trades, were formed from the 12th century. The *livery companies of London are descended from the craft guilds.

guillemot A bird, *Uria aalge*, occurring in coastal regions of the N hemisphere. It is 40 cm long and has a dark-brown plumage with a white belly and wing stripe a slender bill, feeding on fish, shellfish, and worms. The eggs are shaped so that they do not roll off the cliff ledges where they are laid. Family *Alcidae* (auks).

guillotine A device for beheading people. It consists of two vertical posts and a horizontal knife that is dropped onto the victim's neck. Invented by Joseph Ignace Guillotin (1738–1814), it was introduced in France in 1792, during the French Revolution.

Guinea, Gulf of A large inlet of the E Atlantic Ocean, bordering on the Guinea Coast of West Africa.

Guinea, Republic of A country on the coast of West Africa. A coastal plain, partly swamp, rises steeply to plateaus and mountains. The population is mainly Fulani and Mandingo. *Economy*: chiefly agricultural and now largely collectivized. The chief crops are rice and palm oil and nuts, as well as coffee, peanuts, and fruits. Livestock is also important. The principal mineral resources are diamonds, iron ore, and bauxite (alumina is the principal export). *History*: the N formed part of Ghana from the 5th to the 8th centuries AD and of the Mali empire in the 16th century. In 1849 the French established a protectorate over part of Guinea, which became part of French West Africa in 1895. In 1958 French Guinea became an independent republic under President Ahmed Sekon Touré. The army took over following Touré's death in 1984 but a multiparty system was introduced in 1991. Gen Lansana Conté, president since 1984, was re-elected in 1993. In 1996 Sidia Touré became the country's first prime minister, he was succeeded by Lamine Sidime in 1999. Official languages: French and eight local languages. Currency: Guinea franc of 100 centimes. Area: 245 857 sq km (95 000 sq mi). Population (2003): 8 480 000. Capital: Conakry.

Guinea-Bissau, Republic of (name until 1974: Portuguese Guinea) A small country on the coast of West Africa. It consists chiefly of a coastal plain rising to savanna-covered plateau inland. Most of the population are Fulani, Mandyako, and Mandingo. *Economy*: chiefly agricultural, the principal crops being groundnuts (the main export), rice, palm oil, and nuts. Bauxite deposits have also been discovered. *His-*

tory: explored by the Portuguese in the mid-15th century, the area became a centre of the slave trade. It became a Portuguese colony in 1879 and an overseas province of Portugal in 1951. In 1974 it became an independent republic. After a coup in 1980, constitutional rule returned in 1984, with Maj João Bernardo Vieira as elected head of state. The first multiparty elections (1994) were won by the ruling party but Vieira was overthrown in a coup in 1999. Following free elections in 2000 Kumba Ialá became president but he too was deposed by the military in 2003. Official language: Portuguese. Currency: CFA franc of 100 centimes. Area: 36 125 sq km (13 948 sq mi). Population (2003 est): 1 361 000. Capital: Bissau.

g

guinea fowl A bird belonging to an African family (*Numididae*; 7–10 species). About 50 cm long, domesticated guinea fowl are descended from the helmet guinea fowl (*Numida meleagris*), which has a large bony crest, a bare face with red and blue wattles, and a grey white-spotted plumage. Guinea fowl scratch for seeds and insects, especially termites. Order: *Galliformes* (pheasants, turkeys, etc.).

guinea pig A domesticated rodent, *Cavia porcellus*, descended from the *cavy. Guinea pigs were originally bred for food but are now popular as pets.

guinea worm A *nematode worm, *Dracunculus medinensis*, that is a serious parasite of humans in Africa, India, and the Middle East. The larvae are carried by water fleas (genus *Cyclops*) often present in drinking water. When swallowed by humans, they burrow into the tissues and grow to maturity: the females reach a length of up to 120 cm, causing ulcers on the feet and legs.

Guinevere In *Arthurian legend, the wife of King Arthur and lover of *Lancelot. Malory's *Morte d'Arthur* (1485) describes her abduction by Modred and her adulterous love for Lancelot.

Guinness, Sir Alec (1914–2000) British actor. He established his reputation as a stage actor in the 1930s. His films included *Kind Hearts and Coronets* (1949), *The Bridge on the River Kwai* (1957), and *A Passage to India* (1984).

guitar A plucked stringed instrument of Moorish origin, which came to Europe via Spain. The modern Spanish guitar has a flat back, a round sound hole, a fretted fingerboard, and six strings tuned chiefly in fourths. It has a range of over three octaves from the E below the bass stave. Music for it is written an octave higher than it sounds. The electric guitar, which has an electronic pick-up linked to an amplifier rather than a soundbox, was developed in the 1950s.

guitar fish A ray fish, of the family *Rhinobatidae*, that has a flat pointed head with fused pectoral fins and a long muscular sharklike tail. Guitar fish live in shallow waters of tropical and temperate seas and feed on bottom-dwelling animals, especially crustaceans.

Guiyang (*or* **Kuei-yang**) 26 35N 106 40E A city in S China, the capital of Guizhou province. Population (1991 est): 1 530 000.

Gujarat A state in W India, on the Arabian Sea SE of Pakistan. Lowlands merge into hills in the S and E and into marshes in the NW. Cotton, tobacco, peanuts, and other crops are raised. *History*: a flourishing area under Muslim princes (13th–17th centuries), Gujarat was conquered by the Maratha in the 18th century before passing to Britain. In January 2001 a severe earthquake left at least 30 000 dead and 600 000 homeless. Area: 116 024 sq km (44 788 sq mi). Population (2001 est): 50 596 992. Capital: Gandhinagar.

Gujarati An Indo-Aryan language spoken by 20 million people in Gujarat and Maharashtra in India. It is related to Rajasthani, uses a modified Devanagari script, and has a long literary tradition.

Gulf States The nations situated on the Persian Gulf. They are Oman, United Arab Emirates, Qatar, Bahrein, Saudi Arabia, Kuwait, Iraq, and Iran. They comprise the world's major oil-producing area.

Gulf Stream One of the major ocean currents of the world, flowing from the Florida Strait parallel to the North American coast as far as the Newfoundland banks. It bears NE across the Atlantic as the North Atlantic Drift, branching into two main directions, one flowing N towards Spitsbergen and the other flowing S to form the Canary Current. The warm water benefits the climate of NW Europe.

Gulf War 1. (1991) A conflict between Iraq under Saddam *Hussein and a US-led multinational force including troops from the UK, France, Saudi Arabia, Egypt, Syria, Kuwait, and other Arab states. It was precipitated by Iraq's invasion of Kuwait (2 Aug 1990) and refusal to comply with UN resolutions demanding its withdrawal. The coalition nations built up a military force in Saudi Arabia and, when Iraq continued to be defiant, launched air attacks on Baghdad and other targets on 17 Jan 1991.

Iraq responded to the bombing campaign with missile attacks on Israel and Saudi Arabia. On 24 Feb 1991 the coalition forces began a ground attack, overwhelming the Iraqi troops in Kuwait and advancing into southern Iraq. The coalition attack ceased on 28 Feb when Iraq agreed to comply with UN resolutions. However, tensions between Iraq and the West continued, with US bombing raids on Iraqi bases in 1993, 1996, and 1998, and led eventually to the *Iraq War of 2003 (sometimes called the "second Gulf War"). **2.** *See* IRAN-IRAQ WAR.

gulfweed Tropical *brown algae, also called rockweed or sea holly, of the genus *Sargassum*, especially *S. natans*, which forms huge free-floating masses of seaweed in the Sargasso Sea.

gull A seabird belonging to the subfamily *Larinae* (about 40 species), seen mostly in coastal regions. Up to 75 cm long, gulls have long pointed wings and a strong slightly hooked bill. Gulls are typically grey and white. Some gulls feed on fish but most are scavengers. Family: *Laridae* (gulls and terns); order: *Charadriiformes* (gulls, plovers, etc.).

gullet *See* OESOPHAGUS.

gums Adhesive substances exuded by plants. They are odourless tasteless amorphous *carbohydrates that form either clear liquid solutions or gelatinous mixtures with water. **Gum arabic** (*or* gum acacia) is obtained from trees of the genus *Acacia*. **Gum tragacanth** is extracted from shrubs of the genus *Astragalus*.

gum tree A tree of the genus *Eucalyptus* (about 600 species), so called because the whole tree is rich in resin and aromatic oils.

gun metal A type of *bronze containing about 90% copper and sometimes a little zinc, originally used for making cannons. Admiralty gun metal (88% copper, 10% tin, 2% zinc) is used in shipbuilding.

gunnel An eel-like fish of the family *Pholididae* (about 8 species), found in N Atlantic and N Pacific coastal waters, feeding on invertebrates. The rock gunnel (*Pholis gunnellus*), also called butterfish, is 30 cm long and brownish with 9–13 black spots along the dorsal fin. Order: *Perciformes*.

gunpowder An explosive mixture of potassium nitrate, sulphur, and powdered charcoal. Invented by the Chinese many centuries before its description by Roger *Bacon in the 13th century, it has had a profound effect on human conflict.

Gunpowder Plot *See* FAWKES, GUY.

Guomindang (*or* **Kuomintang**) The Na-

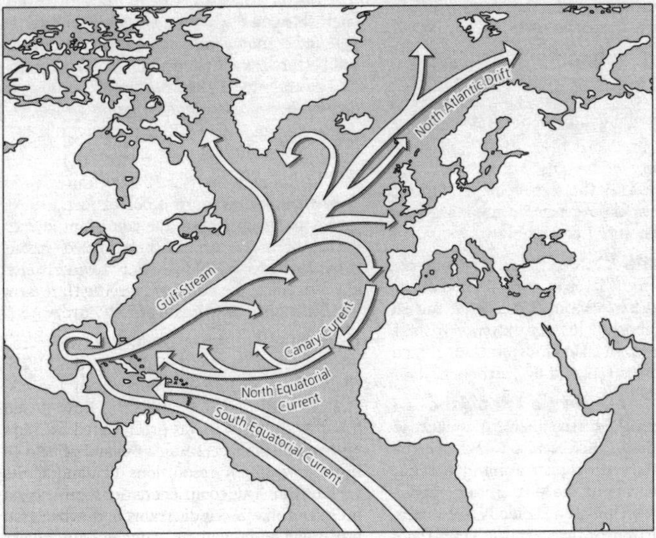

Gulf Stream

tional People's Party of *Taiwan (Republic of China). Organized in 1912 from Sun Yat-sen's Alliance Society, it formed an alliance with the new Chinese Communist Party (CCP) in 1924. Following Sun's death (1925), the Guomindang was led by *Chiang Kai-shek and with the CCP had gained control of most of China by 1926. A break between the two parties (1927) led to civil war until Japanese conquests in China (*see* SINO-JAPANESE WARS) necessitated renewed cooperation in 1937. After Japan's defeat (1945), civil war resumed until a communist victory (1949) drove the Guomindang into exile in Taiwan.

g

guppy A freshwater fish, *Lebistes reticulatus*, native to N South America and the West Indies. Male guppies are up to 4 cm long and brightly coloured. Females produce live young at monthly intervals. Guppies are popular aquarium fish. Family: *Cyprinodontidae*.

Gurkhas Soldiers of Nepalese origin who have served in the British Army since 1815. The name derives from the ruling dynasty of Nepal.

gurnard A carnivorous bottom-dwelling fish, also called sea robin, belonging to a family (*Triglidae*; about 40 species) found in temperate and tropical seas. It has a tapering body, up to 70 cm long, a large armoured head, and produces sound by vibrating its swim bladder. The flying gurnards belong to the family *Dactylopteridae*. Order: *Scorpaeniformes*.

Gutenberg, Johann (c. 1400–c. 1468) German printer, who invented printing with movable metal type. In 1448 he received the financial backing of Johann Fust (1400–66) and by 1455 had produced his great 42-line Bible (the Gutenberg Bible). Fust successfully sued Gutenberg in 1455 for the repayment of his loan and the impoverished Gutenberg was forced to relinquish his machinery.

gutta percha A brownish leathery material obtained from the latex of various trees of the family *Sapotaceae*, especially those of the SE Asian genus *Palaquium*. Once extensively used, for example as an electrical insulator, it has now largely been replaced by synthetics.

Guyana, Cooperative Republic of (name until 1966: British Guiana) A country in the NE of South America, on the Atlantic Ocean. Narrow fertile coastal plains give way to higher undulating areas. Most of the population is of African and East Indian descent. *Economy*: agriculture is important, the main crops being rice and sugar. The most important minerals were formerly gold and diamonds, but these have now been overtaken by bauxite. *History*: the coast was first explored by the Spanish in 1499 and settlements were founded by the Dutch in the 17th century. The area became a British colony, as British Guiana, in 1831. In 1961 it gained internal self-government under Cheddi Jagan. In 1966, as Guyana, it became independent within the British Commonwealth. It is also a member of CARICOM. The Marxist Cooperative Republic of Guyana was formed in 1970. The 1980s saw deepening economic crisis and social unrest; free elections were held in 1992 (the first for 28 years). In 1999 Bharrat Jagdeo became president. Official language: English. Currency: Guyana dollar of 100 cents. Area: 210 000 sq km (83 000 sq mi). Population (2003 est): 778 000. Capital: Georgetown.

Gwalior 26 12N 78 09E A city in India, in Madhya Pradesh. It developed around its impressive fortress, which is believed to date from the 6th century AD. Population (1991): 692 982.

Gwyn, Nell (1650–87) English actress. Originally an orange seller in Drury Lane, she achieved fame as an actress and became Charles II's mistress, bearing him two sons. "Let not poor Nellie starve," are said to have been his last words.

Gwynedd A county of NW Wales, bordering on the Irish Sea. It was created in 1974 from the counties of Anglesey, Caernarfonshire, Merionethshire, and part of W Denbighshire. In 1996 it became a unitary authority; Anglesey was restored as an independent county and the NE became part of the new county borough of Conwy. It is predominantly mountainous, rising to 1086 m (3563 ft) in Snowdon. Area: 1027 sq km (397 sq mi). Population (2001): 116 838. Administrative centre: Caernarfon.

gymnosperms A group of plants, most of which are trees, whose sole consistent characteristic is that their seeds are borne naked, often on *cone scales. They were formerly classified as a class, *Gymnospermae*, but are now generally split into separate phyla: *Coniferophyta* (*see* CONIFER); *Ginkgophyta* (*see* GINKGO); *Cycadophyta* (*see* CYCAD); and *Gnetophyta* (e.g. welwitschia). There are several extinct orders, including the *Cycadofilicales* (*see* SEED FERN) and the *Cordaitales*.

gymnure An insectivorous mammal belonging to the family *Erinaceidae* of SE Asia, also called hairy hedgehog. There are four species, including the *moon rat. Short-legged and flat-footed, 15–60 cm long, they live in thick undergrowth and hunt mainly at night.

gynaecology The branch of medicine and surgery concerned with diseases of women, particularly those affecting the reproductive system. **Obstetrics** deals with the care of women during pregnancy, childbirth, and the period immediately after delivery.

Gypsophila A genus of slender annual or perennial herbs (about 120 species), native to the Mediterranean area. Up to 1.5 m high, they have white or pink flowers. Family: *Caryophyllaceae* (pink family).

gypsum A colourless or white mineral consisting of hydrated calcium sulphate found in clays, shales, and limestones. Rock gypsum is often red-stained, granular, and found in layers. Gypsite is impure and earthy, occurring as surface deposits. Alabaster is a pure compact fine-grained translucent form. Satin-spar is fibrous and silky. Selenite occurs as transparent crystals in clays and mudstones. Gypsum is used in the manufacture of cement, rubber, paper, plaster of Paris, and blackboard chalk.

gypsy moth A moth, *Lymantria dispar*, distributed throughout the N hemisphere. Males are brownish grey and females white. The larvae, which feed on a variety of trees, are a serious pest. *See also* TUSSOCK MOTH.

gyrfalcon The largest *falcon, *Falco rusticolus*, which breeds in N Eurasia, North America, and mountainous regions of Asia. It is 60 cm long and its plumage varies from pure white speckled with black to dark grey with dense black barring. It hunts for hares, rodents, and ground-dwelling birds.

gyrocompass *See* COMPASS.

gyroscope A device consisting of a heavy wheel mounted in a double gimbal so that it is free to rotate about three mutually perpendicular axes. Once spinning, the wheel maintains the same orientation in space, even when the gimbals are turned. It is used as a directional sensor in many instruments (gyrocompass, gyro horizon, automatic pilot).

H

Haakon VII (1872–1957) The first King of Norway (1905–57) following the restoration of Norwegian independence. In 1896 he married Maud (d. 1938), the daughter of Edward VII of the UK. His refusal to abdicate during the German occupation (1940–45) encouraged Norwegian resistance.

Haarlem 52 23N 4 38E A city in the W Netherlands, the capital of North Holland province. It is a major trade centre for bulbs and is noted for its Frans Hals museum and its fine cathedral. Population (1999 est): 148 262.

habeas corpus (Latin: have the body) A remedy against unlawful confinement, consisting of a writ ordering the person alleged to have unlawful custody of a prisoner to produce him or her before the court and to comply with any court orders. The writ may be used to test the legality of imprisonment but not to appeal against a lawful conviction.

Haber-Bosch process A method for the bulk production of ammonia from hydrogen and atmospheric nitrogen. The pure gases are passed over an iron catalyst at about 500°C and a pressure of 500 atmospheres. The process was devised by Fritz Haber (1868–1934) and adapted by Carl Bosch (1874–1940).

Habsburgs (*or* **Hapsburgs**) The most prominent European royal dynasty from the 15th to 20th centuries. The family originated in Switzerland in the 10th century. In 1273 Rudolph I (1218–91) was elected Holy Roman Emperor and consolidated his family's possession of Austria, Carniola, and Styria. The Habsburgs held the imperial title again from 1438 to 1740 and from 1745 to 1806. In 1516 *Charles V inherited the Spanish Crown, adding Spain with its European and American possessions to the Habsburg domains. He left the Spanish Crown to his son, *Philip II, and his Austrian possessions to his brother, Ferdinand I (1503–64). The Spanish branch ruled until 1700; the Austrian Habsburgs became emperors of Austria in 1804 and of *Austria-Hungary in 1867, which they ruled until the end of World War I.

hadal zone *See* ABYSSAL ZONE.

haddock A carnivorous food fish, *Melanogrammus aeglefinus*, related to *cod, that usually occurs in shoals near the bottom of N Atlantic coastal waters. It is up to 1 m long, grey or brown above and silvery below, with two anal and three dorsal fins. It is eaten both fresh and smoked.

Hades (*or* **Pluto**) The Greek god of the dead; also the name of the underworld he ruled. He was the brother of Zeus and Poseidon and husband of *Persephone, whom he abducted. The souls of the dead were ferried to Hades across the River Styx by *Charon.

Hadrian (76–138 AD) Roman emperor (117–38). He was admitted to the imperial household as Trajan's ward in 85 and had a successful military career. On Trajan's death he became emperor and from 120 to 131 toured the provinces. His foreign policy was generally defensive (*see* HADRIAN'S WALL).

Hadrian IV *See* ADRIAN IV.

Hadrian's Wall A Roman frontier defence work. Begun in 122 AD, it was the N frontier of Roman Britain for 250 years. Designed to contain the Scottish tribes, it stretched 120 km (85 mi) from Tyne to Solway. It eventually comprised ditch, stone and turf wall (incorporating forts and signalling turrets), road system, and "vallum" (earthworks delimiting the military area). Substantial portions still stand.

hadron Any elementary particle that takes part in *strong interactions. The group thus includes all baryons and mesons but not leptons or the photon. *See* PARTICLE PHYSICS.

haematite (*or* **hematite**) The principal ore of iron, ferric oxide, varying in colour from red to grey to black. It contains over 70% iron.

It occurs either in crystalline form (specular iron ore) or in massive form.

haematology The study of blood and its diseases. Haematology is concerned particularly with treating *leukaemias, *haemophilia, and rare kinds of anaemia.

haemoglobin The substance, contained within the red blood cells (*see* ERYTHROCYTE), that is responsible for the colour of blood. In humans haemoglobin consists of a protein (globin) combined with an iron-containing pigment (haem). Haem combines with oxygen to form oxyhaemoglobin, which gives arterial blood its bright-red colour and is the means by which oxygen is transported around the body. Oxygen is released at the tissues and the pigment acquires a bluish tinge, responsible for the bluish-red colour of venous blood.

haemophilia A hereditary disease in which the blood does not clot properly due to absence of one of the clotting factors. The disease is almost entirely restricted to boys but is transmitted through the mother. If an affected person (a haemophiliac) cuts himself seriously he needs immediate treatment. The disease can be controlled by administration of Factor VIII, obtained from human blood.

haemorrhoids (*or* **piles**) Swollen (varicose) veins in the anal canal, which may enlarge sufficiently to hang down outside the anus. Piles may cause bleeding from the anus and itchiness; in severe cases they may need to be surgically removed or injected with a sclerosing agent, which makes them shrivel up.

Ha-er-bin (English name: Harbin) 45 45N 126 41E A port in NE China, the capital of Heilongjiang province on the Songhua River. A trading and industrial centre, it was a haven for refugees from the Russian Revolution (1917). Population (1999 est): 2 586 978.

hafnium (Hf) A dense ductile metal, first detected in zircon ($ZrSiO_4$) in 1923 and named after the Latin (Hafnia) for Copenhagen, where it was discovered. It is chemically similar to zirconium. The capacity of hafnium to absorb neutrons is used to control nuclear reactors, especially in submarines. Its compounds include the chloride ($HfCl_4$) and other halides, the oxide (HfO_2), the carbide (HfC), and the nitride (Hf_3N_4). At no 72; at wt 178.49; mp 2331 ± 20°C; bp 4603°C.

Haganah (Hebrew: defence) The irregular organization of the early Jewish settlers in Palestine established in 1920 to counteract the attacks of the Palestinian Arabs. After the partition of Palestine in 1947, the Haganah became the defence force of the Jewish state, and in 1948 the national army of the state of Israel.

hagfish A fishlike vertebrate, 40–80 cm long, sometimes called slime eel, belonging to a family (*Myxinidae*; about 20 species) of *cyclostomes. They occur on or near the sea bottom in cold regions and feed on dead or dying fish. Hagfishes are initially hermaphrodites but develop either male or female sex organs.

Haggard, Sir H(enry) Rider (1856–1925) British novelist. His five years in government service in South Africa provided the background of his first novel, *King Solomon's Mines* (1885), reflecting his own liberal views. Of his many later romances, *She* (1887) is the best known.

haggis A traditional Scottish dish, eaten especially on Burns' Night (25 Jan). Haggis is made from minced sheep's heart, liver, and lungs with onion, oatmeal, suet, and seasonings, all stuffed into a bag made from the sheep's stomach.

Hague, The (Dutch name: 's Gravenhage *or* Den Haag) 52 05N 4 16E The seat of government

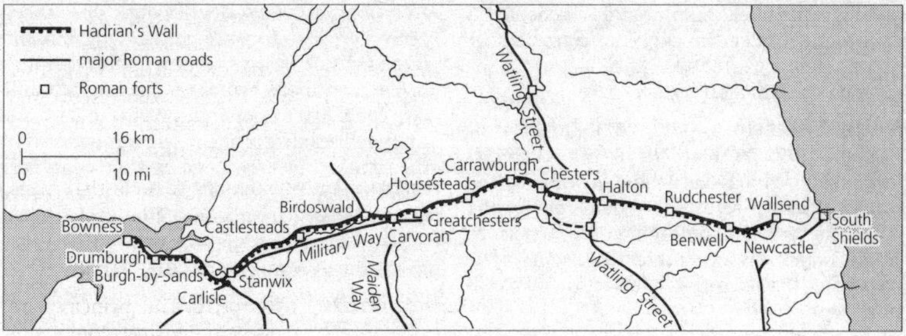

Hadrian's Wall. The most extensive of the Roman remains in the UK.

of the Netherlands and capital of South Holland province. It became the seat of the States General of the seven United Provinces of the Netherlands in the 16th century. It is the residence of the court and the International Court of Justice is located here. Notable buildings include the 13th-century Binnenhof, in which the government is housed. It is a commercial and residential centre with some light industry. Population (1999 est): 440 743.

Hahn, Otto ((1879–1968) German chemist and physicist. With Lise *Meitner he discovered protactinium in 1918. He continued to work with Meitner until she was forced to leave Germany in 1938. Together they discovered the process of nuclear fission. In 1944 he was awarded the Nobel Prize for Chemistry.

h

Hahnemann, Samuel Christian Friedrich (1755–1843) German physician and founder of *homeopathy. Hahnemann's methods aroused controversy among his contemporaries and he was forced to leave his practice in Leipzig, eventually settling in Paris.

hahnium (Ha; element 105) An artificial transuranic element, synthesized in the USA in 1970 by bombarding californium-249 with nitrogen-15 in a particle accelerator and possibly also in the Soviet Union in 1967 by a different method. Named after Otto Hahn. At no 105; at wt (260).

Haifa 32 49N 34 59E A town in NW Israel, on the Mediterranean coast by Mount Carmel. It was the scene of fighting in the 1948–49 Arab-Israeli conflict and has since developed into a manufacturing town. Population (1999 est): 265 700.

Haig, Douglas, 1st Earl (1861–1928) British field marshal. Commander of the first army corps in France and later commander in chief of the British Expeditionary Force during World War I, he was criticized for the appalling losses of the Somme and Passchendaele campaigns. Under the supreme command of *Foch, Haig directed the final victorious assault on the Hindenburg line.

Haile Selassie I (1892–1975) Emperor of Ethiopia (1930–36, 1941–74). In 1936 Haile Selassie fled to England after the invasion by the Italians, but was restored to the throne by the Allies in 1941. He did much to modernize Ethiopia and was a prominent figure in international affairs before his deposition by a military coup.

Hainan Island A Chinese island, the largest in the South China Sea, apart from Taiwan, and separated from the mainland by **Hainan Strait**. Sparsely populated, it is one of China's least developed regions. Rubber and timber are produced and iron ore and other minerals are mined. Area: 33 991 sq km (13 124 sq mi). Population (2000 est): 7 870 000. Capital: Haikou.

Hainaut (Flemish name: Henegouwen; French name: Hainault) A province in SW Belgium, bordering on France. It contains important coalfields and industries include iron and steel processing. Area: 3997 sq km (1466 sq mi). Population (2000 est): 1 279 467. Capital: Mons.

hair Threadlike structures forming the body covering of mammals (*see* SKIN). Each hair grows from the base of a hair follicle embedded in the lower layer (dermis) of the skin and consists of dead cells made largely of the protein *keratin. In most mammals hair forms an insulating and protective coat, which reduces heat loss from the body.

Haiti, Republic of A country in the Caribbean Sea, occupying the W third of the island of Hispaniola. Much of the country is mountainous and forested, with fertile plains lying between the three main mountain ranges. Most of the population is of African descent. *Economy*: mainly agricultural, mostly organized in small farms. The main crops are coffee (the principal export), sugar, rice, bananas, and sisal. Haiti joined the Caribbean Community in 1997. Since the mid-1990s political instability has led to a deepening economic crisis. *History*: the island was discovered by Columbus in 1492 and became a Spanish colony. The E part was ceded to France in 1697, becoming the most prosperous of the French colonies, and the remainder was temporarily ceded between 1795 and 1809. In 1804, under Gen Jean Jacques Dessalines (c. 1758–1806), Haiti gained its independence; a period of unrest was followed by union with the rest of the island (1822–44). For most of the time since it has been a republic; after a series of coups Dr François *Duvalier came to power in 1957 and was succeeded in 1971 by his son, Jean-Claude Duvalier. In 1986 Duvalier's brutal regime fell in a military coup. After elections in 1991 Jean-Bertrand Aristide became president but was deposed by the military. In 1994, aided by US troops, Aristide assumed the presidency. He was succeeded (1996) by René Préval, whose disputes with parliament (1999) led to a constitutional crisis. Aristide was re-elected in 2000 but the result was widely disputed, leading to further unrest. In 2004 rebels advanced on the capital and Aristide went into exile. Official languages: French and Haitian creole. Currency: gourde of 100 centimes. Area: 27 750 sq km (10 700 sq mi). Population (2003 est): 7 528 000. Capital: Port-au-Prince.

hajj The pilgrimage to Mecca that, circumstances permitting, every able-bodied Muslim with adequate means is expected to make at least once in his or her lifetime.

hake A food fish, of the genus *Merluccius*, that is related to *cod and occurs off European, African, and American coasts. Its elongated body, up to about 1 m long, is dark grey above and lighter below, with two dorsal fins.

Haldane, Richard Burdon, 1st Viscount (1856–1928) British army reformer. A Liberal MP (1885–1911), he was secretary for war from 1905 to 1912. He formed the Territorial Force (*see* TERRITORIAL ARMY) and facilitated the mobilization of the British Expeditionary Force at the outbreak of World War I. He became Lord Chancellor in 1912 but was dismissed in 1915 because of accusations that he was pro-German. He also helped to found the London School of Economics (1895). His brother **John Scott Haldane** (1860–1936) was a physiologist, noted for his investigations of human respiration. Haldane established that the rate of breathing was regulated according to the concentration of carbon dioxide in the blood. He also improved mine safety by demonstrating the toxic effects of carbon monoxide. J. S. Haldane's son **John Burdon Sanderson Haldane** (1892–1964) was a geneticist and Marxist philosopher, who contributed to many aspects of biology, including evolution and population genetics.

half-life The time taken for half the atoms in a sample of a radioactive isotope to decay. It is therefore a measure of the activity of an isotope. A very active isotope may have a half-life of only a millionth of a second, whereas some have half-lives of millions of years.

halibut A *flatfish of the genus *Hippoglossus*, especially *H. hippoglossus*—a large food fish, up to about 2 m long, found in N Atlantic coastal waters. The eyed (right) side is brown or dark green with mottling. Family: *Pleuronectidae*.

Halifax 1. 53 44N 1 52W A town in N England, in Calderdale unitary authority, West Yorkshire on the River Calder. Halifax has a strong wool textile tradition going back to the 13th century. Carpets, woollens, and worsteds are manufactured as well as machinery. Population (1991): 91 069. **2.** 44 38N 63 35W A city and major port in E Canada, the capital of Nova Scotia on the Atlantic Ocean. Founded as a British naval base (1749), it dominates the cultural life, commerce, and industry of the *Maritime Provinces. Its industries include shipbuilding, oil refining, steel, and food processing. Population (1996): 113 910.

Hall, Sir Peter (1930–) British theatre director. He was director of the Royal Shakespeare Company from 1960 to 1968 and director of the National Theatre Company from 1973 to 1988. He led his own company from 1988 to 1998 and is now based in the USA.

Halle 51 30N 11 59E A city in central Germany, on the River Saale. The birthplace of Handel, Halle has many fine old buildings. Its industries include sugar refining and coalmining. Population (1999 est): 258 500.

Hallé, Sir Charles (Karl Hallé; 1819–1895) German conductor and pianist. Hallé settled in Britain in 1848 and in 1857 established a series of concerts in Manchester, for which he founded and conducted the **Hallé Orchestra**.

Hall effect If a conductor carrying an electric current is placed in a transverse magnetic field, an electric field appears across the material, perpendicular to both the current and the magnetic field. The charges flowing in the material are displaced to one side thus creating a potential difference. Named after Edwin H. Hall (1855–1938).

Halley, Edmund (1656–1742) British astronomer, who was appointed professor of geometry at Oxford University in 1703. He was the first to realize that *comets have periodic orbits. In 1705 he identified a particular comet, now known as **Halley's comet**, as having a period of 76 years (appearing 1986, 2062, etc.). He also discovered that stars have a proper motion of their own (1718) and was appointed astronomer royal to succeed *Flamsteed (1720).

hallmarks A set of marks stamped onto gold, silver, or (since 1975) platinum objects manufactured in the UK, as a guarantee of purity. Each article has up to five marks: the mark of the assay office (or hall), a standard mark to indicate quality, a date mark, a duty mark (1784–1890) consisting of the sovereign's head showing that the excise duty had been paid, and the maker's mark. Gold articles also have a mark to indicate their purity—in *carats (prior to 1975) and as the number of parts per 1000 thereafter. Since 1999 all articles made of a precious metal in the EU must carry an indication of purity in this numerical form. See illustration on p. 402.

Hallowe'en 31 Oct, the eve of All Saints' Day.

The name is a contraction of All Hallows (hallowed or holy) Eve. In pre-Christian Britain, 31 Oct was the eve of New Year, when the souls of the dead were thought to revisit their homes. Customs include the shaping of a demon's face from a hollow turnip or pumpkin, in which a candle is then placed.

hallucinogens Drugs that produce hallucinations due to their stimulant action on the brain. Such drugs are also described as psychedelic. Hallucinogens, which include *cannabis, *ecstasy, and *LSD, tend to lead to *drug dependence.

halogens The elements forming group VII of the *periodic table: fluorine, chlorine, bromine, iodine, and astatine. In chemical reactions they tend to form negative ions or covalent bonds and they have a valence of 1. All are reactive, particularly fluorine and chlorine. They produce salts on contact with metals ("halogen" means salt-yielding) and react with other nonmetals.

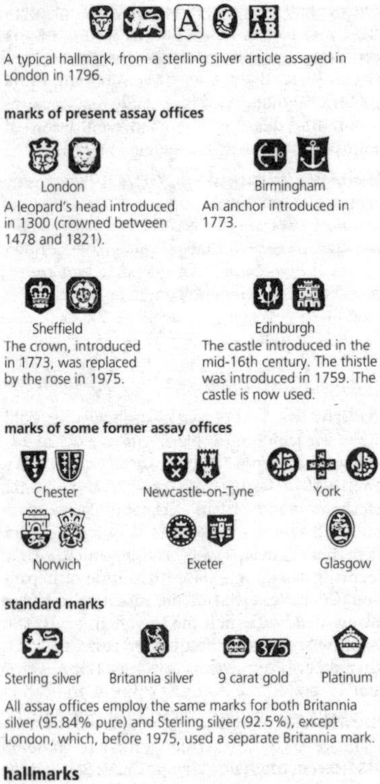
A
PB
AB
A typical hallmark, from a sterling silver article assayed in London in 1796.
marks of present assay offices
London
A leopard's head introduced in 1300 (crowned between 1478 and 1821).
Birmingham
An anchor introduced in 1773.
Sheffield
The crown, introduced in 1773, was replaced by the rose in 1975.
Edinburgh
The castle introduced in the mid-16th century. The thistle was introduced in 1759. The castle is now used.
marks of some former assay offices
Chester
Newcastle-on-Tyne
York
Norwich
Exeter
Glasgow
standard marks
375
Sterling silver
Britannia silver
9 carat gold
Platinum
All assay offices employ the same marks for both Britannia silver (95.84% pure) and Sterling silver (92.5%), except London, which, before 1975, used a separate Britannia mark.

hallmarks

Hals, Frans (c. 1581–1666) Dutch painter of portraits and scenes of everyday life. He was born in Antwerp but worked mainly in Haarlem. Apart from his *Laughing Cavalier* (1624; Wallace Collection, London), he is best known for his group portraits. Later works include *Lady-Governors of the Almshouse at Haarlem* (1664; Frans Hals Museum, Haarlem), influenced by Rembrandt.

Halton A unitary authority in NW England, in Cheshire, consisting of the towns of Widnes and Runcorn. Area: 75 sq km (29 sq mi). Population (2001 est): 118 215.

hamadryas A small *baboon, *Papio hamadryas*, of NE Africa and Saudi Arabia. 100–140 cm long including the tail (40–60 cm), hamadryas baboons have a long silvery-brown mane, pinkish face, and red buttocks. They were sacred animals to the ancient Egyptians.

Hamas An organization formed in 1976 with the aim of creating an Islamic Palestinian state. It became increasingly militant in the 1990s and since 1996 has carried out a series of suicide bombings in Israeli cities. In 2004 its founder and spiritual leader Sheikh Ahmed Yassin was killed by Israeli forces.

Hamburg 53 33N 10 00E A city in N Germany, on the Rivers Elbe and Alster. A major port and leading commercial centre, it is also important for its cultural activity, with a university (1919), art gallery, and opera house (1678). Its many industries include shipbuilding, engineering, and food processing. *History*: its alliance with Lübeck (1241) became the basis of the Hanseatic League. It was a trading centre from the middle ages and the first German stock exchange was established here (1558). It was severely bombed during World War II. Population (1999 est): 1 701 800.

Hamilcar Barca (died c. 229 BC) Carthaginian general and Hannibal's father. Commander in Sicily during the first Punic War, he negotiated peace in 241. After suppressing rebellious mercenaries in Carthage, he invaded Spain. He was drowned after the siege of Helice.

Hamilton 1. 43 15N 79 50W A city and port in central Canada, in S Ontario on Lake Ontario. Canada's main centre of heavy industry, it is particularly important for iron and steel, motor vehicles, machinery, chemicals, and electrical goods. Population (1996): 322 352. **2.** 37 46S 175 18E A city in New Zealand, in N North Island on the Waikato River. It is the most important inland centre and serves a pastoral and lumbering region. The University of Waikato was established in 1964. Population (1999 est): 117 100.

Hamilton, Emma (c. 1761–1815) The mistress of Horatio *Nelson. She was previously the mistress of his uncle Sir William Hamilton (1730–1803), whom she married in 1791. She met Nelson in 1793; they became lovers and in 1801 their daughter Horatia (d. 1881) was born. After Nelson's death (1805), Lady Hamilton squandered her inheritance and fled to Calais (1814), where she died.

Hamito-Semitic languages A language family spoken in N Africa and S Asia. More appropriately known as Afro-Asiatic, it has five branches that descend from an ancestor language, Proto-Hamito-Semitic, which was spoken between the 6th and 8th millenniums BC. The five branches are Egyptian, Berber, Cushitic, Semitic, and Chadic.

Hammarskjöld, Dag (Hjalmar Agne Carl) (1905–61) Swedish international civil servant. The son of Hjalmar Hammarskjöld (1862–1953), who was a prime minister of Sweden (1914–17), he headed the Swedish delegation to the UN and in 1953 became its secretary general. He dealt with the Suez crisis (1956) and the civil war in the Congo (1960). He was killed in a plane crash and awarded the Nobel Peace Prize posthumously in 1961.

hammerhead shark A *shark of the family *Sphyrnidae*, found in warm and temperate salt waters. Up to 4.5 m long, the head is flattened and extended laterally into two hammer- or spade-shaped lobes, which bear the eyes and nostrils. They feed primarily on fish but may attack other animals, including man.

Hammerstein II, Oscar (1895–1960) US lyricist and librettist. With Richard Rodgers he wrote *Oklahoma!* (1943), *Carousel* (1945), *South Pacific* (1949), *The King and I* (1951), and *The Sound of Music* (1959).

hammer throw A field event for men in athletics. The hammer is an iron or brass sphere weighing 16 lb (7.26 kg) attached to a wire handle and grip. It is thrown with both hands within a circle 7 ft (2.13 m) in diameter. The event has been open to women since 1995 (since 2000 in the Olympics). World record: 86.74 m (1986) by Yuri Sedykh (Soviet Union).

Hammett, Dashiell (1894–1961) US novelist. He worked as a private detective for eight years before writing his first detective stories. His novels, the realistic and economical style of which influenced Raymond *Chandler, include *The Maltese Falcon* (1930) and *The Thin Man* (1932).

Hampshire A county of S central England, on the English Channel. Portsmouth and Southampton became independent unitary authorities in 1997. It consists mainly of undulating lowlands, rising to chalk downlands in the N and E. The chief rivers, the Test and Itchen, drain into the Solent, which separates the Isle of *Wight from the mainland. It is predominantly agricultural with dairy and arable farming. Industries, centred on Southampton, include shipbuilding and oil refining and there are important naval bases at Portsmouth and Gosport. Tourism is important in the *New Forest. Area (excluding unitary authorities): 3679 sq km (1420 sq mi). Population (2001, excluding unitary authorities): 1 240 032. Administrative centre: Winchester.

Hampton, Lionel (1913–2002) US Black jazz band leader and vibraphone player, who played with Benny Goodman before forming his own orchestra in 1940. Hampton was the first jazz musician to popularize the vibraphone.

Hampton Court A Tudor and Stuart palace on the River Thames near London. Built by Cardinal Wolsey, it was given in the 1520s to Henry VIII, who made substantial alterations; in the 1690s *Wren began a further rebuilding project for William III. The palace, now open to the public, has an important collection of paintings. In 1986 it was damaged by fire.

hamster A small *rodent of the family *Cricetidae*. The common hamster (*Cricetus cricetus*), native to Europe and W Asia, has a red-brown coat with white patches on the flanks, neck, and cheek. It feeds on seeds and grains. The golden hamster (*Mesocricetus auratus*) is a domestic pet.

Han (206 BC–220 AD) A Chinese dynasty founded by the general Liu Bang (*or* Liu Pang; 256–195 BC), who overthrew the preceding Qin dynasty. The power of the Han was consolidated by the emperor, Wu Di (*or* Wu Ti; 157–87 BC; reigned 140–87), who completed the conquest of a vast empire. Chinese export of silk increased, and a vast canal-building programme was started. Paper was invented by the Han Chinese, who also produced early forms of porcelain. The programme of expansion led to financial difficulties that enabled Wang Mang to usurp the throne in 8 AD. The Han dynasty was subsequently restored for a second period, known as the Later Han (23–220 AD).

handball An indoor game played by two teams of seven, with rules similar to those of Association football. Playing time is 2 x 30 minutes. The game originated in Scandinavia and was further developed in Germany. It has been an Olympic event since 1972 (for women since 1976).

Handel, George Frederick (1685–1759) German composer. He studied in Halle and travelled to Italy, where he became famous as a harpsichordist and as a master of the Italianate style of composition. Handel first visited England in 1712 and became musical director to James Brydges, first duke of Chandos (1673–1744), in 1718. He subsequently became music master to the family of the Prince of Wales and director of the Royal Academy of Music on its foundation in 1720. His Italian operas were successfully produced in London; from 1739 he turned to writing such oratorios as *Saul* (1739), and *Messiah* (1742). In 1751 he began to lose his sight although he continued to compose. His mastery of composition is reflected in the range of his works, which include the *Water Music* (1717), *Music for the Royal Fireworks* (1749), concerti grossi, sonatas, organ concertos, harpsichord suites, and anthems.

h

hang-gliding Unpowered flight in a hang-glider, consisting of a large bat-shaped cloth wing on a light metal framework from which the pilot hangs in a harness, holding a horizontal control bar. In flight, the wing fills to form an aerofoil (*see* AERONAUTICS). The first hang-glider was built by Otto Lilienthal (1848–96), but the prototype for modern design was the sail-wing invented by Frances Rogallo (1912–). Hang-gliding became popular in the late 1960s. In **paragliding** a mattress-like canopy allows greater manoeuvrability.

Hanging Gardens of Babylon Ancient gardens in the palace of Nebuchadnezzar II (604–562 BC) on the E side of Babylon. One of the Seven Wonders of the World, they were built on top of stone arches and watered from the Euphrates by a complicated mechanical system.

Hangzhou (**Hang-chou** *or* **Hangchow**) 30 18N 120 07E A city in E China, the capital of Zhejiang province on Hangzhou Bay, an inlet of the East China Sea. It was the capital (1132–1276) of the Southern Song dynasty. A picturesque tourist centre, its varied industries include silk production. Population (1999 est): 1 346 148.

Hanks, Tom (1956–) US film actor, who made his name in such comedies as *Splash* (1984). Later films include *Philadelphia* (1993) and *Forrest Gump* (1994), both of which earned him Oscars, *Saving Private Ryan* (1998), and *Castaway* (2000).

Hannibal (247–c. 183 BC) Carthaginian general. Appointed commander in Spain in 221, he deliberately provoked the second Punic War with Rome. In 218 he crossed the Alps in winter, losing about 10 000 of his 35 000 men. For two years he devastated Italy, but lost ground in the face of Fabius' guerrilla tactics. Recalled to defend Carthage after Scipio Africanus' invasion of Africa, Hannibal was defeated at Zama (202). Suspected of rebellion, he was forced to flee Roman retribution. He committed suicide to avoid capture.

Hanoi 20 57N 105 55E The capital of Vietnam, in the NE of the country on the Red River. The capital of the Vietnamese empire from the 11th until the 17th centuries, it was occupied by the French in 1873 and became the capital of French Indochina. Following the Japanese occupation in World War II, it became the capital of the Democratic Republic of Vietnam. Many ancient buildings in the Vietnamese quarter remain, together with several imposing buildings in the European quarter built by the French. Population (1993 est, urban area): 2 154 900.

Hanover (German name: Hannover) 52 23N 9 44E A city in N Germany, the capital of Lower Saxony on the River Leine. It is a transshipment port and a commercial and industrial centre. After the destruction of World War II it was largely rebuilt; the Leine Palace (founded 1636) is now the *Land* parliament building. Hanover's manufactures include machinery, rubber, textiles, and motor vehicles. *History*: in 1638 Hanover became the capital of the future electorate and kingdom of Hanover. In 1714 Elector George Louis became George I of Great Britain (*see* SETTLEMENT, ACT OF). He is buried in Hanover. British monarchs were Electors (later Kings) of Hanover until 1837 when Victoria, as a woman, was debarred from succeeding to the Hanoverian throne. Population (1999 est): 515 200.

Hansard The official reports of debates in the UK *parliament. The name, which was officially adopted in 1943, is that of the family that first printed the reports: **Luke Hansard** (1752–1828) and his son **Thomas Curson Hansard** (1776–1833). The Stationery Office published Hansard from 1890.

Hanseatic League An association of N German trading towns (the Hanse) formed in the 13th century to protect their economic interests overseas. By the mid-14th century, the

League, comprising some hundred towns, had become a powerful corporate body and conducted a number of trade wars with Denmark and England. The rise of the non-German Baltic states and changing trade routes contributed to the League's declining influence. It was finally dissolved in 1669.

Hanukka A Jewish festival, commemorating the revolt of the *Maccabees. It falls in midwinter and is celebrated by lighting a lamp each day, traditionally in an eight-branched candelabrum called a **menorah**.

Hanuman In Hindu mythology, a monkey god and one of the principal characters in the *Ramayana*. There are numerous temples dedicated to him in both India and Japan.

hara-kiri The honourable way of death for Japanese *samurai. In its strict form it involved ceremoniously cutting one's stomach open with a dagger before decapitation by the single blow of another samurai's sword. It is still sometimes practised by Japanese suicides, although it is now illegal.

Harald V (1937–) King of Norway (1991–), succeeding his father, Olaf V. Educated at Oxford, he subsequently served in the Norwegian forces.

Harare (name until 1982: Salisbury) 17 50 S 31 02 E The capital of Zimbabwe, on a plateau in the NE. Founded in 1890, it was the capital of the Federation of Rhodesia and Nyasaland (1935–63). It has two cathedrals and is the centre of a tobacco-growing area. Population (1998 est): 1 686 169.

harbour seal The common *seal, *Phoca vitulina*, of coastal Pacific and Atlantic waters. Up to 1.8 m long, with a blotchy grey coat, it inhabits sandbanks and river estuaries, feeding on fish. Family: *Phocidae*.

Hardanger Fjord A fjord in SW Norway, S of Bergen, penetrating inland from the North Sea for 110 km (68 mi).

Hardecanute (*or* **Harthacanute**; c. 1019–42) The last Danish King of England (1040–42), succeeding his illegitimate half-brother Harold I Harefoot, and King of Denmark (1035–42). He razed Worcester after a riot against his tax collectors.

Hardie, J(ames) Keir (1856–1915) British Labour politician. Born in Scotland, he became a coalminer at the age of ten. He founded the Scottish Parliamentary Labour Party in 1888 and, as an Independent Socialist MP (1892–95), he helped to found (1893) the Independent Labour Party. Again an MP (1900–15), he became chairman (1906), of the future *Labour Party.

Hardy, Thomas (1840–1928) British novelist and poet. His major novels, which include *The Return of the Native* (1878), *The Mayor of Casterbridge* (1886), and *Tess of the D'Urbervilles* (1891), are tragic tales set in his native Dorset ("Wessex" in the novels). After public outrage at the alleged immorality of *Jude the Obscure* (1895) he published only verse, beginning with *Wessex Poems* (1898), and an epic drama, *The Dynasts* (1903–08). He was awarded the OM in 1910.

hare A mammal belonging to the widely distributed family *Leporidae* (which also includes the rabbits). Hares are typically larger than rabbits and have long black-tipped ears. They live and breed in the open and are mainly nocturnal, feeding on grass and bark. Chief genus: *Lepus* (about 26 species); order: *Lagomorpha*.

Hare, Sir David (1947–) British playwright. His plays include *Plenty* (1978), *Pravda* (1985), *Racing Demon* (1990), *The Blue Room* (1998), and *The Permanent Way* (2003).

harebell A herbaceous perennial plant, *Campanula rotundifolia*, of N temperate regions, growing to a height of 60 cm. It has rounded leaves and blue bell-shaped flowers. Family: *Campanulaceae*.

Hare Krishna movement (Sanskrit: hail Krishna) A quasi-religious cult, the International Society for Krishna Consciousness (ISKCON), founded in New York in 1966 on Hindu principles by an Indian, Swami Prabhupada (1895–1977). Members are vegetarians; gambling, extramarital sex, and the use of drugs are prohibited. They dress in saffron linen robes and the men have shaved heads. Detractors claim that the sect exploits vulnerable young people.

Hargreaves, James (d. 1778) English inventor, who around 1764 invented the spinning jenny, a machine with which several threads could be spun simultaneously. After local spinners, believing that their jobs were threatened, broke up his machines, Hargreaves set up (1768) a small mill in Nottingham.

Harlech 52 52N 4 07W A historic town in NW Wales, in Gwynedd on Cardigan Bay. It is a resort with a famous ruined castle. Population (1991): 1233.

Harlequin A stock character of the commedia dell'arte. Harlequin began as a comic and covetous servant but developed into the lover of Columbine and the central comic figure of the harlequinade, dressed in a bright diamond-patterned costume, masked, and carrying a wooden club.

harmonica The mouth organ: the smallest member of the reed-organ family; its invention is attributed to Sir Charles Wheatstone (1802–75) in 1829. Notes and chords are obtained by blowing or sucking rows of parallel reeds. The instrument's main exponent was Larry Adler (1914–2001).

harmonium A keyboard instrument of the reed organ family, patented in 1848 by Alexandre Debain (1809–77) in Paris. It is a free *reed instrument, the air being blown by a bellows activated by foot pedals. It may have several stops (*see* ORGAN).

h

harmony In music, the combining of notes into chords, so that they are heard simultaneously. Before about 1650 composers made use of *polyphony; between about 1650 and about 1900 (the **harmonic period**) a system of harmony evolved based on diatonic chords (*see* SCALE). Such chords consist of three notes sounded simultaneously; a note of the scale of the *tonality of the composition and the notes a third and a fifth above it. The constituent notes of any chord can be rearranged to provide variety. A **harmonic progression** consists of a particular sequence of chords, especially one leading (*or* modulating) into another tonality. In the later 19th century harmony became more complex, and tonality ambiguous, in the works of Wagner, Debussy, and others. In the early years of the 20th century Schoenberg first adopted *atonality and subsequently invented *serialism as a substitute for traditional harmony. Other composers of the past hundred years have made use of a wide range of harmonic styles.

Harold I Harefoot (d. 1040) Danish King of England (1037–40). The illegitimate son of Canute, he became king while Hardecanute, Canute's legitimate son, was preoccupied in Denmark. Before Hardecanute could oust him, Harold died.

Harold II (c. 1022–66) The last Anglo-Saxon King of England (1066), reputedly designated heir by the dying Edward the Confessor. After becoming king, he crushed the forces of his brother Tostig (d. 1066) and Harold III Hardraade of Norway (1015–66) at Stamford Bridge (1066). Harold was killed in the battle of *Hastings by the army of William the Conqueror.

harp A plucked stringed instrument of ancient origin, consisting of an open frame with strings of varying length and tension. The modern orchestral harp is triangular in shape with about 45 strings stretched between the soundbox and the neck. The pillar contains a mechanism that enables the player to raise each string by one or two semitones by means of pedals at the base. It gives the harp a full chromatic range of six and a half octaves from the B below the bass stave.

Harpies In Greek mythology, malicious spirits who carried off their victims to their deaths. They were later portrayed as rapacious birds with ugly women's faces.

harpsichord A keyboard instrument with strings plucked by quills, rather than hit by hammers (*see* SPINET; VIRGINALS; *compare* CLAVICHORD; PIANO). In the 16th, 17th, and 18th centuries it was an instrument of great importance. The tone can be changed by the addition of stops, which sound strings an octave below or above the note depressed.

harrier A slender long-legged *hawk belonging to a widely distributed genus (*Circus*). Harriers are about 50 cm long and are usually brown with a small bill and a long tail. They fly low over fields and marshes, searching for frogs, mice, snakes, and insects.

Harris *See* LEWIS WITH HARRIS.

Harrogate 54 00N 1 33W A residential town and former spa in N England, in North Yorkshire. It is an important centre for conferences and trade fairs. Population (1998 est): 70 000.

Harrow A residential borough of NW Greater London. Harrow School, founded by John Lyon in 1571, dominates Harrow-on-the-Hill.

hartebeest A long-faced antelope, *Alcephalus busephalus*, of African plains. About 120 cm high at the shoulder, hartebeests are slender fast-running animals, ranging in colour from dark chestnut to fawn; their horns are generally lyre-shaped.

Hartford 41 45N 72 42W A city in the USA, the capital of Connecticut. Trinity College (1823) and the law and insurance schools of the University of Connecticut are situated here. A commercial, industrial, and financial centre, Hartford is one of the leading insurance centres in the world. Population (2000): 121 578.

Hartlepool 1. 54 41N 1 13W A port in NE England, in Hartlepool unitary authority, Durham. It was originally an old fishing port and medieval walled town. Hartlepool's main industries are engineering, clothing manufacture, and services for North Sea oilfields. Population

(1991): 87 310. **2.** A unitary authority in NE England, in Durham. Area: 93 sq km (36 sq mi). Population (2001): 88 629.

Harvard classification system A system, introduced in the 1890s by astronomers at the Harvard College Observatory (USA), by which stars are classified according to features in their spectra. The stars are grouped into seven major spectral types: O, B, A, F, G, K, and M, in order of decreasing temperature. There are 10 subdivisions for each spectral type, indicated by a digit (0–9) placed after the letter. Stars of one spectral type can be further classified into supergiants, giants, etc., according to their *luminosity. *See also* HERTZSPRUNG-RUSSELL DIAGRAM.

Harvard University The oldest university in the USA (founded 1636), located at Cambridge, Massachusetts. It is named after the clergyman John Harvard (1607–38). The associated women's college, Radcliffe College, dates from 1879.

harvestman An *arachnid, also called harvest spider, belonging to the order *Opiliones* (or *Phalangida*; 2200 species), found in tropical and temperate regions. It has an undivided body, 1–22 mm long, and very long delicate legs.

harvest mite A *mite, also called chigger and scrub mite, belonging to the genus *Trombicula*. Its larvae are parasitic on vertebrates, including man, feeding on skin and causing inflammation.

Harvey, William (1578–1657) English physician and anatomist, who discovered the circulation of the blood. Harvey studied under the great anatomist Fabricius ab Aquapendente (1537–1619) and later became physician to James I and Charles I. His findings were published in *On the Motion of the Heart and Blood in Animals* (1628).

Haryana A state in N India, mostly in the fertile Upper Ganges plain. Predominantly rural, it produces wheat, other grains, cotton, sugar cane, and oilseeds. There is some light industry, including textiles, agricultural implements, and sugar refining. Area: 44 222 sq km (17 070 sq mi). Population (2001 est): 21 082 989. Capital: Chandigarh.

Harz Mountains A mountain range extending about 90 km (56 mi) across Germany W of Halle. They are the northernmost range of the European mountain system. The highest peak is the Brocken.

Hashemites The Arab descendants of the prophet Mohammed, including the fourth caliph *Ali (c. 600–67) and the line of hereditary emirs of Mecca. King Abdullah of Jordan is a modern representative of the line.

Hasidism A Jewish religious movement, founded by the Ba'al Shem Tov (c. 1700–60). Essentially a blend of *kabbalah and popular pietism, Hasidism spread, against strong opposition, throughout the Jewish communities of E Europe in the 18th and 19th centuries. Led by charismatic teachers (*zaddikim*), it stressed simple piety and ecstatic prayer. Most of the Hasidic communities in Europe were wiped out during the *holocaust, but Hasidism still thrives in North America and Israel. Hasidic men are bearded and wear black suits with broad-brimmed hats.

Hastings 50 51N 0 36E A resort town on the S coast of England, in East Sussex. Formerly the chief of the Cinque Ports, it has a ruined castle built by William the Conqueror. Population (1997 est): 82 100. The **Battle of Hastings** between the Normans and the English at Senlac Hill (*see* BATTLE), was fought here on 14 October 1066. William, Duke of Normandy, claiming the English throne, defeated Harold II of England. Both sides suffered heavy losses but the death of Harold allowed William to conquer England (*see* NORMAN CONQUEST) and become its king.

hatchetfish A carnivorous hatchet-shaped fish, up to 10 cm long, belonging to one of two unrelated groups. Deepsea hatchetfish (family *Sternoptychidae*; 15 species) are related to *salmon and occur in warm and temperate waters. The freshwater or flying hatchetfish (family *Gasteropelecidae*; about 9 species) of South America are related to *carp.

Haughey, Charles (1925–) Irish statesman; prime minister of Ireland (1979–81, 1982, and 1987–92). The president of Fianna Fáil (1979–92), he resigned after a series of scandals.

Hauraki Gulf A large inlet of the South Pacific Ocean, in New Zealand on the E coast of North Island. Waitemata Harbour, on which stands Auckland, is situated in the SW. Area: about 2290 sq km (884 sq mi).

Hausa A people of NW Nigeria and S Niger, numbering about nine million. Their language belongs to the Chadic subgroup of the Hamito-Semitic family, but has absorbed many Arabic words and influences. It is an official language of Nigeria and a second language in much of West Africa. The Hausa are mainly Muslim. The economy is based on the cultivation of maize, millet, sorghum, and other crops. Cities, such as *Kano, date from precolonial times but most Hausa live in small rural settlements.

Havana (Spanish name: La Habana) 23 00N 82 30W The capital of Cuba, a port in the NW. It exports sugar, cotton, and tobacco. The university was founded in 1728. *History*: the original settlement was on the S coast, but the inhabitants moved to the city's present site in 1519. It became the capital of Cuba in the late 16th century. Population (1995 est): 2 241 000.

Havel, Václav (1936–) Czech writer; president of Czechoslovakia (1989–92) and of the Czech Republic (1993–2003). The author of such plays as *Largo Desolato* (1984), he was imprisoned (1979–83) for involvement in the dissident Charter 77 movement. In 1989 he took a leading role in the Civil Forum reform movement, and was elected president following the resignation of the Communist government. He resigned as president of Czechoslovakia after failing to prevent its break-up, subsequently becoming president of the Czech Republic.

h

Hawaii (former name: Sandwich Islands) A state in the USA, occupying a chain of over 20 volcanic islands in the central Pacific Ocean. These include the islands of Hawaii (the largest), Maui, Oahu, Kauai, and Molokai. Its population is ethnically diverse. Manufactures include oil and chemical products, steel, textiles, and food. Agriculture is important, the main crops being sugar and pineapples. The principal industry, however, is tourism. There are many US military bases. *History*: first discovered by Capt Cook in 1778, Hawaii remained a kingdom until becoming a republic in 1893. It was annexed by the USA in 1894 and became a territory in 1900. The Japanese attack on Pearl Harbor in 1941 precipitated the entry of the USA into World War II. Hawaii became a state in 1959. Area: 16 641 sq km (6425 sq mi). Population (2000): 1 211 537. Capital: Honolulu.

hawfinch A large *finch, *Coccothraustes coccothraustes*, of Eurasia and N Africa. 18 cm long, it has a reddish-brown plumage with paler underparts, black-and-white wings, and a massive bill.

Haw-Haw, Lord *See* JOYCE, WILLIAM.

hawk A bird of prey belonging to a widely distributed family (*Accipitridae*; 205 species) that includes buzzards, eagles, harriers, kites, and vultures. Hawks have down-curved pointed bills, powerful gripping feet, and good eyesight. They usually nest in trees or crags. Order: *Falconiformes*. *Compare* FALCON.

Hawkesbury River A river in SE Australia, rising in the Great Dividing Range in New South Wales and flowing NE to the Tasman Sea. Length: 472 km (293 mi).

Hawking, Stephen (William) (1942–) British physicist. Although severely handicapped by a progressive nervous disease, he has described the particle emission of black holes (1974) and shown that general relativity supports the big-bang theory. His publications include the best-selling *A Brief History of Time* (1987) and *The Universe in a Nutshell* (2001).

Hawkins, Sir John (1532–95) English navigator. In 1562 he became the first English slave trader, transporting slaves from West Africa to the Spanish West Indies. In 1577 he became treasurer of the navy; he died at Puerto Rico on an expedition with Drake. His son **Sir Richard Hawkins** (c. 1562–1622) served against the Armada and in a subsequent expedition was seized by the Spanish and imprisoned (1594–1602).

hawk moth A moth belonging to the widespread family *Sphingidae* (about 1000 species), also called sphinx moth or hummingbird moth. They have large bodies with relatively small wings (spanning 5–20 cm), which they beat rapidly, hovering over flowers and sipping nectar through their long proboscis.

hawksbill turtle A small sea turtle, *Eretmochelys imbricata*, found in warm waters worldwide. It has hooked jaws, feeds on algae, fish, and invertebrates, and is usually 40–55 cm long. Its shell is used as tortoiseshell.

Hawksmoor, Nicholas (1661–1736) English baroque architect. Hawksmoor was trained by *Wren and collaborated with *Vanbrugh at *Blenheim Palace and Castle Howard. His finest individual work was at Easton Neston (1702), All Souls', Oxford (1729), and St Anne's, Limehouse (1714).

hawthorn A thorny shrub or tree of the N temperate genus *Crataegus* (about 200 species). Hawthorns have lobed leaves, white flowers, and yellow, black, or red fruits. The common hawthorn, or may (*C. monogyna*), is found in hedgerows and thickets in Europe and the Mediterranean. Up to 10 m high, it has red fruits (haws).

Haydn, Franz Joseph (1732–1809) Austrian composer. He became a cathedral chorister in Vienna at the age of eight and subsequently worked as a freelance musician and music teacher. In 1761 he became kapellmeister to the Esterházy family, a post he held for the rest of his life. In 1791 and 1794 he visited London and wrote his last 12 symphonies, which include the *Oxford* and *London* symphonies. Haydn's compositions include piano sonatas, piano trios, string quartets, masses, concertos, 104 symphonies, operas, and the oratorios *The Creation* (1798) and *The Seasons* (1801).

hay fever An *allergy to pollen, which leads to sneezing, a streaming nose, and inflamed eyes. Treatment is by desensitization, with *antihistamines or, in severe cases, with steroids.

hazel A hardy shrub or tree of the N temperate genus *Corylus* (15 species), cultivated since ancient times for its edible nuts, also called cob nuts. The leaves are rounded and toothed. The male flowers are attractive yellow catkins; each female flower develops into a nut. The best-known species is the European hazel (*C. avellana*), up to 12 m high. Family: *Betulaceae* (birch family) or *Corylaceae*.

Hazlitt, William (1778–1830) British critic and essayist. The son of a Unitarian minister, he studied art and philosophy before becoming a journalist. His opinions in politics and literary matters were expressed in brilliant invective. His best-known collections of essays and lectures are *Lectures on the English Poets* (1818) and *The Spirit of the Age* (1825).

Healey, Denis (Winston), Baron (1917–) British Labour politician; chancellor of the exchequer (1974–79). He entered parliament in 1952 and from 1964 to 1970 was defence minister. He was deputy leader of the Labour Party (1981–83).

Heaney, Seamus (Justin) (1939–) Irish poet. His early work reflects his upbringing in rural Northern Ireland. Later volumes include *North* (1975), *Seeing Things* (1991), and *Electric Light* (2001). He was Professor of Poetry at Oxford University (1989–94) and published an acclaimed translation of the Old English *Beowulf* in 1999. He was awarded the Nobel Prize in 1995.

hearing aid A device used by the partially deaf to increase the loudness of sounds. Modern hearing aids are tiny electronic devices, consisting of a microphone, an amplifier, and an earphone. The profoundly deaf may now benefit from electrodes implanted in the inner ear that convey signals from an external microphone directly to the auditory nerve.

heart A four-chambered muscular organ that pumps blood around the body. Two chambers—the left and right atria—dilate to receive oxygen-rich blood from the lungs and oxygen-depleted blood from the rest of the body, respectively (this is called diastole). Contraction of the heart (called systole) starts in the atria, forcing blood into the two ventricles. The left ventricle then contracts to force blood into a large artery—the aorta, which leads from the heart and feeds all the other arteries. The right ventricle pumps blood into the pulmonary artery and to the lungs, where it receives oxygen. Valves between the atria and ventricles and at the arterial exits of the heart prevent the backflow of blood. The rhythm of the heartbeat is maintained by the electrical activity of a group of specialized cells within the heart (*see* PACEMAKER). The muscle of the heart is supplied with blood by the coronary arteries. Atherosclerosis of these arteries may lead to a heart attack (*see* CORONARY HEART DISEASE; MYOCARDIAL INFARCTION). *See also* CIRCULATION OF THE BLOOD.

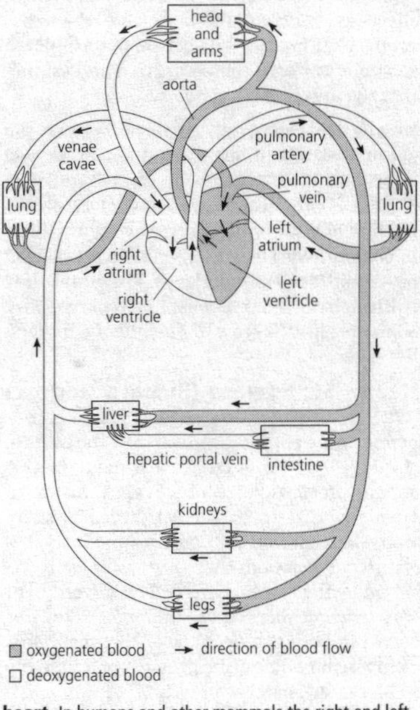

heart. In humans and other mammals the right and left chambers of the heart are completely separate from each other. This ensures that oxygenated and deoxygenated blood do not mix and enables oxygen-depleted blood to receive a fresh supply of oxygen from the lungs before circulating to the rest of the body.

heartsease *See* PANSY.

heat The form of energy that is transferred from one body or region to another at a lower temperature. The amount of heat gained or lost by a body is equal to the product of its *heat capacity and the temperature through which it rises or falls. Heat is measured in joules, but older units, such as calories and British thermal units, are still sometimes used. *See also* HEAT TRANSFER.

heat capacity The amount of heat in joules needed to raise the temperature of a body through one kelvin. For a gas, the heat capacity may be measured under conditions of either constant pressure or constant volume. *See also* SPECIFIC HEAT CAPACITY.

heat death of the universe A hypothetical final state of the universe in which its *entropy is at a maximum and no heat is available to do work. In any closed system the total entropy can never decrease during any process. Thus the entropy of the universe will eventually reach a maximum value and when that happens all matter will be totally disordered and at a uniform temperature. This assumes that the universe is a closed system.

h

heath An evergreen shrub or tree of the genus *Erica* (about 500 species) of Europe and Africa (about 470 species are native to South Africa). Heaths have spikes of bell-shaped or tubular flowers, white, pink, purple, or yellow in colour. Dwarf heaths are abundant on acid peaty soils, such as moorlands. There are many cultivated varieties, popular in rock gardens. Some tree heaths grow to a height of 6 m. Family: *Ericaceae*.

Heath, Sir Edward (Richard George) (1916–) British statesman; Conservative prime minister (1970–74), who took the UK into the EC (1973). He entered parliament in 1950 and assumed cabinet office as minister of labour in 1959. In 1965 he succeeded Douglas-Home as leader of the Conservative Party. His Industrial Relations Act (1971) was badly received by the trade unions and his government was twice challenged by miners' strikes. Defeated in both the elections of 1974 (February, October), he relinquished the party leadership to Margaret Thatcher in 1975.

heather (*or* **ling**) An evergreen shrub, *Calluna vulgaris*, up to 60 cm high, with scaly leaves and clusters of pale-purple bell-shaped flowers. It grows—often with heath—on acid soils of heaths, moors, and bogs throughout Europe and in parts of N Africa and North America. Family: *Ericaceae*.

Heathrow (*or* **London Airport**) 51 28N 0 27W The chief air terminal for the UK, in the Greater London borough of Hounslow. Opened to passengers in 1946, it has an underground railway connection from central London (since 1977).

heat pump A device that extracts heat from one substance at a low temperature and supplies it to another substance at a higher temperature, consuming energy in the process. Heat pumps are used to extract the low temperature heat from rivers, etc., for space- and water-heating units. *See also* REFRIGERATION.

heatstroke A rise in body temperature associated with *dehydration and exhaustion, caused by overexposure to high temperatures. The emergency treatment is to cool the patient down with water or fans.

heat transfer The transference of energy between two bodies or regions by virtue of the difference in temperatures between them. The three methods of transference are: *convection, *conduction, and *radiation. In convection the heat is transferred by a hotter region flowing into a colder region. In conduction, on the other hand, the heat is transferred by direct contact without any apparent relative motion. In radiation the heat is transferred by means of either *infrared radiation or *microwave radiation. Radiation is the only method of transferring heat through a vacuum.

heat treatment The process of heating a metal to a temperature below its melting point and then cooling it in order to change its physical properties. Metals are made up of tiny crystals (grains). Their hardness, strength, and ductility is determined by the concentration and distribution of irregularities (dislocations) in the crystal lattice. Heating creates and redistributes dislocations, relieving any internal stresses that have built up. This makes the metal softer and more ductile; a process known as annealing. Dislocation movement is restricted by the boundaries between grains and by the presence of impurities, which make the metal harder and less ductile. Because both the impurity distribution and the grain structure are affected by heating and the rate of cooling, so also is the metal's strength. In steel manufacture, rapid cooling (quenching) by immersion in water or oil hardens the steel, leaving it brittle. Slow cooling makes it soft and ductile.

heaven In Christian belief, the abode of God in which the souls of the virtuous will be rewarded with everlasting life. The iconography of heaven is based upon the Book of Revelation (*compare* HELL). Analogous concepts exist in other major religions.

heavy water Deuterium oxide (D_2O), the form of water containing the isotope of hydrogen with mass number 2. It is chemically less reactive than normal water and has a relative density of 1.1; its boiling point is 101.42°C. It is present to an extent of 1 part in 5000 in natural water and it is used as a moderator and coolant in some nuclear reactors.

Hebrew A Semitic language. It is written from right to left in an alphabet of 22 letters, all consonants, with vowels indicated by subscript and superscript diacritical marks. The oldest and best-known works of Hebrew literature are those preserved in the *Bible (Old Testament). Hebrew continued to be a literary language throughout the middle ages. In the late 19th century Hebrew was revived as a spoken language, particularly in Russia and Palestine. In 1948 it became an official language of Israel.

Hebrides, the A group of about 500 islands off the W coast of Scotland. The islands are subdivided into the Inner and Outer Hebrides, separated by the Minch. The chief islands of the Outer Hebrides include Lewis with Harris and the Uists; those of the Inner Hebrides include Skye, Mull, Islay, and Jura. The main occupations are stock rearing, fishing, and crofting. Harris tweed is produced, especially in the Uists.

Hebron (Arabic name: Al Khalil) 31 32N 35 06E A town in the S of the *West Bank of the River Jordan. It is one of the oldest continuously inhabited cities in the world and is revered by both Jews and Muslims as the burial place of Abraham. Since 1997 most of the town has been controlled by the Palestinian National Authority. Population (1997): 119 401.

Hecate A primitive Greek fertility goddess and a ruler of the underworld. She was associated with witchcraft and magic and was worshipped at crossroads. She accompanied *Demeter in her search for Persephone.

hectare (ha) A unit of area in the *metric system equal to 100 ares or 10 000 square metres. 1 ha = 2.471 acres.

Hector In Greek legend, the eldest son of Priam, King of Troy, and the chief Trojan warrior. He was the husband of Andromache. He fought Ajax in single combat, killed Patroclus, and was killed in revenge by *Achilles.

Hecuba In Greek legend, the wife of Priam, King of Troy, and mother of *Hector. She was captured by the Greeks after the fall of Troy.

hedgehog A nocturnal prickly-coated insectivorous mammal belonging to the subfamily *Erinaceinae* (15 species). The European hedgehog (*Erinaceus europaeus*) grows up to 30 cm long and has brown and cream spines and soft grey-brown underfur. It feeds on worms, beetles, slugs, and snails. Family: *Erinaceidae.*

hedge sparrow *See* DUNNOCK.

hedonism The ethical theory holding that pleasure is the greatest good. Varying definitions of pleasure distinguished the classical hedonistic schools. Utilitarianism is the most important modern form of hedonism. *Compare* EPICUREANISM.

Hegel, Georg Wilhelm Friedrich (1770–1831) German philosopher, one of the most influential thinkers of the 19th century. His first major work, *The Phenomenology of Mind*, was published in 1807, the *Encyclopedia of the Philosophical Sciences* in 1817, and *The Philosophy of Right* in 1821. Besides these major works, he left voluminous lecture notes on history, religion, and aesthetics. **Hegelianism** is the idealist school of thought based on his philosophy.

Heidegger, Martin (1889–1976) German philosopher. His main philosophical work was *Sein und Zeit* (*Being and Time*; 1927). As rector of Freiburg University (1933–34) he supported Hitler and this association, together with logical flaws in his work, has damaged his reputation.

Heidelberg 49 25N 08 42E A city in SW Germany, in Baden-Württemberg on the River Neckar. A tourist centre, it has a ruined castle (mainly 16th–17th centuries) and the oldest university in Germany (1386). Its varied manufactures include printing presses, cigars, and electrical appliances. *History*: the capital of the Palatinate until 1685, it was devastated during the Thirty Years' War and later by the French. During the 19th century it was the student centre of Germany. In 1952 it became the European headquarters of the US army. Population (1999 est): 139 400.

Heifetz, Jascha (1901–87) Russian-born US violinist. A child prodigy, he entered the St Petersburg conservatoire in 1910, and at the age of 12 began a worldwide career. He commissioned Walton's violin concerto.

Heine, Heinrich (1797–1856) German Jewish poet and writer. His early works include the poetry collection *Buch der Lieder* (1827) and the prose *Reisebilder* (1826–31). From 1831 he lived in

Paris, where he wrote essays on French and German culture and some satirical poetry.

Heisenberg, Werner Karl (1901–76) German physicist, who, with *Schrödinger, was the main architect of quantum mechanics. In 1927 Heisenberg created a mathematical system, known as matrix mechanics, to explain the structure of the hydrogen atom. In the same year he put forward the theory known as the *Heisenberg uncertainty principle, for which he was awarded the Nobel Prize in 1932. During World War II Heisenberg was in charge of Germany's unsuccessful attempts to make an atom bomb at the Max Planck Institute in Berlin. After the war he became director of the Max Planck Institute for Physics in Göttingen.

Heisenberg uncertainty principle If a simultaneous measurement is made of the position and momentum of a particle, there is always an uncertainty in the values obtained. The product of the uncertainties is of the same order as Planck's constant. A similar uncertainty exists with the simultaneous measurement of energy and time. The uncertainty, which is only important at subatomic levels, arises because the act of observing the system interferes with it in an unpredictable way. Named after Werner *Heisenberg.

Hejaz (*or* **Western Province**) A province in Saudi Arabia, bordering on the Red Sea. Its coastal plain supports some agriculture; income is also derived from pilgrims to Mecca and Medina. The largest town is Jidda. Hejaz, formerly independent, joined Najd in a dual kingdom in 1926, and both became part of Saudi Arabia in 1932. Area: about 350 000 sq km (135 107 sq mi). Population (2000 est): 7 304 025.

Helen In Greek legend, the daughter of Zeus and *Leda, famed for her supreme beauty. She married Menelaus, King of Sparta, but later fled to Troy with *Paris, thus precipitating the *Trojan War. After the fall of Troy she was reunited with Menelaus.

Helena, St (c. 248–c. 328 AD) Roman empress, mother of Constantine the Great. A Christian from 313, she made a pilgrimage to the Holy Land (c. 326), where she founded several churches and, according to tradition, rediscovered the cross used at the crucifixion. Feast day: 18 Aug. Emblem: the cross.

Helgoland (*or* **Heligoland**) 54 09N 7 52E A German island in the North Sea, in the North Frisian group. Ceded to Britain in 1814, it was transferred to Germany in exchange for Zanzibar in 1890 and was a major German naval base during both World Wars. Area: about 150 ha (380 acres).

helicopter An aircraft that obtains both its lift and its thrust from aerofoils (rotors) rotating about a vertical axis (*compare* AUTOGIRO). The first successful helicopter was made in 1939 by Igor *Sikorsky in the USA. A helicopter using a single rotor requires an anti-torque tail propeller and some models also use a vertical propeller for forward thrust. Helicopters can rise and drop vertically, hover, and move backwards, forwards, and sideways by control of the pitch of the rotors. First used in World War II, helicopters have since been developed for rescue services, police observation, and urban passenger services.

Helios The Greek sun god, usually represented as a charioteer driving the sun across the sky each day. In later legends he was identified with Hyperion or Apollo.

heliotrope A herb or shrub of the genus *Heliotropium* (220 species), found in tropical and temperate regions and having heads of blue or white flowers. Many horticultural varieties of the cherry-pie plant (*H. peruvianum*) and *H. corymbosa* are used as bedding plants in cooler climates. Family: *Boraginaceae*.

helium (He) The lightest noble gas, first detected in 1868 by Janssen (1838–1904) as an unexpected line in the spectrum of the sun, and named from Greek *helios*, sun. Helium was discovered on earth in 1895 in the uranium mineral, clevite, as a radioactive decay product (*see* RADIOACTIVITY). It is used for filling balloons, as a gas shield in arc welding, and to replace nitrogen in the breathing mixture used by divers. Helium has the lowest melting point of any element. At no 2; at wt 4.0026; mp −272.2°C; bp −268.9°C.

helium dating A method of dating rocks, minerals, and fossils that utilizes the production of helium in the form of *alpha particles during the radioactive decay of uranium-235, uranium-238, or thorium-232. The amount of helium trapped in the sample is a measure of its age.

hell In Christian belief, the place in which the souls of the wicked are imprisoned in everlasting torment. The concept of hell as a dark and fiery pit derives from the Book of Revelation. Some Christians insist upon the physical reality of hellfire but most consider it a metaphor for the misery of being deprived forever of the vision of God. *Compare* PURGATORY.

hellebore A poisonous perennial herb of the

genus *Helleborus* (20 species), of Europe and W Asia. The stinking hellebore (*H. foetidus*) grows to a height of 30–50 cm and bears clusters of cup-shaped purple-edged green flowers. Family: *Ranunculaceae*. *See also* CHRISTMAS ROSE.

Hellen In Greek mythology, the grandson of Prometheus and eponymous ancestor of the Greeks, who called themselves the Hellenes and their country Hellas. The four subgroups of the Hellenes, the Aeolians, Dorians, Ionians, and Achaeans, were named after his sons and grandsons.

Hellenistic age The period, between the death of Alexander the Great of Macedon (323 BC) and the accession of the Roman emperor Augustus (27 BC), when Greek culture spread throughout the Mediterranean. In the Hellenistic period Alexandria in Egypt was the major commercial city and centre of intellectual life, including scholarly literature and grandiose art, *Epicureanism, *Neoplatonism, Stoic philosophy, *Gnosticism, and Christianity. The Koine, common Greek, was the universal language.

Hellespont *See* DARDANELLES.

Helmand, River (**R. Helmund** *or* **R. Hilmand**) The longest river in Afghanistan. Rising in the E of the country, it flows generally SW then N to enter the marshy lake of Halmun Helmand on the Afghan-Iranian border. Length: 1400 km (870 mi).

Helmholtz, Hermann Ludwig Ferdinand von (1821–94) German physicist and physiologist, who made contributions to many fields of science. In physiology his main interest was the sense organs, developing *Young's theory of colour vision (now known as the Young-Helmholtz theory). This work was published in his *Physiological Optics* (1856). He played a considerable part in the development of thermodynamics, especially in formulating the concept of free energy.

Helpmann, Sir Robert (1909–86) Australian ballet dancer, choreographer, and actor. He went to England in 1933 and worked mainly with Sadler's Wells Ballet until 1950. He became artistic director of the Australian Ballet in 1955. His ballets include *Comus* (1942) and *Hamlet* (1942).

Helsingør (*or* **Elsinore**) 56 03N 12 38E A seaport in Denmark, in NE Sjælland situated on the Sound opposite Hälsingborg in Sweden. It contains the fortress of Kronborg (1580), famous as the scene of Shakespeare's play *Hamlet*. Population (2000 est): 116 870.

Helsinki (Swedish name: Helsingfors) 60 13N 24 55E The capital of Finland, a port in the S on the Gulf of Finland. It is the country's commercial and administrative centre; industries include metals, textiles, food processing, and paper. Its famous buildings include the 18th-century cathedral; the city is also renowned for its 20th-century architecture. *History*: founded by Gustavus I Vasa of Sweden in 1550, it replaced Turku as capital of Finland (then under Russian rule) in 1812. Population (2000 est): 551 123.

Hemel Hempstead 51 46N 0 28W A market town in SE England, in Hertfordshire. Designated a new town in 1946, the principal industries include light engineering. Population (1991): 79 235.

Hemichordata A phylum of marine invertebrate animals (about 100 species), found in coastal sand or mud and on the sea bed. The gill slits and nervous system show similarities with those of chordates—hence their name. The group comprises the *acornworms and the pterobranchs (class *Pterobranchia*).

Hemingway, Ernest (1899–1961) US novelist. After World War I he joined the American expatriate community in Paris. In his short stories and novels, which include *The Sun Also Rises* (1926), *To Have and Have Not* (1937), *For Whom the Bell Tolls* (1940), about the Spanish Civil War, and *The Old Man and the Sea* (1952), he celebrated the virtues of courage and stoicism in a forceful economical style. He won the Nobel Prize in 1954. Subject to severe depressions, he committed suicide.

hemiplegia *See* PARALYSIS.

Hemiptera An order of insects (about 50 000 species)—the true bugs—having piercing mouthparts for sucking the juices from plants or animals. The suborder *Heteroptera* includes the plant bugs and the water bugs. The forewings of these insects have both a leathery and a membranous region. The suborder *Homoptera*, including the *froghoppers, *aphids, *cicadas, and *scale insects, are all plant feeders and have uniform front wings.

hemlock **1.** A poisonous biennial plant, *Conium maculatum*, native to Europe, W Asia, and N Africa. It grows in damp places to a height of 2 m and has branching purple-spotted stems that bear much divided leaves and clusters of tiny white flowers. Family: *Umbelliferae*. **2.** A coniferous tree of the genus *Tsuga* (15 species), native to S and E Asia and North America. The narrow bladelike leaves are grouped in two rows along the stems and the cones are brown and egg-shaped. Family: *Pinaceae.*

hemp An annual herb, *Cannabis sativa*, native to central Asia. It grows to a height of 5 m and bears small yellow flowers. Hemp is cultivated in many temperate regions for its fibre. The flowers, bark, twigs, and leaves contain a narcotic resin (*see* CANNABIS). Family: *Moraceae.*

Hengist and Horsa Legendary leaders of the first Anglo-Saxon settlers in Britain. According to the Anglo-Saxon Chronicle (late 9th century AD) Horsa was killed in 455 AD and his brother Hengist ruled over Kent from 455 to 488.

Henley-on-Thames 51 32N 0 56W A town in S central England, in Oxfordshire on the River Thames. It is chiefly a residential and recreational town with an annual Royal Regatta (first held in 1839). Population (1991): 10 558.

henna A shrub, *Lawsonia inermis*, occurring in Egypt, India, and the Middle East. Up to 2 m high, it has fragrant white-and-yellow flowers. The leaves are powdered and used for tinting the hair a reddish colour. Family: *Lythraceae.*

henry (H) The SI unit of inductance equal to the inductance of a closed circuit such that a rate of change of current of one ampere per second produces an induced e.m.f. of one volt. Named after the US physicist Joseph Henry (1797–1878).

Henry I (1069–1135) King of England (1100–35); the youngest son of *William (I) the Conqueror. Henry became king on the death of his brother William Rufus, successfully defending his throne against the claims of his eldest brother Robert II Curthose, Duke of Normandy. In England his reign is notable for important legal and administrative reforms, especially in the Exchequer. Abroad Henry waged several campaigns against Louis VI of France (1081–1137; reigned 1108–37), Fulk V, Count of Anjou (1092–1143), and Norman rebels.

Henry II (1133–89) King of England (1154–89); the son of Matilda and Geoffrey of Anjou and the grandson of Henry I. Henry succeeded Stephen. He married *Eleanor of Aquitaine in 1152 and ruled an empire that stretched from the River Tweed to the Pyrenees. In spite of frequent hostilities and his quarrel with Thomas *Becket, Henry maintained control over his possessions until shortly before his death.

Henry II (1519–59) King of France (1547–59); the husband from 1533 of *Catherine de' Medici. He concluded war against the Emperor *Charles V at Cateau-Cambrésis (1559). An ardent Roman Catholic, he began the systematic persecution of Huguenots, which ultimately led to the *Wars of Religion.

Henry III (1207–72) King of England (1216–72), succeeding his father John. Hubert de Burgh (d. 1243) controlled the government from 1119 to 1232 and Henry's personal government began in 1234. Baronial discontent simmered, boiling over in 1258; reforms—the Provisions of Oxford—were agreed upon but then renounced by Henry. Simon de *Montfort led a rebellion against the king (*see* BARONS' WARS), which was defeated after initial success.

Henry III (1551–89) King of France (1574–89) during the *Wars of Religion. Elected King of Poland in 1573, he abandoned that country on succeeding to the French throne. In France he allied with the Huguenot Henry of Navarre (the future *Henry IV). He was assassinated while besieging Paris.

Henry IV (1366–1413) King of England (1399–1413); the eldest son of *John of Gaunt. As Henry Bolingbroke, he seized the throne from Richard II. In the early years of his reign Henry faced considerable opposition from Richard's supporters and from the Welsh. Successful in defeating his enemies, the costs of these wars and resultant taxation led to protracted struggles between king and parliament for control of royal expenditure.

Henry IV (1553–1610) The first Bourbon King of France (1589–1610), who restored peace and prosperity following the *Wars of Religion. A Protestant, he succeeded his mother to the throne of Navarre in 1572. Shortly afterwards he married Charles IX's sister Margaret of Valois (1553–1615). In 1576 he became a *Huguenot (Protestant) leader in the Wars of Religion. His succession to the throne was secured in 1594, when he became a Roman Catholic; in 1598 he granted the Huguenots freedom of worship by the Edict of *Nantes.

Henry V (1387–1422) King of England (1413–22); the eldest son of Henry IV. He vigorously resumed the *Hundred Years' War, his first campaign culminating in the battle of *Agincourt (1415); by 1420, in alliance with Burgundy, he controlled much of N France. He married Catherine of Valois and gained recognition (1420) as the heir of her father *Charles VI.

Henry VI (1421–71) King of England (1422–61, 1470–71), succeeding his father Henry V. He married *Margaret of Anjou in 1445. His inability to govern led to bitter struggles that culminated in the Wars of the *Roses. Deposed and imprisoned by the Yorkists (1461), he was briefly restored to power (1470–71). A notable patron of learning, he founded Eton College (1440) and King's College, Cambridge (1447).

Henry VII (1457–1509) King of England (1485–1509). As Henry Tudor, Earl of Richmond, he defeated Richard III at Bosworth (1485) and his marriage (1486) to Richard's niece Elizabeth of York (1465–1503) united the Houses of *Lancaster and *York, ending the Wars of the *Roses. His domestic rule was noted for its harsh financial exactions, efficient administration, and growing prosperity. His foreign policy temporarily put an end to war with France.

Henry VIII (1491–1547) King of England (1509–47), who initiated the English *Reformation. In 1512 he joined a European alliance against France and in the same year his army thwarted a Scottish invasion at *Flodden. His desire to make England a notable European power was pursued from 1515 by his Lord Chancellor, Cardinal *Wolsey. From 1527 Henry was preoccupied by his wish to divorce *Catherine of Aragon and marry Anne Boleyn. He blamed Catherine's failure to produce a son on the canonical prohibition against marrying one's brother's widow and sought a papal annulment. Only in 1533, after Thomas *Cromwell had initiated the legislation that made the English Church, under Henry's supreme headship, independent of Rome, could the king marry Anne. In 1536 Anne was executed for adultery; Henry then married Jane *Seymour, who died shortly after giving birth to the future Edward VI (1537). His marriage to *Anne of Cleves was short lived, ending in divorce; shortly afterwards Henry married Catherine *Howard, who was executed in 1542, and finally, in 1543, Catherine *Parr, who outlived him. Henry's last years were dominated by war with France and Scotland.

Henry, O. (William Sidney Porter; 1862–1910) US short-story writer. He adopted his pseudonym while serving a prison sentence for embezzlement. He subsequently worked in New York, where he published *Cabbages and Kings* (1904), the first of many volumes of short stories.

hepatitis Inflammation of the liver, most commonly caused by viruses. The main types of infectious hepatitis are hepatitis A, usually contracted by ingesting the virus from food or drink, and hepatitis B and C, contracted from contaminated hypodermic needles or blood products or sexually transmitted. The patient usually has a fever, loses his appetite, and later becomes jaundiced. Unless chronic disease develops, hepatitis often resolves without specific treatment.

Hepburn, Katharine (1909–2003) US actress. She made several films with Spencer *Tracy, and her other films include *The Philadelphia Story* (1940), *The African Queen* (1952), *The Lion in Winter* (1968), and *On Golden Pond* (1981).

Hepplewhite, George (1727–86) British furniture designer and cabinetmaker, who established a business in London. His neoclassical furniture is a simplified and more functional version of the designs of Robert *Adam, with whom he sometimes collaborated. Usually in inlaid mahogany or satinwood, it is characterized by straight tapering legs and heart- or oval-shaped chairbacks filled with openwork designs.

heptathlon An athletic competition for women, consisting of seven events over two days. They are the 100 m hurdle, high jump, shot put, 200 m sprint, long jump, javelin throw, and 800 m sprint.

Hepworth, Dame Barbara (1903–75) British sculptor. She studied in Leeds and at the Royal College of Art. A friend of Henry *Moore, she was also influenced by *Brancusi and *Arp. Her abstract carving in wood and stone developed after *Pierced Form* (1931), creating massive shapes broken by holes with wires stretched across their openings. She received the DBE in 1965.

Hera In Greek mythology, the daughter of Cronus and Rhea and the sister and wife of Zeus. She was jealous of Zeus' mistresses but gave support to *Jason and *Achilles. She was worshipped as a goddess of women and marriage. She is identified with the Roman *Juno.

Heracles (*or* **Hercules**) A Greek legendary hero, famed for his strength and courage. He was the son of Zeus and Alcmene. After killing his wife and children in a fit of madness, he performed the Twelve Labours in expiation: he killed the Nemean lion and the *Hydra of Lerna, captured the Hind of Ceryneia and the Boar of Erymanthus, cleaned the Augean stables, chased away the Stymphalian birds, captured the Cretan bull and the horses of Diomedes, stole the girdle of Hippolyte, captured the oxen of Geryon, stole the apples of the *Hesperides, and finally captured and bound *Cerberus in Hades.

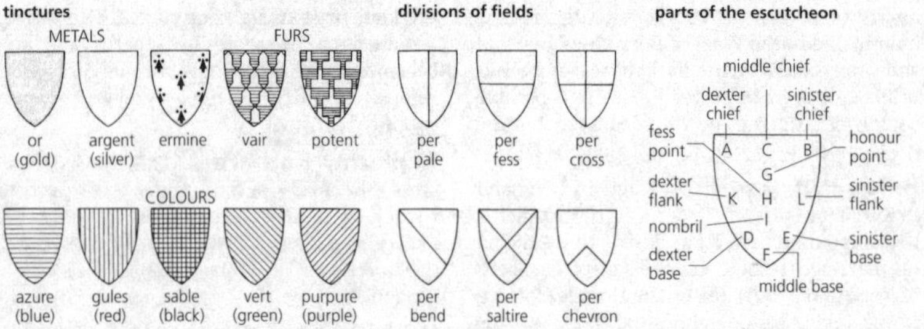

heraldry. The terminology of heraldry, of which a few terms are illustrated, reveals the science's French origins.

heraldry A system of pictorial devices on shields originally used to identify individuals when wearing armour. Personal devices on shields are of great antiquity but in the early 12th century armorial devices became hereditary in Europe. They were also used as *seals. Coats of arms are also granted to institutions. In England heraldry is controlled by the *College of Arms. The Court of the Lord Lyon has a similar function in Scotland. Coats of arms comprise the shield, a helmet surmounted by a crest, a mantling (stylized drapery behind the shield), a wreath, and a motto. The shield bears the heraldic signs (charges), which have ancient fixed meanings. From these heralds can determine genealogy and status.

Herbert, George (1593–1633) English poet. A member of a distinguished family, he was an MP before becoming rector of Bemerton, Wiltshire, in 1630. His religious lyrics, collected in *The Temple* (1633), are among the finest in the language.

herbs and spices The fresh or dried parts of aromatic or pungent plants used in food, drink, medicine, and perfumery. Herbs are generally the leaves of plants growing in temperate zones. Common culinary herbs are *basil, *bay leaves, *marjoram, *mint, *parsley, and *thyme. Spices generally grow in hot countries; they were formerly a valuable trade commodity. Spices are usually dried and may be obtained from the root (e.g. *ginger), bark (e.g. *cinnamon), flower (e.g. *clove), seed pod (e.g. *chilli), or, most commonly, from the seed itself (e.g. *coriander, *cumin, *pepper).

Herculaneum An ancient Italian city near *Naples in Italy. It was destroyed by the same eruption as *Pompeii (79 AD). Entombment beneath solidified volcanic mud makes excavation there very difficult.

Hercules *See* HERACLES.

hercules beetle A giant green and black beetle, *Dynastes herculeus*, occurring in Central and South America. The male may reach a length of 15 cm, nearly two-thirds of which is taken up by an enormous pair of horns, extending from the thorax and head. Family: *Scarabeidae* (*see* SCARAB BEETLE).

Hereford 52 04N 2 43W A city in W England, the administrative centre of Herefordshire on the River Wye. Situated in an important agricultural area, Hereford deals mainly in agricultural produce, manufacturing cider, beer, leather goods, and chemicals. It has given its name to a famous breed of beef cattle. The cathedral, begun in 1079, contains one of the oldest maps (*Mappa Mundi*) in the world (about 1314). Population (1991): 54 326.

Herefordshire A county of W England, on the Welsh border. In 1974 it became part of Hereford and Worcester but in 1998 it was reinstated as an independent unitary authority. Herefordshire consists of a rolling plain separating the Malvern Hills in the E from the Black Mountains in the W. The chief river is the Wye. It is predominantly agricultural, with hops and apples and pears grown. The Hereford breed of cattle is renowned worldwide. Industry is concentrated in Hereford. Area: 2180 sq km (842 sq mi). Population (2001): 174 844. Administrative centre: Hereford.

Herero A group of Bantu-speaking peoples of SW Africa, Botswana, and Angola. They are traditionally cattle, sheep, and goat herders but some adopted agriculture after European contact. Their social organization is based on the common principle of counting descent in the male line for some purposes and in the female line for others.

Hereward the Wake (11th century) Anglo-Saxon thegn, who led a raid on Peterborough Abbey (1070) as a protest against William I's appointment of a Norman abbot. He and other disaffected Anglo-Saxon nobles took refuge on the Isle of Ely until its capture by William (1071).

hermaphrodite (*or* **bisexual**) A plant or animal possessing both male and female reproductive organs. Such organisms may show cross- or self-*fertilization: the latter method is particularly common when the opportunity of finding a mate is remote. True hermaphroditism rarely occurs in humans. More common is **pseudohermaphroditism**, in which an individual develops secondary characteristics appropriate to the opposite sex (e.g breasts in a man), due to hormone imbalance.

Hermes In Greek mythology, the messenger and herald of the gods and the guide of travellers. He was regarded as the god of riches and good luck, the protector of merchants and thieves, and the god of dreams. He was usually portrayed as an athletic youth wearing a cap and winged sandals and carrying a golden staff. He was the son of Zeus and Maia. He is identified with the Roman *Mercury.

hermit crab A *crab with a soft unprotected abdomen, belonging to the worldwide families *Paguridae* and *Coenobitidae*. It lives in portable hollow objects, such as snail shells, for protection. Hermit crabs are found in sandy or muddy-bottomed waters and occasionally on land and in trees. Tribe: *Anomura*.

hernia The protrusion of an organ or tissue through a weak spot in the wall that normally contains it. The most common types are the inguinal hernia (popularly called a rupture), which is a swelling in the groin caused by the protrusion of the abdominal contents, and the hiatus hernia, in which part of the stomach protrudes into the chest cavity. Hernias should usually be surgically repaired or they may become painful and cut off from their blood supply (strangulated).

Hero and Leander Legendary lovers whose story was recounted by the Greek poet Musaeus (4th or 5th century AD). Hero was a priestess of Aphrodite at Sestos and Leander swam to her each night across the Hellespont from Abydos. After a stormy night Hero found her lover's drowned body and in despair drowned herself.

Herod (I) the Great (c. 73–4 BC) King of Judaea (37–4); the son of Antipater the Idumaean (d. 43 BC). Supported by Mark Antony, he became the Romans' king in Judaea. A Jew of Arab origins, he retained power by control of the religious establishment and rigorous suppression of opposition. Shortly before his death he ordered the massacre of the infants of Bethlehem.

Herod Agrippa I (c. 10 BC–44 AD) King of Judaea (41–44); the grandson of Herod the Great. He was educated at the Roman imperial court after the execution of his father by Herod the Great. He intrigued in imperial family politics and helped Emperor Claudius to power, for which he was made King of Judaea. He was a popular ruler but persecuted Christians.

Herod Agrippa II (died c. 100 AD) King of Chalcis (50–c. 100) in S Lebanon; the son of *Herod Agrippa I. He attempted to prevent the Jewish rebellion of 66, during which his troops fought on the Roman side, and helped to take Jerusalem in 70.

Herod Antipas (21 BC–39 AD) Tetrarch (governor) of Galilee (4–39 AD) after the partition of the realm of his father Herod the Great. He divorced his wife to marry his niece Herodias, for which he was censured by John the Baptist. Herodias persuaded her daughter Salome to ask for John's head in return for dancing at Antipas' birthday celebration and John was executed. Jesus Christ was brought before Antipas after his arrest, but Antipas returned him to Pontius Pilate of Judaea without passing judgment.

Herodotus (c. 484–c. 425 BC) Greek historian. Born at Halicarnassus, he was exiled for political reasons and moved first to Samos, then to Athens, and lastly to the Athenian colony of Thurii in S Italy. He was the first historian to subject his material to critical evaluation and research. His narrative account of the wars between Greece and Persia in nine books contains much incidental information gathered on his travels.

heroin (*or* **diamorphine**) A pain-killing drug with a stronger action and fewer side effects than *morphine, from which it is made. Heroin is used to alleviate the suffering of terminal illness. Because the use of heroin can lead to physical dependence its use in medicine is strictly controlled. It is widely abused.

heron A wading bird belonging to a subfamily (*Ardeinae*; 60 species) occurring on lakes and rivers worldwide, especially in the tropics. 75–150 cm long, herons have a slim body, longish legs, broad wings, and a grey, blue, greenish, white, purple, or reddish plumage. Herons hunt by seizing fish and insects with the long pointed bill. Family: *Ardeidae* (herons and bitterns). *See also* EGRET.

herpes A virus of which there are several forms. Herpes zoster virus (*or* varicellazoster) causes chickenpox and shingles. Herpes simplex virus I causes cold sores. Herpes simplex virus II causes the sexually transmitted genital herpes.

Herrick, Robert (1591–1674) English poet. He served as rector of Dean Prior, Devonshire, from 1630 to 1646 and again after the Restoration. The majority of his secular and religious poems, collected in *Hesperides* (1648), are short lyrics influenced by classical models.

herring A food fish, *Clupea harengus*, found mainly in the N Atlantic and the North Sea. It has a slender silvery body, up to about 40 cm long, with a single dorsal fin and feeds on plankton. A related species (*C. pallasi*) occurs in the N Pacific. Herrings are eaten fresh, pickled, and smoked. Smoked herrings, mainly produced in Scotland, are known as kippers. Order: *Clupeiformes*.

herring gull A large grey and white *gull, *Larus argentatus*, occurring around coasts in the N hemisphere. It is omnivorous and is commonly seen scavenging at refuse tips. Adults are 57 cm long and have pink legs and a yellow bill with a red spot on the lower mandible.

Hertford 51 48N 0 05W A market town in SE England, the administrative centre of Hertfordshire on the River Lea. Industries include printing, flour milling, brewing, and brush manufacturing. Population (1991): 21 665.

Hertfordshire A county of S England, bordering on Greater London. It lies mainly in the Lower Thames Basin rising to the Chiltern Hills in the NW and is drained by the Rivers Lea, Stort, and Colne. The chief agricultural activity is arable farming, producing barley for the brewing industry. Dairy farming, market gardening, and horticulture are also important. There is a mixture of modern and traditional industries. Area: 1634 sq km (632 sq mi). Population (2001): 1 033 977. Administrative centre: Hertford.

Hertz, Heinrich Rudolf (1857–94) German physicist, who first produced and detected *radio waves (1888). The SI unit of frequency the **hertz** (Hz), equal to one cycle per second, is named after him.

Hertzog, James Barry Munnik (1866–1942) South African statesman; prime minister of the Union of South Africa (1924–39). In the second Boer War he led the Orange Free State forces. He formed the Afrikaner Nationalist Party in 1914 in opposition to Botha, becoming prime minister in 1924. In 1933 he formed a coalition government with *Smuts, resigning in 1939.

Hertzsprung-Russell diagram A graphic representation of the classification of stars according to spectral type (*see* HARVARD CLASSIFICATION SYSTEM) and brightness—usually absolute *magnitude. The stars are not uniformly distributed. Most lie on a diagonal band, the main sequence, the brightest stars of which are spectral types O and B and the faintest are M stars. The somewhat brighter *giant stars, the even brighter *supergiants, and the faint *white dwarfs fall into their own distinct groupings and are at later stages of evolution. The diagram was originally produced, independently, in 1911 by E. Hertzsprung (1873–1967) and in 1913 by H. N. Russell (1877– 1957).

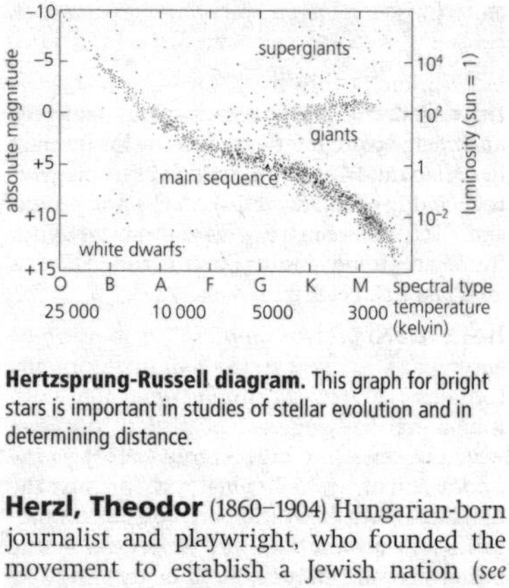

Hertzsprung-Russell diagram. This graph for bright stars is important in studies of stellar evolution and in determining distance.

Herzl, Theodor (1860–1904) Hungarian-born journalist and playwright, who founded the movement to establish a Jewish nation (*see* ZIONISM). A world congress of Zionists in Basle (1897), at which the World Zionist Organization was established, elected Herzl as the first president.

Heseltine, Michael (Ray Dibdin), Baron (1933–) British Conservative politician; deputy prime minister (1995–97); secretary of state for the environment (1979–83; 1990–92), for defence (1983–86), and for trade and industry and president of the board of trade (1992–95). He ran unsuccessfully for the leadership of the Conservative Party in 1990, precipitating the fall of Margaret Thatcher.

Hesperides (Greek: daughters of evening) In Greek mythology, three nymphs who guarded the sacred golden apples of Hera in a garden in the far west. The apples were stolen by *Heracles as one of his Twelve Labours.

Hess, Rudolf (1894–1987) German politician. Hess joined the Nazi Party in 1920, becoming deputy party leader (1933). After his unsuccessful secret mission to Scotland to negotiate a separate peace with Britain (1941) he was imprisoned until 1946, when he was convicted at the Nuremberg war trials and sent to Spandau prison, where he committed suicide.

Hesse (German name: Hessen) A *Land* in central Germany. Formed in 1945, it consists of the former duchies of Hesse-Darmstadt and Nassau. Hilly and forested, it is chiefly agricultural, producing potatoes, sugar beet, and wheat. Industry includes publishing and the manufacture of machinery and chemicals. Iron ore, salt, and coal are mined. Area: 21 112 sq km (8150 sq mi). Population (2000 est): 6 052 000. Capital: Wiesbaden.

Hesse, Hermann (1877–1962) German novelist and poet. He worked as a bookseller until publication of his first novel, *Peter Camenzind* (1904). His early themes of art and self-knowledge were later extended by his interest in Indian mysticism and Jungian psychology, as reflected in *Siddharta* (1922), *Steppenwolf* (1927), and *The Glass Bead Game* (1943). From 1911 until his death he lived in Switzerland. He was awarded a Nobel Prize (1946).

Heyerdahl, Thor (1914–2002) Norwegian ethnologist. He built and sailed the balsa wood raft *Kon-Tiki* from the Pacific coast of South America to Polynesia to show that the pre-Incan inhabitants of Peru might thus have migrated to Polynesia. In 1969–70 he crossed the Atlantic Ocean from Morocco to South America in a papyrus boat—the *Ra*—showing the possibility of Egyptian influence on Precolumbian civilization. Later he led a series of archaeological expeditions to Easter Island (1986–88).

Hiawatha The legendary chief of the Onondaga tribe of American Indians, who was said to have formed the *Iroquois League. His story is the subject of Longfellow's *Song of Hiawatha* (1855).

hibernation A state of *dormancy in winter experienced by many fish, amphibians, reptiles, and mammals of temperate and Arctic regions: it is an adaption to avoid death by heat loss, freezing, or food scarcity. Hibernation involves a period of sleep during which the body temperature drops almost to that of the surroundings, the body processes are slowed, and the hibernator lives on body fat until it awakens in the spring.

Hibiscus A genus of tropical and subtropical herbs, shrubs, and trees (about 150 species). Two popular cultivated shrubs, up to 3 m high, are the Chinese *H. rosa-sinensis* (rose of China), which has red, pink, or yellow flowers, and the Syrian *H. syriacus* (rose of Sharon), which has pink, blue, or white flowers. The genus also includes plants cultivated for their food value (*see* OKRA) and for their fibre. Family: *Malvaceae.*

hickory A tree of the genus *Carya* (20 species), native to E North America and Asia and cultivated for timber, nuts, and ornament. They grow to 30 m and have compound leaves consisting of paired leaflets. Commercially important species are the shagbark (*C. ovata*) and the pecan (*C. illinoensis*). Family: *Juglandaceae.*

hieroglyphics Originally, an Egyptian picture writing in use from about 3000 BC to 300 AD; it now denotes any pictographic or ideographic writing system. The Egyptians used hieroglyphics largely for monumental inscriptions. The characters are reproductions of people, animals, and objects and represent either the objects they portray or the sounds that are featured in the pronunciation of the referent.

hieroglyphics. A picture was used to represent objects, related ideas, and sounds.

Higgs boson A massive *boson the existence of which was proposed by the Scottish physicist Peter Higgs (1929–) to explain the weak interaction (*see* PARTICLE PHYSICS). In his theory Higgs suggested that the nonzero masses of the intermediate vector bosons (the W and Z bosons) are acquired by the particles in interacting with an all-pervading field, known as the **Higgs field**. CERN's large hadron collider (LHC), which is due to be completed in 2006, is being constructed to test this theory.

high jump A field event in athletics in which jumpers compete to clear a horizontal bar. A competitor is allowed three attempts at a height and is eliminated if he fails to clear it.

World records: men: 2.45 m (1993) by Javier Sotomayor (Cuba); women 2.09 m (1987) by Stefka Kostadinova (Bulgaria).

Highland A council area in N Scotland, created in 1975 (as Highland Region) under local government reorganization from the N part of Argyll, Caithness, Inverness, Nairn, Ross and Cromarty, and Sutherland. It became a unitary authority in 1996. The region consists chiefly of glaciated highlands divided from NE to SW by the fault valley, Great Glen, and includes part of the Inner Hebrides. Sheep farming is the main agricultural activity. Industries associated with North Sea oil have developed and aluminium smelting, pulp and paper production, and distilling are all important. Tourism is a major source of revenue. Salmon farming is a growing industry. Area: 25 425 sq km (9814 sq mi). Population (2001): 208 914. Administrative centre: Inverness.

Highland dress The traditional male costume (since the 17th century) of the Scottish Highlands. It consists of the kilt and the plaid (a cloak worn over one shoulder). Accessories include the sporran (a goatskin pouch), cap, kilt pin, and dagger (worn in the right sock). Highland dress was banned for civilian wear (1746–82) following the Jacobite rebellions. **Tartan**, the material used for the kilt and plaid, is a woollen cloth woven into a design of large-meshed cross stripes. The tradition of each clan having its own tartan probably dates from the 17th century.

Highland Games Scottish athletics meetings, usually professional, held in the Highlands. Events include standard track and field events as well as such Scottish sports as caber tossing, and there are also competitions in highland dancing and playing the bagpipes. The Braemar Games can be traced back to the 8th century AD.

High Wycombe 51 38N 0 46W A town in SE England, in Buckinghamshire. It has a long tradition of furniture making and also produces paper, precision instruments, and clothing. Hughenden Manor was the home of Disraeli. Population (1991): 71 718.

Hildegard of Bingen, St (1098–1179) German writer, composer, and mystic. She lived in a convent from the age of eight, becoming a prioress in 1136 and an abbess in 1147. Her writings include works on medicine and science as well as mystical poems, many of which she set to music.

Hillary, Sir Edmund (Percival) (1919–) New Zealand mountaineer and explorer. In 1953 he and *Tenzing Norgay were the first to reach the summit of Mount Everest, for which achievement he was knighted. He was New Zealand High Commissioner in Delhi (1984–89).

Hilliard, Nicholas (1547–1619) English portrait miniaturist, born in Exeter. Like his father, he trained as a jeweller, later becoming court painter to Elizabeth I and James I. Many of his portraits are in the royal collection at Windsor Castle. In his *Treatise on the Art of Limning* (c. 1600), he describes his style and technique of painting miniatures.

Himachal Pradesh A state in NW India, in the W Himalayas beside Tibet's border. Long part of the *Punjab, it was formed by the combination of various hill states (1948). Most of the inhabitants are Pahari-speaking Hindus who farm grains, potatoes, maize, and livestock. The forests yield timber and bamboo, and enormous hydroelectric potential is being exploited. Area: 55 673 sq km (21 490 sq mi). Population (2001): 6 077 248. Capital: Simla.

Himalayas A vast mountain system, the highest in the world, structurally the southern edge of the great plateau of central Asia. They extend about 2400 km (1550 mi) along the N Indian border, reaching 8848 m (29 028 ft) at Mount *Everest. The region is disputed by China, India, and Pakistan.

Himmler, Heinrich (1900–45) German politician. He joined the Nazi Party in 1925 and became head of the SS in 1929. From 1936 he also directed the Gestapo and supervised the extermination of Jews in E Europe. After the Nazi collapse he was captured and committed suicide.

Hindemith, Paul (1895–1963) German composer. He studied in Frankfurt am Main, where he led the opera orchestra (1915–23). His music was banned by the Nazis in 1933; he moved to Turkey and in 1939 went to the USA. His early works were highly dissonant; he later evolved his own system of tonal harmony. Many of his compositions are neoclassical in character; they include the opera *Cardillac* (1926), the ballet *Nobilissima Visione* (1938), concertos, sonatas, and much *Gebrauchsmusik* (German: utility music).

Hindenburg, Paul von Beneckendorff und von (1847–1934) German general, who was recalled from retirement at the outbreak of World War I and with' Erich Ludendorff (1865–1937) won a great victory at Tannenberg (1914). In 1916 Hindenburg became commander in chief and directed the German retreat to the **Hindenburg line** (fortified defence on the Western Front). He became president of Germany in 1925 and was re-elected in 1932.

Hindi The national language of India and the most widely spoken, having approximately 134 million speakers. It is an Indo-Aryan language, showing strong *Sanskrit influence in its written form but with a much simpler grammar. The standard form, written in Devanagari script, is based on the Khari Boli dialect of Delhi.

Hinduism The religious beliefs of about 400 million inhabitants of India and parts of neighbouring countries. The complex result of about 5000 years of cultural development, it includes many diverse traditional beliefs and practices. One of its central concepts is that one's actions in life lead to *reincarnation at a higher or lower level of life (*see* KARMA). The goal of the religion is to find a release from the cycle of rebirth and to return to the ultimate unchanging reality, *Brahman. Release may be sought through good works, devotion to a particular god, or through various types of meditation and asceticism (e.g. samadhi, YOGA). The principle gods are Brahma, Vishnu, and Shiva, together known as the *Trimurti. Popular devotion consists mainly of temple worship and the celebration of numerous festivals. The great Hindu texts, the *Mahabharata* and the *Ramayana*, were composed in the 4th century BC. *See also* VEDANTA.

Hindustani An Indo-Aryan language that originated in the dialect of the Delhi district. The Moguls and the British promoted its use as a lingua franca throughout India. *Urdu and *Hindi are the literary forms developed from it.

hip The part of the body at which the legs are joined to the trunk. The skeleton of the hip consists of the *pelvis and the part of the spine (the sacrum) to which it is attached. The hip joint—the articulation between the pelvis and femur (thigh bone)—is a common site for arthritis: in severe cases the whole joint may be replaced by an artificial one or pins or other devices may be inserted into the damaged parts.

Hipparchus (c. 190–c. 120 BC) Greek astronomer, born in Nicaea. He produced the first accurate map of over 1000 stars, indicating their positions by means of latitude and longitude. He also discovered the precession of the equinoxes and accurately measured the distance to the moon by parallax. In mathematics he invented trigonometry by constructing a table of the ratios of the sides of right-angle triangles.

Hippocrates (c. 460–c. 377 BC) Greek physician and founder of the Hippocratic school of medicine, which greatly influenced medical science until the 18th century. Hippocrates was a prominent physician, who travelled widely in Greece and Asia Minor. His followers believed that health was governed by the balance of four body fluids, or humours: phlegm, blood, black bile, and yellow bile. The Hippocratic Oath, taken by medical students in some countries, was probably not written by Hippocrates.

hippopotamus A large hoofed mammal, *Hippopotamus amphibius*, of tropical Africa. About 150 cm high at the shoulder and weighing around 3.5 tonnes, hippos have dark-brown skin and continuously growing tusks up to 60 cm long. They spend the day in rivers or waterholes, emerging at night to graze on surrounding pasture. Herds usually number 10–15 individuals. Family: *Hippopotamidae*. *See also* PYGMY HIPPOPOTAMUS.

Hirohito (1901–89) Emperor of Japan (1926–89), having been regent for five years after his father Yoshihito (1879–1926) had been declared insane. He married (1924) Princess Nagako Kuai. Ruling as divine emperor until Japan's defeat in World War II, he became no more than a constitutional monarch under the 1946 constitution. He also wrote several books on marine biology.

Hiroshima 34 23N 132 27E A city in Japan, in SW Honshu on the delta of the River Ota. A former military base and important seaport, it was largely destroyed (6 August 1945) by the first atomic bomb to be used in warfare; over 130 000 people were killed or injured. The city was rapidly rebuilt and is now a major industrial centre. An international conference is held here annually to oppose nuclear weapons. Population (1995): 1 108 868.

Hispaniola The second largest West Indian island, in the Greater Antilles. It is politically divided between the *Dominican Republic and *Haiti. Area: 18 703 sq km (29 418 sq mi).

histamine An amine, derived from the amino acid histidine, that is released from body tissues after injury or in an allergic reaction, such as asthma or hay fever. It dilates blood vessels, producing inflammation; contracts smooth muscle, which in the lungs leads to breathing difficulties; and stimulates the secretion of gastric juice. Its effects can be counteracted with *antihistamine drugs.

histology The study of tissues. Originally histology was limited to the study of tissues by light microscopy, but the development of such techniques as electron microscopy, immunofluorescence, and autoradiography has enabled the details of subcellular structure to be revealed. *See also* CYTOLOGY.

history The study that discovers, examines, and interprets the records of past human societies, events, and personalities. It is generally regarded as beginning with the ancient Greeks, among whom *Herodotus, *Thucydides, and *Xenophon were outstanding. Notable Roman historians include *Sallust, *Cicero, *Livy, and *Tacitus. Early Christian history writing (historiography) was influenced by Jewish historians, such as Josephus (c. 38–c. 100). Medieval historiography consisted largely of chronicles, such as those of *Bede and Matthew *Paris; the later middle ages were influenced by Byzantine historians, including Anna Comnena (1083–?1148). The classical interests of early Renaissance scholars (*see* HUMANISM) led to a new concern for textual criticism, which led to the work of *Machiavelli and Francesco Guicciardini (1483–1540) in the early 16th century. Their critical approach to sources was continued by 17th-century historians but the 18th-century Enlightenment enlarged the interests of historians to include a more fundamental study of the pattern of change in human societies. This concern is reflected in the work of the 18th-century British historian Edward Gibbon. In the 19th century, under the influence of such German historians as Leopold von Ranke (1795–1886), history was established as a discipline in the universities. Outstanding British historians of the 19th century included William Stubbs, *Macaulay, and *Carlyle. The scope of historiography widened greatly in the 20th century under the influence of sociology, anthropology, and new techniques, such as the use of computers to analyse statistics.

Hitchcock, Sir Alfred (1899–1980) British film director. He worked almost exclusively in Hollywood from 1940. He specialized in sophisticated thrillers, using calculated effects to create tension and suspense. His films include *The Thirty-Nine Steps* (1935), *Strangers on a Train* (1951), *Psycho* (1960), and *The Birds* (1963).

Hitler, Adolf (1889–1945) German dictator. Born in Austria, he won the Iron Cross in World War I. In 1919 he joined the German Workers' Party, which was renamed the National Socialist (abbreviated to Nazi) Party in 1920. He became its president in 1921 and two years later staged an abortive coup—the Munich Putsch—against the Bavarian Government. During a brief imprisonment he wrote most of *Mein Kampf* (*My Struggle*), based on spurious notions of the superiority of the Aryan race and the culpability of the Jews for Germany's defeat in World War I. In the economic crisis of the late 1920s and early 1930s Hitler's oratory and his anticommunism brought the Nazis increasing support. In 1933 he was offered the chancellorship by *Hindenburg, the German president. He gained a majority in the subsequent elections (in coalition with the Nationalists); and in 1934 assumed the title of Führer (leader). He proceeded to crush his opponents, institute his fanatical persecution of the Jews by the establishment of concentration camps, and launch a massive rearmament programme. He lent support to Mussolini in Italy and Franco in Spain, precipitating *World War II by invading Austria (1938) and Czechoslovakia and Poland (1939). As his dreams of world domination collapsed with Germany's defeat, he committed suicide with Eva *Braun (whom he had married shortly before) in the bunker of the chancellory in Berlin.

Hittites An Indo-European people who appeared in Anatolia around the beginnning of the second millennium BC. By 1340 BC they had emerged as a major power, conquering much of Anatolia and also Syria. In their polytheistic religion, their king was believed to be the representative of god on earth and became a god himself on death. The society was feudal in organization and also upheld the institution of slavery. Their language is extinct, but is known from cuneiform tablets and inscriptions.

hives *See* URTICARIA.

Hizbollah (Arabic: Party of God) A Shiite Muslim organization, based in Lebanon, that became notorious for hijackings, hostage taking, and other terrorist activities in the late 1980s. Hizbollah attacks have provoked Israel to launch several offensives against S Lebanon since 1996.

HMSO *See* STATIONERY OFFICE, THE.

hoatzin A primitive bird, *Opisthocomus hoazin*, that occurs in tropical South American swamps. It is 65 cm long and has a small head with a wispy crest and a long tail. Its plumage is streaked brown with yellowish underparts and it feeds chiefly on flowers and fruit. It is the only member of its family (*Opisthocomidae*). Order: *Galliformes* (pheasants, turkeys, etc.).

Hobart 42 54S 147 18E A city in Australia, the capital and chief port of Tasmania on the Derwent River estuary. Industries include zinc refining and food processing; the chief exports are apples, wool, timber, and dairy produce. The University of Tasmania was established here in 1890. Population (1995 est): 194 700.

Hobbes, Thomas (1588–1679) English political philosopher. Hobbes was a proponent of scientific *materialism, particularly with regard to human nature. His interests lay in mathematics, geography, and the classics until the breakdown of English political and social order in the 1640s inspired him to devise his own political theory. *Leviathan* (1651) argues that because people are inherently selfish they need to be ruled by an absolute sovereign, whose function is to enforce public order.

Hobbs, Jack (Sir John Berry H.; 1882–1963) British cricketer. The world's greatest batsman between *Grace and *Bradman, he played for Surrey and for England in 61 Test matches. During his career (1905–34) he scored 61 237 runs and 197 centuries (98 made after the age of 40). He was the first cricketer to be knighted (1953).

Ho Chi Minh (Nguyen That Thanh; 1890–1969) Vietnamese statesman, who led Vietnam in its struggle for independence from the French. As a young man he lived in France. In 1924 he went to communist-controlled Canton, where he formed the Association of Young Vietnamese Revolutionaries (Thanh Nien), the forerunner of the Indochinese Communist Party (1930). Returning to Vietnam in 1941, he formed the *Viet Minh, which waged the long and ultimately victorious colonial war against the French (1945–54; *see* INDOCHINA). According to the Geneva Accords, which Ho Chi Minh attended, Vietnam was divided on either side of the 17th parallel into North Vietnam, of which Ho became president, and South Vietnam. In 1959 he extended support to the *Viet Cong guerrilla movement in the South (*see also* VIETNAM WAR) with the aim of Vietnamese unification, which was achieved after his death.

Ho Chi Minh City (name until 1976: Saigon) 10 46N 106 43E A city in S Vietnam, on the River Saigon. It is the major commercial and industrial centre of the S, with shipbuilding, metalworking, textile, and chemical industries. *History*: an ancient Khmer town, it was the capital of Cochinchina and then of French Indochina (1887–1902). During the *Vietnam War it was the capital of South Vietnam. Population (1993 est): 4 322 300.

hockey An 11-a-side field game, the object of which is to score goals. It has been played in various forms for at least 4000 years. A team comprises a goalkeeper, two full-backs, three half-backs, and five forwards, each of whom carries a curved stick for hitting the ball. Players dribble the ball with the stick and hit it along the ground or through the air. *See also* ICE HOCKEY.

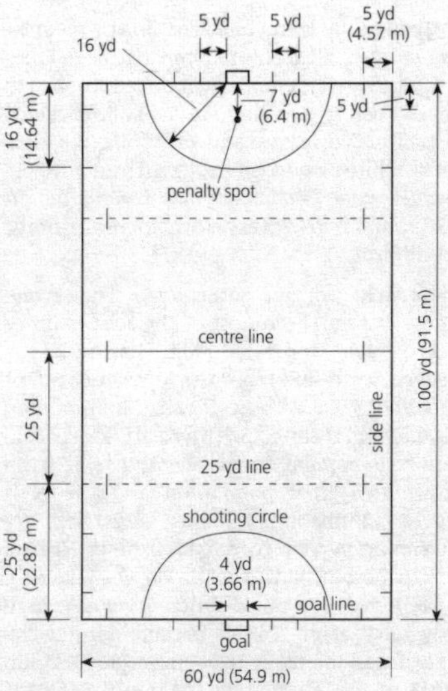

hockey. The dimensions of the pitch.

Hockney, David (1937–) British painter, printmaker, draughtsman, and photographer, born in Bradford. After studying at the Royal College of Art (1959–62), he travelled in the USA, where he developed his witty style, his favourite subjects being figure studies and aquatic themes. Later work includes landscapes. He has also designed stage sets and illustrated books.

Hoffman, Dustin (1937–) US film actor. He made his reputation in the films *The Graduate* (1967) and *Midnight Cowboy* (1969) and won Oscars for *Kramer vs Kramer* (1980) and *Rain Man* (1989). His other films include *Lenny* (1974), *Tootsie* (1982), *Hero* (1992), *Wag the Dog* (1998), and *Goodbye Hello* (2002).

Hogarth, William (1697–1764) British painter and engraver. He established his reputation with the sequence *A Harlot's Progress* (1731–32). He excelled in moralizing social satires in such narrative series as *A Rake's Progress*, *Industry and Idleness*, and the paintings of *Marriage à la Mode* (Tate Gallery), works that led him to campaign for an Engraving Copyright Act (the so-called Hogarth's Act, 1734). The naturalism and vivacity of *Captain Coram* (Foundling Hospital, London) and *Hogarth's Servants* (National Gallery, London) were influential. His artistic theories are expressed in his treatise *The Analysis of Beauty* (1753).

hogweed A biennial herb, *Heracleum sphondylium*, also called cow parsnip, native to Eurasia and N Africa and introduced to North America. Up to 2 m high, it has hollow ridged stems, divided leaves, and umbrella-like clusters of white or pinkish flowers. The giant hogweed (*H. mantegazzianum*) may reach a height of 3.5 m and is grown as an ornamental. Family: *Umbelliferae*.

Hokkaido (former name: Yezo) The second largest and northernmost of the four main islands of Japan, separated from Honshu by the Tsugaru Strait and from the Russian island of Sakhalin by La Perouse Strait. Mountainous, volcanic, and forested, with a relatively cool climate, it is popular for winter sports. It has a sizable aboriginal population and the N is largely uninhabited. Main industries are coalmining, agriculture, and fishing. *History*: the Japanese began to settle on the island in the 16th century but did not develop it seriously until after 1868. It became administratively autonomous in 1885. Area: 78 508 sq km (30 312 sq mi). Population (2000 est): 5 683 000. Capital: Sapporo.

Holbein the Younger, Hans (c. 1497–1543) German painter, born in Augsburg. In 1515 he settled in Basle, where he designed woodcuts. Settling in England in 1532, he painted portraits of merchants before becoming court painter and designer to Henry VIII (1536). His portrait of Henry VIII in a wall painting (destroyed) for Whitehall Palace became the prototype for other paintings of the king. He was also commissioned to paint Henry's prospective wives, including *Anne of Cleves* (Louvre), and established a thriving portrait-painting business, e.g. *The Ambassadors* (National Gallery, London). His father **Hans Holbein the Elder** (c. 1465–1524) was also a painter; he painted the *S Sebastian Altar* (Alte Pinakothek, Munich).

Holiday, Billie (Eleanor Gough McKay; 1915–59) US Black jazz singer, known as "Lady Day." She was discovered in Harlem by Benny Goodman and made her first recording in 1933. She subsequently sang with the bands of Count Basie and Artie Shaw. Addiction to heroin caused her death.

holistic medicine An approach to therapy in which all the physical, mental, and social aspects of the patient's life are taken into account in understanding and curing his or her disease, as opposed to merely treating symptoms. The holistic approach is a basic tenet of *alternative medicine.

Holland The low-lying NW region of the Netherlands, now comprising the provinces of North Holland and South Holland. A county of the Holy Roman Empire from the 12th century, Holland came under Burgundy in the 15th century and then (1500) under the Habsburgs. Prominent in the 16th-century *Revolt of the Netherlands against Spanish Habsburg rule, Holland became the chief province of the independent United Provinces of the Netherlands. When the kingdom of the *Netherlands was established in 1814, its importance diminished. Nevertheless the whole country is still commonly called Holland.

holly A tree or shrub of the widely distributed genus *Ilex* (300 species). The evergreen English holly (*I. aquifolium*) grows to a height of 15 m and has spiny lustrous dark-green leaves and small white flowers; the female flowers develop into red berries. It is widely cultivated for hedging and used for Christmas decorations. Family: *Aquifoliaceae*. *See also* MATÉ.

hollyhock A perennial herb, *Althaea rosea*, native to China but widely cultivated. Up to 3 m high, it bears large white, yellow, or red flowers. Family: *Malvaceae*.

Hollywood 34 00N 118 15W A NW suburb of Los Angeles, in California in the USA. Founded in the 1880s, it is the centre of the US film industry. Population (1996 est): 127 894.

holmium (Ho) A metallic lanthanide element, discovered in 1879 by P. T. Cleve (1840–1905) and named after his native city, Stockholm. Holmium occurs in rare-earth minerals, such as monazite ($CePO_4$). It forms an oxide (Ho_2O_3) and halides (HoX_3), but has few uses. At no 67; at wt 164.93032; mp 1474°C; bp 2700°C.

holocaust The extermination of European *Jews by the Germans (1939–45). Some six million Jews from many countries, two-thirds of European Jewry, were killed in Auschwitz and other *concentration camps.

Holocene epoch The present, or Recent, epoch in geological time, including the last 10 000 years from the end of the Pleistocene. Some authorities consider it to be an interglacial phase of the Pleistocene. At the beginning of the Holocene the rise in sea level resulting from melting ice isolated Britain from the rest of Europe.

holography A method of producing a stereoscopic image without using a camera. A beam of monochromatic coherent radiation from a *laser is split into two using a semitransparent mirror; one beam falls directly onto a photographic film or plate and the other is reflected by the subject onto the film. The two beams form *interference patterns on the film, which is called a hologram. To reconstruct the image, light of the same wavelength from a laser is shone onto the hologram. The interference pattern on the hologram diffracts the beam and splits it into two parts. One part gives a real two-dimensional image and the other gives a virtual three-dimensional image.

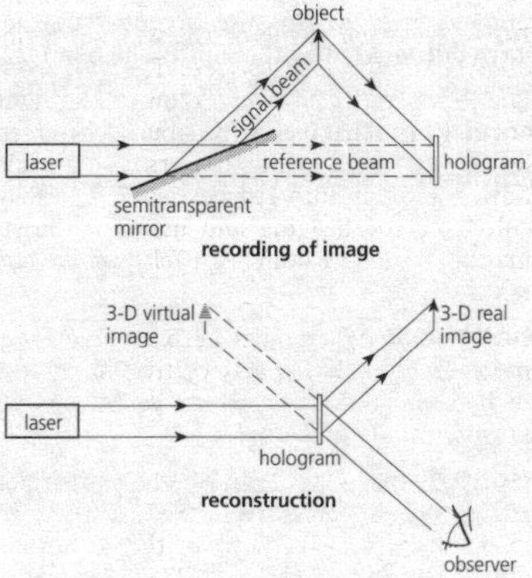

holography. A three-dimensional image formed by two beams of light is recorded as an interference pattern on a single plate. The two images, giving a 3-D effect, are reconstructed by shining a similar beam through the hologram.

Holst, Gustav (Theodore) (1874–1934) British composer. Having studied composition at the Royal College of Music, he taught at the Royal College, Morley College, and St Paul's Girls' School. His interest in oriental philosophy inspired the chamber opera *Savitri* (1908) and other works. Among his most famous compositions are the choral work *The Hymn of Jesus* (1917), the tone poem *Egdon Heath* (1927), and the orchestral suite *The Planets* (1914–16).

Holy Grail In medieval legend, a vessel or dish having supernatural power. Originally the grail may have had some significance in pre-Christian Celtic mythology; but by the 12th century it was associated with the chalice used by Christ at the Last Supper and later given to *Joseph of Arimathea, who received the blood of Christ in it at the crucifixion. Chrétien de Troyes combined the grail legend with the *Arthurian legend, and the knightly quest for the Holy Grail is a dominant theme in many Arthurian romances. According to a passage in William of Malmesbury (c. 1090–c. 1143), Joseph brought the Holy Grail to Glastonbury.

Holy Island 1. (*or* **Lindisfarne**) 55 41N 1 48W An island, in NE England off the NE coast of Northumberland. Its monastery was founded by St Aidan (635 AD); St Cuthbert was a bishop here (685–87). **2.** An island off the NW coast of Anglesey.

holy orders In Christian Churches, specifically those accepting episcopacy, the ranks of bishop, priest, etc., conferred by a bishop. They are traditionally divided into major and minor orders, the former being the ranks of bishop, priest, deacon, and (in the Roman Church) subdeacon. Holy orders are considered a *sacrament by the Orthodox and Roman Catholic Churches. Women priests were first ordained in the Church of England in 1994.

Holy Roman Empire The successor to the western *Roman Empire of antiquity. The institution dates from 800, when *Charlemagne was crowned emperor of the West by Pope Leo III. Its territory came to comprise much of W and central Europe, being centred on Germany and Austria and including areas of E France and N Italy. After the failure of Charlemagne's Carolingian dynasty the imperial title passed (962) to the German kings, who retained it until the Empire's abolition in 1806. Between the 11th and 13th centuries the emperors vied with the popes for dominance in Europe (*see* GUELFS AND GHIBELLINES), a conflict from which the Empire emerged much weakened. It was further undermined by the *Reformation in the 16th century, the *Thirty Years' War in the 17th century, and the rise of Prussia and was finally broken by Napoleon's conquest of imperial territories in the early 19th century.

Holyrood House A palace in Edinburgh, which is the Scottish residence of the British monarch. A medieval building, it was substantially modified in the classical style from 1671 onwards by Sir William Bruce (d. 1710).

Holy Spirit (*or* **Holy Ghost**) In Christian theology, the third person of the Trinity, coequal and of one substance with the Father and the

Son. Old Testament references to the spirit of God are given a more specific application in the New Testament Gospels: in St John's Gospel the Holy Spirit is seen as the "Paraclete" or Comforter; in Acts, the descent of the Holy Spirit upon the Apostles is described. In art, the Holy Spirit is usually symbolized by a dove.

Home of the Hirsel, Alec Douglas-Home, Baron (Alexander Frederick D.-H.; 1903–95) British statesman; Conservative prime minister (1963–64). He was an MP (1931–45, 1950–51) before he became the 14th Earl of Home. After serving as foreign secretary (1960–63), he renounced his peerages to become prime minister. Following the Conservative electoral defeat (1964) he resigned the party leadership (1965). He received a life peerage in 1974.

homeopathy The system of treating illness developed by Samuel *Hahnemann at the end of the 18th century and based on the principle of "like cures like." To treat a disease homeopaths prescribe tiny doses of a drug that in larger quantities would cause the symptoms of the disease.

Homer (8th century BC) Greek epic poet, presumed author of the *Iliad* and *Odyssey*. He is believed to have lived in Ionia in Asia Minor and according to legend was blind. The *Iliad* concerns the Trojan War, and its basic tragic theme is enlivened by the human sympathy of its individual episodes. The *Odyssey* relates the various adventures of *Odysseus during his voyage home from the Trojan War to his kingdom of Ithaca. Both poems have had a profound influence on western culture.

Home Rule An Irish political movement to repeal the Act of *Union with Britain and give Ireland a legislature responsible for domestic affairs. Founded in 1870, the Home Rule movement achieved parliamentary prominence under the leadership of *Parnell from 1880. The Home Rule bills of 1886 and 1893 were defeated; in 1914 the third Home Rule bill was passed but suspended for the duration of the war. A modified act was passed in 1920 providing separate parliaments for northern and southern Ireland. This was accepted by the north but rejected by the south, which in 1922 gained dominion status as the Irish Free State.

homing instinct *See* MIGRATION, ANIMAL.

hominid A member of the *Hominidae* family

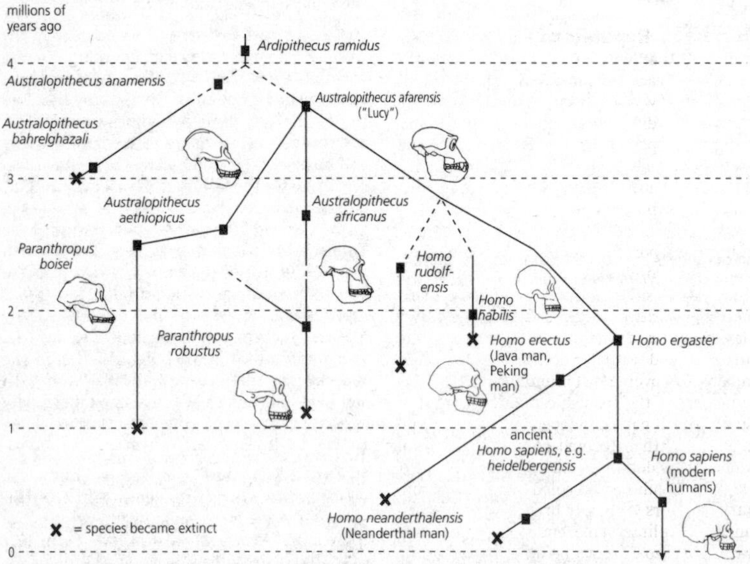

Homo. The human evolutionary tree is still far from complete: the picture is constantly changing as new fossil evidence comes to light. Palaeoanthropologists are still debating many of the relationships shown on this chart (indicated by the broken lines).

of primates, to which humans (*Homo sapiens*) belong. Besides *H. sapiens*, there are no surviving hominids: the others are known only from fossil remains. The *Hominidae* include the genera *Australopithecus*, and *Homo*.

Homo A genus of *hominids characterized by a large cranial capacity, erect posture, bipedal gait, a thumb capable of a precision grip, and the ability to make and use tools. *Homo erectus* (formerly called *Pithecanthropus*) first appeared 1.8 million years ago and made hand axes. A contemporaneous species was *H. ergastes*, which is thought by many authorities to be the earliest direct ancestor of modern humans. *Neanderthal man also belongs to the genus *Homo*, as does *Cro-Magnon man, who was probably an early form of the species *Homo sapiens*. *See also* AUSTRALOPITHECUS.

homosexuality Sexual attraction or relations between persons of the same sex. It is known as lesbianism when the persons involved are females. Homosexual acts between consenting adults in private are now legal in all EU countries. In 1994 the age of consent for homosexual men in the UK was lowered from 21 to 18, and in 2000 the age of consent for both homosexuals and heterosexuals was equalized at 16.

Honduras, Republic of A country in Central America, with a N coastline on the Caribbean Sea and a short S one on the Pacific Ocean. Narrow coastal plains rise to mountainous country, dissected by river valleys. The majority of the population is of mixed Indian and Spanish descent. *Economy*: mainly agricultural, the chief crops are bananas and coffee (the principal exports). Almost half the land is forested, with valuable hardwoods and pine. Fishing is important, especially shrimps for export. The considerable mineral resources include gold, silver, lead, tin and zinc, and mercury. *History*: the area was a centre of Mayan culture from the 4th to the 9th centuries AD and was later occupied by the Lenca Indians. Discovered by Columbus in 1502, it became part of the Spanish captaincy general of Guatemala. It gained independence from Spain in 1821 and then formed part of the Central American Federation (1823–38). For the next 145 years Honduras was ruled by a series of military dictators with only brief periods of civilian rule. Military rule ended in 1982, when Roberto Suazo Córdova became president; the current president is Ricardo Maduro. Honduras suffered its worst natural disaster of modern times in Nov 1998, when torrential rains in the wake of Hurricane Mitch devastated the capital leaving 8000 dead and 250 000 homeless. Honduras is a member of the OAS and the Organization of Central American States. Official language: Spanish. Currency: lempira of 100 centavos. Area: 112 088 sq km (43 227 sq mi). Population (2003 est): 6 803 000. Capital: Tegucigalpa.

Honegger, Arthur (1892–1955) French composer, born in Switzerland. He was a pupil of Widor and d'Indy and one of Les Six. He developed his own polyphonic and dissonant style. His compositions include five symphonies, the stage works *King David* (1921) and *Joan of Arc at the Stake* (1934–35), chamber music, and piano music.

honesty A herbaceous plant of the European genus *Lunaria* (3 species). Up to 1 m high, it is often grown in gardens for its papery seed heads. *L. annua* has white to purple flowers while *L. variegata* has crimson flowers and variegated foliage. Family: *Cruciferae*.

honey A sweet thick yellow syrup collected from the honeycomb of bee hives. Bees suck nectar from flowers and empty it into the cells of their hives, where they convert the sugar it contains from sucrose into dextrose and laevulose. Honey consists of about 70% sugars, 18% water, and small amounts of minerals, pollen, and wax.

honey badger *See* RATEL.

honeybee A social *bee, *Apis mellifera*, also called hive bee. Native to Europe, it is reared worldwide for its *honey and *beeswax. Honeybees have large colonies with 50 000–80 000 workers during the summer and a well-defined caste system. Workers attend to nest building, food gathering, and brood care; they use dances to communicate the location of food sources to other colony members. The queen lays her eggs in wax chambers (cells). Larvae hatching from fertilized eggs and fed on protein-rich "royal jelly" throughout their development become queens. New colonies are formed by a swarm of workers led by the old queen (*compare* BUMBLEBEE); a young queen continues the established colony. Family: *Apidae*.

honeyeater An arboreal songbird belonging to a family (*Meliphagidae*; 160 species) occurring chiefly in SE Asia and Australasia. They are 10 to 35 cm long and have a drab plumage. The slender bill is down-curved and the long extensible tongue has a central trough, through which nectar is drunk, and a brush-like tip for collecting pollen and small insects.

honeysuckle A shrub or twining plant of

the genus *Lonicera* (100 species). The common European honeysuckle (*L. periclymenum*), also called woodbine, is a trailing shrub with clusters of tubular yellowish flowers. Some species are cultivated as ornamentals, including the fragrant climbing honeysuckle (*L. japonica*). Family: *Caprifoliaceae.*

Hong Kong A special administrative region of S China, which until 1 July 1997 was a British crown colony. It consists of the island of Hong Kong, the mainland peninsula of Jiulong, the New Territories, and Stonecutters Island. Much of the land is steep and barren. The majority of the population is Chinese. *Economy*: owing to its strategic position and fine natural harbour, it is an important entrepôt and banking centre. Much of China's foreign trade passes through Hong Kong. The export of manufactured goods has become increasingly important since World War II and the textile and clothing industry accounts for over half the total domestic exports. Electronics and plastics are also important and there is some heavy industry. Tourism is a major source of revenue. A new airport (the world's largest) opened in 1998. *History*: the island was ceded to Britain by China at the end of the first Opium War (1842) and Kowloon (Jiulong) was added in 1860. In 1898 the New Territories were granted on a 99-year lease. Hong Kong was occupied by the Japanese during World War II. The 1980s saw a big influx of refugees from Vietnam (boat people) and the first forced repatriations. The return of the colony to Chinese control in 1997 was agreed between Britain and China in 1984. In 1992 Chris Patten was appointed governor to oversee the transition to Chinese rule. Hong Kong is now governed by an executive council, headed by the chief executive, and an elected legislative council. Official languages: Chinese and English. Currency: Hong Kong dollar of 100 cents. Area: 1031 sq km (398 sq mi). Population (2002 est): 6 785 000. Administrative centre: Victoria.

Honolulu 21 19N 157 50W A city in the USA, the capital of Hawaii on SE Oahu in the central Pacific Ocean. It is the site of three universities and of Iolani Palace, the former royal residence. *Pearl Harbor is still an important naval base. Population (2000): 371 657.

Honshu The largest of the four main islands of Japan, situated between the Pacific Ocean and the Sea of Japan. It is mountainous, volcanic, and prone to earthquakes. The historic centre of Japan, it has been the site of its capital since earliest times. Most of Japan's major ports and cities are here. Rice, fruit, cotton, and tea are grown; mineral wealth includes oil, zinc, and copper. The traditional industry is silk but the many modern industries include shipbuilding, iron and steel, chemicals, and textiles. Area: 230 448 sq km (88 976 sq mi). Population (1995): 100 995 000. Chief town: Tokyo.

Hooch, Pieter de (1629–c. 1684) Dutch painter, born in Rotterdam. Working in Delft, Leiden, and Amsterdam, he excelled in small paintings, such as *The Pantry* (Rijksmuseum, Amsterdam), depicting household tasks in courtyards or dark interiors.

Hood, Samuel, 1st Viscount (1724–1816) British admiral, who achieved eminence in the American Revolution, when he defeated the French off Dominica (1782). In the French Revolutionary Wars he captured Toulon (1793) and destroyed the defences of Corsica (1794).

Hooke, Robert (1635–1703) British physicist and instrument maker. In 1660 he discovered **Hooke's law**, which states that for an elastic body, the stress is directly proportioned to the strain. Many of his microscope studies were published in *Micrographia* (1665). Appointed a city surveyor after the Fire of London, he designed several buildings, including the College of Physicians.

Hook of Holland (Dutch name: Hoek van Holland) 51 59N 4 07E A port in the SW Netherlands, in South Holland province at the North Sea end of the Nieuwe Waterweg (New Waterway). A ferry service operates from here to Harwich, England.

hookworm A parasitic *nematode worm inhabiting the intestine of animals and man. About 1 cm long, hookworms attach themselves to the gut lining and feed by sucking blood and body fluids. The two main species infecting man are *Necator americanus*, of the southern USA and Africa, and the Eurasian *Ancylostoma duodenale.*

Hoover, Herbert (Clark) (1874–1964) US statesman; Republican president (1929–33). As secretary of commerce (1921–29) he was chairman of commissions that initiated construction of the Hoover Dam (named after him) and the St Lawrence Seaway.

hop A perennial climbing herb, *Humulus lupus.* Native to Eurasia, where it grows to a length of 3–6 m in hedges and thickets, it is widely cultivated for its pale yellow-green female flowers ("cones"), which are used in brewing to flavour beer. Family: *Cannabiaceae.*

Hope, Bob (Leslie Townes Hope; 1903–2003) US comedian, born in Britain. He starred in a number of popular films during the 1940s, including *Road to Zanzibar* (1941) and other "Road" films in which he partnered Bing *Crosby. He gave many performances for US troops. He was awarded an honorary British knighthood in 1998.

Hopkins, Gerard Manley (1844–89) British poet. He converted to Roman Catholicism in 1866 and was ordained as a Jesuit priest in 1877. In verse of daring originality he rejected conventional metres in favour of a flexible "sprung rhythm." "The Wreck of the Deutschland" and "The Windhover" are among his best-known poems, which were published posthumously in 1918.

Horace (Quintus Horatius Flaccus; 65–8 BC) Roman poet. Reduced to poverty after fighting for Brutus in the Civil War, he became a leading poet under the emperor Augustus and acquired a farm near Rome, celebrated in his poetry. His *Odes* and his *Satires* and verse *Epistles* vividly portray contemporary Roman society.

hormone A substance that is secreted into the blood in small quantities to cause a response in a specific target organ or tissue of the body. Hormones are produced and secreted by *endocrine glands and by specialized nerve cells (*see* NEUROHORMONE) under the control of the nervous system or in response to changes in the chemical composition of the blood. Hormones regulate short-term physiological processes, such as digestion, and long-term changes, such as those associated with growth and reproduction; they also help to maintain a constant internal environment in the body. The following are some of the more important hormones known in humans: *ACTH, *gonadotrophin, *growth hormone, and *prolactin (secreted by the pituitary); *corticosteroids, e.g. cortisone, and *adrenaline (from the adrenal glands); *androgens and *oestrogens (from the sex glands); thyroid hormone (from the *thyroid gland); *insulin and glucagon (from the pancreas). Chemically, most hormones are proteins or steroids. The study of hormones is called endocrinology.

hornbeam A tree of the genus *Carpinus* (26 species), of N temperate regions. The common Eurasian hornbeam (*C. betulus*) has smooth grey bark, oval pointed leaves with prominent veins, and small nuts with conspicuous winged bracts. It is planted for ornament and for its hard fine-grained timber. Family: *Corylaceae*.

hornbill A bird belonging to a family (*Bucerotidae*; 45 species) occurring in Old World tropical regions. 38–150 cm long, hornbills are characterized by a huge bill, often bearing a large bony "helmet," and feed on fruit and berries. Order: *Coraciiformes* (kingfishers, etc.).

hornblende A mineral of the *amphibole group, which occurs widely in igneous and metamorphic rocks. It consists mainly of silicates of sodium, calcium, magnesium, and iron. It is black or greenish black and occurs in crystalline or massive form.

hornet A social *wasp, *Vespa crabro*, that is common throughout Europe and has spread to North America and elsewhere. 35 mm long, it is tawny-yellow with brown markings and nests in hollow trees. It feeds chiefly on insects, nectar, and fruit juices and its painful sting can be dangerous to humans. Members of the genera *Dolichorespula*, *Paravespula*, and *Vespula* may also be known as hornets.

Horowitz, Vladimir (1904–89) Russian pianist, who settled in the USA in 1940. Horowitz excelled in Russian music and in his own transcriptions.

horse A hoofed mammal, *Equus caballus*, domesticated for pack and draught work, riding, and sport. The earliest horse is believed to have been *eohippus, which is thought to have originated in North America and spread to Asia. Successive larger forms evolved, in which the central toe became enlarged as the hoof; these horses developed from forest browsers to become grazing animals of the plains.

The many breeds of modern horse are grouped into ponies, light horses, and draught horses. They range in size from the tiny Falabella (developed in Argentina from Shetland pony stock) to the massive *Shire horse and are measured in hands (1 hand = 4 in = 10.16 cm) to the top of the shoulders (withers). According to breed, horses mature at 3½–5 years of age and the lifespan is usually 20–35 years. Mares have a gestation period of 11 months, producing usually a single foal. Horses belong to the family *Equidae*, which also includes asses and *zebras. See illustration on p. 430.

horse chestnut A broad spreading tree, *Aesculus hippocastanum*, native to SE Europe and widely planted as an ornamental. It grows to a height of 25 m, producing large compound leaves and white flowers; the green spiny fruits ripen to release large brown shiny seeds (conkers). Family: *Hippocastanaceae*.

horse fly A stout-bodied fly of the genus *Tabanus* (the term is also used loosely for the other genera—*Chrysops* (deerflies) and *Haema-*

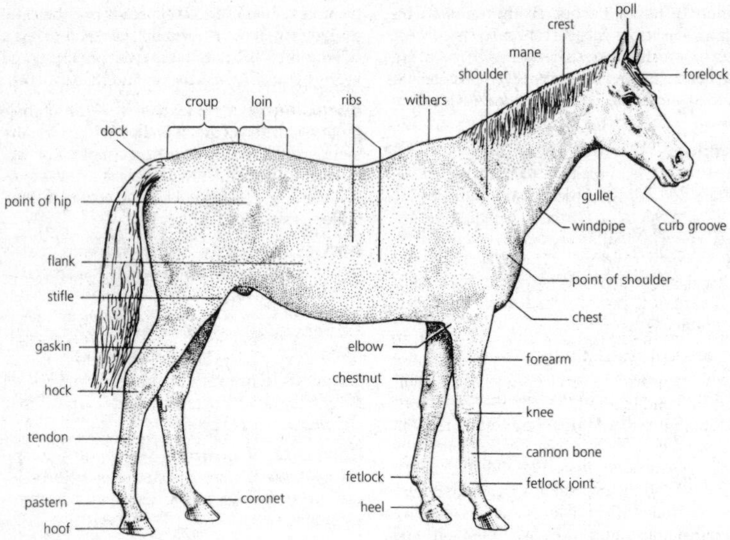

horse. The points of a horse.

topota (cleg flies)—of the family *Tabanidae*; 2500 species). Male horse flies feed on nectar but the females are bloodsuckers and inflict painful bites on man, horses, cattle, etc. A few species transmit diseases, such as tularemia and anthrax.

horsepower (hp) A unit of power equal to 550 foot-pounds per second. It was devised by James *Watt, who found that a strong horse could raise a weight of 150 pounds 4 feet in 1 second. *See also* WATT.

horseradish A perennial herb, *Armoracia rusticana*, probably native to SE Europe and W Asia and widely cultivated. Growing to a height of 125 cm, it has fleshy pungent roots from which horseradish sauce is made and it bears small white flowers. Family: *Cruciferae*.

horseshoe crab A large nocturnal marine *arthropod (up to 50 cm long), also called king crab, belonging to the subclass *Xiphosura*. The two living genera, *Limulus* and *Tachypleus*, are found in shallow waters on the E coasts of North America and Asia respectively. They have a hinged body covered by a brown horseshoe-shaped carapace and a long tail spine. They can swim but usually burrow in sand, feeding on worms and thin-shelled molluscs. Class: *Meristomata*.

horticulture The cultivation of vegetables (also known as market gardening) and fruit for food and of trees, shrubs, and other plants for ornament. Horticulture is both a popular domestic pastime and an important commercial activity. Higher-yielding and more disease-resistant plant varieties, increased mechanization, the use of new cultivation techniques, and the application of fertilizers and pesticides have all contributed to improved productivity and quality.

Horus The Egyptian sun-god, usually portrayed as a falcon or with a falcon's head. He was the son of *Osiris and *Isis. The pharaohs were conceived as the incarnations of Horus as earthly ruler and added the god's name to their titles.

hospice An establishment that provides care for the terminally ill. Hospices specialize in easing the physical and mental distress of the patients and providing support for their families. Most modern hospices are modelled on St Christopher's hospice, founded in London in 1967 by Dame Cicely *Saunders.

hospital An institution providing diagnostic and therapeutic services for the sick on a residential (in-patient) or nonresidential (out-patient) basis. In the ancient world such medical services as existed were provided by religious organizations. In Europe in the middle ages many institutions for the care of the sick were founded by monastic orders and later, during the Crusades, by orders of knighthood. St Bartholomew's (1123) and St Thomas's (1207) in London date back to this period. In the UK, during the 18th and 19th centuries, many new voluntary hospitals were founded by philanthropists and staffed by doctors who gave their services free. Municipal hospitals with paid medical staff arose alongside the voluntary hospitals; both systems were nationalized by the National Health Service Act (1946). Since then all NHS hospitals have provided free services, although some have a small number of paybeds. In the 1990s many hospitals opted to be run by self-governing NHS trusts, obtaining income by providing services to health authorities and fund-holding GPs. In 1999 the Labour government replaced this "internal market" in NHS services with a system under which the trusts contract long-term service agreements with teams of doctors and nurses (primary care groups). Under the Private Finance Initiative (1992), hospitals can now be built, financed, and operated by private interests who lease them to the NHS. From 2004 the best-performing hospitals can apply to become so-called "foundation hospitals," which will enjoy greater administrative autonomy. *See also* NATIONAL HEALTH SERVICE.

Hospitallers (Order of the Hospital of St John of Jerusalem) A religious order of knighthood that began as a hospital for pilgrims to Jerusalem (c. 1070) and during the *Crusades took on a military function. The Hospitallers were the great rivals of the *Templars and immensely wealthy. After the fall of Acre (1291) they established themselves in Cyprus, Rhodes, and finally Malta.

Hosta A genus of perennial herbaceous plants (10 species), native to China and Japan and widely planted in gardens. They are grown chiefly for their often variegated foliage—but they also produce attractive spikes of purplish or white funnel-shaped flowers. Family: *Liliaceae.*

Houdini, Harry (Erich Weiss; 1874–1926) US magician. His ability to escape from handcuffs, straitjackets, and locked containers, even when under water, gained him an international reputation.

housefly A dull-grey fly, *Musca domestica*, that is a worldwide household pest. The adult is 5–7 mm long, with mouthparts used for sucking up organic liquids of all kinds. Through the contamination of food it spreads many serious diseases, such as typhoid, tuberculosis, and dysentery. Family: *Muscidae.*

Houston 29 45N 95 25W A city in the USA, the main port in Texas. Founded in 1836, it is named after the Texan leader Sam(uel) Houston (1793–1863). It expanded rapidly following the building of a canal (1912–14), linking it to the Gulf of Mexico, and the development of coastal oilfields. One of the world's major oil and petrochemical centres, Houston also has shipbuilding and steel manufacture. The Lyndon B. Johnson Space Center is nearby. Population (2000): 1 953 631.

hovercraft (*or* **air-cushion vehicle**) A ship-like vehicle equipped with powerful blowers capable of lifting it off a surface so that it rides on a cushion of air, which is contained within a rubber skirt. It can navigate on almost any kind of surface and is moved forward by propellers. The first hovercraft was built by Christopher *Cockerell in 1959. Hovercraft were used as ferries between England and France but have been superseded by high-speed *hydrofoils, which use less fuel.

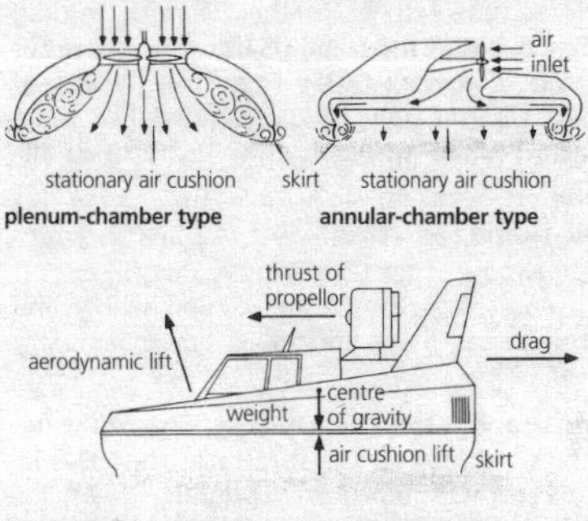

hovercraft. In the plenum chamber the air cushion is produced by a horizontal fan; the cushion in the centre is almost at rest and is surrounded by a fast-moving ring of turbulent air. In the annular chamber the cushion is formed within an annular ring of jets, the nozzles of which are sloped inwards. The lower figure shows the forces acting on a hovercraft.

hoverfly A fly, also called a flowerfly or syrphid fly, belonging to the family *Syrphidae* (about 4000 species). Many species are black and yellow, resembling bees and wasps, but they do not sting. The larvae of many hoverflies are scavengers in decaying organic matter or the nests of ants, termites, or bees.

Howard, Catherine (c. 1520–42) The fifth wife (1540–42) of Henry VIII of England. She was beheaded for treason when Henry learnt of her premarital love affairs.

Howard, Sir Ebenezer (1850–1928) British theorist of town planning. His book *Garden Cities of Tomorrow*, first published under this title in 1902, propounds his concept of ideal spacious suburbs. This was first realized in the planning of Letchworth (1903), Lutyens' design for Hampstead (1908), and Welwyn Garden City (1920).

Howard, John (c. 1726–90) English prison reformer. Horrified by conditions in Bedford gaol, which he inspected while high sheriff of Bedfordshire, Howard campaigned for sanitary improvements and wages for gaolers. An act of 1774 achieved his aims. The **Howard League for Penal Reform**, founded in 1866 as the Howard Association, was named after him.

h

Howard, John (Winston) (1939–) Australian politician; prime minister (1996–). The leader of the Liberal Party from 1985 to 1989 and again from 1995, he led his party to victory in elections in 1996, 1998, and 2001.

Howard, Leslie (Leslie Howard Stainer; 1890–1943) British actor of Hungarian descent. He became famous as the romantic leading man in both British and US films, including *The Scarlet Pimpernel* (1935), *Pygmalion* (1938), and *Gone with the Wind* (1939). He was killed when his aeroplane was shot down by German aircraft.

Howard, Michael (1941–) British politician; leader of the Conservative Party (2003–). He entered parliament in 1983 and held several ministerial posts, including home secretary (1993–97).

Howard, Trevor (1916–88) British actor. After working in the theatre in the 1930s he concentrated on films, including *Brief Encounter* (1946), *The Third Man* (1949), *Mutiny on the Bounty* (1962), *Ryan's Daughter* (1970), and *White Mischief* (1987).

Howe, (Richard Edward) Geoffrey, Baron (1926–) British Conservative politician; chancellor of the exchequer (1979–83); foreign secretary (1983–89). He became deputy prime minister in 1989 but unexpectedly resigned in 1990, contributing to the fall of Margaret Thatcher as prime minister.

howitzer A low-velocity *artillery firearm with a shorter barrel and a larger bore than a gun but a smaller bore and longer barrel than a *mortar. They are often mounted on carriages that enable them to fire either flat gun-type trajectories or arched mortar-type trajectories. They were widely used in World War I. The word comes from the Dutch *houwitzer*, catapult.

howler monkey A large monkey belonging to the genus *Alouatta* (6 species), of Central and South American forests. Howlers are 115–180 cm long including the tail (58–91 cm) and are named after their loud voices. They have beards over their enlarged throats, prehensile tails, and live in groups of up to 40 individuals. Family: *Cebidae*.

Hoya *See* WAXPLANT.

Hoyle, Sir Fred (1915–2001) British astronomer, who with Hermann Bondi (1919–) and Thomas Gold (1920–) proposed the *steady-state theory of the universe. His other theoretical studies were mainly concerned with stellar evolution. He was also a leading science writer and a notable science-fiction writer.

Huancayo 12 05S 75 12W A city in W Peru, the chief commercial centre of the central Andes. It has a cathedral and a university (1962). Population (1998 est): 305 039.

Huang Hai *See* YELLOW SEA.

Huang Ho *See* YELLOW RIVER.

Hubble constant (H_o) The rate at which the velocity of expansion of the universe changes with distance. It relates the recessional velocity, V, of a distant galaxy to its distance, D. **Hubble's law**, proposed in 1929 by the US astronomer Edwin Hubble (1889–1953), states that recessional velocity and distance are directly proportional: $V = H_oD$.

Hubli 15 20N 75 14E A city in India, in Karnataka. Together with Dharwar, it forms one of the state's most populous areas. Industries include cotton and newspapers. Population (1991): 647 640.

Huddersfield 53 39N 1 47W A town in N England, in Kirklees unitary authority, West Yorkshire, at the confluence of the Rivers Colne and Holme. Formerly a major wool textile town, Huddersfield now has important manufacturing and chemical industries; it is also a centre for culture and sport. Population (1991): 143 726.

Hudson, Henry (d. 1611) English navigator. In 1607 he sailed in search of the *Northeast Passage to China, reaching Spitzbergen. He tried again, unsuccessfully, in 1608. On a third voyage, under the auspices of the Dutch East India Company, he sailed some 240 km (150 mi) down what came to be called the Hudson River.

His fourth voyage (1610–11) took him to what is now Hudson Bay, where his men mutinied and cast him adrift.

Hudson Bay A huge shallow oceanic bay in N central Canada, linked to the Atlantic Ocean by Hudson Strait and to the Arctic Ocean by Foxe Channel. Frozen during winter, in summer it carries grain ships from W Canada to Europe.

Hudson River A river in the NE USA, flowing from the Adirondack Mountains to New York Bay, where it forms part of New York Harbor. An important commercial waterway, it is linked by canals with the *Great Lakes and the *St Lawrence River. Length: 492 km (306 mi).

Hudson's Bay Company A fur-trading company, formed in 1670, that was given settlement and trading rights in Canada. It engaged in rivalry with the Northwest Company from the 1780s until 1821, when they were united under the name of the Hudson's Bay Company. In 1870 it sold its territories to Canada but remained a major fur-trading agency with headquarters in London.

Hue 16 28N 107 35E An ancient city in central Vietnam, on the Huong estuary. A commercial centre, Hue has textile, timber, and cement industries. *History*: a Chinese military stronghold from about 200 BC, Hue lat er fell to Champa and after 1635 was the capital of Annam and after 1802 of the short-lived Vietnamese empire. It suffered heavily during the Vietnam War. Population (1992 est): 219 149.

Hughes, Howard (Robard) (1905–76) US aviator, film producer, and multi-millionaire. After founding the Hughes Aircraft Company he broke the landplane speed record in 1935, reaching a speed of 352 mph. His films include *Hell's Angels* (1930), *Scarface* (1932), and *The Outlaw* (1944). From 1950 until his death he lived in seclusion.

Hughes, Ted (1930–98) British poet. His first volume, *The Hawk in the Rain* (1957), contained many poems concerned with the natural world written in a forceful energetic style. The poems in *Crow* (1970) are characterized by increased violence of language and subject matter. He became poet laureate in 1984. Later works include the adaptation *Tales from Ovid* (1997) and *Birthday Letters* (1998), a sequence of poems about his doomed marriage to Sylvia *Plath. He was appointed to the OM in 1998.

Hugo, Victor (Marie) (1802–85) French poet, dramatist, and novelist. After several early novels and volumes of poetry, his leadership of the Romantic movement was confirmed by the success of his drama *Hernani* (1831). During the 1840s he became involved in republican politics and, after the coup d'état by the future Napoleon III in 1851, he went into exile in the Channel Islands until 1870. His later major works included *Les Contemplations* (1856), a volume of poems, and the novel *Les Misérables* (1862).

Huguenots French Protestants. Their name is derived from the Swiss-German *Eidgenoss*, confederate. The Huguenots, chiefly followers of John Calvin, were soon an influential national minority. The rivalry of their leaders with the prominent Roman Catholic Guise family caused the *Wars of Religion (1562–94). The Edict of Nantes (1598) guaranteed the Huguenots freedom of worship but after the revocation of the Edict (1685) over 250 000 Huguenots emigrated.

Hu Jintao (1942–) Chinese politician, who succeeded *Jiang Zemin as general secretary of the Communist Party in 2002 and as president of China in 2003. He was previously vice president (1998–2003).

Hull *See* KINGSTON-UPON-HULL.

humanism **1.** The intellectual movement that formed the basis of Renaissance culture. Humanist scholars were inspired by the rediscovery and study of classical Greek and Roman authors, which had been initiated in Italy by such men as *Petrarch and *Boccaccio. Turning away from the theological bias of their predecessors, they concentrated on human achievements. *Erasmus was the greatest N European humanist. **2.** A 20th-century philosophical viewpoint based on atheism, holding religion to be an outmoded superstition.

human rights Privileges claimed or enjoyed by a human being simply by virtue of being human. The concept developed from Roman ideas of "natural law" entailing "natural rights" to 20th-century liberal acceptance of the idea that human beings should have certain equal civil, political, and economic rights. The UN Universal Declaration of Human Rights (1948), itself not a legally binding code, has spawned various subsequent agreements, such as the Covenants on Civil and Political Rights and on Economic, Social, and Cultural Rights (1966), accepted as binding by 35 states. A UN High Commissioner for Human Rights was appointed in 1994. The European Convention on Human Rights was promulgated in 1950 and the European Court of Human Rights established in 1959. In 1998 the UK parliament passed the Human Rights Act, under which the European convention on Human Rights was incorporated into English law.

Humber An estuary in N England, flowing from the confluence of the Rivers Ouse and Trent to the North Sea past the ports of Kingston-upon-Hull, Immingham, and Grimsby. The **Humber Bridge** (opened 1981) was formerly the world's longest single-span suspension bridge, with a main span of 1410 m (4626 ft). Length: 64 km (40 mi).

Humboldt Current (*or* **Peru Current**) An ocean current constituting part of the South Pacific oceanic circulation system. It flows N off the Peruvian coast of South America. It is a cold current rich in plankton and the fish that feed on them, giving rise to Peru's prosperous fishing industry.

Humboldt Glacier The largest known glacier in the N hemisphere, in NW Greenland. At its end in Kane Basin it is 100 km (60 mi) wide and 91 m (300 ft) high.

Hume, David (1711–76) Scottish philosopher and historian. In *A Treatise of Human Nature* (1739–40) he developed his influential distinction between impressions and ideas. For Hume almost nothing about existence was demonstrable; regarding the existence of God, he maintained an incisive agnosticism. Although an empiricist like *Locke and *Berkeley, Hume modified problematic aspects of their philosophies in favour of psychological explanations. Hume's *History of England* (1754–62) was a best-seller for many years.

Hume, John (1937–) Northern Irish politician; leader of the *Social Democratic and Labour Party (1979–2001). In 1998 he was awarded the Nobel Peace Prize (jointly with David *Trimble) for his role in the peace process that led to the Good Friday Agreement of that year.

humidity A measure of the amount of water vapour in the atmosphere. Absolute humidity is the mass of water vapour in unit volume of air, measured in kilograms per cubic metre. Relative humidity is the ratio of the absolute humidity at a given temperature to the maximum humidity without precipitation at the same temperature, usually expressed as a percentage.

hummingbird A brightly coloured bird belonging to a New World family (*Trochilidae*; 320 species). Hummingbirds are 5.5–20 cm long and have a slender often downcurved bill and a brush-tipped tongue for feeding on nectar and small insects. Hummingbirds can hover, fly backwards, and produce a humming noise by the rapid vibration of their wings during flight. Order: *Apodiformes* (swifts, etc.).

Humperdinck, Engelbert (1854–1921) German composer. He assisted Wagner with the score of *Parsifal* in 1880–81. Of his many operas only *Hänsel und Gretel* (1893) is still popular: it blends German folklore with Wagnerian operatic techniques.

humus The black organic matter in soil resulting from the decomposition of dead plants and animals (humification). It is rich in such elements as carbon, nitrogen, phosphorus, and sulphur, which maintain soil fertility and promote plant growth. Humus also improves water absorption and workability of the soil.

Hundred Years' War (1337–1453) A war between England and France. It was precipitated by Edward III's claim to the French throne. The Treaty of *Brétigny (1360) recognized initial English successes at Sluys (1340), *Crécy (1346), and Poitiers (1356) but thereafter the war was waged intermittently with frequent truces. Henry V of England achieved recognition as heir to the French throne after his victory at *Agincourt (1415), but the more vigorous French prosecution of the war (inspired by *Joan of Arc) reversed his triumph and by 1453 England had been expelled from all French territory except Calais.

Hungarian A language of the Finno-Ugric branch of the Uralic family. It is spoken by 14 million people mainly in Hungary, where it is the official language, and in Slovakia, Romania, and Yugoslavia. It uses a modified Latin alphabet and has borrowed many words from surrounding languages. *See also* MAGYARS.

Hungary, Republic of (Hungarian name: Magyar Köztársasag) A country in central Europe. It lies mainly in the basin of the middle Danube, which forms the NW boundary with Slovakia before running N–S across the centre of the country. To the E of the Danube lies the Great Hungarian Plain; to the W an undulating plain rises to some low hills in the SW and in the NW to the hilly Bakony Forest. The people are mainly Magyars, with minorities of Germans, Slovaks, and others. *Economy*: under communism agriculture was organized collectively and most farms are still cooperatives; the main crops are wheat and maize as well as fruit and vegetables. Mineral resources include bauxite, oil, coal, and natural gas but most fuel supplies come from Russia. After 1949 all industry was nationalized and there was considerable expansion. From 1968 there was a certain amount of decentralization, although overall state control was maintained. In 1992 it was decided that some 75% of industry should be privatized. Exports include transport equipment, computer software, and fruit and vegetables. *History*: the Magyars reached the Danube area in the 9th century AD and settled there. In the 11th century St *Stephen I converted the country to Christianity and became the first Hungarian king. After a long period of dynastic struggles and threats from foreign powers, Hungary was conquered by the Turks in 1526 and in the 17th century it became part of the Habsburg Empire. In 1867 Hungary gained internal self-government as part of the Dual Monarchy of *Austria-Hungary. In 1918 Hungary became a republic but, after a short period of communist rule, a constitutional monarchy was formed. After World War II it became a republic again and in 1949 the communists gained control. In 1956 an anti-Stalinist uprising was crushed by Soviet forces. Pressure for liberal reform led to the introduction of pluralist democracy in 1989; the Communist Party was reformed as the Hungarian Socialist Party, which formed governments in 1994–98 and from 2002. Hungary joined NATO in 1999 and the EU in 2004. Official language: Hungarian (Magyar). Currency: forint of 100 fillér. Area: 93 035 sq km (35 911 sq mi). Population (2003 est): 10 136 000. Capital: Budapest.

Huns Nomadic peoples, originating in Mongolia, who overran much of SE Europe in the late 4th and 5th centuries, overthrowing the *Ostrogoths and then invading the Roman Empire. United under *Attila, the Huns invaded Greece, Gaul, and finally Italy (452). The death of Attila (453) fragmented their empire and they were defeated by a coalition of tribes at Nedao (455).

Hunt, William Holman (1827–1910) British painter. He helped found the *Pre-Raphaelite Brotherhood. His symbolic paintings include *The Light of the World* (Keble College, Oxford) and *The Scapegoat* (Port Sunlight), inspired by a visit to Syria and Palestine (1854).

Huntingdon 52 20N 0 12W A town in E England, in Cambridgeshire on the Great Ouse River. A market town with printing, brewing, and knitwear industries, Huntingdon is the birthplace of Oliver Cromwell. Population (1994): 15 575, with Godmanchester.

hurdling A track event in athletics in which sprinters jump ten hurdles in the course of a race. Distances are 110 m and 400 m for men and 100 m for women. For the 110 m the height of the hurdles is 106.7 cm (3.5 ft), for the 400 m it is 91.4 cm (3 ft), and for the 100 m 84 cm (2.75 ft). Racers are not normally disqualified for knocking hurdles over.

hurling (*or* **hurley**) An Irish 15-a-side stick-and-ball field game similar to *hockey, over 3000 years old. The ball is hit or carried through the air with a broad-bladed curved stick, the hurley (Gaelic word: *caman*), and may be caught in the hand. A goal, hit under the crossbar, scores three points; a hit between the posts but above the bar scores one.

Huron, Lake The second largest of the Great Lakes in North America, situated between the USA and Canada. It is an important shipping route carrying iron ore, coal, grain, and oil. Area: 59 570 sq km (23 000 sq mi).

hurricane **1.** A tropical *cyclone with surface-wind speeds in excess of 64 knots (32.7 m per second) that occurs around the Caribbean Sea and Gulf of Mexico. The centre (eye) of a hurricane is an area of light winds around which strong winds, cloud, and rain bands spiral. **2.** Any wind reaching force 12 on the *Beaufort scale (in excess of 64 knots or 32.7 metres per second).

husky One of several breeds of compact sturdy deep-chested dogs used for pulling sledges in Arctic regions. The Siberian husky has small erect ears, a long muzzle, and a brushlike tail. The dense double-layered coat provides insulation against the severe climate. Height: 51–63 cm. *See also* SAMOYED.

Hussein (ibn Talal) (1935–99) King of Jordan (1952–99). He became king following the deposition because of mental illness of his father Talal. Hussein led Jordan into the 1967 Arab-Israeli War, in which it lost the *West Bank of the River Jordan to Israel. In 1970 he ruthlessly crushed Palestinian guerrillas but in 1974, under pressure from other Arab countries, he accepted the claims of the Palestine Liberation Organization to the West Bank. In the 1990s he took a role in the Arab-Israeli peace process. He was succeeded by his son, Abdullah II.

Hussein, Saddam (1937–) Iraqi statesman; Ba'athist president of Iraq (1979–2003). He repressed such minority groups as the Kurds, established his own personality cult, and led Iraq into the *Iran-Iraq War. His annexation of Kuwait (1990) led to the *Gulf War, in which his forces were routed by a US-led coalition. In the 1990s his defiance of UN ceasefire terms led to further US air raids. Defeat in the 2003 *Iraq

War led to the collapse of his regime; he was subsequently captured by US forces.

Hussites The followers of the Bohemian heretic **Jan Hus** (1372–1415). They demanded a reformed national Church with a vernacular liturgy. In spite of crusades led by the Holy Roman Emperor Sigismund, the Hussites remained undefeated until a compromise was reached at the Council of *Basle in 1433. The moderate Utraquists gained many of their demands and survived until the 17th century.

Huston, John (1906–87) US film director and scriptwriter. His first film as director was *The Maltese Falcon* (1941), and subsequent films included *The Treasure of the Sierra Madre* (1948), for which he wrote the script and in which he also acted, *The African Queen* (1951), *The Misfits* (1960), and *The Dead* (1987). His daughter **Angelica Huston** (1952–) has starred in such films as *The Grifters* (1990), *The Crossing Guard* (1995), and *Blood Work* (2002).

Hutu A Bantu-speaking people, some 9–10 million of whom inhabit Burundi and Rwanda. Although the Hutu form the majority in both countries, they have traditionally been dominated by the **Tutsi** minority. In the 1990s escalating ethnic violence culminated in the slaughter of over half a million Rwandan Tutsis by Hutu militiamen. In the ensuing civil war a flood of Hutu refugees fled to neighbouring countries; this has caused further instability, especially in the Democratic Republic of Congo.

Huxley, Thomas Henry (1825–95) British biologist, whose impact spanned both biology and philosophy. He developed his interest in natural history while serving as a ship's surgeon in the Far East. After valuable work in palaeontology Huxley held numerous public posts and played an important role in educational reform. From 1880 onwards he challenged orthodox theology and coined the term "agnosticism" to describe his own position. Three of his grandsons achieved fame. **Sir Julian Huxley** (1887–1975) was a zoologist and scientific administrator, who also made valuable contributions to the philosophy of science. He was involved in the improvement of the London Zoo at Regent's Park and was appointed first director general of UNESCO (1946–48). His brother **Aldous Huxley** (1894–1964) was a novelist and writer. His witty satirical novels *Antic Hay* (1923) and *Point Counter Point* (1928) were followed by *Brave New World* (1932) and *Eyeless in Gaza* (1936). **Sir Andrew Fielding Huxley** (1917–), half-brother to Sir Julian and Aldous, is a biologist noted for his researches into the mechanisms of nerve-impulse conduction and muscle contraction. Huxley and his collaborator A. L. Hodgkin shared a Nobel Prize (1963) with Sir John *Eccles.

Huygens, Christiaan (1629–95) Dutch astronomer and physicist, who discovered Saturn's rings in 1656. He also built the first pendulum clock and designed an arrangement of lenses called a Huygens eyepiece. He devised a wave theory of light to explain double refraction.

hyacinth A perennial herbaceous plant of the genus *Hyacinthus* (about 30 species), native to the Mediterranean region and tropical Africa. Growing from bulbs, the plants have a dense head of bell-shaped flowers, varying from white to deep purple, and slender leaves. The common garden hyacinths are derived from *H. orientalis*. Family: *Liliaceae*.

hybrid The offspring resulting from the mating of two unrelated individuals. The hybrid offspring often shows greater general fitness than either of the two parents, a phenomenon called hybrid vigour (or heterosis). This is commonly used by plant breeders to produce a generation of crop plants giving higher yields and showing improved resistance to disease.

Hyderabad 17 22N 78 26E One of the largest cities in India, the capital of Andhra Pradesh situated on the River Musi. Formerly the capital of the princely state of Hyderabad, it was founded in 1590 by the Muslim Qutb Shahi sultans. An educational centre, Hyderabad is the site of Osmania University (1918), an agricultural university, and several research institutes. The chief manufactures include bus and railway equipment, textiles, and pharmaceutical goods. Population (1991): 3 145 939.

Hydra (mythology) In Greek legend, a monster with many heads who grew two more whenever one was cut off. It was killed by *Heracles.

Hydra (zoology) A widely distributed genus of solitary freshwater invertebrate animals belonging to an order (*Hydroida*) of *cnidarians. They are flexible *polyps, 10–30 mm long, with the mouth at the top surrounded by 6–10 tentacles. Hydras attach to stones, sticks, or aquatic vegetation and feed on small animals. Class: *Hydrozoa*.

Hydrangea A genus of shrubs (about 80 species) native to Asia and North and South America, including several popular ornamentals. The showy heads of white, pink, or blue flowers may be sterile and sometimes change colour according to the acidity or alkalinity of the soil. Family: *Hydrangeaceae.*

hydraulics The application of hydrostatics (the study of fluids at rest) and hydrodynamics (the study of fluids in motion) to design problems. In civil engineering it is used to study the flow of water in pipes, rivers, canals, etc., especially with reference to the construction of dams, reservoirs, and hydroelectric power stations. In mechanical engineering, applications include the design of machinery involving fluids, such as hydraulic presses, *turbines, propellers, etc.

hydrocarbons Compounds containing carbon and hydrogen. The saturated hydrocarbons are classified as *alkanes. Unsaturated hydrocarbons include the *alkenes and *alkynes. *Aromatic compounds include *benzene and its many derivatives.

hydrochloric acid A solution in water of the colourless pungent gas hydrogen chloride (HCl). It is made by the action of sulphuric acid on salt or by the direct recombination of hydrogen and chlorine from the electrolysis of sea water. It is very soluble in water and forms a strong acid. Concentrated hydrochloric acid contains about 40% HCl by weight and is a clear fuming corrosive liquid. The acid in the human stomach is dilute hydrochloric acid (0.4%).

hydroelectric power Electricity generation using the energy of falling water. The water turns a *turbine connected to an alternator, generating electricity with an efficiency of over 90% at full load. Water is led through pipes from high-level natural or artificial reservoirs to the power station. Hydroelectric power is, therefore, a cheap power source in mountainous areas with high rainfall. In pumped storage stations, electricity is stored by using it to drive pumps that raise the water to a high-level reservoir. In times of high demand this water is run back through the turbines. Hydroelectricity is a renewable energy source causing no pollution; it currently provides 2.4% of world energy needs.

hydrofoil A ship the hull of which is raised out of the water by foils as its speed increases. The foils provide lift in much the same way as an aerofoil; once the hull is clear of the water the drag is greatly reduced and the speed can be increased far above that of a normal ship of the same size and weight. The first hydrofoil was built in 1906 by Enrico Fortanini (1848–1930). Modern craft use a large V-shaped foil, to provide stability in turns or in rough seas, or small totally submerged foils, which support the hull on streamlined struts. Propulsion is by propeller or by pumped-water jet. Hydrofoils of 150 tonnes are in use in many parts of the world, including a cross-Channel service.

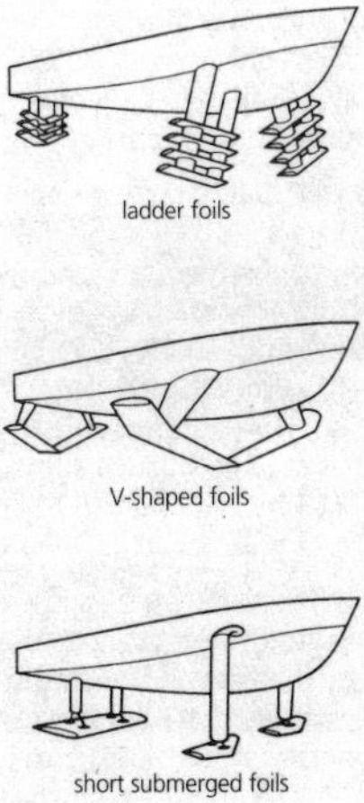

hydrofoil

hydrogen (H) The lightest of all gases, recognized as an element by *Cavendish in 1766 and named by *Lavoisier after water (Greek *hudro*, water). Hydrogen makes up about three-quarters of the mass of the universe. It is the simplest element, its nuclei consisting of one proton. Heavier elements are formed by nuclear fusion (*see* nuclear energy) from hydrogen in stars. The heavier isotope of hydrogen, *deuterium (D *or* ^2H), occurs as about one part in 6000 of ordinary hydrogen. *Tritium (^3H) also occurs but is unstable. As well as the gaseous element (H_2) and water (H_2O), hydrogen occurs in organic compounds and in all inorganic *acids and alkalis. The gas itself is used as a fuel for rockets, in welding, and in chemical manufacture. It combines (explosively if in the right proportions) with oxygen to form water and can be obtained from water by electrolysis. At no 1; at wt 1.00794; mp −259.34°C; bp −252.87°C.

hydrogen bomb *See* NUCLEAR WEAPONS.

hydrology The study of the occurrence and movement of water on the surface of the earth. The **hydrological cycle** is the movement of water from the sea to the atmosphere and back, via precipitation, streams, and rivers. The main

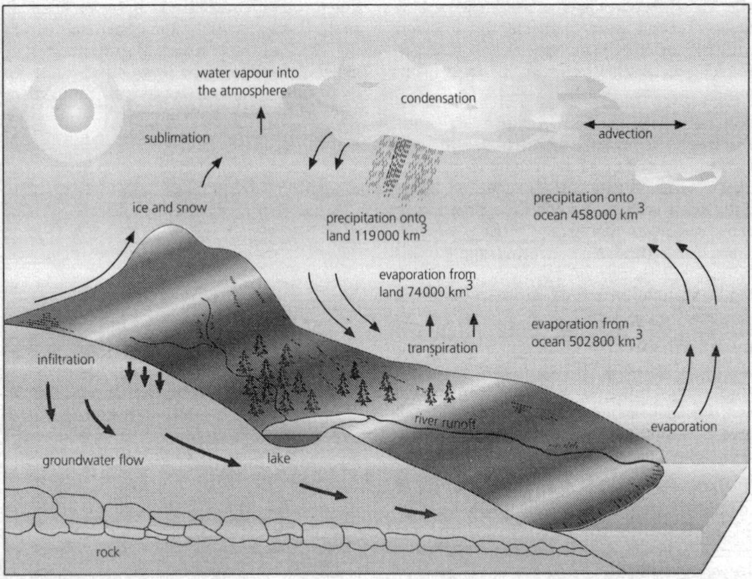

hydrology. The hydrological cycle.

processes with which hydrology is concerned are precipitation, evaporation and transpiration, stream flow, and groundwater flow. It has many important applications, such as flood control and the supply of water for domestic and industrial purposes, irrigation, and hydroelectric power.

hydrophobia *See* RABIES.

hydroponics The cultivation of plants in a liquid nutrient solution instead of soil. An aqueous solution of the nutrients required for healthy growth is used, usually in conjunction with an inert medium, such as sand or gravel, which provides support for the plant-root system. On a small scale, the solution is simply poured over the substrate and the excess allowed to drain into containers for re-use. On a commercial scale, this is achieved by an automatic pumping system in which the solution is monitored to maintain nutrient levels and acidity.

hyena (*or* **hyaena**) A carnivorous mammal of the family *Hyaenidae*. There are three species: the African spotted hyena (*Crocuta crocuta*); the Asian striped hyena (*Hyaena hyaena*); and the brown hyena (*H. brunnea*) of South Africa, also called strandwolf. Hyenas are doglike in appearance, up to 1.5 m long including the tail, and stand about 90 cm high at the shoulder. They hunt in packs, feeding on carrion and killing young or sick animals.

hygrometer An instrument that measures the relative *humidity of the atmosphere. In mechanical hygrometers, a material (usually human hair) is used, the length of which varies with the humidity; the variations being transformed into the movement of a pointer along a scale. In the wet-and-dry bulb hygrometer, two thermometers are placed side by side, one having its bulb covered by a moist cloth. The cooling caused by the evaporation from this wet bulb depends on the atmospheric moisture and thus the difference between the two thermometer readings can be related by standard tables to the relative humidity.

Hymenoptera A large worldwide order of insects (over 100 000 species) including the ants, sawflies, ichneumons, wasps, and bees. Many species show a high degree of social organization. Typically they have two pairs of membranous wings and the first segment of the abdomen is constricted to form a "waist." A tubular egg-laying structure (ovipositor) is generally present and in higher groups is modified for sawing, piercing, or stinging. The larvae (except the sawflies) are legless and have well-developed heads. The males develop from unfertilized eggs. Many species are of benefit to man because they pollinate flowering plants and prey on insect pests.

hyperbola The curve, or pair of curves, formed by a *conic section and defined in Cartesian coordinates (*see* COORDINATE SYSTEMS) by the equation $x^2/a^2 - y^2/b^2 = 1$, where a and b are constants. Its two parts have a common axis and are separated by a minimum distance $2a$ along this axis. As it goes out to *infinity, the curve becomes increasingly close to two straight lines (*asymptotes).

hyperbolic functions A set of mathematical functions written sinh x, cosh x, tanh x, and their inverses csch x, sech x, and coth x respectively. Sinh x is defined as $\frac{1}{2}(e^x - e^{-x})$, where e is the base of natural logarithms; cosh x is $\frac{1}{2}(e^x + e^{-x})$, and tanh x is sinh x/cosh x. Hyperbolic functions are defined by analogy with the trigonometric functions sin x, etc., and are so named because they are related to the *hyperbola in much the same way as the trigonometric functions are related to the circle.

hypermetropia *See* LONGSIGHTEDNESS.

hypertension High *blood pressure. This is a common condition, which can be caused by kidney disease, hormonal disorders, and some congenital diseases; for most cases, however, no cause can be found. Usually there are no symptoms, with the consequent danger that untreated hypertension may lead to heart failure, kidney failure, cerebral haemorrhage, and blindness. It is treated by drugs.

hypnosis The production of a trance state by means of firm suggestion, with the cooperation of the subject. People who have been deeply hypnotized can carry out instructions that would not be possible in a normal waking state. First used for therapeutic purposes by *Mesmer in the 18th century, it was developed (and given the name hypnosis) by James Braid (1795–1860) in the 19th century. By the turn of the century it was established as a means of treating certain psychiatric disorders (especially those of psychosomatic origin).

hypothalamus A part of the *brain, surrounding the lower part of the third ventricle, that is an important coordinating centre for the functions of the autonomic *nervous system. It is particularly involved with the control of body temperature, with regulating how much is eaten and drunk, and with the emotions. It also releases *neurohormones affecting other organs, especially the *pituitary gland.

hypothermia Lowering of the body temperature. This is most commonly seen in old people and young babies—whose body temperature is less well controlled—if they are living in poorly heated rooms. If the body temperature falls very low severe internal changes may occur, but otherwise gentle warming will help the patient to recover.

hyrax An African *mammal belonging to the order *Hyracoidea* (6 species), also called cony. 30–60 cm long, hyraxes are related to ungulates (hooved mammals), having hooflike toes and a two-chambered stomach for digesting their vegetable diet. They are nimble and live in small colonies in trees or among rocks, being most active at twilight.

hyssop A perennial herbaceous plant, *Hyssopus officinalis*, native to S Europe, Asia, and Morocco. It is grown elsewhere as a garden ornamental and was formerly cultivated as a medicinal herb. Growing to a height of 60 cm, it has whorls of violet-blue flowers along the stem. Family: *Labiatae*.

hysterectomy The surgical removal of the womb. A subtotal hysterectomy involves removing the body of the womb but leaving the neck (cervix); in total hysterectomy (or panhysterectomy) the entire womb is removed. It is most commonly performed when the womb contains large fibroids—benign tumours that cause heavy menstrual periods. Other conditions that may require hysterectomy include cancer of the womb or the presence of precancerous cells in the cervix. The operation is usually performed through an incision made in the abdominal wall: it invariably precludes subsequent pregnancy but does not affect sexual activity.

hysteria A neurotic condition of emotional instability and immaturity in which patients are vulnerable to suggestion and develop physical symptoms. Hysterical symptoms are unconsciously adopted by the individual because they bring some gain. The symptoms may be of "conversion hysteria," characterized by physical symptoms, such as paralysis; or of "dissociative hysteria," with changes in thinking, such as multiple personality. Treatment is usually by *psychotherapy.

I

iamb A metrical foot consisting of an unstressed syllable (or in verse based on quantity, a short syllable) followed by a stressed (or long) syllable. Developed by the ancient Greeks, it is the commonest type in English poetry.

Ibadan 7 23N 3 56E The second largest city in Nigeria. It is an important industrial and administrative centre. Population (1996 est): 1 432 000.

Iberian Peninsula A peninsula in SW Europe, occupied by Portugal and Spain. It is separated from the rest of Europe by the Pyrenees and its flora and fauna are similar to those of N Africa. Area: 593 250 sq km (229 054 sq mi).

Iberians A Bronze Age people of S and E Spain in the 1st millennium BC. Their non-Indo-European language, which was displaced by Latin, is known from a variety of inscriptions on stone and other materials. The economic basis was agriculture, mining, and metalworking. The Iberians lost their identity by cultural assimilation to the *Celts in Roman times.

ibex A rare wild *goat, *Capra ibex*, of Eurasian and N African mountains. About 85 cm high at the shoulder, ibexes have backward-curving horns up to 65 cm long and their coat is brownish-grey with variable markings.

ibis A long-necked wading bird belonging to the subfamily *Threskiornithinae* (20 species), distributed worldwide in warm regions. 55–75 cm long, ibises have a slender downcurved bill and unfeathered face or head and neck. Family: *Threskiornithidae* (ibises and spoonbills); order: *Ciconiiformes* (herons, storks, etc.).

Ibiza (**Iviza** *or* **Ivica**) One of the Balearic islands. It is a popular tourist centre, noted for its many nightclubs etc.; exports include almonds, dried figs, apricots, and salt. Area: 541 sq km (209 sq mi). Population (latest est): 45 000. Chief town: Ibiza.

Ibn Saud (c.1880–1953) The first King of Saudi Arabia (1932–53). With the military help of al-Ikhwan, a tribal militia, he extended his territory from the Sultanate of Najd, which he reconquered in 1902, to encompass much of Arabia by 1924, when he took Hejaz. The name Saudi Arabia was adopted in 1932.

Ibo (*or* **Igbo**) A people of SE Nigeria who speak Igbo, a language of the Kwa subgroup of the Niger-Congo family. Subsistence cultivators of yams, cassava, and taro, they traditionally lived in scattered small holdings or village clusters of patrilineal kin headed by the eldest male descendant of the founder. *See also* BIAFRA.

Ibsen, Henrik (1828–1906) Norwegian playwright and poet, the founder of modern prose drama. From 1864 to 1891 he lived in Italy and Germany. His fame as a dramatist grew with *Brand* (1865) and *Peer Gynt* (1867). Later plays explored social issues: women's emancipation in *A Doll's House* (1879), inherited disease and guilt in *Ghosts* (1881), and public corruption in *An Enemy of the People* (1882). In his last plays, *The Master Builder* (1892), *John Gabriel Borkman* (1896), and *When We Dead Awaken* (1899), he turned to the symbolic treatment of autobiographical themes.

Icarus *See* DAEDALUS.

ice Water in its solid (frozen) phase. Pure water at a pressure of 101.3 kilopascal (= 1 atmosphere) freezes at 0° C. Its density at this temperature is 0.92, so that about 8% of a floating piece of ice is above water.

Ice Age A period in the earth's history when ice spread towards the equator with a general lowering of temperatures. The most recent of these was the *Pleistocene epoch ending about 10 000 years ago, during which four major ice advances occurred. Other ice ages occurred in Permo-Carboniferous times about 250 million years ago and in Pre-Cambrian times about 500 million years ago. Between 1550 and 1850 the

Little Ice Age occurred, with a significant lowering of temperatures in the N hemisphere.

iceberg A large mass of ice in the sea that has originated on land. Many result from the breaking off of ice from glaciers. In the N hemisphere icebergs originate chiefly from Greenland, in the S hemisphere most break off from the Antarctic ice.

ice hockey A six-a-side team game played with stick and puck on a rink. It derives from field hockey and was first played by Englishmen on the frozen Kingston Harbour, Ontario (c. 1860). Canada is the true home of the game, but it is widely played in the USA, Russia, and Scandinavia.

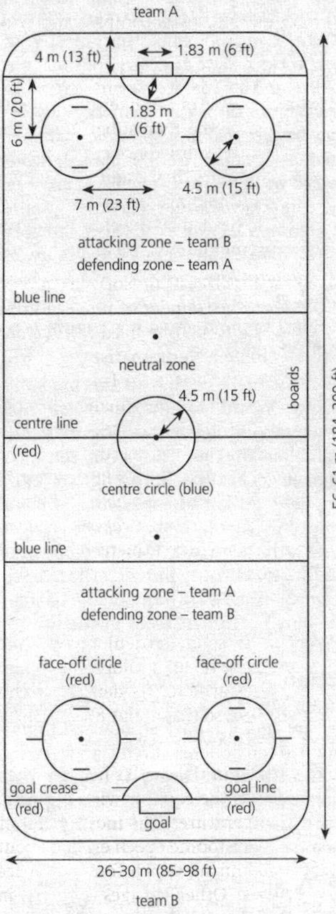

ice hockey. The dimensions of the rink.

Iceland, Republic of (Icelandic name: Ísland) An island country in the N Atlantic, just S of the Arctic Circle, off the SE coast of Greenland. It consists mainly of an uninhabited plateau of volcanoes, lava fields, and glaciers; most of the population live around the deeply indented coast. *Economy*: the main exports are fish, fish products, ferrosilicon, and aluminium. Tourism is of growing importance. Hydroelectricity and geothermal power (from geysers and thermal springs) are important sources of energy. Iceland is a member of the European Free Trade Association. *History*: the Vikings reached Iceland about 874 AD and by the 10th century it had become an independent state with its own parliament, the Althing, considered to be the oldest in the world. In 1264 it came under Norwegian rule and, with Norway, passed to the Danish Crown in 1381. In 1918 it became an independent state under the Danish Crown, attaining full independence as a republic in 1944. Iceland was involved in several Cod Wars with the UK during the 1960s and 1970s; falling fish prices have since created economic strain. In 1995 and 1997 parliamentary elections were won by the Independence Party. Official language: Icelandic. Currency: króna of 100 aurar. Area: 103 000 sq km (39 758 sq mi). Population (2003 est): 290 000. Capital: Reykjavik.

Icelandic A North Germanic language of the Western Scandinavian subgroup, developed from Old Norse. It is the official language of Iceland.

Iceni A British tribe that inhabited the area that is now Norfolk and Suffolk. Under *Boadicea (60 AD) their revolt against Roman rule was brutally suppressed.

ice plant A succulent annual or biennial plant, *Cryophytum crystallinum*, that is covered in glistening papillae and has long prostrate stems reaching 75 cm. Native to South Africa, it is widely grown as a garden or pot plant. Family: *Aizoaceae*.

ice skating The recreation and sport of sliding over ice on steel-bladed skates. The main forms of the sport are speed skating (racing), figure skating (set exercises followed by a freestyle performance to music, either singly or in pairs), and ice dancing (a combination of dancing and pairs figure skating).

ichneumon An insect, also called ichneumon fly and ichneumon wasp, belonging to a family (*Ichneumonidae*; about 40 000 species) occurring in Europe, North America, and elsewhere. About 12 mm long, ichneumons resemble wasps but have longer antennae. They are parasitic upon other insects thereby controlling many insect pests. Order: *Hymenoptera.*

ichthyosaur An extinct dolphin-like marine reptile that lived through much of the Mesozoic era but was most abundant in the Jurassic period (200–135 million years ago). 1–12 m long, it had broad flexible paddles, a large tail fin, and a triangular dorsal fin.

icon A painted or mosaic image of Christ or a saint, peculiar to the Byzantine and Orthodox churches. Unlike other paintings, icons have undergone little stylistic development and are characterized by a symbolic rather than realistic approach to colour, perspective, etc.

id In *psychoanalysis, the part of the unconscious mind that is governed by irrational instinctive forces, such as libido and aggression. These forces seek immediate (actual or symbolic) relief and the id is therefore said to be ruled by the pleasure principle and not by reality or logic. *See also* EGO; SUPEREGO.

Id (*or* **Eid**; Arabic: festival) Either of two annual Muslim festivals, **Id-ul-Adha** (Festival of Sacrifice) held in late February or early March to mark the end of the pilgrimage to Mecca (*see* HAJJ), or **Id-ul-Fitr** (Festival of Fast Breaking) held in early December to mark the end of *Ramadan.

Idaho A state in the NW USA, dominated by the N Rocky Mountains. It is primarily agricultural producing potatoes, wheat, and sugar beet along with beef cattle and sheep. Rich in minerals, Idaho is a leading US producer of silver and antimony. *History*: first settled in the early 19th century, it became a state in 1890. Area: 216 412 sq km (83 557 sq mi). Population (2000 est): 1 293 953. Capital: Boise.

idealism Any philosophical doctrine that equates reality with mind, spirit, person, soul, thought, or, as in *Plato, archetypal ideas. Philosophers who have held various idealist views include Berkeley, Kant, and Hegel.

ideographic writing systems (*or* **ideography**) Writing systems in which each concept is represented by a symbol. All ideographic systems were probably derived from pictographic writing systems, stylized representations of abstract concepts being added to the list of symbols. Languages such as Chinese still use ideographic writing systems.

igloo A temporary dome-shaped dwelling made from blocks of snow by Inuits of the region between the Mackenzie River delta and Labrador in N Canada. The blocks are cut with a long knife and the joints filled with snow. The igloo is entered by a low and narrow semicylindrical passageway.

Ignatius Loyola, St (1491–1556) Spanish founder of the *Jesuits. His interest in religion dated from 1521, when he read the life of Christ while convalescing from a war wound. After visiting the Holy Land (1523), he studied in Spain and in Paris. There, in 1534 he made vows of poverty, chastity, and obedience, with St *Francis Xavier and other followers. He was ordained in 1537 and founded the Society of Jesus with the approval of Pope Paul III in 1540. His *Spiritual Exercises* (1548) has had lasting influence on the Roman Catholic Church. Feast day: 31 July.

igneous rock One of the three major categories of rock (*compare* METAMORPHIC ROCK; SEDIMENTARY ROCK) consisting mostly of crystalline rocks cooled directly from magma. That cooled at the surface forms extrusive rocks—volcanic lavas with small crystals because they have cooled rapidly. Some extrusive rocks, such as obsidian, are like glass. Igneous rocks cooled at depth are called intrusive or plutonic. They have larger crystals, granite being a common example. A third category contains the hypabyssal rocks, cooled in dykes or sills at intermediate depth and usually having intermediate crystal sizes, for example dolerite. Silica is the dominant chemical constituent of igneous rocks.

iguana A lizard belonging to the predominantly New World family *Iguanidae* (700 species), comprising desert-dwelling, arboreal, and amphibious species. The green common iguana (*Iguana iguana*) reaches a length of 1.8 m including the long tail (about 1.3 m) and has a short spiny crest along the back; males have a dewlap beneath the throat. They feed on vegetation and are excellent swimmers. The marine iguana (*Amblyrhynchus cristatus*) of the Galápagos is the only lizard that feeds in the sea. *See also* BASILISK.

Iguanodon A large dinosaur that lived in the Jurassic and Cretaceous periods (200–65 million years ago). It stood on powerful hind legs about 5 m tall and measured 11 m from its head to the tip of its heavy balancing tail. Iguanodons were herbivorous, tearing off leaves with their tongues and cutting them with bladelike teeth. Order: *Ornithischia.*

Illinois A group of Algonquian-speaking North American Indian tribes of Wisconsin, Illinois, Missouri, and Iowa. Their villages were of rush-mat-covered dwellings, each housing several families. Men hunted forest game and prairie bison; women cultivated maize and corn. The Illinois were much reduced in population through wars with other tribes and eventually dispersed from their territory.

Illinois A state in the USA, in the Midwest. It consists largely of flat prairies crossed by the Illinois and Kaskaskia Rivers. Approximately half its population is concentrated in the Chicago metropolitan area, the area to the S being predominantly rural. Illinois is a major producer of soya beans, maize, corn, pork, beef, and dairy products. Manufacturing and coalmining are also important. *History*: the first Europeans to visit Illinois were the French in the 17th century. It formed part of the French province of Louisiana but was ceded to Britain (1763). It came under US control (1783), becoming a territory in 1809 and a state in 1818. Area: 146 075 sq km (56 400 sq mi). Population (2000): 12 419 293. Capital: Springfield.

illuminated manuscripts Manuscripts of gospels, books of hours, prayers, etc., decorated with designs in watercolour and frequently gold leaf. The art was first practised by monastic scribes in the early middle ages, as in the 8th-century Book of Kells. The Duke of Berry's book of hours by the de *Limburg brothers (active c. 1400–c. 1416) is an outstanding example of late medieval illumination.

Illyria The Adriatic coastal region W of the Balkans. Inhabited from the 10th century BC by warlike tribes, Illyria constantly harassed Macedonia and Epirus. Piratical raids in the Adriatic provoked Roman intervention from 228 BC; Illyria became the Roman province of Illyricum in 167 BC.

Iloilo 10 41N 122 33E A port in the central Philippines, in SE Panay. The island's commercial centre, it exports sugar and rice. Population (2000): 365 820.

Ilyushin, Sergei Vladimirovich (1894–1977) Soviet aircraft designer. He first became known for the Il-2 Stormovik dive bomber; he later worked on commercial aircraft, designing the jet airliner Il-62.

imaginary number *See* COMPLEX NUMBERS.

Imagism A literary movement begun in Britain in 1912, dedicated to the concise expression of pure visual images in poetry. Its emphasis on clarity and hardness derived largely from the criticism of T. E. Hulme (1883–1917). *Des Imagistes* (1914), an anthology edited by Ezra *Pound, included poems by Richard Aldington, Hilda Doolittle (H. D.), and Amy Lowell. The movement was shortlived but profoundly influenced British and US poetry.

Immaculate Conception A dogma of the Roman Catholic Church stating that the Virgin Mary was conceived free from original sin. It was opposed by prominent theologians, such as St Bonaventure and St Thomas Aquinas, but was promulgated as dogma in 1854 by Pope Pius IX.

immunity In medicine, resistance to infection, usually that specifically acquired due to the presence of *antibodies. Newborn babies have a temporary passive immunity from antibodies transferred from the mother's blood through the placenta. Active immunity is produced when an individual forms his (or her) own antibodies after exposure to an antigen, such as occurs following an infection. There are two different kinds of immune response produced by antibodies. Cell-mediated immunity is due to activity of the T-lymphocytes (produced by or dependent on the thymus), which produce cells with antibody bound to their surface. They are responsible for such reactions as graft rejection. Humoral immunity is produced by the B-lymphocytes (probably formed by lymphatic tissue in the gut), which produce cells that release free antibody into the blood. Patients whose immune systems have failed to develop completely are said to be **immunodeficient**; those whose immune systems have become deficient, as through AIDS, are **immuncompromised**.

Immunization is the production of immunity by artificial means. This may be achieved by injecting antibodies against specific diseases (e.g. tetanus and diphtheria), providing temporary passive immunity, or by *vaccination to produce active immunity.

immunology The study of the biological processes by which the body reacts to foreign substances. Immunologists are also concerned with disorders of the immune system, including *allergy and *autoimmunity.

immunosuppression The condition in which the *immunity of the body is reduced. This can occur in various diseases (e.g. leukaemia and severe infections) or it may be deliberately induced by certain drugs (e.g. azathioprine and cyclophosphamide). Immunosuppressive drugs are administered after transplant surgery and are also used to treat rheumatoid arthritis and other conditions associated with *autoimmunity.

impala A common antelope, *Aepyceros melampus*, of central and S African savanna. About

100 cm high at the shoulder, impalas have a red-brown coat and white underparts; males have lyre-shaped ridged horns. Impalas are known for their agile springing leaps.

Impatiens A genus of annual and perennial herbaceous plants (about 700 species), widely distributed in temperate and tropical regions. The genus includes touch-me-not (*I. noli-tangere*) and various cultivated species, such as the red-flowered garden *balsam (*I. balsamina*) and busy Lizzies. Family: *Balsaminaceae*.

impeachment In the UK, a prosecution brought by the House of Commons as prosecutor and tried by the House of Lords as judge, especially against a minister of the Crown for a serious public offence. In the USA impeachments are brought by the House of Representatives and tried by the Senate.

impedance A measure of the ability of a circuit to resist the flow of an alternating current. It is given by $Z = R + iX$, where Z is the impedance, R is the *resistance, and X is the reactance. Impedance and reactance are measured in *ohms.

impressionism A French art movement that flourished from the late 1860s to the late 1880s. Its name was derived from Monet's painting *Impression: Sunrise* (1872; Musée Marmottan, Paris), shown at the first of the eight impressionist exhibitions (1874, 1876, 1877, 1879, 1880, 1881, 1882, 1886). The leading impressionists were *Monet, *Pissarro, *Sisley, and *Renoir. They aimed to capture fleeting effects of light and weather with dabs of bright colour and a minimum of drawing.

imprinting In *ethology, a rapid and irreversible form of learning that takes place in some animals in the first hours of life. Animals attach themselves to whatever creatures they are exposed to at that time – usually, but not necessarily, their mothers. This behaviour was first described by Konrad *Lorenz.

Incarnation The central tenet of Christian belief, that the second person of the Trinity took human form and became man. Although in other religions gods temporarily appear in human form (i.e. a theophany), in Christianity the union of the divine and human in Christ is permanent and the integrity of both the divine and human natures is maintained. The doctrine is stated in the opening of the Gospel of St John and in St Paul's Epistle to the Colossians.

Incas A Quechua-speaking South American Indian people of the Peruvian Andes. From their capital of *Cuzco, they established, during the 15th century, an empire extending from Ecuador to central Chile. It was destroyed in the 16th century by the Spaniards. *See also* MACHU PICCHU.

incense A mixture of gums and spices (especially gum benzoin) burnt for its aroma (*see also* FRANKINCENSE). It was employed in pagan rituals in ancient Egypt, Greece, and Rome as well as in Judaic ritual and was a valued trade commodity. In the Book of Revelation it is a symbol of the prayers of saints and has been used in Christian worship since the 6th century AD.

incest Proscribed sexual relations between close kin. The most common and universal prohibitions apply to members of the same nuclear family, such as relations between parents and children and between brothers and sisters. These taboos, founded in folklore, have a sound basis in genetics (unfavourable recessive genes can become dominant when consanguineous relatives breed).

Inchŏn 37 30N 126 38E A city in NW South Korea, Seoul's main seaport on the Yellow Sea. A UN attack here (1950) during the Korean War halted the North Korean invasion. Population (1995): 2 307 618.

income tax A direct tax on income and a major source of government revenue in many countries. In most countries, including the UK, it is a progressive tax (the rate charged increasing with the taxable income) in which a certain amount can be earned without attracting tax.

incunabula Books printed during the infancy of modern printing (before 1500). N European incunabula have a heavy type design known as black letter; Italian books have a more elegant roman typeface.

Independence Day The national holiday in the USA that marks the adoption of the *Declaration of Independence by the Continental Congress on 4 July 1776.

independent school A UK school that is not funded by central government or a local authority. The main groups are the public schools (for 13–17 year olds), the preparatory schools ("prep" schools; 8–13 year olds), and the independent primary schools ("pre-prep" schools; 5–7).

India, Republic of (Hindi name: Bharat) A country in S Asia, the seventh largest in the world and the second most populous. Bordering on Pakistan, China, Nepal, Bhutan, and Myanmar (Burma), it comprises 28 states and 7 Union Territories. The Himalayas, in which the

River Ganges rises, form a natural barrier to the N. Central India consists of a plateau (the Deccan), flanked by the mountains of the Western and Eastern Ghats. N of this lies the Indo-Gangetic plain, with the Thar Desert in the W. The population comprises many ethnic and cultural groups and about 1600 languages and dialects are spoken. The chief religions are Hinduism (83% of the population) and Islam (11%). The *caste system still survives, although untouchability has been officially abolished. *Economy*: 70% of the workforce is engaged in agriculture, with rice, pulses, and cereals as the main food crops; sugar cane, tea, jute, cotton, and tobacco are also important. Mineral resources include iron ore, manganese, bauxite, mica, and ilmenite. Coal is mined, oil is produced from the Arabian Sea, and India also has nuclear power. India is the world's tenth greatest industrial power. Chief exports are cotton goods, tea, leather, iron ore, and jute. The economy has grown rapidly since the early 1990s. *History*: the *Indus Valley was the site of a civilization for a millennium before the invading Aryans established theirs (c. 1500 BC) between the Indus and the Ganges. From this civilization Hinduism emerged as India's dominant religion. The Mauryan Empire followed (c. 320 BC–c. 185 BC), which unified most of India. The 4th–6th centuries AD saw a flowering of Hindu culture in the N under the Gupta dynasty. Muslim raids on the N culminated in the establishment of a Muslim sultanate based on Delhi (1129), under which much of India was again unified. A later Muslim invasion resulted in the magnificent *Mogul Empire (established 1526). At this time Europeans were also arriving. The British *East India Company fought with French traders in the 18th century for a monopoly as the Mogul Empire declined. With Robert Clive's victory at Plassey (1757), the British established their supremacy and power shifted from the East India Company to the British Government. The Indian economy suffered under British trading arrangements, provoking social and political unrest. After the *Indian Mutiny (1857–59) reforms were introduced, including the transfer of the East India Company's administrative powers to the India Office, represented by a viceroy and provincial governors. Subsequent reforms allowed Indians greater involvement in government, and in 1919 a parliament was created. However, the nationalist movement (*see* INDIAN NATIONAL CONGRESS) became increasingly forceful in its demand for home rule and, under Mahatma *Gandhi and Jawaharlal *Nehru, pursued a policy of civil disobedience. Independence was finally achieved in 1947, with Nehru as prime minister, on condition that a separate Muslim state should be established. The creation of *Pakistan (1947) was followed by violence and war between the two countries over Kashmir. Trouble between India and Pakistan erupted again in 1965 and 1971 (*see also* BANGLADESH). Hostility between Hindus and Muslims has been a continuing problem, leading to serious violence in the 1990s. The Kashmir border dispute continues, having led India and Pakistan to the brink of war in 1990, 1999, and 2001–02. India, which became a sovereign state in 1950, has been consolidated by the incorporation of former French and Portuguese territories (1956 and 1961) and Sikkim (1975). Indira *Gandhi (prime minister 1966–77, 1980–84) suppressed a militant Sikh movement, advocating autonomy for the Punjab, in 1984. Later that year she was assassinated; she was succeeded by her son, Rajiv Gandhi (killed by a terrorist bomb in 1991). The late 1990s saw a series of short-lived coalitions until the general election of 1999, which resulted in a clear victory for the militant Hindu BJP under A. B. *Vajpayee. The Congress Party returned to power in 2004, with Dr Manmohan Singh as the country's first Sikh prime minister. Official languages: Hindi and English. Currency: Indian rupee of 100 paise. Area: 3 287 590 sq km (1 269 072 sq mi), including Jammu and Kashmir. Population (2003 est): 1 065 462 000. Capital: New Delhi.

Indiana A state in the USA, forming part of the Mississippi Basin. It is largely undulating prairie with glacial lakes in the N. Agriculture is important in the central plain, the major crops being soya beans, maize, wheat, and vegetables; pigs are the primary livestock. Coal and building stone are also exploited. It is a transport centre with the Ohio River linking Indiana with the Mississippi River. *History*: explored by the French in the 17th century, the area was ceded to Britain in 1763, passing to the USA in 1783. Increased settlement followed the defeat of the Indians (1794) and Indiana became a state in 1816. Area: 93 993 sq km (36 291 sq mi). Population (2000): 5 080 485. Capital: Indianapolis.

Indianapolis 39 45N 86 10W A city in the USA, the capital of Indiana. It is the scene of annual speedway races, including the **Indianapolis 500**, first held in 1911. Population (2000): 791 926.

Indian languages Languages of widely differing origins spoken in the Indian subcontinent. The two major language families are the Indo-European and the Dravidian. On the NW borders of India, Baluchi and Pashto, members of the Iranian subgroup of the Indo-European family, are spoken. Most of the other Indo-European languages of India are of the Indo-Aryan subgroup. This includes the lingua franca Hindustani; *Hindi, the official national language; Rajasthani, Punjabi, *Gujarati, and Sindhi in the west; *Bengali and Bihari in the east; and Kashmiri. Most of S India is covered by the Dravidian language family. In addition to these two large families, there are scattered languages of the Munda group in the NE, and languages of Sino-Tibetan origins are spoken in the Himalayas.

Indian Mutiny (1857–59) A revolt of about 35 000 sepoys (Indian soldiers in the service of the British East India Company), which developed into a bloody Anglo-Indian War. It began with a massacre of Europeans at Meerut in May 1857, following which the mutineers captured Delhi. The sepoys then rose in many other N Indian towns and were joined by local princes. Extensive British reinforcements were able under Colin Campbell (1792–1863) to regain Delhi in Sept and relieve besieged Lucknow in Nov; by July 1858, the revolt had largely been contained.

Indian National Congress The political party, founded in 1885, that governed India after the declaration of independence in 1947. After 1917, under the guidance of Mahatma *Gandhi, it advocated noncooperation with the British and in World War II it refused to support Britain without being promised Indian independence. The party was led by Jawarhalal *Nehru from 1951 to 1964, by Lal Bahadur Shastri (1904–66) until 1966, and then by Indira *Gandhi, under whom it split into two factions. Her son Rajiv Gandhi took over the leadership of the main faction, Congress (I), in 1984 and was succeeded by Narasimha Rao in 1991. The party suffered a heavy electoral defeat in 1996; Sitaram Kesh took over as leader but was succeeded by Sonia Gandhi (Rajiv's widow) in 1998. She led the party to victory in the general election of 2004 but declined the post of prime minister, which was assumed by Dr Manmohan Singh.

Indian Ocean The world's third largest ocean, extending between Asia, Africa, Australia, and Antarctica. Lying mainly in the S hemisphere, most is within the tropical and temperate zones. The ocean floor is extremely rich in minerals.

indicator A substance used to indicate through changes in colour, fluorescence, etc., the presence of another substance or the completion of a chemical reaction. Indicators are usually weak organic acids or bases that yield ions of a different colour to the unionized molecule. For example, litmus is red in the presence of acids but blue in the presence of alkalis.

indium (In) A soft silvery metal, named after the bright indigo line in its spectrum. It is used in making transistors, rectifiers, thermistors, and alloys of low melting point. At no 49; at wt 114.82; mp 156.63°C; bp 2073°C.

Indochina The area of SE Asia comprising Vietnam, Cambodia, Myanmar (Burma), Thailand, Malaysia, and *Laos. During the 19th century the French established control over the region, forming (1887) the Union of Indochina. Its capital was Saigon (now Ho Chi Minh City). During World War II the Japanese occupied all Indochina (1941). Following Japan's defeat, fighting broke out between nationalists (*see* VIET MINH) and the French, bitter conflict continuing until 1954, when the *Geneva Conference ended French control of Indochina (*see also* DIEN BIEN PHU, BATTLE OF).

Indo-European languages The largest language family of the world, sometimes also called Indo-Germanic. Indo-European languages are spoken throughout Europe as well as in India, Iran, and in parts of NW Asia, and the family is generally thought to include the following subgroups: Germanic; Italic; Indo-Iranian; Celtic; Baltic; Slavic (*see* SLAVONIC LANGUAGES); Albanian; Greek; *Armenian; Tocharian; and Anatolian.

Indonesia, Republic of (name from 1798 until 1945: Dutch East Indies) A country in SE Asia, consisting of a series of islands extending E–W for some 5150 km (3200 mi) in the Pacific and Indian Oceans. The main islands are Sumatra, Java and Madura, Bali, Sulawesi, Lombok, and the Moluccas together with the W part of Timor, part of Borneo (Kalimantan), the W half of New Guinea (Irian Jaya). Most of the islands are volcanic. Its ethnically diverse population belongs mainly to the Malaysian race. The Chinese are the largest nonindigenous group. *Economy*: although rich in natural resources, it is a mainly agrarian economy of which the staple crop is rice; cash crops include rubber, palm oil, copra, sugar cane, and coffee. The main exports include crude oil, timber, sand, and rubber. *History*: in the middle ages kingdoms and empires flourished. In the 16th century it was occupied successively by the Portuguese, the British, and the Dutch, and from 1602 to 1798 it was ruled by the Dutch East India Company. It became a colony of the Netherlands and, after Japanese occupation during World War II, declared itself a republic in 1945 under the leadership of Dr Sukarno. The country was formally granted independence in 1949–50. Under Sukarno Irian Jaya was incorporated in 1963 and there was confrontation with Malaysia (1963–66). A military coup in 1966 under the leadership of Gen Suharto established a harsh military dictatorship; left-wing elements were virtually eliminated. In 1975 Indonesia occupied *East Timor, killing thousands of civilians. East Timor was formally annexed in 1976 despite UN opposition. Separatist movements in East Timor and in Irian Jaya were violently suppressed in the 1980s and 1990s. In 1998 Indonesia's economy collapsed and riots ensued. Mass protests led Suharto to resign in favour of his deputy, B. J. Habibie. Disorder continued, with prodemocracy demonstrations, conflict between Muslims and Christians, and ethnic fighting in Kalimantan. East Timor voted for independence in 1999 and became a separate nation in May 2002. Indonesia's first free elections for 45 years took place in June 1999 and the veteran Muslim leader, Abdurrahman Wahid, became president. In 2001 Wahid was impeached for alleged corruption and replaced by Megawati Sukarnoputri, Sukarno's daughter. The general election of 2004 saw a victory for supporters of Suharto. Official language: Bahasa Indonesia. Currency: rupiah of 100 sen. Area: 1 903 650 sq km (735 000 sq mi). Population (2003 est): 219 883 000. Capital: Jakarta.

Indore 22 42N 75 54E A city in India, in Madhya Pradesh. Formerly the capital of the princely state of Indore, it is an important trading centre. Population (1991): 1 086 673.

Indra The principal Hindu deity of the Vedic period, god of war and storm, who slew the dragon Vritra, releasing the fertile water and light necessary to create the universe. He is portrayed as wielding a thunderbolt.

induction The process of making an empirical generalization by observing particular instances of its operation. The conclusion goes beyond the facts, since not all possible instances can be examined. From induction predictions can be made but they are always liable to falsification.

indulgences In the Roman Catholic Church, remissions of the temporal penalties incurred for sins already forgiven by God in the sacrament of penance. The practice of indulgences arose in the early Church when confessors and those about to be martyred were permitted to intercede for penitents and so mitigate the discipline imposed on them. During the later middle ages, indulgences came to command a financial value, which led to widespread abuse and was one of the chief causes of *Luther's attack on the Church at the Reformation. Their sale was prohibited in 1567.

Indus, River A river in S central Asia, one of the longest in the world. Rising in SW Tibet in the Himalayas, it flows NW through Kashmir, then SSW across Pakistan to its large delta near Karachi on the Arabian Sea. Its main tributary is the Panjnad. The Indus Valley contained one of the earliest organized cultures, which lasted from about 2500 until 1700 BC. Length: 2900 km (1800 mi).

Indus Valley civilization A literate urban civilization that flourished in the Indus plain (modern Pakistan) c. 2500–1500 BC. The cities of Harappa and Mohenjo Daro have been excavated.

industrial revolution The process of change that transformed Britain and then other countries from agricultural to industrial economies. The industrial revolution began about 1750 when the *agricultural revolution was well under way. Inventions were made in the textile industry by such men as James *Hargreaves, Richard *Arkwright, and Samuel *Crompton, which made the production of cloth much faster and the yarn produced of better quality. These new machines required factories to house them, at first near rivers for water power and then, when the steam engine was invented, near coalfields. Industrial towns with poor living and working conditions developed, but the belief in *laissez-faire meant little was done to regulate industrial growth. Advances were also made in the production of iron and in communications. The *canals were extended and from about 1830 railways were built. By the mid-19th century British industrial methods had spread to continental Europe and the USA.

inert gases *See* NOBLE GASES.

inertia A property of a body that causes it to resist changes in its velocity or, if stationary, to resist motion. When the body resists changes in its linear motion its mass is a measurement of its inertia (*see* MASS AND WEIGHT). When it resists changes in rotation about an axis its inertia is given by its *moment of inertia.

inertial guidance A means of guiding a missile or submarine without communicating with its destination or point of departure. It consists of a set of three *gyroscopes, with their axes mounted mutually perpendicular to each other, connected to a computer. The gyroscopes provide a frame of reference, which enables the computer to adjust the controls of the vehicle to steer a preset course.

infallibility A dogma of the Roman Catholic Church promulgated at the first Vatican Council (1870). It stated that the pope cannot err in defining the Church's teaching in matters of faith and morals when speaking *ex cathedra* (Latin: from the throne), i.e. when intending to make such a pronouncement.

infection Illness caused by microorganisms, including bacteria, viruses, fungi, and protozoa. Examples of bacterial infections are diphtheria, pneumonia, and whooping cough. Viruses cause influenza, measles, herpes, and AIDS (among others); malaria and sleeping sickness result from protozoan infection, and fungi cause ringworm. Infectious diseases are the commonest cause of sickness and—except in modern industrial societies—have always been the main cause of death. Methods of transmission include direct contact with an infected person, contact with a human or animal carrier or contaminated objects, and contact with infected droplets produced by coughing and sneezing. Antibiotics are active against a wide range of organisms, but as yet there are few effective drugs for viral diseases (*see* VACCINATION), although antiviral drugs have been developed for controlling AIDS and herpes.

inferiority complex An unconscious belief, first described by Alfred *Adler, that one is severely inadequate in some particular way. This leads to defensive behaviour and often to an overcompensation, such as open aggressiveness.

infinity In mathematics, a quantity larger than any that can be specified. The symbols $+\infty$ and $-\infty$ are read as "plus infinity" and "minus infinity" respectively. They indicate infinitely large positive and negative values. $x \rightarrow +\infty$ means that the value of a variable quantity, x, continues to increase and has no maximum.

inflation A general sustained increase in prices resulting from excessive demand for goods (demand-pull inflation), increased pricing by sellers in the absence of increased demand (cost-push inflation), or an expansion of the money supply (monetary inflation). **Deflation** is the opposite process and causes a reduction in both output and employment. Deflation in the 1930s has been followed in the postwar years by a protracted period of inflation. Remedies have varied according to the importance ascribed to each contributory factor: control of wages and prices, increased taxation, control of interest rates, reduced government spending, and a controlled money supply have been among current policies. *Compare* DEPRESSION.

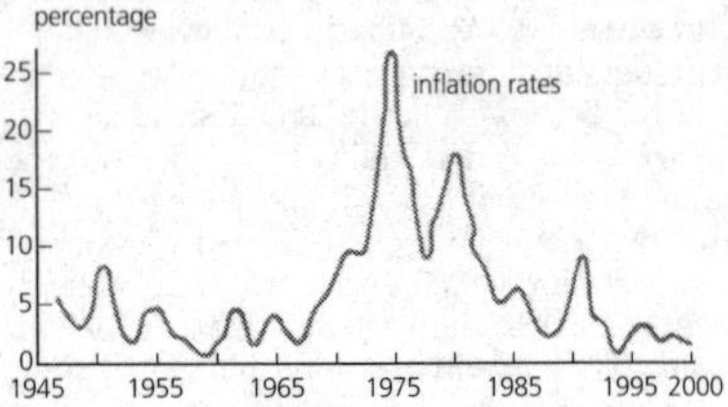

inflation. UK percentages (1948–2000; annual averages).

inflorescence The arrangement of a group of flowers borne on the same main stalk, of which there are two basic types. In a racemose (or indefinite) inflorescence the tip of the main stem continues to grow and flowers arise below it. Examples are the raceme (e.g. foxglove) and the spike (e.g. wheat). A cymose (or definite) inflorescence, or cyme, is one in which a flower is produced at the tip of the main stem, which then ceases to grow. Growth is continued either by one lateral bud below the tip, to produce a monochasium (e.g. buttercup), or by a pair of buds, giving a dichasium (e.g. stitchwort).

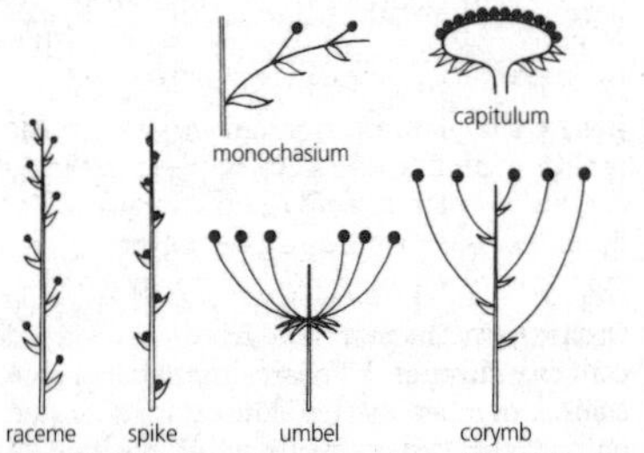

inflorescence. All plants except those with solitary flowers show characteristic arrangements of their flowers on the main flowering stalk. All the types shown here, with the exception of the monochasium, are racemose inflorescences.

information theory The mathematical theory of communication, involving analysis of the information content of messages and the processes used in their transmission, reception, storage, and retrieval. Statistical concepts, such as probability, are used to assess the extra information (redundancy) necessary to compensate for spurious signals (noise) occurring during communication. The *bit is the basic unit of information and the channel capacity is a measure of the ability of the transmission medium.

infrared radiation Electromagnetic radiation with wavelengths between about 750 nanometres and 1 millimetre. In the electromagnetic spectrum it lies between the red end of visible light and microwaves. It was discovered in 1800 by William Herschel (1738–1822).

infrared telescope A reflecting *telescope for detecting and studying infrared radiation from astronomical sources. Semiconductor detectors are used, and these (and in some cases the telescope optics) must be cooled to very low temperatures. Infrared telescopes are normally sited at high altitudes to reduce infrared absorption by the atmosphere or are carried on satellites.

Ingres, Jean-Auguste-Dominique (1780–1867) French painter. His three paintings of the Rivière family (Louvre) established him as a skilled portraitist. Many of his historical and mythological paintings aroused criticism but his *Vow of Louis XIII* (Cathedral, Montauban) established him as an opponent of Romanticism. He is noted for his nudes, e.g. *Valpinçon Bather* (Louvre); his draughtsmanship influenced *Degas and *Picasso.

inheritance tax A UK tax introduced in 1986 to replace capital-transfer tax. The first £263,000 (2004–05) of an inheritance is tax-free, thereafter a flat rate of 40% is applied. The tax on lifetime gifts was replaced with a tapered charge on gifts made within seven years of death.

ink A coloured fluid for writing or printing. Ordinary permanent blue-black writing ink contains ferrous sulphate, mineral organic acid, and other dyes. Coloured inks contain only synthetic dyes, while washable inks use water-soluble synthetic dyes. Marking ink is a mixture of inorganic and organic salts. Indian ink is a black waterproof ink containing carbon black and *shellac. Printing ink consists of pigments suspended in linseed oil, resins, and solvents. Ballpoint pen ink consists of synthetic dye dissolved in organic liquids with a resinous binder.

Inkerman, Battle of (5 November 1854) A decisive battle of the Crimean War, in which the French and British defeated the Russians at Inkerman, near Sevastopol. The Russians lost about 12 000 men, the British, about 2 500, and the French, about 1 000.

Inland Sea (Japanese name: Seto Naikai) A shallow section of the NW Pacific Ocean between the Japanese islands of Honshu, Shikoku, and Kyushu.

Innsbruck 47 17N 11 25E A city in W Austria, the capital of the Tirol on the River Inn. It is a popular tourist and winter-sports centre. Population (2001): 113 826.

Inns of Court Assocations with the exclusive right to confer the rank or degree of *barrister-at-law, known as "calling to the Bar." For the English bar, the Inns are the Honourable Societies of Lincoln's Inn (established 1310), Middle Temple (1340), Inner Temple (1340), and Gray's Inn (1357). Most barristers' offices (known as chambers) in London are in one of the Inns.

Inquisition (*or* **Holy Office**) An institution of the medieval and early modern Church designed to combat heresy and moral offences. Formally instituted (1231) by Pope Gregory IX (c. 1148–1241), it attempted to place all control of heresy in papal hands. The use of torture was authorized in 1252 and trials were held in secrecy; fines and various penances were imposed on those who confessed, while those who refused were imprisoned or executed by burning. Almost entirely confined to S Europe, the Inquisition was revived in Spain in 1478 against apostate Jews, Muslims, and, later, Protestants. The growth of Protestantism also led to the establishment (1542) of a Roman Inquisition by Pope Paul III. In 1965 the Holy Office was renamed the Sacred Congregation for the Doctrine of the Faith; it is now concerned with maintaining Roman Catholic discipline.

INRI Abbreviation for *Iesus Nazarenus Rex Iudeorum* (Jesus of Nazareth King of the Jews). According to St John (19.19–20) this inscription, written in Hebrew, Greek, and Latin, was placed by order of Pilate on the cross upon which Jesus was crucified.

insanity In law (although not a legal term), defect of reason caused by disease of the mind, making a person not responsible for his acts. A person is presumed sane until the contrary is proved. If a jury finds an accused person committed an act as charged but was insane, it must return a verdict of not guilty by reason of insanity. According to **M'Naghten's Rules** an accused person is insane if he was unaware of the nature or quality of his act or did not know it was morally wrong. Insanity may affect a person's capacity to make binding contracts or a will or fitness to stand trial.

insect An invertebrate animal (an arthropod), 0.2–350 mm long, belonging to the largest class in the animal kingdom (*Insecta* or *Hexapoda*; about a million known species). Insects occur throughout the world and account for 83% of all animal life. An insect's body is divided into three sections: the head, which bears a pair of antennae; the thorax, with three pairs of legs and typically two pairs of wings; and the ab-

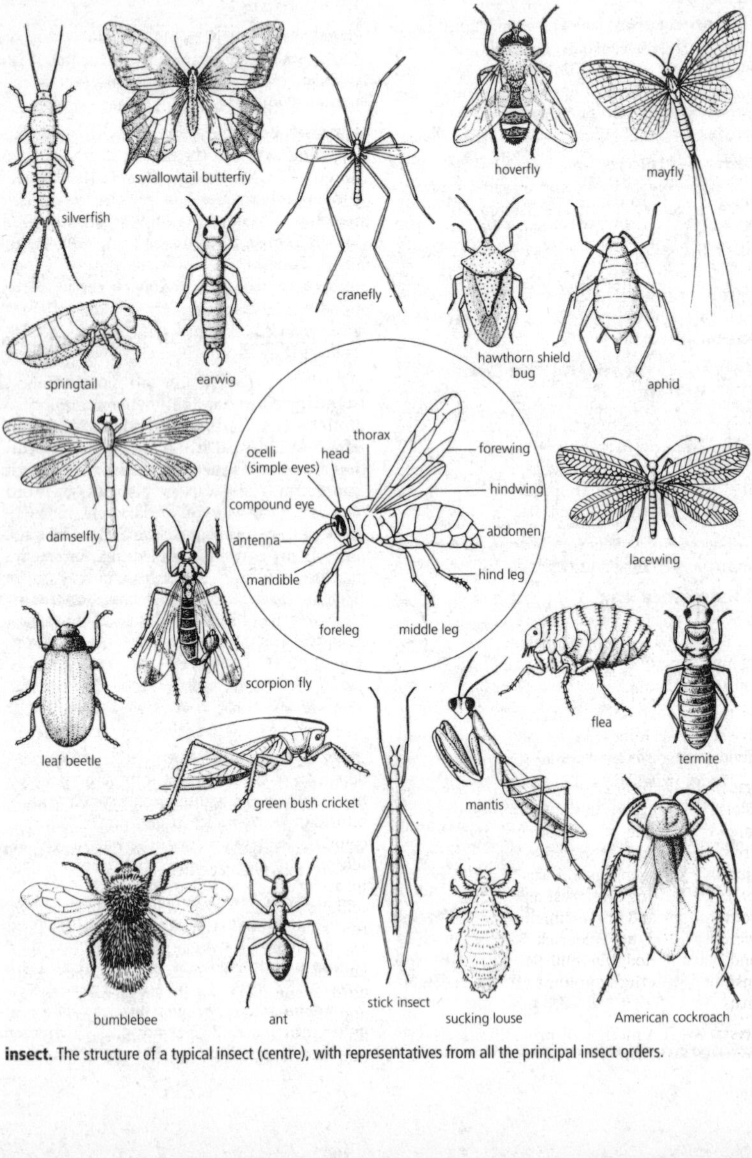

insect. The structure of a typical insect (centre), with representatives from all the principal insect orders.

domen. With biting or sucking mouthparts they feed on almost all plant or animal materials. The majority of insects lay eggs, which go through a series of changes (metamorphosis) to reach the adult stage. Insects play an important role in nature as predators, parasites, scavengers, and as prey, but can also spread disease. Others are useful in pollinating crops or killing insect pests and some produce useful substances, such as honey, beeswax, and silk.

insecticides Substances used to kill insects by chemical action. Previously, strong inorganic poisons, such as arsenic compounds and cyanides, were used but these were also toxic to humans and livestock. Synthetic organic substances, beginning with DDT in 1945, were then widely used. **Contact insecticides** are applied directly to the insects, while **residual insecticides** are sprayed on surfaces that the insects touch. Problems of insect immunity and environmental pollution have encouraged research into alternative methods involving *biological control.

Insectivora The order of *mammals, comprising about 375 species, that includes *shrews, *tenrecs, *hedgehogs, *moles, golden moles, and solenodons. Feeding mainly on invertebrates, insectivores are fairly primitive mammals with narrow snouts and sharp simple teeth. Frequently nocturnal, insectivores are found in nearly all regions; they are absent from the Poles and Australasia.

instinct **1.** A complex pattern of behaviour, the form of which is determined by heredity and is therefore characteristic of all individuals of the same species. Although the behaviour may be released and modified by environmental stimuli, its basic pattern does not depend on the experience of the individual. Birdsong and the complex behaviour of social insects (such as bees) are striking examples. **2.** An innate drive, such as hunger or sex, that urges the individual towards a particular goal.

insulin A protein hormone secreted by the islets of Langerhans in the *pancreas. It stimulates the uptake of glucose and amino acids from the blood by the tissues and the formation of *glycogen. Insulin was first isolated in 1921 by *Banting and *Best and its amino acid composition and three-dimensional structure were revealed by Frederick Sanger (1918–) and Dorothy Hodgkin (1910–94). A deficiency of insulin causes the symptoms of *diabetes mellitus.

insurance A method of providing monetary compensation for a misfortune or loss that may not occur. Events that must occur at some time, such as death, are provided for by assurance. In the UK and some other countries insurance against unemployment, sickness, and retirement is provided by the government (*see* NATIONAL INSURANCE). Other types of insurance are undertaken either by insurance companies or by *Lloyd's. The public does not deal directly with the underwriters (insurers) but arranges to cover a risk through an insurance broker, who works for a commission. The cost to the insured of covering the risk (premium) is calculated by the insurer's *actuary on the basis of the probability of the risk occurring.

integrated circuit (IC) A solid-state *semiconductor circuit contained in a single wafer of semiconductor. ICs are made by a process of etching and diffusing a pattern of impurities into the semiconductor surface, forming tiny p-n junctions, which make up individual diodes, *transistors, etc. Since the 1970s computers have been used to make ICs smaller and more complex. A silicon chip (*or* microchip) is covered with circuits, and computer-controlled microscopic probes search out the best points for connections for each specific device.

intelligence The ability to reason and to profit by experience. An individual's level of intelligence is determined by a complex interaction between his heredity and environment; Jean Piaget (1896–1980) greatly contributed to the understanding of intellectual development. The first **intelligence tests** were devised by Alfred Binet (1857–1911) in 1905. An individual's performance in a test is represented by his **intelligence quotient** (IQ). Tests are constructed so that the average IQ is 100; over 95% of the population come between 70 and 130. However, it is now widely thought that true intelligence can be expressed only through speech and writing (and is therefore inaccessible to testing).

intelligence service The government department responsible for obtaining information about the military and economic capabilities and political intentions of another country (intelligence) or for thwarting the attempts of a foreign country to obtain such information for itself (counterintelligence). Intelligence services existed in antiquity and the first known treatise on the subject is Sun Tzu's *The Art of War* (c. 400 BC). Elizabeth I of England had a notable intelligence service, as did Cardinal de Richelieu in 17th-century France and Frederick the Great in 18th-century Prussia. The first specifically military service was established in France during the Napoleonic

Wars, which the British countered (1808) with the Peninsular Corps of Guides in Spain. A similar corps was set up (1855) during the Crimean War. The subsequent Intelligence Department was active in the second Boer War (1899–1902). In 1909 and 1912 respectively the army general staff's Directorate of Military Operations organized MO-5 (counterintelligence) and MO-6 (intelligence), which soon became MI(Military Intelligence)-5 (the Security Service) and MI-6 (the Secret Intelligence Service). Elsewhere, the best-known intelligence services have included the *Central Intelligence Agency, the Federal Bureau of Investigation (counterintelligence), and the National Security Agency (dealing with cryptology) in the USA and the *KGB in the former Soviet Union.

interactive compact disc (**CD-i**) A *compact disc that stores digitized information, such as text, sound, and pictures, in a form in which the user can interact with it and control it. CD-is are used for education, games, etc. *See also* MULTIMEDIA SYSTEM.

interest The amount of money charged by a lender to a borrower for the use of a loan. The principal (P) is the amount on which interest is calculated; the term (t), the length of time in years for which the money is lent; and the interest rate (r), the annual rate of return per 100 units of principal. In simple interest, the principal each year is the sum originally lent. The lender is paid $Prt/100$ in interest and repaid P after t years. In compound interest, the interest each year is not paid to the lender but is added to the principal, so that the principal for the next year becomes $P + r/100$. After t years the lender is paid $P(1 + r/100)^t$.

interference A wave phenomenon in which two waves combine either to reinforce each other or to cancel each other out, depending on their relative phases. The pattern of light and dark strips so produced is called an **interference pattern** (*or* interference fringe). Interference was discovered in 1801 by Thomas *Young and provided strong evidence for the wave theory of light. An **interferometer** is used to produce interference patterns, mainly for the accurate measurement of wavelengths.

interferon A protein that appears in the plasma during viral infections: it is released from infected cells and inhibits the growth of the viruses. Interferon plays an important role in *immunity because it can enter uninfected cells and render them immune to all viral infections. It was discovered in 1957 by a British virologist, Alick Isaacs (1921–67). Human interferon is now being used to treat certain viral infections (e.g. hepatitis B and C), cancers, and multiple sclerosis.

internal-combustion engine A *heat engine in which fuel is burnt inside the engine, rather than in a separate furnace (*see* STEAM ENGINE). This category includes all piston engines, *jet engines, and *rockets. The first practical internal-combustion engine was patented by N. *Otto in 1876. The modern four-stroke Otto-cycle petrol engine, used to power most road vehicles, has a compression ratio of 8 or 9 to 1, which requires special fuels (*see* TETRAETHYL LEAD) to avoid knocking. A simpler but less efficient variety of the petrol engine is the two-stroke, which is used where low power is required. The main alternative to the petrol engine is the oil engine, based on a cycle invented by the German engineer Rudolf Diesel (1858–1913). In this case the compression ratio has to be 15 or 16 to 1, making the engine considerably heavier and more expensive than the petrol engine. The *gas turbine uses continuous combustion and with a compression ratio of up to 30:1 can reach a working temperature of 1200°C. It is therefore more efficient and creates less pollution than piston engines. Jet engines based on the gas turbine are used in aircraft. *See* ELECTRIC CAR.

International An association of national socialist or labour parties formed to promote socialism or communism. The **First International** was founded in London in 1864 as the International Working Men's Association. Karl Marx soon assumed its leadership and its first congress was held in Geneva in 1866. Although the First International was successful in disseminating socialist ideas among workers, it failed to make any political changes. Its last meeting was held in 1876 in Philadelphia. The **Second International** was founded in Paris in 1889; its headquarters were in Brussels. Its leaders included Ramsay *MacDonald. At the outbreak of World War I, the organization collapsed because of division between pro- and anti-war groups. A postwar attempt to revive it failed. The **Labour and Socialist International** was founded in Vienna in 1921; its goal was to create a socialist commonwealth. It has been called the "second and a half International" because it was composed of those out of sympathy with the Second and Third Internationals. It came to an end following Hitler's invasions in W Europe in 1939. The **Third International** (*or* Comintern), an organization of world Communist Parties, was founded by Lenin in March 1919, to encourage worldwide proletariat revo-

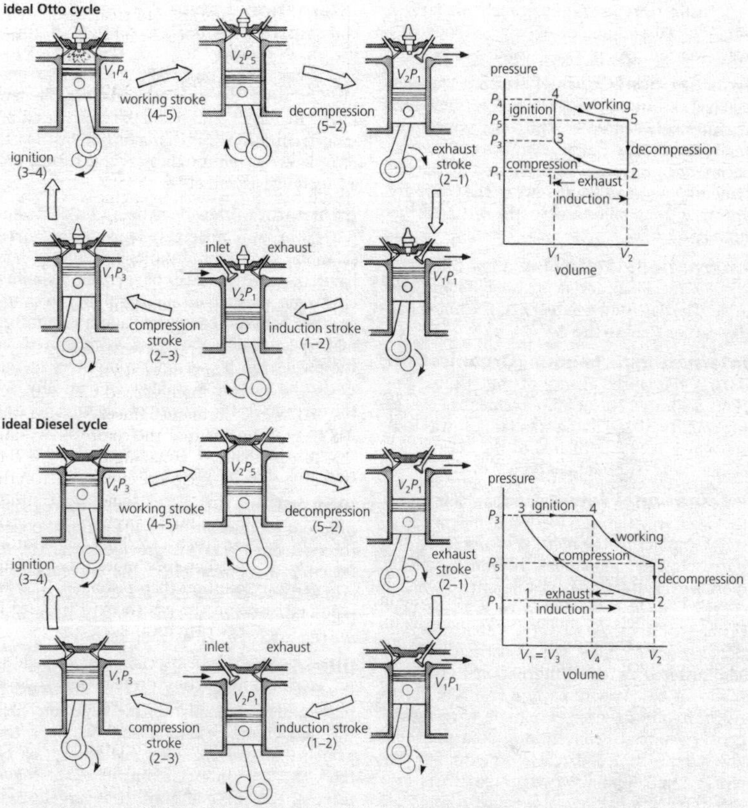

internal-combustion engine. In the ideal Otto-cycle (four-stroke) engine, there are four piston strokes (movements up and down) for explosion. The petrol-air mixture is drawn into the cylinder by the induction stroke (1–2) and compressed by the compression stroke (2–3). A spark then ignites (3–4) the mixture causing the pressure to rise from P_3 to P_4 before the piston descends (combustion at constant volume). The piston then descends in the working stroke (4–5) and rises again in the exhaust stroke (2–1), when the burnt gases are pushed out of the cylinder through the exhaust valve. The graph illustrates the pressure and volume changes during the cycle. In the Diesel cycle, ignition is caused by the high compression achieved by the compression stroke (2–3) and the piston descends, increasing the volume of the burning gas from V_3 to V_4, before the pressure has time to rise (combustion at constant pressure).

lution. Throughout its existence it was influenced by the power struggles within the Soviet party leadership. Stalin dissolved the International in 1943. The **Fourth International** was founded by *Trotsky in Mexico City in 1937 in opposition to Stalin and the Third International. It held its first conference in France in 1938. The **Socialist International** was founded in 1951 as an association of socialist parties that believe in parliamentary democracy and oppose communism. Its headquarters are in London.

International Bank for Reconstruction and Development (**IBRD**) A specialized agency of the *United Nations, known as the World Bank, with headquarters in Washington, DC. It finances development in member countries by making loans to governments or under government guarantee. It was set up by the 1944 Bretton Woods agreements.

International Brigades A volunteer army recruited during the Spanish Civil War (1936–39) by the Comintern to aid the Republicans against Franco. Comprising at its largest some 20 000 volunteers, of which about 60% were communists, it was disbanded in 1938.

International Court of Justice The judicial body set up by the UN to pass judgment on disputes between states. The court, which normally sits at The Hague, comprises 15 judges, each from a different state, elected by the UN General Assembly. Judgments of the court are enforced by application to the UN Security Council.

International Date Line A line following the 180° meridian, deviating to avoid some land areas. The date immediately E of the line is one day earlier than to the W.

International Labour Organisation (**ILO**) A specialized agency of the *United Nations dedicated to the improvement of working conditions and living standards. It was first convened in 1919, affiliated to the *League of Nations, and its headquarters are in Geneva.

international law Rules that determine the legal relationship between independent states (public), or the method of resolving disputes between individuals to which two or more legal systems may be relevant, as when a contract made in one country is to be performed in another (private). Public international law, also called the law of nations and administered by the *International Court of Justice, is based on: (1) natural law, being laws recognized by civilized nations; (2) agreements between states, i.e. conventions; (3) customs followed in practice; and, to a lesser extent (4) the writings and opinions of respected jurists. Private international law, also called conflict of laws, determines the laws of which country should apply.

International Monetary Fund (**IMF**) A specialized agency of the *United Nations, with headquarters in Washington, DC, set up by the 1944 Bretton Woods agreements to stabilize exchange rates and facilitate international trade.

International Organization for Standardization (**ISO**) An organization, situated in Geneva, for establishing and controlling international scientific, industrial, and commercial standards of measurement and design. It was founded in 1946.

International Phonetic Alphabet (**IPA**) An augmented Roman alphabet, developed by the International Phonetic Association in the late 19th century. It attempts to symbolize, on phonetic principles, every sound used in human language.

international style The predominant architectural style of the 20th century. Originating in W Europe and the USA with such architects as *Gropius, *Wright, Behrens, and *Le Corbusier, the style evolved from the new tastes, materials, and technology produced by industrialization. It is characterized by the use of concrete, often roughcast, cubic forms, and a functional asymmetry.

Internet A worldwide network linking computers through modems, telephone lines, optical cables, and communications satellites. Users have access to a number of services, including electronic mail (email) and the ability to transfer files between computers and access information on remote databases. With growth in the ownership of personal computers in the 1990s, the system expanded dramatically. By the early 2000s the growth of the Internet had begun to revolutionize many established practices in the fields of entertainment, information provision, business, and shopping.

Interpol (*Inter*national Criminal *Pol*ice Organization) An association of 169 national police forces, formed in 1923 to provide a means of international cooperation in the prevention of crime. Its major concerns are the exchange of police information and the arrest of those who are the subject of an extradition order.

intestine The part of the digestive tract, in the abdomen, that extends from the stomach to the anus. The small intestine, which includes the duodenum, jejunum, and ileum, is the principal site of digestion and absorption of food. The large intestine consists of the colon, caecum, rectum, and anus. It is largely concerned with the absorption of water from digested food and the formation of faeces, which are expelled from the anus.

intrusive rock *See* IGNEOUS ROCK.

Inuit A Mongoloid people of the Arctic regions of Canada and Greenland. The men are traditionally hunters of seals, whales, walrus, and caribou, using harpoons and canoes. Fishing is also important. Their clothes are made of animal skins. Some construct semisubterranean sod shelters or use snow-covered skin tents, others use igloos. The term "Eskimo" is considered offensive by most Inuit. In 1999 the semiautonomous region of *Nunavut was established in NE Canada as an Inuit homeland.

Inuit-Aleut languages A language group, sometimes included in the classification of American Indian languages. it consists of three distinct languages: Inupik (Inupiaq *or* Inuk), spoken in Greenland and N Canada by Inuit; Yupik, spoken in Siberia and S Alaska; and Aleut, spoken in the Aleutian Islands.

Invar An *alloy of iron with 36% nickel, which expands by only 0.9 mm per km for each centigrade degree temperature rise. It was discovered in 1896 and since then has been used for accurate measuring tapes and chronometer parts.

Inverclyde A council area of W central Scotland, on the firth of Clyde. It was created from part of Strathclyde Region in 1996. The S bank of the Clyde is highly industrialized; inland it is mainly agricultural. Area: 162 sq km (63 sq mi). Population (2001): 84 203. Administrative centre: Greenock.

Inverness 57 27N 4 15W A city in N Scotland, the administrative centre of the Highland council area, at the head of the Moray Firth. It has a 19th-century cathedral and castle. Population (1991): 41 234.

in vitro fertilization *See* TEST-TUBE BABY.

Io A priestess of Hera, loved by Zeus, who transformed her into a heifer to protect her from discovery. Hera ordered Argus, a herdsman with eyes covering his entire body, to guard her, but she escaped with the help of Hermes and was finally restored to Zeus in Egypt.

iodine (I) A purple-black lustrous solid *halogen that evaporates slowly at room temperature to give a purple gas. It was discovered in 1811 by B. Courtois (1777–1838). It is insoluble in water but dissolves readily in organic solvents, such as carbon tetrachloride (CCl_4), to give pink-purple solutions. Potassium iodide (KI) is widely used in photography. The radioactive isotope ^{131}I, with a half-life of 8.1 days, is produced in nuclear reactors. Tincture of iodine is used as an antiseptic. At no 53; at wt 126.904; mp 113.5°C; bp 184.35°C.

ion An atom or group of atoms that has lost or gained one or more electrons and consequently has an electric charge. Positively and negatively charged ions are called **cations** and **anions** respectively. The sign and magnitude of the charge is indicated by a superscript, as in the potassium ion, K^+, or the doubly charged sulphate ion, SO_4^{2-}. Many compounds (electrovalent compounds) are combinations of positive and negative ions; sodium chloride, for example is formed from sodium ions (Na^+) and chloride ions (Cl^-). *See also* CHEMICAL BOND; IONIZATION.

Iona 56 19N 6 25W A small sparsely populated island in NW Scotland, in the Inner Hebrides. St Columba landed here in 563 AD, establishing a monastery that became the centre of the Celtic Church. Area: 854 ha (2112 acres).

Ionesco, Eugène (1912–94) French dramatist, born in Romania. He inaugurated the *Theatre of the Absurd with his first play, *The Bald Prima Donna* (1950). His later plays include *The Lesson* (1951), *Rhinoceros* (1960), and *Man With Bags* (1977).

Ionia In antiquity, the central W coast of Asia Minor and the adjacent islands, settled by Greeks about 1000 BC. Between the 8th and 6th centuries BC *Miletus, Samos, *Ephesus, and other Ionian cities led Greece in trade, colonization, and culture. After 550 BC Ionia passed under the domination of *Lydia and later Persia.

Ionian Islands A group of Greek islands in the Ionian Sea, including Páxos, Lévkas, Ithaca, and Cephalonia. They belonged to Britain from the Treaty of Paris (1815) until 1864, when they were ceded to Greece. Total area: 2307 sq km (891 sq mi). Population (2001): 214 274.

Ionic order *See* ORDERS OF ARCHITECTURE.

ionization The process of producing *ions from neutral atoms or molecules, by solvation (surrounding of an ion by polar solvent molecules), heating (thermal ionization), or bombardment with particles or radiation. The minimum energy required to ionize an atom A (i.e. $A \rightarrow A^+ + e^-$) is called its **ionization potential**, which is usually measured in electronvolts.

ionizing radiation Any radiation that ionizes the atoms or molecules of the matter through which it passes. It may consist of particles (such as *electrons) or it may be electromagnetic radiation (*see* ULTRAVIOLET RADIATION; X-RAYS; GAMMA RADIATION). Ionizing radiation occurs naturally in *cosmic rays and is emitted by radioactive substances. It is also produced artificially in X-ray machines, particle accelerators, nuclear reactors, etc.

ionosphere A region of the upper atmosphere that reflects short radio waves, enabling transmissions to be made round the curved surface of the earth by sky waves. The gases in the ionosphere are ionized by absorption of radiation from the sun. Its existence was suggested in 1902 by A. E. Kennelly (1861–1939) and independently by O. Heaviside (1850–1925). Sir Edward Appleton (1892–1925) provided proof by bouncing radio waves off the different layers of the ionosphere, which vary in behaviour with the position of the sun and with the sunspot cycle. The ionization of the D region, at between 50 and 90 kilometres altitude, disappears during the day. The E region is 90 to 160 kilometres high and the F region (sometimes called the Appleton layer) is from 160 kilometres up to about 400 kilometres.

Iowa A state in the USA, in the Midwest. The land rises slowly from the Mississippi Valley, with higher land in the NW. Iowa is predominantly an agricultural state, famed for its livestock, particularly pigs. Major crops are corn, oats, soya beans, and other fodder crops. There is also some mining for portland cement and gypsum. *History*: explored by the Frenchmen Louis Jolliet (1645–1700) and Jacques Marquette (1637–75) in 1673, it formed part of the Louisiana Purchase (1803) by the USA. It became a territory (1838) and then a state (1846). Area: 145 790 sq km (56 290 sq mi). Population (2000): 2 926 324. Capital: Des Moines.

ipecacuanha A South American herbaceous plant, *Uragoga ipecacuanha*, cultivated in the tropics for its root, which yields medicinal alkaloids used as an expectorant and emetic. Family: *Rubiaceae*.

Iphigenia In Greek legend, the eldest daughter of *Agamemnon and *Clytemnestra. At the beginning of the *Trojan War, Agamemnon was told that Artemis demanded the sacrifice of his daughter before his fleet could sail to Troy. In some versions of the myth, Artemis took pity on Iphigenia and transported her to Tauris, where she became a priestess.

Ipoh 4 36N 101 02E A city in NW Peninsular Malaysia, the capital of Perak state. It is a tin-mining centre and has Chinese rock temples. Population (1991): 382 633.

Ipswich 52 04N 1 10E A town in SE England, the administrative centre of Suffolk at the head of the Orwell estuary. It is a port with various economic activities, including financial services and telecommunications. Cardinal Wolsey was born here. Population (1997): 112 959.

IRA *See* IRISH REPUBLICAN ARMY.

Iráklion (*or* **Herakleion**; Italian name: Candia) 35 00N 25 08E The chief port of the Greek island of Crete, on the N coast. It possesses many Venetian fortifications and is a tourist centre. Exports include raisins, grapes, and olive oil. Population (1991): 117 167.

Iran, Islamic Republic of (name until 1935: Persia) A country in the Middle East lying between the Caspian Sea and the Persian Gulf. Its central plateau, containing deserts and marshes, is surrounded by mountains. The population is mainly Persian with groups of Turks, Kurds, Armenians, Arabs, and such tribes as the Bakhtyari. *Economy*: agriculture supports 75% of the population, although lack of rain hampers productivity. Wheat, rice, tobacco, fruit, sugar beet, and tea are grown; sheep and goats are kept. Oil is the chief source of revenue, the main oilfields being in the Zagros Mountains. Other minerals include coal, copper, iron ore, lead, natural gas, and precious stones. *History*: the Caspian coast and the plateau are among the earliest centres of civilization. Early Persian dynasties include the Achaemenians and the Sasanians (*see also* GREEK-PERSIAN WARS). Arab domination, which established Islam in the area, was followed by that of the Turks and Mongols before the Persian Safavid dynasty (1502–1736) came into power. Following a period of great prosperity (1587–1629) Persia again declined, encroached on by Uzbeks, Arabs, Afghans, Turks, and Russians. The next great dynasty, the Kajar dynasty (1794–1925), was marked largely by rivalry for domination between Britain and Russia. Repressive rule provoked opposition that was intensified by resentment against the concessions granted to Britain and Russia. The Shah was forced to grant a constitution and National Assembly (the Majlis; 1906); his successor disbanded this and was then deposed (1909). Further disorders brought Reza Khan to power (1921), from 1925 as Reza Shah Pahlavi. Under his virtual dictatorship order returned and the country was westernized; he was forced to abdicate in favour of his son *Mohammed Reza Pahlavi (1941). In 1945 the Soviet Union supported an Azerbaidzhani and Kurdish revolt to gain oil concessions (later withdrawn). Oil was also a major issue for the militant National Front movement, which nationalized the oil industry (1951); the British responded with a blockade. The Shah's reform programme, which included in 1963 the enfranchisement of women, the redistribution of land, and compulsory education, led to riots and harsh repression. By 1978 different opposition groups had united under the exiled Muslim leader Ayatollah Ruholla *Khomeini. The Shah fled the country in 1979, later dying in exile (1980), and Ayatollah Khomeini took over the government in the so-called Islamic Revolution, which established a strict Muslim regime. War with Iraq broke out in September 1980 (*see* IRAN-IRAQ WAR). Khomeini died in 1989 and Hashemi Rafsanjani became president. Iran's alleged involvement in international terrorism led to the imposition of US trade sanctions (1995–99). In 1996 Ayatollah Mohammed Khatami was elected president and began a cautious programme of liberal reform, while aiming to normalize Iran's international relations. Although Khatami was re-elected in 2001, the general election of 2004 produced a landslide for hardline elements after many leading reformists were barred from standing. Since 2002 Iran has come under increasing pressure from the USA over its alleged nuclear weapons programme and links with terrorist groups. Official language: Persian (Farsi). Currency: Iranian rial of 100 dinars. Area: 1 648 000 sq km (636 160 sq mi). Population (2003 est): 66 255 000. Capital: Tehran.

Iranian languages A subgroup of the Indo-Iranian language family. Iranian languages are spoken in Iran, Afghanistan, Turkey, and parts of the Caucasus and are closely related to *Sanskrit. Modern Iranian languages include Persian, Kurdish, Pashto, and Ossetic.

Iran-Iraq War (*or* **Gulf War**; 1980–88) An indecisive conflict in the Persian Gulf between Iran and Iraq over border territory. Iraqi forces invaded Iran and a war of attrition developed, with heavy casualties on both sides. Peace was achieved through UN mediation.

Iraq, Republic of A country in the Middle East, bordering on the Persian Gulf. The SE consists of an alluvial plain around the delta of the Rivers Tigris and Euphrates. The W is a vast desert while the N is mountainous. The population is about 90% Muslim divided evenly between Shiite and Sunnite sects. The Kurds, who live in the NE, form about 15–20% of the population. *Economy*: mainly agricultural, the chief crops being wheat, barley, rice, maize, sorghum, sesame, dates, and cotton. The main industry is oil and Iraq is a member of OPEC. Before the UN's imposition of a worldwide ban on Iraqi oil exports in 1990, oil accounted for almost 100% of government revenue. This ban and the damage to industry sustained in the *Gulf War led to economic crisis, further exacerbated in the War of 2003. *History*: as *Mesopotamia, Iraq was the site of the world's first civilization. It was conquered by Arabia and became Muslim in the 7th century AD and was part of the Ottoman Empire from 1534 until World War I, when UK troops expelled the Turks. As a British mandate (1920–32), Iraq became a kingdom (1921); the monarchy was overthrown in 1958. Since the 1960s the Kurds of the NE have been in intermittent rebellion. The Ba'athist leader Saddam *Hussein assumed absolute power in 1979; subsequently he invaded Iranian border territory, provoking the *Iran-Iraq War (1980–88), oppressed the Kurdish and Marsh Arab minorities, and invaded Kuwait (1990). In the ensuing *Gulf War his army was expelled from Kuwait by a US-led military alliance (Feb 1991). Iraq's defiance of UN ceasefire terms provoked further US air raids in 1993, 1996, and 1998. The UN agreed (1996) to a partial lifting of the oil-sales ban on the condition that the revenue was used for humanitarian purposes. In March 2003, arguing that Saddam's regime constituted a threat to international stability, the USA and UK launched the *Iraq War. The Ba'athist government was toppled and a US civil administrator appointed. Moves toward representative government have been hampered by the collapse of Iraq's economy and infrastructure and mounting resistance to the occupiers. Iyad Allawi was named prime minister elect in June 2004. Official language: Arabic. Currency: Iraqi dinar of 1000 fils. Area: 438 446 sq km (169 248 sq mi). Population (2003 est): 24 683 000. Capital: Baghdad.

Iraq War (2003) A conflict between Iraq under Saddam *Hussein on the one hand and the USA and the UK (with some military support from Australia and Poland) on the other. In 2002 President George W. *Bush accused Iraq of developing weapons of mass destruction (WMD) and threatened to remove the Ba'athist regime there as an extension of the USA's *war on terrorism. Although strongly backed by Tony Blair, the proposed military action divided Western opinion and failed to get explicit authorization from the UN. On 20 March 2003 the USA launched an air attack on Baghdad; this was followed by rapid advances into Iraq by US and UK ground forces, accompanied by a continuing aerial bombardment. Basra fell to the invaders on 7 April and Baghdad on 9 April. Although the main phase of the conflict was declared over on 14 April, attacks by Iraqi irregulars (including suicide bombers) have continued, becoming more widespread and concerted in April–May 2004. The fugitive Saddam Hussein was captured by US troops in December 2003. Controversy over the justification for the war has continued, owing mainly to the failure of investigators to find any evidence of WMD in Iraq.

Ireland The second largest island in the British Isles, separated from Great Britain by the North Channel, the Irish Sea, and St George's Channel. It consists of a central lowland area of fertile plains, bogs, and moorland, rising to hills and mountains in the N and S. Since 1920 Ireland has been politically divided, the NE part forming Northern Ireland in the UK and the remainder comprising the Republic of Ireland. *History*: Ireland was invaded in the 4th century BC by the Celts. The country came to be divided into the five tribal kingdoms (the Five Fifths) of Ulster, Meath, Leinster, Munster, and Connaught. In the 5th century the country was converted to Christianity—a process in which St Patrick was the outstanding figure. The 9th and 10th centuries saw Viking invasions; in the mid-12th century Ireland was invaded by the Norman conquerors of England and Henry II gained the allegiance of the Irish kings. English law and administration were introduced in the 13th century and an Irish parliament (composed of the Anglo-Irish and subordinate to the English Crown) began to meet. However, English rule was restricted to the area around Dublin (called the Pale) until the 16th century. Revolts, inspired in part by Roman Catholic opposition to the Reformation, were suppressed and the Plantation of Ireland by English and later by Scottish settlers was begun in Ulster. Irish resistance continued, culminating in the rebellion of 1641, which was not suppressed until Oliver Cromwell's expedition in 1649–50. The subsequent redistribution of the rebels' land among English colonists established the economic and political ascendancy of the Protestant minority in Ireland. It was strengthened by the Restoration settlement, which extended Protestant landholdings, and by William of Orange's defeat (1690) of the Irish supporters of the deposed Catholic king, James II. In the 18th century Ireland's subservience to England was opposed by many Irish Protestants and in 1782, under the leadership of Henry Grattan, the Irish parliament obtained legislative independence. However, the abortive rebellion of 1798 by the Society of United Irishmen persuaded Pitt the Younger of the need for the complete union of Britain and Ireland (1800; *see* UNION, ACTS OF). It also convinced him of the need for *Catholic emancipation, which was not fully obtained until 1829. Attempts by the Young Ireland group to repeal the Act of Union failed, and nationalist agitation was taken up after the Irish (potato) famine, first by the *Fenians and then by the *Home Rule movement. While the Land League pursued agrarian reform with some success, Home Rule, in spite of Gladstone's support, was delayed. Following the proclamation of an Irish republic by *Sinn Féin (1919) and virtual civil war Britain proposed partition (1920), with the establishment of separate parliaments in the predominantly Protestant NE and Catholic S and W, both of which would be self-governing provinces of the UK. This was rejected in the S, where independence was now demanded. Following negotiations between the British government and Republican leaders, the Irish Free State, with dominion status, came into being in 1922. The NE (Northern Ireland) accepted self-government within the UK.

Northern Ireland The province is divided into 26 administrative districts. There are also six nonadministrative traditional counties: Antrim, Armagh, Down, Fermanagh, Londonderry, and Tyrone. *Economy*: since the 1950s, the traditional industries of shipbuilding and linen manufacture have declined and there has been expansion of the service sector. The economy has suffered from the political upheavals of the last 30 years. *History*: following the Government of Ireland Act (1920) and the Anglo-Irish Treaty (1921), which provided for the division of Ireland, six of the nine counties of Ulster became an autonomous province of the UK. From 1922 until 1972 Northern Ireland was governed by a parliament, which met at Stormont Castle in Belfast and had legislative responsibility for most matters. Tension between the Protestant majority who dominated politics and the Catholic minority (most of whom favoured Northern union with the Irish Republic) led to violent conflict in 1969, when a British peacekeeping force was sent in. A terrorist campaign by the IRA led to the imposition (1972) of direct rule from Westminster. In the Downing Street Declaration (1993) the UK and Dublin governments stated their willingness to negotiate with all political parties that renounced violence. Subsequently Sinn Féin announced a complete IRA ceasefire and the Protestant paramilitaries did the same. Talks in 1997–98 led to the **Good Friday Agreement** (April 1998), which proposed the creation of three new bodies: a Northern Ireland assembly with a powersharing executive, a North-South ministerial council, and a "Council of the Isles" with members from the British and Irish governments and devolved bodies within the UK. The agreement, which required the complete decommissioning of all terrorist weapons, was backed in a referendum by 71% of the electorate and David Trimble was elected Northern Ireland's first minister. Following further negotiations an executive including Sinn Féin members was established (December 1999) and power was devolved to the new bodies; however, lack of progress on IRA decommissioning led Britain to suspend the political institutions in February–May 2000. Although the IRA began to decommission its weapons in 2001, evidence of continuing illicit activity by the organization led to a further suspension of devolved government in October 2002. Area: 14 121 sq km (5452 sq mi). Population (2001): 1 685 267. Capital: Belfast.

Republic of Ireland (Irish name: Éire) The country is administratively divided into 26 counties. *Economy*: predominantly agricultural, cattle rearing being of major importance. Dairy farming is also extensively practised. Arable crops include barley, wheat, oats, potatoes, and sugar beet. Tourism is another major source of revenue. Peat is extensively cut as a fuel for power stations and as a household fuel. In 1977 Europe's largest lead-zinc mines were opened at Navan. In the later 1990s the Republic had the fastest growing economy in the developed world. *History*: Republican opposition to partition continued immediately after the establishment of the Irish Free State but was quelled by 1923. In 1932 *De Valera, leader of Fianna Fáil, became prime minister and, in 1937, introduced a new constitution by which the Irish Free State was renamed Éire. In 1949 a coalition took the country, as the Republic of Ireland, out of the British Commonwealth. In 1973 Ireland became a member of the EC (now the EU). Since 1997 the Republic has had a Fianna Fáil government under Bertie Ahern. In a referendum (May 1998) the Irish electorate endorsed the Good Friday Agreement on Northern Ireland, in which the Republic agreed to abandon its constitutional claim to the province. Ireland adopted the European single currency in 1999–2002. Official languages: Irish and English. Currency: euro of 100 cents. Area: 68 893 sq km (26 599 sq mi). Population (2003 est): 3 969 000. Capital: Dublin.

Irian Jaya A province in E Indonesia, comprising W New Guinea. Formerly a Dutch colony, it was incorporated into Indonesia in 1963. Indonesia's exploitation of Irian Jaya's considerable mineral wealth has caused environmental damage and provoked unrest among the indigenous people.

iridium (Ir) A hard brittle metal, discovered in 1803 by C. Tennant (1768–1838), in the residue left after dissolving platinum in aqua regia. Its salts are highly coloured, whence its name (Latin *iris*, rainbow). It is used as a hardening agent for platinum and in electrical contacts. At no 77; at wt 192.22; mp 2477°C; bp 4428°C.

iris (anatomy) The muscular tissue in the eye that surrounds the pupil and is situated immediately in front of the lens: it is responsible for eye colour. Reflex contraction of the muscles in the iris cause it to become smaller in dim light (which enlarges the pupil and allows more light to enter the eye) and larger in bright light (thus decreasing the size of the pupil).

Iris (botany) A genus of perennial herbaceous plants (about 300 species), native to N temperate regions and widely planted in gardens. Irises grow from bulbs or rhizomes (underground stems) and their flowers can be three or more colours. Family: *Iridaceae*. *See also* FLAG.

Iris (mythology) The Greek goddess of the rainbow and messenger of the gods, especially of *Hera. She is portrayed as carrying a herald's staff and often bearing water that could put perjurers to sleep.

Irish Republican Army (**IRA**) A militant organization established in 1919 to fight British rule in Ireland. Under Michael *Collins it fought an effective war against British forces (1919–21) but the subsequent partition treaty was rejected by many IRA members. The antitreaty faction was defeated by Irish government forces by 1923 but continued to press for an all-Ireland republic. The movement was reactivated when the Northern Irish troubles began in 1968. In 1969 both the IRA and *Sinn Féin, to which many IRA members belong, split into the Officials, who abandoned the policy of abstaining from constitutional Irish politics, and the Provisionals, who embarked on a terrorist campaign to expel the British from the North. Subsequent IRA outrages included the attempted assassination of the British prime minister in Brighton (1984) and a mortar attack on 10 Downing St (1991). In 1986 there was a further split into the Provisional IRA/Sinn Féin, who adopted a policy of constitutional activity backed by terrorism, and the Continuity IRA/Republican Sinn Féin, who remain outside politics and committed to violence. Following the Downing Street Declaration of 1993 (*see* (NORTHERN) IRELAND), the Provisional IRA announced a complete ceasefire (abandoned in 1996 but resumed in 1997). Although Sinn Féin accepted the subsequent Good Friday Agreement (1998), the IRA repeatedly refused to begin decommissioning its weapons. The IRA finally announced that some weapons had been put "beyond use" in October 2001, and further acts of decommissioning followed in 2002–03. However, evidence that the organization was still engaged in illegal activities led to a further impasse in the peace process from 2003. The "Real IRA," a splinter group hostile to the Agreement, has continued terrorist activity, most infamously the Omagh bombing (August 1998).

Irish Sea A section of the Atlantic, separating England, Scotland, and Wales from Ireland. Area: about 100 000 sq km (40 000 sq mi). Maximum width: 240 km (149 mi).

Irish wolfhound An ancient breed of large hunting dog originating in Ireland. It has a powerful body and a long narrow head with small ears. The rough wiry coat can be grey, brindle, red, black, white, or fawn. Height: 78 cm minimum (dogs); 71 cm minimum (bitches).

Irkutsk 52 18N 104 15E A city in S Russia. It is the industrial, cultural, and educational centre of E Siberia. Population (1999 est): 596 400.

i

iron (Fe) A metallic transition element that has been used since prehistoric times. It is the fourth most abundant element in the earth's crust, occurring in the ores haematite (Fe_2O_3), magnetite (Fe_3O_4), and siderite ($FeCO_3$). It is obtained from its ores by smelting in a *blast furnace to give pig iron, which is then converted into cast iron, wrought iron, or steel. Iron has two important valence states forming iron II (ferrous) and iron III (ferric) compounds. Common compounds include the sulphates ($FeSO_4$ and $Fe_2(SO_4)_3$), chlorides ($FeCl_2$, $FeCl_3$), and oxides (FeO, Fe_3O_4, Fe_2O_3). Iron is vital to animal life owing to its presence in *haemoglobin. At no 26; at wt 55.847; mp 1538°C; bp 2862°C. *See also* FERROMAGNETISM.

Iron Age The cultural phase during which iron replaced bronze metal technology (*see* BRONZE AGE). Despite spasmodic earlier use of meteoric iron, it was not until about 1500 BC that iron-working techniques were perfected by the *Hittites. It was used in Hallstatt Europe in the 7th century BC. The Chinese were both forging and casting iron about 500 BC, preceding Europe by about 1700 years in casting.

Iroquois North American Indian tribes of the NE region, who spoke the Iroquois language belonging to the Iroquois Caddoan family. These tribes were cultivators and hunters, organized into matrilineal clans. The *Mohawk, Oneida, Onondaga, Cayuga, and Seneca tribes formed the **Iroquois League** during the 16th century, which was allied with the British in wars against the French and, except for the Oneida and Tuscarora (members of the League from 1715), against the colonists in the American Revolution (1775–83).

Irrawaddy River The chief river in Myanmar (Burma), flowing SSW across the country. It enters the Andaman Sea through a swampy delta. Length: 2010 km (1250 mi).

Irving, Sir Henry (John Henry Brodribb; 1838–1905) British actor and manager. He established his reputation in London during the early 1870s and remained the leading actor for the next 30 years. From 1878 to 1902 he was manager of the Lyceum Theatre, where, with Ellen *Terry, he acted in a notable series of Shakespearean productions.

Isabella (I) the Catholic (1451–1504) Queen of Castile (1474–1504). Her marriage (1469) to Ferdinand of Aragon united the two major Spanish kingdoms. The introduction of the Inquisition (1480) and the expulsion of the Jews (1492) were largely due to Isabella's influence. *See also* FERDINAND (V AND II) THE CATHOLIC.

Isabella II (1830–1904) Queen of Spain (1833–68). Her succession was only secured in 1839, after the first Carlist War. Her governments became increasingly unpopular and she was deposed.

Isaiah (8th century BC) Old Testament prophet, influential at the court of Judah until the Assyrian invasion (701 BC). The **Book of Isaiah** contains his prophecies, although chapters 40–66 are now usually ascribed to a later hand. Several passages predict the coming of the Messiah, and these proved important in the development of early Christianity.

Ischia 40 44N 13 57E A volcanic island in Italy, in the Bay of Naples. Area: 47 sq km (18 sq mi). Population (latest est): 16 100. Chief town: Ischia.

Isfahan (*or* **Esfahan**) 32 41N 51 41E A town in central Iran. It has some fine examples of Persian architecture, including the 17th-century royal mosque. Population (1996 est): 1 266 765.

Isherwood, Christopher (1904–86) British novelist. His experiences while teaching in Berlin in the 1930s are described in the novel *Mr Norris Changes Trains* (1935) and in the stories *Goodbye to Berlin* (1939), adapted as the film *Cabaret* (1968). He collaborated with his friend W. H. *Auden on several plays.

Ishtar The supreme Babylonian and Assyrian goddess, the daughter of the sky god Anu or of the moon god Sin. She combined aspects of a beneficent mother goddess and fierce goddess of war and fertility. She descended to the underworld in search of her lover Tammuz.

Isis An Egyptian goddess, the sister and wife

of *Osiris, whose dismembered body she magically restored to life, and mother of *Horus. She was usually portrayed as holding the child Horus and wearing on her head the solar disc and a cow's horns, the same attributes as Hathor.

Islam (Arabic: submission to God) A major world religion, which originated in Arabia in the 7th century AD. The essential creed of Islam, whose adherents are called Muslims, is that there is one God, Allah, and that *Mohammed is his prophet. The revelations received by Mohammed are recorded in the *Koran, which is the basis of Islamic belief and practice (*see also* ISLAMIC LAW). Five fundamental duties are incumbent upon the individual Muslim: expression of belief in Allah and in the prophethood of Mohammed; observance at set times of five daily prayers, which are recited facing towards Mecca; fasting during the month of *Ramadan; payment of a special tax for charitable purposes; and a pilgrimage to Mecca at least once, if means permit. The main sects are the *Sunnites (*or* Sunni) and the *Shiites (*or* Shiah). There are an estimated 800 million Muslims, about one million of whom are UK citizens.

Islamabad 33 40N 73 08E The capital of Pakistan, situated in the N of the country. The site was chosen in 1959 and construction began in 1961. Population (1998): 524 500.

Islamic law The sacred law of Islam, *shari'ah*, prescribes not only religious duties (*see* ISLAM) but covers every aspect of the life of a Muslim. Its basic principles were elaborated in the 9th century AD. The law covers marriage, divorce, and inheritance; it forbids usury, the depiction of living beings, the drinking of alcohol, the eating of pork, etc., and prescribes penalties and punishments for crimes. In modern times most Muslim states have adopted secular legal systems at least in part and especially with regard to criminal, financial, and property law although some have reverted to strict Islamic law.

Islay An island of the Inner Hebrides in the Atlantic Ocean, off the W coast of Scotland. Area: 606 sq km (234 sq mi). Population (latest est): 3500.

Ismaili A *Shiite Muslim sect. In the 8th century AD a group of Shiites recognized Ismail the son of Jafar al-Sadiq as imam, while the rest of the Shiites supported his brother Musa. The Ismaili Fatimids ruled in Egypt and N Africa until 1171, contesting control of the Muslim world with the Abbasid dynasty of Baghdad. Today the best-known Ismaili sect is that headed by the Aga Khan.

ISO *See* INTERNATIONAL ORGANIZATION FOR STANDARDIZATION.

Isocrates (436–338 BC) Athenian teacher of rhetoric and political pamphleteer. His appeals to successive military leaders to unite the feuding Greek states against Persia culminated in the *Philippus* (346 BC), addressed to *Philip of Macedon.

isomers Chemical compounds that have the same molecular formulae but different arrangements of atoms. In **structural isomerism** the molecules have different molecular structures. Thus, ethanol (C_2H_5OH) and dimethyl ether (CH_3OCH_3) both have the molecular formula C_2H_6O, although they are different compounds. Another form occurs when functional groups appear at different positions in the molecule. In **stereoisomerism** the isomers differ in their spatial arrangements. **Cis-trans isomerism** occurs as a result of the positioning of groups in a planar molecule. Since rotation cannot occur about a double bond it is possible to have two isomers in organic compounds containing double bonds: one with groups on the same side of the bond (the cis isomer) and the other with groups on opposite sides of the bond (trans isomer). Another form of stereoiso-

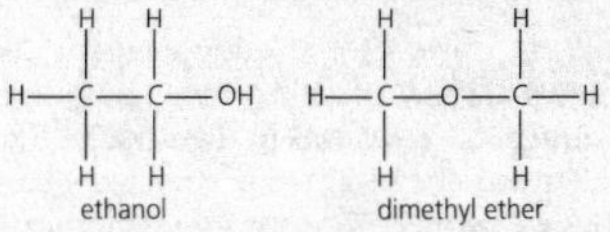

structural isomers. Ethanol and dimethyl ether have the same atoms in the molecule but different functional groups.

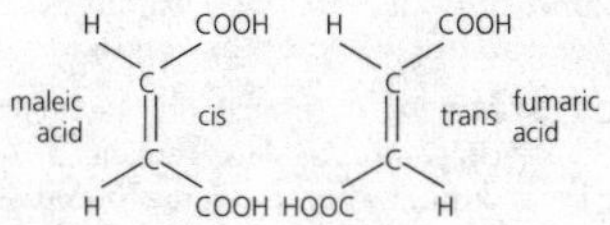

cis-trans isomers. A form of stereoisomerism occurring as a result of a double bond.

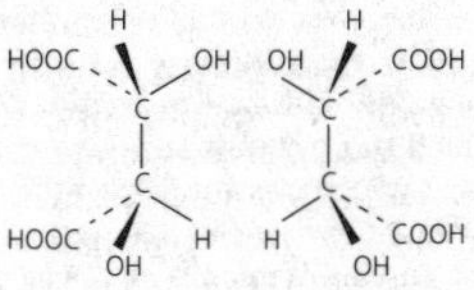

optical isomers. Another form of stereoisomerism in which two forms of tartaric acid have different optical properties.

isomers

merism is **optical isomerism**, in which the two isomeric forms of the molecule are asymmetric and differ in that one molecule is a mirror image of the other; these are optically active, i.e. they rotate *polarized light passed through their solutions. Isomers of all types have different physical properties and, to a greater or lesser extent, different chemical properties. In some cases isomers can exist in equilibrium (**tautomerism**).

Isopoda A widely distributed order of *crustaceans (4000 species). The group includes the most successful terrestrial crustacean—the woodlouse—as well as aquatic forms. Isopods have oval flattened bodies, covered by armour-like plates, and—usually—seven pairs of walking legs. The young develop within a brood pouch on the female.

i

isoprene (CH_2:C(CH_3)CH:CH_2) A colourless volatile liquid. It is made from chemicals extracted from oil, coal, or tar and is used to make synthetic rubber. Natural rubber consists mainly of a polymer of isoprene.

isotherm A line on a map joining points of equal temperature. Corrections are usually made to compensate for the effect of altitude on temperature.

isothermal process Any process that occurs without a change in the temperature of a system (*compare* ADIABATIC PROCESS).

isotopes Atoms of the same element that contain equal numbers of *protons but different numbers of *neutrons in their nuclei. They have identical chemical properties but different physical properties. An isotope is indicated by combining its nucleon number and its name or symbol in various ways, for example uranium-235, U-235, ^{235}U. All naturally occurring elements are mixtures of isotopes.

Israel, State of A country in the Middle East, bordering on the Mediterranean Sea. There are mountains in the N, a narrow coastal plain in the W, and the Negev Desert in the S. The River Jordan flowing through the Great Rift Valley forms part of the E border. The population consists largely of Jews who have immigrated since 1948. Many Palestinian Arabs left the area when Israel was created but some have since returned. The Jews form 82% of the population and the Arabs 16%; immigration is decreasing. Some 3% of the population live in *kibbutzim* (*see* KIBBUTZ) and about 5% live in *moshavim*. *Economy*: both industrial and agricultural output has increased rapidly since 1948, boosted by investments and gifts of capital from abroad. There are resources of copper ore and phosphates; potash and bromine from the Dead Sea are also exploited. Fishing and tourism are also important. 6% of the work force is employed in agriculture, which depends heavily on artificial irrigation. *History*: Israel's history prior to 1948 is that of *Palestine, in which Jewish Zionists had demanded the creation of a Jewish state since the late 19th century. According to a UN recommendation. Palestine was to be divided into a Jewish state, an Arab state, and a small internationally administered zone around Jerusalem. As soon as the state of Israel was proclaimed following British withdrawal (1948), however, Arab forces invaded; by early 1949 Israeli forces had not only repulsed them but had gained control of 75% of Palestine, while the rest had been annexed by Jordan (the *West Bank of the River Jordan) and Egypt (the *Gaza Strip). Jerusalem was divided between Jews and Arabs. In 1956, Israeli forces occupied the Gaza Strip and the *Sinai Peninsula. In the Six Day War (1967) Israel defeated Egypt, Syria, and Jordan and again occupied the Gaza Strip and the Sinai Peninsula as well as the *Golan Heights, the West Bank, and the Arab sector of Jerusalem. A peace agreement with Egypt after the Yom Kippur War (1973; in which the Israelis were taken unawares by Egyptian forces on the Day of Atonement—Yom Kippur), was achieved in 1979 at the Camp David talks, following which Israel withdrew from Sinai (1980–82). In 1982 Israel invaded Lebanon and forced the Palestine Liberation Organization (PLO) to leave West Beirut, withdrawing in 1985. Israel has been criticized for its treatment of Palestinians in the Israeli-occupied territories, which led to violent protests (the *intifada*) in 1988. Israel signed a peace agreement with the PLO in 1993, and in 1994–95 gave autonomous status to the Gaza Strip and Jericho, handing over power to a new Palestinian National Authority. In 1995 the prime minister Yitzhak Rabin was murdered by a Jewish extremist opposed to the peace process. Israel and the PLO signed a further peace agreement in October 1998. In the 1999 general election the right-wing government of Binyamin Netanyahu was heavily defeated by Labour under Ehud Barak. Hizbollah activity forced Israel to withdraw all its forces from S Lebanon in May 2000. That same year talks with the PLO collapsed over the issue of Arab E Jerusalem, leading to violent protests by Palestinians and heavy retaliation by Israel. Barak resigned as prime minister and lost the ensuing elections (2001) to Likud's Ariel *Sharon, widely seen as a hardliner. Violence then escalated sharply. Rising casualties from Arab suicide bombings prompted Israel to reoccupy large areas of the Palestinian West Bank in 2001–02, and to refuse all demands that it should withdraw. In 2004 Sharon announced a new plan to disengage from the Gaza Strip but to retain parts of the West Bank. Official languages: Hebrew and Arabic. Currency: shekel of 100 agora. Area (excluding occupied territories): 20 770 sq km (8018 sq mi). Population (2003 est): 6 473 000. Capital (de facto): Jerusalem (the UN recognizes only Tel Aviv).

Issus, Battle of (333 BC) The battle in which Alexander the Great defeated an enormous Persian army under Darius III, which was caught in a narrow pass.

Istanbul (*or* **Stamboul**) 41 02N 28 57E A city in W Turkey, on both sides of the Bosporus. There are many ancient buildings in the city, including the mainly 6th-century Hagia Sophia the Blue Mosque, and the Topkapi Palace. It is a major port and industrial centre. *History*: ancient Byzantium was renamed Constantinople in 330, when the emperor Constantine I declared it the capital of the Eastern Roman Empire. It was the capital of the Byzantine Empire until its capture by the Ottoman Turks in 1453, although it had been held by Crusaders from 1204 to 1261. The Ottomans made it the capital of their empire in 1457; it was renamed Istanbul in 1926. Population (1997): 8 260 438.

Istria A peninsula in NW Croatia. Passing to Italy at the end of World War I, it was ceded to Yugoslavia (1947) except for the Territory of Trieste, which was divided between Italy and Yugoslavia in 1954. It became part of independent Croatia in 1991.

Italian A language of the Romance family spoken in Italy. The standard literary and official form is based upon the Tuscan dialect of Florence.

Italic languages A subgroup of the Indo-European language family spoken in central and NE Italy in the thousand years before the rise of Rome. A parent of modern *Romance languages, this group comprised four related dialects: Latin, Faliscan, Osco-Umbrian, and Venetic. At the beginning of the 1st millennium BC Osco-Umbrian was the most widely spoken, but with the growth of Roman civilization, Latin replaced it.

italic script A style of handwriting adopted in 15th-century Italy by papal scribes and later (c. 1500) adapted for printing. Italic cursive letters eliminate unnecessary lifts of the pen, permitting rapid legible handwriting. *In print its characteristic sloped letters, such as those used in this sentence, are used mainly for display, emphasis, or to indicate that a word is in a foreign language.*

Italy, Republic of A country in S Europe, occupying a peninsula bordered by the Tyrrhenian Sea (W), the Ionian Sea (S), and the Adriatic Sea (E). The principal offshore islands are Sicily and Sardinia. Except for small coastal areas and the Po Valley in the N, the country is generally rugged and mountainous. The main rivers are the Po, Tiber, Arno, and Adige. *Economy*: agriculture is still important, the main crops being wheat, maize, grapes, and olives. Industry, however, has expanded considerably since World War II. The wine industry is important. Mineral resources are not large and Italy is heavily dependent on imported fossil fuels. Tourism is an important source of revenue. *History*: pre-Roman Italy was inhabited from the 7th century BC by the *Etruscans in the N, Italics and Latins in central Italy, and Greek colonists in the southern mainland and Sicily. By 275 BC most of the peninsula had come under the rule of Rome (*see* ROMAN REPUBLIC). As the western *Roman Empire declined from the 4th century AD, Italy was invaded by a succession of barbarian tribes, including the Visigoths and the Vandals. The last Roman emperor was deposed in 476 by the German king, Odoacer, who in 493 was in turn overthrown by the Ostrogoths. They were expelled in the early 6th century by the Eastern (Byzantine) Roman Empire, which was then threatened from the mid-6th century by successive invasions by the Lombards and the Franks, a period that also saw the origins of the pope's temporal power (*see* PAPAL STATES). The Muslims invaded the S in the 9th and 10th centuries, Magyars, the N in the 10th century, and Normans, the S in the 11th century. The claim of the German kings to rule Italy was established in 962, when Otto the Great was crowned Holy Roman Emperor in Rome. The conflict from the 11th century between successive popes and emperors over the investiture controversy embroiled the Italian city states (notably Milan, Pisa, Genoa, Venice, and Florence), which in the 12th century were further divided by the struggle between *Guelfs and Ghibellines. Many of the Italian cities came to be dominated by single families, such as the Visconti and then the Sforza in Milan and the *Medici in Florence, who during the Renaissance were often outstanding patrons of culture and learning. Following the French invasion of Italy in 1494 Italy became the scene of conflict between France and Spain and from the 16th to early 18th centuries was largely dominated by the latter. During the 18th century control passed to Austria until 1796, when Italy was conquered by Napoleon. After the restoration of Austrian rule the movement for independence and unification (the *Risorgimento) developed. By 1861, under the leadership of King Victor Emmanuel II of Sardinia-Piedmont and his chief minister Cavour, aided by Garibaldi in the S, the Austrians had been expelled and the kingdom of Italy proclaimed with Victor Emmanuel as its first king. In the late 19th century Italy acquired a colonial empire, notably in East Africa. In 1915 Italy entered World War I on the side of the Allies. The postwar rise of fascism brought Mussolini to power in 1922. In 1936 he conquered Ethiopia and in 1939, Albania. In 1940, Mussolini took Italy into World War II on Germany's side. The Allied conquest of Sicily (1943) brought Mussolini's fall and in 1946 Umberto II abdicated. Since the establishment of the Republic there have been nearly 60 governments; political instability has been exacerbated by a stagnating economy, extremist groups such as the *Red Brigades of the 1970s, and widespread corruption. In 1996 elections were won by a left-wing coalition led by Romano Prodi. The general election of 2001 resulted in victory for a right-wing coalition led by the controversial tycoon Silvio *Berlusconi. Italy was a founder member of the EC (now the EU) and adopted the European single currency in 1999–2002. Official language: Italian. Currency: euro of 100 cents. Area: 301 425 sq km (116 350 sq mi). Population (2003 est): 57 033 000. Capital: Rome.

itch mite A parasitic *mite, *Sarcoptes scabei*, that produces *scabies in man and mange in domestic animals. The female burrows into the skin, where it lays eggs and causes irritation. Family: *Sarcoptidae*.

Ivan (III) the Great (1440–1505) Grand Prince of Muscovy (1462–1505). Ivan greatly expanded Muscovite territory and ended Russian subordination to the Tatars. In 1497 he introduced a new legal code. Ivan married (1472) Zoë Palaeologus (d. 1503), the niece of the last Byzantine emperor, and adopted the Byzantine two-headed eagle in his arms.

Ivan (IV) the Terrible (1530–84) Grand Prince of Muscovy (1533–84), who was crowned tsar in 1547. Ivan reformed the legal code and local administration (1555), conquered Kazan and Astrakhan, and established commercial relations with England. After 1560 his reign was marred by his brutality: thousands were executed and in a fit of rage Ivan murdered his son (1581). The effects of his tyranny were aggravated by the financial strains resulting from the abortive Livonian War (1558–82).

Ives, Charles (Edward) (1874–1954) US composer. Noted for his musical inventiveness, he composed more than 500 works. Two of the best known are his second piano sonata, subtitled *Concord, Mass* (1909–15), and *Central Park in the Dark* (1898–1907).

ivory The close-grained white tissue forming the tusks of elephants, walruses, and narwhals and the teeth of hippos. So-called fossil ivory is obtained from mammoths. Ivory carving is a very ancient art; objects from France date to Palaeolithic times and fine examples survive from Egyptian, Minoan, Mycenaean, Assyrian, Greek, and Roman civilizations. India, SE Asia, China, and Japan have ancient traditions of skilled ivory carving. American Eskimo carvings in walrus ivory are greatly prized by connoisseurs. In 1989 many countries banned ivory imports to conserve the African elephant from poachers. Poaching for ivory reduced the numbers of the African elephant from 1.3 million in 1979 to only 600 000 in 1989.

ivy An evergreen woody climbing plant, *Hedera helix*, that has glossy leaves, aerial roots (with which it clings to supports), greenish-yellow flowers, and small round fruits ripening from green to black. Native to Europe and W Asia, it is widely cultivated. Family: *Araliaceae*.

Ivy League A group of prestigious universities in the NE USA. They include Harvard, Yale, and Princeton and are all members of an athletic conference for intercollegiate sports known as the Ivy League (founded 1870s).

Iwo Jima 24 47N 141 19E A Japanese island in the W Pacific Ocean, the largest of the Volcano Islands. Captured by US forces in 1945, it was returned in 1968. Sulphur and sugar are produced. Area: 20 sq km (8 sq mi).

Izmir (former name: Smyrna) 38 25N 27 10E A port in W Turkey, on the Aegean Sea. Much was destroyed by fire in 1922, the rebuilt town being a modern commercial centre. Population (1997 est): 2 081 556.

J

jacana A waterbird belonging to a family (*Jacanidae*; 7 species) occurring in tropical regions worldwide, also called lily trotter. Jacanas are characterized by long legs with elongated toes and claws, which enable them to run over floating vegetation. 25–32 cm long, they are commonly reddish to dark-brown in colour. Order: *Charadriiformes* (gulls, plovers, etc.).

Jacaranda A genus of trees and shrubs (50 species) of South and Central America and the West Indies, often grown as ornamentals. *J. mimosifolia*, up to 15 m tall, and blue or violet tubular flowers. Some species yield valuable timber. Family: *Bignoniaceae*.

jackal A carnivorous mammal of the genus *Canis*, found in Asia and Africa. Jackals are closely related to dogs and have pricked ears and bushy tails. The African black-backed jackal (*C. mesomeles*) is up to 110 cm long including the tail (25–33 cm) and often hunts in packs for carrion. The African side-striped jackal (*C. adustus*) is smaller.

jackdaw An intelligent Eurasian crow, *Corvus monedula*, about 32 cm long, having a black plumage with a grey nape, an erectile crest, and pale-blue eyes. Often found in colonies, jackdaws feed on insects, grain, and carrion.

Jack Russell terrier A breed of dog developed in England from the fox terrier by the Rev John Russell (1795–1883) for flushing foxes from earth. It has a stocky body and a strong muscular head. The short coat is white, black, and tan. Height: up to 38 cm.

Jackson 32 20N 90 11W A city in the USA, the capital of Mississippi. Founded in 1821, it was virtually destroyed by Gen Sherman in 1863. Population (2000): 184 256.

Jackson, Michael (1958–) US pop singer, who established himself as a solo star in the 1980s after success with his brothers as the Jackson Five. His solo albums include the hugely successful *Thriller* (1982), *Bad* (1987), *Dangerous* (1991), and *Invincible* (2001). In 2003 he was charged with several counts of child molestation.

Jackson, Peter (1961–) New Zealand film director, screenwriter, and producer. His early work included *Bad Taste* (1987) and *Heavenly Creatures* (1994), but he is now best known for his spectacular film adaptation of Tolkien's epic trilogy *The Lord of the Rings* (2001–03).

Jackson, Stonewall (Thomas Jonathan J.; 1824–63) US Confederate general in the Civil War. In the first battle of *Bull Run, he and his brigade were described as standing "like a stone wall" in the face of the Federal advance. Jackson was a master of rapid tactical movement, shown particularly in the Shenandoah valley campaign (1862). His accidental death at Chancellorsville left a gap in the Confederate command.

Jack the Ripper An unidentified murderer who killed and mutilated at least six prostitutes in the East End of London in late 1888.

Jacob In the Old Testament, the son of Isaac and Rebekah and the ancestor of the entire Jewish nation. His story is told in Genesis 25–50. His 12 sons gave their names to the 12 tribes of Israel.

Jacobites Supporters of the exiled *Stuart king, James II (Latin name: Jacobus), and his descendants. Between 1688, when the Glorious Revolution overthrew James II, and 1745, the Jacobites (mainly Roman Catholics and/or Tories), were the rallying point for opposition to the Hanoverian monarchs. Two Jacobite rebellions, in 1715 (the "15 Rebellion" led by *James Edward Stuart, the Old Pretender) and 1745 (the "45 Rebellion" led by *Charles Edward Stuart, the Young Pretender), were suppressed and thereafter the movement disintegrated.

Jacob's ladder A perennial herb, *Polemonium caeruleum*, native of Eurasia and widely cultivated as a garden flower. Growing to a height of 90 cm, it has bright-blue flowers. Family: *Polemoniaceae*.

jade A hard semiprecious stone, usually green, consisting of either the rare jadeite, $NaAlSi_2O_6$, or the more common nephrite, $Ca_2(Mg,Fe)_5Si_8O_{22}(OH,F)_2$. It has been used for carved ornaments and jewellery since prehistoric times.

Jaffa *See* TEL AVIV-JAFFA.

Jagannatha A Hindu deity in some contexts synonymous with Krishna. Devotees were alleged to throw themselves under the massive chariot on which his idol is annually wheeled during a festival at Puri, in Orissa, and from which the term "juggernaut" is derived.

Jagger, Sir Mick *See* ROLLING STONES, THE.

j

jaguar The largest New World *cat, *Panthera onca*, found in the southern USA and Central and South America. Up to 2.5 m long including the tail (70–90 cm), it has dark rosette-shaped spots on its yellow coat. Jaguars inhabit forest and scrub and hunt peccaries, turtles, fish, and capybaras and may attack domestic livestock.

jaguarundi A weasel-like *cat, *Felis yagouaroundi*, of Central and South America. Up to 110 cm long, it stands only 28 cm high at the shoulder. It has a red or grey coat, long tail, and small ears.

Jainism The religion of between two and three million Indians, followers of Mahavira (?599–527 BC). Founded in the 6th century BC, Jainism stresses ahimsa, asceticism, and meditation. Right belief, knowledge, and conduct are the means of release from the perpetual round of rebirth caused by *karma. This release is possible only for monks; the laity aim only for a better rebirth. Jainism is atheistic, although lesser spirits and demons proliferate.

Jaipur 26 53N 75 50E A city in India, the capital of Rajasthan. It has many fine buildings built in pink sandstone and is famous for its enamel work and jewellery, textile printing, and stone, marble, and ivory carving. Population (1991): 1 454 678.

Jakarta (*or* **Djakarta**; name until 1949: Batavia) 6 09S 106 49E The capital of Indonesia, in NW Java. It became a commercial centre as the base of the Dutch East India Company. Population (1995 est): 9 160 500.

jalap A climbing plant *Ipomoea purga*, of Mexico and South America, that has crimson flowers. The dried tubers yield a resin that is used medicinally as a laxative. Family: *Convolvulaceae*.

Jamaica An island country in the Caribbean Sea, off the S coast of Cuba. A high plateau is crossed by the Blue Mountains, which reach 2255 m (7400 ft). The population is mainly of African and mixed African and European descent. *Economy*: sugar, bauxite, bananas, and tourism form the basis. Recent industrial developments include the construction of an oil refinery with Mexican aid. *History*: discovered by Columbus in 1494, it was occupied by the Spanish, who exterminated the original Arawak inhabitants. Captured by the British in 1655, it became a colony and a centre of the slave trade. Self-government was introduced in 1944 and in 1962 Jamaica became an independent state within the British Commonwealth. There was considerable political unrest in the 1970s: a state of emergency was imposed in 1976–77 by the socialist prime minister Michael Manley. In the 1989 election Manley became prime minister for the second time, retiring in 1992. He was replaced by Percival J. Patterson, who was re-elected in 1993, 1997, and 2002. Jamaica is a member of the OAS and CARICOM. Official language: English. Currency: Jamaican dollar of 100 cents. Area: 10 991 sq km (4244 sq mi). Population (2003 est): 2 644 000. Capital: Kingston.

James I (1394–1437) King of the Scots (1406–37), whose actual rule began on his release (1424) from English imprisonment. He strengthened royal authority at the expense of the nobles and extended royal control over justice and commerce. He was assassinated by a group of disaffected nobles.

James I (1566–1625) The first Stuart King of England and Ireland (1603–25) and, as James VI, King of the Scots (1567–1625). He succeeded to the Scottish throne after the abdication of his mother Mary, Queen of Scots. As king he reasserted royal authority against the nobility and, less successfully, the Presbyterians. In 1589 he married *Anne of Denmark. In England, James encountered opposition from his parliaments (1604–10, 1614, 1621–22) and was also unpopular for his choice of favourites and for his attempts to obtain a Spanish marriage for his son. One of the great achievements of his reign was the publication (1611) of the *King James Version of the Bible.

James II (1430–60) King of the Scots (1437–60). He established his authority over rival factions and continued the extension of royal control and justice begun by his father James I. He was killed while besieging the English at Roxburgh Castle.

James II (1633–1701) King of England, Scotland, and Ireland (1685–88). The second son of Charles I, James (as Duke of York) escaped to Holland (1648) after his father's defeat in the Civil War and during the 1650s fought for the French and then the Spanish. In 1659 he married the daughter of the Earl of Clarendon, Anne Hyde (1637–71), by whom he had two daughters (later Queens Mary II and Anne). In about 1669 he became a Roman Catholic: consequent attempts to exclude him from the succession failed and in 1685 he became king. The Protestant rebellion of the Duke of *Monmouth was suppressed, Roman Catholics were admitted to public office, and religious freedom for all denominations was announced (1687). In 1688 James prosecuted the Archbishop of Canterbury and six bishops who refused to proclaim religious toleration from the pulpit but lost the case. This defeat and the threat of a Roman Catholic succession with the birth of a son (*see* JAMES EDWARD STUART, THE OLD PRETENDER) to his second wife, Mary of Modena (1658–1718), precipitated the *Glorious Revolution. James fled; in his subsequent attempt to regain the Crown from Ireland he was defeated by William III's forces at the *Boyne (1690) and *Aughrim (1691). He died an exile in France.

James III (1452–88) King of the Scots (1460–88). Until 1469 Scotland was ruled by a regency and his personal rule was marked by baronial revolts. He was killed after defeat by rebel barons near Stirling.

James IV (1473–1513) King of the Scots (1488–1513). In 1503 he married *Margaret Tudor. He defeated the rebels who had killed his father James III, procuring internal stability. Recurrent hostility with England culminated in the invasion of Northumberland (1513) and his defeat and death at *Flodden.

James V (1512–42) King of the Scots (1513–42). During his minority (1513–28) Scotland was controlled by rival pro-French and pro-English factions. He died shortly after the failure of an invasion of England and was succeeded by his daughter Mary, Queen of Scots.

James, Henry (1843–1916) US novelist and critic. He spent much of his childhood in Europe, becoming a British citizen in 1915. His novel *Roderick Hudson* (1875) introduced the theme of Americans confronting European culture that recurred in many of his novels, such as *The Portrait of a Lady* (1881), although he occasionally returned to American settings, as in *The Bostonians* (1886). He wrote more than a hundred shorter works of fiction, including *The Turn of the Screw* (1898). In his later novels, *The Wings of the Dove* (1902), *The Ambassadors* (1903), and *The Golden Bowl* (1904), action is subordinated to psychological analysis. His brother **William James** (1842–1910) was a psychologist and philosopher, who held that a theory was only true if it helped to solve problems. Religious and moral beliefs were treated in the same nondogmatic way, especially in his influential *Varieties of Religious Experience* (1902) and *The Meaning of Truth* (1909).

James, Jesse (Woodson) (1847–92) US outlaw. After the Civil War he formed the James gang and by 1867 was robbing banks, stagecoaches, and trains in his native Missouri and surrounding states. He was shot and killed by Robert Ford, a James gang member who claimed the $10 000 reward.

James, P(hyllis) D(orothy), Baroness (1920–) British novelist, best known for her detective fiction. Her novels include *Death of an Expert Witness* (1977), *Devices and Desires* (1990), *A Certain Justice* (1997), and *The Murder Room* (2003). She received a life peerage in 1991.

James Edward Stuart, the Old Pretender (1688–1766) The son of James II, the deposed Roman Catholic King of England. In exile, he was urged by his supporters, known as *Jacobites, to claim the English throne. After their invasion of Scotland failed in 1715, James abandoned his claim and lived in permanent exile in Rome.

Jammu and Kashmir A state in N India, forming part of the disputed area of *Kashmir. Area: 100 569 sq km (38 820 sq mi). Population (2001): 10 069 917. Capital: Srinagar.

Jamshedpur 22 47N 86 12E A city in India, in Jharkand. Founded in 1907 by the industrialist Dorabji Jamsetji Tata, it is the site of India's principal iron and steel works. Population (1991): 461 212.

Janáček, Leoš (1854–1928) Czech composer. He was over 60 before he gained wide recognition. In his vocal works he attempted to reproduce natural speech rhythms; he was also influenced by folk music. His works include the operas *Jenufa* (1894–1903), *The Excursions of Mr Broucek* (1908–17), and *The Makropulos Case* (1923–25), two string quartets, and the *Glagolitic Mass* (1926).

Jansenism A movement in the Roman Catholic Church in the 17th and 18th centuries based on the teaching of the Dutch theologian Cornelius Jansen (1585–1638). Jansenists emphasized the doctrine of *predestination and rejected some aspects of traditional teaching on the sacraments; this led to conflict with the Jesuits and condemnation from the Church leadership. One of the most famous Jansenists was *Pascal.

Jansky, Karl Guthe (1905–50) US radio engineer, who discovered a source of radio waves outside the solar system (1932), while investigating static interference. Jansky's discovery led to the science of *radio astronomy.

Janus The Roman god of doors, thresholds, and beginnings, after whom the month January is named. He is usually portrayed as having two heads facing forwards and backwards.

Japan (Japanese name: Nippon *or* Nihon) A country in E Asia, consisting of a series of islands lying between the Pacific Ocean and the Sea of Japan. The four main islands are *Honshu, *Kyushu, *Hokkaido, and *Shikoku. Much of the land is mountainous, with the highest mountain, *Fujiyama, rising to 3778 m (12 399 ft). The population is of mixed Malay, Manchu, and Korean descent; the original inhabitants, the Ainu, survive in small numbers on Hokkaido. *Economy*: Japan is a highly industrialized country, manufacturing electronic goods, motor vehicles, and petrochemicals; it now produces about a third of the world's ships. Mineral resources are on the whole sparse. Agriculture is intensive and, although rice is still the main crop, there have been efforts to diversify with such crops as wheat, barley, and soya beans. There is considerable timber production. Japan is also one of the world's leading fishing nations. Japan is now one of the world's foremost financial centres, although it suffered severely in the Asian financial crisis of 1997–98. *History*: about 200 BC the country was united under the Yamato dynasty. Their religion formed the basis of *Shinto and Japanese emperors were regarded as divine descendants of the sun goddess. From 1186 AD real power was in the hands of the military *shoguns until Emperor Mutsuhito (1852–1912) regained power for the House of Yamato in 1867. 1871 saw the end of Hoken Seido (the feudal system) and from the mid-19th century the country was opened up to western communications and ideas. It expanded colonially, especially in successful wars against China and Russia, and it occupied several Asian countries. It fought against the Allies in World War II and surrendered after the dropping of atomic bombs on Hiroshima and Nagasaki in 1945. By a new constitution of 1947 the emperor renounced his former claim to divinity and became a constitutional monarch. The Liberal Democratic Party (LDP) held power from 1955 until 1993, when a coalition government was formed. In 1997–98 Japan's financial system was severely hit by the crisis in SE Asia and the economy entered its worst recession since World War II. A new coalition was formed (1998) under the LDP's Keizo Obuchi. Junichiro Koizumi became prime minister in April 2001. Official language: Japanese. Currency: yen of 100 sen. Area: 372 480 sq km (143 777 sq mi). Population (2003 est): 127 546 000. Capital: Tokyo.

Japan, Sea of A section of the NW Pacific Ocean between Japan and the Asian mainland.

Japanese The language of Japan. Its relationship to other languages is uncertain but it is probably related to *Korean. It is polysyllabic and usually stresses all syllables equally. There are many dialects; the standard form is based on the speech of Tokyo. Japanese writing systems are complex. In about the 5th century the Japanese adopted Chinese ideographic characters (*kanji*), which have both Chinese-like (*on*) and native Japanese (*kun*) pronunciations. About 2000 *kanji* are now used. In about the 9th century the Japanese supplemented the *kanji* by deriving from them two phonetic syllabaries, of 48 symbols each, called *hiragana* and *katakana*. *Hiragana* is mainly used for suffixes and grammatical functions and for words for which there are no *kanji*. *Katakana* is mainly used for foreign names, loanwords, and scientific words.

Japanese cedar A conifer, *Cryptomeria japonica*, native to China and Japan, where it is an important timber tree reaching a height of 55 m; elsewhere it is grown for ornament and rarely exceeds 35 m. Japanese cedar has globular spiny cones, 2 cm across. Family: *Taxodiaceae*.

Japanese maple A *maple tree, *Acer palmatum*, up to 13 m tall, the 5–11 lobed leaves of which turn scarlet in autumn. Native to Japan, it is a popular ornamental in many cultivated varieties, including purple-leaved and dwarf types.

japonica A shrub or tree of the genus *Chaenomeles* (or *Cydonia*), native to Japan but widely cultivated as an ornamental. Flowering quince (*C. japonica*) and Japanese quince (*C. speciosa*) are the most popular species. These have clusters of scarlet five-petalled flowers, 5 cm across. The apple-like fruit is used in marmalade and jelly. Family: *Rosaceae*.

Japurá, River A river in NW South America, rising in SW Colombia and flowing generally SE to join the River Amazon in Brazil. Length: 2800 km (1750 mi).

jasmine A shrub of the genus *Jasminum* (about 300 species), native to tropical and subtropical regions and widely cultivated. Many species yield an essential oil used in perfumery. Two species suitable for temperate gardens are the common jasmine (*J. officinalis*) from S Asia, up to 6 m tall with fragrant white flowers, and the Chinese winter jasmine (*J. nudiflorum*), 3–6 m tall, with yellow flowers. Family: *Oleaceae*.

Jason A legendary Greek hero, heir to the throne of Iolcos in Thessaly. Sent by his uncle, the usurper Pelias, to fetch the *Golden Fleece, he and the *Argonauts underwent many adventures before finally recovering the Fleece from Colchis with the help of *Medea. After many years of wandering he died at Corinth.

jasper An impure variety of *chalcedony, usually red or reddish brown. Slightly translucent, it is regarded as a semiprecious stone. It is an abundant mineral, occurring in veins and in cavities in volcanic rocks.

jaundice Yellowing of the skin and whites of the eyes due to the presence of *bile pigments. Jaundice may result if there is excessive breakdown of red blood cells, as in haemolytic anaemia, or in disease of the liver, such as *hepatitis, or blockage of the bile duct by gallstones.

Java An Indonesian island, the smallest of the Greater *Sunda Islands. Its chain of volcanic mountains has formed exceptionally fertile soil, and its many rivers feed its intensive wet-rice agriculture. Other food crops, sugar cane, and kapok are grown and forest products include teak. Indonesia's administrative and industrial centre, Java is heavily overpopulated. *History*: Indian colonies in the early centuries AD developed into Hindu and Buddhist kingdoms, with Hindu-Javanese culture reaching its height in the 14th century. The Dutch East India Company was centred here from 1619. Many died during anticommunist purges (1965–67). Area: 132 174 sq km (51 032 sq mi). Population (1999 est): 121 193 000, with Madura. Capital: Jakarta.

javelin throw A field event in athletics in which a spearlike javelin is thrown as far as possible. The men's javelin is 2.6–2.7 m (8.5–8.9 ft) long and weighs 800 g (1.8 lb). The women's measures 2.2–2.3 m (7.2–7.5 ft) and weighs a minimum of 600 g (1.3 lb). It is thrown with one hand, over the shoulder, after a run-up of approximately 36 m (120 ft), and the metal head must hit the ground first. Each competitor has six tries.

jay A crow, *Garrulus glandarius*, of Eurasia and N Africa. It is about 34 cm long and brownish pink, with a black tail, white rump, black-barred blue wing patches, and a black-and-white erectile crest. Jays are found mainly in woodland, feeding on insects and larvae in summer and storing seeds for winter food.

Jefferson, Thomas (1743–1826) US statesman; the third president (1801–09) of the USA. A lawyer, Jefferson was elected a delegate to the second Continental Congress in 1775 and was the chief author of the *Declaration of Independence. Jefferson served as governor of Virginia (1779–81), minister to France (1785–89), secretary of state (1789–93), and vice president (1797–1801) under John Adams. During Jefferson's two terms as president, he approved the *Louisiana Purchase (1803) and encouraged US neutrality in the Napoleonic Wars.

Jefferson City 38 33N 92 10W A city in the USA, the capital of Missouri on the Missouri River. Population (latest est): 35 481.

Jeffreys of Wem, George, 1st Baron (c. 1645–89) English judge. A supporter of the Crown, he became a leading prosecutor of suspected traitors following the *Popish Plot and, in 1685, James II's Lord Chancellor. He is notorious for the harsh punishments and death sentences he imposed during the Bloody Assizes, after Monmouth's rebellion (1685). He was captured after the fall of James II and died in the Tower of London.

Jehovah *See* YAHWEH.

Jehovah's Witnesses A religious movement, first known as Bible Students, organized in the early 1870s by Charles Taze Russell (1852–1916) in Philadelphia. Jehovah's Witnesses accept the Bible as their sole authority, worshipping the Creator, Jehovah, and acknowledging Jesus Christ to be God's son and spokesman. They look for the end of the present world order in the near future. They believe that 144 000, the Christian congregation, will rule with Jesus Christ in his heavenly kingdom over the rest of obedient mankind, who will live on a paradise earth. They do not engage in politics and are conscientious objectors.

jellyfish A free-swimming aquatic invertebrate animal belonging to a class (*Scyphozoa*; about 200 species) of cnidarians. The translucent gelatinous body, 1.5–2000 mm in diameter, is bell- or umbrella-shaped, with a central tubular projection that hangs down and bears the mouth. Jellyfish occur in all oceans and usually propel themselves through the water by contracting muscles around the edge of the bell. Stinging tentacles are used to capture and paralyse prey. The term jellyfish is also used for the free-swimming sexual form of any other coelenterate (*see* MEDUSA).

Jena and Auerstädt, Battles of (14 October 1806) Simultaneous battles in which Napoleon defeated the Prussians. Auerstädt and Jena broke Prussia as a military power and left Russia to face Napoleon alone. Prussia remained in the orbit of the French Empire until 1813, when it rejoined the alliance against Napoleon.

j

Jenkins, Roy (Harris), Baron Jenkins of Hillhead (1920–2003) British politician. He became a Labour MP in 1948 and joined the cabinet in 1964. As home secretary (1965–67; 1974–76) he introduced liberal social reforms. After serving as president of the EC Commission (1977–81), he helped to found the Social Democratic Party and became its leader (1982–83). He was noted for his historical biographies.

Jenner, Edward (1749–1823) British physician, who developed the first effective vaccine—against smallpox. Jenner noticed that people who caught the mild disease cowpox never contracted smallpox. In 1796 he inoculated a small boy with cowpox and, two months later, with smallpox. The boy did not develop smallpox. Jenner published his findings in 1798 after which vaccination became a widespread protective measure.

jerboa A small hopping *rodent belonging to the family *Dipodidae* (25 species) of Asian and N African deserts, also called desert rat. Jerboas are 4–15 cm long and have kangaroo-like hind feet, a long balancing tail, and sandy fur. They emerge at night from their burrows to feed on seeds.

Jerez de la Frontera 36 41N 6 08W A city in SW Spain, in Andalusia. It is renowned for its wine industry and gave its name to sherry. Population (1998 est): 181 602.

Jericho 31 52N 35 27E A town in the Jordan Valley, on the Israeli-occupied West Bank. The site of the old city was excavated by Kathleen Kenyon (1906–78), revealing one of the earliest known towns (before 8000 BC); of the Bronze Age city attacked by Joshua (Joshua 6) nothing remains. The ruins of the palace, Khirbat al-Mafjar, built (739–44 AD) by the Umayyad caliph Hisham (d. 743) can still be seen. By the 1993 peace agreement between Israel and the PLO, Palestinian self-rule was granted in Jericho in 1994.

Jerome, St (c. 342–420 AD) Italian biblical scholar; Doctor of the Church and author of the *Vulgate Bible, the first Latin translation of the Bible from the Hebrew. After a period as a hermit, he was ordained by St Paulinus of Nola in Antioch. A secretary to Pope Damasus I, he later settled in Bethlehem, where he established a monastery. Feast day: 30 Sept.

Jersey 49 13N 2 07W The largest of the Channel Islands, in the English Channel. It was colonized from Normandy in the 11th century; French influence remains strong and French is the official language. It consists chiefly of a plateau incised by deep valleys. Agriculture, particularly dairy farming, is important and the famous Jersey cattle are bred for export. Finance and tourism are also major sources of income. Area: 116 sq km (45 sq mi). Population (2001): 89 400. Capital: St Helier.

Jerusalem (Arabic name: El Quds) 31 47N 35 13E The capital of Israel, in the Judaea Heights between the Mediterranean and the Dead Sea. Jerusalem is a religious centre for Christianity, Judaism, and Islam. The modern city spreads to the W of the Old City, which is walled (1537–40) and contains the Western (Wailing) Wall (part of the retaining wall of the second Jewish Temple, consecrated 515 BC), the Dome of the Rock (691 AD; Islamic), and the Church of the Holy Sepulchre, (begun 335 AD on the traditional site of Christ's crucifixion). *History*: Jerusalem was conquered by King David in 1005 BC; it became the capital of Judah in 930 BC. Nebuchadnezzar, King of Babylon, destroyed the city in 586 BC, when the Jewish inhabitants were exiled to Babylon. In 538 BC, 40 000 Jews returned to the city, whose walls were rebuilt under Nehemiah in 445 BC. It was occupied by Alexander the Great (4th century BC) and the Romans (63 BC), under whose fifth procurator, Pontius Pilate, Jesus was put to death. Occupation by the Turks was succeeded by the Kingdom of Jerusalem, a feudal state created in 1099 following conquest by the Crusaders. It was enlarged in the early 12th century by Baldwin I (c. 1058–1118) and his successors, but fell to Saladin in 1187. The Turks retook the city in 1517 and held it until 1917, when it became a British mandate, until 1948. Jerusalem was then divided between the state of Israel, of which it became the capital (1950), and Jordan. Israel occupied the whole city in June 1967, but this annexation is not recognized by the UN. The city has since been troubled by ethnic unrest. Population (1999 est): 653 700.

Jerusalem artichoke A North American perennial herb, *Helianthus tuberosus*, that grows to a height of 2 m, and has edible tubers up to 10 cm long. They bloom only in hot summers. Family: *Compositae*.

Jesuits Members of the Society of Jesus, an order founded by St *Ignatius Loyola in 1533 to propagate the Roman Catholic faith. In addition to vows of chastity, poverty, and obedience, Jesuits were sworn to go wherever the pope might send them. They became one of the dominant forces of the *Counter-Reformation and played a prominent role in missions to the New World and the East. Their power eventually brought them into conflict with civil authorities throughout Europe, and in 1773 Pope Clement XIV suppressed the order. Reinstated in 1814, the order is now active worldwide and is noted for its schools and universities.

Jesus (c. 6 BC–c. 30 AD) The founder of *Christianity; called by his followers the Messiah or Christ (Greek *khristos*, anointed one). According to the New Testament, Jesus, the son of the Virgin *Mary, was born at Bethlehem in the last years of the reign of Herod the Great; Mary's husband, Joseph, was a carpenter of Nazareth who belonged to the tribe of Judah and the family of David. Jesus was baptized in about 27 AD by John the Baptist and began his public ministry in Galilee, preaching largely in parables. His teaching, summarized in the Sermon on the Mount (Matthew 5–7), emphasized the approaching Kingdom of God, the need for repentance, and the importance of charity, faith, and humility. Miracles were attributed to him, including healing and feeding a multitude of 5000. The beginnings of a movement are evident in Galilee when Jesus summoned his 12 disciples, instructing them to preach the imminence of the Kingdom of God. Accompanied by his disciples he travelled to Jerusalem for Passover. There, after betrayal by Judas, he was arrested and condemned to death by the Jewish tribunal, the Sanhedrin, for claiming to be the Messiah. He was crucified according to Roman law as a criminal by order of Pontius Pilate. In the New Testament his death is presented as the fulfilment of a divine purpose, made clear to the disciples at the resurrection (on the next day but one after the crucifixion) and by a number of appearances to individuals and groups of disciples. His ascension into heaven is said to have occurred 40 days after the resurrection.

jet engine A form of *gas turbine (*see also* INTERNAL-COMBUSTION ENGINE) in which part of the fuel energy drives a turbine, which in turn drives a compressor to increase the pressure of the air required for combustion, and part is used as a jet to provide thrust to drive an aircraft. The jet engine was patented in 1930 by Sir Frank *Whittle, the first practical Whittle engine powering a Gloster aircraft in 1941. Thrust is equal to the mass of the gas produced multiplied by its acceleration and is due to the pressure of the expanding gas on the engine itself rather than on the air through which it is flying. It is therefore more efficient at higher altitudes, where the atmosphere is thinner. Early postwar commercial aircraft used a turboprop engine, in which a propeller is driven by the turbine. For greater speed and economy the turboprop has now been replaced by the turbojet or the turbofan. At over twice the speed of sound (Mach 2), the forward pressure of the air is sufficient for the compressor, and the turbine, to be dispensed with. The resulting engine is called a ramjet.

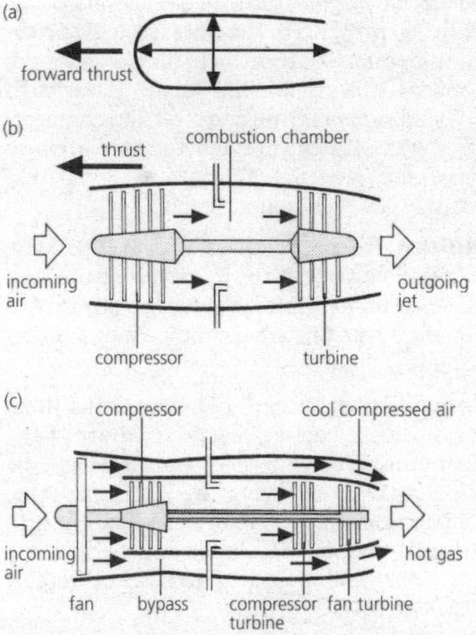

jet engine. (a) The principle: equal pressure from the expanding gas inside the engine meets equal resistance except rearwards. The result is a forward thrust. The lower the outside pressure, the greater the thrust. (b) The turbojet, used for subsonic and supersonic flight (especially with reheat). (c) The turbofan, used for subsonic flight: cool air, compressed by the fan, bypasses the engine and mixes with the hot jet.

The drawback of the ramjet is that it needs a rocket-assisted take-off. Turboshaft engines, similar to the turboprop, are used in helicopters, ships, etc. *See also* ROCKETS.

Jews A predominantly Semitic people, claiming descent from the ancient Israelites and practising *Judaism. They inhabited Israel until the Babylonian exile, returning in 1948. During the intervening 25 centuries they were dispersed (*see* DIASPORA) throughout the world and there are now communities in most countries (*see* ASHKENAZIM; SEPHARDIM). Under Persian, Greek, and Roman rule the Jews gradually evolved a system of communal administration that enabled them to survive as minority communities through many centuries of Christian and Muslim domination, despite frequent persecution. Since the late 18th century they have been accepted in most countries, although the German slaughter of six million Jews in Europe (*see* HOLOCAUST) is one of the ugliest episodes in human history. It did, however, provide the Zionist claim for a national home for the Jews with unanswerable force (*see* ZIONISM).

Jharkand A state of NE India, created in 2000 from part of Bihar. It consists of the E part of the Chota Nagpur plateau, at elevations of about 700 m (2300 ft). The state has India's richest mineral resources, including coal in the Damodar valley and mica in the Hazaribagh area, and supports iron and steel and engineering works. Agriculture and forestry are also important. Area: 74–677 sq km. Population (2001): 26 909 428. Capital: Ranchi.

Jhelum, River A river in India and Pakistan, the most westerly of the five rivers of the Punjab. Rising in Kashmir it flows generally SSW to join the River Chenab. Length: about 720 km (450 mi).

Jiang Zemin (1926–) Chinese Communist statesman. He became general secretary of the Communist Party in 1989 and president of China in 1993, emerging as China's supreme leader on the death (1997) of Deng Xiao Ping. He was succeeded by *Hu Jintao as general secretary (2002) and president (2003) but retains other key posts.

Jiddah (*or* **Jedda**) 21 30N 39 10E A town in Saudi Arabia, on the Red Sea coast. It is a modern industrial city and the chief port for Muslim pilgrims to Mecca. Population (1992 est): 1 500 000.

jimsonweed *See* THORN APPLE.

Jinan (**Chi-nan** *or* **Tsinan**) 36 41N 117 00E A city in E China, the capital of Shandong province. A city since the 8th century BC, it is a cultural centre. Population (1999 est): 1 713 036.

jinja A Shinto shrine dedicated to a deity or nature spirit, situated in a place of exceptional natural beauty. It consists of three parts: the *haiden*, a hall where the laity pray and worship; the *heiden*, where religious ceremonies are performed; and the *honden*, the main inner sanctuary usually accessible only to priests. Before the jinja is a sacred gateway.

Jinnah, Mohammed Ali (1876–1948) Indian statesman, who was largely responsible for the creation of Pakistan. Born in Karachi, he studied law in England. As a member of the Muslim League and the *Indian National Congress he championed Hindu-Muslim unity until 1930, when he resigned from the Congress in opposition to Gandhi's policies. He was president of the League in 1916 and 1920 and from 1934. He advocated a separate state for Indian Muslims, which was achieved with the creation in 1947 of Pakistan, of which he was the first governor general.

Jiulong (*or* **Kowloon**) 22 20N 114 15E A port in SE China, on the Jiulong peninsula, opposite Hong Kong island and from 1860 to 1997 part of the British colony. Population (2001): 2 023 979.

Joan of Arc, St (French name: Jeanne d'Arc; c. 1412–31) French patriot, known as the Maid of Orléans, whose military and moral leadership led to a reversal of French fortunes in the *Hundred Years' War. Of peasant origin, she claimed to have been told by Saints Michael, Catherine, and Margaret that it was her divine mission to expel the English from France and enable Charles VII to be crowned. She persuaded Charles to allow her to lead an army to relieve the besieged city of Orléans. Her success resulted in Charles' coronation at Rheims (July 1429). Other victories followed but she failed to recapture Paris and was subsequently seized by the Burgundians, who sold her to their English allies. They tried her and burned her as a heretic. She was canonized in 1920.

Jocasta *See* OEDIPUS.

Jodrell Bank The site, near Macclesfield, Cheshire (UK), of the Nuffield Radio Astronomy Laboratories of Manchester University. The principal instrument is the 76.2 m (250 ft) fully steerable radio-telescope dish.

Jogjakarta (*or* **Yogyakarta** *or* **Depok**) 7 48S 110 24E A city in Indonesia, in S Java. It was the capital of the 1945–49 Indonesian Republic. A cultural centre, it is rich in Buddhist monuments, notably the temple of Borobudur. Population (1995): 661 495.

Johannesburg 26 10S 28 02E The largest city in South Africa, in the Transvaal. It was founded in 1886 following the discovery of gold in the area. During the second Boer War it was taken by the British (1900). Today it is a major industrial, commercial, and banking centre containing the South African Stock Exchange (1887). Linked to the city is the complex of towns known as *Soweto, inhabited by Black Africans. Population (1996): 1 480 530.

John (1167–1216) King of England (1199–1216), nicknamed John Lackland; the youngest son of Henry II, he succeeded his brother Richard I. His reign saw the renewal of war with *Philip II Augustus of France, to whom he had lost several continental possessions, including Normandy, by 1205. Struggles with Pope Innocent III over John's objection to the election of Stephen Langton (c. 1150–1228) as Archbishop of Canterbury led to the imposition of an interdict over England (1208) and the king's excommunication (1212). He came into conflict with his barons and was forced to endorse the *Magna Carta. His subsequent repudiation of the Charter led to the first Barons' War (1215–17).

John (II) the Good (1319–64) King of France (1350–64), who was taken prisoner by the English at the battle of Poitiers (1356) during the *Hundred Years' War. He remained in captivity in London, where he was forced to sign the unfavourable Treaty of *Brétigny. Released in 1360, he was unable to raise the ransom demanded by the English and was forced to return to London, where he died.

John XXIII (Angelo Roncalli; 1881–1963) Pope (1958–1963). Elected at the age of 77, John was the most popular and innovative pope of modern times. In 1962 he summoned the second Vatican Council. His best-known encyclical, *Pacem in Terris* (*Peace on Earth*; 1963), advocated reconciliation between the western democracies and eastern communist countries.

John, Augustus (Edwin) (1878–1961) British painter, born in Wales. A flamboyant character, he travelled widely, often in Gipsy style. He is known for his strongly characterized portraits of contemporaries, such as James Joyce and T. E. Lawrence. His sister **Gwen John** (1876–1939) was also a painter, noted especially for her portraits of women.

John, Sir Elton (Reginald Kenneth Dwight; 1947–) British rock pianist and singer, who became popular in the early 1970s with such songs as "Rocket Man" and "Daniel." In 1997 a reworking of his hit "Candle in the Wind" was released as a charity tribute to Diana, Princess of Wales, and became the world's biggest-ever selling single.

John, St In the New Testament, one of the 12 Apostles, brother of James. **The Gospel according to St John** is traditionally ascribed to him but is now thought to have been written in the late 1st century AD; it is markedly different in content and style from the other Gospels. The three **Epistles of John** and the Book of *Revelation are also ascribed to John.

John Dory (*or* **dory**) A fish of the family *Zeidae*, found worldwide in moderately deep marine waters. It has a round narrow body with deep sides, each having a black spot surrounded by a yellow ring, and spiny-rayed fins extended into filaments. *Zeus faber*, up to 90 cm long, is a food fish of the Atlantic and Mediterranean. Order: *Zeiformes*.

John of Gaunt (1340–99) The fourth son of Edward III of England; Duke of Lancaster from 1362. After a distinguished career in the *Hundred Years' War he assumed an increasingly important role in domestic government. Never popular, John, who supported *Wycliffe, was opposed by *William of Wykeham (1324–1404). From 1386 to 1389 he attempted without success to realize his claim, through his second wife, to Castile. In 1396 he married his mistress Catherine Swynford, and in 1397 their descendants were legitimized but excluded from the royal succession.

John O'Groats 58 39N 3 02W A village at the NE tip of Scotland, site of the house of John de Groot, a 16th-century Dutch immigrant. John O'Groats is 970 km (603 mi) in a straight line from Land's End, Cornwall.

John Paul II (Karol Wojtyła; 1920–) Pope (1978–). A Pole, he is the first non-Italian pope since 1522 and the longest-serving pontiff of the 20th century. In the early part of his reign he outspokenly defended the Church in communist countries, especially in Poland. His uncompromising position on contraception, abortion, homosexuality, and a celibate clergy has led to considerable opposition. In 1981 he survived an assassination attempt.

Johnson, Amy (1903–41) British aviator. She established several long-distance records with her solo flights to Australia in 1930, to Tokyo in 1932, and to the Cape of Good Hope and back in 1936. In 1932 she married Jim Mollison

(1905–59), another pilot, with whom she flew the Atlantic in 1936. She was killed when her plane crashed into the sea off the Kent coast, possibly as a result of friendly fire from anti-aircraft guns.

Johnson, Lyndon Baines (1908–73) US statesman; Democratic president (1963–69). A Texan, he succeeded to the presidency after *Kennedy's assassination. His Great Society programme initiated broad social reform. He became unpopular for increasing US military involvement in the *Vietnam War.

Johnson, Samuel (1709–84) British poet, critic, and lexicographer. He left Oxford without taking a degree, married a wealthy widow in 1735, and went to London in 1737. His early publications include a long didactic poem, *The Vanity of Human Wishes* (1749). From 1750 to 1752 he produced the weekly *Rambler* almost single handed. His *Dictionary* appeared in 1755 after nine years' work and was well received, but he still relied on hackwork for money, writing *Rasselas* (1759) in a week to pay for his mother's funeral. His last major works were an edition of Shakespeare (1765) and his *Lives of the Poets* (1779–81). From the early 1760s he enjoyed the security of a pension and the friendship of Reynolds, Goldsmith, and his biographer *Boswell.

John the Baptist, St In the New Testament, the son of a priest, Zacharias, and Elizabeth, a relative of the Virgin *Mary. He began in about 27 AD preaching on the banks of the River Jordan, urging repentance and baptism because of the imminent approach of the Kingdom of God (Matthew 3.2). He baptized Christ, recognizing him as the Messiah. He was beheaded by *Herod Antipas, at the request of Salome, for denouncing his second marriage to Herodias. Feast days: 24 June (birth); 29 Aug (beheading).

Johor A swampy forested state in S Peninsular Malaysia. Chief products are rubber, copra, pineapples, palm oil, tin, and bauxite. Area: 18 958 sq km (7330 sq mi). Population (2000): 2 565 701. Capital: Johor Baharu.

Joliot-Curie, Frédéric and Irène *See* CURIE, MARIE.

Jolson, Al (Asa Yoelson; 1886–1950) US popular singer and songwriter, born in Russia. He became famous for his blacked-up face and the song "Mammy." In 1927 he appeared in the first full-length sound film *The Jazz Singer*.

Jones, Inigo (1573–1652) English classical architect. One of the first Englishmen to study architecture in Italy, Jones was particularly influenced by *Palladio in his two best-known buildings, the Queen's House, Greenwich (1616–35), and the Banqueting Hall, Whitehall (1619–22). His career effectively ended with the outbreak of the Civil War in 1642, and his style only became strongly influential in England in the 18th century. With Ben Jonson, he also designed numerous court masques.

jonquil *See* NARCISSUS.

Jonson, Ben (1572–1637) English dramatist and poet. In *Every Man in His Humour* (1598) he introduced the "comedy of humours," each character being driven by a particular obsession. Other major satirical plays include *Volpone* (1606), *The Alchemist* (1610), and *Bartholomew Fair* (1614). In collaboration with Inigo *Jones he produced many court masques. He also published poems and translations and influenced a number of younger poets known as "the Tribe of Ben."

Joplin, Scott (1868–1917) US Black pianist and composer of *ragtime music. Joplin is remembered for such rags as "Maple Leaf Rag" and "The Entertainer." His ragtime operas *A Guest of Honour* (1903), now lost, and *Treemonisha* (1907) were failures and Joplin died in an asylum in poverty.

Jordaens, Jakob (1593–1678) Flemish painter. Although he painted numerous religious altarpieces, influenced by *Rubens, he is best known for his allegorical scenes of merrymaking peasants, such as *The King Drinks* (Brussels).

Jordan, Hashemite Kingdom of A country in the Middle East. It is mainly desert but more fertile in the W and N, where the population is concentrated. The people are Arab; most are Sunnite Muslims, with Christian and other minorities. *Economy*: major industries include the extraction and processing of phosphates, which are exported from Aqaba, oil refining, and tourism. Agriculture is concentrated in the irrigated Jordan Valley. Produce includes cereals, vegetables, wool, and such fruit as melons and olives. There are reserves of natural gas. Tourism is a growing source of revenue. *History*: the area that is now Jordan appears to have flourished in the Bronze Age and was part of the Roman Empire by 64 BC. It was controlled by Arabs from the 7th century, Crusaders in the 11th and 12th centuries, and Turks from the 16th century until 1916. In 1920 the part E of the River Jordan was named Transjordan and a League of Nations mandate for its control was given to the UK.

It became independent in 1946. In the Arab-Israeli War of 1948–49, Jordan overran the *West Bank, but it was occupied by Israel in the Six-Day War of 1967. There followed further bloodshed in the civil war of 1970–71 and the Arab-Israeli War of 1973. Jordan has since recognized the *Palestine Liberation Organization as the body entitled govern the West Bank and in 1988 recognized the West Bank as a state. In 1990–91 Jordan gave political support to Iraq in the Gulf War which caused massive disruption to the Jordanian economy. The first multiparty elections for 37 years were held in 1993. In 1994 Jordan and Israel signed a peace treaty and border agreement ending the state of war existing since 1948. King Hussein (reigned 1952–99) was succeeded by his son, Abdullah II. Official language: Arabic. Currency: dinar of 1000 fils. Area: 89 185 sq km (34 434 sq mi). Population (2003 est): 5 395 000. Capital: Amman.

Jordan, River A river in the Middle East. It rises in Syria and Lebanon and flows due S through the Sea of Galilee, finally entering the Dead Sea. It forms for some of its course part of the border between Israel and Jordan. Length: 320 km (199 mi).

Joseph, St In the New Testament, the husband of the Virgin *Mary. He was a devout Jew belonging to the line of David but worked humbly as a carpenter. He was certainly dead by the time of the crucifixion. Feast day: 19 March.

Joséphine (1763–1814) The wife (1796–1809) of Napoleon Bonaparte and Empress of the French from 1804. Her first husband was Alexandre, Vicomte de Beauharnais (1760–94), who was guillotined in the French Revolution. She presided over a brilliant court until divorced by Napoleon because of their childlessness.

Joseph of Arimathea, St In the New Testament, a man described as a councillor. He asked Pontius Pilate for the body of Christ after the crucifixion and arranged for its burial on the same day. According to medieval legend, he came to England after the crucifixion, bringing with him the *Holy Grail, and built the first English church, at Glastonbury. Feast day: 17 March.

Joshua tree A treelike plant, *Yucca brevifolia*, native to desert regions of the SW USA. Growing to a height of more than 10 m, its branching stem can assume unusual shapes. It has stiff sword-shaped leaves and bears waxy white flowers.

Josquin des Prez (c. 1450–1521) Flemish composer. A pupil of Ockeghem, he served at the courts of Milan, Ferrara, and Rome. His compositions were either elaborately contrapuntal or expressively homophonic; they include masses, motets, and chansons.

joule (J) The SI unit of work or energy equal to the work done when the point of application of a force of one newton moves through a distance of one metre. Named after James *Joule.

Joule, James Prescott (1818–89) British physicist, who performed a series of experiments during the 1840s to determine the mechanical equivalent of heat. His work contributed towards Helmholtz's formulation of the law of conservation of energy. He also investigated the heating effect of an electric current, stating in **Joule's law** that the heat produced is equal to the product of the resistance, the square of the current, and the time for which it flows. With Lord Kelvin he discovered the fall in temperature that occurs when a gas expands adiabatically (the **Joule-Kelvin effect**). The unit of energy is named after him.

Joyce, James (1882–1941) Irish novelist and poet. Accompanied by Nora Barnacle (whom he did not marry until 1931), he left Ireland in 1904, living first in Trieste (until 1915) and later in Zurich during World War I and Paris (1920–40). *Dubliners* (1914), a volume of short stories, was followed by the semiautobiographical novel *Portrait of the Artist as a Young Man* (1916). In 1922 he published *Ulysses*, a stream-of-consciousness epic portraying a single day in the lives of several Dubliners. He carried linguistic experiment to further extremes in *Finnegans Wake* (1939), a dream recounted in puns and word play. Joyce died in Zurich.

Joyce, William (1906–46) Nazi broadcaster, known as Lord Haw-Haw. Born in the USA, he broadcast Nazi propaganda to Britain throughout World War II and was subsequently tried as a British subject for treason and executed.

JP *See* JUSTICE OF THE PEACE.

Juan Carlos (1938–) King of Spain (1975–). The grandson of Alfonso XIII, he was designated heir to the throne by Francisco *Franco and became king when he died, presiding over Spain's peaceful transition to democracy. In 1962 he married Sophia (1938–), daughter of King Paul of Greece.

Juárez, Benito (Pablo) (1806–72) Mexican statesman, who was the first Indian president of Mexico (1861–65, 1867–72). He won popularity by nationalizing ecclesiastical property and led the successful opposition (1864–67) to the French invasion.

Juba, River A river in East Africa. Rising in S central Ethiopia, it flows S across Somalia to the Indian Ocean. Length: 1660 km (1030 mi).

Judaea The southern division of ancient Palestine. The Old Testament kingdom of Judah survived Syrian, Assyrian, and Philistine attacks following Solomon's death but was conquered by *Nebuchadnezzar II of Babylon, when its capital, Jerusalem, was destroyed (586 BC) and the Jews were exiled. Judaea came next under Persian domination, when the Jews were allowed to return and rebuild Jerusalem, but under the Seleucids Antiochus IV Epiphanes' desecration of the temple in 167 BC instigated the Maccabees' revolt. Judaea achieved independence until the Roman conquest in 63 BC. After years of unrest the Roman province of Syria absorbed it in 135 AD.

j

Judaism The religion of the *Jews. Its fundamental tenet is belief in a single, eternal God, who created the world and desires its welfare. Judaism's most sacred text is the *Torah. There is no agreement as to when Judaism began. Biblical tradition attaches importance to *Abraham and *Moses, but many characteristic ideas and institutions emerged much later during the Babylonian exile and the period of the second *Temple of Jerusalem. After the destruction of the temple the *rabbis codified the traditional teachings (*see* MIDRASH; MISHNAH; TALMUD), and in the middle ages the *kabbalah exerted a great influence. The modern enlightenment undermined traditional values and gave rise to several conflicting movements. Orthodox Judaism asserts the supernatural authority of Torah and right behaviour (halakhah), which is challenged by *Reform Judaism. Conservative Judaism and Reconstructionism support a compromise between these extreme views.

Judas tree A shrub or small tree of the genus *Cercis* (7 species), also called redbud, native to S Europe, Asia, and North America, and cultivated for ornament. The pinkish-red clusters of flowers appear before the heart-shaped leaves have opened. The name is used particularly for *C. siliquastrum*, from which Judas Iscariot is said to have hanged himself. Family: *Leguminosae*.

judge An officer who decides legal disputes and passes sentence on offenders. In England and Wales judges try cases in the House of Lords (the Lords of Appeal in Ordinary, or law lords), the Court of Appeal (the Lords Justices), the High Court of Justice (high-court judges), the Crown Court (high-court judges and circuit judges), and County Courts (circuit judges). A judge is appointed by the Crown on the recommendation of the Lord Chancellor (*see* LORD CHIEF JUSTICE; MASTER OF THE ROLLS) and must be a barrister (or a *solicitor) of at least ten years' standing. (A part-time recorder, who must also be a solicitor or barrister of ten years' standing, may be appointed to serve in the Crown Court; a *justice of the peace or stipendiary magistrate serves in Magistrates' Courts.) *See also* COURTS OF LAW.

judo A form of wrestling developed from *jujitsu in Japan by Jigoro Kano (1860–1938). Contestants wear kimonos and coloured belts to indicate their proficiency. The five *kyu* (pupil) grades wear white, orange, green, blue, or brown belts in order of increasing skill, the 12 *dan* (master) grades all wear black belts. Contestants score points by executing prescribed throws, ground holds, and locks. *See also* MARTIAL ARTS.

jujitsu (Japanese name: *yawara*) The form of unarmed self-defence used by the Japanese *samurai. The object was to disable, cripple, or kill an opponent by using his own momentum and strength against him. *Judo, *aikido, and *karate developed from it.

jujube A small thorny tree of the genus *Zizyphus* that produces sweet edible fruit. *Z. jujuba*, native to China, has been widely introduced to other hot dry regions. It grows up to a height of 9 m and has small yellow flowers. Family: *Rhamnaceae*. *See also* CROWN OF THORNS.

Jumna, River (**R. Jamuna** *or* **R. Yamuna**) A river in N India. Rising in Uttar Pradesh, it flows S and SE to the River Ganges near Allahabad. Length: 1385 km (860 mi).

Juneau 58 20N 134 20W A city in the USA, the capital of Alaska. A supply centre for a fur-trading and mining region, it is also an ice-free port. Population (latest est): 26 751.

Jung, Carl Gustav (1875–1961) Swiss psychiatrist and pioneer psychoanalyst. Jung collaborated with Sigmund *Freud until, in 1912, their differences became irreconcilable. Jung originated the concept of introvert and extrovert personalities and made valuable studies of mental disorders, including schizophrenia. In his major work, *Psychology of the Unconscious* (1912), Jung regarded the unconscious part of the mind as containing both the personal experiences of the individual and common inherited cultural experiences (the so-called **collective unconscious**).

Jungfrau 46 33N 7 58E A mountain peak in S central Switzerland, in the Bernese Oberland. Height: 4158 m (13 632 ft).

jungle fowl An Asian forest bird belonging to the genus *Gallus* (4 species). The males have a large fleshy comb and wattles at the sides of the bill and, in the breeding season, fight fiercely using their sharp leg spurs. The red jungle fowl (*Gallus gallus*) is the ancestor of the domestic *fowl. Family: *Phasianidae* (fowl and pheasants).

juniper A coniferous tree or shrub of the genus *Juniperus* (60 species), widely distributed in the N hemisphere. Male and female flowers grow on separate trees. The common juniper (*J. communis*) is native to N Europe, North America, and SW Asia; it rarely exceeds 4 m in height and is often planted for ornament. The cones are used for flavouring gin and foods, as a source of oil, and as a diuretic. Family: *Cupressaceae.*

Juno A principal Roman goddess, the wife of Jupiter. She was concerned with all aspects of women's life and is usually portrayed as a matronly figure. She was identified with the Greek *Hera. The *month June is probably named after her.

Jupiter (astronomy) The largest and most massive planet, orbiting the sun every 11.86 years at a mean distance of 778.3 million km. Its rapid axial rotation (in less than 10 hours) has produced a nonspherical shape: equatorial diameter 142 800 km, polar diameter 135 500 km. Jupiter is composed mainly (99%) of hydrogen and helium (in the ratio 82:17). Ammonia, methane, and other compounds are present in the cloud layers. The planetary interior is liquid hydrogen with possibly a small rocky core. Jupiter radiates heat and is also a source of radio waves. It has a magnetic field and radiation belts of great intensity. The planet has 38 named satellites, including the four large *Galilean satellites, a further 23 minor satellites discovered since 2000, and a satellite ring of rocks.

Jupiter (mythology) The principal Roman god, identified with the Greek *Zeus. Originally a sky god, he controlled the weather and used the thunderbolt as his weapon. His temple on the Capitoline hill was the principal Roman religious structure.

Jura Mountains A mountain range in E France and NW Switzerland. It extends along the border in a NE–SW arc, rising to 1723 m (5653 ft) at Crêt de la Neige.

Jurassic period A geological period of the Mesozoic era, between about 200 and 135 million years ago, following the Triassic and preceding the Cretaceous periods. The dinosaurs and other reptiles flourished and diversified in this period. Fossils of the earliest birds and mammals have also been found in Jurassic rocks.

Juruá, Rio A river in South America, rising in E central Peru and through NW Brazil to the River Amazon. Length: 1900 km (1200 mi).

jury A body of people, usually 12, who have taken an oath to decide questions of fact arising in a court case (now usually a criminal case but occasionally a civil case) according to the evidence before them. To qualify for jury service a person must be a registered elector between 18 and 70 years old and resident in the UK for at least 5 years since the age of 13.

Members of the judiciary and anyone involved in administering justice were formerly ineligible for jury service, but since 2003 this is no longer the case. Others (MPs, medical personnel, etc.) may be excused from jury service, but this right has now been restricted; persons who have received certain types of convictions are disqualified. By the Criminal Justice Act (1967) a majority verdict (normally ten to two) was permitted in criminal trials and the Courts Act (1971) permitted similar verdicts in civil proceedings in the High Court. In 2000 the government introduced legislation to remove a defendant's automatic right to choose jury trial for lesser offences.

justice of the peace (JP) An unpaid *magistrate appointed by the Lord Chancellor to keep the peace within a county, with statutory power to try summarily certain cases in a Magistrates' Court and to commit other more serious cases for trial by a higher court.

Justinian I (482–565 AD) Byzantine emperor (527–65) noted for his legal and administrative reforms, especially the codification of *Roman law in the so-called **Justinian Code**. He also built the great church of *St Sophia. He was greatly influenced by his wife Theodora, a former actress.

jute Either of two Indian annual plants, *Corchorus capsularis* or *C. olitorius*, cultivated in India, Pakistan, and Thailand for their fibres. Growing to a height of 3 m, they have small yellow flowers. The stems are cut, soaked in water, and beaten to remove the fibres, which are processed into cloth, etc. There are many grades, used for ropes, sacks, carpet backings, hessian, and tarpaulin. Family: *Tiliaceae*.

Jutes A Germanic people, probably from Jutland, who invaded Britain together with the *Angles and *Saxons in the 5th century AD. The Jutes settled in what are now Kent, the Isle of Wight, and Hampshire.

Jutland (Danish name: Jylland) A peninsula in N Europe, between the North Sea, the Skagerrak, the Kattegat, and the Little Belt. It is occupied by the continental part of Denmark and part of the German *Land* of Schleswig-Holstein. The Battle of Jutland (1916) was a major naval engagement in World War I.

Juvenal (Decimus Junius Juvenalis; c. 60–c. 130 AD) Roman satirical poet. His 16 *Satires*, probably written 98–128 AD, are savage attacks on the corruption of Roman society and human folly.

K

K2 (*or* **Mt Godwin Austen**) 35 53N 76 32E The second highest mountain in the world (after Mount Everest), in N Pakistan in the Karakoram Range. As it was the second peak to be measured in the range it was given the symbol, K2. The summit was first reached on 31 July 1954, by an Italian team. Height: 8611 m (28 250 ft).

kabbalah (Hebrew: tradition) An esoteric Jewish theosophical system. The classical kabbalistic text is the *Zohar* (*Book of Splendour*), written in Aramaic in 13th-century Spain, but the kabbalah has much older roots. It has strong connections with gnosticism and also with magical practices. An important 16th-century kabbalistic school flourished at Safed, in Galilee, around Isaac Luria (1534–72), and Christian interpretations of the kabbalah blended with *Neoplatonism in the 16th and 17th centuries.

Kabuki A form of Japanese popular theatre that developed from the aristocratic *No theatre during the 17th century. The earliest notable dramatist was Chikamatsu Monzaemon (1653–1724). The plays are performed with musical accompaniment on a wide revolving stage and emphasize visual effects and acting skills.

Kabul 34 30N 69 10E The capital of Afghanistan, situated in the NE of the country at an altitude of 1830 m (6000 ft). It was capital of the Mogul Empire (1504–1738), becoming capital of Afghanistan in 1773. Population (1993 est): 700 000.

Kafka, Franz (1883–1924) Czech writer. Born in Prague (then in Bohemia), the son of German Jewish parents, he wrote fantasies and parables that portray the individual isolated in an incomprehensible and uneasy environment. Most of his work was published posthumously, against his instructions, by his friend Max Brod. Among his best-known writings are the stories *Metamorphosis* (1912) and the novels *The Trial* (1925) and *The Castle* (1926).

Kafue River A river in Zambia, rising on the frontier with the Democratic Republic of Congo and flowing S and E to the Zambezi River. Length: 966 km (600 mi). The **Kafue Dam** (1972) provides about two-thirds of Zambia's hydroelectric power.

Kagoshima 31 37N 130 32E A port in Japan, in S Kyushu. The site of *Francis Xavier's landing in Japan (1549), it has porcelain and textile industries and a naval yard. Population (1995): 546 294.

Kaikoura Ranges Twin mountain ranges in New Zealand, comprising the Inland and the Seaward Kaikouras. They extend SW–NE in NE South Island, reaching 2885 m (9465 ft) at Tapuaenuku in the Inland Kaikouras.

Kalahari Desert A semiarid area in S Africa, chiefly in Botswana. It is sparsely inhabited by nomadic Bushmen, and although its few rivers are generally dry there is some vegetation. Area: about 250 000 sq km (96 505 sq mi).

Kali In Hindu mythology, the goddess of death. The wife of *Shiva in her destructive aspect, she is represented as a hideous four-armed black woman.

Kalimantan The Indonesian part of *Borneo, comprising the SE two-thirds of the island. It is little developed, but its dense forests provide valuable timber. Small-scale agriculture includes the growing of rice, tobacco, sugar cane, coffee, and rubber. Since Indonesian independence in 1949 the province has seen recurrent ethnic and political violence, including the mass slaughter of Muslim Madurese by indigenous Dyaks (from 1997). Area: 550 203 sq km (212 388 sq mi). Population (1999 est): 11 396 100. Chief towns: Banjarmasin and Pontianak.

Kaliningrad (name until 1946: Königsberg) A city in W Russia on the Baltic Sea. Formerly a German naval base, it was annexed by the Soviet Union in 1945. The city and its hinterland forms an exclave of Russia, surrounded by

Lithuania. Industries include shipbuilding, timber, and paper. The economy is depressed and environmental pollution is considerable. Population (1999 est): 427 200.

Kama In Hindu mythology, the god of love. He is the son of *Shiva and his popular epithet of Ananga (bodiless) derives from his having been reduced to ashes by a glance from his father's eye when Kama playfully shot his arrows at him.

Kama, River A river in central Russia, rising in the Ural Mountains and flowing mainly SW to the River Volga. Length: 2030 km (1260 mi).

Kamakura 35 19N 139 33E A city in Japan, in SE Honshu. A former Japanese capital (1192–1333), it is noted for its shrines and for its bronze Buddha, 13 m (43 ft) high. Population (1995 est): 170 319.

Kamchatka A peninsula in the extreme E of Russia. It is about 1200 km (746 mi) long and separates the Sea of Okhotsk from the Bering Sea. Area: about 270 000 sq km (104 225 sq mi).

k

Kamet, Mount 30 55N 79 36E A mountain in N India, in the Himalayas. It was first climbed in 1931. Height: 7756 m (25 446 ft).

Kamikaze A Japanese aircraft crashed deliberately by its pilot into its target. Such suicide missions were first flown at the battle of Leyte Gulf (1944) in World War II; at Okinawa (1945) some 3000 sorties sunk 21 US ships. Kamikaze means divine wind and refers to the typhoon that scattered Kublai Khan's invasion fleet in 1281.

Kampala 0 20N 32 30E The capital of Uganda, N of Lake Victoria. Founded by the British in the late 19th century, it became the capital in 1962. Population (1999 est): 1 154 000.

Kananga (name until 1966: Luluabourg) 5 53S 22 26E A city in the central Democratic Republic of Congo, on the River Lulua. It serves an agricultural and diamond-producing area. Population (1994 est): 393 030.

Kanazawa 36 35N 136 38E A city in Japan, in central Honshu. It is renowned for its landscape garden. Manufactures include textiles, porcelain, and lacquerware. Population (1995): 453 977.

Kandahar (*or* **Qandahar**) 31 36N 65 47E A city in S Afghanistan. Situated on main routes to central Asia and India, it is built on the site of several ancient cities. Population (1993 est): 237 500.

Kandinsky, Wassily (1866–1944) Russian expressionist painter and art theorist. He painted the first purely abstract pictures in European art (c. 1911). These are characterized by freely applied paint and dazzling colours, from which he drew analogies to music in his book *Concerning the Spiritual in Art* (1911). He was a founder of the Neue Künstlervereinigung (1909) and the *Blaue Reiter (1911) and taught at the *Bauhaus school, where his style became more geometrical.

Kandy 7 17N 80 40E A city in central Sri Lanka. Capital of the kingdom of Kandy from 1480 until 1815, when it was occupied by the British, it has a Buddhist temple, Dalada Malagawa, and is the commercial centre for Sri Lanka's major tea-producing region. Population (1997 est): 150 532.

kangaroo The largest *marsupial mammal. There are two species, the red kangaroo (*Macropus rufus*) of Australia and the grey kangaroo (*M. kanguru*) of Australia and Tasmania. Red kangaroos can reach a height of 2 m and a weight of 90 kg. Kangaroos have short front legs and long hind legs and feet: they travel by a succession of leaps. Family: *Macropodidae*. *See also* WALLABY.

Kangchenjunga, Mount (*or* **Mt Kanchenjunga**) 27 44N 88 11E The third highest mountain in the world (after Mount Everest and K2), on the Sikkim (India)–Nepal border in the Himalayas. It was first climbed in 1955. Height: 8598 m (28 208 ft).

Kanpur (former name: Cawnpore) 26 27N 80 14E A city in India, in Uttar Pradesh. Ceded to the British East India Company (1801), it became an important British frontier station and during the Indian Mutiny was the scene (1857) of a massacre of British soldiers. Population (1991): 2 111 284.

Kansas A state in the centre of the USA. It consists mainly of undulating prairie. Its mineral resources include oil, natural gas, coal, sand and gravel. Kansas is the USA's main wheat-growing area; other crops include sorghum grains and hay. *History*: explored by the Spanish in the 16th century, it was claimed by the French (1682) and formed part of the Louisiana Purchase (1803). It became a state (1861) and the arrival of the railway in the late 1860s and 1870s brought many cattlemen. The Mennonites introduced wheat into the area (1874). Area: 213 063 sq km (82 264 sq mi). Population (2000): 2 688 418. Capital: Topeka.

Kansas City 39 05N 94 37W A city in the USA, in Missouri. Settled in 1821, it expanded rapidly with the arrival of the railways in the mid-19th century. Population (2000): 441 545.

Kant, Immanuel (1724–1804) German philosopher. His early works sought to examine metaphysics in the light of the work of *Newton and *Leibniz. Acquaintance with Hume's empiricism, however, initiated his so-called "critical period" in which he evolved his doctrine of transcendental idealism. In the famous *Critique of Pure Reason* (1781) he explored the limitations of reason by which mankind interprets experience. The *Critique of Judgment* (1790) deals with aesthetic and teleological judgments. Reason makes experience possible by imposing upon the raw data supplied by the senses the forms of understanding. Kant identified 12 of these basic forms (which he called "categories"). He maintained that there was an absolute moral law and called the obligation to obey this moral law the "categorical imperative."

Kapitza, Peter Leonidovich (1894–1984) Soviet physicist, who worked with *Rutherford on high transient magnetic fields. After returning to the Soviet Union in 1934 he transferred his attention to low-temperature physics, which led him to the discovery of superfluidity in helium (1941) and also a new liquefaction technique. For this work he was awarded the 1978 Nobel Prize.

kapok The fine silky hairs covering the seeds of the silk-cotton tree (*Ceiba pentandra*), which are used for stuffing mattresses, etc. The tree is native to tropical America and widely cultivated in the tropics. Growing to 35 m, it has white or red flowers. Family: *Bombacaceae*.

Karachi 24 51N 67 02E The largest city and chief seaport in Pakistan, situated on the Arabian Sea just NW of the Indus delta. It became the capital of Pakistan (1947) following partition. The removal of the capital to Islamabad (1959) and the building of new satellite towns has eased overcrowding by refugees. Population (1998 est): 9 269 265.

Karaganda 49 53N 73 07E A city in E Kazakhstan. Founded in 1857, Karaganda grew rapidly as the Karaganda coal basin was exploited. It was one of the largest producers of bituminous coal in the former Soviet Union. Population (1999): 436 900.

Karajan, Herbert von (1908–89) Austrian conductor. Musical director of the Vienna State Opera (1957–64), he founded the Salzburg Easter Festival in 1967 and conducted the Berlin Philharmonic Orchestra (1955–89).

Karakoram Range A mountain range mainly in SW China, NE Pakistan, and NW India. It extends about 450 km (280 mi) between the Pamirs and the Himalayas and includes *K2, the second highest mountain in the world. In 1978 the **Karakoram Highway** was opened connecting China with Pakistan over the Khunjerab Pass, 4933 m (16 188 ft) high.

Kara Kum A desert in Turkmenistan, between the Caspian Sea and the River Amu Darya. Area: about 300 000 sq km (115 806 sq mi).

karate A form of unarmed combat that was systematized in Okinawa in the 17th century and spread to Japan in the 1920s, where it absorbed elements of *jujitsu. Breath-control techniques as well as philosophical attitudes, such as the necessity of mental calm, were taken from Zen Buddhism. The aim is to focus the body's total muscular power in one instant. Hands, feet, elbows, etc., are toughened in stylized training sequences against padded or wooden blocks. In actual fights, however, blows are stopped short before impact. As in *judo, grades are distinguished by coloured belts. *See also* MARTIAL ARTS.

Karelian Isthmus A land bridge in NW Russia, connecting Finland with Russia. It was ceded to the Soviet Union in 1944. It is 40–113 km (25–70 mi) wide and 145 km (90 mi) long and its principal cities are St Petersburg and Vyborg.

Kariba, Lake A reservoir in Zambia and Zimbabwe. It is formed by the Zambezi River above the **Kariba Dam** (completed 1959) and generates hydroelectric power. Length: 282 km (175 mi).

Karlsruhe 49 00N 8 24E A city in SW Germany, in Baden-Württemberg. The capital of the former *Land* of Baden, it is the site of the federal court of justice and has a harbour on the Rhine. Population (1999 est): 276 700.

karma (Sanskrit: action) The sum of all human actions, which according to Hinduism and Jainism is passed from one individual existence to the next and determines the nature of the individual's rebirth. In *Buddhism, karma is associated with mental and physical elements passed on in the cycle of rebirth until the personal self is annihilated in attaining *nirvana.

Karnak 25 44N 32 39E A village near *Thebes (Upper Egypt), the site of the huge temple of Amon, built (c. 1320–1237 BC) mainly by the pharaohs Seti I (reigned 1313–1292) and Ramses II. *See also* LUXOR.

Karpov, Anatoly (1951–) Russian chess player, who became an International Grandmaster at 19 and subsequently world champion (1975). He successfully defended his title against Victor Korchnoi (1931–) in 1978 and 1981 but was defeated by *Kasparov (1985–87, 1990). He regained his title in 1993 (Kasparov did not take part in the championships).

karri A tree, *Eucalyptus diversicolor*, native to SW Australia and cultivated elsewhere. It grows to a height of over 35 m in moist areas and produces good timber.

karting (*or* **go-karting**) A form of *motor racing that originated in the USA in the 1950s. A kart usually has a tubular chassis, no body or suspension system, and a single driving seat. It has a maximum wheelbase of 50 in (1.27 m) and is usually powered by a single-cylinder two-stroke engine. Most karts are capable of about 160 km per hour (100 mph).

Kasai, River A river in central Africa. Rising in Angola, it flows N into the Democratic Republic of Congo to join the Congo River. It forms part of the Angola–Congo border. Length: 2100 km (1300 mi).

Kashmir The northernmost region of the Indian subcontinent, bordered by China to the NE and Afghanistan to the NW. The S Jammu lowlands rise into the Himalaya and Karakoram Mountains. Rice, silk, cotton, fruits, and sheep are farmed. *History*: most Kashmiris became Muslims in the 14th century but in the 19th century Hindu princes won power under British control; violence between Muslims and Hindus continues to the present day. Britain's withdrawal (1947) was followed by fighting between India and Pakistan and resulted in the partition of the region. Sporadic fighting between Indian and Pakistani forces has continued. Pakistan rules 78 932 sq km (30 468 sq mi) of the W and barren N. China occupies 42 735 sq km (16 496 sq mi) in the E. The remainder forms the Indian state of *Jammu and Kashmir. Area (all Kashmir): 222 236 sq km (85 783 sq mi).

Kasparov, Gary (Gary Weinstein; 1963–) Chess player of Armenian origin, born in Azerbaidzhan; the youngest-ever world champion. He won the world championship at the age of 22, beating *Karpov in 1985–87 and 1990. In 1993 he founded the Professional Chess Association with Nigel Short (1965–) and was stripped of his world title by FIDE, the game's ruling body.

Kassel 51 18N 9 30E A city in central Germany, in Hessen. Notable buildings include the Orangery Palace (1701–11). Population (1999 est): 196 700.

Kathmandu (*or* **Katmandu**) 27 42N 85 19E The capital of Nepal, near the confluence of the Rivers Baghmati and Vishnumati. Founded in the 8th century AD, it has many historical buildings and hosts several religious festivals. Population (2000 est): 701 499.

Katmai, Mount An active volcano in the USA, in S Alaska. Following its violent eruption in 1912, the Valley of Ten Thousand Smokes was formed. Height: 2100 m (7000 ft). Depth of crater: 1130 m (3700 ft). Width of crater: about 4 km (2.5 mi).

Katowice (former name (1953–56): Stalinogrod) 50 15N 18 59E A city in S central Poland. It is an important industrial centre within the Upper Silesia coalfield. Population (1999 est): 345 934.

Kattegat A strait between Denmark and Sweden linking the Skagerrak with the Baltic Sea. Length: about 240 km (149 mi).

Katyn Massacre The execution during World War II of 4250 Polish officers in the Katyn forest, near Smolensk in Russia. The bodies of the Poles, who had been interned by the Russians following the Soviet occupation of Polish territory in 1939, were discovered by the Germans in 1943. The Russians did not admit responsibility for the massacre until 1990.

Kauffmann, Angelica (1741–1807) Swiss painter. In England (1765–81) she painted portraits influenced by *Reynolds and was employed on decorative work in country houses designed by Robert and James *Adam.

Kaunas (Russian name: Kovno) 54 52N 23 55E A port in central Lithuania, at the confluence of the Rivers Neman and Viliya. It was held successively by Lithuania, Poland, and Russia. The capital of independent Lithuania from 11918 until 1940, it was occupied by German forces during World War II. Population (2000 est): 412 614.

Kaunda, Kenneth (David) (1924–) Zambian statesman; president (1964–91). In 1958 he founded the militant Zambia African National Congress and was imprisoned for subversion. On his release in 1960 he became president of the United National Independence Party, which took Northern Rhodesia to independence as Zambia in 1964. In 1991 he was defeated in the country's first free elections since 1968. From 1995 until 2000 he was leader of Zambia's main opposition party. He was subsequently stripped of Zambian citizenship as his parents were born in Malawi.

kauri pine A coniferous tree, *Agathis australis*, from New Zealand. Growing to a height of 46 m, it has spherical cones, 5–8 cm in diameter. It yields a resin (kauri copal or gum) used in making varnishes. Its timber is used for building purposes. Family: *Araucariaceae*.

kava A shrub, *Piper methysticum*, of the Pacific Islands and Australia, the ground and fermented roots of which are made into a narcotic drink. The roots are also chewed, and continued use produces inflammation and ulcers of the mouth. It has been used medicinally and as a local anaesthetic. Family: *Piperaceae*.

Kawasaki 35 32N 139 41E A city in Japan, in SE Honshu. It is part of the Tokyo-Yokohama industrial complex. Population (1995 est): 1 202 811.

Kazakhstan, Republic of A republic in central Asia. The Kazakhs comprise some 30% of the population, which includes Russians (43%) and Ukrainians (7%). *Economy*: the area is rich in mineral resources, especially coal, copper, and iron ore. Oil and gas production has expanded greatly in recent years and is now of major importance. The atomic power station on the Mangyshlak peninsula has the world's first industrial fast-breeder reactor. An important agricultural area, Kazakhstan produces cereals, cotton, rice, and fruit and is noted for its sheep. *History*: conquered by Mongols in the 13th century, the region came under Russian rule in the 18th and 19th centuries. It was a constituent republic of the Soviet Union from 1936 until it gained independence in 1991. Although multiparty elections were held in 1994, a subsequent constitution (approved by referendum in 1995) gave President Nursultan Nazarbayev power to dismiss parliament and rule by decree. The country's first contested presidential elections (1999) saw a landslide victory for Nazarbayev, but were deemed unfair by observers. Official language: Kazakh. Currency: tenge of 100 tein. Area: 2 717 300 sq km (1 049 155 sq mi). Population (2003 est): 14 790 000. Capital: Astana.

Kazan (*or* **Kasan**) 53 45N 49 10E A city in E Russia, since 1920 the capital of the Tatar Republic. *History*: founded in the 14th century by the *Tatars, it became the capital of an independent khanate and was captured (1552) by Ivan the Terrible. Its trade and industry developed during the 19th century. Lenin and Tolstoy studied at Kazan's university (1804). Population (1995 est): 1 085 000.

Kazan, Elia (E. Kazanjoglous; 1909–2003) US stage and film director and novelist, born in Turkey of Greek parentage. He helped to found the *Actors' Studio in 1947. For the stage he directed *A Streetcar Named Desire* (1947), *Death of a Salesman* (1949), and other outstanding plays. His films include *On the Waterfront* (1954), *East of Eden* (1955), and *The Arrangement* (1969). In 1999 he was awarded an Oscar for his lifetime's achievement, a controversial decision as he had cooperated with the McCarthy investigations into Hollywood in the 1950s.

Kean, Edmund (c. 1787–1833) British actor. He was particularly successful as Shylock in *The Merchant of Venice*, his first London success in 1814, Richard III, Macbeth, and Iago in *Othello*, all roles suited to his passionate style of acting.

Keating, Paul (1954–) Australian statesman and Labor prime minister (1991–96). As finance minister (1983–91) he introduced sweeping economic reforms. Re-elected in 1993, he was heavily defeated in the 1996 general election.

K

Keaton, Buster (Joseph Francis K.; 1895–1966) US comedian of silent films. He developed his character of the unsmiling and resilient clown in a series of classic silent comedies, including *The Navigator* (1924), *The General* (1926), and *The Cameraman* (1928).

Keats, John (1795–1821) British poet. Despite the failure of his first volume, *Poems* (1817), which contained the sonnet "On First Looking into Chapman's Homer," and the savage criticism directed at his second, *Endymion* (1818), Keats persisted and between 1819 and 1820 wrote most of his best-known poems. His short life was dogged by tragedies, especially the death of his brother from tuberculosis in 1818 and his unrequited love for Fanny Brawne. Such poems as *La Belle Dame Sans Merci*, *The Eve of Saint Agnes*, and the great odes ("To a Nightingale," "On a Grecian Urn," etc.), all published in 1820, eventually established his reputation. He died in Rome in search of a cure for his tuberculosis and was buried there.

Kebnekaise A mountain range in N Sweden. It rises to 2123 m (6965 ft) at Kebnekaise Sydtopp, the highest mountain in Sweden.

Keeshond A breed of dog traditionally used by the Dutch as barge dogs. It has a compact body with a foxlike face and a long thick grey coat with black-tipped hairs. The tail is carried over the back and a dense ruff surrounds the neck. Height: 43–45 cm.

Keitel, Wilhelm (1882–1946) German field

marshal, who was Hitler's chief military adviser throughout World War II. In 1945 in Berlin he confirmed the German surrender. He was hanged for war crimes.

Kekulé von Stradonitz, (Friedrich) August (1829–96) German chemist, whose main interest was in valence. He was the first chemist to establish the valence of the elements and to introduce the notion of single, double, and triple bonds. He went on to deduce the structural formulae of many organic molecules, including that of benzene (**Kekulé formula**), which he claimed to have thought of in 1865 while dozing on a bus. *See also* AROMATIC COMPOUND.

Kelantan A state in central Peninsular Malaysia, bordering on Thailand. Rice is grown on the NE coastal plain, and rubber, copra, and minerals are produced. Area: 14 931 sq km (5765 sq mi). Population (2000): 1 289 199. Capital: Kota Baharu.

k

Kells (Irish name: Ceanannus Mór) 54 48N 6 14W A market town in the Republic of Ireland, in Co Meath. A monastery was founded here in the 6th century AD by St Columba in which *The Book of Kells*, an 8th-century illuminated manuscript of the Gospels, is reputed to have been written. Population (latest est): 2623.

Kelly, Grace (1929–82) US film actress. Her films include *High Noon* (1952), *The Country Girl* (1955), *To Catch a Thief* (1955), and *High Society* (1956). She retired from acting when she married Prince Rainier III of Monaco in 1956. She died following a road accident.

Kelly, Ned (1855–80) Australian outlaw. He and his brother Dan formed a gang in 1878 that became notorious for its daring robberies in Victoria and New South Wales. He was captured and hanged in 1880 after a gunfight with the police in which the other gang members were killed.

kelp A large brown *seaweed belonging to the order *Laminariales* (about 30 genera), found in cold seas, usually below the level of low tide. The giant kelp *Macrocystis*, of the E Pacific coast, reaches a length of 65 m. Its fronds are kept afloat by air bladders. The name kelp is used for the ashes of seaweed, from which potassium and sodium salts and iodine were once obtained.

kelpie A breed of short-haired dog developed in Australia from the Border Collie and used for herding sheep and cattle. Named after a champion sheepdog of the 1870s, the kelpie has a long muzzle and pricked ears. The coat may be black or red (with or without tan), fawn, chocolate, or smoke-blue. Height: 43–50 cm.

kelvin (K) The SI unit of *thermodynamic temperature equal to 1/273.16 of the thermodynamic temperature of the triple point of water. Named after Lord *Kelvin.

Kelvin, William Thomson, 1st Baron (1824–1907) Scottish physicist. Kelvin was the first physicist to take notice of Joule's work. The two physicists then worked together, discovering the Joule-Kelvin effect; both also made great contributions to the new science of thermodynamics. In 1848 Kelvin postulated that there is a temperature at which the motions of particles cease and their energies become zero. He called this temperature *absolute zero and suggested a scale of temperature, now known as the Kelvin scale, in which the zero point is absolute zero. In 1852 he suggested that a *heat pump was a feasible device. During the 1860s he worked on the electrical properties of cables in conjunction with the laying of the first transatlantic cable in 1866. The unit of temperature (*see* KELVIN) is named after him.

Kempis, Thomas à *See* THOMAS À KEMPIS.

Kendal 54 20N 2 45W A town in NW England, in Cumbria, called the Gateway to the Lakes. Catherine *Parr was born in the Norman castle. Population (1991): 25 461.

kendo A Japanese martial art deriving from *samurai sword fighting. Combatants using bamboo staffs or wooden swords try to deliver blows on specified target areas of each other's bodies. Two hits constitute a win.

Kendrew, Sir John Cowdery (1917–97) British biochemist, who shared the 1962 Nobel Prize for Chemistry with Max *Perutz for his discovery of the structure of the myoglobin molecule. Kendrew used the technique of X-ray diffraction, analysing his results with a computer. He was knighted in 1974.

Keneally, Thomas Michael (1935–) Australian writer. He published 16 novels before writing *Schindler's Ark* (1982), which won the 1982 *Booker Prize and was made into the film *Schindler's List* (1994). His other works include *The Chant of Jimmie Blacksmith* (1972), *The Playmaker* (1987), *The Great Shame* (1998), and *The Office of Innocence* (2002).

Kennedy, Charles (Peter) (1959–) British politician, leader of the Liberal Democrats (1999–). An MP from 1983, he is also well known as a journalist and broadcaster.

Kennedy, Joseph Patrick (1888–1969) US businessman and diplomat. He had five daughters and four sons, three of whom entered public life. **John Fitzgerald Kennedy** (1917–63), a Democrat, was the first Roman Catholic president of the USA (1961–63). His liberal domestic polices—the so-called New Frontier—involved tax and social reforms and an extension of racial integration. He also established the Peace Corps. Abroad, he presided over the *Bay of Pigs invasion (1961) and confronted the Soviet Union over its installation of missile bases in Cuba (1962). In 1963 he negotiated the *Nuclear Test-Ban Treaty. Kennedy's presidency also saw the beginning of US military involvement in Vietnam. He was assassinated in Dallas, apparently by Lee Harvey Oswald. In 1953 he married Jacqueline Bouvier (1929–94), who became the wife (1968–75) of Aristotle *Onassis. **Robert Francis Kennedy** (1925–68), attorney general (1961–64) and then a senator (1965–68), campaigned for the Democratic presidential nomination in 1968, during which he too was assassinated. **Edward Moore Kennedy** (1932–) is a lawyer and Democratic Senator.

Kennelly, Arthur Edwin *See* IONOSPHERE.

Kenneth I MacAlpine (died c. 858) King of the Scots of Dalriada (c. 844–c. 858). He formed the kingdom of Alba, the foundation of modern Scotland.

Kensington and Chelsea A royal borough of W central Greater London, created in 1965 from the metropolitan boroughs of Chelsea and Kensington. Kensington Palace was the main royal residence from 1690 to 1760; it was later the birthplace of Queen Victoria and home to Diana, Princess of Wales. The borough is a centre for museums and colleges.

Kent A county of SE England, bordering on the English Channel and Greater London. It consists predominantly of undulating lowlands, crossed by the North Downs from W to E, and rising to the the Weald in the SW. Often called the Garden of England, it is the country's leading fruit- and hop-growing area. Rochester and Gillingham became an independent unitary authority, known as Medway, in 1998. Area (excluding Medway): 3526 sq km (1361 sq mi). Population (2001, excluding Medway): 1 329 653. Administrative centre: Maidstone.

Kent, William (1685–1748) English architect, landscape gardener, and interior designer, a leading exponent of *Palladianism. His buildings include Holkham Hall, Norfolk (1734). His development of landscape gardening was later continued by Capability *Brown.

Kentucky A state in the central USA, lying to the E of the Mississippi River. It consists of the Appalachian Mountains in the E, the Bluegrass region in the centre, an undulating plain in the W, and the basins of the Tennessee and Ohio Rivers in the SW. It is an important coalmining state and also produces petroleum and natural gas. Local timber is used in the furniture and wood industries. Agricultural products include tobacco, corn, hay, soya beans, cattle, sheep, and pigs. It is also an important region for the breeding of thoroughbred horses. *History*: Daniel Boone explored the area (1769) and after rapid settlement it became a state (1792). Area: 104 623 sq km (40 395 sq mi). Population (2000): 4 041 769. Capital: Frankfort.

Kenya, Mount 0 10S 37 30E An extinct volcano in Kenya, the second highest mountain in Africa. Height: 5200 m (17 058 ft).

Kenya, Republic of A country in East Africa, on the Indian Ocean. The land rises gradually from the coast to the highlands of the interior reaching heights of over 5000 m (17 000 ft). Most of the inhabitants are Africans, including *Kikuyu, Luo, *Masai, and Kamba. *Economy*: The chief cash crops are coffee, tea, sisal, and fruit and vegetables; livestock rearing and dairy farming are also important. Forestry is being developed and mineral resources include soda ash, gold, limestone, and salt. Wildlife reserves include the huge Tsavo National Park. Economic problems include widespread poverty and endemic official corruption. *History*: some of the earliest known fossil *hominid remains have been found in the region by the *Leakey family. The coastal area was settled by the Arabs from the 7th century AD and was controlled by the Portuguese during the 16th and 17th centuries. It became a British protectorate (East Africa Protectorate) in 1895 and a colony in 1920. In the 1950s independence movements led to the *Mau Mau revolt. Kenya gained independence in 1963 and in 1964 became a republic within the Commonwealth, with Jomo *Kenyatta as its first president. In 1992 President Daniel arap Moi (1924–) agreed to hold the first multiparty elections since the 1960s. Although he was reelected there were allegations of fraud, causing a political crisis. Elections in 1997 produced another victory for Moi, but the opposition refused to accept the result. In an important constitutional change, parliament voted (1999) to restrict Moi's powers. Following Moi's retirement in 2002, presidential elections were won by the veteran opposition leader Mwai Kibaki. Official languages: Swahili and English. Currency: Kenya shilling of 100 cents. Area: 582 600 sq km (224 960 mi). Population (2003 est): 31 639 000. Capital: Nairobi.

Kenyatta, Jomo (c. 1891–1978) Kenyan statesman; president (1964–78). Son of a poor farmer, he became (1947) president of the Kenya African Union and in 1953 was imprisoned for seven years by the colonial government for his part in the *Mau Mau rebellion (complicity in which he always denied). While in gaol he was elected leader of the Kenya African National Union (1960), which achieved Kenya's independence in 1963. Kenyatta was prime minister before becoming president of a one-party state.

Kepler, Johannes (1571–1630) German astronomer, who was one of the first supporters of Copernicus' heliocentric theory of the solar system. Kepler used Tycho Brahe's observations to deduce the shape of planetary orbits, discovering that they were elliptical. He published this discovery, the first of **Kepler's laws**, together with his second law, stating that orbital velocity decreases with distance from the sun, in *Astronomia Nova* (1609). In 1619 he published his third law relating a planet's year to its distance from the sun. In 1610 he received a telescope built by Galileo, which he used to observe Jupiter. In 1611 he constructed an improved version, now known as a Keplerian *telescope.

k

Kerala A state in SW India. Tropical, beautiful, and poor, it is India's most densely populated state. Rice, tea, coffee, pepper, rubber, nuts, and fruit are farmed. Fishing is also important. *History*: Malayalam-speaking Kerala has traded with the Near and Far East since ancient times, flourishing in the 9th and 10th centuries. Area: 38 855 sq km (14 998 sq mi). Population (2001): 31 838 619. Capital: Trivandrum.

keratin An insoluble fibrous protein that is the major constituent of hair, nails, feathers, beaks, horns, and scales. Keratin is also found in the skin.

Kerguelen Islands 49 30S 69 30E An archipelago in the S Indian Ocean, in the French Southern and Antarctic Territories. Kerguelen Island, the largest, is the site of several scientific bases. Area: 7215 sq km (2786 sq mi).

kermes A scale insect of the genus *Kermes*, especially *K. ilices* of Europe and W Asia, formerly used to produce a red dye. They feed on the small evergreen kermes oak (*Quercus coccifera*), which is native to S Europe, N Africa, and W Asia.

Kern, Jerome (David) (1885–1945) US composer of musical comedies, the most famous of which was *Show Boat* (1927), written in collaboration with Oscar *Hammerstein II. Two of his best-known songs are "Smoke Gets in Your Eyes", and "Ol' Man River"; he also wrote much film music after 1939.

kerosene *See* PARAFFIN.

Kerouac, Jack (1922–69) US novelist. He was a leading figure of the *Beat movement, of which his novel *On the Road* (1957) was a seminal work. Other works include *Big Sur* (1962) and *Desolation Angels* (1965).

Kerr effects Two effects concerned with optical changes produced by magnetic or electric fields. In the magneto-optical effect, plane-polarized light is slightly elliptically polarized when reflected by the pole of an electromagnet. In the electro-optical effect, the plane of polarization of a beam of light is rotated when passed through certain liquids or solids across which a potential difference is applied. This effect is utilized in the **Kerr cell**, which is used as a high-speed shutter and to modu late *laser beams. Named after the discoverer John Kerr (1824–1907).

Kerry (Irish name: Chiarraighe) A county in the SW Republic of Ireland, in Munster. It rises in the S to Macgillycuddy's Reeks and contains the famous Lakes of Killarney. The chief occupations are fishing, farming, and tourism. Area: 4701 sq km (1815 sq mi). Population (2002): 132 424. County town: Tralee.

Kerry, John Forbes US politician. A decorated veteran of the Vietnam War, he was elected to the US Senate in 1984 and was chosen as the Democratic candidate for the presidential election of 2004.

Kesselring, Albert (1885–1960) German general, who commanded the Luftwaffe in the invasions of Poland (1939) and France (1940) and in the battle of Britain (1940). In 1943 he became commander of land and air forces in Italy and in 1945 on the Western Front. His death sentence as a war criminal was commuted to life imprisonment and he was released in 1952.

kestrel A small *falcon characterized by a long tail and the ability to hover before diving on its prey. The common kestrel (*Falco tinnunculus*), 32 cm long, is found in Eurasia and Africa and hunts small rodents, birds, and insects. The female has a brown streaked plumage; the male is blue-grey with black-streaked pale-brown underparts, a black-tipped tail, and a black eye stripe.

Keswick 54 37N 3 08W A town in NW England, in Cumbria. It is one of the main tourist centres of the Lake District. Population (1991): 4836.

ketone A class of organic chemicals having the general formula RCOR′, where R and R′ are hydrocarbon groups. Ketones are prepared by the oxidation of secondary alcohols. Acetone (dimethyl ketone) is a common example.

Kew Gardens The Royal Gardens at Kew, near Richmond, Greater London, which occupy land once owned by the royal family. The first botanic garden was created there in 1759, by Augusta (d. 1772), Princess of Wales, and in the late 18th and early 19th centuries Kew became internationally famous. Between 1848 and 1876 William (1785–1865) and Joseph (1817–1911) Hooker founded the Museum of Economic Botany, the Library, Herbarium, and Jodrell Laboratory.

Keynes, John Maynard, 1st Baron (1883–1946) British economist. After attending the Versailles peace conference Keynes published *The Economic Consequences of the Peace* (1919), which attacked the war reparations imposed on Germany. In his greatest work, *General Theory of Employment, Interest and Money* (1936), he argued that unemployment can only be alleviated by increased public spending.

KGB (Committee of State Security) The former Soviet secret police concerned with internal security and intelligence. It was founded in 1954 to replace the more brutal MGB (Ministry of State Security; 1946–53), which itself replaced the NKVD (People's Commisariat of Internal Affairs; 1934–46). It was abolished in 1991 but formed the basis of separate units responsible for Russian intelligence, counterintelligence, and border control.

Khabarovsk 48 32N 135 08E A port in E Russia, on the River Amur. Situated on the Trans-Siberian Railway, it is a transport centre. Population (1999 est): 614 000.

Khachaturian, Aram Ilich (1903–78) Soviet composer. His music was deeply influenced by Caucasian folk music. His compositions include concertos for piano (1936) and violin (1940) and the famous ballets *Gayaneh* (1942) and *Spartacus* (1954).

Kharkov (*or* **Karkiv**) 50 00N 36 15E A city in E Ukraine. It was almost totally destroyed in World War II. Today, it is an important railway junction and has major engineering industries. Population (1998 est): 1 521 400.

Khartoum (*or* **al-Khurtum**) 15 40N 32 52E The capital of the Sudan, at the confluence of the Blue and the White Nile Rivers. In 1885 *Gordon was besieged and killed here and the town destroyed by the forces of the Mahdi (*see* MAHDI, AL-) but was recaptured by Anglo-Egyptian forces in 1898. It has several cathedrals and two mosques. Population (1993): 924 505.

Khazars A Turkic people who inhabited the lower Volga basin from the 7th to 13th centuries. Noted for their laws, tolerance, and cosmopolitanism, the Khazars embraced Judaism in the 8th century. Slavonic and nomadic Turkic invaders brought the downfall of the Khazars in the 11th century. Itil, near modern Astrakhan, was their capital.

Khmer A people of Cambodia, Thailand, and Vietnam who speak the Khmer language, one of the Austro-Asiatic languages. They are rice cultivators and fishers, living in village communities headed by an elected chief. Their religion is Theravada Buddhism. The Khmer empire was founded in 616 AD and between the 9th and 13th centuries Khmer kings presided over the advanced civilization that was responsible for the great stone buildings of Angkor. The name Khmer was later adopted by the the communist Khmer Rouge movement (*see* CAMBODIA).

Khoisan The racial grouping comprising the Hottentot and Bushmen people of S Africa. The Khoisan languages are noted for their click sounds. Formerly widespread S of the Zambezi River, the Khoisan tribes have been decimated by Bantu and European encroachments since 1700. The Hottentots were nomads, herding sheep and cattle. They were divided into clans, each with its own territory and chief. The Bushmen were traditionally hunters and gatherers, but most are now farm workers. Until the early 2000s some groups in the deserts of W Botswana still roamed in bands, but all have now been forcibly resettled in villages.

Khomeini, Ayatollah Ruholla (1902–89) Iranian Shiite Muslim leader (ayatollah). Following the overthrow of the shah (1979) he returned from 16 years of exile to lead the Islamic Revolution. He imposed strict Islamic law and remained Iran's supreme religious leader until his death. His reactionary anti-Western views incurred international criticism, as in the *Rushdie affair.

Khrushchev, Nikita S(ergeevich) (1894–1971) Soviet statesman; first secretary of the Soviet Communist Party (1953–64) and prime minister (1958–64). Khrushchev was a close associate of Stalin and emerged victorious from the power struggle that followed his death. In 1956 Khrushchev began a programme of destalinization, which gave rise to revolts in other communist countries. Owing to the failure of his economic policies and his unsuccessful foreign policy, notably his attempt to install missiles in Cuba (1962), he was ousted by *Brezhnev and *Kosygin.

Khufu (*or* **Cheops**) King of Egypt (c. 2600 BC) of the 4th dynasty; the father of Khafre (reigned c. 2550 BC). He built the Great Pyramid at *Giza, which took 20 years to construct.

Khyber Pass (**Khaybar Pass** *or* **Khaibar Pass**) 34 06N 71 05E A mountain pass in the Hindu Kush, connecting Afghanistan with Pakistan. Rising to 1072 m (3518 ft), it is of strategic importance.

k

kibbutz An Israeli collective settlement in which land and property are owned or leased by all its members and work and meals are organized collectively. About 3% of the population live in *kibbutzim*. A **moshav** is a smallholders' cooperative in which machinery alone is shared. About 5% of the Israeli population live in *moshavim*.

Kidderminster 52 23N 2 14W A market town in W central England, in Worcestershire. It is famous for carpet manufacture, begun in 1735. Population (1991): 54 644.

Kidman, Nicole (1967–) Australian film actress, born in Hawaii. She made her name in the thriller *Dead Calm* (1989) and starred with her then-husband Tom *Cruise in *Far and Away* (1992) and Kubrick's *Eyes Wide Shut* (1999). Other films include *To Die For* (1995), the musical *Moulin Rouge* (2001), and *The Hours* (2002). Her stage performances include Hare's *The Blue Room* (1998, London).

kidneys The two organs of excretion in vertebrate animals and man, which also regulate the amount of salt and water in the blood. The human kidneys are bean-shaped, each about 12 cm long and weighing about 150 g, and situated on either side of the spine below the diaphragm. They contain millions of tubules, the outer parts of which filter water and dissolved substances from blood supplied by the renal artery. Most of the water and some substances are reabsorbed back into the blood further down the tubules: the remaining fluid (*see* URINE) passes on to the *bladder. If one kidney ceases to function or is removed the other will enlarge and take over its function. Removal of both kidneys requires the use of an artificial kidney machine (*see* DIALYSIS) unless a suitable donor kidney is available for *transplantation.

Kiel 54 20N 10 08E A city in N Germany, the capital of Schleswig-Holstein. A Baltic port, it was the chief naval port of Germany by the late 19th century. It has a 13th-century palace, restored after World War II. It is linked to the North Sea by the Kiel Canal. Population (1999 est): 235 500.

Kierkegaard, Søren (1813–55) Danish philosopher. Although critical of *Hegel, particularly in *The Concept of Irony* (1841), he remained under his influence. Much of his work is poetic and paradoxical even in its titles, for example *Either-Or* (1843) and *Concluding Unscientific Postscript* (1846). Suspicious of both science and the established Church, he saw man as existing in isolation and relating only to God. He greatly influenced 20th-century *existentialism.

Kiev 50 28N 30 29E The capital of Ukraine, on the river Dnepr. Its opera and ballet companies have a worldwide reputation. Outstanding buildings include the 11th-century St Sophia cathedral and the Golden Gate of Kiev. *History*: Kiev, "the mother of cities," was probably founded in the 6th or 7th century AD. Recurrent Tatar attacks virtually destroyed the city, which subsequently passed to Lithuania. Russian rule was established in the 17th century. After the Russian Revolution Kiev became the capital of the short-lived Ukrainian republic and in 1934, the capital of the Ukrainian SSR. In World War II the city was occupied, after a long siege, by the Germans and thousands of its inhabitants were massacred. Population (1998 est): 2 620 900.

Kikuyu A Bantu-speaking tribe of Kenya. They cultivate cereals and sweet potatoes and keep livestock, particularly cattle. Small groups of patrilineal kin occupy scattered homesteads of conical-shaped huts. Age grades are an important basis of social organization, boys being initiated by circumcision. Political authority is held by a council of members of the senior age grade. The largest tribe in Kenya, the Kikuyu were deeply involved in the *Mau Mau movement.

Kildare (Irish name: Contae Chill Dara) A county in the E Republic of Ireland, in Leinster. It consists chiefly of a low-lying plain containing part of the Bog of Allen and the Curragh, an area noted for its racehorse breeding. Cattle rearing and arable farming are also important. Area: 1694 sq km (654 sq mi). Population (2002): 163 995. County town: Naas.

Kilimanjaro, Mount 3 02S 37 20E A volcanic mountain in Tanzania, the highest mountain in Africa. It has two peaks: Kibo at 5895 m (19 340 ft), and Mawenzi at 5273 m (17 300 ft).

Kilkenny (Irish name: Contae Chill Choinnigh) A county in the SE Republic of Ireland, in Leinster. Agriculture is the chief occupation. Area: 2062 sq km (796 sq mi). Population (2002): 80 421. County town: Kilkenny.

Killarney (Irish name: Cill Airne) 52 03N 9 30W A town in the Republic of Ireland in Co Kerry. A tourist centre, it is famous for its scenery. Population (1991): 7250.

killer whale A large toothed whale, *Orcinus orca*, common in Pacific and Antarctic waters but found in all other oceans. Up to 9 m long, killer whales are black above and pure white beneath, with an erect dorsal fin. They are notorious for their voracious appetites. Like other dolphins, they are intelligent and trainable in captivity. Family: *Delphinidae* (dolphins).

Killiecrankie, Pass of 56 43N 3 40W A pass in the Grampian Mountains, Scotland, in Perth and Kinross. It was the scene of a massacre of William III's troops by Jacobite Highlanders (1689).

killifish One of several small elongated fish, also called egg-laying top minnows, belonging to the family *Cyprinodontidae*, especially the genus *Fundulus*. Killifish occur chiefly in tropical America, Africa, and Asia and feed on plant or animal material. Up to 15 cm long, many are brightly coloured and kept as aquarium fish. Similar related fish are the live-bearing top minnows of the family *Poeciliidae*. Order: *Atheriniformes*.

Kilmarnock 55 37N 4 30W An industrial town in SW Scotland, the administrative centre of East Ayrshire. The Burns museum contains many of his manuscripts. Population (1991): 44 307.

kilogram (kg) The SI unit of mass equal to the mass of the platinum-iridium prototype kept at the International Bureau of Weights and Measures near Paris.

kiloton A measure of the explosive power of a nuclear weapon. It is equivalent to an explosion of 1000 tons of trinitrotoluene (TNT).

kilowatt-hour (kW-hr) A unit of energy used in charging for electricity. It is equal to the work done by a power of 1000 watts in 1 hour.

Kimberley 28 45S 24 46E A city in South Africa, in N Cape Province. It was founded (1871) following the discovery of diamonds and is today the world's largest diamond centre. The Kimberley Open Mine, 1.6 km (1 mi) in circumference, was closed in 1915. Population (1996): 170 432.

Kim Dae Jung (1925–) Korean politician; president of South Korea (1997–2002). A leading human-rights campaigner, he was elected to the national assembly in 1961 but was subjected to repeated imprisonment by the authorities. As president, he negotiated (2000) an agreement with North Korea and was awarded the 2000 Nobel Peace Prize.

Kim Il Sung (Kim Song Ju; 1912–94) North Korean statesman; prime minister (1948–72) and then president (1972–94). He became leader of the Soviet-dominated N in 1945: in 1950 he ordered the invasion of South Korea in an unsuccessful attempt to reunite Korea (*see* KOREAN WAR). He was succeeded by his son, **Kim Jong Il** (1942–), who was effectively ruler of the country from 1994 but not declared head of state until 1998.

k

kimono A Japanese floor-length robe, often made of silk, with wide sleeves and a sash tied in a bow at the back. Only the patterns differentiate kimonos for men and for women.

kinetic energy Energy possessed by a body by virtue of its motion. If the body, mass m, is moving in a straight line with velocity v, its kinetic energy is $\frac{1}{2}mv^2$. If it is rotating its rotational kinetic energy is $\frac{1}{2}I\omega^2$, where I is its moment of inertia and ω its angular velocity.

kinetic theory A theory developed in the 19th century, largely by *Joule and *Maxwell, in which the behaviour of gases is explained by regarding them as consisting of tiny dimensionless particles in constant random motion. Collisions, either between the particles or between the particles and the walls of the container, are assumed to be perfectly elastic. The theory explains the pressure of a gas as being due to collisions between the particles and the walls, its temperature as a measure of the *average* *kinetic energy of the particles.

King, Jr, Martin Luther (1929–68) US Black civil-rights leader. An outstanding orator, he followed principles of nonviolent resistance in organizing demonstrations against racial inequality and won the Nobel Peace Prize in 1964.

He was assassinated in Memphis, Tennessee, by James Earl Ray.

King Charles spaniel A breed of *spaniel having a compact body, short legs, a short neck, and a large head with a short upturned nose. There are four colour varieties: Blenheim, ruby, tricolour, and black and tan, the last being associated with King Charles II. Weight: 3.5–6 kg; height: about 25 cm. The Cavalier King Charles spaniel is lighter bodied, with longer legs and a longer muzzle. Weight: 5–8 kg; height: about 30 cm.

king crab *See* HORSESHOE CRAB.

kingcup *See* MARSH MARIGOLD.

kingdom *See* TAXONOMY.

kingfisher A bird belonging to a family (*Alcedinidae*; 85 species) divided into two subfamilies: the *Alcedininae* are narrow-billed and live near water, feeding on small fish; the *Dacetoninae* are broad-billed insectivorous birds not closely associated with water. Kingfishers are 12–45 cm long, with a bright plumage and often brightly coloured bills and usually nest in burrows in banks. Order: *Coraciiformes* (hornbills, kingfishers, etc.).

King James Version The Authorized Version of the English *Bible that appeared in 1611 under the patronage of James I. It was based on the earlier Bishops' Bible (1568), but the translators also consulted and made use of the *Geneva Bible and the *Douai Bible. It was much indebted to the translations of William Tyndale (c. 1494–1536).

Kingsley, Charles (1819–79) British clergyman and writer. In many works, such as *Alton Locke* (1850), he championed various social reforms. His works include the popular children's book *The Water Babies* (1863).

King's Lynn (**Lynn** *or* **Lynn Regis**) 52 45N 0 24E A historic market town in E England, in Norfolk. Its importance as a port has declined since the middle ages. Population (1991): 41 281.

Kingston 17 58N 76 48W The capital and main port of Jamaica, in the SE. Founded in 1692, it became the capital in 1872. In the early 20th century it suffered from hurricanes and an earthquake. Population (1991 est): 103 771.

Kingston-upon-Hull **1.** (*or* **Hull**) 53 45N 0 20W A city and port in NE England, in the East Riding of Yorkshire, on the Humber estuary. An important fishing port, Hull has vast docks and serves as a container port for much of the North and Midlands, with passenger services to the Continent. Industries include food processing, chemicals, and engineering, as well as fish-related industries. Population (1995 est): 268 600. **2.** A unitary authority in NE England, in the East Riding of Yorkshire. Area: 71 sq km (27 sq mi). Population (2001): 243 595.

Kingstown 13 12N 61 14W A port in SW St Vincent, in the West Indies. Exports include bananas, copra, arrowroot, and cotton. Population (1995 est): 15 908.

kinkajou A nocturnal arboreal mammal, *Potos flavus*, of Central and South American forests. Up to 110 cm long including the tail (40–55 cm), it has a soft golden-brown coat, small ears, and a prehensile tail. An agile climber, it feeds mainly on fruit and honey. Family: *Procyonidae* (*see* RACCOON).

Kinnock, Neil (Gordon) (1942–) British politician. As leader of the Labour Party (1983–92) he reunited the Party but failed to win general elections (1987 and 1992). He became a European commissioner in 1995 and vice-president of the Commission in 1999.

Kinshasa (name until 1966: Léopoldville) 4 18S 15 18E The capital of the Democratic Republic of Congo, on the Congo River. It has a long history of human settlement and was occupied by the Humbu when *Stanley discovered it in the late 19th century. Population (1994 est): 4 655 313.

Kintyre A peninsula in W Scotland, in Argyll and Bute between the Atlantic Ocean and the Firth of Clyde. The **Mull of Kintyre** headland forms its most southerly point.

Kipling, (Joseph) Rudyard (1865–1936) British writer and poet. Born in Bombay, he was educated in England, returning to India in 1882 to work as a journalist. After returning to England in 1888, he made his reputation with *Barrack Room Ballads and Other Verses* (1892). From 1892 to 1896 he lived in New England, where he wrote *The Jungle Books* (1894, 1895). *Kim* (1901) is the last novel he wrote with an Indian setting. Among his many other works are *Just So Stories* (1902) and *Puck of Pook's Hill* (1906), both for children. He won the Nobel Prize in 1907.

Kirchhoff, Gustav Robert (1824–87) German physicist. Working with Robert *Bunsen, he invented the technique of spectroscopy and discovered caesium and rubidium in 1861. Kirchoff, working alone, also discovered several elements in the sun, by investigating the solar spectrum. He is also known for **Kirchhoff's laws**, relating to electrical networks.

Kirgizstan, Republic of (*or* **Kyrgyzstan**

or **Kirghizia**) A republic in central Asia. The Kirgiz, a traditionally nomadic Turkic people, comprise over one-half of the population. *Economy*: there are deposits of coal, lead, mercury, and antimony, as well as oil and natural gas. Gold is mined and forms the main export. Industry, which has grown rapidly in recent years, includes the manufacture of machinery and building materials and food processing. Wheat, cotton, and tobacco are grown and livestock, especially cattle, sheep, horses, and yaks, are important. *History*: the Kirgiz came under Russian rule in the 19th century and fought the new Soviet Government after the Russian Revolution. As a result they suffered a famine in 1921–22, in which over 500 000 Kirgiz died. Kirgizstan was a constituent republic of the Soviet Union from 1936 until it became independent on the break-up of the Soviet Union in 1991. A new constitution was approved in 1994 and the country's first multiparty elections were held in 1995. Recent years have seen rising levels of popular unrest and growing government authoritarianism under President Askar Akayev. Official languages: Kirgiz and Russian. Currency: som of 100 tyin. Area: 198 500 sq km (76 642 sq mi). Population (2003 est): 5 059 500. Capital: Bishkek.

Kiribati, Republic of (name until 1979: Gilbert Islands) A country in the S Pacific Ocean comprising the Gilbert Islands, the Phoenix Islands, and some of the Line Islands together with Ocean Island. The majority of the inhabitants are Micronesians. *Economy*: although phosphate mining was discontinued in 1979, proceeds from the industry were placed in a trust fund which remains the country's main source of revenue. The main economic activities are now fishing and subsistence agriculture. Coconuts, copra, and fish are the chief exports. *History*: a centre for sperm whale hunting in the 19th century and part of the British protectorate of the Gilbert and Ellice Islands from 1892, they became a colony in 1915. Links with the Ellice Islands (*see* TUVALU, STATE OF) were severed in 1975 and the remaining islands became independent in 1979 as the Republic of Kiribati. Teburoro Tito has been president since 1993. Official languages: I-Kiribati and English. Currency: Australian dollar of 100 cents. Area: 861 sq km (332 sq mi). Population (2003 est): 87 900. Capital: Bairiki.

Kiritimati *See* CHRISTMAS ISLAND.

Kirkcaldy 56 07N 3 10W A town in E central Scotland, in Fife. It is the birthplace of Adam Smith. Population (1991): 47 155.

Kirklees A unitary authority in N England, in West Yorkshire. Area: 410 sq km (158 sq mi). Population (2001): 388 576.

Kirkwall 58 59N 2 58W A town in NE Scotland, the administrative centre of the island authority of Orkney, on the island of Mainland. Population (1991): 6469.

Kirov (name from 1780 until 1934: Vyatka) 58 38N 49 38E A port in Russia, on the River Vyatka. Founded in 1181, it was renamed after S. M. Kirov (1888–1934). Population (1999 est): 466 100.

Kirov Ballet A Russian ballet company based at the Kirov State Theatre of Opera and Ballet in St Petersburg. The theatre was renamed in honour of the politician S. M. Kirov (1888–1934) in 1935. Some of the Kirov's leading dancers, including Rudolf *Nureyev, Natalia Makarova (1940–), and Mikhail Baryshnikov (1948–), earned international reputations.

Kirovohrad (name until 1924: Yelisavetgrad; name from 1924 until 1936: Zinoviyevsk; name until 1992: Kirovograd) 48 31N 32 15E A city in S central Ukraine. It is a major agricultural centre. Population (1999 est): 270 200.

Kisangani (name until 1966: Stanleyville) 0 33S 25 14E A riverport in the NE Democratic Republic of Congo, on the Congo River. It is an agricultural centre. Population (1994 est): 417 517.

Kish A city of ancient *Sumer, near Babylon. Kish was the pre-eminent centre of civilization until eclipsed by *Ur (c. 2600 BC). Excavated between 1923 and 1933, its site has produced the earliest known example of writing—pictograms dating to soon after 3500 BC.

Kishinev (Romanian name: Chişinău) 47 00N 28 50E The capital of Moldova. Founded in the 15th century, it was under Romanian rule (1918–40). Population (1999 est): 655 000.

Kissinger, Henry (Alfred) (1923–) US diplomat and political scientist; secretary of state (1973–76). Appointed adviser to President Nixon (1969), Kissinger and Le Duc Tho (1911–90) were jointly awarded the Nobel Peace Prize (1973) for helping to negotiate an end to the Vietnam War. Under President Ford he became well known for his flying-shuttle style of diplomacy while negotiating a truce between Syria and Israel (1974).

Kitakyushu 33 52N 130 49E A city in Japan, on the Shimonoseki Strait. Formed in 1963 from the cities of Wakamatsu, Yawata, Tobata, Kokura, and Moji, it is one of Japan's leading trade and deepsea fishing ports. Population (1995 est): 1 019 562.

Kitchener of Khartoum, Horatio Herbert, 1st Earl (1850–1916) British field marshal. Appointed commander in chief of the Egyptian army in 1892, by 1898, with the battle of Omdurman, he had reconquered the Sudan, becoming its governor general (1899). In the second Boer War he suppressed the guerrillas by a scorched-earth policy and the internment of civilians in concentration camps. In 1914, as war secretary, his recruitment campaign was highly successful. He was drowned on his way to Archangel.

kite A *hawk belonging to the subfamily *Milvinae*, which occurs throughout the world, most commonly in warm regions. Typically reddish brown and 52–57 cm long, kites have long narrow wings, a long often forked tail, and a narrow bill and feed on insects, small mammals, and reptiles; some are scavengers.

k

kithara An ancient Greek musical instrument, related to the lyre, with 7–18 strings. It is traditionally believed to have been invented by the god Apollo.

kittiwake A North Atlantic *gull, *Rissa tridactyla*, that is adapted for nesting on narrow cliff ledges. It is 40 cm long and has a white plumage with black-tipped grey wings, short black legs, dark eyes, and a yellow bill. It feeds at sea on fish and offal, going ashore only to breed.

Kitwe 12 48S 28 14E A town in N central Zambia. It is the chief commercial, industrial, and communications centre of the Copperbelt. Population (latest est): 338 207.

kiwi (bird) A secretive flightless bird belonging to a family (*Apterygidae*; 3 species) occurring in forested regions of New Zealand. 25–40 cm long, kiwis have tiny wings hidden in coarse grey-brown plumage and strong legs with large claws. Kiwis are nocturnal and have weak eyes but well-developed hearing; the long bill is used to probe the soil for worms, insect larvae, etc. Order: *Apterygiformes*.

kiwi (plant) A Chinese climbing shrub, *Actinidia chinensis*, also called Chinese gooseberry. It has white or yellow flowers and an edible rough-skinned fruit, up to 5 cm long. Family: *Actinidiaceae*.

Klagenfurt 46 38N 14 20E A city in S Austria, the capital of Carinthia. It has a cathedral (1578–91) and is a tourist centre. Population (1991 est): 89 415.

Klaipeda (German name: Memel) 55 43N 21 07E A port in Lithuania, on the Baltic Sea. It has been occupied at various times by Prussia, France, Russia, and Germany. Population (2000 est): 202 484.

Klee, Paul (1879–1940) Swiss painter and etcher. Working initially as an etcher, influenced by *Beardsley and Goya, he became associated with the *Blaue Reiter group and taught at the *Bauhaus school of design (1920–33). Inspired by a visit to Tunisia (1914), he produced small watercolours in brilliant colours; after 1919 he used oils, incorporating signs and hieroglyphs to create a fantasy world influenced by children's art.

Klein, Melanie (1882–1960) Austrian psychiatrist, who moved to England in 1926. She is noted for her psychoanalytical studies of children, which were influenced by Sigmund *Freud and his associates.

Klein bottle In *topology, a surface that has no edges and only one side. It is made by putting the small end of a tapering tube through the side of the tube, stretching it, and joining it to the large end. It was discovered by the German mathematician Christian Felix Klein (1849–1925).

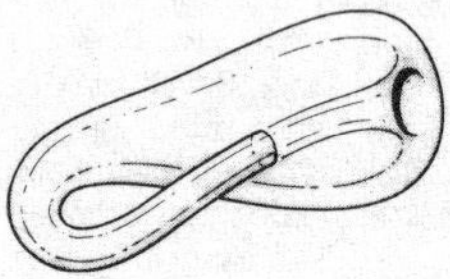

Klein bottle. A solid with no edges and only one side.

Klemperer, Otto (1885–1973) German conductor. He became conductor of the German Opera in Prague on the recommendation of Mahler in 1907. Expelled by the Nazis in 1933, he was principal conductor of the Philharmonia Orchestra from 1959 until his death and is particularly remembered for performances of Beethoven.

Klondike The valley of the Klondike River in NW Canada, in the central *Yukon, where gold was discovered in 1896. The subsequent gold rush opened up the Yukon, although the population dwindled when the gold started to run out (1900).

klystron An electronic device used to generate or amplify *microwaves. It consists of a sealed evacuated tube in which a steady beam of electrons from an electron gun is alternately accelerated and retarded by high-frequency radio waves (velocity *modulation) as it passes through a cavity. The resultant radio-frequency pulses are picked up at a second cavity, either as a voltage oscillation or, if connected to a *waveguide, as electromagnetic waves. The second cavity can be tuned to the input frequency or a harmonic of it. *See also* MAGNETRON.

Kneller, Sir Godfrey (1646–1723) Portrait painter of German birth. He worked successively for Charles II, William III, Queen Anne, and George I, and founded the first English academy of painting (1711). His portraits of the Whig Kit Cat Club (c. 1702–17; National Portrait Gallery), established a standard British portrait type.

Knock A village in the Republic of Ireland, in Co Mayo. Visions of the Virgin Mary were allegedly seen here, the first in 1879, and it has become a place of pilgrimage with its own airport.

Knossos The principal city of Minoan Crete, near present-day Heraklion. It was occupied between about 2500 and 1200 BC. Excavated and reconstructed (1899–1935) by Sir Arthur *Evans, the Palace of Minos was luxurious and sophisticated. About 1450 BC the palace was burnt down.

knot (bird) A short-legged bird, *Calidris canutus*, that breeds in Arctic tundra and winters on southern coasts. 25 cm long, it has a short black bill and its plumage is mottled grey in winter and reddish in summer. In winter, knots probe mud and sand for snails, worms, and crabs. Family: *Scolopacidae* (sandpipers, snipe, etc.).

knot (unit) A unit of speed, used for ships and aircraft, equal to 1 nautical mile per hour (1.15 miles per hour).

knots Fastenings formed by looping and tying pieces of rope, cord, etc. The mathematical theory of knots, a branch of *topology, was developed mainly in the 20th century, and draws on matrix theory, algebra, and geometry. A simple closed curve in space may be knotted in various ways, each with specific topological properties. See illustration on p. 494.

Knowsley A unitary authority of NW England, in Merseyside. Area: 97 sq km (38 sq mi). Population (2001): 150 468.

Knox, John (c. 1514–72) Scottish Protestant reformer. In 1547 he joined the Protestants who had murdered Cardinal Beaton in St Andrew's Castle. The castle was stormed by the French, who imprisoned Knox as a galley slave. After his release (1549) he became a chaplain to Edward VI in England and contributed to the revision of the Second Book of Common Prayer. On the accession of the Catholic Mary I he escaped to the Continent, where he met *Calvin in Geneva. Returning to Scotland in 1559, he became its leading reformer. In 1560 the Scottish parliament adopted the *Confession of Faith* that Knox had compiled. His *First Book of Discipline* (1561) outlined a structure for the reformed Church of Scotland.

Knox-Johnston, Robin (William Robert Patrick K.-J.; 1939–) British yachtsman; the first person to sail alone around the world non-stop (1968–69). In 1981 he set the British transatlantic sailing record (11 days 7 hours 45 mins).

Knoxville 36 00N 83 57W A city in the USA, in Tennessee. It is an inland port and agricultural trading centre. Population (2000): 173 890.

koala An arboreal *marsupial, *Phascolarctus cinereus*, of E Australia. About 60 cm high, koalas have thick greyish fur, tufted ears, a small tail, and long claws. Each adult eats more than 1 kg of eucalyptus leaves every day. The pouch opens towards the female's tail—unusual in herbivorous marsupials. Family: *Phalangeridae*.

kob An African antelope, *Kobus kob*, also called Buffon's kob. Males are about 90 cm high at the shoulder; females are smaller. The coat ranges from orange to nearly black, with white markings on the face, legs, and belly and a black stripe down the foreleg.

Kobe 34 40N 135 12E A major port in Japan, on Osaka Bay. It forms the W end of the Osaka-Kobe industrial area. Population (1995): 1 423 830.

Koblenz (English name: Coblenz) 50 21N 7 36E A city in W Germany, at the confluence of the Rivers Rhine and Moselle. The seat of Frankish kings during the 6th century AD, it was annexed by France in 1798, passing to Prussia in 1815. Notable buildings include the Ehrenbreitstein fortress (c. 1000) and the birthplace of Metternich. Population (1999 est): 108 700.

Kodály, Zoltan (1882–1967) Hungarian composer. In collaboration with Béla *Bartók he collected Hungarian peasant songs, which influenced his style of composition. He achieved international recognition with his *Psalmus Hungaricus* (1923); other works include the opera *Háry János* (1926) and *Dances of Galanta* (1933).

overhand knot This is used either to make a knob in a rope or as the basis for another knot.

reef knot A non-slip knot for joining ropes of similar thickness.

quick release knot A tug on "a" will quickly unfasten this

surgeon's knot The extra twist in the first part of the knot prevents it from slipping loose while the second part is tied.

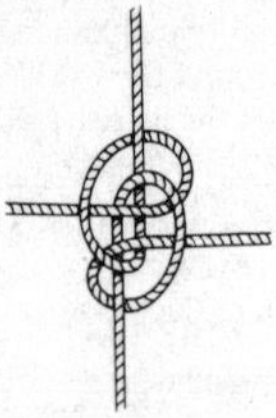

Hunter's bend A strong easily tied knot invented in 1978 by Dr Edward Hunter.

bowline A knot to form a non-slip loop.

running bowline A knot for making a running noose.

sheepshank A means of temporarily shortening a rope.

sheet bend A knot for securely joining two ropes of different thickness.

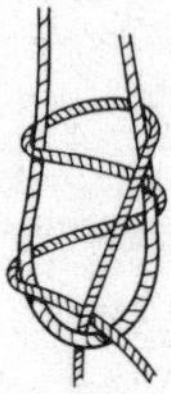

double sheep bend This follows the same principles as the sheet bend.

fisherman's knot Used especially for joining lengths of fishing gut.

carrick bend A knot well suited to tying heavy ropes together.

clove hitch A simple knot for attaching a rope to a ring, rail, etc.

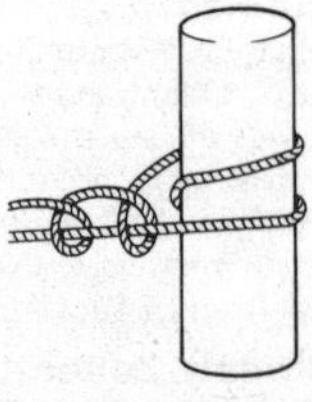

round turn and two half hitches Used for similar purposes as the clove hitch, this knot does not easily work loose.

anchor bend A secure means of attaching a cable to an anchor.

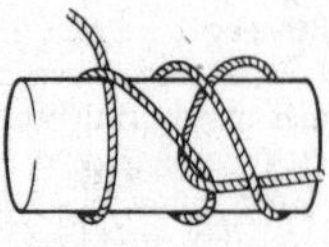

rolling hitch A quickly made and quickly unfastened knot for attaching a rope to a rail or another, standing rope.

knots

Kodiak bear *See* BROWN BEAR.

Koestler, Arthur (1905–83) British writer, born in Hungary. His novel *Darkness at Noon* (1940) called on his own experience as a prisoner in the Spanish Civil War. His nonfiction was concerned with politics (*The Yogi and the Commissar*, 1945), scientific creativity (*The Sleepwalkers*, 1959; *The Act of Creation*, 1964), and parapsychology. He and his wife committed suicide when he became terminally ill.

Koh-i-noor A famous diamond of 108 carats owned by the Mogul dynasty until the Shah of Iran looted it from Delhi (1739). It became Crown property in 1849, when Britain annexed the Punjab. It was set in the coronation crown of George VI's consort, Queen Elizabeth.

Kohl, Helmut (1930–) German statesman; chancellor of West Germany (1982–90) and of Germany (1990–98). A Christian Democrat, he led the opposition in the Bundestag (1976–82). He presided over German reunification, becoming leader of the united country in 1990. Re-elected for a fourth term in 1994, he was defeated by Gerhard Schröder in 1998. In 2000–01 he faced a criminal investigation on charges of accepting illegal party donations; this was dropped when he agreed to pay a large fine.

kohlrabi A variety of *cabbage, sometimes called turnip-rooted cabbage. The green or purple stem base, which swells like a turnip, is used as a vegetable.

Kokoschka, Oskar (1886–1980) Austrian expressionist painter and writer (*see* EXPRESSIONISM). After World War I he taught at the Dresden Academy, later painting landscapes and city views, particularly of London, where he lived (1938–53). From 1953 he lived and worked in Switzerland.

kola (*or* **cola**) Either of two trees, *Cola nitida* or *C. acuminata*, native to West Africa and widely grown in the tropics, that produce **kola nuts**. These are rich in caffeine and chewed in Africa and the West Indies for their stimulating effects. Family: *Sterculiaceae*.

Kola peninsula A peninsula in NW Russia, between the White Sea and the Arctic Ocean, consisting of tundra in the N and taiga in the S. The Murmansk coast has several areas that are ice-free throughout the year and has many military and naval bases. The population consists of immigrant Russians and remains of the Sami (Lapp) aboriginal people. Area: 130 000 sq km (50 182 sq mi). Chief town: Murmansk.

Kolkata *See* CALCUTTA.

Kolyma, River A river in the NE Russia. Rising in NE Siberia, it flows mainly NE to the East Siberian Sea. Length: 2600 km (1615 mi).

Komodo dragon A rare *monitor lizard, *Varanus komodoensis*, which, at 3 m long and weighing 135 kg, is the largest living lizard. It has a stout neck and body, a long powerful tail, and short strong legs and is powerful enough to kill a man. Komodo dragons feed mainly on carrion but also eat smaller monitors. They occur only on Komodo Island and some of the Lesser Sunda Islands of Indonesia.

Konoe Fumimaro, Prince (1891–1945) Japanese noble, who was prime minister three times. His first cabinet (1937–39) escalated the conflict with China; his second (1940–41) took Japan into alliance in World War II with Germany and Italy; and his third (1941) made the decision to attack the USA. After Japan's surrender he committed suicide.

Kon-Tiki The name given by Thor *Heyerdahl to the balsawood raft on which, between 28 April and 7 August 1947, he and five companions travelled the 5000 miles between Peru and the Tuamotu islands near Tahiti to demonstrate that ancient peoples of South America could have reached Polynesia. Kon-Tiki was an older name for the Inca creator god, Viracocha, allegedly known in Polynesia as Tiki.

Konya (ancient name: Iconium) 37 51N 32 30E A town in SW central Turkey. It is the centre of the Whirling Dervish sect and was the capital of the Seljuq kingdom of Rum. Population (1997): 623 333.

kookaburra A large grey-brown Australian *kingfisher, *Dacelo novaeguineae*, also called laughing jackass because of its chuckling call. 43 cm long, it is arboreal and pounces on snakes, lizards, insects, and small rodents from a perch.

Koran (*or* **Quran**) The sacred scripture of Islam. According to tradition, the divine revelations given to *Mohammed (d. 632 AD) were preserved by his followers and collected as the Koran under the third caliph, Uthman (d. 656). The Koran is one of the main sources of the comprehensive system of *Islamic law. Muslims believe that the revelations exist complete in a heavenly book, which contains all that has happened and will happen.

Korda, Sir Alexander (Sandor Kellner; 1893–1956) British film producer and director, born in Hungary. He boosted the British film industry during the 1930s and 1940s with a series of extravagant productions, including *The*

k

Private Life of Henry VIII (1932), *The Scarlet Pimpernel* (1934), and *Anna Karenina* (1948).

kore (Greek: maiden) In archaic Greek sculpture, a draped standing female figure, derived originally (c. 650 BC) from Egyptian models. During the next two centuries the drapery, pose, and expression became increasingly naturalistic. *Compare* KOUROS.

Korea A country in NE Asia, occupying a peninsula between the Sea of Japan and the Yellow Sea, now divided (see below) into the Democratic Republic of Korea (North Korea) and the Republic of Korea (South Korea). Plains in the W rise to mountains in the N and E. Both North and South Koreans are ethnically related to the Mongoloid race. The country long had ties with China but in 1905 became a Japanese protectorate, coming formally under Japanese rule in 1910. In 1945 the Allies divided Korea at the thirty-eighth parallel. The communist Democratic People's Republic of Korea under *Kim Il Sung was established in the Soviet-occupied N and the Republic of Korea under Syngman Rhee in the US-occupied S (1948). Soviet and US troops had withdrawn by 1949 and in 1950 the *Korean War broke out, ending in 1953 with the country still divided. Tensions increased again in the late 1990s, owing to North Korean incursions into South Korean territory. In 2000 the leaders of the two Koreas met for the first time since the conflict and signed a mutual cooperation treaty with peaceful reunification as the ultimate goal.

Korea, Democratic People's Republic of (Korean name: Chosŏn) The division of Korea left the North with almost all the country's mineral wealth and a large proportion of the industries, which had been developed by the Japanese. After the Korean War reconstruction proceeded rapidly; all industry is nationalized and agricultural land was collectivized in the 1950s. In the 1990s the economy suffered from the ending of preferential trading terms with the Soviet Union and China. In 1994 Kim Il Sung handed effective control of the country to his son, Kim Jong Il. North Korea has remained one of the most secretive and authoritarian countries in the world. In 1995 floods left some 500 000 homeless, leading to famine, disorder, and economic collapse: industrial and agricultural output have fallen by two thirds, and the population has decreased by nearly 20%. North Korea's continuing nuclear weapons programme led to rising tension with the USA in the early 2000s. Official language: Korean. Currency: won of 100 jun. Area: 120 538 sq km (46 540 sq mi). Population (2003 est): 22 466 000. Capital: P'yong Yang.

Korea, Republic of (Korean name: Han Kook) The South had been primarily agricultural but US aid led to the predominance of the industrial sector. Mineral resources are not large, although it has one of the world's largest deposits of tungsten. Exports include electrical goods, clothes, textiles, and cars. The corrupt and repressive regime of President Rhee was overthrown in 1960 and the military, headed by General Park Chung Hee, seized power the following year. The 1960s and 1970s saw growing prosperity but continued suppression of dissent. Park Chung Hee was assassinated in 1979 and General Chun Doo Hwan took over in a coup. The 1980s saw remarkable economic growth but increasing political unrest: in 1987 a more democratic constitution was adopted and in 1993 Kim Young Sam became the first civilian president for 32 years. In 1997 the currency and stock market collapsed and the country suffered financial and economic breakdown. The former dissident leader *Kim Dae Jung was elected president in 1997 and succeeded by his supporter Roh Moo Hyun in 2003. In March 2004 Roh was impeached for alleged election violations; however, elections held a month later resulted in a victory for his supporters and the impeachment was overturned. Official language: Korean. Currency: won of 100 chon. Area: 98 447 sq km (38 002 sq mi). Population (2003 est): 47 925 000. Capital: Seoul.

Korean The language of the people of Korea. It may be distantly related to *Japanese. The standard form is based on the dialect of Seoul. It is written in a phonetic script called onmun, devised in the mid-15th century to replace the Chinese characters in use before then.

Korean War (1950–53) An indecisive conflict between communist North Korea and noncommunist South Korea. When North Korean troops crossed the thirty-eighth parallel in 1950, 16 member nations of the UN sent troops, under the supreme command of the US general, Douglas *MacArthur, to support South Korea. The North Koreans were joined by Chinese Communist troops. An armistice was eventually signed on 27 July 1953, by which time some five million people had died.

Kosciusko, Mount 36 28S 148 17E The highest mountain in Australia, in SE New South Wales in the Snowy Mountains. Height: 2230 m (7316 ft).

Kosovo An autonomous province of S Serbia. Kosovo formed the heartland of Serbia in the middle ages but was conquered by the Turks in 1389 and subsequently settled by Muslim Albanians, who now comprise over 90% of the population. After Kosovo declared independence from Serbia (1990), the Serbian government removed its autonomous status. In 1992 unauthorized elections were won by pro-separatists. In 1998 demonstrations by ethnic Albanians led to severe repression by Serb forces and armed retaliation from the Kosovo Liberation Army (KLA). Evidence of "ethnic cleansing" by Serb forces led to NATO air strikes against targets in Yugoslavia in March 1999. The Serbs intensified their campaign against the ethnic Albanians, leading to a mass exodus of refugees to neighbouring countries. In June 1999 the Serbs effectively surrendered, agreeing to a complete withdrawal of their military forces, the presence of peacekeepers, and the return of all refugees. The region's political status remains unresolved. Population (1997 est): 2 227 742. Capital: Priština.

Kosygin, Aleksei Nikolaevich (1904–80) Soviet statesman; prime minister (1964–80). He became prime minister after Khrushchev's fall, initially sharing power with *Brezhnev, but had less influence in the late 1960s.

koto A Japanese stringed instrument of the *zither family. The narrow 2-metre sound board has 13 strings, which the player, sitting on his heels, plucks with plectra.

kouros (Greek: youth) In archaic Greek sculpture, a nude standing male figure, often more than life-size, derived (c. 650 BC) from Egyptian models. The modelling became increasingly naturalistic. *Compare* KORE.

Koussevitsky, Sergei (1874–1951) Russian conductor and composer. He left Russia in 1920 to work in Paris and subsequently in the USA, where he directed the Boston Symphony Orchestra from 1924 to 1949. He founded the Koussevitsky Music Foundation.

Kozhikode (former name: Calicut) 11 15N 75 45E A seaport on the W coast of India, in Kerala. Formerly famous as a cotton-manufacturing centre (Calicut gave its name to calico), it was visited by Vasco da Gama (1498) and in 1664 the British East India Company established a trading post here. Population (1991 est): 420 000.

Kra, Isthmus of The neck of the Malay Peninsula connecting it to the Asian mainland. It is occupied by Burma and Thailand and is 64 km (40 mi) across at its narrowest point.

krait A highly venomous snake belonging to the genus *Bungarus* (12 species) occurring in S Asia. Kraits are usually patterned with blue-and-white or black-and-yellow bands; they prey chiefly on other snakes. The common blue krait (*B. caeruleus*) of India and China is 1.5 m long and its venom can be fatal to humans. Family: *Elapidae* (cobras, mambas, coral snakes).

Kraków (*or* **Cracow**) 50 03N 19 55E The third largest city in Poland, on the River Vistula. It was the capital of Poland from 1305 to 1609 and remains famous as a cultural centre. Notable buildings include the cathedral (14th century). Population (1999 est): 740 666.

Krasnodar (name until 1920: Ekaterinodar) 45 02N 39 00E A city in SW Russia, on the River Kuban. It is the centre of an agricultural region. Population (1999 est): 643 400.

Krasnoyarsk 56 05N 92 46E A city in E central Russia, on the River Yenisei. It developed greatly after the discovery of gold in the region in the 19th century. Population (1999 est): 877 800.

Krebs cycle (**citric acid cycle** *or* **tricarboxylic acid cycle**) The sequence of chemical reactions, taking place in the mitochondria of cells. Named after its principal discoverer, Sir Hans Krebs (1900–81), the cycle involves the conversion of acetyl coenzyme A, derived from the carbohydrates, proteins, and fats of food, into hydrogen atoms or electrons, from which

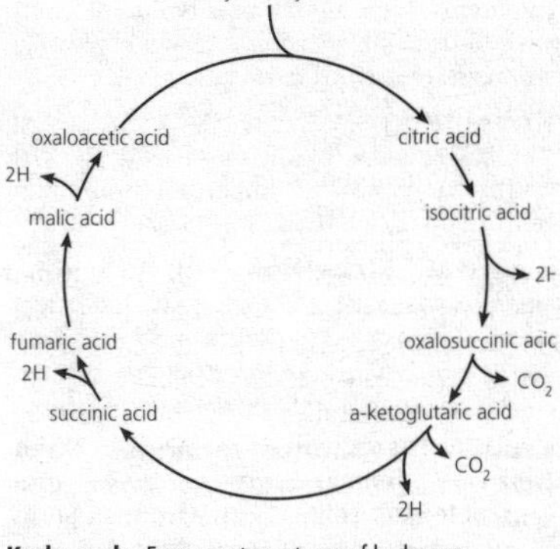

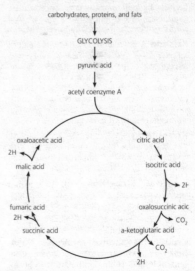

Krebs cycle. For every two atoms of hydrogen transferred, three ATP molecules are generated.

usable energy in the form of *ATP is produced by the cytochrome electron transport chain. Intermediate products are used for the manufacture of carbohydrates, lipids, and proteins by cells.

Krefeld 51 20N 6 32E A city in NW Germany, on the River Rhine. It was the site of a Prussian victory (1758) during the Seven Years' War. Population (1999 est): 242 800.

Kreisler, Fritz (1875–1962) Austrian violinist. A child prodigy, he frequently played his own compositions, written in the style of older composers and (until 1935) ascribed to them.

Kremenchug 49 03N 33 25E A city in E central Ukraine, on the River Dnepr. It has a large hydroelectric station. Population (1998 est): 240 700.

Kremlin The citadel of any Russian city, now referring usually to that of Moscow. Built in 1156 but continually extended, it contains the Cathedral of the Assumption (1475–79), the Cathedral of the Annunciation (1484–89), the Great Kremlin Palace (1838–49), etc. Except for the period between 1712 and 1918 it has served continually as the seat of the Russian government and is now also a museum of Russian architecture.

krill Shrimplike marine *crustaceans, 8–60 mm long, of the order *Euphausiacea* (82 species). Periodically krill swarms occur in certain regions, becoming an important source of food for fishes, birds, and especially baleen whales.

Krishna A popular Hindu deity, the eighth incarnation of *Vishnu. In the *Bhagavadgita* he is revealed as the creator, sustainer, and destroyer of the universe (*see* TRIMURTI). Elsewhere he is worshipped as a fertility god. He is commonly represented as a beautiful youth with bluish skin wearing a crown of peacock feathers. *See also* JAGANNATHA.

Krivoi Rog 47 55N 33 24E A city in SE Ukraine. Founded by the Cossacks in the 17th century, it is now an important ironmining centre. Population (1998 est): 715 400.

Kronstadt Rebellion (1921) An uprising among Soviet sailors in Kronstadt. The sailors, who had supported the Bolsheviks in the Russian Revolution, demanded economic reforms and an end to Bolshevik political domination.

Kruger, (Stephanus Johannes) Paul(us) (1825–1904) Afrikaner statesman; president (1883–1902) of the South African Republic (Transvaal). A farmer of Dutch descent, Kruger settled with his parents in the Transvaal after taking part in the *Great Trek. He led the struggle to regain independence for the Transvaal from the British, achieved in 1881, after the first Boer War. As president he resisted Uitlander (British immigrant) demands for political equality with the Afrikaner, a policy that led to the second Boer War (1899–1902).

Kruger National Park A game and plant reserve with an area of about 21 000 sq km (8106 sq mi) in NE South Africa. In 2002 it was combined with reserves in neighbouring Mozambique and Zimbabwe to form the **Great Limpopo Transfrontier Park**.

krugerrand A South African coin containing one troy ounce of gold, minted since 1967. It has never been a true currency coin and was minted to enable investors to escape restrictions on the private ownership of gold.

Krupp A German family of arms manufacturers. Under **Arndt Krupp** (d. 1624), the family settled in Essen, where in 1811 **Friedrich Krupp** (1787–1826) established a steel factory. His son **Alfred Krupp** (1812–87) diversified the family business into arms manufacture. Under Alfred's son-in-law **Gustav Krupp von Bohlen und Halbach** (1870–1950), the company developed Big Bertha, the World War I artillery piece named after Gustav's wife **Bertha Krupp** (1886–1957). Their son **Alfried Krupp** (1907–67) developed Gustav's ties with the Nazis, employed slave labour, and was imprisoned for war crimes.

krypton (Kr) A noble gas discovered in 1898 by Sir William Ramsay and M. W. Travers (1872–1961), in the residue left after boiling liquid air. Compounds include the fluoride KrF_2 and some clathrates. It is used for filling some fluorescent light bulbs; the *metre was (1960–83) defined in terms of the wavelength of a transition of one of its isotopes. At no 36; at wt 83.80; mp −157.37°C; bp −153.23°C.

Kuala Lumpur 3 10N 101 40E The financial capital of Malaysia, in central Peninsular Malaysia; the administrative capital moved to Putrajaya in 1999. It became capital of the Federated Malay States in 1895 and is a major commercial centre. Population (1991): 1 145 075.

Kuang-chou *See* CANTON.

Kuban, River A river in SW Russia. Rising in the Caucasus Mountains, it flows NW to the Sea of Azov. Length: 906 km (563 mi).

Kublai Khan (1215–94) Emperor of China (1279–94), who founded the Yuan dynasty. Genghis Khan's grandson, Kublai established himself (1259) as chief of the Mongols after years of conflict with his brother Mangu (d. 1259). The acknowledged ruler of all China from 1279, he administered from Peking an empire extending from the River Danube to the East China Sea. More humane than his predecessors, he opened up communications with Europe, largely through Marco *Polo. However, his preoccupation with China and attempts to conquer SE Asia weakened the rest of the empire.

Kubrick, Stanley (1928–99) US film writer, director, and producer. His films, mainly satirical and highly imaginative, include *Lolita* (1962), *2001: A Space Odyssey* (1968), the controversial *A Clockwork Orange* (1971), *The Shining* (1980), *Full Metal Jacket* (1987), and *Eyes Wide Shut* (1999).

kudu A large antelope, *Tragelaphus strepsiceros*, of African bush regions. About 130 cm high at the shoulder, kudus are red-brown with thin white vertical stripes on the flanks. Males have long corkscrew-shaped horns. The lesser kudu (*T. imberbis*) is smaller and found only in NE Africa.

Kufah A town 145 km (90 mi) S of Baghdad, in Iraq. Founded as an Arab garrison town in 638 AD, it is now an archaeological site. Its suburb of Najaf is the burial place of *Ali and a flourishing centre of *Shiite Islam.

Ku Klux Klan (**KKK**) A US secret society active against the Blacks. It originated in Tennessee after the Civil War to deter newly enfranchised Blacks from voting. Klansmen in white cloaks and hoods, burning fiery crosses, killed Blacks and destroyed their property. It was revived in 1915 and again in the 1950s in the South in response to the civil-rights movement. The Un-American Activities Committee investigated its leaders in 1965, but it remains active against minority groups.

Kumamoto 32 50N 130 42E A city in Japan, on the River Shira. One of the strongest centres in feudal Japan, it has a 17th-century castle. Population (1995): 650 322.

Kumasi 6 45N 1 35W The second largest city in Ghana. Formerly the capital of Ashanti, it was taken by the British in 1874. Population (1998 est): 578 000.

kumquat A shrubby plant of the genus *Fortunella* (6 species), of E and SE Asia, with fruits resembling small oranges. They are mainly used for pickling and preserves. Family: *Rutaceae*.

Kundera, Milan (1929–) Czech novelist, living in France since 1975. His ironic sexual comedies include *Life is Elsewhere* (1973), *The Unbearable Lightness of Being* (1984), *Slowness* (1996), and *Ignorance* (2002).

kung fu An ancient Chinese form of combat, mainly for self-defence. Among the other *martial arts it is most closely related to *karate, which possibly developed from it. In the second half of the 20th century the *wing chun* style has become particularly well known.

Kunlun Mountains A mountain system in W China, separating Tibet from the Tarim Basin. It extends 1600 km (1000 mi) E–W, reaching 7723 m (25 378 ft) at Ulugh Muztagh.

Kunming 25 04N 102 41E A city in S China, the capital of Yunnan province. It is noted for its Ming bronze temple. Population (1999 est): 1 350 640.

Kura, River A river in W Asia. Rising in NE Turkey, it flows E through Georgia and Azerbaidzhan to the Caspian Sea. Length: 1515 km (941 mi).

kurchatovium (Ku) An artificial transuranic element and the first transactinide. It was first detected by Soviet scientists in 1964 and named after the Soviet physicist I. V. Kurchatov (1903–60). The claim is disputed by US scientists, who proposed the name **rutherfordium** (Rf) after Lord *Rutherford, following their independent synthesis. At no 104.

Kurdistan An area in the Middle East inhabited by *Kurds, comprising parts of SE Turkey, N Syria, N Iraq, and NW Iran, including the Iranian province of Kordestan. The Turkish part includes a plateau that supports some agriculture, the remainder being mainly mountainous. The area was split at the end of World War I. Since 1992 much of Iraqi Kurdistan has been effectively autonomous, under the control of rival Kurdish militias. Area: 192 000 sq km (74 600 sq mi).

Kurds The major population group in *Kurdistan. Their language, Kurdish, is one of the *Iranian languages and is written in either a modified Arabic or a modified Cyrillic script. The Kurds grow cereals and cotton and are now mostly detribalized but a few nomadic groups still exist. They are Muslims but do not restrict their women to the same extent as other Islamic peoples. Nationalistic rebellions in the 19th and 20th centuries have led to reprisals, especially in Turkey (1925), Iraq, and Iran. Iraq devastated Kurdish villages in 1988 and again following a Kurdish rebellion during the *Gulf War. The later 1990s saw further conflict with Iraqi and Turkish forces.

Kurgan 55 30N 65 20E A city in W Russia, on the River Tobol. Population (1999 est): 367 200.

Kuril Islands A Russian chain of 56 islands extending 1200 km (746 mi) NE–SW between Kamchatka (Russia) and Hokkaido (Japan). Discovered by the Dutch (1634), the islands were Japanese until seized by the Soviet Union (1945); Japan still claims them. The largest are Paramushir, Urup, Iturup, and Kunashir. There are 38 active volcanoes. 200 km (124 mi) to the E is the **Kuril Trench**, maximum depth: 10 542 m (34 587 ft). Area: about 15 600 sq km (6022 sq mi).

Kurosawa Akira (1910–98) Japanese film director. His best-known films are action costume dramas, such as *Rashomon* (1950) and *Seven Samurai* (1954). Other films include the literary adaptations *Throne of Blood* (1957) and *Ran* (1985) (from Shakespeare's *Macbeth* and *King Lear*, respectively) and *Rhapsody in August* (1991).

Kursk 51 45N 36 14E A city in W Russia. Food processing and metallurgy are important. Population (1999 est): 445 400.

k

Kutch, Rann of An area of salt waste in central W India, near the border with S Pakistan. It consists of the Great Rann in the N and the Little Rann in the SE. Total area: about 23 000 sq km (8878 sq mi).

Kuwait, State of A country in the Middle East, in Arabia situated at the head of the Persian Gulf. The country is sandy and barren and has a harsh climate. The inhabitants are predominantly Arab (about half are foreigners); the Kuwaitis are mainly Sunnite or Shiite Muslim. *Economy*: Kuwait is one of the largest oil producers in the world and has one of the highest per capita incomes. Kuwait is a member of OPEC. *History*: Kuwait was originally settled in the early 18th century by nomads from the Arabian interior, who established a sheikdom in 1756. In 1899, to counter German and Ottoman expansionism, Kuwait gave Britain control over its foreign affairs and on the outbreak of World War I it became a British protectorate. Oil was discovered in 1938 and transformed the Kuwaiti economy after World War II. On gaining independence in 1961, Kuwait had to request troops from Britain to avert annexation by Iraq. In August 1990 Iraq invaded, precipitating the *Gulf War of 1991; Iraq's routed army inflicted heavy damage on oil wells and infrastructure. Demands for the restoration of parliamentary democracy under the 1962 constitution, suspended since 1976, led to elections (1992). Official language: Arabic. Currency: Kuwait dinar of 1000 fils. Area: 24 286 sq km (9375 sq mi). Population (2003 est): 2 439 000. Capital: Kuwait City.

Kuwait City 29 20N 48 00E The capital of the sheikdom of Kuwait, on the Persian Gulf. The traditional Islamic town developed into a modern metropolis with growth of the oil industry. It was badly damaged during the Gulf War (1990–91). Population (1995 est): 28 859.

Kwangju 35 07N 126 52E A city in SW South Korea, an ancient administrative and commercial centre. Population (1995): 1 257 636.

kwashiorkor Severe protein deficiency in children under five years. Kwashiorkor occurs in poor countries where the diet does not contain sufficient protein (the name derives from a Ghanaian word). The children fail to grow and succumb to the slightest infection, but recover rapidly with a good diet.

Kyoto 35 2N 135 45E A city in Japan, in S Honshu. It has been a leading cultural centre since early times, when it was the Japanese capital (794–1192 AD) and the old imperial palace and ancient Buddhist temples still remain. Population (1995): 1 463 601.

Kyoto agreement An international agreement to limit the emission of greenhouse gases (*see* GREENHOUSE EFFECT) negotiated between 1997 and July 2001. The agreement committed 38 industrialized countries to reducing their emissions of greenhouse gases by an average of 5.2% from 1990 levels by 2012. However, the USA opted out of the agreement in 2001 and Russia in 2003; as a result the agreement will not now take effect in its original form.

Kyprianou, Spyros (1932–2002) Cypriot statesman; president (1977–88). When Cyprus became independent in 1960 he was appointed minister of justice and then foreign minister (1960–72).

Kyrgyzstan *See* KIRGIZSTAN, REPUBLIC OF.

Kyushu The southernmost of the four main islands of Japan. Mountainous and volcanic, it has hot springs and a subtropical climate and is the most densely populated of the Japanese islands. There is a large rice-growing area in the NW, while heavy industry is centred on the N coalfield. Area: 35 659 sq km (13 768 sq mi). Population (1999 est): 13 462 534. Chief cities: Kitakyushu, Fukuoka, and Nagasaki.

Kyzyl Kum A desert in central Asia, in Kazakhstan and Uzbekistan, lying between the Rivers Amu Darya and Syr Darya. Area: about 300 000 sq km (115 806 sq mi).

L

Labiatae (*or* **Lamiaceae**) A family of herbaceous plants and shrubs (about 3500 species), widely distributed but particularly abundant in the Mediterranean region. They typically have square stems, hairy simple leaves, and clusters of tubular two-lipped flowers. Many of the plants are aromatic and yield useful oils (lavender, rosemary, etc.) and many are used as culinary herbs (marjoram, mint, sage, thyme, etc.).

Labor Party The Australian democratic socialist party, formed in New South Wales in 1891. It first held federal office in the period 1904–16, and subsequently 1929–31, 1939–49, and 1972–75. The most recent Labor premiers have been Bob Hawke (1983–91) and Paul Keating (1991–96). The current leader is Mark Latham.

Labour Day The day on which the labour movement is celebrated. In 1889, the Second International declared an international labour holiday on May Day. In Britain, Labour Day was the first Sunday in May until 1977, when the first Monday of the month was declared a public holiday.

Labour Party The democratic socialist party in the UK. The party was formed in 1900 as the Labour Representation Committee, being renamed the Labour Party in 1906. Its origins lie in the trades-union movement of the 19th century, and the trade unions continue to provide over three-quarters of its funds. The *Fabian Society was also a powerful influence on its formation and political beliefs. In 1922 the Labour Party replaced the divided Liberal Party as one of the two major UK parties (*compare* CONSERVATIVE PARTY) and in 1924 and 1929–31 Labour formed a minority government under Ramsay *MacDonald. It was not until after World War II, when under Clement *Attlee the party won a huge majority in the general election of 1945, that it was able to introduce radical policies. In office from 1945 to 1951, the Labour administration undertook widespread *nationalization and set up a comprehensive system of social security. The party was in office again from 1964 to 1970 and from 1974 to 1979, under Harold *Wilson (1964–76) and then James *Callaghan. Subsequent leaders were Michael Foot (1980–83), Neil *Kinnock (1983–92), and John Smith (1992–94), who died in office. His successor, Tony *Blair, modernized the party's constitution and image, leading it to victory in the general elections of 1997 and 2001.

Labrador (*or* **Coast of Labrador**) A district of NE Canada, on the Atlantic Ocean. Although the coast has belonged to Newfoundland for several centuries, the interior was finally awarded to Newfoundland in 1927. Labrador is mostly a rolling swampy plateau within the Canadian Shield. Generally barren except for forested river valleys, it has vast reserves of high-grade iron ore, which are being mined. Its hydroelectric potential is enormous. Area: 258 185 sq km (99 685 sq mi). Population (latest est): 33 052.

Labrador Current A major ocean current of the N Atlantic, flowing S from the polar seas down the W coast of Greenland and past Newfoundland, until it meets the Gulf Stream and, being cold and dense, sinks beneath it. The Labrador Current carries icebergs S and is a cause of frequent fogs in the region of Newfoundland.

Labrador retriever A breed of dog originating in Newfoundland and brought to Britain by fishermen in the early 19th century. It is solidly built, about 56 cm high, with a tapering otter-like tail and a short dense water-resistant coat, usually black or yellow-brown.

laburnum A tree of the genus *Laburnum*, especially *L. anagyroides*, which is native to mountainous regions of central Europe and widely grown for ornament. Up to 7 m high, its leaves each consist of three dark-green leaflets.

The bright-yellow flowers grow in hanging clusters and produce slender brown pods. All parts of the plant are poisonous, especially the seeds. Family: *Leguminosae.*

labyrinth fish A small elongated laterally compressed fish of the family *Anabantidae* (about 70 species), found in fresh waters of tropical Asia and Africa. They have an accessory respiratory organ (labyrinth) with which they obtain oxygen from air gulped at the surface. Some species are popular aquarium fish. Order: *Perciformes. See also* FIGHTING FISH; GOURAMI.

lace An ornamental network of threads of silk, linen, etc., used mainly for dress collars, cuffs, altar cloths, etc. Needlepoint lace, originating in Italy in the early 16th century, is made with a needle on parchment or fabric. Pillow or bobbin lace, reputedly invented by Barbara Uttmann (b. 1514) in Saxony, is formed by twisting threads around pins stuck in a pillow. The best work was done in Italy, Flanders, France, and England in the 17th and 18th centuries, famous types of lace being Brussels, Valenciennes, Mechlin, and Honiton. Lace making as an art declined in the 19th century after machine manufacture was introduced.

lacewing An insect belonging to one of several families of the suborder *Plannipennia.* Lacewings have delicate net-veined wings and are carnivorous. Green lacewings (*Chrysopidae*), also called golden-eyed lacewings, are about 10 mm long and occur worldwide. Eggs are laid individually on hairlike stalks and the larvae feed on aphids, scale insects, etc. The brown lacewings (*Hemerobiidae*) are smaller and often have spotted wings. Order: *Neuroptera.*

Lachlan River A river in SE Australia, in New South Wales. Rising in the Great Dividing Range it flows generally NW to join the Murrumbidgee River. Length: 1483 km (922 mi).

La Coruña (*or* **Corunna**) 43 22N 8 24W A port in NW Spain, in Galicia on the Atlantic Ocean. The Spanish Armada sailed from here on 26 July 1588, and in 1589 the city was sacked by Sir Francis Drake. It is an important fishing centre. Population (1998 est): 243 134.

lacquer tree A tree, *Rhus vernicifera*, of SE Asia, also called varnish tree. Up to 30 m tall, it has compound leaves, which turn red in autumn. Japanese lacquer is obtained from the milky resin that oozes from cuts in the bark. Family: *Anacardiaceae.*

lacrosse A 10-a-side field game (12 for women) played with a ball and a long-handled stick (the crosse), which has a triangular head with a strung pocket for catching, throwing, and picking up the ball. Of North American Indian origin, it is played mainly in the USA, Canada, Britain, and Australia. The object is to score goals by running with the ball and passing it. Tackling and striking an opponent's stick to dislodge the ball are allowed.

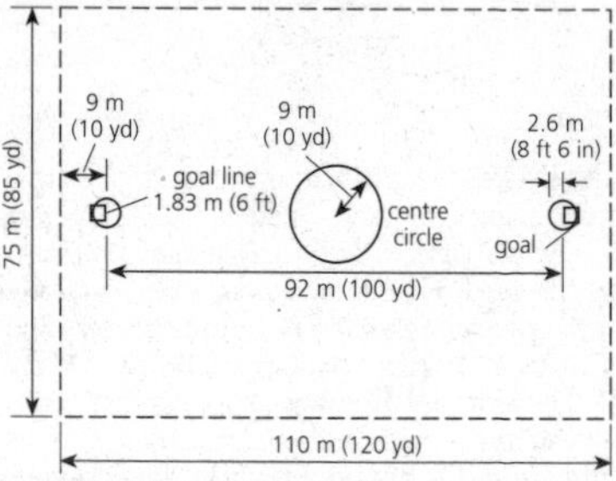

The optimum dimensions of the women's ground, although the game is played with no boundaries.

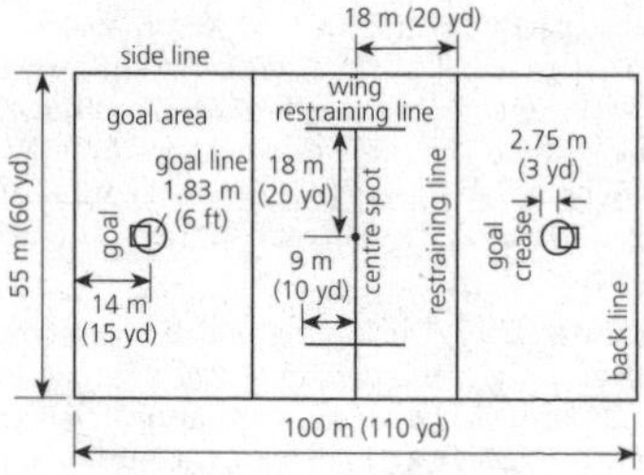

The dimensions of the men's ground.

lacrosse

lactation The secretion of milk from the breasts or mammary glands. In women lactation is controlled by hormones released from the ovary, placenta, and pituitary gland (*see* PROLACTIN) and starts shortly after childbirth, in response to the sucking action of the baby at the nipple: it will continue for as long as the baby is breastfed. A protein-rich fluid called colostrum is secreted in the first few days of lactation, before the milk has been produced. It contains antibodies that give the baby temporary immunity to disease.

Ladakh Range A mountain range mainly in NW India, extending about 370 km (230 mi) between the Karakoram Range and the Himalayas and rising to over 6000 m (19 685 ft).

Ladoga, Lake A lake in NW Russia, the

largest lake in Europe. It discharges via the River Neva into the Gulf of Finland. Area: about 17 700 sq km (6836 sq mi).

ladybird beetle A small round beetle, 8–10 mm long, that belongs to the widely distributed family *Coccinellidae* (5000 species). Most species are red or yellow with black spots. Both the larvae and adults feed on a variety of plant pests, including aphids, scale insects, mealybugs, and whiteflies.

Ladysmith 28 34S 29 47E A town in South Africa, in NW Natal. Founded in 1850, it was besieged for four months (1899–1900) by the Boers during the second Boer War. Population (latest est): 56 599.

lady's slipper A terrestrial orchid, *Cypripedium calceolus*, native to N Europe and Asia. Up to 45 cm high, it has broad leaves and the flowers are grouped singly or in twos and threes. Each flower has small twisted red-brown petals and an inflated yellow slipper-like lip. The lady's slipper is nearly extinct in Britain. *See also* SLIPPER ORCHID.

Lafayette, Marie Joseph Gilbert Motier, Marquis de (1757–1834) French general and politician, prominent at the beginning of the French Revolution. His early career was distinguished by his military successes (1777–79, 1780–82) against the British in the *American Revolution. In France he presented the Declaration of the Rights of Man (1789) and after the storming of the Bastille became commander of the new National Guard. In 1792 the rising power of the radicals threatened his life and he gave himself up to France's enemy, Austria. Lafayette was also prominent in the July Revolution (1830), which overthrew Charles X.

Lagomorpha A world-wide order of mammals (66 species) comprising *pikas, *rabbits, and *hares. Lagomorphs have teeth similar to rodents, with four continuously growing incisors. They are vegetarians and eat their own faecal pellets, thus obtaining the maximum value from their food.

Lagos 6 27N 3 28E The former capital and main port of Nigeria, on Lagos Island on the Bight of Benin. First settled by Yoruba fishermen in the 17th century, it became the centre of the Portuguese slave trade in West Africa and was ceded to Britain in 1861. One of Africa's largest cities, it is an important commercial and industrial centre. Population (1996 est): 1 518 000.

Lahore 31 34N 74 22E The second largest city in Pakistan, near the River Ravi, founded about the 7th century AD. Traditionally the chief city of the Punjab, Lahore is situated close to the Indian border and has been the scene of much bloodshed and violence. It is a major railway, commercial, and political centre and the headquarters of the Muslim League. The famous Shalimar gardens lie to the E of the city. Population (1998): 5 063 499.

laissez-faire The economic theory that governments should not interfere with market forces based on self-interest and the profit motive. The concept, originating in France, was advocated by Adam *Smith and widely accepted until the beginning of the 19th century. By then the growth of capitalism had exposed its principal weaknesses: the rise of monopolies, the grossly inequitable distribution of wealth, and the exploitation of labour. In the 20th century laissez-faire policies were largely abandoned for mixed economies in Western countries. Since the 1970s there has been a revival of free-market ideas.

lake A major body of water that is not a part of the sea. Most lakes are found in the N hemisphere in formerly glaciated areas, where glacial erosion has created a topography favourable to their formation. Lakes have also been formed by faulting of the bedrock, by volcanoes, etc. Most lakes contain fresh water; salt lakes are found mainly in arid areas where evaporation is great and as a rule have no outlet. Some lakes are man made, for water supply, irrigation, and hydroelectric power generation.

Lake District (*or* **Lakeland**) An area in NW England, in Cumbria, a national park since 1951. It consists of a high dome incised by a radial system of glaciated valleys, many of which contain ribbon lakes including Derwentwater, Ullswater, and Windermere. High mountains rise between the valleys, the highest being *Scafell Pike and Helvellyn. It is a major tourist area, with hill walking, rock climbing, and water sports all popular, and has many associations with the so-called Lake Poets (most notably *Wordsworth and *Coleridge). Traditional occupations include hill farming, forestry, and quarrying. Area: about 1813 sq km (700 sq mi).

Lakshmi In Hinduism, the goddess of wealth and happiness, the benign aspect of Shakti, the supreme goddess. As the wife of Vishnu she appears in various forms according to his several incarnations. Many festivals are held in her honour (*see* DIWALI). Lakshmi is also revered by the Jains.

Lalique, René (1860–1945) French *Art Nouveau jeweller and glassmaker. His glassware is characterized by frosted patterns in relief.

Lamarck, Jean-Baptiste de Monet, Chevalier de (1744–1829) French naturalist, noted for his speculations about the evolution of living things, particularly his theory of the inheritance of acquired characteristics (*see* LAMARCKISM), published in 1809. Lamarck also worked on a system of classification for invertebrate animals, published in his *Histoire naturelle des animaux sans vertèbres* (7 vols, 1815–22).

Lamarckism The first theory of *evolution as proposed by Jean-Baptiste *Lamarck in 1809, based on his concept of the inheritance of acquired characteristics. He suggested that an organism develops structural changes during its lifetime as an adaptation to its particular environment and that these features are then inherited by successive generations through sexual reproduction. A classic example of these acquired characteristics is the neck of the giraffe, which he believed became longer through its habit of browsing on tall trees. This now discredited theory has been rejected in favour of Darwin's theory of evolution.

Lamartine, Alphonse de (1790–1869) French poet, one of the major figures of the Romantic movement. He established his reputation with *Méditations poétiques* (1820). In the 1830s he became an active political champion of republican ideals and was briefly head of the provisional government after the Revolution of 1848. His other major works include the narrative poems *Jocelyn* (1836) and *La Chute d'un ange* (1836).

Lamb, Charles (1775–1834) British essayist and critic. He collaborated with his sister Mary (1764–1847) on *Tales from Shakespeare* (1807), a children's book. He is best remembered for his *Essays of Elia* (1822).

Lambaréné 0 41S 10 13E A town in W Gabon, on an island in the River Ogooué. Its hospital (1913) was founded by the missionary Albert *Schweitzer. Population (latest est): 50 800.

lambert A unit of luminance equal to the luminance of a surface that emits one lumen per square centimetre. Named after J. H. Lambert (1728–77).

Lambeth Conferences Assemblies normally convened every ten years under the chairmanship of the Archbishop of Canterbury at Lambeth Palace, London, to which all bishops of the Anglican Church are invited. The first was held in 1867. Although their decisions have no binding power, the conferences are important indications of the Anglican episcopate's views and policies.

laminar flow Fluid flow in which the particles move in parallel layers. A fluid moving slowly along a horizontal straight pipe flows in this way. Above a certain velocity, given by the Reynolds number, the layers no longer remain parallel and the flow becomes turbulent.

lammergeier A large *vulture, *Gypaetus barbatus*, also called bearded vulture because of the long bristles on its chin. It is over 1 m long with a wingspan of 3 m and occurs in mountainous regions of S Europe, central Asia, and E Africa. It is brown with tawny underparts and a black-and-white face.

lamprey A fishlike vertebrate belonging to a family (*Petromyzonidae*; about 22 species) of *cyclostomes. Lampreys have an eel-like body with one or two dorsal fins and seven pairs of gill slits. They occur in fresh or salt water and many are parasitic on fish, attaching themselves with a circular sucking mouth and feeding on the blood and flesh.

lamp shell *See* BRACHIOPODA.

Lanark 55 41N 3 48W A town in S central Scotland, in South Lanarkshire. Nearby New Lanark, founded as a cotton-spinning centre in 1784 by David Dale and Richard Arkwright, is well known for Robert Owen's social experiments there. Population (1991): 8877.

Lanarkshire A historic county of S central Scotland. In 1975 it became part of Strathclyde Region. When this was abolished in 1996, administration passed to three unitary authorities: Glasgow, *North Lanarkshire, and *South Lanarkshire.

Lancashire A county of NW England, bordering on the Irish Sea. It consists of lowlands in the W rising to the high level plateaus of the Pennines in the E, with the chief river, the Ribble, flowing SW to the Irish Sea. The lowlands are important agricultural regions. Industry is based chiefly on textiles (cotton manufacturing being of major importance until recently) and engineering. Tourism is important in the coastal towns of Blackpool and Morecambe. In 1974 it lost the S (including Liverpool and Manchester) to Merseyside and Greater Manchester and the N to Cumbria. Blackburn with Darwen and Blackpool became independent unitary authorities in 1998. Area (excluding unitary authorities): 2889 sq km (1115 sq mi). Population

(2001, excluding unitary authorities): 1 134 974. Administrative centre: Preston.

Lancaster 54 03N 2 48W A town in NW England, in Lancashire on the River Lune, superseded by Preston as the administrative centre of Lancashire. The castle, partly 13th-century and enlarged by Elizabeth I, stands on the site of a Roman garrison. Population (1991): 44 497.

Lancaster A ruling dynasty of England descended from Edmund, the second son of Henry III, who was created Earl of Lancaster in 1267. In 1361 the title passed by marriage to the third son of Edward III, *John of Gaunt. His son seized the throne from Richard II and ruled (1399–1413) as Henry IV. He was succeeded by Henry V, whose son Henry VI led the Lancastrians against the Yorkists (*see* YORK) in the Wars of the Roses (1455–85), in which their emblem was a red rose. At Henry VI's death (1471) the royal dynasty ended.

Lancaster, Duchy of A territory with its own courts and administration created in 1267 by Henry III for his son Edmund (1245–96). After the last Duke of Lancaster became Henry IV in 1399 the Duchy was attached to the Crown, retaining its own jurisdiction. The chancellor of the Duchy of Lancaster is usually a member of the cabinet.

Lancelot In *Arthurian legend, a knight of the Round Table. While a child he was kidnapped by the Lady of the Lake, who educated him and later sent him to serve King Arthur. He was a celebrated warrior but failed in the quest of the *Holy Grail because of his adulterous love for *Guinevere.

lancers Originally foot soldiers armed with a lance, they subsequently became cavalrymen belonging to one of the regiments called lancers, both on the continent and in the UK. The name is retained in some armoured regiments.

Lanchester, Frederick William (1868–1946) British engineer, who built the first British car in 1896. He formed the Lanchester Engine Company producing high-quality vehicles.

Land, Edwin Herbert (1909–91) US inventor of Polaroid, a plastic sheet impregnated with dichroic crystals that produce *polarized light, thus reducing glare. In 1937 he set up the Polaroid Corporation for its manufacture. He also invented (1947) the Polaroid Land Camera, in which pictures are printed almost instantly inside the camera.

land crab A large square-bodied *crab of the tropical family *Gecarcinidae*, specialized for a terrestrial existence. It feeds on plant and animal materials. *Cardiosoma guanhumi*, 11 cm across the back, is found in the West Indies and S North America. Tribe: *Brachyura*.

landlord and tenant The relationship arising from a grant (lease) of exclusive possession of land by a landlord to a tenant for a fixed period and, usually, for a regular payment of rent. The relationship is defined by a *contract, which is contained in the lease or, for short terms, in a tenancy agreement.

Land Registry, HM An official registry of titles to land, established in 1862. This simplifies conveyancing when the property is sold: by searching in the Registry, outstanding leases, mortgages, etc., may be discovered. In England and Wales land registration on sale is now compulsory.

Landseer, Sir Edwin Henry (1802–73) British artist. He achieved success, particularly with Queen Victoria, with his sentimental animal and Highland subjects, notably *Dignity and Impudence*. He sculptured the four bronze lions in Trafalgar Square.

Land's End 50 03N 5 44W The extreme western point of England. A granite headland in Cornwall, it lies at a distance of 970 km (603 mi) from John o'Groats at the N tip of Scotland. The southernmost point of England is the Lizard nearby.

Lang, Fritz (1890–1976) German film director. The best known of a number of influential silent films are *Dr Mabuse the Gambler* (1922), *Metropolis* (1926), and *M* (1931). He went to Hollywood in 1933, where he made commercially successful thrillers and westerns.

Langland, William (c. 1330–c. 1400) English poet. A minor cleric, he is usually considered to be the author of the alliterative allegorical poem *The Vision of Piers Plowman*.

Langtry, Lillie (Emilie Charlotte le Breton; 1853–1929) British actress, known as the Jersey Lily. Having married a wealthy husband she proved that high social position was not incompatible with an acting career. She was noted for her beauty and was a mistress of the Prince of Wales, later Edward VII.

languages, classification of The division of languages into groups. There are three methods of classification. The first method is that of geographical or political division, in which languages are grouped together according to the continent or country in which they occur. Examples of the former include *Indian

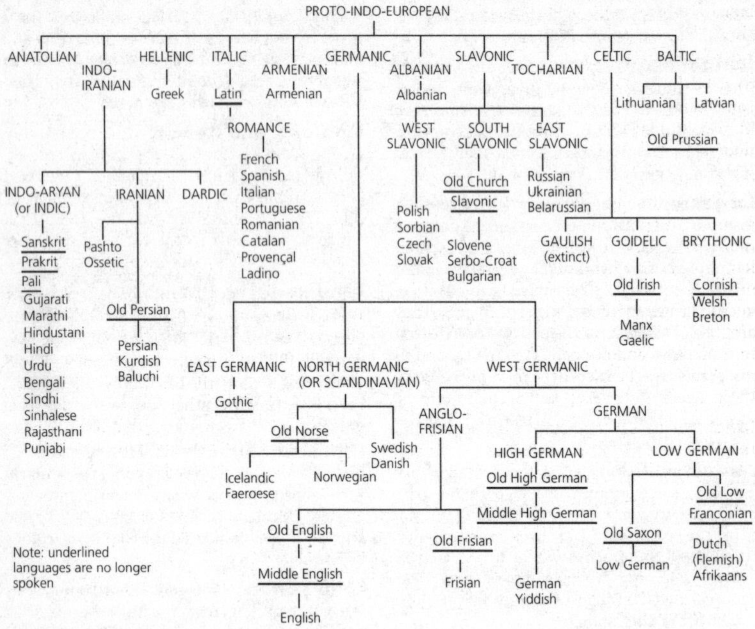

classification of languages. A simplified family tree shows the relationships of the Indo-European languages, spoken by about half the world's population.

languages and European languages. The latter is represented by the similar but politically distinct languages *Swedish, *Danish, and *Norwegian. Such divisions do not always follow the genetic relationships that exist between languages. This relationship forms the basis for the second method of classification, which maps the historical development from one form of the language to another, as in the relation between Old English and modern *English. Further back both these and other languages can be traced to their common Indo-European ancestor. The third possible method of classification is on typological evidence, which depends on the grammatical structure of the language. The original three classes were devised by W. von Humboldt (1767–1835): analytic (or isolating), agglutinative, and inflecting languages. English is an analytic language. **Analytic languages** (e.g. English) show little variation in the forms of words but rely on strict word order to express grammatical relations. In **agglutinative languages** (e.g. Turkish) words have the capacity to be split up into individual components with separate grammatical roles. In **inflecting languages** (e.g. Latin) words are characteristically built up of a root plus a component (morpheme) that represents several different grammatical categories.

Languedoc A former province in S France, on the Gulf of Lions. Its name derived from *langue d'oc*, the language of its inhabitants (*see* PROVENÇAL). It is now incorporated chiefly into the planning region of **Languedoc-Roussillon.** Area: 27 447 sq km (10 595 sq mi). Population (1995 est): 2 221 300.

langur A leaf-eating *Old World monkey of tropical Asia. The largest is the hanuman, or entellus langur (*Presbytis entellus*), 75 cm long with a 95-cm tail. The douc langur (*Pygathrix nemaeus*) of Vietnam is mainly grey with white forearms and is now an endangered species. Chief genera: *Presbytis* (14 species), *Rhinopithecus* (4 species).

lanolin A purified *wax extracted from wool. It is a mixture of cholesterol and other sterols, aliphatic alcohols, and esters. Because it is easily absorbed by the skin, lanolin is used as a base for creams, soaps, and other skin preparations.

lantern fish A deepsea *bony fish belonging to the family *Myctophidae* (about 150 species). Lantern fish have large mouths and eyes and numerous light-producing organs on the head, underside, and base of the tail. Order: *Myctophiformes.*

lanthanides (*or* **rare-earth metals**) A group of 15 transition-metal elements, atomic numbers 57–71, which all have remarkably similar physical and chemical properties as a result of their electronic structures. They occur together in monazite and other minerals. They are used as catalysts in the petroleum industry, in iron alloys and permanent magnets, and in glass polishes. The **rare earths** are the oxides of these metals.

lanthanum (La) The first of the series of lanthanides. At no 57; at wt 138.9055; mp 918°C; bp 3464°C.

Lanzhou (**Lan-chou** *or* **Lanchow**) 36 01N 103 45E A city in N China, the capital of Gansu province at the confluence of the Yellow and Wei Rivers. It is an ancient trade and communications centre and is now an industrial centre. Population (1999 est): 1 429 673.

Laocoon In Greek legend, a Trojan priest of Apollo who warned against accepting the Greek gift of the *Trojan Horse. He and his two sons were killed by sea serpents sent by Apollo or, in some versions, Athena, and the Trojans then opened their gates to the wooden horse.

Laois (*or* **Laoighis** *or* **Leix**; former name: Queen's County) A county in the E central Republic of Ireland, in Leinster. Predominantly low lying with bogs and drained chiefly by the Rivers Barrow and Nore, it rises to mountains in the NW. Agriculture is the main occupation. Area: 1719 sq km (664 sq mi). Population (2002): 58 732. County town: Portlaoise.

Laos, People's Democratic Republic of A landlocked country in SE Asia, between Vietnam and Thailand. Except for the valley of the River Mekong along its western border, the country is mountainous and forested. Over half the population are Lao (descendants of the Thai) and there are minorities of Vietnamese, Chinese, and others. *Economy*: predominantly agricultural. The valuable mineral resources (tin, iron ore, gold, and copper) have yet to be fully exploited. There is little industry and Laos remains one of the world's poorest countries. *History*: the origins of the area as a nation date from the 14th century. European contacts were initiated in the 17th century and in 1893 Laos became a French protectorate. After Japanese occupation (1941–45) the French returned and a constitutional monarchy was formed in 1947. In 1949 Laos became independent within the French Union. In 1953 civil war, which was to last for 20 years, broke out between the government (supported by the USA and by Thai mercenaries) and the communist-led Pathet Lao movement (supported by the North Vietnamese). In 1974 a provisional coalition government was formed but following the collapse of the South Vietnamese the Pathet Lao gained power (December 1975) and the People's Democratic Republic of Laos was formed. In 1991 a new constitution was published, reaffirming the Lao People's Democratic Party (the former Pathet Lao) as the sole legal party. In 1997 Laos was admitted to the Association of South-East Asian States (ASEAN). Recent years have seen border clashes with Thailand. Official language: Laotian. Currency: kip of 100 at. Area: 236 800 sq km (91 429 sq mi). Population (2003 est): 5 657 000. Capital: Vientiane.

Lao Zi (*or* **Lao Tzu**; ?6th century BC) The founder of *Taoism. A shadowy, possibly legendary, figure, he was eventually deified. His purpose, propounded mainly in books compiled about 300 years after his likely date of death, was to reach harmony with the *Tao* (way) by dwelling on the beauty of nature, being self-sufficient, and by desiring nothing.

La Paz 16 30S 68 00W The administrative capital of Bolivia, situated in the W of the country. At an altitude of 3577 m (11 735 ft), it is the world's highest capital. Founded by the Spanish in 1548, it became the seat of government in 1898. Population (2000 est, urban area): 1 000 899. *See also* SUCRE.

lapis lazuli A blue semiprecious stone composed mainly of the sulphur-rich mineral lazurite. It is formed by the metamorphism of limestone. It often contains specks or threads of yellow iron pyrites. Lapis lazuli has been mined in Afghanistan for over 6000 years. The pigment ultramarine was formerly made by grinding up lapis lazuli.

Laplace, Pierre Simon, Marquis de (1749–1827) French mathematician and astronomer. Laplace worked with J. L. Lagrange (1736–1813) on the effects, known as perturbations, of the small gravitational forces that planets exert on each other. They deduced that the perturbations have a minimal effect, thus proving the stability of the solar system. In the published account of their results, *Mécanique céleste* (1799–1825), Laplace speculated that the solar system was formed from a condensing rotating cloud of gas.

Lapland (*or* **Lappland**) A vast region in N Europe, inhabited by the *Lapps and extending across northern parts of Norway, Sweden, Finland, and into the extreme NW of Russia. Lying mainly within the Arctic Circle, it consists of tundra in the N, mountains in the W, and forests in the S; there are many lakes and rivers. For many centuries the Lapps were reduced to virtual slavery by their more powerful neighbours. Subsistence farming, fishing, trapping, and hunting are the principal occupations and reindeer are a particularly important source of income. There are rich deposits of iron ore in Swedish Lapland.

Lapps (*or* **Sami**) A people of N Scandinavia and the Kola peninsula of Russia. They speak a Finno-Ugric language, which differs from the related Finnish and *Estonian mainly in its sound system. There are three major Lapp dialects.

lapwing A Eurasian *plover, *Vanellus vanellus*, also called peewit and green plover. It occurs commonly on farmland, where it feeds on harmful insects. 28 cm long, it has a greenish-black and white plumage and a long crest.

larch A deciduous conifer of the genus *Larix* (10 species), native to the cooler regions of the N hemisphere. Larches have needles growing in bunches on short spurs and produce small woody cones. The common European larch (*L. decidua*), from the mountains of central Europe, is widely cultivated both for timber and ornament. It reaches a height of 40 m. The Japanese larch (*L. kaempferi*) is commonly grown on plantations. Family: *Pinaceae*.

Lares and Penates Roman household gods. The Lares were originally gods of cultivated land who were worshipped at crossroads and boundaries. The Penates were gods of the storeroom. Together with the Manes, they were later worshipped in private homes as guardian spirits of the family, household, and state.

lark A slender long-winged songbird belonging to a family (*Alaudidae*; 75 species) found mainly in mudflats, marshes, grasslands, and deserts of the Old World and characterized by a beautiful song. Larks commonly have a brown or buff streaked plumage that often matches the local soil colour. They have long slender bills and feed on seeds and insects. *See also* SKYLARK.

Larkin, Philip (1922–85) British poet and writer. The poetry in *The Less Deceived* (1955), *The Whitsun Weddings* (1964), and *High Windows* (1974) expresses a wry acceptance of life's limitations. His *Collected Poems* were published in 1988 and his *Selected Letters* in 1992.

Larne 1. A district in Northern Ireland, in Co Antrim. Area: 337 sq km (130 sq mi). Population (2001): 30 832. **2.** 54 51N 5 49W A port in Northern Ireland, in Co Antrim at the entrance to Lough Larne. Larne is a tourist centre and has the shortest searoute between Ireland and Britain (Stranraer). Population (1991): 17 575.

La Rochefoucauld, François, Duc de (1613–80) French moralist. He was born into an ancient aristocratic family and played an active part in intrigues against Richelieu. Thereafter he lived in retirement, writing his *Mémoires* (1664) and compiling his celebrated *Maximes* (1665), a collection of cynical epigrammatic observations on human conduct.

larva The immature form of many animals, which hatches from the egg and often differs in appearance from the adult form. Larvae usually avoid competing for food, etc., with the adults by occupying a different habitat or adopting a different lifestyle. For example, adult barnacles, which are sessile, produce motile larvae, whose role is distribution of the species. Other larvae, such as caterpillars and maggots, are responsible for gathering food reserves for the production of a fully formed adult, whose primary function is to breed. *See also* TADPOLE.

Larwood, Harold (1904–95) British cricketer, who played for Nottinghamshire and England. Larwood was a fast bowler who was at the centre of the bodyline controversy during the 1932–33 tour of Australia.

larynx An organ, situated at the front of the neck above the windpipe (*see* TRACHEA), that contains the **vocal cords.** The larynx contains several cartilages (one of which—the thyroid cartilage—forms the Adam's apple) bound together by muscles and ligaments. Within are the two vocal cords: folds of tissue separated by a narrow slit (glottis). The vocal cords modify the flow of exhaled air through the glottis to produce the sounds of speech, song, etc.

La Scala (*or* **Teatro alla Scala**) The principal Italian opera house, opened in Milan in 1776. It is noted for its varied repertoire and attained its highest reputation under Arturo *Toscanini, director 1898–1907 and 1921–31.

Lascaux Upper *Palaeolithic cave site in the Dordogne (France), discovered in 1940. Lascaux contains rock paintings and engravings of horses, oxen, red deer, and other animals, dating from about 18 000 BC. Deterioration of the paintings caused the cave to be closed again (1963).

Lasdun, Sir Denys (1914–2001) British architect, whose most important works are East Anglia University (1963) and, in London, the National Theatre (1968–76) and the School of African and Oriental Studies (1970–73).

laser (light *a*mplification by *s*timulated *e*mission of *r*adiation) A device that produces a beam of high-intensity coherent monochromatic radiation (light, infrared, or ultraviolet). Stimulated emission is the emission of a photon when an atomic electron falls from a higher energy level to a lower level as a result of being stimulated by another photon of the same frequency. In the laser large numbers of electrons are "pumped" into a higher energy level, an effect called population inversion, and then stimulated to produce a high-intensity beam. Laser beams have been produced from solids, liquids, and gases. The simplest type is the ruby laser, consisting of a cylinder of ruby, silvered at one end and partially silvered at the other. A flash lamp is used to excite chromium ions in the ruby to a high energy level. When the ions fall back to their ground state photons are emitted. These photons collide with other excited ions producing radiation of the same wavelength (monochromatic) and the same phase (coherent), which is reflected up and down the ruby crystal and emerges as a narrow beam from the partially silvered end. Lasers are used in surgery, in *holography, and in compact disc players.

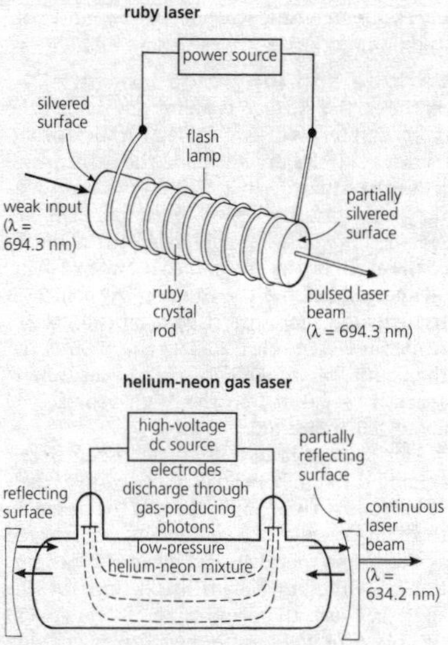

laser. In the solid-state ruby laser, chromium ions are excited by an intense flash of light and then stimulated by weak light of one wavelength to emit a pulse of photons. In the helium-neon gas laser, a continuous laser beam is produced from an electrical discharge through low-pressure gas.

Las Palmas 28 08N 15 27W The largest city in the Canary Islands, the capital of Las Palmas province in Gran Canaria. It is a popular resort. Population (1998 est): 352 641.

La Spezia 44 07N 9 48E A port and resort in Italy, in Liguria on the Gulf of Spezia. It is a major naval base, with the largest harbour in Italy. Population (1992): 100 458.

Lassa fever A severe virus disease occurring in West Africa and first described in 1969 in Lassa, a village in Nigeria. It is a rare and often fatal disease that is transmitted to man by certain species of rat.

Las Vegas 36 10N 115 12W A city in the USA, in SE Nevada. Founded in 1855, it grew rapidly after construction of the nearby Hoover Dam. It is famous for its nightclubs and the Strip (a row of luxury hotels and gambling casinos). Population (2000): 478 434.

La Tène The second phase of the European Iron Age, succeeding Hallstatt from the 5th century BC. Named after the site at La Tène (Switzerland), this recognizably Celtic culture spread throughout Europe, coming into contact with the civilizations of Greece and Rome. Aristocratic chariot burials replaced wagon burials and the geometric patterns of Hallstatt metalwork were superseded by the intricate curvilinear designs of Celtic art. By the 1st century BC Roman expansionism effectively ended coherent La Tène culture. *See also* CELTS.

latent heat The amount of heat absorbed or released by a substance when it undergoes a change of state. For example, a liquid absorbs heat (**latent heat of vaporization**) from its surroundings on evaporation, since energy is needed to overcome the forces of attraction between the molecules as the liquid expands into a gas. Similarly a solid absorbs heat (**latent heat of fusion**) when it melts. The heat absorbed or

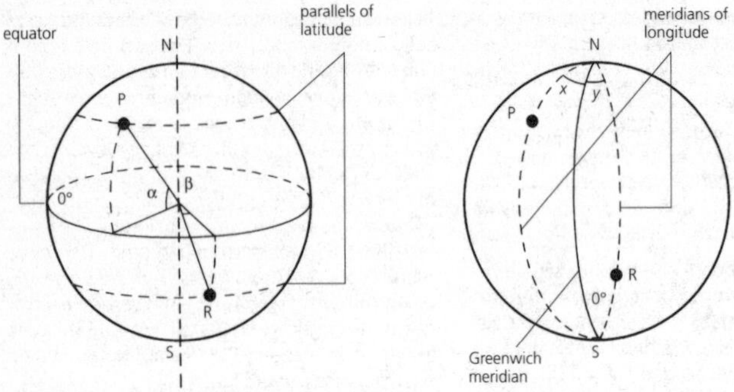

The latitude of P is given by the angle α. In this case it would be α° N. The latitude of R is β° S.

The longitude of P is given by the angle *x*. In this case it would be *x*° W. R has a longitude *y*° E.

latitude and longitude

released per unit mass of substance is called the **specific latent heat**.

Lateran Councils Five ecumenical councils of the Roman Catholic Church convened in the Lateran Palace, Rome, in 1123, 1139, 1179, 1215, and 1512–17. The council of 1215, attended by most major European ecclesiastical and secular powers, proclaimed the fifth Crusade (1217–21) and was enormously influential in its formulations of doctrine and Church organization and law.

Lateran Treaty (1929) An agreement between the Italian government of Mussolini and the Vatican. The Vatican City state was created and the papacy abandoned its claims to the former *papal states.

Latin America The countries of Central and South America in which Romance languages are spoken: mostly Spanish, but also Portuguese and in some areas French and French-derived Creole languages. The populations are mostly mestizo (mixed Indian-European) with minorities of pure Indian or European descent. Brazil and the Caribbean islands have large groups of African origin.

Latin language An Italic Indo-European language, the ancestor of modern Romance languages. First spoken on the plain of Latium near Rome, Latin spread throughout the Mediterranean world as Roman power expanded. An inflected and syntactically complex language, written Latin developed contemporaneously with conversational Latin, although the latter, with its freer syntax and vocabulary, remained less static than the formal language. Colloquial Vulgar Latin used prepositions and conjunctions freely to replace inflected forms and had a simpler word order; it became the Latin of the provinces, contributing to the early development of the Romance languages. As the western Roman Empire's official language, Latin was used in W Europe for religious, literary, and scholarly works until the middle ages.

latitude and longitude Imaginary lines on the earth's surface, enabling any point to be defined in terms of two angles. **Parallels of latitude** are circles drawn round the earth parallel to the equator; their diameters diminish as they approach the Poles. These parallels are specified by the angle subtended at the centre of the earth by the arc formed between a point on the parallel and the equator. All points on the equator therefore have a latitude of 0°, while the North Pole has a latitude of 90°N and the South Pole of 90°S. Parallels of latitude 1° apart are separated on the earth's surface by about 100 km (63 mi).

Meridians of longitude are half great circles passing through both Poles; they cross parallels of latitude at right angles. In 1884 the meridian through Greenwich, near London, was selected as the prime meridian and given the designation 0°. Other meridians are defined by the angle between the plane of the meridian and the plane of the prime meridian, specifying whether it is E or W of the prime meridian. At the equator meridians 1° apart are separated by about 112 km (70 mi).

latitudinarianism An attitude originating with certain 17th-century Anglican clergymen, who deprecated sectarian squabbles over Church government and forms of ritual and considered such matters unimportant in comparison with personal piety and practical morality. Between the 1690s and the rise of the *Oxford Movement in the 1830s latitudinarianism was the predominant tendency in the Church of England.

Latter-Day Saints, Church of Jesus Christ of *See* MORMONS.

Latvia, Republic of A republic in NE Europe, on the Baltic Sea. It is a fertile lowland with extensive forests. Latvians, who comprise approximately 52% of the population, are mainly Lutheran Christians. *Economy*: industries include shipbuilding, engineering, chemicals, and textiles. Fishing plays an important part in the economy and tourism is being developed. *History*: the Latvians were conquered by the Livonian Knights (a German order of knighthood) in the 13th century, passing to Poland in the 16th century, to Sweden in the 17th century, and to Russia in the 18th century. Latvia gained independence in 1918, which was recognized by Soviet Russia in 1920. In 1940 it was incorporated into the Soviet Union as an SSR. It was occupied by Germany in World War II. Independence from the Soviet Union was achieved in 1991. Since independence the main issue has been the status of the large (48%) Russian minority. The draconian citizenship law of 1991, which stripped ethnic Russians of voting and other rights, was subsequently relaxed (1994 and 1998). A centre-right coalition was elected in 2002 but collapsed in 2004, when Indulis Emsis became Europe's first Green prime minister. Latvia joined the EU and NATO in 2004. Official language: Latvian. Currency: lats of 100 santimes. Area: 63 700 sq km (25 590 sq mi). Population (2003 est): 2 324 000. Capital: Riga.

Latvian A language belonging to the E division of the Baltic languages division of the Indo-European family, spoken by about two million Latvians. Most live in Latvia, where Latvian is the official language. Also known as Lettish, it is closely related to *Lithuanian. It is written in a Latin alphabet.

Laud, William (1573–1645) Anglican churchman, with the Earl of Strafford (1593–1641) the chief adviser to Charles I immediately before the *Civil War. Appointed Archbishop of Canterbury (1633–45), he supported Charles I's personal rule and his attempt to enforce liturgical uniformity. His pressure on the Scots to accept the Book of Common Prayer led to the Bishops' Wars and paved the way for the Civil War and his own downfall. He was impeached for high treason by the Long Parliament in 1640 and executed.

Lauder, Sir Harry (Hugh MacLennan; 1870–1950) Scots singer and famous music-hall comedian. His most famous songs included "I Love a Lassie" and "Roamin' in the Gloamin'."

Laughton, Charles (1899–1962) British actor. His international reputation was based on his numerous films, which included *The Private Life of Henry VIII* (1933), *Mutiny on the Bounty* (1935), and *Rembrandt* (1936).

Launceston 41 25S 147 07E A city and port in Australia, in N Tasmania situated at the confluence of the North and South Esk Rivers. Population (1991): 93 347.

Laurasia The supercontinent of the N hemisphere that is believed to have existed prior to 200 million years ago, when the drift of the continents to their present positions began. It probably consisted of Greenland, Europe, Asia (excluding India), and North America. *See also* GONDWANALAND.

laurel One of several unrelated aromatic shrubs or small trees with attractive evergreen leaves. The so-called true laurels (genus *Laurus*) include the *bay tree. Other laurels include the ornamental *cherry laurel (*Prunus laurasocerasus*), the spotted laurels (genus *Aucuba*; family *Cornaceae*), and the mountain laurel (*Kalmia latifolia*; family *Ericaceae*). The spurge laurel is a species of *Daphne*.

Laurel and Hardy US film comedians. **Stan Laurel** (Arthur Stanley Jefferson; 1890–1965), the thin member of the team and originator of the gags, was born in Britain. He joined with **Oliver Hardy** (1892–1957), who played the fat partner, in 1926. They made numerous films in the 1920s and 1930s, including *The Music Box* (1932) and *Way Out West* (1937).

Lausanne 46 32N 6 39E A city and resort in W Switzerland, on the N shore of Lake Geneva. A cultural and intellectual centre, Lausanne is the seat of the Swiss Supreme Court and the headquarters of the International Olympic Committee. Population (1999 est): 114 161.

Lausanne, Conferences of **1.** (1922–23) A conference between the Allied Powers and Turkey that modified the post-World War I Treaty of Sèvres (1920): Turkey regained territory from Greece and the Allies recognized Turkey's right to control its own affairs. **2.** (1932) A conference between the UK, France,

Belgium, and Italy, which ended the payment by Germany of World War I reparations.

lava Magma that has reached the earth's surface through volcanic vents and from which the volatile material has escaped, either molten or cooled and solidified. Basic lavas tend to be liquid and flow over large areas, while acid lavas are viscous.

Laval, Pierre (1883–1945) French statesman. A socialist, Laval was prime minister in 1930, 1931, 1932, 1935, and 1936. After the collapse of France (1940) in World War II, he joined Marshal Pétain's Vichy government, became increasingly powerful, and with the support of Germany gained the virtual leadership of Vichy in 1942. After the liberation of France (1944) he was tried and executed for collaboration.

lavender A small shrub of the genus *Lavandula* (about 8 species), especially *L. vera* and *L. angustifolia* (or *L. officinalis*). 30–80 cm high, it has aromatic narrow grey-green leaves and long-stemmed spikes of small mauve or violet flowers. Native to the Mediterranean area, it is widely cultivated for its flowers, which retain their fragrance when dried, and for its oil, which is used in perfumes. Family: *Labiatae*.

Lavoisier, Antoine Laurent (1743–94) French chemist. He became wealthy by investing in a private tax-collecting company. This enabled him to build a large laboratory where he discovered (1778) that air consists of a mixture of two gases, which he called oxygen and nitrogen. He then went on to study the role of oxygen in combustion, finally disposing of the *phlogiston theory. Lavoisier also discovered the law of conservation of mass and devised the modern method of naming compounds. He was arrested and guillotined during the French Revolution.

law The body of rules that govern and regulate the relationship between one state and another (*see* INTERNATIONAL LAW), a state and its citizens (public law), and one person and another when the state is not directly involved (*see* CIVIL LAW). Two great legal systems are dominant in the western world: *Roman law, as used in most countries of continental Europe and South America, and English law. The laws of England, which are enforceable by judicial process, can be divided into: (1) the *common law, based on judicial decisions, as opposed to law enacted by parliament; (2) *equity, the principles originally applied by the Court of *Chancery; and (3) statute law, embodied in specific Acts of Parliament. *See also* COURTS OF LAW; CRIMINAL LAW.

Law, (Andrew) Bonar (1858–1923) British statesman; Conservative prime minister (1922–23). He fostered the 1916 revolt against Asquith's coalition and in the subsequent coalition led by *Lloyd George became chancellor of the exchequer. He became prime minister after Lloyd George's resignation.

Lawrence, D(avid) H(erbert) (1885–1930) British novelist, poet, and painter. He published his first novel, *The White Peacock*, in 1911. The semiautobiographical *Sons and Lovers* (1913) established his reputation. In 1912 he eloped with Frieda Weekley. Their extensive travels provided material for the novels *Kangaroo* (1923), reflecting a stay in Australia, and *The Plumed Serpent* (1926), set in Mexico. Lawrence explored marital and sexual relations in *The Rainbow* (1915) and *Women in Love* (1921); he treated this subject in more explicit detail in *Lady Chatterley's Lover* (privately printed, Florence, 1928). The novel was not published in Britain in its unexpurgated form until 1961, after a long trial.

Lawrence, Ernest Orlando (1901–58) US physicist, who in 1930 designed and built the first *cyclotron, a type of particle *accelerator. For his invention he received the Nobel Prize in 1939.

Lawrence, T(homas) E(dward) (1888–1935) British soldier and writer, known as Lawrence of Arabia. After the outbreak of World War I he worked for army intelligence in Egypt. In 1916 he joined the Arab revolt against the Turks, leading the Arab guerrillas triumphantly into Damascus in October 1918. His exploits, which brought him almost legendary fame, were recounted in his book *The Seven Pillars of Wisdom* (subscription edition, 1926).

lawrencium (Lr) A synthetic transuranic element discovered in 1961 and named after E. O. *Lawrence. At no 103; at wt (262).

Lawson, Nigel, Baron (1932–) British Conservative politician; chancellor of the exchequer (1983–89) under Margaret *Thatcher. He became an MP in 1974 and was secretary of state for energy (1981–83). His daughter, **Nigella Lawson** (1959–), is a cookery writer and broadcaster.

laxatives (*or* **purgatives**) Drugs used to treat constipation. Osmotic laxatives, such as magnesium sulphate (Epsom salts), mix with the faeces and cause them to retain water, which increases their bulk and makes them easier to pass. Stimulant laxatives, such as senna, stimulate the bowel directly. Bulk-forming laxatives, which include ispaghula husk and bran, both lubricate the faeces and increase their bulk.

lead (Pb) A dense soft bluish-grey metal, occurring in nature chiefly as the sulphide *galena (PbS). The metal is very resistant to corrosion and is used in plumbing (although it is now being replaced by plastics). It is also used to shield X-rays, as ammunition, in crystal glass (as lead oxide), and as an antiknock (as *tetraethyl lead; $(C_2H_5)_4Pb$). Most lead salts are insoluble. At no 82; at wt 207.2; mp 327.502°C; bp 1750°C.

Leadbelly (Huddie Ledbetter; 1888–1949) US Black folksinger and songwriter, noted for his blues and work songs.

leaf An outgrowth from the stem of a plant in which most of the green pigment chlorophyll, used for photosynthesis, is concentrated. Foliage leaves have a large surface area for absorbing light, and they contain pores (stomata) through which exchange of gases and water occurs. They may be simple or compound (composed of a number of leaflets) and with a branching vein system (in *dicotyledons) or parallel veins (in monocotyledons). The spines of cacti and the thorns of gorse are modified leaves.

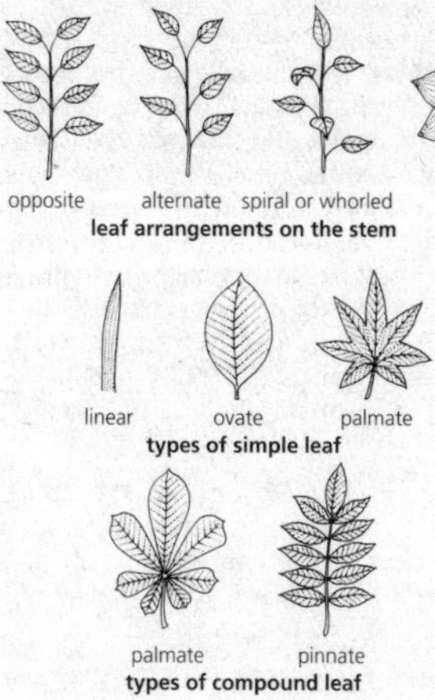

leaf. The type and arrangement of the leaves are characteristic for a particular species of plant. For example, the pear has alternate ovate leaves; the horse chestnut has opposite palmate leaves.

leaf beetle A beetle belonging to a large family (*Chrysomelidae*; 26 000 species) occurring in tropical and temperate regions. Leaf beetles are generally small and brightly coloured. Both the adults and larvae feed on leaves and flowers. Leaf beetles have a wide range of habits; many are serious pests, including the *Colorado potato beetle.

leafcutter bee A solitary *bee, about 10 mm long, belonging to a genus (*Megachile*) of the family *Megachilidae*. It nests in rotten wood and soil, lining the chamber and egg cells with pieces of leaf cut with its strong jaws.

leaf insect A plant-eating insect belonging to the family *Phyllidae*. It is excellently camouflaged against foliage, having a broad leaflike body and wings and leaflike flaps on the legs.

League of Nations An international organization created (1920) after World War I with the purpose of achieving world peace. The USA's failure to ratify the Treaty of *Versailles meant its exclusion from the League. The League failed to deal effectively with the aggression during the 1930s of Japan in China, Italy in Ethiopia (in which the League's use of *sanctions was ineffectual), and Germany, which withdrew from the League in 1933. The UN superseded the League after World War II.

Leakey, Louis Seymour Bazett (1903–72) Kenyan palaeontologist. His work at *Olduvai Gorge uncovered evidence for man's early evolution, notably the *Zinjanthropus* skull dating from 1.75 million years ago. In 1974 his wife **Mary Leakey** (1913–96) unearthed hominid remains at Laetolil (N Tanzania) dating back 3.75 million years. Their son **Richard Leakey** (1944–) made fossil finds around Lake Turkana (N Kenya) and directed Kenya's Wildlife Service (1990–94). In 1995 he formed a new political party to oppose the rule of President Moi.

Lean, Sir David (1908–91) British film director. His early films in collaboration with Noel Coward included *In Which we Serve* (1942) and *Brief Encounter* (1946). Adaptations of Dickens's *Great Expectations* (1946) and *Oliver Twist* (1947) were followed by the classic *The Bridge on the River Kwai* (1957). Later films included *Lawrence of Arabia* (1962), *Dr Zhivago* (1965), and *A Passage to India* (1984).

Leander *See* HERO AND LEANDER.

Lear, Edward (1812–88) British artist and

poet, noted for his four books of nonsense verse for children, beginning with *The Book of Nonsense* (1846). He also popularized a form of the limerick.

leather Specially treated animal skin, chiefly that of cows, sheep, goats, and pigs. The skin is stripped of the fleshy inner and hairy outer layers and then tanned by steeping it in tannin, a preservative, or using chromium salts. Various finishing processes include rubbing to bring out the grain, as in Morocco leather (goatskin); dyeing; oiling; lacquering for patent leather; and sueding to raise a nap. Leather is strong, flexible, waterproof, and permeable to air. Uses range from industrial parts and saddles to clothing and bookbindings.

leatherback turtle The largest living turtle, *Dermochelys coriacea*, found worldwide. Up to 2.1 m long with a weight of 540 kg, it has no horny external shell and its bones are buried in a ridged leathery brown-black skin. It is a strong swimmer and feeds on marine invertebrates, especially large jellyfish.

Lebanon A country in the Middle East, on the E coast of the Mediterranean Sea. It contains two mountain ranges extending N–S separated by the Beqaa Valley. The population is mixed, having Arab, Phoenician, Crusader, and Greek origins. Roughly half are Christian and half Muslim; political and official posts are rigorously divided between the two religions. *Economy*: agriculture, industry, and infrastructure suffered badly during the civil war of 1975–76 and the subsequent violence (1975–92). They are now being rebuilt as part of a long-term reconstruction plan, financed largely by foreign loans. *History*: Lebanon was an early convert to Christianity but in the 7th century broke away from the rest of the Church and was invaded by Muslims. Lebanon was held by the Mamelukes during the 14th and 15th centuries and by the Ottoman Turks from the early 16th century to 1918. France, having invaded Lebanon in 1861 to stop the massacres of Christians by Druses, was given the mandate over Greater Lebanon after World War I. Lebanon became officially independent in 1941, although France retained control until 1945. Lebanon did not fight in the 1967 and 1973 Arab-Israeli Wars, but Israel made raids across the border to eliminate Palestinian guerrillas. In 1975, civil war broke out between Christians and Muslims; after 19 months this was brought to an end by a Syrian-backed Arab Deterrent Force but unrest continued, especially in the S. In 1982 Israel invaded S Lebanon, clashing with Syrian forces in the Beqaa Valley and forcing the Palestine Liberation Organization to leave. Israel withdrew its forces from all but the S border region in 1985 leaving a United Nations force to maintain peace between the Israeli-armed Christians, the Muslims, Druses, and Palestinian guerrillas. In 1987 Syrian troops moved into Beirut but violence continued. Indecisive presidential elections in 1988 resulted in the establishment of rival Christian and Muslim governments. A new Muslim president, René Mouawad, was elected in 1989 but then assassinated. Christian opposition continued under Gen Michel Aoun until he was forced into exile in 1990. Relative peace was established in 1991, when Lebanon agreed to Syria assuming increased responsibility for its affairs. In 1996 hostile activity from Hizbollah fighters provoked an Israeli missile campaign in which hundreds of civilians were killed. A concerted Hizbollah offensive forced Israel to withdraw all its forces from S Lebanon in 2000. Official language: Arabic. Currency: Lebanese pound of 100 piastres. Area: 10 452 sq km (4036 sq mi). Population (2003 est): 3 728 000. Capital: Beirut.

Le Carré, John (David Cornwell; 1931–) British novelist. He served in the foreign service in Germany (1961–64). His novels *The Spy Who Came in from the Cold* (1963), *Tinker, Tailor, Soldier, Spy* (1974), *Smiley's People* (1980), *The Tailor of Panama* (1996), and *Absolute Friends* (2003) are realistic studies of the world of espionage. Other novels include *The Constant Gardener* (2000).

Le Corbusier (Charles-Édouard Jeanneret; 1887–1965) French architect, born in Switzerland, whose buildings and writings have been extremely influential. Until World War II he pioneered a rational form of design, especially with his villas at Garches (1927) and Poissy (1929). Afterwards he became more individual, for example at his extraordinary chapel at Ronchamp (1950). He was also concerned with town planning (e.g. *Chandigarh, 1950s) and large-scale housing projects (L'Unité, Marseilles, 1945).

Leda In Greek myth, the wife of Tyndareus, King of Sparta, and mother, either by her husband or by Zeus, of Clytemnestra, Helen, and Castor and Pollux. Helen was born from an egg after Zeus had visited Leda as a swan.

Lee, Robert E(dward) (1807–70) US Confederate commander in the Civil War. *See* CIVIL WAR, US.

leech A carnivorous aquatic *annelid worm of the class *Hirudinea* (about 300 species).

Leeches inhabit fresh and salt water throughout the world and occur in wet soil and cloud forest. They have one sucker around the mouth and a second at the rear. Leeches can move by "looping," using their suckers. Most feed on the blood of animals and humans, using piercing mouthparts.

Leeds 1. 53 50N 1 35W A city in N England, in Leeds unitary authority, West Yorkshire, on the River Aire. Its traditional industries are clothing, textiles, printing, engineering, chemicals, and leather goods but most employment is now in the service sector. Population (1991): 424 194. **2.** A unitary authority in N England, in West Yorkshire. Area: 562 sq km (217 sq mi). Population (2001): 715 404.

leek A hardy biennial plant, *Allium porrum*, native to SW Asia and E Mediterranean regions and widely grown in Europe as a vegetable. The bulb is hardly differentiated from the stem, which bears long broad leaves. The stems and leaves are eaten in the first year, before flowering. The leek is the emblem of Wales.

Leeuwenhoek, Antonie van (1632–1723) Dutch scientist, noted for his microscopic studies of living organisms. He was the first to describe protozoa, bacteria, and spermatozoa and he also made observations of yeasts, red blood cells, and blood capillaries. Leeuwenhoek also traced the life histories of various animals, including the flea, ant, and weevil.

Leeward Islands 1. A West Indian group of islands in the Lesser Antilles, in the Caribbean Sea extending SE from Puerto Rico to the Windward Islands. **2.** A former British colony in the West Indies (1871–1956), comprising Antigua, St Kitts-Nevis-Anguilla, Montserrat, and the British Virgin Islands. **3.** A group of islands in French Polynesia, in the Society Islands in the S Pacific Ocean.

legionnaires' disease An acute severe pneumonia, caused by the bacterium *Legionella pneumophila*, first described in 1976 after an outbreak among US legionnaires in Philadelphia. Over 30 people died in Stafford, England, as a result of an outbreak in 1985. The disease is treated with the antibiotic erythromycin. The route of transmission is often air-conditioning systems.

Legion of Honour (French name: légion d'Honneur) A French order of knighthood, established by Napoleon in 1802. It has five ranks, to which foreigners are admitted. Its grand master is the president of France.

Leguminosae (*or* **Fabaceae**) A worldwide family of herbs, shrubs, and trees (about 7000 species), which includes many important crop plants, such as peas, beans, clovers, and alfalfa. They all have compound leaves and the fruit is a pod containing a single row of seeds. Both pods and seeds are rich in protein. Most species possess root nodules that contain nitrogen-fixing bacteria and leguminous crops replenish nitrogen in the soil (*see* NITROGEN CYCLE).

Lehár, Franz (Ferencz L.; 1870–1948) Hungarian composer, noted for the composition of operettas, of which *The Merry Widow* (1905) was his greatest success.

Le Havre 49 30N 0 06E A port in N France, in the Seine-Maritime department on the English Channel at the mouth of the River Seine. There is a transatlantic cargo service and a car-ferry service to England. Population (1999): 190 651.

Leibniz, Gottfried Wilhelm (1646–1716) German philosopher and mathematician. He put forward a coherent philosophy, which is summarized in his two philosophical books, *New Essays on the Human Understanding* (c. 1705) and *Theodicy* (1710), and numerous essays. Leibniz' best-known doctrine is that the universe consists of an infinite set of independent substances (monads) in each of which a life force is present. In creating the world, God took account of the wishes of monads and this led to a rational harmony in the "best of all possible worlds." His claim to have invented the calculus was disputed by *Newton.

Leicester 1. (Latin name: Ratae Coritanorum) 52 38N 1 05W A city in central England, in Leicester unitary authority, the administrative centre of Leicestershire. Lying on the Fosse Way, Leicester has Roman remains and the ruins of a Norman castle. The principal industries are hosiery, knitwear, footwear, engineering, and electronics. The National Space Centre, which opened in 2001, is now Leicester's leading tourist attraction. Population (1994 est): 293 400. **2.** A unitary authority in central England, in Leicestershire. Area: 73 sq km (28 sq mi). Population (2001): 279 923.

Leicester, Robert Dudley, Earl of (c. 1532–88) English courtier; the fifth son of the Duke of *Northumberland. Elizabeth I made him Master of the Horse (1558) and then a privy councillor (1559). It was rumoured that he might marry the queen after the death of his wife Amy Robsart (c. 1532–60). His incompetent command (1585–87) of an English force in support of the Revolt of the Netherlands against Spain led to his recall but he retained Elizabeth's favour until his death.

Leicestershire A county in the East Midlands of England. In 1974 it absorbed the small historic county of Rutland: this became an independent unitary authority in 1997, as did Leicester city. The River Soar, flowing N, separates Charnwood Forest from the uplands of the E. Its fertile soil makes it an important agricultural county. Hosiery is the staple industry. Area (excluding unitary authorities): 2084 sq km (804 sq mi). Population (2001, excluding unitary authorities): 609 579. Administrative centre: Leicester.

Leiden (English name: Leyden) 52 10N 4 30E A city in the W Netherlands, in South Holland province. Its university was founded in 1575. During the 17th and 18th centuries it was an artistic and educational centre. Population (1999 est): 117 389.

Leif Eriksson (11th century) Icelandic explorer; the son of Eric the Red (late 10th century). He was converted to Christianity and on his way to promote the faith in Greenland, missed his course and became the first European to reach America (perhaps Newfoundland or Nova Scotia). His story is told in Icelandic sagas.

Leigh, Vivien (Vivien Hartley; 1913–67) British actress. In the theatre, she played many leading Shakespearean roles, frequently appearing with Laurence *Olivier, her husband from 1937 to 1960. Her films include *Gone with the Wind* (1939) and *A Streetcar Named Desire* (1951).

Leinster A province in the SE Republic of Ireland. It consists of the counties of Carlow, Dublin, Kildare, Kilkenny, Laois, Longford, Louth, Meath, Offaly, Westmeath, Wexford, and Wicklow. It incorporates the ancient kingdoms of Meath and Leinster. Area: 19 632 sq km (7580 sq mi). Population (2002): 2 105 449.

Leipzig 51 20N 12 21E A city in E Germany, near the confluence of the Rivers Elster, Pleisse, and Parthe. Leipzig is the country's second largest city and a major industrial and commercial centre. International trade fairs are held here and it is a musical centre. The university was founded in 1409. Population (1999 est): 490 000.

Leitrim A county in the NW Republic of Ireland, in Connacht bordering on Donegal Bay. Mainly hilly, descending to lowlands in the S, it contains several lakes, notably Lough Allen. Area: 1525 sq km (589 sq mi). Population (2002): 25 815. County town: Carrick-on-Shannon.

Lely, Sir Peter (Pieter van der Faes; 1618–80) Portrait painter, born in Germany of Dutch parents. He settled in London (1641), where he was patronized by Charles I and later Cromwell. As court painter to Charles II from 1661, he produced his best-known works, including his *Windsor Beauties* (Hampton Court).

Le Mans 48 00N 0 12E A city in NW France, the capital of the Sarthe department. Its many historical buildings include the cathedral (11th–15th centuries). The Le Mans 24 Hours, a sports-car race, is held here annually. Population (1999): 146 405.

lemming A *rodent belonging to the subfamily *Microtini*, found in northern regions of Asia, America, and Europe. They are 7.5–15 cm long and have long thick fur. When their food of grass, berries, and roots is abundant, they breed at a great rate. When food is scarce they migrate southwards, often in large swarms crossing swamps, rivers, and other obstacles; they sometimes drown through exhaustion. Chief genera: *Dicrostonyx* (collared lemmings; 4 species), *Lemmus* (true lemmings; 4 species). Family: *Cricetidae*.

lemon A small tree or shrub, *Citrus limon*, probably native to the E Mediterranean but widely cultivated in subtropical climates for its fruit. Its fragrant white flowers produce oval fruits with thick yellow skin and acid-tasting pulp rich in vitamin C. The juice is used in cookery and in drinks. Family: *Rutaceae*.

lemon sole A *flatfish, *Microstomus kitt*, found in the NE Atlantic and North Sea. Its upper side is red-brown or yellow-brown with light or dark marbling. It is an important food fish. Family: *Pleuronectidae*.

lemur A small *prosimian primate belonging to the family *Lemuridae* (16 species), found only in Madagascar and neighbouring islands. Lemurs are mostly arboreal and nocturnal and often live in groups. The ring-tailed lemur (*Lemur catta*) is 70–95 cm long including the tail (40–50 cm) and is mainly terrestrial. Dwarf lemurs (subfamily *Cheirogaleinae*) are only 25–50 cm long including the tail (12–25 cm).

Lena, River The longest river in Russia. Rising in S Siberia, W of Lake Baikal, it flows mainly NE to the Laptev Sea. Its large delta is frozen for about nine months of the year. Length: 4271 km (2653 mi).

Lenin, Vladimir Ilich (V.I. Ulyanov; 1870–1924) Russian revolutionary and first leader of communist Russia. In 1893 Lenin, a Marxist, joined a revolutionary group in St Petersburg, where he practised as a lawyer. He was imprisoned in 1895 and exiled to Siberia in 1897. In 1902 he published *What Is to Be Done?*, in which he emphasized the role of the party in effecting revolution. This emphasis led to a split in the Russian Social Democratic Workers' Party between the *Bolsheviks under Lenin and the *Mensheviks. After the failure of the *Revolution of 1905, Lenin again went into exile, settling in Zurich in 1914, where he wrote *Imperialism, the Highest Stage of Capitalism* (1917). In April 1917, after the outbreak of the *Russian Revolution, Lenin returned to Russia. Calling for the transfer of power from the Provisional Government to the soviets (workers' councils), he was forced to flee to Finland. Lenin returned in October to lead the Bolshevik revolution, which overthrew the Provisional Government and established the ruling Soviet of People's Commissars under Lenin's chairmanship. He made peace with Germany and then led the revolutionaries to victory against the Whites in the civil war (1918–20). He founded (1919) the Third *International and initiated far-reaching social reforms. He also introduced the New Economic Policy (1921), which permitted a modicum of free enterprise. A series of strokes from 1922 led to his premature death.

The modified version of *Marxism adopted by Lenin is known as **Leninism** or **Marxist-Leninism**. According to this theory imperialism is an account of the final stage of capitalism, in which it dominates the entire world, decisive control resting with finance capital (banks) as opposed to industrial capital. Because of the worldwide nature of capitalism, socialist revolution becomes possible even in economically underdeveloped countries. In Lenin's theory the revolutionary party, the most conscious element of the proletariat, provides the leadership for the rest of the working class and the peasantry in overthrowing the capitalist class.

Leningrad *See* ST PETERSBURG.

Lenin Peak 39 21N 73 01E The highest mountain in Russia, in the Trans-Altai range. Height: 7134 m (23 406 ft).

Lennon, John (1940–80) British rock musician, a member of the *Beatles. After the group disbanded, he recorded such albums as *Imagine* (1971) and *Walls and Bridges* (1974), often with his wife, the Japanese-born artist Yoko Ono (1933–). He was murdered by a deranged fan.

lens A piece of transparent material, usually glass, quartz, or plastic, used for directing and focusing beams of light. The surfaces of a lens have a constant curvature; if both sides curve outwards at the middle the lens is called convex, if they curve inwards it is concave. The image formed by a lens may be real, in which case the rays converge to the image point (a converging lens), or virtual, in which the rays diverge from the image point (a diverging lens). The focal length of a lens is the distance from the lens at which a parallel beam of light is brought to a focus.

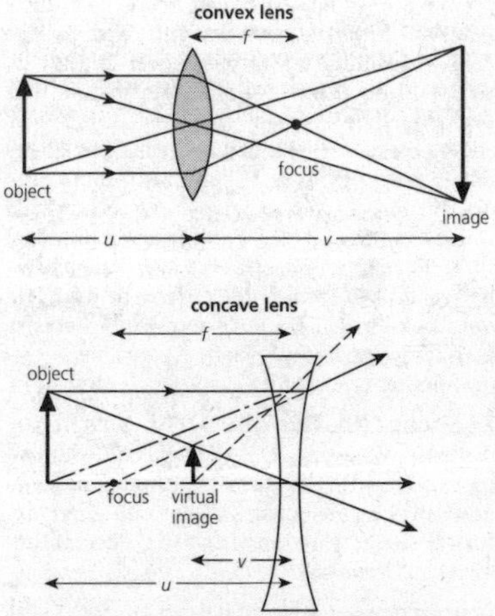

lens. The lines representing light rays show how a convex lens gives a real inverted image and how a concave lens gives an upright virtual image.

Lent The Christian period of fasting and penance preceding Easter. Beginning on *Ash Wednesday, the Lenten fast covers 40 days, in emulation of Christ's 40 days in the wilderness (Matthew 4.2). Since the Reformation the rules of fasting have been generally relaxed in both Roman Catholic and Protestant Churches.

lentil An annual herb, *Lens culinaris*, native to the Near East but widely cultivated. Each pod produces 1–2 flat round green or reddish seeds, which are rich in protein and can be dried and stored for use in soups, stews, etc. Family: *Leguminosae*.

Lenz's law The direction of an induced current in a conductor is such as to oppose the cause of the induction. For example, a current induced by a conductor cutting the lines of flux of a magnetic field would produce a magnetic field of its own, which would oppose the original magnetic field. Named after Heinrich Lenz (1804–65).

Leonardo da Vinci (1452–1519) Italian artistic and scientific genius of the *Renaissance. He trained in Florence under *Verrocchio and in 1482 became painter, engineer, and designer to Duke Ludovico Sforza in Milan, where he painted the fresco of the *Last Supper* and the first version of the *Virgin of the Rocks*. His promised equestrian sculpture glorifying the Duke was never cast but the studies of horses for the project have survived. After the French invasion of Milan (1499), he returned to Florence, becoming military engineer and architect (1502) to Cesare *Borgia. Paintings in this period include *The Virgin and Child with St John the Baptist and St Anne* and the *Mona Lisa*. Some of his paintings were left unfinished and others, because of his experimental techniques, failed to survive. After working again in Milan (1506–13) and in Rome (1513–15), he was invited by Francis I to France (1516), where he died. His notebooks reveal his wide range of interests, including anatomy, botany, geology, hydraulics, and mechanics.

l

Leoncavallo, Ruggiero (1858–1919) Italian composer of operas. Only *I Pagliacci* (1892) has met with continuing success, although he composed over 15, including a trilogy on Italian historical subjects and, a year after Puccini, his own *La Bohème* (1897).

leopard A large spotted *cat, *Panthera pardus*, found throughout Africa and most of Asia. Leopards are slender, up to 2.1 m long including the 90-cm tail, having a yellow coat spotted with black rosettes. Colour variations, such as the *panther, sometimes occur. Leopards are solitary and nocturnal.

leopard lily A perennial herbaceous plant, *Belamcanda chinensis*, native to E Asia and widely planted as a garden ornamental. Growing over 1 m tall from an underground stem (rhizome), it has sword-shaped leaves, orange-spotted red flowers, and blackberry-like clusters of seeds. Family: *Iridaceae*.

leopard seal A solitary Antarctic *seal, *Hydrurga leptonyx*, of the pack ice. Leopard seals are fast agile hunters, feeding mainly on penguins. Grey, with dark spots and blotches, females grow to 3.7 m and males to 3.2 m. Family: *Phocidae*.

Leopold I (1790–1865) The first King of the Belgians (1831–65). He defended Belgium against William III of the Netherlands, who refused to recognize Belgian independence until 1838. A leading diplomat in Europe, at home he encouraged educational and economic reforms. He was briefly (1816–17) married to Charlotte (1796–1817), the daughter of George IV of Great Britain.

Leopold III (1901–83) King of the Belgians (1934–51). He surrendered to the Germans in *World War II, provoking opposition to his return to Belgium in 1945 and forcing his abdication in favour of his son Baudouin.

Lepanto, Battle of (7 October 1571) A naval battle off Lepanto, Greece, in which the Holy League routed the Ottoman navy, which was threatening to dominate the Mediterranean. The Christian force was commanded by John of Austria (1545–78). About 10 000 Christian galley slaves were freed.

leprosy A chronic disease, occurring almost entirely in tropical countries, caused by the bacterium *Mycobacterium leprae* (which is related to the tuberculosis bacillus). Leprosy is contracted only after close personal contact with an infected person. In the lepromatous form of the disease lumps appear on the skin, which—together with the nerves—becomes thickened and progressively destroyed, resulting in deformity. Tuberculoid leprosy usually produces only discoloured patches on the skin associated with loss of sensation in the affected areas. There are now potent antibiotics and sulphones (drugs related to the sulphonamides) available to cure the disease.

lepton A group of elementary particles, consisting of the *electron, *muon, tau particle, *neutrinos, and their antiparticles. They take part only in the weak and *electromagnetic interactions; together with quarks and photons they are thought to be the only truly elementary particles. *See* PARTICLE PHYSICS.

Lermontov, Mikhail (1814–41) Russian poet and novelist. His early Romantic poetry was greatly influenced by *Byron. As an army officer and an observer of high society he developed the cynical attitudes expressed in his novel *A Hero of Our Time* (1840).

Lerner, Alan Jay (1918–86) US lyricist and librettist, who collaborated with the composer Frederick *Loewe in the musicals *Brigadoon* (1947), *My Fair Lady* (1956), and *Camelot* (1960). Lerner also wrote the film scripts for *An American in Paris* (1951) and *Gigi* (1958).

lesbianism *See* HOMOSEXUALITY.

Lesbos (Modern Greek name: Lésvos) A Greek island in the E Aegean Sea, situated close to the mainland of Turkey. Settled about 1000 BC, it is associated with the development of Greek lyric poetry (especially through the work of Alcaeus and Sappho). Lesbos was a member of the Delian League. Area: 1630 sq km (629 sq mi). Population (1991): 105 082.

Lesotho, Kingdom of (name until 1966: Basutoland) A small mountainous country in SE Africa, enclosed by South Africa. Most of the inhabitants are *Sotho. *Economy*: chiefly agricultural; maize, wheat, and sorghum are the main crops. Diamonds, wool, and mohair are exported. *History*: in 1868, following warfare with the Orange Free State, Basutoland came under British protection; direct British administration was imposed in 1884. In 1910 it was placed under the authority of the British High Commission in South Africa and in 1966 became an independent kingdom within the Commonwealth. After a military coup in 1986 Gen Justin Lekhanya came to power. Civilian rule was restored in 1993. Moshoeshoe II was reinstated as king in 1995 and was succeeded by Letsie III in 1996. In 1998 allegations that the general election of that year had been fraudulent led to widespread unrest and military intervention by South Africa. The electoral system was reformed for the 2002 elections, which were agreed to be fair. Official languages: Sesotho and English. Currency: loti of 100 lisente. Area: 30 340 sq km (11 716 sq mi). Population (2003): 1 802 000. Capital: Maseru.

Lesseps, Ferdinand de (1805–94) French diplomat, who supervised the construction of the Suez Canal, which was completed in 1869. A subsequent project to construct the Panama Canal ended in disaster when Lesseps was prosecuted for embezzling funds.

Lesser Antilles (former name: Caribbees) A West Indian group of islands, comprising a chain extending from Puerto Rico to the N coast of Venezuela. They include the Leeward and Windward Islands, Barbados, Trinidad and Tobago, and the Netherlands Antilles.

Lessing, Doris (1919–) British novelist. Born in Iran and brought up in Rhodesia, she came to England in 1949. Political and social themes predominate in her fiction, notably in the sequence of five novels entitled *Children of Violence* (1952–69) and *The Golden Notebook* (1962). Later works include *The Good Terrorist* (1985), *The Fifth Child* (1988), and *The Sweetest Dream* (2001), as well as two volumes of autobiography.

Leto In Greek mythology, a daughter of the *Titans loved by Zeus. She gave birth to Apollo and Artemis.

lettuce An annual herb, *Lactuca sativa*, probably from the Near East and widely cultivated as a salad plant. It has a tight rosette of juicy leaves, rich in vitamin A, and is usually eaten fresh. Cos lettuce has long crisp leaves and oval heads while cabbage lettuce has round heads and often curly leaves. Family: *Compositae*.

leucocyte (*or* **white blood cell**) A colourless blood cell, up to 0.02 mm in diameter, of which there are normally 4000–11 000 per cubic millimetre of blood. There are several kinds, all involved in the body's defence mechanisms. Granulocytes and monocytes ingest and feed on bacteria and other microorganisms that cause infection (*see also* PHAGOCYTE). The lymphocytes are involved with the production of *antibodies.

leucotomy The surgical operation of interrupting the course of white nerve fibres within the brain. It is performed to relieve uncontrollable pain or emotional tension in very severe and intractable psychiatric illnesses, such as severe depression. The original form of the operation—prefrontal leucotomy (*or* lobotomy)—had serious complications. Modern procedures make selective lesions and side effects are uncommon.

leukaemia A disease in which the blood contains an abnormally large number of white blood cells (*see* LEUCOCYTE) that do not function properly. Leukaemia is a type of cancer of the blood-forming tissues. Leukaemias may be acute or chronic, depending on the rate of progression of the disease. They are also classified according to the type of white cell affected. For example, acute lymphocytic leukaemia (affecting the lymphocytes) occurs most commonly in children and young adults; it can now often be controlled by means of radiotherapy or *cytotoxic drugs. Chronic leukaemias occur more often in old people and may not need any treatment.

level An instrument (also called a spirit level) for indicating whether or not a surface is level. It consists of one or more curved or straight glass tubes filled with liquid and containing an air bubble. The level, and therefore the surface on which it rests, is horizontal when the bubble is in the centre of the tube.

Levellers An extremist English Puritan sect, active 1647–49. Led by the pamphleteer John Lilburne (c.1614–57), they campaigned for a written constitution, radical extension of the franchise, and abolition of the monarchy and of other social distinctions (hence their name).

Leven, Loch A lake in Scotland, in SE Tayside Region. It has seven islands, on one of which Mary, Queen of Scots, was imprisoned (1567–68). Length: 6 km (3.7 mi). Width: 4 km (2.5 mi).

lever A simple machine consisting of a bar pivoted at a point on its length (the fulcrum) to move the point of application of a force and to obtain a mechanical advantage. The three orders of lever are shown in the illustration.

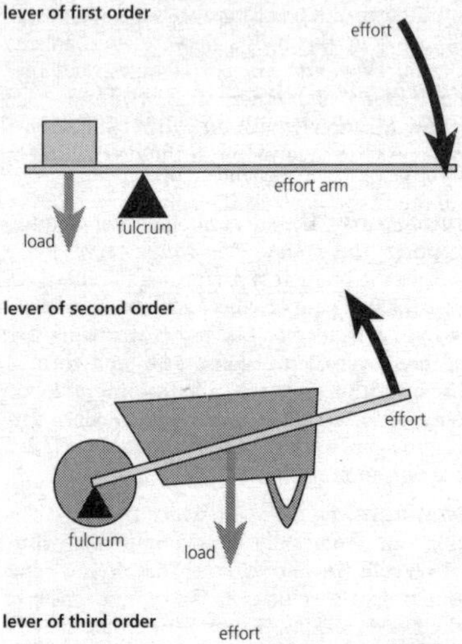

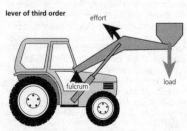

lever. In a first-order lever the fulcrum lies between the load and the effort (as in a pair of scissors). In a second-order lever the load falls between the fulcrum and the effort (as in a wheelbarrow). In a third-order lever the effort lies between the fulcrum and the load (as in a mechanical digger).

Levi, Primo (1919–87) Italian novelist and poet. A Jew, he survived confinement in Auschwitz and described his experiences in *If This Is a Man* (1947). Other works include *The Periodic Table* (1975) and *If Not Now, When?* (1982).

Lévi-Strauss, Claude (1908–) French anthropologist, the founder of structural anthropology (*see* STRUCTURALISM). His works include *The Elementary Structures of Kinship* (1949), *Structural Anthropology* (1958), and *Mythologies* (1964–71).

levodopa (*or* **L-dopa**) A drug used to treat Parkinson's disease, which is caused by a deficiency of dopamine (a chemical secreted at nerve endings when an impulse passes) in the brain. Levodopa is converted to dopamine in the body; it is given in combination with benserazide, which prevents its breakdown in the body before it reaches the brain.

Lewes 50 52N 0 01E A market town in SE England, the administrative centre of East Sussex, on the River Ouse. At the battle of Lewes (1264) Henry III was defeated by the rebel barons under Simon de Montfort. *Glyndebourne is nearby. Population (1991): 15 376.

Lewis, C(live) S(taples) (1898–1963) British scholar and writer. He wrote science-fiction including *Out of the Silent Planet* (1938), children's books chronicling the land of Narnia, and works on religious themes, notably *The Problem of Pain* (1940), *The Screwtape Letters* (1942) and *Mere Christianity* (1952).

Lewis, (Harry) Sinclair (1885–1951) US novelist noted for his social satires, which include *Main Street* (1920), *Babbitt* (1922), *Arrowsmith* (1925), and *Elmer Gantry* (1927). He won the 1930 Nobel Prize.

Lewis, (Percy) Wyndham (1882–1957) British novelist and painter. In many polemical works and brilliant satirical novels, which include *The Apes of God* (1930) and the trilogy *The Human Age* (1928–55), he sustained a continual attack on the liberal cultural establishment. He helped found the art movement *vorticism.

Lewis and Clark expedition (1804–06) A journey of exploration across the American continent by Meriwether Lewis (1774–1809) and William Clark (1770–1838). They ascended the Missouri, crossed the Rockies, and went down the Columbia River to the Pacific, exploring the Yellowstone River on the return journey. Promoted by Thomas Jefferson, the expedition established the US claim to the Louisiana Purchase.

Lewis with Harris The largest island of the Outer Hebrides, separated from the coast of NW Scotland by the Minch. Lewis in the N is linked with Harris by a narrow isthmus. In 1998 a road bridge was opened between Harris and the small island of Scalpay. It is famous for its Harris tweed. Area: 2134 sq km (824 sq mi). Population (latest est): 23 510. Chief town: Stornoway.

lexicography The compilation of dictionaries. Dictionaries can be monolingual (dealing with only one language) or bi- or multi-lingual (giving equivalents of words in other languages). Monolingual dictionaries differ in the style and fullness of the definitions and in the audience for which they are intended (e.g. for native speakers or foreign learners). Some list definitions of a word in historical order while others list definitions in order of current usage. Almost all dictionaries contain information about spelling and meaning; many also offer guidance on pronunciation, usage, inflected forms of words, *etymology, etc. The most famous English dictionaries are Samuel Johnson's *Dictionary* (1755) and the *Oxford English Dictionary on Historical Principles* (1884–1928; chief editor Sir James Murray). The best-known American dictionary is Noah Webster's *American Dictionary of the English Language* (1828).

Leyden *See* LEIDEN.

Lhasa 29 41N 91 10E A city in W China, the capital of Tibet. As the traditional centre of *Tibetan Buddhism, it is the site of many temples, monasteries, and of the Potala, the former palace of the Dalai Lama, the priest-ruler. Since the Chinese occupation (1951) many Tibetans have fled, including the Dalai Lama following the 1959 uprising; there were riots against the Chinese in the late 1980s. Population (1999): 121 568.

libel *See* DEFAMATION.

Liberal Democrats A British political party of the centre, established (as the Social and Liberal Democrats) in 1988 when most of the Social Democratic Party merged with the Liberal Party (the current name was adopted in 1989). Paddy Ashdown was elected as their first leader; he retired in 1999 and was succeeded by Charles *Kennedy. The party advocates proportional representation and closer integration into the EU.

Liberal Party (Australia) A conservative political party, formed in 1944. A Liberal–Country Party coalition won the election of 1949 and under the leadership successively of Robert *Menzies, Harold Holt (1908–67), John Gorton (1911–2002), and William McMahon (1908–88) held office until 1972. The Liberals were again in power from 1975 to 1983 under Malcolm Fraser (1930–) and from 1996 under John *Howard.

Liberal Party (UK) A political party that grew out of the *Whig party. The heyday of the party was from the mid-19th century to World War I, under the prime ministers *Gladstone, *Campbell-Bannerman, *Asquith, and *Lloyd George. Conflict between Asquith and Lloyd George led to a split in the party after World War I, and in 1922 the Labour Party replaced the Liberals as the official opposition. The party forged a political alliance with the newly-formed Social Democratic Party in 1981 and merged with it to become the Social and Liberal Democrats in 1988.

Liberia, Republic of A country in West Africa, on the Atlantic Ocean. Coastal plains rise to higher ground inland and to mountains in the N; much of the land is covered with tropical rainforest. Most of the population belongs to indigenous tribes, including the Kpelle, Bassa, and Kru, with a minority who are descended from American slaves. *Economy*: since the outbreak of civil war in 1990 agriculture has declined to subsistence levels and industry has virtually ceased. The main food crops are rice and cassava; the main cash crop was rubber, some of it grown under concession to US companies. Exploitation of Liberia's mineral resources, especially iron ore and diamonds previously formed the basis of the country's economy. Ships are easily registered in Liberia and, with many foreign vessels, its merchant fleet is the largest in the world. *History*: it was founded in 1822 by the American Colonization Society as a settlement for freed American slaves. In 1847 it became the Free and Independent Republic of Liberia with a constitution based on that of the USA. It has had considerable US aid. Liberia also has close economic ties with Sierra Leone. In 1980 the president Dr William R. Tolbert, Jr (1913–80), was assassinated in a military coup led by Master Sergeant Samuel Doe, who was elected president in 1985. In 1990 rival rebel forces under Charles Taylor and Prince Yormie Johnson seized Monrovia, killing Doe. An interim government was set up but ceasefire agreements failed and fighting continued. A new peace plan was agreed in 1996 and Taylor was elected president in 1997. However, his corrupt and autocratic rule provoked continuing opposition and in August 2003 rebel forces overran Monrovia and forced him into exile. A peace deal was signed and a transitional power-sharing government set up. Official language: English. Currency: Liberian dollar of 100 cents. Area: 111 400 sq km (43 000 sq mi). Population (2003 est): 3 317 000. Capital: Monrovia.

Library of Congress The national library of the USA founded in 1800. First housed in the Capitol, it was moved to its present site in Washington in 1897. It contains over 60 million items, and its system of classification is widely used in academic libraries.

libretto (Italian: little book) The text of an opera or operetta. Dramatists whose plays have been used as libretti include Hugo von Hofmannsthal (1874–1929), *Maeterlinck, and Oscar *Wilde. *Wagner and *Berlioz wrote their own libretti. Notable partnerships between librettists and composers include Lorenzo da Ponte (1749–1838) and Mozart, Arrigo Boito (1842–1918) and Verdi, and Gilbert and Sullivan.

Libreville 0 25N 9 25E The capital of Gabon, a port in the NW on the Gabon Estuary. It was founded by the French in the 19th century, when freed slaves were sent there. Population (1993): 362 386.

Librium *See* BENZODIAZEPINES.

Libya (official name: Great Socialist People's Libyan Arab Republic) A country in N Africa, on the Mediterranean Sea. It consists chiefly of desert, with a narrow coastal plain, rising to the Tibesti Mountains along its southern border and is divided into the three main areas (provinces until 1963) of Cyrenaica, Tripolitania, and Fezzan. The population is mainly of Berber and Arabic origin. *Economy*: between 1955 and 1970 major deposits of oil were discovered, notably at Zelten (1959). Libya is now one of the world's major oil producers and exporters. Subsistence agriculture is important, livestock farming being the main agricultural occupation, nomadic in the S. *History*: during the 16th century the area came under Turkish domination and in 1912 it was annexed by Italy. It was the scene of heavy fighting in World War II; the French occupied Fezzan and the British occupied Cyrenaica and Tripolitania. In 1951 the United Kingdom of Libya was formed from the federation of these three areas and the Emir of Cyrenaica, Mohammed Idris Al-Senussi (1889–1983), became its first king. He was deposed in a coup led by Col Moammar al-*Gaddafi in 1969 and Libya was proclaimed a republic. The Revolutionary Command Council was established to rule the country. In 1973 Gaddafi introduced a cultural revolution based on Islamic principles. Since 1969 Libya has been firmly aligned against Israel and has been accused of using terrorist methods abroad; in 1986 such accusations prompted raids on Libyan cities by US jets. In 1992 UN sanctions were imposed on Libya when Gaddafi refused to extradite two men suspected of involvement in the Lockerbie airliner bombing (1988); they were suspended in 1999 when Gaddafi agreed to a trial in the Netherlands. Decades of isolation were finally ended in 2003–04, when Libya announced that it had abandoned its ambition to build nuclear weapons, paving the way for a state visit from British prime minister Tony Blair (March 2004). Official language: Arabic; Currency: dinar of 1000 dirhams. Area: 1 759 540 sq km (679 216 sq mi). Population (2003 est): 5 551 000. Capital: Tripoli.

lichee *See* LITCHI.

lichens A large group of organisms (about 15 000 species) consisting of two components, an alga or a bacterium (usually a green alga or blue-green bacterium) and a fungus (usually an ascomycete), in a mutually beneficial association. Millions of algal or bacterial cells (the phycobiont) are interwoven with fungal filaments (the mycobiont) to form the lichen body (a thallus), which may be crusty, scaly, leafy, or stalked and shrublike in appearance. Lichens were formerly regarded as plants; they are now classified as fungi. They occur worldwide, mainly on tree trunks, rocks, and soil, and can survive in harsh conditions. They normally reproduce asexually by fragmentation, budding, or by producing special structures (soredia), consisting of a few algal cells enmeshed with fungal threads.

Liechtenstein, Principality of A small country in central Europe, between Switzerland and Austria. Mountains rise from the Rhine Valley to heights of over 2500 m (8000 ft). *Economy*: farming is still important but high-tech engineering is now the mainstay of the economy. Tourism and the sale of postage stamps are also important. *History*: the principality was formed from the union of the counties of Vaduz and Schellenberg in 1719 and was part of the Holy Roman Empire until 1806. It formed a customs union with Switzerland in 1923 and joined EFTA in 1991 and the European Economic Area in 1995. Official language: German. Currency: Swiss franc of 100 centimes. Area: 160 sq km (62 sq mi). Population (2003 est): 34 100. Capital: Vaduz.

lie detector An instrument designed to detect whether a person is lying by measuring such factors as blood pressure, respiration rate, skin conductivity, and pulse rate. A sudden change in these factors in a person being questioned is taken to indicate that he is under stress and may be telling a lie. Lie detectors are not usually accepted in a court of law.

Liège (Flemish name: Luik) 50 38N 5 35E An industrial city in E Belgium, on the River Meuse. It has many old churches, including St Martin's (692 AD). Population (2000 est): 185 638.

life The property that enables a living organism to assimilate nonliving materials from its environment and use them to increase its size and complexity (the process of growth), to repair its existing tissues, and to produce new independent organisms that also possess the properties of life (the process of reproduction). *See also* ANIMAL; PLANT.

Life on earth is thought to have originated between 4500 and 3000 million years ago. The atmosphere then consisted chiefly of methane, hydrogen, ammonia, and water vapour, from which simple organic molecules (such as amino acids, proteins, and fatty acids) were formed as a result of energy supplied by solar radiation, lightning, and volcanic activity. The first cells may have arisen spontaneously as simple envelopes of protein and fat molecules. However, the crucial steps towards life would probably have been the inclusion in such a cell of both the enzyme molecules necessary to perform primitive fermentations and the nucleic acid molecules, such as RNA and DNA, capable of directing the metabolic processes of the cell and of self replication, i.e. passing on this information to succeeding generations. In the course of time increasingly efficient biochemical pathways evolved, including the process of photosynthesis in the first photosynthetic organisms (e.g. blue-green bacteria). This led to the gradual build-up of oxygen in the atmosphere, which started about 2000 million years ago; by about 400 million years ago the *ozone layer in the upper atmosphere was sufficiently dense to shield the land from harmful ultraviolet radiation, enabling plants and animals to survive. With increasing oxygen levels, aerobic respiration—the most efficient method of energy utilization—was adopted by most living organisms.

lifeboat **1.** In the UK, a powerful motorboat, especially designed to right itself in the event of capsize and equipped with safety devices, used by the *Royal National Lifeboat Institution (RNLI) as an emergency vessel in the event of a disaster near the shore. **2.** A boat carried aboard a ship, used for accommodating passengers and crew if the ship has to be abandoned.

Liffey, River A river in the E Republic of Ireland, rising in the Wicklow Mountains and flowing mainly W and NE through Dublin to Dublin Bay. Length: 80 km (50 mi).

ligament A strong fibrous tissue that joins one bone to another at a joint. Ligaments are flexible but inelastic: they increase the stability of the joint and limit its movements to certain directions. Unusual stresses on a joint often damage ("pull") a ligament, as occurs in a "twisted" ankle.

light The form of *electromagnetic radiation to which the eye is sensitive. It forms the part of the electromagnetic spectrum from 740 nanometres (red light) to 400 nanometres (blue light), white light consisting of a mixture of all the colours of the visible spectrum. *Newton supported a corpuscular theory of light in which a luminous body was believed to emit particles of light. This theory adequately explained reflection and geometric optics but failed to explain *interference and *polarized light. The wave theory, supported in the 19th century by Augustin Fresnel (1788–1827) and Jean Foucault (1819–68), adequately explains these phenomena and achieved a mathematical basis when *Maxwell showed that light is a form of electromagnetic radiation. The wave theory, however, does not explain the photoelectric effect and *Einstein reverted to a form of the corpuscular theory in using the *quantum theory to postulate that in some cases light is best regarded as consisting of energy quanta called photons. The present view, expressing Bohr's concept of complementarity, is that both electromagnetic theory and quantum theory are needed to explain light.

light-emitting diode *See* SEMICONDUCTOR DIODE.

lighthouse A tall structure, built on a coastal promontory or cape or on an island at sea, equipped with a powerful beacon, visible at some distance, to mark an obstruction or other hazard. Modern lighthouses are also equipped with radio beacons. Both light and radio signals are emitted in a unique pattern to enable vessels to identify the lighthouse producing them.

lightning An electrical discharge in the atmosphere caused by the build up of electrical charges in a cloud. The potential difference causing the discharge may be as high as one thousand million volts. The electricity then discharges itself in a lightning flash, which may be between the cloud and the ground or, much more commonly, between two clouds or parts of a cloud. Thunder is the noise made by the discharge or its reverberations. *See also* BALL LIGHTNING.

lightning conductor An earthed conducting rod placed at the top of buildings, etc., to protect them from damage by lightning. It acts by providing a low-resistance path to earth for the lightning current.

light year A unit of distance, used in astronomy, equal to the distance travelled by light in one year. 1 light year = 9.46×10^{15} metres or 5.88×10^{12} miles.

lignin A complex chemical deposited in plant cell walls to add extra strength and support. It is the main constituent of *wood cells, allowing the trunk to support the heavy crown of leaves and branches.

lignum vitae Wood from trees of the genus *Guaiacum*, especially *G. officinale*, a tropical evergreen of the New World. Lignum vitae is hard, dense, greenish-brown, and rich in fat (making it waterproof). It was formerly thought to have medicinal properties: its name (from the Latin) means "wood of life." Family: *Zygophyllaceae*.

Liguria A region in NW Italy. It consists of a narrow strip of land between the Apennines and Maritime Alps in the N and the Gulf of Genoa in the S. Industry (including shipbuilding and engineering) and tourism are both important, the region more or less corresponding to the Italian Riviera. Area: 5415 sq km (2091 sq mi). Population (2000 est): 1 625 870. Capital: Genoa.

Ligurian Sea A section of the NW Mediterranean Sea, between Italy (N of Elba) and Corsica.

lilac A deciduous bush or small tree of the genus *Syringa* (30 species), especially *S. vulgaris*, native to temperate Eurasia and often grown as a garden ornamental. It has dense terminal clusters of white, purple, or pink tubular fragrant flowers with four flaring lobes. Family: *Oleaceae*.

Liliaceae A family of monocotyledonous plants (about 250 species), mostly herbaceous and native to temperate and subtropical regions. They usually grow from bulbs or rhizomes to produce six-lobed flowers and three-chambered capsular fruits. The family includes many popular garden plants, including the lilies, tulip, and hyacinth. A few are economically important, for example *Asparagus*. Some authorities include related plants, such as the onion, leek, etc. (*see* ALLIUM), *Agave*, and *Yucca*.

Lille 50 39N 3 05E A city in N France, the capital of the Nord department on the River Deûle. It is at the centre of a large industrial complex. Population (1999): 182 228.

Lilongwe 13 58S 33 49E The capital of Malawi since 1975. Population (1998 est): 435 964.

lily A perennial herbaceous plant of the genus *Lilium* (80–100 species), native to N temperate regions and widely grown for ornament. Lilies grow from bulbs to produce leafy stems with terminal clusters of showy flowers, usually with backward-curving petals. Some popular species are the tiger lily (*L. tigrinum*), from China and Japan, 60–120 cm high with purple-spotted golden flowers; the Eurasian Madonna lily (*L. candida*), 60–120 cm high with pure-white flowers; and the turk's-cap or martagon lily (*L. martagon*), also from Eurasia, 90–150 cm high, the purplish-pink flowers of which are marked with darker spots. There are numerous varieties and hybrids of these and other species. Family: *Liliaceae*.

The name is also applied to numerous other unrelated plants, such as the *arum lily and *leopard lily.

lily-of-the-valley A fragrant perennial herbaceous plant, *Convallaria majalis*, native to Eurasia and E North America and a popular garden plant. Growing from creeping underground stems (rhizomes), its stem bears a cluster of white nodding bell-shaped flowers. Family: *Liliaceae*.

Lima 12 06S 77 03W The capital of Peru, situated in the E of the country near its Pacific port of Callao. Founded by Pizarro in 1535, it became the main base of Spanish power in Peru. Notable buildings include the 16th-century cathedral and university. Lima has expanded rapidly in recent years and now has considerable industry. Population (1998): 316 322.

Lima bean A herb, *Phaseolus lunatus*, also called butter bean or Madagascar bean, native to South America but widely cultivated in the tropics and subtropics as a source of protein. It is easily stored when dry. Family: *Leguminosae*.

Limassol 34 40N 33 03E A town in Cyprus, on the S coast. It is the island's second largest town and a major port. Population (1998 est): 152 900.

Limavady A district in Northern Ireland, in Co Londonderry. Area: 558 sq km (226 sq mi). Population (2001): 32 422.

Limburg 1. A former duchy in W Europe, divided in 1839 between Belgium and the Netherlands. **2.** (French name: Limbourg) A province in NE Belgium, bordering on the Netherlands. The N is an industrial region and the S is chiefly agricultural. Area: 2422 sq km (935 sq mi). Population (2000 est): 1 019 442. Capital: Hasselt. **3.** A province in the SE Netherlands. Coalmining has declined in recent years. Agriculture is varied. Area: 2208 sq km (852 sq mi). Population (2000 est): 1 141 200. Capital: Maastricht.

lime (botany) **1.** A large deciduous tree of the genus *Tilia* (about 30 species), also called linden. Growing to a height of 30 m, it has toothed heart-shaped leaves and fragrant pale-yellow flowers that hang in small clusters on a long winged stalk. The small round fruits remain attached to the papery wing when shed. Family: *Tiliaceae*. **2.** A tree, *Citrus aurantifolia*, growing to a height of about 4 m and cultivated in the tropics for its fruit. Lime fruits have a thick greenish-yellow skin and acid-tasting pulp; the juice is used to flavour food and drinks.

lime (chemistry) Calcium oxide (*or* quicklime; CaO), calcium hydroxide (*or* slaked lime; $Ca(OH)_2$), or, loosely, calcium salts in general. $Ca(OH)_2$ is prepared by reacting CaO with water and is used in *cement. CaO is used in making paper, as a *flux in *steel manufacture, and in softening water.

limerick A short form of comic and usually bawdy verse having five lines of three or two feet and usually rhyming aabba, as in:

> There was a young lady of Lynn
> Who was so uncommonly thin
> That when she essayed
> To drink lemonade,
> She slipped through the straw and fell in.

The form, the origin of which is uncertain, was popularized by Edward *Lear in the 19th century.

Limerick **1.** 52 40N 8 38W A port in the Republic of Ireland, the county town of Co Limerick on the Shannon estuary. Population (2002): 54 058. **2.** A county in the SW Republic of Ireland, in Munster bordering on the River Shannon estuary. It consists chiefly of lowlands rising to hills in the S. Dairy farming is important. Area: 2686 sq km (1037 sq mi). Population (2002): 175 479. County town: Limerick.

limestone A common sedimentary rock consisting largely of carbonates, especially calcium carbonate (calcite) or dolomite. Most limestones were deposited in the sea in warm clear water, but some limestones were formed in fresh water. Organic limestones, including *chalk, consist of fossil skeletal material. Precipitated limestones include evaporites and *oolites (spherically grained calcite). Clastic limestones consist of fragments of pre-existing limestones. Marble is metamorphosed limestone. Limestone is used as a building stone, in the manufacture of cement and glass, for agricultural lime, for road metal, and as a flux in smelting.

limited liability The restriction of a shareholder's obligation to meet company debts in the event of its insolvency. The Companies Act allows the formation of corporations the liability of whose shareholders is restricted either to the nominal amount of their shares ("company limited by shares") or to the amount that they have respectively undertaken to contribute if the company is wound up ("company limited by guarantee").

Limoges 45 50N 1 15E A city in W France, the capital of the Haute-Vienne department on the River Vienne. The centre of the French porcelain industry, it has Roman remains and a cathedral (13th–16th centuries). Population (1999): 133 960.

limpet A marine *gastropod mollusc with a flattened shell and powerful muscular foot for clinging to rocks and other surfaces. The true limpets (superfamily *Patellacea*; about 400 species) are oval-shaped and up to 10 cm long whereas the keyhole limpets (superfamily *Fissurellacea*; several hundred species) have an opening in the shell for expelling wastes and tend to be smaller.

Limpopo River A river in SE Africa. Rising as the Crocodile River in the Witwatersrand, South Africa, it flows generally NE through Mozambique, to the Indian Ocean, forming part of the border between the Transvaal and Botswana. Length: 1770 km (1100 mi).

Lincoln 53 14N 0 33W A city in E central England, the administrative centre of Lincolnshire on the River Witham. The British settlement became Lindum Colonia under the Romans, at the intersection of the important routeways Fosse Way and Ermine Street. The castle was begun in 1068 and the cathedral in 1075. Population (1991): 80 281.

Lincoln, Abraham (1809–65) US statesman; Republican president (1861–65). Lincoln became, in 1847, member of Congress for Illinois. Holding long-standing convictions against slavery, he opposed its extension to the new western states and in 1856 joined the newly formed antislavery Republican Party. Elected president on the slavery issue just before the outbreak of the *Civil War, in 1863 Lincoln proclaimed the freedom of slaves in the South (the Emancipation Proclamation) and gave his famous *Gettysburg Address recalling the principles of equality established by America's founding fathers. He oversaw the 13th amendment prohibiting slavery (1865) and advocated magnanimous *Reconstruction measures but was assassinated a few days after the South surrendered.

Lincolnshire A county in E England, bordering on the North Sea. It is generally low lying, including part of the Fens, with the Lincolnshire Edge (a limestone escarpment) in the W and the Lincolnshire Wolds in the E. It is mainly agricultural producing arable crops and livestock; horticulture is also important. In 1974 it lost the N part to Humberside; when Humberside was abolished in 1996, this area was returned to Lincolnshire for ceremonial purposes but is now administered by the unitary authorities of North Lincolnshire and North East Lincolnshire. Area (excluding unitary authorities): 5880 sq km (2270 sq mi). Population (2001, excluding unitary authorities): 646 646. Administrative centre: Lincoln.

Lind, Jenny (1820–87) Swedish soprano, known as "the Swedish nightingale." She performed in opera and on the concert platform.

Lindbergh, Charles A(ugustus) (1902–74) US aviator who made the first solo nonstop flight across the Atlantic Ocean, from New York to Paris (1927), in the monoplane *Spirit of St Louis*. His two-year-old son was kidnapped and murdered in 1932.

Lindemann, Frederick Alexander, 1st Viscount Cherwell (1886–1957) German-born British physicist, who became Churchill's scientific adviser in World War II. Criticized for advocating mass bombing of civilians, Lindemann was highly praised by Churchill, who made him paymaster-general (1951–53).

Lindisfarne *See* HOLY ISLAND.

Linear A A syllabic script used (c. 1700–1450 BC) to write the lost language of the *Minoan civilization of Crete. It evolved from a pictographic script. Known from fewer than 400 inscriptions, it is still undeciphered, but, like its successor, *Linear B, was mainly used on clay tablets to record inventories.

linear accelerator (*or* **linac**) An *accelerator in which charged elementary particles are repeatedly accelerated along a long straight tube by a radio-frequency electric field. In modern linear accelerators the field is supplied by the electric component of a travelling radio wave in a waveguide. The particles are confined in the tube by a series of magnetic lenses, which focus the beam. The maximum energy attained by a linear accelerator is about 10 GeV for electrons and 2 GeV for protons.

Linear B A syllabic script apparently adapted (c. 1450–1400 BC) from *Linear A by the invading Mycenaeans at *Knossos to write their own language. In 1952 Michael Ventris (1922–56) deciphered this language as an early form of Greek. Several thousand Linear B clay tablets, mainly inventories, survive from Knossos, Pylos, and elsewhere, dating between about 1400 and 1100 BC.

linear motor A form of electric induction motor in which the stator and the rotor are linear instead of cylindrical and parallel instead of coaxial. The development of linear motors as a method of traction for monorail intercity trains has been proposed by E. R. Laithwaite (1921–89). In this arrangement one winding would be in the train and the other on the single rail, thus obviating the need for rotating parts.

linen A fabric manufactured from *flax (*Linum usitatissimum*), probably the first textile of plant origin. Flax growing was brought to Britain by the Romans and in the 16th century a flourishing trade grew up, especially in Scotland and Northern Ireland. Greatly reduced by the 18th-century expansion of the cotton trade, and even more so by the advent of man-made fibres, these strong absorbent fibres now constitute less than 2% of world fibre production.

line of force *See* FIELD.

linguistics The scientific study of language. Modern linguistics has three main branches, corresponding to the three main components of language: *semantics, grammar, and *phonetics. Various specialized interests exist within the field of linguistics. **Comparative linguistics** compares languages either to establish the history of and relationships among related languages (e.g. the Indo-European family) or to test theories about linguistic universals by comparing unrelated languages (*see also* ETYMOLOGY). The main contribution of **structural linguistics**, which developed in the early 20th century, was to free linguistics from the historical and comparative approach, viewing language as a unique relational structure. **Sociolinguistics** deals with social aspects of language, including such matters as how language affects and reflects the role and status of individuals within the community, attitudes to dialect and "correctness," linguistic taboos and preferences, bilingualism, etc. **Psycholinguistics** is the comparatively recent branch of linguistics that deals with psychological aspects of language, including how children acquire language, how language is stored in and generated by the brain, the relationship between meaning and memory, etc.

Linnaeus, Carolus (Carl Linné; 1707–78) Swedish botanist, who established the principles for naming and classifying plants and animals. As a result of his botanical studies, Linnaeus proposed a system for classifying plants based on their flower parts. He published *Systema naturae* in 1735 followed by *Genera plantarum* (1737) and *Species plantarum* (1753). In his system, Linnaeus defined each type of plant by two names: a generic name and a specific name (*see* BINOMIAL NOMENCLATURE). Furthermore he grouped related genera into classes and combined related classes into orders. Linnaeus also applied his system to the animal kingdom.

linnet A small Eurasian *finch, *Acanthis cannabina*, occurring in dry open regions, where it feeds on the seeds of common weed plants. The female has a dull brown-streaked plumage; the male has a crimson crown and breast, a greyish head, and a red-brown back with darker wings and tail. Male linnets have a beautiful flutelike voice.

linseed The flat oval seed of cultivated *flax, which is a source of linseed oil, used in paints, inks, varnishes, oilcloth, and sailcloth. The crushed seed residues form linseed meal, an important protein feed for ruminants and pigs.

Linz 48 19N 14 18E The third largest city in Austria, the capital of Upper Austria on the River Danube. Its many historical buildings include two 13th-century baroque churches. Population (2001): 186 298.

lion A large carnivorous mammal *Panthera leo*, one of the big *cats. Lions are found mainly in Africa (there are a few in India). They are heavily built with sandy-coloured coats: the shaggy-maned males grow to 2.8 m while females lack a mane and are more lightly built. Both sexes have a thin tail with a tuft at the end. Lions inhabit grasslands, living in groups (prides).

Lions, Gulf of (French name: Golfe du Lion) An inlet of the NW Mediterranean Sea, on the coast of central S France between Marseille and the Spanish border.

lipids A group of compounds, generally insoluble in water but soluble in organic solvents, that includes fats, *oils, waxes, phospholipids, sphingolipids, and *steroids. Fats and oils function as energy reserves in plants and animals and form a major source of dietary energy in animals. Phospholipids are important structural components of cell membranes, and sphingolipids are found predominantly in nerve tissues. Steroids have many important derivatives, including cholesterol, bile salts, and certain hormones. Lipids often occur in association with proteins as lipoproteins.

Lipizzaner A breed of horse long associated with the Spanish Riding School in Vienna, where they are trained for spectacular displays. It is named after the stud founded by Archduke Charles at Lipizza, near Trieste, in 1580. The Lipizzaner has a short back, strong hindquarters, a powerful neck, and a small head. Born black, they mature to a grey colour. Height: 1.47–1.52 m.

Lippershey, Hans (died c. 1619) Dutch lens grinder, who built the first *telescope. News of it eventually reached Galileo, who built his own telescope.

Lippi, Fra Filippo (c. 1406–69) An early Renaissance Florentine painter, who was a Carmelite monk from 1421 to about 1432. He was patronized by the Medici but his greatest works are his fresco decorations for the choir of Prato Cathedral (1452–64), showing scenes from the lives of St John the Baptist and St Stephen. He is also noted for his idealized Madonnas. He abducted and later married a nun, Lucrezia Buti; their son, **Filippino Lippi** (1457–1504), was also a painter.

liquefaction of gases Gases are liquefied in several ways. If the temperature of the gas is below its critical temperature (*see* CRITICAL STATE), it can be liquefied simply by compressing it. If the critical temperature is too low for this, the cascade process can be used. In this a gas with a high critical temperature is first liquefied by compression and then allowed to cool by evaporation under reduced pressure. This gas cools a second gas below its critical temperature, so that it in turn can be liquefied, evaporated, and cooled still further. Thus the temperature is reduced in stages. Other methods include cooling by the Joule-Kelvin effect and cooling by adiabatic expansion in which a compressed gas is cooled by performing external work.

liquefied petroleum gas (**LPG**) Propane, propene, butane, butene, or a mixture of any of these. LPG is a product of *oil refining and is also produced from *natural gas. Most of the LPG produced is sold for heating or used as a raw material for chemical manufacture.

liquid crystal A substance exhibiting some liquid properties, especially fluidity, and some crystalline properties, in that large clusters of molecules are aligned in parallel formations. As liquid crystals change their reflectivity when an electric potential is applied to them, they are used in electronic digital displays.

liquids A state of matter between that of *gases and the *solid state. Liquids assume the shape of a container in the same way as gases but being incompressible do not expand to fill the container. Intermolecular forces are considerably stronger than in gases but weaker than in solids. Molecules are only maintained in an orderly arrangement by intermolecular forces over relatively small groups of molecules.

liquorice A perennial herb, *Glycyrrhiza glabra*, native to S Europe but cultivated throughout warm temperate regions. It bears clusters of blue flowers and long flat pods and its sweet roots, up to 1 m long, are a source of flavouring. Family: *Leguminosae*.

Lisbon (Portuguese name: Lisboa) 38 44N 9 08W The capital of Portugal, in the SW on the River Tagus. The country's chief seaport, it has one of the finest harbours in Europe. Lisbon is also a major industrial and commercial centre. Historic buildings include the Tower of Belém and the Jerónimos Monastery; its university was founded in 1290. *History*: a settlement from very early times, it was an organized community under the Roman Empire. It was captured by the Portuguese in the 12th century and became their capital in 1256. It flourished in the 15th and 16th centuries, the great age of Portuguese exploration and colonization, but later suffered a decline. In 1755 it was almost totally destroyed by an earthquake. It has expanded considerably in the 20th century and in 1966 one of the world's longest suspension bridges was opened across the River Tagus. Population (2001, urban area): 3 754 000.

Lisburn A district in Northern Ireland, in Co Antrim and Co Down. Area: 436 sq km (168 sq mi). Population (2001): 108 694.

Lister, Joseph, 1st Baron (1827–1912) British surgeon, who pioneered antiseptic techniques in surgery. In 1865, while surgeon at Glasgow Royal Infirmary, Lister realized the significance of Pasteur's germ theory of disease in trying to prevent the infection of wounds following surgery. Lister devised a means of eliminating contamination and introduced carbolic acid as an antiseptic to dress wounds. His antiseptic procedures eventually became standard practice in hospitals everywhere.

Listeria A genus of rod-shaped bacteria. The single species, *L. monocytogenes*, is a parasite of warm-blooded animals. On transmission to man, especially through eating unpasteurized cheese or yogurt, it may cause **listeriosis**, with symptoms ranging from mild food poisoning to meningitis; in pregnant women it usually results in termination of the pregnancy.

Liszt, Franz (Ferencz L.; 1811–86) Hungarian pianist and composer, considered the greatest performer of his time. As a composer he invented the symphonic poem and made use of advanced harmonies and original forms. His compositions include much piano music (including a sonata in B minor and operatic paraphrases), the *Faust Symphony* (1854–57) and *Dante Symphony* (1855–56), and the symphonic poem *Les Préludes* (1854).

litchi (**lychee** *or* **lichee**) A Chinese tree, *Litchi chinensis*, cultivated in the tropics and subtropics for its fruits. The fruit is almost globular with a warty deep-pink rind and is borne in branched clusters. The white translucent watery flesh has a sweet acid flavour and encloses a single large brown seed. Family: *Sapindaceae*.

lithium (Li) The lightest metal (relative density 0.534), discovered by Arfvedson in 1817. It is an alkali metal. It occurs in nature in various minerals as well as in brine, from which it is extracted commercially by electrolysis of the molten chloride (LiCl). The metal has the highest specific heat capacity of any solid element. It is corrosive, combustible, and reacts with water. Because of its efficiency in reflecting neutrons, lithium has important applications as a blanketing material in both the hydrogen bomb and proposed *thermonuclear reactors. It forms salts, like the other alkali metals, and the hydride LiH. At no 3; at wt 6.941; mp 180.6°C; bp 1342°C.

lithography *See* PRINTING.

Lithuania, Republic of A country in NE Europe, on the Baltic Sea. Most of Lithuania comprises a fertile lowland with forests and peat reserves. Lithuanians comprise about 80% of the population. *Economy*: there are textile, petrochemical, and metalworking industries. Livestock breeding and forestry are important. Tourism is being developed. *History*: one of the largest states in medieval Europe, in the 14th century Lithuania united with Poland under the Jagiellon dynasty. After the partition of Poland in the 18th century it passed to Russia.

It became independent in 1918 but was incorporated into the Soviet Union as an SSR in 1940. It was occupied by Germany during World War II, during which the large Jewish minority was virtually exterminated. It achieved independence from the Soviet Union in 1991. The former communist leader Algirdas Brazauskas was president from 1992 to 1998 and prime minister from 2002. In April 2004 President Rolandas Paksas was impeached by parliament owing to his alleged links with organized crime in Russia. Lithuania joined the EU and NATO in 2004. Official language: Lithuanian. Currency: litas of 100 centas. Area: 65 200 sq km (25 170 sq mi). Population (2003 est): 3 454 000. Capital: Vilnius.

Lithuanian A language belonging to the E division of the Baltic languages division of the Indo-European family, spoken in Lithuania, where it is the official language. Lithuanian is closely related to *Latvian. It is written in a Latin alphabet.

litmus A soluble compound obtained from certain lichens. Litmus turns red in an acid solution and blue in an alkaline solution. It is therefore used as an *indicator, often in the form of **litmus paper**, strips of paper impregnated with litmus.

litre A unit of volume in the *metric system formerly defined as the volume of one kilogram of pure water under specified conditions. This definition still applies for purposes of the UK Weights and Measures Act (1963), but in *SI units the litre is a special name for the cubic decimetre.

Little Bighorn, Battle of the (25 June 1876) The battle fought on the S bank of the Little Bighorn River in which Gen *Custer and his men were massacred by Sioux Indians led by Crazy Horse (?1849–77) and *Sitting Bull (Custer's Last Stand). It was fought to seize the American West for White settlement.

liver A large glandular organ, weighing 1.2–1.6 kg, situated in the upper right region of the abdomen, just below the diaphragm. The liver has many important functions concerned with the utilization of absorbed foods. It converts excess glucose into glycogen, which it stores and reconverts into glucose when required; it breaks down excess amino acids into *urea; and it stores and metabolizes fats. The liver forms and secretes *bile, which contains the breakdown products of worn-out red blood cells, and synthesizes blood-clotting factors, plasma proteins, and—in the fetus—red blood cells. It also breaks down (detoxifies) poisonous substances, including alcohol.

liver fluke A parasitic *flatworm that inhabits the bile duct of sheep, cattle, and man. The common liver fluke (*Fasciola hepatica*) passes its larval stages in a marshland snail before infecting grazing animals (or, rarely, humans). The Chinese liver fluke (*Opisthorchus sinensis*), 1–2 cm long, passes two larval stages in a freshwater snail and fish before maturing in a human host.

Liverpool **1.** 53 25N 2 55W A major city in NW England, in Liverpool unitary authority, Merseyside, on the estuary of the River Mersey. It is the UK's second most important port but has recently suffered industrial decline. Notable buildings include the Royal Liver Building (1910) and the Roman Catholic cathedral (1962–67). *History*: originally trading with Ireland, Liverpool grew rapidly in the 18th and 19th centuries as a result of trade with the Americas and the industrialization of S Lancashire. Britain's first wet dock was built here in 1709. Liverpool is also a cultural centre, with the Walker Art Gallery (built 1876), and the Tate Gallery (opened 1988). Population (1994 est): 474 000. **2.** A unitary authority in NW England, in Merseyside. Area: 113 sq km (44 sq mi). Population (2001): 439 476.

Liverpool, Robert Banks Jenkinson, 2nd Earl of (1770–1828) British statesman; Tory prime minister (1812–27). He was previously foreign secretary (1801–04), home secretary (1807–09), and secretary for war (1809–12). As prime minister he is mainly remembered for his repressive response to the unrest that followed the Napoleonic Wars (*see* PETERLOO MASSACRE).

liverwort A *bryophyte plant of the phylum *Hepatophyta* (c. 6000 species), found growing on moist soil, rocks, trees, etc. There are two groups: leafy liverworts, in which the plant body is differentiated into stems and leaves; and thallose liverworts, which have a flat lobed liverlike body (thallus). The liverwort plant is the gamete-producing phase (gametophyte) and gives rise to a capsule, the spore-producing phase (sporophyte).

livery companies Descendants of the medieval craft *guilds, so called because of the distinctive dress (livery) worn by their members on ceremonial occasions. Some occupy notable buildings in the City of London and some, such as the Mercers, Haberdashers, and Merchant Taylors, have educational interests. In 1878 the livery companies joined the Corporation of the City of London in setting up the City and Guilds of London Institute to promote technical education.

livestock farming (*or* **animal husbandry**) The maintenance and management of domesticated animals for the production of milk, meat, eggs, fibres, skins, etc. Modern improvements in livestock breeds and husbandry techniques have enabled dramatic increases to be made in productivity, nutrition and disease control being essential aspects of management.

Cattle produce milk and beef. Under European conditions, a cow may breed at any time of the year. The gestation period is about 9 months, followed by about 10 months of lactation and a 2-month dry period before calving again. A cow is known as a heifer until her second lactation. Heifers are reared either for beef or as dairy replacements and bull calves are generally castrated and reared for beef, being known as bullocks or steers. Age at slaughter is generally about 18 months. Calves for veal are slaughtered at about 14 weeks.

Sheep are farmed worldwide for meat and wool (and in some countries for milk), often grazing on poor mountainous or arid pastures. Under European conditions, the one or two lambs per ewe are born in early spring. Males are castrated and reared for slaughter at weights of 20–45 kg. Selected females are reared as replacement ewes. Each sheep yields 2–5 kg of wool.

Pigs in modern intensive systems are housed under controlled conditions. Young females (gilts) are first mated at 7–8 months. Following the gestation period of 115 days, an average of 7–9 piglets are born per litter. Pork pigs are slaughtered at 40–50 kg, those reared for bacon at 80–100 kg.

Poultry are now kept indoors in an artificially controlled environment. Chicks are hatched artificially, the female birds starting to lay after about 20 weeks and producing about 250 eggs per year. Laying flocks are kept in "batteries" of cages with 3–5 birds per cage, feeding, cleaning, and egg collection being automatic. Table birds are fed ad lib and reach a weight of around 2 kg in 8–12 weeks. Turkeys are also reared for meat under intensive conditions. *See also* FACTORY FARMING.

Livingstone, David (1813–73) Scottish missionary and explorer of Africa, qualified as a physician. He traced long stretches of the Zambezi, Shire, and Rovuma Rivers, and was the first European to see Lake Ngami (1849), the Victoria Falls (1855), and Lake Nyasa (now Malawi). During an attempt to trace the source of the Nile (1866–73) his famous encounter with Sir Henry Morton *Stanley occurred.

Livingstone, Ken (Kenneth Robert L.; 1945–) British politician; mayor of London (2000–). He became famous as the left-wing Labour leader of the Greater London Council (1981–86). In 2000 he was narrowly defeated in a ballot to decide Labour's candidate for the mayor of London but stood successfully as an independent. In 2003 he introduced a congestion charge to reduce traffic in central London. He won a second term of office in the mayoral elections of 2004, standing as the Labour candidate.

Livy (Titus Livius; 59 BC–17 AD) Roman historian, noted for his monumental history of Rome from its legendary foundation to the death of Drusus in 9 BC. Only 35 of the original 142 books survive.

lizard A *reptile belonging to the suborder *Sauria* (3000 species), occurring worldwide but most abundant in tropical regions. They are mainly terrestrial with cylindrical or narrow scaly long-tailed bodies, some with limbs reduced or absent (*see* GLASS SNAKE; SKINK), and often with crests, spines, and frills. They range in size from the smallest *geckos to the *Komodo dragon. Lizards lay leathery-shelled eggs although certain species of colder regions and many skinks bear live young.

Ljubljana (German name: Laibach) 46 04N 14 30E The capital of Slovenia, situated in the W of the country. Under foreign rule until 1918, it is the centre of Slovene culture. It was largely destroyed by an earthquake in 1895. Population (2000 est): 270 986.

llama A hoofed mammal, *Lama glama*, of S and W South America. Up to 120 cm high at the shoulder, llamas are sure-footed, nimble, and hardy, with thick warm coats. They are now only found in the domesticated state, being used for meat, wool, and as pack animals. Family: *Camelidae* (camels, etc.).

llanos The treeless grasslands of South America that cover about 570 000 sq km (220 000 sq mi) of central Venezuela and N Colombia. Drained by the River Orinoco and its tributaries, the llanos are traditionally a cattle-rearing region but the discovery of oil in the 1930s led to considerable population growth and economic development.

Lloyd, Harold (1893–1971) US film comedian. He appeared as a dogged little man in numerous early silent comedies, most of them characterized by his use of dangerous stunts. His films include *Just Nuts* (1915), *Safety Last* (1923), and *The Freshman* (1925).

Lloyd, Marie (Matilda Wood; 1870–1922) British music-hall entertainer. Her songs, characterized by cockney humour, include "Oh! Mr Porter" and "A Little of What You Fancy."

Lloyd George, David, 1st Earl (1863–1945) British statesman; Liberal prime minister (1916–22). Born in Manchester of Welsh parents, he entered parliament in 1890 and gained a reputation for radicalism as a Welsh nationalist and a supporter of the Afrikaners in the second Boer War (1899–1902). As chancellor of the exchequer (1908–15), he is best known for the so-called People's Budget (1909). This proposed higher death duties, a land value tax, and a supertax; the rejection of this budget by the House of Lords led ultimately to the 1911 Parliament Act, which removed the Lords' veto power. Lloyd George also introduced old-age pensions (1908) and national insurance (1911). In World War I he served as minister of munitions (1915–16) and secretary for war (1916) before succeeding Asquith as prime minister. After the war he continued to lead a coalition government increasingly dominated by the Conservatives. He was criticized for negotiating with Irish militants in the establishment of the Irish Free State (1921) and his government fell when Britain came close to war with the Turkish nationalists. He resigned his parliamentary seat in 1945 on being created an earl.

Lloyd's An association of *insurance underwriters named after the 17th-century London coffee house, owned by Edward Lloyd, where underwriters used to meet. Lloyd's was incorporated by Act of Parliament in 1871. The corporation itself does not underwrite insurance business, which is all undertaken by syndicates of private underwriters, who are wholly responsible for losses. From 1994 private underwriters will include limited companies. There are over 6000 underwriters, none of whom are permitted to deal with the public, all insurance policies with the public being transacted by Lloyd's insurance brokers. **Lloyd's Register of Shipping** is an organization formed by Lloyd's to inspect and list all oceangoing vessels over 100 tonnes. The *Register* gives annual reports on these ships as a result of checks by Lloyd's surveyors. Lloyd's also publishes *Lloyd's List and Shipping Gazette*, giving shipping news for insurance purposes.

Lloyd Webber, Andrew, Baron (1948–) British composer. His earlier musicals, with lyrics by Sir Tim Rice (1944–), included *Joseph and the Amazing Technicolour Dreamcoat* (1968), *Jesus Christ Superstar* (1970), and *Evita* (1978); later works include *Cats* (1981), *The Phantom of the Opera* (1986), and *The Beautiful Game* (2000). He was raised to the peerage in 1997.

Llywelyn ap Gruffudd (Llywelyn II; d. 1282) The only native Prince of Wales (1258–82) to be recognized as such by England. He aided the English barons against Henry III (1263–67) and refused homage to Edward I (1276), who forced Llywelyn into submission. Llywelyn was killed in another revolt.

loach A small freshwater *bony fish of the family *Cobitidae* (over 200 species), found mainly in Asia, but also in Europe and N Africa. Loaches feed at night on bottom-dwelling invertebrates detected by the three to six pairs of barbels around the mouth. Order: *Cypriniformes*.

Lobelia A genus of annual and perennial herbs (about 250 species), found in most warm and temperate regions. The flowers are tubular, with a two-lobed upper lip and a larger three-lobed lower lip. Ornamental species, called cardinal flowers, are usually blue or red. Family: *Lobeliaceae*.

lobotomy *See* LEUCOTOMY.

lobster A large marine *crustacean of the section *Macrura* that has a long abdomen ending in a tailfan. True lobsters (family *Homaridae*) have segmented bodies, a pair of pincers, four pairs of walking legs, and several pairs of swimming legs (swimmerets). They live on the ocean bottom, feeding on seaweed and animals. Many species are important as food, for example *Homarus vulgaris* and *H. americanus*. Order: *Decapoda*.

local government The administration of a locality. In the UK local government has developed from the Anglo-Saxon division of the country into shires, hundreds, and *boroughs but only became systematized in the 19th century. The Municipal Corporation Act (1835) established 178 municipal councils, elected by ratepayers, which in the following decades grew in number and took over a wide range of responsibilities, including the police and public health. County councils were established in 1888. In 1894 the work of local government was distributed by the creation of borough and urban district councils in urban areas and parish councils in rural areas. The Local Government Act (1972; effective 1974) divided England and Wales into 53 *counties. These were divided into districts, and they in turn into parishes or, in Wales, communities. District councils were responsible for a number of important services, including education, housing, and refuse collection. A similar system was established in Scotland in 1973 (effective 1975). Northern Ireland has 26 district councils. In 1996–98 unitary authorities were established to replace the two-tier system of county and district councils in many parts of the UK, including the whole of Scotland and Wales. Local-government spending is financed by the *council tax, business rates, rent, borrowing, and central-government grants.

Locarno Pact (1925) A series of treaties between Germany, France, Belgium, Poland, Czechoslovakia, the UK, and Italy, signed in the Swiss town of Locarno. The most important was an agreement between France, Germany, and Belgium, guaranteed by the UK and Italy, to maintain the borders between Germany and France and Belgium respectively and the demilitarized zone of the Rhineland (violated by Hitler in 1936).

lock A section of a ship canal or a navigable river, enclosed by gates at both ends and with means to regulate the water level. This permits vessels to transfer between sections at different levels, making transshipment unnecessary.

Locke, John (1632–1704) English philosopher. His greatest work, the *Essay concerning Human Understanding* (1690), reveals him as a pioneer of empiricism. It maintains that every one of our ideas comes from sense impressions. Locke's two works *Of Government* (1690) were enormously influential in moulding modern concepts of liberal democracy. He dismissed any divine right to kingship and advocated liberal government.

locomotive An engine that draws a train on a railway. The first locomotives, designed by Trevithick and *Stephenson, were driven by steam engines and steam dominated the railways until the end of World War II. Thousands of steam locomotives are still in use throughout the world. However, the steam engine has a low efficiency (about 8% in a locomotive, which does not use a condenser), it takes a long time to become operational while steam is raised, it uses an awkward and dirty solid fuel (which it has to pull with it in a tender immediately behind the engine), and it creates pollution. For these reasons steam locomotives have largely been replaced in the industrial countries by electric, Diesel-electric, or Diesel trains, all of which have efficiencies of about 22%.

Where the traffic justifies the cost of installing overhead wires or a conductor rail, electric trains are usually preferred, as it is more efficient to generate electricity centrally than in the locomotive. Series-wound direct-current motors are the most widely used, with rectification in the locomotive when the supply is alternating current. When Diesel engines are used, these are either coupled hydraulically to the wheels, using a hydraulic torque converter (or fluid flywheel) and a gearbox, or to an electric generator or alternator, which produces current to power electric motors that drive the wheels. The first Diesel-electric train was used in Sweden in 1912 and the first Diesel-hydraulic in Germany a year later. Because the Diesel provides a very low torque at low speeds, it cannot be used without a hydraulic coupling, but even these units are usually restricted to small trains. *See also* MAGNETIC LEVITATION.

locust (botany) An evergreen Mediterranean tree, *Ceratonia siliqua*, also called carob tree. 12–15 m in height, it produces leathery pods containing a sweet edible pulp and small flat beans. The black locust (*Robinia pseudoacacia*), also called false acacia, is a North American tree widely cultivated for ornament. Up to 24 m tall, it has deeply ridged dark-brown bark, hanging clusters of white flowers, and black pods. Family: *Leguminosae*.

locust (zoology) A *grasshopper that, when environmental conditions are favourable, undergoes sporadic increases in population size to form huge swarms, which migrate long distances and devour all the crops and other veg-

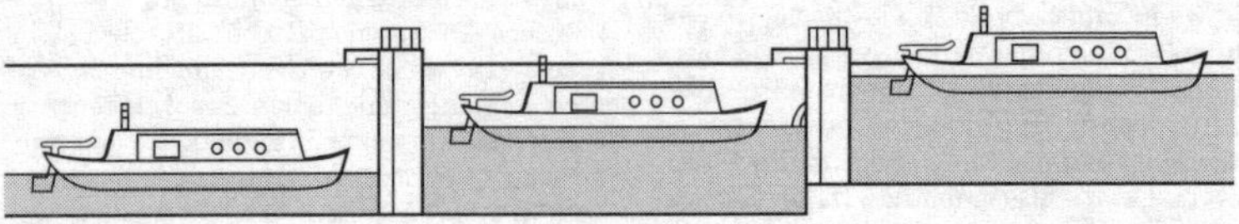

Vessel about to enter lock. Vessel being raised inside lock. Vessel emerging from lock at higher level.

lock

Stephenson's "Rocket" The first locomotive to combine a multi-tubular boiler and a blast pipe, the "Rocket" was designed for the Liverpool to Manchester railway, which opened in 1830.

"General" Typical of the commonest type of US locomotive in the 19th century, the "General" was involved in a dramatic sabotage incident in 1862 during the Civil War. One of this class was the first to run at 100 mph (1893).

C.R. No. 123 Caledonian Railway's famous locomotive, designed by Dugald Drummond, ran the difficult 100.6 miles between Carlisle and Edinburgh in 102.5 minutes in August 1888.

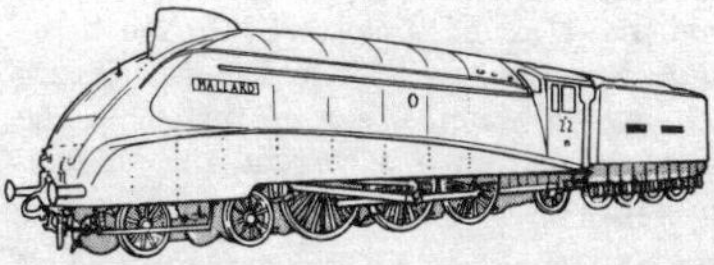

"Mallard" This locomotive, designed by Sir Nigel Gresley, took the world steam traction speed record in July 1938, achieving 126 mph on a brake-test run.

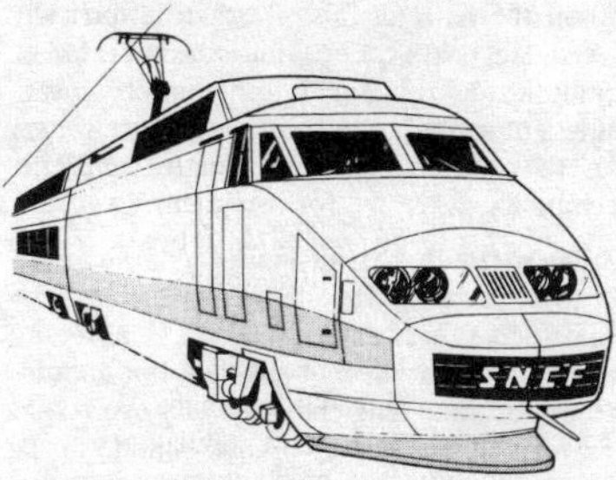

Train à Grande Vitesse (TGV) France's high-speed electric train, which runs on special rails. It established a world record for rail travel of 236 mph in 1981.

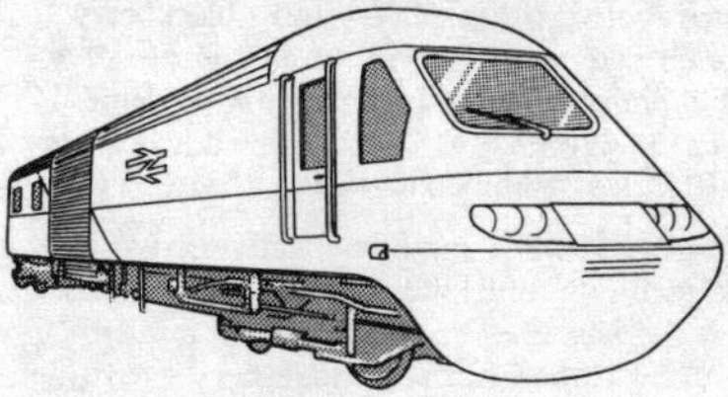

High Speed Train (HST) British Rail's Diesel-electric HST set a world record in1985 for Diesel-powered trains by reaching 144.8 mph. The HST continues to power long-distance services in the UK's privatized system.

locomotive

etation on which they settle. Economically important species include the migratory locust (*Locusta migratoria*), about 55 mm long, found throughout Africa and S Eurasia and eastward to Australia and New Zealand; and the desert locust (*Schistocerca gregaria*), occurring from N Africa to the Punjab.

Lodge, David (John) (1935–) British novelist. His comic novels lampooning academic life include *Changing Places* (1975), *Small World*

(1984), and *Nice Work* (1988); later novels include *Paradise News* (1991), *Therapy* (1995), and *Thinks*... (2001).

Łódź 51 49N 19 28E The second largest city in Poland. It developed during the 19th century and is now a leading industrial centre. Population (1999 est): 806 728.

loess A deposit consisting of wind-born dust from desert or vegetation-free areas at the margins of ice sheets. In Europe loess occurs in Germany, Belgium, and NE France. Deep well-drained soils develop from loess.

Loewe, Frederick (1904–88) Austrian composer of musical comedies, resident in the USA after 1924. He is famous for such musicals as *Brigadoon* (1947), *Paint Your Wagon* (1950), *My Fair Lady* (1956), *Gigi* (1958), and *Camelot* (1960), written with Alan *Lerner.

Lofoten Islands A chain of islands reaching from the coast of N Norway into the N Atlantic, N of the Arctic Circle. The fisheries are rich, but the waters are often turbulent. The fabled Maelstrom is a current, the Moskenstraumen, between two of the outer islands.

log An instrument used to measure a ship's speed through the water. Modern logs are usually propeller or pitot (dynamic pressure-sensing) designs. A logbook, or log for short, is also a ship's diary with notes on positions, etc.

Logan, Mount 60 31N 140 22W The highest mountain in Canada, in SW Yukon in the St Elias Mountains. Height: 6050 m (19 850 ft).

loganberry A bramble-like shrub that is a cross between a raspberry and a blackberry. It bears red fleshy berries, used for preserves, puddings, and wine. It is named after James H. Logan (1841–1928), who first grew it (in California) in 1881. Family: *Rosaceae*.

logarithms A mathematical function used to facilitate multiplication and division. Based on the law that $a^x \times a^y = a^{x+y}$, two numbers p and q can be multiplied together by writing them in the form $p = a^x$ and $q = a^y$ and then adding together the values of x and y (the exponents). x is called the logarithm of p to the base a, i.e. $x = \log_a p$. Pocket calculators have obviated the need for logarithms as a method of computation but they remain useful mathematical functions.

logic In the widest sense, the science of reasoned argument. As a mental discipline, it is concerned not so much with the application of argument in specific instances as with the general rules covering the construction of valid inferences. *Aristotle was the first to make a systematic study of the principles governing rational discourse (also called syllogism). His works were the sourcebooks for medieval logicians. After the Renaissance philosophers became increasingly aware of limitations in the Aristotelian approach. *Leibniz, for instance, was worried by the difference between the logical and grammatical structure of sentences; two grammatically identical sentences may be very different logically. Rules must therefore be found to formalize ordinary language in such a way as to make plain its underlying logical structure, before further rules for the construction of valid arguments can be drawn up. Since the 19th century formulation of such rules has become mainly the province of mathematicians. George *Boole and Gottlob *Frege were important pioneers in what is now called "mathematical logic" to differentiate it from the wider still current sense. *Russell, whose work had important repercussions for *set theory, called "logic...the youth of mathematics, and mathematics...the manhood of logic."

logical positivism A philosophical movement that arose from the *Vienna Circle in the 1920s. Influenced by Ernst Mach (1838–1916) and *Wittgenstein, it insisted that philosophy should be scientific, regarding it as an analytical (rather than a speculative) activity, the purpose of which was clarification of thought. Any assertion claiming to be factual has meaning only if its truth (or falsity) can be empirically tested. Metaphysical propositions and those of aesthetics and religion are consequently meaningless. A secondary goal of logical positivism was the analysis and unification of scientific terminology.

Lohengrin In *Arthurian legend, the son of Percival (Parzival). He champions a young noblewoman, Elsa of Brabant, whom he agrees to marry on condition that she does not enquire into his origins. When her curiosity overcomes her, he is taken back by his swan guide to the castle of the *Holy Grail, whence he came. The story was adapted by *Wagner in the opera *Lohengrin* (1850).

Loire, River The longest river in France. Rising in the Cévennes Mountains, it flows mainly W to the Bay of Biscay at St Nazaire, passing through Orléans, Tours, and Nantes. Its tributaries include the Allier, Vienne, and Maine. The Loire Valley is renowned for its vineyards and chateaux (Amboise, Blois, Chambord, Chaumont, Chenonceaux). It is linked by canal with the River Seine. Length: 1020 km (634 mi).

Loki In Norse mythology, a mischief-making giant with the ability to change his shape and sex, who lived among the gods until imprisoned in a cave for the murder of Balder. His offspring—Hel, the goddess of death, Jörmungandr, the evil serpent surrounding the earth, and Fenris, the wolf—are among the forces of evil, which he leads against the gods at doomsday (Ragnarök).

Lollards The followers of the English religious reformer *Wycliffe. Until his retirement from Oxford in 1378, the preaching of his doctrines was largely confined to the University. Thereafter his teachings were taken up by nonacademics, including merchants, lesser clergy, and a few members of Richard II's court. Henry IV's reign saw considerable repression of the Lollards culminating in the defeat in 1414 of the rebellion led by Sir John Oldcastle (c. 1378–1417). The movement then went underground and became increasingly proletarian. Many of its tenets were adopted by the early Protestants.

Lombardo, Pietro (c. 1438–1515) Italian sculptor and architect. Lombardo worked mainly in Venice, where he was the leading sculptor of his generation. He was frequently assisted by his two sons **Antonio Lombardo** (c. 1458–c. 1516) and **Tullio Lombardo** (c. 1460–1532).

Lombardy A region in N Italy, consisting mainly of mountains in the N and lowlands in the S. It is Italy's most industrialized region. Area: 23 834 sq km (9191 sq mi). Population (2000 est): 9 065 440. Capital: Milan.

Lomond, Loch The largest lake in Scotland, in E Strathclyde Region; it is about 38 km (24 mi) long and 8 km (5 mi) wide. In 2002 Loch Lomond and the Trossachs was designated Scotland's first national park.

London (Latin name: Londinium) 51 30N 0 10W The capital of the UK, in SE England on the River Thames. One of the six largest cities in the world, it comprises a succession of village communities.

London's financial hub is its original nucleus, the **City of London**, roughly a square mile on the N bank of the Thames between Blackfriars Bridge and Tower Bridge. London's **East End**, centring on the borough of Tower Hamlets, has long provided a home for successive immigrant groups. The **West End** comprises the district around Oxford Street (constructed in the 19th century) and is the city's shopping and entertainment centre. London's cultural life is outstanding, with a large number of art galleries, museums, theatres, concert halls, and educational institutions. London is administered (from 2000) by a two-tier system of local government consisting of a Greater London Assembly (with a directly elected mayor) and 32 London borough councils. The City is administered separately by the Corporation of the City of London.

Economy: the City of London is one of the world's greatest banking, commodity, shipping, and insurance centres: the *Bank of England is to be found in Threadneedle Street with the Stock Exchange nearby, while *Lloyd's is in Lime Street. London's commercial development depended to a large extent on its port. However, apart from Tilbury Docks, most of its port area has now been redeveloped for residential and commercial purposes, including Canary Wharf, the tallest building in London and one of the largest office developments in the world.

History: the Romans built London at the highest point at which the Thames could be forded and at the river's tidal limit—on what was later Cornhill and Ludgate Hill. During the reign of William the Conqueror the White Tower (*see* TOWER OF LONDON) was built. London prospered in the middle ages and the Church and the *guilds sponsored exceptional building programmes. Westminster Abbey dates from the 11th century, being largely rebuilt in the 13th century, when Southwark Cathedral was begun. To the 15th century belong the Guildhall and Lambeth Palace and to the 16th century, when London began to extend westwards, St James' Palace. The early Stuart period witnessed the great work of Inigo Jones, notably the Queen's House at Greenwich (1617–35) and the Banqueting Hall in Whitehall (1619–22). London's population was decimated by the Plague (1665) and much of its fabric was destroyed in the Fire of the following year. The greatest loss—Old St Paul's—was replaced by Wren, who was responsible for much of the work of reconstruction, including 49 new parish churches in the City. Many of London's finest squares were built in the late 17th and early 18th centuries; the early 19th century witnessed the work of Nash: Regent's Park and the terraces around it. The 19th century produced the *Palace of Westminster, the Law Courts, and such railway stations as St Pancras. London, especially the City and the East End, was seriously damaged by bomb attacks during World War II and subsequent rebuilding consisted largely of high-rise offices and flats, including the Barbican (1973) and the National Westminster building (1977). Recent development has been concentrated on the old docklands area. Area: 1580 sq km (610 sq mi). Population (2001): 7 172 036.

London, Jack (1876–1916) US novelist, best known for *The Call of the Wild* (1903). His other novels include *White Fang* (1906) and *Martin Eden* (1909).

London Bridge A bridge spanning the River Thames from the City of London to the borough of Southwark. Bridges on this site date back to Roman times. The stone bridge built between 1176 and 1209 had a drawbridge and was surmounted by shops and houses. It was replaced by a new bridge in the 1820s, designed by John Rennie (1761–1821). The present bridge was completed in 1973.

Londonderry (*or* **Derry**) **1.** 55 00N 7 19W A city and port in Northern Ireland, in Co Londonderry on the River Foyle. The City of London Corporation was granted Londonderry and the Irish Society established (1610) to administer it. In a famous siege (1688–89) it held out for 105 days against the forces of James II. Population (1991): 72 334. **2.** A historic county of N Northern Ireland on the Atlantic Ocean. In 1972 its administrative powers were devolved to the new district council of Coleraine, Derry, Limavady, and Magherafelt. Area: 2108 sq km (814 sq mi).

Long Beach 33 47N 118 06W A city and port in the USA, in California on San Pedro Bay. It is a major tourist centre. Population (2000): 461 522.

longbow A bow of straight-grained yew used from about 1400 to about 1600. Originally Welsh, longbows were up to 1.8 m (6 ft) long and could fire a 110 cm (37 in) arrow capable of piercing chainmail and some plate armour at 183 m (200 yd) every 10 seconds.

Longfellow, Henry Wadsworth (1807–82) US poet. He achieved enormous popularity with such narrative poems as *Evangeline* (1847) and *The Song of Hiawatha* (1855).

Longford (Irish name: Longphort) A county in the N central Republic of Ireland, in Leinster, chiefly low lying with areas of bog. Area: 1043 sq km (403 sq mi). Population (2002): 31 127. County town: Longford.

Long Island An island in the USA, in New York state separated from the mainland by Long Island Sound. Chiefly residential with many resorts, it contains the New York City boroughs of Brooklyn and Queens and the international John F. Kennedy Airport. Area: 4462 sq km (1723 sq mi).

longitude *See* LATITUDE AND LONGITUDE.

long jump A field event in athletics. Competitors sprint up a runway and leap into a sandpit from a take-off board. The competitor who makes the longest jump in three or six tries is the winner. World records: men: 8.95 m (1991) by Michael Powell (USA); women: 7.52 m (1988) by Galina Chistyakova (Soviet Union).

Longleat An English country house near Warminster, in Wiltshire, owned by the Marquess of Bath. Dating from 1572, Longleat typifies the Elizabethan style of architecture. The house and its grounds, originally laid out by Capability *Brown and now containing a lion safari park, are open to the public.

Long Parliament (1640–60) The parliament that was summoned by Charles I of England following his defeat in the second Bishops' War. In 1640 it impeached the king's ministers, the Earl of Strafford (1593–1641) and Archbishop *Laud, in 1641 expressed its grievances against Charles in the Grand Remonstrance, and in 1642 assumed control of the militia. Charles' rejection of its demands for reform (Nineteen Propositions) precipitated the outbreak of the Civil War. Its power declined as that of the *New Model Army increased and in 1648 it was purged of its moderate members. The remaining Rump Parliament was dismissed in 1653 by Oliver Cromwell, who established the *Protectorate. The Rump was reinstated in 1659 and the full membership of the Long Parliament was restored by Gen Monck (1608–70) in 1660. Shortly afterwards it dissolved itself, being replaced by the Convention Parliament, which effected the *Restoration.

longship A large sailing vessel equipped with a bank of oars on each side. Longships were used by Scandinavian maritime peoples until the mid-18th century. They had square sails and very high prows and were steered by a long tiller attached to a large rudder.

longsightedness (*or* **hypermetropia**) Inability to see close objects clearly, because the lens of the eye focuses light to a point behind the retina (light-sensitive layer). This is less common than shortsightedness among young people, but, owing to changes in the lens with age, many people need glasses for reading by the time they are 50. This type of longsightedness is known as **presbyopia**.

loofah The fibrous skeleton of the fruit of the tropical dishcloth gourd, or vegetable sponge (genus *Luffa* (6 species), especially *L.*

cylindrica). These vines produce cucumber-like fruits, about 30 cm long. When mature, the pulp and seeds are removed leaving a dense network of fibrous conducting tissue, which is used as a bath sponge, dish washer, and industrial filter. Family: *Cucurbitaceae.*

loquat A small evergreen tree *Eriobotrya japonica*, native to China and Japan but cultivated in Mediterranean countries for its edible fruit. Family: *Rosaceae.*

Lorca, Federico García *See* GARCÍA LORCA, FEDERICO.

Lord Chief Justice The presiding judge of the Queen's Bench Division of the High Court of Justice and the Criminal Division of the Court of Appeal; he is second in the judicial hierarchy to the Lord Chancellor. The present Lord Chief Justice of England (since 2000) is Harry, Baron Woolf (1933–).

Lord Lyon King of Arms The highest authority in the deciding of heraldic matters in Scotland. Originally a herald in the 14th century, the Lord Lyon now heads four heralds and two pursuivants at the Lyon Office where, since 1677, all claims to arms must be registered. Also a judge, the Lord Lyon has jurisdiction over issues of clan chieftainship and pedigrees.

Loren, Sophia (S. Scicoloni; 1934–) Italian film actress, now a French citizen. Her films include *Two Women* (1961), *The Millionairess* (1961), *Marriage Italian Style* (1964), and *Saturday, Sunday, and Monday* (1990).

Lorenz, Konrad (1903–89) Austrian zoologist, who was one of the founders of modern ethology (the study of animal behaviour). In the 1930s Lorenz identified the phenomenon of *imprinting in young chicks. He was concerned with determining the elements of behaviour, how they were stimulated, their development in an individual, and their evolutionary significance. Lorenz wrote several popular books about his work, including *King Solomon's Ring* (1949) and *Man Meets Dog* (1950). He also applied his theories to humans, with controversial implications (*On Aggression*, 1963). He was awarded a Nobel Prize (1973) with Karl von Frisch (1886–1982) and Niko Tinbergen (1907–88).

loris A nocturnal Asian *prosimian primate belonging to the subfamily *Lorisinae* (5 species). Lorises are 20–35 cm long with almost no tail and very large dark eyes. They are generally slow-moving and arboreal. Family: *Lorisidae.*

Lorraine (German name: Lothringen) A planning region and former province in NE France, bordering on Belgium, Luxembourg, and Germany. Its valuable iron-ore deposits are the largest in Europe outside Sweden and the Soviet Union. Disputed between France and the Habsburgs, it was finally incorporated into France, as a province, in 1766. Following the Franco-Prussian War (1871) part of Lorraine (now Moselle department) was lost to Germany and united with *Alsace to form the imperial territory of Alsace-Lorraine. Area: 23 540 sq km (9087 sq mi). Population (1999): 2 310 376.

lory A small brightly coloured *parrot belonging to the subfamily *Loriinae* (62 species), occurring in Australia, New Guinea, and Polynesia. Lories have a slender bill with a brush-tipped tongue and feed on pollen and nectar.

Los Alamos 28 54N 103 00W A town in the USA, in New Mexico. Chosen by the US government (1942) for atomic research, the first atom bombs were made here during World War II. The H-bomb was later developed here by the scientific laboratory of the University of California. Government control of Los Alamos ended in 1962. Population (latest est): 11 455.

Los Angeles 34 00N 118 15W A city and seaport in the USA, in S California on the Pacific coast, founded in 1781 by Franciscan missionaries. It comprises a large industrial and urban complex, with the second largest population in the USA. It is the centre of the US film industry. Industrial pollution, augmented by the high density of cars (Los Angeles has no public transport), is a serious problem. The city was damaged by an earthquake in 1994. Population (2000): 3 694 820.

Los Angeles, Victoria de (1923–) Spanish soprano. She established herself as a popular prima donna, particularly in the title roles of Massenet's *Manon Lescaut* and Puccini's *Madame Butterfly.*

Lotto, Lorenzo (c. 1480–1556) Venetian painter. He travelled extensively but, unable to compete with Titian's success, worked chiefly in Bergamo. He is noted for his altarpieces, e.g. the *Crucifixion* (Monte San Giusto, Bergamo), and the psychological insight of such portraits as *A Young Man* (Kunsthistorisches Museum, Vienna), and *Andrea Odoni* (Hampton Court).

lotus Any of several different water plants. The sacred lotus of ancient Egypt was probably *Nymphaea lotus*, a sweet-scented white night-flowering *water lily with broad petals, or *N. caerulea*, a blue-flowered species. The sacred Indian lotus, *Nelumbo nucifera* (family *Nelum-*

baceae), has roselike pink flowers and edible seeds, called lotus nuts. The genus *Lotus* contains about 70 species of herbs, including the birdsfoot trefoils.

loudspeaker A device for converting electrical signals into sound. It usually consists of a small coil fixed to the centre of a movable diaphragm or cone. The coil lies between the poles of a strong *magnet. An audio-frequency electrical signal fed to the coil creates a varying magnetic field, which interacts with the steady field in the gap. This causes the coil, and the attached cone, to vibrate and produce sound waves of the same frequencies as the electrical signal. Generally, larger cones give a better response at low frequencies and the smaller cones are best at high frequencies; for the best results two or more different-sized cones are therefore used, either in the same or in separate cabinets.

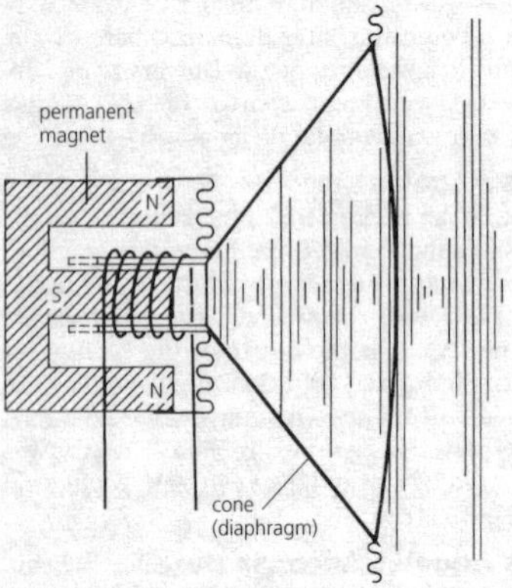

loudspeaker. A moving-coil loudspeaker with a pot-shaped permanent magnet.

Louis (I) the Pious (778–840 AD) Emperor of the West (813–40); son of Charlemagne. He fostered Christianity but imperial unity was undermined by his rebellious sons and after his death the Empire was partitioned.

Louis (VII) le Jeune (c. 1120–80) King of France (1137–80). He was engaged in a bitter struggle with Henry II of England between 1152, when Henry acquired Aquitaine through his marriage to Louis' former wife *Eleanor of Aquitaine, until 1174.

Louis VIII (1187–1226) King of France (1223–26), known as the Lionheart. He was offered the English throne by King John's baronial opponents but his invasion of England was defeated in 1217.

Louis IX, St (1214–70) King of France (1226–70), regarded as the model medieval Christian king. After defeating Henry III of England (1242) he set out as leader of the seventh *Crusade (1248), during which he was captured by the Egyptians. On his return to France he introduced administrative reforms and fostered learning and the arts. He died on a Crusade in Tunisia and was canonized in 1297.

Louis XI (1423–83) King of France (1461–83), who united most of France under his rule and in 1477 finally defeated Charles the Bold of Burgundy. He extended royal authority over the church and encouraged commerce, gaining the support of the middle classes.

Louis XII (1462–1515) King of France (1498–1515). His reign was dominated by the wars that his father Charles VIII had initiated in Italy.

Louis XIII (1601–43) King of France (1610–43), whose reign was dominated by his chief minister Cardinal de *Richelieu. He was the son of the assassinated Henry IV and of Marie de' Medici (1573–1642), who was regent during his minority. In 1617 he exiled Marie from court but mother and son were later reconciled by Richelieu, her adviser, who in 1624 became Louis' chief minister. The king defeated two *Huguenot uprisings (1622, 1628).

Louis XIV (1638–1715) King of France (1643–1715), known as the Sun King because of the splendour of his reign. His minority was dominated by Cardinal Mazarin (1602–61), after whose death Louis allowed no single minister to dominate. He was a firm advocate of the *divine right of kings and is remembered for his protestation *L'état c'est moi* (I am the state). His patronage of artists, including the writers Molière and Racine, enhanced the magnificence of his court. In 1660 he married Maria Theresa (1638–83), the daughter of Philip IV of Spain. His mistresses included Mme de Montespan (1641–1707) and then Mme de Maintenon (c. 1635–1719), whom he secretly married after Maria Theresa's death. Abroad, France became the dominant power in Europe during Louis' reign, although the many wars in which he involved France left it economically weak. France was further weakened by Louis' revocation (1685) of the Edict of Nantes, ending toleration of Protestants and driving many of France's most productive citizens into exile. His reign was nevertheless one of incomparable brilliance.

The **Louis Quartorze style** of late 17th-century interior design was developed in an attempt by Louis XIV and his designers to establish a French national idiom. The formal baroque furniture was sumptuously gilded or veneered for such regal settings as *Versailles.

Louis XV (1710–74) King of France (1715–74), whose weak rule discredited the Crown and contributed to the outbreak of the French Revolution of 1789. His early reign was dominated by Cardinal Fleury (1653–1743), after whose death Louis' indecisiveness and the influence of his mistresses, especially Mme de *Pompadour and, later, Mme *Du Barry, fostered faction and intrigue. The loss of almost all France's colonies in the *Seven Years' War (1756–63) increased his unpopularity, which hasty judicial and financial reforms at the end of his reign did nothing to alleviate.

The **Louis Quinze style** of French interior decoration and furnishing lasted from about 1723 until Louis' death. A sophisticated and informal style, it was a reaction to the formal baroque pomp of Louis XIV's court. *See also* ROCOCO.

Louis XVI (1754–93) King of France (1774–93), who was guillotined during the *French Revolution. The opposition of Louis' wife *Marie Antoinette and the aristocracy thwarted the attempted reforms of his ministers Turgot (1727–81) and Necker (1732–1804). The consequent economic crisis forced the king to summon (1789) the States General, the disaffected Third Estate of which precipitated revolution. The royal family was confined to the Tuileries Palace from which they attempted to flee in 1791, reaching Varennes. Brought back to the Tuileries, Louis was deposed after it had been stormed by the Paris mob. In 1793 he and his wife were guillotined.

The Louis Seize style, a neoclassical French style of furnishing, came into fashion after Louis XVI's accession. It was characterized by rejection of the rococo with straight lines replacing curves and a continuing tendency towards lightness and utility. After the French Revolution (1789–99) this style remained in vogue for some time.

Louis XVII (1785–95) King of France in name (1793–95) following the execution of his father Louis XVI during the French Revolution. He died in prison.

Louis XVIII (1755–1824) King of France, in name from 1795, following the death in prison of his nephew *Louis XVII, and in fact from 1814, following the overthrow of Napoleon. He fled Paris when Napoleon returned from Elba, being restored with diminished prestige after Waterloo (1815). His attempts to be a moderate constitutional monarch were thwarted by the ultraroyalists.

Louis, Joe (Joseph Louis Barrow; 1914–81) US boxer, called the Brown Bomber, who was world heavyweight champion from 1937 to 1948, when he retired.

Louisiana A state in the S USA, on the Gulf of Mexico. Chiefly low lying, it is crossed by the Mississippi River, the delta of which dominates the coastal lowlands in the S. The state produces chemicals and petrochemicals, paper and food products. Oil is exploited throughout the state and there are major deposits of natural gas, sulphur, and salt. New Orleans and Baton Rouge are important ports and tourism is a growing industry. Its favourable climate and fertile soils make it an important agricultural state. *History*: although discovered by the Spanish, it was claimed for France and named after Louis XIV in 1682. It was ceded to Spain (1762) but was restored to France (1800). It was acquired by the USA as part of the Louisiana Purchase (1803), becoming a state in 1812. Area: 125 675 sq km (48 523 sq mi). Population (2000): 4 468 976. Capital: Baton Rouge.

Louisiana Purchase (1803) About 2 144 250 sq km (828 000 sq mi) of land between the Mississippi River and the Rocky Mountains, purchased by the USA from France for $27,267,622. The purchase doubled the size of the USA and established US dominance in North America.

Louis Philippe (1773–1850) King of the French (1830–48), the son of the Duke of *Orléans. He supported the *French Revolution until 1793, when he deserted to the Austrians. He joined the liberal opposition to the restored Louis XVIII and came to the throne after the July Revolution had ousted Louis' successor Charles X. Styled King of the French rather than of France and described by Thiers as the Citizen King, Louis Philippe relied on the support of the middle class. His initial moderation turned to repression in the face of the many rebellions against his rule and he abdicated in the Revolution of 1848.

Lourdes 43 06N 0 02W A town in SW France, in the Hautes-Pyrénées department situated at the foot of the Pyrenees. It has been a major pilgrimage centre for Roman Catholics since **St Bernadette of Lourdes** (1844–79) was led by a vision of the Virgin Mary to the Grotto de Massabielle in 1858. This has been the scene of many reputed cures for a variety of diseases. Population (1995 est): 17 100.

louse A wingless insect parasitic on warm-blooded animals. The sucking lice (order *Anoplura*; 225 species) suck the blood of mammals. They have hairy flattened bodies, 0.5–6 mm long, and claws for attachment to the host. One of the most important species is the human louse (*Pediculus humanus*), of which there are two varieties—the head louse (*P. humanus capitis*) and the body louse (*P. humanus humanus*). Both are transmitted by direct contact and lay their eggs ("nits") on hair or clothing. Body lice are carriers of typhus and related diseases. Biting lice (order *Mallophaga*; 2600 species) resemble sucking lice but have biting mouthparts for feeding on the skin, feathers, etc., of birds—their principal hosts.

Louth (Irish name: Contae Lughbhaidh) The smallest county in the Republic of Ireland, in Leinster bordering on the Irish Sea. It is chiefly low lying. Agriculture is important. Area: 821 sq km (317 sq mi). Population (2002): 101 802. County town: Dundalk.

Louvre The national museum of France containing the art collection of the French kings and housed in the former royal palace and Tuileries palace in Paris. It was opened to the public in 1793.

lovage A perennial herb, *Ligusticum scoticum*, that has large compound leaves with pairs of divided toothed leaflets and clusters of greenish-white flowers. It is native to Europe and used as a pot herb and salad plant. Family: *Umbelliferae*.

lovebird A small brightly coloured *parrot belonging to a genus (*Agapornis*; 9 species) occurring in Africa and Madagascar. Lovebirds typically have a short tail, a red bill, and a prominent eye ring. They often feed in large flocks and may damage crops. They are popular cagebirds.

Lovelace, Richard (1618–57) English Cavalier poet. One of his best-known poems is "To Althea, from Prison." *Lucasta* (1649) contains most of his best lyrics.

love-lies-bleeding *See* AMARANTHUS.

Lowell, Robert (1917–77) US poet. The important collection *Life Studies* (1959) marked a change from his complex and allusive early poetry to a looser, more personal style. Later volumes include *For the Union Dead* (1964). His *Collected Poems* appeared in 2003.

Lower California (Spanish name: Baja California) A peninsula in NW Mexico, between the Gulf of California and the Pacific Ocean. It is chiefly mountainous and arid, with important mineral deposits. Length: 1223 km (760 mi).

Lowry, L(awrence) S(tephen) (1887–1976) British painter, born in Manchester. His most characteristic works are bleak industrial landscapes dotted with matchstick figures.

Lozi A Bantu-speaking people of Zambia, also known as Barotse. They are cereal cultivators on the fertile flood plain of the upper Zambezi, but hunting and animal husbandry are also important. Political authority is vested in a divine king and subordinate queen who rule from separate northern and southern capitals.

LPG *See* LIQUEFIED PETROLEUM GAS.

LSD (lysergic acid diethylamide) A drug that—in very small doses—produces hallucinations, altered sensory perception, and a sense of happiness and relaxation or, in some people, fear and anxiety. Long-term use of LSD can cause a schizophrenia-like illness.

Lualaba, River A river in the SE Democratic Republic of Congo, the headstream of the Congo River. Rising in the Shaba region, it flows N to join the River Luvua and becomes the Congo River at the Boyoma Falls. Length: 1800 km (1100 mi).

Luanda (former name: São Paulo de Loanda) 8 58S 13 09E The capital of Angola, a port in the NW on the Atlantic Ocean. Founded by the Portuguese in 1575, it became a centre of the slave trade to Brazil. Oil was discovered nearby in 1955 and a refinery was established. Population (1999 est): 2 255 000.

Lübeck 53 52N 10 40E A city in N Germany, in Schleswig-Holstein on the Trave estuary. A leading city of the Hanseatic League, it has a cathedral (1173) and city hall (13th–15th centuries). It is a major Baltic port. Population (1999 est): 213 800.

Lubitsch, Ernst (1892–1947) US film director, born in Germany. Following the success of *Madame Dubarry* (1919), a historical romance, he went to Hollywood, where he made sophisticated comedies during the 1920s and 1930s. These include *Forbidden Paradise* (1924), *Bluebeard's Eighth Wife* (1938), and *Ninotchka* (1939).

Lubumbashi (name until 1966: Elizabethville) 11 30S 27 31E A city in the SE Democratic Republic of Congo. Founded in 1910 as a coppermining settlement, it is the industrial centre of an important mining area. Population (1994 est): 851 381.

Lucifer *See* DEVIL.

Lucknow 26 50N 80 54E A city in India, the capital of Uttar Pradesh. Capital of the nawabs of Oudh (1775–1856), it has many notable buildings. The British Residency was besieged in 1857 during the Indian Mutiny. Population (1991): 1 642 134.

Lucretius (Titus Lucretius Carus; c. 95–c. 55 BC) Roman philosopher and poet. His single work, *De rerum natura*, expounds the philosophy of Epicurus (*see* EPICUREANISM), including his atomic theory of phenomena and the belief that the soul was material (and mortal).

Lüda (*or* **Lü-ta**) 38 53N 121 37E A port complex in NE China, at the end of the Liaodong Peninsula. It comprises the two cities **Lüshun** (English name: Port Arthur) and **Dalian** (*or* Ta-lien; English name: Dairen). Lüshun, a major naval base from 1878, served the Russian Pacific fleet during the Russian occupation (1898–1905). The Russians began the construction of the commercial port at Dalian, completed under Japanese occupation (1905–45). Population (1991 est): 2 400 000.

Luddites A group of Nottingham frameworkers, named after their probably mythical leader, Ned Ludd, who destroyed labour-saving machinery in 1811. Luddism, which spread to other parts of industrial England, showed the hostility to the new machines that were taking the men's livelihood from them. It was severely repressed.

Luftwaffe The German air force. The Luftwaffe, which fought in World War I, was further developed by *Göring in the 1930s. In World War II it was involved in the Blitzkreig but was defeated in the battle of Britain.

Lugansk (name from 1935 until 1991: Voroshilovgrad) 48 35N 39 20E A city in E Ukraine. It lies in the coal-producing Donets Basin and has iron, steel, and chemical industries. Population (1998 est): 475 300.

Lugus One of the principal Celtic gods. In Ireland he was called Lug and was skilled in many fields. His Welsh counterpart was Lleu Llaw Gyffes (skilful hand).

lugworm A burrowing *annelid worm, *Arenicola marina*, of Atlantic shores. Up to 40 cm long, lugworms have about 20 segments, with tufts of red gills on all but the last few. They feed on organic material in the mud, leaving casts of egested mud on the surface. Class: *Polychaeta*.

Luke, St New Testament evangelist, traditionally the author of the third Gospel and the Acts of the Apostles. He was apparently a Gentile doctor who accompanied Paul on several missions. **The Gospel according to St Luke** was written in the later 1st century AD with Gentile readers in mind.

lumbar puncture A procedure in which cerebrospinal fluid is withdrawn from the spinal cord by means of a hypodermic syringe. This is done for diagnostic purposes.

lumen (lm) The SI unit of luminous flux equal to the light emitted per second in a cone of one steradian solid angle by a point source of one candela.

luminescence The emission of light by a substance for any reason except high temperature. It occurs as a result of the emission of a *photon by an atom of the substance when it decays from an excited state to its ground state. The atom may be excited by absorbing a photon (photoluminescence), colliding with an electron (electroluminescence), etc. If the luminescence stops as soon as the exciting source is removed, it is known as fluorescence; if it persists for longer than 10^{-8} seconds it is called phosphorescence.

luminosity The intrinsic brightness of an object, such as a star, equal to the total energy radiated per second from the object. A star's luminosity increases both with surface temperature and with surface area: the hotter and larger a star, the greater its luminosity. Stellar luminosity is related (logarithmically) to absolute *magnitude.

luminous flux The rate of flow of light energy, taking into account the sensitivity of the observer or detector to the different wavelengths. For example, the human eye is most sensitive to the colour green. Luminous flux is measured in *lumens.

luminous intensity The amount of light emitted per second by a point source per unit solid angle in a specified direction. It is measured in *candela.

lumpsucker A slow-moving carnivorous *bony fish, also called lumpfish, belonging to the family *Cyclopteridae*, found in cold northern seas. They have a thickset body, sometimes studded with bony tubercles, a cleft dorsal fin, and a ventral sucking disc formed from fused pelvic fins. *Cyclopterus lumpus* is the largest species, reaching 60 cm long. The roe is used as a substitute for caviar. Order: *Scorpaeniformes*.

Lüneburg 53 15N 10 24E A spa in N Germany, in Lower Saxony. There are many fine medieval buildings. **Lüneburg Heath** was the site of the surrender of German troops in 1945 at the end of World War II. Population (latest est): 61 000.

lungfish A freshwater *bony fish belonging to the order *Dipnoi*, now reduced to six species including *Lepidosiren paradoxa* of South America, *Protopterus annectens* of Africa, and the Australian *Neoceratodus forsteri.* Lungfish have slender bodies, narrow paired fins, and tapering tails. Their swim bladders are modified for breathing air, an adaptation for droughts, when some make burrows in the bottom mud, leaving air vents above the mouth. They reemerge in the rainy season to feed and spawn.

lungs The respiratory organs of many air-breathing animals and man. The human lungs are situated within the rib cage on either side of the heart. Each lung is enclosed by a smooth moist membrane (the pleura), which permits it to expand without friction, and contains many tiny thin-walled air sacs (alveoli), through which exchange of oxygen and carbon dioxide takes place during breathing (*see* RESPIRATION). Air to the lungs passes through the *trachea (windpipe) to the two main airways (bronchi), which subdivide into progressively smaller branches that terminate (as respiratory bronchioles) in the alveoli. Diseases affecting the lungs and airways include virus infections, bronchitis, and cancer.

Lupercalia An ancient Roman festival of purification and fertility held annually on 15 Feb. After performing sacrifices, priests carrying whips of goat hide made a circuit of the Palatine. Women struck by their whips were ensured fertility. The ceremony was suppressed in 494 AD by Pope Gelasius.

lupin An annual or perennial herb of the genus *Lupinus* (about 200 species), native to the N hemisphere and widely cultivated for ornament. They have compound leaves with radiating leaflets and dense spikes of flowers. Family: *Leguminosae.*

lupus A skin disease of which there are two forms. Used alone, the term usually refers to **lupus vulgaris**, a tuberculous infection of the skin, which is now readily cured by drugs. **Lupus erythematosus** (LE) is a disease in which inflammation of tissues is brought about by the body's own antibodies. LE can be controlled with steroid drugs.

Lusaka 15 03S 28 30E The capital of Zambia, lying on the Tanzam Railway. It became the capital of Northern Rhodesia in 1935 and of Zambia on independence in 1964. The centre of an important agricultural region, it has expanded rapidly. Population (latest est): 982 362.

Lüshun *See* LÜDA.

lute A plucked stringed instrument of Moorish origin. The European lute, popular during the 15th, 16th, and 17th centuries, had a body in the shape of a half pear, six or more courses of double strings and a fretted fingerboard. The lute was used chiefly as a solo instrument and to accompany singers; it has been revived in the last hundred years.

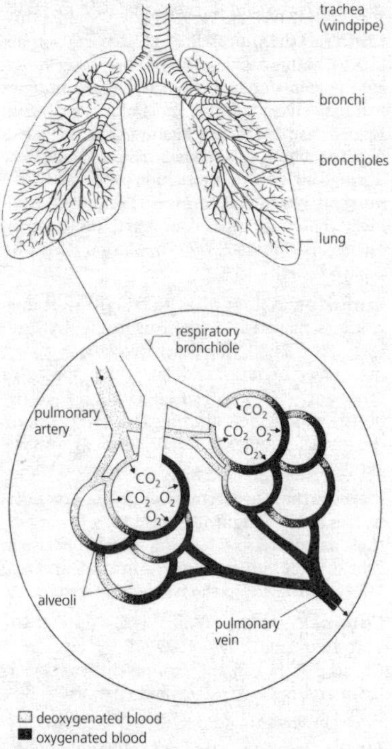

lungs. The air passages in the lungs terminate in millions of tiny air sacs (alveoli), into which blood from the pulmonary artery releases its carbon dioxide. Inhaled oxygen in the alveoli is absorbed by the blood, which is carried back to the heart by the pulmonary vein.

luteinizing hormone *See* GONADOTROPHIN.

lutetium (Lu) The heaviest *lanthanide element named by its discoverer, G. Urbain (1872–1938) after his native Paris (Latin: *Lutetia*).

It was formerly known as **cassiopeium**. At no 71; at wt 174.967; mp 1663°C; bp 3402°C.

Luther, Martin (1483–1546) German Protestant reformer. An Augustinian monk and from 1507 a priest, he became professor of theology at Wittenberg University in 1511. After experiencing a personal revelation he came to believe that salvation could be attained by faith alone. Several visits to Rome convinced him of the corruption of the papacy, and the Dominican monk Johann Tetzel (c.1465–1519), who sold *indulgences on behalf of papal funds, became a particular target for his hostility. In 1517 he nailed his 95 theses against this practice to the church door at Wittenberg. He disobeyed the papal summons to Rome (1518) and further attacked the papal system in his writings. His public burning of a papal bull condemning his theses and writings resulted in his excommunication in 1521. He appeared before Charles V's imperial diet (legislative assembly) at Worms but refused to recant and was declared an outlaw. While in hiding at Wartburg, under the protection of the Elector of Saxony, he completed a German translation of the New Testament. In 1522 he returned openly to Wittenberg, where he led the reform of its church. His original intention was reform not schism, but with the *Augsburg Confession (1530) a separate Protestant church emerged. Subsequently the leadership of the German Reformation was gradually taken over by Philip Melanchthon (1497–1560).

The belief and practice of the Protestant Churches that derive from Luther's teaching is known as **Lutheranism**. There is a wide divergence in matters of belief among Lutherans. Essentially Scripture is taken to be the only rule of faith and conservative Lutherans accept Luther's basic doctrine that redemption is only through faith in Christ. Lutheranism is the national faith in all Scandinavian countries, is the principal Protestant Church in Germany, and is also strong in North America. There are 80 million Lutherans world wide.

Luton 1. 51 53N 0 25W A town in SE England, in Luton unitary authority, Bedfordshire. It has motor-vehicle, mechanical, and electronic engineering industries. Nearby is London's Luton Airport. Population (1995): 181 400. **2.** A unitary authority in SE England, in Bedfordshire. Area: 43 sq km (17 sq mi). Population (2001): 184 390.

Lutuli, Albert (John Mvumbi) (1898–1967) South African Black leader, whose advocacy of nonviolent opposition to racial discrimination won him the Nobel Peace Prize in 1960. A Zulu chief, in 1952 he became president of the African National Congress.

Lutyens, Sir Edwin Landseer (1869–1944) British architect. Known as the last English designer of country houses, he also designed the central square of Hampstead Garden Suburb (1908–10) and the Cenotaph (1919–20) but his most spectacular commission was the layout and viceregal palace of New Delhi (1912–30). His daughter, **Elisabeth Lutyens** (1906–83), was a noted composer.

lux (lx) The SI unit of intensity of illumination equal to the illumination resulting from a flux of one lumen falling on an area of one square metre.

Luxembourg, Grand Duchy of A small country in central Europe, between France and Germany. The generally undulating S with its wide valleys rises to the rugged uplands of the Ardennes Plateau in the N. *Economy*: predominantly industrial; iron and steel are especially important although considerable economic diversification has taken place. Agriculture remains important. The city of Luxembourg is an important international centre with the headquarters of the European Parliament and the European Coal and Steel Community. *History*: with the Netherlands and Belgium it formed part of the so-called Low Countries. It became a grand duchy under the Dutch Crown in 1815 and joined the Belgian revolt against the Netherlands in 1830. Thereafter W Luxembourg joined independent Belgium and the E formed part of the Netherlands until the duchy obtained independence in 1867. In 1921 it formed an economic union with Belgium and in 1948 both joined with the Netherlands to form the *Benelux Economic Union. Luxembourg was a founding member of the EEC (now the EU). In 2000 Grand Duke Jean abdicated in favour of his son Henri. Luxembourg adopted the single European currency in 1999–2002. Official languages: Luxembourgish, French, and German. Currency: euro of 100 cents. Area: 2586 sq km (999 sq mi). Population (2003 est): 453 000. Capital: Luxembourg.

Luxor (*or* **El Aksur**) 25 40N 32 38E A town in central Egypt, on the River Nile. It occupies the S part of the ancient city of *Thebes and has numerous ruins and tombs. Population (1996 est): 360 503.

Luzon A volcanic island in the N Philippines, the largest and most important. Largely mountainous, its central fertile plain is a major grain growing area with rice terraces to the N. Most industry is concentrated around Manila. Area:

108 378 sq km (41 845 sq mi). Population (1995 est): 32 558 000. Chief town: Manila.

Lviv (Russian name: Lvov; German name: Lemberg) 49 50N 24 00E A city in W Ukraine. It is a major industrial and cultural centre. Under Austrian rule from 1772, it was ceded to Poland after World War I and to the Soviet Union in 1939, being occupied by the Germans in World War II; it passed to Ukraine in 1991. Population (1998 est): 793 700.

Lyceum The gardens and gymnasium in ancient Athens in which *Aristotle lectured and which gave their name to the school and research foundation that he established there in about 335 BC. The name is now applied particularly to Aristotle's philosophical doctrines.

lychee *See* LITCHI.

Lydia In antiquity, a region of W Asia Minor with its capital at Sardis. Its last native king, *Croesus (ruled 560–546 BC), enriched by Lydia's alluvial gold, controlled Anatolia eastwards to the River Halys, until his defeat by Cyrus the Great (d. 529 BC). The Lydians invented coined money (c. 700 BC).

lymph A clear colourless fluid, consisting of water and dissolved substances, that is contained in a network of vessels called the **lymphatic system**. It is derived from blood and bathes the cells, supplying them with nutrients and absorbing their waste products, before passing into the lymphatic vessels. Here the lymph passes through a series of small swellings called **lymph nodes**, which filter out bacteria and other foreign particles, before draining into the main lymphatic vessels in the neck. These two vessels are connected to veins in the neck and so drain the lymph back into the bloodstream. The lymph nodes, which also produce lymphocytes (a type of white blood cell), sometimes become enlarged during infections. The lymphatic system is one of the routes by which cancer is spread.

lymphocyte *See* LEUCOCYTE.

lymphoma Cancer of the lymph nodes. There are several different types but the most common is Hodgkin's disease, which can now often be controlled by chemotherapy.

lynx A short-tailed *cat, *Felis lynx*, that inhabits forests of Eurasia and North America. Lynxes are about 1 m long with faintly spotted yellow-brown thick fur; their ears are tipped with black tufts. They hunt at night, usually for small mammals.

Lyon 45 46N 4 50E The third largest city in France, the capital of the Rhône department at the confluence of the Rivers Rhône and Saône. Notable buildings include the cathedral (12th–15th centuries). The focal point of road and rail routes, Lyon is an important financial centre and has been a leading textile centre since the 15th century. Population (1999): 445 257.

lyre An ancient plucked string instrument. It consists of a sound box with two symmetrical arms supporting a cross piece from which strings are stretched to a bridge on the belly.

lyrebird A primitive ground-dwelling passerine bird belonging to a family (*Menuridae*; 2 species) restricted to forests of E Australia. The male superb lyrebird (*Menura superba*) is brown with grey underparts. Its magnificent tail is spread out into a lyre shape during the courtship display. All lyrebirds sing loudly and are excellent mimics.

Lysander (d. 395 BC) Spartan general and politician. He commanded the fleets that defeated the Athenians at Notium (407) and Aegospotami (405) towards the end of the *Peloponnesian War.

Lysenko, Trofim Denisovich (1898–1976) Soviet biologist, who had a damaging influence on Soviet biology. He endorsed *Lamarck's discredited theory of evolution through inheritance of acquired characteristics. This led him to attack Mendelian genetics and the chromosome theory of inheritance, which, in the 1930s, were widely accepted elsewhere. With the backing of Stalin, Lysenko's influence grew, and by 1948, Soviet scientific opposition to his views had been stifled. Lysenko's influence was eclipsed after Stalin's death.

lysergic acid diethylamide *See* LSD.

lysosome A membrane-bounded structure occurring in large numbers in nearly all animal cells and containing enzymes responsible for the breakdown of materials both within and outside the cell. Functions of lysosomes include the destruction of bacteria in white blood cells.

M

Mabinogion, the A collection of eleven medieval Welsh folktales. Drawing on Celtic, Norman, and French legends, it was compiled in the 14th century and contains the earliest known Arthurian romance, *Culhwch and Olwen* (c. 1100).

Mabuse *See* GOSSAERT, JAN.

Macao (Portuguese name: Macáu; Chinese name: Aomen) 22 13N 113 36E A port and special administrative region of S China, across the Zhu estuary from Hong Kong. It was an overseas territory of Portugal until December 1999. The population is mainly Chinese. Industries now include gambling and financial services as well as the traditional textiles and fishing. Tourism is also important. *History*: it was a major trading centre until the 19th century. Immigration of refugees from Communist China was stopped after procommunist riots (1966–67). Sovereignty passed to China in 1999. Official currency: pataca of 100 avos. Area: 16 sq km (6 sq mi). Population (2002 est): 438 000.

macaque An *Old World monkey belonging to the genus *Macaca* (12 species), found mainly in the forests of S Asia. 35–78 cm long, macaques have short legs and areas of hard bare skin on the rump. They are mainly terrestrial, feeding on plant and animal matter. The Barbary ape is a macaque of N Africa. *See also* RHESUS MONKEY.

MacArthur, Douglas (1880–1964) US general. One of the outstanding strategists of World War II, he commanded the occupation of Japan (1945–51) and led the UN forces in the Korean War. His advocacy of active operations against China was contrary to US policy and President Harry S. Truman dismissed him (1951).

MacArthur, Ellen (1976–) British yachtswoman. In 2001 she came second in the Vendée Globe round-the-world race, becoming the youngest person and the fastest woman to circumnavigate the globe single-handed.

Macassar *See* UJUNG PANDANG.

Macaulay, Thomas Babington, 1st Baron (1800–59) British essayist, historian, and poet. He was a leading contributor to the *Edinburgh Review* and had a long career in parliament. His Whig sympathies are evident in his successful *History of England* (5 vols, 1849–61).

macaw A large brightly coloured *parrot belonging to one of two genera (*Ara* and *Anodorhynchos*), ranging from Mexico to Paraguay. Up to 100 cm long, macaws have a long loose tail and a huge hooked bill.

Macbeth (d. 1057) King of Scots (1040–57), after killing Duncan I in battle at Bothnagowan. He was killed by Duncan's son Malcolm.

Maccabees The Hasmonean dynasty founded in Jerusalem by the Jewish fighter Judas Maccabee (d. 161 BC) after a revolt against Syrian (Seleucid) rule. It continued until the capture of Jerusalem by the Romans in 63 BC. The **Books of Maccabees** are four books of the *Apocrypha.

McCarthy, Joseph R(aymond) (1908–57) US Republican senator, who led Senate investigations of supposed communists during the Cold War. His claim to have the names of communist infiltrators into the State Department was not proved and in 1954 his anticommunist witchhunt—commonly known as McCarthyism—came to an end.

McCartney, Sir Paul (1942–) British rock musician and songwriter, formerly with the *Beatles. His subsequent recordings include *Band on the Run* (1973; with Wings) and *Driving Rain* (2001).

Macclesfield 53 16N 2 07W A town in N England, in Cheshire on the W edge of the Pennines. A former centre of the silk industry, it now produces plastics and pharmaceuticals. Population (1998): 50 810.

McConnell, Jack (Wilson) (1960–) Scottish Labour politician; first minister of Scotland (2001–).

McCullers, Carson (1917–67) US novelist and playwright. Her novels, which include *The Heart Is a Lonely Hunter* (1940) and *A Member of the Wedding* (1946), are set in her native South and describe a grotesque world. Other works include *The Ballad of the Sad Café* (1951) and *Clock Without Hands* (1961).

MacDiarmid, Hugh (Christopher Murray Grieve; 1892–1978) Scottish poet. Active both as a nationalist and Marxist, he virtually created the "Scottish Renaissance" in literature. His early work, notably *A Drunk Man Looks at the Thistle* (1926), was written in a Scots language drawn from regional dialects and Middle Scots writers. Most of his later poems are in English.

MacDonald, (James) Ramsay (1866–1937) British statesman; the first Labour prime minister (1924, 1929–31, 1931–35). He joined the Independent Labour Party in 1894. Elected an MP (1906) he became leader of the parliamentary *Labour Party (1911) but resigned in opposition to World War I (1914). Re-elected to parliament in 1922 he again led the Labour Party, becoming prime minister in 1924. His minority government was defeated after a vote of no confidence. His 1929–31 government was broadened into a coalition (1931–35) that was increasingly dominated by the Conservatives.

m

mace *See* NUTMEG.

Macedonia The central region of the Balkans. Inhabited from Neolithic times, Macedonia was settled by many migrating northern tribes. About 640 BC Perdiccas I became the first ruler of the kingdom of Macedon. *Philip II (359–336 BC) quelled the warlike tribes and founded Macedon's military and economic power, which under his son Alexander the Great was extended to the East. After defeat (168 BC) in the Macedonian Wars, Macedonia became a Roman province (146). After World War I the region was divided between S Yugoslavia (*see* MACEDONIA, FORMER YUGOSLAV REPUBLIC OF), N Greece, and SW Bulgaria.

Macedonia, Former Yugoslav Republic of A country in SE Europe, in the Balkans. *Economy*: UN sanctions against Serbia (Macedonia's main trading partner), an economic blockade by Greece (1994–95), and a massive influx of refugees from Kosovo (1999), have had a particularly damaging effect. Mining, metalworking, chemicals, and textiles are the main industries. Agricultural products include tobacco, wheat, and sugar beet. *History*: the country occupies the N part of the region of Macedonia, which was ceded by Turkey to Serbia in 1913. It was a constituent republic of Yugoslavia from 1944 but declared independence in 1991. Greek fears of a possible claim to the Greek region of Macedonia delayed international recognition of the country until 1993, when it agreed to adopt its current name. In 2001 the NE saw mounting violence between Albanian militants and state forces. A peace agreement involving major constitutional reforms was signed in August. Official languages: Macedonian and Albanian. Currency: denar of 100 deni. Area 25 713 sq km (9925 sq mi). Population (2003 est): 2 056 000. Capital: Skopje.

McEnroe, John (Patrick, Jr) (1959–) US tennis player. He won the US singles title in 1979, 1980, 1981, and 1984 and became Wimbledon singles champion in 1981, 1983, and 1984. He retired in 1993.

McEwan, Ian (Russell) (1948–) British novelist and writer, whose books include *First Love, Last Rites* (1975), *The Child in Time* (1987), *Enduring Love* (1997), and *Atonement* (2001).

Macgillicuddy's Reeks A mountain range in the Republic of Ireland, in Co Kerry. It extends W of the Lakes of Killarney, reaching 1041 m (3414 ft) at Carrantuohill.

Machiavelli, Niccolò (1469–1527) Italian political theorist. He served the Florentine republic as statesman and diplomat from 1498 to 1512, when the restoration of the Medici family forced him into exile. In *The Prince* (1532), written in 1513, he argued that all means are permissible to obtain a stable state.

Mach number The ratio of the velocity of a body in a fluid to the velocity of sound in that fluid. The velocity is said to be supersonic if the Mach number is greater than one. If it exceeds five the velocity is said to be hypersonic. Named after the Austrian physicist Ernst Mach (1838–1916).

Machu Picchu A well-preserved 15th-century *Inca town in the Urubamba valley (Peru), discovered in 1911. Sited on a precipitous ridge, Machu Picchu is flanked by extensive agricultural terraces. It contains a central plaza, royal palace, and sun temple, all built of polygonal dressed stone blocks.

McIndoe, Sir Archibald Hector (1900–60) New Zealand surgeon, who pioneered techniques in plastic surgery. He is particularly noted for his work in Britain with badly burnt RAF airmen during World War II.

Macintosh, Charles (1766–1843) Scottish chemist, who invented the waterproof garment known as the "mackintosh." He made his discovery in 1823 by noting that rubber dissolved in naphtha could be used to stick together two pieces of cloth, producing a waterproof layer between them. He also patented a steel-making process (1825).

McKellen, Sir Ian (1939–) British actor, noted for his Shakespearean roles and for the film trilogy *The Lord of the Rings* (2001–03).

Mackenzie River The longest river in Canada, flowing from Great Slave Lake in the North West Territories W and NNW to an extensive delta on the Beaufort Sea. Navigable in summer, it carries oil and minerals from the Arctic Ocean to S Canada. Length: 1705 km (1065 mi).

mackerel An important food and game fish belonging to the genus *Scomber*, related to tuna. Mackerels live in shoals in tropical and temperate oceans, feeding on fish and invertebrates. They have a streamlined body, two dorsal fins, and a forked tail. The common Atlantic mackerel (*S. scombrus*), about 30 cm long, is marked with black and green bands above and is silvery-white below.

McKinley, Mount A mountain in the USA, in S central Alaska in the Alaska Range. The highest peak in North America, it was first successfully climbed in 1913 by a party led by the US explorer Hudson Stuck (1863–1920). Height: 6194 m (20 320 ft).

Maclean, Donald (1913–83) British Foreign Office official and Soviet secret agent. He fled to Russia in company with Guy Burgess (1911–63) in 1951; they were followed by fellow-conspirator Kim Philby (1912–88) in 1963. In 1979 it was revealed that Anthony Blunt (1907–83), a distinguished art historian, was implicated in the affair. The so-called "fifth man" involved was identified in 1991 as John Cairncross.

Macmillan, (Maurice) Harold, 1st Earl of Stockton (1894–1986) British statesman; Conservative prime minister (1957–63). The grandson of the publisher Daniel Macmillan, he first became an MP in 1924. He became minister of housing and local government in 1951 and then minister of defence (1954) and foreign secretary (1955). As chancellor of the exchequer (1955–57) he introduced Premium Bonds (1957). Macmillan succeeded Sir Anthony Eden as prime minister. His "wind of change" speech in Africa in 1958 marked his government's support of independence for African states; he is also remembered for his assertion during the 1959 election that "you've never had it so good." His second ministry was plagued by scandal and suffered a blow when de Gaulle frustrated Britain's attempt to join the EEC (1963). Macmillan became chancellor of Oxford University in 1960, was awarded the OM in 1976, and was granted an earldom in 1984.

MacNeice, Louis (1907–63) Irish-born British poet. He published his first volume of poetry, *Blind Fireworks*, in 1929. Among his other volumes are *Autumn Journal* (1939), *The Burning Perch* (1963), and a distinguished collection of plays for radio, *The Dark Tower* (1947).

Mâcon 46 18N 4 50E A town in E France, the capital of the Saône-et-Loire department on the River Saône. An important trading centre for Burgundy wines, its manufactures include textiles, vats, and agricultural machinery. Population (1995 est): 39 700.

McQueen, Steve (1930–80) US film actor. Following his success in *The Magnificent Seven* (1960) he usually played tough laconic heroes. His later films include *Bullitt* (1968) and *Papillon* (1973).

Madagascar, Republic of (name until 1975: Malagasy Republic) An island country in the Indian Ocean, off the SE coast of Africa. A narrow coastal plain in the E and a broader one in the W rise to central highlands. Most of the inhabitants are Merina, Betsimisaraka, and Betsileo, all speaking Austronesian dialects. *Economy*: chiefly agricultural: the main crops include rice and manioc as well as coffee, sugar, and spices, the main exports. Minerals include graphite, chrome, and ilmenite. Industry, previously based mainly on food processing and tobacco, now includes metals, plastics, paper, and oil refining. The country remains very poor, with a large external debt. *History*: settled by Indonesians from the 1st century AD and by Muslim traders from Africa from the 8th century, it remained a native kingdom until the late 19th century, when the French laid claim to Madagascar and established a protectorate (1896). It became a French overseas territory in 1946 and a republic within the French Community in 1958, gaining full independence in 1960. In 1975 Madagascar became a Marxist republic, with Admiral Didier Ratsiraka (1936–) as its first president. After social unrest, a transitional government was installed in 1991 to

m

oversee constitutional reform. Multiparty elections were held in 1993 and Ratsiraka was re-elected in 1997. Presidential elections in 2001 gave Marc Ravalomanana a narrow victory, which Ratsiraka refused to accept. This led to virtual civil war before Ravalomanana was finally sworn in in 2002. Official languages: Malagasy and French. Currency: Malagasy franc of 100 centimes. Area: 587 041 sq km (229 233 sq mi). Population (2003 est): 16 606 000. Capital: Antananarivo.

Madeira Islands (*or* **Funchal Islands**) A Portuguese archipelago in the Atlantic Ocean, about 640 km (398 mi) off the coast of Morocco. It comprises the inhabited islands of Madeira and Porto Santo and two uninhabited island groups. Madeira, the largest and most important island, is densely vegetated. Its products include basketwork, fruit (such as mangoes), sugar, and the famous Madeira wine. Area: 777 sq km (300 sq mi). Population (2001): 242 603. Capital: Funchal.

Madhya Pradesh A state in central India, stretching N over highlands to the S Ganges plain; it is chiefly agricultural, with rich mineral resources and several industrial cities. The region was under Islamic (11th–18th centuries) and Maratha (18th–19th centuries) rule until Britain took control. Formerly India's largest state, it lost the SE to the new state of *Chhattisgarh in 2000. Area: 308 332 sq km (119 016 sq mi). Population (2001): 60 385 118. Capital: Bhopal.

Madonna (Madonna Louise Veronica Ciccone; 1958–) US pop singer and film actress. Her bestselling records include "Like a Virgin" (1985), "Like a Prayer" (1989), and *Music* (2000).

Madras 13 05N 80 18N A city and major seaport in India, the capital of Tamil Nadu on the Coromandel Coast. Founded (1639) by the British East India Company, the city developed around Fort St George, which is the site of the first English church built in India (1678–80). An important industrial centre, Madras manufactures cars, bicycles, and cement and its chief exports are leather, iron ore, and cotton textiles. Population (1991): 3 795 028.

Madrid 40 27N 3 42W The capital of Spain, situated on a high plateau in the centre of the country on the River Manzanares. Its industries include the manufacture of leather goods, textiles, chemicals, engineering, glassware, and porcelain and the processing of agricultural products. A cultural centre, Madrid possesses a university, notable art galleries, and the national library (founded in 1712). Fine buildings include the former royal palace and the 17th-century cathedral. *History*: Madrid was captured from the Moors in 1083 by Alfonso VI. Philip II established it as the capital in 1561. In the Spanish Civil War Madrid was a Republican stronghold until it fell to the Nationalists in March 1939. In March 2004 nearly 200 people were killed in a bomb attack by Islamic terrorists. Population (1998 est): 2 881 506.

madrigal A secular polyphonic composition (*see* POLYPHONY) for voices, often a setting of a love poem. In 14th-century Florence, Landini wrote madrigals for voices and instruments. The Italian madrigal of the 16th and 17th centuries developed as an aristocratic art form in the complex compositions of Marenzio, Monteverdi, and Gesualdo. The English school (Byrd, Morley, Weelkes, etc.) wrote in a simpler style.

Maeander, River *See* MENDERES, RIVER.

Maes, Nicolas (*or* **N. Maas**; 1634–93) Dutch painter of domestic scenes and portraits. Initially influenced by his teacher Rembrandt, in such paintings as *Girl at the Window* (c. 1655; Rijksmuseum, Amsterdam), he later adopted the style of Flemish portraiture.

Maeterlinck, Maurice (1862–1949) Belgian poet and dramatist. Having established his reputation as a poet he became the leading dramatist of the Symbolist movement with such plays as *Pelléas et Mélisande* (1892). He also wrote several philosophical and mystical prose works. He won the Nobel Prize in 1911.

Mafeking (*or* **Mafikeng**) 25 53S 25 39E A town in South Africa, in Bophuthatswana. It was besieged for 217 days by Boers during the second Boer War (1899–1902) but was held by Col *Baden-Powell until relieved. It was the capital of the protectorate of Bechuanaland (now Botswana) until 1965. Population (latest est): 6775.

Mafia A criminal organization that originated as a secret society in 13th-century Sicily. The word (meaning "swank") was coined in the 19th century, when the Mafia was employed by the great landowners of Sicily to manage their estates. By extortion, "protection," ransom, and blackmail, the Mafia formed an organization so powerful that it virtually ruled Sicily. Italian emigrants took the Mafia to the USA in the early 20th century, where as Cosa Nostra (Our Affair), it has flourished.

Magdalenian A culture of the Upper *Palaeolithic, succeeding the Solutrean in W Europe. Named after La Madeleine cave in the Dordogne (SW France), the Magdalenian is marked by an abundance of bone and antler tools. Dating from about 15 000 to 10 000 BC, it was the heyday of prehistoric art with magnificent cave paintings (e.g. at Altamira).

Magdeburg 52 8N 11 35E A city in E Germany, on the River Elbe. It achieved fame in the middle ages for its judicial system, the "Magdeburg Law," which was used as a model by many other European cities. It was also a leading member of the Hanseatic League. An important inland port, its industries include iron, oil and sugar refining, chemicals, and textiles. Population (1999 est): 238 000.

Magellan, Ferdinand (c. 1480–1521) Portuguese explorer. He undertook many expeditions to India and Africa for Portugal between 1505 and 1516. In 1519, under Spanish patronage, he set off to seek a passage W to the Moluccas. Late in 1520 the expedition sailed through the Strait of Magellan, which separates the mainland of South America from Tierra del Fuego. In the spring of 1521 they reached the East Indies, where Magellan was killed. Only one ship returned to Spain, thus completing the first circumnavigation of the world.

Maggiore, Lake (Latin name: Lacus Verbanus) A long narrow lake in Italy and Switzerland. Sheltered from the N by the Alps, it enjoys a mild climate: the holiday resorts at its edge include Locarno, in Switzerland. Area: 212 sq km (82 sq mi).

Magherafelt A district of Northern Ireland, in Co. Londonderry. Area: 572 sq km (221 sq mi). Population (2001): 39 780.

Magi **1.** In antiquity, the priests of *Zoroaster, renowned for their astronomical knowledge. **2.** The sages who came from the East, following a star, to worship the infant Christ at Bethlehem (Matthew 2.1–12). Early Christian tradition gave them the title of kings and the names of Caspar, Melchior, and Balthazar. Symbolic significance was ascribed to their gifts: gold (kingship), frankincense (divinity), and myrrh (death).

magic A system of beliefs and practices by which it is believed that man may control the natural and supernatural forces that affect his life. Generally regarded as "superstition" in industrial societies, magic plays an important social role in many preindustrial societies. Its practitioners may rank highly, being credited with the ability to communicate with good and evil spirits.

Maginot line Fortifications built (1929–38) to protect the E frontier of France. They were named after André Maginot (1877–1932), French minister of war (1929–32), who authorized its construction.

magistrate An officer who administers the law. In England magistrates are either justices of the peace or stipendiary magistrates, who are appointed to try cases in some metropolitan Magistrates' Courts, have wider powers than justices, and are salaried.

maglev *See* MAGNETIC LEVITATION.

magma Molten rock lying beneath the earth's surface, either in the crust or upper mantle. It may rise to the surface through volcanic fissures and be extruded as lava; if it solidifies under ground it forms intrusive *igneous rock. Magma is a hot largely silicate liquid, containing dissolved gases and sometimes suspended crystals.

Magna Carta (1215) The Great Charter that was sealed at Runnymede by King John of England in response to baronial unrest. The Charter defined the barons' feudal obligations to the monarch and confirmed the liberties of the English Church. Of the four extant originals, two are in the British Library, one is in Salisbury Cathedral, and one is in Lincoln Cathedral.

magnesium (Mg) A light silvery-white reactive metal, first isolated by Sir Humphry Davy in 1808. Magnesium is the eighth most common element in the earth's crust and is a major constituent of the earth's mantle. It is extracted by electrolysis of magnesium chloride ($MgCl_2$), which is obtained from sea water and is responsible for the stickiness of unrefined table salt, since magnesium chloride is deliquescent. Magnesium forms many other ionic salts, such as the sulphate ($MgSO_4$; Epsom salts), the carbonate ($MgCO_3$; magnesite), the oxide (MgO), the nitrate ($Mg(NO_3)_2$), and the hydroxide ($Mg(OH)_2$; milk of magnesia). It also plays a central role in plant life, occurring in *chlorophyll. It has important commercial uses when alloyed with aluminium. At no 12; at wt 24.3050; mp 650°C; bp 1090°C.

magnet A body that has an appreciable external *magnetic field (*see also* MAGNETISM). Every magnet has two distinct areas around which the field is greatest— called the north and south poles. If two magnets are brought together, the like poles repel each other and the opposite poles attract each other. Ferromagnetic materials (*see* FERROMAGNETISM) are attracted to magnets because the magnet induces a field in the material in line with its own field. **Permanent magnets** are made of ferromagnetic materials and retain their magnetism unless they are heated above a certain temperature or are demagnetized by a strong opposing field. **Electromagnets** only function when an electric current flows through their coils.

magnetic constant (μ_0) A constant frequently occurring in magnetic equations in SI units. Also known as the *permeability of free space, its value is $4\pi \times 10^{-7}$ henry per metre. It is related to the *electric constant (ε_0) by $\mu_0\varepsilon_0 = 1/c^2$, where c is the velocity of light.

magnetic declination (*or* **magnetic variation**) The angle between geographical north and the horizontal component of the *geomagnetic field at the same point.

magnetic dip The angle formed between the horizon and a compass allowed to swing freely in the vertical plane. It thus indicates the direction of the vertical component of the *geomagnetic field.

magnetic domain *See* FERROMAGNETISM.

magnetic field The concept, devised by *Faraday, to explain the action-at-a-distance forces produced by a *magnet. The magnet is thought of as being surrounded by a field of force, within which its magnetic properties are effective. The strength and direction of the field is indicated by the lines of force that join the magnet's north and south poles. These lines of force can be seen if a card is laid over a magnet and iron filings sprinkled onto the card; when the card is tapped, the filings congregate along the lines of force. A wire carrying an electric current is also surrounded by a magnetic field, with concentric lines of force. An electromagnet usually consists of a coil of wire, in which the lines of force run through the centre of the coil and around its circumference. *See also* ELECTROMAGNETIC FIELD.

magnetic levitation (or **maglev**) A magnetic method of raising a vehicle above its tracks to provide almost frictionless propulsion. Starting on normal wheels, the train levitates above its elevated track as it gathers speed as a result of the interaction between superconducting magnets buried in the track and those in the base of each coach. Forward propulsion is by linear motor.

magnetic resonance imaging (**MRI**) A technique used in medicine for producing images, in any plane, of soft tissues, especially in the brain and spinal cord. It involves subjecting the tissues to a strong magnetic field and enables a variety of diseases to be diagnosed without exposing the patient to X-rays.

magnetism A phenomenon in which one body can exert a force on another body with which it is not in contact (action at a distance). The space in which such a force exists is called a *magnetic field. Stationary charged particles are surrounded by an *electric field; when these charged particles move or spin, an associated effect, the magnetic field, is created. The behaviour of materials when placed in such a field depends on how the spinning electrons inside its atoms align themselves. *See also* FERRIMAGNETISM; FERROMAGNETISM; PARAMAGNETISM.

magnetite (*or* **lodestone**) A black magnetic mineral, a form of iron oxide (Fe_3O_4). It often has distinct north and south magnetic poles and was known around 500 BC for its use as a compass. It is one of the ores from which iron is extracted.

magneto An alternating-current *electric generator that uses a permanent *magnet, rather than an electromagnet, to create the magnetic field. It usually consists of one or more conducting coils rotating between pairs of magnetic poles. The induced voltage has a frequency equal to the number of magnets times the speed of rotation of the coils. It is used in some small internal-combustion engines to produce the ignition spark.

magnetohydrodynamics (**MHD**) A method of generating electricity in which current carriers in a fluid are forced by an external magnetic field to flow between electrodes placed in the fluid. Usually the fluid is a hot ionized gas or plasma in which the current carriers are electrons. The electron concentration is increased by adding substances of low ionization potential (e.g. sodium or potassium salts) to the flame.

magnetomotive force (mmf) A measure of the magnetic effect of an electric current in a coil. It is analogous to *electromotive force and is measured in ampere-turns, being dependent on the number of turns in the coil.

magnetosphere A region surrounding a planet in which charged particles are controlled by the magnetic field of the planet rather than by the interplanetary magnetic field carried by the *solar wind. Its shape arises from the interaction between solar wind and planetary magnetic field. The earth's magnetosphere, which includes the *Van Allen radiation belts, extends 60 000 km from the sunward side of the planet but is drawn out to a much greater extent on the opposite side.

magnetostriction The mechanical deformation of a ferromagnetic material (*see* FERROMAGNETISM) when it is subjected to a magnetic field.

magnetron An electronic device used to generate and amplify *microwaves. It consists of a sealed evacuated tube that contains a central cylindrical cathode (source of electrons) inside a cylindrical anode to which electrons are drawn by an electrostatic field. A steady magnetic field applied along the axis of the tube deflects the electrons from their radial path and, if strong enough, will cause them to rotate around the cathode setting up microwave-frequency oscillations. It is widely used in radar generators.

magnification In optical systems, the ratio of the width of an object to the width of its image, both being measured perpendicular to the axis of the system. For a single lens this reduces to the ratio of the distances of the image and the object from the lens when the image is in focus. For optical instruments the magnification is defined as the ratio of the size of the image on the retina produced by an object with and without the instrument.

magnitude A measure of the brightness of stars and other astronomical objects. An object's **apparent magnitude** is its brightness as observed from earth and depends primarily on its *luminosity and its distance. An object's **absolute magnitude** is its apparent magnitude if it lay at a distance of 10 parsecs (32.616 light years). Both apparent and absolute magnitude are measured at various specific wavebands in the visible, ultraviolet, and infrared regions of the electromagnetic spectrum.

Magnolia A genus of evergreen or deciduous shrubs and trees (35 species), native to North America and Asia and widely grown as ornamentals. Up to 45 m high, they have large simple leaves and showy white, yellow, greenish, or pink flowers. These produce papery conelike structures containing winged fruits. Family: *Magnoliaceae*.

magpie A noisy black-and-white crow, *Pica pica*, occurring in Eurasia, NW Africa, and W North America. 44 cm long, it has a long wedge-shaped tail. Magpies are omnivorous and notorious predators of eggs and nestlings; they are also attracted to bright objects. The name is also given to Australian songbirds of the family *Cracticidae*, which includes the *currawongs.

Magritte, René (1898–1967) Belgian surrealist painter. Initially a wallpaper designer and commercial artist, he became associated with the Paris surrealists (*see* SURREALISM) in the late 1920s. In his work everyday images are made to appear menacing by unusual juxtapositions.

Magyars The largest ethnic group in Hungary. They originated from mixed Ugric and Turkic stock and migrated from Siberia during the 5th century, reaching their present location during the late 9th century. *See also* HUNGARIAN.

Maharashtra A state in W central India, on the Arabian Sea. Rising from its coastal plain eastwards over the Western *Ghats, it lies mostly on the Deccan plateau. Cotton, millet, wheat, and rice are farmed. The second most industrialized state, it produces textiles, machinery, and oil products. Bauxite, manganese, and iron ore are mined. Area: 307 690 sq km (118 774 sq mi). Population (2001): 96 752 247. Capital: Bombay.

Mahayana (Sanskrit: Great Vehicle) The school of Buddhism dominant in Tibet, Mongolia, China, Korea, and Japan. More evolved, adaptable, and less conservative and academic than the rival school, the Theravada, the Mahayana teaching differs from it primarily in promulgating the ideal of the Bodhisattva—the one who, having gained enlightenment, remains in the world in order to help other beings to their release.

Mahdi, al- (Arabic: the guided one) In Islamic tradition, a messianic leader who will appear shortly before the end of the world and, for a few years, restore justice and religion. According to some *Shiite Muslims, the 12th imam (9th century AD), who is now hidden, will return as the Mahdi. The best-known claimant to the title was the Sudanese leader **Muhammad Ahmad** (1844–85). After a religious experience, he proclaimed himself the Mahdi and led an uprising against the Egyptian Government. In 1885, after a ten-month siege, he captured Khartoum, which was defended by General *Gordon.

mahjong An ancient Chinese game. It is usually played by 4 people using 2 dice and 136 tiles of bone, ivory, or plastic. 108 of the tiles are arranged in 3 suits: circles, bamboos, and characters. There are also four each of red, white, and green dragons and four each of east, south, west, and north winds. The tiles are built into a square of four walls, symbolizing a walled city. Players score by collecting sequences of tiles.

Mahler, Gustav (1860–1911) Austrian composer and conductor. He directed the Viennese Court Opera from 1897–1907. In 1909 he became conductor of the New York Philharmonic Society, but met resistance to his advocacy of modern music. His nine large-scale symphonies (and uncompleted tenth) were written during brief vacations. The second (*Resurrection Symphony*), third, fourth, and eighth (*Symphony of a Thousand*) employ vocal soloists. He also wrote song cycles.

mahogany An evergreen tree of the genus *Swietenia* (7 species), native to tropical America and the West Indies and widely cultivated for timber. Up to about 20 m high, it has large compound leaves, greenish-yellow flower clusters, and fruit capsules containing winged seeds. *S. macrophylla* and *S. mahagoni* are the most important species: their hard red-brown wood is highly valued for furniture. Family: *Meliaceae*.

maidenhair fern An ornamental *fern of the genus *Adiantum* (about 200 species), especially *A. capillus-veneris*, found worldwide in moist warm places. From a creeping rhizome arise delicate brown or black stalks, about 2.5–30 cm high, bearing fan-shaped green leaflets. Clusters of spore capsules (sori) are situated on the leaf margins, which are folded onto the underside. Family: *Adiantaceae*.

m

maidenhair tree *See* GINKGO.

Maidstone 51 17N 0 32E A town in SE England, the administrative centre of Kent on the River Medway. It is an ancient town and the centre of an important fruit- and hop-growing region. There are brewing, paper, cement, confectionery, and engineering industries. Population (1991): 90 878.

Mailer, Norman (1923–) US novelist and journalist. He established his reputation with the World War II novel *The Naked and the Dead* (1948). His concern with American society is expressed in such works as *An American Dream* (1965), *The Armies of the Night* (1968), and *The Executioner's Song* (1979). More recent works include *Ancient Evenings* (1983) and *Harlot's Ghost* (1991); *The Time of Our Time* (1998) is a collection of his journalism.

Main, River A river in central Germany, flowing generally W through Frankfurt to join the River Rhine at Mainz. It is linked by canal with the River Danube. Length: 515 km (320 mi).

Maine A coastal state in the extreme NE USA. The largest of the New England states, it consists of uplands in the W and NW and lowlands along the deeply indented coast in the E. Four-fifths of the state is forested. It is the most sparsely populated state E of the Mississippi. Manufacturing is most important and the major products are paper and pulp, leather goods, food, timber, and textiles. It is an area of considerable mineral wealth; limestone, building stone, sand, and gravel are exploited. The state's major agricultural products are potatoes, poultry, dairying, apples, and beef. *History*: although claimed by both Britain and France, it became a British possession (1763). It entered the Union as part of Massachusetts (1788) and later became a separate state (1820). Area: 86 027 sq km (33 215 sq mi). Population (2000): 1 274 923. Capital: Augusta.

Mainland 1. (*or* **Pomona**) The largest of the Orkney Islands, divided into two main parts by Kirkwall Bay and *Scapa Flow. Area: 492 sq km (190 sq mi). Population (1991): 15 128. Chief town: Kirkwall. **2.** The largest of the Shetland Islands. Area: about 583 sq km (225 sq mi). Population (1991): 17 596. Chief town: Lerwick.

main sequence *See* HERTZSPRUNG-RUSSELL DIAGRAM.

Mainz (French name: Mayence) 50 00N 8 16E A city and port in SW Germany, the capital of Rhineland-Palatinate at the confluence of the Rivers Rhine and Main. Originally a Celtic settlement, it was the first German archbishopric and in the 15th century Gutenberg set up his printing press here. It is a wine-trading centre with varied industries. Population (1999 est): 185 600.

maiolica Italian pottery originating in the 15th century. Made from calcareous clay, the soft buff body is coated with white tin glaze and brilliantly painted in lustre and rainbow colours. Items made include tableware and display ornaments. Principal centres of manufacture were Gubbio, Deruta, Caffaggiolo, and Faenza (*see* FAIENCE).

maize An annual *cereal grass, *Zea mays*, also called Indian corn, sweet corn, or corn, native to the New World and widely cultivated in tropical and subtropical regions. 1–4.5 m high, it bears a tassel of male flowers at the top of the stem and spikes of female flowers in the leaf axils; these develop into cobs, each comprising long parallel rows of grains. Maize is used as a vegetable, in breakfast cereals, flour, and livestock feed and for the extraction of corn oil. It is the third most important cereal crop (after wheat and rice), the USA being the chief producing country.

Major, John (1943–) British Conservative politician; prime minister (1990–97). Having entered parliament in 1979, he served as foreign secretary (1989) and chancellor of the exchequer (1989–90) before succeeding Margaret *Thatcher as premier. Despite success in the 1992 general election, an economic recovery, and a new peace initiative in Northern Ireland, his party was divided over Europe and troubled by scandal. He led the party to a crushing defeat in the 1997 general election.

Majorca (Spanish name: Mallorca) A Spanish island in the Mediterranean Sea, the largest of the Balearic Islands. The chief occupations are agriculture and tourism; cereals, legumes, oranges, olives, and figs are produced and marble is quarried. Area: 3639 sq km (1465 sq mi). Population (latest est): 614 000. Capital: Palma.

Makarios III (Mikhail Khristodolou Mouskos; 1913–77) Cypriot churchman and statesman; archbishop of the Orthodox Church of Cyprus (1950–77) and president of Cyprus (1960–74, 1974–77). In 1956 he was deported to the Seychelles by the British because of his support for Greek-Cypriot union.

Malabo (name until 1973: Santa Isabel) 3 45W 8 48E The capital of Equatorial Guinea, a port in the N of the island of Bioko (formerly Macías Nguema), founded by the British in 1827. Population (1995 est): 47 500.

Malacca (*or* **Melaka**) **1.** 02 14N 102 14E A historic port in W Peninsular Malaysia, the capital of Malacca state. It was colonized successively by the Portuguese, Dutch, and British after 1511. Population (1991): 295 299. **2.** A state in W Peninsular Malaysia, on the Strait of Malacca. Consisting chiefly of a low-lying coastal plain, it produces rice, rubber, copra, tin, and bauxite. Area: 1650 sq km (637 sq mi). Population (2000): 602 867. Capital: Malacca.

malachite An ore of copper consisting of hydrated copper carbonate, $Cu_2(OH)_2CO_3$. It is bright green and is found in deposits of copper minerals. It occurs in massive form, often with a smooth surface.

Málaga 36 43N 4 25W A city in S Spain, in Andalusia on the Mediterranean Sea. Founded by the Phoenicians (12th century BC), it passed successively to the Romans, the Visigoths, and the Moors, before falling to Ferdinand and Isabella in 1487. A major tourist centre and port, it exports olives, almonds, and dried fruits. Population (1998 est): 528 079.

Malamud, Bernard (1914–86) US novelist. With such witty novels as *The Assistant* (1957) and *A New Life* (1961) he built a reputation as a skilful chronicler of Jewish characters and themes. His other novels include *The Tenants* (1971) and *God's Grace* (1982).

malaria An infectious disease caused by protozoa of the genus *Plasmodium*. Malaria is transmitted by the female *Anopheles* mosquito, which lives only in the tropics. There are four species of *Plasmodium* that infect man and cause different types of malaria. Malignant tertian malaria (caused by *P. falciparum*) is the most severe; benign tertian malaria (caused by *P. vivax*) is less often fatal but there are repeated attacks. The parasites invade the red blood cells and cause them to burst. There is always fever and there may be fits, diarrhoea, shock, and jaundice. There are drugs (such as chloroquine) to treat and prevent the disease, but it remains a major cause of death and ill health in the tropics.

Malawi (name until 1963: Nyasaland) A country in SE Africa, between Tanzania, Zambia, and Mozambique. Lake Malawi lies at its E border and the land consists mainly of high plateaus reaching heights of over 3000 m (9800 ft). The majority of the population is Bantu. *Economy*: chiefly agricultural. The main subsistence crop is maize, and cash crops include tobacco, tea, sugar, and groundnuts, which are the chief exports. Mineral resources are sparse. *History*: the area was visited by the Portuguese in the 17th century and, after Livingstone's exploration, became a British protectorate in 1891. In 1953 it was joined with Northern and Southern Rhodesia to form the Federation of Rhodesia and Nyasaland. Nyasaland became independent in 1964. In 1966 it became a republic within the British Commonwealth with Dr Hastings Banda (1905–97) as its first president (subsequently life president). Steps towards implementing multiparty democracy were taken in 1993 and in 1994 Bakili Muluzi was elected president. The early 2000s saw a serious food shortage. In 2004 there were riots when Muluzi's chosen successor, Bingu wa Mutharika, was declared victorious in presidential elections. Official languages: Chichewa and English. Currency: kwacha of 100 tambala. Area: 94 079 sq km (36 324 sq mi). Population (2003 est): 11 651 000. Capital: Lilongwe.

Malay A language of the Indonesian branch of the Austronesian family spoken in SE Asia and Indonesia. The dialect of the S Malay peninsula is the basis of standard Malay. It can be written in Roman or Arabic script. The Malay people probably migrated to this area from China between 2500 and 1500 BC. Since the 15th century Islam has been the accepted religion, but vestiges of former Hinduism survive.

Malay Archipelago (former name: East Indies) An island group in SE Asia, the largest in the world. It lies between the Pacific and Indian Oceans and between the Asian and Australian continents. It comprises the Indonesian, Malaysian, and Philippine islands; New Guinea is sometimes included.

Malay peninsula The land from the *Kra Isthmus (connecting the peninsula to the mainland) to the Strait of Malacca (dividing it from Sumatra). The peninsula is tropical and partly mountainous, and is occupied by the states of Thailand (part of the Kra Isthmus), Malaysia, and Singapore.

Malaysia A country in SE Asia, consisting of the 11 states of Peninsular Malaysia (formerly the Federation of Malaya) and the states of *Sabah and *Sarawak in N Borneo. Peninsular Malaysia consists of coastal plains rising to mountains in the interior. Most of the inhabitants are Malays and Chinese. *Economy*: the country industrialized rapidly in the 1970s and 1980s and now manufactures cars and electronic goods. The resulting economic boom ended abruptly in late 1997, when the stock market and currency collapsed owing to the financial crisis in SE Asia. Malaysia is a major exporter of rubber, tin, and palm oil; rice is the chief food crop. Timber and fishing are also important. Minerals exploited include tin, iron ore, bauxite, ilmenite, and gold. *History*: from the 9th to the 14th centuries the Srivijaya empire dominated the area. In the 14th century it was overrun by Hindu Javanese and in about 1400 Malacca was established as an Islamic centre. In 1511 the port was taken by the Portuguese and in 1641 by the Dutch. British interest in the Malay states began in the 18th century and increased with the opening of the Suez Canal. Following occupation by the Japanese during World War II, the Federation of Malaya was established (1948). Malaya became independent in 1957 and in 1963 part of the federal state of Malaysia. There has been considerable unrest since the 1960s caused mainly by Chinese resentment of Malay dominance in the government. In 1997–98 the severe economic crisis led the government to adopt harsh measures, including the expulsion of some two million foreign workers. In 2003 Dr Mahathir bin Mohamad, prime minister since 1981, stepped down in favour of Abdullah Ahmad Badawi. Official language: Bahasa Malaysia. Currency: ringgit of 100 sen. Area: 329 749 sq km (127 289 sq mi). Population (2003 est): 25 225 000. Capitals: Putrajaya (administrative), Kuala Lumpur (financial).

Malcolm III (c. 1031–93) King of the Scots (1057–93). He became king after killing *Macbeth, the murderer of his father Duncan I (d. 1040; reigned 1034–40). He became a vassal of William the Conqueror (1072) and was murdered during the last of frequent raids into N England.

Malcolm X (1925–65) US militant Black leader. A former member of the *Black Muslims, he founded the rival Organization of Afro-American Unity (1964), which backed violent means of achieving racial equality. He was assassinated while addressing a rally.

Maldives, Republic of (Divehi name: Divehi Raajjeyge Jumhooriyyaa; name until 1969: Maldive Islands) A small country in the Indian Ocean, to the SW of Sri Lanka. It consists of a large number of small coral islands, grouped in atolls, of which just over 200 are inhabited. Most of the population is of mixed Indian, Sinhalese, and Arabic descent. *Economy*: coconuts and fish are the main exports. Other sources of revenue are shipping, tourism, and copra production. *History*: formerly a dependency of Ceylon, the islands were officially under British protection from 1887 to 1965. They were ruled by an elected sultan until 1968, when they became a republic. The Republic of Maldives became a full member of the Commonwealth in 1985. As most of the islands rise less than 1.8 m (6 ft) above sea level, the future of the Maldives is threatened by the ecological changes associated with global warming. Official language: Divehi. Currency: rufiyaa of 100 laari. Area: 298 sq km (115 sq mi). Population (2003 est): 285 000. Capital: Malé.

Mali, Republic of (name until 1959: French Sudan) A large landlocked country in West Africa. It consists largely of desert, the flood plains of the River Niger providing most of the fertile land. The majority of the population are Bambara, Fulani, and Senufo. *Economy*: chiefly subsistence agriculture, especially livestock, including cattle, camels, and sheep. The main crops are rice, millet, cassava, cotton, and groundnuts. Dried and smoked fish, cattle, and groundnuts are the main exports. Industry is based mainly on the processing of food and hides and skins. Mineral reserves of bauxite, uranium, and oil are present but only salt and small quantities of gold are exploited. *History*: from the 4th century AD the area was occupied by successive empires, including those of Ghana, Mali, and Gao. In the late 19th century it was conquered by the French and, as French Sudan, it became part of French West Africa. It achieved internal self-government as part of the French Community in 1958 and became a fully independent republic in 1960. In 1968 the government was overthrown in a military coup led by Lt Moussa Traoré, who became president in 1969. In 1991 social unrest led to his overthrow in a coup led by Amadou Toumani Touré; free elections were held in 1992 and Alpha Konare became president. Konare stepped down in 2002 and the former military ruler Touré was elected president. Official language: French. Currency: CFA franc of 100 centimes. Area: 1 204 021 sq km (464 752 sq mi). Population (2003 est): 11 626 000. Capital: Bamako.

mallard A dabbling duck, *Anas platyrhynchos*, common on ponds and lakes in the N hemisphere. About 55 cm long, females are mottled brown and males greyish with a green head, white collar, reddish breast, black rump, a curly tail, and a broad yellow bill. Both sexes have a purple wing speculum.

Mallarmé, Stéphane (1842–98) French poet. He became a major figure of the Symbolist movement, believing that the function of poetry was to evoke the ideal essences that lay behind the world of actual appearances. His best-known works include *Hérodiade* (1864) and *L'Après-midi d'un faune* (1865).

mallow A herbaceous plant of the genus *Malva* (30 species), native to N temperate regions. Mallows, which may be creeping or erect, grow up to 90 cm tall. They have hairy lobed leaves and five-petalled flowers, which are usually purple, pink, or white. The tree mallow (*Lavatera arborea*) is a shrublike biennial, up to 3 m high, with rose-purple flowers. Family: *Malvaceae*. *See also* MARSH MALLOW.

Malmö 55 38N 12 57E A city and port in S Sweden, on the Sound opposite Copenhagen. It was a prominent trade and shipping centre in the middle ages. Malmö's varied industries include shipbuilding, textiles, and food processing. Population (2000 est): 257 574.

Malory, Sir Thomas (?1400–1471) English writer. He was the author of *Morte d'Arthur* (c. 1469), a narrative in 21 books of the legendary court of King Arthur, drawn mostly from French sources. The work was printed by Caxton in 1485. Malory was probably a Warwickshire knight who had fought in France, became an MP in 1445, and was several times imprisoned.

Malraux, André (1901–76) French novelist and essayist. His career included active service with communist revolutionaries in China in the 1920s, with the Republican forces in the Spanish Civil War, and with the French Resistance in World War II. His novels include *Man's Estate* (1933) and *Days of Hope* (1938). He also wrote on art and produced a volume of memoirs, *Antimémoires* (1967).

Malta, Republic of A small country in the Mediterranean Sea, to the S of Sicily comprising the two main islands of Malta and Gozo and several islets. *Economy*: Malta was previously heavily dependent on British military bases. The naval dockyards have been converted to commercial use and port facilities have been developed; shipbuilding and repair are important. There is some agriculture, both crops and livestock, and fishing. Tourism is now the most important source of revenue. Exports include clothing, textiles, machinery, and food. *History*: occupied successively by the Phoenicians, Greeks, Carthaginians, and Romans, the island was conquered by the Arabs in 870 AD. In 1090 it was united with Sicily and in 1530 was granted to the Knights Hospitallers. In 1798 the island was occupied by the French and then by the British, to whom it was formally ceded in 1814. As a crown colony it became an important naval and air base, showing heroic resistance to German attack in World War II. Malta became fully independent in 1964; in 1974 under Dom Mintoff it became a republic within the British Commonwealth. Malta joined the EU in 2004. Official languages: Maltese and English. Currency: Maltese lira of 100 cents. Area: 316 sq km (122 sq mi). Population (2003 est): 399 000. Capital: Valletta.

Malthus, Thomas Robert (1766–1834) British clergyman and economist, famous for his population theories. In his *Essay on the Principle of Population* (*First Essay*, 1798; *Second Essay*, 1803) Malthus argued that most of mankind is doomed to remain at near-starvation level as growth in food production, which increases at an arithmetical rate, is negated by the geometrical increase in population.

Malvern 52 05N 2 20W A town in W central England, in Worcestershire, consisting of Great Malvern and several villages incorporating the name. Lying on the E slopes of the Malvern Hills, it is a spa town with a famous public school (Malvern College, founded 1863). Population (1991): 31 537.

Malvinas, Islas *See* FALKLAND ISLANDS.

mamba A large agile highly venomous snake belonging to the African genus *Dendroaspis* (4–5 species). The aggressive black mamba (*D. polylepis*) is 4.3 m long, lives in open rocky regions, and preys on birds and small mammals. The smaller arboreal green mamba (*D. angusticeps*) reaches a length of 2.7 m. Mambas are egg-laying snakes. Family: *Elapidae* (cobras, mambas, coral snakes).

mammal. This large and diverse group of animals has succeeded in colonizing almost every available habitat on earth, even the most inhospitable. Representative mammals are shown from eight of the world's major habitats (the animals depicted in each habitat are not necessarily from the same geographical region).

Mamet, David (Alan) (1947–) US playwright, screenwriter, and film director. His plays, which are noted for their naturalistic dialogue, include *American Buffalo* (1975), *Glengarry Glen Ross* (1984), and *Oleanna* (1992).

mammal A warm-blooded animal belonging to the class *Mammalia* (about 4250 species). The evolution of mammals from reptiles involved the development of a temperature-regulation system with an insulating layer of fur and

sweat glands in the skin for cooling. This enabled mammals to become highly active, with well-developed sense organs and brains, and to colonize cold climates. The survival of the young was improved by the evolution of *mammary glands, and in placental mammals a specialized nourishing membrane (the *placenta) in the uterus (womb).

The majority of modern mammalian species are terrestrial, ranging in size from tiny shrews to the elephant. However, bats are flying mammals and whales have adapted to a wholly marine existence.

mammary gland The gland in female mammals that secretes milk. Believed to have evolved from sweat glands, there are one or more pairs on the ventral (under) side of the body. The number of glands is related to the number of young produced at one birth. Each gland consists of branching ducts leading from milk-secreting cells and opening to the exterior through a nipple. In the most primitive mammals (*Monotremata*) there are no nipples and the milk is secreted directly onto the body surface. *See also* LACTATION.

m

mammoth An extinct elephant belonging to the genus *Mammuthus*, whose remains have been found in India, Europe, and North America. Of the four types known, the imperial mammoth (*M. imperator*) was the largest, 4.5 m at the shoulder. The woolly mammoth (*M. primigenius*) had thick body hair and tusks up to 2.5 m long.

Man, Isle of An island in the Irish Sea, between England and Ireland. It has been a British Crown possession since 1828 but is virtually self-governing with its own parliament, the Court of Tynwald. It consists of central hills rising to 620 m (2034 ft) at Snaefell, with lowlands in the N and S. Tourism is the main source of revenue, with attractions including the famous annual Tourist Trophy (TT) motorcycle races. Agriculture is varied; sheep and cattle are raised and produce includes cereals, turnips, and potatoes. *History*: the island was originally inhabited by Celts and the Manx language survived in common usage until the 19th century. The island became a dependency of Norway in the 9th century AD and was ceded to Scotland (1266), coming under English control after 1406. Area: 588 sq km (227 sq mi). Population (2001): 76 315. Capital: Douglas.

Managua 12 06N 86 18W The capital of Nicaragua, on the S shore of Lake Managua. Formerly an Indian settlement, it became capital in 1857. It suffered severe damage from earthquakes in 1931 and 1972 and from the civil war (1979). Population (1995 est, urban area): 1 195 000.

manatee A herbivorous aquatic *mammal belonging to the genus *Trichechus* (3 species), of warm Atlantic waters and coastal rivers of Africa and America. Up to 4.5 m long, manatees have a rounded body with tail fin and flippers and a squarish snout. The American manatee (*T. manatus*) of Florida feeds mainly at night. Family: *Trichechidae*; order: *Sirenia*. *See also* DUGONG.

Manaus (*or* **Manáos**) 3 06S 60 00W A city in NW Brazil, the capital of Amazonas state on the Rio Negro. Founded in 1660, it became the centre of the rubber boom (1890–1920). It remains the chief inland port of the Amazon basin and is accessible to oceangoing steamers. Exports include rubber, brazil nuts, timber, and other forest products. Population (2000): 1 394 724.

Manawatu River A river in New Zealand, in SW North Island flowing generally W and SW to the Tasman Sea NE of Wellington. The surrounding plain is one of New Zealand's most productive farming areas. Length: 182 km (113 mi).

Man Booker Prize *See* BOOKER PRIZE.

Manchester 1. 53 30N 2 15W A city in NW England, in Manchester unitary authority, Greater Manchester, situated on the River Irwell and forming part of a large conurbation. Linked with the Mersey estuary by the Manchester Ship Canal (opened 1894), it is an important port as well as England's second largest commercial centre (banking, insurance). Industries include chemicals, engineering, clothing, printing, paper, rubber, food products, and electrical goods. It is also a cultural and educational centre. The 15th-century parish church became Manchester Cathedral in 1847. *History*: the Roman fort of Mancunium, Manchester developed as a regional market place for raw wool and flax and finished pieces. From the mid-18th century it became the world's main cotton-manufacturing town. Its rapid growth led to industrial discontent and political agitation (*see* PETERLOO MASSACRE). It also nurtured the basic principles of economic and political liberalism, embodied in the **Manchester School** (a group of political economists, the most famous being John *Bright (1811–89) and Richard Cobden (1804–65)). Population (1991): 402 889. **2.** A unitary authority in NW England, in Greater Manchester. Area: 116 sq km (45 sq mi). Population (2001 est): 392 819.

Manchuria A region in NE China bordering

on Russia, roughly comprising the provinces of Heilongjiang, Jilin, and Liaoning. It is mountainous in the E and W with a large central fertile plain, which is a major industrial and agricultural area. Products include timber, minerals, such as coal and iron, and fish. *History*: the area was for centuries inhabited and fought over by the Manchu, Mongols, and Chinese. Their power struggles resulted in empires established over China by the Mongols (1279–1368; *see* YUAN) and Manchus (1644–1912; *see* QING). In the late 19th century it was dominated by Russia (1898–1904) and then by Japan (1905–45). In 1931, following the Mukden Incident (*see* SHENYANG), Japanese forces invaded Manchuria and established the puppet state of Manchukuo. After 1945 the area received much aid from the Soviet Union until the 1960s, when the break between China and the Soviet Union took place. Since then military forces have been massed along the border. Area: about 1 300 000 sq km (502 000 sq mi).

Mandalay 21 57 96 04E A city in Myanmar (Burma), on the Irrawaddy River. The last capital of the Burmese kingdom, it fell to the British in 1885. It has numerous monasteries, temples, and pagodas and is the site of a university (1964). Mandalay is the principal commercial centre of Upper Burma. Population (1995 est): 677 000.

mandarin Chinese bureaucrat, whose appointment in the civil service was by examination. Mandarins occupied a privileged position in society and spoke the Mandarin dialect of *Chinese, which in its standard, Beijing, form is now spoken by 70% of the population.

Mandela, Nelson (Rolihlahla) (1918–) South African statesman; president of South Africa (1994–99). He was a lawyer, practising in Johannesburg, when he was acquitted of treason (1961) but retried (1963–64) and sentenced to life imprisonment; his release was finally achieved in 1990. He became president of the African National Congress in 1991. In 1993 he signed South Africa's new transitional multiracial constitution, which marked the end of apartheid, and was awarded the Nobel Peace Prize with F. W. de Klerk. In the country's first multi-racial election he won an overwhelming victory for the ANC. By the late 1990s, he was an influential and much respected world statesman. His wife, **Winnie Mandela** (1934–), also became active in South African politics but in 1991 she was found guilty on a charge of kidnapping and being accessory to assault. She and her husband separated in 1992 and divorced in 1996.

Mandelson, Peter (Benjamin) (1953–) British politician. He became the Labour Party's director of communications in 1985 and an MP in 1992. He joined the cabinet in 1997 but resigned (1998) when it was revealed that he had failed to disclose a loan from a colleague. In 1999 he became secretary of state for Northern Ireland but in 2001 he was forced to resign again over his intervention in the passport application by an Indian sponsor of the Millennium Dome.

mandolin A plucked musical instrument, generally having four double wire strings tuned as the violin. It is played with a plectrum, using a tremolo to sustain longer notes. It is used in informal music and more rarely as a solo or orchestral instrument.

mandrake A herb of the genus *Mandragora*, especially *M. officinarum*, native to Europe. It has large simple leaves, white flowers, and a thick forked root, which was formerly believed to have healing and aphrodisiac properties. Family: *Solanaceae*.

mandrill A large *Old World monkey, *Mandrillus sphinx*, of West African coastal forests. They are 66–84 cm long including the tail (5–7.5 cm), with red and blue muzzle and buttocks and yellow-brown hair. They live in family groups and forage for plants and insects.

Manet, Edouard (1832–83) French painter. By 1860 he was painting contemporary scenes, but throughout his career he remained indebted to the Old Masters, particularly Velázquez and Hals. He exhibited at the Paris Salon, where such paintings as *Olympia* and *Déjeuner sur l'herbe* (both Louvre) were scorned and derided. In the 1870s he adopted the technique of the impressionists. Such paintings as *The Balcony* (Louvre) and *The Luncheon* (Munich) anticipate 20th-century art by making brushwork, colour, and design more important than the subject matter.

manganese (Mn) A hard grey brittle transition element that resembles iron, first isolated in 1774 by J. G. Gahn (1745–1818). It occurs in nature in many minerals, especially pyrolusite (MnO_2) and rhodochrosite ($MnCO_3$), in addition to the extensive deposits of manganese nodules discovered on the deep ocean floors. It is extracted by reduction of the oxide, with magnesium or aluminium, or by electrolysis. The metal is used in many alloys, particularly in steel, in which manganese improves the strength and hardness. Manganese forms compounds in a number of different *valence states: for example MnO, Mn_3O_4, MnO_2. The permanganate ion (MnO_4^-) is a well-known oxidizing agent. At no 25; at wt 54.9380; mp 1246±3°C; bp 2062°C.

mange A contagious skin disease, caused by mites, that can affect domestic livestock, pets, and man (*see* SCABIES). The parasites bite or burrow into the skin causing hair loss, scaly dry skin, pimples, blisters, and intense itching. Treatment is with a suitable insecticide, such as gamma benzene hexachloride.

mango A large evergreen tropical tree, *Mangifera indica*, native to SE Asia but cultivated throughout the tropics for its fruit. Growing 15–18 m high, it has long narrow leaves and pinkish flowers. The oblong fruit, up to 2.3 kg in weight, has a green, yellow, or reddish skin and contains a stony seed, surrounded by juicy orange edible flesh that has a spicy flavour. Family: *Anacardiaceae*.

mangroves Shrubs and trees forming dense thickets and low forests on coastal mudflats, salt marshes, and estuaries throughout the tropics. Many are evergreen, with shiny leathery leaves and aerial supporting (prop) roots. The main species are the common or red mangrove (*Rhizophora mangle*), the black mangrove (*Avicennia nitida*), and *Sonneratia* species.

manic-depressive psychosis (*or* **bipolar disorder**) A severe mental illness causing repeated episodes of *depression, mania (excessive euphoria and overactivity), or both. Long-term treatment with lithium salts can prevent attacks or reduce their frequency and severity.

Manichaeism A religion influenced by both *Gnosticism and Christianity. It originated in Persia (c. 230 AD), spread throughout Asia and the Roman Empire, and survived in Chinese Turkistan until the 13th century. Its founder, Mani (c. 216–c. 276), was martyred by the adherents of Zoroastrianism (*see* ZOROASTER). Fundamental to his creed was the belief that matter is entirely evil, but within each individual is imprisoned a soul, which is a spark of the divine light.

Manila 14 30N 121 12E The capital and main port of the Philippines, on Manila Bay in Luzon. Founded by the Spanish in 1571, it suffered several foreign occupations over the centuries and the old town was destroyed in World War II. The official capital was transferred to Quezon City on the outskirts (1948–76). An educational centre, it has over 20 universities, including the University of Santo Tomas founded in 1611. It has one of the finest harbours in the world and is also an important industrial centre; its industries include textiles, pharmaceuticals, and food processing. Population (2000): 1 581 082.

manioc *See* CASSAVA.

Manitoba A province of central Canada, in the centre of North America. Although it is one of the Prairie Provinces, only the SW is true prairie. Further to the NE lies the *Red River Valley and three large lakes (Winnipeg, Winnipegosis, and Manitoba) with extensive forests in the N. Manitoba's economy is based on large mechanized farms producing grains and livestock. Forests, fisheries, and hydroelectricity are also important. Manitoba produces copper, gold, zinc, silver, nickel, and oil. Greater *Winnipeg contains over half the population. *History*: originally exploited for furs, Manitoba first attracted dispossessed Scots Highlanders as settlers (1812). Acquisition of the area by Canada (1869) provoked the Riel Rebellion (1869–70), an uprising of French-speaking Métis. Manitoba became a province in 1870. Area: 548 495 sq km (211 774 sq mi). Population (2001 est): 1 150 200. Capital: Winnipeg.

Mann, Thomas (1875–1955) German novelist. Art and the artist are his main themes, in the novella *Death in Venice* (1912), *The Magic Mountain* (1924), and *Doctor Faustus* (1947), a novel about a modern composer of genius. His other works include *Joseph and His Brothers* (1933–44), a series of four novels based on the biblical story of Joseph, and the picaresque *Felix Krull* (1954). Mann opposed Nazism and was forced to emigrate to the USA in the 1930s. He was awarded a Nobel Prize in 1929.

mannerism An art movement dominant in Italy from about 1520 to 1600. Mannerism developed out of the *Renaissance style, some of its characteristics being evident in the late work of *Raphael and Michelangelo. It aimed to surpass the Renaissance style in virtuosity and emotional impact. In painting this led to a distortion of scale, an elongation of form, and dissonance of colour. Leading mannerist painters were Pontormo, Parmigianino, *Vasari, and *Bronzino.

Mannheim 49 30N 8 28E A city in SW Germany, in Baden-Württemberg at the confluence of the Rivers Rhine and Neckar. It was the seat of the Electors Palatine (1720–98) and has a notable baroque castle. It is a major port with an oil refinery and its manufactures include motor vehicles and agricultural machinery. Population (1999 est): 308 400.

manometer An instrument for measuring

pressure differences. The simplest form consists of a U-shaped tube containing mercury, one arm of which is connected to a source of pressure and the other is open. The difference in height of the liquid in the arms is a measure of the pressure difference.

manor The most common unit of agrarian organization in medieval Europe, introduced into England by the Normans. The manor was essentially the lord's landed estate, usually consisting of the lord's own farm (the demesne), and land let out to peasant tenants, chiefly *villeins, who worked for the demesne and were legally dependent upon their lord.

Mansfield, Katherine (Kathleen Mansfield Beauchamp; 1888–1923) New Zealand short-story writer. She came to Europe in 1908 and published her first collection of stories in 1911. *Bliss* (1920) and *The Garden Party* (1922) contain her best-known stories, often compared in stylistic subtlety to those of Chekhov.

manslaughter The crime of killing a person either (1) accidentally by an unlawful act or by culpable negligence or (2) in the heat of passion, after provocation. The second case is closely related to murder, and is possible only if there is no evidence of premeditation.

manta ray A *ray fish, also called devil ray or devil fish, of the family *Mobulidae*. 60–660 cm long, they swim near the surface of warm-temperate and tropical waters, feeding on plankton and small animals swept into the mouth by hornlike feeding fins projecting from the front of the head.

Mantegna, Andrea (c. 1431–1506) Italian Renaissance painter and engraver, born near Vicenza. His marriage (1453) to the daughter of Jacopo *Bellini connected him with the Venetian school. As court painter to the Duke of Mantua from 1459, he painted nine panels depicting *The Triumph of Caesar* (Hampton Court, London). His fresco decorations for the bridal chamber of the ducal palace include portraits of members of the Mantuan court and an illusionistic ceiling, which anticipates the *baroque.

mantis An insect belonging to the family *Mantidae* (2000 species), found in tropical and warm temperate regions. Up to 125 mm long, mantids blend with the surrounding vegetation and are voracious carnivores, using their forelegs to capture insects and other small animals. The "praying" position held by the forelegs at rest accounts for the name praying mantis, applied in particular to *Mantis religiosa*. Order: *Dictyoptera*.

Mantua (Italian name: Mantova) 45 10N 10 47E A city in N Italy, in Lombardy on the River Mincio. Notable buildings include a cathedral (10th–18th centuries) and a 14th-century castle. An important tourist centre, Mantua also has tanning, printing, and sugar-refining industries. Population (latest est): 54 808.

Maori A Polynesian people of New Zealand, who make up about 10% of the population. They trace their origins to migrants, probably from the Cook Islands, who came in canoes around 1350. They were an agricultural people who lived mainly in the North Island in large fortified villages of timber dwellings. The traditional arts of wood carving and dancing still survive but urbanization and Christianization have largely destroyed the Maoris' way of life.

Mao Tse-tung (*or* **Mao Ze Dong**; 1893–1976) Chinese communist statesman. Born into a peasant family, he was a Marxist by 1920 and helped to form the Chinese Communist Party (CCP) in 1921. In 1931 he became chairman of the Jiangxi Soviet. Forced to evacuate Jiangxi in 1934, Mao led the communist forces on the Long March. His arrival in Yan'an in 1935 marked his emergence as a leader of the CCP. Following the defeat of Japan in the Sino-Japanese War of 1937–45, civil war was resumed, ending in communist victory. In 1949 Mao, as chairman of the Communist Party, proclaimed the establishment of the People's Republic of China. Mao's political writings formed the theoretical basis of the new government and led to the founding of communes and the Great Leap Forward. He stepped down as chairman in 1958, but reappeared with greater standing during the *Cultural Revolution.

The modified form of *Marxism developed by Mao is known as **Maoism**. Mao's strategy for revolution in China gave central importance to peasant armies rather than to the action of the industrial working class in urban centres. Similarly, he believed that the socialist revolutions would develop first in the underdeveloped countries rather than in advanced capitalist countries.

maple A shrub or tree of the genus *Acer* (over 200 species), widespread in N temperate regions and often grown for timber and ornament. Growing 6–35 m high, maples usually bear lobed leaves, which turn yellow, orange, or red in autumn, and small yellow or greenish

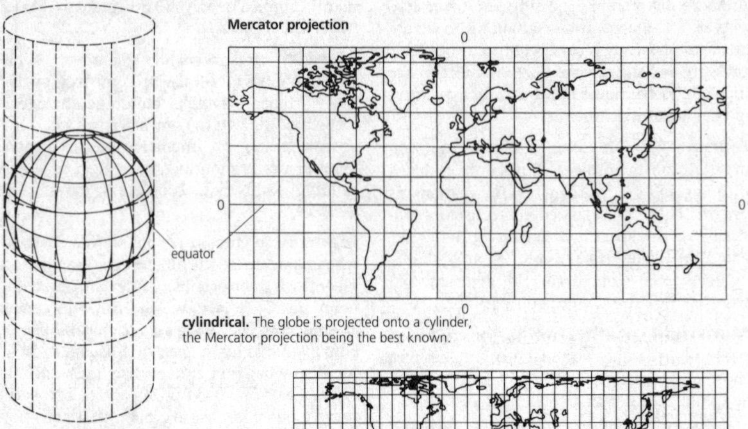

cylindrical. The globe is projected onto a cylinder, the Mercator projection being the best known.

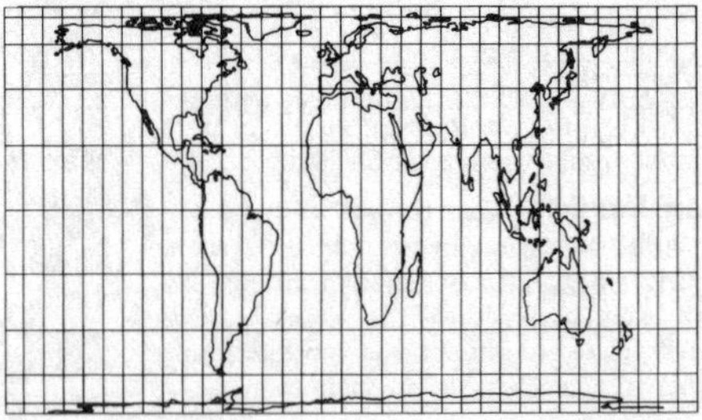

Peters' projection. Designed by the German historian, Arno Peters, in 1973, this modified cylindrical equal-area projection draws attention away from Europe, focusing instead on the developing countries, which are placed prominently in the centre of the map. It aims to show countries more accurately in relation to their true size but has an odd appearance in that land surfaces close to the equator are elongated and those in high latitudes are compressed.

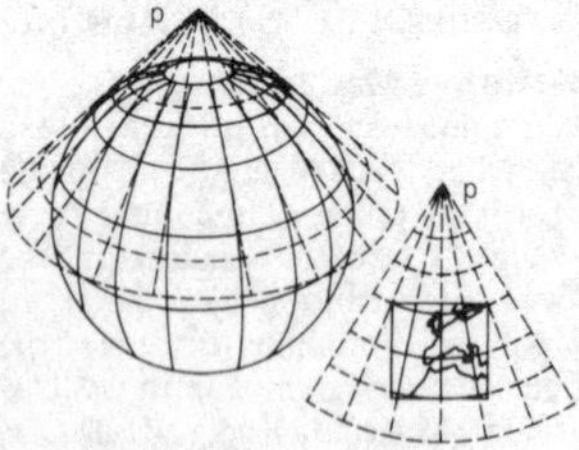

conical. The globe is projected onto the cone as if it contained a source of light casting a shadow of its features onto the cone, resulting in a flat projection when the cone is unfurled. The cone may touch the globe along one parallel of latitude or intersect along two parallels.

orthographic projection

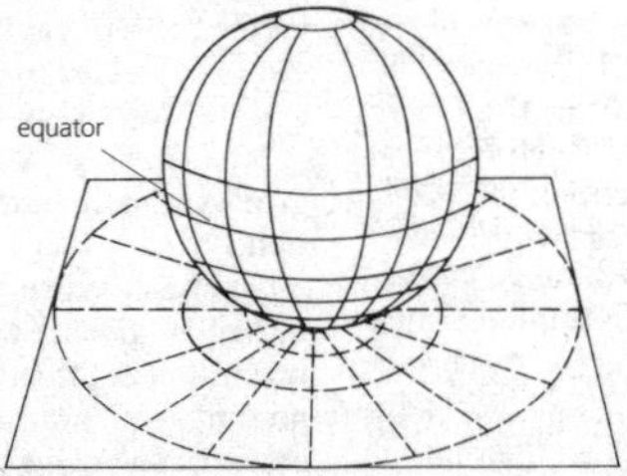

azimuthal (*or* zenithal). The globe is pictured as a flattened disc. It may be projected as if it were seen from a point in the centre of the earth (gnomonic), from a point on the far side of the earth (stereographic), or from a point in space (orthographic).

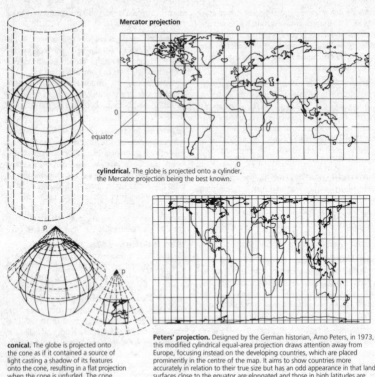

Lambert's azimuthal projection

map projection

flowers, which give rise to paired winged fruits (samaras). The sugar maple (*A. saccharum*) of E North America is the source of maple sugar. Family: *Aceraceae*.

map projection The representation of the curved surface of the earth on a plane surface. The parallels of latitude and meridians of longitude (*see* LATITUDE AND LONGITUDE) are represented as a network of intersecting lines. It is not possible to produce a projection of the earth's surface without some distortion of area, shape, or direction. In the conical projection the globe is projected onto a cone with its point above either the North or the South Pole. In the cylindrical projection the globe is projected onto a cylinder touching the equator; the *Mercator projection is of this type. Part of the globe is projected upon a plane from any point of vision in the azimuthal projection.

Maputo (name until 1975: Lourenço Marques) 25 58S 32 35E The capital and chief port of Mozambique, on Delagoe Bay. It became the capital of Portuguese East Africa in 1907. It is a major East African port, exporting minerals from South Africa, Swaziland, and Zimbabwe. Population (1997): 989 386.

marabou A large African *stork, *Leptoptilus crumeniferus.* It is 150 cm tall with a wingspan of 2.6 m and has a grey-and-white plumage, a bare black-spotted pink head and neck with a pendulous inflatable throat pouch, and a huge straight pointed bill.

Maracaibo 10 44N 71 37W The second largest city in Venezuela, a port on the NW shore of Lake Maracaibo. Its economic importance is based on oil production; industries include petrochemicals. Population (2000 est): 1 764 038.

Marajó Island (Portuguese: Ilka de Marajó) The world's largest fluvial island, in NE Brazil in the Amazon delta. Area: 38 610 sq km (15 444 sq mi).

marasmus *See* KWASHIORKOR.

Marat, Jean Paul (1743–93) French politician, journalist, and physician. He devoted himself to radical journalism during the French Revolution, becoming editor of *L'Ami du peuple.* Elected to the National Convention in 1792, he was murdered by Charlotte Corday (1768–93), a member of the Girondin party, whom Marat had helped to overthrow (1793).

marathon A long-distance running race over 42 195 m (26 mi 385 yd). The marathon derives its name from the story of a soldier who ran from the battlefield of Marathon to Athens with news of the Greek victory. As different courses vary, there is no official world record; the fastest time is 2 hours 6 minutes 50 seconds (1988) by Belanyeh Dinsamo (Ethiopia).

Marathon, Battle of (490 BC) The battle during the *Greek-Persian Wars in which the Athenians under *Miltiades defeated the Persians. *Phidippides was sent to summon Spartan help but the Spartans arrived too late.

marble A rock consisting of metamorphosed limestone, although the term is used of any rock, particularly limestone, that can be cut and polished for ornamental use. Pure marble is white recrystallized calcite, but impurities, such as dolomite, silica, or clay minerals result in variations of colour. Certain quarries in Greece and Italy have been producing large quantities of marble since pre-Christian times.

Marburg disease *See* GREEN MONKEY DISEASE.

marcasite A pale bronze mineral form of *pyrite. It occurs as nodules in sedimentary rocks as a replacement mineral, particularly in chalk. Marcasite jewellery is sometimes pyrite but more often polished steel or white metal.

Marceau, Marcel (1923–) French mime. He began to study mime in 1946 and gradually developed the original character Bip, a white-faced clown. As well as giving solo performances, he formed his own mime company.

Marcellus, Marcus Claudius (d. 208 BC) Roman general in the second Punic War. Chosen to check Hannibal's advance through Italy, he captured Syracuse and harassed the Carthaginian armies in S Italy.

Marches The border areas of England and Wales, conquered between 1067 and 1238 by vassals of the English kings. The so-called **marcher lords** enjoyed enormous powers until the union of Wales and England in the 1530s.

Marciano, Rocky (Rocco Francis Marchegiano; 1923–69) US boxer. He took the world heavyweight championship from Joe Walcott in 1952 and retired undefeated in 1956, after 6 defences. Unbeaten in his 49 professional fights, a record among world heavyweight champions, he was killed in an aircrash.

Marconi, Guglielmo (1874–1937) Italian electrical engineer, who invented, independently of Aleksandr Popov (1859–1905), communication by radio. On reading about the discovery of radio waves, Marconi built a device that would convert them into electrical signals. He then experimented with transmitting and receiving radio waves over increasing distances until, in 1901, he succeeded in transmitting a signal across the Atlantic Ocean. For this work he shared the Nobel Prize for Physics in 1909.

Marcos, Ferdinand E(dralin) (1917–89) Philippine statesman; president (1965–86). In 1972 he declared martial law and assumed dictatorial powers. The murder in 1983 of opposition leader Begnino Aquino Jr, with alleged government complicity, caused unrest that culminated in a popular uprising in 1986, when Marcos was forced to go into exile. In 1988 he and his wife **Imelda Romualdez Marcos** (c. 1930–) were charged in the US courts with embezzlement and fraud. He died before he could be tried; Imelda was cleared in 1990 but found guilty of corruption in 1993.

Marcus Aurelius (121–180 AD) Roman emperor (161–180), in association with Lucius Verus (130–169) from 161 and alone from 169. Although he is known as the philosopher emperor on account of his *Meditations* (12 books of aphorisms in the Stoic tradition), his rule was active.

Marcuse, Herbert (1898–1979) German-born US thinker. His radical anti-authoritarian philosophy evolved from the Frankfurt School of social research. Marcuse attacked both Western positivism and orthodox Marxism in such books as *The Ethics of Revolution* (1966) and *Counter-Revolution and Revolt* (1973).

Marengo, Battle of (14 June 1800) A battle, fought 5 km (3 mi) SE of Alessandria, in Napoleon's Italian campaign (*see* REVOLUTIONARY AND NAPOLEONIC WARS). Napoleon was surprised by the Austrians with his forces divided and only the timely arrival of reinforcements made French victory possible.

Margaret of Anjou (1430–82) The wife (1445–71) of Henry VI of England; their marriage constituted an attempt to cement peace between England and France during the Wars of the *Roses, in which she was one of the most formidable Lancastrian leaders. She was captured and imprisoned after the Lancastrian defeat in the battle of Tewkesbury (1471). After her husband's death she returned to France (1476).

Margaret Tudor (1489–1541) Regent of Scotland (1513–14) for her son James V. The elder daughter of Henry VII of England and the wife of James IV of the Scots (d. 1513), she was ousted from the regency by the English but played an active role in politics until 1534.

margarine A butter substitute that does not contain dairy-product fat. A type of margarine was first produced in France in 1869 from beef tallow. However, vegetable oils were only able to be used extensively after 1910, when a hydrogenation process was developed to solidify the liquid vegetable oils by adding hydrogen to saturate some of the unsaturated fatty-acid residues in the oils. In modern margarine, pasteurized fat-free milk powder is emulsified with water and such refined vegetable oils as soya-bean oil, groundnut oil, and palm-kernel oil. Vitamins A and D are also added. Soft margarines contain only lightly hydrogenated oils, retaining a large part of their unsaturated nature.

Margrethe II (1940–) Queen of Denmark (1972–), who succeeded her father Frederick IX after the Danish constitution had been altered to permit the accession of a woman. In 1967 she married a French diplomat Henri de Laborde de Monpezat (Prince Henrik; 1934–).

marguerite A perennial herb, *Chrysanthemum frutescens*, also called Paris daisy, native to the Canary Isles. Each stem bears a large daisy-like flower. The name is also applied to the *oxeye daisy. *See also* CHRYSANTHEMUM.

Mari An ancient city on the middle Euphrates River in Syria. Commanding major trade routes, Mari throve during the early Sumerian period (*see* SUMER) and under the rule of Akkad (c. 2300 BC). Its archive of 25 000 cuneiform tablets throws light on contemporary diplomacy, administration, and trade.

Mariana Islands (*or* **Ladrone Islands**) A group of mountainous islands in the W Pacific Ocean, comprising the US unincorporated territory of *Guam and the US commonwealth territory of the Northern Marianas. Strategically important, they include the islands of Tinian and Saipan. Discovered in 1521, the islands were colonized by Spanish Jesuits after 1668. Sugar cane, coffee, and coconuts are produced. Area: 958 sq km (370 sq mi). Population (2001 est): 221 400.

Marianas Trench A deep trench in the earth's crust in the W Pacific; it is the greatest known ocean depth (11 033 m). It marks the site of a plate margin (*see* PLATE TECTONICS),

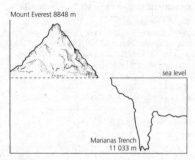

Marianas Trench

where one plate is being submerged beneath another.

Maria Theresa (1717–80) Archduchess of Austria (1740–80). Her father Emperor Charles VI issued the Pragmatic Sanction (1713) to enable Maria Theresa, as a woman, to succeed to his Austrian territories. Her accession nevertheless precipitated the War of the *Austrian Succession (1740–48). Under the influence of Count von Kaunitz (1711–94), Maria Theresa substituted her English alliance with a French coalition but in the subsequent *Seven Years' War (1756–63) Austria suffered resounding defeat. At home she combined absolutism with a measure of reform.

Maribor (German name: Marburg) 46 35N 15 40E A town in N Slovenia, on the River Drava. A former Habsburg trading centre, it is now one of Slovenia's largest industrial centres. Population (1996 est): 134 289.

Marie Antoinette (1755–93) The wife of Louis XVI of France, whose uncompromising attitude to the *French Revolution contributed to the overthrow of the monarchy. The daughter of Emperor Francis I and Maria Theresa, she married the dauphin Louis in 1770. Her extravagance and alleged immorality contributed to the unpopularity of the Crown. After the overthrow of the monarchy and Louis' execution, she was guillotined.

marigold One of several annual herbaceous plants of the family *Compositae*, popular as garden ornamentals. The pot marigold (*Calendula officinalis*), native to S Europe, bears orange or yellow flowers. The African and French marigolds (genus *Tagetes*) have single or double flowers with large outer florets; there are several dwarf varieties. *See also* MARSH MARIGOLD.

marihuana *See* CANNABIS.

Mariner probes A series of successful US planetary probes. Mariners 2 and 5 approached Venus in 1962 and 1967, while Mariner 10 flew past Venus in 1974 and then three times past Mercury in 1974–75. Mariners 4 (1965), 6 and 7 (1969), and 9 (1971–72) investigated Mars, with Mariner 9 going into Martian orbit. Mariners 11 and 12 were renamed the *Voyager probes. Mariners 1, 3, and 8 did not achieve their missions.

Maritain, Jacques (1882–1973) French Roman Catholic thinker. He applied St Thomas *Aquinas' methods to contemporary social problems. *Les Degrés du savoir* (1932) treats mystical, metaphysical, and scientific knowledge as complementary.

Maritime Alps (French name: Alpes Maritimes) A range of mountains in SE France and NW Italy, running about 130 km (81 mi) along the border and constituting the southernmost arm of the Alps. It reaches 3297 m (10 817 ft) at Punta Argentera.

maritime law The branch of law relating to ships and shipping. The Romans, borrowing from the customs of Rhodes, imposed a code in the Mediterranean that was international and uniform in character. This uniformity was preserved until 17th-century nationalism gave rise to various individual codes. The English **Admiralty Court**, established in the 14th century, developed very broad powers in deciding questions of commercial law, but in the 17th century was restricted to matters "done upon the sea." Today the Admiralty Court is mainly concerned with cases involving salvage and collisions at sea. A certain international uniformity has been achieved by the Comité maritime international (CMI), in which 31 member states have agreed and ratified a number of maritime conventions.

Maritime Provinces (**Maritimes** *or* **Atlantic Provinces**) The easternmost provinces of Canada, on the Atlantic coast and the Gulf of St Lawrence. They consist of *New Brunswick, *Nova Scotia, *Prince Edward Island, and usually *Newfoundland and lie in the Appalachian Highlands.

marjoram One of several aromatic perennial herbs or small shrubs of the Eurasian genera *Origanum* (about 13 species) or *Majorana* (about 4 species). Wild marjoram (*O. vulgaris*), is a hairy plant, 30–80 cm tall, bearing clusters of small tubular pinkish-purple flowers. Sweet marjoram (*M. hortensis*), is widely cultivated for its aromatic leaves and flowers, which are used as culinary flavouring. Family: *Labiatae*.

Mark, St A New Testament evangelist, traditionally the author of the second Gospel. A cousin of *Barnabas, he went with him and Paul on their first mission. Subsequently he seems to have assisted Paul in Rome, where he also acted as interpreter for Peter. Feast day: 25 April. **The Gospel according to Mark** is the earliest of the Gospels, written c. 65–70 AD.

Mark Antony (Marcus Antonius; c. 83–31 BC) Roman general and statesman. Following Julius Caesar's assassination, Antony came into conflict with Octavian (*see* AUGUSTUS) but they were later reconciled and formed the second

Triumvirate with Lepidus (43). In 42 Antony defeated his opponents, Brutus and Cassius, at *Philippi. In 37 he abandoned his wife Octavia (Octavian's sister) to live with Cleopatra in Egypt. In 32 the Senate declared war on Egypt and Antony was defeated at *Actium. Both he and Cleopatra committed suicide.

markhor A large wild *goat, *Capra falconeri*, of the Himalayas. Over 100 cm tall at the shoulder, markhors are red-brown in summer and grey in winter and have massive corkscrew-like horns.

Markova, Dame Alicia (Lilian Alicia Marks; 1910–) British ballet dancer. She joined Diaghilev's Ballets Russes in 1925 and the Vic-Wells Ballet in 1931. Her dancing was noted for its lightness and delicacy, particularly evident in her performances in *Giselle*, *Swan Lake*, and *Les Sylphides*.

marl A calcareous clay that is soft and plastic when wet; consolidated marl is usually called marlstone. Marls are deposited in water, either fresh or marine. Marls and marlstones are used in the manufacture of cement.

Marlborough, John Churchill, 1st Duke of (1650–1722) British general. He suppressed Monmouth's rebellion against James II (1685) but subsequently supported the *Glorious Revolution (1688) against James. As commander in chief in the War of the *Spanish Succession, he won the great victories of *Blenheim (1704), Ramillies (1706), Oudenaarde (1708), and Malplaquet (1709). A *Whig, his political importance owed much to the influence of his wife **Sarah Churchill** (*born* Jennings; 1660–1744), a confidante of Queen Anne. Following Sarah's fall from favour, he was charged with embezzlement and dismissed (1711). *See also* BLENHEIM PALACE.

marlin A large game fish, also called spearfish, belonging to the genus *Tetrapturus* (or *Makaira*). It has an elongated body, up to 2.5 m long, a cylindrical spearlike snout, and a long rigid dorsal fin. Marlins are fast swimmers, occurring in all seas. Family: *Istiophoridae*; order: *Perciformes*.

Marlowe, Christopher (1564–93) English dramatist and poet. His involvement in secret political activity while a student at Cambridge may have had some bearing on his death in a tavern fight in Deptford. His development of blank verse and dramatic characterization in his plays, which include *Tamburlaine the Great* (written about 1587) and *Faustus* (probably 1592), prepared the way for the achievements of Shakespeare.

Marmara, Sea of A sea lying between European and Asian Turkey and between the Bosporus and the Dardanelles. In it lies the island of Marmara, where marble and granite have long been quarried. Area: 11 474 sq km (4429 sq mi).

marmoset A small South American monkey belonging to the genera *Callithrix* (9 species) and *Cebuella* (one species—the pygmy marmoset), with claws instead of fingernails. Marmosets are 20–90 cm long including the tail (10–38 cm) and have silky fur, often strikingly marked, and long balancing tails. They feed on fruit, insects, eggs, and small birds. Family: *Callithricidae*.

marmot A large ground squirrel belonging to the genus *Marmota* (8 species), also called groundhog, of Europe, Asia, and North America. Marmots are 30–60 cm long and inhabit mountainous areas. The woodchuck (*M. monax*) lives in North American woodlands.

Marne, River A river in NE France. Rising on the Plateau de Langres, it flows N and W to join the River Seine near Paris. Linked by canal to the Rivers Rhine, Rhône, and Aisne, it was the scene of two unsuccessful German offensives during *World War I (1914, 1918). Length: 525 km (326 mi).

Marquesas Islands A group of 12 volcanic islands in the S Pacific Ocean, in French Polynesia (annexed 1842). Nuku Hiva is the largest. Mountainous and fertile, the islands export copra, cotton, pearls, and vanilla. Area: 1287 sq km (497 sq mi). Population (1996 est): 8064. Capital: Atuona, on Hiva Oa.

Marrakech (*or* **Marrakesh**) 31 49N 8 00W The second largest city in Morocco. Founded in 1062, it was for a time the capital of the Moorish kingdom of Morocco. It is an important commercial centre, producing carpets and leather goods. Population (1994 est): 621 914.

marram grass A coarse perennial *grass of the genus *Ammophila* (2 species), also called beach grass or sand reed, which grows on sandy coasts of temperate Europe, North America, and N Africa. About 1 m high, it has tough scaly underground stems, which can spread over large areas. It is used to stabilize sand dunes.

Marranos *See* CONVERSOS.

marrow (botany) A trailing or climbing vine, *Cucurbita pepo*, probably native to the Americas and including several varieties cultivated as vegetable crops. Marrows bear yellow or orange cup-shaped flowers and large long fleshy fruits, which have orange, green, or yellow skins. Family: *Cucurbitaceae*. *See also* COURGETTE.

marrow (zoology) The soft tissue contained in the central cavities of bones. In early life the marrow of all bones is engaged in the manufacture of blood cells: it is called red marrow. In adult life the marrow of the limb bones becomes filled with fat cells and ceases to function: this is yellow marrow.

Mars (astronomy) The fourth planet from the sun, orbiting the sun every 687 days at a mean distance of 227.9 million km. Its diameter is 6794 km and its period of axial rotation 24 hours 37 minutes 23 seconds. It has two small *satellites. The Martian atmosphere is 95% carbon dioxide and is very thin (surface pressure 7 millibars). The dry reddish dust-covered surface is heavily cratered in the S hemisphere while N regions show signs of earlier volcanic activity. In 2001 NASA launched the Mars Odyssey Probe, which subsequently orbited the planet 400 km (250 mi) above the surface, carrying out detailed chemical and geological surveys. Two NASA Mars Exploration Rovers were successfully landed on the planet in 2004.

Mars (mythology) The Roman war god, the son of Juno. He was identified with the Greek *Ares and is usually portrayed as an armed warrior. Originally a god of agriculture, he was later worshipped at Rome as a major deity and protector of the city.

Marsala (ancient name: Lilybaeum) 37 48N 12 27E A port in Italy, in W Sicily. Founded in 397 BC as a Carthaginian stronghold, it has ancient remains and a baroque cathedral. Marsala wine, grain, and salt are exported. Population (1998 est): 80 177.

Marseillaise, La The French national anthem, written in 1792 by Claude Rouget de l'Isle (1760–1836). Originally a patriotic song entitled "Le Chant de guerre de l'armée du Rhin," it was taken up by a group of republican soldiers from Marseille, who were prominent in the storming of the Tuileries, and became the revolutionary anthem.

Marseille (English name: Marseilles) 43 18N 5 22E The principal seaport in France, the capital of the Bouches-du-Rhône department. Founded about 600 BC, it was destroyed by the Arabs in the 9th century AD, redeveloped during the Crusades, and came under the French Crown in 1481. Most industry is associated with its large world trade and includes oil refining at Fos. Population (1990): 1 231 000.

Marshall, George C(atlett) (1880–1959) US general and statesman. As army chief of staff (1939–45) he organized the build-up of US forces, contributing greatly to the Allied victory. As secretary of state (1947–49) he devised the **Marshall Plan**, or European Recovery Programme, in which the USA provided economic aid to Europe after World War II. For this he won a Nobel Peace Prize (1953).

Marshall Islands, Republic of the A country in the central Pacific Ocean. *Economy*: coconut oil and copra are the main exports; fishing is important. *History*: formerly part of the UN Trust Territory of the Pacific Islands, the country became self-governing in 1979 and its independence was recognized by the UN in 1990. The islands are threatened by global warming as a 1 m rise in sea levels would submerge 80% of the land. Official language: English. Currency: US dollar of 100 cents. Area: 181 sq km (70 sq mi). Population (2003 est): 56 400. Capital: Majuro.

marsh mallow A stout perennial herb, *Althaea officinalis*, of marshy coastal areas of Eurasia. 60–90 cm high, it has lobed leaves and flesh-coloured flowers. The fleshy roots yield a mucilage that was formerly used to make marshmallow. Family: *Malvaceae*.

marsh marigold A stout perennial herb, *Caltha palustris*, also called kingcup, growing in marshes and wet woods throughout arctic and temperate Eurasia and North America. It has erect or prostrate stems, up to 80 cm long, bearing round leaves and bright golden flowers. Family: *Ranunculaceae*.

Marston Moor, Battle of (2 July 1644) The battle in the English *Civil War in which the parliamentarians and the Scots decisively defeated the royalists at Marston Moor, W of York. The parliamentary victory destroyed the king's hold on N England.

marsupial A primitive *mammal belonging to the order *Marsupialia* (176 species). Most marsupials are found in Australia and New Guinea and include the *kangaroos, *bandicoots, and *phalangers. The only New World marsupials are the *opossums. Marsupials have small brains and lack a placenta. Young marsupials, which are born in a very immature state, complete their development in a pouch of skin on the mother's belly surrounding the teat, from which they are fed until fully formed.

Martello towers Fortifications containing cannons built in S Britain, Ireland, and Guernsey from 1804 to 1812. The towers were intended to check the potential invasion of Britain by Napoleon—which never materialized. They were named after the single tower mounting cannon at Mortella Point, Corsica.

marten A carnivorous mammal belonging to the genus *Martes* (8 species), of Eurasian and North American forests. Up to 90 cm long including the tail (15–30 cm), martens are arboreal agile hunters with dark lustrous fur. The two European species are the *pine marten and the smaller stone marten (*M. foina*). The fur of the American marten (*M. americana*) is called American *sable. Family: *Mustelidae*.

martensite The hard brittle form of *steel produced after rapid quenching in *heat treatment. When steel is heated to red heat (750°C), the carbon in it forms a solid solution in the iron. On quenching the carbon is frozen into this configuration and the crystal structure of the steel has internal strains, which cause its hardness. Named after Adolph Martens (1850–1914).

martial arts Styles of armed and unarmed combat developed in the East. The Japanese forms, such as *karate, *judo, and sumo, derive largely from the fighting skills of the *samurai. Since the late 19th century they have become forms of sport, as has the Chinese style, *kung fu. *See also* BUSHIDO.

martin A bird belonging to the *swallow family (*Hirundidae*; 78 species). The brown sand martin (*Riparia riparia*) is about 12 cm long and has white underparts with a brown breast band. It nests in colonies in tunnels excavated in sand or clay banks. The black-and-white Old World house martin (*Delichon urbica*), about 13 cm long, commonly nests beneath the eaves of houses.

Martin, Pierre-Émile (1824–1915) French engineer, who invented the Siemens-Martin process of producing steel. In this process Martin employed the open-hearth furnace developed in 1856 by Sir William Siemens (1823–83) but adopted his own steel-producing process, which utilized pig iron and scrap steel.

Martin, St (c.316–97 AD) A patron saint of France; Bishop of Tours (372–97). A soldier in the imperial army, he later settled at Poitiers and nearby founded the first monastery in Gaul. His military cloak, part of which he reputedly gave to a naked beggar, has become a symbol of charity. Feast day: 11 Nov.

Martinique A French overseas region in the West Indies, in the Windward Islands of the Lesser Antilles. It consists of a mountainous island of volcanic origin. Agriculture is of importance, the chief exports being sugar, bananas, and rum. *History*: colonized by the French in 1635, it became a French overseas department in 1946. Area: 1090 sq km (420 sq mi). Population (2002 est): 386 000. Capital: Fort-de-France.

Martinů, Bohuslav (1890–1959) Czech composer. During World War II he settled in the USA. Largely self-taught, he composed many works, including symphonies, concertos, the ballet *La Revue de cuisine* (1927), and the opera *Julietta* (1936–37).

Marvell, Andrew (1621–78) English poet. He was employed as tutor by Cromwell and Fairfax and as secretary by Milton. From 1659 until his death he served as MP for Hull. He published several satires and pamphlets attacking religious intolerance and government corruption. His poems, noted for their combination of intelligent argument and lyricism, include "To his Coy Mistress" and "The Garden."

Marx, Karl (Heinrich) (1818–83) German philosopher, economist, and revolutionary. In 1842 Marx became the editor of a radical paper; after its suppression he left Germany and spent the rest of his life in exile. In Paris he met Friedrich *Engels, who later collaborated in many of Marx's writings and provided him with substantial financial support. While in Brussels, Marx's association with a group of German handicraftsmen led to *The Communist Manifesto* (1848). In 1849 Marx moved to London, where he remained for the rest of his life, publishing *A Contribution to the Critique of Political Economy* (1859) and other works. Following the establishment of the International Working Men's Association in 1864, Marx devoted many years to the affairs of the First *International. The first volume of *Das Kapital* was published in 1867. *See also* MARXISM.

Marx brothers A US family of comic film actors: **Chico** (Leonard M.; 1886–1961), **Harpo** (Adolph M.; 1888–1964), **Groucho** (Julius M.; 1890–1977), and, until 1933, **Zeppo** (Herbert M.; 1901–79). Their film comedies included *Horse Feathers* (1932), *Duck Soup* (1933), and *A Night at the Opera* (1935). The team disbanded in 1949.

Marxism The theory of scientific socialism introduced by Karl Marx and Friedrich Engels, which explains the origin, historical development, and demise of the capitalist economic system. It relies heavily on the philosophy of

Hegel (*see* DIALECTICAL MATERIALISM). Marxism developed the theory of proletarian revolution. The transition to a socialist and eventually a classless society would involve the violent overthrow of the state power of the bourgeois class. The working class would have to establish its own state power, which would be more democratic because it would be the rule of the majority of the population. As classes gradually disappeared, however, state power would also wither away. The classless society of the future would allow the fullest developments of individuals through social cooperation. Since World War I many different versions of Marxism have been expounded, notably the Marxist-Leninism of V. I. *Lenin. *See also* COMMUNISM.

Mary I (1516–58) Queen of England and Ireland (1553–58), succeeding her half-brother *Edward VI. The daughter of Henry VIII and Catherine of Aragon, Mary became queen after the failure of a conspiracy to place Lady Jane *Grey on the throne. Her singleminded aim was to restore Roman Catholicism in England: Edward's Protestant legislation was repealed and in 1554 the heresy laws were reintroduced, resulting in almost 300 deaths at the stake and the queen's nickname, Bloody Mary. Her marriage (1554) to Philip II of Spain led to England's entanglement in Philip's foreign policy and the loss in 1558 of its last possession on the Continent, Calais.

Mary II (1662–94) Queen of England, Scotland, and Ireland (1689–94), joint monarch with her husband William III. Daughter of James II, she was brought up as a Protestant and came to the throne after the enforced abdication of her Roman Catholic father during the *Glorious Revolution.

Mary, Queen of Scots (1542–87) The daughter of James V and Mary of Guise (1515–60), she succeeded to the throne shortly after her birth. From 1547 Mary, a Roman Catholic, lived at the French court, where in 1558 she married the dauphin (later Francis II). After Francis's death (1561) Mary returned to Scotland and in 1565 married, unpopularly, her cousin Lord *Darnley. In 1566 she gave birth to the future James VI (James I of England). In 1567 Darnley was murdered by *Bothwell, who subsequently married Mary. A rebellion of Scottish nobles defeated Mary and Bothwell at Carberry Hill (1567) and Mary was forced to abdicate in favour of her son. After fleeing to England, where her claim to the English succession had long been an embarrassment to Elizabeth I, she was held prisoner for the rest of her life. She became the focus of a series of plots against Elizabeth and was finally tried for complicity in the conspiracy of Anthony Babington (1561–86) and executed.

Mary, the Virgin In the New Testament, the mother of *Jesus Christ. The fullest accounts of Mary are contained in the birth stories in Luke and Matthew. John (19.25) reports that she was present at the crucifixion. Luke records the Annunciation; her betrothal to *Joseph; her meeting with her cousin Elizabeth; and her song of praise (the Magnificat) when Elizabeth had greeted her as the mother of the Lord. The Gospels also state that she was a virgin. Mary's *Immaculate conception has been recognized as a dogma of the Roman Catholic Church since 1854 and the belief that she was taken into heaven (the Bodily Assumption) was defined as doctrine in 1950.

Mary Magdalene, St In the New Testament, the first person to see Jesus after the resurrection. Jesus cured her of possession by evil spirits. She aided his work in Galilee and was present at the crucifixion and burial. Medieval scholars associated her with the repentant prostitute who annointed Jesus' feet, mentioned in Luke's Gospel. Feast day: 22 July.

Maryland A state on the E seaboard of the USA. It consists of the Atlantic Coastal Plain, split by Chesapeake Bay into a low flat plain in the E and uplands in the W, and an area of higher ground, part of the Alleghenies in the N and W. Manufacturing is important, with primary metals, metal products, food processing, transportation and electrical equipment, printing and publishing, and textiles. The state's farmers produce livestock, poultry, dairy products, corn, tobacco, soya beans, and vegetables. *History*: one of the 13 original colonies, it was first settled by the English. It was named after Henrietta Maria, wife of Charles I. Area: 27 394 sq km (10 577 sq mi). Population (2000). 5 296 486. Capital: Annapolis.

Mary Rose A Tudor warship (Henry VIII's flagship), which sank in 1545 in Portsmouth Harbour while sailing into battle. The wreck was positively identified in 1971. The ship's contents, most of which were remarkably preserved, were raised during the following ten years and the hull itself was lifted in 1982 and placed in dry-dock in Portsmouth. The Mary Rose Trust, of which the Prince of Wales is president, was formed in 1979.

Masaccio (Tommaso di Giovanni di Simone Guidi; 1401–28) Florentine painter of the early Renaissance. He collaborated with Masolino

(1383–?1447) on the *Madonna and Child with St Anne* (Uffizi) and other works. His independent paintings include the *Trinity* (Sta Maria Novella, Florence). Masaccio initiated the use of linear perspective and a single light source in painting.

Masada 31 19N 35 21E A precipitous rocky hilltop near the W shore of the Dead Sea, in S Israel. The site of one of Herod the Great's fortified palaces, it was later a centre of the *Essene sect and a stronghold of the Jews in their revolt against Rome (66 AD). In the last action of the war (73 AD) the defenders committed mass suicide rather than surrender. The site is an Israeli national monument.

Masai A Nilotic people of Kenya and Tanzania who speak a Sudanic language. They are nomads with little centralized political organization. Milk and blood from cattle form an important part of their diet, the blood being drawn from a vein in the animal's neck without killing it. Tall and active, the Masai highly value courage in their warriors.

Masaryk, Tomáš (Garrigue) (1850–1937) Czechoslovak statesman, who was one of the founders of Czechoslovakia. In Paris, during World War I, he and *Beneš founded the Czechoslovak National Council. When Austria-Hungary fell in November 1918, Masaryk was elected Czechoslovakia's first president; he was re-elected in 1920, 1927, and 1934.

m

Mascagni, Pietro (1863–1945) Italian opera composer. His fame rests chiefly on his one-act opera *Cavalleria Rusticana* (1889), written as an entry for a competition in which it won first prize.

Masefield, John (1878–1967) British poet. His first volume, *Salt-Water Ballads* (1902), reflects his experiences in the merchant navy. He also wrote narrative poems, such as *Reynard the Fox* (1919), and several children's books, including *The Midnight Folk* (1927). He became poet laureate in 1930.

maser (*m*icrowave *a*mplification by *s*timulated *e*mission of *r*adiation) A device that works on the same principle as the *laser, the radiation produced being in the *microwave region instead of in the visible spectrum. Masers are used as oscillators (e.g. the ammonia clock; *see* ATOMIC CLOCK) and amplifiers.

Maseru 29 19S 27 29E The capital of Lesotho, near the South African border. It was founded in 1869. The University of Botswana, Lesotho, and Swaziland was established nearby in 1966. Population (1996 est): 160 100.

masochism Sexual pleasure obtained from the experience of pain. The condition is named after an Austrian writer, Leopold von Sacher-Masoch (1835–95), whose novels depict it. It is often associated with a strong need to be humiliated by and submissive to one's sexual partner.

mason bee A solitary *bee belonging to the genus *Osmia* and related genera, occurring in Europe, Africa, and elsewhere. It builds nests of soil cemented together with saliva in hollows in wood or stones. Family: *Megachilidae*.

Mason-Dixon line A line drawn in 1767 by two surveyors, Charles Mason and Jeremiah Dixon, to settle the conflict over borders between Pennsylvania and Maryland. Until the Civil War it also represented the division between southern proslavery and northern free states. It has remained a symbolic boundary between the North and South.

masque A form of dramatic court entertainment popular in England during the late 16th and early 17th centuries. It consisted of a combination of verse, dance, and music, usually with a slight dramatic plot based on a mythological theme. The form was perfected in the collaborations of Ben *Jonson and Inigo *Jones.

mass *See* MASS AND WEIGHT.

Massachusetts A state on the NE coast of the USA, in New England. The uplands in the W, which are cut N–S by the Connecticut River, are separated from the lowlands of the Atlantic Coastal Plain and Cape Cod Peninsula. A major manufacturing state, its industries produce electrical and communications equipment, instruments, chemicals, textiles, and metal and food products. Boston is an important financial and service centre. Its farmers produce dairy products, eggs, poultry, cranberries, and horticultural goods. Massachusetts is an important centre in the educational and cultural life of the USA. *History*: one of the 13 original colonies, the arrival of the Pilgrim Fathers (1620) heralded major settlement. It was a centre for opposition to British colonial policy leading to the American Revolution and became prominent following statehood (1788). Area: 21 386 sq km (8257 sq mi). Population (2000): 6 349 097. Capital: Boston.

mass action, law of The rate of a chemical reaction for a uniform system at constant temperature varies as the concentration of each reacting substance, raised to the power equal to the number of molecules of the substance appearing in the balanced equation. Thus, for the reaction $2H_2 + O_2 = 2H_2O$ the speed of the forward reaction is proportional to the concentration of O_2 (written $[O_2]$) and to $[H_2]^2$; the reverse reaction depends on $[H_2O]^2$.

mass and weight Two physical quantities used to express the extent to which a substance is present; they are sometimes confused. The mass of a body was defined by *Newton as the ratio of a force applied to the body to the acceleration it produces. This is now called the **inertial mass. Gravitational mass** is defined in terms of the gravitational force between two bodies in accordance with Newton's law of gravitation. Lóránt Eotvos (1848–1919) showed experimentally that inertial mass and gravitational mass are equal.

Weight is proportional to gravitational mass, being the force by which an object is attracted to the earth. It is therefore equal to the product of the mass and the *acceleration of free fall (i.e. $W = mg$). Thus, the weight of a body may vary according to its position; the mass is a constant.

mass defect The difference between the total mass of the constituent protons and neutrons in an atomic nucleus and the mass of the nucleus. This defect is equal to the *binding energy of the nucleus.

mass-energy equation *See* RELATIVITY.

Massenet, Jules (1842–1912) French composer. He studied at the Paris conservatoire and won the Prix de Rome in 1863. Massenet wrote 27 operas, of which *Manon* (1884) and *Werther* (1892) are still performed today.

Massey, William Ferguson (1856–1925) New Zealand statesman; prime minister (1912–25). He entered parliament in 1894 and became (1903) leader of the Conservative opposition, which in 1909 he named the Reform Party. His administration, in coalition (1915–19) with the Liberals during World War I, supported agrarian interests.

Massif Central A plateau area in S central France. Generally considered to be that area over 300 m (984 ft) high, it rises to 1885 m (6188 ft) at Puy de Sancy. The central N area is also known as the Auvergne and the SE rim as the Cévennes. There is dairy and arable farming as well as heavy industry. Area: about 90 000 sq km (34 742 sq mi).

Massine, Léonide (Leonid Miassin; 1896–1979) Russian ballet dancer and choreographer.He choreographed for many companies, notably the Ballet Russe de Monte Carlo. Most controversial were his innovatory symphonic ballets *Les Présages* (1933) and *Symphonie Fantastique* (1936).

mass number (*or* **nucleon number**) The total number of protons and neutrons in the *nucleus of an atom.

mastectomy Surgical removal of a breast, usually for the treatment of breast cancer. In a partial mastectomy (or lumpectomy) only the tumour is removed, while in a total mastectomy the entire breast is removed. A radical mastectomy involves removal of the breast together with the lymph nodes in the armpit and the chest muscles associated with it.

Master of the Queen's (*or* **King's**) **Music** An English court post established in the reign of Charles I. It is now an honorary position held by a composer who may be called upon to write music for ceremonial occasions. The present holder is Sir Peter Maxwell Davies (2004–).

Master of the Rolls The presiding judge of the Civil Division of the Court of Appeal. The office originated as the guardian of all charters, patents, etc., entered upon parchment rolls. Judicial adviser to the Lord Chancellor, the Master of the Rolls became a full judge in 1729 and a member of the Court of Appeal in 1881. As his legal responsibilities increased he became less involved in record-keeping.

mastic An evergreen shrub, *Pistacia lentiscus*, up to 1.8 m high, native to the Mediterranean region. An aromatic yellowish-green resin obtained from the bark is used to make varnishes and as an adhesive. Family: *Anacardiaceae*. The name is also applied to other resin-yielding trees.

mastiff An ancient Eurasian breed of large dog long used as a guard dog and for bull- and bear-baiting. It is powerfully built with a large head and a short deep muzzle. The short smooth coat may be apricot, silver, or fawn; the muzzle, ears, and nose are black. Height: 76 cm (dogs); 69 cm (bitches). *See also* BULL MASTIFF.

mastodon An extinct elephant that originated in Africa 34 million years ago and spread throughout Europe, Asia, and America. Early mastodons were small and had two pairs of tusks; later forms were larger. The American mastodons survived until about 8000 years ago.

Mastroianni, Marcello (1924–96) Italian actor, who became one of the best-known international film stars of the 1960s. He appeared in Visconti's *White Nights* (1957), Fellini's *La dolce vita* (1960) and *Intervista* (1987), and *Dark Eyes* (1987).

Matabeleland An area in W Zimbabwe, between the Limpopo and Zambezi Rivers. It was named after the Ndebele tribe. Consisting chiefly of extensive plains, the area has important gold deposits. Area: 181 605 sq km (70 118 sq mi).

Mata Hari (Margaretha Geertruida Zelle; 1876–1917) Dutch courtesan and secret agent. She lived in Indonesia with her husband, a Dutch colonial officer, from 1897 to 1902. She became a professional dancer in Paris in 1905 and probably worked for both French and German intelligence services. She was executed by the French in 1917.

maté The dried leaves of a *holly shrub or tree, *Ilex paraguariensis*, native to Paraguay and Brazil. They are roasted, powdered, and infused with water to make a stimulating greenish tealike beverage.

materialism In classical metaphysics, materialism is the doctrine of *Democritus and Leucippus (5th century BC) that everything in the universe is matter or stuff. By contrast *Plato sought to establish the existence of some incorporeal objects and *Aristotle believed that the soul was immaterial. Marx's economic materialism took the form of *dialectical materialism. In all these senses materialism is a metaphysical doctrine. More popularly, the term has also been used to signify worldly outlooks and behaviour.

m

mathematics The logical study of numerical and spatial relationships. It is usually divided into pure and applied mathematics. In pure mathematics the general theoretical principles are studied, often in abstract. Its branches are *arithmetic, *algebra, *calculus, *geometry, and *trigonometry. The ancient Egyptians, Sumerians, and Chinese were all using a form of *abacus to carry out calculations for thousands of years before the Christian era. But it was not until the 9th century AD that *al-Khwarizmi introduced the idea of writing down calculations. The Venetian mathematicians of the 11th and 12th centuries were largely responsible for the introduction of these methods to the West. However, the application of mathematics to the physical sciences was largely a 16th-century development inspired by Galileo. It was from this development that applied mathematics grew. It is now largely concerned with *mechanics and *statistics.

Matilda (*or* **Maud**; 1102–67) The daughter of Henry I of England, who designated her his heir. On his death (1135), his nephew Stephen seized the throne and Matilda invaded England (1139) inaugurating a period of in conclusive civil war. She captured Normandy and in 1152 the Treaty of Wallingford recognized her son Henry as Stephen's heir.

Matisse, Henri (1869–1954) French painter and sculptor. Matisse initiated *fauvism in the early 1900s with his boldly patterned and vibrantly coloured still lifes, portraits, and nudes, notably the controversial *Woman with the Hat* (1905). He was also inspired by Islamic art. A stained glass design for the Dominican chapel at Vence (S France) was among his last works.

Matsuyama 33 50N 132 47E A port in Japan, in NW Shikoku on the Inland Sea. It is an agricultural and industrial centre, with a university (1949). Population (1995): 460 870.

Matterhorn (French name: Mont Cervin; Italian name: Monte Cervino) 45 59N 7 39E A mountain in Europe, on the Swiss-Italian border in the Alps near Zermatt. First climbed in 1865 by the British mountaineer, Edward Whymper, it is conspicuous because of its striking pyramidal shape. Height: 4478 m (14 692 ft).

Matthew, St In the New Testament, one of the 12 *Apostles. He was a tax collector until he became a follower of Jesus. According to tradition, he preached in Judaea, Ethiopia, and Persia and suffered martyrdom. Feast day: 21 Sept. **The Gospel according to St Matthew** is generally believed to have been written some time after St Mark's Gospel, from which it drew material.

Maud *See* MATILDA.

Maugham, W(illiam) Somerset (1874–1965) British novelist and dramatist. He qualified in medicine but abandoned it after the success of his first novel, *Liza of Lambeth* (1896). His later fiction includes *Of Human Bondage* (1915), *The Moon and Sixpence* (1919), and *Cakes and Ale* (1930). He wrote popular comedies of manners, such as *The Circle* (1921), and many short stories.

Mau Mau A secret organization among the Kikuyu people of Kenya, which led a revolt (1952–57) against the British colonial government. Secret oaths were administered to participants, who committed appalling atrocities against Whites and uncooperating Blacks. Jomo *Kenyatta was thought to be a Mau Mau leader.

Maundy Thursday The Thursday before *Good Friday. Its name derives from Latin *mandatum*, commandment, and its traditional foot-washing and almsgiving ceremonies originated at the Last Supper (John 13). The British sovereign's annual distribution of special Maundy money is a survival of these rites.

Maupassant, Guy de (1850–93) French short-story writer and novelist. Introduced into literary circles by Flaubert, he joined Zola's group of naturalist writers (*see* NATURALISM). Following the phenomenal success of "Boule de Suif" (1880), he wrote about 300 short stories and 6 novels, including *Une Vie* (1883) and *Bel-Ami* (1885). He suffered from syphilis and died in an asylum.

Mauriac, François (1885–1970) French novelist. His novels, which include *Thérèse Desqueyroux* (1927) and *Le Noeud de vipères* (1933), characteristically portray the conflict between worldly passions and religion in provincial marital and family relationships. He also wrote plays and polemical criticism and journalism. He won the Nobel Prize in 1952.

Mauritania, Islamic Republic of (French name: Mauritanie; Arabic name: Muritaniyah) A country in West Africa, with a coastline on the Atlantic Ocean. The N part is desert while the S is mainly fertile. Most of the inhabitants are Arabs and Berbers with a Negro population, mainly Fulani, in the S. *Economy*: chiefly agricultural. Livestock, especially cattle, are important and the main crops are millet, sorghum, beans, and rice. Fishing is important and fish processing is one of the main industries. Iron ore and copper are exploited. *History*: Mauritania was dominated by Muslim Berber tribes from about 100 AD; the coast was visited by the Portuguese in the 15th century and by the Dutch, English, and French in the 17th century. The area became a French protectorate in 1903 and a colony in 1920 achieving internal self-government within the French Community in 1958. It subsequently joined the Arab League and the Arab Common Market. In 1976, with Morocco, it took over Western Sahara, prompting guerrilla attacks from the Polisario, the Western Saharan independence movement. In 1979 Mauritania withdrew from all but the southern tip of Western Sahara. The country was under military rule from 1978 until 1992, when Col Maaouya Ould Sidi Ahmed Taya, president since 1984, won free elections. However, these and subsequent elections were marred by accusations of fraud. Official languages: French and Arabic. Currency: ouguiya of 5 khoums. Area: 1 030 700 sq km (397 850 sq mi). Population (2003 est): 2 696 000. Capital: Nouakchott.

Mauritius, Republic of An island country in the Indian Ocean, about 800 km (500 mi) to the E of Madagascar. It is mainly hilly and subject to tropical cyclones. The majority of the population are of Indian descent. *Economy*: it is dependent primarily on sugar production, although manufacturing is of rising importance. Fishing is being developed, as is tourism. *History*: the island was settled by the Dutch in 1598. In 1715 it came under French rule as Île de France and in 1814 it was ceded to Britain. After riots in 1968 it became independent within the British Commonwealth. It became a republic in 1992. Sir Aneerood Jugnauth of the Mauritius Socialist Party has been prime minister since 1982. Official languages: English and French. Currency: Mauritius rupee of 100 cents. Area: 1843 sq km (720 sq mi). Population (2003 est): 1 221 000. Capital: Port Louis.

maxwell The unit of magnetic flux in the *c.g.s. system equal to the flux through 1 cm^2 perpendicular to a field of one gauss. Named after James Clerk *Maxwell.

Maxwell, James Clerk (1831–79) Scottish physicist, who achieved the unification of electricity, magnetism, and light into one set of equations (known as **Maxwell's equations**). These equations, published in their final form in 1873, enabled Faraday's lines of force to be treated mathematically by introducing the concept of the electromagnetic field. Maxwell observed that the field radiated outwards from an oscillating electric charge at the speed of light, which led him to identify light as a form of electromagnetic radiation. Maxwell also made important advances in the kinetic theory of gases by introducing Maxwell-Boltzmann statistics, developed independently by Ludwig Boltzmann (1844–1906).

Maya An American Indian people of Yucatán (Mexico) Guatemala, and Belize. There are a number of languages in the Totonac-Mayan language family (*see* MESOAMERICAN LANGUAGES). Today the Maya live mainly in farming villages, but between 300 and 900 AD they had established an advanced civilization. They developed hieroglyphic writing and had considerable knowledge of astronomy and mathematics. Their elaborate ritual and ceremonial life was centred on such sites as *Chichén Itzá and Tikal, where large pyramid temples were constructed for the worship of the sun, moon, and rain gods.

Mayer, Louis B. (1885–1957) US film producer, born in Russia. In 1924 he founded the Metro-Goldwyn-Mayer (MGM) production company, whose films were largely determined by his personal taste for lavish but uncontroversial entertainment.

Mayflower The ship that carried the *Pilgrim Fathers to America. The *Mayflower* reached Plymouth (Massachusetts) in December 1620. There, the Pilgrims drew up the **Mayflower Compact**, which based their government on the will of the colonists, not the English Crown.

mayfly A slender insect of the order *Ephemeroptera* (1500 species), found near fresh water. Up to 40 mm long, mayflies are usually brown or yellow with two unequal pairs of membranous wings. The adults only live long enough to mate and lay eggs. The aquatic nymphs feed on plant debris and algae.

Mayo (Irish name: Contae Mhuigheo) A county in the W Republic of Ireland, in Connacht bordering on the Atlantic Ocean. Mountainous in the W, it contains several large lakes. Cattle, sheep, and pigs are raised and potatoes and oats are grown. Area: 5397 sq km (2084 sq mi). Population (2002): 117 428. County town: Castlebar.

m

mayor The chief officer of a municipal council. In the UK a mayor or mayoress is the chairman or chairwoman of a district council having *borough status. The mayor's counterpart in Scotland is called a provost. The mayor of the City of London and certain other cities is called a **Lord Mayor** (Lord Provost in Scotland). A directly elected mayor was instituted in London in 2000 and in several other UK cities in 2002.

Mazu (*or* **Ma-tsu**) 26 10N 119 59E A Taiwanese island in the East China Sea. It is near the Chinese mainland, from which it was bombed in 1958, causing an international incident. Area: 44 sq km (17 sq mi). Population (latest est): 8200.

Mbabane 26 30S 31 30E The capital of Swaziland, in the Mdimba Mountains. Tourism is important and nearby there is a large iron mine. Population (1998 est): 60 000.

MBE *See* ORDER OF THE BRITISH EMPIRE, THE MOST EXCELLENT.

Mbeki, Thabo (1942–) South African politician; president (1999–). A leading ANC activist, he took a prominent role in the negotiations that effected South Africa's transition to multi-racial democracy (1991–93). Deputy president to Nelson Mandela (1994–99), he succeeded him as president of the ANC (1997) and as national president in May 1999. He was reelected in 2004.

Mc– Names beginning Mc are listed under Mac.

mead An alcoholic drink of fermented honey and water. The honey is dissolved in water and boiled with spices. When cool, after brewer's yeast has been added, the mead ferments in barrel. It was drunk in Anglo-Saxon England and, called hydromel, by the ancient Romans.

meadowsweet A perennial herb, *Filipendula* (or *Spiraea*) *ulmaria*, common in damp places throughout temperate Eurasia. 60–120 cm high, it has large compound leaves, and small creamy-white fragrant flowers. An oil distilled from the flower buds is used in perfumes. Family: *Rosaceae*.

mealworm *See* DARKLING BEETLE.

meander A curve in a river. Meandering is common in rivers flowing across plains. Because erosion is concentrated on the outside of the bends and deposition occurs on the inside, the curvature of the meander increases progressively, until the ends of the curve meet, the river takes a shorter path, and the process starts anew. The cut-off loop forms a stagnant oxbow lake.

mean life (*or* **lifetime**) The average time for which a radioactive isotope, elementary particle, or other unstable state exists before decaying. *See* RADIOACTIVITY.

measles A highly infectious viral disease, which usually affects children. After an incubation period of about two weeks the child becomes irritable and fevered and has a running nose and inflamed eyes. Two or three days later a rash appears on the head and face and spreads over the body. Usually the child recovers after a week. *Compare* GERMAN MEASLES.

Meath (Irish name: Contae na Midhe) A county in the E Republic of Ireland, in Leinster bordering on the Irish Sea. Consisting chiefly of fertile glacial drifts it is important for agriculture; cattle are fattened and oats and potatoes grown. Area: 2338 sq km (903 sq mi). Population (2002): 133 936. County town: Trim.

Mecca (Arabic name: Makkah) 21 26N 39 49E A city in W Saudi Arabia, in a narrow valley surrounded by barren hills. Every Muslim is expected to visit Mecca at least once in his or her lifetime unless circumstances make this impossible; nonbelievers are not allowed to enter the city. It has been a holy city since ancient times, but was also the birthplace of Mohammed (c. 570). Population (1992): 965 697.

mechanics The study of the motion of bodies and systems and the forces acting on them. The subject is traditionally divided into statics, the study of bodies in equilibrium, and dynamics, the study of forces that affect the motion of bodies. Dynamics is further divided into kinetics, the effects of forces and their moments on motion, and kinematics, the study of velocity, acceleration, etc., without regard to the forces causing them. Aristotelian (*see* ARISTOTLE) mechanics was based on the erroneous concept that a force is required to maintain motion. Newtonian mechanics recognizes that once a body is moving a force is required to stop it but no force is needed to keep it moving. The more general relativistic mechanics is applicable to systems moving at speeds comparable to that of light (it reduces to Newtonian mechanics at velocities that are small compared to that of light). Fluid mechanics is the application of mechanical principles to fluids, both stationary (hydrostatics) and flowing (hydrodynamics).

Medawar, Sir Peter Brian (1915–87) British immunologist, noted for his investigation of the development of the immune system in embryonic and young animals, including the phenomenon of acquired immunological tolerance to foreign tissue grafts. Medawar shared the 1960 Nobel Prize with Sir Macfarlane *Burnet.

Medea In Greek legend, a sorceress, the daughter of King Aeetes of Colchis and niece of *Circe. She helped *Jason steal the *Golden Fleece. When Jason deserted her for Glauce, daughter of the Corinthian King Creon, she killed Glauce, Creon, and her own two children.

Media An ancient region SW of the Caspian Sea settled by seminomadic tribes of Medes. Between the 8th and 6th centuries BC they began to unite against Assyria and in 612 destroyed Nineveh and overthrew the Assyrian empire.

median 1. The line joining the vertex of a triangle to the midpoint of the opposite side. **2.** The middle value of a set of numbers arranged in order of magnitude. For example, the median of 2, 3, 3, 4, 5 is 3.

Medici A family that dominated Florence from 1434 to 1737 (as grand dukes from 1532). The Medici, who were merchants and bankers, dominated the government of Florence in the 15th century by manipulating elections to the key magistracies. The family's power was established by **Cosimo de' Medici** (1389–1464), who also initiated the Medici tradition of artistic patronage. His son **Piero de' Medici** (1416–69) succeeded to his position, which then passed to **Lorenzo the Magnificent** (1449–92). An outstanding patron of Renaissance artists (Botticelli, Ghirlandaio, Michelangelo) and scholars (Ficino, Pico della Mirandola, Politian), Lorenzo tended to neglect the family business, which declined in the late 15th century. He was succeeded by his son **Piero de' Medici** (1472–1503), who was forced to flee Florence in a revolt incited by *Savonarola. Piero's brother **Giovanni de' Medici** (1475–1521) was restored to Florence in 1512, a year before he became Pope Leo X (1513–21). **Alessandro de' Medici** (1511–37) became the first Duke of Florence; subsequent grand dukes included **Cosimo I** (1519–74), **Francesco I** (1541–87), and **Ferdinando I** (1549–1609).

Medina (Arabic name: Al Madinah) 24 30N 39 35E A city in W Saudi Arabia, N of Mecca. The tomb of Mohammed is in the mosque at Medina, the second most holy Muslim city after Mecca. Date-packing supplements the city's income from pilgrims, and the Islamic University was founded in 1961. Population (1992): 608 295.

Mediterranean Sea An almost landlocked sea extending between Africa and Europe to Asia. It connects with the Atlantic Ocean at Gibraltar, the Black Sea via the Sea of Marmara, and the Red Sea via the Suez Canal. Fed continuously by the Atlantic and to a lesser extent by the Black Sea, it is saltier and warmer than the oceans; pollution is a serious problem. Tidal variation is insignificant.

m

medlar A thorny shrub or tree, *Mespilus germanica*, native to SE Europe and central Asia and cultivated for its fruit. Growing to a height of 6 m, it bears white five-petalled flowers. The brownish fruit has an opening at the top through which the five seed chambers can be seen. Medlars are eaten when partly decayed; they can also be made into jelly. Family: *Rosaceae*.

medulla oblongata *See* BRAIN.

medusa The free-swimming sexual form that occurs during the life cycle of many animals of the phylum *Cnidaria*. Medusae resemble small *jellyfish and have separate sexes, releasing eggs and sperm into the water. The ciliated larvae settle and develop into the sedentary asexual forms (*see* POLYP). *See also* CNIDARIAN.

Medusa In Greek mythology, the only mortal *Gorgon. Athena, angered by her love affair with Poseidon, made her hair into serpents and her face so ugly that all who saw it were turned to stone. She later sent *Perseus to behead her. From her blood sprang *Pegasus and Chrysaor, her children by Poseidon.

Medway A unitary authority in SE England, in Kent. Administrative centre: Gillingham. Area: 204 sq km (79 sq mi). Population (2001): 249 502.

Medway, River A river in SE England. Rising in Sussex, it flows N and E through Kent to join the River Thames by a long estuary. It passes through Tonbridge, Maidstone, Rochester, Chatham, and Gillingham. Length: 113 km (70 mi).

meerkat A small carnivorous mammal, *Suricata suricata*, also called suricate, of South African grasslands. It is about 60 cm long including the tail (17–25 cm), and lives in shallow burrows. Meerkats feed on insects, grubs, reptiles, birds, and small mammals. Family: *Viverridae*.

Meerut 29 00N 77 42E A city in India, in Uttar Pradesh. The scene of the first uprising (1857) of the Indian Mutiny, Meerut is an important army headquarters and has diverse industries. Population (1991): 753 778.

m

megalith (Greek: large stone) A large stone particularly favoured for building monuments in the *Neolithic and *Bronze Age. Megaliths could be placed singly, in lines, or in simple or complex circles as at *Stonehenge. Megaliths were also used for tombs and temples in Malta, Egypt, and elsewhere.

megapode A bird belonging to a family (*Megapodiidae*; 12 species) ranging from Australia to Peninsular Malaysia. 48–70 cm long, megapodes are fowl-like and ground-dwelling with brownish or black plumage and build a large nest mound in which the eggs are incubated by the heat of fermenting plant material, the sun, or volcanic heat. They include the mallee fowl and the brush turkeys (e.g. *Alectura lathami*). Order: *Galliformes* (pheasants, turkeys, etc.).

megaton A measure of the explosive power of a nuclear weapon. It is equivalent to an explosion of one million tons of trinitrotoluene (TNT).

Megiddo An ancient site in N Israel. Continuously occupied between about 3000 and 350 BC, Megiddo was strategically positioned on the route between Egypt and Syria and was the scene of many battles. Megiddo is identified with the biblical Armageddon (Revelation 16.16).

meiosis The process by which the nucleus of a germ cell divides prior to the formation of gametes (such as sperm, pollen, or eggs). Meiosis consists of two successive divisions during which one cell with the normal duplicate (diploid) set of chromosomes gives rise to four cells each with only one chromosome of each type (haploid). Meiosis differs from *mitosis in that the chromosomes of each pair become closely associated, enabling the interchange of genetic material between maternal and paternal chromosomes. There is no duplication of chromosomes between the two divisions of meiosis.

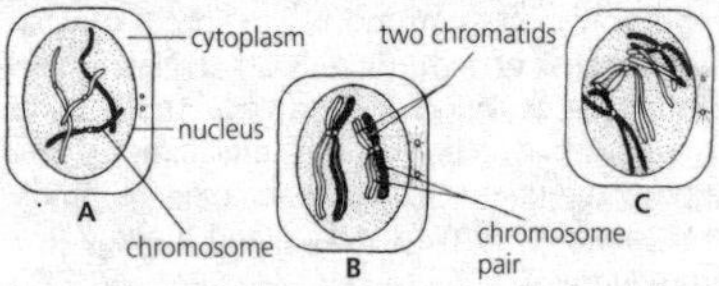

prophase I. The four chromosomes appear as thin threads (A), which form pairs (B). Each chromosome divides into two chromatids and exchange of genetic material occurs between the chromatids of each pair (C).

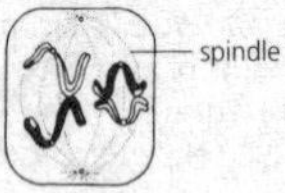

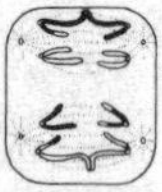

metaphase I. The chromosomes of each pair separate from each other and move to opposite poles of the spindle.

metaphase II. Two new spindles form and the chromatids of each group separate from each other.

telophase II. Four new nuclei form, each containing two chromosomes.

meiosis. The formation of four egg or sperm cells from one parent cell takes place in two divisions, each of which is divided into several phases. Only four phases are shown here.

Meir, Golda (1898–1978) Israeli stateswoman, born in Russia; prime minister (1969–74). A founder member of the Israeli Workers' Party (Mapai) she was its secretary general (1966–68). She was minister of labour (1949–56) and minister of foreign affairs (1956–66) before becoming prime minister. She resigned after Israel had been taken unawares in the 1973 Yom Kippur war.

Meissen porcelain The first hard-paste porcelain made in Europe following discovery

(1709) in Dresden of the technique by the alchemist J. F. Böttger (1682–1719) under the patronage of the Elector of Saxony. The manufacture moved to Meissen, a town on the River Elbe, in E Germany, in 1710. There followed extensive ranges of domestic ware, figures, chinoiseries, small boxes, seals, and painted ornaments.

Meitner, Lise (1878–1968) Austrian physicist. She worked with Otto *Hahn in Berlin (1907–38); together they discovered protactinium (1918) and caused the first fission of a uranium atom by neutron bombardment (1934). Expelled by the Nazis, she moved to Stockholm, becoming a Swedish citizen in 1949.

Mekong, River A major SE Asian river, rising in Tibet and flowing generally SE through China, Laos, Kampuchea, and Vietnam to the South China Sea. The extensive delta is one of the greatest Asian rice-growing areas. Length: about 4025 km (2500 mi).

Melanesia A division of Oceania in the SW Pacific Ocean, consisting of an arc of volcanic and coral islands NE of Australia. It includes the Bismarck Archipelago, the Solomon, Admiralty, and D'Entrecasteaux Islands, Vanuatu Republic, New Caledonia, and Fiji. *See also* MICRONESIA, FEDERATED STATES OF; POLYNESIA.

Melanesians The people of the Melanesian islands. The term also covers similar peoples of New Guinea, though these are also often known as Papuan. They are of Oceanic Negroid race and speak languages of the Austronesian family. The Melanesians cultivate yams, taro, and sweet potatoes and live in small, usually dispersed, homesteads. In coastal areas fishing is important.

melanin A pigment, varying from brown-black to yellow, that occurs in hair, skin, feathers, and scales. Derived from the amino acid tyrosine, its presence in the skin helps protect underlying tissues from damage by sunlight. Melanin is also responsible for colouring the iris of the eye.

melanoma A form of cancer, mainly affecting the skin, that arises in the cells producing the pigment *melanin. Most melanomas develop from an existing *mole, and excessive exposure to sunlight is known to be a contributory factor.

Melba, Dame Nellie (Helen Porter Armstrong; 1861–1931) Australian soprano. She made her debut in 1887 as Gilda in Verdi's opera *Rigoletto*. Her worldwide career culminated in a number of farewell performances in 1926.

Melbourne 37 45S 144 58E The second largest city of Australia, the capital of Victoria on Port Phillip Bay. It is a major commercial centre. Port Melbourne is sited 4 km (2.5 mi) away, on the mouth of the Yarra River; exports include wool, scrap metal, and dairy products. The chief industries are heavy engineering, food processing, and the manufacture of textiles and clothes. A cultural centre, Melbourne possesses three universities and the new Arts Centre of Victoria. The Melbourne Cricket Ground, founded in 1853, is world famous. *History*: founded in 1835, it developed rapidly following the 1851 gold rush. It was the capital of the Commonwealth of Australia from 1901 until 1927. Population (1998 est): 2 865 329.

Melbourne, William Lamb, 2nd Viscount (1779–1848) British statesman; Whig prime minister (1834, 1835–41). He was chief secretary for Ireland (1827–28) and then home secretary (1830–34), when he dealt harshly with the *Tolpuddle Martyrs. During his second ministry his attempted resignation (1839) precipitated Victoria's *Bedchamber Crisis. In 1805 he married Lady Caroline Ponsonby (1785–1828). As **Lady Caroline Lamb**, she had a love affair with Lord Byron (1812–13); because of her increasing mental instability, she separated from Lord Melbourne in 1825.

m

melon An annual tropical African vine, *Cucumis melo*, widely cultivated for its fruits. Melon plants have hairy leaves, yellow or orange cup-shaped flowers, and round or oval fruits, up to 4 kg in weight, with tough skins and sweet juicy flesh surrounding a core of seeds. Varieties include the muskmelon, with a net-veined skin and pinkish flesh; the honeydew melon, with smooth skin and light-green flesh; and the canteloupe, with rough warty skin and orange flesh. Family: *Cucurbitaceae*. *See also* WATERMELON.

Melos (*or* **Mélos**) A Greek island in the Aegean Sea, one of the Cyclades. The famous statue, the *Venus de Milo*, was discovered here in 1820. Area: 150 sq km (58 sq mi). Population (latest est): 4555.

Melville, Herman (1819–91) US novelist. In 1841 he joined the crew of a whaler; his experiences in the South Seas form the raw material of his works. His masterpiece, *Moby Dick* (1851), is a narrative about whaling with an underlying philosophical theme on the nature of evil. *Billy Budd*, published in 1924 after his death, formed the basis of a libretto for an opera by Benjamin Britten.

memory The recollection of experiences from the past. Three processes are required: registration, in which an experience is received into the mind; retention, in which a permanent memory trace, or engram, is preserved in the brain; and recall, in which a particular memory is brought back into consciousness. Short-term memories are forgotten with the passage of time unless they are registered in the long-term memory. Failure of memory (*see* AMNESIA) is a common consequence of diseases of the brain. An abnormally good memory (hypermnesia) can sometimes be produced by hypnosis.

memory, computer The part of a computer that stores information. It usually refers to the computer's internal store, in which the programs and data are held; this is under the direct control of the central processing unit. In some computers, a high-speed buffer store holds information in active use by the central processing unit, while longer-term storage is provided by the slower main store. Solid-state electronic memory devices, which operate at very high speeds but lose their contents when the machine is turned off, are used for the internal memory. Slower devices, such as magnetic disks, provide permanent storage but their contents cannot be accessed directly by the central processing unit; these are sometimes called the external memory.

Memphis 35 10N 90 00W A city and port in the USA, in Tennessee situated above the Mississippi River. It is a major cotton, timber, and livestock market and its manufactures include textiles and chemicals. Memphis is associated with W. C. Handy, the composer of the blues. Population (2000): 650 100.

Memphis An ancient city of Lower Egypt, S of modern Cairo. Memphis was founded as the capital of all Egypt after its unification by Menes (c. 3100 BC), remaining the capital until supplanted by *Thebes (c. 1570 BC). The necropolis of Saqqarah and the *pyramids and sphinx at Giza formed part of its extensive complex of monuments.

Menai Strait A channel separating the island of Anglesey from the mainland of NW Wales. It is crossed by a notable suspension bridge designed by Thomas Telford (1819–26). The Britannia railway bridge, built by Robert Stevenson (1850) and seriously damaged by fire in 1970, has been rebuilt.

Menander (c. 341–c. 290 BC) Greek dramatist. The leading exponent of the New Comedy, he wrote sophisticated comedies on romantic and domestic themes with strongly individualized characters. His single surviving complete play is the *Dyscolus*.

Mendel, Gregor Johann (1822–84) Austrian botanist, who discovered the fundamental principles governing the inheritance of characters in living things (*see* GENETICS). Mendel was a monk with a scientific education. In 1856 he began to inbreed lines of pea plants to study the characters of tallness and dwarfness. Mendel concluded that such characteristics were determined by factors of inheritance (now called alleles of the gene) that were contributed equally by both parents and that sorted themselves among the offspring according to simple statistical rules. He summarized these findings in his Law of Segregation and Law of Independent Assortment (**Mendel's laws**). Mendel reported his findings in 1865 but his achievement was not appreciated until the rediscovery of his work by C. E. Correns (1864–1933), Hugo de Vries (1848–1935), and E. von Tschermak (1871–1962) in 1900.

mendelevium (Md) A synthetic element, first produced in 1955 by Ghiorso and others, by bombarding einsteinium with helium ions; it is named after the chemist Mendeleyev. At no 101; at wt (258).

Mendeleyev, Dimitrii Ivanovich (1834–1907) Russian chemist, who was professor at St Petersburg (1866–90). In 1869 he arranged the elements in order of increasing atomic weights so that those with similar properties were grouped together (*see* PERIODIC TABLE).

Mendelssohn, Felix (Jacob Ludwig Felix Mendelssohn-Bartholdy; 1809–47) German composer. A child prodigy, he demonstrated his precocious brilliance in his overture to *A Midsummer Night's Dream* (1826). In 1836 he became conductor of the Leipzig Gewandhaus orchestra and subsequently founded the Leipzig conservatoire. His compositions include five symphonies, overtures, the oratorios *St Paul* (1836) and *Elijah* (1846), chamber music, and piano music.

Menderes, River (ancient name: R. Maeander; Turkish name: Büyük Menderes) A winding river in W Turkey, flowing WSW into the Aegean Sea. Its ancient name gave rise to the term meander. Length: 400 km (249 mi).

Mendes, Sam (Samuel Alexander M.; 1965–) British theatre and film director. He achieved celebrity as the young director of London's Donmar Warehouse Theatre (1992–2002) before making the films *American Beauty* (1999), which earned five Academy Awards, and *Road to Perdition* (2002).

Mendip Hills (*or* **Mendips**) A range of limestone hills in SW England, in N Somerset, extending NW–SE between Axbridge and the Frome Valley, reaching 325 m (1068 ft) at Blackdown. Its many limestone features include Cheddar Gorge and the caves of Wookey Hole.

Mendoza 32 48S 68 52W A city in W Argentina. It is the commercial centre of an irrigated area specializing in wine production. Population (1999 est): 119 681.

Menelaus A legendary Spartan king and husband of *Helen. He served under his brother Agamemnon in the *Trojan War and after the fall of Troy won Helen back.

Menelik II (1844–1913) Emperor of Ethiopia (1889–1913). He greatly expanded Ethiopia, limited the power of the nobility, and modernized the administration.

Mengele, Josef (1894–?1979) German medical scientist, notorious for atrocities committed in the Nazi concentration camp at Auschwitz. Known as "the Angel of Death," he was camp doctor at Auschwitz from 1943 to 1945 and was subsequently held responsible for the deaths of 400 000 people, mostly Jews, many of whom died in bizarre medical experiments. In 1985 a body exhumed in Brazil was identified as his.

meningitis Inflammation of the meninges—the membranes that surround the brain. This is usually caused by bacteria or viruses and occurs most commonly in children. Symptoms include headache, vomiting, stiff neck, intolerance to light, tiredness, irritability, and fits. Treatment for bacterial meningitis is with antibiotics and the patient usually recovers rapidly, but meningococcal meningitis, a severe form caused by the meningococcus (*Neisseria meningitidis*), develops rapidly and can be fatal within a week unless diagnosed and treated promptly. The Hib vaccine protects children against bacterial meningitis caused by *Haemophilus influenzae* type B. Viral meningitis is often mild but may have serious effects.

menopause The change of life: the time in a woman's life when the menstrual periods become irregular and finally cease because egg cells are no longer produced by the ovaries. The menopause can occur at any age between the late 30s and late 50s. Some women may experience symptoms, including flushing ("hot flushes"), palpitations, and irritability, due to reduced secretion of oestrogens. These can be relieved by **hormone replacement therapy** with oestrogens (and progestogens to prevent damage to the womb lining that oestrogens alone may cause).

Menotti, Gian Carlo (1911–) Italian-born US composer. Among his compositions are the operas *The Medium* (1946) and *The Saint of Bleecker Street*, both of which won Pulitzer Prizes, and the television opera *Amahl and the Night Visitors* (1951). In 1958 he founded the Spoleto Festival.

Mensheviks One of the two factions into which the Russian Social Democratic Workers' Party split in 1903 in London. Unlike the rival *Bolsheviks, the Mensheviks (meaning those in the minority) believed in a large and loosely organized party. They supported Russia's participation in World War I and were prominent in the Russian Revolution until the Bolsheviks seized power in October 1917. They were finally suppressed in 1922.

menstruation The monthly discharge of blood and fragments of womb lining from the vagina. This is part of the **menstrual cycle**—the sequence of events, occurring in women from puberty to the menopause, by which an egg cell is released from the ovary. Menstruation is the stage at which the egg cell (with blood, etc.) is expelled from the womb if conception has not occurred. Ovulation occurs at around the middle of the cycle.

menthol ($C_{10}H_{20}O$) A white crystalline solid. It is a constituent of peppermint oil and is responsible for the characteristic smell of the mint plant, but can also be prepared synthetically. Menthol is used as an analgesic and in flavouring for sweets and cigarettes.

Menuhin, Yehudi, Baron (1916–99) British violinist, born in the USA of Russo-Jewish parentage. A pupil of Georges Enesco, he became famous in boyhood. From 1959 to 1968 Menuhin was director of the Bath Festival, where he also participated as a conductor. He founded the Yehudi Menuhin School for musically gifted children in 1963.

Menzies, Sir Robert Gordon (1894–1978) Australian statesman; prime minister as leader of the United Australia Party (1939–41) and then of the Liberal Party (1949–66). He was attorney general (1934–39) before becoming prime minister. He resigned in 1941 and formed the Liberal Party in 1944. As Liberal prime minister he increased US influence in Australian affairs and was strongly anticommunist.

Mercator, Gerardus (Gerhard Kremer; 1512–94) Flemish geographer, best known for the Mercator projection. Prosecuted for heresy in 1544, he emigrated to Protestant Germany in 1552, where he was appointed cartographer to the Duke of Cleves. The **Mercator projection** first used in 1569, is a cylindrical map projection. The parallels of latitude are represented as being straight lines of equal length to the equator. The meridians are equally spaced and intersect at right angles. The correct ratio between latitude and longitude is maintained by increasing the distance between the parallels away from the equator causing increased distortion towards the Poles.

merchant banks Financial institutions that became acceptance houses as a result of their foreign trading as merchants. They are now involved in a variety of other businesses, including: the issue, placing, and underwriting of shares and debentures for firms; the issue of long-term loans for governments and institutions abroad; advising on the investment of funds and the management of portfolios; advising on and managing takeover bids; and dealings in foreign exchange.

m

Mercia A kingdom of Anglo-Saxon England. The Mercians were *Angles and their territory embraced most of central England south of the Humber between Wales and East Anglia. Mercia achieved pre-eminence under *Offa (757–96); thereafter it declined and was merged in the 9th century into a united England under Wessex.

mercury (botany) An annual or perennial herb of the genus *Mercurialis* (8 species), native to Eurasia and N Africa. The perennial dog's mercury (*M. perennis*) of woodland areas has an evil smell and is poisonous to grazing animals. Growing 15–40 cm high, it has large toothed leaves and small green flowers. The annual mercury (*M. annua*) occurs on wasteland and as a garden weed. Family: *Euphorbiaceae*.

mercury (Hg) The only common metal that is liquid at room temperature (it has a high relative density of 13.546). It occurs chiefly as the sulphide cinnabar (HgS), from which mercury is obtained simply by heating in a current of air. Mercury is used in thermometers, barometers, and batteries and as an amalgam in dentistry. Compounds include the oxide (HgO), mercurous and mercuric chlorides (Hg_2Cl_2, $HgCl_2$), and the explosive mercury fulminate ($Hg(ONC)_2$), which is widely used as a detonator. Mercury and its compounds are highly poisonous and are only slowly excreted by the human body. At no 80; at wt 200.59; mp −38.87°C; bp 356.58°C.

Mercury (astronomy) The innermost and second smallest (4880 km diameter) planet, orbiting the sun every 88 days at a mean distance of 57.9 million km. Its long period of axial rotation, 58.6 days, is two-thirds of its orbital period. Like the moon, Mercury exhibits *phases. Its surface is heavily cratered, with intervening lava-flooded plains. It has only a very tenuous atmosphere, mainly helium and argon.

Mercury (mythology) The Roman god of merchants and commerce and of astronomy who was also the messenger of the gods. He is usually portrayed as holding a purse, and with a cap, winged sandals, and staff. He was identified with the Greek god Hermes.

Meredith, George (1828–1909) British poet and novelist. His long poem sequence *Modern Love* (1862) was partly based on his unhappy marriage. His novels include *The Egoist* (1879) and *The Tragic Comedians* (1880).

merganser A *duck belonging to a genus (*Mergus*) of the N hemisphere, also called sawbill. 40–57 cm long, mergansers have a long serrated bill for feeding on worms, fish, and eels. Males have a dark-green double-crested head, a chestnut breast, and a grey-and-white back; females are brown with a white wing bar.

Mérida 20 59N 89 39W A city in E Mexico. It is the commercial and industrial centre for an agricultural area specializing in henequen (a fibre) production. It has a 16th-century cathedral and is the site of the University of Yucatán (refounded 1922). Population (2000): 660 848.

Merino A breed of sheep from Spain, noted for its long thick high-quality white fleece. Merinos have been exported to many parts of the world, especially Australia.

meristem An area of actively dividing plant cells responsible for growth in the plant. The main meristematic regions in dicotyledon plants are the shoot tip and root tip (apical meristems) and the *cambium (lateral meristem).

merlin A small *falcon, *Falco columbarius*, occurring in moorland and heathland regions of the N hemisphere. The female is 32 cm long and is dark brown with heavily streaked underparts; the male is 26 cm long and has a grey-blue back and tail.

Merlin In *Arthurian legend, the wizard who counsels and assists Arthur and his father, Uther Pendragon. There are various accounts of Merlin's life in *Geoffrey of Monmouth and later writers. He helped Uther to win Igraine, Arthur's mother, made the Round Table, cared for Arthur as a child, and armed him with the sword Excalibur.

Meroë An ancient city, capital of a Nubian kingdom in present Sudan, founded c. 600 BC. The Iron Age culture was a mixture of local and Egyptian traditions.

Merovingians The first Frankish ruling dynasty (*see* FRANKS). It was founded by Merovech, King of the Salian Franks, in the mid-5th century AD. His grandson Clovis (reigned 481–511) greatly extended Merovingian possessions and the kingdom reached its zenith in the mid-6th century. The last Merovingian king, Childeric III, was deposed in 751 by the Carolingian Pepin the Short.

Mersey, River A river in NW England. Formed by the confluence of the Rivers Goyt and Tame at Stockport, it flows W to enter the Irish Sea by way of a 26 km (16 mi) long estuary, with the ocean ports of *Liverpool and Birkenhead on its banks. Length: 113 km (70 mi).

Merseyside A metropolitan county of NW England, created in 1974 from SW Lancashire and NW Cheshire. In 1986 its administrative powers were devolved to the unitary authorities of Sefton, Liverpool, St Helens, Knowsley, and Wirral. Area: 648 sq km (250 sq mi).

Merthyr Tydfil (Welsh name: Merthyr Tudful) **1.** 51 46N 3 23W A town in SE Wales, in Merthyr Tydfil county borough on the River Taff. Formerly a world iron and steel centre based on the surrounding coalfields, it now has light and electrical engineering. Population (1991 est): 39 482. **2.** A county borough in SE Wales, created from part of Mid Glamorgan in 1996. Area: 111 sq km (43 sq mi). Population (2001): 55 983.

mescaline A hallucinogenic drug obtained from the *peyote cactus of Mexico, where it was once widely used in religious ceremonies. Mescaline does not cause serious dependence and the hallucinations are mostly visual.

Mesmer, Franz Anton (1734–1815) German physician, who claimed to cure diseases by correcting the flow of "animal magnetism" in his patients' bodies. Investigation of "mesmerism" concluded that any cures were due to the powers of suggestion, but Mesmer's claims stimulated serious study of hypnosis.

Mesoamerican languages A geographical classification of the languages spoken by the American Indian peoples of Mexico, Guatemala, Honduras, Belize, El Salvador, and Nicaragua. It includes around 70 languages belonging to a number of families, such as the Uto-Aztecan, Otomangean, and Tarascan.

Mesolithic The middle division of the *Stone Age, especially in N Europe, where a distinct cultural stage, the Maglemosian, intervened between the last ice age and the evolution of farming communities. Generally, the Mesolithic is characterized by production of microliths (very minute stone tools), which were hafted into wooden, bone, or other handles.

mesons A group of unstable elementary particles (lifetimes between 10^{-8} and 10^{-15} second) that are classified as hadrons; each meson is believed to consist of a quark-antiquark pair (*see* PARTICLE PHYSICS).

Mesopotamia The region between the Rivers Tigris and Euphrates. The Sumerians settled in S Mesopotamia about 4000 BC: they established the world's first civilization and founded city states, such as *Ur, *Kish, and *Uruk. *Babylon became Mesopotamia's capital under Hammurabi (d. 1750 BC). After his death Mesopotamia was overrun successively by Kassites, Assyrians, and Persians.

Mesozoic era The geological era following the Palaeozoic and preceding the Cenozoic. It contains the Triassic, Jurassic, and Cretaceous periods, and lasted from about 240 to 65 million years ago. The reptiles were at their greatest development during this era but became extinct before the end of it.

Messerschmitt, Willy (1898–1978) German aircraft designer. He is best known for his World War II military planes, particularly the Me-109 fighter (1935) and the Me-262, the first jet fighter.

Messiaen, Olivier (1908–92) French composer, organist, and teacher. In 1931 he was appointed organist of La Trinité in Paris. His works, heavily influenced by Catholic mysticism and eastern music, include *La Nativité du Seigneur* (1935), the symphony *Turangalîla* (1948), *La Transfiguration* (for chorus and orchestra; 1965–69), and the opera *St Francis d'Assise* (1986).

Messina 38 13N 15 33E A port in Italy, in NE Sicily on the Strait of Messina. Successively occupied by Greeks, Carthaginians, Mamertines, Romans, Saracens, Normans, and Spaniards, in 1860 it became the last city in Sicily to be made part of a united Italy. Its manufactures include macaroni, chemicals, and soap. Population (2000 est): 259 156.

metabolism The sum of the processes and chemical reactions that occur in living organisms in order to maintain life. It can be divided into two components. **Anabolism** involves building up the tissues and organs of the body using simple substances, such as amino acids, simple sugars, etc., to construct the proteins, carbohydrates, and fats of which they are made. These processes require energy, which is provided by the oxidation of nutrients or the body's own food reserves. Oxidation and all other processes involving the chemical breakdown of substances with the production of waste products are known collectively as **catabolism**. Basal metabolism is the energy required to maintain vital functions (e.g. respiration, circulation) with the body at rest. It is measured by estimating the amount of heat produced by the body and is controlled by hormones from the thyroid gland.

metal An element that is usually a hard crystalline solid, a good conductor of heat and electricity, and forms a salt and hydrogen when reacted with an acid. Not all metals have these properties, however: mercury is a liquid at normal temperatures and sodium is soft. The most important are the heavy metals (iron, copper, lead, and zinc) used in engineering and the rarer heavy metals (nickel, chromium, tungsten, etc.) used in alloys. Other important metals are the noble metals (gold, silver, and platinum), and the light metals (aluminium and magnesium). Chemically important metals include the *alkali metals (sodium, potassium, and lithium), the *alkaline-earth metals (calcium, barium, etc.), and the rare-earth metals (*see* LANTHANIDES). Uranium is important in the nuclear power industry (*see* NUCLEAR ENERGY). Most metals occur in the earth's crust in the combined state and have to be mined before being extracted from their ores (*see* METALLURGY).

metallography The study of the crystalline structure of metals. It includes various techniques and is used to test the quality of steel after *heat treatment. Usually a small sample is taken from a batch and polished before being examined under a microscope for cracks, impurities, or holes. The polished surface may also be treated chemically to show up the different constituents of an alloy or to highlight cracks. The technique of X-ray diffraction developed by Max von Laue (1879–1960) is used to examine metallic crystals.

metalloids Elements displaying the physical and chemical properties both of *metals and nonmetals. Examples of metalloids are arsenic and germanium, which both have metallic and nonmetallic allotropes. They may form positive ions as well as covalently bonded compounds. The metalloid elements are often *semiconductors.

metallurgy The science and technology of producing metals. It includes the extraction of metals from their ores, alloying to form materials with specific properties, and *heat treatment to improve their properties.

metamorphic rock One of the three major rock categories (*compare* IGNEOUS ROCK; SEDIMENTARY ROCK) consisting of rocks produced by the alteration of existing rocks by heat, pressure, and chemically active fluids. Contact (*or* thermal) metamorphism occurs around igneous intrusions and results from heat alone. Regional metamorphism results from the heat and pressure created by crustal deformation. Dislocation metamorphism results from localized mechanical deformation, as along fault planes. Metamorphic rocks often form upland masses. Marble is a metamorphic rock formed from recrystallized limestone.

metamorphosis The process in animals by which a *larva changes into an adult. This radical change of internal and external body structures may be gradual or abrupt. Certain insects, such as dragonflies, undergo incomplete metamorphosis, during which successive stages (known as nymphs) become increasingly like the adult through a series of moults. In complete metamorphosis, seen in such insects as butterflies and houseflies, the larva passes into a quiescent pupal stage, during which the adult tissues are developed. Metamorphosis also occurs in amphibians (*see* FROG). The process in insects and amphibians is controlled by hormones.

metaphysical poets A group of 17th-century English poets whose work was characterized by intellectual wit and ingenuity, especially in their use of elaborate figures of speech. The leading poet was John *Donne, and his successors included George Herbert (1593–1633), Henry Vaughan (c. 1622–95), Andrew *Marvell, and Abraham Cowley (1618–67). They frequently employed colloquial speech rhythms in both their secular and their religious verse.

metaphysics The study of existence or being in general. The term derives from the title given to a group of Aristotle's writings.

The status of metaphysics has been much debated; *Kant thought this kind of investigation impossible because our minds can only cope with the phenomenal world or the world of appearances and *Ayer used the word as a pejorative term to indicate the meaninglessness of much traditional philosophy. However, metaphysics is still held to be one of the main divisions of philosophy.

Metazoa In traditional classification systems, a subkingdom of animals whose bodies consist of many cells differentiated and coordinated to perform specialized functions. It excludes the single-celled *protozoa and the *Parazoa* (*see* SPONGE). In modern classifications, the animal kingdom is divided into the subkingdoms *Parazoa* and *Eumetazoa*.

metempsychosis *See* REINCARNATION.

meteor A streak of light seen in the night sky when a **meteoroid**—an interplanetary rock or dust particle enters and burns up in the earth's atmosphere. A decaying *comet gradually produces a **meteor stream** of meteoroids around its orbit. When the earth passes through a meteor stream, an often spectacular **meteor shower** is observed. A **meteorite** is a large piece of interplanetary debris (mass usually over 100 kg) that falls to the earth's surface. Its composition is either principally iron or stone or an intermediate mixture.

meteorology The study of the physics, chemistry, and movements of the *atmosphere and its interactions with the ground surface. The troposphere and stratosphere, the lower layers of the atmosphere in which most weather phenomena occur, are the chief focuses of meteorology. **Weather** is the state of atmospheric conditions (including temperature, sunshine, wind, clouds, and precipitation) at a particular place and time. A **weather forecast** is a prediction of what weather conditions will be over a stated future period; it is made by studying weather maps, especially those obtained from satellites. Weather forecasts are essential to shipping and aviation and are of use to many other bodies, as well as to farmers. See illustration on p. 584.

methane (CH_4) A colourless odourless flammable gas that is the main constituent of *natural gas. It is the simplest member of the *alkane series and is used as a fuel and a source of other chemicals. Methane is produced in nature by the decay of vegetable matter under water, rising in bubbles from marshes as **marsh gas**. Coal gas also contains methane. Recently the generation of methane from sewage has been investigated as an *alternative energy source. It burns with a clear blue flame.

methanol (**methyl alcohol** *or* **wood alcohol**; CH_3OH) A colourless poisonous flammable liquid. Originally produced by distillation of wood, it is now usually made from hydrogen and carbon monoxide by high-pressure *catalysis. It is used as a solvent, antifreeze, and a raw material for making other chemicals. *See also* METHYLATED SPIRITS.

Methodism The Christian denomination that developed out of the religious practices advocated by the *Wesley brothers. Methodism evolved its own church organization during the 1790s. The supreme decision-making body is the Conference; local societies (congregations) are highly organized and pastoral and missionary work are major concerns. Methodism in the USA accounts for 80% of all Methodists.

methylated spirits A form of *ethanol (ethyl alcohol) that has been made unsuitable for drinking by the addition of about 9.5% of methanol (methyl alcohol), about 0.5% of pyridine, and a methyl violet dye. In this form it has many household uses, especially as a fuel for spirit burners. Industrial methylated spirits (IMS) consists of ethanol with about 5% of methanol and no pyridine. It is used as a solvent for varnishes, etc.

metre (m) The unit of length in the *metric system. Originally defined in 1791 as one ten-millionth of the length of the quadrant of the earth's meridian through Paris, it was redefined in 1927 as the distance between two marks on a platinum-iridium bar. It is now defined (General Conference on Weights and Measures, 1983) as the length of the path travelled by light in a vacuum in 1/299 792 458 second, which replaces the 1960 definition based on the emission of a krypton lamp.

metre (poetry) The rhythmic pattern of a line of verse measured in terms of basic metrical units or feet. In accentual verse, as in English, a foot consists of various arrangements of stressed (´) and unstressed (˘) syllables. In classical Greek and Latin verse, the quantity or length rather than the stress of syllables determines the foot. In English the most common feet are the *iamb (˘´), the trochee (´˘), the anapaest (˘˘´), the dactyl (´˘˘), and the spondee (´´). Most traditional poetic forms, such as the *sonnet, are written according to strict metrical patterns.

metric system A system of measurement

weather conditions

● rain ✶ snow ⌒ dew

● drizzle ▲ hail ≡ fog

▽ showers ⊿ ice pellets ℞ thunderstorm

cloud cover

○ clear

◑ 1 okta

◗ 2

◗ 3

◖ 4

◕ 5

● 6

◕ 7

● 8

⊗ sky obscured (1 okta = ⅛ of the sky)

wind. The arrow points in the direction from which the wind is blowing.

knots

◎ calm

○— 1–2

○—' 3–7

○—/ 8–12

○—⁄ 13–17

○—// 18–22

○—/// 23–27

○—/// 28–32

○—/// 33–37

○—//// 38–42

○—///// 43–47

○—▲ 48–52

weather map The numbers at the stations show temperature (0°C). Isobars show atmospheric pressure in millibars.

fronts

▼▼▼ **cold front** boundary between overtaking cold air mass and warm air mass.

●●● **warm front** boundary between overtaking warm air mass and cold air mass.

▼●▼ **stationary** boundary between air masses of similar temperature.

▲●▲● **occluded** line where a cold front overtakes a warm front.

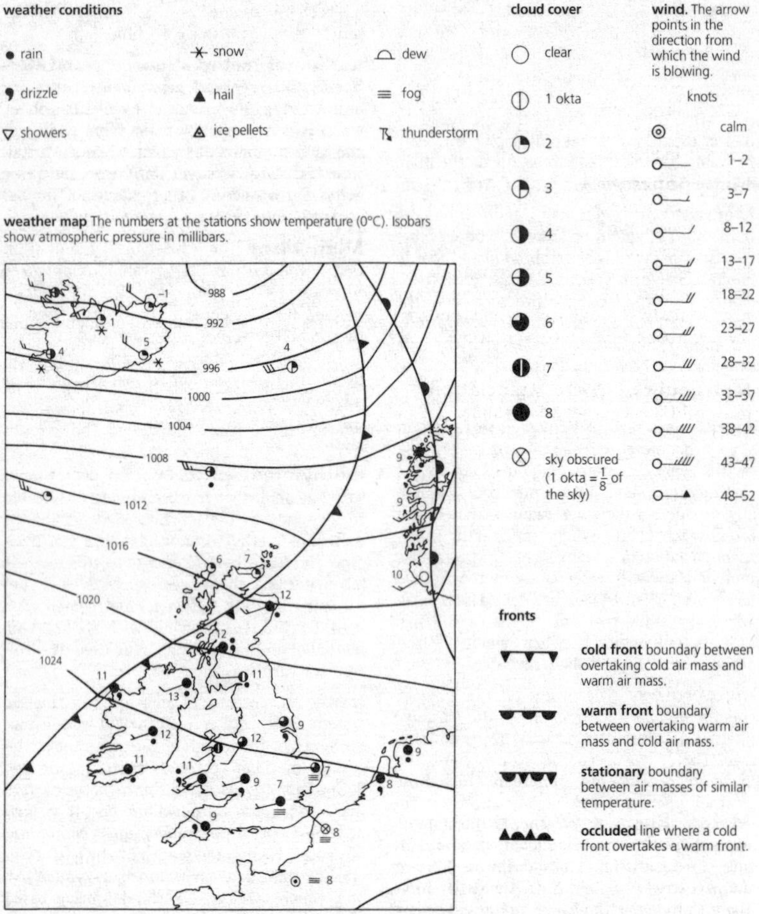

meteorology. Internationally agreed symbols are used throughout the world by meteorological stations to represent current weather conditions. These are plotted on weather maps from which forecasts can be made.

based on the decimal system. First suggested in 1585, it was not given formal acceptance until 1795, when a French law provided definitions for the *metre, *are, stere, *litre, and gram. However, this form of the metric system was not widely used, even in France, until the third decade of the 19th century; during this period it was also adopted by most European countries. Although the metric system was authorized in the UK in 1864, British reluctance to abandon its own "Imperial units" did not weaken until 1963, when the Imperial yard and

pound were given legal definitions in terms of metric units. The **Metrication Board,** set up in 1969, was disbanded in April 1980. From 1 January 2000 an EU regulation was adopted into British law, making it illegal to sell goods in any measure other than grams, kilograms, millimetres, and metres (with exceptions for beer and milk).

For scientific purposes, former metric systems (such as the *c.g.s. system) have been replaced by *SI units.

metronome A small device consisting of a

pendulum with a small sliding weight on it, which can be regulated to make the pendulum beat at a desired number of beats per minute. The most common type is the clockwork metronome invented by J.N. Maelzel (1770–1838); electric metronomes also exist. Metronome markings are often given in musical scores to indicate the exact speed of the music.

Metropolitan Museum of Art The principal museum in New York City and one of the most important in the world. Founded in 1870, it was opened in its present premises in Central Park in 1880. Its enormous collection comprises paintings, drawings, sculptures, ceramics, furniture, etc., from many periods and countries, including China, ancient Egypt, Greece, and Rome.

Metropolitan Opera Association The principal US opera company, founded in New York in 1883. Enrico Caruso (1873–1921) sang regularly with the company from 1904 to 1921. The company occupied the Metropolitan Opera House until 1966, when it moved into the Lincoln Centre for the Performing Arts, the original building being demolished.

Metternich, Klemens Wenzel Nepomuk Lothar, Fürst von (1773–1859) Austrian statesman, the leading figure in European diplomacy from the fall of Napoleon (1815) until the Revolutions of 1848. As foreign minister (1809–48) he sought to maintain the balance of power in Europe, supporting dynastic monarchies and suppressing liberalism. His policies dominated the Congresses of *Vienna (1814–15), Aix-la-Chapelle (1818), Troppau (1820), Laibach (1821), and Verona (1822).

Meuse, River (Dutch and Flemish name: Maas) A river in W Europe. Rising in NE France and flowing mainly N past Liège in Belgium and Maastricht in the S Netherlands, it enters the North Sea at the Rhine Delta. It was the scene of heavy fighting in World War I (1914) and World War II (1940). Length: 926 km (575 mi).

Mexican War (1846–48) The war between Mexico and the USA over disputed border territory. Military operations began when Gen Zachary *Taylor invaded New Mexico and ended with the fall of Mexico City (1847). Peace was concluded with the Treaty of Guadalupe-Hidalgo.

Mexico, United States of A country in North America between the Gulf of Mexico and the Pacific Ocean. Narrow coastal plains rise to high mountain ranges in the interior. Much of the N is arid with tropical forest in the S, especially in the Yucatán Peninsula in the SE. Most of the population is of mixed Indian and Spanish descent. *Economy*: Mexico now ranks among the world's main oil-producing countries. It also has large reserves of natural gas and there are substantial deposits of uranium. Other minerals extracted include iron ore, zinc, sulphur, silver, and copper, and Mexico is the world's largest producer of fluorite and graphite. Manufacturing is increasingly important. Agriculture remains relatively underdeveloped: maize is the main food crop; cash crops include cotton, sugar, coffee, and fruit and vegetables, as well as sisal in Yucatán. Fishing has been developed considerably and tourism is an important source of foreign currency. *History*: Mexico was the site of the Mayan civilization from the 2nd to the 13th centuries AD, and between the 8th and the 12th centuries the *Toltecs flourished. The 14th century saw the rise of the *Aztecs. The Aztecs were conquered by the Spanish under Cortés in 1521 and Mexico became part of the viceroyalty of New Spain. The struggle for independence from Spain was achieved in 1821. A turbulent period dominated by *Santa Anna was followed by the *Mexican War (1846–48), in which territory was lost to the USA. The Mexican Revolution (1910–40) produced the constitution of 1917, the democratic goals of which have been the declared aims of subsequent governments. Mexican politics is dominated by the Party of Institutionalized Revolution (PRI), which remained the governing party from 1929 until 2000, despite repated allegations of electoral fraud. Economic pressures in the 1980s led to high inflation, devaluation of the peso, and austerity measures. In 1994 there was an armed uprising of indigenous peoples from the poverty-stricken southern states. Inflation, unmanageable debt levels, and a soaring trade deficit recurred in the mid- and late 1990s. Mexico is a member of the OAS and a signatory of NAFTA. Official language: Spanish. Currency: peso of 100 centavos. Area: 1 967 183 sq km (761 530 sq mi). Population (2003 est): 100 588 000. Capital: Mexico City.

Mexico City (Spanish name: Ciudad de México) 19 25N 99 10W The capital of Mexico, in the S of the high central plateau at a height of 2380 m (7800 ft), surrounded by mountains. The 14th-century Aztec city of Tenochtitlán was destroyed by Cortés in 1521. A new Spanish city was built on the site and it rapidly became the most important in the New World. It was captured by the USA and then by France in the 19th century and in the 20th century was the centre of several revolutions. It now has considerable industry. It is the site of the National Autonomous University of Mexico (founded in 1551), the national library, the museum, and the Palace of Fine Arts Theatre. In 1985 the city and surrounding areas were devastated by an earthquake. It suffers atmospheric pollution. Population (2000 est): 8 591 309.

Miami 25 45N 80 15W A city and port in the USA, in Florida on Biscayne Bay. A tourist resort and retirement centre, it grew during the Florida land boom of the 1920s. It produces citrus fruit and winter vegetables. Industries include aircraft repairing, sponge fisheries, clothing, and concrete. Population (2000): 362 470.

micas A group of common rock-forming silicate minerals with a layered structure and complex composition. The group includes muscovite, $K_2Al_4(Si_6Al_2)O_{20}(OH,F)_4$, a white mica and economically the most important; it occurs in granitic rocks (often pegmatites), gneisses, and schists. The other principal micas are phlogopite (amber), biotite (dark), paragonite, margarite, zinnwaldite, and lepidolite (a source of lithium). Since it is a good insulator and can withstand high temperatures, mica has many electrical uses and is used for furnace windows.

m

Michaelmas daisy *See* ASTER.

Michelangelo Buonarroti (1475–1564) Italian sculptor, painter, architect, and poet. Working in Rome from 1496 until 1501, he produced his first major sculptures, notably the *Pietà* (St Peter's, Rome). This was followed (1501–05) by his work in Florence, including *David* (Accademia, Florence) and the painting of the *Holy Family* (Uffizi). The celebrated Sistine Chapel ceiling (1508–12), in the Vatican, established his reputation as the greatest painter of his day. Returning to Florence (1516), Michelangelo became the architect and sculptor of the Medici funerary chapel (1520–34) in the church of San Lorenzo and he also designed the Laurentian Library. These architectural projects and the fresco of the *Last Judgment* (1534–41) for the Sistine Chapel were his first major works in the new mannerist style (*see* MANNERISM). In his last years he worked mainly as an architect, becoming in 1547 chief architect of St Peter's, Rome, in which capacity he designed its great dome.

Michelson, Albert Abraham (1852–1931) US physicist, born in Germany. He designed an accurate interferometer known as the Michelson interferometer and used it to measure precisely the speed of light. He used it in the **Michelson-Morley experiment**, with the US chemist E. W. Morley (1838–1923) in 1881; they tried to show that luminiferous ether existed by measuring the earth's velocity relative to it. The negative result led to the downfall of the ether theory and was explained by Einstein's theory of *relativity in 1905.

Michigan A state in the N central USA, bordered largely by water (Lakes Superior, Huron, Michigan, Erie, and St Clair). It is divided by the Straits of Mackinac into the Lower Peninsula in the S and the Upper Peninsula in the N. Most of Michigan's population and industry is concentrated in the Lower Peninsula. Manufacturing is important; other industries include machinery, iron and steel, and chemicals. It has large mineral reserves of gypsum, calcium, and magnesium compounds, natural gas, and oil. *History*: explored by the French in the 17th century, it remained under French control until it was acquired by the British (1763) as part of Canada. It came under American control (1783), becoming a state in 1837. Area: 150 779 sq km (58 216 sq mi). Population (2000): 9 938 444. Capital: Lansing.

Michigan, Lake The third largest of the Great Lakes in North America, wholly in the USA. It is linked with Lake Huron via the Straits of Mackinac; Chicago is on its S bank. Area: 58 000 sq km (22 400 sq mi).

microbiology The study of microorganisms, or microbes—organisms that are invisible to the naked eye, including bacteria, small fungi (e.g. yeasts and moulds), algae, protozoa, and viruses. Microorganisms bring about decomposition and the recycling of nutrients. They are vital to many industries, including brewing, dairying, and food processing, and they have revolutionized medical treatment with the discovery of antibiotics. Some microorganisms cause disease (*see* INFECTION).

microchip *See* INTEGRATED CIRCUIT.

microcomputers Small but sophisticated *computers designed for a single user and often for a specific application. The central processing unit is a *microprocessor. Laptop and handheld computers are very small and portable.

microcopy A greatly reduced photographic copy of a printed page, drawing, or other image. **Microfilm** is a strip of standard-width film containing microcopies. It was introduced in the 1920s for use in banks and is now widely used for compact storage and ready reference to documents. Special enlarging viewers can rapidly wind the film to the correct page. **Microfiche** is a similar system on cards holding a single film negative, with even greater reduction of the pictures. The viewers often have a printer attached to reproduce paper copies.

microlight aircraft A small powered aircraft of minimal weight. These aircraft were developed in the 1980s, when such models as the British Optica were considered for traffic monitoring and other roles. Some models can be folded up for ease of transport.

micrometer An instrument for measuring small lengths with great accuracy. The object to be measured is held between the jaws of a C-shaped metal piece, one jaw of which can be adjusted by a screw. The screw is turned by rotating a drum with a vernier scale marked on it, from which the required dimension can be read.

Micronesia, Federated States of A country in the W Pacific Ocean, consisting of 600 of the Caroline Islands, including Chuuk, Yap, Pohnpei, and Kosrae. *Economy*: the main exports are copra and fish. *History*: formerly part of the UN Trust Territory of the Pacific Islands, the country became self-governing in 1986 and was recognized as independent by the UN in 1990. Official languages, English and local languages. Currency: US dollar of 100 cents. Area: 700 sq km (270 sq mi). Population (2003 est): 112 000. Capital: Palikir.

microphone A device that converts sound into electrical signals. A telephone mouthpiece usually consists of a carbon microphone in which the sound waves exert a varying pressure on carbon granules, so varying their electrical resistance. In capacitor microphones, used in music recording, a diaphragm forms one plate of a capacitor, across which the sound waves produce a fluctuating potential difference. Crystal microphones rely on the *piezoelectric effect. Ribbon microphones have a highly directional response. They consist of a thin strip of aluminium alloy in a strong magnetic field.

microprocessor The central processing unit of a *microcomputer. Its development was made possible in the 1970s by advances in solid-state electronics, in particular the design of integrated circuits of such complexity that all the main calculating functions can be carried out by a single silicon chip (*see* INTEGRATED CIRCUIT).

microscope An optical instrument used for producing a magnified image of a small object. There are several distinct types, the most common being the compound microscope, which contains an objective lens system and an eyepiece system. It was invented in 1609 by a Dutch spectacle maker Zacharias Janssen (1580–c. 1638) and his father, but Robert *Hooke gave the first extensive description of its use in biology in his *Micrographia* (1665). In a compound microscope the objective produces a real magnified image, which is further magnified by the eyepiece. The magnification, which may be up to a thousand, is limited by the *resolving power of the lenses; the smallest detail capable of resolution by an optical microscope is about 0.2 micrometre. This can be increased by using an oil-immersion lens (*see also* ULTRAMICROSCOPE). Still higher magnifications are obtained by using shorter wavelength radiations, as in the *electron microscope.

microwave background radiation *See* BIG-BANG THEORY.

microwaves Electromagnetic radiation with wavelengths between 1 and 300 millimetres, lying between infrared rays and radio waves in the electromagnetic spectrum. They are used in *radar and **microwave heating**. This method is used in the rapid cooking of food as the radiation penetrates to the interior of the food. The microwave photon is the same order of magnitude as the vibrational energy of atoms and molecules and therefore heats the interior directly, rather than by conduction from the surface. Microwaves are generated by such devices as *magnetrons and *klystrons.

Midas In Greek legend, a king of Phrygia whose wish that everything he touched be turned to gold was granted by Dionysus in gratitude for his hospitality to the satyr *Silenus. In another legend, Midas was asked to judge between the music of Pan and Apollo and chose the former. Apollo punished his tactlessness by changing his ears into those of an ass.

middle ages The period of European history that is generally regarded as commencing in the 5th century with the fall of the western Roman Empire and ending with the Renaissance. This period begins with the creation of the barbarian kingdoms, which developed into the nation states of W Europe. In Church history, the period covers the rise to supremacy of the Roman Catholic Church. Socially and economically the period saw the rising power of the great landed magnates and the creation of a feudal society, while urban growth and the development of trade reached unprecedented heights.

Middlesbrough **1.** 54 35N 1 14W A town in NE England, in Middlesbrough unitary authority, North Yorkshire, on the Tees estuary. Local iron ore and local coking coal gave Middlesbrough early industrial advantages. Until the recessions of the 1980s and 1990s iron and steel, petrochemicals, and constructional engineering were major industries. The economy is now mainly based on the service sector. Population (1998 est): 145 000. **2.** A unitary authority in NE England, in North Yorkshire; formerly (1974–96) part of the county of Cleveland. Area: 54 sq km (21 sq mi). Population (2001): 134 847.

midge A small fly, also called a nonbiting midge, belonging to the family *Chironomidae* (over 2000 species). It resembles a mosquito but is harmless. Midges are found near fresh water, often in large swarms. The wormlike aquatic larvae are often red.

The term is also applied loosely to similar but unrelated flies.

Midlothian A council area of SE Scotland. Under local government reorganization in 1975 the historic county of Midlothian, including the city of Edinburgh, was absorbed into Lothian Region. In 1996 a much smaller area, excluding Edinburgh, became an independent unitary authority. Midlothian is mainly hilly and the chief activity is agriculture. Area: 356 sq km (137 sq mi). Population (2001): 80 941. Administrative centre: Dalkeith.

midnight sun The sun when it remains above the horizon all night in places poleward of the Arctic and Antarctic Circles, for periods around the summer solstice (amounting to one night on the Circles and to six months at the Poles). A corresponding period of "noon darkness" occurs during the winter.

Midrash (Hebrew: enquiry, exposition) Exposition of the Bible, and more particularly a book consisting of such exposition. There are many Midrashim, mostly dating from the early middle ages, and they are a valuable source for the religious ideas of the Jews of the time. The *Talmuds also contain a great deal of Midrash.

Midway Islands A group of atolls approximately in the middle of the Pacific Ocean. They are under US administration, the only inhabitants being US military personnel. A US–Japanese air battle near Midway in June 1942 was the first major Japanese setback in World War II.

Mies van der Rohe, Ludwig (1886–1969) German architect. A pioneering architect of the 1920s and 1930s, Mies first achieved fame with his glass skyscrapers (1919–21). However, his most influential building was the glass, steel, and marble German pavilion at the Barcelona international exhibition (1929). In 1937 he moved to the USA, where he designed such buildings as the Illinois Institute of Technology (1939) and the Seagram building, New York (1958).

migraine Recurrent headaches, usually affecting one side of the head and thought to be caused by contraction and then dilation of the arteries in the brain. The attacks are often preceded by blurring of vision and flickering lights (called an aura). During the headache itself vomiting commonly occurs.

migration, animal The periodic movement of animal populations between one region and another, usually associated with seasonal climatic changes or breeding cycles. Migration is best known among birds, but the phenomenon is seen in many other animals, including fish (notably salmon), butterflies, bats, lemmings, and whales. The mechanism of navigation and homing is not completely understood. In birds it seems to involve sighting of visible landmarks, as well as a compass sense, using the sun or the stars as bearings. Other animals are thought to use similar methods.

Míkonos (*or* **Mykonos**) A Greek island in the S Aegean Sea, one of the Cyclades. It is popular with tourists and is noted for having a large number of churches. Area: 90 sq km (35 sq mi). Population (latest est): 5503.

Milan (Italian name: Milano; Latin name: Mediolanum) 45 28N 9 12E A city in N Italy, the capital of Lombardy on the River Olona. Milan is the chief commercial and industrial centre of Italy. Its manufactures include motor vehicles, machinery, silk and other textiles, and chemicals and it is a major publishing centre. Milan has a gothic cathedral (duomo), the Brera Palace (containing the city's chief art collection), and the opera house of *La Scala. *History*: founded by the Gauls about 600 BC, it was captured by the Romans in 222. After the 12th century it enjoyed considerable economic prosperity. Having fallen to Spain in 1535, it was under Austrian rule (1713–96) and in 1797 Napoleon made it capital of the Cisalpine Republic (1797) and capital of the kingdom of Italy (1805–14). Population (2000 est): 1 300 977.

mildew Any fungus that grows as dense filaments forming visible white patches. Many fungal diseases of plants are called mildews: powdery mildews are infestations by fungi of the order *Peronosporales*, while downy mildews are due to infection by fungi of the family *Erysiphaceae*.

mile A unit of length traditionally used in the UK and USA. A statute mile is equal to 1760 yards. A nautical mile (UK) is equal to 6080 feet; a nautical mile (international) is equal to 1852 metres (6076.12 ft). The unit is based on the Roman mile of 1000 paces.

Miletus An ancient Greek city in *Ionia, founded about 1000 BC. Commercially active from Italy to Egypt, Miletus exemplified Ionian energy and enterprise. Milesians were prominent among the 6th-century Ionian thinkers, and even after destruction by Persia (494 BC) Miletus remained commercially important until its harbours silted up.

Milhaud, Darius (1892–1974) French composer, a member of Les Six. He made use of polytonality and jazz in many of his compositions. With Jean Cocteau he wrote the ballets *Le Boeuf sur le toit* (1919) and *Le Train bleu* (1924); with Paul Claudel he wrote the opera *Christophe Colomb* (1928). His other works include 12 symphonies, 15 string quartets, concertos, and Jewish liturgical music.

milk A fluid secreted by the *mammary glands of mammals to feed their young. Cows' milk consists typically of about 87% water, 3.6% fat, 3.3% protein, 4.7% lactose (milk sugar), small quantities of minerals (mainly calcium and phosphorus), and vitamins (mainly vitamins A and B). (Human milk, in contrast, contains less protein and more lactose.) Milk forms a well-balanced and highly nutritious food. In the UK most milk is sold, after *pasteurization, in bottles or cartons, with daily doorstep deliveries. Sterilized and UHT (ultraheat-treated) milk both have a longer shelf-life.

milkweed A herb of the genus *Asclepias* (120 species), native to North America and often grown in the tropics and subtropics for ornament. Up to 1.2 m high, it bears umbrella-shaped clusters of orange, purple, pink, or red flowers and yields a milky latex. Family: *Asclepiadaceae*.

Milky Way The diffuse band of light that is seen, on a clear moonless night, stretching across the sky. It is composed of innumerable stars that are too faint to be seen individually. They lie around the sun in the flattened and densely populated disc of our *Galaxy.

Mill, John Stuart (1806–73) British economist and philosopher. His *Principles of Political Economy* (1848) is little more than a restatement of the ideas of Adam Smith and Ricardo. *On Liberty* (1859) shows that he was concerned for the rights of the individual, and he believed strongly in the equality of the sexes, publishing his views in *Subjection of Women* (1869). A prolific journalist, he edited the *London Review* during the period 1835–40.

Millais, Sir John Everett (1829–96) British painter. He was one of the founders of the *Pre-Raphaelite Brotherhood, the principles of which he applied to his best paintings, notably the controversial *Christ in the House of His Parents* (1850) and *Ophelia* (1852; both Tate Gallery). After abandoning Pre-Raphaelitism in the 1860s, he painted more popular and sentimental works, such as *Bubbles* (1886), a portrait of his grandson.

Millennium Dome A large dome erected in Greenwich, Greater London, to house a multimedia exhibition celebrating the year 2000. With a circumference of over 1 km (1099 yds) and a height of 50 m (164 ft), it is the world's largest dome. Designed by the Richard Rogers Partnership, the Dome cost £750 m to build; as the exhibition failed to attract the expected interest it then required an additional £600 M of lottery money to keep open for 1 year. Subsequently it remained empty, finally (2002) being given away to a developer, who will stage entertainments and sports events and develop the surrounding land.

Miller, Arthur (1915–) US dramatist. As a Jewish liberal intellectual he has played an active role in political life. His plays include *All My Sons* (1947), *Death of a Salesman* (1947), which won a Pulitzer Prize, *The Crucible* (1953), concerning the Salem witch trials of the 1690s, *After the Fall* (1964), which is in part a portrait of his late wife Marilyn *Monroe, *The Ride Down Mt Morgan* (1991), and *Mr Peter's Connections* (1998).

Miller, Glenn (1904–44) US jazz trombonist and band leader, known for such popular songs as "Moonlight Serenade" and "In the Mood." Miller's band, assembled in 1938, recorded many hit swing tunes and entertained the troops during World War II.

millet One of various grasses or their seeds, cultivated in Asia and Africa as a cereal crop and in parts of Europe and North America chiefly as a pasture grass and fodder crop. It grows 30–130 cm high and the flowers form spikes or branched clusters. Common or broomcorn millet (*Panicum miliaceum*) is used for poultry feed or for flour milling. Pearl millet (*Pennisetum glaucum*) is grown as a food grain, Italian millet (*Setaria italica*) as a grain crop, and Japanese millet (*Echinochloa crus-galli* var. *frumentacea*) mainly for fodder. A variety of sorghum (durra) is also known as millet.

Millet, Jean François (1814–75) French painter of peasant origin. He studied in Cherbourg and in Paris, achieving acclaim in 1844. After settling in Barbizon (1849), he became associated with the Barbizon school and painted melancholy and sometimes sentimental agricultural scenes, notably *The Gleaners* (1857) and *The Angelus* (1859; both Louvre).

millipede A slow-moving *arthropod of the widely distributed class (or subclass) *Diplopoda* (about 8000 species). Its slender cylindrical body, 2–280 mm long, is covered by a calcareous cuticle and consists of 20–100 segments, most of which bear two pairs of legs (*compare* CENTIPEDE). Millipedes live in dark humid places as scavengers of dead plant and animal materials. In defence they secrete a toxic fluid containing cyanide and iodine.

Milne, A(lan) A(lexander) (1882–1956) British novelist and dramatist. He is best known for his books for and about his son Christopher Robin. These include two collections of verse and two books about toy animals, *Winnie-the-Pooh* (1926) and *The House at Pooh Corner* (1928).

m

Milošević, Slobodan (1941–) Serbian politician; president of Serbia (1989–97) and of the Federal Republic of Yugoslavia (1997–2000). He supported Bosnian Serb aggression in Bosnia-Hercegovina (1992–95) and led repression of the ethnic Albanians in *Kosovo, provoking NATO airstrikes. He was swept from power in 2000 and handed over to the war crimes tribunal in the Hague, where he is standing trial for genocide.

Miltiades (c.550–489 BC) Athenian general and statesman. Sent to govern the Thracian peninsula in Athenian interests, he ruled as tyrant and fought with Darius I of Persia (c.558–486 BC) in Scythia. Appointed a general in 490, he devised the strategy by which the Greeks decisively defeated the Persians at the battle of *Marathon.

Milton, John (1608–74) English poet. His early works include the poems *L'Allegro* and *Il Penseroso* (1632), the masque *Comus* (1633), and the elegy *Lycidas* (1637). During the 1640s and 1650s he actively supported the Puritan revolution and wrote many polemical pamphlets, notably *Areopagitica* (1644), a defence of free speech. In 1649 he was appointed Latin Secretary to the Council of State, but his eyesight began to fail and he had become totally blind by 1652. After the Restoration he retired from public life to write his great epic poem *Paradise Lost* (1667), its sequel *Paradise Regained* (1677), and the dramatic poem *Samson Agonistes* (1671).

Milton Keynes 1. 52 02N 0 42W A city in S central England, in Milton Keynes unitary authority, Buckinghamshire. Developed since 1967 as a new town around the old village of Milton Keynes, it is the headquarters of the Open University (1969) and has varied light industries. The UK's only multidenominational cathedral opened here in 1993. Population (1991): 156 148. **2.** A unitary authority in S central England, in Buckinghamshire. Area: 310 sq km (119 sq mi). Population (2001): 207 063.

Milwaukee 43 03N 87 56W A city and port in the USA, in Wisconsin on Lake Michigan. The state's largest city and a major shipping centre, Milwaukee is a leading producer of heavy machinery, electrical equipment, and diesel and petrol engines. Population (2000): 596 974.

mime Acting without words by physical gestures alone. It was practised in ancient Greek and Roman drama and was an important constituent of the *commedia dell'arte in the 16th century. Exponents of modern mime include Jean-Louis Barrault (1910–94) and Marcel *Marceau.

mimesis (Greek: imitation) A philosophical concept introduced by *Aristotle in the *Poetics*. He argues that imitation is the basis of all the arts but they differ as to the means they use and the objects they imitate. Imitation in the arts does not refer to a simple realistic rendering of detail but to the poet's (or artist's) ability to select and present his material so as to express essential truth.

mimicry The phenomenon of two or more organisms (commonly different species) resembling each other closely, which confers an advantage—usually protection—to one or both of them. In **Batesian mimicry**, named after H. W. Bates (1825–92), a poisonous or inedible species (the model) has a conspicuous coloration, which acts as a warning to predators. This coloration is adopted by a harmless edible species (the mimic), which derives protection against the same predators. In **Müllerian mimicry**, first described by the German naturalist Fritz Müller (1821–97), two or more species—all inedible—have the same warning coloration.

After a predator has associated this pattern with an inedible species it will learn not to select similarly coloured species.

Mimosa A genus of trees, shrubs, and herbs (450–500 species), mostly native to tropical and subtropical America. They have feathery compound leaves and fluffy round catkins of yellow flowers. The genus includes the sensitive plants, *M. pudica* and *M. sensitiva*. Florists' mimosas are species of *Acacia* (*see* WATTLE). Family: *Leguminosae*.

minaret The tower of a mosque, from which the muezzin calls the faithful to prayer. Turkish minarets are typically slender; other shapes have been used in Persia and Arabia.

Mind (National Association for Mental Health) A voluntary British organization founded in 1946 to provide for the needs of the mentally ill and distressed. It campaigns for better services for the mentally ill, runs advice centres, generally encourages an understanding of mental illness, and promotes mental health.

Mindanao An island in the S Philippines, the second largest. Hemp, maize, pineapples, timber, nickel, and gold are the chief products. Its Muslim population has resisted Spanish, US, and now Philippine rule. Area: 101 919 sq km (39 351 sq mi). Population (1995): 14 262 000. Chief towns: Davao and Zamboanga.

minerals Naturally occurring substances of definite chemical composition (although this may vary within limits). Some consist of a single element but most are compounds of at least two. Strictly defined, minerals are solid (except native mercury) and are inorganically formed, although the constituents of organic limestones, for instance, are considered minerals. The term is used loosely for any naturally occurring material that is of economic value. Almost all true minerals are crystalline; a few, such as opal, are amorphous. Minerals are identified by the following properties: crystal system (e.g. cubic) and habit or form (e.g. fibrous), hardness (*see* MOHS' SCALE), relative density, lustre (e.g. metallic), colour, streak (colour when finely divided), *cleavage, and fracture. Rocks are composed of mixtures of minerals. The study of minerals is called **mineralogy**.

Minerva A Roman goddess originally of the arts and crafts of wisdom, later identified with the Greek *Athena. As goddess of war she almost equalled Mars.

minesweeper A vessel equipped to cut the cables of floating mines. Partially submerged cables are towed through a minefield so that the cable, passing under the mines, cuts their anchor chains, allowing the mines to float so that they can be detonated by gunfire. Mines laid on the seabed are detected by a submersible mine-finder.

Ming (1368–1644) A native Chinese dynasty, which succeeded the Mongol Yuan dynasty. It was founded by Hong-wu (1328–98), the first of 17 Ming emperors. The Ming provided an era of stable government personally controlled by the emperor. Painting and pottery, especially blue and white porcelain, flourished under the Ming.

miniature painting The art of painting on a very small scale, using watercolour on a vellum, card, or ivory base. The medieval Persian and Indian miniatures are the first great examples of the art. In Europe it flourished in the form of oval, circular, and occasionally rectangular portraits from the 16th to mid-19th centuries. There it developed from the medieval art of manuscript illumination and *Renaissance portrait medals. Nicholas *Hilliard was the first major specialist of the art in England. Other famous British miniaturists were Isaac Oliver (?1556–1617), Samuel Cooper (1609–72), and Richard Cosway (1742–1821).

minicomputer A small *computer, especially one that fits into a single cabinet. Compared with a large mainframe computer it is slower, has a smaller memory, and is considerably cheaper. The term is no longer used specifically as minicomputers have been superseded by microcomputers.

minimal art An abstract style of painting and sculpture developed in New York in the 1960s. In reaction to *abstract expressionism, it aimed to eliminate self-expression by using simple geometrical shapes and unmodulated colours. Leading minimalists include the painters Kenneth Noland (1924–) and Frank Stella (1936–) and the sculptor Carl André (1935–).

minivet An Asian songbird of the genus *Pericrocotus* (10 species), occurring in forests, where it hunts for insects in small flocks. Male minivets, about 17 cm long, have a black-and-red plumage; the females are yellowish grey. Family: *Campephagidae* (cuckoo-shrikes and minivets).

mink A small carnivorous mammal belonging to the genus *Mustela* (weasels, stoats, etc.), prized for its fur. The American mink (*M. vison*) is the largest species (about 70 cm long) and has the most valuable fur. They are nocturnal, semi-aquatic, and prey on fish, rodents, and waterfowl. Family: *Mustelidae*.

Minneapolis 45 00N 93 15W A city in the USA, in Minnesota on the Mississippi River. Adjacent to St Paul, the Twin Cities comprise the commercial, industrial, and financial centre of a large grain and cattle area; flour milling is the main industry. The University of Minnesota was established here in 1851. Population (2000): 382 618.

Minnesota A state in the USA, bordering on Canada in the N and Lake Superior in the NE. It consists of rolling prairies rising to the heavily forested Superior Highlands in the N and contains many lakes. Manufacturing industries (especially food processing) now form the most important sector of the economy, but mining is still important. Agriculture produces maize and soya beans. *History*: part of the Louisiana Purchase in 1803, it became a state in 1858. During the 1880s many Scandinavians settled in Minnesota. Area: 217 736 sq km (84 068 sq mi). Population (2000): 4 919 479. Capital: St Paul.

minnow One of several fish of the family *Cyprinidae*, especially *Phoxinus phoxinus*, found in clear fresh waters of Europe and N Asia. Its slim body is usually about 7.5 cm long, has small scales, and ranges in colour from gold to green. Order: *Cypriniformes*. The name is also applied to various other small fish.

Minoan civilization The civilization of Bronze Age Crete, named by Sir Arthur *Evans after the legendary King *Minos. The most advanced Aegean civilization, the Minoan arose after 2500 BC. It is conventionally divided into three phases: Early (2500–2000), Middle (2000–1700), and Late (1700–1400). During the Middle period palace building at *Knossos, Mallia, and Phaistos attests Crete's growing wealth. Around 1700 these structures were replaced by grander ones, the centres of power in a marine empire covering the S Aegean. A catastrophic eruption on Thera (c. 1450) may have ended Minoan prosperity, although this is controversial. Three scripts were used: hieroglyphics (c. 1900–1700), *Linear A (c. 1700–1450), and *Linear B (c. 1450–1400).

Minorca (Spanish name: Menorca) A Spanish island in the Mediterranean Sea, the second largest of the Balearic Islands. It is generally low lying and dry and agriculture is limited. Shoe manufacture is important and it has an expanding tourist industry. Area: 702 sq km (271 sq mi). Population (latest est): 55 500. Chief town: Mahón.

minor planet (*or* **asteroid**) A small nonluminous rocky body that orbits a star. Over 100 000 orbit the sun, mostly (probably 95%) in a main belt between the orbits of Mars and Jupiter, 2.17–3.3 astronomical units from the sun. The smallest minor planets are less than 1 km across with only about 200 exceeding 100 km: the largest is *Ceres (1003 km). They are probably debris from collisions of bodies that formed between Mars and Jupiter.

Minos A legendary king of Crete, son of Zeus and Europa. Although usually regarded as a good ruler, the Athenians portrayed him as a tyrant, who exacted an annual tribute of seven youths and seven maidens who were fed to the *Minotaur.

Minotaur In Greek legend, a Cretan monster with a bull's head and a man's body. It was the offspring of Pasiphae, wife of *Minos, and a bull with which Poseidon had caused her to become enamoured. *Theseus killed it with the help of Ariadne.

Minsk 53 51N 27 30E The capital of Belarus, in the centre of the country. Dating from at least the 11th century, it came under Lithuanian and then Polish rule; it was restored to Russia in 1793. It was virtually destroyed in World War II. Its varied industries include machine and vehicle manufacturing, textiles, and food processing. Population (1998 est): 1 717 000.

mint An aromatic perennial herb of the genus *Mentha* (about 25 species), native to Eurasia and Australia and widely distributed throughout temperate and subtropical regions. It has creeping roots from which arise square stems, bearing simple toothed leaves and terminal clusters of purple, pink, or white flowers. Many species are grown for their fragrance or as culinary herbs, especially *peppermint and *spearmint. Family: *Labiatae*.

Mintoff, Dom(inic) (1916–) Maltese statesman; Labour prime minister (1955–58, 1971–84). He was an active proponent of Maltese independence.

Miocene epoch *See* TERTIARY PERIOD.

Mir A space station launched into earth orbit by the Soviet Union in 1986. The first permanently manned space station, it was a refinement of the earlier Salyut stations. Following its collision with an unmanned ship in 1997, Mir was abandoned; its remains were brought back to earth in 2001.

Mirabeau, Honoré Gabriel Riquetti, Comte de (1749–91) French statesman. In 1789 he was elected to the States General, championing the cause of the Third Estate at the outbreak of the Revolution. However, he was out of sympathy with the growing republicanism, advocating the establishment of a constitutional monarchy on the British model, and came under increasing attack from the extremist Jacobins.

miracle plays Medieval European dramas based on religious themes. In England, they flourished particularly in the 14th and early 15th centuries. A distinction between **mystery plays** (based on episodes in the Bible) and miracle plays (based on the lives of saints) is often made with regard to French examples of the genre but in England the terms are used interchangeably. Originally performed in churches, they became increasingly secular in form and content and were eventually performed on mobile stages in public marketplaces.

Miró, Joan (1893–1983) Surrealist painter, born in Barcelona. He moved to Paris (1919) and began painting in a childlike style. His "savage" paintings, expressed the horrors of the Spanish Civil War; his *Constellations* were painted (during World War II) with his characteristic amoebic shapes intertwined with threadlike lines.

mirrors Devices for reflecting light, usually consisting of a sheet of glass with one surface silvered. A plane mirror, in which the sheet is flat, forms a laterally inverted virtual image. Spherical mirrors, concave or convex, magnify or reduce the image. To avoid spherical aberration, parabolic mirrors are used in reflecting *telescopes.

miscarriage *See* ABORTION.

Mishnah (Hebrew: instruction) An early code of Jewish law. Written in Hebrew, it is traditionally thought to have been based on earlier compilations and edited in Palestine by the ethnarch Judah I in the early 3rd century AD. It consists of halakhah on a wide range of subjects, derived partly from biblical law as interpreted by the early rabbis (called *Tannaim*) and partly from customs that had grown over a long period. *See also* TALMUD.

Mississippi A state in the S central USA, on the Gulf of Mexico. Mainly low lying, it consists of the cotton-producing alluvial plain of the Mississippi River in the W, extensive swamps in the SW, and low hills in the E and NE. The predominantly rural population has a large Black community. Still an important agricultural state, its main products are cotton, soya beans, poultry, eggs, and livestock. Ship construction and repair, timber and paper products, textiles, chemicals, and food processing are important industries. Petroleum is the main mineral but natural gas, clay, and sand and gravel are also exploited. Mississippi remains, however, one of the country's poorest states. *History*: explored by the Spanish, it was later claimed for France and was ceded to Britain (1763). Colonization followed and the area came under US control (1783). Made a state in 1817, it became a leading cotton producer and slave state until the US Civil War. Area: 123 584 sq km (47 716 sq mi). Population (2000): 2 844 658. Capital: Jackson.

Mississippian period *See* CARBONIFEROUS PERIOD.

Mississippi River A river in the central USA, the second longest river in North America. Rising in N Minnesota, it flows generally S into the Gulf of Mexico, through several channels (known as the Passes). Famous for its steamboats, it is now one of the world's busiest commercial waterways, with major ports at St Louis and New Orleans. Length: 3780 km (2348 mi).

Missolonghi (Modern Greek name: Mesolóngion) A town in W Greece, on the Gulf of Patras. It is famous for its defence against the Turks during the War of Greek Independence (1821–29) and as the death place of Lord Byron (1824). Population (latest est): 10 164.

Missouri A state in the central USA, lying immediately W of the Mississippi River. It is divided by the Missouri River into fertile prairies and rolling hills in the N and W and the hills of the Ozark plateau in the S. Manufacturing dominates the economy, with transport and aerospace equipment, food processing, chemicals, and printing and publishing. The leading lead producer in the USA, it also exploits barytes, iron ore, and zinc deposits. Agriculture is diversified producing livestock and dairy products, soya beans, corn, wheat, cotton, and sorghum grains. *History*: explored by the French from Canada and claimed for France (1682), it was ceded to Spain (1783) before returning to France in 1800. It formed part of the Louisiana Purchase (1803) by the USA, becoming a state in 1821. Area: 180 486 sq km (69 686 sq mi). Population (2000): 5 595 211. Capital: Jefferson City.

Missouri River A river in the central USA, the longest river in North America and chief tributary of the Mississippi River. Rising in the Rocky Mountains, it flows N and E through Montana, then SE across North and South

Dakota before joining the Mississippi at St Louis. Length: 4367 km (2714 mi).

mistle thrush A heavily built thrush, *Turdus viscivorus*, of Eurasia and NW Africa. It is about 28 cm long and has a greyish-brown upper plumage with a thickly speckled yellowish breast and white underwings. It feeds on berries (especially mistletoe—hence its name), snails, and worms.

mistletoe A semiparasitic evergreen shrub of the temperate and tropical family *Loranthaceae* (1300 species), growing on the branches of many trees. The Eurasian mistletoe (*Viscum album*) occurs mainly on apple trees, poplars, willows, and hawthorns. It has rootlike suckers and woody branching stems, 60–90 cm long, bearing oval leathery leaves and yellow flowers. The female flowers give rise to white berries.

Mistletoe was once believed by the Druids to have magic powers and medicinal properties and is a traditional Christmas decoration.

mite A tiny *arachnid (up to 6 mm long) comprising—with the ticks—the worldwide order *Acarina* (or *Acari*; over 20 000 species). It has an unsegmented body and eight bristly legs. Mites occur in a wide range of habitats, including soil, stored foods, water, and plants; some are parasitic on animals. They may transmit diseases (including typhus). *See also* HARVEST MITE; ITCH MITE.

Mithraism A mystery religion that worshipped Mithra, the Persian god of the sun who represented justice and goodness. It spread through Asia Minor, finally reaching Rome in about 68 BC. Here Mithra was known as Mithras and was worshipped widely among Roman soldiers. He was regarded as the eternal enemy of evil, whose sacrifice of a bull symbolized the regeneration of life. Mithraism rivalled Christianity until its decline in the 3rd century AD.

mitochondria Granular rod-shaped structures that occur in the cytoplasm of nearly all cells. They contain various enzymes that function in cellular *respiration and the metabolism of fat, glycogen, proteins, etc., to produce energy. Therefore in very active cells (i.e. those requiring more energy), such as heart muscle, mitochondria are large and numerous.

mitosis The process by which the nucleus of a somatic cell (i.e. any cell that is not a germ cell) duplicates itself exactly, producing two daughter nuclei with chromosomes that are identical to those of the parent nucleus. This nuclear division involves the separation of the two chromatids of each chromosome, which move apart to form two groups at opposite ends of the cell. In the final phase each group becomes enclosed in a new nuclear membrane. After this the cytoplasm usually divides to form two new cells. Mitosis occurs in most animals and plants during the normal growth and repair of tissues. *Compare* MEIOSIS.

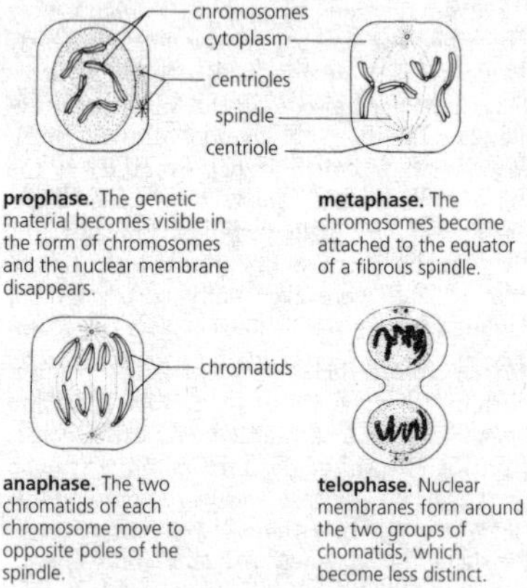
chromosomes
cytoplasm
centrioles
spindle
centriole
prophase. The genetic material becomes visible in the form of chromosomes and the nuclear membrane disappears.
metaphase. The chromosomes become attached to the equator of a fibrous spindle.
chromatids
anaphase. The two chromatids of each chromosome move to opposite poles of the spindle.
telophase. Nuclear membranes form around the two groups of chomatids, which become less distinct.

mitosis. Division of the nucleus of an animal cell takes place in four phases, which grade into each other.

Mitterrand, François (Maurice) (1916–96) French socialist politician; president (1981–95). He assumed leadership of the newly unified Socialist Party in 1971. After two unsuccessful runs for the French presidency (1965, 1974), in 1981 he became the first socialist president in 35 years. He assumed a leading role in the formation of EC policy.

Mizoram A state in NE India, in tropical hills between Bangladesh and Myanmar (Burma). Its largely Christian tribes are subsistence farmers of rice, sugar, and potatoes. Mizoram was separated from Assam in 1972 and became a state in 1986. Area: 21 230 sq km (8195 sq mi). Population (2001): 891 058. Capital: Aijal.

M'Naghten's Rules *See* INSANITY.

Mnemosyne In Greek mythology, a daughter of the *Titans Uranus and Gaea. She is the personification of memory. After sleeping with Zeus for nine consecutive nights she gave birth to the *Muses.

moa An extinct flightless bird belonging to an order (*Dinornithiformes*; about 25 species) that occurred in New Zealand. Moas were 60–300 cm tall and had a small head, a long neck, and long legs. They were fast runners but were hunted by early Polynesian settlers.

Moabites A highly civilized Semitic tribe living E of the Dead Sea from the late 14th century BC. They successfully rebelled against Israelite occupation in the 9th century BC. In 582 BC, according to Josephus, they were conquered by the Babylonians.

mobile phone A small battery-operated telephone that uses the cellular network to connect to other mobiles or to the main telephone system. So-called second generation models also enable up to 160 characters of text to be sent; **texting** in this way is now widespread and has its own shorthand. Third generation models allow photographs and video images to be sent and have many computer functions.

Mobutu Sese Seko (Joseph-Désiré M.; 1930–97) Dictator (1965–97) of Zaïre (the Democratic Republic of Congo). As commander-in-chief of the Congo army he seized power in 1960 and again in 1965. In 1970 he became president and changed the country's name to Zaïre. By the 1990s his authoritarian rule faced mounting opposition and he was deposed (1997) by rebels under Laurent Kabila.

mockingbird A songbird that belongs to an American family (*Mimidae*; 30 species) and is noted for its ability to mimic sounds. Mockingbirds live on or near the ground, feeding on insects and fruit. The common mockingbird (*Mimus polyglottus*), which ranges from S Canada to S Mexico, is about 25 cm long with a grey plumage and white wing bars.

mock orange A shrub, also called syringa, belonging to the genus *Philadelphus* (75 species), native to N temperate regions and commonly cultivated for ornament. They have simple leaves and fragrant white flowers resembling orange blossom. *P. coronarius* is the only native European species. Family: *Philadelphaceae*.

Modena (ancient name: Mutina) 44 39N 10 55E A city in N Italy, in Emilia-Romagna. Ruled by the Este family (1288–1860), it has an 11th-century romanesque cathedral, several palaces, and an ancient university (1175). The centre of a rich agricultural area, its industries include agricultural engineering, textiles, and motor vehicles. Population (2000 est): 176 022.

modes Musical scales derived from ancient Greek music, on which European music was based up to the 16th century. Each mode consists of a different pattern of the five tones and two semitones of the octave; the patterns can be clearly demonstrated using the white notes of the piano keyboard. Two of the most common modes were the Ionian (C-C) and the Aeolian (A-A), which became the basis of the major and minor scales.

Modigliani, Amedeo (1884–1920) Italian painter and sculptor. His mature work, executed in Paris (1906–20), was influenced by *Cézanne and *Brancusi and, in its angular and elongated character, by Negro masks. From 1909 to 1915 he worked chiefly on sculptures; from 1915 until his death he painted many nudes and portraits.

modulation A method of carrying information (the signal) on an electromagnetic wave or an oscillating electric current. In **amplitude modulation** (AM) the amplitude of a carrier wave is changed according to the magnitude of the signal. This is used in medium-wave sound broadcasting in which audio-frequencies (50–20 000 hertz) are carried on radio waves with a frequency of about one megahertz. In **frequency modulation** (FM) the frequency of the carrier wave is changed within a small bandwidth of the reference frequency. FM is used in VHF *radio (about 100 megahertz). Its main advantage over AM is its better signal-to-noise ratio. In **pulse modulation** the carrier is a series of pulses. It is used in digital equipment, such as computers, and in telegraphy and telemetry. A continuous signal alters the height in pulse-amplitude modulation, the width in pulse-duration modulation, or the time between pulses in pulse-position modulation. Pulse-code modulation uses a coded pattern of pulses to carry the signal, e.g. in *Morse code.

Mogadishu (*or* **Mogadiscio**) 2 01N 45 25E The capital and main port of Somalia, on the Indian Ocean. It was founded as an Arab settlement in the 10th century and sold to Italy in 1905 becoming the capital of Italian Somaliland. In 1991 the city was reduced to ruins during the prolonged civil war. Population (1999 est): 1 162 000.

Moguls An Indian Muslim dynasty, descended from the Mongol leader *Genghis Khan, that ruled from 1526 until 1858. Its founder was Babur (reigned 1526–30); he and the first 5 of his 18 successors are known as the Great Moguls, and by the time of Aurangzeb (1658–1707) the Empire spread from the far N to the far S of India. During the late 17th and the 18th centuries Mogul power declined; the last emperor, Bahadur Shah II (reigned

1837–58), was deposed after the *Indian Mutiny.

Mohammed (*or* **Muhammad**; c.570–632 AD) According to Muslims, the last of the prophets and preacher of *Islam to the Arabs. Mohammed is said to have been born in Mecca. In 610 he received revelations from God and called upon his pagan fellow townsmen to prepare for the Last Day and to repent. The Meccans rejected him and in 622 he fled to Yathrib, where he established the first Muslim community and began to spread Islam. By 629 the Muslims in Yathrib, now called Medina, were strong enough to obtain control of Mecca. By the time of Mohammed's death, Islam had begun to spread throughout Arabia. Mohammed's revelations were collected after his death to form the *Koran.

Mohammed Reza Pahlavi (1918–80) Shah of Iran (1941–79). He became shah when the Allies forced his father, Reza Shah Pahlavi, to abdicate in World War II. In 1979 civil war forced him into exile and an Islamic republic was established in Iran under the leadership of Ayatollah Khomeini.

Mohawk An Iroquoian-speaking American Indian tribe of New York state. They were one of the five tribes that formed the league of the *Iroquois, said to have been founded by the Mohawk chief *Hiawatha.

Mohican An Algonkian-speaking American Indian tribe of New England. Primarily cultivators, they lived in fortified communities or in enclosed villages, but were displaced by wars with the Mohawks.

Mohorovičić discontinuity The boundary between the earth's crust and upper mantle, marked by a sudden increase in velocity in seismic waves at the denser mantle. It lies at a depth of 33–35 km (20–22 mi) beneath the continents and 5–10 km (3–6 mi) beneath the oceans. It is named after the Croatian scientist, Andrija Mohorovičić (1857–1936), who discovered it in 1909.

Mohs' scale A scale of hardness of minerals named after the mineralogist Friedrich Mohs (1773–1839). The ten standard minerals of increasing hardness, are: 1. talc, 2. gypsum, 3. calcite, 4. fluorite, 5. apatite, 6. orthoclase feldspar, 7. quartz, 8. topaz, 9. corundum, and 10. diamond. Each can be scratched by any mineral higher up the scale, and other minerals can be assigned numbers according to which materials will scratch them.

Mojave Desert (*or* **Mohave Desert**) A desert area in the USA, in S California. It comprises part of the *Great Basin. Area: 38 850 sq km (15 000 sq mi).

Moldavia A former principality in SE Europe. It was occupied by the Mongols in the 13th century, becoming independent in the 14th century. It became an Ottoman vassal state in the 16th century, losing Bessarabia to Russia in the 19th century (*see* MOLDOVA, REPUBLIC OF). In 1859 Moldavia and Walachia formed Romania.

Moldova, Republic of A republic in SE Europe. *Economy*: industries include wine making, tobacco processing, and food canning; the land is very fertile, producing wheat, maize, fruit, and vegetables. *History*: as the Moldavian Soviet Socialist Republic, it was formed in 1940, mainly from Russian Moldavia (*see* MOLDAVIA). It became an independent republic in 1991. Separatist aspirations in the mainly Russian and Ukrainian Dnestr region led to fierce fighting in 1992. Union with Romania was rejected in a 1994 referendum and that year Moldova joined the Commonwealth of Independent States. The republic's first multiparty elections were held in 1994 and free presidential elections in 1997. The Communists were voted back into power in 2001 but their attempts to limit opposition led to mass protests in 2002. Official language: Moldovan (a form of Romanian). Currency: leu. Area: 33 670 sq km (13 000 sq mi). Population (2003 est): 4 267 100. Capital: Kishinev.

mole (medicine) An area of darkly pigmented skin, known medically as a naevus. *See also* MELANOMA.

mole (metrology; symbol mol) The SI unit of amount of substance equal to the amount of substance that contains the same number of entities as there are atoms in 0.012 kg of carbon-12. One mol of any substance contains $6.022\,52 \times 10^{23}$ entities (*see* AVOGADRO). The entities may be atoms, molecules, ions, electrons, etc.

mole (zoology) A burrowing mammal of the family *Talpidae*, of Europe, Asia, and North America. The common Eurasian mole (*Talpa europaea*) is about 14 cm long including its small bristly tail. It is thickset, with black fur, and has long-clawed digging forefeet. Moles make a system of underground tunnels, feeding on earthworms. They are practically blind above ground. Order: *Insectivora*.

molecular biology The scientific discipline that deals with the molecular basis of living processes. Molecular biology involves both *biochemistry and *biophysics: its growth since the 1930s has been made possible by the development of such techniques as chromatography, *electron microscopy, and X-ray diffraction, which have revealed the structures of biologically important molecules, such as DNA, RNA, and enzymes.

molecule The smallest portion of a compound that can exist independently and retain its properties. The atoms that make up a molecule are either bonded together covalently, e.g. CO_2, or electrovalently, e.g. NaCl. However, in crystalline substances the bonds extend throughout the whole crystal structure and the molecule has only a notional existence. In covalent gases and liquids, however, the molecule actually exists. **Molecular weight** (*or* relative molecular mass) is the ratio of the average mass per molecule to one-twelfth of the mass of a carbon-12 atom.

Molière (Jean-Baptiste Poquelin; 1622–73) French dramatist, the father of modern French comedy. He toured the provinces with his theatrical company from 1645 to 1658. His plays include *Tartuffe* (1664), *Le Misanthrope* (1666), *L'Avare* (1668), and *Le Malade imaginaire* (1673). His ridicule of hypocrisy and his vigorous satire of contemporary manners and types brought him into constant conflict with the religious authorities. He frequently acted in his own productions.

mollusc An invertebrate animal belonging to the phylum *Mollusca* (about 50 000 species). Molluscs occupy marine, freshwater, and terrestrial habitats, being especially common on rocky coasts. They have a soft unsegmented body with a muscular foot, variously modified for crawling, burrowing, or swimming, and a thin dorsal mantle that secretes a shell of one, two, or eight parts. The shell is usually external, as in snails, but it may be internal, as in cuttlefish, or absent, as in slugs. Most molluscs are herbivores, with some carnivores and scavengers. *See also* BIVALVE; CEPHALOPOD; GASTROPOD.

moloch A grotesque desert-dwelling Australian lizard, *Moloch horridus*, also called thorny devil. Its yellow-and-brown body is covered in spines, which provide camouflage. Ants are its chief food. Family: *Agamidae*.

Moloch A Semitic god whose worship involved the sacrificial burning of children. There are several biblical references to his worship by the Israelites during the period of the Kings (c. 961–c. 562 BC).

Molotov, Vyacheslav Mikhailovich (V. M. Scriabin; 1890–1986) Soviet statesman. As prime minister (1930–41) and foreign minister (1939–49, 1953–56), Molotov signed the Soviet-German nonaggression treaty in 1939; after the German invasion in 1941, he negotiated alliances with the Allies. His subsequent attitude to the West contributed to the Cold War. The **Molotov cocktail** is a home-made incendiary hand device, consisting of a bottle full of inflammable liquid.

Moluccas (*or* **Maluku**) An Indonesian group of islands between Sulawesi and West Irian. It includes the islands of Ambon, Halmahera, and Ceram. Mountainous and volcanic, most are fertile and humid. The indigenous population fishes, hunts, and collects sago; spices, fish, and copra are exported. *History*: before the Portuguese arrival (1512), the islands were ruled by Muslims and known as the Spice Islands. Dutch control was established in the 19th century. With Indonesian independence (1949) the S Moluccas fought to secede but were subjugated by the new government (1950–56). Rioting between Muslims and Christians caused hundreds of deaths in 1999–2000. Area: about 74 504 sq km (28 766 sq mi). Population (1999 est): 2 223 000. Chief town: Ambon.

molybdenum (Mo) A very hard silvery-grey metal of high melting point, it was first prepared in 1782 by P. J. Hjelm (1746–1813). It occurs in nature as molybdenite (MoS_2) and as wulfenite (lead molybdenate; $PbMoO_4$). It is extracted by the reduction of molybdenum trioxide (MoO_3). Molybdenum is used in high-temperature filaments and as an alloying agent in the production of high-strength steels. At no 42; at wt 95.94; mp 2623°C; bp 4639°C.

Mombasa 4 04S 39 40E A port in Kenya, on an island in an inlet of the Indian Ocean. It was an important port for Arab traders and was taken in the 16th and 17th centuries by the Portuguese. The modern deepwater port at Kinlindini handles most of Kenya's trade; industries include oil refining. Population (1999): 461 753.

moment The product of a force and its perpendicular distance from the axis about which it acts. A moment produces a turning effect and is sometimes called a torque. The inertia of a body to a torque is called its **moment of inertia**. This quantity is equal to mr^2 for a single mass (m) rotating about an axis at a distance r from the axis. The moment of inertia of a system of masses is equal to the sum of these products.

momentum The linear momentum of a body is the product of its mass and its linear velocity. The angular momentum of a body is the product of its *moment of inertia and its angular velocity. During any process the total momentum of the system always remains constant (the law of conservation of momentum).

Monaco, Principality of A small country on the Mediterranean Sea, an enclave within French territory. It consists of three principal localities: the business district around the ports, Monte Carlo, and the capital Monaco. *Economy*: the main sources of revenue are real estate, financial services, tourism, and the sale of postage stamps. *History*: ruled by the house of Grimaldi since 1297, it has been under French protection since 1641. Rainier III has been prince since 1949. Official language: French. Currency: euro of 100 cents. Area: 1.96 sq km (0.76 sq mi). Population (2003 est): 32 400. Capital: Monaco-Ville.

Monaghan (Irish name: Contae Mhuineachain) A county in the NE Republic of Ireland, in Ulster. It is generally low lying and undulating. Agricultural produce includes oats and potatoes; cattle rearing and dairy farming are also important. Area: 1551 sq km (499 sq mi). Population (2002): 52 772. County town: Monaghan.

mona monkey *See* GUENON.

monarch A widespread American butterfly, *Danaus plexippus*. Light brown with black borders and white dots, the adults migrate southwards for the winter. In spring they move north, breeding on the way. The caterpillars are green with black and yellow bands and feed on milkweed. Family: *Danaidae*.

monazite A rare-earth mineral of composition $(Ce,La,Y,Th)PO_4$; yellow to reddish-brown in colour, it is found as an accessory in acid igneous rocks and as placer deposits. Monazite is usually obtained as a by-product of titanium and zircon mining; it is the most common source of the rare earths.

Mönchengladbach (*or* **München Gladbach**) 51 12N 6 25E A city in W Germany, in North Rhine-Westphalia. It is the centre of the German textile industry and headquarters of the NATO forces in N central Europe. Population (1999 est): 264 100.

Mond, Ludwig (1839–1909) German industrial chemist, who lived in Britain from 1862. He discovered nickel carbonyl and its application to the extraction of platinum from its ores, a method now known as the **Mond process**.

Mondrian, Piet (Pieter Cornelis Mondriaan; 1872–1944) Dutch painter. While in Paris (1912–14) he came under the influence of *cubism. His first abstract compositions (1917) used only horizontal and vertical lines, primary colours, and black and white. During this period he helped to launch the art movement of de Stijl. After 1919 his style, known as neoplasticism, influenced the *Bauhaus school.

Monet, Claude (1840–1926) French impressionist painter. Initially influenced by the Barbizon school, in the late 1860s he developed the impressionist technique in views of Paris and in the 1870s in boating scenes at Argenteuil. He excelled in his series of the same scenes painted at different times of day, e.g. *Gare St Lazare*, *Haystacks*, *Rouen Cathedral*, and the *Poplars*, the last of which anticipates *abstract art.

monetarism A revision of old-established economic theories that rivals Keynesianism. Monetarism's most celebrated proponent is the US economist Milton *Friedman. Monetarists regard responsible regulation of the money supply as essential to the wellbeing of the economy, advocating a gentle expansion of the money supply at roughly the rate of growth of the economy. Monetarists blame *inflation on overexpansion of the money supply.

money A medium of exchange. To be an efficient medium of exchange, money should be divisible (for small transactions), have a high value-to-weight ratio, and be not easily counterfeited. Money also functions as means of credit and a store of wealth, for which purposes its value must remain stable. Money was reputedly invented by the Lydians in the 7th century BC. It originally took the form of something intrinsically valuable (such as a precious metal) but, so long as it is generally acceptable, this is not necessary. Indeed, most money is now in the form of paper.

The total stock of money in the economy is known as the **money supply**. In the UK two definitions of the money supply are used: the narrow M1 (essentially, the total amount of cash and current accounts) and the broad M3 (essentially, the total amount of cash plus both current and deposit accounts).

money spider A tiny *spider of the family *Liniphiidae* (over 250 species). It has a reddish or black body and occurs in fields, etc. Money spiders build sheetlike webs on vegetation to which they cling upside down, waiting to catch insects that drop onto the web.

moneywort A perennial herb, *Lysimachia nummularia*, also called creeping jenny, native to damp places in Europe. It has a creeping stem, up to 60 cm long, shiny heart-shaped leaves, and yellow flowers. Family: *Primulaceae*.

Mongolia, State of A country in NE central Asia, between Russia and China. It rises to the Altai and Khangai mountains in the W and extends into the Gobi Desert in the S. *Economy*: with its nomadic-pastoral tradition, it is still mainly dependent on livestock rearing, with recent attempts to increase crop growing. Copper mining is being introduced and other minerals include coal, oil, gold, tungsten, lead, and uranium. There is some light industry. Exports include cattle and horses, wool, and hair. In the early 1990s the end of special trading arrangements with communist East Europe led to considerable economic hardship. In 1996–2000 the government implemented IMF-backed policies of restructuring and deregulation. *History*: in the 13th century Genghis Khan ruled the Mongol empire from Karakoram in the N. As Outer Mongolia, the area was a province of China from 1691 to 1911, when it became an autonomous monarchy under Russian protection. Again under Chinese influence from 1919 to 1921, it then became independent and the Mongolian People's Republic was declared in 1924. In 1990 the Communist Party renounced its monopoly of power and a multi-party system was introduced. In 1996 the Democratic Union formed a government pledged to radical free-market reforms but elections in 2000 resulted in a landslide for the former Communists under Nambariyn Enkhbayar. Official language: Khaikha Mongolian. Currency: tugrik of 100 möngö. Area: 1 565 000 sq km (604 095 sq mi). Population (2003 est): 2 493 000. Capital: Ulan Bator.

Mongolian languages A group of languages that, together with Turkic and Manchu-Tungus, constitute the Altaic language family. Western Mongolian languages are spoken in SE Russia, the Republic of Mongolia, and Afghanistan; Eastern Mongolian is spoken in China and the Republic of Mongolia. There are more than three million speakers of these languages, the majority of which remain unwritten.

Mongoloid The racial grouping comprising the populations of E Asia and the Arctic region of North America. They have medium skin pigmentation, the epicanthic fold of the upper eyelid, straight coarse black hair, a rather flat face with high cheekbones, and slight facial and body hair.

Mongols An Asiatic people united in the early 13th century by *Genghis Khan, who built up an empire that encompassed much of central Asia. The Mongols ruled China as the *Yuan dynasty until 1368. They were subsequently confined to the area approximating to the present-day State of Mongolia.

mongoose A carnivorous mammal belonging to the family *Viverridae*, found in warm regions of the Mediterranean, Africa, and Asia. There are about 40 species, ranging in size from 50 to 100 cm including the long tapering furry tail (25–50 cm), with short legs, small ears, and long coarse grey-brown fur. Mongooses are renowned for catching snakes and rats and also eat eggs, small mammals, frogs, and birds. Chief genera: *Galidictis*, *Herpestes*, *Helogale*.

monitor lizard A lizard belonging to the Old World family *Varanidae* (30 species), occurring in tropical and subtropical regions. 0.2–3 m long, monitors have an elongated body and well-developed legs. They feed on mammals, snakes, lizards, eggs, and carrion. *See also* KOMODO DRAGON.

monkey A tree-dwelling *primate. Monkeys are 20–110 cm long and most have a long balancing tail of up to 100 cm used in climbing, although some are tailless. Agile and intelligent, they have fingernails and an opposable thumb enabling manual dexterity. Most monkeys are omnivorous but they prefer fruit, nuts, and other vegetation. *See also* NEW WORLD MONKEY; OLD WORLD MONKEY.

monkey puzzle A coniferous tree, *Araucaria araucana*, also called Chile pine, native to Chile and Argentina and widely grown as an ornamental. Up to 30 m high, it has whorled horizontal branches covered with leathery prickly overlapping leaves, 3–4 cm long. The globular spiny cones, 10–17 cm long, break up to release large seeds that are edible when roasted. Family: *Araucariaceae*.

monkfish A *shark belonging to the family *Squatinidae*. It has a broad flattened head, an elongated tapering body, winglike pectoral fins, two dorsal fins, and no anal fin. Monkfish occur in tropical and temperate seas and feed on bottom-dwelling fish, molluscs, and crustaceans. A species of *anglerfish, *Lophius piscatorius*, is also called monkfish.

monkshood *See* ACONITE.

Monmouth, James Scott, Duke of (1649–85) The illegitimate son of Charles II of England and Lucy Walter (d. 1658), who led the Monmouth rebellion against his uncle James II. A focus of the opposition to the succession of the Roman Catholic James, he was banished (1684) after being implicated in the Rye House Plot of 1683, a failed attempt to murder Charles and James. After James's accession (1685), Monmouth landed at Lyme Regis to raise a rebellion and was defeated at *Sedgemoor, captured, and beheaded.

Monmouthshire A county of SE Wales bounded by the Bristol Channel in the S and the English border in the E. Under local government reorganization in 1974 it was mainly absorbed into Gwent. When Gwent was abolished in 1996, administration passed to a reduced Monmouthshire and four county boroughs (Blaenau Gwent, Newport, Torfaen, and Caerphilly). Monmouthshire consists of undulating country, rising to the Black Mountains in the N. It is chiefly agricultural with tourism and light industry. Area: 851 sq km (329 sq mi). Population (2001): 84 879. Administrative centre: Cwmbran.

m

monoclonal antibody A type of pure antibody that can be produced artificially in large quantities and used, for example, to distinguish the major blood groups and to treat certain disorders, including some types of cancer. Mouse lymphocytes producing the required antibody are fused with mouse cancer cells; the resulting hybrid cells multiply rapidly and all produce the same type of antibody as their parent lymphocytes.

monocotyledons The smaller of the two main groups of flowering plants, which includes the palms, bananas, orchids, grasses, lilies, and many garden bulbs and corms (*compare* DICOTYLEDONS). Monocots have a single seed leaf (cotyledon) in the embryo. Typically the flower parts are in threes (or multiples of three) and the leaves have parallel veins. *See also* ANGIOSPERM.

monomer A simple molecule or group of atoms forming a repeated unit in a dimer (two molecules), trimer (three molecules), or polymer (*see* POLYMERIZATION).

monopoly An industry in which the market is supplied by one supplier. The monopolist can obtain a high profit by restricting supply and demanding a high price. In the public sector of a mixed economy monopolies for the supply of public services are commonplace. In the private sector they are usually restricted by legislation. In the UK the **Monopolies Commission**, the duties of which are set out in the Fair Trading Act (1973), conducts investigations into monopolies and mergers.

monorail A railway using a single rail, either from which to suspend a carriage or over which a carriage is straddled. The former type was first used in 1884, consisting of an electrically driven truck running on a single rail from which was suspended a load-carrying car (called a **telpher**). The latter type has been demonstrated at Birmingham's National Exhibition Centre, using magnetic levitation. Monorail systems are expensive to instal.

monosaccharide (*or* **simple sugar**) A *carbohydrate consisting of a single sugar unit and possessing either a keto group (C=O) or an aldehyde group (CHO). Monosaccharides are classified according to the number of carbon atoms they possess—the most common being pentoses (with five) and hexoses (with six)—and they can exist as either straight-chain or ring-shaped structures. The most widely occurring are *glucose and *fructose.

monotreme A primitive *mammal of the order *Monotremata*, found only in Australia and New Guinea. Monotremes have a single vent for passing urine, faeces, and eggs or sperm. They lay eggs, suckling their young after these hatch. The only living monotremes are the *echidnas and *duck-billed platypus.

Monroe, James (1758–1831) US statesman; president (1817–25). He was minister to France (1794–96) and Britain (1803–07) before becoming secretary of state (1811). His two peaceful terms as president saw the opening of the West and the acquisition of Spanish Florida. The **Monroe Doctrine** (1823) warned European powers not to intervene in the Americas.

Monroe, Marilyn (Norma Jean Baker *or* Mortenson; 1926–62) US film actress. Promoted as a sex symbol, in such films as *Niagara* (1952) and *Gentlemen Prefer Blondes* (1953), she later developed a real acting talent and ability as a comedienne. Her third husband was Arthur *Miller, and her last film appearance was in *The Misfits* (1961), which he wrote. She died from an overdose of barbiturates.

Monrovia 6 20N 10 46W The capital and main port of Liberia, on the Atlantic Ocean. Founded in 1822 as a settlement for freed slaves, it was named after President Monroe of the USA. The University of Liberia was founded in 1851. Population (1999 est): 479 000.

monsoon A seasonal large-scale reversal of

winds in the tropics, resulting chiefly from the differential heating of the land and oceans. The term is now commonly applied to the rainfall that accompanies the wind reversals, especially in S Asia (April to September).

Montaigne, Michel de (1533–92) French essayist. In 1568 he resigned his position as magistrate in Bordeaux and began composing his *Essais*. In 1580 he travelled extensively in Europe and was mayor of Bordeaux from 1581 to 1585. His *Essais*, which inaugurated a new literary genre, expressed his mature humanistic philosophy and constitute a moving self-portrait. They were published in two editions in 1580 and 1588, and a posthumous edition incorporated his final revisions.

Montana The fourth largest state in the USA, bordering on Canada. It is mountainous and forested in the W, with the rolling grasslands of the Great Plains in the E. Its economy is predominantly agricultural, cattle ranching and wheat production being of greatest importance. Other crops include barley and sugar beet. It possesses important mineral resources, notably copper (at Butte) and coal. There are several Indian reservations within the state. *History*: it formed part of the Louisiana Purchase in 1803. During the mid-19th century a gold rush caused an influx of immigrants. During the Indian wars the battle of *Little Bighorn (Custer's Last Stand) took place (1876). Area: 377 070 sq km (145 587 sq mi). Population (2000): 902 195. Capital: Helena.

Mont Blanc (Italian name: Monte Bianco) 45 50N 6 52E The highest mountain in the Alps, on the French–Italian border. It was first climbed in 1786. A road tunnel (1958–62) beneath it, 12 km (7.5 mi) long, connects the two countries. Height: 4807 m (15 771 ft).

montbretia A perennial herb, *Crocosmia crocosmiflora* (a hybrid between *C. pottsii* and *C. aurea*), native to South Africa but naturalized in Europe and often grown as a garden ornamental. Up to 1 m high, it has long stiff sword-shaped leaves and orange-red funnel-shaped flowers. The name is also applied to the similar and related flowering herbs of the South African genus *Montbretia* (or *Tritonia*). Family: *Iridaceae*.

Monte Bello Islands 20 30S 115 30E A group of uninhabited coral islands in the Indian Ocean, off the W coast of Western Australia. They were used for testing British nuclear weapons in 1952 and 1956.

Monte Carlo 43 44N 7 25E A resort in the principality of Monaco, on the Riviera. It is famous for its casino, motor rally, and other cultural and sporting events. Population (latest est): 12 000.

Montenegro (Serbo-Croat name: Crna Gora) The smaller of the two republics in the Union of *Serbia and Montenegro, on the Adriatic. It is mountainous and forested. It was declared a kingdom in 1910, becoming a province of the kingdom of the Serbs, Croats, and Slovenes (later Yugoslavia) in 1918. Following the disintegration of Yugoslavia (1991–92), Montenegro and Serbia formed the Federal Republic of Yugoslavia. The later 1990s saw growing opposition to the federation with Serbia, exacerbated by Belgrade's repressive policy in Kosovo and the resultant war with NATO (1999). Tensions rose (1999–2000) as the Montenegrin parliament announced plans to withdraw from the federation. However, there has been a rapprochement with Serbia since the fall of the *Milošević regime in 2000; in 2002 the federation was replaced with a new Union of Serbia and Montenegro. Area: 13 812 sq km (5387 sq mi). Population (2001 est): 658 000. Capital: Podgorica.

Monterrey 25 40N 100 20W One of the largest cities in Mexico. Founded in 1579, it has many notable buildings. Monterrey is a major industrial centre specializing in metallurgy. Population (2000 est): 1 108 400.

Montessori system A system of education for young children devised by the Italian doctor Maria Montessori (1870–1952). It emphasizes development of the senses and envisages a limited role for the teacher as the child learns by itself through the use of didactic materials.

Monteverdi, Claudio (1567–1643) Italian composer. From 1613 until his death he was maestro di cappella at St Mark's Cathedral, Venice. He was the first great composer of *opera; enlarging the orchestra, he employed a new range of instrumental effects and made use of an innovatory harmonic style to achieve dramatic effects. Works include the operas *Orfeo* (1607) and *The Coronation of Poppea* (1642), a set of *Vespers* (1610), and madrigals.

Montevideo 34 55S 56 10W The capital and main port of Uruguay, in the S on the Río de la Plata. Founded in 1726 by the Spanish, it became capital of Uruguay in 1828. In the 20th century it has developed rapidly, as both an industrial and a communications centre, and it is now one of South America's largest cities. Population (1996): 1 378 707.

Montezuma II (1466–c. 1520) The last Aztec Emperor of Mexico (1502–20). During his reign his empire was weakened by tribal warfare, which enabled the Spaniards, led by Hernán *Cortés, to establish themselves in Mexico.

Montfort, Simon de, Earl of Leicester (c. 1208–65) English statesman, born in Normandy. After serving Henry III of England in Gascony, he joined the antiroyalist faction that demanded greater control of the government, becoming the barons' leader in the subsequent Barons' War. Initially successful, he became virtual ruler of England, summoning a parliament in 1265. In the same year, however, he was defeated and killed at Evesham.

Montgolfier, Jacques-Étienne (1745–99) French balloonist, who with his brother **Joseph-Michel Montgolfier** (1740–1810) invented the hot-air balloon, which was publicly launched in 1782. A much larger balloon, which rose 2000 m, was demonstrated in June 1783 and in October a series of passenger-carrying ascents were made. The Montgolfiers' experiments aroused enormous interest in flying.

m

Montgomery, Bernard Law, 1st Viscount Montgomery of Alamein (1887–1976) British field marshal. In World War II he became commander of the Eighth Army (1942) and after the battle of Alamein drove *Rommel back to Tunis and surrender (1943). Having played a major role in the invasion of Italy (1943), he became chief of land forces in the 1944 Normandy invasion. He helped plan the Arnhem disaster (September 1944), but pushed back the subsequent German offensive, receiving Germany's surrender. After the war he was chief of the imperial general staff (1946–48) and deputy commander of NATO forces (1951–58).

month The time taken by the moon to complete one revolution around the earth. The complicated motion of the moon requires the starting and finishing points of the revolution to be specified. The length of the month depends on the choice of reference point. The **sidereal month**, of 27.32 days, is measured with reference to the background stars. The **synodic month**, of 29.53 days, is measured between two identical phases of the moon.

Montpellier 43 36N 3 53E A city in S France, the capital of the Hérault department. A Huguenot stronghold, it was besieged and captured by Louis XIII in 1622. It trades in wine and brandy and has numerous manufacturing industries. Population (1999): 225 392.

Montreal 45 30N 73 36W A city and port in E Canada, in Quebec on Montreal Island at the junction of the Ottawa and St Lawrence Rivers. Canada's second largest city, it is a major transportation, trade, and manufacturing centre. Industries include oil refining, meat packing, brewing and distilling, food processing, textiles, and aircraft. Housing four universities, Montreal is a forum for politics, broadcasting, theatre, film, and publishing. Two-thirds of the population is French-speaking. *History*: founded as Ville-Marie (1642), Montreal quickly became a commercial centre. Captured by Britain (1760), it acquired an English-speaking merchant community that has dominated Quebec's economy ever since. Population (1996): 1 016 376.

Montserrat A British overseas territory comprising one of the Leeward Islands, in the Caribbean Sea to the SE of Puerto Rico. It is largely mountainous with active volcanoes. *Economy*: chiefly agricultural; the main exports are cotton, coconuts, fruit and vegetables, and cattle. Forestry is being developed. *History*: discovered by Columbus in 1493, it was colonized by the Irish in the 17th century. Formerly administratively joined to the Leeward Islands, it became a separate colony in 1960. In 1997 a huge volcanic eruption made two-thirds of the island uninhabitable (including the capital, Plymouth). Half the population have fled, with Britain offering help with voluntary resettlement. The future of the island is uncertain. Official language: English. Currency: East Caribbean dollar of 100 cents. Area: 106 sq km (40 sq mi). Population (2001 est): 4500.

Mont St Michel 48 38N 1 30W A granite islet in NW France, in the Manche department in the Bay of St Michel. The islet is connected to the mainland by a causeway. It is about 78 m (256 ft) high and is crowned by a Benedictine monastery (founded 966 AD).

moon The natural satellite of the earth. It orbits the earth every 27.32 days at a mean distance of 384 400 km, keeping more or less the same face (the nearside) towards the earth. As it revolves, different *phases can be seen from earth, together with up to two or three lunar *eclipses per year. The moon is only 81 times less massive than the earth and has a diameter of 3476 km.

The major surface features are the light-coloured highlands and the much darker lava plains—the maria. The surface is heavily cratered with roughly circular walled depressions produced by impacting bodies from space. The extremely tenuous atmosphere exposes the surface to considerable temperature extremes (−180°C to +110°C). The first landing on the moon was made by Neil *Armstrong and Edwin *Aldrin on 20 July 1969. *See* APOLLO MOON PROGRAMME.

moonfish A deep-bodied fish, also called opah, belonging to the genus *Lampris* and family *Lamprididae*, widely distributed in warm seas. Up to 2 m long, its body is coloured blue above, rose-pink below, and is spotted with white; the fins are scarlet. Order: *Lampridiformes*.

Moonies *See* UNIFICATION CHURCH.

moonstone A semiprecious stone; a translucent form of feldspar.

Moore, G(eorge) E(dward) (1873–1958) British philosopher. Moore's work centred around language and the analysis of its meaning. His books include *Principia Ethica* (1903) and *Ethics* (1912). He was professor of mental philosophy and logic at Cambridge (1925–39) and editor of the journal *Mind* (1921–47).

Moore, Henry (1898–1986) British sculptor. His fascination with primitive African and Mexican art moulded the development of his two characteristic themes: mother and child sculptures and reclining figures. The latter, a lifelong preoccupation, reached its apogee in the sculpture for UNESCO in Paris (1956–57). After devoting himself to abstract work in the 1930s, Moore reverted to the humanist tradition in the early 1940s with his celebrated drawings of sleeping figures in air-raid shelters.

moorhen A grey-brown to black waterbird, *Gallinula chloropus*, also called common gallinule and waterhen, occurring worldwide except for Australia. It is 32 cm long and has a red bill and forehead and a white patch beneath the tail. It breeds in thick vegetation near ponds and marshes and feeds on seeds, water plants, and aquatic invertebrates. Family: *Rallidae* (rails, etc.).

Moors The conventional European name for the *Arab and *Berber inhabitants of NW Africa and, by extension, for the 8th-century Muslim conquerors of the Iberian peninsula. The Moors were the dominant power in Spain until the 11th century. A highly civilized people, they played a major role in transmitting classical science and philosophy to W Europe.

moose *See* ELK.

moraine Crushed rock and clay etc., ground, transported, and deposited by glaciers, ice sheets, and glacial streams. A glacier often exhibits midline and lateral moraines on its surface, and deposits end moraines. Formerly glaciated areas usually have soils and land forms dominated by moraines (eskers, drumlins, etc.).

Moravia (Czech name: Morava; German name: Mähren) An area of the Czech Republic, formerly (1918–49) a province of Czechoslovakia. Lying chiefly in the basin of the River Morava, it rises in the N to the Sudeten Mountains and in the E to the Carpathian Mountains. It contains important mineral deposits, including coal and iron ore. *History*: settled by Slavic tribes in the late 8th century AD, it formed the centre of an important medieval kingdom (Great Moravia). It was part of the Republic of Czechoslovakia from 1918 until the end of 1992. Chief town: Brno.

Moravia, Alberto (Alberto Pincherle; 1907–90) Italian novelist. His early novels criticized fascism and the corrupt middle-class society that allowed it to flourish. His later works, which include *The Woman of Rome* (1947), *The Lie* (1966), and *Erotic Tales* (1985) concern themes of social alienation and the futility of sexual relationships.

Moray A council area of NE Scotland, on the Moray Firth and the North Sea. In 1975 the historic county of Moray was expanded to form a district of Grampian region; in 1996 this became an independent unitary authority. It consists mainly of hills and moors, rising to the Cairngorm Mountains in the S. Agriculture, fishing, forestry, and whisky distilling are important. Area: 2238 sq km (864 sq mi). Population (2001): 86 940. Administrative centre: Elgin.

moray eel A thick-bodied *eel of the family *Muraenidae* (over 80 species). Up to 1.5 m long, it is brightly coloured and lacks pectoral fins. Moray eels live in rock crevices and reefs of warm and tropical seas.

Moray Firth An inlet of the North Sea in NE Scotland, extending SW from a line between Tarbat Ness in the Highland Region and Burghead in Grampian Region. Length: about 56 km (35 mi).

More, Sir Thomas (1477–1535) English lawyer, scholar, and saint. He joined Henry VII-I's Privy Council in 1518 and succeeded Wolsey as chancellor in 1529. He resigned the chancellorship in 1532 in opposition to Henry's assumption of the supreme headship of the English Church. In 1534 More was imprisoned after refusing to swear to the new Act of Succession. He was brought to trial for treason in 1535, convicted on false evidence, and beheaded. His best-known scholarly work is *Utopia* (1516).

morel A fungus belonging to the genus *Morchella*. Morels are typically club-shaped with the surface of the cap pitted like a honeycomb. The edible common morel (*M. esculenta*) has a yellowish-brown cap, 4–8 cm high, and a stout whitish stalk. Phylum: *Ascomycota*.

Morgan, John Pierpont (1837–1913) US financier, who founded (1895) J. P. Morgan and Co, one of the most powerful banking corporations in the USA. During the 1880s he reorganized many foundering railway companies and later financed such consolidations as the US Steel Corporation and General Electric. His son **John Pierpont Morgan, Jr** (1867–1943) succeeded him and helped to organize the credit requirements of the Allies in World War I.

Morgan le Fay In *Arthurian legend, an evil sorceress who plotted the overthrow of her brother King Arthur. According to Malory's *Morte d'Arthur* (1485) she betrayed Guinevere's adultery to Arthur. However, in the earlier *Vita Merlini* (c. 1150) by *Geoffrey of Monmouth she is a benevolent figure.

m

Moriscos *See* CONVERSOS.

Morley, Thomas (1557–1603) English composer, music printer, organist of St Paul's Cathedral, and member of the Chapel Royal. A pupil of Byrd, he wrote madrigals, canzonets, songs, church music, and the textbook *A Plaine and Easie Introduction to Practicall Musicke* (1597).

Mormons Adherents of the Christian sect that is formally called the Church of Jesus Christ of Latter-Day Saints, founded in 1830 by Joseph Smith in New York state. Smith claimed to have discovered golden tablets that contained the sacred Book of Mormon. After Smith's murder by a mob, the persecuted Mormons moved W under Brigham Young, establishing their headquarters at Salt Lake, Utah, in 1847. Mormons have no professional clergy, reject infant baptism, abstain from alcohol and other stimulants, and run educational and missionary programmes.

morning glory A trailing or twining plant of the genus *Ipomoea*, native to tropical America and Australia and cultivated for its beautiful flowers. The leaves are often heart-shaped and the trumpet-shaped flowers, up to 12 cm across, are deep blue, purple, pink, or white. Popular species are *I. purpurea* and *I. alba* (the moonflower). The seeds of certain varieties contain hallucinogens. Family: *Convolvulaceae*.

Moro, Aldo (1916–1978) Italian statesman; Christian Democratic prime minister (1963–68, 1974–76) and foreign minister (1965–66, 1969–72, 1973–74). In 1978 he was kidnapped and then murdered by the *Red Brigades.

Morocco, Kingdom of A country in NW Africa, bordering on the Atlantic Ocean and Mediterranean Sea. The Atlas Mountains crossing the centre of the country separate the Atlantic coastal area from the Sahara. The population is mainly of Berber and Arabic origin. *Economy*: the chief occupations are agriculture and mining. Wheat, barley, maize, and citrus fruits are grown; livestock is also important. Morocco is a leading exporter of phosphates; other mineral resources are iron ore, coal, lead, zinc, cobalt, and manganese. Industries include food processing, textiles, and traditional handicrafts. There is a thriving fishing industry, sardines and tuna being the chief catch. It is also a popular tourist centre. *History*: part of the Roman province of Mauretania, it fell to the Vandals in the 5th century AD. Its strategic importance was recognized by the European powers in the 19th century, French and Spanish interests conflicting with those of Germany. In the early 20th century Morocco was partitioned into French and Spanish protectorates (1912) and the international zone of Tangier (1923). In 1956 the protectorates were relinquished and Morocco became a sultanate, later a kingdom (1957) under King Mohammed V; his son, Hassan II, acceded to the throne in 1961. In 1976 *Western Sahara was partitioned between Morocco and Mauritania; when Mauritania withdrew in 1979 the area came under Moroccan occupation, with active opposition from the pro-independence Polisario Front. Following elections to a new national assembly (1998), a socialist government came to power (re-elected in 2002). Hassan II was succeeded by his son Mohammed VI in 1999. Official language: Arabic. Currency: dirham of 100 centimes. Area: 458 730 sq km (144 078 sq mi). Population (2003 est): 30 097 000. Capital: Rabat.

morphine A *narcotic analgesic drug obtained from *opium and used in medicine for the relief of severe pain. Its depressant effect on the brain accounts for the pain-killing properties; in high doses it also inhibits the breathing and cough centres. Morphine is an addictive drug and readily leads to severe physical dependence.

morphology The study of the form and structure of plants, animals, and microorganisms. Anatomy is often used synonymously with morphology but in the former the emphasis is on the gross and microscopic structure of organs and parts.

Morris, William (1834–96) British designer, artist, and poet. Associated with the *Pre-Raphaelite Brotherhood, he later started a firm of decorators and designers (1861). He designed stained glass, carpets, and furniture, and his wallpaper designs are still used. His Kelmscott Press, founded in 1890, influenced book design and printing generally. He was also one of the founders of British socialism.

Morris dance A ritual English folk dance performed by groups of white-clad men wearing bells and often carrying sticks or handkerchiefs. A common theme is fertility through death and rebirth. Similar dances are found throughout Europe, India, and the Americas, often featuring animal characters or the black-faced Morisco (Moor), whence the name Morris is thought to derive.

Morse, Samuel Finley Breese (1791–1872) US inventor, who erected the first telegraph line, between Washington and Baltimore (1844). Messages were sent by **Morse code**, a system in which each letter of the alphabet and number has a characteristic sequence of dots and dashes (short and long pulses).

letters

A	•—	N	—•
B	—•••	O	———
C	—•—•	P	•——•
D	—••	Q	——•—
E	•	R	•—•
F	••—•	S	•••
G	——•	T	—
H	••••	U	••—
I	••	V	•••—
J	•———	W	•——
K	—•—	X	—••—
L	•—••	Y	—•——
M	——	Z	——••

numbers / punctuation marks

1	•————	.	•—•—•—
2	••———	,	——••——
3	•••——	:	———•••
4	••••—	?	••——••
5	•••••	'	•————•
6	—••••	-	—•••—
7	——•••	/	—••—•
8	———••	(or)	—•——•—
9	————•	"	•—••—•
0	—————		

Morse code

mortar (building material) A mixture of sand, hydrated lime, and Portland cement, used to bind together building bricks, etc. It is applied wet as a paste, which sets to a durable solid.

mortar (weapon) A short-barrelled muzzle-loading artillery piece with a low-velocity high-angled trajectory. In World War II the largest Allied mortar had a calibre of 4.2 inches (107 mm), the German version being 8.3 inches (210 mm) with six barrels. Mortars are principally used to fire high-explosive and smoke bombs.

mortgage Rights in property (usually land, buildings, etc.) given by a borrower (mortgagor) to a lender (mortgagee) as security for a loan. In the UK building societies lend money for house purchase in return for a legal charge on the property, which gives them the right to sell it to recover their debt if the borrower defaults. When all the money borrowed and the interest due under the mortgage have been repaid, it is redeemed.

Mortimer, Sir John Clifford (1923–) British barrister and playwright. He is best known for the televised tales of Horace Rumpole, a barrister. Other works include the novels *Paradise Postponed* (1985) and *The Sound of Trumpets* (1998) and the autobiographical play *A Voyage Round My Father* (1970). He was knighted in 1998.

Morton, Jelly Roll (Ferdinand Joseph La Menthe; 1885–1941) US Black jazz pianist and composer, who made recordings in the 1920s with the group Morton's Red Hot Peppers. Claiming that he "invented jazz in 1902," his reputation has been the subject of controversy.

mosaic A picture or ornamental design made from small coloured cubes of glass, stone, tile, etc. Mosaics were common in ancient Greece, where they were principally used for floors and made from coloured pebbles. During the Roman Empire mosaics of glass became popular for wall and vault decoration, a development that reached its peak in the early Christian churches in Byzantium and Italy. The 6th-century decorations in S Vitale, in Ravenna, are among the most famous mosaics of the middle ages.

Moscow (Russian name: Moskva) 55 45N 37 42E The capital of Russia and of the Moscow autonomous region (*oblast*), on the River Moskva. It is the economic and political centre of Russia and an important transportation centre. Industries include heavy engineering, cars, textiles, electronics, chemicals, publishing, and food processing. The city is based on a radial plan; the *Kremlin (citadel) and Red Square are at its heart. The Kremlin, triangular in shape, encloses a number of notable ecclesiastical buildings. Red Square is the traditional setting for military parades and demonstrations. Moscow is a major cultural centre; its many educational institutions include the University of Moscow (1755) and the Academy of Sciences. Other famous institutions include the Bolshoi Theatre of Opera and Ballet (1780), the *Moscow Art Theatre, and the Moscow State Circus. *History*: first documented in 1147, settlement actually dates back to prehistoric times. By the beginning of the 13th century it was the centre of the Muscovy principality and became the seat of the metropolitan of the Russian Orthodox Church in 1326. The city was invaded by Napoleon (1812) and the ensuing fire destroyed much of the city. In March 1918, it became the capital of the RSFSR and following the arrival of Lenin and other communist leaders (1922) the capital of the Soviet Union. Development resumed after World War II, since when Moscow has developed an important tourist industry. Population (1999 est): 8 389 000.

Moselle, River (German name: R. Mosel) A river in W Europe, flowing N from NE France to join the River Rhine at Koblenz. It forms part of the border between Germany and Luxembourg. Its valley is one of the main wine-growing areas of Germany. Length: 547 km (340 mi).

m

Moses In the Old Testament, the lawgiver of Israel, who led the people from slavery in Egypt (Exodus) and brought them close to the Promised Land. As a child in Egypt (according to the Old Testament), Moses was saved from the slaughter of all Hebrew male children ordered by Pharaoh by being hidden in bulrushes on the Nile. On Mt Sinai he was given the Ten Commandments by Jehovah. He died at the age of 120.

Moses, Grandma (Anna Mary Robertson M.; 1860–1961) US primitive painter, born in Greenwich, New York (*see* PRIMITIVISM). Entirely self-taught, she only turned seriously to painting at the age of 67. She specialized in naive and nostalgic scenes of farm life.

Mosley, Sir Oswald Ernald (1896–1980) British fascist. He was a Conservative MP (1918–22), an Independent MP (1922–24), and then a Labour MP (1924, 1926–31), serving as chancellor of the Duchy of Lancaster (1929–30). In 1932 he established the British Union of Fascists, which incited antisemitic violence, especially in the East End of London. In World War II he was interned (1940–43) and in 1948 founded the Union Movement.

mosque A Muslim place of worship. It evolved in various styles from a simple rectangular building, such as the first mosque built by Mohammed at Medina in 622 AD. Prayers are said in a large covered area on the side facing Mecca, the direction being indicated by a niche (*mihrab*) in the wall. Mosques are often domed and have minarets (tall slender towers). The mosque has traditionally been the centre of Muslim life, intellectual and social as well as religious.

mosquito A small fly belonging to a family (*Culicidae*; about 2500 species) of almost worldwide distribution, being especially abundant in the tropics. It has long legs, elongated mouthparts, and a long slender abdomen. In most species the males feed on plant juices, while the females bite and suck the blood of mammals, often transmitting serious human and animal diseases. The three important genera are *Anopheles*, *Aedes*, and *Culex* (including the common gnat, *C. pipiens*).

moss A flowerless plant of the phylum *Bryophyta* (about 15 000 species; *see* BRYOPHYTES), growing worldwide (except in salt water) on moist soil, trees, rocks, etc. The moss plant is differentiated into stems and leaves and produces sex cells (gametes), which give rise to a spore capsule that grows from the plant on a long stalk. *Sphagnum*, responsible for peat formation, is economically important.

The name is also applied to several unrelated plants, for example *Spanish moss.

moss animal *See* BRYOZOA.

Mössbauer effect The emission of a gamma ray (*see* GAMMA RADIATION) by an excited nucleus in a solid. Generally such an emission causes the nucleus to recoil, thus reducing the energy of the gamma ray. In the Mössbauer effect the recoil is distributed throughout the solid. The gamma ray therefore loses no energy and may then raise other nuclei into the same excited state. It was discovered by the German physicist Rudolph Mössbauer (1929–   ) and enables the structure of nuclei and molecules to be examined.

moss pink *See* PHLOX.

motet A polyphonic composition (*see* POLYPHONY) for voices, generally unaccompanied. In the medieval motet the fundamental tenor (holding) part was based on a slow-moving plainchant or popular song while the upper triplex (treble) and motetus (worded) parts had a different text and a quicker rhythm. The 16th-century motet with Latin text, used during church services but not a part of the liturgy, is found in its purest form in the works of Palestrina. Since the 17th century the word has been used to describe a serious but not necessarily religious choral work.

moths *See* BUTTERFLIES AND MOTHS.

Motion, Andrew (1952–) British poet and writer. His publications include the poetry collections *Pleasure Steamers* (1978), and *Public Property* (2001), biographies of Larkin (1982) and Keats (1998), and the historical novel *Wainewright the Poisoner* (2000). He was appointed poet laureate in 1999.

motmot A bird of the tropical American family *Motmotidae* (8 species). 16–50 cm long, motmots have short rounded wings, short legs, and long tails with elongated central feathers. The bill is broad and serrated and the plumage is green, blue, brown, and black. Motmots live in forests and prey on insects, spiders, worms, etc. Order: *Coraciiformes* (kingfishers, etc.).

motorcycle racing Racing single-seater motorcycles or sidecar combinations, in classes according to engine capacity. In **road racing**, run usually on special circuits, the main classes are 125, 250, 350, and 500 cc. World championships are awarded according to points won in Grand Prix and other races, such as the Tourist Trophy (TT) races on the Isle of Man (first held in 1907). **Motorcycle trials** are usually events in which a cross-country course has to be completed within a certain time, with points lost for stopping, touching the ground, etc. **Moto-cross** (*or* scrambling) takes place on a circuit marked out across rough country. *See also* DRAG RACING.

motorcycles Two-wheeled engine-powered vehicles. The concept of a steam-powered bicycle was first realized by S. H. Roper in the USA in the 1860s. However, the true forerunner of the modern motorcycle was Gottlieb Daimler's 1885 bicycle powered by an *Otto four-stroke engine. The first production model was Hildebrand and Wolfmüller's 1894 *Pétrolette*. By 1900 there were some 11 000 motorcycles in France and by the start of World War I over 100 000 were registered in the UK. During the war, motorcycles were extensively used by both sides. The interwar period—the great era of the motorcycle—saw the development of many classic designs: the Harley-Davidson in the USA; the Brough Superior, Triumph Speed Twin, and Ariel Square Four in the UK; and the German DKW two-stroke and BMW four-stroke. All these were in military use in World War II. During and after the war some innovations were made but the basic design remained unchanged. In the 1950s and 1960s interest in motorcycles in Europe and the USA declined; the motor scooter, a low-powered Italian-originated version of the motorcycle, and the moped, an engine-assisted bicycle, acquired some popularity. In the 1970s, the Japanese, exploiting the closure of European factories, developed a whole new range of motorcycles, based on European designs.

motor racing Racing in cars, from family saloons at club level to highly specialized Grand Prix vehicles. Early races, such as the 1895 race from Paris to Bordeaux and back, were held on roads, but since 1903 they have usually been held on closed-circuit courses, the first of which in England was Brooklands (1907) in Surrey. The most prestigious form of racing is Grand Prix (Formula One) racing, for which specially built single-seater vehicles are raced by professional drivers for manufacturers or private owners. The Drivers' World Championship (instituted in 1950) is awarded according to points won in certain Formula One races. **Sports-car racing** is for production-type or modified sports cars; the most famous sports-car race is the Le Mans 24 Hours. **Indy Car** racing originated with the Indianapolis 500 in 1911. **Autocross** races are amateur races over grass, while **rallycross** is a similar but more professional form, with races held on circuits that are half grass and half tarmac. *See also* DRAG RACING; KARTING.

mouflon A wild sheep, *Ovis musimon*, native to Corsica and Sardinia and introduced to other parts of Europe and to North America. Mouflons are about 65 cm high at the shoulder and males have large curved horns, a rump patch, and a white saddle on the back.

mould Any fungus that forms a fine woolly mass growing on food, clothing, etc. Examples are the bread mould and species of *Aspergillus* and *Penicillium*. *See also* SLIME MOULDS.

mountain ash A tree, *Sorbus aucuparia*, also called rowan, native to temperate Eurasia and commonly cultivated as an ornamental. Up to 15 m high, it has long leaves with numerous paired leaflets and large clusters of small cream flowers, which give rise to bright-scarlet berries with a bitter acid taste, used to make wine and jelly. The similar and related American species is *S. americana*. Family: *Rosaceae*.

mountain lion *See* COUGAR.

Mountbatten, Louis, 1st Earl Mountbatten of Burma (1900–79) British admiral and colonial administrator; son of Prince Louis of Battenberg (1854–1921) and of Princess Victoria of Hesse-Darmstadt, the granddaughter of Queen Victoria. In World War II he was supreme Allied commander in SE Asia (1943–45), retaking Burma. As viceroy of India (1947) he presided over the transfer of power to India and Pakistan and was then governor general of India (1947–48). He was subsequently commander in chief of the Mediterranean fleet (1952–54) and first sea lord (1955–59), becoming an admiral in 1956. He died in Ireland, the victim of an IRA bomb.

Mounties *See* ROYAL CANADIAN MOUNTED POLICE.

Mount of Olives The highest point in a small range of four summits situated just E of Jerusalem. It features in the Old and New Testaments. Its W slope was the site of the Garden of Gethsemane. According to the Acts of the Apostles (1.2–12), Christ ascended to heaven from the Mount of Olives.

Mount Rushmore National Memorial The gigantic sculpture of the heads of four US presidents—Washington, Jefferson, Lincoln, and Theodore Roosevelt—carved (1927–41) to the design of the sculptor Gutzon Borglum (1871–1941) on the NE cliffs of Mount Rushmore, South Dakota. Each head is about 18 m (60 ft) high.

mouse A *rodent belonging to the suborder *Myomorpha*. The house mouse (*Mus musculus*) is common in buildings worldwide. Greyish brown, it is 14–16 cm long including its tail (7–8 cm) and feeds on a variety of foods, from sugar and grain to oil-based paints and putty. Most mice—together with the rats—are grouped into the subfamilies *Murinae* of the Old World and *Cricetinae* of the New World (which also includes hamsters). There are separate subfamilies for African tree mice (*Dendromurinae*; 7 species), jumping mice (*Zapodinae*; 3 species), dormice, and other small groups.

mouse deer *See* CHEVROTAIN.

Mousterian A stone-tool industry of the Middle *Palaeolithic, associated with *Neanderthal man. Named after caves at Le Moustier in the Dordogne (SW France), the Mousterian occurs, with variants, throughout Eurasia from France to China and in N Africa. Spanning roughly the period of 70 000 to 35 000 BC, it is characterized by a wide variety of hand axes, scrapers, points, and blades.

mouthbrooder A fish belonging to one of several genera of *cichlid fishes. The eggs are carried in the mouth of the parent, usually the female, until they hatch. Chief genera: *Tilapia*; *Haplochromis*; *Pelmatochromis*. Other mouthbrooders include certain *fighting fish, *catfish, and cardinal fish.

mouth organ *See* HARMONICA.

Moyle A district in Northern Ireland, in Co Antrim. Area: 494 sq km (191 sq mi). Population (2001): 15 933.

Mozambique, Republic of (Portuguese name: Moçambique) A country in S East Africa, bordering on the Indian Ocean. Extensive coastal plains rise to plateaus inland with mountains reaching over 2000 m (6500 ft). The chief rivers, notably the Zambezi and Limpopo, flow E and provide both irrigation and hydroelectric power. Most of the population is African, mainly Bantu. *Economy*: chiefly agricultural, the staple food crops being rice and maize. The main cash crops of cashew nuts, cotton, and sugar are also the principal exports. Industry is based largely on food processing and textiles. Mineral resources, including natural gas and high-grade iron ore, are largely unexploited except for coal and bauxite. By the late 1990s government moves to deregulate the economy and attract foreign investment had resulted in a spectacular burst of growth. However, these gains were largely reversed by the floods of 2000. *History*: the N coast was settled by Arabs from the 10th century and was explored by Vasco da *Gama in 1498, becoming a Portuguese colony in the early 16th century. In 1951 it became an overseas province of Portugal. From 1963 FRELIMO (Frente de Libertação de Moçambique) waged a guerrilla campaign that achieved the establishment (1975) of an independent socialist republic under Samora Machel (1933–86). From 1977 the South African-backed Mozambique National Resistance (Renamo) applied military pressure in Mozambique; it was recognized as a legitimate political party in 1991, following the introduction of multiparty democracy (1990). A peace treaty ending the civil war was concluded in 1992. Mozambique joined the Commonwealth in 1996, the first member state to have no historic links with the UK. In 2000 and 2001 Mozambique was devastated by cyclones and flooding that left about one million people homeless. Official language: Portuguese. Currency: metical of 100 centavos. Area: 784 961 sq km (303 070 sq mi). Population (2003 est): 18 568 000. Capital: Maputo.

Mozart, Wolfgang Amadeus (1756–91) Austrian composer, born in Salzburg, the son of the violinist and composer Leopold Mozart (1719–87). Mozart exhibited extraordinary musical talent at the age of four; in 1762 his father took him on a tour of Germany and to Paris and London, where he received adulation for his abilities. After a period of unhappy service with the Archbishop of Salzburg (1779–81) he settled in Vienna as a freelance musician and teacher, composing such masterpieces as the operas *The Marriage of Figaro* (1786) and *Don Giovanni* (1787). Mozart achieved a fusion of the Germanic and Italianate styles of composition and his immense productivity enriched almost every musical genre. He composed 49 symphonies, over 40 concertos, 6 string quintets, 26 string quartets, numerous divertimenti, piano sonatas, violin sonatas, and much other music. Some of his finest works, such as the operas *Così fan tutte* (1790) and *The Magic Flute* (1791) and the *Jupiter* symphony (1788), were written in the last years of his life.

MRI *See* MAGNETIC RESONANCE IMAGING.

Mubarak, (Mohammed) Hosni (Said) (1928–) Egyptian statesman; president (1981–). A general, he commanded (1972–75) the Egyptian air force in the Yom Kippur War against Israel (1973). He became vice president to Anwar *Sadat in 1975 and succeeded him on his assassination. A modernizing pragmatist, he has contained inflation and improved relations with the USA and Arab countries.

mucous membrane A moist membrane that lines the digestive and respiratory tracts and the nasal sinuses. It is a type of epithelium containing cells that secrete **mucus**, a slimy substance that protects its surface and—in the digestive tract—also lubricates the passage of food and faeces. In the bronchi the mucus traps dust particles and bacteria that are inhaled with air.

Mudéjars (Arabic: vassal) The Muslims (*see* MOORS) of Spain who had, by the 13th century, become subject to Christian rule during the reconquest of the Iberian peninsula. Many were of mixed *Berber and Spanish descent and continued to preserve their Islamic religion and customs. They created an architectural style notable for its ornamental brickwork and use of ceramic tiling. Many examples survive in Castile and Aragon.

mudskipper A fish of the subfamily *Periophthalminae*, especially the genus *Periophthalmus*, found in swamps, estuaries, and mud flats of Africa, Polynesia, and Australia. Mudskippers have an elongated body, up to 30 cm long, a blunt head, and dorsally protruding eyes. They are able to climb and walk over land using their limblike pectoral fins. Family: *Gobiidae* (*see* GOBY).

Mugabe, Robert (Gabriel) (1925–) Zimbabwean statesman; prime minister (1980–87); president (1988–). He helped found the Zimbabwe African National Union (ZANU) in 1963 and, after ten years' (1964–74) detention in Rhodesia, formed the Patriotic Front (PF) with Joshua Nkomo, leader of the Zimbabwe African People's Union (ZAPU). They waged guerrilla warfare against the governments of Ian Smith and then Bishop Muzorewa until the peace talks of 1979–80. His party's election victory (1980) brought Mugabe the leadership of Zimbabwe. Subsequently he restricted opposition, creating (1987) a one-party state. In the late 1990s his authoritarian rule and deepening recession provoked protests. His policy of condoning the illegal seizure of White-owned farms by Black militants led to international criticism in 2000; he was re-elected amid accusations of fraud in 2002.

Muhammad *See* MOHAMMED.

Muir, Edwin (1887–1959) Scottish poet. Born in Orkney, he moved to Glasgow in 1901 and to London in 1919. During the 1930s he and his wife Willa moved to Prague, where they translated the novels of Franz *Kafka. His reputation as a poet was established with *The Voyage* (1946) and *The Labyrinth* (1949).

m

mulberry A tree of the genus *Morus* (12 species), native to N temperate and subtropical regions. The black mulberry (*M. nigra*) is the species most commonly cultivated for its fruit. About 12 m high, it has toothed heart-shaped leaves and round green flower clusters (catkins). The female flowers give rise to a blackberry-like fruit, which is used in jellies, desserts, etc. The leaves of the white mulberry (*M. alba*) are the staple food of silkworms. Family: *Moraceae*.

mule The sterile offspring of a female horse and a male ass. Mules are useful pack and draught animals, being sure-footed and strong but smaller than horses.

Mull An island off the W coast of Scotland, in the Inner Hebrides. It is chiefly mountainous; some sheep and cattle are raised. Other occupations include fishing, forestry, and tourism. Area: 909 sq km (351 sq mi). Population (1991): 2708. Chief town: Tobermory.

mullein A biennial or perennial herb of the genus *Verbascum* (about 300 species), native to N temperate Eurasia. The biennial common mullein (*V. thapsus*), also called Aaron's rod, occurs in dry limy regions. 0.6–2 m tall, it bears woolly leaves and yellow flowers. Some species, including the European dark mullein (*V. nigrum*), are garden plants. Family: *Scrophulariaceae*.

mullet A food fish, also called grey mullet, belonging to the genus *Mugil* (about 70 species), found in temperate and tropical coastal waters and estuaries. It has a slender silvery-green or grey large-scaled body, 30–90 cm long, with two dorsal fins. Family: *Mugilidae*; order: *Perciformes*.

multimedia system A computer system capable of producing high-quality moving pictures and sound, as well as text, usually from information stored on a compact disc.

multiple sclerosis A chronic and usually progressive disease of the nervous system in which the fatty sheaths that surround the nerves in the brain or spinal cord are destroyed. The disease is also called disseminated sclerosis, as its effects are disseminated in different parts of the body. It usually begins in young adults, and the commonest initial symptoms are sudden severe blurring of the vision or weakness in one limb. The disease usually recurs, causing permanent handicap.

m

Mumbai *See* BOMBAY.

mummers' play An English folk drama based on the legend of St George and the Seven Champions of Christendom; it was a dumb show (*mummer*, from Middle English *mum*, silent), traditionally enacted on Christmas Day by masked performers.

mummy A human or animal body prepared and embalmed for burial according to ancient Egyptian religious practice. The internal organs were extracted and sealed in Canopic jars and the body was desiccated by packing in dry natron, anointed, and encased in linen bandages.

mumps An acute virus infection that usually occurs in children. After an incubation period of 12 to 20 days the child develops headache and fever; later, the parotid salivary glands (situated under the ear) become tender and swollen. The disease is usually mild and resolves rapidly. In adult male patients the infection may spread to the testicles, which may occasionally lead to sterility.

Munch, Edvard (1863–1944) Norwegian painter and printmaker, who was a major influence on 20th-century German *expressionism. His symbolic paintings of love, death, and despair, including the famous *Cry* (1893; Nasjonalgalleriet, Oslo), reflect the pessimism caused by family tragedy.

München Gladbach *See* MÖNCHENGLADBACH.

Münchhausen, Karl Friedrich, Freiherr von (1720–97) German soldier and raconteur. His hyperbolic accounts of his feats passed into legend and were the subject of a series of adventure tales, *The Adventures of Baron Münchhausen* (1793), written by R.E. Raspe (1737–94).

mung bean A *bean plant, *Phaseolus aureus*, also known as green gram, native to India and cultivated in tropical and subtropical regions chiefly as a vegetable crop. The slender pods contain up to 15 small edible seeds, which can be dried and stored or germinated in the dark to produce bean sprouts. Family: *Leguminosae*.

Munich (German name: München) 48 08N 11 35E A city in S Germany, the capital of Bavaria on the River Isar. It has a 15th-century cathedral and many baroque and rococo buildings. It is also noted for its annual Oktoberfest (beer festival). A centre of commerce, industry, and tourism, its manufactures include precision instruments, electrical goods, chemicals, and beer. *History*: Munich was from 1255 the residence and from 1506 the capital of the Dukes of Bavaria (from 1806 Kings). The Nazi movement began here in the 1920s. Population (1999 est): 1 193 600.

Munich Agreement (1938) The settlement, resulting from the conference between Neville Chamberlain (UK), Daladier (France), Hitler (Germany), and Mussolini (Italy), that recognized Hitler's territorial claims to the *Sudetenland. Described by Chamberlain as achieving "peace in our time," it was followed in March 1939 by Hitler's invasion of Czechoslovakia and in Sept by World War II.

Münster 51 58N 7 37E A city and port in NW Germany, in North Rhine-Westphalia on the Dortmund-Ems Canal. It was a member of the Hanseatic League and the capital of the former province of Westphalia. It has a 13th-century cathedral and a university (1773). Service industries provide employment for most of the workforce. Population (1999 est): 264 700.

Munster A province and ancient kingdom of the SW Republic of Ireland. It consists of the counties of Clare, Cork, Kerry, Limerick, Tipperary, and Waterford. Area: 24 125 sq km (9315 sq mi). Population (2002): 1 101 266.

muntjac A small deer belonging to the subfamily *Muntiacinae* (6 species), occurring in forests of Asia, Sumatra, Java, and Borneo. The Indian muntjac (*Muntiacus muntjak*), also called barking deer or rib-faced deer, is 55 cm high at the shoulder with short unbranched antlers and short sharp fangs. Muntjacs are mainly solitary and nocturnal.

muon A negatively charged unstable elementary particle (lifetime 2×10^{-6} second; mass 207 times that of the electron) that decays into an electron and two *neutrinos. It has a corresponding antiparticle. The muon was originally thought to be a meson (and was called the mu-meson) but is now classified as a lepton. *See* PARTICLE PHYSICS.

mural painting The decoration of walls and ceilings by such varied techniques as encaustic, tempera, and *fresco painting. *Renaissance painters often used perspective and architecture in their murals to create the illusion that the painted walls or ceilings were space extensions of the real architecture. Mural painting was revived during the 20th century, principally by the Mexican painters *Rivera, Orozco, and Siqueiros, who used it to reach a wider public with their social and political subject matter.

Murdoch, Dame Iris (1919–99) British novelist and philosopher. Born in Dublin, she studied and taught philosophy at Oxford; her philosophical works include *Sartre* (1953) and *Metaphysics as a Guide to Morals* (1992). Her novels, which explore moral and philosophical dilemmas, include *The Bell* (1958), *A Severed Head* (1961), *The Sea, the Sea* (1978), which won the Booker Prize, *The Good Apprentice* (1985), and *Jackson's Dilemma* (1995). Her last years were clouded by Alzheimer's disease.

Murdoch, (Keith) Rupert (1931–) US media entrepreneur, born in Australia. His News International Group owns *The Times* and *The Sun*. He is also chairman of 20th Century-Fox, HarperCollins publishers, and British Sky TV.

murex A *gastropod mollusc belonging to the family *Muricidae* (about 1000 species), mainly of tropical seas. Murex shells are elaborately ornamented with spines and frills; the snail feeds on other molluscs by drilling holes in their shells and extracting the flesh with its long proboscis.

Murillo, Bartolomé Esteban (1617–82) Spanish painter. He spent most of his life in Seville, working for the religious orders and helping to found the Spanish Academy (1660), of which he became first president. After abandoning his early realism, he painted urchins and religious scenes in an idealized style influenced by Rubens and the Venetians.

Murmansk 68 59N 33 08E A port in NW Russia, on the Kola inlet of the Barents Sea (*see* KOLA PENINSULA). Its ice-free harbour was formerly an important fishing base but has now declined. The surrounding area is amongst the most polluted in the world, having served as a dump for nuclear waste. Population (1999 est): 382 700.

Murphy-O'Connor, Cormac, Cardinal (1932–) British Roman Catholic churchman. He succeeded Basil Hume as Archbishop of Westminster in 2000 and was created a cardinal in 2001.

Murray, Sir James (Augustus Henry) (1837–1915) British lexicographer. After joining the Philological Society and editing some early English texts, he was in 1878 appointed editor of the *New English Dictionary on Historical Principles* (later called the *Oxford English Dictionary*), to which he devoted the rest of his life.

Murray River The chief river in Australia. Rising near Mount Koscuisko, in New South Wales, it flows generally W and S forming the boundary between Victoria and New South Wales. It enters Encounter Bay on the Indian Ocean through Lake Alexandrina. The main tributaries are the Darling and Murrumbidgee Rivers; it also receives water from the Snowy Mountains hydroelectric scheme. Length: 2590 km (1609 mi).

Murrumbidgee River A river in SE Australia, rising in the Eastern Highlands in New South Wales and flowing through the Australian Capital Territory before entering the Murray River. Length: 1690 km (1050 mi).

Muscat 23 37N 58 38E The capital of Oman, on the Gulf of Oman. Most port traffic is now handled at Matrah to the NW. There is an oil terminal to the W. Population (1993): 51 969.

muscle Tissue that is specialized to contract, producing movement or tension in the body. It contains long spindle-shaped cells (muscle fibres) that convert chemical energy (*see* ATP) into mechanical energy. Most of the body's musculature consists of voluntary muscle, which is consciously controlled via the central nervous system. It is also known as skeletal muscle (because it is attached to the bones) and striated (or striped) muscle (because of its banded appearance under the microscope). Individual muscles are made up of bundles of fibres enclosed in a strong fibrous sheath and attached to bones by tendons. Involuntary muscle occurs in the walls of hollow organs, such as blood vessels, intestines, and the bladder. It is responsible for movements not under conscious control and is regulated by the autonomic nervous system. Cardiac muscle is a special type of muscle found only in the heart: its rhythmic contractions produce the heartbeat.

muscovite *See* MICAS.

muscular dystrophy A group of chronic and progressive disorders characterized by wasting and weakening of the muscle fibres. The disease is inherited and the commonest type, Duchenne muscular dystrophy, affects predominantly boys. There is no specific treatment but physiotherapy and orthopaedic measures can help.

Muses In Greek mythology, the nine patrons of the arts and sciences, daughters of Zeus and *Mnemosyne. Calliope was the muse of epic poetry; Clio, history; Euterpe, flute playing and music; Erato, love poetry and hymns; Terpsichore, dancing; Melpomene, tragedy; Thalia, comedy; Polyhymnia, song and mime; and Urania, astronomy.

mushroom The umbrella-shaped spore-forming body produced by many fungi. (Sometimes the word toadstool is used for those species that are inedible or poisonous, mushroom being restricted to the edible species.) It consists of an erect stem (stipe) and a cap, which may be flat, conical, spherical, or cylindrical and has numerous radiating gills on its undersurface in which the spores are produced. The well-known edible mushrooms belong to the genus *Agaricus*; they have a smooth white or scaly brown cap with gills that become deep brown at maturity.

musical instruments Devices used to produce music. In the orchestra musical instruments are grouped into families. The *stringed instruments (*or* strings) include the violin, viola, cello, double bass, and harp (*see also* PIANO). The wind instruments are divided into the woodwind (flute, clarinet, oboe, and bassoon) and brass (horn, trumpet, trombone, and tuba). The percussion instruments include the triangle, cymbals, xylophone, timpani, and other instruments. Many instruments are used chiefly in jazz or pop (e.g. guitar, vibraphone, and maracas) while others, such as the Indian sitar, feature predominantly in the music of particular countries.

music hall In England, a type of popular entertainment featuring a variety of performers including singers, dancers, comedians, and conjurors. It attained its greatest popularity at the end of the 19th century and declined in the 1920s and 1930s with the rise of the cinema and the radio. Notable music-hall performers included Marie *Lloyd, Vesta Tilley, and Harry *Lauder. The US equivalent was known as vaudeville. Celebrated vaudeville performers included W. C. *Fields and Will Rodgers (1879–1935).

musk A perennial plant, *Mimulus moschatus*, native to North America and grown as an orna-

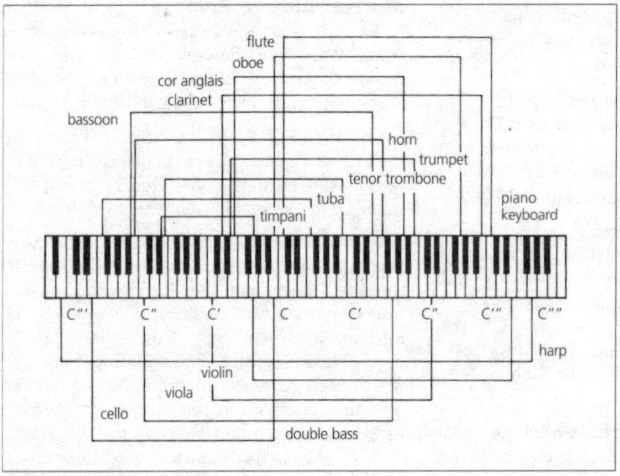

musical instruments. The range of some musical instruments shown on a piano keyboard.

mental for its musky fragrance. 20–60 cm tall, it has oval leaves and tubular yellow flowers. The name is also applied to several other plants with a musky odour including the musk mallow (*Malva moschata*) and musk rose (*Rosa moschata*).

musk deer A small solitary deer, *Moschus moschiferus*, found in mountain forests of central Asia. Musk deer are about 60 cm high at the shoulder with long hind legs; males have no antlers but grow long fangs. The secretion of their musk gland is used in the manufacture of perfumes.

musket A smoothbore firearm fired from

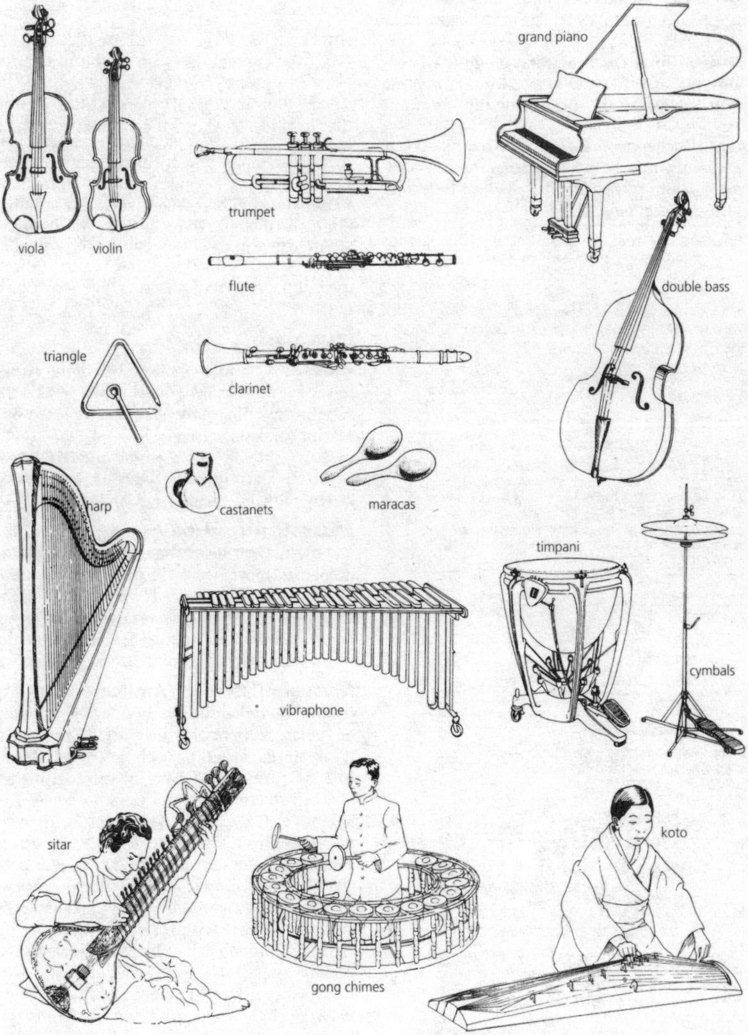

musical instruments

m

the shoulder. The earliest form, known as a harquebus (*or* arquebus) evolved in the 15th century as the first hand-held form of the *cannon. In the second half of the 16th century a Spanish general invented a heavy shoulder weapon with a sufficiently large charge to penetrate armour. This musket still relied on the matchlock, it was not until the mid-17th century that wheellocks and flintlocks were adopted for military use. The next landmark in the development of the musket was the percussion cap at the beginning of the 19th century, which led to the breech-loading musket with cartridge and percussion-cap ammunition. Muskets were superseded by *rifles in the mid-19th century.

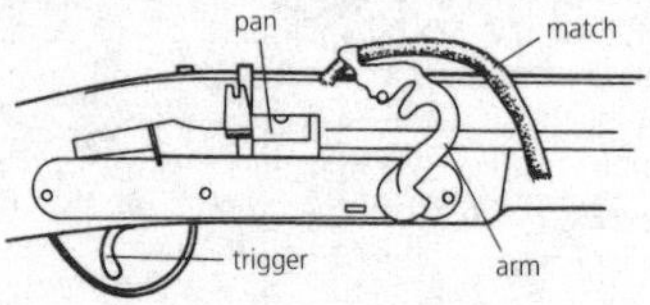

In the matchlock, a slow-burning match was forced into the powder pan by the arm when the trigger was pressed.

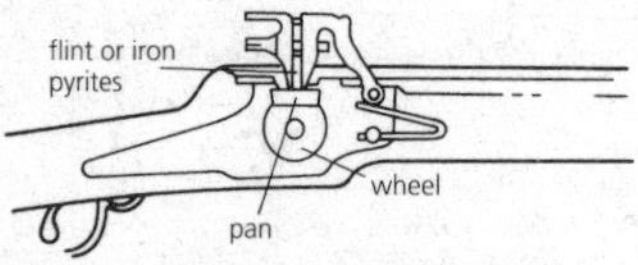

In the wheellock, the flint or iron pyrites was lowered onto a serrated wheel when the trigger was pressed. The sparks produced ignited the charge in the pan. The wheel, wound up by a key, also rotated when the trigger was pressed.

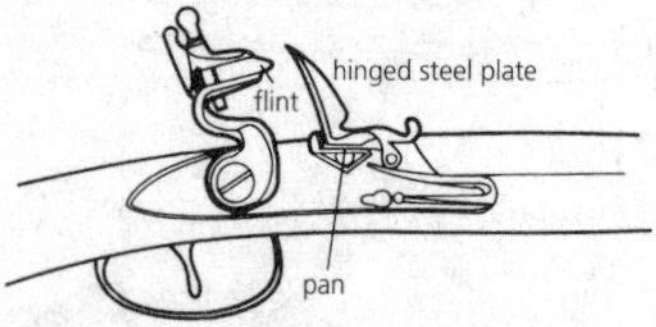

In the flintlock, pressing the trigger caused the flint to strike a hinged steel plate, forcing it back to expose the powder in the pan to the sparks.

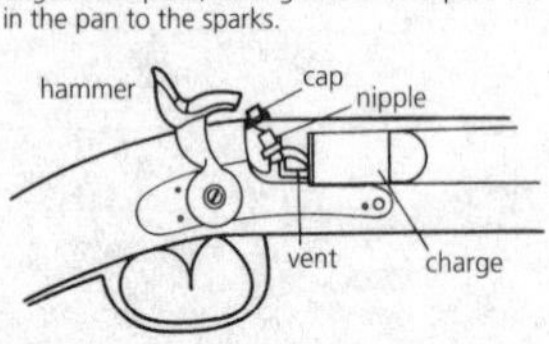

The percussion cap, containing mercury fulminate, was struck by the hammer when the trigger was pressed. The flame produced passed through the hollow nipple into the vent, where it fired the main charge.

musket. The types of lock mechanism used in muzzle-loaders.

musk ox A large hoofed mammal, *Ovibos moschatus*, inhabiting the Arctic tundra of North America. About 150 cm high at the shoulder, musk oxen have long dark shaggy hair and prominent curved horns. Bulls have a strong musky scent in the rutting season. Family: *Bovidae*.

muskrat A large North American water *vole, *Ondatra zibethica*, also called musquash. It grows up to 35 cm long, excluding its black hairless tail, and its soft glossy coat is used in the fur trade. Muskrats inhabit marshland and feed on water plants, mussels, and crayfish. Family: *Cricetidae*.

muslin A smooth delicately woven cotton fabric. Originally made in Mosul in Mesopotamia (hence its name), it is used for dresses and curtains. In the USA coarser cotton fabrics used for shirts and sheeting are also called muslins.

musquash *See* MUSKRAT.

mussel A *bivalve mollusc belonging either to the family *Mytilidae* (marine mussels) or the superfamily *Unionacea* (freshwater mussels). Marine mussels have wedge-shaped shells measuring 5–15 cm. The edible mussel (*Mytilus edulis*) is an important seafood. Freshwater mussels inhabit ponds, lakes, and streams.

Musset, Alfred de (1810–57) French poet and dramatist, one of the major figures of the Romantic movement. He published his first volume of poetry, *Contes d'Espagne et d'Italie*, at the age of 20. His autobiographical *La Confession d'un enfant du siècle* (1836) includes an account of his love affair with George *Sand.

Mussolini, Benito (Amilcare Andrea) (1883–1945) Italian fascist dictator. His support of Italian participation in World War I led to his expulsion from the Socialist Party (1915). In 1919 he formed the Fasci di combattimento (Blackshirts) in Milan and came to power following the March on Rome (1922). He was prime minister but gradually (1924–29) established a dictatorship. As *duce* ("leader") his policies initially impressed the Italian people. However, his expansionist foreign policy, especially his alliance with Hitler, brought him increasing unpopularity. In 1939 he annexed Albania and after the outbreak of World War II he declared war on France and Britain (June 1940). The Italian war effort was disastrous; following the Allied invasion of Sicily, Mussolini was forced to resign (July 1943). Rescued by the

Germans to head a new fascist republic in N Italy, he was subsequently captured and shot by Italian partisans.

Mussorgski, Modest Petrovich (1839–81) Russian composer. An army officer and civil servant, he had little formal training. His masterpieces are the opera *Boris Godunov* (1868–72), the piano work *Pictures at an Exhibition* (1874), and the orchestral tone poem *A Night on the Bare Mountain* (1860–66).

mustang The wild horse of North America. Mustangs are descended from the domesticated European stock of Spanish settlers and have become tough and small in the harsh conditions. Many were caught and tamed by cowboys and Indians, including the Mustang tribe.

mustard Any of various annual herbs of the genus *Brassica* and closely related genera, native to Europe and W Asia and cultivated chiefly for their seeds—source of the condiment mustard. They have deeply lobed leaves and terminal clusters of yellow flowers. The leaves may be used as fodder, fertilizer, vegetables, or herbs. The main species are the white or yellow mustard, *Sinapis alba* (or *B. hirta*), black or brown mustard (*B. nigra*), and Indian mustard (*B. juncea*).

mutation A change in the hereditary material (*see* DNA) of an organism, which results in an altered physical characteristic. A mutation in a germ cell is inherited by subsequent generations of offspring; a change in any other cell (somatic cell) affects only those cells produced by division of the mutated cell. Gene mutations result from a change in the bases of the DNA molecule; chromosome mutations may be due to the addition or subtraction of bases and can usually be seen under a microscope. Both types of mutation affect the *genetic code and hence the corresponding function of the genes.

Very occasionally, mutations occur spontaneously and at random. They can also be induced by certain chemicals, ionizing radiation (such as X-rays), and by ultraviolet light. Most nonlethal mutations are of no benefit to the organism, but they do provide an important source of genetic variation in the population on which natural selection can act, which eventually results in the *evolution of new species.

mute swan An Old World *swan, *Cygnus olor*, found in marshy areas and estuaries and, as a semidomesticated ornamental bird, on rivers and lakes. It is 160 cm long and has a long neck, white plumage, black legs, and an orange bill with a black base. It is less vocal than other swans.

mutualism *See* SYMBIOSIS.

MX missile A US nuclear strategic missile with a range of 9650 km (6000 mi). Carrying 10 warheads, the MX missile was developed in response to the vulnerability of the concrete underground silos in which other ICBMs are housed. The MX missile can be launched from ships, aircraft, submarines, mobile land launchers, or from specially reinforced silos.

Myanmar, Union of (name until 1989: Socialist Republic of the Union of Burma) A country in SE Asia, on the Bay of Bengal and the Andaman Sea. The majority of the population is Burmese, but there are several minorities, including the Shan, Karen, and Chachin peoples. *Economy*: the main crop is rice. Half the land is under forest and teak is a valuable export: other exports are rice and rice products, rubber and jute. Myanmar is thought to be the world's largest producer of opium. There is some mining, especially lead and zinc, and petroleum is produced and refined. Tourism increased tenfold during the 1990s. *History*: by the 13th century the Burmese had developed a civilization based on Hinayana Buddhism. After successive wars Burma came under British rule in 1885 as part of British India. In 1937 it attained a measure of self-government and was separated from India. In World War II it was occupied by Japanese forces. In 1948 it became a republic outside the Commonwealth. In 1962 parliamentary democracy was overthrown in a military coup led by Gen U Ne Win and since 1988 strict martial law has been enforced. The 1990 elections were won by the National League for Democracy, led by *Aung San Suu Kyi, who had been held under house arrest since 1989. However, the military refused to hand over power and suppressed opposition activity. Repeatedly released and rearrested since 1995, Suu Kyi has continued to campaign for political change. Myanmar was admitted to the Association of South-East Asian States in 1997. Official language: Burmese. Currency: kyat of 100 pyas. Area: 678 000 sq km (261 789 sq mi). Population (2003 est): 42 511 000. Capital: Rangoon.

Mycenae An ancient citadel in the Peloponnese (S Greece). Famed in legend as the home of *Agamemnon, Mycenae attained its zenith between 1600 and 1200 BC. Massive fortifications attest Mycenae's military readiness and exquisite bronze, gold, and silver articles from its royal graves indicate affluence.

Mycenaean civilization The civilization of Bronze Age Greece. It developed after about 1650 BC in mainland centres, such as *Mycenae and Pylos, and after 1450 BC its influence extended to Crete. The Mycenaeans were a warrior aristocracy. They spoke a form of Greek, used *Linear B script, and lived in palaces decorated with frescoes and equipped with luxury goods. About 1200 BC the palaces were destroyed, but Mycenaean culture survived until about 1100 BC.

mycology The branch of biology dealing with the study of fungi. Mycology was established as a separate discipline in the early 19th century, when the Swedish botanist Elias Fries (1794–1878) published the first scientifically based classification of the fungi (1821–32).

mycorrhiza A close association between a fungus and the roots of a higher plant that is beneficial to both participants (*see* SYMBIOSIS). The plant benefits by more efficient uptake of nutrients, and the fungus obtains carbohydrates and other nutrients from the plant.

mynah A songbird belonging to a genus (*Acridotheres*) native to SE Asia. Mynahs usually have a dark plumage with bright wattles on the face. They feed chiefly on the ground and eat the insects found on cattle. The common mynah (*A. tristis*) has become a pest in some regions. The popular cagebird that mimics human speech is a related species, the hill mynah (*Graculus religiosa*). Family: *Sturnidae* (starlings).

myocardial infarction Death of part of the heart muscle: the cause of what is popularly described as a heart attack. This usually results from *atherosclerosis. The patient usually experiences sudden severe central chest pain, which may spread to the neck and arms and is usually accompanied by sweating and nausea.

myopia *See* SHORTSIGHTEDNESS.

Myron (5th century BC) Athenian sculptor. His *Discus-Thrower* and *Marsyas*, described by ancient critics, are known through Roman copies.

myrrh An aromatic yellow to red gum resin obtained from small tropical thorny trees of the genus *Commifera*, especially *C. myrrha*, *C. molmol*, and *C. abyssinica*, native to Africa and SW Asia. It is used in incense, perfumes, cosmetics, dentistry, and pharmaceuticals. Family: *Commiphoraceae*.

myrtle An evergreen shrub of the genus *Myrtus* (over 100 species). The common myrtle (*M. communis*), native to the Mediterranean area and W Asia, may grow to a height of 5 m. It has aromatic dark-green shiny leaves, fragrant five-petalled white flowers, and blue-black berries. Its oil is used in perfumery. Family: *Myrtaceae*. Other plants known as myrtle include the sweet gale.

Mysore 12 18N 76 37E A city in India, in Karnataka. Industries include textiles, chemicals, and food processing and it has a university (1916). Population (1991): 480 692.

mystery plays *See* MIRACLE PLAYS.

mysticism Belief in a type of religious experience in which the individual claims to achieve immediate knowledge of or temporary union with God. Mysticism is an element in most theistic traditions. The usual preliminary is strict asceticism. St *Francis of Assisi, St *Teresa of Avila, and Julian of Norwich (c. 1342–c. 1413) are among the many famous Christian mystics. Official Church attitudes have alternated between regarding mysticism as a special spiritual grace and suspecting it of verging on *Gnosticism, *pantheism, or *Neoplatonism.

mythology Imaginative poetic stories, traditions, etc., concerning religious beliefs, gods, and supernatural and heroic human beings. Mythology often involves a cosmogony—an attempted explanation of the origin of the universe, of mankind, or of a particular race or culture. The term also refers to the formal study of such stories, traditions, etc. Anthropology and psychoanalysis have thrown new light on the function of myths. Among primitive peoples they serve to provide an explanation or justification for social institutions. They also appear to embody universal values or patterns with regard to human psychology. The mythologies of particular cultures have provided the material of much of the world's great literature and art.

myxomatosis An infectious disease of rabbits and hares that is caused by a virus. Symptoms include swollen eyes, nose, and muzzle, closed eyelids, and fever. The disease, which is usually fatal, was introduced to the UK and Australia during the 1950s as a pest-control measure.

N

Nabis (Hebrew: prophets) A group of French artists formed in Paris in 1888. The leading members—Paul Sérusier (1863–1927), Maurice Denis (1870–1943), Pierre *Bonnard, and Édouard Vuillard (1868–1940)—were united by their admiration for *Gauguin and Japanese prints. They disbanded in 1899.

Nabokov, Vladimir (1899–1977) US novelist, born in Russia. He achieved popular success with *Lolita* (1955), whose academic antihero lusts after young girls. His other novels include *The Defence* (1930), one of several originally written in Russian, *Pale Fire* (1962), and *Ada* (1969).

Na-Dené languages An American Indian language group. It includes the Athabascan, Tlingit, Haida, and Eyak subgroups.

nadir *See* ZENITH.

NAFTA *See* NORTH AMERICAN FREE TRADE AGREEMENT.

naga In Hindu mythology, one of a race of minor serpent deities. Vishnu is often portrayed sleeping on the naga Sesha, and there is a Buddhist legend of a naga raising the Buddha on its coils above a flood sent to prevent his attaining enlightenment. Nagas are depicted as half-snake and half-human, as many-headed cobras, or in human form posed beneath a canopy of cobras.

Nagasaki 32 45N 129 52E A port in Japan, in W Kyushu. On 9 August 1945, the second atomic bomb was dropped on Nagasaki, killing or wounding about 75 000 people. Population (1995): 438 724.

Nagorno-Karabakh An administrative region in Azerbaidzhan. Formed in 1923, it is populated by Christian Armenians (76%) and Muslim Azerbaidzhanis. It has metal and mineral deposits but is chiefly agricultural. In the late 1980s the Armenians' agitation for union with Armenia led to riots and the declaration of a state of emergency (1990). In 1991 fighting broke out between Armenian and Azerbaidzhani forces; a ceasefire was agreed in 1994 but peace talks have yet to produce any significant result. Area: 4400 sq km (1700 sq mi). Population (latest est): 193 300. Capital: Stepanakert.

Nagoya 35 8N 136 53E A port in Japan, in SE Honshu. The fourth largest city in the country, it was rebuilt after bombing in 1945. Population (1995): 2 152 258.

Nagpur 21 10N 79 12E A city in India, in Maharashtra. Founded in the early 18th century, it fell under British control in 1853. Population (1991): 1 622 225.

Nagy, Imre (1896–1958) Hungarian statesman, who led the revolutionary government of 1956. As prime minister (1953–55) Nagy promised numerous reforms. Opposed by Hungary's Stalinists, he was demoted and in 1956 expelled from the Communist Party. In the subsequent *Hungarian Revolution Nagy once more became prime minister but was deposed and executed by the Soviets.

Nahuatl The most widely used American Indian language of the Uto-Aztecan family, spoken in Mexico. It was the language of the *Aztecs and *Toltecs. The Nahua people are slash-and-burn cultivators, growing maize, beans, tomatoes, and chilis.

Naipaul, Sir V(idiadhur) S(urajprasad) (1932–   ) British novelist and writer, born in the West Indies. A witty ironic tone characterizes such early novels as *A House for Mr Biswas* (1961). Later novels include *A Bend in the River* (1979), *The Enigma of Arrival* (1987), and *Half a Life* (2001). Non-fiction works include *A Turn in the South* (1989) and *Beyond Belief* (1998). He was awarded the Nobel Prize for Literature in 2001.

Nairobi 1 17S 36 50E The capital of Kenya, situated just S of the equator. It is the trading centre of a fertile agricultural region. Population (1999): 2 143 254.

Namib Desert A desert chiefly in W Namibia, extending some 1600 km (994 mi) along the Atlantic coast. It is almost devoid of population.

Namibia, Republic of (name until 1968: South West Africa) A country in SW Africa. The narrow coastal plains of the Namib Desert rise to the central plateau, with the Kalahari Desert to the N. The majority of the population is African, the largest group being the Ovambo. *Economy*: chiefly subsistence agriculture. Fishing is important, especially for pilchards. Rich mineral resources include diamonds (the main export), uranium, copper, lead, and zinc. The economy remains highly dependent on South Africa. *History*: a German protectorate from 1884, during World War I it surrendered (1915) to South Africa, which administered South West Africa under a League of Nations mandate. In 1966 South Africa refused to acknowledge that the mandate was at an end and was condemned by both the UN and the South West Africa People's Organization (SWAPO) for illegally occupying the territory. In 1985 South Africa installed an interim administration in Namibia as a first step towards granting independence (achieved in 1990); Walvis Bay was returned to Namibia in 1994. SWAPO candidates won multiparty elections held in 1989 and Sam Nujoma became president. Namibia joined the Commonwealth in 1990. Official languages: Afrikaans and English. Currency: Namibian dollar of 100 cents. Area: 824 269 sq km (318 261 sq mi). Population (2003 est): 1 927 000. Capital: Windhoek.

n

Nanak (1469–1539) Indian founder of *Sikhism. Born near Lahore, he settled finally in Kartarpur, where he attracted a large community of disciples. His teachings are contained in a number of hymns.

Nancy 48 42N 6 12E A town in NE France, on the River Meurthe. The former capital of the Dukes of Lorraine, it passed to France in 1766. Population (1999): 103 605.

Nanjing (**Nan-ching** *or* **Nanking**) 32 05N 118 55E A port in E China, on the Yangtze River. An ancient cultural centre, it was the centre of the Taiping Rebellion (1851–64). Population (1999 est): 2 388 915.

Nansen, Fridtjof (1861–1930) Norwegian explorer, zoologist, and statesman. In 1888 he led an expedition across the Greenland icefield and in 1893, in the *Fram*, set sail across the Arctic. In 1895, with F. J. Johansen (1867–1923), he left the ship and reached 18 14N, the nearest point to the North Pole then attained. He contributed to the League of Nations and pioneered the **Nansen passport**, an identification card for displaced persons (1922). He won the Nobel Peace Prize (1923).

Nantes 47 14N 1 35W A major port in W France, on the Loire estuary. It was here that the **Edict of Nantes**, guaranteeing religious toleration, was signed in 1598. Population (1999): 268 695.

Nantucket An island in the USA, off SE Massachusetts. A former whaling centre, it is now chiefly a resort. Length: 24 km (15 mi). Width: 5 km (3 mi). Population (latest est): 6012.

napalm An inexpensive jelly consisting of a mixture of the aluminium salts of *na*pathenic acid and *palm*itic acid used to thicken petrol so that it can be used in incendiary bombs and flame-throwers. It was used in World War II, the Korean War, and in Vietnam.

naphthalene ($C_{10}H_8$) A white crystalline aromatic hydrocarbon that occurs in coal tar. **Naphthol** ($C_{10}H_7OH$) is the hydroxy derivative. It consists of two isomers; the most important, beta-naphthol, is used in antioxidants for rubbers and dyes and in drugs.

Napier 39 29S 176 58E A port in New Zealand, in E North Island. It is the most important centre of New Zealand's wool trade. Population (1995 est): 53 500.

Napier, John (1550–1617) Scottish mathematician, who invented *logarithms. In 1614 he published a table of logarithms to the base e, now known as Napierian logarithms. Napier also produced an elementary calculating machine, known as **Napier's bones**.

Naples (Italian name: Napoli; ancient name: Neapolis) 40 50N 14 15E A city in S Italy, overlooking the Bay of Naples. It is an important port and a centre of tourism. Its many historic buildings include medieval castles, a gothic cathedral (13th–14th centuries), the 17th-century Royal Palace, and the university (1224). *History*: founded by Greek colonists about 600 BC, it fell to Rome in 326. It was under Byzantine rule (6th–8th centuries AD) and in 1139 it became part of the Norman kingdom of Sicily. Following the revolt known as the *Sicilian Vespers (1282), the Italian peninsula S of the Papal States became known as the kingdom of Naples (with Naples as its capital) until it fell to Garibaldi (1860) and was united with the rest of Italy (*see also* SICILY). From this time Naples lagged economically behind the N, resulting in considerable poverty. The city was badly damaged during World War II. Population (2000 est): 1 002 619.

Napoleon I (1769–1821) Emperor of the French (1804–15). Born Napoleon Bonaparte in Corsica, he became an artillery officer and rose to prominence in 1795, when he turned the guns of the Paris garrison on a mob. Shortly afterwards he married Josephine de Beauharnais and was appointed to command the French army in Italy (*see* REVOLUTIONARY AND NAPOLEONIC WARS). His Italian campaign (1796–97) brought the conquest of Milan and Mantua. Napoleon then obtained the Directory's support for his plan to break British imperial power by conquering Egypt and India. In Egypt his great victory of the Pyramids was undermined by Nelson's annihilation of a French fleet at the Battle of the Nile (1798) and in 1799 he returned unobtrusively to France. In the coup d'état of 18 Brumaire (9–10 November 1799) he became first consul; in 1802 he became consul for life and in 1804 had himself proclaimed emperor. His outstanding domestic achievement was the *Code Napoléon*, but Napoleon achieved immortal fame with his exploits abroad. In 1802 he negotiated the Treaty of Lunéville, which marked his defeat of the Austrians at Marengo, and the Treaty of Amiens with the British. Despite the disaster at *Trafalgar (1805), which forced him to abandon his plan for the invasion of Britain, his land victories, especially at *Austerlitz (1805), Jena (1806), and Friedland (1806), drew almost every continental power within the French orbit. However, an attempt to break the British by blockade (the Continental System) failed and the protracted *Peninsular War (1808–14) drained French resources. In 1812 Napoleon invaded Russia with half a million men, of whom nearly 400 000 died in the Russian winter. In 1813 Europe rose against Napoleon, inflicting a massive defeat at Leipzig that forced his abdication and exile to Elba. In 1815, however, he returned to France and attempted in the Hundred Days to regain his former greatness. He suffered a decisive defeat at *Waterloo and spent the rest of his life on St Helena. Napoleon's claim to the French Crown was pursued after his death by the son of his second marriage, to Marie Louise of Austria, who styled himself Napoleon II.

Napoleon III (1808–73) Emperor of the French (1852–70); nephew of Napoleon I. Napoleon used the prestige of his name to win the presidential election after the Revolution of 1848. By a coup d'état at the end of 1851, he dissolved the legislative assembly and, a year later, declared himself emperor. His domestic policies fostered industry and transformed Paris. Abroad, his diplomacy embroiled France in the Crimean War (1854–56), in war against the Austrians in Italy (1859), and in a conflict in Mexico (1861–67). Finally, his aggressive stance towards Bismarck helped to cause the *Franco-Prussian War, in which the Second Empire was destroyed and Napoleon was driven into exile.

Napoleonic Wars *See* REVOLUTIONARY AND NAPOLEONIC WARS.

Narayan, R(asipuram) K(rishnaswamy) (1906–2001) Indian novelist and short-story writer. Writing in English and setting his stories in imaginary Malgudi, Narayan published such works as *Swami and Friends* (1935), *The Man-Eater of Malgudi* (1961), *Under the Banyan Tree* (1985), and *The Grandmother's Tale* (1993).

Narcissus (botany) A genus of perennial herbaceous plants (about 40 species), native to Eurasia and N Africa and widely planted in gardens and parks. Growing from bulbs, they produce erect flower stalks up to 30 cm high. The *daffodils (*N. pseudonarcissus*) have large solitary yellow flowers with trumpet-shaped crowns; the jonquils (*N. jonquilla*) have smaller pale-yellow flowers with small cuplike crowns. Family: *Amaryllidaceae*.

Narcissus (Greek mythology) A beautiful youth who was punished for rejecting the love of the nymph Echo by being made to fall in love with his own reflection in a pool. He died and was transformed into a flower.

narcotics Drugs that cause stupor or sleep and relieve pain by depressing activity of the brain. The term is used particularly for *opium and its derivatives (opiates), including morphine and codeine. Synthetic narcotics include heroin, methadone, and pethidine.

narwhal A gregarious Arctic toothed *whale, *Monodon monoceros*, up to 5 m long and feeding on fish and squid. Male narwhals have a long straight spirally twisted tusk that grows to a length of 3 m; its function is unknown. Family: *Monodontidae*.

NASA (National Aeronautics and Space Administration) The US civilian agency, formed in 1958, that is responsible for all nonmilitary aspects of the US space programme. Its major projects have included the manned *Apollo moon programme, the manned space station

Skylab (launched 1973), reusable *space shuttles, and successful planetary probes.

Naseby, Battle of (14 June 1645) The battle in the English Civil War that decided Charles I's defeat. The *New Model Army under Fairfax and Oliver Cromwell routed Prince Rupert's royalist forces at Naseby, near Market Harborough, Leicestershire.

Nash, John (1752–1835) British architect of the Regency period. Under the patronage of the Prince of Wales (later George IV), Nash redeveloped parts of London, laying out Regent's Park as a formal park surrounded by curved terraces of houses with stucco façades. Regent's Street (1825) was designed to link the park with Westminster. In London Nash also built Carlton House Terrace (1833), laid out Trafalgar Square and St James's Park (1829), and redesigned *Buckingham Palace with the triumphal Marble Arch (1828) as its gateway. In Brighton he redesigned the Royal Pavilion as an oriental fantasy.

Nash, Paul (1889–1946) British painter. He became known for his symbolic war landscapes during World Wars I and II, the finest example being *Totes Meer* (1940–41; Tate Gallery). Nash was also a leading member of Unit One (1933), a group of artists dedicated to promoting modern art. His brother **John Nash** (1893–1977) produced fine watercolour landscapes and botanical illustrations.

Nashville 36 10N 86 50W A city in the USA, the capital of Tennessee. Founded in 1779, it is a centre of country and western music. Population (2000, with Davidson): 545 524.

Nasik 20 00N 73 52E A city in India, in Maharashtra. It is a major Hindu pilgrimage centre. Population (1991): 648 896.

Nassau 25 2N 77 25W The capital of the Bahamas, a port on New Providence Island. Built in 1729, it is an important tourist centre. Population (1999 est): 114 000.

Nasser, Gamal Abdel (1918–70) Egyptian statesman; prime minister (1954–56) and president (1956–70). An army officer, he helped to found the nationalist Free Officers group, which overthrew the monarchy in 1952. He became prime minister and then president of Egypt (United Arab Republic from 1958). His nationalization of the Suez Canal led to an unsuccessful Israeli and Anglo-French attack on Egypt (1956).

nasturtium An annual garden plant of the genus *Tropaeolum* (90 species), also called Indian cress, native to Central and South America. It has orange, yellow, pink, or red flowers. *T. majus* is the most popular ornamental species. Family: *Tropaeolaceae*.

Natal 1. 5 46S 35 15W A port in NE Brazil, near the mouth of the Rio Potengi. It exports sugar, cotton, and carnauba wax. Population (2000, urban area): 709 422. **2.** A former province in South Africa, extending from the Indian Ocean in the E to the Drakensberg Mountains in the W. Sugar cane is the major crop and timber is also important. Durban is the main industrial centre and port. Coal is the chief mineral. *History*: the Boers attempted to establish a republic in Natal (1838) but this was annexed by Britain in 1843 and with additions became a province of the Union of South Africa (1910). In 1994 it was replaced by the new region **KwaZulu/Natal**.

Natchez A Muskogean-speaking North American Indian tribe of the Lower Mississippi. They were cultivators who, like the *Creeks, built mound temples and worshipped the sun.

National Aeronautics and Space Administration *See* NASA.

National Curriculum The curriculum of subjects taught in state schools in England and Wales. Established by the Education Reform Act 1988, it comprises ten foundation subjects (eleven in Wales), three of which (the core subjects – English, maths, science) must be studied by all children from the age of five and taken at GCSE. Of the remaining subjects, design and technology, history or geography, and a modern language are a compulsory part of secondary education; music and art are optional. Physical education is also taught. Children are formally tested at the ages of 7, 11, 14, and 16. In addition to the National Curriculum, all schools must provide religious education and (from 2002) lessons in citizenship.

national debt The money that a government borrows; together with the revenue from taxation it makes up the government's income. In the UK, the funded debt consists of money that the government does not have to repay on a fixed date; it makes up about 10% of the national debt. The unfunded debt consists of the floating debt (e.g. treasury bills), gilt-edged securities, and such savings as Savings Bonds. Money borrowed as unfunded debt has to be repaid on a fixed date.

National Gallery An art gallery in Trafalgar Square (London), containing the largest collection of paintings in the UK. Founded for the nation in 1824, it was housed in Pall Mall until William Wilkins (1778–1839) built the present premises (1832–38). An extension, designed by Robert Venturi, opened in 1991.

National Health Service (NHS) A comprehensive medical service in the UK, financed primarily by taxation. The National Health Service Act (1946), implemented in 1948, covered all aspects of health care except that of the school child and the worker. Complaints that the structure and policies of the NHS did not facilitate medical advance, together with rising costs, led to substantial reorganization of the Service in 1974, 1982, 1988, 1990, 1999, and 2003. In England overall responsibility lies (from 1988) with the secretary of state for health. The service is administered (since 1996) by Health Authorities, which combine the functions of the old District Health Authorities and Family Health Service Authorities. In Wales and Scotland responsibility now lies (since 1999) with the devolved bodies, while administration lies with Health Authorities (in Wales) or Health Boards (in Scotland). In 1990 legislation was passed enabling hospitals to opt to be run by self-governing NHS trusts, which are funded by selling their services to Health Authorities and fund-holding GPs. In 1999 the Labour government replaced GP fund-holding with a system of primary care groups (*see* HOSPITAL). Long waiting lists, a shortage of nurses, and the dilapidated state of some hospitals have led many to conclude that after 50 years the NHS is no longer working as it should. Plans to increase annual spending on the NHS by 43% within five years were announced in 2002.

National Insurance A UK insurance scheme providing funds to pay for the National Health Service and social security benefits. Contributions from employees, employers, the self-employed, and the government are paid into the National Insurance Fund, from which the benefits (including income support, maternity, and child benefits as well as retirement pensions) are paid. Under the State Earnings-Related Pension Scheme (SERPS) of 1978, contributions to retirement pensions are related to earnings, and pensions are index-linked. In 2020 the pension age will be equalized at 65. In 2001 the government introduced "stakeholder" pensions as an alternative to SERPS for those without occupational or personal pensions; these are administered by the private sector but regulated by government.

nationalization The policy of taking into public ownership industries that were privately owned. In the UK after World War II, Attlee's Labour government (1945–51) nationalized those industries in which competition appeared wasteful and those war-damaged enterprises needing huge injections of capital (e.g. coal, railways). Most of these industries were returned to the private sector in the 1980s and 1990s by Conservative governments.

National Portrait Gallery An art gallery in London founded in 1856 to house portraits that are authentic likenesses of famous personalities in British history. The main gallery is in St Martin's Place, adjacent to the National Gallery, and there are annexes in Carlton House Terrace and at Montacute House, Somerset. A major extension opened in 2000.

Nationals An Australian political party, founded in 1919 as the Country Party, to represent the interests of farmers. It was subsequently renamed the National Country Party and then the National Party, adopting its current name in 2003. It has held office only in coalition with the Liberal Party.

National Theatre *See* ROYAL NATIONAL THEATRE COMPANY.

National Trust An independent charity in the UK, founded in 1895, that acquires and preserves country houses, castles, gardens, and places of interest or natural beauty. Properties bequeathed to the Trust are exempt from inheritance tax but must be self-supporting or accompanied by an endowment.

NATO *See* NORTH ATLANTIC TREATY ORGANIZATION.

natterjack A short-legged European *toad, *Bufo calamita*. About 7 cm long when fully grown, the natterjack has a yellow stripe down its back. If alarmed, it raises its inflated body on its hind legs to appear larger to the enemy.

natural gas A naturally occurring mixture of gaseous hydrocarbons consisting mainly of methane with smaller amounts of heavier hydrocarbons. It is obtained from underground reservoirs, often associated with *oil deposits. Like oil it originates in the bacterial decomposition of animal matter. It also contains nonhydrocarbon impurities, the most important being helium, which is extracted commercially.

Natural History Museum *See* BRITISH MUSEUM.

Naturalism A literary and artistic movement of the late 19th century characterized by the use of realistic techniques to express the philosophical belief that all phenomena can be explained by natural or material causes. It was influenced by the biological theories of *Darwin, the philosophy of *Comte, and the deterministic theories of the historian Hippolyte Taine (1828–93). Its literary manifesto was *Le Roman expérimentale* (1880) by *Zola.

natural selection *See* DARWINISM.

Nauru, Republic of (*or* **Naoero**; former name: Pleasant Island) A small country in the central Pacific Ocean, NE of Australia comprising a coral island. The small population consists mainly of Nauruans and other Pacific islanders. *Economy*: based entirely on the mining of phosphates, the only export. The phosphates are expected to run out early in the 21st century, therefore Nauru has made investments abroad and is developing as a transport centre and tax haven. *History*: discovered by the British in 1798, it was under British mandate from 1920 to 1947, when it came under the joint trusteeship of Australia, New Zealand, and the UK. In 1968 it became an independent republic and a special member of the British Commonwealth. Nauru received some £50 million compensation from Australia in 1993 for environmental damage and loss of mining profits while it was a trusteeship. Official language: English. Currency: Australian dollar of 100 cents. Area: 21 sq km (8 sq mi). Population (2003 est): 12 600. Capital: Yaren.

nautilus One of several cephalopod molluscs with external shells. The pearly nautiluses (genus *Nautilus*; 3 species) live near the bottom of the Pacific and Indian Oceans. Up to 20 cm across, they have 60–90 tentacles surrounding a horny beak and live in the outermost chamber of their flat coiled shells. The others serve as buoyancy chambers. The paper nautilus (*Argonauta argo*) is found in the Atlantic and Pacific Oceans. The female, 20 cm long, secretes from one of its tentacles a papery boat-shaped shell in which the eggs develop. The male is much smaller (about 2 cm long).

Navajo A North American Indian Athabascan-speaking people of New Mexico, Arizona, and Utah. Like their relatives, the *Apache, they migrated from the far north, probably during the 17th century. They are farmers and herders and now the most numerous North American Indian tribe.

Navarino, Battle of (20 October 1827) A naval battle during the War of Greek Independence. French, Russian, and British ships destroyed an Ottoman-Egyptian fleet in the Bay of Navarinou in the Peloponnese. This was the last fleet action fought wholly under sail.

Navarre A former kingdom in N Spain, corresponding to the present-day Spanish region of Navarra and part of the French department of Basses-Pyrénées. S Navarre was conquered by Ferdinand the Catholic of Aragon in 1512 and united with Castile in 1515. French Navarre passed to the French Crown in 1589.

Navratilova, Martina (1956–) Czech-born tennis player who defected to the USA in 1975. She was Wimbledon singles champion 1978–79, 1982–87, and 1990 and doubles champion 1976, 1979, 1981–86. She also holds a record of 74 consecutive wins. She retired in 1994.

Náxos A Greek island in the S Aegean Sea, the largest in the Cyclades. Náxos is traditionally the place where Theseus abandoned Ariadne. Area: 438 sq km (169 sq mi). Population (latest est): 14 000. Chief town: Náxos.

Nazareth 32 41N 35 16E A town in N Israel, between Haifa and the Sea of Galilee. The city's many churches commemorate its associations with the early life of Jesus Christ. Population (latest est): 51 000.

Nazi Party (*Na*tionalso*zi*alistische Deutsche Arbeiterpartei) The National Socialist German Workers' Party, founded in 1919 as the German Workers' Party and led from 1921 until 1945 by Adolf *Hitler. *See also* FASCISM.

N'djamena (name until 1973: Fort Lamy) The capital of Chad, a port in the SW. It was founded by the French in 1900. Population (1993): 530 965.

Ndola 13 00S 28 39E A city in N Zambia, near the border with the Democratic Republic of Congo. It is an important commercial centre for the Copperbelt. Population (latest est): 376 300.

Neagh, Lough A lake in Northern Ireland, divided between Co Antrim, Co Armagh, and Co Tyrone. It is the largest lake in the British Isles. Area: 388 sq km (150 sq mi).

Neanderthal man An extinct *hominid race that inhabited Europe and the adjacent areas of Africa and Asia between about 150 000 and 30 000 years ago. Characterized by heavy brow ridges, receding forehead, heavy protruding jaw, and robust bone structure, Neanderthal man had a large cranial capacity and upright posture. They were cave-dwelling hunters; and are generally regarded as a distinct species (*Homo neanderthalensis*), rather than a subspecies of *Homo sapiens*, and may have evolved from *Homo heidelbergensis* (*see* HOMO).

Neath Port Talbot (Welsh name: Castell-Nedd Port Talbot) A county borough in S Wales, created from part of West Glamorgan in 1996. Area: 442 sq km (170 sq mi). Population (2001): 134 471. Administrative centre: Port Talbot.

Nebraska A state in the N central USA, lying W of the Missouri River. Part of the Central Lowlands cover the eastern third of the state, with the higher Great Plains in the W. Traditionally an agricultural state, it is still a leading producer of cattle, corn, and wheat. Most of the population is situated in the industrial E. *History*: explored by the French and Spanish, it formed part of the Louisiana Purchase (1803). It became a state in 1867. Area: 200 018 sq km (77 227 sq mi). Population (2000): 1 711 263. Capital: Lincoln.

Nebuchadnezzar II (*or* **Nebuchadrezzar**; c. 630–562 BC) King of *Babylon (605–562). Nebuchadnezzar extended Babylonian power in Elam, N Syria, and S Asia Minor. He captured Jerusalem in 597 and again in 586, when he destroyed the city and forced the Jews into exile.

nebula A cloud of interstellar gas and dust that becomes visible for one of three reasons. In an **emission nebula** the gas is ionized by ultraviolet radiation and light (predominantly red and green) is emitted. In a **reflection nebula** light from a nearby star is reflected in all directions by dust in the cloud, thus illuminating the cloud. The dust in a **dark nebula** reduces the amount of light passing through it (by absorption and scattering) and a dark region is seen against a brighter background.

nectar A sugary solution produced by glandular structures (nectaries) in flowers pollinated by animals. Nectar attracts insects, birds, or bats to the flower and encourages pollination as the animal collects nectar from different sources.

needlefish A carnivorous fish, also called garfish, belonging to the family *Belonidae* (about 60 species), that occurs in tropical and warm-temperate seas. It has a slender silvery-blue or green body, up to 1.2 m long, with elongated jaws and numerous sharp teeth. Species include the European garfish (*Belone belone*). Order: *Atheriniformes*.

Nefertiti (died c. 1346 BC) The cousin and chief wife of Akhenaton (1379–1362 BC) of Egypt. Her portrait bust is perhaps the best-known work of Egyptian art.

Negev A desert in S Israel. In recent decades large areas have been irrigated by pipeline from the River Jordan. Area: about 12 000 sq km (4632 sq mi).

Negro, Río 1. (Portuguese name: Rio Negro) A river in NE South America. Rising in E Colombia as the Guainía, it joins the River Amazon about 16 km (10 mi) below Manaus. Length: about 2250 km (1400 mi). **2.** A river in S Argentina, rising in the Andes and flowing generally SE to the Atlantic Ocean. Length: 1014 km (630 mi).

Negros A volcanic island in the central Philippines. The chief industry is sugar production. Area: 12 704 sq km (4904 sq mi). Population (latest est): 3 168 000. Chief town: Bacolod.

Nehru, Jawaharlal (1889–1964) Indian statesman; the first prime minister of independent India (1947–64). He was elected president of the *Indian National Congress in 1929 in succession to his father Motilal Nehru (1861–1931). Between 1921 and 1945 he served nine prison sentences for participating in the movement of noncooperation against the British. After World War II he helped negotiate independent India. As premier, he carried through many social reforms and maintained a policy of nonalignment with foreign powers. His daughter was Indira *Gandhi.

Neisse, River 1. (*or* **Glatzer Neisse**; Polish name: Nysa) A river in SW Poland, flowing NE to the River Oder. Length: 244 km (159 mi). **2.** (*or* **Lusatian Neisse**) A river rising in the N Czech Republic and flowing mainly N to the River Oder in Poland. Length: 225 km (140 mi).

nekton An ecological division of aquatic animals that includes all those swimming actively in the open waters of a sea or lake (*compare* PLANKTON). The nekton includes fishes, squids, turtles, seals, and whales.

Nelson, Horatio, Viscount (1758–1805) British admiral. At the outbreak of the French Revolutionary Wars he was given a command in the Mediterranean. In 1794, at Calvi, he lost the sight in his right eye but went on to play an important part in the victory off Cape St Vincent (1797). Shortly afterwards he lost his right arm in action but in 1798 he destroyed France's naval power in the Mediterranean by his great victory in the battle of the *Nile. Nelson spent the following year in Naples, where, although married, he fell in love with Emma, Lady *Hamilton. Subsequently he was given command in the Baltic and was responsible for the victory at Copenhagen (1801). In 1803 he became commander in the Mediterranean. He block-

n

aded Toulon for 18 months but in 1805 the French escaped; the ensuing chase culminated in the battle of *Trafalgar (1805). Nelson directed this British triumph from aboard the *Victory* but was himself mortally wounded.

Neman, River (*or* **R. Nyeman**) A river in E Europe. Rising in Belarus, it flows mainly NW through Lithuania to the Baltic Sea. Length: 937 km (582 mi).

nematode A spindle-shaped colourless worm, also called roundworm, belonging to the phylum *Nematoda* (over 10 000 species). Nematodes live almost everywhere in soil, fresh water, and the sea. Some are parasites of plants or animals; others feed on dead organic matter. *See also* FILARIA; GUINEA WORM; HOOKWORM; PINWORM.

Nemertina *See* RIBBONWORM.

Nemesia A genus of annual herbs native to South Africa. They are up to 30 cm tall, with showy white, yellow, red, pink, or purple two-lipped flowers. Family: *Scrophulariaceae*.

Nemesis In Greek mythology, a goddess personifying the gods' anger at and punishment of human arrogance or hubris.

neoclassicism 1. In art and architecture, a style dominant in Europe from the late 18th to mid-19th centuries. Although essentially a revival of classical art and architecture, it was distinguished from similar revivals by its scientific approach to the recreation of the past. This was largely stimulated by archaeological discoveries at *Pompeii, *Herculaneum, and elsewhere. Key figures in the early development of neoclassicism were the art historian Johann Winckelmann (1717–68) and Giambattista Piranesi (1720–78). Early neoclassical painters included Jacques Louis *David and *Ingres. Other leading neoclassicists were the sculptors Antonio Canova (1757–1822) and Bertel Thorvaldsen (1768–1844) and the architects Robert *Adam and Jacques Soufflot (1713–80). *See also* EMPIRE STYLE. **2.** A style of musical composition originating in the 1920s. It was characterized by the use of counterpoint and the revival of 18th-century forms. The leading practitioners were *Stravinsky and *Hindemith.

neodymium (Nd) A *lanthanide element, occurring in the mineral monazite. It is used with lanthanum in misch metal and, as the oxide (Nd_2O_3), together with praseodymium, to produce special dark glasses used in welding goggles. At no 60; at wt 144.24; mp 1021°C; bp 3074°C.

Neolithic The final division of the *Stone Age. It is characterized by the development of the earliest settled agricultural communities and increasing domestication of animals (*see* JERICHO). Although man still used only stone tools and weapons, he evolved improved techniques of grinding stone and the invention of pottery facilitated food storage and preparation.

neon (Ne) A noble gas present in very small amounts in the earth's atmosphere, discovered in 1898 by Ramsay and M. W. Travers (1872–1961) by fractional distillation of liquid air. It is commonly used in advertising signs and voltage indicator lamps. At no 10; at wt 20.179; mp −248.67°C; bp −246.08°C.

Neoplatonism The philosophy, formulated principally by *Plotinus, that emphasizes an eternal world of order, goodness, and beauty, of which material existence is a weak and unsatisfactory copy. The chief influences were Plato's *Symposium* and the *Phaedo*.

neoteny The condition in which larval characteristics persist in an animal when it reaches sexual maturity. The *axolotl is a neotenous salamander that rarely assumes the typical adult form under natural conditions. Neotony is also known in certain primitive marine chordates.

Nepal, Kingdom of A landlocked country in the Himalayas, between China (Tibet) and India. Most of the country consists of a series of mountain ranges, with some of the world's highest peaks, including Mount Everest, along its northern border. Its predominantly Hindu population is of Mongoloid stock, the Gurkhas having been the dominant group since 1769. *Economy*: chiefly agricultural, with rice, maize, millet, and wheat as the main crops. Mineral resources are sparse. Tourism is the main source of revenue. *History*: the independent principalities that comprised the region in the middle ages were conquered by the Gurkhas in the 18th century and Nepal was subsequently ruled by the Shah family and then by the Rana, who continue to reign. An elected parliament was set up in 1959 but abolished by the king in 1962. In 1990 mass unrest led to the restoration of parliamentary democracy under a new constitution. A communist-led government held power in 1994–96. In 2001 King Birendra, his queen, and six other members of the royal family were shot dead by Crown Prince Dipendra, who then killed himself. Dipendra's brother Gyanendra then assumed the throne. A guerrilla campaign by Maoist insurgents, which began in 1996, escalated dramatically in 2002. Further unrest was provoked by King Gyanendra's appointment (2003) of an unelected royalist government. Official language: Nepali. Currency: Nepalese rupee of 100 paisa. Area: 141 400 sq km (54 600 sq mi). Population (2003 est): 24 172 000. Capital: Kathmandu.

nephritis (*or* **Bright's disease**) Inflammation of the kidneys. It may result from infection, as in pyelitis, or from a disorder of the body's system that affects the kidneys (called glomerulonephritis), which causes protein, cells, and blood to appear in the urine and swelling of the body tissues (*see* OEDEMA).

Neptune (astronomy) The most distant giant planet, orbiting the sun every 165 years at a mean distance of 4497 million km. It is smaller (48 600 km in diameter) and more massive (17.2 earth masses) than *Uranus, but is thought to be almost identical to it in structure. It has 11 *satellites. Discovered in 1846 by J.G.Galle, it was circumnavigated by Voyager 2 in 1989.

Neptune (mythology) The principal Roman sea god, identified with the Greek *Poseidon. He is usually portrayed holding a trident and riding a dolphin.

neptunium (Np) The first synthetic transuranic element, produced in 1940 at Berkeley, USA, by bombarding uranium with neutrons. It is available in small quantities in nuclear reactors and forms halides (for example NpF_3, $NpCl_4$) and oxides (for example NpO_2). At no 93; at wt (237); mp 639°C; bp 3902°C.

Neri, St Philip (1515–95) Italian mystic, who founded the Congregation of the Oratory. Over the nave of the Church of San Girolamo he built an oratory to hold religious meetings and concerts of sacred music, from which both the name of Neri's order and the word *oratorio* derive. Feast day: 26 May.

Nero (Claudius Caesar) (37–68 AD) Roman emperor (54–68), notorious for his cruelty. His early reign was dominated by his mother Agrippina the Younger, Seneca, and Sextus Afranius Burrus but by 62 Nero had thrown off these influences: Agrippina was murdered (59), Burrus died, perhaps by poison (62), and Seneca retired (62). Also in 62, he murdered his wife Octavia in order to marry Poppaea, who herself died in 65 after being kicked by her husband. A conspiracy to assassinate him, after which Seneca was forced to kill himself, failed in 65. In 68, however, revolts in Gaul, Spain, and Africa and the mutiny of his palace guard precipitated his suicide.

Neruda, Pablo (Ricardo Reyes; 1904–73) Chilean poet and diplomat. His volumes include *Residencia en la tierra* (1925–31) and the long poem *Canto general* (1950). He was awarded the Nobel Prize in 1971.

nerve *See* NEURONE.

nerve gases War gases that inhibit the transmission of impulses from nerve to nerve or muscle. Death results from paralysis of the diaphragm leading to asphyxiation. Most nerve gases are derivatives of phosphoric acid.

Nervi, Pier Luigi (1891–1979) Italian engineer and architect, famous for his inventive use of reinforced concrete. In 1949 he designed the great exhibition hall in Turin and in 1953 was one of the architects of the UNESCO building in Paris.

nervous system The network of nervous tissue in the body. This comprises the central nervous system (CNS), i.e. the *brain and *spinal cord, and the peripheral nervous system. The latter includes the cranial and spinal nerves with their ganglia and the autonomic nervous system (ANS). The ANS controls unconscious body functions, such as digestion and heartbeat, and is coordinated by the *hypothalamus. The nervous system is chiefly responsible for communication both within the body and between the body and its surroundings. Incoming information passes along sensory *neurones to the brain, where it is analysed and compared with *memory; nerve impulses then leave the central nervous system along motor nerves.

Ness, Loch A deep lake in N Scotland, in the Highland Region in the Great Glen. The sight of a monster (the **Loch Ness monster**) has frequently been reported. Length: 36 km (22 mi). Depth: 229 m (754 ft).

netball A seven-a-side court game adapted from *basketball. The court is 100 × 50 ft (30.5 × 15.25 m), divided into three equal zones. The goal is a net mounted 10 ft (3.05 m) above the ground. The game is played by throwing the ball; players may not run with it.

Netherlandic A subgroup of the Western *Germanic languages. It is spoken in Holland and Belgium, where it is called Dutch and Flemish respectively. It is the parent language of Afrikaans.

Netherlands, Kingdom of the A country in NW Europe, on the North Sea. It is almost entirely flat except for some low hills in the SE, and considerable areas of land have been reclaimed from the sea. *Economy*: banking and commerce are important sources of income. Highly developed industries include engineering, petrochemicals, plastics, electronics, and food processing. Agriculture is highly mechanized and market gardening is important. *History*: until 1581 the Netherlands formed with present-day Belgium and Luxembourg the region often referred to as the Low Countries. It was under Roman occupation from the 1st century BC to the 4th century AD. It was then overrun by German tribes. After the partition of the Frankish empire in 843 the region was called Lotharingia. The following centuries saw the rise of powerful principalities, notably the bishopric of Utrecht and the counties of Holland and Guelders, which came under the influence of Burgundy and then Spain. In 1581, during the *Revolt of the Netherlands, the seven northern provinces—Holland, Zeeland, Utrecht, Overijssel, Gröningen, Drenthe, and Friesland—proclaimed their independence as the United Provinces of the Netherlands under the leadership of William the Silent. War with Spain continued intermittently until, at the conclusion of the Thirty Years' War, Spain recognized the independence of the Dutch Republic in the Peace of Westphalia (1648). In the 17th century the Netherlands reached a peak of prosperity and international prestige, forming a considerable overseas empire. In 1795, however, it fell to Revolutionary France and in 1806 Napoleon made his brother Louis Bonaparte King of Holland. Following Napoleon's defeat the former Dutch Republic was reunited with the southern provinces to form the Kingdom of the Netherlands (1814). In 1830 the S revolted against the union, forming Belgium (1831), and in 1867 Luxembourg became an independent state. The Netherlands remained neutral in World War I but in World War II was occupied by Germany (1940–45). In 1948 the Netherlands joined with Belgium and Luxembourg to form the *Benelux economic union; it is now a member of the European Union. The immediate postwar period was dominated by the Dutch colony of Indonesia's fight for independence. In 1980 Queen Juliana abdicated and was succeeded as head of state by her daughter Princess Beatrix. The Netherlands adopted the European single currency in 1999–2002. A centre-left coalition under Wim Kok (1938–) governed from 1994 until 2002, when a right-wing government was formed under Jan Peter Balkenende. Official language: Dutch. Currency: euro of 100 cents. Area: 41 160 sq km (15 892 sq mi). Population (2003 est): 16 238 000. Capitals: Amsterdam (legal and administrative); The Hague (seat of government).

Netherlands Antilles (Dutch name: Nederlandse Antillen) Two groups of West Indian islands in the Lesser Antilles, in the Caribbean Sea some 800 km (497 mi) apart. The S group lies off N Venezuela and consists of *Curaçao and Bonaire; the N group (geographically part of the Leeward Islands) consists of St Eustatius, Saba, and the S part of *St Martin. Aruba, geographically part of the S group, became a separate Dutch territory in 1986. Under Dutch control since the 17th century, the islands became self-governing in 1954. The economy is based chiefly on oil refining and ship repairing. Currency: Netherlands Antilles guilder of 100 cents. Area: 996 sq km (390 sq mi). Population (2002 est): 175 000. Capital: Willemstad.

nettle An annual or perennial herb of the genus *Urtica* (about 30 species), found in temperate regions worldwide. Up to 1.5 m in height, it may have stinging hairs. Family: *Urticaceae*. Dead-nettles are annual or perennial herbs of the genus *Lamium* (about 40 species), occurring in Europe, temperate Asia, and N Africa. They lack stinging hairs. Family: *Labiatae*.

nettle rash *See* URTICARIA.

Neuchâtel (German name: Neuenburg) 47 00N 6 56E A city in W Switzerland, on Lake Neuchâtel. Industries include watchmaking and chocolate production. Population (latest est): 32 509.

Neumann, John von (1903–57) US mathematician, born in Hungary. He invented *game theory and set quantum theory upon a rigorous mathematical basis.

neurohormone A chemical (*see* HORMONE) that is secreted by nerve cells and modifies the function of other organs in the body. The *hypothalamus, for example, releases several hormones that cause the *pituitary gland to secrete its own hormones, the kidney to retain water in the body, and the breast to produce milk.

neurology The study of the structure (neuroanatomy), function (neurophysiology), and diseases (neuropathology) of the *nervous system. A neurologist specializes in the diagnosis and treatment of nervous diseases.

neurone (*or* **nerve cell**) The functioning unit of the *nervous system. A neurone consists of a cell body, containing the nucleus; small irregular branching processes called dendrites; and a single long nerve fibre, or axon, which may be ensheathed by layers of fatty material (myelin) and either makes contact with other neurones at *synapses or ends at muscle fibres or gland cells. When a neurone is stimulated from outside or by another neurone, a nerve impulse is transmitted electrochemically down the axon. Bundles of nerve fibres are bound together to form **nerves**, which transmit impulses from sense organs to the brain or spinal cord (sensory nerves) or outwards from the central nervous system to a muscle or gland (motor nerves).

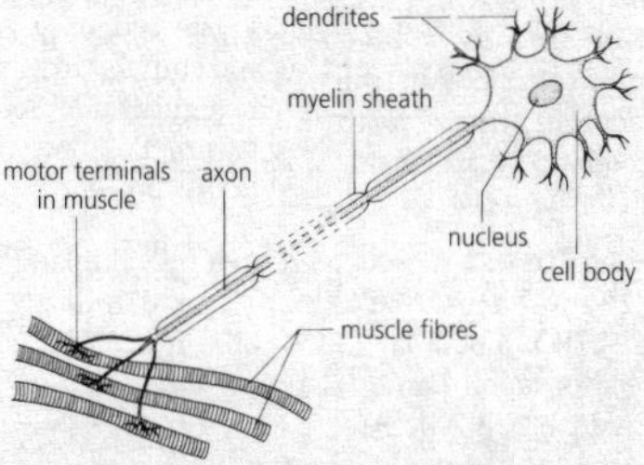

neurone. When a nerve impulse transmitted down the axon of a neurone reaches the motor terminals in muscle fibres, the muscle is stimulated to contract.

Neuroptera An order of slender carnivorous insects (4500 species) with long antennae and two similar pairs of net-veined wings. The order includes the *alderflies, snakeflies, and dobsonflies (suborder *Megaloptera*) and the *lacewings and *antlions (suborder *Plannipennia*).

neurosis (*or* **psychoneurosis**) A mental illness in which insight is retained but behaviour is disordered, causing suffering to the patient (*compare* PSYCHOSIS). The symptoms include a pathologically severe emotional state, as in anxiety or *depression; distressing behaviour and thoughts, as in *phobias or obsessions; and physical complaints, as in *hysteria. Neuroses are now often referred to as **anxiety disorders**. Treatment can include *tranquillizers, *psychotherapy, and behaviour therapy (*see* BEHAVIOURISM).

neutrinos A group of three elementary particles and their antiparticles. They are classified as leptons, have no charge, and are probably massless. One type of neutrino is associated with the *electron, one with the *muon, and one with the tau particle.

neutron An elementary particle that is a constituent of all atomic nuclei except hydrogen-1. It has no electric charge and its mass is slightly greater than that of the *proton. Inside the nucleus the neutron is stable but when free it decays, with a mean life of 12 minutes, by the *weak interaction to a proton, an electron, and an antineutrino (*see* BETA DECAY). The neutron was discovered by *Chadwick in 1932. *See also* PARTICLE PHYSICS.

neutron bomb *See* NUCLEAR WEAPONS.

neutron star A star that has undergone *gravitational collapse to the extent that most of the protons and electrons making up its constituent atoms have coalesced into neutrons. The density is extremely high (about 10^{17} kg m^{-3}) and the pressure exerted by the densely packed neutrons can support the star against further contraction. Neutron stars are thought to form when the mass of the stellar core remaining after a *supernova exceeds about 1.4 times the sun's mass. *See also* PULSAR.

Nevada One of the mountain states in the W USA. Lying almost wholly within the Great Basin, most of the state consists of a vast plateau with several mountain ranges. Most of its population and manufacturing industry is located in the two main cities of Las Vegas and Reno. Tourism is by far the most important industry. *History*: ceded by Mexico to the USA in 1848, it became a state (1864) during a mining boom (1860–80). Area: 286 297 sq km (110 540 sq mi). Population (2000): 1 998 257. Capital: Carson City.

Nevis *See* ST KITTS-NEVIS, FEDERATION OF.

Newark 40 44N 74 11W A city in the USA, in New Jersey on Newark Bay. Founded in 1666, it attracted several inventors, whose developments included patent leather (1818), malleable cast iron (1826), the first photographic film (1888), and electrical measuring instruments (1888). Population (2000 est): 273 546.

New Britain A volcanic island in the SW Pacific Ocean, in Papua New Guinea, the largest of the Bismarck Archipelago. Copra and some minerals are exported. Area: 36 520 sq km (14 100 sq mi). Population (1999 est): 435 307. Chief town: Rabaul.

New Brunswick A province of E Canada, on the Gulf of St Lawrence. Heavily forested, it consists of rugged uplands with fertile river valleys. There is some mixed farming and fishing is important along the Bay of Fundy. Lead, zinc, and some copper are mined at Bathurst. *History*: settlement by French peasants ended shortly after Britain's control of the coastal areas was confirmed in 1713. Colonization from

Britain and New England followed, and New Brunswick became a separate colony (1784). It was a founding member of the Dominion of Canada (1867). Area: 72 092 sq km (27 835 sq mi). Population (2001 est): 757 100; approximately 30% are French speaking. Capital: Fredericton.

New Caledonia (French name: Nouvelle Calédonie) An island in the SW Pacific Ocean. Together with its dependencies (the Isle of Pines, the Loyalty Islands, and others) it forms a French overseas territory. The main industries are nickel mining and processing and meat preserving. Violence in the 1980s led to a referendum (1987) on the issue of independence; the people voted to remain under French sovereignty. Area: 19 103 sq km (7374 sq mi), with dependencies. Population (2002 est): 218 000. Capital: Nouméa.

Newcastle 32 55S 151 46E A city in Australia, in New South Wales. Iron and steel industries are important. In 1989 it was hit by Australia's first fatal earthquake, killing 12 people. Population (1998 est): 139 171.

Newcastle, Thomas Pelham-Holles, 1st Duke of (1693–1768) British statesman; Whig prime minister (1754–56, 1757–62). He resigned as prime minister in 1756 because of early reverses in the *Seven Years' War but returned in 1757 with foreign affairs in the hands of Pitt the Elder. His brother **Henry Pelham** (1696–1754) was prime minister (1743–54).

Newcastle upon Tyne 1. 54 59N 1 35W A city in NE England, in Newcastle upon Tyne unitary authority, Tyne and Wear, on the River Tyne. It is the principal port and regional centre of NE England, with a 14th-century cathedral and two universities; cultural institutions include the Baltic Centre for Contemporary Art (2000). Industries include marine and electrical engineering. *History*: founded as a Roman settlement (Pons Aelius), Newcastle was the site of George Stephenson's iron works, established in 1823. Population (1991): 189 150. **2.** A unitary authority in NE England, in Tyne and Wear. Area: 112 sq km (43 sq mi). Population (2001): 259 573.

Newcomen, Thomas (1663–1729) English blacksmith, who in 1712 constructed an early steam engine. It was based on Thomas Savery's engine and was widely used for pumping water out of mines.

New Deal (1933–41) Legislation introduced by the US president, F. D. Roosevelt, to ameliorate the effects of the Depression and to initiate social and economic reforms. Emergency legislation enabled sound banks to reopen and regulated credit, currency, and foreign exchange; the gold standard was abandoned and the dollar devalued. Loans on crops, credit, and refinancing of debts and mortgages supported farmers, while the unemployed were helped by direct relief and civil-works programmes.

New England 1. An area in the extreme NE USA, bordering on the Atlantic Ocean. It consists of the states of Maine, New Hampshire, Vermont, Massachusetts, Rhode Island, and Connecticut. Explored and named by Capt John Smith (1614), it was first settled by the Puritans (1620). Area: about 164 000 sq km (63 300 sq mi). **2.** A district of Australia, in New South Wales. Predominantly agricultural, it occupies the N Tableland between the Moonbi Range and the Queensland border.

New Forest A woodland area in S England, in Hampshire. Originally an ancient hunting forest, it is a popular tourist area, noted for its breed of small ponies. It was designated a national park in 2001. Area: 336 sq km (130 sq mi).

Newfoundland A province of E Canada, consisting of the sparsely populated Coast of *Labrador on the Atlantic Ocean and the triangular island of Newfoundland. Pulp and paper has replaced the declining fisheries as the major industry. *History*: discovered by John Cabot (1497), Newfoundland won representative government (1832) and developed steadily until World War I, when it became a dominion. In 1927 it won possession of Labrador's interior and in 1949 became the newest Canadian province. Area: 370 485 sq km (143 044 sq mi). Population (2001 est): 533 800. Capital: St John's.

Newfoundland dog A breed of working dog originating in Newfoundland. The heavy dense black, brown, or black-and-white coat enables them to withstand icy water. Height: 71 cm (dogs); 66 cm (bitches).

New Guinea An island in the SW Pacific Ocean, separated from Australia by the Torres Strait. It consists of the Indonesian province of Irian Jaya in the W and *Papua New Guinea in the E. Mountainous and forested, it is largely undeveloped and is famed for its unique species of butterflies and birds. Its linguistically diverse tribal population consists of Melanesian, Negrito, and Papuan ethnic groups. *History*: known to Europeans from 1511, the island was colonized by the Dutch in the 18th century. The W part became part of Indonesia in 1963. The SE was colonized by Britain and the NE by Germany in the late 19th century. Area: 775 213 sq km (299 310 sq mi). Population (2002 est): 7 646 934.

New Hampshire A state in the NE USA, in New England. It is generally hilly, with many lakes. Manufacturing is the principal source of employment. Tourism is the other major industry. *History*: one of the 13 original colonies, it was first settled by English colonists about 1627, becoming a royal province in 1679. One of the first states to declare its independence, it became a state in 1788. Area: 24 097 sq km (9304 sq mi). Population (2000): 1 235 786. Capital: Concord.

New Haven 41 18N 72 55W A city and seaport in the USA, in Connecticut on Long Island Sound. It is best known as the site of Yale University (1701). Population (2000): 123 626.

New Jersey A state in the NE USA, on the mid-Atlantic coast. The Kittatinny Mountains extend across the NW corner of the state, SE of which lies a belt of lowland containing most of New Jersey's major cities. One of the most highly urbanized and densely populated states, it is a major industrial centre. Agriculture is also well developed. Its beaches, forests, and mountain regions form the basis of a thriving tourist industry. *History*: one of the original 13 colonies, it was first settled by the Dutch in the 1620s, coming under British control in 1664. It became a state in 1787. Area: 20 295 sq km (7836 sq mi). Population (2000): 8 414 350. Capital: Trenton.

Newman, John Henry, Cardinal (1801–90) British churchman, a leader of the *Oxford Movement until his conversion to Roman Catholicism (1845). He wrote many tracts, including the controversial *Tract 90*, which argued that the Thirty-Nine Articles were not incompatible with Roman Catholicism. Later works include his spiritual autobiography, *Apologia pro vita sua* (1864). He was made a cardinal in 1879. In 1991 he was awarded the title 'venerable', the first step towards canonization.

Newman, Paul (1925–) US film actor. He has frequently played the roles of cynical and witty heroes, notably in *Hud* (1963), *Butch Cassidy and the Sundance Kid* (1969), and *The Sting* (1973); among his other films are *The Verdict* (1982), *The Color of Money* (1986), and *Road to Perdition* (2002).

Newmarket 52 15N 0 25E A market town in E England, in Suffolk. It is the centre of British horse racing. Population (1991): 16 498.

New Mexico One of the mountain states in the SW USA. There are three main physical regions: a flat tableland in the E, a central mountainous region cut N–S by the Valley of the Rio Grande, and a region of mountains and plains in the W. Its oil and natural-gas deposits are important. Problems of irrigation are mitigated by the Rio Grande and the Pecos rivers. Tourism is an important source of revenue. *History*: a Spanish possession from the 16th century, it was under Mexican rule when it was annexed by the USA in 1848. Following a period of Indian wars and land disputes, it became a state (1912). Area: 315 113 sq km (121 666 sq mi). Population (2000): 1 819 046. Capital: Santa Fe.

New Model Army The parliamentary army formed in 1645 during the English *Civil War. Organized by Sir Thomas Fairfax (1612–71), its core comprised the forces of the Eastern Association led by Oliver *Cromwell. It wielded increasing political power after its success at *Naseby (1645). In 1650 Cromwell became its commander in chief.

New Orleans 30 00N 90 03W A city and major port in the USA, in Louisiana. It is one of the leading commercial and industrial centres of the South. The Vieux Carré (French Quarter) has many historic buildings. The famous Mardi Gras festival is held here annually. *History*: founded in 1718, New Orleans became the capital of the French colonial region of Louisiana before passing to Spain in 1763. It returned briefly to France in 1803 but passed to the USA in the same year. Jazz originated among Black musicians of New Orleans during the late 19th century. Population (2000): 484 674.

New Plymouth 39 03S 174 04E A port in New Zealand, in W North Island. New Zealand's chief natural gas field is nearby, at Kapuni. Population (1995 est): 49 800.

Newport 50 42N 1 18W A market town and port in S England, the administrative centre of the Isle of Wight. Nearby are Carisbrooke Castle and Parkhurst Prison. Population (1991): 20 574.

Newport (Welsh name: Casnewydd ar Wysg) **1.** 51 35N 3 00W A port in SE Wales, in Newport county borough. Its parish church became the cathedral for the Monmouth diocese in 1921. Population (1991): 115 522. **2.** A county borough in SE Wales, created in 1996 from part of Gwent. Area: 190 sq km (73 sq mi). Population (2001): 137 017.

Newry 54 11N 6 20W A port in Northern Ireland, in County Down on Carlingford Lough. Close to the border with the Republic, it has suffered from sectarian violence. It was granted city status in 2002. Population (1991): 82 943.

Newry and Mourne A district in Northern Ireland, in Co Down. Area: 886 sq km (342 sq mi). Population (2001): 87 058.

New Siberian Islands (Russian name: Novosïbirskiye Ostrova) A Russian archipelago off the N coast, between the Laptev Sea and the East Siberian Sea. There is no permanent population. Total area: 35 100 sq km (13 549 sq mi), including the Lyakhov Islands.

New South Wales A state of SE Australia, bordering on the Pacific Ocean. It consists of extensive plains in the W, separated from the narrow coastal belt by the *Great Dividing Range with the *Snowy Mountains and part of the Australian Alps in the SE. Agricultural products include beef cattle, cereals, fruit and vegetables, wool, and dairy produce. Fishing and forestry are also important. Minerals extracted include coal, silver, lead, zinc, and copper. Over half the population live in Sydney, where most of the industries are located. Area: 801 428 sq km (309 433 sq mi). Population (1999 est): 6 441 680. Capital: Sydney.

newt A salamander belonging to a family (*Salamandridae*) occurring in Europe, Asia, and North America. The European smooth newt (*Triturus vulgaris*) is greenish brown with dark-brown spots and has a black-spotted orange belly. It grows to a length of 10 cm (including a 5 cm tail). Newts live mainly on land, hibernating under stones in winter and returning to water to breed in spring. The European fire salamander (*Salamandra salamandra*) bears live young and produces a poisonous skin secretion when harmed.

New Testament The 27 books that constitute the second major division of the Christian *Bible. Written in Greek, the New Testament has four divisions: the four Gospels (*Matthew, *Mark, *Luke, and *John); the Acts of the Apostles; the *Epistles, mainly written by St Paul; and the Book of *Revelation. It was written between about 50 and 100 AD.

newton (N) The SI unit of force defined as the force required to give a mass of one kilogram an acceleration of one metre per second per second. Named after Sir Isaac *Newton.

Newton, Sir Isaac (1642–1727) British physicist and mathematician. His first discovery was the law of gravitation, apocryphally inspired by the realization that an apple falling from a tree is attracted by the same force that holds the moon in orbit. Gravitation required a precise definition of force, and this Newton also supplied in his laws of motion (*see* NEWTONIAN MECHANICS). Newton's second major work was the invention of the calculus; *Leibniz and Newton bickered for some years as to who had the idea first. His third contribution was in optics: he recognized that white light is a mixture of coloured lights, which can be separated by refraction. His incorrect belief that this effect could not be corrected, when it occurs as the chromatic aberration of a lens, inspired him to invent the reflecting telescope. Newton's principal publications were *Philosophiae naturalis principia mathematica* (1686–87) and *Optics* (1704), which held that light is a corpuscular phenomenon. He was president of the Royal Society from 1703 until his death.

Newtonian mechanics The branch of *mechanics concerned with systems in which the results of *quantum theory and the theory of *relativity can be ignored. It is based on Newton's three laws of motion. The first law states that a body remains at rest or moves with constant velocity in a straight line unless acted upon by a *force. The second law states that the *acceleration (a) of a body is proportional to the force (f) causing it. The constant of proportionality is the mass (m) of the body: $f = ma$. The third law states that the action of a force always produces a reaction in the body. The reaction is of equal magnitude but opposite in direction to the action.

Newton's rings A series of light and dark rings formed in a plano-convex lens if monochromatic light is shone onto the lens when it rests on a plane mirror. First observed by *Newton, they are caused by *interference between light reflected by the mirror and light reflected at the curved surface of the lens.

Newtownabbey A district in Northern Ireland, in Co Antrim. Area: 156 sq km (60 sq mi). Population (2001): 79 995.

New Wave (*or* **Nouvelle Vague**) A movement in French cinema that began in the late 1950s, characterized by a rejection of Hollywood conventions. Directors associated with the movement include *Godard, *Chabrol, and *Truffaut.

New World A name for the American continent, used especially by early emigrants from Europe and in describing the geographical distribution of plants and animals. By contrast, Europe, Africa, and Asia are sometimes referred to as the **Old World**.

New World monkey A *monkey native to the Americas. There are two families: the *Cebidae* (37 species) including uakaris, sakis, titis, howlers, capuchins, *squirrel monkeys, spider monkeys, woolly monkeys, and the douroucouli; and the *Callithricidae* (33 species) containing *marmosets and *tamarins.

New York 1. 40 45N 74 00W The largest city in the USA, situated in New York state at the mouth of the Hudson River. Divided into five boroughs—Manhattan, Brooklyn, the Bronx, Queens, and Richmond (coextensive with Staten Island), it is the nation's leading seaport. As one of the world's financial centres (*see* WALL STREET), it is the site of many large corporations and the New York and American Stock Exchanges. Notable features include Central Park, the fashionable shops of Fifth Avenue, the *Statue of Liberty, Times Square, Greenwich Village, the Brooklyn Bridge (1883), Rockefeller Center, St Patrick's Cathedral (1858–79), and a large number of skyscrapers, such as the Empire State Building (1931) and the United Nations Headquarters (1951). As well as the Broadway theatre district, there are numerous museums, art galleries, and libraries. *History*: on 3 September 1609, Henry Hudson sailed into New York Bay and his glowing reports attracted its founding Dutch colonists, who arrived in 1620. In 1625 New Amsterdam, situated at the S tip of Manhattan, became the capital of the newly established colony of New Netherland and the following year the whole island was bought from the Indians for the equivalent of $24. In 1664 the city was captured by the English for the Duke of York and promptly renamed. From 1789 until 1790 it was the first capital of the USA. The opening of the Erie Canal in 1825 ensured its pre-eminence as a commercial city and seaport. Early in the 20th century the arrival of millions of European immigrants supplied New York with limitless cheap labour. During the mid-1970s New York was narrowly saved from bankruptcy by emergency loans. In the 1970s and 1980s it acquired a reputation for street violence, but this was reduced in the later 1990s. On *September 11 2001 New York saw the destruction of one of its great landmarks, the *World Trade Center, in a terrorist outrage that cost nearly 3000 lives. Population (2000): 8 008 278. **2.** A state in the NE USA. It is basically an upland region, dissected by the valleys of the Mohawk and Hudson Rivers. New York is the chief manufacturing state in the USA. The presence of New York City also makes it the commercial, financial, and cultural centre of the nation. The most important agricultural activity is dairying. *History*: one of the 13 original colonies, it was first settled by the Dutch in the early 17th century. It became an English colony in 1664 and later played a prominent role in the American Revolution. Area: 128 402 sq km (49 576 sq mi). Population (2000): 18 976 457. Capital: Albany.

New Zealand A country in the Pacific Ocean, to the SE of Australia. It consists of *North Island and *South Island, together with several smaller islands. Most of the population is of British descent with a large Maori minority. *Economy*: the main basis of the economy is livestock rearing, especially sheep farming. Mineral resources include coal, gold, limestone and silica sand. Tourism is the fastest growing economic activity. *History*: from about the 14th century the islands were inhabited by the Maoris, a Polynesian people. The first European to discover New Zealand was Tasman in 1642, who called it Staten Land, later changed to Nieuw Zealand; in 1769 the coast was explored by *Cook. During the early part of the 19th century it was used as a whaling and trading base. By the Treaty of *Waitangi in 1840 the Maori chiefs ceded sovereignty to Britain and a colony was established. After two wars with the Maoris over land rights, peace was reached in 1871. New Zealand was made a dominion in 1907 and became fully independent by the Statute of Westminster in 1931. Since World War II New Zealand has played an increasing role in international affairs, especially in the Far East. In 1985 relations with the USA were strained when the Labour government prohibited nuclear vessels from entering New Zealand waters. In 1990 the National Party was returned to office under James Bolger, who retained the premiership until 1997. The 1999 and 2002 general elections saw a victory for the Labour Party, led by Helen Clark. Official languages: English and Maori. Currency: New Zealand dollar of 100 cents. Area: 268 704 sq km (103 719 sq mi). Population (2003): 4 001 000. Capital: Wellington.

Nguni A division of the Bantu-speaking peoples of S Africa. It includes the *Swazi, *Xhosa, and *Zulu.

Niagara Falls Two waterfalls on the US–Canadian border, on the Niagara River. The American Falls, 51 m (167 ft) high and 300 m (1000 ft) wide, are straight while the Horseshoe Falls (Canada), 49 m (162 ft) high and 790 m (2600 ft) wide, are curved.

Niamey 13 32N 2 05E The capital (since 1926)

of Niger, on the River Niger. Population (1995 est): 495 000.

Nicaea, Councils of Two ecumenical councils of the Christian Church held at Nicaea, now Iznik (Turkey). **1.** (325) The council summoned by the Byzantine emperor Constantine to establish Church unity and suppress Arianism. The *Nicene Creed was the major doctrinal formulation. **2.** (787) The council summoned by the Byzantine empress Irene to condemn iconoclasm.

Nicaragua, Republic of A country in Central America between the Caribbean Sea and the Pacific Ocean. Swamp and dense tropical forest on the Caribbean coast, and a broader plain with lakes to the W, rise to a central mountain range. The population is mainly of mixed Indian and Spanish descent. *Economy*: chiefly agricultural, the main crops being cotton, coffee, peanuts, sugar, rice, and maize. Minerals include gold, silver, and copper. Oil and gas deposits are being explored. Economic hardship resulting from the civil war of the 1980s has continued to the present; there is a large external debt. *History*: sighted by Columbus in 1502, it was colonized by Spain from 1522, becoming part of the captaincy general of Guatemala. It broke away from Spain in 1821 and formed part of the Central American Federation until 1838, when Nicaragua became a republic. From 1933 the government was dominated by the Somoza family, opposition to which culminated in a civil war that forced (1979) the resignation of the president, Gen Anastasio Somoza Debayle (1925–80). The victorious Sandinista National Liberation Front (FSLN) under Daniel Ortega instituted socialist policies. Accusing the Sandinistas of supplying arms to the rebels in El Salvador, the USA supported an army of 'Contras' who attacked Nicaragua from neighbouring states. In 1990 Violeta Chamorro (1929–   ), heading the UNO coalition party, won an election against Ortega. A ceasefire was signed with the Contras in 1994. In late 1998 the country was devastated by Hurricane Mitch. Enrique Bolaño, a liberal, was elected president in 2002. Nicaragua is a member of the OAS and the Central American Common Market. Official language: Spanish. Currency: córdoba of 100 centavos. Area: 148 000 sq km (57 143 sq mi). Population (2003 est): 5 482 000. Capital: Managua.

Nice 43 42N 7 16E A city in SE France, the capital of the Alpes-Maritimes department. Ceded by Sardinia to France in 1860, it is one of the leading resorts of the French Riviera. Population (1999): 342 738.

Nicene Creed The statement of Christian belief accepted as orthodox by the first Council of *Nicaea (325). The Nicene Creed used in the *Eucharist service of Orthodox, Roman Catholic, and Protestant Churches is a version of this creed.

Nicholas I (1796–1855) Emperor of Russia (1825–55), notorious as an autocrat. Nicholas' accession was followed by the *Dekabrist revolt, which hardened his conservatism. His ambitions in the Balkans precipitated the *Crimean War.

Nicholas II (1868–1918) The last Emperor of Russia (1894–1917). Nicholas' ambition in Asia led to the unpopular *Russo-Japanese War, which in turn precipitated the *Revolution of 1905. Forced to accept the establishment of a representative assembly, Nicholas nevertheless continued attempts to rule autocratically. In 1915 he took supreme command of Russian forces in World War I, leaving Russia to the mismanagement of the Empress *Alexandra and *Rasputin. Following the Russian Revolution in 1917, Nicholas was forced to abdicate (March). He and his family were imprisoned by the Bolsheviks and executed at Ekaterinburg.

Nicholas, St (4th century AD) The patron saint of Russia, sailors, and children. He is thought to have been Bishop of Myra in Asia Minor. Legends telling of his gifts of gold to three poor girls for their dowries gave rise to the practice of exchanging gifts on his feast day, 6 Dec. This now happens on 25 Dec in most countries.

Nicholson, Ben (1894–1982) British artist. Some of his best abstract works were produced in the 1930s, while he was a member of the British art group Unit One (*see* NASH, PAUL). These include white-painted plaster reliefs of rectangles combined with circles.

Nicholson, Jack (1937–   ) US film actor. After success in *Easy Rider* (1969), he became a leading star. His films include *Chinatown* (1974), *Prizzi's Honour* (1985), *Batman* (1989), and *About Schmidt* (2002). He won Oscars for *One Flew Over the Cuckoo's Nest* (1976), *Terms of Endearment* (1983), and *As Good as It Gets* (1998).

nickel (Ni) A hard silvery metal similar to iron, discovered in 1751 by A.F. Cronstedt (1722–65). It occurs in nature chiefly as pentlandite, NiS, and pyrrhotite, (Fe,Ni)S. It is chemically similar to cobalt and copper, and forms a green oxide (NiO), the chloride ($NiCl_2$), the sulphate ($NiSO_4$), and other compounds. It is used widely in alloys, such as stainless steel, and in coinage. At no 28; at wt 58.6934; mp 1455°C; bp 2914°C.

Nicklaus, Jack William (1940–) US golfer, who has won more major titles than any other, including six Masters championships.

Nicopolis, Battle of (25 September 1396) The battle in which a coalition of Crusaders under Emperor Sigismund were defeated by the Turks under Sultan Bayezid I (1347–1403; reigned 1389–1403).

Nicosia (Greek name: Leukosía; Turkish name: Lefkosa) The capital of Cyprus, on the River Pedieas. Originally known as Ledra, it has been successively under Byzantine, Venetian, Turkish, and British control. Its many old buildings include the Cathedral of St Sophia (completed 1325). Population (1998 est): 230 935.

Nicotiana A genus of poisonous herbs (over 100 species), native to Central and South America and Australia. 30–300 cm in height, they bear large funnel- or bell-shaped flowers. Many species are cultivated for ornament and certain species are grown commercially for *tobacco. Family: *Solanaceae*.

nicotine ($C_{10}H_{14}N_2$) A toxic colourless oily liquid alkaloid that rapidly turns brown on exposure to air. It is obtained from the dried leaves of the tobacco plant and is present in small quantities in cigarettes. It is also used as an insecticide.

nicotinic acid *See* VITAMIN B COMPLEX.

Nielsen, Carl (August) (1865–1931) Danish composer and conductor. Nielsen developed the principle of progressive tonality in his six symphonies, of which the fourth, entitled *The Inextinguishable* (1914–16), and the fifth (1922) are the best known.

Niemeyer, Oscar (1907–) Brazilian architect. A disciple of *Le Corbusier, Niemeyer made a major contribution to the development of modern architecture in Brazil. His designs for Brasília include the president's palace (1959) and the cathedral (1964) and for Rio de Janeiro the Museum of Contemporary Arts (2001).

Niemöller, Martin (1892–1984) German Lutheran pastor and Protestant leader. A U-boat commander in World War I, he became head of the Pastors' Emergency League, which became the Confessing Church, and opposed the nazification of the Church in Germany. In 1937 he was sent to a concentration camp, where he remained until the end of the war.

Nietzsche, Friedrich (1844–1900) German philosopher. His first book, *The Birth of Tragedy* (1872), argued that Wagnerian opera was the successor to Greek drama. Nietzsche rejected Christian morality and argued that the "will to power" was the crucial human characteristic. In *Thus Spake Zarathustra* (1883–92), he eulogizes the man who is free, titanic, and powerful, an ideal adopted by the Nazis for the Aryan superman. After 1889 he was permanently insane.

Niger, Republic of A large landlocked country in West Africa, lying mainly in the Sahara. Approximately half the population are Hausa, with large porportions of Zerma, Songhai, and Fulani. *Economy*: agriculture, particularly livestock raising, is important but has suffered from repeated droughts. Mineral resources include salt, natron, tin, and uranium. The main exports are uranium, groundnuts, and livestock. *History*: occupied by France (1883–99), it became a territory of French West Africa in 1904. It won independence in 1960 and Hamani Diori became president. The country was under military rule from 1974 until 1993, when Mohamane Ousmane was elected president in free elections. In 1996 he was overthrown in a military coup; elections later that year were won by the coup leader, Brig Gen Ibrahim Barre Mainassara. In 1999 Mainassara was assassinated, parliament was suspended, and military rule imposed. Following elections in November, Tandja Mamadou became president. Official language: French. Currency: CFA franc of 100 centimes. Area: 1 186 408 sq km (458 075 sq mi). Population (2003 est): 11 380 000. Capital: Niamey.

Niger, River The third longest river in Africa. Rising in the S highlands of Guinea, it flows NE and then SE to the Gulf of Guinea. Length: 4183 km (2600 mi).

Niger-Congo languages An African language family spoken in central and S Africa. It is subdivided into six groups: the *West Atlantic languages; the Mande languages; the Voltaic languages; the Kwa languages; the Benue-Congo group, which includes the *Bantu languages; and the Adamawa-Eastern group.

Nigeria, Federal Republic of A large country in West Africa, on the Gulf of Guinea. Mangrove swamps along the coast give way to tropical rain forest inland, rising to open savanna-covered plateaus and mountains in the E. The inhabitants are mainly Hausa and Fulani in the N, Yoruba in the W, and Ibo in the E. *Economy*: oil production accounted for about

90% of exports in the late 1970s but declined dramatically thereafter, causing serious economic problems; Nigeria is a member of OPEC and still the world's fifth largest producer. There are also important reserves of natural gas, tin, coal, iron ore, and columbite. Agriculture is important; the main cash crops are groundnuts and cotton in the N and palms, coconut, and rubber in the S. *History*: in the middle ages there were highly developed kingdoms in the area, such as those of the Hausa in the N and the Yoruba in the SW. The coast was explored in the 15th century by the Portuguese, who developed the slave trade, in which the Dutch and English also participated. In 1861 Lagos was annexed by Britain and in 1886 the Royal Niger Company was incorporated to further British interests. By 1906, the British were in control of Nigeria, which was divided into the protectorate of Northern Nigeria and the colony (of Lagos) and protectorate of Southern Nigeria. These were united in 1914. Nigeria became a federation in 1954, gained independence in 1960, and became a republic within the Commonwealth in 1963. In 1967 the eastern region withdrew to form the Republic of *Biafra. Civil war followed, lasting until Biafra's surrender in 1970. A coup in 1985 brought Maj Gen Ibrahim Babangida to power. Democratic elections held in 1993 were annulled by Babangida, provoking a political crisis. Gen Sana Abacha subsequently seized power and abolished all democratic institutions. In 1995 Nigeria was suspended from the Commonwealth (until 1999). Following Abacha's death (1998) Gen Abdulsalam Abubakar became president, promising to restore civilian rule. Presidential elections in 1999 resulted in victory for Gen Olusegun Obsanjo amid claims of fraud; he was re-elected in 2003. Recent years have seen escalating ethnic and religious strife. Official language: English. Currency: naira of 100 kobo. Area: 923 773 sq km (356 669 sq mi). Population (2003 est): 125 275 000. Capital: Abuja.

nightingale A plump woodland bird, *Luscinia megarhynchos*, that winters in tropical Africa and breeds in S Europe and Asia Minor during the summer. It is about 16 cm long with reddish-brown plumage and pale underparts and feeds on ground insects and spiders. Nightingales are noted for their beautiful song. Family: *Turdidae* (thrushes).

Nightingale, Florence (1820–1910) British hospital reformer and founder of the nursing profession. On the outbreak of the Crimean War, in 1854, she volunteered to lead a party of nurses to work in the military hospitals. She set about transforming the appalling conditions, earning herself the title Lady with the Lamp from her patients. In 1860, she established the Nightingale School for Nurses at St Thomas's Hospital—the first of its kind.

nightjar A nocturnal bird belonging to a subfamily (*Caprimulginae*; 60–70 species) occurring in most temperate and tropical regions, also called goatsucker. About 30 cm long, nightjars have a soft mottled grey, brown, and rufous plumage and a long tail. Its short bill has a wide gape surrounded by long sensitive bristles enabling it to catch insects in flight. Family: *Caprimulgidae*; order: *Caprimulgiformes* (frogmouths, nightjars, etc.).

nightshade One of several plants of the family *Solanaceae*. The most notorious is *deadly nightshade (*or* belladonna). The **woody nightshade**, or bittersweet (*Solanum dulcamara*), is a scrambling shrubby perennial, up to 2 m tall, of Eurasia and N Africa. It has small purple-lobed flowers and its red berries are poisonous. The **black nightshade** (*S. nigrum*) is an annual, up to 50 cm high. It has poisonous black berries. The unrelated **enchanter's nightshade** (*Circaea lutetiana*), of Eurasia, is a herbaceous perennial of shady places. Up to 60 cm tall, it has a terminal spike of tiny white flowers. Family: *Onagraceae*.

nihilism A political or philosophical view that rejects all traditional values and institutions. *Turgenev invented the label in his *Fathers and Sons* (1861).

Niigata 37 58N 139 2E A city in Japan, in NW Honshu. It is the main port for the Sea of Japan. Population (1995): 494 785.

Nijinsky, Vaslav (1890–1950) Russian ballet dancer. In 1909 he joined Diaghilev's company in Paris, and quickly achieved an international reputation. Michel *Fokine created *Petrushka*, *Scheherazade*, and other ballets for him, and from 1913 he also began to choreograph himself. He retired in 1919 suffering from schizophrenia.

Nikolaev 46 57N 32 00E A port in S Ukraine, at the confluence of the Rivers Bug and Ingul. Long a naval base, it has important shipbuilding industries. Population (1998 est): 517 900.

Nile, Battle of the (1 August 1798) A naval battle in which the British, under *Nelson, defeated the French during Napoleon's invasion of Egypt (*see* REVOLUTIONARY AND NAPOLEONIC WARS). This engagement gave Britain control of the Mediterranean.

Nile, River A river in N Africa, the longest in the world. The longest of its three main tributaries, the White Nile, rises in Burundi and flows N through Lake Victoria and Lake Mobutu. At Khartoum it is joined by the Blue Nile (which rises in the Ethiopian highlands) and later by the River Atbara before flowing through a broad delta into the Mediterranean Sea. The Nile's annual floodwaters have supported cultivation on its floodplains since ancient times. Vast dams have also been constructed, including the Aswan Dam and *Aswan High Dam. Length: 6741 km (4187 mi).

Nilo-Saharan languages A widely varied family of African languages. It includes the Nilotic languages of the Chari-Nile group, such as Dinka and Nuer.

nimbostratus A form of *cloud common in temperate latitudes. Dark grey and solid in appearance it has a low base but may show extensive vertical development. Precipitation of snow or rain is often prolonged although not usually heavy.

Nîmes 43 50N 4 21E A city in S France, the capital of the Gard department. An important Roman settlement, it was a Protestant stronghold (16th–17th centuries). Population (1999): 133 424.

Nimrod A legendary biblical figure described in Genesis as a mighty hunter. He founded a Mesopotamian kingdom that included the cities of Babel, Erech, and Akkad and is credited with building the cities of Nineveh and Kalhu (modern Nimrud).

Nimrud An Assyrian capital (ancient Kalhu) near Mosul (Iraq). Founded about 1250 BC it was destroyed by the Medes in 612 BC. Excavations (1845–51) by Sir Austen Layard (1817–94) of the 9th-century city yielded gigantic sculptures and *cuneiform tablets.

Nineveh An Assyrian capital (modern Kuyunjik) near Mosul (Iraq). Nineveh was made cocapital with Nimrud by Sennacherib (c. 700 BC). The Medes sacked it in 612 BC. Sir Austen Layard's great find here was the library of Ashurbanipal.

Ningbo (*or* **Ning-po**) 29 54N 121 33E A river port in E China, in Zhejiang province. Important for overseas trade (5th–9th centuries), it was also a religious centre. Population (1999 est): 704 819.

Niobe In Greek mythology, the daughter of Tantalus and wife of the King of Thebes. After her many children were killed by Apollo and Artemis, she was changed by Zeus into a stone column or statue, the face of which was said continually to shed tears.

niobium (Nb) A soft ductile white metal, discovered in 1801. It was formerly known as columbium in the USA. Niobium is used in specialist alloys in spacecraft, and at low temperatures it has superconducting properties. Its compounds include the white oxide (Nb_2O_5) and the volatile fluoride and chloride (NbF_5, $NbCl_5$). At no 41; at wt 92.9064; mp 2469 ± 10°C; bp 4744°C.

nirvana The supreme goal of Buddhism, in which liberation from the limitations of existence and rebirth are attained through the extinction of desire. In Hinduism nirvana also means spiritual release in the sense of freedom from reincarnation or union with God or the Absolute.

Niš 43 20N 21 54E A city in Serbia and Montenegro, in E Serbia. For five centuries to 1877 it was a centre for Serbian resistance to Turkish control. Population (2000 est): 182 583.

Nishinomiya 34 44N 135 22E A city in Japan, in S Honshu. It is traditionally known for its *sake* (rice wine). Population (1995): 390 388.

Niterói 22 54S 43 06W A city in SE Brazil, opposite the city of Rio de Janeiro. It is a popular resort. Population (2000): 458 465.

nitric acid (HNO_3) A fuming corrosive liquid made by the oxidation of ammonia by air in the presence of a platinum catalyst or the action of sulphuric acid on sodium or potassium nitrate. It is used in the manufacture of fertilizers and explosives.

nitrogen (N) A colourless odourless gas, discovered by D. Rutherford (1749–1819) in 1772. It makes up 78% of the earth's atmosphere by volume. The element exists as diatomic molecules (N_2) bonded very strongly together. It forms a range of chemical compounds including ammonia (NH_3), the oxides (N_2O, NO, N_2O_3, NO_2, N_2O_5), nitric acid (HNO_3), and many nitrates (for example $NaNO_3$). Liquid nitrogen has a wide range of cryogenic applications. Ammonia (NH_3) and nitrates are of great importance as fertilizers. At no 7; at wt 14.0067; mp −210.0°C; bp −195.8°C.

nitrogen cycle The sequence of processes by which nitrogen and its compounds are utilized in nature. Nitrogen gas in the air is converted (fixed) to ammonia by certain soil bacteria and fertilizer manufacturers (*see* NITROGEN FIXATION). Nitrifying bacteria in the roots of leguminous plants convert ammonia

n

to nitrites and then to nitrates, which are used by plants to manufacture amino acids. When animals eat plants some of this nitrogenous plant material is incorporated into animal tissues. Nitrogenous excretory products and dead organic matter decompose to produce ammonia, so completing the cycle.

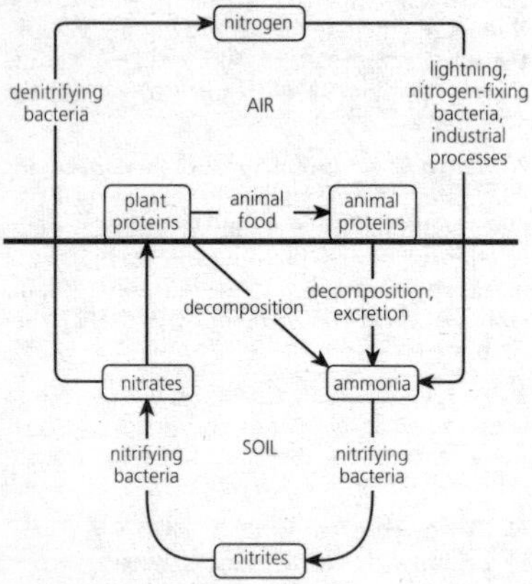

nitrogen cycle

n

nitrogen fixation The conversion of atmospheric nitrogen gas into nitrogen compounds. The process occurs naturally by the action of bacteria in the roots of leguminous plants (*see* NITROGEN CYCLE). Industrial methods of fixing atmospheric nitrogen are of immense importance in the manufacture of nitrogen fertilizers.

nitroglycerin ($C_3H_5(NO_3)_3$) A yellow oily highly *explosive liquid. It is used as an explosive either alone or as *dynamite or *gelignite.

Niven, David (1909–83) British film actor. His early films include *The Prisoner of Zenda* (1937) and *Wuthering Heights* (1939), and he later appeared in many stylish comedies and action films, including *Separate Tables* (1958). He published two volumes of autobiography, *The Moon's a Balloon* (1972) and *Bring on the Empty Horses* (1975).

Nixon, Richard Milhous (1913–94) US statesman; Republican president (1969–74). He contributed to *McCarthy's anticommunist investigations and was Eisenhower's vice president from 1953 until 1960, when he became the Republican presidential candidate. As president he reduced US troop commitments abroad and in 1973 ended US military involvement in Vietnam. In 1972 he paid a successful visit to the People's Republic of China. Participation in illegal efforts to ensure re-election in 1972 and the subsequent cover-up attempt led to the *Watergate scandal. Under threat of impeachment he became the first president to resign office.

Nizhnii Novgorod (name from 1932 until 1991: Gorkii) 56 20N 44 00E A city in central Russia on the Rivers Oka and Volga. It is an important industrial city and was renamed in 1932 in honour of the writer Maksim Gorki. Population (1999 est): 1 364 900.

Nizhnii Tagil 58 00N 59 58E A city in Russia, on the E slopes of the Ural Mountains. Its metallurgical industries arise from the surrounding ironmining region. Population (1999 est): 395 800.

Nkrumah, Kwame (1909–72) Ghanaian statesman; prime minister (1957–60) and then president (1960–66). He formed (1949) the Convention People's Party, which with a policy of noncooperation with the British took the Gold Coast to independence as Ghana in 1957. Nkrumah was deposed by a military coup in 1966.

No A form of Japanese theatre. It is performed with a minimum of scenery and properties and is characterized by the use of dance, mime, and masks. The acting is highly stylized.

Nobel, Alfred Bernhard (1833–96) Swedish chemist and businessman. From his invention of dynamite (1866) and a smokeless gunpowder (1889) and his exploitation of the Baku oilfields he amassed a considerable fortune, leaving £1.75 million as a foundation for the **Nobel Prizes**. There are now six awards: for physics, chemistry, physiology or medicine, literature, peace, and economics.

nobelium (No) A synthetic transuranic element discovered in 1957 by bombarding curium with carbon ions in an accelerator. Five isotopes with short half-lives have been discovered. Named after Alfred Nobel. At no 102; at wt (259).

noble gases (*or* **inert gases**) The elements forming group O of the *periodic table: helium, neon, argon, krypton, xenon, and radon. All are colourless odourless tasteless gases, which are slightly soluble in water. For many years they were thought to be chemically inert. The first compound of xenon was discovered in 1962, since when fluorides and oxygen fluorides of xenon, krypton, and radon have been prepared.

noctule An insect-eating *bat, *Nyctalus noc-*

tula, of Eurasia. About 12 cm long, it has bright-chestnut fur and long narrow wings. Noctules hibernate only from Dec to Jan. Family: *Vespertilionidae*.

Nolan, Sir Sidney (1917–92) Australian painter. He is known for his paintings of Australian historical figures, such as Ned *Kelly, and landscapes of the outback.

Nonconformists In its original early-17th-century sense, the term referred to members of the Church of England who did not conform with its rituals. After the Act of Uniformity (1662), the term's scope widened to include members of dissenting Protestant sects, such as the Quakers and Methodists.

noradrenaline (*or* **norepinephrine**) A hormone secreted by the core (medulla) of the adrenal glands. A *catecholamine, structurally similar to *adrenaline, it produces different effects in certain target organs, especially the heart, the rate of which it decreases. Noradrenaline is stored by cells of the sympathetic nervous system and released by nerve endings to excite adjacent nerves in the transmission of impulses. In the hypothalamus it is thought to inhibit transmission of impulses.

Norfolk 1. 36 54N 76 18W A seaport in the USA, in Virginia on Hampton Roads. Founded in 1682, it suffered considerable damage in the American Revolution and the US Civil War. Population (2000): 243 403. **2.** A county of E England, in East Anglia. It is mainly low lying, with fens in the W and the Norfolk *Broads in the E. It is mainly agricultural. Tourism is important. Area: 2763 sq km (1067 sq mi). Population (2001): 796 733. Administrative centre: Norwich.

Norfolk, Thomas Howard, 3rd Duke of (1473–1554) English statesman. He became president of the privy council in 1529 and in 1536 suppressed the *Pilgrimage of Grace. He lost power after the execution of his niece Catherine Howard (1542) and was imprisoned (1546–53) for involvement in the alleged treason (1546) of his son Henry Howard, Earl of *Surrey. Surrey's son **Thomas Howard, 4th Duke of Norfolk** (1538–72) was imprisoned (1559–60) by Elizabeth I for planning to marry Mary, Queen of Scots. He subsequently plotted against Elizabeth and was executed.

Norfolk Island 29 05S 167 59E A mountainous Australian island in the SW Pacific Ocean, formerly a British penal colony. Area: 36 sq km (14 sq mi). Population (1993): 2665. Chief town: Kingston.

Norman conquest (1066–72) The conquest of England by William, Duke of Normandy (*see* WILLIAM (I) THE CONQUEROR). After defeating Harold II at the battle of Hastings (1066), William captured London and was crowned. English risings were suppressed by 1070 and with the defeat of the Scots in 1072 the conquest was complete. The English lay and ecclesiastical aristocracy was replaced by Normans and other continentals and *feudalism was introduced. Latin became the language of government and Norman French, the literary language; Norman influence was also felt in church and architecture.

Normandy (French name: Normandie) A former province in N France, on the English Channel. *History*: during the medieval period Normandy flourished. William II, Duke of Normandy, conquered England (1066) to become William I of England. Subsequently disputed between England and France, it finally reverted to France in 1449. During World War II it suffered severe damage.

Normans Viking settlers in N France (later Normandy) whose rule, under their leader Rollo, was formally recognized (911) by Charles the Simple (879–929; reigned 898–923). By the end of the 11th century they had also conquered England (*see* NORMAN CONQUEST) and much of S Italy and Sicily and had established crusading states in the E, besides gaining a foothold in Wales and Scotland. Noted for their military inventiveness, they adopted and adapted existing administrative practices in countries they conquered with great success.

Norrköping 58 35N 16 10E A port in SE Sweden, on an inlet of the Baltic Sea. Population (2000 est): 122 212.

North, Frederick, Lord (1732–92) British statesman; prime minister (1770–82). As prime minister, he was criticized for precipitating the *American Revolution (1775–83), and eventually resigned.

North America The N part of the American double continent. For purposes of natural geography, this comprises the whole continent as far S as the Isthmus of Panama, including the Caribbean and the Canadian Arctic islands and Greenland. The W part is occupied by mountain chains (the Cascades, Rocky Mountains, Sierra Madre) surrounding arid high plateaus. The central part is the Great Plains and Mississippi basin. The Appalachian Mountains in the E are separated from the Canadian Shield by the Great Lakes. Area: over 24 000 000 sq km (9 500 000 sq mi). Population (2000 est): 440 000 000.

North American Free Trade Agreement (NAFTA) A treaty signed in 1993 by the USA, Canada, and Mexico to establish free trade with each other. All trade tariffs will be removed, those on certain agricultural products being gradually phased out.

North American Indian languages A geographical classification of the languages of the indigenous peoples of North America. It is estimated that these languages originally numbered about 300. Edward Sapir (1884–1939) arranged them into six phyla (1929): Eskimo-Aleut; Algonkian-Wakashan; Na-Dené; Penutian; Hokan-Siouan; and Aztec-Tanoan.

North American Indians A group of peoples of North America, mistakenly believed to be inhabitants of the Indian subcontinent when first encountered by Columbus. In common with other American Indians, they are probably descended from migrants who arrived from Asia some 20 000 years ago. Their traditional cultures range from that of warlike hunters and gatherers to peaceful cultivators. Social organization is usually based on kinship.

Northampton 52 14N 0 54W A town in England. Administrative centre of Northamptonshire, it is a centre of the footwear industry. Population (1997 est): 193 000.

n

Northamptonshire (*or* **Northants**) A county in the East Midlands of England. A ridge of gentle hills runs NE–SW. It is predominantly agricultural. Industry includes shoe making, food processing, and engineering. Area: 2367 sq km 915 sq mi). Population (2001 est): 629 676. Administrative centre: Northampton.

North Atlantic Treaty Organization (NATO) An alliance formed in 1949 by Belgium, Canada, Denmark, France, Iceland, Italy, Luxembourg, the Netherlands, Norway, Portugal, the UK, and the USA; Greece and Turkey joined in 1952, West Germany in 1955, Spain in 1982, and the united Germany in 1990. It was formed during the *Cold War to guard against possible Soviet aggression. All member states are bound to protect any member against attack. Its secretariat headquarters is in Brussels and its military headquarters in Norfolk, Virginia, and near Mons, Belgium. In 1991 NATO began to forge links with the former Eastern-bloc nations, many of which joined a "partnership for peace." In 1997 Russia gained a voice in NATO in return for accepting NATO's expansion into eastern Europe. The Czech Republic, Poland, and Hungary joined in 1999; Bulgaria, Estonia, Latvia, Lithuania, Romania, Slovakia, and Slovenia joined in 2004. In 1995 NATO carried out air strikes against Serb positions around Sarajevo, its first-ever aggressive action; in 1999 it undertook a major air campaign against Serbia (*see* KOSOVO).

North Ayrshire A council area of W central Scotland on the Firth of Clyde, comprising part of the historic county of Ayrshire, including the Isle of Arran. Absorbed into Strathclyde Region in 1975, it became an independent unitary authority in 1996. Tourism and fishing are important. Area: 884 sq km (341 sq mi). Population (2001): 135 817. Administrative centre: Irvine.

North Carolina A state in the USA, on the S Atlantic coast. The extensive coastal plain stretches westwards to the Piedmont Plateau and the Appalachian Mountains in the E. It is heavily populated and the leading industrial state in the South. *History*: one of the 13 original colonies, it shares its early history with South Carolina. It was made a separate colony in 1713 and it became a state in 1789. It was a supporter of the Confederate cause in the US Civil War. Area: 136 197 sq km (52 586 sq mi). Population (2000): 8 049 313. Capital: Raleigh.

North Dakota A state in the N central USA. It comprises three main physical regions: the Red River Valley along the E border, the Central Lowlands just W of this strip, and the Great Plains in the SW. Agriculture and mining are the two principal economic activities. *History*: early attempts to settle were made by Scottish and Irish families at Pembina in 1812. It formed part of the territory of Dakota from 1861 until 1889 when it was made a separate state. Area: 183 022 sq km (70 665 sq mi). Population (2000): 642 200. Capital: Bismarck.

North Down A district in Northern Ireland, in Co Down. Area: 82 sq km (32 sq mi). Population (2001): 76 323.

Northeast Caucasian languages A group of about 25 languages of the NE region of the Caucasus, also called the Nakho-Dagestanian family. Chechen, the most important, is part of the Nakh subdivision.

North East Lincolnshire A unitary authority in NE England, in Lincolnshire; formerly (1975–96) part of the county of Humberside. Area: 192 sq km (74 sq mi). Population (2001): 157 983.

Northeast Passage (Russian name: Severny Morskoy Put) The sea route along the N Eurasian coast, kept open in summer by Soviet icebreakers. It was first traversed by the Swedish explorer, Niels Nordenskjöld (1878–79). *See also* NORTHWEST PASSAGE.

Northern Ireland *See* IRELAND.

Northern Lights *See* AURORA.

Northern Territory An administrative division of N central Australia. It consists chiefly of a plateau with Arnhem Land in the N and the Macdonnell Ranges in the S. Close to the geographical centre of the continent stands *Ayers Rock. The main agricultural activity is the rearing of beef cattle. Minerals are important, especially uranium, iron ore, manganese, copper, gold, and bauxite. In 1978 the Northern Territory became an independent state, but the federal government retained control over uranium. Area: 1 346 200 sq km (519 770 sq mi). Population (1999 est): 192 880. Capital: Darwin.

Northern War, Great (1700–21) The war fought for Baltic supremacy between Russia, Denmark, and Poland on one side, and Sweden on the other. After the death of Charles XII of Sweden (1718), the war between Denmark, Poland, and Sweden was ended by the Treaties of Stockholm (1719–20). The Treaty of Nystad (1721) between Russia and Sweden marked Russia's emergence as the major Baltic power.

North Island The most northerly of the two principal islands of New Zealand, separated from South Island by Cook Strait. Area: 114 729 sq km (44 281 sq mi). Population (2001): 2 849 724.

North Korea *See* KOREA.

North Lanarkshire A council area of central Scotland, consisting mainly of the NE part of the historic county of Lanarkshire. Absorbed into Strathclyde Region in 1975, it became an independent unitary authority in 1996. Industries include engineering, metal working, and electronics. Area: 1771 sq km (684 sq mi). Population (2001): 321 067. Administrative centre: Motherwell.

North Lincolnshire A unitary authority in NE England, in Lincolnshire; formerly (1975–96) part of the county of Humberside. Area: 1497 sq km (578 sq mi). Population (2001): 152 839.

North Sea A section of the Atlantic Ocean in NW Europe, between the British Isles and the continent N of the Strait of Dover. The entire floor is part of the continental shelf, with an average depth of about 300 m (914 ft). Recent exploitation of *North Sea oil and natural-gas finds have increased its economic importance.

North Somerset A unitary authority of SW England, in Somerset; formerly (1974–96) part of the county of Avon. Area: 375 sq km (145 sq mi). Population (2001): 188 556.

North Star *See* POLARIS.

North Tyneside A unitary authority in NE England, in Tyne and Wear. Area: 84 sq km (32 sq mi). Population (2001): 191 663.

Northumberland The most northerly county of England. It consists of a coastal plain rising to the Cheviot Hills in the N and the Pennines in the W. The main river is the Tyne. There are outstanding Roman remains, notably Hadrian's Wall. The chief agricultural activity is sheep farming. The industrial SE became part of Tyne and Wear in 1974. Area: 5033 sq km (1944 sq mi). Population (2001): 307 186. Administrative centre: Morpeth.

Northumberland, John Dudley, Duke of (1502–53) English statesman, who was virtual ruler of England (1549–53) under Edward VI. He replaced the Duke of Somerset as head of the regency council in 1549, securing his execution in 1552. In 1553 he married his son to Lady Jane *Grey, whom he persuaded the king to name as his heir. On Edward's death Jane was proclaimed queen but lack of support forced Northumberland's surrender to Mary (I) and he was executed.

Northumbria A kingdom of Anglo-Saxon England north of the Humber. Northumbria became politically pre-eminent in England in the 7th century under *Edwin, Saint *Oswald, and Oswiu (d. 670). Northumbrian scholarship was also unrivalled, boasting such great names as *Bede. By 829, however, Northumbria had recognized the overlordship of Wessex and in the late 9th century its unity was destroyed by the Danes.

Northwest Caucasian languages A group of languages of the NW region of the Caucasus, also called the Abkhazo-Adyghian family. It includes Abkhaz, Abaza, Adyghian, Kabardian (Circassian), and Ubykh.

North-West Frontier Province A province in NW Pakistan, SE of Afghanistan. Its Pathan inhabitants mostly herd livestock or cultivate grains, fruit, sugar cane, and tobacco. Over the centuries several great powers have sought to control the province, but it has usually remained semiautonomous because of its rugged terrain and fierce inhabitants. Since the early 1980s over a million refugees have fled here from the civil wars in Afghanistan. Area: 74 522 sq km (28 773 sq mi). Population (1998): 17 555 000. Capital: Peshawar.

Northwest Passage The sea route along

the coast of North America, between the Atlantic and Pacific Oceans. It was first traversed by Roald Amundsen (1903–06). *See also* NORTHEAST PASSAGE.

Northwest Territories A territory of NW Canada. It formerly occupied a vast area stretching from 60°N to the North Pole and from Baffin Island in the E to the Yukon border in the W. In 1999 a large area of the NE became the new territory of *Nunavut, a semiautonomous homeland for the Inuit peoples. The remainder, which is the more developed part of the Canadian north, continues to be known as the Northwest Territories, although new names have been proposed. It is rich in mineral resources and mining is important. The vast oil reserves are being explored. Area: 2 082 910 sq km (804 003 sq mi). Population (1999 est): 41 800. Capital: Yellowknife.

North Yorkshire A county in N England. In 1996 the post-1974 county of Cleveland was abolished and those districts historically belonging to Yorkshire were restored to the county for ceremonial purposes: they are now administered by the unitary authorities of Langbaurgh, Middlesbrough, and Stockton-on-Tees. The city of York also became a unitary authority. The Pennines rise to the W of the Vale of York, while the Cleveland Hills and North York Moors, rise to the E. It is chiefly agricultural, with some industrial activity in the larger towns. Tourism is centred on Harrogate and Scarborough. Area (excluding unitary authorities): 8037 sq km (3102 sq mi). Population (2001 est, excluding unitary authorities): 569 600. Administrative centre: Northallerton.

Norway, Kingdom of (Norwegian name: Norge) A country in N Europe occupying the W part of the Scandinavian Peninsula. It is largely mountainous, reaching heights of almost 2500 m (8000 ft), with a heavily indented coastline. Glaciers and forests cover approximately one-quarter of the country. The archipelago of Svalbard and Jan Meyen Island are also part of Norway together with the dependencies of Bouvet Island, Peter I Island, and Queen Maud Land. *Economy*: abundant hydroelectric power has enabled Norway to develop as an industrial nation. Norway is also one of the world's great fishing nations. Forestry is a major source of wealth and revenues from tourism are important. Minerals include iron ore, limestone, coal, copper, zinc, and lead. *History*: its early history was dominated by the Vikings. The many local chieftains were not subjected to a single ruler until the reign of Harold I Haarfager (died c. 930). Christianity was introduced in the 10th century. During the reign (1204–63) of Haakon IV Haakonsson Norway acquired Iceland and Greenland and in the 14th century it was united with Sweden and Denmark. Sweden broke free in 1523 but Norway remained under Danish domination until 1814, when it was united with Sweden, while maintaining internal self-government. Only in 1907 was full independence achieved. Norway declared its neutrality in both World Wars but from 1940 to 1945 was occupied by the Germans, who established a government under Quisling. After World War II, Norway joined the UN and NATO. Norway has a highly developed social-welfare system. In a referendum (1994) Norwegians voted against joining the EU. Following elections in 2001 Kjell Magne Bondevik formed a centre-right government. Official language: Norwegian. Currency: krone of 100 øre. Area: 323 886 sq km (125 053 sq mi). Population (2003 est): 4 569 000. Capital: Oslo.

Norwegian A North Germanic language of the West Scandinavian division, spoken in Norway. There are two distinct forms known as Dano-Norwegian (Bokmål or Riksmål) and New Norwegian (Nynorsk or Landsmål).

Norwegian Antarctic Territory The area in Antarctica claimed by Norway, consisting mainly of Queen Maud Land and adjacent islands. There have been many research stations along the mountainous coast.

Norwich 52 38N 1 18E A city in E England, the administrative centre of Norfolk. Towards the end of the 16th century many weavers from the Netherlands settled in the city and it became a major textile centre; engineering and financial services are now important. Population (1993 est): 128 100.

nose The organ of smell, which is also an entrance to the respiratory tract. It leads to the nasal cavity, which is lined by *mucous membrane, extends back to the pharynx and windpipe, and is connected to the air sinuses of the skull. Hairs in the nostrils filter particles from inhaled air, which is further cleaned, warmed, and moistened in the nasal cavity. The membrane at the top of the nasal cavity contains olfactory cells, which are sensitive to different smells and are connected to the brain via the olfactory nerve.

Nostradamus (Michel de Notredame; 1503–66) French physician and astrologer, famous for his *Centuries* (1555–58), in which he made a number of prophecies in the form of rhyming quatrains. His prophecies are obscure and open to various interpretations.

notochord A flexible skeletal rod that runs along the length of the body in the embryos of all animals of the phylum Chordata (including vertebrates). In primitive chordates, such as the lancelets and lampreys, the notochord remains the main axial support.

Notre-Dame de Paris The gothic cathedral built (1163–1345) on the Île de la Cité, Paris, to replace two earlier churches. The nave, choir, and west front were completed by 1204; the innovatory flying buttresses and the great rose windows are notable features. Damaged during the French Revolution, Notre-Dame was fully restored (1845–64) by Eugène Viollet-le-Duc (1814–79).

Nottingham 1. 52 58N 1 10W A city in N central England, in Nottingham unitary authority, the administrative centre of Nottinghamshire. Charles I raised his standard here in 1642 at the outbreak of the Civil War. Notable buildings include the "Trip to Jerusalem," reputed to be the oldest inn in England. It was once famous for its lace. Population (1995 est): 283 800. **2.** A unitary authority in N central England, in Nottinghamshire. Area: 78 sq km (30 sq mi). Population (2001): 266 995.

Nottinghamshire A county in the East Midlands of England. It consists mainly of lowlands, crossed by the River Trent, with Sherwood Forest (famous for the Robin Hood legend) in the SW. Agriculture is important with arable and dairy farming, orchards, and market gardening. The main town, Nottingham, became an independent unitary authority in 1998. Area (excluding Nottingham): 2086 sq km (805 sq mi). Population (2001, excluding Nottingham): 748 503. Administrative centre: Nottingham.

Nouakchott 18 09N 15 58W The capital of Mauritania, in the W near the Atlantic coast. A small village until the 1950s, it was developed as the capital after independence in 1960. Population (1999 est): 881 000.

Nouméa 22 16S 166 26E The capital of New Caledonia. A port, it exports nickel, chrome, manganese, and iron. Population (1996): 76 293.

nova A *binary star that suddenly increases in brightness by perhaps 10 000 times or more and then fades over months or years, usually to its original brightness. Nova eruptions occur in close binary systems comprising a *white dwarf with a nearby companion star that is expanding and is losing matter to the white dwarf.

Nova Scotia A province of E Canada. It consists of a peninsula protruding into the Atlantic Ocean and *Cape Breton Island. Mostly rolling hills and valleys, Nova Scotia was originally covered by mixed forest but has been largely replanted with conifers. Coal output is down significantly, but Nova Scotia also mines gypsum, salt, and copper. Agriculture includes dairying, mixed farming, livestock, and fruit. *History*: from the first colonization (1605), Britain and France contested the area, Britain eventually gaining possession (confirmed by the Treaty of Paris in 1763). Since joining Canada (1867), its economy has lagged. Area: 52 841 sq km (20 402 sq mi). Population (2001): 942 700. Capital: Halifax.

Novaya Zemlya A Russian double island in the Arctic Ocean. It is mountainous with wild steep coasts. There is no permanent population, apart from weather stations. Soviet nuclear tests were formerly conducted here. Area: 83 000 sq km (32 040 sq mi).

Novello, Ivor (David Ivor Davies; 1893–1951) British composer, dramatist, and actor. He composed the World War I song "Keep the Home Fires Burning" and such romantic musicals as *Careless Rapture* (1936).

Novosibirsk 55 04N 83 05E A city in W central Russia, on the River Ob and the Trans-Siberian Railway. Population (1999 est): 1 402 400.

Nu, U (*or* **Thakin Nu**; 1907–95) Burmese statesman; prime minister (1948–56, 1957–58, 1960–62). A leading nationalist, he first became prime minister on independence.

Nubia A region of NE Africa, between Aswan (Egypt) and Khartoum (Sudan). Much of Nubia is now drowned by Lake Nasser. From about 2000 BC the Egyptians gradually occupied Nubia, which they called Cush. As Egyptian power waned, Nubian kings, based at Napata and Meroë, became influential, even dominating Egypt itself (c. 730–670). Their independent culture lasted until the 4th century AD.

Nubian Desert A desert in the NE Sudan, between the River Nile and the Red Sea. It consists of a sandstone plateau with peaks of up to 2259 m (7411 ft). Area: about 400 000 sq km (154 408 sq mi).

nuclear energy The energy evolved by nuclear fission or nuclear fusion. The energy is liberated in fission when a heavy atomic nucleus, such as uranium, splits into two or more parts, the total mass of the parts being less than the mass of the original nucleus. This difference in mass is equivalent to the *binding energy of the nucleus and most of it is converted into the kinetic energy of the components formed in the reaction. In a fusion reaction, two light nuclei, such as hydrogen, combine to form a stable nucleus, such as helium; with light nuclei the nucleus formed has a lower mass than the sum of the component nuclei, again energy is released. In the case of fission, when a nucleus of uranium-235 is struck by a neutron, a U-236 nucleus is formed,

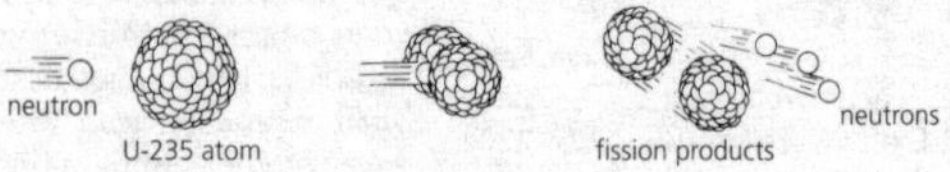

nuclear fission

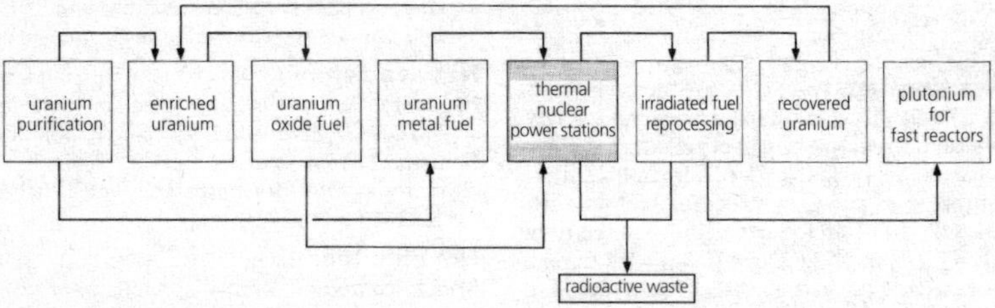

nuclear fuel cycle

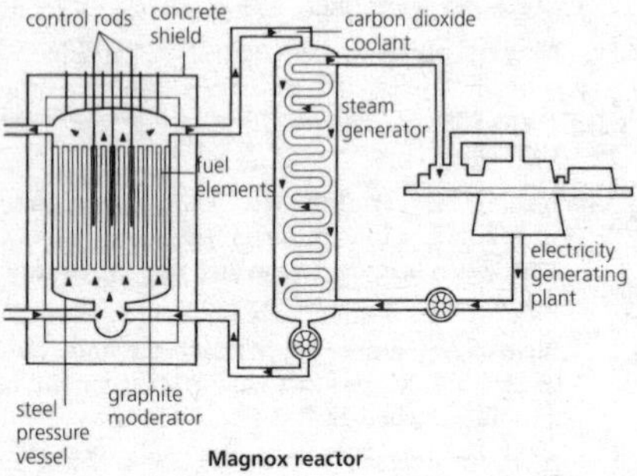

Magnox reactor

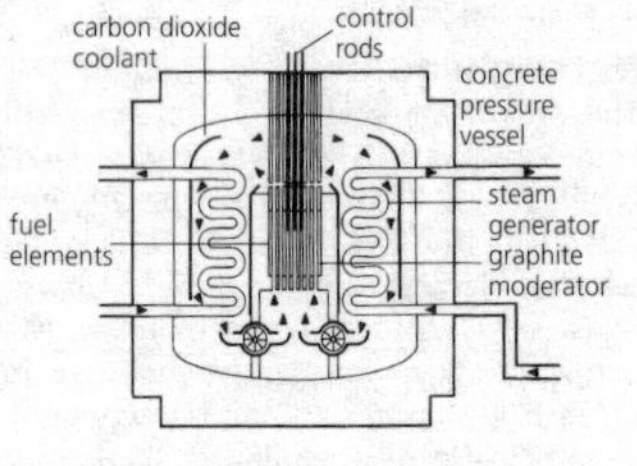

advanced gas-cooled reactor (AGR)

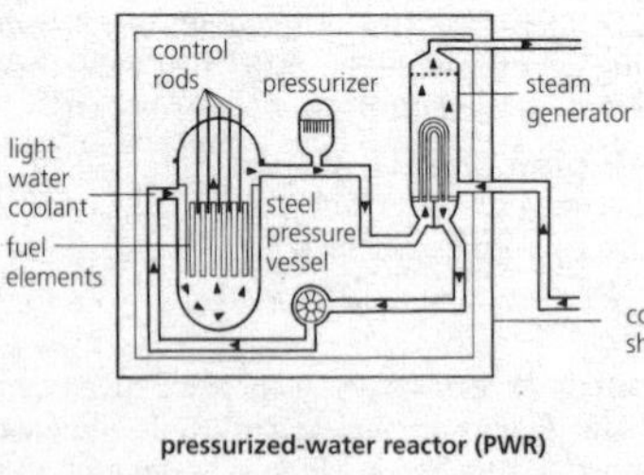

pressurized-water reactor (PWR)

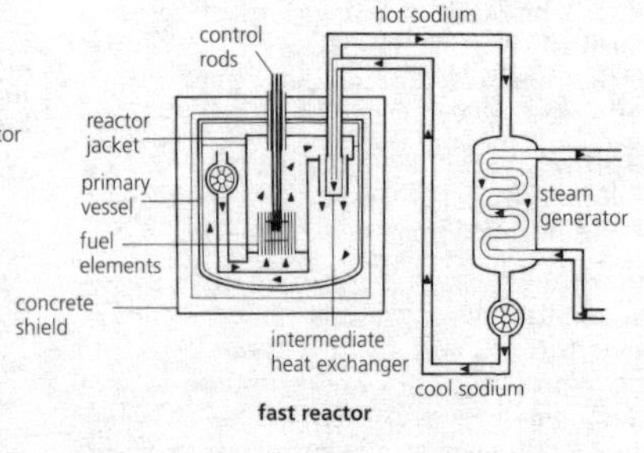

fast reactor

nuclear energy. Natural uranium metal fuel clad in Magnox (magnesium alloy) is used in Magnox thermal reactors. Enriched uranium dioxide pellets clad in steel are used in AGR and PWR fuel elements. Plutonium for fast reactors and recycled enriched uranium is obtained by reprocessing spent fuel from thermal reactors. The electricity generating plant is similar with all reactor types.

which immediately splits into two roughly equal parts. Two or three neutrons are produced at the same time. As these neutrons can cause further fissions, a chain reaction builds up and a lump of U-235 will disintegrate almost instantaneously with enormous explosive power, provided that it is in excess of the critical mass (*see* NUCLEAR WEAPONS). In nuclear power stations the fission reaction is harnessed to produce heat at a controlled rate (to raise steam to drive a turbine). They use natural uranium, which contains only 0.7% of the fissionable U-235 isotope, nearly all of the rest being the isotope U-238. The U-238 isotope absorbs the fast-moving neutrons emitted by the fission of U-235 and prevents a chain reaction from occurring in natural uranium. There are, however, two ways of producing a chain reaction. One is to use a moderator to slow down the fast neutrons so that they are not absorbed by U-238 nuclei (*see* THERMAL REACTOR). The other is to enrich the natural uranium with extra quantities of U-235 (or plutonium-239) so that there are sufficient neutrons to sustain the chain reaction in spite of absorption by U-238 (*see* FAST REACTOR). Most present commercial reactors are thermal, although fast reactors are now operating in the UK, France, and the former Soviet Union.

The fusion process is the basis of the hydrogen bomb (*see* NUCLEAR WEAPONS; THERMONUCLEAR REACTOR).

nuclear fission *See* FAST REACTOR; NUCLEAR ENERGY; NUCLEAR POWER; NUCLEAR WEAPONS; THERMAL REACTOR.

nuclear fusion *See* NUCLEAR ENERGY; NUCLEAR WEAPONS; THERMONUCLEAR REACTOR.

nuclear medicine The use of radioisotopes in the study of disease. It is widely used in heart disease (**nuclear cardiology**): a gamma-emitting nuclide (e.g. thallium-201) is injected into the blood, enabling a computerized gamma camera to record images of the working heart.

nuclear power The generation of electricity using nuclear energy. The nuclear power industry expanded rapidly from the 1960s: by the 1990s it provided some 22% of world electricity, 30% of Europe's electricity, and 28% of UK electricity. However, the disaster (1986) at *Chernobyl caused universal concern over nuclear safety. The Soviet design of the Chernobyl reactor, using a single shell building, is now considered unsafe, unlike the US water-cooled reactors using double-walled buildings, which prevented disaster at Three Mile Island in 1979. In addition to safety fears, the cost of disposing of radioactive waste and high decommissioning costs have made the price of nuclear-generated electricity uncompetitive with fossil fuels. This has been especially so in the UK since privatization of the industry in 1996, when the £1 bn per year subsidy raised by the **nuclear levy** came to an end. Once regarded as the energy source of the future, nuclear power is now becoming, in the UK at least, a thing of the past. Most countries have reconsidered their plans for expansion and in the UK the 15 remaining plants will be closed during the next 20 years. This position has been reached in spite of a strong lobby that regards nuclear power as essential in view of diminishing fossil fuel reserves and the global warming they cause (*see* GREENHOUSE EFFECT). *See also* FAST REACTOR; THERMAL REACTOR; THERMONUCLEAR REACTOR.

nuclear reactor A device for producing *nuclear energy in a usable form. *See* FAST REACTOR; NUCLEAR POWER; THERMAL REACTOR; THERMONUCLEAR REACTOR.

Nuclear Test-Ban Treaty (1963) A treaty banning nuclear testing by its signatories on the ground, in the atmosphere, in space, and under water. The signatories were the Soviet Union, the UK, and the USA; many other countries agreed to adhere to the treaty. Subsequent disarmament talks led to a comprehensive test-ban treaty (1996) but this will only come into force when signed and ratified by all 44 countries deemed to have nuclear potential. So far it has been signed by all but India, Pakistan, and North Korea but ratified only by France and the UK.

nuclear waste *See* RADIOACTIVE WASTE.

nuclear weapons Missiles, bombs, or mines that use nuclear fission or fusion (*see* NUCLEAR ENERGY) yielding enormous quantities of heat, light, blast, and radiation. The first **atomic bomb** (*or* fission bomb), manufactured by the USA in World War II, was dropped on Hiroshima in 1945. It consisted of two small masses of uranium-235 forced together by a chemical explosion to form a supercritical mass, in which an uncontrolled chain reaction occurred. The bomb had an explosive power equivalent to 20 000 tons of TNT. Later models used plutonium-239 to even greater effect.

The **hydrogen bomb** (fusion bomb *or* thermonuclear bomb) consists of an atom bomb surrounded by a layer of hydrogenous material, such as lithium deuteride. The atom bomb creates the necessary temperature (about 100 000 000°C) needed to ignite the fusion reaction (*see* THERMONUCLEAR REACTOR). Hydrogen bombs have an explosive power measured in tens of megatons (millions of tons) of TNT. The first hydrogen bomb was exploded by US scientists on Eniwetok Atoll in 1952.

The **neutron bomb** (*or* enhanced radiation bomb) is a nuclear weapon designed to maximize neutron radiation. It is lethal to all forms of life but, having reduced blast, leaves buildings, etc., relatively undamaged.

nucleic acids Organic compounds, found in the cells of all living organisms, that consist of a mixure of nitrogenous bases (purines and pyrimidines), phosphoric acid, and a pentose sugar. The sugar is ribose in the ribonucleic acids (*see* RNA) and deoxyribose in the deoxyribonucleic acids (*see* DNA). Nucleic acids store genetic information in living organisms and interpret that information in protein synthesis. *See also* NUCLEOPROTEIN.

nucleolus A small dense body, one or more of which can be seen within the *nucleus of a nondividing cell. It contains RNA and protein and is involved in the synthesis of *ribosomes.

nucleon A collective name for a proton or neutron. *See also* MASS NUMBER.

nucleoprotein A compound consisting of a nucleic acid associated with one or more proteins. The nucleoprotein of cell nuclei—the chromosomes—consists of DNA and proteins, mainly histones; cytoplasmic nucleoproteins—the ribosomes—are ribonucleoproteins comprising some 60% protein and 40% RNA. Viruses also consist of nucleoprotein.

nucleus (biology) A large granular component of nearly all cells. It is usually spherical or ovoid in shape and is surrounded by a nuclear membrane, which is perforated with pores to allow exchange of materials between the nucleus and cytoplasm. The nucleus contains the *chromosomes, made up of the hereditary material (DNA), and is therefore essential for the control and regulation of cellular activities, such as growth and metabolism. During cell division the chromosomes are involved in the transfer of hereditary information (*see* MEIOSIS; MITOSIS).

nucleus (physics) The central core of the atom (*see* ATOMIC THEORY) discovered by Lord Rutherford in 1911. All nuclei consist of protons and neutrons (jointly called nucleons), except for hydrogen, which consists of a single proton. The constituent nucleons are held together by the *strong interaction. The number of protons in the nucleus determines its charge and atomic number; the number of neutrons (in addition to the number of protons) determines the mass number and the isotope. **Nuclear physics** is the study of the structure and reactions of the nucleus. *See also* PARTICLE PHYSICS.

Nuffield, William Richard Morris, 1st Viscount (1877–1963) British car manufacturer and philanthropist. He established a car factory in Cowley, near Oxford, which in 1913 produced the first Morris Oxford, soon followed by the Morris Cowley. He founded Nuffield College, Oxford, the Nuffield Trust, and the Nuffield Foundation.

Nuku'alofa 21 09S 175 14W The capital of Tonga in the S Pacific, in N Tongatabu. It is the site of the Royal Palace (1865–67) and Royal Tombs. Population (1999 est): 37 000.

Nullarbor Plain A plain of SW South Australia and SE Western Australia, bordering on the Great Australian Bight. It consists of a treeless arid plateau. Area: 260 000 sq km (100 000 sq mi).

numbat A rat-sized *marsupial, *Myrmecobius fasciatus*, of SW Australia, also called marsupial (*or* banded) anteater. It is slender and rust-coloured, with white stripes across the back and a long tail, and it feeds on ants and termites with its long sticky tongue. Numbats have no pouch. Family: *Dasyuridae.*

number theory The study of the properties of numbers. It includes various theorems about *prime numbers, many of which are unproved but apparently true, and the study of Diophantine equations (named after the 3rd-century Greek mathematician Diophantus of Alexandria), i.e. equations that have only integer solutions. Fermat's last theorem deals with the solution of one of these equations and is a famous unproved theorem. It now includes analytic number theory, originated by Leonhard Euler (1707–83) in 1742; geometric number theory, which uses such geometrical methods of analysis as Cartesian coordinates (*see* COORDINATE SYSTEMS), *vectors, and matrices; and probabilistic number theory, based on *probability theory.

Numidia An ancient kingdom of N Africa, W of *Carthage. Its *Berber population was nomadic until Masinissa (c. 240–149 BC) promoted agriculture and urbanization. After supporting Pompey against Julius Caesar (46 BC), Numidia lost its monarchy and became part of the Roman province of Africa.

Nunavut (Inupik: Our Land) A territory of NE Canada, created in 1999 from part of the Northwest Territories as a semiautonomous homeland for the Inuit peoples. It extends from 60° N to the North Pole and incorporates most of Canada's Arctic islands. Although the territory is rich in mineral resources (including copper, silver, zinc, and iron), these remain largely unexploited owing to the severe climate and lack of infrastructure. Elections to the new territorial assembly took place in 1999 and Paul Okalik became premier. The territory has severe economic and social problems. Area: 2 093 190 sq km (808 185 sq mi). Population (2001): 26 745. Capital: Iqaluit.

Nuneaton 52 32N 1 28W A town in central England, in Warwickshire. It has textile and light-engineering industries. Population (1991): 66 715.

Nuremberg (German name: Nürnberg) 49 27N 11 05E A city in S Germany, in Bavaria, with metal-working and electrical industries. It was severely bombed during World War II. *History*: it was the centre of the German Renaissance, when the mastersingers' contests were held here. It was the site of the Nazi Party congresses (1933–38) and the war-crime trials after World War II. Population (1998 est): 489 758.

Nureyev, Rudolf (1938–93) Russian ballet dancer. He danced with the Leningrad Kirov Ballet from 1958 until 1961, when he defected from Russia. In 1962 he joined the Royal Ballet, where he partnered Margot *Fonteyn in such ballets as *Giselle* and *Swan Lake*. He was artistic director of the Paris Opéra Ballet from 1983 until 1989.

nurse shark A *shark, *Ginglymostoma cirratum*, that occurs in warm shallow waters of the Atlantic Ocean. Yellow-brown or grey-brown and up to 4.2 m long, it is considered dangerous to man only when provoked. Family: *Orectolobidae*.

Nusa Tenggara (former name: Lesser *Sunda Islands) A volcanic island group E of Java, mostly in Indonesia; the chief islands are Bali, Lombok, Sumbawa, Sumba, Flores, and Timor. Area: 73 144 sq km (28 241 sq mi). Population (1995 est): 7 237 600.

nut Loosely, any edible nonsucculent fruit, including the peanut and brazil nut. Botanically, a nut is a large dry fruit containing a single seed that is not released from the fruit at maturity. An example is the chestnut.

nutcracker A songbird of the genus *Nucifraga* found in coniferous forests of E Europe and Asia. The common nutcracker (*N. caryocatactes*) is dark brown speckled with white, about 32 cm long, and cracks open pine cones with its sharp bill to extract the seeds. Family: *Corvidae* (crows, jays, magpies).

nuthatch A small stocky bird belonging to a family (*Sittidae*: 30 species) occurring everywhere except South America and New Zealand. Nuthatches have long straight bills, for hammering open nuts, and long-clawed toes, for running up and down tree trunks in search of insects. The European nuthatch (*Sitta europaea*), about 14 cm long, has a blue-grey upper plumage with paler underparts and a black eyestripe.

nutmeg A fragrant tropical evergreen tree, *Myristica fragrans*, native to Indonesia but widely cultivated in SE Asia and the West Indies. Growing to 20 m high, it has tiny male and female flowers borne on separate trees. The yellow fleshy fruit, about 3 cm across, splits when ripe to expose the seed, which has a red fleshy covering (aril). The dried aril (mace) and whole or ground seeds (nutmeg) are used as spices. Family: *Myristicaceae*.

nutria *See* COYPU.

Nuuk (name until 1979: Godthåb) 64 10N 51 40W The capital of Greenland, a port at the mouth of Godthåb Fjord. Population (2000 est): 13 838.

nyala An antelope, *Tragelaphus angasi*, of SW Africa. About 100 cm high at the shoulder, nyalas are shy and nocturnal and have spiral-shaped horns and a greyish-brown coat with vertical white stripes on the flanks. The mountain nyala (*T. buxtoni*) lives in mountainous regions of S Ethiopia.

Nyeman, River *See* NEMAN, RIVER.

Nyerere, Julius (Kambarage) (1922–99) Tanzanian statesman; president (1962–85). In 1954 Nyerere formed the Tanganyika African National Union, which led the fight for independence (achieved in 1960). He became chief minister (1960), prime minister (1961), and then president of Tanganyika, which was renamed Tanzania in 1964 after union with Zanzibar. He was instrumental in the overthrow of Amin in Uganda in 1979.

nylon A synthetic material with a translucent creamy white appearance, widely used both in fibre form and in solid blocks because of its lightness, toughness, and elasticity. It is made by *polymerization of diamine with *fatty acid or by polymerizing a single monomer, in both cases to form a polyamide. Nylon is used to make small engineering components and is also spun and woven into fabrics for clothing, etc., and can be coloured with pigments. Introduced commercially in 1938, nylon was the first truly synthetic fibre.

nymph A stage in the life cycle of insects that show incomplete *metamorphosis, including dragonflies, grasshoppers, and bugs. The egg hatches into a nymph, which undergoes a series of moults to form a line of nymphs that show increasing similarity to the adult.

nymphalid butterfly A butterfly belonging to the widely distributed family *Nymphalidae*, also called brush-footed butterfly. Nymphalids are characterized by small hairy forelegs, useless for walking. Many, including the migratory *red admiral and *painted lady, are strong fast fliers.

nymphs In Greek mythology, female spirits of nature, often portrayed as youthful and amorous dancers or musicians. The several classes of nymphs associated with particular natural phenomena include the dryads, the naiads, and the nereids.

Nyoro A Bantu-speaking people of the western lakes region of Uganda. They were traditionally divided into the Bito clan from whom the hereditary paramount chief (Mukama) always came, the aristocratic Huma pastoralists, and the subordinate Iru cultivators. They are a patrilineal people who live in small scattered settlements.

O

Oahu A US island in Hawaii, the most populous and the administrative centre. The Japanese attack on *Pearl Harbor (1941) was decisive in bringing the USA into World War II. Area: 1584 sq km (608 sq mi). Population (latest est): 836 231. Chief town: Honolulu.

oak A deciduous or evergreen tree or shrub of the genus *Quercus* (over 800 species), found in N temperate and subtropical regions. The simple leaves usually have lobed or toothed margins. The fruit—an acorn—is a hard oval nut partly enclosed by a round cup. Often 30–40 m high, many species are important timber trees, especially the common or pedunculate oak (*Q. robur*) and the durmast oak (both Eurasian). Several are planted for ornament, including the Mediterranean holm oak. Family: *Fagaceae*.

oarfish A fish of the genus *Regalecus*, especially *R. glesne*, found in all seas. It has a long silvery ribbon-like body, up to 9 m long, a long red dorsal fin, long red oarlike pelvic fins situated near the pectoral fins, and no anal or tail fins.

OAS *See* ORGANISATION DE L'ARMÉE SECRÈTE; ORGANIZATION OF AMERICAN STATES.

oasis An area within a desert where water is available for vegetation and human use. It may consist of a single small spring around which palms grow or be an extensive area where the water table is at or near the ground surface.

Oates, Lawrence Edward Grace (1880–1912) British explorer and a member of R.F. *Scott's expedition to the Antarctic (1910–12). After reaching the Pole Oates, fearing that his lameness (resulting from frostbite) might hinder the already struggling expedition on the return journey, walked out into the blizzard to die. His gallant act, related in Scott's diaries, failed to save his companions.

Oates, Titus *See* POPISH PLOT.

oats Annual grasses belonging to the genus *Avena* (10 species), native to temperate regions. The common oat (*A. sativa*) was first cultivated in Europe and is grown widely in cool temperate regions. The grain is used as a livestock feed, especially for horses, and for oatmeal, breakfast cereals, etc. The straw is used for livestock fodder and bedding. Wild oats, especially *A. fatua*, can be a serious weed in cereal crops.

Ob, River A river in N central Russia, flowing N from the Altai Mountains to the **Gulf of Ob** on the Kara Sea. One of the world's largest rivers, its drainage basin covers an area of about 2 930 000 sq km (1 131 000 sq mi). Length: 3682 km (2287 mi).

OBE *See* ORDER OF THE BRITISH EMPIRE, THE MOST EXCELLENT.

obelisk A stone monument consisting of a tapering pillar with a pyramid-shaped top. Erected by the ancient Egyptians as cult objects, they were covered by hieroglyphs and dedicated to the sun god. Some later obelisks were erected as memorials to rulers. Many obelisks were carried away by conquerors; two famous specimens in Rome were taken there in antiquity and there are now 14 in the city. Their transport and erection were considerable engineering feats. Obelisks misnamed "Cleopatras needles" are found in both London and New York.

Oberammergau 47 35N 11 07E A town in S Germany, in the Bavarian Alps. It is noted for its passion play, performed every ten years following a vow made by the villagers (1633) when they were saved from the plague. Population (latest est): 4740.

obesity The condition of being seriously overweight, usually defined as having a body mass index (BMI) of 30 or more (BMI = weight (in kilograms) divided by height (in metres) squared). It is caused by the consumption of more food than is required to supply a person's energy needs. Obesity, the most common nutritional disorder in the developed world, increases the body's susceptibility to disease and reduces life expectancy.

oboe A woodwind instrument with a double reed, made in three jointed sections and having a conical bore and small belled end. It derives from the ancient shawm. It has a range of about three octaves above the B flat below middle C and because of its constant pitch usually gives the A to which other orchestral instruments tune.

Obote, (Apollo) Milton (1925–) Ugandan statesman; prime minister (1962–66) and president (1966–71, 1980–85). On independence he became prime minister and in 1966 deposed Mutesa II of Buganda (1924–69). Overthrown by *Amin in 1971, he was re-elected in 1980 but deposed in a military coup in 1985.

obsidian A black glassy volcanic rock with a conchoidal fracture. It is formed by the rapid cooling of acid lava.

obstetrics *See* GYNAECOLOGY.

O'Casey, Sean (1880–1964) Irish dramatist. His early realistic tragicomedies include *The Shadow of a Gunman* (1923) and *Juno and the Paycock* (1924). His later work, which includes *The Silver Tassie* (1929) and *Red Roses for Me* (1943), is usually considered inferior.

O

Occitan *See* PROVENÇAL.

occultation The temporary disappearance of one astronomical body behind another, as when the moon passes in front of and obscures a star. *See also* ECLIPSE.

occupational therapy The ancillary medical specialty concerned with restoring the physical and mental health of the sick and disabled. The occupational therapist plays an important role in keeping long-stay hospital patients interested and usefully occupied, helps them gain confidence to return to work, and trains disabled persons for new employment. *See also* GERIATRICS.

Oceania The islands of the Pacific Ocean, usually taken to exclude Japan, Indonesia, Taiwan, the Philippines, and the Aleutian Islands, but often including Australasia.

Ocean Island (*or* **Banaba**) 00 52S 169 35E An island in the SW Pacific Ocean, in Kiribati. Rich deposits of phosphate were mined to exhaustion by the UK (1900–79). During the Japanese occupation (1942–45) Banabans were deported to Fiji; the remainder were massacred in 1945. In 1965 surviving Banabans were paid compensation for overmining and in 1979 they were given dual Kiribati and Fijian nationality. Area: about 5 sq km (2 sq mi). Population (latest est): 284.

oceanography The study of the oceans, particularly their origin, structure, and form, the relief and sediments of the sea floor, the flora and fauna they contain, and the properties of sea water, waves, currents, and tides.

oceans The large areas of water (excluding lakes and seas) covering about 70% of the earth's surface. The oceans are the Pacific (covering about one-third of the world), Atlantic, Indian, and Arctic; the Southern Ocean (waters south of 40°S) is sometimes distinguished. Major structural features are the continental margins (continental shelf and slope), mid-ocean ridges, ocean basins, and trenches.

ocelot A *cat, *Felis* (*Panthera*) *pardalis*, of Central and South American forests. 100–150 cm long including the tail (30–50 cm), it has a black-spotted buff coat with stripes on the legs. It frequently hunts by night.

Ockham's Razor The metaphysical principle, associated with the English medieval philosopher William of Ockham (c. 1285–1349), that "Entities should not be multiplied unnecessarily." In analysing a problem one should always choose the hypothesis that makes the least number of assumptions; only indispensible concepts are real.

O'Connell, Daniel (1775–1847) Irish politician. As a Catholic, his election as an MP in 1828 forced the government to concede Catholic Emancipation. A popular speaker known as the Liberator, he subsequently campaigned for the repeal of the union with Britain.

octane number A measure of the extent to which a fuel causes knocking in a petrol engine. It is the percentage by volume of *iso*-octane (C_8H_{18}) in a mixture of *iso*-octane and *n*-heptane (C_7H_{16}), which has the same knocking characteristics as the fuel under specified conditions.

Octavian *See* AUGUSTUS.

octopus An eight-armed *cephalopod mollusc belonging to the genus *Octopus*, found in most oceans. The common octopus (*O. vulgaris*) has a pair of well-developed eyes, a ring of tentacles around its horny beak, and a saclike body. Octopuses feed mainly on crabs and lobsters and may eject a cloud of ink when alarmed. Family: *Octopodidae*; order: *Octopoda*.

Oder, River A river in E Europe. Rising in the Oder Mountains of the Czech Republic, it flows N and W through Poland and enters the Baltic Sea at Szczecin. Linked by canals to both E and W Europe, it is of great commercial importance. Length: 886 km (551 mi).

Oder-Neisse Line The boundary between Germany and Poland, following the Rivers Oder and Neisse. Confirmed by the Allies at the *Potsdam Conference (1945) at the end of World War II, it was recognized by East Germany and Poland in 1950 but not by West Germany until 1970.

Odessa 46 30N 30 46E A port in S Ukraine, on the Black Sea. Founded in the 14th century as a Tatar fortress, it passed to Russia in 1791 and

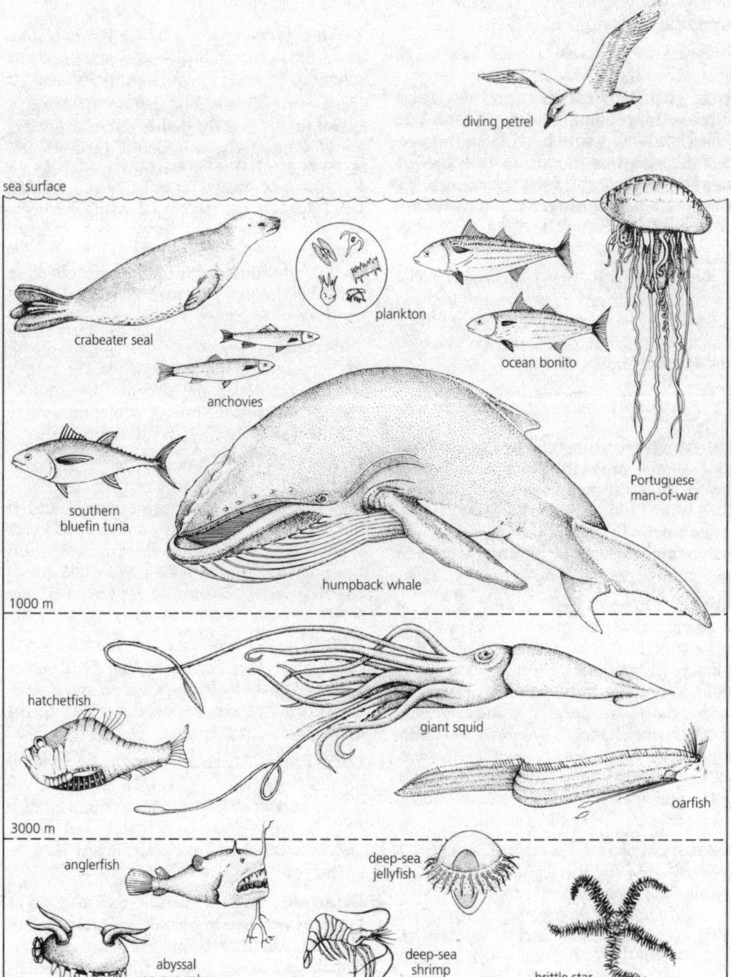

oceans. A selection of animals and plants found at different depths of the ocean.

became a naval base. It was the scene (1905) of the mutiny on the *Potemkin*. Population (1998 est): 1 027 400.

Odin The principal god of the Teutonic peoples, the husband of *Frigga and, according to some legends, the father of *Thor. Also known as Woden and Wotan, he was the god of war, learning, and poetry and possessed great magical powers. He was the protector of slain heroes, who were brought to *Valhalla by his servants the *Valkyries.

Odysseus (*or* **Ulysses**) A legendary Greek king of Ithaca and hero of Homer's *Odyssey*, notable for his cunning. His many adventures during his voyage home from the *Trojan War included encounters with the Cyclops Polyphemus, the enchantress *Circe, and the goddess Calypso, with whom he lived for eight years. Having reached Ithaca, he was reunited with his faithful wife *Penelope after killing her suitors with the help of his son Telemachus.

Oë, Kenzaburo (1935–) Japanese novelist and writer. In such novels as *Our Age* (1959) and *The Silent Cry* (1967) he explored the spiritual confusion of postwar Japan. He was awarded the Nobel Prize in 1994.

OECD *See* ORGANIZATION FOR ECONOMIC COOPERATION AND DEVELOPMENT.

oedema The accumulation of fluid in body tissues, leading to swelling, popularly known as dropsy. There are many causes of oedema, including heart failure, kidney failure, liver failure, and malnutrition. Diuretic drugs can usually resolve oedema by causing the patient to pass more urine.

Oedipus In Greek legend, a king of Thebes who unwittingly fulfilled the prophecy of the oracle at Delphi that he would kill his father and marry his mother. He was brought up by Polybus, King of Corinth. He killed his true father, Laius, in a roadside quarrel, and after winning the throne of Thebes by solving the riddle of the *sphinx he married his mother, the widowed Jocasta. When they discovered the truth, Jocasta committed suicide and Oedipus blinded himself and went into exile.

Oedipus complex The unconscious sexual feelings of a boy for his mother, which are accompanied by aggressive feelings for his father. According to psychoanalysis this is a normal desire, made unconscious by *repression. The female equivalent (in which a girl desires her father) is called the **Electra complex**.

Oersted, Hans Christian (1777–1851) Danish physicist. He discovered the magnetic effect of an electric current and thus established the relationship between electricity and magnetism.

oesophagus The gullet: a muscular tube, about 25 cm long, running from the pharynx at the back of the mouth to the stomach. Contractions of the oesophagus propel swallowed food towards the stomach: the food is lubricated with mucus secreted by the walls of the oesophagus.

oestrogens A group of steroid hormones that function principally as female sex hormones. The most important oestrogens in mammals are oestradiol and oestrone. Produced by the ovaries, they promote the development of the reproductive organs and secondary sexual characteristics (such as enlargement of breasts) at puberty and regulate the changes of the menstrual cycle. Oestrogens are also produced by the placenta, adrenal glands, and testes. Synthetic oestrogens are used to treat menstrual and menopausal disorders; they are also constituents of *oral contraceptives.

oestrus The period of "heat" in the sexual cycle of female mammals, when the female will attract males and permit copulation. It corresponds to the time of ovulation, so that mating is most likely to result in pregnancy.

Offa (d. 796) King of Mercia (757–96) and overlord of all England S of the Humber. He accepted greater papal control of the Church, introduced a new currency, and devised a code of laws. **Offa's Dyke**, an earthwork dividing England from Wales, built c. 784–c. 796, marks the frontier established by his wars with the Welsh.

Offaly (Irish name: Uabh Failghe) A county in the central Republic of Ireland, in Leinster, bordered in the W by the River Shannon. Area: 2000 sq km (770 sq mi). Population (2002): 63 702. County town: Tullamore.

Offenbach, Jacques (J. Eberst; 1819–80) German composer of French adoption. He wrote a series of popular operettas, including *Orpheus in the Underworld* (1858), and *La Vie Parisienne* (1866), and one grand opera, *The Tales of Hoffman* (produced posthumously; 1881).

Ogaden, the A semidesert area in E Ethiopia, enclosed by Somalia except to the W. The nomadic inhabitants are chiefly Muslim Somalis and in the 1960s a claim to the area by Somalia provoked border clashes. Somalia invaded the Ogaden in 1977 but withdrew in 1978. Guerrilla fighting has continued.

O'Higgins, Bernardo (?1778–1842) Chilean national hero of Irish descent, who fought with José de *San Martin against Spain and liberated Chile. He was made dictator of the country in 1817 but his wide-ranging reforms created much resentment and he was deposed.

Ohio A state in the USA, in the Midwest situated to the S of Lake Erie. The flat or rolling land of W Ohio gives way in the E to the hill and valley region of the Appalachian Plateau. A major industrial state, it lies at the centre of the most industrialized area of the USA and is strategically located near many rich markets. Agriculture is important, especially livestock. Ceded to Britain in 1763 and to the USA in 1783, it became a state in 1802. Area: 106 764 sq km (41 222 sq mi). Population (2000): 11 353 140. Capital: Columbus.

Ohio River A river in the USA flowing mainly SW from Pittsburgh in W Pennsylvania to join the Mississippi (in Illinois) as its main E tributary. Length: 1577 km (980 mi).

ohm (Ω) The SI unit of electrical resistance equal to the resistance between two points on a conductor when a potential difference of one volt between the points produces a current of one ampere. Named after Georg *Ohm.

Ohm, Georg Simon (1787–1854) German physicist, who discovered in 1827 that the current flowing through a wire (or circuit element) is directly proportional to the potential difference between its ends (**Ohm's law**). The constant of proportionality is the resistance of the wire or element. The unit of resistance is named after him.

oil There are three types of oil: lipids (*see* FATS AND OILS), *essential oils, and mineral oil. Petroleum (*or* rock oil) is the thick greenish mineral oil that occurs in permeable underground rock. It consists mainly of *hydrocarbons derived from the remains of living organisms deposited many millions of years ago with rock-forming sediments. Under the effects of heat and pressure this organic material passed through a number of chemical and physical changes ending up as droplets of petroleum, which migrated through porous rocks and fissures to become trapped in large underground reservoirs, often floating on a layer of water and held under pressure beneath a layer of natural gas (mostly methane). The modern oil industry began when oil was discovered in Pennsylvania in 1859 and has grown with the development of the internal-combustion engine, which is entirely dependent on it as a fuel. Once the presence of oil has been detected and its extent determined, the oil well is made by drilling through the rock; a specially prepared mud is pumped through the hollow bit to collect the debris, which is forced back up the shaft around the drilling bit. Drilling for oil below the sea is achieved in a similar manner, except that the drilling rig has to be supported on a base, which has legs sunk into the sea bed.

Petroleum has no uses in its crude form and has to be refined by fractional distillation (i.e. separating the components according to their boiling points) before it is of commercial value. Natural gas is widely used as a substitute for coal gas. Products made by blending the distillation fractions include aviation spirit, petrol, kerosene, Diesel oil, lubricating oil, paraffin wax, and petroleum jelly. Catalytic reforming is used to make a number of valuable chemicals (petrochemicals), which are required to manufacture detergents, plastics, fibres, fertilizers, drugs, etc.

The price, conservation, and political significance of oil are extremely controversial issues. In 1961 the *Organization of Petroleum Exporting Countries (OPEC) was set up to protect producing countries from exploitation. Its advent ended the era of cheap energy and prices for petroleum products rose sharply during the ensuing decade. In 1974 the International Energy Agency (IEA) was established to protect consumers.

oil palm A *palm tree, *Elaeis guineensis*, native to tropical West Africa and cultivated in Africa, Indonesia, Malaysia, and tropical America as the source of palm oil. The small fleshy fruits contain a white kernel within a hard black shell. Palm oil is extracted from the pulp and kernel and used in making soaps, margarine, lubricants, etc. The residual meal from the kernels is a valuable livestock feed.

oilseeds Oil-bearing seeds of plants from which the edible oil is extracted for making margarine, soaps, etc. Examples include rapeseed, cottonseed, groundnuts, and soya beans. The oil is obtained from the seeds by expelling it under pressure or by extracting it using a solvent; the **oilcake** remaining after most of the oil has been removed is widely used as animal feed.

Ojibwa A North American Indian people of the Great Lakes region, who speak a language of the Algonkian family. They are also known as Chippewa.

okapi A hoofed mammal, *Okapia johnstoni*, of central African rain forests. Okapis have a dark-brown coat with horizontal black and white stripes on the legs and rump. The smaller male has short bony backward-pointing horns. Family: *Giraffidae* (giraffes).

Okeechobee, Lake A large freshwater lake in the USA, in S Florida. It drains into the Atlantic Ocean through the Everglades. Area: 1813 sq km (700 sq mi).

Okinawa A mountainous Japanese island, the main one of the Ryukyu group. Captured by the USA in World War II, it was returned to Japan in 1972, the USA retaining military bases there. Area: 1176 sq km (454 sq mi). Population (1995): 1 273 508. Capital: Naha.

Oklahoma A state in the S central USA with a diverse landscape of hills and plains. An oil-rich state, agriculture (especially cattle) remains a major source of revenue. Most industry is located around Oklahoma City and Tulsa (one of the world's leading oil centres). Oklahoma formed part of the Louisiana Purchase in 1803. It was reserved as Indian territory (1828) but after the US Civil War White settlement began and it became a state in 1907. Area: 181 089 sq km (69 919 sq mi). Population (2000): 3 450 654. Capital: Oklahoma City.

Oklahoma City 35 28N 97 33W A city in the USA, the capital of Oklahoma on the North Canadian River. Founded in 1889, it expanded rapidly following the discovery of oil (1920s). Today it is a commercial, industrial, and distribution centre for an oil-producing and agricultural area. In 1995 a right-wing extremist bombed a government office building, killing 168 people. Population (2000): 506 132.

okra An annual African herb, *Hibiscus esculentus*, also called lady's fingers or gumbo, widely cultivated in the tropics and subtropics. It has five-petalled yellow flowers with a crimson centre and edible pods. The seeds are a coffee substitute. Family: *Malvaceae*.

Old Catholics Christian Churches from several European countries that separated from the Roman Catholic Church at various times and in 1932 entered into communion with the Church of England. They comprise the Church of Utrecht (1724), the Old Catholic Churches of Germany, Switzerland, and Austria (1870), the National Polish Church (established 1897), and the Yugoslav Old Catholic Church (1924).

Old English sheepdog A breed of working dog originating in England. It has a compact body and a long dense shaggy coat that may be grey or blue-grey with white markings. Their tails are docked at birth. Height: 55–66 cm.

Oldham **1.** 53 33N 2 07W A town in N England, in Oldham unitary authority, Greater Manchester. Formerly a cotton-spinning town, Oldham now has electronics, plastics, and clothing industries. Population (1991): 103–991. **2.** a unitary authority in N England, in Greater Manchester. Area: 141 sq km (54 sq mi). Population (2001): 217 393.

Old Norse A North Germanic language formerly spoken in Iceland and Norway (c. 1150–c. 1350). It was closely related to the contemporary speech of Denmark and Sweden. From this group the modern Scandinavian languages are derived.

Old Testament The collection of 39 books that forms the first of the two major divisions of the Christian *Bible (the second being the *New Testament). The same writings (traditionally divided into 24 books) form the whole of the Hebrew Bible, the sacred scriptures of Judaism. The Christian title derives from the Latin word for *covenant and refers to the pact between God and Israel. The books claim to cover the period from the creation of the universe and man (Adam) to about 400 BC. They are traditionally divided into three parts: the Law or *Torah, the first five books, traditionally ascribed to Moses and often called the Pentateuch; the Prophets, bearing the names of individual prophets and containing much historical information; and the Writings or Hagiographa, the latest books admitted to the Hebrew Old Testament (c. 100 AD).

Olduvai Gorge A site in N Tanzania yielding an important sequence of Lower *Palaeolithic fossils and tools, many found by the *Leakey family.

Old Vic A London theatre built in 1818 and named the Royal Victoria in 1833. It became famous for music hall and, after Lilian Baylis (1874–1937) became manager in 1912, for productions of Shakespeare. It was the temporary home of the National Theatre Company (1963–76; *see* ROYAL NATIONAL THEATRE COMPANY). It was saved from closure in 1998–2000 and the US film star Kevin Spacey was appointed artistic director in 2002.

Old World *See* NEW WORLD.

Old World monkey A *monkey belonging to the family *Cercopithecidae* (58 species), native to Africa or Asia. There are both terrestrial and arboreal species, active mainly by day and either omnivorous or vegetarian. They inhabit

1896	Athens	1960	Rome
1900	Paris	1964	Tokyo
1904	St Louis	1968	Mexico City
1908	London	1972	Munich
1912	Stockholm	1976	Montreal
1920	Antwerp	1980	Moscow
1924	Paris	1984	Los Angeles
1928	Amsterdam	1988	Seoul
1932	Los Angeles	1992	Barcelona
1936	Berlin	1996	Atlanta
1948	London	2000	Sydney
1952	Helsinki	2004	Athens
1956	Melbourne	2008	Beijing
Winter Olympics			
1924	Chamonix	1972	Sapporo
1928	St Moritz	1976	Innsbruck
1932	Lake Placid	1980	Lake Placid
1936	Garmisch-Partenkirchen	1984	Sarajevo
1948	St Moritz	1988	Calgary
1952	Oslo	1992	Albertville
1956	Cortina d'Ampezzo	1994	Lillehammer
1960	Squaw Valley	1998	Nagano
1964	Innsbruck	2002	Salt Lake City
1968	Grenoble	2006	Turin

Venues of Olympic Games since 1896

forest, savannah, swamps, and rocks. *See also* BABOON; GUENON; LANGUR; MACAQUE.

oleander A poisonous evergreen shrub, *Nerium oleander*, also called rosebay, native to the Mediterranean region and widely cultivated in warm regions for its attractive flowers. Up to 7 m high, it has long narrow leaves, clusters of white, pink, or purplish five-petalled flowers (up to 7.5 cm across), and dangling pods. Family: *Apocynaceae*.

oleaster A shrub or tree, *Elaeagnus angustifolia*, found throughout S Europe. It has ornamental silvery foliage and small fragrant yellowish flowers. The edible olive-shaped yellowish fruits have a silvery scaly coat. Family: *Elaeagnaceae*.

olefines *See* ALKENES.

Oligocene epoch *See* TERTIARY PERIOD.

olive An evergreen tree, *Olea europaea*, native to W Asia but cultivated throughout Mediterranean and subtropical regions for its fruits. It has a gnarled grey trunk, grey-green leaves, and fleshy oval berries. Unripe green olives and ripe black olives are usually pickled for use in hors d'oeuvres and other dishes. **Olive oil**, pressed from the fruit, is one of the finest edible oils. It is also used in soaps, cosmetics, and textiles. Family: *Oleaceae*.

Olives, Mount of (*or* **Olivet**) 31 47N 35 15E A hill to the E of the old city of Jerusalem. Near its foot is the Garden of Gethsemane, the scene of the betrayal of Christ (Mark 14.26–50) and it is the traditional site of Christ's Ascension (Acts 1.2–12).

Olivier, Laurence (Kerr), Baron (1907–89) British actor. He played many Shakespearean roles while with the Old Vic Theatre Company, 1937–1949, and a number of outstanding modern roles, including Archie Rice in *The Entertainer* (1957). His films include the Shakespeare adaptations *Henry V* (1944), *Hamlet* (1948), and *Richard III* (1956). While director of the National Theatre Company (1961–73), he played many leading roles. His second marriage to Vivien *Leigh ended in divorce; in 1961 he married Joan Plowright (1929–).

olivine A group of greenish rock-forming silicate minerals, with a conchoidal fracture, that occur in igneous rocks. Peridot is a pale green gem variety. Olivine may be a major constituent of the earth's upper mantle.

Olympia A sanctuary of *Zeus, established about 1000 BC in the NW *Peloponnese, in W Greece. From 776 BC until at least 261 AD it was the venue of the *Olympic Games. The temple of Zeus in the Altis (sacred grove), which later held Phidias' famous statue, was completed in 457 BC. The sanctuary was closed by the Christian Emperor Theodosius (390 AD).

Olympic Games A quadrennial international amateur sports contest. The modern games derive from the ancient Greek athletic festival held at *Olympia. They were revived at Athens in 1896. The Winter Olympics were first held in 1924. The Games are governed by the International Olympic Committee (IOC). Although officially a contest between individuals, hosted by a particular city, the Games are often seen as a competition between countries; they have sometimes been disrupted by international political tensions. See table on p. 653.

Olympus, Mount 40 05N 22 21E A group of mountains in NE central Greece, held in ancient times to be the home of the gods. Highest point: 2917 m (9570 ft).

Om In Indian religions, the greatest of the mantras or mystical sounds embodying spiritual power. In Sanskrit *Om* comprises three sounds *A, U, M* (the vowels being equivalent to *O*), which represent the three Vedic scriptures, the three worlds (earth, atmosphere, heaven), the *Trimurti or some other triple, and ultimately the essence of the universe.

Omagh A district in Northern Ireland, in Co Tyrone. Area: 1123 sq km (434 sq mi). Population (2001): 47 952.

O

Oman, Sultanate of (name until 1970: Muscat and Oman) A country in the Middle East, in E *Arabia on the Gulf of Oman. It is mainly flat with coastal mountains in the N. The majority of the population is nomadic Arab and Ibadhi Muslim by religion. *Economy*: oil, which has been extracted since 1967, accounts for about 90% of the country's revenue. *History*: Oman was settled by the Portuguese, Dutch, and English in the 16th century. Since the 19th century Britain has been influential; it supported the present sultan's overthrow of his father in 1970 and helped to defeat a Marxist insurgency in 1975. Although a State Advisory Council and a Council of State were established in the 1990s, Oman remains an absolute monarchy. Official language: Arabic. Currency: rial Omani of 1000 baiza. Area: 300 000 sq km (120 000 sq mi). Population (2003 est): 2 621 000. Capital: Muscat.

Omar (*or* **Umar**) (d. 644 AD) The second caliph (634–44), regarded by Islam as the founder of the Muslim state. Omar continued the Muslim conquests and in 638 visited Jerusalem after its capture. He was murdered.

'Omar Khayyam (?1048–?1122) Persian poet, mathematician, and astronomer. His poems, characterized by an agnostic and hedonistic philosophy, were written in the form of *ruba'is* (quatrains). The free translation of 75 of them by Edward *Fitzgerald in 1859 became popular; more recent translations have also been made.

Omayyads *See* UMAYYADS.

ombudsman A person appointed to investigate grievances against maladministration. The post originated in Sweden in 1809. In the UK an ombudsman (the parliamentary commissioner for administration) was first appointed in 1967 to investigate complaints against central government departments; complaints against health authorities are investigated by Health Service Commissioners, appointed since 1973; there have been ombudsmen for local government since 1974. In the 1980s and 1990s various financial ombudsmen were set up to investigate complaints against banks, insurance companies, pension managers, etc.

Omdurman 15 37N 32 29E A city in the Sudan, on the River Nile. The Mahdi made it his capital in 1885 but his successor, the Khalifa, was defeated by Anglo-Egyptian forces under Lord Kitchener in the battle of Omdurman (1898). Population (1993): 1 267 077 (urban area).

Omsk 55 00N 73 22E A port in W central Russia, at the confluence of the Rivers Irtysh and Om. Also on the Trans-Siberian Railway, it has important engineering industries and oil refineries. Population (1999 est): 1 157 600.

Onassis, Aristotle Socrates (1906–75) Greek businessman, who owned one of the largest independent shipping lines in the world and during the 1950s became one of the first to construct supertankers. In 1968 he married Jacqueline Kennedy, his second wife, after a long relationship with Maria *Callas.

oncogene A gene responsible for turning a normal cell into a cancerous cell. Several viruses (called oncogenic viruses) are known to carry oncogenes; when such a virus infects a host cell the oncogene directly transforms it into a cancer cell without altering the host cell's genes.

Onega, Lake A lake in NW Russia, the second largest in Europe. It forms part of the water route from the Gulf of Finland to the White Sea. Area: 9887 sq km (3817 sq mi).

O'Neill, Eugene (1888–1953) US dramatist. His plays include *Beyond the Horizon* (1920), *Anna Christie* (1921), the trilogy *Mourning Be-*

comes Electra (1931), *The Iceman Cometh* (1946), and the autobiographical *Long Day's Journey into Night* (1956). He won the Nobel Prize in 1936.

onion A hardy herbaceous perennial plant, *Allium cepa*, probably native to central or W Asia but now cultivated worldwide, mainly in temperate regions, for its edible bulb. The mature plant has a long leafless stalk, which bears a round head of small white flowers, and six long slender leaves growing directly from the bulb. Immature bulbs, together with their leaves, are eaten raw in salads, etc.: these are spring onions. Family: *Liliaceae*.

Ontario A province of Canada, the most populous and wealthy, stretching from the Great Lakes N to Hudson Bay. It lies mainly on the mineral-rich Canadian Shield, a rocky forested plateau with many lakes and rivers. Most of the population live in the fertile lowlands near the S Great Lakes, dominated by the highly industrialized belt stretching from Toronto to Windsor. Manufacturing and mining are both important. Penetrated by French explorers and fur traders in the 17th century, Ontario became British (1763) and was settled by expatriate Americans loyal to Britain after the American Revolution. Area: 891 194 sq km (344 090 sq mi). Population (2001 est): 11 874 400. Capital: Toronto.

Ontario, Lake A lake in E North America, the smallest and easternmost of the Great Lakes. It is fed by the Niagara River and empties into the St Lawrence River. Area: 18 941 sq km (7313 sq mi).

ontogeny *See* PHYLOGENY.

ontology The branch of philosophy that deals with the theory of being. Ontological theories may assert that only minds exist (extreme idealism), or that only physical objects do (*see* MATERIALISM).

onyx A semiprecious stone consisting of a variety of *chalcedony characterized by straight parallel bands, often distinctly coloured. Onyx occurs in the lower part of steam cavities in igneous rocks.

oolite A variety of *limestone consisting mainly of beds of ooliths, spherical concretions of calcite accumulated in concentric layers around a nucleus (for example a grain of sand or fragment of a shell). Although most oolites are calcareous, oolitic ironstones also occur.

opal A semiprecious stone consisting of a hydrous amorphous variety of silica. The precious variety, used as a gem, shows a characteristic internal play of colours (opalescence) resulting from internal reflection and refraction of light. It occurs in cavities in many rocks, deposited by percolating silica-bearing water.

OPEC *See* ORGANIZATION OF PETROLEUM EXPORTING COUNTRIES.

open-hearth process A technique for making *steel from *pig iron, scrap steel, and iron ore, developed in the 1850s. The process uses gaseous fuel, which is preheated by the exhaust gases from the furnace. The molten metal lies in a pool at the bottom or hearth of the furnace.

Open University (**OU**) A nonresidential university in the UK, established in 1969 to provide further education on a part-time basis for adults by means of correspondence courses and radio and television programmes, supported by a tutor-counselling service at regional centres throughout the country. It is open to anyone regardless of previous qualifications, age, or school attended. The first courses started in 1971. More recently the OU has moved into nondegree forms of continuing education.

opera A staged dramatic work in which all or most of the text is set to music. Opera originated in Florence in the early 17th century as the result of attempts to revive Greek tragedy and to reproduce its musical elements. These became the aria, recitative, and chorus of operatic convention. The earliest opera still in the modern repertory is Monteverdi's *Orfeo* (1607). Opera seria is the Italian style of opera developed by such composers as Scarlatti and Handel and characterized by a heroic or mythological plot. Opera buffa is a form of comic opera containing some spoken dialogue. It developed in the early 18th century and was originally performed between the acts of opera seria. At the end of the 18th century Mozart perfected opera buffa. In the early 19th century the influence of Romanticism gave rise to the works of Weber and Meyerbeer, while the Italian bel canto ("beautiful singing") tradition was maintained by Bellini, Rossini, and Donizetti. In the mid-19th century the musical and dramatic elements of opera were integrated by Wagner in his opera cycle *Der Ring des Nibelungen* (1869–76) and his subsequent operas. Verdi extended the emotional and dramatic range of Italian opera. The realism of Bizet's *Carmen* (1875) influenced Leoncavallo, Mascagni, and Puccini. In the 20th century a wide variety of operatic styles flourished, including the dramatic realism of Janáček and the neoclassicism of Stravinsky. Richard Strauss's operas were greatly influenced by

Wagner. Other important operatic composers of the past hundred years include Prokofiev, Britten, Henze, and Tippett.

ophthalmology The medical specialty concerned with the study, diagnosis, and treatment of diseases of the eye. Ophthalmologists are doctors specializing in this. **Optometry** is the assessment and correction of visual defects, and opticians are not doctors: ophthalmic opticians (*or* optometrists) both test eyesight and prescribe suitable lenses; dispensing opticians make and fit glasses.

opium The dried juice obtained from the seed capsule of the *opium poppy, *Papaver somniferum*, an annual cultivated in N temperate and subtropical regions. Opium is extracted from the latex of the plant, which exudes from notches made in the half-ripened capsule. A narcotic drug, opium has been used for centuries in medicine for the relief of pain. Although still sometimes given in the form of laudanum (tincture of opium), its main legitimate uses today include the extraction of its active ingredients—*morphine (first isolated in 1803), codeine, papaverine, etc.—and preparation of their derivatives (e.g. heroin). Because opium causes *drug dependence and overdosage can be fatal, its preparation and use are strictly controlled. (Illegal trading continues however.) India, Turkey, and Afghanistan are the main opium-producing countries.

O

Opium Wars 1. (1839–42) The war between Britain and China precipitated by the confiscation by the Chinese Government of British opium stores in Canton and the murder of a Chinese by British sailors. The British victory led to five treaty ports being opened to British trade and residence. **2.** (1856–60) The war between Britain and France, on one side, and China. Its immediate cause was the boarding of the British *Arrow* by Chinese officials. The allied victory opened further ports to western trade and led to the legalization of opium.

Oporto 41 09N 8 37W The second largest city in Portugal, on the River Douro near the Atlantic coast. Built on terraces, it has many tall granite houses and a modernized 13th-century cathedral. It is famous for the export (chiefly to Britain) of its port wine. Population (2000): 262 928.

opossum A New World *marsupial belonging to the family *Didelphidae* (65 species). Opossums are the only marsupials outside Australasia. The common, or Virginian, opossum (*Didelphys marsupialis*) is cat-sized, with a large pouch containing up to 16 teats.

Oppenheimer, J. Robert (1904–67) US physicist, who contributed to quantum mechanics and particle physics. In 1943 he was put in charge of the development of the atom bomb at Los Alamos, New Mexico. After the war he opposed the development of the hydrogen bomb and was labelled a security risk by Senator Joseph McCarthy's committee.

opposition An alignment of two celestial bodies in the solar system, usually the sun and a planet, that occurs when they lie directly opposite each other in the sky. The angle planet-earth-sun is then 180°.

optical activity The rotation of the plane of polarization of plane *polarized light as it passes through certain solutions and crystals. The angle through which the plane is rotated is directly proportional to the path length of the light in the substance and, in the case of a solution, to its concentration. If the plane is rotated clockwise (looking at the oncoming light) the substance is said to be dextrorotatory. Laevorotatory substances rotate the plane anticlockwise.

optics The branch of physics concerned with *light and vision. Optics is divided into two major branches: geometrical optics studies the geometry of light rays as they pass through an optical system; physical optics concerns light's properties (e.g. *diffraction, *interference, and polarization) and its interaction with matter (e.g. in *refraction, scattering, and absorption).

oracle A response given by a deity, usually through the medium of a priest or priestess, to an individual's inquiry; also, the sacred place at which such responses were sought. Although occurring in Egyptian and other ancient civilizations, the best-known oracles were those of classical Greece, especially the oracle of Apollo at Delphi.

oral contraceptive A hormonal drug—usually a mixture of an *oestrogen and a synthetic progesterone—taken in the form of tablets ("the Pill") by women to prevent conception. Oral contraceptives act by preventing the monthly release of an egg cell from the ovary. They may cause depression, high blood pressure, weight gain, and in rare cases thrombosis.

Oran 35 45N 0 38W A port in Algeria, on the Mediterranean Sea. Under intermittent Spanish occupation from the 16th to the 18th centuries, it was occupied by France from 1831 until Algerian independence (1962). Population (1998): 692 516.

orange One of several small evergreen trees or shrubs of the genus *Citrus*, native to SE Asia but cultivated throughout the tropics and subtropics. They have thick shiny leaves and clusters of fragrant white flowers. The globular fruit has a dimpled orange or yellow rind and a juicy pulp. Fruit of the sweet orange (*C. sinensis*) is eaten fresh while that of the Seville orange (*C. aurantium*) is used to make marmalade. Oranges are also used in soft drinks and confectionery. Family: *Rutaceae*. *See also* TANGERINE.

Orange The ruling dynasty of the Netherlands since 1815. In the 16th century the Princes of Orange, in S France, married into the House of *Nassau. William the Silent (1533–84), Prince of Orange-Nassau, led the Revolt of the Netherlands against Spain. He and his descendants (one of whom became William III of England) were stadholders (chief magistrates) of the United Provinces of the Netherlands until its collapse in 1795. In 1815 the family were restored as monarchs of the newly established kingdom of the Netherlands.

Orange Free State (Afrikaans name: Oranje Vrystaat) A former province in South Africa, consisting mainly of the undulating plain of the Highveld. Agriculture is the leading economic activity. Mining has developed recently; diamonds, gold, uranium, and coal are produced. The province has a strong Afrikaner culture. First settled by Voortrekkers in the early 19th century, the area was under British rule from 1848 until an independent Orange Free State was recognized in 1854. It joined the Union of South Africa in 1910. In 1994 it became the **Free State** region as part of administrative reorganization. Area: 129 152 sq km (49 886 sq mi). Population (2002 est): 2 859 081. Capital: Bloemfontein.

Orange Order An Irish sectarian society, named after William III of England (previously William of Orange), pledged to maintain the Protestant succession. Formed in 1795, following William's defeat of the Roman Catholic former king James II, it provided the backbone of Ulster resistance to the *Home Rule movement and remains the embodiment of Protestant Unionism.

Orange River A river in SW Africa. Rising in NE Lesotho, it flows mainly W across the South African plateau to the Atlantic Ocean. The largest river in South Africa, it forms part of the border between South Africa and Namibia. In 1963 the **Orange River Project** was begun to provide, through a series of dams, irrigation and hydroelectric power. Length: 2093 km (1300 mi).

orang-utan A long-armed great *ape, *Pongo pygmaeus*, of Borneo and Sumatra. Orang-utans grow up to 120 cm tall, have long coarse reddish-brown hair, and are mainly vegetarian. They are the only great apes outside Africa.

oratorio A musical composition, usually on a religious subject, for soloists, chorus, and orchestra. The name derives from the Oratory of St Philip Neri in 16th-century Rome where semidramatized versions of biblical stories were performed with musical accompaniment. Among notable oratorios are the *St Matthew* and *St John Passions* of J. S. Bach, Handel's *Messiah*, Haydn's *The Creation*, Mendelssohn's *Elijah*, Elgar's *Dream of Gerontius*, and Tippett's *A Child of Our Time*.

orbital An atomic orbital is the region around the nucleus in which there is an appreciable probability that an electron will be found. Each orbital has a fixed energy and a shape determined by three *quantum numbers, one (n) indicating the most probable distance of the electron from the nucleus, one (l) giving its angular momentum, and one (m) giving the orientation of the orbital if it is not spherical. In the formation of a covalent bond between two atoms, a molecular orbital containing two electrons is formed. *See also* WAVE MECHANICS.

orchestra A large instrumental ensemble. The modern symphony orchestra, which evolved during the 18th and 19th centuries, has string, wind (brass and woodwind), and percussion sections. The Greek word *orkestra* originally referred to the round space between the stage and the auditorium in ancient Greek theatres, which was occupied by the chorus, musicians, and dancers.

orchid A herbaceous perennial plant of the family *Orchidaceae* (about 20 000 species), found worldwide, especially in damp tropical regions. Most temperate orchids grow normally in the soil; while tropical orchids tend to grow nonparasitically on trees (i.e. as epiphytes) and form pseudobulbs (storage organs) at the base of the stem. Each flower consists of three petal-like sepals and three petals—the lowest (labellum) being very distinctive. The one or two stamens and stigma are fused to form a central column that bears pollen grains grouped into masses (pollinia), which are transferred to other flowers by insects. The flowers of many species are adapted to receive only a particular species of insect; examples are the bee, fly, and spider orchids (genus *Ophrys*). Many orchids are cultivated for ornament (*see* CYMBIDIUM; SLIPPER ORCHID); one genus—**Vanilla*—is of commercial importance as the source of vanilla flavouring.

Order of Merit (OM) A British order of chivalry, instituted in 1902. It comprises the sovereign and not more than 24 men and women of great eminence.

Order of the British Empire, The Most Excellent A British order of knighthood, instituted in 1917 and having five classes: Knights or Dames Grand Cross (GBE); Knights or Dames Commanders (KBE or DBE); Commanders (CBE); Officers (OBE); and Members (MBE).

orders of architecture The fundamental elements of classical *architecture, comprising five main types of supportive column—Doric, Tuscan, Ionic, Corinthian, and Composite. The column was developed by the Greeks and Romans to such an extent that the proportions between its constituent parts determined the proportions of the entire building. Each order usually consists of four main parts, the base, shaft, capital, and entablature, these having individual shapes and types of decoration.

Ordnance Survey The official map-making body of the UK. Established in 1791, following the mapping of Scotland (1726–90), it published its first map in 1801. Maps ranging from the large-scale 1:1250 (for major areas) to the small-scale 1:1 000 000have since been produced. The original scale to be used, the 1:63 360 (1 in:1 mi) was converted to the metric scale of 1:50 000 in the 1970s. The First Series of the 1:50 000 was completed in 1976; this has now been replaced by a Second Series with redrawn maps (the "Landranger" series), completed in 1988. Some 80% of the Survey's income now comes from the supply of mapping information in digital form. *See also* DIGITAL MAPPING.

Ordovician period A geological period of the Lower Palaeozoic era, between the Cambrian and Silurian periods. It lasted from about 515 to 445 million years ago. It is divided into the Upper and Lower Ordovician.

ore A rock body or mineral deposit from which one or more useful materials, usually metals, can be economically extracted. The gangue is the waste material left when the desired mineral has been extracted.

oregano An aromatic perennial herb, *Origanum vulgare*, native to the Mediterranean and W Asia. The dried leaves and flowers are used as a culinary flavouring and the plant is a source of essential oils. Family: *Labiatae*.

Oregon A state in the USA, on the NW Pacific coast. The Cascade Range extends N–S dividing the state between the valleys of the W and the dry plateau areas of the E. The economy is based predominantly on agriculture and forestry. Oregon is the nation's leading timber state and approximately half its area is forested; the Douglas fir is especially important. Oregon became a state in 1859, following considerable migration of White settlers from the Midwest during the 19th century. Area: 251 180 sq km (96 981 sq mi). Population (2000): 3 421 399. Capital: Salem.

Orestes In Greek legend, the son of *Agamemnon, King of Mycenae, and *Clytemnestra. Encouraged by his sister *Electra, he avenged his father's murder by killing his mother and her lover Aegisthus.

Orff, Carl (1895–1982) German composer, teacher, conductor, and editor. He developed a monodic style of composition characterized by lively rhythms; his best-known work is the oratorio *Carmina Burana* (1935–36).

organ A musical wind instrument of early origin. The modern organ consists of a large number of graduated pipes, some of which contain reeds, fitted over a wind chest and blown by manual or electric bellows. The pipes are made to sound by depressing keys or pedals. Each pipe sounds one note, but groups of duplicate pipes, called stops, can be made to sound together or successively. Different stops have different tone colours, many of which resemble orchestral instruments. An organ console may have as many as five keyboards, as well as pedals. Each keyboard has a separate range of stops and different characteristics. The action linking keys and pipes consists of a series of rods called a tracker action or wires conveying electrical impulses. The modern **electronic organ** consists of a series of electronic oscillators to produce notes, which are then amplified.

organic farming *See* FERTILIZERS.

Organisation de l'Armée secrète (OAS) An organization of French settlers in Algeria opposed to Algerian independence from France. The OAS was established in 1961 and led by General Raoul Salan (1899–1984). Its campaign of terrorism in Algeria and France included the attempted assassination in September 1961, of the French president, de Gaulle, who by March 1962 had reached agreement with the Algerian nationalists (*see* FRONT DE LIBÉRATION NATIONALE). Salan was captured (imprisoned 1962–68) and the OAS collapsed.

Organization for Economic Cooperation and Development (**OECD**) An international organization founded in 1961 to further world trade and coordinate aid to developing countries. It succeeded the organization set up in 1948 to coordinate the *Marshall Plan for European economic recovery after World War II. The headquarters are in Paris.

Organization of African Unity (OAU) *See* AFRICAN UNION.

Organization of American States (**OAS**) A body founded in 1948 to foster mutual understanding and cooperation between American republics and collective security. It is based on the *Monroe Doctrine, which discouraged European intervention in the Americas. Cuba was expelled in 1962.

Organization of Central American States (**OCAS**) An international organization founded in 1951. Its members include Costa Rica, El Salvador, Guatemala, Honduras, and Nicaragua, and its headquarters are in Guatemala City. Its aim is to promote social, cultural, and economic development through joint action.

Organization of Petroleum Exporting Countries (**OPEC**) An organization founded in 1960 to represent the interests of the chief oil-exporting nations (Algeria, Indonesia, Iran, Iraq, Kuwait, Libya, Nigeria, Qatar, Saudi Arabia, United Arab Emirates, and Venezuela) in dealings with the major oil companies. Since the mid-1970s OPEC has been less effective in controlling the price of oil due to internal dissension and increased supplies from non-OPEC sources. Ecuador left in 1992 and Gabon in 1995.

orienteering A navigational sport, held over rugged country, that originated in Sweden in 1918 and is designed to test both intellectual and athletic ability. Using a map and compass, competitors run round a series of control points in a prescribed sequence.

Orinoco, River The third largest river system in South America. Rising in S Venezuela, it flows in an arc forming part of the Venezuela–Colombia border before entering the Atlantic Ocean via an extensive delta region. Drainage basin area: 940 000 sq km (365 000 sq mi). Length: about 2575 km (1600 mi).

oriole A songbird belonging to an Old World family (*Oriolidae*; 28 species) occurring mainly in tropical forests. Orioles generally have a black-and-yellow plumage, measure 18–30 cm, and feed on fruit and insects. The golden oriole (*Oriolus oriolus*) is the only species reaching Europe. American orioles belong to the family *Icteridae* (87 species). They usually have a black plumage with red, yellow, or brown markings.

Orion A very conspicuous constellation that can be seen from most parts of the world. The brightest stars, Rigel and *Betelgeuse, lie at opposite corners of a quadrilateral of stars with Bellatrix and Saiph at the other corners. Inside the quadrilateral three 2nd-magnitude stars form **Orion's Belt**, S of which lies the **Orion nebula**.

Orkney Islands (*or* **Orkneys**) A group of about 70 islands off the N coast of Scotland, separated from the mainland by the Pentland Firth. The chief ones are Mainland (Pomona), South Ronaldsay, Westray, Sanday, and Hoy. The population is of Scandinavian descent, reflecting the Islands' long connections with Norway and Denmark. The group became an island authority in 1975. Agriculture is of major importance; the Islands also serve as a base for the exploitation of North Sea oil with a pipeline from the Piper field. Area: 974 sq km (376 sq mi). Population (2001): 19 245. Administrative centre: Kirkwall.

Orléans 47 54N 1 54E A city in N France, the capital of the Loiret department on the River Loire. In 1429, during the Hundred Years' War, the strategically important city was delivered from the English by Joan of Arc. Its cathedral, which was destroyed by the Huguenots in 1568, was rebuilt in the 17th century. The focal point of road and rail routes, Orléans has an extensive trade in wine, brandy, and agricultural produce. Population (1999): 112 833.

Orléans, Louis Philippe Joseph, Duc d' (1747–93) French revolutionary. A cousin of Louis XVI of France, he nevertheless supported the dissident Third Estate at the beginning of the *French Revolution, joining the radical Jacobins in 1791. He was executed after his son (later King Louis Philippe) had joined the Austrian coalition against France.

ormolu (French: *d'or moulu*, powdered gold) Ornamental gilded bronze used as embellishment on furniture, especially French 18th- and 19th-century furniture.

Ornithischia An order of herbivorous *dinosaurs that lived in the Jurassic and Cretaceous periods (200–65 million years ago). They had hip bones arranged like those of birds (the name means "bird hips") and a horny beak at the front of the jaw (teeth were present only at the rear). Some were bipedal while others evolved to become quadrupedal and heavily armoured. There were both amphibious and terrestrial forms. *See* IGUANODON; STEGOSAURUS; TRICERATOPS.

ornithology The study of *birds. Ornithology is a popular pastime as well as a branch of zoology; the records of bird spottings made by amateur ornithologists can be valuable in helping to determine the ecology and behaviour of bird populations. Recovery of rings used in bird-ringing experiments provides information regarding the dispersion and migration of birds. Many species are protected by legislation, and bird sanctuaries have been established.

orogeny A period of mountain building. Several major orogenies have occurred in the earth's geological history, major ones since the Precambrian including the Caledonian (in the Lower Palaeozoic) and the Alpine (in the Tertiary). **Orogenesis** is the process of mountain building, including folding, faulting, and thrusting, resulting from the collision of two continents, which compresses the sediment between them into mountain chains (*see* PLATE TECTONICS).

Orpheus A legendary Greek poet and musician, the son of the muse Calliope by either Apollo or Oeagrus, King of Thrace. After sailing with the *Argonauts he married *Eurydice. After her death, he descended to Hades to recover her. *Persephone, charmed by his playing on the lyre, released Eurydice but Orpheus lost her when he disobeyed the gods' command not to look back at her. He was murdered by the Maenads, followers of *Dionysus.

orrisroot The fragrant rhizome (underground stem) of several European plants of the genus *Iris.* It is dried and ground for use in perfumes and medicines.

orthoclase An alkali potassium *feldspar, $KAlSi_3O_8$, found in acid igneous rocks and in many metamorphic rocks. It is white, pink, or greenish grey, and is softer than quartz. Commercially, orthoclase is frequently obtained from pegmatites; it is used in the manufacture of glass, ceramic glazes, and enamels.

Orthodox Church The federation of self-governing Churches historically associated with the eastern part of the Roman Empire and separated from the Latin Church since 1054; also called the Eastern Orthodox Church. The four ancient patriarchs of Orthodoxy are of Constantinople (which has primacy of honour), Alexandria, Antioch, and Jerusalem; in addition there are patriarchs of Moscow, Georgia, Serbia, Bulgaria, and Romania. Independent Orthodox Churches exist in Greece, Cyprus, Albania, the Czech Republic, and Poland. There are also congregations in other countries, many established by Russian immigrants after the Revolution. Government is by bishops, who must be unmarried, priests, and deacons, who play an important liturgical role. The Orthodox Church claims the authority of *apostolic succession and regards itself as the one true Church, accepting as doctrine only the *Nicene Creed. Its worship is sacramental and centred on the Eucharist and the ancient liturgies of St John Chrysostom and St Basil, which are always solemnly celebrated and sung without accompaniment. The veneration of *icons is a distinctive feature of Orthodox worship; statues and other three-dimensional images are forbidden. Easter is the main feast of the Church year. *See also* GREEK ORTHODOX CHURCH; RUSSIAN ORTHODOX CHURCH.

orthopaedics The medical specialty concerned with treating deformities caused by disease of and injury to the bones and joints. This includes the use of surgery (especially for artificial hip joints), manipulation, traction, etc., in correcting deformities and fractures, together with rehabilitation of patients.

Orthoptera A mainly tropical order of generally large stout-bodied insects (15 000 species), including the *grasshoppers and *crickets. The hind legs are enlarged and specialized for jumping and the large blunt head has biting jaws for feeding on vegetation. Few species are good fliers. Many species produce sounds by rubbing one part of the body against another (stridulation).

ortolan A Eurasian *bunting, *Emberiza hortulana*, about 16 cm long, having a brown-streaked plumage with a yellow throat and pinkish belly. Large numbers are trapped as table delicacies on their autumn migration to N Africa and the Middle East.

Orton, Joe (Kingsley) (1933–67) British dramatist, whose black comedies on themes of sexual perversion and corruption included *Loot* (1966) and *What the Butler Saw* (1969). A homosexual, he was murdered by his lover.

Orwell, George (Eric Blair; 1903–50) British novelist and writer, born in India. His nonfiction includes *Down and Out in Paris and London* (1933), *The Road to Wigan Pier* (1937), and *Homage* *to Catalonia* (1936). *Animal Farm* (1945) is an anti-Stalinist allegory and *Nineteen Eighty Four* (1949) a pessimistic view of a totalitarian future.

oryx A desert antelope, *Oryx gazella*, which comprises two races, beisa and gemsbok, of S and E Africa. Oryxes have long slender straight horns and are greyish brown with black markings on the face and legs. The Arabian oryx (*O. leucoryx*) and the N African scimitar-horned oryx (*O. tao*) are both endangered species.

Osaka 34 40N 135 30E A port in Japan, in SW Honshu on the Yodo delta. The third largest city in Japan, it was a leading commercial centre by the 17th century. It is also a cultural centre. Together with Kobe, Kyoto, and several small cities it forms the important **Osaka-Kobe** industrial area. Population (1995): 2 602 352.

Osborne, John (1929–94) British dramatist, one of the original Angry Young Men, best known for his play *Look Back in Anger* (1956). His criticism of contemporary Britain continued in such plays as *The Entertainer* (1957), *A Patriot for Me* (1965), and *West of Suez* (1971). Other plays include *Luther* (1960), *Inadmissible Evidence* (1964), and *Déjà Vu* (1992).

Oscar *See* ACADEMY OF MOTION PICTURE ARTS AND SCIENCES.

Osiris The Egyptian god of the dead, the brother and husband of *Isis; as the father of *Horus (the sun), he was also the god of renewal and rebirth. He was killed by his evil brother *Set. After Isis had magically reconstructed his body, he became ruler of the underworld. Dead pharaohs became identified with Osiris.

Oslo (former name (1877–1925): Kristiania) 59 56N 10 54E The capital and main port of Norway, situated in the SE at the head of Oslo Fjord. It is the financial and industrial centre of Norway and is also a cultural centre. Founded in the 11th century, Oslo became capital in 1299 and developed into an important trading post under the influence of the Hanseatic League. Population (2000 est): 507 467.

osmiridium A naturally occurring alloy consisting mainly of osmium and iridium. It is hard and resistant to wear.

osmium (Os) An extremely hard bluish-silver metal of the platinum group. It is one of the densest elements known (relative density 22.6). Its major use is in the production of hard alloys with other noble metals, for pen nibs and electrical contacts. At no 76; at wt 190.2; mp 3033 ± 20°C; bp 5012 ± 100°C.

osmosis The passage of a solvent from a less concentrated into a more concentrated solution through a semipermeable membrane (one allowing the passage of solvent, but not solute, molecules). Osmosis stops if the pressure of the more concentrated solution exceeds that of the less concentrated solution by an amount known as the **osmotic pressure** between them. In living organisms the solvent is water and osmosis plays an important role in effecting the distribution of water in plants and animals, causing water to pass into and out of cells.

osprey A large *hawk, *Pandion haliaetus*, also called fish hawk, occurring worldwide (except in South America) around coasts and inland waters. It is 65 cm long and its plumage is brown above and white below. It feeds mostly on pike and trout, caught in its talons, which are covered in rough spikes to help grasp prey.

Ostend 1 13N 2 55E A seaport and coast in NW Belgium, on the North Sea. Ostend is the headquarters of the country's fishing fleet and maintains a cross-Channel ferry service to Dover, England. Population (1995 est): 68 858.

osteoarthritis A disease of the joints, mainly back, hips, and knees, in which their internal surfaces are rubbed away and they become swollen and painful. This becomes increasingly common as people age. Drugs can reduce the pain as can surgically installed artificial hips and knees. *See also* ARTHRITIS.

osteopathy A system of healing by manipulation and massage, based on the theory that nearly all diseases are due to the displacement of bones, especially the bones of the spine. Osteopathy is of use in relieving disorders of the joints, bones, and muscles, especially those causing back pain.

Ostia A town of ancient Rome, at the mouth of the River Tiber. A major naval base under the Republic, its prosperity was greatest in the 2nd century AD, when it was an important commercial centre.

ostrich A fast-running flightless African bird, *Struthio camelus*, occurring in open grassland and semidesert regions. It is the largest living bird. Males may reach 2.5 m tall and are black with white wing and tail plumes; females are smaller and mainly brown. Ostriches have a long almost naked neck, a small head, and a ducklike bill used to feed on plant material. Order: *Struthioniformes*.

Ostrogoths A branch of the *Goths, forced W of the River Dniester by the *Huns (375 AD). In the 6th century they frequently invaded N

Italy and captured much of the Balkans. Between 493 and 526 Theodoric (c. 445–526), their leader, ruled Italy. The Roman Empire, subsequently destroyed the Ostrogoths (562).

Oswald, Saint (c. 605–41) King of Northumbria (634–41) after defeating and killing the Welsh king, Cadwallader. He restored Christianity in Northumbria with the help of St *Aidan. Oswald was killed in battle by Penda. Feast day: 5 Aug.

Oświęcim (German name: Auschwitz) 50 02N 19 11E A town in S Poland, site of a notorious Nazi extermination camp during World War II. Between two and four million people (mostly Jews) were systematically murdered here. Parts of the site are preserved as a monument. Population (latest est): 45 200.

Ottawa 45 25N 75 43W The capital of Canada, in SE Ontario on the Ottawa River. It is two-thirds English speaking and one-third French speaking. Founded in the early 19th century as a lumbering centre, it became national capital in 1867. Population (1996): 323 340.

Ottawa River A river in central Canada, rising in W Quebec and flowing W, then SE down the Ontario-Quebec border to join the St Lawrence River, as its chief tributary, at Montreal. It is linked with Lake Ontario by the Rideau Canal. Length: 1120 km (696 mi).

otter A semi-aquatic carnivorous mammal belonging to the subfamily *Lutrinae* (18 species), distributed worldwide except in Polar regions, Australasia, and Madagascar. Otters have a cylindrical body, waterproof fur, short legs, partially webbed feet, and a thick tapering tail. The Eurasian otter (*Lutra lutra*) is about 1.2 m long. Chief genera: *Lutra*, *Paraonyx*; family: *Mustelidae*. *See also* SEA OTTER.

Otto (I) the Great (912–73 AD) Holy Roman Emperor (936–73; crowned 962). He subdued his rebellious vassals, defeated a Hungarian invasion at the great victory of Lechfeld (955), and extended his influence into Italy.

Otto, Nikolaus August (1832–91) German engineer, who in 1876 devised the four-stroke cycle, known as the Otto cycle, for the *internal-combustion engine. His engine made the development of the motor car possible.

Ottoman Empire A Turkish Muslim empire ruling large parts of the Middle East as well as territories in Europe from the 14th to the 20th centuries. Its capital was *Istanbul (formerly Constantinople) and its rulers descendants of its founder Osman I (c. 1258–c. 1326). Originating around 1300 as a small Turkish state in Asia Minor, in 1453 the Ottomans captured Constantinople and destroyed the Eastern Roman (Byzantine) Empire. Ottoman power culminated in the 16th century with the conquest of Egypt and Syria (1517) and, under Suleiman the Magnificent, Hungary (1529) and territories in the Middle East and N Africa. From the 17th century the Empire declined. In World War I the Ottomans supported Germany and defeat brought the loss of territories outside Asia Minor. The subsequent nationalist revolution of Kemal *Atatürk replaced the Ottoman Empire with the state of Turkey (1922).

Ouagadougou 12 25N 1 30W The capital of Burkina Faso, founded in the 11th century as the centre of a Mossi empire. Population (1993 est): 690 000.

Oudry, Jean-Baptiste (1686–1755) French *rococo painter and tapestry designer, head of the *Beauvais (1734) and Gobelin (1736) tapestry works. His illustrations to La Fontaine's *Fables* are particularly well known.

Ouse, River The name of several rivers in England, including: **1.** A river in NE England, flowing mainly NE through Yorkshire to join the River Trent, forming the Humber estuary. Length: 92 km (57 mi). **2.** A river in S England, flowing E and S across the South Downs to the English Channel at Newhaven. Length: 48 km (30 mi). *See also* GREAT OUSE RIVER.

ovary 1. The organ of female animals in which the *egg cells (ova) are produced. In mammals (including women) there are two ovaries close to the openings of the Fallopian tubes, which lead to the uterus (womb). They produce both eggs and steroid hormones (*see* OESTROGENS; PROGESTERONE) in a regular cycle (*see* MENSTRUATION). **2.** The part of a flower that contains the *ovules. It is situated at the base of the carpel(s) and becomes the fruit wall after fertilization.

Ovid (Publius Ovidius Naso; 43 BC–17 AD) Roman poet. His poems include the *Amores* and the *Ars amatoria*, on his characteristic theme of love. His greatest work, the *Metamorphoses*, is a poem in 15 books including mythological and historical tales. In 8 AD he was exiled by the emperor Augustus to the Black Sea.

ovule The structure within the ovary of a *flower that contains an egg cell and nutritive tissue. After fertilization it develops into the *seed containing the embryo.

ovum *See* EGG.

Owen, David (Anthony Llewellyn), Baron (1938–) British politician. As a Labour

MP (1966–81), he was foreign secretary (1977–79). A cofounder of the Social Democratic Party (SDP), he became leader in 1983 but resigned in 1987 when the party merged with the Liberals.

Owen, Robert (1771–1858) British philanthropist and manufacturer. In 1800 he became manager of the mills at New Lanark, Scotland, where he established a model community with improved housing and working conditions. He later established cooperative societies for the unemployed and cofounded the Grand National Consolidated Trades Union in 1834.

Owen, Wilfred (1893–1918) British poet. His poetry written during World War I includes "Strange Meeting" and "Anthem for Doomed Youth." He was killed in action. His friend Siegfried *Sassoon edited his *Poems* (1920).

Owens, Jesse (John Cleveland O.; 1913–80) US Black athlete. In 1935 he set six world records in 45 minutes (in the long jump, 100 yards, 220 yards, 220 metres, 220 yards hurdles, and 220 metres hurdles). At the Berlin Olympics (1936) he won four gold medals.

owl A nocturnal bird of prey belonging to an order (*Strigiformes*) of worldwide distribution. There are two families: *Strigidae* (typical owls) and *Tytonidae* (barn and bay owls). Owls have a large head with large forward facing eyes surrounded by a facial disc of radiating feathers, soft plumage, usually brown and patterned, and a short sharp hooked bill. Owls hunt mammals, birds, and insects. They range in size from 16 cm (pygmy owls; genus *Glaucidium*) to 70 cm (eagle owls; genus *Bubo*). *See* BARN OWL; TAWNY OWL.

oxalic acid (*or* **ethanedioic acid**; $(COOH)_2$) A colourless poisonous soluble crystalline solid. Potassium and sodium salts are found in plants. Oxalic acid is used as a metal cleaner and for bleaching textiles and leather.

oxeye daisy A perennial herb, *Chrysanthemum leucanthemum*, also called moon daisy or marguerite, found in grassland and wasteland throughout Europe. It has large solitary flower heads with long white rays surrounding a yellow central disc. Family: *Compositae*.

OXFAM A British charity founded in 1942, and registered in 1948 as the Oxford Committee for Famine Relief. Its purpose is to relieve suffering throughout the world. Its long-term projects include medical, social, and economic research and training schemes.

Oxford 51 46N 1 15W A city in S central England, the administrative centre of Oxfordshire on the Rivers Thames and Cherwell. It is the site of the **University of Oxford**, one of the oldest universities in Europe, dating from the 12th century. The University is organized as a federation of colleges, which are governed by their own teaching staff ("fellows"). The first college, University College, was founded in 1249. Other notable colleges include All Souls (1438), Christ Church (1546), and Lady Margaret Hall (1878), which was the first women's college. In the Civil War Oxford was the royalist headquarters. College buildings dominate the city centre, with business parks on the outskirts. The motor-car works at Cowley now employs only a fraction of its former workforce. Oxford has one of the world's great libraries (the Bodleian Library, 1602). Population (1991): 127 600.

Oxford, Provisions of (1258) The scheme of constitutional reform imposed upon Henry III by his barons at Oxford following their opposition to excessive taxation. His repudiation of the Provisions (1261) led to the Barons' War.

Oxford Movement A movement within the Church of England emphasizing the Catholic principles on which it rested. Led by *Newman, John Keble (1792–1866), Edward Pusey (1800–82), and James Froude (1818–94) of Oxford University, it was initiated in 1833 and greatly invigorated Anglicanism. *See also* ANGLO-CATHOLICISM.

Oxfordshire A county in the S Midlands of England. In 1974 it gained a large part of NW Berkshire. It consists mainly of a broad vale, crossed by the River Thames, with the *Chiltern Hills in the SE and the *Cotswold Hills in the NW. It is chiefly agricultural; industries include light manufacturing, electronics, and tourism (centred on Oxford). Area: 2611 sq km (1008 sq mi). Population (2001): 605 492. Administrative centre: Oxford.

oxidation and reduction Oxidation is the chemical combination of a substance with oxygen. An example is the combustion of carbon to carbon dioxide: $C + O_2 \rightarrow CO_2$. The converse process, removal of oxygen, is known as reduction; e.g. the reduction of iron oxide to iron: $Fe_2O_3 + 3C \rightarrow 2Fe + 3CO$. Reduction also refers to reaction with hydrogen and oxidation to removal of hydrogen. More generally, an oxidation reaction is one involving loss of electrons and reduction a gain of electrons. Usually oxidation and reduction reactions occur together. Thus, in the reaction of ferric ions (Fe^{3+}) with stannous ions (Sn^{2+}), the ferric ions are reduced to ferrous ions (Fe^{2+}) and the stannous ions oxidized to stannic ions (Sn^{4+}). Reactions of this type are called **redox reactions**.

oxidation number (*or* **oxidation state**) The number of electrons that would have to be added to an atom to neutralize it. Thus Na^+, Cl^-, and He have oxidation numbers of 1, −1, and 0, respectively. Rules have been developed for assigning oxidation numbers to covalently bound atoms depending on the electric charge that the atom would have if the molecule ionized.

oxpecker An African songbird, genus *Buphagus*, that feeds on ticks and maggots pecked from the hides of cattle and game animals. Family: *Sturnidae* (starlings).

oxygen (O) A colourless odourless gas discovered by J. *Priestley. The element exists in two forms—the diatomic molecule (O_2), which constitutes 21% of the earth's atmosphere, and trace amounts of the highly reactive triatomic allotrope, ozone. Oxygen is very reactive and forms oxides with most elements. In addition to its vital importance for plants and animals, its major use is in the production of steel in blast furnaces. It is obtained by the distillation of liquid air. At no 8; at wt 15.9994; mp −218.79°C; bp −182.97°C.

oxygen cycle The process by which oxygen—present in the atmosphere or dissolved in water—is taken in by plants and animals for use in *respiration (intercellular combustion of food materials to provide energy) and released into the environment as a waste product, mostly in the form of free oxygen (by plants in photosynthesis). Oxygen is often combined in organic and inorganic compounds, which may also be considered as part of the cycle. *See also* CARBON CYCLE; NITROGEN CYCLE.

oyster A sedentary *bivalve mollusc belonging to the family *Ostreidae* (true osyters), of temperate and warm seas. The lower plate (valve) of the shell is larger and flatter than the upper valve; they are held together by an elastic ligament and powerful muscles. Edible oysters are cultivated for their white flesh; pearl oysters (family *Aviculidae*) are cultivated for their pearls, which they make by coating a grain of sand lodged inside their shell with calcareous material.

oystercatcher A black or black-and-white wading bird of a family (*Haematopodidae*; 4 species) occurring in temperate and tropical coastal regions. 40–50 cm long, oystercatchers have a flattened orange-red bill specialized for opening bivalve molluscs and probing in mud. Order: *Charadriiformes*.

ozone (O_3) A pale blue gaseous form of *oxygen, formed by passing an electrical discharge through oxygen (O_2). Ozone is a poisonous unstable gas. It is used as an oxidizing agent, for example in water purification. It is present in small amounts in the atmosphere, mostly in the **ozone layer**, which forms 11–26 km (7–16 mi) above the earth's surface as a result of dissociation by solar ultraviolet radiation of molecular oxygen into single atoms, some of which then combine with undissociated oxygen molecules. The ozone layer absorbs in the 230–320 nm waveband, protecting the earth from dangerous excessive ultraviolet radiation. In the 1980s holes in the ozone layer were detected over both poles, prompting the EU to phase out the use of harmful CFCs (*see* FLUOROCARBONS) by 1997, while other countries agreed to limit such emissions in the Montreal Pact (1990). *See also* GREENHOUSE EFFECT.

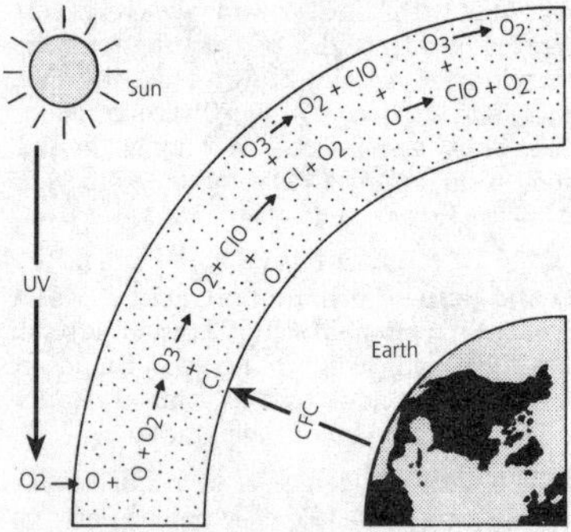

ozone layer. Solar ultraviolet radiation breaks up oxygen molecules (O_2) into atoms, some of which recombine with oxygen molecules to form ozone (O_3). Chlorine atoms from stable CFCs combine with O_3 to form chlorine monoxide (ClO), which reacts with atomic oxygen to form O_2 and chlorine atoms again. These Cl atoms react again with O_3. Each chlorine atom can react 20 000 times with ozone causing a severe drop in the concentration of ozone in the ozone layer.

P

pacemaker A small section of specialized heart muscle that initiates heartbeat. It is situated in the right atrium and contracts spontaneously: the impulse to contract is transmitted from the pacemaker to both atria and then to the ventricles. If the pacemaker ceases to function (heart block) it may be replaced by a battery-operated device that stimulates the heart to contract.

Pacific Ocean The world's largest and deepest ocean, covering a third of its surface. It extends between Asia, Australia, Antarctica, and America. It reaches its maximum depth in the *Marianas Trench. The S and E have a uniform climate with steady winds, but the W is known for its typhoons, which cause coastal flooding. The Pacific has some diurnal and mixed tides, while Tahitian tides follow the sun and not the moon.

Pacino, Al (1940–) US actor, best known for his film roles, often as violent but brooding antiheroes. His films include *The Godfather* (1972) and its sequels, *Scent of a Woman* (1992), which earned him an Oscar, and *Insomnia* (2002).

Padang 1 00S 100 21E A port in Indonesia, in W Sumatra. An early Dutch settlement, it flourished when railways were built in the 19th century. It exports coal, cement, coffee, copra, and rubber. Population (1995 est): 721 500.

Paderewski, Ignacy (Jan) (1860–1941) Polish pianist, composer, and statesman. He achieved an international reputation as a performer and composed a piano concerto and many solo pieces. He was the first prime minister (1919) of newly independent Poland but resigned after ten months to return to his musical career.

Padua (Italian name: Padova) 45 24N 11 53E A city in NE Italy, near Venice. An important city in Roman and Renaissance times, it has several notable buildings; in front of the Basilica of St Anthony stands Donatello's equestrian statue of Gattamelata. Machinery and textiles are produced. Population (2000 est): 211 391.

paediatrics The medical specialty concerned with the problems and illnesses of infants and children from birth to adolescence. Paediatricians must have a detailed knowledge of obstetrics, genetics, and psychology. Their work includes the management of handicaps as well as the treatment and prevention of childhood diseases.

Paestum The Roman name for Posidonia, a Greek colony founded about 600 BC on the SW coast of Italy. The remains of three great Doric temples still stand there. Named after the Greek sea god *Poseidon, it was conquered by Rome in 273 BC.

Paganini, Niccolò (1782–1840) Italian virtuoso violinist. After an adventurous youth he toured Europe, astonishing audiences with his techniques. He composed six violin concertos, showpieces for violin, including a set of variations on the G string, and 24 caprices.

pagoda A Buddhist shrine in the form of a tower for housing relics of the Buddha. Pagodas originated in India, where their standardized form of a basic unit repeated vertically in diminishing sizes was evolved. The pagoda spread to Sri Lanka, SE Asia, China, and Japan. See illustration on p. 666.

Paine, Thomas (1737–1809) British political writer. In 1774 he went to America, where his *Common Sense* (1776) initiated the movement towards independence. Back in England, he published *The Rights of Man* (1791–92) in defence of the French Revolution. Indicted for treason, he fled to France, where he wrote *The Age of Reason* (1796), a deist manifesto. He died in poverty in America.

paint A finely powdered insoluble pigment suspended in a binding medium; on application to a surface the volatile components of the binding medium evaporate, the drying oils

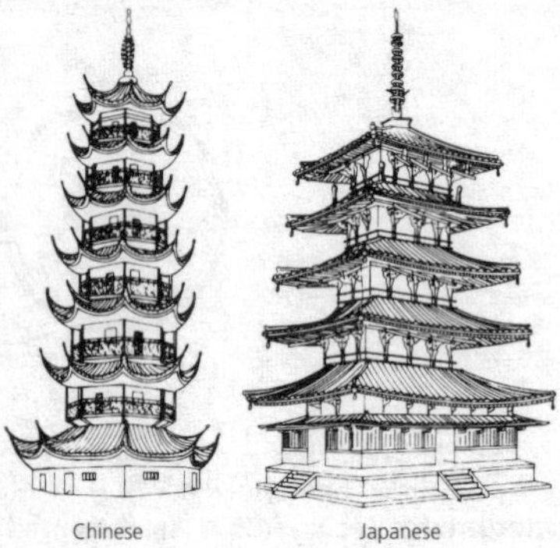

pagoda. The exuberantly curving roofs of the typical multistoreyed Chinese pagoda contrast with the more restrained Japanese form.

oxidize, and the resins polymerize, leaving a decorative or protective skin. The binding medium consists of a drying oil (e.g. linseed oil or tung oil), a resin (rosin or a synthetic alkyd), a thinner (turpentine, benzene, etc.), and a drier (e.g. lead linoleate) to accelerate film formation. Water-based emulsion paints consist of emulsions of a synthetic resin in water.

painted lady An orange, black, and white butterfly, *Vanessa cardui*, of worldwide distribution. It cannot survive cold winters but migrates from warmer regions each year. The caterpillars feed mainly on thistles and nettles.

Paisley 55 50N 4 26W A town in W central Scotland, in Strathclyde Region near Glasgow. Famous for shawls in the 19th century, Paisley's textile industry is still important. The abstract design used for the shawls is still known as **paisley pattern**. Dyeing, bleaching, engineering, and starch and cornflour manufacturing are also important. Population (1991): 75 526.

Paisley, Ian (1926–) Northern Irish politician. A minister of the Free Presbyterian Church of Ulster from 1946, he was a Protestant Unionist member of the Northern Irish parliament (1970–72) before becoming (1974–85; 1986–) a Democratic Unionist MP in the House of Commons, an MEP (1979–2004), and a member of the Northern Ireland assembly (1998–). He is a leading opponent of the Good Friday Agreement (1998).

Pakistan, Islamic Republic of A country in S Asia, bordering on Iran, Afghanistan, China, and India. The W is mountainous and the E has areas of desert, while the River Indus rises in the Himalayas in the N and flows S to the Arabian Sea. The population is a mixture of many Asian and Middle Eastern racial groups. 97% of the population is Muslim. *Economy*: mainly agricultural, producing cotton, rice, wheat, and sugar cane. Pakistan has become a major exporter of cotton and cotton yarn and cloth. Chemical fertilizers, cement, sugar, and handicrafts are also produced, and a steel industry is being developed. Fishing is increasingly important. Resources include coal, iron ore, copper, limestone, oil, and large quantities of natural gas. *History*: the history of Pakistan is that of *India until 1947, when it was created to satisfy the Muslim League's demand for a separate state for the Muslim minority. It consisted then of two separate areas; West Pakistan comprised Baluchistan, the Northwest Frontier, West Punjab (now Punjab province), and Sind, while East Pakistan was formed from East Bengal. The most serious problem has been the unification of Pakistan's diverse population groups. The unifying force of the common religion has not been able to contain demands for regional autonomy and increased democracy. Thus each of Pakistan's three constitutions (1956, 1962, 1973) has been replaced by martial law (an amended version of the 1973 constitution was restored in 1985 and suspended in 1999). The electoral victory in East Pakistan of the Awami League (1970), which demanded regional autonomy, led to its secession as *Bangladesh (1971). From 1972 to 1989 Pakistan withdrew from the Commonwealth. Unrest followed the disputed 1977 elections, leading finally to a military coup by Gen Zia ul-Haq. The former prime minister, Zulfikar Ali Bhutto, was executed for conspiracy to murder (1979). Zia became president in 1978; after he was assassinated in 1988 Bhutto's daughter Benazir Bhutto became prime minister. In 1990, in the wake of ethnic violence, Bhutto was dismissed. Her successor, Nawaz Sharif, was dismissed in 1993 following accusations of corruption; Bhutto was re-elected but in 1996 was again dismissed on grounds of corruption. Sharif was re-elected in 1997 but faced constitutional disputes, ethnic violence, and deepening economic crisis. In 1999 Sharif was deposed in a military coup led by Gen Pervaiz Musharraf, who subsequently appointed himself president. Musharraf's supporters won elections held in 2002, but these were widely seen as flawed. The long-running border dispute with India over Kashmir escalated sharply in 2002 but there have since been peace talks. Official language: Urdu. Currency: Pakistan rupee of 100 paisa. Area (excluding Jammu and Kashmir): 803 943 sq km (310 322 sq mi). Population (2003 est): 149 030 000. Capital: Islamabad.

Palace of Westminster The British parliamentary buildings in Westminster, London, containing the House of Commons and the House of Lords (*see* PARLIAMENT). It is also known as the Houses of Parliament. A royal palace of medieval construction until the 16th century, when it assumed its present function, it was largely burnt down in 1834, only the Great Hall surviving. It was rebuilt in the gothic revival style by *Barry and *Pugin. *See also* BIG BEN.

Palaeocene epoch *See* TERTIARY PERIOD.

Palaeolithic The earliest division of the *Stone Age. It extends roughly from the emergence of man to the end of the last ice age. The Palaeolithic has three phases: Lower, beginning as much as 3 500 000 years ago and characterized by pebble-tool manufacture; Middle, beginning about 70 000 years ago and associated with *Neanderthal man; and Upper, beginning about 40 000 years ago and associated with *Cro-Magnon man.

palaeomagnetism The history of the earth's magnetic field (*see* GEOMAGNETIC FIELD) as determined from the remanent magnetism of rocks. The study assumes that the principal component of igneous and sedimentary rocks' magnetism was determined at or near to the time at which the rocks were formed. Palaeomagnetism provides evidence for continental drift (*see* PLATE TECTONICS) and the movement of the magnetic poles.

palaeontology The study of ancient organisms from their *fossil remains in the rocks. Fossils are used to correlate bodies of rock and establish their stratigraphic relationships with each other; this field is called biostratigraphy. The study of ancient microscopic organisms (microfossils) is called **micropalaeontology**.

Palaeozoic era The era of geological time between the Precambrian and the Mesozoic, lasting from about 590 to 240 million years ago. It is divided into the Lower Palaeozoic, which contains the Cambrian, Ordovician, and Silurian periods, and the Upper Palaeozoic, containing the Devonian, Carboniferous, and Permian. It is the first era of Phanerozoic time.

palate The roof of the mouth, which is divided into two parts. The soft palate at the back of the mouth is composed of mucous membrane and prevents food passing into the nose during swallowing. The hard palate, further forward, is composed of two fused halves made up of the palatine bone and part of the maxillary (upper jaw) bones.

Palatinate Two regions of W Germany: the Lower (*or* Rhenish) Palatinate is now in Rheinland-Pfalz, Baden-Württemberg, and Hessen and the Upper Palatinate is now in Bavaria. In 1156 the title of count palatine was bestowed by Emperor Frederick I on his half-brother Conrad, whose territories included what later became the Rhenish Palatinate. When, in 1214, it passed to the Wittelsbach family, their lands in Bavaria became the Upper Palatinate. From 1356 the counts palatine were electors of Holy Roman Emperors. The two Palatinates were separated from 1648 until 1777. In the early 19th century the Lower Palatinate was divided between France and various German states and the Upper Palatinate passed to Bavaria.

Palau *See* BELAU, REPUBLIC OF.

Palermo 38 08N 13 23E A port in Italy, the capital of Sicily. Founded by the Phoenicians in the 8th century BC, it became the chief town of the island under the Arabs (9th–11th centuries). Buildings include the gothic cathedral and the Norman palace. It has shipbuilding and textile industries. Population (2000 est): 683 794.

Palestine (*or* **Holy Land**) A historic area in the Middle East, consisting of the area between the Mediterranean Sea and the River Jordan. It now comprises *Israel and the Israeli-occupied territories. Sacred to Jews, Christians, and Muslims alike, the area has been much fought over. Towards the end of the 2nd millennium BC it was settled by the Hebrew people, and in about 1000 BC a Hebrew kingdom was founded by Saul. Following the reign of Solomon it was split into Israel, later conquered by the Assyrians, and Judah (*see* JUDAEA), later conquered by the Babylonians. From the late 4th century AD many Jews left Palestine, which became a centre first for Christian and later for Muslim pilgrimage (following Arab conquest in 636 AD). Christianity was reinstated in the area by the conquest of the Crusaders (1099 until the 13th century). After a period of Egyptian rule it fell to the Ottoman Turks (1516), who ruled it until World War I. From the mid-19th century Jews returned from the Diaspora to settle in Palestine. The late 19th century saw the beginning of *Zionism and in 1909 Tel Aviv, the first new Jewish city, was founded. In 1918 Palestine was captured by the British, who supported the Jewish demand for a Jewish nation in Palestine. This provoked unrest and terrorism among the Arab population, who felt increasingly threatened by Jewish immigration. In 1947 the problem was referred to the UN, which decided to divide Palestine into two separate states, Jewish and Arab. As this was accepted by the Jews but not the Arabs, Britain renounced its mandate in 1948. The state of Israel was then proclaimed and immediately attacked by the surrounding Arab countries. They were repulsed and Israel greatly expanded its territory; the rest of Palestine was divided between Jordan (the West Bank) and Egypt (the Gaza strip). In 1995, following a peace agreement with the *Palestine Liberation Organization, Israel handed over the administration of the Gaza Strip and parts of the West Bank to a new Palestinian National Authority. Yassir *Arafat was elected (1996) first president of the Authority. Further progress was hampered by continuing Arab violence and delays in Israeli troop withdrawals. In 2001–02 rising casualties from Arab suicide bombings led the Israeli military to occupy large areas of Palestinian territory.

Palestine Liberation Organization (**PLO**) An organization of various Palestinian groups opposed to Israel, led by Yassir Arafat's al-*Fatah. It was founded in 1964. Terrorist actions carried out by the PLO include the murder of 11 Israeli athletes at the Munich Olympics (1972). In 1982 PLO forces were expelled from Lebanon when Israel invaded. In 1988 the PLO set up a parliament in exile (in Tunis) for the newly declared state of Palestine. In the same year Arafat adopted a more peaceful policy. A peace agreement was signed in 1993 by Arafat and Yitzhak Rabin. The PLO renounced terrorism and recognized Israel's right to exist; Israel offered to withdraw its troops from the Gaza Strip and the West Bank. The Palestinians, under PLO leadership, gained effective autonomy in these areas in 1995. However, the peace process then stalled, owing to violence from extreme Arab factions and Israeli reluctance to withdraw troops. A further land-for-security deal was signed by Israel and the PLO in 1998 but US-brokered talks in 2000 ended in bitter failure. The result was rising violence on both sides. Claims that the PLO was colluding in Arab suicide bombings were used to justify Israel's reoccupation of Palestinian cities in 2002.

Palestrina, Giovanni Pierluigi da (?1525–94) Italian composer. He spent most of his life in Rome, as chorister, choirmaster, or maestro at churches including St Peter's. One of the greatest masters of *polyphony, he composed 93 masses, 179 motets, and other pieces.

Palladio, Andrea (1508–80) Italian architect, born in Padua. Palladio is famous for developing the architectural style now known as **Palladianism**; based on classical Roman public architecture, it was introduced into England in the early 17th century by Inigo Jones. Palladio's first job was the remodelling of the basilica in Vicenza (begun 1549) and from that emerged a hugely successful career. He produced villas, palaces, and churches, the most famous being S Giorgio Maggiore in Venice (begun 1566).

palladium (Pd) A silvery-white noble metal of the platinum group, discovered by W. H. Wollaston (1766–1828) in 1803, and named after the asteroid Pallas. It readily absorbs hydrogen and is used as a catalyst for hydrogenation reactions; it is alloyed with gold to form white gold. At no 46; at wt 106.4; mp 1555°C; bp 2964°C.

palm A monocotyledonous plant of the family *Palmae* (or *Arecaceae*; about 2500 species), occurring in tropical and subtropical regions. 1 to 60 m in height, palms have an unbranched trunk crowned with a cluster of large leaves, which are fan-shaped or feather-like. The flowers give rise to berries or drupes (stone fruits). Palms are important as a source of food (*see* COCONUT; DATE; SAGO), oil (*see* OIL PALM), wax, fibres, and building materials.

Palma (*or* **Palma de Mallorca**) 39 35N 2 39E The capital of the Spanish Balearic Islands, in Majorca. Its historic buildings include the gothic cathedral (1230–1601) and the 14th-century Bellver Castle. A noted tourist resort, it is also a port and commercial centre; industries include textiles, footwear, and crafts. Population (1995 est): 318 030.

palm civet A mammal of the family *Viverridae*, smaller than true civets and more omnivorous than *genets. Most palm civets are Asian (the two-spotted palm civet (*Nandinia binotata*) is the only African species). The masked palm civet (*Paguma larvata*) of SE Asia is up to 140 cm long including the tail (50–65 cm) and is mainly arboreal, feeding on fruit, insects, and vertebrates.

Palmer, Samuel (1805–81) British landscape painter and etcher. His best landscapes, which were either in sepia or watercolour, were painted during his association (1826–35) with a group of painters in Shoreham, who shared Palmer's admiration for William *Blake.

Palmerston, Henry John Temple, 3rd Viscount (1784–1865) British statesman; foreign secretary (1830–34, 1835–41, 1846–51) and Liberal prime minister (1855–58, 1859–65). He entered parliament in 1807 as a Tory, serving as secretary for war from 1809 to 1828, but by 1830 he had joined the Whigs. His markedly nationalistic foreign policy sought to defend constitutional states and prevent a Franco-Russian combination. As prime minister Palmerston supported the Confederacy in the US Civil War but was dissuaded from actively involving Britain.

palmyra A *palm tree, *Borassus flabellier*, cultivated in India and Sri Lanka. The timber is used for construction and the leaves are used for thatch and made into a type of paper. The sugary sap from the flower heads is fermented to give palm wine and the kernels of the fruits are eaten.

Palmyra (*or* **Tadmor**) 34 36N 38 15E An ancient Syrian desert city on the route of the E–W caravan trade in the 2nd and 3rd centuries AD. The ruins of the ancient city include the remains of the Temple of Bel (Palmyra's chief deity). Inscriptions in the Palmyric alphabet provide important information on Palmyra's trade.

Palomar, Mount A mountain in the USA, in California. It is the site of the Mount Palomar Observatory. Its 508 cm (200 in) reflecting telescope is among the largest in the world. Height: 1870 m (6140 ft).

Paltrow, Gwyneth (Kate) (1973–) US film actress. Her films include *Emma* (1996), *Shakespeare in Love* (1998), which earned her an Oscar, and *Sylvia* (2003), in which she played Sylvia Plath.

Pamirs (*or* **Pamir**) A mountainous area of central Asia, situated mainly in Tadzhikistan. It consists of a complex of high ranges, with the Tian Shan in the N, the Kunlun and Karakoram in the E, and the Hindu Kush in the W. Its highest point in Tadzhikistan is Communism Peak, at 7495 m (24 590 ft). In China it reaches 7719 m (25 326 ft) at Kungur.

Pampas The flat treeless plains of Argentina. They are of major agricultural importance in the E, producing wheat, corn, and beef in particular.

pampas grass A perennial *grass of the genus *Cortaderia*, native to South America and widely cultivated as an ornamental. *C. argentea* grows in dense clumps, with leaves up to 2 m long and flowering stems exceeding 3 m in length. The flowers form silvery-white plumes.

Pamplona 42 49N 1 39W A city in NE Spain, in the Basque Provinces. It has a cathedral and holds a renowned fiesta (during which bulls are driven through the streets to the bullring). It is an agricultural centre and its industries include traditional crafts and chemicals. Population (1998 est): 171 150.

Pan The Greek god of shepherds and their flocks, the son of Hermes. He is usually portrayed with the legs, ears, and horns of a goat. He lived in the mountains and was associated especially with Arcadia, where he played his pipes (*see* PANPIPES).

Panama, Republic of A country in Central America, occupying the Isthmus of Panama. Narrow coastal plains rise to volcanic mountains. The population is largely of mixed Indian, European, and African descent. *Economy*: considerable revenue comes from receipts from the Panama Canal and from international capital. The main agricultural products are bananas, rice, sugar, and maize; fishing (especially for shrimps) is growing in importance. Industries include cement production and paper and food processing; oil refining has declined. Tourism is now the main source of foreign revenue. *History*: the original inhabitants were destroyed following Panama's discovery by Columbus in 1502 and Spanish colonization. Panama later became part of the viceroyalty of Peru and then of New Granada. In 1821 it became part of newly independent Colombia, from which it broke free in 1903 after a revolution supported by the USA. A military coup in 1968 brought Gen Omar Torrijos (1929–81) to power; in 1978 he retired as head of state. In 1981 Gen Manuel Noriega (1938–) took effective control. His alleged involvement in drug-dealing and refusal to relinquish power prompted the USA to send a military task force (1989); he was deposed and taken to the USA, where he was convicted on drug charges (1992). In 1991 a new constitution abolished the armed forces. In 1999 Mireya Moscoso became Panama's first woman head of state; Martin Torrijos, son of the former dictator Omar Torrijos, was elected president in 2004. Official language: Spanish. Currency: balboa of 100 centésimos. Area: 78 046 sq km (30 134 sq mi). Population (2003 est): 3 116 000. Capital: Panama City.

Panama Canal A canal across the Isthmus of Panama connecting the Atlantic and Pacific Oceans. Some 82 km (51 mi) long, it was begun in 1880 by the French Panama Canal Company under Ferdinand de *Lesseps. In 1903 the USA acquired the construction rights from Panama and the canal was opened to commercial traffic in 1914. The USA also acquired sovereignty in perpetuity over the **Panama Canal Zone**, a region extending 8 km (5 mi) on either side of the canal. In 1977–78 two treaties restored Panamanian sovereignty over the canal and the Zone (from 1979), while also ensuring their neutrality and the USA's continued use of its bases. Full control of the canal reverted to Panama on 31 December 1999. Area: 1676 sq km (647 sq mi).

Panama City 5 58N 79 31W The capital of Panama. Founded by the Spanish in 1519 on the site of an Indian fishing village, it was destroyed in 1671 and rebuilt two years later 8 km (5 mi) to the SW. It became capital of the newly independent Panama in 1904. The University of Panama was founded in 1935 and that of Santa Maria de la Antigua in 1965. Population (2000): 415 964.

pancreas A gland, about 15 cm long, situated in the abdomen behind the stomach. When food passes into the intestine the pancreas secretes several digestive enzymes that drain into the intestine through the pancreatic duct. In addition, small clusters of cells (called islets of Langerhans) scattered throughout the pancreas secrete the hormones *insulin and glucagon.

panda A bearlike mammal of the family *Procyonidae*. The giant panda (*Ailuropoda melanoleuca*) is rare; it lives in the cold bamboo forests of central China, feeding on young bamboo shoots. Giant pandas are up to 1.6 m long and have bold black and white markings. The red panda (*Ailurus fulgens*), also called the lesser panda, lives in the forests of the Himalayas and W China. 80–110 cm long including the bushy tail (30–50 cm), it is red-brown with black markings on its white face. It feeds on roots, nuts, lichens, and bamboo shoots.

Pandora In Greek mythology, the first woman, fashioned by Hephaestus and invented by Zeus. She married Epimetheus, brother of Prometheus. Her dowry was a box, which, when opened, released all the varieties of evil and retained only hope.

pangolin An armoured mammal belonging to the genus *Manis* and order *Pholidota* (7 species), of Africa and S Asia, also called scaly anteater. 30–80 cm long with long prehensile tails, pangolins are covered on their backs with overlapping horny scales. Toothless, with a long sticky tongue, they feed at night on ants and termites.

Pankhurst, Emmeline (1858–1928) British suffragette, who founded, in Manchester, the Women's Social and Political Union (1903). Imprisoned several times, she underwent hunger strikes and forcible feeding. During World War I, she encouraged the industrial recruitment of women. Her daughters **Dame Christabel Pankhurst** (1880–1958) and **Sylvia Pankhurst** (1882–1960) were also suffragettes.

panpipes (*or* **syrinx**) An ancient musical instrument consisting of a row of small graduated pipes bound together. According to Greek legend it was invented by *Pan, who pursued the nymph Syrinx. When she was changed into a reed by Apollo, Pan made the instrument from the reed stem.

pansy A popular garden plant that is a hybrid of the wild pansy (*Viola tricolor*), developed in the early 19th century. There are now many varieties, up to 20 cm high, with (usually) yellow, orange, purple, brown, or white flowers. The wild pansy, or heartsease, found throughout Eurasia, has small flowers coloured purple, yellow, and white. Family: *Violaceae*. *See also* VIOLET.

pantheism Any belief or doctrine presenting the natural world, including man, as part of the divine. Pantheism is a predominant tendency in Hinduism but is frowned on by orthodox Christianity.

Pantheon **1.** A temple dedicated to the worship of many gods. The most famous is that in Rome begun in 27 BC but rebuilt about 118 AD. A circular design topped by a huge concrete dome, in 609 AD it became the Church of Sta Maria Rotonda. **2.** A building honouring the famous. The best known is that in Paris designed by Jacques Soufflot (1713–80) in 1759.

panther A colour variety of leopard that has a great deal of black pigmentation. Panthers can occur among a litter of normally spotted leopards.

pantomime A British form of dramatic entertainment for children, traditionally performed at Christmas. Although the word also refers to several other dramatic forms, such as mime plays and dumbshows, children's pantomime developed during the 19th century from the harlequinade (*see* HARLEQUIN). Based on fairy tales, pantomimes include popular songs and slapstick comedy. The principal boy is traditionally played by a girl, and the dame, a comic old woman, by a man.

papal states The central Italian states under papal sovereignty between 756 and 1870. They included parts of Emilia-Romagna, Marche, Umbria, and Lazio. A major obstacle to the 19th-century movement for Italian unification (*see* RISORGIMENTO), they were finally annexed in 1870. The popes refused to recognize their loss of temporal power until the *Lateran Treaty (1929) established the Vatican City as an independent papal state.

papaw (*or* **papaya**) A small tropical American tree, *Carica papaya*, cultivated throughout the tropics. About 7.5 m tall, it has lobed toothed leaves and fragrant creamy-white flowers. The yellowish fruit resembles an elongated melon: its succulent pinkish or orange flesh encloses a mass of seeds. The fruits are eaten fresh, boiled, and in preserves or pickles and are a commercial source of the enzyme papain, used as a meat tenderizer. Family: *Caricaceae.*

Papeete 17 32S 149 34W The capital of French Polynesia, in NW Tahiti. A tourist centre, it is a stop on many Pacific routes. Population (1996, urban area): 121 000.

paper A substance in sheet form made from the pulped cellulose fibres of wood, grass, cotton, etc., and used for writing and printing on, wrapping, cleaning, etc. The Chinese invented paper (c. 2nd century BC). Foreign competition meant a slow start to British paper making, the first successful mill being set up about 1589. All early paper was handmade; a machine for making paper in a continuous roll was not invented until 1798, in France. Brought to England in 1803 by Henry Fourdrinier (1766–1854), this machine picked up the pulp on a travelling wire mesh and shook it until the fibres were interlaced and the water drained off, before passing it through pressing and drying rollers. The **pulp** for papermaking is obtained chiefly from wood, but also from esparto grass and rags (for strong durable high-quality paper), and increasingly from recycled wastepaper.

papilloma A harmless tumour that grows from the surface of the skin or from the lining of a hollow organ, for example the bladder, womb, or lungs. Warts and *polyps are types of papilloma.

paprika *See* CAPSICUM.

Papua New Guinea, State of A country in the Pacific Ocean, E of Indonesia. It consists of the E part of *New Guinea and several islands, including the Bismarck Archipelago, the N part of the Solomon Islands, and the Admiralty Islands. Most of the population are Melanesians. *Economy*: subsistence agriculture and the growing of cash crops, such as coconuts, cocoa, coffee, and rubber, are the chief occupations. The chief mineral resource and export is copper; mining on *Bougainville was halted by secessionist violence in 1989. Other exports include gold, coffee, cocoa, timber, and copra. *History*: the SE part of the island of New Guinea was annexed by Queensland in 1883, becoming a British colony in 1888, known as the Territory of Papua. The NE part came under Australian rule in 1914 as the Trust Territory of New Guinea. In 1921 the two territories including their islands were merged, later becoming a UN Trusteeship under Australia. It was renamed Papua New Guinea in 1971, achieved self-government in 1973, and became fully independent in 1975. In 1990 rebels on Bougainville declared independence and fighting broke out; a permanent ceasefire was signed in 1998 and a political settlement agreed in 2001. Official languages: English, pidgin, and Motu. Currency: kina of 100 toea. Area: 462 840 sq km (178 656 sq mi). Population (2003 est): 5 583 000. Capital: Port Moresby.

papyrus An aquatic reedlike plant, *Cyperus papyrus*, up to 3 m tall, originally cultivated in the Nile delta of Egypt and now growing wild in parts of Africa and in Syria. It was used by the ancient Egyptians to make paper, and also for rope, mats, sails, and shoes. The pith was a common food. Family: *Cyperaceae.*

parabola The curve, formed by a conic section, in which the distance from a fixed point (focus) and a fixed line (directrix) are equal. In Cartesian coordinates (*see* COORDINATE SYSTEMS) a standard form of its equation is $y^2 = 4ax$, for a parabola that is symmetrical about the *x*-axis and cuts it at the origin (vertex).

Paracelsus (Theophrastus Bombastus von Hohenheim; 1493–1541) Swiss physician, whose radical ideas influenced the development of

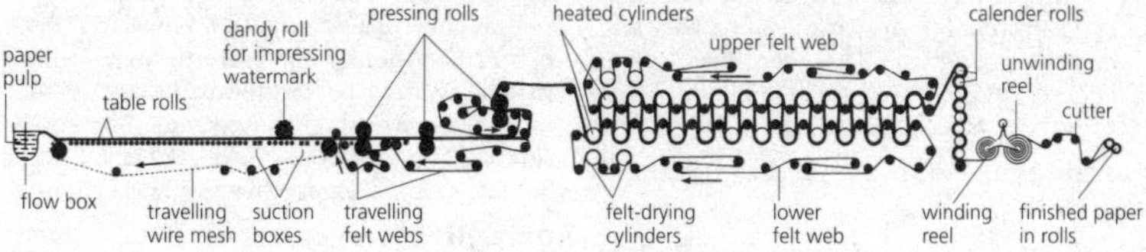

paper. The Fourdrinier paper-making machine is one of the longest machines in use.

medicine during the Renaissance. He stressed the importance of chemical compounds in treating disease, refuted the notion that mental illness was caused by demons, and linked goitre with minerals in drinking water.

paraffin 1. (*or* **kerosene**) A mixture of hydrocarbons that boil in the range 150–300°C and have a relative density of 0.78–0.83. It is obtained from crude *oil by distillation and is used as a fuel for domestic heating and for aircraft. **2.** *See* ALKANES.

paraffin wax A wax obtained during the refining of crude *oil. Fully refined, it is a white tasteless solid (mp 50–60°C) consisting of higher *alkanes; it is used in the manufacture of waxed papers, candles, and polishes.

Paraguay, Republic of A landlocked country in the centre of South America. It is divided by the River Paraguay into two zones: an area of fertile plains and hills to the E and the semidesert of the Gran Chaco to the W. The great majority of the population is of mixed Spanish and Guaraní Indian descent. *Economy*: chiefly agricultural; livestock rearing is of particular importance. Meat packing is one of the main industries. Exports include meat, cotton, oilseed, and timber. The main crops are cotton, soya beans, cassava, and sugar cane. Hydroelectricity is a major source of power. *History*: explored and colonized by the Spanish in the 16th century, it became independent of Spain in 1811. In 1814 José Gaspar Rodríguez de Francia (1766–1840) was elected dictator. The population suffered great losses in the War of the *Triple Alliance (1865–70) against Brazil, Argentina, and Uruguay and again in the Chaco War (1932–35) with Bolivia. In 1954 Gen Alfredo Stroessner (1912–) seized power and became president; he was overthrown in a coup in 1989. In 1993 Paraguay's first democratic elections were held and a civilian, Juan Carlos Wasmosy, was elected president. In 1998 presidential and legislative elections resulted in victory for Raúl Cubas Gran and his Colorado Party. However, in 1999 he resigned and fled abroad after his supporters murdered a political rival. Nicanor Duarte Frutos was elected president in 2003. Paraguay is a member of the OAS and LAIA. Official languages: Spanish and Guaraní. Currency: guaraní of 100 céntimos. Area: 406 752 sq km (157 042 sq mi). Population (2003 est): 5 642 000. Capital: Asunción.

Paraguayan War *See* TRIPLE ALLIANCE, WAR OF THE.

parakeet A small seed-eating *parrot characterized by a long tapering tail and a predominantly green plumage and found especially in SE Asia and Australia. Brightly coloured species are popular as cagebirds. *See also* BUDGERIGAR; ROSELLA.

paralysis Failure of a muscle or a group of muscles to work. This is commonly caused by damage to the nerve (and its connections) supplying the muscle, as resulting from injury or infection (*see* POLIOMYELITIS), but may also be due to failure of the nerve impulse to be transmitted to the muscle (as in myasthenia gravis) or by wasting of the muscle (as in *muscular dystrophy). A *stroke causes damage to the part of the brain that controls movement and may result in **hemiplegia**, i.e. half of the body and face becomes paralysed. **Paraplegia** (paralysed legs) results from injury to the spinal cord. **Quadriplegia** (paralysed legs and arms) results when the spinal cord is damaged close to the brain.

paramagnetism A form of *magnetism caused by the presence in atoms or molecules of electrons with unpaired spins. The atom or molecule therefore acts like a tiny magnet (*see* FERROMAGNETISM). In the presence of an external magnetic field these microscopic magnets tend to align with the field, reinforcing it. The effect is destroyed by random thermal motion and, except at low temperatures and high field strengths, the *permeability (a measure of the extent of alignment) is inversely proportional to the temperature.

Paramaribo 5 52N 55 14W The capital and main port of Suriname, in the N on the River Suriname. Founded by the French (1540), it was later under English and then Dutch rule. The University of Suriname was founded in 1968. Population (1999 est): 233 000.

Paraná, Rio (Spanish name: Río Paraná) A river in South America. Formed by the confluence of the Rio Grande and Rio Paranaíba in SE central Brazil, it flows generally S for 2900 km (1800 mi) to join the River Uruguay and form the Río de la Plata. The Itaipu Dam, which is sited at Foz do Iguaçu near the Paraguayan border, was opened in 1982.

paranoia A mental disorder in which the patient is governed by a rigid system of irrational beliefs (delusions). The sufferer may believe that he is being persecuted by others, or that he is overwhelmingly important. The condition can result from *schizophrenia, *alcoholism, or manic-depressive psychosis.

paraplegia *See* PARALYSIS.

parasite An organism living in or on another

organism of a different species (called the host), from which it obtains food and protection: the relationship may or may not be harmful to the host. Many parasites have complex life cycles, with one or more intermediate hosts (of different species) supporting the parasite in the immature stages of its development. The study of parasites—**parasitology**—is of great importance in medicine since many parasites, such as bacteria, ticks, and fleas, either cause or transmit disease. Many plants are either partly or completely parasitic: mistletoe is a partial parasite.

parathyroid glands Two pairs of small endocrine glands lying immediately behind the thyroid gland. These glands secrete **parathyroid hormone** in response to a reduction in the level of calcium in the blood. This hormone causes the release of calcium from the bones and its transfer to the blood. Deficiency of parathyroid hormone results in muscle spasms and cramps (tetany).

parchment Animal skin, usually of the goat, sheep, or calf, treated for writing on. It derives its name from Pergamum, where in the 2nd century BC improved methods of treating skins were developed. It was used for manuscripts and early bound books. More delicate skin from young animals is called vellum. *See also* LEATHER.

Paris 48 52N 2 18E The capital of France and a department of the Paris Region, situated in the N of the country on the River Seine. The administrative, commercial, and cultural centre of France, Paris is also an important industrial base, and many international organizations, including UNESCO, have their headquarters here. At the heart of the city, the Île de la Cité contains the cathedral of Notre-Dame. On the Left Bank lie Montparnasse and the Latin Quarter, which is known for its associations with writers and artists. On the Right Bank stands the Palais du Louvre, one of the world's most important museums. Further W is a series of radiating boulevards meeting at the Place Charles de Gaulle. The Champs Élysées runs from the *Arc de Triomphe at the centre of the Place Charles de Gaulle to the Place de la Concorde. Further N lies Montmartre, dominated by the Basilica of the Sacré Coeur (1919). To the S of the Seine stands the *Eiffel Tower. *History*: the earliest known settlement was on the Île de la Cité in Roman times. In the 6th century Clovis made it the capital of his Frankish kingdom but it later suffered attacks from Vikings. It regained importance as the capital under the Capetians. Since the storming of the Bastille (1789), heralding the beginning of the French Revolution, it has been the scene of many revolts, such as the July Revolution (1830) and the Revolution of 1848. Population (1999): 2 123 261.

Paris In Greek legend, a son of *Priam and Hecuba. His abduction of *Helen with the help of Aphrodite caused the *Trojan War, during which he killed Achilles and was himself killed by Philoctetes. *See also* ERIS.

parity In physics, the concept of left- and right-handedness. According to the law of conservation of parity, no fundamental distinction exists between left and right. In 1957 this principle was shown to be violated in *weak interactions. For example, when a neutron decays the electron produced is always left-polarized (i.e. spins in a direction opposite to that of its motion), whereas if parity was conserved there would be equal numbers of left- and right-polarized electrons. This lack of parity provides a fundamental distinction between left and right. The parity of elementary particles is expressed as a *quantum number.

Park, Mungo (1771–c. 1806) Scottish explorer. In 1795–96 he ascended the Niger from the mouth of the River Gambia, crossed the Senegal Basin, and was imprisoned by Arabs. His *Travels in the Interior Districts of Africa* (1797) related his adventures. In 1805, under government patronage, he resumed his exploration. The expedition was attacked by Africans and Park died.

Parker, Charlie (Christopher) (1920–55) US Black jazz saxophonist and composer, known as "Bird" or "Yardbird." With Dizzy *Gillespie he originated the *bop style of jazz in New York in the 1940s. His early death was hastened by heroin addiction and alcoholism.

Parkinson's disease A chronic disease affecting the part of the brain controlling voluntary movement, first described in 1817 by a British physician, James Parkinson (1755–1824). The symptoms are tremor of the hands and mouth, stiffness, and difficulty in initiating movements. Sometimes this group of symptoms, known as **parkinsonism**, may result from infection, side effects of drugs, or injury. It is treated with drugs, including levodopa.

parliament The legislative assembly of a country. In the UK parliament is the supreme legislature; it consists of the sovereign, the House of Lords, and the House of Commons; its seat is the *Palace of Westminster. Parliament developed in the 13th century from the *Curia

Regis (King's Court), in which the monarch consulted with his barons. In 1213, 1254, and 1258 representatives of the shires were also summoned to attend parliament and in 1265 the parliament summoned by Simon de *Montfort included borough representatives—the origins of the House of Commons. By the reign of Edward III (1327–77) Lords and Commons, meeting separately, were recognized constituents of government. Parliament's conflict with James I and Charles I led to the Civil War (1642–51) and the establishment of republican government under Cromwell. Following the Restoration in 1660, the attempts of James II to rule arbitrarily led to the Glorious Revolution (1688), which achieved the beginning of parliamentary ascendancy over the Crown. The 18th century saw the emergence of party politics and of a *prime minister and the development of *cabinet government.

Until the present government began its reform of the House of Lords it had some 1300 members, including over 750 hereditary peers (*see* PEERAGE). In 1999 the hereditary peers were removed except for a rump of 92, who will remain until further reform has been completed. Although it is envisaged that the reformed second chamber should have about 600 members, there is no agreement as to whether these should be wholly appointed, wholly elected, or some combination of the two. In 2003 MPs voted to reject all of a series of options submitted to them, leaving the reform process in disarray. The House of Commons has (1999) 659 members of parliament (MPs), each representing a geographical constituency, and is regulated by the *Speaker of the House of Commons. Parliamentary legislation is introduced in the form of private or public bills. After a first reading a bill will be printed and then debated in a second reading. It is then referred to a committee by which it may be amended. Its amendments are considered by the whole house and it then receives a third reading after which it is sent to the other house, where it goes through a similar procedure. After passing both houses the bill receives the royal assent and becomes an Act of Parliament.

Parma 44 48N 10 19E A city in N Italy, in Emilia-Romagna. Dating from Roman times, it became an important cultural centre in the middle ages. Its university was established in 1222 and it has a romanesque cathedral and a 16th-century palace. Industries include the manufacture of Parmesan cheese, perfume, fertilizers, and glass. Population (2000 est): 168 717.

Parnassus, Mount (Modern Greek name: Parnassós) 38 32N 22 41E A mountain in S central Greece, held in ancient times as sacred to the god Apollo and the Muses. Height: 2457 m (8061 ft).

Parnell, Charles Stewart (1846–91) Irish politician, who in 1880 became the leader of the *Home Rule party in the British House of Commons. Parnell, an MP from 1875, reconciled constitutional and radical forces and enjoyed widespread popular support in Ireland. He allied his party with the Liberals in 1886, when Gladstone introduced the Home Rule bill. Parnell remained a dominant political figure until 1890, when he fell from grace after being cited in a divorce case.

Parr, Catherine (1512–48) The sixth wife (1543–47) of Henry VIII of England. After Henry's death, she married (1547) Thomas, Baron Seymour of Sudeley (d. 1549).

parrot A bird belonging to the family (*Psittacidae*; 300 species) occurring worldwide in warm regions. 10–100 cm long, parrots have a compact body, a short neck, and strong rounded wings. The plumage is typically brightly coloured and the short stout hooked bill is used to open nuts and to feed on fruits and seeds. Most are arboreal and excellent climbers, having clawed feet with rough scaly toes. They have a harsh screaming voice. Order: *Psittaciformes*. *See also* COCKATOO; LORY; LOVEBIRD; MACAW; PARAKEET.

parrot fish A fish, also called parrot wrasse, belonging to the family *Scaridae* found among tropical reefs. The teeth are fused to form a hard beak, which is used to feed on coral, molluscs, and seaweed. Order: *Perciformes*.

Parry, Sir (Charles) Hubert (Hastings) (1848–1918) British composer of operatic, orchestral, choral, chamber, and solo works, the best known of which is the song *Jerusalem* (1916). He was the director of the Royal College of Music (1894–1918) and professor of music at Oxford University (1900–08).

parsec A unit of distance, used in astronomy, corresponding to a parallax of one second of arc. 1 parsec = 3.26 light-years or 3.084×10^{16} metres.

Parseeism The religion of the descendants of Persians who fled their country in the 8th century AD to avoid persecution following the Arab conquest. Mostly located in Bombay, Madras, Calcutta, and Karachi, they continue to practise Zoroastrianism (*see* ZOROASTER) in two sectarian forms.

parsley A fragrant biennial herb, *Petroselinum crispum*, native to the Mediterranean region but widely cultivated. The compound leaves have an aromatic flavour. They are used fresh or dried in fish and meat dishes, soups, garnishes, and bouquets garnis. The flowering stems, up to 1 m high, bear yellowish flowers. Family: *Umbelliferae*.

parsnip A hairy strong-smelling biennial plant, *Pastinaca sativa*, native to Eurasia and widely cultivated for its large starchy white taproot, which is eaten as a vegetable or used as cattle feed. The leaves consist of paired lobed toothed leaflets on a long furrowed stalk and the clusters of tiny yellow flowers are borne on stems up to 150 cm high. Family: *Umbelliferae*.

parthenogenesis A method of reproduction in which the egg develops without *fertilization to produce an individual usually identical to the parent. It occurs commonly among lower plants and animals, particularly aphids, ants, bees, and wasps.

Parthenon A temple on the hill of the Acropolis in Athens dedicated to the goddess Athena. Built between 447 and 432 BC, it represents the summit of classical Greek architecture. Its rectangular colonnaded exterior of Doric columns originally contained a walled chamber with Phidias' gold and ivory statue of Athena. In the 5th century AD it became a Christian church and in the 15th century a mosque. Later used as a magazine by the Turks, it blew up during a bombardment by the Venetians in 1687. *See also* ELGIN MARBLES.

Parthia The region S of the Caspian Sea approximating to present-day Khorasan (NE Iran). Inhabited by seminomadic tribes, Parthia controlled a great empire from about 250 BC to 224 AD with its capital at Ctesiphon. Parthia's famous cavalry and mounted archers overwhelmed Crassus' army in a humiliating defeat at Carrhae in 53 BC. In 224 AD the Parthian empire was conquered by the Sasanians of Persia.

particle physics The study of elementary particles and their interactions. The existence of the electron (J. J. Thomson; 1897) and the discovery of the *proton (Rutherford; 1911) made it clear that the atom had an internal structure. When the *neutron was discovered (Chadwick; 1932), it appeared that the whole universe was constructed of just these three particles. The outstanding problem was the nature of the force that held neutrons and protons together in the atomic nucleus. The only two fundamental forces known at that time were the gravitational force and the electromagnetic (em) force: the gravitational force was too weak to account for the great stability of the nucleus and the em force had no effect on the electrically uncharged neutron.

In 1935 *Yukawa suggested that there might be in nature a short-lived particle (later called the meson) that jumped between protons and neutrons and held them together. This concept of exchange forces and the subsequent discovery of short-lived particles led to intensive research into particle physics throughout the world (*see* ACCELERATORS). By the 1960s some 200 "elementary" particles had been identified and it became clear that there were four basic types of force; in addition to gravitational and em forces there were *strong interactions (100 times more powerful than em forces) and *weak interactions (10^{10} weaker than em forces). There are now believed to be two classes of particles: leptons (the electron, muon, tau particle, and neutrinos), which interact by the em or the weak forces and have no apparent internal structure; and hadrons (including the proton, neutron, pion, etc.), which interact by the strong interaction and do appear to have an internal structure.

The current model of the hadron is based on Murray Gell-Mann's concept of the quark, introduced in 1963. In this model, hadrons themselves are divided into two classes: baryons, which decay into protons; and mesons, which decay into leptons and *photons or into proton pairs. Baryons consist of three quarks and mesons consist of a quark-antiquark pair. Thus all the matter in the universe is now seen as being made of leptons and quarks. Quark theory is fairly elaborate; quarks have fractional electronic charges (+2/3 or −1/3 of the electronic charge) and come in six "flavours" called up (u; +2/3), down (d; −1/3), charmed (c; +2/3), strange (s; −1/3), top (t; +2/3), and bottom (b; −1/3). For each flavour there is an equivalent antiquark ($\bar{u}$, $\bar{d}$, etc.). The proton consists of uud ($2/3 + 2/3 - 1/3 = 1$) and the neutron consists of udd ($2/3 - 1/3 - 1/3 = 0$).

In this limited form quark theory conflicted with the *Pauli exclusion principle and it therefore became necessary to introduce the concept of "colour." Thus each flavour of quark can have one of the three colours red, yellow, or blue, with antiquarks having the corresponding anticolours. "Colour" in this sense has no connection with visual colour but the analogy is useful. All hadrons are regarded as white and baryons must consist of a red, a blue, and a yellow (since these visual colours produce white); mesons consist of a quark of any colour and its corresponding anticolour. This interpretation of the nature of matter is known as the **standard model**; the one missing particle required to complete the integration of the weak interaction into this model is the *Higgs boson (*see* CERN). *See also* ANTIMATTER; CHARM; STRANGENESS.

partridge A small gamebird native to the Old World but widely introduced elsewhere. Partridges are 25–40 cm long and have rounded bodies with short rounded wings. The European partridge (*Perdix perdix*) is a common farmland bird and has a greyish plumage with a red face and tail. Family: *Phasianidae* (pheasants, quail, partridges).

pascal (Pa) The SI unit of pressure equal to one newton per square metre. Named after Blaise *Pascal.

Pascal, Blaise (1623–62) French mathematician, physicist, and theologian. He invented Pascal's triangle for calculating the coefficients of a binomial expansion. He also made discoveries in *fluid mechanics, notably that the pressure in a fluid is everywhere equal (**Pascal's principle**). In 1641 he invented the first calculating machine. At the age of 31 he had a mystical experience; he became a Jansenist and his *Lettres provinciales* (1656–57) defended *Jansenism against the Jesuits. His greatest work was *Pensées sur la religion* (1669), a metaphysical treatise on human nature.

Passchendaele *See* WORLD WAR I.

passerine bird A bird belonging to the order *Passeriformes*, which includes over half (about 5100) of all bird species. Passerines—the perching birds—are characterized by their feet, which are specialized for gripping branches, and stems. They are the most highly evolved birds and occur in almost every habitat, although few live or feed in water. There are both migratory and sedentary species. The order is divided into four major groups (suborders): *Eurylaimi* (broadbills); *Tyranni* (includes manakins, ovenbirds, pittas, and tyrant flycatchers); *Menurae* (lyrebirds and scrubbirds); and—the largest and most advanced group—*Oscines* (*see* SONGBIRD).

passionflower A climbing plant of the genus *Passiflora* (500 species), native chiefly to tropical and subtropical America and cultivated for ornament. The leaves may be simple or deeply lobed. The distinctive flowers each consist of a cup-shaped base with five coloured sepals and petals at its upper edge surmounted by a coloured fringe. The fruit is a berry or capsule, which in some species (e.g. *P. quadrangularis*) is edible (passionfruits *or* granadillas). Family: *Passifloraceae*.

Passion plays Religious dramas concerning the crucifixion and resurrection of Christ. They were performed on Good Friday throughout medieval Europe. The Passion play at *Oberammergau in W Germany has been performed every ten years since 1634.

Passover (Hebrew word: *Pesah*) One of the three biblical pilgrimage festivals (the others are Weeks and Tabernacles). It commemorates the Exodus from Egypt and also incorporates a spring harvest festival. In Judaism, it is celebrated for seven or eight days, beginning on the eve of the first day with a formal meal. In Christianity it has been replaced by *Easter.

Pasternak, Boris (1890–1960) Russian poet and novelist. He published several volumes of Symbolist poetry between 1917 and 1923. His epic novel *Dr Zhivago* was banned in Russia but became internationally successful after its publication in Italy in 1957. Under severe political pressure, he declined the Nobel Prize in 1958.

Pasteur, Louis (1822–95) French chemist and microbiologist, who made great advances in the prevention and treatment of diseases caused by microorganisms. In 1854 Pasteur was appointed dean of sciences at Lille University. He found that fermentation was caused by microorganisms and that by excluding these, souring or decay could be prevented (*see* PASTEURIZATION). By 1881 he had devised a means of safely inducing immunity to anthrax by injecting a vaccine of heat-treated (attenuated) live anthrax bacilli. Pasteur also produced a vaccine for chicken cholera and an effective rabies vaccine. The Pasteur Institute was founded in 1888 to treat rabies and has since developed into a world centre for biological research.

pasteurization Heat treatment used to destroy the microorganisms in milk. The method involves heating milk for 30 minutes at 60°C, which kills the tuberculosis bacteria without damaging the milk protein. Named after Louis *Pasteur.

Patagonia A geographic area of S South America in Argentina and Chile, extending S of the River Colorado to the Strait of Magellan. It consists chiefly of an arid plateau rising to the Andes. Sheep raising is the principal economic activity. It contains the major oilfield of Comodoro Rivadavia and the Río Turbio coalfield. Area: about 777 000 sq km (300 000 sq mi).

pathology The branch of medicine concerned with the study of disease and disease processes in order to understand their causes and nature. The specialty originated in the mid-19th century, with the work of Virchow, Pasteur, and Koch on the bacterial cause of disease, but it was not until the beginning of the 20th century that the knowledge gained in the laboratory was applied to the treatment and prevention of disease in patients. Examples of early work in the science of clinical pathology include Schick's test for diphtheria and Wasserman's test for syphilis. Chemical pathology developed notably with the work of Banting and Best on the importance of insulin in diabetes and contributions from such haematologists as Landsteiner in the discovery of the blood groups. Today pathology includes studies of the chemistry of blood, urine, faeces, and diseased tissue, together with the use of X-rays and many other investigative techniques.

Patna 25 37N 85 12E A city in India, the capital of Bihar on the River Ganges. It was founded in 1541 on the former site of Pataliputra, ancient capital of the Maurya and Gupta empires. Population (1991): 916 980.

Patras (*or* **Pátrai**) 38 14N 21 44E A port in W Greece, in the N Peloponnese on the Gulf of Patras. The War of Greek Independence began here in 1821. Exports include currants, sultanas, tobacco, and olive oil. Population (1991): 172 763.

patricians The hereditary aristocracy of ancient Rome. Originally the sole holders of political and religious offices, the patricians were gradually forced during Republican times to admit *plebeians to political offices and their privileged position was eroded.

Patrick, St (c. 390–c. 460 AD) The patron saint of Ireland. A local chief's slave in Antrim, he later escaped to Gaul, finally returning to Ireland as a missionary. He established an archiepiscopal see at Armagh and by the time of his death had firmly established Christianity in Ireland. His only certain works are a spiritual autobiography, the *Confession*, and the *Epistle to Coroticus*. Feast day: 17 March.

Paul VI (Giovanni Battista Montini; 1897–1978) Pope (1963–78). Succeeding *John XXIII, Paul continued his predecessor's policies of reform, reconvening the second Vatican Council after his election. His encyclical *Humanae Vitae* (1968) affirmed the Church's opposition to birth control.

Paul, St (c. 3–c. 64 AD) Christian Apostle, born Saul of Tarsus, who spread Christianity among the Gentiles; the 13 Epistles attributed to him form a major part of the New Testament. The son of a Pharisee, he was initially anti-Christian, having participated in the martyrdom of St *Stephen. While travelling to Damascus, he had a vision that led to his conversion to Christianity. He began his activity as an Apostle in Damascus, later joining the other Apostles in Jerusalem. His missionary work consisted of three journeys in which he travelled to Cyprus, Asia Minor, Macedonia, Greece, Ephesus, and elsewhere. Arrested by Roman soldiers on his return to Jerusalem, he eventually appealed to Caesar and, as a Roman citizen, was taken to Rome for trial. He was imprisoned for two years; here the New Testament account ends. Feast day: 29 June.

Pauli, Wolfgang (1900–58) US physicist, born in Austria, who in 1925 formulated the Paulis exclusion principle, that no two fermions may exist in the same state, for which he received the 1945 Nobel Prize. In 1931 he postulated that some of the energy of a *beta decay was carried away by massless particles, which *Fermi named neutrinos.

Pauling, Linus Carl (1901–94) US chemist, who originated and developed important concepts concerning the structure of molecules. Using new analytical techniques, Pauling elucidated the nature of chemical bonding in both simple and complex molecules, publishing *The Nature of the Chemical Bond* in 1939. He received the Nobel Prize for Chemistry (1954) and the Nobel Peace Prize (1962) for his stance against the use of nuclear weapons.

Pavarotti, Luciano (1935–) Italian operatic tenor. He made his debut at La Scala, Milan, in 1966. He specializes in the works of Bellini, Verdi, and Puccini. His rendering of "Nessun Dorma" became a bestseller in 1990 and he is now known worldwide as one of the "Three Tenors," the others being Placido Domingo and José Carreras.

Pavlov, Ivan Petrovich (1849–1936) Russian physiologist, best known for his studies of digestion and his demonstration of the *conditioned reflex. Pavlov showed how heartbeat is regulated by the vagus nerve and how eating stimulates secretion of digestive juices by the stomach. He extended his theories of reflex behaviour to cover aspects of human behaviour, such as learning. He was awarded the 1907 Nobel Prize.

Pavlova, Anna (1885–1931) Russian ballet dancer. She joined Diaghilev's company in Paris in 1909, and from 1914 she devoted her career to international tours with her own company. She created the chief role in *Les Sylphides* and was especially associated with *Le Cygne*, choreographed for her by *Fokine in 1907.

Paxton, Sir Joseph (1801–65) British architect. Initially a gardener, Paxton experimented with new techniques of construction in building greenhouses at Chatsworth. This experience culminated in the design of the revolutionary *Crystal Palace for the Great Exhibition of 1851.

pea An annual herb of the genus *Pisum* (about 6 species), native to the Mediterranean area and W Asia, especially the widely cultivated *P. sativum*. The leaves consist of paired oval leaflets and have curling tendrils used for climbing. The edible round seeds are contained in an elongated pod and are an important source of protein for man and livestock. Family: *Leguminosae*.

Peace River A river in W Canada, whose headstreams (Finlay and Parsnip Rivers) rise in the British Columbia Rockies. Flowing generally NE across the N Alberta plains, it empties into the Slave River. It is mostly navigable and is also tapped for hydroelectricity. Its valley is fertile farmland, with important oil and timber reserves. Length: 1923 km (1195 mi), including Finlay River.

peach A small tree, *Prunus persica*, probably native to China but widely cultivated in Mediterranean and warm temperate regions. Up to 6 m high, it has glossy green leaves and pink flowers. The round fleshy fruit (a *drupe) has thin velvety skin, yellowish with a crimson tinge. The sweet white or yellow flesh encloses a wrinkled stone. Peaches are eaten fresh, canned, or in preserves. Nectarines (*P. persica* var. *nectarina*) are varieties with smooth-skinned fruits. Family: *Rosaceae*.

Peacock, Thomas Love (1785–1866) British satirical novelist. He worked for the East India Company from 1819 to 1856 and was a close friend of Shelley. His seven novels, which include *Nightmare Abbey* (1818) and *Gryll Grange* (1860), satirize contemporary fashions and ideas.

peacock butterfly A common Eurasian *nymphalid butterfly, *Inachis io*. The adults are brownish purple with a bright eyespot on each wing. They fly from early spring well into summer. The black spiny caterpillars feed on stinging nettles.

peafowl An Old World gamebird belonging to a genus (*Pavo*; 2 species) native to lowland forests of India and SE Asia. Peafowl are 75 cm long and the female (peahen) has a green-brown plumage; males (peacocks) have elaborate lacy tails, 150 cm long, the feathers of which are tipped by blue-and-bronze markings and raised over the body during display. Family: *Phasianidae* (pheasants, partridges, etc.); order: *Galliformes* (pheasants, turkeys, etc.).

Peak District A hilly area and national park in N central England, mainly in Derbyshire, at the S end of the Pennines. It reaches 727 m (2385 ft) at Kinder Scout and contains many limestone caves.

peanut *See* GROUNDNUT.

pear A tree of the genus *Pyrus* (about 20 species), native to temperate Eurasia. The numerous cultivated varieties are derived from *P. communis*. Up to 13 m high, it has oval leaves and white flowers. The fruit, which narrows towards the stalk, has sweet gritty flesh; it is eaten fresh or canned. The wood is used for furniture making. Family: *Rosaceae*.

pearl A natural calcareous concretion formed around a foreign body in certain bivalve molluscs popularly known as pearl oysters or pearl mussels. Used for jewellery since earliest times, pearls are usually white or bluish grey and of globular, oval, pear-shaped, or irregular form. It consists of concentric films of nacre, consisting of aragonite, which also forms the smooth lustrous lining (mother-of-pearl) in the shells of pearl-bearing molluscs. Cultured pearls are beads of mother-of-pearl artificially inserted into the mollusc, where they are left for three to five years. Birthstone for June.

Pearl Harbor An inlet of the Pacific Ocean in the USA, in Hawaii on Oahu Island. On 7 December 1941, the Japanese launched an air attack on US military installations in Hawaii. This action precipitated US involvement in World War II. It is now a naval shipyard, supply centre, and submarine base.

Pearson, Lester B(owles) (1897–1972) Canadian statesman and diplomat; Liberal prime minister (1963–68). Ambassador to the USA (1945–46), chairman of NATO (1951), and delegate to the UN, Pearson played a key role in settling the Suez crisis (1956), which earned him the Nobel Peace Prize in 1957.

Peary Land An area in N Greenland, between Victoria Fjord and the Greenland Sea. It is the most northerly land area in the world and was named after the Arctic explorer, Robert

E. Peary (1856–1920), who first explored it in 1892.

Peasants' Revolt (1381) The only major popular revolt in England during the middle ages. It was occasioned by heavy poll taxes and reflected a general discontent with government policies. The peasants, led by Wat *Tyler and John Ball (d. 1381), marched on London. They achieved initial success, but the revolt soon collapsed and its supporters were ruthlessly suppressed.

peat Partially decomposed dark-brown or black plant debris laid down in waterlogged conditions in temperate or cold climates. The remains of *Sphagnum* (peat or bog moss) are important constituents. Peat is the starting point for coal formation and is itself used as a fuel.

peccary A small gregarious hoofed mammal belonging to the genus *Tayassu* (2 species) of South and Central American forests. Resembling a pig, the collared peccary (*T. tajacu*) is dark grey with a light stripe from chest to shoulder and grows to a length of 90 cm. It has two pairs of short tusks. The white-lipped peccary (*T. albirostris*) is darker and larger and has a white patch on the snout. Both are omnivorous. Family: *Tayassuidae*.

pectin A carbohydrate found combined with cellulose in the cell walls of plants. Ripening fruits change any other pectic compounds present into jelly-like pectin—an essential ingredient for the gelling of jam.

Peel, Sir Robert (1788–1850) British statesman; Conservative prime minister (1834–35, 1841–46). Elected to parliament in 1809, he was twice home secretary (1822–27, 1828–30), introducing prison and criminal-law reforms and founding the Metropolitan Police (1829). In the Tamworth manifesto (1834), he stated a programme of reform that clearly identified the *Conservative Party. He is best remembered for the repeal of the *Corn Laws (1846).

peerage In the UK and Ireland, the temporal hereditary nobility and the life peers, comprising (since 1876) the Lords of Appeal in Ordinary (law lords) and (since 1958) those created in recognition of public service. The five ranks of the hereditary peerage are, in descending order, duke, marquess, earl, viscount, and baron. A life peer has the rank of baron. Until recently all peers were permitted to sit in the House of Lords but were not allowed to be MPs (although from 1963 peers were able to disclaim their titles for life to enable them to sit in the Commons). In 1999 the hereditary peers (except a transitional rump of 92) were deprived of the right to sit in the Lords. Under a White Paper (2001), newly created life peers would no longer have a seat in the Lords and the existing life peers would gradually be replaced with new appointees (who would have no title). Plans to abolish the law lords were announced in 2003.

peewit *See* LAPWING.

Pegasus (astronomy) A large constellation in the N sky that contains the **Square of Pegasus**, formed from three 2nd- and 3rd-magnitude stars in the constellation together with the 2nd-magnitude star Alpheratz in Andromeda.

Pegasus (Greek mythology) A winged horse that sprang from the blood of *Medusa. It carried the legendary hero Bellerophon in his battles. It became a constellation and the bearer of thunderbolts for Zeus.

Pei, Ieoh Ming (1917–) US architect, born in China. He moved to the USA in 1935 and became a US citizen in 1954. His buildings include the John Hancock Tower (1973) in Boston, a glass and steel pyramid at the Louvre, Paris (1989), and the Rock and Roll Hall of Fame in Cleveland (1995).

Peking *See* BEIJING.

Pekingese An ancient breed of toy dog originating in China and brought to the West by British forces who sacked the Imperial Palace, Peking (Beijing), in 1860. It has a long straight coat forming a luxuriant mane on the shoulders and a black short-muzzled face. Height: 15–23 cm.

Peking man A type of fossil *hominid belonging to the species *Homo erectus* (*see* HOMO); it is represented by skeletal remains found at Chou-K'ou-Tien (Zhou kou tian) cave near Peking (Beijing). Formerly known as *Pithecanthropus*, Peking man lived during the middle Pleistocene period (c. 500 000 years ago).

Pelagius (c. 360–c. 420 AD) The originator of the heretical Christian doctrine known as Pelagianism. He rejected original sin and predestination, believing in man's free will and inherent capacity for good.

Pelargonium *See* GERANIUM.

Pelé (Edson Arantes do Nascimento; 1940–) Brazilian Association footballer. The greatest inside forward of his time, he became a world star at 17 when Brazil first won the World Cup (1958). He scored over 1300 goals. In 1994 he was appointed special minister for sports and in

1997 he was awarded an honorary British knighthood.

Pelham, Henry *See* NEWCASTLE, THOMAS PELHAM-HOLLES, 1ST DUKE OF.

pelican A large waterbird belonging to a family (*Pelecanidae*; 7 species) occurring on lakes, rivers, and coasts of temperate and tropical regions. 125–180 cm long, pelicans have short legs, a short tail, and very large wings. Their long straight pointed bills have a distensible pouch underneath, in which fish are held before being swallowed. Order: *Pelecaniformes* (gannets, pelicans, etc.).

pellagra A disease caused by deficiency of nicotinic acid (*see* VITAMIN B COMPLEX). It occurs mainly in poor countries in people whose diet consists predominantly of maize. The disease causes dermatitis, diarrhoea, and delirium or depression.

Peloponnese (Modern Greek name: Pelopónnesos) The S peninsula of Greece, joined to central Greece by the Isthmus of Corinth. It includes the towns of Corinth, Patras (the chief port), and *Sparta. It was linked to W Greece by bridge in 2004. Area: 21 637 sq km (8354 sq mi). Population (2001): 1 632 955.

Peloponnesian War (431–404 BC) The conflict between Athens and Sparta and their allies, in which Sparta was finally victorious. Sparta's superior infantry invaded Athens in 431 while Athens, under Pericles, attacked at sea. In 415 Athens led by *Alcibiades set out to conquer Sicily, which retaliated with Spartan help and destroyed the Athenian fleet (413). The war continued until Sparta under *Lysander besieged Athens, which then surrendered (404).

Pelops The legendary Greek founder of the Pelopid dynasty of Mycenae, a son of Tantalus. He won his bride Hippodamia by winning a chariot race with the help of his driver Myrtilus. When Myrtilus demanded his reward, Pelops refused and drowned him. The curse pronounced by the dying Myrtilus was passed on to all his descendants until it was exorcized by the purification of Orestes.

Peltier effect *See* THERMOELECTRIC EFFECTS.

pelvis A basin-like structure composed of the hip bones and lower part of the spine. It protects the soft organs of the lower abdomen and provides attachment for the bones and muscles of the legs.

Pembrokeshire A county in SW Wales, on the Irish Sea and the Bristol Channel. In 1974 it became part of Dyfed but it was reinstated in 1996. It consists of a peninsula with a spectacular indented coast, rising to the Prescilly Hills in the N. Agriculture, fishing, and tourism are important; oil-refining has developed around Milford Haven. Area: 1593 sq km (615 sq mi). Population (2001): 112 901. Administrative centre: Haverfordwest.

Penal Laws (1571, 1581, 1593) A series of Acts passed during the reign of Elizabeth I to punish those (recusants), especially Roman Catholics, who refused to attend Church of England services. Recusants were fined, imprisoned, banished, or executed and suffered civil disabilities, such as loss of property. The Laws were repealed in 1829 (*see* CATHOLIC EMANCIPATION). *See also* TEST ACTS.

Penang A state in NW Peninsular Malaysia, on the Strait of Malacca, consisting of Penang island and Province Wellesley on the mainland. The island was the first British settlement in Malaya. The main products are rice, rubber, and tin. Area: 1031 sq km (398 sq mi). Population (2000): 1 225 501. Capital: Georgetown.

Penates *See* LARES AND PENATES.

Penderecki, Krzysztof (1933–) Polish composer. His music, for which he has devised a special system of notation, is characterized by unusual sound effects. His works include *Threnody for the Victims of Hiroshima* (for strings; 1960), five symphonies, four operas, and the *Polish Requiem* (1983–84).

pendulum A device in which a mass (the bob) swings freely about a fixed point with a constant period. In the ideal simple pendulum the bob is connected to the fixed point by a length (l) of weightless string, wire, etc. Its period is $2\pi(l/g)^{1/2}$, where g is the *acceleration of free fall, and is independent of the mass of the bob. Pendulums are used to regulate a clock mechanism and in instruments that determine the value of g.

Penelope In Homer's *Odyssey*, the wife of *Odysseus. During her husband's absence she put off her many suitors by saying that she must first make a shroud for her father-in-law Laertes. Each night she unravelled what she had woven by day.

penguin A flightless black-and-white seabird belonging to a family (*Spheniscidae*; 14–18 species) occurring on cold coasts of the S hemisphere. Penguins are adapted for aquatic life, having wings reduced to narrow flippers giving fast propulsion. 40–120 cm long, they have dense plumage enabling them to tolerate extreme cold. Order: *Sphenisciformes*. *See also* EMPEROR PENGUIN.

penicillins A group of *antibiotics. The first penicillin was discovered in the mould *Penicillium notatum*, in 1929, by Sir Alexander *Fleming but was not used to treat infections in humans until 1941. Natural penicillins include benzylpenicillin (*or* penicillin G), which is usually administered by injection, and phenoxymethylpenicillin (*or* penicillin V), which is administered orally. Semisynthetic penicillins (e.g. flucloxacillin, methicillin) are effective against infections resistant to naturally occurring penicillins. Penicillins can cause severe allergic reactions in susceptible patients.

Peninsular War (1808–14) That part of the Napoleonic Wars fought in Spain and Portugal. The French took Portugal in 1807 and in 1808 Napoleon's brother, Joseph Bonaparte (1768–1844), replaced Ferdinand VII as King of Spain. Popular revolts broke out and turned into a vicious guerrilla war. British troops under the command of the Duke of *Wellington eventually liberated the Peninsula.

penis The male copulatory organ of mammals, some reptiles, and a few birds. In humans (and other mammals) it contains a tube (urethra) through which both semen and urine can be discharged. Erectile tissue making up the bulk of the penis becomes engorged with blood during sexual excitement. The corresponding part in women is the **clitoris**, a small erectile mass of tissue situated in front of the urinary opening.

Penn, William (1644–1718) English Quaker and founder of Pennsylvania, son of Admiral Sir William Penn (1621–70). In 1668 he was imprisoned in the Tower, where he wrote *No Cross, No Crown* (1669), a classic of Quaker practice. From 1682 he was involved in the establishment of Quaker settlements in America, including Pennsylvania.

Pennines (*or* **Pennine Chain**) An upland range in N England. It extends from the Cheviot Hills in the N to the valley of the River Trent in the S. Sometimes known as the "backbone of England," it is the watershed of the chief rivers in N England. It rises to 893 m (2930 ft) at Cross Fell.

Pennsylvania A state in the E USA, dominated by the uplands of the Appalachian Plateau. It is a leading iron and steel producer and provides nearly all the country's hard coal. Oil is important and the world's first oil well was drilled near Titusville in 1859. Dairy farming predominates in the NE, while the fertile lands of the SE yield cereals, fruit, and vegetables. *History*: one of the 13 original colonies, it was first settled by Swedes, who were soon dispossessed by the Dutch (1655). In 1681 the area was given to William Penn by Charles II of England as a haven for Quakers. It became a state in 1787. Area: 117 412 sq km (45 333 sq mi). Population (2000): 12 281 054. Capital: Harrisburg.

Pennsylvanian period *See* CARBONIFEROUS PERIOD.

Pentagon The headquarters of the US Defense Department, a massive five-sided building in Virginia built (1941–43) during World War II. It houses all three services and is the largest office building in the world, extending over 14 hectares (34 acres). The terrorist attack on *September 11, 2001 left some 180 workers dead and seriously damaged the building.

pentathlon An athletic competition comprising five events, the winner being the competitor with the highest total. It originated in an Olympic contest instituted in 708 BC. The current women's version, an Olympic event since 1964, consists of the 100 m hurdles, shot put, high jump, long jump, and 800 m run. The men's pentathlon has been replaced in major competitions by the *decathlon. The **modern pentathlon** is a sporting competition comprising five events: a 5000 m cross-country ride (on horseback), fencing, pistol shooting, a 300 m swim, and a 4000 m cross-country run. It was first included in the Olympic Games in 1912.

Pentecost *See* WHIT SUNDAY.

Pentecostal Churches A Christian movement originating in revivalist meetings in the USA in 1906. In Pentecostal assemblies people seek spiritual renewal through baptism by the Holy Spirit, as took place on the first Pentecost (Acts 2.1–4).

pentlandite The principal ore mineral of nickel, (Ni,Fe)S, found in association with pyrrhotite and chalcopyrite in basic and ultrabasic igneous rocks. It is mined in Canada, Australia, and the republics of the former Soviet Union.

peony A large perennial herb or shrub of the genus *Paeonia* (33 species) of N temperate regions, often cultivated for its showy flowers. It has large glossy leaves and solitary white, pink, crimson, or yellow flowers, about 10 cm across, with incurving petals and a fleshy central disc. The fruit is a large leathery pod containing black seeds. Family: *Paeoniaceae*.

Pepin the Short (d. 768 AD) King of the

Franks (751–68) after overthrowing the *Merovingians. Founder of the Carolingian dynasty, Pepin checked Lombard expansion and in 756 presented Pope Stephen II with the nucleus of the *papal states.

pepper A condiment derived from a perennial climbing vine, *Piper nigrum*, native to India. Up to 10 m high, it bears chains of up to 50 inconspicuous flowers that form berry-like fruits (or peppercorns), about 5 mm in diameter. Family: *Piperaceae*. The fleshy red and green peppers are the fruits of *Capsicum* species (*see* CAPSICUM).

peppered moth A European *geometrid moth, *Biston betularia*, the typical form of which has a similar coloration to the lichen-encrusted tree bark on which it rests. During the past century a dark form, var. *carbonaria*, has become common in sooty industrial areas.

peppermint A perennial herb, *Mentha* × *piperata*: a hybrid between water mint (*M. aquatica*) and *spearmint. It has dark-green leaves and reddish-lilac flowers and is the source of oil of peppermint, used as a flavouring.

pepsin A protein-digesting enzyme found in gastric juice. The inactive form, pepsinogen, is secreted by glands in the stomach wall and converted to pepsin by the hydrochloric acid in the stomach. Pepsin is a powerful coagulant of milk.

p

peptic ulcer An inflamed eroded area in the wall of the stomach (**gastric ulcer**) or, more commonly, the duodenum (**duodenal ulcer**). Ulcers are more common in people who secrete excessive amounts of stomach acid. They may cause abdominal pain, nausea, and vomiting. Serious complications occur when the ulcer bleeds or perforates (bursts). Evidence suggests that infection with *Helicobacter pylori* must be controlled by antibiotics to avoid recurrence of ulcers.

peptide A chemical compound comprising a chain of two or more *amino acids linked by peptide bonds (–NH–CO–) formed between the carboxyl and amino groups of adjacent amino acids. Polypeptides, containing between three and several hundred amino acids, are the constituents of *proteins. Some peptides are important as hormones and as antibiotics.

Pepys, Samuel (1633–1703) English diarist. He was secretary to the Admiralty (1669–88), an MP, and president of the Royal Society. His *Diary*, which extends from 1660 to 1669 and includes descriptions of the Restoration, the Plague, and the Fire of London, was written in code.

perch One of two species of freshwater food and game fish belonging to the genus *Perca*. The common perch (*P. fluviatilis*) of Eurasia has a deep elongated body, usually about 25 cm long, and is greenish in colour, with dark vertical bars on its sides and a spiny first dorsal fin. Perch usually live in shoals, feeding on fish and invertebrates. Family: *Percidae*; order: *Perciformes*. *See also* SEA BASS.

percussion instruments Musical instruments struck directly with the hand or with a hand-held implement. The main categories are idiophones, in which the entire instrument body vibrates (gong, xylophone, cymbals, rattles) and membranophones, in which the sound is emitted by a tensioned membrane (most drums, kettledrums, tambourines). Another distinction is between instruments with a defined pitch (kettledrums, bells, xylophone) and those without a defined pitch (bass and marching drums, triangles).

Percy, Sir Henry (1364–1403) English rebel, called Hotspur. Together with his father, Henry, 1st Earl of Northumberland (1342–1408), he led the most serious revolt against Henry IV, whom they had helped to the throne in 1399. He appears in Shakespeare's *Henry IV, Part I*.

peregrine falcon A large powerful *falcon, *Falco peregrinus*, occurring in rocky coastal regions worldwide. It is 33–48 cm long and has long pointed wings and a long tail. The male is blue-grey with black-barred white underparts; females are browner. It feeds mainly on ducks, shorebirds, and mammals.

Pereira 4 47N 75 46W A city in W Colombia. An agricultural trading centre, it has coffee-processing, brewing, and clothing industries. Population (1999 est): 381 275.

perennials Plants that can live for many years. In herbaceous perennials aerial parts die down each winter and the plants survive in the form of underground organs (rhizomes, bulbs, corms, etc.). Woody perennials have woody stems, which overwinter above ground.

Peres, Shimon (1923–) Israeli statesman, prime minister (1984–86; 1995–96); foreign minister (1986–88; 1992–95; 2001–02); finance minister (1988–90). Born in Poland, Peres emigrated to Palestine in 1934. He became head of the navy in 1948 and was defence minister from 1974 to 1977. In 1994 he was awarded the Nobel Peace Prize with Yassir Arafat and Yitzhak

Rabin for his part in securing the Israeli–PLO peace agreement.

perestroika *See* GLASNOST.

Pergamum An ancient city of W Asia Minor. After about 230 BC it became capital of a powerful Hellenistic kingdom. Pergamum became rich largely from *parchment and luxury textiles mass-produced by slave labour. The last king bequeathed his realm to Rome (133 BC).

Pericles (c. 495–429 BC) Athenian statesman, who presided over Athens' golden age. Pericles became leader of the democratic party in 461 and secured power shortly afterwards. He dominated Athens until 430 by virtue of his outstanding oratory and leadership and his reputation for honesty. Under Pericles, Athens asserted its leadership of the *Delian League and revolts among its members were suppressed. By 431, rivalry between Athens and Sparta had led to the outbreak of the *Peloponnesian War. Pericles' strategy was undermined by the plague of 430 and he briefly lost office. He died shortly after his reinstatement.

peridotite An ultrabasic coarse-grained igneous rock consisting mainly of olivine. The earth's mantle is sometimes called the peridotite shell. Peridotites occur beneath many mountains and islands.

perigee The point in the orbit of the moon or of an artificial satellite around the earth at which the body is nearest the earth. *Compare* APOGEE.

Perigordian A culture of the Upper *Palaeolithic. Perigordian is the preferred French designation for the pre-Solutrean industries in W Europe, excluding the typologically different Aurignacian. Upper Perigordian is approximately equatable with *Gravettian.

Périgueux 45 12N 0 44E A town in SW France, the capital of the Dordogne department. It is renowned for its *pâté de foie gras*, truffles, and wine. Manufactures include hardware and chemicals. Population (latest est): 32 850.

perihelion The point in the orbit of a body around the sun at which the body is nearest the sun. The earth is at perihelion on 3 Jan. *Compare* APHELION.

periodic table A tabular arrangement of the chemical *elements in order of increasing atomic number, such that physical and chemical similarities are displayed. The earliest version was devised in 1869 by D. *Mendeleyev, who predicted the existence of several elements from gaps in the table. The rows across the table are known as periods and the columns as groups. The elements in a group all have a similar configuration of outer electrons and therefore show similar chemical behaviour. Across each period, atoms are electropositive (form positive ions) to the left and electronegative to the right. Atomic theory explains this behaviour using the concept of electron shells, corresponding to different energy levels of the atomic electrons. Atoms combine in order to form complete outer shells. The shells are built up by filling the lower energy states (inner shells) first. The first shell takes two electrons, and the second, eight. In larger atoms, the inner electrons screen the outer electrons from the nucleus, resulting in a more complex shell-filling sequence. The short periods are from lithium (Li) to neon (Ne) and from sodium (Na) to argon (Ar). The *noble gases in column 0 have complete outer shells and are generally chemically inactive. See table on p. 684.

periodontal disease Disease of the gums and other structures surrounding the teeth, formerly known as pyorrhoea. Caused by the action of bacteria on food debris that forms a hard deposit (calculus) in the spaces between the gums and teeth, it results in swelling and bleeding of the gums: eventually—if untreated—the teeth become loose and fall out. Periodontal disease is the major cause of tooth loss in adults: it may be prevented (and the early stages treated) by regular brushing, scaling, and polishing, to remove the calculus. Advanced cases require surgery.

periscope An optical device consisting, typically, of a tube in which mirrors or prisms are arranged so that light passing through an aperture at right angles to the tube is reflected through the length of the tube to emerge at an aperture at the other end also at right angles to the tube. Extendible periscopes are used by submerged submarines to see above the surface of the water.

Perissodactyla An order of hoofed mammals (16 species) that includes *horses, *tapirs, and rhinoceroses. The name—meaning odd-toed—reflects the fact that the weight of the body is carried mainly by the central (third) digit of the foot. They are herbivorous, but have only a single stomach, which is less efficient than the digestive system of *ruminants. *Compare* ARTIODACTYLA.

peritonitis Inflammation of the peritoneum—the membrane that lines the abdom-

periodic table

Period \ Group	1	2	3	4	5	6	7	8	9	10	11	12	13	14	15	16	17	18
1	1 H																	2 He
2	3 Li	4 Be											5 B	6 C	7 N	8 O	9 F	10 Ne
3	11 Na	12 Mg											13 Al	14 Si	15 P	16 S	17 Cl	18 Ar
4	19 K	20 Ca	21 Sc	22 Ti	23 V	24 Cr	25 Mn	26 Fe	27 Co	28 Ni	29 Cu	30 Zn	31 Ga	32 Ge	33 As	34 Se	35 Br	36 Kr
5	37 Rb	38 Sr	39 Y	40 Zr	41 Nb	42 Mo	43 Tc	44 Ru	45 Rh	46 Pd	47 Ag	48 Cd	49 In	50 Sn	51 Sb	52 Te	53 I	54 Xe
6	55 Cs	56 Ba	57–71 La–Lu	72 Hf	73 Ta	74 W	75 Re	76 Os	77 Ir	78 Pt	79 Au	80 Hg	81 Tl	82 Pb	83 Bi	84 Po	85 At	86 Rn
7	87 Fr	88 Ra	89–103 Ac–Lr	104 Rf	105 Db	106 Sg	107 Bh	108 Hs	109 Mt	110 Ds	111 Uuu	112 Uub	113 Uut	114 Uuq	115 Uup	116 Uuh	117 Uus	118 Uuo

Period																
6	**Lanthanoids**	57 La	58 Ce	59 Pr	60 Nd	61 Pm	62 Sm	63 Eu	64 Gd	65 Tb	66 Dy	67 Ho	68 Er	69 Tm	70 Yb	71 Lu
7	**Actinoids**	89 Ac	90 Th	91 Pa	92 U	93 Np	94 Pu	95 Am	96 Cm	97 Bk	98 Cf	99 Es	100 Fm	101 Md	102 No	103 Lr

inal cavity. This results from the bursting of an abdominal organ (such as the appendix) or of a peptic ulcer. Alternatively it may result from bacterial infection. An immediate operation is essential to repair the perforated organ and to cleanse the inside of the abdomen; antibiotics are also given.

periwinkle (botany) An evergreen creeping shrub or perennial herb of the genus *Vinca* (5 species), native to Europe and W Asia. The attractive solitary flowers are blue or white and the fruit is usually a long capsule. They are cultivated as ornamentals: *V. major* is an important species. Family: *Apocynaceae*.

periwinkle (zoology) A *gastropod mollusc belonging to the family *Littorinidae*, also called winkle. The common edible winkle (*Littorina littorea*) of European seashores is about 2 cm high and has a dark-green rounded shell with a pointed spire and grazes on algae.

Perkin, Sir William Henry (1838–1907) British chemist, who in 1856 synthesized the first artificial dye, aniline purple. The following year he built a factory to manufacture the dye but he later returned to chemical research and the synthesis of many compounds.

Perm (name from 1940 until 1957: Molotov) 58 01N 56 10E A port in W Russia, on the River Kama. Its varied industries include engineering, chemical manufacturing, and oil refining. The *Permian period was first identified here. Population (1999 est): 1 017 100.

permafrost The permanent freezing of the ground, sometimes to great depths, in areas bordering on ice sheets. During the summer season the top layer of soil may thaw and become marshy, while the frozen ground below remains an impermeable barrier.

permeability, magnetic (μ) A measure of the response of a material to a *magnetic field equal to the ratio of the magnetic *flux induced in the material to the applied magnetic field strength. The relative permeability, μ_r, is the ratio of μ in the medium to that in a vacuum, μ_0 (*see* MAGNETIC CONSTANT). Paramagnetic materials have a μ_r greater than unity because they reinforce the magnetic field. Ferromagnetic materials can have a μ_r as high as 100 000. Diamagnetic materials have a μ_r of less than one.

Permian period The last geological period of the Palaeozoic era, between the Carboniferous and Triassic periods, lasting from about 280 to 240 million years ago. The period was marked by an increasingly dry climate that continued into the Triassic, and the two periods are often linked together as the Permo-Triassic.

permittivity (ε) The absolute permittivity of a medium is the ratio of the electric displacement to the electric field at the same point. The absolute permittivity of free space is called the *electric constant. The relative permittivity (or dielectric constant) ε_r of a capacitor is the ratio of its capacitance with a specified dielectric between the plates to its capacitance with free space between the plates.

Perón, Juan (Domingo) (1895–1974) Argentine statesman; president (1946–55, 1973–74). Elected in 1946 after winning popular support as head of the labour secretariat, his position was strengthened by the popularity of his second wife, **Evita Perón** (María Eva Duarte de P.; 1919–52), who was idolized by the poor for her charitable work. After her death, support for Perón waned and he was deposed. He was re-elected president in 1973.

Perpendicular The style of gothic architecture predominant in England between about 1370 and the mid-16th century. The name derives from the panel-like effect of the window design, with its pronounced vertical mullions broken regularly by horizontal divisions. King's College chapel, Cambridge (1446–1515) and St George's chapel, Windsor (begun 1481) are masterpieces of the Perpendicular style.

Perpignan 42 42N 2 54E A city in S France, the capital of the Pyrénées-Orientales department situated near the Spanish border. The capital of the former province of Roussillon in the 17th century, it has a gothic cathedral and a 13th-century castle. Perpignan is a tourist and commercial centre, trading in wine, fruit, and vegetables. Population (1999): 105 115.

Persephone (Roman name: Proserpine) Greek goddess of the underworld, daughter of Zeus and *Demeter. She was abducted by *Hades, who made her queen of the underworld. Zeus allowed her to spend part of each year on earth, symbolizing the regeneration of natural life in the spring.

Persepolis An ancient Persian city in Fars province, Iran. Darius I (reigned 522–486 BC) planned Persepolis as the ceremonial capital of his empire and its wealth and splendour were legendary. Alexander the Great destroyed Persepolis in 330 BC.

Perseus In Greek mythology, the son of Zeus and Danae. One of the greatest Greek heroes, he beheaded the *Medusa with the help of

Athena, who gave him a mirror to avoid looking at the Gorgon and being turned to stone. He married Andromeda, daughter of the Ethiopian king.

Pershing missile A US army two-stage solid-fuelled nuclear surface-to-surface missile launched from mobile launcher vehicles and having a range of 740 km (460 mi). Several improved versions of the missile have been produced. It is named after Gen J. J. Pershing (1860–1948).

Persian cat A domesticated cat, also called a Longhair, having a long flowing coat with a ruff or frill around the neck. The coat may be of any colour, although the Blue Persian is most popular.

Persian Gulf An arm of the Arabian Sea, extending some 950 km (590 mi) NW beyond the Gulf of Oman. The large offshore oil deposits are exploited by the surrounding *Gulf States. Area: 233 000 sq km (89 942 sq mi).

persimmon A tree of the genus *Diospyros* that produces edible fruits. These are the Japanese persimmon (*D. kaki*), the American persimmon (*D. virginiana*), and the Asian date plum (*D. lotus*). They have dark-green oval leaves and produce round orange, yellow, or red fruits, 5–8 cm across. Persimmons are eaten fresh, cooked, or candied. Family: *Ebenaceae*.

Perspex (polymethyl methacrylate) A colourless transparent thermoplastic material made by *polymerization of methyl methacrylate. It can be extruded and moulded and coloured, for use in light fittings, aircraft parts, and car parts. It is widely used as an unbreakable substitute for glass.

Perth 1. 56 24N 3 28W A city in E Scotland, the administrative centre of Perth and Kinross on the River Tay. It was an early capital of Scotland. There are dyeing, textiles, whisky distilling, and carpet industries and it is a popular tourist centre. Population (1991): 41 453. **2.** 31 58S 115 49E The capital of Western Australia, on the Swan River. Founded in 1829, it expanded following the discovery (1893) of gold. Its port, Fremantle, is a growing industrial centre. Population (1995 est): 1 262 600.

Perth and Kinross A council area of central Scotland. In 1975 the historic county of Perthshire was abolished; the greater part combined with the county of Kinross to form Perth and Kinross district in Tayside Region. In 1996 this became an independent unitary authority. It is chiefly mountainous. Agriculture is concentrated in the SE lowlands. Tourism and forestry are important. Area: 5231 sq km (2019 sq mi). Population (2001): 134 949. Administrative centre: Perth.

Peru, Republic of A country in the NW of South America, on the Pacific Ocean. Narrow coastal plains rise to the Andes, reaching heights of over 6500 m (21 000 ft). The land descends again to the tropical forests of the Amazon basin. Most of the population is of Indian or mixed Indian and European descent. *Economy*: Peru is one of the world's leading fishing countries, the main product being fishmeal. Agriculture is important, and the main crops include maize, rice, sugar cane, cotton, and coffee. Livestock is particularly important, especially the production of wool. Rich mineral resources include copper, silver, lead, zinc, and iron; oil was discovered in the 1970s but production has since declined. With its rain forests and relics of ancient civilizations, Peru has a valuable tourist trade. The main exports include minerals and metals and fishmeal. *History*: Peru's precolonial history encompasses the civilization of the Chimú and that of the *Incas, who were conquered by the Spanish under Pizarro in 1533. Peru was the last of Spain's American colonies to declare its independence (1821) and the Spanish were finally defeated in 1824. Political stability was achieved by Gen Ramón Castilla (1797–1867), who developed Peru's economy. However, the country's prosperity was undermined by the War of the Pacific (1879–83). In the 1960s and 1970s there was a series of coups. In 1980, in Peru's first elections to be held in 17 years, the former civilian president Fernando Belaúnde Terry was re-elected. The 1980s and 1990s saw terrorist outrages by left-wing insurgents and human-rights abuses by the military. Alberto Fujimori was elected president in 1990 and enhanced his powers in a new constitution (1993). Peru's long-standing border dispute with Ecuador (which had led to war in 1941, 1981, and 1995) was finally settled in 1998. In 2000 Fujimori was elected to a third term amid accusations of fraud; protests and a corruption scandal led him to stand down and go into exile. He has since been charged with murder and kidnapping. In 2001 Alejandro Toledo was elected president, becoming the first Indian to hold the post. Peru is a member of the OAS and LAIA. Official languages: Spanish, Quechua, and Aymará. Currency: nuevo sol of 100 céntimos. Area: 1 285 215 sq km (496 093 sq mi). Population (2003 est): 27 148 000. Capital: Lima.

Perugia 43 07N 12 23E A city in Italy, the capital of Umbria. Originally an Etruscan city, it has 13th-century city walls, a 14th-century cathedral, and a university (1200). Perugia is an agricultural trading centre and its manufactures include furniture and textiles. Population (2000 est): 156 673.

Perutz, Max Ferdinand (1914–2002) British chemist, born in Austria, who developed X-ray diffraction to determine the molecular structure of haemoglobin. He shared a Nobel Prize (1962) with J. C. *Kendrew.

Peshawar 34 01N 71 40E A city in N Pakistan, situated at the E end of the Khyber Pass. It is one of the oldest cities in Pakistan. Industries include textiles, shoes, and pottery. Population (1998): 988 055.

Pestalozzi, Johann Heinrich (1746–1827) Swiss educationalist, pioneer of mass education. His book *Wie Gertrud ihre Kinder lehrt* (1801) reflected his ideas on the intuitive method of education. Pestalozzi's work is commemorated in the **Pestalozzi International Children's Villages**, the first of which was established in 1946 for war orphans at Trogen (Switzerland).

Pétain, (Henri) Philippe (1856–1951) French general and statesman. In World War I he distinguished himself at the defence of Verdun (1916), becoming marshal of France (1918). In World War II, when France was on the verge of defeat (1940), Pétain became prime minister. In June 1940, he signed an armistice with Hitler that allowed for a third of France to remain unoccupied by Germany. Pétain was sentenced to death in 1945 for collaboration but reprieved.

Peter (I) the Great (1672–1725) Tsar (1682–1721) and then Emperor (1721–25) of Russia, who established Russia as a major European power. Peter travelled in W Europe in the late 1690s, acquiring knowledge of western technology. He instituted many reforms in government and administration, trade and industry, and in the army. In the Great Northern War (1700–21), he acquired Livonia, Estonia, and also Ingria, where in 1703 he founded St Petersburg. He campaigned less successfully against the Turks (1710–13) but gained territory in the Caspian region from war with Persia (1722–23).

Peter, St In the New Testament, one of the 12 Apostles. He was a fisherman until called by Jesus. Although his faith often wavered, notably at the crucifixion, when he denied Christ three times, Peter was named as the rock upon which the Church was to be built. After Christ's death, he dominated the Christian community for 15 years, undertaking missionary work despite imprisonment. Feast day: 29 June.

Peterborough 1. 52 35N 0 15W A city in E central England, in Peterborough unitary authority, Cambridgeshire, on the River Nene. The cathedral was begun in the 12th century. Designated a new town in 1967, it is an important marketing centre for the surrounding agricultural area. Population (1991): 134 788. **2.** A unitary authority in E central England, in Cambridgeshire. Area: 402 sq km (155 sq mi). Population (2001): 156 060.

Peterloo Massacre (1819) The name given, by analogy with the battle of Waterloo, to the violent dispersal of a political meeting held in St Peter's Fields, Manchester. A peaceful crowd had gathered to hear Henry Hunt (1773–1835) speak on parliamentary reform. The magistrates called in local troops, the cavalry were ordered to charge, and 11 people were killed.

Petition of Right (1628) A parliamentary declaration accepted by Charles I. It made illegal imprisonment without trial, taxation without parliamentary approval, and the billeting of soldiers on private individuals.

Petra An ancient town in S Jordan. It was the capital of the Nabataeans, nomadic Arabs who settled along the caravan routes from Arabia to the Mediterranean. Petra was a great trading centre from the 3rd century BC. It was incorporated in the Roman Empire in 106 AD and was superseded by *Palmyra in the 2nd century. Accessible only through a narrow gorge, Petra is renowned for its rock-cut temples and dwellings.

Petrarch (Francesco Petrarca; 1304–74) Italian poet. He travelled widely in Europe and in 1341 was crowned as poet laureate in Rome. His works of scholarship anticipated the Renaissance in their combination of classical learning and Christian faith. He is remembered chiefly for the *Canzoniere*, a series of love poems addressed to Laura.

petrel A marine bird belonging to a widely distributed family (*Procellariidae*; 55 species) characterized by thick plumage, webbed feet, and a hooked bill. 27–90 cm long, petrels feed on fish and molluscs. Diving petrels belong to a family (*Pelecanoididae*; 5 species) occurring in the S hemisphere; they are 16–25 cm long and feed mostly on crustaceans. Order: *Procellariiformes*. *See also* FULMAR; PRION; SHEARWATER; STORM PETREL.

petroleum *See* OIL.

petrology The study of rocks, including

their formation, structure, texture, and mineral and chemical composition. **Petrogenesis** is the origin or mode of formation of rocks; **petrography** is the description and classification of rocks from hand specimens or thin sections.

Petunia A genus of tropical American herbs (about 40 species), cultivated for their showy funnel-shaped flowers. Ornamental species include *P. integrifolia*, with pink, blue, or purple flowers, the white-flowered *P. axillaris*, and hybrids between them. Family: *Solanaceae*.

pewter An *alloy of tin (80–90%) and lead (20–10%) with small amounts of antimony to harden it or copper to soften it. It was formerly used for plates, spoons, and other utensils but now only beer mugs are made from it.

peyote A blue-green *cactus, *Lophophora williamsii*, also called mescal, native to Mexico and the SW USA. It bears white to pink flowering heads, which, when dried, are known as "mescal buttons." They contain the alkaloid *mescaline, which produces hallucinations when chewed.

pH A measure of the acidity or alkalinity of a solution, equal to the logarithm to the base 10 of the reciprocal of the number of moles per litre of hydrogen ions it contains. In neutral solutions, therefore, the hydrogen ion concentration is 10^{-7} and the pH is consequently 7. In acid solutions the pH is less than 7; alkaline solutions have pH values greater than 7. The pH scale is logarithmic; for example, a solution with a pH of 2 is ten times more acidic than one with a pH of 1. *See also* ACIDS AND BASES.

p

Phaedra In Greek mythology, the daughter of *Minos and Pasiphaë and the wife of Theseus. She fell in love with her stepson Hippolytus. When he rejected her, she hanged herself, after writing a letter to Theseus accusing Hippolytus of having seduced her.

phagocyte A cell that engulfs and then digests particles from its surroundings: this process is called phagocytosis. Many protozoans are phagocytic, but the word specifically refers to certain white blood cells that protect the body by engulfing bacteria and other foreign particles.

phalanger A small herbivorous *marsupial of the family *Phalangeridae* (48 species), occurring in woodlands of Australia and New Guinea. They are adapted for climbing trees, having strong claws and prehensile tails. The family includes the cuscuses, flying phalangers, *honey mouse, *koalas, and *possums.

phalarope A lightly built migratory shorebird belonging to a family (*Phalaropodidae*; 3 species) in which the female courts the male, which rears the young. 20–25 cm long, phalaropes have a slim neck, lobed toes, and a grey and red-brown plumage. Two species breed in the Arctic and one inland in North America.

pharaoh The title of ancient Egyptian rulers. The word derives via Hebrew from the Egyptian for great house. The royal cobra, the sun god Ra's symbol, signified divinity; pharaoh represented Ra reigning on earth. The first dynasty, or line of pharaohs, was founded about 3200 BC.

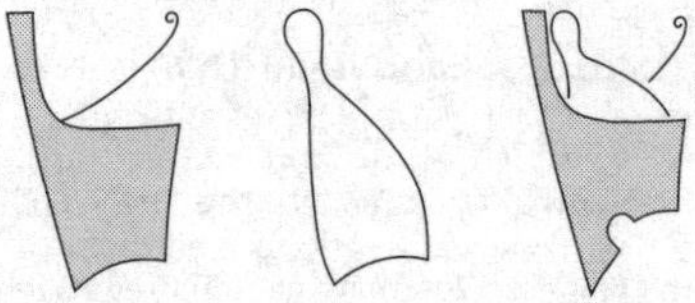

pharaoh. The pharaoh's double crown, combining the red crown of Lower Egypt with the white crown of Upper Egypt, symbolized the unification of the two lands (c. 3100 BC).

Pharisees An ancient Jewish religious and political party. The party originated in the 2nd century BC and vied for political influence with the *Sadducees. In the *Gospels they are frequently criticized by Jesus, although his own teachings are very close to theirs.

pharmacology The study of the action of drugs on living organisms. Pharmacologists examine the uptake of drugs after administration, their subsequent effects, their unwanted side effects, the interaction between different drugs, etc. **Pharmacy** is the science concerned with the preparation, manufacture, packaging, quality, and supply of medicinal drugs. The practice of pharmacy should conform to the standards laid down in the official **pharmacopoeia**, a government-approved list giving details of the manufacture, dosage, uses, and characteristics of drugs.

Pharos of Alexandria An ancient lighthouse, one of the *Seven Wonders of the World. Built in about 280 BC by Sostratus of Cnidos for Ptolemy II of Egypt, it was over 135 m (440 ft) high. It was demolished in the 13th century AD.

Pharsalus, Battle of (48 BC) The decisive encounter near present-day Fársala (Greece) in the Roman civil war, in which Julius Caesar defeated Pompey. Pompey's defeat opened the way to Caesar's dictatorship.

pharynx The muscular tract, lined with mucous membrane, between the back of the mouth and oesophagus (gullet) and larynx. It acts as a passageway for food and it also conducts air from the nasal cavity to the larynx and windpipe. Inflammation of the pharynx (pharyngitis) is a common cause of a sore throat.

phase (astronomy) The fraction of the face of the moon or a planet that is illuminated at a particular time in its orbit. Lunar phases vary from new moon (unilluminated) through a waxing crescent, first quarter, a waxing gibbous moon, to full moon, followed by a waning gibbous moon, last quarter, a waning crescent, and the next new moon.

phase (physics) **1.** The fraction of its whole cycle that a periodically varying system has completed. For example, two *alternating currents of the same frequency are **in phase** if they reach their maximum values at the same instant. In an electricity-supply system there are usually three phases. **2.** Any portion of a system that is physically distinct, is homogeneous throughout, and can be mechanically separated from other phases. For example, a salt solution is a one-phase system, whereas a mixture of ice and water is a two-phase system.

pheasant A long-tailed gamebird belonging to an Old World subfamily (*Phasianinae*; 50 species) occurring in open or woodland regions. Pheasants have short wings, a short bill, and strong claws for scratching up grain, roots, and grubs. Males are brightly coloured, with bright fleshy wattles and long tail feathers. Family: *Phasianidae* (pheasants, quail, partridges); order: *Galliformes* (pheasants, turkeys, etc.).

phenols A class of organic compounds with the general formula ROH, in which the –OH group is linked directly to a carbon atom in an aromatic ring. The simplest example, phenol itself (or **carbolic acid**), C_6H_5OH, is a white deliquescent solid used as a disinfectant and in the production of drugs, weedkillers, and synthetic resins.

phenylketonuria A genetic disease that leads to mental deficiency if untreated. Patients are unable to metabolize the amino acid phenylalanine, which is a normal constituent of diet; the amino acid and its derivatives accumulate in the body and prevent proper mental development. Phenylketonuria can now be easily detected at birth by a routine test. Babies with the disease need a special diet that contains little phenylalanine, which should be maintained until adolescence.

pheromone A chemical substance produced by animals to communicate with others of the same species. The best-known pheromones are the sex attractants secreted by moths to attract mates. Pheromones are also used by ants to lay trails and by mammals to mark out territories.

Phidias (c. 490–c. 417 BC) Athenian sculptor, one of the most influential artists of his time. Phidias designed and supervised the sculptures of the *Parthenon (*see* ELGIN MARBLES). His works included two famous chryselephantine statues: Athena in the Parthenon and *Zeus at Olympia.

Phidippides (5th century BC) Greek runner who ran 241 km (150 mi) from Athens to Sparta in two days to ask for help against the Persians before the battle of Marathon in 490 BC. The modern *marathon race derives from this feat.

Philadelphia 40 00N 75 10W A city in the USA, situated on the Delaware River in Pennsylvania at the junction of the Schuylkill River. Founded in 1681 by the Quaker, William Penn, it has many historic buildings, including Independence Hall (1732–59), where the Declaration of Independence was adopted. It is the USA's fourth largest city and has the world's largest freshwater port. Industries include oil refining, textiles, and shipbuilding. Population (2000): 1 517 550.

Philip (II) of Macedon (382–336 BC) King of Macedon (359–336), who founded the Macedonian empire. Philip unified Macedonia, expanded the economy, and trained a professional army. Despite the resolute opposition of *Demosthenes at Athens, the Greeks were defeated at the battle of Chaeronea (338). Philip planned to lead a combined force against Persia but he was assassinated.

Philip II Augustus (1165–1223) King of France (1179–1223), who destroyed the Angevin empire of the English kings. He waged war with Henry II (1187–89), Richard Lionheart (1194–99), and John; he took Normandy in 1204, followed by Maine, Touraine, and Anjou (1204–05), and in 1214 defeated an English-imperial alliance at Bouvines.

Philip II (1527–98) King of Spain (1556–98). He married Mary I of England in 1554. Philip faced the *Revolt of the Netherlands and the Turkish threat in the Mediterranean, suppressed the Moriscos (*see* CONVERSOS), launched the *Spanish Armada against Protestant England (1588), and intervened in the French *Wars of Religion against the Huguenots.

Philip V (1683–1746) The first Bourbon King of Spain (1700–24, 1724–46). The grandson of Louis XIV of France, his accession instigated the War of the *Spanish Succession. He abdicated in 1724 in favour of his son Luis (1707–24) but returned to the throne when Luis died.

Philip, Prince, Duke of Edinburgh (1921–) The husband (from 1947) of Elizabeth II of the United Kingdom. The son of Prince Andrew of Greece, he assumed the name Mountbatten in 1947, when he took British citizenship. In 1956 he introduced the **Duke of Edinburgh's Award Scheme** to encourage the leisure activities of young people between the ages of 14 and 25.

Philippi, Battle of (42 BC) The battle in which Mark Antony and Octavian (later Emperor *Augustus) defeated *Brutus and *Cassius Longinus in the Roman civil war.

Philippines, Republic of the A country in SE Asia, consisting of an archipelago of over 7000 islands between the Pacific Ocean and the South China Sea. There are few extensive lowlands, most of the larger islands, being mountainous and volcanic. Most of the inhabitants are Filipinos. *Economy*: based principally on agriculture, forestry, and fishing. The production of the staple crops of rice and maize and the main cash crops (sugar, coconuts, bananas, and pineapples) is concentrated around the central plain of Luzon. The country has a wide range of metallic minerals, including copper, gold, iron ore, manganese, molybdenum, zinc, lead, and silver. Forests cover over half the land, providing gums and resins, bamboo, and dyes in addition to good-quality hardwoods. The main industries are electronics, food processing, textiles, and wood processing. *History*: colonized by Spain in 1565, the islands were ceded to the USA in 1898 following the Spanish-American War. They became independent in 1946. Following the election of President *Marcos in 1965 rapid economic development and a greatly improved infrastructure brought increased prosperity to the Philippines. During the early 1970s growing communist guerrilla activity in the N and a Muslim separatist movement in the S led to the declaration of martial law (1972). This was lifted in 1981 but unrest increased when the exiled opposition leader Benigno S. Aquino was assassinated in 1983. After elections in 1986, Marcos went into exile and Corazon Aquino, widow of Benigno, became president. She was succeeded by Fidel Ramos in 1992. In 1996 he signed a peace agreement with Muslim rebels, which created an autonomous Muslim region in the S. The left-wing populist Joseph Estrade was elected president in 1998 but forced to resign in 2001 after allegations of financial misconduct. The vice-president Gloria Macapagal-Arroyo succeeded him as president and was re-elected in 2004. Official languages: Filipino (a new language based on Tagalog) and English. Currency: Philippine peso of 100 centavos. Area: 300 000 sq km (115 830 sq mi). Population (2003 est): 81 161 000. Capital: Manila.

Philistines A non-Semitic people, who were driven from Egypt about 1200 BC and settled in Canaan; the region took the name Palestine from its new settlers. A warlike seafaring people, without cultural pretensions (hence the derogatory word philistine), they were largely absorbed into the kingdom of Israel under King David about 1000 BC.

Philodendron A genus of woody, usually climbing, plants (275 species), native to tropical America. They cling to trees or other supports by means of aerial roots growing from their stems. Cultivated as ornamental house plants for their foliage, *P. andreanum* and *P. erubescens* are among the most popular species. Family: *Araceae.*

philosopher's stone A hypothetical substance sought by alchemists for its ability to turn less valuable minerals into gold. In alchemical literature it is also called the elixir, the tincture, and of other names. It was sometimes credited with the power of curing all diseases and of making its possessors immortal. *See* ALCHEMY.

phloem Plant tissue specialized to transport synthesized foods, mainly sugars, around the plant. It consists principally of tubelike cells that lack nuclei, the end of one cell being linked to the next by means of a porous wall (sieve plate). The cells are controlled by small neighbouring cells, known as companion cells.

phlogiston theory An 18th-century theory of combustion based on the belief that all combustible substances contain phlogiston, which is liberated when the substance is heated, leaving calx or ash. The more combustible the substance, the more phlogiston it contains. The theory was finally overthrown in the late 18th century by A. *Lavoisier, who correctly explained combustion in terms of oxidation.

Phlox A genus of ornamental herbs (about 65 species), mostly native to North America. The flowers have five white, pink, red, or purple spreading petals. The creeping phlox, or moss pink (*P. subulata*), forms carpets of flowers in rock gardens. *P. drummondii* is the source of most garden varieties. Family: *Polemoniaceae*.

Phnom Penh (*or* **Pnom Penh**; Cambodian name: Phnum Pénh) 11 35N 104 55E The capital of Cambodia, a port at the head of the Mekong delta. The capital since about 1432, it is now the site of the royal palace, many museums and pagodas, and several universities. The country's commercial centre, its industries include textiles and food processing. Population (1999 est): 938 000.

phobia A pathologically strong fear of a particular situation or thing. The main kinds are agoraphobia (fear of public places and open spaces); claustrophobia (fear of enclosed places); specific phobias of individual things, such as sharp knives; social phobias of encountering people; and animal phobias, as of spiders, rats, or snakes. Phobias are sometimes learned after a frightening incident, sometimes acquired in childhood from other people, and sometimes result from *depression.

Phoenicia A group of city states on the coastal plain of Syria N of ancient *Canaan. Semitic peoples settled here sometime before 1800 BC and after about 1000 BC they became outstanding navigators and merchants, establishing trading posts all over the E Mediterranean and beyond. Their major cities were *Tyre, Sidon, and *Byblos. The Phoenician alphabet was the ancestor of all western alphabets. Phoenicia was attacked by Alexander the Great (332 BC), becoming part of the Hellenistic and later the Roman Empires.

phoenix A fabulous bird associated with sun worship, especially in Egypt, and representing resurrection and immortality. It was like an eagle in size and shape, had red and golden plumage, and lived for 500 years. The dying phoenix was consumed by fire in a nest of aromatic materials and from its ashes a new bird arose.

Phoenix 33 30N 112 03W A city in the USA, the capital of Arizona on the Salt River. The state's largest city, the commercial centre for a cotton and farming region, its industries include the manufacture of aircraft and textiles. Population (2000): 1 321 045.

phonetics The study of the production and perception of sounds in languages. Sounds are classified in terms of the way in which they are produced by the speech organs. The study of the system of sounds within any given language is called **phonology** and the individual sounds are called phonemes. Phonetics also includes the study of stress and intonation.

phosphorescence *See* LUMINESCENCE.

phosphorus (P) A nonmetallic solid element discovered by H. Brand (died c. 1692) in 1669. It exists in at least four forms: white (α and β), red, and black. White phosphorus is a waxy solid, which ignites spontaneously in air to form the pentoxide (P_2O_5). Red phosphorus, a more stable allotrope, is formed when white phosphorus is heated to 400°C; it is used in matches. Black phosphorus is also stable and forms when white phosphorus is heated to 200–300°C. Phosphorus exists in nature chiefly as the mineral *apatite ($Ca_3(PO_4)_2$), from which the element is obtained, either by reduction with carbon or reaction with silica at high temperatures. Phosphates are used extensively as fertilizers (mainly as "superphosphate"—calcium hydrogen phosphate) but find other uses in detergents, water softeners, and specialist glasses. Some organo-phosphorus compounds are extremely toxic and are used as nerve gases. At no 15; at wt 30.9738; mp (white) 44.1°C; bp (white) 280°C.

photocell (*or* **photoelectric cell**) A device that makes use of a photoelectric effect to measure or detect light or other electromagnetic radiation. In the photoemissive cell, a photosensitive cathode emits electrons when it is illuminated; these photoelectrons constitute a current when they flow to the positive anode of the cell. In solid-state devices the light changes the behaviour of a p–n junction (as in the photodiode), creating a potential difference by the photovoltaic effect. In the conductivity cell, the resistance of a substance, such as selenium, changes when light falls on it as a result of photoconductivity. Photocells are widely used in light-operated controls, such as fire alarms; they are also used in solar cells (*see* SOLAR POWER) and photographic light meters. See illustration on p. 692.

photocopying machine A device that prints copies of documents, drawings, etc., from an optical image. The most common technique is a dry electrostatic process known as xerography. A pattern of electric charge is induced by light falling on a layer of *semiconductor material on a conducting surface. Toner powder is sprayed or rolled onto this material, so that it sticks to the highly charged areas. The image so formed is printed onto charged paper, where it is fixed by heating to produce the final copy.

photoelectric effects A number of

effects in which electromagnetic radiation interacts with matter, frequently with the emission of electrons. These effects include photoconductivity, the photovoltaic effect, and the *Compton effect and the Auger effect. The frequency of the radiation (f) has to be such that the energy of the photon (hf, where h is Planck's constant) is sufficient to liberate the electron. For solids, the minimum energy required is called the work function; for free atoms or molecules it is equal to the first *ionization potential, the effect then being known as photoionization. For most substances, an ultraviolet frequency is needed to eject an electron, but for some metals, such as caesium, visible light is sufficient. *See* PHOTOCELL.

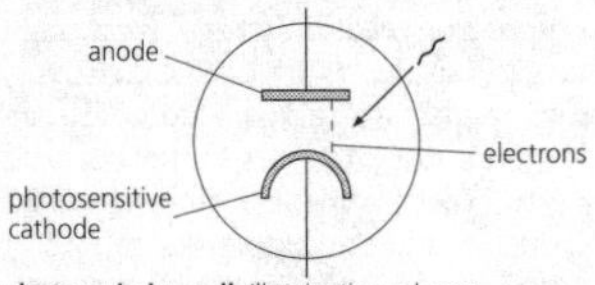

photoemissive cell. Illumination releases electrons from the cathode.

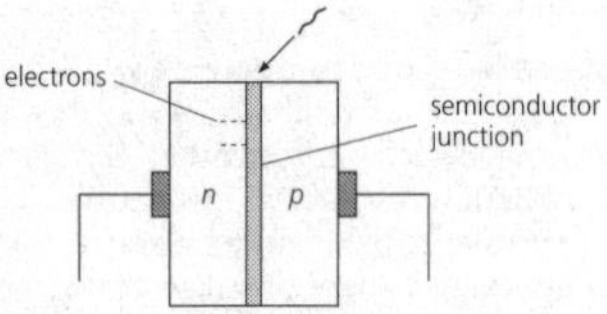

photovoltaic cell. Illumination creates a potential difference at a p–n semiconductor junction.

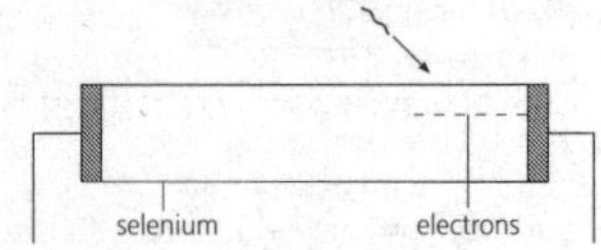

photoconductivity cell. Illumination increases the conductivity of a semiconductor, such as selenium.

photocell

photography The recording of images on sensitized material, by means of visible light, X-rays, or other radiation, and the subsequent chemical processing. The first photograph was taken in 1826 by Joseph Nicéphore Niépce (d. 1833). In 1839 *Daguerre introduced the daguerrotype, a positive image of milky white on a silver background, produced directly from silver iodide emulsion on plates exposed inside a simple *camera. Modern photography involves a negative made by the development of *film coated with silver salts. The positive picture is obtained by shining light through the negative onto light-sensitive paper with a coating similar to that on the original film. Lenses can be used to enlarge or reduce the size of the final image on the print. Transparencies, for use with a slide projector, may also be made. Film is usually developed and printed in a darkroom by dipping it in baths of chemicals. Polaroid photography, however, produces positive pictures directly from the camera in one stage. This system was invented by Edwin *Land in 1947 and is used for instant pictures for security passes, laboratory records, etc.

photolysis The breaking of a chemical bond by absorbed electromagnetic radiation. The photon energy of the radiation must exceed the bond energy, and photolytic reactions can be produced by light, ultraviolet radiation, and X-rays. Examples occur in *photosynthesis, suntan, and photography. **Flash photolysis** is a technique for identifying and studying unstable reaction intermediates. The intermediates are produced in a gas by an intense brief flash of light, and their reactions are followed by spectroscopy.

photometry The branch of physics concerned with measuring quantities related to the intensity of light. If the intensity is measured in terms of the energy of the light, they are known as radiant quantities. They may also be measured in terms of their visual effect; they are then known as luminous quantities.

photon The quantum of *electromagnetic radiation, having an energy hf, where h is the *Planck constant and f is the frequency of the radiation. It may also be regarded as an elementary particle with *spin 1 and zero mass that travels at the speed of *light.

photosphere The boundary between the atmosphere of a star and its much denser interior. The sun's photosphere is several hundred kilometres thick. Almost all the energy emitted by the sun is radiated from the photosphere. Its temperature falls from about 6000°C at the convective zone to about 4000°C where the photosphere merges with the *chromosphere. *See also* SUNSPOTS.

photosynthesis The means by which plants and certain bacteria produce carbohydrates from carbon dioxide and a hydrogen source. The energy for the process is provided by light absorbed by the green pigment chlorophyll, which is contained in the *chloroplasts. Plants use water (H_2O) as the hydrogen source and release its oxygen as a by-product. Photosynthesis comprises two sets of reactions. One set, which requires light, produces energy-storing and reducing compounds; the other reactions use these compounds to add hydrogen atoms to carbon dioxide and make carbohydrates. The overall reactions can be summarized by the equation $6CO_2 + 6H_2O \rightarrow C_6H_{12}O_6 + 6O_2$.

Phrygia The central and W areas of Asia Minor inhabited after the Hittite empire collapsed (12th century BC) by Thracian migrants. The shortlived Phrygian kingdom, centred on its capital Gordium, reached its peak in the late 8th century. The legendary *Midas was King of Phrygia. The Phrygians are reputed to have invented embroidery.

phylloxera A plant-eating insect belonging to the family *Phylloxeridae*, closely related to the *aphids. The grape, or vine, phylloxera (*Phylloxera vitifoliae* or *Viteus vitifolii*) is a notorious pest of grapevines. The insect forms galls on the leaves and roots, which damage the plant. The grape phylloxera almost destroyed the wine industry in France in the 19th century.

phylogeny The history of the *evolution of a species or other group of organisms. By studying the fossil record, comparative anatomy, embryology, biochemistry, and geographical distribution of the groups involved, one can establish the probable lines of descent and degrees of relationship between broad groups of plants or animals to produce a phylogenetic tree. Phylogeny forms the basis for the classification of organisms (*see* TAXONOMY). It should be distinguished from **ontogeny**, the succession of developmental stages through which an individual organism passes during its lifetime.

phylum A major unit of classification for living organisms (*see* TAXONOMY). Organisms belonging to the same phylum share basic features but are divided into classes, orders,

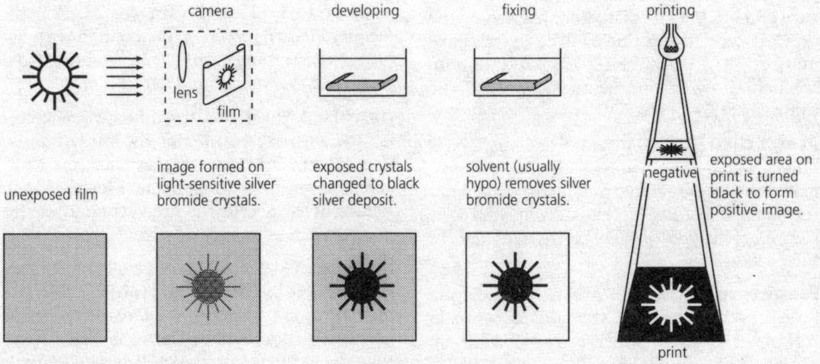

black and white photography. The stages in making a photographic print.

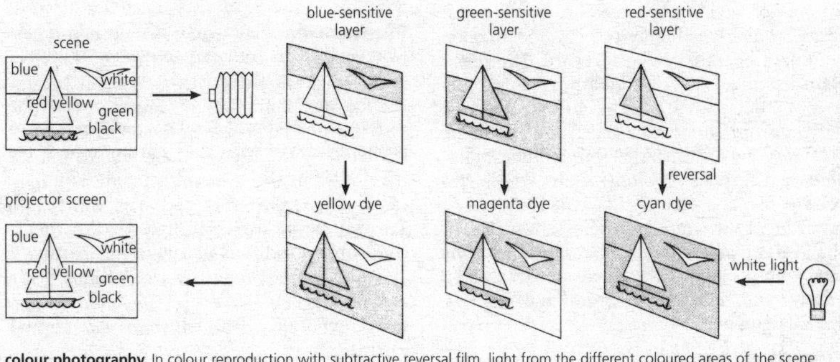

colour photography. In colour reproduction with subtractive reversal film, light from the different coloured areas of the scene forms negatives for each primary colour. These are dyed to form filters that subtract colours from white light to reconstruct the original picture.

photography

genera, and species according to their supposed degrees of relationship. In traditional plant-classification systems the equivalent term is division.

physics The study of the interrelationship between matter and energy, without reference to chemical change. Traditionally the subject was divided into the study of mechanics, electricity and magnetism, heat and thermodynamics, optics, and acoustics. More modern aspects of the subject include quantum mechanics, relativity, nuclear physics, particle physics, solid-state physics, and astrophysics.

physiology The study of the functioning of living organisms and their constituent parts. Physiology is closely linked with both *anatomy (the study of structure) and *biochemistry (the chemical reactions that play a vital role in many physiological processes).

pi In mathematics, the ratio of the circumference of a circle to its diameter, denoted by the Greek letter π. It was proved to be an irrational number by J. H. Lambert (1728–77) and transcendental by F. Lindemann (1852–1939). Its value is 3.14159....

Piaf, Edith (Edith Giovanna Gassion; 1915–63) French cabaret and music-hall singer. Originally a street singer, her small size earned her the nickname "piaf" (French slang: sparrow). Her songs include "Je ne regrette rien" and "La Vie en rose."

p

Piaget, Jean (1896–1980) Swiss psychologist, noted for his studies of thought processes in children. His books, which include *The Origins of Intelligence in Children* (1954), have had a major influence on educational practice.

piano A musical instrument consisting of a number of wire strings stretched over a metal frame, which are hit by felt-covered wooden hammers operated by a keyboard. The piano was invented by Bartolommeo Cristofori (1655–1731) in the early 18th century; the name derives from the Italian *pianoforte*, soft-loud, referring to the variation in volume obtainable on the piano in contrast to the earlier *clavichord and *harpsichord. In the modern instrument the frame is either horizontal, as in the **grand piano**, or vertical, as in the **upright piano**. The piano has a compass of seven and a quarter octaves and the largest repertory of any instrument.

Picardy (French name: Picardie) A planning region and former province in N France. It was incorporated into France in 1477 by Louis XI of France. During World War I it was the scene of heavy fighting. Area: 19 411 sq km (7493 sq mi). Population (1999): 1 857 834.

Picasso, Pablo (1881–1973) Spanish artist, born in Malaga. Picasso trained in Barcelona but worked chiefly in Paris after 1900. Although his most popular paintings are those of his blue (1901–04) and rose (1905–08) periods, his most original work began with *Les Demoiselles d'Avignon* (1907), influenced by Cézanne and African sculpture, and resulted in his development of *cubism with *Braque. One of his major works, *Guernica* (1937), is a horrific depiction of the destruction of the Basque capital during the Spanish Civil War.

Piccard A family of Swiss scientists and explorers. **Auguste Piccard** (1884–1962) and his twin **Jean-Félix Piccard** (1884–1963) pioneered the scientific study of the stratosphere in balloons, reaching a height of 16 940 metres in 1932. In 1948 Auguste designed a bathyscaphe, using it to explore the sea depths. His son **Jacques Piccard** (1927–) collaborated with his father in designing bathyscaphes and reached a depth of 10 917 metres in 1960.

piccolo A woodwind instrument, the smallest and shrillest member of the *flute family. It is pitched an octave higher than the flute and its music is written an octave lower than it sounds. It is used in the orchestra and in the military band.

Picts (painted people) The Roman name (referring to their tattoos) for all Scottish tribes living N of the *Antonine Wall. Perpetually hostile to the Romans, the Picts had forced them to withdraw behind *Hadrian's Wall by 200 AD, and remained independent until Kenneth I MacAlpine unified S Scotland in the 9th century.

Piedmont (Italian name: Piemonte) A region in NW Italy. Associated with the House of Savoy since the early 11th century, it became the nucleus of Italian unification in the mid-19th century. It consists of the upper Po Valley, bordered by the Alps in the N and W and the Apennines in the S. Manufacturing is important, with engineering and steel centred on Turin; other industries include textiles, chemicals, rubber, and food products. Agriculture is also important, producing rice, cereals, wine, and dairy products. Area: 25 400 sq km (9807 sq mi). Population (2000 est): 4 287 465. Capital: Turin.

Piero della Francesca (c. 1420–92) Italian Renaissance painter. *The Baptism of Christ* (National Gallery, London) shows his monumental figure style. He frequently worked at the court of Urbino, where he painted the double portrait of the duke and his wife in profile (Uffizi). His interest in perspective is reflected in his fresco cycle *The Legend of the True Cross*, painted for the church of S Francesco, Arezzo, and in his treatise *On Perspective in Painting*.

Pietermaritzburg 29 36S 30 24E A city in South Africa, the capital of KwaZulu/Natal. It was founded by Boers (1838) and named after their leaders, Piet Retief and Gert Maritz, massacred by the Zulus. It is the centre of a rich farming area. Population (1996): 378 126.

piezoelectric effect The production of electric charges on the opposite faces of certain asymmetric crystals when they are compressed or expanded. The charges are of equal magnitude but opposite in sign on the two faces, the sign on each face depending on whether the crystal is expanded or compressed. Such piezoelectric crystals include quartz and Rochelle salt. In the converse effect a voltage applied across a piezoelectric crystal causes it to expand or contract. The effect is used in the piezoelectric oscillator, the crystal microphone, and the piezoelectric loudspeaker.

pig A hoofed mammal belonging to the Old World family *Suidae* (8 species). Also called hogs or swine, pigs have a stocky body with short legs, a short neck, and a large head with a long cylindrical snout used for digging up roots, seeds, small animals, etc., from soil. Modern breeds are reared for pork and bacon (*see* LIVESTOCK FARMING). Other members of the pig family include the babirusa and *warthog. *See also* PECCARY; WARTHOG.

pigeon A bird belonging to a family (*Columbidae*; 300 species) occurring worldwide except in the coldest regions; the smaller long-tailed forms are called doves. 17–75 cm long, pigeons have soft plumage, a plump body, a small head, short bill and legs, and a characteristic cooing call. Pigeons feed mainly on seeds and other plant material. They are often fast fliers and some are highly migratory, domesticated breeds being used as messengers and for racing. Order: *Columbiformes* (pigeons and sandgrouse). *See also* WOOD PIGEON.

Piggott, Lester Keith (1935–) British jockey, who rode his first winner at the age of 12 (1948). Champion jockey eleven times and Derby winner a record nine times, he became a trainer in 1985. He was gaoled (1987–88) for tax evasion but returned to win his 30th classic race in 1992.

pig iron The type of iron produced by *blast furnaces, and used as the first stage in *steel making. It has a high carbon content (about 4% by weight) and contains impurities, including some slag, which make it brittle. *See also* CAST IRON.

pigmies *See* PYGMIES.

pika A small mammal belonging to the genus *Ochotona* (14 species), of Asia and North America, also called mouse hare, cony, and rock rabbit. 12.5–30 cm long and resembling large short-tailed mice, pikas live in cold rocky areas above the tree line. Family: *Ochotonidae*; order: *Lagomorpha*.

pike A freshwater fish of the genus *Esox* found in temperate regions of Eurasia and America. It has a broad flat snout, and a large mouth with strong teeth. It feeds voraciously on fish and other animals. The common pike (*E. lucius*) is olive-grey above with silvery underparts and pale spots. Family: *Esocidae*; order: *Salmoniformes*.

Pilate, Pontius (1st century AD) Roman governor. As procurator of Judaea and Samaria (26–36) he condemned Christ to death but, according to the New Testament Gospels, did so reluctantly, fearing the outcome of any other course. He came into frequent conflict with the Jews and was finally dismissed for his cruel suppression of a Samaritan rebellion.

pilchard An important food fish, *Sardina pilchardus*, related to the herring and sprat, that occurs in abundance in the Mediterranean, E Atlantic, and English Channel. Its slender body, 25–35 cm long, is bluish green above and whitish below and it swims in large shoals feeding on crustaceans and fish eggs. Pilchards up to one year old are called *sardines. Pilchards are eaten fresh and tinned.

piles *See* HAEMORRHOIDS.

Pilgrimage of Grace (1536) A revolt in N England against the government of Henry VIII. The rebels were united by their opposition to the recent *Reformation legislation and the dissolution of the monasteries as well as by economic grievances. Under Robert Aske (c. 1500–37) they seized York but were persuaded to surrender. However, some 230 men, including Aske, were executed.

Pilgrim Fathers The 102 English colonists who established the first settlement in New England in 1620. They included 35 Puritans, escaping persecution in England, and sailed in the *Mayflower* to New Plymouth, Massachusetts.

Pill, the *See* ORAL CONTRACEPTIVE.

Pillars of Hercules Two promontories at the entrance to the Mediterranean Sea, known in ancient times as Calpe (modern Gibraltar) and Abyla (modern Jebel Musa, at Ceuta, Morocco). According to one legend, the promontories were joined until Heracles tore them apart.

pilot fish A fish, *Naucrates ductor*, that has a pale-blue elongated body marked with dark vertical bands. It is found in warm and tropical seas, accompanying ships and large fish, especially sharks, to feed on parasites and scraps of food. Family: *Carangidae*; order: *Perciformes*.

Piltdown man Skeletal remains once thought to be those of a fossil *hominid, found on Piltdown Common, near Lewes (England), in 1912. In 1953–54 the "find" was shown to be a hoax or fraud.

pimpernel A slender herb of the genus *Anagallis* (about 20 species), found in Eurasia, Africa, and America, especially the annual scarlet pimpernel (*A. arvensis*). Growing 5–30 cm tall, pimpernels have simple leaves and small red, pink, blue, or white bell-shaped flowers. The fruit is a capsule, which opens by a round lid. The yellow pimpernel (*Lysimachia nemorum*) belongs to a closely related genus. Family: *Primulaceae*.

p

Pindar (518–438 BC) Greek poet. Of his 17 books of choral lyrics only 4 survive. These contain Epinician Odes written in honour of victors of athletic games and noted for their exalted style and religious feeling.

pine A coniferous tree of the genus *Pinus* (about 80 species), widely distributed in the N hemisphere. Pines have long slender needles and hanging cones made up of overlapping woody scales. Pines are important softwoods: the timber is easily worked and yields turpentine, tar, pitch, and other resinous products. Commercially important and widely planted species include the Scots pine (*P. sylvestris*), of N and W Europe and Asia, up to 40 m high and the maritime pine (*P. pinaster*), of W Mediterranean regions and N Africa, up to 35 m high. These and other species are also planted for shelter and ornament and some species have edible seeds (*see* STONE PINE). Family: *Pinaceae*. *See also* BRISTLECONE PINE.

A number of other unrelated conifers are called pines, including species of *Araucaria*, the *cypress pine, and the *kauri pine.

pineal gland A small gland within the brain. In some lower animals, for example certain lizards, it is receptive to light and is visible externally as a third eye (pineal eye); in man its function is unknown, although it may help to regulate the onset of puberty.

pineapple A perennial herbaceous plant, *Ananas comosus*, native to tropical and subtropical America and cultivated in many warm and tropical regions for its fruit. It reaches a height of 1 m. Purplish flowers occur at the centre of a rosette of leaves and—with their bracts—fuse to form the composite fruit, which ripens 5–6 months after flowering begins and can weigh up to 10 kg. The major producing countries are the Hawaiian Islands, Brazil, Mexico, Cuba, and the Philippines. Family: *Bromeliaceae*.

pine marten A European carnivorous mammal, *Martes martes*. About 70 cm long, it inhabits dense evergreen forests, preying on squirrels, birds, insects, and eggs. As with other *martens, the female has a litter (2–5 cubs) only every second year.

pink One of several usually perennial herbaceous plants derived from *Dianthus plumarius* and often grown as fragrant garden ornamentals. They have long slender leaves and showy white, pink, or red flowers, often with fringed petals. Family: *Caryophyllaceae*.

Pinochet, Augusto (1915–) Chilean general and head of state (1973–90). He led the military coup that overthrew Salvador *Allende and became the head of a repressive military junta. He relinquished office in 1990 but remained head of the army until 1998, when he was made a senator for life. That year he was arrested while visiting London, pending extradition to Spain to answer charges of murder and torture of Spanish nationals during his presidency. After a lengthy legal battle the home secretary authorized Pinochet's release (2000) on medical grounds. After his return to Chile he was charged with murder and kidnapping but was eventually (2001) found mentally unfit to stand trial.

pintail A *duck, *Anas acuta*, occurring in the N hemisphere, that breeds on inland waters and winters in coastal areas. The male has a dark-brown head and neck with a white band down the neck, grey flanks, and long black central tail feathers. Females have mottled brown plumage and both sexes have a blue-grey bill.

Pinter, Harold (1930–) British dramatist. In his plays, which include *The Birthday Party* (1958), *The Caretaker* (1960), *The Homecoming*

(1965), *Betrayal* (1978), *Mountain Language* (1988), *Ashes to Ashes* (1996), and *Celebration* (2000), he uses elliptical dialogue to evoke an atmosphere of tension and ambiguity. He has also written film scripts and directed plays.

pinto A horse whose coat consists of sharply defined patches of white and a darker colour—either black (piebald pattern) or brown, bay, dun, or roan (skewbald pattern). Pintos were commonly used by American Indians. Height: 1.42 m minimum (14 hands).

pinworm A slender parasitic *nematode worm, *Enterobius vermicularius*, also called seatworm or threadworm. Up to 1 cm long, pinworms are white and inhabit the human intestine; they are common in Europe and America. Female worms migrate to the anus to lay thousands of eggs, causing itching, especially at night.

Pinyin *See* CHINESE.

pion A group of three elementary particles (*see* PARTICLE PHYSICS) classified as *mesons (symbol: π). The charged pions (π^+ and π^-) have a mass of 139.6 MeV, the neutral pion (π°) a mass of 136 MeV. The *strong interaction can be represented by the exchange of virtual pions between particles (*see* VIRTUAL PARTICLE).

Piper, John (1903–92) British painter and writer. He painted abstract works in the 1930s and was an official war artist in World War II. Best known for his watercolours and aquatints of architecture, he also designed stained glass, notably for Coventry Cathedral, and stage sets.

pipistrelle A small insect-eating *bat belonging to the genus *Pipistrellus* (50 species) with a worldwide distribution. The Eurasian pipistrelle (*P. pipistrellus*) is about 3.5 cm long with a 20-cm wingspan. Pipistrelles have a prehensile tail, used when crawling into crevices to roost. Family: *Vespertilionidae*.

pipit A small insectivorous songbird of the genus *Anthus* (30 species), 14–16 cm long with a brown-streaked plumage and paler speckled underparts. The meadow pipit (*A. pratensis*) occurs on moors and downs in Britain. The water pipit (*A. spinoletta*) inhabits the high mountains of Eurasia and North America; it is also found in coastal regions, when it is known as the rock pipit. Family: *Motacillidae* (wagtails and pipits).

Piraeus (Modern Greek name: Piraiévs) 37 57N 23 42E The chief port of Greece, SW of Athens on the Saronic Gulf. It was founded during the 5th century BC as the port of Athens. Industries include shipbuilding, oil refining, and chemicals. Its exports include wine and olive oil. Population (1991): 169 622.

Pirandello, Luigi (1867–1936) Italian dramatist and novelist. Born in Sicily, he studied philology in Germany. His writing was greatly influenced by life with his insane wife. He gained international success with his plays exploring the nature of reality and illusion, notably *Six Characters in Search of an Author* (1921) and *Henry IV* (1922). He won the Nobel Prize in 1934.

piranha A freshwater fish, also called caribe and piraya, belonging to a genus (*Serrasalmus*) found in South America. It has a deep body, ranging from silver to black in colour, strong jaws, and razor-sharp teeth. Piranhas swim in groups and feed on other fish; they also attack larger animals, including man. Family: *Characidae*.

Pisa 43 43N 10 24E A city in Italy, in Tuscany on the River Arno. Dating from Etruscan times, it developed into a thriving maritime republic (11th–12th centuries) but declined after it fell to the Florentines in 1509. Its most famous building is the Leaning Tower, which is 59 m (194 ft) high and about 5 m (17 ft) out of perpendicular. Machinery, textiles, bicycles, and glass are manufactured. Population (1998 est): 93 133.

Pisano, Nicola (c. 1220–c. 1278) Italian sculptor. He initiated the revival of antique Roman forms that led eventually to Renaissance sculpture, beginning with his pulpit in the Baptistry, Pisa. Later works reveal the cooperation of his son **Giovanni Pisano** (c. 1250–1314). Giovanni introduced French gothic elements into his sculptures for the façade of Siena Cathedral.

Pissarro, Camille (1830–1903) French impressionist painter, born in the West Indies. Chiefly influenced by *Corot, he was more interested in landscape structure than the other impressionists. He is noted for his encouragement of younger painters, especially *Cézanne and *Gauguin. In the 1880s he experimented with *pointillism.

pistachio A small aromatic tree, *Pistacia vera*, native to central Eurasia and cultivated in Mediterranean regions for its edible green kernels ("nuts"). Growing 7–10 m high, it has compound leaves and drooping spikes of small male and female flowers. The oval white fruits, 1.5–2 cm long, often split to expose the kernels, which are used as dessert nuts and for flavouring confectionery, cakes, etc. Family: *Anacardiaceae.*

pistil The part of a flower consisting of the female reproductive organs. It consists of one or more *carpels, which may be united into a single structure. Some plants, such as the cucumber, have separate male and female flowers: the latter are described as pistillate.

pistol A short-range small arm that can be used with one hand. Pistols fall into two classes: the *revolver and the automatic. The first successful revolver was the Colt of 1835, in which a magazine chamber revolves behind a single barrel. The first automatics (1893) combined a box magazine in the butt with a recoil loading action. The Luger 9 mm automatic went into service with the German navy in 1904. Both revolvers and automatics are still in military and police use throughout the world.

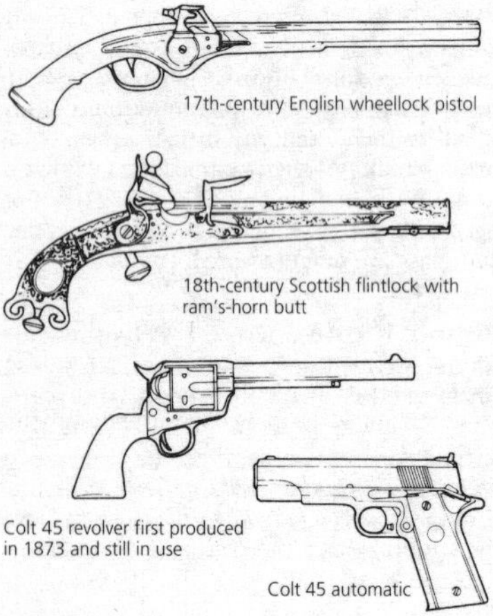

17th-century English wheellock pistol

18th-century Scottish flintlock with ram's-horn butt

Colt 45 revolver first produced in 1873 and still in use

Colt 45 automatic

pistol

pit bull terrier *See* BULL TERRIER.

Pitcairn Islands A small island group in the central S Pacific Ocean, a United Kingdom overseas territory, consisting of Pitcairn Island and three uninhabited islands. Subsistence agriculture is the chief occupation. Pitcairn Island was occupied in 1790 by mutineers from the *Bounty* and women from Tahiti. By 1856 the island was overpopulated and the inhabitants were moved to Norfolk Island; some later returned. Area: 4.6 sq km (1.75 sq mi). Population (1999 est): 54. Sole town: Adamstown.

pitch A black or dark-brown residue resulting from the partial evaporation or fractional distillation of coal tars or tar products. The term is sometimes used for the residue obtained from petroleum distillation (bitumen) or for the naturally occurring petroleum residue (asphalt). Bitumen is a mixture of heavy hydrocarbons with a high proportion of free carbon. It is used as a binding agent (it is the main constituent of road tars), as a protective coating in bituminous paints, in roofing felts, and as a fuel.

pitchblende The chief ore of uranium, a massive form of uraninite, UO_2, a black radioactive mineral found in hydrothermal veins and as an accessory mineral in acid igneous rocks.

pitcher plant Any *carnivorous plant with pitcher-shaped leaves, belonging mainly to the families *Nepenthaceae* and *Sarraceniaceae*. The pitcher is often brightly coloured and secretes nectar to attract insects, which often fall inside and drown in the digestive juices at the bottom of the pitcher.

Pitman, Sir Isaac *See* SHORTHAND.

pitot tube A type of anemometer for measuring the velocity of a fluid, invented by Henri Pitot (1695–1771). It consists of an L-shaped tube placed in the moving fluid; the vertical limb of the tube has an opening facing into the flow. The difference in pressure between the interior of the tube and the surroundings enables the velocity of the fluid to be calculated. The device is used to measure the velocity of liquids, aircraft airspeeds, etc.

Pittsburgh 40 26N 80 00W A city in the USA, in Pennsylvania at the confluence of the Allegheny and Monongahela Rivers, which here form the Ohio River. It is the site of several colleges and universities, including the University of Pittsburgh (1787) and the famous Carnegie Institute. Pittsburgh has grown as a major centre of the steel industry and is the country's largest inland port. Other manufactures include machinery, petroleum, coal, glass, and chemicals. Population (2000): 334 563.

Pitt the Elder, William, 1st Earl of Chatham (1708–78) British statesman, known as the Great Commoner. Having entered parliament in 1735, he established a reputation as an outstanding orator. He became secretary of state and leader of the House of Commons in 1756, was dismissed in 1757, and then recalled to form a ministry with *Newcastle. In charge of foreign affairs, he was largely responsible for British victory in the *Seven Years' War, reorganizing the militia and navy and rallying public opinion.

His second son **William Pitt the Younger** (1759–1806) was twice prime minister (1783–1801, 1804–06), the youngest in British history. As prime minister he inherited an enormous public debt, which he reduced by a fiscal policy influenced by Adam *Smith. He also reformed the Indian administration. Pitt negotiated the first (1793) and second (1798) coalitions against France (*see* REVOLUTIONARY AND NAPOLEONIC WARS) and resolved the crisis caused by the Irish rebellion in 1798 by union of Britain and Ireland in 1800. His second ministry was marked by an alliance with Russia, Sweden, and Austria against Napoleon, which collapsed shortly before his death in office.

pituitary gland A small endocrine gland, about 12 mm by 8 mm, lying within the skull close to the centre of the head. The anterior (front) lobe produces *growth hormone, *prolactin, and hormones that regulate the function of other glands. The posterior (back) lobe is a downgrowth from the *hypothalamus and stores various neurohormones that are synthesized in this part of the brain. Neural control of the entire endocrine system is effected from the pituitary gland.

Pius V, St (Michele Ghislieri; 1504–72) Pope (1566–72). A Dominican friar, he enforced the decrees of the Council of *Trent and expanded the activities of the *Inquisition. He excommunicated the Protestant Elizabeth I of England in 1570. He was canonized in 1712. Feast day: 30 April.

Pius IX (Giovanni Maria Mastai-Ferretti; 1792–1878) Pope (1846–78). At first sympathetic to liberal and nationalist movements, he abandoned radicalism for reaction after the Revolution of 1848, in which he fled Rome. He refused to acknowledge the newly established kingdom of Italy, into which Rome was incorporated in 1870. He defined the dogmas of the Immaculate Conception (1854) and papal infallibility (1869–70).

Pizarro, Francisco (c. 1475–1541) Spanish conquistador. In the 1520s he explored the NW coast of South America. In 1531 he crossed the Andes to Cajamarca, where he treacherously murdered the Inca king, Atahuallpa. Over the next nine years he consolidated the Spanish conquest of the Inca empire, founding Lima in 1535.

placenta **1.** An organ formed within the womb of mammals and other viviparous animals during pregnancy, composed of fetal and maternal tissues. Via the placenta the fetus receives nutrients, oxygen, and antibodies from the mother's blood and its waste products are absorbed into the mother's circulation. The fetus is attached to the placenta by the umbilical cord. **2.** A tissue in plants that connects the ovules (later the seeds) to the ovary (later the fruit wall).

plague An infectious disease caused by the bacterium *Yersinia pestis*, which is transmitted to man by rat fleas. There are three forms of the disease, the most common of which is bubonic plague, in which fever, vomiting, and headache are accompanied by swollen inflamed lymph nodes (buboes). Epidemics of plague afflicted Europe throughout the middle ages, the *Black Death of 1348 being the most devastating. The **Great Plague of London** (1665–66) claimed an estimated 70 000 lives. Today plague is usually restricted to areas of poor sanitation in tropical countries.

plaice A commercially important *flatfish, *Pleuronectes platessa*, that occurs in the N North Atlantic and British coastal waters. It is usually 25–40 cm long and is coloured brown with bright-red or orange spots above and white beneath.

Plaid Cymru A political party, founded in 1925, dedicated to the achievement of Welsh independence from the UK. The party won its first parliamentary seat in 1966 (in 2001 it won four seats). Plaid Cymru currently holds 12 of the 60 seats in the Welsh assembly (established 1999), making it the main opposition to Labour. The current leader is Ieuan Wyn Jones.

Planck, Max Karl Ernst Ludwig (1858–1947) German physicist; the originator of *quantum theory. In 1900 Planck solved the problem of black-body radiation by assuming that the radiation was emitted in discrete amounts (quanta) known as *photons. The energy (E) of a photon is related to the frequency (f) of the radiation by the equation $E = hf$, where h is known as **Planck's constant** (which has the value $6.626\,196 \times 10^{-34}$ J s). For this work he received the Nobel Prize in 1918.

planet A celestial body that moves around a star and shines by light reflected from its surface. The only known planets are those orbiting the sun (solar system): there are nine major planets and numerous *minor planets. The major planets in order from the sun are *Mercury, *Venus, *earth, and *Mars (the **terrestrial planets**), *Jupiter, *Saturn, *Uranus, and *Neptune (the **giant planets**) and, usually outermost, *Pluto.

plane tree A large tree of the genus *Platanus* (10 species), native to the N hemisphere and often grown for shade and ornament. Up to 50 m tall, the trees have patchy peeling bark, large lobed leaves, and separate round clusters (catkins) of male and female flowers: the female flowers give rise to bristly round fruits. The London plane (*P.* × *acerifolia*) is a hybrid between the Oriental plane (*P. orientalis*) and North American buttonwood (*P. occidentalis*). The timber is a valuable hardwood used in carpentry. Family: *Platanaceae.*

plankton Minute or microscopic animals (zooplankton) and plants (phytoplankton) that float and drift in the open waters of a sea or lake. The phytoplankton carry out *photosynthesis in the surface waters. The zooplankton include protozoa, small crustaceans, and larvae. Plankton are of great ecological and economic importance as a food source for fish and whales.

plant A living organism belonging to the kingdom *Plantae*, of which there are some 280 000 or so species. Plants are typically immobile and most manufacture their own food from simple inorganic nutrients by *photosynthesis, trapping the energy required for the process in the green pigment chlorophyll. Plant cells have rigid cell walls, providing support, and growth occurs from specialized zones of tissue (*see* MERISTEM), continuously or periodically throughout life. Plants lack specialized sense organs and a nervous system; response to external stimuli is usually slow and often permanent. Green plants are the primary source of food and oxygen for all animals.

Plantagenet The surname of the Angevin, Lancastrian, and Yorkist Kings of England (1154–1485). They were descended from Queen Matilda and Geoffrey Martel, Count of Anjou (d. 1151), who was nicknamed Plantagenet because he wore a sprig of broom (*plante genêt*) in his cap. The name was not formally adopted until the 15th century.

plantain 1. An annual or perennial herb of the genus *Plantago* (about 50 species), occurring in temperate regions and on mountains in the tropics, often as a troublesome weed. Plantains have a basal rosette of simple leaves from which arises a stalk bearing a dense terminal head of inconspicuous green, white, yellow, or brown flowers with protruding stamens. Family: *Plantaginaceae.* **2.** *See* BANANA.

plasma (anatomy) The fluid constituent of *blood, in which the blood cells are suspended. Plasma consists of a solution of various salts, sugars, etc., and contains numerous proteins, including those involved in *blood clotting and the immunological response to infection (i.e. antibodies). It is obtained by centrifuging unclotted blood. *Compare* SERUM.

plasma (physics) A gas the atoms of which have been completely ionized. Sometimes called the fourth state of matter, plasmas occur at enormously high temperatures and are also created in *thermonuclear reactors.

Plasmodium A genus of parasitic single-celled animals (*see* PROTOZOA) that cause *malaria in humans. *Plasmodium* undergoes the sexual phase of its development in blood-sucking mosquitoes of the genus *Anopheles*, through which it is transmitted to man. Four species cause different forms of malaria: *P. falciparum*, *P. vivax*, *P. malariae*, and *P. ovale*. Class: *Apicomplexa* (*see* SPOROZOAN).

broad category	*major groups (phyla)*	*important classes*	*representative members*
nonvascular plants (bryophytes)	Hepatophyta		liverworts (e.g. *Pellia*)
	Bryophyta		mosses (e.g. *Sphagnum*)
	Anthocerophyta		hornworts (e.g. *Anthoceros*)
vascular plants (tracheophytes)	Lycophyta		clubmosses (e.g. *Lycopodium*)
	Sphenophyta		horsetails (*Equisetum*)
	Filicinophyta		ferns (e.g. *Pteridium*)
	Coniferophyta (conifers)		pines, larches, spruces, firs, yews
	Anthophyta (flowering plants)	Monocotyledoneae (monocotyledons)	grasses, palms, orchids, lilies
		Dicotyledoneae (dicotyledons)	daisies, roses, buttercups, hardwood trees (oak, beech, etc.)

plant. A simplified classification of the plant kingdom.

plaster of Paris A hydrated form of calcium sulphate ($CaSO_4.\frac{1}{2}H_2O$) made by partial dehydration of *gypsum by heating. When mixed with water it sets into a hard mass by formation of the dihydrate ($CaSO_4.2H_2O$). It is used for casts for broken limbs and for modelling.

plastics Synthetic materials that consist of polymers, which are moulded during manufacture. Plastics are made from synthetic *resins. **Thermosetting plastics** harden on heating to give a rigid product that cannot then be softened. Polyurethanes, *polyesters, and *epoxy resins all form thermosetting plastics. **Thermoplastic materials** soften when heated and harden again when cooled. These include der-

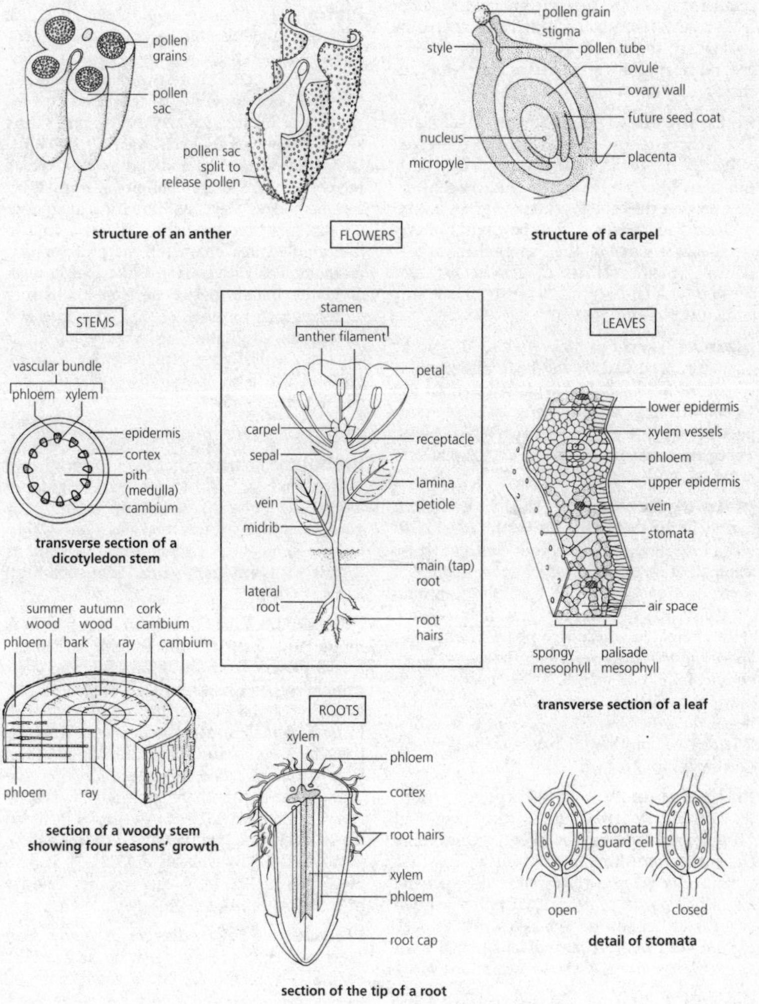

plant. Structure of a flowering plant.

ivatives of *cellulose and *polythene, and other polymers, which contain a reactive double bond.

The first synthetic material was Celluloid, made in 1870 from cotton and camphor. This highly inflammable substance was replaced during World War I by cellulose acetate and casein products. These materials were all based on naturally occurring large molecules. The first polymers to be made by joining together smaller mole cules were the phenol-formaldehyde resins (trade name Bakelite) invented in 1908 by Leo Baekeland (1863–1944). Since then a vast number of different resins have been synthesized.

Plata, Río de la (English name: River Plate) The estuary of the Río Paraná and the River Uruguay, on the Atlantic coast of SE South America between Uruguay and Argentina. Montevideo, the capital of Uruguay, lies on the N shore and Buenos Aires, the capital of Argentina, is situated on the S shore. A naval battle was fought off its mouth in 1939 (*see* WORLD WAR II). Length: 275 km (171 mi). Width (at mouth): 225 km (140 mi).

platelet A small particle, 0.001–0.002 mm in diameter, produced by the bone marrow and found in the blood. Platelets are essential for *blood clotting, accumulating in large numbers at the site of an injured blood vessel. There are normally 150 000 to 400 000 platelets per cubic millimetre of blood.

p

plate tectonics The theory, developed mainly in the 1960s, that the earth's crust is divided into rigid plates (oceanic, continental, or a combination of both), which move about the earth's surface at rates of 1–9 cm per annum. At constructive plate margins new oceanic crust is created where two plates are moving apart and magma rises to fill the gap; this occurs at midocean ridges. At destructive plate margins two plates collide and one dips beneath the other, producing deep-sea trenches. Where two continental plates collide, mountain chains are formed.

Plath, Sylvia (1932–63) US poet and writer. In 1956 she married the British poet Ted *Hughes, whom she had met at Cambridge University. The disciplined poems of her first volume, *The Colossus* (1960), contrast with the anguished poems of *Ariel* (1965), published two years after her suicide. She also wrote a novel, *The Bell Jar* (1966). Her journals and her *Collected Poems* (1981) were published posthumously.

platinum (Pt) A precious silver-white noble metal. It is malleable, ductile, and has a high melting point. Platinum is found in nature in nickel ore. It can absorb large quantities of hydrogen and is used as a catalyst, particularly in contact process for making sulphuric acid. It is also used in thermocouple wires and in jewellery. Although unreactive, platinum also forms other compounds, including the hexafluoride (PtF_6), one of the most powerful oxidizing agents known. At no 78; at wt 195.08; mp 1769°C; bp 3827 ± 100°C.

Plato (429–347 BC) Greek philosopher. An Athenian nobleman, he became a devoted follower of *Socrates, after whose death he travelled widely. In 387 he returned to Athens and founded his *Academy, to which he devoted the rest of his life. Some of Plato's poetry and all his prose works survive. Apart from 13 possibly spurious letters and the *Apology*, which purports to be Socrates' defence of himself before his judges, they are dramatic dialogues of outstanding literary merit. The early ones illustrate Socrates' character and philosophical methods. The *Phaedo*, *Symposium*, and *Republic* of Plato's middle period develop his mature views on such topics as metaphysics, love, and government, notably his theory of ideas (Forms), the perfect spiritual entities or prototypes of which the physical world is a feeble and imperfect copy.

platypus *See* DUCK-BILLED PLATYPUS.

plebeians Romans other than the privileged *patricians. At first without civil rights, in 493–92 the plebeians forced the Senate to appoint their own tribunes and an assembly. During the subsequent two centuries of conflict, the plebeians gradually gained admission to all Roman offices.

Pléiade, La A group of seven French writers in the 16th century who sought to liberate French poetry from medieval tradition. Their principles, deriving from the study of Greek, Latin, and Italian literature, were expounded in *Défense et illustration de la langue française* (1549) by Joachim du Bellay (1522–60), and their innovations included the introduction of the sonnet, the ode, and the alexandrine. Led by Pierre de Ronsard (1524–85), the group included du Bellay, J.-A. de Baïf (1532–89), Étienne Jodelle (c. 1532–73), Rémy Belleau (c. 1528–77), Pontus de Tyard (c. 1522–1605), and Jacques Peletier (1517–82) or Jean Dorat (1508–88).

Pleiades (*or* **Seven Sisters**) A young open *star cluster in the constellation Taurus that contains several hundred stars, of which six are clearly visible to the naked eye. They were named after the seven daughters of *Atlas, who were changed by the gods into stars while being pursued by Orion.

Pleistocene epoch The epoch of geological time between the Pliocene and the Holocene, at the beginning of the Quaternary period. It lasted from about 1.8 million to 10 000 years ago. It is often called the *Ice Age because during this time the earth experienced great fluctuations in temperature. Fossils from the Pleistocene include horses, pigs, and elephants.

plesiosaur A widely distributed marine reptile of the Jurassic and Cretaceous periods (200–65 million years ago). Up to about 12 m long, plesiosaurs had broad turtle-like bodies with paddle-like limbs, a long flexible neck, and jaws armed with sharp teeth used to catch fish.

pleurisy Inflammation of the pleura—the membrane that covers the lungs and lines the chest cavity. The commonest cause of pleurisy is bacterial or viral infection. The patient will often have a fever, a pain in the chest that is worse on coughing or taking a deep breath, and a cough.

Plimsoll line A series of lines painted on the outside of a cargo ship's hull showing the various safe levels to which the ship can be loaded. The measure was introduced in the UK as a result of the Merchant Shipping Act (1876) at the instigation of the MP Samuel Plimsoll (1824–98).

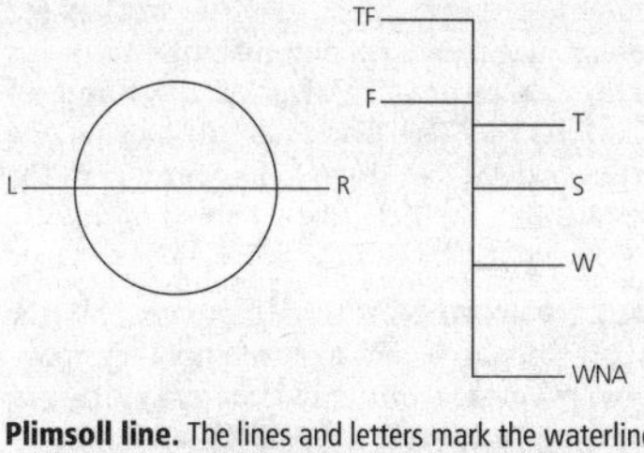

Plimsoll line. The lines and letters mark the waterline under various conditions. TF = fresh water in the tropics; F = fresh water; T = salt water in the tropics; S = salt water in the summer; W = salt water in the winter; WNA = winter in the N Atlantic. LR represents Lloyd's Register.

Pliny the Elder (Gaius Plinius Secundus; 23–79 AD) Roman scholar, whose universal encyclopedia, *Natural History*, was a major source of scientific knowledge until the 17th century. During his military career, Pliny assembled material from numerous sources on a wide range of disciplines, including astrology, geography, agriculture, medicine, zoology, and botany. He finally completed this work of 37 volumes in 77 AD. His nephew and adopted son **Pliny the Younger** (Gaius Plinius Caecilius Secundus; c. 61–c. 113 AD) held various administrative posts and was a prominent legal orator. His ten volumes of private letters constitute an intimate unofficial history of his time.

Pliocene epoch *See* TERTIARY PERIOD.

PLO *See* PALESTINE LIBERATION ORGANIZATION.

Plotinus (205–70 AD) Greek philosopher and founder of *Neoplatonism. Born in Egypt, he studied at Alexandria, and finally settled in Rome. Developing Plato's mysticism, he taught that the immaterial impersonal indescribable "One" is the ground of all existence and value. From it emanate successively mind, soul, and nature. By rejecting material nature and cultivating the intellect man may briefly become mystically united with the One.

Plovdiv (former name: Philippopoli) 42 08N 24 45E A city in S central Bulgaria, on the River Maritsa. Bulgaria's second largest city, its industries include food processing and carpet manufacture. Population (1999 est): 342 584.

plover A bird belonging to a widely distributed family (*Charadriidae*; 56 species) occurring in open regions and along shores. Plovers have brown or grey plumage, often mottled, with white underparts. They feed on insects and other small invertebrates and nest on the ground. Order: *Charadriiformes* (gulls, plovers, etc.). *See also* LAPWING.

plum A small tree, *Prunus domestica*—a natural hybrid between the *blackthorn and the cherry plum (*P. cerasifera*), native to SW Asia and cultivated in most Mediterranean and N temperate regions for its fruit. It has oval toothed leaves and white flowers. The fruit is round or oval and has a dark-red to blue-black skin (when ripe), enclosing a sweet greenish-yellow pulp and a central oval stony seed. Plums are eaten fresh, cooked in desserts, canned, or dried as prunes. Family: *Rosaceae*. *See also* DAMSON.

Plumbago A genus of herbaceous plants, shrubs, and climbers (12 species), native to warm regions and including a number of ornamentals. They have simple leaves and terminal clusters of white, blue, violet, pink, or red flowers. *P. auriculata*, with pale-blue flowers, and *P. rosea*, with red flowers, are popular greenhouse plants. Some species are used for medicinal purposes. Family: *Plumbaginaceae*.

Plutarch (c. 46–c. 120 AD) Greek biographer and essayist. He was a citizen of both Athens and Rome and a priest of Delphi. His *Parallel Lives* consists of biographies of 23 pairs of Greek and Roman statesmen and soldiers. The *Moralia* contain 83 essays on ethical, scientific, and literary topics.

Pluto (astronomy) The smallest and usually outermost planet, orbiting the sun every 248 years at a mean distance of 5900 million km. Pluto was discovered in 1930 but little was known about it until its satellite was discovered in 1978. It is a very cold low-density body about 3000 km in diameter.

Pluto (mythology) *See* HADES.

plutonic rock *See* IGNEOUS ROCK.

plutonium (Pu) An important synthetic transuranic element discovered in 1940. Trace quantities exist in natural uranium ores. It is produced in large quantities in nuclear reactors by beta-decay from uranium-239. Plutonium is fissile and was used in the atomic bomb dropped on Nagasaki in 1945 (*see* NUCLEAR WEAPONS). It forms oxides (PuO, PuO_2), halides (for example PuF_3), and other compounds. It is used in *fast reactors and small power units for spacecraft. At no 94; at wt (244); mp 640°C; bp 3230°C.

Plymouth 1. 50 23N 4 10W A port in SW England, in Plymouth unitary authority, Devon, on Plymouth Sound between the Tamar and Plym estuaries. On Plymouth Hoe Drake is reputed to have finished his game of bowls while the Spanish Armada approached; the *Mayflower* embarked from here for America in 1620 (*see* PILGRIM FATHERS). Plymouth is an important naval base with associated marine industries. Clothing, radio equipment, and processed foods are manufactured. Population (1991): 245 991. **2.** A unitary authority in SW England, in Devon. Area: 76 km (30 sq mi). Population (2001): 240 718.

Plymouth Brethren An austere Protestant sect founded at Plymouth in 1830 by a former Anglican priest, J.N. Darby (1800–82). The Brethren have strict standards of behaviour and shun many secular trades and professions. Small groups exist throughout the world, often as active missionaries.

pneumoconiosis Chronic lung disease caused by inhaling dust, most commonly coal dust (causing coalworkers' pneumoconiosis) and silica (causing silicosis). Considerable coal dust may be taken into the lungs without causing much damage, but later progressive massive fibrosis may develop. *See also* ASBESTOSIS.

pneumonia Inflammation of the lungs, mostly caused by infection. Pneumonia may arise in only one lobe of the lung (lobar pneumonia) or in patches in both lungs (bronchopneumonia). The infective organisms may be streptococci, viruses, tubercle bacilli, or other organisms, such as mycoplasmas. The patient has a fever, cough, and pain in the chest and may be breathless.

Po, River (Latin name: Padus) The longest river in Italy rising in the Cottian Alps and flowing mainly ENE through Turin to enter the Adriatic Sea by way of a large delta in the E. The Po Valley is the most fertile and economically important region in Italy. Length: 652 km (405 mi).

pochard A large-headed *duck, *Aythya ferina*, occurring in temperate inland waters of Eurasia. It has grey legs and a grey-blue bill; males have a reddish head, black breast, and grey body; females are brown. It feeds on water plants and small aquatic invertebrates.

podzol A type of *soil typical of many cool temperate humid zones especially with coniferous vegetation, as in the taiga of Russia and North America. It is characterized by an ashen-coloured upper layer (A horizon) and an underlying layer (B horizon) of redeposition humus and iron, which may develop into an impermeable pan.

Poe, Edgar Allan (1809–49) US poet, short-story writer, and critic. After publishing two volumes of poetry (1827, 1829), he worked for literary magazines. Among his prose tales and horror stories are "The Fall of the House of Usher" (1839), "The Black Cat" (1843), and the first ever detective story, "The Murders in the Rue Morgue" (1841). His best-known poems are "The Raven" (1845) and *The Bells* (1849).

poet laureate A title bestowed by the British monarch on a contemporary poet, whose traditional duties include the writing of commemorative odes on important public occasions. The first official poet laureate was John Dryden, who served from 1668 to 1688, and his most recent successors include John Betjeman (1972–84), Ted Hughes (1984–98), and Andrew Motion (1999–). Until 1999 the title was bestowed for life and the holder was rewarded with an annual present of wine; it is now a salaried post with a fixed tenure of 10 years.

Poincaré, Raymond (1860–1934) French statesman; president (1913–20) and prime minister (1912–13, 1922–24, 1926–29). His foreign policy aimed to prevent French isolation in the face of possible German aggression. His postwar economic policy brought a period of stability to France. His cousin **Jules Henri Poincaré** (1854–1912) was a mathematician, regarded by some as the last universal mathematician. Poincaré wrote important treatises on the nature of mathematical creativity, emphasizing its intuitional aspects.

poinsettia An ornamental shrub, *Euphorbia pulcherrima*, native to Mexico and tropical America and a popular pot plant at Christmas in Europe and North America. It has simple dark-green leaves and clusters of tiny greenish-yellow flowers surrounded by large scarlet bracts, up to 14 cm long, which resemble petals. Family: *Euphorbiaceae*.

pointer A breed of sporting dog originating in England and named after its habit of pointing its nose towards game. It is lithely built with a long tapering tail, a long muzzle, and drooping ears. The short smooth coat is white combined with yellow, orange, liver, or black. Height: 63–68 cm (dogs); 61–66 cm (bitches).

pointillism A style of painting using dots of pure colour. The pointillists applied primary colours to the canvas in dots and allowed the colours to be mixed by the eye. It was developed by *Seurat in France in the 1880s.

Poisson, Siméon Dénis (1781–1840) French mathematician. He made important contributions to the mathematical theory of electricity, magnetism, and mechanics. His work on electricity led him in 1837 to discover Poisson's equation, which describes the electric field created by an arbitrary charge density. Poisson's distribution is widely used in probability calculations and **Poisson's ratio** (the ratio of the lateral strain to the longitudinal strain in a stretched wire) is used by engineers in studying the elongation of structural members.

poker A card game, usually for five to seven players. In the standard version each player receives five cards, with the option of discarding and replacing up to five of them. Each player makes bets on his or her hand before and after discarding until a limit is reached or no one wishes to bet further. The object is to make the best hand (i.e. the one containing the highest-ranking combination of cards) or to bluff one's opponents that one has the best hand.

Poland, Republic of A country in N Europe, on the Baltic Sea. Wide plains in the N rise to the Carpathian Mountains in the S, which reach heights of over 2500 m (8000 ft). About 90% of the inhabitants are Roman Catholic. *Economy*: Poland is one of the world's leading agricultural nations. The chief crops are rye, wheat, oats, sugar beet, and potatoes. Its mineral wealth includes deposits of coal, copper, and sulphur; natural gas has been found as well as some oil. Poland's industries include shipbuilding, textiles, engineering, steel, cement, chemicals, and food products. *History*: Poland first became a separate state in the 10th century, which also saw the introduction of Christianity. From the 14th to 16th centuries its power was extended under the Jagiellon dynasty. Foreign intervention in the 18th century culminated in partition by Russia, Austria, and Prussia (in 1772, 1793, and 1795). At the Congress of Vienna in 1815 the *Congress Kingdom of Poland was created under the Russian Crown. After World War I independence was declared under Józef Piłsudski (1867–1935), who ruled as a dictator from 1927. In 1939 Poland was invaded by Germany; some six million Poles, including three million Jews, died during the occupation. Polish resistance contributed to the Allied victory, and in 1945 Poland was occupied by the Russians. The first postwar elections, in 1948, brought a communist-controlled government to power under Władysław Gomułka (1905–82). Unrest in 1970 led to his enforced resignation and he was succeeded by Edward Gierek (1913–). In December 1981, the independent trade union *Solidarity, led by Lech *Wałęsa, was outlawed and martial law was declared by Gen Wojeiech Jaruzelski. Following mass demonstrations, Solidarity was relegalized in 1989 and allowed to contest a general election; it won all but two of the seats contested and led the new government with Wałęsa as president from 1990. The 1990s saw continuing economic crisis and a series of shortlived governments. In 1995 Aleksander Kwasniewski, a former communist, defeated Wałęsa in presidential elections. In 1997 Poland adopted a new constitution that removed the last traces of communism. Poland joined NATO in 1999 and the EU in 2004. Official language: Polish. Currency: złoty of 100 groszy. Area: 312 677 sq km (120 624 sq mi). Population (2003 est): 38 623 000. Capital: Warsaw.

Polanski, Roman (1933–) Polish film director, born in Paris. His films include *Repulsion* (1965), *Rosemary's Baby* (1968), *Tess* (1979), *Frantic* (1988), *Death and the Maiden* (1995), and *The Pianist* (2002).

polar bear A white bear, *Thalarctos maritimus*, living on the shores of the Arctic Ocean. Up to 2.5 m long and weighing 500–700 kg (depending on the season), polar bears prey on seals, fish, and birds.

Polaris (*or* **North Star**) A remote cream *supergiant, apparent magnitude 2.0 and about 650 light years distant, that is the brightest star in the constellation Ursa Minor. It is the present *pole star, lying about 1° from the N celestial pole. It is a *Cepheid variable and is the primary component of a multiple star.

Polaris missile A US navy two-stage solid-fuelled nuclear strategic missile launched from a submarine and having a range of 4500 km (2800 m). Travelling at speeds of over mach 10, some versions (Poseidon) are capable of delivering 10 separately guided 15-*kiloton warheads. When fired from below the surface, the missile is ejected from the vessel by compressed gas, its rocket firing at the surface. Firing is by two-key control, linked directly to Washington. In the UK Polaris was replaced by the Trident missile in the 1990s.

polarized light Light in which the direction of vibration is restricted. In ordinary light (and other types of *electromagnetic radiation) the transverse vibrations of the electric and magnetic fields are at right angles to each other in all possible planes. In **plane-polarized light** the vibrations of the electric field are confined to one plane and the magnetic field to one at right angles to it. Plane-polarized light can be produced by reflection at a certain angle or by passing light through such doubly refracting substances as Polaroid (a plastic sheet impregnated with tiny crystals of a dichroic substance orientated parallel to each other). **Circularly** and **elliptically polarized light** occur when the electric vector describes a circle or an ellipse round the direction of the light beam.

polder An area of low-lying land reclaimed from the sea or other water, often for agricultural purposes. Polders are usually formed by constructing dykes around the area, which is then drained. The most notable polders are those of Holland, next to the IJsselmeer.

polecat A carnivorous mammal, *Mustela putorius*, found in woods and grassland throughout Europe, Asia, and N Africa. About 50 cm long, it has a dark-brown coat with yellowish patches on the face and ears. Polecats are nocturnal, foraging for rodents and insects. They eject a pungent fluid when alarmed. Family: *Mustelidae* (weasels, etc.). *See also* FERRET.

Poles, North and South The most northerly and southerly points of the earth's surface and the ends of the earth's axis, about which it rotates. The magnetic north and south poles are the points to which a magnetic compass needle points and where the lines of force of the earth's magnetic field are vertical. They do not coincide with the geographical poles and their positions slowly change. *See also* ARCTIC CIRCLE; ANTARCTICA.

pole star Either of two stars that are nearest the N or S celestial pole. The poles are not fixed in position but, owing to precession of the earth's axis, trace out two circles in the sky over a period of 25 800 years. There is thus a sequence of stars that slowly, in turn, become the N or S pole star. *See also* POLARIS.

pole vault An event in athletics, in which competitors use a fibreglass pole to vault a horizontal bar. A competitor is allowed three tries at each height. The height is increased until only one competitor is left. The event was opened to women in 1995 (2000 in the Olympics). World record: 6.14 m (1994) by Sergei Bubka (Ukraine).

poliomyelitis A viral infection of the central nervous system that may result in muscle paralysis. It was formerly known as infantile paralysis, because children were most commonly affected. In most cases the infection is mild, but sometimes a more severe illness develops, which may lead to severe pain in the limbs followed by permanent paralysis. A vaccine is available that gives complete protection (*see* SABIN VACCINE; SALK VACCINE).

Polish (*or* **Lekhitic**) A West Slavonic language spoken in Poland and closely related to *Czech, *Slovak, and Sorbian. It is written in a Latin alphabet and the standard form is based on the dialect of Poznań.

polka A Bohemian folk dance in 2/4 time, which became a ballroom dance in 19th-century Europe and rivalled the waltz in popularity. It is characterized by three steps and a hop.

pollen The male gametes of seed plants, which are produced in the *stamens of flowering plants and in the male *cones of conifers and other gymnosperms. To ensure fertilization, the pollen must be transferred to the stigma (in flowering plants) or the female cone (in conifers)—the process of **pollination**. Many flowers are cross-pollinated, i.e. the pollen from one plant is deposited on the stigma of another of the same species by means of insect carriers, wind, or water. Some flowers are self-pollinated, the pollen being transferred from the anthers to the stigma of the same plant: the stamens are usually bent over the stigma to assist the process. After pollination, a pollen tube grows down from the pollen grain into the pistil of the pollinated flower until it reaches the ovule. Two pollen nuclei travel down this tube: one fertilizes the egg cell, which develops into the embryo plant in the seed; the other fuses with a nucleus in the ovule to become food for the seed.

Pollock, Jackson (1912–56) US painter. By 1947 he had developed a style of *abstract expressionism to express feelings and unconscious thoughts through the act of painting itself (*see* ACTION PAINTING). He dripped paints onto very large canvases to form patterns of interweaving lines.

poll tax A levy on individuals (*poll*, head), regardless of means. First levied regularly in England in 1377, it was a direct cause of the Peasants' Revolt in 1381 and was abolished in 1698. A poll tax (the **community charge**) replaced domestic rates in 1989–90; following public opposition, it was replaced by *council tax in 1993.

pollution The addition to the environment of substances that cannot be rendered harmless by normal biological processes. Modern industrial and agricultural activities have led to pollution by either man-made toxic substances (such as pesticides and fertilizers) or by the overproduction of naturally occurring substances (such as carbon dioxide gas). Current problems include the disposal of radioactive wastes; increasing amounts of heavy metals (such as lead), carbon dioxide, carbon monoxide, etc., in the atmosphere; the disposal of human refuse and sewage; and unacceptable noise levels. *See also* ACID RAIN; GREENHOUSE EFFECT; OZONE.

polo A four-a-side stick-and-ball game, in which the players are mounted on specially bred ponies. It was played in Persia by 600 BC and was rediscovered by British officers in India in the 19th century. The riders use long sticks with mallet heads to hit a solid wooden ball, with the object of scoring goals. A game consists of up to eight seven-minute periods, or "chukkas," after each of which mounts are changed.

Polo, Marco (c. 1254–1324) Venetian traveller. His father and uncle travelled to Beijing in 1271 at the request of the Mongol emperor, Kublai Khan, taking Marco with them. Having learned Mongolian, he entered Kublai's service, conducting missions as far as S India, until leaving China in 1292. He subsequently fought for the Venetians against the Genoese and was captured. In prison (1296–98) he dictated an account of his travels.

polonium (Po) A highly radioactive element discovered in 1898 by Marie Curie in minute amounts in pitchblende. It is 5000 times as radioactive as *radium and liberates considerable amounts of heat. Polonium has 27 isotopes, more than any other element. It is used in compact radiation and thermoelectric power sources. At no 84; at wt (209); mp 254°C; bp 962°C.

Pol Pot (1925–98) Cambodian politician; head of state of Democratic Kampuchea (1975–79). He launched an armed revolution in 1968 and commanded the victorious Khymer Rouge movement in the ensuing civil war (1970–75). He then began a radical restructuring of Cambodian society, having hundreds of thousands killed in labour camps. In 1979 his regime fell but he maintained influence over Khmer Rouge guerrillas in Cambodia from his exile in Thailand. In 1997 he was captured and sentenced to life imprisonment by former Khmer Rouge colleagues.

polyanthus A hardy perennial, *Primula × polyanthus*, derived from a cross between the common primrose and the cowslip. There are many varieties, with yellow, brown, blue, or red flowers. *See also* PRIMULA.

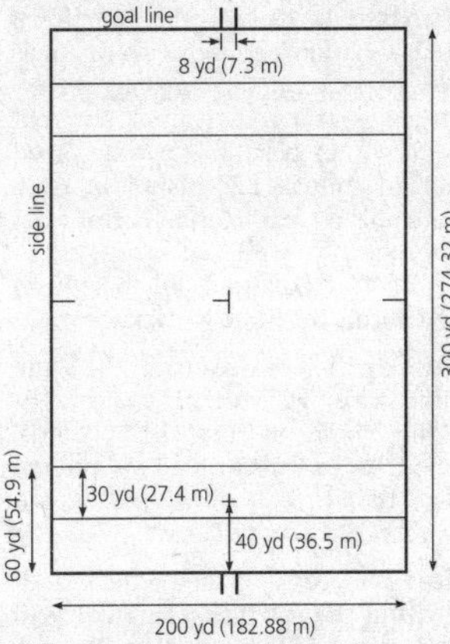

polo. The dimensions of the ground. If the side lines are boarded, the width is 160 yd (146.4 m) and there is a safety area extending 10 yd (9 m) beyond each side line and 30 yd (27 m) beyond each goal line.

polyesters Synthetic resins or *plastics that are polymers of *esters. Saturated polyesters (i.e. those with no double bonds), made by a condensation reaction, are widely used in such synthetic fibres as Dacron and Terylene. Unsaturated polyesters are used as resins to make thermosetting plastics.

Polygonum A genus of annual or perennial herbs (about 75 species), found worldwide. 10 to 200 cm in height, they bear simple leaves and small white or pink flowers. Family: *Polygonaceae*.

polyhedron A solid body bounded by plane polygons constituting its faces. Three or more edges meet at a vertex. The five regular polyhedrons (known as Platonic solids) have equal faces that are regular polygons. They are the regular tetrahedron, hexahedron, octahedron, dodecahedron, and icosahedron with 4, 6, 8, 12 and 20 faces respectively.

polymerization The chemical combination of simpler molecules (monomers) to form long chain molecules (**polymers**) of repeating units. In **addition polymerization**, the monomers simply add together and no other compound is formed. Polythene is made from ethylene in this way. In **condensation polymerization**, water, alcohol, or some other small molecule is formed in the reaction, as in the production of *nylon.

polymethyl methacrylate *See* PERSPEX.

polymorphism In biology, the functional or structural variation between two or more members of a species, determined by differences in either genetic constitution, environmental conditions, or both. It is a widespread phenomenon in animals and plants. In **transient polymorphism** two different forms exist together temporarily, while one form is replacing the other; in **balanced polymorphism** the different forms continue to coexist.

Polynesia A division of Oceania in the S and central Pacific Ocean. The volcanic and coral islands include those of French Polynesia, Hawaii, Samoa, Tonga, Tuvalu, Kiribati, and the Line and Cook Islands. *See also* MELANESIA; MICRONESIA, FEDERATED STATES OF.

Polynesian The people of the Pacific islands contained within the roughly triangular area between and including Hawaii, New Zealand, and Easter Island. They are seafarers, with considerable skill in navigation. Fishing and cultivating are also important. The Polynesian languages belong to the Oceanic branch of the Austronesian family and include Samoan, *Maori, Tongan, Tahitian, and Hawaiian.

polyp (biology) A sedentary form that occurs during the life cycle of many animals of the phylum *Cnidaria*. It has a cylindrical stalklike body attached at the base, with the mouth at the free end surrounded by tentacles bearing stinging cells (nematocysts). Polyps occur singly or in colonies; colonial polyps are modified for different functions, such as feeding, reproduction, and protection. *See* CNIDARIAN.

polyp (*or* **polypus**) (medicine) A growth that has a narrow base or stalk. Polyps may occur in the bowel, the nose, the womb, the larynx, and other sites. They often cause obstruction or infection and some forms may become cancerous.

polyphony (Greek: many voices) Music that consists of a horizontal combination of melodic strands rather than a series of vertical chords. The high point of the polyphonic style was reached in the 16th century with Palestrina's church music, the Italian *madrigal, the English madrigal, and the church music of Tallis and Byrd. *See* COUNTERPOINT; HARMONY; MODES.

polypropylene A thermoplastic material made by *polymerization of propylene (CH_2:$CHCH_3$). It is similar to high-density *polythene but stronger, lighter, and more rigid. Polypropylene products, such as beer crates, luggage, and hinges, are injection moulded. Fibres, which are used to make sacks and carpet backings, are made by extrusion.

polysaccharide A complex carbohydrate comprising chains of between three and several thousand linked *monosaccharide units. Polysaccharides, such as *starch, *glycogen, and *cellulose, are important as energy reserves and structural components of plants and animals.

polytetrafluoroethene (**PTFE**) A synthetic material produced by the *polymerization of tetrafluoroethene (F_2C:CF_2). It can withstand temperatures of up to 400°C and has a very slippery surface. PTFE is used to coat nonstick cooking utensils and in gaskets, bearings, and electrical insulation. It is sold under the tradenames Teflon and Fluon.

polythene (**polyethylene** *or* **polyethene**) A white translucent thermoplastic material made by *polymerization of *ethene. **Low-density polythene** is made at high pressure and is a soft material used for flexible pipes, sheets, and bags. **High-density polythene** is made at lower pressures, is more rigid, and softens at a higher temperature. It is used for moulded articles.

polyurethane A synthetic polymer the molecules of which contain the –NH.CO.O– group. Some polyurethanes form thermosetting resins and others, thermoplastic resins. They have a wide range of properties and are used in paints, adhesives, moulded articles, rubbers, lacquers, and foams.

polyvinyl chloride (PVC) A vinyl *resin or plastic produced by *polymerization of vinyl chloride (chloroethene; CH_2:CHCl), a toxic gas. Rigid PVC products are made by moulding. The addition of a plasticizer produces flexible PVC. PVC is tough, nonflammable, and a good electrical insulator.

pomegranate A shrub or small tree, *Punica granatum*, native to W Asia and widely cultivated in the tropics and subtropics for its fruit. 5–7 m tall, it has narrow pointed leaves and orange-red flowers. The large round fruit has a thick yellowish-reddish skin and contains several chambers, each containing many seeds coated with a pinkish juicy pulp. Pomegranates are eaten fresh or used in beverages or wines. The seeds are used in preserves and syrups. Family: *Punicaceae*.

Pomeranian A breed of toy dog, developed in Pomerania, a region of NE Europe now divided between Poland and E Germany. Its ancestors are thought to have been Scandinavian sledge dogs. The Pomeranian has a compact body and foxlike head with small erect ears. The short undercoat is covered by a long straight outercoat and the fluffy tail is held over the back. The coat may be any recognized colour, including white, black, brown, or reddish. Height: 14–18 cm.

Pompadour, Mme de (Jeanne Antoinette Poisson, Marquise de P.; 1721–64) The mistress of Louis XV, who exerted considerable political influence from 1745 until her death. She influenced the negotiation of an Austrian alliance against Prussia and was blamed for French defeats in the subsequent *Seven Years' War. She was a notable patron of artists and scholars.

Pompeii An ancient city near Naples, in Italy. It was buried four to six metres deep under volcanic ash by the eruption of Mount *Vesuvius (79 AD)and rediscovered in 1748. Pompeii provides unparalleled evidence for daily life in Roman times: buildings, with extensive wall paintings and graffiti; food and wooden furniture, preserved by the ash; and personal possessions abandoned by the fleeing inhabitants.

Pompey (Gnaeus Pompeius; 106–48 BC) Roman general and statesman, called Pompeius Magnus (Pompey the Great). In 60 he joined Julius Caesar and Crassus in the first Triumvirate, marrying Caesar's daughter Julia (d. 54) in 59, but in 50 he supported the Senate's demand for Caesar to resign his armies. In the civil war that followed Pompey was defeated by Caesar at Pharsalus (48) and fled to Egypt, where he was murdered.

Pompidou, Georges (Jean Raymond) (1911–74) French statesman; prime minister (1962–68) and president (1969–74). He served under de Gaulle during World War II and was his personal assistant in 1958–59, when he helped draft the constitution of the Fifth Republic. He negotiated a settlement with the Algerians (1961) and with the students in the revolt of May 1968.

Pondicherry A Union Territory in SE India, on the Coromandel Coast. Founded by the French in 1674, it was their chief settlement in India until transferred to Indian administration in 1954. Rice and millet are the chief products. Area: 479 sq km (185 sq mi). Population (2001 est): 973 829. Capital: Pondicherry.

pond skater (*or* **water strider**) A water bug belonging to the family *Gerridae* with over 300 species. They have a slender body and long legs, feed on small insects, and walk on the surface of stagnant water, supported by surface tension.

pondweed A usually perennial aquatic herb of the genus *Potamogeton* (100 species), found worldwide in fresh water. It has submerged or floating oblong or pointed leaves and tiny greenish flowers. Family: *Potamogetonaceae*.

The Canadian pondweed (*Elodea canadensis*) has submerged stems, up to 3 m long, with whorls of narrow backward-curving dark-green leaves. Native to North America, it is naturalized in Europe and used in aquariums. Family: *Hydrocharitaceae*.

Ponte Vecchio A bridge over the River Arno in Florence. Topped by buildings, it was designed by Taddeo *Gaddi and finished in 1345. It was a highly advanced structure for its period.

Pontianak 0 05S 109 16E A port in Indonesia, in W Kalimantan on the Kapuas delta. Formerly Borneo's main gold town, its chief industries are shipbuilding and rubber, palm oil, sugar, and timber processing. Population (1995 est): 449 100.

pontoon (*or* **vingt-et-un**) A card game in which the objective is to score 21, counting court cards as 10 and the ace as 1 or 11. One card is dealt to each player, who puts up a stake accordingly; a second card is then dealt. Players then have the option of "sticking" (keeping the cards they have), buying another card face down, or "twisting" (accepting another card face up at no cost). Hands scoring more than 21 lose their stakes (go "bust"). The winner is the player with the score nearest to 21. Players scoring exactly 21 win double their stakes.

Blackjack is a variant on pontoon played by a croupier and six punters in a casino, using four standard packs.

pony A *horse that does not exceed 1.47 m (14½ hands) in height at maturity, measured from the top of the shoulders (withers). The many modern breeds of pony are thought to have developed from one or two original types. Ponies have traditionally been used by man as pack animals and for riding. Today, they are especially popular as children's mounts and for pony trekking.

poodle A breed of dog of uncertain origins but long associated with France and Germany. The poodle is an active intelligent dog with a long straight muzzle, drooping ears, and a docked tail. The dense coat was originally clipped to enable them to swim and retrieve in water. The miniature poodle and toy poodle are derivative breeds of the standard poodle. Height: 38 cm minimum (standard); 28–38 cm (miniature); under 28 cm (toy).

p

Poole 1. 50 43N 1 59W A resort and port in S England, in Poole unitary authority, Dorset; it stands on **Poole Harbour**, one of the world's largest natural harbours, and has boatbuilding, engineering and pottery industries. Population (1991): 138 479. **2.** A unitary authority in S England, in Dorset. Area: 37 sq km (14 sq mi). Population (2001): 138 299.

Poona (*or* **Pune**) 18 34N 73 58E A city in India, in Maharashtra. Capital of the Marathas in the late 18th century, it was taken by the British in 1817. A commercial, manufacturing, and military centre, it has cotton textiles, rubber, paper, and munitions industries. Population (1991): 1 559 558.

Poor Laws The laws that governed assistance to the poor in Britain. From the 16th century parishes were responsible for providing for their poor and from 1572 levied a rate for poor relief. The Poor Law Amendment Act of 1834 abolished such outdoor relief and those seeking assistance had to enter a *workhouse. The Poor Law system was not abolished until 1947.

pop art A US and British art movement of the 1950s and 1960s characterized by the use of techniques and subject matter from popular mass culture (television, comics, advertising, etc.). Leading pop artists included Andy *Warhol, Roy Lichtenstein (1923–97), Richard Hamilton (1922–), and Peter Blake (1932–).

Pope, Alexander (1688–1744) British poet. He established his reputation as a poet of biting wit and skill, especially in his masterly use of the heroic couplet, with *An Essay on Criticism* (1711) and the mock epic *The Rape of the Lock* (1712–14). His other works include translations of Homer's *Iliad* (1715–20) and *Odyssey* (1725–26), the mock epic *The Dunciad* (1728; revised 1742–43), the philosophical poem *An Essay on Man* (1733–34), and poems modelled on the satires of Horace.

Popish Plot (1678) A supposed conspiracy invented by Titus Oates (1649–1705) and Israel Tonge. They alleged the existence of a plot to assassinate Charles II and place his Roman Catholic brother, James, on the throne. The anti-Catholic passions Oates and Tonge thus aroused led to the execution of 35 suspects and the exclusion of Catholics from parliament (*see* TEST ACTS).

poplar A shrub or tree of the genus *Populus* (about 30 species), native to N temperate regions and grown for wood pulp, shade, and ornament. Up to 40 m tall, the trees may have a broad spreading crown, as in the European black poplar (*P. nigra*), or a tall slender one, as in the Lombardy poplar (*P. nigra* var. *italica*). The poplar has oval, triangular, or heart-shaped leaves and drooping catkins. The seeds have tufts of silky white hairs. Family: *Salicaceae*. *See also* ASPEN.

Popper, Sir Karl (Raimund) (1902–94) British philosopher, born in Austria. In *The Logic of Scientific Discovery* (1935) he argued that the basic procedure of science was the falsification, rather than the verification, of hypotheses by observation. In *The Open Society and Its Enemies* (1942) and *The Poverty of Historicism* (1957) he defended liberal individualism against Marxism.

poppy An annual, biennial, or perennial plant of the genus *Papaver* (about 120 species), native mainly to the N hemisphere and often grown for ornament. It yields a milky sap (latex) and bears large lobed or divided leaves and showy white, pink, or red flowers with 4–6 petals surrounding a dense whorl of stamens. The fruit is a capsule with pores through which the seeds are dispersed. Species include the *corn poppy and *opium poppy. Family: *Papaveraceae*. *See also* WELSH POPPY.

porcelain White vitrified ceramic evolved by Chinese potters about 900 AD. It was not invented but developed out of stoneware pottery. There are three kinds of porcelain: hard-paste or true porcelain, soft-paste or artificial, and English bone china. Hard-paste porcelain consists of china clay (kaolin) and fusible feldspathic rock (petuntse) finely mixed and fired to about 1400°C. This forms a translucent white resonant vitreous body, which is usually glazed with pure petuntse during the firing. Soft-paste porcelain differs from hard-paste in that the clay or kaolin is mixed with an artificial flux, such as sand with lime, flint, soda, etc. The mixture is fired at about 1100°C and the glaze, usually of glass, is applied in a second firing at about 1000°C. Bone porcelain is an 18th-century English invention using bone ash as a flux.

porcupine A large herbivorous spiny *rodent belonging to either of the families *Erethizontidae* (New World porcupines; 11 species) or *Hystricidae* (Old World porcupines; 15 species). American porcupines tend to be arboreal and have prehensile tails. The North American porcupine (*Erethizion dorsatum*) is about 75 cm long and grows a soft winter coat that almost conceals its covering of quills. Old World porcupines are mainly ground-dwelling. The Indian crested porcupine (*Hystrix indica*) grows to 1 m in length and may have spines 35 cm long. Porcupines respond to a threat by turning their backs and raising their spines.

porphyria A group of genetic disorders in which there is an accumulation in the body of one or more porphyrins—precursors of the red blood pigment—due to an enzyme defect. The disease affects the digestive tract, causing abdominal pain, vomiting, and diarrhoea; the nervous system, causing psychotic disorder, epilepsy, and weakness; the circulatory system, causing high blood pressure; and the skin, causing photosensitivity.

porphyry An igneous rock, usually hypabyssal, containing numerous large crystals called phenocrysts set in a finer-grained, or sometimes glassy, groundmass. The term porphyry is often given with the name of the prophyritic mineral, for example quartz porphyry.

porpoise A small toothed *whale belonging to the family *Phocoenidae* (7 species), of coastal waters. The common, or harbour, porpoise (*Phocoena phocoena*) of the N Atlantic and Pacific, has a rounded body, tapering towards the tail, blue-grey above and pale grey beneath. It feeds on fish, squid, and crustaceans.

port A fortified usually dessert *wine from Oporto (N Portugal). The grapes grown on the Douro hillsides are trodden in stone presses. Fermentation is halted by adding brandy. Subsequently the wine is taken to the lodges near Oporto, where it matures in wood.

Port-au-Prince 18 40N 72 20W The capital of Haiti, a port in the SW on the Gulf of Gonaïves. Its main exports are coffee and sugar. The University of Haiti was founded here in 1944. Population (1997 est): 917 112.

Porter, Cole (Albert) (1893–1964) US composer of musical comedies and popular songs. He wrote a series of musicals, including *The Gay Divorcee* (1932), *Anything Goes* (1934), *Kiss Me Kate* (1948), and *Can Can* (1953). His songs included "Night and Day" and "Begin the Beguine."

Portland, Isle of A peninsula in S England, in Dorset, connected to the mainland by Chesil Bank. It contains Portland Castle, built by Henry VIII (1520). The Portland stone quarried here has been used in many London buildings, notably St Paul's Cathedral.

Port Louis 20 10S 57 30E The capital of Mauritius, in the NW of the island. Founded in about 1736, it is the site of two cathedrals. Sugar is exported. Population (1999 est): 147 648.

Port Moresby 9 30S 147 07E The capital and main port of Papua New Guinea, on the Gulf of Papua. It was an important Allied base in World War II. Population (1999 est, urban area): 298 145.

Pôrto Alegre 30 03S 51 10W A city in S Brazil, the capital of Rio Grande do Sul state on the Lagôa (Lagoon) dos Patos. It is a major commercial and industrial centre; industries are chiefly related to agriculture and include meat processing, tanning, and the manufacture of textiles. Population (2000): 1 320 000.

Port-of-Spain 10 38N 61 31W The capital and main port of Trinidad and Tobago since 1783, on the W coast of Trinidad. Notable buildings include the Anglican and Roman Catholic cathedrals. Petroleum products, sugar, and rum are among the main exports. Population (1996 est): 43 396.

Porto Novo 6 30N 2 47E The capital of Benin, on the Gulf of Guinea. A former centre of the slave trade with the Portuguese, it came under French rule in the late 19th century. Trade includes palm oil and cotton. Population (1994 est): 200 000.

Port Said (*or* **Bur Said**) 31 17N 32 18E A major port in Egypt, situated at the Mediterranean entrance to the Suez Canal. Founded in 1859, it became an important fuelling point but suffered from the closure of the Suez Canal (1967–75) and Israeli occupation of the E bank. Population (1996): 469 533.

Portsmouth 1. 50 48N 1 05W A port in S England, in Portsmouth unitary authority, Hampshire, at the entrance to Portsmouth Harbour. Landmarks include Nelson's flagship HMS *Victory*. The chief naval base in the UK, Portsmouth is also a commercial port. Population (1991): 174 690. **2.** A unitary authority in S England, in Hampshire. Area: 37 sq km (14 sq mi). Population (2001): 186 704.

Port Sudan 19 38N 37 07E A port in the Sudan, on the Red Sea. It handles much of the country's trade; exports include cotton, gum arabic, and sesame seeds. It also has an important salt-panning industry. Population (1993): 305 385.

Portugal, Republic of A country in SW Europe, occupying the W section of the Iberian Peninsula and bordering on the Atlantic Ocean. The *Madeira Islands are an integral part of Portugal. Coastal plains rise to mountains, reaching 1935 m (6352 ft) in the N. *Economy*: traditionally agricultural but now moderately industrialized. Portugal's principal exports include motor vehicles and components, textiles, clothing, cork, wood products, sardines, and fortified wines. Rich mineral resources include coal, copper pyrites, kaolin, haematite and hydroelectricity is a valuable source of power. Tourism is important. *History*: the early history of the region is that of the rest of the Iberian Peninsula (*see* SPAIN, KINGDOM OF). Portugal as a distinct Christian territory dates from 868. It became a kingdom in 1139 under Alfonso I (1112–85) and its long alliance with England began in the 14th century. From the 15th century Portuguese explorers opened up new trade routes, allowing for the establishment of an extensive overseas empire. The country was under Spanish domination from 1580 to 1640, when the Braganzas came to power. In 1807 Portugal was invaded by the French, who were defeated in the subsequent *Peninsular War. A revolution in 1910 overthrew the monarchy and established a republic. A period of political instability culminated in a military coup in 1926. A prominent role in the new government was played by António *Salazar, who became prime minister in 1932. His long dictatorship saw colonial wars in Africa and economic decline. In 1974 Salazar's successor, Marcello Caetano (1906–80), was overthrown in a military coup. Constitutional government was restored in 1976. In 1986 Portugal joined the EC. The current president, Jorge Sampaio, was elected in 1996. Following elections in 2002 a centre-right coalition was formed under José Manuel Durão Barroso. Portugal adopted the single European currency in 1999–2002. Official language: Portuguese. Currency: euro of 100 cents. Area: 91 631 sq km (34 861 sq mi). Population (2003 est): 10 181 000. Capital: Lisbon.

Portuguese A Romance language spoken in Portugal, Galicia (Spain), Brazil, Madeira, and the Azores. Brazilian Portuguese differs slightly in grammar and sound system. A notable characteristic of Portuguese is the use of nasal vowel sounds.

Portuguese man-of-war A colonial marine invertebrate animal belonging to a genus (*Physalia*) of cnidarians found mainly in warm seas. It has a translucent bladder-like float (pneumatophore), pink, blue, or violet in colour. Attached underneath are *polyps bearing stinging tentacles, up to 50 m long, which paralyse fish and other prey. Order: *Siphonophora*; class: *Hydrozoa*.

Poseidon The Greek god of the sea and earthquakes, brother of Zeus and Hades. His many offspring included Theseus, Polyphemus, and the winged horse Pegasus. He was usually portrayed with a trident and dolphin. He was identified with the Roman *Neptune.

positron The antiparticle of the *electron, having the same mass and *spin as the electron but opposite electric charge. A positron and an electron annihilate each other on collision, producing two gamma-ray photons.

possum The most common Australian *marsupial, *Trichosurus vulpecula*, also called brush-tailed phalanger. Nocturnal and arboreal, it is cat-sized and has a soft greyish coat and bushy tail. It feeds mainly on buds, leaves, and fruit, and occasionally fledgling birds. The name possum is often used for other members of the family *Phalangeridae*.

postimpressionism The art of the late 19th-century French painters *Cézanne, *Seurat, *Van Gogh, *Gauguin, *Toulouse-Lautrec, and their followers whose work developed out of and, to some extent, in reaction to *impressionism. The term was coined by the British art critic, Roger *Fry.

postmortem *See* AUTOPSY.

potassium (K) A reactive alkali metal discovered by Sir Humphry Davy in 1807. It is a common constituent of the earth's crust; forming *feldspars ($KAlSi_3O_8$), clays, and evaporite minerals. The metal is prepared by electrolysis of the molten hydroxide. It is soft, easily cut with a knife, and reacts readily with water, catching fire and liberating hydrogen. It oxidizes rapidly in air and must therefore be stored under oil. The element is highly electropositive and its chemistry is dominated by its ability to form ionic salts (e.g. KCl). Its largest use is in fertilizers, potassium being essential for plant growth. Alloys of potassium and sodium have been proposed as heat transfer media in nuclear reactors, since the lowest melting alloy melts at −12.3°C. One of the three isotopes (^{40}K) is radioactive with a half-life of 1.3×10^9 years and is used in *potassium-argon dating. The metal and its salts impart a lilac colour to flames. At no 19; at wt 39.0938; mp 63.71°C; bp 759°C.

potassium-argon dating A method of radiometric dating of geological specimens based on the decay of the radioactive isotope potassium-40, which is present to a small extent in all naturally occurring potassium. Its half-life is 1.3×10^9 years and it decays to argon-40; thus an estimate of the ratio of the two isotopes in a specimen of rock gives an indication of its age.

potato A perennial herbaceous plant, *Solanum tuberosum*, native to the Andes but cultivated throughout the world, especially in temperate regions, as an important vegetable crop. Potatoes were first introduced to England in the late 16th century by Sir Walter Raleigh. The plants grow to a height of 50–100 cm, with compound leaves and clusters of white and purple flowers. The tubers have a thin brownish-white, white, yellow, or pinkish skin and are rich in starch; there are several varieties, up to 1.5 kg in weight, and they are eaten cooked or ground into flour. Family: *Solanaceae*. *See also* SWEET POTATO.

potential, electric A measure of electrical work. The potential at a point in an *electric field is one volt when one joule of energy is needed to bring a positive charge of one coulomb to that point from infinity. Usually the potential difference between two points, rather than the absolute potential, is used. *See also* ELECTROMOTIVE FORCE.

potential energy Energy stored in a body by virtue of its position or configuration. Thus a body, mass m, at a height h above the ground has a potential energy equal to mgh, where g is the *acceleration of free fall, relative to the ground. A compressed spring and an electrically charged body also store potential energy.

Potentilla A genus of mostly perennial herbs (500 species), found mainly in N temperate and arctic regions. It includes several species and hybrids grown as ornamentals. They have erect or creeping stems, 5–70 cm long, bearing compound leaves and yellow, white, or red flowers. The fruit is a group of seedlike achenes. Family: *Rosaceae*.

potholing *See* SPELEOLOGY.

pot marigold A herb, *Calendula officinalis*, native to S Europe and cultivated in temperate regions as an ornamental. About 30–35 cm tall, it bears simple oblong leaves and yellow or orange daisy-like flowers, often double in cultivated varieties. The fresh petals may be eaten in salads or puddings or are dried and used in medicines. Family: *Compositae*.

Potomac River A river in the E central USA, rising in the Appalachian Mountains of W Virginia and flowing generally NE through Washington, DC, to Chesapeake Bay. Length: 462 km (287 mi).

Potsdam 52 19N 13 15E A city in E Germany, on the River Havel adjoining Berlin. It was the residence of Prussian kings and German emperors. Notable buildings include the Brandenburg Gate (1770) and the Sanssouci Palace (1745–47). An industrial city, Potsdam has many scientific institutes. After the end of World War II in Europe, Truman, Stalin, and Churchill (and then Attlee) met here at the **Potsdam Conference**. Population (1999 est): 129 500.

Potter, Beatrix (1866–1943) British children's writer and illustrator. *The Tale of Peter Rabbit* (1900) was the first of a series of famous children's books concerning such animals as Jemima Puddle-Duck and Mrs Tittlemouse.

potter wasp A solitary *wasp belonging to the genus *Eumerus*, common in North America and Europe. It constructs juglike nests of mud or clay, cemented by saliva and attached to plant stems. A single egg is laid in each nest.

Poulenc, Francis (1899–1963) French composer, a member of Les Six. He produced a wide variety of compositions, including the song cycle *Le Bestiaire* (1919), the operas *Les Mamelles de Tirésias* (1944) and *Les Dialogues des Carmélites* (1953–56), and the ballet *Les Biches* (1923).

Pound, Ezra (1885–1972) US poet and critic. He went to Europe in 1908 and became a dynamic propagandist for modernist literary and artistic movements in London (*see* IMAGISM; VORTICISM). His early poetry included *A Lume Spento* (1908), his first volume, and the long poems *Homage to Sextus Propertius* (1917) and *Hugh Selwyn Mauberly* (1920). He moved to Paris and, in 1924, to Italy, where he worked on the *Cantos* (1925–69). His pro-fascist broadcasts during World War II led to his confinement in a mental hospital in the USA (1946–58), after which he returned to Italy.

Poussin, Nicolas (1594–1665) French painter, regarded as one of the greatest exponents of *classicism. Poussin lived in Rome from 1624 until his death, apart from two years in France. His representation of religious themes, such as *The Martyrdom of St Erasmus* (1628; Vatican), gave way to an interest in mythology and the Old Testament, for example *The Worship of the Golden Calf* (c.1635; National Gallery, London). The classicism of his second Roman period is exemplified in *Landscape with Diogenes* (1648; Louvre).

powder metallurgy The shaping of metals by pressing powdered metal into blocks, heating, and stamping. The method is used for working metals, such as platinum and tungsten, that are difficult to shape by other means. It leaves no scrap and is suitable for intricate shapes. Nonmetal additives can be easily included, such as the graphite lubricant in self-lubricating bearings.

p

Powell, Anthony (1905–2000) British novelist. His novel sequence *A Dance to the Music of Time* comprises 12 social comedies beginning with *A Question of Upbringing* (1951) and ending with *Hearing Secret Harmonies* (1975). He also wrote memoirs and diaries.

Powell, Colin (Luther) (1937–) US Republican politician and soldier. A general, he was appointed chairman of the Joint Chiefs of Staff in 1989, the first Black American to hold the post. He became US secretary of state under George W. Bush in 2001.

Powell, (John) Enoch (1912–98) British politician. He became a Conservative MP in 1950. From 1960 to 1963 he was minister of health, his only cabinet post, and in 1968 he was dismissed from Edward Heath's shadow cabinet following a controversial speech against immigration. From 1974 to 1987 he was the Ulster Unionist MP for South Down.

power The rate at which a body or system does work. It is measured in watts or horsepower.

power station An electricity generating plant that forms part of the *electricity supply system. In **thermal power stations**, heat from the burning of fossil fuels (oil, coal, and gas) or from thermal nuclear reactors is used to generate steam. The steam drives *turbines connected to alternating-current generators (turbo-alternators), thus converting heat into electricity. Gas turbines are also used, missing out the steam-generation stage. They are easy to build and flexible to run, but have an efficiency of only about 25%. Sometimes the exhaust gas is used to help generate steam for a steam turbine, in order to increase the station's overall efficiency. Usually in a steam-turbine thermal station about 30 to 40% of the heat is converted to electricity, most of the rest being lost when steam is condensed to water before it is returned to the boilers. Hydroelectric power stations are more efficient (up to 90%) and provide about 0.2% of UK electricity supplies. *See also* ENERGY.

Powys A county of E Central Wales, bordering on England. It was formed in 1974 from Montgomeryshire, Radnorshire, and most of Breconshire. It is generally mountainous, rising to 886 m (2907 ft) in the Brecon Beacons. Agricultural activities include sheep, cattle, dairy, and arable farming. Tourism is important. Area: 5077 sq km (1960 sq mi). Population (2001): 126 344. Administrative centre: Llandrindod Wells.

Prado An art gallery in Madrid. Designed originally as a natural-history museum by Juan de Villanueva (1739–1811), the art gallery was founded in 1818 by Ferdinand VII. Most of its collection consists of paintings collected by the Spanish monarchs from the 16th century onwards. It includes works by Vélazquez, Goya, *El Greco, *Titian, and *Bosch.

Praetorian Guard The official bodyguard of the Roman emperors created by Augustus in 27 BC. Composed of up to 16 long-serving infantry divisions each of 500–1000 men, and stationed as a single unit in Rome, the Guard and its commanders developed great political influence; as senatorial power diminished emperors came to rely upon Praetorian support and in later imperial times the emperor's position and even his life depended on the Guard's favour.

Prague (Czech name: Praha) 50 8N 14 25E The capital of the Czech Republic, in the centre of the country on the River Vltava. The industrial and commercial centre of the country, it manufactures machinery, cars, aircraft, food products, clothing, and chemicals. Notable buildings include Hradčany Castle and the mainly gothic Cathedral of St Vitus. *History*: in the middle ages it was the seat of the Přemyslid kings of Bohemia. Under Habsburg rule from the 16th century, it was made the capital of newly independent Czechoslovakia in 1918. In 1968 the city was occupied by Soviet troops; in 1989 it witnessed mass demonstrations leading to the fall of the Communists. Population (2000 est): 1 186 855.

prairie dog A large ground squirrel, *Cynomys ludovicanis*, of North America, also called black-tailed prairie marmot. Heavily built animals, about 30 cm long, prairie dogs feed on grass and have been treated as pests by cattle ranchers.

prairies The extensive grasslands of the interior of North America. They occupy a broad N–S belt extending from Alberta and Saskatchewan through the Midwest into Texas, reaching as far W as the Rocky Mountains. Little of the original true prairie now remains, having been extensively ploughed for wheat production. *See also* STEPPES.

praseodymium (Pr) A *lanthanide element, which was separated from its mixture with neodyminium by von Welsbach in 1885. It forms trihalides (for example $PrCl_3$) and an oxide (Pr_2O_3), which is used to give a strong yellow colour to glass. At no 59; at wt 140.9077; mp 931°C; bp 3520°C.

prawn A large shrimplike *crustacean (up to 20 cm long), belonging to the suborder *Natantia*. The antennae are longer than the body and a forward projection of the carapace forms a spike (rostrum) between the eyes, bearing six or more teeth. The second pair of appendages are enlarged to form pincers (*compare* SHRIMP). The common edible prawn (*Leander serratus*) occurs in temperate coastal waters and is 5–8 cm long.

Praxiteles (mid-4th century BC) Athenian sculptor, renowned for his handling of marble. His statue of Hermes, discovered at *Olympia in 1877, exemplifies the sensuous grace and repose of his work.

Precambrian Geological time from the formation of the earth's crust, about 4500 million years ago, to about 590 million years ago when the Palaeozoic era began. Precambrian rocks lie below the Cambrian system. Most are metamorphosed and have undergone one or more Precambrian mountain-building periods as well as later ones. The largest areas of exposed Precambrian rocks are the *shield areas.

precession A circular motion described by the axis of a rotating object, such as a spinning top. The earth's axis exhibits a slow precession around the pole of the ecliptic, of about 50 seconds of angle a year.

precession of the equinoxes The gradual westward motion of the equinoxes around the *ecliptic in a period of about 25 800 years. It is caused by the precession of the earth's axis of rotation, which results mainly from the gravitational pull of the sun and moon on the equatorial bulge of the nonspherical earth. As the axis precesses, slowly tracing out a cone in the sky, the celestial equator moves relative to the ecliptic. The points of intersection, i.e. the equinoxes, thus continuously change.

predestination In Christian doctrine, God's foreordaining of salvation for certain people. The idea is propagated by St *Paul in the Epistles and was later developed systematically by St Augustine and *Calvin. It raises enormous problems about the nature of divine justice and the role of the human will and endeavours, problems that Christian philosophers have never satisfactorily solved.

pregnancy The period in humans during which a fetus develops in the womb, usually lasting for about 266 days from conception to delivery of the baby. A pregnancy can be confirmed after the first missed period with the aid of a pregnancy test, usually based on the presence of the hormone human chorionic *gonadotrophin in the urine.

premium bond A UK government security, held in numbered units of one pound, the interest on which is put into a fund and allocated to bond holders by a monthly lottery, as tax-free prizes. The numbers of winning bonds are selected by Electronic Random Number Indicator Equipment (ERNIE). Premium bonds were introduced in 1956.

Pre-Raphaelite Brotherhood A group including the British painters Dante Gabriel *Rossetti, John Everett *Millais, and William Holman *Hunt, who joined together in 1848 in reaction to the banality of contemporary British painting and its enthusiasm for *Raphael. Signing all their works PRB, they sought to emulate Italian painters earlier than Raphael and to paint subjects of a moral or religious character. The PRB had a strong influence on such artists as William *Morris and Edward *Burne-Jones.

presbyopia *See* LONGSIGHTEDNESS.

Presbyterianism A Protestant church organization based on government by elders. These elders determine Church policy through a hierarchical system of presbyteries, synods, and general assemblies. Presbyterianism originated with the 16th-century followers of *Calvin. In Scotland the tenets of Presbyterianism were formulated (1560) by *Knox and it became the established church in 1696.

Prescott, John (Leslie) (1938–) British Labour politician; deputy prime minister (1997–). His cabinet posts include secretary of state for local government and the regions (2002–).

Presley, Elvis (Aaron) (1935–77) US popular singer, whose fusion of Black and White styles effectively created modern pop music. His first big hit, "Heartbreak Hotel" (1956), was followed by "Hound Dog," "Suspicious Minds," and numerous others, making him the best-selling recording artist in history. His early death was accelerated by drug dependence.

Press Complaints Commission An organization founded in 1991 to deal with complaints of invasion of privacy and unfair treatment by the press and to ensure that the press maintains high professional standards. It replaced the **Press Council**, founded in 1953 to defend press freedom.

press gang A band of men employed to force paupers, vagabonds, or criminals into the army or navy. This system of impressment, common throughout the world in the 18th century, ceased when improved pay and conditions in the army and navy increased voluntary recruitment.

pressure Force per unit area. For a liquid, density *d*, the pressure at a depth *h* is *hdg*, where *g* is the *acceleration of free fall. Pressure is usually measured in pascals, millimetres of mercury, or millibars.

pressure gauge An instrument for measuring the pressure of a fluid. Atmospheric pressure is measured with a mercury *barometer or an aneroid barometer. Pressures above atmospheric pressure are usually measured with a Bourdon gauge, which consists of a flattened curved tube that tends to straighten under pressure. Low pressures are measured with such vacuum gauges as the McLeod gauge or Pirani gauge.

Preston 53 46N 2 42W A city in NW England, the administrative centre of Lancashire on the River Ribble. It has plastics, chemical, motor-vehicle and aircraft construction, and electronics industries as well as the traditional cotton and engineering works. It was granted city status in 2002. Population (1991): 177 660.

Pretender, Old *See* JAMES EDWARD STUART, THE OLD PRETENDER.

Pretender, Young *See* CHARLES EDWARD STUART, THE YOUNG PRETENDER.

Pretoria 25 36S 28 12E The administrative capital of South Africa. Founded in 1855, it became the capital of the Union of South Africa in 1910. The University of South Africa was founded here in 1873. Industries include iron and steel processing, engineering, and food processing. Population (1996): 1 104 479.

Priam In Greek legend, the last king of Troy, husband of Hecuba. As an old man he witnessed the deaths of many of his 50 sons in the *Trojan War.

Priapus A Greek fertility god associated with gardens, son of Dionysus and Aphrodite. He was usually portrayed as a comic ugly figure with an enormous phallus. The donkey, symbol of lust, was sacrificed to him.

price index A single figure used to measure the average percentage change in the price of a set of goods over a period of time, taking a base figure of 100 for a specified year. The best-known indexes are the Wholesale Price Index and the Retail Price Index, the latter providing a reliable guide to the cost of living. Some wages, salaries, and costs are **index-linked** (i.e. increase in proportion to a specified price index) to cover the devaluation of money as a result of *inflation. **Indexation** is commonly used in agreements that extend over a long period during which inflation is expected to be a significant factor.

prickly pear A *cactus of the genus *Opuntia*, native to North and South America and introduced to Australia and South Africa. It has flat jointed spiny stems bearing large orange or yellow flowers, which give rise to edible pear-shaped fruits. The seeds are used to produce an oil and the shoots are eaten as vegetables or used as animal feed.

Priestley, J(ohn) B(oynton) (1894–1984) British novelist and dramatist. He first won popular success with his picaresque novel *The Good Companions* (1929). His plays include *An Inspector Calls* (1946) and several mildly experimental dramas exploring the nature of time, including *Time and the Conways* (1937).

Priestley, Joseph (1733–1804) British chemist and one of the discoverers of oxygen, together with Carl Scheele (1742–86). Priestley, being a firm believer in the *phlogiston theory, named his gas dephlogisticated air and first prepared it in 1774 by heating mercuric oxide. In 1778–79 *Lavoisier demolished the phlogiston theory and named the gas oxygen. Priestley also produced and studied several other gases, including ammonia, sulphur dioxide, and hydrogen chloride. He invented the method of collecting them over mercury, since some of these gases dissolved in water.

primary colours The minimum number of *colours that, when mixed in the correct proportions, are capable of giving all the other colours in the visible spectrum. When light of three **primary additive colours** (usually red, green, and blue) is mixed in equal intensities, white light results. This principle is used in colour television and colour *photography. Any particular colour can also be obtained by subtracting from white light a mixture of three **primary subtractive colours**, usually cyan (blue-green), magenta (purplish red), and yellow, which are complementary to red, green, and blue. Adding pigments of these in equal proportions gives black pigment.

primate A mammal belonging to the order *Primates* (about 195 species), which includes the *prosimians, monkeys, *apes, and humans. Primates probably evolved from insectivorous climbing creatures like *tree shrews and have many adaptations for climbing, including five fingers and five toes with opposable first digits (except in the hind feet of man). They have well-developed sight and hearing and enlarged cerebral hemispheres of the brain.

prime minister A head of government. In the UK the post developed in the 18th century. Sir Robert *Walpole is generally regarded as the first prime minister (1721–42) but the post was not formally recognized until 1905. The prime minister is customarily a member of the House of Commons and is head of government by virtue of being the leader of the dominant political party in the Commons.

prime number An integer greater than one that has no integral factors except itself and one; for example 2, 3, 5, 7, 11, 13, 17. Every natural number can be expressed uniquely as a product of prime numbers; for example $1260 = 2^2 \times 3^2 \times 5 \times 7$.

primitivism In art, the style of untrained artists who ignore or are ignorant of both traditional aesthetic standards and avantgarde trends. Its chief characteristics are meticulous detail, brilliant colours, childlike representation, and faulty perspective. The best known primitive is the French painter Henri *Rousseau; others include the American Grandma *Moses. The term is also sometimes applied to African and Polynesian indigenous art.

primrose A perennial herbaceous plant, *Primula vulgaris*, growing in woodlands and hedge banks in Europe and N Africa. It has a basal rosette of puckered spoon-shaped leaves, with solitary pale-yellow flowers. Family: *Primulaceae*. *See also* EVENING PRIMROSE.

Primula A genus of perennial plants (about 500 species), native mainly to N temperate regions and often grown as ornamentals. They have a basal rosette of leaves and five-petalled flowers, red, pink, purple, blue, white, or yellow in colour and usually with a different coloured centre. The fruit is a capsule. The genus also includes the *cowslip and *primrose. Family: *Primulaceae*.

Prince Edward Island An island province of E Canada, in the S Gulf of St Lawrence. Its small farms produce potatoes, grains, dairy cattle, and other livestock. Tourism and fishing are also important. *History*: discovered (1534) and colonized (1720) by France, the island was captured (1758) and resettled by Britain. In 1873 it joined Canada. Area: 5657 sq km (2184 sq mi). Population (2001 est): 138 500. Capital: Charlottetown.

Prince of Wales A title customarily conferred on the eldest son of the British sovereign. It was a native Welsh title until 1301, when Edward I, following his annexation of Wales, bestowed it on his son, the future Edward II. The present holder of the title is Prince Charles.

Príncipe Island *See* SÃO TOMÉ AND PRÍNCIPE.

printed circuit An electronic circuit in which the connections between components are formed by a pattern of conducting film on a board, instead of by wires. The method greatly facilitates mass-production. An insulating board is coated with a conducting material, such as copper, and a protective pattern is deposited on it using photographic techniques. The unprotected metal is then etched away and components are soldered in place.

printing The production of multiple copies of text or pictures, usually on paper. The oldest method, in use in China and Japan before 800 AD, is **letterpress**, in which the raised surfaces of etched, engraved, or cast material are inked and pressed onto the paper. This method was revolutionized by the invention of movable type in the 15th century. Early printing presses were of the hand-operated platen variety in which the type stands on a horizontal surface and the paper is pressed onto it from above. Faster production became possible on the power-driven presses of the 19th century: first the cylinder press, and later the rotary press.

In **lithography**, a method invented by Aloys Senefelder (1771–1834) in 1798, the printing surface is smooth, the printing and nonprinting areas being made greasereceptive and grease-repellent respectively. Greasy ink rolled over the entire area is taken up only by the grease-receptive areas; the ink is then transferred by rolling onto the paper. **Offset printing**, involves an intermediate rubber-covered cylinder that transfers the ink from plate to paper. In **gravure printing**, the small square etched holes (cells) in the copper printing plate are filled with a free-flowing ink, the rest of the plate is wiped clean, and the plate is rolled against the paper, which absorbs the ink out of the cells.

Letterpress and offset lithography are used for almost all types of printing job; gravure is limited to long runs, such as cheap illustrated magazines, postage stamps, and packaging. Direct lithography has been used almost exclusively by artists. In **silk-screen printing** (screen-process printing *or* serigraphy), a piece of taut open-weave silk, metal, or synthetic fabric carries the negative of the desired image in an impervious substance, such as glue; ink is forced through the clear (printing) areas by a squeegee onto the paper, glass, fabric, or other material, behind. It is used for printing posters, electronic circuit boards, labelling on bottles, etc.

Full-colour reproduction is achieved by **colour-process printing**, in which all colours can be produced from combinations of three primary colours—yellow, cyan (blue), and magenta.

prion A *petrel belonging to a genus (*Pachyptila*; 4 species) found in Antarctica and nearby islands. Prions have a blue-grey plumage with white underparts. The flattened bill has a fringe of strainers with the floor of the mouth forming a small pouch; it feeds by skimming over the sea and straining out small invertebrates.

prism A piece of glass or other transparent material having parallel polygonal ends, with a number of rectangular surfaces meeting them at right angles. They are used in optical instruments, such as cameras and binoculars, for changing the direction of light, either by refraction or by reflection from their walls. They

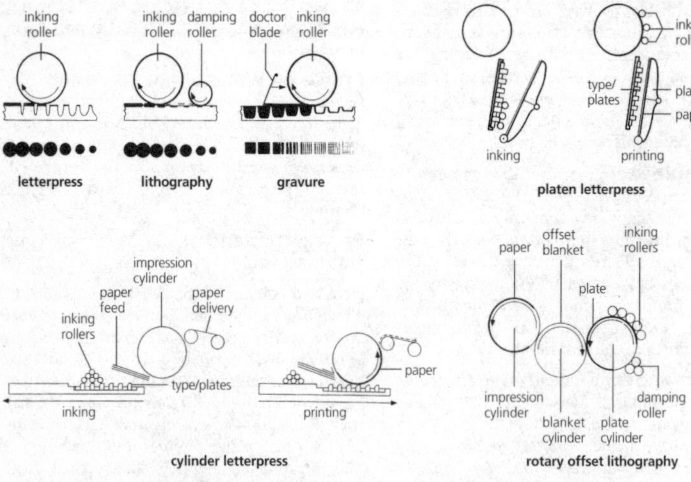

printing. Principles of three major printing processes and the three major designs of printing press.

are also used for splitting light into its component colours as a result of double refraction.

prisons Institutions for confining convicted criminals (*see* CRIMINAL LAW). In primitive societies, and throughout much of history, prisons were primarily places in which people were held until other punishments could be carried out. It was not until the 18th century that the main purpose of prisons became custodial. The appalling prison conditions at this time led to the reform movements of John *Howard and Elizabeth *Fry. During the 19th century a massive prison-building programme was carried out in the UK, modelled on Pentonville (1842), the structure of which was based on the principle of solitary confinement. Reforms since have changed the emphasis in penal institutions from retribution to correction and rehabilitation. The first "open prison," in which prisoners are permitted some personal freedom, was opened in 1936. *See also* COMMUNITY SERVICE; ELECTRONIC TAGGING.

Pristina 42 39N 21 10E A city in S Serbia and Montenegro, the capital of *Kosovo. It was the capital of medieval Serbia, until captured by the Turks in a decisive battle (1389). In 1999 it was severely damaged by Serb forces engaged in "ethnic cleansing" of Muslim Albanians, who make up the majority of the population. Population (2000 est): 186 611.

Pritchett, Sir V(ictor) S(awden) (1900–97) British short-story writer and critic. He travelled widely in Europe during the 1920s and wrote frequently about Spain. He published critical works, volumes of stories including his *Complete Short Stories* (1990), and two much acclaimed autobiographical books, *A Cab at the Door* (1968) and *Midnight Oil* (1971).

privatization The sale of a public corporation to the private sector. Conservative governments of the 1980s and 1990s sold interests in British Telecom, British Gas, and British Rail, etc., to private investors to increase the efficiency of these organizations and the number of shareholders in the community. Similar policies have been implemented by the formerly communist countries of E Europe and by developing countries in Africa and Asia. *See* NATIONALIZATION.

privet An evergreen or deciduous shrub or small tree of the genus *Ligustrum* (40–50 species), native to Eurasia and Australia and widely used for ornamental hedges, especially the European common privet (*L. vulgare*). Growing up to about 5 m high, it has simple oval leaves and small creamy flowers, which give rise to black berries. Family: *Oleaceae*.

Privy Council A body advising the British monarch, now having chiefly formal functions. It consists of all cabinet ministers, the Archbishops of Canterbury and York, the speaker of the House of Commons, and senior British and Commonwealth statesmen, who are all addressed as the Right Honourable.

probability The mathematical concept concerned with the effects of chance on an event, experiment, or observation. It originated in 1654, when the mathematicians *Pascal and *Fermat worked on problems sent to them by a gambler. If an event can occur in n ways and r is the number of ways it can occur in a specified way, then the **mathematical probability** of it occurring in the specified way is r/n. For example, the probability of the number 5 coming up on a six-faced dice in one throw is 1/6. The probability of a 5 coming up x times in x throws is obtained by multiplication, i.e. it is $(1/6)^x$. Probabilities are expressed as numbers between 1 (a certainty) and 0 (an impossibility). If an event has occurred n times and failed m times, the **empirical probability** of success in the next trial is $n/(n + m)$. Actuarial tables of life expectancy are based on empirical probabilities.

probation In English law, a court order, given instead of a sentence, requiring an offender of or over 17 years of age to be under the supervision of a probation officer for between 6 months and 3 years. Failure to comply with the order makes the offender liable to be sentenced for the original offence.

proboscis monkey A large leaf-eating *Old World monkey, *Nasalis larvatus*, of Borneo. Up to 1.5 m tall, proboscis monkeys have a protruding nose and live in groups in forests, feeding on young palm leaves.

progesterone A steroid hormone secreted mainly by the corpus luteum of the mammalian ovary following ovulation. It prepares the womb for implantation of the embryo and maintains this state during pregnancy. Progestogens—synthetic steroids with progesterone-like actions—are constituents of *oral contraceptives.

program, computer A series of instructions that directs a computer to perform a particular operation. The programs executed by the computer are in a machine code, which has the form of a series of numbers that the device interprets as either instructions or data. Programming languages simplify the programmer's task. Low-level languages are those that resemble closely the logic of the machine; high-level languages, such as Basic, Fortran, Cobol, Algol, and Pascal, use abstract constructs more suited to human thought and are independent of any particular machine. *See also* SOFTWARE.

Prohibition (1919–33) A period during which the manufacture, sale, and transportation of alcoholic drinks were prohibited in the USA by the 18th Amendment to the constitution. The temperance movement, combined with the wartime need to divert grain from distilleries to food manufacture, led to national prohibition. It was repealed by the 21st Amendment.

Prokofiev, Sergei (1891–1953) Soviet composer and pianist. He lived abroad from 1918 to 1933 and in 1948 was officially condemned for "undemocratic tendencies" in his music. His work includes seven symphonies, five piano concertos, two violin concertos, the opera *The Love of Three Oranges* (1919), the ballet *Romeo and Juliet* (1935–36), and *Peter and the Wolf* (1936) for speaker and orchestra.

prolactin A protein hormone, produced by the pituitary gland, that initiates and maintains lactation in mammals. In other animals, it has a variety of functions, being involved in growth and the balance of water and salts, as well as reproduction. *See also* GONADOTROPHIN.

p

proletariat Originally, the lower class of Rome and other ancient states, the term was later used to refer to the lower class of any community. *Marx defined the proletariat as the wage labourers of capitalist economies. *See* MARXISM.

promenade concerts Originally, concerts in which the audience was free to walk about, now a series of concerts organized by the BBC, which were started by Henry *Wood in 1895. The BBC Promenade Concerts (the Proms) have been held in the Royal Albert Hall since the original venue, the Queens Hall, was destroyed by bombs in World War II.

Prometheus (Greek: forethought) In Greek mythology, the son of a Titan and Themis who created man and endowed him with reason. He also stole fire from heaven to give to man. Zeus chained him to a rock in the Caucasus and sent an eagle each day to devour his liver, which grew again by night.

promethium (Pm) A radioactive element, not known on earth but identified by its spectrum in the light from stars, in which it is continuously being formed by nuclear reactions. The most stable isotope has a half-life of 17.7 years. Promethium salts exhibit bluish-green *luminescence and can be used in photoelectric cells. It is obtained from nuclear reactors. At no 61; at wt (145); mp about 1042°C.

propellant 1. A solid or liquid substance used to provide thrust in a rocket engine or gun. Propellants utilize very fast exothermic chemical reactions to produce large quantities of expanding gas quickly. Generally, they are explosive substances or mixtures. **2.** The pressurized inert liquids used to drive an *aerosol from its container.

propeller A device for converting the rotation of a shaft into thrust in the direction of its axis. A **marine propeller** has between two and six blades, shaped as part of a helical surface. It acts as a screw, accelerating a column of water rearwards. An **air propeller** (*or* airscrew) has longer thinner blades (usually two or four) and a higher rotational speed. It, too, accelerates a mass of air rearwards thrusting the aircraft forwards.

proportional representation (**PR**) A voting system that aims to reflect accurately the wishes of the electorate and to ensure that votes for unsuccessful candidates are not wasted. In the system of PR known as the **single transferable vote** electors indicate their preferences among the candidates by numbering them on their ballot paper. Those candidates who obtain a required quota of first-choice votes are elected to represent the constituency. First-choice votes in excess of the quota are then redistributed to the voter's second-choice, as are those for the least successful candidate. The **alternative vote** system is similar but takes place in single-member constituencies. Under the **additional member** system people vote separately for a candidate and a party. Parties are awarded additional MPs if the number of constituencies they win does not reflect their share of the overall vote. In the **party-list system** (introduced for the UK's elections to the European Parliament in 1999) electors vote for a party, which is then allocated seats in proportion to its total vote. Elections to the devolved bodies in Scotland and Wales use a combination of the traditional "first-past-the-post" and the additional member system; those to the Northern Ireland assembly use the single transferable vote.

Proserpine *See* PERSEPHONE.

prosimian A *primate of the suborder

Prosimii (53 species), including the *lemurs, indris, sifakas, lorises, *bushbabies, *tarsiers, *tree shrews, and the aye-aye. Prosimians are mainly arboreal.

Prost, Alain (1955–) French motor racing driver. He is the most successful Formula One driver ever, having won 51 Grand Prix races. He won the World Championship in 1985, 1986, 1989, and 1993, the year he retired.

prostaglandins Compounds derived from long-chain (essential) fatty acids and found in mammalian body tissues. Their effects include stimulation of contraction in the womb, dilation of blood vessels, and modification of hormonal activity. They are released at sites of inflammation following tissue damage and the pain-relieving properties of such drugs as aspirin are due to their inhibition of prostaglandin synthesis.

prostate gland A gland in men, situated just beneath the bladder. It secretes an alkaline fluid during ejaculation that forms part of the semen. Enlargement of the prostate commonly occurs in elderly men, obstructing the bladder and preventing urination. It is usually treated by drugs, a surgical transurethral resection of the prostate (TURPS), or in extreme cases by removal of the gland (prostatectomy).

protactinium (Pa) A radioactive *actinide element, first identified in 1913. It is present in pitchblende as a member of the uranium decay series. The oxide (Pa_2O_5) and iodide (PaI_5) have been produced. The latter decomposes on heating to give the metal. At no 91; at wt (231); mp 1572°C.

Protea A genus of evergreen shrubs and trees (over 100 species), native to S and central Africa. They have small white, pink, yellow, or orange flowers that are grouped in clusters. The flowers are a national emblem of South Africa. Family: *Proteaceae*.

Protectorate (1653–59) The period during which England was governed by Oliver *Cromwell. The Instrument of Government (1653) vested executive authority in the Lord Protector (Cromwell) and a state council and legislative authority in the Protector and a triennial parliament. The Instrument was modified by the Humble Petition and Advice (1657), which gave more power to parliament. Cromwell's relations with parliament subsequently deteriorated and he dismissed it in 1658.

protein A complex organic compound that consists of one or more chains of *amino acids linked by *peptide bonds (–NH–CO–). These chains are variously coiled, wound, and cross-linked to form a three-dimensional molecular structure that determines the biological properties of the protein. Proteins are manufactured by cells according to the genetic information carried in the chromosomes and the specific function of the cell (*see* DNA; RNA). Proteins fulfil many important biological roles: some, including *collagen and *keratin, are important structural materials of body tissues, while the proteins of muscle—actin and myosin—are responsible for its contractile properties. Proteins vital to the functioning of the body include enzymes, *antibodies, and many *hormones.

Protestantism The movement for Church reform that arose in the Western Church in the 16th century and led to the establishment of the Reformed Churches. The word derives from the *protestatio* of the dissident reforming minority at the Diet of Speyer (1529). The early leaders of the Reformation—*Luther, *Calvin, and Ulrich Zwingli (1484–1531)—each promoted his own brand of Protestantism. Under Elizabeth I Protestantism finally became the established religion in England.

There are many doctrinal divisions among Protestants, but all reject a varying number of tenets and practices retained in Catholicism. In general Protestants rely less upon ecclesiastical tradition, believing the Bible to be the sole source of truth. They deny papal authority and admit a variety of forms of Church government. Transubstantiation, *purgatory, special veneration of the Virgin Mary, and invocation of saints are all repudiated. The importance of the sacraments is minimized, with only baptism and the *Eucharist being accorded widespread acceptance. The preaching and studying of God's word in the Bible is conversely important.

Proteus A Greek sea god who served Poseidon as a shepherd of seals. He had prophetic powers but used his ability to change his form to avoid communicating his knowledge.

proton A positively charged elementary particle classified as a baryon (*see* PARTICLE PHYSICS). It forms part of all atomic nuclei, a single proton being the nucleus of the hydrogen atom. It is a stable particle, 1836 times heavier than the electron.

protostar An embryonic star that has formed out of a contracting cloud of interstellar gas and dust. It continues to contract, the density and temperature at its centre rising until they are sufficiently high to cause energy-releasing thermonuclear reactions to begin in the central core. The collapse is then halted, and the object becomes a luminous star.

protozoa A large and diverse group of typically microscopic single-celled organisms, traditionally classified as simple animals but now assigned to a variety of phyla that are usually placed in the kingdom *Protoctista*. Widely distributed in moist and watery places, including mud, soil, fresh waters, and oceans, protozoans range in size from 0.1 mm to several centimetres. They may have one or several nuclei and a variety of specialized structures, including a contractile vacuole for regulating the water content and cilia or flagella for movement and feeding. The cell may be fairly rigid, with a stiff cell wall (pellicle) or skeletal elements, or flexible and variable. Some protozoans contain pigment and obtain food by photosynthesis in the same way as plants. However, most forms take in dissolved nutrients or solid food particles (detritus, bacteria, etc.). Asexual reproduction is by means of simple division of the parent cell (binary fission) or by budding to form new cells; various forms of sexual reproduction occur, including *conjugation. Protozoans can survive dry or adverse conditions by forming resistant cysts or spores. Some are important parasites of humans and animals, including species of *Plasmodium*, which cause malaria, and trypanosomes, which cause sleeping sickness.

Proust, Joseph-Louis (1754–1826) French chemist, who demonstrated by accurate analysis that compounds always contain fixed proportions of elements. This is now known as the law of definite proportion or sometimes as Proust's law. This work contributed to Dalton's atomic theory.

Proust, Marcel (1871–1922) French novelist. In the 1890s he became a socialite in the most fashionable aristocratic circles in Paris but from 1905 he dedicated his life to writing. In 1912 he published the first volume (*Swann's Way*) of what was to become his masterpiece, *In Search of Lost Time*. The second volume, *Within a Budding Grove* (1919), won the Prix Goncourt; it was followed by *The Guermantes Way* (1920–21) and *Cities of the Plain* (1921–22). Proust managed to complete but not revise the final three volumes before his death. *In Search of Lost Time* is a detailed portrait of the society that Proust had abandoned, recreated through

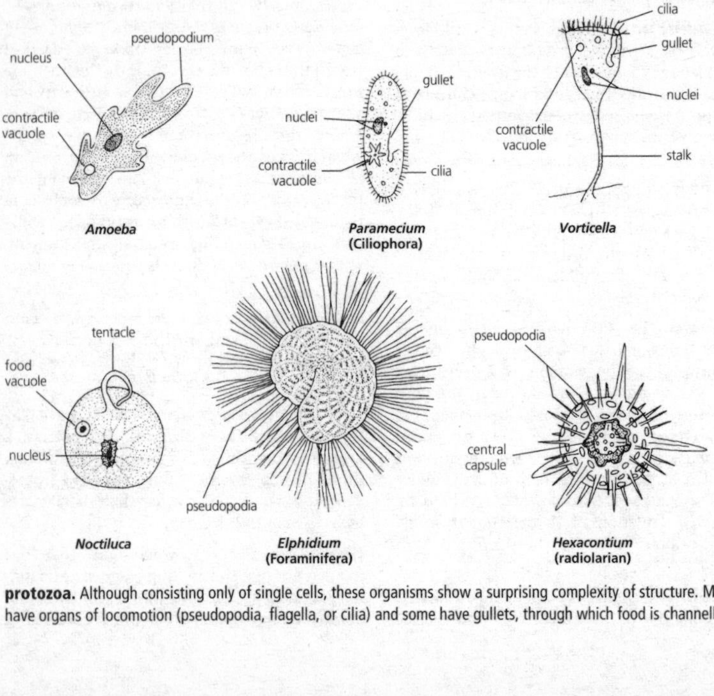

protozoa. Although consisting only of single cells, these organisms show a surprising complexity of structure. Many have organs of locomotion (pseudopodia, flagella, or cilia) and some have gullets, through which food is channelled.

the involuntary workings of memory. There is a strong autobiographical element.

Provençal A Romance language, strictly the dialect of *Provence, but also used to refer to the dialects of various regions of S France and in this broad sense often called Occitan. These dialects are also collectively described as the *langue d'oc*, in contrast to the *langue d'oïl* spoken in northern and central areas of France (*oc* and *oïl* being the medieval forms for *yes* in these two dialect areas). About nine million people still speak it.

Provence A former province in SE France, bordering on Italy and the Mediterranean Sea. A kingdom during the 9th century AD, it became part of France in 1481 and now forms the modern planning region of **Provence-Côte-d'Azur**. Chiefly mountainous, its fertile river valleys produce grapes, olives, and mulberries. It contains the French *Riviera along the S coast. Area: 31 435 sq km (12 134 sq mi). Population (1995 est): 4 428 000.

Prunus A genus of deciduous or evergreen shrubs and trees (over 200 species), mostly native to N temperate regions. It includes the *plums, *almonds, *apricots, peaches, and *cherries as well as many ornamental species. They have oval toothed leaves, and white or pink flowers. They produce stone fruits (*see* DRUPE), often with edible flesh or kernels. Family: *Rosaceae*.

Prussia A former state in N Germany on the NE Baltic coast. Established in the 13th century by the Teutonic Knights, Prussia became a duchy in 1525 under Hohenzollern rule. United with Brandenburg in 1618, it became the most powerful N German state. In the 18th century, under Frederick the Great, Prussia annexed Silesia and parts of Poland and became a major European power. Under *Bismarck's leadership, Prussia defeated Austria and Austria's German allies (1866), acquiring *Schleswig-Holstein and forming the North German Confederation. Following Prussia's victory in the *Franco-Prussian War (1870–71) the German Empire was proclaimed under Prussian leadership. Prussia was abolished by the Allies after World War II.

Przewalski's horse The single surviving species of wild horse, *Equus przewalskii*, discovered in Mongolia in about 1880 by the Russian explorer Nicolai Mikhailovich Przewalski (1839–88). It is sturdily built with a short erect dark-brown mane and a dark dorsal stripe. The coat is reddish brown. Height: 1.22–1.42 m (12–14 hands).

pseudopodium A temporary extension of the cytoplasm found in some protozoa and used for locomotion and for engulfing food particles. In *Amoeba*, the pseudopodia are blunt lobular processes but in other protozoa they may be slender, filamentous, or branching.

Psilocybe A genus of mushrooms growing in soil and dung. The Mexican species *P. mexicana* contains the hallucinogenic compounds psilocin and psilocybin. It was regarded as a sacred mushroom in Mexico and eaten during religious ceremonies. Mushrooms of the liberty cap fungus (*P. semilanceolata*) are common in pastures and lawns, having greyish-brown or olive-green conical caps.

psittacosis (*or* **parrot disease**) An infectious illness caused by a microorganism of the *Chlamydia* group, which is caught from birds, particularly parrots. The severity of the disease varies, but usually it causes pneumonia.

psoriasis A chronic recurring skin disease marked by excessive scaling of the skin. It begins with small red patches covered in scales and may spread extensively. The knees, elbows, lower back, scalp, and nails are most commonly affected.

psychedelic drugs *See* HALLUCINOGENS.

psychiatry The study and treatment of mental disorders. A psychiatrist is a medically qualified physician specializing in mental illness. The range of mental disorders includes *psychosis, *neurosis, psychosomatic disorders, *drug dependence, and mental retardation. Within psychiatry there are several specialities, notably child psychiatry, *psychotherapy, and geriatric psychiatry (psychogeriatrics).

psychoanalysis A school of *psychology and a method of treating mental disorders based upon the teachings of Sigmund *Freud (*see also* ADLER, ALFRED; JUNG, CARL GUSTAV). Psychoanalysis stresses the dynamic interplay of unconscious mental forces and the way in which the adult personality is determined by the course of sexual development in childhood. The chief techniques of psychoanalysis are free association and the recall of dreams in the course of intensive psychotherapy, the object being to bring repressed conflicts into consciousness so that they can be resolved. *See also* EGO; ID; OEDIPUS COMPLEX; REPRESSION; SUPEREGO.

psychology The scientific study of the behaviour of man and animals. Different schools of psychology use differing methods and have different theories. These include *behaviourism; experimental psychology; *Gestalt psychology; associationist psychology; and *psychoanalysis. Clinical psychology applies these approaches to the understanding and treatment of mental illness (*see also* PSYCHIATRY). Educational psychology studies the ways in which children learn, in order to intervene as problems arise. Occupational psychology studies people in their working environment. *See also* ETHOLOGY.

psychosis A severe mental illness in which the sufferer loses contact with reality. Organic psychoses are caused by diseases affecting the brain, such as epilepsy, alcoholism, and dementia; functional psychoses have no known physical cause. The major functional psychoses are *schizophrenia and manic-depressive psychosis. All psychoses can cause hallucinations, delusions, and altered thought processes.

psychotherapy Psychological methods of treatment for mental disorders. There are many different approaches to psychotherapy, including *psychoanalysis and *group therapy. In client-centred therapy the therapist refrains from giving any direct advice. Family therapy involves several members of a family meeting together with a therapist to improve their relationships. All these approaches share the goal of helping self-understanding and personal development through the relationship between the client and the therapist.

ptarmigan A grouse, *Lagopus lagopus*, found in Arctic tundra and mountain regions. 35 cm long, it has white wings and a mottled blackish-brown body that changes to white in winter. Its feet are covered with feathers and it feeds on shoots and fruits in summer and on lichens and leaves dug from the snow in winter.

pteridophyte A flowerless perennial vascular plant that shows a distinct *alternation of generations with the asexual spore-bearing (sporophyte) generation predominating. The sporophyte plant consists typically of leaves, stems, and roots and bears spores in special capsules (sporangia), which are often arranged in clusters (sori) on the leaves. Pteridophytes were formerly classified together in the division *Pteridophyta*, but in most modern classification systems they are assigned to separate divisions (or phyla). They include the clubmosses (*Lycophyta*), horsetails (*Sphenophyta*), whisk ferns (*Psilophyta*; mostly extinct), and ferns (*Filicinophyta*).

pterosaur (*or* **pterodactyl**) An extinct flying reptile that lived during the Jurassic and Cretaceous periods (200–65 million years ago). A thin wing membrane stretched from the elongated fourth finger of the fore limb along the body to the knee; a second membrane stretched to the neck. It had long slender hind limbs, probably used to cling, batlike, to rocks and trees. Its light bones and toothless beaked jaw resembled those of modern birds.

Ptolemaic system A theory concerning the motions of the sun, moon, and planets that was originally advanced in Greece in the 3rd century BC and was completed by *Ptolemy in the 2nd century AD. It was a geocentric system in which the moon, Mercury, Venus, Sun, Mars, Jupiter, and Saturn moved around the earth. Ptolemy proposed that each orbiting body moved in a small circle (an epicycle) the centre of which moved in a larger circle (a deferent) around the earth. The Ptolemaic system was finally abandoned when the heliocentric system of *Copernicus was accepted.

Ptolemy (*or* **Claudius Ptolemaeus**; 2nd century AD) Egyptian mathematician, astronomer, and geographer. The foremost of his works outlines the *Ptolemaic system of astronomy and was known to Arab astronomers by the Greek superlative *Megiste*, which took the Arab form *Almagest*, the name by which it is still known. His other works include *Analemma* and *Planisphaerium* on geometry and *Geographike hyphegesis*.

Ptolemy I Soter (?367–?283 BC) The first Macedonian King of Egypt and founder of the Ptolemaic dynasty. He was a general of Alexander the Great, after whose death he became governor of Egypt. He conquered Palestine, Cyprus, and much of Asia Minor, taking the title of king in 304. He made *Alexandria his capital, and wrote a history of Alexander's campaigns.

ptomaines Compounds formed during the bacterial decomposition of proteins in animal and plant tissues. Most are amines, such as diethylamine, putrescine, and cadaverine, and they may be poisonous, although the symptoms ascribed to "ptomaine poisoning" are usually due to bacterial toxins in contaminated food.

public school In the UK a fee-paying independent school, usually a boarding school with an established reputation. Although traditionally male preserves, most public schools now admit girls, especially at sixth-form level, and a number of well-known independent girls' schools were established in the 19th century; entrance is usually at 13. Any school the headteacher of which is a member of the Headmasters' and Headmistresses' Conference, the Governing Bodies Association, or the Governing Bodies of Girls' Schools Association is now usually regarded as a public school, making the total number about 200, although this includes many of the former direct-grant schools (state-assisted schools that have either been incorporated into the state system or become totally independent).

public sector Those parts of the economy that are financed out of taxation, are under state control, or both. It usually embraces central and local government, education, health and social services, and any nationalized industries. In the UK and many other countries certain businesses essential to the life of the community, such as the public utilities, were formerly nationalized but are now privately owned (*see* PRIVATIZATION). The amount by which the receipts of the public sector, including taxation, fall short of public expenditure constitutes the Public Sector Borrowing Requirement.

Puccini, Giacomo (1858–1924) Italian opera composer. His first major success was *Manon Lescaut* (1893). The operas that followed established Puccini as the master of the *verismo* (Italian: realism) style: *La Bohème* (1896), *Tosca* (1900), and *Madame Butterfly* (1904). *La fanciulla del West* (1910) and the three one-act operas of *Il Trittico* (1918) were less successful; his final masterpiece, *Turandot*, was produced posthumously in 1926.

Pueblo Indians North American Indian tribes of the SW region including the Tewa, Keres, Hopi, and Zuni. Their collective name derives from the Spanish term for their villages—*pueblos*. They began to abandon their hunting existence and adopt their present farming economy about 1600 years ago. They were always extremely peaceful peoples, much given to ritual and ceremonial pursuits. Communities were traditionally governed by a council of the heads of the various secret religious societies. The diversity of Pueblo languages indicates different origins.

Puerto Rico, Commonwealth of (name from 1898 until 1932: Porto Rico) An island and self-governing commonwealth in association with the USA. It is in the West Indies, the smallest and most easterly island in the Greater Antilles. It is largely mountainous, rising to over 1200 m (3937 ft), and supports one of the densest populations in the world. *Economy*: industrialization has transformed the economy since World War II. Manufacture (chemicals, textiles, plastics, food processing) is the main source of income, while in the agricultural sector income from dairy and livestock farming has overtaken that of sugar, the principal crop. *History*: discovered by Columbus in 1508, it was under Spanish rule for nearly 400 years until ceded to the USA in 1898. Full US citizenship was granted in 1917 and it attained its present status in 1952. Since the mid 1970s there has been militant pressure for the independence of Puerto Rico but also a strong lobby arguing for its incorporation as a state of the USA. In 1993 and 1998 Puerto Ricans voted against both these options, choosing to maintain their present status. Official languages: Spanish and English. Currency: US dollar of 100 cents. Area: 8674 sq km (3349 sq mi). Population (2002 est): 3 856 000. Capital: San Juan.

puff adder A large stout-bodied highly venomous *adder belonging to the genus *Bitis* (8 species), occurring in semiarid areas of Africa and characterized by its habit of hissing loudly and inflating its body in a threatening posture. Puff adders are brown or grey with yellow chevron patterning.

puffball The globular or pear-shaped fruiting body of certain fungi. As it matures, the outer layer cracks and sloughs off; the spongy interior produces powdery spores. The greyish-white giant puffball (*C. giganteum*) occurs in pastures, woodlands, and road verges and may reach over 1 m across. Phylum: *Basidiomycota*.

puffer A fish, also called globefish, belonging to the family *Tetraodontidae*, that inflates its body with air or water when disturbed. The tough spiny skin contains a highly toxic chemical (tetraodontoxin), which can be fatal. Puffers live mainly in tropical and subtropical seas, feeding on corals, molluscs, and crustaceans. Order: *Tetraodontiformes*.

puffin A N Atlantic seabird, *Fratercula arctica*. 29 cm long, it is black with a white face and underparts, red legs, and a blue ring around the eye. Its large triangular bill is striped red, yellow, and blue in the breeding season. It feeds at sea on fish and molluscs and breeds in disused rabbit burrows. Family: *Alcidae* (auks).

pug A breed of toy dog originating in China and introduced to Britain from Holland in the 17th century. It is stockily built, and has a wrinkled skin and a large head with a short square muzzle. The short smooth coat can be silver, black, or apricot-fawn with a black mask on the face. Height: 25–28 cm.

Pugin, Augustus Welby Northmore (1812–52) British architect and theorist. Pugin was the most vocal exponent of the English gothic revival. His most influential book, *Contrasts* (1836), exalted the English *Decorated style (late 13th to early 14th centuries) above all others. He was most accomplished at designing churches, such as Nottingham Cathedral (1842), but is best known for his collaboration with *Barry on the *Palace of Westminster, being responsible for the interior design.

Pulitzer Prizes Annual awards endowed by the US publisher Joseph Pulitzer (1847–1911) for achievements in journalism and literature. The prizes for journalism and for literature were first awarded in 1917. Since 1943 a prize for musical composition has also been awarded.

Pullman, Philip (1946–) British author. He writes primarily for older children, but has attracted readers of all ages. He is best known for *His Dark Materials*, a trilogy of fantasy novels comprising *Northern Lights* (1997), *The Subtle Knife* (1999), and *The Amber Spyglass* (2000).

pulsar A celestial object that emits extremely regular pulses of radiation and is almost certainly a rotating *neutron star. Pulsars were originally discovered, in 1967, at radio wavelengths. The Crab and Vela pulsars also emit pulses at optical and gamma-ray wavelengths. The pulses arise when a beam of radio waves emitted by the rotating star sweeps ast the earth. The radiation (synchrotron radiation) is generated by electrons moving in the star's strong magnetic field; the emission site is still uncertain. Pulsars are thought to originate in supernovae.

pulsating stars *See* VARIABLE STARS.

puma *See* COUGAR.

pumice A volcanic rock derived from acidic lava. It resembles sponge in having many cavities produced by bubbles of gas trapped on rapid solidification. Pumice is light in colour and weight and often floats on water.

pumpkin The fruit of certain varieties of *Cucurbita pepo* and *C. maxima*, small bushes or trailing vines cultivated in North America and Europe. The fruit is large and round, up to 30 kg in weight with a lightly furrowed yellow rind surrounding an edible fleshy pulp and numerous seeds. It is cooked and eaten as a vegetable, in pies, puddings, and soups or used as animal feed. Family: *Cucurbitaceae*.

Punic Wars Three wars between Rome and Carthage, which gave Rome control of the Mediterranean. The first Punic (from the Latin *Punicus*, Carthaginian) War (264–241 BC) was provoked by Roman intervention in Sicily and was marked by the emergence of Roman naval power: its newly built fleet was victorious off the Aegates Insulae (241), which brought the war to an end. The second Punic War (218–201) was instigated by Hannibal's capture (219) of Saguntum, a Roman ally in Spain. His advance into Italy was eventually checked by *Fabius Maximus and Scipio Africanus, who defeated Hannibal at Zama (202). Roman fears of a resurgence of Carthaginian power caused the third Punic War (149–146), in which Carthage was destroyed and its territory became the Roman province of Africa.

Punjab A region of the NW Indian subcontinent, in India and Pakistan below the Himalayan foothills on the flat alluvial plain of five Indus tributaries. Hot and dry, it produces grain surpluses with irrigation. Pulses, cotton, sugar cane, oilseeds, fruit, and vegetables are also grown. Industries include textiles, bicycles, electrical and metal goods, machinery, and food products. Its population is 60% Sikh in India's Punjab state, and almost entirely Muslim in Pakistan's Punjab province. *History*: the Punjab was conquered by Muslims (11th century) but eventually became a Sikh stronghold until Britain established control (19th century). On the partition of India and Pakistan (1947), the Punjab was divided on a religious basis. The W section became the Pakistan province of West Punjab (renamed Punjab in 1949), with an area of 205 346 sq km (79 284 sq mi) and its capital at Lahore; its population in 1998 was 72 585 000. The Indian section was reorganized in 1966 on a linguistic basis when the Punjabi-speaking state of Punjab was created, 50 376 sq km (19 445 sq mi), with its capital at Chandigarh; its population in 2001 was 24 289 296.

pupa A stage in the life cycle of certain insects, including flies, butterflies, ants, bees, and beetles, during which complete *metamorphosis from larva to adult takes place. The adult emerges by cutting or digesting the pupal case after a period of a few days to several months.

pupil *See* EYE; IRIS.

Purcell, Henry (1659–95) English composer and organist. In 1677 he was appointed composer to the orchestra of the Chapel Royal and, in 1682, organist there. He wrote keyboard pieces, sonatas, anthems, songs, cantatas, and much music for the stage, including incidental music for *King Arthur* (1691) and *The Fairy Queen* (1692) and one opera, *Dido and Aeneas* (1689).

purgatory In Roman Catholic doctrine, the state in which souls are purified after death to make them fit for heaven. Masses or prayers for the dead are believed to shorten a soul's purgatorial sufferings. The doctrine of purgatory was officially adopted by the Church in the late 6th century, but at the Reformation the Protestants rejected the concept.

Purim A Jewish festival, commemorating the frustration of an attempt to exterminate the Jews of the Persian Empire (473 BC), as narrated in the book of Esther. It is celebrated on the 14th Adar (Feb–March), with lighthearted festivities and charitable gifts.

purine An organic nitrogenous base ($C_5H_4N_4$) consisting of a two-ringed molecule of carbon and nitrogen atoms. The derivatives adenine and guanine are constituents of the nucleic acids *DNA and *RNA. Uric acid and *caffeine are also purines.

Puritanism A movement among Protestants in 16th- and 17th-century England. The term originally denoted members of the Church of England in Elizabeth I's reign who wished to eliminate elements in the Church's liturgy and hierarchy that were reminiscent of Roman Catholicism. In the 17th century the Puritans, many of them now forming extremist sects (*see* LEVELLERS), became associated with the parliamentarian side in the Civil War. After the Act of Uniformity (1662) the term *Nonconformists became generally applied to the sects of Puritan origin that survived.

Pusan 35 05N 129 02E A port in SE South Korea, on the Korea Strait, capital of South Kyongsang province and South Korea's second largest city. Its industries include shipbuilding. Population (1995): 3 813 814.

Pushkin, Aleksandr (1799–1837) Russian poet, novelist, and dramatist. In 1820 he was exiled to the southern provinces for his political verse. In exile he began the epic verse novel *Eugene Onegin* (1833), on which Tchaikovsky based his opera (1877–78). In 1824 he was transferred to NW Russia, where he wrote the historical drama *Boris Godunov* (1831). He returned to Moscow in 1826. During his last years he wrote the epic poem *The Bronze Horseman* (1837) as well as lyrical poetry and several prose works. He died of injuries sustained in a duel.

puss moth A moth, *Cerura vinula*, of Europe, Asia, and N Africa. The adult has a fat white hairy body with black spots. The caterpillar is green with black markings and when alarmed it presents a grotesque appearance with the head and tail appendages raised up. It feeds on sallow, willow, and poplar.

Putin, Vladimir (Vladimirovich) (1952–) Russian statesman; president of the Russian Federation (2000–). A former KGB colonel, he became head of Russia's security services in 1998 and prime minister in 1999. Appointed acting president on Yeltsin's resignation (31 December 1999), he became full president following elections in March 2000. His ruthless crushing of the revolt in *Chechenia (1999–2000) was criticized in the West but highly popular in Russia. He was re-elected in 2004.

Putrajaya 2 80N 101 40E The capital of Malaysia since 1999, in the SW Malay Peninsula. Construction of this high-tech garden city is expected to be complete in 2010, when it will house over 300 000 people.

Puttnam, David (Terence), Baron (1941–) British film producer, who was chairman (1986–87) of Columbia Pictures. His films include *Midnight Express* (1978), *Chariots of Fire* (1981), *The Killing Fields* (1984), *The Mission* (1986), and *My Life So Far* (1999). He was made a life peer in 1997.

PVC *See* POLYVINYL CHLORIDE.

Pygmalion In Greek mythology, a legendary king of Cyprus who made an ivory statue and fell in love with it. When he prayed for a wife who would be as beautiful as the statue, Aphrodite gave the statue life.

p

Pygmies Peoples of the tropical forest region of Africa, who are much smaller in stature than their Bantu neighbours. The males are less than 150 cm (4 ft 11 in) in height. They are nomadic hunters and gatherers, wandering in small and basically patrilineal exogamous bands of around 30 members. They speak various Bantu languages.

pygmy hippopotamus A small *hippopotamus, *Choeropsis liberiensis*, of West African forests. Up to 100 cm high at the shoulder and weighing about 200 kg, pygmy hippos frequent river banks, sleeping during the day and feeding in the forest at night.

P'yŏngyang 39 00N 125 47E The capital of the Democratic People's Republic of (North) Korea, in the NW on the River Taedong. Reputedly the oldest city in Korea, it is a major industrial as well as administrative centre. Population (1996 est): 2 500 000.

Pyracantha A genus of thorny evergreen shrubs (about 10 species), known as firethorns, native to SE Eurasia and widely cultivated as garden shrubs. A commonly grown species is *P. coccinea*. It has finely toothed leaves and white or pinkish-yellow flowers. The round scarlet berries may last all winter. Family: *Rosaceae*.

pyramids Royal funerary monuments in ancient Egypt. The greatest are the pyramids of *Khufu, Khafre, and Menkaura (Greek name: Mycerinus) at Giza (built c. 2600–2500 BC), the only survivors of the *Seven Wonders of the World. Pyramids were also built in ancient Mexico.

Pyramus and Thisbe Legendary lovers in a Babylonian story retold by *Ovid. The couple were forbidden to marry by their parents but exchanged vows through a chink in the wall between their houses. They arranged a secret meeting. Thisbe arrived first at the meeting place, which was near a mulberry tree; but she was frightened by a lion and fled, dropping her veil. Pyramus, finding her veil and thinking her dead, stabbed himself, and when Thisbe returned she killed herself also. The mulberry tree has borne blood-red fruit ever since. The rustics' farce in Shakespeare's *A Midsummer Night's Dream* is based on this story.

Pyrenean mountain dog (*or* **Great Pyrenees**) A breed of large dog, possibly of Asian origin, used in Europe for over 3000 years to guard shepherds and their flocks. They are massively built with drooping ears. The long thick slightly wavy coat is white, with or without grey or brown patches. Height: 71 cm (dogs); 66 cm (bitches).

Pyrenees (French name: Pyrénées; Spanish name: Pirineos) A mountain range in SW Europe. It extends between the Bay of Biscay in the W and the Mediterranean Sea in the E, forming a barrier between France and Spain. The entire republic of Andorra lies within the range, which rises to 3404 m (11 168 ft) at Pico de Aneto.

pyrethrum A perennial plant, *Chrysanthemum coccineum* (or *Pyrethrum roseum*), with finely divided leaves and showy red, pink, lilac, or white flowers. It is native to Persia and the Caucasus and widely cultivated for ornament in temperate regions. An insecticide is prepared from its dried flower heads. Family: *Compositae*.

Pyrex The trade name for a heat-resistant glass containing borosilicate. It is also resistant to many chemicals and is an electrical insulator. Pyrex is used in laboratory glassware, ovenware, and large telescopes.

pyridine (C_6H_5N) A hygroscopic colourless liquid, with a strong odour, which boils at 115°C. It is a basic aromatic compound with a six-membered heterocyclic molecule, made by passing tetrahydrofurfuryl alcohol and ammonia over a catalyst at 500°C. It is used as an industrial solvent and in the manufacture of various drugs and pesticides.

pyridoxine *See* VITAMIN B COMPLEX.

pyrimidine An organic base ($C_4H_4N_2$) consisting of a six-membered ring of carbon and nitrogen atoms. Its derivatives cytosine, thymine, and uracil are constituents of the nucleic acids *RNA and *DNA.

pyrite (*or* **iron pyrites**) A pale brassy yellow mineral, FeS_2, the most common sulphide mineral. It occurs as an accessory mineral in igneous rocks, in hydrothermal veins, in contact metamorphic rocks, and in sediments laid down in anaerobic conditions. It is usually mined for its sulphur, used for the manufacture of sulphuric acid, or for the gold and copper found in association with it. Because of its colour it has been called fool's gold.

pyroelectricity The development of opposite electric charges on opposite faces of asymmetric crystals when they are heated. The charges occur on those faces that are responsible for the crystal's asymmetry. Quartz and tourmaline have pyroelectric properties. *See also* PIEZOELECTRIC EFFECT.

pyrometer An instrument used for measuring high temperatures. The two most important types are the optical pyrometer and the radiation pyrometer. In the optical pyrometer a filament, heated to a known temperature, is viewed with the hot body in the background. The temperature of the filament is adjusted until it appears to vanish, at which point its temperature is the same as the temperature to be measured. In the radiation pyrometer, radiant heat from the hot body is focused into a *thermocouple, which develops a potential difference proportional to the temperature.

pyroxenes A group of ferromagnesian rock-forming silicate minerals. They usually occur in basic and ultrabasic igneous rocks but also in some metamorphosed rocks. Those of orthorhombic crystal structure are orthopyroxenes and those of monoclinic structure are clinopyroxenes. Orthopyroxenes vary in composition between the end-members enstatite ($MgSiO_3$) and orthoferrosilite ($FeSiO_3$). Clinopyroxenes, the larger group, include diopside, hedenbergite, augite, pigeonite, aegirine, jadeite, and spodumene (a source of lithium).

Pyrrhus (319–272 BC) King of Epirus (307–303, 297–272). Having secured his throne (297), Pyrrhus pursued an adventurous policy of expansion but his empire was short-lived: in support of Tarentum against Rome he won victories that cost much in loss of life ("Pyrrhic" victories), and he was forced to withdraw.

pyruvic acid An organic acid ($CH_3COCOOH$). Its anion, pyruvate (CH_3–CO–COO^-), is an important intermediate compound in the carbohydrate metabolism of living organisms.

Pythagoras (6th century BC) Greek philosopher and religious leader. Born at Samos, he migrated in about 530 BC to Crotone (S Italy), where he founded a religious society that governed Crotone for many years until its suppression (460–440 BC). Its members followed an ascetic regime aimed at purifying the soul and releasing it from "entombment" in successive bodies. Pythagoras probably discovered the geometrical theorem named after him and certainly discovered the arithmetical ratios governing musical intervals, which led him to interpret the universe in terms of mathematics alone. Pythagoreans were pioneers in several branches of science. *See also* ALCMAEON.

python A large *constrictor snake belonging to the Old World subfamily *Pythoninae* (20–25 species), occurring in tropical and temperate regions. Pythons usually live near water and tend to be sluggish, catching prey—which may include goats, pigs, and deer—by ambush. The reticulated python (*Python reticulatus*) is the largest of all constrictors, reaching 10 m in length. Family: *Boidae*.

Q

Qatar, State of A country in the Middle East, in Arabia. The native population is mainly Arab and Wahhabi Sunnite Muslim, but over 80% of workers are immigrants from other countries. *Economy*: oil extraction accounts for some 90% of the national income and Qatar is a member of OPEC. The export of natural gas is of growing importance. *History*: Qatar relied on Britain for most of the 19th and 20th centuries, becoming a protectorate in 1916; it became independent in 1971. In 1995 Sheikh Hamad bin Khalifa al-Thani became emir after ousting his father. Qatar was an absolute monarchy until 2003, when an elected national body was created. That same year a new constitution gave women the right to vote and hold office. Official language: Arabic. Currency: Qatar riyal of 100 dirhams. Area: 11 000 sq km (4246 sq mi). Population (2003 est): 626 000. Capital: Doha.

Qin (*or* **Ch'in**; 221–206 BC) The dynasty under which China became a unified empire. The first Qin emperor, Shi Huangdi (*or* Shih Huang Ti; c. 259–210 BC), consolidated his vast conquest by unifying weights, measures, and coinage and by creating one system of writing for the whole empire. It was during the Qin reign that much of the *Great Wall of China was built.

Qing (*or* **Ch'ing**; 1644–1911) A Manchu dynasty, founded by Nurhachi (1559–1626), that ruled China from the fall of the Ming dynasty until 1911. At its height in the 18th century under Qian Long (1711–99), the dynasty ruled a vast empire that included Outer Mongolia, Tibet, and Turkistan. Trade and commerce flourished, as did cultural life and learning. Bureaucratic conservatism, however, resisted modernization, corruption became rife, and China suffered a series of defeats by foreign powers (e.g. the *Opium Wars) as well as internal rebellions (e.g. the *Taiping Rebellion) that culminated in the overthrow of the Qing in 1911.

Qingdao (Ch'ing-tao *or* Tsingtao) 36 04N 120 22E A port in E China, in Shandong province on the Yellow Sea. From 1898 to 1922 it was under German and then Japanese control. Population (1999 est): 1 702 108.

Qom (*or* **Qum**) 34 39N 50 57E A city in central Iran, S of Tehran. It is the burial place of many Islamic saints. Population (1996): 777 677.

quadratic equation An algebraic equation in which the greatest power of the variable is two. It is usually written in the form $ax^2 + bx + c = 0$, in which the two *roots are given by $x = [-b \pm \sqrt{(b^2 - 4ac)}]/2a$. Both of these roots are real numbers when the quantity under the square-root sign is greater than or equal to zero. They are equal when that quantity is zero. If it is less than zero the roots are complex numbers.

quadriplegia *See* PARALYSIS.

Quadruple Alliances 1. (1718) The alliance formed by Britain, France, the Holy Roman Emperor, and the Netherlands to maintain the Treaties of *Utrecht (1713–14), which had been repudiated by Spain. **2.** (1814) The alliance formed by Britain, Austria, Prussia, and Russia against Napoleon. **3.** (1834) The alliance between Britain, France, Spain, and Portugal that sought to maintain constitutional monarchy in Spain and Portugal.

quail A round-bodied short-tailed gamebird of open grassland and farmland. Old World quail (subfamily *Perdicinae*; 95 species) are 13–20 cm long, have a smooth-edged bill and leg spurs, and are usually sandy in colour. New World quail (subfamily *Odontophorinae*; 36 species) are up to 30 cm long and have a strong serrated bill, no leg spurs, and are brightly coloured and patterned. Family: *Phasianidae* (pheasants, partridges, and quail).

Quakers The Christian sect, formally known as the Religious Society of Friends, founded in England by George *Fox in the late 1640s. They suffered violent persecution for many years and in 1682 William *Penn led a colony of Friends to *Pennsylvania. In the USA they were leaders in the fight against *slavery. The early Quakers adopted an unostentatious dress and way of life. They were (and remain) pacifists, refused to take oaths, and rejected the use of titles.

quaking grass An annual or perennial *grass of the genus *Briza* (about 20 species), mostly native to South America. Their long slender flower stalks bear spikelets of open flower clusters, which quiver in the wind. *B. media* is native to temperate Eurasia and grows 20–50 cm high.

quantity theory of money A theory that seeks to explain how the money supply (*see* MONEY) affects the economy. Originally put forward in the 17th century, it has been restated in its modern form by the US economist Milton *Friedman. It states that if there is a change in the money supply, either the price level will change or the supply of goods in the economy will alter.

quantum number An integral or half-integral number (0, ½, 1, 1½, 2, ...) that gives the possible values of a property of a system according to the *quantum theory. For example, in Bohr's atomic theory the angular momentum of an electron moving in orbit round an atomic nucleus can only have the values $nh/2\pi$, where n is a quantum number specifying these values and h is Planck's constant. Bohr's theory has now been replaced by the more versatile *wave mechanics, but the concept of quantum numbers is useful in some contexts. It is also used to quantify the properties of elementary particles (*see* PARTICLE PHYSICS).

quantum theory The theory first developed by Max *Planck in 1900 to explain the distribution of wavelengths of electromagnetic radiation emitted by a *black body. The experimental observations could only be explained when Planck assumed that the radiation was emitted and absorbed in discrete amounts, which he called quanta. The energy of each quantum has the value hf, where h is a universal constant (now known as the Planck constant) and f is the frequency of the radiation. Planck's theory was used by *Einstein to explain the photoelectric effect and in 1913 by Niels *Bohr to explain the spectrum of hydrogen. **Quantum mechanics** is the application of quantum theory to the mechanics of atomic systems; **quantum electrodynamics** is the theory of *electromagnetic interactions between elementary particles.

quarantine The period during which a person or animal suspected of carrying an infectious disease is kept in isolation. The term was originally applied to the 40-day period (French: *quarantaine*) during which ships suspected of carrying infected people were prevented from communicating with the shore. The quarantine period is now slightly longer than the incubation period of the disease. Until 2000 all domestic animals entering the UK had to undergo a six-month quarantine to prevent the importation of rabies. Under the new "passport for pets" scheme, this quarantine requirement has been lifted for animals from rabies-free countries with proof of vaccination and a fixed microchip to identify them.

quarter days In law, days in each quarter of the year on which rent and other dues on land were traditionally paid. In England they are 25 March (Lady Day), 24 June (Midsummer Day), 29 Sept (Michaelmas Day), and 25 Dec (Christmas Day).

quartz The commonest of all minerals, consisting of crystalline *silica. It occurs in many rocks, particularly acid igneous rocks (such as granite), many metamorphic rocks (such as gneisses), and in sands and gravels, which form sandstones on consolidation. Pure quartz is colourless and is known as rock crystal; it is used in glassmaking, in jewellery, and (because of its piezoelectric properties) in making electrical oscillators. Some coloured varieties, such as amethyst (violet), rose quartz (pink), and citrine (yellow), are used as gemstones.

quartzite A resistant pale-coloured rock consisting almost wholly of quartz. It is formed by the metamorphism of a pure sandstone, the original quartz grains being recrystallized and interlocking.

quasar (*quasi*-stell*ar* object; **QSO**) A class of celestial objects discovered in 1964–65. They appear as starlike points of light but are each emitting more energy than several hundred giant galaxies. Quasar *redshifts are extremely large and indicate that quasars are the most distant and hence the youngest extragalactic objects known. The prodigious energy could result from matter spiralling into a supermassive *black hole (maybe 10^9 solar masses) lying at the centre of a galaxy.

Quasimodo, Salvatore (1901–68) Italian poet. His early work, such as *And Suddenly It's Night* (1942), was evocative and private, but after World War II his poetry, as in *Il falso e vero verde* (1956), expressed his active concern for social issues. He won the Nobel Prize in 1959.

Quassia A genus of tropical Asian trees and shrubs (40 species). Bitterwood (*Q. amara*) is an attractive shrub with red flowers. The heartwood is a source of quassiin, used in medicine. Family: *Simaroubaceae*.

Quaternary period The most recent period of geological time, from the end of the Tertiary (about 1.8 million years ago) to the present day. It includes the Pleistocene (Ice Age) and *Holocene epochs.

Quebec 1. 46 50N 71 15W A city and port in E Canada, the capital of Quebec. First settled in 1608, it is strategically located above a sudden narrowing of the St Lawrence River. Quebec was the key to New France until captured by Britain (1759). Most of the workforce is employed by government and service industries. The Plains of *Abraham lie to the SW of the city. Population (1996): 167 264. **2.** The largest province of Canada, stretching from the *St Lawrence River N to Hudson Bay and Strait. Most of the population lives in the St Lawrence valley. The SE strip of Quebec enters the fertile Appalachian Highlands. The province's highly industrialized economy is based on its abundant natural resources. Asbestos, iron-ore, copper, zinc, gold, and other minerals are mined. Fishing, farming, and tourism are also important. *History*: claimed by France (1534), Quebec or New France was a French colony (1608–1763) until ceded to Britain. French-Canadian culture was preserved after the formation of Canada (1867). In 1995 a proposal that Quebec should become a sovereign state was very narrowly rejected in a referendum within the province. Area: 1 356 791 sq km (523 858 sq mi). Population (2001 est): 7 410 500; over 80% are French speaking. Capital: Quebec. *See also* MONTREAL.

Quechua The language of the *Incas and of the present-day American Indian peoples of the central Andean highlands. The people are nominally Roman Catholic but many pagan beliefs and rituals survive.

Queen Anne style An English architectural and decorative style with some baroque elements, dating from about 1700 to 1715. Beautiful walnut veneered furniture was made, enhanced by the restrained use of herringbone inlays. Chairs became lighter, more comfortable, and invariably had cabriole legs. Plateglass wall mirrors in gilt frames decorated panelled rooms.

Queen Charlotte Islands An archipelago of W Canada, in British Columbia 160 km (100 mi) off the Pacific coast. Mountainous with lush vegetation, the islands are mostly inhabited by Haida Indians engaged in fishing and forestry. Area: 9596 sq km (3705 sq mi). Population (1991): 5316.

Queen's Award An award to industry in the UK, instituted in 1965 and made on the birthday (21 April) of Queen Elizabeth II. Awarded to firms, rather than individuals, it entitles holders to make use of a special emblem for five years.

Queen's Counsel (**QC**) A barrister appointed to senior rank as counsel to the English queen on the recommendation of the Lord Chancellor. Such a barrister is a **King's Counsel** during the reign of a king. QCs have no special duties to the Crown; they wear a silk gown, sit within the Bar of the court, and take precedence over the "utter barristers" (i.e. the outer barristers, who sit outside the Bar).

Queensland The second largest state of Australia, situated in the NE. The *Great Dividing Range separates the hilly coastlands from the vast inland plain and the *Great Barrier Reef runs parallel to the Pacific coast. The area is rich in natural resources, which form the basis of Queensland's rapid economic progress. Coal is the most important mineral. Other minerals include copper, bauxite, lead, silver, and zinc; oil production began in 1964; natural gas is piped to Brisbane. Beef, sugar, and wool are major industries. Another growing industry is tourism. Area: 1 728 000 sq km (667 000 sq mi). Population (1999 est): 3 512 360. Capital: Brisbane.

quelea A small brown African weaverbird, *Quelea quelea*, about 13 cm long, also called the red-billed dioch. Queleas live in vast colonies: they destroy grain crops, frequently causing famine, and also damage the trees in which they roost.

Quemoy (Chinese name: Jinmen) A Chinese island near the coast of the mainland, held by Taiwan but contested by the People's Republic who bombed it in 1958. Area: 130 sq km (50 sq mi). Population (1996 est): 53 237.

Quetta 30 15N 67 00E A city in W central Pakistan, at an altitude of 1650 m (5500 ft). The chief town of Baluchistan, it was badly damaged by an earthquake in 1935. Population (1998): 560 387.

quetzal A Central American bird, *Pharomachus mocinno*, that lives in cloud forests and feeds on fruit, insects, tree frogs, and lizards. The male reaches 1.3 m in length, including its curved ornamental tail feathers; its plumage is iridescent green, red, and white. Family: *Trogonidae* (trogons).

Quetzalcoatl A Mexican wind and fertility god, usually portrayed as a feathered snake. During the Aztec period (14th–16th centuries) he was identified with the planet Venus, symbol of death and resurrection.

Quezon City 14 39N 121 01E A city in the N Philippines, in S Luzon near to Manila. It was the nation's former capital (1948–76). Population (2000): 2 173 831.

quillwort A small perennial nonvascular flowerless plant of the genus *Isoetes* (about 60 species), which grows mainly in swampy cooler regions of N North America and Eurasia. Tufts of stiff spiky quill-like leaves, about 5–18 cm long, grow from a short stout rhizome that bears numerous roots. The common Eurasian quillwort (*I. lacustris*) is aquatic. Order: *Isoetales*; phylum: *Lycophyta* (clubmosses, etc.).

quince A small tree or shrub, *Cydonia vulgaris*, probably native to W Asia but cultivated in temperate regions for its fruit. 4.5–6 m high, it has white or pink flowers, 5 cm across. The pear-shaped fruit is 7.5–10 cm long with a golden-yellow skin and many pips. Family: *Rosaceae*.

quinine The first drug used to treat malaria. Quinine, which is obtained from the bark of *Cinchona* trees, has now been largely replaced by other drugs (e.g. chloroquine), which have fewer side effects and are less toxic. Quinine-like compounds (e.g. quinidine) are used to treat abnormal heart rhythms.

quinone ($O:C_6H_4:O$) An *aromatic compound with two hydrogen atoms in the benzene ring replaced by two oxygen atoms. Quinones are used in photography and dye manufacture. They are also found in plants.

quinsy An abscess in the tissue surrounding a tonsil. This arises from infection of the tonsils and may be a complication of tonsillitis. The patient has a sore throat and difficulty in swallowing. Quinsy is sometimes treated by surgical draining of the abscess.

Quisling, Vidkun (Abraham Lauritz Jonsson) (1887–1945) Norwegian army officer and Nazi collaborator, whose name is a synonym for "traitor." After serving as a diplomat, Quisling formed (1933) the fascist National Union Party in Norway. He encouraged the Nazi occupation of Norway (1940), and as "minister president" in the occupation government, sent a thousand Jews to concentration camps. Arrested in 1945, he was found guilty of war crimes and executed.

Quito 0 20S 78 45W The capital of Ecuador, on the slopes of the volcano Pichincha at an altitude of 2850 m (9350 ft). It was the capital of the Inca kingdom of Quito until 1534, when it was captured by the Spanish. It contains many Spanish-colonial churches. Population (1997 est): 1 487 513.

Qumeran, Khirbat The site on the NW shore of the Dead Sea in Israel, where a Jewish sect called the *Essenes lived from about 125 BC to 68 AD. The community produced the *Dead Sea Scrolls, found by Bedouin shepherds in 1947 in nearby caves.

R

Ra (*or* **Re**) The Egyptian sun god and lord of creation, portrayed with a falcon's head bearing a solar disc. During the 18th dynasty (1567–1320 BC) he became identified with the Theban god Amon as Amon-Ra.

Rabat (Arabic name: Ribat) 34 00N 6 42W The capital of Morocco, near the Atlantic coast. Founded in the 12th century, it became the capital under the French protectorate in the early 20th century. Population (1994 est): 623 457.

rabbi A Jewish scholar and religious authority. For a long time the rabbinate was not a salaried office; the title indicated scholarly achievement and legal competence. In modern Jewish communities rabbis are community leaders, preachers, and pastoral workers.

rabbit A burrowing *mammal belonging to the family *Leporidae* (which also includes the hares). The European rabbit (*Oryctolagus cuniculus*) grows to about 45 cm; it has long ears, a short tail, and soft grey-brown fur. Rabbits are gregarious, living in large warrens and feeding on grasses and vegetation. Order: *Lagomorpha*.

Rabelais, François (1483–1553) French satirist. He became a Franciscan and then a Benedictine monk, left the monastery to practise medicine, and visited Italy. His humanism is expressed in his works of inventive and often coarse comic satire, *Pantagruel* (1532), *Gargantua* (1534), *Tiers Livre* (1546), and *Quart Livre* (1552). The classic English translation of his works is by Sir Thomas Urquhart (1653).

rabies An acute viral infection of the brain that can affect all warm-blooded animals and may be transmitted to man through the bite of an infected animal (usually a dog). Symptoms, which appear after an incubation period of from ten days to two years, include painful spasms of the throat on swallowing. Later, the very sight of water induces convulsions and paralysis (hence the alternative name of the disease—hydrophobia, literally "fear of water") and the patient eventually dies in a coma. Antirabies vaccine and rabies antiserum given to patients immediately after they have been bitten may prevent the infection from developing. In the UK there are strict quarantine regulations for imported domestic animals to prevent the disease from reaching Britain.

Rabin, Yitzhak (1922–95) Israeli politician; Labour prime minister (1974–77, 1992–95). He was a chief of staff of the Israeli army (1964–68) and minister of defence (1984–90). In 1993 he signed a peace agreement with Yassir *Arafat of the PLO; he shared the Nobel Peace Prize in 1994 with Arafat and Shimon Peres. He was assassinated by a right-wing Jewish extremist.

raccoon An omnivorous mammal belonging to the genus *Procyon* (7 species), of the Americas. About 1 m long, raccoons are stockily built, with long hind legs and short forelegs. A black patch across the eyes and a striped tail contrast with the grey coat. Family: *Procyonidae*; order: *Carnivora*.

Rachmaninov, Sergei (1873–1943) Russian composer, pianist, and conductor. He spent most of the rest of his life (from 1917) in the USA. His works include four operas, three symphonies, four piano concertos (which he also recorded), the *Rhapsody on a Theme of Paganini* (1934), and *The Bells* (1910).

Racine, Jean (1639–99) French dramatist. His major classical verse tragedies, which were influenced initially by those of Pierre *Corneille, include *Andromaque* (1667), *Britannicus* (1669), *Bérénice* (1670), and *Phèdre* (1677). In 1677 he retired, married, and accepted a post at the court of Louis XIV. His final works were two religious dramas, *Esther* (1689) and *Athalie* (1691).

rad The unit of absorbed dose of ionizing radiation in the *c.g.s. system equal to an energy

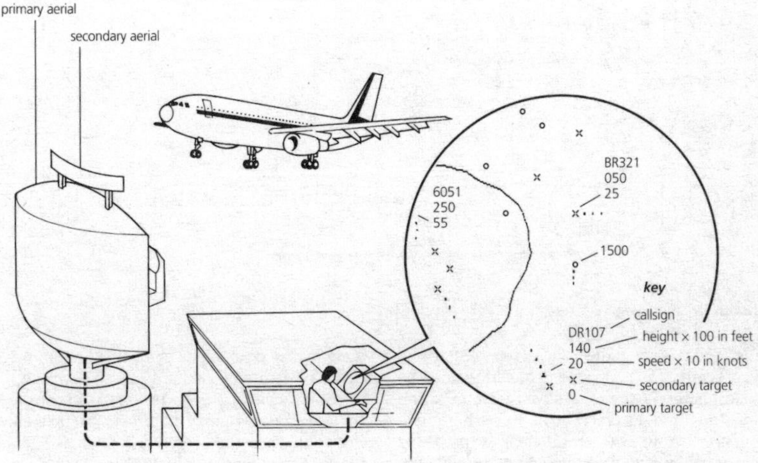

radar. The high-frequency pulses sent out by the transmitting aerial are reflected back by the target and displayed on a screen. The typical air-traffic control picture seen here shows East Anglia (only a few of the targets are labelled, for clarity).

absorption of 100 ergs per gram of irradiated material.

radar (*ra*dio *d*etection *a*nd *r*anging) A method of locating distant objects used in military surveillance, air traffic control, and navigation; it was developed before World War II by a British team led by Sir Robert *Watson-Watt. High-frequency (300 to 30 000 megahertz) radio waves are sent out in pulses from a powerful rotating transmitter and are reflected back by any object they encounter. The reflected signal is picked up by a receiver antenna and is used to deflect the electron beam in a *cathode-ray tube. The beam scans the screen of the tube by rotating at the same speed as the antenna, so that its angular position indicates the direction of the located object. The distance from the centre of the screen shows the distance away of the object.

radian (rad) The SI unit of plane angle equal to the angle subtended at the centre of a circle by an arc equal in length to the radius of the circle.

radiation The propagation of energy by means of beams of particles or waves. It includes all electromagnetic waves, beams of elementary particles, ions, etc., and sound waves.

radiation sickness Illness caused by exposure to *ionizing radiation. Short-term effects include nausea and diarrhoea, while long-term effects include sterility and cancer (especially leukaemia).

radical A group of atoms in a chemical compound that behaves as a unit in chemical reactions. For example, the methanol molecule (CH_3OH) can be considered as a methyl radical (CH_3.) and a hydroxyl radical (.OH) which is the functional group of alcohols. **Free radicals** are groups existing independently. Because they have unpaired electrons they are usually extremely reactive transient species.

radio The transmission of sound or other information by radio-frequency (3 kilohertz to 300 gigahertz) electromagnetic waves. The use of radio waves for communication was pioneered by *Marconi in 1895, although their existence had been postulated by *Maxwell in 1873 and demonstrated by *Hertz in 1888.

A **radio transmitter** generates a radio-frequency electrical signal (carrier wave) in an oscillator and superimposes the sound signal on it by a *modulation process. The composite signal is then fed to an aerial, which transmits electromagnetic waves. Transmission beyond the horizon is made possible by the ionosphere, a layer of the upper atmosphere that reflects radio waves in the long and medium wavebands. Long-wave (30 to 300 kilohertz) and medium-wave (300 to 3000 kilohertz) radio is used for direct (ground-wave) transmission in amplitude-modulated (AM) sound broadcast-

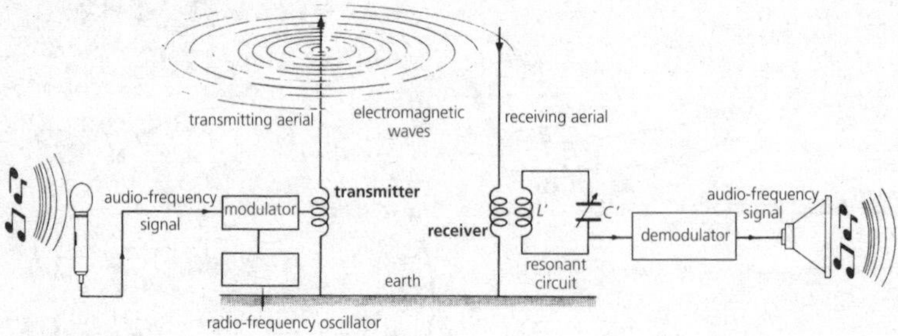

radio. The transmission and reception of radio broadcasts.

ing. Short-wave radio is used for AM sound broadcasting over longer distances using the ionosphere (sky waves) and for communication to ships and aircraft. VHF (very high frequency; 30 to 300 megahertz) is used for *stereophonic sound broadcasting in frequency modulated (FM) transmissions. Television uses mostly UHF (ultrahigh frequency). Neither VHF nor UHF are reflected by the ionosphere, but can be relayed by *communications satellites. All **radio receivers** consist of an *aerial, a resonant circuit, a demodulator, an amplification system, and one or more *loudspeakers,

radioactive tracer A radioactive *isotope used for following the course of a substance during a physical, biological, or chemical process. A nonradioactive isotope in the substance is replaced by a radioactive isotope of the same element, which can then be detected by observing its radiation with a *Geiger counter.

radioactive waste Waste products from nuclear reactors, uranium processing plants, etc., that are radioactive. Because the radioactivity of some materials persists for many years, their disposal is controlled. High-level waste (spent nuclear fuel, etc.) needs artificial cooling and is stored by its producers for decades before disposal. Intermediate-level waste (reactor components, etc.) is mixed with concrete and stored in steel drums prior to burial in deep mines or beneath the seabed in concrete chambers. Low-level waste in the UK is disposed of by Nirex Ltd in steel drums in concrete trenches at Driggs, Cumbria. Disposal of wastes in the Atlantic was banned in 1983. Some low-level gaseous and liquid wastes are discharged into the air.

radioactivity The spontaneous emission of a particle by an atomic nucleus. The emitted particle may be an alpha particle (a helium nucleus consisting of two protons and two neutrons), in which case the process is known as alpha decay; or it may be a beta particle (an electron), when the process is known as *beta decay. Highly energetic X-rays (*see* GAMMA RADIATION) may also be emitted simultaneously. In both alpha and beta decay the nucleus changes into that of another element. Radioactive decay is a random process and its occurrence for a single nucleus can be neither predicted nor controlled. However, for a large number of nuclei the time taken for a certain fraction of nuclei to decay can be accurately predicted as either its *mean life or *half-life. These quantities vary from about 10^{-8} second to 10^{10} years depending on the isotope. The phenomenon was first discovered in 1898 by *Becquerel in uranium.

radio astronomy The study of celestial objects by means of the radio waves they emit. This radio emission was first noticed by K.G. *Jansky in 1932 and now forms an important branch of *astronomy. It has enabled the evolution of the universe to be studied from its creation (*see* BIG-BANG THEORY).

radiocarbon dating A method of estimating the age of a material, such as wood, that was once living. All living things absorb a small proportion of carbon-14 from atmospheric carbon dioxide, however, once dead, the level of carbon-14 falls as a result of *beta decay. By measuring the radioactivity of a material, the concentration of carbon-14 and hence its age can be estimated.

radio galaxy A *radio source that lies beyond our Galaxy, is identified with an optical *galaxy, and the radio-power output of which greatly exceeds that of a normal galaxy. A massive *black hole at the galaxy centre has been postulated as a possible energy source.

radiography The technique of examining the internal structure of a solid body by passing *X-rays or *gamma radiation through it to produce an image on a photographic film or fluorescent screen. It is used in medicine (*see* RADIOLOGY) and in industry to find structural defects.

radio interferometer *See* RADIO TELESCOPE.

radioisotope (*or* **radioactive isotope**) An *isotope that is radioactive. Radioisotopes are used in the production of *nuclear energy, in *radiotherapy, as *radioactive tracers, and in dating techniques. Some are naturally occurring (those with mass numbers in excess of 208) while others can be made radioactive by neutron bombardment.

radiolarian Any one of a group of single-celled marine organisms (*see* PROTOZOA), traditionally regarded as a class or order, *Radiolaria*, but now usually classified in several different classes, occurring chiefly as a component of plankton. Radiolarians are spherical, 0.1 mm to several millimetres in diameter, with a siliceous skeleton of radiating spines from which long thin pseudopodia extend to capture food particles. The skeletal remains of radiolarians form radiolarian ooze. Phylum: *Actinopoda*.

radiology The branch of medicine concerned with the use of radiation in the diagnosis and treatment of disease. A radiologist is a doctor specialized in the interpretation of X-ray photographs and films. *See also* RADIOTHERAPY; TOMOGRAPHY.

radio source A celestial object that emits radio waves. The sun and Jupiter are solar-system sources. Other radio sources within our Galaxy are pulsars, supernova remnants, interstellar hydrogen clouds, and the galactic centre. Extragalactic sources include spiral galaxies, radio galaxies, and some quasars.

radio telescope An instrument for detecting and measuring the radio emissions from celestial *radio sources. It consists of an antenna, or system of antennas, the radio-frequency signals of which are carried by wires or waveguides to one or more receivers. The antenna may be a large metal parabolic or spherical dish, usually steerable, that brings radio waves from a radio source to a focus on a secondary antenna. Alternatively simple dipole antennas may be used. The **radio interferometer**, in two separate units, has a very much greater resolving power than a single antenna. The largest single radio telescope dish in the world is that at Arecibo, Puerto Rico; it measures 305 m (1000 ft) across. The best-known radio telescope in the UK is that at Jodrell Bank.

radiotherapy The use of X-rays and other forms of radiation for treating disease. The radiation may be directed at the target organ from a distance or radioactive needles, wires, pellets, etc., may be implanted in the body. Radiation is used in treating various forms of *cancer and overactivity of the thyroid gland.

radish An annual or biennial herb, *Raphanus sativus*, widely grown for its edible root, which may be red, white, or purple. The plant bears white flowers. Family: *Cruciferae*.

radium (Ra) A metallic element, discovered in pitchblende in 1898 by Pierre and Marie Curie. It is a divalent alkaline-earth element, forming a number of simple salts, such as the chloride ($RaCl_2$). It decays to form the noble gas radon and is used in radiotherapy. At no 88; at wt (226); mp 700°C; bp 1140°C.

radon (Rn) The heaviest noble gas, produced by the decay of radium, thorium, and actinium. It is radioactive, the longest-lived isotope (^{222}Rn) having a half-life of 3.825 days. Like the other noble gases, Rn forms clathrates and fluorides. At no 86; at wt (222); mp −71°C; bp −61.8°C.

raffia (*or* **raphia**) A *palm tree of the genus *Raphia*, especially *R. pedunculata* (or *R. ruffia*), native to Madagascar. Its leaves, up to 20 m long, are composed of 80–100 leaflets from which the fibre is torn in thin strips and dried in the sun. Raffia is woven into mats and baskets and used in horticulture, etc.

Rafflesia A genus of Malaysian parasitic herbs (12 species). The monster plant (*R. arnoldii*) has the world's largest flower—up to 45 cm across and weighing up to 10 kg. It smells of rotten meat and attracts carrion flies, which act as pollinators. The genus was named after Sir Stamford Raffles (1781–1826). Family: *Rafflesiaceae*.

Raglan, FitzRoy James Henry Somerset, 1st Baron (1788–1855) British field marshal. In 1854 he became commander in the *Crimean War and, in spite of success at *Inkerman, his strategy was much criticized (*see also* BALACLAVA, BATTLE OF). The Raglan sleeve is named after him.

Ragnarök In Norse mythology, doomsday, when a catastrophic battle between the gods and the forces of evil will occur. After the defeat of the gods everyone will be destroyed except for Lif and Lifthrasir, a man and woman who will subsequently found a new race.

ragtime A precursor of New Orleans style jazz. Ragtime was characterized by syncopation in the melody against a marchlike accompaniment and was popular from the 1890s. Scott *Joplin was the first ragtime composer to write down his music.

ragworm A marine *annelid worm, *Nereis cultrifera*, also called chainworm, of European coastal waters. 5–10 cm long, ragworms swim by means of paddle-like structures occurring in pairs on each body segment. Most live in burrows in sand or mud or among stones, feeding on dead organisms and detritus. Class: *Polychaeta.*

rail A slender secretive ground-dwelling bird belonging to a widely distributed family (*Rallidae*; about 300 species), occurring mostly in swamps, marshes, and fresh waters. 11–45 cm long, rails have short rounded wings, a short tail, and typically a dull grey or brown plumage, often barred for camouflage. Order: *Gruiformes* (cranes, rails, etc.). *See also* COOT; CORNCRAKE; GALLINULE.

railway A permanent track, consisting of parallel steel rails laid on sleepers of wood or concrete, on which *locomotive-drawn or self-propelled trains for freight or passengers travel. The normal gauge of the track is 1435 mm, in Russia and Finland 1676 mm, in Ireland 1600 mm, and in Spain and Portugal 1524 mm. Narrow gauge railways of 600–1200 mm gauge are common in Japan, parts of South America, and Africa. Trains were originally powered by steam, but are now nearly exclusively drawn by diesel or electric locomotives. The first passenger service was opened in 1825 between Stockton and Darlington in England. Railway building on the European continent and in Scandinavia started in the mid-1850s. The first Pacific railway in the USA was finished in 1869, the Trans-Siberian in Russia in 1905. From the 1950s, railways met increased competition from road and air travel, many railways being abandoned, or services curtailed. More recently increasing congestion on the roads has led to new opportunities for the railways. In the UK special passenger trains attain speeds of over 200 km per hr (125 mph), while in Japan and France speeds reach over 300 km per hr (186 mph). The USA has 338 000 km (209 000 mi) of railway, India 60 200 km (37 400 mi), and Australia 41 500 km (25 800 mi).

rain A form of precipitation composed of liquid water drops ranging in size from about 0.5 to 5 mm diameter. Minute droplets of water in clouds may coalesce to form larger drops; if these are sufficiently heavy they will fall as rain. The amount of rain, together with other forms of precipitation, that falls in a specific time is usually measured with a **rain gauge**. This is a cylindrical container with a funnel of standard diameter into which the rain falls. The water collected is periodically measured and recorded.

rainbow An optical phenomenon consisting of an arc of light across the sky composed of the colours of the spectrum. It is caused by the refraction of sunlight through falling water drops; the larger the drops the stronger the colours.

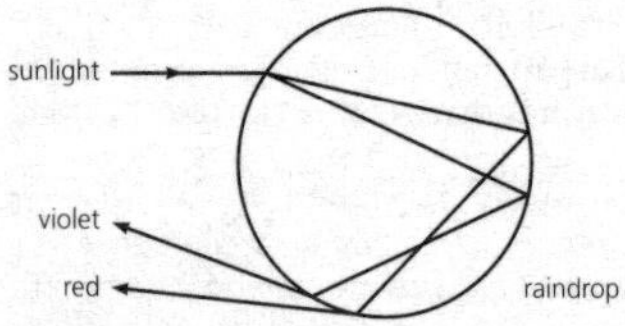

rainbow. The refraction of light by a raindrop.

rain forest *See* FOREST.

Rainier III (1923–) Prince of Monaco (1949–). He repudiated the principle of the *divine right of kings in a new constitution (1962). In 1956 he married Grace *Kelly. Their three children are Prince Albert (1958–), Princess Caroline (1957–), and Princess Stephanie (1965–).

Rajkot 22 18N 70 53E A city in India, in Gujarat. It is a commercial and industrial centre. Population (1991): 556 137.

Rajput A group of clans in N and central India, now numbering about 11 million people. Descended from invading tribes from Central Asia, they were once included within the Ksatriya (warrior) caste of Hindu society. The Rajput states resisted the Muslim invaders, maintaining their independence in Rajasthan. They acknowledged the overlordship of the Moguls in the 16th century, the Marathas in the 18th century, and the British in 1808.

Raleigh, Sir Walter (1554–1618) British explorer and writer; a favourite of Elizabeth I. Unsuccessful in founding (1584–89) a colony in Virginia, he brought back the potato and tobacco plant from America. In 1595–96 he led an expedition to South America, which he described in *The Discoverie of Guiana* (1596), and in 1596 took part in the sack of Cádiz. At James I's accession (1603) he stood trial for treason, but the death sentence was commuted to imprisonment; while in the Tower of London he wrote *The History of the World* (1614). He was released in 1616 to search for gold along the Orinoco but his mission was a failure and after his return he was executed.

Rama The seventh incarnation of *Vishnu, appearing as a hero in the epics the *Ramayana* and *Mahabharata*. In the *Upanishads* and elsewhere he appears as a god. He is usually represented holding a bow and arrow and attended by his wife.

Ramadan The ninth month of the Muslim year. It is a time of atonement, and every Muslim is required to observe a strict fast daily from dawn to dusk until the new moon of the next month is visible.

Ramapithecus A genus of fossil *hominids that lived during the late Miocene and early Pliocene. They were about the size of a gibbon, possibly walked erect, and may represent the early ancestors of modern man.

Ramayana (Sanskrit: romance of Rama) Hindu epic poem in seven books. It tells the story of *Rama and his devoted wife Sita, her abduction by the demon king Ravana, and Rama's struggle to recover her with the aid of *Hanuman.

Rambert, Dame Marie (Cyvia Rabbam, later Miriam Rambach; 1888–1982) British ballet dancer and choreographer, born in Poland. As director of the Carmargo Society, which in 1935 became the Ballet Rambert, she trained and encouraged many young British dancers and choreographers.

Rameau, Jean Philippe (1683–1764) French composer. He wrote a *Traité de l'harmonie* (1722), before beginning to compose. His works include chamber, keyboard, and vocal music, as well as 24 operas and opera-ballets, including *Les Indes galantes* (1735) and *Castor et Pollux* (1737).

Ramillies, Battle of (23 May 1706) The battle in the War of the *Spanish Succession in which Marlborough defeated the French 21 km (13 mi) N of Namur. The victory gave much of the Spanish Netherlands to the allies.

Ramsay, Sir William (1852–1916) Scottish chemist, whose work on the *noble gases earned him the 1904 Nobel Prize for Chemistry. In 1894, Ramsay, working with Rayleigh, discovered argon. By fractionally distilling argon, Ramsay isolated neon, xenon, and krypton in 1898. In 1895 he had discovered the inert gas, helium, being given off by the mineral cleveite.

Ramses (II) the Great King of Egypt (1304–1237 BC) of the 19th dynasty. His warfare against the Hittites ended in lasting peace around 1284. Ramses also built the temple complex of *Abu Simbel. He is probably the pharaoh who oppressed the Israelites.

Rangoon (name from 1989: Yangon) 16 47N 96 10E The capital of Myanmar (Burma), a port in the S on the River Rangoon. Industry has increased greatly since independence in 1948. *History*: a settlement grew up in very early times around the Shwe Dagon Pagoda, which is the focal point of Burmese religious life. Twice captured by the British in the 19th century, it became the capital of all Burma in 1886. It was badly damaged in World War II. Population (1995): 3 851 000.

Ranunculaceae A family of herbaceous and woody plants (about 1300 species), found all over the world but most abundant in N temperate and Arctic regions. The family includes many garden flowers, such as *Anenome*, *Aquilegia*, *Clematis*, and *Delphinium*, as well as common weeds, e.g. buttercup (genus *Ranunculus*).

rape An annual or biennial herb, *Brassica napus* var. *arvensis*, also called oilseed rape or coleseed, that grows to a height of 1 m and has yellow flowers. It is widely cultivated for its seeds, which yield an edible oil. Family: *Cruciferae*.

Raphael (Raffaello Sanzio; 1483–1520) Italian Renaissance painter and architect. He trained in Perugia before moving to Florence in 1504. There, influenced by Leonardo and Michelangelo, he painted numerous Madonnas and also the portraits of Angelo and Maddalena Doni (Palazzo Pitti, Florence). Settling in Rome in 1508, he decorated the papal apartments in the Vatican with frescoes. He painted his patron Pope Julius II (Palazzo Pitti) and the *Sistine Madonna* (Dresden). In 1514 he succeeded Bramante as architect of St Peter's. In 1515 he designed tapestries for the Sistine Chapel. His last work, the *Transfiguration* (Vatican Museum), anticipates *mannerism.

Rarotonga 21 15S 159 45W A mountainous island in the SW Pacific Ocean, the administrative centre of the *Cook Islands. Copra and citrus fruit are exported. Area: 67 sq km (26 sq mi). Population (latest est): 9281. Chief town: Avarua.

raspberry A prickly woody perennial plant,

Rubus idaeus, native to Eurasia and North America. Up to 1.5 m high, it produces red sweet fruits. Upright canes grow from basal buds and bear fruit in their first autumn or second summer. Family: *Rosaceae*.

Rasputin, Grigori Yefimovich (c. 1872–1916) Russian mystic, who was a favourite of Emperor *Nicholas II and *Alexandra. A Siberian peasant, Rasputin's apparent ability to ease the bleeding of the haemophiliac crown prince brought him considerable influence over the royal family. His unpopularity, aggravated by his debauchery, led to his murder by a group of nobles: when poison inexplicably failed he was shot and thrown into the River Neva.

Rastafarians Members of a West Indian religious and political sect, who believe that Ras Tafari Makonnen (*Haile Selassie) will arrange for the deliverance of the black races by procuring for them a homeland in Ethiopia. Rastafarian men wear their hair in long matted curls (dreadlocks).

rat A *rodent belonging to the suborder *Myomorpha*, distributed worldwide. Typical rats belong to the Old World genus *Rattus* (137 species) The black rat (*R. rattus*), originally Asian, has spread to most regions of the world, living in human habitations and sewers. The brown rat (*R. norvegicus*) is larger, measuring 30–45 cm including its tail (15–20 cm), and tends to live outdoors in burrows. Both species eat a wide variety of plant and animal materials, often causing serious damage and transmitting disease. *See also* MOUSE.

ratel An omnivorous mammal, *Mellivora capensis*, also called honey badger, of Africa and S Asia. About 70 cm long, grey above and black underneath, it lives in thick woods. Family: *Mustelidae*.

rationalism A philosophical movement stemming from 17th-century attempts to study the universe using reason rather than sense-experience. *Descartes, for example, tried to deduce what God's world is like from the axioms of divine existence and goodness. Conflict between the new sciences and religion is reflected in the work of *Spinoza, Antoine Arnauld (1612–94), and *Leibniz.

rat kangaroo A *marsupial belonging to the subfamily *Potoroinae* (9 species), of Australia (including Tasmania). Two species are commonly known as boodies and two others as potoroos. Measuring 23–44 cm excluding the tail (15–38 cm), rat kangaroos are related to kangaroos and have a narrow ratlike face. They forage at night for grubs and tubers. Family: *Macropodidae*.

rattan The stems of climbing *palms of the genus *Calamus* (375 species), native to Old World tropical regions. Up to 130 m long, the stems are used in furniture, matting, etc.

Rattigan, Sir Terence (1911–77) British dramatist. His highly successful plays include upper-class comedies (*French without Tears*, 1936), more ambitious studies of human relationships (*The Deep Blue Sea*, 1952), and studies of historical characters (*Ross*, 1960).

Rattle, Sir Simon (1955–) British conductor. He was principal conductor (1980–91) and musical director (1991–98) of the City of Birmingham Symphony Orchestra. In 2002 he became chief conductor of the Berlin Philharmonic.

rattlesnake A pit viper belonging to either of two genera, *Sisturus* (2 species) or *Crotalus* (28 species), and characterized by having a rattle composed of loosely connected horny tail segments. Rattlesnakes occur in both North and South America and are 0.3–2.5 m long with dark diamond, hexagonal, or spotted markings on a pale background. *See also* SIDEWINDER.

Ravel, Maurice (1875–1937) French composer of the impressionist school. His works include, for piano, *Pavane pour une infante défunte* (1899), *Valses nobles et sentimentales* (1911), and *Le Tombeau de Couperin* (1914–17), the suite *Gaspard de la nuit* (1908), and two piano concertos; for orchestra, *La Valse* (1920), *Boléro* (1927), and the ballet *Daphnis and Chloe* (1909–12); the opera *L'Enfant et les sortilèges* (1920–25); and many songs.

raven A large glossy black crow, *Corvus corax*, about 63 cm long with a massive bill and a wedge-shaped tail. It feeds on carrion, small animals, seeds, and fruits and often roosts in large colonies. Ravens occur in mountain and moorland regions of the N hemisphere.

Ravenna 44 25N 12 12E A city and port in N Italy, connected to the Adriatic Sea by canal. Ravenna was the capital of the western Roman Empire (402–76 AD), of the Ostrogothic kings (476–526), and of the Byzantine exarchate (military governorship) from 584 to 751. It is noted for its mosaics. Population (2000 est): 138 418.

Ravi, River A river in NW India and Pakistan. Rising in the Himalayas, it flows W and SW to the River Chenab. Length: 724 km (450 mi).

Rawalpindi 33 40N 73 08E A city in N Pakistan. From 1959 until 1969 it served as the interim capital while the new capital at Islamabad was being built. Population (1998): 1 406 214.

ray A predominantly marine *cartilaginous fish of the worldwide order *Batoidea* (or *Rajiformes*; about 350 species). Rays have a flattened head and body with greatly enlarged winglike pectoral fins; the tapering tail often bears sharp poison spines. Rays are generally bottom-dwelling and feed mainly on fish and invertebrates. Subclass: *Elasmobranchii*.

Ray, Satyajit (1921–92) Indian film director. He achieved an international reputation with *Pather Panchali* (1955), *The Unvanquished* (1956), and *The World of Apu* (1959), a trilogy of films about social change in India; his other films include *Charulata* (1964) and *The Stranger* (1992).

Rayleigh, John William Strutt, 3rd Baron (1842–1919) British physicist. His work on black-body radiation was upset by Planck's discovery of the quantum theory but he did much valuable work in optics, hydrodynamics, and the theory of electrical units. He was awarded the 1904 Nobel Prize for his discovery of argon, in conjunction with Sir William *Ramsay.

rayon A textile fibre or fabric made from *cellulose. **Viscose rayon** is made by dissolving wood pulp in a mixture of sodium hydroxide and carbon disulphide. The fibres are reconstituted in an acid bath. **Acetate rayon** is made by mixing wood pulp with acetic anhydride, acetic acid, and sulphuric acid to form cellulose acetate, which is then dissolved in a solvent and forced through fine holes to form fibres as the solvent evaporates.

razorbill A black-and-white *auk, *Alca torda*, that breeds around N Atlantic coasts and winters in the Mediterranean. 40 cm long, it has a laterally compressed bill. It dives to catch fish, shellfish, and worms.

razor shell A burrowing *bivalve mollusc of the family *Solenidae* (about 40 species), also called a jack-knife clam, of Atlantic and Pacific coasts. The common razor (*Ensis siliqua*), about 15 cm long, has a narrow shell with squared ends; its curved foot burrows into sand.

reactance *See* IMPEDANCE.

Reading 1. 51 28N 0 59W A town in S England, in Reading unitary authority, Berkshire. It is the headquarters of several international industries. Population (1991): 134 600. **2.** A unitary authority in S England, in Berkshire. Area: 37 sq km (14 sq mi). Population (2001): 143 124.

Reagan, Ronald (1911–2004) US statesman; Republican president (1981–89). He was a film actor before entering politics. In 1981 he survived an assassination attempt. As president he cut taxes, increased defence spending, and approved the US invasion of Grenada (1983) and CIA operations in Nicaragua, despite Congress opposition. He agreed the Intermediate Nuclear Forces (INF) Treaty with the Soviet Union in 1987 and improved US–Soviet relations after *Gorbachov came to power.

realism 1. The medieval philosophical theory that general terms (called universals) have a real existence, that is that there is some abstract entity that corresponds with the term. *Plato and *Aristotle were realists in believing that the universe contained universals in addition to particulars. *Aquinas and *Duns Scotus were leading realists. **2.** In modern philosophy, a stance opposed to *idealism. Realists, such as G. E. *Moore, assert that objects exist independently of being perceived.

real tennis A racket-and-ball indoor court game, which originated in France in the 12th–13th centuries; it was originally played with the bare hand. Many other handball and racket-and-ball court games developed from it. Its world championships date back to about 1750, although it is now very much a minority sport. The stone or concrete floor area is approximately 29 × 10 m (96 × 32 ft). The cloth ball is hit over a central net, as in *tennis, but it also bounces off the side walls, as in *squash rackets.

Réaumur, René-Antoine Ferchault de (1683–1757) French physicist, whose work on thermometers led him to devise the temperature scale that bears his name. On this scale water freezes at 0° and boils at 80°.

received pronunciation (**RP**) The pronunciation of English most generally accepted as standard or correct. The term was coined in 1926 by Daniel Jones (1881–1967) to describe the characteristic accent of the public schools and universities. Historically, it is derived from Middle English spoken in the London area.

recessive gene The *allele of a gene the function of which is hidden when the organism concerned is crossed with one carrying a different allele (called the dominant allele) for the same gene.

Recife (*or* **Pernambuco**) 8 06S 34 53W A port in NE Brazil, on the Atlantic Ocean. It is a major port. Population (1995): 3 168 000.

recombinant DNA technology *See* GENETIC ENGINEERING.

Reconstruction (1865–77) The period after the US *Civil War in which the defeated Confederate states were brought back into the Union. The new state governments were dominated by Whites prepared to compromise, newly enfranchised Blacks, and northern carpetbaggers, but after the withdrawal of Federal troops in 1877 White supremacists were restored to power.

recorder A woodwind instrument of medieval origin. The recorder is end-blown, through a whistle mouthpiece mounted in a block (*or* fipple). The holes are covered with the fingers; the tone is quieter than that of the flute.

rectifier A device that allows electric current to flow in one direction only; it is generally used to convert alternating current to direct current. Semiconductor diodes have now replaced thermionic valves (diodes) for lower voltage applications. For power supplies of several megawatts, mercury-arc rectifiers are used.

rectum *See* INTESTINE.

red admiral A butterfly, *Vanessa atalanta*, found throughout Europe, Asia, and North America. The wings are black with red and white markings. Red admirals migrate to northern regions for the summer. The caterpillars feed mainly on stinging nettles. Family: *Nymphalidae*.

red algae Algae of the phylum *Rhodophyta* (about 3000 species), which are usually red or blue in colour due to the presence of the pigments phycoerythrin (red) or phycocyanin (blue), which mask the green chlorophyll. They range from small unicellular or filamentous forms to branching or sheetlike *seaweeds. Reproduction is asexual or sexual.

Red Brigades (Italian name: Brigate Rosse) A group of Italian terrorists formed in 1969 and dedicated to the violent overthrow of capitalist society. They were responsible for the murder of Aldo *Moro in 1978.

Redcar and Cleveland A unitary authority in NE England, in North Yorkshire; part of Cleveland county from 1974 to 1996. Area: 240 sq km (93 sq mi). Population (2001): 139 141.

Red Cross, International An organization founded by the Geneva Convention of 1864 to provide care for the casualties of war. Inspired by Henri Dunant (1828–1910), its headquarters are in Geneva and its emblem, the red cross, represents the Swiss flag with its colours reversed. Muslim countries have generally adopted the crescent as their emblem. The International Red Cross has twice won the Nobel Peace Prize, in 1917 and 1944.

redcurrant A shrub of the genus *Ribes* (*see* CURRANT), cultivated for its red fruits, which may be made into jellies, jams, etc. Cultivated redcurrants have been derived from *R. rubrum* of Eurasia, *R. sativum* of W Europe, and *R. petraeum* of central and S Europe.

red deer A large reddish-brown deer, *Cervus elaphus*, of European and Asian woodlands. Over 120 cm high at the shoulder, males have spreading branched antlers up to 125 cm long; females are more lightly built. Stags and hinds come together in the autumn for the rut, when mature males compete to gather hinds.

Redford, Robert (1936–) US film actor and director. He costarred with Paul *Newman in *Butch Cassidy and the Sundance Kid* (1969) and *The Sting* (1973). His other films include *All the President's Men* (1976), *Out of Africa* (1986), *Indecent Proposal* (1993), and *Spy Game* (2001). Films that he has directed include *Ordinary People* (1980) and *The Horse Whisperer* (1998), in which he also starred.

red giant A greatly distended cool but very luminous *giant star. It is one of the final evolutionary stages of a normal *star, attained when its central hydrogen has been converted to helium. As it evolves it may change to a hotter more compact type of giant and then swell back to a red giant.

Redgrave, Sir Michael (1908–85) British Shakespearean actor, who also performed in and directed modern plays. His films included *The Browning Version* (1951) and *The Go-Between* (1971). His daughter **Vanessa Redgrave** (1937–) has acted on stage and in films, including *Blow-Up* (1966), *Julia* (1977), *Comrades* (1987), and *Mrs Dalloway* (1998). She is well known for her left-wing political activities, as is her brother **Corin Redgrave** (1939–), who is also an actor. His daughter **Lynn Redgrave** (1943–) is also an actress. Vanessa Redgrave's daughters **Natasha Richardson** (1963–) and **Joely Richardson** (1965–) have also appeared on stage and in films.

red grouse A *grouse, *Lagopus lagopus scoticus*, found on moorlands of Great Britain and Ireland, where it is managed as a gamebird. 34–37 cm long, it feeds on ling heather. The male is red-brown with red wattles above the eyes and the female is browner and barred.

Red Guards High-school and university students organized by Mao Tse-tung during the *Cultural Revolution The Red Guards destroyed property, humiliated foreign diplomats, and attacked those officials who opposed Mao's policies.

red-hot poker A plant of the African genus *Kniphofia*, cultivated as garden plants. 45–120 cm tall, they have tubular flowers, usually scarlet and/or yellow. Family: *Liliaceae*.

redox reactions *See* OXIDATION AND REDUCTION.

Red River (Vietnamese name: Song Hong) The chief river of N Vietnam, rising in S China and flowing SE to the Gulf of Tonkin. Length: 500 km (310 mi).

Red River of the North (*or* **Red River**) A river in central North America, rising in W Minnesota and flowing N into Canada. Length: 1000 km (621 mi).

Red Sea A long narrow arm of the Indian Ocean between Africa and Asia, extending some 2400 km (1491 mi) NNW beyond the Gulf of Aden and the Bab el-Mandeb. In the N, it is connected to the Mediterranean Sea by the Suez Canal. Area: 438 000 sq km (169 076 sq mi).

redshank An Old World *sandpiper, *Tringa totanus*, that breeds in cool marshy regions of Eurasia. 30 cm long, it has long reddish legs, a black-tipped red bill, and a brown-grey plumage with a white rump. It winters on mudflats of Africa and Asia, feeding on crustaceans, molluscs, and ragworms.

redshift An overall displacement towards larger wavelengths of the spectral lines of a celestial object. Its astronomical significance was suggested by Edwin Hubble (1889–1953) in 1929, when it was used as the basis of the theory that the universe is expanding (*see* EXPANDING UNIVERSE). A redshift usually arises from the *Doppler effect, that is from recession of a celestial object. It increases as the object's radial velocity increases and for an extragalactic body can be used as a measure of distance. A **gravitational redshift** occurs whenever radiation is emitted by a body.

red squirrel A tree *squirrel, *Sciurus vulgaris*, of Eurasia. About 20 cm long with a 20-cm tail, red squirrels have dark glossy red fur and tufted ears. They feed mainly on seeds and nuts.

redstart A small Eurasian thrush of the genus *Phoenicurus*, about 14 cm long with a sharp bill. The male European redstart (*P. phoenicurus*) is grey with a russet breast and a red tail, which it fans out in its courtship display to the yellow and brown female. It is found in woodland and heathland.

reduction *See* OXIDATION AND REDUCTION.

redwood A coniferous tree, *Sequoia sempervirens*, thought to be the tallest tree in the world and one of the longest lived: a specimen in California is over 111 m tall and some Californian trees are over 2000 years old. Also called coast redwood, it is native to the Pacific coast between Oregon and California and is an important timber tree. It has brown-red fibrous bark and red-brown globular cones, about 2 cm long. Family: *Taxodiaceae*. *See also* SEQUOIA.

reed Any of several species of tall aquatic grasses, especially those of the genus *Phragmites* (2–3 species). The common reed (*P. communis*) has a creeping underground stem (rhizome) and grows worldwide along the margins of marshes, lakes, streams, and fens.

Reed, Sir Carol (1906–76) British film director. His best-known films include *The Fallen Idol* (1948) and *The Third Man* (1949) both with screenplays by Graham *Greene. His later films include *The Agony and the Ecstasy* (1965) and *Oliver!* (1968).

reedbuck An African antelope belonging to the genus *Redunca* (3 species). The common reedbuck (*R. arundinium*) grows to 90 cm high at the shoulder and has a stiff grey coat and slender ridged horns and inhabits lush grassland. The bohor reedbuck (*R. redunca*) is smaller and lives in swampy regions, while the gregarious mountain reedbuck (*R. fulvorufula*) lives in hilly areas.

reedling A Eurasian bird, *Panurus biarmicus*, about 16 cm long, also called bearded tit. It lives in reedbeds, feeding on insects and seeds. The plumage is brown with pale underparts: the male has a grey head with a black moustache of feathers. Reedlings belong to the babbler family.

reedmace A widely distributed perennial herbaceous plant, *Typha latifolia*, also called bulrush or cat's-tail, growing in reed swamps. It has an erect stem, 1.5–2.5 m high, bearing cylindrical fruit. There are several other reedmaces of the genus *Typha*. Family: *Typhaceae*.

reed warbler An acrobatic *warbler, *Acrocephalus scirpaeus*, about 12 cm long with a reddish-brown plumage, pale underparts, and a pale eyestripe. It winters in SE Africa and breeds in European reedswamps.

referendum and initiative Votes on specific legislation by the whole electorate. In the UK referendums have been held concerning membership of the EC (1975) and *devolution for Scotland and Wales (1979 and 1997). Initiatives are proposals, drafted by a citizen or group of citizens, that by virtue of attaining a requisite number of signatures on a petition are put to the electorate for acceptance or rejection.

reflection The rebounding of a wave of light or other radiation when it strikes a surface. Reflected light obeys two laws: first, the normal (an imaginary line vertical to the surface at the point of impact), the incident ray, and the reflected rays all lie in the same plane; second, the angle between the incident ray and the normal is equal to the angle of reflection. *See also* MIRRORS.

reflex An automatic and involuntary response by an organism to a change in the environment, which occurs before the brain has had time to convey the necessary information to the muscles involved. *See also* CONDITIONED REFLEX.

Reform Acts The legislation that reformed the British parliamentary system. The Reform Act of 1832 gave many more people the right to vote, disenfranchised some rotten and pocket boroughs, and gave parliamentary representation to new industrial towns. The 1867 Reform Act gave the vote to many working-class householders for the first time. The 1884 Reform Act made the county franchise the same as that in the towns, thus increasing the electorate to about five million.

Reformation A religious movement in 16th-century Europe that began as an attempt to reform the *Roman Catholic Church and ended with the establishment of independent Protestant Churches (*see* PROTESTANTISM).

The Reformation began on 31 October 1517, when Martin *Luther nailed his 95 theses on the door of the castle church at Wittenburg. Luther's attack on the sale of *indulgences and, subsequently, on papal authority and the *sacraments (save baptism and the Eucharist) was condemned by the pope and the Holy Roman Emperor but gained the support of several German princes. The consequent conflict (*see* CHARLES V) was not resolved until 1555 (*see* AUGSBURG, Peace of).

In Switzerland, the Reformation was initiated by Ulrich Zwingli (1484–1531) in Zurich in 1520, spreading to Basle, Berne, and also to Geneva, where it was led by John *Calvin. In France, where Protestants were called Huguenots, the Reformation became involved in a political struggle for control of the Crown, giving rise to the *Wars of Religion, and in the Low Countries it fired the *Revolt of the Netherlands against Spanish rule.

In England, the Reformation had three stages. Under Henry VIII papal authority in England was destroyed. Thomas Cromwell's legislation (1529–36) culminated in Henry's divorce from Catherine of Aragon and the Act of Supremacy (1534), which proclaimed the king supreme head of the English Church; in 1536 the dissolution of the monasteries was authorized. Under Edward VI Protestantism was established by the 1552 Book of *Common Prayer, the accompanying Acts of *Uniformity, and the 42 Articles (1553). Protestantism finally became the established *Church of England under Elizabeth I and a new Act of Supremacy was passed (1559). In Scotland, the Reformation was influenced by John *Knox and *Presbyterianism was established in 1592. *See also* COUNTER-REFORMATION.

Reform Judaism A religious movement attempting to adapt traditional Judaism to modern circumstances. It began in Germany in the early 19th century. The first Reform synagogue in England was established in 1840; the Liberal movement (founded 1903) instituted more radical reforms typical of US Reform Judaism. The World Union for Progressive Judaism was founded in London in 1926 (it is now based in Jerusalem). The reforms include abolition of many of the ritual laws, acceptance of modern biblical criticism, vernacular services, and full equality for women.

refraction The bending of a beam of radiation as it passes from one medium onto another. For a light ray the amount by which it is bent depends on the angle of the incident ray and on the refractive indices of the two media, the exact dependence being given by *Snell's law. Refraction is caused by the difference in the velocity of the radiation in the two media. The ratio of the velocity of light in the two media is known as the **refractive index**.

refrigeration The process of lowering the temperature inside a closed insulated container. In the domestic refrigerator the method most commonly used is the vapour-compression cycle in which a liquid refrigerant, such as Freon (a compound of chlorine, fluorine, and carbon), is pumped through cooling coils formed into the ice-making compartment. In these coils the refrigerant evaporates, taking the latent heat required to make it into a gas from the surroundings. It is then passed to an electrically driven compressor; after compression it condenses back to liquid, when the absorbed heat is given out (usually at the back of the refrigerator). This cycle is repeated over and over again until the required temperature (about 1–2°C in the food chamber and −15°C in the deep-freeze compartment) is achieved. *See also* FREEZING.

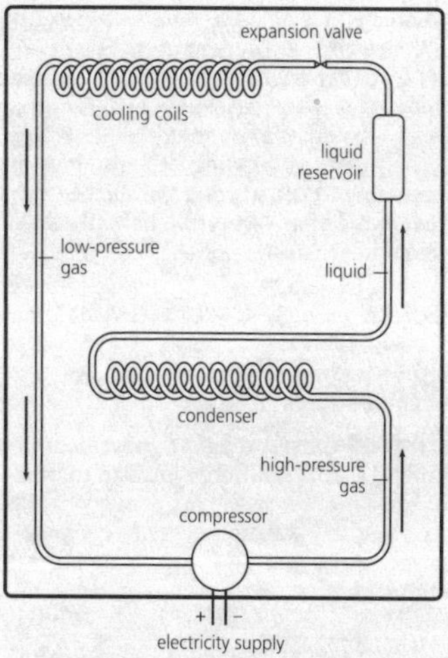

refrigeration. The vapour–compression cycle commonly used in domestic refrigerators. The energy for the cycle is supplied by the mains electricity.

Regency style An English decorative style fashionable from about 1800 to 1830 and influenced by the French *Empire style. Dark woods and veneers were popular and were set off by ormolu mounts. Concurrently there was a vogue for oriental motifs (*see* CHINOISERIE) and some magnificent lacquer was produced, for example for the Prince Regent's Pavilion at Brighton.

regeneration In biology, the regrowth and development of tissues or organs lost through injury, as a normal process (e.g. during moulting), or by any other means. It is particularly well developed in plants and simple animals. Thus, whole plants can regenerate from stem and leaf cuttings and simple animals, such as sponges and planarians, can develop from minute fragments. More complex animals, such as crustaceans, replace lost appendages, while lizards can grow new tails. In mammals regeneration is limited to wound healing and regrowth of peripheral nerve fibres.

Regina 50 30N 104 38W A city in W Canada, the capital of Saskatchewan. Founded in 1882, it has expanded rapidly since 1945. Population (1996): 180 400.

Reichstag (Imperial Diet) The legislative assembly of the German Empire (1871–1918) and the Weimar Republic (1919–33). Its origins lay in the diet of the Holy Roman Empire. It was divided into an electoral college, a college of princes, and a college of cities. It was revived by Bismarck in 1867 as the representative assembly of the North German Confederation. In 1933 the Reichstag building was burnt out; Nazi allegations of communist responsibility provided an excuse to ban opposition parties. In the late 1990s the Reichstag building was radically restored to provide a new seat for the German government (from 1999).

Reign of Terror (1793–94) The most violent period of the French Revolution. Dominated by *Robespierre, the governing Committee of Public Safety took severe measures against the Revolution's opponents. About 1400 were summarily guillotined. Public reaction contributed to Robespierre's downfall and execution in July 1794.

Reims (*or* **Rheims**) 49 15N 4 02E A city in NE France, in the Marne department. An important Roman town, it was the scene of the coronations of most of the French kings. The magnificent gothic cathedral was badly damaged in World War I. Population (1999): 187 206.

reincarnation (*or* **metempsychosis**) The migration of the soul from one body at death and its re-entry into another (human or animal) body. The cycle of reincarnation (*samsara*) is fundamental to Hindu, Buddhist, and Jain conceptions of the world, all spiritual effort being directed towards release (*moksa*) from the cycle. Orthodox Christianity rejected it as contrary to belief in the resurrection of the body.

reindeer A large deer, *Rangifer tarandus*, of European and North American tundra (in America it is called a caribou). About 125 cm high at the shoulder, reindeer have a grey-brown coat and spreading branched antlers (the antlers of males are larger). Reindeer feed mainly on lichens (*reindeer moss) but also eat dwarf willow and other shrubs.

reindeer moss A grey tufted *lichen, *Cladonia rangiferina*, that is very abundant in Arctic regions. Up to 8 cm high, it serves as the major food source for reindeer, moose, musk oxen, etc.

Reinhardt, Django (Jean Baptiste R.; 1910–53) Belgian jazz guitarist of gipsy origin. He injured his hand in a fire at the age of 18 but developed an original guitar technique. From 1934 to 1939 he led the quintet of the Hot Club de France with Stephane *Grappelli.

Reith, John Charles Walsham, 1st Baron (1889–1971) British administrator. His severe moral principles greatly influenced the early development of the BBC, of which he was director general from 1927 to 1938. The Reith lectures, broadcast annually, were named in his honour.

relativistic mass The mass of a body that is moving at a velocity comparable to the *velocity of light. According to the theory of *relativity, if the velocity of the body is v then its mass is $m_0(1 - v^2/c^2)^{-1/2}$, where c is the velocity of light and m_0 the rest mass (the mass when stationary).

relativity The first part of the theory, published by Albert Einstein in 1905 and known as the special theory, applies only to motion in which there is no acceleration. Up to this time it was thought that light travelled through a stationary medium, called the ether, at a constant speed and that its speed relative to an observer could be calculated in the same way as the relative speed of any two moving objects. For example, if one car (A) travelling at 90 mph on a motorway overtakes another (B) travelling at 70 mph, the speed of the two cars relative to each other is 20 mph. In talking about relative speeds it is necessary to be precise about what a particular speed is relative to. Car A's speed relative to car B is 20 mph, but relative to the earth it is 90 mph. Relative to the sun it is about 24 million mph. Because two American scientists, Michelson and Morley, had shown that light travelled at the same speed whether measured in the direction of the earth's rotation or at right angles to this direction, Einstein suggested that the restriction about relative motion does not apply to light. It always has the same speed of 2.998×10^8 metres per second (186 000 miles per second), irrespective of the motion of the observer.

In his special theory Einstein suggested that as bodies increase in speed they become shorter and heavier. This effect is only noticeable as the speed of light is approached. An electron travelling at 99% of the speed of light becomes seven times heavier than its mass at rest. Einstein also showed that no body could actually travel at the speed of light itself. If it did it would be infinitely heavy and have zero length.

The increase in mass and decrease in length that a body undergoes when moving at high speeds led Einstein to the conclusion that an energy (E) has a mass (m); they are related by the simple equation $E = mc^2$, where c is the velocity of light. The atom bomb and *nuclear energy both depend on this equation.

In the general theory of 1916, Einstein considered accelerated relative motion, especially as it is concerned with gravitation. The gravitational force experienced by a body is treated as a property of space and time, which Einstein suggested was "curved" by the presence of the mass. The observed bending of light rays as they pass close to the sun and the shift of certain lines in the solar *spectrum have provided experimental verification of the theory.

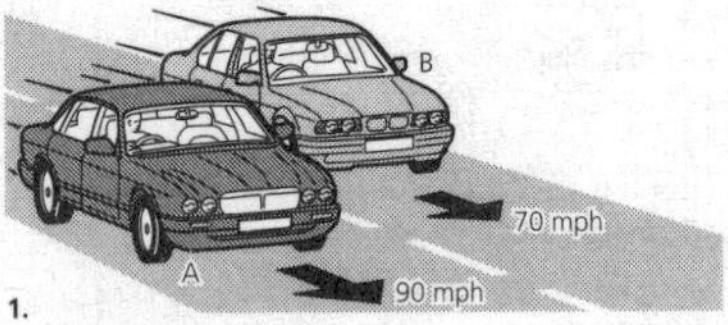

1.

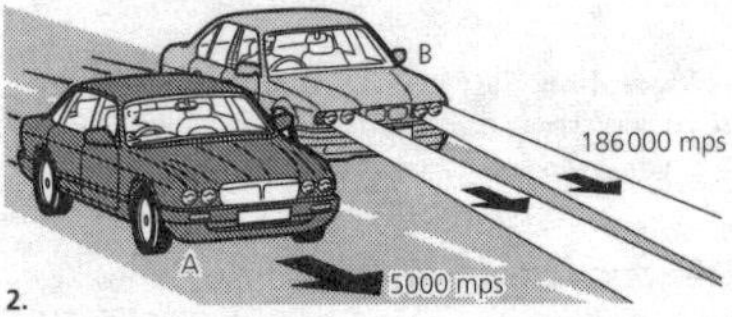

2.

relativity. 1. Two cars, A and B, travelling along a motorway. The speed of car A relative to the earth is 90 mph. The speed of car B relative to the earth is 70 mph. The speed of car A relative to car B is 90–70 = 20 mph. 2. Car B is now stationary; its headlight beams are turned on as supercar A passes, travelling at 5000 miles per second. The speed of car B's headlight beam relative to car A is 186 000 miles per second (not 186 000–5000 miles per second). The speed of light is absolute.

relay, electric An electrical switching device in which one circuit is controlled by a separate circuit, often to avoid the danger of direct contact with high-voltage supplies or to reduce the length of high-current cable needed. Relays may involve mechanical movement and an electromagnetic connection between the two circuits or be controlled entirely by solid-state electronic components.

reluctance (*or* **magnetic resistance**) The ratio of the *magnetomotive force in a material to the total magnetic flux induced by it. It is analogous to electrical *resistance.

Rembrandt (Harmenszoon) van Rijn (1606–69) Dutch painter and etcher. Settling permanently in Amsterdam (1631), he made his name as a portrait painter with *The Anatomy Lesson of Dr Tulp* (1632; The Hague). It was followed by many other portraits, including those of his wife Saskia and culminating in the famous group portrait, *The Nightwatch* (1642; Rijksmuseum, Amsterdam). He also treated dramatic mythological and biblical subjects and excelled as a landscapist. His etchings are among the finest ever produced. He eventually had financial difficulties and became bankrupt.

Remembrance Sunday The day on which the British remember the dead of both World Wars. Since 1956 it has been observed on the second Sunday of November. A two-minute silence marks the time, 11 am, of the signing of the Armistice on 11 November 1918 and wreaths of Flanders poppies are laid at the Cenotaph in Whitehall, London, and at other war memorials.

remora A dark slender elongated fish, 30–90 cm long, belonging to a family (*Echeneidae*; 8–10 species) found in warm marine waters. The dorsal fin is modified to form a flat oval sucking disc on its head by which it attaches itself to various marine animals or ships to feed on scraps of food or the hosts' parasites. Order: *Perciformes*.

Renaissance (French: rebirth) An intellectual and cultural movement that began in Italy in the 14th century, spread to N Europe, and flourished until the late 16th century. Fundamental to the Renaissance were the revival of classical learning, art, and architecture and the concept of the dignity of man, which characterized *humanism. Great writers of the Italian Renaissance included *Petrarch, *Dante, *Boccaccio, *Machiavelli, and *Ariosto.

The first painter to mirror these new ideals was *Giotto. He was followed in the 15th century by *Masaccio, *Uccello, *Piero della Francesca, *Mantegna, and others, who introduced the use of linear perspective. The High Renaissance denotes the period between about 1500 and about 1520, when the artists *Leonardo da Vinci, *Raphael, and *Michelangelo perfected the harmony and balance associated with classical art.

In sculpture the major figures were Nicola *Pisano, *Donatello, *Ghiberti, *Verrocchio, and Michelangelo. In building Brunelleschi was the first to revive the classical use of the *orders of architecture. Later architects, such as *Alberti, Donato Bramante (1444–1514), and *Palladio, also revived ancient temples and domed structures.

In the 16th century the Renaissance spread to N Europe, where it manifested itself in the art of *Dürer, the scholarship of *Erasmus, the plays of *Shakespeare, and particularly in the courts of such rulers as Elizabeth I of England.

Renfrewshire A council area of W Scotland, on the Clyde Estuary W of Glasgow. In 1975 the historic county of Renfrewshire was absorbed into Strathclyde Region. In 1996 Strathclyde was abolished and the unitary authorities of Inverclyde, Renfrewshire, and East Renfrewshire were established. The main economic activities are engineering, textiles, and agriculture. Area: 216 sq km (101 sq mi). Population (2001): 172 867. Administrative centre: Paisley.

Reni, Guido (1575–1642) Italian painter. In Rome (c. 1600–14) he established a studio and painted his masterpiece, the ceiling fresco of *Aurora* (Palazzo Rospigliosi). Later, in Bologna, his highly idealized style became somewhat sentimental.

renin An enzyme, secreted by the kidneys, that breaks down a liver protein to form the peptide angiotensin I. This is converted to angiotensin II, which constricts blood vessels—causing a rise in blood pressure—and increases the secretion of aldosterone from the adrenal glands.

Rennes 48 06N 1 40W A city in NW France, in the Ille-et-Vilaine department. The capital of of Brittany, it was badly damaged by fire in 1720. It is now the main commercial centre of W France. Population (1999): 206 229.

rennet An extract, prepared from cows' stomachs, that contains the milk-coagulating enzyme rennin. It is used in the manufacture of cheese and junket.

Renoir, Pierre Auguste (1841–1919) French impressionist painter, born in Limoges. He exhibited at the first three impressionist exhibitions but later abandoned impressionism. Increasingly crippled by arthritis, he spent his last years in the south of France, painting many sensuous nudes. His best-known works include *Les Parapluies* (National Gallery, London) and *Le Moulin de la Galette* (Louvre). His son **Jean Renoir** (1894–1979) was a film director whose best-known films are the social satires *La Grande Illusion* (1937) and *La Règle du jeu* (1939). During World War II he went to Hollywood but he returned to Europe to make *French Can-can* (1955) and other films.

Representatives, House of *See* CONGRESS.

repression In *psychoanalysis, the process of excluding unacceptable ideas from consciousness. Repressed wishes and thoughts continue to exist in the unconscious mind and may give rise to symptoms. One of the goals of psychoanalytic treatment is to bring repressed material back into conscious awareness so that it can be coped with rationally.

reproduction The generation of new individuals of the same species. In **asexual reproduction** individuals are derived from one parent; the simplest form is *fission, occurring mostly in unicellular organisms. Simple multicellular organisms, such as sponges and cnidarians, reproduce by budding: a new individual arises as an outgrowth (bud) from the parent. In plants a common form of asexual reproduction is **vegetative reproduction** (*or* vegetative propagation), in which new individuals develop from such structures as bulbs, corms, rhizomes, and tubers, which become detached from the parent plant. Most animals and plants, however, reproduce by **sexual reproduction**, which involves specialized reproductive cells (*see* GAMETE)—typically male and female—that fuse to produce a new individual with a different genetic makeup. This process occurs in its simplest form in *conjugation. In more complex organisms the gametes are produced in special organs, e.g. the carpel and stamen in flowering plants and the ovary and testis in animals. The importance of sexual reproduction is that it allows genetic variation in a population, enabling it to adapt to the changing environment.

r

reptile A vertebrate animal belonging to the class *Reptilia* (about 6000 species), which includes *crocodiles, *turtles, *lizards, *snakes, and the *tuatara. Reptiles, which evolved from amphibians, occur in terrestrial, freshwater, and marine habitats, chiefly in tropical regions. They have a covering of horny scales and are cold-blooded. Fertilization of the egg takes place within the female, unlike fish and most amphibians. The large egg has a leathery shell, enabling it to be laid on land. In some lizards and snakes the eggs are retained inside the female and live young are born. Young reptiles resemble their parents and—unlike amphibians—do not undergo metamorphosis.

Republican Party One of the two major political parties of the USA (*compare* DEMOCRATIC PARTY). The name was used by Jefferson's Republican Democrats (formed in 1792), but the modern Republican Party originated in 1854 as an alliance of those opposed to the extension of slavery in the new territories in the W USA. After the election of the first Republican president, Lincoln, in 1860, the Republicans were usually the ascendant party until the 1930s. Recent Republican presidents include *Nixon, *Reagan, and *Bush (father and son).

requiem shark A *shark of the family *Carcharhinidae* (over 60 species), found worldwide mainly in warm oceans. 1.5–5.5 m long, they have two dorsal fins and are carnivorous, feeding on fish and invertebrates. Some species, such as the *tiger shark, are dangerous to humans.

resins Adhesive nonflammable organic polymers, usually insoluble in water but soluble in organic solvents. **Natural resins**, such as *rosin and *shellac, are exuded by plants and insects. **Synthetic resins** are made by modifying natural polymers or by polymerization of petrochemicals. Thermosetting resins, those that harden on heating, include epoxy and some *polyurethane resins. Thermoplastic resins, those that soften on heating, include *polythene, *polyvinyl chloride, and *polypropylene.

resistance The property of all materials, except superconductors (*see* SUPERCONDUCTIVITY), that reduces the flow of electricity through them. It is defined by Ohm's law as the ratio of the potential difference between the ends of a conductor to the current flowing through it (*see also* IMPEDANCE).

resolving power 1. The ability of a *microscope to produce separate images of two neighbouring points; the closer the points, the greater the resolving power of the microscope. The resolving power may be increased by using shorter wavelength radiation (e.g. ultraviolet radiation) or by using very short wavelength electrons (as in the *electron microscope). Alternatively the refractive index of the medium between the specimen and the objective lens may be increased, as in the oil-immersion lens. **2.** A measure of the ability of a *telescope to distinguish detail, usually the smallest angle between two point objects that produces distinct images.

resonance (chemistry) The existence of a compound with a molecular structure intermediate between two or more conventional structures. For example, the polar molecule HCl, can be regarded as a **resonance hybrid** between two structures. One is the covalent molecule H–Cl and the other the ionic compound H^+Cl^-.

resonance (physics) The sympathetic oscillation of a system in response to an external excitation. A wire under tension, for example, will not respond to an external vibration unless the vibration is at the natural frequency of oscillation of the wire. A **resonant circuit** consists of a capacitance in parallel with an inductance. When the capacitor discharges through the inductor an induced emf is produced, which again charges the capacitor (in the opposite sense). The circuit will then continue to oscillate, provided that energy is supplied from an outside source. Such circuits, feeding an aerial, are used in *radio transmitters to generate

reptile. Some representative reptiles.

radio-frequency oscillations and in receivers to detect incoming signals.

Respighi, Ottorino (1879–1936) Italian composer. He wrote several operas, the symphonic poems *The Fountains of Rome* (1917) and *The Pines of Rome* (1924), the orchestral suite *The Birds* (1927), and ballets, including *La Boutique fantasque* (1919).

respiration The process by which an organism takes up oxygen from its environment and discharges carbon dioxide into it. In man and most air-breathing animals the organs through which this takes place are the *lungs (aquatic animals use *gills; insects use tracheae). Oxygen-depleted blood is pumped from the *heart to the air sacs (alveoli) of the lungs, where it receives oxygen (from inhaled air) and releases carbon dioxide (which is exhaled). Oxygen in the blood is carried to the tissues and cells, where it oxidizes foodstuffs to produce energy.

respirator A machine used to maintain breathing in patients whose respiratory muscles are paralysed. The cabinet respirator (iron lung) encloses the patient in a sealed container from the neck down; by lowering the pressure in the cabinet the chest expands and draws air into the lungs. A positive-pressure respirator pumps air at regular intervals into the lungs through a tube placed in the windpipe.

Restoration (1660) The re-establishment of the monarchy in England following the fall of the *Protectorate. The Restoration of Charles II, whose father Charles I had been executed (1649) during the Civil War, was engineered by General Monck (1608–70). In April 1660, the Convention Parliament accepted Charles' Declaration of Breda, in which he promised religious toleration and an amnesty to all but 57 of those who had fought the Crown.

retina The light-sensitive layer that forms the inner surface of the eye. Light is focused by the lens onto the retina, which contains numerous interconnecting light-sensitive cells (rods and cones) that send signals to the visual centre of the brain via the optic nerve. The rods are responsible for vision in dim light and the cones are sensitive to colour and visual detail. *See also* DETACHED RETINA.

retriever A large strongly built sporting dog descended from the Labrador and characterized by a "soft" mouth and good swimming ability. The flat-coated retriever has a dense coat while the curly-coated retriever has a coat of small tight curls, indicating possible poodle ancestry. Height: 56–68 cm. *See also* GOLDEN RETRIEVER.

Réunion A volcanic island and French overseas department in the W Indian Ocean, in the Mascarene Islands. It was settled in about 1642 by the French with their African and Indian slaves. Sugar, rum, and molasses are exported. Area: 2512 sq km (970 sq mi). Population (2002 est): 743 000. Capital: Saint-Denis.

Revelation, Book of A prophetic book, the last in the New Testament, written perhaps about 90–95 AD by "John the Divine," who is often identified with the apostle John. It consists of seven highly symbolic visions that trace the fortunes of the Christian Church from its inception to the end of the world.

Revere, Paul (1735–1818) American silversmith and revolutionary. On 18 April 1775, he rode out to warn the people of Massachusetts that the British troops were on the march. The next morning the American Revolution began with shots at the British at Lexington. Revere's ride is celebrated in a poem by Longfellow.

Revolt of the Netherlands The rebellion against Spanish rule in the Netherlands, inspired by political and economic grievances and resentment at the suppression of Protestantism. The revolt broke out in 1568 but the independence of the United Provinces of the Netherlands was not acknowledged until 1648, when the Peace of Westphalia was signed.

Revolutionary and Napoleonic Wars (1792–1815) A series of European wars precipitated by the *French Revolution and *Napoleon I's ambitions for the conquest of Europe. War broke out as a result of the hostile reaction of Austria and Prussia to the arrest of Louis XVI. Initial French success prompted Britain, the Netherlands, and Spain to close ranks with Austria and Prussia in the first coalition (1793). Hard pressed, France created a citizen army and achieved a series of victories. In 1795 Prussia, the Netherlands, and Spain sued for peace and, following Napoleon's first Italian campaign (1796–97), Austria followed suit. French supremacy was thwarted only by British naval strength and Nelson's great victory of the *Nile (1798). In 1798–99 the second coalition of Britain, the Ottoman Empire, Naples, Portugal, and Austria was formed but collapsed (1801) in the face of Napoleon's victories, especially at Hohenlinden (1800), and the Revolutionary Wars ended with the uneasy Treaty of Amiens (1802) between Britain and France.

Napoleon's aggression, including his imposition of the Continental System of trade blockades against Britain, led to the resumption of naval war between Britain and France. In 1805 Pitt the Younger negotiated a third coalition against Napoleon, who was defeated by Nelson at *Trafalgar. Napoleon now defeated Austria and Russia at *Ulm and *Austerlitz (1805), Prussia at *Jena and Auerstadt (1806), and Russia again at Friedland (1807). With the failure of the Continental System and Wellington's victories in the *Peninsular War, Napoleon's dominance diminished. Following his disastrous Russian campaign (1812) the allies were able to defeat him at *Leipzig (1813) and later, after his return from exile, at *Waterloo (1815). The post-Napoleonic settlement of Europe was decided at the Congress of *Vienna.

Revolution of 1905 An insurrection in Russia, an expression of the widespread discontent that culminated in the *Russian Revolution of 1917. It began on 22 January 1905 (*Bloody Sunday), when a group of workers marched peacefully on the Winter Palace in St Petersburg and were fired on by troops. The massacre precipitated nationwide strikes, uprisings, and mutinies (including the mutiny on the battleship *Potemkin*). The Revolution was crushed by the end of December.

Revolutions of 1848 A series of revolutions in continental Europe caused by economic distress and liberal agitation. The first revolution broke out in France, where the insurgents overthrew the July Monarchy of Louis Philippe, but a split in their ranks led to the suppression of the Left and the election of Louis Napoleon (later *Napoleon III) as president. In the Italian states the revolution formed part of the movement against the Austrian presence in Italy (*see* RISORGIMENTO). In the Austrian Empire revolts in Vienna secured the resignation of Metternich and the summoning of a constituent assembly. In Prussia, Frederick William IV was forced to convene a constituent assembly. By December, however, the revolutions there and in other German states had been suppressed. The revolutions were all quelled but not without some concessions to liberal and nationalist movements.

revolver A short-range small arm having a revolving cylinder containing the rounds behind the barrel. Calibres range from .21 inches to .455 inches. The first successful revolver was the Colt. *See also* PISTOL.

Reykjavík 64 10N 21 53W The capital of Iceland, an important fishing port, on Faxa Fjord in the SW. Founded by the Vikings in 874 AD, it became the seat of parliament (the Althing) in 1843 and capital of Iceland in 1918. Population (1999 est): 109 184.

Reynolds, Sir Joshua (1723–92) British portrait painter. Using the techniques of the Old Masters in such paintings as *Sarah Siddons as the Tragic Muse* (San Marino, California), Reynolds aimed to give portraits the prestige of history paintings. In 1768 he became the first president of the *Royal Academy, where he delivered the *Discourses* containing his artistic theories.

rhea A large flightless bird of a family (*Rheidae*; 3 species) occurring in South America. 120 cm tall, rheas have a brownish plumage and long legs with three toes. They live in flocks, feeding on leaves, roots, seeds, insects, and small vertebrates. Order: *Rheiformes*.

Rhea In Greek religion, a Titan, daughter of Uranus and Gaea. Her consort *Cronus swallowed her children, fearing that they would overthrow him. Rhea substituted a stone for one child, *Zeus, who eventually overthrew Cronus and forced him to disgorge the other children.

Rhee, Syngman (1875–1965) Korean statesman; president of South Korea (1948–60). He became leader of South Korea in 1945 during the US occupation and as its first president claimed his government's right to rule over all Korea. Popular unrest unseated him in 1960.

rhenium (Re) A dense (relative density 21.02) silvery-white transition metal with a very high melting point. The metal is very ductile and is used to alloy with tungsten. Alloys with molybdenum are superconducting. The metal is obtained as a by-product of molybdenum refining. At no 75; at wt 186.2; mp 3186°C; bp 5596°C.

rhesus factor (**Rh factor**) A blood protein present on the red cells in 83% of the population: the presence or absence of the Rh factor is the basis of the Rh *blood group system, people with the factor being described as Rh positive and those without as Rh negative. If a Rh-negative woman has a Rh-positive baby she may produce anti-Rh antibodies that will react against subsequent Rh-positive pregnancies. The affected baby's blood cells may be destroyed by these antibodies, leading to the severe anaemia of haemolytic disease of the newborn. The incidence of this disease has been reduced by taking steps to prevent the formation of maternal anti-Rh antibodies soon after delivery of the first baby.

rhesus monkey A *macaque monkey, *Macaca mulatta*, of S Asia, widely used in medical research. In the wild, rhesus monkeys live in large colonies in forests or on hillsides.

rheumatic fever A disease of children that occurs (rarely) after infection with a streptococcus bacterium. The symptoms develop 10–14 days after the original infection (which is usually of the throat) and include fever, aching joints, chorea (involuntary movements), and inflammation of the heart, which—in a few cases—may lead to chronic heart disease. Treatment is with bed rest, penicillin, aspirin, and sometimes steroids.

rheumatism Any condition involving pain in the joints. This may be caused by a simple strain or by rheumatoid *arthritis, *osteoarthritis, *gout, or *rheumatic fever.

Rhine, River (German name: Rhein; Dutch name; Rijn) A river in central and W Europe. Rising in SE Switzerland, it flows N along the Swiss-German border, the Franco-German border and into Germany and the Netherlands before entering the North Sea. The main tributaries are the Rivers Ruhr, Main, Moselle, and Neckar. It is W Europe's main navigable waterway. Length: 1320 km (820 mi).

rhinoceros A large hoofed mammal belonging to the family *Rhinocerotidae* (5 species), of Asia and Africa. Rhinos have a massive virtually naked dark-skinned body with short thick legs, a short neck, and a large head. The Indian rhinoceros (*Rhinoceros unicornis*) has a single horn; all other rhinos have two horns. Rhinos range in size from the large rare African white rhinoceros (*Diceros simus*), up to 2 m high and weighing 3.5 tonnes, to the Sumatran rhinoceros (*Didermocerus sumatrensis*), which is up to 150 cm high and weighs 500–1000 kg. Rhinos are generally solitary grazers. All are now endangered species.

rhizome An underground plant stem producing aerial leaves and shoots. It may extend some distance below ground and can be fleshy (as in the iris) or wiry (as in couch grass). Rhizomes can function both as organs of vegetative reproduction and as overwintering structures.

Rhode Island The smallest state in the USA, indented by Narragansett Bay. One of the New England states, it is the second most densely populated US state. It is highly industrialized and has important naval installations. It is famous for its poultry. *History*: settled in 1636, it was the first colony to declare its independence from Britain. Area: 3144 sq km (1214 sq mi). Population (2000): 1 048 319. Capital: Providence.

Rhode Island Red A breed of domestic fowl developed on Rhode Island farms in the 19th century. It has a deep broad long body with a nearly horizontal back and a slightly curved beak. The plumage is red. Weight: 3.8 kg (cocks); 3.0 kg (hens).

Rhodes (Modern Greek name: Ródhos) A Greek island in the SE Aegean Sea, the largest of the Dodecanese group. It has a mountainous interior with fertile coastal strips, producing cereals, fruit, and wine. Tourism is important. *History*: colonized by Dorians before 1000 BC, Rhodes entered its period of greatest prosperity in the 3rd century BC. It suffered several earthquakes, one of which destroyed the *Colossus of Rhodes in 244 BC. It was occupied by the Knights *Hospitallers from 1282 until 1528, when it became part of the Ottoman Empire. Conquered by Italy in 1912, it was ceded to Greece in 1947. Area: 1400 sq km (540 sq mi). Population (latest est); 40 392. Capital: Rhodes.

Rhodes, Cecil (John) (1853–1902) South African financier and statesman. Born in Britain, he went to South Africa in 1870. In 1888 his company bought up the Kimberley mines and in 1889 he gained a charter to develop the territory that in 1895 was named Rhodesia in his honour. He became prime minister of Cape Colony in 1890 but was forced to resign in 1896 over the abortive Jameson raid into the Transvaal. Rhodes endowed 170 Rhodes scholarships at Oxford University for students from the British Empire, the USA, and Germany.

rhodium (Rh) A metal of the platinum group, discovered in 1803 by W. H. Wollaston (1766–1828). It is a very hard highly reflective metal and is used to plate jewellery and optical instruments. At no 45; at wt 102.905; mp 1963 ± 3°C; bp 3697 ± 100°C.

Rhododendron A genus of small trees and shrubs (about 250 species), mainly of N temperate regions. They have leathery often evergreen leaves, large scaly winter buds, and colourful fragrant bell- or funnel-shaped flowers. Many, including *azaleas, are cultivated as ornamentals. Family: *Ericaceae*.

Rhondda, Cynon, Taff A county borough in S Wales, created in 1996 from part of Mid Glamorgan. Area: 558 sq km (215 sq mi). Population (2001): 231 952. Administrative centre: Rhondda.

Rhône, River A major river in W Europe. Rising in the Rhône Glacier in Switzerland, it flows through Lake Geneva to enter France, flowing generally SW. Since 1976 the River Rhône has been canalized from Lyon to the Mediterranean Sea. Length 812 km (505 mi).

rhubarb A perennial plant, *Rheum rhaponticum*, possibly of Asian origin, widely cultivated for its juicy red or green leafstalks, up to 1 m high, which are cooked in sugar. The leaves are poisonous. Family: *Polygonaceae.*

rib A curved bone, 12 pairs of which make up the rib cage, enclosing and protecting the heart and lungs. Each rib articulates with the *spine, permitting movement of the rib cage during breathing. The other ends of the upper seven ribs (the so-called true ribs) are fixed directly to the breastbone by means of a cartilage. Each of the next three pairs (the "false" ribs) is connected by the cartilage to the rib above it, and the two lowest ribs (the floating ribs) end in the muscles of the body wall.

Ribbentrop, Joachim von (1893–1946) German Nazi politician and diplomat. From 1936 to 1938 he was ambassador to the UK and then became Hitler's foreign minister. He was arrested in 1945 and hanged for war crimes.

ribbonworm A long flat wormlike animal, also called proboscis worm, belonging to the invertebrate phylum *Nemertina* (about 600 species). Ranging in length from 1 mm to 30 m, ribbonworms live in shallow seas, feeding on annelid worms, molluscs, and crustaceans.

Ribeirão Prêto 21 09S 47 48W A city in S Brazil, in São Paulo state. It is the centre of a coffee- and sugar-growing area. Population (2000): 502 333.

Ribera, José de (*or* **Jusepe R.**; 1591–1652) Spanish-born painter and etcher. He settled in Naples (1616), where he was known as Lo Spagnoletto (Little Spaniard). He painted chiefly religious subjects and some everyday life scenes and portraits, the best examples of which are *The Martyrdom of St Bartholomew* (Prado) and *Clubfooted Boy* (Louvre).

riboflavin *See* VITAMIN B COMPLEX.

ribonucleic acid *See* RNA.

ribose A simple sugar ($C_5H_{10}O_5$). Ribose and its derivative deoxyribose are important constituents of *RNA and *DNA respectively.

ribosome A granular particle present in enormous numbers in the cytoplasm of nearly all *cells. Ribosomes are composed of *RNA and protein and are the site of protein synthesis.

rice An annual cereal *grass, *Oryza sativa*, or its edible grain, probably native to India but widely cultivated throughout tropical, subtropical, and warm temperate regions. Seedlings are generally transplanted to flooded paddy fields, although varieties of upland rice do not require flooding. The field is drained to enable mechanical harvesting. Milling the grain removes either the outer husk alone, resulting in brown rice, or both the husk and the bran layer, resulting in vitamin-B-deficient white rice.

Richard (I) the Lionheart (1157–99) King of England (1189–99); a hero of medieval legend, he spent all but six months of his reign abroad. The third son of Henry II and *Eleanor of Aquitaine, he joined the third Crusade in 1189 and conquered Messina and Cyprus before arriving in the Holy Land. His victory at Arsuf gained Joppa (1191). On his way home he was captured in Austria and was only released after payment of an enormous ransom (1194). He died campaigning in France.

Richard II (1367–1400) King of England (1377–99). Succeeding his grandfather Edward III, as a minor, government was largely in the hands of his uncle *John of Gaunt. Factional struggles culminated in the banishment in 1398 of Gaunt's son Henry Bolingbroke. He returned in 1399, while Richard was in Ireland, and seized the throne as Henry IV. Richard died shortly afterwards at Pontefract Castle in mysterious circumstances.

Richard III (1452–85) King of England (1483–85). He was the youngest brother of Edward IV, on whose death in 1483 he became protector for Edward V, a minor. After destroying the power of the Woodville faction, Richard imprisoned Edward and his brother and seized the throne. It is alleged that Richard murdered the boys, who disappeared in August 1483. As king, he made important administrative and financial reforms but faced opposition, first from Henry Stafford, 2nd Duke of Buckingham (executed in October 1483), and then from Henry Tudor (subsequently *Henry VII), by whom Richard was defeated and killed at Bosworth.

Richardson, Sir Ralph (1902–83) British actor. He established his reputation as an actor of Shakespearean roles while working with the Old Vic Company during the 1930s and 1940s. He also acted in modern plays, such as David Storey's *Home* (1970) and Harold Pinter's *No Man's Land* (1976) and made many films.

Richardson, Samuel (1689–1761) British

novelist. His pioneering novel *Pamela* (1740) evolved from a publisher's commission for a book of model letters for inexperienced writers. His acute psychological characterization was further developed in *Clarissa* (1748).

Richelieu, Armand Jean du Plessis, Cardinal de (1585–1642) French statesman, who greatly increased the absolute authority of the Crown and France's power in Europe. He rose to prominence as adviser to Louis XIII's mother Marie de' Medici (1573–1642), becoming Louis' chief minister in 1629. He ruthlessly suppressed the *Huguenots and by means of an extensive secret service thwarted a series of aristocratic conspiracies against himself. He directed France with brilliance in the Thirty Years' War and founded the French Academy.

Richmond 37 34N 77 27W A city and port in the USA, the capital of Virginia. Richmond was the capital of the Confederate states during the US Civil War. Population (2000): 197 790.

Richmond-upon-Thames A mainly residential borough of SW Greater London. It contains Richmond Park, Hampton Court Palace, and Kew Gardens.

Richter scale A scale of earthquake magnitude devised in 1935 by C. F. Richter (1900–85). It is a logarithmic scale from 0–9, the largest earthquakes having the highest numbers. The strongest earthquake so far recorded had a Richter scale value of 8.6.

Richthofen, Manfred, Freiherr von (1892–1918) German air ace of World War I, who shot down 80 Allied aircraft before being killed himself in action. His nickname, the Red Baron, referred to the colour of his plane.

rickets A disease of children affecting the bones and caused by *vitamin D deficiency. With a poor diet and/or inadequate sunshine the bones become soft and do not grow properly.

rickettsia A minute organism belonging to a phylum of bacteria that cannot reproduce outside the bodies of their hosts. They infect arthropods (especially ticks and mites) and can be transmitted to humans, in whom they cause such diseases as *typhus. All species live within living cells: they were formerly regarded as intermediate between bacteria and viruses. The name derives from the principal genus (*Rickettsia*), which was named after the US pathologist H. T. Ricketts (1871–1910).

Ridgeway A prehistoric trackway in S England. It runs along the scarp of the Berkshire Downs, linking the *Avebury region with the Thames.

Rif A *Berber people of N Morocco. Most of the 19 tribes speak the Rif dialect of the Berber language but a few speak Arabic. Many are light skinned and have blue or grey eyes. The Rif are Muslims and are renowned for their warrior tradition.

rifle A shoulder small arm with a spiral groove inside its long barrel to make the projectile spin during its trajectory. Invented in the 15th century, the rifle superseded the *musket during the 18th and 19th centuries. During the 1880s breech-loading rifles became capable of firing more than one cartridge without reloading. These were the immediate predecessors of the modern repeating rifle. *See also* BROWNING AUTOMATIC RIFLE.

riflebird A large *bird of paradise having a black plumage with iridescent throat patches and small ornamental plumes. The magnificent riflebird (*Craspedophora magnifica*) is about 30 cm long with a slender curved bill, a glossy green crown, and a purplish throat. The male performs its courtship display on fiercely defended perches.

rift valley A steep-sided valley with a flat floor formed as a result of the valley floor subsiding between two roughly parallel faults. The most notable example is the vast Great Rift Valley in Africa.

Riga 56 53N 24 08E The capital of Latvia, a port on the Baltic Sea. It is an industrial and cultural centre. *History*: the order of Livonian Knights was founded here in 1201, and in 1282 Riga became a member of the Hanseatic League. It then passed to Poland (1581), to Sweden (1621), and to Russia (1710). The capital of independent Latvia (1918–40 and from 1991) and of the Latvian SSR (1940–91), it was occupied by the Germans (1941–44) in World War II. Population (2000 est): 788 283.

right ascension An angular distance, analogous to terrestrial longitude, that is used with **declination** to specify the position of an astronomical body on the *celestial sphere. It is measured eastwards along the celestial equator from the vernal *equinox. Declination is the angular distance of the body N or S of the celestial equator.

Rights of Man and of the Citizen, Declaration of the (1789) The formal expression of the ideals of the *French Revolution. Comprising 17 articles, it was drafted by the National Assembly to preface the constitution of 1791. Incorporating *Enlightenment theories and both English and American precedents (*see* BILL OF RIGHTS), the Declaration asserted that "all men are born free and equal in rights."

right whale A *whale of the family *Balaenidae* (5 species), so called because they were the right whales to catch (by whalers). Up to 18 m long and weighing over 20 tonnes, they are large-headed slow-moving plankton feeders.

Rijeka (Italian name: Fiume) 45 20N 14 27E The chief seaport in Croatia on the Adriatic Sea. Made a free port in 1723, it was annexed by Hungary in 1779. In 1919, Gabriele D'Annunzio (1863–1938) led a force to capture it for Italy. It again became a free port in 1920, reverted to Italy in 1924, came to Yugoslavia in 1947, and finally became part of independent Croatia in 1991. Population (2001): 147 709.

Rijksmuseum A museum and art gallery in Amsterdam, housing the national collection of the Netherlands. It originated in 1808 as the Royal Museum and became the Rijksmuseum in 1817. Its paintings of the Dutch school include the celebrated *Night Watch* by Rembrandt.

Rijswijk, Treaty of (1697) The treaty that ended the War of the Grand Alliance between France and England, Spain, Austria, and the Netherlands. Louis XIV of France surrendered most of the territories he had conquered, recognized William III as King of England, and granted trading concessions to the Dutch.

Rilke, Rainer Maria (1875–1926) Austrian poet, born in Prague. Paris is the setting for the meditative prose of *Die Aufzeichnungen des Malte Laurids Brigge* (1910). In his poetry, the mysticism of *Das Stunden-Buch* (1905) develops into a pantheistic celebration of life in the *Duino Elegies* (1923) and the *Sonnets to Orpheus* (1923).

Rimbaud, Arthur (1854–91) French poet. He was welcomed to Paris in 1871 by *Verlaine, with whom he formed a tempestuous relationship that eventually ended in a violent quarrel. His visionary theories about poetry were expressed in *Une Saison en enfer* (1873) and *Les Illuminations* (1886). At the age of 20 he renounced poetry and wandered in Europe and the Near East, eventually becoming a gun-runner in Ethiopia.

Rimini (Latin name: Ariminium) 44 03N 12 24E A town and resort in Italy, on the N Adriatic coast. It has various Roman and medieval remains. Population (2000 est): 131 062.

Rimsky-Korsakov, Nikolai (1844–1908) Russian composer. He was a member of the group of nationalist composers known as the Mighty Five. He wrote 15 operas, including *The Snow Maiden* (1880–81) and *The Golden Cockerel* (1906–07), such orchestral works as *Scheherazade* (1888), chamber music, and songs.

ringlet A *satyrid butterfly characterized by brownish wings marked with small white rings. The larval food plants are mainly grasses. Chief genera: *Aphantopus*, *Cacnonympha*, *Erebia*.

ring ouzel A shy songbird, *Turdus torquatus*, of mountainous regions. The male is black with a broad white crescent around the throat; the female is dark brown with less distinct markings. Family: *Turdidae* (thrushes).

ringworm A highly infectious disease of the skin, hair, and nails that is caused by various fungi: it is known medically as tinea. Ringworm is usually transmitted by direct contact. The affected area is typically ring-shaped (especially on the scalp). Infections are treated with a variety of antifungal drugs, applied locally or taken by mouth.

Rio de Janeiro 22 53S 43 17W The chief port in Brazil, the capital of Rio de Janeiro state. Discovered by the Portuguese in 1502, it was the capital of Brazil from 1763 until 1960. It is renowned for its spectacular setting backed by mountains, the most famous of which is the conical Sugar Loaf Mountain. Another famous landmark is the giant figure of Christ standing on the highest peak. It is an important port and trading centre. Population (2000): 5 850 544.

Rio Grande (Spanish names: Río Bravo; Río Bravo del Norte) The fifth longest river of North America. Rising in the Rocky Mountains, it forms the entire border between Texas (USA) and Mexico. Length: 2040 km (1885 mi).

Risorgimento (Italian: resurgence) The nationalist movement in 19th-century Italy that achieved the country's independence and unification. Secret societies, such as the Carbonari and Young Italy, encouraged Italian patriotism after 1815. In 1859, the Piedmontese prime minister *Cavour freed Lombardy and in 1860 Garibaldi surrendered to Piedmont the conquests made in the S by his Expedition of the Thousand. Tuscany, Modena, Parma, Bologna, and Romagna then accepted entry into the kingdom of Italy under the House of Piedmont, proclaimed in 1861. Unification was completed by Italy's annexation of Venetia in 1866 and of the papal states in 1870.

Rivera, Diego (1886–1957) Mexican mural painter. In Mexico in the 1920s, he revived the old techniques of *fresco and encaustic painting. His communist-inspired subject matter made him notorious in the USA. His wife **Frida Kahlo** (1907–54) was also a noted painter.

Riverina A district of Australia, in S New South Wales. It consists chiefly of flat alluvial plains. Area: 68 658 sq km (26 509 sq mi).

Riviera (French name: Rivière) The narrow Mediterranean coastal belt of France and Italy, extending roughly between Toulon and La Spezia. Its climate, scenery, and beaches have made it a long-standing cosmopolitan resort.

Riyadh 24 39N 46 46E A city in Saudi Arabia, in the centre of the Arabian Peninsula. Riyadh and Mecca are joint capitals of the kingdom. Population (1996 est): 2 800 000.

RNA (*or* ribonucleic acid) A nucleic acid that is important in the synthesis of proteins by living organisms. In some viruses RNA is the genetic material. Structurally, it is similar to *DNA but usually occurs as a single-stranded molecule with the sugar ribose and the base uracil replacing the deoxyribose and thymine of DNA. There are three main types of RNA: ribosomal (r) RNA, messenger (m) RNA, and transfer (t) RNA. mRNA contains the genetic code necessary for protein synthesis. It is transcribed from DNA in the nucleus and then moves to the ribosomes, where the genetic information encoded within it is translated into a particular polypeptide chain. The amino acids making up the protein are brought to their correct positions in the chain by tRNA.

roach One of several freshwater fish related to carp, especially *Rutilus rutilus*, a game fish found in N Europe. It has an elongated body, 15–45 cm long, olive-green to grey-green above and silvery white below with reddish fins and red eyes. It lives in shoals, feeding on small animals and plants.

Robert (I) the Bruce (1274–1329) King of the Scots (1306–29). After a long career of rebellion against the English Crown Robert seized the Scottish throne in 1306. Although immediately forced into exile by Edward I of England, on the accession of Edward II he slowly recovered the kingdom, decisively defeating the English forces at Bannockburn (1314).

Robert II (1316–90) The first *Stuart King of the Scots (1371–90). He was three times regent of Scotland (jointly 1334–35; alone 1338–41 and 1346–57) while his uncle David II (1324–71) was imprisoned or in exile. His own rule, as an old man, was of little consequence.

Roberts, Julia (1967–) US film actress, who rose to stardom in *Pretty Woman* (1990). Later films include *Notting Hill* (1999), *Erin Brockovich* (2000), which earned her an Oscar, and *Mona Lisa Smile* (2003).

Robeson, Paul (1898–1976) US Black actor and singer of Negro spirituals. His stage performances include the title role of Othello, and he actively campaigned for Black civil rights.

Robespierre, Maximilien François Marie Isidore de (1758–94) French revolutionary. A lawyer, Robespierre was elected to the States General in 1789 and became one of the leaders of the radical Jacobins. After the execution of Louis XVI he was instrumental in the overthrow of the Girondins (1793). He subsequently wielded supreme power on the Committee of Public Safety, instituting the *Reign of Terror. In 1794 his cult of the Supreme Being became unpopular: he was denounced in the Legislative Assembly and guillotined.

robin A small Eurasian songbird, *Erithacus rubecula*. About 13 cm long, it has an olive-brown plumage with an orange-red breast, throat, and forehead and feeds on insects, earthworms, fruit, and seeds. A robin defends its territory fiercely, using its song to warn off intruders. Family: *Turdidae* (thrushes).

Robin Hood An English outlaw, probably legendary, who figures in a series of medieval ballads. According to the *Lytell Geste of Robyn Hoode* (c. 1495) he killed the evil sheriff of Nottingham, was visited in his forest home by the king, and was then employed in the royal household.

Robinson, Sugar Ray (Walker Smith; 1921–89) US boxer, world welterweight champion (1946–51) and five times middleweight champion (twice in 1951, 1955, 1957, 1958–60). He fought 202 professional bouts, of which he lost only 19.

robotics The study of automatic machines that are capable of simulating and replacing human activities. Some robotic machines have sensory devices and can make decisions based on a sensory input and a self-programming facility. However, most robots in current industrial use carry out a fixed sequence of computer-controlled operations.

Rob Roy (Robert Macgregor; 1671–1734) Scottish outlaw, whose violent life was romanticized in Sir Walter Scott's novel *Rob Roy* (1818). He became a bandit after losing his family fortunes in 1712.

Robson, Dame Flora (1902–84) British actress. She was successful in both comedy, as in *Captain Brassbound's Conversion* (1948), and in serious drama, such as Ibsen's *Ghosts* (1958) and *John Gabriel Borkman* (1963). In her many films she usually played character parts.

Rochdale A unitary authority in N England, in Greater Manchester. Area: 159 sq km (61 sq mi). Population (2001): 205 233.

Rochester 1. 43 12N 77 37W A city in the USA, in New York state on Lake Ontario. Founded in 1789, its industries include the manufacture of photographic equipment. Population (2000): 219 773. **2.** 51 24N 0 30E A city and port in SE England, in Medway unitary authority, Kent on the Medway estuary. It was a Roman stronghold. Population (1994 est): 146 200.

rock A solid mixture of *minerals forming part of the earth's crust. Rocks are classified according to their formation (*see* IGNEOUS ROCK; METAMORPHIC ROCK; SEDIMENTARY ROCK), their age (*see* STRATIGRAPHY), and their composition. The principal minerals in rocks are the silicates (including silica), carbonates, and oxides. The essential minerals in a rock are those that determine its classification; accessory minerals are those that do not affect its classification. Petrology is the study of rocks.

rock crystal *See* QUARTZ.

Rockefeller, John D(avison) (1839–1937) US industrialist, who founded the monopolistic oil-refining company, Standard Oil (1870). A philanthropist, he founded the University of Chicago in 1891 and, with his son **John D(avison) Rockefeller, Jr** (1874–1960), established the Rockefeller Institute for Medical Research (now Rockefeller University) in 1901. The latter's nephew, **Nelson A(ldrich) Rockefeller** (1908–79), was Gerald Ford's vice-president (1974–77).

rockets Vehicles or missiles powered by jet propulsion that carry their own fuel and oxidizer and can therefore travel both in space and in the atmosphere. Rockets have no lift surfaces (*see* AERONAUTICS), obtaining both lift and thrust from their propulsive jets. Solid-fuel firework rockets were known to the Chinese in the 13th century; the first liquid-fuelled rocket to fly was designed by the American R. H. Goddard (1882–1945) in 1926. This achievement attracted little interest, except in Germany, where the Peenemünde rocket research station was set up. It was here that Werner *von Braun produced the *V-2 rocket in World War II. Intercontinental *ballistic missiles (with nuclear warheads) developed from this model. These rockets, in turn, led to the space rockets that carried man to the moon.

Space rockets are built in stages, a high-thrust vehicle providing lift-off and acceleration into the thinner atmosphere, where this first stage is jettisoned and the second stage takes over. The world's biggest rocket, the US Saturn V, is a three-stage rocket weighing 3000 tonnes fully laden. The first stage burns kerosene and the second and third stages burn liquid hydrogen. Liquid oxygen (lox) is the oxidizer for all stages.

rockrose A small spreading shrub, *Helianthemum chamaecistus*, up to 30 cm high with bright-yellow flowers; it is found in grassland and scrub of Europe and W Asia. Family: *Cistaceae*.

Rocky Mountains (*or* **Rockies**) The chief mountain system in North America. It extends roughly N–S for about 4800 km (3000 mi) between New Mexico (USA) and the Yukon (Canada), forming the Continental Divide. It rises to 4399 m (14 431 ft) at Mount Elbert.

rococo A style dominant in the fine and decorative arts of France between about 1700 and 1750. Developing in reaction to the *baroque pomp of the Louis XIV period, it was characterized by curved forms, slender proportions, asymmetry, pastel colours, and a general effect of gaiety and delicacy. Rococo artists include the painters *Fragonard, *Boucher, and *Watteau and the sculptor Clodion (1738–1814). The style spread to Austria and Germany, where the leading exponent was the architect Balthazar Neumann (1687–1753).

rodent A mammal belonging to the order *Rodentia* (over 1700 species). Rodents are distributed worldwide and occupy a wide range of habitats. They range in size from about 7.5 cm (the smallest mice) to 130 cm (the capybara). Rodents have distinctive teeth. The single pairs of chisel-like incisors in each jaw continue to grow throughout life, as they are worn away by gnawing. There are no second incisor or canine teeth, leaving a gap between the front teeth and cheek teeth. Rodents are divided into three suborders: *Hystricomorpha* (porcupines, cavies, chincillas, etc.; 180 species); *Sciuromorpha* (squirrels, beavers, marmots, chipmunks, etc.; 366 species); and *Myomorpha* (rats, mice, lemmings, voles, etc.; 1183 species).

Rodgers, Richard Charles (1902–79) US composer of musical comedies. With the lyricist Lorenz Hart (1895–1943) he wrote such works as *The Girl Friend* (1926) and *Pal Joey* (1940). After Hart's death he collaborated with Oscar *Hammerstein II on *Oklahoma* (1943), *The King and I* (1951), *The Sound of Music* (1959), and other musicals.

Rodin, Auguste (1840–1917) French sculptor. He produced his first major work, *The Age of Bronze* (1877), after visiting Italy (1875), where he was influenced by the work of Michelangelo and Donatello. *The Burghers of Calais* (1884–86), his nude monument of Victor Hugo, and his dressing-gowned Balzac were all initially rejected. Nevertheless, by 1900 Rodin had established an international reputation, his bronze portrait busts and his marble *The Kiss* (1886; Tate Gallery), being particularly admired. His most personal work, *The Gates of Hell*, was left unfinished at his death.

Rodney, George Brydges, 1st Baron (1719–92) British admiral. He wrecked (1759–60) a French invasion fleet during the Seven Years' War and won victories (1780–82) against the powers that supported the American Revolution. His victory over the French off Dominica (1782) helped Britain to gain favourable terms in the concluding Peace of Versailles (1783).

Rodrigo, Joaquín (1902–99) Spanish composer, blind since the age of three. His works include the *Concierto de Aranjuez* (for guitar and orchestra; 1940) and *Concierto Pastorale* (for flute and orchestra; 1978).

roe deer A small deer, *Capreolus capreolus*, of temperate Eurasian forests. About 70 cm high, roe deer have a dark-brown winter coat, a red-brown summer coat, and a large white rump patch; males have small antlers. They feed at night on leaves, shoots, and berries.

r

roentgen A unit of dose of ionizing radiation equal to the dose that produces ions of one sign carrying a charge of 2.58×10^{-4} coulomb in air.

Roentgen, Wilhelm Konrad (1845–1923) German physicist. In 1895 Roentgen was investigating the *luminescence that cathode rays produce in certain substances and discovered that the luminescence persisted when the cathode rays themselves were blocked by cardboard. He correctly concluded that some other type of radiation was coming from the cathode-ray tube. He named the radiation X-rays.

Rogers, Ginger (Virginia McMath; 1911–95) US actress and singer. During the 1930s she partnered Fred *Astaire in film musicals, including *Top Hat* (1935), *Swing Time* (1936), and *Follow the Fleet* (1936).

Rogers, Richard, Baron (1933–) British architect, born in Italy. With his first wife Su he formed Team 4 with Norman and Wendy *Foster (1963–67). His buildings include the Pompidou Centre in Paris (1971–77; with Renzo Piano), Lloyd's in London (1986), the European Court of Human Rights, Strasbourg (1989–95), and the *Millennium Dome, Greenwich.

Rolland, Romain (1866–1944) French novelist, dramatist, and essayist. His best-known novel, *Jean Christophe* (1904–12), concerns a German composer. He won the Nobel Prize in 1915.

Rolling Stones, the A British rock group, formed in 1962. Their early hits included "The Last Time" and "Satisfaction". Later albums include *Beggar's Banquet* (1968), *Exile on Main Street* (1972), and *Some Girls* (1978). The original members were Mick *Jagger (1944–), Keith Richard (1943–), Bill Wyman (1936–), Charlie Watts (1941–), and Brian Jones (1942–69).

Roman Catholic Church The Christian Church of which the pope is the temporal leader. After the split with the Eastern Orthodox Churches (1054), Roman Catholicism was the unchallenged spiritual authority in W Europe. In the early 16th century the rising tide of *Protestantism demonstrated the need for urgent reforms within the Church. The Council of Trent (1545–63) has largely determined the present dogmatic, disciplinary, and liturgical character of Roman Catholicism (*see also* COUNTER-REFORMATION), although important reforms were initiated by the second Vatican Council. The Church organization is centralized and hierarchical and the pope's decisions are reinforced by the doctrine of *infallibility. Other accepted doctrines include *transubstantiation and *purgatory. The number of the *sacraments has been fixed at seven since the 12th century. The cult of the Virgin Mary, which flourished in the middle ages, underwent a major revival in the 19th century. Until the mid-20th century Latin was the sole language of the Mass. Roman Catholicism has spread worldwide due to strenuous missionary efforts since the 16th century (*see* JESUITS) and is the largest Christian denomination. Some modernization of the Church has taken place (the use of the vernacular in the Mass, etc.), although traditional teachings on such issues as abortion, contraception, divorce, and female and married priests have been maintained.

Romance languages Descendants of the Italic language group, in particular of the spoken form of Latin, called Vulgar Latin. The group consists of modern *French, *Italian,

*Spanish, *Portuguese, *Romanian, *Catalan, the Rhaetian (*see* ROMANSCH) group of dialects, Sardinian, and the now extinct Dalmatian. They are classified as a group on the basis of a shared section of basic vocabulary, which originated in the influence of the language of the Roman conquerors of the Mediterranean.

Roman Curia (Latin: *Curia Romana*) The papal court, comprising the chief judicial and administrative bodies of the *Roman Catholic Church. Extensively reformed in 1967 by Pope Paul VI, it consists of three tribunals, which are mainly concerned with judicial matters; five offices, including the Chancery, which issues papal bulls, and the offices of the Palatinate Secretaries; and nine Roman Congregations, which are permanent commissions of cardinals having specific tasks.

Roman Empire The imperial period of ancient Roman history from 27 BC, when Octavian became emperor as *Augustus, until 476 AD. Under imperial government many of the political institutions of the *Roman Republic, notably the Senate, continued to function, although Augustus and his successors enjoyed supreme power as *princeps* (chief citizen). Augustus fostered peace and prosperity, which continued, despite outbreaks of rebellion, under the paternalistic rule of the Flavian (69–96 AD: Vespasian, Titus, and Domitian) and Antonine (96–180: Nerva, Trajan, Hadrian, Antoninus Pius, Marcus Aurelius) emperors. Civil war, however, followed the death of Commodus (193). Order was briefly restored by Lucius Septimus Severus (reigned 193–211), who openly acknowledged his dependence on military might. The 3rd century saw a rapid succession of army-nominated emperors, while Rome's frontiers were threatened by the Sasanians and the Goths. Diocletian (reigned 284–305) countered these attacks with the reorganization of the Empire between East (*see* EASTERN ROMAN EMPIRE) and West (293). It was reunited (324) under *Constantine the Great, who founded a new imperial capital at Constantinople (*see* ISTANBUL). Civil war and economic decline followed his death and the western Empire fell prey to barbarian invasions. In 476 the last Roman emperor of the West, Romulus Augustulus (b. ?461), was deposed by the German king Odoacer. The Eastern Roman, or Byzantine, Empire survived until 1453. See p. 618.

Romanesque art The dominant style of building, art, and furniture from the end of the 10th century until the emergence of the Gothic style around 1200. The buildings are characterized by the round arch, inherited from the Romans, which is used for doorways, windows, and friezes; vaulting, when used, is often barrel vaulting. The pictorial art is often severe and stylized, while furniture is more robust than elegant.

Romania, Republic of A country in SE Europe, on the Black Sea. The Carpathian Mountains and the Transylvanian Alps separate the plains in the E and S from the Transylvanian plateau in the NW. *Economy*: the main crops are maize, wheat, potatoes, sugar beet, and fruit. Livestock is also important. Minerals include oil and gas, salt, lignite, iron, and copper. The industrial sector is based on heavy industries such as minerals and metals and stands in need of modernization. There is a considerable timber industry and wine-making is of growing importance. Soaring inflation and a depreciating currency in the mid-1990s obliged the government to introduce free-market reforms. *History*: formed in 1861 from the principalities of *Moldavia and *Walachia, Romania gained independence from the Ottoman Empire in 1878 and in 1881 became a kingdom under Carol I. Romania joined (1916) the Allies in World War I and was occupied by the Germans. In 1918 it obtained Bessarabia, Bukovina, and Transylvania, which it was forced to relinquish to the Axis Powers in 1940. Shortly afterwards Carol II abdicated in favour of his son Michael and the fascist Ion *Antonescu came to power. He gave military support to Germany until Soviet forces entered the country and his government was overthrown (1944). After World War II a communist-dominated coalition was established (1945) and in 1947 Michael abdicated. Elections in 1948 resulted in a clear communist victory. Under the totalitarian regime of President Nicolae Ceauşescu (from 1967) all dissent was suppressed and living standards plummeted. In 1989 mass demonstrations in Bucharest, Timişoara, and elsewhere culminated in a full-scale revolution. Ceauşescu was executed and a new administration installed. A new constitution enshrining a multiparty system and free-market reforms was approved in a national referendum (1991) but the government continued to be dominated by the ex-communists and President Ion Iliescu was accused of blocking reform. Demonstrations against the government were repressed. In 1996 non-communists were victorious in presidential and parliamentary elections but elections in 2000 saw the return of Iliescu and the ex-communists. Romania was invited to join NATO in 2002 and a new constitution, based on EU law, was adopted in 2003. Official language:

Romanian. Currency: leu of 100 bani. Area: 237 500 sq km (91 699 sq mi). Population (2003 est): 21 616 000. Capital: Bucharest.

Romanian A Romance language, the main form of which (Daco-Romanian) is spoken in Romania and Moldova. Other forms are Aromanian or Macedo-Romanian (Greece, Macedonia, Serbia, Albania, and Bulgaria); Megleno-Romanian (N Greece); and Istro-Romanian (Istrian peninsula).

Roman law The body of laws compiled by the Romans, which forms the basis of the *civil law of many modern countries. Before about 150 BC the laws of the Twelve Tables (450 BC) were elaborated as the *jus civile* (civil law), i.e. the law applicable exclusively to Roman citizens. With increasing interests abroad, another system, the *jus gentium* (law of nations), was also applied by Roman courts. This system of international law derived from the philosophical concept of natural law (i.e. a law common to all men and to nature) and was used in cases involving provincial Roman subjects of different states and in suits between a foreigner or provincial and a Roman citizen. As Roman law developed there arose a number of anomalies, until the Byzantine emperor *Justinian I sponsored the *Corpus Juris Civilis* (Body of Civil Law) or Justinian Code, published between 529 and 565 AD. This consisted of four parts: (1) the *Codex Constitutionum*, a chronological collection of the ordinances (*constitutiones*) of the emperors, with all anomalies eliminated; (2) the *Digest*, a collection of statements by jurists on points of law; (3) the *Institutes*, a textbook explaining legal institutions; and (4) the *Novellae* or *Novels*, the new ordinances issued by Justinian after the publication of the *Codex*. The most influential modern codification based on it was the *Code Napoléon*.

Roman numerals The system of numbers used by the Romans, based on letters of the alphabet: I = 1, V = 5, X = 10, L = 50, C = 100, D = 500, and M = 1000. Intermediate numbers are given by the sum of a larger number and the smaller number that follows it (e.g. VI = 6) or the difference between a larger number and the smaller number that precedes it (IV = 4, IX = 9)

Roman Republic (510–27 BC) The period of ancient Roman history between the expulsion of *Tarquin the Proud and the proclamation of *Augustus as the first Roman emperor. Republican government comprised two chief magistrates (later *consuls) elected annually, an increasing number of subordinate magistrates, the *Senate, and popular assemblies. Power lay in the hands of the *patricians until the *plebeians, after two centuries of struggle, achieved access to all state offices.

Roman dominance over the rest of Italy was achieved by the early 3rd century. By the mid-2nd century Cisalpine *Gaul had been subdued and the *Punic Wars with Carthage brought control of the Mediterranean (146) and Rome's first overseas provinces. Concomitantly, dominance over Greece was achieved and control of much of Asia Minor. In the mid-1st century *Caesar completed the conquest of Transalpine Gaul. The Republic was gradually undermined, however, by provincial unrest, which, together with the military ineptness of the Senate in the late 2nd century, brought a series of ambitious army commanders to the fore.

The first of these, Marius (c. 157–86 BC), lost a bloody power struggle to the aristocrat, *Sulla, whose dictatorship (83–79) was marked by legislation to strengthen the Senate. This was revoked in 70 by *Pompey and *Crassus, who ten years later formed the so-called first Triumvirate with Caesar. The death of Crassus (53) and Pompey's intrigues with Caesar's senatorial enemies brought civil war. Caesar's victory and subsequent short-lived dictatorship rang the knell of the Roman Republic, which was finally destroyed by Octavian's defeat of *Mark Antony and his assumption of absolute power as Augustus. *See also* ROMAN EMPIRE.

Romansch A Romance language belonging to the Rhaetian group, spoken in N Italy and in the Rhine Valley in Switzerland.

Romanticism A fundamental development in western art, literature, music, and their related fields of theory in the late 18th and early 19th centuries. Romanticism constituted a reaction against the unquestioned authority of reason and tradition (*see* CLASSICISM) and an affirmation of faith in man's innate powers of creativity. Its various manifestations included a passionate concern with the relationship between man and his natural environment and a new interest in the primitive and the irrational. In literature, English Romanticism is usually dated from the publication of *Lyrical Ballads* by Wordsworth and Coleridge in 1798 and is associated with the poetry of Byron, Shelley, and Keats.

Romany The language spoken by Gipsies. It is related to *Sanskrit and the Indo-Aryan languages of N India but diverged from these about 1000 AD, when the Gipsies began their nomadic way of life. Romany has been greatly influenced in vocabulary by the languages spoken in regions the Gipsies have passed through, resulting in many different dialects.

Rome (Italian name: Roma) 41 53N 12 33E The capital of Italy, on the River Tiber. It is an administrative and cultural centre and, with the *Vatican City within its boundaries, the focal point of the Roman Catholic Church. Relics of classical times include the Forum, the *Pantheon, and the *Colosseum. There are many ancient churches the origins of which go back to the early Christian era. The Renaissance produced not only many outstanding buildings, such as St Peter's Basilica, but also the paintings and sculpture of such artists as Michelangelo and Raphael. *History*: according to legend Rome was founded on the Palatine Hill in 753 BC by Romulus, its first king. Seven kings were followed by the *Roman Republic, and the *Roman Empire was founded in the 1st century BC. As the Empire declined in the 5th century AD Rome was sacked by Germanic tribes. From the 6th century it regained importance, this time as an ecclesiastical power. In 800 Charlemagne was crowned emperor here. It remained under papal control until 1871, when it became capital of the newly unified Italy. The popes however refused formally to relinquish their temporal power until the Lateran Treaty of 1929, when their jurisdiction was confined to the Vatican City. Mussolini's March on Rome in 1922 marked the beginning of his fascist rule; the city was occupied by the Allies in World War II. Population (1996): 2 654 187.

Rome, Treaties of (1957) Two treaties signed in Rome, which led to the establishment of the *European Economic Community and the *European Atomic Energy Community.

Rommel, Erwin (1891–1944) German general, known as the Desert Fox. In 1940 he became commander of the Seventh Panzer Division and, in 1941, of the Afrika Corps. In N Africa he was hailed as a liberator by the Arabs and gained the respect of the enemy but in 1943, after his defeat at Alamein (1942), he was recalled and became commander of the Channel defence. His involvement in the attempt to assassinate Hitler in 1944 (*see* STAUFFENBERG, CLAUS, GRAF VON) led to his suicide, under pressure from Hitler.

Romney, George (1734–1802) British portrait painter. He attracted a fashionable clientele and rivalled Reynolds when he moved to London in 1762. He is best known for his numerous portraits of Emma, Lady *Hamilton.

Romulus and Remus The legendary founders of Rome, the sons of Mars and Rhea Silvia, daughter of Numitor, King of Alba Longa. Amulius, who had deposed Numitor, threw the twin babies into the Tiber. They were washed ashore and suckled by a she-wolf. They eventually founded Rome at the place where they had been rescued.

rondo A musical form in which a recurring theme alternates with contrasting episodes. In its simplest form it consists of the pattern ABACADA, A being the rondo theme and B, C, and D the episodes.

Ronsard, Pierre de *See* PLÉIADE, LA.

rook A large blue-black Eurasian crow, *Corvus frugilegus*, about 45 cm long and having a narrow grey bill with pale patches of bare skin at its base. Rooks are highly gregarious and feed on earthworms, larvae, carrion, and grain.

Roosevelt, Franklin D(elano) (1882–1945) US statesman; Democratic president (1933–45). He was paralysed from the waist down by poliomyelitis in 1921 but despite this disability became the only US president to be elected four times. He helped US recovery from the Depression with the *New Deal relief programmes. In World War II he introduced lend-lease aid to the Allies and, after the Japanese bombing of Pearl Harbor (1941), took the USA into the war. He attended the *Tehran and *Yalta Conferences but died in office before the conclusion of the war.

Roosevelt, Theodore (1858–1919) US statesman; Republican president (1901–09). A rancher and big-game hunter, he led the Rough Riders (1st Volunteer Cavalry) in the 1898 war with Cuba. As president he introduced his *Square Deal programme for social reform. Roosevelt's foreign policy was to "speak softly and carry a big stick." He established US control over the building of the Panama Canal and made the USA a policing power in the Americas.

root (algebra) **1.** One of the equal factors of a number. The square root is one of two equal factors; for example $\sqrt{9} = \pm 3$; the rth root of a number n is the number that when raised to the rth power gives n. **2.** The solution of an equation, i.e. the values of the variable that will satisfy the equation. *See* QUADRATIC EQUATION.

root (botany) The part of a plant that provides anchorage and enables the uptake of water and nutrients from the soil. Some plants, such as the dandelion, have one main root with smaller branches—a tap root system; others, such as grasses, have a mass of similar-sized roots—a fibrous root system. Roots can act as food-storage organs, as in the carrot and turnip (tap roots); fibrous roots that become swollen with food are called tuberous roots. Some roots act as supports.

root-mean-square value (**rms value**) The square root of the arithmetic average of the squares of a set of numbers; for example the rms of 2, 4, 5, 6 is $[(2^2+4^2+5^2+6^2)/4]^{1/2} = 4.5$. The rms value is useful in continuous quantities, such as alternating electric current, in which the heating effect is proportional to the current squared.

Roque de los Muchachos Observatory An international observatory on the island of La Palma in the Canaries at an altitude of 2400 m, set up in the 1980s by Britain, Denmark, Spain (who owns the site), and Sweden.

rorqual A small-headed fast-moving whalebone *whale of the family *Balaenopteridae* (6 species). The common rorqual (*Balaenoptera physalus*), also called fin whale or razorback, grows up to 25 m long; it has a dark back, shading to white underneath, and a small dorsal fin. *See also* BLUE WHALE.

Rorschach test A psychological test intended to measure aspects of personality. Devised by the Swiss psychiatrist Hermann Rorschach (1884–1922), it consists of ten inkblots in complex shapes. The way in which the subject describes these pictures suggests his or her character.

Rosaceae A cosmopolitan family of trees, shrubs, and herbs (about 2000 species). They include important fruit trees (cherries, apricots, apples, plums, etc.) and ornamentals (notably roses).

r

Rosario 33 00S 60 40W The second largest city in Argentina, on the Río Paraná. It is an industrial and commercial centre and the terminus of the pampas railways. Population (1999 est): 1 000 000.

Roscommon (Irish name: Ros Comáin) A county in the N Republic of Ireland, in Connacht. It has many lakes and extensive bogs. Agriculture is the chief occupation. Area: 2463 sq km (951 sq mi). Population (2002): 58 803. County town: Roscommon.

rose A prickly shrub or climber of the genus *Rosa* (200–250 species), native to N temperate regions but widely cultivated. The flowers are usually white, yellow, pink, or red and the fruits are red, yellow, or black hips containing many seeds. Modern hybrid roses—usually with double flowers—include the hybrid teas, derived from the tea rose (*R. odorata*), and the floribundas. Wild species include *dog rose and *sweet briar. Family: *Rosaceae*.

rosella A brightly coloured *parakeet belonging to a genus (*Platycercus*; 7 species) occurring in Australia and New Zealand. 18 cm long, rosellas have a long broad tail, which is usually blue or green edged with white, black shoulders, and distinctive face and throat markings. They are largely ground-dwelling.

rosemary An evergreen shrub, *Rosmarinus officinalis*, native to the Mediterranean region and W Asia. Up to 2 m high, it has bluish flowers. It is widely cultivated for its oil and for its leaves, which are used as a culinary herb. Family: *Labiatae*.

rose of Jericho A perennial herb, *Anastatica hierochuntica*, also called resurrection plant, native to W Asia. During the dry season the leaves are shed and the whole plant forms a wickerwork-like ball that is blown by the wind. When moistened, the plant regains its shape and produces tiny white flowers. Family: *Cruciferae*.

rose of Sharon *See* HIBISCUS; ST JOHN'S WORT.

Roses, Wars of the (1455–85) The civil wars between the Houses of *Lancaster (the red rose) and *York (the white rose) for possession of the English Crown. The Lancastrian Henry VI's incompetent rule resulted in factional struggles led by the Lancastrian Beauforts and Richard Plantagenet, Duke of *York, and the Earl of *Warwick (the Kingmaker). Open warfare broke out in 1455. York was killed in 1460 and his son seized the Crown in 1461, becoming Edward IV, and crushed the Lancastrians. In 1470–71 Henry VI was briefly restored by disaffected Yorkists but Edward returned after his victory at Tewkesbury and ruled until 1483. He was succeeded by his brother Richard III, whose reign ended with his defeat by Henry (VII) at Bosworth (1485). The remaining Yorkists were finally overcome at Stoke in 1487.

Rosetta Stone An inscribed stone slab discovered (1799) at Rosetta (Arabic name: Rashid), near Alexandria (Egypt). It carries a decree (196 BC) of Ptolemy V Epiphanes (reigned 205–180) in Egyptian *hieroglyphic and demotic, and Greek. The repetition of Ptolemy's name in the different scripts gave Thomas *Young the clue to deciphering hieroglyphs.

rosewood An attractive hardwood, usually dark reddish and often rose-scented, derived from several tropical evergreen trees of the genus *Dalbergia* (family *Leguminosae*). These in-

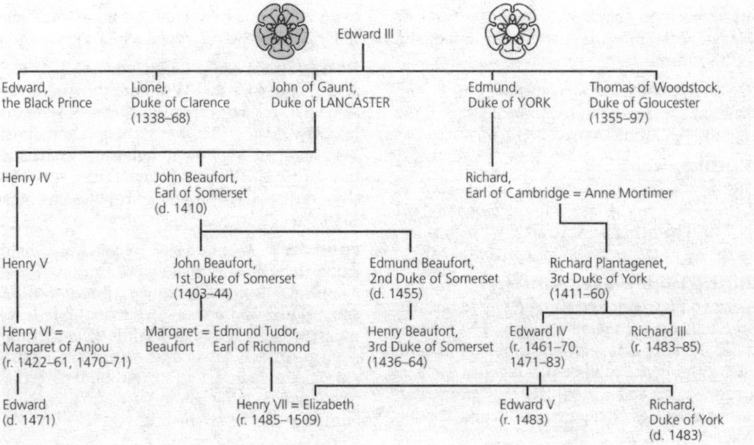

Wars of the Roses. The rival Houses of Lancaster and York.

clude Brazilian rosewood, or blackwood (*D. nigra*), used for veneers and cabinetwork; Honduras rosewood (*D. stevensoni*), used for musical instruments; and East Indian rosewood (*D. latifolia*).

Rosh Hashana (Hebrew: beginning of the year) The Jewish New Year festival, celebrated in Sept or Oct. It is regarded as a time of penitence and preparation for *Yom Kippur. A ram's horn (*shofar*) is blown in the synagogue.

Rosicrucianism An esoteric movement for spiritual renewal that originated in Protestant Germany in the early 17th century. Its manifesto traces its source to a fictitious brotherhood that was founded by a certain Christian Rosenkreuz in 1484. *See also* FREEMASONRY.

rosin (*or* **colophony**) A yellowish *resin obtained as a residue from the distillation of *turpentine. It is used in varnishes, soaps, soldering *flux, and to rub on violin bows.

Rossetti, Dante Gabriel (Gabriel Charles Dante R.; 1828–82) British painter and poet. In 1848 Rossetti joined with *Millais, *Hunt, and others to found the *Pre-Raphaelite Brotherhood. He founded the shortlived Pre-Raphaelite journal *The Germ* (1850–51) and later published several volumes of poetry and translations, including *Poems* (1870) and *Ballads and Sonnets* (1881). His sister **Christina Georgina Rossetti** (1830–74), a poet, was influenced by the *Oxford Movement. *Goblin Market and Other Poems* (1862), her first published volume, gave literary expression to Pre-Raphaelite ideals.

Rossini, Gioacchino Antonio (1792–1868) Italian composer. He wrote 36 highly successful operas, including *Tancredi* (1813), *The Italian Girl in Algiers* (1813), *The Barber of Seville* (1816), *The Thieving Magpie* (1817), and *William Tell* (1829). He also invented a number of recipes, including Tournedos Rossini.

Ross Island 77 40S 168 00E A volcanic island in the W Ross Sea, at the edge of the **Ross Ice Shelf**, a vast mass of permanent ice.

Ross Sea A large inlet of the S Pacific Ocean, in the Antarctic continent between Victoria Land and Byrd Land.

Rostock 54 03N 12 07E A city and Baltic port in NE Germany. Its fine medieval buildings have been restored following damage during World War II. Population (1999 est): 205 900.

Rostov-na-Donu 47 15N 39 45E A port in S Russia, on the River Don. Its importance owes much to its position on the route from the W to the Caucasus. Population (1999 est): 1 017 300.

Rostropovich, Mstislav (1927–) Soviet-born cellist. He left the Soviet Union in 1975 and now lives in London. Prokofiev, Britten, and Shostakovich all wrote cello works for him.

Roth, Philip (1933–) US novelist. Middle-class Jewish themes predominated in his early works including *Portnoy's Complaint* (1969). In subsequent novels, such as *The Anatomy Lesson* (1983) and *Operation Shylock* (1993), the targets of his satire are more various. His latest novels, which include *American Pastoral* (1997) and *The Human Stain* (2000), show a further broadening of his range.

Rotherham A unitary authority in N England, in South Yorkshire. Area: 283 sq km (109 sq mi). Population (2001): 248 176.

Rothko, Mark (Marcus Rothkovitch; 1903–70) Russian-born painter, who emigrated to the USA in 1913. In the late 1940s he pioneered colour-field painting, an abstract style using large expanses of colour, often in horizontal bands.

Rothschild, Mayer Amschel (1744–1812) German merchant and banker, whose business in Frankfurt prospered during the Napoleonic Wars, making loans to the various combatants and trading in high-demand goods such as arms, wheat, and cotton. His sons later established branches of the firm in Vienna, London, Naples, and Paris.

rotifer A tiny invertebrate animal belonging to the phylum *Rotifera* (about 2000 species), also called wheel animalcule, found mainly in fresh water. Rotifers vary in shape and range between 0.1 and 0.5 mm in length. Each has a ring of cilia (corona) for wafting food particles into the mouth and providing a means of locomotion in active species.

Rotorua 38 07S 176 17E A spa city in New Zealand, in N North Island. A Maori centre, situated within a volcanic area with hot springs, it has been developed as a health resort. Population (1994): 54 700.

Rotterdam 51 55N 4 29E The chief port and second largest city in the Netherlands, on the New Meuse River. It became important during the 19th century, mainly with the opening of the 35 km (12 mi) long Nieuwe Waterweg (New Waterway) in 1872 linking it to the North Sea. During World War II the city centre was destroyed; it has since been rebuilt. Buildings include the restored Groote Kerk (Great Church). Population (1999 est): 592 665.

r

Rottweiler A breed of working dog developed originally in Rottweil, Germany, with a reputation for aggression. It has a broad round body, a strong neck, and a large head with a deep muzzle. The coarse short coat is black with tan markings. Height: 63–68 cm (dogs); 58–63 cm (bitches).

Rouault, Georges (Henri) (1871–1958) French artist. A major 20th-century religious artist, he executed many paintings of clowns and prostitutes, which expressed his sympathy with social outcasts. As a graphic artist his main achievement was his series of etchings (1916–27), entitled *Miserere* and *Guerre*.

Rouen (Latin name: Rotomagus) 49 26N 1 05E A city and port in NW France, on the River Seine. The ancient capital of Normandy, it was here that Joan of Arc was tried and burned in 1431. Many of its notable buildings, including the cathedral (13th–16th centuries), survived the damage of World War II. Population (1999): 106 035.

rounders A nine-a-side bat-and-ball field game, which is probably the prototype of *baseball. The two teams take turns at batting and fielding and a match consists of two innings per team. The hard ball is delivered underarm to each batsman in turn until all are out. The batsmen try to score rounders by hitting it and running round the four bases without being caught or run out.

Roundheads The parliamentary party during the English *Civil War. The name referred originally to the short haircuts of the apprentices who demonstrated against the king at Westminster in 1640.

roundworm *See* NEMATODE.

Rousseau, Henri (1844–1910) French painter. From 1886 he exhibited at the Salon des Indépendants but his work, resembling folk art in technique (*see* PRIMITIVISM), was ridiculed. After 1894, when he exhibited *War* (Louvre), followed by the *Sleeping Gypsy* (1897; New York), he received more serious attention. The childlike quality of his jungle landscapes influenced many 20th-century painters.

Rousseau, Jean Jacques (1712–78) French philosopher and writer. Through his acquaintance with *Diderot, Rousseau joined the *Encyclopedists. In the *Discourse on the Origin and Foundations of Inequality amongst Men* (1754) he argued that man's perfect nature is spoiled by corrupt society. *Émile* (1762), a novel on education, expanded his views on ideal unfallen human nature. Such political works as *Du contrat social* (1762) found favour with the French revolutionaries. His romantic outlook inspired Shelley, Byron, and Wordsworth.

rowan *See* MOUNTAIN ASH.

rowing A sport using narrow light boats propelled by oars and often steered by a coxswain. It arose in its modern form in England during the 18th century; Olympic rowing events began in 1900. Each rower sits on a mobile slide, enabling leg, back, and arm muscles to be used. In sculling boats (single, double, four) each rower has two oars. **Sculling** is a form of rowing for one, two, or four people per boat, each person controlling two oars.

Rowlandson, Thomas (1756–1827) British caricaturist. Using a reed pen and delicate washes of colour, he produced the satirical *Dr Syntax* series (1812–21) and the *English Dance of Death* (1815–16). He also illustrated books by Smollett, Goldsmith, and Sterne.

Rowling, J(oanne) K(athleen) (1965–) British children's writer, whose stories about the boy wizard Harry Potter—*The Philosopher's Stone* (1997), *The Chamber of Secrets* (1998), *The Prisoner of Azkaban* (1999), *The Goblet of Fire* (2000), and *The Order of the Phoenix* (2003)—became a publishing phenomenon.

Royal Academy An art society in Burlington House, London, that holds annual summer exhibitions of contemporary British art, as well as loan exhibitions of modern artists and the old masters. Founded in 1768, it moved to its present premises in 1867.

Royal Academy of Dramatic Art (**RADA**) The leading British school of acting, founded in London in 1904 by Sir Herbert Beerbohm *Tree. It has received a government subsidy since 1924.

Royal Air Force (**RAF**) A British armed service formed in 1918 by the amalgamation of the Royal Flying Corps (1912) with the Royal Naval Air Service (1914). It contributed to the final operations on the western front in World War I and played a decisive role in *World War II. It is now divided into Strike Command (the operational command), Maintenance Command, and Training Command and is administered by the Air Force Department of the Ministry of Defence. The **Women's Royal Air Force** was formed in 1949 in succession to the Women's Auxiliary Air Force (WAAF) of World War II and the short-lived Women's Royal Air Force (1918–20). *See also* AIRCRAFT.

royal antelope The world's smallest antelope, *Neotragus pygmaeus*, of West African forests. 25–30 cm high, it is red-brown with white underparts; males have short spiky horns. They are nocturnal.

Royal Ballet The leading British ballet company and school, founded by Dame Ninette de Valois in 1931. Based at the Royal Opera House, Covent Garden, since 1946, it was known as the Sadler's Wells Ballet until 1956. Anthony Dowell was its director from 1986 until 2001; the current director is Monica Mason.

Royal British Legion An organization for ex-servicemen and women, founded in 1921 largely through the efforts of Douglas *Haig. It provides assistance with housing or employment problems and runs homes for the sick and aged. It also manufactures the Flanders poppies sold before *Remembrance Sunday.

Royal Canadian Mounted Police (*or* **Mounties**) Canadian police force. Founded in 1873 as the North West Mounted Police, it has become famous for the efficiency of its members, dressed in their distinctive scarlet tunics, blue breeches, and wide-brimmed hats.

Royal Geographical Society A British learned society, established in 1830 and incorporated in 1859, for the advancement of geographical knowledge. Among other functions it provides grants to finance expeditions. Two Royal Medals are awarded annually by the Queen to geographers recommended by the Society.

Royal Greenwich Observatory An observatory founded in 1675 by Charles II at Greenwich, London, in a building designed by Sir Christopher Wren. The meridian through Greenwich (0°) was internationally adopted as the prime meridian in 1884. The observatory was based at Herstmonceux, Sussex (1948–86), before its main telescope was moved to the new *Roque de los Muchachos Observatory in the Canary Islands; the observatory moved to Cambridge in 1990.

Royal Horticultural Society A society in the UK that exists to further interest in vegetables and ornamental plants. Founded in 1804, it now has its headquarters in Vincent Square, London. The society promotes new varieties and rare plants at various shows, the most famous being the annual Chelsea Flower Show.

Royal Institution One of the first scientific research centres, founded by Benjamin Thompson, Count *Rumford, in 1799. Several famous scientists have worked at its premises in Albermarle Street, London, including *Davy, *Faraday, and *Bragg.

Royal Marines A corps of troops, founded in England in 1664, which serves on land, at sea, or in the air. Their ranks correspond to those of the army but they are administered by the Navy Board. They served in both World Wars, in the Korean War and in Northern Ireland.

Royal Mint The factory in which the UK's coins are made. It was formerly in the Tower of London, moving to Tower Hill in 1811 and to Llantrisant, South Wales, in 1968. In 1999 the government announced that it would be semi-privatized.

Royal National Lifeboat Institution (**RNLI**) A voluntary organization, founded in 1824, that operates a 24-hour *lifeboat service around British coasts. Each lifeboat has a full-time mechanic but the other crew members are volunteers.

Royal National Theatre Company A British government-subsidized theatre company established as the National Theatre Company in 1963. Laurence Olivier, its first director, was succeeded by Peter Hall in 1973, Richard Eyre in 1988, Trevor Nunn in 1996, and Nicholas Hytner in 2003. The company's building, designed by Sir Denys Lasdun and opened in 1976, comprises an open-stage theatre called the Olivier, a proscenium-stage theatre called the Lyttleton, and a studio theatre for experimental plays called the Cottesloe. The prefix Royal was added in 1988.

Royal Navy (**RN**) The senior of Britain's three armed services. Founded in the 9th century by Alfred the Great, the RN emerged as "the wooden walls of England" in the 16th century with such victories as that over the Spanish *Armada (1588). The 17th century saw further victories against the Dutch, but little improvement in the lot of the sailors ("Jack Tars"). Mutiny finally broke out at the Nore and Spithead (1797) even as the RN entered its greatest era with a series of victories under *Nelson against Napoleonic France. The supreme sea power during the 19th century, the RN fought its last set-piece battle at Jutland (1916) during World War I. The modern RN is probably the most efficient navy in the world and undertakes fishery protection, mine sweeping, and NATO roles.

Royal Opera The leading British opera company, based at the Royal Opera House in Covent Garden. The company acquired its present name in 1969. Conductors with the Royal Opera have included Sir Thomas Beecham, Karl Rankl, and Sir Georg Solti. The Royal Opera House also houses the Royal Ballet. Chairman: Dame Judith Mayhew.

Royal Shakespeare Company (**RSC**) A British theatre company, founded in 1960 from the company at the Shakespeare Memorial Theatre in Stratford-upon-Avon. Peter Hall, its first director, was succeeded in 1968 by Trevor Nunn, who was joined by Terry Hands in 1978. Adrian Noble became director in 1991 but his plans to restructure the company and rebuild the main Stratford theatre caused opposition; he was replaced by Michael Boyd in 2002. The company performs Shakespeare and modern plays at Stratford and in London and tours frequently.

Royal Society The oldest and most important scientific society in the UK. It originated in 1645 and was incorporated by royal charter in 1662, early members including Sir Christopher *Wren and Samuel *Pepys. With the presidency from 1703–27 of Isaac *Newton, the Royal Society achieved great standing and financial security. The Society publishes scientific papers in the *Proceedings* and the *Philosophical Transactions*, maintains a large library, disburses grants, and awards medals for scientific achievement.

Royal Society for the Prevention of Cruelty to Animals (**RSPCA**) A British charity founded in 1824 to investigate reports of cruelty to animals. Funded by voluntary contributions, it has branches in the Commonwealth.

Royal Society for the Protection of Birds (**RSPB**) A British charity founded in 1889 to protest against the wholesale killing of birds for their plumage. Since then it has promoted the conservation of wild birds throughout Britain.

Royce, Sir (Frederick) Henry (1863–1933) British car manufacturer, who founded, with Charles Rolls (1877–1910), Rolls-Royce Ltd (1906). In 1884 Royce opened an engineering business in Manchester and in 1904 began to build cars, which much impressed Rolls and led to the merger of their businesses. Royce and his team designed many famous cars and the aeroengine that became the Merlin (used in Spitfires and Hurricanes in World War II).

Ruapehu, Mount 39 18S 175 36E An active volcano in New Zealand, the highest peak in North Island. Height: 2797 m (9175 ft).

Rub' al-Khali The S part of the Arabian Desert, mainly in Saudi Arabia. It constitutes the largest continuous area of sand in the world. Area: about 800 000 sq km (308 815 sq mi).

rubber A synthetic or natural organic polymer that is elastic and tough. The name comes from its ability to erase pencil marks. **Natural rubber**, which consists mainly of polyisoprene—$(CH_2CH{:}C.CH_3{:}CH_2)_n$—is made from the latex of the *rubber tree (*Hevea brasiliensis*) grown in SE Asia. The rubber is coagulated from latex (using acids) and pressed into sheets. Vulcanization increases its durability. **Synthetic rubbers** are made from petrochemicals (*see* OIL). Styrene-butadiene rubber (SBR), now the commonest synthetic rubber, was introduced during World War II.

rubber plant A tree, *Ficus elastica*, native to India and Malaysia, where it grows to a height of 35 m in forests. Its latex is the source of Assam or India rubber. Family: *Moraceae.*

rubella *See* GERMAN MEASLES.

Rubens, Peter Paul (1577–1640) Flemish painter, who lived chiefly in Antwerp. The greatest of the *baroque artists, Rubens first worked for the Mantuan court in Italy (1600–08). Returning to Antwerp, he painted his first major works, *The Raising of the Cross* and *Descent from the Cross* (both Antwerp Cathedral). Many commissions followed, including a cycle for Marie de' Medici (Louvre) and the ceiling of the Banqueting House, Whitehall, for Charles I. His most personal works are his portraits of his family, notably *Helena Fourment with a Fur Cloak* (Kunsthistorisches Museum, Vienna), and such landscapes as *The Château de Steen* (National Gallery, London).

Rubicon A stream in N central Italy, which formed the boundary between Italy and Cisalpine Gaul in the time of the Roman Republic. In 49 BC Julius Caesar precipitated civil war by leading his army across the Rubicon into Italy, an illegal act. Hence "crossing the Rubicon" has come to mean taking an irrevocable step.

rubidium (Rb) A highly electropositive alkali metal, discovered spectroscopically by R.W. Bunsen and G. R. Kirchhoff in 1861. The element is soft and silvery-white. It ignites spontaneously in air and reacts violently with water. The isotope ^{87}Rb is radioactive with a half-life of 5×10^{11} years and is used in *rubidium-strontium dating. Rubidium forms ionic salts and four oxides (Rb_2O, Rb_2O_2, Rb_2O_3, RbO_2). At no 37; at wt 85.47; mp 39.48°C; bp 688°C.

rubidium-strontium dating A method of radiometric dating, used mainly for rocks, fossils, etc. It utilizes the fact that naturally occurring rubidium contains about 28% of the radioactive isotope rubidium-87, which undergoes *beta decay to strontium-87. Thus by measuring the ratio of rubidium-87 to strontium-87 in the sample, its age may be estimated.

Rubinstein, Artur (1888–1982) Polish-born US pianist. He acquired a worldwide reputation, particularly as a performer of Chopin.

ruby A red transparent variety of *corundum, the colour being due to traces of chromium. It is used as a gemstone and in lasers, watches, and other precision instruments. Prior to the 14th century rubies were called carbuncles.

rudd A game fish, *Scardinius erythrophthalmus*, found in fresh waters of Europe and W Asia. It has a stout body, 35–40 cm long, golden- or olive-brown above and silvery white below, deep-red fins, and golden eyes.

rue An evergreen shrub, *Ruta graveolens*, also known as herb of grace, native to S Europe. 90 cm high, it has yellow flowers. The leaves yield a bitter oil, once used as a spice and in medicines. Family: *Rutaceae.*

ruff An Old World *sandpiper, *Philomachus pugnax*, that breeds in coastal wetlands of N Eurasia and winters on mudflats of South Africa and S Asia. The female (called a reeve) is 25 cm long and has a grey-brown plumage; the larger male has a double crest and a multicoloured collar in the breeding season.

Rugby 52 23N 1 15W A town in the English Midlands, in Warwickshire. According to tradition the game of rugby football originated here in 1823 at the famous public school (1567), which was described in *Tom Brown's Schooldays.* Rugby's industries include engineering and cement. Population (1997 est): 87 500.

Rügen A German island in the Baltic Sea, 2.5 km (1.5 mi) off Stralsund, to which it is connected by a road and rail causeway. Area: 926 sq km (358 sq mi). Population (latest est): 84 500.

Ruhr, River A river in W Germany, rising in the Sauerland and flowing NW and W to the River Rhine. The Ruhr Valley (German name: Ruhrgebiet) is the centre of the German iron and steel industry. Length: 235 km (146 mi).

Ruisdael, Jacob van (?1628–82) The greatest of Dutch landscape painters. His baroque compositions are noted for their dramatic contrasts of light and shade. *The Jewish Cemetery* (c. 1660) is a striking evocation of human mortality.

rum A colourless spirit distilled from molasses derived from sugar cane. Better-quality rums are aged in oak casks for several years.

Rumford, Benjamin Thompson, Count (1753–1814) American-born scientist, who spied for the British in the American Revolution. In England he carried out scientific research in ballistics and the theory of heat. Suspected of spying for the French, he left England in 1785 for Paris and then Bavaria, where he became a count of the Holy Roman

Empire. In 1795 he returned to England, where he helped to found the *Royal Institution (1799).

ruminant A hoofed mammal belonging to the suborder *Ruminantia* (about 175 species), which includes deer, cattle, antelopes, sheep, and goats. Ruminants are characterized by possession of a four-chambered stomach. Ruminants regurgitate their food periodically to "chew the cud," which helps to break up the plant cell walls.

Rump Parliament *See* LONG PARLIAMENT.

Rum Rebellion (1808) A rebellion in Australia in which William *Bligh, governor of New South Wales, was imprisoned by officers of the New South Wales Corps. It was incited by Bligh's suppression of the rum traffic.

Rundstedt, (Karl Rudolf) Gerd von (1875–1953) German field marshal, who was recalled from retirement at the outbreak of World War II, becoming (1942) commander in chief in France. He was captured in 1945 but his ill health secured his release.

runic alphabet An alphabetical writing system used for Norse and certain other Germanic languages. It originated, probably as a modified version of the Etruscan or the Roman alphabet, in the 2nd or 3rd century AD, and went out of use gradually after the 14th century. The runes were always associated with magical powers.

runner bean A climbing plant, *Phaseolus coccineus*, also known as scarlet runner, native to South America and widely cultivated as an annual vegetable crop. Growing up to 3 m high, it bears usually red flowers, which give rise to bean pods, 20–60 cm long, that are eaten cooked. Family: *Leguminosae*. *See also* BEAN.

Runnymede (*or* **Runnimede**) 51 26N 0 33W A meadow in SE England, on the S bank of the River Thames near Windsor. The Magna Carta was granted here by King John (1215).

Runyon, Damon (1884–1946) US humorous writer. His stories about New York characters were first collected in *Guys and Dolls* (1932).

Rupert, Prince (1619–82) Cavalry officer, who fought for the Royalists in the Civil War; he was the son of Frederick the Winter King of the Palatinate and Elizabeth, daughter of James I of England. A charismatic leader, he lacked the ability to maintain control when battle commenced. He was defeated at *Marston Moor (1644) and *Naseby (1645) and after Charles' surrender was banished from England. He returned at the Restoration (1660) and served as an admiral in the *Dutch Wars.

rupture *See* HERNIA.

rush A grasslike plant of the genus *Juncus* (over 300 species), found worldwide in damp temperate and cold regions. Rushes have tufts of slender rigid stalks, up to about 1 m high, bearing long flat leaves and produce many-seeded capsules. Family: *Juncaceae*. The name is also applied to similar plants, including the *bulrush, *flowering rush, and woodrush.

Rushdie, Salman (1947–) British novelist, born in India, who now lives in the USA. His first novel, *Grimus* (1975), was followed by the Booker prizewinner *Midnight's Children* (1981), *Shame* (1983), and *The Satanic Verses* (1988), which many Muslims interpreted as blasphemous. After Ayatollah *Khomeini's fatwa demanding the death of the author, he went into hiding. In 1998 the Iranian government formally dissociated itself from the fatwa, effectively ending his ordeal. His most recent novels are *The Ground Beneath Her Feet* (1999) and *Fury* (2001).

Ruskin, John (1819–1900) British art and social critic. He wrote *Modern Painters* (1843–60) to defend the paintings of J. M. W. Turner. In *The Stones of Venice* (1851–53) he promoted the gothic style in architecture. In *Unto This Last* (1862) and other volumes of social criticism he denounced materialism and laissez-faire economics. During his last years he became insane.

Russell, Bertrand Arthur William, 3rd Earl (1872–1970) British philosopher. His first major philosophical work, *Principia Mathematica* (1910–13), written with A. N. *Whitehead, presented pure mathematics as a development of *logic. *Our Knowledge of the External World* (1914) attempted a new approach to epistemology. From his pupil *Wittgenstein, he also acquired a lasting interest in language. He was imprisoned (1918) for his outspoken pacifism and again in 1961 for civil disobedience during the Campaign for Nuclear Disarmament. He was awarded the Nobel Prize for Literature in 1950.

Russell, Ken (1927–) British film director. His films include *Women in Love* (1969) and controversial biographical films, such as *The Music Lovers* (1970), about Tchaikovsky, *Mahler* (1974), and *Valentino* (1977).

Russian The main language of Russia, belonging to the East Slavonic family. It is a highly inflected language and is written in the *Cyrillic alphabet. The standard form is based on the dialect of Moscow.

Russian Federation (*or* **Russia**) The world's largest country, covering N Eurasia. It consists of 21 constituent republics, 11 national-territorial formations, 6 territorial formations, 49 regions, and 2 federal cities (Moscow and St Petersburg). The area W of the River Yenisei consists of vast plains and depressions, dissected by the Ural Mountains, while the E consists mainly of mountains and plateaus. *Economy*: Russia's mineral resources include iron ore, coal, oil, gold, platinum and copper. Industrial products include heavy machinery, electronic equipment, textiles, and chemicals. The main agricultural products are wheat, cotton, fruit and vegetables, tobacco, and sugar beet. In 1991 the new Russian state inherited economic troubles created over many years under the Soviet Union. Mass privatization began in 1992, as did reorganization of agriculture. Initially there was instability and hyperinflation but the economy has grown steadily since the financial crisis of 1998–99. *History*: little is known of the region's history until the 8th century AD, when European and Middle Eastern traders began its exploration. Control of the area between the Baltic and Black Seas was established by Scandinavian adventurers by 1000. Dominated by Kiev from the mid-10th to mid-11th centuries, these Varangian principalities submitted (after 1223) to the overrule of the Mongol Golden Horde. By the time of the Horde's collapse in the 14th century, Moscow, ruled by Rurik princes, had emerged as a powerful principality, becoming the capital of a united Russia under Ivan the Great in the 15th century. Contact with W Europe was established in the late 17th century by Peter the Great, who also established the Russian bureaucracy and educational system and built a new capital, St Petersburg. By the 19th century Russia had been greatly extended but its bureaucracy had grown unwieldy and oppressive, and its Romanov emperors (tsars) were opposed to any political change. Revolutionary activity began with the Dekabrists' conspiracy, uncovered in 1825; although serfdom was abolished in 1861, its abolition was achieved on terms unfavourable to the peasants and served to encourage revolutionaries, a group of whom assassinated Alexander II in 1881. Following the *Revolution of 1905, a parliament, the Duma, was established in 1906, but political unrest continued and was aggravated during World War I by military defeat and food shortages. The February and October Revolutions (*see* RUSSIAN REVOLUTION) were followed by civil war (1918–22), after which communist control was complete. Russia itself became the Russian Soviet Federal Socialist Republic (RSFSR), forming the major part of the Soviet Union. The independent Russian Federation was created in 1991 with Boris *Yeltsin as its first president. In 1993 Yeltsin's economic reforms were endorsed in a referendum and he secured their implementation by ordering the military to act against a defiant parliament. A new constitution was endorsed by referendum that same year. In 1995 the Communists became the largest party in the Russian parliament. The republic of *Chechenia achieved *de facto* independence following a fierce struggle between separatists and Russian troops (1994–96), but was reoccupied by Russian forces (1999–2000). Yeltsin was re-elected (1996) and a further power struggle followed in which he sacked the whole government four times in 18 months. Vladimir *Putin succeeded Yeltsin as president in 2000 and was re-elected in 2004. Official language: Russian. Currency: rouble of 100 kopeks. Area: 17 074 984 sq km (6 592 658 sq mi). Population (2003 est): 144 893 000. Capital: Moscow.

Russian Orthodox Church An offshoot of the Greek Orthodox Church, dating from the baptism of the emperor Vladimir (later St Vladimir) in 988. Since 1328 the metropolitan see has been at Moscow.

Russian Revolution (1917) The revolution between March and November (Old Style February and October) 1917, that established the world's first communist state. It began with the February Revolution, when riots in Petrograd led to the establishment of a provisional government of Duma deputies, which forced *Nicholas II to abdicate. The failure of Prince Lvov and then Aleksandr Kerenski (1881–1970) to end Russia's participation in World War I and to deal with food shortages led to the October (*or* Bolshevik) Revolution, in which *Lenin seized power and established the Soviet of People's Commissars. In the subsequent civil war (1918–21) the Red Army was ultimately victorious against the anticommunist White Russians but with the loss of some 100 000 lives.

Russo-Japanese War (1904–05) A confrontation arising from conflicting Japanese and Russian interests in Manchuria. In 1904 Japan attacked Port Arthur (now Lüda), which fell in January 1905. In May a Japanese fleet destroyed Russia's Baltic Fleet in the Tsushima Straits, forcing Russia's surrender.

rust A reddish-brown solid consisting of hydrated iron oxide. Rusting is a special case of corrosion; the mechanism involves the setting up of a cell in which iron is the anode and a metal impurity the cathode. Both water and oxygen must be present for rust to form although the most serious damage, pitting, is always found in an oxygen-free portion of metal.

rust fungi Fungi, belonging to the order *Uredinales*, that are parasites of plants, forming spots, blotches, and pustules on the stems and foliage of their hosts. Several are important pests of cereal crops, including black rust (*Puccinia graminis*) of wheat. Other important wheat rusts include yellow rust (*P. striiformis*) and brown rust (*P. recondita*). Phylum: *Basidiomycota*.

Ruth, Babe (George Herman R.; 1895–1948) US baseball player. Known as the "Sultan of Swat," he became the top player of the 1920s.

ruthenium (Ru) A hard metal of the platinum group, first separated in 1844 by K. K. Klaus (1796–1864). It is used to harden platinum and palladium in electrical contacts and as a catalyst. The tetroxide (RuO_4) is toxic. The element shows a wide range of *valence states. At no 44; at wt 101.07; mp 2334°C; bp 4150°C.

Rutherford, Ernest, 1st Baron (1871–1937) English physicist, born in New Zealand. He made fundamental discoveries concerning the nature of *radioactivity, distinguishing between the three types of radiation, which he named alpha, beta, and gamma rays. Working with Hans Geiger (1882–1945) he discovered that alpha radiation consisted of positively charged helium atoms. In 1906, he deduced the existence of a heavy positively charged core in the atom, which he called the *nucleus. In 1908, Rutherford received the Nobel Prize for Chemistry.

rutherfordium *See* KURCHATOVIUM.

rutile A brown to black form of natural titanium dioxide, TiO_2. It is found in igneous and metamorphic rocks, in veins, and as fibres in quartz, known as Venus' hair.

Rutland A historic county in the East Midlands of England. The smallest county in England, it became part of *Leicestershire in 1974 but was reinstated as an independent unitary authority in 1997. Rutland Water is one of the largest artificial reservoirs in the UK. Area: 394 sq km (152 sq mi). Population (2001): 34 560. Administrative centre: Oakham.

Rwanda, Republic of A small landlocked country in E central Africa. Lake Kivu forms most of its W boundary and the land is chiefly mountainous. Most inhabitants are Bantu-speaking Hutu, with a Tutsi minority. *Economy*: chiefly subsistence agriculture. The principal cash crop is coffee. Methane gas has been found under Lake Kivu. *History*: a Tutsi kingdom from the 16th century, the area came under German East Africa in 1890. From 1919, it was administered by Belgium as N Ruanda-Urundi. In 1959 the Tutsi kingdom was overthrown by the Hutu, who declared Rwanda a republic (1961); independence was recognized by Belgium (1962). In 1973 the Hutu Maj Gen Juvénal Habyarimana (1937–94) came to power in a coup. Uganda-based Tutsi rebels, the Rwandan Patriotic Front (RPF), invaded in 1990 but were contained by troops from France, Belgium, and Zaïre (now Democratic Republic of Congo). A transitional multiparty government was formed in 1992 but in 1994 Habyarimana was assassinated and some half a million Tutsi were massacred. In the ensuing civil war the RPF gained control and about two million Hutus fled into exile; a broad-based government was established under President Paul Kagame but ethnic violence has continued. The late 1990s saw the repatriation of refugees and the establishment of a UN International Criminal Tribunal to prosecute those responsible for genocide. Official languages: Kinyarwanda and French. Currency: Rwanda franc of 100 centimes. Area: 26 330 sq km (10 166 sq mi). Population (2003 est): 8 387 000. Capital: Kigali.

Ryazan 54 37N 39 43E A city in W central Russia. Founded in 1095, it was the capital of a principality until annexed by Russia in 1521. Population (1999 est): 531 300.

Rybinsk (name from 1946 until 1958: Shcherbakov; name from 1984 until 1991: Andropov) 58 01N 38 52E A port in W central Russia, on the River Volga. It is situated below the **Rybinsk Reservoir**, an artificial lake of 5200 sq km (2000 sq mi) created in 1941. Population (1999 est): 241 800.

Ryder, Sue *See* CHESHIRE, (GEOFFREY) LEONARD, BARON.

Ryder Cup A biennial golf tournament between teams from Europe and the USA. It was first played between members of the British and US Professional Golfers' Associations, in 1927. In 1979 the British team was opened to continental golfers. The cup was won by Europe in 1995 and 1997, by the USA in 1999, and by Europe in 2002.

rye A cereal *grass, *Secale cereale*, native to W Asia but widely cultivated in cool temperate and upland regions. 1–2 m high, it bears a terminal spike, 10–15 cm long. The grain is milled to produce a dark-coloured flour, used in making black bread or for livestock feed.

Ryle, Gilbert (1900–76) British philosopher. His philosophy centred on detailed analysis of mental concepts. *The Concept of Mind* (1949) argued against Descartes' idea of the human being consisting of mind and body ("the ghost in the machine").

Ryle, Sir Martin (1918–84) British astronomer; astronomer royal (1972–84). A pioneer of radio telescopy, his most important work was the development of a technique for studying distant radio sources. In 1974 he shared the Nobel Prize for Physics.

Ryukyu Islands A group of volcanic and coral islands in the W Pacific Ocean, extending almost 650 km (400 mi) from Kyushu to N Taiwan. A kingdom until the 14th century, the islands were dominated by the Chinese before becoming a part of Japan (1879). They were under US control (1945–72). Area: 2196 sq km (849 sq mi). Population (2000 est): 1 318 000. Chief city: Naha (on Okinawa).

S

Saarbrücken 49 15N 6 58E An industrial city in SW Germany, the capital of Saarland on the River Saar near the French border. A centre of the iron and steel industry, it was under French administration in 1801–15, 1919–35, and 1945–57. Population (1999 est): 186 402.

Saarinen, Eero (1910–61) US architect, born in Finland. His most famous building is the Trans World Airlines terminal at Kennedy Airport, New York (1956–62), which has reinforced concrete vaults spreading outwards to suggest flight.

Saarland A state (*Land*) in W Germany, around the River Saar, a tributary of the Moselle. The area has often passed between France and Germany but plebiscites (1935 and 1955) led to union with Germany. Rich in coal, it has a large steel industry. Area 2569 sq km (992 sq mi). Population (2000 est): 1 071 500. Capital: Saarbrücken.

Sabah (former name: North Borneo) A state in Malaysia, in NE *Borneo. Forested and mountainous, it is largely undeveloped, but on the western coastal plain rice and rubber are grown. Copper and oil resources are being exploited; timber, rubber, and copra are exported. *History*: North Borneo was first colonized by the British in 1877, becoming a protectorate in 1882. In 1963 it joined Malaysia under its present name. Tension between Muslims and the government led to violence in the 1980s. Area: 76 115 sq km (29 388 sq mi). Population (2000): 2 603 485. Capital: Kota Kinabalu.

Sabines The peoples of the scattered hilltop communities NE of ancient Rome. The legendary abduction of the Sabine women by Roman settlers indicates the early interbreeding of Sabines with Romans. Sabine influence on Roman religion was especially strong. They became Roman citizens in 268 BC.

Sabin vaccine A vaccine that prevents poliomyelitis, developed by a US virologist, A. B. Sabin (1906–93). It contains a weakened polio virus that stimulates the body's defence against polio without causing the disease. Sabin vaccine is given by mouth (often on a sugar lump) in three consecutive doses. *See also* SALK VACCINE.

sable A carnivorous mammal, *Martes zibellina*, native to N Eurasia. It is less than 50 cm long and has thicker legs and longer ears than other *martens. Its coat is thick, soft, and glossy and is valued as fur (Siberian sable).

sabre-toothed tiger An extinct *cat that lived 30 million years ago and became extinct in the Pleistocene epoch (1 million years ago). *Smilodon*, a Pleistocene form, was about the size of a tiger, with very long upper canine teeth used to pierce the thick hide of its prey.

saccharin An organic compound ($C_7H_5NO_3S$) used as a sweetening agent in the food industry and as a sugar substitute. It has about five hundred times the sweetening power of table sugar.

Sacks, Jonathan (Henry) (1948–) British rabbi. An academic philosopher by training, he became a rabbi in 1978 and Commonwealth chief rabbi in 1991. His books include *The Persistence of Faith* (Reith Lectures; 1991).

sacrament In Christian theology, a ritual having a special significance as a visible sign of an inner grace in its participants. The *Roman Catholic Church and Orthodox Churches accept seven sacraments: baptism, confirmation, penance, the *Eucharist, marriage, holy orders, and anointing of the sick (formerly extreme unction). Baptism and the Eucharist are the only commonly accepted sacraments among the Protestant Churches.

Sacramento 38 32N 121 30W A city in the USA, the capital of California on the Sacramento River. Founded in 1839, it grew after the discovery of gold nearby in 1848. Linked by canal (1963) to San Francisco Bay, it is a deepwater port and serves an extensive agricultural area. Population (2000): 407 018.

sacred ibis An African ibis, *Threskiornis aethiopica*, that was revered in ancient Egypt. 75 cm long, it is pure white except for dark ornamental plumes on its back, dark wing tips, and a black head, neck, and bill. It feeds in flocks along rivers.

Sadat, Anwar (1918–81) Egyptian statesman; president (1970–81). Sadat was twice vice president (1964–66, 1969–70) before becoming president on *Nasser's death. He moved Egypt away from the Soviet Union and towards the USA, under the influence of which he negotiated a peace agreement with Israel in 1979. He shared the 1978 Nobel Peace Prize with Israel's President Begin. He was assassinated (1981) by Islamic extremists.

Sadducees An ancient Jewish religious and political party. They formed a conservative and aristocratic group centring on the priesthood in Jerusalem. With the destruction of the temple the party ceased to exist. *See also* PHARISEES.

Sade, Donatien Alphonse François, Marquis de (1740–1814) French novelist. Most of his works of sexual fantasy and perversion, which include *Justine* and *Les 120 Journées de Sodome*, were written in the 1780s and 1790s, during his many years of imprisonment for sexual offences. The sexual perversion "sadism," in which sexual pleasure is derived from causing or observing pain, is named after him.

Sadler's Wells Theatre A theatre in London where Lilian Baylis (1874–1937) established an opera and ballet company in 1931. From the 1680s the medicinal wells on the site were exploited and its owner, Mr Sadler, later erected a music hall. In 1753 this became a theatre, which closed (1878) but was restored by Baylis. Its ballet and opera companies later transferred to the West End, becoming the *Royal Ballet and English National Opera respectively. In 1998 Sadler's Wells reopened as a high-tech "dance theatre for the millennium" after a multimillion-pound redevelopment.

saffron The dried orange-yellow stigmas of the saffron crocus (*C. sativa*), used for flavouring and colouring foods and liqueurs and formerly as a fabric dye. The crocus, which has purple flowers, is cultivated mainly in France, Spain, and Italy. About 100 000 flowers are needed to produce 1 kg of saffron.

sagas Heroic prose narratives in Old Norse, the best of which were written down in Iceland in the 12th and 13th centuries. Characteristic subject matter was drawn from ancient Scandinavian oral traditions and included fictionalized accounts of the deeds of Norwegian kings, for example *Heimskringla* by Snorri Sturluson (1178–1241), and heroic legends of the pagan past.

sage A perennial herb or shrub, *Salvia officinalis*, native to the Mediterranean region and widely cultivated for its leaves, which are used for flavouring foods. It has blue, pink, or white flowers. *See also* SALVIA.

sage grouse A large grouse, *Centrocercus urophasianus*, occurring in sagebrush deserts of western USA. It is 75 cm long and the male has ornamental wattles and a long slender tail, which is fanned out during its courtship display.

sago A starchy food obtained mainly from the Indonesian sago *palms (*Metoxylon sagu* and *M. rumphii*), cultivated in Malaysia. It is extracted from the pithy stems.

Sahara The largest desert in the world, covering most of N Africa. The terrain consists chiefly of a plateau with central mountains rising to 3415 m (11 204 ft) and some areas of sand dunes, such as the Libyan Desert in the NE. The vegetation is sparse. Geological evidence shows that the Sahara was once well vegetated and that parts were formerly under the sea. There are large deposits of oil and gas in Algeria and Libya and phosphates in Morocco and Western Sahara. Rainfall is minimal and irregular, but there are numerous scattered oases. Area: about 9 000 000 sq km (3 474 171 sq mi).

saiga A small antelope, *Saiga tatarica*, of Asian deserts and steppes. Saigas are slightly built with a pale woolly coat and a remarkable swollen snout with convoluted nasal tracts, thought to be an adaptation for warming inhaled air or to be related to their keen sense of smell. Males have straight ridged horns. Saigas form large herds to migrate southwards in winter.

Saigon *See* HO CHI MINH CITY.

Saimaa, Lake A lake in SE Finland. It is the primary lake in a system spread over most of S Finland. Area: about 1760 sq km (680 sq mi).

saint In Christian belief, a person characterized by special holiness. In the *Roman Catholic Church saints formally admitted to the calendar of saints by *canonization can be invoked as intercessors. *Protestantism rejects the invocation of saints, although the *Church of

England's calendar recognizes a number of saints' days.

St Albans 51 46N 0 21W A city in SE England, in Hertfordshire. Here stood the important Romano-British town of Verulamium, site of the martyrdom of St Alban; Roman remains include a theatre and mosaic pavement. The abbey, founded in honour of the saint in 793 AD, was made a cathedral in 1877. Population (1991): 80 376.

St Andrews 56 20N 2 48W A resort in E Scotland, in Fife Region on St Andrews Bay. An ancient ecclesiastical centre, its university (1412) is the oldest in Scotland. The famous Royal and Ancient Golf Club was founded here in 1754. Population (1991): 11 136.

St Bartholomew's Day Massacre The slaughter of *Huguenots that began on 24 August 1572, in Paris. The massacre was ordered by Charles IX of France under the influence of his mother, Catherine de' Medici. Some 3000 Huguenots died in Paris and many more were murdered in the provinces.

St Basil's Cathedral The cathedral of the Russian Orthodox Church in Moscow built between 1554 and 1560 for Ivan the Terrible. It is named after the Russian saint, who was buried there at the end of the 16th century.

St Bernard A breed of large working dog developed in Europe from Asian ancestors and employed as a rescue dog by the hospice of St Bernard in the Swiss Alps since the 17th century. It is massively built, having a large head with drooping ears. The coat is white marked with red-brown or brindle. Height: 65 cm minimum.

St Catherines 43 10N 79 15W A city and port in E Canada, in S Ontario at the entrance to the Welland Ship Canal linking Lakes Erie and Ontario. Founded in 1790, it is a fruit-farming and industrial centre and houses Brock University (1962). Population (1996): 130 926.

St Croix (*or* **Santa Cruz**) A West Indian island, the largest of the US Virgin Islands. The economy is based on tourism and agriculture. Area: 207 sq km (80 sq mi). Population (2000): 53 234. Chief town: Christiansted.

St David's (Welsh name: Tyddewi) 51 54N 5 16W A village in SW Wales in Pembrokeshire, the smallest cathedral city in Britain. The 12th-century cathedral, the largest in Wales, was an important medieval pilgrimage centre for the shrine of St David. Population (1991): 1627.

St Dunstan's (full name: St Dunstan's for Men and Women Blinded on War Service) A British organization for the training, settlement, and lifelong care of those blinded in war. It was founded in 1915 by a blind newspaper proprietor, Sir Arthur Pearson (1866–1921).

St Elmo's fire A small electrical discharge, with a luminous appearance, that is associated with stormy weather and seen around the extremities of tall objects, such as the tops of trees and mastheads.

Saint-Exupéry, Antoine de (1900–44) French novelist and aviator. His novels include *Night Flight* (1931) and *Wind, Sand and Stars* (1939). He also wrote a fable for children, *The Little Prince* (1943).

St George's 12 04N 61 44W The capital of Grenada, on the SW coast, both a port and tourist resort. Founded by the French in the 17th century, it was capital of the British Windward Islands from 1885 to 1958. Population (1991): 4439.

St George's Channel A channel between SE Ireland and Wales, linking the Irish Sea with the Atlantic Ocean. Length: about 160 km (100 mi). Maximum width: 145 km (90 mi).

St Helena 15 58S 5 43W A mountainous island in the S Atlantic Ocean, a British dependent territory. Napoleon I was exiled here (1815–21). Area: 122 sq km (47 sq mi). Population (1994 est): 5157. Capital: Jamestown.

St Helens 1. 53 28N 2 44W A town in NW England, in St Helens unitary authority, Merseyside. It has an important glass industry, besides brick and tile manufacturing, engineering, and brewing. Population (1991): 106 293. **2.** A unitary authority in NW England, in Merseyside. Area: 130 sq km (50 sq mi). Population (2001): 176 845.

St Helens, Mount 46 12N 122 11W A volcano in the USA, in SW Washington state in the S Cascade Range. Dormant since 1857, the mountain erupted in May 1980, causing widespread destruction in which more than 50 people died. Height: 2950 m (9677 ft).

St Helier 49 12N 2 07W A market town and resort in the Channel Islands, on the S coast of Jersey. There is a substantial trade in early vegetables and Jersey cattle. Population (1996): 27 523.

St James's Palace A royal palace in Pall Mall, in London, built for Henry VIII on the site of an 11th-century hospital. It was the principal London residence of the monarch from 1697, when Whitehall was burnt down, until superseded by Buckingham Palace in 1837. Much of the original building was destroyed by fire in 1807.

St John River A river in E North America. Rising in Maine, USA, it flows NE to New Brunswick, Canada, and then SE to the Bay of Fundy, where high tides cause the river to reverse its course at the famous Reversing Falls. Length: 673 km (418 mi).

St John's 47 34N 52 41W A city in E Canada, the capital and commercial centre of Newfoundland. Settled in the 16th century, it is located beside a huge protected harbour. Population (1996): 101 936.

St John's wort A perennial herb or shrub, genus *Hypericum* (400 species), found in temperate regions. They have yellow five-petalled flowers with many stamens and many species are cultivated for ornament, including *H. calycinum* (also known as rose of Sharon). Family: *Guttiferae*.

St Kilda 57 49N 8 34W A group of three small mountainous islands off the Scottish mainland, the most westerly of the Outer Hebrides. Evacuated in 1930, they are now a nature reserve. Area: about 16 sq km (6 sq mi).

St Kitts-Nevis, Federation of (*or* **St Christopher-Nevis**) A country in the West Indies, in the Leeward Islands in the E Caribbean Sea. *Economy*: primarily agricultural; sugar, molasses, cotton, and coconuts are the main products. Tourism is important. *History*: from 1967 it was a UK associated state consisting of three islands: St Kitts, Nevis, and Anguilla. Anguilla became a separate British dependency in 1980. St Kitts-Nevis became fully independent within the British Commonwealth in 1983. Although the Nevis parliament announced (1997) plans to secede from the Federation, a referendum in 1998 failed to secure the two-thirds majority required for independence. Area: 262 sq km (101 sq mi). Population (2003 est): 46 400. Capital: Basseterre, on St Kitts.

Saint-Laurent, Yves (1936–) French fashion designer, who trained with Christian Dior and took over his fashion house (1957), opening his own in 1962. He established his reputation as the first designer to produce ready-to-wear clothes for the mass market; he has also produced clothes for men and a range of perfumes.

St Lawrence River A river in North America that belongs to one of the world's greatest water systems, draining the *Great Lakes into the Atlantic Ocean. From Lake Ontario it flows NE along the Canadian-US border through the Thousand Islands, a major tourist district. Above Montreal it enters Canada and passes through rapids where hydroelectricity is produced. At Quebec it broadens into a long estuary that merges with the Gulf of St Lawrence, an arm of the Atlantic Ocean and a major fishing ground. The St Lawrence valley is an important agricultural and industrial belt as well as a rail, water, and road corridor. The **St Lawrence Seaway** is a navigable waterway through the St Lawrence River and the Great Lakes, completed in 1959. With a season of over eight months, it admits ships of up to 9000 tons. Length: Lake Ontario to Quebec 480 km (298 mi); St Louis River headwaters to Anticosti Island 3395 km (2110 mi).

St Louis 38 40N 90 15W A city and port in the USA, in Missouri on the Mississippi River. A major centre in the colonization of the West, it is now a large industrial and university city and an important agricultural market. Population (2000): 348 189.

St Lucia An island country in the West Indies, in the Windward Islands in the E Caribbean Sea. It is a mountainous island of volcanic origin. The population is mainly of African descent. *Economy*: mainly agricultural, the main crops being bananas and coconuts; there is a growing tourist industry. *History*: St Lucia was colonized by the French in the 17th century and ceded to Britain in 1814. It became internally self-governing in 1967 and fully independent within the British Commonwealth in 1979. Official language: English. Currency: East Caribbean dollar of 100 cents. Area: 616 sq km (238 sq mi). Population (2003 est): 162 000. Capital: Castries.

St Mark's Cathedral The cathedral church of Venice since 1807. It was built in the 9th century to house the relics of St Mark but rebuilt in the 11th century after a fire. Designed as a Greek cross surmounted by five domes, it is strongly influenced by Byzantine art and is famous for its opulent mosaic and sculptural decoration.

St Moritz 46 30N 9 51E A resort in SE Switzerland, on St Moritz Lake. A renowned winter-sports centre, its Cresta Run (for bobsleds) dates from 1885. Population (latest est): 5335. Altitude: 1822 m (5978 ft).

St Paul 45 00N 93 10W A city in the USA, the capital of Minnesota on the Mississippi River adjacent to Minneapolis; the Twin Cities comprise the commercial and industrial centre of an extensive grain and cattle area. Population (2000): 259 606.

St Paul's Cathedral The cathedral of the diocese of London; there have been five cathedrals on this site, the first three of which were Saxon. The present building was designed by Sir Christopher *Wren and replaced the Norman structure burnt down in the Great Fire. It features a traditional cruciform plan, a classical two-tiered portico, a great dome, and flanking towers.

St Peter's Basilica The basilica in the Vatican City, Rome. It dates from the 16th century and replaced the original gothic building. It is the largest church in the world. Its general shape was determined by Donato Bramante (1444–1514), although it was designed together with its enormous dome by *Michelangelo. Giacomo da Vignola (1507–73) continued the work and the nave and façade were added by Carlo Maderna (1556–1629). *Bernini completed the building in the 17th century.

St Petersburg (name from 1914 until 1924: Petrograd; name from 1924 until 1991: Leningrad) 59 55N 30 25E The second largest city in Russia and the capital of an autonomous region (*oblast*), at the head of the Gulf of Finland on the River Neva. It is a major industrial and commercial centre and its port, although frozen between January and April, is one of the largest in the world. Buildings include the Peter-Paul Fortress, the Winter Palace, and the Gostiny Dvor. *History*: the city was founded (1703) by Peter the Great and was the capital of Russia from 1712 until 1918, replacing Archangel as Russia's main seaport. In the late 19th century it developed as an important industrial centre. St Petersburg was prominent in both the *Revolution of 1905 and the 1917 revolution (*see* RUSSIAN REVOLUTION). During World War II the city withstood a siege by the Germans (8 September 1941–27 January 1944), in which nearly a million people perished. Population (1999 est): 4 169 400.

S

Saint-Saëns, Camille (1835–1921) French composer, conductor, pianist, and organist. His compositions include 12 operas, five symphonies, *The Carnival of the Animals* (published posthumously; 1922) for two pianos and orchestra, and five piano concertos.

St Sophia (*or* **Hagiá Sophia**) A building in Istanbul. In 537 *Justinian I erected a Byzantine church of great size and beauty to replace an earlier church (326) founded by Constantine I. In 1453, after the Turkish conquest, this became a mosque with added minarets. It was converted into a museum in 1935.

St Thomas 18 22N 64 57W A West Indian island in the US Virgin Islands, in the Lesser Antilles, once a major sugar producer and slave-trading centre. Tourism is of major importance. Area: 83 sq km (28 sq mi). Population (2000): 51 181. Capital: Charlotte Amalie.

St Vincent, Cape 37 01N 8 59W A promontory in the extreme SW of Portugal, in the Algarve on the Atlantic Ocean. Several naval battles have been fought off the cape, including the British defeat (1797) of the Spanish fleet during the Napoleonic Wars.

St Vincent and the Grenadines A country in the E Caribbean Sea, in the Windward Islands of the Lesser Antilles. It consists of the principal island of St Vincent and its dependencies of the Grenadine islets. *Economy*: based on agriculture; bananas, taro, and sweet potatoes are the main products. *History*: a British possession since 1763, it became fully independent within the Commonwealth in 1979. Area: 390 sq km (150 sq mi). Population (2003 est): 113 000. Capital: Kingstown.

saké (*or* **rice wine**) An alcoholic drink made in Japan from steamed rice, to which a special yeast is added, and slowly fermented. It resembles a light sherry in taste and is served warm.

Sakhalin A Russian island, mountainous and forested, between the Sea of Okhotsk and the Sea of Japan, divided from the mainland by the Tatar Strait. The island has coal, iron, and fisheries; major off-shore reserves of gas and oil were discovered in the 2000s. It has also been used as a place of exile. At times it belonged to Japan but was re-annexed by the Soviet Union in 1945. Area: 76 000 sq km (29 300 sq mi). Population (2000 est): 598 000. Main town: Yushno Sakhalinsk.

Sakharov, Andrei Dimitrievich (1921–89) Soviet physicist. After helping to develop the Soviet hydrogen bomb during the 1940s and 1950s he spoke out against nuclear weapons in the 1960s and argued for freedom of speech in the Soviet Union. He was awarded the Nobel Peace Prize in 1975. His exile to Gorkii (Nizhnii Novgorod) in 1980 aroused international protest and ended in 1986. In 1989 he was elected to the new Soviet People's Congress of Deputies.

Saki (H(ector) H(ugh) Munro; 1870–1916) British writer. Born in Burma, he settled in London in 1908. He published several volumes of humorous short stories, many of which featured his fastidious and snobbish heroes Clovis and Reginald. He was killed in action in World War I.

Saladin (?1137–93) The leader of the Muslims against the Crusaders in Syria. He obtained control over the Muslim lands in Egypt, of which he became sultan in 1175, and Syria. He then captured the Kingdom of Jerusalem following his great victory over the Crusaders at the battle of Hattin (1187). During the third *Crusade he won his legendary reputation as a chivalrous warrior.

Salam, Abdus (1926–96) Pakistani physicist, who became professor of physics at Imperial College, London, in 1957. He was also director of the International Centre for Theoretical Physics in Trieste. In 1979 he shared the Nobel Prize with the US physicists Sheldon Glashow (1932–) and Steven Weinberg (1933–) for their work on *weak interactions.

Salamanca 40 58N 5 40W A city in central Spain, in Salamanca. During the Peninsular War the battle of Salamanca was fought here on 22 July 1812, in which Wellington secured a decisive victory over the French. An intellectual centre of Renaissance Europe, Salamanca remains an important cultural centre with a university (founded 1218). Its many notable old buildings include two cathedrals and it has a fine Roman bridge. Population (1998 est): 158 457.

salamander A tailed *amphibian belonging to a widely distributed order (*Urodela* or *Caudata*; about 225 species). Salamanders have short legs and long bodies and move by bending the body from side to side to give as wide a movement as possible for their feet. They usually hide in damp places when not hunting small worms and insects. Their habits range from wholly aquatic to wholly terrestrial. *See also* NEWT.

Salazar, António de Oliveira (1889–1970) Portuguese dictator, prime minister from 1932 to 1968. His New State repressed opposition and fought long colonial wars in Africa, which gravely impeded the country's economic development.

Salerno 40 40N 14 46E A port in Italy, in Campania on the Gulf of Salerno. Founded by the Romans in 197 BC, its medical school flourished in the middle ages. It was the scene of heavy fighting during World War II (1943). Population (2000 est): 142 055.

Salford 1. 53 30N 2 16W A city in NW England, in Salford unitary authority, Greater Manchester, on the River Irwell and the Manchester Ship Canal. The docks have been redeveloped for business and leisure. The Lowry, a major art gallery and cultural centre named in honour of L. S. *Lowry, opened in 2000. Population (1991): 227 400. **2.** A unitary authority in NW England, in Greater Manchester. Area: 97 sq km (37 sq mi). Population (2001): 216 119.

Salic Law The law of the Salian *Franks issued under Clovis in the early 6th century. Owing little to other contemporary law codes or to Roman law, it is concerned with both criminal and civil law. Its importance for later periods lies in its prohibition against women inheriting land. This canon was invoked in France in 1316 and 1321 to prevent a woman from succeeding to the throne and, in 1328, Edward III's claim to the French Crown was rejected on the grounds that his claim was by female descent.

Salieri, Antonio (1750–1825) Italian composer and conductor in Vienna from 1766. His pupils included Beethoven, Schubert, and Liszt. Because of his rivalry with Mozart, he was fancifully credited with having poisoned him.

Salinger, J(erome) D(avid) (1919–) US novelist, who achieved success with his novel of adolescent alienation *The Catcher in the Rye* (1951). Later works include *Franny and Zooey* (1961), and *Seymour, An Introduction* (1963), but he subsequently became a recluse and published very little.

Salisbury 51 05N 1 48W A city in S England, in Wiltshire at the confluence of the Rivers Avon and Wylye. Its 13th-century cathedral has the highest spire in the country, 123 m (403 ft). Industries include light engineering and tourism. Nearby is Old Sarum, the site of an Iron Age hill fort with extensive earthworks; settlement here continued until the 13th century. Population (1996): 39 431.

Salisbury, Robert Cecil, 1st Earl of *See* BURGHLEY, WILLIAM CECIL, LORD.

S

Salisbury, Robert Arthur Talbot Gascoyne-Cecil, 3rd Marquess of (1830–1903) British statesman; Conservative prime minister (1885–86, 1886–92, 1895–1902). Elected an MP in 1853, he became Disraeli's foreign secretary in 1878. As prime minister he served as his own foreign secretary (except in 1886 and 1900–02) and his policy has been characterized as one of "splendid isolation."

saliva The fluid secreted by three pairs of **salivary glands** around the mouth in response to the sight, smell, taste, or thought of food. Its major role is to bind the food particles and to lubricate the mouth and gullet.

Salk vaccine The first successful antipolio

vaccine. Given by injection, it was developed by the US virologist J. E. Salk (1914–95) and first used in 1954. It has been replaced by the Sabin vaccine in many countries.

Sallust (Gaius Sallustius Crispus; c. 86–c. 34 BC) Roman politican and historian. Expelled from the Senate for alleged immorality, he supported Julius Caesar in the war against Pompey and became governor of Numidia. He was accused of corruption and extortion and retired from politics in about 44 BC. His best-known works are the monographs *Bellum Catilinae* and *Bellum Jugurthinum*.

salmon One of several fish of the genera *Oncorhynchus* or *Salmo*, especially the Atlantic salmon (*S. salar*)—a valuable food and game fish. It has an elongated body, up to 150 cm long, and two dorsal fins. Salmon live mainly in the sea, feeding on other fish, but migrate into fresh water to spawn. The spawned fish (kelts) either die or return to the sea and spawn in successive years. On hatching the young fish are known as parr once they start feeding. At about two years the coat becomes silver and the fish (smolt) migrate to the sea to reach maturity. After about two to three years they return to their native spawning waters as grilse, guided upstream by their sense of smell. Family: *Salmonidae*; order: *Salmoniformes*.

Salmonella A genus of rod-shaped bacteria that are parasites of animals and man and cause several diseases: *S. typhi* and *S. paratyphi* cause *typhoid fever in humans while *S. typhimurium* is a common cause of food poisoning.

salsify A biennial herb, *Tragopogon porrifolius*, native to the Mediterranean region. It is cultivated in temperate regions for its fleshy white root, supposed to taste like oysters when cooked. The plant has long narrow leaves, used in salads, a head of purple flowers surrounded by stiff pointed green sepals. Family: *Compositae*.

salt 1. (sodium chloride; NaCl) The crystalline solid that is used for seasoning and preserving food and is present in sea water and halite, which are its chief sources. It has an important function in the human body and is used in the manufacture of many chemicals, such as soap, fertilizer, and ceramics. **2.** Any similar compound formed, together with water, when an acid reacts with a base.

Salt Lake City 40 45N 111 55W A city in the USA, the capital of Utah near Great Salt Lake. Founded in 1847 by the Mormons under the leadership of Brigham Young, it is the world headquarters of the Mormon Church. Population (2000): 181 743.

saltpetre (**potassium nitrate** *or* **nitre**; KNO_3) A white crystalline solid used as a fertilizer, a food preservative, and in *gunpowder and fireworks.

saltwort An annual or perennial herb belonging to the widely distributed genus *Salsola* (50 species), found on seashores and salt marshes. They have fleshy spiked leaves. Family: *Chenopodiaceae*.

saluki An ancient breed of hunting dog. It has a slender body with long legs, giving speed and agility, and a small head with a long narrow muzzle. The smooth soft coat can be of various colours. Height: 50–70 cm.

Salvador (*or* **Bahia**) 12 58S 38 29W A port in NE Brazil, the capital of Bahia state on the Atlantic Ocean. It has a fine natural harbour. Population (2000): 2 439 881.

Salvation Army The international Christian organization founded in 1865 in London by William *Booth. Its members wear a characteristic uniform on public occasions. It is famous for its social and evangelistic work.

Salvia A genus of perennial herbs and shrubs (about 700 species), widely distributed in temperate and tropical regions. Many are cultivated for ornament, including the Brazilian scarlet sage (*S. splendens*) and the blue-flowered *S. patens*. Common *sage is the culinary herb. Family: *Labiatae*.

Salyut A series of manned Soviet space stations first launched into earth orbit in 1971. Crews were conveyed to and from the orbiting laboratory by Soyuz spacecraft. They lived in weightless conditions, sometimes for very long periods, conducting a variety of experiments and observations. The series was superseded by the *Mir space stations.

Salzburg 47 54N 13 03E A city in central Austria, the capital of Salzburg. It has many fine buildings. Mozart was born here and a famous musical event, the Salzburg Festival, is held annually. Population (2001): 144 816.

Samar The third largest island in the Philippines, in the Visayan Islands linked by bridge to Leyte. Its frequent typhoons restrict agriculture; the chief products are rice, coconuts, and hemp. Copper and iron ore are mined. Area: 13 415 sq km (5181 sq mi). Population (latest est): 1 300 000. Chief town: Catbalogan.

Samara (name from 1935 until 1991: Kuibyshev) 53 10N 50 10E A port in SW central Russia, on the River Volga. Population (1999 est): 1 168 000.

Samaritans 1. A people of ancient Samaria (now in N Israel), with a religion closely akin to Judaism but much disliked by the Jews. They declined under Muslim rule. **2.** A British telephone and e-mail service for the suicidal and despairing, started in 1953 by the Rev Chad Varah (1911–) in a London church (St Stephen Walbrook). A nonreligious charity, it offers a nonprofessional, confidential, and anonymous service to anyone in distress through over 200 UK branches. Many overseas branches belong to the associated Befrienders International.

samarium (Sm) A *lanthanide element, discovered 1879, that occurs naturally, with other lanthanides, in monazite ($CePO_4$). At no 62; at wt 150; mp 1074°C; bp 1794°C.

Samarkand 39 40N 66 57E A city in E Uzbekistan. It was the chief junction of the ancient *Silk Road between China and the Mediterranean and, conquered by the Arabs in the 8th century, became the Abbasids' capital (9th–10th centuries) and a great Islamic centre. In the 14th century it became the capital of Timur's mighty empire, coming later under the rule of the Uzbek people (16th–19th centuries). The city's remarkable historic buildings include Timur's mausoleum. Population (1998 est): 388 000.

Samoa, American An incorporated US territory in the S central Pacific, consisting of Tutuila and several smaller islands in the E Samoan archipelago. Agriculture is the main occupation; canned tuna is an important export. An elected legislature with limited law-making powers was established under the constitutions of 1960 and 1967. Area: 197 sq km (76 sq mi). Population (2001): 58 000. Capital: Pago Pago.

Samoa, Independent State of (name until 1997; Western Samoa) A country in the S central Pacific; the main islands are Savai'i and Upolu. *Economy*: subsistence agriculture is the main occupation; exports include copra, bananas, and cocoa. Food processing, fishing, and tourism are also important. *History*: a German protectorate until World War I, Western Samoa was subsequent under New Zealand control until it became independent in 1962. The following year Susuga Malietoa Tanumafili II (1913–) became head of state for life. Universal adult suffrage was introduced in 1990. The Human Rights Protection Party under Tofilau Eti Alesana has played the leading role in government since 1996. Official languages: Samoan and English. Currency: tala (Samoa dollar) of 100 sene. Area: 2842 sq km (1097 sq mi). Population (2003 est): 179 000. Capital: Apia.

Samoyed (dog) A breed of dog developed in Siberia and used by the Samoyed tribesmen as a sledge dog. It is robustly built with husky-like features; the white or cream coat consists of a short soft undercoat and a long coarse outer coat. Height: 51–56 cm (dogs); 46–51 cm (bitches).

Samoyed (people) A group of Siberian peoples of the tundra and N forest region of central Russia. They were traditionally nomadic reindeer hunters and fishers, but are now mainly settled as reindeer breeders. Shamanism dominates their religious life. The five Samoyed languages belong to the Uralic family, only Nenets (*or* Yurak) having a considerable number of speakers.

Sampras, Pete (1971–) US tennis player who was Wimbledon singles champion in 1993–95 and 1997–2000. He won the US Open in 1990, 1993, 1995, and 1996.

samurai The provincial warriors who rose to power in Japan in the 11th century. Most became the vassals of *daimyo* (feudal lords). The samurai class was sharply divided from other classes by its superior status and marked distinctions also existed within its own ranks. After the Meiji restoration (1868) the samurai lost their special position but ex-samurai became leaders in various areas of modern Japanese life.

Sana'a 15 23N 44 14E The capital of Yemen, in the west of the country. Notable buildings include the Great Mosque, where there is a sacred Muslim shrine. Population (1995): 972 000.

San Andreas Fault A fault in the earth's crust, 1200 km (750 mi) in length, running along the margin between the Pacific tectonic plate (*see* PLATE TECTONICS) and the North American plate in NW California. In 1906 a horizontal displacement between the plates of about 6 metres and a lateral displacement of 1 metre caused an earthquake that devasted San Francisco; in 1989 and 1994 earthquakes caused further damage to the city. It is named after San Andreas Lake, through which it passes.

San Antonio 29 25N 98 30W A city in the USA, in Texas. Founded in 1718, it was the scene of the Mexican attack on the *Alamo (1836) during the Texan revolution. San Antonio has several military bases and is a commercial and industrial centre for a large agricultural region. Population (2000): 1 144 646.

sanctions Penalties imposed for breaking a law, especially international law. They were first imposed by the *League of Nations on Italy following its invasion of Ethiopia. More recent examples of economic sanctions were those imposed by the UN against South Africa (1985–94); Iraq (1990–2003); and Serbia (1992–2000).

sand Unconsolidated grains of rock, varying in size from 0.06 to 2.00 mm in diameter. Consolidated sands form *sandstones; grits are coarse sandstones with angular grains. Most sands consist mainly of quartz, derived from the weathering of quartz-bearing rocks. Sand is used in glass and cement production, and as an abrasive.

Sand, George (Aurore Dupin, Baronne Dudevant; 1804–76) French novelist. Her first book, *Indiana* (1832), the first of an enormous number of successful novels. Among her many lovers were Alfred de Musset and Frédéric Chopin.

sandalwood An evergreen tree belonging to the genus *Santalum* (about 25 species), native to SE Asia and the Pacific Islands. The true sandalwood (*S. album*) is partially parasitic on the roots of other trees. Its white wood is used to make boxes and furniture and, when distilled, yields sweet-scented sandalwood oil. Family: *Santalaceae.*

sand dollar A marine invertebrate animal belonging to an order (*Clypeastroida*) of *echinoderms. Its round flat rigid body is covered with small spines and saclike organs (tube feet). Sand dollars live on the sea bed and sift minute food particles from the sand in which they burrow. Class: *Echinoidea.*

S

sanderling A bird, *Calidris alba*, that nests on Arctic coasts and winters on shores worldwide. 20 cm long, it has a rust-coloured upper plumage, changing to pale-brown in winter, and a long white wing stripe. It feeds on shrimps, sandhoppers, and molluscs with its straight slender bill. Family: *Scolopacidae* (sandpipers).

sandfly A small fly belonging to the widely distributed genus *Phlebotomus.* Sandflies are among the worst pests of the tropics: the bloodsucking females can give a painful bite and several species are carriers of serious human diseases. The name has also been used for many bloodsucking *gnats and *midges of sandy places.

sand hopper A small terrestrial jumping *crustacean, also called beach hopper and sand or beach flea, belonging to the family *Talitridae.* Its body is laterally flattened and lacks a carapace. During the day it is buried in sand but at night it emerges to feed on organic debris under stones, etc. Order: *Amphipoda.*

Sandhurst 51 02N 0 34E A village in SE England, in Bracknell Forest unitary authority, Berkshire. The Royal Military Academy (1799) for training officers moved to nearby Camberley, Surrey, in 1946 but is still known as Sandhurst. Population (1991): 19 153.

San Diego 32 45N 117 10W A city in the USA, in California on San Diego Bay. It has a US naval base and naval air service facilities and is the site of a scientific research centre. Population (2000): 1 223 400.

sand lizard A slender long-tailed European lizard, *Lacerta agilis,* occurring in sandy regions. It has white-centred dark spots along its pale-brown or grey back. Family: *Lacertidae.*

sandpiper A wading bird belonging to a family (*Scolopacidae*; 82 species) occurring chiefly in the N hemisphere, breeding in northerly latitudes and migrating south to winter. Sandpipers typically have long legs, long wings, a mottled brown or grey plumage, which commonly changes colour seasonally, and a long slender bill. They nest in marshy regions or on mud flats. Order: *Charadriiformes* (gulls, plovers, etc.).

Sandringham 52 49N 0 30E A village in E England, in Norfolk. The Sandringham estate was bought by Queen Victoria for the Prince of Wales (later Edward VII) in 1861. Sandringham House remains a royal residence. Population (latest est): 440.

sandstone A sedimentary rock consisting of consolidated *sand, cemented mainly by calcareous, siliceous, or ferruginous minerals. They may be deposited by wind action in deserts or in shallow seas, estuaries and deltas, and along low-lying coasts by water. Sandstones vary in colour from red to yellow to white according to the presence of other minerals in addition to the quartz.

Sandwell A unitary authority in W central England, in West Midlands. Area: 86 sq km (33 sq mi). Population (2001): 282 901.

San Francisco 37 40N 122 25W A city in the USA, in California situated on a peninsula between San Francisco Bay and the Pacific Ocean. It is a major seaport, a financial and insurance centre, and a major cultural centre. Landmarks include the San Francisco–Oakland Bay Bridge (1936), the Golden Gate Bridge (1937), Chinatown, and the city's cable cars. Founded by the Spanish in 1776, it was captured by the USA (1846) during the Mexican War. It expanded rapidly following the discovery of gold in California (1848) and it was during this period that the first Chinese settled in the city. In 1906 movement in the San Andreas Fault led to devastation of the city by an earthquake and three-day fire. In 1989 another earthquake caused about 70 deaths. Population (2000): 776 733.

Sanhedrin The highest court of the Jews, which met in Jerusalem. Its composition and its jurisdiction varied with its history. In New Testament times, the high priest was president and its functions were administrative, judicial, and religious.

San José 37 20N 121 55W A city in the USA, in California on the S arm of San Francisco Bay. Founded in 1777, it was the first city in California and state capital (1849–51). Situated in the fertile Santa Clara Valley, it has many food-processing plants and wineries as well as aerospace and electronics industries. Population (2000): 894 943.

San José 9 50N 84 02W The capital of Costa Rica, situated in the centre of the country in a high fertile valley. It was founded in 1736; a university was established in 1843. Population (2000 est): 344 349.

San Juan 18 29N 66 08W The capital and main port of Puerto Rico, in the N. Founded by the Spanish in 1508, it was captured by the US navy in 1898. It expanded considerably in the 20th century and is now also an industrial and tourist centre. Population (2000): 421 958.

San Marino, Republic of A small independent republic, an enclave in Italian territory, situated on the slopes of the Apennines mountain range, SW of Rimini. *Economy*: farming, winemaking, tourism, and the sale of postage stamps are the main sources of income. *History*: dating from the 4th century AD, it was an independent commune by the 12th century. In 1862, the newly established kingdom of Italy guaranteed San Marino's independence and a customs union. Executive power lies in the Congress of State and two regents elected by the Great and General Council. Official language: Italian. Currency: euro of 100 cents. Area: 61 sq km (24 sq mi). Population (2003 est): 29 200. Capital: San Marino.

San Martín, José de (1778–1850) South American soldier and statesman; the national hero of Argentina. After participating in the struggle of Buenos Aires against the Spanish, he raised an army in Argentina (1814–16), which he led across the Andes; with Bernardo *O'Higgins he defeated the Spanish at Chacubuco (1817) and Maipo (1818), achieving the liberation of Chile. In 1821 he entered Lima, proclaimed the independence of Peru, and became its "protector." He resigned in 1822, after differences with Bolívar.

San Salvador 13 59N 89 18W The capital of El Salvador, situated in the centre of the country. Founded by the Spanish in 1525, it become capital in 1839. It has suffered severe earthquakes, most recently in 1986, and in 1989 witnessed conflict between rebel and government forces. Population (1992): 422 570.

San Sebastián 43 19N 1 59W A seaside resort in N Spain, in the Basque Provinces on the Bay of Biscay. It possesses a cathedral and palace. Population (1991): 169 933.

Sansevieria A genus of herbaceous perennial plants (60 species) native to tropical and S Africa and S Asia. They have a basal rosette of stiff swordlike leaves arising from thick creeping underground stems (rhizomes). *S. trifasciata* var. *laurentii* (mother-in-law's tongue) is a popular house plant with long leaves, striped green and yellow. The leaves of several species yield a fibre used for ropes, mats, etc. Family: *Liliaceae*.

Sanskrit The classical literary language of the Hindu scriptures, belonging to the Indo-Aryan family. From it the Prakrits and modern N Indian languages developed. It was spoken in NW India from 1500 BC, becoming a scholarly language in the 5th century BC, and is still used as a sacred language. It is highly complex and is written in the Devanagari script.

Sansovino, Jacopo (Jacopo Tatti; 1486–1570) Florentine sculptor and architect. From 1527 he introduced the High Renaissance style to Venice, serving as the city's chief architect until his death. His works include the library of St Mark's Cathedral (from 1537) and the gigantic statues of *Neptune* and *Mars* in the Doge's Palace (from 1554).

Santa Anna, Antonio López de (1794–1876) Mexican soldier and statesman; president (1833–36) and dictator (1839, 1841–45). He dominated Mexican politics from 1823 until driven into exile in 1845. He is best known for his defeat of Texan forces at the *Alamo (1836).

Santa Cruz 17 45S 63 14W A city in SE Bolivia. It is the commercial centre for an area producing chiefly sugar cane, rice, and coffee. Major industries include the manufacture of cigarettes and sugar refining. Population (2000 est): 1 016 137.

Santayana, George (1863–1952) Spanish-born US philosopher and poet. His philosophy was set out in *Realms of Being* (1927–40). His witty and urbane works include *The Life of Reason* (1905–06), *Scepticism and Animal Faith* (1923), and *The Last Puritan* (1935).

Santiago (*or* **Santiago de Chile**) 33 35S 70 40W The capital of Chile, situated in the centre of the country at the foot of the Andes. It was founded by the Spanish in 1541 and is now a major industrial centre. Population (1999 est): 4 640 635.

Santo Domingo 18 32N 69 50W The capital of the Dominican Republic, a port on the S coast. Founded by Columbus in 1496, it became the capital of the first Spanish colony in the Americas and is the site of the first cathedral (1521) and the first university (1538) in the New World. It became capital of the new Dominican Republic in 1844. Population (1993): 1 555 656.

Santos 23 56S 46 22W A city in SE Brazil, in São Paulo state on the Atlantic Ocean. It is the leading coffee port of the world. Population (2000): 415 553.

São Luís 2 34S 44 16W A port in N Brazil, the capital of Maranhão state. The chief exports are babaçu palm products, cotton, sugar, and balsam. It is the site of the University of Maranhão (1966). Population (2000, urban area): 834 968.

Saône, River A river in E France, rising in Lorraine and flowing mainly S to join the River Rhône at Lyons. It is linked by canal to the Rivers Moselle, Rhine, Loire, Seine, and Meuse. Length: 480 km (298 mi).

São Paulo 23 33S 46 39W The largest city in Brazil, the capital of São Paulo state. Founded in 1554, it grew rapidly after 1880 with the development of coffee plantations. Coffee remains important but its industries have diversified and it is now the fastest-growing city in Brazil. Population (2000): 9 785 640.

São Tomé and Príncipe, Democratic Republic of A small island country off the coast of West Africa, in the Gulf of Guinea. It comprises the two main islands, which have coastal plains rising to volcanic mountains in their interiors, together with two islets. Most of the population is descended from African slaves and southern Europeans. *Economy*: chiefly agricultural; the main crops are cocoa, copra, palm oil and kernels, and coffee. *History*: discovered by the Portuguese in 1471, the islands came under Portuguese rule in 1522. They became an overseas province in 1951 and gained independence in 1975. The 1990s saw an ongoing power struggle between parliament and the president. Fradique de Menezes was elected president in 2001. Official language: Portuguese. Currency: dobra of 100 centavos. Area: 964 sq km (372 sq mi). Population (2003 est): 142 000. Capital: São Tomé.

sap The fluid found in the vascular (conducting) system of plants. It consists of water and minerals, absorbed from the soil and transported through the plant in the *xylem, and sugars, made in the leaves and distributed in solution in the *phloem.

sapodilla An evergreen tree, *Achras sapota*, native to Central America but cultivated elsewhere in the tropics. It produces large edible brown rounded fruits, with a juicy pulp surrounding black seeds. Milky latex from the bark is a source of chicle gum, used in chewing gum. Family: *Sapotaceae*.

sapphire A transparent variety of *corundum that may be any colour except red (*see* RUBY) due to traces of iron and titanium. It is used as a gemstone and in record-player styluses. Sapphires occur in igneous and metamorphic rocks but most are obtained from detrital gravels.

Sappho (c. 612–c. 580 BC) Greek lyric poet, contemporary with Alcaeus. Her passionate poetry, which has survived in fragments, was written for her group of female admirers on the island of Lesbos (from which the term "lesbianism" is derived).

Sapporo 43 5N 141 21E A city in Japan, in SW Hokkaido. It is the island's main administrative and educational centre. It is also a ski resort, site of the 1972 winter Olympics. Population (1995): 1 756 968.

saprotroph (*or* **saprophyte**) An organism that obtains its energy by feeding on dead or decaying tissue. Bacteria and fungi are important saprotrophs, using enzymes to break down organic material and release nutrients into the soil, which can be used by plants.

Sarajevo 43 52N 18 26E The capital of Bosnia-Hercegovina, an industrial and cultural centre. It was here that the heir apparent of Austria-Hungary, *Francis Ferdinand, was assassinated

(28 June 1914), precipitating World War I. In 1992 fierce fighting broke out between Bosnian Serbs and Muslims following Bosnia-Hercegovina's declaration of independence from Yugoslavia. From April 1992 it was besieged and bombarded by Bosnian Serb forces; NATO airstrikes on their positions finally ended their grip on the city in 1995. Following the signing of the Bosnian peace accord (Dec 1995), Sarajevo was reunited under Bosnian government control. Population (1997 est): 360 000.

Saratoga, Battles of (19 September and 7 October 1777) Two battles fought near Saratoga, New York, which formed the turning point of the *American Revolution. The second ended with the surrender of Gen Burgoyne to the Americans. The outcome of the battles helped persuade the French to recognize and support the USA.

Sarawak A state in Malaysia, in NW *Borneo on the South China Sea. It has a mountainous forested interior with a swampy coastal plain, where rubber, pepper, sago, and rice are grown. Oil production is of prime importance. It was given in 1841 by the sultan of Brunei to the British explorer James Brooke, the "white rajah." Made a British protectorate in 1888, it was ruled by the Brooke family until World War II, when it was occupied by the Japanese. Ceded to Britain in 1946, it joined Malaysia in 1963. Area: 124 970 sq km (48 250 sq mi). Population (2000): 2 012 616. Capital: Kuching.

sardine A young *pilchard or any of several species of food fish of the family *Clupeidae*, especially members of the genera *Sardina*, *Sardinops*, and *Sardinella*.

Sardinia The second largest island in the Mediterranean Sea, comprising an autonomous region of Italy. It is largely mountainous. Agriculture is important, especially on the fertile alluvial plain in the SW. Its major industry is mineral production, especially lead, zinc, coal, fluorspar, and sea salt. First settled by the Phoenicians, it was ceded to Savoy by Austria (1720) in exchange for Sicily and formed the kingdom of Sardinia with Piedmont, which formed the basis of a unified Italy. Area: 23 813 sq km (9194 sq mi). Population (2000 est): 1 651 888. Capital: Cagliari.

Sargasso Sea An elliptical section of the N Atlantic Ocean between latitudes 20°N and 35°N and longitudes 30°W and 70°W. Contained within a current system, it is still and warm. It takes its name from the floating brown seaweed of the genus *Sargassum* (*see* GULFWEED), found in it.

Sargent, Sir Malcolm (1895–1967) British conductor and organist. He was chief conductor at the London Promenade Concerts (1948–1967) and conductor of the BBC Symphony Orchestra (1950–57).

Sark 49 26N 2 22W The smallest of the four main Channel Islands. It consists of Great Sark and Little Sark, connected by a narrow isthmus. It is governed by a hereditary seigneur or dame in a semifeudal system. Cars are prohibited here. Area: 5 sq km (2 sq mi). Population (1996): 550.

sarsaparilla An extract of the roots of several perennial climbing or trailing vines of the genus *Smilax*, especially *S. aristolochiaefolia*, cultivated in Central and South America. The dried roots are used as a tonic and as flavouring for medicines and beverages. Family: *Smilacaceae*.

Sartre, Jean-Paul (1905–80) French philosopher, novelist, dramatist, and critic. A leading existentialist, his major works of philosophy include *Being and Nothingness* (1943). His novels include *Nausea* (1938) and the trilogy *The Roads to Freedom* (1945–49). Among his plays are *In Camera* (1944) and *Altona* (1959). He had a close association with Simone de *Beauvoir.

SAS *See* SPECIAL AIR SERVICE.

Saskatchewan A province of W Canada, on the Great Plains. The N is covered by forest with lakes and swamps. The S is open prairie and is one of the world's most important wheatlands. The province is rich in minerals, including uranium, oil, natural gas, potash, zinc, and copper; associated industries are important. Explored in the 17th and 18th centuries, Saskatchewan was first exploited for furs. Agricultural settlement began slowly (1870s) but sped up in the decade before 1914. Area: 570 269 sq km (220 181 sq mi). Population (2001 est): 1 015 800. Capital: Regina.

Saskatchewan River A river in W Canada, rising in two separate branches in the Rocky Mountains and flowing generally E through prairie grainlands to unite in central Saskatchewan. The river then continues to Lake Winnipeg. Length: 1940 km (1205 mi).

sassafras A tree, *Sassafras albidum*, native to North America. It bears clusters of yellow flowers and dark-blue berries. The aromatic roots are dried for use in medicines and also yield oil of sassafras, which is used in perfumes and as flavouring for beverages. Family: *Lauraceae*.

Sassoon, Siegfried (1886–1967) British

poet and writer. In 1917 his disgust with the progress of World War I led him to make a public refusal to serve, for which he was sent to a military hospital where he met Wilfred *Owen. His antiwar poetry appeared in *The Old Huntsman* (1917) and *Counterattack* (1918) and he wrote several volumes of memoirs.

Satan *See* DEVIL.

satellite 1. A celestial body orbiting a *planet. The planets of the solar system have at least 50 known satellites, ranging greatly in size. The small bodies comprising the rings of Saturn, Uranus, and Jupiter may also be regarded as satellites. Mercury and Venus have no satellites. Spacecraft have sent back information on various satellites, including the earth's moon, the four large Galilean satellites of Jupiter, Saturn's rings and its largest satellite Titan, and the satellites of Uranus and Neptune. In recent years many small satellites have been discovered by these spacecraft, notably a further six moons of Uranus, a further 12 moons of Saturn, and a further 45 moons of Jupiter, most of which remain unnamed. **2.** A spacecraft that is launched into orbit around the earth or enters an orbit around some other solar-system body. It may be a *communications satellite, retransmitting radio signals from one location on earth to another. Alternatively, its instruments may gather information from earth or from other celestial objects and transmit it, by radio signals, to ground-based receiving stations. This information is used, for example, in weather forecasting, navigation, scientific and astronomical research, and for military purposes.

Satie, Erik (1866–1925) French composer. He turned away from impressionism towards a clear-textured style that admitted humour. His works include the ballet *Parade* (1916),

planet & satellite	*diameter (km)*	*distance from primary (1000 km)*	*year of discovery*
EARTH			
Moon	3476	384.40	—
MARS			
Phobos	22	9.38	1877
Deimos	13	23.46	1877
JUPITER			
Metis	40	128	1979
Adrastea	20	129	1979
Amalthea	190	181	1892
Thebe	100	222	1979
Io	3630	422	1610
Europa	3138	671	1610
Ganymede	5262	1070	1610
Callisto	4800	1883	1610
Leda	16	11094	1974
Himalia	185	11480	1904
Lysithea	36	11720	1938
Elara	76	11737	1905
Ananke	30	21200	1951
Carme	40	22600	1938
Pasiphae	50	23500	1908
Sinope	36	23700	1914
SATURN			
Pan	20	134	1991
Atlas	30	138	1980
Prometheus	105	139	1980
Pandora	90	142	1980
Janus	90	151	1966
Epimetheus	120	151	1966
Mimas	390	186	1789
Enceladus	500	238	1789
Tethys	1050	295	1684
Telesto	30	295	1980
Calypso	25	295	1980
Dione	1120	377	1684
Helene	30	377	1980
Rhea	1530	527	1672
Titan	5150	1222	1655
Hyperion	290	1481	1848
Iapetus	1440	3561	1671
Phoebe	220	12952	1898
URANUS			
Cordelia	26	50	1986
Ophelia	30	54	1986
Bianca	42	59	1986
Cressida	62	62	1986
Desdemona	54	63	1986
Juliet	84	64	1986
Portia	108	66	1986
Rosalind	54	70	1986
Belinda	66	75	1986
Puck	154	86	1985
Miranda	472	129	1948
Ariel	1158	191	1851
Umbriel	1172	266	1851
Titania	1580	436	1787
Oberon	1524	584	1787
NEPTUNE			
Naiad	54	48	1989
Thalassa	80	50	1989
Despina	150	53	1989
Galatea	160	62	1989
Larissa	200	74	1989
Proteus	420	118	1989
Triton	2700	354	1846
Nereid	340	5511	1949
PLUTO			
Charon	1186	19	1978

The principal planetary satellites

piano pieces, including *Trois Gymnopédies* (1888), and many songs.

satinwood A tree, *Chloroxylon swietenia*, native to S India and Sri Lanka. Its wood is valued in cabinetmaking for its fine golden-yellow finish. The wood of certain West Indian species is also known as satinwood. Family: *Meliaceae*.

satsuma *See* TANGERINE.

Saturn (astronomy) The second largest planet, orbiting the sun every 29.5 years at a mean distance of 1427 million km. The most oblate planet, its equatorial diameter is 120 000 km. The dominant feature is **Saturn's rings**, lying in the equatorial plane and tilted at 27° to the orbital plane. There are six rings, differing considerably in brightness and width but are all composed of small icy chunks. The overall diameter is almost 600 000 km but the thickness is only a few hundred metres. The main rings, C, B, and A, were discovered in the 17th century. The outermost, A, is separated from the brightest ring, B. Saturn also has at least 30 *satellites. Saturn is made up primarily of hydrogen and helium.

Saturn (mythology) The Roman god of agriculture and father of the gods, identified with the Greek *Cronus. Various aspects of the **Saturnalia**, his annual festival held in December, at which presents were exchanged and normal social rules relaxed, were taken over by the Christian festival of Christmas.

saturniid moth A moth belonging to the mainly tropical family *Saturniidae* (about 800 species). They are usually large with a transparent eyespot on each wing. Their cocoons can be a source of silk.

satyrid butterfly A butterfly of the worldwide family *Satyridae*. The wings are mainly brownish with a few or numerous eyespots. The forelegs are rudimentary and the flight weak and fluttering. Satyrids hide when alarmed, folding the forewings inside the camouflaged hindwings.

Satyrs and Sileni In Greek mythology, male fertility spirits of the woods and fields, usually portrayed with goats' legs and pointed ears or horns. Associated with *Dionysus, they were typically drunk and lustful. *See also* SILENUS.

Saudi Arabia, Kingdom of A country in the Middle East comprising most of Arabia, bordering on the Red Sea and the Persian Gulf. In the W a line of mountains runs close to the Red Sea, while the Najd, the central plateau, slopes downwards W–E. In the N and SE are large areas of desert. The population, densest in the SW, is mainly Sunnite Muslim. About 27% are nomads. *Economy*: based on oil in the Persian Gulf, exploited since 1938. The country, a member of OPEC, is the world's greatest exporter of oil. Income is also derived from pilgrims visiting Mecca, Medina, and Jiddah. *History*: the establishment of Saudi Arabia (1932) under *Ibn Saud followed the 19th-century struggle by the Saud family to dominate the warring tribes of the peninsula and take overall control from Turkey. Asir was incorporated in 1934. Saudi Arabia became a founding member of the Arab League (1945). Under Ibn Saud's son, *Faisal Ibn Abdul Aziz, there was economic development, Faisal using the oil crisis of the early 1970s to increase Saudi holdings in oil operations. The present king, since 1982, is a brother of Faisal, Fahd Ibn Abdul Aziz. Saudi Arabia is an absolute monarchy with a constitution and legal system based on the Koran and Islamic law. An appointed council was established in 1993 and local elections were held for the first time in 2003. Official language: Arabic. Currency: riyal of 100 halalah. Area: 2 400 000 sq km (927 000 sq mi). Population (2003 est): 24 008 000. Capital: Riyadh.

Saul In the Old Testament, the first King of Israel, who reigned in the 11th century BC. He was anointed king by the prophet Samuel and began his reign with a great victory over the Ammonites, followed by many battles against the Philistines. His last years were marked by a growing enmity with *David.

Sault Ste Marie 46 32N 84 20W A city in E Canada, in NW Ontario on the St Mary's River opposite Sault Ste Marie, USA. Its canal allows ships to bypass local rapids. Population (1996): 88 054.

Saunders, Dame Cicely Mary Strode (1918–) British philanthropist. In 1967 she founded St Christopher's Hospice in London for the care of the terminally ill, which specializes in the relief of pain and support for the families. Her books include *Living with Dying* (1983).

Saurischia An order of *dinosaurs dominant in the Jurassic period (about 195–130 million years ago). They had hip bones like those of modern lizards (the name means "lizard hips") and were mostly bipedal carnivores, although some were quadrupedal herbivores. *See also* ALLOSAURUS; APATOSAURUS; TYRANNOSAURUS.

saury A marine fish, also called skipper, belonging to the family *Scomberesocidae* (about 4 species). It has a long slim body, blue or olive above and golden or silvery below, with beaklike jaws. Sauries occur in large shoals in tropical and temperate surface waters, and are often seen leaping or skipping over the surface to escape predators. Order: *Atheriniformes*.

Saussure, Ferdinand de (1857–1913) Swiss linguist, whose posthumously published *Course in General Linguistics* (1916) is usually regarded as the foundation of modern linguistics. His conception of languages as self-contained systems of arbitrary signs formed the basis of *structuralism.

savanna (*or* **savannah**) The extensive tropical grasslands, bordering on the equatorial rain forests in both the N and S hemispheres. They cover extensive areas in N Australia, Africa, and South America (where they are known as the *llanos in Venezuela and Colombia and the campos in Brazil). The vegetation of savannas is dominated by tall grasses, such as elephant grass, interspersed with low often flat-topped trees and bushes. Grazed by herds of hooved animals, savannas are ideal cattle-rearing areas.

Savonarola, Girolamo (1452–98) Italian religious reformer. A Dominican prior in Florence from 1491, he began a crusade against religious and political corruption, centring his attacks on the papacy and the *Medici. He became the virtual ruler of Florence when the Medici were expelled by the populace in 1494. Excommunicated in 1497, he was hanged and burned for heresy.

savory A herb belonging to the genus *Satureja*, of warm and temperate regions. Summer savory (*S. hortensis*) is an annual, native to central Europe and Asia. Both the dried leaves and the oil extract are used for flavouring foods. The perennial winter savory (*S. montana*) is also a culinary herb. Family: *Labiatae*.

S

Savoy An Alpine frontier region of SE France corresponding to the present-day departments of Savoie and Haute-Savoie. Strategically important for its mountain passes, the county of Savoy was founded in 1034. Piedmont was acquired in the 14th century and Sardinia in 1720; Savoyard dukes then took the title King of Sardinia, which in 1748 became the kingdom of Piedmont-Sardinia. Savoy (but not Sardinia) was annexed by France during the Revolutionary Wars but restored in 1815 and Piedmont-Sardinia became the leading spirit in the movement for Italian unification (*see* RISORGIMENTO). Savoy became part of France in 1860, but the House of Savoy ruled the newly formed kingdom of Italy (1861–1946).

sawfly An insect belonging to the widely distributed suborder *Symphyta*. The female possesses a needle-like tubular ovipositor, used to insert eggs into foliage and timber. The larvae, resembling caterpillars, damage trees. Chief families: *Argidae, Siricidae, Cimbicidae, Diprionidae, Tenthredinidae*; order: *Hymenoptera*.

saxifrage A perennial herb belonging to certain genera of the family *Saxifragaceae*, found in cold and temperate regions. The leaves may either form a basal rosette or occur in pairs along the stem and the flowers are white, yellow, purple, or red.

Saxons A Germanic people who, during the 5th century AD, expanded from their Baltic coastal homelands to other areas of N Germany, the coast of Gaul (France), and (with the *Angles and *Jutes) to Britain. Charlemagne eventually defeated the continental Saxons in the 8th century and converted them to Christianity. *See also* ANGLO-SAXONS.

Saxony (German name: Sachsen) **1.** An ancient NW German duchy. Named after its original inhabitants, the *Saxons, it was incorporated into Charlemagne's empire and subsequently became a duchy. In the 13th century Saxony became an electorate and in the 16th and 17th centuries a leading German Protestant state. In 1697 Elector Frederick Augustus I (1670–1733) became King of Poland and Saxony's subsequent involvement in Polish affairs kept it apart from German power struggles until the 19th century. Conquered by Napoleon in 1806, N Saxony was annexed by Prussia in 1815 and in 1866 joined the Prussian-dominated North German Confederation. The remainder of Saxony joined the German Empire in 1871. **2.** A *Land* in E Germany, formerly part of East Germany. Area: 18 413 sq km (7109 sq mi). Population (2000 est): 4 459 700. Capital: Dresden.

saxophone A woodwind instrument with a brass body, keys, and a single reed mouthpiece similar to that of a *clarinet. It was invented by the Belgian Adolphe Sax (1814–94) and patented in France in the 1840s. The most common sizes of saxophone are the soprano, alto, tenor, and baritone. They are most commonly used as solo instruments in jazz.

Sayers, Dorothy L(eigh) (1893–1957) British writer, best known for her series of detective novels, beginning with *Whose Body?* (1923), featuring the erudite detective Lord Peter Wimsey.

scabies A contagious skin infection caused by the *itch mite, which tunnels and breeds in the skin, causing intense itching. Treatment is by application of benzylbenzoate cream.

scabious An annual or perennial herb belonging to the genus *Scabiosa* (80–100 species), native to the Mediterranean region and temperate parts of Eurasia and Africa. The small scabious (*S. columbaria*) is widely distributed on chalky soils. It has small bluish-lilac flowers on a long stalk. The field scabious, *S.* (or *Knautia*) *arvensis*, is similar. Family: *Dipsacaceae*.

Scafell Pike 54 28N 3 12W The highest peak in England, in Cumbria, in the Lake District. Height: 978 m (3210 ft).

scalar quantity A quantity that is represented by magnitude only. Unlike a *vector quantity, a scalar quantity has no direction. Examples include mass, time, and speed.

scale An ascending or descending succession of notes, characterized by a fixed succession of intervals between the notes that constitute it. Many thousands of different scales exist; all the major musical traditions are based upon them. In Western music there are three **diatonic scales**: the major scale, the harmonic minor scale, and the melodic minor scale. The octave is divided into 12 notes and any of these scales may be constructed on these notes. The version of the scale produced is associated with a particular *tonality. The **chromatic scale** includes all 12 semitones of the octave.

scale insect An insect belonging to the superfamily *Coccoidea* (about 4000 species), abundant in warm and tropical regions. Scale insects are usually small and the females are often legless, wingless, and eyeless and covered by a waxy scale or mass of threads. They become encrusted on plants and suck the juices, often becoming serious pests. Other species are of value by producing *shellac, *cochineal, and various waxes. Suborder: *Homoptera*; order: *Hemiptera*.

scallop An edible *bivalve mollusc belonging to the family *Pectinidae* (about 400 species), of warm and temperate seas. The valves of the shell are broad, flattened, and deeply fluted, and the animal swims by flapping them with a single powerful muscle.

Scandinavia Geographically, a peninsula in NW Europe, comprising Sweden and Norway. Culturally and historically, it also includes Denmark, Iceland, the Faeroes, and Finland.

Scandinavian languages A subgroup of the Germanic group of languages consisting of *Swedish, *Norwegian, *Danish, *Icelandic, and Faeroese. The first three are similar enough to be mutually intelligible, their separateness being imposed by their history and political boundaries. They all developed from a common Scandinavian ancestor, which originally used the *runic alphabet (*see also* OLD NORSE). This language spread with the Vikings to Iceland, the Faeroes, and elsewhere.

scandium (Sc) The first transition metal, predicted by Mendeleyev and discovered in 1879. It is trivalent, light (relative density 2.989), and has a high melting point. At no 21; at wt 44.956; mp 1541°C; bp 2836°C.

Scapa Flow A section of the Atlantic Ocean off the N coast of Scotland, in the Orkney Islands. It was the main base of the British Grand Fleet in World War I. Following its surrender, the German fleet scuttled itself here (1919). Length: 24 km (15 mi). Width: 13 km (8 mi).

scarab beetle A beetle belonging to the worldwide family *Scarabaeidae* (over 19 000 species). Scarabs show a great variety in size and form: the largest beetles—the goliath and *hercules beetles—are scarabs, while other species have developed extraordinary horns. The family has two main groups—the *dung beetles and *chafers. Certain dung-rolling beetles, especially *Scarabaeus sacer*, were the sacred scarabs of the ancient Egyptians.

Scarborough 54 17N 0 24W A resort in NE England, on the North Yorkshire coast. The promontory is the site of a prehistoric settlement, a Roman signal station, and a 12th-century castle. There is fishing, tourism, and manufacturing. Population (1995): 44 930.

Scarlatti, Domenico (1685–1757) Italian composer and noted harpsichordist and organist, working in Lisbon from 1720 and in Madrid from 1729. Besides some operas and church music, he wrote over 600 harpsichord sonatas, many of which were highly innovative. His father **Alessandro Scarlatti** (1660–1725) was also a composer, working chiefly in Rome and Naples. His works include over a hundred operas, 600 chamber cantatas, 200 masses, 12 chamber symphonies, and 14 oratorios.

scarlet fever A highly infectious disease of children caused by streptococcus bacteria. The child develops a sore throat, fever, and headache, and 24–48 hours later a red rash spreads from the chest over the whole body. Before antibiotics scarlet fever killed many children or left them disabled with *rheumatic fever, kidney disease, or ear infections; it can now be rapidly cured with penicillin.

Schama, Simon (Michael) (1945–)

British historian and art writer, based in the USA. His books include *The Embarrassment of Riches* (1987), *Citizens* (1989), and *Landscape and Memory* (1995). He is also well known for presenting the television series *A History of Britain* (2000–02).

Scheldt, River A river in W Europe. Rising in NE France, it flows generally NNE through W Belgium to Antwerp, then NW to the North Sea in the SW Netherlands. Canals connect it to the Rivers Somme, Seine, Sambre, Meuse, and Rhine. Length: 435 km (270 mi).

Schiller, (Johann Christoph) Friedrich (von) (1759–1805) German dramatist, poet, and writer. His first play, *Die Räuber* (1781), typifies the **Sturm und Drang* call for political freedom. With Goethe's encouragement, Schiller turned from historical and academic studies to produce brilliant dramas: the trilogy *Wallenstein* (1798–99), *Maria Stuart* (1800), *Die Jungfrau von Orleans* (1801), and *Wilhelm Tell* (1804). His nondramatic works include poems and an important essay on aesthetics.

schistosomiasis (*or* **bilharziasis**) A widespread disease of the tropics caused by blood flukes of the genus *Schistosoma* (or *Bilharzia*). It is contracted by bathing in water contaminated by snails, which harbour the larvae of the parasite. The larvae penetrate the skin and—when mature—settle in the blood vessels of the intestine or bladder. Symptoms, caused by the release of eggs by adult flukes, include anaemia, inflammation, and diarrhoea and dysentery, or cystitis and blood in the urine. The disease is treated by drugs that destroy the parasite.

schizophrenia A severe mental disorder characterized by disintegration of the processes of thinking, contact with reality, and emotional responsiveness. Delusions and hallucinations are common, especially those that produce the feeling of a loss of personal identity. Treatment consists of administration of drugs (*see* ANTIPSYCHOTICS) and vigorous psychological and social rehabilitation. *See also* PARANOIA; PSYCHOSIS.

Schleswig-Holstein A low-lying *Land* in N Germany bordering on the North Sea, the Baltic Sea, and Denmark. During the 19th century Denmark and the Austrian-led German confederacy both laid claim to the two duchies of Schleswig and Holstein. The duchies were eventually annexed to Prussia in 1866, the *Land* being formed in 1949. Area: 15 696 sq km (6059 sq mi). Population (2000 est): 2 777 300. Capital: Kiel.

Schliemann, Heinrich (1822–90) German archaeologist. After a successful business career, Schliemann retired (1863) to search for Homeric *Troy. He excavated Hissarlik on the Asia Minor coast of Turkey, finding ruins of nine consecutive cities. His spectacular finds at *Mycenae (1874–76), Orchomenos in Boeotia (1880), and Tiryns (1884–85) established him as the discoverer of *Mycenaean civilization.

Schmidt, Helmut (1918–) German statesman; Social Democratic chancellor of West Germany (1974–82). Entering Federal politics in 1953, he was minister of defence (1969–72) and for finance (1972–74) before becoming chancellor.

Schmidt telescope A *telescope that uses a thin "correcting" lens in front of the spherical primary mirror. It was developed by the Estonian instrument maker Bernard Voldemar Schmidt (1879–1935). It produces very sharp photographic images of celestial objects over a very wide angle of sky.

schnauzer A breed of dog originating in Germany and used as a guard dog. Strongly built with a docked tail, it has a square muzzle with long sidewhiskers. The coat is black or light grey and brown. Two varieties are the giant schnauzer bred for farm and police work and the miniature schnauzer. Height: 33–35 cm (miniature); 45–48 cm (standard); 54–65 cm (giant).

Schoenberg, Arnold (1874–1951) Austrian-born composer. Forced as a Jew to leave Berlin (1933), he became a US citizen in 1941. His early compositions, in a late Romantic style, include two string quartets and the symphonic poem *Pelleas und Melisande* (1902–03). Later works were characterized by *atonality. In 1924 Schoenberg developed the theory and technique of *serialism, which he employed in most of his subsequent works, including a violin concerto (1936), a piano concerto (1942), and the unfinished opera *Moses und Aaron* (begun 1932).

scholasticism The intellectual discipline comprising all the philosophical and theological activities pursued in the medieval universities (schools). As the international philosophy of Christendom it respected orthodoxy and was concerned with the philosophies of *Plato and *Aristotle. For scholastics, such as *Abelard and *Aquinas, religion was predominant and it was by theology that the selection of problems for study and the scope of scientific enquiry were to be decided. After Aquinas, scholasticism became virtually synonymous with *Aristotelianism.

Schopenhauer, Arthur (1788–1860) German philosopher. He placed emphasis upon the human will as a means to understanding. *The World as Will and Idea* (1818) sets out his principal ideas and pessimistic conclusions. He was distrustful of rationalism and the scientific method, believing that contemplative freedom could be achieved through art.

Schröder, Gerhard (1944–) German politician; chancellor (1998–). A Social Democrat, he defeated Helmut *Kohl and the CDU in the elections of 1998. He was re-elected in 2002.

Schrödinger, Erwin (1887–1961) Austrian physicist, who worked in Dublin, 1940–56. He shared the 1933 Nobel Prize with *Dirac for his development of the form of the *quantum theory known as *wave mechanics.

Schubert, Franz (Peter) (1797–1828) Austrian composer, who achieved little recognition before his premature death. Schubert's melodic genius is evident in his 600 *Lieder*, which include "Death and the Maiden" and "The Trout." Some of his greatest songs are to be found in the song-cycles *Die Schöne Müllerin* (1823) and *Die Winterreise* (1827). His other compositions include nine symphonies (of which one is lost and the eighth is unfinished), string quartets, piano trios, an octet, two quintets, piano sonatas, and choral music.

Schumacher, Michael (1969–) German motor-racing driver. He was Formula One world champion in 1994, 1995, 2000, 2001, 2002, and 2003. He has won more Grand Prix races and more world championships than any other driver.

Schumann, Robert (Alexander) (1810–56) German composer. Almost all his musical compositions up to 1840 were for the piano, including *Kreisleriana* (1838). His works also include four symphonies and many songs. He wrote much as a critic, founding and editing (1835–44) a musical journal. Insanity developed in later life and he died in an asylum. His wife **Clara Schumann** (1819–96) was a famous pianist, teacher, and composer, and became a great interpreter and editor of her husband's works.

Schuschnigg, Kurt von (1897–1977) Austrian statesman; chancellor (1934–38). He tried in vain to prevent the Nazi *Anschluss* and was forced to resign, being imprisoned by Hitler throughout World War II. On his release he taught in the USA until 1967, when he returned to Austria.

Schwarzenegger, Arnold (1947–) US film actor and politician, born in Austria. A former bodybuilder, he later starred in hugely successful action films such as *Terminator* (1984) and *Total Recall* (1990). In 2003 he was elected Republican governor of California.

Schwarzkopf, Dame Elisabeth (1915–) German soprano, especially noted for her interpretation of Mozart and Richard Strauss.

Schweitzer, Albert (1875–1965) Alsatian-born theologian, medical missionary, and organist. From 1913 until his death, Schweitzer practised as a doctor in the hospital he founded in Gabon at the jungle village of Lambaréné. In 1952 he received the Nobel Peace Prize.

Science Museum A museum in South Kensington, London, devoted to the history and development of science, engineering, and industry. Its full name is the British National Museum of Science and Industry. It was separated from the Victoria and Albert Museum in 1909. The National Railway Museum, York, (opened 1975) is an outstation.

Scilly, Isles of (*or* **Scillies**) A group of about 140 islands and islets in the Atlantic Ocean, off the extreme SW coast of England. Only five are inhabited, namely St Mary's (the largest), Tresco, St Martin's, St Agnes, and Bryher. Their mild climate has been exploited to produce early spring flowers for the UK market. Agriculture is intensive. Area: 16 sq km (6 sq mi). Population (2001): 2153. Chief town: Hugh Town.

sclerosis Stiffening and hardening of the tissues. This is a feature of many diseases. *See* MULTIPLE SCLEROSIS; ARTERIOSCLEROSIS; ATHEROSCLEROSIS.

S

Scofield, (David) Paul (1922–) British actor. His major theatrical roles include Hamlet (1948, 1955), Lear (1962), Prospero (1976), and Othello (1980). His best-known film performance was as Sir Thomas More in *A Man for All Seasons* (1966).

Scone 56 25N 3 24W A parish in E central Scotland, in Perth and Kinross. It consists of the villages of New Scone and Old Scone, the Pictish and later Scottish capital where most Scottish kings were crowned. The coronation stone was taken from here by Edward I in 1296 and placed in Westminster Abbey. It was removed by Scottish nationalists in 1950 but later recovered. In 1996 it was moved to Edinburgh castle.

scops owl A small *owl of the mainly tropical genus *Otus*, also called screech owl because of its call. Scops owls are mostly arboreal, with camouflaging plumage resembling bark.

scorpion An *arachnid of the order *Scorpionida* (about 800 species), found in warm dry regions. The second pair of appendages form large pincers and the elongated abdomen curls upwards and bears a poisonous sting, which can be fatal to man. They prey at night, mainly on insects and spiders.

scorpion fish A carnivorous fish, often called rockfish or zebra fish, belonging to the family *Scorpaenidae*, found mainly on rocky beds of tropical and temperate coastal waters. It has a stout body, up to 1 m long, a large spiny head, and strong fin spines, which can inflict painful wounds and may be venomous. Order: *Scorpaeniformes*.

scorpion fly An insect of the order *Mecoptera* (400 species), so called because the males of many species curl the abdomen over the body, like a scorpion. Scorpion flies have long legs and antennae and, typically, two similar pairs of net-veined wings. Larvae and adults feed on dead animals and plants.

Scorsese, Martin (1942–) US film director, noted for tough urban dramas such as *Mean Streets* (1973), *Taxi Driver* (1976), *Raging Bull* (1980), *Goodfellas* (1990), and *Gangs of New York* (2002).

Scotland A country occupying the N part of Great Britain and comprising a political division of the *United Kingdom. Most of the population lives in a narrow lowland belt, which runs E–W across the country and separates the lower hills of the S from the higher mountains of the N (including the Grampian and Cairngorm Mountains). There are many islands off the N and W coasts, including the Hebrides to the W and the Orkneys and Shetlands to the N. The principal rivers are the Clyde, Forth, Tay, and Spey. There are many lochs in the northern mountains. Administratively, Scotland is divided into 32 council areas. *Economy*: the central belt of the country is highly industrialized. However the traditional industries of coalmining and shipbuilding are now almost extinct. Whisky, for which Scotland is internationally famous, is produced in Highland, Moray, and Aberdeenshire. The discovery of oil in the North Sea has led to a boom on the E coast. Agriculture remains important and includes sheep farming in the upland areas, dairying in the SW, beef production in the E and NE lowlands, and market gardening. Forestry has grown in importance. Fishing is a major source of revenue and salmon farming is a growing industry. *History*: Scotland was never completely subdued by the Romans, but the barbaric northern tribes were kept N of *Hadrian's Wall and, for some 40 years, the more northerly Antonine Wall. The diverse peoples (Picts, Scots, Britons, and Angles) of Scotland gradually united, helped by the spread of Christianity, and Kenneth I MacAlpine (died c. 858) is regarded as their first king. During the middle ages there was recurrent war between England and Scotland. In 1296 Edward I of England declared himself King of Scotland but after his death Robert the Bruce reasserted Scottish independence, which was recognized by England in 1328. The 14th century saw the establishment of a long-standing alliance between France and Scotland and the succession of the *Stuart dynasty. Under the influence of John *Knox the Scottish Church became Presbyterian (*see* CHURCH OF SCOTLAND) during the reign of Mary, Queen of Scots. In 1603 her son James VI succeeded as James I to the throne of England but political union was not established until 1707 (*see* UNION, ACTS OF). After the Hanoverian succession the Stuart cause was kept alive by the *Jacobites, who staged two unsuccessful rebellions (1715, 1745). Scotland experienced rapid industrialization in the 19th century. Following the parliamentary Reform Act (1832) a tradition for Liberalism was established but Labour gained dominance in the 20th century. Nationalism became a growing force in the 1970s but devolution plans failed to attract sufficient support in a referendum in 1979. In 1997, however, 74.3% of voters backed proposals to establish a Scottish parliament. Elections for the parliament took place in 1999. The current first minister is Labour's Jack *McConnell. Area: 78 769 sq km (30 405 sq mi). Population (2001): 5 062 011. Capital: Edinburgh.

Scots law Originally Scots law differed little from English law, but from the beginning of the 16th century there was a tendency to introduce elements of *Roman law, especially as embodied in the *civil law of France and the Netherlands. This resulted in marked differences from English law, the preservation of which was guaranteed by the Treaty of Union with England in 1707. An example is the Scots law of *contract, in which the principle of "consideration" does not have the importance it has in English law. Modern statutes have, however, introduced many new laws that are the same for both countries.

Scott, Sir George Gilbert (1811–78) British architect. An advocate of the gothic revival style, Scott was a noted designer, restorer of medieval buildings, and author. He renovated many churches and cathedrals, including Westminster Abbey. His original buildings include the Albert Memorial (1864) and St Pancras station (1865). His grandson **Sir Giles Gilbert Scott** (1880–1960) was also an architect. He designed the Anglican Cathedral in Liverpool (begun 1904), the new Bodleian Library, Oxford (1936–46), and the new Waterloo Bridge (1939–45).

Scott, Sir Ridley (1937–) British film director, who established himself in the cinema with the science-fiction films *Alien* (1979) and *Blade Runner* (1982). Later films include the feminist road movie *Thelma and Louise* (1991), the epic *Gladiator* (2000), which won five Academy Awards, and *Hannibal* (2001).

Scott, Robert Falcon (1868–1912) British explorer and naval officer. He led two expeditions to the Antarctic, 1900–04 and 1910–12. With a party of four he reached the South Pole on 17 January 1912, only to find that *Amundsen had preceded them. Delayed by illness and blizzards they perished only a few miles from safety. His son **Sir Peter Markham Scott** (1909–89) was a noted ornithologist and wildlife painter. In 1946 he founded the Wildfowl Trust (renamed the Wildfowl and Wetlands Trust in 1989) based at Slimbridge, Gloucestershire, for the study and conservation of birds.

Scott, Sir Walter (1771–1832) Scottish novelist and poet. His early works included a collection of border ballads (1802–03) and the popular narrative poem *The Lay of the Last Minstrel* (1805). *Waverley* (1814) was the first of a series of successful historical novels that included *Old Mortality* (1816) and *The Heart of Midlothian* (1818).

Scottish Borders A council area in SE Scotland, bordering on England. Created in 1996, it has the same boundaries as the former Borders Region. It is mainly hilly, with sheep farming and forestry; tweed and knitwear are manufactured. Area: 4734 sq km (1827 sq mi). Population (2001): 106 764. Administrative centre: Newtown St Boswells.

Scottish National Party (**SNP**) A political party, founded in 1928, dedicated to achieving Scottish independence from the UK. The party secured 11 seats and 30.4% of the Scottish vote in the 1974 parliamentary election, but in 1979 held only two seats. After the 1997 election it held six seats (five from 2001), thereby becoming the main opposition to Labour in Scotland. It also forms the official opposition in the Scottish parliament, holding 27 of the 129 seats. The current leader is .

Scottish terrier A breed of dog, originally called Aberdeen terrier, used to chase foxes from earth. It is thickset with short legs, a short erect tail, and pricked ears. The long muzzle has characteristically long whiskers and the wiry coat is usually black. Height: 25–28 cm.

Scout Association An association founded by Robert Baden Powell in 1908 to encourage boys to become enterprising members of society. It includes Cub Scouts (for boy aged 8 to 11), Scouts (11–16), and Venture Scouts (16–29). Girl Scouts were first admitted in the UK in 1990. *See also* GUIDES ASSOCIATION.

screech owl *See* SCOPS OWL.

screw pine A treelike plant of the genus *Pandanus* (about 150 species), native to the Old World tropics. The name derives from the spiral arrangement of the leaves. Stout aerial prop roots grow down from the stem into the ground: the part of the stem below these roots decays, so that the plant is supported entirely by the prop roots. The leaves are used for matting and weaving. The flowers grow in large heads enclosed in leafy structures (spathes) and the fruits of some species are edible. Family: *Pandanaceae*.

Scriabin, Alexander (1872–1915) Russian composer and pianist. His mature compositions were characterized by chords built on the interval of the fourth. His works include three symphonies, a piano concerto (1894), ten piano sonatas, and *Prometheus* or *The Poem of Fire* (1909–10).

scrofula Ulceration of a lymph node infected with *tuberculosis, seen most commonly in the neck. This form of tuberculosis is now uncommon in developed countries. Treatment is with antibiotic drugs and surgery.

Scunthorpe 53 36N 0 38W A town in NE England, in North Lincolnshire unitary authority, Lincolnshire. The service sector has risen in importance as iron and steel have declined. Population (1991): 75 982.

scurvy A disease caused by deficiency of *vitamin C (which is present in most fresh fruits and vegetables). In the past scurvy was common among sailors on long voyages, but it is now rarely seen.

Scylla and Charybdis In Greek mythology, two sea monsters on opposite sides of the

Strait of Messina who menaced *Odysseus, the *Argonauts, and other legendary heroes. Scylla was a monster with six heads and a pack of baying hounds, while Charybdis was a raging whirlpool.

Scythians An Indo-European people who temporarily settled in Asia Minor before settling in what is now S Russia in the 6th century BC. The true Scythians, called Royal Scyths, established a kingdom N of the Black Sea. Their skill as horsemen and archers halted Persian and Macedonian invasions but they disappeared from history during the Gothic onslaughts of the 3rd century AD.

sea anemone A sedentary marine invertebrate animal of a worldwide order (*Actiniaria*; over 1000 species) of *cnidarians. It has a soft columnar body (*see* POLYP) with a mouth at the top surrounded by rings of tentacles, which—when expanded—give the animal a flower-like appearance. Sea anemones are often found attached to rocks and weeds. They feed mainly on fish and other animals. Class: *Anthozoa*.

sea bass A carnivorous fish, also called sea perch, of the family *Serranidae* (about 400 species), found mainly in coastal waters of tropical and temperate seas. Its elongated body ranges up to 3.75 m long and varies in colour with the species. They may be active or sedentary and certain species are *hermaphrodite while others, such as *groupers, are able to change sex. Many are valued food and game fish. Order: *Perciformes*. *See also* BASS.

sea bream A fish, also called porgy, belonging to a family (*Sparidae*; about 400 species) found mainly in shallow waters of tropical and subtropical seas. It has a deep laterally flattened body covered with large scales, a single long dorsal fin, and well-developed teeth. It lives in shoals and feeds by scraping algae and small animals off rocks.

S

sea cow *See* DUGONG.

sea cucumber A marine invertebrate animal belonging to a worldwide class (*Holothuroidea*; 1100 species) of *echinoderms. At one end of its leathery cucumber-shaped body there is a mouth surrounded by a ring of tentacles. It crawls sluggishly on the sea bottom or burrows in sand or mud.

sea-floor spreading A concept developed in the 1960s that provides a mechanism for *continental drift. Magma rises from the earth's mantle to the surface along midocean ridges (constructive plate margins; *see* PLATE TECTONICS), cools to form new oceanic crust, and displaces the older material sideways at an average rate of 4 cm per year. Magnetic reversals recorded in the rocks in approximately symmetrical strips at each side of the mid-ocean ridges provide strong evidence.

sea eagle An eagle of the widely distributed genus *Haliaeetus*. The European sea eagle, *H. albicilla* may have a wingspan up to 2.4 m. They have a wedge-shaped tail and feed mainly on fish.

seagull *See* GULL.

sea horse One of several small bony-plated marine fish of the family *Syngnathidae*, especially the genus *Hippocampus*, that lives in shallow warm waters. The horselike head with its long tubular snout is set at an angle to the body. They use the prehensile tail to cling to seaweed and swim in a vertical position by undulating the dorsal fin. Order: *Gasterosteiformes*.

seal A carnivorous marine mammal belonging to the order *Pinnipedia* (32 species). Seals have a streamlined body with a smooth rounded head and an insulating layer of blubber under the sleek-coated skin. Both pairs of limbs flatten into flippers. They feed mainly on fish and breed on land or ice.

There are two main families: the *Otariidae* (eared seals; 13 species) including fur seals and *sealions, which have external ears and can turn their hind flippers forward for walking on land; and the *Phocidae* (true seals; 18 species), which lack external ears and have trailing hind flippers. *See also* *walrus.

sealion A large *seal belonging to the family *Otariidae*. Californian sealions (*Zalophus californianus*) of the Californian coast grow to 2 m and live in groups with a definite social hierarchy. Steller's sealion (*Eumetopias jubatus*) is the largest species, growing to over 3 m.

Sealyham terrier A breed of dog developed (1850–91) on the Sealyham estate, Haverfordwest, Wales, for hunting foxes and badgers. It is sturdily built with short legs, drooping ears, and a short thin tail. White with darker markings, Sealyhams have a soft under coat and a wiry outer coat. Height: 27–30 cm.

sea otter A marine *otter, *Enhydra lutris*, of the N Pacific, living in colonies of up to 90 individuals. Sea otters feed on molluscs, crustaceans, and fish and can crack open shells using a pebble. Once hunted for their valuable fur, they are now a protected species.

Sea Peoples The seafaring tribes, uncertainly identified, who colonized Asia Minor, the

Aegean, and N Africa in the 13th and 12th centuries BC, destroying the *Hittite empire. About 1170 they were almost annihilated by Rameses III of Egypt and those that survived scattered.

sea slug A marine *gastropod mollusc of the order *Nudibranchia*. Sea slugs have exposed feathery gills, two pairs of tentacles, and no shell. They browse on sponges, sea anemones, and corals and are often brightly coloured.

sea snake A venomous fish-eating snake belonging to the family *Hydrophiidae* (50 species) occurring mainly in coastal waters of Australasia and SE Asia. Sea snakes are adapted to an underwater life by having a flattened body with an oarlike tail and valvelike closures in the nostrils. Most produce live young (rather than eggs).

Seattle 47 35N 122 20W A city and port in the USA, in Washington state between the Puget Sound and Lake Washington. A port of entry to the Klondike, it became a boom town with the 1897 Alaska Gold Rush. There are large timber mills and various forest-based industries. Population (2000): 563 374.

sea urchin A marine invertebrate animal, belonging to the class *Echinoidea*, with a typically spherical rigid body covered by long movable spines. Sea urchins live on shores and ocean floors and use a complex feeding apparatus to masticate algae and other organic material scraped off rocks. Phylum: *Echinodermata* (*see* ECHINODERM).

sea water The water constituting the world's oceans and seas. It is usually saline, average salinity being about 35 g per kg of sea water. The principal dissolved salts are sodium chloride (2.8%), magnesium chloride (0.4%), and magnesium sulphate (0.2%). Where evaporation is high, salinity is increased, as in the Red Sea. *See also* DESALINATION).

seaweed Large multicellular red, brown, or green marine *algae that are generally found attached to the sea bed, rocks, or other solid structures by rootlike structures called holdfasts. The plants have stemlike stalks and fronds, which may be flat and undivided, threadlike, or branched, sometimes with small air bladders for buoyancy. Seaweeds often occur in dense aggregations along shores. Many are of commercial importance as food (e.g. carrageen, laver, and sea lettuce), as fertilizers, in chemical and pharmaceutical products, etc. *See also* KELP; WRACK.

Sebastian, St (3rd century AD) Roman martyr, killed by archers. According to tradition, he was an officer of the Praetorian Guards until his Christianity was discovered by Diocletian. Feast day: 20 Jan.

Sebastiano del Piombo (S. Luciano; c. 1485–1547) Venetian painter. Although he was a pupil of Giovanni Bellini, his early works, notably *St John Chrysostom* (c. 1509; S Giovanni Crisostomo, Venice), were influenced by Giorgione. Moving to Rome in 1511, he painted decorations in the Farnesina with *Raphael, whose *Transfiguration* he directly challenged with his *Raising of Lazarus* (1517–19; National Gallery, London). He was also known as a portraitist; his sitters included Christopher Columbus and Pope Clement VII, who appointed him keeper of the papal seals (*piombi*) in 1531—hence his nickname.

second 1. (s) The SI unit of time equal to the duration of 9 192 631 770 periods of the radiation corresponding to a specified transition of the caesium-133 atom. **2.** A unit of angle equal to one-sixtieth of a minute.

secondary education Education for adolescent children, aged approximately from 11 to 18. In the UK the Education Act (1944) introduced universal secondary education (compulsory to the age of 15, extended to 16 in 1972). Initially a tripartite system (comprising *grammar schools for more academic pupils, secondary modern schools, and technical schools) was implemented in England and Wales, selection being based upon the eleven-plus examination. This exam has since been largely phased out and a widespread system of *comprehensive schools introduced.

secondary emission The ejection of electrons from the surface of a metal when it is bombarded with charged particles of sufficient energy. When the bombarding particles are themselves electrons, these are known as primary electrons and the ejected electrons are called secondary electrons. The effect is used in such devices as the electron multiplier.

secretary bird A large long-legged terrestrial bird of prey, *Sagittarius serpentarius*, that lives in dry uplands of Africa. It has a hawklike face and a grey plumage with a long pair of central tail feathers and a black crest of quills behind its head—hence its name. Order: *Falconiformes* (falcons, hawks, etc.).

Sedan, Battle of (1 September 1870) The battle in the *Franco-Prussian War in which German forces, invading NE France, defeated the army of Napoleon III. This precipitated revolution in Paris and marked the end of the Second Empire.

sedatives Drugs that relieve restlessness, anxiety, and tension. Most drugs that depress the activity of the nervous system have this effect (including barbiturates and narcotics), but the most widely used sedatives are the *benzodiazepines.

sedge A perennial herbaceous grasslike plant of the genus *Carex* (about 2000 species), growing throughout the world, mainly in swampy places. Sedges have solid triangular stems, with long narrow leaves and small male and female flowers usually grouped into separate clusters (spikes). Family: *Cyperaceae*.

Sedgemoor, Battle of (6 July 1685) The battle, E of Bridgwater, Somerset, in which the forces of James II of England defeated the rebellion of his nephew, the Duke of *Monmouth.

sedimentary rock One of the three major categories into which rocks are divided (*compare* IGNEOUS ROCK; METAMORPHIC ROCK). Sedimentary rocks are deposited mainly under water, usually in approximately horizontal layers (beds). **Clastic sedimentary rocks** are formed from the erosion and deposition of pre-existing rocks and are classified according to the size of the particles: those with sand-grade particles include the sandstones; those with silt- or clay-grade particles include siltstones and mudstones; those with gravel-grade and larger fragments include the breccias, conglomerates, etc. Organically formed sedimentary rocks are derived from the remains of plants and animals, for example limestone and coal. Chemically formed sedimentary rocks result from natural chemical processes and include sedimentary iron ores. Many sedimentary rocks show complex internal structures, formed during or after deposition.

S

Seebeck effect *See* THERMOELECTRIC EFFECTS.

seed The reproductive structure formed after pollination and fertilization in higher plants. In flowering plants (angiosperms) the seed begins to develop after the *pollen nucleus has fused with the egg. In gymnosperms (conifers and related plants) the ovule begins dividing before pollination. All seeds contain an embryo and usually a food store, which is mobilized on germination. Angiosperm seeds are surrounded by a seed coat and contained within a *fruit; gymnosperm seeds are naked (*see* CONE). The development of the "seed habit" has given the higher plants a marked advantage over the ferns, mosses, algae, and fungi. Water is not needed for fertilization, and therefore the plants can colonize arid habitats. In addition, seeds—unlike the spores of lower plants—can survive adverse conditions.

seed fern A fernlike *gymnosperm plant belonging to the extinct order *Cycadafilicales* (or *Pteridospermales*), abundant during the Carboniferous and Permian periods (370–240 million years ago). Seed ferns—unlike ferns—produced seeds, in cuplike structures.

Sefton A unitary authority in NW England, in Merseyside. Area: 150 sq km (58 sq mi). Population (2001): 282 956.

Segovia, Andrés (1893–1987) Spanish guitarist, who revived the popularity of the guitar as a concert instrument.

Seine, River A river in N France. Rising on the Plateau de Langres, it flows mainly NW through Paris to the English Channel, S of Le Havre. It is the second longest river in France, linked by canal with the Rivers Somme, Scheldt, Meuse, Rhine, Saône, and Loire. Length: 776 km (482 mi).

seismic belts (*or* **seismic zones**) The narrow distinct belts on the earth's surface that are subject to frequent earthquakes. They usually follow the line of plate boundaries (*see* PLATE TECTONICS), especially along midocean ridges, island arc systems, and major *faults.

seismic wave An elastic shock wave emanating from the focus of an *earthquake or explosion. When seismic activity is recorded, several types of wave can be identified: longitudinal P (*primae*) waves and transverse S (*secundae*) waves are small rapid vibrations that come directly through the earth's interior in the preliminary tremor of an earthquake. The main earthquake consists of large slow L (*longae*) waves travelling along the surface. The study of seismic waves has provided much of our knowledge of the earth's interior.

seismology The branch of geophysics concerned with the study of *earthquakes: their origin, the waves they produce (*see* SEISMIC WAVE), their effects, their distribution, and their prediction and modification. The instruments used are the **seismograph**, which records the magnitude of the oscillations during an earthquake, and the **seismometer**, which detects and records the motions of the earth in a particular direction (usually used in sets of three).

Selene The Greek moon-goddess, daughter of

the Titan Hyperion and sister of Helios (the sun) and Eos (dawn). She became identified with the later Greek goddess *Artemis and with the Roman *Diana.

selenium (Se) A chemical element that is a member of the sulphur family and exists in several forms, including deep-red crystals, but the commonest allotrope is grey. The element has photovoltaic properties and is used in photocells, light meters, and in photocopying machines. It is a semiconductor and is widely used in rectifiers. At no 34; at wt 78.96; mp 221°C; bp 685°C.

Seleucids A Middle Eastern dynasty of the Hellenistic age (323–27 BC) founded by Seleucus I Nicator (c. 356–280 BC), the Macedonian general who, after Alexander the Great's death, became governor and then ruler (312) of Babylonia. He extended his kingdom to the frontiers of India in the east and then into Syria in the west but his successors failed to maintain his conquests. Antiochus the Great (reigned 223–187) briefly restored Seleucid power in the east but could not prevent Rome's Mediterranean expansion. The empire was further weakened by the revolt of the *Maccabees, who were repressed, and the failure to push back the Parthians precipitated its final disintegration. In 64 BC Pompey annexed what was left of it to form the Roman province of Syria.

Sellers, Peter (1925–80) British comic actor. He made his name in the 1950s with the BBC radio comedy series *The Goon Show*. His films include *I'm All Right, Jack* (1959), *Dr Strangelove* (1963), *What's New, Pussycat?* (1965), The Pink Panther series (1963–77), and *Being There* (1980).

Selznick, David O(liver) (1902–65) US film producer. In 1936 he formed his own production company and produced *A Star Is Born* (1937) and *Gone with the Wind* (1939) among other films. His later films included *Duel in the Sun* (1946) and *A Farewell to Arms* (1957).

semantics The branch of *linguistics concerned with the meaning of individual words; also, in logic and philosophy, the study of the relationship between words and the objects or concepts they refer to. There can be problems in explaining such a relationship when a word has no concrete referent (e.g. "honesty").

semaphore 1. A visual method of communication between ships at sea, used mainly by

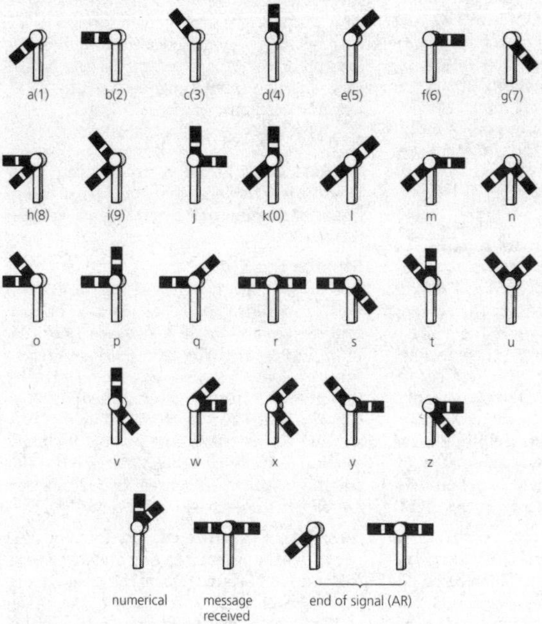

semaphore

warships wishing to maintain radio silence, and consisting of a pattern of signalling by the use of two flags, held by a signalman, their relative positions symbolizing an alphabetical or numerical character. **2.** A mechanical railway signalling device, consisting of a movable steel arm.

Semarang 6 58S 110 29E A port in Indonesia, in central Java on the Java Sea. A commercial centre with textile and shipbuilding industries, it exports sugar, rubber, coffee, kapok, and copra. The port is sometimes disrupted by the monsoon. Its university was established in 1960. Population (1995 est): 1 366 500.

semiconductor A crystalline material in which the electrical conductivity increases with temperature and is between that of a conductor and an insulator. The conductivity is also sensitive to minute quantities of impurities in the crystal lattice. Some (donor) impurities increase the number of negative charge carriers (electrons), creating what is known as an n-type semiconductor. Other (acceptor) impurities increase the number of positive charge carriers (holes), creating a p-type semiconductor. The introduction of these impurities is called doping. Solid-state electronic components, such as diodes, *transistors, and *integrated circuits depend on the properties of junctions between p-type and n-type regions in the same piece of semiconductor crystal (p-n junctions). Metal oxide semiconductor (MOS) devices also use the properties of a thin layer of insulating oxide on the semiconductor surface. The element silicon is now the most widely used semiconducting material.

semiconductor diode A solid-state electronic device with two electrodes. It consists of a single p-n junction (*see* SEMICONDUCTOR). When the p-region is at a more positive voltage than the n-region (forward bias), the current flow increases exponentially as the voltage rises. In reverse bias, very little current flows until a sufficiently high reverse voltage has built up to cause breakdown; the current then increases sharply. The diode is, therefore, commonly used as a rectifier. Semiconductor diodes are also used to generate microwaves by the Gunn effect, to detect light in *photocells, and to emit light in low-voltage displays (**light-emitting diodes**; LEDs).

Semites A group of peoples, including the *Jews and *Arabs, said in the Bible to be descended from Shem, Noah's eldest son. The Babylonians, Assyrians, Canaanites, and Phoenicians were ancient Semitic peoples.

Semitic alphabets The earliest known truly alphabetic writing systems, developed among the Semitic peoples of the E Mediterranean around 2000 BC. From them all the major alphabets of today are derived: the south Semitic version gave rise to the modern Amharic script of Ethiopia; from North Semitic were derived Greek (and from Greek came the Roman, Cyrillic, runic, and other alphabets), Phoenician, and Aramaic (from which came the scripts of Hebrew, Arabic, and Devanagari in India).

Semitic languages A subgroup of the Hamito-Semitic language family spoken in a large area of N Africa, extending through Palestine to the SW corner of Asia. The Semitic languages originated in Mesopotamia in the 3rd millennium BC and are recorded in Sumerian *cuneiform inscriptions. Although many, including Aramaic, Assyrian, and Babylonian are now extinct, examples of living Semitic languages are *Hebrew, modern *Arabic, and Maltese.

Senate In ancient Rome, the state council. During Republican times it was largely composed of ex-magistrates and, although its role was primarily to advise the magistrates, it carried much weight, especially in foreign policy, finance, and religion. Under the Empire membership of the Senate became largely hereditary and its chief function was to ratify imperial decisions.

Senate, US *See* CONGRESS.

Sendai 38 16N 140 52E A city in Japan, in NE Honshu. It is the largest city of N Japan and an important commercial centre. Population (1995 est): 971 297.

Seneca the Elder (Marcus Annaeus Seneca; c.55 BC–c.41 AD) Roman rhetorician, born at Córdoba (Spain). Parts of his work on oratory, addressed to his sons, have survived. One of his sons, **Seneca the Younger** (Lucius Annaeus Seneca; c.4 BC–65 AD), was an author and politician. He was tutor and later chief minister to Nero. Retiring in 64 AD, he was accused of treason and forced to commit suicide. His philosophical writings advocate *Stoicism. His nine tragedies, which influenced the Elizabethan dramatists, also survive.

Senegal, Republic of A country in West Africa, on the Atlantic Ocean. The River Senegal forms its N boundary and the River Gambia flows E–W through the country to the border of The Gambia, which forms an enclave within Senegalese territory. Senegal consists chiefly of level plains rising to a dissected plateau in the SE. Most of the population are Wolof, Serer, and Tukolor. *Economy*: chiefly agricultural, the production of groundnuts being dominant. Phosphates, iron ore, and offshore oil and natural gas have been found in significant quantities. There is a large foreign debt. *History*: the French extended their control in the mid-19th century over most of the region. The country achieved self-government in 1958 as a member of the French Community and in 1959–60 briefly formed the Federation of Mali with Sudan. Senegal became a separate independent republic in 1960, with Leopold Senghor (1906–2002) as president. From 1982 until 1989 it formed the Senegambia Confederation with The Gambia, with each country retaining its independence but having joint defence, foreign, and monetary policies. Abdou Diouf (1935–) succeeded Senghor as president in 1981. The 1990s saw rising ethnic tensions, including a virtual frontier war with Mauritania (1989–92). In 2000 40 years of socialist rule came to an end when President Diouf was defeated by Abdoulaye Wade. Official language: French. Currency: CFA franc of 100 centimes. Area: 197 722 sq km (76 320 sq mi). Population (2003 est): 10 095 000. Capital: Dakar.

senna *See* CASSIA.

sensitive plants *See* MIMOSA.

Seoul 37 30N 127 00E The capital of the Republic of (South) Korea, in the NW on the River Han near the coast. It was the capital of Korea from 1394. Population (1995): 10 229 262.

Sephardim (Hebrew *Sepharad*: Spain) Jews who went to Spain and Portugal in the *diaspora. When the Jews were expelled from Spain in 1492 they spread to many parts of the world, preserving their customs and their language, Ladino. The first Jewish settlers in England were Marranos from Spain. In the 17th century the Sephardim came from Holland; they opened their first synagogue in 1657, which was replaced in 1701 by a synagogue in Bevis Marks in the City of London, which is still in use. The term is now sometimes applied, especially in Israel, to all non-*Ashkenazim.

September 11 The day in 2001 that saw the worst terrorist atrocity in history, directed at targets in New York and Washington. Four passenger airliners were hijacked by Islamic terrorists: two were flown into the twin towers of the *World Trade Center in New York, causing their collapse, a third was crashed into the *Pentagon, while the fourth hit the ground near Pittsburgh, apparently as a result of a fight-back by passengers. A total of 265 people (including 19 terrorists) died in the hijacked aeroplanes, over 2600 died in the collapse of the World Trade Center, and a further 180 were killed in the Pentagon, bringing the total death toll to about 3195. Evidence was soon found to confirm suspicions that the *al-Qaida terrorist network led by Osama *Bin Laden was responsible. In October, the USA launched its so-called *war on terrorism with air strikes against al-Qaida and *Taleban targets in Afghanistan.

sequoia Either of two Californian coniferous trees, the *redwood (*Sequoia sempervirens*), the world's tallest tree; or the giant sequoia, *Sequoiadendron giganteum* (formerly *Sequoia gigantea*), also called wellingtonia. The latter forms natural forests in California's Sierra Nevada, where some trees are over 3000 years old, with a height of over 80 m and a girth of over 24 m. The red-brown bark is soft and fibrous and the shoots are covered with pointed scalelike leaves. Family: *Taxodiaceae*.

seraphim *See* CHERUBIM AND SERAPHIM.

Serbia (Serbo-Croat name: Srbija) A constituent republic of the Union of *Serbia and Montenegro, incorporating the autonomous regions of *Vojvodina and *Kosovo. It is mountainous in the S, descending in the N to the Danube basin. Agriculture is important as is mining, especially for copper, antimony, coal, and chrome. In the 1990s the economy was devastated by the imposition of economic sanctions and NATO bombing (1999). *History*: first settled by the Serbs in the 7th century AD, it later came under Turkish control (1389–1804), finally regaining its independence in 1878. It played a major role in events leading up to World War I, Austria accusing Serbia of direct involvement in the assassination of Archduke Francis Ferdinand. In 1918 Serbia became the leading partner in the kingdom of Serbs, Croats, and Slovenes, later renamed *Yugoslavia. In 1991 Serbia under Slobodan *Milošević attempted unsuccessfully to prevent the break-up of Yugoslavia by military action against Slovenia and Croatia. Serbia was also condemned for its involvement in the civil war in Bosnia-Hercegovina (1992–95). In 1992 Serbia and Montenegro formed a new Federal Republic of Yugoslavia. Serbia's attempt to suppress ethnic Albanian separatists in Kosovo through a campaign of "ethnic cleansing" led to NATO airstrikes in 1999. Popular discontent with the authoritarian rule of Milošević culminated (October 2000) in a bloodless revolution in which he was replaced by the opposition leader, Vojislav Kostunica. A new agreement with Montenegro, establishing the Union of Serbia and Montenegro, was signed in 2002 and ratified in 2003. Area: 88 361 sq km (34 107 sq mi). Population (2001 est): 9 993 000. Capital: Belgrade.

Serbia and Montenegro, Union of A country in SE Europe, consisting of the republic of *Serbia and its much smaller neighbour *Montenegro. It is chiefly mountainous, descending to the fertile Danube plains in the N. There is a short Adriatic coastline in Montenegro. *Economy*: the country is self-sufficient in food production and livestock-raising. Forestry and wine-making are important. The economy is slowly beginning to recover from Serbia's international isolation (1990s) and NATO bombing (1999). *History*: following the break-up of *Yugoslavia (1991–92), Serbia and Montenegro announced the formation of a new federal Republic of Yugoslavia in 1992 (not recognized by the UN until 2000). Slobodan *Milošević became president in 1997. His nationalist and authoritarian policies, together with deepening economic crisis, led to a growing movement for separatism in Montenegro in the late 1990s. Following Serbia's defeat by NATO in the *Kosovo War, Milošević was deposed (2000). His successor, Vojislav Kostunica, moved to restore relations with both the West and Serbia's Balkan neighbours, including Montenegro. In 2002–03 the existing federation was replaced by a new Union of Serbia and Montenegro. The two republics now have a joint foreign and defence policy but virtual autonomy in domestic and economic matters. The final status of Kosovo is unresolved; it remains nominally part of Serbia but is administered separately by the UN. Official language: Serbo-Croatian. Currency: new dinar of 100 paras in Serbia; euro of 100 cents in Montenegro and Kosovo. Area: 102 173 sq km (39 440 sq mi). Population (2003 est): 10 527 000. Capital: Belgrade.

S

Serbo-Croat The language of the Serbs and Croats of the former Yugoslavia. Serbian and Croatian differ little in terms of vocabulary and not at all in grammar but Serbian is written in Cyrillic and Croatian in Latin script.

serf An unfree peasant of the middle ages. Serfdom was characteristic of the manorial economic system (*see* MANOR). A serf was bound to the soil he tilled, paying his lord a fee and providing service in return for the use of his land. Serfs had their own homes, plots, and livestock and enjoyed customary rights. While serfdom declined in W Europe in the late middle ages, it continued in E Europe until the 19th century.

serialism (*or* **twelve-tone music**) A method of composing music using all 12 notes of the chromatic scale equally, invented by Arnold *Schoenberg in the 1920s. Schoenberg sought an alternative to chromaticism and *atonality by using a fixed sequence of 12 notes (called a **series** or **tone row**) as a source of melody and harmony. The series could be transposed so as to begin on any degree of the scale and could also be inverted and used in a retrograde form. In strict serialism no single note of the row could be repeated until the other 11 had occurred in melody or harmony.

series The sum of the terms in a sequence, written as $a_1 + a_2 + a_3 + ...a_r + ...$ The partial sum to the nth term is denoted by S_n. A series is convergent if S_n approaches a particular value as n increases and divergent if it increases without limit. A geometric series has the general form $a + an + an^2 + ...$, where a and n are constant. A power series has the general form $a_0 + a_1x + a_2x^2 + a_3x^3 + ...$, where x is a variable.

serpentine A group of minerals consisting mainly of hydrous magnesium silicates, with a layered structure. They are usually green or white, and often streaked or mottled like a snake's skin. They occur in igneous rocks. Rock consisting mainly of serpentine is sometimes quarried for ornamental stone.

serum The fluid that remains after blood has been allowed to clot. It can be obtained by centrifuging clotted blood and is similar in composition to plasma, except that it lacks the factors, such as fibrinogen, that are involved in blood clotting.

serval A slender long-legged *cat, *Felis serval*, of the African bush. It is about 1.25 m long including the tail and has large ears and a spotted coat. Servals hunt birds and small mammals, mainly at night.

service tree A tree, *Sorbus domestica*, about 15 m high, native to S Europe, W Asia, and N Africa and commonly grown for ornament. Related to the *mountain ash, it has compound leaves and its small green fruits are used for making wine. Family: *Rosaceae*.

sesame An annual herb, *Sesamum indicum*, cultivated in Central and South America, the Middle East, and SE Asia for its seeds, which are used in confectionery and as food flavouring. An edible oil is extracted from the seeds; the residue is used as cattle feed. Family: *Pedaliaceae*.

Set An Egyptian deity. Originally a sun and sky god, he murdered his brother *Osiris and so came to represent all evil. He was killed by *Horus, son of Osiris.

setter One of three breeds of sporting dog with a lean deep-chested body and drooping ears. Setters are named after their habit of squatting flat ("setting") after finding game. The English setter has a long white silky coat flecked with darker markings. The heavier Gordon setter is black with chestnut markings, while the Irish, or red, setter has a flat silky chestnut coat. Height: 61–69 cm.

set theory The study, founded by Georg *Cantor, of the logical and mathematical laws of sets. A set is a defined collection of objects or elements; for example the set of odd integers between 0 and 10 is 1, 3, 5, 7, 9. The empty or null set has no elements. All sets are contained in the universal set E. The relationships between sets can be illustrated in a Venn diagram, named after the British logician John Venn (1834–1923), or shown by symbols. $a \in A$ means the element a is a member of the set A. $A \subset B$ means set A is contained in set B. $A \cup B$ means the union of A and B. $A \cap B$ means the intersection of A and B, i.e. those elements in both. A^c or A' is the complement of A, all elements in E but not in A.

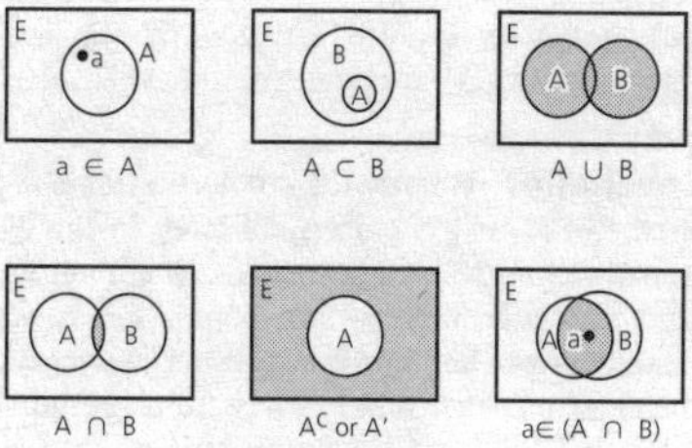

set theory. Venn diagrams.

Settlement, Act of (1701) The Act that established the Hanoverian succession to the English throne. In the absence of heirs to William III or Anne, the Crown was to pass to James I's granddaughter Sophia (1657–1714), Electress of Hanover, or to her Protestant descendants. The Act stipulated that the monarch must be a Protestant and that foreigners must not hold public office or enter parliament. Anne was succeeded by the first Hanoverian king, George I, in 1714.

Seurat, Georges (1859–91) French painter who developed neoimpressionism, popularly called *pointillism. Although he finished only seven paintings in this style, for example *Sunday Afternoon on the Island of the Grande Jatte* (1884–86), his work was very influential.

Sevastopol (English name: Sebastopol) 44 36N 33 31E A port in S Ukraine, in the Crimean *oblast* (region) on the Black Sea. It is a popular seaside resort. Founded in 1783, after Russia's annexation of the Crimea it became an important naval base and, later, a commercial port. It was besieged by the British and French during the Crimean War, falling after 11 months. Population (1996 est): 365 000.

Seven Deadly Sins Pride, covetousness, lust, envy, gluttony, anger, and sloth. The traditional Christian list was already established by the 6th century.

Seven Wonders of the World The supreme man-made structures of the ancient world. They were the Pyramids of Egypt, the *Colossus of Rhodes, the *Hanging Gardens of Babylon, the Mausoleum of Halicarnassus, the statue of *Zeus at Olympia, the temple of *Artemis at Ephesus, and the *Pharos of Alexandria. Only the Pyramids have survived.

Seven Years' War (1756–63) The war between Prussia, Britain, and Hanover on one side and France, Austria, Russia, and Spain on the other. The war had two main aspects: the rivalry between Austria and Prussia for domination of Germany and the struggle between France and Britain for overseas supremacy. The war was precipitated by Austria's desire to regain Silesia, lost to Frederick the Great of Prussia in the War of the *Austrian Succession, and began with Frederick's invasion of Saxony. Russia's defection (1762) to Prussia enabled Frederick ultimately to emerge victorious and Prussian ascendancy was confirmed by the Peace of Hubertusberg. Overseas, the British despite initial reverses won a series of spectacular victories in India (by *Clive) and Canada (by Wolfe). By the Treaty of *Paris (1763) Britain was confirmed as the supreme world power.

Severn, River (Welsh name: Hafren) The longest river in the UK, rising in central Wales and flowing NE and E into England, then S to the Bristol Channel. It passes through Shrewsbury, Worcester, and Gloucester. It is spanned near its estuary by the **Severn Bridges**. The first of these, a suspension bridge 988 m (3240 ft) long, was built in the 1960s. However, its vulnerability to high winds led to frequent closure and a second bridge, mainly cantilevered and with a much greater wind resistance, was opened in 1996; this now takes the majority of the traffic. Length: 365 km (227 mi).

Seville (Spanish name: Sevilla) 37 24N 5 59W A city and port in SW Spain, in Andalusia on the River Guadalquivir. Now a major industrial centre, it was important during Roman times, thrived under the Moors (711–1248) as a cultural centre, and became a major port in the 16th century. There is a university (founded 1502) and a cathedral (1401–1591). Population (1998 est): 701 927.

Sèvres porcelain The finest French porcelain, first produced in Vincennes in 1738 and still made. The factory moved to Sèvres near *Versailles in 1756. It always enjoyed royal patronage. Early output was soft-paste porcelain but from 1768 hard-paste was made. Products were figures, vases, ornaments, and table services with blue, rose Pompadour, yellow, or green grounds richly gilded for royal taste.

sex chromosome A *chromosome that carries the genes for determining the sex of an individual. In humans there are two types of sex chromosomes, called X and Y. The body cells of normal males possess one X and one Y chromosome while those of normal females have two X chromosomes. Human sperm is therefore either "male" or "female" depending on whether it carries an X or a Y chromosome. The sex of the embryo is determined by which type of sperm fertilizes the female egg (which always carries an X chromosome). Abnormal numbers of sex chromosomes cause a range of disabilities, including physical abnormalities, mental retardation, and sterility.

sex hormones Hormones that regulate the growth, development, and functioning of the reproductive organs and determine external sexual characteristics. The major female sex hormones are the *oestrogens, *progesterone, and *prolactin while the *androgens are the principal male ones. Their production is regulated by *gonadotrophins from the pituitary gland.

sextant An instrument used primarily in navigation for determining latitudes by measuring the angle subtended by some celestial body to the horizon. Thomas Godfrey of Philadelphia and John Hadley of London, working independently, discovered the sextant's principle in 1730. The graduated metal strip, shaped in an arc of the sixth part of a circle, gave the instrument its name. In use the movable index arm is slid along the scale until the image of the reference star as viewed in the half-silvered index mirror is aligned with the horizon. The reading on the scale then indicates the angle subtended.

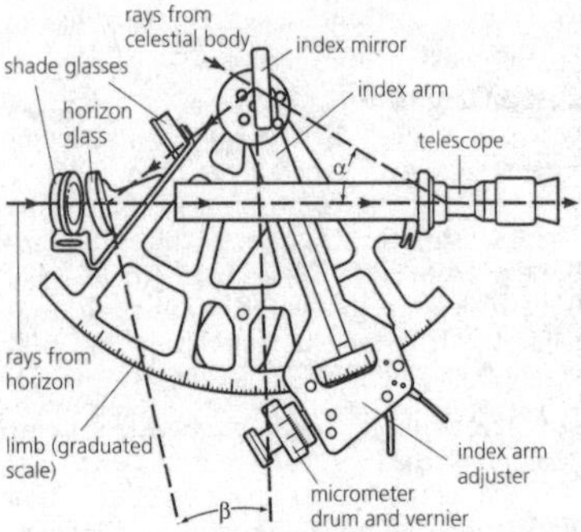

sextant. Angle α measures the angle between horizon and reference arm; β is the angle between index mirror and horizon glass, marked by the angular movement of the index arm along the limb. $\alpha = 2\beta$, therefore the graduations marked on the scale are twice the actual angular movement.

sexton beetle *See* BURYING BEETLE.

sexually transmitted disease (STD) Any disease transmitted by sexual intercourse, also known as venereal disease (VD). Among the most prevalent STDs today are genital herpes, nonspecific urethritis (NSU; caused by *Chlamydia*), and AIDS; syphilis and gonorrhoea—the former scourges—are now treatable with antibiotics.

Seychelles, Republic of A country consisting of 87 widely scattered islands in the W Indian Ocean, NE of Madagascar. The main island is Mahé. Most of the population is of mixed African and European descent. *Economy*: the chief products and exports are fish, copra, and cinnamon bark. Tourism is important, as is offshore banking and finance. *History*: the uninhabited islands became a French colony in the mid-18th century as a spice plantation. Captured by the British in 1794, they were a dependency of Mauritius from 1814 until 1903, when they became a British crown colony. In 1976 the country became an independent republic within the Commonwealth. Multiparty elections held in 1993 resulted in victory for Albert René and his ruling party; he was re-elected in 2002. Official languages: English and French; the majority speak Creole. Currency: Seychelles rupee of 100 cents. Area: 444 sq km (171 sq mi). Population (2003 est): 81 500. Capital: Victoria.

Seymour, Jane (c. 1509–37) The third wife (1536–37) of Henry VIII of England. A lady in waiting to Anne Boleyn, she married Henry 11 days after Anne's execution. Jane died shortly after the birth of a son, Edward VI.

's Gravenhage See HAGUE, THE.

Shackleton, Sir Ernest Henry (1874–1922) British explorer. He accompanied Scott's expedition of 1901–04 and on his own expedition in 1908–09 nearly reached the South Pole. In an expedition of 1914–16 his ship, the *Endurance*, was marooned but he and his men reached Elephant Island by sledge and boats. With five others he then journeyed 1300 km (800 mi) to find relief. He died on his fourth expedition.

shad A food fish, belonging to a genus (*Alosa*) related to herrings, that occurs in the N Atlantic, Mediterranean, and North Sea. It has one or a succession of black spots along each side and a notch in the upper jaw. They migrate in large shoals to spawn in fresh waters.

Shaffer, Peter (1926–) British dramatist. His plays include *Five-Finger Exercise* (1958), *The Royal Hunt of the Sun* (1964), *Equus* (1973), *Amadeus* (1979), *Yonadab* (1985), *Lettice and Lovage* (1987), and *The Gift of the Gorgon* (1992).

Shaftesbury, Anthony Ashley Cooper, 7th Earl of (1801–85) British reformer. He became an MP in 1826 and campaigned successfully for reform of the lunacy laws (1845), a ten-hour day for factory workers (1847), and an end to the employment of children in coal mines (1842) and as chimney sweeps (1840).

Shah Jahan (1592–1666) Emperor of India (1628–58) of the Mogul dynasty; the son of Jahangir (1569–1627). His reign was as ruthless as his means of attaining it; he put his nearest relatives to death in 1628. His passion for fine architecture produced such monuments as the *Taj Mahal and the Delhi Red Fort. He was deposed by his son Aurangzeb (1618–1707).

Shakespeare, William (1564–1616) English dramatist, universally recognized as the greatest English writer. Born in Stratford-upon-Avon, he married in 1582 a local girl, Anne Hathaway, by whom he had three children. Soon afterwards he went to London, where he became an actor in the leading theatrical company, the Lord Chamberlain's Men (called the King's Men after 1603). The three parts of *Henry VI* and *Richard III* were his first plays (1589–92). His poems *Venus and Adonis* (1593) and *The Rape of Lucrece* (1594) were dedicated to his patron Henry Wriothesley, 3rd Earl of *Southampton. His *Sonnets* (1609) were probably written at this time. His early comedies (1593–95) were *Love's Labour's Lost*, *The Two Gentlemen of Verona*, and *The Taming of the Shrew*. These were followed (1595–1600) by *A Midsummer Night's Dream*, *The Merchant of Venice*, *Much Ado About Nothing*, *Twelfth Night*, and *As You Like It*. During this period he also wrote his first significant tragedy, *Romeo and Juliet*, as well as *Richard II* and *Julius Caesar*. In 1597 he bought New Place, a large house in Stratford, and later became a shareholder in the Globe Theatre in London. The two parts of *Henry IV* were completed before *Hamlet*, *Othello*, *King Lear*, and *Macbeth*, his major tragedies (1600–06). His final experimental plays included *The Winter's Tale* (c. 1610) and *The Tempest* (c. 1611). In about 1611 he retired to Stratford, where he died. The first collected edition of his works, known as the First Folio and containing 36 plays, was published in 1623. His other plays were: *The Comedy of Errors*, *Titus Andronicus*, *King John*, *Henry V*, *The Merry Wives of Windsor*, *Antony and Cleopatra*, *Coriolanus*, *Troilus and Cressida*, *Measure for Measure*, *All's Well That Ends Well*, *Timon of Athens*, *Pericles*, *Cymbeline*, and, with John Fletcher (1579–1625), *Henry VIII* and *The Two Noble Kinsmen*.

shale A fine-grained *sedimentary rock that splits easily along the closely spaced bedding planes as a result of the alignment of the clay mineral particles parallel to the bedding planes. Shales may disintegrate in water. They are softer and lighter than slate, which is a fine-grained *metamorphic rock.

shallot A hardy perennial herbaceous plant, *Allium ascalonium*, probably of Asiatic origin. Its small hollow cylindrical leaves are often used for dressing food and in salads. Its small angular bulbs occur in garlic-like clusters and are used for flavouring and pickling. Family: *Liliaceae*.

shamanism The religious beliefs and practices common in certain tribal societies of Asia, such as the *Samoyed. The term is also applied to North American Indian practices. The shaman is a tribal priest generally felt to be possessed by a spirit or deity and hence to have supernatural powers. He may also act as the tribal ruler and judge.

Shamir, Yitzhak (1915–) Israeli statesman, born in Poland; prime minister (1983–84, 1986–92). He led the Israeli Freedom Fighters (1940–41), served in Israel's secret service (1955–65), and was foreign minister (1980–83, 1984–86). In 1984–88 he had a special power-sharing agreement with Shimon *Peres. His government collapsed in 1992 over peace talks with Palestinian leaders.

shamrock Any of several plants bearing leaves with three leaflets, especially various *clovers, black medick (*Medicago lupulina*), and *wood sorrel (*Oxalis acetosella*). The shamrock is worn on St Patrick's Day.

Shanghai 31 13N 121 25E An administratively autonomous port in E China, on the Yangtze estuary. The largest city in China, it is its chief port and industrial city. It grew rapidly after it was opened to foreign trade in 1842, coming under British, US, and French rule until World War II. Population (1999 est): 8 937 175.

Shankar, Ravi (1920–) Indian *sitar player who popularized Indian music in the West.

Shannon, River The longest river in the Republic of Ireland. Rising in NW Co Cavan, it flows S to Limerick and then W to the Atlantic. Length: 386 km (240 mi).

shari'ah *See* ISLAMIC LAW.

Sharjah *See* UNITED ARAB EMIRATES.

shark A *cartilaginous fish belonging to the worldwide order *Selachii* (about 250 species). Ranging in size from the smallest *dogfish to the enormous *whale shark, they have a torpedo-shaped body with a muscular tail used in swimming, five to seven pairs of gill slits on the sides of the head, and numerous sharp teeth. They are chiefly marine and carnivorous. Subclass: *Elasmobranchii*.

Sharon, Ariel (1928–) Israeli soldier and politician; prime minister (2001–). An Israeli army officer, he became a national hero in the Yom Kippur War (1973). As defence minister he organized Israel's invasion of Lebanon (1982) but was sacked (1983) when it was found that he had connived in the massacre of Palestinian refugees by right-wing Lebanese forces. He later emerged as a leading critic of the Palestinian peace process and served as foreign minister (1998–99). He became leader of Likud (2000), taking the party to victory in the 2001 elections. In 2001–02 he responded to Arab suicide bombings by ordering the reoccupation of much of the West Bank, a move that incurred much criticism from abroad.

Sharpeville A Black African town in South Africa, in the S Transvaal near Vereeniging. It was the scene of a riot on 21 March 1960, in which African demonstrators were fired on by the police. Over 60 of the demonstrators were killed and many others wounded. There were riots on the anniversary in 1984 and 1985, when 19 died.

Shaw, George Bernard (1856–1950) Irish dramatist, critic, and writer, born in Dublin. He went to London in 1876, becoming a music and drama critic, an active socialist, and a founder of the Fabian Society. He wrote more than 40 plays, the Prefaces indicating at length the social and moral issues involved. *Plays Pleasant and Unpleasant* (1898) included *Mrs Warren's Profession* (on prostitution), and the comedies *Arms and the Man* and *Candida*. His *Three Plays for Puritans* (1901) included *Caesar and Cleopatra* and *Captain Brassbound's Conversion*. The epic comedy of ideas, *Man and Superman* (1903), was followed by *John Bull's Other Island* (1904), *The Doctor's Dilemma* (1906), *Misalliance* (1910), and *Pygmalion* (1913), an outstanding commercial success. Later works include *Heartbreak House* (1917), the series of plays entitled *Back to Methuselah* (1921), and the historical drama *St Joan* (1924). In 1925 he was awarded the Nobel Prize.

shear stress *See* STRESS.

shearwater One of a group of birds (about 15 species) of the oceanic family *Procellariidae*. Shearwaters have a dark plumage (some species have white underparts), long narrow wings, and slender bills; they feed on fish from the sea surface. The great shearwater (*Puffinus gravis*) breeds in the South Atlantic, migrating to spend summer and autumn in the North Atlantic. The Manx shearwater (*P. puffinus*) breeds off British and Mediterranean coasts and winters in E South America and Australia. Order: *Procellariiformes*. *See also* PETREL.

sheep A hoofed *ruminant mammal belonging to the genus *Ovis* (7 species), native to mountainous regions of Eurasia and North America. Related to goats, sheep are generally 75–100 cm tall at the shoulder. They have a compact body with slender legs and a short tail and the coat ranges from white to brown in colour. Males (rams) have large spiralled horns; females (ewes) have smaller less curved horns. There are over 200 breeds of domestic sheep (*O. aries*), which are reared worldwide for meat, wool, and milk (*see* LIVESTOCK FARMING). Family: *Bovidae*. *See also* AOUDAD; BIGHORN; MOUFLON.

sheepdog A dog used for handling sheep, such as the *collie, *German shepherd dog, *Old English sheepdog, and *Shetland sheepdog, as well as crossbred derivatives.

Sheffield **1.** 52 23N 1 30W A city in N England, in Sheffield unitary authority, South Yorkshire on the River Don. It is world famous for steel, produced here since the mid-18th century. Population (1991): 431 607. **2.** A unitary authority in N England, in South Yorkshire. Area: 368 sq km (142 sq mi). Population (2001): 513 234.

shelduck A large *duck, *Tadorna tadorna*, found around coasts of W and central Eurasia. It is 65 cm long and has black-and-white plumage with a green head, chestnut shoulders, and a red bill.

shellac A natural thermoplastic *resin made from the secretions of the lac insect, *Laccifer lacca*, which is parasitic on certain trees in India and Thailand. Its solution in alcohol is used as a varnish and in lacquers.

Shelley, Percy Bysshe (1792–1822) British poet. He wrote the revolutionary poem *Queen Mab* in 1813 and in 1816 he met and befriended Byron in Switzerland. From 1818 until his death he lived in Italy, where he wrote the verse drama *Prometheus Unbound* (1818–19), the elegy *Adonais* (1821) prompted by the death of Keats, and much lyrical poetry. He was drowned in a sailing accident off the Italian coast. His second wife **Mary Wollstonecraft Shelley** (1797–1851) is best known for her novel *Frankenstein: the Modern Prometheus* (1818).

shells The hard casings secreted by some animals to protect themselves or their eggs. The term usually refers to the shells of molluscs, which consist largely of calcium carbonate and come in a wide variety of shapes and sizes. They may be spiralled or flat, with one valve (in gastropods, such as snails) or two (in bivalves, such as mussels). The pearly nautilus has a many chambered shell, which provides buoyancy.

Shelter (National Campaign for the Homeless) A British organization, founded in 1966, to raise funds for housing projects and housing aid centres for the homeless and to campaign for more and better housing.

Shenyang (former name: Mukden) 41 50N 123 26E A city in NE China, on the River Hun, the capital of Liaoning province. China's fourth largest city, it is a major industrial centre. Population (1999 est): 3 876 289.

Sheraton, Thomas (1751–1806) British furniture designer, who made his name with the designs in his *Cabinet-Maker and Upholsterer's Drawing Book* (1791–94). Influenced by *Adam and contemporary French styles, these designs were characterized by elegance, delicacy, straight lines, and inlaid decoration.

Sheridan, Richard Brinsley (1751–1816) Anglo-Irish dramatist, who lived in England

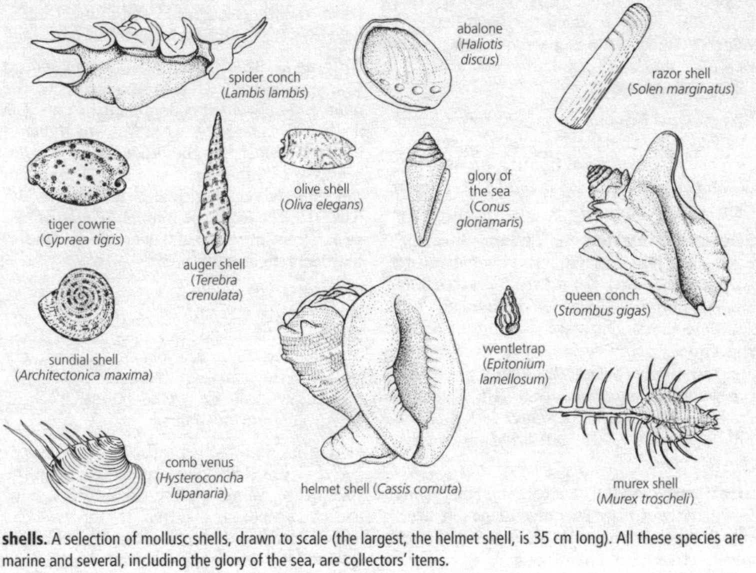

shells. A selection of mollusc shells, drawn to scale (the largest, the helmet shell, is 35 cm long). All these species are marine and several, including the glory of the sea, are collectors' items.

from childhood. He wrote witty comedies of manners, of which the best known are *The Rivals* (1775) and *School for Scandal* (1777). A Whig MP from 1780 to 1812, he was recognized as being one of the great parliamentary orators.

sheriff An official with administrative and judicial responsibilities in England, Scotland, and the USA. Originating in the 10th century as the king's representative in the shire and at the shire court, the sheriff continued in this role under the Normans, who expanded his judicial competence. The sheriffs' powers were reduced by Henry II and succeeding kings and became little more than ceremonial in the 16th century. Sheriffs in England and Scotland are normally appointed by the Crown to each county. In Scotland sheriffs are also the chief county judges. In the USA they are elected and are the principal law enforcement officers in a county.

Sherpa A people of Nepal who speak a dialect of Tibetan. They often act as porters for Himalayan expeditions. With Edmund Hillary, the Sherpa *Tenzing Norgay reached the summit of Everest in 1953.

sherry A fortified *wine, originally made around Jerez de la Frontera (whence its name) in S Spain. There are two basic types of sherry: fino is a pale dry wine on which the *flor* (flower or yeast) has developed fully; oloroso is a rich full-bodied wine on which the *flor* is little developed. Amontillado is a strong dark derivative of a fino and cream sherry is a heavily sweetened oloroso.

Sherwood Forest An ancient forest in the Midlands of England, in Nottinghamshire. Once an extensive royal hunting ground, it is now much reduced; it is famous for its associations with Robin Hood.

S

Shetland Islands (*or* **Shetland**; official name until 1974: Zetland) A group of about 100 islands in the North Sea, off the N coast of Scotland. The largest islands include Mainland, Yell, and Unst. Shetland is best known for its ponies and knitted goods (especially in the Shetland and Fair Isle patterns). The islands are a base for North Sea oil exploitation with a pipeline from the Brent field. Area: 1427 sq km (551 sq mi). Population (2001): 21 988. Administrative centre: Lerwick.

Shetland pony The smallest British pony breed, native to the Shetland Islands. It has a sturdy compact body with short legs and a relatively large head. The mane and tail are profuse and the coat becomes thick in winter. Height: up to 1.05 m (10½ hands).

Shetland sheepdog (*or* **Sheltie**) A breed of dog developed in the Shetland Islands for working sheep. Related to and resembling the *collie, it has a soft undercoat and a long outer coat and may be black, brown, or blue-grey, with white and tan markings. Height: about 35 cm.

Shevardnadze, Eduard (1928–) Georgian statesman; president (1992–2003). As Soviet minister for foreign affairs (1985–90, 1991) he played a key role in arms negotiations with the USA. He was re-elected in 1995 and 2000 but resigned in Nov 2003, following mass protests accusing him of rigging parliamentary elections.

shield An extensive rigid block of Precambrian rocks. Shields are the oldest continental regions, frequently of igneous granite or metamorphic gneiss. The shields were once the site of Precambrian mountain belts, although the mountains have been completely eroded. The **Canadian** (*or* **Laurentian**) **Shield** is the largest, covering several million square kilometres of NE North America.

Shih tzu A breed of small dog originating in Tibet and introduced to the UK in the 1930s. It has a long body with short legs, a short muzzle, and drooping ears. The long straight coat can be of various colours and the plumed tail is held over the back. Height: about 26 cm.

Shiites (*or* **Shiah**) The general term applied to a number of different Muslim sects, the main body of which is dominant in Iran. The distinctive belief of the Shiites, which differentiates them from the other major Muslim group, the *Sunnites, is that *Ali, the fourth caliph, is the only legitimate successor of Mohammed. The leader of Islam, the imam, must be a descendant of Ali and has authority in secular and religious matters.

Shikoku The smallest of the four main islands of Japan, separated from Honshu and Kyushu by the Inland Sea. Its population is concentrated on the coastal plains, with industry mainly in the N. Area: 17 759 sq km (6857 sq mi). Population (2000 est): 4 154 000. Chief cities: Matsuyama and Takamatsu.

shingles An infection caused by the *herpes zoster virus, which lodges in nerve cells in the spinal cord. Shingles affects adults who have had chickenpox as children. It usually starts with pain along the course of a sensory nerve, followed by a band of blisters round half of the body or face. The rash usually eventually disappears but the patient may be left with severe neuralgia.

Shinto The native religion of Japan. Shinto is primarily an attitude of nationalistic and aesthetic reverence towards familiar places and traditions, rather than a set of religious beliefs. However, the central themes are the belief in numerous usually amoral *kamis* or nature spirits, together with ancestor worship and an ideal of military chivalry. The two principal *kamis* are the sun-goddess (reputedly mother of the emperor) and her brother the storm-god. The conflict between them expresses the creative and destructive forces of nature. After World War II, Shinto was disestablished as the state religion.

ships Early mariners included the Egyptians, Chinese and Phoenicians. The short broad Phoenician merchant ships of the 13th century BC were propelled by oars and a single square sail to catch the prevailing wind.

The Greeks developed biremes (with two banks of oars) and triremes (with three banks) as warships, especially strengthened for ramming enemy vessels. The Romans also relied on oars, but their larger grain ships had a number of square sails. In the N the double-ended longships of the Vikings were designed to cope with the rough and windy North Sea. Developed in the 8th century AD and propelled by sail and oars, ships of this kind brought William the Conqueror to England. It was not until the 12th century and the stimulus of the Crusades that the art of using sails was sufficiently developed for oars to be dispensed with. Sailing into the wind was originally pioneered by the Chinese in their junks, but it was the Arabs who perfected the lateen sail, which made it a reliable means of propulsion for large ships. By the 14th century sailing ships were commonplace. The warships of the period had "castles" built at each end to house fighting men, and guns were usually carried on the forecastle. By the end of the 15th century the heavy muzzle-loading cannons were carried in gun ports low in the hull. During this period, too, the single-master with one large heavy sail gave way to the three-master with more manageable small sails and full rigging. During the next 300 years sailing ships developed in many ways, usually with the merchantmen following the innovations in hull design and rigging made by the designers of warships. Sailing ships reached their zenith in the 19th-century clippers, which remained supreme until the *steam engine revolutionized seafaring. The first steamer to cross the Atlantic (in April 1827) was the Dutch *Curaçao* (built 1826), the first British ship to do so (in April 1838) being Brunel's *Great Western*, a wooden paddle steamer. In the next century the propeller completely replaced the paddle and Parson's steam *turbine largely replaced the reciprocating engine. Passenger travel across the Atlantic has now been captured by the airlines; shipbuilding concentrates on cargo vessels, especially oil *tankers.

Warships in the age of steam were largely modelled on the turbine-driven battleship *Dreadnought* (1906), which together with the *cruiser, *destroyer, frigate, and *submarine dominated naval warfare in World War I. By World War II the *aircraft carrier had evolved and with its long-range striking power became the supreme weapon of the war at sea. However, the strength of navies is now judged by their missile- and aircraft-carrying capabilities, as well as by numbers of nuclear-powered submarines. See illustrations on pp. 806–07.

Shire horse A breed of draught horse descended from the English warhorse and one of the world's largest horses. It is massively built with characteristic long white hair (called feathering) covering the lower parts of the legs. The coat is grey, bay, or black. Height: about 1.73 m (17 hands).

Shiva (*or* **Siva**) The third member of the Hindu trinity, the *Trimurti. He is known as the Destroyer, but represents the principle of generation symbolized by the lingam or phallus. His female counterpart is Parvati, also known in her more ominous aspects as Kali and Durga. He is often portrayed in human form with four arms, a third eye in the centre of the forehead, and sometimes wearing a necklace of skulls. His most famous depiction is as *Nataraja* (king of dancing), his dance symbolizing the cosmic rhythm of creation and destruction. The worship of Shiva is characterized by an asceticism that contrasts with the gentler worship of *Vishnu.

shock **1.** A severe condition resulting from failure of the circulatory system, when the blood supply to the tissues is inadequate. The shock may be caused by failure of the heart to pump sufficiently strongly, for example after a heart attack; by loss of blood fluid, for example through haemorrhage or burns; or by widening of the blood vessels so that there is not enough blood to fill them, for example after injury or during a very severe infection. **2.** Injury resulting from electrocution. The extent of the injury depends on the current pass-

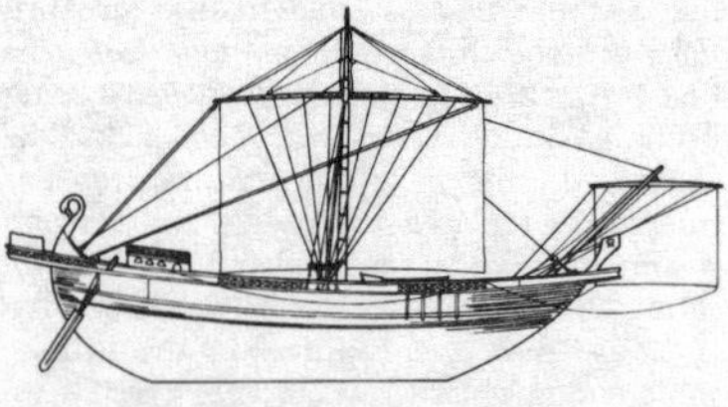

Roman merchantman (c. 100 AD) The Romans' need to transport grain from N Africa to Europe encouraged the building of imposing ships up to 55 m (180 ft) long.

Portuguese caravel (c. 1450) Although it was only a little longer than a large rowing boat, the caravel took part in most of the 15th-century voyages of discovery. The lateen sail, derived from Arab examples, enabled it to sail against the prevailing winds.

Cutty Sark (1869) The 19th-century clippers were renowned for their speed and grace. The *Cutty Sark*, built to bring tea from China, was one of the fastest and most consistent sailing ships of its time. It is now permanently moored at Greenwich.

Great Britain (1843) The second steam ship designed by I. K. Brunel, the *Great Britain* was the first all-iron propeller-driven ship to cross the Atlantic, taking 15 days between Liverpool and New York. Wrecked off the Falkland Islands in 1937, it was restored in the 1970s in Bristol, where it is kept in dry dock.

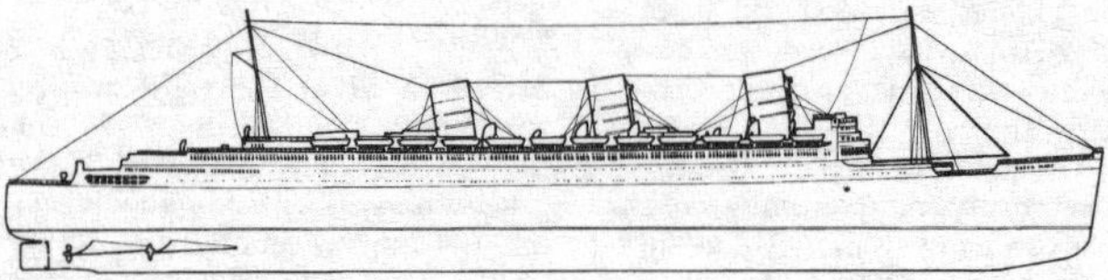

Queen Mary (1934) In 1938 this British passenger liner captured the Blue Riband for the fastest Atlantic crossing with a time of 3 days 20 hours 42 minutes. In 1967 it was anchored off Long Beach, California, as a tourist centre.

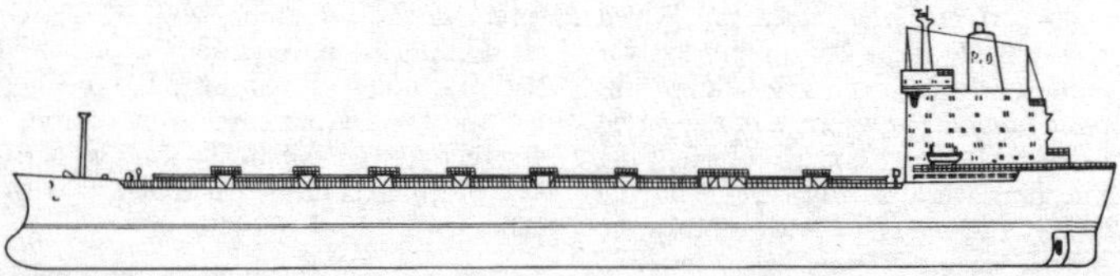

oil tanker (1968) The largest vessels afloat today, some of these giant ships have a deadweight capacity of over 300 000 tonnes.

ships

ing through the body, which is related to the voltage and the skin resistance. As skin resistance is greatly reduced when it is wet, mains voltage (240 V) can cause a lethal current (about 15 milliamps) to flow through the body if live terminals are touched with wet hands.

Shockley, William Bradfield (1910–89) British-born US physicist, who shared the 1956 Nobel Prize with John *Bardeen and Walter *Brattain for their discovery of the *transistor at the Bell Telephone laboratories (1948).

shock wave A narrow region of a high pressure in a fluid, created when a fast-moving body passes through the fluid. The waves are

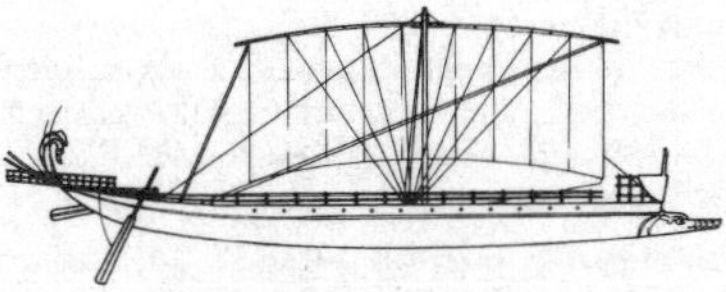

Greek bireme (c. 500 BC) Propelled during an attack by its two ranks of oars, the bireme was strongly built round a keel to support the strain of the ram attached to its bows.

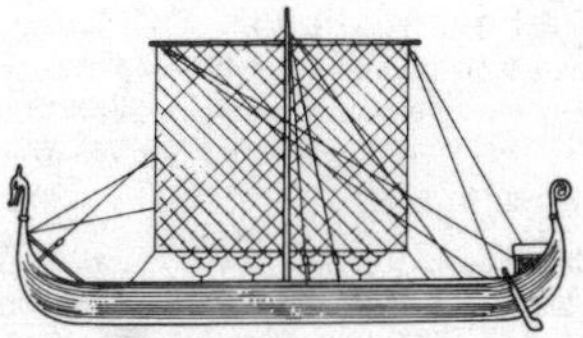

Viking longship (c. 1000 AD) The clinker-built, double-ended longship, propelled by oars and sail, was used mainly to transport fighting men.

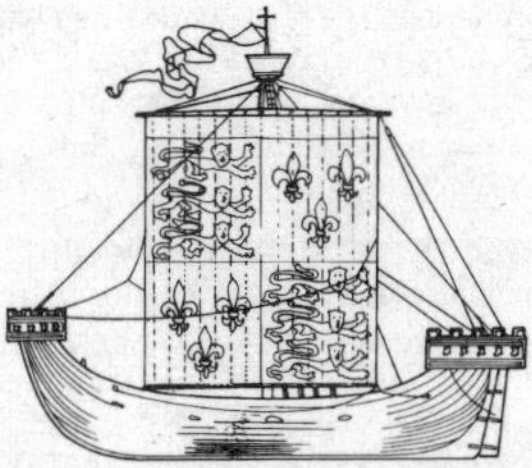

medieval nef (c. 1400) This single-masted vessel had platforms (castles) for fighting men at either end and one on the mast (topcastle) from which missiles could be hurled.

Victory (1759–65) Nelson's flagship at the battle of Trafalgar (1805), the *Victory* carried 100 guns and a crew of 850. It is now preserved at Portsmouth.

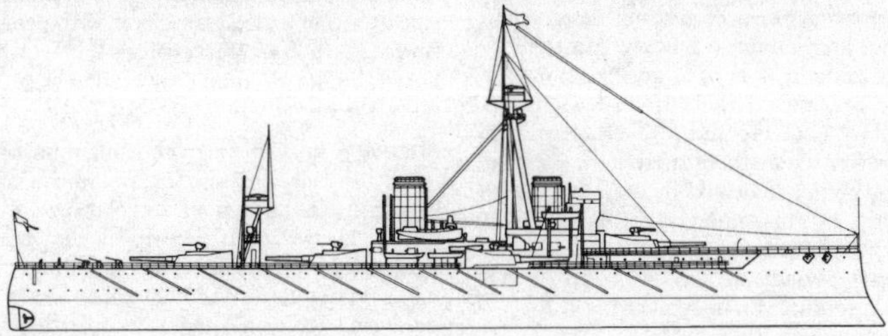

Dreadnought (1906) The design of the British *Dreadnought* became the model for battleships in a period in which a country's naval strength was reckoned in terms of how many battleships it possessed. The *Dreadnought* carried ten 12-inch guns, 27 smaller guns, and five underwater torpedo tubes.

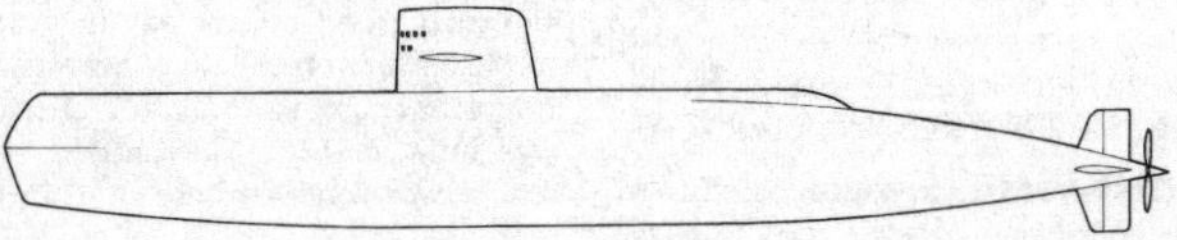

Nautilus (1954) The first nuclear-powered warship, the US *Nautilus* heralded an era in which naval strength is reckoned in terms of nuclear submarines. They are armed with torpedoes and long- and short-range missiles carrying nuclear warheads, all of which can be fired while the vessel is submerged.

warships

propagated outwards from the body and occur, for example, when an aircraft passes through the *sound barrier.

shogun A hereditary military title held by the heads of three families; they were the rulers of Japan, although the emperors retained formal sovereignty. The shogunate was secured for the Minamoto from the emperor in 1192 after Minamoto Yoritomo's victory over the Taira league. From 1338 to 1573 the Ashikaga family held the title and in 1603 Tokugawa Ieyasu (1542–1616), who claimed Minamoto ancestry, revived it. The last shogun was Tokugawa Keiki (1827–1913; ruled 1867–68).

Sholokhov, Mikhail (1905–84) Soviet novelist. His first major novel (1928–40) was translated in two parts as *And Quiet Flows the Don* and *The Don Flows Home to the Sea*. He won the Nobel Prize in 1965.

shooting Discharging a weapon at a target or at game. The two main categories of **target shooting** for rifles are small bore (.22 calibre) at ranges of 25–200 m (27–219 yd), and full bore (7.62 calibre) at ranges of 200–1200 yd (183–1097 m); full-bore courses are fired from standing, sitting, kneeling, and prone positions. Weapons for pistol shooting range from the .177 air pistol to the .45 pistol, with ranges between 10 and 50 yd (9–45 m). In **clay-pigeon shooting** (*or* trap-shooting) clay discs are mechanically flung into the air and fired at with shotguns. In **grouse shooting** (in the UK permitted only from 12 Aug to 10 Dec), **pheasant shooting** (1 Oct to 1 Feb), and **partridge shooting** (1 Sept to 1 Feb) the birds are either driven by a semicircle of beaters towards the shooters in butts or are flushed out by hunting dogs and beaters for a moving party of shooters.

shorthand A form of writing designed to record spoken language quickly. Most forms use only as many sounds as are necessary for accurate reading. In the Pitman System (devised by Sir Isaac Pitman; 1813–97) characters are based on segments of a circle or straight lines; vowels are indicated by dots; voicing of consonants by thickening of strokes. The US system was invented by John Robert Gregg (1867–1948). Shorthand speeds of up to 300 words per minute can be achieved.

Shorthorn A breed of cattle originating in NE England and formerly popular for both beef and dairy purposes. Stocky, with short legs, Shorthorns range from red to white with various mottled mixtures. They have been replaced by specialist beef and dairy breeds.

S

shortsightedness (*or* **myopia**) Inability to focus on distant objects. This is the commonest kind of visual defect and commonly runs in families: it is due to a slightly misshapen eyeball, in which the light rays are focused in front of the retina (light-sensitive layer). It is corrected by wearing glasses with concave lenses or contact lenses.

Shoshoni A group of North American Indian tribes of the Great Basin region who spoke a language of the Uto-Aztecan family. Some acquired horses and moved onto the Plains, including the *Comanche.

Shostakovich, Dmitri (1906–75) Russian composer. His 15 symphonies include the wartime seventh symphony (*The Leningrad*; 1941). He also composed two concertos each for piano, violin, and cello, 15 string quartets, and the operas *The Nose* (1927–28) and *Lady Macbeth of Mtsensk* (1930–32).

shot put (*or* **putting the shot**) A field event in athletics, in which an iron or brass sphere is thrown as far as possible. It weighs 7.26 kg (16 lb) for men and 4 kg (8.8 lb) for women. It is thrown, or put, one-handed from in front of the shoulder and the putter must stay within a circle 2.1 m (7 ft) in diameter. World records: men: 23.12 m (1990) by Eric Randolph Barnes (USA); women: 22.63 m (1987) by Natalya Lisovskaya (USSR).

shoveler duck A *duck, *Spatula clypeata*, found in the N hemisphere, having a large bill for feeding on water plants and invertebrates. 50 cm long, it has a blue wing flash; the male has a green head, white breast, and chestnut underparts and the female is brown.

showjumping Competitive jumping by horse and rider across a course of artificial obstacles, either against the clock (with penalties for faults) or as *puissance* contests, in which the horse's ability to jump over a number of high objects is tested.

shrew A small insectivorous mammal of the family *Soricidae* (265 species), found worldwide except in Australasia and the Polar regions. The dwarf shrew (*Suncus etruscus*) is the smallest mammal in the world, weighing 2 g and measuring 7–8 cm. The common shrew (*Sorex araneus*) eats its own weight in food every 24 hours. Order: *Insectivora*.

Shrewsbury 52 43N 2 45W A market town in W central England, the administrative centre of Shropshire on the River Severn. It achieved importance as a gateway to Wales, and a castle was built in 1070. The famous boys' public school was founded here in 1552. Population (1996 est): 97 371.

shrike A predatory songbird of a family (*Laniidae*; 74 species) occurring in Eurasia, Africa, and North America and also called butcherbird. Shrikes dive on insects and vertebrates from the air, killing them with their hooked bills.

shrimp A *crustacean, usually 4–8 cm long, belonging to a worldwide suborder (*Natantia*; about 2000 species) that occurs in fresh and salt water. Shrimps have a semitransparent body with long slender legs (the first pair pincer-like), a fanlike tail, and long whiplike antennae. They feed on small animals or plants. Many species, including the European *Crangon vulgaris*, are commercially important as food. Order: *Decapoda*.

Shropshire (name 1974–80: Salop) A county in the W Midlands of England, bordering on Wales. The River Severn separates the lowlands in the N and E from the uplands in the S and W. During the 18th century it became the main iron-producing county in England; the world's first cast-iron bridge was built at Ironbridge in 1779. It is now chiefly agricultural. The rapidly developing area around Telford new town became an independent unitary authority (as Telford and Wrekin) in 1998. Area (excluding Telford and Wrekin): 3201 sq km (1236 sq mi). Population (2001, excluding Telford and Wrekin): 283 240. Administrative centre: Shrewsbury.

Shroud of Turin A relic believed by some to be the linen cloth used to wrap Christ's body for burial. It bears impressions of a human body marked with wounds consonant with Christ's at the crucifixion. It has been kept in Turin since 1578, but there are gaps in its history prior to the 14th century. Carbon dating in 1988 indicated that it had been woven from flax gathered between 1260 and 1390 but this finding has been called into question by later tests.

Shrove Tuesday The day before the beginning of Lent (*see* ASH WEDNESDAY), so called from the "shriving" (i.e. confession and absolution) of the faithful that was customary before the Lenten season. In many countries carnivals are held and in England pancakes are traditionally eaten—hence the popular name Pancake Day.

sial The earth's continental crust, which is composed of granitic rocks rich in silicon (Si) and aluminium (Al). It is less dense than the underlying layer of *sima and much thicker.

siamang The largest of the *gibbons, *Hylobates syndactylus*, found in Malaya and Sumatra. Up to 90 cm tall, with arms spanning 150 cm, siamangs have a large naked vocal sac on the throat, which expands to give volume to their cries.

Siamese cat A breed of short-haired cat, originating from SE Asia. The Siamese has a slender body, slanted blue eyes, large pointed ears, and a long slim tapering tail. The fur on the body is cream-coloured or off-white, shading into one of several colours (most popularly seal-brown or blue-grey) on the ears, mask, paws, and tail (the "points").

Siamese twins Identical twins who are fused together, usually at the head or along the trunk. They can sometimes be surgically separated, providing that vital organs are not involved in the point of union. The original Siamese twins, Chang and Eng (1811–74), were born in Siam; they were joined at the hip and remained fused.

Sibelius, Jean (Johan Julius Christian S.; 1865–1957) Finnish composer. Many of his works have Finnish associations and many were inspired by the epic poem, the *Kalevala*. They include seven symphonies, symphonic poems such as *The Swan of Tuonela* (1893) and *Finlandia* (1899–1900), a violin concerto, and many songs.

Siberia A region chiefly in Russia, extending into N Kazakhstan. Corresponding to N Asia, it is bordered on the W by the Ural Mountains, on the N by the Arctic Ocean, on the E by the Pacific Ocean, and on the S by Mongolia and China. Siberia comprises three geographical areas—the West Siberian Plain, the Central Siberian Plateau, and the Far East. It is notorious for its long harsh winters. Its outstandingly rich mineral resources include coal and petroleum. Forestry is also important and Siberia's many rivers (notably the Ob, Yenisei, and Lena) are harnessed for hydroelectric power. Russian settlement was intermittent until the building (1891–1905) of the Trans-Siberian Railway. Siberia has long been a place of exile for Russian criminals and political prisoners. Area: about 13 807 037 sq km (5 330 896 sq mi).

Sibyl In Greek and Roman mythology, any of various divinely inspired prophetesses, the most famous of which was the Sibyl of Cumae, near Naples. Three books of these Sibylline prophecies were preserved in the Temple of Jupiter on the Capitoline hill at Rome and were consulted in national emergencies.

Sicilian Vespers (1282) The massacre of 2000 French residents of Palermo that began the Sicilian revolt, backed by Pedro III of Aragon (1236–85; reigned 1276–85), against the oppressive regime of the Angevin Charles I. Aragonese control was finally established in 1302 under Pedro's son Frederick II (1272–1337).

Sicily The largest island in the Mediterranean Sea, which together with adjacent islands comprises an autonomous region of Italy. It is separated from the mainland by the Strait of Messina. Sicily is largely mountainous (highest point Mount Etna) and underdeveloped. The mining industry is important, especially oil.

History: occupied by the Greeks, Carthaginians, Romans, and later the Arabs, in 1060 the Norman conquest of Sicily began. In 1266 Charles I became the first Angevin King of Sicily. The island was conquered by Aragon in 1284 following the revolt (called the *Sicilian Vespers) in 1282 against Charles' oppressive regime. In 1734 Don Carlos of Bourbon (later Charles III of Spain) became Charles IV of Naples and Sicily, which formally became the Kingdom of the Two Sicilies in 1815 under Ferdinand I. After conquest by Garibaldi (1860), Sicily was united with the rest of Italy. Since then Sicily's history has been one of trouble and discontent as a result of an ailing economy, widespread poverty, and the influence of the *Mafia. Area: 25 710 sq km (9927 sq mi), with adjacent islands. Population (2000 est): 5 087 794. Capital: Palermo.

Sickert, Walter (Richard) (1860–1942) British impressionist painter and etcher, born in Munich of Danish and Irish parentage. His paintings of Venice and Dieppe (1895–1905) and scenes from the music hall and domestic life are distinguishable from French *impressionism chiefly by their sombre colours.

sickle-cell disease A condition resulting from the production of an abnormal form of haemoglobin (the pigment of red blood cells). The disease is hereditary and affects only Blacks. When the blood is deprived of oxygen the abnormal haemoglobin crystallizes and distorts the red cells into a sickle shape: these sickle cells are removed from the blood by the spleen, which leads to *anaemia. Those less severely affected survive and even tend to have some built-in resistance to malaria.

Siddons, Sarah (*born* Kemble; 1755–1831) English actress, acclaimed at her London debut in 1782 as the leading tragic actress of her time.

S

sidereal period The time taken by a planet or satellite to return to the same point in its orbit, i.e. to complete one revolution, with reference to the background stars.

sidewinder A small nocturnal *rattlesnake, *Crotalus cerastes*, occurring in deserts of the S USA and Mexico, that has a sideways looping method of locomotion enabling it to move quickly over loose sand.

Sidney, Sir Philip (1554–86) English poet and courtier. His works include the prose romance *Arcadia* (1580), the sequence of Petrarchan sonnets, *Astrophel and Stella* (1591), and an important work of critical theory, *The Defence of Poesy* (1595). He served as a diplomat in Europe and was killed while fighting the Spanish in the Netherlands.

Siegfried A hero of Germanic legend, who also appears in early Scandinavian legend as Sigurd. In the Germanic *Nibelungenlied*, Siegfried wins *Brunhild for his brother-in-law Gunther, but a quarrel between Brunhild and Siegfried's wife Kriemhild leads to Siegfried's death by treachery. In the Old Norse *Volsungasaga*, Sigurd is betrothed to Brynhild but is tricked (by a magic potion) into forgetting her and marries Gudrun. He then wins Brynhild for his brother-in-law Gunnar; later Brynhild incites Gunnar to kill him. Siegfried is the hero of the last two operas of Wagner's *The Ring of the Nibelung*.

siemens (S) The SI unit of conductance between two points on a conductor when a potential difference of one volt between the points causes a current of one ampere to flow. Named after the German electrical engineeer Ernst Werner von Siemens (1816–92).

Siena 43 19N 11 19E A city in central Italy, in Tuscany. Founded by the Etruscans, it was a commercial and artistic centre in the middle ages. Its fine buildings include a 13th-century cathedral, a university (1240), and several palaces. Population (latest est): 58 728.

Sierra Leone, Republic of A country in West Africa, on the Gulf of Guinea. Coastal plains, fringed by mangrove swamps, rise to higher land in the interior. The main ethnic groups are Mende and Temne. *Economy*: chiefly agricultural, with fishing, forestry, and mining industries. Minerals, including diamonds, are the main exports. The economy has been severely disrupted by the recent political instability. *History*: in 1787 local chiefs ceded to Britain a piece of land along the coast for the settlement of slaves freed in the colonies. In 1896 the region became a British protectorate, gaining independence within the Commonwealth in 1961. In 1971 Sierra Leone became a republic and in 1978 one-party government was introduced. Plans for a multiparty system were approved in 1991 but suspended when Capt Valentine E. M. Strasser staged a coup in 1992. In 1996 free presidential elections resulted in a victory for Ahmad Tejan Kabbah, but he was overthrown in a further coup the following year. President Kabbah was restored in 1998 but savage fighting broke out again when members of the deposed junta joined with left-wing rebels to attack Freetown. Following talks, a power-sharing government was established (late 1999) and a UN peace-keeping force deployed. When rebel violence erupted once more in 2000, British troops were sent in to support UN forces. In 2002 Kabbah won a landslide victory in elections called to draw a line under 10 years of civil war. Official language: English; Krio is widely spoken. Currency: leone of 100 cents. Area: 73 326 sq km (27 925 sq mi). Population (2003 est): 4 971 000. Capital: Freetown.

Sierra Madre The chief mountain system of Mexico. It extends for about 2500 km (1500 mi) SE from the US border, reaching 5699 m (18 697 ft) at Citlaltépetl.

Sierra Nevada **1.** A mountain range in the USA. It extends generally NW–SE through California, reaching 4418 m (14 495 ft) at Mount Whitney. It contains the famous Yosemite National Park. **2.** A mountain range in S Spain. It rises to 3481 m (11 421 ft) at Mulhacén, the highest point in Spain.

Sihanouk, Norodom (1923–) King (1941–55, 1993–) of Cambodia; head of state (1975–76, 1991–93). Following World War II, Sihanouk achieved Cambodia's independence from France (1953). Abdicating in 1955, he dominated Cambodian politics as prime minister until 1970, when he was overthrown in a coup. He returned briefly (1975–76) as head of state but was again deposed. From 1982 he led Cambodia's government in exile, returning as head of state in 1991. In 1993 a new constitution made him king again.

sika A deer, *Cervus nippon*, also called Japanese deer, native to S Asia, Japan, and Taiwan and introduced to New Zealand and Europe. Grey-brown in winter and chestnut with white spots in summer, its shoulder height is 70–100 cm. Stags have slender eight-pointed antlers about 80 cm long.

Sikhism The religion of some nine million Indians, most of whom live in the Punjab. Founded in the 15th century by the Guru *Nanak, Sikhism combines Hindu and Islamic ideas. The Hindu concepts of *karma and rebirth are accepted, but the caste system is rejected. Sikhs believe that god is the only reality and that spiritual release can be obtained by taming the ego. The guidance of the guru, or spiritual teacher, is essential. The concept of Khalsa, a chosen race of warrior-saints, is central, as are the so-called five Ks: *kangha* (comb); *kacch* (shorts); *kirpan* (sword); *kara* (steel bracelet); and *kes* (uncut hair and beard). The occupation of the Sikh Golden Temple at Amritsar by Indian troops in 1984 led to the assassination a few months later of the Indian prime minister Indira *Gandhi by Sikh members of her bodyguard. Violent reprisals against Sikhs followed throughout India.

Sikorski, Władysław (1881–1943) Polish general and statesman; prime minister (1922–23) and then minister of military affairs (1924–25). After Poland's collapse in 1939, he became prime minister of the Polish government-in-exile in London. He was killed in a plane crash near Gibraltar.

Sikorsky, Igor Ivan (1889–1972) US aeronautical engineer, born in Russia, who invented the helicopter. He produced the S-1 biplane in 1910. After moving to the USA (1919) he completed the first successful helicopter, the VS-300, in 1939.

Silbury Hill A prehistoric mound in S England, near *Avebury, Wiltshire. Begun about 2150 BC, it is the largest man-made hill in Europe, standing 40 m (130 ft) high.

Silenus In Greek mythology, an elderly *Satyr, companion of the god *Dionysus. He was famed for his wisdom and prophetic powers as well as his drunkenness. The Sileni were his fellow nature spirits.

Silesia A region of E central Europe now in the Czech Republic and Poland. Because of its geographical position, mineral wealth, and industrial potential, Silesia has been disputed territory since the 17th century, when it was claimed by both Austria and Prussia. The seizure of most of it by Prussia was finally recognized by Austria in 1763, after the *Seven Years' War. After World War I it was divided between Czechoslovakia, Germany, and Poland and after World War II, between Czechoslovakia and Poland.

silica The mineral silicon dioxide, SiO_2, the most abundant of all minerals. There are three main forms of silica: *quartz, tridymite, and cristobalite, the last two occurring in acidic volcanic rocks. Silica content is used to classify igneous rocks. In one scheme the rocks are divided into acidic (over 65% silica), intermediate (52–66% silica), basic (45–52% silica), and ultrabasic (under 45% silica) varieties; these terms do not reflect pH value.

silicon (Si) The second most abundant element in the earth's crust, after oxygen. It is a major constituent of almost all rock-forming minerals. Pure silicon is of great importance in the electronics industry as a semiconductor. Silicates have been important for centuries as the main constituents of pottery, glasses, and many building materials. Silicon carbide (*see*

CARBORUNDUM) is a widely used abrasive, refractory, and semiconductor. Organic silicon compounds are known as *silicones. At no 14; at wt 28.086; mp 1414°C; bp 3267°C.

silicon chip *See* INTEGRATED CIRCUIT.

silicones Synthetic polymers consisting of chains of alternating silicon and oxygen atoms, with organic groups attached to the former. Silicones include fluids, greases, rubbers, and resins. All have similar chemical properties: stability to heat, oxidation, many chemicals, and oils. The main applications are in adhesives, paints, elastomers, and waterproofing agents.

silicosis A lung disease caused by prolonged inhalation of silica dust: an occupational disease of stone cutters, quarry workers, etc. The air sacs of the lungs become thickened and scarred, causing breathlessness and coughing. There is no specific treatment so prevention is essential. *See also* PNEUMOCONIOSIS.

silk The thread produced by the caterpillar of the *silkworm moth and the luxury fabric woven from it. The cocoons are unravelled and the filaments from several twisted together; processing this raw silk includes combining these strands and washing away the sticky secretion. China, where silk production was first practised, and Japan are the leading producers of pure silk; wild silk, produced by silkworms that feed on leaves other than mulberry or by uncultivated silkworms, includes a coarser brown Indian silk. Silk is lustrous, elastic, absorbent, and very strong.

Silk Road A trade route, 6400 km (4000 mi) long, that connected China with the Mediterranean. It was most used in antiquity, when silk was taken westwards and wool and precious metals eastwards, but was again travelled in the later middle ages, notably by Marco Polo.

silkworm A caterpillar that spins a silken cocoon, especially one that is suitable for commercial silk production. The commonest is the Chinese silkworm (*Bombyx mori*), which feeds on mulberry leaves. The pupae are killed by heat and the silken thread, up to 900 m long, is then unwound. The Japanese oak silkmoth (*Antherea yamanai*) and the Chinese species *A. pernyi* are also used.

silky oak One of two species of Australian trees. *Grevillea robusta*, of E Australia, has fern-like leaves. It is widely cultivated in the tropics as an ornamental or shade tree. The northern silky oak (*Cardwellia sublimis*) has pinkish soft wood and is an important timber tree.

sill A horizontal or near-horizontal sheetlike mass of intrusive igneous rock. Most sills consist of medium-grained hypabyssal rock, the commonest being dolerite.

silt A fine-grained sedimentary deposit, the rock particles of which range from 0.002 to 0.06 mm in diameter. Silts consist mainly of clay minerals, with iron oxides and hydroxides and silica. They collect in sheltered marine environments, such as estuaries, which makes dredging necessary. Consolidated silts form siltstones.

Silurian period A geological period of the Lower Palaeozoic era between the Ordovician and Devonian periods, lasting from about 445 to 415 million years ago. Conditions were mainly marine and the first true fish appeared. The first evidence of land plants also comes from Silurian rocks. The Caledonian period of mountain building reached its peak.

silver (Ag) A metallic element that occurs in nature as the metal, as argentite (Ag_2S), and in lead, zinc, and copper ores. Pure silver has the highest electrical and thermal conductivity known. In air, silver tarnishes forming a coating of the black sulphide (Ag_2S). Sterling silver (92.5% pure) is used for jewellery. Although not a reactive metal, silver forms many compounds including the oxide (Ag_2O), the nitrate ($AgNO_3$), and halides (for example AgCl, AgBr). Silver salts are of great importance in photography since they are light sensitive. At no 47; at wt 107.868; mp 961.93; bp 2163°C.

silverfish A widely distributed primitive wingless insect, *Lepisma saccharina*. One of the three-pronged *bristletails, it is covered with silvery scales and is common in buildings, feeding on starchy materials, including books and fabrics. Family: *Lepismatidae*.

silverplate Any object that is plated with silver rather than being solid silver. So-called Sheffield plate, in which silver is fused onto copper, was first produced in 1742. In 1840 the advent of *electroplating brought silverplated domestic articles to a much wider public. Many silverplated articles are marked EPNS (electroplated nickel silver)—nickel silver itself is an alloy of copper, nickel, and zinc and contains no silver; in this process a layer of silver is electroplated onto the nickel-silver base.

sima The earth's oceanic crust, which is composed of basaltic rocks rich in silica (Si) and magnesium (Mg). It is denser than the *sial of the continental crust and is believed to continue beneath it.

Simbirsk (former name: Ulyanovsk) 54 19N

48 22E A port in W central Russia, on the River Volga. In 1924 it was renamed in honour of Lenin (originally V. I Ulvanov), who was born here. Population (1999 est): 671 700.

Simenon, Georges (1903–89) Belgian novelist. The best known of his several hundred novels feature the Parisian *commissaire de police*, Maigret.

simple harmonic motion Any oscillation performed by a body about some reference point so that the restraining force is directly proportional to its displacement from that point. Examples include a *pendulum swinging through a small angle and a vibrating string. The displacement, x, at a time t is represented by the equation $x = A\sin\omega t$, where A is the amplitude (maximum displacement) and ω the angular frequency, which is related to the period of oscillation T by $\omega = 2\pi/T$.

Simplon Pass An alpine pass linking Brig in Switzerland with Iselle in Italy. Built 1800–07 it reaches 2009 m (6590 ft). The **Simplon Tunnel** was, at 20 km (12 mi), the longest rail tunnel in the world until 1979.

Simpson Desert (*or* **Arunta Desert**) A desert of central Australia, mainly in Northern Territory. Area: about 77 000 sq km (29 723 sq mi).

Sinai A desert peninsula in Egypt, bounded by Israel and the Gulf of Aqaba to the E and the Gulf of Suez and mainland Egypt to the W. Mount Sinai, 2285 m (7497 ft) high, is in the mountain range in the S. The N half of the desert is plateau. The chief resources of the region are manganese and the oil deposits in the W, based on Sudr. Sinai was occupied by Israel in the 1956 and 1967 Arab-Israeli Wars and following the 1973 war Egyptian and Israeli lines were established on either side of a UN buffer zone. Under the 1979 Egyptian-Israeli agreement a large proportion of the area was returned to Egypt.

Sinatra, Frank (Francis Albert S.; 1915–98) US singer and film actor, who recorded his first hit, "All or Nothing at All," in 1943. His role in the film *From Here to Eternity* (1953), earned him an Oscar; he subsequently appeared in such films as *Guys and Dolls* (1955) and *The Manchurian Candidate* (1962). Later recorded hits include "Strangers in the Night" (1966) and "My Way" (1969).

Singapore, Republic of A republic in SE Asia, off the S tip of the Malay Peninsula, consisting of the island of Singapore and over 58 islets. The city of Singapore, located in the S, occupies a substantial part of the island's area. The majority of the diverse population is Chinese with minorities of Malays, Indians, and others. *Economy*: Singapore is one of the world's busiest ports and lies on a major sea route. It is a major commercial and financial centre and in recent decades industry has been expanded and diversified, electronics, telecommunications, shipbuilding, and oil refining being important. *History*: although a prosperous trading centre in the middle ages, the island was largely uninhabited in 1819 when Sir Stamford Raffles established a station of the British East India Company here. In 1824 it was ceded to Britain. During World War II it was occupied by the Japanese (from 1942). It became a British crown colony in 1946 and gained its independence in 1959. It joined the Federation of Malaysia on its formation (1963) but broke away in 1965 and formed an independent republic. The People's Action Party has governed continuously since 1965; Lee Kuan Yew was prime minister until 1990, when he was succeeded by Goh Chok Tung. Official languages: Chinese, English, Malay, and Tamil. Currency: Singapore dollar of 100 cents. Area: 639 sq km (247 sq mi). Population (2003 est): 4 233 000.

Singer, Isaac Bashevis (1904–91) Polish-born US writer. His novels and stories, written in Yiddish and frequently dramatizing Jewish life in Poland, include *Gimpel the Fool* (1957), *The Slave* (1960), *Shosha* (1978), *Old Love* (1979), and *The King of the Fields* (1989). He won the Nobel Prize in 1978.

Sinhalese The major ethnic group in Sri Lanka. They speak an Indo-Aryan language that has been much influenced by Pali and the Dravidian languages, particularly *Tamil. They are descended from migrants from Bengal who colonized Sri Lanka during the 5th century BC. An agricultural people, they base their social organization on caste and practise Theravada Buddhism.

Sinn Féin (Irish: We Ourselves) An Irish political party committed to the establishment of an Irish republic to include Northern Ireland. It was founded by Arthur *Griffith in 1905. In 1918, under Eamon *De Valera, it won a majority of the Irish seats in the British parliament, declared independence, and began a campaign of guerrilla warfare through its military wing, the *Irish Republican Army. However, the creation of the Irish Free State in 1922 split the party and it dwindled into an insignificant rump. It became prominent again as the political wing of the republican movement after the outbreak of the Northern Irish "Troubles" in 1968. IRA ceasefires were announced by Sinn Féin president Gerry *Adams in 1994 and 1997. Subsequently Sinn Féin voted to back the Good Friday Agreement (1998) and its representatives were included in the assembly and the power-sharing executive established under the agreement (suspended from Oct 2002).

Sino-Japanese Wars **1.** (1894–95) The war between China and Japan resulting from rivalry in Korea. China, heavily defeated, was forced to pay a large indemnity and cede Taiwan, the Pescadores, and the Liaodong peninsula. **2.** (1937–45) The war between China and Japan brought about by Japanese expansion into China in the 1930s. The Japanese had established a puppet state in Manchuria in 1932 but only after internal nationalist-communist cooperation against Japan did full war break out. The Japanese took Shanghai and Nanchang in 1937 and Wuhan and Canton in 1938. Their position remained strong until the USA entered World War II (1941) and gave China assistance. After Japan's surrender (1945) China regained Manchuria, Taiwan, and the Pescadores.

Sino-Tibetan languages A group of languages spoken in E Asia. It includes all the *Chinese dialects (which use the same alphabet but differ substantially in sound), the Tibeto-Burman languages (Tibetan, Burmese, and many related languages of the Himalayas), and probably the Tai languages, such as Siamese, Laotian, and Shan. The main characteristic is the monosyllabic nature of the vocabulary of these languages and their use of tonality to differentiate otherwise similar words. They all use word order, not inflection, to determine grammatical relations.

Sintra (former name: Cintra) 38 48N 9 22W A town in central Portugal. The many notable buildings include the royal palace (14th–15th centuries) in Moorish and gothic styles. It is a tourist and agricultural centre. Population (latest est): 20 574.

sinus A hollow cavity, especially one in a bone. The term usually refers to the air sinuses of the head, which are cavities in the facial bones; all have connections to the nasal cavity and they are susceptible to infection and inflammation (**sinusitis**).

Siouan languages A family of North American Indian languages including Dakota *Sioux, Crow, and several others. Most are spoken by Plains tribes.

Sioux A confederation of North American Plains Indian tribes, also known as the Dakota. They fought fiercely against White encroachments upon their territories and defeated Gen Custer at the battle of the *Little Bighorn (1876) under their leaders Sitting Bull and Crazy Horse. They were ultimately subdued, one group making a last stand at *Wounded Knee (1890).

Sirens In Greek mythology, female creatures, sometimes portrayed with birdlike features, who lured sailors to their island by their singing and then destroyed them. *Odysseus saved himself by tying himself to the mast of his ship and filling the ears of his crew with wax. The *Argonauts were protected by the superior singing of *Orpheus.

sirocco (*or* **scirocco**) A southerly wind occurring in N Africa, Sicily, and S Italy. Hot and dry on the N African coast, it picks up moisture as it crosses the Mediterranean Sea bringing extensive cloud to S Italy.

sisal A perennial plant, *Agave sisalana*, native to central America and cultivated throughout the tropics for its fibre, which is extracted from the leaves. It is used in shipping, general industry, and agriculture.

Sisley, Alfred (1839–99) Impressionist painter, born in Paris of British parents. In 1862 he met *Monet and *Renoir and later exhibited with them. In the 1870s he produced some of his best landscapes, for example *Misty Morning*, and three pictures of the *Floods at Port-Marly*.

Sistine Chapel The principal chapel of the Vatican, built for Pope Sixtus V (1473) by Giovanni dei Dolci. It is famous for its Renaissance interior decoration, with murals by Perugino (c. 1450–1523), *Botticelli, and *Ghirlandaio and the roof and ceiling by *Michelangelo.

Sisyphus A legendary Greek king of Corinth. For various offences he was condemned in the underworld eternally to roll a boulder to the top of a hill, from whence it always rolled down again.

sitar An Indian long-necked *lute with a resonating body made from a large gourd, seven metal strings stopped against movable arched frets, and a series of sympathetic strings.

Sitting Bull (c. 1834–93) American Sioux Indian chief. Resisting US expansion into the Plains, Sitting Bull led the massacre of Gen Custer and his men at the *Little Bighorn (1876). After an amnesty he settled on a Dakota reservation but was killed during further hostilities.

SI units (Système International d'Unités) An international system of units, used for all scientific purposes. It has seven base units (metre, kilogram, second, ampere, kelvin, candela, and mole) and two supplementary (or dimensionless) units (radian and steradian). All physical quantities are expressed in these units or in derived units consisting of combinations of these units, 18 of which have special names and agreed symbols. Decimal multiples of all units are expressed by a set of prefixes, such as kilo-, milli-, and mega-. See Appendices (Units of Measurement).

Six Day War *See* ISRAEL, STATE OF.

Sjaelland (Danish name: Sjælland) The most westerly and the largest of the major Danish islands, between Great Belt (Store Bælt) in the west and the Sound (Øresund), and Sweden in the east. Area: 7016 sq km (2709 sq mi). Population (latest est): 1987549. Chief town: Copenhagen.

Skagerrak A channel in N Europe, lying between Denmark and Norway and connecting the Kattegat to the North Sea.

skate A large *ray fish belonging to the family *Rajidae* (over 100 species), especially the genus *Raja*. 50–200 cm long, skates have a diamond-shaped flattened body with spiny or thorny structures on the upper surface and often an extremely long snout.

skeleton The rigid supporting framework of an animal's body. In such animals as *arthropods it lies outside the body (exoskeleton) and must be shed periodically during growth. Vertebrates, including humans, have a skeleton (endoskeleton) of *bones and cartilage that is entirely within the body and grows with age. The human skeleton is made up of over 200 bones, which are connected to each other at joints and held together by ligaments. The skeleton protects and supports the soft tissues of the body and provides a firm surface for the attachment of muscles and a system of levers that are essential for movement.

skiing A means of locomotion over snow. Although skis have been used in Scandinavia since the Stone Age, skiing as a sport did not develop until the 19th century. It is divided into Alpine or downhill skiing ('straight' downhill, giant and special slalom, and the combined Super G), and Nordic skiing (cross-country races over various distances and ski jumping). To these has been added freestyle skiing (ski acrobatics). Recreational skiing has become a vast holiday industry.

skimmer A black-and-white bird belonging to a family (*Rhynchopidae*; 3 species) occurring chiefly around western Atlantic coasts and African and Asian rivers. The skimmer fishes by flying close to the water, shearing the surface with the lower mandible and snapping the bill shut as soon as a fish is caught.

skin The tissue that covers the body. The outer layer (epidermis) consists of several layers of cells: the outermost layer contains dead cells made of keratin, which are constantly sloughed off and replaced by the deeper layers of continuously dividing cells. The inner layer of skin (dermis) contains *connective tissue with blood vessels, sensory nerve endings, *sweat glands, sebaceous glands (which secrete an oily substance, sebum, that protects the skin surface), and hair follicles. The skin protects the body from external injury and desiccation, assists in regulating body temperature (e.g. by sweating), and is sensitive to touch, temperature, and pain. The branch of medicine concerned with the diagnosis and treatment of skin disorders is called **dermatology**. Skin grafting is one of the most important and successful *transplantation operations.

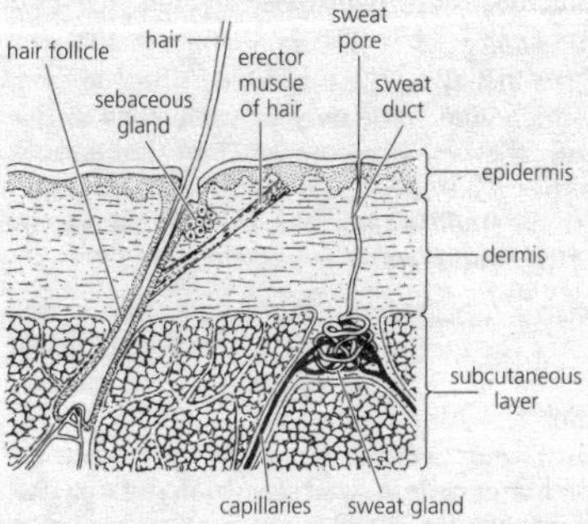

skin. A vertical section through the human skin shows its microscopical structure. The subcutaneous layer of fat cells provides insulation.

skink A lizard belonging to the family *Scincidae* (600 species), occurring throughout the tropics and in temperate North America. Skinks are well adapted for burrowing: they have cylindrical streamlined bodies with smooth scales, internal eardrums, a transparent covering over the eye, and often reduced limbs. Many have an elongated tail and move with sideways undulations of the body.

Skinner, Burrhus Frederic (1904–90) US

S

psychologist and advocate of *behaviourism. Many of Skinner's experiments involved teaching simple actions to animals by reinforcing the desired action with rewards of food. He developed equipment, including the Skinner box, in order to standardize the teaching of animals and applied his principles to human educational aids. His books include *The Behaviour of Organisms* (1938), *Science and Human Behaviour* (1953), and *Beyond Freedom and Dignity* (1971).

Skopje (Turkish name: Usküb) 42 00N 21 28E The capital of the Former Yugoslav Republic of Macedonia, on the River Vardar. It was burned down in 1689 to stop a cholera epidemic and almost completely destroyed by an earthquake in 1963. Population (1994): 541 280.

skua A large hook-billed seabird belonging to a family (*Stercorariidae*; 4 species), breeding in Arctic and Antarctic regions and wintering in warmer latitudes. Skuas are strong fliers and have a dark plumage with two long central tail feathers. They scavenge around seabird colonies, feeding on eggs, chicks, and food scraps. Order: *Charadriiformes* (gulls, plovers, etc.).

skull The skeleton of the head, made up of 22 bones of varying shapes and sizes. The cranium consists of eight flat platelike bones that surround and protect the brain. The remaining 14 bones, including the mandible, form the face: the mandible is the only movable bone in the skull; the rest are connected by immovable joints called sutures. Numerous holes puncture the skull to allow blood vessels and nerves to pass to and from the brain.

skunk A black and white carnivorous mammal of the family *Mustelidae* that is known for its defensive habit of ejecting a foul-smelling fluid. The nine species are found in North, South, and Central America. The nocturnal North American striped skunk (*Mephitis mephitis*) inhabits woodland.

S

Skye The largest and most northerly island of the Inner Hebrides group, off the W coast of Scotland. It is mountainous, with an economy based on crofting and tourism. A toll bridge linking Skye with the mainland was opened in 1996. Area: 1735 sq km (670 sq mi). Population (1994 est): 8139. Chief town: Portree.

Skye terrier A small (height: 25 cm) terrier originating on the island of Skye in the Hebrides. It has a long protective outer coat. The colour may be grey, fawn, cream, or black.

skylark A *lark, *Alauda arvensis*, occurring in Eurasia and N Africa and noted for its sustained warbling flight song. It is about 17 cm long, with brown plumage, a small crest and a white stripe above the eye.

slander *See* DEFAMATION.

slate A fine-grained rock produced by the low-grade metamorphism of mudstone, siltstone, or other argillaceous sediments. Its perfect cleavage is due to the parallel alignment of crystals of mica and chlorite. Slate is used as a constructional material.

slavery The condition in which human beings are owned by others as chattels. In ancient Greece and early Rome captives from conquered lands were the chief source of slaves, who often had special skills, were well treated, and might be freed (manumission). The condition of slaves in later Roman times greatly worsened. Slaving became a lucrative business in the 16th century, when European traders began to transport thousands of Africans to the Americas. By the early 19th century humanitarians, such as William *Wilberforce, had begun to attack slavery on moral grounds and it was abolished in all British territories by 1834. In the USA, slavery in the South became one of the causes of the Civil War. In 1863 Abraham *Lincoln liberated all slaves in the southern states (*see* EMANCIPATION PROCLAMATION); in 1865 the Constitution was amended to abolish slavery. The UN estimates that there are still some 200 million slaves (including bonded labourers) in the developing world.

Slavonic languages A subgroup of the Indo-European language family. Native to E Europe and NW Asia, they are often classified into three groups: South Slavonic (including *Serbo-Croat, Slovene, *Bulgarian, and Macedonian); West Slavonic (including Czech, *Slovak, Sorbian, and Polish); and East Slavonic (Russian, Belarussian, and Ukrainian). All the dialects are linked historically and all developed from a common ancestor, Proto-Slavonic. The peoples who originally settled in these regions migrated from Asia during the second or third millennium BC. The present Slav nations began to emerge around the 5th and 6th centuries AD, when there was further westward movement. Most Slavs speak Russian, many learning it as a second language.

sleep A naturally occurring state of unconsciousness. Orthodox sleep occurs in four stages, which vary in depth. The electrical activity of the brain continues but is more rhythmical than when awake and and reacts less to outside stimuli. It is periodically interrupted by paradoxical sleep, in which the eyes move rapidly and the brain is more active, but the muscles are especially relaxed. Paradoxical sleep is particularly associated with dreams. Sleep is biologically necessary and probably helps to control physical growth; individuals' needs vary widely between three and ten hours a night. Insomnia can be caused by changes of routine, anxiety, *depression, and by many drugs.

sleeping sickness A disease caused by infection with a protozoan of the genus *Trypanosoma*, which is transmitted by the tsetse fly and occurs only in East, central, and West Africa: it is the African form of trypanosomiasis. Initial symptoms are swelling of the lymph nodes and fever, which persists for several months. The brain is then infected, causing lethargy, weakness, and depression: without treatment the patient dies.

sleepy sickness A highly infectious viral disease of the brain. Known medically as encephalitis lethargica, it is marked by drowsiness leading eventually to coma.

Sligo (Irish name: Contae Shligigh) A county in the NW Republic of Ireland, in Connacht bordering on the Atlantic Ocean. Chiefly hilly, much of the land is devoted to pasture; cattle rearing and dairy farming are important. Area: 1795 sq km (693 sq mi). Population (2002): 58 178. County town: Sligo.

Slim, William Joseph, 1st Viscount (1891–1970) British field marshal. In World War II he commanded the 14th Army (the "forgotten army") in Burma (1943). After successful operations against the Japanese he became commander in chief of Allied land forces in SE Asia. In 1948 he became chief of the imperial general staff and was then governor general of Australia (1953–60).

slime moulds Organisms traditionally regarded as fungi (since they produce fruiting bodies) but having affinities with the protozoa; they are now usually classified in the kingdom *Protoctista*. The so-called true slime moulds (*Myxomycota*) are found beneath logs and in other damp places. They consist of slimy sheets of protoplasm that engulf bacteria, wood particles, etc. The cellular slime moulds (*Acrasiomycota*) are single-celled amoeba-like organisms found in soil. The parasitic slime moulds (*Plasmodiophora*) live in the tissues of plants.

slipper orchid A terrestrial *orchid of the tropical Asian genus *Paphiopedilum* (about 50 species) and the related genera *Cypripedium* and *Phragmipedium*. Popular ornamentals, they are characterized by their flowers, which have a pouched slipper-shaped lip and are usually borne singly or in clusters of two or three.

sloe *See* BLACKTHORN.

sloth A primitive arboreal *mammal belonging to the family *Bradypodidae* (7 species) of Central and South America, also called ai or unau. 50–65 cm long, sloths are slow-moving and hang upside down from branches, feeding on leaves and fruit. Their greyish-brown fur lies so that rain runs off easily and is often greenish from algae. Order: *Edentata*.

Slough 1. 51 31N 0 36W A town in SE England, in Slough unitary authority, Berkshire. It grew rapidly after a large trading estate was built here in the 1920s and now has a great variety of light industries. Population (1998 est): 108 000. **2.** A unitary authority in SE England, in Berkshire. Area: 28 sq km (11 sq mi). Population (2001): 119 070.

Slovak A Western Slavonic language, closely related to *Czech. It is spoken mainly in Slovakia, where it is the official language, and written in the Latin alphabet.

Slovakia, Republic of A country in central Europe. Lying mainly within the Carpathian Mountains, it descends SW to the plains of the Danube Valley. *Economy*: mainly agricultural; products include cereals, wines, and tobacco. There is heavy industry in most of the larger towns. *History*: conquered by the Magyars in the 10th century, it was part of Hungary until 1918 when it became a province of Czechoslovakia. As such it was under communist control from 1948 to 1990. Slovakia became an independent republic on the dissolution of Czechoslovakia (1 Jan 1993). In 1997 Slovakia was refused EU membership owing to concerns about human-rights abuses under the government of Vladimir Meciar. In 1998 a new coalition was formed under Mikulas Dzurinda, who promised economic and social reforms. Slovakia joined both the EU and NATO in 2004. Official language: Slovak. Currency: koruna of 100 hellers. Area: 49 039 sq km (18 934 sq mi). Population (2003 est): 5 402 000. Capital: Bratislava.

Slovenia, Republic of (Serbo-Croat name: Slovenija) A republic in S central Europe. It is mountainous. *Economy*: mainly agricultural, but manufacturing has expanded and diversified. Slovenia has important deposits of coal, mercury, and zinc. *History*: chiefly under Habsburg rule from the 14th century, it was incorporated (1918) into the kingdom of Serbs,

Croats, and Slovenes, later renamed *Yugoslavia. It declared independence in 1991, leading to a brief war with the Serb-led Yugoslav army, and achieved international recognition in 1992. The Liberal Democracy Party of Janez Drnovšek won election victories in 1996 and 2000; Drnovšek was elected president in 2002. Slovenia joined the EU and NATO in 2004. Official language: Slovenian. Currency: tolar. Area: 20 251 sq km (7819 sq mi). Population (2003 est): 1 971 000. Capital: Ljubljana.

slowworm A legless lizard, *Anguis fragilis*, also called blindworm, occurring in heaths and open woodlands of Europe. It is about 30 cm long, usually brown, grey, or reddish, and feeds on snails, slugs, and other soft-bodied invertebrates. Family: *Anguidae*.

slug A *gastropod mollusc of the order *Stylommatophora*, widely distributed in moist terrestrial habitats. Slugs have slimy soft bodies with the shell vestigial or absent. They range in colour from yellow through red-brown to black. Some are carnivorous or scavenging while others feed on soft plant tissues. Subclass: *Pulmonata*. *Compare* SEA SLUG.

smallpox A highly infectious virus disease marked by a skin rash that leaves permanent pitted scars. Smallpox is transmitted by direct contact; the initial symptoms of fever, prostration, severe headache, and backache are followed by the rash on the face and limbs. Secondary infection with staphylococci is often fatal. After a worldwide vaccination programme sponsored by the World Health Organization smallpox was officially declared to have been eradicated in 1979.

smelt A slender food fish of the genus *Osmerus* and family *Osmeridae*, occurring in coastal and estuarine waters of Europe and North America. It migrates to fresh water to spawn. The European smelt (*O. eperlanus*), up to about 30 cm long, is greenish grey above and silvery below. Order: *Salmoniformes*.

smelting The extraction of a metal from its ore by heating. The method used depends on the metal, the type of ore, and the melting points of both. The smelting takes place either in a *blast furnace (e.g. to extract iron) or a reverberatory furnace (e.g. to extract copper).

Smetana, Bedřich (1824–84) Bohemian composer. In 1859 he joined a group of composers in Prague who were establishing a national opera. *The Brandenburgers in Bohemia* (1862–63) and *The Bartered Bride* (1863–66) were composed for it. Despite becoming totally deaf in 1874 he wrote the four symphonic poems *Má Vlast* (1874–79) and a string quartet (1876).

Smith, Adam (1723–90) Scottish moral philosopher and political economist. In 1776, he published *An Enquiry into the Nature and Causes of the Wealth of Nations*, an attack on mercantilism that was to become the bible of the free-trade movement. He held that employment, trade, production, and distribution are as much a part of a nation's wealth as its money. An individual allowed to promote his own interests freely within the law often promotes the interests of society as a whole.

Smith, Ian (Douglas) (1919–) Prime minister (1964–79) of Rhodesia (now Zimbabwe). An advocate of White supremacy, he demanded full independence for Southern Rhodesia in 1964 but opposed Britain's stipulation that Black majority rule be prepared for. In 1965 he made a unilateral declaration of independence (UDI), maintained until 1976 when he agreed to the principle of Black majority rule.

Smith, John (1938–94) British politician; leader of the Labour Party (1992–94). He entered parliament in 1970, becoming shadow chancellor (1987–92).

Smith, Joseph (1805–44) US founder of the *Mormons. Smith announced in 1827 his discovery of the sacred *Book of Mormon*, which he claimed to have translated from two gold tablets. His new church, founded in Fayette, New York (1830), grew rapidly but attracted opposition. While in jail on charges of conspiracy, Smith was killed by an angry mob. The Mormons migrated westward to Utah under Brigham *Young.

Smith, Dame Maggie (1934–) British stage and screen actress. Her films include *The Prime of Miss Jean Brodie* (1969), which earned her an Oscar, *A Room with a View* (1986), *The Secret Garden* (1993), and *Gosford Park* (2001).

Smith, Stevie (Florence Margaret S.; 1902–71) British poet, whose deceptively simple poetry blends tenderness, toughness, and humour. The best known of her idiosyncratic novels is *Novel on Yellow Paper* (1936). Her *Collected Poems* (1975) were published posthumously.

Smithsonian Institution A research institution in Washington, DC, founded in 1846 with a bequest from the Englishman James Smithson (1765–1829). It has carried out important scientific work and explorations throughout the world, and administers a number of important museums, including the National

Air and Space Museum and the National Collection of Fine Arts.

smoke tree (*or* **smoke bush**) One of several species of trees and shrubs having a whitish cloudy appearance at some stage of the season. The American smoke tree (*Cotinus obovatus*) grows to a height of 9 m and has a smokelike mass of whitish flower heads, as does the Australian smoke bush (*Conospermum stoechadis*). *Rhus cotinus* is the common smoke bush native to the Mediterranean area and parts of Asia.

Smolensk 54 49N 32 04E An industrial city in W Russia, on the River Dnepr. Dating back to at least the 9th century, it was long disputed between Lithuania and Russia, falling to the latter in 1654. It saw fierce fighting in World War II. Population (1999 est): 355 700.

Smollett, Tobias (George) (1721–71) Scottish writer. His lively picaresque novels include *Roderick Random* (1748), *Peregrine Pickle* (1751), and *Humphry Clinker* (1771).

smooth snake A widespread Eurasian snake, *Coronella austriaca*, that has smooth glossy scales and is brown or reddish with a pale belly and dark spots along its back and tail. Up to 65 cm long, it favours sandy heathlands. Family: *Colubridae*.

smut A disease affecting flowering plants, particularly the cereals and grasses, caused by various basidiomycete fungi of the genus *Ustilago*. Infection is not usually apparent until spore formation, when dark powdery masses of spores are released over the flower head. Stinking smuts are caused by fungi belonging to the related genus *Tilletia*. Both are controlled by spraying crops with fungicide and treating seed before sowing.

Smuts, Jan (Christiaan) (1870–1950) South African statesman and general; prime minister (1919–24, 1939–48). He led commandos in the second Boer War (1899–1902) but thereafter worked for reconciliation with Britain. He played an important part in achieving responsible government for the Transvaal (1906) and the Union of South Africa (1910), becoming a minister in Louis Botha's government (1910–19) and succeeding him as prime minister. During his second premiership he led South Africa into World War II and strove to maintain links with the British Commonwealth.

snail A *gastropod mollusc with a spirally coiled shell, including terrestrial, freshwater, and marine forms. The common garden snail (*Helix pomatia*) is active at night, feeding on vegetation and sheltering by day in crevices.

snake A legless *reptile belonging to the suborder *Serpentes* (about 3000 species), occurring worldwide but especially common in the tropics. Snakes range from 0.12–10 m in length and grow throughout their lives, periodically shedding the skin in one piece. They feed chiefly on other vertebrates, which they swallow whole. Prey may be killed by constriction, by engulfing it alive, or by the injection of venom by means of hollow or grooved fangs. The major families are the *Boidae* (pythons, boas, etc.), the *Colubridae* (typical snakes, e.g. the grass snake), the *Elapidae* (cobras, coral snakes, etc.), and the *Viperidae* (vipers, etc.). Order: *Squamata* (lizards and snakes).

Snake River A river in the NW USA. Rising in the Yellowstone National Park in Wyoming, it flows W through Idaho to join the Columbia River in Washington State. Length: 1670 km (1038 mi).

snapdragon *See* ANTIRRHINUM.

snapper A carnivorous shoaling fish of the family *Lutjanidae* (about 250 species), found in tropical seas. It has an elongated body, a large mouth, and sharp teeth. Some are valuable food fish, especially the red snapper (*Lutjanus blackford*); others are poisonous.

Snell's law When a ray of light passes from one medium to another the angle (r) between the refracted ray and a line normal to the interface between the media is related to the angle (i) of the incident ray, also taken to the normal, by the equation $\sin i/\sin r = n$, where n is the relative refractive index of the media (*see* REFRACTION). It is named after the Dutch astronomer Willebrord Snell (1591–1626).

snipe A *sandpiper belonging to a subfamily (*Scolopacinae*; 10 species) occurring in wet areas of warm and temperate regions. Snipe have a long flexible bill used to probe for worms, and a barred and striped brown, black, and white plumage. The common snipe (*Gallinago gallinago*) is popular gamebird.

snooker A game, deriving from *billiards, that arose among British officers in India (1875). It is played by two players or pairs of players on a billiards table. There are 22 balls: 1 white cue ball, 15 red balls (value 1 point each), and 6 coloured balls—yellow (2 points), green (3), brown (4), blue (5), pink (6), black (7). The object is to pocket a red ball and a coloured ball alternately, each time returning the coloured ball to its prescribed spot on the table. The red balls are not replaced. When all the red balls have been potted the colours are potted.

snow A solid form of precipitation composed of ice crystals or snowflakes. Ice crystals occur when temperatures are well below freezing point; with temperatures nearer to 0°C (32°F) snowflakes develop through the clustering together of crystals.

snowball tree *See* GUELDER ROSE.

Snowdon (Welsh name: Yr Wyddfa) 53 04N 4 05W The highest mountain in Wales, in Gwynedd. The surrounding area, **Snowdonia**, was designated a national park in 1951. Height: 1085 m (3560 ft).

snowdrop A small early spring-blooming herbaceous plant of the genus *Galanthus* (about 10 species) native to Europe and W Asia. They grow from bulbs to produce grasslike leaves and slender stems bearing solitary nodding white flowers, tipped with green or yellow. There are over 50 cultivated varieties. *G. nivalis* is the common European snowdrop. Family: *Amaryllidaceae*.

snow goose An Arctic *goose, *Anser caerulescens*. It is either pure white with black wingtips, pink legs, and a red bill or blue-grey with a white head. Snow geese winter in the southern USA, Japan, and China.

snow leopard A big *cat, *Panthera* (or *Uncia*) *uncia*, also called ounce, found in the mountains of central Asia. It is 1.9 m long, with a thick ash-grey coat marked with dark rosettes.

Snowy Mountains A mountain range in Australia. It lies in New South Wales, and contains Australia's highest mountain, Mount *Kosciusko.

soaps Salts of *fatty acids. Household soap (**hard soap**) is a mixture of sodium stearate, oleate, and palmitate. It is made by the hydrolysis of fats with caustic soda (sodium hydroxide), thus converting the glycerides of stearic, oleic, and palmitic acids into sodium salts and glycerol. **Soft soap** is made with potassium hydroxide instead of sodium hydroxide. Soaps have a cleansing action because they contain negative ions composed of a long hydrocarbon chain (which has an affinity for grease and oil) attached to a carboxyl group (which has an affinity for water). Particles of grease or oil are therefore emulsified in soapy water. *See also* DETERGENTS.

soapstone *See* TALC.

Soares, Mario (1924–) Portuguese statesman; prime minister (1976–79; 1983–85); president (1986–96). He was a critic of *Salazar and lived in exile from 1970 to 1974, when he became foreign minister in the new military government. He became prime minister as leader of the Portuguese Socialist Party.

Sobers, Garry (Sir Garfield Saint Auburn S.; 1936–) West Indian cricketer, who captained the West Indies and Nottinghamshire. One of the greatest all-rounders, he played in 93 Test matches, scoring 8032 runs, including 26 centuries, and taking 235 wickets and 110 catches.

Social Democratic and Labour Party (**SDLP**) A British political party, active in Northern Ireland. Founded by John *Hume and others in 1970, it supports peaceful union with Ireland. Its leader in the Northern Ireland assembly is Mark Durkan (1960–).

Social Democratic Party (**SDP**) A British political party of the centre, formed in 1981 by the "gang of four" labour dissidents: Roy Jenkins, Shirley Williams, David Owen (leader 1983–87), and William Rodgers. The SDP formed a political alliance with the Liberal Party in 1981; in 1988 the party merged with the Liberals, forming the Social and Liberal Democrats (subsequently renamed the *Liberal Democrats).

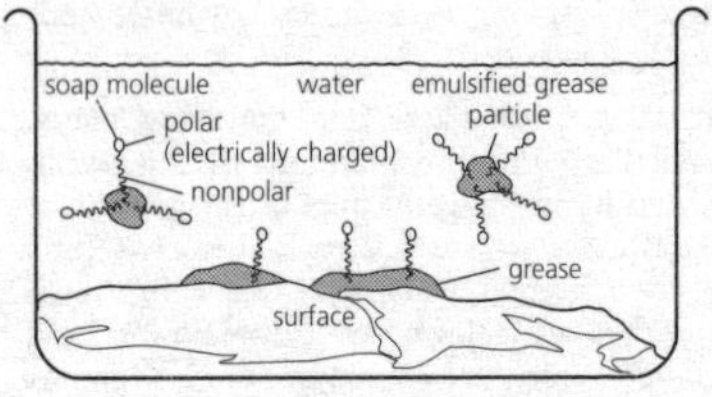

soaps. The action of soap in emulsifying grease. The nonpolar hydrocarbon end of the soap molecule attaches itself to the grease. The attraction of the polar end to water breaks up the grease and distributes it throughout the solution.

socialism A concept, resulting in diverse political movements, that emphasizes cooperation rather than competition as the basis of society. In the 19th century one sense of the word implied reform of the social system to develop liberal values and end class privileges. Socialism in a second sense was explicitly contrasted with competitive individualism; practical cooperation could not be achieved until a society based on private property was replaced by one based on social ownership and control. In 1848 Marx and Engels laid down the principles of scientific socialism in *The Communist Manifesto* and *Marxism became the theoretical basis for most socialist thought. The British

*Fabian Society (founded 1884) revived a variant of the first sense of the term, which later found political expression in the *Labour Party. It was the split in Russia, however, between the revolutionary *Bolsheviks and the reformist *Mensheviks that led to the decisive distinction between the terms *communism and socialism as they are now generally understood, socialists being those who seek change by peaceful reform and communists being those dedicated to change by revolution. In the late 20th century many socialist parties abandoned or revised traditional socialist ideas in response to the collapse of Marxist systems and the apparent triumph of global capitalism.

Society Islands An archipelago in French Polynesia, discovered in 1767. It consists of two mountainous island groups, the **Windward Islands** (including Tahiti and Moorea) and the **Leeward Islands** (including Raiatea and Huahine). The capital of French Polynesia, Papeete, is on Tahiti. Area: 1595 sq km (616 sq mi). Population (1996): 189 524.

Society of Friends *See* QUAKERS.

Society of Jesus *See* JESUITS.

sociology The systematic study of the development, organization, functioning, and classification of human societies. Its growth was stimulated by the rapid industrial and social change in Europe in the early 19th century. It has employed techniques of participant observation, the systematic comparison of different societies, and surveys of social conditions, attitudes, and behaviour. Contemporary sociology is divided into several specialized subdisciplines including demography, political, educational, and urban sociology as well as sociological studies of deviance, religion, and culture.

sockeye salmon A *salmon, *Oncorhynchus nerka*, also called red salmon or blueback, that lives in the N Pacific and spawns in Canadian fresh waters.

Socrates (c. 469–399 BC) Athenian philosopher, whose ideas, integrity, and courage are known through his disciples *Plato and *Xenophon. Socrates diverted philosophy from physical speculations about the universe towards *ethics. His insistence upon thorough critical analysis of ethical concepts also marked the beginning of *logic. The "Socratic method" of teaching was by eliciting answers from interlocutors to reveal inconsistencies in accepted opinions. He was tried on charges of atheism and "corrupting the youth" and condemned to die by drinking hemlock.

Soddy, Frederick (1877–1956) British chemist, who worked under *Rutherford and *Ramsay and went on to win the 1921 Nobel Prize for his discovery of *isotopes.

sodium (Na) A highly reactive alkali metal, long-recognized in compounds but first isolated as the element by Sir Humphry Davy in 1807. It is obtained commercially by electrolysis of common salt (NaCl). It occurs naturally in some silicate minerals (for example *feldspars; $NaAlSi_3O_8$), as well as in salt deposits and in the oceans. The metal is soft, bright, and less dense (relative density 0.97) than water, with which it reacts violently, liberating hydrogen. It is a highly electropositive element, forming many ionic salts of great importance, such as the chloride (common salt; NaCl), the carbonate (soda ash; Na_2CO_3), the bicarbonate (baking-soda; $NaHCO_3$), various phosphates, and the nitrate ($NaNO_3$). At no 11; at wt 22.9898; mp 97.8°C; bp 882.9°C.

sodium bicarbonate (**sodium hydrogen carbonate** *or* **bicarbonate of soda**; $NaHCO_3$) The white soluble powder that is a constituent of *baking powder and is used to make fizzy drinks and as an antacid in medicine.

sodium carbonate (Na_2CO_3) A white soluble salt. The commercial form (**soda ash**) is a white anhydrous powder and is used in making glass, soap, paper, as well as other chemicals. **Washing soda**, its hydrated form, is a white crystalline solid used as a domestic cleanser and water softener.

sodium hydroxide (*or* **caustic soda**; NaOH) A white solid that is strongly alkaline in aqueous solution and is very corrosive to organic tissue. It is used in making rayon, paper, detergents, and other chemicals.

Sodom and Gomorrah In the Old Testament, two cities of Palestine, known as the "cities of the plain," sited S of the Dead Sea. According to Genesis (18, 19), they were destroyed by fire and brimstone from heaven because of the utter depravity of their inhabitants.

Sofia 42 40N 23 18E The capital of Bulgaria, situated on a plateau in the W of the country. Sofia came under the Byzantine Empire in the 6th century and was taken over by the Bulgars in the 9th century. Under Turkish rule from 1382, the city was liberated by the Russians in 1878 and became the national capital (1879). Population (1999 est): 1 122 302.

software The suite of programs that sets up

a computer system for operation, as distinct from the physical equipment (hardware). Software supplied by the computer manufacturer controls various parts of the system and provides facilities for further programming. Additional programs are purchased separately or written by the user. *See also* PROGRAM, COMPUTER.

Sogne Fjord The longest and deepest fjord in Norway, extending 204 km (127 mi) inland N of Bergen. It is flanked by spectacular mountain scenery.

soil The mixture of unconsolidated mineral particles, derived from weathered rock, and organic matter (humus), derived from the breakdown of plant tissue by living organisms, that covers much of the earth's land surface and provides a medium for plant growth. Soils are characterized by their texture, which depends on particle sizes (*see* SAND; SILT; CLAY), and their structure, which depends on the way the particles are bound into aggregates (e.g. crumbs, granules, flakes, etc.). These are important factors in determining the fertility of the soil, particularly its moisture and air content, susceptibility to leaching (the removal of nutrients to deeper levels by percolating water), and ease of cultivation. Soils are also classified according to their profiles—the arrangement of the layers (horizons) between the ground surface and the bedrock. *See also* CHERNOZEM; PODZOL.

sol *See* COLLOID.

Solanaceae A family of herbaceous plants and shrubs (about 2000 species), widely distributed but chiefly tropical. Their flowers have five fused sepals and petals. The family includes several commercially important species (e.g. the potato, tomato, pepper, and tobacco) and some ornamentals (e.g. *Petunia*); various other members are poisonous (e.g. the nightshades).

solar constant The total amount of solar energy passing perpendicularly through unit area per unit time at a particular distance from the sun. It is about 1.36 kW m^{-2} at the earth's mean orbital distance.

solar flare A sudden brightening, within minutes, of areas in the sun's atmosphere, resulting from an explosive release of energetic particles and radiation. Flares often occur above *sunspot groups. Large flares affect radio transmission on earth and produce *auroras.

solar power The use of the sun's energy to provide heating or to generate electricity. Solar energy is most commonly converted into heat by direct heating of water flowing through special panels on the roof of a building. The temperature rise produced is fairly small but it reduces the energy required from other sources for hot water and space heating. Higher temperatures, sufficient to form steam for electricity generation, are possible using large mirrors to collect and focus the sun's rays. Direct conversion of solar radiation into electrical energy is possible with **solar cells**. These are semiconductor devices sensitive to the photovoltaic effect. The method is used mainly in small-scale specialized applications, for example powering remote monitoring equipment, spacecraft, marine beacons, etc.

solar system A system comprising the *sun and the astronomical bodies gravitationally bound to the sun, that is the nine major *planets, their *satellites, and the immense numbers of *minor planets, *comets, and meteoroids. Almost all the mass of the solar system (99.86%) resides in the sun. The planets orbit the sun in the same direction and, with the exception of Pluto, move in paths close to the earth's orbital plane. The solar system formed some 4600 million years ago, following the contraction and subsequent flattening of a rotating cloud of interstellar gas and dust.

solar wind An almost radial outflow of charged particles discharged from the sun's corona into interplanetary space. The particles, mainly protons and electrons, are moving at speeds between 200 and 900 km per second in the vicinity of the earth's orbit. They interact with the earth's *magnetosphere.

solder An *alloy that is melted to form a joint between other metals or, occasionally, nonmetals. The surfaces to be joined are heated by a soldering iron or by a flame, but are not melted. **Soft solder** is usually made of lead and tin and melts in the range 200–250°C. It cannot be used for joints that have to stand up to stress or heat, but is used for making secure electrical connections. **Brazing**, also called **hard soldering**, uses a harder alloy with a higher melting temperature (850–900°C), usually a *brass with 60% zinc and 40% copper. **Silver solder** has a slightly lower melting point (630–830°C) than brass, and often contains antimony or other metals but no longer contains silver. Like brazing, its strength makes it useful in engineering applications. A flux of zinc chloride or a resin is applied to the hot surfaces

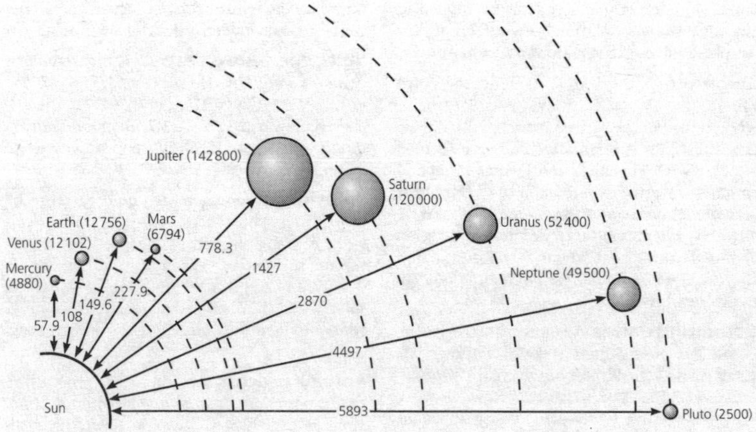

solar system. The planets with their equatorial diameters in kilometres (in brackets after the planet's name) and their distance from the sun in millions of kilometres (not to scale).

before soldering to clean them and to enable the solder to flow.

sole An elongated *flatfish of the family *Soleidae* (over 100 species), found in temperate and tropical seas. The common European sole (*Solea solea*), also called Dover sole, is a valuable food fish and has a blotchy brown body with a black spot on each pectoral fin. *See also* LEMON SOLE.

solenoid A coil of wire usually forming a long cylinder. When electric current flows through it a *magnetic field is created. This field can be used to move an iron rod placed on its axis. Solenoids are often used to operate mechanical valves attached to the iron rod by switching on or off the current.

Solent, the A channel between the coast of Hampshire in S England and the Isle of Wight. It is an important shipping route between Southampton and the English Channel.

solicitor In the UK, a member of the legal profession qualified to give legal advice to clients, to present clients' cases in Magistrates' Courts, County Courts, and (since 1971) higher courts (provided that they have obtained the necessary advocacy qualification), and to undertake other legal work, such as the transfer of property (conveyancing). They are eligible for appointment as circuit judges and recorders, but are not eligible for the higher judiciary. A barrister must always be instructed through a solicitor.

Solidarity (Polish name: Solidarnosc) A Polish trade union. Formed in Gdansk (1980) and led by Lech *Wałęsa, it became a focus of resistance to General Jarulzelski's Soviet-dominated government and was outlawed from 1982 until 1989. In June 1989 the movement triumphed in elections, forming the first noncommunist government in the communist world. By 1993, the movement had split into several political groupings, only one of which retained the name Solidarity.

solid state One of the four states of matter and that to which all substances, except helium, revert at sufficiently low temperatures. It is distinguished from the other states by being the only one in which matter retains its shape, as a result of the stronger intermolecular forces.

solid-state devices Electronic devices made with solid *semiconductor components. They have no moving parts and depend for their operation on the movement of charges within a crystalline solid. Solid-state devices are compact, robust, and easily mass-produced. *See also* SEMICONDUCTOR DIODE; TRANSISTOR.

Solihull A unitary authority in central England, in West Midlands. Area: 180 sq km (70 sq mi). Population (2001): 199 521.

solmization A method of teaching sight-singing that eliminates learning to read music notation from the stave. In the tonic sol-fa system the notes of the rising major scale are represented by the syllables doh, ray, me, fah, soh, lah, ti, and doh. The system can be applied in any key, and modulation to a different key simply involves shifting doh to another pitch.

Solomon In the Old Testament, the third King of Israel, son of *David and Bathsheba, who reigned in the 10th century BC. During his peaceful reign foreign alliances were formed (notably with Phoenicia and Egypt), trade and commerce were expanded, and the *Temple of Jerusalem and many palaces were built. To realize his schemes he imposed heavy taxation and used compulsory labour, which resulted in the revolt of N Israel. He is traditionally famous for his wisdom.

Solomon Islands A country in the Pacific Ocean, E of New Guinea. It consists of over 900 small islands, the largest of which are *Guadalcanal, Malaita, San Cristobal, New Georgia, Santa Isabel and Choiseul. The larger islands are mainly forested and mountainous, with some active volcanoes. Most of the population are Melanesian, with Polynesian and Micronesian minorities. *Economy*: the main industries are fishing, mining, forestry and tourism. The economy has been severely affected by recent political disorders. *History*: inhabited from about 2000 BC, the islands were visited by the Spanish in 1568. The four main islands became a British protectorate in 1893 and others were added in 1898–99. They achieved self-government in 1976 and became independent within the Commonwealth in 1978. Ethnic fighting erupted on Guadalcanal in 1998 and culminated in a coup (2000) deposing prime minister Bartholomew Ulufa'ulu. Although a peace deal was signed (Oct 2000), violence and disorder continued, leading to the despatch of Australian peacekeepers in 2003. Official language: English. Currency: Solomon Islands dollar of 100 cents. Area: 29 785 sq km (11 500 sq mi). Population (2003 est): 450 000. Capital: Honiara.

Solon (6th century BC) Athenian statesman, who laid the foundations of Athenian democracy. As archon (c.594–593), Solon cancelled debts for which land or liberty was the security and introduced a new coinage and weights and measures. He also instituted a new constitution and a more lenient legal code.

solstice Either of two points on the *ecliptic, midway between the equinoxes, at which the sun reaches its greatest angular distance above or below the celestial equator (*see* CELESTIAL SPHERE). In the N hemisphere the sun's northernmost position occurs at the **summer solstice**, usually on 21 June, when daylight hours are at a maximum. Its southernmost position occurs at the **winter solstice**, usually on 22 December, when daylight hours are minimal.

Solti, Sir Georg (1912–97) Hungarian-born British conductor. He was conductor of the Royal Opera, Covent Garden (1961–71), the Orchestre de Paris (1972–75), the London Philharmonic Orchestra (1979–83), and the Chicago Symphony Orchestra (1969–91).

solution A homogenous liquid mixture of two or more substances. Solutions, unlike *colloids, contain no identifiable particles of different substances. When a solid or gas is dissolved in a liquid, the liquid is known as the solvent and the dissolved material the solute. If the components are all liquid, the one in excess is the solvent.

Solvay process An industrial process for the production of sodium carbonate. Limestone is first heated strongly to produce calcium oxide and carbon dioxide, which is then passed through brine saturated with ammonia, precipitating sodium hydrogencarbonate ($NaHCO_3$). This, on mild heating, yields sodium carbonate and some carbon dioxide, which is recycled. The ammonia is also recovered. Named after E. Solvay (1833–1922).

solvent abuse The sniffing of organic solvents in glue, cleaning fluids, aerosols, etc., especially by adolescents. The practice has grown up as an offshoot of the drug culture and is highly dangerous. In the UK there are now restrictions on the sale of materials containing solvents to children.

Solzhenitsyn, Aleksandr (1918–) Russian novelist. After World War II he was held in prison camps until 1956. In 1974 he left the Soviet Union and moved to the USA. His major works include *Cancer Ward* (1968), *The First Circle* (1968), and *The Gulag Archipelago* (1974–78). He won the Nobel Prize in 1970. He returned to Russia in 1994.

Somali An E African people occupying Somalia, Djibouti (where they are called Issas), Ethiopia, and NW Kenya. There are many tribes. Some Somalis are nomadic herdsmen while others dwell in towns and along the coast as traders and farmers. Their language belongs to the Cushitic branch of the Hamito-Semitic family.

Somalia (official name: Somali Democratic Republic) A country in East Africa, occupying most of the Horn of Africa between the Gulf of Aden and the Indian Ocean. Coastal plains rise in the N to a high plateau. Most of the inhabitants are nomadic *Somalis with minorities of

Sab, Bantu, and others. *Economy*: chiefly agricultural, livestock raising being especially important. *History*: British and Italian *Somaliland gained independence as Somalia in 1960. In 1969, after a military coup, a Supreme Revolutionary Council was established under Gen Mohammed Siad Barré. The country has had serious territorial disputes with Ethiopia (*see* OGADEN, THE), which has a considerable Somali population. Barré was replaced as president in a coup in 1991 by Ali Mahdi Mohammed. His rule was rejected by several factions, and in 1991 the N of the country declared itself independent as the Somaliland Republic. Civil war broke out in the S, exacerbating famine conditions; UN troops intervened in 1992 but failed to maintain a ceasefire and withdrew in 1995. Confused factional fighting continued until Dec 1997, when 26 of the warring militias agreed to establish a national transitional government. This was inaugurated in 2000 but failed to take effective control owing to continuing opposition from some factions. In Jan 2004 a further peace deal was signed proposing the establishment of a new parliament and president. Official language: Somali; Arabic, Italian, and English are used extensively. Currency: Somali shilling of 100 centesemi. Area: 700 000 sq km (270 000 sq mi). Population (2003 est): 8 025 000. Capital: Mogadishu.

Somaliland A region corresponding to present-day Somalia and Djibouti. Between the 7th and 12th centuries AD the coast was occupied by Muslim traders while the N was settled from the 10th century by nomadic Somalis. During the 19th century the region was divided between France, Britain, and Italy. Italian Somaliland was united with Ethiopia by Mussolini (1935) and became an Italian trust territory after World War II. British and Italian Somaliland united to become Somalia in 1960 and the French territory, Afars and Issas, as Djibouti in 1977.

somatotrophin *See* GROWTH HORMONE.

Somerset A county of SW England, bordering on the Bristol Channel. In 1974 it lost the NE part to Avon; in 1996 the administration of this area passed to two unitary authorities, Bath and North East Somerset and North Somerset, which are considered part of Somerset for ceremonial purposes. It consists mainly of a flat plain enclosed by the Quantock Hills and Exmoor in the W, the Blackdown Hills in the S, and the Mendip Hills in the N. It is predominantly agricultural, with dairy farming and the traditional cider making. Tourism is also important. Area (excluding unitary authorities): 3452 sq km (1332 sq mi). Population (1996 est, excluding unitary authorities): 482 700. Administrative centre: Taunton.

Somme, River A river in N France, rising in the Aisne department and flowing mainly W through Amiens and Abbeville to the English Channel. It was the scene of extensive fighting in *World War I (1916). Length: 245 km (152 mi).

sonar *See* ECHO SOUNDING.

sonata (Italian: sounded, as opposed to *cantata*, sung) A piece of music for one or more instruments. The name has been used of a variety of abstract musical forms. **Sonata form**, the normal structure of the first movement of the classical sonata, was based on the exposition, development, and recapitulation of two contrasting themes. It was applied to the first movement of the *symphony and of *chamber music compositions as well as the sonata proper. Beethoven and his successors enlarged the formal boundaries of the sonata; Liszt evolved a single-movement form out of the three or four movements of the classical sonata.

Sondheim, Stephen (Joshua) (1930–) US composer, who studied with Oscar Hammerstein. He wrote the lyrics for *West Side Story* (1957) and both words and music for *Sweeney Todd* (1979), *Sunday In the Park with George* (1989), and *Assassins* (1992).

songbird A *passerine bird belonging to the suborder *Oscines* (about 4000 species), in which the vocal organ (syrinx), at the junction of the trachea (windpipe) and bronchi, is highly developed. The flow of air vibrates the vocal membranes; muscles alter their tension and so produce the different notes. Bird song communicates the identity and whereabouts of an individual to other birds and also signals alarm and sexual intentions; it is especially important in birds that feed or migrate in flocks.

sonnet A poem of 14 lines originating in Italy in the 13th century and introduced into England in the 16th century by Sir Thomas *Wyatt. Its two principal variations are the Petrarchan sonnet, usually divided into an octet rhyming *abbaabba* and a sestet rhyming *cdecde*, and the Shakespearean sonnet, usually rhyming *abab cdcd efef gg*.

Sophists The Greek sages of the 5th and early 4th centuries BC who were itinerant experts on various subjects including public speaking, grammar, ethics, literature, mathematics, and elementary physics. In philosophy they tried to explain the phenomenal world.

Their educational programme centred on the belief that virtue can be taught. From their opponent *Plato, they acquired a bad name as philosophical tricksters.

Sophocles (c. 496–406 BC) Greek dramatist; with Aeschylus and Euripides, one of the three great Athenian tragic dramatists. He developed the more static drama of Aeschylus by introducing a third actor and by reducing the role of the chorus. Of his 123 plays, 7 survive, including *Electra*, *Oedipus Rex*, and *Antigone*. He led an active public life, holding several important civil and military administrative posts.

soprano (Italian: upper) The highest female singing voice. Range: middle C to the C above the treble stave. The **mezzo-soprano** voice lies between the soprano and the contralto. Range: A below middle C to F an octave and a sixth above.

Sorghum A genus of annual or perennial grasses (about 30 species), native to Africa, especially *S. vulgare*, of which there are several varieties, such as sweet sorghum and durra, widely cultivated as cereal crops. They have rigid stalks, long flat leaves, and terminal flower clusters bearing 800–3000 starch-rich seeds. The seeds are used as grain for making bread, etc., and as a source of edible oil, starch, and sugar. The stalks are used as fodder or sometimes for syrup manufacture.

sorrel A tall perennial herb, *Rumex acetosa*, common throughout temperate Eurasia and North America. It bears numerous small red flowers. The tangy-tasting leaves are used as a culinary flavouring and in salads. Family: *Polygonaceae*. *See also* WOOD SORREL.

Sotho A large group of Bantu-speaking peoples of S Africa. The term applies in a general sense to the peoples of Botswana, Lesotho, and the Transvaal (South Africa), but, more specifically, to one of the four main divisions of these peoples, the Sotho of Lesotho. The other branches are the Tswana, Pedi, and Venda, each with many tribes.

sound A disturbance propagated through a medium by longitudinal waves. Strictly the term applies only to those waves that are audible to the human ear, i.e. with frequencies between about 20 and 20 000 hertz, those with higher frequencies being called ultrasound. Sound is propagated by vibrations of molecules in the medium, producing fronts of compression and rarefaction. Sound waves are longitudinal as the molecules vibrate in the direction of propagation; the speed of sound in air at 0°C is about 332 metres per second (760 mph). The three principal characteristics of a sound are its pitch (the frequency of the wave), loudness (the amplitude of the wave), and *timbre (the extent to which it contains harmonics of the fundamental frequency). *See also* ACOUSTICS; SOUND INTENSITY.

sound barrier An obstacle experienced by subsonic *aircraft attempting to fly at or above the speed of sound. Drag increases sharply, lift falls off, and the aircraft becomes difficult to control (*see* AERONAUTICS). At subsonic speeds the pressure waves created by the aircraft as it flies through the air are able to move ahead of the aircraft; at supersonic speeds they cannot escape in a forward direction as the source is moving faster than the pressure waves themselves. Thus shock waves build up on the aircraft's wings and fuselage, creating an apparent barrier to supersonic flight. Many aircraft are now capable of supersonic flight (including Concorde) by greater streamlining, sweptback wings, and more powerful engines. As these aircraft cross the sound barrier a **sonic boom** is heard. This is created by a shock-wave cone with the nose of the aircraft at its vertex. In level flight the intersection of this cone with the ground produces a hyperbola at all points along which the boom is heard.

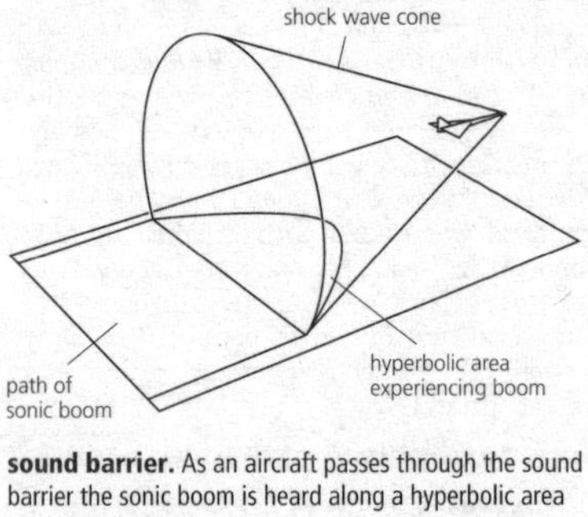

sound barrier. As an aircraft passes through the sound barrier the sonic boom is heard along a hyperbolic area on the ground.

sound intensity The rate at which sound energy is propagated through a unit area perpendicular to the direction of propagation. It is measured in watts per square metre. The intensities of two sound levels are compared by a unit called the *decibel. The intensity of sound is not the same as its loudness, the latter being the magnitude of the sensation produced by the human ear, which is dependent on the frequency of the sound.

Sousa, John Philip (1854–1933) US composer and bandmaster. He wrote military marches including "The Stars and Stripes Forever," "The Washington Post," and "Liberty Bell" and invented the **sousaphone**, a tuba-like band instrument with a forward-facing bell.

souslik (*or* **suslik**) A nocturnal ground squirrel belonging to the genus *Citellus* (34 species), of E Europe, Asia, and North America (where it is sometimes called a gopher). The European souslik (*C. citellus*) is yellowish brown with large eyes and small ears. *See also* CHIPMUNK.

South Africa, Republic of (Afrikaans name: Suid-Afrika) A country occupying the S tip of Africa. Narrow coastal plains rise to plateaus in the interior, with the Drakensberg mountains in the E. The N is mainly desert. The Limpopo, Molopo, and Orange Rivers mark the N boundary. The Vaal, a tributary of the Orange, is another important river. The majority of the inhabitants are Africans (71%) with White, Coloured, and Asian (mostly Indian) minorities. *Economy*: although South Africa is highly industrialized, agriculture (including citrus fruits) is still important. South Africa is the world's biggest producer of gold, diamonds, platinum, and chrome; uranium, coal, manganese, phosphates, and iron are also mined. Industries include metals, machinery, chemicals, food processing, and textiles. Wine making is of growing importance, as is tourism. *History*: Bantu-speaking tribes arrived from the north between 1000 and 1500. The Portuguese under Bartolomeu Dias (c. 1450–c. 1500) first sighted the Cape of Good Hope in 1488 but made no permanent settlement. The Dutch East India Company settlement (1652) at Table Bay (Cape Town) expanded into the interior. During the Napoleonic Wars Britain acquired the Cape Colony for strategic reasons, a possession confirmed in 1814. In the 1830s increasing numbers of Dutch farmers (or Boers, forebears of the modern Afrikaners) moved E and N to escape British rule, clashing with the *Bantu peoples who were then migrating southwards (*see* GREAT TREK). The Boers founded two independent republics, the Orange Free State and the Transvaal, but their republic in Natal was soon annexed by the British (1843), who were also expanding the Cape Colony. *Kruger's assertion of Boer independence led to war with the British (1880–81, 1899–1902) (*see* BOER WARS). The need for cooperation led the two former Boer republics and the two British colonies to combine in the Union of South Africa (1910). In both World Wars South Africa, under J. C. *Smuts, enthusiastically supported Britain, but in 1948 Smuts was ousted by the anti-British Afrikaner National Party and in 1961 South Africa became a republic outside the Commonwealth. From 1910 until 1994 the treatment of the non-White majority was the crucial political issue (*see* APARTHEID). In 1976 the *Transkei became the first independent Bantu Homeland (Bantustan); these areas were abolished in 1994. South Africa intervened in Angola (1976) and Namibia, and supported the White minorities in Zimbabwe and Mozambique. Some non-Whites received limited parliamentary power under a new tricameral constitution (1984). In the face of rising unrest a state of emergency was declared in 1985, leading the USA and EC to impose economic sanctions. In 1989 P. W. Botha was replaced as president by F. W. de Klerk, who legalized the banned African National Congress, released Nelson *Mandela from prison, and began to dismantle apartheid. Classification by race was ended in 1991. In 1993 the government was replaced by a multiracial multiparty Transitional Executive Council (TEC), which devised an interim constitution. In 1994 the ANC won multiracial elections and Mandela became president. South Africa then rejoined the Commonwealth. A permanent constitution was adopted in 1996. Mandela retired in 1999 and, following elections, Thabo *Mbeki became president. Official languages: Afrikaans, English, and African languages. Currency: rand of 100 cents. Area: 1 221 042 sq km (472 359 sq mi). Population (2003 est): 45 349 000. Capitals: Pretoria (administrative), Bloemfontein (judicial), Cape Town (legislative).

South America The fourth largest continent, lying chiefly in the S of the W hemisphere between the Pacific and Atlantic Oceans. It is linked to the continent of North America by the Isthmus of Panama. An ancient shield occupies much of the NE part of the continent and forms the Brazilian and Guiana Highlands. These are separated by the vast basins of the Orinoco, Amazon, and Paraná–Paraguay river systems. In the extreme W, beyond a series of plains, rise the mountains and high plateaus of the *Andes. South America's climate varies considerably, largely because of its length, but much is tropical with vast areas of tropical rainforest (selva). The population consists chiefly of the indigenous Indians, Europeans (especially Spanish and Portuguese), and mestizos together with large numbers of Negroids. *History*: the flourishing kingdoms of South America (such as those of the *Incas and Chibchas), were vanquished by the Spanish conquistadors. The entire continent was divided—

Portugal taking the NE portion (now Brazil) and Spain the remainder—during the 16th century. With the collapse of the Spanish Empire during the early 19th century, there followed struggles for independence under national leaders, who included *Bolívar and *San Martin. Large-scale European immigration occurred in the 19th century. During the 20th century the constituent nations became increasingly industrialized and saw rapid rises in their populations. Although political and economic instability was endemic for most of the century, democratic government is now in place in every country and several (notably Chile and Brazil) have achieved prosperity. Area: 17 767 331 sq km (6 858 527 sq mi). Population (1996 est): 317 846 000.

Southampton 1. 50 55N 1 25W A city in S England, in Southhampton unitary authority, Hampshire on Southampton Water (an inlet of the English Channel). It is the UK's principal passenger port, used by the largest transatlantic liners, and has four tides daily. It is also an industrial centre with a large oil refinery at Fawley. Population (1991): 210 138. **2.** A unitary authority in S England, in Hampshire. Area: 49 sq km (19 sq mi). Population (2001): 217 478.

Southampton, Henry Wriothesley, 3rd Earl of (1573–1624) English courtier, famous as the patron of Shakespeare. He was involved in the Earl of Essex's conspiracy against Elizabeth I (1600), sentenced to death, but pardoned by James I (1603).

South Australia A state of S central Australia, on the Indian Ocean and Great Australian Bight. It consists chiefly of low-lying plains with the *Great Victoria Desert in the W, rising in the NW to the Musgrave Ranges and in the SE to the Flinders Range. The only major river is the Murray. Intensive agriculture is restricted to the S. The vineyards of the fertile Barossa Valley are important, producing almost half of Australia's wine. Mineral resources include iron ore, coal, large natural gas fields in the N, and opals. Industry is concentrated in Adelaide. Area: 984 377 sq km (380 070 sq mi). Population (1999 est): 1 493 070. Capital: Adelaide.

South Ayrshire A council area in SW Scotland on the Firth of Clyde, comprising part of the historic county of Ayrshire. Absorbed into Strathclyde Region in 1975, it became an independent unitary authority in 1996. South Ayrshire is mainly agricultural, but fishing and tourism are also important. Area: 1202 sq km (464 sq mi). Population (2001): 112 097. Administrative centre: Ayr.

South Carolina A state in the SE USA, on the Atlantic coast. Lowlands make up two-thirds of the state rising to uplands in the NW. The large areas of woodland supply the furniture industries and the large textile and clothing industries are based on the region's cotton crop. One of the 13 original colonies, it became separate from North Carolina in 1713 and was the first state to secede from the Union (1860). Area: 80 432 sq km (31 055 sq mi). Population (2000): 4 012 012. Capital: Columbia.

South Caucasian languages A group of languages, also known as the Kartvelian languages, spoken by the people of W Transcaucasia and adjacent regions. It includes *Georgian, Svan, Mingrelian, and Laz. Only Georgian possesses a literary tradition.

South China Sea A section of the W Pacific Ocean, between SE Asia, Borneo, the Philippines, and Taiwan. A monsoon area, it is heavily fished.

South Dakota One of the Plains states in N central USA. The Missouri River separates the arid Badlands, the Black Hills, and the Great Plains in the W from the flat fertile prairie in the E, which forms the basis of South Dakota's predominantly agrarian economy. Livestock and livestock products are the chief source of revenue. Part of the Louisiana Purchase (1803), the gold rush and land boom of the 1880s brought many settlers and South Dakota became a state in 1889. Area: 199 551 sq km (77 047 sq mi). Population (2000): 754 844. Capital: Pierre.

Southend-on-Sea 1. 51 33N 0 43E A resort in SE England, in Southend-on-Sea unitary authority, Essex, on the lower Thames estuary. It is the nearest seaside resort to London and has the world's longest pleasure pier. Population (1991 est): 158 517. **2.** A unitary authority in SE England, in Essex. Area: 42 sq km (16 sq mi). Population (2001): 160 256.

Southern Alps The highest range of mountains in New Zealand. It extends SW–NE through South Island and contains many peaks over 3000 m (10 000 ft), including Mount *Cook. Glaciers, fed by the central snowfields, flank the mountains. It is an important winter-sports area.

South Georgia An island in the S Atlantic Ocean, a UK overseas territory. It has no permanent population but there is a British Antarctic Survey base. With the Falkland Islands, it was invaded by Argentina (1982) but was soon recaptured. Area: 3755 sq km (1450 sq mi).

South Gloucestershire A unitary authority of SW England, in Gloucestershire; it was part of Avon county from 1974 to 1996. Area: 510 sq km (197 sq mi). Population (2001): 245 644.

South Island The larger of the two principal islands of New Zealand, separated from North Island by Cook Strait. It is generally mountainous, including the *Southern Alps in the W, with coastal plains.

South Lanarkshire A council area of S Scotland, consisting of the S part of the historic county of Lanarkshire. Absorbed into Strathclyde Region in 1975, it became an independent unitary authority in 1996. It consists of the valley of the River Clyde and is mainly agricultural. Forestry and market gardening are also important. Area: 1771 sq km (684 sq mi). Population (2001): 302 216. Administrative centre: Hamilton.

South Pole *See* ANTARCTICA.

Southport 53 39N 3 01W A town and resort in NW England, in Sefton unitary authority, Merseyside, on the Irish Sea. Its annual flower show is famous. Population (1991): 90 959.

South Sea Bubble (1720) The collapse of the British market in South Sea stocks that had far-reaching political repercussions. The South Sea Company was founded in 1711 to trade with Spanish America and in 1718 George I became its governor. A boom in South Sea stock was followed by collapse and the subsequent inquiry revealed corruption among ministers and even touched the king. The day was saved by Sir Robert *Walpole, who transferred the South Sea stocks to the Bank of England and the East India Company.

South Shields 55 00N 1 25W A port in NE England, in South Tyneside unitary authority, Tyne and Wear, on the Tyne estuary opposite North Shields. Industries include petrochemicals and paint manufacture; shipbuilding has declined. The first lifeboat was built here (1790). Population (1991): 83 704.

South Tyneside A unitary authority in NE England, in Tyne and Wear. Area 64 sq km (25 sq mi). Population (2001): 152 785.

South Yorkshire A metropolitan county of N England, created in 1974 from the S part of the West Riding of Yorkshire and a small part of NE Derbyshire. In 1986 the county council was abolished and administrative powers were devolved to the districts of Sheffield, Rotherham, Doncaster, and Barnsley. Agriculture is important on the Pennines in the W and on the lowlands in the E. The main industrial activities include iron and steel and engineering. Area: 1562 sq km (603 sq mi).

Soutine, Chaim (1893–1943) Lithuanian-born painter, who emigrated to Paris in 1913. Using thickly applied paint, intense colour, and distorted and writhing forms, he was, together with *Chagall, the leading representative of French expressionism.

soviet A government council in the Soviet Union. Soviets originated as committees of workers' deputies in the *Revolution of 1905 and were again established in the *Russian Revolution of 1917. The Supreme Soviet was in theory the supreme organ of government in the Soviet Union; soviets were also elected at the local, provincial, and republican levels. Candidates, one for each deputy, were selected by the Communist Party.

Soviet Union (official name: Union of Soviet Socialist Republics) A former country in E Europe and N Asia. It was a federal state comprising 15 constituent republics: the Armenian, Azerbaidzhan, Belarussian, Estonian, Georgian, Kazakh, Kirgiz, Latvian, Lithuanian, Moldavian, Russian Soviet Federal, Tadzhik, Turkmen, Ukrainian, and Uzbek Soviet Socialist Republics. Administrative subdivisions included 20 Autonomous Soviet Socialist Republics and, within some of these, 8 autonomous regions (Russian *oblast*, region). The population included over a hundred national groups. The most numerous were the Russians, Ukrainians, Uzbeks, Belarussians, Tatars, and Kazakhs. *Economy*: formerly based on state ownership and controlled through Gosplan (the State Planning Commission) and Gosbank (the State Bank), it began a programme of liberalization in the late 1980s, with privatization of state monopolies and new pricing policies. Such a system was designed to replace the five-year plans, under which the economy had been directed since 1928. The country possessed vast natural resources. The Soviet Union was the world's leading producer of oil, coal, iron ore, cement, and steel; manganese, gold, and natural gas were also of major importance. Industry was concentrated on the production of capital goods. Agriculture, which was organized in a system of state and collective farms, was highly mechanized but not very productive. Fishing, forestry, and dependent industries were also important. *History*: the February and October Revolutions in Russia (*see* RUSSIAN REVOLU-

TION) were followed by civil war (1918–22), after which communist control was complete. The Soviet Union was created in 1922 from the union of Russia, Ukraine, Belarussia, and Transcaucasia. After *Lenin's death (1924) *Stalin had emerged as leader by 1928, having ousted Trotsky. Under Stalin the Soviet Union became a major industrial power but a totalitarian state, with effective political opposition eliminated during the 1930s by purges. World War II established the Soviet Union as one of the two major superpowers with effective control over much of E Europe (*see* WARSAW PACT). Relations with the other superpower, the USA, became tense during the *Cold War and again following the Soviet invasion of Afghanistan (1979). The Soviet Government used military force to crush the Hungarian Revolution (1956) and the Czechoslovakian liberalization programme (1968). In 1982 the Soviet leadership directed the suppression of the Solidarity trade union in Poland. Internal dissent was suppressed until the mid-1980s, when more liberal policies were adopted under *Gorbachov (*see* GLASNOST). A parliament of approved elected representatives called the Congress of People's Deputies was established in 1989 and in 1990 the Communists voted to give up their guaranteed right to rule, to create a strong new executive presidency, and to allow private property ownership. Relations with the West improved greatly with important agreements on disarmament. In 1989 the Soviet Union did not intervene when Communist regimes throughout E Europe were replaced by multiparty systems. The 1980s also saw growing separatist movements in many of the Soviet Union's constituent republics. In 1991 Communist Party rule in the Soviet Union collapsed following the failure of an anti-Gorbachov coup by Communist hardliners. The constituent republics asserted their independence and the Soviet Union ceased to exist in December 1991. In the same month the *Commonwealth of Independent States, a looser organization with responsibility for economic and military cooperation, was formed.

S

Soweto 26 10S 28 02E A large urban area in South Africa, in the Transvaal forming a suburb of Johannesburg. It is inhabited by Black Africans and comprises 36 townships, divided into tribal areas. In June 1976, it was the scene of serious rioting by African students during which over a hundred people died; there were further riots in 1985. Population (1996): 1 098 094.

soya bean (*or* **soybean**) An annual plant, *Glycine max*, widely cultivated for its seeds. The many commercial varieties produce clusters of pods, each containing two or three seeds. The ripe seeds contain 35% protein. Soya-bean oil is extracted for use in making margarines, cooking oils, resins, and paints and for many other foods, chemicals, and textiles. The meal residue is an important protein food for livestock and a meat substitute for man. The beans are also eaten whole, ground into flour, and as soy sauce. Family: *Leguminosae*.

Soyinka, Wole (1934–) Nigerian dramatist and writer. His works include the plays *The Lion and the Jewel* (1963) and *A Scourge of Hyacinths* (1992), the novel *The Interpreters* (1965), and essays in *The Burden of Memory, the Muse of Forgiveness* (1998). He was imprisoned during the Nigerian civil war (1967–69) and later exiled (1993–98). He won the 1986 Nobel Prize.

Soyuz *See* SALYUT.

spacecraft A vehicle designed to be launched into space and to function effectively for a considerable period in space. Unmanned craft include several thousand *satellites of diverse functions and planetary probes. Space stations and *space shuttles carry crews.

space shuttle One of a series of manned reusable US space transportation systems developed by *NASA. First launched in April 1981 it was operational by 1982. It consists of a delta-wing Orbiter that has three powerful rocket engines, a large cargo bay, and living space. Satellites and other craft can be launched from the cargo bay. Having completed its mission (7–30 days), the shuttle enters the earth's atmosphere in a shallow dive and makes an unpowered landing. Flights were suspended following the explosion of the shuttle *Challenger* (1986) but resumed in 1988. A further disaster occurred in 2003, when the shuttle *Columbia* disintegrated as it re-entered the earth's atmosphere, killing all seven astronauts. The first reusable Soviet shuttle, *Buran*, was launched in 1988.

space station A large orbiting spacecraft on which people can live and work in weightless conditions. The first space station was the Soviet Salyut–1, launched in 1971; America's Skylab was orbited in 1973. The USA, in cooperation with 14 other nations, plans to launch an international space station in the early 21st century. *See also* MIR.

space-time continuum A coordinate system that has four dimensions, three representing physical space and the fourth time. It is used in *relativity.

Spain, Kingdom of A country in SW Europe, occupying over four-fifths of the Iberian Peninsula. The Balearic and Canary Islands are also part of Spain. It consists mainly of a high plateau, rising over 3000 m (10 000 ft) in the Pyrenees in the NE. *Economy*: although traditionally agricultural, the industrial sector had begun to predominate by the early 1970s. Tourism is a major source of foreign currency. Forestry, fishing, and wine are important and there are rich mineral resources. *History*: early inhabitants included Iberians, Celts, Phoenicians, and Greeks; the Carthaginians conquered most of the Iberian peninsula in the 3rd century BC but were expelled by the Romans in the second Punic War (218–201 BC). Christianity was introduced in the 1st century AD and by the 5th century the Romans had given way to German tribes, including the Vandals and then the Visigoths. The Visigothic kingdom collapsed (711) in the face of Muslim invaders, who dominated most of the centre and S under a series of powerful dynasties. The reconquest of Muslim Spain was pursued throughout the middle ages by the Christian kingdoms in the N and was completed in 1492 with the conquest of Granada by Ferdinand of Aragon and Isabella of Castile. The union of Spain, begun by the union of Aragon and Castile, was now complete. The year 1492 also saw the expulsion from Spain of the Jews, who were followed after much persecution (1609) by the Muslims; the influence of both peoples on Spanish culture was enormous. The 16th century was Spain's golden age. Overseas exploration led to the formation of an empire in the New World, which brought great wealth to Spain. The country's prestige and power, as well as its possessions, in Europe were furthered by the Habsburg kings Charles I (who as *Charles V was also Holy Roman Emperor) and his son Philip II but the latter's reign witnessed the beginnings of decline. The *Revolt of the Netherlands against Spanish rule led to the secession (1581) of the northern Dutch provinces and in 1588 Spain suffered the humiliating defeat of the Armada by the English. Following the Thirty Years' War Spain lost to France its position as the leading European power (1659). The death in 1700 of the last Habsburg king (Charles II), without an heir, led to the War of the *Spanish Succession (1701–14). This confirmed the Bourbon succession and also deprived Spain of the Spanish Netherlands, Milan, Naples, Sardinia, and Sicily. In the second half of the 18th century Spain's decline was arrested by reform, especially under Charles III, but in 1808 Napoleon established his brother Joseph Bonaparte on the Spanish throne. The Spanish resistance to their French conquerors contributed to the defeat of Napoleon (*see* PENINSULAR WAR) and in 1814 the Bourbon Ferdinand III (1716–88) was restored. Conflict between supporters and opponents of the pretender Don Carlos (1788–1855) and subsequently between monarchists and republicans dominated the 19th century, during which Spain lost its last American possessions. It was neutral in World War I, following which Miguel Primo de Rivera (1870–1930) established a military dictatorship that undermined the position of the monarchy. In 1931 Alfonso XIII abdicated and the Second Republic was established. The electoral victory of the Popular Front in 1936 precipitated a military revolt led by Gen *Franco that became the *Spanish Civil War (1936–39). Franco's victory initiated over three decades of Nationalist dictatorship. Following Franco's death in 1975, the monarchy was restored and Juan Carlos de Borbón became king. The return to democracy proceeded rapidly. In 1978 provisional regional self-government was granted to Catalonia, Valencia, the Canary Islands, Aragon, Galicia, and the Basque provinces, although terrorist activities by Basque separatists have continued. Spain's first Socialist government in nearly 50 years was elected in 1982 under Felipe González. In the 1996 elections José María Aznar led the right-wing Popular Party to victory. In March 2004 nearly 200 people were killed in a bomb attack on Madrid, presumed to be the work of *al-Qaida. The bombing, and the government's response to it, produced a surprise victory for the Socialists under José Luis Rodriguez Zapatero in that month's general election. Spain joined NATO in 1982 and the EC (now the EU) in 1986. It adopted the European single currency in 1999–2002. Official language: Spanish. Currency: euro of 100 cents. Area: 504 879 sq km (194 883 sq mi). Population (2003 est): 42 600 000. Capital: Madrid.

spaniel One of several breeds of sporting dogs developed in Britain and thought to have originated in Spain. The English springer spaniel is typical, having a lean compact body, long muzzle, and drooping ears. It is longer in the leg than the similar *cocker spaniel but has the same flat wavy weather-resistant coat. It is generally black and white or liver and white, while the smaller Welsh springer spaniel is always red and white. Height: 51 cm (English springer). *See also* KING CHARLES SPANIEL.

Spanish A Romance language spoken in

Spain, Latin America, the Philippines, and elsewhere by about 308 million people. The standard form is based on the Castilian dialect.

Spanish Civil War (1936–39) The civil war in Spain precipitated by a military revolt on 18 July 1936, led by the Nationalist Gen *Franco, against the Republican Government of Manuel Azaña (1880–1940). By the end of 1936 the Nationalists had gained control of most of W and S Spain, while the Republicans held the urban areas of the E and N, including Madrid, Valencia, Barcelona, and Bilbao. During 1937 the Nationalists, with Italian and German help, failed in their attempt to take Madrid but captured Bilbao. In 1938, in spite of the assistance of the *International Brigade and the Soviet Union, the Republican front was broken and early in 1939 Barcelona, Valencia, and then Madrid fell. The Republican cause rallied liberals throughout Europe against fascism.

Spanish moss **1.** An epiphytic plant, *Tillandsia usneoides* (or *Dendropogon usneoides*), found in warm regions of America. Its seeds are windblown to trees, where they germinate and grow downwards in large silvery-grey beardlike masses, 6–7.5 m long. It is covered in hairlike scales, which absorb water from the air. Family: *Bromeliaceae*. **2.** A tropical lichen, *Usnea longissima*, which resembles *T. usneoides*.

Spanish Riding School A centre for classical horsemanship in Vienna, originally sited in the Habsburg imperial palace and probably founded in the late 16th century. The purest *haute école* *dressage of the 16th and 17th centuries is practised. The white *Lipizzaner stallions used here have been bred from horses imported from Spain in the 16th century—hence the title "Spanish."

S

Spanish Succession, War of the (1701–14) The third of the European wars caused by Louis XIV's attempts to increase French power. The immediate cause of conflict was the succession to the Spanish throne. Following the death of the childless Charles II, Louis proclaimed the succession of his grandson as Philip V. England felt menaced, and with the Dutch Republic and the Holy Roman Emperor formed an alliance against France in 1701; they were joined by most German states upon the outbreak of general hostilities (1702). Spain, Bavaria, Portugal, and Savoy supported France. The English won a series of brilliant victories under the Duke of *Marlborough but pressed for peace in 1712, when a Spanish-Austrian union threatened. The Treaties of *Utrecht (1713–14) concluded the war.

Spark, Dame Muriel (1918–) British novelist, who achieved success with a series of witty satirical novels including *Memento Mori* (1959) and *The Prime of Miss Jean Brodie* (1961). Her later novels include *The Abbess of Crewe* (1974), *A Far Cry from Kensington* (1988), *Reality and Dreams* (1996), and *The Finishing School* (2004).

sparrow A small thick-billed member of the *weaverbird family. Sparrows are generally brown and grey in colour, often with black or bright yellow patches. They are mostly tropical Old World species but also occur in Eurasia; the Eurasian house sparrow (*Passer domesticus*) has been introduced to North America, where it is now a pest. Sparrows eat seeds, etc., feeding on the ground. Subfamily: *Passerinae*.

sparrowhawk A small woodland *hawk, *Accipiter nisus*, occurring in Eurasia and NW Africa. It has a long tail and short rounded wings and the male (27 cm long) is grey with brown-barred white underparts; females (38 cm long) are brown above. It hunts small birds.

Sparta 37 05N 22 25E In ancient Greece, the capital of Laconia on the River Eurotas in the S Peloponnese. Having developed during the 10th century BC, Sparta controlled much of Laconia and Messenia by 700 BC. It became an austere militaristic state, where weaker boys were abandoned at birth and those that survived were subjected to a rigid military training. Its military strength brought conflict in the 5th century with Athens, and ultimate victory (404) in the consequent *Peloponnesian War: defeat by the Thebans at Leuctra (371) marked the beginning of Spartan decline. The ancient city was destroyed by the Visigoths in 396 AD.

Spartacus Thracian gladiator, who led a slave revolt against Rome in 73 BC. After defeating the Romans in five separate engagements in Italy, he moved N to Cisalpine *Gaul. When his followers refused to disperse, Spartacus marched S again and was defeated by Marcus Licinius *Crassus (71). He and his followers were crucified.

Spartina A genus of grasses (16 species), known as cordgrass, found on salt marshes and tidal flats of North America, Europe, and Africa. They have stiff erect stems and yellowish flower spikes. Townsend's cord grass (*S. townsendii*) has been used extensively to help reclaim coastal land.

Speaker of the House of Commons The presiding officer of the lower chamber of the British parliament. Elected by each new parliament, a Speaker or his deputy regulate with impartiality all the debates and proceedings of the House, except for proceedings in committee. The current Speaker (since 2000) is Michael Martin.

spearmint An aromatic perennial herb, *Mentha spicata*, native to central and S Europe and widely cultivated as a culinary herb. The oil extract from the leaves is used to flavour sweets, etc. Family: *Labiatae*.

Special Air Service (**SAS**) A specialist division of the British army, formed in 1942. The unit is highly trained in operations behind enemy lines and is the most secretive of the British forces. Its motto is "Who dares wins."

species A unit of classification of living organisms. Individuals of the same species usually resemble one another closely and can breed among themselves to produce fertile offspring that resemble the parents. Some species are subdivided into subspecies and varieties. Breeds of domestic animals and cultivated varieties of plants have been specially developed by man for economic or other purposes and are all derived from a few wild species. Those originating from the same species can interbreed, despite obvious differences in character. All breeds of domestic dog, for instance, belong to the same species—*Canis familiaris*—and can breed together.

specific gravity *See* DENSITY.

specific heat capacity (*c*) The quantity of heat needed to raise a unit mass of substance by 1 K. It is measured in joules per kelvin per kilogram. For gases, the specific heat capacity at constant pressure (c_p) exceeds that at constant volume (c_v) as heat is required to do work against the surroundings during the expansion.

spectacles Lenses worn in frames in front of the eyes to correct defective vision. Convex lenses bend parallel light rays inward; they are used by those unable to focus on close objects (*see* LONGSIGHTEDNESS). Concave lenses have the opposite effect and are used by those unable to focus on distant objects (*see* SHORTSIGHTEDNESS). Astigmatism is treated by wearing lenses that produce a compensating distortion of the light rays. Bifocal spectacles have convex lenses consisting of upper and lower parts of different curvatures, for focusing on distant and near objects, respectively: they are worn for presbyopia. *See also* CONTACT LENSES.

spectral type *See* HARVARD CLASSIFICATION SYSTEM.

spectrum In general, the way in which a particular property of a system is distributed over its components. The visible spectrum, for example, is observed in a *rainbow, which shows the distribution of frequencies when sunlight is split up into its components by raindrops. The visible spectrum, however, is only a small part of the electromagnetic spectrum, which ranges from gamma rays to radio waves. **Spectroscopy** is concerned with analysing the emission and absorption of electromagnetic energy by atoms and molecules. Atoms emit and absorb radiation at characteristic frequencies, which show up as lines in their spectrum and can be used to identify particular elements.

speedwell An annual or perennial herbaceous plant of the genus *Veronica* (about 200 species), occurring throughout temperate regions. The flowers are usually blue. The fruit is a flattened heart-shaped capsule. Family: *Scrophulariaceae*.

Speke, John Hanning (1827–64) British explorer. He accompanied Richard Burton (1821–90) on the expeditions (1855, 1857–58) to discover the source of the Nile. They discovered Lake Tanganyika and then Speke went on alone to discover Lake Victoria, which on a second visit in 1860 he established to be the source of the Nile. Burton disputed Speke's claim.

speleology (*or* **spelaeology**) The study and exploration of *caves and underground water courses. This includes the survey of caves and the study of their formation, plant and animal life (past and present), and geology. Potholing—or descending through potholes into underground drainage passages in order to follow the course of underground streams—is a popular activity.

Spence, Sir Basil (1907–76) British architect, who became internationally known with his design for rebuilding Coventry Cathedral (consecrated 1962). Later buildings included Sussex University and the British Embassy in Rome (completed 1971).

Spencer, Herbert (1820–1903) British philosopher, an influential exponent of *laissez-faire. He believed that state intervention limited progress and he developed this idea fully in his popular *The Man versus the State* (1884). Spencer's other writings include works on psychology, ethics, and sociology. He supported Darwin's theory of evolution and applied evolutionary ideas to social development.

Spencer, Sir Stanley (1891–1959) British painter. He is known for his religious subjects, often depicted in the everyday setting of his native village of Cookham, Berkshire.

Spenser, Edmund (c. 1552–99) English poet. His major work, *The Faerie Queene*, a long moral allegory in nine-line "Spenserian" stanzas, was dedicated to Elizabeth I and published in six books in 1590 and 1596. His other works include *The Shepheardes Calendar* (1579) and the *Epithalamion* (1595), celebrating his second marriage.

sperm (*or* **spermatozoon**) The reproductive cell of male animals, which is formed in the *testis and fertilizes an egg cell during sexual reproduction. A sperm usually has a head region, containing the genetic material, and a tail, by means of which it swims to the egg. In men, sperms develop and mature in the testes. At ejaculation they are mixed with secretions from various glands (including the *prostate gland) to form semen.

sperm whale A large toothed *whale, *Physeter cathodon*, also called cachalot. It is 18 m long, grey-blue above and pale beneath, with tiny flippers and large tail flukes. Family: *Physeteridae*.

Spey, River A fast-flowing river in NE Scotland, flowing mainly NE through the Grampian Mountains to Spey Bay. It is known for its salmon fishing. Length: 172 km (107 mi).

Sphagnum A widely distributed genus of mosses (over 300 species), called bog or peat moss, forming dense raised clumps in bogs and other waterlogged places. Green to dark red in colour, the fine stems bear clusters of thread-like branches, densely clothed with tiny leaves, and globular spore capsules. The ability of the stems and leaves to retain water means that these mosses can drain very wet ground and form bogs. The dead remains form peat. Family: *Sphagnaceae*.

sphinx A mythological creature with a lion's body and a human head, occurring in the art and legends of most ancient Near and Middle Eastern civilizations. The most famous representation is the Great Sphinx at Giza, Egypt, dating from the 3rd millennium BC. In Greek legend, the Sphinx was a female monster that preyed on travellers going to Thebes. She killed those who could not answer her riddle, which was finally solved by *Oedipus.

sphygmomanometer A device for measuring arterial *blood pressure. It consists of an inflatable arm cuff connected via a rubber tube to a column of mercury with a graduated scale or an aneroid device. The cuff is inflated until the pulse cannot be detected (using a stethoscope) and then slowly deflated until the systolic and then the diastolic pressure can be recorded as the pulse returns.

spices *See* HERBS AND SPICES.

spider An *arachnid belonging to the worldwide order *Araneae* (or *Araneida*; over 30 000 species). The body of a spider consists of a cephalothorax and an abdomen separated by a narrow "waist." There are eight walking legs, up to eight eyes, and several pairs of spinnerets, which produce silk used for making webs, egg cocoons, etc. Spiders are predominantly terrestrial and prey mainly on insects, hunting them or trapping them in their webs. The victims are killed with poison-bearing fangs; in a few species the poison is harmful to man. The female is generally larger than the male, which she sometimes kills and eats after mating. *See also* BLACK WIDOW; TARANTULA; WATER SPIDER; WOLF SPIDER.

spider crab A marine *crab belonging to the widely distributed family *Maiidae*, especially one of the genus *Libinia*. It has a thick rounded body with long spindly legs and generally moves slowly. Most spider crabs are scavengers, especially of dead animals.

spider monkey A monkey belonging to the genus *Ateles* (4 species), of Central and South American forests. Spider monkeys have very long legs and a long prehensile tail, which is capable of supporting their weight. They live in family groups in thick forest, feeding on seeds and leaves. Family: *Cebidae*.

spider plant A plant of the genus *Chlorophytum*, especially *C. elatum*, native to South Africa and widely grown as a house plant. It has long green and white leaves and periodically produces a stem bearing small white flowers or young plantlets. Family: *Liliaceae*.

spiderwort *See* TRADESCANTIA.

Spielberg, Steven (1946–) US film director, whose hugely successful adventure and fantasy films include *Jaws* (1975), *ET* (1982), and *Jurassic Park* (1993). *The Color Purple* (1986), *Schindler's List* (1994), and *Saving Private Ryan* (1998) have more serious themes. In 1996 he set up Dream Works, his own Hollywood studio.

spin A property possessed by elementary particles as a result of which they possess a constant angular momentum that is independent of their motion. The spin is quantized and labelled by a spin *quantum number (symbol: s), which may be integral or half-integral.

spina bifida A defect, present at birth, in

which the backbone fails to fuse properly, leaving the spinal cord and its coverings exposed. Commonly the child has paralysed legs and disordered bladder and bowel function. Intelligence is often normal. The condition can be diagnosed during pregnancy (*see* AMNIOCENTESIS), and is less likely to occur if pregnant women take extra folic acid.

spinach An annual herbaceous plant, *Spinacia oleracea*, native to Asia and widely cultivated as a vegetable. Its edible leaves are rich in iron and vitamins A and C. Family: *Chenopodiaceae*.

spinal cord An elongated part of the central *nervous system, running downwards from the base of the brain and consisting of a core of grey matter (nerve cell bodies) surrounded by white matter (nerve fibres). It is surrounded and protected by the spine and is enclosed in membranes (meninges). It gives off spinal nerves, usually in pairs, and ends in a bundle of nerves supplying the legs and lower part of the body. Through it run the nerve fibres between the brain and the body; injury can therefore cause paralysis and loss of sensation.

spine In anatomy, the backbone, or vertebral column: a series of small bones (vertebrae) that runs up the centre of the back. The spine encloses and protects the spinal cord, articulates with the skull, ribs, and pelvis, and provides attachment for muscles of the back. There are 26 vertebrae in the adult spine. The vertebrae are connected by tough discs of cartilage (intervertebral discs), which absorb the shock produced by running and other movements.

spinet A plucked keyboard instrument of the *harpsichord family that superseded the *virginals in the 17th century. It is wing shaped, the strings (one to each note) being at an angle of 45° to the keyboard.

spinning The process of converting cleaned and straightened fibres into yarn by twisting overlapping fibres together. Yarn was made originally by drawing out a length of fibre from the mass and attaching it to a vertically hanging stick (spindle) that was weighted to help it spin round. This process was mechanized first by the spinning wheel (in Europe not until the 14th century). The inventions of *Hargreaves, *Arkwright, and *Crompton in the late 18th century industrialized the process. Modern spinning machines produce thousands of metres of yarn every hour. As applied to synthetic fibres, spinning is the extrusion of viscous solutions to form continuous filaments.

Spinoza, Benedict (*or* **Baruch de S.**; 1632–77) Dutch philosopher and theologian of Jewish parentage. Influenced by the writings of *Descartes, *Hobbes, and Giordano Bruno (1548–1600), Spinoza rejected the concepts of the personal nature of God and the immortality of the soul. The Jewish community of his native Amsterdam expelled him in 1656 on account of his unorthodoxy and his *Tractatus Theologico-Politicus* (1670) was furiously attacked by Christian scholars. The idea of God as the basis of all things was, however, central to his philosophy. His major work, generally known as the *Ethics*, could only be published posthumously in 1677.

Spiraea A genus of shrubs (about 100 species), widely distributed in N temperate regions. Many are cultivated as ornamentals, including the willow spiraea (*S. salcifolia*), which bears dense clusters of small pink flowers. Family: *Rosaceae*.

spirochaete A bacterium belonging to the order *Spirochaetales*. Spirochaetes are corkscrew-shaped and flexible: they swim by means of bending and looping motions, achieved by contraction of a bundle of fibrils within the cell. Some spirochaetes cause diseases, including syphilis and yaws in humans.

Spirogyra A genus of *green algae, also called mermaid's tresses or pond scum, in the form of threadlike strands of connected cells up to about 30 cm long. Large masses may be found floating near the surface of quiet fresh waters. Reproduction is asexual (by fragmentation) or sexual (*see* CONJUGATION).

Spitsbergen *See* SVALBARD.

spitz One of a group of dog breeds originating in N Eurasia and having a thick coat, small pricked ears, and a brushlike tail carried over the back. The Finnish spitz, bred in Finland as a hunting and guard dog, has a reddish-brown or yellowish-red coat.

spleen A rubbery dark-red organ, about 14 cm long, situated in the abdomen just beneath the lower border of the left side of the rib cage. The spleen assists in the body's defence mechanisms by producing antibodies in newborn babies and by absorbing and digesting bacteria in the bloodstream. It also removes worn-out and abnormal red blood cells and other particles from the circulation. The spleen becomes enlarged in some diseases, including liver disease and severe infections.

Split (Italian name: Spalato) 43 31N 16 28N A port in SE Croatia, on the Adriatic Sea. The vast

3rd-century AD Palace of Diocletian contains the present-day city centre, including the cathedral, which was Diocletian's mausoleum. It has a university (1974) and diverse industries. Population (2001): 173 692.

sponge An aquatic invertebrate animal belonging to the phylum *Porifera* (about 5000 species). Most sponges are marine, found attached to rocks or the sea bed, and measure up to several metres across: they may be treelike, cylindrical, or flat irregular masses. Sponges have an internal skeleton of lime, silica, or a fibrous protein (spongin). Bath sponges are spongin skeletons without the living animals. The simplest type of sponge has a vase-shaped body with a pore at the top and smaller pores in the sides. The inside is lined with special cells, which maintain a flow of water in through the side pores and out at the top. Food particles in the water are extracted by these cells; other cells in the body wall digest food, secrete the skeleton, and produce eggs and sperm. Fertilized eggs are dispersed in the water current and the free-swimming larvae eventually settle and become new sponges. The animals can also reproduce asexually, by budding or fragmentation.

spoonbill A long-legged wading bird belonging to a subfamily (*Plataleinae*; 6 species) occurring around estuaries and lakes in tropical and subtropical regions worldwide. 60–80 cm long, spoonbills are usually entirely white, often with a naked head. They feed on fish and crustaceans picked up by sweeping the large spatulate bill from side to side in mud or shallow water. Family: *Threskiornithidae* (ibises and spoonbills); order: *Ciconiiformes* (herons, storks, etc.).

spore The small, often single-celled, reproductive unit of plants, algae, fungi, protozoa, and bacteria, which may serve either as a rapid means of propagation or as a dormant stage in the life cycle. Spores may be produced sexually or asexually, i.e. fusion of sex cells (gametes) may or may not occur before their formation. In plants exhibiting an *alternation of generations spores are formed by the sporophyte following meiosis and give rise to the gametophyte, which produces the sex cells.

sporophyte *See* ALTERNATION OF GENERATIONS.

sporozoan A microscopic single-celled organism of the phylum *Apicomplexa* (formerly *Sporozoa*; *see* PROTOZOA), all of which are parasites with complex life cycles involving asexual and sexual forms of reproduction. They are often found in the intestinal tracts or blood of animals and form resistant spores or cysts, which can remain dormant until entering a suitable host.

sprat A small food fish, *Clupea* (*Sprattus*) *sprattus*, that is similar and related to the herring. It lives in shoals in the E Atlantic, N Mediterranean, and British coastal waters. The young are known as whitebait.

springbok A rare antelope, *Antidorcas marsupialis*, inhabiting arid regions of S Africa. It has a white face with a black line along each side of the muzzle and a patch of white hairs on the rump, which can be flashed as an alarm signal.

Springsteen, Bruce (1949–) US rock singer and guitarist. Born in New Jersey, he built up a huge following with songs describing working-class US life and with his energetic live performances; his albums include *Born to Run* (1975), *Born in the USA* (1984), *The Ghost of Tom Joad* (1995), and *The Rising* (2002).

spruce A coniferous tree of the genus *Picea* (about 50 species), widely distributed in the N hemisphere. Its needles grow in spirals and leave peglike projections on the shoots when they fall. The woody cones hang down from the branches. An important and widely grown timber tree is the Norway spruce (*Picea abies*), from N and central Europe; the timber is known as white wood or deal. Young specimens are used as Christmas trees in Britain. Family: *Pinaceae*.

spurge *See* EUPHORBIA.

Sputnik A series of Soviet unmanned satellites, the first of which was the first spacecraft to be launched (4 October 1957).

Square Deal A programme of economic and social reform intended by Theodore *Roosevelt (president 1901–09) to benefit the "plain man" in the USA. It sponsored improved labour conditions, regulations regarding food, and antimonopoly legislation.

squash The fruit of certain plants belonging to the genus *Cucurbita* (15 species), especially *C. maxima*. Native to the New World, squash plants are widely cultivated, producing fleshy edible fruits. They are usually served as a cooked vegetable. Family: *Cucurbitaceae*. *Compare* GOURD; PUMPKIN.

squash rackets A racket-and-ball game played in a four-walled court. Players hit the ball with the object of making a shot that the opponent cannot return. (When the ball is played it must hit the front wall of the court

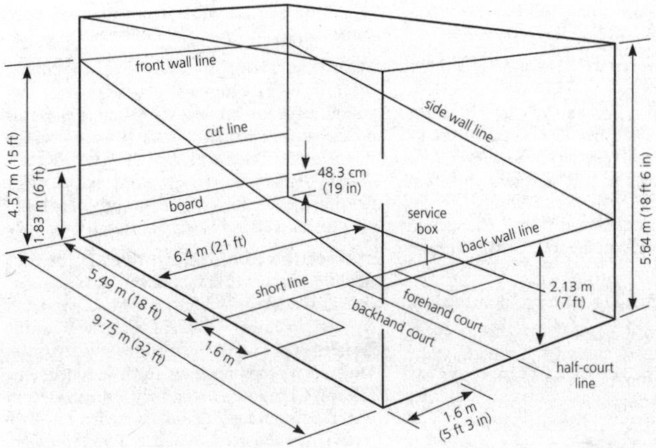

squash rackets. The dimensions of the court.

and may hit any other wall.) The service goes to the winner of the previous point. The British competitive version is a singles game going to nine or sometimes more points and only the server may score.

squid A *cephalopod mollusc of the order *Decapoda*. Surrounding the mouth, squids have ten arms bearing suckers; two arms are long tentacles used for capturing prey. Their tapering bodies have fins on either side. Squids feed on fish and molluscs, using a siphon to produce a jet of water to dart forwards. The giant squid (genus *Architeuthis*) can reach 20 m in length.

squint (*or* **strabismus**) A condition in which both the eyes cannot focus on the same object at the same time. This may be caused by paralysis of one of the nerves moving the eye, in which case the squint is often temporary. Nonparalytic squints are often seen in children and may be corrected.

squirrel A *rodent belonging to the family *Sciuridae*, which includes ground squirrels, *flying squirrels, and tree squirrels, distributed worldwide. The grey squirrel (*Sciurus carolinensis*), native to North America but now found in most parts of the world, is an agile climber with a long bushy balancing tail. Grey squirrels feed chiefly on nuts, berries, and buds and have become a pest of orchards and gardens. *See also* RED SQUIRREL.

Sri Lanka, Democratic Socialist Republic of (name until 1972: Ceylon) An island country in the Indian Ocean, to the E of the S tip of the Indian subcontinent. Broad coastal plains rise to mountains in the S central part of the island. There are two main groups: the Sinhalese majority, who are mainly Buddhists, and the Tamils, who are chiefly Hindus. *Economy*: predominantly agricultural, the chief activities being the processing and export of tea, rubber, and coconuts. The industrial sector has recently expanded. *History*: in 1505 the Portuguese established settlements in the W and S, which passed to the Dutch in the mid-17th century and to the British in 1798. In 1802 the island was made a separate crown colony. Following World War II Ceylon became a dominion (1948) within the British Commonwealth and in 1972 Sri Lanka became a republic under Sirimavo *Bandaranaika. Tension between the Sinhalese and Tamil communities erupted into open war in 1983, when the Tamil Tigers, a separatist militia, began to take control of the N and E. A Tamil separatist was responsible for the assassination of President Ranasinghe Premadasa in 1993. In 1994 Chandrika Kumaratunga was elected president and reinstated her mother, Sirimavo Bandaranaika, as prime minister. Ramasiri Wicknemanayake became prime minister following elections in 2000. A ceasefire with the Tamil Tigers was agreed in 2002 but the peace process was plunged into crisis in late 2003, when Kumaratunga suspended parliament and refused to implement plans giving the Tamil areas greater autonomy. Official language: Sinhala. Currency: Sri Lanka rupee of 100 cents. Area: 65 610 sq km

S

(25 332 sq mi). Population (2003 est): 19 665 000. Capital: Colombo.

SS (German: Schutzstaffel, Defence Squad) The Nazi military corps created in 1925 as Hitler's bodyguard and commanded by Heinrich Himmler from 1929. The SS, or Blackshirts, by the mid-1930s controlled the Nazis' security system, including the *Gestapo, concentration camp guards, and the Waffen SS, an elite corps of combat troops in World War II. The activities of the SS were condemned at the Nuremburg trials (1946).

St Names beginning St are listed under Saint.

Staffordshire A county in the Midlands of England. It consists mainly of undulating lowlands rising to moorlands in the N, with the River Trent flowing SE. Agriculture is important, especially dairy farming. Industries include the manufacture of pottery, which became famous during the 18th century, especially through the work of Josiah *Wedgwood. Coalmining was formerly important. In 1974 the industrial area in the S passed to the new metropolitan county of the West Midlands. Stoke-on-Trent became an independent unitary authority in 1997. Area (excluding Stoke-on-Trent): 2624 sq km (1013 sq mi). Population (2001, excluding Stoke-on-Trent): 806 737. Administrative centre: Stafford.

Staffordshire bull terrier A breed of dog developed from a bulldog-terrier cross as a pit dog. It is stockily built with a broad deep head and a short smooth coat that may be of various colours. Height: 35–40 cm (English).

stag beetle A beetle belonging to a family (*Lucanidae*; about 900 species) occurring mostly in the tropical regions. The males have well-developed mandibles that in many species resemble antlers. They are used during combat with other males. Most stag beetles are black or brown, although tropical species are often more colourful.

S

stagecoach A large horse-drawn coach for four or six horses (mules in some countries) used for scheduled transport of passengers and mail in W Europe and in America from the second half of the 18th century. Stagecoaches disappeared with the advent of rail travel.

staghorn fern A *fern of the genus *Platycerium*, which grows upon other plants but is not a parasite. The fronds fork repeatedly into long pointed leaflets, resembling antlers, and the spore capsules are borne on their undersides. The fern, which is native to most warm regions, is cultivated as a pot plant. Family: *Polypodiaceae*.

stainless steel An alloy *steel containing up to 20% chromium and 10% nickel. It is corrosion resistant because the oxide that forms on the surface remains intact and protects the metal, unlike other steels in which it flakes off. Stainless steel is used in a wide variety of engineering applications where this property is important, as well as in kitchen utensils.

stalactites and stalagmites Deposits of calcium carbonate in limestone caves; stalactites are conical or cylindrical projections from the cave roof, while stalagmites grow upwards from the floor and are generally more stumpy. They sometimes meet to form a continuous column. They are gradually formed from water containing calcium bicarbonate dripping from the roof. When the water evaporates a solid residue of calcium carbonate is left.

Stalin, Joseph (J. Dzhugashvili; 1879–1953) Soviet statesman. Born in Georgia, Stalin (whose adopted name means "man of steel") became a Marxist in the 1890s. In 1903 he joined the *Bolsheviks under *Lenin and in the years preceding the Russian Revolution (1917) was repeatedly imprisoned and exiled. In 1922 he became general secretary of the Communist Party. After Lenin's death in 1924 Stalin struggled to eliminate his rivals, above all *Trotsky, and emerged as supreme dictator in 1929. He abandoned Lenin's New Economic Policy, initiating a series of five-year plans to enforce, with great brutality, the collectivization of industry and agriculture. The 1930s saw a reign of terror, culminating in the great purge, in which Stalin sought to remove his real, or imagined, rivals. In World War II, Stalin became chairman of the Council of People's Commissars and, following Hitler's invasion of the Soviet Union (1941), reversed the German alliance of 1939. He attended Allied conferences at Tehran (1943) and at Yalta and Potsdam (1945). In the postwar years, when Stalin's autocracy intensified, he pursued a foreign policy of imperialism towards the communist countries of E Europe and unremitting hostility towards the noncommunist world. After his death many of Stalin's policies were denounced by the Soviet regime.

Stalingrad, Battle of (1942–43) A battle in World War II, in which the German 6th Army under Friedrich Paulus (1890–1957), having entered Stalingrad (now Volgograd), surrendered to the Russians under *Zhukov. The Germans lost 200 000 men.

stamen The part of a flower that produces the *pollen (male gametes). It comprises an anther, a lobed structure consisting of four pollen sacs, borne on a stalk (filament). The pollen develops within the sacs, which split open to release it. In self-pollinated flowers, the stamens open inwards, towards the pistil, but in cross-pollinated flowers they open outwards. *See also* FLOWER.

Stamford Bridge 53 59N 0 55W A village in N England, in the East Riding of Yorkshire on the River Derwent. Here King Harold defeated his brother Tostig and King Harald of Norway in 1066, three weeks before his own defeat at Hastings by William the Conqueror. Population (1991): 3099.

Stamp Act (1765) The first British Act that imposed direct taxes on documents, newspapers, and dice in the American colonies. Parliament was forced by colonial hostility to repeal the Act but asserted its right to impose laws on the colonies (Declaratory Act, 1766), thus aggravating the opposition that led to the *American Revolution.

standard deviation *See* VARIANCE.

Stanislavsky, Konstantin (K. Alekseyev; 1863–1938) Russian actor and theatre director. As director of the Moscow Art Theatre, which he cofounded in 1898, he developed an innovatory style of naturalistic production. His theories about acting, later developed in the USA as "method" acting at the *Actors' Studio, emphasized the actor's complete identification with his or her character.

Stanley 51 45S 57 56W The capital of the Falkland Islands, in NE East Falkland Island on the Atlantic Ocean. It was the focal point of the Falklands War of 1982. Population (1991): 1643.

Stanley, Sir Henry Morton (1841–1904) British explorer and journalist. He went to the USA in 1859, joined the *New York Herald*, and in 1871 was sent to search for David *Livingstone in Africa. Having found him at Ujiji, the two men explored Lake Tanganyika together. On a second expedition (1874–77) Stanley followed the Congo River to its mouth. By obtaining Belgian sponsorship for exploration in the Congo he was instrumental in securing Belgian sovereignty over the Congo Free State.

Stansted 51 54N 0 12E A village in SE England, E of London in Essex. It is the site of London's third airport. Population (1991): 4943.

Staphylococcus A genus of spherical bacteria. *S. aureus* is responsible for boils and mastitis, *S. pyogenes* infects wounds, and certain strains cause acute food poisoning.

star A luminous celestial body that is composed of gas and that derives its energy from thermonuclear reactions in its hot dense core. The sun is a typical star: stellar mass usually ranges from about 0.05 to 60 times the sun's mass. The higher the mass, the brighter, hotter, and larger the star and the shorter its life. Young stars evolve from the *protostar stage when they begin to generate energy by the thermonuclear fusion of hydrogen to form helium. This continues for some 10^{10} years for stars of solar mass but for only a few million years for the most massive stars. When the hydrogen is exhausted, stars evolve into *giant stars, those of near solar mass becoming *red giants, and further thermonuclear reactions occur. A low-mass star finally evolves to a *white dwarf. More massive stars explode as supernovae. Stars are not distributed uniformly throughout the universe, but are grouped into enormous assemblies, called *galaxies, as a result of gravitational forces. The nearest star to the sun is 4.3 light years away.

starch A carbohydrate that is an important storage product of many plants. Chemically it consists of linked glucose units. Starch occurs naturally as white powdery granules that are insoluble in cold water but form a gelatinous solution in hot water. Plants manufacture starch by photosynthesis and it is a major constituent of seeds, fruits, roots, and tubers and a major source of dietary energy for animals and man.

Star Chamber, Court of A court, originating in the king's council of medieval England, that met in the Star Chamber at Westminster Palace. It was concerned chiefly with breaches of the peace. Its misuse by Charles I to enforce his unpopular policies led to its abolition (1641) by the *Long Parliament on the eve of the Civil War.

starfish A marine invertebrate animal belonging to a worldwide class (*Asteroidea*; 1800 species) of *echinoderms. Its fleshy star-shaped body is covered with a spiny skin and has five or more radiating arms. Starfish occur on shores and ocean floors and move slowly, using saclike tube feet on the underside of the arms. They feed mainly on molluscs and other invertebrates.

starling A noisy sharp-winged songbird, *Stur-*

nus vulgaris, having a black plumage speckled with iridescent purple, green, and white. It is a versatile bird, common on farmland, where it probes the soil for insects, and also in cities, where it is a scavenger. It is gregarious and commonly nests in flocks. Family: *Sturnidae*.

star-of-Bethlehem A spring-blooming perennial plant, *Ornithogalum umbellatum*, native to the Mediterranean and grown in gardens. Growing from a bulb, it has clusters of star-shaped white flowers striped with green. Family: *Liliaceae*.

star of David (Hebrew *magen David*; shield of David) A six-pointed star or hexagram, composed of two equilateral triangles. Widely used from antiquity as an ornament or magical sign, it has been regarded since the 17th century as a Jewish symbol, and was imposed on the Jews as a "badge of shame" by the Nazis. In 1897 it was officially adopted as an emblem of Zionism and it now appears on the flag of Israel.

States General In France, the assembly of representatives of the three estates—clergy, nobility, and the Third Estate or commons. It did not meet after 1614 until summoned by Louis XVI in 1789 on the eve of the *French Revolution. The Third Estate declared itself a National Assembly, which replaced the States General.

states of matter Matter has traditionally been seen as occurring in three states or phases, depending on temperature: in the *solid state mutual forces hold individual atoms firmly in place; in *liquids thermal movement partially overcomes these binding forces, so that the substance has no intrinsic shape; and in *gases molecules and individual atoms fly apart; the gas fills all the available volume. A fourth state is **plasma*, in which even atoms are dissociated into electrons and nuclei. In the universe as a whole, plasma is by far the most common state, as it occurs in stars and in galactic space. Transitions between phases may occur at distinct temperatures, melting/freezing points and evaporation/condensation points.

static electricity The effects created by electrical charges at rest. Current electricity is an effect resulting from a flow of electrons; in static electricity electrons from one object are pulled onto another object, usually by rubbing them together, but they do not flow. The effect can be observed with many nonconducting materials, for example a comb passing through dry hair. A force exists between two charged bodies (*see* ELECTRIC FIELD), attractive if they have opposite charges, repulsive if the charges are similar; the magnitude of the force is given by Coulomb's law (*see* ELECTRIC CHARGE).

statics *See* MECHANICS.

Stationery Office, The (**TSO**) The UK company that supplies all the stationery, office supplies, office machinery, and printing and binding needed for use in the civil service. It also publishes and sells government publications, including Acts of Parliament. Formerly known as Her Majesty's Stationery Office (HMSO), it was privatized in 1996.

Stations of the Cross A series of 14 pictures or images depicting the final events in the life of Christ, beginning at Pontius Pilate's house, where he was condemned to death, and concluding at the sepulchre. They are usually arranged on the walls of a church and form the basis of a devotion in which prayers are recited as each station is visited in turn. The devotion was popularized in the middle ages by the Franciscans but derived from the early custom of pilgrims who followed the Way of the Cross (Via Dolorosa) in Jerusalem.

statistics The study of methods for collecting and analysing quantitative data. The data measure certain characteristics of a group of people or objects, called the population; usually the whole population cannot be observed, often because it is too large, so data are collected from a representative sample of the population. The sample is analysed and conclusions are inferred about the whole population, using *probability theory because the inferences cannot be certain.

Statue of Liberty A statue of a woman 46 m (152 ft) high holding a torch in her raised right hand, on Liberty Island in New York harbour. Designed by Frédéric *Bartholdi, it was given to the Americans by the French in 1884 to commemorate the French and American Revolutions. Unveiled and dedicated in 1886, it has been a US national monument since 1924.

Stauffenberg, Claus, Graf von (1907–44) German army officer, who attempted to assassinate Hitler in 1944. Stauffenberg served in N Africa, where he was badly wounded. He tried to eliminate Hitler by bombing his headquarters at Rastenburg. He and his fellow conspirators were executed.

steady-state theory A cosmological theory proposed in 1948 by Hermann Bondi (1919–), Fred *Hoyle and Thomas Gold (1920–) in which the universe is regarded as having always existed in a steady state. The expansion of the universe is compensated by the continuous creation of new matter. On the present evidence this theory has been discredited in favour of the *big-bang theory.

steam engine A heat engine in which heat from a furnace is used to raise steam, the expansion of which forces a piston to move up and down in a cylinder to provide mechanical energy. A primitive steam engine was invented in 1698 by a Capt Savery to pump water from mines. In 1711 *Newcomen improved on this design but still relied on cooling the cylinder with a jet of water after each stroke. Watt's single-acting steam engine, patented in 1769, was the first to use a separate condenser. Watt went on to invent the double-acting engine, the crank and crosshead mechanism, and the governor. It was largely this engine that created the *industrial revolution. The steam engine was the supreme prime mover of railways throughout the world from 1829 (when *Stephenson built his first *locomotive) until after World War II, when steam was largely replaced by electric and Diesel-electric trains. From the beginning of the 19th century steam engines were also widely used in place of sails in *ships. Moreover, it was the steam engine that drove the first electricity generators for public supply. However, the more compact and efficient steam *turbine has now replaced the steam engine for this purpose.

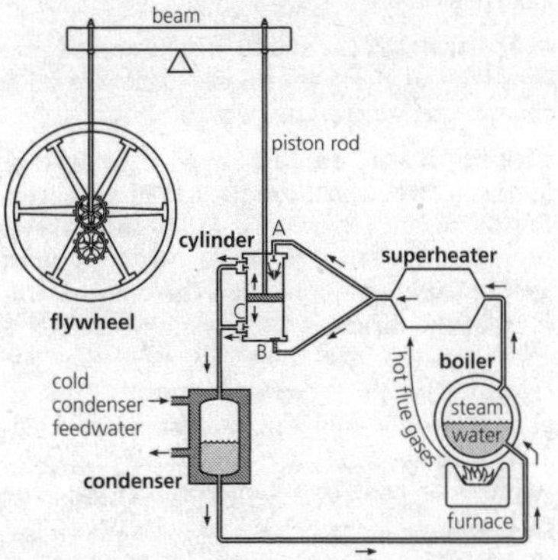

steam engine. The principle of a double-action beam engine of the kind patented by James Watt. During the first half of the cycle, valve A opens, steam flows in and pushes the cylinder down, and steam flows out to the condenser through valve C. During the second half of the cycle, B opens and the steam pushes the piston the other way.

steel An *alloy of iron containing a small carefully controlled proportion of carbon, usually less than 1%. Carbon steels contain principally iron and carbon. Alloy steels have other metals added. Steel products form the basis of modern technology and steel production is therefore a key factor in the world economy. For many engineering products the starting material is **mild steel**, a carbon steel with between 0.2% and 0.8% carbon and sometimes a little manganese or silicon. It can be further improved by *heat treatment. Alloy steels, such as *stainless steel, are usually more expensive to produce. They are used where special hardness, strength, or corrosion resistance are needed.

Steel is made by *smelting iron ore in a blast furnace to produce pig iron, which is added to melted down scrap iron before being converted by the basic-oxygen process, or formerly by the *Bessemer process, the open-hearth furnace, or the electric-arc furnace.

Steel, David (Martin Scott), Baron (1938–) British politician; leader of the Liberal Party (1976–88). He entered parliament in 1964 and succeeded Jeremy Thorpe as Liberal leader. In the 1980s he headed the SDP-Liberal Alliance alongside the SDP leader, David Owen. He was raised to the peerage in 1997 and elected presiding officer of the new Scottish parliament (1999–2003).

Steele, Sir Richard (1672–1729) British essayist and dramatist. He is best remembered for his essays in *The Tatler* (1709–11) and *The Spectator* (1711–12), periodicals that he founded and on which he collaborated with Joseph *Addison.

steeplechase 1. A form of horse race that grew out of *foxhunting, in which horses jump artificial hedges and ditches. Hurdling is a less taxing version over lower lighter fences and shorter distances. Point-to-points are steeplechases for amateur riders. **2.** A track event for men in athletics over a 3000 m course that includes 28 hurdles 91 cm (3 ft) high and seven water jumps 3.66 m (12 ft) across per lap. World record: 8 minutes 2.08 seconds (1992) by Moses Kiptanui (Kenya).

Stegosaurus A dinosaur of the late Jurassic period (about 150–135 million years ago). 7 m long and weighing 1.75 tonnes, it had a double row of large triangular plates arranged in pairs along its back. It fed on soft plants. Order: *Ornithischia*.

Steinbeck, John (1902–68) US novelist. The

majority of his novels, notably *Of Mice and Men* (1937) and *The Grapes of Wrath* (1939), deal with the social and economic conditions of his native California. *East of Eden* (1952) is the most ambitious of his later novels. He won the Nobel Prize in 1962.

stem cells Simple cells in the body that give rise to specialized cells when stimulated by growth factors and other chemical signals produced by the body. Stem cells occur in the embryo, where they continually divide to produce all the many different tissues required by the developing embryo. They are also found at various sites in the adult body (including skin, bone, muscle, and intestine) to provide replacement cells for the repair of tissues at those sites. For example, stem cells in the bone marrow are active throughout life, providing a continual supply of new blood cells as the old ones wear out. Much interest now focuses on the potential of stem cells to treat disease or repair injured tissue. Adult stem cells, such as bone marrow cells, are already used in treating leukaemia and other diseases of blood cells, by forming new healthy cells to replace the defective ones, as are tissue-matched cord-blood stem cells, taken from the umbilical cord of a new-born baby. Other disorders that might benefit from stem-cell therapy include diabetes, Parkinson's disease, and spinal injury. Embryonic stem cells are particularly attractive since they can produce many different types of cells and – triggered by the appropriate chemical signals—begin producing the required tissue cells wherever they are inserted. Human embryos cloned from a person's cells could, in theory, provide genetically identical therapeutic stem cells that would not be rejected by that person's immune system. But technical hurdles and ethical objections lie in the way of attaining this goal. In 2002 the UK became one of the first countries to license stem-cell research, subject to strict guidelines. This would include the use of spare embryos generated by IVF techniques as well as—if there is an exceptional need—embryos produced by therapeutic cloning.

Stendhal (Henri Beyle; 1783–1842) French novelist and critic. His two major novels, *Le Rouge et le noir* (1830) and *La Chartreuse de Parme* (1839), blend romantic vigour with dispassionate and often ironical psychological analysis.

Stentor A genus of tiny single-celled organisms (*see* PROTOZOA) occurring in fresh water. They are trumpet-shaped, with tracts of hair-like cilia over the body surface, and are often attached by a stalk to the substrate. Phylum: *Ciliophora*.

Stephanotis A genus of evergreen climbing shrubs (5 species), native to Madagascar, and including some ornamental species. *S. floribunda* is a popular greenhouse plant with small fragrant white waxy flowers. Family: *Asclepiadaceae*.

Stephen (c. 1097–1154) King of England (1135–54); grandson of William the Conqueror. Stephen seized the throne from Henry I's daughter Matilda, who invaded England in 1139. Civil war followed. In 1152, after much of the country had been ravaged in factional fighting and the royal administration had broken down, Stephen recognized Matilda's son Henry (later Henry II) as heir to the throne.

Stephenson, George (1781–1848) British engineer, who developed a greatly improved steam locomotive. Stephenson became interested in locomotives in 1813 and two years later built the *Blucher*, which could draw 30 tons of coal at 4 mph. He assisted his son **Robert Stephenson** (1803–59) on his famous locomotive the *Rocket*, built in 1829. It carried passengers at a speed of 36 mph on the new Liverpool–Manchester line and stimulated railway development throughout Europe and in North America.

steppes The midlatitude grasslands of Eurasia extending in a broad belt from Ukraine to SW Siberia. They consist chiefly of level, virtually treeless, plains.

steradian (sr) The SI unit of solid angle equal to a solid angle that encloses a surface on a sphere equal to the square of its radius.

stereophonic sound Sound reproduction in which two signals are used to give a directional quality. It results in more realistic reproduction than a single signal system (monophonic sound) because the brain distinguishes the direction by assessing the difference between the sound in each ear. For recording, either two directional *microphones at right angles in one place or two separated microphones are needed. Playing back requires at least two *loudspeakers, one for each signal.

sterility Inability to produce offspring by sexual reproduction. Sterility (*or* infertility) in men may be caused by various conditions in which the sperms are deficient in numbers or defective in quality. It may also result from psychological problems causing impotence. In women sterility may be due to disease of the womb, blockage of the Fallopian tubes leading from the ovaries to the womb, or failure of the ovaries to produce egg cells. *See also* STERILIZATION.

sterilization The surgical technique or any other means used to induce *sterility. Surgical sterilization may be performed for contraceptive purposes or when pregnancy would damage the health of the woman. For men, the operation—vasectomy—involves cutting and tying the duct (vas deferens) that conveys sperm from the testicle. In women the Fallopian tubes are clipped or tied (tubal ligation), which prevents the passage of the egg cells to the womb. Neither operation affects sexual desire or the ability to satisfy it. Sterilization should be considered as irreversible. *See also* CASTRATION.

Stern, Isaac (1920–2001) Russian-born US violinist, who became a world-famous soloist and toured extensively.

Sterne, Laurence (1713–68) Irish-born British novelist and clergyman, best known for his eccentric comic novel *Tristram Shandy* (1759–67). *A Sentimental Journey* (1768) was based on his travels on the Continent.

steroids A class of organic chemical compounds with a basic structure of three six-membered carbon rings joined to a five-membered ring. Steroids and their hydroxy derivatives (**sterols**) fulfil many biological roles in plants and animals and include the *sex hormones, *corticosteroids, *bile acids, and *vitamin D. Cholesterol is an important precursor in the synthesis of many steroids.

stethoscope An instrument widely used by doctors to listen to sounds within the body. Modern instruments consist of two earpieces joined by two tubes to a head, which is placed on the body. The head usually has a diaphragm (for high-pitched sounds) and a bell (for low-pitched sounds). More sophisticated stethoscopes are fitted with electronic amplification devices.

Stevenage 51 55N 0 14W A town in SE England, in Hertfordshire. The first of the new towns (1946) to be developed after World War II, it is now a centre for electrical and aerospace industries. Population (1997 est): 78 114.

Stevens, Wallace (1879–1955) US poet. In such poems as "The Man with the Blue Guitar" (1937) he explores the relationship between reality and imagination. His poems were collected in *Collected Poems* (1954) and *Opus Posthumus* (1957).

Stevenson, Adlai E(wing) (1900–65) US Democratic politician, governor of Illinois (1949–53). He twice ran for the presidency (1952, 1956) but was defeated on both occasions by Eisenhower. He helped to found the UN, to which he was later US delegate (1961–65).

Stevenson, Robert Louis (1850–94) Scottish novelist. After travels in Europe and the USA, he published several novels that remain among the best-known in the language: *Treasure Island* (1883), *Kidnapped* (1886), and *The Strange Case of Dr Jekyll and Mr Hyde* (1886). Constantly troubled by respiratory disease, he travelled to the South Seas in 1888. His other works include the unfinished masterpiece *Weir of Hermiston* (1896).

Stewart, James (Maitland) (1908–97) US film actor. He established himself as an incorruptible hero with a distinctive drawl in such films as *Mr Smith Goes to Washington* (1939), *The Philadelphia Story* (1940), and *It's a Wonderful Life* (1946); later films include Hitchcock's *Vertigo* (1958).

stick insect An insect belonging to the family *Phasmidae.* It has a twiglike body and long spindly legs and the wings are reduced or absent. Males are rare; the females live in trees or shrubs, producing eggs that drop to the ground and develop without fertilization (*see* PARTHENOGENESIS). Order: *Phasmida* (stick and leaf insects).

stickleback A fish of the family *Gasterosteidae* (about 12 species), found in both fresh and salt water in temperate regions of the N hemisphere. Sticklebacks have a row of spines along the back. The male builds a nest for the eggs and guards the young. Order: *Gasterosteiformes.*

stigma The part of the pistil of a flower that is specialized to receive *pollen. In flowers pollinated by insects the stigma is sticky, whereas wind-pollinated flowers have large feathery stigmas.

stimulants A large group of drugs that stimulate activity of the nervous system. Caffeine (in tea and coffee) and nicotine (in cigarettes) are stimulants used widely to reduce feelings of tiredness and to improve concentration. Hallucinogens, *amphetamine, and *cocaine are also stimulants. Stimulants may affect other parts of the body, particularly the heart.

stingray A round or diamond-shaped *ray fish belonging to a family (*Dasyatidae*; 89 species) found mainly in warm shallow ocean waters. Most species have a whiplike tail armed with one or more saw-edged venomous spines, which can inflict an intensely painful wound causing paralysis and occasionally death.

stinkhorn A fungus of the order *Phallales*, producing a phallus-shaped fruiting body. This consists of a stout whitish stalk arising from a basal egg-shaped structure and bearing a thimble-shaped cap containing spores. When the spores are ripe the cap produces a strong-smelling secretion that attracts flies, which disperse the spores. Phylum: *Basidiomycota*.

Stirling 1. 56 07N 3 57W A city in Scotland, the administrative centre of Stirling council area on the River Forth. It was once a residence of the Scottish kings and the first Scottish parliament was held here in 1326. The castle occupies a prominent position. Stirling is a market town with financial and other services. It was granted city status in 2002. Population (1997 est): 30 791. **2.** A council area of central Scotland. In 1975 the historic county of Stirling was abolished; most of it was incorporated into a new Stirling district in Central Region. In 1996 this district became an independent unitary authority. Agriculture has declined but is still important; coal is no longer mined. The main economic activities are now administration, finance, and tourism. Area: 2173 sq km (839 sq mi). Population (2001): 86 212. Administrative centre: Stirling.

Stirling engine An external combustion piston engine using heated air as the working fluid. Heat is transferred to the cylinders by heat exchangers. The engine is silent and vibration-free, uses many types of fuel economically, and can produce clean exhaust gases. It was invented in 1816 by the clergyman Robert Stirling (1790–1878), but was not put to practical use until the 1960s, when it was used as an auxiliary engine in submarines.

stoat A small carnivorous mammal, *Mustela erminea*, of Europe, Asia, and North America. About 35 cm long, with a long sinuous body, flattish head, and short legs, it can be distinguished from a *weasel by its black-tipped tail. Stoats prey mainly on rabbits.

stock One of several herbaceous plants of the genus *Matthiola* that are cultivated as ornamentals. Many garden varieties, including ten-week stocks and Brompton stocks, are derived from the European biennial *M. incana*, which has clusters of purple flowers. The night-scented stock (*M. bicornis*) has small lilac flowers that emit their fragrance at night. Family: *Cruciferae*.

stock exchange A market in which securities are bought and sold. The three largest stock exchanges are in London, New York, and Tokyo. A stock exchange is an essential part of the capital market, providing capital for industry and a form of investment for savers. Members of the London Stock Exchange, founded in 1773, were formerly either stockbrokers or stockjobbers, but this distinction ceased to exist with the change in City practices known as the "Big Bang" (October 1986). Thereafter the market became a highly computerized free-for-all, in which commissions were negotiable. The **Alternative Investment Market** (AIM), established in 1995, deals with smaller and newer company shares.

Stockhausen, Karlheinz (1928–) German composer. He rejected traditional forms and techniques, developing a concept of music as a sequence of sound "events" in such works as *Gruppen* (for three orchestras; 1955–57) and *Kontra-Punkte* (for ten instruments; 1962). Such works as *Mantra* (for two pianos and percussion; 1970) were influenced by Indian mysticism. Later works include the operas *Donnerstag* (1978–80), *Montag* (1988), *Dienstag* (1991), and *Freitag* (1996).

Stockholm 59 20N 18 95E The capital of Sweden, built on several islands between Lake Mälar and the Baltic Sea. It is the country's second largest port. The old town contains many buildings erected in the middle ages and in the 16th and 17th centuries. A settlement from very early times, Stockholm became the capital in 1436. Population (2000 est): 743 703.

Stockport 1. 53 25N 2 10W A town in N England, in Stockport unitary authority, Greater Manchester, on the River Mersey. Traditionally a textile town (particularly for cotton), Stockport now has engineering, electronics, and high-tech industries. Population (1991): 132 813. **2.** A unitary authority in N England, in Greater Manchester. Area: 126 sq km (49 sq mi). Population (2001): 284 544.

stocks and shares Documents representing money invested in industrial and commercial corporations or loaned to a government. In the UK stocks represent fixed-interest loans made to the government (*see* GILT-EDGED SECURITY), foreign governments, local authorities, or companies (*see* DEBENTURE STOCK). Shares represent equal amounts of capital subscribed to a company in return for membership rights. Ordinary shareholders are the last to receive their *dividends, which fluctuate according to the level of profits. They usually have voting rights in the company. Shares in public companies can be bought and sold on a *stock exchange. In the USA ordinary shares are called common stock.

Stockton-on-Tees 1. 53 34N 1 19W A town in NE England, in Stockton-on-Tees unitary authority, Co Durham, on the River Tees. The first passenger railway was built from here to Darlington in 1825, and it was once an important port. Now retail and services are the chief employers. Population (1996 est): 82 800. **2.** A unitary authority in NE England, in Co Durham and North Yorkshire; from 1974 to 1996 it was part of the county of Cleveland. Area: 195 sq km (75 sq mi). Population (2001): 178 405.

Stoicism The philosophical school founded about 300 BC in Athens by *Zeno of Citium. Stoics believed that God (identified with reason) was the basis of the universe, that human souls were sparks of the divine fire, and that the wise man lived "in harmony with nature." Knowledge of virtue was all-important. Stoicism was subsequently modified to stress the primacy of active virtue and duty. Its doctrines influenced many later thinkers.

Stoke-on-Trent 1. 53 00N 2 10W A city in N central England, in Stoke-on-Trent unitary authority, Staffordshire, on the River Trent. Formed in 1910 by the amalgamation of five towns, the area is known as the Potteries and is the centre of the British ceramic industry. Population (1991): 266 543. **2.** A unitary authority in N central England, in Staffordshire. Area: 93 sq km (36 sq mi). Population (2001): 240 643.

stomach A muscular sac, just beneath the diaphragm, that opens from the oesophagus (gullet) and leads to the duodenum (part of the small intestine). The stomach secretes gastric juice, containing hydrochloric acid and the enzyme *pepsin, which continue the digestion of food that started in the mouth. Release of acid is triggered in response to the presence of food. The churning action of the stomach ensures constant mixing of the food and its secretions.

Stone Age The cultural phase during which man relied on stone, supplemented by wood, bone, or antler, as material for weapons and tools. It is the earliest phase in a system devised (1816) for classifying human technological progress (*compare* BRONZE AGE; IRON AGE). The Stone Age is subdivided into Old (*see* PALAEOLITHIC), Middle (*see* MESOLITHIC), and New (*see* NEOLITHIC).

stonechat A small *chat, *Saxicola torquata*, occurring in Eurasia and N Africa and feeding chiefly on insects and their larvae. The male has a dark-brown head and back, chestnut underparts, and white rump; the female is a drabber brown. Stonechats favour dry heathland regions.

stonecrop An annual or perennial herb belonging to the genus *Sedum* (600 species), found in N temperate regions and also in Central and South America. They have white, pink, or yellow flowers. Some are popular ornamentals. Family: *Crassulaceae*.

stone curlew A ground-nesting bird belonging to a widely distributed family (*Burhinidae*; 9 species) characterized by thickened tarsal joints, also called thickknee. Stone curlews are typically nocturnal, feeding on beetles, worms, etc. Order: *Charadriiformes* (gulls, plovers, etc.).

stonefly An insect of the order *Plecoptera* (3000 species), 6–60 mm long with long antennae and two pairs of membranous wings. The short-lived adults rarely feed and are found near fresh water. The aquatic *nymphs feed on plants, decaying organic material, or other insects.

Stonehenge A famous megalithic structure on Salisbury Plain in Wiltshire (England). Sarsens and bluestones, the latter probably brought from S Wales, are set upright in concentric circles and horseshoes the orientation of which suggests one purpose as being sun and moon observation. It was erected in three main phases between c. 3000 and c. 1600 BC. The alleged "Druid" connection dates only from the 18th century AD. See illustration on p. 846. *See also* MEGALITH.

stone pine A *pine tree, *Pinus pinea*, native to SW Europe and Asia but planted throughout Mediterranean regions since Roman times for its edible seeds. Up to 30 m high, it has cones about 12.5 cm long.

Stopes, Marie (Charlotte Carmichael) (1880–1958) British birth-control campaigner. She worked as a botanist until the failure of her first marriage turned her attention to sexual problems. In 1921 she opened the first birth-control clinic in Britain. Her books include *Married Love* (1918) and *Contraception: Its Theory, History, and Practice* (1923).

Stoppard, Sir Tom (Thomas Straussler; 1937–) British dramatist, born in Czechoslovakia. He achieved international success with *Rosencrantz and Guildenstern Are Dead* (1967). In *Jumpers* (1972), *Travesties* (1975), *The Real Thing* (1982), *Arcadia* (1993), and *The Invention of Love*

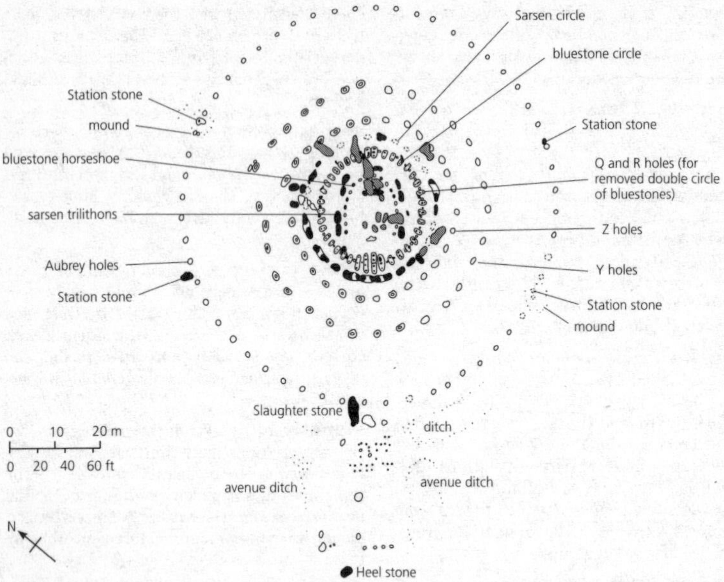

Stonehenge. The plan reveals features of consecutive building phases that may no longer be visible to the visitor to the site.

(1997) he explored philosophical ideas with wit and great verbal facility. His most recent work is the trilogy *The Coast of Utopia* (2002). He has also written television, radio, and film scripts, including *Shakespeare in Love* (1999; with Marc Norman). Stoppard was appointed to the OM in 2000.

storax A tree or shrub belonging to the genus *Styrax* (130 species), occurring in warm and tropical regions. They have small white flowers and several species are cultivated as ornamentals. The resin storax, used in cough mixtures, pastilles, etc., is extracted from trees of the genus *Liquidambar* (sweet gums). Family: *Styracaceae.*

stork A large bird belonging to a widely distributed family (*Ciconiidae*; 17 species) occurring in warm and temperate regions. 60–150 cm tall, storks have long necks, legs, and bill and are white with black markings. They feed chiefly on fish, frogs, molluscs, and insects and build a large nest platform of twigs in a tree or on a rooftop. Order: *Ciconiiformes* (herons, storks, flamingos). *See also* ADJUTANT STORK; MARABOU.

storksbill A herb of the genus *Erodium* (about 90 species) occurring in Eurasia, Australia, and South America. The common storksbill (*E. cicutarium*) grows to a height of 60 cm and has purplish-pink flowers. Family: *Geraniaceae.*

Stormont The seat of the government of Northern Ireland, in Belfast; the site includes Stormont Castle, Parliament House (1932), and Dundonald House (1963). From 1921 until 1972 it housed the parliament of Northern Ireland and the residence of its prime minister and was a symbol of Protestant domination. Since 1998 Parliament House has been the seat of the Northern Ireland Assembly, set up under the Good Friday Agreement of that year.

storm petrel A small seabird belonging to a family (*Hydrobatidae*; 20 species) occurring in all oceans. 13–25 cm long, storm petrels have dark-grey or brown plumage, often with paler underparts. Species of southern oceans feed by "walking" on the water with wings outstretched, picking up plankton. Northern species feed by swooping on fish. Order: *Procellariiformes* (petrels).

Stornoway 58 12N 6 23W A port in NW Scotland, in the Outer Hebrides, on the Isle of

S

Lewis. It is the administrative centre of the Western Isles Islands Area. Population (1991): 5975.

Stowe, Harriet Beecher (1811–96) US novelist. She was the daughter of Lyman Beecher (1775–1863), a famous preacher. Her *Uncle Tom's Cabin* (1852) greatly stimulated antislavery feeling.

Strabane A district in Northern Ireland, in Co Tyrone. Area: 861 sq km (332 sq mi). Population (2001): 38 248.

strabismus *See* SQUINT.

Stradivari, Antonio (?1644–1737) Italian violin maker. He was a pupil of Niccolò *Amati. From 1666 he and two of his sons made outstanding violins, violas, and cellos at their workshop in Cremona.

strain In physics, the deformation of a body when it is subjected to a *stress. **Longitudinal strain** is the extension per unit length when a body is stretched; **bulk strain** is the volume change per unit volume when a body is compressed; and **shear strain** is an angular measure of deformation.

strangeness A property of matter, expressed as a *quantum number (*s*), postulated to account for the unusually long lifetime of some *hadrons. In the quark model (*see* PARTICLE PHYSICS) strange hadrons contain the strange quark or its antiquark.

Strasbourg (German name: Strassburg) 48 35N 7 45E A city in NE France, on the River Ill. An important inland port, it is famous for its *pâté de foie gras*. *History*: made a free imperial city in the 13th century, it was ceded to France in 1697. Captured by the Germans (1871), it was returned to France after World War I. Population (1999): 263 940.

Stratford-on-Avon 52 12N 1 41W A town in central England, in Warwickshire on the River Avon. It is the birthplace of William Shakespeare. The Royal Shakespeare Theatre (opened in 1932) stages mainly Shakespeare's plays. Population (1991): 22 231.

stratigraphy The branch of geology concerned with the formation, composition, sequence in time, and spatial correlation of stratified rocks. **Lithostratigraphy** involves the lithological and spatial relations of rock units. **Biostratigraphy** utilizes fossils in calibrating rock successions. **Chronostratigraphy** studies rock bodies according to the time of their formation (*see* GEOLOGICAL TIME SCALE).

stratocumulus cloud (Sc) A low type of *cloud composed of dark grey globular masses, often forming extensive sheets.

stratosphere *See* ATMOSPHERE.

stratus cloud A low type of *cloud forming below 2400 m (7874 ft), having a grey uniform appearance; it may actually occur at ground level as hill fog.

Strauss, Richard (1864–1949) German composer and conductor. Strauss was much influenced by *Wagner, whose use of leitmotifs he adopted. From 1887 to 1899 Strauss wrote a series of symphonic poems, including *Death and Transfiguration* (1889), *Also sprach Zarathustra* (1895–96), and *Ein Heldenleben* (1898). He then turned to opera, writing 15 works, including *Salome* (1905), *Elektra* (1906–08), *Der Rosenkavalier* (1909–10), and *Ariadne auf Naxos* (1912).

Strauss the Younger, Johann (1825–99) Austrian violinist, conductor, and composer. He wrote a great many waltzes, such as "The Blue Danube" and "Tales from the Vienna Woods," as well as polkas and marches. He also wrote 16 operettas, including *Die Fledermaus* (1874) and *The Gipsy Baron* (1885). His father **Johann Strauss the Elder** (1804–49) composed 152 waltzes as well as quadrilles, marches (including the "Radetzky March"), galops, etc.

Stravinsky, Igor (1882–1971) Russian-born US composer. He became famous with a series of ballet scores commissioned by *Diaghilev, including *The Firebird* (1910), *Petrushka* (1911), and *The Rite of Spring* (1913), which provoked demonstrations at its premiere and had a strong influence on 20th-century music. Stravinsky subsequently developed a neoclassical style (*see* NEOCLASSICISM) in such works as the oratorio *Oedipus Rex* (1927). Towards the end of his life Stravinsky adopted *serialism in such works as *Canticum Sacrum* (1955).

Straw, Jack (John Whitaker S.; 1946–) British Labour politician; home secretary (1997–2001) and foreign secretary (2001–). He entered parliament in 1979 and was shadow home secretary (1994–97).

strawberry A perennial herb belonging to the genus *Fragaria* (15 species), native to N temperate regions and widely cultivated for its edible fruit. Most of the commercial varieties are hybrids derived from the European hautbois strawberry (*F. moschata*), the Chilean strawberry (*F. chiloensis*), and the North American scarlet strawberry (*F. virginiana*). The plants are low growing, with white flowers. Family: *Rosaceae*.

strawberry tree *See* ARBUTUS.

Streep, Meryl (Mary Louise S.; 1949–) US actress. After appearing in *The Deerhunter* (1978) she became the leading US film actress of the 1980s in such films as *Kramer vs. Kramer* (1980), *The French Lieutenant's Woman* (1981), *Sophie's Choice* (1982), and *Out of Africa* (1986). Later films include *The River Wild* (1994) and *The Hours* (2002).

Streptococcus A genus of spherical anaerobic bacteria many of which live as parasites in the respiratory and digestive systems of animals and humans. *S. pyogenes* causes scarlet fever in humans.

streptomycin An *antibiotic, obtained from the bacterium *Streptomyces griseus*, that revolutionized the treatment of tuberculosis. It is usually administered (by injection) in combination with other antibiotics.

stress The force per unit area that causes a deformation (or *strain) in a body. **Tensile stress** tends to stretch a body; **bulk stress** tends to compress it; and **shear stress** tends to twist it.

strike A form of industrial action in which a group of employees, usually organized in a trade union (or unions), withdraws its labour in order to achieve its demands. A strike is the last resort in the process of collective bargaining: it may prompt a settlement either because it proves that neither side is bluffing or because the costs involved (in terms of lost pay and profits) force a compromise. As future orders and job security may be jeopardized by a strike, responsible unions only resort to the measure in extreme cases. An official strike is one that is recognized by a trade union, whereas an unofficial (or wildcat) strike is a walkout organized by shopfloor workers without union backing. The Trade Union Act (1984) provides for compulsory ballots in connection with strikes and other industrial actions.

S

Strindberg, August (1849–1912) Swedish dramatist and writer. His unhappy childhood and three unsuccessful marriages gave rise to mental instability and a violent hatred of women. This is reflected in the plays *The Father* (1887) and *Miss Julie* (1888), and the autobiographical prose works *Confessions of a Fool* (1912) and *Inferno* (1897). Other works include *The Dance of Death* (1900), the symbolistic *Easter* (1901), and *A Dream Play* (1901). His late chamber plays, such as *The Ghost Sonata* (1907), combine irrational elements with realistic settings.

stringed instruments Musical instruments in which notes are produced by the vibration of stretched strings. The strings may be plucked, bowed, plucked mechanically, struck mechanically, or played with hammers.

stroke (*or* **apoplexy**) Sudden loss of consciousness with weakness or paralysis of one side of the body, caused by interruption of the blood supply to the brain. This may be due to a blood clot in one of the arteries of the brain (*see* EMBOLISM; THROMBOSIS) or to the rupture of a blood vessel in the brain (cerebral haemorrhage). With careful nursing and physiotherapy many patients recover completely.

Stromboli An Italian island in the Tyrrhenian Sea, in the Lipari Islands. Its active volcano produces a stream of lava.

strong interaction One of the four basic forces in the universe; it occurs between the class of elementary particles called hadrons. It is the strongest of the four (100 times stronger than the electromotive interaction) but effective only over about 10^{-15} metre. It is the force that holds the protons and neutrons together in the nucleus and is thought to occur as the result of the exchange of gluons between quarks. *See* PARTICLE PHYSICS.

strontium (Sr) A reactive alkaline-earth metal, discovered by Sir Humphry Davy in 1808 and named after Strontian, a town in Scotland where the carbonate ($SrCO_3$) is found. It also occurs as the sulphate, celestine ($SrSO_4$). It is a highly reactive metal, being more electropositive than calcium and reacting vigorously with water to liberate hydrogen. The isotope ^{90}Sr is produced in nuclear fallout. At no 38; at wt 87.62; mp 769°C; bp 1384°C.

structuralism An approach to the study of culture that seeks to uncover underlying patterns and structures and the basic elements from which these are constructed. The leading figure of this school was the anthropologist Claude *Lévi-Strauss, whose work on kinship, ritual, and religion sought to elucidate universal laws of human thought. This approach was stimulated by the structural school in *linguistics, as originated by *Saussure, which maintains that linguistic signs achieve meaning only through their structural relationships with other signs in the same system. In the 1960s a structuralist approach to literary criticism and popular culture was pioneered by French critics, such as Roland *Barthes, and became influential in the humanities. During the 1970s structuralism evolved into so-called **post-structuralism** in the work of Jacques Derrida (1930–) and others.

strychnine An alkaloid poison derived from plants of the genus *Strychnos*. It acts on the central nervous system, causing convulsions and ultimately death.

Stuarts (*or* **Stewarts**) The ruling dynasty of Scotland from 1371 to 1714 and of England from 1603 to 1714. The first Stuart king was Robert II (crowned 1371) of Scotland. The direct male line ended with the death of James V in 1542, when the throne passed to his daughter Mary, Queen of Scots, and following her abdication (1567) to her son James VI, who inherited the English Crown (1603) as James I. He was succeeded by Charles I, Charles II, James II, Mary II (and her husband William III), and Anne (d. 1714). The Crown then passed to the Hanoverians (*see* SETTLEMENT, ACT OF) but the Stuart claim was kept alive by *James Edward Stuart, the Old Pretender, and his son, *Charles Edward Stuart, the Young Pretender. The last royal Stuart was Henry Stuart, Cardinal York (d. 1807).

Stubbs, George (1724–1806) British animal painter. He is best known for his horse paintings, such as *Mares and Foals in a Landscape* (Tate Gallery), but he also painted portraits and farming scenes.

stupa A Buddhist shrine, originally a reliquary mound. It is usually surrounded by a processional path and a wall, and is often crowned with sculpted parasols representing the heavens. The stupa is the origin of the *pagoda.

sturgeon A *bony fish belonging to a family (*Acipenseridae*; about 24 species) found in N temperate waters. Sturgeons have a large sharklike body, up to 8.4 m long, with five longitudinal rows of sharp bony plates, a small ventral mouth, and four sensory barbels. Eggs are laid in fresh water and are commercially important as caviar. *See also* BELUGA.

Sturm und Drang (German: Storm and Stress) A German literary movement of the late 18th century that anticipated many aspects of Romanticism. Its influence is most notable in the drama, where it led to a rejection of neoclassical conventions.

Stuttgart 48 47N 9 12E A city in SW Germany, on the River Neckar. It became the capital of Württemberg in 1482. It was largely destroyed in World War II. Population (2000): 581 200.

stylops A minute insect of the order *Strepsiptera* (about 400 species), which is parasitic on bees and other insects. The grublike female lives permanently inside the host's body; the winged male, often less than 4 mm long, leaves its host to find and fertilize a female.

Styx In Greek mythology, the main river of Hades across which the souls of the dead were ferried by *Charon. It was sometimes personified as the daughter of Oceanus.

sublimation In chemistry, the evaporation of a solid without melting. For any substance the liquid phase only occurs within certain limits of temperature and pressure—if the pressure is low enough, heating a solid will result in sublimation. Substances that sublime at atmospheric pressure include carbon dioxide (dry ice) and iodine.

submarine A warship designed for sustained operation under water. The earliest record of a submarine craft is that developed by Cornelis Drebbel (1572–1634) of Holland in 1620. A more practical model, the "Turtle," was invented by David Bushnell (1742–1824) of Connecticut in 1776, and saw limited use in the American Revolution. Submarines, called **U-boats** (German name: *Unterseeboot*, undersea boat), were first used extensively by the German navy in World War I. They became an important armament in World War II. Modern submarines may be powered by nuclear reactors and can remain submerged for months at a time. These vessels also carry one or more guns mounted on deck, torpedoes for firing under water, and missiles that can be launched when the submarine is submerged.

substitution reaction A type of chemical reaction in which one atom or group of atoms is displaced by another. An example is the reaction of methyl chloride (CH_3Cl) with hydroxide ions (OH^-) to give methanol (CH_3OH) and chloride ions (Cl^-). The hydroxide ion, in this case, is referred to as the substituent.

succession In ecology, the process of continual change that takes place in the composition of a *community of organisms occupying a particular habitat from the time of its initial colonization to the establishment of a stable climax community.

Sucre 19 00S 65 15W The capital of Bolivia, in the S at an altitude of 2790 m (9153 ft). It was founded by the Spanish in 1538. The seat of government was moved to La Paz in 1898. Population (2000 est): 192 238.

sucrose (**cane sugar** *or* **beet sugar** *or* **saccharose**) A carbohydrate consisting chemically of one molecule each of *glucose and *fructose linked together. It is commercially the most important of the *sugars.

S

Sudan, Democratic Republic of the A large country in NE Africa, bordering on the Red Sea. It consists chiefly of a vast plateau rising to mountains in the S and W. The main rivers are the Blue Nile and White Nile. About half the population are Arabs, and there are minorities of *Dinka, Nubians, and others. *Economy*: chiefly agricultural, the main cash crop and export being cotton. Livestock rearing is also important. Forest products include gum arabic. Since the mid-1980s the economy has been devastated by drought, famine, US sanctions (1996–99), and continuous civil war. *History*: the NE was part of ancient *Nubia. The region was Christianized in the 6th century and invaded from the N in the 13th century, after which it was converted to Islam. In 1821 it was conquered by the Egyptians, against whom a revolt under the Mahdi took place in 1881. In 1898 an Anglo-Egyptian force under Kitchener subdued his followers and in 1899 an Anglo-Egyptian condominium was established. In 1956 the Sudan became an independent republic. A coup in 1969 brought Col Jaafar al Nemeiry to power. In 1972 he negotiated an end to the fighting between the mainly Muslim N and the mainly animist and Christian S that had raged since independence. However, new violence in the S erupted in 1983, with the Sudanese People's Liberation Army taking over large areas. During widespread famine in 1985, Nimeiry was overthrown and civilian rule re-established. A further military coup was led by Lt Gen Omar Hassan Ahmad al-Bashir, who established an Islamic state. The new government's abuse of human rights and alleged support for Islamic terrorism led to its international isolation in the 1990s. In 1996 al-Bashir and his supporters were victorious in parliamentary and presidential elections. Peace talks in 2002–04 produced an agreement under which the S would enjoy near autonomy, with the option of formal secession after six years. A further conflict erupted in the western Darfur region in 2003, where government-backed Arab militias have carried out brutal ethnic cleansing of Black Africans. War and war-related food shortages are thought to have claimed over 2 million lives since 1983. Official language: Arabic; English is widely spoken. Currency: Sudanese dinar of 10 pounds. Area: 2 500 000 sq km (967 500 sq mi). Population (2003 est): 38 114 000. Capital: Khartoum.

Sudbury 46 30N 81 01W A city in E Canada, in Ontario. Established in 1883, it is one of the world's greatest mining cities. Population (1996): 92 059.

sudden infant death syndrome (**SIDS**) *See* COT DEATH.

Sudetenland A mountainous region in the W Czech Republic. Incorporated in Czechoslovakia in 1919, it was reoccupied by Germany in 1938. After World War II Czechoslovakia regained the Sudetenland and expelled the Sudeten Germans.

Suez (Arabic name: As-Suways) 29 59N 32 33E A port in Egypt, near the mouth of the Suez Canal. An important refuelling station, it was rebuilt after the Arab-Israeli War of 1967. Population (1996): 417 610.

Suez Canal A canal in Egypt connecting the Mediterranean Sea and the Red Sea. Running between Port Said in the N and Suez in the S, it is 165 km (103 mi) long. It was designed by the French engineer Ferdinand de Lesseps and was opened in 1869. In 1888 it became a neutral zone, with Britain the guarantor of its status. In 1956 President Nasser nationalized the canal, provoking an Anglo-French attack on Egypt. However, Britain and France withdrew within a few days in the face of international censure. The canal was closed from 1967 to 1975 because of Arab-Israeli hostilities.

Suffolk A county in E England, on the North Sea. It consists of undulating lowlands. It is mainly agricultural, producing cereals and sugar beet, and is noted for its horse breeding (Suffolk Punches). Area: 3800 sq km (1467 sq mi). Population (2001): 668 548. Administrative centre: Ipswich.

Sufism (Arabic *sufi*: wearer of a woollen cloak, mystic) A mystical movement arising within Islam in the 8th and 9th centuries AD. The goal of the Sufis was mystical union with God achieved by fervent worship. Later Sufism shows the influence of Neoplatonism and Hindu asceticism.

sugar beet A biennial herb derived from the European sea *beet (*Beta vulgaris*). Sugar beet is widely cultivated for the sucrose content of its large roots. Family: *Chenopodiaceae*.

sugar cane A perennial grass of the tropical genus *Saccharum* (5 species), especially *S. officinarum*, which is cultivated for its sugar content. The clumps of stalks (canes), 3–8 m high, may bear dense woolly clusters of female flowers. Usually, the canes are crushed to extract the sugary liquid. This is concentrated and refined to produce table sugar, etc. The remaining liquor (molasses) is used for animal feedstuffs, industrial alcohol, etc. The fibrous residue (bagasse) is used as fuel, cattle feed, etc.

sugars A class of sweet-tasting *carbohydrates, classified chemically as *monosaccharides or disaccharides. The sugar widely used to sweeten food, drinks, and confectionery is the disaccharide *sucrose, derived from sugar cane (11–15% sucrose) and from sugar beet (17% sucrose). Sugar manufacture is believed to have originated in India (Sanskrit *sarkara*, sand) around 3000 BC; it was taken to the New World by Christopher Columbus in 1493. Sucrose is extracted from raw sugar cane by pressure, the extract being crystallized by evaporation. It is extracted from beet by hot water. Raw cane sugar and beet sugar are further refined to produce granulated, caster, icing, and cube sugars. By-products include molasses and sugar-beet pulp, both of which are used in animal feedstuffs.

Suharto (1921–) Indonesian statesman and general; president (1967–98). He gained prominence in the struggle for Indonesian independence and came to power in the gradual overthrow (1965–68) of *Sukarno. Following the collapse of Indonesia's economy (1997), there were mass protests leading to his resignation (1998). He was charged with corruption (2000) but escaped trial owing to ill health.

Sukarno (1901–70) Indonesian statesman; president (1945–67). He helped to found the Indonesian Nationalist Party in 1927 and was Indonesia's main resistance leader during the Japanese occupation (1942–45). When Indonesia was declared independent he became president. From 1965 he effectively lost power to the army under *Suharto. His daughter, **Megawati Sukarnoputri** (1947–), became president of Indonesia in 2001.

Sulawesi (former name: Celebes) An island in Indonesia, off E Borneo. It is mountainous and forested. Area, including adjacent islands: 189 033 sq km (72 986 sq mi). Population (1999 est): 14 768 400. Chief towns: Ujung Pandang and Menado.

Suleiman (I) the Magnificent (?1494–1566) Ottoman sultan (1520–66), under whom the Ottoman Empire reached its peak. Suleiman captured Belgrade in 1521 and Rhodes in 1522. In 1526 he defeated the Hungarians at Mohács and annexed large parts of Hungary. In 1529 he besieged Vienna. In campaigns against Persia he made many conquests and the Ottoman navy, under Barbarossa (d. 1546) and others, controlled the E Mediterranean.

Sulla, Lucius Cornelius (c. 138–78 BC) Roman dictator; an opponent of Gaius Marius (c. 157–86 BC) and *Cinna. Enraged because his command against Mithridates, King of Pontus, was transferred to Marius, he stormed Rome (87), forcing Marius and Cinna to flee. Although outlawed when his rivals returned, he successfully concluded the campaign against Mithridates and in 83 invaded Italy. Elected dictator, Sulla butchered his opponents. After restoring the Senate's constitutional powers, he retired (79).

Sullivan, Sir Arthur (1842–1900) British composer. He is best known for his collaboration with the librettist W. S. *Gilbert in such comic operas as *The Pirates of Penzance* (1879), *The Mikado* (1885), and *The Yeomen of the Guard* (1888).

sulphonamides (*or* **sulpha drugs**) A group of drugs, derived from sulphanilamide, that prevent the growth of bacteria. Sulphonamides are used to treat a wide variety of infections, particularly those of the urinary tract and the eye. Sulphonamides are also combined with the antibiotic trimethoprim, which improves their effectiveness. In some patients sulphonamides may cause severe allergic disorders.

sulphur (S) A yellow nonmetallic solid element, occurring in various crystalline and amorphous forms. Sulphur was known in ancient times as brimstone. It is found near volcanoes and in large deposits associated with oil trapped against salt domes. Extraction is by the Frasch process, in which the sulphur is melted and pumped to the surface. Sulphur reacts readily with many elements to form sulphides, sulphates, and oxides. The oxides SO_2 and SO_3 are acidic gases that dissolve in water to form sulphurous acid (H_2SO_3) and sulphuric acid (H_2SO_4). At no 16; at wt 32.066; mp 115.22°C; bp 444.674°C.

sulphuric acid (H_2SO_4) A colourless oily liquid that has a great affinity for water and is used as a drying agent. H_2SO_4 is made by the contact process, in which sulphur dioxide is heated and passed through columns of platinized asbestos catalyst to produce sulphur trioxide (SO_3). The SO_3 is then dissolved in water to form H_2SO_4. Adding further SO_3 to H_2SO_4 produces fuming sulphuric acid (oleum; $H_2S_2O_7$), a fuming liquid that forms a crystalline solid on cooling. Sulphuric acid is one of the most important industrial chemicals.

Sulu Archipelago An island group in the SW Philippines. The most important of its 400 islands are Basilan and Jolo. Area: 2815 sq km (1087 sq mi). Population (latest est): 555 239. Chief town: Jolo.

sumach (*or* **sumac**) A tree or shrub of the genus *Rhus* (250 species), native to warm temperate and subtropical regions. The leaves of the Sicilian sumach (*R. coraria*) yield a substance used in tanning and dyeing. Several species are cultivated as garden ornamentals. Some species are poisonous and irritate the skin on contact, particularly the American poison ivy and poison sumach (*R. vernix*). Family: *Anacardiaceae*. *See also* LACQUER TREE.

Sumatra (*or* **Sumatera**) The second largest Indonesian island, separated from Peninsular Malaysia by the Strait of Malacca. The mountainous volcanic spine descends in the NE to swamps. It is Indonesia's chief rubber and oil producer. Crops include coffee, tea, and pepper. *History*: the Buddhist kingdom of Sri Vijaya (7th–13th centuries) was based in Palembang. During the 15th century the Islamic influence became dominant, resisting Dutch domination in the N until 1908. Since 1949 there has been considerable separatist activity. Area: 524 097 sq km (202 311 sq mi). Population (1999 est): 24 284 400. Chief towns: Palembang and Medan.

Sumer The area in S Mesopotamia in which the earliest civilization evolved during the 4th millennium BC. The fertile natural environment encouraged settlements that grew into such politically independent cities as *Ur. After 2000 BC Sumer was absorbed into *Babylonia.

sumo *See* WRESTLING.

sun The nearest star, lying at an average distance of 149.6 million km from earth at the centre of the *solar system. It has a diameter of 1 392 000 km, a mass of 1.99×10^{30} kg, and rotates on its axis in a mean period of 25.38 days. A typical yellow (G2) main-sequence star, it is composed primarily (99%) of hydrogen and helium in the approximate ratio 3:1 by mass. In its hot central core, about 400 000 km in diameter, energy is generated by nuclear fusion reactions. The surface, called the *photosphere, is the boundary between the opaque outer (convective) zone of the sun's interior and its transparent atmosphere. The atmosphere comprises the *chromosphere and the inner and outer *corona. There are regions of intense localized magnetic fields on the sun, where *sunspots, solar prominences, and *solar flares occur. *See also* SOLAR WIND.

sun bear A *bear, *Helarctos malayanus*, of tropical forests of Asia, Sumatra, and Borneo. It is the smallest bear, (110–140 cm long) and climbs well, hunting for small vertebrates, fruit, and honey.

sunbird An arboreal bird belonging to a tropical family (*Nectariniidae*; 104 species) ranging from Africa to Australasia. Sunbirds are 9–15 cm long and have a brilliant metallic plumage, slender down-curved bills, and long extensible tongues for feeding on nectar.

Sunda Islands An Indonesian group of islands, between the Indian Ocean and South China Sea. It consists of the **Greater Sunda Islands** (including Sumatra, Java, Borneo, and Sulawesi) and *Nusa Tenggara.

Sunderland 1. 54 55N 1 23W A port in NE England, in Sunderland unitary authority, Tyne and Wear, at the mouth of the River Wear. Sunderland exported coal from the Durham coalfield from the 14th century until the late 20th century, when the last deep pit closed. The main industries are now car manufacture (Nissan), engineering, and chemicals. Sunderland was given city status in 1992. Population (1991): 183 310. **2.** A unitary authority in NE England, in Tyne and Wear. Area: 138 sq km (53 sq mi). Population (2001): 280 807.

sundew A perennial or annual *carnivorous plant of the genus *Drosera* (about 100 species), of temperate and tropical regions. Sundews have a basal rosette of leaves covered in sticky reddish gland-tipped hairs, used to trap insects. Family: *Droseraceae*.

sunfish An omnivorous fish of the family *Molidae*, especially *Mola mola*, found in all tropical and temperate seas. It has a disc-shaped laterally flattened body, up to 3 m long, with the tail fin reduced to a wavy frill attached to the triangular dorsal and anal fins. Order: *Tetraodontiformes*.

The name is also applied to several carnivorous freshwater food and game fish of the North American family *Centrarchidae*. They have deep laterally flattened bodies, 2.5–80 cm long, and a single long dorsal fin. Order: *Perciformes*.

sunflower A herbaceous plant of the genus *Helianthus*, native to North and South America. *H. annuus* is about 3 m high with yellow flower heads, up to 35 cm in diameter. It is cultivated both for ornament and for its seeds, from which oil is obtained. Perennial sunflowers include *H. salicifolius* and *H. decapetalus*. Family: *Compositae*.

sunn An annual herb, *Crotalaria juncea*, cultivated in India for its stem fibres. It grows to a height of 2–3 m and produces small yellow flowers. The fibres are used for netting, canvas, yarns, and in certain paper products. Family: *Leguminosae.*

Sunnites (*or* **Sunni**; Arabic *sunna*: custom) The larger of the two main Muslim Sects. In contrast to the *Shiite Muslims, the Sunnites accept the first three caliphs as Mohammed's legitimate successors. They are strictly orthodox in their obedience to the Koran. They form the majority party in most Islamic countries except Iran.

sunspots Comparatively dark markings on the sun's *photosphere, typically a few thousand kilometres across with the central region being darkest and coolest. They can influence the climate on earth. They are centres of intense localized magnetic fields. The number of sunspots seen in a year, and their mean solar latitude, varies in a cycle of about 11 years, known as the **sunspot cycle**.

sunstroke A form of *heatstroke caused by overexposure to the sun. **Sunburn** is damage to the skin resulting from overexposure to the sun's rays. This may vary from slight reddening to large painful blisters.

superconductivity A phenomenon in which the electrical resistance of certain metals vanishes when they are cooled to very low temperatures. The temperature below which superconductivity occurs is called the transition temperature and varies for different substances. If a loop of a superconducting substance is cooled to below its transition temperature, a current will flow through the loop indefinitely. Ceramic conductors have now been found that operate at higher temperatures than the metal conductors first used.

supercooling The reduction in the temperature of a liquid below its freezing point without its solidification. This can only be achieved by slow and continuous cooling with pure liquids. A supercooled liquid is in a metastable state and any disturbance will cause solidification.

superego In *psychoanalysis, the part of the mind that acts as a moral conscience. It was believed by *Freud to result from the incorporation of the parent's instructions into a child's mind. *See also* EGO; ID.

superfluid A fluid that exhibits a very high thermal conductivity and virtually no friction at temperatures close to absolute zero. Such a fluid will flow up the sides and out of an open container.

supergiant The largest and most luminous type of star. They evolve from very massive but more compact stars. Rigel, *Betelgeuse, and Antares are examples. *See also* GIANT STAR.

superheterodyne A system widely used in radio receivers; the incoming radio-frequency signal is combined with a locally generated carrier wave to give an intermediate frequency between radio- and audio-frequency (*see* MODULATION). The intermediate frequency is easier to amplify than radio-frequency.

Superior, Lake The largest of the Great Lakes in North America, situated between the USA and Canada. The lake is important for shipping. Area: 82 362 sq km (31 800 sq mi).

supernova A cataclysmic stellar explosion, seen as a sudden increase in a star's brightness. Most or all of the star's substance is blown off at high velocity, forming an expanding gas shell—the **supernova remnant**. If the star's core survives, it will most probably end up as a *neutron star or *black hole. *See also* CRAB NEBULA.

superphosphates Phosphorus-containing fertilizers that are highly active. Single superphosphate is made by reacting sulphuric acid with insoluble calcium phosphate rock to form calcium sulphate and soluble calcium hydrogen phosphate $Ca(H_2PO_4)_2$. Often the process is carried out under pressure. Triple superphosphate is more concentrated.

Supreme Court of the United States The highest law court in the USA, comprising the chief justice and eight associate justices appointed for life by the president. Its main functions include interpreting and safeguarding the constitution. It also decides disputes between states and between one state and the citizens of another and hears appeals from state and federal courts.

Surabaja 7 14S 112 45E A port in Indonesia, in E Java. It is Indonesia's second largest city and chief naval base. Population (1995 est): 2 701 300.

Surakarta (*or* **Solo**) 7 32S 110 50E A city in Indonesia, in central Java. A cultural centre noted for its shadow plays, it is the site of a sultan's palace (1745). Population (1995 est): 516 500.

Surat 21 10N 72 54E A city in India, in Gujarat on the River Tapti. It was the Mogul Empire's chief port (16th–17th centuries). It was the headquarters of the East India Company until 1687. Population (1991): 1 496 943.

surface tension A force occurring on the surface of a liquid that makes it behave as if the surface has an elastic skin. It is caused by forces between the molecules of the liquid:

only those at the surface experience forces from below, whereas those in the interior are acted on by intermolecular forces from all sides. Surface tension causes a meniscus to form, liquids to rise up capillary tubes, paper to absorb water, and droplets and bubbles to form. It is defined as the force acting tangentially to the surface on one side of a line of unit length (newtons per metre) or as the work required to produce unit increase in surface area (joules per square metre).

surfactant A substance that lowers the surface tension of a liquid, thus allowing easier penetration and spreading. For this reason they are often known as **wetting agents**. Surfactants are widely used in *detergents, emulsifiers, paints, adhesives, inks, etc.

surgeonfish A tropical marine fish, also called tang, belonging to the family *Acanthuridae* (about 100 species). Its deep laterally flattened body, up to about 50 cm long, is often brightly coloured, with a single long dorsal fin, and a sharp bladelike spine on each side of the tail. They feed mainly on algae. Order: *Perciformes.*

Suriname, Republic of (name until 1948: Dutch Guiana) A country on the N coast of South America, largely covered by tropical forest. The population is ethnically very diverse. *Economy*: based on bauxite, the chief industry being aluminium processing. Fishing is important, as is production of rice. *History*: it was sighted by Columbus in 1498 and the first permanent settlement was established by the English in 1650. It was ceded to the Netherlands in 1667. During the Revolutionary and Napoleonic Wars it was again (1799–1802, 1804–16) under British rule. In 1949 it gained a measure of self-government, subsequently becoming an autonomous part of the Netherlands (1954) and an independent republic (1975). The military took over in 1980; although democracy was ostensibly restored in 1988, Lt Col Désiré Bouterse remained the real leader until the free elections of 1991, which resulted in the opposition leader Runaldo Venetiaan becoming president. Venetiaan was again president from 2000. Crime, corruption, and the drug trade are endemic problems. Suriname is a member of the OAS and the Caribbean Community. Official language: Dutch; English, Hindustani, and Javanese are widely spoken; Surinamese (Sranang Tongo) is used as a lingua franca. Currency: Suriname guilder of 100 cents. Area: 163 265 sq km (63 020 sq mi). Population (2003 est): 435 000. Capital: Paramaribo.

S

surrealism A European movement in art and literature of the 1920s and 1930s. Surrealism began as a literary movement, when its leader, the poet André *Breton, published the surrealist manifesto in Paris (1924). It aimed, under the influence of *Freud, to embody in art and poetry the irrational forces of dreams and the subconscious mind. Other leading surrealists were the poets Louis *Aragon and Paul Eluard (1895–1952) and the painters *Ernst, *Miró, *Dali, *Magritte, Paul Delvaux (1897–1994), and Yves Tanguy (1900–55).

Surrey A county in SE England, bordering on Greater London. The North Downs run E–W across the middle of the county. Although it has developed primarily as a residential area, agriculture is important in the S. Area: 1679 sq km (648 sq mi). Population (2001): 1 059 015. Administrative centre: Kingston-upon-Thames.

Surrey, Henry Howard, Earl of (1517–47) English poet. The son of the Duke of Norfolk, he led a precarious life in the service of Henry VIII, and was finally executed on a charge of treason. He pioneered the use of blank verse in his translation of Virgil's *Aeneid* (1557), and, with Sir Thomas *Wyatt, was responsible for introducing Italian forms into English poetry.

Surya In Hindu mythology, the sun-god. He appears as a major deity in the *Vedas* and remained prominent as patron of numerous Hindu royal dynasties.

Susa (*or* **Shushan**) An ancient city in SW Iran. Occupied since the 4th millennium BC, it was a capital of Elam. Susa's heyday was as administrative capital of the Achaemenian kings of Persia (521–331).

Susquehanna River A river in the E USA. It rises in New York State and flows mainly S to Chesapeake Bay. Length: 715 km (444 mi).

Sussex *See* WEST SUSSEX; EAST SUSSEX.

Sutherland, Graham (Vivian) (1903–80) British artist. He turned to painting in 1935, specializing in disturbing landscapes and scenes of war desolation. Also well known are his *Crucifixion* (1946; St Matthew's, Northampton), his tapestry for Coventry Cathedral, and his portraits, e.g. of Somerset Maugham (Tate Gallery).

Sutherland, Dame Joan (1926–) Australian operatic soprano. She established her reputation at Covent Garden in 1959 in the title role of Donizetti's *Lucia di Lammermoor* and retired in 1990.

Sutlej, River A river in India and Pakistan.

Rising in SW Tibet, it flows mainly SW across the Punjab plain into Pakistan, where it joins the River Chenab. Length: 1368 km (850 mi).

suttee An ancient Hindu custom of self-immolation of widows on their husbands' funeral pyres. It was officially abolished in India by the British in 1829.

Sutton Coldfield 52 34N 1 48W A town in England, in Birmingham unitary authority, West Midlands, a mainly residential suburb of Birmingham. Population (1992 est): 103 097.

Sutton Hoo The site of a Saxon ship burial near Woodbridge, in Suffolk (E England). Excavations in 1939 revealed the remnants of a 38-oar boat containing a magnificent treasure hoard. The mound is thought to be a cenotaph to King Raedwald (died c. 625 AD).

Suu Kyi, Aung San *See* AUNG SAN.

Suva 18 08S 178 25E The capital of Fiji, on the S coast of Viti Levu. Its industries include tourism and the production of coconut oil and soap. Population (1996 est): 167 421.

Suwannee River (*or* **Swanee R.**) A river in the SE USA, flowing from the Okefenokee Swamp in SE Georgia across Florida to the Gulf of Mexico. Length: 400 km (200 mi).

Suzhou (**Su-chou** *or* **Soochow**) 31 21N 120 40E A city in E China, on the Yangtze delta. Famed for its beautiful canals and gardens, it is a centre of culture and the silk industry. Population (1999 est): 845 687.

Svalbard (*or* **Spitsbergen**) A Norwegian archipelago in the Arctic Ocean. Following disputes over their sovereignty, they were granted to Norway in 1920. Covered largely by icefields and glaciers their major importance is as a source of coal. Area: 62 050 sq km (23 958 sq mi). Population (latest est): 3544. Chief town: Longyearbyen.

Swabia (German name: Schwaben) A former region in SW Germany now divided between Germany, Switzerland, and France. Swabia was one of the leading German duchies in the middle ages. Napoleon finally partitioned Swabia among neighbouring states in 1807.

Swahili (*or* **Kiswahili**) A Bantu language of East Africa and the lingua franca of Tanzania, Kenya, the Democratic Republic of Congo, and Uganda. There are three main dialects.

swallow A songbird belonging to a cosmopolitan family (*Hirundidae*; 78 species) of acrobatic fliers that catch insects on the wing. Swallows are 10–22 cm long, with short necks, long pointed wings, short legs, and often forked tails. All temperate swallows migrate to hot climates for the winter. *See also* MARTIN.

swallowtail butterfly A papilionid butterfly having long swallow-like tails on the hindwings. Many species are tropical and brightly coloured, with the sexes often of different colours. The caterpillars give off a strong odour if they are disturbed. Family: *Papilionidae*.

swamp cypress A deciduous conifer, *Taxodium distichum*, also called bald cypress, native to swampy regions of the SE USA and grown for its timber and as an ornamental. In waterlogged soils its roots protrude above the water. Up to 45 m high, it has globular cones, 2.5 cm across. Family: *Taxodiaceae*.

swan A large waterbird belonging to a genus (*Cygnus*; 7–8 species) occurring worldwide on fresh waters or sheltered coasts and estuaries. 100–160 cm long, swans are usually white with black legs and have large feet, a long neck, and a powerful spatulate bill, which they use to feed on underwater plants. Immature swans have a mottled brown plumage. *See also* MUTE SWAN. Family: *Anatidae* (ducks, geese, swans).

Swansea (Welsh name: Abertawe) **1.** 51 38N 3 57W A city and port in Swansea county, South Wales. It is the second-largest city in Wales and a major industrial centre, with metals, chemicals, and oil refining. Population (1991): 181 906. **2.** A county in S Wales on the Bristol Channel, created in 1996 from part of West Glamorgan. It includes the Swansea conurbation, the Gower Peninsula, and some hillier country in the N. The economy is based on heavy industry and port facilities in Swansea and tourism in the Gower. Area: 378 sq km (146 sq mi). Population (2001): 223 293. Administrative centre: Swansea.

swastika An ancient symbol of uncertain origin, generally held to signify prosperity and creativity. It is a cross, the four arms of which are deflected at right angles either clockwise or anticlockwise. It has been revered by Buddhists, Hindus, Celts, and North American Indians. The Nazis adopted the symbol, mistakenly believing it to be of pure Aryan origins.

Swazi A Bantu-speaking people who occupy Swaziland and adjacent areas of South Africa. They are an agricultural and pastoral people. Polygyny is practised by senior men. Traditionally ancestor worship, witchcraft, and magic were prominent in religious life.

Swaziland, Kingdom of A small country

in SE Africa between South Africa and Mozambique. It consists of *veld. *Economy*: chiefly agricultural, the main food crop being maize. The chief cash crop is sugar. Rich mineral resources include iron ore, asbestos, and coal. Manufacturing has developed rapidly since the late 1980s. *History*: the *Swazi occupied the area in the late 18th century. It became a South African protectorate in 1894 and, in 1902, after the Boer War it came under British rule. It became an independent kingdom within the Commonwealth in 1968. Under a new constitution (1978) political parties were banned; there is a partly elected House of Assembly but the country is effectively an absolute monarchy under King Mswati III. Economic crisis led to a growth in pro-democracy activism in the 2000s. Official languages: Siswati and English. Currency: lilangeni of 100 cents; South African currency is also legal tender. Area: 17 400 sq km (6705 sq mi). Population (2003 est): 1 077 000. Capital: Mbabane.

sweat (*or* **perspiration**) A watery fluid, consisting mainly of sodium chloride and urea in solution, that is secreted by the sweat glands in the skin. Sweating is a means of excreting nitrogenous waste products, but is more importantly a means of temperature regulation.

swede An annual or biennial herbaceous plant, *Brassica napus napobrassica*, growing to a height of 1 m, with yellow flowers. It is cultivated for its fleshy edible taproot; this is eaten as a vegetable and also fed to livestock. Family: *Cruciferae*.

Sweden, Kingdom of (Swedish name: Sverige) A country in N Europe occupying the E part of the Scandinavian peninsula. Undulating land in the S rises to mountains in the N. There are numerous lakes and forests. *Economy*: Sweden is rich in mineral resources, notably iron ore, which forms the basis of the country's heavy industry and is a major export. The large forests support important pulp and paper industries. There is a thriving fishing industry. Agricultural activities are concentrated in the S. *History*: the area was inhabited from early times by German tribes, the Swedes in the N and the Goths in the S, and its people participated in the exploits of the Vikings. Christianity was introduced in the 9th century. Finland was acquired in the 13th century and the 14th century saw the Kalmar Union of Sweden with Denmark and Norway. Independence was achieved in 1523 under Gustavus I Vasa, during whose reign Lutheranism was introduced. In the 17th century, under Gustavus Adolphus, Sweden emerged from the *Thirty Years' War as a major European power, a position undermined by the Great *Northern War (1700–21). In 1809, during the Napoleonic Wars, Finland was surrendered to Russia. In 1814 Norway was ceded to Sweden, the two countries remaining united until 1905. Sweden remained neutral in both World Wars. From 1932 to 1976 politics was dominated by the Social Democrats, who created a highly developed welfare state (this has been cut back since the 1990s). On the accession of Carl XVI Gustaf in 1975 a new constitution reduced the power of the monarchy. The Social Democrat prime minister Olof Palme was assassinated in 1986. There was a centre-right government from 1991 to 1996, when the Social Democrats returned under Göran Persson (re-elected 1998, 2002). Sweden joined the EU in 1995. In 2003 Sweden rejected the euro in a referendum marked by the assassination of the pro-euro foreign minister Anna Lindh. Official language: Swedish. Currency: krona of 100 øre. Area: 449 964 sq km (173 732 sq mi). Population (2003 est): 8 958 000. Capital: Stockholm.

Swedish A language belonging to the Scandinavian branch of the North Germanic group. It is the official language of Sweden and is spoken by a minority in Finland. The standard literary form is based mainly on the dialect of Stockholm.

sweet briar A branched prickly fragrant *rose, *Rosa rubiginosa* (or *R. eglanteria*), also called eglantine. Found in scrub and chalk grassland across the N hemisphere, it grows to a height of 2 m and has pink flowers.

sweet corn *See* MAIZE.

sweet pea An annual climbing herb, *Lathyrus odoratus*, native to Sicily and widely cultivated as a garden ornamental. Flower colours include shades of red, purple, blue, white, and yellow. Family: *Leguminosae*.

sweet potato An annual herb, *Ipomoea batatas*, native to tropical America and widely cultivated for its starchy edible tubers, which are reddish-brown with white or orange flesh. Family: *Convolvulaceae*.

sweet william A usually biennial herb, *Dianthus barbatus*, native to S Europe and widely cultivated as a garden ornamental. Growing to a height of 30–70 cm, sweet williams produce flowers of red or pink in the wild but of various shades and patterns in cultivated varieties. Family: *Caryophyllaceae*.

swift A bird belonging to a widely distributed family (*Apodidae*; 75 species). 9–23 cm long, swifts have grey or brown plumage with white markings; a wide slightly curved bill, and forked tail. With scimitar-shaped wings and a high-speed flight they capture insects and even mate and sleep on the wing. Order: *Apodiformes* (swifts, hummingbirds, etc.).

Swift, Jonathan (1667–1745) Anglo-Irish clergyman, poet, and satirist. Born in Dublin, he lived as a young man in England, where he wrote the satire *A Tale of a Tub* (1704). In 1714 he returned to Dublin, where he became dean of St Patrick's Cathedral, attacked English misrule in a series of pamphlets, and wrote his satirical masterpiece, *Gulliver's Travels* (1726).

swiftlet A small *swift belonging to a genus (*Collocalia*; 15–20 species) occurring in SE Asia and Australia. 9–15 cm long, swiftlets use echolocation to navigate in the caves where they nest.

Swinburne, Algernon Charles (1837–1909) British poet. His poetry, especially in the first volume of *Poems and Ballads* (1866), is characterized by sensuous flowing rhythms. He supported republican movements in Europe and rebelled against conventional British morality.

Swindon 1. 5134N 147W A town in S England, in Swindon unitary authority, Wiltshire. It developed around the workshops of the former Great Western Railway. Railway engineering is still a major employer but there are now diverse industries as well as financial and other services. Population (1991 est): 145 236. **2.** A unitary authority in S England, in Wiltshire. Area: 230 sq km (89 sq mi). Population (2001): 180 061.

swine fever An infectious virus disease of pigs. In young pigs the disease is usually acute, resulting in death. Animals are treated with antiserum and antibiotics to combat secondary infection. In the UK infected animals are slaughtered.

Swithin, St (d. 862) English churchman. He was appointed Bishop of Winchester in 852. His tomb in Winchester Cathedral has become a famous shrine and according to legend the weather conditions on his feast day, 15 July, continue for 40 days.

Switzerland, Confederation of (French name: Suisse; German name: Schweiz; Italian name: Svizzera) A small landlocked country in central Europe. Undulating land in the N rises to the Jura Mountains in the W and the Alps in the S. The majority of the population is German, with large French and Italian minorities. *Economy*: although lacking in mineral wealth, Switzerland owes much of its prosperity to its terrain and central European position. The latter has led to its development as a centre for trade, banking, and insurance, while the magnificent scenery has long been a major tourist attraction. The principal exports are machinery, watches, chemicals, and textiles. *History*: its Celtic inhabitants (the Helvetii) were conquered by the Romans in the 1st century BC and the region was overrun by German tribes in the 5th century AD, becoming part of the Holy Roman Empire in the 10th century. In 1291 Uri, Schwyz, and Nidwalden formed the Everlasting League, which is traditionally regarded as the origin of the Swiss Federation. By 1499 the Federation had achieved virtual independence and in the 16th century it became an important centre of the Reformation. In 1648 its independence was formally recognized by the European powers. The French conquered Switzerland in 1798, but after Napoleon's fall (1815) the Congress of Vienna guaranteed Swiss neutrality. Religious conflict led to a modified constitution (1848) by which Switzerland became a unified federal state. It maintained its neutrality through both World Wars and has become the headquarters of many international organizations. Switzerland is a member of the European Free Trade Association but the electorate rejected membership of the European Economic Area in 1992 and voted against joining the EU in 2001. In 2002 Switzerland ended its long tradition of isolationism by joining the UN. Official languages: French, German, Italian, and Romansch. Currency: Swiss franc of 100 centimes. Area: 41 288 sq km (15 941 sq mi). Population (2003 est): 7 336 000. Capital: Bern.

swordfish A food and game fish, *Xiphias gladius*, related to tuna and found in all tropical and temperate seas. It has an elongated body, up to 4.6 m long, a triangular front dorsal fin, no pelvic fins, and an elongated swordlike snout used to slash at shoaling fish on which it feeds. It is the only member of its family (*Xiphiidae*).

swordtail A tropical freshwater fish of the genus *Xiphophorus*, especially *X. helleri*. It has an elongated body, up to 13 cm long, and males have a long swordlike extension of the lower lobe of the tail fin. Swordtails are naturally green with a red strip on each side, but have been bred in many colours for aquaria. Family: *Poeciliidae*; order: *Atheriniformes*.

sycamore A large *maple tree, *Acer pseudoplatanus*, native to central and S Europe and widely grown elsewhere. Up to 30 m tall, it produces winged fruits. The wood is used for violin cases, carvings, and furniture.

Sydney 33 55S 151 10E The oldest and largest city in Australia, the capital of New South Wales, situated on Port Jackson inlet. It is a commercial, cultural, and financial centre. The N side of Port Jackson is predominantly residential, industry being located to the S. The two shores are connected by Sydney Harbour Bridge (1932), the second largest single span bridge in the world. Cultural centres include the Sydney Opera House (opened 1973). *History*: a penal settlement was established at Port Jackson in 1788. Under the governorship of Lachlan Macquarie (1810–21), it developed into a thriving town. Area: 1735 sq km (670 sq mi). Population (1998 est): 3 276 207.

syenite A range of coarse-grained intrusive rocks (*see* IGNEOUS ROCK) consisting mainly of alkali feldspar or feldspathoids, together with hornblende and biotite.

syllabaries Writing systems in which each symbol represents a syllable in the language rather than a concept (*compare* IDEOGRAPHIC WRITING SYSTEMS). The only major language using a syllabary today is Japanese.

symbiosis Any close relationship between individuals of two different species of organisms. The term can therefore include parasitism (*see* PARASITE), *commensalism, and inquilinism (in which one organism shares the nest of the other), but is often restricted to—and used synonymously with—**mutualism**, in which both partners (symbionts) benefit from the association. An example of such a symbiotic relationship is provided by a sea anemone (*Adamsia paliata*), which lives attached to the snail shell inhabited by the hermit crab (*Eupagurus prideauxii*). The anemone protects the crab, from which it receives food and transport.

S

symphonic poem (*or* **tone poem**) A one-movement orchestral composition based on a literary, dramatic, or pictorial theme. The symphonic poem was invented by *Liszt, who composed a series of such works.

symphony An orchestral composition, usually in four movements. The classical symphony evolved in the mid-18th century and was perfected by Haydn and Mozart: the fast first movement was generally in *sonata form, the second was slow and expressive, the third a minuet and trio, and the fourth fast. Beethoven extended the formal and emotional range of the symphony, introducing a chorus and soloists in the last movement of his ninth symphony. In the hands of such composers as Bruckner and Mahler the symphony underwent further enlargement: Mahler's eighth symphony (1907) requires a thousand performers. Sibelius developed a concentrated approach to symphonic writing: his seventh symphony (1924) is in one movement. In the 20th century Nielsen, Shostakovich, Vaughan Williams, and others all developed the symphony in differing ways.

synagogue A Jewish place of worship. The synagogue probably originated during the Babylonian exile as a substitute for the Temple at Jerusalem. In antiquity it was a public meeting place, devoted mainly to the reading and exposition of the *Torah. It is now primarily a house of prayer. The principal piece of furniture is the cupboard (Ark) containing the Torah scrolls.

synapse The meeting point between one nerve cell and another (*see* NEURONE). The nerve impulse, as it arrives at the end of one nerve process, causes a chemical neurotransmitter (e.g. *acetylcholine or noradrenaline) to be released. This reaches receptors on the opposite neurone and produces a new nerve impulse.

synchrocyclotron A type of *cyclotron in which the frequency of the accelerating electric field can be varied to compensate for the relativistic increase in the mass of the accelerated particles. This enables energies of up to 500 MeV to be obtained.

synchrotron A particle *accelerator, similar to the *cyclotron, in which protons or electrons are accelerated in a circular path by an alternating electric field. The frequency of the field is synchronized with the energy of the particles to counteract their relativistic increase in the mass. Proton energies of several hundred GeV have been attained in these devices.

synchrotron radiation Electromagnetic radiation emitted in certain directions by a charged particle when the presence of a magnetic field confines its motion to a circle. The particle has to be moving at speeds comparable to that of light for a noticeable amount of radiation to be emitted. Therefore a high magnetic field is needed. Such fields are used in *synchrotrons.

syncline A trough-shaped fold or downfold in folded rock strata, the strata dipping towards a central axis (*compare* ANTICLINE). The youngest rocks occur in the core unless very complex deformation has occurred. Where the strata dip inwards from all directions the resulting feature is called a structural basin.

syndicalism A type of *socialism, advocated by Georges Sorel (1847–1922), under which the workers, not the state, would take over the productive resources of industry. Syndicalists were widely influential in Europe from the late 19th century until World War I.

Synge, John Millington (1871–1909) Irish dramatist. Most of his plays, which contributed greatly to the Irish Literary Renaissance, were inspired by his experience of life in an isolated Irish community, recorded in *The Aran Islands* (1907). His best-known play, *The Playboy of the Western World* (1907), caused riots at its first performance.

synodic period The average time taken by a planet or satellite to return to the same point in its orbit, relative to the sun, as seen from earth or from the satellite's primary (i.e. the body it orbits). It is therefore the interval between *oppositions or between identical *phases.

synthesizer A device that can reproduce the sounds of conventional instruments electronically or produce a variety of artificial tones. Electronic oscillators produce a range of signals, which after amplification and appropriate filtering are converted to sound waves. Individual circuits can be plugged in and out by the player, enabling a wide range of sounds to be produced.

syphilis A sexually transmitted disease caused by the *spirochaete bacterium *Treponema pallidum*. In primary syphilis chancres (hard ulcers) appear after about 25 days at the site of infection (usually the genitals). Weeks or months later the rash of secondary syphilis occurs. Arthritis, meningitis, and hepatitis may also occur at this stage. Without treatment the tertiary stage of syphilis may appear up to 30 years later and give rise to a variety of symptoms, including large tumour-like masses (gummas) in many organs, heart disease, blindness, and madness and paralysis. Syphilis can be treated with antibiotics. Several blood tests are available for diagnosing the disease.

Syracuse (Italian name: Siracusa) 37 04N 15 18E A seaport in Italy, in SE Sicily. Founded by Greeks in 734 BC, it became an important cultural centre in the 5th century. In 212 BC Syracuse fell to the Romans after a three-year siege. Ancient remains include a Greek temple, a Roman amphitheatre, and a fortress. Population (2000 est): 126 282.

Syr Darya, River (ancient name: Jaxartes) A river in central Asia, rising in the Tian Shan and flowing mainly W to the Aral Sea. Length: 2900 km (1800 mi).

Syria (official name: Syrian Arab Republic) A country in the Middle East, on the Mediterranean. In the W the Ghab depression runs N–S. To the E of this is steppe and desert with some mountains. The main fertile areas are the coastal strip and the basin of the River Euphrates (*see* FERTILE CRESCENT). The population is predominantly Muslim (mainly Sunnites). *Economy*: largely agricultural. Natural resources include oil, natural gas, phosphates, and salt. Syria has a planned socialist economy; much of its industry is nationalized, and land has been redistributed in favour of the peasants. *History*: before the 20th century Syria extended over much of the Middle East, including Palestine and Lebanon. In ancient times the *Amorites settled here and later *Phoenicia flourished. Islam was introduced by conquering Arabs (c. 640 AD) and the caliphate established at Damascus. From the 11th century, it was the site of battles with the Crusaders. From 1517 until World War I it was part of the Ottoman Empire. In 1920 it became part of a French mandate. Demands for Syrian independence were finally satisfied in 1946. It united briefly with Egypt in the United Arab Republic (1958–61). In 1971 Syria, Libya, and Egypt united loosely in the Federation of Arab Republics. From 1976 Syria intervened in Lebanon, at first as a mediator but later as an active supporter of certain Muslim factions. Syria's military presence in Lebanon was formalized by treaty in 1991. Although formerly friendly with the Soviet Union and implacably hostile towards Israel, Syria has more recently improved relations with the West. A tentative rapprochement with Israel has also begun. Syria is a member of the Arab League. Syria was ruled by President Hafiz al-*Assad from 1971 until his death in 2000, when he was succeeded by his son, Bashar al-Assad. Official language: Arabic. Currency: Syrian pound of 100 piastres. Area: 185 680 sq km (71 772 sq mi). Population (2003 est): 17 586 000. Capital: Damascus.

Syriac A Semitic language based on the dialect of *Aramaic spoken in Edessa (now Urfa, SE Turkey). It became an important literary and liturgical language during the 3rd to the 7th centuries AD.

syringa *See* LILAC; MOCK ORANGE.

syrinx The vocal organ of birds, located at the base of the windpipe. Air from the lungs vibrates membranes within a resonating chamber. Muscular tension alters pitch, and the two halves of the syrinx can produce different notes simultaneously.

Syros (Modern Greek name: Síros) A Greek island in the S Aegean Sea. The chief town, Hermopolis, is the capital of the Cyclades. Area: 85 sq km (33 sq mi). Population (1991 est): 16 008.

systole *See* BLOOD PRESSURE; HEART.

Szczecin (German name: Stettin) 53 25N 14 32E A city in NW Poland, on the River Oder. It is a major port, the chief export being coal. *History*: it became a member of the Hanseatic League in 1360. Seized by the Swedes (1648) it passed to Prussia in 1720, remaining under German control until it was ceded to Poland in 1945. It suffered severe damage during World War II. Population (1999 est): 416 988.

Szilard, Leo (1898–1964) US physicist, born in Hungary, who in 1934, while working in England, conceived the idea of a self-sustaining nuclear chain reaction. He joined *Teller in persuading Einstein to write to Roosevelt to warn him of the possibility that Germany might make an atom bomb first. During World War II he actually worked on the atom bomb, but later pressed for the abolition of all nuclear weapons.

S

T

tabasco A hot red pepper or sauce made from the entire fruits of a variety of the South American plant *Capsicum frutescens* and used to flavour soups, stews, curries, etc. Family: *Solanaceae*.

table tennis (*or* **Ping-Pong**) An indoor game for two or four players that originated in England in the late 19th century from *real tennis. It is played on a table 2.74 m (9 ft) long and 1.52 m (5 ft) wide, divided across its width by a net 15.25 cm (6 in) high. The players hit a small hollow plastic ball with a rubber-faced wooden bat. A point is scored when the opponent fails to return the ball after it has bounced once. The winner of a game is the first to reach 21 points with at least a two-point lead.

Tabriz 38 05N 46 18E A city in NW Iran. The most notable buildings are the Blue Mosque (15th century) and the citadel; it is famous for its carpets and has an airport and important rail connections. Population (1996): 1 191 043.

Tacitus, Cornelius (c. 55–c. 120 AD) Roman historian. He established his reputation as a public orator in Rome and became consul in 97 AD; in 112–13 he was governor of Asia. In 98 he wrote two historical monographs, *Germania* and *Agricola*, the latter an account of his father-in-law's career. His major works, the *Histories* and the *Annals*, survey Roman history during the periods 69–96 AD and 14–68 AD.

tadpole The aquatic larva of frogs and toads. The newly hatched tadpole feeds on vegetation but later becomes carnivorous. The external gills of the young tadpole are gradually replaced by internal gills, and after about ten weeks the limbs start to appear, the tail degenerates, the lungs develop, and the circulatory system changes to enable the adult to lead a terrestrial life.

Tadzhikistan, Republic of (*or* **Tajikistan**) A republic in central Asia. Largely mountainous, it contains the Pamir and Altai ranges. Some 53% of the population are *Tadzhiks, with Uzbek and Russian minorities. *Economy*: primarily agricultural, although there are mining, engineering, and textile industries. Health resorts have grown up around its mineral springs. The economy suffered badly from the civil war of the 1990s. *History*: the region converted to Islam in the 7th century. Ruled by the Uzbeks from the 15th century, Tadzhikistan was taken by Russia in the 1860s. It was a constituent republic of the Soviet Union from 1924 until it gained independence in 1991. A violent struggle between the ex-communist government and Muslim rebels broke out in 1992; a ceasefire was signed in 1994 but subsequent elections were boycotted by the opposition and fighting recurred. Peace was secured by a further agreement (1997), which involved a degree of power sharing. Tadzhikistan's cooperation with the USA in its *war on terrorism (2001) in neighbouring Afghanistan has led to closer relations with the West. Official language: Tadzhik. Currency: somoni of 100 dinars. Area: 143 100 sq km (55 240 sq mi). Population (2003 est): 6 535 000. Capital: Dushanbe.

Tadzhiks An Iranian Muslim people of Afghanistan and parts of Turkistan. They practise agriculture, growing cereal and fruit trees, and are traditionally traders, because of their position on the caravan routes between China, India, and Persia. They speak Tadzhik, a form of Persian.

Taegu 35 52N 128 36E A city in SE South Korea, the capital of North Kyongsang province. An old cultural centre, it has an important textile industry. Population (1995): 2 249 139.

Taft, William Howard (1857–1930) US statesman; Republican president (1909–13). Taft's conservative presidency was characterized by antitrust legislation and high protective tariffs, which split the Republican vote and lost the 1912 election to the Democrats.

Tagore, Rabindranath (1861–1941) Indian poet, philosopher, and teacher. He resigned his knighthood in 1919 as a protest against the *Amritsar massacre. He advocated cultural links between the East and the West and won the Nobel Prize for Literature in 1913 after the publication in English of *Gitanjali* (1912), a volume of spiritual poetry.

Tagus, River (Portuguese name: Tejo; Spanish name: Tajo) A river in SW Europe. Rising in E central Spain, it flows NW and then SW to the Atlantic Ocean at Lisbon. Length: 1007 km (626 mi).

Tahiti The largest of the Society Islands in the S central Pacific Ocean, in French Polynesia. Mountainous and famous for its beauty, it was *Gauguin's home for two years (1891–93). Settled by Polynesians in the 14th century, it was first visited by Europeans in 1767. It became French in 1842. Tourism is important, and copra, sugar cane, vanilla, and coffee are exported. Area: 1005 sq km (388 sq mi). Population (latest est): 116 000. Chief town: Papeete.

Tai Peoples of SE Asia and China who speak a group of related languages probably belonging to the Sino-Tibetan family. They are traditionally rice cultivators and Theravada Buddhists Major groupings are the Thai or Siamese, the Lao, Shan, and Lu.

taiga The coniferous forests, composed chiefly of spruces, pines, and firs, in the N hemisphere in subpolar latitudes. It extends from Norway across Sweden, Finland, and Russia (including Siberia). The coniferous forests of North America are also known as taiga.

tailorbird A S Asian *warbler belonging to the genus *Orthotomus* (9 species), named after its habit of sewing the edges of a large leaf together to form a bag in which the nest is built.

Tainan 23 01N 120 14E A city in SW Taiwan. It is the island's former capital (1683–1891). Population (2000 est): 728 060.

taipan A small-headed *cobra, *Oxyuranus scutellatus*, that occurs in NE Australia and New Guinea. Up to 3.3 m long, it has a ridged brown back and a yellow belly. Its venom contains a blood-clotting agent that is fatal within a few minutes.

Taipei (*or* **Taibei**) 25 00N 121 32E The capital of Taiwan, in the N of the island. Founded in the 18th century, it was under Japanese occupation (1895–1945) and became the seat of the Nationalist Government (*see* GUOMINDANG) in 1949. Population (2000 est): 2 641 312.

Taiping Rebellion (1851–64) A peasant rebellion in China that seriously undermined the Qing dynasty. In 1851 a Hakka peasant, Hong Xiu Quan, raised an army of rebels and marched N, capturing Nanjing in 1853. They then marched on Beijing but imperial forces, and cold weather, drove them back. When Nanjing fell, Hong and his followers committed mass suicide.

Taiwan (official name: Republic of China) An island off the SE coast of mainland China. Together with several nearby islands, including the Penghu Islands and the islands of Jinmen and *Mazu, it comprises the so-called Republic of China. Taiwan Island is largely mountainous, and two-thirds of the land is under forest. The people are predominantly Chinese. *Economy*: the balance of the economy has shifted from agriculture to industry and services. Iron and steel are important and the large volume of exports also includes television and radio sets, mass-produced plastic goods, chemicals, and textiles. As well as coal, gold, and other minerals, oil, and natural gas have been found, although timber remains the main natural resource. The chief crops are sugar cane, rice, and sweet potatoes. *History*: the island, named Formosa ("beautiful") by the Portuguese, who discovered it in 1590, was ceded by China to Japan in 1897. It surrendered to Gen *Chiang Kai-shek in 1945 and after the defeat of his Nationalist (*Guomindang) government by the Chinese Communists he fled here in 1949. Following threats by the People's Republic of China, the USA undertook in 1955 to protect Taiwan from attack. However, Taiwan's importance in international affairs diminished, and in 1979 the USA established diplomatic relations with mainland China and severed those with Taiwan. Taiwan is now recognized by less than 40 countries. Relations with China improved in the early 1990s but declined in 1995–96, when Taiwan embarked on democratic elections and China carried out military exercises in the Taiwan Strait. The Goumindang's 50-year domination of Taiwanese politics ended in 2000, when Chen Shui-Bian of the Democratic Progressive Party was elected president; he was narrowly re-elected in 2004. Official language: Mandarin Chinese. Currency: new Taiwan dollar of 100 cents. Area: 35 981 sq km (13 892 sq mi). Population (2003): 22 569 000. Capital: Taibei.

Taiyuan 37 50N 112 30E A city in NE China, the capital of Shanxi province. An ancient fortified city, it is a centre of technology, coalmining, and heavy industry. Population (1991 est): 1 960 000.

Tajikistan *See* TADZHIKISTAN, REPUBLIC OF.

Taj Mahal The mausoleum in Agra (N India) built (1631–53) for Mumtaz-i-Mahal, wife of the Mogul emperor, *Shah Jahan, who is also buried here. Set in formal gardens, the Taj Mahal is built mainly of white marble, delicately carved and inlaid with precious stones.

talapoin The smallest *guenon monkey, *Cercopithecus talapoin*, of central West Africa, also called pygmy guenon. Only 30 cm long, it has slightly webbed fingers and inhabits swampy forests. It has olive-green fur and conspicuously swollen genitals.

talaq An Islamic extra-judicial law of divorce enabling a husband to unilaterally divorce his wife by repudiating her three times. The marriage is then dissolved, unless the husband revokes the pronouncement during the next three months or, if the wife is pregnant, before the child is born.

talc A white or green mineral of hydrated magnesium silicate, $Mg_3(Si_4O_{10})(OH)_2$, with a layered structure. It is soft (hardness 1 on *Mohs' scale) and greasy. Soapstone (steatite) is a rock consisting almost wholly of talc. Besides its use as talcum powder, it is used as a filler, lubricant, and soft abrasive.

Taleban (Pashto: seeker) A militant Sunni Muslim organization that controlled most of Afghanistan from 1996 until late 2001. It imposed strict Islamic law, proscribing nearly all Western influences and denying women access to education and paid work. In Oct 2001 the Taleban's links with *al-Qaida prompted massive US air strikes (*see* WAR ON TERRORISM) and the regime collapsed within weeks.

talipot palm A *palm tree, *Corypha umbraculifera*, cultivated in India and Burma. Its trunk bears fan-shaped leaves up to 5 m in diameter. The pyramid-shaped flower cluster, more than 7 m tall, is the largest in the plant kingdom. The seeds are used for buttons and ornaments and the leaves for matting, fans, and thatching.

Talleyrand (Charles Maurice de Talleyrand-Périgord; 1754–1838) French politician and diplomat. He was foreign minister from 1797 until 1807, and again under the restored Louis XVIII. He represented France at the *Congress of Vienna and was ambassador to Great Britain (1830–34).

Tallinn (German name: Reval) 59 22N 24 48E The capital of Estonia, a port on Tallinn Bay in the Gulf of Finland. Its varied industries include shipbuilding. A member of the Hanseatic League, it was a prominent trading centre in the middle ages. Population (2000 est): 404 000.

Tallis, Thomas (c. 1505–85) English composer. He was joint organist of the Chapel Royal with his pupil Byrd. In 1575 he and Byrd produced *Cantiones Sacrae*, a collection of their motets. Tallis' most famous works are *The Lamentations of Jeremiah* and *Spem in Alium.*

Talmud Two of the most important works of Jewish religious literature: the Babylonian and the Palestinian (or Jerusalem) Talmud. Both Talmuds have the same form: they are written in a mixture of Hebrew and Aramaic and are presented as a commentary (*gemara*) on the *Mishnah. They contain records of rabbinic discussions, concentrating especially on halakhah. The rabbis mentioned in the Talmuds are called *Amoraim*; the Palestinian *Amoraim* flourished in the 3rd and 4th centuries AD; the Babylonian *Amoraim* continued to about 500.

tamarin A South American monkey found in open woodland and forests, closely related to *marmosets. Tamarins have tusklike lower canine teeth and feed on fruit, insects, eggs, etc. Chief genera: *Leontocebus* (21 species), *Leontideus* (3 species); family: *Callithricidae.*

tamarind An evergreen tree, *Tamarindus indica*, cultivated in tropical regions for its fruit. It bears clusters of yellow flowers. The fruit is a plump pod containing seeds and a bittersweet pulp, which is used in chutneys, curries, and medicines. Family: *Leguminosae.*

tamarisk A tree or shrub belonging to the genus *Tamarix* (90 species), native to W and S Europe, central Asia, and India. Tamarisks have small scalelike leaves, feathery clusters of small pink flowers, and deep roots. They have been widely planted to stabilize sand dunes. *T. mannifera* of the Middle East and central Asia exudes a sweet white edible substance (manna) from the stems. The false tamarisks (genus *Myricaria*; 10 species) are native to temperate Eurasia. Family: *Tamaricaceae.*

t

Tambo, Oliver (1917–93) South African politician; president of the African National Congress (1977–91). A lawyer, he was arrested with Nelson *Mandela in 1956, but released a year later. From 1960 to 1990 he directed ANC activities from outside South Africa.

Tamerlane *See* TIMUR.

Tameside A unitary authority in NW England, in Greater Manchester. Area: 103 sq km (40 sq mi). Population (2001): 213 045.

Tamil A Dravidian language of S India and Sri Lanka. It is the official language of the state of Tamil Nadu. There are several regional dialects. It is written in a script known as Vattelluttu and there are marked differences between the written and spoken forms. Tamil society, mainly Hindu, is stratified into caste groups.

Tampere (Swedish name: Tammerfors) 61 32N 23 45E The second largest city in Finland. It has a 20th-century cathedral and a university (1925). Its manufactures include railway rolling stock, textiles, wood pulp, paper, and footwear. Population (2000 est): 193 174.

Tampico 22 18N 97 52W A port and winter resort in SE Mexico, on the Río Panuco. Oil refining is the chief industry. Population (2000 est): 294 789.

tanager A brightly coloured songbird belonging to a family (*Thraupidae*; 222 species) occurring in tropical and subtropical America. Tanagers are 10–20 cm long, plumpish, with a short neck and a conical bill. They live mainly in forests and feed on fruit, nectar, and insects.

Tang (*or* **T'ang**; 618–906 AD) A Chinese dynasty that established an empire extending over much of central Asia and Korea. In Tang times foreign trade was encouraged and many Chinese scientific inventions, such as gunpowder, spread to the West. Arts, especially poetry, flourished, printing was invented, and paper money was used for the first time. In 751 Arab forces recaptured Turkestan and the Tang empire began to disintegrate. Two rebellions finally led to the collapse of the dynasty.

Tanganyika, Lake A lake in E central Africa, in Democratic Republic of Congo, Burundi, Tanzania, and Zambia. It is drained intermittently to the W by the River Lukuga. Area: about 33 000 sq km (12 738 sq mi).

tangent A straight line touching a curve at one point only or a plane touching a curved surface at one point only.

tangerine The fruit of a tree, *Citrus reticulata*, also called mandarin, native to SE Asia and cultivated in the S USA and the Mediterranean region. The orange fruit, which peels easily and readily splits into segments, is usually eaten fresh. Many varieties have been developed, including the satsuma and clementine.

Tangier (*or* **Tangiers**) 35 48N 5 45W A port in N Morocco, on a bay on the Strait of Gibraltar. An important Roman town, it was established as an international zone in 1923. Its international status was abolished on Moroccan independence (1956). Its industries include cigarette and textile manufacture, fishing, and market gardening, and it is also a tourist centre. Population (1994 est): 521 735.

tank An armour-plated military vehicle that is self-propelled on caterpillar tracks and typically armed with a gun (usually turret-mounted) and machine guns. Tanks are classified as main battle tanks (MBTs), for independent operation, and light tanks, for reconnaissance and other specialized uses. Based on a design of Sir Ernest Swinton (1868–1951), they were first used during the Somme offensive in September 1916. In World War II tank battles across Europe and N Africa replaced the static trench warfare of World War I. Modern tank development has concentrated on improving weapons, armour, and computer-aided navigation and fire control.

tanker A seagoing vessel equipped with a large cargo tank for transporting liquids, especially oil. The forerunner of the modern tanker was built in 1885; modern **supertankers** with a carrying capacity of 75 000 tonnes were developed after World War II. Ultra-Large Crude Carriers (ULCCs) have deadweights of up to nearly half a million tonnes.

Tannhäuser (c. 1200–c. 1270) German poet, a Minnesinger several of whose lyrics survive. Wagner's opera is based on the legend of his seduction by Venus, his life of sensuality at her court, and his pilgrimage to seek papal forgiveness.

tannin (*or* **tannic acid**) One of a group of phenol derivatives present in the bark, leaves, fruits, and galls of many plants. Tannins are used as mordants for many dyes, in tanning leather, and in making ink.

tansy A perennial herb, *Tanacetum* (or *Chrysanthemum*) *vulgare*, native to temperate Eurasia. It has flat-topped clusters of yellow flowers and was formerly cultivated for its aromatic leaves, used for cooking and medicinal purposes. Family: *Compositae*.

tantalum (Ta) A very hard grey dense metallic element, discovered in 1802 by A. K. Ekeberg (1767–1813). It is similar to niobium (Nb) and is difficult to separate from it. Tantalum occurs naturally in the ore columbite ($Fe(Nb,Ta)_2O_6$). It is resistant to chemical attack and is used in alloys, for example in surgical materials for implantation in the body and in incandescent filaments. The oxide (Ta_2O_5) is used in special glass, with high refractive index, for camera lenses. At no 73; at wt 180.948; mp 3020°C; bp 5458 ± 100°C.

Tantalus A legendary Greek king of Lydia, son of Zeus and Pluto and father of *Niobe and *Pelops. In Hades he was punished for certain offences against the gods by being made to stand within reach of water and fruits that moved away whenever he tried to drink or eat.

Tantras A group of Sanskrit religious texts written in India in the 5th century AD. They form the basis of esoteric systems of meditation in both Hinduism and Buddhism. In the **Tantric yoga** of Hinduism, two principles are postulated: Shiva and Shakti, male and female, mind and creative energy. The object of tantric practices is to arouse the female element and ultimately to unite it with the male principle. **Tantric Buddhism** involves an elaborate system of meditation by means of mudras (gestures), mantras (symbolic sounds), and mandalas (diagrams). The imagery of sexual union is the distinctive feature of both systems.

Tanzania, United Republic of A country in East Africa, on the Indian Ocean. It consists of a mainland area (formerly the republic of Tanganyika) and the islands of *Zanzibar and Pemba, as well as some smaller islands. The land rises from the coast through plateaus to mountains, especially in the N, with Mount Kilimanjaro at 5950 m (19 520 ft). The majority of the population is African, mainly of Bantu origin. *Economy*: chiefly agricultural, with much subsistence farming. In mainland Tanzania the chief crops are cotton, maize, and cassava. Zanzibar (with Pemba) is the world's largest producer of cloves, with coconuts as the second cash crop. Food crops include rice, bananas, and cassava. Minerals include diamonds, gold, tin, and salt; coal and iron have been found, as has offshore gas. There is little industry and Tanzania remains one of the world's poorest countries. *History*: important prehistoric remains have been found by the *Leakey family. Tanganyika was occupied by the Germans in the 1880s, becoming a German protectorate in 1891. After World War I it was under British rule. It gained independence in 1961 and in 1962 became a republic within the Commonwealth with Julius Nyerere as its first president. In 1964 Tanganyika and Zanzibar joined to form the United Republic of Tanganyika and Zanzibar, now known as Tanzania. In 1977 it became a one-party state. Plans to create a multiparty system were endorsed in 1992. In 1995 elections resulted in victory for the ruling party of the Revolution and Benjamin Mkapa became president. Recent years have seen a growing separatist movement in Zanzibar. Official languages: Swahili and English. Currency: Tanzanian shilling of 100 cents. Area: 945 087 sq km (364 900 sq mi). Population (2003 est): 35 078 000. Capital: Dodoma.

Taoism Emerging in the 6th century BC, Taoism is one of the two great native Chinese religio-philosophical systems (the other is Confucianism) and a major influence in the development of Chinese culture. The goal of Taoism as a philosophy is joyful, mystical, and practical harmony with the universe. *Yin* (the feminine) balances *yang* (the masculine). *Te* (virtue) and *ch'i* (energy) represent the power of effortless action accessible to the Taoist. Taoism emphasizes breath control, diet, exercises, sexual continence, and chemical elixirs as a means of achieving immortality. Since the Cultural Revolution (1966–68) religious Taoism survives mainly in Taiwan. Western interest has been aroused by philosophical Taoism, especially by the *I Ching*, an oracular work that claims to demonstrate purpose in chance events.

tape recorder A device for recording and playing back sound stored on magnetic tape, which is usually wound into cassettes or cartridges. In recording, the sound is converted to an electrical signal by a *microphone, amplified, then fed to an electromagnet in the recording head. The varying field of the magnet leaves a pattern of magnetization in the iron (or sometimes chromium) oxide coating of the tape. To play back, the magnetized tape induces a current in a coil as it passes the reproducing head. The coil current is then amplified and fed to loudspeakers.

tapeworm A parasitic hermaphrodite *flatworm of the class *Cestoda* (about 3000 species). Tapeworms range from 20 mm to 15 m in length and anchor themselves inside the intestine of their host by means of hooks and suckers on the head. The body consists of a chain of progressively large segments through which food is absorbed. The terminal segments—full of eggs—are regularly shed, passing out of the host's body to infect a secondary host, where larvae invade muscle tissue. Species infecting man include the beef tapeworm (*Taenia saginata*) and the pork tapeworm (*T. solium*).

tapir A shy nocturnal hoofed mammal belonging to the genus *Tapirus* (4 species). The largest species is the black and white Malayan tapir (*T. indicus*), reaching about 1 m at the shoulder and weighing up to 350 kg. Other species are brown. All have a large head with a short fleshy snout. Young tapirs are marked with white spots and stripes. Tapirs inhabit forests near water, feeding on leaves and shoots. Family: *Tapiridae*; order: *Perissodactyla*.

tar A thick black semisolid substance of organic origin, especially coaltar obtained when coal is heated to over 1000°C in the absence of air (1 kg of coal yielding about 50 g of tar). Tar can be used as it is, or can be distilled to produce a wide range of organic chemicals including benzene, naphthalene, and anthracene and their derivatives. The substance remaining is called pitch.

Tara 53 34N 6 35W A village in the Republic of Ireland, in Co Meath. The Hill of Tara was the ancient religious and political centre of Ireland and here the early Irish Kings lived and were crowned.

Tarantino, Quentin (1963–) US film director and screenwriter, noted for his violent stylish crime dramas, which include *Reservoir Dogs* (1993), *Pulp Fiction* (1994), and the two parts of *Kill Bill* (2003, 04).

tarantula A large dark hairy spider (up to 75 mm long) of the family *Theraphosidae*, found in tropical America. Many tarantulas live on trees or in burrows in the soil, feeding mainly at night on insects and occasionally frogs, toads, mice, and small birds. Their poisonous bite is painful but not fatal to man. The name was originally given to a *wolf spider (*Lycosa tarentula*) of Taranto (Italy).

taro A perennial herbaceous plant, *Colocasia esculenta*, also known as eddo, dasheen, and elephant's ear, native to tropical Asia and widely cultivated in tropical and subtropical areas for its edible tubers. The tubers, which are large, starchy, and spherical, contain more protein than potatoes and are eaten cooked as vegetables or made into puddings or bread. Family: *Araceae*.

t

tarot A pack of 78 cards used primarily in fortune telling, although they are also the forerunners of modern playing cards. They originated in 14th-century Italy. The original pack is now known as the Greater Arcana; this consists of 22 cards (believed to correspond to the letters of the Hebrew alphabet)—21 numbered cards representing natural elements, vices, and virtues and a "Fool" (the original joker). During the 14th century these were combined with 56 cards, now known as the Lesser Arcana, in 4 suits: cups, swords, coins, and rods, representing clergy, nobility, merchants, and peasants. Each suit consists of number cards from one to ten and four court cards: king, queen, knave, and knight.

Tarquin the Proud (Tarquinius Superbus) The last King of Rome, who ruled, according to Roman tradition, from 534 to 510 BC. Tarquin is probably a historical figure but many myths evolved to account for the nickname Superbus.

tarragon A perennial herb, *Artemisia dracunculus*, native to central Asia and widely cultivated. It has slender leaves and flowers, which are often dried and used in salads, sauces, pickles, etc. It also yields an essential oil used in cooking and perfumery. Family: *Compositae*.

tarsier A small nocturnal *prosimian primate belonging to the genus *Tarsius* (3 species), of Sumatra, Borneo, Celebes, and the Philippines. 22–43 cm long including the naked tail (13–27 cm), tarsiers have enormous eyes, large hairless ears, and gripping pads at the end of their digits. They are mainly arboreal. Family: *Tarsiidae*.

Tarsus 36 52N 34 52E A town in central S Turkey, near Adana. The first known settlement here was Neolithic; it was Assyrian for many centuries and an important town in the Roman and Byzantine Empires. St Paul was born here. Population (1997): 190 184.

Tashkent 41 16N 69 13E The capital of Uzbekistan. It is the oldest and largest city of central Asia, being a major communications, industrial, and cultural centre. Textiles, food- and tobacco-processing, and chemical industries are important. *History*: dating from at least the 1st century BC, it fell successively to the Arabs (7th century) and the Turks (12th century). It was captured by Russia in 1865. Population (1998 est): 2 124 000.

Tasmania An island state of Australia, separated from the SE corner of the mainland by Bass Strait. Discovered by the Dutch navigator Abel Tasman (c. 1603–c. 1659) in 1642, it was called Van Diemen's Land, after Tasman's patron, until 1856. Agriculture is important with dairy farming, sheep rearing, and apples and hops. More than 40% of the island is covered by forest and the export of wood chips to Japan is a significant industry. Large mineral deposits include tin, iron ore, zinc, lead, and copper. Area: 68 332 sq km (26 383 sq mi). Population (1999 est): 470 260. Capital: Hobart.

Tasmanian devil A carnivorous marsupial, *Sarcophilus harrisi*, now restricted to Tasmania. About 1 m long, it is black with a large head and wide jaws containing doglike teeth. Strong and heavily built, it feeds on wallabies, birds, and lizards and fights ferociously when cornered. Family: *Dasyuridae* (dasyures).

Tasman Sea A section of the SW Pacific Ocean, lying between SE Australia and Tasmania on the W and New Zealand on the E. Area: about 2 300 000 sq km (900 000 sq mi).

Tasso, Torquato (1544–95) Italian poet. He joined the court of the Este family at Ferrara where he wrote *Aminta* (1573) and his major work, the epic *Gerusalemme Liberata* (1575; published 1581). He later suffered from mental instability.

Tatars A mainly Muslim people, living mainly in the Tatar Republic of Russia, who belong to the NW division of the Turkic-speaking peoples. They traditionally lived by farming and herding. The Tatars are descended from peoples associated with the Mongol empire and the name was often used to refer to all the nomadic Turkic and Mongol peoples of the steppes.

Tate Galleries Two art galleries in London. The original Tate Gallery was built on Millbank in 1897 with the financial support of the sugar merchant and philanthropist Sir Henry Tate (1819–99). Highlights are its Pre-Raphaelite works and paintings by Turner, housed in the Clore Gallery since 1987. New branches were opened in Liverpool (1988) and in St Ives, Cornwall (1993). In 1999–2000 the former Bankside power station, on the S bank of the Thames, was converted into **Tate Modern**; this now holds the collection of international modern art, leaving the Millbank gallery (Tate Britain) for British works.

Tatra Mountains Two mountain ranges in central E Europe: the **High Tatras**, which extend 90 km (56 mi) E–W along the Polish-Slovakian border and constitute the highest area of the *Carpathian Mountains, and, to the S, the **Low Tatras**, which run parallel for some 150 km (93 mi) and rise to 2043 m (6703 ft).

Taunton 51 01N 3 06W A market town in SW England, the administrative centre of Somerset. The Great Hall in the 12th-century castle was the scene of Judge Jeffreys' Bloody Assizes (1685). Service industries now predominate; there is also precision engineering and the traditional cider making. Population (1996): 60 300.

Taupo, Lake (*or* **Taupomoana**) The largest lake in New Zealand. It lies on the volcanic plateau of central North Island and is drained by the Waikato River. Area: 616 sq km (238 sq mi).

tautomerism *See* ISOMERS.

Tavener, Sir John (1944–) British composer. His earlier compositions include the cantata *The Whale* (1966) and the opera *Thérèse* (1979). Later works, such as *The Protecting Veil* (1989) and *Mary of Egypt* (1992), are influenced by the liturgy of the Russian Orthodox Church.

Taverner, John (c. 1495–1545) English composer. He became choirmaster at Cardinal College (later renamed Christ Church) Oxford, in 1526. In 1528 he was imprisoned for heresy and left Oxford in 1530. He became a paid agent of Thomas Cromwell and gave up music. He left 28 motets, a *Te Deum*, 8 masses, and some instrumental music.

tawny owl A common *owl, *Strix aluco*, occurring in Europe and SE Asia. It has short rounded wings, dark-brown eyes, a mottled brown plumage, and lacks ear tufts.

taxidermy The art of making lifelike zoological models of creatures by preserving their skins and mounting them on suitable dummies. Taxidermy dates from the 17th century; improved technology and the use of plastic body forms have resulted in greater degrees of realism.

taxis The movement of a living organism or cell in response to an external stimulus: the movement is either towards or away from the stimulus, i.e. a positive or negative taxis. **Chemotaxis** is the response to a change in the concentration of a chemical. Many insects, for example, respond chemotactically to the scents emitted by the opposite sex. **Phototaxis** is the response to light: cockroaches are negatively phototactic. *Compare* TROPISM.

taxonomy The study of the classification and nomenclature of organisms. The principles of taxonomy were established in the 18th century by the work of *Linnaeus (*see also* BINOMIAL NOMENCLATURE). As far as possible, organisms are arranged into a hierarchy of groups (called taxa) based on degrees of relationship (*see* PHYLOGENY). When knowledge of the evolution of a group is lacking, taxonomy is based on structural and other similarities. The basic unit of classification is the *species. Related species are grouped into genera, which are arranged into orders and then classes, phyla, and finally kingdoms. In most modern classifications five kingdoms are recognized: *Animalia* (animals), *Plantae* (plants), *Fungi*, *Bacteria* (or *Prokaryotae*), and *Protoctista* (which includes algae, protozoa, and slime moulds).

Tay, River The longest river in Scotland, rising in the Grampian Mountains and flowing through Loch Tay. It enters the North Sea through the Firth of Tay. Length: 193 km (120 mi).

Taylor, Dame Elizabeth (1932–) US film actress, born in England. She began her career as a child star, notably in *National Velvet* (1944). Her other films include *Cleopatra* (1962) and *Who's Afraid of Virginia Woolf?* (1966), in both of which she costarred with Richard *Burton, to whom she was twice married; she has had six other husbands. She was created a DBE in 2000.

Taylor, Zachary (1784–1850) US statesman and general; president (1849–50). In the *Mexican War (1846–48) he won the victory of Buena Vista although his forces were outnumbered by four to one.

Tbilisi (former name: Tiflis) 41 43N 44 48E The capital of Georgia (Asia), on the River Kura. Engineering and the manufacture of textiles, wine, and food are the principal economic activities. *History*: founded in the mid-5th century, it fell successively to the Persians, Byzantines, Arabs, Mongols, Turks, and (in 1801) to the Russians. Population (1997 est): 1 398 968.

Tchaikovsky, Peter Ilich (1840–93) Russian composer. He became professor at the Moscow conservatoire in 1866. After the success of his first piano concerto, Tchaikovsky was offered financial support from Nadezhda von Meck (1831–94), a wealthy widow, whom he never met. Among his compositions are six symphonies, including the *Pathétique* (1893), three piano concertos (one unfinished), a violin concerto, string quartets, the opera *Eugene Onegin* (1877–78), and the ballets *Swan Lake* (1876–77) and the *Nutcracker* (1891–92).

tea The dried leaves and shoots of the evergreen shrub or tree, *Camellia sinensis*, which yield a beverage when infused with water. Native to parts of India and China, the tea plant has three major varieties—China, Assam, and Cambodia—and numerous hybrids. The shoots and young leaves are picked by hand and left to wilt before being lightly rolled and dried. The major tea exporters are India and Sri Lanka; most of China's production goes for home consumption. Tea is usually sold in the form of chopped leaves—loose or contained in small porous paper bags (tea bags). Its stimulating effect is due to the caffeine content (about 3.5%); flavour depends on the presence of volatile oils, and tannins are responsible for its colour. Family: *Theaceae*.

teak A tropical tree, *Tectonia grandis*, native to SE Asia and cultivated for its timber. It has small white flowers and fleshy fruits. The aromatic golden-yellow heartwood becomes brown when seasoned and is very hard and durable, being used for furniture, door and window frames, etc. Burma is the major teak exporter. Family: *Verbenaceae*.

teal A small dabbling duck, *Anas crecca*, of the N hemisphere, nesting on marshes and wintering on mudflats and estuaries. It feeds on water plants and aquatic invertebrates. Drakes are grey and have a chestnut head and a white wing stripe; females are mottled brown and both sexes have a green-and-black wing patch.

tear gas (*or* **lachrymator**) A substance, generally an atomized liquid rather than a gas, that is used to control crowds by causing acute eye irritation with temporary blindness and copious flow of tears. Chloroacetophenone (Mace) is the best-known example.

teasel A biennial herb, *Dipsacus fullonum*, native to Europe, W Asia, and N Africa. The prickly stems grow to a height of 2 m and bear conical heads of blue, purple, or white flowers with stiff hooked bracts. The flower heads of fuller's teasel (*D. fullonum sativus*) were formerly used to tease fabrics. Family: *Dipsacaceae*.

technetium (Tc) A silvery-grey radioactive element that was the first to be produced artificially. It does not occur naturally on earth but has been observed spectroscopically in a number of stars. It is chemically similar to rhenium and the compound $KTcO_4$ is a remarkable corrosion inhibitor in steels. At no 43; at wt (98); mp 2204°C; bp 4265°C.

tectonics The study of the major structural features of the earth's crust and the processes by which they are constructed. *See also* PLATE TECTONICS.

Tedder, Arthur William, 1st Baron (1890–1967) British air marshal. He joined the Royal Flying Corps in 1916. In World War II he was appointed (1940) to command the RAF in the Middle East and then (1943) in the Mediterranean. He became Eisenhower's deputy in 1944 and contributed to the success of the Normandy landings.

Tees, River A river in N England. Rising in the Pennines in Cumbria, it flows E through Co Durham to join the North Sea in the Teesmouth estuary. **Teesside** is the industrial district on the estuary, consisting of Stockton-on-Tees and Middlesbrough. Length: 113 km (70 mi).

teeth Hard structures in the mouth, embedded in the jaws, used for biting and chewing food. The human adult (permanent) dentition consists of 32 teeth, including incisors (8), canines (4), premolars (8), and molars (12), which replaces the milk (deciduous) dentition of young children. The third molars (wisdom teeth) do not normally appear until the age of about 20. The crown of a tooth consists of very dense hard enamel (largely *apatite) overlying the yellow bonelike dentine, which is slightly spongy and very sensitive to touch, temperature, and pain. The pulp at the centre contains blood vessels and nerve fibres. *See also* DENTISTRY.

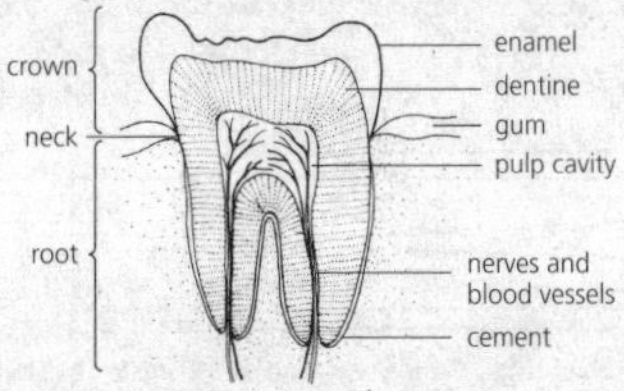

molar tooth The root of the tooth is anchored into the socket by a bonelike substance, cement.

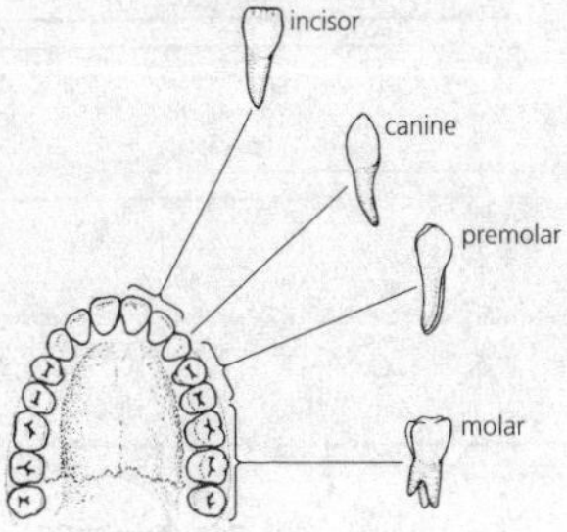

teeth in the adult upper jaw The incisors and canines are used principally for biting; the premolars and molars are used for grinding and chewing. The lower jaw contains the same number and type of teeth.

teeth

Tegucigalpa 14 20N 87 12W The capital of Honduras, situated in the centre of the country in a high valley. Founded in 1579, it was an important centre of gold and silver mining. It became the capital in 1824. Population (1999 est): 988 400.

Tehran (*or* **Teheran**) 35 40N 51 26E The capital of Iran, in the N centre of the country at the foot of the Elburz Mountains. Tehran is the commercial, industrial, administrative, and cultural centre of the country, with six universities (oldest 1934). It became the capital in 1788 and was greatly enlarged during the 20th century. Population (1996): 6 758 845.

Tehran Conference (1943) The conference in World War II attended by F. D. Roosevelt (USA), Stalin (Soviet Union), and Churchill (UK). Its chief purpose was to coordinate Allied strategy in W and E Europe.

Te Kanawa, Dame Kiri (1944–) New Zealand soprano. She made her major debut in the *Marriage of Figaro* at Covent Garden in 1971. She was made a DBE in 1982.

tektites Small glassy objects, which have been found in certain parts of the earth, often stewn over immense areas. They are apparently composed of rapidly cooled molten material, probably terrestrial in origin and formed during the impact of giant meteorites.

Tel Aviv-Jaffa 32 05N 34 46E A city in central Israel, on the Mediterranean coast. It is the largest city in Israel, and the country's commercial, industrial, and cultural centre. The city's port is at Ashdod, to the S. *History*: Tel Aviv was originally a suburb to the N of Jaffa, founded in 1909 to relieve the overpopulation of the Jewish quarter. Following tension between Arabs and Jews, the two towns were separated in 1921. Almost the entire Arab population fled Jaffa on its capture by Jewish forces in 1948, and the two cities were reunited in 1950. Population (1999 est): 348 100.

Telemann, Georg Philipp (1681–1767) German composer. Whilst studying law at Leipzig University he taught himself to play various instruments and to compose. He held musical posts in various cities, including Frankfurt and Hamburg (1721). His output was very large and included operas, oratorios, church music, and much chamber music.

teleost Any *bony fish belonging to the infraclass *Teleostei* (over 20 000 species), which includes nearly all the important food and game fish and many aquarium fish. Teleosts have a symmetrically divided (homocercal) tail fin and an air-filled swim bladder. Most lay eggs on rocks or plants, or freely in the water, although some bear live young. Chief orders: *Clupeiformes* (*see* HERRING; ANCHOVY), *Salmoniformes* (*see* SALMON; TROUT; PIKE), *Cypriniformes* (*see* CARP), *Gadiformes* (*see* COD; HAKE), *Perciformes* (*see* PERCH; MACKEREL), *Pleuronectiformes* (*see* FLATFISH); subclass: *Actinopterygii*.

telepathy *See* EXTRASENSORY PERCEPTION.

telescope An optical instrument that produces a magnified image of distant objects. The

refracting telescope was invented in 1608 by *Lippershey in Holland and developed by Galileo as an astronomical instrument a year later. The light in the refracting telescope falls on a converging long-focus objective lens. The resulting image is then magnified by the short-focus eyepiece to produce the final image. An example is the **Keplerian telescope**. Refractors are also used as terrestrial telescopes, usually containing an additional lens or a prism to cause the inverted image to be seen erect. The first **reflecting telescope** was produced by *Newton in 1668. In the reflecting telescope the light from an object is collected by a concave, usually paraboloid, mirror of long focal length. This primary mirror reflects the lights into a secondary optical system, which in turn reflects it into a short-focus eyepice. The eyepiece lenses produce a magnified image that can be viewed or photographed. Depending on the secondary optics, reflectors are called **Gregorian, Newtonian, Cassegrain,** or **coudé telescopes.** *See also* SCHMIDT TELESCOPE; RADIO TELESCOPE.

teletext An information service in which pages of text are transmitted for display on a domestic television set. The system utilizes two of the unused lines between picture frames. All the stored information, which may be weather reports, news flashes, sports results, etc., is sent out continuously in a cycle. The required pages are selected for display by keypad. The two systems originally developed in the UK were Ceefax, run by the BBC, and Oracle, run by the Independent Broadcasting Authority; Oracle was replaced by a new system provided by Teletext Ltd in 1992 and Ceefax was gradually phased out in favour of a digital text service from 2001. *See also* VIEWDATA.

television (**TV**) The broadcasting of pictures and sound by *radio waves or electric cable. Television was invented by John Logie *Baird in 1926. A television *camera converts the picture into an electrical signal. In most of Europe the picture consists of 625 lines made by an electron beam scanning the screen of a *cathode-ray tube, 25 such pictures being formed every second. In the USA and Japan, 525 lines and 30 frames per second are used. High-definition television (HDTV) employs pictures with up to 1125 lines in a wide-screen format. A brightness signal and a synchronization signal (to form the lines and frames of the picture) make up the picture signal, which is used to modulate (*see* MODULATION) a VHF or UHF carrier wave and is broadcast with the modu-

refractors

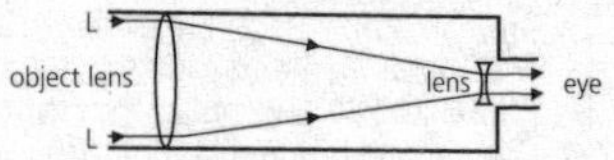

Galilean. The simplest practical form of refracting telescope was developed by Galileo in about 1609 from Lippershey's invention.

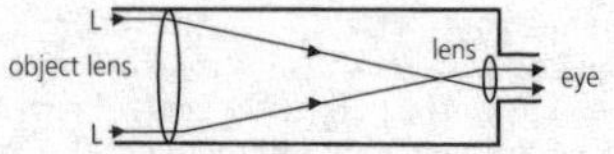

Keplerian. Kepler's arrangement produces an inverted image but was much used for astronomical observations in which the inversion did not matter.

reflectors

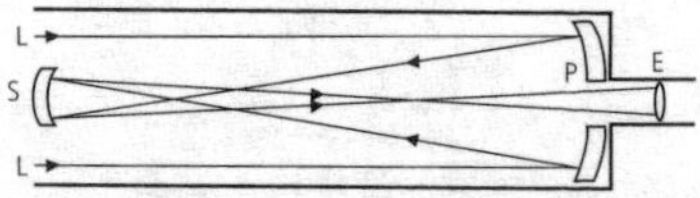

Gregorian. James Gregory proposed this design in 1663 but it has had little general application.

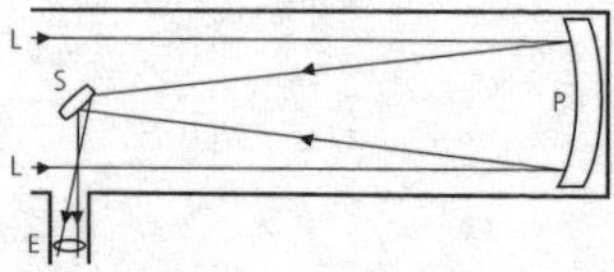

Newtonian. In Newton's 1671 design the secondary mirror is placed at an angle of 45° to the axis of the beam.

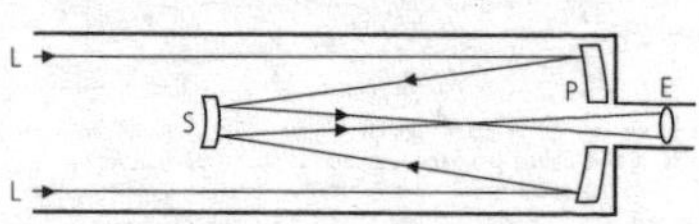

Cassegrain. Widely used, this form was invented by the obscure French astronomer N. Cassegrain in 1672.

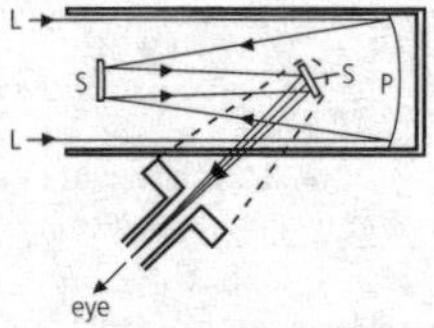

Condé (French: angled). This arrangement is valuable in larger telescopes as it increases their focal length.

L = light rays P = primary mirror
E = eyepiece S = secondary mirror

telescope

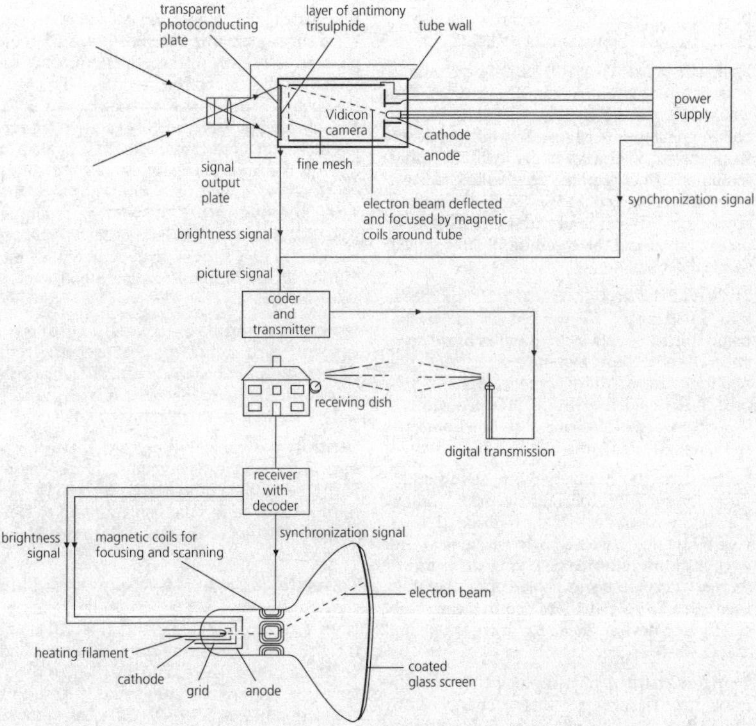

television

lated sound carrier wave (which has a slightly different frequency).

The aerial or dish (for satellite broadcasts) of the TV receiver detects the broadcast radio waves and the picture and sound signals are separated within the receiver. The picture signal is demodulated, and the resulting current is used to control the electron beam in a cathode-ray tube so that the picture is reconstructed.

In a colour television camera light from the scene to be televised is filtered into three primary colour components: red, green, and blue. Light of each colour goes to a separate image tube. There are three systems in use for encoding colour picture information for transmission, all of which combine colour and intensity information with sound and synchronization in a similar way to black-and-white television. The colour television receiver splits the signal into red, green, and blue components and applies these to three separate electron guns. The beam from each gun activates a set of phosphor dots of that colour on the screen, thus reconstructing the red, green, and blue components of the picture.

Since the late 1990s there has been a growing use of digital systems in which the signal is sampled up to 30 000 times per second and the characteristics of the sampled signal are represented by digits, which are then transmitted and reconstituted in the receiver. The digital process ensures that no distortion or interference occurs. In the UK there are plans to complete the switch to digital by 2010, when all viewers will require a set-top decoder or an integrated digital TV.

Telford, Thomas (1757–1834) British civil engineer. His suspension bridge over the Menai Strait, completed in 1825, is 177 metres long. Telford also designed some 1500 kilometres of roads, many bridges and aqueducts, canals, and St Katherine's Dock in London.

Telford and Wrekin A unitary authority in

W central England, in Shropshire. Area: 289 sq km (112 sq mi). Population (2001): 158 285.

Tell, William A Swiss national hero who is first mentioned in a 15th-century chronicle and who, in Schiller's play *Wilhelm Tell* (1804), embodies the Swiss struggle for independence from the Austrian Habsburgs. After refusing to do homage as required by Gessler, the Austrian governor, Tell was ordered to shoot an apple from his son's head with a crossbow at 80 paces. He passed this test and later killed Gessler.

Teller, Edward (1908–2003) US physicist, born in Hungary. He worked on the fission bomb during World War II and subsequently on the fusion bomb, making a significant contribution to its development. Teller's unfavourable evidence in J.R. *Oppenheimer's security-clearance hearing lost him some respect among scientists.

tellurium (Te) A silvery-white semiconductor of the sulphur group, discovered by Müller von Reichenstein in 1782. The hydride (H_2Te) is volatile and toxic, with a powerful smell of bad eggs. Bismuth telluride (BiTe) is used as an effective thermoelectric cooler. The metal is used in some special alloys and in some semiconducting devices. At no 52; at wt 127.60; mp 449.5 ± 0.3°C; bp 988°C.

temperature A physical quantity that is a measure of the average *kinetic energy of the constituent particles of a body. It determines the direction in which *heat flows when two bodies are in contact, the body with the higher temperature losing heat to that with the lower. The temperature of a body is measured in kelvins, degrees Celsius, or degrees Fahrenheit.

Templars (Poor Knights of Christ and of the Temple of Solomon) A religious order of knighthood founded (c. 1120) in Jerusalem by a group of French knights. The Templars were, with the *Hospitallers, the most important military order of the *Crusades. Accused of heresy and immorality by Philip IV of France, the Templars were suppressed by the papacy in 1312.

Temple, Shirley (1928–) US film actress, who featured as a child star in such films as *Little Miss Marker* (1934) and *Heidi* (1937). She won a special Academy Award in 1934. She was subsequently appointed US ambassador to Ghana (1974–76) and to Czechoslovakia (1989–92).

Temple of Jerusalem The ancient centre of Jewish religious life. The first Temple was built by King Solomon (c. 950 BC) and destroyed by Nebuchadnezzar in 586 BC. The second Temple was built later in the 6th century BC, restored by the *Maccabees and later by Herod the Great, and destroyed by the Romans in 70 AD. An attempt was made to rebuild the Temple under the Roman emperor Julian (362 AD) but it was abandoned. Both temples were built on the same walled platform, known as the Temple Mount; part of the western retaining wall of this structure is the **Western (Wailing) Wall**, still a holy site for Jews. Since 691 AD the Muslim Dome of the Rock has stood on the Temple Mount.

tench An elongated fish, *Tinca tinca*, that is related to *carp and occurs in European fresh waters. Its slimy body is greenish or blackish above with lighter undersides. It lives in quiet waters, feeding on small animals and plants.

tendon A strong fibrous cord that joins a muscle to a bone. The tendon fibres merge with the muscle fibres and extend to the fibrous tissue lining the bone, serving to concentrate the pull of the muscle on a small part of the bone.

Tenerife 28 15N 16 35W A Spanish island in the Atlantic Ocean, the largest of the Canary Islands. Its Pico de Teide mountain is, at 3710 m (12 172 ft), the highest in Spain. Early fruit and vegetables are produced and the island is popular for holidays. Area: 2020 sq km (780 sq mi). Population (latest est): 771 000. Chief town: Santa Cruz de Tenerife.

Tennessee A state in the S central USA. In the E there is a region of thickly wooded mountains, while further W an area of upland plateau and rolling hills gives way to lowland plains and swamps situated between the Tennessee and Mississippi Rivers. An agriculturally poor state, its major crops are tobacco, soya beans, and cotton. Beef and dairy products are also important. The leading industries produce chemicals, food products, machinery, and textiles. The state is an important hardwood producer. It is the USA's largest producer of zinc and the extraction of stone is a major source of revenue. *History*: disputed by the English and French in the 17th century, it was under British rule during the American Revolution. The area became a territory in 1790 and a state in 1796. Area: 109 411 sq km (42 244 sq mi). Population (2000): 5 689 283. Capital: Nashville.

Tennessee River A river in SE USA. It follows a U-shaped course from E Tennessee, flowing through NE Alabama before returning across Tennessee to join the Ohio River at Paducah, Kentucky. **The Tennessee Valley Authority**, created in 1933, built dams along the river to control floods, arrest soil erosion, and generate electricity. Length: 1049 km (652 mi).

Tenniel, Sir John (1820–1914) British cartoonist and book illustrator. He worked for *Punch* from 1851 to 1901 but is best known for his illustrations for *Alice in Wonderland.*

tennis (*or* **lawn tennis**) A game for two or four players using rackets to hit a cloth-covered rubber ball on a grass or hard court. It originated in England in the mid-19th century. A match lasts a maximum of five sets for men and three for women and the minimum number of games per set is six. A lead of two games is usually needed to win a set. The scoring system derives from *real tennis and a minimum of four points is needed for a game: 15, 30, 40, and game; a lead of two points is also needed to win a game. To win points players must return the ball over the net either before it bounces (volley) or after the first bounce, positioning it so that their opponents cannot return it. The game is popular at all levels, from the local club to the All England Championships at Wimbledon. Other highly prized trophies are the *Davis Cup and the Wightman cup.

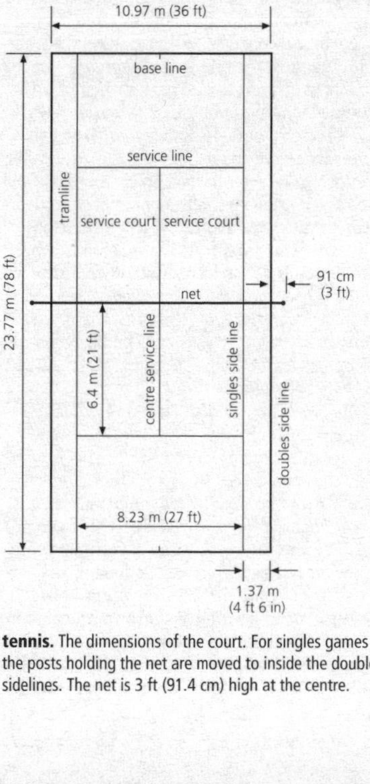

tennis. The dimensions of the court. For singles games the posts holding the net are moved to inside the doubles sidelines. The net is 3 ft (91.4 cm) high at the centre.

Tennyson, Alfred, Lord (1809–92) British poet. He published volumes in 1830 and 1832 but gained general acclaim only with his 1842 volume, which included "Morte d'Arthur." In 1850 he married, became poet laureate, and published *In Memoriam*, a sequence of elegaic lyrics mourning the death of his close friend Arthur Hallam (1811–33). He reinforced his popularity with *Idylls of the King* (1859) and other poems. He accepted a peerage in 1884.

tenor A high adult male singing voice. The word comes from the Latin *tenere*, to hold; in Renaissance polyphonic music the tenor part held the melody on which the music was based. Range: C on the bass stave to C two octaves above.

tenrec An insect-eating mammal belonging to the family *Tenrecidae* (30 species), found only in Madagascar and the Comoro Islands. Tenrecs measure 5–40 cm, some with long tails and some tailless, and generally have a brownish coat of bristly hairs or spines. Most tenrecs live in burrows and are nocturnal, feeding mainly on small invertebrates with some plant material. Order: *Insectivora*.

Tenzing Norgay (c. 1914–86) Sherpa mountaineer, who, with Sir Edmund *Hillary, was the first man to reach the summit of Mount Everest (1953). He later became a director at the Himalayan Mountaineering Institute, Darjeeling.

tequila A Mexican spirit made of the fermented juice of an agave plant (*see* AGAVE), water, and, sometimes, sulphuric acid and yeast. The spirit is distilled twice in potstills then may be aged in casks. It is produced near the town of Tequila.

terbium (Tb) A *lanthanide element, discovered in 1843 by C. G. Mosander (1797–1858) and named after the village Ytterby in Sweden. It is obtained from monazite ($CePO_4$), and the brown oxide (Tb_2O_3) is used as a phosphor in colour-television tubes. The metal is silvery-grey and can be cut with a knife. At no 65; at wt 158.92; mp 1356°C; bp 3230°C.

terebinth A small tree, *Pistacia terebinthus*, native to the Mediterranean region. It has small flowers producing purple fruit and was formerly an important source of turpentine. Family: *Pistaciaceae*.

Teresa, Mother (Agnes Gonxha Bejaxhui; 1910–97) Indian nun born in Yugoslavia of Albanian parents, who founded the Order of the Missionaries of Charity (Calcutta; 1948) to help lepers, the poor, and the aged and dying throughout the world. She received the 1979 Nobel Peace Prize, became an honorary OM (1983), and was beatified (2003) only six years after her death.

Teresa of Ávila, St (1515–82) Spanish nun and mystic, who reformed the Carmelite order. She joined the Carmelites at Ávila in 1533 and in 1555 experienced a spiritual awakening followed by several visions. She founded the Convent of St Joseph in Ávila in 1562 and later other religious houses with the help of St John of the Cross (1542–91). Her books, which include her *Life* (1562–65) and *The Way of Perfection* (after 1565), are regarded as classics of mysticism.

Teresina 5 09S 42 46W A city in NE Brazil, the capital of Piauí state on the Rio Parnaíba. It is a commercial centre; exports include cattle, hides, cotton, rice, and manioc. Population (2000): 676 596.

termite A social insect, also called white ant (although unrelated to the ants), belonging to the mainly tropical order *Isoptera* (2000 species). Termite colonies nest in tunnels and galleries in wood, soil, or earth mounds (termitaria). There are three major castes: winged reproductives, workers, and soldiers. The reproductives found new colonies; the workers construct galleries, feed the colony, and care for the young; while the soldiers are concerned with defence. Termites eat cellulose and are very destructive when they invade houses and attack wood products.

tern A seabird belonging to a subfamily (*Sterninae*; 35–40 species) occurring around coasts and inland waters worldwide. Terns have long wings, short legs, usually a forked tail, and their plumage is white, black-and-white, or almost totally black. They feed on fish and crustaceans and often migrate long distances. Family: *Laridae* (gulls and terns).

terracotta (Italian: baked earth) A fired clay, usually reddish in colour, used to make sculpture, tiles, bricks, containers, etc. Terracotta figurines, often painted, were very common in ancient Greece and Rome. The art was revived during the Renaissance.

terrapin A small edible turtle belonging to the family *Emydidae*, occurring chiefly in the New World. The diamondback terrapin (*Malaclemys terrapin*), which occurs in coastal waters and salt marshes of North America, has diamond-shaped patterns on its dark carapace and is yellow with black speckles underneath. It is regarded as a table delicacy.

terrier One of about 20 breeds of dog characterized by their small compact sturdy build and traditionally used for hunting vermin and rousing foxes and badgers from cover. The Scottish breeds, such as the *cairn terrier, *Scottish terrier, *Skye terrier, and West Highland white terrier, tend to be smaller and longer haired than other terriers.

Territorial Army A British force of volunteers, created as the Territorial Force in 1907 and renamed in 1922. Between 1967 and 1979 it was known as the Territorial Army Volunteer Reserve. Its 84 000 men constitute a pool of trained and equipped reinforcements for the regular army.

terrorism The use of violence and intimidation to achieve an objective that is usually, but not always, political. The targets may be members of a government or organization who are known to be antagonistic to the terrorists' cause or ordinary members of the public. In the latter case the motive is usually an attempt to generate publicity through outrage, or to put pressure on governments by arousing public alarm and concern. Indiscriminate shooting, bombing, hostage-taking, kidnapping, and hijacking of aircraft are all part of the terrorists' armoury. The psychology of terrorists clearly varies widely; while in some cases their behaviour defies rational understanding, other groups can be seen to have made a calculating use of terrorist methods as part of a political strategy and have disbanded when these objectives were achieved. Terrorist groups whose motivation is not strictly or wholly political include those motivated by racism (e.g. Nazi *Brownshirts, the US *Ku Klux Klan), a religious belief (e.g. *Hamas, *al-Qaida), or an extreme minority cause (e.g. militant animal rights movements).

The containment of terrorism is usually extremely difficult, not least because many of the organizations involved are financed, abetted, and protected by sympathetic governments. International collaboration against terrorism has rarely proved effective, owing to the different interests of the governments and police authorities involved. Following the terrorist attacks on the USA on *September 11, 2001 (the most murderous and spectacular in history), President George W. Bush announced a concerted *war on terrorism in which US military force would be used against international terrorist networks and those regimes found to be harbouring them.

Terry, Dame Ellen (Alice) (1847–1928) British actress. A member of a large and talented family of actors, from 1878 to 1898 she acted with Sir Henry *Irving at the Lyceum Theatre, achieving particular success in the major Shakespearean roles.

Tertiary period The first geological period of the Cenozoic era, following the Cretaceous period and preceding the Quaternary. It lasted from about 65 to 1.8 million years ago and contains the Palaeocene, Eocene, Oligocene, Miocene, and Pliocene epochs, in ascending order. Modern invertebrates and mammals evolved and became increasingly abundant; the modern angiosperms became the dominant plants. The Alpine period of mountain formation reached its peak in the Miocene. The climate began to deteriorate in the Oligocene, finally leading to the Ice Age of the Pleistocene.

tesla (T) The SI unit of magnetic flux density equal to one weber per square metre. Named after Nikola Tesla (1856–1943), US engineer.

Test Acts **1.** In England, the Acts stipulating that public office holders must take Holy Communion in the Church of England (1673) and excluding all Roman Catholics except the Duke of York (later James II) from parliament (1678). They were not formally repealed until the mid-19th century. **2.** In Scotland, the Act (1681) that forced all public office holders to declare their belief in Protestantism; it was repealed in 1889.

testis The organ of male animals in which *sperm is produced. In men there is a pair of testes, or testicles, which produce both sperm and sex hormones (*see* ANDROGENS). Before birth the testicles descend into the scrotum—a sac of skin outside the abdominal cavity—since sperms require a temperature lower than that of the body to mature. The sperms complete their development in a convoluted tube (epididymis) outside the testis.

testosterone A steroid hormone—the most important of the *androgens—first isolated from bull testes in 1935. Synthetic testosterone has various medical uses, including treatment of certain forms of sterility in men.

test-tube baby A baby produced by fertilizing the mother's egg cell with sperm from the father in a test tube (*in vitro* fertilization): the fertilized egg is then implanted surgically into the mother's womb. It is a means of overcoming sterility in a woman due to blocked Fallopian tubes or any similar defect. The first test-tube baby was born in July 1978, and the first from a frozen embryo in 1988. *See also* ARTIFICIAL INSEMINATION.

tetanus A serious disease caused by the bacterium *Clostridium tetani* entering wounds and producing a powerful toxin (poison) that irritates the nerves supplying muscles. After an incubation period of seven–ten days, stiffness, spasm, and rigidity of the muscles affects the jaw (hence the popular name—lockjaw) and spreads to other muscles. The disease can be prevented by completing a full course of antitetanus immunization.

tetracyclines A group of *antibiotics derived from *Streptomyces* bacteria. Tetracyclines are active against a large number of different bacteria. Taken by mouth, they may cause the side effects of diarrhoea, nausea, and discoloration of growing teeth and bones.

tetraethyl lead ($Pb(C_2H_5)_4$) A colourless poisonous oily liquid. It is made by treating lead-sodium alloys with chloroethane and is added to petrol to prevent knocking in internal-combustion engines. However, lead-free petrol is now being widely promoted to reduce lead pollution of the atmosphere.

Teutonic Knights A religious knightly order founded in the Holy Land in 1191 which subsequently (from 1211) moved its activities to the Baltic area. The Order ruled the coastal lands S and SE of the Baltic in the 13th and 14th centuries, presiding over an intense German colonization, in which the indigenous peoples were reduced to serfdom. A defeat by the Poles and Lithuanians at Tannenberg in 1410 halted its expansion. After the Reformation the order was dissolved and in 1525 the last Grand Master became the secular ruler of Prussia and the founder of the dynasty of Hohenzollern. One branch of the order survived in Germany until it was dissolved in 1809 by Napoleon.

Texas The second largest and the third most populous state in the USA, in the SW of the country. It consists of four main physical regions: the West Gulf Coastal Plain in the SE; the Central Lowland; the Great Plains; and the Trans-Pecos or mountainous area in the W. It leads the nation in the production of oil and natural gas and is also a major producer of sulphur. Oil-related industries dominate the manufacturing sector, the most important being the chemical industry. There is an important space centre at Houston and Dallas is a major commercial and industrial centre. Texas also produces a variety of crops, especially cotton, sorghum grains, rice, and peanuts, and is a leading livestock producer. *History*: it was colonized by the Spanish in 1682, the first permanent Anglo-American settlement being established in 1821. In 1836 the Texans set up a provisional government in opposition to the Mexican dictatorship of Antonio López de Santa Anna; following the heroic defence of the *Alamo, the revolutionary army finally defeated Mexican forces. A republic was established and Texas remained independent for almost a decade until annexation by the USA was agreed upon and Texas became a state. Area: 692 402 sq km (267 338 sq mi). Population (2000): 20 851 820. Capital: Austin.

Thackeray, William Makepeace (1811–63) British novelist and journalist. After publishing several novels under pseudonyms, he won fame and financial success with *Vanity Fair* (1847–48), which he followed with the semiautobiographical *The History of Pendennis* (1848–50) and the historical *Henry Esmond* (1852). In his last years he edited the *Cornhill Magazine* (1860–62).

Thailand, Kingdom of (name until 1939: Siam) A country in SE Asia, on the Gulf of Thailand. Fertile plains and hills in the S rise to mountains in the N. Most of the population is Thai. *Economy*: the chief food crop and main export is rice. Forests cover 60% of the land but export of hardwoods has been banned. Mineral resources include tin, manganese, antimony, and zinc. The cement, textiles, and motor vehicle industries are important; other manufactures include electronic equipment and computers. Tourism is now the main source of foreign revenue. The rapid economic growth of the 1990s came to a sudden end with the collapse of the currency and stock market (mid-1997). *History*: by the 6th century AD the Thais had reached the area from the N. They conquered the Mons to the S and in succeeding centuries were involved in struggles with the Burmese and Khmers. In the 19th century they lost territory to the French and the British but remained independent. In 1932 the absolute monarchy was replaced by a constitutional monarchy, since when civil and military governments have alternated, often through violent upheavals. In 1992 mass protests led to the removal of the unelected prime minister Gen Suchinda Kraprayoon and, following free elections, the creation of a reformist coalition under Chuan Leekpai. The financial crisis of 1997 led to the virtual collapse of the economy and the fall of the government of Chavalit Yongchaiyudh. The telecommunications tycoon Thaksin Shinawatra was elected prime minister in 2001. Official language: Thai. Currency: baht of 100 satang. Area: 514 000 sq km (198 250 sq mi). Population (2003 est): 64 022 000. Capital: Bangkok.

Thales (c. 624–547 BC) The first of the Greek speculative scientists. Born at Miletus, he used the data from Babylonian astronomers to predict the solar eclipse of 28 May, 585 BC, advised on stellar navigation, and introduced Egyptian methods of land measurement. He held that all things derive from water and set the Presocratics on their quest for the basic substance of the universe.

thalidomide A sedative drug that was found to cause severe developmental defects in the fetus when taken during pregnancy. The most common abnormality induced by thalidomide is phocomelia, in which feet and hands develop normally without corresponding growth of the bones of the arms and legs. Between 1959 and 1962 some 500 deformed babies were born in the UK and over 2000 in West Germany.

thallium (Tl) A metallic element, discovered spectroscopically by Sir William Crookes in 1861 and named after the Greek *thallos*, a green shoot, because of its bright-green spectral line. The metal is soft and malleable and reacts easily to form numerous salts. It occurs in sulphide ores of lead and zinc and in iron pyrites (FeS_2). At no 81; at wt 204.38; mp 304°C; bp 1473 ± 10°C.

Thallophyta In traditional plant classification systems, a subkingdom containing all those plants that lack true stems, leaves, and roots, i.e. the algae, fungi, and lichens. The plant body is a thallus, conducting tissue. Although this subkingdom is no longer used in modern classifications, the term "thallus" is still used for the body of algae and some lower plants.

Thames, River The longest river in England. Rising in the Cotswold Hills near Cirencester, it flows mainly ESE through Oxford, Reading, and London to enter the North Sea at the Nore. A tidal barrier was constructed below London to reduce the danger of flooding. Length: 346 km (215 mi).

Thanet, Isle of 51 22N 1 15E An island in SE England, separated from the Kent mainland by two channels of the River Stour. It contains the resorts of Ramsgate and Margate. Area: 109 sq km (42 sq mi).

Thanksgiving Day A national holiday in

the USA, celebrated on the fourth Thursday in November. Thanksgiving Day was originally observed by the Pilgrim Fathers, who in 1621 celebrated their first harvest in North America. It became a national holiday in 1863. It is also celebrated in Canada, on the second Monday in October.

Thatcher, Margaret (Hilda), Baroness (1925–) British stateswoman; Conservative prime minister (1979–90). She entered parliament in 1959 and became secretary of state for education and science (1970–74). She succeeded Edward Heath as Conservative leader in 1975 and in 1979 became the first woman prime minister of the UK. In office she introduced montarist economic policies, cut government spending, and used military force to retain control of the Falkland Islands (1982). Following a landslide victory in 1983, she pursued policies of *privatization and curbing union powers. A further victory in 1987 led to her becoming the longest serving UK prime minister of the century. However, discontent with her style of leadership and her attitude to the EC led to the resignations of her chancellor, Nigel Lawson (1989), and her deputy prime minister, Sir Geoffrey Howe (1990). Implementation of the *poll tax also lost her popularity. Failure to win outright victory in a leadership ballot in 1990 precipitated her resignation. She left the House of Commons and was made a life peer in 1992.

Theatre of the Absurd A theatrical genre popularized in the 1950s and 1960s in which the human condition is presented as absurd. It includes the plays of Eugene *Ionesco, Samuel *Beckett, Arthur Adamov (1908–70), and others, which rejected established theatrical conventions and used comic effects in developing pessimistic philosophical themes.

Thebes 1. An ancient city in Upper Egypt and capital of all Egypt (c. 1570–c. 1085 BC). Thebes' power was linked with the supremacy of its god Amon in the Egyptian pantheon. **2.** 88 19N 23 19E A town in Boeotia, in central Greece. It was founded in Mycenaean times and its legendary history was a favourite theme in Greek drama. Thebes briefly became the leading Greek state after defeating the Spartans at Leuctra (371). Population (latest est): 18 712.

theft The offence of dishonestly appropriating property belonging to another with the intention of permanently depriving the other person of it. The earlier offence of larceny was until 1827 divided into Grand Larceny and Petty Larceny. It was replaced by theft as defined by the Theft Act (1968), as were embezzlement, fraudulent conversion, and related offences.

thegn A person in Anglo-Saxon England who held land from his lord in return for service. The status of thegn (meaning one who serves) was hereditary. The king's thegns, who were the most important, had military and administrative duties and attended the *witan (king's council). Their importance declined in the early 11th century, when the Danish kings introduced their housecarls, and the thegns died out as a clan after the Norman conquest.

theism The belief in a personal God as creator and preserver of the universe, who reveals himself by supernatural means to his creatures. Apparently coined (1678) by Ralph Cudworth (1617–88) as an opposite to *atheism, the word has been refined in meaning to exclude both *pantheism and *deism.

Themistocles (c. 528–462 BC) Athenian statesman. Themistocles persuaded Athens to expand its navy (483) and to transfer its port from Phaleron to the more defensible Piraeus. These policies, and his leadership at the battle of Salamis, saved Greece from Persia (480) (*see* GREEK-PERSIAN WARS). Themistocles also argued successfully for the fortification of Athens.

theodolite An instrument used in surveying to measure horizontal and vertical angles. It consists of a telescope, with crosshairs in the eyepiece for focusing on the target, that can swivel on horizontal and vertical axes, which pass through two circular scales. It has a spirit level to indicate when the instrument is horizontal.

Theodosius (I) the Great (347–95 AD) Roman emperor in the East (379–94) and sole emperor (394–95). Theodosius allowed the Visigoths independence on Roman territory by a treaty in 382. A devout and orthodox Christian, he imposed Christianity on the Empire in 391, closing pagan temples and forbidding sacrifices.

theology Literally, the study of God. Christian theology includes within its scope the nature of God, His relationship with the universe, His providence regarding man, and the teachings of the Church. Different traditions exist within the Roman Catholic, Orthodox, and Protestant communions, but typical subdivisions of theology are dogmatic, historical, and pastoral theology.

Thera (*or* **Santorini**; modern Greek name: Thira) A volcanic island, the most southerly of the Greek Cyclades. A Minoan city existed here but was destroyed in a volcanic explosion in the 15th century BC, in which much of the island sank into the sea. The cataclysm is thought to have been a severe blow to the Minoan civilization in Crete, and some scholars believe it to be the foundation of the legend of Atlantis. Rich archaeological finds have been made here.

Thérèse, St (Marie Françoise Thérèse Martin; 1873–97) French nun, known as the Little Flower of Jesus. She entered the Carmelite convent at Lisieux when only 15 and died there 9 years later of tuberculosis. Her fame rests on her spiritual autobiography, *Histoire d'une âme* (1898). She was canonized in 1925. Feast day: 3 Oct.

thermae Roman baths. The Roman citizen spent much of his or her afternoon in the thermae, moving between its three main rooms—the *frigidarium* (cold), the *tepidarium* (tepid), and the *calidarium* (hot); this could be supplemented by a dip in the indoor pool, exercises in the gym, or a stroll in the gardens. The thermae were also cultural institutions, with libraries, concerts, and lecture halls. Established by the munificence of the rulers, they were free to Roman citizens. Impressive ruins remain, especially in Rome (the Baths of Caracalla).

thermal reactor A nuclear reactor (*see* NUCLEAR ENERGY) in which natural or enriched uranium is used with a moderator so that the velocities of the emitted neutrons are comparable to the velocities of gas molecules ("thermal" velocities). The reactor core consists of fuel rods made of uranium metal or oxide surrounded by a moderator, the heat of the reaction being removed by a coolant. After leaving the core, the coolant passes to a heat exchanger in which steam is raised. The rate of reaction is controlled by a series of control rods, which can move in and out of the core: the rods contain a neutron-absorbing element, such as boron. Early British reactors (Magnox) used natural uranium; the next generation (advanced gas-cooled reactor; AGR) used enriched uranium dioxide and CO_2 as a coolant. The US-designed pressurized-water reactors (PWR), using ordinary water as both moderator and coolant are now widely used. *Compare* FAST REACTOR.

thermionic valve A device consisting of an evacuated glass or metal tube, into which two or more electrodes are inserted. One heated electrode, the cathode, emits electrons, which are attracted to the positively charged anode, forming an electric current. This current flows in one direction only and can be controlled by the voltage applied at one or more other electrodes (called grids). The **diode valve** was invented in 1904 by Sir John Ambrose Fleming. The **triode valve** with one grid was invented in 1910 by Lee De Forest; it was the first to function as an amplifier. The weak signal fed to the grid produces a stronger signal in the anode circuit. Diode and triode valves made possible the development of radio transmitters and receivers, although now *semiconductor diodes and *transistors have replaced them.

thermistor A *semiconductor device with an electrical resistance that decreases sharply as temperature increases. It is used in temperature-control circuits and can be calibrated for use as a thermometer.

thermocouple A type of thermometer consisting of an electric circuit formed by two dissimilar metals joined at each end. One junction is exposed to the temperature to be measured, a voltage being generated between it and the other (reference) junction as a result of the temperature difference between them (*see* THERMOELECTRIC EFFECTS). The output is usually displayed on a *galvanometer. Copper-constantan junctions are used up to 500°C and platinum-rhodium alloy up to 1500°C. A **thermopile** consists of several thermocouples connected in series.

thermodynamics The study of *heat and its relationship with other forms of energy. Thermodynamics is primarily a statistical subject, thermodynamic quantities, such as *temperature and *entropy, being dependent on the statistical behaviour of the particles that comprise a system. There are three fundamental laws of thermodynamics. The first law states that the energy of a closed system remains constant during any process. The second law states that heat cannot flow from a cold body to a hot body without the expenditure of external work; or, that the entropy of a closed system can never decrease. The third law states that as the thermodynamic temperature of a system aproaches *absolute zero, its entropy approaches zero. *See* HEAT DEATH OF UNIVERSE.

thermoelectric effects The effects of changes of temperature on electric circuits or devices. The **Seebeck effect**, named after Johann Seebeck (1770–1831), provides the basis for the *thermocouple; it occurs when a circuit has two junctions between dissimilar metals. If the junctions are maintained at different temperatures, a voltage is generated between them. The **Peltier effect**, named after Jean Peltier (1785–1845), is the converse of this. One junction heats up and the other cools down when a steady current flows through such a circuit. In the **Thomson** (*or* **Kelvin**) **effect**, named after Lord *Kelvin, a temperature gradient along a single metal conductor causes a current to flow through it.

thermometer An instrument used for measuring temperature. Thermometers make use of some property of a substance that varies uniformly with temperature, most commonly the expansion of a liquid, such as mercury. A clinical thermometer is a typical mercury-in-glass thermometer; more accurate thermometers use the expansion of a gas, which is much greater than that of a liquid. Other thermometers include the resistance thermometer, which depends on the variation in the resistance of a wire (usually platinum); the bimetallic strip, which makes use of the unequal expansion of two metals welded together; and the thermistor, in which the change in conductivity of a semiconductor is used as a measure of temperature. High temperatures are measured by a *pyrometer.

thermonuclear reactor A reactor in which a fusion reaction (*see* NUCLEAR ENERGY) takes place with the controlled release of energy. The most readily achieved fusion reaction is the combination of deuterium and tritium to form helium ($^2_1H + ^3_1H = ^4_2He + n + 17.6$ MeV). To overcome the electrostatic repulsion between nuclei a temperature of about 40 million °C is needed. Containing the *plasma (as the high-temperature ionized gas is called) is the central problem. In magnetic containment a high current passed through the plasma creates a magnetic bottle that keeps the plasma away from the containing walls. To produce useful power gain at this temperature, the product of the plasma density and the containment time must exceed 10^{14} particle seconds per cm^3. In magnetic containment the plasma is kept away from the containing walls by magnetic fields generated by electric currents flowing through external coils as well as the plasma itself. Toroidal tokamak devices, which originated in the Soviet Union, have approached this figure but problems of magnetic instabilities and impurity control have not yet been solved. Other possible techniques include inertial confinement, in which a pellet of fuel is exposed to *laser or particle beams to produce adiabatic compression (to 100 times solid density), which causes ignition. The outstanding problems relate to the efficient generation of high-power beams (ultraviolet, X-ray, or proton) and to maintaining symmetry during compression.

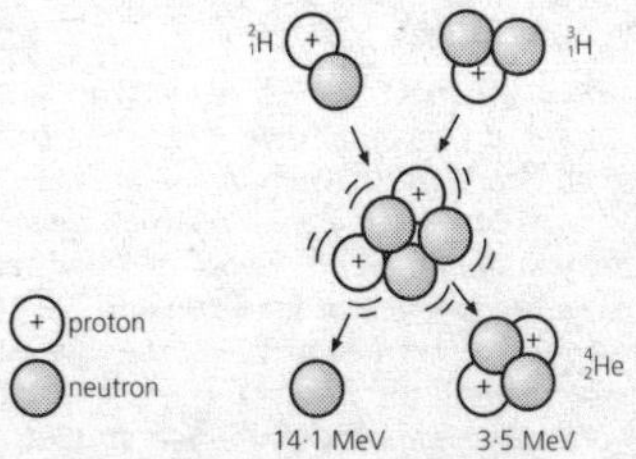

deuterium-tritium fusion reaction

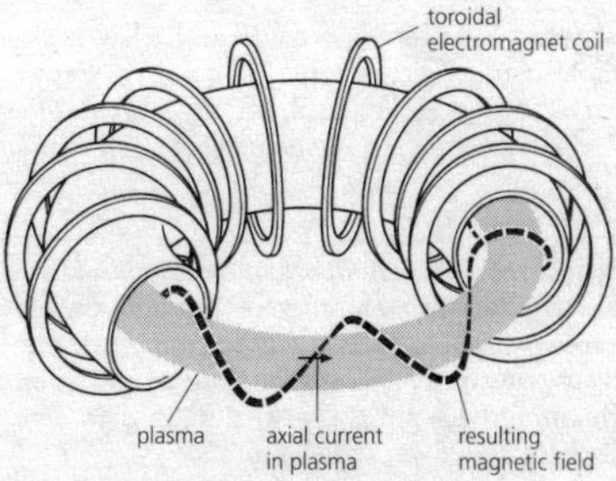

fusion reactor experiment

thermonuclear reactor. The combination of deuterium (^2_1H) and tritium (^3_1H) in a fusion reaction that forms helium. This is being attempted using a toroidal electromagnet to contain plasma consisting of deuterium and tritium nuclei.

Thermopylae, Battle of (480 BC) The battle in which the Greeks under the Spartan king, Leonidas (reigned ?490–480), attempted to hold the pass of Thermopylae in E central Greece against the Persians. After the main Greek force had retreated the Spartans and Thespians, surrounded and outnumbered, fought to the death.

Thermos flask *See* DEWAR FLASK.

Theseus A legendary Greek hero. He freed the Athenians from their annual tribute to *Minos by killing the *Minotaur. He extended the rule of Athens to various communities and was the subject of many legends.

Thessaloníki (English name: Salonika) 40 38N 22 58E The second largest port in Greece, in Macedonia on the Gulf of Salonika. Founded in 315 BC, it became the capital of Macedonia. It was captured by the Turks (1430) and remained in the Ottoman Empire until ceded to Greece (1913). The port handles about one-third of Greek exports. Industries include the manufacture of textiles and food processing. Population (1991): 377 951.

Thessaly (Modern Greek name: Thessalía) A region of E central Greece, bordering on the Aegean Sea. In the 4th century BC it fell to Philip of Macedon. Freed from Macedonian rule by Rome in 196 BC, it was incorporated in the Roman province of Macedonia in 148 BC. It subsequently formed part of the Byzantine Empire, falling to Turkey in the late 14th century AD. It was annexed by Greece in 1881. Population (2001): 754 893.

thiamine *See* VITAMIN B COMPLEX.

thiazine An organic compound that has a molecular structure containing a ring of four carbon atoms and two sulphur atoms. Thiazine derivatives are used in such drugs as tranquillizers, antihistamines, and antibiotics, as well as in various dyes.

thiazole (C_3H_3NS) An organic compound that has a molecular structure containing a ring of three carbon atoms, one sulphur atom, and one nitrogen atom. Thiazole derivatives occur in thiamine (vitamin B_1), penicillin, and in synthetic drugs, dyes, and chemicals.

Third Reich (1933–45) The Nazi regime in Germany. The name refers to the Nazi ambition to revive the medieval Holy Roman Empire (the first Reich) and the German Empire (the second Reich; 1871–1918). The Third Reich ended with Germany's defeat in World War II.

Thirty-Nine Articles (1563) A set of formulations defining the historic doctrine of the *Church of England. They were derived from Thomas Cranmer's 42 Articles (1553), which had been revoked by Mary I in re-establishing Roman Catholicism in England. The Articles do not represent a creed; rather they deal with specific points that were matters of controversy and give in broad terms the Anglican position. The clergy of the Church of England are no longer required to subscribe formally to the Articles but only to promise not to contradict them.

Thirty Years' War (1618–48) The conflict between rival dynastic and religious interests in the Holy Roman Empire that escalated into a major European war. It was caused by the revolt of Protestants in Bohemia against the Counter-Reformation policies of the imperial government at Prague. Although imperial forces defeated the Bohemians in 1620, the revolt spread. With the Edict of Restitution (1629) Emperor Ferdinand II dispossessed many German Protestants. In 1635 France, hoping to contain the power of Spain and the Empire, entered the conflict. The war ended with the Peace of *Westphalia (1648), although the Franco-Spanish conflict continued until 1659. The war caused serious economic and demographic reverses in Germany.

Thisbe *See* PYRAMUS AND THISBE.

thistle A prickly-leaved herb belonging to one of several genera of the family *Compositae*, especially *Carduus* (120 species), *Cirsium* (120 species), *Carlinus* (20 species), and *Onopordum* (20 species), distributed through out the N hemisphere. Thistles characteristically have heads of small purple flowers and spiny stems. The perennial creeping thistle (*Cirsium arvense*) grows to a height of 1 m and is a persistent weed.

thixotropy A property possessed by certain gels as a result of which they become liquid when stirred and return to a gel-like state when left to stand. Thixotropic gels are used in nondrip paints. Certain types of quicksand are naturally thixotropic.

Thomas, Dylan (1914–53) Welsh poet. Born in Swansea, he moved to London after the publication of *18 Poems* in 1934 and worked for the BBC. *Deaths and Entrances* (1946) contains many of his best-known poems. In 1949 he returned to Wales, where he wrote his popular radio play *Under Milk Wood* (1954). Alcoholism precipitated his death.

Thomas, Edward (1878–1917) British poet and writer, whose work reflects his love of the English countryside. He was killed in action in World War I.

Thomas, R(onald) S(tuart) (1913–2000) Welsh poet. Earlier volumes, such as *Song at the Year's Turning* (1955), draw on his work as a clergyman in rural Wales. His *Collected Poems* appeared in 1993.

Thomas, St In the New Testament, one of the 12 Apostles. He is known as "Doubting Thomas" because he refused to believe in the resurrection until he had seen and touched Christ. Feast day: 21 Dec.

Thomas à Kempis (Thomas Hemmerken; c. 1380–1471) German spiritual writer and monk. He spent most of his life writing and teaching at the Augustinian convent of Agnietenberg near Zwolle (Netherlands). His fame rests on his devotional treatise, *The Imitation of Christ*.

Thompson, Emma (1959–) British actress. Her films include *Howards End* (1992), which earned her an Oscar, *Sense and Sensibility* (1995), for which she also wrote the Oscar-winning screenplay, *Primary Colors* (1998), and *Love Actually* (2003). She was married to Kenneth *Branagh.

Thomson, Sir Joseph John (1856–1940) British physicist, who discovered the *electron. In 1897 he succeeded in deflecting cathode rays by an electric field, thus showing that they consisted of negatively charged particles. He also measured the ratio of their charge to mass and deduced that electrons were about 2000 times lighter than the hydrogen atom. Thomson thought that atoms consist of electrons embedded in a positively charged sphere, a concept that was superseded by Rutherford's model. He was awarded the Nobel Prize in 1906.

Thomson, William *See* KELVIN, WILLIAM THOMSON, 1ST BARON.

Thomson effect (*or* **Kelvin effect**) *See* THERMOELECTRIC EFFECTS.

Thor The Teutonic god of thunder, in some legends the son of *Odin. He presided over the home and controlled the weather and crops; he was also worshipped as a god of war. His name survives in *Thursday*.

thorax In mammals (including humans), the region of the body between the diaphragm and the neck, which contains the lungs and heart and their associated vessels. The skeleton of the thorax is formed by the breastbone at the front, the spine at the back, and the ribs at the sides. In arthropods the thorax is between the head and abdomen.

thorium (Th) A naturally occurring radioactive metal. It is possible that thorium-fuelled nuclear reactors may be developed in the future, since it is more abundant than uranium and does not produce plutonium-239 in appreciable quantities (*see* URANIUM). Thorium oxide (ThO_2) has one of the highest known melting points (3300°C), which led to its use in gas mantles, as it glows white when heated. At no 90; at wt 232.038; mp 1755°C; bp 4788°C.

thorium series One of three naturally occurring series of radioactive decays. The thorium series is headed by thorium-232, which undergoes a series of decays ending with the stable isotope lead-208. *See also* ACTINIUM; URANIUM SERIES.

thorn apple An annual herb, *Datura stramonium*, also called jimsonweed, occurring in N temperate and subtropical regions. It has white trumpet-shaped flowers producing a fruit with a spiny capsule that splits to release the black seeds. All parts of the plant are very poisonous, containing the alkaloids hyoscyamine, hyoscine, and scopolamine. Family: *Solanaceae*.

thornbill A drab-coloured Australian bird belonging to one of three genera, especially *Acanthiza*. The yellow-tailed thornbill (*A. chrysorrhoea*) builds a very long oval nest with several nest chambers. Family: *Muscicapidae* (*see* FLYCATCHER).

Thrace The Balkan region bordered by the Black Sea, the Aegean, Macedonia, and the River Danube. From the 8th century BC Greek cities colonized the coasts, while the inland tribes were an easy target for invaders—the Persians in about 516 BC and then Philip II of Macedon in the mid-4th century. Having come under the influence of Rome in 168 BC, it became a Roman province in 46 AD. Famous for its horses and horsemen, and for ecstatic religious rituals, Thrace was traditionally the birthplace of the mysteries associated with the worship of Dionysus. It is now divided between Turkey, Greece, and Bulgaria.

threadworm *See* PINWORM.

thrift A perennial herb, *Armeria maritima*, also called sea pink, native to mountains, salt marshes, and sandy coastal regions of N Europe. The flower stem rises from a basal tuft of long narrow grasslike leaves and bears a cluster of rose-pink or white flowers. Family: *Plumbaginaceae*.

thrips A minute insect, also called thunder fly, belonging to the order *Thysanoptera* (about 3000 species). Thrips have dark slender bodies, 0.5–5 mm long, and usually two pairs of narrow fringed wings. Many species suck the juices of flowering plants, often causing serious damage and spreading plant diseases.

thrombosis The formation of a blood clot inside a blood vessel, which often obstructs the flow of blood. Thrombosis is more likely to occur if the blood vessel is damaged or if the blood flow is very slow. The commonest site of thrombosis is in the veins of the legs. This is particularly likely to occur if a person is bedridden for a long time. The clot may become detached and carried to the lungs, causing pulmonary *embolism.

Thrombosis can also occur in the arteries

supplying the heart (coronary thrombosis), causing a heart attack (*see* MYOCARDIAL INFARCTION), or the brain, causing *stroke.

thrush (bird) A songbird belonging to a family (*Turdidae*; 300 species) found throughout the world but predominantly in Old World regions. Thrushes are slender billed and usually brown—often with speckling or patches of red, yellow, or blue. They feed chiefly on insects and fruit and often have melodious songs, as in the song thrush (*Turdus philomelus*). Northern species are migratory. *See also* BLACKBIRD; MISTLE THRUSH; RING OUZEL.

thrush (disease) *See* CANDIDIASIS.

Thucydides (c. 460–c. 400 BC) Greek historian. He served as an Athenian general in the Peloponnesian War but was banished in 424 BC for allowing the Spartan general Brasidas to capture the colony of Amphipolis. His eight-volume *History of the Peloponnesian War* is notable for its political, moral, and psychological analysis.

thulium (Tm) The least abundant of the *lanthanide elements, discovered in 1879 by P. T. Cleve (1840–1905). Radioactive ^{169}Tm is used in portable X-ray generators. At no 69; at wt 168.934; mp 1545°C; bp 1950°C.

Thurber, James (1894–1961) US humorous writer and cartoonist. An early and continuing contributor to the *New Yorker*, he satirized intellectual fashions and domestic habits with irony and sophistication. His essays and stories are collected in *The Thurber Carnival* (1945) and other volumes.

Thurrock A unitary authority in SE England, in Essex. Area: 163 sq km (63 sq mi). Population (2001): 143–042.

Thutmose III (d. 1450 BC) King of Egypt (c. 1504–1450) of the 18th dynasty, who ruled Egypt at its most powerful and prosperous. In 1468 he defeated Syrian rebels at Megiddo and in later campaigns advanced beyond the River Euphrates. He organized the country's complicated administration and was an outstanding athlete and big-game hunter and a patron of art and architecture.

thylacine The largest carnivorous *marsupial, *Thylacinus cynocephalus*, also called Tasmanian wolf or tiger and now probably extinct. About 1.5 m long, it resembles a dog with dark stripes across its grey-brown back. Family: *Dasyuridae*.

thyme A small shrub belonging to the genus *Thymus* (about 50 species), native to temperate Eurasia. Garden thyme (*T. vulgaris*) is cultivated for its fragrant leaves, which are dried and used as a herb. An oil extract is used in perfumes and medicines. The common wild thyme (*T. drucei*) has a creeping stem and clusters of rose-purple flowers. Family: *Labiatae*.

thymus An organ situated at the base of the neck, above the heart. The thymus grows until puberty, after which it shrinks and ceases to function. During infancy the thymus produces lymphocytes that form the *antibodies associated with allergic responses and the rejection of transplanted tissues and organs. *See also* IMMUNITY.

thyristor A solid-state electronic device, also called a semiconductor or silicon-controlled rectifier; it consists of four layers of *semiconductor forming three p-n junctions. It acts as a switch, blocking the current through two terminals until it has been turned on by a pulse applied to the third terminal. This pulse can be initiated by light or a temperature change. Thyristors can pass currents ranging from milliamperes to several hundred amperes, often replacing gas-filled valve relays.

thyroid gland An endocrine gland situated at the base of the neck, in front and on either side of the windpipe. It secretes the hormone thyroxine, which controls the basal metabolism of the body; thyroxine secretion is regulated by thyroid-stimulating hormone, which is released from the *pituitary gland. Because thyroxine production requires iodine, deficiency of iodine causes the thyroid to enlarge in an attempt to produce adequate amounts of the hormone (*see* GOITRE).

Tiber, River (Italian name: Tevere; Latin name: Tiberis) A river in central Italy, rising in the Apennines of Tuscany and flowing mainly S through Rome to the Tyrrhenian Sea near Ostia. Length: 405 km (252 mi).

Tiberius (42 BC–37 AD) Roman emperor (14–37 AD). Tiberius was recognized by his stepfather, Emperor Augustus, as his successor in 4 AD. As emperor his policies were unambitious though sound but he faced the Senate's hostility, family intrigue, and military rebellion. He retired to Capri in 26 AD, where he gained a reputation for depravity.

Tibet (Chinese name: Xizang Autonomous Region) An administrative region in W China, bordering on India, Nepal, Bhutan, and Burma. It consists of a high plateau and is surrounded by mountains, including the Himalayas and the Kunlun Mountains. Most agriculture and the country's cities are in the river valleys. The area is rich in minerals. *History*: Buddhism, introduced in the 7th century AD, has exerted a profound influence on Tibetan history. The lamas (priests) of *Tibetan Buddhism attained political power in the 13th century. In 1642, the fifth *Dalai Lama became ruler of all Tibet. In 1720 the Chinese Qing dynasty established a control over Tibet that lasted until 1911. Independence was declared, but in 1950 Tibet again fell to the Chinese. An uprising in 1959 was brutally suppressed. There were further riots in the 1980s, leading to the imposition of martial law (1989–90). China has been widely accused of violating Tibetans' human and religious rights. In 1997 an International Commission of Jurists denounced Chinese rule and called for a UN-monitored referendum to decide Tibet's future. Area: 1 221 601 sq km (471 660 sq mi). Population (2000 est): 2 620 000. Capital: Lhasa.

Tibetan Buddhism (*or* **lamaism**) A form of Mahayana Buddhism practised in Tibet and Mongolia. Introduced into Tibet in the 7th century AD, it has a complex symbolic literature and monastic discipline. The guru, or venerated spiritual teacher, is of prime importance; some are held to be reincarnations of previous lamas. Until 1959, the *Dalai Lama was temporal and spiritual head of the state.

tick A parasitic *arachnid of the worldwide suborder *Metastigmata* (850 species), which sucks the blood of birds and mammals and may transmit such diseases as *typhus and relapsing fever. Its round unsegmented body, up to 30 mm long, bears eight bristly legs. After feeding, the adults drop off the host and lay eggs on the ground. The larvae attach themselves to a suitable victim, feed, then drop off and moult into nymphs, which repeat the procedure. Order: *Acarina* (or *Acari*). *Compare* MITE.

tides The regular rising and falling of seawater resulting from the gravitational attraction between the earth, sun, and moon. Most parts of the world experience semidiurnal tides (occurring twice per tidal day—24 hours 5 minutes). Tidal currents are periodic horizontal flows of water resulting from the rise and fall of the tide. Near the coast they are usually perpendicular to it and reversing, but in the ocean they flow in a rotary manner around a series of nodal points.

Tiepolo, Giovanni Battista (1696–1770) Venetian *rococo painter. His early sombre style evolved into the exuberance of his first major frescoes, for the Archbishop's Palace at Udine (1725–29). These were followed by decorations for many N Italian palaces and churches. Abroad he decorated the Residenz Palace, Würzburg (1750–53) and the Royal Palace in Madrid (1762–66).

Tierra del Fuego An archipelago separated from the mainland of S South America by the Strait of Magellan. The W and S belong to Chile, the E to Argentina. Sheep farming and oil production are the principal economic activities. Chief towns: Punta Arenas (Chile); Ushuaia (Argentina).

tiger A large *cat, *Panthera tigris*. Tigers are usually about 3 m long, but the race of Siberian tigers can reach 4 m. Tigers evolved in Siberia and have spread south to most of Asia; they shed their coat seasonally and shelter from hot sun during the day. They hunt (mainly antelope) at night.

tiger moth A moth belonging to the family *Arctiidae*, occurring in Eurasia, N Africa, and North America. The adults have a stout body and are brightly coloured, often orange and black. The hairy larvae, commonly called woolly bears, are seldom destructive.

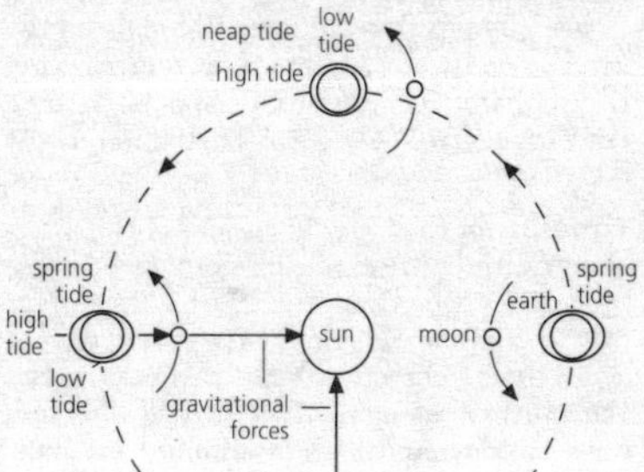

tides. The force of gravity between the earth and the moon pulls the waters of the seas towards the moon, creating high tides once a day. The second daily high tide occurs because the moon pulls the earth itself away from the water on the far side of the moon. Exceptionally high spring tides occur twice monthly when the gravitational force of the moon is in line with that of the sun. The lower neap tides occur when these two forces are at right angles.

tiger shark A large *requiem shark, *Galeocerdo cuvieri*, that lives mainly in tropical seas. It has a greyish-brown body, up to about 5.5 m long, patterned with vertical bars and a lighter underside. It eats virtually anything, including mammals, birds, fish, invertebrates, refuse, and man.

Tigris, River A river in SW Asia, rising in SE Turkey and flowing SE through Diyarbakir, along the Turkish-Syrian border, and into Iraq. It joins the River Euphrates to form the Shatt al-Arab. Length: 1850 km (1150 mi).

Tijuana 39 29N 117 10W A city in NW Mexico, on the US border. Tijuana is the main entry point to Mexico from California and is a popular tourist resort. Population (2000 est): 1 150 000.

timbre A quality in the sound of a musical instrument, voice, etc., that distinguishes it from others. Thus a violin and a clarinet sound different even when they are playing the same note. The difference arises because each type of instrument produces different overtones in different strengths when a note is played. The production of overtones is controlled by the way the note is produced (plucking, blowing, etc.) and by the characteristics of the individual instrument.

Timbuktu (French name: Tombouctou) 16 49N 2 59W A town in E central Mali, on the River Niger. It was an important centre on the trans-Saharan caravan route and an Islamic cultural centre (1400–1600). Population (latest est): 31 925.

time One of the four dimensions of the space-time continuum of the Einsteinian universe (the others being the three spatial dimensions of *Newton's world). Unlike the spatial dimensions, time is directional and passively carries the universe along with it in one direction only. To Newton, time was absolute and independent of the spatial dimensions, which are also absolute. In relativity, all dimensions are interdependent.

t

time dilation An effect predicted by Einstein's special theory of *relativity. If two observers, A and B, are moving at a velocity v relative to each other, it will appear to A that B's clock will show that time is running more slowly; thus a time t measured on A's clock will be $t(1-v^2/c^2)^{1/2}$ on B's clock, where c is the velocity of light.

time zones North-south zones of standardized time. Astronomical noon travels continuously around the globe, but for convenience, equalized times are applied in the 24 zones, starting at the International Date Line (180° W and E). Each is normally 15° = 1 hour wide.

Timor The largest island of the *Nusa Tenggara group. Mountainous and dry, it is largely undeveloped. Crops include coffee, coconut, and sandalwood. *History*: in 1859 it was divided between Portugal and Holland. West (Dutch) Timor was included in independent Indonesia (1949). Although *East Timor was subsequently (1975–76) annexed by Indonesia, this was not accepted by the UN. Demonstrations against Indonesian rule in 1991 were severely repressed. Indonesia finally withdrew its troops in 1999, leaving a UN administration to oversee the transition to full nationhood in May 2002. Area: 39 775 sq km (11 883 sq mi). Chief towns: Kupang and Dili.

Timor-Leste *See* EAST TIMOR.

Timothy, St In the New Testament, a disciple of *Paul, whom he accompanied on many missions. According to tradition he was martyred in Ephesus. Feast day: 6 Feb.

timpani (*or* **kettledrums**) Drums with a large bowl-shaped body and a single head. They have a musical pitch, which can be altered by keys round the circumference or a pedal. The military kettledrums used in mounted bands are attached to a horse in pairs, tuned to two fixed tones.

Timur (*or* **Tamerlane**; c. 1336–1405) Mongol conqueror, a descendant of Genghis Khan. After winning control of Turkestan in central Asia, Timur swept ruthlessly through Mongolia, Persia, Turkey, Russia, and India, leaving death and destruction behind him. Paradoxically, he spared and encouraged all kinds of artists.

tin (Sn) A silvery-white metal known to the ancients. Its principal ore is the oxide cassiterite (SnO_2), often found in alluvial concentrations. The element exists as at least two allotropes—the grey alpha-tin, and beta-tin, which is the common form above 13.2°C. At low temperature beta-tin slowly changes into alpha-tin causing **tin plague**. It is obtained by reduction with coal in a reverberatory furnace. The major use of tin is in tinplate. It alloys with copper to form *bronzes and with niobium to give a superconducting composition, which is used in electromagnets. At no 50; at wt 118.710; mp 231.9°C; bp 2603°C.

tinamou A solitary ground-dwelling bird belonging to a family (*Tinamidae*; 50 species) occurring in Central and South America. Well camouflaged with a mottled grey or brown plumage, tinamous have small wings and a very short tail and are poor fliers. They feed on seeds, fruit, and insects.

tineid moth A moth of the widespread family *Tineidae*. The adults are usually small with a golden or silvery sheen and frequently do not feed. The caterpillars feed on a variety of plant and animal matter. *See clothes moth.*

Tintagel 50 40N 4 45W A village and resort in SW England, on the N coast of Cornwall. On the rugged promontory of Tintagel Head are the ruins of Tintagel Castle, reputedly the birthplace of King Arthur.

Tintoretto (Jacopo Robusti; 1518–94) Venetian painter, whose nickname, meaning "little dyer," derived from his father's profession of silk dyeing. His three paintings of the *Miracles of St Mark* (1562–66) for the Confraternity of S Marco were followed by his series of the life of Christ (1564–87; Scuola di S Rocco) and his paintings for the Doge's Palace, including the enormous *Paradise*. As a portraitist, he was particularly adept at painting old men, for example *Bearded Man with Fur* (Kunsthistorisches Museum, Vienna).

Tipperary (Irish name: Contae Tiobraid Árann) A county in the S Republic of Ireland, in Munster. It contains part of the Golden Vale (one of the most fertile areas in Ireland) in the SW. Predominantly agricultural, dairy farming is especially important. Area: 4255 sq km (1643 sq mi). Population (2002): 140 281. County town: Clonmel.

Tippett, Sir Michael (1905–98) British composer. He wrote five operas, including *The Midsummer Marriage* (1947–52), *The Knot Garden* (1966–70), and *New Year* (1989). His other works include four symphonies, five string quartets, four piano sonatas, and the oratorio *A Child of Our Time* (1940). In 1983 he was appointed a member of the OM.

Tirana (Albanian name: Tiranë) 41 20N 19 49E The capital of Albania, situated on a fertile plain in the centre of the country. Founded in the 17th century, it became the capital in 1920. There has been considerable industrial expansion since World War II. Population (1999 est): 279 000.

Tiresias In Greek legend, a blind Theban seer who lived for seven generations. *Oedipus learned from him of his own patricide and incest and *Odysseus consulted him in the underworld, where he retained his prophetic powers.

Tirich Mir, Mount 36 18N 71 55E A mountain in NW Pakistan, the highest in the Hindu Kush. Height: 7692 m (25 236 ft).

Tirol (*or* **Tyrol**) A mountainous federal state in W Austria, bordering on Germany and Italy. It has an international reputation for winter sports, especially at Kitzbühel, and tourism is important throughout the year. The chief occupations are agriculture and forestry, with some mining and manufacturing industries. Area: 12 648 sq km (4883 sq mi). Population (2001): 675 063. Capital: Innsbruck.

Tisza, River (Slavonic and Romanian name: Tisa) A river in S central Europe. Rising in the W Ukraine, it flows across the Hungarian Plain to join the River Danube below Novi Sad in Serbia. It is a source of irrigation and power, especially in NE Hungary. Length: 980 km (610 mi).

tit A small acrobatic songbird (also called titmouse) belonging to a family (*Paridae*; 65 species) occurring in Eurasia, North America, and Africa. Tits frequent woodlands and gardens, feeding chiefly on insects. Their soft plumage is usually grey or black, often with blue and yellow markings. *See also* BLUETIT.

Titanic A luxury passenger ship that on 14–15 April 1912, struck an iceberg near Newfoundland on its maiden voyage and sank with the loss of 1513 lives. Because of its special design it was thought to be unsinkable. As a result of the disaster safety rules for ships at sea were drawn up. The wreck of the Titanic was located (1985) and subsequently salvaged.

titanium (Ti) A relatively light strong transition metal discovered in 1791 by W. Gregor (1761–1817). It occurs in nature in the minerals rutile (TiO_2), ilmenite ($FeTiO_3$), sphene ($CaTiO_3$), and in some iron ores. The dioxide (TiO_2) is used in white paint as it has excellent opacity. The metal is as strong as steel but 45% lighter (relative density 4.54) and 60% heavier than aluminium but twice as strong. It is used in alloys for missiles and aircraft. At no 22; at wt 47.88; mp 1670°C; bp 3289°C.

Titans In Greek mythology, 12 primeval gods and goddesses, the children of *Uranus and *Gaia. They were Oceanus, Coeus, Crius, Hyperion, Iapetus, Cronus, Thea, Rhea, Themis, Mnemosyne, Phoebe, and Tethys. They were overthrown by Zeus and the Olympian gods.

tithes The tenth part of an income allotted to religious purposes. Originating in the offering of the "first fruits" as a divine sacrifice, tithes were decreed by Mosaic law, which demanded payment in kind from all agricultural produce. Christian ecclesiastical law also enjoined tithes to maintain churches and clergy. Tithes were abolished in Britain in 1936.

Titian (Tiziano Vecellio; c. 1488–1576) Venetian painter of the High Renaissance. He collaborated with Giorgione on frescoes for the façade of the German Exchange (1508). In his *Assumption of the Virgin* (Sta Maria dei Frari) his monumental style links him with such Florentine painters as Raphael. His greatest works for the Habsburgs, who patronized him from 1530 onwards, were the equestrian portrait of Emperor Charles V at Mühlberg (1548; Prado) and *Philip II* (1550–51; Prado). His mythological works include *Bacchus and Ariadne* (National Gallery, London).

Titicaca, Lake A lake in South America, between Peru and Bolivia, in the Andes. At an altitude of 3809 m (12 497 ft) it is the world's highest lake navigable to large vessels. Area: 8135 sq km (3141 sq mi). Depth: 370 m (1214 ft).

Tito (Josip Broz; 1892–1980) Yugoslav statesman; president (1953–80). Tito was captured by the Russians in World War I and subsequently fought with the Red Army in the Russian civil war. He returned to Yugoslavia in 1920 and joined the Communist Party. In World War II he led the resistance to the German occupation, becoming a marshal in 1943. He became Yugoslavia's postwar leader and introduced the policy of decentralization to workers' councils. Following Yugoslavia's expulsion (1948) from the Cominform, Tito successfully maintained his country's independence from Soviet interference, pursuing a foreign policy of nonalignment.

Titus (Flavius Vespasianus) (39–81 AD) Roman emperor (79–81). He fought with his father Vespasian in Judaea and ended the Jewish revolt (70) by capturing Jerusalem. Titus was a popular emperor; when Vesuvius erupted (79), he aided the victims generously. At his death he was deified.

Tivoli 41 58N 12 48E A town in central Italy, in Lazio. A summer resort in Roman times, it possesses the remains of Hadrian's villa and the Renaissance Villa d'Este, with its terraced water gardens. Population (latest est): 55 030.

Tlingit A North American Indian people of the NW Pacific coast in SE Alaska. There were 14 tribes divided into independent matrilineal clans, each headed by a chief. They lived by salmon fishing and hunting. Their language belongs to the Na-Dené group.

TNT (trinitrotoluene; $C_6H_2(NO_2)_3CH_3$) A highly explosive yellow crystalline solid prepared from toluene treated with concentrated sulphuric and nitric acids. It is used in shells, bombs, and blasting explosives.

toad A tail-less amphibian belonging to a widely distributed order (*Anura*; about 2600 species). Toads have long hind legs and short forelegs; they swim by means of partially webbed feet. They have a long sticky tongue that can extend very rapidly to capture flying insects. *See also* NATTERJACK; TREE FROG.

toadfish A bottom-dwelling carnivorous *bony fish of the order *Batachoidiformes* (about 45 species), found mainly in tropical and subtropical seas. It has a heavy brownish body and makes grunting or croaking sounds resembling a toad.

toadstool *See* MUSHROOM.

tobacco A plant belonging to the genus *Nicotiana*, especially *N. tabacum* and *N. rustica*, which are cultivated for their leaves, used to make cigarettes, cigars, snuff, etc. Commercial tobacco plants grow to a height of 1–3 m and bear pink, white, or greenish flowers. After harvesting, their large sticky leaves are slowly dried and then fermented. The main growing regions are the USA, China, India, Russia, and Georgia. Tobacco contains about 2–4% nicotine, which produces its stimulant and addictive properties. Family: *Solanaceae*.

Tobata *See* KITAKYUSHU.

Toc H An interdenominational Christian fellowship devoted to social service. It was founded in 1915 in Belgium by the Rev P. B. Clayton (1885–1972), a Church of England chaplain, as a military chapel and club; it was named Talbot House in memory of Gilbert Talbot (1891–1915), a British lieutenant, killed in action. Its name derives from army signallers' designations of the initials *T H*.

toga The formal outer garment of the Roman citizen, worn over a tunic. It was originally worn by both sexes but later only by patrician males. The toga was an oval sheet of linen, draped across the left shoulder, and forced the wearer to comport himself in a dignified manner. Senators, high officials, and emperors wore togas edged with purple, while candidates for office wore their togas in the Forum whitened with chalk (the *toga candida*).

Togo, Republic of (French name: République Togolaise) A small narrow country in West Africa, on the Gulf of Guinea between Ghana and Benin. The majority of the population is African. *Economy*: chiefly agricultural; food crops consist mainly of cassava, maize, and rice and cash crops include cocoa, coffee, and cotton. Forests produce not only timber but oil palms and dyewoods. There are rich deposits of phosphates, which are the main export. Bauxite was found in the 1950s. Industry includes food processing, a large cement plant, and an oil refinery. *History*: settled by the Ewe in the 12th and 13th centuries, the area was raided for slaves from the 17th to 19th centuries. From 1884 to 1914 Togoland was a German protectorate and after World War I it was divided between France and the UK. The French territory gained full independence in 1960. (The British part joined Ghana in 1957.) A coup in 1967 brought Lt Col (later Gen) Etienne Gnassingbé Eyadéma to power. Following prodemocracy riots, a multiparty constitution was approved in 1992. Eyadéma was re-elected president in 1993, 1998, and 2003 but these polls were widely condemned as fraudulent. Opposition parties gained a majority in legislative elections (1994) but the government continued to be dominated by Eyadéma's supporters. Further elections (1999 and 2002) were boycotted by the opposition. Official language: French. Currency: CFA franc of 100 centimes. Area: 56 000 sq km (21 616 sq mi). Population (2003 est): 5 429 000. Capital: Lomé.

Tokyo 35 40N 139 45E The capital of Japan, in E central *Honshu on Tokyo Bay (an inlet of the Pacific). Administratively joined to its port Yokohama and to the industrial centre of Kawasaki, Greater Tokyo is the world's largest city. It has over 100 universities. *History*: the village of Edo was founded in the 12th century. As Tokyo, it replaced Kyoto as imperial capital in 1868. It was badly damaged by an earthquake in 1923 and by bombing during World War II, since when its industrial growth has been dramatic. Population (1995): 7 966 195.

Toledo 1. 41 40N 83 35W A city in the USA, in Ohio on Lake Erie at the mouth of the River Maumee. It is a major Great Lakes port, shipping oil, coal, and farm products. Industrial activities include shipbuilding and oil refining. Population (2000): 313 619. **2.** 39 52N 4 02W A city in central Spain, in New Castile on the River Tagus. It was formerly the capital of Spain. Famous for its swords and knives, it produces metalwork engraved in the Moorish tradition. Population (1991): 63 560.

Tolkien, J(ohn) R(onald) R(euel) (1892–1973) British scholar and writer. His trilogy *The Lord of the Rings* (1954–59; filmed 2001–03), in which he created a richly detailed fantasy world, became a bestseller. Related works include *The Hobbit* (1937) and *The Silmarillion* (1977).

Tolpuddle Martyrs Six members of the Friendly Society of Agricultural Labourers of Tolpuddle, Dorset, founded in 1833. The six were unfairly charged with administering unlawful oaths and transported to Australia. They were pardoned in 1836.

Tolstoy, Leo (Nikolaevich), Count (1828–1910) Russian writer and moralist. Following his marriage in 1862 he wrote two novels, *War and Peace* (1865–69), concerning the Napoleonic War, and *Anna Karenina* (1875–77), both acknowledged masterpieces of Russian literature. Around 1879 he underwent a spiritual crisis from which he emerged with a faith in an extreme form of Christian anarchism. He worked and dressed as a peasant, became a vegetarian and pacifist, repudiated his literary works, and gave his property to his family.

Toltecs An Indian people who dominated central Mexico between the 10th and 12th centuries AD. Their language, *Nahuatl, was also spoken by the Aztecs. A militaristic people, they created an empire and introduced the cult of *Quetzalcoatl. The *Aztecs destroyed their capital of Tula in the mid-12th century.

tomato An annual plant, *Lycopersicon esculentum*, native to South America and widely cultivated for its fleshy red fruit. In warm temperate regions, tomatoes are grown in fields and are low branching plants; the hothouse tomatoes of cooler regions often grow a single erect fruiting stem. The yellow flowers produce rounded or pear-shaped fruits which are eaten fresh or canned and made into purée, pickles, etc. Family: *Solanaceae*.

tomography The technique, used in medicine for diagnosis, of producing an image of a selected plane of the body using X-rays or other radiation. In **computerized tomography** (CT), a ring-shaped X-ray machine (CT scanner) is rotated around the patient and records different planes of the body. The information obtained is assembled by the scanner's computer into a three-dimensional representation of the body.

Tomsk 56 30N 85 05E A port in central Russia, on the River Tom. Industries include engineering and it has a university (1888). In 1993 an explosion at a nuclear reprocessing plant resulted in radioactive contamination of the surrounding region. Population (1999 est): 481 400.

ton An Imperial unit of weight equal to 2240 lb (long ton) or 1016 kilograms. In the USA a unit equal to 2000 lb (short ton) is also used.

The metric ton (or **tonne**) is equal to 1000 kilograms.

tonality The presence of a tonal centre or key in a musical composition. Musical compositions from at least the early 17th century to about 1900 are in distinct keys. These are based on individual scales, in which certain notes (the tonic and dominant degrees) form tonal centres to which the music periodically returns. Music in which tonal centres are deliberately avoided exhibits *atonality. *See also* SERIALISM.

Tonga, Kingdom of (*or* **Friendly Islands**) A country in the SW Pacific Ocean, E of Fiji. It consists of 169 small islands. *Economy*: agricultural, the main products being copra, vanilla beans, and fruit. Fishing and tourism are important. *History*: the islands were visited by Captain Cook in 1773. Under King Taufa'ahau Tupou (George I; 1797–1893) Tonga became a united kingdom and converted to Christianity. The country became a British protectorate in 1900, and an independent state within the Commonwealth in 1970. There is a partly elected assembly but considerable power remains with the king (since 1965 King Taufa'ahau Tupou IV). Official languages: Tongan and English. Currency: pa'anga of 100 seniti. Area: 700 sq km (270 sq mi). Population (2003 est): 102 000. Capital: Nuku'alofa.

tongue A muscular organ situated in the floor of the mouth. The root of the tongue is attached by muscles to the U-shaped hyoid bone in the neck. The tongue is the main organ of taste: its surface is covered by taste buds, which detect sweet, sour, salt, and bitter tastes. It also manipulates food during chewing and swallowing and plays an important role in the articulation of speech.

tonsils Patches of tissue situated on each side at the back of the mouth. They produce lymphocytes, which protect the body against infection. Inflammation of the tonsils (tonsillitis) may be caused by a variety of infections.

topaz A mineral consisting of a hydrous fluosilicate of aluminium, $Al_2SiO_4(OH,F)_2$. It occurs in acidic igneous rocks, in pegmatites and veins. It is usually colourless or yellow, and when cut and polished it is used as a gemstone. The finest specimens come mainly from the Urals, Brazil, and Ceylon. Birthstone for November.

topology The branch of *geometry concerned with the properties of an object that do not change under homeomorphisms, i.e. when the object is bent, stretched, or shrunk but not torn or deformed so that several points on it are fused. Topology is often called rubber-sheet geometry; it was formerly called analysis situs. One application is in networks in which the topological properties depend on the so-called Euler characteristic, named after Leonhard Euler (1707–83), $V - E + F$, where V is the number of vertices in the network, E the number of edges, and F the number of areas enclosed by the edges.

Torah (Hebrew: instruction) The five books of Moses (Genesis, Exodus, Leviticus, Numbers, and Deuteronomy), which constitute the first of the three divisions of the Hebrew *Bible. In Judaism, the term is also applied more widely to the whole body of religious teachings, viewed as the revealed word of God and including both the written and the oral Torah.

Torbay A unitary authority in SW England, in S Devon, consisting of **Torquay** with two neighbouring seaside resorts. Area: 63 sq km (24 sq mi). Population (2001): 129 702.

Torfaen A county borough of SE Wales, created in 1996 from part of Gwent. Area: 290 sq km (112 sq mi). Population (2001): 90 967.

Tories A British political group that became the *Conservative Party under Robert *Peel in the 1830s; Tory is still used synonymously with Conservative. Originally an Irish name for a Roman Catholic outlaw, it was applied in 1679 to a supporter (in opposition to the *Whigs) of the succession to the throne of the Roman Catholic Duke of York (later James II). The Tories were later associated with the rebellious Jacobites and were excluded from politics until the 1780s, when they re-emerged. They represented the interests of the country gentry, merchants, and Anglicans.

tornado A violently rotating column of air, small in diameter, characterized by a funnel-shaped cloud, which may reach ground surface. Wind speeds of up to 200 knots (100 m per second) have been experienced. Occurring over land, tornadoes cause large-scale destruction and are a considerable problem in the central USA and Australia.

Toronto 43 42N 79 25W A city and port in E Canada, the capital of Ontario on Lake Ontario. It is Canada's largest city, housing a stock exchange and many business headquarters. Its diversified industries include heavy engineering, electrical, chemical, and wood products, foods, clothing, sporting goods, publishing, and films. *History*: established as Upper Canada's capital and military centre (1793), Toronto was scene of the Mackenzie Rebellion (1837) against oligarchic government. It became an industrial and commercial centre with the development of railways (1850s). Population (1996): 4 338 400 (metropolitan area).

torpedo (armament) A self-propelled guided underwater missile carrying a high-explosive warhead. They can be launched by ships or aircraft but have been used most successfully by submarines. Designed in 1866 by a British engineer, Robert Whitehead (1823–1905), they were used to sink 25 million tons of Allied shipping in World Wars I and II. Modern torpedos are driven by steam turbines or by battery-powered electric motors and have sophisticated active or passive acoustic homing systems.

torpedo (fish) *See* ELECTRIC RAY.

Torquemada, Tomás de (1420–98) Spanish Dominican friar and Grand Inquisitor. Confessor to Ferdinand and Isabella, he was appointed head of the Spanish *Inquisition in 1483. His sentences were extremely harsh and he was responsible for the expulsion of the Jews from Spain in 1492.

Torres Strait A channel between New Guinea and Cape York Peninsula, N Australia, linking the Arafura Sea and Coral Sea. It was discovered (1606) by the Spaniard Luis Vaez de Torres. Width: 145 km (90 mi).

Torricelli, Evangelista (1608–47) Italian physicist. He discovered that the atmosphere exerts a pressure and demonstrated it by showing that it could support a column of mercury in a tube, thus inventing the mercury barometer (1643). He also created the first man-made vacuum in his simple barometer, the space above the mercury still being called a Torricellian vacuum.

tort In law, a civil wrong that constitutes a breach of a duty established by law rather than by *contract. It is distinguished from a crime in that it affects the interests of the injured person rather than of the state.

Tortelier, Paul (1914–90) French cellist. He won first prize at the Paris conservatoire at the age of 16. After playing in orchestras in the USA he began a career as a soloist, composer, and teacher.

tortoise A slow-moving herbivorous reptile belonging to the family *Testudinidae* (40 species). Tortoises have a protective high-domed shell, tough scaly legs, and range in size from about 10 cm to 1.5 m (*see* GALÁPAGOS ISLANDS). Tortoises lay eggs and have long lifespans, reputedly up to 150 years. *Compare* TURTLE; TERRAPIN.

tortoiseshell butterfly A *nymphalid butterfly whose wings are mainly orange with black markings. Tortoiseshells are found in Europe, Asia, and North America. The caterpillars feed mainly on nettles and willows. Chief genera: *Aglais, Nymphalis.*

Toscanini, Arturo (1867–1957) Italian conductor. He made his debut in 1886 and subsequently conducted at La Scala, Milan, and at the Metropolitan Opera in New York. From 1937 until his death he conducted the NBC (National Broadcasting Company) Symphony Orchestra.

toucan A noisy forest-dwelling bird belonging to a family (*Ramphastidae*; 37 species) occurring in tropical America. Toucans have huge brightly coloured bills and typically black plumage with a brightly coloured breast. They feed on fruit. Order: *Piciformes* (woodpeckers, etc.).

touchstone A black or grey flintlike stone, formerly used for testing the purity of gold and silver. The metal to be tested and one of known purity are both rubbed with the touchstone and compared. The colour of the marks left indicates the impurities present.

Toulon 43 07N 5 55E A port in SE France, in the Var department on the Mediterranean Sea. Toulon is one of France's principal naval bases and has marine engineering, chemical, oil, and textile industries. Population (1999): 159 389.

Toulouse 43 33N 1 24E A city in S France, the capital of the Haute-Garonne department on the River Garonne. A major commercial and industrial centre, it has aircraft, armaments, chemical, and textile industries. It is also an important agricultural trading centre. Notable buildings include the basilica (11th–13th centuries), the gothic cathedral, and the university (1230). Population (1999): 390 413.

Toulouse-Lautrec, Henri (Marie Raymond) de (1864–1901) French artist. Stunted by a childhood accident, he settled in Paris, where he led an unconventional life among the music halls and cafés of Montmartre. His sympathetic studies of entertainers, circus life, and prostitutes in posters, lithographs, and paintings were influenced by *Degas and Japanese prints. Characteristic paintings are *At the Moulin Rouge* (Art Institute of Chicago) and *La Toilette* (Louvre).

Tour de France The main Continental professional cycling race. Founded in 1903, the road race lasts three weeks or more and has a maximum length of approximately 4000 km (2480 mi). The race starts in a different town each year but always ends in Paris.

tourmaline A group of minerals composed of complex cyclosilicates containing boron. There are numerous varieties, some being used as gemstones and some for their piezoelectric and polarizing properties. Tourmalines are found in veins and pegmatites, in granite rocks.

Tours 47 23N 0 42E A city in central France, the capital of the Indre-et-Loire department situated between the Rivers Loire and Cher. Notable buildings include the gothic cathedral, the archiepiscopal palace (17th–18th centuries), and the university (1970). Tours is a tourist centre for the Loire Valley and has varied manufacturing industries. Population (1999): 132 820.

Tower Bridge A bridge over the River Thames, next to the *Tower of London. Built in 1894 in the gothic style, it has a central portion that lifts to allow large ships to pass through it into the Pool of London.

Tower of London A royal fortress on the N bank of the River Thames, to the E of the City of London. It was begun in the 11th century and added to in subsequent centuries. It was a royal palace until the 17th century and a state prison. It is now a barracks, armoury, and museum, containing the British crown jewels.

toxaemia The presence of bacterial toxins in the blood. Formerly, the term was used to describe a condition affecting pregnant women thought to be due to toxins but now known to be caused by *hypertension (raised blood pressure).

toxin A poison produced by a living organism. Many microorganisms, including bacteria and fungi, produce toxins. In diphtheria and tetanus the toxin is produced by the bacteria within the infected person; in botulism the toxin is produced in contaminated food. Some toxins are useful: penicillin is a toxin that kills bacteria.

Trabzon (former name: Trebizond) 41 00N 39 43E A port in NE Turkey, on the Black Sea. It was the capital of the Comnenian empire (1204–1461) and has a university (1963). Population (1997): 182 552.

tracery Decorative stonework supporting the segments of leaded stained glass in the windows of Gothic and Gothic-revival buildings. It was often very elaborate, especially in the late Gothic *Flamboyant (Continental) and *Perpendicular (English) styles. *See* GOTHIC ART AND ARCHITECTURE.

trachea **1.** The windpipe: a tube that conducts air from the larynx to the left and right bronchi, which continue to the *lungs. The trachea is lined by *mucous membrane and supported by hoops of cartilage in its wall. **2.** One of the air passages in insects, which lead directly to the tissues. Each trachea has an external opening (spiracle) that can be opened and closed.

trachoma An eye disease that occurs in dry poor parts of the world and is caused by a virus-like bacterium of the genus *Chlamydia*. It is a severe form of *conjunctivitis in which the membrane lining the eyelids becomes scarred and shrunken. Trachoma is the world's most common cause of blindness.

Tracy, Spencer (1900–67) US film actor. He began his film career in the 1930s by playing gangsters, but later costarred with Katherine *Hepburn in nine films, including *Adam's Rib* (1949) and *Guess Who's Coming to Dinner* (1967). Other notable films include *The Old Man and the Sea* (1958) and *Judgement at Nuremberg* (1961).

trade cycle The repeated cycle of boom, recession, *depression, recovery, and boom in an economy. In the UK in the 19th century, the trade cycle displayed remarkable regularity and stability; in the last hundred years it has fluctuated more. The *Depression of the 1930s was a severe and protracted world slump followed, after World War II, by a period of boom, interrupted by only minor recessions, which persisted until another depression was entered in the 1970s and another in the early 1990s. The causes of the cycle are uncertain, but it may result from the regular cycle of electoral politics or from erratic shocks to the economy, such as wars or rises in the prices of essential commodities (such as oil).

trademarks Distinctive emblems owned by a manufacturer or trader and applied to his goods to identify them as produced or sold by him. The owner of a trademark has the right to its exclusive use in connection with the goods associated with it. Any trademark can be protected against infringement by legal action and registered trademarks enjoy additional statutory protection.

Tradescantia A genus of flowering plants (about 60 species), native to North and Central America and popular as ornamentals. Varieties of the wandering jew (*T. fluminensis*) are popular house plants, having oval green leaves, tinged with pink or with silver stripes. Spiderworts, derived from *T. virginiana*, have three-petalled blue, red, or white flowers and grasslike leaves; they are attractive border plants. Family: *Commelinaceae*.

trade union An organization of employees joined together to present a collective front in negotiations with an employer and to provide a measure of security for its members. The origins of trade unions lie in the local clubs of skilled craftsmen in 18th-century Britain. Robert *Owen's Grand National Consolidated Trades Union (1834), the first attempt to unite skilled and unskilled workers, collapsed following the transportation of the *Tolpuddle Martyrs. In 1851 the first successful national trade union, the Amalgamated Society of Engineers, was formed and in 1868 the Trades Union Congress (TUC) met for the first time. Granted legal status in 1871, trade unions began to be formed by unskilled workers. Unions in the UK finally became secure with the passing of the Trade Disputes Act (1906), which prevented employers from suing unions for damages after a *strike. The failure of the *General Strike (1926) was a blow to the trades union movement in Britain and the consequent Trade Disputes Act (1927) made general strikes illegal. This was repealed by the postwar Labour Government. In the 1960s and 1970s trade unions became an important political force, but their power was subsequently curbed by the Employment Acts (1980, 1982, 1988) and the Trade Union Act (1984) passed by the Thatcher Government. The Labour Party has loosened its traditional links with the trade unions since the mid-1990s.

The first international trade union was the first *International (1864); the international trades union movement is now represented by the World Federation of Trade Unions and the *International Confederation of Free Trade Unions.

trade winds (*or* **tropical easterlies**) The predominantly easterly winds that blow in the tropics. They blow from the NE in the N hemisphere and from the SE in the S hemisphere, converging towards the equator.

Trafalgar, Battle of (21 October 1805) The naval battle in the Napoleonic Wars in which the British under Nelson (in the *Victory*) defeated the French W of Cape Trafalgar, between Cádiz and Gibraltar (SW Spain). The British success, which was tragically marred by Nelson's death in the hour of victory, ended the threat of a French invasion of Britain.

Trafford A unitary authority in NW England, in Greater Manchester. Area: 106 sq km (41 sq mi). Population (2001): 210 135.

tragedy A form of drama recounting the fall (usually, the death) of a noble protagonist. The form evolved in ancient Greece and was fully developed in the plays of Aeschylus, Sophocles, and Euripides. Little tragic drama of worth was then written until the tragedies of Shakespeare and his contemporaries. In 17th-century France the neoclassical tragedies of Racine and Corneille were carefully based on principles derived from Aristotle's *Poetics*. Ibsen and Strindberg in Europe and Eugene O'Neill in the USA contributed to the development of tragic drama in the 19th and 20th centuries.

tranquillizers Drugs used to relieve anxiety and tension. They include the *benzodiazepines. The powerful drugs used in the treatment of schizophrenia and other mental disorders were formerly known as major tranquillizers but are now known as antipsychotic drugs (*see* ANTIPSYCHOTICS).

transformer A device for converting alternating current from one voltage to another. The input is fed to a primary winding, a coil of wire round a soft iron core, creating an oscillating magnetic field in the core. This field induces a secondary current of the same frequency in the secondary winding wound on the same core. The ratio of primary to secondary voltage is equal to the ratio of the number of turns in the secondary coil to that in the primary. The device is widely used both in electronic circuits and in the transmission and distribution of electric power (*see* ELECTRICITY SUPPLY).

transistor A *semiconductor device with three or more electrodes. Transistors form the basic elements of electronic *amplifiers and logic circuits, often combined with other components in *integrated circuits. They were first developed in 1948 by William *Shockley and his coworkers at the Bell Telephone Co and now replace *thermionic valves in most applications. A **bipolar junction transistor** consists of two junctions between p-type and n-type semiconductors forming either a p-n-p or n-p-n structure. Current is carried across these junctions by both negative and positive charge carriers (electrons and holes). Depending on how it is connected into a circuit, the junction transistor can act as a voltage or current amplifier in much the same way as a triode valve.

Originally, junction transistors were made by alloying the impurity metal onto the semiconductor crystal or by adding impurities as the crystal was being grown. Now the doping is diffused in as a gas, introduced by ion implantation, or, more commonly, achieved by a combined process of etching and diffusion, known as the planar process.

The **field effect transistor** (FET) is a unipolar device, in which current is carried by only one type of charge. There are two types: the junction FET (JFET) has a region of semiconductor of one doping type flanked by two highly doped layers of the opposite type. Current flows parallel to the junctions, between the so-called source and drain electrodes, through a narrow channel between the highly doped regions (the gate); it is controlled by the electric field arising from the gate input voltage, which alters the width of the conducting channel. The JFET is used as a separate component in amplifiers and switches. In the insulated-gate FET (IGFET) the source and drain electrodes are highly doped regions in a substrate of the opposite type. The gate electrode is a conductor separated from the substrate by a thin insulating layer across the surface. The electric field caused by the gate voltage controls the source-drain current on the other side of the insulator. The IGFET is used mainly in metal-oxide semiconductor (MOS) integrated circuits. It is smaller than the equivalent bipolar junction transistor and uses less power. The first plastic transistor was built in 1988.

transition elements A large group of metallic elements, including most of the commonly used metals, the inner electron shells of which are incomplete. The *lanthanides and the *actinides are sometimes included in this definition. The elements show considerable similarities to their horizontal neighbours in the *periodic table. In general, they are hard, brittle, high-melting, and excellent conductors of heat and electricity. They have multiple valencies and form coloured compounds.

t

Transkei, Republic of A former Bantu homeland in South Africa, consisting of three separate areas. Most of the population was *Xhosa. Created in 1963, as the first of the Bantu Homelands, it became nominally independent in 1976. All Black Africans of Transkeian origin became its citizens, simultaneously losing their South African citizenship. Its independence was only recognized by South Africa. In 1994, following the adoption of a multiracial constitution, the Bantu Homelands were reintegrated into South Africa and South African citizenship granted to their inhabitants.

transmutation The conversion of one element into another. An early (unfulfilled) aim of alchemy was the transmutation of base metals into gold. Transmutations were achieved in the 20th century by bombarding elements with *alpha particles or *neutrons.

transpiration The loss of water vapour from the surface of a plant, which occurs primarily through small pores (stomata) in the leaves but also (slowly) through the cuticle of the *epidermis. The rate of water loss is controlled by the opening and closing of the stomata, greater loss occurring during the day than at night.

transplantation The surgical implantation of a tissue or organ derived either from another part of the patient's body or from another individual (the donor). Skin grafting is an example of the former: it is used particularly to repair damage and disfigurement caused by burns and other injuries. Transplantation of donor organs requires careful matching of the donor's and recipient's tissues together with the use of drugs that suppress the recipient's immune responses (*see* IMMUNOSUPPRESSION). The first successful heart transplant operation was performed by Christiaan *Barnard in 1967; other organs that have been transplanted include the kidneys, lungs, liver, and pancreas. The first implantation of an artificial heart, made of titanium, took place in 1988.

transportation In law, the practice of sending a convicted criminal to some place outside Britain, usually to one of the colonies, to be kept in hard labour. Transportation dates back to the reign of Elizabeth I; it ceased in the 19th century.

Trans-Siberian Railway The world's longest railway, running 9335 km (5800 mi) from Moscow to Vladivostok. Double track, largely electrified, has replaced the original single track line built between 1891 and 1905. The complete journey with nearly a hundred stops takes nine days.

transubstantiation In Roman Catholic theology, the doctrine that the substance of the elements of bread and wine in the *Eucharist is changed at consecration into the substance of the body and blood of Christ. Only the accidents (i.e. the qualities apparent to the senses) of the bread and wine remain.

transuranic elements Elements with higher atomic number than uranium. Apart from traces of neptunium and plutonium, none of them has ever been detected in nature,

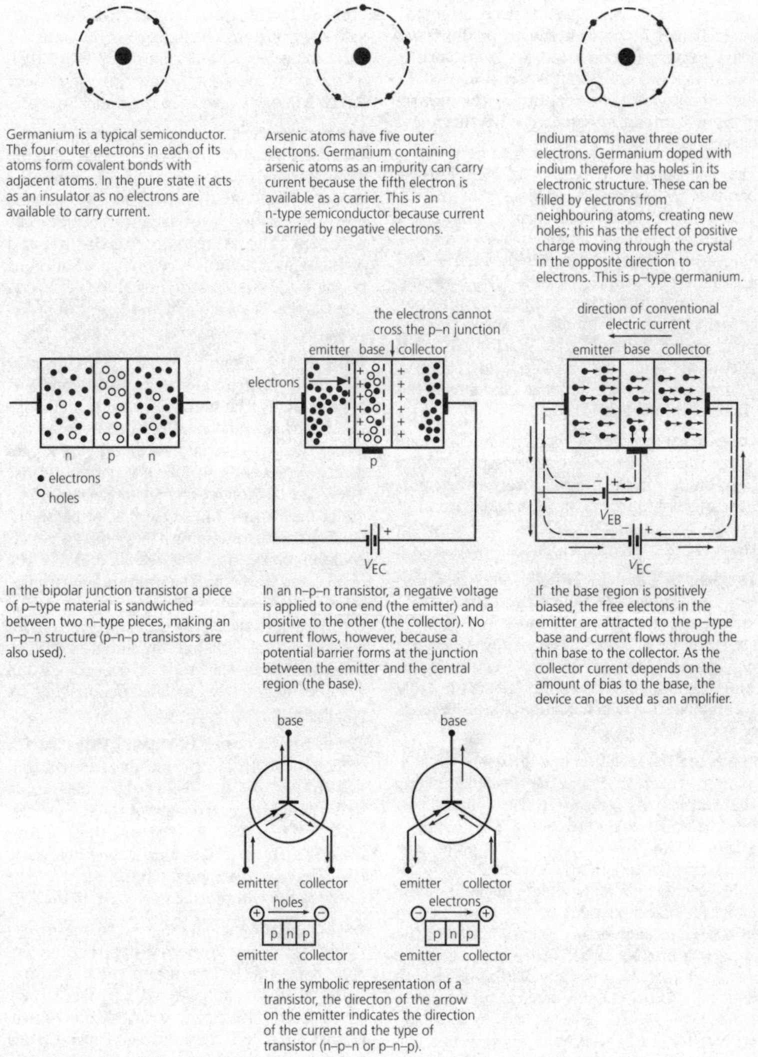
Germanium is a typical semiconductor. The four outer electrons in each of its atoms form covalent bonds with adjacent atoms. In the pure state it acts as an insulator as no electrons are available to carry current.
Arsenic atoms have five outer electrons. Germanium containing arsenic atoms as an impurity can carry current because the fifth electron is available as a carrier. This is an n-type semiconductor because current is carried by negative electrons.
Indium atoms have three outer electrons. Germanium doped with indium therefore has holes in its electronic structure. These can be filled by electrons from neighbouring atoms, creating new holes; this has the effect of positive charge moving through the crystal in the opposite direction to electrons. This is p–type germanium.
n p n
electrons
holes
the electrons cannot cross the p–n junction
emitter base collector
electrons
p
V_{EC}
direction of conventional electric current
emitter base collector
V_{EB}
V_{EC}
In the bipolar junction transistor a piece of p–type material is sandwiched between two n–type pieces, making an n–p–n structure (p–n–p transistors are also used).
In an n–p–n transistor, a negative voltage is applied to one end (the emitter) and a positive to the other (the collector). No current flows, however, because a potential barrier forms at the junction between the emitter and the central region (the base).
If the base region is positively biased, the free electons in the emitter are attracted to the p–type base and current flows through the thin base to the collector. As the collector current depends on the amount of bias to the base, the device can be used as an amplifier.
base
emitter collector
holes
p n p
emitter collector
base
emitter collector
electrons
p n p
emitter collector
In the symbolic representation of a transistor, the directon of the arrow on the emitter indicates the direction of the current and the type of transistor (n–p–n or p–n–p).

transistor. The operation of the bipolar junction transistor.

since no isotopes of sufficient *half-life exist; they have been created since 1940 in nuclear reactions. *See also* ACTINIDES.

Transvaal A former province in South Africa. Heavily populated in the S, it contains the country's main industrial area, centred on the Witwatersrand; iron, steel, and chemicals are produced. Mineral deposits include gold, diamonds, uranium, coal, chromite, tin, and platinum. It has a well-developed agriculture producing maize, wheat, peanuts, citrus fruit, cotton, and tobacco; sheep and cattle are raised.

Forestry is also important. *History*: originally an Afrikaner republic, it fought in the *Boer Wars against Britain (1880–81, 1899–1902). It joined the Union of South Africa in 1910. In 1994 the province was replaced by the new regions of **Gauteng**, **Mpumalanga**, **Northern**, and parts of **Northwest**.

Transylvania A region of SE Europe, bounded by the Carpathian Mountains and the Transylvanian Alps. Transylvania retained its distinctive character under successive Roman, Magyar, and Hungarian rulers; during the 16th and 17th centuries, it was a self-governing princedom within the Ottoman Empire. Restored to Hungary in 1687, Transylvania became part of Romania after World War I. In a 1996 treaty Hungary renounced any claim to Transylvania, while Romania guaranteed the rights of ethnic Hungarians.

trap-door spider A *spider, especially one of the family *Ctenizidae*, that constructs a silk-lined burrow in the ground covered by a tight-fitting silk-hinged door. Ctenizids are dull brown, with short stout legs. They occur in tropical and subtropical regions.

Trappists A Roman Catholic monastic order, officially known as the *Cistercians of the Strict Observance. It was founded in 1664 at the abbey of La Trappe in Normandy; there are now monasteries in Britain, Ireland, North America, and elsewhere. The order is notable for its austerity, which includes the observance of strict silence.

treason The violation by a citizen of his allegiance to the sovereign or the state. In England, the Statute of Treasons (1352) defined two kinds of treason: high treason was (1) to plot to kill or maim the sovereign; (2) to wage war against him or to join his enemies; (3) to kill his eldest son or heir; (4) to violate his wife, eldest daughter (if unmarried), or heir's wife; (5) to kill the chancellor, or any judge while he or she is performing his or her office; petty treason, abolished in 1828, was the violation of private allegiance. Until 1999 all forms of high treason carried the death penalty; this is now restricted to treason in time of war or imminent war.

t

treasure trove Formerly, gold or silver items of unknown ownership found hidden in a concealed place. In England it belonged to the Crown provided it had been deliberately concealed rather than abandoned or lost. The finder of treasure trove was rewarded the value of the property found, unless he concealed it, in which case he was liable to imprisonment. The Treasure Act (1996) redefined treasure as any item (excluding single coins) at least 300 years old and containing more than 5% precious metal. It belongs to the Crown, which will pay a reward to the finder.

Treasury The UK government department, established in 1653, that is responsible, with the *Bank of England, for the management of the economy and the allocation of the available government money between the spending departments. The prime minister is the first lord of the treasury, but it is run by the chancellor of the exchequer, assisted by the chief secretary to the Treasury and the financial secretary.

tree A tall perennial woody plant, usually with a single main stem (the trunk) and secondary stems (the branches) arising some distance above ground level. Most tree species are either *dicotyledons (angiosperms)—the broad-leaved trees—or *conifers (gymnosperms). These are of economic importance as producers of hardwoods and softwoods, respectively. Other groups containing trees are the cycads (gymnosperms), monocotyledons (notably the palms), and the ferns. The conifers and tropical trees are mostly *evergreen plants, while broad-leaved trees growing in regions with marked seasonal changes in climate are typically deciduous. The study of the ecology and classification of trees is called **dendrology**. *See also* FOREST.

Tree, Sir Herbert (Draper) Beerbohm (1853–1917) British actor and theatre manager, halfbrother of the writer Max Beerbohm (1872–1956). He was manager of the Haymarket Theatre from 1887 to 1899 and then of Her Majesty's Theatre, where he staged many lavish Shakespearean productions. In 1904 he founded the *Royal Academy of Dramatic Art.

treecreeper A small songbird belonging to a family (*Certhiidae*; 5 species) occurring in Europe, Asia, and North America. It has a brownish streaked plumage with pale silvery underparts, long claws, and a slender down-curved bill. The European treecreeper (*Certhia familiaris*) occurs mainly in coniferous woods, where it creeps up tree trunks to probe for small beetles, spiders, woodlice, etc.

tree frog A small toad belonging to a widely distributed family (*Hylidae*; about 500 species). They have adapted to living in trees and have adhesive pads on their toes that enable them to cling to leaves and branches, leaping acrobatically to capture insects.

tree

tree of heaven A tree, *Ailanthus altissima*, native to central Asia and planted elsewhere as an ornamental. Growing to a height of 30 m, it has compound leaves, up to 1 m, composed of paired leaflets. Its flowers form greenish-white clusters; the female flowers produce winged fruits. Family: *Simaroubaceae.*

tree-ring dating *See* DENDROCHRONOLOGY.

tree shrew A mammal belonging to the order *Scandentia* (19 species), found in Java, Borneo, Sumatra, the Philippines, and S Asia. The common tree shrew (*Tupaia glis*) is 30–45 cm long including the tail (15–23 cm) and has a slender pointed face. It darts among the branches, feeding on insects, fruit, and seeds.

Trenchard, Hugh Montagne, 1st Viscount (1873–1956) The first British air marshal. As commander of the Royal Flying Corps during World War I, he was chiefly responsible for the establishment of the RAF (1918).

Trent, Council of (1545–63) The 19th general council of the Roman Catholic Church, an expression of the *Counter-Reformation, which was summoned by Pope Paul III to strengthen the Church in its confrontation with Protestantism. It was held in Trento (N Italy). There were three sessions (1545–47, 1551–52, 1562–63), which clarified doctrine and instituted reforms; the Council condemned Luther's doctrine of justification by faith alone and defined *transubstantiation. It effectively determined the structures, teachings, and liturgy of the Church until the Second *Vatican Council 400 years later.

Trent, River A river in central England. Flowing mainly NE from Staffordshire through Nottingham, it joins the River Ouse to form the Humber estuary. The Midlands' main river, it is linked to the Mersey by the Trent, Mersey, and Grand Union Canals. Length: 270 km (170 mi).

Trento (German name: Trent) 46 04N 11 08E A city in N Italy, the capital of Trentino-Alto Adige on the River Adige. Dating from pre-Roman times, it has a romanesque cathedral (12th century) and the 16th-century Church of Sta Maria Maggiore, where the Council of *Trent met. Population (2000 est): 104 906.

triangle A geometric figure bounded by three straight sides meeting in three corners called the vertices (singular: vertex). In a plane triangle, the sum of the internal angles is always 180°; in non-Euclidian geometries the sum may be more (spherical triangles) or less.

t

Triassic period (*or* **Trias**) A period of geological time at the beginning of the Mesozoic era, lasting from about 240 to 200 million years ago. The rocks of the period were laid down mainly under continental conditions. The dinosaurs, ichthyosaurs, and plesiosaurs appeared in the Triassic.

tribes of Israel In the Bible, the Hebrew people. The 12 tribes, descended from the sons of Jacob, were Reuben, Simeon, Judah, Issachar, Zebulun, Benjamin, Dan, Naphtali, Gad, Asher, Levi, and Ephraim and Manasseh. These last two were usually counted as one. After the death of Solomon, ten of the tribes broke away from Benjamin and Judah to form the northern kingdom of Israel; they are known as the Ten Lost Tribes of Israel.

tribune In ancient Rome, a plebeian magistrate appointed to protect plebeians' rights. Instituted during the 5th-century political struggles between *patricians and plebeians, the tribunes could veto legislative proposals of the Senate or popular assemblies and could propose legislation without senatorial approval.

Triceratops A three-horned dinosaur of the late Cretaceous period (about 100–65 million years ago). 8 m long and weighing 8.5 tonnes, it had an enormous head with one horn on the snout and one over each eye. It also had a large bony neck frill and browsed on tough plants. Order: *Ornithischia.*

Trident missile A US navy three-stage solid-fuelled nuclear strategic missile launched from a submarine and having a range of 7800 km (4800 mi). Designed as a replacement for the Poseidon missile, Trident missiles, first deployed in the early 1980s, are capable of great accuracy at increased distances and carry a new stellar-inertial guidance system. They replaced the UK's Polaris systems in 1994–96. The UK launched its fourth and last Trident submarine in 1998.

Trier (French name: Trèves) 49 45N 6 39E A city in SW Germany, in Rhineland-Palatinate on the River Moselle. Founded by the Emperor Augustus, it has important Roman remains. It is a wine-trading and industrial centre. Population (1991): 98 750.

Trieste (Serbo-Croat name: Trst) 45 39N 13 47E A seaport in Italy, the capital of Friuli-Venezia Giulia, situated on the Gulf of Trieste at the head of the Adriatic Sea. An important transit port for central Europe, it has shipyards, oil refineries, and a steel industry. *History*: an important Roman port in the 1st century AD, it passed to Austria in 1382. It expanded rapidly in the 19th century and in 1920 was ceded to Italy. Following World War II it became the capital of the Free Territory of Trieste. In 1954 most of the N of the Territory (including Trieste) passed to Italy and the remainder to Yugoslavia. Population (2000 est): 216 459.

triggerfish A shallow-water fish, of a family (*Balistidae*) related to *puffers, that occurs in tropical seas. Its deep laterally flattened body is covered with large scales. The strong spine of the first dorsal fin is erected and locked into position by the second dorsal fin, forming a "trigger" that wedges the fish into crevices.

trigonometry A branch of mathematics founded by Hipparchus in the mid-2nd century BC, concerned originally with the measurement of triangles. The ratios of the lengths of the sides of a right-angled triangle are used to define the sine, cosine, and tangent of one of the angles of the triangle. Trigonometry deals with the properties of these and related functions.

trilobite An extinct marine *arthropod belonging to a subphylum (*Trilobita*; over 4000 species) that flourished 500–200 million years ago. Trilobite fossils are abundant in rocks of this period. Its flattened oval body, 10–675 mm long, was divided by two longitudinal furrows into three lobes. The head bore a pair of antennae and two eyes and each segment of the thorax and tail region carried a pair of forked appendages.

Trimble, (William) David (1944–) Northern Irish politician, leader of the Ulster Unionist Party (1995–). An MP from 1990, he was a leading participant in the multiparty talks that led to the Good Friday Agreement of 1998 and became Northern Ireland's first minister later that year. In 1998 he was awarded the Nobel Peace Prize jointly with John *Hume.

Trimurti The Hindu triad of gods, *Brahma, *Vishnu, and *Shiva, representing the creative, sustaining, and destructive aspects of reality respectively, sometimes portrayed as one body with three heads.

Trinidad and Tobago, Republic of A country off the N coast of South America, consisting of the islands of Trinidad and Tobago. Both are hilly and wooded. Most of the population is of African and East Indian descent. *Economy*: oil has replaced cocoa and sugar as the main source of wealth and reserves of offshore gas have also been discovered. Other industrial developments include aluminium smelting, plastics, electronics, iron and steel, and chemicals. Tourism is growing. The republic is a member of CARICOM. *History*: Trinidad was inhabited by Arawak and Carib Indians when it was discovered by Columbus in 1498. It was a Spanish colony from the 16th century until 1802, when it was ceded to Britain; it joined with Tobago in 1809. The country became an independent state within the Commonwealth in 1962 and a republic in 1976. Legislative elections in 2001 produced a straight tie between the main parties, causing a constitutional crisis that was not resolved until the following year. Official language: English. Currency: Trinidad and Tobago dollar of 100 cents. Area: 5128 sq km (1980 sq mi). Population (2003): 1 279 000. Capital: Port-of-Spain.

Trinity, the A central doctrine of Christian theology, stating that God is one substance but with three distinct, coequal, and coeternal "persons," the Father, the Son, and the *Holy Spirit. It was given a first formal definition by the Council of *Nicaea (325).

triode *See* THERMIONIC VALVE.

Triple Alliance (1882) An alliance between Germany, Austria-Hungary, and Italy, which with the opposing *Triple Entente shaped European diplomacy before World War I. At the outbreak of war (1914) Italy declared its neutrality, thus breaking the alliance.

Triple Alliance, War of the (*or* **Paraguayan War**; 1865–70) The war between Paraguay and a coalition of Argentina, Brazil, and Uruguay. Conflict was precipitated by the belligerent diplomacy of Paraguay's dictator, F. S. López (1826–70), towards Argentina, which with Brazil and Uruguay invaded Paraguay. López waged a guerrilla war until captured (1870).

Triple Entente An informal combination of France, Russia, and Britain resulting from the Franco-Russian alliance (1893), the Franco-British Entente Cordiale (1904), and the Anglo-Russian agreement (1907). It was formed in opposition to the *Triple Alliance.

triple jump (former name: hop, step, and jump) A field event in athletics, similar to the long jump but executed as a continuous series of three jumps. The jumper lands first on the takeoff foot and then on the other, which becomes the takeoff foot for the final jump. The event was opened to women in 1990 (1996 for the Olympics). World record: 17.97 m (1985) Willie Banks (USA).

Tripoli 1. (Arabic name: Tarabulus al-Gharb) 32 58N 13 12E The capital and main port of Libya, on the Mediterranean Sea. Originally founded as Oea by the Phoenicians, it became the capital of Libya on independence in 1951. Exports include fruit and olive oil and it is a transshipment centre. Population (1991 est): 1 000 000. **2.** (Arabic name: Tarabalus ash-sham) 34 27N 35 50E A port in NW Lebanon, on the Mediterranean Sea. It was the capital of a Phoenician federation of three other cities. Iraqi oil is brought by pipeline to the refinery here. Population (1991 est): 240 000.

trireme *See* SHIPS.

Tristan The tragic hero of several medieval romances. After accidentally drinking a magic love potion, he becomes the lover of Iseult (Isolde), who is betrothed to his uncle, King Mark of Cornwall. He later renounces Iseult and goes to Brittany, where he marries. Dying from a wound, he sends for Iseult; she arrives too late and dies of grief at his side. Of Celtic origin, the legend appeared in a French poem, written in about 1150. Other versions include Gottfried von Strassburg's *Tristan und Isolde*, the source of Wagner's opera. In the 13th century the story was incorporated into the *Arthurian legend.

Tristan da Cunha 37 15S 12 30W A group of four small islands in the S Atlantic Ocean, a dependency of St Helena. The only settlement, Edinburgh, is on Tristan (the largest island). In 1961 the inhabitants were evacuated to the UK to escape a volcanic eruption but most chose to return in 1963. The economy is based on crawfish canning and postage stamps. Area: about 100 sq km (40 sq mi). Population (latest est): 313.

tritium (T *or* ^{3}H) A radioactive isotope of hydrogen, the nucleus of which contains one *proton and two *neutrons. It does not occur naturally but is produced in nuclear reactors and is used as a radioactive tracer and in nuclear weapons. Tritium decays with a half-life of 12.3 years, emitting beta-rays.

triton shell A *gastropod mollusc of the family *Cymatiidae* (about 100 species), occurring mainly in tropical seas. Triton trumpets (genus *Charonia*) grow to 40 cm and have ribbed shells, often with prominent knobs. They feed on molluscs and echinoderms.

triumvirate In Roman affairs, a board of three men officially appointed for special administrative duties. The so-called first Triumvirate (60 BC) of Caesar, Pompey, and Crassus was merely a private arrangement. The triumvirate, or triple dictatorship, of Mark Antony, Lepidus, and Octavian was unique; appointed in 43 BC to maintain public order in Rome, they held office with absolute powers until Lepidus was ousted in 36.

Troilus In Greek mythology, a son of King Priam of Troy who was killed by Achilles. The story of his love for Cressida, who deserted him for the Greek Diomedes, first appeared in the *Roman de Troie* by the 12th-century French poet Benoît de Sainte-Maure. Later versions include those by Chaucer and Shakespeare.

Trojan Horse In Greek legend, a gigantic hollow wooden horse used in the *Trojan War. The Trojans hauled it inside their city, believing it to be a gift to Athena, and Greek warriors then emerged from it to open the gates to their army.

Trojan War In Greek legend, a ten years' war waged by the Greeks against *Troy after the abduction of *Helen by Paris. Its history, probably based on an actual war fought in the 12th century BC, is related in Homer's *Iliad*. The Greeks were led by *Agamemnon and their champions included *Achilles, Diomedes, and *Odysseus. The chief Trojan warriors were *Hector and *Paris, sons of King Priam. The war culminated in the capture of Troy by the stratagem of the *Trojan Horse.

troll In Scandinavian folklore, originally a gigantic ogre-like creature imagined as guarding treasure, inhabiting a castle, and stalking through the forest at night. In later folklore, trolls were conceived as dwarflike cave- and mountain-dwellers who were skilled craftsmen.

Trollope, Anthony (1815–82) British novelist. He worked for the General Post Office from 1834 until he retired in 1867. He established his reputation with a series of novels, including *The Warden* (1855) and *Barchester Towers* (1857), set in the imaginary county of Barsetshire with a cast of predominantly clerical characters. A second series of novels, set against a political background, includes *Phineas Finn* (1869) and *The Eustace Diamonds* (1873).

trombone A brass musical instrument, consisting of a cylindrical tube, about 3 m (9 ft) long, turned back upon itself, a cup-shaped mouthpiece, and a flaring bell. By means of a slide and by varying lip pressure, a chromatic range of almost three octaves can be produced. The trombone has been part of the symphony orchestra since the late 18th century and is frequently used in jazz. The old English name for the trombone was the **sackbut**.

Trondheim 63 36N 10 23E A city and seaport in W Norway on Trondheim Fjord. It has a famous cathedral (12th–14th centuries) where Norwegian sovereigns have been crowned since early times and two universities. Industries include shipbuilding and fishing. Population (2000 est): 148 859.

trooping the Colour Traditionally, the parade of the British sovereign's flag, or Colour, displayed so that foreign mercenaries would recognize it in battle. It is now a military parade held on the Horse Guards parade ground in Whitehall, London, on the sovereign's official birthday.

tropic bird A white seabird belonging to a family (*Phaethontidae*; 3 species) occurring in tropical and subtropical waters. Tropic birds have black eye and wing markings and are up to 50 cm long excluding the long streamer-like tail feathers. Order: *Pelecaniformes* (cormorants, pelicans, etc.).

tropics The area of the earth's surface lying roughly between the Tropic of Cancer on the 23°30′N parallel of latitude and the Tropic of Capricorn on the 23°30′S parallel.

tropism The growth of a plant or sedentary animal in response to a directional external stimulus: a growth movement towards the stimulus is a positive tropism; the opposite response is a negative tropism. For example, positive **hydrotropism** is growth towards water; negative **geotropism** is growth away from the pull of gravity.

troposphere *See* ATMOSPHERE.

Trotsky, Leon (Lev Bronstein; 1879–1940) Russian revolutionary and Marxist theorist. Trotsky became a Marxist in the 1890s and was imprisoned and exiled for revolutionary activities. He lived in W Europe until the Revolution of 1905, when he was again imprisoned and exiled. On the outbreak of the Russian Revolution, he returned to Russia and abandoned his *Menshevik loyalities to become a *Bolshevik. He played a major role in the October Revolution and during the civil war (1918–20) directed the Red Army to victory. Under Lenin, Trotsky was Russia's second most powerful man but he lost to Stalin the power struggle that followed Lenin's death and was banished. He was murdered, probably by a Soviet agent. The form of Marxism developed by Trotsky, who advocated world revolution in opposition to the view that socialism could be achieved in one country, is known as **Trotskyism**.

troubadours Provençal poets of the 12th to 14th centuries whose lyric poetry had a profound influence on both the subject matter and form of subsequent European verse. Both poets and composers, the troubadours wrote songs introducing a new concept of love, later labelled courtly love. The earliest troubadour was Guillaume, 9th Duc d'Aquitaine (1071–1127). Other famous troubadours included Vicomte de Hautefort (c. 1140–c. 1207); Arnaut Daniel (c. 1180), who was credited with inventing the *sestina*; and Bernard de Ventadour (late 12th century), in whose lyrics the conventions of courtly love were most clearly developed.

trout One of several predatory fish belonging to the family *Salmonidae*, especially the genus *Salmo*, that are native to the N hemisphere but introduced elsewhere as food and game fish. It has a stout body with a blunt head and varies in colour from blackish to light olive with characteristic black or red spots or X-shaped markings. Trout occur mainly in fresh water. The common European brown trout (*S. trutta*) has a migratory variety called the sea trout. The North American rainbow trout (*S. gairdneri*) is distinguished by a broad purple band along its sides. Order: *Salmoniformes*.

Troy An ancient city in Asia Minor, near the Dardanelles. According to legend, when the Trojan prince *Paris abducted *Helen, *Agamemnon led a Greek force to recover her and captured Troy (*see* TROJAN WAR). Schliemann's excavations (1870) identified Troy at Hissarlik. Excavations have revealed nine superimposed cities, the seventh of which was contemporary with the legendary siege. *See also* HOMER.

Trudeau, Pierre Elliott (1919–2000) Canadian statesman; Liberal prime minister (1968–79, 1980–84). A French Canadian, he nevertheless opposed French separatism and in 1970 briefly introduced martial law to deal with separatist agitation in Quebec. He retired from office in 1984 and his Liberal party lost the subsequent general election.

Truffaut, François (1932–84) French film director and critic, an influential member of the *New Wave. His films, noted for their visual charm and elegance, include *Le Quatre Cent Coups* (1959), *Jules et Jim* (1961), *L'Enfant sauvage* (1970), *Day for Night* (1973), and *Le Dernier Métro* (1980).

truffle A fungus belonging to the order *Tuberales*. Up to 10 cm across, truffles are rounded and occur in chalky soils, usually in association with tree roots. Several species are regarded as delicacies, including the black Périgord truffle (*Tuber melanosporum*) and the white Piedmont truffle (*T. magnatum*), both of France. They are collected in oak woods using trained pigs or dogs. The bluish-black English truffle (*T. aestivum*) is found mainly in beech woods. Phylum: *Ascomycota*.

Trujillo 8 06S 79 00W A city in Peru, situated 13 km (8 mi) from its port, Salaverry, on the Pacific coast. Founded in 1535, Trujillo is the commercial centre for an area producing sugar cane and rice. Population (1998 est): 603 657.

Truman, Harry S. (1884–1972) US statesman; Democratic president (1945–53). One of his first acts as president was to order the atomic bombing of Hiroshima and Nagasaki to end the war with Japan. In the **Truman Doctrine** he announced economic and military aid to countries thought to be vulnerable to communist takeover or influence. His administration saw the establishment of the *North Atlantic Treaty Organization (1949). In domestic politics his Fair Deal programme promised social reform.

trumpet A brass musical instrument. The modern trumpet consists of a cylindrical tube, 1.5 m (5 ft) long, turned back on itself, a cup-shaped mouthpiece, and a flaring bell. Three valves alter the effective length of the tube; with varying lip pressure the B flat trumpet has a chromatic range of two and a half octaves.

trunkfish A tropical fish, also called boxfish or cowfish, belonging to a family (*Ostraciidae*) related to *puffers, that occurs in the Atlantic and Pacific Oceans. Its body is often brightly coloured and encased in a boxlike shell of fused bony plates with spaces for the fins, etc.

Truro 50 16N 5 03W A cathedral city in SW England, the administrative centre of Cornwall. It is a small port and market town, with pottery and biscuit manufacturing. Population (1991): 18 966.

trypsin A digestive enzyme, secreted by the pancreas, that breaks down dietary proteins in the small intestine. It is secreted in an inactive form, which is converted to trypsin by the enzyme enterokinase in the intestine.

tsetse fly A fly, 6–16 mm long, belonging to a genus (*Glossina*; 22 species) restricted to tropical Africa. Both sexes bite and suck the blood of mammals; *G. palpalis* transmits sleeping sickness to man and *G. morsitans* transmits nagana to cattle. Family: *Muscidae*.

Tuamotu Archipelago A chain of about 80 coral atolls in the S Pacific Ocean, in French Polynesia. Rangiroa is the largest island and Fakarava, the most important economically. French nuclear tests were held here during the 1960s. Mother-of-pearl, phosphate, and copra are produced. Area: 860 sq km (332 sq mi). Population (1996): 15 370. Administrative centre: Apataki atoll.

tuatara A lizard-like reptile, *Sphenodon punctatus*, that is the only living representative of the primitive order *Rhynchocephalia*, which lived 200 million years ago. It is found only on islands off the North Island of New Zealand and has a brown-black to greenish body with a crest of spines running from head to tail; up to 70 cm long, it may live 100 years. Tuataras live in burrows during the day and emerge at night to feed on spiders, insects, and birds' eggs.

tuba A valved brass instrument with a conical bore and low pitch, derived originally from the saxhorn. Various types of tuba exist under a variety of names; the instrument is used in the symphony orchestra as well as in the military band.

tuber A swollen underground plant stem in which carbohydrates (often in the form of starch) are stored. Some tubers, for example potatoes and yams, are important human foods. Tuber-bearing plants may reproduce vegetatively from buds on the tuber, and tuber crops are usually grown from tubers rather than seed.

tuberculin A protein derived from tuberculosis bacilli that have been killed. In the Mantoux test tuberculin is injected into the skin to test whether a person has been in contact with tuberculosis. The appearance of an inflamed patch (a positive reaction) indicates previous exposure to the bacilli.

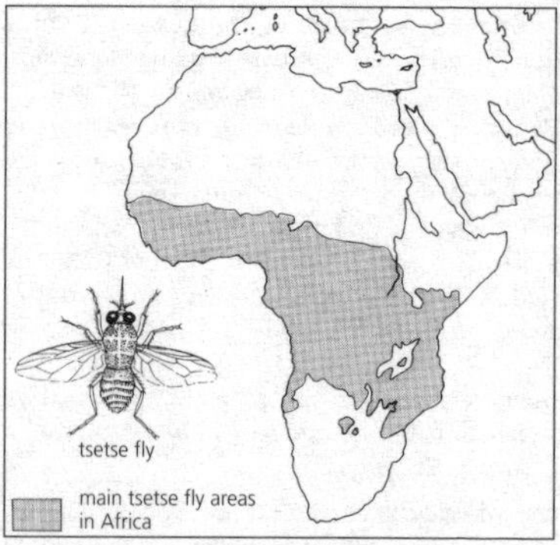

tsetse fly. Several species of tsetse fly carry the parasites causing sleeping sickness in humans and cattle. The tsetse areas in Africa correspond to the areas where sleeping sickness is endemic.

tuberculosis An infectious disease caused by the bacillus *Mycobacterium tuberculosis* (which was first recognized by the bacteriologist Robert Koch (1843–1910) in 1882). In pulmonary tuberculosis the bacillus is inhaled into the lungs, where it forms a primary tubercle that usually heals without trouble. Alternatively the disease may smoulder for months without showing any symptoms. Reactivation of the primary disease, or reinfection, may lead to active tuberculosis ("consumption"), characterized by a cough, fever, lassitude, weight loss, and breathlessness. The TB bacillus can also enter the body through drinking infected cows' milk. Improved environmental conditions, pasteurization of milk, X-ray screening, and *BCG vaccinations have all reduced the incidence of TB in developed countries.

tubifex A freshwater *annelid worm, also called bloodworm, belonging to the widely distributed family *Tubificidae*. Found along muddy rivers and estuaries, the most common species is the bright-red extremely active *Tubifex tubifex*, up to 85 mm long. Class: *Oligochaeta*.

Tucson 32 15N 110 57W A city and health resort in the USA, in Arizona. Its growth came with the arrival of the Southern Pacific Railroad (1880) and the discovery of silver at nearby Tombstone. Tucson is an industrial centre for the surrounding agricultural and mining district. Population (2000): 486 699.

Tudjman, Franjo (1922–99) Croatian soldier and politician, president of Croatia (as a federal republic of Yugoslavia 1990–92, as an independent state 1992–99). In 1991–92 he led the Croatian struggle against the Serb-led Yugoslav army and in 1992–95 he involved his country's forces in the civil war in Bosnia-Hercegovina. His regime was nationalistic and authoritarian.

Tudors The ruling dynasty of England from 1485 to 1603. Owen Tudor (c. 1400–61), a Welshman, entered the service of Henry V and married (1422) his widow Catherine of Valois (1401–37). Their eldest son Edmund, Earl of Richmond (c. 1430–56), married Margaret Beaufort (1443–1509), the great-great-granddaughter of Edward III, and their son became the first Tudor monarch, Henry VII. Subsequent Tudor monarchs were Henry VIII, Edward VI, Mary I, and Elizabeth I.

tulip A perennial herbaceous plant of the genus *Tulipa* (about 100 species), native to the Old World but widely cultivated for ornament. Growing from bulbs, most tulips have a solitary bell-shaped flower, with bluish-green leaves clustered at the base of the plant. There are nearly 4000 varieties of garden tulips: the older varieties are descended from *T. gesneriana* and *T. suaveolens*; the newer ones often have *T. kaufmanniana*, *T. greigi*, or *T. fosteriana* as one of the parent species. Family: *Liliaceae*.

tulip tree A tree, *Liriodendron tulipifera*, native to E North America and widely planted for ornament. Reaching a height of 58 m in the wild, it has three-lobed leaves and large tulip-like flowers, greenish white or yellow, produce papery cones containing winged fruits. The wood, known as white wood, is used for furniture, plywood, paper, and boxes. The Chinese tulip tree (*L. chinense*) is similar but smaller. Family: *Magnoliaceae*.

Tull, Jethro (1674–1741) English agriculturist, best known for his invention in 1701 of the seed drill. He made many other innovations in agricultural methods.

Tulsa 36 07N 95 58W A city in the USA, in Oklahoma on the Arkansas River. Oil was discovered in 1901 and today over 800 oil companies have established plants here. Population (2000): 393 049.

tumour Any swelling in the body caused by the abnormal proliferation of cells. Tumours that do not spread to other parts of the body (i.e. are noncancerous) are described as benign. They are usually harmless. Tumours that destroy the tissue in which they arise and spread to other parts of the body are described as malignant (*see* CANCER).

tuna A carnivorous food and game fish, sometimes called tunny, belonging to a family (*Scombridae*) found in warm seas. Its elongated robust body is generally dark above and silvery below. The large bluefin tuna (*Thunnus thynnus*) reaches 4.3 m in length. Large quantities of tinned tuna are consumed throughout the world. Order: *Perciformes*. *See also* ALBACORE.

Tunbridge Wells (*or* **Royal Tunbridge Wells**) 51 08N 0 16E A town in SE England, in Kent. Visited for its medicinal waters since the 17th century, it became a fashionable health resort. Population (1991): 45 155.

tundra The level, virtually treeless, areas in the N hemisphere (in Eurasia and North America) lying between the most northerly region in which trees grow and the polar regions of perpetual snow and ice. Winters are long and severe with brief summers in which temperatures remain below 10°C (50°F); *permafrost is a feature. Vegetation includes mosses, lichens, dwarf shrubs, herbaceous perennials, and a few stunted trees.

tungsten (*or* **wolfram**; W) A grey brittle metal with the highest melting point of any element. It was discovered in 1779 and is obtained from the ores wolframite ($FeWO_4$) and scheelite ($CaWO_4$) by reduction with hydrogen or carbon.

t

It oxidizes readily when heated, forming the oxide WO_3. The metal is used as filaments in electric light bulbs, in television tubes, contact breakers, and X-ray tubes, and in many hard alloys for high-speed cutting tools. Tungsten carbide (WC) is very hard and is used for tipping drill bits. At no 74; at wt 183.85; mp 3422 ± 20°C; bp 5555°C.

tunicate A small marine animal belonging to the phylum (*or* subphylum) *Urochordata* (or *Tunicata*; about 2000 species). Tunicates range from several millimetres to over 30 cm in size. They have a saclike cellulose tunic covering the body; food particles are filtered from water drawn in through a siphon at the top and expelled through a second siphon. The free-swimming tadpole-like larvae show the major characteristics of all chordates; they subsequently metamorphose to the adult form and lose their chordate features. Sea squirts (class *Ascidacea*) live attached to rocks, etc., singly or in colonies, while the salps (class *Thaliacea*) float in the sea, sometimes as chains of several hundred individuals.

Tunis (Arabic name: Tunus) 36 48N 10 13E The capital of Tunisia, on the Gulf of Tunis. It was developed by the Arabs in the 7th century AD. It came under French rule in the late 19th century, and became the capital on independence in 1956. Industries include chemicals, lead smelting, and textiles. Population (1994): 674 100.

Tunisia, Republic of (Arabic name: al-Jumhuriyah at-Tunisiyah) A small country in N Africa, bordering on the Mediterranean Sea. Its narrow coastal zone extends into desert in the S and rises to uplands in the N. The population is largely Arabic. *Economy*: predominantly agricultural, with wheat, olive oil, citrus fruits, dates, and wine among the chief products; livestock is also important. Tunisia is one of the world's largest producers of phosphates. Oil reserves were discovered in 1964 and exploitation began in 1972; iron ore and lead are also mined. Manufacturing industry includes oil refining, cement, and steel processing. Fine beaches and notable architecture contribute to Tunisia's popularity with tourists. *History*: first settled by the Phoenicians, it developed into the empire of Carthage and was later absorbed into the Roman Empire. Under the dynasty of the Berber Hafsids (1207–1574) it became powerful. It became a French protectorate in 1883, gaining its independence in 1956. Habib Bourguiba was elected president in 1957; he was replaced in a bloodless coup by Zine al-Abidine Ben Ali in 1987. Elections in 1989 and 1994 were won by President Ben Ali and his supporters. Recent years have seen concerns about Tunisia's human-rights record. Official language: Arabic. Currency: Tunisian dinar of 1000 millimes. Area: 164 150 sq km (63 362 sq mi). Population (2003 est): 9 888 000. Capital: Tunis.

tunnel effect The passage of an electron or other particle through a potential barrier when, according to classical mechanics, it has insufficient energy to do so. It is explained by *wave mechanics on the basis that the electron is not completely localized in space, part of the energy of the associated wave being able to tunnel through the barrier. The effect has a negligible probability in large-scale systems, but a finite probability in microscopic systems. It is made use of in the **tunnel diode**, a semiconductor device that has a negative resistance over part of its operating range.

Tupi A group of South American Indian peoples and languages including the *Guarani. They are mainly a tropical rainforest people; they also fish in the rivers and off the coast where their villages are located. Cannibalism was common. Culture varied considerably from one region to another. Religion emphasized nature spirits.

Tupolev, Andrei Nikolaievich (1888–1972) Soviet designer of the first supersonic passenger aircraft, the TU-144, tested in 1969. He also designed supersonic bombers, such as the TU-22, and swing-wing bombers. His TU-104, first produced in 1955, was one of the first passenger jet aircraft.

turaco (*or* **touraco**) A brightly coloured arboreal bird belonging to a family (*Musophagidae*; 18 species) occurring in Africa. Turacos have short rounded wings, a short downcurved bill, and are often crested. Most species have a greenish plumage. Order: *Cuculiformes* (cuckoos and turacos).

turbine A device in which a moving fluid drives a wheel or motor, converting the kinetic energy of the fluid into mechanical energy. In its simplest form it is known as a **water wheel**, which has been in use since ancient times to drive mills, pumps, etc. The principle of the water wheel forms the basis of the hydraulic turbine, used in the generation of hydroelectricity. The Pelton wheel (patented in 1889 by L.A. Pelton) consisting of a ring of buckets or bucket-shaped vanes arranged around the periphery of a wheel, is known as an impulse turbine as it is only the impulse of the water that makes the wheel turn. The Francis turbine (designed in 1849 by J. B. Francis), with its outer ring of stationary guide vanes and inner ring of curved vanes on the surface of one side of the wheel, is a reaction turbine; part of the energy is derived from the impulse of the water and part from the reaction between the water and the blades.

The steam-driven turbine was invented in the 1st century AD by the Greek engineer and mathematician Hero of Alexandria. However, the first practical turbine to be driven by steam was a reaction device with several rows of turbine wheels (enabling the energy of the expanding steam to be utilized in stages) invented in 1884 by the British engineer, Sir Charles Parsons (1854–1931). An impulse turbine using several steam nozzles was invented by Carl de Laval (1845–1913) in the 1890s. Since the beginning of the 20th century steam turbines based on these designs have replaced the *steam engine as the prime mover in *power stations. See illustration on p. 904. *See also* GAS TURBINE.

turbot A *flatfish, *Scophthalmus maximus*, that occurs off European shores. It has a broad circular body, up to 1 m long, which is usually light- or grey-brown on the upper (left) side and whitish underneath. It is a valuable food fish. Family: *Bothidae*.

Turgenev, Ivan (1818–83) Russian novelist. His *Sportsman's Sketches* (1852) was followed by such works as the novel *Fathers and Sons* (1862) and the long story *The Torrents of Spring* (1872). He also wrote poetry and plays, notably *A Month in the Country* (published 1870). A lifelong admirer of Western society, he went into self-imposed exile in Baden Baden (1862–70) and Paris (1871–83).

Turin (Italian name: Torino) 45 04N 7 40E A city in NW Italy, the capital of Piedmont on the River Po. Dating from Roman times, it was the first capital (1861–65) of united Italy. Notable buildings include a 15th-century cathedral and a 17th-century palace. Turin's industries include engineering, publishing, and the manufacture of motor vehicles, textiles, paper, chocolate, wine, and leather goods. Population (2000 est): 903 703.

Turkana, Lake (name until 1979: Lake Rudolph) A lake in Kenya and Ethiopia. Since it has no outlet, it has become increasingly saline through evaporation. Significant fossil finds have been made here by Richard Leakey. Area: about 6405 sq km (2473 sq mi).

turkey A large terrestrial bird belonging to a family (*Meleagrididae*; 2 species) native to North and Central American woodlands. Wild turkeys have green-bronze plumage, a warty red neck, and a long fleshy bill ornament and throat wattle. The common turkey (*Meleagra gallopavo*) was brought to Europe in the 16th century and is now farmed for its flesh. Order: *Galliformes* (pheasants, turkeys, etc.).

Turkey, Republic of A country in the Middle East. The large Asian area, Anatolia, lies between the Mediterranean Sea and the Black Sea. The small European area, Thrace, is bordered by Greece and Bulgaria. Anatolia consists of a semiarid plateau surrounded by mountains. The coastal areas are the most populous. 98% of the population is Muslim. *Economy*: mainly agricultural. Wheat, barley, sugar beet, potatoes, and rice are grown in the interior, and cotton, tobacco, and citrus fruit are grown for export around the coast. Cattle, sheep, and goats are kept. Copper, chromium, borax, coal, bauxite, and oil are produced. The main industries are steel, cement, textiles, and fertilizers. Turkey is an associate member of the EU. *History*: Anatolia, formerly known as *Asia Minor, was dominated by the Seljuqs (1055–1243) and later became the core of the *Ottoman Empire (c. 1300–1922). Under Kemal *Atatürk, who ruled as a virtual dictator, the new Republic of Turkey (declared 1923) was rapidly westernized. After the death of Kemal (1938) and World War II, Turkey became less stable politically. The Democratic Party came to power in 1950 but grew increasingly reactionary; unrest increased until a military coup took place in 1960. The army again intervened in 1971, when martial law was imposed (until 1973). Rivalry with Greece over Cyprus almost resulted in war in 1974, when the island was invaded by Turkish troops. In 1980 a military coup overthrew the government of Suleiman Demirel (1924–). A state of emergency was imposed until 1991, when Demirel returned as prime minister, subsequently becoming president (1993–2000). The later 1990s saw a growing challenge to Turkey's secular constitution from Muslim fundamentalists. In 1987 Turkey applied to join the EC (now the EU), but this application has been frozen until Turkey improves its poor human-rights record. There has been fighting between Kurdish separatist guerrillas and government troops since 1984. In August 1999 the NW was hit by Turkey's worst post-war earthquake, in which over 17 000 died. Official language: Turkish. Currency: Turkish lira of 100 kurus. Area: 779 452 sq km (330 883 sq mi). Population (2003 est): 70 597 000. Capital: Ankara.

Turkic languages A group of languages of the Altaic language family, related to Mongo-

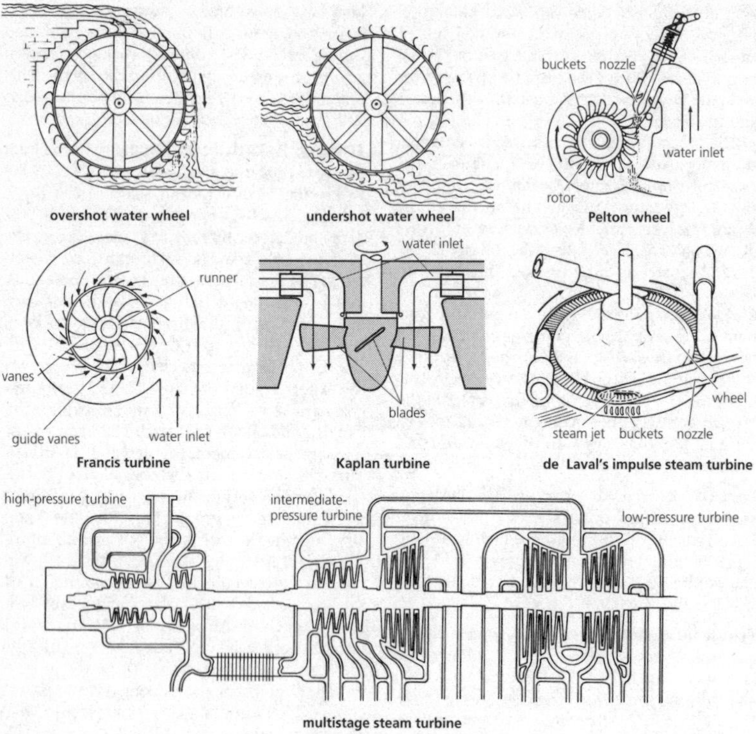

turbine

lian and Manchu-Tungus. Spoken by more than 66 million people, the languages are spread over a geographical area extending from Turkey to Siberia. Originally written in the Arabic script in the 9th century, the languages are now written in the *Cyrillic alphabet in the republics of the former Soviet Union and in Latin script in Turkey.

Turkish A Turkic language, spoken mainly in Turkey. Since 1929 it has been written in a modified Latin alphabet, replacing Arabic script. Its grammatical system is based on the use of suffixes.

Turkistan (*or* **Turkestan**) A region of central Asia, now comprising the Xinjiang Uygur AR of the People's Republic of China and Kazakhstan, Turkmenistan, Tadzhikistan, Kirgizstan, and Uzbekistan. W Turkistan was ruled by the Persians from the 6th century BC, Islam from the 7th century AD, and the Russians from the 18th century. The E was long disputed between Chinese dynasties and nomadic tribes.

Turkmen (*or* **Turkoman**) A people of SW Asia speaking a language that is part of the Turkic language group (it is the official language of Turkmenistan). Most are settled farmers in Turkmenistan, but groups in Iran, Afghanistan, E Turkey, N Syria, and N Iraq retain their traditional nomadic life. They are Sunni Muslims.

Turkmenistan, Republic of A republic in central Asia. Some 90% comprises desert, including the Kara Kum or semidesert; 66% of the population are Turkmen. *Economy*: the country is only economically viable owing to its large deposits of oil and natural gas. The principal occupation is agriculture (cotton, wool, and karakul pelts). There is some heavy industry. *History*: Turkmenistan was gradually taken over by Russia during the 19th century. The Turkmen SSR was established in 1924 and became independent as Turkmenistan in 1991. Power has remained in the hands of the former Communist Party and President Sapamurad Niyazov, whose executive powers were extended to the point of virtual dictatorship by the new constitution of 1992. Niyazov was declared president for life in 2002. Official language: Turkmen. Currency: manat of 100 tenesi. Area: 488 100 sq km (186 400 sq mi). Population (2003 est): 4 867 000. Capital: Ashkhabad.

Turks and Caicos Islands A UK overseas territory consisting of a series of over 30 islands in the Atlantic Ocean, to the SE of the Bahamas. The most important are Grand Turk, Grand Caicos, and Salt Cay. Most of the inhabitants are of African descent. *Economy*: mainly based on fishing and offshore finance; exports include conchs, conch shells, crawfish, salt, and fishmeal. Tourism is an important source of revenue. *History*: the islands were discovered by the Spanish in 1512 but remained uninhabited until 1678. A dependency of Jamaica (1874–1959), they became a British crown colony in 1962 and gained internal self-government in 1976. Official language: English. Currency: US dollar of 100 cents. Area: 430 sq km (192 sq mi). Population (1999 est): 23 000. Capital: Grand Turk.

turmeric A perennial herbaceous plant, *Curcuma longa*, native to S India and Indonesia and cultivated for its underground rhizomes. It has narrow leaves and yellow flowers. The rhizomes are boiled and dried in the sun for 5–7 days, then polished and usually sold in ground form. Turmeric is used as a spice in curries, etc., and as a yellow dye. Family: *Zingiberaceae*.

Turner, Joseph Mallord William (1775–1851) British landscape and marine painter. After painting many watercolours, he achieved success in the late 1790s with his landscapes in oil. In 1802 he made the first of several continental tours, which provided him with such scenic subjects as the Alps, Venice, and Rome. In the 1810s his style evolved into a romantic vision of colour, light, and weather; such late paintings as *Rain, Steam, and Speed* (National Gallery, London) and *Interior at Petworth* (Tate Gallery) anticipate French *impressionism.

turnip A biennial plant, *Brassica rapa*, probably native to Asia and widely cultivated for its thick fleshy root, which is used as a vegetable. An erect branching stem grows out of the basal leaf rosette and produces bright-yellow flowers. Family: *Cruciferae*.

turnstone A small *plover, *Arenaria interpres*, that breeds around Arctic coasts and migrates to the S hemisphere to winter. It has a black-and-brown upper plumage, becoming tortoiseshell in summer, and white underparts. Turnstones have short black bills used to turn over pebbles and shells in search of molluscs, small fish, and sandhoppers.

turpentine An oily liquid extracted from pine resin. Its main constituent is pinene ($C_{10}H_{16}$); it is used as a solvent for paints.

Turpin, Dick (1706–39) British highwayman. He was hanged at York for murder and horse stealing. The story of his ride from London to York on his horse Black Bess, popularized in Harrison Ainsworth's novel *Rookwood* (1834), is probably based on a much older legend.

turquoise An opaque greenish-blue mineral used as a gem. It consists of a basic aluminium phosphate, traces of copper providing the colour. Birthstone for December.

turtle An aquatic reptile belonging to the order *Chelonia*, which includes *tortoises and *terrapins. 10–200 cm long, turtles have broad paddle-like flippers and a streamlined shell and occur in most seas. Their diet consists of worms, snails, crustaceans, and fish. Some turtles live in fresh water. *See also* GREEN TURTLE; LEATHERBACK TURTLE.

turtle dove A small dove, *Streptopelia turtur*, occurring in S Europe and N Africa, visiting N Europe in the summer. It has a chequered red-brown back, grey wings, a pink breast, a black-and-white striped neck patch, and a long white-tipped tail. Family: *Columbidae* (pigeons).

Tuscany (Italian name: Toscana) A region in N central Italy, consisting mainly of hills and mountains with coastal lowlands in the W. It is predominantly agricultural, producing cereals, wines (Chianti), olives, and fruit. Tourists are attracted by the scenery and the cultural centres of Florence, Siena, and Pisa. The major industries are iron and steel and mining and quarrying. Area: 22 989 sq km (8876 sq mi). Population (2000 est): 3 536 392. Capital: Florence.

Tussaud, Marie (Marie Grosholtz; 1761–1850) French wax modeller, who went to London in 1802, where she founded (1835) the waxworks museum known as Madame Tussaud's.

tussock moth A moth of the family *Lymantriidae*, occurring in both the Old and New Worlds and including the vapourers, tussocks, and *gypsy moths. The caterpillars, cocoons, and adults are typically hairy, frequently causing skin irritation and swelling if handled.

Tutankhamen King of Egypt (c. 1361–1352 BC) of the 18th dynasty. Tutankhamen became king at the age of 11. He abandoned Akhenaton's worship of the sun-god Aton, reinstating that of Amon and transferring the capital once more to Thebes. His splendid tomb was discovered by Howard Carter (1874–1939) in 1922.

Tutu, Desmond (1931–) South African clergyman, noted for his opposition to *apartheid. Ordained in 1960, he became the first Black general secretary of the South African Council of Churches (1979), Anglican Bishop of Johannesburg (1984), and Archbishop of Cape Town (1986). In 1996 he retired and was appointed head of the Truth and Reconciliation Commission set up to investigate crimes of apartheid, which presented its report in 1998. He won the Nobel Peace Prize in 1984.

Tuvalu, State of (name until 1976: Ellice Islands) A small country in the SW Pacific Ocean. It consists of a group of nine islands, the main one being Funafuti. Most of the population is Polynesian. *Economy*: coconut growing and fishing are the chief occupations. The only export is copra. Since 1993 the main source of revenue has been a deal whereby Tuvalu allows its national Internet suffix (.tv) to be used by a US television company. *History*: formerly part of the Gilbert and Ellice Islands colony, it became a separate colony in 1974, gaining independence in 1978. It is a member of the Commonwealth. As most of the islands rise less than 3m (11.5 ft) above sea level, their future is threatened by rising sea levels. Official language: Tuvalu. Currency: Australian dollar of 100 cents. Area: 24 sq km (9.5 sq mi). Population (2003 est): 10 200. Capital: Fongafale.

Twain, Mark (Samuel Langhorne Clemens; 1835–1910) US novelist. He worked as a steamboat pilot on the Mississippi before gaining a national reputation for humorous journalism. He wrote several works based on his early life, notably *Life on the Mississippi* (1883) and his masterpiece *The Adventures of Huckleberry Finn* (1884).

Tweed, River A river in SE Scotland and NE England. Flowing E from the Tweedsmuir Hills to the North Sea at Berwick, it forms part of the border between England and Scotland. Length: 156 km (97 mi).

twelve-tone music *See* SERIALISM.

twins Two individuals born from the same pregnancy. Identical twins are produced when a fertilized egg splits in two and develops as two fetuses of the same sex. More commonly, nonidentical (or fraternal) twins are produced when two eggs are fertilized at the same time; they may be of different sexes. *See also* SIAMESE TWINS.

Tyburn A stream in SE England, in London. It now flows underground from Hampstead to the River Thames. The London gallows, known as the Tyburn Tree (1571–1759), stood at the W end of Oxford Street.

Tyler, Wat (d. 1381) English rebel, who led the *Peasants' Revolt (1381). He was murdered during negotiations with Richard II at Smithfield.

Tyne, River A river in N England. Flowing E from the SW Cheviot Hills to the North Sea at Tynemouth, it passes through Newcastle, Gateshead, and Jarrow. Length: 48 km (30 mi).

Tyne and Wear A metropolitan county of NE England, created in 1974 from SE Northumberland and NE Durham. In 1986 the county council was abolished and administrative powers passed to the unitary authorities of Newcastle upon Tyne, North Tyneside, Gateshead, South Tyneside, and Sunderland. Industries grew up along the River Tyne owing to the large coalfields; in the 19th century the development of the shipyards was especially important. During the Depression of the 1930s and the recessions of the 1980s and early 1990s it suffered severely owing to its dependence on heavy industry. The last 15 years has seen considerable diversification of industry. Area: 540 sq km (208 sq mi).

typewriter A hand-operated machine for producing printed symbols. The first machine was invented in the USA in 1867 but the commercial success of the typewriter began in 1874 with the machines produced by Remington and Sons. This design, with the paper held in a moving platen, remained the basis of the typewriter until the advent of electric golf-ball machines, with a stationary platen, in the early 1960s. Typewriters have now been superseded by computer-controlled *word processors.

typhoid fever An infectious disease of the digestive tract caused by the bacterium *Salmonella typhi*. This disease (and paratyphoid fever) are usually contracted by drinking infected water. The symptoms include fever, headache, cough, loss of appetite, and constipation; a characteristic red rash may appear. If untreated, the patient may develop bowel haemorrhage or perforations.

typhoon A tropical cyclone or *hurricane with winds above force 12 on the *Beaufort scale occurring in the China Sea and the W Pacific Ocean. The name is derived from a Chinese word meaning great wind.

typhus An infection caused by certain parasitic bacteria (*see* RICKETTSIA), which are transmitted to humans by lice, fleas, mites, or ticks. The many different forms of typhus share the symptoms of fever, headache, pains in muscles and joints, delirium, and a rash. Treatment is with tetracycline antibiotics or chloramphenicol.

Tyr (Old English name: Tiw) In Teutonic mythology, the god of war; with *Odin and *Thor, he is one of the three main Germanic gods. His name is linguistically related to *Zeus* and survives in *Tuesday*.

Tyrannosaurus A huge bipedal dinosaur that lived in North America during the late Cretaceous period (about 100–65 million years ago). This animal was 15 m long, stood 6.5 m tall, and weighed up to 10 tonnes. It had a massive body with a short thick neck supporting a large head, large muscular hind limbs with clawed feet, and tiny fore legs. It was a carnivore with long dagger-like teeth. Order: *Saurischia*.

tyrant flycatcher A passerine bird belonging to the New World family *Tyrannidae* (365 species), ranging from 9–27 cm in length and generally grey, brown, or olive-coloured with paler underparts. They are typically arboreal and dart out from a perch to seize flying insects. Tyrant flycatchers will attack large birds that enter their breeding territories. *Compare* FLYCATCHER.

Tyre (modern name: Sur) 33 12N 35 11E A port in SW Lebanon, on the Mediterranean Sea. It was important to the Phoenicians for several centuries and was taken by Alexander the Great in 322 BC and by the Romans in 68 BC. The city was long held by the Crusaders but fell to Muslim forces in 1291. Population (1991 est): 70 000.

Tyrol *See* TIROL.

Tyson, Mike (1966–) US boxer. He won the World Boxing Championship title and the World Boxing Association's title in 1986, subsequently adding the International Boxing Federation title (1988). In 1992 he was gaoled for rape. After his release (1995) he regained both the WBC and WBA titles. In a fight with Evander Holyfield (1997) he was banned from the ring (until 1998) for biting off part of his opponent's ear.

t

U

Uccello, Paolo (P. di Dono; 1397–1475) Florentine painter. His frescoes for Sta Maria Novella, Florence, include the famous *Flood*, which shows his preoccupation with perspective. In the three paintings of the Battle of San Romano, he combines a geometric structure with aspects of the international gothic style.

Ufa 54 45N 55 58E A city in W central Russia. Situated in the Ural Mountains, it has oil refineries. Population (1999 est): 1 088 900.

Uffizi An art gallery in Florence, containing the art treasures of the Medici. Built by *Vasari, the Uffizi was opened as a museum in 1765. The major part of its collection comprises Italian Renaissance paintings.

Uganda, Republic of A landlocked country in East Africa. It consists chiefly of a high plateau rising to mountains; a large part of the total area is occupied by lakes, notably Lake Victoria. The majority of the population is African, especially *Ganda. *Economy*: chiefly agricultural. Food crops include plantains and maize; cash crops include coffee, cocoa, vanilla, and tea. Livestock is also important, as is freshwater fishing. The chief mineral resource is copper. *History*: the area was dominated by the kingdom of *Buganda before it became a British protectorate in 1894. It became an independent state within the Commonwealth in 1962; the following year a republic was established with *Obote as prime minister. In 1971 a military coup brought Gen Idi *Amin to power. His repressive regime was overthrown in 1979, by Ugandan exiles aided by Tanzanian troops. In 1986, after a further series of coups, Yoweri Museveni came to power. A referendum in 2000 resulted in a large vote against returning to multiparty politics; however, this poll was boycotted by most opposition supporters. In 2001 Museveni won presidential elections. Ugandan troops have been involved in the conflict in the Democratic Republic of Congo since 1998. Official language: English. Currency: Ugandan shilling of 100 cents. Area: 236 860 sq km (91 343 sq mi). Population (2003 est): 25 437 000. Capital: Kampala.

ugli A hybrid cross between a *grapefruit and a *tangerine. The fruit has brownish-yellow warty skin and orange flesh. It is grown in the West Indies.

Uist Two islands in NW Scotland, in the Outer Hebrides. North Uist is separated from South Uist by the island of Benbecula.

Ujjain 23 11N 75 50E A city in India, in Madhya Pradesh. One of the seven sacred Hindu cities, it is the scene of the 12-yearly bathing festival (Kumbh Mela). Population (1991): 366 787.

Ujung Pandang (**Makassar** *or* **Macassar**) 5 09S 119 08E A port in central Indonesia, in SW Sulawesi. Its exports include coffee, copra, and vegetable oils. Population (1995 est): 1 091 800.

UKAEA *See* ATOMIC ENERGY AUTHORITY.

Ukraine A republic in SE Europe. Very fertile and wooded, it was the economically most important Soviet republic after Russia. Some 96% of the population are Slavs, mostly Ukrainians. *Economy*: Major coalfields and iron-ore mines support a large ferrous metallurgical industry. The machine-building, chemical, consumer-goods, and food industries are also important. Crops include wheat, sugar beet, cotton, and tobacco. The economy came close to collapse in the years after independence but has since improved, owing partly to a treaty of economic cooperation with Russia (1998). *History*: it was dominated by the Khazars from the 7th to the 9th centuries and then by the Rurik princes of Kiev. In the 13th century the Golden Horde overran the region, which subsequently came under the rule of Lithuania and, in the 16th century, Poland. Polish domination was followed by Russian rule. After a national and cultural revival in the late 19th century the Ukraine declared independence in 1918 but became a constituent republic of the Soviet

Union in 1922. It achieved independence on the break-up of the Soviet Union in 1991. The largely Russian region of Crimea declared itself independent in 1992; Crimeans were subsequently given dual citizenship. Until 1994, Post-independence governments were dominated by the authoritarian president, Leonid Kravchuk; he was succeeded by the reformist Leonid Kuchma. A new constitution consolidating democracy was adopted in 1996 but the legislature remained dominated by communists, leading to persistent conflict with the presidency. From 2001 Kuchma faced demands for his resignation following allegations that he had ordered the murder of a hostile journalist. Official languages: Ukrainian and Russian. Currency: hyrvna of 100 kopiykas. Area: 603 700 sq km (231 990 sq mi). Population (2003 est): 47 856 000. Capital: Kiev.

Ulan Bator (*or* **Ulaanbaatar**; former name: Urga) 47 54N 106 52E The capital of the Republic of Mongolia, situated on a plateau in the N of the country. Built around a monastery, in the 17th century it developed as a centre of trade between China and Japan. It became the capital when Outer Mongolia declared its independence in 1911. Population (2000 est): 691 000.

Ulbricht, Walter (1893–1973) East German statesman. Ulbricht was the leading architect of the German Democratic Republic after World War II. He was general secretary of the Socialist Unity Party from 1950 and in 1960 became chairman of the newly established council of state. In 1961 he erected the Berlin Wall.

ulcer An inflamed eroded area of skin or mucous membrane. There are many forms of ulcer, one of the most prevalent being *peptic ulcers, which affect the stomach and duodenum. Ulcers may also occur in the colon (*see* COLITIS). Varicose ulcers may develop in the skin of patients with chronic *varicose veins.

Ulm, Battle of (25 September–20 October 1805) A battle in which Napoleon with 210 000 men defeated 72 000 Austrians in Bavaria.

Ulster A province and former kingdom of N Ireland. The land passed to the English Crown in 1461. It was partitioned in 1921, six counties forming Northern Ireland and the counties of Cavan, Donegal, and Monaghan forming the province of Ulster, part of the Republic of Ireland. Area (province in Irish Republic): 8013 sq km (3094 sq mi). Population (province in Irish Republic; 2002): 246 571.

Ulster Democratic Unionist Party (**DUP**) A British politicial party, active in Northern Ireland. Founded in 1969, it strongly opposes any weakening of the province's links with the UK and is hostile to the Good Friday Agreement of 1998. It became the largest unionist party following the 2003 elections to the Northern Ireland Assembly. Its leader is Ian *Paisley.

Ulster Unionist Party (**UUP**) A British political party, active in Northern Ireland. Its leader, David *Trimble, was a chief architect of the Good Friday Agreement of 1998. It was the largest unionist party until 2003, when it was overtaken at the polls by the Ulster Democratic Unionist Party.

ultramicroscope A type of microscope, invented by Richard Zsigmondy (1865–1929) in 1902, used to study colloidal particles in a liquid medium. A beam of light illuminates the particles from the side, the scattered light enabling the movements of the particles to be observed as flashes against a dark background (dark-field illumination).

ultrasonics The study of *sound waves the frequencies of which are too high to be audible to the normal human ear, i.e. above about 20 000 hertz. Ultrasound waves may be produced by *magnetostriction or by applying a rapidly alternating voltage across a piezoelectric crystal. Ultrasound is used in medical diagnosis in place of X-rays.

ultraviolet radiation Electromagnetic radiation with frequencies between the violet end of the visible spectrum and *X-rays, i.e. between about 380 and 5 nanometres. Ultraviolet radiation is produced during arc discharges and by gas-discharge tubes. It is also produced in large quantities by the sun, although the radiation below 200 nm is absorbed by the *ozone layer of the atmosphere.

Ulysses *See* ODYSSEUS.

Umayyads (*or* **Omayyads**) The first dynasty of caliphs, which ruled Islam from 661 to 750 AD. The dynasty reached its peak with 'Abd al-Malik (reigned 685–705). They were overthrown by a rebellion of discontented Arabs and pious Muslims. In Muslim Spain, an Umayyad, 'Abd ar-Rahman, seized power in 756 and established a dynasty that ruled until 1030.

Umbelliferae (*or* **Apiaceae**) A widely distributed family of plants (2850 species), most abundant in N temperate regions. Most species are herbaceous, with much divided leaves and umbrella-shaped heads of tiny flowers. The family includes vegetables, such as the carrot, celery, and parsnip, and many culinary herbs and spices.

Umberto I (1844–1900) King of Italy (1878–1900). He commanded with distinction in the war against the Austrians (1866). As king he led Italy into the *Triple Alliance (1882) and encouraged Italian colonialism in Africa. Two unsuccessful attempts on Umberto's life were followed by his assassination at Monza.

Umberto II (1904–83) The last King of Italy (1946), following the abdication of his father Victor Emmanuel III. He too was forced to abdicate after a referendum approved the establishment of republican government.

umbilical cord The structure, about 50 cm long, that connects a fetus to the *placenta in the womb. It contains three blood vessels (two arteries and one vein) that convey blood to and from the placenta. At birth the umbilical cord is tied off and cut.

Un-American Activities Committee US House of Representatives committee established in 1935 to investigate subversive organizations in the USA. Spurred on by Senator *McCarthy, it blacklisted several Hollywood writers and directors and investigated government officials. Its influence declined after 1954 and it was abolished in 1975.

UNESCO *See* UNITED NATIONS EDUCATIONAL, SCIENTIFIC AND CULTURAL ORGANIZATION.

uniat churches Various churches of Eastern Orthodox Christianity that are in full communion with the Roman Catholic Church. They retain their own traditional liturgies and canon law.

UNICEF *See* UNITED NATIONS INTERNATIONAL CHILDREN'S EMERGENCY FUND.

Unification Church A religious sect founded in South Korea in 1954 by a millionaire Korean businessman, Sun Myung Moon (1920–). Absolute obedience is demanded of members ('Moonies'), who spend most of their waking hours earning money for the organization. Moon was imprisoned for tax evasion in 1984–85.

unified field theory A theory that encompasses the four fundamental interactions—strong, weak, electromagnetic, and gravitational—in terms of a single field, analogous to the electromagnetic or gravitational fields. Einstein failed to unify gravitation and electromagnetism, although a measure of unification has been achieved between the weak and electromagnetic fields.

Uniformity, Acts of A series of Acts (1549, 1552, 1559, 1562) that enforced the use of the Book of *Common Prayer in England during the *Reformation.

Union, Acts of **1.** The Acts (1536–43) uniting England and Wales. They imposed English law and administration on Wales, made English the language of officialdom, and provided for Welsh representation in parliament. **2.** The Act (1707) uniting England and Scotland to form Great Britain. Scotland retained its legal system and Presbyterian Church and was to be represented in parliament by 16 peers and 45 MPs. **3.** The Act (1800) that united Great Britain and Ireland to form (1801) the United Kingdom. It provided for Irish representation in parliament (4 spiritual peers, 28 life peers, 100 MPs).

Union of Soviet Socialist Republics *See* SOVIET UNION.

Unitarians A group of Christians who reject the doctrine of the Trinity and the divinity of Christ, believing instead in the single personality of God. Modern Unitarian thought dates from the Reformation, but congregations were first formed in Britain and the USA in the 18th century.

United Arab Emirates (**UAE**; former name: Trucial States) A federation of seven sheikdoms in the Middle East, in *Arabia, comprising Abu Dhabi, Ajman, Dubai, Fujairah, Ras al-Khaimah, Sharjah, and Umm al-Qaiwain. The population is mainly Arab and Sunnite Muslim. The terrain is flat sandy desert. *Economy*: the oil of Abu Dhabi and Dubai is the chief product and export. Fishing and pearls are still important, as are financial services. Tourism is expanding. *History*: the sheikdoms signed several common treaties with Britain from 1820; that of 1892 made them protectorates—the Trucial States. The federation was formed in 1971 (Ras al-Khaimah joined in 1972) and is a member of OPEC. The UAE is governed by a supreme council consisting of the seven ruling sheikhs; there is also an appointed federal council. Official language: Arabic. Currency: dirham of 100 fils. Area: 83 650 sq km (32 290 sq mi). Population (2003 est): 3 818 000. Capital: Abu Dhabi.

United Kingdom (**UK**) A country in N Europe, consisting of *England, *Scotland, *Wales, and Northern Ireland (*see* IRELAND). The UK does not include the Channel Isles and the Isle of Man, which are direct dependencies of the Crown. *History*: The United Kingdom of Great Britain and Ireland was formed in 1801 (*see* UNION, ACTS OF), since when the histories of the member countries have been inextricably linked (for history prior to 1801, *see* ENGLAND; SCOTLAND; WALES). With the Industrial Revolution the UK evolved from an agricultural to an industrial economy; during the long reign of Victoria there was agitation for an extension of the franchise (*see* REFORM ACTS) and a shift in political influence from the landowners to the urban middle class. The growing power of the Trade Unions led to the formation in 1900 of the *Labour Party. The 19th century also saw the heyday of the British *Empire and the beginning of colonial rivalry with Germany, which was a significant factor in the outbreak of *World War I. In 1922, following the creation of the Irish Free State, the UK was retitled the United Kingdom of Great Britain and Northern Ireland. The interwar years were dominated by the Depression and the growing threat of fascism, which culminated in *World War II. 1945 saw the return of a Labour government, which established a Welfare State and began a programme of nationalization. The Conservatives returned to power (1951–64) before the return of Labour (1964–70; 1974–79). From 1979 to 1997 the Conservatives presided over extensive privatization and a recession followed by economic recovery. Labour returned with a landslide victory (1997) and Tony Blair became prime minister. Devolution for Scotland and Wales was put into effect in 1999. Hopes for a solution to the long-running problem of Northern Ireland were raised by the Good Friday Agreement (1998). The general election of 2001 was won by Labour. Official languages: English, Welsh, and Gaelic languages. Currency: pound sterling of 100 pence. Area: 244 014 sq km (94 214 sq mi). Population (2003 est): 59 164 000. Capital: London.

United Kingdom Overseas Territories (former names: British Dependent Territories *or* Crown dependencies) Overseas territories for which constitutional responsibility rests with the UK Foreign and Commonwealth Office. There are currently 13 such territories: Anguilla, Bermuda, British Antarctic Territory, British Indian Ocean Territory, British Virgin Islands, Cayman Islands, Falkland Islands, Gibraltar, Montserrat, Pitcairn Islands, St Helena and Dependencies, South Georgia and South Sandwich Islands, and Turks and Caicos Islands. Full British citizenship (revoked in most cases during the 1980s) was restored to their inhabitants in 2002.

United Nations (UN) An organization established to maintain international peace and to foster international cooperation in the resolution of economic, social, cultural, and humanitarian problems. The UN was founded on 24 October 1945 (United Nations Day). There were 51 founder members; most countries are now members of the UN, the chief exception being *Taiwan, which lost its seat to China in 1971. Monaco joined in 1993 and Switzerland in 2002. The headquarters of the UN are in New York. The organization's main deliberative organ is the **General Assembly**. Each member state has one equal vote in the Assembly, which cannot impose its will upon members. The **Security Council** bears the chief responsibility for maintaining international peace. Its permanent members are China, France, Russia (until 1991 the Soviet Union), the UK, and the USA; a further ten members are elected by the General Assembly for two-year terms. Decisions, except on procedure, must be agreed by nine members, including all the permanent members (the so-called veto privilege). In the event of a breach of international peace the Council may commit military forces to re-establish peace. The **Economic and Social Council** (ECOSOC) coordinates the economic and social work of the UN. The principal judicial organ of the UN is the *International Court of Justice. The **Secretariat**, headed by the secretary general (currently Kofi Annan), is responsible for administration.

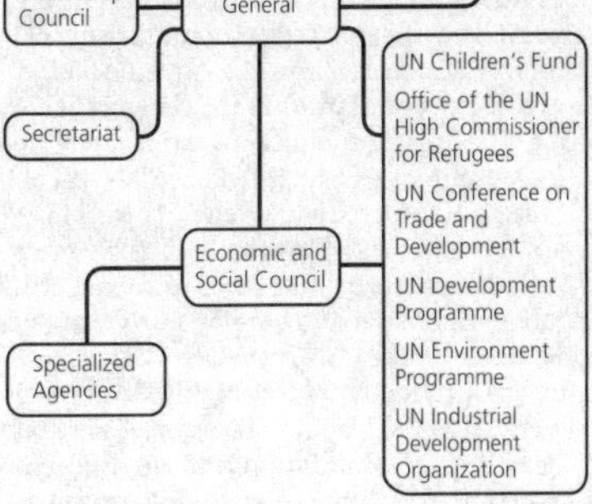

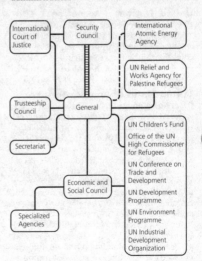

United Nations. The structure of the organization.

Other UN bodies are the **United Nations Development Programme** (UNDP), which fosters the economic growth of the *developing countries; the **United Nations Conference on Trade and Development** (UNCTAD), which encourages international trade; the **United Nations Industrial Development Organization** (UNIDO), which promotes industrial development; and the **United Nations Environment Programme** (UNEP), which is concerned with the protection of the environment. Other specialized agencies include the *Food and Agriculture Organization, *International Labour Organisation, *International Monetary Fund, *United Nations Educational, Scientific and Cultural Organization, *International Bank for Reconstruction and Development, and the *World Health Organization.

United Nations Educational, Scientific and Cultural Organization (UNESCO) A specialized agency of the *United Nations established in 1945 to promote international cooperation in education, science, and culture. Its headquarters are in Paris. Objecting to inefficiency and political bias, the USA withdrew in 1984 and the UK in 1985–97.

United Nations High Commissioner for Refugees, Office of the (UNHCR) A *United Nations body established in 1950 to provide international protection for refugees. Its headquarters are in Geneva. It won the Nobel Peace Prize in 1981.

United Nations International Children's Emergency Fund (UNICEF) A *United Nations body established in 1946. It is chiefly concerned with providing health care, education, and improved nutrition to *developing countries. Its headquarters are in Geneva. It won the Nobel Peace Prize in 1965.

United States of America (USA) A country in North America, the fourth largest in the world. It is a federal republic comprising 50 states, including Alaska, in the extreme NW of the continent, and Hawaii, in the central Pacific Ocean. The Pacific mountain system and the Rocky Mountains extend N–S in the W with an arid area between, while the Appalachian Mountains extend N–S in the E. In the centre lie vast plains. The population is of mixed ethnic stock, the majority being of European descent. *Economy*: the USA is the world's greatest industrial producer, with a highly diversified economy. It is the leading producer of natural gas, lead, copper, aluminium, and sulphur and of electrical and nuclear energy. Farming is highly mechanized and 15% of exports are agricultural products. Cereals, soya beans, cotton, and tobacco are the main crops. Other exports include motor vehicles, aircraft, machinery, computers, electrical components, and chemicals. *History*: the first inhabitants probably came from Asia about 30 000 years ago. Following the voyage of Columbus in 1492, America was settled by Europeans, with the British colonies in the E becoming the most successful. During the 18th century conflict developed between local colonial assemblies and their British governors, particularly over taxation. The colonists' confidence was strengthened by their success in the *French and Indian Wars (1754–63) and the 13 colonies finally won independence in the *American Revolution (1775–83). The USA was rapidly expanding W at this time and through the *Mexican War (1846–48) acquired California; the discovery of gold there (1848) further encouraged settlement in the W. By 1820 conflict was developing between the cotton-growing states of the South (where African slaves had worked since the late 17th century) and the commercial North (where slavery was opposed). This led to the *Civil War (1861–65), which ended in victory for the North and the abolition of slavery. It was followed by a period of rapid industrial and economic expansion, while territorial expansion continued with the purchase of Alaska (1867), the annexation of Hawaii (1898), and the Spanish-American War (1898), in which the USA acquired the Philippines, Puerto Rico, Guam, and a measure of control over Cuba.

Intervention in Colombia led to the construction of the Panama Canal (opened 1914). The status of the USA as a world power was confirmed by its role in World War I, which it entered reluctantly in 1917. The 1920s saw another economic boom, which ended in the *Depression that followed the Crash of 1929. The USA was again reluctant to enter World War II but was forced to do so by the Japanese bombing of Pearl Harbor in Hawaii (December 1941). Postwar fear of Soviet expansion resulted in the Marshall Plan (1947), designed to render Europe less susceptible to communism, in the *Cold War, and in the harassment of supposed communists at home (*see also* MCCARTHY, JOSEPH R(AYMOND); UN-AMERICAN ACTIVITIES COMMITTEE). Fear of the spread of communism led also to intervention in Korea (1950–53), Cuba (1961–62), and Vietnam (1961–75). After 1963 relations with the Soviet Union improved and diplomatic relations were established with China in 1979. Domestic problems of the 1960s and 1970s included difficulties in effecting racial integration and opposition to the *Vietnam War. The *Watergate affair (1972–74) undermined confidence in US institutions and the postwar economic boom was followed by decline in the 1970s. There was considerable tension in US relations with Iran and Libya during the 1980s. Relations with the USSR deteriorated once more after the Soviet invasion of Afghanistan (1979) but subsequently improved with the arrival of the reformist Soviet leader Gorbachov. The collapse of the Soviet Union in 1991 left the USA as the world's only superpower. In 1991 US forces led a military alliance against Iraq in the *Gulf War. The 1990s saw US airstrikes against targets in Iraq (1996, 1998) and Yugoslavia (1999) during the presidency of Bill Clinton; there was also a prolonged economic boom. In 2001 George W. Bush became president following a disputed election that was only resolved by a Supreme Court ruling. Following the terrorist attack of *September 11 Bush declared a *war on terrorism and sent US forces into action in Afghanistan. In 2003 the USA invaded and occupied Iraq, deposing the regime of Saddam Hussein (*see* IRAQ WAR). Official language: English. Currency: US dollar of 100 cents. Area: 9 363 123 sq km (3 614 343 sq mi). Population (2003 est): 291 587 000. Capital: Washington, DC.

unit trust An organization that uses funds raised by selling "units" to the public to buy and sell securities in order to make profits for distribution to unit holders. Securities are held in the names of trustees, usually banks. The small investor has the advantages of a professionally managed widespread portfolio.

Universal Decimal Classification (*or* **Brussels Classification**) A system of library classification developed in 1895 in Brussels. It extends the division of the *Dewey Decimal Classification, on which it is based.

Upanishads About 200 prose and verse metaphysical commentaries on the *Vedas*, dating from around 400 BC. They deal with the nature of *Brahman and the soul and are reputedly divinely inspired.

Updike, John (Hoyer) (1932–) US novelist and short-story writer. In such novels as *Rabbit, Run* (1960) and *Couples* (1968) he explored the moral confusions of contemporary US society. *Rabbit is Rich* (1981) and *Rabbit at Rest* (1990) won Pulitzer Prizes. Later novels include *Bech at Bay* (1998) and *Seek My Face* (2003).

Uppsala 59 55N 17 38E A city in E central Sweden. It has Sweden's oldest university (1477), where *Linnaeus taught. Population (2000 est): 188 478.

Ur An ancient city of *Sumer (S Iraq). Sir Leonard *Woolley's excavations (1922–34) made famous the rich royal burials of about 2500 BC and seemed to provide historical evidence for Noah's flood. The leading city in Sumer when it was sacked by barbarians about 2000 BC, Ur was superseded by *Babylon.

uraemia The accumulation of *urea in the blood due to kidney failure. Kidney failure can occur suddenly due to shock, obstruction of both ureters, injury, or acute kidney disease or it may arise slowly due to *nephritis or other diseases. The kidneys will often recover after *dialysis. In chronic conditions a kidney transplant is preferred.

Ural, River A river in central Russia and W Kazakhstan, rising in the S Ural Mountains, and flowing S to the Caspian Sea. Length: 2534 km (1575 mi).

Uralic languages A major language family comprising two related groups of languages, the Finno-Ugric and the Samoyedic (*see* SAMOYED). The two branches of the Uralic language family have developed into multiple forms covering an extensive area.

Ural Mountains A mountain range in W central Russia. It extends 2000 km (1243 mi) N–S from the Kara Sea to the steppes NE of the Caspian Sea. The highest point is Mount Narodnaya, in the N, at 1894 m (6214 ft).

uranium (U) A radioactive metallic element (*see* NUCLEAR ENERGY). It is a silvery-white metal, almost as hard as steel and very dense (relative density 18.95), and has the highest atomic number of the naturally occurring elements. It was first isolated in 1841 by E. Péligot (1811–90), although it had been identified before this in pitchblende. Natural uranium contains three isotopes: ^{238}U (99.283%), ^{235}U (0.711%), and ^{234}U (0.006%). ^{238}U has a half-life of 4.51×10^9 years and is useful in dating rocks, as well as in fuel for fast reactors. ^{235}U is used in *thermal reactors. Some reactors use uranium dioxide (UO_2). Other oxides include U_3O_8 and UO_3. At no 92; at wt 238.0289; mp 1135°C; bp 4134°C.

uranium-lead dating A group of methods of radiometric dating certain rocks, depending on the decay of the radioactive isotope uranium-238 to lead-206 or of uranium-235 to lead-207.

uranium series One of three naturally occurring series of radioactive decays. The uranium series is headed by uranium-238, which undergoes a series of alpha and beta decays ending with the stable isotope lead-206. *See also* ACTINIUM; THORIUM SERIES.

Uranus (astronomy) A giant planet, orbiting the sun every 84 years (between Saturn and Neptune) at a mean distance of 2870 million km. It is somewhat larger (50 800 km in diameter) than Neptune and exhibits a similar greenish featureless disc in a telescope. In its equatorial plane lie at least 21 moons and about 20 rings. Its atmospheric and interior structure are thought to be almost identical to those of Neptune. Uranus was discovered telescopically in 1781 by Sir William Herschel.

Uranus (Greek mythology) The personification of Heaven. He was the son of Gaea (Earth), and his children by her included the *Titans and the *Cyclops. He was castrated by his son Cronus and his genitals were thrown into the sea, which gave birth to *Aphrodite.

Urdu An Indo-Aryan language of N India and Pakistan. Like *Hindi it arose from *Hindustani. It is written in a modified Arabic script.

urea (*or* **carbamide**) A white crystalline compound ($CO(NH_2)_2$) derived from ammonia and carbon dioxide. It is used as a nitrogen fertilizer, a feed supplement for ruminant animals, and in industry. Urea is present in *urine.

urea-formaldehyde resins Synthetic thermosetting resins that are made by the condensation in aqueous solution of urea and formaldehyde with an ammonia catalyst. Cellulose filler is added to produce a moulding powder. This powder is used to make cups, bathroom fittings, etc.

urethane A white crystalline solid, $CO(NH_2)(OC_2H_5)$, made by heating ethanol with urea nitrate. It is used to make *polyurethane foam.

uric acid A compound ($C_5H_4N_4O_3$) formed during the nitrogen metabolism of animals. In man, raised levels of uric acid in the blood are associated with gout.

urine The fluid that is formed by the kidneys and contains the waste products of metabolism and surplus water and salts. In man the kidneys produce 0.9–1.5 l of urine per day.

Urmia, Lake A shallow lake in NW Iran, the largest in the country, lying 1300 m (4265 ft) above sea level. It has no outlet and varies in size. Average area: 5000 sq km (1930 sq mi).

Ursa Major (Latin: Great Bear) A large conspicuous constellation in the N sky. The seven brightest stars form the Plough.

Ursa Minor (Latin: Little Bear) A constellation in the N sky that contains the N celestial pole. The brightest star is *Polaris.

urticaria (*or* **hives**) An acute or chronic allergic disorder in which itching white raised patches surrounded by red areas appear on the skin: they resemble nettle stings (hence the alternative name—nettle rash). Acute urticaria usually arises from allergy to food or drugs and usually disappears quickly if the cause is removed. Chronic urticaria occurs in young people and its cause is not certain.

Uruguay, Oriental Republic of A country in SE South America. Coastal plains rise to higher ground, especially in the N. Most of the population is of Spanish and Italian descent. *Economy*: the traditional livestock industry was badly affected by the 1974 EC ban on meat imports, although new markets have since been found. The cultivation of wheat, barley, and rice has been intensified and the fishing industry has been expanded. The principal industries include food processing, hides and leather, textiles, construction, metallurgy, and rubber. Winemaking is of growing importance. *History*: Charrúa and Chaná Indians inhabited Uruguay before its exploration by the Spanish in the 16th century. Its subsequent history was one of rivalry between Spanish and Portuguese settlements. In 1776 it became part of the Spanish viceroyalty of the Río de la Plata. Under the leadership of José Gervasio Artigas (1764–1850), Uruguay joined Argentina in the struggle for independence from Spain but was subsequently fought over by Argentina and Brazil. In 1828, with British help, Uruguay achieved independence. The late 19th century saw considerable immigration from Europe. In 1973 the army took over, imposing repressive measures that led to international protests. Military rule officially ended in early 1985, when Julio Sanguinetti became president; he lost power in 1989 but was re-elected in 1995. Legislative elections (2000) resulted in victory for the left, while the conservative Jorge Batlle was elected president. The country suffered a severe economic and financial crisis in 2002, leading to a general strike and social unrest. Uruguay is a member of the OAS and LAIA. Official language: Spanish. Currency: Uruguayan peso of 100 centésimos. Area: 186 926 sq km (72 172 sq mi). Population (2003 est): 3 380 000. Capital: Montevideo.

Uruguay, River (Portuguese name: Rio Uruguai; Spanish name: Río Uruguay) A river in South America. Rising in S Brazil, it flows SW forming the Argentina–Brazil and Argentina–Uruguay borders before joining the Rio Paraná. Length: about 1600 km (1000 mi).

Uruk (biblical name: Erech; modern name: Warka) An ancient city in S Mesopotamia. The site testifies to the beginnings of Sumerian civilization in the 4th millennium BC. Supplanted by *Ur (c. 2100), Uruk nevertheless remained inhabited until the early Christian era.

USSR *See* SOVIET UNION.

Ussuri River A river in E Asia, rising in the extreme E of Russia and forming part of the border with China as it flows N to the River Amur. Length: about 800 km (500 mi).

Utah One of the mountain states in the SW USA. The Wasatch Range of the Rocky Mountains divides the state into two arid regions: the Great Basin and the Great Salt Lake Desert in the W and the Colorado Plateau in the E. Livestock raising is the principal agricultural activity. There are significant deposits of copper, oil, natural gas, and uranium. Scenic attractions make it a popular tourist area. *History*: the Mormons began major settlements here in 1847 and continue to dominate the life of the state. Ceded to the USA by Mexico in 1848, Utah was finally admitted to the Union in 1896. Area: 219 931 sq km (84 916 sq mi). Population (2002 est): 2 233 169. Capital: Salt Lake City.

uterus *See* WOMB.

utilitarianism An ethical doctrine holding that the best action is the one that will result in the greatest happiness and least pain for the greatest number of people. Utilitarianism flourished in Britain from the mid-18th century to the mid-19th century. *Hume, *Bentham, and James *Mill (1773–1836) propounded it and John Stuart Mill defended it.

utopianism A programme of total social and political reform with the object of establishing a perfect society. The term derives from the imaginary state depicted in Thomas More's *Utopia* (1516). Utopian experiments have included the New Lanark community established by Robert *Owen. Utopianism advocates a communistic organization of society, but the concomitant authoritarianism reveals that no way has been found of reconciling individual freedom and happiness with social justice.

Utrecht 52 06N 5 07E A city in the central Netherlands. The Union of Utrecht (1579) united the northern provinces of the Netherlands against Spain. The **Treaties of Utrecht** (1713–14), ending the War of the Spanish Succession, were concluded here. Its notable buildings include the gothic cathedral (14th century). Population (1999 est): 232 718.

Utrillo, Maurice (1883–1955) French painter. For almost his entire life, he suffered from alcoholism and drug addiction. He specialized in painting street scenes, notably of Montmartre, which are distinguished by their near-monochrome colours and precise drawing.

Uttar Pradesh A state in N India, consisting mainly of the Upper Ganges plain. India's most populous state, it produces grains, pulses, tea, and timber; there is little industry. Uttar Pradesh was the core of the Mogul Empire and the centre of the Indian Mutiny (1857–59) and the 20th-century independence movement. The NW Himalayan region became the new state of **Uttaranchal** in 2000. Area: 243 350 sq km (93 933 sq mi). Population (2001): 166 052 859. Capital: Lucknow.

Uzbekistan A republic in central Asia, formerly a constituent republic of the Soviet Union. The NW is desert but fertile land is found in the SE. The Uzbeks, Turkic-speaking Sunnite Muslims, make up two-thirds of the population. *Economy*: based on intensive agriculture. Cotton is the chief crop; rice and fruit are also grown. However, the extensive use of chemical pesticides and industrial pollution have caused serious environmental problems, which have affected agricultural production in recent decades. Uzbekistan is rich in oil, coal, and copper, and has more than 20 hydroelectric plants and 3 natural gas pipelines in operation. Industries include mining, chemicals, and metals. *History*: the region was invaded by the Persians under Darius I, the Macedonians under Alexander the Great, and then by the Arabs (8th century AD) and the Mongols (13th century). In the 16th century the Uzbeks dominated the region, which was annexed by Russia in the 19th century. The Uzbek SSR was formed in 1924. Uzbekistan achieved independence on the break-up of the Soviet Union in 1991. The Communist Party has remained in power under the maverick President Islam Karimov. Despite the introduction of a multiparty constitution (1992), political opposition is effectively banned and the country's human-rights record has been severely criticized. There have also been ethnic clashes between Uzbeks and Tadzhiks. In 2001 Uzbekistan provided operational support for the USA's military action in Afghanistan (*see* WAR ON TERRORISM), leading to closer relations with the West. Official language: Uzbek. Currency: som. Area: 449 600 sq km (173 546 sq mi). Population (2003 est): 25 640 000. Capital: Tashkent.

V

V-1 A German World War II unguided missile, also called a flying bomb. Powered by an air-breathing type of ramjet, it carried about 2000 pounds (900 kg) of high explosive. Some 8000 were launched against London between June 1944 and March 1945, killing 5500 civilians.

V-2 A German World War II ballistic missile powered by a rocket engine using alcohol and liquid oxygen as fuel. It carried about 2000 pounds (900 kg) of high explosive and had a preset guidance system. Some 4000 were used against Britain and the Low Countries in 1944 and 1945. It became the basis for both US and Soviet postwar rocket design.

Vaal River A river in South Africa, rising in the SE Transvaal. It flows generally W and SW, to join the Orange River and forms part of the Orange Free State–Transvaal border. Length: 1210 km (750 mi).

vaccination (*or* **inoculation**) The introduction of inactivated or dead disease-causing microorganisms (vaccine) into the body to stimulate the formation of *antibodies to these agents (*see also* IMMUNITY). The first vaccination (against smallpox) was performed by Edward *Jenner in 1798. Vaccines are usually given by injection but some can be administered through skin scratches and some are taken by mouth.

vacuum A region of space that contains no matter. In practice, a perfect vacuum is impossible to obtain. In technical work a soft (*or* low) vacuum goes down to a pressure of 10^{-2} pascal, a hard (*or* high) vacuum is between 10^{-2} and 10^{-7} pascal, and an ultrahigh vacuum is below 10^{-7} pascal. Vacuum technology is used in making cathode-ray tubes, light bulbs, etc., and is used in food preservation.

vacuum flask *See* DEWAR flASK.

Vadodara (former name: Baroda) 22 19N 73 14E. A city in India, in Gujarat. The siting of an oil refinery at nearby Kouali has helped to promote Vadodara's industrial growth and its chief products include petrochemicals, cotton textiles, wood, and tobacco. Population (1991): 1 021 084.

Vaduz 47 08N 9 32E The capital of Liechtenstein. Its castle (restored 1905–16) is the residence of the ruling prince. Population (2000 est): 5043.

vagina The part of the reproductive tract of women and other female mammals into which the *penis is inserted during sexual intercourse. It connects the womb to the exterior and is readily distensible to allow for childbirth.

vagus nerve An important nerve that connects the brain with the throat, larynx, heart, lungs, stomach, and gut. Surgical cutting of a branch of the vagus nerve (**vagotomy**) may be done to treat a peptic ulcer.

Vajpayee, A(tal) B(ihari) (1926–) Indian politician; prime minister (1996, 1998–2004). He became leader of the Hindu nationalist Bharatiya Janata Party (BJP) in 1980. His premiership saw a rise in tensions with Pakistan but subsequent peace talks (2004).

valence (*or* **valency**) The combining power of an atom, ion, or radical. It is equal to the number of hydrogen atoms that the atom, ion, or radical can combine with or replace in forming compounds. Many elements have more than one valence. A **valence electron** is an electron in the outer shell of an atom that participates in forming chemical (valence) bonds. *See also* ENERGY BAND.

Valencia 1. 39 29N 0 24W The third largest city in Spain, on the Guadalaviar estuary. In 1021 it became the capital of the Moorish kingdom of Valencia. El Cid took the city from the Moors in 1094. Its many notable buildings include the cathedral (1262–1482) and a scientific and cultural complex by Santiago Calatrava (1998–2002). Population (1998 est): 739 412. **2.**

10 14N 67 59W The third largest city in Venezuela. It is the focus of the country's chief agricultural area and an industrial centre. Population (2000 est): 1 338 833.

Valentine, St (died c. 269) Roman priest and martyr, known as the patron of lovers. The customs practised on his feast day (14 Feb) have no connection with his life.

Valentinian I (d. 375 AD) Western Roman emperor (364–75). He fought campaigns in the north of the Empire, restoring the Rhine frontier and Hadrian's Wall.

Valentino, Rudolf (Rodolpho Gugliemi di Valentina d'Antonguolla; 1895–1926) US film actor, born in Italy. His performances in *The Sheik* (1921), *Blood and Sand* (1922), *Son of the Sheik* (1926), and other silent romantic dramas established him as a leading cinema idol of the 1920s.

Vale of Glamorgan A county borough of S Wales, created in 1996 from parts of Mid Glamorgan and South Glamorgan. Area: 295 sq km (114 sq mi). Population (2001): 119 293. Administrative centre: Barry.

Valéry, Paul (1871–1945) French poet, essayist, and critic. *Cahiers* (29 vols, 1957–60) is a record of his metaphysical speculations from 1894 until his death. His later poetry in *La Jeune Parque* (1917) and *Charmes* (1922) combines sensuous lyricism with intellectual force.

Valhalla In Teutonic mythology, one of the three homes of *Odin. Half of the warriors who die in battle are brought by the *Valkyries to Valhalla, where they spend their days in battle and their nights in feasting and listening to songs of their heroic exploits.

Valkyries In Teutonic mythology, beautiful maidens, who are the personal attendants of *Odin. They wear armour and, led by *Freyja, ride on horseback over battlefields in order to carry away the slain warriors whom Odin has chosen to live with him in *Valhalla.

Valladolid 41 39N 4 45W A city in central Spain, in Old Castile. It was formerly the capital of Castile and León (14th–15th centuries). It has a 16th-century cathedral and contains Cervantes' house; Christopher Columbus died here (1506). Population (1998 est): 319 946.

Valletta 35 54N 14 32E The capital of Malta. Founded (1566) by the Knights of St John, it was formerly an important British naval base. Population (1999 est): 7100, with a conurbation of 102 000.

valley An elongated depression in the earth's surface. Valleys have various origins but the common **V-shaped valley** is formed as the result of erosion by a river. Those that originated through glacial erosion are **U-shaped valleys**, with steep sides and broad floors, often occupied by deep lakes (*see* FJORD). *See also* RIFT VALLEY.

Valley of the Kings The cemetery of the Egyptian pharaohs from about 1580 to about 1085 BC, near *Thebes. All the tombs were robbed, except that of *Tutankhamen.

Valois The royal dynasty of France from 1328 to 1589. The *Hundred Years' War (1337–1453) nearly destroyed Valois power, which was saved by *Charles VII (reigned 1422–61). Charles VIII (reigned 1483–98) and *Louis XII waged disastrous wars in Italy, where they opposed the *Habsburgs. The last Valois were victims of rival religious factions (*see* WARS OF RELIGION).

Valparaíso 33 05S 71 40W The second largest city in Chile, on the Pacific Ocean. Founded by the Spanish (1536), Valparaíso is a major port. Population (1999 est): 283 489.

value-added tax (**VAT**) An indirect tax on goods calculated by adding a percentage to the value of a product as it increases at each stage of production; the whole cost is eventually passed on to the consumer. The tax was introduced in the UK in 1973. It is charged at a rate of 17.5% on all goods and services except those that are zero-rated, exempt, or taxed at a special rate.

vampire bat A bat of the family *Desmodontidae* (3 species), of Central and South America. The most common species is *Desmodus rotundus*, 7.5–9 cm long. Vampire bats feed on the blood of mammals or birds. Although too small to cause serious blood loss to their host, they can transmit dangerous diseases.

vanadium (V) A transition metal, named after the Norse goddess Vanadis. The metal is isolated by reduction of the trichloride (VCl_3) with magnesium or of the pentoxide (V_2O_5) with calcium. At no 23; at wt 50.9415; mp 1910 ± 10°C; bp 3409°C.

Van Allen radiation belts Two regions of charged particles in the earth's *magnetosphere. The toroidal inner belt lies 1000–5000 km above the equator; the outer belt lies 15 000–25 000 km above the equator, curving down towards the earth's magnetic poles. The belts were discovered in 1958 by the US physicist James Van Allen (1914–).

Vanbrugh, Sir John (1664–1726) English architect, soldier, and playwright. His plays included *The Relapse* (1697) and *The Provok'd Wife* (1697). He was England's most successful *baroque architect, his buildings including Castle Howard (1699–1726) and *Blenheim Palace (begun 1705), on which he collaborated with *Hawksmoor.

Van Buren, Martin (1762–1862) US statesman; Democratic president (1837–41) and a founder of the Democratic Party. He came to power during the economic crisis of 1837 but his adherence to laissez-faire principles led to his defeat in 1840.

Vancouver 49 13N 123 06W A city and port in W Canada, in British Columbia. Established in 1862 at the S end of the Coast Mountains, Vancouver is the commercial and industrial centre of British Columbia. Population (1996): 514 008.

Vancouver Island A Canadian island off the Pacific coast of British Columbia. Its E coastal plain rises to glaciers and forested mountains. The economy depends on timber, mining, fishing, and tourism. Area: 32 137 sq km (12 408 sq mi). Population (latest est): 461 573. Chief town: Victoria.

Vandals A Germanic tribe that during the first four centuries AD migrated southwards from Scandinavia and the S Baltic coast. In 455 they sacked Rome. The devastation they caused gave rise to the term vandalism.

Van de Graaff generator A type of electrostatic generator, invented by the US physicist Robert Jemison Van de Graaff (1901–67), that produces static potentials of millions of volts. Charge from an external source is fed onto a continuously moving belt, which transfers it to the inside of a large hollow conducting sphere. The charge moves to the outer surface of the sphere, leaving the inside neutral and able to collect more charge.

Van der Waals' equation A modification of the ideal gas equation, $pV = RT$, where p is the pressure exerted by a gas with volume V and thermodynamic temperature T. R is the gas constant. Van der Waals adjusted V to $(V - b)$ to take account of the volume occupied by the molecules. He also assumed that forces (**Van der Waals' forces**) exist between the molecules and therefore adjusted the pressure term to $(p - a/V^2)$. Both a and b are constant for a particular gas.

van de Velde A family of 17th-century Dutch painters. **Willem van de Velde the Elder** (1611–93) and his eldest son **Willem van de Velde the Younger** (1633–1707) were both marine artists, living in England after 1672. His younger son **Adriaen van de Velde** (1636–72) was a landscape painter. **Esaias van de Velde** (c. 1591–1630), the landscape painter, was probably the brother of Willem van de Velde the Elder.

Van Dyck, Sir Anthony (*or* **Vandyke**; 1599–1641) Flemish *baroque painter. Working chiefly in England, he painted many religious and mythological subjects, although his reputation rests largely on his portraits of the English court. *Charles I on Horseback* (National Gallery, London) demonstrates the elegance and grandeur of his style.

Vänern, Lake The largest lake in Sweden. It drains into the Kattegat via the River Göta. Area: 5546 sq km (2141 sq mi).

van Eyck, Jan (c. 1390–1441) Flemish painter. He is noted for his realistic portraits, particularly *The Arnolfini Marriage* and *Man in a Red Turban* (both National Gallery, London). He certainly perfected and possibly invented the Flemish technique of oil painting, in which the pigment is mixed with oil and turpentine and applied in thin glazes. The famous *Adoration of the Lamb* altarpiece in Ghent was probably begun by his elder brother **Hubert van Eyck** (d. 1426) and completed by Jan.

Van Gogh, Vincent (1853–90) Dutch postimpressionist painter. His early works were chiefly drawings of peasants. On moving to Paris (1886) he briefly adopted the style of *impressionism. In Arles in 1888 he painted his best-known works—orchards, sunflowers, and the local postman —but only one painting was sold during his lifetime. The visit of *Gauguin ended in a quarrel during which Van Gogh cut off part of his own left ear. In 1889 he entered a mental asylum at Saint-Rémy. *Wheatfield with Crows* (Stedelijk Museum, Amsterdam) was painted shortly before his suicide.

Vanilla A genus of climbing *orchids (about 90 species), native to tropical Asia and America. They have long fleshy stems attached to trees by aerial roots and produce large white and yellow flowers. Several species are cultivated commercially for the flavouring agent vanilla.

Van't Hoff, Jacobus Henricus (1852–1911) Dutch chemist, who pioneered the field of stereoisomerism, showing that the bonds of a carbon atom are arranged in a tetrahedron. This enabled him to explain *optical activity in terms of molecular structure. He also contributed to chemical thermodynamics and to the theory of solutions, for which he won the 1901 Nobel Prize.

Vanua Levu A volcanic island in the S Pacific Ocean, the second largest in Fiji. Sugar, copra, and gold are exported. Area: 5535 sq km (2137 sq mi). Population (latest est): 909. Chief town: Lambasa.

Vanuatu, Republic of (name until 1980: New Hebrides) A country in the SW Pacific Ocean comprising a chain of about 80 forested volcanic islands, the largest of which is Espíritu Santo. *Economy*: copra, cocoa, coffee, and beef are exported. Tourism and financial services have also developed. *History*: sighted by the Portuguese (1606), the islands were later charted (1774) by James Cook. In the 19th century thousands of the indigenous inhabitants were forcibly removed to sugar plantations in Australia. From 1906 the islands were jointly administered by France and the UK. In 1980 they became independent. Official languages: French, English, and Bislama. Currency: vatu of 100 centimes. Area: about 14 760 sq km (5700 sq mi). Population (2003 est): 204 000. Capital: Vila.

Varanasi (*or* **Benares**) 25 20N 82 00E A city in India, on the River Ganges. A major place of pilgrimage for Hindus, Jains, Sikhs, and Buddhists, it has 5 km (3 mi) of ghats (steps), from which thousands of Hindus bathe in the sacred river. Population (1991): 925 962.

Vargas Llosa, Mario (1936–) Peruvian novelist and politician. His novels include *The City and the Dogs* (1963), *The War of the End of the World* (1981), and *The Notebooks of Don Rigoberto* (1998).

variable stars Stars the brightness of which varies with time. In regular variables the brightness completes a cycle of changes in a period ranging from minutes to years. The brightness variation can be up to several *magnitudes. The three major groups are: eclipsing *binary stars, cataclysmic variables, and pulsating stars.

variance In a set of numbers, usually measurements, the quantity obtained by summing the squares of the differences between each number and the average value of the set and then dividing by the number of members of the set. Variance and, more often, its square root, called the **standard deviation**, are used to estimate scatter or random error in experimental results.

varicose veins Swollen tortuous veins in the legs caused by malfunctioning of the valves in the veins, which obstructs blood flow. Varicose veins tend to run in families and are commoner in older and fat people, women, and those who are constantly standing.

Varna 43 12N 27 57E A city and port in E Bulgaria, on the Black Sea. Founded in the 6th century BC, it finally passed to Bulgaria in 1878. In the **Battle of Varna** (10 November 1444) a Hungarian force was decisively defeated by the Turks, who were thus enabled to expand further into the Balkans. Population (1999 est): 299 801.

varnish A resinous solution in oil or alcohol that dries to a hard transparent coating on wood, metal, etc. Natural resins include *shellac, copal, dammar, and congo. Polyurethane is a durable and chemical-resistant synthetic resin. Polyesters and alkyds are also used.

varve dating A technique used in geology and archaeology to give the age of a sediment and to provide information about the climate during which it was formed. Varves are layers of claylike sediment deposited from a melting glacier into a lake. Each varve represents a single year's deposition.

Vasa The ruling dynasty of Sweden (1523–1818) and of Poland (1587–1668) founded by Gustavus I Vasa (1496–1560). The best-known Vasa monarchs in Sweden were Gustavus II Adolphus (1594–1632) and Christina (1626–89).

Vasari, Giorgio (1511–74) Italian painter, architect, and writer. In Florence he painted fresco cycles and built the *Uffizi, both works showing his respect for *mannerism. However he is best known for his *Lives of the Most Eminent Italian Architects, Painters, and Sculptors*, tracing the history of Renaissance art.

Västerås 59 36N 16 32E A city in central Sweden, on Lake Mälar. An important city in medieval times, it has a 12th-century castle. Population (1997 est): 124 084.

VAT *See* VALUE-ADDED TAX.

Vatican City, State of the A small independent state within the city of Rome, the seat of government of the Roman Catholic Church. It came into being in 1929, when Pius XI signed the *Lateran Treaty with Mussolini. The state is governed by a commission appointed by the pope. Official language: Italian. Currency: euro of 100 cents. Area: 44 hectares (109 acres). Population (2003 est): 900.

Vatican Councils Two ecumenical councils of the Roman Catholic Church, held in Rome. **1.** (1869–70) The council that was convoked by *Pius IX, resulting in the promulgation of the doctrine of papal *infallibility. **2.** (1962–65) The council that was convoked by *John XXIII and continued by *Paul VI. It reformed the liturgy and established an atmosphere in which progressive critics could freely express their views.

Vaughan Williams, Ralph (1872–1958) British composer. Influenced by English folksong and Tudor music, he developed a modal style that found its first full expression in *Fantasia on a Theme by Tallis* (for string orchestra; 1910). His works include nine symphonies, the ballet *Job* (1931) and the opera *The Pilgrim's Progress* (1951).

vector (mathematics) A quantity that has both magnitude and direction. Examples of vectors include velocity, force, magnetic flux density, etc. A vector needs three numbers (called components) to be defined, each number representing its magnitude in one of three mutually perpendicular directions.

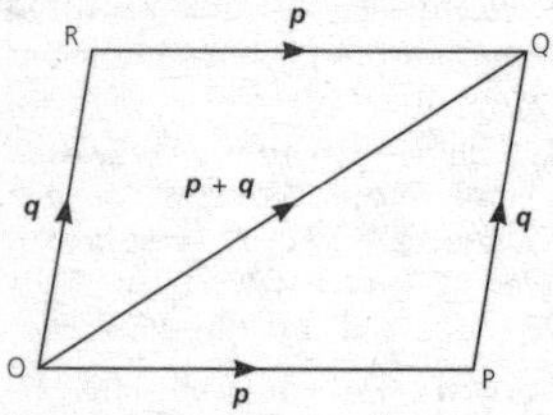

vectors. The two vectors OP (***p***) and PQ (***q***) add to give the resultant vector OQ (***p*** + ***q***). OR = PQ = ***q***, OP = RQ = ***p***. OQP is a vector triangle and ORQP is a parallelogram of vectors.

vector (medicine) An organism that is capable of transmitting a disease-causing organism (pathogen) from one organism to another. Transmission may be accidental or the vector may play a significant role in the life cycle of the pathogen, for example the malarial parasite spends part of its life cycle in the mosquito, which transmits it to man.

Vedanta The various philosophical schools of Hinduism, which derive from the commentaries on the *Vedas*, especially the **Upanishads*, the *Brahmasutras*, and the **Bhagavadgita*. The schools have in common the belief in reincarnation, the truth of the *Vedas*, the law of *karma, and the need for spiritual release. Believing Brahman to be the cause of the world, they condemn Buddhism and Jainism.

Vedas (Sanskrit: divine knowledge) The basic Hindu scriptures, written in archaic Sanskrit (Vedic) around 1500 BC. They comprise hymns, invocations, mantras, spells, and rituals, mostly concerning the sacrificial worship of gods representing various natural forces.

Vega A conspicuous white star, apparent magnitude 0.03 and 26.5 light years distant, that is the brightest star in the constellation Lyra.

Vega (Carpio), Lopé Felix de (1562–1635) Spanish dramatist and writer. After serving with the Spanish Armada he settled in Madrid and was ordained (1614). His numerous plays include *Fuenteovejuna* (1612–14) and *El caballero de Olmedo* (1615–26).

vegetarianism The practice of abstaining from eating animal flesh for ethical, religious, or nutritional reasons. Some vegetarians will not eat any animal products, including milk, cheese, eggs, etc., and are called **vegans**. Vegetarianism occurs in many religious traditions, including Buddhism, Jainism, and Hinduism, and it was advocated by Pythagoras, Plato, and many other thinkers. Vegetarians, especially vegans, can suffer from anaemia unless their diet includes sufficient vitamin B_{12}.

vein A thin-walled blood vessel that carries oxygen-depleted blood from the tissues to the *heart. The veins opening directly into the heart are the superior and inferior vena cavae and the pulmonary veins from the lungs, which are unique in carrying oxygenated blood.

Velázquez, Diego Rodriguez de Silva (1599–1660) Spanish painter. Influenced by Titian, he specialized initially in religious subjects and still-lifes. Later (1623) he became court painter to Philip IV and painted many portraits of the royal family and courtiers. Other works include *Pope Innocent X* (Rome), the *Rokeby Venus* (National Gallery, London), and the group portrait *Las Meninas* (Milan).

veld (*or* **veldt**) A tract of open grassland on the plateau of S Africa. It includes the Highveld (over 1500 m), Middleveld (1500–900 m), and Lowveld (below 900 m).

velocity The rate of change of a body's position in a given direction. The speed of a body is not in a specified direction. Velocity is thus a *vector quantity and speed is a scalar quantity. **Angular velocity** is the rate of change of a body's motion about an axis. It is measured in radians per second.

venereal disease *See* SEXUALLY TRANSMITTED DISEASE.

Venezuela, Bolivaran Republic of A country on the N coast of South America. The plains of the Orinoco basin in the N rise to the

Guiana Highlands in the SE, and in the NW the N end of the Andean chain reaches heights of over 5000 m (16 000 ft). Most of the population is of mixed European and Indian descent. *Economy*: based chiefly on oil, although production has declined since the 1970s. Efforts are being made to diversify the economy. Venezuela's rich mineral deposits include iron ore, bauxite, diamonds, gold, zinc, copper, and lead. Agriculture remains underdeveloped. Prolonged recessions in the 1980s and early 1990s led to the introduction of radical free-market reforms. *History*: sighted by Columbus in 1498, it was visited in 1499 by Vespucci, who named it Venezuela ("Little Venice") on seeing Indian villages built on stilts over Lake Maracaibo. Spanish settlement began in 1520 and Venezuela remained under Spanish rule until liberated by Bolívar in 1821. It then formed part of Colombia until 1830. Independent Venezuela was ruled by a succession of dictators until the post-World War II period, which has seen more democratic governments. Economic crisis in the late 1980s and early 1990s led to rising unrest. The 1998 presidential elections saw victory for the radical populist Lt Col Hugo Chávez Frias. A new constitution was introduced in 1999. That same year Venezuela suffered its worst natural disaster of the century, when at least 30 000 died in flooding and mud slides. The period 2001–04 saw deepening economic crisis, an abortive military coup (April 2002), and growing demands that the unpopular and authoritarian Chávez stand down. Venezuela is a member of the OAS, LAIA, and OPEC. Official languages: Spanish and indigenous languages. Currency: bolívar of 100 céntimos. Area: 912 050 sq km (352 143 sq mi). Population (2003 est): 25 699 000. Capital: Caracas.

Venice (Italian name: Venezia) 45 26N 12 20E A city in NE Italy. It is a seaport built on over 100 islands in the Lagoon of Venice. Venice is a centre of commerce and tourism and its manufactures include glassware, textiles, and lace. The Grand Canal and about 170 smaller canals provide waterways for water buses (*vaporetti*) and gondolas. Famous bridges include the Rialto Bridge and the *Bridge of Sighs. At the centre of Venice is St Mark's Square (Piazza San Marco) overlooked by *St Mark's Cathedral, the Campanile, and the Doge's Palace. The Accademia houses a unique collection of Venetian paintings; the Lido, a seaside resort, is 3 km (2 mi) to the SE. *History*: originally settled by refugees fleeing barbarian invasions (5th century AD onwards), Venice was united under the first *doge in 697. It became an independent republic and a great maritime power from the 14th century. It came under Austrian control in 1797 and became part of Italy in 1866. Venice is now threatened by subsidence and there are plans to build a flood barrier in the lagoon by 2010. Population (2000 est): 277 305.

Venn diagram *See* SET THEORY.

Venturi tube A device consisting of an open-ended tube with a central constriction, used to measure the rate of flow of a fluid, which can be calculated from the pressure difference between the centre and the ends. It is used to measure the airspeed of aircraft. Invented by G. B. Venturi (1746–1822).

Venus (goddess) A Roman goddess originally of gardens and fertility who became identified with the Greek *Aphrodite as goddess of love.

Venus (planet) The second planet in order from the sun, orbiting the sun every 225 days at an average distance of 108 million km. It is 12 102 km in diameter and has an extremely long period of axial rotation (243 days). It can be one of the most brilliant objects in the sky, reaching a *magnitude of −4.4, and like the moon exhibits *phases. Its surface is totally obscured by dense clouds of sulphuric acid droplets and sulphur particles. The atmosphere is primarily (98%) carbon dioxide. Planetary probes have shown that the surface temperature is a hostile 470°C.

Venus flytrap A *carnivorous plant, *Dionaea muscipula*, native to the eastern USA. The upper part of each leaf is hinged at the midrib and an alighting insect triggers the leaf to snap shut, thus trapping the prey. Family: *Droseraceae*.

Venus's girdle A marine invertebrate animal, *Cestum veneris*, belonging to an order (*Cestida*) of *ctenophores. Its transparent ribbon-like body is about 5 cm wide and 1 m or more long. It occurs in the Mediterranean Sea and Atlantic Ocean.

Veracruz (*or* **Veracruz Llave**) 19 11N 96 10W A major port in E Mexico, on the Gulf of Mexico. Population (2000 est): 410 000.

Verbena A genus of herbaceous plants or dwarf shrubs (about 250 species), chiefly native to North and South America. Lemon verbena (*Lippia citriodora*) is a related shrub from tropical America, the leaves of which yield an oil used in perfumery. Family: *Verbenaceae*.

Verde, Cape *See* CAPE VERDE, REPUBLIC OF.

Verdi, Giuseppe (1813–1901) Italian composer of operas. His first mature work was *Rigoletto* (1851); this was quickly followed in

1853 with *La Traviata* and *Il Trovatore*. In 1869 he wrote *Aida* (1871). His last works were the *Requiem* (1874) and the operas *Otello* (1887) and *Falstaff* (1893).

verdigris A green copper acetate used as a paint pigment. The term is also applied to the green coating, consisting of copper sulphate or carbonate, that forms on copper roofs, etc.

Verdun 49 10N 5 24E A fortified town in NE France, on the River Meuse. It was the scene (1916) of the longest battle of *World War I. Population (latest est): 23 430.

Verlaine, Paul (1844–96) French poet. His tempestuous relationship with *Rimbaud, who influenced his experimental *Romances sans paroles* (1874), resulted in the break-up of his marriage, and in 1873 he was imprisoned for shooting and wounding Rimbaud. After the publication of *Les Poètes maudits* (1884) Verlaine was the acknowledged leader of the Symbolist poets.

Vermeer, Jan (1632–75) Dutch painter, who spent his entire life in Delft. His paintings of everyday scenes, which are remarkable for their motionless figures and use of light, include *The Milkmaid* (Rijksmuseum, Amsterdam), *The Lacemaker* (Louvre), and *Allegory of Painting* (Kunsthistorisches Museum, Vienna), showing himself at work.

vermiculite A clay mineral with the property of expanding up to 22 times its original thickness on heating. Vermiculite results from the hydrothermal alteration of biotite and the intrusion of acid magma into basic rock.

vermilion Red mercuric sulphide (HgS). It sublimes readily on heating and occurs naturally as the mineral cinnabar. It is used as a pigment.

Vermont A state in the NE USA, in New England. The extensively forested Green Mountains run N–S through the centre of the state. Small manufacturing industries, mining, and tourism are important. The state's farmers produce dairy products, hay, potatoes, corn, and maple syrup. *History*: settled by the British in 1724, it declared its independence in 1777 and joined the Union in 1791. Area: 24 887 sq km (9609 sq mi). Population (2002 est): 608 827. Capital: Montpelier.

Verne, Jules (1828–1905) French writer. Verne's *Voyages extraordinaires* introduced such technological marvels as the submarine, space travel, and television. They included *Journey to the Centre of the Earth* (1864) and *Twenty Thousand Leagues Under the Sea* (1873). Other stories included *Around the World in Eighty Days* (1873).

Vernier scale A device for measuring subdivisions of a scale, such as those on a pair of calipers. The auxiliary Vernier scale is divided so that ten of its subdivisions correspond to nine of those on the main scale. Named after Pierre Vernier (1580–1637).

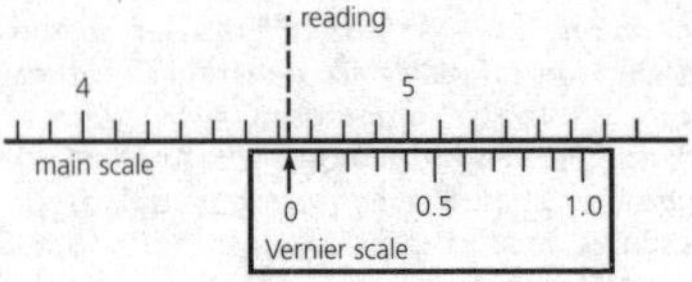

Vernier scale. An auxiliary scale used to measure accurately to two places of decimals.

Verona 45 26N 11 00E A city in N Italy, on the River Adige. A tourist centre, it possesses a Roman amphitheatre, a 12th-century cathedral, and the medieval Castelvecchio. Population (2000 est): 255 268.

Veronese, Paolo (P. Caliari; 1528–88) Italian painter of the Venetian school. In the Villa Barbaro at Maser, designed by *Palladio, he painted illusionistic landscapes, mythological scenes, and portraits. His religious works, for example *Marriage at Cana* (Louvre), were often pretexts for depicting contemporary banquets in impressive architectural settings.

Verrocchio, Andrea del (Andrea del Cione; c. 1435–88) Florentine Renaissance sculptor, painter, and goldsmith. Verrocchio's best-known sculptures are the *David* in Florence and the equestrian monument of Bartolommeo Colleoni in the Campo SS Giovanni e Paolo, Venice.

Versailles 48 48N 2 08E A town in N central France, famous for its baroque palace, the residence of the French kings from 1678 to 1769. Historic events enacted at the palace include Britain's recognition of American independence (1783), the crowning (1871) of William I as German emperor, and the signing of the **Treaty of Versailles** (1919), which imposed reparations on Germany after World War I and established the League of Nations. Population (latest est): 91 029.

vertebra *See* SPINE.

Vertebrata (*or* **Craniata**) A subphylum (or phylum) of animals that includes the fish, amphibians, reptiles, birds, and mammals. They are characterized by a backbone consisting of interlocking vertebrae, which forms the main support for the body and protects the nerve cord (spinal cord). *See also* CHORDATE.

Verwoerd, Hendrik Frensch (1901–66) South African statesman; prime minister (1958–66). The chief architect of the *apartheid system, he took South Africa out of the Commonwealth in 1960. He was assassinated in parliament.

Vesalius, Andreas (1514–64) Flemish anatomist, whose major work, *The Seven Books on the Structure of the Human Body* (1543), contained some of the first accurate descriptions of human anatomy.

Vespasian (9–79 AD) Roman emperor (69–79). Vespasian's decisive policies brought an end to civil war and he increased taxes and reformed the army. He was deified after his death.

Vespucci, Amerigo (1454–1512) Italian navigator, after whom America is named. In 1499 and 1501 he explored the E coast of South America.

Vesta The Roman goddess of the hearth, identified with the Greek Hestia. She was worshipped in private households, and her annual festival, the Vestalia, was held in June. The **Vestal Virgins**, her priestesses, tended the eternal fire at her shrine in Rome.

Vesuvius 40 49N 14 26E A volcano in S central Italy, near Naples. In 79 AD it engulfed *Herculaneum and *Pompeii; the last eruption was in 1944. Average height: 1220 m (4003 ft).

vetch A climbing or trailing annual or perennial herb of the genus *Vicia* (about 150 species), native to N temperate regions and South America. Some species are grown as fodder crops. Family: *Leguminosae*.

Vibrio A genus of freshwater and marine bacteria. They are rod-shaped, either straight or curved, and swim by means of whiplike flagella. *V. cholerae* causes *cholera in humans.

Viburnum A genus of shrubs and small trees (about 200 species), mostly native to N temperate regions. They have white or pink flowers. Many are grown as ornamentals, including the snowball tree (*see* GUELDER ROSE) and laurustinus. Family: *Caprifoliaceae*.

Vicenza 45 33N 11 33E A city in NE Italy. It was the home of the 16th-century architect Andrea Palladio. Population (1996 est): 107 786.

Vichy 46 07N 3 25E A spa in central France, on the River Allier. From 1940 until 1944, it was the seat of the pro-German puppet government of Marshal *Pétain. Its waters, which were known to the Romans, are bottled and exported worldwide. Population (latest est): 30 554.

Victor Emmanuel II (1820–78) King of Italy (1861–78). As king of Sardinia-Piedmont (from 1849) he fought the Austrians, supported the nationalist goals of *Cavour, and coordinated with *Garibaldi in the campaign that freed S Italy. As King of Italy he acquired Venetia (1866) and Rome (1870), which he made the Italian capital.

Victor Emmanuel III (1869–1947) King of Italy (1900–46) following the assassination of his father Umberto I. He acquiesced in Mussolini's seizure of power (1922) and after Mussolini's fall (1943) relinquished his powers to his son Umberto II.

Victoria 1. A state of SE Australia. It consists of central uplands, descending to plains in the N and S. Gippsland is a noted dairying area. Cattle production is now concentrated in S Victoria. Brown coal is mined in Central Gippsland and gas and oil are piped from the Bass Strait. Industry is concentrated on Melbourne. Area: 227 600 sq km (87 884 sq mi). Population (1999 est): 4 712 170. Capital: Melbourne. **2.** 22 16N 114 13E An urban district in S China, the administrative centre of Hong Kong, situated on the N of the island. Population (latest est): 590 771.

Victoria (1819–1901) Queen of the United Kingdom (1837–1901). The daughter of George III's fourth son Edward, Duke of Kent (1767–1820), Victoria succeeded her uncle William IV. In 1840 she married her cousin Prince *Albert of Saxe-Coburg-Gotha; they had nine children. Albert's death in 1861 was a severe blow to Victoria and she resolved thereafter to act exactly as he would have wished. She had an exalted view of the monarch's role in government, failing to appreciate the limitations of constitutional monarchy. Her refusal to dismiss her Whig ladies of the bedchamber when the Tory, Robert Peel, was attempting to form a ministry caused the *Bedchamber Crisis (1839). Her close friendship with *Disraeli, who made her Empress of India (1876), contrasted with her strained relations with his rival *Gladstone. In the last years of her reign, especially after her Golden Jubilee (1887), she enjoyed enormous popularity.

Victoria, Lake (*or* **Victoria Nyanza**) The largest lake in Africa, in Uganda, Tanzania, and

Kenya. It was discovered for Europeans in 1858 by Speke. Area: 69 485 sq km (26 826 sq mi).

Victoria and Albert Museum A London museum founded in 1853 to house examples of applied arts of all periods and cultures. Originally at Marlborough House, it moved to South Kensington in 1857.

Victoria Cross (VC) The highest British decoration for "bravery...in the presence of the enemy." Instituted by Queen Victoria in 1856, VCs were formerly cast from the metal of Russian guns taken during the Crimean War (1854–56).

Victoria Falls 17 55S 25 52E A waterfall in the Zambezi River on the border of Zimbabwe and Zambia. The river drops as much as 128 m (420 ft), and then flows through a narrow gorge known as the **Boiling Pot**.

vicuna A hoofed mammal, *Vicugna vicugna*, of high Andean plateaus. Resembling a small camel, the vicuna is 75 cm high and has a tawny-brown coat with a white bib and underparts. Aggressively territorial, they are valued for their wool. Family: *Camelidae* (camels, etc.).

video recording The storage of a *television programme or prerecorded film on magnetic tape. Because the demodulated video (vision) signal can have frequencies in the megahertz range, the signal is recorded diagonally on the tape (each diagonal line representing one line of the picture) and the tape is run slowly over a drum on which the recording and reading heads rotate at high speeds. Since the late 1990s DVDs (*see* COMPACT DISC) have increasingly replaced video tape as a means of storing prerecorded films.

Vienna (German name: Wien) 48 12N 16 20E The capital of Austria, on the River Danube. With its musical and theatrical life, its museums, and parks, it is a popular tourist attraction. Trade and industry, however, form the basis of the economy. Most of the chief buildings lie on or within the Ringstrasse, the boulevard built in 1857 to replace the old city ramparts. *History*: seat of the Habsburgs (1278–1918) and residence of the Holy Roman Emperor (1558–1806), Vienna became an important cultural centre in the 18th and 19th centuries, having associations with Haydn, Mozart, Beethoven, Schubert, and the Strauss family. It suffered damage during World War II and was jointly occupied by the Allied Powers (1945–55). Population (2001): 1 562 676.

V

Vienna, Congress of (1814–15) A conference of European powers that met following the fall of Napoleon. Its Final Act created a kingdom of the Netherlands, a German confederation of 39 states, Lombardy-Venetia subject to Austria, and the Congress Kingdom of Poland. Legitimate monarchs were restored in Spain, Naples, Piedmont, Tuscany, and Modena, and Louis XVIII was confirmed as King of France.

Vienna Circle The group of scientific philosophers who developed the doctrine of *logical positivism. Founded by Moritz Schlick (1882–1936) in 1924, the Vienna Circle flourished until 1939. Members included *Carnap, Kurt Gödel (1906–78), and Otto Neurath (1882–1945). *See also* AYER, SIR ALFRED (JULES).

Vienne, River A river in W central France, flowing mainly NNW to the River Loire. Length: 354 km (220 mi).

Vientiane 18 06N 102 30E The capital of Laos, a port on the River Mekong. Founded in the 13th century, it came under Siamese control in the 18th century and was destroyed (1828) following a revolt against Siamese rule. It became capital of the French protectorate of Laos in the late 19th century. Population (1999 est): 540 000.

Viet Cong Communist guerrillas who fought in the *Vietnam War (1954–75). In 1960 they established the National Liberation Front, which amalgamated the various groups opposed to the South Vietnamese government.

Viet Minh The Vietnam League for Independence, formed in 1941 by *Ho Chi Minh to create an independent Vietnamese republic. After World War II, in which it resisted the Japanese occupation, the Viet Minh played a prominent role in the *Indochina war against France (1946–54).

Vietnam, Socialist Republic of A country in SE Asia, occupying the E part of the Indochina peninsula. Fertile coastal lowlands rise to forested plateaus and mountains, the most populated areas being around the Mekong delta in the S and the Red River delta in the N. The inhabitants are mainly Vietnamese, with minorities of Chinese and others. *Economy*: agriculture remains the most important sector. Rice is grown extensively and is now a major export. Teak and bamboo are the chief forest products and fishing is also important. Industrial developments have been concentrated mainly in the N. Offshore oil production is increasing and crude petroleum is exported. Other exports include garments, footwear, and coffee. *History*: the northern kingdom of Nam

Viet was conquered in 111 BC by the Chinese. In 939 AD it broke free and resisted further Chinese invasions until the 15th century, when it was again briefly occupied. Its southward expansion culminated in the establishment (1802) of a united Vietnamese empire, which lasted until the establishment of the Union of *Indochina by the French (1887). Vietnam was occupied by the Japanese in World War II. France's refusal in 1945 to recognize Ho Chi Minh's government led to war (1946–54) after which, following defeat at Dien Bien Phu, the French withdrew. The Geneva Conference (1954) divided Vietnam along the 17th parallel into communist North Vietnam and noncommunist South Vietnam, between which civil war ensued. In 1961 the USA extended assistance to the South and remained involved in the conflict until 1973 (*see* VIETNAM WAR). In 1976 the victorious North proclaimed the reunited Socialist Republic of Vietnam. Vietnamese troops invaded Cambodia in December 1978 and did not withdraw until 1989. The 1980s saw a massive increase in the number of refugees, known as the Boat People, attempting to leave Vietnam by small craft across the South China Sea. A new constitution was adopted in 1992, endorsing the free-market reforms of the previous decade. Official language: Vietnamese. Currency: dong of 100 xu. Area: 329 466 sq km (127 180 sq mi). Population (2003 est): 81 377 000. Capital: Hanoi.

Vietnam War (1954–75) The war between communist North Vietnam, aided by *Viet Cong guerrillas, and South Vietnam, aided from 1961 by the USA. It resulted in communist victory and the union (1976) of North and South Vietnam. Some 900 000 Viet Cong and North Vietnamese, 50 000 Americans, and some 400 000 South Vietnamese died in the war. *See also* INDOCHINA.

viewdata An information storage and retrieval system in which pages of text are transmitted as coded signals along telephone wires and displayed on a domestic television receiver. The user has direct access to a central computer store via a keypad. *See also* TELETEXT.

Vigny, Alfred de (1797–1863) French poet, novelist and dramatist. He associated with many Romantic writers while serving (1814–27) as an army officer. His works include the historical novel *Cinq-Mars* (1826) and the play *Chatterton* (1835).

Vigo 42 15N 8 44W A port and naval base in NW Spain, on the Atlantic coast. In 1702 an English-Dutch fleet sank a Spanish treasure fleet here. Population (1998 est): 283 110.

Vijayawada (former name: Bezwada) 16 34N 80 40E A city in India, on the River Krishna. Industries include engineering and rice milling. Population (1994 est): 288 573.

Viking probes Two identical US spacecraft that went into orbit around Mars in 1976. The Lander sections landed on the surface in July and September and performed various experiments. The Orbiter sections took extensive measurements and photographs of Mars' surface and two satellites.

Vikings Scandinavian sea warriors active from the late 8th to the mid-11th centuries. They established settlements in the British Isles (especially at York and Dublin), where an Anglo-Danish dynasty was founded (1016) by Canute, and in Normandy. They also settled in the E Baltic, *Vinland, and Greenland. Viking literature (the sagas) and art are noted for their vitality.

Villa, Pancho (Francesco V.; 1878–1923) Mexican revolutionary. Villa supported successive revolts against Mexican governments and came to dominate the north with an irregular army. In 1916 he raided Texas and New Mexico. After an agreement with the Mexican Government in 1920, he disbanded his army. He was later assassinated.

Villa-Lobos, Heitor (1887–1959) Brazilian composer. He toured Brazil collecting folksongs and in 1945 founded the Brazilian Academy of Music. His vast output includes 12 symphonies, *Bachianas Brasileiras* (1930–45), *Rudepoema* (1921–26) for piano, and the ballet *Uirapurú* (1917).

Villanovan The earliest Iron Age culture of N Italy, named after the site of Villanova near Bologna. Emerging in the 9th century BC Villanovan culture is characterized by sophisticated metalworking.

villein The unfree peasant of medieval Europe, holding land from the lord of the *manor in return for labour. Many villeins acquired written titles to their holdings following the *Peasants' Revolt.

Villeneuve, Pierre (1763–1806) French admiral during the Napoleonic Wars. He was defeated by Nelson at Trafalgar (1805) and taken prisoner. After his release he committed suicide.

Villon, François (1431–?1463) French poet. He led a life of vagrancy and crime and was condemned to be hanged in 1463 but was banished instead. The ballades and other poems in his *Lais* and *Grand Testament* are characterized by compassion, irony, and a fascination with death and decay.

Vilnius (Polish name: Wilno) 54 40N 25 19E The capital of Lithuania, on the River Neris. *History*: the capital of Gediminas, who founded Lithuania in the 14th century, it was ceded to Russia in 1795. After World War I it was given to newly independent Lithuania but was seized by Poland in 1922. It then became part of the Soviet Union (1940–91). The Germans occupied Vilnius in World War II, when its large Jewish population was virtually exterminated. Population (2000 est): 577 969.

Vimy *See* WORLD WAR I.

vinegar A dilute solution of acetic acid, produced from soured wine, beer (malt vinegar), or other dilute alcoholic liquids. It is used in salad dressings, preserving, etc.

Vinland The Viking name for the area of NE America, probably Newfoundland, discovered, explored, and briefly settled by *Leif Eriksson (c. 1000). The area was possibly visited a decade earlier by Bjarni Herjolfsson.

viol A bowed stringed instrument, common from the 15th until the early 18th centuries, when it was eclipsed by the *violin. Viols have six strings, tuned mainly in fourths, and are held between the knees when played. The bass viol acquired the name **viola da gamba** from the Italian *gamba*, leg.

viola A musical instrument of the *violin family. It is similar to the violin, although larger in size, having thicker strings and a heavier bow. It has a range of over four octaves from the C below middle C; its strings are tuned C, G, D, A.

violet A perennial herb of the genus *Viola*, up to 40 cm tall, whose solitary flowers are usually blue, purple, or white. The sweet-scented garden violets are derived from the Eurasian sweet violet (*V. odorata*). The dog violet (*V. canina*) is another common species, and the genus also includes the *pansies. Family: *Violaceae*.

V

violin A bowed string instrument, the soprano member of the family that includes the viola, cello, and double bass. It has four strings tuned in fifths (G, D, A, E), an arched bridge, and a smooth fingerboard. It has a range of over four octaves from the G below middle C. It is played with a bow strung with horsehair; the strings can also be plucked. The design of the violin was perfected by the Amati, Guarneri, and Stradivari families in Italy between the mid-16th and early 18th centuries.

viper A venomous snake, belonging to the family *Viperidae* (150 species), that has long erectile fangs. 0.3–3 m long, vipers feed on small animals. Most give birth to live young. Old World vipers (subfamily *Viperinae*) are stout-bodied and broad-headed and mostly grounddwelling. New World vipers (subfamily *Crotalinae*) are known as pit vipers.

Virgil (Publius Vergilius Maro; 70–19 BC) Roman poet. Reacting against a troubled political background, he described in his *Eclogues* (42–37 BC) an idealized pastoral landscape. His more practical vision of Italy in the *Georgics* (36–29 BC) is informed by his interest in agriculture. During his final years he worked on the *Aeneid*, a national epic describing the wanderings of Aeneas, and the founding of Rome and extolling Augustus. The supreme poet of imperial Rome, Virgil became the object of superstitious reverence to later generations.

virginals A keyboard instrument of the 16th and 17th centuries, the earliest and simplest form of the *harpsichord. It was often made in the form of a box, which could be set on the table; the strings ran parallel to the keyboard.

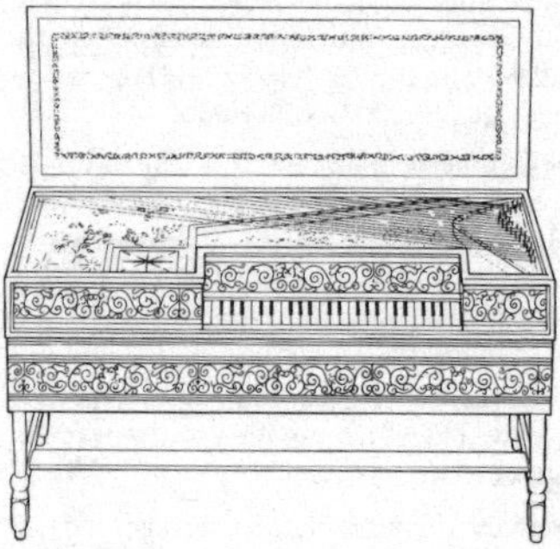

virginals

Virginia A state on the mid-Atlantic coast of the USA. The low-lying coastal plain rises to the forested Appalachian Mountains in the W. The principal industries are chemicals and tobacco processing. Fishing, tourism, and mining are also significant. The state produces tobacco, hay, corn, apples, and peaches. *History*: one of the 13 original colonies, it was named after Elizabeth I of England, the Virgin Queen. It became a state in 1788. Area: 105 716 sq km (40 817 sq mi).

Population (2000 est): 7 078 515. Capital: Richmond.

Virginia creeper A climbing shrub, also called woodbine, of the genus *Parthenocissus*, especially *P. tricuspidata* of SE Asia and *P. quinquefolia* of North America. It clings by means of branched tendrils. Family: *Vitaceae*.

Virgin Islands A group of approximately 100 small islands in the Caribbean, in the Lesser Antilles. **The British Virgin Islands** consist of about 40 islands, the largest being Tortola. They became a British crown colony (now a United Kingdom overseas territory) in 1956. Area: 153 sq km (59 sq mi). Population (2001 est): 20 000. Capital: Road Town. **The Virgin Islands of the United States** consist of three main islands, the largest being *St Croix, and about 50 smaller ones. They were purchased from Denmark in 1917. Area: 344 sq km (133 sq mi). Population (2002 est): 110 000. Capital: Charlotte Amalie.

Virgo (Latin: Virgin) A large equatorial constellation on the *zodiac between Libra and Leo. The brightest star is Spica. The constellation contains the **Virgo cluster** of galaxies, which contains over 2500 members.

virtual particle A short-lived particle that is used in quantum mechanics to represent the interaction between stable particles. In quantum mechanics the electromagnetic interaction would be represented by the exchange of virtual photons between them. The *strong interaction is represented by the exchange of virtual pions, the *weak interaction by the exchange of intermediate vector bosons, and the *gravitational interaction by the exchange of virtual gravitons.

virtual reality A computer-generated environment that simulates the real world or creates realistic fantasy worlds. Virtual reality machines provide sounds and images of the artificial environment through eyescreens and headphones. The computer is linked to movement sensors and other, often manual, controls: the images change in response to the movements of the user. Virtual reality technology has been developed for such uses as flight simulation but can also be used for games.

virus A minute noncellular particle that can reproduce only in living cells. Viruses consist of a core of nucleic acid (either *DNA or *RNA), surrounded by a protein coat (capsule) and, in some types, a lipid-containing envelope. Viruses alternate between an inert virion stage and an infective stage, in which the capsule binds to the host cell and the viral nucleic acid (containing its genes) enters the cell and directs the components of the host cell to assemble replica viruses. These are finally liberated, often with damage to or death of the host cell. Viruses are responsible for a wide range of diseases in plants and animals.

viscacha A gregarious South American *rodent, *Lagostomus maximus*, related to *chinchillas. Over 50 cm in length, viscachas live in warrens of 12–15 burrows. They are nocturnal and feed on grasses, roots, and seeds. Family: *Chinchillidae*.

Visconti, Luchino (1906–76) Italian film director. Born into a noble family, he became a committed Marxist. Early films, such as *Ossessione* (1942), are neorealist in style but later films are characterized by elaborate visual composition. They include *The Leopard* (1963), *The Damned* (1970), and *Death in Venice* (1971).

viscosity A measure of the degree to which a fluid resists a deforming force. It is defined by Newton's law of viscosity: if two layers of a fluid, area A and distance x apart, flow with a relative velocity v, there is a force between them equal to $\eta Av/x$. η is the coefficient of viscosity. Viscosity is measured in newton seconds per square metre. The **kinematic viscosity** is the coefficient of viscosity divided by the density of the fluid.

Vishakhapatnam 17 42N 83 24E A city in India, on the Bay of Bengal. It is an important port; India's first steamer was launched here in 1948. Population (1991): 750 024.

Vishnu The second member of the Hindu trinity, the *Trimurti. He is known as the Preserver and is married to *Lakshmi. He has ten avatars or manifestations, the most famous of which are *Rama and *Krishna. He is often portrayed as lying asleep on a seven-headed snake.

Visigoths A branch of the *Goths. Forced by the *Huns across the Danube (376 AD), they destroyed a Roman army at Adrianople (378) and, under Alaric I (c. 370–410 AD), sacked Rome in 410.

Vistula, River (Polish name: Wisła) The longest river of Poland, rising in the Carpathian Mountains and flowing N and NW to enter the Baltic Sea near Gdańsk. Length: 1090 km (677 mi).

vitamin An organic compound, other than a protein, fat or carbohydrate, that is required in small amounts by living organisms for normal growth and maintenance of life. Vitamins function as *coenzymes in many metabolic reactions.

vitamin A (*or* **retinol**) A fat-soluble vitamin and an essential constituent of the visual pigments of the eyes. It also functions in the maintenance of healthy mucous membranes. Sources include liver, fish-liver oils, and egg yolk.

vitamin B complex A group of water-soluble vitamins that are all constituents of *coenzymes involved in metabolic reactions. Thiamine (B_1) occurs in cereal grains, beans, peas, and pork. Deficiency leads to *beriberi. Riboflavin (B_2) is found in yeast, liver, milk, and green leafy plants. Nicotinamide (nicotinic acid *or* niacin) can be synthesized from the amino acid tryptophan; liver is a rich source of the vitamin and milk and eggs of tryptophan. Vitamin B_6 (pyridoxine) is widely distributed in yeast, liver, milk, beans, and cereal grains. Also common in many foods are pantothenic acid, a constituent of coenzyme A; biotin, which is synthesized by intestinal bacteria; and choline, a precursor of *acetylcholine (which transmits nervous impulses). Folic acid and vitamin B_{12} (cyanocobalamin) can be synthesized by intestinal bacteria. Liver is a good source of vitamin B_{12}.

vitamin C (*or* **ascorbic acid**) A water-soluble compound that is required especially for the maintenance of healthy connective tissue. It cannot be synthesized by man and certain animals. Fruit and vegetables, especially citrus fruits, are good sources. Deficiency of vitamin C leads to *scurvy.

vitamin D A fat-soluble vitamin consisting of several related compounds (sterols), chiefly cholecalciferol (D_3) and ergocalciferol (D_2). Vitamin D is important in calcium and phosphorus metabolism. Vitamin D_3 is produced by the action of sunlight on skin. Fish and fish-liver oils are the main natural sources, while vitamin D_2 is added to margarine. Deficiency in infants causes *rickets.

vitamin E A vitamin consisting of a group of related compounds that function as biological antioxidants. The most potent form of vitamin E is alpha-tocopherol, found in green leafy plants, cereal grains, and eggs.

vitamin K A vitamin consisting of a group of quinone-based compounds that are necessary for the formation of prothrombin, important in blood clotting. Vitamin K occurs in vegetables, cereals, and egg yolk and can be synthesized by intestinal bacteria.

Viti Levu The largest Fijian island, in the S Pacific Ocean. Mount Victoria rises to 1302 m (4341 ft). Sugar, pineapples, cotton, and rice are produced. Area: 10 386 sq km (4010 sq mi). Population (latest est): 340 561. Chief settlement: Suva.

Vitoria 42 51N 2 40W A city in N Spain. Wellington defeated the French here (1813). Population (1998 est): 216 527.

Vitruvius (Marcus Vitruvius Pollio; 1st century BC) Roman architect and military engineer. His *De architectura* describes all aspects of Roman architecture. It strongly influenced architects in Renaissance Italy.

Vivaldi, Antonio (1678–1741) Italian composer and violinist, based mainly in Venice. Besides operas and sacred music, Vivaldi wrote over 450 concertos for various instruments, including a set of four violin concertos entitled *The Four Seasons*.

Viverridae A family of mammals of the order *Carnivora*. The 82 species include the genets, civets, linsangs, and mongooses. Viverrids typically have a long body and tail and short legs.

viviparity A reproductive process in animals in which the embryo develops within the maternal body. Viviparity occurs in most mammals—the embryos being nourished through the placenta—and in some snakes, lizards, and sharks.

vivisection The use of live animals for experiments, either to determine the effects of drugs, cosmetics, food additives, and other chemicals on living organisms, or in medical and biological research. In the UK experimenters are licensed by the Home Office. Alternatives to live animals include the use of test-tube (*in vitro*) techniques, tissue cultures, and computer-based mathematical models.

Vladikavkas (name from 1944 until 1954: Dzaudzhikau; name from 1954 until 1991: Ordzhonikidze) 43 02N 44 43E A city in S Russia, the capital of the North Ossetian Republic. An important road and rail junction, it has metallurgy and food processing industries. Population (1999 est): 310 600.

Vladivostok 43 09N 131 53E A port in SE Russia, on the Sea of Japan. It is the terminus of the Trans-Siberian Railway and a major Russian naval base. Population (1999 est): 613 100.

Vltava, River A river in the Czech Republic,

rising in the Forest of Bohemia and flowing mainly SE then N to join the River Elbe. Length: 434 km (270 mi).

vodka A spirit distilled from potatoes, rye, barley, or malt, usually in E Europe. Being colourless and without a distinctive flavour, vodka is used in many mixed drinks.

Vojvodina An autonomous province of NE Serbia and Montenegro, in N Serbia. Low lying and fertile, it produces cereals, fruit, and vegetables. With a large Hungarian minority, it became a focus of ethnic unrest in the late 1980s; in 1990 it was stripped of its autonomous status but this was restored in 2002. Area: 22 489 sq km (8683 sq mi). Population (2001 est): 1 937 000. Capital: Novi Sad.

volcanoes Vents or fissures in the earth's surface through which magma rises from the earth's interior and erupts lava, gases, and pyroclastic material. Basaltic lava tends to produce gently sloping cones, the lava flowing over a wide area, whereas the more viscous acid lava produces a steeper-sided cone. Volcanic cones are often topped by craters, created by volcanic explosions. The world's highest volcano (extinct) is Aconcagua (6959 m) in the Andes.

vole A small short-tailed *rodent belonging to the subfamily *Microtinae*. Voles are found in Europe, Asia, and North America and range in size from 7 to 35 cm. They have blunt noses and their cheek teeth grow continuously. The common field voles (genus *Microtus*; 42 species) eat nearly their own weight in seeds, roots, and leaves every 24 hours. Family: *Cricetidae*.

Volga, River A river in W Russia, the longest river in Europe. Rising in the Valdai Range, it flows mainly E and S to the Caspian Sea. Length: 3690 km (2293 mi).

Volgograd (name until 1925: Tsaritsyn; name from 1925 until 1961: Stalingrad) 48 45N 44 30E A city in SW Russia, on the River Volga. It has been rapidly redeveloped since World War II (*see* STALINGRAD, BATTLE OF). Population (1999 est): 1 000 000.

volleyball A six-a-side court game invented in the USA in 1895, in which an inflated ball is hit with the hands or arms. After the service each team is allowed to hit the ball three times before it crosses the net. A rally ends when the ball touches the ground or is not returned correctly. A game goes to 15 points and a 2-point lead is required to win.

volt (V) The SI unit of potential, potential difference, or electromotive force equal to the potential difference between two points on a conductor carrying a steady current of one ampere when the power dissipated is one watt. Named after the Italian physicist Alessandro Volta (1745–1827).

Volta, River A river in West Africa. Its headstreams, the Black Volta and White Volta Rivers, join in N central Ghana to form the River Volta, which then flows S to enter the Bight of Benin. Length: 480 km (300 mi).

Voltaire (François-Marie Arouet; 1694–1778) French writer, philosopher, and moralist, whose versatile work epitomizes the age of Enlightenment. An outspoken opponent of political and religious tyranny, he was obliged to spend most of his later life in exile. His voluminous writings include the satirical fable *Candide* (1759), *Traité de la tolérance* (1763), the *Dictionnaire philosophique* (1764), and histories of Peter the Great and Louis XV.

voltmeter A device for measuring voltage. In the direct-current moving-coil voltmeter the magnetic force on a coil in a magnetic field is used to deflect a needle, the high impedance needed being provided by a high resistance in series with the coil. Cathode-ray oscilloscopes and digital voltmeters are used for both direct and alternating current.

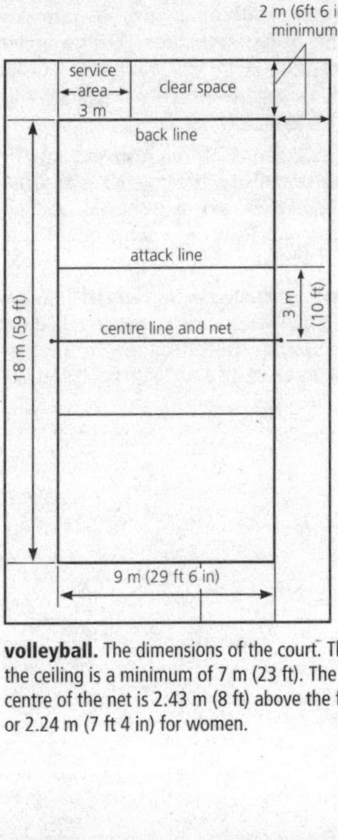

volleyball. The dimensions of the court. The height of the ceiling is a minimum of 7 m (23 ft). The top of the centre of the net is 2.43 m (8 ft) above the floor for men or 2.24 m (7 ft 4 in) for women.

Volturno, River A river in S central Italy, flowing SE and SW to the Tyrrhenian Sea. In 1860 it was the scene of a battle in which Garibaldi defeated the Neapolitans (*see* RISORGIMENTO). Length: 175 km (109 mi).

Voluntary Service Overseas (**VSO**) A British organization founded in 1958 by Alexander Dickson (1914–94) to send skilled volunteers at the request of overseas governments to work as teachers and doctors or on agricultural, industrial, or business schemes.

von Braun, Wernher (1912–77) US rocket engineer, born in Germany. He was director of the German Rocket Test Centre at Peenemünde during World War II, when the *V-2 rocket was built. After the war von Braun worked on US space rockets (*see* ROCKETS).

voodoo Magical and animistic cults of West African origin, practised in the Caribbean and in parts of South America. Trances induced by spirit possession are central to voodoo ritual. Other elements in the nocturnal rites are animal sacrifice, drum beating, dancing, and debased elements of Roman Catholic liturgy.

Voronezh 51 40N 39 13E A city in W Russia. It is at the centre of an agricultural region. Population (1999 est): 908 000.

Vorster, Balthazar Johannes (1915–83) South African statesman; prime minister (1966–78) and briefly president (1978). Vorster was known for his strict enforcement of racial policies. He retired during investigations of financial irregularities.

Vorticella A genus of microscopic aquatic single-celled organisms (*see* PROTOZOA). 0.05–0.15 mm long, they are bell-shaped and attached to the substrate by a long coiled contractile stalk. Phylum: *Ciliophora*.

Vorticism A British art movement inaugurated in 1913 by Wyndham *Lewis. It called for an art expressing the advanced technology and pace of modern life. Its journal, *Blast*, included contributions from Ezra *Pound and T.S. *Eliot. The sculptors Jacob *Epstein and Henri Gaudier-Brzeska (1891–1915) were also associated with the movement.

Vosges A range of mountains in NE France. It extends roughly N–S to the W of the River Rhine, rising to 1423 m (4672 ft).

Voyager probes Two US planetary probes launched in 1977. Voyager 1 approached Jupiter in 1979 then flew towards Saturn, which it reached in 1980. Voyager 2 flew past Jupiter in 1979, Saturn in 1981, Uranus in 1986, and reached Neptune in August, 1989.

VSO *See* VOLUNTARY SERVICE OVERSEAS.

Vulcan The Roman god of fire. He became patron of smiths and metalworkers after his identification with the Greek Hephaestus, whose myths he assumed.

vulcanization A process in which sticky natural rubber is made into a harder useful material by heating it with sulphur. Vulcanization involves the formation of sulphur bridges (–S–S–) between the polymer chains. An inert filler is incorporated at the same time.

Vulgate The Latin translation of the Bible made by St Jerome in the 4th century AD. The oldest surviving translation of the whole Bible, it was adopted by the Council of Trent (1546) as the official version of the Roman Catholic Church.

vulture A large carrion-eating bird belonging to the order *Falconiformes*. 60–100 cm long with a wingspan of up to 270 cm, vultures have a fleshy naked head. New World vultures (family *Cathartidae*; 6 species) have a slender hooked bill, large feet, and are voiceless. *See also* CONDOR. Old World vultures (subfamily *Aegypiinae*; 20 species) are widely distributed in open temperate and tropical regions and have a feathered ruff at the base of the neck. Family: *Accipitridae* (hawks and eagles). *See also* GRIFFON VULTURE; LAMMERGEIER.

W

Wabash River A river of the E central USA, flowing from W Ohio to the Ohio River. Length: 765 km (474 mi).

wadi A normally dry valley in a desert area. It will occasionally contain water following the infrequent violent downpours of rain that occur in these areas.

Wagner, (Wilhelm) Richard (1813–83) German composer. His early operas *Rienzi* (1842) and *The Flying Dutchman* (1843) led to his appointment as conductor at the Dresden opera house. In 1845 his opera *Tannhäuser* was successfully performed there but in 1848, after the failure of the May uprising, Wagner fled to Zürich, where he began the opera cycle *Der Ring des Nibelungen*, an epic treatment of German mythology. In this work and in *Tristan und Isolde* (1865) Wagner developed the use of leitmotifs to integrate music and drama in opera. In 1868 he produced his comic opera *Die Meistersinger von Nürnberg*; he also raised money to build a theatre in Bayreuth for the first performance of the *Ring* cycle (1876). His last opera, *Parsifal*, was produced in Bayreuth in 1882.

Wagram, Battle of (5–6 July 1809) The battle in which Napoleon finally defeated the Austrians. Fought NE of Vienna, Wagram witnessed the largest recorded concentration of field artillery.

wagtail A songbird noted for its constantly bobbing tail. The pied wagtail (*Motacilla alba*) is black, grey, and white, and about 18 cm long. The larger grey wagtail (*M. cinerea*) lives near streams, catching flying insects. The yellow wagtail (*M. flava*) visits Britain in the summer. Family: *Motacillidae* (wagtails and pipits).

Waikato River The longest river in New Zealand, in North Island. Rising in Mount Ruapehu, it flows NW to the Tasman Sea. Length: 350 km (220 mi).

Waitangi, Treaty of (1840) A treaty between the British Government and 46 Maori chiefs in New Zealand, which gave the Maori full rights and confirmed their possession of their lands. Its infringement by settlers led to the *Maori Wars. The signing of the treaty on 6 Feb is a national holiday in New Zealand (**Waitangi Day**).

Wakashan languages A group of *North American Indian languages of the NW Pacific coast, including Nootka and Kwakiutl.

Wakefield 1. 53 42N 1 29W A city in N England, in Wakefield unitary authority, West Yorkshire on the River Calder. A battle was fought here in 1460 during the Wars of the Roses. Population (1995 est): 75 900. **2.** a unitary authority in N England, in West Yorkshire. Area: 333 sq km (129 sq mi). Population (2001): 315 173.

Walachia (*or* **Wallachia**) A principality in SE Europe. Founded in 1290, it was a Hungarian fief until 1330. In the late 14th century it came under Turkish domination. In 1859 Walachia united with *Moldavia to form Romania, independent from 1878.

Walcheren An island in the SW Netherlands, in the Scheldt estuary. Protected from the sea by dykes, it produces sugar beet and vegetables. Area: 212 sq km (82 sq mi). Chief towns: Flushing and Middelburg.

Walcott, Derek (1930–) St Lucian poet and playwright. His volumes include *Collected Poems* (1986), the epic *Omeros* (1991), and *The Bounty* (1997). He received the Nobel Prize in 1992.

Waldheim, Kurt (1918–) Austrian diplomat and statesman; secretary general of the UN (1972–81), president of Austria (1986–92). He became president despite controversy over his war record as a Nazi army officer.

Wales (Welsh name: Cymru) A principality in the W of Great Britain, comprising a political division of the *United Kingdom. It is bordered by England to the E, the Irish Sea to the N, St George's Channel to the W, and the Bristol Channel to the S. Much of the country is covered by hills and mountains. Most of the population lives in the S and along the coastal strip in the N. Wales is administered by 22 unitary authorities (10 counties and 12 boroughs). *Economy*: the valleys and coastal plain in the S became highly industrialized in the 19th century, owing to the coal found there; however, there is now only one working pit. Wales still accounts for about half the UK's production of steel sheet and almost all its production of tinplate. Since the decline of traditional industries in the 1980s, South Wales has become one of Europe's chief centres for the manufacture of electrical goods and components (mostly Japanese and Korean-owned companies). Milford Haven, in the far SW, is used for the importing of oil, which has given rise to oil refining and associated petrochemical industries. Tourism, forestry, and sheep rearing are also important. *History*: the Celts living in Wales were little affected by the Roman occupation and were christianized in the 3rd century AD. King *Offa of Mercia built a great dyke (8th century) stretching from sea to sea, behind which the Welsh kingdoms were contained. Temporary unity was achieved by Hywel the Good (d. 950) but subsequent disunity enabled Edward I of England to defeat Llywelyn ap Gruffud (d. 1282) and establish English supremacy. Owen Glendower's revolt in the early 14th century was also crushed and English rule was formalized with the Acts of *Union (1536–43). Wales adopted Protestantism in the 16th century and has been a centre of Nonconformity since the 18th century. The early 19th century was characterized by rural overpopulation and near famine; Wales also suffered during the Depression of the 1930s. Welsh nationalism (*see* PLAID CYMRU) became a growing force in the 1960s and the 1970s, although *devolution plans were rejected in a referendum in 1979. A further referendum (1997) resulted in a small majority in favour of a Welsh assembly. This was established in May 1999. Area: 20 767 sq km (8016 sq mi). Population (2001): 2 903 085. Capital: Cardiff.

W

Wałęsa, Lech (1943–) Polish statesman and trade unionist; president of Poland (1990–95). An electrician at the Gdansk shipyard, he became leader of the independent trade union *Solidarity from its establishment (1980). He was awarded the 1983 Nobel Peace Prize for his efforts to ensure workers' rights. As president he faced economic crisis and political instability.

walking (*or* **race walking**) In athletics, a form of racing in which a particular gait is used; the advancing foot must touch the ground before the other leaves it.

wallaby A herbivorous marsupial belonging to the *kangaroo family (*Macropodidae*). Hare wallabies (genus *Lagorchestes*; 3 species) are the smallest, measuring up to 90 cm in length. Rock wallabies (genus *Petrogale*; 6 species) have rough-soled feet for negotiating rocky ground. Scrub wallabies (genus *Protemnodon*; about 11 species) inhabit brush or open forest.

Wallace, Alfred Russel (1823–1913) British naturalist, who formulated a theory of evolution by natural selection independently of Charles *Darwin. Wallace spent eight years (1854–62) assembling evidence in the Malay Archipelago, sending his conclusions to Darwin in England. He also proposed an imaginary line (**Wallace's line**) dividing the fauna of Asia and Australia.

Wallace, Sir William (c. 1270–1305) Scottish hero who resisted English rule in the 1290s. In 1297 he captured Stirling Castle and was proclaimed warden of Scotland. However, in 1298 he was defeated by Edward I at Falkirk and he was later captured and hanged.

Wallace Collection An art museum in Manchester Square, London. The collection, which was given to the nation in 1897, was formed by the 4th Marquess of Hertford and his half-brother Sir Richard Wallace (1818–90). It includes 18th-century French paintings and furniture, armour, and *The Laughing Cavalier* by *Hals. A large extension opened in 2000.

wallcreeper A Eurasian songbird, *Tichodroma muraria*, about 17 cm long and having a grey plumage with broad black wings patched with red. It climbs rock faces clinging with its sharp claws and probing crevices for insects. Family: *Sittidae* (nuthatches).

Wallenberg, Raoul (1912–?1947) Swedish diplomat. Sent to Hungary in 1944 as a special envoy, he helped thousands of Jews to escape the Nazis, issuing them with Swedish passports. In 1945 he was arrested by the Soviet authorities and disappeared. Although the Russian government has stated that he died in 1947 in prison, there is considerable uncertainty as to his fate.

Waller, Fats (Thomas W.; 1904–1943) US Black jazz musician and songwriter. An exceptional pianist, he recorded many of his own compositions, including "Honeysuckle Rose" and "Ain't Misbehavin'."

wallflower An annual or perennial herb of the genera *Cheiranthus* (about 10 species), native to Eurasia and North America, or *Erysimum* (about 80 species), native to Eurasia. Wallflowers have orange, yellow, red, or brown flowers. Many varieties of *C. cheiri* are cultivated as garden ornamentals. The Siberian wallflower (*E.* × *marshallii*) has brilliant orange or yellow flowers. Family: *Cruciferae*.

Wallis, Sir Barnes (Neville) (1887–1979) British aeronautical engineer. He designed the airship R100 and geodetic constructions, which he used in his Wellington bomber. He also invented the swing-wing aircraft but is best known for his invention in 1943 of the bouncing bomb, used to destroy the Ruhr dams in Germany.

Wallis and Futuna A French overseas territory in the SW Pacific Ocean comprising two small groups of islands. The chief of the **Wallis Islands** is Uvéa, while the **Futuna Islands** (*or* Îles de Horne) consist of Futuna and Alofi. Copra and timber are produced. Area: 275 sq km (106 sq mi). Population (1993 est): 14 400. Capital: Matautu, on Uvéa.

Walloons The French-speaking inhabitants of Belgium, living mainly in the S and E of the country. They are descended from the northernmost group of *Franks who adopted the Romance speech. *Compare* FLEMINGS.

Wall Street The centre of the financial district in New York City, in which the New York Stock Exchange is situated. Wall Street, often known as the Street, is synonymous with the stock exchange.

walnut A tree of the genus *Juglans* (about 17 species), especially the Eurasian species *J. regia*, which produces the best quality nuts. Up to 30 m tall, it has grey furrowed bark. The plum-sized green fruits each contain an edible kernel enclosed in a wrinkled pale-brown shell. The whole fruits may be eaten pickled. The timber of this species and of the American black walnut (*J. nigra*) is valued for furniture. Family: *Juglandaceae*.

Walpole, Sir Robert, 1st Earl of Orford (1676–1745) British statesman, regarded as the first prime minister (1721–42). He became a Whig MP in 1700 and was secretary for war (1708–10) and treasurer of the navy (1710–11). In 1712 he was impeached for corruption but came back into the government (1715–17) as first lord of the treasury and chancellor of the exchequer. He became paymaster general in 1720, and returned to the treasury after his effective handling of the *South Sea Bubble crisis (1721). His power was subsequently maintained by the adroit use of patronage. However, conflict with Spain led to the War of Jenkins' Ear and Walpole was forced to resign. His fourth son, **Horace Walpole, 4th Earl of Orford** (1717–97), was a writer. Strawberry Hill, his villa at Twickenham, became a showpiece of the gothic architectural revival. He wrote the popular gothic novel, *The Castle of Otranto* (1765) and numerous letters.

walrus A large *seal, *Odobenus rosmarus*, of coastal Arctic waters. Males are up to 3.7 m long and weigh about 1400 kg. Walruses have tusks—elongated upper canine teeth up to 1 m long—used in digging for molluscs on the sea bed and for fighting and display. Family: *Odobenidae*.

Walsall 1. 52 35N 1 58W An industrial town in central England, in Walsall unitary authority, West Midlands. Population (1991): 174 739. **2.** A unitary authority in W central England, in West Midlands. Area: 106 sq km (41 sq mi). Population (2001): 253 502.

Walton, Ernest Thomas Sinton (1903–95) Irish physicist, who shared the 1951 Nobel Prize with Sir John *Cockcroft for their invention in 1929 of the first particle accelerator.

Walton, Izaak (1593–1683) English writer best-known for *The Compleat Angler* (1653), an entertaining treatise on fishing. He also wrote biographies of John Donne (1640), George Herbert (1670), and other churchmen.

Walton, Sir William (Turner) (1902–83) British composer. He first became well known through *Façade* (1922), a setting of poems by Edith Sitwell. Later works include two symphonies (1932–35, 1960), the opera *Troilus and Cressida* (1954), concertos for viola (1929), violin (1939), and cello (1957), the oratorio *Belshazzar's Feast* (1931), and music for Laurence Olivier's films of *Hamlet*, *Henry V*, and *Richard III*.

Wankel engine A four-stroke rotary *internal-combustion engine. It consists of a triangular-shaped rotating piston, with outward curved sides and rounded corners. This rotates in an oval-shaped chamber, which has inlet and exhaust ports and a sparking plug. The small number of moving parts and the lack of vibration are the chief advantages of this engine, but gas leakage has been the principal problem. It was invented by the German engineer Felix Wankel (1902–88). See illustration on p. 934.

Wannsee Conference (early 1942) The

conference held at Wannsee, near Berlin, at which the Germans formulated their plan to exterminate all European Jews. Chaired by Reinhard Heydrich, the conference appointed Adolf *Eichmann to organize the logistics of the "final solution." *See also* HOLOCAUST.

WAP (wireless application protocol) A standard protocol for data transmission used in connecting mobile telephones to the Internet. WAP phones are capable of sending and receiving e-mails and accessing a limited range of Internet services.

wapentake Any of the medieval administrative subdivisions into which the parts of England settled by the Danes (*see* DANELAW) were divided. They corresponded to the hundreds found in the rest of England.

Warbeck, Perkin (c. 1474–99) Flemish-born impostor, the focus of a Yorkist plot against Henry VII of England. Pretending to be the Duke of York (presumed murdered in 1483) he landed in Cornwall in 1497 but he and his 6000 followers fled in the face of Henry's troops. Captured at Beaulieu, he was hanged.

warble fly A parasitic fly belonging to the family *Oestridae*, widespread in Europe and North America. *Hypoderma boris* and *H. lineatum* attack cattle: eggs are laid on the legs and the larvae burrow into the tissue. When mature the larvae leave the host and pupate in the ground.

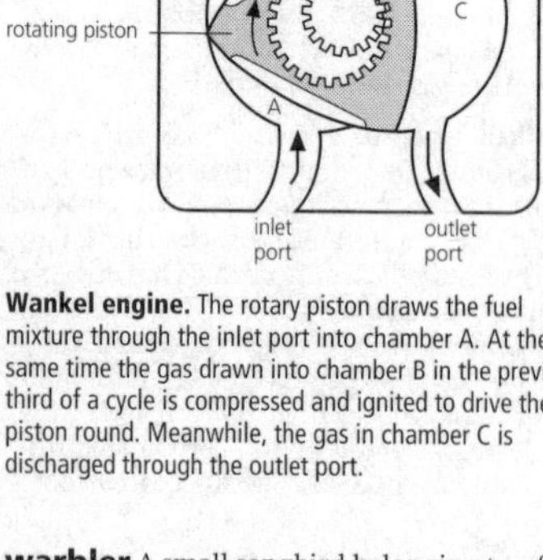

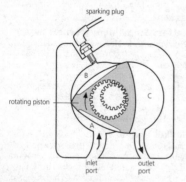

Wankel engine. The rotary piston draws the fuel mixture through the inlet port into chamber A. At the same time the gas drawn into chamber B in the previous third of a cycle is compressed and ignited to drive the piston round. Meanwhile, the gas in chamber C is discharged through the outlet port.

warbler A small songbird belonging to a family (*Sylviidae*; 400 species) widely distributed in Old World regions. 9–25 cm in length, warblers have slender bills, soft thick plumage, and feed on insects and berries. They are usually drab brown or olive in colour. *See* BLACKCAP; CHIFFCHAFF; REED WARBLER; WHITETHROAT.

Ward, Sir Joseph George (1856–1930) New Zealand statesman; Liberal (1906–12) and United Party (1928–30) prime minister. He advocated unity within the British Empire in foreign affairs and led the Liberals in the coalition government (1915–19) under W. F. Massey, before becoming leader of the United Party.

Wardrobe A royal administrative department in medieval England. Originally the room in which the king kept his clothes and jewels, it became a government department in the late 12th century. Controlled by the king, it was used by Henry III to counterbalance the Exchequer. It declined in importance during the 14th century.

Warhol, Andy (Andrew Warhola; 1926–87) US *pop artist and film producer. He achieved notoriety in the early 1960s with paintings of soup cans and portraits of film stars made with the silk-screen printing technique. His films include *The Chelsea Girls* (1966).

War of 1812 (1812–14) The war declared on Britain by the USA in response to Britain's impressment of sailors from US ships and its blockade on US shipping during the Napoleonic Wars. The USA was also incensed by British assistance to Indians harassing NW settlements. The war was inconclusive but helped forge US unity.

war on terrorism The "war" against international terrorism announced by President George W. *Bush in the wake of *September 11, 2001. Bush declared that the USA would use military force to destroy international terrorist networks and any regimes found to be harbouring them. Several countries, including the UK, offered military assistance while others pledged operational support. Blame for the September 11 attacks was quickly pinned on the *al-Qaida network controlled by Osama *Bin Laden, which was based in Afghanistan and known to have links with the *Taleban regime. Accordingly, the USA began air strikes on Afghan targets in early October 2001, leading to the total collapse of Taleban power by mid-November. US forces then concentrated on the Tora Bora, a cave complex in the S Afghan mountains believed to be the stronghold of Bin Laden. This resulted in the death or capture of many al-Qaida fighters but Bin Laden is assumed to have survived. Although sporadic fighting has recurred, al-Qaida's Afghan operation had been effectively destroyed by the end of 2001. US attention then focused on the aim of destroying the regime of Saddam *Hussein in Iraq (*see* IRAQ WAR).

Warrington 1. 53 24N 2 37W An industrial town in NW England, in Warrington unitary authority, Cheshire. It was designated a new town in 1968. Population (1991 est): 81 812. **2.** A unitary authority in NW England, in N Cheshire. Area: 176 sq km (68 sq mi). Population (2001): 191 084.

Warrumbungle Range A mountain range of Australia. It lies in N New South Wales and contains the Breadknife, a rock 90 m (300 ft) high but only 1.5 m (5 ft) wide.

Warsaw (Polish name: Warszawa) 52 15N 21 00W The capital of Poland, on the River Vistula. It became the capital in 1611. It was occupied by Russia in 1794 and later by France and Prussia. After German occupation in World War I, it became the capital once more when independence was achieved (1918). During the German occupation in World War II, a ghetto was established (1940) for 400 000 Jews and in February 1943, the survivors (about 100 000) staged an uprising, after which they were put to death. After the war much of the old town was faithfully reconstructed. It is now an important industrial and communications centre. Population (1999 est): 1 618 468.

Warsaw Pact (*or* **Warsaw Treaty Organization**) A military treaty signed in 1955 by the Soviet Union, Albania (until 1968), Bulgaria, Czechoslovakia, East Germany, Hungary, Poland, and Romania. Formed as a communist counterpart to NATO, it was dissolved in 1991.

Wars of Religion (1562–98) French civil wars arising out of the struggle of the *Huguenots (French Protestants) for religious liberty and the rivalry between Protestants and Roman Catholic nobles. The wars ended in the victory of the Huguenot leader Henry of Navarre (subsequently Henry IV), who in 1598 issued the Edict of *Nantes, giving the Huguenots religious freedom.

wart A small leathery growth on the skin, caused by human papillomaviruses. Warts are common in children and usually appear on the hands and on the soles of the feet (plantar warts *or* verrucae). Genital warts are often associated with other infections of the genital area. Warts appear suddenly and may disappear without treatment. Persistent warts can be treated by cauterization, freezing, or with drugs.

warthog A wild pig, *Phocochoerus aethiopicus*, of tropical African woodland. Short-legged, with a large head, bulging eyes, and long curved tusks, warthogs grow to about 75 cm high. They are grey-brown with sparse body hair and feed during the day on roots, grass, etc.

Warwick 52 17N 1 34W A town in central England, the administrative centre of Warwickshire on the River Avon. It is a historic town with a 14th-century castle. Population (1994): 22 600.

Warwick, Richard Neville, Earl of (1428–71) English statesman, known as the Kingmaker. A supporter of the Yorkists in the Wars of the Roses, he was responsible for the seizure of the Crown in 1461 by Edward, Duke of York (Edward IV). In 1470, he changed sides and briefly restored Henry VI to the throne. After the Lancastrians were routed (1471), he was killed, at Barnet.

Warwickshire A county in the Midlands of England. It consists mainly of undulating countryside, drained to the SW by the River Avon. It is predominantly agricultural, having lost the industrial NW (including Birmingham and Coventry) to West Midlands in 1974. Area: 1981 sq km (765 sq mi). Population (2001): 505 885. Administrative centre: Warwick.

Wash, the A shallow inlet of the North Sea, in E England between Lincolnshire and Norfolk. Length: about 30 km (19 mi). Width: 24 km (15 mi).

Washington One of the Pacific states in NW USA. Mountains ring the state, including Mount *St Helens, and the Columbia Basin covers much of the central area. The state's major manufacturing industry is the construction of aircraft. Attempts to diversify the economy have led to a growing tourist industry and significant mineral extraction, especially of gold, silver, and uranium. *History*: the British Hudson Bay Company dominated the area until the 1840s. In 1846 the boundary between Washington and Canada was agreed and the state (1889) was named after George Washington. Area: 176 616 sq km (68 192 sq mi). Population (2000): 5 894 121. Capital: Olympia.

Washington, DC 38 55N 77 00W The capital of the USA, in the E on the Potomac River. Coextensive with the District of Columbia, it is the centre of the government of the USA. Its many notable landmarks include the Washington Monument, the Lincoln Memorial, the Capitol, the White House, the *Pentagon, the Library of Congress, the Smithsonian Institution, and the Vietnam Veterans Memorial. *History*: its location was chosen by George Washington and approved by Congress in 1790. Planned by the French engineer, Pierre L'Enfant (1754–1825), its first constructions date from 1793. Population (2000): 572 059.

Washington, George (1732–99) US statesman and general; the first president of the USA (1789–97). Washington gained a high reputation in the *French and Indian War before becoming a leading opponent of British rule. On the outbreak of the *American Revolution (1775–83) he was appointed commander in chief of the American forces. After winning the final victory at Yorktown (1781), Washington presided over the Constitutional Convention (1787) and was unanimously elected president.

wasp A stinging insect, 6–40 mm long, belonging to the order *Hymenoptera*. The common European wasps (genus *Vespula*) are typical social wasps, forming colonies that consist of a queen, males, and workers. The adults feed on nectar, ripe fruit, insects, etc. New colonies are established by young fertilized queens—the only individuals to survive the winter. Certain parasitic wasps lay their eggs in the nests of other wasps. Solitary wasps (family *Sphecidae*) lay their eggs in individual nests. *See also* GALL WASP; HORNET; POTTER WASP.

Wassermann, August von (1866–1925) German bacteriologist, who invented the Wassermann test for detecting *syphilis. Wassermann also developed a test for tuberculosis and an antitoxin against diphtheria.

watch A timepiece small enough to be worn by a person. Watches first came into use in the 16th century with the invention by Peter Henlein (1480–1542) of the mainspring. Based on a verge escapement, watches were then bulky devices worn on the girdle. The invention of the balance spring (claimed by both *Hooke and *Huygens) in 1675 converted the watch into an article that could be concealed in the pocket. By the 18th century pocket watches had attained a high degree of accuracy. At the beginning of the 20th century wrist watches were introduced. Between the wars these became smaller and cheaper and incorporated such features as rust and shock resistance, luminous dials, or self-winding mechanisms. In

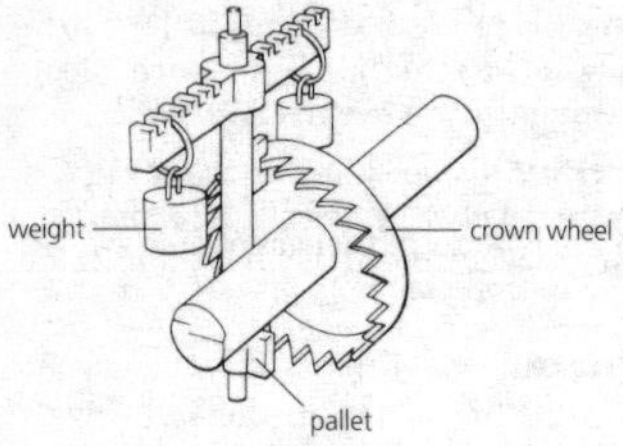

verge escapement

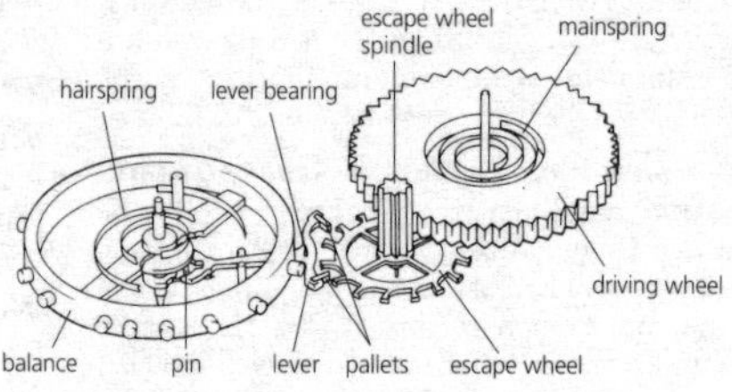

balance wheel and lever escapement

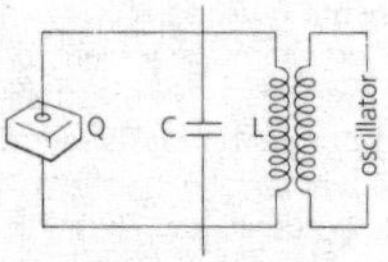

quartz-crystal watch A crystal of quartz (Q) uses the piezoelectric effect accurately to control the frequency of an oscillating electronic circuit consisting of a capacitor (C) and inductance (L).

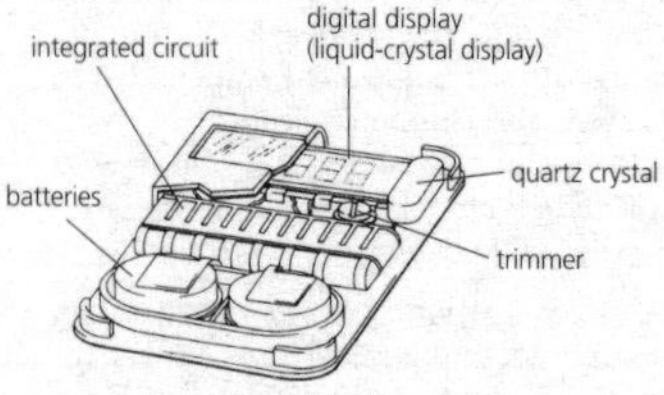

digital watch

watch. Early watches used the verge escapement of clocks. The balance wheel and lever escapement dominated watch design until the quartz crystal and digital watch emerged in the 20th century.

the early 1950s electromagnetic watches were developed, but it was not until the late 1960s that the first electronic watch appeared. In the 1970s quartz watches were developed without moving parts, the dial and hands being replaced by a digital display. Digital wrist watches now often incorporate additional functions, such as a tiny calculator.

water (H_2O) A colourless odourless tasteless liquid consisting of eight parts of oxygen to two parts of hydrogen by weight. Water covers 72% of the earth's surface and is found in all living matter, in minerals, and as a small but important constituent of the atmosphere. The solid form of water (ice) is less dense (916.8 kg/m^3) than the liquid at 0°C (999.84 kg/m^3), which is why ice floats and frozen water pipes burst. The maximum density (999.97 kg/m^3) occurs at 3.98°C, unlike most liquids in which the maximum density occurs at the melting point. The molecules of water are polar, i.e. they have a positive electric charge at one end and a negative at the other. This makes it an excellent solvent.

water beetle A beetle of the family *Dytiscidae*—the so-called true water beetles. The name is also used loosely for any aquatic beetle, including the *whirligig beetles (family *Cyrinidae*); the water scavenging beetles (family *Hydrophilidae*); and the crawling water beetles (family *Haliplidae*).

water boatman A *water bug belonging to the cosmopolitan family *Corixidae* (over 300 species). It has a flattened boat-shaped body with fringed oarlike hind legs and feeds on plant debris and algae, scooped up by the spoon-shaped front legs.

water buffalo A large buffalo, *Bubalus bubalis*, also called Asiatic buffalo or carabao, found wild in swampy land of SE Asia and widely domesticated throughout Asia. Up to 180 cm at the shoulder and heavily built, water buffaloes are grey-black with long backward-curving horns. Domestic breeds are used for milk and as draught animals.

water bug An insect of the suborder *Heteroptera* (*see* HEMIPTERA) that lives in or on fresh or brackish water. True water bugs include the *backswimmer and *water boatman. The surface water bugs include the pond skater (*Gerridae*), water cricket (*Vellidae*), and water measurer (*Hydrometridae*).

water chestnut An annual aquatic plant of the genus *Trapa*, especially the Eurasian species *T. natans*, which has floating leaves, feathery submerged leaves, and small white flowers. The hard spiny dark-grey fruit, up to 5 cm across, contains edible seeds. Family: *Trapaceae*. The Chinese water chestnut is the edible tuber of an E Asian sedge, *Eleocharis tuberosa*. Family: *Cyperaceae*.

watercress Either of two perennial herbs, *Nasturtium officinale* or *N. microphyllum × officinale*, native to Eurasia and widely cultivated for the peppery young shoots, which are used in salads. Watercress grows submerged or floating in streams or on mud. Family: *Cruciferae*.

water flea A small freshwater *crustacean of the suborder *Cladocera* (about 430 species). Its compact body, usually 1–3 mm long, is covered, behind the head, by a laterally flattened transparent carapace, which encloses 4–6 pairs of appendages. Common genera: *Daphnia*, *Leptodora*; subclass: *Branchiopoda*.

Waterford (Irish name: Port Lairge) **1.** 52 15N 7 06W A city and port in the SE Republic of Ireland, the county town of Co Waterford. It has Protestant and Roman Catholic cathedrals and is famous for its glass making. Population (2002): 44 564. **2.** A county in the S Republic of Ireland, in Munster. Chiefly hilly, it is drained by the Rivers Blackwater and Suir. The traditional glass-making industry is of note. Area: 1838 sq km (710 sq mi). Population (2002): 101 518. County town: Waterford.

water gas A mixture of equal amounts of hydrogen and carbon monoxide made by passing steam over red hot coke: $H_2O + C \rightarrow H_2 + CO$. The mixture is a useful fuel gas. Water gas can be made in conjunction with an exothermic reaction—that between air and carbon: $O_2 + 4N_2 + 2C \rightarrow 2CO + 4N_2$. The mixture of carbon monoxide and nitrogen is called **producer gas**. It has a lower calorific value than water gas. The heating value of water gas can be improved by passing it through petroleum while hot (carburetting).

Watergate A building complex in Washington, DC, that gave its name to a political scandal culminating in the resignation of President Richard *Nixon. The *Washington Post* exposed the involvement of presidential officials in a burglary of Democratic Party headquarters at the Watergate during the 1972 presidential election, and in subsequent attempts to cover the matter up. Following the prosecution of top White House staff, Nixon resigned under the threat of impeachment (1974).

water glass (*or* **sodium silicate**) A mixture of silicates with the general chemical formula

$x\text{Na}_2\text{O}.y\text{SiO}_2$, forming a clear viscous solution in water. It is made by fusing *sodium carbonate and sand (*silica) in an electric furnace and is used in making silica gel, detergents, and textiles.

Waterhouse, Alfred (1830–1905) British architect of the gothic revival. His early work was done in Manchester and included the Assize Court (1859; demolished 1959) and the Town Hall (1868). In London he built the Natural History Museum (1881) and the now demolished gothic redbrick St Paul's School (1885) and City and Guilds College (1879).

water lily An annual or perennial freshwater plant of the family *Nymphaeaceae* (75 species), native to temperate and tropical regions. Water lilies have round wax-coated leaves floating on the water surface and borne on long stalks arising from creeping stems buried in the mud below. The large flowers are cup-shaped, usually white, yellow, pink, red, blue, or purple in colour. *See also* LOTUS.

Waterloo, Battle of (18 June 1815) The battle in which Napoleon was finally defeated by British, Dutch, Belgian, and German forces commanded by Wellington and the Prussians under von Blücher. Napoleon caught Wellington 5 km (3 mi) S of the village of Waterloo (Belgium) in isolation from the Prussians and attempted to smash his army by a direct offensive. However, British lines held until the Prussians arrived, when a concerted charge brought victory.

watermark A distinctive mark produced in *paper during manufacture by making it slightly thinner in some places than in others. In handmade paper, the watermark is formed by the wires in the bottom of the mould. In machine-made paper the mark is put in by a roller.

watermelon The fruit of an annual climbing plant, *Citrullus vulgaris*, native to Africa but widely cultivated. The plant produces large oval fruits, up to 25 cm across, with a shiny dark-green rind and red, yellow, or white flesh, which is juicy and sweet-flavoured. Family: *Cucurbitaceae*. *See also* MELON.

water polo A ball game played seven-a-side (with four substitutes), usually in a swimming pool. It originated in England in the 1870s, with players riding floating barrels to resemble horses and hitting the ball with paddles; in the modern game players swim.

water rat A large aquatic *rodent belonging to the subfamily *Hydromyinae* (13 species) found in Australia, New Guinea, and the Philippines. The Australian water rat (*Hydromys chrysogaster*) is about 35 cm long and has otter-like fur and a white-tipped tail. Family: *Muridae*. Water voles and *muskrats are also known as water rats.

water skiing Planing on water on wooden skis while being towed by a motorboat. Speeds of at least 25 km per hour (15 mph) are required. Competitive water skiing includes jumping, slalom, and trick riding.

water spider A European freshwater *spider, *Argyronecta aquatica*, that lives under water in a bell-shaped structure constructed from silk and plant material and filled with bubbles of air. It feeds inside on small animals. The male (15 mm long) is—usually—larger than the female (10 mm long).

waterspout A funnel-shaped cloud extending from the base of a cumulonimbus cloud to the surface of the sea. It is a small-scale intense low-pressure system, characterized by intense rotating winds.

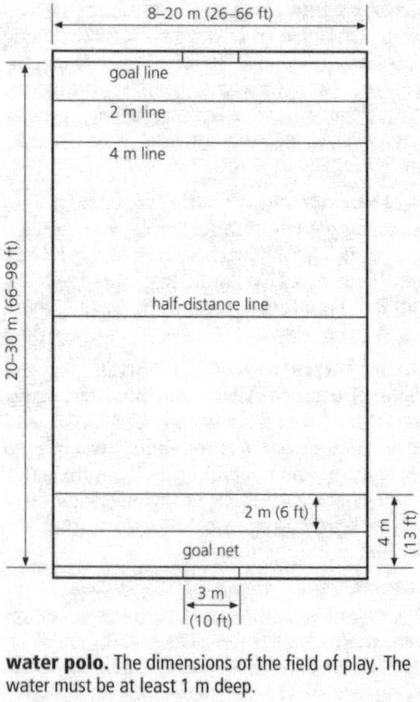

water polo. The dimensions of the field of play. The water must be at least 1 m deep.

water table The upper level of the water that has percolated into the ground and become trapped in permeable rocks. The level varies with topography and rainfall. *See also* ARTESIAN WELL.

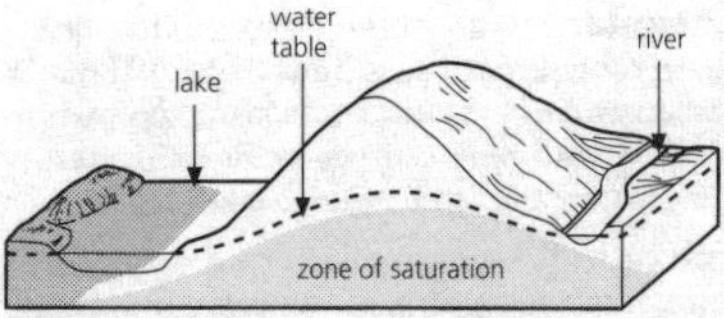

water table

water vole A large *vole, *Arvicola terristris*, of Europe and Asia. 15–20 cm long, they are heavily built with light-brown to black fur. Water voles burrow into river banks and feed on aquatic vegetation.

water wheel *See* TURBINE.

Watford 51 40N 0 25W A town in SE England, in Hertfordshire. Industries include light engineering, computer software, and financial services. It is also a dormitory town for London. Population (1998 est): 80 000.

Watling Street The Roman road that traversed Britain from London to Wroxeter, with a branch to the legionary fortress at Chester.

Watson, James Dewey (1928–) US geneticist, who (with Francis *Crick) proposed a model for the molecular structure of *DNA (1953). Watson later investigated aspects of the *genetic code. He received a Nobel Prize (1962) with Crick and Maurice *Wilkins.

Watson, John Broadus (1878–1958) US psychologist and founder of the US school of *behaviourism. Watson declared that speculations about animal behaviour should be based entirely on observations made under laboratory conditions. In *Psychology from the Standpoint of the Behaviourist* (1919), Watson applied his principles to human behaviour.

Watson-Watt, Sir Robert Alexander (1892–1973) Scottish physicist, who pioneered the development of *radar. In 1935 the British Government put him in charge of a research team, which enabled radar to be used by the Allies in World War II ahead of the Axis powers.

watt (W) The SI unit of power equal to one joule per second. In electrical terms it is the energy per second expended by a current of one ampere flowing between points on a conductor between which there is a potential difference of one volt. Named after James *Watt.

Watt, James (1736–1819) British engineer, whose development of the steam engine contributed to the *industrial revolution. He realized that the Newcomen engine could be made more efficient if the steam was condensed in a separate chamber. Watt's steam engine, completed in 1769, soon replaced the Newcomen engine. By 1800 some 500 stationary Watt engines were in use. He later invented the centrifugal governor and devised the unit "horsepower."

Watteau, (Jean) Antoine (1684–1721) French rococo painter. Despite his early death from tuberculosis, he achieved fame with his charming *fêtes galantes* (scenes of gallantry) and paintings of comedians, notably *L'Embarquement pour l'île de Cythère* and the portrait of the clown *Gilles* (both Louvre).

wattle Any of various Australian trees and shrubs, especially those of the genus *Acacia*, used for fencing, turnery, etc. The commonest are the black wattle (*A. binervata*), the golden or green wattle (*A. pycnantha*), and the silver wattle (*A. dealbata*), which has globular yellow flower heads and is used by florists under the name of mimosa.

wattmeter An instrument for measuring electrical power. The most common type has two conducting coils connected in series, one fixed and one movable. The magnetic forces between them produce a deflection of the movable coil proportional to the square of the current, which is in turn proportional to the power.

Waugh, Evelyn (Arthur St John) (1903–66) British novelist. With *Decline and Fall* (1928), *Vile Bodies* (1930), *A Handful of Dust* (1934), and other novels, he established his reputation as a brilliant social satirist. After his conversion to Roman Catholicism in 1930, religious themes played an increasing part in his novels, especially in *Brideshead Revisited* (1945). Later novels include his *Sword of Honour* trilogy about World War II (1952–61).

wave Any periodic change in a property of a system that is propagated through a medium (or through space). Waves are classified according to the curve produced when their magnitude is plotted against time on a graph. If the wave is shaped like a sine curve, it is known as a sine (*or* sinusoidal) wave. Examples include electromagnetic waves and sound waves. A wave is characterized by amplitude, the maximum displacement of the wave; *wavelength; and *frequency. The wave may propagate energy, in which case it is known as a travelling wave, or it may not, when it is known as a standing or stationary wave. **Wavelength** is the distance between successive peaks (or troughs) of a wave. It is equal to the velocity of the wave divided by its frequency.

Wavell, Archibald Percival, 1st Earl (1883–1950) British field marshal. In World War II, as commander in chief in the Middle East, he defeated the Italians in N and East Africa. After the failure of his offensive against *Rommel in June 1941, he was transferred to SE Asia, where he was again replaced after failing to halt the Japanese advance. He was viceroy of India from 1943 to 1947.

wave mechanics A branch of *quantum theory in which elementary particles are treated as *de Broglie waves. Systems of particles are described by a wave equation, known as the *Schrödinger equation. The solutions of this equation give the allowed values of the energy of each particle (eigenvalues) and the associated wave functions (eigenfunctions); the wave functions provide a measure of the probability that each particle will appear at different points in space. The theory, first proposed by de Broglie, was developed by Erwin Schrödinger.

wave power The use of the energy of wave motion in the sea to generate electricity. Generators of various types have been developed, the best known being the "nodding-duck" type, a string of floats that bob up and down in the waves, thus turning a generator. It is estimated that there are between 50 and 100 kilowatts of power per metre in the waves off the coast of Britain, a total of 120 gigawatts over all the suitable sites. The main disadvantages of wave power are that it is variable and unpredictable; that, since it is sited off the coast, it may be obstructive to shipping; and that the design and construction of generators to work at sea present a formidable engineering problem. Nevertheless, research into wave power has been intensified in the UK as a result of the renewables obligation (*see* ALTERNATIVE ENERGY).

wax A smooth substance of low melting point (40–80°C) obtained from plants (e.g. carnauba wax) or animals (e.g. *beeswax, *lanolin) or made synthetically. They consist of esters of higher fatty acids than are found in fats, usually with monohydric alcohols. Mineral waxes include paraffin wax, which is obtained from the distillation of petroleum. Waxes are used in making polishes, candles, mouldings, etc., and in modelling.

W

waxbill A bird of the *weaverfinch family having a stout waxy-red conical bill. Most waxbills inhabit open grassy regions of Africa. They are 7.5 to 15 cm long and typically grey or brown with red, yellow, or brown markings and fine barring on the wings.

waxplant An evergreen climbing plant, *Hoya carnosa*, native to China and Australia. It produces clusters of large fragrant waxy white flowers with pink centres and is cultivated as an ornamental. Family: *Asclepiadaceae*.

waxwing A broad-billed fruit-eating songbird, *Bombycilla garrulus*, occurring in N coniferous forests and birch woods. It has a soft plumage, liver-coloured above with a reddish crest, a yellow-banded tail, and a black throat and eyestripe. The red tips of the flight feathers resemble sealing wax. Family: *Bombycillidae* (9 species).

Wayland (*or* **Weland**) In Teutonic mythology, a skilled smith with supernatural powers. He was captured and lamed by King Nidudr who kept him on an island, where he was forced to practise his metalworking. Wayland murdered the king's sons and made ornaments of their skulls before escaping by magic. In England an ancient site near White Horse Hill on the Berkshire Downs is known as Wayland's Smithy.

Wayne, John (Marion Michael Morrison; 1907–79) US film actor. Following his success in *Stagecoach* (1939) he played the tough hero of numerous classic westerns including *Red River* (1948), *The Searchers* (1956), *True Grit* (1969), and *The Shootist* (1976).

weak interaction One of the four fundamental interactions between elementary particles (*see* PARTICLE PHYSICS). The weak interaction is about 10^{10} times weaker than the electromagnetic interaction. It is believed to be generated by the exchange of *virtual particles known as intermediate vector bosons.

weasel A small carnivorous mammal, *Mustela nivalis*, of Europe, Asia, N Africa, and New Zealand. Growing to about 25 cm long, it is long-bodied and short-legged, bright red-brown above with white underparts. Weasels feed on rats, mice, and voles. They swim well but do not climb. Family: *Mustelidae*.

weaverbird A small songbird belonging to a mainly tropical Old World family (*Ploceidae*; 132 species). Most species build elaborate domed nests. The communal nest of the sociable weaver (*Philetairus socius*) houses 20–30 pairs of birds. Weavers are seed eaters with stout conical bills and variously coloured plumage. *See also* SPARROW; QUELEA.

weaverfinch A small finchlike seed-eating songbird belonging to a family (*Estrildidae*; 108 species) occurring in tropical regions of Africa, SE Asia, and Australasia. Weaverfinches have large conical bills and are usually brightly coloured. *See* GRASSFINCH; WAXBILL; ZEBRA FINCH.

weaving The process of interlacing two or more yarns at right angles to produce a fabric. The equipment used is called a loom, which is first set up with a series of longitudinal threads (warp). In plain weave, alternate warp threads are raised and lowered by means of wires or cords (heddles) to allow the crosswire threads (weft), wound onto a bobbin (shuttle), to pass between them. Different kinds of weave, such as twill and herringbone, are made by altering the pattern of interlacing. Power looms were invented by Edmund *Cartwright in 1786.

Webb, Sidney (James), Baron Passfield (1859–1947) British economist and socialist. He helped to organize the *Fabian Society in 1884 and was one of the founders of the London School of Economics (1895). He initiated educational reforms as a member of the London County Council (1892–1910) and later held various government posts. His wife **Beatrice (Potter) Webb** (1858–1943), collaborated with him on a number of books, including *The History of Trade Unionism* (1894) and *Industrial Democracy* (1897).

weber (Wb) The SI unit of magnetic flux equal to the flux linking a circuit of one turn that produces an electromotive force of one volt when reduced uniformly to zero in one second. Named after Wilhelm Weber (1804–91).

Weber, Carl Maria von (1786–1826) German composer. His most successful opera, *Der Freischütz* (1821), based on a German fairy story, was the first opera in the German Romantic tradition.

Weber, Max (1864–1920) German sociologist, one of the founders of modern sociology. His major works include *The Protestant Ethic and the Spirit of Capitalism* (1904–05) and *Economy and Society* (1922).

Webern, Anton von (1883–1945) Austrian composer, a pupil of *Schoenberg. His compositions, which employ the technique of *serialism, include a concerto for nine instruments (1934) and a string quartet (1938). He was killed by a US soldier during the occupation of Vienna.

Webster, John (c. 1580–c. 1625) English dramatist, whose major plays are *The White Devil* (1612) and *The Duchess of Malfi* (c. 1613). Despite their violence and morbidity, the plays are distinguished by their poetic intensity and psychological insight.

Weddell Sea A large inlet of the S Atlantic Ocean in Antarctica, between the Antarctic Peninsula and Coats Land. It is named after the British explorer James Weddell (1787–1834).

Wedgwood, Josiah (1730–95) British potter, industrialist, and writer. Trained under his brother Thomas, he opened his own factory at Burslem, Staffordshire. In 1769 he opened a new factory (Etruria), where he also built a village for his workmen, displaying his interest in social welfare. Employing such leading artists as John Flaxman (1755–1826), Wedgwood popularized the neoclassical taste in pottery. His high-quality ceramics perfected creamware and developed basalt and jasperware; they also brought transfer printing to Staffordshire.

weevil A beetle, also called a snout beetle, belonging to the largest family (*Curculionidae*; about 60 000 species) in the animal kingdom. Most weevils are small (less than 6 mm) and their mouthparts are at the tip of a beaklike rostrum, which can sometimes exceed the body length. Many species are serious pests.

weight *See* MASS AND WEIGHT.

weight lifting A sport in which men and women compete to lift weighted barbells. In the most common form of competition contestants make three attempts in each of two styles, the snatch and the clean and jerk.

Weil, Simone (1909–43) French philosopher. An active socialist in the 1930s, she served in a nonmilitary capacity in the Spanish Civil War. After a mystical experience she became a convinced Roman Catholic, although she refused baptism. During World War II she worked for the Free French Resistance in London. Her writings on spiritual and social themes include *Waiting for God* (1951) and *The Need for Roots* (1952).

Weill, Kurt (1900–50) German composer. His collaboration with Bertolt *Brecht began with the opera *The Rise and Fall of the City of Mahagonny* (1927), a satirical portrayal of American life. Their most famous work was *The Threepenny Opera* (1928), a modern version of John Gay's *The Beggar's Opera*.

Weimar 50 59N 11 15E A city in central Germany, on the River Ilm. It was the capital of the grand duchy of Saxe-Weimar-Eisenach (1815–1918). In 1919 the German National Assembly met in the city and drew up the constitution of the new *Weimar Republic. Population (1991): 59 100.

Weimaraner (*or* **Weimeraner**) A breed of dog developed in Weimar, Germany, for hunting and retrieving game. It has drooping ears and a short slender tail; the short sleek coat is silver-grey or mouse-grey. Height: 61–69 cm (dogs); 56–64 cm (bitches).

Weimar Republic The government of Germany from 1919 to 1933. Named after the town in which the new German constitution was formulated, the Republic faced political and economic crises and was finally overthrown by Hitler.

Weismann, August Friedrich Leopold (1834–1914) German biologist, who (in 1883) proposed that heredity was based upon the transfer, from generation to generation, of a substance—germ plasm—with a definite molecular constitution. Weismann is regarded as one of the founders of modern genetics.

Weizmann, Chaim (Azriel) (1874–1952) Israeli statesman; the first president of Israel (1949–52). A leader of the British Zionist movement, his discovery (1916) of a process for the production of acetone, which contributed to the British war effort, facilitated the negotiations that led to the *Balfour Declaration (1917). As president (1920–31, 1935–46) of the World Zionist Movement he played an important part in the establishment of Israel in 1948.

Weldon, Fay (Franklin Birkinshaw; 1931–) British writer. Her novels include *The Fat Woman's Joke* (1967), *Praxis* (1978), *The Life and Loves of a She-Devil* (1983), and *Big Women* (1998). She has also written plays, including many for radio and television.

Welles, (George) Orson (1915–85) US film actor and director. After establishing his reputation in the theatre and on radio he went to Hollywood in 1940. His first film, *Citizen Kane* (1941), became one of the most famous of all time. His other films include *The Magnificent Ambersons* (1942), *A Touch of Evil* (1958), and *Chimes at Midnight* (1966). As a film actor he is best remembered for *The Third Man* (1949).

Wellington 41 17S 174 47E The capital of New Zealand, a port in S North Island. It became the seat of central government in 1865 and is now the commercial and communications centre of New Zealand. Population (1999 est): 166 700.

W

Wellington, Arthur Wellesley, 1st Duke of (1769–1852) British general and statesman, known as the Iron Duke; prime minister (1828–30). Born in Dublin, he went to India in 1799, where he held command against Tipu Sahib (1749–99) and became governor of Mysore. In the Napoleonic Wars he was responsible for victory (1814) in the *Peninsular War and commanded at Waterloo (1815), where he and Marshal Blücher (1742–1819) finally defeated Napoleon. He served in Lord Liverpool's Tory government and represented Britain at the Congresses of Aix-la-Chapelle (1818) and Verona (1822). As prime minister he introduced *Catholic emancipation but opposed parliamentary reform, leading to his resignation. He subsequently served as foreign secretary (1834–35) and was commander in chief of the British army (1827–28, 1842–52).

Wellingtonia *See* SEQUOIA.

Wells, Henry (1805–78) US businessman, who with **William Fargo** (1818–81) and others founded Wells, Fargo and Company (1852). An express business, it carried mail to and from the newly developed West. It also controlled banks and later ran a stagecoach service.

Wells, H(erbert) G(eorge) (1866–1946) British novelist. He found success with *The Time Machine* (1895) and other science-fiction novels and with a series of comic social novels, including *Kipps* (1905) and *The History of Mr Polly* (1910). A member of the Fabian Society, he engaged in frequent controversy with G. B. Shaw. His nonfiction works include *The Outline of History* (1920) and *The Shape of Things to Come* (1933).

wels A large nocturnal predatory *catfish, *Silurus glanis*, also called waller, found in fresh waters of Europe and W Asia. Up to 4.5 m long, it has three pairs of barbels, a long anal fin, and is usually mottled olive-green to blue-black with a paler belly.

Welsh A Celtic language of the Brythonic group. Some 19% of the Welsh population (about 600 000 people) speak Welsh as their first or favoured language; it is taught as a compulsory part of the National Curriculum in Welsh schools and is the general teaching language in some schools. For convenience Welsh speakers usually use English words and phrases for modern concepts. Road signs and other public notices throughout Wales are provided in both English and Welsh.

Welsh pony One of two breeds of pony originating in Wales. The Welsh Mountain pony, used for riding and draught work, has a compact muscular body with short strong legs and a profuse mane and tail. The larger Welsh riding pony is a popular children's mount. Both may be any solid colour. Height: Mountain pony: up to 1.22 m (12 hands); riding pony: up to 1.37 m (13½ hands).

Welsh poppy A perennial herbaceous plant, *Mecanopsis cambrica*, up to 38 cm tall and found in damp regions of W Europe. It bears solitary yellow flowers, up to 7.5 cm across.

welwitschia An unusual *gymnosperm plant, *Welwitschia mirabilis*, confined to the deserts of SW Africa. The very short stem bears two strap-shaped waxy leaves, up to 1 m long. The small conelike flowers produce winged seeds. Individual plants may live for more than a hundred years. Phylum: *Gnetophyta*.

Welwyn Garden City 51 48N 0 13W A town in SE England, in Hertfordshire. Founded in 1919 by Sir Ebenezer *Howard, it became a new town in 1948. Population (1991): 41 710.

Wenceslas, St (d. 929 AD) Duke of Bohemia (?924–29), famous for his piety. Wenceslas' unpopular submission to the German king Henry the Fowler gave rise to a conspiracy of nobles, who incited Wenceslas' brother to assassinate him. He became Bohemia's patron saint.

wentletrap A *gastropod mollusc of the worldwide family *Epitoniidae* (about 200 species). 2–10 cm long, wentletraps have shells with long spires; that of the precious wentletrap (*Epitonium scalare*) is prized by collectors. They can produce a purple substance used as a dye.

wergild The sum payable as compensation in Anglo-Saxon England to the family of a slain man by his assassin or the latter's kin. The amount was regulated according to the status and nationality of the victim.

Weser, River A river in NW Germany. It flows NW from Münden, through Bremen, to the North Sea. Length: 477 km (296 mi).

Wesker, Arnold (1932–) British dramatist best known for the trilogy of plays *Chicken Soup with Barley* (1958), *Roots* (1959), and *I'm Talking about Jerusalem* (1960). Later plays include *Chips with Everything* (1962), *The Merchant* (1976), and *Break My Heart* (1997).

Wesley, John (1703–91) British religious leader, founder of *Methodism. As a student, Wesley was one of a group nicknamed "Methodists," who sought to live disciplined religious lives. His brother **Charles Wesley** (1707–88) was also a member. The brothers, both ordained, sailed to Georgia as missionaries in 1735, but returned disillusioned in 1738. In the same year both experienced a spiritual awakening while attending meetings of the Moravians, as a result of which they toured the country preaching a message of repentance, faith, and love. They did not intend to form a new denomination, the Wesleyan Methodist Church being organized only after their death. John travelled the country on horseback preaching thousands of sermons. Charles was the author of many well-known hymns.

Wessex The kingdom of the West *Saxons, under which Anglo-Saxon England was united in the 9th century. Egbert, King of Wessex (802–39), destroyed Mercian ascendancy in 825 and made possible the subsequent union of England under Alfred the Great.

West, Mae (1892–1980) US actress. She became an international sex symbol during the 1930s. Her films, many of which she wrote, include *She Done Him Wrong* (1933) and *My Little Chickadee* (1939).

West Atlantic languages A subgroup of the Niger-Congo family, spoken in Guinea and Senegal. It includes the languages Wolof and *Fulani.

West Bank A territory in the Middle East, on the W bank of the River Jordan. It comprises the hills of Judaea and Samaria. Formerly part of *Palestine, it was left in Arab hands after partition (1948), became part of Jordan following the ceasefire of 1949, and was occupied by Israeli forces in 1967. Israel has since been under pressure to withdraw and allow an autonomous Palestinian state to be set up, especially following the Camp David agreement (1978). In 1988 Jordan relinquished claims to the area and the PLO declared a Palestinian state, unrecognized by Israel. In 1993 Israel agreed to withdraw its troops from certain areas as part of a peace settlement with the PLO. The Palestinian National Authority assumed control of the Jericho area in 1994–95 but Israel postponed further withdrawals on security grounds. Mounting frustration on the West Bank erupted into open violence in 2000; this escalated sharply during 2001–02, provoking Israel to reoccupy large parts of the territory. Area: about 6000 sq km (2320 sq mi). Population (2000 est): 1 949 000.

West Berkshire A unitary authority of S England, in Berkshire. Area: 705 sq km (272 sq mi). Population (2001): 144 445.

West Bromwich 52 31N 1 59W An industrial town in central England, in Sandwell unitary authority, West Midlands. Population (1992 est): 154 531.

West Dunbartonshire A council area of W

central Scotland on the Clyde estuary, part of the historic county of Dunbarton. Absorbed into Strathclyde Region in 1975, it became a unitary authority in 1996. The main economic activities are engineering, whisky distilling, and agriculture; there is marine engineering in Clydebank. Area: 162 sq km (63 sq mi). Population (2001): 93 378.

Western Australia The largest state of Australia, bordering on the Indian Ocean, Timor Sea, and Great Australian Bight. It is mainly an arid undulating plateau with the Great Sandy Desert, the Gibson Desert, and the Great Victoria Desert in the interior. In the SW is the Darling Range; the Kimberleys are in the N. Agricultural activities include dairy farming, lumbering, and the cultivation of citrus fruits, wheat, and vines in the extreme SW. Mineral resources include bauxite, nickel, oil, gold, and huge deposits of ferrous minerals. Industry is located chiefly around Perth. Area: 2 527 621 sq km (975 920 sq mi). Population (1999 est): 1 755 000. Capital: Perth.

Western European Union An organization formed in 1955 by the UK, Belgium, France, Italy, Luxembourg, the Netherlands, and West Germany to coordinate defence policy and to cooperate in political and other spheres. Portugal and Spain joined in 1988 and Greece joined in 1995. In 1991 the WEU was designated as the future defence component of the European Union. All the other EU states now have some form of associate membership, as do Bulgaria, Iceland, Norway, Romania, and Turkey.

Western Isles Islands Area (official Gaelic name: Eileen Siar) An administrative area of NW Scotland consisting of the Outer Hebrides (*see* HEBRIDES, THE). Area: 2901 sq km (1120 sq mi). Population (2001): 26 502. Administrative centre: Stornoway.

Western Sahara (name until 1975: Spanish Sahara) A territory in NW Africa, bordering on the Atlantic Ocean, Mauritania, and Morocco. It consists chiefly of desert. *History*: in 1884 Spain claimed a protectorate over the area and in 1958 it became a province of Spain as Spanish Sahara. In 1976 this was partitioned between Mauritania and Morocco; Morocco occupied the whole area when Mauritania withdrew in 1979. The Polisario Front, a guerrilla organization seeking to establish an independent Saharan Arab Democratic Republic, violently opposes the Moroccan occupation, with backing from Algeria. A UN peacekeeping force has been in occupation since 1991 but attempts to settle the status of the region have not succeeded. Area: 266 000 sq km (102 680 sq mi). Population (1993 est): 214 000.

Western Wall (*or* **Wailing Wall**) *See* TEMPLE OF JERUSALEM.

West Indies An archipelago extending for over 2400 km (1500 mi) from Florida to Venezuela enclosing the Caribbean Sea. It is subdivided into the *Greater Antilles, the *Lesser Antilles, and the *Bahamas. The islands are chiefly volcanic but some are composed of coral. Hurricanes occur frequently. The people are of mixed origin but the descendants of African slaves form the largest group. The original Arawak and Carib Indians have virtually disappeared. *Economy*: sugar-cane cultivation has been important since the beginning of colonization. Many islands also grow tobacco, bananas, spices, or coffee. Mineral deposits are scarce. *History*: Columbus discovered the archipelago in 1492 and named it in the belief that he had found the west route to India. The Spanish (the first Europeans to settle) introduced sugar cultivation and imported African slaves to work the plantations. The slave trade was maintained until the 19th century. Britain created the Federation of the West Indies in 1958 but this collapsed in 1962. Jamaica and Trinidad and Tobago then became independent nations within the Commonwealth, as did Barbados in 1966. The status of British associated state was adopted by Antigua, Dominica, Grenada, St Kitts-Nevis-Anguilla, and St Lucia in 1967 and St Vincent in 1969. Grenada became independent in 1974, Dominica in 1978, St Lucia and St Vincent in 1979, Antigua (and Barbuda) in 1981, and St Kitts-Nevis in 1983. Area: over 235 000 sq km (91 000 sq mi).

West Lothian A council area of SE Scotland, on the Firth of Forth. In 1975 the historic county of West Lothian was abolished; its boundaries were adjusted to form a district of the same name, in Lothian Region. In 1996 this district became an independent unitary authority. Oil refining is an important industry. Area: 425 sq km (164 sq mi). Population (2001): 158 714. Administrative centre: Livingstone.

Westmeath (Irish name: Contae Na Hiarmhidhe) A county in the central Republic of Ireland, in Leinster. It is predominantly low lying with areas of bog; much of the land is under pasture. Area: 1764 sq km (681 sq mi). Population (2002): 63 000. County town: Mullingar.

West Midlands A metropolitan county in the West Midlands of England, created in 1974 from parts of Staffordshire, Warwickshire, and Worcestershire. In 1986 the county council was abolished and administrative power devolved to the districts of Wolverhampton, Walsall, Dudley, Sandwell, Birmingham, Solihull, and Coventry. Area: 899 sq km (347 sq mi).

Westminster, City of A borough of central Greater London, on the N bank of the River Thames. The heart of London's West End, it contains many famous theatres, restaurants, and shops. Historic buildings include *Buckingham Palace, the Palace of Westminster, and *Westminster Abbey. It also contains St James's Park, Green Park, Hyde Park, and Regent's Park.

Westminster, Statutes of **1.** (1275, 1285, 1290) Legislation initiated by Edward I of England. The first Statute dealt principally with criminal law and procedures for the improvement of royal justice while the second dealt with rights of inheritance. The Statute of 1290 prohibited subinfeudation of land (i.e. the granting of portions of a knight's estate), which had occasioned considerable loss of feudal dues. **2.** (1931) The Statute that established the *Commonwealth of Nations.

Westminster Abbey A historic abbey church at Westminster, London. The present building, begun (1245) by Henry III, replaces one dedicated (1065) by Edward the Confessor, whose shrine the abbey still houses. Since William I, every English monarch (except Edward V and Edward VIII) has been crowned in Westminster Abbey and many are buried there in magnificent tombs. The Coronation Chair was first used in 1307. Other features include Poets' Corner, where Chaucer, Spenser, Dryden, Tennyson, Dickens, and many others are buried or have memorials.

Westphalia A region of NW Germany, approximating to present-day Nordrhein-Westfalen. By the 12th century Westphalia comprised many small principalities and in the 18th century it came largely under Prussian control. In 1807–13 Prussian Westphalian territories became the kingdom of Westphalia. The Congress of Vienna (1815) restored most of Westphalia to Prussia.

Westphalia, Peace of (1648) The agreements, negotiated in Osnabrück and Münster (Westphalia), that ended the *Thirty Years' War. The peace marked the end of the supremacy in Europe of the Holy Roman Empire. It recognized the sovereignity of the German states, the Swiss Confederation, and the Netherlands, and granted W Pomerania to Sweden. Lutherans, Calvinists, and Roman Catholics were given equal rights.

West Point 41 23N 73 58W A military reservation in the USA, in New York state. It is the site of the United States Military Academy (1802).

West Sussex A county of S England, formerly part of Sussex, bordering on the English Channel. It is mainly low lying, rising in the S to the South Downs. It is predominantly agricultural. Tourism is important in the coastal resorts. Area: 1989 sq km (768 sq mi). Population (2001): 753 612. Administrative centre: Chichester.

West Virginia A state in the E central USA. It consists of a ridge and valley region (the Great Appalachian Valley) in the E and the Appalachian Plateau. Although predominantly a rural state, manufacturing and mining (especially of coal) are important. *History*: originally part of Virginia, it joined the Union as a separate State in 1863. Area: 62 628 sq km (24 181 sq mi). Population (2000 est): 1 808 344. Capital: Charleston.

Westwood, Vivienne (1941–) British fashion designer. With Malcolm McLaren (1941–) she pioneered the punk look of the late 1970s. Her highly original designs won her the Designer of the Year award in both 1990 and 1991.

West Yorkshire A metropolitan county of NE England, created in 1974 from the W part of the West Riding of Yorkshire. In 1986 the county council was abolished and administrative power devolved to the districts of Bradford, Leeds, Calderdale, Kirklees, and Wakefield. West Yorkshire remains the centre of the English wool textile industry. Area: 2039 sq km (787 sq mi).

wet rot The decay that affects timber with a relatively high moisture content, caused by the cellar fungus (*Coniophora cerebella*) and characterized by the formation of a dark surface mass. Treatment is by drying affected timbers. *Compare* DRY ROT.

Wexford (Irish name: Contae Loch Garman) A county in the SE Republic of Ireland, in Leinster. It was the first Irish county to be colonized from England (1169). Lowlands rise to mountains in the W. Area: 2352 sq km (908 sq mi). Population (2002): 116 543. County town: Wexford.

Weyden, Rogier van der (c. 1400–64) Flemish painter of portraits and religious altarpieces. The influence of the Master of *Flémalle is evident in *The Deposition* (Prado). In 1450 he visited Italy and paintings from this period, for example the *Entombment* (Uffizi), show Italian influences.

Weymouth 50 36N 2 28W A town in S England, on the coast of Dorset. It is a resort and port. Population (1991): 46 065.

whale A large marine mammal belonging to the order *Cetacea*. Whales have no hind limbs; their forelimbs are flippers and their tails are horizontally flattened to form a pair of flukes. They breathe through a blowhole on top of the head. Whales are insulated by a thick layer of blubber under the skin. The whalebone whales (*Mysticetae*; 12 species)—including the *rorquals, *blue whale, and *right whales—are large and slow-moving and feed on krill. Toothed whales (*Odontocetae*; 80 species)—including the *dolphins, *narwhal, and *sperm whale—are smaller and more agile. They feed on fish and squid and are often gregarious. *See also* WHALING.

whaling The hunting of whales for their carcasses. Modern whaling fleets comprise a mother factory ship and a fleet of small hunter vessels equipped with harpoon guns and winches. The carcasses are a source of meat, fats, oils, and other chemicals. Whaling has depleted whale populations to the point that some species are in danger of extinction. The International Whaling Commission has called for a complete ban on commercial whaling.

Whangarei 35 43S 174 20E A city in New Zealand, in North Island. It is the site of New Zealand's only oil refinery (1964). Population (1994): 44 800.

Wharton, Edith (Newbold) (1862–1937) US novelist, who lived in Paris from 1907. Her novels, which are mainly about New York society, include *The House of Mirth* (1905), *Ethan Frome* (1911), and *The Age of Innocence* (1920).

wheat A cereal *grass belonging to the genus *Triticum*, native to W Asia but widely cultivated. With the exception of einkorn (*T. monococcum*), most commercial wheats are hybrids with the genus *Aegilops*. The stems, up to 1 m high, each bear a cylindrical head of up to a hundred flower clusters. The grain of bread wheat (*T. aestivum*) is milled to produce flour. Hard or durum wheat (*T. durum*) is used to make pasta and semolina. Surplus grain, bran, etc., is fed to livestock. Wheat is also a commercial source of alcohol, dextrose, gluten, malt, and starch.

Wheeler, Sir (Robert Eric) Mortimer (1890–1976) British archaeologist. Wheeler's skill in interpreting archaeological strata was renowned. He excavated Romano-British sites, including Maiden Castle.

whelk A *gastropod mollusc of the family *Buccinidae* (over 400 species), of warm and cold seas. 4–12 cm long, whelks feed on molluscs and worms. The common northern whelk (*Buccinum undatum*), 5 cm long, has a drab yellow-brown shell and edible flesh. Tropical species are more colourful.

Whigs Members of a British political group that became the *Liberal Party after about 1868. Originally an abusive Scottish name for a horsethief, it was later applied to one who wished to exclude the Roman Catholic Duke of York (later James II) from the succession. The Whigs dominated politics in the first half of the 18th century. Identifying with industrialist, Nonconformist, and reforming interests, they became the Liberal Party under *Gladstone.

whimbrel A *curlew, *Numenius phaeopus*, that breeds on Arctic tundra and winters in Africa, South America, and S Asia. 40 cm long, it has a streaked brown plumage and a dark crown with a pale central stripe. It feeds on insects, spiders, worms, and snails.

whinchat A migratory *chat, *Saxicola rubetra*, common on open farmland. It winters in Africa and breeds in Eurasia, feeding on flies and moths. The male has a streaked brown plumage, pale chestnut breast, white wingbars, and a white eyestripe; the female is duller.

whip In the UK, an official of a political party responsible for ensuring that the party's MPs vote according to its leadership's policies. The term also refers to the summons to vote sent by whips to MPs, a crucial summons being underlined three times (three-line whip).

whippet A breed of dog developed in England during the 19th century from terrier and greyhound stock and used for coursing and racing. It has a slender streamlined build. The fine short coat can be any mixture of colours. Height: 46 cm (dogs); 43 cm (bitches).

whip snake A slender arboreal snake belonging to the genus *Zamenis* (5 species). The common European speckled grey whip snake (*Z. gemonensis*) feeds on other snakes and lizards. The green whip snakes (genus *Dryophis*; 8 species) occur in tropical Asia and Australasia. Family: *Colubridae*.

whirligig A dark shiny *water beetle belonging to the widely distributed family

Gyrinidae (about 700 species). It spins around on the surface of still or slow-moving fresh water, feeding on insects or other small animals. If disturbed, whirligig beetles exude a foul-smelling milky liquid.

whirlwind A small revolving column of air, which whirls around a low-pressure centre produced by local heating and convectional uprising. It may pick up small pieces of debris and dust and in desert areas may cause sandstorms.

whisky A spirit distilled from malted barley or other grain. The word comes from the Gaelic *uisgebeatha*, water of life. The milled grain is mixed with water to form a mash, which must be converted to sugar before fermentation; the resulting alcoholic liquid is distilled and then aged in the cask for at least three years.

Whistler, James (Abbott) McNeill (1834–1903) US painter. He specialized in portraits and landscapes dominated by one or two colours, the best known being *The Artist's Mother* (Louvre) and *Nocturne in Blue and Gold* (Tate Gallery). In 1877 *Ruskin described one of Whistler's works as "flinging a pot of paint in the public's face" and was sued for libel (1878). Whistler was also famous as a wit.

Whitbread Book of the Year Award An annual literary award of £23,000. Announced in 1985, it is open to both fiction and non-fiction, but the author must live in the UK or Ireland. The prize is administered by the Booksellers Association of Great Britain. Winners include Seamus Heaney for *The Spirit Level* in 1996 and *Beowulf* in 1999, Ted Hughes for *Tales from Ovid* in 1997 and *Birthday Letters* in 1998, Philip Pullman for *The Amber Spyglass* in 2001, and Mark Haddon for *The Curious Incident of the Dog in the Night-Time* (2003).

Whitby, Synod of (663 AD) A council convened at Whitby, Yorkshire, by King Oswy of Northumbria to decide whether to adopt Roman or Celtic Church usages in Britain. The Roman view triumphed and the English Church was brought into line with the Continent.

White, Patrick (1912–90) Australian novelist. He explored the national consciousness in his epic novels *The Tree of Man* (1955) and *Voss* (1957). His other works include *A Fringe of Leaves* (1976) and *Netherwood* (1983). He won the Nobel Prize in 1973.

whitebeam A tree, *Sorbus aria*, up to 15 m tall and found mainly in S and central Europe. Swedish whitebeam (*S.* × *intermedia*), a hybrid between whitebeam and *mountain ash, is often planted in parks. Family: *Rosaceae*.

white dwarf A very small faint low-mass star (less than 1.44 solar masses) that has undergone *gravitational collapse following exhaustion of its nuclear fuel. Electrons are stripped from the constituent atoms, and it is the pressure exerted by these densely packed electrons that eventually halts the star's contraction. The density is then 10^7–10^{11} kg m^{-3}.

whitefish A slender fish, belonging to a genus (*Coregonus*) related to trout, that occurs mainly in deep northern lakes and rivers of Europe, Asia, and North America. It has a small mouth, minute teeth, and a covering of large silvery scales. Whitefish feed on insects and other small animals.

white fly A small winged insect of the mainly tropical family *Aleyrodidae*. 2–3 mm long, it is covered with a mealy white powder and resembles a minute moth. White flies suck plant juices and exude honeydew on which a black mould grows, often damaging crops. Suborder: *Homoptera*; order: *Hemiptera*.

Whitehall A street in Westminster, London, where many government offices are located; the name is often applied to the civil service. The Cenotaph is also in Whitehall.

Whitehead, A(lfred) N(orth) (1861–1947) British philosopher and mathematician. Whitehead's first major work, the *Principia Mathematica* (1910–13), was written with Bertrand *Russell. In *Principles of Natural Knowledge* (1919) and *The Concept of Nature* (1920), he explored the relationships between concepts and sense perception.

White Horse, Vale of the A valley in S England, in Oxfordshire. Its name derives from the Uffington White Horse, the figure of a horse 110 m (361 ft) long cut in the chalk of the Berkshire Downs.

White House The official residence of the president of the USA. In Washington, DC, the building was burnt (1814) by the British during the *War of 1812 but was subsequently restored, being painted white to hide the smoke stains.

Whitelaw, William (Stephen Ian), 1st Viscount (1918–99) British Conservative politician. He was deputy leader of the Conservative Party (1975–88), home secretary (1979–83), and leader of the House of Lords (1983–88) under Margaret Thatcher.

White Russians The Russians who fought

against the Soviet Red Army in the civil war (1917–21) that followed the *Russian Revolution. The name derives from that of the royalist opponents to the French Revolution, called Whites because they adopted the white flag of the French Bourbon dynasty.

White Sea (Russian name: Beloye More) A gulf of the Arctic Ocean in NW Russia. It gives access to Archangel and Kandalaksha.

white shark A dangerous man-eating *mackerel shark, *Carcharodon carcharias*, that occurs in tropical and temperate seas. Its heavy body, up to 11 m long, is grey-brown to slate-blue with light-grey undersides.

whitethroat An Old World *warbler, *Sylvia communis*, that breeds in N Eurasia and winters in central Africa. It is about 14 cm long. The male is russet brown with a greyish head and white throat and performs a tumbling courtship display in flight. The female is a duller brown.

white whale A small Arctic toothed *whale, *Delphinapterus leucas*, also called beluga. Young white whales are blue-grey, but change to white as they mature. About 4.5 m long with a rounded head, they feed mainly on fish. Family: *Monodontidae*.

whiting A marine food and game fish belonging to the genus *Gadus* (or *Merlangius*), especially *M. merlangus* found in shallow European waters. It has a slender body, up to 70 cm long, which is olive, sandy, or bluish above and silvery white below, and three dorsal and two anal fins.

Whitlam, (Edward) Gough (1916–) Australian statesman; Labor prime minister (1972–75). He ended conscription, relaxed rules on immigration, and tried to lessen US influence. In 1975 he was dismissed by the governor, Sir John Kerr (1914–91).

Whitman, Walt (1819–92) US poet. He expressed his democratic idealism in the revolutionary free-verse poems of *Leaves of Grass* (1855), revised and enlarged in nine editions during his lifetime. During the Civil War he nursed wounded soliders. His later works include the prose *Democratic Vistas* (1871).

Whit Sunday (*or* **Pentecost**) The seventh Sunday after Easter, a Christian festival commemorating the descent of the Holy Spirit on the Apostles on the 50th day after Easter (Acts 2.1). Whit Sunday became a time for baptisms, hence its name ("White" Sunday), referring to the white baptismal robes.

Whittington, Dick (Richard W.; d. 1423) English merchant, who was three times Lord Mayor of London (1397–98, 1406–07, 1419–20). The legend of Whittington and his cat dates from the early 17th century.

Whittle, Sir Frank (1907–96) British aeronautical engineer who designed and flew the first British jet aircraft. The engine was fitted into a specially constructed Gloster E28/39; its maiden flight took place on 15 May 1941.

WHO *See* WORLD HEALTH ORGANIZATION.

whooping cough A respiratory infection of children caused by the bacterium *Bordetella pertussis*. After an incubation period of 7–14 days, the child develops a cough, a nasal discharge, and low fever, followed by paroxysms of coughing accompanied by a characteristic whooping sound. A vaccine is available but its use is controversial, since rare cases of brain damage in immunized children have been attributed to it.

whooping crane A rare bird, *Grus americana*, that breeds in NW Canada and winters in SE Texas: 150 cm tall with a wingspan of 210 cm, it has a white plumage with black-tipped wings, black legs, and a bare red face and has a loud whooping call. Family: *Gruidae* (cranes).

whydah (*or* **whidah**) A small *weaverbird belonging to the genus *Vidua* (11 species), also called widowbird and occurring in open grassy regions of Africa. The males have long tail feathers used in the courtship display and the females lay their eggs in the nests of *waxbills, which rear their young.

Wichita 37 43N 97 20W A city in the USA, in Kansas. Founded in 1864, it is the state's largest city. Population (2000): 344 284.

Wicklow (Irish name: Contae Chill Mhantáin) A county in the E Republic of Ireland, in Leinster. Fertile lowlands rise to the central Wicklow Mountains. Agriculture is the chief occupation. Area: 2025 sq km (782 sq mi). Population (2002): 114 719. County town: Wicklow.

Wiener, Norbert (1894–1964) US mathematician, who pioneered the mathematics of information and communication, which he called *cybernetics. After World War II, during which he worked on anti-aircraft guns, Wiener spent the rest of his life writing about the social problems resulting from automation.

Wiesbaden 50 05N 8 15E A spa city in SW Germany, on the River Rhine. Its hot saline springs have made it a popular resort since Roman times. Population (1999 est): 268 200.

Wiesenthal, Simon (1908–) Austrian investigator of Nazi crimes against the Jews. Since World War II, during which he was held in concentration camps, he has tracked down over 1000 war criminals, including *Eichmann. He was founder (1961) and head of the Jewish Documentation Centre in Vienna.

Wigan 1. 53 33N 2 38W A town in NW England, in Wigan unitary authority, Greater Manchester. It is an industrial and market town. Population (1991): 85 819. **2.** A unitary authority in NW England, in Greater Manchester. Area: 199 sq km (77 sq mi). Population (2001): 301 417.

wigeon A fast-flying *duck, *Anas penelope*, that breeds in N Eurasia and winters as far south as Africa and S Asia. 45 cm long, males have a chestnut head with a yellowish crown and grey back, while females are brown with a white belly and white shoulders.

Wight, Isle of (Latin name: Vectis) 50 40N 1 15W An island and county in S England, separated from the mainland by the Solent. It consists chiefly of chalk downs; the Needles, a group of chalk rocks, stand off the W coast. Tourism is important. The annual Cowes Regatta Week is famous. Area: 380 sq km (147 sq mi). Population (2001): 132 719. Administrative centre: Newport.

Wigner, Eugene Paul (1902–95) US physicist, born in Hungary, who worked out the theory of neutron absorption by nuclei and discovered that solids change their size under radiation (Wigner effect). He won a share of the 1963 Nobel Prize for his work on nuclear physics.

wigwam The dome- or tunnel-shaped hut of the North American Woods Indians, covered with bark on a light wooden frame. The conical tent of the Plains Indians, the **teepee**, has often been incorrectly called a wigwam.

Wilberforce, William (1759–1833) British philanthropist. As an MP (1780–1825) he led the parliamentary campaign to abolish the slave trade (achieved in 1807) and then to emancipate existing slaves (achieved a month after his death).

wildcat A *cat, *Felis sylvestris*, of Europe and W Asia. About 75 cm long, it has a bushy rounded tail and thick striped coat. Wildcats inhabit dense woodland and breed once a year. They may interbreed with domestic cats.

Wilde, Oscar (Fingal O'Flahertie Wills) (1854–1900) Anglo-Irish dramatist and writer. He dazzled London society with his wit and became a leading figure of the *Aesthetic movement. His works include a novel, *The Picture of Dorian Gray* (1891), and a series of brilliant social comedies: *Lady Windermere's Fan* (1892), *A Woman of No Importance* (1893), *An Ideal Husband* (1895), and *The Importance of Being Earnest* (1895). Socially and financially ruined by a trial in 1895 arising from his homosexual relationship with Lord Alfred Douglas (1870–1945), he was imprisoned for two years. In exile in France he produced his best-known poem, *The Ballad of Reading Gaol* (1898).

wildebeest *See* GNU.

Wilder, Billy (Samuel W.; 1906–2002) US film director and screenwriter, born in Austria. His films include *Double Indemnity* (1944), *Sunset Boulevard* (1950), *Some Like It Hot* (1959), *The Apartment* (1960), and *The Front Page* (1974).

Wilder, Thornton (1897–1975) US novelist and dramatist. His best-known plays are *Our Town* (1938) and *The Skin of Our Teeth* (1942); novels include *The Bridge of San Luis Rey* (1927).

Wilhelmina (1880–1962) Queen of the Netherlands (1890–1948), who encouraged Dutch resistance in World War II. She abdicated in favour of her daughter Juliana.

Wilhelmshaven 53 32N 8 07E A seaport in NW Germany, on the North Sea. It was founded in 1869 as the main Prussian (later German) naval base. Population (1991): 91 150.

Wilkes, John (1725–97) British journalist and politician. He was a member of the Hellfire Club of debauchees and founded the weekly *North Briton*, in which he attacked George III's ministers. Issue No 45 (1763) accused the government of lying in the king's speech and Wilkes was arrested for libel. Outlawed in 1764 and three times expelled from the House of Commons, he was at last permitted to take his seat in 1774.

Wilkins, Maurice Hugh Frederick (1916–) New Zealand physicist, who worked on the atom bomb during World War II. After the war, he assisted James *Watson and Francis *Crick in determining the structure of DNA. These three scientists shared the 1962 Nobel Prize.

Willemstad 12 12N 68 56W The capital and main port of the *Netherlands Antilles, on the SE coast of Curaçao. Population (1999 est): 123 000.

William (I) the Conqueror (c. 1028–1087) Duke of Normandy (1035–87) and the first Norman King of England (1066–87). He claimed to have been named by Edward the Confessor as heir to the English throne. When Harold II succeeded Edward, William invaded England, defeated and killed his rival at the battle of Hastings, and became king. His administration relied upon Norman and other foreign personnel, especially his Archbishop of Canterbury, Lanfranc (c. 1010–89). In 1085 William commissioned the *Domesday Book.

William (I) the Lion (1143–1214) King of the Scots (1165–1214). After his capture in a revolt against *Henry II of England in 1174, he became a vassal of the English throne. On Henry's death in 1189 he regained independence for his kingdom in return for a payment to Richard I.

William (I) the Silent (1533–84) The leader of the *Revolt of the Netherlands against Spanish rule. When open revolt broke out in 1568, William soon emerged as its leader and in 1576 succeeded in uniting the Roman Catholic south with the Protestant north. This union was short lived, however, and in 1579 the northern provinces declared independence with William as their first stadholder (chief magistrate). He was assassinated by a Spanish agent.

William II Rufus (c. 1056–1100) King of England (1087–1100), succeeding his father William the Conqueror. His harsh rule aroused baronial and ecclesiastical opposition, notably from Anselm. He made several attempts to recover Normandy from his elder brother Robert (d. 1134) and was killed by an arrow while hunting in the New Forest.

William III (1650–1702) King of England (1689–1702) and Stadholder (chief magistrate) of the United Provinces (1672–1702), known as William of Orange. Grandson of Charles I of England and son of William II, Prince of Orange (1626–50), he married James II of England's daughter Mary in 1677. In 1688 he was invited to invade England by James's opponents and in 1689 he was proclaimed joint sovereign with his wife, Mary II (*see* GLORIOUS REVOLUTION). William defeated the former king at the *Boyne in 1690. On the Continent he was successful in the War of the Grand Alliance (1689–97) against France.

William IV (1765–1837) King of England and Hanover (1830–37), known as the Sailor King. He served in the Royal Navy from 1778 to 1790. He had ten illegitimate children by the Irish actress Dorothea Jordan before marrying (1818) Adelaide of Saxe-Meiningen (1792–1849). William was succeeded in England by his niece Victoria.

William and Mary style An English derivative (1689–1702) of the *Louis XIV style of furniture. The cabriole leg was a typical innovation replacing the preceding twist turned legs. Rich gilding was common and some important furniture was made of cast silver. Cabinet furniture was finely veneered with marquetry or lacquered and gilded.

William of Ockham *See* OCKHAM'S RAZOR.

William of Wykeham (1324–1404) English churchman and statesman. Bishop of Winchester from 1366 and Lord Chancellor (1367–71, 1389–91), he founded New College, Oxford (1379), and Winchester College (1382).

Williams, Rowan (Douglas) (1950–) British churchman; Archbishop of Canterbury from 2002. He was previously Archbishop of Wales (2000–02).

Williams, Tennessee (1911–83) US dramatist. *The Glass Menagerie* (1945), his first major success, introduced his recurrent themes of family tensions and sexual frustration, which were treated with increasing violence in *A Streetcar Named Desire* (1947) and *Cat on a Hot Tin Roof* (1955).

Williams, Venus (1980–) US tennis player, whose titles include the US Open (2000, 2001), and Wimbledon (2000, 2001). Her sister **Serena Williams** (1981–), also a tennis player, won the US Open in 1999 and 2002 and Wimbledon in 2002 and 2003.

Williams, William Carlos (1883–1963) US poet. His free-verse poems are noted for their directness and use of natural speech rhythms. His volumes include *Collected Poems* (1934), *Pictures from Brueghel* (1963), and the epic *Paterson* (1946–58).

Williamson, Malcolm (1931–2003) Australian composer, living in the UK from 1953. His works include an organ concerto (1961), the operas *Our Man in Havana* (1963) and *The Violins of St Jacques* (1966), and eight symphonies. He was Master of the Queen's Music from 1975.

willow A tree or shrub of the genus *Salix* (about 300 species), native to temperate and arctic regions. Male and female catkins are borne on separate trees and open before the leaves. Willows are common in wet places and some are grown as ornamentals, especially the weeping willow (*S. babylonica*), with its slender drooping branches, and the bay willow (*S. pentandra*). Family: *Salicaceae*.

willowherb A tall perennial herb of subarctic and temperate regions, growing profusely in forest glades and in meadows, especially on ground recently cleared (and sometimes therefore called *fireherb*). The flowers, often light purple, are grouped in high spikes. The approximately 170 species belong to two genera, *Epilobium* and *Chamaenerion*.

willow pattern A *chinoiserie pattern attributed to Thomas Minton and introduced about 1780. The elements are a willow tree, pagoda, figures on a river bridge, and two flying birds in an elaborate border.

willow warbler A small inconspicuous warbler, *Phylloscopus trochilus*, which is probably the most common of all birds in Eurasian deciduous forests.

Wilson, Charles Thomson Rees (1869–1959) British physicist, who won the 1927 Nobel Prize for his invention of the Wilson *cloud chamber. He discovered that moisture condensed in the presence of ions and, when X-rays and radioactivity were discovered, applied his discoveries to invent the cloud chamber.

Wilson, (James) Harold, Baron (1916–95) British statesman; Labour prime minister (1964–70, 1974–76). He was a government economist during World War II, after which he became an MP (1945) and president of the Board of Trade (1947). He succeeded Gaitskill as Labour leader in 1963 and achieved electoral victory in 1964. His statutory incomes policy and plans for industrial-relations reform were unpopular and he lost the 1970 election. His second ministry saw the renegotiation of the UK's terms of membership to the EC, which was confirmed by a referendum in 1975. In 1976 Wilson unexpectedly resigned. He was made a life peer in 1983.

Wilson, (Thomas) Woodrow (1856–1924) US statesman; Democratic president (1913–21). In his first term as president he introduced progressive reforms. In World War I, Wilson declared war on Germany (1917) in response to its unrestricted submarine campaign. Wilson's Fourteen Points (1918) proposed a basis on which peace might be settled and contained a plan for a League of Nations that was incorporated into the Treaty of Versailles.

Wiltshire A county of S England. It consists of a rolling chalk plateau, bordered by lowlands in the NW and SE. It is predominantly agricultural. Prehistoric sites include *Stonehenge and *Avebury. Swindon became a unitary authority in 1997. Area (excluding Swindon): 3481 sq km (1344 sq mi). Population (2001, excluding Swindon): 432 973. Administrative centre: Trowbridge.

Winchester 51 04N 1 19W A city in S England, the administrative centre of Hampshire. As capital of Saxon Wessex, it rivalled London. The cathedral, built in the 11th century on earlier Saxon foundations, contains many royal tombs. Winchester College (1382), founded by *William of Wykeham, is England's oldest public school. Population (1991): 36 121.

wind A general horizontal movement of the atmosphere, as distinct from strictly local turbulence. In principle, winds blow from high to low pressure areas, but the direction is usually changed due to the earth's rotation. In the N hemisphere winds are forced to deviate to the right, in the S to the left. Wind speeds are measured in metres per second or may be classified by the *Beaufort scale.

Windermere The largest lake in England, in Cumbria in the Lake District. The lake is extensively used for watersports. Length: 17 km (10.5 mi).

Windhoek 22 34S 17 06E The capital of Namibia. It is the centre of the world's karakul (Persian lamb) skin industry. Population (1997 est): 169 000.

wind instruments Musical instruments in which the sound is produced by a vibrating column of air. *Brass instruments are activated by lip pressure; **reed instruments**, such as the clarinet, oboe, and bassoon, employ double or single reed mouthpieces; the *flute is side blown; the *recorder has a mouthpiece; *organ pipes have air blown into them by mechanically activated bellows. *Compare* PERCUSSION INSTRUMENTS; STRINGED INSTRUMENTS.

windmills Machines in which the wind turns a set of vanes or sails mounted on a horizontal shaft, the rotation of which is transmitted by gearing to working machinery. Windmills had appeared by 1150 in NE Europe and were used for grinding corn, pumping water, and powering light industry. Two common designs were the Dutch mill, in which only the sails and the conical roof moved to catch the wind, and the German post mill, in which the whole millhouse rotated around a central supporting pole. The modern metal windmill with multiple-bladed sails is found world wide in rural areas.

wind power The use of wind energy to generate electricity. Because of the world shortage of conventional energy resources, wind turbines (aerogenerators) have now become more

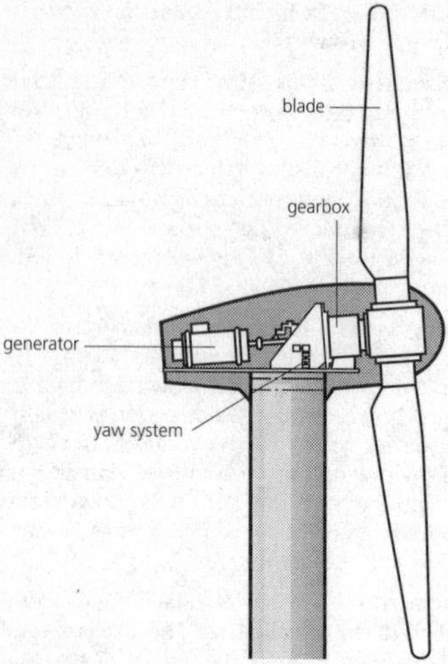

wind power. A typical aerogenerator with a horizontal axis. The blades, rotated by the wind, drive the gearbox, which increases the number of revolutions to an efficient rate for the production of electricity by the generator. The yaw system turns the top of the structure to obtain the maximum amount of energy from the wind.

attractive economically. Advantages of wind power are that it is free from pollution and uses no fuel. There are several different designs of aerogenerator: some with a horizontal axis and blades like the familiar *windmill; some with specially shaped aerofoil blades rotating on a vertical axis. A considerable number of large wind turbines and wind farms (groups of up to a few hundred machines) now supply the grid in the UK, USA, and elsewhere. In the UK the renewables obligation (*see* ALTERNATIVE ENERGY) will require a major increase in the number of wind farms.

Windsor 51 29N 0 38W A town in SE England, in Windsor and Maidenhead unitary authority, Berkshire on the River Thames. **Windsor Castle**, a royal residence, dominates the town. It was begun by William the Conqueror as a stockaded earthwork. Many additions were made by subsequent monarchs, notably the keep by Henry III, St George's Chapel, an example of the *Perpendicular style, by Edward IV, and the Albert Memorial Chapel (so called by Queen Victoria) by Henry VII. Population (1991): 31 225.

Windsor, House of The name of Britain's royal family from 1917, when it replaced that of House of Saxe-Coburg-Gotha, of which Prince *Albert had been a member. In 1960 Elizabeth II declared that those of her descendants in the male line who were not princes or princesses would take the surname Mountbatten-Windsor.

Windsor and Maidenhead A unitary authority in SE England, in Berkshire. Area: 197 sq km (76 sq mi). Population (2001): 133 606.

Windward Islands (Spanish name: Islas de Barlovento) A West Indian group of islands forming part of the S Lesser Antilles. They comprise the islands of Martinique, St Lucia, St Vincent, the N Grenadines, and Grenada.

wine An alcoholic drink made from fermented grape juice. The grapes are first crushed, traditionally by treading, now generally by machine. This process brings the yeast on the grapeskins, visible as the "bloom," into contact with the sugar in the juice, which it then converts into ethanol (ethyl alcohol). Depending upon when the fermentation is stopped, the resulting wine is dry, medium, or sweet. Table wines contain about 9–13% alcohol. Fortified wines (e.g. *port, *sherry) contain about 16–23% alcohol. The bubbles in sparkling wines are caused by a secondary fermentation in the bottle (*see also* CHAMPAGNE). Red wines are made from whole grapes; for white wines the grapeskins are removed at an early stage in production. True rosé wines are made from the grenache grape, from which the skins are removed before the juice is deeply stained by them. The variety of grape, the soil of the vineyard, and the local climate govern a wine's quality. The appellation "vintage" is now used to designate a wine of outstanding quality.

Wingate, Orde Charles (1903–44) British soldier, who led the *Chindits. A Zionist, he organized Jewish guerrillas in Palestine (1936–39). In World War II, after taking Addis Ababa from the Italians (1941), he formed the Chindits to disrupt communications behind the Japanese lines in Burma. He was killed in an aircrash.

Winnipeg 49 53N 97 10W A city in S Canada, capital of Manitoba. Established as a fur-trading post (1806), it expanded with the growth of farming and the arrival of the railway (1881) from E Canada. Population (1996): 618 477 (metropolitan area).

Winnipeg, Lake A lake in S Canada, in S Manitoba. Emptying into Hudson Bay, it drains much of the Canadian prairies. Area: 24 514 sq km (9465 sq mi).

wintergreen An evergreen creeping perennial herb or small shrub of the family *Pyrolaceae* (about 35 species), found in N temperate and arctic regions. The flowers are white or pale-pink and the fruit is a capsule. Oil of wintergreen is extracted from the leaves of the winterberry (*Gaultheria procumbens*), a North American shrub; the common wintergreen (*Pyrola minor*) is a herb of Eurasia and North America.

Winter War *See* RUSSO-FINNISH WAR.

Wirral A unitary authority in NW England, in Merseyside. Area: 158 sq km (61 sq mi). Population (2001): 312 289.

Wirral Peninsula A peninsula in NW England, in Merseyside and Cheshire. Chiefly low-lying, it serves mainly as a residential area for Liverpool.

Wisconsin A state in the N central USA. The Central Lowlands give way in the N to the Superior Upland, which contains many forests and lakes. Manufacturing is the state's major economic activity. *History*: ceded to the USA by the British in 1783, large-scale immigration in the 1820s led to its organization as a territory (1836) and it became a state in 1848. Area: 145 438 sq km (56 154 sq mi). Population (2000): 5 363 675. Capital: Madison.

Wisteria A genus of twining usually woody vines (10 species), native to E Asia and North America and grown as ornamentals, especially *W. floribunda* from Japan, which may reach a height of 30 m. Family: *Leguminosae*.

witan A body of 30 to 40 high-ranking laymen and ecclesiastics, which advised Anglo-Saxon kings on such major policy matters as foreign policy and taxation. It met only at the king's will and had no fixed procedure.

witchcraft The supposed manipulation of natural events by persons using supernatural means. In Europe the biblical injunction "Thou shalt not suffer a witch to live" (Exodus 22.18) sanctioned widespread persecution. Social and religious upheavals in the 16th and 17th centuries brought an upsurge in witch hunts; the famous outbreak at Salem, Massachusetts (1692), is a paradigm case of witch hysteria. Witches were accused of worshipping the devil at nocturnal orgies (sabbaths), of keeping evil spirits (familiars), and of killing livestock, wrecking crops, and causing barrenness, impotence, and fits. Many traditional African communities hold witchcraft accountable for similarly inexplicable misfortunes.

witch hazel A shrub or small tree of the genus *Hamamelis* (6 species), native to E Asia and North America, especially the American *H. virginiana*, which is the source of witch-hazel lotion used in pharmacy. This and several other species are often grown as ornamentals. Family: *Hamamelidaceae*.

Wittenberg 53 00N 11 41E A town in E Germany, on the River *Elbe. The Reformation began here on 31 October 1517, when Martin Luther nailed his 95 theses to the door of All Saints Church. Population (1991): 87 000.

Wittgenstein, Ludwig (1889–1951) Austrian philosopher. His two major works are the *Tractatus Logico-philosophicus* (1921) and the posthumously published *Philosophical Investigations* (1953). In his earlier work he developed the "picture theory" of language—words represent things by established conventions—but later he considered actual usage to be more important than set convention.

Witwatersrand (*or* **the Rand**) A ridge of hills in NE South Africa. It extends about 160 km (99 mi) chiefly W of Johannesburg. It has been worked for gold since the 1880s.

woad A branching perennial or biennial herb, *Isatis tinctoria*, native to central and S Europe. Formerly cultivated for the blue dye extracted from its crushed leaves, it is now rare. Up to 120 cm tall, it has tiny yellow flowers. Family: *Cruciferae*.

Wodehouse, Sir P(elham) G(renville) (1881–1975) British-born writer, who became a US citizen in 1955. In his many comic novels featuring Bertie Wooster and his manservant Jeeves, including *The Inimitable Jeeves* (1923) and *The Code of the Woosters* (1938), he portrayed an English upper-class society fixed forever in the 1920s.

Woden *See* ODIN.

Wokingham A unitary authority in SE England, in Berkshire. Area: 179 sq km (69 sq mi). Population (2001): 150 257.

wolf A wild *dog, *Canis lupus*, of Eurasia and North America. Wolves are 140–190 cm long including the tail (30–55 cm). They live in packs of 5–30 and feed mainly on mice, fish, and carrion but also attack deer. Mating is often for life. Wolves in colder climates are generally larger and shaggier. There is an almost white N Siberian race, while the Indian pale-footed wolf is small and grey. *See also* TIMBER WOLF.

Wolf, Hugo (1860–1903) Austrian composer. He wrote 300 *Lieder*, the opera *Der Corregidor* (1895), and an *Italian Serenade* for string quartet. He died insane.

Wolfe, James (1727–59) British soldier. After the outbreak of the Seven Years' War he was sent to Canada, where he excelled in the capture of Louisberg (1758). The following year he besieged the Marquis de Montcalm (1712–59) in Quebec. His forces scaled the undefended Heights of Abraham and a pitched battle ensued in which both commanders were killed. Wolfe's victory established Britain's supremacy in Canada.

wolfhound *See* BORZOI; IRISH WOLFHOUND.

Wolfit, Sir Donald (1902–68) British actor and manager. He acted all the major Shakespearean roles, receiving especial acclaim for his Lear, first performed in 1943.

wolframite The principal ore of tungsten, consisting of ferrous tungstate, (Fe,Mn)WO_4. It is brown, black, grey, or reddish in colour and is found particularly in quartz veins associated with granitic rocks.

Wolfram von Eschenbach (c. 1170–c. 1220) German poet. His great romance, *Parzifal* (c. 1212), is the first German work to use the story of the Holy Grail and is the basis of Wagner's opera.

wolf spider A *spider, also called hunting spider, belonging to a widespread family (*Lycosidae*; over 175 species). Wolf spiders, up to 25 mm long, are dark brown with long stout legs and are usually active at night, hunting prey rather than trapping it in webs. The female carries the eggs and young.

Wollongong, Greater 34 25S 150 52E A city in Australia, in New South Wales. It includes the towns of Wollongong, Bulli, and Port Kembla. Population (1991): 236 010.

Wollstonecraft, Mary (1759–97) British writer. In 1797 she married the social philosopher William Godwin (1756–1836). Her best-known work is *A Vindication of the Rights of Women* (1792), which argued for equal opportunities for all in education. She died after giving birth to her daughter Mary, who married *Shelley.

Wolsey, Thomas, Cardinal (c. 1475–1530) English churchman and statesman; Lord Chancellor (1515–29) under Henry VIII. As chancellor he interfered unsuccessfully in the conflict between Francis I of France and Emperor *Charles V. Wolsey's attempts to raise taxes to pay for his foreign policy encountered violent opposition. He fell from power after failing to persuade the pope to annul Henry's marriage to Catherine of Aragon and died on his way to face trial in London.

Wolverhampton 1. 52 36N 2 08W A town in central England, in Wolverhampton unitary authority, West Midlands. Metalworking and engineering are the principal industries. Population (1996 est): 244 500. **2.** A unitary authority in W central England, in West Midlands. Area: 69 sq km (27 sq mi). Population (2001): 236 573.

wolverine A carnivorous mammal, *Gulo gulo*, also called glutton, inhabiting northern evergreen forests of Europe, Asia, and America. It is heavily built, about 1 m long and weighing about 25 kg, and hunts lemmings and hares. Family: *Mustelidae*.

womb (*or* **uterus**) The part of a woman's reproductive tract in which the fetus develops. The womb is a hollow muscular organ, connected by the vagina to the outside and to the ovaries by the Fallopian tubes. In a nonpregnant woman the lining of the womb is shed at monthly intervals (*see* MENSTRUATION). During childbirth the womb, which is greatly enlarged (about 30 cm long), undergoes strong contractions to expel the baby.

wombat A bearlike *marsupial belonging to the family *Phascolomidae* (2–3 species), of Australia (including Tasmania). The coarse-haired wombat (*Phascolomis ursinus*) is about 1 m long and has strong claws, which it uses for tunnelling. It feeds on grass, roots, and tree bark.

Women's Institutes, National Federation of A British organization founded in 1915 to develop the quality, chiefly through further education, of rural life for women. Local institutes meet monthly to hear talks on a wide range of subjects.

Women's Royal Voluntary Service A British organization founded in 1938 as the Women's Voluntary Service (WVS). Its members perform many voluntary welfare services, including Meals on Wheels.

wood The hard tissue of the stems and branches of trees and shrubs, beneath the bark, consisting of *xylem cells strengthened with deposits of lignin. The central part of the trunk—heartwood—consists of dead xylem. Conifers are referred to as softwoods because the xylem is porous; broad-leaved (angiosperm) trees, which are called hardwoods, contain more fibres and are therefore stronger.

Wood A family of English architects, known for their contribution to town planning and urban architecture. They mainly worked in Bath, which **John Wood the Elder** (1704–54) began to develop in the late 1720s. His work was continued by his son **John Wood the Younger** (1728–81), who designed the famous Royal Crescent (1767–75) and the Assembly Rooms (1769–71).

Wood, Sir Henry (Joseph) (1869–1944) British conductor. He is remembered for the London Promenade concerts, which he established at the Queen's Hall, London, and which continued at the Albert Hall after the Queen's Hall was bombed in World War II.

woodbine *See* HONEYSUCKLE; VIRGINIA CREEPER.

woodcock A Eurasian gamebird, *Scolopax rusticola*, occurring in woodland and generally active at night. It has a stocky body, 34 cm long, and a russet plumage with a dark-barred head and a white-tipped tail. Woodcocks have long bills and feed on worms and insect larvae. Family: *Scolopacidae* (sandpipers, snipe).

woodcut A relief *printing technique. The design is drawn on the surface of a block of medium soft wood, sawn along the grain, and all the undrawn parts are cut away. The design is then transferred to paper by pressing the inked block onto the paper. The woodcut was used in China (c. 5th century AD) for textile design but its history in Europe dates from the 14th century. Leading 16th-century German artists, such as *Dürer and *Holbein the Younger, used the medium to supreme effect.

wood engraving A technique of printing images, refined in the 18th century by Thomas Bewick (1753–1828). The surface of a hardwood block, sawn against the grain, is cut away with engraving tools to leave raised areas which, when treated with ink, will appear dark when printed, in contrast to the white line of the incised areas.

woodlouse A terrestrial crustacean of the suborder *Oniscoidea*, found in damp shady places under stones, logs, etc. Woodlice have a body covering of armour-like plates. A common species is the pill bug or woodlouse (*Armadillidium vulgare*), about 17 mm long, which rolls into a ball when disturbed. Common genera: *Oniscus*, *Porcellio*; order: *Isopoda*.

woodpecker A bird belonging to a family (*Picidae*; about 220 species) occurring worldwide except Madagascar, Australia, and New Zealand. 9–57 cm long, woodpeckers have multicoloured plumage, often barred or spotted. Most are exclusively arboreal, chiselling through bark with their long straight bills in search of insects.

wood pigeon A large Eurasian *pigeon, *Columba palumbus*, which is a serious pest on farmland. 40 cm long, it has a predominantly grey plumage with a black-tipped tail, brownish back and wings, white wing patches, and a green, purple, and white neck patch.

Woods, Tiger (Eldrick W.; 1975–) US golfer. In 1997 he became (at 21) the youngest Masters champion and the first Black golfer to win a major championship. In 2000 he became the youngest player to win all four major competitions and in 2001 the only player to hold all four titles at once.

wood sorrel A herbaceous plant of the genus *Oxalis* (about 800 species), of temperate and tropical regions, especially *O. acetosella*, of Europe. This species has solitary white flowers. Some species, including the vegetable oca (*O. tuberosa*), have edible tubers. Family: *Oxalidaceae*.

woodwasp A *sawfly belonging to the families *Xiphydriidae* (Europe and North America), *Sytexidae* (North America), or *Orussidae* (worldwide). *Xiphydriidae* larvae bore into deciduous trees. *Sytexidae* are restricted to the incense cedar tree. *Orussidae* larvae are external parasites on wood-dwelling beetle larvae.

woodwind instruments Blown musical instruments in which a column of air is made to vibrate either by blowing across a mouth hole, as in the flute, or by making a single or a double reed vibrate, as in the oboe, bassoon, clarinet, and saxophone.

woodworm A wood-boring beetle of the genus *Anobium*, especially the furniture beetle (*A. punctatum*), 5 mm long, which damages furniture and old buildings. The larvae bore into wood and emerge when adult. Family: *Anobiidae*.

wool Fibres obtained from the fleeces of domestic sheep. Elastic, resilient, and absorbent, it is also an excellent insulator. *Merino wool is the best in quality. Wools from the 26 British breeds vary widely, while New Zealand sheep are crossbreeds of merino and British. The wool of Asian sheep and mountain breeds is used chiefly for carpets. Since World War II, synthetic fibres have been mixed with wool.

Woolf, (Adeline) Virginia (*born* Stephen; 1882–1941) British novelist, a central figure of the *Bloomsbury group. Her novels in which she used an impressionistic style to capture the fluidity of existence, include *Mrs Dalloway* (1925), *To the Lighthouse* (1927), and *The Waves* (1931). She also wrote biographies and criticism, including the essays in *The Common Reader* (1925–32), and voluminous diaries. She committed suicide by drowning. Her husband **Leonard (Sidney) Woolf** (1880–1969), with whom she founded the Hogarth Press in 1917, was literary editor of the *Nation* (1923–30) and wrote five volumes of autobiography (1960–69).

Woolley, Sir Leonard (1880–1960) British archaeologist. He worked at Carchemish and Tell el-Amarna but is famous chiefly for his excavations at *Ur (1922–34).

woolly rhinoceros A rhinoceros belonging to the extinct genus *Coelodonta*, which inhabited Eurasia and North Africa during the Pleistocene epoch (2.5 million to 10 000 years ago). Well-preserved specimens show that it was a large shaggy-coated animal with two horns.

Woomera 31 11S 136 54E A town in central South Australia. The Anglo-Australian Long Range Weapons Establishment was founded here in 1947 and the site has subsequently been used as a test range for missiles and other weapons and a launching base for space satellites. Population (latest est): 1805.

Worcester 52 11N 2 13W A city in W central England, the administrative centre of Hereford and Worcester on the River Severn. The cathedral, begun in 1084, dates mainly from the 14th century. At the battle of Worcester (1651) Charles II was defeated by Cromwell. It is traditionally associated with porcelain and gloves but now has a diverse service-based economy. Population (1997): 93 500.

Worcestershire A county in W central England. In 1974 it was absorbed into the new county of Hereford and Worcester and lost part of the N to the West Midlands: it was reinstated as a county in 1998. It is mainly agricultural, with cattle breeding and fruit growing. Industries include engineering and chemicals. Area: 1742 sq km (674 sq mi). Population (2001): 542 107. Administrative centre: Worcester.

word processor A software package for a computer enabling documents, letters, etc., to be created, edited, printed, and stored. Modern word processors enable text to be justified and correctly hyphenated, a variety of fonts and weights of typefaces to be used, tables and footnotes to be automatically generated, and graphics to be incorporated. Most word processors are now capable of producing print-quality documents.

W

Wordsworth, William (1770–1850) British poet. Born in Cumberland, he became an enthusiastic republican during a visit to Revolutionary France (1791–92). In 1795 he met S. T. *Coleridge, with whom he collaborated on *Lyrical Ballads* (1798), a seminal work of the Romantic movement. In 1799 he settled in the Lake District, where, cared for by his wife Mary and his sister Dorothy, he completed his masterpiece, a verse autobiography entitled *The Prelude* (completed 1805; published 1850). In this and other poems he described his feelings of union with nature. Dorothy's journals provide details of their life in the Lake District.

work The product of a force and the distance through which it causes a body to move in the direction of the force. Work, like energy, is measured in *joules.

workhouses Institutions set up in the 17th century in Britain and elsewhere to provide employment and shelter for paupers. The 1834 Poor Law Amendment Act made it necessary for anyone seeking assistance to enter a workhouse, which because of their inhuman rules soon became dreaded places.

World Bank *See* INTERNATIONAL BANK FOR RECONSTRUCTION AND DEVELOPMENT.

World Council of Churches An organization of more than 200 Protestant and Orthodox churches. A product of the ecumenical movement, it was founded at Amsterdam in 1948, with headquarters at Geneva.

World Cup An international association football competition held first in 1930 and thereafter every four years (except during World War II). It is organized by the Féderation Internationale de Football association (FIFA). The winners have been Uruguay (1930, 1950), Italy (1934, 1938, 1982), West Germany (1954, 1974, 1990), Brazil (1958, 1962, 1970, 1994, 2002), England (1966), Argentina (1978, 1986), and France (1998).

World Health Organization (WHO) A specialized agency of the *United Nations established in 1948. WHO supports programmes to eradicate diseases, carries out and finances epidemiological research, trains health workers, strengthens national health services, and has established international health regulations; it also provides aid in emergencies. Its headquarters are in Geneva.

World Meterological Organization (WMO) A specialized agency of the *United Nations established in 1951 with the aim of standardizing international meteorological observations and improving the exchange of weather information. Its headquarters are in Geneva.

World Trade Center (**WTC**) A building complex, designed by Minotu Yamasaki, that formerly stood in New York's Manhattan district. When the building opened (1974), its 417 m (1368 ft) and 415 m (1362 ft) towers were the tallest in the world. In the infamous terrorist attack of *September 11, 2001, each of the towers was struck by a hijacked airliner, caught fire, and collapsed from the top downwards. Around 2800 people were killed, including several hundred emergency workers and all 156 passengers and crew on the aircraft.

World Trade Organization (**WTO**) An organization set up to succeed the General Agreement on Tariffs and Trade (GATT) from 1 Jan, 1996. Its aim is to raise standards of living worldwide by liberalizing international trade. There are currently 108 member states. The secretariat is based in Geneva.

World War I (1914–18) The Great War between the Allied Powers including countries of the British Empire, France, Russia, Belgium, Japan, Serbia, Italy (from May 1915), Portugal (from March 1916), Romania (from August 1916), the USA (from April 1917), and Greece (from July 1917) on one side, and the Central Powers, including Germany, Austria-Hungary, Turkey (from November 1914), and Bulgaria (from October 1915) on the other. Its causes included fear of the German Empire's European and colonial ambitions. Tensions among European powers were expressed by the formation of the *Triple Alliance and of the *Triple Entente. The immediate cause of the war lay in the conflict of interests between Russia and Austria-Hungary in the Balkans. On 28 June 1914, the heir to the Austro-Hungarian throne, Archduke Francis Ferdinand, was assassinated at Sarajevo by a Serbian nationalist and on 28 July Austria-Hungary, with German support, declared war on Serbia. On 29 July Russia mobilized its forces in support of Serbia; on 1 August Germany declared war on Russia and on 3 August, upon France. Germany's invasion of Belgium brought the UK into the war at midnight on 4 August.

Western Front: German strategy at the start of the war was based on the Schlieffen plan, which envisaged a rapid flanking movement through the Low Countries. The German forces under von Moltke advanced rapidly through Belgium until they were forced by the British Expeditionary Force (BEF) and the French under Joffre, at the first battle of the Marne (5–9 Sept), to retreat across the River Aisne. Germany's effort to reach the Channel was thwarted at the first battle of Ypres (12 Oct–11 Nov) and the combatants settled to futile trench warfare. 1915 saw inconclusive battles at Neuve-Chapelle (March), again at Ypres (April–May), where the Germans used poison gas for the first time, and at Loos (Sept). On 21 February 1916, the Germans launched a crippling attack on the French at Verdun but on 1 July Haig, who had succeeded Sir John French as commander of the BEF, opened the battle of the Somme, during which *tanks were used (by the British) for the first time; the Allies lost some 600 000 men and the Germans about 650 000. In early 1917 the Germans under Ludendorff withdrew behind the *Hindenburg line; in April Haig took Vimy Ridge (with the loss of 132 000 men); but the French campaign in Champagne was disastrous and command passed to Pétain. With the USA (incensed by German *submarine warfare) now participating, on 31 July Britain launched the third battle of Ypres and by 6 November had taken Passchendaele (with 245 000 British losses). In spring 1918 Germany thrust a bulge in the Allied line, which the Allied commander in chief, Foch, wiped out at the second battle of the Marne. In September the Hindenburg line was broken by Haig between Saint Quentin and Cambrai. By October Germany was suing for peace.

Eastern Front and Balkans: in August 1914 the Russians advanced into E Prussia but were defeated at Tannenberg. When late in 1914 Turkey attacked Russia in the Caucasus, the Allies launched the **Gallipoli campaign**, in which Australian and New Zealand forces played a major part (*see* ANZAC). It failed to break through the Dardanelles and by January 1916, the Allies had withdrawn. Germany's offensive in the summer of 1915 secured Poland, most of Lithuania, and Serbia. Meanwhile, the Allies landed at Salonika, the ensuing **Macedonian campaign** continuing until Bulgaria capitulated in September 1918. Russia collapsed following the Russian Revolution (March 1917) and signed the Treaties of Brest-Litovsk.

Middle East: the **Mesopotamian campaign**, intended to protect oil installations, was launched on 6 November 1914. However, the Allies failed to take Baghdad (November 1915) and in April 1916 they lost Kut al-Amara to the Turks. In February 1917 it was retaken and in March Baghdad fell. Meanwhile the Allies had invaded Palestine and, aided by the Arab revolt, Allenby took Jerusalem in December 1917; his victory at Megiddo (September 1918) and capture of Damascus and Aleppo finally crushed the Turks.

Italy: the Italian front was maintained along

the River Isonzo through 11 battles until 1917, when the Italians were defeated by Austria-Hungary at Caporetto (Oct–Nov). In October 1918 Austria-Hungary was defeated at Vittorio-Veneto and in November capitulated.

War at sea and in the air: at sea the larger British navy was dominant in the North Sea. German raids on the English coast were repudiated by Beatty's victory at Dogger Bank in January 1915. The indecisive battle of Jutland (31 May 1916) was the only engagement between the main fleets. The real threat to the Allies at sea came from the German U-boats, which sunk some 6000 ships, including the *Lusitania*. World War I was the first war in which aircraft were used: in 1915 German Zeppelins began to attack British cities and in 1917 aircraft were also thus employed. Some air combat took place on the Western and Eastern Fronts and towards the end of the war the newly established Royal Air Force was bombing German cities.

Conclusion: with the defeat of the Turks and Bulgarians in September 1918 and of Germany on the Western Front and Austria-Hungary in Italy in October, revolt broke out in Germany. On 9 November the German emperor, William II, fled and on 11 November Germany signed the armistice. On 18 January 1919 the Allies met at the *Paris Peace Conference to determine the peace settlement, which was signed by Germany (the Treaty of Versailles) on 28 June. The Allies lost some 5 million lives (of which 3 million were French and Russian) in the war; the Central Powers lost some 3.5 million (of which 3 million were German and Austro-Hungarian). 21 million combatants were wounded.

World War II (1939–45) The war between the Allied Powers, including countries of the Commonwealth, France, the Soviet Union (from June 1941), the USA (from December 1941), and China (from December 1941) on one side, and the *Axis Powers, including Germany, Italy (from June 1940), and Japan (from December 1941) on the other. The war was caused by the failure of the Paris Peace Conference to provide for international security and by the territorial ambitions of Nazi Germany under Adolf Hitler. In March 1938 Germany annexed Austria (*see* ANSCHLUSS) and in September, following the *Munich Agreement, the *Sudetenland. In March 1939 Hitler occupied the rest of Czechoslovakia. On 23 May Hitler came to an agreement with Mussolini's Italy, which in April had conquered Albania. Hitler's and Stalin's nonaggression pact followed on 23 August and Britain, France, and Poland made an agreement of mutual assistance on 25 Aug. On 1 September Germany invaded Poland and two days later Britain and France declared war on Germany.

Western Europe (1939–41): by 27 September Poland had succumbed to the German Blitzkreig. The Soviet invasion of Finland (*see* RUSSO-FINNISH WAR) brought Finnish capitulation by March 1940 and in April Germany invaded Denmark and Norway. The Allied failure in Scandinavia led to Neville Chamberlain's resignation and on 10 May, the day that Germany invaded Belgium and the Netherlands, Churchill became Britain's prime minister. The German advance outflanked the *Maginot line and split the Allied forces; on 26 May an Allied evacuation from the Continent was ordered. Between 29 May and 4 June some 338 226 Allied troops were rescued from Dunkirk. On 22 June Pétain signed the French armistice with Germany, following which French resistance to the Axis Powers was directed by de Gaulle from London, where he organized the Free French.

Britain now faced an imminent German invasion. In August and September 1940, the *Luftwaffe attacked SE England and then London in a series of daytime raids. In October German bombing was carried out at night and extended to other British cities. The Luftwaffe failed to cripple the RAF and by the end of October the battle of Britain had been won by the RAF under Dowding. The RAF lost 915 aircraft in the conflict and the Luftwaffe some 1733.

Africa and the Middle East (1940–43): in September 1940 Italy advanced from Libya into Egypt but was forced to retreat by Wavell's troops. By 6 February 1941 the Allies had captured 113 000 Italian soldiers but their success was undermined by the arrival in N Africa of Rommel and the German Afrika Corps. In March Wavell's force was weakened by the dispatch of troops to aid Greece (Yugoslavia and Greece fell in April, and Crete in May) and retreated to the Egyptian border.

In November Auchinleck (who had replaced Wavell in July) launched an offensive against Rommel but by January 1942 had been forced to take up a defensive position at El-Alamein, inside the Egyptian frontier. In August Auchinleck was replaced by Alexander and Montgomery became commander of the Eighth Army. In the decisive battle of Alamein (23 Oct–4 Nov) Montgomery defeated Rommel, forcing his retreat along the N African coast. On 8 November an Anglo-US force under Eisenhower landed on the coast of French N Africa. The French under Darlan surrendered and the Allies advanced through Tunisia to meet (7 April 1943) with Montgomery's Eighth Army.

On 7 May the Allies took Bizerta and Tunis and on 13 May the Axis forces surrendered (some 248 000 troops were captured).

In East Africa, Wavell had taken Addis Ababa from the Italians in April 1941 and had secured Ethiopia and British Somaliland (captured by Italy in August 1940) by May. In the Middle East, in April Britain occupied Iraq, by June Lebanon and Syria were in Allied hands, and in August the Allies gained control of Iran.

Italy (1943–45): on 10 July 1943 Alexander's army group (the Eighth under Montgomery and the US Fifth Army), under the supreme command of Eisenhower, landed in Sicily. On 25 July Mussolini fell and on 3 Sept the Italian armistice was signed and the Allies landed on the Italian mainland. The Germans held back the Allies at the Ortona-Garigliano line until an Allied offensive, launched on 12 May 1944 succeeded in breaking through to Rome (4 June). Bologna and then Milan were taken in April 1945 and on 2 May Trieste fell.

Eastern Front (1941–45): Germany, with Finland, Hungary, and Romania, invaded the Soviet Union on 22 June 1941. The Axis forces took the Crimea and the Ukraine in the S, besieged Leningrad (St Petersburg) in the N, and by November were in sight of Moscow. The Soviets staged an effective counterattack in the winter of 1941–42 but Germany retaliated in June and by August the battle of *Stalingrad had begun. Following this heroic Soviet victory, the Germans launched a new offensive in July but were gradually forced back until expelled from Soviet soil in August 1944. On 23 August the Soviet Union secured a Romanian armistice and on 19 Sept, a Finnish armistice. Also in September Bulgaria declared war on Germany and the Germans evacuated Greece. On 5 October Belgrade fell following collaboration between the Red Army and Tito's Partisans. In October Soviet troops invaded Germany and in January 1945 launched a final offensive, taking Poland, Austria, and Hungary and entering Czechoslovakia. Berlin fell on 2 May, shortly after Hitler's suicide.

Western Front (1944–45): on 6 June 1944, D-Day, the Allied invasion of Normandy began under Eisenhower. The RAF Bomber Command had prepared the way with heavy strategic bombing, including the bombing of German cities. By 2 July one million US and British troops had landed. The British under Montgomery took Caen and US troops, after capturing St Lô (July), invaded Brittany. The Canadians took Falaise on 17 August, shortly after US and French troops had landed in the South of France from the Mediterranean. On 25 August Paris fell to the Allies, who now advanced into the Ruhr.

At the battle of Arnhem in September airborne troops were withdrawn after sustaining heavy losses. That December the Germans launched a counteroffensive (the battle of the Bulge) in the Ardennes region of S Belgium. US troops forced the Germans to retreat in January 1945 and the final Allied offensive was launched. The Rhine was crossed in March and by 1 April the Ruhr was encircled. On 4 May Montgomery accepted the surrender of German forces in NW Germany, Holland, and Denmark at Lüneburg Heath. On 7 May the Germans signed a general surrender at Reims, which was ratified two days later in Berlin.

War at sea: The battle for control of the sea routes, known as the **battle of the Atlantic**, was fought from December 1939, when the German *Graf Spee* inflicted considerable damage on HMS *Exeter* in the battle of the River Plate in the S Atlantic. In November 1940 a successful naval air attack was launched on Taranto and in March 1941 at Cape Matapan the British Mediterranean fleet thwarted an Italian attempt to prevent the transfer of British troops from Egypt to Greece. In May the *Hood* was sunk by the *Bismarck* and, three days later, the *Dorsetshire* sunk the *Bismarck*. However, as in World War I, the major threat was posed by the German U-boats. These were most effective early in 1943 but by the summer, partly owing to the introduction of Allied escort carriers, 37 U-boats had been sunk and the battle of the Atlantic was over.

Asia (1941–45): the Japanese attack on Pearl Harbor on 7 December 1941 initiated a truly "world" war. On 10 December Germany and Italy declared war on the USA and the second Sino-Japanese War became part of the wider conflict.

Japan invaded Malaya on 8 December and captured Hong Kong (25 Dec), Manila (3 January 1942), and Singapore (15 Feb). The Dutch East Indies fell on 10 March and the Philippines and Burma in May. However, the US naval and air victories of the *Coral Sea (4–8 May), Midway Island (4–6 June), and *Guadalcanal (Aug) then halted Japan's eastward expansion. In October 1944 the Japanese fleet was decisively defeated at Leyte Gulf and the Allied conquest of Manila (February 1945), the Philippines (June), and Borneo (May–June) followed. Burma was reconquered by the 14th ("forgotten") Army under Slim (January–May 1945). Japanese resistance was finally ended by the atomic bombing on 6 and 9 August respectively of Hiroshima and

Nagasaki, and Japan formally surrendered on 14 August.

Conclusion: in May 1945, with the fall of Berlin, the war in Europe was over. The postwar settlement was decided at the *Potsdam Conference in July and August (*see also* TEHRAN CONFERENCE; YALTA CONFERENCE).

In the course of the war Germany lost some 3.5 million combatants and 780 000 civilians. In contrast the UK lost some 264 443 combatants and 92 673 civilians. The Soviet Union lost 11 million combatants and 7 million civilians; the Japanese 1.3 million and 672 000 respectively; and the USA, 292 131 and 6000. In addition some 5.7 million Jews died in Nazi concentration camps.

World Wide Fund for Nature (WWF) An international organization dedicated to the conservation of endangered species and their natural habitats. Founded in 1961 as the World Wildlife Fund, it has financed projects both in Britain and abroad. The international president is HRH the Duke of Edinburgh.

worm A soft-bodied elongated invertebrate. The term is applied to members of several different groups, especially *earthworms and various parasitic species, and sometimes the larvae of insects. *See also* ANNELID WORM; FLATWORM; NEMATODE; RIBBONWORM.

Worms 49 38N 8 23E A town in SW Germany, on the River Rhine. Heavily bombed during World War II, it has an 11th-century cathedral and synagogue (1034). *History*: in the 5th century AD it was the capital of Burgundy. Among the imperial diets (assemblies) held here was that of 1521 at which Luther refused to recant. It was annexed by France in 1797 and passed to Hesse-Darmstadt in 1815. Population (1991): 77 430.

wormwood An aromatic herb or shrub of the worldwide genus *Artemisia* (about 200 species), especially *A. absinthium*, which is found in grasslands of the N hemisphere and is the source of absinthe. Up to 80 cm high, it has small yellow flowers. Family: *Compositae*.

Worthing 50 48N 0 23W A resort in S England, on the West Sussex coast. Nearby on the South Downs is the neolithic Cissbury Ring. Population (1991): 95 732.

W

Wotan *See* ODIN.

Wounded Knee The site in SW South Dakota (USA) of the last confrontation (29 December 1890) between the Indians and US troops. Fearing an uprising among the discontented Sioux, troops killed over 200 men, women, and children at Wounded Knee creek. In 1973 two Indians were killed when the American Indian Movement occupied the village of Wounded Knee in protest against government Indian policies.

wrack A large brown *seaweed of the order *Fucales*, found almost worldwide on rocky shores. Leathery branching fronds arise from a circular rootlike anchor (holdfast), often bearing air bladders to aid flotation. Examples are bladderwrack (*Fucus vesiculosus*) and serrated wrack (*F. serratus*).

wrasse A fish of the family *Labridae* (300 species) found near rocks or coral reefs in shallow tropical and temperate seas. It has a slender often brilliantly coloured body, 5–200 cm long, long dorsal and anal fins, and thick lips. Order: *Perciformes*.

wreckfish A carnivorous fish, *Polyprion americanus*, also called stone bass, found in Mediterranean and Atlantic offshore waters. It has a deep heavy body, up to 2 m long, dark brown above and yellowish below, a large head, and a jutting lower jaw. Family: *Serranidae*; order: *Perciformes*.

wren A small brown bird belonging to a family (*Troglodytidae*; 63 species) found chiefly in South America. Wrens are 9–22 cm long with sharp slender bills and short cocked tails. The only Eurasian species, *Troglodytes troglodytes*, is about 10 cm long and has a reddish-brown plumage with barring on the wings and tail. The name is also given to the families *Maluridae* (Australian wrens) and *Xenicidae* (New Zealand wrens).

Wren, Sir Christopher (1632–1723) English architect. He was a founder member of the Royal Society and later its president (1680–82). His first designs were for Pembroke College chapel, Cambridge (1663) and the Sheldonian Theatre, Oxford (1664). Within days of the *Fire of London Wren produced a new plan for the whole City; although this was rejected he was commissioned to rebuild 51 City churches and some 36 company halls. Basing many of his designs for the churches on Vitruvius' Roman basilica, Wren showed enormous ingenuity in fitting his buildings into the old sites. His design for St Paul's Cathedral was accepted, after many modifications, in 1675. His later buildings include the Greenwich Hospital (begun in 1694).

wrestling A form of unarmed combat, in which two people attempt to throw and hold each other down. It first became an Olympic sport in 704 BC. In **Graeco-Roman wrestling** holds on the body below the waist and the use of legs to hold or trip are not allowed. They are, however, allowed in **freestyle wrestling**. In both styles a wrestler wins a match by securing a fall (throwing his opponent onto his back and pinning both shoulders to the mat for one second) or by accumulating the most points according to a complex scoring system. **Sumo** is the highly popular Japanese style in which the wrestlers, usually weighing around 130 kg (20 stone), attempt to force each other out of the ring. *See also* JUDO.

Wrexham 1. 53 03N 3 00W A town in North Wales, in Wrexham county borough. It is a market town, manufacturing chemicals and metal goods. Population (1991): 40 614. **2.** A county borough in N Wales, created in 1996 from part of Clwyd. Area: 500 sq km (93 sq mi). Population (2001): 128 477.

Wright, Frank Lloyd (1869–1959) US architect. He first demonstrated his originality in a series of Chicago houses between 1900 and 1909, the most famous being the Robie house (1909). Later buildings include the Johnson Wax factory at Racine, Wisconsin (1936–39), Taliesin West (1938), his winter home in the Arizona desert, and the Guggenheim Museum (1959).

Wright, Orville (1871–1948) US aviator, who with his brother **Wilbur Wright** (1867–1912) is usually considered to have made the first powered and controlled flights (17 December 1903). They took place near Kitty Hawk, North Carolina, and in the second, lasting about a minute, the aircraft flew 250 metres.

Wrocław (German name: Breslau) 51 05N 17 00E A city in SW Poland, on the River Oder. Founded during the 10th century, it suffered severe damage in World War II under siege from the Soviet armies (1945). Population (1999 est): 637 877.

wrought iron An almost pure form of iron, often with less than 0.1% carbon. It was originally produced by repeatedly hammering and folding hot *pig iron to squeeze out the impurities. The puddling process has now superseded hand working.

Wuhan 30 35N 114 19E A port in E central China, at the confluence of the Yangtze and Han Rivers. Formed by the amalgamation (1950) of the ancient cities of Hankou (*or* Hankow), Hanyang, and Wuchang, it is the commercial and industrial centre of central China. Population (2000): 3 911 824.

Wuppertal 51 05N 7 10E A city in NW Germany, in the *Ruhr. It was formed in 1929 from six towns, including Elberfeld, and was heavily bombed in World War II. Population (1999 est): 370 700.

Würzburg 49 48N 9 57E A city in SW Germany, on the River Main. The former episcopal residence (1720–44), containing frescoes by Tiepolo, was damaged in World War II but later restored. Population (1999 est): 126 000.

Wuxi (*or* **Wu-hsi**) 31 35N 120 19E A city in E China, on the *Grand Canal. A major grain market since the 7th century AD, it is also an industrial centre. Population (1999 est): 940 858.

Wyatt, Sir Thomas (1503–42) English poet. With Henry Howard, Earl of *Surrey, he introduced Italian verse forms and metres, notably the Petrarchan sonnet, into English poetry. 96 of his poems, together with 40 by Surrey, were included in *Tottel's Miscellany* (1557).

Wycherley, William (1640–1716) English dramatist. He wrote four comedies, notably *The Country Wife* (1675) and *The Plain Dealer* (1676), adapted from Molière's *Le Misanthrope*. His plays are more fiercely satirical than those of his fellow Restoration dramatists.

Wycliffe, John (c. 1329–84) English religious reformer. An Oxford philosopher, he made increasingly radical criticisms of the Church, resulting in his condemnation as a heretic. He attacked the doctrine of transubstantiation and emphasized the importance of the Bible, of which he supervised the first English translation from the Latin. Wycliffe's adherents, the *Lollards, were forerunners of English Protestantism.

Wye, River A river in E Wales and W England. Flowing mainly SE from Plynlimmon it joins the River Severn near Chepstow. Length: 210 km (130 mi).

Wyoming One of the mountain states in the NW USA. Its natural resources include oil, natural gas, uranium, coal, trona, bentonite clay, and iron ore. Livestock production dominates farming. Tourism is significant with such attractions as the Yellowstone National Park. *History*: part of the territory acquired from France by the Louisiana Purchase (1803), the arrival of the Union Pacific Railway (1867–69) brought settlement in the S and the area became a state in 1890. Area: 253 596 sq km (97 914 sq mi). Population (2000): 493 782. Capital: Cheyenne.

X

xenon (Xe) A noble gas, present in the atmosphere and discovered in 1898 by Sir William Ramsay and M. W. Travers (1872–1961), in the residue of distilled liquid air. The first noble gas compounds were discovered by Neil Bartlett (1932–), by reacting xenon with dioxygenyl platinum hexafluoride ($O_2^+PtF_6^-$) to form $Xe^+PtF_6^-$. Xenon is used in special lamps and the radio-active isotope ^{133}Xe is produced in nuclear reactors. It is a "poison," i.e. a neutron absorber, and is a crucial factor in the control of the chain reaction (*see* NUCLEAR ENERGY). At no 54; at wt 131.3; mp −111.76°C; bp −108°C.

Xenophon (c. 430–c. 354 BC) Greek historian and soldier. He was born in Athens and became a disciple of Socrates. In 410 he led a group of 10 000 Greek mercenaries in a heroic retreat through the hostile Persian Empire to the Black Sea, after their commander, Cyrus, was killed in battle. This feat formed the subject of his best-known work, the *Anabasis*. His other works include *Memorabilia*, *Apology*, and *Symposium*, which deal with Socrates.

xerophyte A plant that lives in a hot dry climate and is adapted for conserving water. Cacti, for example, often have spiny leaves (to prevent water loss) and green succulent stems (in which water is stored). A **xeromorph** is a plant that shows some of the features of xerophytes but may not live in desert areas.

Xerxes I (d. 465 BC) King of Persia (486–465). Having brutally repressed revolts in Egypt, he invaded Greece (*see* GREEK-PERSIAN WARS) in 480. However, defeat at Salamis (480), Plataea and Mycale (479), and the consequent revolt of the Asiatic Greeks forced him to withdraw. This tyrannous ruler and compulsive builder was assassinated in a court intrigue.

Xhosa A Bantu people of the *Transkei region of South Africa. Many Xhosa are migrant labourers in other areas of South Africa. Their language employs click sounds borrowed from the *Khoisan languages.

Xi An (Hsi-an *or* Sian) 34 16N 108 54E A city in central China, on the Wei Ho (River). It contains many Tang pagodas and a noted museum. *History*: as a Tang capital (618–906 AD) it attracted many Buddhist, Muslim, and Christian missionaries. After 1935 it was a Guomindang (Nationalist) base. It is now an industrial centre. Population (1999 est): 2 294 790.

Xi Jiang (*or* **Hsi Chiang**) The most important river in S China, rising in Yunnan province and flowing E to form the densely populated Canton delta and the Zhu Jiang. Length: about 1900 km (1200 mi).

Xingu, River (Portuguese name: Rio Xingu) A river in central Brazil, rising on the Mato Grosso plateau and flowing generally N to enter the Amazon delta. Length: 1932 km (1200 mi).

Xiong Nu (*or* **Hsiung-nu**) Turkish and Mongol tribes on the N and NW borders of China, which threatened Chinese security from about 500 BC. The Chinese attempted to control the Xiong Nu by building the Great Wall of China, marrying their daughters to Xiong Nu leaders, and trading with them.

Xochimilco 19 08N 99 09W A town in central Mexico, on Lake Xochimilco. It is famous for its floating gardens, which originated as soil-covered rafts and have since become islands. Population (latest est): 271 000.

X-ray diffraction The *diffraction of *X-rays when they strike a crystal. The angle through which the X-rays are diffracted depends on the spacing between the different planes in the crystal in a manner given by *Bragg's law. The technique is used in studying crystal structure.

X-rays Electromagnetic radiation lying between ultraviolet radiation and gamma rays in the electromagnetic spectrum. X-rays may have wavelengths between 10^{-9} metre and 10^{-11} metre. Discovered by Wilhelm *Roentgen in

1895, they are produced when heavy metal atoms are struck by sufficiently energetic electrons, as in an **X-ray tube**. The electrons in an X-ray tube are produced by a heated cathode in an evacuated tube and accelerated to the heavy-metal anode by an electric field. The collisions knock inner electrons from the atoms, X-rays being emitted when the vacancy is filled by outer electrons. X-rays cause ionization in gases and penetrate matter. X-rays have many uses in medical diagnosis, *radiotherapy, structural analysis, and the study of crystals (X-ray diffraction).

xylem A plant tissue specialized for the transport of water and salts. The main cells are tubelike, with their walls strengthened by deposits of *lignin. In trees and shrubs the lignin deposits eventually block the tubes completely: this tissue forms *wood, and new secondary xylem is produced.

xylene (*or* **dimethyl benzene**; $C_6H_4(CH_3)_2$) A colourless toxic flammable liquid consisting of a mixture of three isomers. It is obtained by fractional distillation of petroleum and is used as an aviation fuel and as a solvent.

xylophone A pitched percussion instrument, consisting of a frame on which wooden bars in the pattern of a keyboard are fixed, each with a tubular metal resonator beneath it. It is played with two sticks. Orchestral xylophones usually have a compass of three octaves.

Y

Yahweh The conjectural pronunciation of one of the Hebrew names of God. The name YHWH (the Tetragrammaton or "four-letter" name) occurs often in the Bible; out of reverence it was traditionally not pronounced except by the high priest when he entered the Holy of Holies. "Jehovah" represents another attempt to pronounce this name.

yak A shaggy-coated wild ox, *Bos grunniens*, inhabiting mountain pastures of central Asia. Yaks have long been domesticated for draught purposes and milk; their dung is used as fuel. Wild yaks, up to 2 m high with long upward-curving horns, are larger than domestic yaks and are always black.

Yale University One of the oldest universities in the USA (founded 1701), situated at New Haven, Connecticut. It is named after Elihu Yale (1648–1721), who donated his books to the college.

Yalta Conference (1945) The conference, held at the Black Sea port of Yalta, towards the end of World War II attended by F. D. Roosevelt (USA), Stalin (Soviet Union), and Churchill (UK). They agreed upon the postwar occupation of Germany and decided that German surrender must be unconditional. Stalin also gave assurances (subsequently broken) that free elections would be held in Poland and other countries of E Europe occupied by the Red Army.

yam A twining herbaceous plant of the genus *Dioscorea*, cultivated in wet tropical regions for its edible tubers. Tubers can reach a length of 2.6 m and a weight of 45 kg; species commonly cultivated are *D. alata* (white yam), *D. rotundata* (white guinea yam), *D. batatas* (Chinese yam), and *D. cayenensis* (yellow yam). Family: *Dioscoreaceae*.

Yamasaki, Minoru (1912–86) US architect. His earliest buildings, such as Missouri's St Louis airport (1953–55), were remarkable for their simple but dramatic elegance. However, later works, such as the *World Trade Center in New York (1970–77), employed controversial pseudo-Gothic elements.

Yamoussoukro 6 49N 5 17W The capital of Côte d'Ivoire. Yamoussoukro was chosen as an inland replacement for the old capital of Abidjan in 1983. It includes the largest basilica in the world, completed in 1989. Population (1995 est): 110 000.

Yang, Chen Ning (1922–   ) US physicist, born in China, who shared the 1957 Nobel Prize with his countryman Tsung-Dao Lee (1926–   ) for their theoretical work suggesting that parity would not be conserved in the *weak interaction. This was quickly confirmed by observations of beta decay.

Yangtze River (Chinese name: Chang Jiang *or* Ch'ang Chiang) The longest river in China and the third longest in the world. Rising in mountains on the Tibetan borders, it flows E to the East China Sea via an extensive delta. The Yangtze is one of China's main transport routes. Work on the **Yangtze dam**, the world's biggest hydroelectric and flood-control project near Yichang, began in 1994 and is due to be completed in 2010. There are also plans to divert some 10% of the Yangtze's waters to desert areas thousands of miles to the N. Length: 6380 km (3964 mi).

Yaoundé (*or* **Yaunde**) 3 51N 11 31E The capital of Cameroon. Founded in 1888, it has been capital of Cameroon since 1922 (except during World War II). Population (1992 est): 800 000.

yarrow (*or* **milfoil**) A medium-sized perennial herb, *Achillea millefolium*, with small white flowers, common in pastures in temperate Eurasia. Family: *Compositae*.

yaws A chronic tropical disease caused by a *spirochaete bacterium, *Treponema pertenue*. It occurs mostly among poor children and is spread by skin contact. After an incubation period of three to four weeks a growth appears on the thighs or buttocks; later, multiple growths appear all over the skin. If not treated the disease can be very disfiguring. Treatment with penicillin is highly effective.

year The time taken by the earth to complete one revolution around the sun. This is equal to the period of the sun's apparent motion around the *ecliptic. The **tropical year**, of 365.2422 days, is the interval between two successive passages of the sun through the vernal *equinox. The **sidereal year**, of 365.2564 days, refers to successive passages of the sun through a point relative to the background stars. These periods differ because of the *precession of the equinoxes. *See also* CALENDAR.

yeast A single-celled fungus that is capable of fermenting carbohydrates and that reproduces asexually by budding new cells from its surface. Strains of *Saccharomyces cerevisiae* are widely used to cause *fermentation in baking, brewing, etc. Yeast extracts are used as a food for their high vitamin B content. Phylum: *Ascomycota.*

Yeats, William Butler (1865–1939) Irish poet and dramatist. His best-known poems, many of which appeared in *The Tower* (1928) and *The Winding Stair* (1929), are mainly tragic meditations on personal and political themes. Among them are "Easter, 1916," "The Second Coming," and "Sailing to Byzantium." He was an admirer of the Irish nationalist Maud Gonne (1866–1953), who inspired many of his love poems, and with Lady Gregory (1852–1932) he founded (1904) the Abbey Theatre, Dublin. He was a senator of the Irish Free State (1922–28) and won the Nobel Prize in 1923. His brother **Jack Butler Yeats** (1871–1957) was a noted painter.

yellow fever An acute viral infection transmitted by female mosquitoes of the genus *Aëdes*, which occur in tropical rain forests. After an incubation period of 3–14 days the patient develops a fever with aching muscles. In severe cases the virus affects the liver causing jaundice (hence the name), the kidneys, and the heart; death may result from liver or heart failure. There is no specific treatment but two kinds of vaccine can prevent it.

yellow-green algae Algae of the phylum *Chrysophyta* (about 6000 species), which are yellow-green to brown in colour. Most are unicellular or colonial and they form a major constituent of plankton (*see also* DIATOMS). Most reproduce asexually by spores.

yellowhammer A Eurasian *bunting, *Emberiza citrinella*, that occurs on farmland and roadsides, where it feeds on grain and seeds. About 16 cm long, the male has a bright-yellow head and underparts, chestnut rump, and a brown-streaked back; females are less colourful.

Yellow River (Chinese name: Huang He *or* Huang Ho) A river in China, rising in the W and flowing E to the Gulf of Chihli via a fertile delta. Its diversion during the Japanese invasion (1938) caused the death of 900 000 people. Length: about 4350 km (2700 mi).

Yellow Sea (Chinese name: Huang Haï) A large shallow inlet of the W Pacific Ocean, bordered by China and Korea. It is so called because of the yellowish silt deposited by the Chinese rivers.

Yellowstone National Park The largest national park in the USA, chiefly in NW Wyoming but extending into S Montana and E Idaho. Its active geysers include Old Faithful. Area: 8956 sq km (3458 sq mi).

Yellowstone River A river in the W USA, rising in NW Wyoming and flowing N through the *Yellowstone National Park then E to join the Missouri River. Length: 1080 km (671 mi).

Yeltsin, Boris (1931–) Russian politician; president of the Russian Federation (1991–2000). A former first secretary of the Moscow Communist Party (1985–87), he was elected president of the Russian SFSR in 1990, becoming the chief political rival to Gorbachov. In 1991 he led resistance to the failed coup by Communist hardliners and became president of Russia on the break-up of the Soviet Union. His economic reforms met with opposition from parliament, leading to a brief military confrontation in 1993. His handling of the crisis in Chechenia (1994–96) led to international criticism. Although he was re-elected in 1996, his authority was already in decline owing to ill health.

Yemen Republic A country in the Middle East, in S *Arabia bordering on the Red Sea, the Gulf of Aden, and the Arabian Sea. It includes several islands, including Kamaran and Perim Island. It consists of narrow dry coastal plains rising to upland valleys and mountains in the W (the wettest and most fertile in Arabia) and desert in the N and E. The population is chiefly Arab and Sunnite Muslim. *Economy*: agriculture was the basis of the economy until oil production began in 1986. Subsistence farming remains the chief occupation. Cotton is the main crop: others include cereals, coffee, fruit and vegetables, tobacco, and the narcotic qat.

Livestock are kept and sardine fishing is important. The S and E have almost no industry outside Aden. The economy relies on foreign aid and money received from Yemenis who work abroad. *History*: ruled by Muslim imams (priest-kings) from the 9th century, Yemen (excluding Aden) was nominally part of the Ottoman Empire from the 16th century to 1918. Aden was captured from the Turks in 1839 and occupied by the British East India Company. The British made protectorate treaties with other local rulers (1886–1914), finally uniting them under the Aden Protectorate (1937). The state of North Yemen, in the NW of present-day Yemen and with its capital at Sana'a, was established in 1934. It joined the Arab League (1945) and the UN (1947) and was loosely allied with Egypt and Syria (1958–61) in the United Arab Republic. In 1963 the Aden Protectorate and adjoining sheikdoms formed the Federation of South Arabia. This collapsed in 1967 and South Yemen became an independent socialist republic, with its capital at Aden. In North Yemen, civil war (1962–70) ended with the recognition of a republican regime. Successive heads of state were assassinated in 1977 and 1978. The history of South Yemen was dominated by border disputes with North Yemen and with Oman (until 1976). In 1986 foreign nationals were evacuated during a violent military coup. Plans for union between the two Yemens were implemented in 1990, but a civil war broke out (1994) in which the northern forces defeated the southern seccessionists. Multiparty elections were held in 1997; Yemen's first direct presidential elections, held in 1999, were won by the incumbent, President Ali Abdullah Saleh. Official language: Arabic. Currency: riyal of 100 fils. Area: 531 870 sq km (205 311 sq mi). Population (2003 est): 12 010 000. Capital: Sana'a (administrative) and Aden (commercial).

Yenisei, River A river in central Russia, rising in the Sayan Mountains and flowing N to **Yenisei Bay** on the Kara Sea. Length: about 4000 km (2485 mi).

Yeomen of the Guard The bodyguard of the British sovereign established by Henry VII in 1485. Their last appearance in battle was at Dettingen in 1743. They are often confused with the Yeoman Warders of the Tower of London who wear a similar red and gold uniform. The nickname Beefeaters (of disputed origin) is popularly applied to both units but disliked by the Yeomen of the Guard.

Yerevan (Russian name: Erevan) 40 10N 44 31E The capital of Armenia. The city dates from at least the 7th century AD. A commercial centre, it has chemical, textile, and food-processing industries. Population (1995 est): 1 248 700.

Yeti *See* ABOMINABLE SNOWMAN.

Yevtushenko, Yevgenii (1933–) Russian poet. His implicit criticism of the Soviet authorities in such poems as *Babi Yar* (1961) gained him wide popularity among both Soviet and Western readers. His more recent works include *Farewell to Red Banner* (1992).

yew A coniferous tree or shrub of the genus *Taxus* (10 species), native to the N hemisphere. Male and female flowers, which produce bright-red berries, grow on separate trees. The berries are attractive to birds but the seeds and leaves are poisonous. The most widespread species is the common yew (*T. baccata*), of Europe, SW Asia, and N Africa. Family: *Taxaceae*.

Yggdrasill In Norse mythology, an evergreen ash tree embracing the whole universe. Its three roots join the underworld, the land of giants, and the home of the gods (Asgard). The maypole and the Christmas tree are possibly symbolic derivatives of Yggdrasill.

Yiddish A language used by *Ashkenazim (East European) Jews and based on a dialect of High German. It emerged during the 9th century and has absorbed many Slavonic and other influences. It is written in the *Hebrew alphabet. After the holocaust it yielded its place as the principal literary language of the Jews to Hebrew. Over the last hundred years many Yiddish words have entered American English.

yield point The point at which a body becomes permanently deformed when subjected to a sufficiently large stress. Below the yield point the body is elastic, above the yield point it becomes plastic.

yin and yang Contrasting but complementary principles at the root of traditional Chinese cosmology. Yin is the negative feminine mode, associated with the earth, darkness, and passivity. Yang is the positive dynamic principle of masculine energy associated with heaven and light.

yin and yang. The symbols are interlocked and each contains a tiny portion of the other.

YMCA *See* YOUNG MEN'S CHRISTIAN ASSOCIATION.

yoga The principles and practice of self-training that permeate all Indian philosophical traditions. The methods used include physical control and meditative techniques. Physical control is stressed in Hindu yoga; in the Buddhist practice contemplative methods predominate; in Jainism asceticism is emphasized. Usually the aim is a state of release and liberation from the material world. The yoga fashionable in the West is often hatha-yoga, which involves physical exercises to bring peace and insight.

Yokohama 35 28N 139 28E The second largest city of Japan, a port in SE Honshu. Together with Tokyo it forms Japan's greatest urban area. *History*: it grew rapidly after 1859, but was almost destroyed by the 1923 earthquake and bombed during World War II. Population (1995): 3 307 408.

Yokosuka 35 18N 139 39E A port in Japan, in SE Honshu on Tokyo Bay. William Adams (d. 1620), the first Englishman to visit Japan (1600), is buried here. It has a major naval base and its chief industry is shipbuilding. Population (1995): 432 202.

Yom Kippur (Hebrew: Day of Atonement) A Jewish holy day, falling nine days after Rosh Hashanah. It is a day of penitence and cleansing from sin and is marked by 24 hours' total fast.

Yom Kippur War *See* ISRAEL, STATE OF.

Yonkers 40 56N 73 54W A city in the USA, in New York state on the Hudson River. Manufactures include elevators, carpets, and chemicals. Population (2000): 196 086.

York 1. (Latin name: Eboracum) 53 58N 1 05W A city in N England, in York unitary authority, North Yorkshire on the River Ouse. It was the principal Roman garrison in Britain and was for long regarded as the northern capital. The cathedral (Minster), seat of the Archbishop of York, the second of the two archbishops of England, was begun in 1154. The medieval walls and four city gateways remain. It is an educational and tourist centre with various light industries. Population (1994 est): 104 100. **2.** A unitary authority in N England. Area: 272 sq km (105 sq mi). Population (2001): 181 131.

York A ruling dynasty of England descended from Edmund, Duke of York (1342–1402), the fourth son of Edward III. Richard Plantaganet, Duke of *York, led the opposition to Henry VI in the Wars of the Roses (1455–85), in which the Yorkist emblem was the white rose. His son Edward IV established the royal dynasty. After the brief rule of his son Edward V and the overthrow of Richard III (1485) the Crown passed to Henry VII, the first *Tudor monarch, who married Edward IV's daughter Elizabeth.

York, Richard Plantagenet, 3rd Duke of (1411–60) English magnate. His claim to the throne against Henry VI resulted in the outbreak of the Wars of the Roses in 1455. He was killed in a skirmish at Wakefield. His sons became Edward IV and Richard III.

Yorkshire A historic county in NE England. It was traditionally divided into North, West, and East Ridings (thirds). It was reorganized in 1974 to form the counties of *North Yorkshire, *West Yorkshire, and *South Yorkshire, and parts of Humberside and Cleveland. When Humberside and Cleveland were abolished (1996), the *East Riding was reinstated as a unitary authority and parts of the NE were returned to North Yorkshire for ceremonial purposes.

Yorkshire terrier A breed of toy dog developed in N England during the 19th century. It is small and compact with a very long straight coat that trails on the ground. This is black at birth but matures to steel-blue with tan on the head and chest. Height: 20–23 cm.

Yosemite National Park A national park in the USA, in central California. The scenic Yosemite Valley contains the world's three largest monoliths of exposed granite. Its many lakes, rivers, and waterfalls include the Yosemite Falls. Area: 3061 sq km (1182 sq mi).

Young, Brigham (1801–1877) US Mormon leader, who succeeded Joseph *Smith. A former Methodist, Young joined the new church in 1832. After Smith's death he led the major migration to Salt Lake City, Utah (1846–47).

Young, Thomas (1773–1829) British physician and physicist. He identified astigmatism and described the ciliary muscles of the eye. He demonstrated the interference of light and suggested a wave theory of light in opposition to Newton's corpuscular theory. As a result of his work on the elasticity of materials, the ratio of stress to strain is known as Young's modulus (*see* ELASTIC MODULUS). Also an Egyptologist, he helped decipher the Rosetta Stone.

Young Men's Christian Association (**YMCA**) A Christian organization for young men and, since 1971, young women, founded in 1844 by George Williams (1821–1905). Its aim is to encourage Christian morality and qualities of leadership.

Young Women's Christian Association (YWCA) A Christian organization for women (to which men may now also belong). It was founded in 1855 by Emma Robarts and Mary Jane Kinnaird to promote unity among Christians and understanding between different faiths.

Youth Hostels Association (YHA) A British organization, founded in 1930, to promote a greater understanding of the countryside, especially by providing hostels where young people of limited means may stay. There are over 250 hostels in England and Wales.

Ypres (Flemish name: Ieper) 50 51N 2 53E A town in W Belgium, on the River Yperlee. Its many medieval buildings were almost completely destroyed during the three battles of Ypres in World War I. Population (1991 est): 21 400.

ytterbium (Yb) A lanthanide element, named after Ytterby in Sweden. It forms trivalent compounds, including the oxide (Yb_2O_3) and trihalides (for example $YbCl_3$). At no 70; at wt 173.04; mp 819°C; bp 1196°C.

yttrium (Y) A lanthanide element, discovered in 1794 by J. Gadolin (1760–1852). It is widely used as the oxide (Y_2O_3) to make red television-tube phosphors. At no 39; at wt 88.906; mp 1522°C; bp 3338°C.

Yuan (1279–1368) A Mongol dynasty that ruled China after overthrowing the Song dynasty. The first and strongest Mongol ruler was Kublai Khan, who held the empire together by military force.

Yucatán A peninsula of Central America, chiefly in SE Mexico but extending into Belize and Guatemala, separating the Gulf of Mexico from the Caribbean Sea. It was a centre of Maya civilization. Area: about 181 300 sq km (70 00 sq mi).

Yucca A genus of succulent plants (about 40 species), native to S North America and varying in height from small shrubs to 15-m-high trees. Most are stemless and have a rosette of stiff sword-shaped leaves crowded on a stout trunk. The waxy white bell-shaped flowers are pollinated by female yucca moths (genus *Pronuba*). Family: *Agavaceae*. *See also* JOSHUA TREE.

y

Yugoslavia, Federal Republic of A former country in SE Europe, on the Adriatic Sea. Yugoslavia was originally created in 1918 as a homeland mainly for South (Jugo) Slavic peoples (Serbs, Croats, Slovenes, and Macedonians). Until its violent break-up in 1991–92, it comprised the area now occupied by the nations of Croatia, Slovenia, Bosnia-Hercegovina, the former Yugoslav Republic of Macedonia, and the Union of *Serbia and Montenegro. *Economy*: agriculture was important. Forestry and wine-making were major sources of revenue and there were also rich mineral resources. Industry developed rapidly in the decades after World War II but in the 1990s the economy was devastated by civil war, UN sanctions on Serbia, and NATO bombing in the *Kosovo war (1999). *History*: Yugoslavia was so named in 1927, having been formed in 1918 as the Kingdom of Serbs, Croats, and Slovenes. The Serbian king, Alexander I (1888–1934), assumed absolute power in 1929 but was assassinated by extreme nationalist Croatians (Ustashi) in 1934. In 1941 Yugoslavia was attacked and occupied by the Germans and Italians. Croatia was put under the rule of the Ustashi, who committed atrocities against Serbs, Jews, and others. Internal resistance was divided between the Chetniks and the communist Partisans under *Tito. After the war Tito established a communist dictatorship. In 1948 Tito broke with Stalin and Yugoslavia became a leader of the nonaligned countries in foreign affairs. After Tito's death, the country struggled with economic and political crises. Croatia and Slovenia declared independence in 1991; military action by the Serb-led Yugoslav Army failed to subdue them. The independence of Slovenia and Croatia was recognized by EC and other states in January 1992 and that of Bosnia-Hercegovina in March. The latter descended into savage civil war (1992–95) between Bosnian Serbs, Muslims, and Croats. In April 1992 Macedonia declared independence but this was not recognized until 1993. That same month the Belgrade government announced the formation of a new Federal Republic of Yugoslavia comprising Serbia and Montenegro; this was not generally recognized until 2000. The Serbian leader Slobodan *Milošević became president of this rump Yugoslavia in 1997. From 1998 Serbian forces attempted to crush separatism in Kosovo by large-scale "ethnic cleansing." In response NATO bombed military and economic targets throughout Serbia until it withdrew its forces in June 1999. Following elections in 2000, Milošević refused to accept his defeat by the opposition candidate Vojislav Kostunica. He was subsequently deposed by a mass uprising and Kostunica became president. The name Yugoslavia was finally consigned to history in February 2002, when the Federal Republic of

Yugoslavia was replaced by a new Union of *Serbia and Montenegro.

Yukawa, Hideki (1907–81) Japanese physicist, who postulated (1935) that the *strong interaction could be accounted for by the exchange of *virtual particles. He calculated the mass of the particle involved. Confirmation came in 1947, when Cecil Powell (1903–69) discovered the pion. Yukawa won a Nobel Prize in 1949.

Yukon A territory of NW Canada, on the Beaufort Sea. It is covered by tundra in the N. Poor soils and low precipitation produce only sparse vegetation, except in S valleys. The population is concentrated on the central plateau, where silver, lead, zinc, copper, and asbestos are mined. There is some lumbering and tourism. The Yukon was first opened up by the *Klondike gold rush (1897–99). Area: 531 844 sq km (205 345 sq mi). Population (2001 est): 29 900. Capital: Whitehorse.

Yukon River A river in NW North America. Rising in NW Canada, it flows N through Alaska, USA, then SW into the Bering Sea. Length: 3185 km (1979 mi).

YWCA *See* YOUNG WOMEN'S CHRISTIAN ASSOCIATION.

Z

Zagreb 45 48N 15 58E The capital of Croatia, on the River Sava. A cultural centre of the Croats since the 16th century, it possesses a gothic cathedral. Population (2001): 682 598.

Zagros Mountains A mountain system in W Iran, extending 1600 km (994 mi) NW–SE between the Turkish border and the Strait of Hormuz. It rises to 4811 m (15 784 ft) at Sabalan.

Zaïre, Republic of *See* CONGO, DEMOCRATIC REPUBLIC OF.

Zambezi River A river in S Africa. Rising in NW Zambia, it flows generally S through E Angola before re-entering Zambia and curving E along the frontier of Namibia. It then forms the Zambia–Zimbabwe border, the *Victoria Falls and Kariba Dam being located along this course, before flowing SE to enter the Indian Ocean. It has a drainage area of about 1 347 000 sq km (520 000 sq mi). Length: 2740 km (1700 mi).

Zambia, Republic of (name until 1964: Northern Rhodesia) A landlocked country in S central Africa. It consists chiefly of low undulating plateaus and is drained along its southern border by the Zambezi River; other main rivers are the Kafue and Luangwa. The population is largely Bantu, with European, Asian, and Chinese minorities. *Economy*: copper accounts for about 96% of the total mineral production and comes mainly from the Copperbelt. Lead and zinc are also important, some coal is mined, and there are extensive iron-ore deposits, as yet unexploited. Agriculture is a major occupation; the chief subsistence crop is maize. Cash crops include cotton and tobacco but commercial agriculture has declined since the 1970s. Livestock and forestry are also important. There is a large foreign debt. *History*: the area had already been occupied by Bantu peoples when it was raided by Arab slave traders in the 18th century. In the 19th century British missionaries, notably David *Livingstone, paved the way for Cecil *Rhodes, who incorporated the region into a territory named Rhodesia and administered by the British South Africa Company. Constituted as Northern Rhodesia in 1911, it became a British protectorate in 1924. It formed part of the Federation of Rhodesia and Nyasaland (1953–63), obtaining internal self-government and then full independence within the Commonwealth as the Republic of Zambia (1964). *Kaunda became president on independence. In 1972 a new constitution led to one-party rule. After the legalization of opposition parties, Kaunda was defeated in free elections in 1991 and Frederick Chiluba became president. He was re-elected in 1996 amid accusations of fraud. An attempted coup led the government to impose a state of emergency in 1997–98. In January 2002 Levy Mwanawasa became president following elections; Chiluba and several of his ministers were subsequently charged with corruption. Official language: English. Currency: kwacha of 100 ngwee. Area: 752 262 sq km (290 586 sq mi). Population (2003 est): 10 812 000. Capital: Lusaka.

Zanzibar An island in Tanzania, off the NE coast of the mainland. It came under Arab influence early in its history and was, together with Pemba, a sultanate from 1856 to 1964. It was under British rule from 1890 until it became independent within the Commonwealth in 1963. In 1964 the Sultan was exiled and Zanzibar united with Tanganyika to form Tanzania. It exports mainly cloves and copra. Recent years have seen a growing movement for independence. Area: 1658 sq km (640 sq mi). Population (2002 est): 604 910. Chief town: Zanzibar.

Zapata, Emiliano (?1877–1919) Mexican revolutionary, who championed the cause of agrarian reform. By late 1911 he controlled the state of Morelos, where he carried out land reforms, chasing out the estate owners and dividing their land amongst the peasants. In 1919 he was tricked into an ambush and assassinated.

Zaporozhye (name until 1921: Aleksandrovsk) 47 50N 35 10E A city in E Ukraine, on the River Dnepr. A large hydroelectric station, built here in the years 1927–32, was destroyed in World War II but subsequently rebuilt. Population (1998 est): 863 100.

Zapotecs An American Indian people of the Oaxaca valleys (S Mexico). Their traditional culture, emerging about 300 AD, developed into one of the classic Mesoamerican Indian civilizations. Monte Alban, their chief city, declined under pressure from the Mixtecs (c. 900–50).

Zaragoza (English name: Saragossa) 41 39N 0 54W A city in NE Spain, in Aragon on the River Ebro. During the Peninsular War it heroically resisted a French siege until about 50 000 of its defenders had died (1808–09). It has two cathedrals and a university (founded 1533). An industrial centre, Zaragoza produces paper and wine. Population (1998 est): 603 367.

Zealots A Jewish political party of the 1st century AD. They were bitterly opposed to Roman rule in Judaea, and played a leading part in the revolt of 66 AD. Their last stronghold, *Masada, fell in 73. After the war their influence in Judaea was minimal but they may have been responsible for the further revolts in Egypt, Libya, and Cyprus in 115 AD.

zebra An African wild horse having characteristic black and white stripes covering part or all of the body. There are three races of the plains zebra (*Equus burchelli*), distinguished by the extent and nature of their stripes. The mountain zebra (*E. zebra*) has very bold stripes and a dewlap on the throat, while Grévy's zebra (*E. grevyi*) is the largest species, standing over 1.5 m at the shoulder with narrow stripes.

zebra finch An Australian *grassfinch, *Taeniopyga castanotis*, occurring in large flocks in the interior grasslands. The males are grey above with white underparts, reddish flanks, and black-and-white barred throat, breast, and tail. Zebra finches are popular cagebirds and have been bred to produce a white form with the black-and-white barring.

zebra fish A tropical freshwater fish, *Brachydanio rerio*, also called zebra danio, found in E India and popular in aquaria. It has a shiny blue body, up to 4.5 cm long, with four longitudinal yellowish gold stripes along its sides. *See also* SCORPION FISH.

zebu The domestic cattle of Asia and Africa, *Bos indicus*, also called Brahmin (*or* Brahman). Larger and leaner than western cattle, zebus have a distinctive hump over the shoulders, a large dewlap under the throat, and long horns. Zebus are no longer found in the wild and have been exported to hot countries for their heat tolerance and insect resistance in crosses with beef breeds.

Zeebrugge 51 20N 3 13E A small port in NW Belgium, on the North Sea, connected by ship canal (1907) to Bruges. A German submarine base in World War I, the canal was blocked by British naval forces in 1918. In 1987 the British ferry *Herald of Free Enterprise* capsized here, with the loss of 193 lives.

Zeeman, Pieter (1865–1943) Dutch physicist, who discovered (1886) the splitting of the spectral lines of a substance when placed in a magnetic field (**Zeeman effect**). It is caused by changes in the energy levels of the electrons of the emitting atoms as a result of interaction between the magnetic moment of the orbit and the external field. For this discovery he shared the 1902 Nobel Prize with Hendrik Lorentz (1853–1928).

Zeffirelli, Franco (1923–) Italian film and theatre director and stage designer. Having started in the theatre, he went on to direct films, including *The Taming of the Shrew* (1966), *Romeo and Juliet* (1968), *La Traviata* (1983), *Hamlet* (1990), and *Tea with Mussolini* (1999). He has also directed operas, plays, and the television series *Jesus of Nazareth* (1975).

Zen Buddhism (Japanese *Zen*, meditation) In China and Japan, a Buddhist school emphasizing the transmission of enlightenment from master to disciple without reliance on the scriptures. It derives from the teaching of Bodhidharma, who came to China in 520 AD. The two major sects, Soto and Rinzai, stress meditation and the use of logical paradoxes (*koans*) respectively, in order to confound the rational mind. Many aspects of Japanese and Chinese art, music, and literature, as well as calligraphy, the tea ceremony, the martial arts, etc., express the spontaneous Zen attitude to life. More recently Zen has gained followers in the West, where its opposition to rationalism has popular appeal.

zenith The point in the sky lying directly above an observer and 90° from all points on his horizon. The (unobservable) point diametrically opposite the zenith is the **nadir**.

Zenobia (3rd century AD) The wife of Odaenathus of Palmyra, whom she may have murdered (267) and whom she succeeded as regent for their son. Zenobia occupied Syria, Egypt, and much of Asia Minor before the Roman emperor Aurelian (c. 215–275 AD) defeated and captured her in 272. She enjoyed a reputation for beauty and intelligence.

Zeno of Citium (c. 335–262 BC) Greek philosopher, who was born in Cyprus of Phoenician stock, came to Athens in 313 BC, and attended lectures at Plato's Academy. He was influenced by various philosophical schools, including the *Cynics, before evolving his own doctrine of *Stoicism.

Zeno of Elea (born c. 490 BC) Greek philosopher. Zeno's paradoxes are the first dialectic arguments, eliciting contradictory conclusions from an opponent's hypotheses. These paradoxes include: Achilles and the tortoise—if space is infinitely divisible, once Achilles has given the tortoise a start he cannot overtake it, for whenever he arrives where the tortoise was it has already moved on; the flying arrow—if space is divisible into finite parts, a moving arrow at each moment of its flight is opposite a particular piece of ground and therefore stationary.

zeolites A group of complex silicate minerals containing loosely held water. They are divided into three groups: fibrous (natrolite, mesolite, scolecite), platy (heulandite, stilbite), and equant (harmatome, chabazite). Most occur in cavities in basic volcanic rocks. They are usually colourless or white and are relatively soft. Because of their property of base exchange they were used as water softeners before the introduction of artificial substitutes. They are also used as molecular sieves in the petroleum industry and as drying agents.

Zeppelins *See* AIRSHIPS.

Zeus The Greek sky and weather god, the supreme deity, identified with the Roman *Jupiter. He was the son of Cronus and Rhea, and brother of Poseidon and Hades. His defeat of Cronus and the *Titans represents the triumph of the Olympian deities over their predecessors. His offspring included *Athena, *Apollo, and *Dionysus and from his many love affairs, which excited the jealousy of his wife, *Hera, were produced numerous other divine and semidivine children. He was usually portrayed as a bearded man, with thunderbolts and the eagle as his attributes.

Zeus, statue of The chryselephantine statue designed by the Greek sculptor *Phidias in about 430 BC for the temple of Zeus at Olympia. One of the *Seven Wonders of the World, it was 12 m (40 ft) high and covered with jewels and gold. It was destroyed in the 5th century AD.

Zhangjiakou (*or* **Chang-chia-k'ou**; Mongolian name: Kalgan) 40 51N 114 59E A city in NE China, in Hebei province near the Great Wall. It was historically important for defence against and trade with the Mongols and is the site of two forts (1429, 1613). Population (1990): 529 136.

Zhengzhou (*or* **Cheng-chou**) 34 35N 113 38E A city in E China, the capital of Henan province. An old administrative centre, it has many industries developed since 1949. Population (1990): 1 159 679.

Zhou (?1027–221 BC) The earliest Chinese dynasty of which there is accurate knowledge. The dynasty was founded in the area now called Shenxi after the Zhou ruler, Wu Wang, had annihilated the armies of the preceding Shang dynasty and set up a system of government under feudal rulers. These undermined Zhou authority in the so-called Warring States period (481–221), after which the *Qin emerged to unite China. Under the Zhou human sacrifice was abolished and the Chinese idea of ancestor worship came into being. The late Zhou was also the great period of Chinese philosophy, when Taoist and Confucian thought first emerged.

Zhukov, Georgi Konstantinovich (1896–1974) Soviet marshal. An expert on armoured warfare, he became chief of the army general staff (1941). He planned or commanded almost every major Soviet military operation in World War II. Under Khrushchev he became defence minister and a member of the presidium of the Communist Party.

Ziegfeld, Florenz (1867–1932) US theatrical producer. The *Ziegfeld Follies*, lavish revues modelled on the *Folies-Bergère, appeared annually from 1907 until his death. He also created such hits as *Show Boat* (1927) and *Bitter Sweet* (1929) and launched Will Rogers, W. C. Fields, and others on their careers.

Ziegler, Karl (1898–1973) German chemist, who shared the 1963 Nobel Prize with Giulio Natta (1903–79) for their work on plastics and polymers. Ziegler showed that certain organometallic compounds (**Ziegler catalysts**) would catalyze the *polymerization of ethylene giving unbranched polymers that were tougher and had a higher melting point than those previously obtainable.

ziggurat A type of ancient Mesopotamian brick-built temple tower. Ziggurats were constructed of rectangular terraces of diminishing size, generally with a shrine for the god on top. They existed in every major Sumerian,

Babylonian, and Assyrian centre, the one at Babylon being the probable original of the Tower of Babel.

Zimbabwe, State of (name until 1979: Rhodesia) A landlocked country in SE Africa. It is bounded in the N by the Zambezi River and in the S by the Limpopo River. Much of the land consists of plateau, generally over 1000 m (3300 ft), with extensive areas of savanna. Most of the population is Bantu with small minorities of Europeans, Asians, and others. *Economy*: agriculture is the major source of employment. Tobacco production has fallen since the colonial period and a diversification to cotton and cattle has taken place; other cash crops include sugar and citrus fruit. The chief subsistence crops are maize, millet, and groundnuts. Forestry and fishing are important. Zimbabwe has gold, copper, asbestos, chrome, and nickel resources, but no oil reserves. Industry is mainly limited to the processing of food and minerals. An economic growth crisis in the late 1980s and 1990s, exacerbated by a financial crisis in 1998–99 and the government policy of seizing White-owned farms, has led to the virtual collapse of the economy in the early 2000s. Commercial food production has dropped sharply, leaving some 70% of the population below the breadline. *History*: ruins at *Great Zimbabwe attest the existence of a medieval Bantu civilization in the region. In 1837 its Mashona inhabitants were conquered by the Matabele and later in the 19th century it was explored by European missionaries, notably *Livingstone. In 1889 Cecil *Rhodes obtained a charter for the British South Africa Company, which conquered the Matabele and their territory, named Rhodesia (1895) in Rhodes' honour. In 1911 it was divided into Northern Rhodesia (now *Zambia) and Southern Rhodesia, the latter becoming a self-governing British colony in 1922. In 1953 the two parts of Rhodesia were reunited in the Federation of Rhodesia and Nyasaland, and after its dissolution in 1963 the Whites demanded independence for Southern Rhodesia (Rhodesia from 1964). The UK's refusal to permit independence without a guarantee of majority rule led the prime minister Ian *Smith to issue a unilateral declaration of independence (UDI) in 1965. Both the UK and the UN imposed economic sanctions but these proved fruitless. In 1970 Rhodesia declared itself a republic. In 1974 the Rhodesian government opened negotiations with the Zimbabwe African People's Union (ZAPU) and the Zimbabwe African National Union (ZANU), which had pursued guerrilla activities since the 1960s. Smith failed to negotiate an agreement with the Black nationalists, who remained divided under the umbrella of the Patriotic Front. In 1978, following the intervention of the UK (1977), agreement was reached on a transitional government leading to Black majority rule. However, when this government under Bishop Muzorewa failed to obtain the support of the Patriotic Front, an all-party conference was called in London (1979–80). Here Lord Soames (1920–87) was appointed governor to oversee the holding of elections (which brought Robert *Mugabe, leader of ZANU (PF), to power) and the granting of independence to Zimbabwe as a member of the Commonwealth (1980). In 1987 ZAPU and ZANU were unified under Mugabe, effectively creating a one-party state. Since 1997 Mugabe has faced protests over food prices, corruption, and the lack of political reform. The government has responded with authoritarian measures. With Mugabe's collusion, a campaign of violent seizure of White farms by squatters began in 2000. Despite widespread intimidation, elections in June 2000 resulted in massive gains for the opposition. Although Mugabe won presidential elections in 2002, the result was condemned as a fraud by foreign observers. State violence and repression led to Zimbabwe's suspension from the Commonwealth in 2002. Official language: English. Currency: Zimbabwe dollar of 100 cents. Area: 390 622 sq km (150 820 sq mi). Population (2003 est): 11 719 000. Capital: Harare.

zinc (Zn) A bluish-white metal known in antiquity in India and the Middle East. It occurs in nature principally in the ores calamine ($ZnCO_3$), zincite (ZnO), and zinc blende (ZnS). Zinc is widely used to make *galvanized steel and forms a number of useful low-melting alloys, including *brass. The sulphide (ZnS) is a phosphor and is used in making television screens and fluorescent tubes. Zinc oxide (ZnO) is widely used as a pigment and in medicines, batteries, cosmetics, plastics, and other products. Trace amounts of zinc are also important for growth in animals, including human beings. At no 30; at wt 65.37; mp 419.58°C; bp 907°C.

Zinnia A genus of herbs and shrubs (about 15 species), mostly native to North America. They have stiff stems, oval to heart-shaped leaves, and daisy-like flower heads with variously coloured ray florets. Cultivated zinnias are hybrids derived from the Mexican species *Z. elegans*. Family: *Compositae*.

Zinoviev, Grigori Yevseevich (1883–1936) Soviet politician. Zinoviev became a member of the politburo (1918) and chairman of the

Comintern (1919) but was expelled from the Communist Party in 1927. In 1935 he was accused of complicity in the murder of Sergei *Kirov (1888–1934) and was executed. A letter allegedly written by Zinoviev, in which the British Communist Party was urged to revolt, contributed to the defeat of the Labour Government in 1924. This was subsequently (1966) exposed as a forgery.

Zion (*or* **Sion**) A stronghold (II Samuel 5.6–7) on the SE hill of Jerusalem, captured by David, who made it the centre of his capital (Jerusalem). In the Old Testament it is another name for Jerusalem, or the place in which God dwells and reigns. In the New Testament and in later Christian writings, it symbolizes heaven.

Zionism A Jewish nationalist movement. It emerged during the 19th century on a tide of European antisemitism and was formally established at the First Zionist Congress (Basle, 1897). The Congress defined its political aim as the establishment of a Jewish national home in Palestine; the World Zionist Organization was set up, with Theodor *Herzl as its first president. Jewish immigration into Palestine (*aliyah*) was encouraged, especially through the Jewish National Fund (founded 1901) and the Jewish Agency for Palestine (1929). It was also supported by the Balfour Declaration, facilitated by Chaim *Weizmann's relationship with the British government. After World War II, the holocaust provided Zionism with an unanswerable case. Since the establishment of *Israel in 1948 the Zionist movement has continued to foster *aliyah*; the conflict between this principle and the rights of Palestinians has not, however, been resolved.

zircon A mineral consisting of zirconium silicate, found as an accessory mineral in intermediate and acid igneous rocks. It is usually colourless or yellowish. Gem varieties include hyacinth (red) and jargoon (colourless or smoky grey). It is the chief ore of zirconium and is used as a refractory material.

zirconium (Zr) A grey high-melting-point transition metal, isolated by J. J. Berzelius in 1824. It occurs in nature as zircon (zirconium silicate; $ZrSiO_4$), which is used as a gemstone. The dioxide (zirconia; ZrO_2) has a high melting point (2715°C) and is used as a refractory and crucible material. The metal is used in cladding fuel elements in nuclear reactors. At no 40; at wt 91.22; mp 1855 ± 2°C; bp 4409°C.

zither A plucked stringed instrument of ancient origin, consisting of a flat resonating box fitted with 30 to 40 strings, approximately 5 of which lie across a fretted fingerboard for playing the melody. The rest are used for playing accompanying chords.

zodiac A zone of the heavens extending about 8° on either side of the *ecliptic. Within it lies the apparent annual path of the sun, as seen from the earth, and the orbits of the moon, and major planets, apart from Pluto. The 12 constellations in the zodiac are known as "signs" or "houses" to astrologers, who believe them capable of stamping their individual dispositions upon those born under their influence (*see* ASTROLOGY). The 12 signs and their astrologically effective dates (different from their astronomical periods on account of precession) are: Aries, the Ram 21 Mar–19 Apr; Taurus, the Bull 20 Apr–20 May; Gemini, the Twins 21 May–21 June; Cancer, the Crab 22 June–22 July; Leo, the Lion 23 July–22 Aug; Virgo, the Virgin 23 Aug–22 Sept; Libra, the Scales 23 Sept–23 Oct; Scorpio, the Scorpion 24 Oct–21 Nov; Sagittarius, the Archer 22 Nov–21 Dec; Capricornus, the Goat 22 Dec–19 Jan; Aquarius, the Water-carrier 20 Jan–18 Feb; and Pisces, the Fish 19 Feb–20 Mar.

Zog I (1895–1961) King of Albania (1928–39). Zog was proclaimed king after serving as prime minister (1922–24) and president (1925–28). He let Albania fall under Italian economic domination and when Mussolini invaded Albania (1939) he fled into exile.

Zohar (Hebrew: splendour) The classical text of the *kabbalah. Written in Aramaic, it purports to be a mystical commentary on the *Torah and a collection of theosophical discussions dating from the time of the *Mishnah. It was actually written about 1280 by the Spanish kabbalist Moses de Leon, although it contains some later additions.

Zola, Émile (1840–1902) French novelist, the leading exponent of literary *naturalism. Following the success of his first major novel, *Thérèse Raquin* (1867), he conceived the plan for the series of 20 novels entitled *Les Rougon-Macquart* (1871–93). *L'Assommoir* (1877), describing the disintegration of a working-class family, *Nana* (1880), concerning a girl from the slums, *Germinal* (1885), about a mining community, and *La Terre* (1887), about the life of peasants, are among his powerful exposés of social problems. He fled to England after defending *Dreyfus in an open letter, *J'accuse* (1898), but was welcomed back as a hero after Dreyfus had been cleared.

Zollverein A customs union of 18 German states formed under Prussian dominance in

1834. By 1867 all German states except Hamburg and Bremen had joined. This commercial union helped pave the way for German unification under Prussian leadership (1871).

zoogeography The study of the geographical distribution of animals. It is based mainly on the work of A. R. *Wallace, who divided the world into a number of zoogeographical regions, each with a distinctive fauna. The present-day distribution of animals reflects both their evolutionary history and the movements of the land masses in past geological ages (*see* CONTINENTAL DRIFT). Thus the concentration of marsupials in the Australasian region is explained by the fact that the separation of Australia from the Asian mainland coincided with the evolutionary radiation of this group. The Australian marsupials therefore avoided competing with the more efficient placental mammals, which subsequently evolved on the mainland.

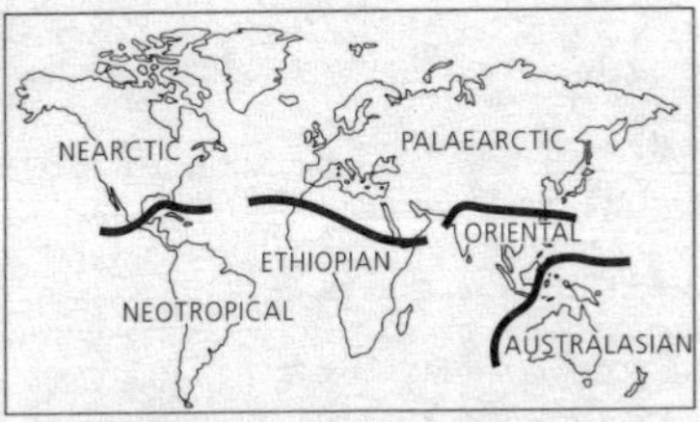

zoogeography. The world can be divided into six regions according to the distribution of its animals. Since some animals are less fixed in their habitats than others and may be found in more than one region, the divisions between the regions are somewhat arbitrary. For example, Wallace's line, separating the Oriental and Australasian regions, has been modified since Wallace proposed it.

zoology The branch of biological sciences specializing in the scientific study of animals. This includes their classification, anatomy, physiology, ecology, behaviour, evolution, etc. The importance of animals as food producers, pests, etc., in relation to man makes many aspects of zoology economically significant. *See also* ENTOMOLOGY; ORNITHOLOGY.

Zoroaster (*or* **Zarathustra**; c. 628–c. 551 BC) Iranian prophet, founder of **Zoroastrianism**, a dualistic religion that recognizes two principles, good and evil, as personified by Ahura Mazda and Ahriman. Probably born near Tehran, he is believed to have been a priest in the ancient polytheistic religion when he received a vision of Ahura Mazda, who exhorted him to preach a new faith based on his worship. Zoroaster abolished orgiastic rituals, although animal sacrifice and the ancient fire cult continued to be practised. The teachings attributed to him are preserved in the Gathas (hymns) in the *Avesta. Zoroastrianism survives in some parts of Iran and in India among the Parsees (*see* PARSEEISM).

Zuccarelli, Francesco (1702–88) Italian painter. He worked chiefly in Venice (after 1732) and in England (1752–62, 1765–71). A founding member of the Royal Academy and a favourite painter of George III, he specialized in picturesque landscapes.

Zuider Zee A former inlet of the SE North Sea, within the Netherlands. The N part, the Waddenzee, is separated from the S part (now the IJsselmeer) by a huge dam (completed 1932).

Zululand An area of SE South Africa. The home of the *Zulu people, it became a powerful state during the 1820s under their king Shaka (c. 1787–1828). Following conflict with the Boers the Zulus, under Cetshwayo (c. 1826–84), were defeated by the British (1879) and Zululand was incorporated into the former province of Natal in 1897. It comprised part of the *Bantu Homeland of KwaZulu and is now part of the KwaZulu/Natal region, which was created in 1994.

Zulus A Bantu people of SE South Africa. They are traditionally cattle herders and cattle are still a prestige possession. Polygyny is practised by important men. In the 19th century, under Shaka (c. 1787–1828), the Zulus conquered an extensive empire until eventually defeated in wars with the Europeans. Their highly efficient military organization was based on the age-set system; warriors could not marry until they attained a certain grade. Ancestor worship and witchcraft were prominent in their religious beliefs and the king had important ritual functions. Today, many Zulus are migrant labourers. In 1994 the status of the Zulu king was enshrined in South Africa's constitution.

Zurbarán, Francisco de (1598–1664) Spanish painter. In his earlier career, when he was based in Seville, he specialized in scenes from the lives of the saints, portraits, and still-lifes. The paintings of his later years, when he lived in Madrid, are characterized by a sentimental piety and are now considered inferior.

Zürich 47 23N 8 33E The largest city in Switzerland, on Lake Zürich. It is the commercial and industrial centre of Switzerland. Zürich's Alpine setting has contributed to the rise of its tourist industry. The Romans occupied the site in the 1st century BC. During the middle ages it became the most important Swiss town and joined the Swiss confederation in 1351. A leading centre of the Reformation, Zürich became a refuge for those persecuted in the Counter-Reformation. Population (1999 est): 336 821.

Zwingli, Ulrich (1484–1531) Swiss Protestant reformer. A priest in the minster at Zürich, he welcomed *Luther's writings and had established a reformed church by 1525. He separated from Luther over the latter's Eucharistic doctrine, which he saw as a persistence of Roman doctrine.

zygote *See* FERTILIZATION.

Appendices

Units of Measurement

SI units (Système International d'Unités) are now widely used throughout the world, especially for scientific purposes. SI units are metric units, based on the metre, kilogram, and second.

The base units are:

PHYSICAL QUANTITY	SI UNIT	SYMBOL
length	metre	m
mass	kilogram	kg
time	second	s
electric current	ampere	A
thermodynamic temperature	kelvin	K
luminous intensity	candela	cd
amount of substance	mole	mol
plane angle (supplementary unit)	radian	rad
solid angle (supplementary unit)	steradian	sr

The derived units with special names are:

PHYSICAL QUANTITY	SI UNIT	SYMBOL
frequency	hertz	Hz
energy	joule	J
force	newton	N
power	watt	W
pressure	pascal	Pa
electric charge	coulomb	C
electric potential difference	volt	V
electric resistance	ohm	W
electric conductance	siemens	S
electric capacitance	farad	F
magnetic flux	weber	Wb
inductance	henry	H
magnetic flux density (magnetic induction)	tesla	T
luminous flux	lumen	lm
illuminance	lux	lx
absorbed dose	gray	Gy
activity	becquerel	Bq
dose equivalent	sievert	Sv

SI units are used in decimal multiples, e.g. 1 km = 1000 metres, often written 10^3 m ($1 \times 10^3 = 10 \times 10 \times 10 = 1000$); 1 cm = 1/100 of a metre, often written 10^{-2} m ($1 \times 10^{-2} = 1 \div (10 \times 10) = 1/100$).

The following prefixes are used:

SUBMULTIPLE	PREFIX	SYMBOL	MULTIPLE	PREFIX	SYMBOL
10^{-1}	deci-	d	10	deca-	da
10^{-2}	centi-	c	10^2	hecto-	h
10^{-3}	milli-	m	10^3	kilo-	k
10^{-6}	micro-	m	10^6	mega-	M
10^{-9}	nano-	n	10^9	giga-	G
10^{-12}	pico-	p	10^{12}	tera-	T
10^{-15}	femto-	f	10^{15}	peta-	P
10^{-18}	atto-	a	10^{18}	exa-	E
10^{-21}	zepto-	z	10^{21}	zetta-	Z
10^{-24}	yocto-	y	10^{24}	yotta-	Y

These prefixes are used with all SI units.

Unit Conversion Tables

LENGTH

	METRE	CENTIMETRE	INCH	FOOT	YARD
1 metre	1	100	39.3701	3.28084	1.09361
1 centimetre	0.01	1	0.393701	0.0328084	0.0109361
1 inch	0.0254	2.54	1	0.0833333	0.0277778
1 foot	0.3048	30.48	12	1	0.333333
1 yard	0.9144	91.44	36	3	1

	KILOMETRE	MILE	NAUTICAL MILE
1 kilometre	1	0.621371	0.539957
1 mile	1.60934	1	0.868976
1 nautical mile	1.85200	1.15078	1

AREA

	M^2	CM^2	IN^2	FT^2
1 square metre	1	10^4	1550	10.7639
1 square centimetre	10^{-4}	1	0.155	1.07639×10^{-3}
1 square inch	6.4516×10^{-4}	6.4516	1	6.94444×10^{-3}
1 square foot	9.2903×10^{-2}	929.03	144	1

	M^2	KM^2	YD^2	MI^2	ACRE
1 square metre	1	10^{-6}	1.19599	3.86019×10^{-7}	2.47105×10^{-4}
1 square kilometre	10^6	1	1.19599×10^6	0.386019	247.105
1 square yard	0.836127	8.36127×10^{-7}	1	3.22831×10^{-7}	2.06612×10^{-4}
1 square mile	2.58999×10^6	2.58999	3.0976×10^6	1	640
1 acre	4.04686×10^3	4.04686×10^{-3}	4840	1.5625×10^{-3}	1

VOLUME

	M^3	CM^3	IN^3	FT^3	GALLONS
1 cubic metre	1	10^6	6.10236×10^4	35.3146	219.969
1 cubic centimetre	10^{-6}	1	0.0610236	3.53146×10^{-5}	2.19969×10^{-4}
1 cubic inch	1.63871×10^{-5}	16.3871	1	5.78704×10^{-4}	3.60464×10^{-3}
1 cubic foot	0.0283168	28316.8	1728	1	6.22882
1 gallon (UK)	4.54609×10^{-3}	4546.09	277.42	0.160544	1

MASS

	KG	G	LB
1 kilogram	1	1000	2.20462
1 gram	10^{-3}	1	2.20462×10^{-3}
1 pound	0.453592	453.592	1

ENERGY AND WORK

	J	CAL_{IT}	KWHR	BTU_{IT}
1 joule	1	0.238846	2.77778×10^{-7}	9.47813×10^{-4}
1 calorie (IT)	4.1868	1	1.16300×10^{-6}	3.96831×10^{-3}
1 kilowatt hour	3.6×10^6	8.59845×10^5	1	3412.14
1 British Thermal Unit (IT)	1055.06	251.997	2.93071×10^{-4}	1

PRESSURE

	N/M^2(PA)	KG/CM^2	LB/IN^2	ATMOS
1 newton per square metre (pascal)	1	1.01972×10^{-5}	1.45038×10^{-4}	9.86923×10^{-6}
1 kilogram per square centimetre	980.665×10^2	1	14.2234	0.967841
1 pound per square inch	6.89476×10^3	0.0703068	1	0.068046
1 atmosphere	1.01325×10^5	1.03323	14.6959	1

Prime Ministers of Great Britain (from 1721)

NAME	TERM
Robert Walpole	1721–42
Spencer Compton, Earl of Wilmington	1742–43
Henry Pelham	1743–54
Thomas Pelham-Holles, Duke of Newcastle	1754–56
William Cavendish, Duke of Devonshire	1756–57
Thomas Pelham-Holles, Duke of Newcastle	1757–62
John Stuart, Earl of Bute	1762–63
George Granville	1763–65
Charles Watson-Wentworth, Marquis of Rockingham	1765–66
William Pitt, Earl of Chatham	1766–68
Augustus Henry Fitzroy, Duke of Grafton	1768–70
Frederick North	1770–82
Charles Watson-Wentworth, Marquis of Rockingham	1782
William Petty, Earl of Shelburne	1782–83
William Henry Cavendish Bentinck, Duke of Portland	1783
William Pitt (son of Earl of Chatham)	1783–1801
Henry Addington	1801–04
William Pitt	1804–06
William Wyndham Grenville, Baron Grenville	1806–07
William Bentinck, Duke of Portland	1807–09
Spencer Perceval	1809–12
Robert Banks Jenkinson, Earl of Liverpool	1812–27
George Canning	1827
Frederick John Robinson, Viscount Goderich	1827–28
Arthur Wellesley, Duke of Wellington	1828–30
Charles Grey, Earl Grey	1830–34
William Lamb, Viscount Melbourne	1834
Robert Peel	1834–35
William Lamb, Viscount Melbourne	1835–41
Robert Peel	1841–46
John Russell	1846–52
Edward George Geoffrey Smith Stanley, Earl of Derby	1852
George Hamilton Gordon, Earl of Aberdeen	1852–55
Henry Temple, Viscount Palmerston	1855–58
Edward Stanley, Earl of Derby	1858–59
Henry John Temple, Viscount Palmerston	1859–65
John Russell, Earl Russell	1865–66
Edward Stanley, Earl of Derby	1866–68
Benjamin Disraeli	1868
William Ewart Gladstone	1868–74
Benjamin Disraeli, Earl (1876) of Beaconsfield	1874–80
William Ewart Gladstone	1880–85
Robert Gascoyne-Cecil, Marquis of Salisbury	1885–86
William Ewart Gladstone	1886
Robert Gascoyne-Cecil, Marquis of Salisbury	1886–92
William Ewart Gladstone	1892–94
Archibald Philip Primrose, Earl of Rosebery	1894–95
Robert Gascoyne-Cecil, Marquis of Salisbury	1895–1902
Arthur James Balfour	1902–05
Henry Campbell-Bannerman	1905–08
Herbert Henry Asquith	1908–16
David Lloyd George	1916–22
Andrew Bonar Law	1922–23
Stanley Baldwin	1923–24
James Ramsay MacDonald	1924
Stanley Baldwin	1924–29
James Ramsay MacDonald	1929–35
Stanley Baldwin	1935–37
Neville Chamberlain	1937–40
Winston Churchill	1940–45
Clement Richard Attlee	1945–51
Winston Churchill	1951–55
Anthony Eden	1955–57
Harold Macmillan	1957–63
Alec Douglas-Home	1963–64
Harold Wilson	1964–70
Edward Heath	1970–74
Harold Wilson	1974–76
James Callaghan	1976–79
Margaret Thatcher	1979–90
John Major	1990–97
Tony Blair	1997–

Presidents of the United States of America

NAME	TERM	NAME	TERM
George Washington	1789–97	Benjamin Harrison	1889–93
John Adams	1797–1801	Grover Cleveland	1893–97
Thomas Jefferson	1801–09	William McKinley	1897–1901
James Madison	1809–17	Theodore Roosevelt	1901–09
James Monroe	1817–25	William Howard Taft	1909–13
John Quincy Adams	1825–29	Woodrow Wilson	1913–21
Andrew Jackson	1829–37	Warren Gamaliel Harding	1921–23
Martin Van Buren	1837–41	Calvin Coolidge	1923–29
William Henry Harrison	1841	Herbert Clark Hoover	1929–33
John Tyler	1841–45	Franklin Delano Roosevelt	1933–45
James Knox Polk	1845–49	Harry S. Truman	1945–53
Zachary Taylor	1849–50	Dwight David Eisenhower	1953–61
Millard Fillmore	1850–53	John Fitzgerald Kennedy	1961–63
Franklin Pierce	1853–57	Lyndon Baines Johnson	1963–69
James Buchanan	1857–61	Richard Milhous Nixon	1969–74
Abraham Lincoln	1861–65	Gerald Rudolph Ford	1974–77
Andrew Johnson	1865–69	James Earl Carter	1977–81
Ulysses Simpson Grant	1869–77	Ronald Wilson Reagan	1981–89
Rutherford Hayes	1877–81	George Herbert Walker Bush	1989–93
James Abram Garfield	1881	William Jefferson Clinton	1993–2001
Chester Alan Arthur	1881–85	George Walker Bush	2001–
Grover Cleveland	1885–89		